ENCYCLOPEDIA OF
Special Education

THIRD EDITION

Encyclopedia of Special Education, THIRD EDITION

Cecil R. Reynolds and Elaine Fletcher-Janzen, Editors

CONTRIBUTING EDITORS

KIMBERLY F. APPLEQUIST
University of Colorado at Colorado Springs
Colorado Springs, Colorado

RANDALL L. DE PRY
University of Colorado at Colorado Springs
Colorado Springs, Colorado

RON DUMONT
Fairleigh Dickinson University
Teaneck, New Jersey

SAM GOLDSTEIN
University of Utah
Salt Lake City, Utah

JAMES C. KAUFMAN
California State University, San Bernardino
San Bernardino, California

TOM OAKLAND
University of Florida
Gainesville, Florida

CYNTHIA RICCIO
Texas A&M University
College Station, Texas

RACHEL TOPLIS
Falcon School District 49
Colorado Springs, Colorado

LEE SWANSON
University of California, Riverside
Riverside, California

JOHN O. WILLIS
Rivier College
Nashua, New Hampshire

RON ZELLNER
Texas A&M University
College Station, Texas

ENCYCLOPEDIA OF
Special Education

A Reference for the Education
of Children, Adolescents,
and Adults with Disabilities and
Other Exceptional Individuals

Edited by

Cecil R. Reynolds

Elaine Fletcher-Janzen

JOHN WILEY & SONS

CONTRIBUTORS

Susanne Blough Abbott
Bedford Central School District
Mt. Kisco, New York

Marty Abramson
University of Wisconsin at Stout
Menomonie, Wisconsin

Patricia Ann Abramson
Hudson Public Schools
Hudson, Wisconsin

Salvador Hector Achoa
Texas A&M University
College Station, Texas

Patricia A. Alexander
University of Maryland
College Park, Maryland

Vincent C. Alfonso
Fordham University
New York, New York

Nancy Algert
Texas A&M University
College Station, Texas

Thomas E. Allen
Gallaudet College
Washington, DC

Marie Almond
The University of Texas of the
    Permian Basin
Odessa, Texas

Geri R. Alvis
Memphis State University
Memphis, Tennessee

Daniel G. Amen
University of California School of
    Medicine
Irvine, California

C. H. Ammons
*Psychological Reports / Perceptual
    and Motor Skills*
Missoula, Montana

Carol Anderson
Texas A&M University
College Station, Texas

Kari Anderson
University of North Carolina at
    Wilmington
Wilmington, North Carolina

Peggy L. Anderson
University of New Orleans,
    Lakefront
New Orleans, Louisiana

Candace Andrews
California State University, San
    Bernardino
San Bernardino, California

Jean Annan
Massey University
New Zealand

J. Appelboom-Fondu
Université Libre de Bruxelles
Brussels, Belgium

James M. Applefield
University of North Carolina at
    Wilmington
Wilmington, North Carolina

Pauline F. Applefield
University of North Carolina at
    Wilmington
Wilmington, North Carolina

Kimberly F. Applequist
University of Colorado at Colorado
    Springs
Colorado Springs, Colorado

Anna M. Arena
Academic Therapy Publications
Novato, California

John Arena
Academic Therapy Publications
Novato, California

Julie A. Armentrout
University of Colorado at Colorado
    Springs
Colorado Springs, Colorado

Patricia Ann Arramson
Hudson Public Schools
Hudson, Wisconsin

Gustavo Abelardo Arrendondo
Monterrey, Mexico

Bernice Arricale
Hunter College, City University of
    New York
New York, New York

H. Roberta Arrigo
Hunter College, City University of
    New York
New York, New York

Alfredo J. Artiles
University of California, Los Angeles
Los Angeles, California

Maria Arzola
University of Florida
Gainesville, Florida

Michael J. Ash
Texas A&M University
College Station, Texas

Adel E. Ashawal
Ain Shams University
Cairo, Egypt

Shannon Atwater
Branson School Online
Branson, Colorado

William G. Austin
Cape Fear Psychological Services
Wilmington, North Carolina

Anna H. Avant
University of Alabama
Tuscaloosa, Alabama

Dan G. Bachor
University of Victoria
Victoria, British Columbia, Canada

John Baer
Rider University
Wenonah, New Jersey

Rebecca Bailey
Texas A&M University
College Station, Texas

Timothy A. Ballard
University of North Carolina at
    Wilmington
Wilmington, North Carolina

Melanie Ballatore
University of Texas
Austin, Texas

Tanya Y. Banda
Texas A&M University Press
College Station, Texas

Deborah E. Barbour
University of North Carolina at
    Wilmington
Wilmington, North Carolina

Russell A. Barkley
University of Massachusetts Medical
    Center
Worchester, Massachusetts

Charles P. Barnard
University of Wisconsin at Stout
Menomonie, Wisconsin

David W. Barnett
University of Cincinnati
Cincinnati, Ohio

Ellis I. Barowsky
Hunter College, City University of
    New York
New York, New York

Lyle E. Barton
Kent State University
Kent, Ohio

Vicki Bartosik
Stanford University
Stanford, California

Paul Bates
Southern Illinois University
Carbondale, Illinois

Anne M. Bauer
University of Cincinnati
Cincinnati, Ohio

Elizabeth R. Bauerschmidt
University of North Carolina at
    Wilmington
Wilmington, North Carolina

Michael Bauerschmidt
Brunswick Hospital
Wilmington, North Carolina

Monique Banters
Centre d'Etude et de Reclassement
Brussels, Belgium

John R. Beattie
University of North Carolina at
    Charlotte
Charlotte, North Carolina

George R. Beauchamp
Cleveland Clinic Foundation
Cleveland, Ohio

Mellisa Beckham
The Citadel
Charleston, South Carolina

Ronald A. Beghetto
University of Oregon
Eugene, Oregon

Julie Bell
University of Florida
Gainesville, Florida

Ana Yeraldina Beneke
University of Oklahoma
Norman, Oklahoma

Randy Elliot Bennett
Educational Testing Service
Princeton, New Jersey

Richard A. Berg
West Virginia University Medical
    Center, Charleston Division
Charleston, West Virginia

John R. Bergan
University of Arizona
Tucson, Arizona

Dianne E. Berkell
C.W. Post Campus, Long Island
    University
Greenvale, New York

Gary Berkowitz
Temple University
Philadelphia, Pennsylvania

Shari A. Bevins
Texas A&M University
College Station, Texas

John Bielinski
AGS Publishing
St. Paul, Minnesota

Kristan Biernath
The Hughes Spalding International
    Adoption Evaluation Center
Atlanta, Georgia

Erin D. Bigler
Brigham Young University
Provo, Utah

Tia Billy
Texas A&M University
College Station, Texas

Roseann Bisighini
The Salk Institute
La Jolla, California

Kendra J. Bjoraker
University of Northern Colorado
Greeley, Colorado

Jan Blacher
University of California, Riverside
Riverside, California

Gérard Bless
University of Fribourg
Fribourg, Switzerland

L. Worth Bolton
Cape Fear Substance Abuse Center
Wilmington, North Carolina

Gwyneth M. Boodoo
Texas A&M University
College Station, Texas

Nancy Bordier
Hunter College, City University of
New York
New York, New York

Jeannie Bormans
Center for Developmental Problems
Brussels, Belgium

Morton Botel
University of Pennsylvania
Philadelphia, Pennsylvania

Daniel J. Boudah
Texas A&M University
College Station, Texas

Michael Bourdot
Centre d'Etude et de Reclassement
Brussels, Belgium

Bruce A. Bracken
University of Memphis
Memphis, Tennessee

Mary Brady
Pennsylvania Special Education
Assistive Device Center
Elizabethtown, Pennsylvania

Janet S. Brand
Hunter College, City University of
New York
New York, New York

Don Braswell
Research Foundation, City
University of New York
New York, New York

T. Berry Brazelton
Children's Hospital
Boston, Massachusetts

Warner H. Britton
Auburn University
Auburn, Alabama

Debra Y. Broadbooks
California School of Professional
Psychology
San Diego, California

Melanie L. Bromley
California State University, San
Bernardino
San Bernardino, California

Michael G. Brown
Central Wisconsin Center for the
Developmentally Disabled
Madison, Wisconsin

Robert T. Brown
University of North Carolina at
Wilmington
Wilmington, North Carolina

Ronald T. Brown
Emory University School of Medicine
Atlanta, Georgia

Tina L. Brown
Memphis State University
Memphis, Tennessee

Robert G. Brubaker
Eastern Kentucky University
Richmond, Kentucky

Catherine O. Bruce
Hunter College, City University of
New York
New York, New York

Andrew R. Brulle
Wheaton College
Sycamore, Illinois

Laura Kinzie Brutting
University of Wisconsin at Madison
Madison, Wisconsin

Donna M. Bryant
University of North Carolina at
Chapel Hill
Chapel Hill, North Carolina

Milton Budoff
Research Institute for Educational
Problems
Cambridge, Massachusetts

Carolyn L. Bullard
Lewis & Clark College
Portland, Oregon

Thomas R. Burke
Hunter College, City University of
New York
New York, New York

Alois Bürli
Swiss Institute for Special Education
Lucerne, Switzerland

Jason Burrow-Sanchez
University of Utah
Salt Lake City, Utah

Thomas A. Burton
University of Georgia
Athens, Georgia

Michelle T. Buss
Texas A&M University
College Station, Texas

James Button
United States Department of
Education
Washington, DC

Claudia Camarillo-Dievendorf
Pitzer College, Claremont
Claremont, California

Anne Campbell
Purdue University
West Lafayette, Indiana

Frances A. Campbell
University of North Carolina at
Chapel Hill
Chapel Hill, North Carolina

Steven A. Carlson
Beaverton Schools
Beaverton, Oregon

Douglas Carnine
University of Oregon
Eugene, Oregon

Deborah Birke Caron
St. Lucie County School District
Ft. Pierce, Florida

Janet Carpenter
University of Oklahoma
Norman, Oklahoma

Edward G. Carr
State University of New York at
Stony Brook
Stony Brook, New York

Tracy Calpin Castle
Eastern Kentucky University
Richmond, Kentucky

John F. Cawley
University of New Orleans
New Orleans, Louisiana

Christine D. Cde Baca
University of Northern Colorado
Greeley, Colorado

Constance Y. Celaya
Irving, Texas

James C. Chalfant
University of Arizona
Tucson, Arizona

Elaine A. Cheesman
University of Colorado at Colorado
   Springs
Colorado Springs, Colorado

Rebecca Wing-yi Cheng
The University of Hong Kong
Hong Kong, China

Chris Cherrington
Lycoming College
Williamsport, Pennsylvania

Robert Chimedza
University of Zimbabwe
Harare, Zimbabwe

Kathleen M. Chinn
New Mexico State University
Las Cruces, New Mexico

Elaine Clark
University of Utah
Salt Lake City, Utah

LeRoy Clinton
Boston University
Boston, Massachusetts

Renato Cocchi
Pesaro, Italy

Cynthia Price Cohen
Child Rights International Research
   Institute
New York, New York

Shirley Cohen
Hunter College, City University of
   New York
New York, New York

Ginga L. Colcough
University of North Carolina at
   Wilmington
Wilmington, North Carolina

Christine L. Cole
University of Wisconsin at Madison
Madison, Wisconsin

Rhonda Collins
Florida State University
Tallahassee, Florida

Jennifer Condon
University of North Carolina at
   Wilmington
Wilmington, North Carolina

Jane Close Conoley
University of Nebraska–Lincoln
Lincoln, Nebraska

Clayton R. Cook
University of California, Riverside
Riverside, California

Krystal T. Cook
Texas A&M University
College Station, Texas

Vivian I. Correa
University of Florida
Gainesville, Florida

Barbara Corriveau
Laramie County School District # 1
Cheyenne, Wyoming

Lawrence S. Cote
Pennsylvania State University
University Park, Pennsylvania

Kathleen Cotton
Northwest Regional Educational
   Laboratory
Portland, Oregon

Katherine D. Couturier
Pennsylvania State University
King of Prussia, Pennsylvania

J. Michael Coxe
University of South Carolina
Columbia, South Carolina

Julia Coyne
Loyala University, Chicago
Chicago, Illinois

Anne B. Crabbe
St. Andrews College
Laurinburg, North Carolina

Lindy Crawford
University of Colorado at Colorado
   Springs
Colorado Springs, Colorado

Sergio R. Crisalle
Medical Horizons Unlimited
San Antonio, Texas

Chara Crivelli
Vito de Negrar
Verona, Italy

John Crumlin
University of Colorado at Colorado
   Springs
Colorado Springs, Colorado

Jack A. Cummings
Indiana University
Bloomington, Indiana

Jacqueline Cunningham
University of Texas
Austin, Texas

Susan Curtiss
University of California, Los Angeles
Los Angeles, California

Rik Carl D'Amato
University of Northern Colorado
Greeley, Colorado

Elizabeth Dane
Hunter College, City University of
   New York
New York, New York

Craig Darch
Auburn University
Auburn, Alabama

Barry Davidson
Ennis, Texas

Jacqueline E. Davis
Boston University
Boston, Massachusetts

Raymond S. Dean
Ball State University
Indiana University School of
   Medicine
Muncie, Indiana

Jozi De Leon
New Mexico State University
Las Cruces, New Mexico

Bernadette M. Delgado
University of Nebraska–Lincoln
Lincoln, Nebraska

Allison G. Dempsey
University of Florida
Gainesville, Florida

Jack R. Dempsey
University of Florida
Gainesville, Florida

Randall L. De Pry
University of Colorado at Colorado
   Springs
Colorado Springs, Colorado

Lizanne DeStefano
University of Illinois, Urbana-
   Champaign
Champaign, Illinois

S. De Vriendt
Vrije Universiteit Brussel
Brussels, Belgium

Caroline D'Ippolito
Eastern Pennsylvania Special
   Education Resources Center
King of Prussia, Pennsylvania

Mary D'Ippolito
Montgomery County Intermediate
   Unit
Norristown, Pennsylvania

Roja Dilmore-Rios
California State University, San
   Bernadino
San Bernadino, California

Jeffrey Ditterline
University of Florida
Gainesville, Florida

Marilyn P. Dornbush
Atlanta, Georgia

Amanda Jensen Doss
Texas A&M University
College Station, Texas

Susann Dowling
University of Houston
Houston, Texas

Sharon Duffy
University of California, Riverside
Riverside, California

Jengjyh Duh
National Taiwan Normal University
Taipei, Taiwan

Ron Dumont
Fairleigh Dickinson University
Teaneck, New Jersey

Brooke Durbin
Texas A&M University
College Station, Texas

Mary K. Dykes
University of Florida
Gainesville, Florida

Alan Dyson
University of Manchester
Manchester, England

Peg Eagney
School for the Deaf
New York, New York

Ronald C. Eaves
Auburn University
Auburn, Alabama

Jana Echevarria
California State University, Long
   Beach
Long Beach, California

Danielle Edelston
University of California, Riverside
Riverside, California

Amita Edran
California State University, Long
   Beach
Long Beach, California

John M. Eells
Souderton Area School District
Souderton, Pennsylvania

Cassie Eiffert
University of Florida
Gainesville, Florida

Stephen N. Elliott
University of Wisconsin at Madison
Madison, Wisconsin

Julie Ellis
University of Florida
Gainesville, Florida

Ingemar Emanuelsson
Goteburg University
Goteburg, Sweden

Petra Engelbrecht
University of Stellenbosch
Stellenbosch, South Africa

Carol Sue Englert
Michigan State University
East Lansing, Michigan

Chaz Esparaza
California State University, San
   Bernardino
San Bernardino, California

Christine A. Espin
University of Minnesota
Minneapolis, Minnesota

Michelle Evans
California State University, San
   Bernardino
San Bernardino, California

Rand B. Evans
Texas A&M University
College Station, Texas

Rose Fairbanks
Temecula, California

Sarah Fairbanks
University of Connecticut
Storrs, Connecticut

Katherine Falwell
University of North Carolina at
   Wilmington
Wilmington, North Carolina

Judith L. Farmer
New Mexico State University
Las Cruces, New Mexico

Stephen S. Farmer
New Mexico State University
Las Cruces, New Mexico

Peter Farrell
University of Manchester
Manchester, England

MaryAnn C. Farthing
University of North Carolina at
  Chapel Hill
Chapel Hill, North Carolina

Lisa Fashnacht-Hill
Children's Hospital
Los Angeles, California

Mary Grace Feely
School for the Deaf
New York, New York

John F. Feldhusen
Purdue University
West Lafayette, Indiana

Britt-Inger Fex
University of Lund
Lund, Sweden

Donna Filips
Steger, Illinois

Marni R. Finberg
University of Florida
Gainesville, Florida

Krista Finstuen
Texas A&M University
College Station, Texas

Sally L. Flagler
University of Oklahoma
Norman, Oklahoma

Dawn P. Flanagan
St. John's University
Jamaica, New York

Dennis M. Flanagan
Montgomery County Intermediate
  Unit
Norristown, Pennsylvania

David Fletcher-Janzen
Colorado Springs, Colorado

Elaine Fletcher-Janzen
University of Colorado at Colorado
  Springs
Colorado Springs, Colorado

Wendy L. Flynn
Staffordshire University
England

Cindi Flores
California State University, San
  Bernardino
San Bernardino, California

Constance J. Fournier
Texas A&M University
College Station, Texas

Rollen C. Fowler
Eugene 4J School District
Eugene, Oregon

Emily Fox
University of Michigan
Ann Arbor, Michigan

Thomas A. Frank
Pennsylvania State University
University Park, Pennsylvania

Leslie Coyle Franklin
University of Northern Colorado
Greeley, Colorado

Mary M. Frasier
University of Georgia
Athens, Georgia

Joseph L. French
Pennsylvania State University
University Park, Pennsylvania

Alice G. Friedman
University of Oklahoma Health
  Services Center
Norman, Oklahoma

Douglas L. Friedman
Fordham University
Bronx, New York

Douglas Fuchs
Peabody College, Vanderbilt
  University
Nashville, Tennessee

Lynn S. Fuchs
Peabody College, Vanderbilt
  University
Nashville, Tennessee

Gerald B. Fuller
Central Michigan University
Mt. Pleasant, Michigan

Rosemary Gaffney
Hunter College, City University of
  New York
New York, New York

Jason Gallant
University of Florida
Gainesville, Florida

Diego Gallegos
Texas A&M University
College Station, Texas

Clarissa I. Garcia
Texas A&M University
College Station, Texas

Shernaz B. Garcia
University of Texas
Austin, Texas

Katherine Garnett
Hunter College, City University of
  New York
New York, New York

Melissa M. George
Montgomery County Intermediate
  Unit
Norristown, Pennsylvania

Phil Bless Gerard
University of Fribourg
Fribourg, Switzerland

Verena Getahun
AGS Publishing
St. Paul, Minnesota

Violeta Gevorgianiene
Vilnius University
Vilnius, Lithuania

Harvey R. Gilbert
Pennsylvania State University
University Park, Pennsylvania

Grazina Gintiliene
Vilnius University
Vilnius, Lithuania

Elizabeth Girshick
Montgomery County Intermediate
    Unit
Norristown, Pennsylvania

Joni J. Gleason
University of West Florida
Pensacola, Florida

Sharon L. Glennen
Pennsylvania State University
University Park, Pennsylvania

Sam Goldstein
University of Utah
Salt Lake City, Utah

Rick Gonzales
Texas A&M University
College Station, Texas

Libby Goodman
Pennsylvania State University
King of Prussia, Pennsylvania

Carole Reiter Gothelf
Hunter College, City University of
    New York
New York, New York

Steve Graham
University of Maryland
College Park, Maryland

Jeffrey W. Gray
Ball State University
Muncie, Indiana

P. Allen Gray, Jr.
University North Carolina at
    Wilmington
Wilmington, North Carolina

Darielle Greenberg
California School of Professional
    Psychology
San Diego, California

Jacques Grégoire
Catholic University of Louvain
Louvain, Belgium

Laurence C. Grimm
University of Illinois
Chicago, Illinois

Lindsay S. Gross
University of Wisconsin
Milwaukee, Wisconsin

Suzanne M. Grundy
California State University, San
    Bernardino
San Bernardino, California

Nonna Guerra
Texas A&M University
College Station, Texas

John Guidubaldi
Kent State University
Kent, Ohio

J. C. Guillemard
Dourdan, France

Deborah Guillen
The University of Texas of the
    Permian Basin
Odessa, Texas

Steven Gumerman
Temple University
Philadelphia, Pennsylvania

Thomas Gumpel
The Hebrew University of Jerusalem
Jerusalem, Israel

Rumki Gupta
Indian Statistical Institute
Kolkata, India

Terry B. Gutkin
University of Nebraska–Lincoln
Lincoln, Nebraska

Patricia A. Haensly
Texas A&M University
College Station, Texas

George James Hagerty
Stonehill College
North Easton, Massachusetts

Robert Hall
Texas A&M University
College Station, Texas

Winnifred M. Hall
University of West Indies
Kingston, Jamaica

Lindsay Halliday
California State University, San
    Bernardino
San Bernardino, California

Richard E. Halmstad
University of Wisconsin at Stout
Menomonie, Wisconsin

Glennelle Halpin
Auburn University
Auburn, Alabama

Donald D. Hammill
PRO-ED, Inc.
Austin, Texas

Monika Hannon
Colorado Springs, Colorado

Harold Hanson
Southern Illinois University
Carbondale, Illinois

Elise Phelps Hanzel
California School of Professional
    Psychology
San Diego, California

Jennifer Harman
University of Florida
Gainesville, Florida

Janice Harper
North Carolina Central University
Durham, North Carolina

Gale A. Harr
Maple Heights City Schools
Maple Heights, Ohio

Karen L. Harrell
University of Georgia
Athens, Georgia

Frances T. Harrington
Radford University
Blacksburg, Virginia

Karen R. Harris
University of Maryland
College Park, Maryland

Kathleen Harris
Arizona State University
Tempe, Arizona

Patti L. Harrison
University of Alabama
Tuscaloosa, Alabama

Beth Harry
University of Miami
Miami, Florida

Stuart N. Hart
University of Victoria
Victoria, British Columbia, Canada

Lawrence C. Hartlage
Evans, Georgia

Patricia Hartlage
Medical College of Georgia
Evans, Georgia

Dan Hatt
University of Oklahoma
Norman, Oklahoma

Anette Hausotter
Bis Beratungsstelle Fur Die
    Intergration
Germany

Leanne S. Hawken
University of Utah
Salt Lake City, Utah

Krista D. Healy
University of California, Riverside
Riverside, California

Jeff Heinzen
Indianhead Enterprise
Menomonie, Wisconsin

Floyd Henderson
Texas A&M University
College Station, Texas

Rhonda Hennis
University of North Carolina at
    Wilmington
Wilmington, North Carolina

Latanya Henry
Texas A&M University
College Station, Texas

Arthur Hernandez
Texas A&M University
College Station, Texas

E. Valerie Hewitt
Texas A&M University
College Station, Texas

Julia A. Hickman
Bastrop Mental Health Association
Bastrop, Texas

Craig S. Higgins
Stonehill College
North Easton, Massachusetts

Alan Hilton
Seattle University
Seattle, Washington

Delores J. Hittinger
The University of Texas of the
    Permian Basin
Odessa, Texas

Harold E. Hoff, Jr.
Eastern Pennsylvania Special
    Education Resources Center
King of Prussia, Pennsylvania

Elizabeth Holcomb
*American Journal of Occupational
    Therapy*
Bethesda, Maryland

E. Wayne Holden
University of Oklahoma Health
    Sciences Center
Norman, Oklahoma

Ivan Z. Holowinsky
Rutgers University
New Brunswick, New Jersey

Thomas F. Hopkins
Center for Behavioral Psychotherapy
White Plains, New York

Robert H. Horner
University of Oregon
Eugene, Oregon

Wayne P. Hresko
Journal of Learning Disabilities
Austin, Texas

Charles A. Hughes
Pennsylvania State University
University Park, Pennsylvania

Jan N. Hughes
Texas A&M University
College Station, Texas

Kay E. Hughes
The Riverside Publishing Company
Itasca, Illinois

Aimee R. Hunter
University of North Carolina at
    Wilmington
Wilmington, North Carolina

Nancy L. Hutchinson
Simon Fraser University
Buraby, British Columbia

Beverly J. Irby
Sam Houston State University
Huntsville, Texas

Paul Irvine
Katonah, New York

Lee Anderson Jackson, Jr.
University of North Carolina at
    Wilmington
Wilmington, North Carolina

Elisabeth Jacobsen
Copenhagen, Denmark

Markku Jahnukainen
University of Helsinki
Finland

Diane Jarvis
State University of New York at
    Buffalo
Buffalo, New York

Phillip Jenkins
University of Kentucky
Lexington, Kentucky

Jacqueline Jere
University of Zambia
Lusaka, Zambia

Olga Jerman
University of California, Riverside
Riverside, California

Brian Johnson
University of Northern Colorado
Greeley, Colorado

Elizabeth Jones
Texas A&M University
College Station, Texas

Gideon Jones
Florida State University
Tallahassee, Florida

Philip R. Jones
Virginia Polytechnic Institute and
    State University
Blacksburg, Virginia

Shirley A. Jones
Virginia Polytechnic Institute and
    State University
Blacksburg, Virginia

Diana Joyce
University of Florida
Gainesville, Florida

Araksia Kaladjian
University of California, Riverside
Riverside, California

James W. Kalat
North Carolina State University
Raleigh, North Carolina

Maya Kalyanpur
Towson University
Towson, Maryland

Randy W. Kamphaus
University of Georgia
Athens, Georgia

Harrison Kane
University of Florida
Gainesville, Florida

Stan A. Karcz
University of Wisconsin at Stout
Menomonie, Wisconsin

Maribeth Montgomery Kasik
Governors State University
University Park, Illinois

Jen Katz-Buonincontro
University of Oregon
Eugene, Oregon

Alan S. Kaufman
Yale University School of Medicine
New Haven, Connecticut

James C. Kaufman
California State University, San
    Bernardino
San Bernardino, California

Nancy J. Kaufman
University of Wisconsin at Stevens
    Point
Stevens Point, Wisconsin

Scott Barry Kaufman
Yale University
New Haven, Connecticut

Kenneth A. Kavale
Regent University
Virginia Beach, Virginia

Hortencia Kayser
New Mexico State University
Las Cruces, New Mexico

Forrest E. Keesbury
Lycoming College
Williamsport, Pennsylvania

Barbara Keogh
University of California, Los Angeles
Los Angeles, California

Leanne Ketterlin-Gellar
University of Oregon
Eugene, Oregon

Kay E. Ketzenberger
The University of Texas of the
    Permian Basin
Odessa, Texas

Eve Kikas
University of Tartu
Tartu, Estonia

Peggy Kipping
PRO-ED, Inc.
Austin, Texas

Gonul Kircaali-Iftar
Anadolu University
Turkey

Bob Kirchner
University of Northern Colorado
Greeley, Colorado

Margie K. Kitano
New Mexico State University
Las Cruces, New Mexico

Howard M. Knoff
University of South Florida
Tampa, Florida

Tim Knoster
Bloomsburg University
Bloomsburg, Pennsylvania

Brandi Kocian
Texas A&M University
College Station, Texas

F. J. Koopmans-Van Beinum
Amsterdam, The Netherlands

Mark A. Koorland
Florida State University
Tallahassee, Florida

Peter Kopriva
Fresno Pacific University
Fresno, California

L. Koulischer
Institut de Morphologie
    Pathologique
Belgium

Martin Kozloff
University of North Carolina at
    Wilmington
Wilmington, North Carolina

Thomas R. Kratochwill
University of Wisconsin at Madison
Madison, Wisconsin

James P. Krouse
Clarion University of Pennsylvania
Clarion, Pennsylvania

Louis J. Kruger
Tufts University
Medford, Pennsylvania

Miranda Kucera
University of Colorado at Colorado
   Springs
Colorado Springs, Colorado

Loni Kuhn
University of Utah
Salt Lake City, Utah

Timothy D. Lackaye
Hunter College, City University of
   New York
New York, New York

Shui-fong Lam
The University of Hong Kong
Hong Kong, China

C. Sue Lamb
University of North Carolina at
   Wilmington
Wilmington, North Carolina

Gordon D. Lamb
Texas A&M University
College Station, Texas

Nadine M. Lambert
University of California, Berkeley
Berkeley, California

Louis J. Lanunziata
University of North Carolina at
   Wilmington
Wilmington, North Carolina

Rafael Lara-Alecio
Texas A&M University
College Station, Texas

Franco Larocca
The University of Verona
Verona, Italy

Kerry S. Lassiter
The Citadel
Charleston, South Carolina

Jeff Laurent
University of Texas
Austin, Texas

Mark M. Leach
University of Southern Mississippi
Hattiesburg, Mississippi

Samuel LeBaron
University of Texas Health Science
   Center
San Antonio, Texas

Yvan Lebrun
School of Medicine
Brussels, Belgium

Jillian N. Lederhouse
Wheaton College
Sycamore, Illinois

Linda Leeper
New Mexico State University
Las Cruces, New Mexico

Ronald S. Lenkowsky
Hunter College, City University of
   New York
New York, New York

Mary Louise Lennon
Educational Testing Service
Princeton, New Jersey

Carmen Léon
Andrés Bello Catholic University
Caracas, Venezuela

Richard Levak
California School of Professional
   Psychology
San Diego, California

Allison Lewis
University of North Carolina at
   Wilmington
Wilmington, North Carolina

Collette Leyva
Texas A&M University
College Station, Texas

Elizabeth O. Lichtenberger
The Salk Institute
La Jolla, California

Ping Lin
Elmhurst College
Elmhurst, Illinois

Janet A. Lindow
University of Wisconsin at Madison
Madison, Wisconsin

Ken Linfoot
University of Western Sydney
Sydney, Australia

Daniel D. Lipka
Lincoln Way Special Education
   Regional Resources Center
Louisville, Ohio

Cornelia Lively
University of Illinois, Urbana-
   Champaign
Champaign, Illinois

Lisa A. Lockwood
Texas A&M University
College Station, Texas

Jeri Logemann
Northwestern University
Evanston, Illinois

Charles J. Long
University of Memphis
Memphis, Tennessee

Linda R. Longley
University of North Carolina at
   Wilmington
Wilmington, North Carolina

Emilia C. Lopez
Fordham University
New York, New York

Esmerelda Lopez
Texas A&M University
College Station, Texas

Patricia A. Lowe
University of Kansas
Lawrence, Kansas

Michael T. Lucas
California State University, San
   Bernardino
San Bernardino, California

Marsha H. Lupi
Hunter College, City University of
   New York
New York, New York

Ann E. Lupkowski
Texas A&M University
College Station, Texas

Pat Lynch
Texas A&M University
College Station, Texas

Loleta Lynch-Gustafson
California State University, San
Bernardino
San Bernardino, California

Philip E. Lyon
College of St. Rose
Albany, New York

James Lyons
University of California, Riverside
Riverside, California

John W. Maag
University of Nebraska–Lincoln
Lincoln, Nebraska

Charles A. MacArthur
University of Maryland
College Park, Maryland

John MacDonald
Eastern Kentucky University
Richmond, Kentucky

Taddy Maddox
PRO-ED, Inc.
Austin, Texas

Danielle Madera
University of Florida
Gainesville, Florida

Ghislain Magerotte
Mons State University
Mons, Belgium

Susan Mahanna-Boden
Eastern Kentucky University
Richmond, Kentucky

Charles A. Maher
Rutgers University
Piscataway, New Jersey

Elba Maldonado-Colon
San Jose State University
San Jose, California

David C. Mann
St. Francis Hospital
Pittsburgh, Pennsylvania

Douglas L. Mann
V. A. Medical Center, Medical
University of South Carolina
Charleston, South Carolina

Lester Mann
Hunter College, City University of
New York
New York, New York

Donald S. Marozas
State University of New York at
Geneseo
Geneseo, New York

Ellen B. Marriott
University of North Carolina at
Wilmington
Wilmington, North Carolina

James E. Martin
University of Oklahoma
Norman, Oklahoma

Tamara J. Martin
The University of Texas of the
Permian Basin
Odessa, Texas

Patrick Mason
The Hughes Spalding International
Adoption Evaluation Center
Atlanta, Georgia

Margo A. Mastropieri
Purdue University
West Lafayette, Indiana

Deborah C. May
State University of New York at
Albany
Albany, New York

Joan W. Mayfield
Baylor Pediatric Specialty Service
Dallas, Texas

Liliana Mayo
Centro Ann Sullivan
Lima, Peru

James K. McAfee
Pennsylvania State University
University Park, Pennsylvania

Eileen F. McCarthy
University of Wisconsin at Madison
Madison, Wisconsin

Elizabeth McClellan
Council for Exceptional Children
Reston, Virginia

Dalene M. McCloskey
University of Northern Colorado
Greeley, Colorado

George McCloskey
Philadelphia College of Osteopathic
Medicine
Philadelphia, Pennsylvania

Laura S. McCorkle
Texas A&M University
College Station, Texas

Linda McCormick
University of Hawaii, Manoa
Honolulu, Hawaii

Paul A. McDermott
University of Pennsylvania
Philadelphia, Pennsylvania

Kevin S. McGrew
St. Joseph, Minnesota

Phillip J. McLaughlin
University of Georgia
Athens, Georgia

James A. McLoughlin
University of Louisville
Louisville, Kentucky

James K. McMee
Pennsylvania State University
King of Prussia, Pennsylvania

Paolo Meazzini
University of Rome
Rome, Italy

Frederic J. Medway
University of South Carolina
Columbia, South Carolina

Brenda Melvin
New Hanover Regional Medical
Center
Wilmington, North Carolina

Marissa I. Mendoza
Texas A&M University
College Station, Texas

James F. Merritt
University of North Carolina
Wilmington, North Carolina

Judith Meyers
San Diego, California

Danielle Michaux
Vrije Universiteit Brussel
Brussels, Belgium

Jennifer Might
University of North Carolina
Wilmington, North Carolina

Stephen E. Miles
Immune Deficiency Foundation
Towson, Maryland

Susie Miles
University of Manchester
Manchester, England

James H. Miller
University of New Orleans
New Orleans, Louisiana

Kevin Miller
University of Central Florida
Orlando, Florida

Ted L. Miller
University of Tennessee
Chattanooga, Tennessee

Norris Minick
Center for Psychosocial Studies
The Spencer Foundation
Chicago, Illinois

Anjali Misra
State University of New York
Potsdam, New York

Andrew A. Mogaji
University of Lagos
Lagos, Nigeria

Lisa Monda
Florida State University
Tallahassee, Florida

Lourdes Montenegro
Andrés Bello Catholic University
Caracas, Venezuela

Judy K. Montgomery
Chapman University
Irvine, California

Linda Montgomery
The University of Texas of the
    Permian Basin
Odessa, Texas

Hadley Moore
University of Massachusetts
Boston, Massachusetts

Melanie Moore
University of North Carolina at
    Wilmington
Wilmington, North Carolina

Luis Benites Morales
Universidad San Martin de Porres
Lima, Peru

Marianela Moreno
Andrés Bello Catholic University
Caracas, Venzuela

Richard J. Morris
University of Arizona
Tucson, Arizona

Lonny W. Morrow
Northeast Missouri State University
Kirksville, Missouri

Sue Ann Morrow
EDGE, Inc.
Bradshaw, Michigan

Elias Mpofu
Pennsylvania State University
Harrisburg, Pennsylvania

Tracy Muenz
Alliant International University
San Diego, California

Mary Murray
Journal of Special Education
Ben Salem, Pennsylvania

Gladiola Musabelliu
University of Tirana
Tirana, Albania

Magen M. Mutepfa
Zimbabwe Schools Special Services
    and Special Education Department
Zimbabwe

Jack Naglieri
The Ohio State University
Columbus, Ohio

Sigamoney Naicker
Western Cape Educational SI
    Department
South Africa

Michael Nall
Louisville, Kentucky

Nicole Nasewicz
University of Florida
Gainesville, Florida

Robert T. Nash
University of Wisconsin at Oshkosh
Oshkosh, Wisconsin

Bonnie K. Nastasi
Kent State University
Kent, Ohio

Cameron L. Neece
University of California, Los Angeles
Los Angeles, California

Thomas Neises
California State University, San
    Bernardino
San Bernardino, California

Joyce E. Ness
Montgomery County Intermediate
    Unit
Norristown, Pennsylvania

Ulrika Nettelbladt
University of Lund
Lund, Sweden

Robert C. Nichols
State University of New York at
    Buffalo
Buffalo, New York

Etta Lee Nurick
Montgomery County Intermediate
    Unit
Norristown, Pennsylvania

Christopher Oakland
New York City, New York

Thomas Oakland
University of Florida
Gainesville, Florida

Festus E. Obiakor
Emporia State University
Nigeria

Hector Salvia Ochoa
Texas A&M University
College Station, Texas

Joy O'Grady
University of Memphis
Memphis, Tennessee

Masataka Ohta
Tokyo Gakujei University
Tokyo, Japan

John O'Neill
Hunter College, City University of
New York
New York, New York

Robert O'Neill
University of Utah
Salt Lake City, Utah

Alba Ortiz
University of Texas
Austin, Texas

Samuel O. Ortiz
St. John's University
Jamaica, New York

Andrew Oseroff
Florida State University
Tallahassee, Florida

Lawrence J. O'Shea
University of Florida
Gainesville, Florida

Marika Padrik
University of Tartu
Tartu, Estonia

Doris Paez
New Mexico State University
Las Cruces, New Mexico

Ellis B. Page
Duke University
Durham, North Carolina

Kathleen D. Paget
University of South Carolina
Columbia, South Carolina

Douglas J. Palmer
Texas A&M University
College Station, Texas

Hagop S. Pambookian
Elizabeth City, North Carolina

Ernest L. Pancsofar
University of Connecticut
Storrs, Connecticut

Sara Pankaskie
Florida State University
Tallahassee, Florida

Linda H. Parrish
Texas A&M University
College Station, Texas

Daniel R. Paulson
University of Wisconsin at Stout
Menomonie, Wisconsin

Nils A. Pearson
PRO-ED, Inc.
Austin, Texas

Mary Leon Peery
Texas A&M University
College Station, Texas

Kathleen Pelham-Odor
California State University, San
Bernardino
San Bernardino, California

Shelley L. F. Pelletier
Dysart Unified School District
El Mirage, Arizona

Michelle Perfect
University of Texas
Austin, Texas

Olivier Périer
Université Libre de Bruxelles
Centre Comprendre et Parler
Brussels, Belgium

Joseph D. Perry
Kent State University
Kent, Ohio

Richard G. Peters
Ball State University
Muncie, Indiana

Faith L. Phillips
University of Oklahoma Health
Sciences Center
Norman, Oklahoma

Jeffry L. Phillips
University of North Carolina at
Wilmington
Wilmington, North Carolina

Kathleen M. Phillips
University of California, Riverside
Riverside, California

Lindsey A. Phillips
University of Utah
Salt Lake City, Utah

Yongxin Piao
Beijing Normal University
Beijing, China

Sip Jan Pijl
Gion University of Groningen
Groningen, The Netherlands

John J. Pikulski
University of Delaware
Newark, Delaware

Sally E. Pisarchick
Cuyahoga Special Education Service
Center
Maple Heights, Ohio

Brenda M. Pope
New Hanover Memorial Hospital
Wilmington, North Carolina

John E. Porcella
Rhinebeck County School
Rhinebeck, New York

James A. Poteet
Ball State University
Muncie, Indiana

Michelle W. Potter
University of California, Riverside
Riverside, California

Shawn Powell
United States Air Force Academy
Colorado Springs, Colorado

Kristiana Powers
California State University, San
    Bernardino
San Bernardino, California

David P. Prasse
University of Wisconsin
Milwaukee, Wisconsin

Jennifer Dawn Pretorius
Vaal University of Technology
South Africa

Marianne Price
Montgomery County Intermediate
    Unit
Norristown, Pennsylvania

Elisabeth A. Prinz
Pennsylvania State University
University Park, Pennsylvania

Philip M. Prinz
Pennsylvania State University
University Park, Pennsylvania

Antonio E. Puente
University of North Carolina at
    Wilmington
Wilmington, North Carolina

Krista L. Puente
University of North Carolina at
    Wilmington
Wilmington, North Carolina

Nuri Puig
University of Oklahoma
Norman, Oklahoma

Elizabeth P. Pungello
University of North Carolina at
    Chapel Hill
Chapel Hill, North Carolina

Shahid Waheed Qamar
Lahore, Pakistan

Jennifer M. Raad
University of Kansas
Lawrence, Kansas

Linda Radbill
University of Florida
Gainesville, Florida

Paige B. Raetz
Western Michigan University
Kalamazoo, Michigan

Katrina Raia
University of Florida
Gainesville, Florida

Craig T. Ramey
University of North Carolina at
    Chapel Hill
Chapel Hill, North Carolina

Sylvia Z. Ramirez
University of Texas
Austin, Texas

Noe Ramos
Texas A&M University
College Station, Texas

Arlene I. Rattan
Ball State University
Muncie, Indiana

Gurmal Rattan
Indiana University of Pennsylvania
Indiana, Pennsylvania

Anne Reber
Texas A&M University
College Station, Texas

Robert R. Reilley
Texas A&M University
College Station, Texas

Fredricka K. Reisman
Drexel University
Philadelphia, Pennsylvania

Kimberly M. Rennie
Texas A&M University
College Station, Texas

Daniel J. Reschly
Peabody College, Vanderbilt
    University
Nashville, Tennessee

Cecil R. Reynolds
Texas A&M University
College Station, Texas

Robert L. Rhodes
New Mexico State University
Las Cruces, New Mexico

William S. Rholes
Texas A&M University
College Station, Texas

Cynthia A. Riccio
Texas A&M University
College Station, Texas

James R. Ricciuti
United States Office of Management
    and Budget
Washington, DC

Teresa K. Rice
Texas A&M University
College Station, Texas

Paul C. Richardson
Elwyn Institutes
Elwyn, Pennsylvania

Sylvia O. Richardson
University of South Florida
Tampa, Florida

Pamela M. Richman
University of North Carolina at
    Wilmington
Wilmington, North Carolina

Bert O. Richmond
University of Georgia
Athens, Georgia

Richard Rider
University of Utah
Salt Lake City, Utah

Michelle Ries
University of Memphis
Memphis, Tennessee

Catherine Hall Rikhye
Hunter College, City University of
    New York
New York, New York

T. Chris Riley-Tillman
East Carolina University
Greenville, North Carolina

Selina Rivera-Longoria
Texas A&M University
College Station, Texas

Gary J. Robertson
American Guidance Service
Circle Pines, Minnesota

Kathleen Rodden-Nord
University of Oregon
Eugene, Oregon

Olga L. Rodriguez-Escobar
Texas A&M University
College Station, Texas

Jean A. Rondal
University of Liege
Liege, Belgium

Sheldon Rosenberg
University of Illinois
Chicago, Illinois

Bruce P. Rosenthal
State University of New York
New York, New York

Eric Rossen
University of Florida
Gainesville, Florida

Beth Rous
University of Kentucky Human
   Development Institute
Lexington, Kentucky

Amy Loomis Roux
University of Florida
Gainesville, Florida

Kathy L. Ruhl
Pennsylvania State University
University Park, Pennsylvania

Joseph M. Russo
Hunter College, City University of
   New York
New York, New York

Robert B. Rutherford, Jr.
Arizona State University
Tempe, Arizona

Kim Ryan-Arredondo
Texas A&M University
College Station, Texas

Anne Sabatino
Hudson, Wisconsin

David A. Sabatino
West Virginia College of Graduate
   Studies
Institute, West Virginia

Susan Sage
Dysart Unified School District
El Mirage, Arizona

Monir Saleh
Beheshti University
Tehran, Iran

Lisa J. Sampson
Eastern Kentucky University
Richmond, Kentucky

Alfred Sander
Universitat des Saarlandes
Saarbruecken, Germany

Tiffany D. Sanders
University of Florida
Gainesville, Florida

Polly E. Sanderson
Research Triangle Institute
Research Triangle Park, North
   Carolina

Scott W. Sautter
Peabody College, Vanderbilt
   University
Nashville, Tennessee

Robert F. Sawicki
Lake Erie Institute of Rehabilitation
Lake Erie, Pennsylvania

Patrick J. Schloss
Pennsylvania State University
University Park, Pennsylvania

Ronald V. Schmelzer
Eastern Kentucky University
Richmond, Kentucky

Carol S. Schmitt
Eastern Kentucky University
Richmond, Kentucky

Sue A. Schmitt
University of Wisconsin at Stout
Menomonie, Wisconsin

Lyle F. Schoenfeldt
Texas A&M University
College Station, Texas

Jacqueline S. Schon
University of Kansas
Lawrence, Kansas

Eric Schopler
University of North Carolina at
   Chapel Hill
Chapel Hill, North Carolina

Fredrick A. Schrank
Olympia, Washington

Louis Schwartz
Florida State University
Tallahassee, Florida

Adam J. Schwebach
University of Utah
Salt Lake City, Utah

Krista Schwenk
University of Florida
Gainesville, Florida

June Scobee
University of Houston, Clear Lake
Houston, Texas

Thomas E. Scruggs
Purdue University
West Lafayette, Indiana

Denise M. Sedlak
United Way of Dunn County
Menomonie, Wisconsin

Robert A. Sedlak
University of Wisconsin at Stout
Menomome, Wisconsin

Katherine D. Seelman
University of Pittsburgh
Pittsburgh, Pennsylvania

John D. See
University of Wisconsin at Stout
Menomonie, Wisconsin

Sandra B. Sexson
Emory University School of Medicine
Atlanta, Georgia

Susan Shandelmier
Eastern Pennsylvania Special
    Education Regional Resources
    Center
King of Prussia, Pennsylvania

Alison Shaner
University of North Carolina at
    Wilmington
Wilmington, North Carolina

Deborah A. Shanley
Medgar Evers College, City
    University of New York
New York, New York

William J. Shaw
University of Oklahoma
Norman, Oklahoma

Susan M. Sheridan
University of Wisconsin at Madison
Madison, Wisconsin

Naoji Shimizu
Tokyo Gakujei University
Tokyo, Japan

Ludmila Shipitsina
International University for Family
    and Child
Russia

Edward A. Shirkey
New Mexico State University
Las Cruces, New Mexico

Gerald L. Shook
Behavior Analyst Certification Board
Tallahassee, Florida

Dakum Shown
University of Jos
Jos, Nigeria

Almon Shumba
University of KwaZulu-Natal
South Africa

Lawrence J. Siegel
University of Texas Medical Branch
Galveston, Texas

Rosanne K. Silberman
Hunter College, City University of
    New York
New York, New York

Brandi Simonsen
University of Connecticut
Storrs, Connecticut

Lissen Simonsen
University of North Carolina at
    Wilmington
Wilmington, North Carolina

Paul T. Sindelar
Florida State University
Tallahassee, Florida

Jennie Kaufman Singer
California Department of
    Corrections, Region 1 Parole
    Outpatient Clinic
Sacramento, California

Jerry L. Sloan
Wilmington Psychiatric Associates
Wilmington, North Carolina

Julie E. Smart
Utah State University
Logan, Utah

Craig D. Smith
Georgia College
Milledgeville, Georgia

E. S. Smith
University of Dundee
Dundee, Scotland

Maureen A. Smith
Pennsylvania State University
University Park, Pennsylvania

Judy Smith-Davis
Counterpoint Communications
    Company
Reno, Nevada

Latha V. Soorya
Binghamton University
The Institute for Child Development
Binghamton, New York

Cesar Merino Soto
University Privada San Juan
    Bautista
Lima, Peru

Jane Sparks
University of North Carolina at
    Wilmington
Wilmington, North Carolina

Barbara S. Speer
Shaker Heights City School District
Shaker Heights, Ohio

Harrison C. Stanton
Las Vegas, Nevada

Shari A. Stanton
Las Vegas, Nevada

J. Todd Stephens
University of Wisconsin at Madison
Madison, Wisconsin

Bernie Stein
Tel Aviv, Israel

Cecelia Steppe-Jones
North Carolina Central University
Durham, North Carolina

Linda J. Stevens
University of Minnesota
Minneapolis, Minnesota

Rachael J. Stevenson
Bedford, Ohio

Mary E. Stinson
University of Alabama
Tuscaloosa, Alabama

Roberta C. Stokes
Texas A&M University
College Station, Texas

Doretha McKnight Stone
University of North Carolina at
    Wilmington
Wilmington, North Carolina

Eric A. Storch
University of Florida
Gainesville, Florida

Laura M. Stough
Texas A&M University
College Station, Texas

Michael L. Stowe
Texas A&M University
College Station, Texas

Edythe A. Strand
University of Wisconsin at Madison
Madison, Wisconsin

Elaine Stringer
University of North Carolina at
  Wilmington
Wilmington, North Carolina

Dorothy A. Strom
Ball State University
Indiana University School of
  Medicine
Muncie, Indiana

Sheela Stuart
Georgia Washington University
Washington, DC

Sue Stubbs
Save the Children Fund
London, England

George Sugai
University of Connecticut
Storrs, Connecticut

Jeremy R. Sullivan
University of Texas at San Antonio
San Antonio, Texas

Kathryn A. Sullivan
Branson School Online
Branson, Colorado

Shelley Suntup
California School of Professional
  Psychology
San Diego, California

Emily G. Sutter
University of Houston, Clear Lake
Houston, Texas

Lana Svien-Senne
University of South Dakota
Vermillion, South Dakota

H. Lee Swanson
University of California, Riverside
Riverside, California

David Sweeney
Texas A&M University
College Station, Texas

Mark E. Swerdlik
Illinois State University
Normal, Illinois

Thomas G. Szabo
Western Michigan University
Kalamazoo, Michigan

Henri B. Szliwowski
Hôpital Erasme, Université Libre de
  Bruxelles
Brussels, Belgium

Pearl E. Tait
Florida State University
Tallahassee, Florida

Paula Tallal
University of California, San Diego
San Diego, California

Mary K. Tallent
Texas Tech University
Lubbock, Texas

C. Mildred Tashman
College of St. Rose
Albany, New York

James W. Tawney
Pennsylvania State University
University Park, Pennsylvania

Joseph R. Taylor
Fresno Pacific University
Fresno, California

Therese Tchombe
University of Yaounde 1
Cameroon

Ellen A. Teelucksingh
University of Minnesota
Minneapolis, Minnesota

Tirussew Teferra
Addis Ababa University
Ethiopia

Cathy F. Telzrow
Kent State University
Kent, Ohio

Yolanda Tenorio
California State University, San
  Bernardino
San Bernardino, California

Carol Chase Thomas
University of North Carolina at
  Wilmington
Wilmington, North Carolina

Jo Thomason
Council of Administrators of Special
  Education
Fort Valley, Georgia

Bruce Thompson
Texas A&M University
College Station, Texas

Spencer Thompson
The University of Texas of the
  Permian Basin
Odessa, Texas

Sage Thornton
University of California, Riverside
Riverside, California

Eva Tideman
Lund University
Lund, Sweden

Steven R. Timmermans
Mary Free Bed Hospital and
  Rehabilitation Center
Grand Rapids, Michigan

Gerald Tindal
University of Oregon
Eugene, Oregon

Francine Tomkins
University of Cincinnati
Cincinnati, Ohio

Carol Tomlinson-Keasey
University of California, Riverside
Riverside, California

Rachel M. Toplis
Falcon School District 49
Colorado Springs, Colorado

Keith. J. Topping
University of Dundee
Dundee, Scotland

Raymond Toraille
Public Education
Paris, France

Jose Luis Torres
Texas A&M University
College Station, Texas

Stanley O. Trent
University of Virginia
Charlottesville, Virginia

David M. Tucker
Austin, Texas

Timothy L. Turco
Louisiana State University
Baton Rouge, Louisiana

Lori E. Unruh
Eastern Kentucky University
Richmond, Kentucky

Susan M. Unruh
University of Kansas
Wichita, Kansas

Marilyn Urquhart
University of South Dakota
Vermillion, South Dakota

Cynthia Vail
Florida State University
Tallahassee, Florida

Greg Valcante
University of Florida
Gainesville, Florida

Hubert B. Vance
East Tennessee State University
Johnson City, Tennessee

Aryan Van Der Leij
Free University
Amsterdam, The Netherlands

Heather S. Vandyke
Falcon School District 49
Colorado Springs, Colorado

K. Sandra Vanta
Cleveland Public Schools
Cleveland, Ohio

Rebeccas Vaurio
Austin, Texas

Don Viglione
California School of Professional
    Psychology
San Diego, California

Judith K. Voress
PRO-ED, Inc.
Austin, Texas

Emily Wahlen
Hunter College, City University of
    New York
New York, New York

Christy M. Walcott
East Carolina University
Greenville, North Carolina

Deborah Klein Walker
Harvard University
Cambridge, Massachusetts

Donna Wallace
The University of Texas of the
    Permian Basin
Odessa, Texas

Raoul Wallenberg
International University for Family
    and Child
Russia

Marjorie E. Ward
The Ohio State University
Columbus, Ohio

Nicole R. Warnygora
University of Northern Colorado
Greeley, Colorado

Sue Allen Warren
Boston University
Boston, Massachusetts

John Wasserman
The Riverside Publishing Company
Itasca, Illinois

Sharine Webber
Laramie County School District #1
Cheyenne, Wyoming

Lauren Webster
University of North Carolina at
    Wilmington
Wilmington, North Carolina

Danny Wedding
Marshall University
Huntington, Virginia

Frederick F. Weiner
Pennsylvania State University
University Park, Pennsylvania

Marjorie Weintraub
Montgomery County Intermediate Unit
Norristown, Pennsylvania

Bahr Weiss
University of North Carolina at
    Chapel Hill
Chapel Hill, North Carolina

Shirley Parker Wells
University of North Carolina at
    Wilmington
Wilmington, North Carolina

Louise H. Werth
Florida State University
Tallahassee, Florida

Catherine Wetzburger
Hôpital Erasme, Université Libre de
    Bruxelles
Brussels, Belgium

Jessi K. Wheatley
Falcon School District 49
Colorado Springs, Colorado

Larry J. Wheeler
Southwest Texas State University
San Marcos, Texas

Annika White
University of California, Riverside
Riverside, California

Susie Whitman
Immune Deficiency Foundation
Towson, Maryland

Thomas M. Whitten
Florida State University
Tallahassee, Florida

J. Lee Wiederholt
PRO-ED, Inc.
Austin, Texas

Lisa Wildmo
Bryan, Texas

Saul B. Wilen
Medical Horizons Unlimited
San Antonio, Texas

Greta N. Wilkening
Children's Hospital
Denver, Colorado

C. Williams
Falcon School District 49
Colorado Springs, Colorado

L. Williams
Falcon School District 49
Colorado Springs, Colorado

Mary Clare Williams
Ramey, Pennsylvania

Diane J. Willis
University of Oklahoma Health
Sciences Center
Oklahoma City, Oklahoma

John O. Willis
Rivier College
Nashua, New Hampshire

Victor L. Willson
Texas A&M University
College Station, Texas

John D. Wilson
Elwyn Institutes
Elwyn, Pennsylvania

Margo E. Wilson
Lexington, Kentucky

Kelly Winkels
University of Florida
Gainesville, Florida

Britt L. Winter
Western Michigan University
Kalamazoo, Michigan

Joseph C. Witt
Louisiana State University
Baton Rouge, Louisiana

Bencie Woll
University of Bristol
Bristol, England

Bernice Y. L. Wong
Simon Fraser University
Buraby, British Columbia

Mary M. Wood
University of Georgia
Athens, Georgia

Diane E. Woods
World Rehabilitation Fund
New York, New York

Lee L. Woods
University of Oklahoma
Norman, Oklahoma

Frances F. Worchel
Texas A&M University
College Station, Texas

Patricia Work
University of South Dakota
Vermillion, South Dakota

Eleanor Boyd Wright
University of North Carolina at
Wilmington
Wilmington, North Carolina

Logan Wright
University of Oklahoma
Norman, Oklahoma

Karen F. Wyche
Hunter College, City University of
New York
New York, New York

Martha Ellen Wynne
Loyola University, Chicago
Chicago, Illinois

James E. Ysseldyke
University of Minnesota
Minneapolis, Minnesota

Roland K. Yoshida
Fordham University
New York, New York

Thomas Zane
Johns Hopkins University
Baltimore, Maryland

Ronald Zellner
Texas A&M University
College Station, Texas

Lonnie K. Zeltzer
University of Texas Health Sciences
Center
San Antonio, Texas

Paul M. Zeltzer
University of Texas Health Sciences
Center
San Antonio, Texas

Xinhua Zheng
University of California, Riverside
Riverside, California

Walter A. Zilz
Bloomsburg University
Bloomsburg, Pennsylvania

Kenneth A. Zych
Walter Reed Army Medical Center
Washington, DC

PREFACE TO THE THIRD EDITION

It has been 20 years since we first set foot on the journey that has become the third edition of the *Encyclopedia of Special Education*. If someone has told us then that we would end up chronicling the evolution of special education, we probably would not have believed him or her. It was enough, at that time, to have created the first *Encyclopedia of Special Education;* nearly 2,000 pages, thousands of entries, and more than 400 authors coming together to cement this fledgling field that was full of hope and imagination.

So, here we are more than 20 years later, near the end of our guardianship of the *Encyclopedia.* It is our old friend, and it has been our mentor, our judge, and our inspiration. During the editing of the second and third editions, we are well aware of how life, research, and standards have changed for those of us who practice in special education. It is an interesting process to look back and see how the *Encyclopedia* has changed over the years and how it has really provided a mirror of the zeitgeist of the times in which we live.

The first edition was full of new ideas such as profile analysis, direct instruction, and terms such as "trainable" and "educable." The field had license to imagine and try ways to rewire the brain that was having trouble in school. Not so now! The third edition clearly marks the federal and state demands for evidence-based practices, perhaps reflecting the end of imagination and the beginning of an era of proof or accountability. Hence, we see behavioral terms and behavioral-oriented credentials enjoying resurgence because they allow for documentation of behaviors that are easy to observe. Accountability is a force to be noticed as it infiltrates and guides current practice.

The first edition was full of laws that were still new and somewhat unexplored: We were still trying to interpret Public Law 94-142! Now we have visited those laws, reauthorized (and revised) them many times, and joined them with support such as the ADA and Technology acts. Individuals with disabilities have never enjoyed the protections of as many laws and regulations as we have today. There are also so many more consumer protection groups and organizations around today that fight for the rights of those who have disabilities. In fact, current beliefs about advocacy are also focusing on assisting full participation by the individual with the disability in planning and transitions. Years ago, parents got together and had to forge an organization and eventually laws that gave their children the right to an appropriate education. Their voices were heard and their legacy has been grand indeed as we see the very same children advocating for themselves.

The advocacy network that surrounds special education students today is vast, connected, and accessible. The Internet has exponentially changed the individual's abilities to learn about support organizations and to reach out to others who have similar concerns and conditions. This movement is not just on a national level, the World Health Organization is rallying the international community to connect the daily living experiences of individuals with disabilities in the *International Classification of Functioning, Disability, and Health.* This classification system was designed to describe the *individual* with a disability, not just to classify the disability itself. Indeed, we remember that in the first edition of the *Encyclopedia,* it was acceptable to label individuals via the disability; therefore, individuals with Schizophrenia were schizophrenics and individuals with Mental Retardation were the mentally retarded. The disability came first and the individual came second. In the second edition of the *Encyclopedia,* we remember stressing heavily with all of our editors and authors that all language referring to clinical populations would have to reflect the individual first and his or her handicapping condition second. This was a major literary turn at the time!

Many years ago, special education students were all too often relegated to isolated classrooms in secluded areas of school buildings. Not so now. The third edition (and somewhat in the second edition) of the *Encyclopedia* fully reflects that concepts such as "mainstreaming" are now archaic. Inclusion is the rule unless it is not in the best interests of the student. Disability and ability now live side by side. Humanness is central and our similarities outweigh our differences, even in special education.

The three editions of the *Encyclopedia* have also reflected the evolution of test construction and interpretation. The level of psychometric design is outstanding right now. Consumers have come to enjoy new tests that have specificity, such as tests about executive functions, trauma, study skills, and so on. The major broadband assessment batteries that measure cognitive abilities and psychological constructs are excellent, theory-based measures that have imaginative and careful design. Therefore, our ability to include well-designed tools in the assessment process has never been better. The third edition of the *Encyclopedia* catalogues many new tests and revisions of old and true instruments.

The demand for "countable" accountability of special education outcomes is upon these days. For the past 20 years, the *Encyclopedia* reflected exploration, and now exploration is passé and counting and demanding results is the zeitgeist of the times. Renegades as we are, we have included more and more neuropsychological principles and terms into the various editions of the *Encyclopedia* as we have paid homage to the vast mystery of the human brain and personality that will most likely never be reduced down to accountable facts. Herein lies the rub for those with interests in brain-behavior relationships, the very thing that we seek is unattainable and therein provides continuous wonder, curiosity, and frustration! We are confident that the most important aspect of future research that seeks to improve the daily lives of children with disabilities lies in the study of the brain and its relationship to learning and daily living skills. This process will always be a study of one, and not given to group statistics. Therefore, regardless of the political zeitgeist, we have expressed our desire to support clinical excellence throughout the third edition of the *Encyclopedia* and minimize old ideas that have been parceled out as new and redesigned to fit ends that are not apolitical. The original *Encyclopedia* was bursting with curiosity and wonder about a new field. We wish to maintain this tribute in the current edition and support the continued innocence of true scientific exploration.

So, what is new in the third edition of the *Encyclopedia*? Very little information these days is entirely new; however, there are some entries that reflect a resurgence or future directions, such as Response to Intervention, Highly Qualified Teachers, Diffusion Tensor Imaging, and Positive Behavior Supports. Tom Oakland, our "International Special Education entries" Contributing Editor provided us with many entries from new areas of the world such as Estonia, Albania, sub-Saharan Africa, and other exciting places reflecting his expertise in international special education and the trend of professionals to think more globally these days.

All of the laws and legal entries were completely and competently updated by our Contributing Editor, Kimberly Applequist, JD. The final regulations for the Individuals with Disabilities Education Improvement Act of 2004 are not out at this time and so the exact nature of the guidelines is not known, but we look forward to seeing how they take shape. Randall DePry updated many entries related to teaching and behavioral supports and provided new entries on the exacting process of applied behavior analysis. Lee Swanson focused on entries pertaining to the latest developments in reading and reading remediation. These entries will provide the reader with the most up-to-date information on a topic that is being urgently stressed all over the United States at this time. His expertise is very evident in these entries.

Rachel Toplis spent many hours updating information on organizations and journals so the readers will be able to get current information that they can apply immediately. She also wrote to all of the biographees and asked what they had been up to for the past few years. It was nice to have contact with them again.

Ron Zellner and Cynthia Riccio were Contributing Editors hailing from Texas A&M University who provided us with current information on technology, assistive, devices, and current trends in special education guidelines. Contributing Editor Sam Goldstein brought us up to date on the latest imaging devices that are assisting in the investigation of autism spectrum disorders, reading interventions, and learning in general. In addition, James Kaufman had a very creative time refreshing entries on theories of creativity and intelligence; the reader will enjoy his unique perspectives on these topics. Last but not least, the Drs. Ron Dumont and John Willis provided a completely new thread of reviews of standardized assessments throughout the *Encyclopedia*; their expertise in assessment reviews are legendary and we are please to have them as part of our effort.

Please allow us to apologize to our authors if their affiliations or names have changed over the past 20 years and the most recent changes are not incorporated into the third edition. We have tried to keep up with the changes but are sure that we have missed a few and promise to remediate in future editions! We also had to make editorial decisions about giving credit where credit was due for updates of entries. Therefore, the reader will notice that we have taken painstaking efforts to list the authors and to which editions they contributed. In some cases, an entry needed some tiny editing and in that case, Cecil and Elaine took tiny liberties and corrected dates or added a current reference here and there. We, again, apologize if our tiny contributions were bigger than the author would wish. In most of these cases, the article was so well written it would have been a waste of time to try to rewrite.

There are, as usual, many individuals to thank for assisting with the creating and preparation of this volume of work. First, let us thank the contributing editors to the previous and current editions. These individuals took on the responsibilities of looking at where the field has been and where it is going in their respective areas of expertise. They then shepherded many authors into taking on smaller parts to reflect important aspects of the basics and documenting growth. Without their commitment and dedication, we would be bereft of hope for a renovation of this size of work! We would also like to thank the individual authors for their cheerful attitude and dedication to their contributions: They are representatives of the best the field has to offer and we are very grateful for their efforts.

Cecil would like to thank Julia, as he does so untiringly, for her support in so many ways, and his long-deceased Dad, who gave him the gift of a model of service. Elaine would like to take this opportunity to thank David, Emma, and Leif for putting up with her being obsessed one more time; and her father, Peter C. Fletcher, who has modeled insatiable curiosity and a love of life's work that will stay with her always.

Lastly, we would like to thank the editors at John Wiley & Sons, Inc., Tracey Belmont and Lisa Gebo for their supervision of the work, and publisher Peggy Alexander for making a lifetime commitment to this endeavor. What started as a description of the field of special education became a history of special education and a chronicle of its life and times. We have been honored to witness this process and, as always, look forward to future growth.

A

AAAS

See AMERICAN ASSOCIATION FOR THE ADVANCEMENT OF SCIENCE.

AAMR, AMERICAN ASSOCIATION ON MENTAL RETARDATION

The AAMR promotes progressive policies, sound research, effective practices, and universal human rights for people with intellectual and developmental disabilities. It has been a major force in recent years in shaping current beliefs about all aspects of Mental Retardation. In terms of AAMR's principles, it has adopted a 13-point set of principles to accomplish the mission:

- Achieving full societal inclusion and participation of people with intellectual and developmental disabilities
- Advocating for equality, individual dignity, and other human rights
- Expanding opportunities for choice and self-determination
- Influencing positive attitudes and public awareness by recognizing the contributions of people with intellectual disabilities
- Promoting genuine accommodations to expand participation in all aspects of life
- Aiding families and other caregivers to provide support in the community
- Increasing access to quality health, education, vocational, and other human services and supports
- Advancing basic and applied research to prevent or minimize the effects of intellectual disability and to enhance the quality of life
- Cultivating and providing leadership in the field
- Seeking a diversity of disciplines, cultures, and perspectives in our work
- Enhancing skills, knowledge, rewards, and conditions of people working in the field

- Encouraging promising students to pursue careers in the field of disabilities
- Establishing partnerships and strategic alliances with organizations that share our values and goals

The AAMR's goals specify how the general policy directions of the organization's mission will be carried out by (1) building association capacity, (2) building capacity to serve professionals who work with individuals with intellectual and developmental disabilities, and (3) building societal capacity. The AAMR can be reached online at http://www.aamr.org. It has an excellent web site for professionals, families, and individuals with Mental Retardation that promotes conferences, publications, policies, and other helpful sources of information.

STAFF

AAMR CLASSIFICATION SYSTEMS

Founded in 1876, the American Association on Mental Retardation (AAMR) is the world's oldest and largest interdisciplinary organization of professionals concerned about Mental Retardation. With headquarters in Washington, DC, the AAMR has a constituency of more than 50,000 people and an active core membership in the United States and in 55 other countries. The mission of the AAMR is to promote progressive policies, sound research, effective practices, and universal rights for people with intellectual disabilities. The AAMR has led the field of developmental disabilities by officially defining the condition known as *Mental Retardation*. A diagnostic and classification system remains important in today's society because it is used to determine who can access publicly funded services and supports.

The AAMR has updated the definition of *Mental Retardation* 10 times since 1908. Changes in the definition have occurred when there is new information, or there are changes in clinical practice or breakthroughs in scientific research. The 10th edition of *Mental Retardation: Definition, Classification, and Systems of Supports* (AAMR, 2002) contains a comprehensive update to the landmark 1992 system and provides important new information, tools, and strategies for the field and for anyone concerned about people with mental retardation. The 10th edition discusses the 2002 AAMR definition and classification system in great detail. It presents the latest thinking about Mental Retardation and includes important tools and strategies to determine if an individual has Mental Retardation along with detailed information about developing a personal plan of individualized supports. It is available from the AAMR through their web site at http://www.aamr.org/bookstore/ or by calling 301-604-1340.

The overall AAMR definition of *Mental Retardation* is that it is a disability characterized by significant limitations both in intellectual functioning and in adaptive behavior as expressed in conceptual, social, and practical adaptive skills. This disability originates before the age of 18. The AAMR considers five assumptions that are essential to the application of this definition:

1. Limitations in present functioning must be considered within the context of community environments typical of the individual's age peers and culture.
2. Valid assessment considers cultural and linguistic diversity as well as differences in communication, sensory, motor, and behavioral factors.
3. Within an individual, limitations often coexist with strengths.
4. An important purpose of describing limitations is to develop a profile of needed supports.
5. With appropriate personalized supports over a sustained period, the life functioning of the person with Mental Retardation generally will improve (AAMR, 2002).

A complete and accurate understanding of Mental Retardation involves realizing that *Mental Retardation* refers to a particular state of functioning that begins in childhood, has many dimensions, and is affected positively by individualized supports. As a model of functioning, it includes the contexts and environment within which the person functions and interacts and requires a multidimensional and ecological approach that reflects the interaction of the individual with the environment and the outcomes of that interaction with regards to independence, relationships, societal contributions, participation in school and community, and personal well-being.

Adaptive behavior is the collection of conceptual, social, and practical skills that people have learned so they can function in their everyday lives. Significant limitations in adaptive behavior impact a person's daily life and affect the ability to respond to a particular situation or to the environment. Limitations in adaptive behavior can be determined by using standardized tests that are normed on the general population, including people with disabilities and people without disabilities. On these standardized measures, sig-

Table 1 Specific examples of adaptive behavior skills

Conceptual Skills
- Receptive and expressive language
- Reading and writing
- Money concepts
- Self-directions

Social Skills
- Interpersonal
- Responsibility
- Self-esteem
- Gullibility (likelihood of being tricked or manipulated)
- Naiveté
- Follows rules
- Obeys laws
- Avoids victimization

Practical Skills
- Personal activities of daily living such as eating, dressing, mobility, and toileting.
- Instrumental activities of daily living such as preparing meals, taking medication, using the telephone, managing money, using transportation, and doing housekeeping activities.

Occupational skills
- Maintaining a safe environment

nificant limitations in adaptive behavior are operationally defined as performance that is at least 2 standard deviations below the mean of either (1) one of the following three types of adaptive behavior: conceptual, social, or practical, or (2) an overall score on a standardized measure of conceptual, social, and practical skills (AAMR, 2002). Table 1 includes some specific examples of adaptive behavior skills.

The concept of supports originated about 15 years ago with the AAMR, and it has revolutionized the way habilitation and education services are provided to persons with Mental Retardation. Rather than mold individuals into preexisting diagnostic categories and force them into existing models of service, the supports approach evaluates the specific needs of the individual and then suggests strategies, services, and supports that will optimize individual functioning. The supports approach also recognizes that individual needs and circumstances will change over time. Supports were an innovative aspect of the 1992 AAMR manual, and they remain critical in the 2002 system. In 2002, they have been dramatically expanded and improved to reflect significant progress over the last decade.

Supports are defined as the resources and individual strategies necessary to promote the development, education, interests, and personal well-being of a person with Mental Retardation. Supports can be provided by a parent, friend, teacher, psychologist, and doctor or by any appropriate person or agency. Providing individualized supports can improve personal functioning, promote self-determination and societal inclusion, and improve personal well-being of a person with Mental Retardation. Focusing on supports as the way to improve education, employment, recreation, and living environments is an important part of person-centered approaches to providing supports to people with Mental Retardation.

The AAMR recommends that an individual's need for supports be analyzed in at least nine key areas: human development, teaching and education, home living, community living, employment, health and safety, behavioral, social, and protection and advocacy. Some specific examples of supports areas and support activities can be found in Table 2.

The AAMR has recently published the Supports Intensity Scale (SIS), a planning tool that assesses the practical supports requirements of a person with an intellectual disability. The SIS is directly related to the 2002 classification system and therefore allows seamless transition from assessment to intervention (AAMR, 2005). Contact information for the AAMR is as follows:

American Association on Mental Retardation
444 North Capitol Street
Washington, DC 20001-1512
Phone: 202-387-1968
Fax: 202-387-2193
Web site: http://www.aamr.org

Table 2 Specific examples of support areas and support activities

Human Development Activities
- Providing physical development opportunities that include eye-hand coordination, fine motor skills, and gross motor activities
- Providing cognitive development opportunities such as using words and images to represent the world and reasoning logically about concrete events
- Providing social and emotional developmental activities to foster trust, autonomy, and initiative

Teaching and Education Activities
- Interacting with trainers and teachers and fellow trainees and students
- Participating in making decisions on training and educational activities
- Learning and using problem-solving strategies
- Using technology for learning
- Learning and using functional academics (reading signs, counting change, etc.)
- Learning and using self-determination skills

Home Living Activities
- Using the restroom or toilet
- Laundering and taking care of clothes
- Preparing and eating food
- Housekeeping and cleaning
- Dressing
- Bathing and taking care of personal hygiene and grooming needs
- Operating home appliances and technology
- Participating in leisure activities within the home

Community Living Activities
- Using transportation
- Participating in recreation and leisure activities
- Going to visit friends and family
- Shopping and purchasing goods
- Interacting with community members
- Using public buildings and settings

Employment Activities
- Learning and using specific job skills
- Interacting with coworkers
- Interacting with supervisors
- Completing work-related tasks with speed and quality
- Changing job assignments
- Accessing and obtaining crisis intervention and assistance

Health and Safety Activities
- Accessing and obtaining therapy services
- Taking medication
- Avoiding health and safety hazards
- Communicating with health care providers
- Accessing emergency services
- Maintaining a nutritious diet
- Maintaining physical health
- Maintaining mental health and emotional well-being

Behavioral Activities
- Learning specific skills or behaviors
- Learning and making appropriate decisions
- Accessing and obtaining mental health treatments
- Accessing and obtaining substance abuse treatments
- Incorporating personal preferences into daily activities
- Maintaining socially appropriate behavior in public
- Controlling anger and aggression

Social Activities
- Socializing within the family
- Participating in recreation and leisure activities
- Making appropriate sexual decisions
- Socializing outside the family
- Making and keeping friends
- Communicating with others about personal needs
- Engaging in loving and intimate relationships
- Offering assistance and assisting others

Protection and Advocacy Activities
- Advocating for self and others
- Managing money and personal finances
- Protecting self from exploitation
- Exercising legal rights and responsibilities
- Belonging to and participating in self-advocacy or support organizations
- Obtaining legal services
- Using banks and cashing checks

Please note that the information contained in this entry was taken directly from the AAMR web site with gracious permission from the AAMR. Personal communications with Anu Prabhala (June 15 through June 23, 2005) in the AAMR office of publications greatly enhanced the breadth and depth of this entry, and we thank her for her time and consideration.

REFERENCES

American Association on Mental Retardation (AAMR). (2002). *Mental Retardation: Definition, classification, and systems of supports* (10th ed.). Washington, DC: Author.

American Association on Mental Retardation (AAMR). (2005). *Definition.* Retrieved June 23, 2005, from http://www.aamr.org

AAMR STAFF

AAMR, AMERICAN ASSOCIATION ON MENTAL RETARDATION
MENTAL RETARDATION

AAMR ADAPTIVE BEHAVIOR SCALES–RESIDENTIAL AND COMMUNITY: SECOND EDITION

The AAMR Adaptive Behavior Scales–Residential and Community: Second Edition (ABS-RC:2; Nihira, Leland, & Lambert, 1993) is intended to assess adaptive behaviors and gauge how people cope with natural and social demands of their environment. The ABS-RC:2 measures skills and abilities necessary to perform tasks of daily living and to participate in social activities. This measure is intended to assess the behavior of institutionalized persons with Mental Retardation and those in community settings who previously had been classified at different adaptive behavior levels according to the AAMR's Classification in Mental Retardation (Grossman, 1983). It is also intended to be used to assess the adaptive behavior levels in public school populations. Designed for mentally handicapped persons aged 18 to 80, this measure is individually administered in an interview format based on the informant's knowledge of the individual being assessed. Testing time is estimated at 15 to 30 minutes.

Originally published in 1969, the ABS-RC has undergone many alterations and intensive item analyses. Items that were carried over from the previous version were identified on the basis of their interrater reliability and their ability to discriminate between the two groups mentioned (i.e., those previously classified in an institutionalized setting and those classified in a public school population).

Domain raw scores are converted to standard scores (M = 10, SD = 3) and percentiles. Factor raw scores are used to generate quotients (M = 100, SD = 15) and percentiles. The normative sample for the ABS-RC:2 consists of over 4,000 persons with developmental disabilities in the community or in residential settings. It was selected to represent the national population with developmental disabilities. Persons included in the sample had additional disabilities (e.g., blindness, deafness, emotional disturbance, learning disability, physical impairments, and speech or language impairments; Carey, 1998). Internal consistency reliabilities and stability for all scores exceed .80. Further evidence supporting the scale's statistical adequacy is provided in the manual.

The manual is clearly written. It provides appendixes that include norm tables for converting raw scores to standard scores, percentiles ranks, and age equivalents. A software-based scoring and reporting system is available from the publisher. Some reviewers have criticized the ABS-RC:2 for being overly similar to the AAMR Adaptive Behavior Scales–School: Second Edition (Harrison, 1998). This point may be important to consider if questions exist regarding the more appropriate measure for a particular individual.

REFERENCES

Carey, K. T. (1998). Review of the AAMR Adaptive Behavior Scales–Residential and Community: Second Edition. In J. C. Impara & B. S. Plake (Eds.), *The thirteenth mental measurements yearbook* (pp. 41–46). Lincoln, NE: Buros Institute of Mental Measurements.

Grossman, H. J. (Ed.). (1983). *Classification in Mental Retardation.* Washington, DC: American Association on Mental Retardation.

Hatton, C., Emerson, E., & Robertson, J. (2001). The Adaptive Behavior Scales–Residential and Community (Part I): Towards the development of a short form. *Research in Developmental Disabilities, 22,* 273–288.

Harrison, P. L. (1998). Review of the AAMR Adaptive Behavior Scale–Residential and Community: Second Edition. In J. C. Impara & B. S. Plake (Eds.), *The thirteenth mental measurements yearbook* (pp. 39–41). Lincoln, NE: Buros Institute of Mental Measurements.

Nihira, K., Leland, H., & Lambert, N. (1993). *AAMR Adaptive Behavior Scales–Residential and Community* (2nd ed.). Austin, TX: PRO-ED.

RON DUMONT
Fairleigh Dickinson University

JOHN O. WILLIS
Rivier College

AAMR CLASSIFICATION SYSTEMS
MENTAL RETARDATION
VINELAND ADAPTIVE BEHAVIOR SCALES–SECOND EDITION

AAMR ADAPTIVE BEHAVIOR SCALE–SCHOOL: SECOND EDITION

The AAMR Adaptive Behavior Scale–School: Second Edition (ABS-S:2; Lambert, Nihira, & Leland, 1993) was designed to assess the current functioning of children being evaluated for evidence of Mental Retardation, for evaluating adaptive behavior characteristics of children with autism, and for differentiating children with behavior disorders who require special education assistance from those with behavior problems who can be educated in regular class programs (Harrington, 1998).

The ABS-S:2 was developed in its first-edition original form by Nihira, Foster, Shellhaas, and Leland (1969) and was revised and standardized in 1974 by Nadine Lambert, Myra Windmiller, and Linda Cole. It was revised and standardized once again in 1981 by Nadine Lambert and Myra Windmiller. This second and most recent edition was published in 1993. It is intended for use with children and adolescents ages 3:0 through 18:11. The ABS-S:2 is administered individually in an interview format. Testing time is estimated at 15 to 30 minutes.

The current scale is divided into two parts. In part one, skills are grouped into nine behavior domains: independent functioning, physical development, economic activity, language development, numbers and time, prevocational/vocational activity, self-direction, responsibility, and socialization. These skills focus on personal independence and evaluate the coping skills considered important to independence and responsibility in daily living.

The behaviors in part two are grouped into seven domains, which assess adaptive behaviors that relate to the manifestation of personality and behavior disorders: social behavior, conformity, trustworthiness, stereotyped and hyperactive behavior, self-abusive behavior, social engagement, and disturbing interpersonal behavior.

Domain raw scores are converted to standard scores (M = 10, SD = 3) and percentiles. Factor raw scores are used to generate quotients (M = 100, SD = 15) and percentiles. The standardization sample for the ABS-S:2 included 2,000 persons with developmental disabilities attending public schools and 1,000 with no disabilities (Harrington, 1998).

Stinnett, Fuqua, and Coombs (1999) examined the construct validity of the AAMR ABS-S:2 (Lambert et al., 1993) through exploratory factor analyses and reported that "results indicated the ABS-S:2 is a two-factor instrument both for children with and without mental retardation." Factor 1 items were related to personal independence, and factor 2 items were related to social behavior. "Because the data strongly indicated a 2-factor model for both the MR and Non-MR samples, users should be cautious in interpreting ABS-S:2 results in terms of the five-factor model presented by the test's authors" (Stinnett et al., 1999, p. 43).

REFERENCES

Harrington, R. L. (1998). Review of AAMR Adaptive Behavior Scale–School: Second Edition. In J. C. Impara & B. S. Plake (Eds.), *The thirteenth mental measurements yearbook* (pp. 389–393). Lincoln, NE: Buros Institute of Mental Measurements.

Lambert, N., Nihira, K., & Leland, H. (1993). *AAMR Adaptive Behavior Scale–School* (2nd ed.). Austin, TX: PRO-ED.

Nihira, K., Foster, R., Shellhaas, M., & Leland, H. (1969). *AAMR Adaptive Behavior Scale.* Washington, DC: American Association on Mental Deficiency.

Stinnett, A. T., Fuqua, D. R., & Coombs, W. T. (1999). Construct validity of the AAMR Adaptive Behavior Scale–School: 2. *School Psychology Review, 28,* 31–43.

Watkins, M. W., Ravert, C. M., & Crosby, E. G. (2002). Normative factor structure of the AAMR Adaptive Behavior Scale–School (2nd ed.). *Journal of Psychoeducational Assessment, 20,* 337–345.

RON DUMONT
Fairleigh Dickinson University

JOHN O. WILLIS
Rivier College

ADAPTIVE BEHAVIOR
MENTAL RETARDATION

AB DESIGN

The AB design is one of several single-subject or single-case research designs that are used by behavior analysts and special education researchers (Kennedy, 2005; Tawney & Gast, 1984). Single-subject research methodologies are derived from the study of applied behavior analysis (Baer, Wolf, & Risley, 1968). Like qualitative and quantitative research, single-subject research relies on specific rules and assumptions for conducting an experimental study, including carefully defined variables, systematic observation in both baseline and intervention conditions, experimental control, and visual analysis of data.

The name AB design describes how the study will be conducted. The letter *A* designates the baseline phase of the study, and the letter *B* designates the intervention phase of the study. The baseline phase includes repeated measurement of the "natural frequency" of the targeted behavior that is being measured under nonintervention conditions (Barlow & Hersen, 1984, p. 142). The targeted behavior is also known as the *dependent variable*. The intervention phase consists of the introduction of the intervention or treatment along with repeated measurement of the dependent variable. The intervention or treatment is known as the *independent variable*.

For example, a researcher might be interested in studying the effect of self-monitoring on measures of academic engagement for a middle school student with emotional or behavioral disorders. The researcher first operationally defines academic engagement and selects a method for data collection (e.g., duration recording). Next, the researcher systematically collects data on academic engagement during the baseline phase. When the researcher has demonstrated data stability (e.g., trend and variability), he or she would then introduce the self-monitoring procedure. Self-monitoring would be taught to the participant, and data would continue to be collected by the researcher on the measure of academic engagement. Upon conclusion of the data collection, the researcher would analyze the graphed data on academic engagement during baseline and intervention conditions (see Figure 1 for sample AB graph). If the data shows increases in academic engagement during the intervention phase, the researcher can *infer* that the intervention influenced the change in the dependent variable. However, making an inference and demonstrating causality are very different constructs.

The AB design allows for inferences to be made because changes in the dependent variable are "*presumed* to be a function of the independent variable" (Tawney & Gast, 1984, p. 191). Because the effect is not replicated as part of the AB design it is impossible to demonstrate that the intervention, and only the intervention, *caused* the change in the dependent variable. Using our example from the preceding, the self-monitoring procedure may have resulted in increased access to positive adult attention, increases in instructional feedback, or other variables that may have influenced the change in academic engagement demonstrated as part of the experiment.

The AB design is the most basic single-subject design. While it doesn't permit the demonstration of a functional relationship between the independent and dependent variables, it has proven to be a useful tool for understanding behavioral change in educational settings where a comprehensive experimental procedure is not warranted or possible. Teachers and researchers that have used the AB design have found the procedures to be both effective and useful for the evaluation of academic and behavioral interventions in applied settings.

REFERENCES

Baer, D. M., Wolf, M. N., & Risley, T. R. (1968). Some current dimensions of applied behavior analysis. *Journal of Applied Behavior Analysis, 8,* 387–398.

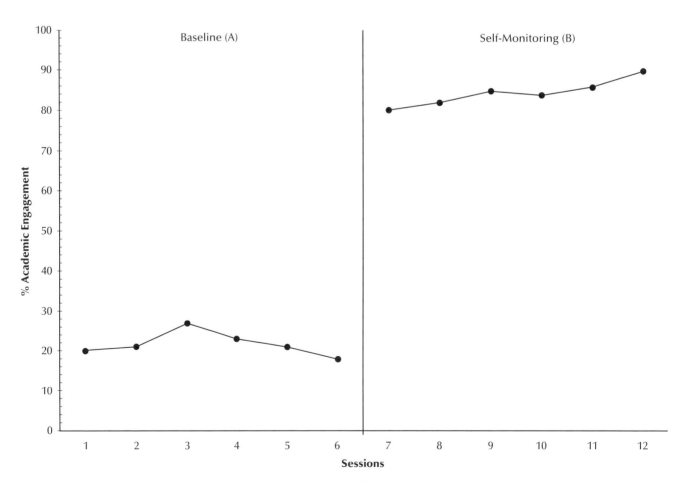

Figure 1 Sample AB graph

Barlow, D. H., & Hersen, M. (1984). *Single case experimental designs: Strategies for studying behavior change* (2nd ed.). New York: Pergamon.

Kennedy, C. H. (2005). *Single-case designs for educational research.* Boston: Allyn & Bacon.

Tawney, J. W., & Gast, D. L. (1984). *Single subject research in special education.* New York: Merrill.

RANDALL L. DEPRY
*University of Colorado at
Colorado Springs*

RESEARCH IN SPECIAL EDUCATION

ABAB DESIGN

The ABAB design is one of the oldest and most widely used single-case designs developed in behavioral psychology. It was initially used in laboratory studies with animals (Sidman, 1960); however, as the applied behavior analysis movement got under way (Baer, Wolf, & Risley, 1968), it became a prototype for applied behavioral investigations conducted in the natural environment. Although the number of single-case designs has increased markedly since the early days of applied behavior analysis (e.g., Kazdin, 1980; Kratochwill, 1978), the ABAB design still occupies a prominent place in applied behavioral research. Moreover, because of the high degree of experimental control that it provides, it has been widely used with individuals manifesting various types of handicaps (Bergan, 1977). For example, the ABAB design has been particularly useful in studying environmental variables affecting language acquisition in retarded children (Bergan, 1977).

The ABAB design is intended to reveal a functional relationship between an experimental treatment and a behavior targeted for change. For example, it might be used to establish a functional relationship between the use of the plural form of a noun and a treatment such as praise following the occurrence of a plural noun. The demonstration of a functional relationship between praise and plural nouns would require an association between the frequency of plural-noun production and the occurrence of verbal praise. Given that a functional relationship were established, verbal praise could be assumed to function as a positive reinforcer increasing the probability of occurrence of plural nouns by the subject or subjects participating in the experiment.

The ABAB technique has often been referred to as a single-case design (e.g., Kratochwill, 1978). However, it may be applied with more than one subject. Thus, the term single case is a bit misleading. Glass, Wilson, and Gottman (1975) among others called attention to the fact that the ABAB design is a time-series design in that it reflects an effort to determine changes in behavior occurring across a series of points in time. Recognition of the ABAB design as a time-series design opened the way for linking the design to the statistical procedures associated with time-series analysis (see, for example, Glass, Wilson, & Gottmann, 1975). Application of time-series analysis procedures affords a statistical test for hypotheses that may be investigated with the ABAB design. However, despite this advantage, time-series techniques have not been widely used in applied investigations involving the ABAB design. There are a variety of reasons for this. Among them is the fact that the graphing techniques suggested by behavioral psychologists (e.g., Parsonson & Baer, 1978) as an alternative to statistical analysis are easier to implement and to interpret than time-series statistics. Nonetheless, time-series procedures constitute a potentially powerful tool for applied behavioral research and their use can be expected to increase in the future.

As the letters in its name suggest, the ABAB design includes four phases. The initial A phase is a baseline period that records behavior across a series of points in time in the absence of intervention. The length of the baseline period varies depending on the variability of the behavior being recorded. If the behavior is highly variable, a longer baseline is required than if the behavior is highly stable. More data are required to get a sense of the fluctuations that may be expected without intervention for a highly variable behavior than for a highly stable behavior. The second phase, denoted by the letter B, is a treatment phase. During this phase the treatment is introduced. The treatment may be implemented in accordance with a variety of different schedules. For example, treatment may be implemented with every occurrence of the target behavior. For instance, praise might be given following every occurrence of a plural noun. On the other hand, treatment might be implemented in accordance with one of the many available partial reinforcement schedules. Thus, praise might be given after every third occurrence of a plural noun. The third phase, also denoted by the letter A, constitutes a return to baseline. The return to baseline may be brought about by various means. One is to withdraw the treatment. For instance, praise might not be given following plural-noun utterances during the return-to-baseline phase. Another procedure is to introduce another treatment intended to bring the target behavior back to baseline level. For example, reinforcement of a behavior that is incompatible with the target behavior may be introduced during the return-to-baseline phase. The final phase in the ABAB design, denoted by the second occurrence of the letter B, is a second implementation of the treatment. The second implementation is intended to demonstrate treatment control over the target behavior by minimizing the possibility that environmental influences occurring coincidentally with the treatment could be responsible for the observed behavior change.

The major advantage of the ABAB design lies in the fact that it minimizes the likelihood of coincidental environmental influences on the target behavior. There are two potential disadvantages to the approach (Kazdin, 1973). One is that some behaviors are not easily reversed. For example, a skill that has been well-learned may not be easy to unlearn. The second disadvantage is that there are cases in which it may not be practical to carry out a return-to-baseline even if it is possible to do so. For instance, a teacher may not want to return a child's performance of an academic skill to baseline even for a short period of time. Despite these shortcomings, the ABAB design has been shown to be useful in establishing a functional relationship between a treatment and behavior in countless applications. It is truly a mainstay in applied behavioral research and will continue to be used widely.

REFERENCES

Baer, D. M., Wolf, M. M., & Risley, T. R. (1968). Some current dimensions of applied behavior analysis. *Journal of Applied Behavior Analysis, 8,* 387–398.

Bergan, J. R. (1977). *Behavioral consultation.* Columbus, OH: Merrill.

Glass, G. V., Wilson, V. L., & Gottman, J. M. (1975). *Design and analysis of time-series experiments.* Boulder: Colorado Associated University Press.

Kazdin, A. E. (1973). Methodological and assessment considerations in evaluating reinforcement programs in applied settings. *Journal of Applied Behavior Analysis, 6,* 517–531.

Kazdin, A. E. (1980). *Research design in clinical psychology.* New York: Harper & Row.

Kratochwill, T. R. (1978). *Single-subject research: Strategies for evaluating change.* New York: Academic.

Parsonson, B. S., & Baer, D. M. (1978). The analysis and presentation of graphic data. In T. R. Kratochwill (Ed.), *Single-subject research: Strategies for evaluating change.* New York: Academic.

Sidman, M. (1960). *Tactics of scientific research.* New York: Basic.

JOHN R. BERGAN
University of Arizona

RESEARCH IN SPECIAL EDUCATION

THE ABECEDARIAN PROJECT

In the 1960s and 1970s, a number of early childhood programs were provided for children born into poverty in the hope that enhancement of their early environments would increase the likelihood of academic success in later years. Head Start was the largest of these, but many other investigators mounted studies designed to learn what sorts of preschool programs would best prepare poor children for school. The timing, duration, and service delivery models for these intervention programs varied. Most were 1- or 2-year preschools offered for part days during the school year or in the summertime, others were delivered through visits to the home, and some were child-care based. Some taught children directly, while others concentrated more on showing parents how to provide cognitive stimulation for their young children. However, all addressed issues related to educational environments that would support cognitive development and the acquisition of school-related skills. Unfortunately, many of these programs lacked scientifically acceptable control groups that would have enabled truly empirical evaluations of their impact on children's development. In addition, many did not follow up on participants to learn how enduring their effects might be. Accordingly, many educators and policymakers doubted the wisdom of using scarce resources for early childhood programs as a means of improving academic performance among poor children.

To address the ensuing controversy, a consortium was formed by the investigators of 11 independent programs whose designs permitted a scientific examination of child outcomes. This Consortium for Longitudinal Studies (Lazar, Darlington, Murray, Royce, & Snipper, 1982) located and followed up on their study participants several years after treatment ended to learn what long-term benefits could fairly be claimed. Across all studies, they found that treated children made better school progress (fewer grade retentions and assignments to special education), surpassed control children on standardized cognitive tests for a few years after programs ended, and had more positive attitudes toward academic achievement. In addition, their parents displayed higher aspirations for their children (Lazar et al., 1982). As important as this landmark work proved to be, few of the programs included in the Consortium had data on their participants in adulthood. As Haskins (1989) pointed out, the real worth of early childhood programs lies in their potential for improving the life circumstances of treated individuals. Such early benefits as boosts in IQ test scores or enhanced academic performance in elementary and secondary school need to be linked to real-life achievements in later years.

The Abecedarian Project to be described in this entry offers one of the best opportunities to examine the magnitude and duration of effects of early childhood intervention programs. Founded too late for inclusion in the Consortium described in the preceding, the Abecedarian study was a randomized control trial of early childhood educational intervention with a sample of sufficient size to permit reliable comparisons between treated and control participants. Unlike most other early childhood programs, this project involved intensive child care-based treatment that was provided year round from early infancy to age 5 when the children entered kindergarten. A second phase of treatment was then offered to half of those with preschool treatment and half of those without, enabling a test of the relative efficacy of preschool and early elementary school intervention as they related to early and lasting academic outcomes for treated children. Long-term follow-up data are also available, with participants assessed at ages 12, 15, and 21 years. Attrition has been low, increasing confidence in the findings based on long-term outcomes. The randomized study design justifies attributing treatment or control differences to treatment itself given that relevant background predictors should have been the same in both treated and control participants. The intensity and duration of the early treatment, the low attrition, and the long-term follow-up information available distinguish this study among other investigations of early childhood intervention.

Long-term outcomes from the Abecedarian study can be particularly informative for two reasons. First, of the earlier programs reporting comparable long-term outcomes—the Perry Preschool Project (Schweinhart, Barnes, & Weikart, 1993), the Early Training Project (Gray, Ramsey, & Klaus, 1982), and a comparison of outcomes in Head Start children whose classrooms had differing levels of structure (Karnes, Shwedel, & Williams, 1983)—none provided preschool treatment as intensive, in terms of its duration (full days) and length (5 years starting in infancy), as that of the Abecedarian study. Second, the two other programs that did provide high-risk children with equally intensive and long-lasting preschool programs—the Syracuse Family Development Research Program (Lally, Mangione, & Honig, 1988) and the Milwaukee Project (Garber, 1988)—did not track their graduates into adulthood.

The specific aims of the Abecedarian early childhood program were (1) to determine whether developmental delay and school failure could be ameliorated in children from high-risk backgrounds (i.e., low-income families), (2) to learn whether a follow-through program in early elementary school was necessary to maintain preschool program gains, and (3) to learn whether an elementary school program alone could significantly improve intellectual and school performance in poor children. Follow-up studies have been designed to learn in what domains and how long early benefits can be detected.

Preschool Program

Starting with pilot research in 1971 and enrollment of subjects in 1972, the Abecedarian Project provided a prospective, in-depth study of the lives of multirisk families and their children. The preschool program was designed by Craig T. Ramey and his colleagues at the Frank Porter Graham Child Development Center, then directed by James J. Gallagher at the University of North Carolina in Chapel Hill. Local social service agencies and prenatal clinics helped to identify potential participants. Selection criteria were based on 13 sociodemographic factors that were weighted and combined to create a High-Risk Index (Ramey & Smith, 1977). In addition, infants had to appear free of biological conditions associated with mental, sensory, or motor disabilities.

Four cohorts of families were enrolled in the study between 1972 and 1977. Randomization was through matching with replacement, that is, recruited pairs were matched on High-Risk Index scores, then assigned to preschool treatment or control status on the basis of a table of random numbers. If a family refused its assignment, a replacement family was given that slot. Of the 120 families screened and randomized, 109, to whom 111 infants (one set of identical twins, one sibling pair) were born, agreed to take part. Fifty-seven infants (28 females and 29 males) were assigned to the Experimental (E) group and 54 (31 females and 23 males) to the Control (C) group. The characteristics of families in the two groups were very similar. All families met poverty guidelines. The typical mother was young (M = 20 years old), had less than a high school education (M = 10 years), was unmarried, lived in a multigenerational household, and reported no earned income. Approximately one-third of the mothers were receiving public assistance. Ethnicity was not a selection factor, but of those who took part, 98 percent were African American.

Early Childhood Procedures

The service delivery model was child-centered, with treated children having full-day child care year-round. A systematic curriculum was provided by Joseph Sparling and Isabel Lewis that included gamelike educational activities extending down to the earliest months of life. Eclectic in nature, these Learningames fostered cognitive, language, and adaptive behavior skills (Sparling & Lewis, 1979, 1984, 2000). The activities involved simple, age-appropriate, adult-child interactions such as talking to an infant, showing toys or pictures, and offering infants a chance to react to sights or sounds in the environment. Activities were individualized for each child by the staff. As children grew, the educational content became more conceptual and skill-based. The curriculum was more group-oriented for older preschoolers. Language development was especially emphasized. However, children always had freedom to choose activities, and the emphasis on individual development was paramount throughout.

Control infants had nutritional supplements (iron-fortified formula) for the first 15 months of life because treated infants received much of their nutrition at the child care facility and the original investigators wanted to control for the effect of early nutrition on brain development. Families in both the treated and control groups received supportive social services as needed. Although control group children did not receive systematic educational intervention (e.g., Ramey et al., 1976; Ramey & Campbell, 1984, 1987), a number of them attended other child care centers, some entering in infancy, others later in the preschool years (Burchinal, Lee, & Ramey, 1989). Thus, the treatment and control comparisons were between children who had the Abecedarian educational child care and others reared either at home or in the variety of child care settings utilized by local low-income families, that is, the natural ecology of low-income families at that place and time. For ethical reasons, control group children whose development appeared to lag were referred to community service agencies for further assessment and preschool services as recommended. Thus, the comparisons made between treatment and control children are conservative.

Standardized intellectual tests were a major outcome measure for the preschool years. Mother-infant interactions were filmed on a regular basis. Family demographics were monitored across time, and during the preschool years annual visits were made to each child's home to measure the educational stimulus value of that environment (Caldwell & Bradley, 1984). Children's attachment to their mothers was also studied in a series of mother-infant interaction studies.

Preschool Outcomes

In brief, assessment of preschool cognitive development in the Abecedarian sample showed that cognitive test performance in treated children was significantly enhanced; after the age of 18 months, treated children earned significantly higher scores on standardized intellectual measures during the preschool years (Ramey & Campbell, 1984). During the preschool treatment phase, the treatment effect size averaged 1.75 if the pooled sample standard deviation is the denominator (Campbell, Pungello, Miller-Johnson, Burchinal, & Ramey, 2001). Concerning effects of child care on the mother-child relationship, the preschool program did not appear to reduce the infants' attachment to their mothers. Despite being in full-time child care, young children overwhelmingly turned to their mother rather than a child care provider in a laboratory situation where they needed adult help to accomplish a task (Farran & Ramey, 1977).

School-Age Procedures

Based on the 48-month cognitive test score, pairs of children were matched within the preschool treatment and control groups, then randomly assigned to school-age treatment and control groups. Permanent attrition at that point included the four children who were deceased, one who proved to have a biological condition undetected at birth that obviated inclusion, and one who was withdrawn from the study. In addition, several children did not have full preschool data primarily because of family mobility. For these reasons, only 96 of the original 111 infants received school-age assignments. The rerandomizing process created four treatment conditions: children with 8 years of intervention (5 in preschool plus 3 at school age) designated as Experimental-Experimental (EE); those with 5 years (preschool alone) designated as Experimental-Control (EC); those with 3 years of intervention (elementary school alone) designated as

Control-Experimental (CE); and those who were untreated in both phases, designated as Control-Control (CC).

Families treated in the school-age phase were assigned a Home School Resource Teacher (HST) who served as a liaison between the school and the home for the first 3 years the child attended public school, typically kindergarten through second grade. The goal was to increase parental involvement in the children's learning. To focus parental efforts, individualized curriculum packets were devised for each child based on the child's needs as identified by the classroom teacher. These activities were delivered to the home every other week. Parents were encouraged to use them at least 15 minutes each day with the children. Feedback was sought as to the success of each activity as new ones were delivered. Most parents rated the activities highly and said they used them regularly. Because regular meetings with classroom teachers and parents took place, the HST was able to enhance communication between families and schools. She (only females were hired for these positions) also supported families through counseling or by referrals in situations that compromised the parent's ability to concentrate on the child's school progress (Ramey & Campbell, 1991).

Intellectual measures and individually administered academic tests were administered to all children in each of the first 3 years in school. Teachers rated classroom adjustment and learning style each year. Academic tests administered in the spring of the third year and intellectual tests administered that summer constituted an endpoint evaluation. Also at the end point, family circumstances were again assessed through parent interviews and a parent completed the Child Behavior Checklist (Achenbach & Edelbrock, 1983) for each child.

School-Age Outcomes

Multivariate analysis of variance for repeated measures was used to analyze school-age intellectual test scores. The results indicated that children with preschool treatment earned significantly higher intellectual test scores across the 3-year span from age 5 to 8, $F(1, 83) = 6.90, p < .01$, but no effect was seen for the school-age phase on intellectual test scores. With respect to academic scores at the end point, age-referenced standardized reading test scores showed a linear relationship between the number of years of treatment and reading scores. That is, those who had the full 8 years had the highest average score, outscoring the group with 5 years in preschool only, which in turn outscored those with 3 years in elementary school only. The group not treated in either phase had the lowest average score of all, $F(1, 79) = 11.09, p < .001$. The same analysis of mathematics scores also showed a linear increase as a function of years of treatment, but the trend was less striking, $F(1, 79) = 4.05, p < .05$. Fewer of the children with preschool treatment were retained in grade during the primary years. Thus, the school-age outcomes indicated that school-age treatment seemed to have no effect on intellectual test scores and that preschool treatment was more powerful than school-age treatment in enhancing academic performance.

Early adjustment to primary school was not always smooth for the children. Early cohorts of children with preschool treatment showed more physical and verbal aggression than did children from the preschool control cohorts (Haskins, 1985). Further analyses of teacher ratings of classroom adjustment, based on ratings of the ratings of Considerateness, Verbal Intelligence, and Extraversion scales from the Classroom Behavior Inventory (Schaefer, Edgerton, & Aaronson, 1977) showed that, averaged across the primary years (Kindergarten through second grade) scores, did not significantly increase as a function of the number of years of treatment. There was a trend for teachers to rate children higher on Verbal Intelligence as the number of years of educational intervention increased, $F(1, 83) = 3.09, p = .08$. Otherwise, teacher and parent ratings of child behavior at age 8 were essentially similar irrespective of early intervention (Ramey & Campbell, 1991).

Later Follow-Up Data

Abecedarian follow-up studies were conducted at three points: when children had been in school for 7 years and should have completed elementary school (then sixth grade); after 10 years in school, the point when they should have completed ninth grade; and in young adulthood when they were 21 years of age. At all three points, standardized measures of intelligence and academic achievement were collected. School records were collected for as many participants as possible to learn full details about retentions, special class placements, and high school graduation. In young adulthood, particular emphasis was placed on post-secondary school, jobs, and the establishment of families.

During the school-age phase of treatment and for the two follow ups conducted during later public school years (age 12 and age 15 years), analyses were generally based on four-group comparisons that permitted tests of the relative strength of intervention effects during each phase. However, those children whose early attrition precluded their having random school-age assignments were nevertheless invited to participate in all follow ups, and most of them did so. In young adulthood, 105 of the original 111 infants admitted to the study were still living and eligible for inclusion. Of the 105 who might have been included as young adults, 104 took part in the follow-up study.

Long-term intellectual development.
Figure 1, taken from Campbell et al. (2001), illustrates longitudinal intellectual test scores. Because earlier analyses showed that the school-age phase of treatment had no effect on intellectual test scores, the model tested here considered only the preschool group assignment of the individual. Missing data points

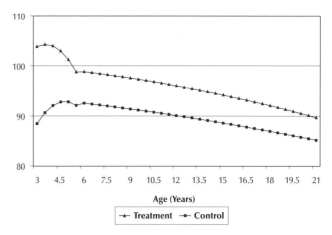

Figure 1 Cognitive growth curves as a function of preschool treatment

were estimated by participants who missed testing occasions over the years. Across this 18-year time span Hierarchical Linear Modeling (HLM) analysis showed a significant main effect for preschool treatment group, with individuals who had early educational treatment earning higher IQ scores overall than those in the control group. A main effect was also found for change over time, indicating that IQ scores across all subjects were characterized by a linear decline. In addition, a significant main effect was found for the test administered, indicating that participants scored higher on the Stanford-Binet administered to them at ages 36 and 48 months than on the Wechsler scales (administered from age 5 to age 21).

These main effects were qualified by significant higher-order interactions. The magnitude of the difference between the treatment and control groups varied as a function of time of assessment, as indicated by a significant two-way interaction of treatment group by time of assessment (i.e., during treatment versus after treatment). Although the treatment or control mean difference was greater while treated children were still receiving the intervention, treatment differences were significant both during the preschool period and in the follow-up period. A significant two-way interaction was also found for time of assessment and quadratic age, indicating that across all subjects, significantly more curvature existed during the preschool period than in the post-preschool period. Finally, these two-way interactions were qualified by a significant three-way interaction found for treatment group by time of assessment by linear age. As can be seen in Figure 1, a greater treatment or control group was found during the preschool period than in later years, and the linear decline in the two groups was greater during the treatment years than during the follow-up period. That is, not only the size of the group difference was larger during the early years, but the pattern of change over time differed between the groups during treatment. After treatment, a similar parallel decline in intellectual test scores was seen in both groups.

Academic Achievement. To examine the long-term effects of both phases of treatment on academic test scores, young adult reading and mathematics scores were first analyzed as a function of both treatment phases. The model contrasted the effects of preschool treatment and school-age treatment and the interaction between the two. The data are age-referenced standardized tests for reading and math from the Woodcock-Johnson (WJ) Tests of Achievement (Woodcock & Johnson, 1977; 1989) as earned at ages 8, 12, 15, and 21 years. Because testing this four-group model precluded estimating missing data, power to detect differences was reduced accordingly. Neither of the aggregate WJ scores, Broad Reading or Broad Mathematics, showed significant preschool effects, school-age effects, or preschool by school-age treatment effects when the four-group models were tested, but disaggregating the Broad scores showed trends toward preschool effects on Letter-Word Identification, $F(1, 91) = 2.88, p < .10$, and Calculation $F(1, 91) = 3.58$, $p < .10$. In terms of effect sizes, however, striking treatment effects can be seen across the age span from 8 to 21 years, especially in reading. Effect sizes were calculated by subtracting the mean of the CC group from that of each of the other groups and dividing the remainder in each instance by the standard deviation of the CC group. According to Cohen (1988), an effect size of .20 is considered "small" but may be meaningful, an effect size of .50 is "medium," and one of .80 is "large" (p. 40).

Judging from effect sizes, the Abecedarian treatment influenced reading achievement more strongly than mathematics achievement. Through age 21, large to medium effect sizes for the full 8 years of treatment were found for reading (ranging from 1.04 at age 8 to .79 at age 21). The effect size for preschool treatment alone varied from medium to small (.75 at age 8 to .28 at age 21), suggesting that adding the primary grade component helped to maintain an advantage in reading skills. In contrast, effect sizes for school-age treatment alone (CE group) were all in the small range or less (from .28 at age 8 to .11 at 21). For mathematics, effect sizes for the full 8 years of treatment were medium (ranging from .64 at age 8 to .42 at age 21), whereas those for preschool treatment alone varied from small to large (ranging from .27 at age 8 to .73 at age 21). Effect sizes for school-age treatment alone on mathematics were small (ranging from .11 at age 8 to .26 at age 21). These effect sizes suggest that having the full 8 years of treatment did persistently enhance reading scores through young adulthood over and above the positive effects of preschool treatment, but the school-age benefit for mathematics performance did not persist (EC group outscored the EE group in mathematics in later years). The school-age program alone did not have lasting effects on mathematics performance. Although at the point that school-age treatment ended those who had school-age

intervention added to preschool treatment outscored those with preschool only in math, this effect was not seen by age 12 or thereafter.

Collapsing the four groups back into the original two-group preschool treatment or control allows for a more stringent test of preschool effects on long-term academic outcomes. Using a once-randomized–always-analyzed model gives increased power to detect differences because more individuals can contribute data. On the other hand, it may dilute treatment or control differences because some treated individuals will contribute actual and estimated data even though they did not have the same amount of treatment. Thus, the once-assigned–always-analyzed model is probably a conservative test of treatment. The metric was again age-referenced standardized reading and mathematics scores.

Taken in isolation, young adult academic test data showed that individuals assigned to preschool treatment earned significantly higher scores on Broad Mathematics, $F(1, 100) = 4.13, p < .05$. Examining the components of the Broad Mathematics score indicated that the preschool advantage was significant for Calculation, $F(1, 100) = 5.92$, $p < .05$, but not for Applied Problems. For Broad Reading, the preschool effect approached significance, $F(1, 100) = 3.78, p = .055$. Disaggregating this score showed that the treatment and control groups differed significantly on Letter-Word Identification $F(1, 100) = 5.43, p < .05$, but not on Passage Comprehension. No significant main effect for gender nor any group by gender interaction was found for either subject.

Grade-equivalent academic scores earned by young adults provide another comparison between those with preschool treatment and those without. By this metric, significant preschool treatment effects were found for both subjects, $F(1, 100) = 6.48, p < .05$ for reading and $F(1, 100) = 4.12, p < .05$ for math. Those with preschool treatment earned grade equivalent scores almost 2 years higher than those of preschool controls (Campbell, Ramey, Pungello, Miller-Johnson, & Sparling, 2002).

Longitudinal analyses of reading and mathematics scores the treatment control differences and the patterns of change over time were also calculated, again considering only the preschool group assignment. The results showed that those with preschool treatment earned consistently higher reading scores across the 13-year span from age 8 to 21, $F(1, 187) = 8.34, p < .004$, but the trajectories were essentially flat across time, showing only a very small increase in standardized scores from age 8 to 21, and the patterns were parallel in both groups. In contrast, although mathematics scores also showed a significant main effect for preschool group, $F(1, 187) = 6.02, p < .015$, a striking decline took place after age 8, $F(1, 104) = 79.015, p < .0001$. Again, this pattern was the same in both groups. Contrasting the 8-year-old achievement scores in reading and math showed that math scores were higher in elementary school but fell sharply thereafter, whereas reading scores were initially lower but the relative levels were maintained and even increased very slightly (but not significantly) through young adulthood (Campbell et al., 2001).

Life-Success

Young adult educational attainment, employment, self-sufficiency, parenthood, and social adjustment were examined as a function of whether the young adult had been assigned to the preschool treated or control group. The findings, summarized in the following are reported in Campbell et al. (2002).

Educational Attainments. Individuals treated in preschool completed significantly more years of education by age 21 than did those in the control group, $F(1, 99) = 5.00, p < .05$. Those with preschool treatment had attained more years of education (M = 12.2 years, SD = 1.5 years) than those in the preschool control group (M = 11.6 years, SD = 1.4 years). This finding was modified by a gender by preschool treatment interaction. Although there was not a significant main effect for gender, the interaction of treatment by gender was significant, $F(1, 99) = 4.19, p < .05$. Females with preschool treatment earned 1.2 more years of education (M = 12.6 years, SD = 1.6 years) than did females in the control group (M = 11.3 years, SD = 1.4 years). Males, in contrast, earned almost identical amounts of education irrespective of early childhood treatment (M = 12.0 years, SD = 1.5 years for those with early treatment; M = 11.9 years, SD = 1.3 years for those without). Individuals with preschool treatment were also more likely to be in school at age 21. A significantly higher percentage of those with preschool treatment were currently in school (42 percent) than was true for preschool controls (20 percent), $\chi^2(1, N = 104) = 5.85, p < .05$. Moreover, almost three times as many individuals in the treated group (35.9 percent) compared to the control group (13.7 percent) had attended, or were still attending, a 4-year college, $\chi^2(1, N = 104) = 6.78, p < .01$. Figure 2 illustrates this important point.

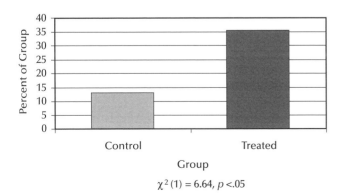

$\chi^2 (1) = 6.64, p < .05$

Figure 2 Percent attending a 4-year college by preschool treatment group

Skilled employment. Individuals in the preschool treated and control groups did not differ significantly in the percent employed but did differ significantly in the level of employment they reported. Based on Hollingshead scores of 4 or higher, young adults with preschool treatment were more likely to be engaged in skilled jobs: 47 percent of treated individuals compared with 27 percent of the controls, $\chi^2(1, N = 100) = 4.50, p < .05$. Electrician is one example of a job rated 4 on the Hollingshead scale.

Self-sufficiency. The treated and control groups did not differ significantly in the degree to which they had attained economic self-sufficiency, here defined by four indices of independent living: not requiring financial support from others, maintaining a home of their own, having their own means of transportation, and having medical coverage. Descriptively, fewer young adults who experienced the early childhood program were living in homes of their own at age 21 (19 percent compared to 29 percent of preschool controls). Few at this age were rated as maintaining full support for themselves and any dependents (9 percent of the preschool treatment group compared with 6 percent of controls). Those with preschool treatment were slightly more likely to have medical coverage than those in the preschool control group (45 percent compared with 31 percent). About half of each preschool group had cars of their own by age 21.

Parenthood. Although few of the young adults interviewed at age 21 indicated they were married (7 out of 104), 46 individuals reported having one or more children (number of children reported ranged from one child to three born by age 21). Within this sample, females had more children than males (40 in all reported by females compared to 24 reported by males, $F(1, 103) = 3.09, p < .10$. Analysis of variance showed no significant preschool effect for having a child, nor was there a significant gender by preschool interaction for the number of children born. Descriptively, however, females in the treatment group had delayed having children to some extent: 56 percent of them reported none by age 21, compared with 43 percent of control females. It is also noteworthy that fewer second or third births were reported by treated females. Almost twice as many children were born to females in the preschool control group (26 in all) as to females with preschool treatment (14 children in all). In contrast, the percent of treatment and control group males who reported being parents at age 21 was very similar in the treated and control groups: 36 percent of treated males compared with 39 percent of control group males. Twelve children in all were born to 10 treated males, and 12 were born to 9 control males.

Among those who did have children by age 21, preschool treatment was associated with a significant delay in the average age at first birth. The mean age at the birth of a first child was significantly higher for those in the preschool treatment group (M = 19.1 years, SD = 2.1 years) than for those in the preschool control group (M = 17.7 years, SD = 1.5 years), $F(1, 41) = 5.26$, $p < .05$. However, the youngest parent in both groups was 15 years old when she or he reported having a child. Defining a *teen parent* as one aged 19 or younger when a first child was born, preschool treatment was associated with a significant reduction in teen parenthood (26 percent of those treated compared with 45 percent of controls had children as teens), $\chi^2(1, N = 104) = 3.96$, $p < .05$.

Social adjustment. Indices of social adjustment included self-reported use of legal and illegal substances, substance abuse, violence, and crime. Marijuana use within the past 30 days was significantly less among the treated individuals. Eighteen percent cited some level of usage during that period, compared to 39 percent of controls, $\chi^2(1, N = 102) = 5.83$, $p < .05$. Early treatment had no significant impact on reports of the use of cocaine or other controlled substances, which was extremely rare within this sample. Cocaine use was admitted by only three persons in the sample. Alcohol use was common and comparable among those with and without preschool treatment; 73 percent of the controls and 76 percent of the treated individuals indicated that they had one or more drinks within the past 30 days. *Alcohol Abuse,* here defined as binge drinking (five or more drinks in a row within the past 30 days), was admitted by approximately one-third of the participants, 37 percent of those responding in the treated group and 27 percent of the control group; this difference was not significant. There was a tendency toward a reduction in smoking for those with preschool treatment—39 percent of the treated group and 55 percent of the controls described themselves as regular smokers, $\chi^2(1, N = 102) = 2.52$, $p = .11$. (Two individuals in the treated group chose not to complete the Risk Behavior Survey from which the substance use statistics were taken.)

The percentages of treated and control participants who admitted to carrying a weapon or violent behavior during the past month were virtually identical; 33 percent of the control participants and 35 percent of those treated in preschool responded yes to any instance of either kind of behavior. With respect to criminal convictions, females had fewer than males. Only one treatment group female reported a misdemeanor conviction compared to four in the control group. No female in either group reported a felony conviction. For males, the number reporting misdemeanor convictions was the same for both groups ($N = 5$), whereas six control group males and four treated group males reported felony convictions. These differences are not statistically significant.

A cost-benefit analysis has been independently conducted on the Abecedarian data considering the cost of the preschool program and the likely savings to society based on age 21 outcomes. Masse (2003) estimated that, conservatively, society may potentially save $3.66 for every dollar spent on the early childhood program, based on the reduction in special education placements, on higher projected lifetime earnings for the study participants and for the mothers of children who benefited from having 5 years of free child care, and on better health related to the reduction in regular smoking reported by young adults who had preschool treatment.

Current Work

Because the timing of the young adult follow up meant that those attending college or other postsecondary training had not had a chance to complete their educations or to graduate, it was important to learn more about future life success within this study sample. Funds were secured for an age-30 follow up, an age when, for most of the sample, formal education was likely to have been completed and long-term vocations begun. For 30-year-olds, data collection is being concentrated on questions of final educational attainments, vocational histories, economic status, the establishment of families, and social adjustment. Data are also being collected on children (those aged 3 and older) born to the study participants. The adults' ideas about parenting, their sense of parenting efficacy, their beliefs about their role in their child's education, and the home environments they provide their children are being assessed. Standardized achievement tests (or readiness tests) in reading and math are being administered to children. It will be important to learn if any transfer of benefit to the next generation can be detected.

Conclusion

On the whole, findings from the Abecedarian Project were quite positive. Early enhancements of cognitive skills were instrumental in better scholastic achievement in later years (Campbell et al., 2001). As young adults, those in the preschool treatment group were more likely to be still in school or to be employed at a better than minimal-level job. A very encouraging indicator of future self-sufficiency was the increased likelihood of a young adult who had experienced the preschool educational program enrolling in a 4-year college or university. The probability of attaining this goal was almost three times greater for those who had been in the preschool treated group. Given that all enrolled infants were from high-risk backgrounds, this improvement in the odds of going to college is striking and encouraging. Trends toward life-altering positive choices, such as delaying parenthood or choosing not to smoke, were also seen among those with preschool treatment. On balance, getting a good start through a cognitively stimulating and stable child care environment during the early years seems to have had far reaching implications for this sample of children born into poverty.

REFERENCES

Achenbach, T. M., & Edelbrock, C. (1983). *Manual for the Child Behavior Checklist and Revised Behavior Profile.* Burlington: Department of Psychiatry, University of Vermont.

Burchinal, M., Lee, M., & Ramey, C. (1989). Type of day-care and intellectual development in disadvantaged children. *Child Development, 60,* 128–137.

Caldwell, B. M., & Bradley, R. H. (1984). *Home Observation for Measurement of the Environment (HOME)–Revised Edition.* Little Rock, AR: University of Arkansas at Little Rock.

Campbell, F. A., Pungello, E. P., Miller-Johnson, S., Burchinal, M., & Ramey, C. T. (2001). The development of cognitive and academic abilities: Growth curves from an early childhood educational experiment. *Developmental Psychology, 37,* 231–242.

Campbell, F. A., Ramey, C. T., Pungello, E. P., Miller-Johnson, S., & Sparling, J. J. (2002). Early childhood education: Young adult outcomes from the Abecedarian Project. *Applied Developmental Science, 6,* 42–57.

Cohen, J. (1988). *Statistical power analysis* (2nd ed.). Hillsdale, NJ: Erlbaum.

Farran, D. C., & Ramey, C. T. (1977). Infant day care and attachment behavior toward mothers and teachers. *Child Development, 48,* 1112–1116.

Gray, S. W., Ramsey, B. K., & Klaus, R. A. (1982). *From 3 to 20: The Early Training Project.* Baltimore: University Park Press.

Garber, H. L. (1988). *The Milwaukee Project: Prevention of Mental Retardation in children at risk.* Washington, DC: American Association on Mental Retardation.

Haskins, R. (1985). Public school aggression among children with varying daycare experience. *Child Development, 56,* 689–703.

Haskins, R. (1989). Beyond metaphor: The efficacy of early childhood education. *American Psychologist, 44*(2), 274–282.

Karnes, M. B., Shwedel, A. M., & Williams, M. B. (1983). A comparison of five approaches for young children from low-income homes. In Consortium for Longitudinal Studies (Ed.), *As the twig is bent: Lasting effects of preschool programs* (pp. 133–169). Hillsdale, NJ: Erlbaum.

Lally, J. R., Mangione, P. L., & Honig, A. S. (1988). The Syracuse University Family Development Research Program: Long-range impact on an early intervention with low-income children and their families. In I. E. Sigel (Series Ed.) & D. R. Powell (Vol. Ed.), *Annual advances in applied developmental psychology: Vol. 3. Parent education as early childhood intervention: Emerging directions in theory, research, and practice* (pp. 79–104). Norwood, NJ: Ablex.

Lazar, I., Darlington, R., Murray, H., Royce, J., & Snipper, A. (1982). Lasting effects of early education: A report from the Consortium for Longitudinal Studies. *Monographs of the Society for Research in Child Development, 47*(2–3, Serial No. 195).

Masse, L. N. (2003, April). A benefit-cost Analysis of the Carolina Abecedarian Preschool Program presentation. In F. A. Campbell (Chair), *What's a good early childhood education worth and why?* Paper symposium presented at the Biennial Meeting of the Society for Research in Child Development, Tampa, FL.

Ramey, C. T., & Campbell, F. A. (1984). Preventive education for high-risk children: Cognitive consequences of the Carolina Abecedarian Project. *American Journal of Mental Deficiency, 88,* 515–523.

Ramey, C. T., & Campbell, F. A. (1987). The Carolina Abecedarian Project: An educational experiment concerning human malleability. In J. Gallagher & C. T. Ramey (Eds.), *The malleability of children* (pp. 115–126). Baltimore: Paul H. Brookes.

Ramey, C. T., & Campbell, F. A. (1991). Poverty, early childhood education and academic competence: The ABC experiment. In A. Houston (Ed.), *Children in poverty* (pp. 190–221). New York: Cambridge University Press.

Ramey, C. T., Collier, A. M., Sparling, J. J., Loda, F. A., Campbell, F. A., Ingram, D. L., & Finkelstein, N. W. (1976). The Carolina Abecedarian Project: A longitudinal and multidisciplinary approach to the prevention of developmental retardation. In T. Tjossem (Ed.), *Intervention strategies for high-risk infants and young children* (pp. 629–665). Baltimore: University Park Press.

Ramey, C. T., & Smith, B. (1977). Assessing the intellectual consequences of early intervention with high-risk infants. *American Journal of Mental Deficiency, 81,* 318–324.

Schaefer, E., Edgerton, M., & Aaronson, M. (1977). *Classroom Behavior Inventory.* (Available from the Frank Porter Graham Child Development Institute, University of North Carolina at Chapel Hill, Chapel Hill, NC 27599.)

Schweinhart, L. J., Barnes, H. V., & Weikart, D. P. (1993). *Significant benefits: The High Scope / Perry Preschool Study through age 27.* (Monographs of the High Scope Educational Research Foundation No. 10). Ypsilanti, MI: High/Scope Educational Research Foundation.

Sparling, J., & Lewis, I. (1979). *Learningames for the first three years: A guide to parent-child play.* New York: Walker.

Sparling, J., & Lewis, I. (1984). *Learningames for threes and fours: A guide to adult and child play.* New York: Walker.

Sparling, J., & Lewis, I. (2000). Learningames: The Abecedarian curriculum. Hillsborough, NC: MindNurture.

Woodcock, R. W., & Johnson, M. B. (1977). *Woodcock-Johnson Psycho-Educational Battery: Part 2. Tests of Academic Achievement.* Boston: Teaching Resources Corporation.

Woodcock, R. W., & Johnson, M. B. (1989). *Woodcock-Johnson Psycho-Educational Battery–Revised.* Allen, TX: DLM.

FRANCES A. CAMPBELL
ELIZABETH P. PUNGELLO
University of North Carolina at Chapel Hill

EARLY CHILDHOOD, CULTURALLY AND LINGUISTICALLY DIVERSE ISSUES IN HEAD START

ABILITY TRAINING, EARLY EFFORTS IN

Many educators believe that most academic and social learning is based on factors such as student aptitudes or abilities, instructional environment, and teaching methodology. While these three variables do not form a complete structure capable of containing all those factors contributing to learning, they certainly account for many of the variables educators would agree are important to success in school.

Learner aptitudes or abilities are those personological variables that frequently are called intelligence(s), traits, gifts, and characteristics. Frequently, educators will talk about a child's potential to learn, using the term ability as if it were a predetermined factor waiting to be drawn on at some point. The logic, then, is that if learning is a result of the presence and development of certain mental abilities, school failure (both academic and social) may be the result of disabilities, with disability implying an academic or social handicap.

If regular (elementary and secondary) educators teach to the abilities of students to learn, then special educators may direct more of their instruction to the disabilities that inhibit learning, hence the term and concept of ability training. How valid is this construct of ability training? A short response to that question is impossible. Any field involving relatively newly defined services to persons, especially children, in particular handicapped children, will generate professional controversy. Any field struggling with the pressures associated with economic, political, social, legislative, litigative, and basic human rights and values will face diversity. Any field that requires its many disciplines to unite in purpose will experience communicative stress. But, few professionals will purposely question their field's major methodology to the degree special and remedial educators have, for the period of time they have done so, and in the face of such a degree of controversy.

Some special educators believe avidly in ability training of all types; some reject it totally; but almost all, no matter what they believe, practice ability training. The truth in that observation is vividly displayed when we recognize that the value of ability training to handicapped persons has been questioned repeatedly for over the last 100 years. What then is in ability training that has caused the field of special education to tenaciously and steadfastly maintain its cause? Ability training is routed in the historic search for the structure and function of the mind. Educators, in particular special educators, have sought to diagnose specific abilities and provide remediation to those abilities, or disabilities as the case may be.

Mental ability (aptitude), concerns those components that are assumed to constitute the mind, and therefore explain learning. Mental-ability structures, in more scientific parlance, may be referred to as information-processing behaviors. Mental processes or information processes are those theoretical or conceptual acts (processes) by which information is transmitted from the peripheral (to the central nervous system) sensory organs (i.e., eyes, ears, fingers [tactile], muscles [kinesthetic]) perceived, labeled, stored, provided mediated meaning, conceptually associated, and expressed as language or motoric responses. It is not unusual for practitioners to reference most psychological functions synonymously with mental abilities. Hence, the very definition of learning disabilities refers to "basic psychological processes."

The history of man, at least those aspects related to the structures of the mind, how it works, and therefore how these processes can be measured, begins with the early Greek philosophers. Pythagoras placed the "mind" in the brain in the sixth century BC. Most of the processes described then were hypotheoretical, related to this assumed function. Therefore, the names given these processes sometimes sound as if they had been isolated neurologically or psychoneurologically. The truth is that the majority of the commonly referenced mental processes, that is, perception and language, are not simple, easily explained constructs. They are complex concepts that may contain hundreds of component subparts. The major issues relating to ability training have been the long-standing arguments regarding the mind, its disabilities, and the habilitation or rehabilitation needed. A case in point is that while simple tests are designed to ascertain visual perceptual-motor development, visual perception is not a simple discriminate function. In a general sense, perception requires the discrimination of distinctive features, wherein a specific symbolic meaning can be assigned each distinct stimuli. Logically then, once perceptual information has been discriminated, it may be stored for some short-term reference, or it may be assigned a permanent symbolism, then converted to a language concept. Logically then, too, there may be both visual and auditory perception. These two processes may need to be coordinated when auditory and visual information is presented in an integrated manner. Perception, however, is not logically complex in contrast to the explanations of the structure and function of language.

A mental ability may also be referred to as a faculty. Mann (1979) credits Aristotle for establishing the basis for modern faculty psychology. The Romans further refined and added descriptors such as intellect, attention, and language. St. Thomas Aquinas, during the Middle Ages, although poorly credited, began to amplify and extend faculty psychology by dividing it into two parts: the *intellectus,* which carries out abstractions and functions of the possible intellect; and the *ratio,* which is directed toward understanding, judgment, and reasoning. The intellect is active and creative, the ratio, passive and receptive, that is, sensory stimuli must be perceptually assigned symbolic meaning/value before they have intellectual meaning.

Faculty psychology, the theoretical basis for mental process, was soundly criticized by many of the seventeenth-, eighteenth-, and nineteenth-century scholars. Hobbes

(1558–1679) displaced it with his theories of automotion in the brain set off by sensory stimulation. Locke (1632–1704) was a sensationalist, and an arch antifaculist. Hume (1715–1776), also a sensationalist in the British tradition, condemned faculties, basing mental response solely in sensory stimulation. By the mid-nineteenth century, the psychologist and educator Herbart attempted to destroy for all time the residual of faculty psychology.

One of the predominate figures in mental measurement, Spearman, writing in 1927, notes that faculty psychology seems to persist, no matter what the criticism.

> One curious feature about these formal faculties has yet to be mentioned. The doctrine loses every battle—so to speak—but always wins the war. It will bend to the slightest breath of criticism; but not the most violent storm can break it. The attacks made long ago by the Herbartians appeared to be irresistible; no serious defense was even attempted. Yet the sole permanent effect of these attacks was only to banish the word "faculty," leaving the doctrine represented by this word to escape scot free. (pp. 38–39)

However, other early forces in the field such as Thorndike continued to be critical. As a quote from Mann (1979) notes,

> The science of education should at once rid itself of its conception of the mind as a sort of machine, different parts of which sense, perceive, discriminate, imagine, remember, conceive, associate, reason about, desire, choose, form habits, attend to. . . . There is no power of sense discrimination to be delicate or coarse. . . . There are only the connections between separate sense stimuli and our separate senses and human judgments thereof. . . . There is no memory to hold in a uniformly tight and loose grip the experiences of the past. There are only the particular connections between particular mental events and others. (Klein, 1970, p. 662)

Though an out-and-out antifaculist, Thorndike, interestingly enough, could not shake the ingrained habit of his times of speaking about "faculties." Thus, he described his bonds as faculties in the 1903 edition of *Education Psychology* (p. 30) "the mind is a host of highly particularized and independent faculties" (Spearman, 1927, p. 36).

Yet, it is faculty psychology that provided the definition for twentieth-century mental measurement. On the basis of his inquiries, Galton described what, in essence, is a superfaculty, which he called "general ability," assigning to this faculty the name intelligence (a term popularized by Spencer). Galton distinguished this superfaculty from special aptitudes. He was more interested in the first, since he believed that general ability inevitably set a limit to accomplishment of any kind. He complained that most writers emphasized specific aptitudes or skill, that they

> lay too much stress upon apparent specialties, thinking that because a man is devoted to some particular pursuit, he could not have succeeded in anything else; they might as well say that,

because a youth has fallen in love with a brunette, he could not possibly have fallen in love with a blonde. He may or may not have had any more natural liking for the former type of beauty than for the latter; but it is as probable as not that the affair was mainly or wholly due to a general amorousness. It is just the same with intellectual pursuits. (Burt, 1955, p. 85)

Galton most certainly did not deny the existence of special capacities or their potential importance. He cited instances in which memory, musical ability, and artistic and literary talent ran within several members of the same family. Home environment or family tradition could not explain all such cases, for example, "prodigies of memory." However, his studies in the main had convinced him "in how small a degree intellectual eminence can be considered as due to purely special powers" (Burt, 1955, p. 85).

As to the measurement of both general and special abilities, Galton suggested that individual differences in both are distributed in accordance with the normal curve, much as other human characteristics such as size or height are distributed. He printed a tabular classification of frequencies which he held "may apply to special just as truly as to general ability" (Burt, 1955, p. 85). Thus we see the beginnings of psychometric assessment of both general ability and specific abilities.

About 1880, the German psychiatrist Kraeplin, one of Wundt's students, began to use different tests to describe higher cognitive functions (Guilford, 1967). His testing interests were directed to such processes as general memory, specific memory, attention, and task-directed behaviors. However, it was James McKeen Cattell who first formulated the term "mental tests." Cattell's extension of Galton's simple tests began the modern practice of psychometrics as we know it today. Others such as DeSanctis attacked the realms of higher cognitive functioning. DeSanctis published a series of six tests including (1) memory for colors, (2) recognition of forms, (3) sustained attention, (4) reasoning involving relations, (5) following instructions, and (6) thinking.

At the turn of the twentieth century, the French Minister of Public Instruction was still wrestling with an age-old problem: how to consistently identify the handicapped. Having agreed on the terminology to be used (idiot for the lowest level; imbecile for the intermediate level; and moron for the mildly mentally retarded), a psychologist, Alfred Binet, and physician, Theodore Simon, were commissioned to develop a consistent means of classifying children. Binet and Simon (1905, 1908) produced, through a standardized procedure of observation, a psychological classification of quantifiable differences in children's intellectual characteristics (traits). By 1905 Binet and Simon had developed 29 such tests designed to measure specific traits; by 1908 they had developed a classification of tests beginning at age three and continuing through age 13. Thus, the work preceding 1905 established human intelligence as a comprehensive integration of several traits including memory, attention, comprehension, muscular coordination, spatial relations, judgment, initiative, and ability to adapt. Further, the criteria for measurement of these traits were standardized at various chronological age levels. From this procedure the measurement of human performance took a great leap forward.

Binet carried his interest in higher processes into his work of developing mental tests for use in Paris schools. He and his associates criticized tests of the Galton type as being too simple, too sensory-motor, and too dependent on associationistic dogma. They expressed their own preference for the complex cognitive functions, proposing that 10 categories be explored by mental tests: (1) memory, (2) imagery, (3) imagination, (4) attention, (5) comprehension, (6) suggestibility, (7) aesthetic appreciation, (8) moral sentiment, (9) muscular force, force of will, and motor skill, and (10) judgment of visual space.

Modern psychoeducational assessment and remedial practices, indeed the very content of most perceptual, motor, language, vocational, and academic remedial curricula, are based on Binet's work. Two of the major issues are the specificity with which mental ability processes can reliably be ascertained and the desirability of remediating the specific perceptual or language processes in terms of their transferability and ultimate academic and social learning transfer.

But, it is clear that abilities had been identified by tests and that ability training was to become a crucial issue facing the twentieth century. The main philosophic question is, do mental abilities really exist in nature? The second question is, do they respond to specific training once they are described, measured, observed, and, in short, isolated as specific mental abilities? These two questions constitute the major issues facing special educators today. Since mental abilities are developmentally linked to chronological growth, culture, and experience, they may be encouraged by structured educational experiences. Conversely, when developmentally arrested, culturally neglected, or denied sequenced experiential practice, they may become deficient. Mental ability deficiencies may then be the principal characteristics associated with handicapping conditions such as learning and behavioral disorders. The entire nervous system develops only when each aspect or component necessary to successfully decode information (perceive its symbolic features) provides that symbol a language construct and a mechanism by which encoding of the mediated concept through motoric or verbal language permits communication. Therefore, specific reference is made in the definition of mental retardation and learning disabilities, two of the largest categories of handicapping conditions, to dysfunction of perceptual, perceptual-motor, or language abilities.

Philosophically, then, it appears that a leap in logic is *not* required to assume that if a disability exists, relative to causing a handicap, it should be corrected. That is exactly what ability training implies. It would appear that it was incorrectly named to begin with. It should be called disability training.

The history of ability training parallels that of the field of special education. The pioneers in ability training were the pioneers of the field. Itard, Howe, Sequin, Montessori, Binet, Wepman, Kirk, Strauss, Fernald, Frostig, and Cruickshank were all advocates of special education as it grew, and responsible for advancing ability training simultaneously. Tests used to describe a disability were followed by commercially prepared curricula to train the ability and remove the disability. The logic is obvious. The problem is in the scientific validation, or lack of it.

The early 1960s brought with it a concern for neurologically impaired children. The mid-1960s added the term learning disabled as a category of handicapping conditions. Both of these conditions required an increased emphasis on psychoneurological and psychoeducational assessment. Those that developed psychoeducational and psychoneurological tests to diagnose these conditions fueled the fire for ability training by describing conditions which, by their description, must exist.

Curricula designed to modify and treat patterns of disability were soon commercially available. Whole classes of children were exposed to Montessori, Frostig, and Fernald techniques, and administered Frostig, Kephart, and Delaccato assessment procedures. Tests such as the Illinois Test of Psycholinguistic Abilities became commonplace, much as the Woodcock-Johnson test batteries of today. The prevailing belief was that specific mental processes must be diagnosed in order for modification of a specific disability to result in quantum jumps in academic remedial achievement and potential normalization. Thus, the so-called diagnostic-prescriptive process is one form of ability training.

What then is the difficulty with visual and auditory perceptual training, perceptual motor training, language training, and the other forms of sensory, motor, perceptual, and language ability training? The problem is that data arrived at through quasi-scientific means are controversial concerning the results of ability training. There are data to support ability training, if the objective to be achieved is a change in an ability, and that ability alone. There are relatively few data to support that transfer of training occurs between training of a perceptual or cognitive ability and an academic achievement skill, for instance reading.

The overall interaction among these abilities being trained and other abilities remains unknown, except it does seem that auditory perceptual training is related to language growth much more than visual perceptual training. Language training seemingly has the greatest transference to academic remediation. But even the search for generalities would produce only controversy. The fact is, ability training makes sense logically but has not been sufficiently researched devoid of other educational practices with school-age children to permit definitive statements.

And yet, the practice does not only continue, it continues to thrive.

REFERENCES

Binet, A., & Simon, T. (1905). Methodes nouvelles pour le diagnostic du niveau intellectuel des anomaux. *L'anne psychologique, 11,* 191–244.

Binet, A., & Simon, T. (1908). Le developpement de l'intelligence chez les infants. *L'anne psychologique, 14,* 1–94.

Burt, C. (1955). The evidence for the concept of intelligence. *British Journal of Educational Psychology, 25,* 158–177.

Klein, D. B. (1970). *A history of scientific psychology.* New York: Basic Books.

Mann, L. (1970). *On the trail of process.* New York: Grune & Stratton.

Spearman, C. (1927). *The abilities of man: Their nature and measurement.* London: Macmillan.

DAVID A. SABATINO
*West Virginia College of
Graduate Studies*

DIAGNOSTIC PRESCRIPTIVE TEACHING
FERNALD METHOD
ILLINOIS TEST OF PSYCHOLINGUISTIC ABILITIES
INTELLIGENCE
REMEDIATION, DEFICIT-CENTERED MODELS OF

ABNORMALITIES, NEUROPHYSIOLOGICAL

The human nervous system consists of the brain, the spinal cord, and an intricate network of nerve fibers projecting from the brain and spinal cord. Structurally, the brain is differentiated into the two cerebral hemispheres, the brain stem, and the cerebellum. The brain, together with the spinal cord, traditionally has been conceptualized as the central nervous system (CNS). The entire network of nerve fibers is then referred to as the peripheral nervous system (PNS). The brief discussion regarding normal neurological structure and function that follows is meant as an aid in the appreciation of neurophysiological disorders. The intent here is to offer an overview; for a more detailed account of the nervous system, the reader is referred to one of a number of neurophysiological texts (e.g., Bickerstaff, 1978; Lindsley & Holmes, 1984; Swaiman & Ashwal, 2006).

Peripheral nerves are referred to by the direction the impulses flow and the site of their termination. Specifically, the direction of the impulses carried in relation to the CNS, the originating structure, or final destination of the impulse, and the nature of the impulse itself, are used to classify peripheral nerves. For instance, the PNS contains sensory nerves that carry impulses from the sense organs (eyes, ears, nose, etc.) to the CNS. By way of contrast, the motor nerves travel from the CNS to the periphery, exciting both skeletal (voluntary) and smooth (involuntary) muscle into movement. Included in PNS, the cranial nerves arise from or travel to the brain stem (connecting structure between spinal cord and cerebrum). Similarly, the spinal nerves travel to or from the spinal cord. The group of peripheral nerves that carry impulses to smooth muscle (causing involuntary movements of the intestines, heartbeat, constriction of the pupils, etc.) and those that incite the secretion of glands cause automatic changes in the body. These peripheral nerves are sometimes referred to collectively as the autonomic nervous system.

Functionally, the fundamental building block of the nervous system is the neuronal circuit. The simplest neuronal circuit contains only two interconnected nerve cells, involving an input and an output cell (e.g., simple knee jerk reflex). Local circuits exist at all levels of the nervous system and, in fact, such circuits in the spinal cord connect the cerebral cortex, brain stem, and cerebellum. These connections can function as modules in more complex circuits. Indeed, these integrated networks are capable of sustaining complex behavior (Gaddes, 1985; Kandel, Schwartz, & Jessell, 1991).

As an example, sensory impulses traveling from the various sense organs to the brain are integrated, recorded, recognized, stored or remembered, as interpreted by the cerebral cortex. Moreover, skeletal movement may be affected by motor nerves traveling by way of the spinal cord. Generally, the entire system works to regulate and coordinate bodily responses to both internal and external changes in the environment (Taber, 1970). A malfunctioning neurological system results in an impaired capacity for responding adaptively to a changing environment.

Neurophysiological abnormality may occur by means of many agents and during various stages of the life process; some stages offer more vulnerability than others. Antenatal agents (occurring before birth) described by Nelson (1969) include genetic factors, chromosomal aberrations, placental disease, maternal complications, number of previous pregnancies, age of both mother and father, intrauterine infection, toxic agents (including certain drugs and alcohol), and radiation. Various organ systems begin and end their prenatal development at different times, therefore their sensitivity to agents varies with maturity of the fetus. The most vulnerable period for the brain is from 15 to 25 days of gestation but, clearly, damage can occur at any time during the development of the nervous system (Hetherington & Parke, 1979).

Perinatal (occurring just before or after birth) vulnerability to neurological insult is accentuated by premature birth. Inadequate oxygen during this stage, hemorrhage, trauma, and infection are the principal offenders (Nelson, 1969). Postnatal (occurring after birth) damage to the neurological system may include damage incurred after birth, during childhood, or throughout the various stages of adulthood. Infections, principally meningitis and encephalitis, injuries, and degenerative neurological disease have also been implicated (Nelson, 1969).

Weller, Swash, McLellan, and Scholtz (1983) estimated that 40 percent of developmental malformations of the CNS arise from genetic abnormality. The most common genetic abnormality is Down's syndrome. This disorder is associated with a group of chromosomal aberrations involving the 21st chromosome pair. In the great majority of cases, a failure to join occurs during the meiosis process, resulting in a trisomy (additional chromosome) of the 21st chromosome pair. Translocation and mosaician represent less frequently occurring aberrations of the 21st chromosome pair, also associated with Down's syndrome (Kopp & Parmelee, 1979).

The incidence of Down's syndrome is between one and two per thousand live births for all races and ethnic groups (Gillberg, 1995; Norman, 1963). Although there is some variability in incidence, most researchers cite an increase in relation to maternal age (Benda, 1960; Lawrence, 1981; Weller et al., 1983). A gradual increase begins with maternal age of 35 and escalates drastically after 40. Metabolic or environmental factors in the mothers' ovaries have been suggested as causes for the syndrome (Benda, 1960; Lawrence, 1981; Nelson, 1969; Norman, 1963; Weller, Swash, McLellan, & Scholtz, 1983). Structural inspection of the Down's syndrome brain suggests impairment of both growth and differentiation (Benda, 1960). The brain is generally low in weight and the normal convolutional pattern of the brain is simplified. The density of the nerve cells in the cerebral cortex is reduced (Weller et al., 1983).

Rate of mental development is not only slower than normal but also deteriorates progressively with age in Down's syndrome (Cornwell & Birch, 1969; Dicks-Mireaux, 1972; Gillberg, 1995). Many explanations, including neurophysiologic changes, have been offered as explanation for this progressive deterioration. Weller et al. (1983) noted that the microscopic study of brain tissue of Down's syndrome victims during autopsy reveals patterns of neurofibrillary tangles, senile plaques, and granulovacular degeneration such as are found in Alzheimer's disease (deteriorative disease of the elderly involving degeneration of the smaller blood vessels of the brain). Kopp and Parmelee (1979) suggest that the severe limitations in higher level integrative abilities evident in Down's syndrome may cause deficits in information processing (e.g., use of language) that could have progressive detrimental effects on the child's intellectual development over time. The child's capacity for responding adaptively to changing stimulus conditions, a necessity for proper intellectual development, may be impaired directly by the nature of the syndrome. However, the nature of the environment in which these children find themselves, whether it is enriched or impoverished, also can affect development.

In contrast to Down's syndrome, which is genetically related, spina bifida seems to be more influenced by environmental factors. Although genetic factors are suggested by the higher incidence in infants born to parents with a family history of such lesions, it seems that racial, geographical, and even seasonal factors also may be implicated (Kopp & Parmelee, 1979; Weller et al., 1983). Clearly, the interaction of genetic and environmental factors has recently been given prominence. Genetic predisposition combined with certain environmental factors may be the causal condition for spina bifida occurrence (Carter, 1974).

Spina bifida represents a malformation of the nervous system that appears to be more localized and variable in effect than that of Down's syndrome. This defect occurs as a result of faulty prenatal development, in which the lower end of embryotic CNS fails to close. The contents of the spinal column (nerve fibers, meninges, and fluid) may protrude from the lower back in a sac (meningomyelocele). Individual defects vary depending on the extent of damage to the nerve fibers and the existence of other associated conditions (Kleinberg, 1982). The spinal cord is frequently abnormal above and below the level of the spina bifida (Weller et al., 1983). Hydrocephalus, abnormal accumulation of cerebral spinal fluid, frequently is associated with spina bifida. Untreated hydrocephalus creates severe enlargement of the head, increased pressure, and subsequent damage to the brain (Kleinberg, 1982).

Intellectual levels of victims with spina bifida are variable, ranging from an IQ of 137 to severe subnormality (Gillberg, 1995; Hunt, 1981). More specifically, Spain (1974) associates mental retardation with protrusion of a portion of the brain (cranial meningocele and cephalocele), whereas infants with other forms are considered to have potentially normal intellect. Many individuals with spina bifida are incontinent of urine and feces, and have weakness of their legs with sensory loss below the level of the lesion (Kleinberg, 1982). Owing to the presence of the typical locomotor problems in spina bifida, it is unclear whether some deficits are due to neurological impairment or environmental influence. Spain's (1974) longitudinal spina bifida studies have revealed significant deficits in spatial and manipulative development. The fact that the disorder limits the individual's experience may, in fact, cause or influence the specific deficits in spatial and manipulative development. Among the educational problems noted are difficulties with arithmetic and perseveration in language, as well as emotionality and poor motivation (Kopp & Parmelee, 1979).

Primary disorders of the CNS, like Down's syndrome and spina bifida, represent a relatively small proportion of the neurological problems in infants (Horwitz, 1973). More frequently, the genetic programs for potentially normal neurological development are subverted by adverse prenatal or birthing conditions such as lack of oxygen (hypoxia). Cerebral hemorrhage often occurs during prolonged hypoxia. The accumulation of stagnate blood that follows circulatory collapse may cause bleeding and ultimate damage to brain tissue (Weller et al., 1983). Premature infants are especially vulnerable to hypoxia. Since the respiratory system is not fully perfected until the last four to six weeks of gestation, these infants are often born without an optimally functioning respiratory system. Postmortem studies on premature children show that the bleeding usually occurs within one of the cavities of the brain or the space below the arachnoid membrane that contains cerebrospinal fluid (subarachnoid space [Horwitz, 1973]). Later complications of such subarachnoid hemorrhage involve epilepsy, dementia, and hydrocephalus (Weller et al., 1983). Full-term infants are more likely to suffer from hemorrhage in the mid-brain stem (pons) and the posterior portion of the cerebral cortex (hippocampus). Cause for these differences are not, as yet, fully understood.

The location and size of brain lesions at or soon after birth are the primary determinants of the extent of nervous system impairment. The results may range from a gross alteration of brain organization to more minimal effects such as motor overactivity, shortened attention span, or slight muscle impairment (Pincus & Tucker, 1974; Teberg et al., 1982). Large injuries in infants tend to produce more widespread deficits in intellectual abilities than similar injuries in adults. Dulling of many areas of intellectual functioning, as opposed to having an effect in specific functioning (e.g., language development, visual-spatial relationship comprehension), is also a hallmark effect of the diffuse damage that follows hypoxia (Rapin, 1982).

Neurological deficiencies from early injury are difficult to predict. The nervous system of the newborn infant is extremely immature, functioning largely at brain stem and spinal cord level. The neurologic reflexes such as Moro, grasping, and stepping represent primitive neuronal function that is largely uninhibited by higher cerebral control. Changes in these reflexes are usually not helpful in localizing the lesion, and may occur with either cortical or subcortical dysfunction (Horwitz, 1973). Damage to the cerebral cortex, for instance, may not be evident until the age when behavior dependent on the damaged part makes its developmental appearance. Thus, pathology of fine motor coordination, speech, and cognition is unlikely to be diagnosed in infancy (Rapin, 1982). However, changes in reflexes and disorganized activity of the subcortical structures expressed as a movement disorder or spasticity continue to be used as indicators of neurological damage. In Teberg et al.'s study of low birth weight infants (1982), spastic quadriplegia did, in fact, emerge as the indicative diagnosis of neurological handicap. Churchill, Masland, Naylor, and Ashworth (1974) support this finding.

Turkewitz (1974) contended that the standard methods used for the early identification of neurologic handicaps are insensitive to many forms of neurological involvement. Infants who have had difficulties shortly before or during the birth process frequently appear to recover in a few days. However, abnormalities in motor, language, and intellectual functioning become apparent later in infancy and childhood. Studies using indicators of higher levels of neurological

organization (e.g., left/right preference) are being investigated in an effort to identify infants who have experienced neurological damage that is normally not expressed until later in life. However, normative patterns of left/right preference for infants must be established first, before atypical patterns can be interpreted.

The possibilities for neurophysiological dysfunction are limitless; the pathologies presented should not be considered as inclusive by any means. However, it is hoped that an appreciation of the complexity of cerebral neural structure and the corresponding intricacies of impairment resulting from neurophysiological dysfunction will encourage the reader to treat each impaired patient as a unique individual, for heterogeneity of outcome is common (Gaddes, 1985; Goldstein & Reynolds, 1999; Kopp & Parmelee, 1979).

REFERENCES

Benda, C. E. (1960). *The child with mongolism (congenital acromicria)*. New York: Grune & Stratton.

Bickerstaff, E. R. (1978). *Neurology* (3rd ed.). Bungay, England: Chaucer.

Carter, C. O. (1974). Clues to the aetiology of neural tube malformations: Studies in hydrocephalus and spina bifida. *Developmental Medicine and Child Neurology, 16*(Suppl. 32), 3–15.

Churchill, J. A., Masland, R. L., Naylor, A. A., & Ashworth, M. R. (1974). The etiology of cerebral palsy in pre-term infants. *Developmental Medicine and Child Neurology, 16,* 143–149.

Cornwell, A. C., & Birch, H. G. (1969). Psychological and social development in home-reared children with Down's syndrome (mongolism). *American Journal of Mental Deficiencies, 74,* 341–350.

Dicks-Mireaux, M. J. (1972). Mental development of infants with Down's syndrome. *American Journal of Mental Deficiencies, 77,* 26–32.

Gaddes, W. H. (1985). *Learning disabilities and brain function: A neuropsychological approach* (2nd ed.). New York: Springer-Verlag.

Gillberg, C. (1995). *Clinical child neuron psychiatry*. Cambridge, England: Cambridge University Press.

Goldstein, S., & Reynolds, C. R. (1999). *Handbook of neurodevelopmental and genetic disorders of children*. New York: Guilford.

Hetherington, E. M., & Parke, R. D. (1979). *Child psychology: A contemporary viewpoint* (2nd ed.). New York: McGraw-Hill.

Horwitz, S. J. (1973). Neurologic problems. In M. H. Klaus & A. A. Fanaroff (Eds.), *Care of the high risk neonate* (pp. 287–300). Philadelphia: Saunders.

Hunt, G. (1981). Spina bifida: Implications for 100 children at school. *Developmental Medicine and Child Neurology, 23,* 160–172.

Kandel, E., Schwartz, J., & Jessell, T. (1991). *Principles of neural science*. New York: Elsevier.

Kleinberg, S. B. (1982). *Educating the chronically ill child*. Rockville, MD: Aspen Systems.

Kopp, C. B., & Parmelee, A. H. (1979). Prenatal and perinatal influences on infant behavior. In J. D. Osofsky (Ed.), *Handbook of infant development* (pp. 29–75). New York: Wiley.

Lawrence, K. M. (1981). Abnormalities of the central nervous system. In A. P. Norman (Ed.), *Congenital abnormalities in infancy* (pp. 21–81). Oxford, England: Blackwell.

Lindsley, D. F., & Holmes, J. E. (1984). *Basic human neurophysiology.* Amsterdam: Elsevier Science.

Nelson, W. E. (Ed.). (1969). *Textbook of pediatrics* (9th ed.). Philadelphia: Saunders.

Norman, A. P. (1963). *Congenital abnormalities in infancy.* Philadelphia: Davis.

Pincus, J. H., & Tucker, G. J. (1974). *Behavioral neurology.* New York: Oxford University Press.

Rapin, I. (1982). *Children with brain dysfunction: Neurology, cognition, language and behavior.* New York: Raven.

Spain, B. (1974). Verbal performance ability in pre-school children with spina bifida. *Developmental Medicine and Child Neurology, 16,* 773–780.

Swaiman, K. F., & Ashwal, S. (2006). *Pediatric neurology principles and practice* (4th ed.). St. Louis: Mosby.

Taber, C. W. (1970). *Taber's cyclopedic medical dictionary* (11th ed.). Philadelphia: Davis.

Teberg, A. J., Wu, P. Y. K., Hodgman, J. E., Mich, C., Garfinkle, J., Azen, S., & Wingert, W. A. (1982). Infants with birth weight under 1500 grams: Physical, neurological and developmental outcome. *Critical Care Medicine, 10,* 10–14.

Turkewitz, G. (1974). The detection of brain dysfunction in the newborn infant. In D. P. Purpura & G. P. Reaser (Eds.), *Methodological approaches to the study of brain maturation and its abnormalities* (pp. 125–130). Baltimore: University Park Press.

Weller, R. O., Swash, M., McLellan, D. S., & Scholtz, C. L. (1983). *Clinical neuropathology.* New York: Overwallop, Great Britain: BAS.

DOROTHY A. STROM
RAYMOND S. DEAN
Ball State University
Indiana University School of
Medicine

ADAPTED PHYSICAL EDUCATION
HEALTH MAINTENANCE PROCEDURES
PHYSICAL ANOMALIES

ABPP

See AMERICAN BOARD OF PROFESSIONAL PSYCHOLOGY.

ABROMS, KIPPY I. (1942–   )

Kippy I. Abroms received her BA in psychology from the University of New Hampshire in 1962, MEd in reading from

Kitty I. Abroms

Tulane University in 1973, and PhD in special education from the University of South Mississippi in 1977. Abroms also completed post doctoral training at the University of California, Riverside in 1977 where she worked with Jane Mercer on the System of Multiple Pluralistic Assessment (SOMPA). Abroms is presently an associate professor at Tulane University where she has been teaching since 1975. She has directed several projects for the Office of Special Education and Rehabilitation Services and the Bureau of Education for the Handicapped.

Abroms conducted research with J. W. Bennett (1981) that dispelled the well-entrenched notion of exclusive maternal etiology in Down's syndrome. Abroms and Bennett found that in a significant number of cases the extra 21st chromosome, the immediate cause of Down's syndrome, comes from the sperm. Thus there can be a maternal or paternal contribution to the etiology of Trisomy 21.

Her research has included a longitudinal study on the social development of preschool gifted children, and, as a member of the cranio-facial team at Tulane University Medical Center, she has been involved in investigations of the relationship between cognitive functioning, self-concept, and cranio-facial intervention. She has also become interested in how genetic disorders are manifested in children, and especially in facial deformities that are obvious in the classroom (Abroms, 1987).

REFERENCES

Abroms, K. (1987). Genetic disorders underlying facial deformities. *Topics in early childhood special education, 6,* 92–100.

Abroms, K. I., & Bennett, J. W. (1981). Parental contributions to Trisomy 21: Review of recent cytological and statistical findings.

In P. Mittler (Ed.), *Frontiers of knowledge in mental retardation, Vol. 2. Biomedical aspects* (pp. 149–157). Baltimore: University Park.

ELAINE FLETCHER-JANZEN
*University of Colorado at
Colorado Springs*

ABSENCE OF SPEECH

See SPEECH, ABSENCE OF.

ABSENCE SEIZURES

Absence seizures (previously referred to as *petit mal epilepsy*) are characterized by impaired consciousness that is unaccompanied by large convulsive movements. Individuals with absence seizures describe them as "brief flashes of blackouts," "like in a daze," or "getting into a trance" (Panayiotopoulos et al., 1992). While absence seizures are nonconvulsive during the seizure, some movement (e.g., eye-blinking, staring) and other minor facial movements (e.g., twitching) may be present. An observer also may notice body limpness and the arrest of activity, such as the dropping of an item.

There is a lack of aura (i.e., a sensation that it is about to occur) prior to the onset of an absence seizure as well as an absence of a postictal period (post seizure confusion) following the seizure's termination. Absence seizures are characterized by their brevity; although they may last up to 1 minute, they typically last for 5 to 10 seconds. The term *pyknolespy* (*pyknos* refers to overcrowding) is frequently used to describe absence seizures as they have a tendency to occur in rapid succession. Prolonged periods of impaired consciousness due to consecutive absence seizures may lead to considerable dysfunction in school activities and others that require concentration and comprehension. For example, if absence seizures occur while a teacher is discussing novel material, impaired consciousness may cause the child to miss important instructional objectives that may not be addressed again during the academic school year (Leppik, 2000). Therefore, academic deficits are not uncommon in children who experience absence seizures.

Absence seizures are generalized. They involve abnormal activity throughout the brain, and their genesis is not in a discrete (focus) part of the brain. A distinction is made between typical and atypical absence seizures. Electroencephalograms (EEGs) show that typical absence seizures are characterized by an abrupt and synchronous onset and termination of both hemispheres and by a characteristic three-cycle-per-second spike and wave pattern. Structural abnormalities typically are not noted during neurological exams or the use of computerized axial tomographic scans.

Absence seizures occur in 2 percent to 10 percent of children with epilepsy. The age of onset typically is between 5 and 15 and is more common in girls. Typical absence seizures are frequently idiopathic (genetic) and remit in 40 percent of patients (Leppik, 2000). Hyperventilation, and, less commonly, photic stimulation may facilitate the spike discharges associated with absence seizures (Panayiotopoulos et al., 1992).

Atypical absence seizures are more complex than typical absence seizures. During atypical absence seizures, children can retain some ability for purposive movement and speech. Electroencephalogram results show a gradual onset and offset with less symmetrical synchrony between the hemispheres (Nolan, Bergazar, Chu, Cortez, & Snead, 2005). Furthermore, the predominant frequency tends to be less than a three-cycle-per-second wave pattern (Nolan et al., 2005). Like typical absence seizures, atypical absence seizures occur more frequently in females and present prior to adolescence. However, compared to typical absence seizures, atypical absence seizures tend to occur with greater frequency, are more prolonged, and commonly are combined with other seizure types. Children with atypical absence seizures demonstrate significantly higher rates of Mental Retardation and tend to have a higher incidence of global cognitive deficits. This seizure type tends to be expressed as a nonspecific symptom of brain injury during development.

Valproate (Depakene) and ethosuximide are the most commonly prescribed drugs for absence seizures. Childhood absence seizures are frequently benign, therefore, ethosuximide usually is recommended first; valproate is reserved for when ethosuximide is insufficient or when the child also has generalized tonic-clonic seizures. Lamotragine formerly was considered a second line drug; however, its use has increased significantly over time (Posner, Mohamed, & Marson, 2005).

REFERENCES

Leppik, I. L. (2000). *Contemporary diagnosis and management of the patient with epilepsy.* Newton, PA: Handbooks in Health Care.

Meeren, H., van Luijtelaar, G., Lopes da Silva, F., & Coencen, A. (2005). Evolving concepts of pathophysiology of absence seizures. *Archives of Neurology, 62,* 371–376.

Nolan, M., Bergazar, M., Chu, B., Cortez, M. A., & Snead, O. C. (2005). Clinical and neurophysiologic spectrum associated with atypical absence seizures in children with intractable epilepsy. *Journal of Child Neurology, 20*(5), 404–410.

Panayiotopoulos, C. P., Chroni, E., Daskslopoulos, C., Baker, A., Rowlinson, S., & Walsh, P. (1992). Typical absence seizures in adults: Clinical EEG, video-EEG findings and diagnostic/syndromic considerations. *Journal of Neurology, Neurosurgery, and Psychiatry, 55,* 1002–1008.

Posner, E. B., Mohamed, K., & Marson, A. G. (2005). A systematic review of treatment of typical absence seizures in children and adolescents with ethosuximide, sodium valproate, or lamotrigine. *Seizure, 14,* 116–122.

NICOLE NASEWICZ
University of Florida

ELECTROENCEPHALOGRAPH
GRANDE MAL SEIZURES
SEIZURE DISORDERS

ABSENTEEISM/ATTENDANCE OF CHILDREN WITH DISABILITIES

Compulsory school attendance laws have been enacted in all states. The scope of those laws was narrowed in most states by the introduction of exemption clauses. These clauses excuse children considered unfit or uneducable because of physical or mental handicaps from school attendance. Legal challenges by handicapped children for extension and protection of the right established under state law of equal access to educational opportunity ensued during the early 1970s. Those cases were followed by federal and state laws that mandate free appropriate public education to handicapped children and ensure their right to attend school regardless of the severity or type of their disability.

Under IDEA and Section 504 of the Rehabilitation Act of 1973, a handicapped child must be educated in the least restrictive environment his or her needs allow. Children with serious, often chronic, health impairments who require special education and related services may receive instruction in hospitals or in the home. Schools use various approaches, including home visitations, school-to-home telephone communication, and interactive television to connect a homebound or hospitalized student with the classroom. Federal law recognizes that there are instances when, because of the nature or severity of a child's handicap, the child must be educated in a setting other than the regular classroom. However, the least restrictive environment provisions prohibit placement of a child on homebound instruction or other exclusion from the regular educational environment solely because the child has disabilities. Homebound instruction may not be appropriate for the instructional needs of that child.

There have been few studies of program and school attendance as a factor in the achievement of students with disabilities. There is some evidence that handicapped students attending regular schools are no more likely to be absent from school than nonhandicapped students (Sullivan & McDaniel, 1983). High rates of school attendance do not necessarily ensure high rates of program attendance or achievement. Sullivan and McDaniel (1983) concluded that children served in resource rooms may be receiving up to one-quarter less schooling time than is prescribed in their individualized education programs because of competing school activities and absences of either the resource room teacher or the student during a scheduled period. In various studies involving children with and without disabilities (Ivarie, Hogue, & Brulle, 1984; Rosenshine, 1979), investigators in the area of academic learning time as it relates to academic achievement have found a positive correlation between the learning of basic skills and the number of minutes students spend on academically relevant tasks. Researchers are continuing their study of increased active learning time as a powerful intervention technique for all students.

Under the IDEA and Section 504, mandatory procedural safeguards exist that allow parents to challenge school disciplinary actions that would interrupt a handicapped child's education. Expulsions, suspensions, and transfers to settings outside a regular classroom or school are considered placement changes because such measures remove students from their current school program or curtail attendance (Simon, 1984). A series of court decisions on this sensitive area have provided important guidelines for determining when and for what length of time handicapped students may be expelled or suspended under federal law (Reschly & Bersoff, 1999; Simon, 1984).

REFERENCES

Ivarie, J., Hogue, D., & Brulle, A. (1984). Investigation of mainstream teacher time spent with students labeled learning disabled. *Exceptional Children, 51,* 142–149.

Reschly, D., & Bersoff, D. (1999). Law and school psychology. In C. R. Reynolds & T. B. Gutkin (Eds.), *The handbook of school psychology* (3rd ed., pp. 1077–1112). New York: Wiley.

Rosenshine, B. V. (1979). Content, time, and direct instruction. In P. L. Peterson & H. J. Walberg (Eds.), *Research on teaching* (pp. 28–56). Berkeley, CA: McCutchan.

Simon, S. G. (1984). Discipline in the public schools: A dual standard for handicapped and nonhandicapped students? *Journal of Law & Education, 13,* 209–237.

Sullivan, P. D., & McDaniel, E. A. (1983). Pupil attendance in resource rooms as one measure of the time on task variable. *Journal of Learning Disabilities, 16,* 398–399.

SHIRLEY A. JONES
*Virginia Polytechnic Institute
and State University*

HOMEBOUND INSTRUCTION
INDIVIDUALS WITH DISABILITIES EDUCATION
   IMPROVEMENT ACT OF 2004 (IDEIA)
SUMMER SCHOOL FOR INDIVIDUALS WITH DISABILITIES

ABSTRACTION, CAPACITY FOR

Abstract reasoning refers to the ability to identify common features of two or more concepts, and has been considered an essential component of intelligence (e.g., Thorndike, 1927). Abstract reasoning ability can be assessed through at least three types of tasks: those which require a person to identify a general concept common to several exemplars, for example, sorting objects according to categories; to state common features among different concepts, for example, the Similarities subtest of the Wechsler Intelligence Scale for Children–IV, or to state examples or features of a given concept (Burger, Blackman, Clark, & Reis, 1982).

While general abstraction ability varies across persons, ability to reason abstractly in specific tasks appears to vary with subject area expertise. For example, in studying the superior memory of chess masters for the configuration of briefly presented game arrangements, Chi, Glaser, and Rees (1981) suggest that experts form abstract, organized representations of the field of play, while novices retain only the surface features of the problem. Adelson (1984) found that novice computer programming students actually had better recall for the details of a briefly presented program than did expert programmers, but that the experts had better recall for what the programs were designed to do. Ability to make abstractions about information seems to improve with experience; as one gains more experience with an area of knowledge, one becomes familiar with the organization of it, and is able to integrate new information with greater success.

Burger et al. (1982) found that educable mentally retarded (EMR) adolescents could be trained to improve their abstract reasoning abilities. Context and instructional support also influence the application of abstract thinking skills (Alexander & Murphy, 1999; Gopnik, Glymour, Sobel, Schulz, Kushnir, & Danks, 2004).

REFERENCES

Adelson, B. (1984). When novices surpass experts: The difficulty of a task may increase with expertise. *Journal of Experimental Psychology: Learning, Memory, and Cognition, 10*, 483–495.

Alexander, P. A., & Murphy, P. K. (1999). What cognitive psychology has to say to school psychology: Shifting perspectives and shared purposes. In C. R. Reynolds & T. B. Gutkin (Eds.), *The handbook of school psychology* (3rd ed., pp. 167–193). New York: Wiley.

Burger, A. L., Blackman, L. S., Clark, H. T., & Reis, E. (1982). Effects of hypothesis testing and variable format training on generalization of a verbal abstraction strategy by EMR learners. *American Journal on Mental Deficiency, 86*, 405–413.

Chi, M. T. H., Glaser, R., & Rees, E. (1981). Expertise in problem solving. In R. Sternberg (Ed.), *Advances in the psychology of human intelligence* (Vol. 1, pp. 7–75). Hillsdale, NJ: Erlbaum.

Gopnik, A., Glymour, C., Sobel, D. M., Schulz, L. E., Kushnir, T., & Danks, D. (2004). A theory of causal learning in children: Causal maps and Bayes nets. *Psychological Review, 1*, 3–32.

Thorndike, E. L. (1927). *The measurement of intelligence.* New York: Bureau of Publications, Teachers College, Columbia University.

JOHN MACDONALD
Eastern Kentucky University

INTELLIGENCE TESTING
MENTAL RETARDATION

ABSTRACT THINKING, IMPAIRMENT IN

Those who work with children having learning problems are interested in trying to understand their thinking processes. Three groups of children have been of particular interest—deaf, mentally retarded, and learning disabled. Children with these disorders have all exhibited difficulty acquiring academic skills. One hypothesis for their difficulty is that they may not be processing information normally. Some assert these children have deficiencies in abstract reasoning.

A theory of abstract reasoning hinges on the notion that human thinking is a process of conceptualization. Concept formation is the organization of data into categories. To know a concept is to know the characteristics of an entity that either include it or exclude it from a category. To know the concept of "dog" is to know that animals with four legs, hair, and the ability to bark belong together in a category. Some argue that forming a concept is a process of abstracting. To learn the concept of dog requires noticing common characteristics of different dogs, as well as noticing that cats have some characteristics that eliminate them from that category. However, not all concepts are created equally. Some are based on immediate, sensory experience. For example, a child may form a category of "doggy" by directly experiencing dogs and pictures of dogs. This is considered to be a concrete concept. On the other hand, there are concepts that are built from other concepts, for example, the notion of "mammal." A concept even further removed from direct experience is "democracy." The more removed the concept from direct experience, the more abstract it is. The term *abstract*, then, is used in two different ways. On the one hand, it is used to mean the process by which the salient characteristics of entities are identified in order to form concepts. On the other hand, it is used in contrast with the term *concrete* to indicate the role of direct experience.

Another factor related to abstract reasoning is the role of symbolization. Luria (1961) stated that the development of more abstract concepts was dependent on symbolization—more specifically the use of language. In fact, he felt that higher level concept formation was probably dependent on the mediation of language. For example, Luria would contend that a concept such as democracy more than likely requires language for acquisition.

Those dealing with children having difficulties with learning have tried to understand the role of conceptualization and symbolization in the development of abstract reasoning. Johnson and Myklebust (1967) were particularly interested in the conceptualization problems of learning-disabled children. They asserted that some have difficulties in the process of concept formation itself. They argued that any deficit in the processes of perception, imagery, symbolization, or abstracting could interfere with conceptualization. Others have difficulty not so much in the process of conceptualization as in dealing with the more abstract concepts. As Johnson and Myklebust point out, an individual with disturbances in the processes of abstracting or conceptualizing may be identified as a concrete thinker.

Myers and Hammill (1982) note that children who cannot form abstract concepts are generally labeled as being mentally retarded rather than learning disabled. Nonetheless, learning-disabled children are often described as having "concrete behavior characterized by a dependence upon immediate experience as opposed to abstract behavior that transcends any given immediate experience and results in the formation of conceptual categories" (p. 39). Many would argue that the difficulty exhibited by learning-disabled children is caused by a developmental lag and is not a permanent problem. In the case of mentally retarded children, however, the conceptualization problem may be permanent. Further, a body of research has been dedicated to trying to determine whether the conceptual behavior of mentally retarded children represents simply a delay or difference (Zigler & Balla, 1982; Robinson, Zigler, & Gallagher, 2000). To understand this problem researchers may, for example, look at how mentally retarded children use the role of language as a mediation device for concept formation (Field, 1977).

It is not uncommon for those working with hearing-impaired children to describe their cognitive behavior as being concrete (Johnson & Myklebust, 1967). There are several difficulties with this notion, however. Hearing-impaired children, because of their limited input, may simply not have had a sufficient experiential base to adequately form concepts that would be expected of hearing children. Another problem in understanding the hearing-impaired child's conceptualization is that these children live in a visual linguistic world. What may appear to be concrete behavior on the part of the child may simply be an artifact of one of the underlying rules of natural sign language systems. The rule is that the structure of an utterance cannot violate the visual world. For example, the word order of the structure "I finished my work, then watched television" is directly translatable into American Sign Language. "I watched television after I finished my work" is not, because it violates the visual sequence of events. Difficulties that hearing-impaired children have with the latter structure,

when encountering it in English, are sometimes interpreted as evidence that the child is a concrete thinker. In truth, it may be simply that the child is having difficulty in dealing with a structure that violates the child's linguistic rules (also see Braden, 1994).

It is important to note that the relationship between sensory information, concept formation, and symbolization is not well understood. Research has given us only the most sketchy idea of what the relationship among the three might be. One field of philosophy, epistemology, has been dedicated to trying to understand these relationships. Introspection and logical reasoning remain the most powerful tools available to both psychology and philosophy for describing concept development and abstract reasoning.

In summary, the notion of abstract reasoning is used in two different ways. It can mean the process by which one identifies the salient characteristics in entities for purposes of categorization. Abstract reasoning can also be the process by which individuals deal with concepts that are based on other concepts, rather than concepts that are based on direct experience. Children with learning problems can have difficulties with either type of abstract reasoning. When difficulties are exhibited, the question arises as to whether the difference is simply developmental delay or a difference in cognitive processing. Some people working with learning-disabled children contend that they eventually outgrow problems in these areas. Mentally retarded children may not necessarily do so. Children who are hearing impaired have also been described as "concrete" learners. However, their difficulties may be a result of too little experience and their use of visually based linguistic rules.

REFERENCES

Braden, J. P. (1994). *Deafness, deprivation, and IQ*. New York: Plenum Press.

Field, D. (1977). The importance of verbal content in the training of Piagetian conversation skills. *Child Development*, 1583–1592.

Johnson, D. J., & Myklebust, H. R. (1967). *Learning disabilities: Educational principles and practices*. New York: Grune & Stratton.

Luria, A. R. (1961). *The role of speech in the regulation of normal and abnormal behavior*. New York: Liveright (Pergamon Press).

Myers, P. I., & Hammill, D. D. (1982). *Learning disabilities: Basic concepts, assessment practices, and instructional strategies*. Austin, TX: PRO-ED.

Robinson, N. M., Zigler, E., & Gallagher, J. J. (2000). Two tails of the normal curve: Similarities and differences in the study of mental retardation and giftedness. *American Psychologist, 55*, 1413–1424.

Zigler, E., & Balla, D. (1982). *Mental retardation: The developmental-difference controversy*. Hillsdale, NJ: Erlbaum.

CAROLYN BULLARD
Lewis & Clark College

CONCRETE OPERATIONS
DEAF
LEARNING DISABILITIES

ABUSED CHILDREN, PSYCHOTHERAPY WITH

Today abused children are typically regarded as suffering from a primary illness (Quirk, 1980). A primary illness refers to the notion that living with a certain circumstance for a prolonged period of time creates a situation in the victim requiring primary treatment. The primary illness of child abuse has identifiable symptoms and etiology along with an official diagnosis and prescribed treatments.

An orderly treatment for abused children and adults who were abused as children involves the ability of the clinician to identify and diagnose properly the dilemma and its ramifications and to facilitate the natural healing process from trauma. Thus the first step in treatment is proper identification of child abuse as the problem to be treated.

Children who have been abused relive their abuse over and over in clear or symbolic ways. They dream abusive dreams, remember abusive situations, and in adulthood go so far as to recreate abusive relationships. They manifest little positive affect in interpersonal relationships, dissociative symptoms, and they lack intimacy and express difficulty in trusting others (Herman, 1981; Thomas, 2005). They are depressed and have difficulty in developing meaningful relationships or experiences in their lives. Adults who were abused children are often defensive, suspicious, nervous, and overly alert. They seem to be preoccupied with their bodily functions and are frequently labeled hypochondriacs. Insomnia is another frequently reported symptom, even in the absence of distressing nightmares. Abused children are also guilt-ridden, and experience much shame and self-hatred. Concentrating and following a task through to its completion is another problem area for this population (American Psychiatric Association, 1994; Mrazek & Kempe, 1981; Williams & Money, 1980).

Acting out the abuse in self-destructive ways such as drug abuse is frequently observed in this population, which is disproportionately represented in chemical dependency treatment facilities. As teenagers, abused children often become runaways and act out their rage in criminal behavior. Abused children are also disproportionately represented in facilities for delinquents. A disproportionately large group in this population may attempt suicide, hallucinate, manifest seizures, and ultimately be placed in psychiatric hospitals. While these obvious problematic behaviors will occur at high rates, another observed phenomena of this population is the frequency with which they become quiet, good children who then marry an abusive partner. Other compulsive behaviors are frequently manifested by these children and subsequently they will be found as adults

in Al-Anon, Alcoholics Anonymous, Narcotics Anonymous, Overeaters Anonymous, Gamblers Anonymous, and other self-help treatment programs.

Abused children as adults have difficulty with parenting. Appropriate discipline is difficult for them because it is too restimulating. Consequently, they will abdicate their parenting until the children eventually become abusive toward them (Justice & Justice, 1976). This promotes another likely place for adult abused children to reflect inadequacies—as parents of children in trouble. On the other hand, adult abused children may become abusive parents themselves. The inordinate numbers of child abusers that were themselves abused has been widely documented.

Because young and abused children live and grow with a wounded and fragmented personality, they often need intensive treatment efforts. The client who clings or annoys the clinician, reporting that something is missing from treatment, will often be a person who was abused. This person will often complain about the deficiencies of treatment and report that he or she has not been responded to reasonably. This type of reporting should be expected in view of the fact that abused children are wounded people who will have difficulty objectifying their relations: after all, their primary objects, mom or dad, abused them.

Treatment programs and clinicians should routinely be sensitive in recognizing and treating child abuse. When working with clients the following questions should be a routine part of the interview. What was your childhood like? How did your parents treat you? How were you disciplined? What were the punishments employed by your parents? Were you ever raped or seduced? Those who report having difficulty recalling all or crucial parts of their childhood should definitely be regarded as potentially having been abused. This self-induced amnesia, or dissociation, is a primitive form of defense against the pain and discomfort resulting from recall of an abusive situation. Naturally, this needs to be dealt with in a sensitive manner by the clinician, and the client should not be prematurely pushed into acknowledging information or feelings they are not prepared to confront.

Abused children often feel at fault for their experience of child abuse. They live with much guilt, shame, self-blame, and self-loathing. Often their abusers told them it was their fault. Child molesters use guilt as a tool with their victims in order to keep the secret, while parents who physically beat their children do so in the name of discipline. Yet, abused children mentally make their parents correct and good. Generally, therapists should enjoy relationships with people, but it is even more important for therapists of abused children to like their clients: While one might think that all therapists would like their clients, fragile clients often find themselves disliked by their therapists. Since they do not grow as the therapist expects, they experience rejection in the context of the therapeutic relationship.

Adults who were abused in childhood have unusual difficulty in establishing trust with the therapist, identifying and discussing feelings, and cooperating with the therapeutic process. Because their tormentors were often people they trusted (e.g., parents), abused children may recoil at the need to trust the therapist. Therefore, an unusually long working-through process is frequently required. This is often difficult for the novice therapist, educator, or other professional lacking information about child abuse and its symptoms.

Most children learn to cope by making decisions separate from the influence of their parents. Abused children have more to cope with, and fewer skills to do so. Reparenting applies here also. Regardless of age, abused children need to learn to live and cope in the real world, and come to recognize that not all people are as threatening as their abusive parents. Therefore, learning coping skills is essential to any successful treatment program. The following are examples of important coping skills to be addressed: learning to trust one's own instincts; learning to identify one's own needs; and learning to proceed to satisfy those needs. Another essential component to treatment is the development of an ability to identify and avoid close contact with abusive people.

Because abuse occurs in the context of an interpersonal relationship, the environment of a therapeutic group has proven itself a particularly helpful treatment modality. In view of the characteristics of this population, the following are important considerations for the leader of a group of abused children. The group should be initially supportive, gentle, homogeneous, and closed to new members after the group has begun. These elements are necessary to address the difficulty in trusting manifested by this population. The group needs to project an image of safety and members must be monitored from inappropriately expressing the rage some may possess. Confrontation must be kept well managed to further reduce regression that may be promoted by some of the more fragmented members. The group leader must monitor the development of any situation that may resemble the childhood abuse of any member in the group. A primary goal of the group is to develop understanding of the personal dynamics of abuse and coping skills that may prevent the development of similar abusive situations in the future.

REFERENCES

American Psychiatric Association. (1994). *Diagnostic and statistical manual of mental disorders* (4th ed.). Washington, DC: Author.

Herman, J. L. (1981). *Father-daughter incest.* Cambridge, MA: Harvard University Press.

Justice, B., & Justice, R. (1976). *The abusing family.* New York: Human Sciences.

Mrazek, P. B., & Kempe, C. H. (Eds.). (1981). *Sexually abused children and their families.* New York: Pergamon.

Quirk, J. P. (Ed.). (1980). *Reading in child abuse.* Guilford, CT: Special Learning.

Thomas, P. M. (2005). Dissociation and internal models of protection: Psychotherapy with child abuse survivors. *Psychotherapy: Theory, Research, Practice, Training, 42,* 20–36.

Williams, J. W., & Money, J. (Eds.). (1980). *Traumatic abuse and neglect of children at home.* Baltimore: Johns Hopkins University Press.

CHARLES P. BARNARD
University of Wisconsin at Stout

ACTING OUT
CHILD ABUSE
ETIOLOGY

ACADEMIC ASSESSMENT

The global function of achievement testing is to assess a student's attainment of academic content areas. Reading, written language, and mathematical functioning are the major domains under the rubric of academic achievement. Anastasi (1982) notes that traditionally academic assessment has been differentiated from aptitude/ability testing by the degree to which a measure is designed to assess uniform versus diverse antecedent experiences. To be categorized as a measure of academic achievement, a measure is designed to test a fairly uniform previous experience (e.g., first grade instruction in reading). In contrast, an aptitude test would be designed to assess the impact of multiple or diverse antecedent experiences. Contemporary measurement specialists recognize that both achievement and aptitude tests assess acquired knowledge, but differ on the degree of specificity and abstraction.

Salvia and Ysseldyke (1981) have described four functions that achievement tests fulfill within the schools. They are used for screening students who may need more in-depth assessment to determine whether special services are appropriate; determining whether a child is eligible for placement in a special education class based on local criteria; assessing a child's strengths and weaknesses to facilitate decisions regarding his or her placement in an instructional sequence; and determining the impact of educational intervention on a class or group of students.

Achievement testing may be conceptualized along several lines: norm-referenced versus criterion referenced; individual versus group administered; and informal teacher-constructed versus standardized instruction. Each of these dimensions will be discussed to highlight the multifaceted construct of academic achievement assessment.

Norm-referenced testing (NRT) began to play a prominent role in American education after World War I. Army Alpha and Beta tests were used for the classification of recruits during the war. The Otis Group Intelligence Scale was published in 1918 by the World Book Company. This scale employed such advances as multiple choice questions, answer sheets, test booklets, and improved normative sampling procedures (Cunningham, 1986). These advances were adapted for the first norm-referenced, standardized measure of academic achievement, the Stanford Achievement Test, published in 1923.

The most salient characteristic of norm-referenced achievement tests is that an examinee's performance on the test is interpreted by comparing his or her relative standing to a given reference group. The reference group or standardization sample is usually composed of representative peers of the same chronological age, or peers in the same grade placement. Performance on a norm-referenced test is typically expressed in scores based on the normal curve such as stanines, T-scores, and/or standard scores (which usually have a mean of 100 and a standard deviation of 15, or sometimes 16). Performance on a norm-referenced test may also be expressed in percentiles, which tell a student's standing relative to a hypothetical group of 100 children. For instance, a score at the 86th percentile indicates that the examinee scored better than 86 out of 100 of his or her hypothetical same-aged peers.

The major norm-referenced group achievement tests include the California Achievement Test (CTB/McGraw-Hill, 1985); the Comprehensive Test of Basic Skills (CTB/McGraw-Hill, 1981); the Iowa Test of Basic Skills (Hieronymus, Lindquist, & Hoover, 1983); the Metropolitan Achievement Test (Barlow, Farr, Hogan, & Prescott, 1978); and the Standard Achievement Test (Gardner, Rudman, Karlsen, & Merwin, 1982).

These group-administered tests have multiple levels, each designated for a specified grade range. For instance, the Stanford Achievement Test series has six levels: Primary Level 1 for grades 1.5–2.9; Primary Level 2 for 2.5–3.9; Primary Level 3 for 3.5–4.9; Intermediate Level 1 for 4.5–5.9; Intermediate Level 2 for 5.5–7.9; and Intermediate Level 3 for 7.0–9.9. Generally, these tests have gone through several revisions. The Stanford Achievement Test, for example, is in its seventh revision and has been in use in the public schools for over 60 years.

A primary difference between norm-referenced and criterion-referenced tests lies in the way they are interpreted. As noted, the norm-referenced achievement test is designed to give information on a given student's performance relative to a representative group of same-aged peers. In contrast, the criterion-referenced achievement test is designed to give information on a given student's performance in terms of whether he or she has learned a given concept or skill. Thus, the criterion-referenced measure is designed to tell what the student can and cannot do. For instance, the student can add single digit numerals with sums less than 10, but has not learned to regroup or perform simple

subtraction problems. Since discrimination among students is not the purpose of a criterion-referenced test, the difficulty level of items and the power of items to separate students are not as important as they are in norm-referenced measures. The major issue in criterion-referenced measurement is whether items reflect a specified instructional domain. Most of the major group-administered achievement tests have been adapted to yield criterion-referenced information. The problem with adapting norm-referenced tests is that there are a multiplicity of instructional objectives (Cunningham, 1986). Since each objective requires several test items to achieve an adequate level of reliability, the length of the test becomes unmanageable.

Up to this point group-administered measures have been used to illustrate the norm- versus criterion-referenced dimensions of academic assessment. Academic achievement testing may also be examined from the viewpoint of the administration format, either individual or group. While group achievement tests are usually given to a whole class by the regular education teacher, individual achievement measures are administered by specially trained personnel (special education teachers, educational diagnosticians, and school psychologists) to a child on a one-to-one basis. Typically, the child has been referred for testing because of academic or behavioral problems manifested in the regular classroom. A general distinction between group and individual measures relates to their use in the decision-making process. Group measures are designed to make decisions about groups, while individual tests are more appropriate for decisions concerning an individual. Therefore, caution must be exercised when attempting to interpret the results of a single child's performance on a group-administered measure. There are many variables that may influence a child's performance on a group-administered measure and result in an inaccurate portrayal of that child's academic skills. Misunderstanding instructions, fatigue, random guessing, class distractions, looking on a neighbor's response sheet, and so on, may invalidate a child's scores. When a child is being considered for placement in a special education program, a poor performance on a group-administered measure should be followed up with an individual assessment.

Finally, the academic achievement test may be approached by examining the degree to which the directions to students are standardized. The standardized test is one where the instructions and test questions are presented in the same manner to all examinees. On the other hand, in the teacher-constructed test, there is unlimited latitude in the construction and administration of test items. Both standardized and informal teacher-made tests have advantages and disadvantages. However, they should share certain attributes, that is, clear directions to students, careful development of items based on a table of specifications, and the type or format of test items.

Whether the directions to an achievement test are standardized or constructed by the teacher, building a table of specifications represents the first step in test construction. A table of specifications contains a listing of instructional objects as well as the relative emphasis to be assigned to each objective. For standardized measures of achievement, the table of specification is based on an examination of major textbook series used across the country. For instance, when reading subtests are constructed, the most widely used basal reading series are reviewed by the test developer. Note is taken at what point in the curricula various concepts are introduced. Invariably, decisions and compromises have to be made regarding content, because all basal reading series are not identical. As such, the consumer of both individual and group standardized achievement tests must examine the available measures, not just in terms of quality of standardization and reliability, but also with respect to the match between the concepts assessed by the test and those taught within the framework of the local curriculum. See Table 1 for selected objectives covered by Forms E and F of the California Achievement Test.

A major difference between standardized and informal, teacher-developed tests is that the former usually represents many more hours of item development, refinement, empirical tryouts, and final selection of test items. In developing standardized achievement tests, considerable weight is placed on both content validity (the representativeness of the items to the domain being tested, and the appropriateness of the format and wording of items relative to the age level of the prospective examinees), and the empirical tryout of the items in terms of reliability. The advantage of the standardized test lies in its documented reliability (presented in an accompanying technical manual), and its ability to compare a student's performance with that of a reference group or specified criterion. Whereas standardized tests measure content that is common to reading and mathematics programs from around the country, the teacher-constructed tests can be specifically targeted to the content of the local curriculum, or to a specific teacher's class.

In addition to defining informal assessment as the administration of a teacher-constructed measure, the term may also be applied to diagnostic processes. These include error analysis, behavioral observation, and the learner's relations to various instructional strategies (Sedlak, Sedlak, & Steppe-Jones, 1982). This last process is flexible and dynamic. A psychoeducational examiner presents tasks to the student in a branching manner similar to the operation of a branching computer-assisted instructional program. Information about the student's mastery of various skills is gleaned from analysis of his or her errors. Error analysis has been applied to reading, writing, mathematics, second language learning, and spelling (Bejar, 1984). The analysis is usually conducted within a "content" framework, such as an educational taxonomy.

Mathematical functioning is a key area where error analysis has been profitably employed (Brown & VanLehn,

Table 1 Selected objectives from the California Achievement Tests, Forms E and F

Visual Recognition
  1. Single letters
  2. Upper, lowercase letters
  3. Letter combinations

Sound Recognition
  4. Initial consonant sounds
  5. Final consonant sounds
  6. Rhyming

Word Analysis
  7. Single consonants/oral
  8. Consonant clusters, diagraphs/oral
  9. Consonant clusters
  10. Variant consonant sounds
  11. Long vowels/oral
  12. Long vowels
  13. Short vowels/oral
  14. Short vowels
  15. Diphthongs, variant vowel sounds
  16. Sight words
  17. Compound words
  18. Root words/affixes

Reading Comprehension
Literal Comprehension
32. Passage details
33. Stated main ideas
Inferential Comprehension
34. Passage analysis/oral
35. Character analysis
36. Central thought
37. Interpreting events
Critical Comprehension
38. Forms of writing
39. Writing techniques

Spelling
40. Vowel sounds
41. Consonant sounds
42. Structural units

1982). Ashlock (1976) offers useful exercises in a semiprogrammed text to help detect common error patterns in computation. See Table 2 for exemplars of common errors that give insight into the students' problems. Lankford (1974) demonstrated the value of having a student think aloud while solving arithmetic problems. Thus, when an error is made, the computation strategy used by the student becomes apparent. Roberts (1968) has noted four common error categories for arithmetic computation: selecting the wrong operation; erring in recalling a specific arithmetic fact; attempting the correct operation but using an inappropriate algorithm; and random responding that has no apparent relationship to the problem.

Another strategy that has a long history of success for assessment of academic skills is curriculum-based assessment

Table 2 Samples of common arithmetic error patterns that give insight into the student's incorrect problem-solving strategy

Addition

```
   56              24
 +  7            +  5
 ─────          ─────
  513             11
```

(Addition of all numerals without regard for place value)

Subtraction

```
   53
 -  5            522
 ─────         - 101
   52           ─────
                 401
```

(Failure to group)

(Misunderstanding of zero as a subtrahend)

Multiplication

```
   34
 ×  3             93
 ─────          ×  8
  122            ─────
                 101
```

(Addition of the regrouped number prior to multiplication)

(Use of inappropriate algorithm)

Division

```
      21                5
    2)24             3)18
     20
    ────
      4
```

(A right to left recording pattern is employed)

(Basic fact mistake)

(CBA; Fuchs, Fuchs, Prentice, Hamlett, Finelli, & Courey, 2004). CBA attempts to link assessment more directly to classroom instruction and to provide a more direct assessment of a student's instructional needs (Shapiro & Elliott, 1999). Although touted as an alternative to traditional norm-referenced testing, CBA and NRT are seen best as complementary models, and not as competitive ones.

In summary, academic achievement assessment is used to make decisions about students. These decisions may be made from a normative perspective or in terms of students' mastery of a specified skill. Depending on the administration, format decisions can be made for an individual student or for groups of students. Norm-referenced achievement tests provide information about a student's relative standing compared with that of a reference group, while criterion-referenced tests and informal assessments may be used to make informed decisions about a student's future instructional needs. Specific achievement tests are described throughout this work.

REFERENCES

Anastasi, A. (1982). *Psychological testing* (5th ed.). New York: Macmillan.

Ashlock, R. B. (1976). *Error patterns in computation: A semi-programmed approach* (2nd ed.). Columbus, OH: Merrill.

Barlow, I. H., Farr, R., Hogan, T. P., & Prescott, G. A. (1978). *Metropolitan Achievement Tests* (5th ed.). New York: Psychological Corp.

Bejar, I. I. (1984). Educational diagnostic assessment. *Journal of Educational Measurement, 21,* 175–189.

Brown, J. S., & VanLehn, K. (1982). Toward a generative theory of "bugs." In T. P. Carpenter, J. M. Moser, & T. A. Romberg (Eds.), *Addition and subtraction: A cognitive perspective.* Hillsdale, NJ: Erlbaum.

CTB/McGraw-Hill. (1981). *The Comprehensive Tests of Basic Skills.* New York: Author.

CTB/McGraw-Hill. (1985). *California Achievement Tests.* New York: Author.

Cunningham, G. K. (1986). *Educational and psychological measurement.* New York: Macmillan.

Fuchs, L. S., Fuchs, D., Prentice, K., Hamlett, K., Finelli, R., & Courey, S. J. (2004). Enhancing mathematical problem solving among third-grade students with schema-based instruction. *Journal of Educational Psychology, 96,* 635–647.

Gardner, E. G., Rudman, H. C., Karlsen, B., & Merwin, J. C. (1982). *Stanford Achievement Test* (1982 ed.). New York: Psychological Corp.

Hieronymus, A. N., Lindquist, E. F., & Hoover, H. D. (1983). *Iowa Tests of Basic Skills.* Chicago: Riverside.

Jastak, S., & Wilkinson, G. S. (1984). *The Wide Range Achievement Test–Revised* (1984 revised ed.). Wilmington, DE: Jastak Associates.

Lankford, F. G. (1974). What can a teacher learn about a pupil's thinking through oral interviews? *Arithmetic Teacher, 21,* 26–32.

Roberts, G. H. (1968). The failure strategies of third grade arithmetic pupils. *Arithmetic Teacher, 15,* 442–446.

Salvia, J., & Ysseldyke, J. E. (1981). *Assessment in special and remedial education* (2nd ed.). Boston: Houghton Mifflin.

Sedlak, R. A., Sedlak, D. M., & Steppe-Jones, C. (1982). Informal assessment. In D. A. Sabatino & L. Mann (Eds.), *A handbook of diagnostic and prescriptive teaching.* Rockville, MD: Aspen Systems.

Shapiro, E., & Elliott, S. N. (1999). Curriculum based assessment and other performance based assessment strategies. In C. R. Reynolds & T. B. Gutkin (Eds.), *The handbook of school psychology* (3rd ed., pp. 383–408). New York: Wiley.

JACK A. CUMMINGS
Indiana University

ACHIEVEMENT TESTS
CRITERION-REFERENCED TESTING
CURRICULUM-BASED ASSESSMENT
NORM-REFERENCED TESTING

See also SPECIFIC TEST NAMES.

ACADEMIC LANGUAGE

Academic language (instructional discourse, cognitive-academic language, or school language) is the way teachers and students organize their communication interactions within educational environments. The purpose is to transmit scientific or logically based knowledge and skills. In contrast, everyday discourse (conversation, social discourse, or basic interpersonal communication) has as its general purpose the regulation of social interaction or interpersonal functions (Chamot & O'Malley, 1994; Wallach & Butler, 1994; Wallach & Miller, 1988; Westby, 1985).

Comprehending and producing academic language requires more cognitive and linguistic complexity than using social language. The transition from oral communication to literate communication marks the need for increased cognitive and linguistic complexity in the teaching-learning process (Cummins, 1983; Larson & McKinley, 1995; Merritt & Culatta, 1998; Naremore, Densmore, & Harman, 1995; Nelson, 1998; Ripich & Creaghead, 1994; Westby, 1997, 1998). Major cognitive, linguistic, and contextual characteristics of academic language include:

Cognitive: abstract concepts; cognitively demanding tasks (critical thinking [analytical and creative], problem solving, decision making); language-thinking and executive functions that are stabilizing (Nelson, 1998; Wallach & Butler, 1994; Wallach & Miller, 1988; Westby, 1998).

Linguistic: complex morphological markers, syntactic transformations, and semantic relationships and networks with explicit vocabulary, resulting in increased oral and text cohesion and coherence; the ability to project, predict, and infer; increased demand for oral and text *form* (pronunciation, spelling, punctuation, organization), *content* (accuracy, synthesis cohesion, and coherence), and *style* (advanced narrative levels and expository genres) (Hedberg & Westby, 1993; Hughes, McGillivray, & Schmidek, 1997; Naremore et al., 1995; Nelson, 1998; Tough, 1979; Wallach & Butler, 1994; Wallach & Miller, 1988).

Contextual: reduced contextual clues; indeterminate audience diffuse in time and space; often physical and temporal separation between sender (writer, speaker) and receiver (listener, reader) (Merritt & Culatta, 1998; Nelson, 1998; Wallach & Butler, 1994; Wallach & Miller, 1988).

Academic communication-learning problems are associated with many developmental and acquired disorders. Academic language use and rules vary from culture to culture (Solomon & Rhodes, 1996) and are now also influenced by technology (Cummins, 2000). However, the consensus is that to succeed in mainstream educational settings in the course of life students must be able to understand and use the cognitive, linguistic, and contextual conventions associated with academic language.

REFERENCES

Chamot, A. U., & O'Malley, J. M. (1994). *The CALLA handbook: Implementing the cognitive academic language learning approach.* Reading, MA: Addison-Wesley.

Cummins, J. (1983). Language proficiency and academic achievement. In J. W. Oller, Jr. (Ed.), *Issues in language testing research.* Rowley: Newbury House.

Cummins, J. (2000). Academic language learning, Transformative Pedagogy, and Information Technology: Towards a critical balance. *TESOL Quarterly, 34,* 537–547.

Hedberg, N. L., & Westby, C. E. (1993). *Analyzing storytelling skills: Theory to practice.* Tucson, AZ: Communication Skill Builders.

Hughes, D., McGillivray, L., & Schmidek, M. (1997). *Guide to narrative language.* Eau Claire, WI: Thinking Publications.

Larson, V. L., & McKinley, N. (1995). *Language disorders in older students: Preadolescents and adolescents.* Eau Claire, WI: Thinking Publications.

Merritt, D. D., & Culatta, B. (1998). *Language intervention in the classroom.* San Diego, CA: Singular Publishing Group.

Naremore, R. C., Densmore, A. E., & Harman, D. R. (1995). *Language intervention with school-aged children: Conversation, narrative, and text.* San Diego, CA: Singular Publishing Group.

Nelson, N. W. (1998). *Childhood language disorders in context: Infancy through adolescence* (2nd ed.). Boston: Allyn & Bacon.

Ripich, D. N., & Creaghead, N. A. (Eds.). (1994). *School discourse problems* (2nd ed.). San Diego, CA: Singular Publishing Group.

Solomon, J., & Rhodes, N. (1996). Assessing academic language: Results of a survey. *TESOL Journal, 5,* 5–8.

Tough, J. (1979). *Talk for teaching and learning.* Portsmouth, NJ: Heinemann.

Wallach, G. P., & Butler, K. G. (1994). *Language learning disabilities in school-age children and adolescents: Some principles and applications.* New York: Merrill/Macmillan College Publishing.

Wallach, G. P., & Miller, L. (1988). *Language intervention and academic success.* San Diego, CA: College-Hill/Little, Brown.

Westby, C. E. (1985). From learning to talk to talking to learn: Oral-literate language differences. In C. Simon (Ed.), *Communication skills and classroom success: Therapy methodologies for language-learning disabled students.* San Diego, CA: College-Hill.

Westby, C. E. (1997). There's more to passing than knowing the answers. *Language, Speech and Hearing Services in the Schools, 28,* 274–287.

Westby, C. E. (1998). Communicative refinement in school age and adolescence. In W. O. Haynes & B. B. Shulman (Eds.), *Communication development: Foundations, processes, and clinical applications* (pp. 311–360). Baltimore: Williams and Wilkins.

STEPHEN S. FARMER
New Mexico State University

DISCOURSE
LANGUAGE ASSESSMENT

ACADEMIC SKILLS

While to some individuals the definition of academic skills conjours up the three Rs, to others the delineation of the academic skills most important to the process of special education is a task that poses an awesome definitional problem. To the preschool special educator, for example, certain fine motor skills may be defined as important academic skills. On the other hand, for the special educator working at the secondary level, the ability to accept positive and negative feedback (social skills), driving skills, or home economics may be considered important academic skills that warrant inclusion in the secondary special education curriculum.

A comprehensive sourcebook on research on teaching presents detailed analyses of seven academic skill areas: written composition, reading, mathematics, natural sciences, arts and aesthetics, moral and values education, and social studies (Wittrock, 1986). At least a few of these areas would be considered by most individuals to be core or basic academic skills. The fact that these academic skill areas have entire chapters devoted to them also indicates that there is enough research, theory, or perhaps controversy regarding them as to allow them to be studied and discussed extensively.

Beyond the issue of defining academic skills are the related issues of the rise and fall of skills across generations (which is constantly addressed by the popular media), and equally important, the procedures by which these skills are taught and acquired by students in special education. Cartwright, Cartwright, and Ward (1981) list several approaches used by special education teachers to impart academic skills; these include the diagnostic teaching model, remedial and compensatory education models, direct instruction, task analysis, perceptual-motor training, inquiry, modeling, media-based instruction, education games, and computer-assisted and computer-managed instruction. Two additional instructional approaches that were popularized in the 1970s include mastery learning and cooperative learning (Stallings & Stipek, 1986). In any case, current instructional methodology requires evidence-based instruction for any academic skill and in any setting (Lerman, Vorndran, Addison, & Contrucci, 2004; Odom, Brantlinger, Gersten, Horner, & Thompson, 2005).

With regard to learner characteristics that affect the acquisition of academic skills, Wittrock (1986) suggests the following broad categories for consideration: students' perceptions and expectations, attention, motivation, learning and memory, comprehension and knowledge acquisition, learning strategies, and metacognitive processes. In summary, special educators must first define the academic skills that their students must acquire and then consider instructional, student, and other variables in planning for the optimal acquisition of academic skills.

REFERENCES

Cartwright, P. G., Cartwright, C. A., & Ward, M. E. (1981). *Educating special learners.* Belmont, CA: Wadsworth.

Lerman, D. C., Vorndran, C. M., Addison, L., & Contrucci, S. (2004). Preparing teachers in evidence-based practices for young children. *School Psychology Review, 34,* 510–526.

Odom, S. L., Brantlinger, E., Gersten, R., Homer, R. H., & Thompson, B. (2005). Research in special education: Scientific methods and evidence-based practices. *Exceptional Children, 71,* 137–148.

Stallings, J. A., & Stipek, D. (1986). Research on early childhood and elementary school teaching programs. In M. C. Wittrock (Ed.), *Handbook of research on teaching.* New York: Macmillan.

Wittrock, M. C. (1986). Students' thought processes. In M. C. Wittrock (Ed.), *Handbook of research on teaching.* New York: Macmillan.

RANDY W. KAMPHAUS
University of Georgia

ACHIEVEMENT TESTS
MEMORY DISORDERS
METACOGNITION

ACADEMIC THERAPY

Academic Therapy was the first journal designed for specialists (special education teachers, educational diagnosticians, psychologists, resource room specialists, practitioners in speech, language, communication, vision, and hearing) who are in direct contact with children manifesting learning, language, and communication difficulties. Since 1965, it has established a reputation for easy-to-read and practical articles that focus on "what works" in the special clinical, therapeutic, or classroom setting. Contributors are teachers, professors, and specialists. Articles are short and are selected on the basis of their usefulness and ability to be put into immediate use by the journal reader. Each issue includes listings of new materials, current news on the national level, and ideas for home management. *Academic Therapy* is published five times during the year: September, November, January, March, and May.

JOHN ARENA
Academic Therapy Publications

ACADEMIC THERAPY PUBLICATIONS

Since 1965, Academic Therapy Publications (ATP) has served specialists, diagnosticians, private clinics and schools, teachers in mainstream and self-contained classes, and others who work in special settings. It has a wide variety of publications designed to address classroom aids, auditory learning, language, math, vocational/career, secondary/adult, professional texts, parent brochures, and reading programs. Academic Therapy Publications has a computer software division for students and professionals, and a test division which offers diagnostic instruments for assessing academic achievement. The *Directory of Facilities and Services for the Learning Disabled* was published every two years for 34 years. The 17th edition, published in 1997, marked the *Directory*'s last and final publication.

Presently ATP offers a range of assessments and supplementary educational materials to include publications that can be used by regular classroom teachers, special education teachers, parents, educational therapists, ESL teachers, and specialists in all fields working with persons with reading, learning, and communication disabilities.

Attention is focused on the inefficient learner who, although intellectually capable, is unable to achieve academically by traditional methods. ATP's materials are divided between two catalogs: *Academic Therapy* and *High Noon Books*. Academic Therapy features professional tests and reference books, curriculum material, teacher/parent resources, and visual/perceptual training aids.

High Noon Books publishes high-interest low-level mystery novels, written on a first through third/fourth grade reading level for individuals ages 10 through adult who have reading difficulties or limited English proficiency. Activity workbooks are also available.

REFERENCES

Kratowille, B. L. (Ed.). (1997). *Directory of facilities and services for the learning disabled* (17th ed.). Novato, CA: Academic Therapy.

Academic Therapy Publications web site: sales@academictherapy.com

ANNA M. ARENA
Academic Therapy Publications
First edition

RACHEL M. TOPLIS
Falcon School District 49
Colorado Springs, Colorado
Third edition

ACALCULIA

The ability to complete calculations often is impaired in individuals with traumatic brain injury (TBI) or other focal brain damage (Ardila & Rosselli, 1994) and represents a loss in function rather than a failure to develop. For example, consider a fourth grader who has already mastered basic operations and basic facts, can do grade-appropriate calculation, and is meeting expectancy in the classroom. An accident occurs, and there is brain damage, and one of the residual problems from the brain damage is that the child can no longer recall basic facts or complete basic computational problems. Originally referred to in this way by Henschen in 1925 (Ardila & Rosselli, 2002), this loss of ability attributed to brain injury or damage is called *acalculia* (Loring, 1999).

Although calculation abilities are routinely included as part of psychoeducational and neuropsychological assessments, there is limited research specific to acalculia. Ardila and Rosselli (2002) reviewed the existing research and offered a conceptualization of acalculia that is dissociated from language disorders. They concluded that arithmetic skills are associated with a range of other ability domains, including verbal memory, visuospatial ability, visual perception, constructional abilities, as well as language. Each of these is associated, in turn, with differing structures of the brain; as such, the location(s) of the injury or damage result(s) in a variety of calculation disorders. Most often indicated in calculation are the left prefrontal areas and posterior superior temporal gyrus (Burbaud et al., 1995; Sakurai, Momose, Iwata, Sasaki, & Kanazawa, 1996). Further, calculation ability is highly related to overall intellectual functioning and the ability to manipulate acquired knowledge (Mandell, Knoefel, & Albert, 1994); functional magnetic resonance imaging (MRI) and positron emission tomography (PET) reveal a complex pattern of brain activity to be involved in completing arithmetic operations (Burbaud et al., 1995; Sakurai et al., 1996).

There are different forms of acalculia (e.g., Ardila & Rosselli, 1990; Grafman, 1988). *Primary acalculia* is said to occur when the primary deficit is in arithmetic skills. In contrast, acalculia that is secondary to some other disorder, such as a language disorder, is referred to as *secondary acalculia* (Ardila & Rosselli, 1990). Individuals with primary acalculia have difficulty with numerical concepts, with the concept of quantity, with numerical signs, with magnitude estimation, and with syntactic operations (e.g., regrouping, borrowing). For primary acalculia, the deficits are evident regardless of modality of presentation of the math task or output. Abilities such as counting and rote fact learning may not be impaired (Ardila & Rosselli, 1994). Primary acalculia is associated with damage to the left angular gyrus (e.g., Gerstmann, 1940; Levin et al., 1993) or the left parietal area (Rosselli & Ardila, 1989). Acalculia frequently co-occurs with acquired language disorder or aphasia. In particular, individuals with acalculia also may evidence difficulty in anomia, word-finding difficulties, and language comprehension problems. This is not surprising in that numbers are encoded verbally, and some mathematical tasks (e.g., word problems) require language.

Assessment for acalculia is intended to determine (1) if the individual is experiencing significant difficulty in calculation following brain injury or damage, (2) to determine the pattern of difficulties (i.e., through error analysis) the individual is evidencing, (3) to identify any collateral or related deficits, and (4) to develop a rehabilitation program (Ardila & Rosselli, 2002). Available measures for such assessment are limited to specific subtests of broad measures of cognitive ability and achievement tests. Curriculum-based measures of mathematical skills also may be helpful in identifying subtle deficits. In all, assessment for acalculia should include a variety of tasks such as counting, enumeration, reading numbers, writing numbers, reading and writing arithmetical signs, rote learning, magnitude comparison (i.e., which is greater?), arithmetic operations, aligning numbers in columns, mental calculation, and so on (Ardila & Rosselli, 2002). Determination of the types of errors (e.g., errors in signs, errors in algorithms, errors in borrowing or carrying over) can be useful in determining the intervention plan. Multiple techniques have been used successfully to address acalculia (see Ardila & Rosselli, 2002).

REFERENCES

Ardila, A., & Rosselli, M. (1990). Acalculias. *Behavioral Neurology, 3,* 39–48.

Ardila, A., & Rosselli, M. (1994). Spatial acalculia. *International Journal of Neuroscience, 78,* 177–184.

Ardila, A., & Rosselli, M. (2002). Acalculia and dyscalculia. *Neuropsychology Review, 12,* 179–231.

Burbaud, P., Degreze, P., Lafon, P., Franconi, J. M., Bouligand, B., Bioulac, B., et al. (1995). Lateralization of prefrontal activation during internal mental calculation: A functional magnetic resonance imaging study. *Journal of Neurophysiology, 74,* 2194–2200.

Gerstmann, J. (1940). The syndrome of finger agnosia, disorientation for right and left, agraphia, and acalculia. *Archives of Neurology and Psychiatry, 44,* 398–404.

Grafman, J. (1988). Acalculia. In F. Boller, J. Grafman, G. Rizzolatti, & H. Goodglass (Eds.), *Handbook of neuropsychology* (Vol. 1, pp. 121–136). Amsterdam: Elsevier.

Levin, H. S., Goldstein, F. C., & Spiers, P. A. (1993). Acalculia. In K. M. Heilman & E. Valenstein (Eds.), *Acalculia in clinical neuropsychology* (pp. 91–122). New York: Oxford University Press.

Loring, D. W. (Ed.). (1999). *INS dictionary of neuropsychology.* New York: Oxford University Press.

Mandell, A. M., Knoefel, J. E., & Albert, M. L. (1994). Mental status examination in the elderly. In A. L. Albert & J. E. Knoefel (Eds.), *Clinical neurology of aging* (pp. 277–313). New York: Oxford University Press.

Rosselli, M., & Ardila, A. (1989). Calculation deficits in patients with right and left hemisphere damage. *Neuropsychologia, 27,* 607–618.

Sakurai, Y., Momose, T., Iwata, M., Sasaki, Y., & Kanazawa, J. (1996). Activation of prefrontal and posterior superior temporal areas in visual calculation. *Journal of Neurological Science, 39,* 89–94.

CYNTHIA A. RICCIO
Texas A&M University

ARITHMETIC REMEDIATION
DYSCALCULIA
TRAUMATIC BRAIN INJURY
TRAUMATIC BRAIN INJURY IN CHILDREN

ACCELERATION OF GIFTED CHILDREN

Acceleration is the term used for the process through which a child makes educational progress at a pace that is more rapid than usual. It can be measured by the child's actual achievement or by advancement in school grade (Ward, 1980). Currently, a variety of options exist through which a child can accelerate his or her learning and achievement, given the child is of advanced intellectual functioning or demonstrates an exceptional aptitude in one or more areas. The types of acceleration can be grouped into two general categories: grade-based acceleration and subject-based acceleration (Rogers, 2002).

The distinction between the two is that while grade-based acceleration is designed to shorten the time it takes for the intellectually advanced child to progress from kindergarten through the 12th grade in a traditional school setting, subject-based acceleration involves presenting the child with materials and skills that are more advanced than those traditionally expected to be mastered by children of the same age or grade level. Generally, grade-based acceleration is employed when the child exhibits above average general intellectual functioning, while subject-based acceleration is traditionally used when the child demonstrates exceptional aptitude in a particular area (Rogers, 2002).

Grade-based acceleration can be performed in a variety of ways, including the following options:

1. Grade skipping in which a child is promoted 2 or more years in the normal progression of kindergarten through 12th grade.
2. Placing the child in a classroom in which the curriculum is presented in a format that is undifferentiated by grade level or in a nongraded classroom.
3. Grade telescoping, which involves fast-paced progress through the completion of 3 years of coursework within 2 years or 4 years of coursework in 3 years (Fox, 1979).

4. Early admission programs in which an intellectually advanced student is allowed to enroll in college without completing high school or when a child is admitted into kindergarten or first grade at an age that is lower than usual.

5. Radical acceleration in which a combination of grade-based acceleration strategies are employed (Rogers, 2002).

The methods of subject-based acceleration include the following:

1. Early admission to formal schooling.

2. Presenting the child with a *compacted curriculum,* in which the student can demonstrate mastery of the curriculum and continue to learn at his or her own pace in the regular classroom setting.

3. Concurrent enrollment, which involves enrollment in classes at two different levels. This can be illustrated by the case in which a student may be enrolled in college courses while still attending high school.

4. Mentorship by an expert in a certain area.

5. Credit by examination to test out of courses.

6. Subject acceleration, in which the curriculum for certain subjects is presented at a more rapid pace than usual.

7. Advanced placement programs in which a student is learning college-level material while still in high school and is waived out of such courses when admitted to college.

8. Completing coursework via correspondence programs in which the material is presented to the student either through the mail or (more recently) over the Internet, and course credit is awarded following an examination over the material.

Historically, the practice of acceleration has generated much controversy, due to the general public opinion that it would result in the social maladjustment of the accelerated child. It was believed that removing the gifted and talented child from the presence of his or her peers would place the child at a disadvantage in learning appropriate social skills for his or her social and emotional developmental level (Gallagher, 1996; Whitmore, 1980). As a result, the practice of acceleration in the school systems has undergone many cycles of popularity. However, recent research suggests otherwise. A study entitled "A Nation Deceived: How Schools Hold Back America's Brightest Students" (The Templeton National Report on Acceleration) investigated hundreds of past studies on many different forms of acceleration, finding that those students who were accelerated were able to achieve at a much higher level than those of their peers who were not accelerated and suffered little to no psychological maladjustment at all (Colangelo, Assouline, & Gross, 2005).

REFERENCES

Colangelo, N., Assouline, S., & Gross, M. (2005). *A nation deceived: How schools hold back America's brightest students* (The Templeton National Report on Acceleration). Retrieved August 16, 2005, from http://nationdeceived.org/

Fox, L. H. (1979). Programs for the gifted and talented. In A. H. Passow (Ed.), *The gifted and talented: Their education and development* (pp. 104–126). Chicago: National Society or the Study of Education.

Gallagher, J. (1996). Educational research and educational policy: The strange case of acceleration. In C. P. Benbow & D. J. Lubinski (Eds.), *Intellectual talent: Psychometric and social issues* (pp. 83–92). Baltimore: Johns Hopkins University Press.

Kulik, J. A., & Kulik, C. C. (1984). Effects of accelerated instruction on students. *Review of Educational Research, 54,* 409–425.

Rogers, K. B. (2002). Effects of acceleration on gifted learners. In M. Neihart & S. Reis (Eds.), *The social and emotional development of gifted children: What do we know?* (pp. 3–12). Waco, TX: Prufrock Press.

Ward, V. (1980). *Differential education for the gifted.* Ventura, CA: Ventura County Schools.

Whitmore, J. R. (1980). *Giftedness, conflict, and underachievement.* Boston: Allyn & Bacon.

Krista Finstuen
Texas A&M University

GIFTED AND TALENTED CHILDREN
GIFTED CHILDREN

ACCESS BOARD

The Access Board (formerly the Federal Architectural and Transportation Barriers Compliance Board) is a federal commission responsible for accessibility issues of federal facilities. According to their statement of purpose, the Access Board

> is an independent Federal agency devoted to accessibility for people with disabilities. Created in 1973 to ensure access to federally funded facilities, the Board is now a leading source of information on accessible design. The Board develops and maintains design criteria for the built environment, transit vehicles, telecommunications equipment, and for electronic and information technology. It also provides technical assistance and training on these requirements and on accessible design and continues to enforce accessibility standards that cover federally funded facilities. (United States Access Board, 2005a)

The Access Board was instituted as a result of an increasing need for federal coordination of access issues in communication, architecture, and transportation settings. In recent years, many of its efforts have focused on information, specifically communications accessibility. In 1990, the Access

Board published a set of communication guidelines that covered the accessibility of software applications and operating systems, web-based intranet and Internet information and applications, telecommunications products, video and multimedia products, self contained or closed products, and desktop and portable computers. Of particular interest are the web-based accessibility guidelines. More commonly known as the *508 Guidelines,* these guidelines provide a concise set of web accessibility standards that have been adopted by numerous entities that may not specifically fall under the Access Board's purview. For example, there are numerous examples of the 508 Guidelines being applied to the web sites of institutions of higher education (e.g., http://rules.tamu.edu/saps/300/330499M501.htm; Texas A&M University, 2005).

Other areas of responsibility for the Access Board include the Americans with Disabilities Act (ADA) Accessibility Guidelines for Transportation Vehicles (United States Access Board, 2005c) and the Telecommunications Act Accessibility Guidelines (United States Access Board, 2005b).

More information can be found on the Internet at http://www.access-board.gov/

REFERENCES

Texas A&M University. (2005). *Web accessibility and usability procedures.* Retrieved October 10, 2005, from http://rules.tamu.edu/saps/300/330499M501.htm

United States Access Board. (2005a). About the Access Board. Retrieved October 10, 2005, from http://www.access-board.gov/about.htm

United States Access Board. (2005b). Telecommunications Act Accessibility Guidelines. Retrieved October 10, 2005, from http://www.access-board.gov/telecomm/rule.htm

United States Access Board. (2005c). Transportation vehicles. Retrieved October 10, 2005, from http://www.access-board.gov/transit/index.htm

DAVID SWEENEY
Texas A&M University

ACCESSIBILITY OF PROGRAMS
AMERICANS WITH DISABILITIES ACT

ACCESSIBILITY OF BUILDINGS

The accessible building is a structure that is readily usable by individuals possessing a wide range of physical disabilities or other limitations (such as sensory handicaps). Although estimates vary widely as to the number of citizens whose temporary or permanent impairments inhibit their mobility, the U.S. Department of Housing and Urban Development (1978) projects that at least 30 million people possess conditions that demand barrier-free facilities. A building or other site designed to accommodate ambulant or sensorily disabled persons is equally convenient and accessible to the nonhandicapped population. The design criteria used to meet the needs of handicapped populations are essentially no different from those of the general, nondisabled citizenry; they are only more pronounced.

The generally accepted minimum standards for ensuring the accessibility of buildings are incorporated in the American National Standards Institute (ANSI) specifications. Originally adopted in 1961 and subsequently revised and expanded during 1970s, the ANSI standards serve as a foundation for state laws and federal guidelines concerning building accessibility. A federal entity, the National Commission on Architectural Barriers (CAB), was created by an act of Congress to promote and evaluate voluntary and, in the case of federally owned or subsidized buildings, mandatory compliance with the ANSI standards.

The CAB's primary function has been to oversee the implementation of the Architectural Barriers Act of 1968 and related federal legislation designed to foster the accessibility of buildings and other environments.

The economic and human benefits of a site design that is barrier free are substantial. Data from the U.S. Office of Housing and Urban Development (1978) suggest that the initial costs of remodeling existing structures or designing and constructing new, fully accessible facilities are minimal when compared with the benefits derived by the disabled, their families, friends and colleagues, educational and other service agencies, and employers. The initial, one-time investment in a barrier-free design provides long-term benefits in terms of personal comfort, mobility, maximization of educational, social and employment options, and (particularly important for business) an expansion in the pool of active consumers.

Guided by the ANSI standards, architects and facility planners must ensure that the entrances to and the interiors of buildings allow for the uninhibited mobility, orientation, comfort, and performance of all facility users. As reviewed by Cotler and DeGraff (1976), the structural dimensions, interior design, entranceways, and the layout of furniture in all buildings should be integrated to accommodate the physical limitations in mobility, reach and posture experienced by most wheelchair users and individuals aided by crutches, walkers, and canes. It is of equal importance to the sensorily handicapped population (e.g., individuals who are blind or deaf) that building environments offer a simple, regular, well-lighted, and marked design that enhances orientation and ready access to sources of visual, aural, and tactile information.

REFERENCES

Cotler, S. R., & DeGraff, A. H. (1976). *Architectural accessibility for the disabled on college campuses.* Albany, NY: State University Construction Fund.

U.S. Department of Housing and Urban Development. (1978). *Access to the environment.* Washington, DC: U.S. Government Printing Office.

GEORGE JAMES HAGERTY
Stonehill College

AMERICANS WITH DISABILITIES ACT
ARCHITECTURAL BARRIERS
ARCHITECTURE AND INDIVIDUALS WITH DISABILITIES

ACCESSIBILITY OF PROGRAMS

Section 504 of the Rehabilitation Act of 1973, as amended by the Rehabilitation Act Amendments of 1998, provides that

> no otherwise qualified individual with a disability . . . shall, solely by reason of her or his disability, be excluded from participation in, be denied the benefits of, or be subjected to discrimination under any program or activity receiving Federal financial assistance or under any program or activity conducted by any Executive agency or the United States Postal Service.

The substantive provisions apply to two distinct sets of entities: recipients of federal financial assistance (federally assisted programs) and the operations of government agencies (federally conducted programs). Requirements of program accessibility were extended under the Americans with Disabilities Act in 1990 to apply to all public entities, including public schools, regardless of such entities' status as recipients (or nonrecipients) of federal funds.

The concept of program accessibility is a key requirement of the implementing regulations for both federally assisted and federally conducted programs (U.S. Government, 1985, 1987). In both cases, the requirement is not that every existing building or classroom be physically accessible, but rather that "the program or activity, when viewed in its entirety, is readily accessible to and usable by handicapped persons" (28 CFR 41.57[a]). All new buildings and facilities must be designed and constructed to be readily accessible to and usable by persons with disabilities.

Since the late 1970s, federal court decisions and regulatory policy have interpreted and qualified the precise requirements of program accessibility. Of particular importance is the U.S. Supreme Court Decision in *Southeastern Community College v. Davis* (1979), which held that the school was not required to modify a nurse training program as sought by a hearing-impaired individual because such modification would constitute "a fundamental alteration in the nature of the program." In discussing program modification, the Court also referenced attaining desirable goals "without imposing undue financial and administrative burdens" (pp. 410, 412).

In its own regulations on federally funded programs, the Department of Justice employs criteria from the *Davis* decision. The program accessibility requirement for existing programs explicitly does not "require the agency to take any action that it can demonstrate would result in a fundamental alteration in the nature of the program or activity or in undue financial and administrative burdens" (28 CFR 39.150[a][2]). Notes accompanying this regulation explain that the Department of Justice's position is that "judicial interpretation of Section 504 [including circuit court decisions following *Davis*] compels it to incorporate the new language" and that the regulations for federally assisted programs must now be interpreted consistent with the federally conducted rule and *Davis*.

A good discussion of these issues is in the editorial note to 28 CFR 39 (U.S. Government, 1985). Other precedents have established the rights of all students to accessibility of educational programs (Sales, Krauss, Sacken, & Overcast, 1999).

REFERENCES

Sales, B., Krauss, D. A., Sacken, D., & Overcast, T. (1999). The legal rights of students. In C. R. Reynolds & T. B. Gutkin (Eds.), *The handbook of school psychology* (3rd ed., pp. 1113–1144). New York: Wiley.

Southeastern Community College v. Davis. (1979). United States Supreme Court, 442 U.S. 397.

U.S. Government. (1985). Code of Federal Regulations Title 28, Part 39. *Enforcement of Non-Discrimination on the Basis of Handicap in Programs or Activities Conducted by the Department of Justice.*

U.S. Government. (1987). Code of Federal Regulations Title 28, Part 41. *Implementation of Executive Order 12250, Non-Discrimination on the Basis of Handicap in Federally Assisted Programs.*

JAMES R. RICCIUTI
United States Office of
Management and Budget
First edition

KIMBERLY F. APPLEQUIST
University of Colorado at
Colorado Springs
Third edition

ACCESSIBILITY OF BUILDINGS
AMERICANS WITH DISABILITIES ACT
REHABILITATION ACT OF 1973, SECTION 504

ACCESSIBILITY OF WEB SITES

See WEB ACCESSIBILITY.

ACCESSIBILITY RESOURCES IN STANDARD COMPUTER SYSTEMS

In addition to being able to incorporate a wide range of special accessibility hardware and software resources, today's major computer operating systems (Windows and Mac OS) contain a number of built-in options to provide accessibility in relation to a variety of disabilities. The two major platforms available in schools have similar assistive features to help empower many disabled students without the need for additional expense, hardware, or materials.

Apple OS X Accessibility

Macintosh OS X Tiger provides features for individuals with vision, hearing, and motor skills disabilities. Universal Access provides numerous modification capabilities that work with basic computer functions as well as with many applications. Because OS X allows settings for multiple users, the same computer can be preset to provide personalized interaction for any number of individual students or groups with similar needs.

Vision

Numerous options are provided to help individuals see the screen contents. The screen text and graphics can be easily magnified up to 20 times without distracting pixilation. As the cursor is moved about, the screen adjusts and follows to automatically display the desired content. The cursor itself is resizable to help the viewer keep oriented. The screen contrast and color range can also be adjusted to any individual preferences.

This system has an integrated screen reader called VoiceOver; any activity on the screen is narrated to the user to provide a full verbal description of the actions. The audio narration content can also be displayed simultaneously in a fully configurable, large-print text caption panel. The system also reads the content of documents and provides full keyboard navigation for control of the computer.

Hearing

For hearing difficulties, the system can be set to flash the screen to alert the user as an alternative to the audio alerts. Quick-access key commands can also be used to adjust the system volume, choose a custom system beep alert, set the alert beep volume independent of the system volume setting, and play unique sounds that identify various system events.

Motor Skills

Students having difficulty with motor skills will often have problems using the mouse. MouseKeys let you adapt the numeric keypad to move the mouse cursor, click, double-click, and drag. The StickyKeys option lets the student create multiple key controls, such as Shift-Option-8, as a sequence of key presses. Key commands can be used to navigate menus, windows, the Dock, and other interface elements using Full Keyboard Access; this feature can also be assigned to work within specific applications. A parallel assistive function uses the built-in speech recognition system to allow the student to speak commands instead of having to type them. Standard features include keyboard control over key repeat and delay rates and control of the mouse tracking and double-click speeds. Individualization of all key shortcuts is also available. Handwriting recognition capability is also built-in using Ink and can be used for text input. Most dialog boxes have buttons that can be selected and activated by keystrokes instead of by the standard mouse click.

Windows XP Accessibility Features

Windows XP contains a number of built-in accessibility features and is compatible with more than a dozen assistive technology products by working closely with assistive technology vendors to serve the needs of users with vision, hearing, mobility, and cognitive disabilities.

Vision

Windows XP has Magnifier, a display utility that makes the screen more readable by students with vision problems by magnifying a portion of the screen in a separate window. The screen display can be customized by changing features such as position, size, and window color. The magnification level and magnifier tracking options can also be controlled. Narrator is a text-to-speech utility for individuals who are blind or have limited vision. Using its built-in internal driver, TTS engine, it reads the contents of the active window, menu options, or text that has been typed. It is specialized to only some applications—Notepad, WordPad, Control Panel Programs, Internet Explorer, the Windows Desktop, and some other parts of Window setup. Narrator has many options that allow the user to customize the way screen elements are read by setting them to announce events on the screen, to read typed characters, to move the mouse pointer to active item, and to adjust voice options. The user can select alternate voices and control the speed, volume, and pitch of the narration.

ToggleKeys provides audio cues when certain keys are pressed. A predefined set of mouse pointers can be chosen to increase visibility of the cursor location. Windows XP can be set to display pointer trails and change the length of the pointer trail for better visibility of mouse pointer. When working with a document while typing with an enlarged mouse pointer, the user can hide mouse pointer for better visibility. The relative speed of the cursor movement can also be adjusted. A SnapTo feature moves the cursor to the default button and selected by the Enter key.

Hearing

Windows XP provides a feature, SoundsEntry, to change the settings to generate visual warnings, such as a blinking title bar or screen flash for people who have difficulty hearing computer system sounds. Visual warnings can be chosen for sounds made by windowed programs or full-screen text programs. The Show Sounds feature instructs programs that usually convey information only by sound to also provide all information by displaying text captions or informative icons.

Motor Skills

On-Screen Keyboard, one of the built-in utilities, displays a virtual keyboard on the computer screen that allows users who have mobility disabilities to type data by using a pointing device or joystick. Different options can be accessed by changing font settings of the keys to make them more legible, using Click Sound to add an audible click, using Clicking Mode to select the on-screen keys to type text, and enabling Hovering Mode to use a mouse or joystick to point to a key image for a predefined period of time to type the character. StickyKeys allows users to press keys one at a time in sequence rather than need to hold them all at once. FilterKeys adjusts the keyboard repeating rate. Also, Windows XP can be set to display pointer trails and change the length of the pointer trail for better tracking and visibility of the mouse pointer. Additionally, Mouse Keys can be activated to provide use of the numeric keypad for both navigation and data entry.

REFERENCES

Apple Computer, Inc. (2005). *Apple-Mac OS X—Universal access.* Retrieved September 1, 2005, from http://www.apple.com/macosx/features/universalaccess/

Microsoft Corporation. (2005). *Windows XP accessibility tips and how-to articles.* Retrieved September 1, 2005, from http://www.microsoft.com/windowsxp/using/accessibility/default.mspx

RON ZELLNER
Texas A&M University

ACCESSIBLE MEDIA PLAYERS

With the promulgation of specifications for accessible electronic formats such as the DAISY-NISO digital talking book (DTB) standard (DAISY Consortium, 2005) and the Open eBook Publication Structure (International Digital Publishing Forum, 2005), a new group of accessible media players has recently emerged. These media players are primarily designed to facilitate reading of accessible materials by people with disabilities. The technology can also be used to advantage by people without disabilities. The term *accessible media player* refers to the greater accessibility of the media itself and also to the accessibility of the playback devices that may incorporate accessible features such as Brailled buttons and audio navigation menus.

Accessible media players provide a more efficient replacement of traditional materials recorded to audio cassette. They operate by facilitating playback of digital audio, usually contained on digital compact discs, through a software program or a dedicated hardware playback device similar to a compact disc player. They provide fairly granular navigation capabilities, allowing direct access of the desired information, unlike traditional audio cassette recordings that use a tone mechanism paired with fast-forward and rewind functions. Materials created in these formats usually contain a digital table of contents, which can be accessed using accessible media players and is much more efficient at locating the desired material when compared to cassettes. Another advantage of accessible media players over traditional books on cassette is that a single compact disc can currently hold up to 40 hours of audio, while a cassette is limited to 4 hours. The new digital media also support comprehensive digital rights management (DRM) structures, protecting copyrighted material from being reproduced or distributed.

A fairly comprehensive list of players can be found on the DAISY Consortium's web site (http://www.daisy.org/tools/playback.asp).

REFERENCES

DAISY Consortium. (2005). *DAISY / NISO standard—formally ANSI / NISO z39.86 specifications for the digital talking book.* Retrieved September 5, 2005, from http://www.daisy.org/z3986/default.asp

International Digital Publishing Forum. (2005). *Open ebook publication structure specification version 1.2.* Retrieved September 5, 2005, from http://www.openebook.com/oebps/oebps1.2/index.htm

DAVID SWEENEY
Texas A&M University

ACCESSIBILITY OF PROGRAMS
COMPUTER USE WITH STUDENTS WITH DISABILITIES

ACCOMMODATION

Accommodation is one of two complementary processes proposed by Jean Piaget to account for an individual's adaptation to the environment; its counterpart is assimilation. Accommodation involves changing or transforming cognitive or sensorimotor schemes according to the demands of the environment; assimilation involves incorporating external elements into existing conceptual schemes.

The difference between accommodation and assimilation can be illustrated by an example of an infant's response to a rattle (Ginsburg & Opper, 1969). When a rattle suspended from an infant's crib begins to shake after the infant's arm movement causes it to move, the infant looks at and listens to the toy rattling, assimilating the event into his or her schemes of looking and listening. To repeat the movement of the rattle, the infant must make the necessary hand and arm movements, accommodating his or her actions according to the demands of the situation.

Assimilation and accommodation were viewed by Piaget as inseparable aspects of a single process of adaptation, separable only for purposes of discussion (Brainerd, 1978). Assimilation and accommodation occur simultaneously; a balance between the two is necessary for adaptation. A scheme must accommodate itself to the specific characteristics of the object or event it is attempting to assimilate; accommodation guides the eventual change in structures (Gelman & Baillargeon, 1983).

REFERENCES

Brainerd, C. J. (1978). *Piaget's theory of intelligence.* Englewood Cliffs, NJ: Prentice Hall.

Gelman, R., & Baillargeon, R. (1983). A review of some Piagetian concepts. In P. H. Mussen (Ed.), *Handbook of child psychology: Vol. III. Cognitive development* (pp. 167–230). New York: Wiley.

Ginsburg, H., & Opper, S. (1969). *Piaget's theory of intellectual development: An introduction.* Englewood Cliffs, NJ: Prentice Hall.

LINDA J. STEVENS
University of Minnesota

ASSIMILATION
COGNITIVE DEVELOPMENT
PIAGET, JEAN

ACCOMMODATIONS

Accommodations change the way instruction is provided or assessment tasks are administered to students with disabilities. These changes reduce the impact of physical, cognitive, or sensory barriers that may prevent students from gaining access to the targeted domain or expressing their knowledge and skills. For example, a student with a hearing impairment may need test directions presented in sign language to understand the information. Without this accommodation, the student would not be able to perform the tasks necessary to demonstrate his or her abilities. As such, accommodations allow students with disabilities to meaningfully interact with curricular materials, thereby increasing their participation in the general education environment.

Changes to the presentation, response, setting, and timing of materials are acceptable accommodations provided they do not change or interfere with the targeted construct. Maintaining the integrity of the construct allows for valid interpretations of student knowledge and skills. If the construct is altered, however, similar interpretations of student ability are not possible.

Presentation accommodations change the format of information that is presented to the student. Such accommodations include, but are not limited to, presenting material in Braille, sign language, high or low contrast, and visual magnification of text or response forms. Other presentation accommodations include reading the directions or questions aloud to students, simplifying the language used in the directions or questions, or reducing the amount of text on a page.

Response accommodations change the format in which responses are recorded or the method in which the student responds to questions or tasks. Format changes include allowing students to use additional space on the paper; record answers directly on a test booklet; or use different types of paper, such as graph or lined paper. Examples of changes to the method of response include providing assistive devices such as word processors or Braillers. Scribes as well as audio recording responses for transcription are also classified as response accommodations. Allowing students to check spelling or grammar is appropriate as long as these skills are not part of the targeted construct.

Setting accommodations change the environment in which instruction is presented or assessment tasks are administered. Setting accommodations include working with the student in a separate location or in a small group, reducing the distractions in a typical setting, or providing assistive furniture. Finally, timing accommodations change the amount of time allocated to the tasks. Examples include providing additional time to complete tasks, allowing the student to complete work during multiple short sessions within or across days, providing frequent breaks, presenting materials at specific times of the day, or changing the schedule to accommodate special needs. Again, it is important to note that any of these accommodations are appropriate if they do not interfere with the targeted construct.

Accommodated materials are created by retrofitting existing activities or embedding changes within the design of new materials. Retrofitting materials allows teachers and other educators to use already created instructional activities and assessment tasks, thereby avoiding the costs of designing new forms. However, changing existing materials can be costly and may result in less than ideal conditions, which may compromise the goal of the accommodation. As an example, imagine creating a Braille version of an existing science test that included multiple graphical representations. Each image would be redesigned in order to be converted to Braille, or the image would be omitted from the Braille version. In any case, the student would not receive the same materials as sighted students.

To avoid the drawbacks incurred when retrofitting existing materials, accommodations can be embedded during the design and construction phases of materials development (Ketterlin-Geller, 2003). For example, the science test discussed in the previous example would be created with simple graphic images that display only the necessary information. When a Braille version is created, the images are easily converted so that all students receive the same materials. By considering the characteristics of the target population when materials are created, developers can include accommodations from the beginning. This circumvents the costs associated with accommodating existing materials.

Once accommodated materials are created, students with disabilities are assigned accommodations that will reduce the sources of error that are caused by the disability. An individualized educational program (IEP) team is responsible for making decisions about assignment of accommodations for an individual student. Input from a variety of sources including parent preference, teacher's experience and observations, and inferences about student performance is considered when determining the use of accommodations (Fuchs & Fuchs, 1999). Care must be taken to assign appropriate accommodations based on the student's characteristics. For accommodations to be beneficial, format changes must be specific to the individual's characteristics and needs (Helwig & Tindal, 2003). For example, a student with a visual impairment may benefit from information presented in large text or Braille. However, this same student may be distracted or confused by materials constructed using simplified language.

Additionally, for accommodations to effectively support students with disabilities and provide meaningful opportunities for these students to participate in the general education curriculum, they must be applied in both instructional and assessment settings. Without the use of accommodations in instruction, students are denied the opportunity to learn the material and are subsequently penalized on assessments. When unfamiliar accommodations are introduced during testing, they may provide additional sources of irrelevant variance in the students' score.

REFERENCES

Fuchs, L. S., & Fuchs, D. (1999). Fair and unfair testing accommodations. *School Administrator, 56*(10), 24–29.

Helwig, R., & Tindal, G. (2003). An experimental analysis of accommodation decisions on large-scale mathematics tests. *Exceptional Children, 69,* 211–225.

Ketterlin-Geller, L. R. (2003). *Establishing a validity argument for universally designed assessments.* Unpublished doctoral dissertation, University of Oregon, Eugene.

LEANNE KETTERLIN-GELLER
University of Oregon

AMERICAN SIGN LANGUAGE

See TEST ANXIETY

ACETYLCHOLINE

Acetylcholine (ACh) is a neurotransmitter, a chemical that is released from one neuron to pass a message to another neuron. Acetylcholine is naturally synthesized in living cells in cholinergic nerve terminals that are located primarily in the autonomic nervous system. It also is evident at parasympathetic postganglionic synapses, and at neuromuscular junctures (Cooper, Bloom, & Roth, 1982).

The autonomic nervous system is involved in what appears to be functionally reflexive responses directed toward energy conservation or preparation for possible trauma. Thus, with cholinergic stimulation, pupils contract, heart rate slows, and muscular contraction is facilitated (Katzung, 1982). Experimental work by Deutsch (1984) suggests the possibility of an indirect, environmental role for ACh in the development of memories. Results of animal studies indicate that drugs that block cholinergic action tend to increase low rates of response and decrease high rates of response among behaviors that were maintained through food reinforcers (Seiden & Dykstra, 1977). Such findings are consistent with the likelihood that ACh plays a role in creating a chemical environmental context for learning by mediating autonomic responsiveness and attention (Himmelheber, Sarter, & Bruno, 2001). A role in pain perception also has been postulated (Cooper et al., 1982). Myasthenia gravis, a disease characterized by fluctuating muscle weakness, especially in muscles innervated by the motor nuclei of the brain stem (Adams & Victor, 1981), is a model of ACh dysfunction. Observed involvement of cholinergic systems in tardive dyskinesia, Huntington's chorea, and Alzheimer's dementia has led to experimental administration of drugs that facilitate ACh; however, no consistent results have been observed in such studies (Cooper et al., 1982).

REFERENCES

Adams, R. D, & Victor, M. (1981). *Principles of neurology.* New York: McGraw-Hill.

Cooper, J. R., Bloom, F. E., & Roth, R. H. (1982). *The biochemical basis of neuropharmacology.* New York: Oxford University Press.

Deutsch, J. A. (1984). Amnesia and a theory for dating memories. In G. Lynch, J. L. McGaugh, & N. M. Weinberger (Eds.), *Neurobiology of learning and memory* (pp. 105–110). New York: Guilford.

Himmelheber, A., Sarter, M., & Bruno, J. P. (2001). *Cognitive Brain Research, 12,* 353–370.

Katzung, B. G. (1982). *Basic and clinical pharmacology.* Los Altos, CA: Lange Medical Publications.

Seiden, L. S., & Dykstra, L. A. (1977). *Psychopharmacology: A biochemical and behavioral approach.* New York: Van Nostrand Reinhold.

ROBERT F. SAWICKI
*Lake Erie Institute of
Rehabilitation*

CENTRAL NERVOUS SYSTEM NEUROLOGICAL ORGANIZATION

ACHENBACH CHILD BEHAVIOR CHECKLIST

The purpose of the Child Behavior Checklist (CBCL 6–18; Achenbach & Rescorla, 2001) is to quickly collect standardized ratings on a broad spectrum of competencies and problems for children aged 6 to 18 years as reported by the child's parent or others that are involved with the child within the home environment. For the 120 behavioral, emotional, and social problem statements, the respondent is directed to answer all items as best as possible even if they do not seem applicable to the child. The instructions to the respondent are located on the CBCL booklet and are written on a fifth-grade reading level. If the respondent cannot read, the CBCL can be administered in an alternate format where the examiner reads the items and records the responses of the respondent.

The CBCL measures competencies using a Total Competence Score, which represents a parent's perception of the child's performance on an Activities scale, a Social scale, and a School scale.

Problems are measured on the CBCL's Syndrome scales. These represent the parents' perception of their child's behavior based on eight statistically derived categories (factors): Anxious/Depressed, Withdrawn/Depressed, Somatic Complaints, Social Problems, Thought Problems, Attention Problems, Rule-Breaking Behavior, and Aggressive Behavior.

The Anxious/Depressed, Withdrawn/Depressed, and Somatic Complaints scales constitute the Internalizing Problems scale score, and the Rule-Breaking Behavior and Aggressive Behavior scales combine to yield the Externalizing Problems scale scores. Adding the Social Problems, Thought Problems, and Attention Problems scales to the

Internalizing and Externalizing Problem scales generates a Total Problem scale score.

In addition, problems on the CBCL have been categorized into six DSM-oriented scales: Affective Problems, Anxiety Problems, Somatic Problems, Attention Deficit/Hyperactivity Problems, Oppositional Defiant Problems, and Conduct Problems.

Scoring the CBCL is easy, and responses are directly recorded from the CBCL booklet. Scoring can be done in one of three ways: by hand, by computer, or by scanner. The hand-scoring method is time consuming, and the many calculations leave room for frequent errors. Although the computer-scoring and scanning methods are initially more costly, they reduce time spent scoring and are more accurate.

Males and females have separate norms based on age. The two age ranges used for each gender are 6 to 11 and 12 to 18. Normative data are provided only on the hand-scoring profiles. No other printed norm tables are available at this time. The computer-generated profile does not provide the examiner with such data.

The t scores and percentiles are calculated for each scale for comparative purposes. For each scale, t scores are further categorized as being within normal limits, within the borderline range, or within the clinical range. The value of t scores for each range varies depending on the scale. On the Competence scales and Total Competence scale, higher t scores are associated with normal functioning. On the Syndrome scales, Internalizing, Externalizing, Total Problem, and DSM-oriented scales, lower t scores are associated with normal functioning.

The CBCL also allows for multiple respondent comparisons to be made using another CBCL, the Teacher Report Form (TRF) or the Youth Self-Report (YSR).

The CBCL sample consisted of 1,753 children. The demographics in the manual indicate that 914 boys and 839 girls were used. There were 387 boys in the 6 to 11 age group and 527 boys in the 12 to 18 age group. There were 390 girls in the 6 to 11 age group and 449 girls in the 12 to 18 age group. The number of participants for each year (i.e., number of 6-year-olds, number of 7-year-olds, etc.) was not presented in the manual. For the sample, socioeconomic status was broken down to three levels with the following results: upper (33 percent), middle (51 percent), and lower (16 percent). In terms of ethnicity, 60 percent were non-Latino White, 20 percent were African American, 9 percent were Latino, and 12 percent were mixed or other. There were 100 sampling sites in 40 states and the District of Columbia. Of the participants, 17 percent were from the Northeast, 20 percent were from the Midwest, 40 percent were from the South, and 24 percent were from the West. Overall, the sample procedures appear to be adequate and fairly representative.

Internal consistency or *split-half reliability* was moderately high and ranged from .55 to .75. For the empirically based problem scales (Syndromes, Internalizing, Externalizing, and Total Problem), reliabilities were high, ranging from .78 to .98. In all cases, Total scores have the highest internal consistency. For the DSM-oriented scales, alphas were high as they ranged from .72 to .91. Test-retest reliability was high for most of the scales, with a range of .80 to .94. The test-retest interval was 8 to 16 days, and the sample included children who had been referred for mental health services and those who had not.

The CBCL is very user friendly. It is easy to administer and take. A big drawback for the examiner is the time requirement and inaccuracy of hand-scoring procedures. If the computer-scoring system is used, scoring is also relatively easy.

REFERENCES

Achenbach, T., & Rescorla, L. A. (2001). *Child behavior checklist.* Burlington, VT: ASEBA.

Belter, R. W., Foster, K. Y., & Imm, P. S. (1996). Convergent validity of select scales of the MMPI and the Achenbach Child Behavior Checklist—Youth Self-Report. *Psychological Reports, 79,* 1091–1100.

Biederman, J., Monuteaux, J. C., Greene, R. W., Braaten, E., Doyle, A. E., & Faraone, S. V. (2001). Long-term stability of the Child Behavior Checklist in a clinical sample of youth with Attention-Deficit Hyperactivity Disorder. *Journal of Clinical Child Psychology, 30,* 492–502.

Impara, J. C., & Plake, B. S. (Eds.). (1998). *The thirteenth mental measurements yearbook* (pp. 933–937). Lincoln, NE: Buros Institute of Mental Measurements.

RON DUMONT
Fairleigh Dickinson University

JOHN O. WILLIS
Rivier College

ACHIEVEMENT NEED

Achievement need is also known as achievement motivation, the need for achievement, and n:Ach. The concept was first defined by Murray (1938) as the need "to overcome obstacles, to exercise power, to strive to do something difficult as well and as quickly as possible" (pp. 80–81). Murray, however, chose not to attempt to conduct applied research in achievement motivation and the concept did not receive much attention until McClelland (1951) developed a cognitive theory of motivation in which the need for achievement is one element. McClelland's theory states that a person's tendency to approach a task (effort) is a function of the strength of the achievement need, the strength of the need to avoid failure, the person's subjective belief about the probability of success or failure, and the value of the incentives associated with either success or failure. According to McClelland (1951) and Atkinson (1964), achievement need is intrinsic. It is not associated with extrinsic rewards that accrue as a result of achievement. Achievement need is generally measured through the Thematic Apperception Test (TAT), although Hermans (1970) developed a paper and pencil test for this purpose called *n:Ach.*

Many researchers have attempted to determine how achievement need develops. Crandall (1963) discovered that children with high achievement needs had mothers who rewarded achievement and achievement activities at an early age. These mothers also did not attend to their children's pleas for help when the children faced a difficult problem. Crandall further concluded that middle- and upper-class parents were more likely to engage in behaviors that develop achievement motivation than were parents of lower economic status. Currently, parental involvement to assist achievement need is taking center stage as an educational improvement strategy (Hara & Burke, 1998).

A number of studies have been conducted to determine the effects of achievement on task performance and personality. Weiner (1970) found that high-need achievement persons persist in the face of failure while low-need achievement persons become more inhibited in their responses. He further found that low-need achievement persons will engage in achievement activity when success and reinforcement rates approach 100 percent, but high-need achievement persons work best when reinforcement is attained approximately 50 percent of the time. Weiner and Kukla (1970) related achievement need research to Rotter's (1966) research in locus of control. Using elementary school children, they concluded that high-need achievement children viewed their successes as resulting from their effort. Both high- and low-achievement need children attributed failure to themselves, but high-need achievement children attributed failure to lack of effort while low-achievement children attributed it to lack of ability.

REFERENCES

Atkinson, J. W. (1964). *An introduction to motivation.* Princeton, NJ: Van Nostrand.

Crandall, V. J. (1963). Achievement. In H. W. Stevenson (Ed.), *Child psychology* (pp. 416–459). Chicago: University of Chicago Press.

Hara, S. R., & Burke, D. J. (1998). Parent involvement: The key to improved student involvement. *School Community Journal, 8,* 9–19.

Hermans, H. J. M. A. (1970). A questionnaire measure of achievement motivation. *Journal of Applied Psychology, 54,* 353–363.

McClelland, D. C. (1951). *Personality.* New York: Dryden.

Murray, H. A. (1938). *Exploration in personality.* New York: Oxford University Press.

Rotter, J. B. (1966). Generalized expectancies for internal versus external control of reinforcement. *Psychology Monographs, 80.*

Weiner, B. (1970). New conceptions in the study of achievement motivation. In B. A. Maher (Ed.), *Progress in experimental personality research* (Vol. 5). New York: Academic.

Weiner, B., & Kukla, A. (1970). An attributional analysis of achievement motivation. *Journal of Personality and Social Psychology, 15,* 1–20.

JAMES K. MCAFEE
Pennsylvania State University

LEARNED HELPLESSNESS
MOTIVATION
SELF-CONCEPT
SELF-CONTROL CURRICULUM

ACHIEVEMENT TESTS

Achievement tests are individually- or group-administered standardized instruments intended to measure the effectiveness of former training. Achievement tests are the dominant form of standardized assessment in education. Measures of achievement have been used to evaluate student performance, school instruction efficacy, candidates for scholarship awards, admission to academic programs, and applicants for industrial and government employment. Group administered achievement tests are more likely to be employed for the evaluation of a scholastic program, whereas individually administered achievement tests are typically used to assist in appropriate grade placement in schools and the identification and diagnosis of learning disabilities.

Traditional achievement tests were based on the principle of comparing examinees to their peers, or normative testing (classical test theory). Some more contemporary achievement tests are based on the premise that a prediction can be made about the performance of a person with a specified ability in regard to that person's probable success or failure on an item of specified difficulty (Anastasi, 1988). In other words, as the level of ability increases, the probability that an examinee will give a correct response increases (Hambleton, Swaminathan, & Rogers, 1991). Given the special characteristics of item response theory (IRT), computer adaptive testing is a desirable method to select different sets of items for each subject.

Some examples of commonly used normative achievement tests and their publishers include: Comprehensive Tests of Basic Skills (CTB/McGraw-Hill), Iowa Tests of Basic Skills (Riverside Publishing Company), Kaufman–Test of Educational Achievement Second Edition (American Guidance Service), Stanford Test of Academic Skills (Psychological Corporation), and Tests of General Educational Development (GED Testing Service of the American Council on Education).

The use of computer aided testing and IRT represents a new era in achievement testing. For example, the ACCU-PLACER (College Board online administration) computerized battery of achievement tests for college level placement is implemented in the placement of hundreds of thousands of students during each school year (Cole, Muenz, & Bates, 1998).

REFERENCES

Anastasi, A. (1988). *Psychological testing* (6th ed.). New York: Macmillan.

Cole, J. C., Muenz, T. A., & Bates, H. G. (1998). Age in correlations between ACCUPLACER's reading comprehension subtest and GPA. *Perceptual and Motor Skills, 86,* 1251–1256.

Hambleton, R. K., Swaminathan, H., & Rogers, H. J. (1991). *Fundamentals of item response theory.* London: Sage.

TRACY A. MUENZ
*California School of
Professional Psychology*

CRITERION-REFERENCED TESTS
NORM-REFERENCED TESTS

ACHONDROPLASIA

Achondroplasia, also called chondrodystrophy, refers to a defect in the formation of cartilage in the epiphyses of long bones, such that a type of dwarfism results. This most common form of dwarfism is usually inherited as an autosomal dominant trait, or it may result from spontaneous mutation (Avioli, 1979; Magalini, 1971). Clinical features of achondroplasia include absolute diminution of extremities; normal trunk and head size; a prominent, bulging forehead; and a flattened, saddle nose. Hands and feet typically are short, and fingers tend to be nearly equal in length (trident hands). Adult height generally does not exceed 1.4 meters. Achondroplasia occurs with equal frequency in females and males and affects approximately 1 in 25,000 children in the United States (Toplis, 2003).

The intelligence of affected persons is reported to be normal (Avioli, 1979; Lubs, 1977), although there is evidence of occasional neurologic complications during early adulthood (Magalini, 1971). The fertility of achondroplastic dwarfs is reported to be 30 percent of normal. Of offspring of two affected persons, two-thirds will exhibit the syndrome (Lubs, 1977). In educational settings, afflicted children may require adaptive equipment to accommodate their short stature. While there is no evidence to suggest that achondroplasia places individuals at increased risk for learning problems, a multifactored evaluation is appropriate for children who experience difficulty in school.

REFERENCES

Avioli, L. V. (1979). Diseases of bone. In P. B. Beeson, W. McDermott, & J. B. Wyngaarden (Eds.), *Cecil textbook of medicine* (pp. 2225–2265). Philadelphia: Saunders.

Lubs, M. (1977). Genetic disorders. In M. J. Krajicek & A. I. Tearney (Eds.), *Detection of developmental problems in children* (pp. 55–77). Baltimore: University Park Press.

Magalini, S. (1971). *Dictionary of medical syndromes.* Philadelphia: Lippincott.

Toplis, R. (2003). Achondroplasia. In E. Fletcher-Janzen & C. R. Reynolds (Eds.), *Childhood disorders diagnostic desk reference* (p. 3). New York: Wiley.

CATHY F. TELZROW
Kent State University

CONGENITAL DISORDERS
MINOR PHYSICAL ANOMALIES

ACTING OUT

Acting out has been defined by Harriman (1975) as the "direct expression of conflicted tensions in annoying or antisocial behavior in fantasies" (p. 30). A child who exhibits acting-out behavior is one who cannot easily accept structural limits and is difficult to manage in the classroom. Acting-out behaviors are similar to conduct disorders or externalizing behaviors, but not necessarily as severe. One reason for the similarity is that acting-out behavior is one of the characteristics clustered under the broader grouping of conduct disorders. Acting-out behaviors usually are of high frequency and of significant duration, and do not include minor daily misbehavior.

Usually, when a behavior is identified as an acting-out behavior, it is operationally defined, observed, and recorded by the classroom teacher in specific and observable terms. Some of the behaviors that can be identified as acting-out behaviors include fighting, lying, temper tantrums, pouting, stealing, hyperactivity, threatening, and bullying (Quay, 1979).

Acting out, or externalizing behaviors are linked to persistant poverty (Eamon, 2000) and observed more frequently in males (Wicks-Nelson & Israel, 2000).

REFERENCES

Eamon, M. K. (2000). Structural model of the effects of poverty on externalizing and internalizing behaviors of four to five-year-old children. *Social Work Research, 24,* 143–154.

Harriman, P. L. (1975). *Handbook of psychological terms.* Totowa, NJ: Littlefield, Adams.

Quay, H. C. (1979). Classification. In H. C. Quay & J. S. Werry (Eds.), *Psychopathological disorders of childhood* (2nd ed.). New York: Wiley.

Wicks-Nelson, R., & Israel, A. C. (2000). *Behavior disorders of childhood.* Upper Saddle River, NJ: Prentice Hall.

MARIBETH MONTGOMERY KASIK
Governors State University

APPLIED BEHAVIOR ANALYSIS
CONDUCT DISORDER

ADAPTED PHYSICAL EDUCATION

Adapted physical education is a

> diversified program of developmental activities, games, sports, and rhythms suited to the interests, capacities, and limitations of students with disabilities who may not safely and successfully engage in unrestricted participation in vigorous activities of the general physical education program. (Hurley, 1981, p. 43)

The focus of adapted physical education is on the development of motor and physical fitness and fundamental motor patterns and skills in a sportslike environment (Sherrill, 1985).

Adapted physical education implies the modification of physical activities, rules, and regulations to meet existing limiting factors of specific handicapped populations. By definition, adapted physical education includes activities planned for persons with learning problems owed to mental, motor, or emotional impairment, disability, or dysfunction; planned for the purpose of rehabilitation, habilitation, or remediation; modified so the handicapped can participate; and designed for modifying movement capabilities.

Adapted physical education primarily occurs within a school setting, but it may also occur in clinics, hospitals, residential facilities, daycare centers, or other centers where the primary intent is to influence learning or movement potential through motor activity (AAHPER, 1952).

In the school setting, adapted physical education differs from regular physical education in the following manner. It has a federally mandated base through IDEA 2004. It serves students who are primarily identified as having a handicapping condition but may serve students such as the obese, who are not identified as handicapped but are in need of physical activity modification within a restricted environment. Adapted physical education classes are usually separate and educationally distinct from regular physical education owing to the need to modify the curriculum to suit the individual interests and capabilities of the student.

The basic elements in curriculum planning are individuality, flexibility, and educational accountability. Because of the intra- and intervariability of individual differences within and across handicaps, activities must be designed and programmed to fit each child's motor capabilities. For instance, children within a particular handicapped group may be able to throw a ball, but each within the group, because of motor limitations, may throw the ball differently while still achieving the objective of distance and accuracy. Second, adapted physical education activities are designed to be flexible enough to achieve educational goals. For instance, for basketball, a smaller ball is provided and baskets are lowered so that students may be able to score more baskets in a game, thereby increasing their enjoyment in the sport (Auxter & Pyer, 1985).

Adapted physical education for students classified as handicapped implies accountability via the individualized educational plan (IEP). Objectives stated on an IEP ensure that the student is receiving instruction in activities where there is the greatest physical, motor, and social need. The student is evaluated periodically to assess progress toward the short- and long-term goals stated in the IEP.

REFERENCES

AAHPER. (1952, April). *Guiding principles for a physical education journal of health, physical education, recreation.* Author.

Auxter, D., & Pyer, J. (1985). *Adapted physical education.* St. Louis, MO: Mosby.

Hurley, D. (1981). Guidelines for adapted physical education. *Journal of Health, Physical Education, Recreation, and Dance,* 43–45.

Sherrill, C. (1985). *Adapted physical education and recreation* (3rd ed.). Dubuque, IA: Brown.

THOMAS R. BURKE
Hunter College, City University of New York

MOTOR LEARNING
PHYSICAL EDUCATION FOR STUDENTS WITH
   DISABILITIES

ADAPTIVE BEHAVIOR

Adaptive behavior, or the daily activities required for personal and social sufficiency, is an integral part of the evaluation and planning for handicapped and nonhandicapped individuals. It is not a new concept and has its roots in historical views concerning the treatment of the mentally retarded. The increased emphasis now placed on the use of the adaptive behavior concept in special education and programs for the handicapped is resulting in attempts to better understand the characteristics of adaptive behavior and in the publication of many new instruments for measuring adaptive behavior (Meyers, Nihira, & Zetlin, 1979).

Present concepts of adaptive behavior are traced to early attempts to describe the mentally retarded (Harrison, 1985). As early as the Renaissance and Reformation, language and law defined mental retardation in terms of adaptive behavior, or a person's ability to take care of himself or herself and get along with others. Legal reforms for the mentally retarded during the 1800s resulted in continued attention to adaptive behavior. However, in the early 1900s, the development of the Binet intelligence scales and its counterparts led to a prevalent practice of defining mental retardation solely in terms of IQ; this practice continued for many years.

Edgar Doll, the major pioneer in adaptive behavior assessment, disagreed with the use of IQs only, and, in the 1930s, indicated that a person's social competence, or adaptive behavior, should be the first and most important criterion for mental retardation. It was not until 1959 that the American Association on Mental Deficiency published its official manual and formally included deficits in adaptive behavior, in addition to low intelligence, as an integral part of the definition of mental retardation (Heber, 1961). Subsequent editions of the manual have further emphasized the importance of adaptive behavior.

Several issues in the 1960s and 1970s precipitated an upsurge of interest in adaptive behavior and adaptive behavior assessment (Witt & Martens, 1984). A concern arose about "6-hour retarded children" or minority group and low socioeconomic status children who were labeled as retarded in the public schools but exhibited adequate adaptive behavior at home and in the community (Mercer, 1973). This concern eventually led to litigation such as the Guadalupe and Larry P. cases and court decisions that indicated that results of intelligence tests cannot be the primary basis for classifying children as mentally retarded and that adaptive behavior must be assessed. The 1960s and 1970s saw a trend toward the normalization of handicapped individuals and the awareness that effective programs for teaching adaptive skills allow handicapped individuals to participate as fully as possible in normal environments. A third issue was the need for a nonbiased and multifaceted assessment of all children with disabilities to facilitate the fairness of decisions based on the results of tests and to investigate functioning in all areas related to a particular handicap.

The passage of the Education of All Handicapped Children Act of 1975 (Public Law 94-142) represented the culmination of the issues of the 1960s and 1970s. Public Law 94-142 and its latest revision, the current Individuals with Disabilities Education Act, commonly known as IDEIA, 2004, have stringent guides for the assessment of children with disability and stipulates that deficits in adaptive behavior must be substantiated before a child is classified as mentally retarded. Further, it recognizes the importance of adaptive behavior assessment for children with disabilities other than the mental retardation. Since the passage of the law, most states have developed guidelines for adaptive behavior assessment (Patrick & Reschley, 1982) and many have strict criteria for the types of adaptive behavior instruments and scores to be used.

Sparrow, Balla, and Cicchetti (1984, 2005) discuss several characteristics that are inherent in concepts of adaptive behavior. Adaptive behavior is an age-related construct; as normally developing children grow older, adaptive behavior increases and becomes more complex. Adaptive behavior is determined by the standards of other people, those who live, work, play, teach, and interact with an individual. Finally, adaptive behavior is defined as what an individual does day by day, not by an individual's ability or what he or she can do. If a person has the ability to perform a daily task, but does not do it, adaptive behavior is considered to be inadequate.

An important issue in the description of adaptive behavior is the distinction between adaptive behavior and intelligence (Meyers, Nihira, & Zetlin, 1979). Adaptive behavior and intelligence have several important differences. First, adaptive behavior focuses on everyday behavior and intelligence on thought processes. Adaptive behavior is based on concrete environmental demands while intelligence focuses on academic demands. Adaptive behavior assessment involves common, typical, and everyday behaviors, whereas intelligence scales attempt to measure a person's potential, or his or her best possible performance.

Since the passage of Public Law 94-142, a large number of adaptive behavior scales have been published. Most adaptive behavior scales are administered to a respondent such as a parent or teacher who is familiar with the daily activities of the person. Some are administered directly to the person whose adaptive behavior is being assessed. The Vineland Adaptive Behavior Scales (Sparrow, et al., 1984, 2005) measure adaptive behavior in the areas of communication, daily living skills, socialization, motor skills, and maladaptive behavior. The Adaptive Behavior Inventory for Children (Mercer & Lewis, 1977) assessed a child's adaptation to family, community, and peer social systems. The AAMR Adaptive Behavior Scale (Lambert, Nihira, & Leland, 1993) evaluates personal sufficiency, social sufficiency, responsibility, and personal and social adjustment. The Scales of Independent Behavior revised (Bruininks, Woodcock, Weatherman, & Hill, 1996) include measures of motor skills, social interaction and communication, personal and community independence, and problem behaviors. The Children's Adaptive Behavior Scale (Richmond & Kicklighter, 1980) contains scales for language, independent functioning, family roles, economic vocational activity, and socialization. The Adaptive Behavior Assessment System–Second Edition (Harrison & Oakland, 2003) assesses conceptual social and practical areas of adaptive behavior cited by the AAMR.

REFERENCES

Bruininks, R. J., Woodcock, R. W., Weatherman, R. F., & Hill, B. K. (1996). *Scales of Independent Behavior Revised.* Itasca, IL: Riverside Publishing.

Harrison, P. L. (1985). *Vineland Adaptive Behavior Scales, Classroom Edition Manual.* Circle Pines, MN: American Guidance Service.

Harrison, P., & Oakland, T. (2003). *Adaptive Behavior System–Second Edition.* San Antonio, TX: PsychCorp.

Heber, R. F. (1961). A manual on terminology and classification in mental retardation (Monograph Suppl.). *American Journal of Mental Deficiency.*

Lambert, N., Nihira, K., & Leland, H. (1993). *AAMD Adaptive Behavior Scale (ABS-S:2).* Austin, TX: PRO-ED.

Mercer, J. R. (1973). *Labeling the mentally retarded.* Berkeley, CA: University of California Press.

Mercer, J. R., & Lewis, J. E. (1977). *Adaptive Behavior Inventory for Children.* New York: Psychological Corporation.

Meyers, C. E., Nihira, K., & Zetlin, A. (1979). The measurement of adaptive behavior. In N. R. Ellis (Eds.), *Handbook of mental deficiency: Psychological theory and research* (2nd ed., pp. 215–253). Hillside, NJ: Erlbaum.

Patrick, J. L., & Reschley, D. J. (1982). Relationship of state educational criteria and demographic variables to school system prevalence of mental retardation. *American Journal of Mental Deficiency, 86,* 351–360.

Richmond, B. O., & Kicklighter, R. H. (1980). *Children's Adaptive Behavior Scale.* Atlanta: Humanities Limited.

Sparrow, S. S., Balla, D. A., & Cicchetti, D. V. (1984). *Vineland Adaptive Behavior Scales.* Circle Pines, MN: American Guidance Service.

Sparrow, S. S., Balla, D. A., & Cicchetti, D. V. (2005). *Vineland Adaptive Behavior Scales–II.* Circle Pins, MN: AGS.

Witt, J. C., & Martens, B. K. (1984). Adaptive behavior: Test and assessment issues. *School Psychology Review, 13,* 478–484.

PATTI L. HARRISON
University of Alabama

AAMR CLASSIFICATION SYSTEMS
MENTAL RETARDATION
VINELAND ADAPTIVE BEHAVIOR SCALES–SECOND EDITION

ADAPTIVE BEHAVIOR ASSESSMENT SYSTEM–SECOND EDITION

The Adaptive Behavior Assessment System–Second Edition (ABAS-II; Harrison & Oakland, 2003a) is a revision of an earlier test, the Adaptive Behavior Assessment System (ABAS; Harrison & Oakland, 2000). The purpose of the

ABAS-II is to assess adaptive and behavior skills useful for the diagnosis and classification of disabilities, identification of strengths and limitations, and documentation and monitoring of progress in individuals from birth through the age of 89. Information from the ABAS-II can be combined with other evaluation information to form a more complete assessment as well as make diagnoses and plan services, including interventions, for individuals with disabilities, disorders, and health conditions including Mental Retardation, developmental disabilities and delays, emotional and Learning Disorders, and Dementias.

The ABAS-II offers five forms: Parent/Primary Caregiver Forms (ages 0–5), Teacher/Day Care Provider Forms (ages 2–5), Parent Forms (ages 5–21), Teacher Forms (ages 5–21), and Adult Forms, which rate the individual on the daily behavioral frequency of various adaptive skills on a four-point Likert scale (*not able, never, sometimes,* and *always*).

The ABAS-II is the only measure that assesses adaptive behavior consistent with the model advocated by the American Association on Mental Retardation (2002). Standard scores from the Conceptual, Social, and Practical domain combine to provide a General Adaptive Composite (GAC) standard score as well as 10 adaptive skills: communication, community use, functional academics, health and safety, home/school living, leisure, self-care, self-direction, social, and work (for adults) as well as motor skills (for young children). These skills are specified by the *Diagnostic and Statistical Manual of Mental Disorders,* fourth edition, text revision (*DSM-IV-TR*) as important to the assessment of Mental Retardation (American Psychiatric Association, 2000).

The standardization sample is representative of U.S. Census data in reference to gender, race or ethnicity, parental education, and proportion of individuals with disabilities (Harrison & Oakland, 2003b). Internal consistency is high. Reliability coefficients for all age groups range from .97 to .99 for the GAC, .91 to .98 for the three adaptive domains, and .85 to .97 for the 10 skill areas. Test-retest reliability coefficients are in the .90s for the GAC and in the .80s to .90s for the skill areas (Rust & Wallace, 2004). Inter-rater reliability ranges from the .60s to the .80s for the skill areas and is in the .90s for the GAC. The correlation between the school-age Teacher Form GAC and the Vineland Adaptive Behavior Scales–Classroom Edition Adaptive Behavior Composite is .82 (Harrison & Oakland, 2003b). The scale's clinical validity also is highly evident, with different profiles displayed by children and adults who have been diagnosed with autism, Attention Deficit/Hyperactivity Disorder, emotional or behavioral disorders, learning disabilities, Mental Retardation, and physical impairment.

The Buros evaluation recommends the use of the ABAS-II with few reservations. The measure is deemed theoretically sound and "(i)t would be difficult to find a measure of adaptive behavior with more convincing data regarding clinical validity" (Spies & Plake, 2005, p. 210). One noted weakness is that more than one form is appropriate for individuals who are 5 years old and those who are 16 to 21 years old. However, the ABAS-II is technically superior to its competitors and is valuable in the complete assessment of an individual's adaptive functioning.

REFERENCES

American Association on Mental Retardation. (2002). *Mental retardation: Definition, classification, and systems of support.* Washington, DC: Author.

American Psychiatric Association. (2000). *Diagnostic and statistical manual of mental disorders* (4th ed., text revision). Washington, DC: Author.

Harrison, P. L., & Oakland, T. (2000). *Adaptive Behavior Assessment System.* San Antonio, TX: Psychological Corporation.

Harrison, P. L., & Oakland, T. (2003a). *Adaptive Behavior Assessment System* (2nd ed.). San Antonio, TX: Psychological Corporation.

Harrison, P. L., & Oakland, T. (2003b). *Technical report: Adaptive Behavior Assessment System–Second edition.* San Antonio, TX: Psychological Corporation.

Rust, J. O., & Wallace, M. A. (2004). Test review: Adaptive Behavior Assessment System–Second edition. *Journal of Psychoeducational Assessment, 22,* 367–373.

Spies, R. A., & Plake, B. S. (Eds.). (2005). *The sixteenth mental measurements yearbook.* Lincoln, NE: Buros Institute of Mental Measurements.

JEFFREY DITTERLINE
University of Florida

ADAPTIVE BEHAVIOR SCALE

See VINELAND ADAPTIVE BEHAVIOR SCALES–SECOND EDITION.

ADAPTIVE DEVICES

See ASSISTIVE DEVICES.

ADAPTIVE TECHNOLOGIES AND PROGRAMS, WEB SITES RELATED TO

Each of the following web sites provides valuable information and resources for individuals who are interested in adaptive or assistive technologies and programs.

ABLEDATA URL: http://www.abledata.com/

ABLEDATA is a site maintained for the National Institute on Disability and Rehabilitation Research (NIDRR: http://www.ed.gov/about/offices/list/osers/nidrr/index.html) of the U.S. Department of Education. ABLEDATA is a source for assistive technology (AT) information and provides objective information about assistive technology products and rehabilitation equipment available from domestic and international sources. The ABLEDATA site provides information centers that provide Internet resources on a number of disability issues. Links provided relate to national and regional organizations; related online publications; information on related conferences, meetings, and other public events; companies that sell disability products; and access to a database for assistive products. Issues covered include extensive coverage in each of the following categories: AT and disability services (e.g., AT training, legal services), consulting services, general disability resources (e.g., accessible housing, information technology and web accessibility), people (e.g., caregivers, veterans), research on AT and disability (e.g., AT outcomes, program evaluation), resources for specific disabilities (e.g., amputees, deaf and hard of hearing), state and local resources, U.S. government resources, and workplace resources. ABLEDATA also provides a consumer forum that provides evaluations of products for people with disabilities from regular consumers as well as professionals in AT.

American Association of People with Disabilities (AAPD) URL: http://www.aapd-dc.org/

The AAPD is a national organization dedicated to promoting the economic and political empowerment of all people with disabilities. The AAPD is "the largest national nonprofit cross-disability member organization in the United States, dedicated to ensuring economic self-sufficiency and political empowerment for the more than 56 million Americans with disabilities." The AAPD mentoring effort promotes nationwide career development for students and job seekers with disabilities through job shadowing and hands-on career exploration. The Disability Vote Project addresses the fundamental inequalities faced by this nation's voters with disabilities and works in a nonpartisan manner to ensure they are provided full accessibility to all polling places and voting equipment. The AADP promotes bipartisan legislation and policy that will further the ability of people with disabilities to live independently, contribute to society, pursue meaningful careers, and enjoy self-determination and maintains a Listserv dedicated to this purpose.

Apple Computer Accessibility in Education URL: http://www.apple.com/education/accessibility/

The Apple site provides resources for educators in relation to a number of accessibility issues. The site provides five sections that focus on specific areas: vision, hearing, physical and motor, literacy and learning, and language and communication. While much of the information is related to features of Apple's hardware and software accessibility resources, links are readily available that lead to related philosophical, research, funding, and general support resources. The main strength of the site is that it organizes the technical information around the various categories of disability solutions. Each area leads to expanded pages that provide detailed information on the resources and solutions related to that topic. In many instances, pdf files are available for download to provide more detailed information. In addition, links to third-party hardware and software are provided to present a full range of resources available in any of the disability areas. Both hardware and software components are presented with brief descriptions and links to the appropriate manufacturer's web site. The literacy and learning and language and communication pages provide more academic, skill-building resources. There is also a section that is devoted to web accessibility concerns and features information on a server-based application that automatically converts and renders web pages into text-only pages to make them more accessible and easier to navigate. This section also provides technical information as well as links to general implementation resources.

Assistive Tech Net URL: http://assistivetech.net/

Assistive Tech Net provides "a diverse resource for assistive technology (AT) and disability-related information." Assistivetech.net maintains an online searchable database that helps the user target solutions, determine costs, and find vendors of AT products for people with disabilities, family members, service providers, educators, and employers. The database can be searched by function, activity, or vendor. Searches can also be associated with specific discussion groups or Assistive Technology Act of 1998 projects. The assistivetech.net site is supported by the Center for Assistive Technology and Environmental Access, the National Institute on Disability and Rehabilitation Research, and the Rehabilitation Services Administration.

Center for Applied Special Technology (CAST) URL: http://www.cast.org/

Founded in 1984, CAST "has earned international recognition for its development of innovative, technology-based educational resources and strategies based on the principles of Universal Design for Learning (UDL)." The CAST is a nonprofit organization focused on expanding learning opportunities for all individuals, especially those with disabilities. The CAST's research and development of innovative, technology-based educational resources and strategies is conducted by specialists in education research and policy, neuropsychology, clinical or school psychology, technology, engineering, curriculum development, kindergarten through 12th grade professional development, and more. The CAST supports universal design for learning, which includes multiple means of representation, multiple means of expression, and multiple means of engagement. The CAST has been involved in the creation or codevelopment of initiatives to develop and promote a National Instructional Materials Accessibility Standard (NIMAS), as well as innovative software such as Thinking Reader, WiggleWorks, and Bobby. Also, NIMAS provides a guide to the production and electronic distribution of curricular materials in accessible, student-ready versions, including Braille and Digital Talking Books. The NIMAS Development Center is focused on improving the standard by monitoring relevant research and technological advances. The NIMAS Technical Assistance Center advises educators and publishers on the production and distribution of NIMAS-compliant materials. Teachers and administrators can access support through The CAST UDL Center, which provides access to a professional development network, consultation, publications, and online resources.

Center for Assistive Technology and Environmental Access (CATEA) URL: http://www.catea.org/

The CATEA, a unit of the College of Architecture at the Georgia Institute of Technology, maintains research projects on accessibility and usability through two research foci:

Development, evaluation, and utilization of assistive technology
Design and development of accessible environments

The CATEA supports individuals with disabilities of any age through expert services, research, design and technological development, information dissemination, and educational programs.

Council for Exceptional Children (CEC) URL: http://www.cec.sped.org/

The CEC "is the largest international professional organization dedicated to improving educational outcomes for individuals with exceptionalities, students with disabilities, and/or the gifted." In addition to a number of general programs and resources for special education in general, CEC has the Technology and Media Division (TAM; http://www.tamcec.org/) that "addresses the need, availability and effective use of technology and media for individuals with disabilities and/or who are gifted." The TAM hosts a national conference and publishes the *Journal of Special Education Technology* (JSET) and the *TAM Connector* newsletter. The TAM is focused on providing mentoring, technical assistance, and relevant information. Development of technical standards and advocating for funds and policies is also

stressed. The site provides access to a number of publications, products, and links to web sites providing information on the selection and use of ATs. The JSET is an e-journal: an online publication of the Technology and Media Division of the CEC (http://www.jset.unlv.edu). The JSET is a refereed professional journal presenting information and opinions about issues, research, policy, and practice related to the use of technology in the field of special education. Articles are indexed by publication date and accessed as web pages.

The International Center for Disability Resources on the Internet (ICDRI) URL: http://www.icdri.org/

The ICDRI is a nonprofit center based in the United States that is focused on "the equalization of opportunities for persons with disabilities." The center is organized by and for people with disabilities and seeks to increase opportunities for people with disabilities by "identifying barriers to participation in society and promoting best practices and universal design for the global community." The ICDRI gathers and maintains a collection of disability resources and best-practices. This collection is available on their web site to provide education, outreach, and training opportunities. The ICDRI also provides disability rights education and customized programs to the international community for public policy strategic planning.

Job Accommodation Network (JAN) URL: http://www.jan.wvu.edu/

The JAN is a free service of the Office of Disability Employment Policy, U.S. Department of Labor, that offers assistance "designed to increase the employability of people with disabilities by: 1) providing individualized worksite accommodations solutions, 2) providing technical assistance regarding the ADA and other disability related legislation, and 3) educating callers about self-employment options." The JAN offers assistance to employers, people with disabilities, rehabilitation professionals, and people affected by disability. The JAN web site offers a small business and self-employment service, a searchable online accommodation resource, a library of presentations on specific topics, and an online newsletter and consultant resources. A variety of downloadable resources and publications are available that provide information or materials related to accommodation needs and services. Links to several employment and informational web sites are also provided. In addition, links related to specific disability legislation, specific disability resources, and all levels of government resources are presented.

National Association for State Directors of Special Education, Inc. (NASDSE) URL: http://www.nasdse.org/

The NASDSE is "dedicated to, and focused on, continuously improving educational services and outcomes while ensuring a balance of procedural guarantees for our children and youth with disabilities and their families." The NASDSE provides support in the delivery of quality education to children and youth with disabilities through training, technical assistance, research, policy development, and powerful collaborative relationships with other organizations. The NASDSE markets a number of publications and assistive technology instruction to professionals through either distance (online) education or face-to-face (on-site) instruction. Its web site describes these products in detail and also provides links to a wide range of related organizations and resources.

National Center to Improve Practice (NCIP) URL: http://www2.edc.org/NCIP/

The NCIP was funded by the U.S. Department of Education, Office of Special Education Programs from 1992 to 1998. Its goal is to "promote the effective use of 4qrf technology to enhance educational outcomes for students with sensory, cognitive, physical and social/emotional disabilities."

To support this goal, the NCIP has worked to facilitate the exchange of information and build knowledge through collaborative dialogue, particularly through a series of facilitated discussion forums and online workshops. The NCIP has gathered, synthesized, and disseminated information about technology, disabilities, practice, and implementation through a variety of efforts:

NCIP Library. A collection of resources about technology and special education

Video Profiles. Short videos with supporting print materials that illustrate students using assistive and instructional technologies to improve their learning

NCIP Guided Tours: Early Childhood. Presents tours of two exemplary early childhood classrooms

Spotlight on Voice Recognition. Demonstrates the use of voice recognition technology to address writing difficulties

Online Workshops and Events. Contains archives of NCIP's online workshops and events held from 1996 to 1998

The NCIP site provides links to other special education and technology resources with a focus on relevant organizations and technology companies. Links to sites for special education and universities with special education resources are also provided. The disability resources highlighted include those for sensory, physical, and speech impairments as well as learning disabilities, cognitive or developmental disabilities, Asperger's Syndrome, ayperlexia, autism, Attention Deficit Disorder, and Attention Deficit/Hyperactivity Disorder. Family and parent support resources are also identified.

National Institute on Disability and Rehabilitation Research (NIDRR) URL: http://www.ed.gov/about/offices/list/osers/nidrr/about.html

The NIDRR is a national leader in sponsoring research and is intended to generate, disseminate, and promote new knowledge to improve the options available to disabled persons. The NIDRR is a component of the United States Department of Education Office of Special Education and Rehabilitative Services (OSERS). The NIDRR conducts programs of research and related activities for the benefit of individuals of all ages with disabilities. Their goal is to maximize their full inclusion, social integration, employment, and independent living. The NIDRR's focus includes research in areas such as employment, health, and function as well as technology for access and function, independent living, and community integration. The NIDRR attempts to support the scientific community in relation to rehabilitation medicine, engineering, psychosocial rehabilitation, integration, vocational outcomes, and the virtual and built environments. The NIDRR's consumer support is based in its efforts to integrate disability research into national policies.

Quality Indicators for Assistive Technology (QIAT) URL: http://sweb.uky.edu/~jszaba0/QIAT.html

The QIAT Consortium is a "nationwide grassroots group that includes hundreds of individuals who provide input into the ongoing process of identifying, disseminating, and implementing a set of widely-applicable Quality Indicators for Assistive Technology Services in School Settings." The resources are intended for use by school districts to provide quality AT services, AT service providers to evaluate and improve their services, consumers of AT services to find adequate AT services, universities and professional developers to develop AT service competencies, and policy makers. The QIAT Consortium provides quality indicators for AT services in school settings and forums for professional involvement, sharing, and discussion.

Rehabilitation Engineering and Assistive Technology Society of North America (RESNA) URL: http://www.resna.org

The RESNA is an "interdisciplinary association of people with a common interest in technology and disability" dedicated to the use of technology for the improvement of the potential of people with disabilities so they may achieve their goals. The RESNA promotes research, development, education, advocacy, and provision of technology and also supports the people who are engaged in such activities.

The RESNA publishes the *Assistive Technology Journal,* hosts annual conferences, and maintains active international affiliations. To ensure consumer safeguards and increase consumer satisfaction, the RESNA maintains a credentialing program for professionals in three applied areas:

Assistive Technology Practitioner (ATP). For service providers who are involved in analysis of a consumer's needs and training in the use of a particular AT device

Assistive Technology Supplier (ATS). For service providers who are involved with the sale, including determination of consumer needs and service of rehabilitation equipment, of AT and commercially available products and devices

Rehabilitation Engineering Technologist (RET). For service providers who apply engineering principles to the design, modification, customization or fabrication of AT for persons with disabilities

Rehabilitation Services Administration (RSA) URL: http://www.ed.gov/about/offices/list/osers/rsa/index.html

The RSA is a component of the U.S. Department of Education of Special Education and Rehabilitative Services (OSERS). The RSA "oversees formula and discretionary grant programs that help individuals with physical or mental disabilities to obtain employment and live more independently through the provision of such supports as counseling, medical and psychological services, job training and other individualized services." One of the RSA's major goals is enhancing the connection between vocational rehabilitation agencies and employers.

REFERENCES

American Association of People with Disabilities. (2005). *American Association of People with Disabilities.* Retrieved September 10, 2005, from http://www.aapd-dc.org/

Apple Education Solutions. (2005). *Accessibility in education.* Retrieved October 15, 2005, from http://www.apple.com/education/accessibility/

Assistive Tech Net. (2004). *assistivetech.net: Your global assistive technology explorer.* Retrieved September 10, 2005, from http://assistivetech.net/

Center for Applied Special Technology. (2005). *CAST: Center for Applied Special Technology.* Retrieved September 10, 2005, from http://www.cast.org/

Center for Assistive Technology and Environmental Access. (2004). *Center for Assistive Technology and Environmental Access (CATEA).* Retrieved September 10, 2005, from http://www.catea.org/

Council for Exceptional Children. (2005). *Council for Exceptional Children.* Retrieved September 5, 2005, from http://www.cec.sped.org/

Job Accommodation Network. (2005). *Job Accommodation Network home page.* Retrieved September 5, 2005, from http://www.jan.wvu.edu/

National Association for State Directors of Special Education, Inc. (2005). *NASDSE: Home page.* Retrieved September 5, 2005, from http://www.nasdse.org/

National Center to Improve Practice. (1998). *NCIP home.* Retrieved September 11, 2005, from http://www2.edc.org/NCIP/

National Institute on Disability and Rehabilitation Research. (2005a). *NIDRR: About NIDRR.* Retrieved September 5, 2005, from http://www.ed.gov/about/offices/list/osers/nidrr/about.html

National Institute on Disability and Rehabilitation Research. (2005b). *Welcome to ABLEDATA.* Retrieved September 10, 2005, from http://www.abledata.com/

Quality Indicators for Assistive Technology. (2005). *QIAT home page.* Retrieved September 10, 2005, from http://sweb.uky.edu/~jszaba0/QIAT.html

Rehabilitation Engineering and Assistive Technology Society of North America. (2005). *RESNA.* Retrieved September 5, 2005, from http://www.resna.org

Rehabilitation Services Administration. (2005). *Rehabilitation Services Administration (RSA)—home page.* Retrieved September 3, 2005, from http://www.ed.gov/about/offices/list/osers/rsa/index.html

RONALD ZELLNER
Texas A&M University

ADDERALL

Adderall is a stimulant medication that is a different mixture of amphetamine isomers than the common stimulants such as dexedrine, benzedrine, methamphetamine, methylphenidate, and magnesium pemoline. It is available in 5, 10, 20, and 30 mg tablets. Adderall is used primarily in the treatment of attention-deficit hyperactivity disorder (ADHD) and narcolepsy. It has also been used in the treatment of obesity (Konopasek, 2003). Adderall has been shown in clinical trials to increase alertness, improve attention span, decrease distractibility, and increase the ability to follow directions among children ages 3 years and up.

Adderall is popular among many children and families because it may need to be taken only once or twice a day, eliminating the need for dosing at school. Since it is a different chemical preparation, Adderall has been found to be effective with patients who do not respond to more popular stimulant treatments, such as Ritalin. However, Adderall may take as long as 3 to 4 weeks to become effective, while other stimulants tend to take effect more immediately. Adderall has a similar side-effect profile to other common stimulants, the most common of those being appetite suppression, growth retardation, insomnia, and headache. Less frequent side effects of this drug class include tics, dry mouth, irritability, cardiovascular acceleration, and, at high dosages, hallucinations and a disorder characterized as amphetamine psychosis. Adderall also interacts with a variety of drugs used in the treatment of depression and with drugs used to treat psychotic symptoms. Certain foods, especially those at extremes of acidity or alkalinity, may also alter dosage effects of Adderall.

Adderall may be habit-forming and has a high potential for abuse (Konopasek, 2003). Monitoring of dose response, side effects, and polypharmacy by a physician is crucial to safe use of Adderall and other drugs in its class. Additional information is available in Arky (1998) and Cahill (1997).

REFERENCES

Arky, R. (1998). *Physicians desk reference.* Montvale, NJ: Medical Economics Data Production.

Cahill, M. (Ed.). (1997). *Nursing 97 drug handbook.* Springhouse, PA: Springhouse Corporation.

Konopasek, D. E. (2003). *Medication fact sheets.* Longmont, CO: Sopris West.

CECIL R. REYNOLDS
Texas A&M University

STIMULANT DRUGS
ATTENTION-DEFICIT/HYPERACTIVITY DISORDER

ADDITIVE-FREE DIETS

Feingold (1976), a pediatrician and allergist, reported an observed decrease in hyperactivity in many of the adults and children who adhered to his strict additive-free Kaiser-Permanente diet. The Kaiser-Permanente diet was designed to eliminate salicylates (which are related to compounds in aspirin) and synthetic, and thus nonnutritive, food dyes and flavors from the diets of people who showed adverse somatic reactions to the additives (e.g., rashes). Feingold inferred that some nonnutritional food dyes and flavors, as well as the salicylates, may have an effect similar to pharmacological compounds and alter the brain's chemistry of those that ingest them. He suggested these alterations in neurological functioning may result in behavioral changes, including increases in hyperactive behavior. Thus, Feingold believed that an additive-free diet, in which children avoid all foods with artificial dyes, flavors, and salicylates (i.e., features that characterize the Feingold diet), may be an appropriate intervention for children that demonstrate hyperactive behavior.

The Feingold diet recommends that parents with concerns about their children's hyperactive behavior should eliminate all artificial colors, flavors, sweeteners, and preservatives as well as salicylates that can be found in many fruits and vegetables (e.g., raisins and berries) from their diet. Recommendations include avoiding the use of products (e.g., toothpastes, vitamins, medications, food and beverage items) that contain any of the nonnutritive additives or salicylates. After a child has strictly adhered to the diet for 4 to 6 weeks and demonstrates improvements in behavior, food items containing salicylates can be added slowly back into the diet.

Studies that have examined the effectiveness of the Feingold diet on hyperactive behavior in children have produced mixed results. For instance, many studies have produced results that suggest that the Feingold diet is an effective intervention for children with hyperactive behavior. Feingold (1976) found that children that adhered to an additive-free diet demonstrated marked decrease in hyperactive behavior and improvement in scholastic achievement, according to teacher report, within 3 weeks of beginning the diet. Bateman and colleagues (2004) found that a diet that eliminated artificial food coloring and preservatives significantly reduced hyperactive behavior in 3-year-old children, regardless of whether they met criteria for a diagnosis of Attention-Deficit/Hyperactivity Disorder (ADHD).

In contrast, Holborow, Elkins, and Berry (1981) found that when the diet was administered to children with and without hyperactive behavior, children with hyperactive behavior did not show significant levels of decreased hyperactivity. However, children who ingested the highest levels of synthetic food colors and flavors before beginning the diet showed greater improvements in behavior than their peers, regardless of whether they demonstrated significant levels of hyperactivity before the diet.

However, many researchers have been unable to produce findings in support of the Feingold diet. Mattes (1983) conducted multiple studies and did not find the diet significantly improved behavior in hyperactive children. Thus, he concluded that, while the diet may be effective for a small percentage of children, it is not an effective intervention to treat the majority of hyperactive children.

Critics of the Feingold diet argue that Feingold and other researchers who found support of the additive-free diet did not utilize rigorous scientific methods to measure changes in behavior and instead relied on anecdotal observations from parents and teachers. Furthermore, they attribute the reported decreases in hyperactivity to the increased attention parents focused on their children during the implementation phase, instead of the direct effects of the diet. Some scholars attribute the lack of consistent findings to support the Feingold diet to the methods implemented in the research studies.

Thus, these findings suggest that the Feingold diet may be an effective treatment for a small proportion of children who demonstrate hyperactive behavior, perhaps 10 to 15 percent, but is not an effective intervention for the majority of children with hyperactive behavior (Schnoll, Burshteyn, & Cea-Aravena, 2003). Additionally, the diet seemingly is more effective for children in early childhood rather than during the elementary years and older.

REFERENCES

Bateman, B., Warner, J. O., Hutchinson, E., Dean, T., Rowlandson, P., Gant, C., et al. (2004). The effects of a double blind, placebo controlled artificial food colourings and benzoate preservative challenge on hyperactivity in a general population sample of preschool children. *Archives of Disease in Childhood, 89,* 506–511.

Feingold, B. F. (1976). Hyperkinesis and learning disabilities linked to artificial food flavors and colors. *Journal of Learning Disabilities, 9,* 551–559.

Holborrow, P., Elkins, J., & Berry, P. (1981). The effect on the Feingold diet on "normal" school children. *Journal of Learning Disabilities, 14,* 143–147.

Rimland, B. (1983). The Feingold diet: An assessment of the reviews by Mattes, by Kavale and Forness and others. *Journal of Learning Disabilities, 16,* 331–333.

Mattes, J. A. (1983). The Feingold diet: A current reappraisal. *Journal of Learning Disabilities, 16,* 319–323.

Schnoll, R., Burshteyn, D., & Cea-Aravena, J. (2003). Nutrition in the treatment of Attention-Deficit/Hyperactivity Disorder: A neglected but important aspect. *Applied Psychophysiology and Biofeedback, 28,* 63–75.

ALLISON G. DEMPSEY
University of Florida

ATTENTION-DEFICIT/HYPERACTIVITY DISORDER
FEINGOLD DIET
HYPERACTIVITY

ADJUSTMENT OF INDIVIDUALS WITH DISABILITIES

By virtue of their "differentness," individuals with disabilities and their families must make certain special adjustments to lead fulfilling and satisfying lives. The most obvious and important of these adjustments is the appraisal and acceptance of the condition itself. Such acceptance is prerequisite to seeking and obtaining appropriate care and services.

Another necessary adjustment requires recognizing and dealing with influences of a disability on all aspects of the individual's development. For example, a physical handicap affects social development and interactions in ways that have only recently been addressed scientifically and professionally, but have long been sources of confusion and frustration.

It has become fashionable among educators and developmental psychologists to refer to the "whole child" in nurturing and/or describing the development of "normal," that is, nonhandicapped, children. Some (e.g., Shontz, 1980) have advocated this integrated approach in understanding the development of children and adolescents. However, two factors make it especially difficult to grasp specific implications of particular handicapping conditions for domains not directly affected by the conditions. One difficulty is that the interrelationships among the various developmental domains are subtle and complex; another is that the exceptional child's development is affected by special social and internal forces. Therefore, our ability to recommend theoretically based prescriptions for professional and parenting practices that will promote maximal development in indirectly affected domains is limited by the lack of empirical evidence comparing particular approaches to raising, treating, and educating the "whole" child.

The development of the child with a disability occurs along the same lines as that of the child without a disability. However, an individual child's development will exhibit qualitative variations from the norm. The specific deviations from typical development depend both on the nature and severity of the condition and on the level of adjustment achieved by the child and his or her family and teachers.

Normal personal-social development includes the emergence of the individual's self-concept and self-esteem. These beliefs about one's characteristics, relative worth, and competence are acquired by internalizing an image of one's self as it is reflected by important adults and peers. Bartel and Guskin (1980) emphasize that the feedback one receives from the social environment is a crucial factor in the development of a positive self-concept and high self-esteem, for it creates an expectation and interpretive schema for self-evaluation of one's abilities and efforts. The self-concept of a child with disabilities is at risk because society's negative evaluations of individuals who are different from the norm are systematically, if unconsciously, transmitted to him or her (Gliedman & Roth, 1980). Because the development of high self-esteem is based on what an individual *can* do, a handicapping condition may endanger a child's self-esteem by focusing attention on what the child cannot do.

A disability may limit a child's or adolescent's physical activities. The handicap may impose restrictions owing to physical limitations or medical complications that limit freedom to get about in the environment. Physical and/or medical limitations may reduce opportunities for interaction and exploration in both the physical and social realms and thus curtail experiences that stimulate and promote cognitive growth and personal-social development. Children with disabilities must be encouraged not to retreat from any activities that are accessible, although inconvenient, because of physical restrictions. Professionals and others can help them to participate in an adapted way, if necessary, in order not to deprive them of beneficial experiences.

Children with disabilities may have to adjust medical interventions or therapies such as drugs, braces, physical therapy, surgical procedures, hearing appliances, and so on. The child's adjustment to the medical aspect of his or her program is absolutely essential because the child must cooperate in order to achieve the maximum benefits of the prescribed treatment(s).

An exceptional child is very likely to have to make an

adjustment involving his or her educational programs. The adjustment may range from simply modifying his or her study habits or methods to full-time participation in a special self-contained program. Professionals who work with the child should strive to minimize whatever educational disadvantage(s) may be imposed by the handicap. The goals of the child's educational program should emphasize activities to compensate for and/or overcome his or her disability.

The effectiveness of the child's program will be amplified by the active involvement of parents in consistently following through on behavioral and educational interventions in the home environment. Concrete benefits are derived from the parents' participation. Parents are able to provide additional reinforcement and practice for skills learned during the school day, helping their child consolidate gains more rapidly. In addition, their involvement is a signal to the child of their commitment to his or her development and the high value they place on educational achievement. These attitudes are highly motivating and will help see the child through difficult periods.

Parents who do not accept and adjust to the child's handicap escalate their child's difficulties. Maladaptive behavior patterns that emerge in the relationship between parents and their handicapped child can arise from either of two opposite, but equally harmful, reactions. Parents may either overestimate or underestimate their child's abilities and potential. Overestimates may be due to parents' denial of their child's problems. Such parents are prone to establish unreasonably high standards for their child's behavior or development. Because the child wants to please the parents but is not capable of fulfilling their expectations, he or she continually faces feelings of frustration, inadequacy, and other negative emotions such as guilt, disappointment, and uncertainty as to his or her place in the affections of the parents. On the other hand, some parents seem to overcompensate for their handicapped child. Some typical behaviors of these parents include setting goals that are too easily attained, praising or rewarding the child for work that is below his or her level of functioning, and intervening unnecessarily when the child is working on difficult tasks. Such behaviors convey the message, albeit indirectly, that the parents do not recognize or appreciate the child's actual abilities. These signals undermine the development of high self-esteem and a positive self-concept. Of course professionals helping parents of children with disabilities need to make sure that support programs are culturally sensitive (Lian & Fantanez-Phelan, 2001).

Adjusting to the child's disability is difficult, but Kogan (1980) has shown that parents can learn and use techniques for interacting with their child in ways that promote an adaptive relationship. General guidelines for parents in nurturing optimum development include realistically accepting the child, including abilities and disabilities. Parents should be sympathetic, but must encourage independence in order to enhance the child's self-esteem and promote his or her success in the "real" world.

Parents also have a crucial role in setting the stage for good sibling relationships. They must not show favoritism toward any of their children. Although they may enjoy different activities with their individual children, they should not give their attention preferentially to any single child. In particular, parents must avoid making comparisons among their children, and instead emphasize each child's individual strengths. All children will benefit when parents provide experiences and delegate responsibilities in accordance with each child's developmental level and needs.

Due to increasing recognition of social and emotional problems that may be secondary to other disabilities, the IDEIA requires a behavioral assessment of all children with a disability, regardless of their handicapping condition. It has become commonplace to use objective behavior rating scales and personality assessments during the initial referral and evaluation process (e.g., Reynolds & Kamphaus, 1992). Also, as a direct result of recognition of behavioral and emotional concomitants of various disabilities, IDEIA now requires a behavioral assessment prior to disciplining a child with a disability, so that it can be determined whether the behavior of concern is a result of the child's disability. When behavioral problems are disability-related, children must be treated, not punished. Teachers will have the primary role to play in such interventions at school.

Over and above the special methods and materials teachers use in working with the handicapped child, perhaps the most important element of the handicapped child's educational experience is a positive social climate. Teachers can provide a model for accepting individual differences in general and specifically valuing each child's, including the child with disabilities, abilities and contributions. The child's classmates will imitate the teacher and assimilate the underlying nondiscriminatory attitudes (Hunt, Doering, Hirose-Hatae, Maier, & Goetz, 2001). Being accepted by one's teachers and classmates nourishes the handicapped child's self-concept and self-esteem, thereby promoting not only social development, but also cognitive growth and educational achievement.

REFERENCES

Bartel, N. R., & Guskin, S. L. (1980). A handicap as a social phenomenon. In W. M. Cruickshank (Ed.), *Psychology of exceptional children and youth* (pp. 45–73). Englewood Cliffs, NJ: Prentice Hall.

Field, T. (1980). Self, teacher, toy, and peer-directed behaviors of handicapped preschool children. In T. Field, S. Goldberg, D. Stern, & A. M. Sostek (Eds.), *High risk infants and children: Adult and peer interactions* (pp. 313–326). New York: Academic.

Gliedman, J., & Roth, W. (1980). *The unexpected minority: Handicapped children in America.* New York: Harcourt Brace Jovanovich.

Hunt, P., Doering, K., Hirose-Hatae, A., Maier, J., & Goetz, L. (2001). Across-program collaboration to support students with and without disabilities in a general education classroom. *Journal of the Association of Persons with Severe Handicaps, 26,* 240–256.

Kogan, K. L. (1980). Interaction systems between preschool handicapped or developmentally delayed children and their parents. In T. Field, S. Goldberg, D. Stern, & A. M. Sostek (Eds.), *High risk infants and children: Adult and peer interactions* (pp. 227–247). New York: Academic.

Lian, M. J., & Fantanez-Phelan, S. M. (2001). Perceptions of Latino parents regarding cultural and linguistic issues and advocacy for children with disabilities. *Journal of the Association for Persons with Severe Handicaps, 26,* 189–194.

Novak, M. A., Olley, G., & Kearney, D. S. (1980). Social skills of children with special needs in integrated separate preschools. In T. Field, S. Goldberg, D. Stern, & A. M. Sostek (Eds.), *High risk infants and children: Adult and peer interactions* (pp. 327–346). New York: Academic.

Reynolds, C. R., & Kamphaus, R. W. (1992). *Behavior assessment system for children.* Circle Pines, MN: American Guidance Service.

Shontz, F. C. (1980). Theories about adjustment to having a disability. In W. M. Cruickshank (Ed.), *Psychology of exceptional children and youth* (pp. 3–44). Englewood Cliffs, NJ: Prentice Hall.

PAULINE F. APPLEFIELD
University of North Carolina at Wilmington

ADAPTIVE BEHAVIOR
BEHAVIOR ASSESSMENT SYSTEM FOR CHILDREN
FAMILY COUNSELING
FAMILY RESPONSE TO A CHILD WITH DISABILITIES
HANDICAPISM
INDIVIDUALS WITH DISABILITIES EDUCATION IMPROVEMENT ACT OF 2004 (IDEIA)
TEACHER EXPECTANCIES

ADLER, ALFRED (1870–1937)

Alfred Adler, an Austrian psychiatrist, severed an early connection with Freudian psychoanalysis to develop his more socially oriented Individual Psychology, which was a powerful influence in the development of the field of social psychology. Adler's work in education and child guidance is less well known, but it contributed greatly to the development of school services in Austria and it had worldwide significance for the education and treatment of children.

At the Pedagogical Institute of the City of Vienna, he helped to train thousands of teachers and established the first child guidance clinics in the Vienna school system. In 1935, with the coming of a fascist regime in Austria, Adler left Vienna for the United States, where he established a private practice and served as professor of medical psychology at the Long Island College of Medicine.

REFERENCES

Ansbacher, H. L., & Ansbacher, R. (1956). *The individual psychology of Alfred Adler.* New York: Basic Books.

Watson, R. I. (1963). *The great psychologists.* New York: Lippincott.

PAUL IRVINE
Katonah, New York

ADMINISTRATION OF SPECIAL EDUCATION

Prior to the advent of public school programs for individuals with disabilities in the late nineteenth and early twentieth centuries, administration of special education programs was usually executed by persons who were not administrators. Because many of the early programs were provided by religious organizations (Hewett & Forness, 1977), the earliest administrators were probably monks, nuns, or other religious figures (e.g., Pedro Ponce deLeon, a Spanish monk who worked with the deaf in the sixteenth century). During the late eighteenth and early nineteenth centuries, philosophical changes and a new attention to science changed attitudes toward the handicapped and their treatment. These changes, evidenced in the French and American revolutions, created a reverence for the individual and a belief that the lives of handicapped persons could be significantly improved through the application of science. Thus a new wave of administrators arose. These administrators were not interested primarily in running a program, but in teaching, scientific inquiry, and having an impact on contemporary thought through their writings. Thus a time was born in which most programs were managed by scientists, physicians, and philosophers such as Edouard Sequin, Valentin Hauy, and Samuel Gridley Howe. During the nineteenth century a great number of public and private residential schools/institutions were developed. For the most part, these institutions (which remained the dominant force in special education until the middle of the twentieth century) were administered by physicians. This was especially true for institutions for the mentally retarded, the emotionally disturbed, and the physically handicapped.

Public school services for exceptional children began in the latter part of the nineteenth century (Gearheart & Wright, 1979). By the middle of the twentieth century, public school classes became the primary mode of education for exceptional children. With this change, the administration of special education programs fell to educators and school psychologists. Although special education programs were held in public school buildings, they were usually separate, and writers of the time advocated separate administration and supervision systems (Ayer & Barr, 1928).

The rise of special education administration as a discipline occurred simultaneously with the rise of segregated public school programs. Special education administrators during the first quarter of the twentieth century were not trained generally as administrators; it was not until 1938 that any professional identity was established. In that year, the National Association of State Directors of Special Education was founded (Burrello & Sage, 1979). In 1951 the Council of Administrators of Special Education (CASE) convened as a special interest group within the Council for Exceptional Children (Burrello & Sage, 1979).

During the 1950s, 1960s, and 1970s, special education administration grew as a result of the increase in public special-education programs brought about by the increased federal role in programs for the handicapped. In the 1950s, the U.S. Office of Education conducted several large-scale studies of special education and special-education administration (Mackie & Engel, 1956; Mackie & Snyder, 1957). These studies helped to establish the roles of administrators of programs for exceptional children and the need for professional training. Many more studies were conducted during the 1960s and 1970s (e.g., Kohl & Marro, 1971; Sage, 1968; Wisland & Vaughan, 1964). It was, however, the passage of PL 94-142, The Education of All Handicapped Children Act of 1975, that brought special education administration to its current state. This legislation, and others that followed, together with numerous lawsuits, created a demand for administrators who were specifically trained to manage special-education programs, a demand that has grown with subsequent programs (e.g., IDEA).

Although special education administration has developed a uniqueness and identity, there is considerable variety within the discipline. This variety is expressed across governmental levels and organizational arrangements. There are three governmental levels in special education administration: federal, state, and local. Within each level the tasks of the administrator may vary considerably depending on the specific role of the administrator, the organization of the agency for which the administrator works, and the ways in which the agency delivers services.

Presently, the federal role in special education administration is executed primarily by the Office of Special Education and Rehabilitation of the U.S. Department of Education. The administrative roles of this office include monitoring state compliance with IDEIA; generating research; providing public information; formulating regulations; promoting personnel development; and drafting legislation. As a result of PL 94-142, IDEA, and IDEIA the federal role in administration of special education has grown substantially. Nearly every administrative decision in special education must be made with consideration for the regulations propagated by IDEIA. Because of this, the majority of the administrators at the federal level are involved in activities related to providing services to the states in order that they may carry out the provisions of IDEIA, or in evaluating/monitoring the state's efforts.

Administration of special education programs at the state level occurs in three places: at the state education agency (SEA); at state-operated schools; and at state-operated regional centers. At the SEA, the roles of administration are to develop legislation; to develop state plans; to obtain and administer financial resources; to develop personnel preparation systems and standards; to develop plans for improving instruction; to enforce and monitor regulations; and to develop public relations (Gearhart & Wright, 1979; Podemski, Price, Smith, & Marsh, 1984). The SEAs also directly administer programs such as state schools for the deaf or blind (e.g., Pennsylvania). These programs are usually for low-incidence populations. In Georgia, the SEA administers both state schools and regional centers that provide direct service to low-incidence populations, especially in rural areas. Regional centers also serve as resource centers for local education agencies (LEAs).

Some state-operated programs in special education are not administered by the SEA. These programs usually serve persons with mental retardation or emotional disturbance and may be managed by state agencies such as a department of mental retardation, mental health, and juvenile services. Such programs are generally subject to the same regulations as programs operated by the SEA. In many instances, however, the programs are not managed by educators. The practice of employing physicians, psychologists, or social workers to manage state residential programs is a vestige of a tradition in state institutions and is justifiable for programs that are not chiefly educational.

At the local level, there are a number of different administrative arrangements and even more varied service delivery arrangements (Burrello & Sage, 1979). The simplest administrative arrangement is the LEA. The LEA, also known as the local school district, provides direct services to exceptional children through various delivery systems. Administration at the local level may be centralized or decentralized. In a centralized system, persons (i.e., teachers) who provide services to exceptional children are managed by a district-wide special education director (coordinator). The special education director in a centralized system exercises a great amount of control over special education personnel and programs. In a decentralized system, the special education administrator serves in a coordinating/supporting/advising role. This administrator may have some authority over personnel but it is generally a building administrator (principal) who oversees daily operations.

More complex local administrative arrangements include intermediate educational units (IEU) and cooperative programs. Intermediate units exist in approximately 35 states (Podemski et al., 1984). In some states (e.g., Georgia) these units may be state-operated regional programs. In other states (e.g., New York, Texas, Wisconsin, Pennsylvania) the intermediate units are administered as a separate level of education agency. Intermediate units may be known by several names (e.g., Board of Cooperative Educational Services in New York, Regional Education Service Centers in Texas). According to Podemski et al. (1984), intermediate units were developed to pool resources and to share costs. In some states (e.g., Pennsylvania) intermediate units provide more than special education services and were developed for political as well as educational reasons during a time of district consolidation. Intermediate units have been criticized as arrangements that violate the principle of least restrictive environment because their services often require removing a child from his or her home school. Among the problems facing administrators of intermediate units are competition with LEAs for funds and students, potential conflict in lines of authority, communication gaps with the LEA, and salary variations that influence competition with LEAs for teachers.

Many rural school systems and suburban systems enter into cooperative agreements in order to provide more cost-effective programs, especially for low-incidence populations (Howe, 1981). Cooperative programs engender the same problems as do IEUs. Additionally, they must often contend with long distances for busing students.

The competencies of LEA and IEU special education administrators are similar. The differences are probably in terms of the amount of time devoted to different tasks rather than the tasks themselves. This may be true also for administrators of state-operated direct service programs (e.g., state schools). The competency areas for such administrators include organization theory and behavior; budget development; curriculum development; supervision; personnel administration; community relations; community resources; change processes; physical plant management; research; professional standards; and policy development.

Specialized graduate training for administrators of programs for exceptional children began in 1965. The impetus for such training was provided by a journal article by Milazzo and Blessing (1964). Subsequent to the publishing of that article, the U.S. Office of Education awarded grants to universities for the purpose of developing training programs (Burrello & Sage, 1979). Although most states do have certification requirements for special education leadership positions, requirements can be met with a general administrative certificate or a collection of courses and experience.

Special education administrators now have organized to promote and shape special education policies. The Council of Administration of Special Education (CASE) promotes leadership and provides special education administrators with opportunities for personal and professional advancement. CASE is a special interest division of the Council for Exceptional Children (CEC; 2005). The web site for CASE has extensive resources for administrators and reflects an international presence.

REFERENCES

Ayer, F. C., & Barr, A. S. (1928). *The organization of supervision.* New York: Appleton.

Burrello, L. C., & Sage, D. D. (1979). *Leadership and change in special education.* Englewood Cliffs, NJ: Prentice Hall.

Council for Exceptional Children (CEC). (2005). *Special interest divisions.* Retrieved June 17, 2005, from http://www.cec.sped.org/dv/

Gearheart, B. R., & Wright, W. S. (1979). *Organization and administration of educational programs for exceptional children* (2nd ed.). Springfield, IL: Thomas.

Hewett, F. M., & Forness, S. R. (1977). *Education of exceptional learners.* Boston: Allyn & Bacon.

Howe, C. (1981). *Administration of special education.* Denver: Love.

Kohl, J. W., & Marro, T. D. (1971). *A normative study of the administrative position in special education.* Grant No. OEG-0-70-2467 (607), U.S. Office of Education, Pennsylvania State University.

Mackie, R. P., & Engel, A. M. (1956). *Directors and supervisors of special education in local school systems.* U.S. Office of Education Bulletin 1955, No. 13. Washington, DC: U.S. Government Printing Office.

Mackie, R. P., & Snyder, W. E. (1957). *Special education personnel in state departments of education.* U.S. Office of Education Bulletin 1956, No. 6. Washington, DC: U.S. Government Printing Office.

Milazzo, T. C., & Blessing, K. R. (1964). The training of directors and supervisors of special education programs. *Exceptional Children, 31,* 129–141.

Podemski, R. S., Price, B. J., Smith, T. E. C., & Marsh, G. E. (1984). *Comprehensive administration of special education.* Rockville, MD: Aspen.

Sage, D. D. (1968). Functional emphasis in special education administration. *Exceptional Children, 35,* 69–70.

Wisland, M. V., & Vaughan, T. D. (1964). Administrative problems in special education. *Exceptional Children, 31,* 87–89.

JAMES K. MCAFEE
Pennsylvania State University

INDIVIDUALS WITH DISABILITIES EDUCATION IMPROVEMENT ACT OF 2004 (IDEIA)
POLITICS AND SPECIAL EDUCATION
SPECIAL EDUCATION PROGRAMS
SUPERVISION IN SPECIAL EDUCATION

ADOPTEES

The practice of adoption is centuries old, but our understanding of the impact of this form of child care continues to be without definitive answers. At the theoretical level, adoption has often been associated with increased risk for psychological maladjustment. Psychoanalytic theory, for example, suggests that the experience of adoption sets the stage for disturbances in personality and identity development. This is especially true because of doubt surrounding the true circumstances of the child's origins, and because the child has two sets of parents instead of one with whom to identify. Bowlby's work (1969) suggests that adopted children are at risk for emotional problems, but only in cases where there is disruption in the development and continuity of primary attachment relationships. Consequently, infants adopted soon after birth and cared for continually by affectionate and competent parents would not be viewed as being at risk in terms of possible maladjustment. However, individuals raised by multiple caregivers, or separated from caregivers after a secure attachment has developed, would be perceived as being at risk.

In contrast to the theoretical literature, the results of empirical research have produced an inconsistent picture of the effects of adoption on an individual's psychological development. After reviewing the social work literature on the success of adoption placements, both Mech (1973) and Kadushin (1974) concluded that the majority of placements were satisfactory and this has been supported in recent studies (Feigelman, 2001) of domestic adoptions but not so much with international adoptions (Tieman, van der Ende, & Verhulst, 2005). However, an examination of the records of mental-health clinics reveals that adopted children are referred to these clinics at disproportionate rates. Mech (1973) reported that while adopted children reared by nonrelatives constitute approximately 1 percent of the population, they account for over 4 percent of the children seen in clinics. Researchers have also reported that there are differences in types of problems presented by adopted children versus those who are nonadopted. Adopted children typically manifest more aggressive and acting-out problems, as well as learning-related difficulties (Simmel, Brooks, Barth, & Hinshaw, 2001). In fact, a study has even reported an elevated number of pediatric health conditions among adopted children (Dalby, Fox, & Haslam, 1982).

While there are those studies available that validate these findings, there are also those such as Aumend and Barrett's (1984) that provide a contrary set of findings. In their study of adult adoptees they reported the following: the majority of those in their study scored above the 60th percentile on the Tennessee Self Concept Scale; had positive scores on the Attitude Toward Parents Scales; were happy growing up, with only 12 percent reporting that they were unhappy; and did not report revelation of their adoptive status as being disruptive or traumatic. These findings were consistent with those of Norvell and Guy (1977), who determined there were no significant differences between self-concepts of an adopted and nonadopted population, aged 18 to 25. They concluded that problems of a negative

identity seemed to stem more from problems within the home, rather than an association with adoption.

Because of a lack of definitive empirical information, the issue of open records, or allowing adopted children to learn about their biological parents at a particular point in time, continues to be controversial. There have been recent calls for unconditional release of records (Miall & March, 2005). Another issue unique to adoption is when children should be informed of their adoptive status. Currently, most specialists on adoption advocate telling children before they are 5 years of age. The specialists believe this promotes the development of a trusting relationship within the context of a warm and supportive family and eliminates the possibility that the child will hear of his or her unique family status from nonfamily members under less than desirable conditions. While many advocate telling the child during the preschool years, recent studies such as that by Brodzinsky, Schechter, Braff, and Singer (1984) suggest that a child's cognitive development during the preschool years may mitigate against his or her understanding of the nature of adoption. Their concern is that parents may relate this information to children and then feel the "job is done," failing to understand that advanced stages of cognitive development call for further explanations and sequential exploration of concerns the child might harbor. Finally, the most sensational adoption issue is currently being debated and that is of gay adoption. At this time, large surveys questioning same-sex adoption indicate approximately half for and half against (Miall & March, 2005).

While the data are not as definitive as might be liked, it certainly seems that adoption is a legitimate way of building families and caring for young children. It is superior to alternatives such as serial placements in a number of homes, or large-scale institutional care. Assuming the family is capable of providing a stable environment that is free of debilitating or otherwise pathological features, and relates the information on adoption in a facilitative fashion, there seems to be little reason to expect greater childhood problems than experienced in biologically created families. In families where psychological attachment between adoptee and parent fails, increased emotional and behavioral problems will occur (Ziegler, 1994).

REFERENCES

Aumend, S. A., & Barrett, M. C. (1984). Self-concept and attitudes toward adoption: A comparison of searching and nonsearching adult adoptees. *Child Welfare, 63,* 251–259.

Bowlby, J. (1969). *Attachment and loss: Volume 1 attachment.* New York: Basic Books.

Brodzinsky, D. M., Schechter, D. E., Braff, A. M., & Singer, L. M. (1984). Psychological and academic adjustment in adopted children. *Journal of Consulting and Clinical Psychology, 52,* 582–589.

Dalby, J. T., Fox, S. L., & Haslam, R. H. (1982). Adoption and foster care rates in pediatric disorders. *Developmental and Behavioral Pediatrics, 3,* 61–64.

Kadushin, A. (1974). *Child welfare services.* New York: Macmillan.

Mech, E. V. (1973). Adoption: A policy perspective. In B. Caldwell & H. Ricuitti (Eds.), *Review of child development research* (Vol. 3). Chicago: University of Chicago Press.

Miall, C. E., & March, K. (2005). Social support for changes in adoption practice: Gay adoption, open adoption, birth reunions and the release of confidential identifying information. *Families in Society, 86,* 83–92.

Norvell, M., & Guy, R. F. (1977). A comparison of self concept in adopted and nonadopted adolescents. *Adolescence, 12,* 443–448.

Simmel, C., Brooks, D., Barth, R. P., & Hinshaw, P. (2001). Externalizing symptomatology among adoptive youth: Prevalence and preadoptive risk factors. *Journal of Abnormal Child Psychology, 29,* 57–69.

Tieman, W., van der Ende, J., & Verhulst, C. (2005). Psychiatric disorders in young adult Intercountry Adoptees: An epidemiological study. *American Journal of Psychiatry, 162,* 592–598.

Ziegler, D. (1994). Adoption and adjustment. In B. James (Eds.), *Handbook for treatment of attachment-trauma problems in children* (pp. 256–266). New York: Lexington Books.

CHARLES P. BARNARD
University of Wisconsin at Stout

CHILD GUIDANCE CLINIC
POST-INSTITUTIONALIZED CHILDREN

ADULT PROGRAMS FOR INDIVIDUALS WITH DISABILITIES

There are numerous programs of several types that serve adults with disabilities. Many such programs are financed by federal, state, and local governments; many others are funded by private business, private nonprofit organizations, and charities. The following is a summary of major programs organized by function and financing source. It will not capture the complexity and breadth of these programs, especially at the state and local level.

The Social Security Act authorizes several major programs providing cash payments and health insurance to adults on the basis of disability. The disability insurance (DI) program replaces in part income lost when a person with a work history can no longer work because of a physical or mental impairment. Many individuals, of course, have separate commercial disability insurance policies provided by an employer or purchased on their own. After receiving Social Security DI benefits for 24 months, regardless of age, an individual becomes eligible for government-provided health insurance under the Medicare program, which normally covers persons 65 and over. The Social Security Act also contains the Supplemental Security Income (SSI) program, which provides cash income support payments to needy individuals who are aged, blind, or disabled. Income is provided regardless of work history to those who meet means and asset requirements. In most states, with SSI eligibility comes eligibility for the Medicaid program (federal-state matching required), which provides health insurance for low-income individuals. Included in Medicaid is support for intermediate care facilities for the mentally retarded (ICFs/MR), which provide residential care and service programs. Many disabled individuals benefit from programs for which they may be eligible without regard to their disability, for example, Social Security Old Age and Survivors insurance payments and Medicare (persons 65 and older).

Finally, there are four other major federal programs of this type for special groups of disabled individuals. Veterans with service-connected disabilities are eligible for special cash payments under the Veterans Compensation program. Veterans of wartime service with nonservice-connected disabilities are eligible for a special pension program. Coal miners disabled by black lung or other lung disease are eligible for one of two separate special payment programs (one administered by the Social Security Administration, the other by the Labor Department), depending on circumstances.

Special programs of postsecondary education for the deaf and hearing impaired, supported with significant federal funding, are provided at Gallaudet College, the National Technical Institute for the Deaf, and four special regional postsecondary institutions. In addition, educational programs that are recipients of federal financial assistance at public and private colleges and universities must be accessible to and usable by individuals with disabilities of all types. Some schools are making adaptations and providing support services that go beyond legal requirements.

Rehabilitation and job training services are available from a number of sources. Under Title I of the Rehabilitation Act, the federal government and the states provide vocational rehabilitation services such as physical restoration, job training, and placement to persons with mental and physical disabilities, regardless of prior work history. Physical rehabilitation is covered by most accident and health insurance policies; vocational rehabilitation is sometimes covered. Rehabilitation is available and in fact required under some state workers' compensation laws. Rehabilitation services financed by various forms of insurance are provided by private, for-profit companies and facilities, private nonprofit agencies, and state agencies. Provision of rehabilitation services by private, profit-making (proprietary) firms has been a growing phenomenon (Taylor et al., 1985) for many years now.

Private nonprofit entities play a significant role in providing job training, rehabilitation, and other skill development to adults with disabilities. Included in this group are organizations such as the Association for Retarded Citizens, Easter Seals, Goodwill Industries, and United Cerebral Palsy. Some activities of these organizations are financed by the government; others are funded by contracts with businesses for work performed.

Major employers, faced with rising costs of disability, will find it in their interest to pay greater attention to management, rehabilitation, and disability prevention (Schwartz, 1984). Many are increasing efforts in these areas, including rehabilitation, job, and work-site modification efforts to facilitate entry or return to jobs by individuals with disabilities. Contracts with the federal government of more than $2500 must operate with an affirmative action program to employ and advance individuals with disabilities.

Self-help, referral, and training services are available to people with very severe disabilities to improve their capacity for independent living. These services are available through a network of community-based nonprofit centers and from state rehabilitation agencies. In addition, supported employment is an important new program for individuals with disabilities so severe they were previously thought incapable of working. These individuals (especially those with mental impairments) are likely to need continual support, but they are able to work on regular jobs in integrated settings if given a highly structured training program and some support on the job site (Mank, 1986).

Special housing and transportation programs are available for individuals with disabilities, financed by both the federal government and states and localities. The same is true for special recreation programs for the disabled, in which local governments, service organizations, charities, and private businesses play a large role. Therapeutic recreation is also part of some rehabilitation programs. In addition, many local recreation facilities and organizations, including those involved with the arts, are adapting programs so that the disabled can participate or attend with the general public.

REFERENCES

General Services Administration. (1985). *Catalog of federal domestic assistance.* Washington, DC: U.S. Government Printing Office.

Mank, D. (1986). Four supported employment alternatives. In W. Kiernan & J. Stark (Eds.), *Pathways to employment for developmentally disabled adults.* Baltimore: Brooks.

National Council on the Handicapped. (1986). *Toward independence: An assessment of federal laws and programs affecting persons with disabilities.* Washington, DC: U.S. Government Printing Office.

Schwartz, G. (1984, May). Disability costs: The impending crisis. *Business and Health,* 25–28.

Taylor, L. J., Golter, M., Golter, G., & Backer, T. (Eds.). (1985). *Handbook of private sector rehabilitation.* New York: Springer.

James R. Ricciuti
*United States Office of
Management and Budget*

ACCESSIBILITY OF PROGRAMS
AMERICANS WITH DISABILITIES ACT
HABILITATION OF INDIVIDUALS WITH DISABILITIES
REHABILITATION

ADVANCED PLACEMENT PROGRAM

The Advanced Placement Program was established in 1955 as a program of college-level courses and examinations for secondary school students. It is administered by the College Board, a nonprofit membership organization composed of public and private secondary schools, colleges, and universities. This program gives high school students the opportunity to receive advanced placement and/or credit on entering college.

The essential premise of the Advanced Placement Program is that college-level courses can be successfully taught to high school students by high school teachers on high school campuses (College Entrance Examination Board, 2005). Descriptions and examinations on 34 introductory college courses in 19 fields are disseminated. These fields include art, biology, chemistry, computer science, English, French, German, government and politics, history, Latin, mathematics, music, physics, and Spanish. Course descriptions are prepared, with the help of the Educational Testing Service, by working committees of school and college teachers appointed by the College Board. Exams are administered by the Educational Testing Service.

Most participating high schools, offering one or more advanced placement courses (called AP courses) are larger schools with enough students to qualify for a class. Smaller schools usually provide independent study for those students wishing to take advanced placement exams. The AP course teachers are provided with course descriptions and teachers' guides that state curricular goals and suggest strategies to achieve them. Teachers are not required to follow a detailed plan of assignments and classroom activities; however, seven Advanced Placement Regional Offices and Advanced Placement Program conferences are available to assist teachers.

Advanced Placement courses offer demanding academic opportunities for abler students. Students who complete these courses are not required to take advanced placement examinations, but those who choose to take them and who receive a passing score, have the opportunity to receive advanced placement and/or credit on entering college.

REFERENCES

College Entrance Examination Board (2005). *About AP.* Retrieved June 19, 2005, from http://www.collegeboard.com

AP Services
P.O. Box 6671
Princeton, NJ 08541-6671
Phone: (888) 225-5427

MARY K. TALLENT
Texas Tech University

ACCELERATION OF GIFTED CHILDREN
GIFTED AND TALENTED CHILDREN

ADVANCE ORGANIZERS

Advance organizers are general overviews or conceptual models of new information presented to learners immediately prior to receiving new information. Ausubel (1960) originally proposed the concept of the advance organizer for use with reading material. The principle of advance organizers is that learning is enhanced when information is linked to learners' existing cognitive structures, thereby enabling the learner to organize and interpret new information (Mayer, 1979). Thus advance organizers prepare the learner for the meaningful reception of new learning. They can either present salient prerequisite knowledge not known to the learner (known as expository organizers), or help the learner establish connections between relevant dimensions of existing knowledge and the new information (known as comparative organizers; Ausubel, Novak, & Hanesian, 1979).

Expository organizers draw the learner's attention to the internal organization of the body of new information by means of a rough overview that briefly presents general topics and concepts and how they are related. Outlines, models, and introductory paragraphs may serve this purpose. With comparative organizers, students' previous experiences or prior learning is tapped in such a way as to identify major points or dimensions of similarity between the new information and existing understandings. By providing external organization, or how new information is related to what students already know, comparative organizers establish a meaningful learning set.

Advance organizers may be either verbal or graphic, and can take a variety of formats, including overviews, outlines, analogies, examples, thought-provoking questions, concrete models, and figures such as cognitive maps (Alexander, Frankiewicz, & Williams, 1979; Mayer, 1984; Zook, 1991). Although originally conceptualized as abstract introduc-

tions, advance organizers tend to be more effective if they are concrete and if they are both familiar to the learner and well-learned. In this way, advance organizers provide frameworks or cognitive maps for new content. Corkill (1992) also emphasizes the importance of using examples that enable learners to identify the relationship between ideas in the organizer and the new information.

Eggen and Kauchak (1996) use the following example of an advance organizer from an elementary social studies lesson on governments.

> The organization of a government is like a family. Different people in the government have different responsibilities and roles. When all the people work together, both families and governments operate efficiently. (p. 214)

Current schema theory provides a theoretical basis for advance organizers, whose function can be viewed as both activating relevant schemata for to-be-learned material and revising the activated schemata to promote assimilation of the new material (Derry, 1984; Glover, Ronning, & Bruning, 1990). Advance organizers will benefit learners most when students lack the prerequisite knowledge for understanding, and when the transfer of learning to new problems is the desired outcome. To be maximally effective, they should be easy to acquire, as concrete as possible, integrated with technology, and offer an integrated overview or model of the new material (Jordan School District, 2005; Mayer, 1987).

REFERENCES

Alexander, L., Frankiewicz, R., & Williams, R. (1979). Facilitation of learning and retention of oral instruction using advance and post organizers. *Journal of Educational Psychology, 71,* 701–707.

Ausubel, D. P. (1960). The use of advance organizers in the learning and retention of meaningful verbal material. *Journal of Educational Psychology, 51,* 267–272.

Ausubel, D. P., Novak, J. D., & Hanesian, H. (1979). *Educational psychology: A cognitive view* (2nd ed.). New York: Holt, Rinehart & Winston.

Corkill, A. (1992). Advance organizers: Facilitators of recall. *Educational Psychology Review, 4,* 33–67.

Derry, S. J. (1984). Effects of an organizer on memory for prose. *Journal of Educational Psychology, 76,* 98–107.

Eggen, P. D., & Kauchak, D. P. (1996). *Strategies for teachers: Teaching content and thinking skills* (3rd ed.). Boston: Allyn & Bacon.

Glover, J. A., Ronning, R. R., & Bruning, R. H. (1990). *Cognitive psychology for teachers.* New York: Macmillan.

Jordan School District. (2005). *Transforming teaching through technology.* Retrieved June 19, 2005, from http://www.t4.jordan .k12.ut.us/teacher_resources/inspiration_templates/

Mayer, R. E. (1979). Can advance organizers influence meaningful learning? *Review of Educational Research, 49,* 371–383.

Mayer, R. E. (1984). Aids to text comprehension. *Educational Psychologist, 19,* 30–42.

Mayer, R. E. (1987). *Educational psychology: A cognitive approach.* Boston: Little, Brown.

Zook, K. B. (1991). Effects of analogical processes on learning and misrepresentation. *Educational Psychology Review, 3,* 41–72.

JAMES M. APPLEFIELD
University of North Carolina at Wilmington

DIAGNOSTIC PRESCRIPTIVE TEACHING
DIRECT INSTRUCTION

ADVENTITIOUS DISABILITIES

Disabilities may present themselves at birth or be acquired through disease or accident. Those acquired later in life are known as adventitious disabilities. Among these is brain damage produced by extremely high and consistent temperatures or a lack of needed oxygen to the brain. Adventitious disabilities may also be a consequence of trauma to the brain or injury to other parts of the body. A major cause of adventitious disabilities is child abuse (Gilles, 1999). Child abuse is emotionally or physically damaging and can cause durable learning problems. An area of childhood exceptionality often associated with an adventitious disability is hearing impairment or deafness (Rapin, 1999). Hearing losses may be present at birth or adventitiously acquired later on in life through disease or accident. Adventitious disabilities and congenital disabilities that appear similar (but are obviously of different etiologies) may well have different outcomes.

REFERENCES

Gilles, E. E. (1999). Nonaccidental head injury. In K. F. Swaiman & S. Ashwal (Eds.), *Pediatric neurology* (3rd ed., pp. 898–914). St. Louis, MO: Mosby.

Rapin, I. (1999). Hearing impairment. In K. F. Swaiman & S. Ashwal (Eds.), *Pediatric neurology* (3rd ed., pp. 77–95). St. Louis, MO: Mosby.

STAFF

BRAIN DAMAGE/INJURY
CHILD ABUSE
POST-INSTITUTIONALIZED CHILDREN

ADOCACY FOR CHILDREN WITH DISABILITIES

Advocacy for children with disabilities has become a multifaceted reality in today's world of concern about the legal rights of those with disabilities. The term actually has a variety of meanings, depending on who is providing the advocacy. In its essence, advocacy refers to attempts by an individual handicapped person, by another person, or by a group to guarantee that all rights due a handicapped person are realized. Roos (1983) traces the origins of the advocacy movement to the 1930s, when parents of mentally retarded children began to react against neglectful or inappropriate actions by professionals who claimed to be helping these children and their families. Frustrated with the professionals' response, parents turned to each other for help.

In 1933, the Cuyahoga County (Ohio) Council for the Retarded Child was founded by parents as the forerunner of today's Association for Retarded Citizens (ARC). Other local, grass-roots organizations sprang up in different communities, and later, in 1950, joined together to form what was then known as the National Association of Parents and Friends of Mentally Retarded Children. At that time, similar organizational activity sprung up with parents of children with cerebral palsy.

Recently groups have been formed to advocate the interests of learning disabled, deaf, blind, and autistic children, and those with a variety of medical and physical anomalies. The early parent movements had at least three effects in the 1950s, at the same time as they formed a base on which later governmental and judicial action would be built. First, local ARCs extended emotional support to families with retarded members, providing information about available resources and bringing the issue of mental retardation into public view. This helped remove some of the stigma of having a handicapped child. Second, they encouraged state legislatures to adopt mandatory legislation for public school programs for retarded children, to enforce existing legislation, and to increase state appropriations for publicly funded programs. Third, parents developed preschool, school-age, and adult programs that became models for professionals, and public education and voluntary agencies (Lippman & Goldberg, 1973).

The role of ARC as a direct service provider has declined recently. Greater emphasis is now placed on information and public education services, advocacy, legislation, and funding (Roos, 1983). Advocacy efforts by ARC and other such groups today focus on citizen advocacy and self-advocacy. Professionals and volunteers have joined with parents to change the makeup of many groups formerly consisting exclusively of parents of handicapped children. Various advocacy groups and professional associations have formed coalitions to increase their political and public influence, with many organizations maintaining full- or part-time offices in Washington, DC, as well as in state capitals (Consortium for Citizens with Disabilities, 2005). These groups may be closely linked with legal advocacy agencies and may be represented on state and national advisory panels, accrediting boards, and monitoring bodies, often by state or federal regulation or court order. Advocacy groups have been instrumental in initiating litigation, often through the use of class-action suits, to guarantee that the existing rights of handicapped persons are safeguarded, to obtain new rights or services, or to enhance currently available programs. In some cases, international societies have been formed by national advocacy groups representing several nations (Roos, 1983).

Herr (1983) describes several different kinds of advocacy that have evolved from earlier movements. Though definitions and actual practice may vary, the following types of advocacy approaches for the handicapped can be identified:

1. *Self-advocacy:* "part consciousness-raising, assertiveness-training . . . and springboard to direct consumer involvement" (Herr, 1983).

2. *Family advocacy:* the oldest and most well understood.

3. *Friend advocacy:* personal, voluntary assistance by altruistic citizens; also referred to as *citizen advocacy.*

4. *Disability rights advocacy:* trained advocacy specialists dealing with individual needs and human service systems.

5. *Human rights advocacy:* usually citizen review committees composed of volunteers and professionals.

6. *Internal advocacy:* individuals within, rather than external to, human service agencies who attempt to guarantee clients' rights (sometimes referred to as ombudsmen).

7. *Legal advocacy:* primarily nonprofit, public-interest law projects, including some private or government lawyers (Herr, 1983).

Although individual special educators, acting alone or through professional organizations, may also view themselves as advocates for the handicapped children they serve, there may be inherent conflicts in attempting to play the two roles simultaneously (Bateman, 1982). Special educators must keep current on ethical practices and legal developments in their field, and on law and education in general.

REFERENCES

Bateman, B. (1982). Legal and ethical dilemmas of special educators. *Exceptional Education Quarterly, 2*(4), 57–67.

Consortium for Citizens with Disabilities. (2005). About CCD. Retrieved June 19, 2005, from http://www.c-c-d.org/about.htm

Herr, S. S. (1983). *Rights and advocacy for retarded people.* Lexington, MA: Lexington Books.

Lippman, L., & Goldberg, I. I. (1973). *Right to education: Anatomy of the Pennsylvania case and its implications for exceptional children.* New York: Teachers College Press.

Roos, P. R. (1983). Advocate groups. In J. L. Matson & J. A. Mulick (Eds.), *Handbook of mental retardation.* New York: Pergamon.

JOHN D. WILSON
Elwyn Institutes

AAMR, AMERICAN ASSOCIATION ON MENTAL RETARDATION
CONSORTIUM FOR CITIZENS WITH DISABILITIES

ADVOCACY GROUPS, CITIZEN

A citizen advocacy group may be defined in general as any organization that has as its purpose to increase the quality of life for a specified handicapped population. Two examples of citizen advocacy groups containing both parents and professionals, and formally organized, are the Association for Children With Learning Disorders (ACLD) and the American Association on Mental Deficiency. These two groups have national headquarters but are organized state by state, having local chapters at county, city, or regional levels. They are not, however, classified as grass-roots advocacy groups.

An example of an informal organization is Youth Advocacy in the Washington, DC, area, a group of citizens (nonparents), with paid professional leadership, that provides services for adjudicated youths. They may represent an alternative to incarceration, providing community-based rehabilitation and supporting school, work, and living arrangements for youths in the area. Another example of a grass-roots nationally organized group is the Association for Autistic children. The chief characteristic of the organization is that the majority of local support groups are informally organized, and indeed are parents, while the leadership has national consolidation. There are formal and informal advocacy groups at national, regional, and local levels serving handicapped students representing all disability groups. The purposes for each group may vary considerably, depending on the perceived needs of the group.

The work of advocacy groups includes seeking federal or state legislation, developing policy or ordinances at the community level, supporting parental work, and intervening directly for students. One example of a community-based advocacy group is the Lion's Club, which supports the visually handicapped. Other social clubs support the hearing impaired (Rotary), the mentally retarded (Civitan), or orthopedically impaired (Shriners) by paying for services, prostheses, or therapy. Another example is the Junior Chamber of commerce, a group that raises partial or full support for group homes, sheltered employment centers, or residential or day schools for the emotionally disturbed.

Providing funds for services or a community-support base are two of the major purposes of advocacy organizations. The definition of a community-support base varies with the particular advocacy group and community. Certainly, providing emotional support for parents is a major consideration. Obtaining legislation also is a primary function, given the fact that all legislation for the handicapped was provided and obtained by parents, not professionals. Advocacy groups may purchase direct services or even provide direct services, but that has not been their major role in the past.

It is becoming more of a major role though, and represents a trend toward advocacy in the United States.

DAVID A. SABATINO
*West Virginia College of
Graduate Studies*

ADVOCACY ORGANIZATIONS

Advocacy organizations are organizations that devote themselves to advocacy for individuals or groups who have needs for which their own resources may not be sufficient. The establishment of these organizations has proceeded on "the assumption that classes of persons exist with similar needs and similar inability to speak effectively for themselves" (Sage & Burrello, 1986).

Many, if not most, of the services currently available to handicapped children and adolescents either began or succeeded because of the efforts of advocacy groups. Much of special education history represents the efforts of advocacy groups, including church, parent, and charitable groups. The Association for Retarded Citizens, in its national, state, and local forms, is an example of an advocacy organization that has altered educational practices in major ways.

Increasing growth in all sorts of advocacy groups has taken place since the 1960s, with an acceleration in the last decade. Not all groups, of course, deal with the handicapped. There are environmental advocacy groups, groups concerned with product safety, with the elimination of drunk driving, and so forth. However, advocacy groups for the handicapped have been among the most vociferous and successful.

Many of these advocacy groups began and sustained themselves through grants from the federal government. This was particularly true during the 1960s and 1970s, when they were financially encouraged as part of the social legislation of the times. Some were started or supported through funds provided by foundations or their own fundraising activities.

The nature of advocacy is such that agencies are likely to be activist, to aggressively seek to achieve long-range changes in the social system to benefit their clients, and to immediately help those clients. Thus they often seek to influence legislation. Some advocacy agencies have special service missions, but modern agencies are more likely to intercede with a particular service or political system so as to obtain services and other needed benefits for their clients rather than provide those benefits themselves. They also make efforts to educate both their clients and the systems with which they interact so as to facilitate their working relationships. Professional advocacy groups usually assume major informational roles. They provide forums for speakers and disseminate information and literature, including manuals that assist their audiences to assist themselves in achieving their goals.

Advocacy organizations often have been successful in obtaining services for their clients, either through their own intercessions or by educating and supporting the services' "consumers" or their representatives so as to make them more effective. Such organizations as Closer Look Information Center for the Handicapped and the National Center for Law and the Handicapped have been instrumental in making public schools more responsive to the needs of handicapped students. They also have played major roles in disseminating information to the individuals whose advocacies they are assuming, to the general public, and to the legislative bodies whose laws and regulations may affect their constituencies.

REFERENCE

Sage, D. D., & Burrello, L. C. (1986). *Policy and management in special education.* Englewood Cliffs, NJ: Prentice Hall.

LESTER MANN
*Hunter College, City University
of New York*

AFFECTIVE DISORDERS

Affect is the externally observable, immediately expressed component of human emotion (e.g., facial expression, tone of voice). Mood is considered to be a sustained emotion that pervades an individual's perception of the world. Affective disorders, as defined by the American Psychiatric Association (1994) are the class of mental disorders where the essential feature is a disturbance of mood.

Emotions and their expression are an integral part of human experience. It is only under certain conditions that the expression of emotion is considered maladaptive; in some instances, in fact, a lack of affect might be viewed as abnormal. It is only when an emotional reaction is disproportionate to the event, when the duration of the reaction is atypical, or when it interferes with a person's psychological, social, or occupational functioning that an emotional response may be labeled symptomatic of an affective disorder.

Affective disorders are comprised of two basic elements, depression and mania, which can be conceptualized as opposite ends of a continuum paralleling the normal happiness/sadness continuum. Both depression and mania have their counterparts in everyday life: The parallels for depression are grief and dejection; the experience corresponding to mania is less clear-cut, but probably could be described as the feverish activity with which people sometimes respond to stress.

Formally, both mania and depression can be characterized by symptoms at the emotional, cognitive, and somatic/

motivational levels. The major emotional components of depression are sadness and melancholy, often accompanied by feelings of guilt and worthlessness. These emotions permeate the individual's total experience of life. Cognitively, depressed persons are characterized by a negatively distorted view of themselves, the world, and the future. Their outlook is generally one of unrealistic hopelessness. In terms of their physical functioning, depressed persons frequently suffer appetite and sleep disturbances, fatigue, apathy, and a general loss of energy.

In certain aspects, the symptoms of mania could be viewed as opposite to those of depression. For instance, people suffering a manic episode often are in a highly elevated mood, seeming to experience life with an intense euphoria. However, it generally takes little frustration to shift this elated enthusiasm to irritability or tears, which suggests that mania may be closer to depression than initially seems apparent. In fact, it has been suggested by a number of theorists that mania is a defense against depression, that it is an attempt to ward off depressive feelings through feverish activity.

Cognitively manic individuals characteristically show wildly inflated self-esteem, believing themselves to be capable of great accomplishments or possessed of exceptional talent. Manic individuals act on their high opinion of themselves. They behave recklessly, involving themselves in unwise business deals or sexual liaisons, wasting large sums of money on shopping sprees or gambling. When experiencing a manic episode, individuals often have a decreased need for sleep, sometimes going for days without rest.

Within the affective disorders, there are two major syndromes: major depression (or unipolar depression as it has traditionally been called) and bipolar disorder (formerly manic-depressive disorder). In unipolar depression, an individual experiences one or more episodes of depression without ever experiencing an episode of mania. Approximately half of the people who suffer major depression will undergo only one episode of depression: Their first episode will be their last. In general, even without intervention, most people will recover from an occurrence of unipolar depression within 3 to 6 months.

In bipolar disorder, an individual experiences both manic and depressive episodes. In rare cases, an individual vacillates between manic and depressive episodes without an intervening period of normal functioning. More often, there are periods of normality interspersed between the manic and/or depressive episodes. There is no separate diagnostic category for persons who experience only manic episodes; this occurs only rarely. In such instances, an assumption is made that the person will ultimately experience a depressive episode, and a diagnosis of bipolar disorder will be made.

Of the two disorders, bipolar disorder is typically, but not always, the more serious and debilitating. People with bipolar disorder, in comparison with those with unipolar disorder, experience more episodes, and their interepisode functioning is worse. Further, such people are more likely to have serious alcohol abuse problems and attempt and commit suicide at a higher rate than persons with unipolar disorder.

Mood disorders have long been the most common of mental illnesses, but they are on the increase in modern society (Keller & Baker, 1992). Depression has been referred to as the common cold of mental illness. Around 10 percent of the males and perhaps 22 percent of the females living in the United States will at some point in their lives experience an episode of major depression. This one-to-two ratio has been found in many different cultures, in Europe and Africa as well as North America. (There are, however, a few notable exceptions such as the Amish in Pennsylvania.) It has been hypothesized that more women experience depression than men because it is more socially acceptable for women to respond to negative life experiences with passive, depressive symptoms. Men may be less likely to experience or express depressive symptoms because they may receive more social rejection (or less social reinforcement) than women for acting depressed. Instead, men may respond to stressful events more actively, with substance abuse (e.g., alcoholism) or antisocial behavior.

Bipolar disorder is much less common than unipolar disorder; slightly less than 1 percent of the U.S. population will experience bipolar disorder at some point in their lives. Unlike unipolar disorder, bipolar disorder occurs with approximately the same frequency in men as in women. Both unipolar and bipolar disorder tend to run in families, though bipolar disorder probably has a significantly larger genetic component than unipolar disorder. At present, the nature of the genetic mechanisms underlying the affective disorders is not clear. It is known, however, that in both mania and depression there are abnormalities in the level of neurotransmitters in the brain.

Beyond the possibility noted that mania is a defense against depression, there has been relatively little psychological theorizing about the causes of mania and bipolar disorder. This is not the case with unipolar depression, for which a number of etiological theories have been developed. From a Freudian perspective, depression is viewed as the punishment an overly punitive superego inflicts on the ego for the ego's failure to properly treat a lost love. The superego's harshness is seen also as a means of preventing the ego's feelings of anger and aggression from being expressed (Freud, 1917).

From a more behavioral perspective, Lewinsohn (1974) has hypothesized that depression is the result of a low rate of response-contingent reinforcement, caused by either a lack of social skills or a deficient environment, which results in the person experiencing behavioral extinction. Rather than being a function of the rate of reinforcement, Seligman and colleagues (Abramson, Seligman, & Teasdale, 1978) believe that it is the individual's lack of control over his or her environment and the attributions that this person makes about this lack of control that results in depression. Seligman believes that a lack of control that is attributed to causes that are internal (the self), global (some general quality), and stable (not likely to change) will result in depression.

Most theorists believe that the cognitions that depressed persons experience are a consequence of depression. Beck (1967), however, believes that negative cognitions and thought patterns are the cause of unipolar depression rather than a consequence of depression. He has proposed that individuals prone to depression have negative schema that are activated by stress. Once activated, the individual tends to interpret his or her experience in the worst possible light, using errors of logic (e.g., drawing sweeping conclusions based on one or two events) to do so. This negative interpretation occurs even when more plausible explanations for experiences are available; the person chooses his or her explanation on the basis of its negativity rather than its validity.

From the viewpoint of the individual working with children, what may be most important regarding affective disorders is an awareness of and ability to recognize signs of childhood affective disorders. It should be noted first that it is rare for children, particularly prior to puberty, to experience manic episodes. When a young child exhibits overactive behavior that appears manic, it is probably more appropriately considered a symptom of hyperactivity. (It is also possible for overactive behavior to result from an endocrine dysfunction.) Depressivelike syndromes, on the other hand, have been reported in children 3 years of age and younger. The symptoms of these syndromes vary in part as a function of age; the older a depressed child, the more closely his or her symptoms will parallel those of adults. Consequently, this discussion will focus on the symptoms of younger school-aged children (i.e., approximately ages 6 to 14).

A major distinction between depressed children and adults is that children, in contrast to adults, seldom seek help or complain about feelings of depression. Instead, they may become apathetic regarding school or socially withdrawn, sometimes preferring to remain in their rooms at home rather than playing with friends. They may make vague physical complaints about head or stomach pains, seem overly self-conscious, and cry inexplicably. Older children may see themselves as bad kids—incompetent in school and unworthy of the love of adults or the friendship of other children. Some, but not all, depressed children may simply look sad, particularly in their facial expressions, for extended periods of time with little apparent fluctuation in mood. Overall, a child will usually exhibit only some of the symptoms noted, and the symptom pattern may vary across a period of weeks.

Such symptoms are expressed in what is essentially a passive manner. Though there is far from universal agreement on the issue, certain professionals believe that in some instances children may express depression through aggressive misbehavior. While it is usually difficult to distinguish between genuine misbehavior and misbehavior that is an expression of so-called masked depression, children who are acting out as a symptom of depression often are more responsive to firm (but not overly authoritarian) limit-setting than children who are misbehaving for other reasons.

A technique that is sometimes useful in determining if a child is feeling depressed is to ask the child where he or she stands on a scale of 1 to 10, with 10 being children who are very happy, and 1 being children who are very sad. (This technique presupposes a certain level of cognitive development in the child.) On an informal level, there are several things a teacher can do for a depressed child. With children who appear apathetic and low in self-esteem, it may be useful to set lower standards for praising their accomplishments in school, or to praise them for their efforts in addition to their finished products. It is important, however, to strike a balance between setting criteria that allow an increase in praise and avoiding reinforcement of the child's symptoms. The latter may lead to the child using the symptoms as an excuse to perform at a level significantly below his or her ability level. Children may also respond to messages from the teacher that suggest that the child is an important, valued person. Overall, it is important to make sure that such interactions with the child are honest and nonpatronizing; if it is not possible to do something in this manner, it is probably better not to do it. Psychologists use a variety of objective testing methods to assess the presence, absence, and degree of depression. Objective testing is necessary for accurate diagnosis.

If a teacher feels that a child needs more assistance than the teacher has the training or experience to render, there is a wide range of professional treatments for depression, many with proven efficacy (though the majority of treatment research has focused on adults rather than children). These treatments range from medication to psychotherapy and behavior therapy. Antidepressants are often prescribed in the treatment of unipolar depression, and they tend to be quite effective. Lithium carbonate is usually prescribed for bipolar disorder in adults; it has an effect on both the depressive and manic symptoms, and is probably the treatment of choice for bipolar disorder. The exact mechanism for lithium's action is unknown. In a few instances, lithium may be used to successfully treat adult unipolar depression.

The variety of psychological and behavioral therapies used in the treatment of depression is vast. Techniques such as social skills training, modification of negative cognitions through cognitive restructuring and reality testing, and the teaching of self-control strategies (to name just a few) have been used. Treatment may occur individually or in groups and many of the therapies have been empirically tested, often with results supporting their value as treatments for depression. Cognitive-behavioral therapies have the greatest support in the scientific literature (e.g., Knell, 1998).

REFERENCES

Abramson, L. Y., Seligman, M. E. P., & Teasdale, J. D. (1978). Learned helplessness in humans: Critique and reformulation. *Journal of Abnormal Psychology, 87,* 49–74.

American Psychiatric Association. (1994). *Diagnostic and statistical manual of mental disorders* (4th ed.). Washington, DC: Author.

Beck, A. T. (1967). *Depression: Clinical, experimental, and theoretical aspects.* New York: Harper & Row.

Freud, S. (1976). Mourning and melancholia. In J. Strachey (Ed. and Trans.), *The complete psychological works.* New York: Norton. (Original work published 1917)

Keller, M., & Baker, L. (1992). The clinical course of panic disorder and depression. *Journal of Clinical Psychiatry, 53,* 5–8.

Knell, S. M. (1998). Cognitive-behavioral play therapy. *Journal of Clinical Child Psychology, 27,* 28–33.

Lewinsohn, P. M. (1974). A behavioral approach to depression. In R. J. Friedman & M. Katz (Eds.), *The psychology of depression: Contemporary theory and research.* Washington, DC: Winston-Wiley.

BAHR WEISS
University of North Carolina at Chapel Hill

CHILDHOOD NEUROSIS
CHILDHOOD PSYCHOSIS
DEPRESSION, CHILDHOOD AND ADOLESCENT
PSYCHONEUROTIC DISORDERS

AFFECTIVE EDUCATION

Affective education promotes emotional development by educating students about attitudes, thoughts, values, feelings, beliefs, and interpersonal relationships (Morse, Ardizzone, Macdonald, & Pasick, 1980). Through it, students are provided experiences in which cognitive, motor, social, and emotional elements are interrelated and balanced (Morse et al., 1980), leading to the enhancement of self-concept (what one is) and self-esteem (how one feels about what one is) and the development of social skills essential to meeting basic needs in a satisfying and socially responsible way (Wood, 1982). Affective education helps youngsters to establish value systems, morals, independence, a sense of responsibility, and self-direction (Morse et al., 1980; Wood, 1982). Although the need for affective education is not limited to students in special education programs, it is especially relevant for them because social skills are essential for success in mainstream placements.

Although most educators agree on the importance of affective education and understand its general purpose, there is less agreement among them on the specific objectives or how best to realize them. In part, this ambiguity derives from the persistent difficulty of defining such terms as self-concept, self-esteem, affect, and attitude. The general lack of systematic programming should not, however, be an indication that affective goals are unimportant (Francescani, 1982). Affective education is commonplace in regular education classrooms and is routinely addressed in teacher education programs (e.g., Woolfolk, 1995). Morse et al. (1980) have argued that affective education represents serious obligation and is an essential component of special education. Essentially, all children deserve the right to more "systematic assistance with their affective growth" (Morse et al., 1980, p. 6).

Nonetheless, affective goals are often subordinated to academic objectives, as the following example (Reinert, 1982) illustrates. Ann, age 10, was known by her teacher to display many different types of inappropriate behavior in the classroom. She talked out loud, pushed and shoved other children, would not share, and cried for no apparent reason. During evaluation, it was discovered that Ann was reading and spelling on a kindergarten level and her arithmetic skills were two years below grade level. In addition, Ann's parents were divorced and she was often absent from school because she had to babysit for her younger sister while her mother worked. She seldom came to school appropriately groomed or attired. Ann was either unwilling or unable to speak to adults or peers in a normal, conversational tone of voice; she had a poor self-concept and relatively few friends. Upon staffing, her Individual Education Plan (IEP) prescribed 60 minutes in a resource room for remedial help in arithmetic and reading skills, but no emphasis on affective problems. Although affective needs should be a part of an IEP, they are seldom systematically delineated.

Systematic instruction in the affective domain is especially important for emotionally handicapped students like Ann. Emotionally handicapped students include those who have not learned essential skills for social and emotional growth, or how to control their behavior in times of stress, how to communicate their feelings and needs in a socially acceptable manner, how to bring interpersonal problems to a satisfying solution, or how to encounter others without conflict (Francescani, 1982). It is difficult to imagine how a student with deficits as pervasive as these can survive in an environment for which he or she is so poorly equipped. Yet it is in the highly socialized classroom world in which affective education must occur, and most proponents recognize the need to integrate affective learning into everyday classroom life.

Integrated affective learning lies at one end of the intrinsic/extrinsic dimension of affective education. Morse et al. (1980) defined this dimension as the extent "to which (affective education) grows naturally out of what is going on in the educational life space versus how much is added as a special function" (p. 16). Ideally, affective lessons should derive naturally from school activities, using materials already in the curriculum in harmony with the philosophy of the program (Morse et al., 1980; Schlindler, 1982). Teachers should capitalize on naturally occurring opportunities spending time motivating the uninvolved student, resolving peer conflicts, encouraging a reluctant student to join in group activity, or trying to enliven a depressed student. A teacher should not rely on an added-on or extrinsic curriculum to accomplish affective goals.

Affective educators stress the need for developing empathetic relationships between teachers and students in order to convey fundamental human relationships where the "sense of relationship dominates authoritarianism" (Morse et al., 1980, p. 15). Teachers and students share responsibilities, goals, and rules for living together (Morse et al., 1980; Reinert, 1982; Sarason, 1971).

However, to expect all teachers to act at all times with the spontaneity, sensitivity, and astuteness that the ideal intrinsic approach requires is unrealistic. This expectation belies the human limitations of teachers and assumes a degree of training rare if not unknown in teacher preparation programs. Approximations to this intrinsic ideal may be found in curricular approaches to affective education and in strategies such as role playing and socio-drama (Wood, 1982) that allow for the exploration of new solutions to familiar problems.

Among the most popular and widely used curricula is DUSO (Developing Understanding of Self and Others). It is designed to be used by teachers or counselors as an add-on to the academic curriculum. Throughout the school year, eight themes (e.g., Developing Self-Concept, Understanding Peers) are explored through listening, modeling, discussion, and role-playing activities. Everyday problems of classroom life are described through pictures, stories, and puppetry, and solutions are discussed, modeled, and role played. The elements of the lessons are carefully prescribed and the materials are attractive and engaging to a primary-aged audience. Although the curriculum is extrinsic, it does provide a structure through which problems may be simulated and the values of alternative solutions weighed.

Only one of many such curricula, DUSO is singled out here for illustration only. Suffice it to say that they are diverse in objectives, activities, and the sophistication of their intended audiences. It is difficult to compare extrinsic programs because the materials themselves provide content and continuity in their individual components (Reinert, 1982). Most seek to enhance self-concept, encourage positive socialization, recognize and understand basic feelings, and model appropriate responses to given situations through practice and role playing. Few have substantial data bases.

Affective education has grown out of the school mental health movement, but has not yet evolved into a well-formulated program intrinsic to the ongoing school process (Morse, 1980). Instead it tends to be relegated to the periphery of the basic curriculum. If affective education is to realize its potential, deliberate efforts must replace the haphazard, casual, and indirect approaches currently in operation.

REFERENCES

Francescani, C. (1982). M A R C: An affective curriculum for emotionally disturbed adolescents. *Teaching Exceptional Children, 14,* 217–222.

Morse, W. C., Ardizzone, J., Macdonald, C., & Pasick, P. (1980). *Affective education for special children and youth.* Reston, VA: Council for Exceptional Children.

Reinert, H. R. (1980). *Children in conflict* (2nd ed.). St. Louis, MO: Mosby.

Reinert, H. R. (1982). The development of affective skills. In T. L. Miller & E. E. Davis (Eds.), *The mildly handicapped student* (pp. 421–451). New York: Grune & Stratton.

Sarason, S. B. (1971). *The culture of schools and the problem of change.* Boston: Allyn & Bacon.

Schlindler, P. J. (1982). Affective growth in the preschool years. *Teaching Exceptional Children, 14,* 226–232.

Wood, F. H. (1982). Affective education and social skills training. *Teaching Exceptional Children, 14,* 212–216.

Woolfolk, A. E. (1995). *Educational Psychology* (6th ed.). Boston: Allyn & Bacon.

LOUISE H. WERTH
PAUL T. SINDELAR
Florida State University

BEHAVIORAL DEFICIT
SELF-CONCEPT

AFRICA: EAST AND SOUTHERN, SPECIAL EDUCATION IN

A brief history, statements on current status, and the future prospects of special education in twelve East and Southern African countries are presented here. The countries discussed include Botswana, Ethiopia, Eriteria, Kenya, Lesotho, Malawi, Namibia, Swaziland, Tanzania, Uganda, Zambia, and Zimbabwe. The availability of information on the aforementioned topics and between these countries differs widely. Thus, some countries are discussed in greater detail (Tanzania, Uganda, and Zimbabwe) than others (Eriteria, Malawi, and Swaziland).

Incidence of Handicapping Conditions within This Region

Reliable data on the incidence of childhood disorders within this region are unavailable. Various problems associated with incidence surveys preclude obtaining accurate data.

Parents may need to register their disabled children in special centers, and they often are reluctant to admit their children display handicapping conditions (Kisanji, 1997; Whyte & Ingstad, 1995). Also, community attitudes toward the handicapped often are negative (Devlieger, 1995; Jackson & Mupedziswa, 1989). These and other qualities are believed to contribute to grossly underestimated incidence figures for handicapping conditions.

This large region in East and Southern Africa is home to an estimated 59,800,000 children. Population details for children ages 5 to 16 years for the year 1996 are provided below (UNICEF, 1996):

Botswana	700,000
Ethiopia	15,600,000
Eritrea	1,600,000
Kenya	12,100,000
Lesotho	600,000
Malawi	3,200,000
Namibia	700,000
Tanzania	8,700,000
Uganda	10,500,000
Zambia	2,900,000
Zimbabwe	3,200,000

If we accept the World Health Organization's general incidence estimate that 10 percent of a country's population is likely to be handicapped, almost six million children in this region can be expected to have one or more handicapping conditions. We believe this estimate substantially underestimates the number of handicapped children, given the region's sub-standard medical, health, and early childhood education facilities. Among children with handicaps, less than 1 percent attend formal school (Kann, Mapolelo, & Nleya, 1989; Tungaraza, 1994).

General History of Educational Services for Handicapped Children

The availability of special education services and other resources for children with physical, sensory, and cognitive disabilities occurred recently. Historically, native African societies integrated learning and other developmental activities within their everyday home and community activities (Kisanji, 1997). Home- and community-based activities provide various advantages: a favorable ratio between the young and elders, accommodations to match the child's developmental levels, and utilization of the child's natural milieu within which to promote development and transfer of training. The extent to which homes and communities provide appropriate adaptations to accommodate children with disabilities is unknown. The beneficial effects that professional services can have on children with disabilities are well-established.

The introduction and evolution of professional services for these children in East and Southern Africa closely follows a pattern found in other developing areas: first, national or regional institutions, often residential in nature and initiated by religious, humanitarian, and philanthropic agencies, are established. Professional services for middle-class children then develop in metropolitan centers. The widespread provision of services to children with disabilities in public schools occurs only after general education services, at least through the elementary level, are well-developed and nationally available. Children with handicapping conditions who reside in rural areas are least likely to receive professional services. Stronger special education services generally are found in countries with stronger and well-established regular education programs (Saigh & Oakland, 1989).

The majority of countries in this region have inadequate basic education programs (UNICEF, 1991, 1994), lack formal special education policies, and experience school dropout rates in the range of 15 percent to 60 percent involving disadvantaged children, which includes those with disabilities (Kann et al., 1989; Stubbs, 1997; UNICEF, 1994).

The Role of Missionaries

Christian missionaries, often from Western Europe, initiated and provided almost all formal education within African communities during the colonial period. The development of special education services in this region is closely associated with their work. Trends in the development of special education facilities within individual countries generally followed a consistent pattern: Services were provided first for those with visual handicaps, and then for those with auditory, physical, and mental handicaps. This trend probably reflected the missionaries' beliefs as to the resources (like teaching expertise and materials) needed to serve each of these groups, as well as the family's willingness to admit one or more members have a disability. Because of their normal hearing ability, persons with visual impairments may have been thought to respond more favorably to the use of conventional instructional methods.

In Botswana, German missionaries opened special schools for the visually handicapped at Linchwe (in Mochudi) and the hearing impaired at Ramotswa (in Ramotswa) in the 1950s. A German couple opened residential centers named Rankoromane based on the Waldorf School model to educate children with mental handicaps in a number of towns in the late 1960s (Ingstad, 1995).

In Ethiopia, the Christofeblinden Mission opened a school for the blind and a training program for teachers of the visually handicapped in the early 1950s. Finnish missionaries were involved in developing Ethiopia's special education programs, and they opened a school for the deaf at Keren in the 1950s. The Church of Christ established the Mekanissa School for the Deaf in 1964. The Baptist Mission created the Alpha School for the Deaf in Addis Ababa in 1967. The Ethiopian Evangelical Mekaneyesus Church started the Hossana School for the Deaf in 1981.

In Eriteria, French Catholic, Swedish Lutheran, and Italian Catholic churches provided school education to the natives since 1890 (Miran, 1998). The role of these organizations in founding schools for persons with disabilities could not be established. Eriteria, now an independent nation, was once a province of Ethiopia.

The first school in Kenya for the visually impaired, the Thika School, was opened by the Salvation Army in 1946 (Kristensen, 1987). Kenya's first full-time program to prepare teachers of students with visual handicaps and a school for deaf-blind children were founded by the Christofeblinden Mission in the 1980s.

In Malawi, education for the blind was started during the early 1940s when two primary residential special schools were established by missionaries at Kasungu and Lulwe. The Catholic Order of the Immaculate Conception (of the Netherlands) developed a program in 1964 that integrated students with and without visual impairments into regular classrooms within ordinary schools; resource rooms provided supportive services to the visually impaired. Fourteen resource rooms serving about 100 blind students were in operation by 1983 (Ross, 1988). The program at Montfort College, organized by the Catholic teaching brothers of the Order of the Immaculate Conception, prepared teachers for students with auditory and visual impairments for Malawi and some neighboring countries (namely, Lesotho, Swaziland, Tanzania, Zimbabwe, and Zambia) in the 1970s.

Tanzania established its first special education facility in 1950 when the Anglican Church opened a school for the blind, the Buigiri School. Two additional schools for the blind followed this school, one opened by the Swedish Free Mission, the Furaha, in 1962, and another by the Lutheran Church, the Irente School, in Lushoto in 1963. The first Tanzanian school for the hearing impaired, the Tabora Deaf-Mute Institute, was opened by the Roman Catholic Church in 1963. The Salvation Army opened the first school in Tanzania for the physically handicapped in 1967.

In Zambia, missionaries again pioneered special education services in the region (Csapo, 1987a). The Dutch Reformed Church established the first school for the deaf (Sichula, 1990) and one for the blind (Csapo, 1987a) at Magwero Mission in 1955. The Christian Mission of Zambia opened another school for the blind at Mambiling soon after. Other special schools were opened by missionaries and continue to exist today.

In Zimbabwe, the Dutch Reformed Church opened the Margaret Hugo School for The Blind, at Masvingo in 1927 (Peresuh, Adenigba, & Ogonda, 1997). Two schools for the hearing impaired opened in 1947, one in Loreto and another in Pamushana, founded by the Catholic Dominican Sisters and the Dutch Reformed Church respectively (Chimedza, 1994).

Information on missionary work and the opening of special education facilities in Lesotho, Namibia, Swaziland, and Uganda could not be located. However, the Dutch Reformed Church appears to have been involved in Namibia, and the Roman Catholic Church and Church of Uganda may have been involved in Uganda. Margaret Brown of the Church Missionary Society initiated Uganda's in-service teacher education for children with hearing impairment in 1962. Although Islam has a substantial following in some East African countries (namely, Tanzania, Uganda, Kenya, and Ethiopia), its role in establishing special education facilities in these countries could not be ascertained.

The Role of International Nongovernmental Organizations and Local Organizations

International nongovernmental organizations and local organizations advocating on behalf of students with disabilities also have had strong roles in developing and providing special education services. Their importance exceeds that of the colonial governments. The Danish International Development Agency (DANIDA), UNESCO Sub-Regional Project for Special Education in Eastern and Southern Africa, Swedish International Development Agency (SIDA), Royal Commonwealth Society for the Blind (now called the Sight Savers), International League for Persons with Mental Handicaps, and the British Red Cross are among the international agencies that have played significant roles in establishing special education programs in East and Southern Africa. DANIDA has been actively involved in promoting special education advising in Kenya, Uganda, and Zimbabwe for at least the past decade. SIDA has been involved in developing special education programs in all twelve Eastern and Southern African countries which comprise the focus of this paper. It helped establish Braille printing presses in Tanzania in 1971 (Tungaraza, 1994) and in Zimbabwe in 1994. In the early 1960s the Royal Commonwealth Society for the Blind started a rehabilitation center at Salama (in Uganda) for adults with visual impairments (Onen & Njuki, 1998).

Information on the involvement of local organizations in founding special education facilities in the East and Southern African countries is quite sparse. The Botswana Red Cross, with support from the Norwegian Red Cross, established a vocational training center for persons with physical disabilities in 1981. The Botswana Council for the Disabled has been unable to implement programs that enable children with disabilities to attend school (Ingstad, 1995). In Ethiopia, the Haile Selassie One Foundation established two special schools for blind students. They became government schools in the 1980s.

In Kenya, local voluntary organizations established two special schools for the mentally handicapped at St. Nicholas and Aga Khan in the late 1950s. These schools amalgamated in 1968 to form the Jacaranda School (Ross, 1988). The Kenya Society for the Mentally Handicapped and The Parents and Friends of Handicapped Children were formed by parents of children with disabilities to promote the education of persons with disabilities, improve the preparation for teachers of children with disabilities, and consolidate schools. The Tanzania Society for the Deaf established the first school for the hearing impaired at Buguruni in 1974. In 1955, the first school for children with visual impairment and blindness was started at Madera in Eastern Uganda by the joint effort of the then-local education committee (Teso education committee), the Ministry of Education, and Uganda Foundation for the Blind. The Uganda government later asked the Catholic Church to administer the school.

With the assistance of the Uganda Society for the Deaf, Sherali Bendali Jafer, Peter Ronald, and Mr. Semmpebwa were closely involved in developing awareness throughout Uganda of the need to educate children with hearing impairment (Onen & Njuki, 1998). As a result of their efforts, an integration unit for children with hearing impairment was started at Mengo Primary School. Subsequently, the Uganda School for the Deaf was started on Namirembe Hill in 1968. The following year, Ngora School for the Deaf was established.

Ugandan educational services for children with physical disabilities and mental handicaps both began in 1968, and both were largely the results of efforts of local self-help organizations. For instance, the Uganda Spastic Society was formed in 1968. Its membership consisted mainly of parents of children with spastic conditions and polio, and medical professionals. The society played a key role in the establishment of a school for the physically handicapped at Mengo (Onen & Njuki, 1998). Services for children with mental disabilities were available through the Uganda Association for Mental Health (UAMH). This association, established in 1968 by the Ministry of Health, had a short life due to the political turmoil in the country at the time and in subsequent years. In 1983, the Uganda Association for the Mentally Handicapped was founded, and it has been instrumental in the founding of many resource units for children with mental handicaps.

In Zimbabwe, the Jairos Jiri Association founded the Narran Center School for the Deaf and the Blind in Gweru in 1968, a school for the visually impaired at Kadoma in 1981, and a number of other schools for children with various physical, mental, and multiple handicaps at Bulawayo, Gweru, and Harare in the 1970s (Farquar, 1987). Zimbabwe's Council for the Blind has been involved in providing structural facilities and equipment to school-based integration units for children with visual disabilities since about 1980. Its Zimcare Trust has been actively involved in providing education for Zimbabwean children with mental handicaps since the 1980s.

Zambia's Council for the Handicapped has conferred with teachers and the Zambian government to promote effective ways of teaching children with disabilities since the 1970s. However, its role in the establishment of special education facilities in that country is unclear.

Information on the involvement of international non-governmental agencies and local organizations advocating for those with disabilities and the establishment of special education facilities in Eriteria, Malawi, Namibia, and Swaziland could not be located.

The Role of Postcolonial Governments

Support for the development of special education by the postcolonial governments in each of the twelve East and Southern African countries differs widely. Support is strongest when elementary and secondary education is widely available and a commitment to the principle of universal education is widely held. Countries recently ravaged by civil war (Uganda, Eriteria, Ethiopia) currently are attempting to re-establish basic elementary and secondary education programs. Their programs in special education are in initial stages of development and support. In contrast, countries that have enjoyed relative political stability (Kenya, Tanzania, Zimbabwe) tend to have stronger regular education programs, as well as a longer history and stronger support for special education programs.

Although Botswana's National Development Plans (1973–1978; 1991–1997) identify the needs of disabled persons as a national priority (Ingstad, 1995), the government historically has viewed educational support to children with disabilities as a family responsibility rather than a state obligation (Ingstad, 1995; Kann et al., 1989). Children with disabilities are conspicuous in their absence from Botswana schools (Kann et al., 1989). Nonetheless, a special education unit was established within the Botswana Ministry of Education in 1984 with the support of SIDA. The University of Botswana has complemented government efforts by offering a two-year diploma course for specialist teachers for children with mental, visual, hearing, and learning handicaps, and is expected to launch a bachelor's degree in special education in August, 1998 (C. Abosi, pers. comm., February 2, 1998).

The Kenya government, through the Kenya Institute of Education, launched special needs teacher education programs at Jacaranda and Highridge Teachers Colleges in 1966–67 (Peresuh et al., 1997). The Kenya Institute of Special Education (KISE), founded by the Kenyan government with the assistance of DANIDA, has assumed responsibility for these programs. More than one thousand teachers have graduated from the KISE teacher education programs since 1987. KISE also is responsible for the educational placement of children with disabilities, community education, and teacher in-service education programs on disabilities.

Lesotho's government became involved in special education in 1987 when its Ministry of Education, with the financial support from the United States Agency for International Development (USAID), commissioned a comprehensive study of its special education programs and accompanying guidelines for its development (Csapo, 1987b). The report recommended the infusion of special needs components to both pre- and in-service teacher preparation programs, adoption of an integration (resource room) model for educating children with special needs, and full community involvement in establishing and supporting special education facilities. The Lesotho Ministry of Education, Lesotho National Federation of Disabled People, Ministry of Social Welfare and Health, and Save the Children Fund (UK) created ten integration units. A special education unit was established in the Lesotho Ministry of Education in 1991 to coordinate the opening of integration units. The Lesotho National Teacher Training College assumed responsibility for introducing special education components in its pre-service programs in 1996, and the abovementioned special education unit within the Ministry of Education assumed responsibility for in-service education programs for teachers (Pholoho, Mariga, Phachaka, & Stubbs, 1995).

Namibia became politically independent in 1990 after a legacy of colonial rule under apartheid from South Africa, which left most of its Blacks with little or no education. Thus, the history of educating children with disabilities in Namibia is recent and short. According to Bruhns et al. (1995), Namibia established its first school for children with disabilities, the Dagbreek Special School, in 1970 as a racially segregated facility for White children. The school opened its doors to disabled students of other races after Namibia become independent. The Eluwa School for blind and deaf students was established at Ongwediva in 1973 with 20 deaf and 20 blind students. By 1995 the school enrolled 172 deaf, 70 blind, and eight physically disabled students. The Moreson School for children with severe learning difficulties was established by the Association of the Handicapped in 1976 and became a government school in 1990. It had 60 students along with seven teachers in 1995.

The Tanzania government, with the help of the Royal Commonwealth Society for the Blind, established the country's first integrated education program for children with visual handicaps, Uhuru Co-education School, in 1966, followed by a similar program for children with mental handicaps in 1982 (Tungaraza, 1994). The government also established a diploma-level teacher education program in 1976 and one for teachers of pupils with mental handicaps in 1983 at the Tabora Teacher Training College. In addition, the Mpwapwa Teacher Training College prepares teachers to work with students with visual handicaps. The number of special needs teachers who have graduated from the two Tanzania colleges could not be established.

Uganda's government involvement in special education came earlier than others in the region because of the lobbying efforts of Sr. Andrew Cohen, then-Governor of Uganda, to educate a blind relative (Atim, 1995). Government support to educate the blind was established through an act of Parliament in 1952. The first trial to integrate children with visual impairment was launched in 1962 at Wanyange Girls School in Eastern Uganda. In July 1973, a department of special education was established at the Uganda Ministry of Education headquarters in Kampala. This department was created to coordinate special education services in the Ministry and to work with other governmental and nongovernmental organizations providing services for persons with disabilities. The head start Uganda enjoyed in developing its special education programs was severely thwarted during two decades of dictatorships and civil war. Special education programs in Uganda began to rebuild after 1991.

The Ugandan government, with the help of DANIDA, founded the Uganda National Institute of Special Education (UNISE) in 1991 and gave it the responsibility for coordinating the country's special education programs and teacher education programs at certificate, diploma, and degree levels. So far, about 255 teachers have received specialist training and attended awareness seminars, which are offered to ordinary primary school teachers in the districts throughout the country. The Special Education/Educational Assessment and Resource Services of Uganda (EARS-U) was formed in 1992. EARS-U, a division within the Uganda Ministry of Education, is responsible for evaluating programs for children with hearing, speech, learning, visual, mental, and physical impairments. EARS-U also is responsible for coordinating educational placements of children with disabilities, counseling services to their parents, community education, and prevention programs.

The Zimbabwe government, with the assistance of SIDA, established a Department of Special Education within the Ministry of Education in 1982, with its primary responsibility being educational placement of children with disabilities, pre-service and in-service training of teachers on special educational needs, and community education programs on disabilities. A teacher education program for teachers of children with visual, mental, hearing, and speech and language impairments was established by the government at the United College of Education in Bulawayo in 1983. About 300 special needs teachers graduated from the United College of Education since the establishment of its special education teacher education program. A two-year, post-diploma bachelor's degree in special education was launched at the University of Zimbabwe in 1993 and has graduated about 75 teachers of special needs children. The Zimbabwe Ministry of Education also has issued a number of documents to guide special education programs in the schools (Mpofu & Nyanungo, 1998).

Government involvement in special needs programs in Zambia, Ethiopia, Eriteria, Malawi, and Swaziland could not be ascertained. However, respondents to a recent survey of special needs experts in these countries suggested that special education facilities in these countries are quite limited (Mpofu, Zindi, Oakland, & Peresuh, 1997).

Current Status of Special Education in East and Southern Africa

Special education services in East and Southern Africa generally follow a functional integration (resource room) model in which children with disabilities attend class part-time to full-time with their non-disabled peers and receive support of a full-time specialist teacher (Charema & Peresuh, 1997). Specialist teachers maintain the resource room, provide intensive individualized instruction to children with disabilities, and work closely with mainstream teachers in planning and effecting integration strategies for children with disabilities. A functional integration model generally is preferred for children with mild to moderate sensory, physical, and cognitive handicaps. Children with more severe handicaps generally attend special schools and rehabilitation centers, typically those residential in nature, which provide more specialized resources. With few exceptions, most integration units for the visually handicapped and hearing impaired are residential, whereas those for children with moderate to mild physical and cognitive handicaps are nonresidential.

Compared to current needs and potential demand, special education facilities in the twelve East and Southern countries of this survey are severely limited. Botswana has approximately 20 special schools and resource units for children with visual, auditory, mental, and physical handicaps (C. Abosi, pers. comm., February 2, 1998). Current enrollment figures by handicapping condition were unavailable. However, previous enrollment was vision (35 students), hearing (88), mental (176), and physical (18) (Kann et al., 1989). There are no facilities in the country for children with severe disabilities.

Lesotho has twelve special schools (Stubbs, 1997). Enrollment figures by handicapping condition were unavailable. Lesotho's Ministry of Education, with support from international nongovernmental organizations and United Nations agencies, recently opened integration units for children with a variety of handicaps in eight of the country's ten districts.

Namibia's school for children with visual impairments has 71 students and its school for the hearing impaired has 185 students (Bruhns et al., 1995). Twenty-four specialist teachers work in these schools. Two schools and 15 specialist teachers serve 125 children with severe learning disabilities. Two additional schools staffed by 67 teachers provide instruction to 733 children with mild learning difficulties. Twelve schools and 16 teachers offer remedial education to 385 children with specific learning disabilities. Namibia also has 28 integration units attended by 507 children with moderate to mild disabilities and taught by 40 teachers.

In Tanzania, services for students with visual impairments are provided in twelve special schools and 23 integrated (18 primary, 5 secondary) schools that offer education to 979 children with visual disabilities (Possi & Mkaali, 1995; Tungaraza, 1994). Sixty-four specialist teachers and 157 regular education teachers provide education to children with visual handicaps. Services for children with auditory impairments are provided through 14 special schools and three integrated primary (one residential and two nonresidential) schools to approximately 980 pupils and staffed by 100 specialist and 26 regular class teachers. In addition, 6 schools serve 305 deaf-blind students. About 930 children

with physical disabilities attend 61 specialist and integration units staffed by 185 specialist and regular class teachers. The vast majority of children with physical disabilities either attend schools in their communities or do not attend school at all. Tanzania also has four residential special schools for children with moderate mental handicaps and 15 nonresidential integrated units that serve 980 children with moderate to mild mental handicaps. Sixty-seven specialist and 128 regular class teachers teach these children. Twelve children with autism and 14 with cerebral palsy attend four units taught by 6 specialist teachers. Thousands of children with severe mental handicaps do not receive any schooling. In contrast, more than 90 percent of Tanzanian children with epileptic conditions attend ordinary schools (Whyte, 1995).

Uganda has at least 6 special schools and one integration unit which serve about 500 children with visual impairments, two special schools for 150 children with hearing impairments, and one special school for 124 students with physical handicaps (Ross, 1988). An estimated 32,134 children with mild to moderate disabilities are attending ordinary schools (Onei & Njuki, 1998). The Ugandan government's goal was to have the country's estimated 325,000 children with disabilities attend school in 1997 (Kristensen, 1997; Uganda Ministry of Education, 1992). However, the country lacked the resources for meeting this highly ambitious target then, and it still does today (Mpofu et al., 1997).

Zimbabwe's twenty special schools provide educational and rehabilitation services to 5,000 children with visual, hearing, physical, and mental disabilities. The country also has 162 integrated resource units: 69 for those with hearing disabilities, 46 with mental disabilities, and 47 with visual disabilities. A total of 1,315 children with disabilities are served by the integrated resource units: 552 with hearing impairments, 409 with mental impairments, and 354 with visual impairments. Additionally, about 4,300 children with moderate to mild generalized learning difficulties attend 270 part-time special classes in regular education settings. At least 50,000 children with learning difficulties receive part-time remedial education in classes or clinics in general education schools.

The current status of special education programs in Swaziland, Eriteria, Kenya, and Zambia is unknown. However, information from respondents to a survey on school psychology practices in these countries (Mpofu et al., 1997) suggests special education programs may be better established in Kenya than in other East and Southern African countries. Such programs generally are limited to urban areas in Zambia, and may not exist to any significant degree in Swaziland and Eriteria.

Although the need for more special education facilities in all of the East and Southern African countries is quite apparent, a paradox exists in that attendance is below capacity in many existing special education schools and units in some countries, including Tanzania and Lesotho (Kisanji, 1995; Stubbs, 1997). This under-utilization exists because the facilities are not well-known to parents of children with disabilities and parents in some rural communities are suspicious of their intended purposes. In addition, government departments and international aid agencies often established special education schools and units in certain communities in response to requests by local politicians or parochial interest groups, but without adequate consultation with traditional and other community leaders. Thus, resistance to utilizing these facilities often occurs regardless of their need.

Some countries in this region have mounted comprehensive community outreach programs aimed at educating citizens on the nature of disabilities, their prevention, and appropriate educational interventions. In addition, teachers have walked from village to village to locate children with disabilities to attend school (Kisanji, 1995). The teachers' door-to-door, village-to-village approach can effectively reach families and significant community leaders, and it often yielded larger enrollments of children with disabilities in areas that seem to have few if any such children.

Future Prospects of Special Education in East and Southern Africa

Nearly all countries in East and Southern Africa provide some forms of special education programs. The work of Christian missionaries and nongovernmental agencies often resulted in the establishment of special education programs. The continued involvement of missionaries, although desired, is unlikely to match prior levels of involvement. Nongovernmental agencies increasingly are recognized by international agencies (like the United Nations and the World Bank) as effective implementers of needed social programs. Although their involvement is likely to continue for some years, their resources also are limited in time. Thus, special education programs in this large and important region must depend more heavily, if not exclusively, on local and regional resolve and resources.

A government's involvement in special education programs and teacher preparation programs (through policies enacted and funded by its legislature and implemented by its ministries of education) provides demonstrable evidence that they support special education as an essential component of its national education program. Although the degree to which federal governments are involved in special education programs differs among the twelve countries within this region, all are involved to some degree. However, beneficial policies often are enacted and either not funded or not implemented by ministries of education. For example, the governments of Uganda and Botswana both established policy underscoring the importance of school attendance among children with disabilities as a national priority. However, this policy remains to be implemented.

The adoption of the principle of universal primary education by these governments implicitly recognizes children with disabilities as having the right to education. This, and other positive trends in educational thinking, eventually can be expected to translate into more favorable policies and practices governing special education programs. Moreover, most governments continue to support the further development of their elementary and secondary regular education programs—conditions prerequisite to the strong support of special education programs. Thus, prospects for the continued growth and availability of special education programs in these countries are somewhat encouraging.

However, one should not underestimate impediments to the further development of sustainable special education programs in East and Southern Africa. These impediments include inadequate personnel and financial resources for the provision of basic and regular education and inadequate leadership from advocacy groups.

Given other pressing responsibilities, federal governments in this region are unlikely to prioritize special education programs without some form of external support. Uncertainty exists as to the willingness and commitment of some governments to fund special education programs at current or higher levels than that currently provided by international development agencies (like DANIDA and SIDA).

The sustainability of donor-supported special education programs in East and Southern Africa will depend on the extent to which donor agencies build into their aid packages policies and practices that cultivate a cadre of local personnel willing to lobby for future programs, to implement genuine partnerships with federal and regional government to establish and maintain special education programs, to employ phased donor-funding withdrawal, and to help developing vibrant self-advocacy organizations at the local and national levels. For example, the Swedish Federation for the Blind has financed an advisory project in Eastern Africa aimed at improving the organization and self-advocacy of persons with disabilities (Ross, 1988).

Greater involvement of parents and community members in founding special education schools and integration units would strengthen a sense of ownership for special education facilities in communities, leading to greater attendance and school retention. In addition, the importance of community education programs on disabilities to the future of special education programs in East and Southern Africa cannot be over-emphasized. Most parents of children with disabilities are not involved with any special interest groups or agencies providing special education services (Kisanji, 1995; Ross, 1988).

The significantly limited material and manpower resources within most of these countries constrain the establishment and growth of special education programs (Ross, 1988; Tungaraza, 1994). Most countries are grappling with the provision of basic education and health facilities. The countries have very few personnel specifically prepared to work with children with disabilities in either special or mainstream school settings. The future of special education programs in the region could be considerably enhanced if countries pooled resources to promote professional preparation and research on effective methods to promote basic education of students in special education.

REFERENCES

Atim, S. (1995). *Special education in Uganda.* Paper presented at the South-South-North Workshop. Kampala, Uganda.

Bruhns, B., Murray, A., Kanguchi, T., & Nuukuawo, A. (1995). *Disability and rehabilitation in Namibia: A national survey.* Windhoek: The Namibian Economic Policy Research Unit.

Farquhar, J. (1987). *Jairos Jiri–the man and his works.* Gweru, Zimbabwe: Mambo.

Charema, J., & Peresuh, M. (1997). Support services for special needs educational needs: Proposed models for countries south of the Sahara. *African Journal of Special Needs Education, 1,* 76–83.

Chimedza, R. (1994). Bilingualism in the education of the hearing impaired in Zimbabwe: Is this the answer? *Zimbabwe Bulletin of Teacher Education, 4,* 1–11.

Csapo, M. (1987a). *Perspectives in education and special education in southern Africa.* Vancouver, British Columbia, Canada: Center for Human Development and Research.

Csapo, M. (1987b). *Basic, practical, cost-effective education for children with disabilities in Lesotho.* Vancouver, British Columbia, Canada: University of British Columbia.

Devlieger, P. (1995). Why disabled? The cultural understanding of physical disability in an African society. In B. Ingstad & S. R. Whyte (Eds.), *Disability and culture* (pp. 94–106). Berkeley: University of California Press.

Ingstad, B. (1995). Public discourses on rehabilitation: From Norway to Botswana. In B. Ingstad & S. R. Whyte (Eds.), *Disability and culture* (pp. 174–195). Berkeley: University of California Press.

Jackson, H., & Mupedziswa, R. (1989). Disability and rehabilitation: Beliefs and attitudes among rural disabled people in a community based rehabilitation scheme in Zimbabwe. *Journal of Social Development in Africa, 1,* 21–30.

Kann, U., Mapolelo, D., & Nleya, P. (1989). *The missing children: Achieving basic education in Botswana.* Gaborone: NIR, University of Botswana.

Kisanji, J. (1995). Interface between culture and disability in the Tanzania context: Part 1. *International Journal of Disability, Development and Education, 42,* 93–108.

Kisanji, J. (1997). The relevance of indigenous customary education principles in the education of special needs education policy. *African Journal of Special Needs Education, 1,* 59–74.

Kristensen, K. (1997). School for all: A challenge to special needs education in Uganda—A brief country report. *African Journal of Special Needs Education, 2,* 25–28.

Miran, J. (1998). *Missionaries, education and the state in the Italian colony of Eriteria 1980–1936.* Paper presented at the Third Annual Midwest Graduate Student Conference in African Studies. University of Wisconsin-Madison, February 27–March 1.

Mpofu, E., & Nyanungo, K. R. (1998). Educational and psychological testing in Zimbabwean schools: Past, present and future. *European Journal of Psychological Assessment.*

Mpofu, E., Zindi, F., Oakland, T., & Peresuh, M. (1997). School psychological practices in East and Southern Africa. *Journal of Special Education, 31,* 387–402.

Murray, J. L., & Lopez, A. D. (1996). *Global health statistics: A compendium of incidence, prevalence and mortality estimates for over 200 conditions.* Cambridge, MA: Harvard University Press.

Onen, N., & Njuki, E. P. (1998). *Special education in Uganda.* Unpublished manuscript.

Peresuh, M., Adenigba, S. A., & Ogonda, G. (1987). Perspectives on special needs education in Nigeria, Kenya, and Zimbabwe. *African Journal of Special Needs Education, 2,* 9–15.

Pholoho, K., Mariga, L., Phachaka, L., & Stubbs, S. (1995). Schools for all: National planning in Lesotho. In B. O'Tootle & R. McConkey (Eds.), *Innovations in developing countries for people with disabilities.* Lancashire, England: Lisieux Hall Publications.

Possi, M. K., & Mkaali, C. B. (1995). *A brief report on special education services in Tanzania.* Paper presented at the South-South-North Workshop. Kampala, Uganda.

Ross, D. H. (1988). *Educating handicapped young people in Eastern and Southern Africa.* Paris: UNESCO.

Saigh, P. A., & Oakland, T. (Eds.). (1989). *International perspectives on school psychology.* Hillsdale, NJ: Erlbaum.

Sichula, B. (1990). *East African sign language report.* Helsinki, Finland: Finnish Association of the Deaf.

Stubbs, S. (1997). Lesotho integrated education programme. *African Journal of Special Needs Education, 1,* 84–87.

Tungaraza, F. D. (1994). The development and history of special education in Tanzania. *International Journal of Disability, Development, and Education, 41,* 213–222.

Uganda Ministry of Education. (1992). *Government white paper on the education policy review commission report.* Kampala, Uganda: Author.

UNICEF. (1991). *Children and women in Zimbabwe: A situation analysis update, July 1985–July 1990.* Republic of Zimbabwe: Author.

UNICEF. (1994). *The state of the world's children: 1994.* Oxford, England: Oxford University Press.

UNICEF. (1996). *The state of the world's children: 1996.* Oxford, England: Oxford University Press.

Whyte, S. R. (1995). Constructing epilepsy: Images and contexts in East Africa. In B. Ingstad & S. R. Whyte (Eds.), *Disability and culture* (pp. 226–245). Berkeley: University of California Press.

Whyte, S., & Ingstad, B. (1995). Disability and culture: An overview. In S. Whyte & B. Ingstad (Eds.), *Disability and culture* (pp. 3–22). Berkeley: University of California Press.

ELIAS MPOFU
Pennsylvania State University

THOMAS OAKLAND
University of Florida

ROBERT CHIMEDZA
University of Zimbabwe

AFRICA, SPECIAL EDUCATION IN

Special education is relatively new in most African countries. The need for a major commitment to special education by African countries to provide handicapped learners with a variety of programs and services has been recognized for some time now (Anderson, 1983; Joy, 1979; Shown, 1980; UNESCO, 1979, 1986), though progress toward realization has been slow and halting. The UNESCO definition of special education is one that generally adheres to western European and American expectations. Thus the Nigerian National Policy on Education (1981) has defined special education as "education of children and adults who have learning difficulties as a result of not coping with the normal school organization and methods" (Nigerian Year Book, 1984). In Nigeria's Plateau State (Nigeria), special education is defined as including "the course and content of education, including specially defined classroom, material, and equipment designed to meet the unique needs of a handicapped child" (Shown, 1986).

Despite such broad perspectives, special education in Africa is more likely to be concerned with children who are physically and sensorially handicapped rather than suffering from mild cognitive deficits. Children with more severe cognitive deficits are likely to be cared for in other contexts than those of formal special education. Expressing this fact, Shown observes: "To acquire education in the modern sense one must possess and make full use of all his senses. This is beside being fully mobile" (Shown, 1980). Sambo (1981) has pointed out "when one loses two or more of these senses, then the acquisition of education in the normal sense becomes a problem entirely different from those problems normally encountered in the acquisition of education. For such a person, there is a need for a viable alternative for educating him."

Anderson (1973) observed that the majority of African teachers were not familiar with the special techniques and methods required to assist handicapped students to become educationally competent. Furthermore, as Shown (1986) has pointed out, a lack of clear educational objectives has hampered the delivery of educational services to handicapped learners.

Because most African nations have faced major fiscal difficulties for many years, improvements in special education have been difficult to achieve. Nations like Nigeria have, however, made serious efforts at both federal and local levels to teach the elements of special education in teacher training institutions (Nigeria Federal Ministry, 1977). Nigeria has established training programs at the universities of Jos and Ibadan. These universities provide training and research on scientific education of the handicapped at undergraduate and graduate levels.

In most places in Africa, there are not likely to be clearly defined admission policies for the handicapped or age limits for education of the handicapped as it now exists in Africa.

It is not uncommon, therefore, to find a handicapped adult in a special education class with much younger students. Furthermore, the personnel providing special education services are likely to come from the middle or lower ranks of school staffs rather than the higher. The burden of education for handicapped students is thus frequently carried by less well-trained aides and members of the local community, rather than by highly skilled teachers.

Special education teachers working in regular school settings have been reported to be facing emotional and psychological problems (Joy, 1972). They may face neglect and even hostility on the part of other teachers who resent having handicapped students and special education teachers in regular schools. Also, nonspecialist teachers are often resentful of the fact that special education teachers receive extra pay.

Many of the special education services provided in Africa on a noninstitutional basis must be on an itinerant basis because of the scarcity of educational facilities able to serve handicapped students. A dearth of itinerant teachers has limited the extent and effectiveness of such education. Recent efforts have been made in certain African countries to mainstream handicapped students. Thus the Federal Ministry of Information, Lagos, Nigeria (1977) mandates that handicapped school children, where possible, should be mainstreamed along with their nonhandicapped peers. Some African educators have expressed disagreement with this policy (Shown, 1980). There is concern about the dangers that the physical hazards of African terrain may pose for mainstreamed handicapped students who are not carefully supervised, for example, most parts of Nigeria have dangerous structures and hazards such as rocks, forests, and rivers. Also, the application of mainstreaming policies in Africa places an inordinate burden on most handicapped students unless they are able to use the same materials as their nonhandicapped peers or can be assisted to achieve comparable levels of attainment; this is difficult to achieve in light of the current dearth of trained professionals and the lack of proper facilities and materials. As UNESCO has pointed out (1979), mere physical placement in a mainstreamed school environment is not an answer to providing services to handicapped African children. Provisions at African colleges for handicapped students are essentially nonexistent. There are no ramps, suitable steps elevators, or toilet facilities with special accommodations.

Despite efforts to improve the education of the handicapped, the outlook of Africans respecting the needs of handicapped students and adults is not such as to raise hopes for serious concern regarding their transition into productive roles in society. As Shown has observed regarding the largest nation in Africa, "Nigerians are immensely practical people calling something or someone only if it is seen to be economically useful. With this in mind, the outlook for the handicapped would seem to be bleak" (Shown, 1980).

REFERENCES

Anderson, E. (1983). *The disabled school child. A study in integration.* Open University Set Book, Jos, Nigeria.

Federal Government of Nigeria. (1984). *Nigerian year book:* Lagos, Nigeria: Author.

Joy, D. C. (1979, August 9). Experiment with blind children. *New Nigerian.*

Nigeria Federal Ministry of Information. (1977). *The republic of Nigeria national policy on education.* Lagos, Nigeria: Author.

Sambo, E. W. (1981, April). *What is special education?* Paper presented at the workshop on the integration of elements of special education into teachers education curriculum in Plateau State, University of Jos, Jos, Nigeria.

Shown, D. G. (1980). *A study of effectiveness of mainstreaming of visually handicapped children in Plateau State of Nigeria with a view toward determining quality education for these children.* Jos, Nigeria: University of Jos.

Shown, D. G. (1986, April). *Integrating handicapped children in Plateau State.* Paper presented at the workshop on the integration of elements of special education into teachers education curriculum in Plateau State, University of Jos, Jos, Nigeria.

UNESCO. (1979, October 15–20). Expert meetings of special education, UNESCO headquarters, Paris. *Final Report.*

UNESCO. (1981, July 20–31). *Sub-regional seminar on planning for special education.* Nairobi, Kenya.

UNESCO. (1986, April). *Expert meeting on special education.* Plateau State, Nigeria: University of Jos.

DAKUM SHOWN
University of Jos, Nigeria

NIGERIA, SPECIAL EDUCATION IN

AFRICA, SUB-SAHARAN, SPECIAL EDUCATION IN

Special education is a recognized educational service by a majority of the national governments of the 36 countries of sub-Saharan Africa. National governments in sub-Saharan Africa consider special education as the provision of access to the regular educational curriculum through the adaptation or modification of methods, equipment, and physical environment to meet the unique learning needs of students with disabilities (Mpofu, Oakland, & Chimedza, 2000). They also define *special education* to include the provision of special or modified curriculum and appropriate intervention to modify the social structure and emotional climate in which education takes place (Jere, 2005).

Definitions of *special educational needs* by the national governments in sub-Saharan African countries tend to be inclusive of the effects of socioeconomic deprivation experienced by millions of African children who may not necessarily have physical, sensory, or cognitive impairments. For example, the South African Department of Education has adopted barriers to learning and development as a perspective to understanding special educational needs. The barriers to learning perspective focus on person-environment interactions to special needs education. It considers special educational needs to be located in the child (e.g., a disability), within the school (e.g., lack of resources, lack of trained teachers) or within the broader social, economic, and political context (e.g., poverty; Department of Education, 1997; Engelbretcht, 2005; Muthukrishna & Schoeman, 2000).

The governments of Cameroon and Ethiopia consider special needs to include the habilitation and rehabilitation of children in poverty, including street children (Tchombe, 2005; Teferra, 2005). However, regardless of any differences in the definition of *special educational needs* among African countries, students with physical, sensory, or cognitive impairments are more likely to receive special needs education in school and other community settings (Mpofu et al., 2000). Children with emotional-behavioral disorders or giftedness tend to not be recognized by the national governments as having special educational needs and are not well served (Jere, 2005; Mpofu, Mutepfa, Chireshe, & Kasayira, in press; Mpofu, Peltzer, Shumba, Serpell, & Mogaji, 2005; Tchombe, 2005).

There are no reliable national disability prevalence data in all countries in sub-Saharan Africa (Mpofu et al., 2000). We estimate that less than 1 percent of students with disabilities in sub-Saharan Africa receive special education services. For example, about 14,000 of 1.5 million children of school-going age receive special education services in Zambia, 70,000 of about 3 million students in Zimbabwe, and 5,000 of 1.2 million students in Cameroon. Sub-Saharan Africa has an estimated total population of 682 million people, about two-thirds (or about 400 million) of which are children under the age of 15 (United Nations Population Division, 2004). The World Health Organization (WHO; 1980) estimates that 10 percent of the general population or 70 million citizens of sub-Saharan Africans have significant disabilities. At least 42 million of people with disabilities in sub-Saharan are children under the age of 15.

A majority of the national governments in sub-Saharan Africa have adopted policies on special needs education. Variability among the countries in this region in the development of special needs policies is considerable. Countries that have relatively more advanced formal education systems (e.g., Kenya, Nigeria, South Africa, Zimbabwe) tend to have more elaborate special education policies than those with relatively less-developed education systems (e.g., Angola, Democratic Republic of the Congo, Somalia; Mpofu, Zindi, Oakland & Peresuh, 1997; Mpofu et al., 2005). None of the countries in sub-Saharan Africa has special education or other legislation mandating that students with special educational needs receive the services they need. Thus, despite the fact that national governments in sub-Saharan Africa have adopted special education policies, special education services are not available to the vast majority of children in the region.

Assessment services for special educational needs are barely available to children with special needs in sub-Saharan Africa (Mpofu, 2001, 2004; Mpofu et al., 1997). The few children born at hospitals may have their disability noted by a physician. However, that information may not be available to the teachers at school enrollment, and, often, the physician's diagnosis does not address any education related issues. Traditional midwives in the villages deliver the vast majority of children born in sub-Saharan Africa, and the children's special education needs may go unnoticed or be ascribed by family to metaphysical forces that require spiritual assistance (Mpofu, 2003). A tiny minority of children with disabilities in countries with more-developed special education services (e.g., South Africa, Zambia, Zimbabwe) receive psychoeducational assessment from professionals (Mpofu, 1996, 2004; Mpofu et al., 1997, 2005; Mpofu & Nyanungo, 1998). Parents of students with special education needs are often minimally involved in both the assessment and subsequent education intervention (Mpofu et al., 1997; Oakland, Mpofu, Glasgow, & Jumel, 2003). In many cases, the parents defer to the special education and allied professionals who they accord the same respect as medical doctors or traditional healers (Mpofu, 2000, 2001, 2003).

Where special education services are available, they are offered at special day schools, residential special schools, special classes in regular schools, integrated schools, or other inclusive settings (Mpofu et al., 1997, 2000; Teferra, 2005). The schools and the classes are typically overcrowded, ill equipped, and understaffed (Mutepfa, 2005; Teferra, 2005; Tchombe, 2005). The vast majority of teachers providing education to children with special educational needs in sub-Saharan Africa are not trained in special needs education. Most of the countries in sub-Saharan Africa have no teacher education programs in special needs education, and those that do (e.g., Ethiopia, Kenya, Nigeria, South Africa, Zambia, and Zimbabwe) qualify a very small number relative to need. A good starting point in making special needs education training available to a majority of teachers in sub-Saharan Africa would be through the infusion of special needs education into all preservice teacher education programs and provision of certificate courses in special education to teachers already in service.

Special education services in sub-Saharan Africa barely exist. The limited services available are likely to be found in the few countries with better-developed educational infrastructures. The fact that most national governments in the region have special education policies suggests that the long-term prospects for the development of special education in sub-Saharan Africa are good.

REFERENCES

Department of Education. (1997). Quality education for all. Overcoming barriers to learning and development. *Report of the National Commission on Special Needs in Education and Training (NCSNET) and National Committee on Education Support Services (NCESS).* Pretoria, South Africa: Government Printers.

Engelbretcht, P. (2005). *Inclusive education in South Africa.* Unpublished manuscript.

Jere, J. (2005). *Special education in Zambia.* Unpublished manuscript.

Kasonde-Ng'andu, S., & Moberg, S. (2001). *Moving towards inclusive education: A baseline study of the special educational needs in the North-Western and Western provinces of Zambia.* Lusaka, Zambia: Ministry of Education and Ministry for Foreign Affairs of Finland.

Mpofu, E. (1996). The differential validity of standardized achievement tests for special educational placement purposes: Results and implications of a Zimbabwean Study. *School Psychology International, 17,* 81–92.

Mpofu, E. (2000). Rehabilitation in international perspective: A Zimbabwean experience. *Disability and Rehabilitation, 23,* 481–489.

Mpofu, E. (2001). Mental retardation in cross-cultural perspective: Implications for education. In R. Chimedza & S. Peters (Eds.), *Special education in an African context: Putting theory into practice from the perspective of different voices* (pp. 98–136). Harare, Zimbabwe: College Press.

Mpofu, E. (2003). Conduct Disorder: Presentation, treatment options and cultural efficacy in an African setting. *International Journal of Disability, Community and Rehabilitation, 2,* 44–49. http://www.ijdcr.ca/VOL02_01_CAN/articles/mpofu.shtml.

Mpofu, E. (2004). Learning through inclusive education: Practices with students with disabilities in sub-Saharan Africa. In C. de la Rey, L. Schwartz, & N. Duncan (Eds.), *Psychology: An introduction* (pp. 361–371). Cape Town, South Africa: Oxford University Press.

Mpofu, E., Mutepfa, M., Chireshe, R., & Kasayira, J. M. (in press). School psychology in Zimbabwe. In S. Jimerson, T. Oakland, & P. Farrell (Eds.), *Handbook of international school psychology.* Thousand Oaks, CA: Sage Publications.

Mpofu, E., & Nyanungo, K. R. L. (1998). Educational and psychological testing in Zimbabwean schools: Past, present and future. *European Journal of Psychological Assessment, 14,* 71–90.

Mpofu, E., Oakland, T., & Chimedza, R. (2000). Special education in East and Southern Africa: An overview. In C. R. Reynolds & E. Fletcher-Janzen (Eds.), *Encyclopedia of special education* (pp. 1678–1686). New York: Wiley.

Mpofu, E., Peltzer, K., Shumba, A., Serpell, R., & Mogaji, A. (2005). School psychology in sub-Saharan Africa: Results and implications of a six country survey. In C. R. Reynolds & C. Frisby (Eds.), *Comprehensive handbook of multicultural school psychology* (pp. 1128–1151). New York: Wiley.

Mpofu, E., Zindi, F., Oakland, T., & Peresuh, M. H. (1997). School psychology practices in East and Southern Africa: Special educators' perspective. *Journal of Special Education, 31,* 387–402.

Mutepfa, M. M. (2005). *Special education in Zimbabwe.* Unpublished manuscript.

Muthukrishna, N., & Schoeman, M. 2000. From "special needs" to "quality education for all": A participatory, problem-centered approach to policy development in South Africa. *International Journal of Inclusive Education, 4*(4), 315–335.

Oakland, T., Mpofu, E., Glasgow, K., & Jumel, B. (2003). Diagnosis and administrative interventions for students with Mental Retardation in Australia, France, United States and Zimbabwe 98 years after Binet's first intelligence test. *International Journal of Testing, 3*(1), 59–75.

Tchombe, T. (2005). *Special education in Cameroon.* Unpublished manuscript.

Teferra, T. (2005). *Special education in Ethiopia.* Unpublished manuscript.

United Nations Population Division. (2004). *Sub-Saharan Africa demographic trends.* Retrieved September 9, 2005, from http://www.unfa.org/africa/demographic.htm

World Health Organization (WHO). (1980). *International classification of impairments, disability and handicaps: A manual of classifications relating to the consequences of disease.* Geneva, Switzerland: Author.

ELIAS MPOFU
Pennsylvania State University

PETRA ENGELBRETCHT
University of Stellenbosch

JAQUELINE JERE
University of Zambia

MAGEN M. MUTEPFA
*Zimbabwe Schools Special
Services and Special
Education Department*

ALMON SHUMBA
University of KwaZulu-Natal

THERESE TCHOMBE
University of Yaounde 1

TIRUSSEW TEFERRA
Addis Ababa University

AGE-APPROPRIATE CURRICULUM

An age-appropriate curriculum is a special-education curriculum that consists of activities that are matched to both the students' chronological ages and their developmental or skill levels. This match has been difficult to achieve, especially for older trainable and severely handicapped students who continue to function on preschool levels. The older students with severe handicaps often need continued training in fine motor, cognitive, and language skills but also need to acquire skills that can be used immediately and will transfer to later community and vocational placements (Drew, Logan, & Hardman, 1984).

The Education for All Handicapped Children Act (P.L. 94-142), and its successor, the Individuals with Disabilities Education Act, has mandated an appropriate education for all handicapped students, but wide differences remain when defining this term. The justification for using an age-appropriate education lies in the principle of *normalization,* which Nirje (1979) has defined as follows: "Making available to all mentally retarded people patterns of life and conditions of everyday living which are as close as possible to the regular circumstances of society" (p. 73). Although it may appear unrealistic to teach age-appropriate behaviors to students with severe developmental delays, Larsen and Jackson (1981) argue that this is the mission of special education: "No, we will not be completely successful (but) . . . our goals for students will stress skills relevant to the general culture, rather than skills that have a proven value only in special-education classrooms" (p. 1).

Our current knowledge of developmental milestones, task analysis procedures, and behavior modification principles can be used in adopting this approach if we also examine the age-appropriateness of the materials, skills, activities, environments, and reinforcers used during instruction. For example, in learning visual discrimination of shapes, elementary-age students may use form boards and shape sorters, while older students use community signs and mosaic art activities. For other skills, calculators may be used instead of number lines, colored clothing can be sorted rather than colored cubes, and the assembly of vocational products may replace peg boards and beads (Bates, Renzaglia, & Wehman, 1981).

Because there are many skills that older severely handicapped youths will never acquire (e.g., reading a newspaper and buying groceries), the curriculum focuses on those abilities that can be learned (e.g., reading survival signs or following directions). To identify these skills for each group of students, Brown et al. (1979) employ an ecological inventory approach listing the environments and subenvironments where the students currently (or will eventually) function. An inventory of the activities in each environment and a listing of skills needed to participate in those activities provide the framework for selecting curriculum goals. In this approach, for example, the basic skill of matching pictures leads to finding grooming items in a drugstore, and identifying different foods leads to ordering in a fast-food restaurant.

Classroom design and decor also should reflect the chronological age of the students. For older youths, pictures of teen activities and movie celebrities are more age-appropriate decorations than cartoon characters. Many special-education classrooms have moved into secondary buildings, opening up opportunities to use age-appropriate training sites, such as home economics rooms.

Severely handicapped students may have extremely slow learning rates and much difficulty in generalizing learning skills to new situations. Therefore, their education must include the teaching of critical skill clusters and opportunities to practice functional skills in natural settings, such as sheltered workshops, supermarkets, and public transportation. For a more-detailed description of curricular approaches to teaching functional skill clusters, see Guess and Noonan (1982).

REFERENCES

Bates, P., Renzaglia, A., & Wehman, P. (1981). Characteristics of an appropriate education for severely and profoundly handicapped students. *Education & Training of the Mentally Retarded, 16,* 142–149.

Brown, L., Branston, M. B., Homre-Nietupski, S., Pumpian, I., Certo, N., & Grunewald, L. (1979). A strategy for developing chronological age appropriate and functional curriculum content for severely handicapped adolescents and young adults. *Journal of Special Education, 13,* 81–90.

Drew, C. J., Logan, D. R., & Hardman, M. L. (1984). *Mental Retardation: A life cycle approach* (3rd ed.). St. Louis, MO: Times Mirror/Mosby.

Guess, D., & Noonan, M. J. (1982). Curricula and instructional procedures for severely handicapped students. *Focus on Exceptional Children, 14,* 9–10.

Larsen, L. A., & Jackson, L. B. (1981). Chronological age in the design of educational programs for severely and profoundly impaired students. *PRISE Reporter, 13,* 1–2.

Nirje, B. (1979). Changing patterns in residential services for the mentally retarded. In E. L. Meyen (Ed.), *Basic readings in the study of exceptional children and youth* (pp. 139–149). Denver: Love.

KATHERINE D. COUTURIER
Pennsylvania State University
Second edition

KIMBERLY F. APPLEQUIST
*University of Colorado at
Colorado Springs*
Third edition

ADAPTIVE BEHAVIOR
FUNCTIONAL INSTRUCTION
FUNCTIONAL SKILLS TRAINING
MENTAL RETARDATION

AGE AT ONSET

Age at onset refers to the point in an individual's life when a specific condition began. Age at onset can be compared with a child's chronological age to establish the duration of a condition. It is a significant variable in making diagnostic judgments and prognostic statements. Within a school setting, age at onset is typically a consideration in: (1) understanding behavioral disorders; (2) understanding the prognosis for adequate intellectual and learning performance in children with neurologic and chronic medical conditions; and (3) assessing and programming for children with learning disabilities.

In the assessment of behavioral difficulties, it is important to have an adequate history of the disorder, including an estimate of when the child began experiencing difficulties. Knowledge of age at onset allows one to assess the relationship between behavioral changes and other significant occurrences in the child's life (e.g., Did difficulties start when a sibling was born? When the child entered school?). Different psychopathologic conditions have different histories, ages at onset, and significance. For example, infrequent nightmares are not pathognomonic, in fact, they are normal in a three-year-old child (Lowrey, 1978). Infantile autism, by definition, has an age of onset prior to 30 months of age (American Psychiatric Association, 1994). For many disorders, age of onset will influence diagnostic decisions, treatment choices, and prognostications.

REFERENCES

American Psychiatric Association. (1994). *Diagnostic and statistical manual of mental disorders* (4th ed.). Washington, DC: Author.

Lowrey, G. H. (1978). *Growth and development of children.* New York: Year Book Medical.

GRETA N. WILKENING
Children's Hospital

MEDICAL HISTORY
MENTAL STATUS EXAMS

AGGRESSION

Research investigating aggression offers various overlapping definitions of the word *aggression*. Most researchers agree that an aggressive act is an intentional behavior that is harmful, either mentally or physically, and aversive to the victim (Crick, Casas, & Mosher, 1997; Dodge, 1980; Goldstein & Conoley, 1997; Jewett, 1992; Landers, 1991; McEvoy, Estrem, Rodriguez, & Olson, 2003).

Various forms of aggression exist. Direct, overt aggression occurs when both the perpetrator and the victim are present (e.g., acts of physical aggression as when a child physically hits another child). Indirect, covert aggression includes the presence of a third person who acts as a facilitator of the aggressive act (e.g., a child who starts a rumor about another child; Juvonen & Graham, 2001).

Aggression also may be thought of as including physical, relational, or verbal aggression. Physical aggression includes acts completed with physical force (e.g., to hit someone, to throw something, to kick something, or to push someone). Verbal aggression includes acts of saying something harmful directly to someone (e.g., insulting someone or saying "I hate you!"). Relational aggression uses peer relationships as ammunition for the aggressive act (e.g., telling someone that he or she cannot be one's friend; Juvonen & Graham, 2001; Monks, Ruiz, & Val, 2002).

Physical aggression may be thought of as reactive or proactive aggression. Specifically, reactive physical aggression refers to an immediate display of violent behavior in response to another's actions. It is sometimes characterized as hot-blooded aggression because it does not involve premeditated planning. Proactive physical aggression is planned aggression (Clarke, 2004; Conner, Steingard, Anderson, & Melloni, 2003; Vitaro, Brendgen, & Tremblay, 2002).

Those who engage in physical aggression are more likely to be males (Juvonen & Graham, 2001; McEvoy et al., 2003; Monks et al., 2002), older, and physically larger than their victims. However, controversy exists regarding the extent to which victims are physically weaker than their attackers (Juvonen & Graham, 2001; Monks et al., 2002). Some research found that victims of physical aggression are not physically weaker than nonvictims (Monks et al., 2002), while other studies found that victims are physically weaker than nonvictims (Juvonen & Graham, 2001).

Aggressive acts are common among very young children. For instance, toddlers will often push, bite, shove, or hit other children when they become angry. As individuals move into the preschool years, they tend to exhibit more verbal aggression, including yelling at other children and displaying temper tantrums (Coie & Dodge, 1997). Aggressive and violent behavior could lead to a diagnosis of and are characteristic of Disruptive Behavior Disorders (DBD; e.g., Oppositional Defiant Disorder, Conduct Disorder) or juvenile delinquency. More specifically, the stability of atypical behavior problems in early childhood appears to be a precursor to the later development of or continued maintenance of a DBD (Lavigne, Cicchetti, Gibbons, Binns, Larsen, & Devitto, 2001; Pierce, Ewing, & Campbell, 1999).

Oppositional Defiant Disorder (ODD) behaviors are more severe and frequent than typical childhood disobedience, and Conduct Disorder (CD) behaviors are more severe than those associated ODD. In early childhood, ODD is characterized by frequent, severe temper tantrums and an intolerance of frustration. A preschool or kindergarten child diagnosed with ODD typically has difficulty delaying gratification, is often extremely hostile and vocal when frustrated, and commonly kicks, thrashes, struggles for power, and destroys property (Kronenberg & Meyer, 2001). Thus, children who have been diagnosed with ODD commonly exhibit severe and frequent aggression (Lumley, McNeil, Herschell, & Bahl, 2002).

In young children, females tend to exhibit more relational aggression than males and to exhibit more relational aggression than physical aggression. Males tend to exhibit more physical aggression than relational aggression (Crick, 1996; Crick et al., 1997; Juvonen & Graham, 2001; McEvoy et al., 2003). Young females often exhibit more relational aggression than physical or verbal aggression (e.g., verbal threats). Females are more physically aggressive than verbally aggressive. Likewise, males engage in physical aggression most often and verbal aggression least often (Monks et al., 2002). After age 3, boys are more likely than girls to engage in both aggressive and nonaggressive antisocial behaviors (National Institute of Mental Health, 2006).

Perpetrators and victims of aggression are at risk for negative outcomes. For example, young children who engage in aggressive acts tend to be less socially accepted than their less aggressive peers (Monks et al., 2002). Similarly, according to the National Institute of Mental Health (NIMH), one's peer group influences his or her engagement in youth violence. Home factors also can contribute to youth violence (http://www.nimh.nih.gov/publicat/violenceresfact.cfm).

Aggression reflects social and personal problems that have the potential for serious negative outcomes. Aggression imposes a grave personal cost to the individual and a great expense to the community and society. Some aggressive children display higher rates of delinquency, lower academic achievement, and poorer peer relationships. These personal difficulties can develop into serious social problems such as criminal acts, school dropout, poor community bonds, and mental illness (Brophy, 1983; Ensminger & Slusarckick 1992; Kupersmidt & Coie, 1990; Meyer, 1985).

The majority of aggressive children do not mature into aggressive adults. A limited number of children who display aggressive behavior maintain the pattern into adolescence and adulthood and often display these behaviors in multiple settings. These children commonly are identified as early starters, that is, those who display a developmental trajectory of increasing severity and escalation of problem behaviors (Moffitt, 1993; Taylor, Iacono, & McGue, 2000).

REFERENCES

Brophy, J. (1983). Research of the self-fulfilling prophecy and teacher expectations. *Journal of Educational Psychology, 75,* 631–661.

Clarke, N. M. (2004). Aggression and antisocial behavior in children and adolescents: Research and treatment. *Bulletin of the Menninger Clinic, 68*(2), 192.

Coie, J. D., & Dodge, K. A. (1997). Aggression and antisocial behavior. In W. V. Damon (Ed.), *Handbook of child development: Social, emotional, and personal development* (5th ed.) New York: Wiley.

Conner, D. F., Steingard, R. J., Anderson, J., & Melloni, R. H. (2003). Gender differences in reactive and proactive aggression. *Child Psychiatry and Human Development, 33*(4), 279–294.

Crick, N. R. (1996). The role of overt aggression, relational aggression, and prosocial behavior in the prediction of children's future social adjustment. *Child Development, 67,* 2317–2327.

Crick, N. R., Casas, J. F., & Mosher, M. (1997). Relational and overt aggression in preschool. *Developmental Psychology, 33*(4), 579–588.

Dodge, K. A. (1980). Social cognition and children's aggressive behavior. *Child Development, 51,* 162–170.

Goldstein, A. P., & Conoley, J. C. (1997). In A. P. Goldstein & J. C. Conoley (Eds.), *School violence intervention: A practical handbook* (pp. 3–22). New York: Guilford.

Jewett, J. (1992). Aggression and cooperation: Helping young children develop constructive strategies. *Eric Digest.* Retrieved February 29, 2005, from http://www.ericfacility.net/ericdigests/ed351147.html

Juvonen, J., & Graham, S. (Eds.). (2001). *Peer harassment in the schools: The plight of the vulnerable and victimized.* New York: Guilford.

Kupersmidt, J. B., & Coie, J. D. (1990). Preadolescent peer status, aggression, and school adjustment as predictors of externalizing problems in adolescence. *Child Development, 61,* 1350–1362.

Landers, C. (1991). The development of aggression and prosocial behavior in early childhood. *Coordinator's Notebook: The Consultative Group on Early Childhood Care and Development, 10,* 1–4.

Lavigne, J. V., Cicchetti, C., Gibbons, R. D., Binns, H. J., Larsen, L., & DeVito, C. (2001). Oppositional Defiant Disorder with onset in preschool years: Longitudinal stability and pathways to other disorders. *Journal of American Academy of Child and Adolescent Psychiatry, 40*(12), 1393–1400.

Lumley, V. A., McNeil, C. B., Herschell, A. D., & Bahl, C. B. (2002). An examination of gender differences among young children with Disruptive Behavior Disorders. *Child Study Journal, 32*(2), 89–99.

McEvoy, M. A., Estrem, T. L., Rodriguez, M. C., & Olson, M. L. (2003). Assessing relational and physical aggression among preschool children: Intermethod agreement. *Topics in Early Childhood Special Education, 23*(2), 53–64.

Meyer, W. J. (1985). Summary, integrations, and prospective. In J. B. Dusek (Ed.), *Teacher expectancies* (pp. 353–370). Hillsdale, NJ: Erlbaum.

Meyer, H. A., Astor, R. A., & Behre, W. J. (2002). Teacher's reasoning about school violence: The role of gender and location. *Contemporary Educational Psychology, 27*(4), 499–528.

Moffitt, T. E. (1993). Adolescence-limited and life-course-persistent antisocial behavior: A developmental Taxonomy. *Psychological Review, 100,* 674–701.

Monks, C., Ruiz, R. O., & Val, T. (2002). Unjustified aggression in preschool. *Aggressive Behavior, 28,* 458–476.

National Institute of Mental Health. (2005). *NIMH: Child and Adolescent Violence Research at the NIMH.* Retrieved May 20, 2006, from http://www.nimh.nih.gov/publicat/violenceresfact.cfm.

Pierce, E. W., Ewing, L. J., & Campbell, S. B. (1999). Diagnostic status and symptomatic behavior of hard-to-manage preschool children in middle childhood and early adolescence. *Journal of Clinical Child Psychology, 28*(1), 44–57.

Taylor, J., Iacono, W. G., & McGue, M. (2000). Evidence for a genetic etiology of early-onset delinquency. *Journal of Abnormal Psychology, 109,* 634–643.

Vitaro, F., Brendgen, M., & Tremblay, R. E. (2002). Reactively and proactively aggressive children: Antecedent and subsequent characteristics. *Journal of Child Psychology and Psychiatry, 43*(4), 495–506.

JENNIFER HARMAN
LINDA RADBILL
University of Florida

BEHAVIOR DISORDER
COGNITIVE BEHAVIOR THERAPY
CONDUCT DISORDER

AGRAPHIA

The *Cyclopedia of Education* (1915) defined *agraphia* as a disorder of the associations of speech in which there is a partial or complete inability to express ideas by means of written symbols in an individual who had previously acquired this mode of speech expression. More recent definitions describe agraphia as the loss or impairment of the ability to produce written language and is the result of a central nervous system dysfunction (Acree & Johnson, 2003). Agraphia is often associated with apraxia and with so-called motor aphasia.

Orton (1937) distinguished between motor agraphia and development agraphia, or special writing disability. Orton defined motor agraphia as the loss of ability to write restricted to the motor component of writing. Orton attributed this problem to dysfunction in relevant motor control areas of the brain without accompanying dysfunction in nearby speech functioning areas. Developmental agraphia was said to manifest itself in one of two ways: the first instance characterized by an unusually slow rate of writing; the second characterized by quality of writing. Orton suggested that "shifted sinistrals," or enforced training of the right hand in left-hand children, may result in slow writing. In other cases, the lack of dominant handedness was said to result in writing problems.

Strauss and Werner (1938) suggested that finger agnosia (inability to recognize one's own fingers) may be related to agraphia. Terms such as agraphia have declined in popularity in recent years, partly as a result of a trend toward the use of more educationally relevant orientations (see Hallahan,

Kauffman, & Lloyd, 1985, for a historical overview). Deficits in writing performance are best defined and remediated in terms of task-specific behaviors (Mercer, 1979). Recent and future trends in remediation and adoption include neuroimaging to identify different types of agraphia and technology to assist writing abilities (Acree & Johnson, 2003).

REFERENCES

Acree, W. M., & Johnson, B. D. (2003). Agraphia. In E. Fletcher-Janzen & C. R. Reynolds (Eds.), *Childhood disorders diagnostic desk reference* (pp. 17–19). New York: Wiley.

Cyclopedia of Education (1915). New York: Macmillan.

Hallahan, D. P., Kauffman, J. M., & Lloyd, J. W. (1985). *Introduction to learning disabilities*. Englewood Cliffs, NJ: Prentice Hall.

Mercer, C. (1979). *Children and adolescents with learning disabilities*. Columbus, OH: Merrill.

Orton, S. T. (1937). *Reading, writing, and speech problems in children*. New York: Norton.

Strauss, A. A., & Werner, H. (1938). Deficiency in finger schema in relation to arithmetic disability (finger agnosia and acalculia). *American Journal of Orthopsychiatry, 8,* 719–724.

THOMAS E. SCRUGGS
MARGO A. MASTROPIERI
Purdue University

DYSGRAPHIA
HANDWRITING

AICARDI SYNDROME (CALLOSAL DYSGENESIS)

Aicardi syndrome is a rare genetic disorder that was first reported in 1965 by Jean Aicardi (Steinman, 2003). Aicardi Syndrome is the most common of syndromes involving agenesis or dysgenesis of the corpus callosum and is sometimes used interchangeably with the designation *callosal dysgenesis*. The corpus callosum is the largest of the cerebral commissures and is the major communication link between the left and the right hemispheres of the brain.

Depending upon the level of dysgenesis, symptoms may vary considerably in their severity but among the most common are: mental retardation, autistic syndromes, severe obsessive compulsive disorders, seizure disorder, and macrocephaly (Gillberg, 1995). When limited to the extreme posterior portions of the corpus callosum, ADHD is a more common result. Girls tend to be overrepresented in callosal dysgenesis syndromes and in Aicardi Syndrome proper, only girls occur since it is an X-linked, dominant mutation. As, among the callosal dysgenesis syndromes, is among the most severe and typically results in moderate to severe mental retardation and numerous physical abnormalities,

especially of the spine and the orofacial area. Diagnosis is by CAT scan or MRI. Neuropsychological testing is recommended due to the possible range of reaction.

Treatment is entirely symptomatic and virtually all such children will require special education services and may qualify under multiple areas of disability. In less severe cases of callosal dysgenesis, asymptomatic presentations have been reported, emphasizing the need for ongoing neuropsychological follow-up and periodic reassessment of intervention plans. Symptoms not appearing by puberty typically do not occur and the disorder is not progressive. In the most severe forms of callosal agenesis, death in infancy is common.

REFERENCES

Gillberg, C. (1995). *Clinical child neuropsychiatry*. Cambridge, England: Cambridge University Press.

Steinman, D. (2003). Aicardi syndrome. In E. Fletcher-Janzen, & C. R. Reynolds (Eds.), *Childhood disorders diagnostic desk reference* (pp. 19–20). New York: Wiley.

CECIL R. REYNOLDS
Texas A&M University

NEUROLOGICAL ORGANIZATION

AIDES TO PSYCHOLINGUISTIC TEACHING

Psycholinguistics focuses on the interactions and psychological functions underlying communication. It attends to the processes by which a speaker or writer emits signals or symbols, and the interpretation of those signals by the receiver (Hammill & Larsen, 1974).

Language programs and assessment techniques have been derived from these psycholinguistic principles and have been applied to education. A basic tenet of psycholinguistics is that language is made up of discrete components that may be identified and measured; further, it is assumed that if one is deficient in a given component, the deficiency can be remediated. This leads to two more assumptions, that a child's failure to learn stems from his or her own weaknesses, and that strengthening weak areas will result in improved classroom learning (Hammill & Larsen, 1974). If these assumptions are valid, programs aimed at mitigating psycholinguistic weaknesses are both necessary and desirable. If the assumptions are invalid, however, a great deal of time and money is being wasted on the application of these programs in educational settings.

In their review of research, Hammill and Larsen (1974) showed that the efficacy of psycholinguistic training had not been adequately demonstrated. They pointed out that many exceptional children are being provided with training programs aimed at increasing their psycholinguistic competencies. On the basis of their review, the authors claimed that it is essential to determine whether the constructs are trainable by present programs. It is also necessary, they said, to identify the children for whom such training would prove worthwhile.

Arter and Jenkins (1977), in their examination of the benefits and prevalence of modality considerations in special education, concluded that research evidence failed to support the practice of basing instructional plans on modality assessment. Thirteen of the 14 studies they reviewed indicated that students were not differentially assisted by instruction congruent with their modality strengths. Further, they stated that "increased efforts in research and development of test instruments and techniques may be warranted but, as far as the practitioner is concerned, advocacy of the (modality) model cannot be justified" (p. 295).

Reviews using a quantitative statistic known as effect size (ES) have been conducted to summarize educational research. This statistic is computed to quantitatively determine how much improvement occurs across different investigations, based on two indices: the direction of improvement (+ or −) and the amount of improvement with an ES of 1.00 revealing a 34 percent improvement. Kavale and Glass (1982) refer to a meta-analysis performed by Kavale in 1981 that investigated the effectiveness of psycholinguistic training. Kavale's studies yielded 240 effect sizes with an overall ES of 0.39. Kavale and Glass conclude by asserting that there are specific situations where psycholinguistic training is effective and that it should be included within a total remedial program. The findings from this research should be qualified, however, because of the lack of consideration of research methodologies across the different investigations. Furthermore, the outcome measures were based on performance on the process tests (i.e., Illinois Test of Psycholinguistic Abilities—ITPA), not on academic tests. Further analyses of studies using achievement outcomes have found negligible effect sizes. It remains open to question whether such improvement on psycholinguistic process tasks would translate into improved performance on academic tasks in the classroom.

REFERENCES

Arter, J. A., & Jenkins, J. R. (1977). Examining the benefits and prevalence of modality considerations in special education. *Journal of Special Education, 11*(3), 281–298.

Hammill, D. D., & Larsen, S. C. (1974). The effectiveness of psycholinguistic training. *Exceptional Children, 41*, 5–14.

Kavale, K. A., & Glass, G. V. (1982). The efficacy of special education interventions and practices: A compendium of meta-analysis findings. *Focus on Exceptional Children, 15*(4), 1–16.

KATHLEEN RODDEN-NORD
GERALD TINDAL
University of Oregon

FERNALD METHOD
ORTON-GILLINGHAM METHOD
PSYCHOLINGUISTICS

AIDS

See PEDIATRIC ACQUIRED IMMUNE DEFICIENCY SYNDROME.

AIDS DYSMORPHIC SYNDROME

The National Organization for Rare Disorders (2000) describes AIDS dysmorphic syndrome (ADS) as a rare disorder of infancy that can result from a mother's infection with the human immunodeficiency virus (HIV) during pregnancy. HIV is the retrovirus that causes acquired immune deficiency syndrome (AIDS). This syndrome has many synonyms, such as dysmorphic AIDS, fetal AIDS infection, HIV embryopathy, and perinatal AIDS. ADS is caused by the transmission of HIV-1 or HIV-2, both forms of the human immunodeficiency virus. The transmission can occur during fetal development or during the birth of the child. Current data suggest that the most likely time for transmission of HIV between mother and infant occurs late in pregnancy or during delivery (Milosevic, 1998).

Most infants born to HIV-positive mothers have passively acquired maternal antibodies against this virus. An infant with passive antibodies is protected because the antibodies help fight the infection by neutralizing or destroying certain foreign proteins called antigens, thus fighting off HIV. If the antibodies prevent the infant from getting ADS, they will no longer be present in the infant's bloodstream by about 12 to 16 months of age. ADS can be accurately diagnosed when the infant is 18 months of age and the presence or absence of the passive antibodies can be clearly tested (National Organization for Rare Disorders [NORD], 2000). NORD (2000) reports that current estimates suggest that the risk of an infant's contracting HIV from his or her infected mother is approximately 13–39 percent of infants who are born to HIV-positive mothers in developed countries who have not undergone treatment with antiviral medications during pregnancy. Milosevic (1998) reports that the incidence of perinatal transmission of ADS varies from 25–48 percent for developing countries. ADS is believed to affect equal numbers of male and female infants (NORD, 2000). Statistics provided from Centers for Disease Control and Prevention (CDC) show that in the early 1990s, approximately 1,000–2,000 new cases of ADS were contracted each year in the United States. Between 1992 and 1998, these numbers have declined 75 percent in the United States, largely because of utilized preventive measures unknown prior to the later 1990s. CDC (1999) also reports that HIV transmission from infected mother to infant during pregnancy, during labor, during delivery, or by breastfeeding has accounted for 91 percent of reported AIDS cases in children in the United States. These children are differentially affected by racial background. CDC (1999) reports that 84 percent of children with AIDS were African American and Hispanic. This number is particularly concerning because only 31 percent of the U.S. population of children are African American or Hispanic.

Characteristics

1. Unusually small head (microencephaly with a prominent boxlike forehead
2. Prominent and widely set eyes (ocular hypertelorism)
3. Flattened nasal bridge and shortened nose
4. An unusual bluish tint to the tough, outermost layer of the eyes (sclerae)
5. An unusually pronounced vertical groove (philtrum) in the center of an abnormally prominent upper lip

The best treatment for ADS is the use of preventive measures (CDC, 1999; Milosevic, 1998; NORD, 2000). These measures would include utilizing or creating programs that would work to prevent infection in women. These programs would dispense knowledge of how to have safe sex and avoid activities such as needle sharing if a woman is an intravenous drug user. After a woman is infected with HIV, education can help her understand the risks of pregnancy and help with birth control methods. If a woman is both infected with HIV and pregnant, the best treatment is early prenatal care, which would include HIV testing, counseling, and treatment with AZT and additional antiviral medications. In addition, delivery by cesarean section may reduce the risk of transmission of HIV to the newborn. The mother would also be told to refrain from breast-feeding her child, and the child would receive AZT during the first 6 weeks of life.

HIV-infected mothers with newborns should consult specialists in infants and children with HIV. Specific drug therapies suggested for the child may include AZT, didanosine (ddI), or lamivudine (3TC; nucleoside analog reverse transcriptase inhibitors) in combination with protease inhibitors. The child will need continued monitoring to assess the effectiveness of the drug therapy.

Teachers working with students affected with ADS will have to be aware of these children's potential for lowered intelligence and problems in psychomotor functioning. Special education teachers should help students with ADS learn skills that will help them with activities requiring a coordination between physical and mental tasks. Children with ADS who are performing below grade level would be good referrals to school psychologists who could assess the child's intellectual, psychomotor, and psychological functioning. The psychological reports can aid teachers in developing a better learning program by utilizing a child's strengths to combat his or her weaknesses.

Children with ADS may look smaller and more immature than their classmates; they may also need a referral to a school counselor or social worker in order to help them develop better social skill so that they can fit in better with same-age peers. Aside from their potentially small stature, their facial abnormalities may prompt severe teasing from their peers. Teasing can be extremely hurtful, and counseling may help the child build necessary coping skills.

Children with ADS are at chronic risk for developing life-threatening illnesses such as non-Hodgkins B-cell lymphoma, brain lymphoma, and Pneumocystis carinii pneumonia (NORD, 2000). An exact percentage of how many ADS children survive into adulthood and older age is unknown. Survival depends on medication therapy and individual treatment for all infections that are likely to assault the child's immune system. Future research should also focus on exactly how and when transmission occurs and on improving methods for preventing transmission between HIV-positive mothers and their infants. Most beneficially, however, future research should focus on continued efforts to find better treatment medications until a cure or vaccine for HIV is developed.

REFERENCES

Center for Disease Control and Prevention (CDC). (1999). *Status of perinatal HIV prevention: U.S. declines continue.* Atlanta, GA: Author.

Milosevic, S. (1998). Perinatal infection with the human immunodeficiency. *Medicinski Pregled, 51,* 325–328.

National Organization for Rare Disorders (NORD). (2000). *Aids dysmorphic syndrome.* New Fairfield, CT: Author.

JENNIE KAUFMAN SINGER
*California Department of
Corrections, Region 1 Parole
Outpatient Clinic
Sacramento, California*

AKINETON

Akineton is the proprietary name of *biperiden,* a skeletal muscle relaxant used in the treatment of Parkinson's disease (Modell, 1985). It is available in tablet and ampul form. Akineton is used in the treatment of all forms of parkinsonism, and it helps reduce movement disorders associated with this condition. It also is used in conjunction with antipsychotic drugs such as the phenothiazines to control extrapyramidal disturbances. Safe, effective use in children has not been established. Possible side effects associated with Akineton include dryness of the mouth, drowsiness, blurred vision, and urinary retention. Extreme adverse effects include mental confusion, agitation, and disturbed behavior. Teachers who have students with juvenile Parkinsonism may encounter those side effects in their students.

REFERENCES

Modell, W. (Ed.). (1985). *Drugs in current use and new drugs* (31st ed.). New York: Springer.

Physician's desk reference (59th ed.). (2005). Oradell, NJ: Thompson.

CATHY F. TELZROW
Kent State University

CHOREA
PHENOTHIAZINES

AL-ANON

Al-Anon (which includes Alateen for younger members) originally was an adjunct of Alcoholics Anonymous, but in 1954 it incorporated as a separate fellowship. The central headquarters, known as the World Service Office (WSO), serves Al-Anon groups all over the world. The WSO is guided by a voluntary board of trustees, a policy committee, and an executive committee that makes administrative decisions. There is a paid staff with an executive director. Although there is a central headquarters, all local groups operate autonomously. The only requirement for membership is the belief that one's life has been or is being deeply affected by close contact with a problem drinker.

Al-Anon groups help those affected by someone else's drinking to:

Learn the facts about alcoholism as a family illness

Benefit from contact with members who have had the same problem

Improve their own attitudes and personalities by the study and practice of the "twelve steps"

Reduce tensions and improve the attitudes of the family through attendance at Al-Anon meetings

Al-Anon is primarily a self-help/support group that focuses on assisting family members in dealing with the problems that an alcoholic brings to the family. It is based on anonymity and sharing.

Al-Anon is not allied with any sect denomination, political entity, organization or institution; does not engage in any controversy; and neither endorses or opposes any cause except to help families of alcoholics (Al-Anon, 2005).

REFERENCE

Al-Anon. (2005). *About us.* Retrieved June 19, 2005, from http://www.al-anon.alateen.org/about.html

PHILIP E. LYON
College of St. Rose

ALATEEN

Alateen is a self-help, self-support group for young Al-Anon members whose lives have been affected by someone else's drinking. Each Alateen group has an active, adult member of Al-Anon who serves as a sponsor and who is responsible for guiding the group and sharing knowledge of the twelve steps and traditions. The basic purpose of this group is to help Alateens to cope with the turmoil created in their lives by someone else's drinking. Meetings are voluntary and generally are held in community buildings. Alateen members openly discuss their problems, share experiences, learn effective ways to cope with their problems, encourage one another, and help each other to understand the principles of the Al-Anon program.

In a survey conducted by World Service Office it was found that 46 percent of the Alateens held membership for between 1 and 4 years, 57 percent were female, most were children of alcoholics, 27 percent were the brother, sister, or other relative of an alcoholic, and the average age of a member was 14, with 71 percent between the ages of 13 and 17. Furthermore, 31 percent of the Alateen members had participated in treatment/counseling before or since coming to Alateen. Fully 94 percent of the Alateen respondents indicated that personal influences were responsible for their attendance at their first Alateen meeting, with Alcoholics Anonymous members, Al-Anon/Alateen members, or family members being the most frequently identified influence.

REFERENCE

Alateen. (2005). *Alateen's purpose.* Retrieved June 19, 2005, from http://www.al-anon.alateen.org/alateen.html

PHILIP E. LYON
College of St. Rose

AL-ANON
ALCOHOL AND DRUG ABUSE PATTERNS
SUBSTANCE ABUSE

ALBANIA, SPECIAL EDUCATION IN

Special education in Albania began in 1963 with the opening of an institute for children with visual and auditory disorders in Tirana, the capital of Albania, and remains the only institute that provides services to children with this disability. After 1970, the first schools for children with mental disorders (mainly mild and moderate levels of retardation) were opened in some of the cities where psychiatric hospitals already existed. Special schools for children with Mental Retardation were opened in Durres in 1974, in Tirana in 1979, in Vlore in 1983, and in Elbasan in 1984. Other schools were opened after 1990. Albania have two national institutions, six special schools, and four day centers. These 12 institutions have 77 classes whose 184 teachers serve 800 students (35 percent female) with special needs in three categories: visual, auditory, or mental disorders (i.e., only Mental Retardation).

Most (75 percent) teachers completed a 4-year university teacher education program, while others completed a high school teacher preparation program. None specialized in working with special needs children except for very few professionals who obtained a psychology degree from a university abroad. Years of experience and their desire and will to help these children have guided their work.

In 1995, a law on preuniversity education (Ministry of Education, 1995) required special education services to be offered to children from ages 6 through 19. Children with Mental Retardation may enroll in public nurseries and kindergartens. However, their numbers are small. Parents generally do not want to publicly admit that their child has a problem and prefer to keep them at home. In addition, teachers of young children are not prepared to work with children with special needs.

The Ministry of Education and Science is responsible for creating special schools. All special schools are public. Some nongovernmental organizations in the larger cities have opened a few day centers for special needs children and provide community-based services, which include counseling with family members, raising awareness in the community about the needs of these children, educating disabled children, and integrating them in public schools and community. The state does not adequately attend to the needs of children with disabilities and does not support programs that other organizations recently have implemented in Albania.

The curricula used for special education generally is consistent with that used in the normal schools with some changes and adoptions according to the disorders that children manifest. Also for children with mental and auditory disorders, vocational training was added recently to the curricula, with the desire to prepare them for employment and to integrate them into society.

REFERENCE

Ministry of Education. (1995). *About the preuniversity education system: Education of students with special needs.* Retrieved July 2005, from www.mash.gov.al

GLADIOLA MUSABELLIU
University of Tirana

ALBINISM

Albinism encompasses a group of disorders that are inherited and characterized by lack of or not enough melanin production. It does not only affect the pigmentation of the skin but also may evidence itself in the skin, hair, and eyes (oculocutaneous albinism) or may only affect the eyes (ocular albinism; Kodsi, Rubin, & Wolf, 2005). Of the variations of albinism, four types are common. In Type I albinism, the body cannot metabolize tyrosine. This deficit blocks the channel for the conversion of tyrosine, an amino acid, to melanin (Barsh, 1996). Type II albinism is an autosomal recessive disorder of pigmentation set apart by a reduced amount of pigmentation in the skin, hair, and eyes. This type of albinism is usually considered less severe than Type I albinism (Brondum-Nielsen et al., 1997). In oculocutaneous albinism, there is a lack of melanin production in the skin, hair, and eyes as stated earlier. People with this type of albinism have an increased sensitivity to ultraviolet light and a predisposition to skin cancer (King & Oetting, 1999). Ocular albinism is when only the eyes are affected by a lack of melanin production. In turn, the lack of melanin in the developing eye contributes to abnormal routing of the optic nerves. This abnormal form of routing is the cause of nystagmus, strabismus, and reduced visual acuity common to all types of albinism (King & Oetting, 1999). The needs of a person with albinism are dependent on their type of albinism. However, the most common special services needed are related to their visual acuity. Some may benefit from counseling if they are experiencing emotional sensitivity or psychological stress due to their phenotypical traits.

REFERENCES

Barsh, G. S. (1996). The genetics of pigmentation: From fancy genes to complex traits. *Trends in Genetics, 12,* 299–305.

Brondum-Nielsen, K., Chitayat, D., Fukai, K., Lee, S., Lipson, M. H., et al. (1997). Novel mutations of the P gene in Type II oculocutaneous albinism (OCA2). *Human Mutation, 10,* 175–177.

King, R. A., & Oetting, W. S. (1999). Molecular basis of albinism: Mutations and polymorphisms of pigmentation genes associated with albinism. *Human Mutation, 13,* 99–115.

Kodsi, S. R., Rubin, S. E., & Wolf, A. B. (2005). Comparison of clinical findings in pediatric patients with albinism and different amplitudes of nystagmus. *Journal of the American Association for Pediatric Ophthalmology and Strabismus, 9,* 363–368.

SELINA RIVERA-LONGORIA
Texas A&M University

CONGENITAL DISORDERS
VISUAL ACUITY
VISUAL IMPAIRMENT

ALBRIGHT'S HEREDITARY OSTEODYSTROPHY (PSEUDOHYPOPARATHYROIDISM)

Albright's hereditary osteodystrophy (AHO) is believed to be an X-linked inherited disorder that results in a low level of calcium and a high level of phosphorus in the blood. Varying degrees of mental retardation, ranging from slight to severe, are associated with the condition, and hearing and vision problems are found in a number of afflicted children. At times, hyperthyroidism is associated with Albright's, therefore alterations in personality and behavior may be seen (Carter, 1978).

Children with this condition are usually short and stocky with skeletal abnormalities often observed in both upper and lower extremities and prominent foreheads. Calcium deposits may be present in the brain, skin, and organs. Calcification is often found in hands, wrists, and feet. Toes and fingers are short and stubby. There may be impairment in the sense of sour and bitter taste and the sense of smell. Glandular disorders may be seen and sexual glands may be poorly developed (Lemeshaw, 1982).

AHO is a rare disorder and the incidence is unknown at this time. There is a female-to-male sex ratio of 2:1 (Davidson & Mayfield, 2003). Neurological, sensory, and motor problems often accompanying this syndrome will require related attention. Developmental and mental status evaluations will be necessary to measure the degree of disability each child has. Because seizures may be present, drug therapy may be necessary and must be known and monitored.

REFERENCES

Carter, C. (Ed.). (1978). *Medical aspects of mental retardation* (2nd ed.). Springfield, IL: Thomas.

Davidson, B. H., & Mayfield, J. W. (2003). Albright hereditary osteodystrophy. In E. Fletcher-Janzen & C. R. Reynolds (Eds.), *Childhood disorders diagnostic desk reference* (pp. 23–24). New York: Wiley.

Lemeshaw, S. (1982). *The handbook of clinical types in mental retardation.* Boston: Allyn & Bacon.

Stonburg, J., & Wyngaarden, J. (1978). *Metabolic basis of inherited disease.* New York: McGraw-Hill.

SALLY L. FLAGLER
University of Oklahoma

HYPERTHYROIDISM
PHYSICAL ANOMALIES

ALCOHOL AND DRUG ABUSE PATTERNS

Alcohol and drug abuse patterns in contemporary American society should be viewed from many perspectives in an effort to understand the multidimensional nature of the problem. Patterns of alcohol and drug use, abuse, and dependence, particularly among adolescents, have changed radically in past years. Rates of use, abuse, and dependence have all increased at an alarming rate, as has the variety of substances indulged in by young and old alike. Satre (2003)

states that prevalence increases with age, leveling off in the early 20s. For example, a large national survey conducted in 2000 found that 14 percent of eighth graders and 30 percent of 12th graders reported binge drinking in the preceding two weeks. Many theories have been developed as social scientists seek to understand and explain the upsurge in adolescent alcohol and drug use.

To explore and explain fully the complex nature of alcohol and drug use among youths, one must look at the theoretical constructs of anthropology, economics, medicine, politics, psychology, and sociology. In a review of the many determinants of alcohol and drug use, Galizio and Maisto (1985) call for a "biopsychosocial" model. Given the alarming rate of acceleration in alcohol and drug use and the complexity of the issue, such a model would allow theorists and scientists from varying disciplines to study and collaborate in an effort to understand and intervene in this escalating social issue.

The fourth edition of the *Diagnostic and Statistical Manual of Mental Disorders* (American Psychiatric Association, 1994) clearly distinguishes among the terms, use, abuse, and dependence. Although each category of psychoactive drug use (e.g., alcohol, barbiturate, opioid, cocaine, amphetamine, phencyclidine, hallucinogen, cannabis, and tobacco) is separated within the manual, the more general term substance use, is employed when referencing the disorder as a whole. Substance use is defined as a pattern of consumption of a psychoactive substance (i.e., one that has a mechanism of action in the brain) that does not meet the definitive criteria that follow for abuse or dependence. Substance abuse is a pattern of pathological use (i.e., impairment in social or occupational functioning that is related to the use of the substance) that lasts at least 1 month. Substance dependence is defined by the presence of body tolerance to the drug, or evidence of withdrawal symptoms (e.g., runny nose, goose flesh, fevers and chills, gastrointestinal discomfort, muscle cramping) after cessation of use. Tolerance is defined as a state of use in which larger and larger amounts of the particular substance are required to produce the user's desired outcome. Withdrawal symptoms can be physiological, psychological, or both; several drugs, notably alcohol, heroin, opioids, barbiturates, sedatives, and some types of stimulants, frequently create both. This point is significant regarding the establishment and maintenance of specific patterns of alcohol and drug use. Cessation of use by a chemically dependent person may create such great discomfort that the user feels compelled to return to use for relief.

Patterns of alcohol and drug use among adolescents are strongly linked with delinquent behavior. Indeed, delinquent behavior and substance abuse are consistently correlated (Elliott & Ageton, 1976). At the least, use of alcohol, illicit drugs, or prescription drugs not prescribed for the individual using them is illegal. Further, other unconventional or nonconforming actions such as sexual experiences, attenuated academic performance, and flagrant violations of minor and major laws often precede involvement with illicit substances. Not all youths who experiment with alcohol and other drugs will manifest the problems associated with chronic or continued substance abuse, but current research supports a high correlation between continuing drug and alcohol use and delinquent behavior (Clayton, 1981). Initial, or trial, use of alcohol and drugs is likely to occur in youths who have already participated in other minor deviant activities; those who choose a high level of peer group involvement; and those who have seen both parent and peer use. Huba, Wingard, and Bentler (1980) found that prior behavior is a much stronger predictor of intended drug behavior than is either expressed interest or desire. This factor is significant in understanding the causal relationship between criminal behavior and drug and alcohol use. Initial research suggested that drug use precedes other forms of juvenile delinquent behavior (Single & Kandel, 1978), but more recent studies indicate that delinquent subgroups establish group acceptance of continued alcohol and drug use beyond the level of what could be considered normal adolescent experimentation and curiosity (Clayton, 1981).

Initiation of alcohol and drug use can be seen as either a developmental issue of adolescence (Kandel, 1975; NIAAA, 2005) or as an abnormal adaptation to frustration (Hendin, 1980), among other possibilities. Numerous theories have been posited about the initial or trial stage of drug use. However, consensus has been reached as to the critical role of peer-group pressure and the addictive nature, physically and/or psychologically, of the substances used in maintaining drug use. Thus regardless of the reason for beginning drug use, acceptance and support by peers to continue use, tolerance, and aversive withdrawal symptoms are essential factors in understanding the use, abuse, and dependence continuum. The addictive potential of the substance used, amount used, frequency and duration of use, and route of administration are key factors influencing adolescent's ability to start and stop their alcohol and drug use.

Adolescents seem to follow a predictable pattern in their continued alcohol and drug use. The use of legal drugs usually precedes the use of illegal drugs, irrespective of what age the use of illegal drugs is begun. Similarly, the use of illicit drugs like marijuana rarely takes place without prior experimentation or use. However, no evidence indicates that anything inherent in the pharmacologic properties of any substance necessarily leads from use of one to the use of another (the stepping stone theory of addition). That is, the use of tobacco leads to alcohol, alcohol to marijuana, marijuana to stronger drugs, and finally addiction and dependency. Factors such as parental role models, peer pressure, and availability and access seem to be more important than anything pharmacological (Kandel, 1975; NIAAA, 2005).

A further complication is that adolescents who use and abuse substances that can produce tolerance may suffer the biomedical consequences of lifelong chemical affinity for continued abuse and dependency (Cohen, 1981). Also, evidence of a biogenetic predisposition to drug dependency can be seen in patterns of use and abuse in the offspring of alcoholics and, to a lesser degree, other substance-addicted parents (Crabbe, McSwigan, & Belknap, 1985). Children of addicted parents may become addicted with fewer episodes of intoxication, smaller amounts of substances, and fewer of the factors noted previously for adolescents. A word of caution is offered by Schuckit (1980), who states that even when a predisposition or affinity for substances is noted in an adolescent, the final picture must involve not only genetics but also the careful consideration of environment, culture, and other social factors.

The range and variation of the adolescent experience is an important final concern in understanding adolescent patterns of alcohol and drug use. The period of chronological growth beginning at age 12 and continuing through age 21 is marked by great physical, emotional, and intellectual development. Early, middle, and late phase adolescents respond differently to issues such as opportunity for first use, continued use, decision making, the ability to make choices, stress and anxiety, and prevalent patterns of communication within a given peer network. Cohen (1983) and Kandel (1975) substantiate concerns about the impact of the age of first use moving downward. Data on age of admission to treatment centers and survey responses both suggest that a large number of adolescents will become dependent at an earlier age. Further research is needed to determine the impact of this trend on the rapidly developing, but fragile, systems of young people. Although some studies suggest a decline in the frequency of adolescent drug and alcohol use in this society (Johnston, Bachman, & O'Malley, 1982), more specific information is needed about high-risk youths from isolated populations that are not routinely surveyed in national studies (e.g., high school dropouts, younger members of the armed forces, and residents of college dorms). Miller (1981) indicates that the "surveillance function of epidemiological research" will best be served by closer attention to special "pockets" of substance-abusing youths who have escaped close scrutiny in the recent past, and research that points to effective prevention (Satre, 2003).

REFERENCES

American Psychiatric Association. (1994). *Diagnostic and statistical manual of mental disorders* (4th ed.). Washington, DC: Author.

Clayton, R. R. (1981). The delinquency and drug use relationship among adolescents: A critical review. In D. J. Lettieri & J. P. Lundford (Eds.), *Drug abuse and the American adolescent* (pp. 82–98). Rockville, MD: National Institute on Drug Abuse.

Cohen, S. (1981). Adolescence and drug abuse: Biomedical consequences. In D. J. Lettieri & J. P. Ludford (Eds.), *Drug abuse and the American adolescent* (pp. 104–109). Rockville, MD: National Institute on Drug Abuse.

Cohen, S. (1983). *The alcoholism problems.* New York: Haworth.

Crabbe, J. C., McSwigan, J. D., & Belknap, J. K. (1985). The role of genetics in substance abuse. In M. Galizio & S. A. Maisto (Eds.), *Determinants of substance abuse* (pp. 13–54). New York: Plenum.

Elliott, J. D. S., & Ageton, A. R. (1976). The relationship between drug use and crime among adolescents. In Research Triangle Institute, *Appendix to drug use and crime: Report of the Panel on Drug Use and Criminal Behavior* (pp. 297–322). Springfield, VA: National Technical Information Service.

Galizio, M., & Maisto, S. A. (1985). Toward a biopsychosocial theory of substance abuse. In M. Galizio & S. A. Maisto (Eds.), *Determinants of substance abuse* (pp. 425–427). New York: Plenum.

Hendin, H. (1980). Psychosocial theory of drug abuse. In D. J. Lettieri, M. Sayers, & H. W. Pearson (Eds.), *Theories on drug abuse* (pp. 195–200). Rockville, MD: National Institute on Drug Abuse.

Huba, G. J., Wingard, J. A., & Bentler, P. M. (1980). Framework for an interactive theory of drug use. In D. J. Lettieri, M. Sayers, & H. W. Pearson (Eds.), *Theories on drug abuse* (pp. 95–101). Rockville, MD: National Institute on Drug Abuse.

Johnston, L. D., Bachman, J. G., & O'Malley, P. M. (1982). *Student drug use, attitudes, and beliefs: National trends 1975–82.* Detroit, MI: Institute of Social Research.

Kandel, D. (1975). Stages in adolescent involvement in drug use. *Science, 190,* 912–914.

Lettieri, D. J., Sayers, M., & Pearson, H. W. (Eds.). (1980). *Theories on drug abuse: Selected contemporary perspectives.* Rockville, MD: National Institute on Drug Abuse.

Maisto, S. A., & Caddy, G. R. (1981). Self-control and addictive behavior: Present status and prospects. *International Journal of the Addictions, 16,* 109–133.

Miller, J. D. (1981). Epidemiology of drug use among adolescents. In D. J. Lettieri & J. P. Ludford (Eds.), *Drug abuse and the American adolescent* (pp. 25–35). Rockville, MD: National Institute on Drug Abuse.

National Institute on Alcohol Abuse and Alcoholism (NIAAA). (2005). *Frequently asked questions.* Retrieved June 19, 2005, from http://www.niaaa.nih.gov/faq.htm

Roebuck, J., & Kessler, R. (1972). *The etiology of alcoholism.* Springfield, IL: Thomas.

Satre, D. D. (2003). Alcohol abuse. In E. Fletcher-Janzen & C. R. Reynolds (Eds.), *Childhood disorders diagnostic desk reference* (p. 24). New York: Wiley.

Schuckit, M. A. (1980). A theory of alcohol and drug abuse: A genetic approach. In D. J. Lettieri, M. Sayers, & H. W. Pearson (Eds.), *Theories on drug abuse* (pp. 297–302). Rockville, MD: National Institute on Drug Abuse.

Single, E., & Kandel, D. (1978). The role of buying and selling in illicit drug use. In A. Trebach (Ed.), *Drugs, crime and politics.* New York: Praeger.

L. Worth Bolton
Cape Fear Substance Abuse Center

CHEMICALLY DEPENDENT YOUTHS
DRUG ABUSE
SUBSTANCE ABUSE

ALEXANDER GRAHAM BELL ASSOCIATION FOR THE DEAF

The Alexander Graham Bell Association for the Deaf is a nonprofit membership organization established in 1890. The Association's mission is to empower persons who are hearing impaired to function independently by promoting universal rights and optimal opportunities to learn, use, maintain, and improve all aspects of their verbal communications, including their abilities to speak, speechread, use residual hearing, and process both spoken and written language. Towards this end, the Association strives to promote (1) better public understanding of hearing loss in children and adults, (2) detection of hearing loss in early infancy, (3) prompt intervention and use of appropriate hearing aids, (4) dissemination of information on hearing loss, including causes and options for treatment, and (5) inservice training for teachers of children who are deaf or hard of hearing. The organization also collaborates on research relating to auditory/verbal communication and with physicians, audiologists, speech/language specialists, and educators to promote educational and social opportunities for individuals of all ages who are hearing impaired.

To accomplish these objectives, a wide variety of member-oriented programs, publications, and financial aid programs are offered, including school-age financial aid awards, scholarships, aid to parents of infants diagnosed with moderate to profound hearing loss, and arts and sciences awards.

The Alexander Graham Bell Association for the Deaf may be contacted by writing P.O. Box 235, Irvington, NY 10533 or by calling (914) 591-4565 or e-mail agbell@agbellny.org

REFERENCE

Alexander Graham Bell Association for the Deaf. (1996). Washington, DC: Author.

Tamara J. Martin
The University of Texas of the Permian Basin

ALEXIA

Alexia is an acquired neuropsychological disorder of reading in which premorbidly literate adults exhibit severe reading impairments in the absence of other obvious language deficits (McKeeff & Behrmann, 2004). This disorder has been characterized as occurring secondary to a lesion in the left occipito-temporal region. The hallmark of this deficit is the word-length effect: the naming latencies of patients increase dramatically with increasing numbers of letters in the word (Montant & Behrmann, 2000). Alexia also may be known by other names, such as *letter-by-letter reading, alexia without agraphia, spelling dyslexia, verbal dyslexia, word blindness,* or *letter-by-letter dyslexia.*

There are several types of alexic disorders, which are characterized by the types of paralexias (incorrect production of words in oral reading) produced and by the properties of words that tend to affect reading performance. These properties include letter length, orthographic regularity, part of speech, concreteness, and familiarity (Friedman & Lott, 2000). The alexic disorders that have been identified and commonly agreed upon are pure alexia, surface alexia, phonological alexia, and deep alexia.

Pure alexia was first described by Déjerine. Déjerine described pure alexia as a disconnection syndrome that isolates the "center for the optic images of letter," situated in the left angular gyrus, from both visual cortices. Because this language center cannot be accessed through visual stimulation, the patients cannot read (Montant & Behrmann, 2000). Individuals with this condition are able to write (thus no agraphia) but are unable to read anything (alexia). This includes words that they have just finished writing; they almost always have a right homonymous hemianopia as well (Nolte, 1993). Although patients with pure alexia have great difficulty recognizing written words, they are able to identify words that are spelled aloud to them. These individuals retain their ability to speak, write, and understand speech because the lesion, or combination of lesions, affects input from the visual cortex to the left angular gyrus, which itself remains intact. As a result, the language areas (in particular the left angular gyrus) are cut off from all visual input, the destroyed left visual cortex can supply no visual input, but the language areas remain undamaged and still connected to the motor cortex; therefore, verbal and written languages can still be produced (Nolte, 1993). Alexia without agraphia occasionally results following a stroke that involves the left posterior cerebral artery if it causes destruction of the left visual cortex (hence the hemianopia) and of the splenium of the corpus callosum (Nolte, 1993).

Surface alexia has been identified as a variant of alexia. Individuals with surface alexia appear to rely upon the pronunciations of written words in order to ascertain their meanings (Friedman, 2005). Patients with this disorder display an inability to distinguish between homophonic words, such as *threw, through,* and *thru.* The ability to correctly pronounce the words remains intact, but there is an inability to denote which word is on the page.

Phonological alexia is sometimes viewed as the antithesis to surface alexia. While patients with surface alexia tend to depend upon a sounding out process for reading, patients with phonological alexia are unable to read via this mechanism (Friedman & Lott, 2000). This disorder if characterized by the ability of individuals to recognize and read words that are known well, but unknown words and unpronounceable words cannot be read.

Deep alexia features the production of semantic paralexias when reading aloud. A semantic paralexia is a type of reading error in which the word produced is related in meaning to the written target word (Friedman, 2005). Friedman notes that individuals with deep alexia demonstrate difficulty in reading words with affixes, and derivational paralexias are produced in which word endings are added, deleted, or substituted for one another (Friedman & Glosser, 1998).

REFERENCES

Friedman, R. B. (2005). *Alexia by R. B. Friedman.* Retrieved September 8, 2005, from http://gumc.georgetown.edu/departments/neurology/friedman/alexia.html

Friedman, R. B., & Glosser, G. (1998). Aphasia, alexia, and agraphia. In H. S. Friedman (Ed.), *Encyclopedia of mental health* (pp. 137–148). San Diego: Academic Press.

Friedman, R. B., & Lott, S. N. (2000). Rapid word identification in pure alexia is lexical but not semantic. *Brain and Language, 72,* 219–237.

McKeeff, T. J., & Behrmann, M. (2004). Pure alexia and covert reading: Evidence from stroop tasks. *Cognitive Neuropsychology, 21,* 443–458.

Montant, M., & Behrmann, M. (2000). Pure alexia. *Neurocase, 6,* 265–294.

Nolte, J. (1993). *The human brain* (3rd ed.). St. Louis, MO: Mosby Year Book.

CYNTHIA RICCIO
FLOYD HENDERSON
Texas A&M University

DYSLEXIA
TRAUMATIC BRAIN INJURY

ALGOZZINE, BOB (1946–)

After receiving a BS in economics in 1968 from Wagner College in New York, Bob Algozzine earned his MS in educational psychology from the State University of New York, Albany in 1970 and his PhD in the education of exceptional children from Pennsylvania State University in 1975. He was a professor at the University of Florida where he was involved with training regular class teachers to work with exceptional students. Currently, he is professor at the University of North Carolina Charlotte, in the Department of Educational Leadership.

In the past, Algozzine's main interest was in working with students who fail to profit in regular classes. Much of his work was focused on the similarities between learning-disabled (LD) and low-achieving students. Algozzine contended that LD was a sophisticated term for low achievement and that it represented an oversophistication of a concept (Algozzine, Ysseldyke, & Shinn, 1982). He has shown that few differences exist in test profiles of LD and low-achieving students and that performance profiles of many normal students evidence significant discrepancies as well. He believes that schools need to spend less energy trying to identify exceptional students and place more effort on determining what to do with all students who fail to profit from their current educational placement (Algozzine & Ysseldyke, 1983).

Currently Algozzine's interests are behavioral instruction in the total school, positive behavioral interventions and support, and effective teaching (personal communication, August 2005).

Algozzine has written over 200 articles, research reports, monographs, final reports, and books. He has been a member of the Council for Exceptional Children, the American Educational Research Association, and the North Carolina Council for Children with Behavior Disorders.

He is a former co-editor of the journal *Exceptional Children* and is currently co-editor of *Teacher Education and Special Education* with Fred Spooner and *Career Development for Exceptional Individuals* with David Test.

REFERENCES

Algozzine, B., & Ysseldyke, J. E. (1983). Learning disabilities as a subset of school failure: The oversophistication of a concept. *Exceptional Children, 50,* 242–246.

Algozzine, B., Ysseldyke, J. E., & Shinn, M. (1982). Identifying children with learning disabilities: When is a discrepancy severe? *Journal of School Psychology, 20,* 299–305.

E. Valerie Hewitt
Texas A&M University
First edition

Kay E. Ketzenberger
*The University of Texas of the
    Permian Basin*
Second edition

Rachel M. Toplis
*Falcon School District 49
    Colorado Springs, Colorado*
Third edition

ALLERGIC DISORDERS

An allergy is a hypersensitivity to a specific substance (an antigen) that in a similar quantity does not affect other people. The abnormal reactions are usually in the form of asthma, hay fever, eczema, hives, or chronic stuffy nose (allergic rhinitis). Technically, the use of the term should be limited to those conditions in which an immunological mechanism can be demonstrated (Hourmanesh & Clark, 2003). Allergies are common to 20 to 25 percent of the chil-

dren in the United States and are inherited (NIAID, 2005). The tendency to develop allergies is present at birth but may appear at any age.

Allergies can be classified into two types: immediate hypersensitivity (such as allergic rhinitis, asthma, and food allergies) and delayed hypersensitivity (such as reactions to poison ivy). Patients with the former have more of the antibody IgE in their systems. This antibody reacts with whatever patients are allergic to, whether it is something that they breathe, eat, or have skin contact with. This reaction causes certain cells in the body to release chemical mediators such as histamine and serotonin. These chemicals cause the dilation of the small blood vessels, increased secretion from the mucous glands, and smooth muscle contractions that produce the allergy symptoms.

Allergic rhinitis is the commonest cause of nasal congestion in children. Epidemiological data indicate that in the United States alone allergic rhinitis occurs in 59.7 cases per 1,000, accounting for 2 million days lost from school (Shapiro, 1986). An important complication of perennial allergic rhinitis is otitis media with effusion, an accumulation of fluid behind the eardrum in the middle ear. Patients usually have at least an intermittent loss of hearing and may complain of a sensation of fullness or popping and cracking noises.

Allergies often play a role in the etiology of asthma, especially in childhood (Hourmanesh & Clark, 2003). The chemical mediators released upon the allergic reaction cause contraction of the smooth muscles in the walls of the bronchial airways, swelling of the bronchial tubes, and an increase in the rate of secretion of mucous by submucosal glands. This produces obstruction and causes the characteristic wheezing and shortness of breath. Asthma may be mild (one or two mild attacks per year) or severe with intractable wheezing daily. The severe form may greatly restrict physical activity and make school attendance difficult for school-age children. Physical exertion may precipitate wheezing and become a problem in physical education classes.

Skin allergies are common, especially in younger children. Atopic dermatitis (eczema) may occur in 3 to 4 percent of infants and result in a dry, scaly, itchy rash involving the cheeks and extremities. While most children outgrow the rash, over 50 percent of them tend to develop respiratory allergies. Another common rash with an allergic origin is urticaria or hives. Possible causes are allergies to drugs like aspirin or penicillin and to foods.

Food allergies are perhaps the most controversial area of allergy study. Some allergists feel that allergic reactions to foods are rare, while others feel they are a common cause of illness. However, the National Institute of Allergy and Infectious Diseases (NIAID, 2005) state that 150 Americans, usually adolescents and young adults, die annually from food induced anaphylaxis. The frequency of food allergy seems to decrease as children grow older. The most common symptoms of food allergy include gastrointestinal symptoms such as abdominal pain, vomiting and diarrhea, and rashes such as hives. Food may play a role in other allergic conditions such as allergic rhinitis, asthma, and eczema, especially during the first 3 or 4 years of life. The most serious allergic reaction to foods and drugs is an anaphylactic one, in which the person experiences a shocklike reaction that can result in death. Any food can cause an allergic reaction, but the foods most apt to cause one in children include milk, eggs, fish, wheat, corn, peanuts, soy, pork, and chocolate.

Stinging insect allergies may cause a severe anaphylactic reaction to the sting of a bee, wasp, hornet, or yellow jacket. The reaction may occur within minutes after the sting and allergic persons need immediate medical attention.

A thorough history and physical examination are important components of a diagnosis. Seasonal patterns of symptoms, exposure to animals, and usual diet are useful information in identifying causes. Laboratory analysis of nasal secretions, sputum, and blood may establish the presence of eosinophil cells that appear in increased numbers with allergic reactions. Pulmonary function tests are also helpful. Scratch and intradermal skin tests for the suspected allergens can confirm a diagnosis. Another tool is the radio-allergoabsorbant (RAST) test, which measures the level of IgE in the blood for a particular allergen (Hourmanesh & Clark, 2003). The elimination-challenge diet is used for suspected food allergies; after avoiding a particular food for two to three weeks, the patient consumes it and is observed for reactions. Awareness of environmental conditions from change of seasons, foliage in different parts of the country, and environmental factors in homes, schools, and the work place also assists the diagnostician.

While there is no cure for allergies, symptoms may be controlled in a variety of ways. First, symptomatic treatment involves using medication. Antihistamines are the most commonly prescribed drugs for the treatment of allergic reactions. They inhibit some of the actions of histamine but frequently have negative side effects such as sedation, excitation, and insomnia. Antihistamines are often combined with decongestant drugs. Asthmatics are usually treated with bronchodilator drugs that cause relaxation of the smooth muscle surrounding the bronchial tubes. Acute asthmatic attacks and anaphylactic reactions are frequently treated with epinephrine. Both drugs may have negative side effects. For severe allergic problems, corticosteroids may be used, but on a limited basis because of adrenal suppression and limitation of physical growth in children.

The second method of treatment is environmental control, that is, removal of troublesome antigens such as pet hair, dust, and pollen. Good housekeeping practices, use of air conditioning at home and in the car, and other careful planning can prevent many allergic problems. A third and related approach is to teach self-regulation strategies to persons with asthma and other types of allergies. They include relaxation training, biofeedback procedures to modify physiological reactions, and general education about the medical condition (Creer, Marion, & Harm, 1988). A fourth treatment is immunotherapy, which involves injecting the patient with small amounts of an antigen that has been processed into a dilute form. These injections stimulate the immune system to produce another type of antibody that inhibits the reaction between the allergic antibody and the antigen. While initially the shots are taken once or twice a week, the regimen is gradually phased out over a 2- to 3-year period (Patterson et al., 1978).

Allergies have been connected with specific learning disabilities through analyses of case studies (Rapaport & Flint, 1976). Allergic children are rated lower in reading, auditory perception, and visual perception (Harvard, 1975). Teacher and parent ratings as well as test scores indicated lower proficiency among allergic students in some areas (Rawls, Rawls, & Harrison, 1971). Learning-disabled students with recurrent otitis media may have more problems with allergies and verbal skills than non-disabled children (Loose, 1984). Geschwind and Behan (1982) associate left-handedness with reports of learning problems and immunological diseases such as thyroid and bowel disorders.

However, McLoughlin et al. (1983) found no differences in parent reports concerning academic achievement, diagnosis for disabilities, and behavioral problems of allergic and nonallergic students. There was a tendency for children with asthma and chronic rhinitis to be rated lower in listening skills. Additionally, a comparison of group achievement scores of allergic and nonallergic students indicated no interaction of exceptional conditions and allergies (McLoughlin, Nall, & Petrosko, 1985). Some lower estimates of allergic children's school performance seem confused with the effects of socioeconomic factors.

Higher rates of school absenteeism are reported for asthmatic children and those with chronic rhinitis (Shapiro, 1986). Asthmatic children may be absent 10 percent of the time; such absenteeism is a direct cause of school problems. Additionally, the seasonal occurrence of allergic reactions (especially in the fall) and the typical pattern of frequent, brief absences are disruptive to classroom performance, attending skills, and social development. Milder forms of allergies may not cause significant school absenteeism, particularly with improved medical treatment, self-management programs, and parent education (McLoughlin et al., 1985). Furthermore, some previous estimates of higher absenteeism of allergic children may have been confused with the effects of socioeconomic status.

Hearing difficulties are frequently associated with otitis media resulting from allergies (Northern, 1980). Among allergic students, Szanton and Szanton (1966) found many cases of intermittent hearing loss that had been undetected on screening measures. Articulation and/or vocal quality problems have also been reported among allergic students (Baker & Baker, 1980). Recurrent otitis media among three year olds has been associated with lower speech and language performance (Rapin, 1999; Teele et al., 1984).

Allergy history seems present among cases of behavioral and emotional disorders (Mayron, 1978). King (1981) estimated that 70 percent of students with such disorders have personal or family allergy histories; cognitive-emotional symptoms were noted after allergic exposure under double-blind conditions. Psychological and personality changes are frequently reported by asthmatic children and their parents (Creer, Marion, & Creer, 1983). However, comparisons of reports and ratings of behavioral problems, placement in services for behavior disorders, and school suspensions between allergic and nonallergic students have not yielded significantly different profiles (McLoughlin et al., 1985).

Allergy medication may have adverse effects on behavior and exacerbate existing behavioral problems (Hourmanesh & Clark, 2003; McLoughlin et al., 1983). Theophylline has been significantly correlated with inattentiveness, hyperactivity, irritability, drowsiness, and withdrawal behavior; the negative side effects increase with length of use. Furakawa and his colleagues (1984) found decreased test performances under the influence of theophylline. Terbutaline created socially inappropriate behavior in a comparison group (Creer, 1979), and corticosteroids negatively affected academic performance (Suess & Chai, 1981). Ladd, Leibold, Lindsey, and Ornby (1980) also reported euphoria, insomnia, and visual disturbances with corticosteroids. Antihistamines may cause sedation, dry mouth, and irritability (Weinberger & Hendeles, 1980). Visual hallucinations occur among some children receiving decongestants (Sankey, Nunn, & Sills, 1984).

Allergic disorders have important implications for the professional assessment and intervention of exceptionalities as well as for parental involvement. Certain types of allergies and/or the side effects of medication may be contributing factors in behaviors of concern and may require special consideration when designing special services. The self-monitoring and management skills taught in special education may be mutually beneficial in coping with this medical condition.

REFERENCES

Baker, M., & Baker, C. (1980). Difficulties generated by allergies. *Journal of School Health, 50,* 583–585.

Creer, T. L. (1979). *Asthma therapy.* New York: Springer.

Creer, T. L., Marion, R. J., & Creer, P. P. (1983). The asthma problem behavior checklist: Parental perceptions of the behavior of asthmatic children. *Journal of Asthma, 20,* 97–104.

Creer, T. L., Marion, R. J., & Harm, D. L. (1988). Childhood asthma. In D. K. Routh (Ed.), *Handbook of pediatric psychology* (pp. 162–189). New York: Guilford.

Furakawa, C. T., Shapiro, G. G., DuHamel, T., Weimer, L., Pierson, W. E., & Bierman, C. W. (1984, March). Learning and behavior problems associated with theophylline therapy. *Lancet,* 621.

Geschwind, N., & Behan, P. (1982). Left-handedness: Association with immune disease, migraine, and developmental learning disorders. *Proceedings of the National Academy of Science, USA, 79,* 5097–5100.

Harvard, J. G. (1975). Relationship between allergic conditions and language and/or learning disabilities. *Dissertation Abstracts International, 35,* 6940.

Hourmanesh, N., & Clark, E. (2003). Allergy disorders. In E. Fletcher-Janzen & C. R. Reynolds (Eds.), *Childhood disorders diagnostic desk reference* (pp. 27–28). New York: Wiley.

King, D. S. (1981). Can allergic exposure provoke psychological symptoms? *Biology Psychiatry, 16,* 3–19.

Ladd, F. T., Leibold, S. R., Lindsey, C. N., & Ornby, R. (1980). RX in the classroom. *Instructor, 90,* 58–59.

Loose, F. F. (1984). *Educational implications of recurrent otitis media among children at risk for learning disabilities.* Unpublished doctoral dissertation, Michigan State University.

Mayron, L. (1978). Ecological factors in learning disabilities. *Journal of Learning Disabilities, 11,* 40–50.

McLoughlin, J. A., Nall, M., Isaacs, B., Petrosko, J., Karibo, J., & Lindsey, B. (1983). The relationship of allergies and allergy treatment to school performance and student behavior. *Annals of Allergy, 51,* 506–510.

McLoughlin, J. A., Nall, M., & Petrosko, J. (1985). Allergies and learning disabilities. *Learning Disability Quarterly, 8,* 255–260.

NIAID. (2005). *National Institute of Allergy and Infectious Diseases allergy statistics.* Retrieved June 19, 2005, from http://www.niaid.nih.gov/factsheets/allergystat.htm

Northern, J. L. (1980). Diagnostic tests of ear disease. In C. Bierman & D. Pearlman (Eds.), *Allergic diseases of infancy, childhood and adolescence* (pp. 492–501). Philadelphia: Saunders.

Patterson, R., Lieberman, P., Irons, J., Pruzansky, J., Melam, H., Metzger, W. J., & Zeiss, C. R. (1978). Immunotherapy. In E. Middleton, Jr., C. Reed, & E. Ellis (Eds.), *Allergy principles and practice* (Vol. 2, pp. 877–897). St. Louis: Mosby.

Rapaport, H. G., & Flint, H. (1976). Is there a relationship between allergy and learning disabilities? *Journal of School Health, 46,* 139–141.

Rapin, I. (1999). Hearing impairments. In R. F. Swaiman & S. Ashwal (Eds.), *Pediatric neurology* (pp. 77–95). St. Louis, MO: Mosby.

Rawls, D. J., Rawls, J. R., & Harrison, D. W. (1971). An investigation of 6 to 11 year old children with allergic disorders. *Journal of Consulting and Clinical Psychology, 36,* 260–264.

Sankey, R. J., Nunn, A. J., & Sills, J. A. (1984). Visual hallucinations in children receiving decongestants. *British Medical Journal, 288,* 1369.

Shapiro, G. (1986). Understanding allergic rhinitis. *Pediatrics in Review, 7,* 212–218.

Suess, W. M., & Chai, H. (1981). Neuropsychological correlates of asthma: Brain damage or drug effects? *Journal of Consulting and Clinical Psychology, 49,* 135–136.

Szanton, V. J., & Szanton, W. C. (1966). Hearing disturbances in allergic children. *Journal of Asthma Research, 4,* 25–28.

Teele, D. W., Klein, J. O., Rosner, B. A., & the Greater Boston Otitis Media Study Group. (1984). *Pediatrics, 74,* 282–287.

Tuft, L. (1973). *Allergy management in clinical practice.* St. Louis, MO: Mosby.

Weinberger, M., & Hendeles, L. (1980). Pharmacologic management. In C. Bierman & D. Pearlman (Eds.), *Allergic diseases of infancy, childhood and adolescence* (pp. 311–332). Philadelphia: Saunders.

JAMES A. McLOUGHLIN
University of Louisville

MICHAEL NALL
Louisville, Kentucky

ASTHMA
CHRONIC ILLNESS IN CHILDREN

Alley, G., & Foster, C. (1979). *Instructional planning for exceptional children.* Denver: Love.

Lenz, B. K., & Alley, G. R. (1983). *The effect of advance organizers on learning and retention of learning disabled adolescents within the context of a cooperative planning model.* Lawrence, KS: Florida Atlantic University/Kansas University.

ROBERTA C. STOKES
Texas A&M University

TAMARA J. MARTIN
The University of Texas of the Permian Basin

ALLEY, GORDON R. (1934–1999)

Gordon R. Alley received his BA (1959) from Augustina, Illinois, later earning his MA (1961) in Psychology and his doctorate (1967) in Special Education and School Psychology from the University of Iowa. Alley's contributions to the field of education include his service as teacher of the mentally retarded, school psychologist, and director of special education. He taught at the University of Utah (1967–1970), and was professor of special education and a lecturer in pediatrics at the University of Kansas from 1970. Alley was invited to present his papers to regional and national gatherings on numerous occasions.

Alley's work emphasized learning strategies associated with the developmental characteristics of adolescents, with his research promoting alternatives to the traditional tutorial and remedial approaches to interventions for students with learning disabilities. As a cofounding member of the Institute for Research in Learning Disabilities at the University of Kansas, Alley published many of his writings pursuant to his interests, including a chapter in *Instructional Planning for Exceptional Children* (1979). Other important publications are his 1979 work, *Teaching the Learning Disabled Adolescent* and *The Effect of Advance Organizers on the Learning and Retention of Learning Disabled Adolescents within the Context of a Cooperative Planning Model,* a study conducted by Alley and Keith Lenz in 1983. Alley's study investigated whether advance organizers would help learning disabled adolescents process information on selected academic tasks more effectively. Results of the research indicated the efficacy of their use in secondary classrooms.

REFERENCES

Alley, G., & Deshler, D. D. (1979). *Teaching the learning disabled adolescent: Strategies and methods.* Denver: Love.

ALPHABETIC METHOD

The alphabetic method of teaching children to read is historically connected with the development of an alphabet. Once letters and sounds were fixed in a structure (an alphabet), a method to master this structure emerged. The first recorded use of the alphabetic method was in ancient Greek and Roman civilizations. Reading instruction began by teaching children all the letters in their proper alphabetical order. After a complete mastery of the alphabet, children learned to group the letters to form syllables, words, and finally sentences. Reading instruction was considered primarily an oral process; the child recited the spelling of each syllable or word and then pronounced it. This progression of teaching letters, syllables, words, and sentences was the predominant method of teaching reading from Greek and Roman times until the late 1800s (Huey, 1908).

In using this method, sixteenth- and seventeenth-century teachers drilled children unmercifully on the names of the letters (Matthews, 1966). Instructional materials that presented lists of letters, syllables, and words to be memorized before advancing to the text were developed. The *New England Primer* was one of the most widely used reading texts in seventeenth-century America. Each reading selection focused on a moral or religious lesson, and was preceded by an alphabet, lists of the vowels and consonants, and lists of syllables such as ab, eb, and ib. The lists of words for spelling began with one-syllable words and progressed to two- and three-syllable words (Huey, 1980).

As the English language evolved, letter names no longer directly represented speech sounds; therefore, children became more and more confused as they tried to read modern literature by simply reciting the names of the letters. Realizing that this confusion hindered efforts to teach reading effectively, the alphabetic method was gradually replaced by phonetically based methods of reading instruction. By the beginning of the twentieth century, the classic alphabetic method was seldom used.

REFERENCES

Huey, E. B. (1908). *The psychology and pedagogy of reading.* New York: Macmillan.

Matthews, M. M. (1966). *Teaching to read.* Chicago: University of Chicago Press.

CHRIS CHERRINGTON
Lycoming College

DISTAR
READING REMEDIATION
WHOLE WORD TEACHING

ALTERNATING TREATMENTS DESIGN

The alternating treatments design is a variation of the multielement designs (Kennedy, 2005). Unlike the multielement design, the alternating treatments design can include a baseline phase; an intervention phase, where two or more independent variables are alternated in a similar fashion as in the multielement design; and a third phase, where the independent variable that was most effective is continued (see Figure 1).

In order to demonstrate a functional relationship, this design requires that responding in one condition is demonstrably different than in the other conditions that are under investigation. In other words, "if response differentiation occurs between the A and B conditions, then a functional relation has been demonstrated" (Kennedy, 2005, p. 137). The inclusion of a baseline phase and a third phase are considered limitations to this research design. For example, baseline data is difficult to interpret because they are not collected (replicated) in subsequent phases. In addition, data in the third phase are also difficult to interpret due to the lack of any experimental manipulation (Kennedy, 2005). Like the multielement design, the alternating treatments design is susceptible to sequence or interaction effects (Sulzer-Azaroff & Mayer, 1991), and the researcher should attempt to control for this using strategies such as randomization or counterbalancing (Barlow & Hersen, 1984; Cooper, Heron, & Heward, 1987).

The alternating treatments design has been used to examine the effect of interspersing easier problems into standard mathematics seatwork for a student with high levels of off-task behavior (McCurdy, Skinner, Grantham, Watson,

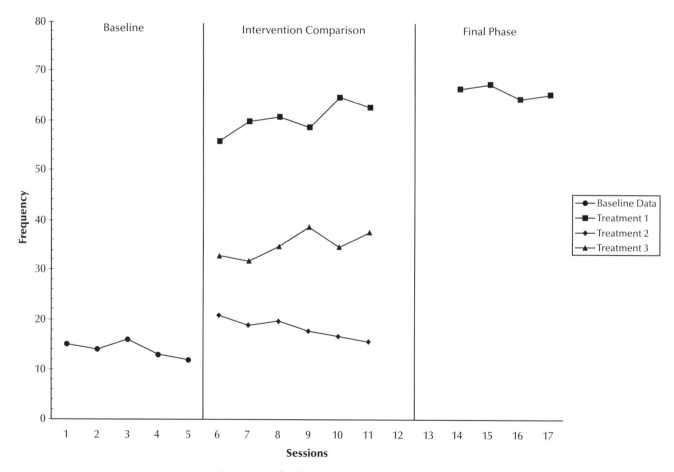

Figure 1 Baseline/intervention comparison/final phase

& Hindman, 2001) and to compare instructional strategies (i.e., response cards, numbered heads together, and whole group questions and answers) on quiz and pre- to posttest scores for students in sixth grade chemistry (Maheady, Michielli-Pendi, Mallette, & Harper, 2002). This design is useful for situations where the withdrawal of the treatment would be inappropriate, such as in the ABAB design and when the researcher is interested in comparing the effects of multiple independent variables.

REFERENCES

Barlow, D. H., & Hersen, M. (1984). *Single case experimental designs: Strategies for studying behavior change* (2nd ed.). New York: Pergamon.

Cooper, J. O., Heron, T. E., & Heward, W. L. (1987). *Applied behavior analysis.* New York: Macmillan.

Kennedy, C. H. (2005). *Single-case designs for educational research.* Boston: Allyn & Bacon.

Maheady, L., Michielli-Pendi, J., Mallette, B., & Harper, G. F. (2002). A collaborative research project to improve the academic performance of a diverse sixth grade science class. *Teacher Education and Special Education, 25,* 55–70.

McCurdy, M., Skinner, C. H., Grantham, K., Watson, T. S., & Hindman, P. M. (2001). Increasing on-task behavior in an elementary student during mathematics seatwork by interspersing additional brief problems. *School Psychology Review, 30,* 23–32.

Sulzer-Azaroff, B., & Mayer, G. R. (1991). *Behavior analysis for lasting change.* Fort Worth, TX: Harcourt Brace.

RANDALL L. DE PRY
*University of Colorado at
Colorado Springs*

ABAB DESIGN
RESEARCH IN SPECIAL EDUCATION

ALTERNATIVE ASSESSMENTS

See ASSESSMENTS, ALTERNATIVE.

ALTERNATIVE COMMUNICATION METHODS IN SPECIAL EDUCATION

Individuals with severe communication disorders are those who may benefit from AAC (augmentative and alternative communication)—those for whom gestural, speech, and/or written communication is temporarily or permanently inadequate to meet all of their communication needs. For those individuals, hearing impairment is not the primary cause for the communication impairment. Although some individuals may be able to produce a limited amount of speech, it is inadequate to meet their varied communication needs. Numerous terms that were initially used in the field but are now rarely mentioned include speechless, nonoral, non-vocal, nonverbal, and aphonic. (ASHA, 1991, p. 10)

Beukelman and Ansel (1995) estimate 8 to 12 persons per 1,000 in the United States are in need of augmentative and alternative communication (AAC).

In the mid 1970s, alternative methods of communication began to be explored with the nonspeaking population. These methods are termed augmentative communication systems. They are currently being used with children and adults who have physical, mental, emotional, and linguistic handicaps. The American Speech-Language-Hearing Association (ASHA; 1991) defines an AAC system as "an integrated group of components, including the symbols, aids, strategies, and techniques used by individuals to enhance communication" (p. 10). Unaided communication systems use only the physical body for communication. They include sign languages, gestures, and facial expressions. Aided systems require additional equipment for communication. There are many advantages to using unaided systems for communication. Social interaction is enhanced because the rate of communication is typically fast. Speaker-listener eye contact is maintained when using unaided systems. The meaning of many signs and gestures are concrete, making learning and recall of vocabulary easier. In addition, during training, sign and gesture response can be physically prompted and shaped by the instructor.

Sign languages such as American Sign Language (ASL) were originally developed for the hearing-impaired population. They are separate languages and not simply word-for-word manual translations of spoken English or other oral languages. Educational sign systems, or pedagogical sign systems, are designed to be manual equivalents of spoken English. Signed English is an educational sign system that is used frequently with the nonspeaking population (Bryen & Joyce, 1985). The differences between true sign languages and educational sign systems include differences in word order and sign representations and changes in grammatical structures. To use sign systems as an augmentative communication system, the nonspeaking person should have good motor control of the hands, arms, and face, along with good visual acuity and spatial orientation (Beukelman & Mirenda, 1998). Persons who routinely interact with a signing communicator will also need to learn the system (ASHA, 2005). Gestures and facial expressions typically require less motor control than sign-language systems. Pantomime and natural gestures can often be used and understood without extensive training. Skelly and Schinsky (1979) developed a comprehensive gestural system known as Amer-Ind; it is based on American Indian hand talk. While gesture systems are initially less complex to learn, the information that can be conveyed is often constrained. Gestures and facial expressions are typically used as supplements to other communication systems, or as temporary communication methods.

Aided communication systems require additional devices

A Hierarchy of Aided Communication Symbol Systems

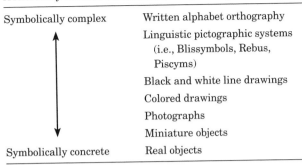

Symbolically complex	Written alphabet orthography
	Linguistic pictographic systems (i.e., Blissymbols, Rebus, Piscyms)
	Black and white line drawings
	Colored drawings
	Photographs
	Miniature objects
Symbolically concrete	Real objects

or equipment for communication. Computers, writing with pen and paper, and communication boards are all examples of aided communication systems. An aided communication system consists of a communication aid, which is the mechanism used for communication, and a symbol system, which is the language used for communication.

The communication aid can consist of three major components: the interface, the communication device, and the output system. Complex electronic systems usually have all three components. Simple communication boards may consist of the communication device alone. The interface is used to control the system. A head stick, joystick, or computer keyboard are examples of interfaces. They are used to select symbols on the communication device. Direct selection allows the user to directly choose symbols for communication. Scanning systems present symbol choices to the user, who then activates a response when the desired symbol is reached. A scanning system resembles an advanced form of the guessing game "Twenty Questions." The communication device can display all of the available vocabulary options, or it can display a few symbols that are combined into codes to access vocabulary. Electronic devices often indicate, by small lights or LCD display screens, which symbol has been selected. Once the entire message to be communicated is completed, an output device such as a speech synthesizer, computer modem, or printer is used to convey the message to others.

Many symbol systems have been developed for use in aided communication systems. Symbol systems can be hierarchically ordered from linguistically simple concrete systems to complex written languages (see Table). Concrete linguistic systems are the easiest to learn. However, linguistically complex systems allow greater flexibility for communicative expression. The advantage of aided communication systems is flexibility. The communication aid and symbol system can be adapted to meet the physical and mental skills of almost any person. The symbol system can be permanently displayed to enhance symbol recall and memory. In addition, most aided communication systems can be easily understood by others without extensive listener training.

There are also many disadvantages to using aided communication systems. The devices themselves are often physically cumbersome and difficult to transport. Communication through a mechanical device also reduces speaker-listener

eye contact and affects the location and distance from the speaker or a listener.

Before an augmentative communication system can be developed, a complete evaluation of the user's physical, linguistic, cognitive, and academic skills must be completed (ASHA, 2005). This requires a team of professionals including speech-language pathologists, physical therapists, occupational therapists, and school psychologists. The physical evaluation should determine the user's gross motor skills, range of motion, adaptive posturing and seating, fine motor accuracy, and speed of movement. An evaluation of language skills should determine the user's current communication strategies and receptive language skills, and the communicative needs of the user (Beukelman & Mirenda, 1998). Academic and cognitive skills should be evaluated with a language specialist to determine a language symbol system that is within the user's capabilities. In addition, the academic and vocational skills and needs of the user should be identified. The evaluation results are then used to determine the communication aid, or unaided system, and symbolic system that best fits the user's needs.

When an aided communication system is being developed, the system should be designed to increase communication speed. Message cost can be used to analyze the communication speed of augmentative communication systems (Goodenough-Trepagnier, Tarry, & Prather, 1982; Higgenbotham, 1992). Message cost equals the number of separate motor movements necessary to encode a message. For example, the message cost of letter-by-letter encoding for "I want to go to the store" equals 25 when blank spaces between words are included. By using whole word symbols, message cost is reduced to seven. If unnecessary words are eliminated (i.e., "I want go store"), message cost is further reduced to four. Any system that requires more motor movements to encode messages will not result in effective communication.

Once an augmentative system is developed, extensive user training is required. There are two components to the training process. The first is augmentative system training. The user needs to learn how the augmentative system functions. Communication aid operation, vocabulary training, and the production of phrases and sentences are aspects of system training. The second component is communication training. Studies have documented that many nonspeaking persons who are trained to use their augmentative communication systems are unable to communicate effectively (Calculator & Bredosian, 1988; Light, 1988; Romski & Sevcik, 1988). Normal children learn how to interact communicatively and socially with others through experience. Nonspeaking persons have limited interactive experiences and need modeling of communicative and social interaction skills. Communication programming should concentrate on establishing the natural communication skills for the natural setting, in the same settings in which they will ultimately be used (ASHA, 2005; Goosens, Crain,

& Elder, 1995). Nonspeaking persons also need to learn how to respond to others, how to maintain conversations, and how to increase intelligibility in various contexts.

The ability to communicate with others is a binding element within members of a society. The development of augmentative communication systems has opened many avenues of communication for the nonspeaking population. While most augmentative systems are not yet perfect replacements for oral speech, they do provide a means of communication and interaction with others.

REFERENCES

American Speech-Language-Hearing Association (ASHA). (1991). Report: Augmentative and Alternative Communication. *ASHA, 33*(Suppl. 5), 9–12.

ASHA. (2005). *American Speech-Language-Hearing Association introduction to augmentative and alternative communication.* Retrieved June 19, 2005, from http://www.asha.org/public/speech/disorders/augmentative-and-alternative.htm

Beukelman, D., & Ansel, B. (1995). Research priorities in augmentative and alternative communication. *Augmentative and Alternative Communication, 11,* 131–134.

Beukelman, D., & Mirenda, P. (1998). *Augmentative and alternative communication.* Baltimore: Paul H. Brookes.

Bryen, D., & Joyce, D. (1985). Language intervention with the severely handicapped: A decade of research. *Journal of Special Education, 19,* 7–39.

Calculator, S., & Bredosian, J. H. (1988). *Communication assessment and intervention for adults with mental retardation.* San Diego, CA: College-Hill Press.

Goldman-Eisler, F. (1986). *Cycle linguistics: Experiments in spontaneous speech.* New York: Academic Press.

Goodenough-Trepagnier, C., Tarry, E., & Prather, P. (1982). Derivation of an efficient nonvocal communication system. *Human Factors, 24,* 163–172.

Goosens, C., Crain, S., & Elder, P. (1995). *Engineering the preschool environment for interactive symbolic communication.* Birmingham: Southeast Augmentative Communication Conference Publications.

Higgenbotham, D. J. (1992). Evaluation of keystroke savings across five assistive communication technologies. *Augmentative and Alternative Communication, 8,* 258–272.

Light, J. (1988). Interaction involving individuals using augmentative and alternative communication systems: State of the art and future directions. *Augmentative and Alternative Communication, 4,* 66–82.

Romski, M., & Sevcik, R. (1988). Augmentative and alternative communication systems: Considerations for individuals with severe intellectual disabilities. *Augmentative and Alternative Communication, 4,* 83–93.

SHARON L. GLENNEN
Pennsylvania State University

SHEELA STUART
George Washington University

COMMUNICATION BOARDS
COMMUNICATION DISORDERS

ALTERNATIVE FORMATS OF INFORMATION

An alternative format is produced when information in one medium is transformed into a different medium while maintaining as much of the original meaning as possible. The form and format of the information may change, but the conservation of the original information is usually the goal of such conversions. For example, a printed textbook (original medium) may be converted into a Braille book (new medium). When applied to special education, alternative formats usually refer to media conversions done to make information available to a student with a disability. Although *alternative formats* have traditionally referred to media used to accommodate students with sensory impairments (e.g., Braille, taped texts, tactile graphics, refreshable Braille), the term is today being applied to alternative formats used to accommodate students with cognitive impairments such as learning disabilities and Attention-Deficit/Hyperactivity Disorder. These populations of students frequently take advantage of taped text materials, text-to-speech technology, cognitive mapping technology, audio files of text materials, and others.

It is important to note that conversion of material into an alternative format does not necessarily equate to accessibility. For example, conversion of a textbook into Braille may provide access to the material by a Braille reader, but ironically the accessibility of the alternative format has decreased since the population of people who can access the format has been reduced. On the other hand, conversion of printed material into an electronic format such as hypertext markup language (HTML) or extensible markup language (XML) may increase accessibility.

When material is converted into an alternative format, some of the original meaning may be lost. For example, in most modern textbooks, desktop publishing techniques can convey meaning by the relative position and size of text elements, coloring and shading, as well as graphic information. When converting these materials into a linear format such as Braille, much of the original message may be altered or lost. The degree of loss in translation varies widely based upon the nature of both the material and inherent strengths and weaknesses of the original and final formats. It is a myth that materials can be converted into an alternative format with no loss of meaning or information. This is an important concept for the practitioner.

The following are some examples of alternative formats:

- *Braille.* Both literary and scientific (Nemeth) Braille are common. Less common is music Braille.

- *Taped Texts.* Organizations such as Recordings for the Blind and Dyslexic (Recording for the Blind and Dyslexic, 2005) provide a wide range of text materials on tape.
- *Digital Talking Books (DTBs).* These consist of analog recordings of material with digital indexing and search capabilities.
- *Tactile Graphics.* These can be made with a variety of technologies, including tactile embossers such as the Tiger Advantage system (Viewplus Technologies, 2005).
- *Large Print.* This is defined as nonserif print of 16-point size or larger.

REFERENCES

Recording for the Blind and Dyslexic. (2005). *Welcome to recording for the blind and dyslexic.* Retrieved October 10, 2005, from http://www.rfbd.org/

Viewplus Technologies. (2005). *ViewPlus Tiger Braille printers.* Retrieved October 10, 2005, from http://www.viewplus.com/products/braille-embossers/

DAVID SWEENEY
Texas A&M University

BRAILLE
RECORDING FOR THE BLIND

AMAROUTIC FAMILIAL IDIOCY

See TAY-SACHS SYNDROME.

AMBLYOPIA

Amblyopia, also called suppression blindness (Harley & Lawrence, 1977), is a visual condition that occurs when an anatomically healthy eye cannot see because of some other defect (Eden, 1978). Amblyopia is commonly called "lazy eye"; however, this is a misnomer (Eden, 1978) because it implies that amblyopia results from a muscular problem. Actually, amblyopia can have a number of causes. For example, strabismus (a condition in which the two eyes are not parallel when viewing an object) can lead to amblyopia. The brain ignores the visual signals of one of the two eyes to reduce the annoyance of double vision. Other factors such as astigmatism can also lead to amblyopia.

The degree of visual impairment associated with amblyopia can vary a great deal from losses that are just below normal to those in which only large objects can be identified. Treatment of amblyopia consists of treating the causal factors. It must be accomplished early in life (before the age of six) because the child is likely to permanently lose the ability to process a 20/20 image from the affected eye.

REFERENCES

Eden, J. (1978). *The eye book.* New York: Viking.

Harley, R. K., & Lawrence, G. A. (1977). *Visual impairment in the schools.* Springfield, IL: Thomas.

Toplis, R. (2003). Amblyopia. In E. Fletcher-Janzen & C. R. Reynolds (Eds.), *Childhood disorders diagnostic desk reference* (pp. 33–34). New York: Wiley.

THOMAS E. ALLEN
Gallaudet College

BLIND
CATARACTS

AMERICAN ACADEMY FOR CEREBRAL PALSY AND DEVELOPMENTAL MEDICINE

The American Academy for Cerebral Palsy, founded in 1947, changed its name in 1976 to the American Academy for Cerebral Palsy and Developmental Medicine (AACPDM). This is a professional organization that was originally composed of physicians, diplomates of specialty boards, and persons holding a PhD degree in specialties concerned with diagnosis, care, treatment, and research into cerebral palsy and developmental disorders.

The scope of the Academy's interests has expanded from an initial focus on cerebral palsy into related areas of developmental medicine, including spina bifida, neuromuscular disease, traumatic brain injury and other acquired disabilities, genetic disorders, communications problems, and specific learning disabilities.

The AACPDM's activities and services include the presentation of awards and grants for research, demonstration, and personnel preparation. The organization also supports or conducts continuing education activities. The AACPDM holds an annual convention. The office address is 6300 N. River Road, Suite 727, Rosemont, IL 60018. Telephone: (847) 698-1635.

SHIRLEY A. JONES
*Virginia Polytechnic Institute
and State University*
First edition

KAY KETZENBERGER
*The University of Texas of the
Permian Basin*
Second edition

RACHEL M. TOPLIS
*Falcon School District 49
Colorado Springs, Colorado*
Third edition

AMERICAN ANNALS OF THE DEAF

The American *Annals of the Deaf* is a professional journal dedicated to quality in education and related services for hearing impaired children and adults. First published in 1847, the publication is the oldest and most widely read English language journal dealing with deafness and the education of deaf persons. The *Annals* is the official organ of the Convention of American Instructors of the Deaf and the Conference of Educational Administrators of Schools and Programs for the Deaf. Members of the executive committees of both organizations comprise the Joint *Annals* Administrative Committee charged with the direction and administration of the publication.

For 150 years, the *Annals* has primarily focused on the education of deaf students as well as dissemination of information for professionals associated with the educational development of this population. Concurrently, the *Annals* extends its range of topics beyond education, incorporating the broad interests of educators in the general welfare of deaf children and adults, and representing the diverse professional readership of the publication. Topics covered include communication methods and strategies, language development, mainstreaming and residential schools, parent-child relationships, and teacher training and teaching skills.

Four literary issues are published by the journal each year in March, July, October, and December. An annual reference issue, a comprehensive listing of schools and programs in the United States and Canada for students who are deaf or hard of hearing and their teachers, is also published by the *Annals*. In addition to the listings, the reference issue provides demographic, audiological, and educational data regarding students who are deaf and hard of hearing and the schools they attend. The data are compiled annually by the Center for Assessment and Demographic Studies, a component of the Gallaudet Research Institute.

CONFERENCE OF EDUCATIONAL
ADMINISTRATORS OF SCHOOLS
AND PROGRAMS FOR THE DEAF

AMERICAN ASSOCIATION FOR THE ADVANCEMENT OF SCIENCE

The American Association for the Advancement of Science (AAAS) was founded in Philadelphia in 1848, making it one of the oldest professional societies in the United States. AAAS is a nonprofit society dedicated to the advancement of scientific and technological quality across all fields of science, and to increasing the general public's understanding of science and technology. The mission of the organization, according to its Constitution, is to "further the work of scientists, facilitate cooperation among them, foster scientific freedom and responsibility, improve the effectiveness of science in the promotion of human welfare, advance education in science, and increase the public's understanding and appreciation of the promise of scientific methods in human progress" (AAAS, 1995).

Today AAAS's membership is international, and is composed of over 143,000 scientists, science educators, engineers, and interested others; membership is open to anyone interested in scientific and technological progress. There are 285 scientific and engineering societies that have chosen to affiliate themselves with the AAAS, and they include 238 other societies, 44 state and regional academies of science, and 3 city academies. AAAS is thus the world's largest federation of professional scientific organizations. The association is organized into 24 sections which represent the various fields of interest of members, and four regional divisions. Programs fall into one of three directorates: Education and Human Resources, International, and Science and Policy.

The Association publishes many science books and reference works, the most prestigious being the weekly *Science,* a highly respected publication which disseminates state-of-the-art scientific research.

REFERENCE

American Association for the Advancement of Science (AAAS). (1995). *General information.* Retrieved from http://www.aaas.org/aaas/geninfo.html

KAY E. KETZENBERGER
*The University of Texas of the
Permian Basin*

AMERICAN ASSOCIATION FOR THE SEVERELY HANDICAPPED

See TASH

AMERICAN ASSOCIATION OF COLLEGES FOR TEACHER EDUCATION

The American Association of Colleges for Teacher Education (AACTE) is a national, voluntary association of colleges and universities with undergraduate and/or graduate programs committed to the preparation of professional educators, including teachers and other educational personnel. The Association is composed of over 700 member institutions representing both private and public colleges and universities of every size and located in every state, the District of Columbia, Puerto Rico, the Virgin Islands, and Guam.

As a group, the AACTE institutions produce more than 85 percent of new educators each year.

The Association encourages major initiatives and innovations in teacher education, and serves as advocate for the profession on issues of interest to the membership, particularly in areas of certification, accreditation, and assessment. AACTE is a major influence in helping form federal and state educational policy, and is recognized as the primary representative of teacher education interests before Congress, state legislatures, other governmental agencies, and the media. The Association continues to advise the National Council for Accreditation of Teacher Education (NCATE) on issues of institutional standards and accreditation. AACTE publishes the biweekly newsletter *Briefs,* which reports on current happenings in the education, public policy, and government arenas to the teacher education community.

AACTE offices are located at 1307 New York Ave. N.W., Suite 300, Washington, DC 20005. Telephone: (202) 293-2450.

KAY E. KETZENBERGER
*The University of Texas of the
Permian Basin*

AMERICAN ASSOCIATION FOR MARRIAGE AND FAMILY THERAPY

The American Association for Marriage and Family Therapy (AAMFT), founded in 1942, is the national organization representing marriage and family therapists. The association seeks to (1) advance marriage and family therapy through increased understanding, research, and treatment, (2) establish and maintain standards for the education and training of marriage and family therapists, and (3) promote professional development, ethics, and conduct among marriage and family therapists. The AAMFT has over 23,000 members and offers four membership categories. Clinical, Associate, and Student members are mental health therapists or therapists-in-training who have met varying levels of AAMFT credential standards. Affiliate members are individuals in allied mental health professions who are interested in marriage and family therapy.

The AAMFT publishes three periodicals and a variety of books, videotapes, and brochures. The *Journal of Marital and Family Therapy* (the official journal of the association) offers current research findings in marriage and family therapy. The *Family Therapy News* provides the latest updates in the field of marriage and family therapy and *Practice Strategies* assists with practice management information and advice.

Each year the AAMFT sponsors an Annual Conference in early fall for training in family systems theory, practice, and research. Also, Summer Institutes are held for continued learning and professional development in marriage

and family therapy. The association offices are located at 112 South Alfred Street, Alexandria, VA 22314. Telephone: (703) 838-9808.

LINDA M. MONTGOMERY
*The University of Texas of the
Permian Basin*

AMERICAN ASSOCIATION ON MENTAL RETARDATION

The American Association on Mental Retardation (AAMR) was founded in 1876, and claims over 9,500 members both in the United States and throughout the world. Its membership is composed of professionals from a large variety of academic disciplines who are interested in the field of mental retardation, as well as nonprofessionals who are involved in and care about mental retardation. One of its primary goals is to expand the possibilities for people with mental retardation to live fulfilling and productive lives.

The AAMR offers strong support to research in mental retardation in the service of increasing the knowledge and skills of all who are involved in the field of mental retardation, through the publication of two professional journals and the Association's newspaper *News and Notes.* The *American Journal on Mental Retardation* is a scholarly research journal, and *Mental Retardation* includes research, book reviews, and conceptual articles aimed at practitioners.

The AAMR is organized into 10 regions that cover the United States, Canada, and parts of the Pacific, and contains over 85 local, state, or provincial chapters. There are 16 divisions, the topics of which include, among others, administration, communication disorders, legal process and advocacy, medicine, psychology, occupational and physical therapy, and vocational rehabilitation. The Association also offers eight special interest groups, focused on creative arts therapies, direct support professionals, Down Syndrome, families, health promotions, mental health services, multicultural concerns, and sexual/social concerns. Membership in the American Association on Mental Retardation is open to anyone concerned about mental retardation.

KAY E. KETZENBERGER
*The University of Texas of the
Permian Basin*

AMERICAN BOARD OF PROFESSIONAL PSYCHOLOGY

Originally named the American Board of Examiners in Professional Psychology, this organization was renamed the American Board of Professional Psychology (ABPP) in

1968. Founded in 1947 with the support of the American Psychological Association, it is comprised of a board of 15 trustees with headquarters in Savannah, Georgia. This certification board conducts oral examinations and awards specialty certification in eleven specialties: behavioral psychology, clinical psychology, clinical neuropsychology, counseling psychology, family psychology, forensic psychology, health psychology, industrial/organizational psychology, psychoanalysis in psychology, rehabilitation psychology, and school psychology. Necessary for certification is 5 years of qualifying experience in psychological practice.

The ABPP annually presents the Distinguished Professional Achievement Award. This and other awards are presented at the annual convention of the American Psychological Association in August. Publications of the ABPP include the *Specialist* newsletter and the *Directory of Diplomates* (biannual).

MARY LEON PEERY
Texas A&M University
First edition

KAY E. KETZENBERGER
*The University of Texas of the
Permian Basin*
Second edition

AMERICAN BOARD OF PROFESSIONAL NEUROPSYCHOLOGY

The American Board of Professional Neuropsychology (ABPN) is a credentialing board that examines doctoral-level psychologists with specialized training in the field of clinical neuropsychology and awards diplomas if examination performance is satisfactory. Examinations consist of an essay exam concerning clinical casework, a work sample examination (wherein examinees submit for scrutiny two actual cases from their practice), and a 3-hour oral examination. Additionally, documentation of appropriate credentials and training is required. Incorporated in 1982, ABPN was the first (and as of this writing, the only) psychology credentialing board that has applied to be approved and certified by the National Commission of Certifying Agencies, the certification arm of the National Organization for Competency Assurance, an organization charged by the federal government with oversight and accreditation of health care certification bodies. The ABPN central office address is Care of the Executive Director, Dr. Michael Raymond, John Heinz Institute of Rehabilitation Medicine, Neuropsychology Services, 150 Mundy Street, Wilkes-Barre, PA 18702.

CECIL R. REYNOLDS
Texas A&M University

AMERICAN CANCER SOCIETY

The American Cancer Society (ACS) is a voluntary organization committed to the elimination and control of cancer. This nationwide effort is conducted through 58 largely state-incorporated divisions and is accomplished through four major activities: (1) the public education program, which emphasizes regular, preventive care for adults, attention to specific warning signals, and information regarding positive outcomes when prompt diagnosis and preventive measures are adopted; (2) a comprehensive professional education program designed to stimulate health professionals to use the best cancer detection, diagnostic, and patient management techniques available, to exchange knowledge on the latest cancer-fighting techniques, and to disseminate new ideas and developments in the community; (3) a wide range of volunteer-based service and rehabilitation programs to assist cancer patients and their families with the necessary practical and emotional support so vital to coping with the wide-ranging effects of the disease; and (4) research into all aspects of cancer, from direct clinical investigations and training to prospective cancer prevention studies.

The ACS began in 1913, when fifteen physicians and business leaders gathered in New York City and founded the American Society for the Control of Cancer (ASCC). The Society's founders were aware that the disease, steeped in a climate of fear and denial, must be brought to the attention of the people. Articles were written for popular magazines and professional journals, a monthly bulletin providing information about cancer was published, and physicians were recruited throughout the United States in an attempt to increase public awareness.

In 1936, Marjorie G. Illig, an ASCC field representative and chair of the General Federation of Women's Clubs Committee on Public Health, proposed the creation of a legion of volunteers, with the sole purpose of waging war on cancer. The Women's Field Army, as this organization came to be known, was the driving force behind the agency's move to the forefront of voluntary health organizations.

Today, the core of the organization's effort resides in its 2 million volunteers who implement the society's public and professional education programs, service programs for patients and families, and raise funds for research programs.

The ASCC was reorganized in 1945, becoming the American Cancer Society (ACS), today's leader in the fight against cancer through its programs in research, patient services, prevention, detection and treatment, and advocacy. The Society strives to achieve this goal by promoting the early detection of cancer through education, intervention, and programs such as the Breast Cancer Network and Man to Man, a prostate cancer education and support group. In conjunction with these efforts, the ACS has increased its effort to protect children through comprehensive school health education and similar programs designed to discourage tobacco use and promote healthy living.

Scientists supported by ACS have successfully established the link between cancer and smoking, demonstrated the effectiveness of the Pap smear, developed cancer-fighting drugs and biological response modifiers, dramatically increased the cure rate for leukemia, and proved the safety and effectiveness of mammography. The American Cancer Society has committed almost $2 billion to research and funded 28 Nobel Prize winners.

CRAIG S. HIGGINS
Stonehill College
First edition

TAMARA J. MARTIN
The University of Texas of the Permian Basin
Second edition

AMERICAN COUNCIL ON RURAL SPECIAL EDUCATION

The American Council on Rural Special Education (ACRES) was founded in 1981 by a group of individuals interested in the unique challenges of rural students and individuals needing special services. The goals of ACRES are to (1) foster quality education and services for individuals with exceptional needs living in rural America; (2) promote cultural diversity and the empowerment of minorities and members of traditionally underrepresented groups in providing services to individuals with exceptional needs, their families, and service providers; (3) promote national recognition for rural special education, health, and human services; (4) promote collaborative partnerships with organizations interested in special education, health, and human services; and (5) disseminate information concerning promising practices and research for improving education and services for individuals with disabilities living in rural communities.

Today, ACRES is the only national organization devoted entirely to special education issues that affect rural America. The geographically diverse membership of ACRES is representative of all regions of the country and comprises special educators, general educators, related service providers, administrators, teacher trainers, researchers, and parents who are committed to the enhancement of services to students and individuals living in rural America. This fact is especially important as rural issues are not only different from urban issues but also may vary among specific rural settings. The members of ACRES strive to provide leadership and support to enhance services for individuals with exceptional needs, their families, the professionals

who work with them, and for the rural communities in which they live.

The ACRES publishes the only national scholarly journal solely devoted to rural special education issues, *Rural Special Education Quarterly (RSEQ)*. The purpose of *RSEQ* is to disseminate information and research concerning rural special education, federal, and other events relevant to rural individuals with disabilities, progressive service delivery systems, reviews of relevant publications, and resources for rural special educators.

Each year, ACRES sponsors an annual conference in March. It is the only national conference devoted entirely to rural special education issues. Topic strands include administration, at-risk issues, collaborative education models, early childhood, gifted and talented, multicultural issues, parents and families, professional development, technology, transition, and related services. Annually, ACRES awards a scholarship to provide a practicing rural teacher an opportunity to pursue education and training that would not otherwise be affordable within his or her district and presents the Exemplary Rural Special Education Program Award to exemplar programs providing services in rural settings. Additional information on the American Council on Rural Special Education is provided on the web site at http://www.acres-sped.org.

KEVIN J. MILLER
University of Central Florida

AMERICAN EDUCATIONAL RESEARCH ASSOCIATION

The American Educational Research Association (AERA) was founded in 1915 as the National Association of Directors of Educational Research. The AERA is an international organization of educators, professors, research directors, specialists, and graduate students interested in educational research. The objectives of AERA include improving the status and quality of research and promoting application and findings of research to educational problems (American Education Research Association, undated).

The AERA is divided into 12 divisions: administration, counseling and human development, curriculum studies, education in the professions, educational policy and politics, history and historiography, instruction and learning, measurement and research methodology, postsecondary education, school evaluation and program development, social context of education, and teaching and teacher education.

Journals published by the AERA include the American Educational Research *Journal, Educational Evaluation and Policy Analysis, Journal of Educational and Behavioral Statistics, Review of Educational Research, Educational Researcher, Review of Research in Education* (annual), *Encyclo-*

pedia of Educational Research, and *Handbook of Research on Teaching* (both revised every 10 years).

The AERA holds an annual convention for the presentation of reports, papers, and awards. It also holds research training programs and monitors federal educational research activities.

REFERENCE

American Educational Research Association (AERA). (Undated brochure). *American Educational Research Association: A membership for your discipline.* Washington, DC: Author.

Douglas L. Friedman
Fordham University

AMERICAN FOUNDATION FOR THE BLIND

The American Foundation for the Blind (AFB), a nonprofit organization, was founded in 1921 to serve as the national partner of local services for the blind and visually impaired. The organization is a leading national resource for people who are blind or visually impaired, the organizations that serve them, and the general public. The mission of the organization is to enable people who are blind or visually impaired to achieve equality of access and opportunity in order to ensure freedom of choice in their lives.

The AFB traces its origins to a meeting of a group of professionals in Vinton, Iowa, in the summer of 1921 (Koestler, 1976). This meeting, comprised primarily of officers of the American Association of Workers for the Blind (AAWB), resulted in the recognition of the pressing need for a national organization that was not affiliated with special interest groups, professional organizations, or any local, regional, or state organization currently serving the needs of the blind (Hagerty, 1987).

Helen Keller was closely identified with AFB from the early 1920s until her death, and the organization is recognized as her cause in the United States. Working with AFB for over 40 years, she represented the organization in their efforts to educate legislators and the public about services needed for people who are blind.

AFB fulfills its mission through four primary areas of activity regarding the nonmedical aspects of blindness and visual impairment. Development, collection, and dissemination of information are accomplished by responding annually to 100,000 inquiries from people who are blind or visually impaired, their family and friends, professionals in the blindness field, and the general public requesting information about AFB's programs, services, and other topics related to blindness and visual impairment.

AFB activities in this area also include the publication of books, pamphlets, videos, and periodicals about blindness for professionals and consumers. The AFB publishes the leading professional journal of its kind, *Journal of Visual Impairment and Blindness.* In addition, the organization is responsible for maintaining and preserving the Helen Keller Archives, an invaluable collection of personal material donated by Helen Keller. AFB also houses the M. C. Migel Memorial Library, one of the world's largest collections of print materials on blindness.

Identification, analysis, and resolution of issues critical to people who are blind or visually impaired is achieved by setting priorities, analyzing policy options, and promoting feasible solutions in conjunction with experts and constituents in the field of blindness. Expertise is offered in program areas such as education, employment, aging, and technology; and policy research that positively affects the quality of life of people who are blind or visually impaired is conducted, evaluated, and published by the AFB. The organization also serves as an advocate for and evaluator of the development of assistive products and technology. Maintenance of the Careers & Technology Information Bank, a network of individuals who are blind from all 50 states and Canada who use assistive technology at home, school, or work and are able and willing to serve as mentors to others, is another function of the AFB.

In the accomplishment of its mission, the AFB also strives to educate policymakers and the public as to the needs and capabilities of people who are blind or visually impaired. Consulting on legislative issues and representing blind and visually impaired persons before Congress and government agencies accomplishes this goal. Corporate and public awareness of the capabilities of people who are blind or visually impaired is also increased through publications, audio/visual presentations, exhibits, and public service announcements.

AFB production and distribution of books and other audio materials includes recording and duplicating Talking Books under contract to the Library of Congress. The organization also records and duplicates annual reports and other publications for various corporations and nonprofit organizations, thus making them accessible to print-handicapped employees, clients, and shareholders.

For more information about AFB, write the American Foundation for the Blind, 11 Penn Plaza, Suite 300, New York, NY 10001 or call 1-800-AFB-LINE (232-5463); in New York State, (212) 502-7600.

REFERENCES

Hagerty, S. J. (1987). American Foundation for the Blind. In C. R. Reynolds & L. Mann (Eds.), *Encyclopedia of special education* (1st ed.). New York: Wiley.

Koestler, F. A. (1976). *The unseen minority.* New York: McKay.

Tamara J. Martin
*The University of Texas of the
Permian Basin*

AMERICAN GUIDANCE SERVICE

American Guidance Service, Inc. (AGS) is an educational publishing company founded in 1957, and is an employee-owned company that encourages partnership and ongoing dialogue with the professionals that use its products. AGS publishes a wide variety of norm-referenced assessment instruments for the identification of special needs students, focusing primarily on cognitive ability, achievement, behavior, and personal and social adjustment, with many publications also available in Spanish. Their better-known tests include the Peabody Picture Vocabulary Test (PPVT-III), Vineland adaptive behavior scales, second edition (Vineland II), Kaufman Assessment Battery for Children, second edition (K-ABC II), Kaufman Test of Educational Achievement, second edition (K-TEA II), the Developmental Indicators for the Assessment of Learning, third edition (DIAL III), and the Behavioral Assessment System for Children, second edition (BASC 2).

In addition to testing materials, AGS publishes a great many instructional materials, including over 900 textbooks, as well as programs for parenting and family living. Much of their material is focused on children with learning/emotional problems or in special education, though they also publish material geared to all ages. AGS can be reached at 4201 Woodland Road, Circle Pines, MN 55014-1796, or by phone at (800) 328-2560 or (651) 287-7220.

TAMARA J. MARTIN
*The University of Texas of the
Permian Basin*

AMERICAN INSTITUTE—THE TRAINING SCHOOL AT VINELAND

The American Institute—The Training School at Vineland, is located in Vineland, New Jersey (Main Road and Landis Avenue, Vineland, NJ 08360). The school and training facility were founded in 1887; they are under the supervision and administrative management of Elwyn Institutes. The facility serves children and adults who are mentally retarded, brain damaged, emotionally disturbed, physically handicapped, and learning disabled.

The school programs are ungraded at the elementary and secondary levels. The school features education and training programs that are designed to train young people to return to the community. The training programs serve mildly handicapped to the severely retarded students. The range of educational programs and vocational training experiences are developed with individualized educational plans and rehabilitation services. The facility is internationally recognized for the pioneering works of Binet and Doll. The Stanford Binet tests were translated and norms were developed at the school. Dr. Edward Doll is recognized

as the pioneer in the development of the Vineland Social Maturity Scale.

REFERENCE

Sargent, J. K. (1982). *The directory for exceptional children* (9th ed.). Boston, MA: Porter Sargent.

PAUL C. RICHARDSON
Elwyn Institutes

AMERICAN JOURNAL OF MENTAL RETARDATION

Originally known as the *American Journal of Mental Deficiency, AJMR* is published on a bimonthly basis by the American Association on Mental Retardation (AAMR). The original title reflected the original name of the sponsoring organization, which was changed from the American Organization on Mental Deficiency (AOMD) to its current name in 1987. The primary purpose of the journal is to publish theoretical manuscripts and research in the area of mental retardation, with an emphasis on material of an objective, scientific, and experimental nature. Book reviews are included. The journal address is P.O. Box 1897, Lawrence, KS 66044. Telephone: (785) 843-1235; e-mail: AJMR@allenpress.com.

STAFF

AMERICAN JOURNAL OF OCCUPATIONAL THERAPY

The *American Journal of Occupational Therapy (AJOT)* is an official publication of the American Occupational Therapy Association. *AJOT* is published monthly except for July/August and November/December, when it appears in bimonthly issues. Manuscripts are subjected to anonymous peer review. Accepted articles pertain to occupational therapy and may include reports of research, educational activities, or professional trends; descriptions of new occupational therapy approaches, programs, or services; review papers that survey new information; theoretical papers that discuss or treat theoretical issues critically; descriptions of original therapeutic aids, devices, or techniques; case reports that describe occupational therapy for a specific clinical situation; or opinion essays that discuss timely issues or opinions and are supported by cogent arguments. In addition, the journal contains letters to the editor, publication reviews, and product advertising.

AJOT is abstracted or indexed by Applied Science Index and Abstracts, Behavioral Medicine Abstracts, Cumulative

Index to Nursing and Allied Health Literature, Exceptional Child Education Resources, Excerpta Medica, Inc., Hospital Literature Index, Index Medicus, Institute for Scientific Information, MEDLINE, OT BibSys, Psychological Abstracts, and Social Sciences Citation Index. Microfilms of complete volumes can be obtained from University Microfilms, Inc.

ELIZABETH HOLCOMB
American Journal of
Occupational Therapy

AMERICAN JOURNAL OF ORTHOPSYCHIATRY

The *American Journal of Orthopsychiatry (AJO)*, is the quarterly journal of the American Orthopsychiatric Association. The association was founded in 1926 and began publication of *AJO* in 1930. The *AJO* is a quarterly, refereed, scholarly journal written from a multidisciplinary perspective. The *AJO* is dedicated to public policy, professional practice, and information that relates to mental health and human development. Clinical, theoretical, research, review, and expository papers are published in *AJO*. These papers are essentially synergistic and directed at concept and theory development, reconceptualization of major issues, explanation, and interpretation.

The *AJO* concentrates on many topics of concern to special educators. During its lifetime, *AJO*'s articles have centered around the topics of social issues and the handicapped, childhood psychosis, psychopharmacology, school phobia, depression, suicide, child abuse, mental retardation, and treatment of all of these disorders. The contributors' list and editorial board have, over the years, featured some of the finest scholars from developmental medicine, developmental psychopathology, child development, school psychology, clinical psychology, special education, neurology, psychiatry, and related mental health fields. The *AJO* is an influential journal that publishes top scholars' writing on special education.

CECIL R. REYNOLDS
Texas A&M University

AMERICAN ORTHOPSYCHIATRIC ASSOCIATION

AMERICAN JOURNAL OF PSYCHIATRY

The *American Journal of Psychiatry* began publication in 1844 as the *American Journal of Insanity*, changing to its current title in 1921. It is the official journal of the American Psychiatric Association, and is the most widely read psychiatric journal in the world. Published monthly, the *American Journal of Psychiatry* publishes peer-reviewed research studies and articles that focus on developments in the biological aspects of psychiatry, on treatment issues and innovations, and on forensic, ethical, social, and economic topics. Letters to the editor, book reviews, and official American Psychiatric Association reports are also included. Of special interest to many readers are the overview and special lead articles, which address major psychiatric syndromes and issues in depth.

KAY E. KETZENBERGER
The University of Texas of the
Permian Basin

AMERICAN OCCUPATIONAL THERAPY FOUNDATION

The American Occupational Therapy Foundation was founded in 1965 as the American Occupational Therapy Association's (AOTA) philanthropic sister organization. The foundation has devoted its energies to raising funds and resources in three program areas—publications, research, and scholarships—associated with the profession of occupational therapy and health-care delivery.

The foundation's publication program aims to increase public knowledge and understanding of the occupational therapy profession. In addition to various reports and documents, it publishes *The Occupational Therapy Journal of Research,* and has produced a major bibliography of completed research in the field. The foundation supports the Occupational Therapy Library, which supplies requested materials through interlibrary loan.

A research program is conducted through the foundation's Office of Professional Research Services. Program services include the Academy of Research, support of researchers through grant awards (in association with the AOTA), and doctoral and postdoctoral fellowship awards to support researchers. The foundation widely disseminates scholarship information for undergraduate and graduate students in occupational therapy publications and through occupational therapy schools.

The American Occupational Therapy Foundation is located at 4720 Montgomery Lane, P.O. Box 31220, Bethesda, MD 20824.

SHIRLEY A. JONES
Virginia Polytechnic Institute
and State University
First edition

KAY KETZENBERGER
The University of Texas of the
Permian Basin
Second edition

AMERICAN ORTHOPSYCHIATRIC ASSOCIATION

The American Orthopsychiatric Association (Ortho) was formed at the invitation of Herman Adler and Karl Menninger at the Institute for Juvenile Research in Chicago in 1924 under the name of the Association of American Orthopsychiatrists. The group operated informally, debating its name and purpose and finally founding Ortho a year later. In 1926 Ortho amended its constitution, which limited membership to physicians, to redefine membership to include psychiatrists, psychologists, social workers, and other professional persons "whose work and interests lie in the study and treatment of conduct disorders." According to Eisenberg and DeMaso (1985), the first published membership roster, published October 1, 1927, included 45 psychiatrists, 12 psychologists, 5 social workers, and several lawyers and penologists. Ortho had as its purpose the centralization of the techniques, objectives, and aspirations of psychiatrists, psychologists, and related mental health workers whose primary interests were in the area of human behavior, providing a common meeting ground for students of behavior problems and for fostering scientific research and its dissemination. The early membership included names familiar to special educators, including such notables as Edgar Doll, Lightner Witmer, and Carl Murchison.

Lightner Witmer, noted among historians of psychology as the man who coined the term clinical psychology, founded school psychology and established the first psychological clinic; he also coined the term orthogenics and established the team approach to children's problems when he invited neurologists to collaborate on case studies (Eisenberg & DeMaso, 1985). Ortho subsequently became a major force in the establishment of the child guidance movement in the early 1900s. In 1930 Ortho established the *American Journal of Orthopsychiatry,* a widely read and respected journal that in its early years vigorously debated the roles and functions of various professionals (e.g., psychiatrists, psychologists, social workers, etc.) in the treatment of childhood mental health disorders.

Presently, many special educators belong to Ortho. It is a large, robust organization of more than 10,000 members. It is involved in social, scientific, and public policy issues, including diagnosis, evaluation, and treatment, relevant to the improvement of the lives of the handicapped. The *American Journal of Orthopsychiatry* is provided as a benefit of membership; it contains many articles of interest to special educators. The association is located at Department of Psychology, Box 871104, Arizona State University, Tempe, AZ 85287. Telephone: (480) 727-7518.

REFERENCES

American Orthopsychiatric Association (Ortho). (1998). *About Ortho.* Retrieved from http://www.amerortho.org/ortho2.htm

Eisenberg, L., & DeMaso, D. R. (1985). Fifty years of the *American Journal of Orthopsychiatry:* An overview and introduction. In E. Flaxman & E. Herman (Eds.), *American Journal of Orthopsychiatry: Annotated index: Vols. 1–50. 1930–1980.* Greenwich, CT: JAI.

CECIL R. REYNOLDS
Texas A&M University

AMERICAN JOURNAL OF ORTHOPSYCHIATRY
WITMER, LIGHTNER

AMERICAN PHYSICAL THERAPY ASSOCIATION

The American Physical Therapy Association (APTA) endeavors to improve physical therapy services and education through accrediting academic programs in physical therapy; assisting states in preparing certification examinations; and offering workshops and continuing education courses for therapists at the national and local level. Information is available about careers in physical therapy, accredited preparation programs, sources of student financial aid, and employment opportunities. A variety of pamphlets are available on prevention of injuries and chronic or degenerative conditions. The association publishes a newsletter and journal. Bibliographies have been prepared on topics including resources for stroke victims, quadriplegics, paraplegics, amputees, parents, and educators. Members benefit from information on questions regarding practice and disabilities. The association also serves as a referral source for individuals who require physical therapy services. Association offices are located at 1111 North Fairfax Street, Alexandria, VA 22314. Telephone: (703) 684-2782; e-mail: www.apta.org.

PHILIP R. JONES
*Virginia Polytechnic Institute
and State University*

AMERICAN PRINTING HOUSE FOR THE BLIND

The American Printing House for the Blind (APH), the oldest private, nonprofit institution for the blind in the United States, was founded in Louisville, Kentucky in 1858. It is the world's largest company devoted solely to creating products and services for people who are visually impaired. The Act to Promote the Education of the Blind, mandated by Congress in 1879, enabled the APH to receive grants for education texts and aids for those with visual impairments from the federal government. Funds appropriated under the Act are used by each state to purchase educational materials from APH for their blind students below the college level (APH, 1998).

The Company's mission is to promote the independence of blind and visually impaired persons by providing special media, tools, and materials needed for education and life. A wide variety of products and services are available through APH, including braille, large type, recorded, computer disk, and tactile graphic publications as well as a wide assortment of educational and daily living products. Various services designed to assist consumers and professionals in the field of vision are also offered, including *Louis,* a database listing materials available from accessible media across North America and *Patterns,* a reading instruction program developed through APH research.

APH's Talking Books on cassette tape, produced in agency recording studios, are a popular reading medium for blind and visually impaired people of all ages. Fiction and nonfiction topics, ranging from romance to cookbooks, are produced by professional narrators who are also teachers, actors, and media personalities. Most Talking Books can be obtained on a free loan basis from the National Library for the Blind and Physically Handicapped, a division of the Library of Congress. Three magazines are offered by APH directly to eligible blind readers. They include *Readers Digest, Newsweek,* and *Weekly Reader.*

In addition to the publications and products provided to those who are visually impaired, APH maintains a national center for research and development, focusing on the creation of products for blind students and adults, and a museum, offering a look at the history of education of blind people.

REFERENCE

American Printing House for the Blind (APH). (1998). *What is the American Printing House for the Blind?* Louisville, KY: Author.

TAMARA J. MARTIN
*The University of Texas of the
Permian Basin*

AMERICAN PSYCHIATRIC ASSOCIATION

The American Psychiatric Association was founded in 1844 as the Association of Medical Superintendents of American Institutions for the Insane, and changed to its current name in 1921. The Association is a national medical specialty society that had over 35,000 U.S. and international members in 2005; members are physicians who specialize in the diagnosis and treatment of mental, emotional, and substance abuse disorders. The Association's major focus areas include mental health, psychopharmacology, psy-

chotherapy, and health professions development, and its primary objectives include the advancement and improvement of care for people with mental illnesses through the provision of nationwide education, public information, and awareness programs and materials.

The Association publishes the *American Journal of Psychiatry* (its official monthly journal), *Hospital and Community Psychiatry* (monthly), and *Psychiatric News* (twice monthly). The Association offers many continuing education workshops, seminars, and courses, as well as library services for members. The Association can be contacted at their national offices at 1000 Wilson Boulevard, Suite 1825, Arlington VA 22209. Tel: (703) 907-7322 or (800) 368-5777.

KAY E. KETZENBERGER
*The University of Texas of the
Permian Basin*

AMERICAN PSYCHOLOGICAL ASSOCIATION

The American Psychological Association (APA) is the nation's major psychology organization. The APA works to advance psychology as a science and a profession, and to promote human welfare. When the APA was established in 1892, psychology was a new profession and the organization had fewer than three dozen members. Over the years the organization has grown rapidly: In 1998 the APA had more than 155,000 members, 51 divisions in specialized subfields and interest areas, and 58 affiliated state, provincial, and territorial psychological associations.

The growth of the science and profession of psychology is reflected in the development of diverse programs and services administered by the association. These programs aim to disseminate psychological knowledge, promote research, improve research methods and conditions, and develop the qualifications and competence of psychologists through standards of education, ethical conduct, and professional practice.

The program and business activities of the APA are coordinated at the association's central office in Washington, DC. These offices are headquarters for APA's programs in governance affairs, national policy studies, public affairs, communications, and financial affairs. Through these programs, the central office staff provides information to members, other professionals, students, and the public through the publication of books, major journals, pamphlets, the monthly APA *Monitor* newspaper, and a growing spectrum of bibliographic and abstracting services covering the literature of psychology.

The affairs of the association are administered by the Board of Directors, which is responsible for the work of an executive officer who administers the affairs of the central office. The Board of Directors is composed of a president, past president, and president-elect, all of whom are elected by APA members at large, and a treasurer, a secretary, and six board members who are elected by the Council of Representatives. The Council of Representatives is composed of members of the association who are elected by their division and state members in proportion to the annual assignment of seats by the membership. The Council of Representatives sets policy for the association, and those policies are administered by the Board of Directors through the executive officer and the staff of the central office.

The governance affairs office of the association coordinates and directs psychology programs and activities such as accreditation of doctoral programs in professional psychology and predoctoral internship sites; supervision of educational affairs aimed at identifying and analyzing developments in higher education and training of psychologists; setting standards for scientific and professional ethics, professional affairs, scientific affairs, social and ethical responsibility of psychologists, and overseeing special issues concerning minority groups and women's programs.

The national policy studies of APA help to formulate and implement federal policy and legislative activities of the association. The Public Policy Office develops advocacy positions, informs Congress and federal agencies of psychology's concerns, keeps the APA membership and governance structure informed of related policy issues, and develops working coalitions with outside organizations on common legislative issues.

The Public Affairs Office works to provide overall direction on the ways organized psychology is presented to its national and international public. The office works with television, radio, and print media to demonstrate the contributions psychologists make to society and to improve public understanding of psychology's broad scope and application.

The APA publishes more than 30 periodicals and a variety of books, brochures, and pamphlets. Among these are *American Psychologist,* the official journal of the association, and *Psychological Abstracts,* which contains abstracts of the world's literature on psychology and related disciplines.

Each year more than 12,000 psychologists and other individuals attend the APA convention in late summer. This is the world's largest meeting of psychologists and one of the largest professional conventions in the United States. The week-long program features more than 3,000 presentations through symposiums, lectures, invited addresses, specialized workshops, and other forums. Through the convention, practitioners and the public are given the opportunity to learn of the latest findings from psychological research, their applications in society, and other professional, scientific, and educational issues.

From energy conservation and industrial productivity to child development, aging, and prevention of stress and related illness, hardly a personal or national problem exists that does not demand an understanding of human behavior. Even modern technological innovations emerge from the ability of the mind to transform observations and data into action. Because of their fundamental understanding of behavior, psychologists are increasingly consulted for ways to increase human progress and well-being. APA can be contacted at 750 First St., N.E., Washington, DC 20002. Telephone: (800) 374-2721.

NADINE M. LAMBERT
University of California, Berkeley

AMERICAN PSYCHOLOGIST

American Psychologist is the official journal of the American Psychological Association. Published monthly, it is the most widely circulated psychological journal in the world, going out to the more than 155,000 members of the Association around the globe. It is a primary source of discussion on cutting-edge issues in psychology, and it publishes empirical, theoretical, and practical articles on broad aspects of psychology. It is indexed in over 20 abstracting/indexing services, including PsychINFO, Index Medicus, Academic Index, Social Sciences Index, and Applied Social Science Index & Abstracts, making its contents easily discoverable and thus highly available to users. As the official journal of the association, it contains archival documents, including the minutes of the annual business meeting, and reports of the officers, directorates, and committees whose work involves policies and practices affecting members of the association. The journal also publishes a commentary section, obituaries of well-known psychologists, and (in each year's December issue) a listing of all APA-approved doctoral training programs in clinical, counseling, and school psychology in the United States and Canada.

In setting forth general editorial policy for the *American Psychologist,* past and present editors have agreed that the journal should (1) contribute to enlightened participation in the profession of psychology and thereby to effective function of the association, (2) provide a forum for the examination of the relationship between psychology and society, especially as historical, cultural, and societal influences have an impact on the science and practice of psychology, (3) foster the development of the diverse applications of psychological knowledge, and (4) present and disseminate psychological knowledge in a form and style suitable to the general membership and to the interested public.

The current editor is Norman B. Anderson. All submissions for publication are mask reviewed in a peer-review process. The journal's offices are housed within the American

Psychological Association's national headquarters, located at 750 First Street, NE, Washington, DC, 20002-4242.

NADINE M. LAMBERT
University of California
First edition

KAY E. KETZENBERGER
*The University of Texas of the
Permian Basin*
Second edition

AMERICAN SIGN LANGUAGE

American Sign Language (ASL), Pidgin Signed English (PSE), and Signed Exact English (SEE) are a few of the many alternative forms of sign communication taught to either deaf or hearing individuals (Marschark, 1997). Only ASL is discussed in detail.

American Sign Language is a complex visual-spatial language used by the deaf community (Daniels, 2001; Drasgow, 1998; Marschark, 1997; Moores, 2001). American Sign Language is a complete nonauditory yet verbal language that is independent of English (Drasgow, 1998; Marschark, 1997; Moores, 2001), one that is a linguistically complete and natural (Daniels, 2001; Drasgow, 1998; Moores, 2001). American Sign Language is the native language of many individuals who are deaf as well as some hearing children born into deaf families (Moores, 2001; Nakamura, 2000). As many as 15 million people in North America communicate to some degree using ASL, thus making it the third most commonly used language in the country (Daniels, 2001).

Like other verbal languages, ASL contains many properties (e.g., phonology, morphology). Its structure can be divided into five components: phonology, morphology, syntax, space, and nonmanual characteristics (Daniels, 2001). The first three will be compared to the English language.

In English, phonology refers to the use of vocal organs. In contrast, the phonological properties of ASL require manual expression and movement that are significant to the visual system.

The four gestural components are location (i.e., the placement of the produced signs at approximately 20 distinct locations on the signer's body), hand shapes (i.e., the shape of each hand when producing the approximate 40 handshapes), movement (i.e., the motion of the hands from one point to another in the signing space), and orientation (i.e., the direction of the hands in relation to approximately 10 distinct orientations to the body; Daniels, 2001; Drasgow, 1998).

Morphology refers to the structure of word, including changes in them by adding prefixes or suffixes. In English, this process generally emerges in a sequential manner (Daniels, 2001; Drasgow, 1998). For example, the letter /s/ at the end of a noun generally makes it plural. In contrast, morphology in ASL is organized in a simultaneous rather than a sequential fashion. That is, rather than adding prefixes or suffixes to a word stem, ASL morphology operates by nesting the sign stem within active movement contours (Daniels, 2001; Drasgow, 1998). For example, the word *improve* (a verb) requires a single slow movement, while the word *improvement* (a noun) requires a faster, more dynamic movement (Daniels, 2001; Drasgow, 1998).

Syntax refers to word order. The word order in English usually is subject-verb-object. Word order is important in English because there are few inflections to show grammatical relationships (Daniels, 2001; Drasgow, 1998). In contrast, ASL is more variable in word order. Although ASL often uses a subject-verb-object sequence, this sequence does not dominate and instead grammatical facial expressions, spatial syntax, and other nonmanual features are used (Daniels, 2001; Drasgow, 1998). *Topicalization,* the process of using facial expressions and head position to alter word order by putting the most important information at the beginning of the sentence, is common in ASL.

The final two components of ASL, space and nonmanual characteristics, are not evident in English. In ASL, space plays a large and complex role as it is used to indicate verb tenses and for indexing (Daniels, 2001; Drasgow, 1998). The notion of tense is represented by an imaginary time line that surrounds the signer's body, where the past is represented by the space behind the signer, the future is represented by the space in front of the signer, and the present is represented by the space nearest to the signer's upper body (Daniels, 2001). *Indexing* refers to pointing to designated locations within the signing space. A signer may place a referent, such as a person or object, in a designated space and then refer to that space later in time (Daniels, 2001; Drasgow, 1998).

Nonmanual characteristics in ASL involve movements of the eyes, mouth, face, hand, and body posture. The purpose of these characteristics is to serve as intonation acts in a spoken language or as punctuation acts in a written language (Daniels, 2001). Alterations in the behavior of the body determine the meaning or emphasis of a specific sign (Daniels, 2001).

Children can acquire and retain considerable knowledge by learning ASL and spoken English simultaneously (Daniels, 1997). Gallaudet believed that employment of sign language as an additional sensory channel provided a stronger language base for young hearing learners (Daniels, 1997). The basic motor control of one's hands occurs before the use of one's voice. Therefore, the use of sign language with young children has various advantages (Bonvillian & Floven, 1993). For example, the use of both a written alphabet and sign language provides an early and convenient form of writing for young children "who are able to finger spell far sooner than they acquire the manual dexterity to write words with paper and pencil" (Daniels, 1997, p. 29). In addition, as Daniels (1997) states, using sign language "literally allows a child to feel language" (p. 29).

American Sign Language has been incorporated in many programs and research studies that have investigated language acquisition and development (Birke, 2003; Carney, Cioffi, Raymond, & Floven, 1985; Daniels, 1993, 1994, 1996a, 1996b; deViveiros & McLaughlin, 1982; Griffith, 1985; Holmes & Holmes, 1980; Orlansky & Bonvillian, 1985; Prinz & Prinz, 1981; Weller & Mahoney, 1983). Findings show that learning ASL and spoken English simultaneously allows children to acquire a greater language base (Daniels, 1997); basic motor control of the child's hands occurs before the voice; therefore, the use of ASL by young children is favored over the use only of voice (Bonvillian & Floven, 1993); signing helps children expand their vocabulary (Stewart & Luetke-Stahlman, 1998); and ASL improves receptive and expressive language of hearing kindergarten children with no hearing impairments (Birke, 2003; Daniels, 1996b; deViveiros and McLaughlin, 1982).

The literature supports the premise that simultaneously presenting words visually, kinesthetically, and verbally enhances vocabulary development in kindergarten students. The assumption that the use of various modalities when teaching language, including ASL, enriches the language acquisition is reasonable (Birke, 2003; Daniels, 1997). Moreover, their simultaneous use holds promise as an effective multisensory method to use with language-delayed children.

REFERENCES

Birke, D. E. (2003). *The effect of exposure to American Sign Language on receptive and expressive vocabulary skills of hearing kindergarten children.* Unpublished master's thesis, University of Florida, Gainesville.

Bonvillian, J. D., & Floven, R. J. (1993). Sign language acquisition: Developmental aspects. In M. Marschark & M. D. Clark (Eds.), *Psychological perspectives on deafness* (pp. 229–265). Hillsdale, NJ: Erlbaum.

Carney, J., Cioffi, G., Raymond, M., & Floven, R. (1985). Using sign language for teaching sight words. *Teaching Exceptional Children, 17*(3), 170–175.

Daniels, M. (1993). ASL as a factor in acquiring English. *Sign Language Studies, 78,* 23–29.

Daniels, M. (1994). Words more powerful than sound. *Sign Language Studies, 83,* 156–166.

Daniels, M. (1996a). Bilingual, bimodal education for hearing kindergarten students. *Sign Language Studies, 90,* 25–37.

Daniels, M. (1996b). Seeing language: The effect over time of sign language on vocabulary development in early childhood education. *Child Study Journal, 26*(3), 193–208.

Daniels, M. (1997). Teacher enrichment of prekindergarten curriculum with sign language. *Journal of Research in Childhood Education, 12*(1), 27–33.

Daniels, M. (2001). *Dancing with words: Signing for hearing children's literacy.* Westport, CT: Bergin & Garvey.

deViveiros, C. E., & McLaughlin, T. F. (1982). Effects of manual sign use to the expressive language of four hearing kindergarten children. *Sign Language Studies, 35,* 169–177.

Drasgow, E. (1998). American Sign Language as a pathway to linguistic competence. *Exceptional Children, 64*(3), 329–343.

Griffith, P. L. (1985). Mode switching and mode finding in a hearing child of deaf parents. *Sign Language Studies, 35,* 195–222.

Holmes, K. M., & Holmes, D. W. (1980). Signed and spoken language development in a hearing child of hearing parents. *Sign Language Studies, 28,* 239–254.

Marschark, M. (1997). *Raising and educating a deaf child: A comprehensive guide to the choices, controversies, and decision faced by parents and educators.* New York: Oxford University Press.

Moores, D. F. (2001). *Educating the deaf: Psychology, principles, and practices* (5th ed.). Princeton, NJ: Houghton Mifflin.

Nakamura, K. (2000). *The deaf resource library.* Retrieved October 1, 2001, from http://www.deaflibrary.org

Orlansky, M. D., & Bonvillian, J. D. (1985). Sign language acquisition: Language development in children of deaf parents and implications for other populations. *Merrill-Palmer Quarterly, 31*(2), 127–143.

Prinz, P., & Prinz, E. (1981). Acquisition of ASL and spoken English by a hearing child of a deaf mother and a hearing father: Phase II, Early combinatorial patterns. *Sign Language Studies, 30,* 78–88.

Stewart, D., & Luetke-Stahlman, B. (1998). *The signing family: What every parent should know about sign communication.* Washington, DC: Gallaudet University Press.

Weller, E. L., & Mahoney, G. J. (1983). A comparison of oral and total communication modalities on the language training of young mentally handicapped children. *Education and Training of the Mentally Retarded, 18*(2), 103–110.

DEBORAH BIRKE CARON
St. Lucie County School District,
St. Lucie County, Florida

ALTERNATIVE COMMUNICATION METHODS IN SPECIAL
    EDUCATION
DEAF
GALLAUDET COLLEGE

AMERICAN SOCIETY FOR DEAF CHILDREN

The American Society for Deaf Children (ASDC) is a national nonprofit organization of parents and families of deaf or hard of hearing children, founded in 1967. Its stated purpose is to provide support, encouragement, and information to families of deaf children, and to advocate for their total high-quality participation in education and the community. ASDC furnishes information upon request to help families base their decisions on current and accurate information, supports the use of signing, and promotes a positive attitude toward deaf culture.

The ASDC operates a Parents Hotline at (800) 942-ASDC, and their national offices are located at P.O. Box 3355, Gettysburg, PA 17325. Telephone: (717) 334-7922.

KAY E. KETZENBERGER
*The University of Texas of the
Permian Basin*

AMERICAN SPEECH-LANGUAGE-HEARING ASSOCIATION

The American Speech-Language-Hearing Association (ASHA) is the professional and scientific association for more than 118,000 speech-language pathologists, audiologists, and speech, language, and hearing scientists in the United States as well as internationally. Its stated mission is to promote the interests of professionals in audiology and speech-language pathology, and work for the provision of the highest quality services for people with communication disorders.

In the early 1900s, a number of practitioners were actively engaged in the treatment of communication disorders. Unfortunately, there were also a few unscrupulous individuals who made claims about their ability to cure communication disorders for exorbitant fees. Those involved in the ethical treatment of speech disorders saw an immediate need to protect the public from this small minority of opportunistic individuals. This became the prime motivation for forming an organization of speech and hearing professionals.

The ethical practitioners of speech correction began working in public schools and publishing the results of their clinical work in the 1920s, with most belonging to the National Association of Teachers of Speech (NATS). They published in the *Quarterly Journal of Speech Education* and met as a special interest group at NATS meetings.

In 1925, a small group interested in communication disorders met in Iowa City, Iowa, to create an organization devoted entirely to the study and treatment of communication disorders, naming it the American Academy of Speech Correctionists. In 1935, the group's 87 members changed its name to the American Speech Correction Association. In 1947 the name was changed again, to the American Speech and Hearing Association (ASHA). The current name of the organization, American Speech-Language-Hearing Association, was adopted in 1978.

One of ASHA's most important actions was the development of standards for a Certificate of Clinical Competence in Speech Pathology (CCC-SP) and Audiology (CCC-A). Professionals in communication disorders must meet stringent training and experience standards in order to qualify for these prestigious certifications. ASHA continues to work actively with state governments on licensing procedures for communication disorder professionals, and remains the voice of the professions of speech-language pathology and audiology.

The ASHA offices are located at 10801 Rockville Pike, Rockville, MD 20852, and may be reached by telephone at (800) 498-2071, for hearing impaired individuals at (301) 897-5700 (TTY), or by fax at (301) 571-0457.

REFERENCE

Paden, E. P. (1970). *A history of the American Speech and Hearing Association, 1925–1958.* Washington, DC: American Speech and Hearing Association.

FREDERICK F. WEINER
Pennsylvania State University
First edition

KAY E. KETZENBERGER
*The University of Texas of the
Permian Basin*
Second edition

AMERICANS WITH DISABILITIES ACT

The Americans with Disabilities Act of 1990 (ADA) is a comprehensive civil rights law designed to prohibit discrimination against people with disabilities. The ADA is a civil rights law; therefore, it preempts any other local, state, or federal law that grants lesser rights to individuals with disabilities (National Association of State Directors of Special Education [NASDSE], 1992), although states may in some instances grant rights in excess of those mandated by the ADA. Federal funding is not provided to carry out the ADA mandates; however, a wide range of public and private institutions, including educational institutions, are required to comply with the ADA provisions. The purpose of ADA is

(1) to provide a clear and comprehensive national mandate for the elimination of discrimination against individuals with disabilities; (2) to provide clear, strong, consistent, enforceable standards addressing discrimination against individuals with disabilities; (3) to ensure that the federal government plays a central role in enforcing the standards established in this Act on behalf of individuals with disabilities; and (4) to invoke the sweep of congressional authority, including the power to

enforce the 14th Amendment, to address the major areas of discrimination faced by people with disabilities. (42 U.S.C. §§ 12101 Sec 2 [b][1–4])

The ADA derives its substance from Section 504 of the Rehabilitation Act of 1973, but its procedures from Title VII of the Civil Rights Act of 1964, amended in 1991 (First & Curcio, 1993).

In 1988, the ADA bill was first introduced in Congress in response to mounting evidence that Americans with disabilities, over 40 million strong, faced an inordinate number of inequities in different spheres of life (Jacob-Timm & Hartshorne, 1995). Moreover, congressional testimony had documented a strong link between disability and economic and social hardships and limited educational opportunities (Burgdorf, 1991). Based on these inequities and disadvantages, congressional legislative action was taken to bring individuals with disabilities into the American social and economic mainstream through the enactment of the ADA. The U.S. Congress approved the final version of the bill on July 13, 1990, and President George Bush signed it into law on July 26, 1990.

The ADA consists of five titles. The areas addressed in these five titles include employment, public services, public accommodations, telecommunications, and miscellaneous provisions. Title I prohibits discrimination in employment of persons with disabilities. Under this title, employers must reasonably accommodate the disabilities of the otherwise qualified applicants or employees unless undue hardship would result. An example of an undue hardship would be a significant difficulty or excessive expense to the employer associated with making alterations or modifications at the job site to accommodate a qualified applicant who is also an individual with a disability. All school districts, regardless of the number of personnel employed, are subject to Title I standards.

Title II prohibits discrimination in programs, activities, and services provided by state and local governments and their instrumentalities. Title II applies to all public entities, including public schools, regardless of federal funding status. Under Title II, school facilities, whether existing facilities or under construction, must meet accessibility requirements for individuals with disabilities consistent with Section 504 of the Rehabilitation Act (First & Curcio, 1993). Public transportation, like buses and rail vehicles, must also meet accessibility requirements. Title II requires school districts to provide appropriate aids so that individuals with disabilities have equal opportunities to participate in available programs and services. Likewise, districts are required to give primary consideration to disabled individuals requests and to ensure that individuals with hearing or visual impairments receive information in an appropriate and understandable format about available programs and services. Examples of public school programs, services, and activities covered by Title II include public entertainment or lectures sponsored by the school district, after-school activities and social events offered by the schools, parent-teacher conferences, classroom activities, field trips, and any other service provided for students or staff (Office of Civil Rights [OCR], 1996).

Title III prohibits discrimination based on disability in privately owned public accommodations. Nonsectarian private schools and school bus transportation, as well as other privately owned public accommodations, must make reasonable alterations in policies, practices, and procedures to avoid discrimination. Nonsectarian private schools must provide auxiliary aids and services to individuals with visual or hearing impairments. In addition, physical barriers must be removed unless readily unachievable. If not readily achievable, alternate methods of providing services must be offered. All new construction and alterations in existing facilities must be handicap accessible. School bus transportation services, such as bus routes, must be comparable in duration and distance for disabled and nondisabled individuals.

Title IV requires telephone companies to provide telecommunication relay services for hearing- and speech-impaired individuals. Closed-captioned public service announcements must also be provided. Under Title IV, schools must ensure that communication with disabled individuals is just as effective as communication with nondisabled individuals.

Title V consists of a variety of provisions. The title identifies the federal agencies responsible for the enforcement and technical assistance related to the ADA. The federal agency responsible for the enforcement of Title II, Subtitle A, programs, activities, and services provided by state and local governments and their instrumentalities, which extends to all public school systems, is the Office of Civil Rights (OCR) in the Department of Education. The OCR not only enforces the ADA provisions under Title II, Subtitle A but it also handles complaints filed with regard to alleged violations of this title. Title V also dictates that state governments are not immune from legal actions related to the ADA. In addition, individuals with disabilities have the right to accept or reject accommodations and services offered under the ADA. Furthermore, individuals with or without disabilities cannot be coerced or retaliated against for exercising their rights under the ADA. The title also addresses the relationship between the ADA and other laws and its impact on insurance providers and benefits.

In examining the relationship between the ADA and other federal laws affecting persons with disabilities, ADA is viewed as a complementary law (Cunconan-Lahr, 1991). The ADA does not diminish any of the rights of disabled individuals under the Civil Rights Act of 1964, as amended in 1991, Individuals with Disabilities Education Act (IDEA), or Section 504 of the Rehabilitation Act of 1973 (NASDSE, 1992).

Section 504 and the ADA espouse the same underlying principle, which is that entities under their jurisdiction cannot discriminate against individuals with disabilities in their programs, activities, and services (Cunconan-Lahr, 1991). To eliminate discrimination, both laws stress the importance of equal opportunity, not just equal treatment, for disabled and nondisabled individuals. However, the ADA does create a higher standard of nondiscrimination than does Section 504 in several respects. First, Section 504 applies only to recipients of federal funding, whereas the ADA applies to employment, public services, public accommodations, and transportation, regardless of whether federal funding is received. Second, Section 504 covers qualified individuals with disabilities, whereas the ADA extends protection to a person without a disability who is related to or associated with an individual with a disability (OCR, 1996).

With the aforementioned exceptions, Title II of the ADA, which extends to public schools, does not impose any new major requirements on school districts (OCR, 1996). Much of the language in Title II and Section 504 are similar, and school districts that receive federal funding have been required to comply with Section 504 for over 30 years. In the area of education, nondiscrimination requirements related to disabled individuals are detailed more specifically under Section 504 than under Title II. However, Title II requirements are not to be interpreted as applying a lesser standard or degree of protection for disabled individuals. In fact, if a rule issued under Section 504 imposes a lesser standard than the ADA regulation, the language in the ADA statute replaces the language in Section 504 (NASDSE, 1992).

The ADA statute does not directly specify procedural safeguards related to special education, evaluation and placement procedures, due process procedures, and responsibility and requirements under the provision of a free, appropriate public education (FAPE) as does Section 504 and IDEA. The ADA incorporates the specific details of these concepts from Section 504 and IDEA into Title II, Subtitle A. The ADA also provides additional protection in combination with the actions brought under Section 504 and IDEA. For example, reasonable accommodations must be made for eligible individuals with disabilities to perform essential functions of a job. Special education programs that are community-based and involve job training or placement are covered under the ADA statute. The ADA protections are also applicable to nonsectarian private schools but not to organizations or entities controlled by religious affiliations (Henderson, 1995).

Section 504 and IDEA provide specific details regarding procedural safeguards, whereas the ADA does not. Procedural safeguards involve notification to parents regarding identification, evaluation, and placement of a child in special education programs and related services. The ADA, on the other hand, specifies administrative requirements, complaint procedures, and consequences for noncompliance related to services (Henderson, 1995).

The ADA does not specify evaluation and placement procedures as does Section 504 and IDEA. However, the ADA does require reasonable accommodations for individuals with disabilities across educational settings and activities. Reasonable accommodations are not limited to, but may include, modifying equipment, hiring one-on-one aids, modifying tests, providing alternate forms of communication, relocating services in more accessible areas, altering existing facilities, and constructing new facilities (Henderson, 1995).

The ADA does not delineate specific due process procedures; however, IDEA and Section 504 do. Section 504 and IDEA require local educational agencies (LEAs) to provide hearings for parents who disagree with the identification, evaluation, or placement of a child. With the passage of the 1997 Amendments to IDEA, parents and LEAs or state educational agencies (SEAs) are strongly encouraged to participate in voluntary mediation to resolve disputes prior to conducting due process hearings. According to the ADA, individuals with disabilities who are discriminated against in an educational setting have the same recourse that is available under Title VII of the Civil Rights Act of 1964, as amended in 1991. Individuals may file complaints with the OCR or sue in federal court. The OCR encourages informal mediation and voluntary compliance (Henderson, 1995). However, administrative remedies do not have to be exhausted prior to filing a lawsuit (28 C.F.R. § 35.172). Federal funds may be removed from schools for noncompliance with the ADA mandates, and individuals with disabilities may be awarded attorney fees if they prevail in any action filed under the ADA (28 C.F.R. § 35.175).

Title II, Subtitle A of the ADA is the section of the statute pertaining to public schools. The statute prohibits discrimination against any "qualified individual with a disability." The ADA's definition of an *individual with a disability* is essentially the same as Section 504's definition. The ADA definition of a *disability* consists of three prongs. The ADA defines a *disability*, with respect to an individual, as "a physical or mental impairment that substantially limits one or more of the major life activities of such individual, a record of such an impairment, or being regarded as having such an impairment" (42 U.S.C. § 12102 [2]).

The first prong of the ADA definition, which is a physical or mental impairment, includes physiological disorders, cosmetic disfigurement, or anatomical loss that affects body systems as well as mental or psychological disorders (28 C.F.R. § 35.104 [1][i]). Examples of physical or mental impairments under the ADA definition of a *disability* are epilepsy; muscular dystrophy; multiple sclerosis; cancer; heart disease; diabetes; Mental Retardation; emotional illness; specific learning disabilities; drug addiction; HIV disease (symptomatic or asymptomatic); alcoholism; and orthopedic, visual, speech, and hearing impairments (OCR, 1996). The preceding examples are not an exhaustive list of physical and mental impairments under the ADA definition of a *disability*.

Another key concept in the ADA definition of a *disability*

is "a substantial limitation in a major life activity." A major life activity refers to a basic activity that the "average person performs with little or no difficulty" such as walking, speaking, seeing, breathing, working, and learning (28 C.F.R. § 35.104). A person who has a substantial limitation that is determined by the nature, severity, duration, and long-term or permanent impact of the impairment on a major life activity is protected under the ADA (OCR, 1996).

In the second prong, a person with a record or history of an impairment that substantially limits a major life activity also meets the ADA's definition of an *individual with a disability* (28 C.F.R. § 35.104 [3]). Examples include a person who has a history of a mental or emotional illness, drug addiction, alcoholism, heart disease, or cancer. An individual who has been misclassified as having an impairment, (such as a person misdiagnosed as being mentally retarded or emotionally disturbed) is also protected under the ADA (OCR, 1996).

The third prong of the definition of a *disability* under ADA protects a person who has an impairment that does or does not substantially limit a major life activity but is perceived by the public or public entity as being substantially limiting (28 C.F.R. § 35.104 [13]). For example, a girl who walks with a limp but is not substantially limited in her ability to walk is not allowed to participate on the school's soccer team out of fear by school personnel that she will be injured. Under the ADA, the third prong of the definition of an *individual with a disability* applies and thus protects the girl. The third prong of the definition of a *disability* also protects an individual who does not have an impairment but who the public or public entity perceives as having an impairment (28 C.F.R. § 35.104 [3]).

An individual who is covered under the second or third prong of ADA's definition of a *disability* is not necessarily entitled to special education and related services or regular education with supplementary services. If a student is protected under the second or third prong, but not under the first prong, then the student is not eligible for special education and related services. For example, if a student has an Attention Deficit Disorder (ADD) but is performing well in the classroom, then an evaluation for special education and related services at the present time is not needed. On the other hand, if a student's mental or physical impairment substantially limits the student's ability to learn in the classroom, then the student would be entitled to an evaluation, and special education and related services or regular education with supplementary services may follow (OCR, 1996).

Title II and Section 504 use the three-prong definition of a *disability,* whereas IDEA uses the 13 recognized disability categories and the *need* criteria. In other words, there must be a need for special education and related services. Based on these differences in the definition of a *disability,* there may be some students who qualify for regular or special education and related services under Section 504 and Title II but do not have one of the 13 disabilities recognized by IDEA (OCR, 1996).

Protection under Title II, Subtitle A is afforded to qualified individuals with disabilities. An individual with a disability is qualified to receive services or participate in an elementary and secondary education program if the student meets the eligibility requirements of a qualified individual with a disability established under Section 504. As previously mentioned, Title II incorporates the more specific details and standards in Section 504. A qualified individual with a disability is an individual who has a disability and is of the appropriate age (school-aged), and

> who, with or without reasonable modifications to rules, policies, or practices, the removal of architectural, communication, or transportation barriers, or the provision of auxiliary aids and services, meets the essential eligibility requirements for the receipt of services or the participation in programs or activities provided by a public entity. (28 C.F.R. § 35.104)

Parents or other associates of a student who are disabled themselves and who are invited to attend a school event or choose to participate in a school event open to the public are also qualified as individuals with disabilities and are protected under the ADA. Under these circumstances, the school district must ensure program accessibility and provide auxiliary aids and services to ensure effective communication for these individuals with disabilities. For example, if a parent is deaf and is invited to attend a parent-teacher conference for his or her child, who may or may not be a student with a disability under the ADA, then the school is responsible for providing an interpreter at the parent's request in order for the parent to participate in the meeting (OCR, 1996).

Title II also extends protection to, but does not provide accommodations for, an individual who is not disabled but who assists or lives with someone with a disability (28 C.F.R. § 35.130 [g]). Family members, friends, or any other person or entity who associates with an individual with a disability are protected under this federal regulation. Likewise, Title II extends protection to an individual with or without a disability who takes action to oppose any act or practice prohibited by the statute or assists or encourages others to exercise their rights under the ADA regulations (28 C.F.R. § 35.134). For example, if an educator encourages a family to exercise their rights under the ADA regarding a school policy, then the educator and the family, including the individual with the disability, are protected under ADA from any coercion or retaliation from the school district.

To bring a school district into compliance with the ADA statute, five action steps must be taken by the district. First, the school district must designate a responsible employee to coordinate ADA compliance. Under Title II, if the school district has 50 or more employees, then at least one coordinator must be designated (28 C.F.R. § 35.107 [a]). The ADA coordinator's role includes planning and coordinating compliance efforts, implementing and ensuring completion of the five action steps, and receiving and investigating complaints of possible discrimination against individuals with disabilities. Second, the school district, regardless of size, must provide notice of the ADA requirements to all interested parties including participants, beneficiaries, employees, applicants, and the public. Specific information on how Title II requirements apply to particular programs, services, and activities must be included (28 C.F.R. § 35.106). Appropriate methods to disseminate this information include publications, public posters, or media broadcast. The most effective methods for making people aware of their rights and protections under the ADA, however, are determined by the head of the school district or delegated to the ADA coordinator. Third, school districts with 50 or more employees must adopt and publish grievance procedures providing for prompt and equitable resolution of complaints alleging violations of the ADA (28 C.F.R. § 35.107). These grievance procedures are available to school district employees, students, or the public. Fourth, every school district, regardless of size, must conduct a self-evaluation of its policies and practices, including communications and employment, and correct any inconsistencies in its policies and practices in relation to the ADA statute (28 C.F.R. § 35.105 [a]). However, if the school district has received federal funding and has conducted a self-evaluation as required under Section 504, then only those programs and new or modified policies or practices since the Section 504 self-evaluation must be reviewed and corrections made to be consistent with the ADA regulations (28 C.F.R. § 35.105 [c]). School districts should have completed Title II self-evaluations by January 26, 1993 (28 C.F.R. § 35.105 [c]) for current programs, policies, and practices in existence at that time. Fifth, a transition plan must be developed to bring existing facilities into structural compliance with the ADA statute. A transition plan is needed to ensure that programs, services, or activities are accessible to individuals with disabilities (28 C.F.R. § 35.150 [di [1]). Structural changes outlined in the transition plan should have been completed by January 26, 1995 for existing facilities (28 C.F.R. § 35.150 [c]).

Nondiscrimination requirements are used to analyze the policies, programs, and practices of a public school district. Specific nondiscrimination requirements imposed on a school district under Section 504 are applicable under Title II. According to Section 504, a school district is obligated to provide a free, appropriate public education (FAPE) to school-aged children with disabilities. The school district's responsibilities are specifically described under Section 504 and are incorporated into the general provisions of Title II (28 C.F.R. § 35.130; 28 C.F.R. § 35.103 [a]; see 34 C.F.R. §§ 104.31-104.37).

Title II also requires a school district to ensure that qualified individuals with disabilities are not excluded from participation in or denied any benefits from the district's programs, services, or activities based on their disability (28 C.F.R. § 35.130 [a]). This requirement applies to programs, services, and activities operated or provided directly by the district as well as those operated or provided by another entity on behalf of the district under contractual agreement or other arrangements (28 C.F.R. § 35.130 [h]). For example, if a student with a disability is excluded from bus service by a private school bus company that is under contract with the school district to provide this service, then the school district would be liable for the alleged discriminatory act under Title II (OCR, 1996).

The school district must also ensure that qualified individuals with disabilities have an equal opportunity to participate in the district's programs as do nondisabled individuals. Likewise, individuals with disabilities must have an equal opportunity to benefit from any aids, benefits, or services provided by the school district as do nondisabled individuals. For example, if a student with a severe visual impairment is evaluated and it is determined, in order to provide FAPE, visual aids and services must be provided, and the school district refuses to pay for the visual aids, citing expenses, then under these circumstances, the school district is in violation of Title II standards because the district has denied related aids and services to the student. As a result, the student does not have an equal opportunity as does a nondisabled student to participate in or receive benefits from the school program (OCR, 1996). Similarly, a school district's benefits and services must be effective enough to afford equal opportunity to obtain the same results, benefits, or levels of achievement for both individuals with and without disabilities.

Under Title II, a school district may not operate different or separate programs or provide different or separate benefits or services, unless the programs, benefits, or services are needed to provide equal benefits to individuals with disabilities (28 C.F.R. § 35.103 [a]; 28 C.F.R. § 35.130 [b1[1] [iv]). If separate or different programs, services, or benefits are needed, then the school district must provide them in the most integrated setting for individuals with disabilities (28 C.F.R. § 35.103 [a]; 28 C.F.R. § 35.130 [d]). However, in the establishment of separate or different programs, services, or benefits, individuals with disabilities may not be denied participation in the regular programs or access to regular benefits and services.

Another nondiscrimination requirement under Title II includes the prohibition of surcharges. A school district is not allowed to place a surcharge on an individual with a disability to cover the costs of measures that are necessary to provide nondiscriminatory treatment (28 C.F.R. § 35.130 [f]). For example, if an evaluation is conducted and it is determined that a student with a disability should be placed in a regular education program with related aids and services, including a computer, then the school district cannot charge the student or his or her parents for the use of the computer as the computer is a necessary aid in order to provide FAPE. Similarly, modifications that would fundamentally alter a specific benefit, program, service, or activity are prohibited. On the other hand, if failure to modify a specific benefit, program, service, or activity results in the denial of FAPE, then the school district must make modifications. However, a school district is not required to provide a personal device, such as a wheelchair, or service of a personal nature, such as toileting, unless the device or service is necessary to provide FAPE to the student.

Nondiscriminatory requirements also apply to eligibility criteria. A school district may not use eligibility criteria to screen out individuals with disabilities from participation in its programs or receipt of its benefits or services (28 C.F.R. § 35.103 [a]; 28 C.F.R. § 35.130 [b][8]). However, a school has the right to impose legitimate safety requirements needed for the safe operation of its services, benefits, or programs, but these safety requirements must be based on actual risks, not stereotypes. For example, if a school offers a course in scuba diving and demonstrates that a certain level of swimming ability is needed for safe participation in the class, then those individuals who cannot pass a swimming test, including some individuals with disabilities, could be screened out without violating the law (OCR, 1996).

Besides nondiscriminatory requirements, a school district must ensure that their programs, services, and activities are accessible to individuals with disabilities. This includes not only students, but also parents, guardians, and members of the public with disabilities. According to Title II, two standards are used to determine program accessibility. One standard deals with existing facilities and the other standard deals with new construction and alterations. For existing facilities, when viewed in their entirety, the program or activity must be accessible to and usable by individuals with disabilities, unless a fundamental alteration in the program or undue financial or administrative burden would result (28 C.F.R. § 35.130). The burden of proof, according to Title II, is placed on the school district. For new or altered facilities, the same standard applies; however, the fundamental alteration or undue burden is not applicable.

Based on the program accessibility standard, numerous misconceptions have evolved, such as the view that buildings must be completely accessible and barrier free. As long as the program, class, or function is accessible, Title II does not require that existing buildings offer a barrier-free environment. In other words, if the program can be held in another classroom or building, and this classroom or building meets accessibility requirements, then the school district's fundamental alteration in the program is in compliance with the standards set forth under Title II (OCR, 1996).

In addition to program accessibility requirements, transition services are also addressed under Title II as well as Title III of ADA. Transition services are defined as "a set of coordinated activities that promote movement from school to postschool activities" (Jacob-Timm & Hartshorne, 1995, p. 379). Transition services for youth with disabilities are provided in more specific details under IDEA. The enactment of the ADA is expected to lead to the expansion of opportunities for youth with disabilities in their transition to postschool activities (American Council on Education, 1993). Postschool activities may include vocational training, continuing education, integrated employment, independent living, community participation, and postsecondary education.

For postsecondary education, the enactment of the ADA has translated into renewed attention focused on disability access to facilities and programs as well as employment and promotion issues. In addition, the ADA has resulted in a greater number of opportunities for students with disabilities due to increased access to employment, public accommodations, transportation, and telecommunications. Thus, an expanded pool of qualified college-educated disabled workers is expected in the future to address anticipated manpower shortages in the next decade (American Council on Education, 1993).

Numerous implications exist for education officials under Title H. First, local agencies may witness an increase in the number of requests for public hearings to determine student eligibility for special education. A potential increase in the number of students served may occur. Second, parents and other adults' requests to participate in school activities may increase. Because public schools offer programs and opportunities to the community, many adults with disabilities may desire greater participation due to the enactment of the statute. As a result, the public school's responsibilities may increase in meeting program accessibility, service, and benefit requirements. Third, the ADA encourages full participation in society of individuals with disabilities. Thus, parents' requests for their children with disabilities to participate in school activities (e.g., athletic events, field trips, recreational offerings, etc.) may increase, and transportation issues will also need to be addressed (NASDSE, 1992).

The implementation of the ADA has expanded the role of the schools in the preparation of students with disabilities to take full advantage of employment opportunities, to participate more fully in school programs, to achieve greater independence through the use of public transportation, and to learn and to communicate more effectively through the use of telecommunication systems (First & Curcio, 1993). The ADA encourages the education system to become more actively involved in the lives of individuals with disabilities and to assist in the empowerment of students with disabilities. Educators and parents are challenged to bring real meaning into the lives of students with disabilities and to the school environment, not only for the students' benefit, but also for the benefit of all people.

REFERENCES

American Council on Education. (1993). *Americans with Disabilities* (Report No. H030C3002-94). Washington DC: HEATH Resource Center. (ERIC Reproduction Document Service No. ED 381 919)

Americans with Disabilities Act of 1990, 28 C.F.R. § 35; 34 C.F.R. §§ 104.31–404.37 (1993).

Americans with Disabilities Act of 1990, 42 U.S.C. § 12101 *et seq.* (West 1994).

Burgdorf, R. L. (1991). The Americans with Disabilities Act: Analysis and implications of a second-generation civil rights statute. *Harvard Civil Rights—Civil Liberties Law Review, 26,* 413–522.

Cunconan-Lahr, R. (1991). *The Americans with Disabilities Act: Educational implications and policy considerations.* (ERIC Document Reproduction Service No. Ed 333 665)

First, P. F., & Curcio, J. L. (1993). *Individuals with disabilities: Implementing the newest laws.* Newbury Park, CA: Corwin.

Henderson, K. (1995). *Overview of ADA, IDEA, and Section 504* (Report No. EDO-EC-94-8). Washington, DC: Office of Educational Research and Improvement. (ERIC Document Reproduction Service No. ED 389 142)

Jacob-Timm, S., & Hartshorne, T. (1995). *Ethics and law for school psychologists.* Brandon, VT: Clinical Psychology.

National Association of State Directors of Special Education (NASDSE). (1992). The Americans with Disabilities Act: New challenges and opportunities for school administrators. *Liaison Bulletin, 18*(4), 1–11.

Office of Civil Rights (OCR). (1996). *Compliance with the Americans with Disabilities Act: A self-evaluation guide for public elementary and secondary schools.* Washington, DC: U.S. Government Printing Office.

PATRICIA A. LOWE
CECIL R. REYNOLDS
Texas A&M University
Second edition

KIMBERLEY F. APPLEQUIST
*University of Colorado at
Colorado Springs*
Third edition

ARCHITECTURAL BARRIERS
INDIVIDUALS WITH DISABILITIES EDUCATION IMPROVEMENT ACT OF 2004 (IDEIA)
REHABILITATION ACT OF 1973, SECTION 504

AMES, LOUISE BATES (1908–1996)

Born in Portland, Maine, Louise Ames received her BA in 1930 from the University of Maine. She then went on to receive her MA in 1933 and PhD in 1937 in experimental

Louise Bates Ames

psychology from Yale University, where she studied with Arnold Gesell. Her relationship with Gesell resulted in the founding of the Gesell Institute in 1950, a project where Dr. Ames collaborated with Dr. Frances Ilg and Dr. Janet Learner. Ames was also an instructor. She was assistant professor at Yale Medical School (1936–1950) and curator of the Yale Films of Child Development (1944–1950).

Working with Frances Ilg and Arnold Gesell, Dr. Ames developed the important developmental theory that patterned, predictable behaviors are associated with chronological age, with the explicit implication that human development unfolded in discrete, recognizable stages. Such ideas were relatively novel at the time and have had great impact since their development. Her career interests and research in the behavior and development of normal children resulted in the development of standard references for psychologists working with children, and served to educate nonprofessionals as well through its coverage by the popular media.

Dr. Ames' greatest impact was in teaching parents and teachers about the course of child development, primarily through her prolific publications, which included *Infant and Child in the Culture of Today* (1940), *School Readiness* (1956), the syndicated newspaper column "Child Behavior" in collaboration with her colleagues (which later became a weekly half-hour television show in the 1950s), *Child Behavior* (1981), and *Don't Rush Your Preschooler* (1980), co-authored with her daughter Joan Ames Chase. Ames also had a strong interest in projective assessment and provided normative data in *Child Rorschach Responses* (1974). This interest extended to assessment of the elderly (*Rorschach Responses in Old Age*) and a series of articles developing test batteries for assessing deterioration of functions in old age.

Over her long career, Dr. Ames authored some 300 articles and monographs, co-authored/collaborated on 25 books, and received honorary degrees and many awards for service. One of the most publicized women in psychology, Louise Bates Ames died of cancer in November, 1996, at the age of 88.

REFERENCES

Ames, L. B. (1940). *Infant and child in the culture of today.* New York: Harper & Row.

Ames, L. B. (1974). *Child Rorschach responses.* New York: Brunner/Mazel.

Ames, L. B. (1981). *Child behavior.* New York: Harper Perennial.

Ames, L. B., & Chase, J. A. (1980). *Don't rush your preschooler.* New York: Harper & Row.

Ames, L. B., & Ilg, F. (1956). *School readiness.* New York: Harper & Row.

Ames, L. B., Metraux, R. W., Rodell, J. L., & Walker, R. W. (1973). *Rorschach responses in old age.* New York: Brunner/Mazel.

ELAINE FLETCHER-JANZEN
*University of Colorado at
Colorado Springs*
First edition, Third edition

KAY E. KETZENBERGER
*The University of Texas of the
Permian Basin*
Second edition

AMNESIA

Amnesia is a disorder of memory that occurs in the absence of gross disorientation, confusion, or dementia. Amnesia may be retrograde, where the individual has difficulty remembering events and information learned prior to the onset of the amnesia, or it may be anterograde, where the individual is unable to learn new information from the point of onset of the amnesia. Amnesics do not have difficulty with immediate memory. Digit span and immediate repetition are intact. Rather, individuals with amnesia are unable to remember after a delay filled with interference.

Amnesia is fascinating because observation of amnesics may help us understand how new information is learned (e.g., what brain structures are involved and what processes facilitate new learning). Amnesics are also of interest because the sense of continuity and time passing, remembering experiences, and hence, self-identity (Walton, 1977) depend on continuous access to information about the remote and recent past. The difficulties that amnesic patients encounter in awareness of their own experiences emphasizes just how important memory is.

Amnesia as an isolated neurologic symptom can be mistaken for a psychiatric disorder (DeJong, Itabashi, & Olson, 1969). There are hysterical amnesias that are a consequence of psychiatric distress alone. Fugue states are 20 dissociative episodes during which an individual forgets his or her identity and past. Hysterical amnesia is discriminable from neurologic conditions causing amnesia in that the total loss of self-identity rarely occurs in neurologically based amnesias, and because the end of the fugue state is abrupt. In the neurologically based amnesias that remit, the cessation of memory loss is gradual, with the period of time for which the individual is amnesic shrinking only gradually.

Transient amnesia is a known consequence of electroconvulsive therapy (ECT shock treatment). Individuals receiving ECT have both retrograde amnesia for events occurring just prior to treatment, and anterograde amnesia for what happens subsequent to treatment. When compared with their own performance after recovery from amnesia, patients who are amnesic after receiving ECT forget more easily and at an abnormal rate (Squire, 1981). This suggests a deficit in consolidation and elaboration of memory. There is some disagreement as to whether memory loss secondary to ECT is cumulative. Transient amnesia also may occur when an individual receives general anesthesia.

Anterograde amnesia that gradually remits is a frequent occurrence after closed head injuries (Levin, Benton, & Grossman, 1982; Reynolds & Fletcher-Janzen, 1997). There often is a more limited retrograde amnesia for the period just prior to the injury. Anterograde amnesia secondary to closed head injury (also called posttraumatic amnesia) is a good index of the severity of the injury and useful in the prediction of long-term recovery. After the amnesia has remitted, there is often a residual memory disorder.

Transient global amnesia is a neurologic condition that is now assumed to be a consequence of transient ischemia (Heathfield, Croft, & Swash, 1973). The presentation of an individual with transient global amnesia is characteristic. There is an abrupt onset of amnesia, both retrograde and anterograde, with perhaps only initial, mild clouding of consciousness, and no change in cognition or speech. Episodes typically last for several hours only, and the retrograde amnesia gradually shrinks, leaving individuals amnesic only for the period during which they had anterograde amnesia (Hecaen & Albert, 1978).

Amnesia is the hallmark of Korsakoff's disease (an entirely adult disease induced by alcohol consumption). Patients with Korsakoff's have a profound anterograde amnesia. Though immediate repetition is intact, remembering what they have been told after an interference (e.g., a brief conversation) is impossible. Patients hospitalized with Korsakoff's often reintroduce themselves to their physicians when the physician who has been caring for them reenters the room after a short interval. Korsakoff's patients are notable for their tendency to confabulate (i.e., fill in the blanks in their memory with imaginary accounts). The most common etiology of Korsakoff's is thiamine deficiency as a consequence of alcoholism. Head injury, anoxia, carbon monoxide poisoning, tumors, and other pathologies involving the same brain structure are other causes of the disorder (Walton, 1977).

A great deal has been learned about amnesia and memory through the study of groups of patients with unremitting forms of amnesia: amnesia secondary to Korsakoff's syndrome, amnesia secondary to neurosurgery for control of epilepsy, traumatic brain lesions resulting in amnesia, and generalized dementing processes (especially Huntington's disease and Alzheimer's disease) in which memory deficits are disproportionately problematic (at least during specific stages of the disease). Careful investigation of these patients clearly reveals that though the average clinician thinks of memory as a unitary phenomenon, memory loss is a multidimensional symptom with different etiologies resulting in characteristic, discriminable patterns of memory loss and skill (Butters, 1984).

One pattern of amnesia reflects hemispheric differences. Individuals with amnesia secondary to isolated damage to the right hemisphere have deficient skills in nonverbal memory when the information is presented visually. Those amnesic secondary to isolated left hemisphere damage have greater difficulty with verbal memory. Verbal memory deficits are seen regardless of the sensory modality used to present the information; for example, visual presentation of verbal information (Hecaen & Albert, 1978).

The pattern of retrograde amnesia is not the same across all amnesic populations. Butters (1984) compared remote memory functioning in Huntington's disease, Korsakoff's disease, and normal subjects by assessing their ability to recall famous people and events from past decades. Korsakoff's patients had more severe difficulties recalling past events, but there was a normal gradation in their ability to remember, with events that occurred further in the past recalled better than more recent past experiences. The Huntington's disease patients demonstrated a flat pattern. They were equally unable to remember any past event. This pattern of remote recollection occurs across the stages of Huntington's disease, though the severity increases as the disease progresses.

Amnesic patients of differing etiologies demonstrate differential responses to manipulations aimed at facilitating memory. For example, Korsakoff's amnesics are assisted in memorization by increasing rehearsal time, intertrial rest intervals, and a structured orientation procedure. They are not aided, however, by the provision of verbal mediation. Conversely, Huntington's disease patients are not assisted as are Korsakoff's patients; neither increased rehearsal

time, increased intertrial intervals, nor does general orientation aid their performance. They are assisted, however, by verbal mediation. Patients with Alzheimer's disease are not assisted by verbal mediation.

Another difference between amnesic syndromes is related to the ability to acquire procedural versus declarative memories (Squire, 1982). Declarative memory pertains to specific facts and data. Procedural memory refers to the rules for completing a specific type of task. Studies of amnesic patients indicate that patients with amnesia secondary to Korsakoff's disease acquire procedural information but have great difficulty in learning declarative data. Huntington's disease patients do not remember procedural rules, but do learn (or at least recognize) previously presented data of a declarative type.

The study of patient populations with known etiologies has been useful in increasing our understanding of what brain structures are involved in the elaboration and retrieval of memory. Evidence from neurosurgical intervention to control severe epilepsy has demonstrated that damage to the medial aspects of both temporal lobes, especially the hippocampus, results in profound amnesia (Hecaen & Albert, 1978; Squire, 1982). This amnesia is distinguished by rapid and abnormal forgetting. Other amnesics appear to have diencephalic damage with some disagreement as to exactly which structures are affected. The mammillary bodies and dorsal-medial nucleus of the thalamus are involved, though the relative contributions of either structure are not known. Damage to the dorsal-medial nucleus appears sufficient to cause amnesia (Squire, 1982). Amnesia secondary to diencephalic damage is notable for a normal forgetting curve, but difficulty with encoding. Identification of structures involved in memory is useful not only in terms of understanding specific syndromes, but also in considering pharmacologic manipulations to assist in treatment.

With the exception of posttraumatic amnesia, amnesia in its pure form is not reported to occur in children. Subsequent to head injuries, children do exhibit posttraumatic amnesia and have difficulty learning new information in school and remembering what they learned just prior to their injuries. Consequently, they will be confused in the school setting. Posttraumatic amnesia generally will remit. Such children should be allowed to recover after their injuries (with the most rapid recovery occurring in the first 6 months; Pompa, 2003) without the expectation that by studying harder they will remember significantly better. Once the major recovery period is over (after 6 to 9 months), cognitive rehabilitation programs aimed at providing strategies to assist in memory may be useful. There are limited data available on how generalizable the effect of cognitive rehabilitation is in the adult population, and less data regarding children.

It should be clear that the short-term memory impairments described in the learning of disabled children bear little resemblance to amnesic disorders. Amnesic patients are capable of short-term memory performance. Children with severe brain injury may become amnesic, but it is most often within the context of general dementia with difficulties in a variety of areas.

REFERENCES

Butters, N. (1984). The clinical aspects of memory disorders: Contributions from experimental studies of amnesia and dementia. *Journal of Clinical Neuropsychology, 6,* 17–36.

DeJong, R. N., Itabashi, H. H., & Olson, J. R. (1969). Memory loss due to hippocampal lesion. *Archives of Neurology, 20,* 339–348.

Heathfield, K. W. G., Croft, P. B., & Swash, M. (1973). The syndrome of transient global amnesia. *Brain, 96,* 729–731.

Hecaen, H., & Albert, M. L. (1978). *Human neuropsychology.* New York: Wiley.

Levin, H. S., Benton, A. L., & Grossman, R. G. (1982). *Neurobehavioral consequences of closed head injury.* New York: Oxford University Press.

Milner, B., Corkin, S., & Teuber, H. L. (1968). Further analysis of the hippocampal amnesic syndrome: A 14-year follow-up study of H. M. *Neuropsychologia, 6,* 215–234.

Pompa, J. (2003). Amnesia. In E. Fletcher-Janzen & C. R. Reynolds (Eds.), *Childhood disorders diagnostic desk reference* (pp. 34–35). New York: Wiley.

Reynolds, C. R., & Fletcher-Janzen, E. (Eds.). (1997). *Handbook of clinical child neuropsychology.* New York: Plenum Press.

Squire, L. (1981). Two forms of human amnesia: An analysis of forgetting. *Journal of Neurosciences, 1,* 635–640.

Squire, L. (1982). The neuropsychology of human memory. *Annual Review of Neurosciences, 5,* 241–273.

Walton, J. N. (1977). *Brain's diseases of the nervous system.* Oxford, England: Oxford University Press.

GRETA N. WILKENING
Children's Hospital

MEMORY DISORDERS
TRAUMATIC BRAIN INJURY

AMNIOCENTESIS

Amniocentesis is the sampling of amniotic fluid surrounding a fetus. A physician anesthetizes a small area of the pregnant woman's abdomen, inserts a small needle through the abdominal wall, and, with the aid of ultrasonography, enters the amniotic sac and removes 30 ccs (approximately 1 oz) of fluid. It is performed most frequently between 15 and 18 weeks gestation to detect hereditary disease or congenital defects in the fetus. One disadvantage is that analysis of the fluid takes 2 to 4 weeks. Damage to the fetus also may occur, but the risk is small (1 in 200; March of Dimes, 2005).

Midtrimester amniocentesis plays an important role in genetic and other prenatal counseling by providing potential parents with reproductive options. It should be considered when the pregnant woman is over 35, or a family history of genetic or congenital disorders is apparent (Kaback, 1979; March of Dimes, 2005). Cytogenetic analysis of fetal fluid leads to prevention of birth of approximately 15,000 chromosomally abnormal infants each year in the United States alone (Pritchard, MacDonald, & Gant, 1985).

Amniocentesis allows identification of about 300 chromosomal, single-gene, and other congenital abnormalities (Pritchard et al., 1985). The list grows with the discovery of new markers. Chromosomally based disorders are identified through karyotyping and resultant abnormal appearance of one or more chromosomes; other disorders are identified through elevated or reduced levels of particular substances. Among the disorders that can be reliably diagnosed are (1) all chromosomally based disorders such as Down's syndrome and cri du chat; (2) about 75 inborn errors of metabolism, including galactosemia, Tay-Sachs disease, and Lesch-Nyhan syndrome (X-linked), but not phenylketonuria; (3) some central nervous system defects including meningocele (a form of spina bifida) and anencephaly; (4) some fetal infections (cytomegalovirus, herpes simplex, and rubella); (5) and some hematologic disorders (e.g., sickle-cell anemia; Pritchard et al., 1985).

The widespread availability of amniocentesis forces many women to confront the decision to terminate an advanced pregnancy. Attachment grows throughout pregnancy, and confronting the decision of choosing termination at a late stage can be emotionally painful (Brewster, 1984). Many women are unprepared for the anxiety associated with both waiting several weeks for results of their amniocentesis and choosing between life and quality of life. Optimally, women in high-risk groups should weigh this decision and discuss other reproductive options with a genetic counselor prior to conception. Some counselors suggest that health caregivers be sensitive to pregnant women's emotional reactions and not use measures such as a doppler to hear the fetus's heartbeat or ultrasonography to take pictures of the fetus, that promote maternal attachment prior to amniocentesis (Brewster, 1984).

A new diagnostic technique, chorion-villus biopsy, usable as early as 8 weeks gestation, may be preferable in some cases because of the emotional and medical problems presented with a midtrimester abortion.

REFERENCES

Brewster, A. (1984). After office hours: A patient's reaction to amniocentesis. *Obstetrics & Gynecology, 64,* 443–444.

Kaback, M. M. (1979). Predictors of hereditary diseases or congenital defects in antenatal diagnosis (National Institute of Child Health and Human Development, U.S. Department of HEW, NIH Publication No. 79-1973). *Antenatal Diagnosis,* 39–42.

March of Dimes. (2005). *What's inside*. Retrieved June 19, 2005, from http://www.marchofdimes.com/pnhec/159_520.asp.

Pritchard, J. A., MacDonald, C., & Gant, N. F. (Eds.). (1985). *Williams obstetrics* (17th ed., pp. 267–293). Englewood Cliffs, NJ: Appleton-Century-Crofts.

BRENDA M. POPE
*New Hanover Memorial
Hospital*

CHRONIC VILLUS SAMPLING
GENETIC COUNSELING
INBORN ERRORS OF METABOLISM

AMPHETAMINE PSYCHOSIS

Amphetamine psychosis results from the neurochemical and behavioral interaction of large doses of amphetamines. The toxic reaction, induced by chronic amphetamine abuse or by an acute overdose, leads to transitory symptoms that are clinically indistinguishable from those of paranoid schizophrenia. Such symptoms, occurring as early as 36 to 48 hours after a large dosage, include vivid auditory, visual, and tactile hallucinations, changes in affect, loosening of associations with reality, and paranoid thought processes (Gilman, Goodman, & Gilman, 1980). Affected individuals may also show behavioral stereotypes such as continuous rocking or polishing motions, repetitive grooming activities (rubbing or picking of the skin), and other locomotor irregularities. Biochemical correlates of amphetamine psychosis, including increased dopaminergic activity, are similar to those of schizophrenia (Kokkinidis & Anisman, 1980).

In addition to reducing amphetamine intake, treatment includes sedatives, psychotherapy, and custodial care. Acidification of the urine will speed excretion of the amphetamines. The psychotic state usually clears in about a week after beginning treatment, with hallucinations being the first symptom to disappear (American Medical Association, 1980). However, some confusion, memory loss, and delusional ideas commonly persist for months (Merck, 2005).

REFERENCES

American Medical Association. (1980). *AMA drug evaluations* (4th ed.). New York: Wiley.

Gilman, A. G., Goodman, L. S., & Gilman, A. (1980). *Goodman and Gilman's pharmacological basis of therapeutics* (6th ed.). New York: Macmillan.

Kokkinidis, L., & Anisman, H. (1980). Amphetamine models of paranoid schizophrenia: An overview and elaboration of animal experimentation. *Psychological Bulletin, 88,* 551–579.

Merck Manual. (2005). *Amphetamine dependence*. Retrieved June 19, 2005, from http://www.merck.com/mrkshared/mmanual/section15/chapter195/195g.jsp.

VICKI BARTOSIK
Stanford University

CHILDHOOD SCHIZOPHRENIA
DRUG ABUSE
LSD
PSYCHOTROPIC DRUGS

AMSLAN

See AMERICAN SIGN LANGUAGE.

ANASTASI, ANNE (1908–2001)

Anne Anastasi obtained her BA from Barnard College in 1928 and her PhD from Columbia University in 1930 at the age of 21. Influenced by H. L. Hollingworth and articles about early precursors of factor analysis by C. Searman, Anastasi changed her orientation from mathematics to psychology. She also extended her study of individual differences to include major group differences. These changes began her association with the development of differential psychology. Her major areas of study are the nature and identification of psychological traits, test construction and evaluation, and interpretation of test results with specific reference to the role of cultural factors in individual and group differences.

Anastasi's publication of *Psychological Testing,* in the most recent edition, continues to stress the responsibility of the test administrator in selecting appropriate tests and

Anne Anastasi

methods of testing, interpreting test scores, and using and communicating test results. Other major publications include *Differential Psychology* and *Fields in Applied Psychology*. She has published more than 170 journal articles and monographs and was the only author who has contributed to every edition of the *Mental Measurements Yearbook* since its inception in 1938.

Anastasi received several honorary degrees and many awards such as the 1977 Educational Testing Service Award for Distinguished Service to Measurement, the E. L. Thorndike Award for Distinguished Psychological Contributions to Education (from APA Division 15), the American Psychological Association Distinguished Scientific Award for the Application of Psychology, the American Psychological Foundation Gold Medal, and the AERA award for Distinguished Contributions to Research in Education. In 1987 she was presented with the National Medal of Science by President Ronald Reagan. Anastasi was also professor emeritus at Fordham University and was esteemed as the third female president of the American Psychological Association. Anne Anastasi was known and seen by her peers as the prominent woman in psychology up until her death in the year 2001.

REFERENCES

Anastasi, A., & Urbina, S. (1997). *Psychological testing* (7th ed.). Upper Saddle River, NJ: Prentice Hall.

Anastasi, A. (1979). *Fields of applied psychology* (2nd ed.). New York: McGraw-Hill.

Anastasi, A. (1958). *Differential psychology* (3rd ed.). New York: Macmillan.

ELAINE FLETCHER-JANZEN
*University of Colorado at
Colorado Springs*
First edition

DEBORAH B. GUILLEN
*The University of Texas of the
Permian Basin*
Second edition

RACHEL M. TOPLIS
*Falcon School District 49,
Colorado Springs, Colorado*
Third edition

ANASTASIOW, NICHOLAS J. (1924–)

Though he retired as Thomas Hunter professor at Hunter College, City University of New York, in 1992, Nicholas Anastasiow maintains his principal interest in early childhood special education and child development. He began his career as an elementary school teacher in the early 1950s and garnered various educational certifications until he

Nicholas J. Anastasiow

received his PhD in child development and guidance from Stanford University in 1963. In 1967, he completed postdoctoral courses in neurology at Columbia University.

Anastasiow believes that "many at risk children can lead normal lives when they are provided remediation as well as support and education for their parents" (personal communication, August 2, 1985). This belief is well represented in the 200 articles, reports, and books he has published on a vast array of subjects such as language development. Some of his titles are *Language and Reading Strategies for Poverty Children* (Anastasiow, Hanes, & Hanes, 1982), *The At Risk Infant* (Harel & Anastasiow, 1984), and *Development and Disabilities* (Anastasiow, 1986). He currently has finished the 11th revision of the classic textbook *Educating Exceptional Children,* which he co-authors with Samuel Kirk and Jim Gallagher.

Anastasiow is also interested in the "prevention of at risk children by educating future parents in knowledge of child development and the skills and strategies of parenting before they become parents" (personal communication, August 2, 1985). He has encouraged schools to establish child development courses for sixth and seventh graders in publications such as *The Adolescent Parent* (1982).

Anastasiow has served as a consultant to the Assistant Secretary on Human Development, the White House Conference on the Handicapped, and the President's Council for Exceptional Children—Early Childhood Division, and as an exchange delegate to the USSR.

REFERENCES

Anastasiow, N. J. (1982). *The adolescent parent.* Baltimore: Brookes.

Anastasiow, N. J. (1986). *Development and disabilities.* Baltimore: Brookes.

Anastasiow, N. J., Hanes, M. L., & Hanes, M. (1982). *Language and reading strategies for in text poverty children.* Austin, TX: PRO-ED.

Anastasiow, N. J., & Harel, S. (Eds.). (1993). *The at risk infant.* Baltimore: Brookes.

Harel, S., & Anastasiow, N. J. (Eds.). (1984). *The at risk infant.* Baltimore: Brookes.

ELAINE FLETCHER-JANZEN
*University of Colorado at
Colorado Springs*

ANDERSON, META L. (1878–1942)

Meta L. Anderson, while a teacher in the New York City public schools, enrolled in a course in the education of mentally retarded children at The Training School at Vineland, New Jersey. There, Edward R. Johnstone and Henry H. Goddard, recognizing her unusual ability, recommended her to the Newark, New Jersey, Board of Education, which employed her to begin special classes for mentally retarded children. In 1910 she established two special classes and Newark joined the handful of school systems that provided special programs for handicapped students.

Anderson developed an instructional approach based on careful analysis of the abilities and limitations of each student and devised trade classes and a work experience program to provide vocational preparation. Her book, *Education of Defectives in the Public Schools* (1917), described the program and added impetus to the growing special class movement in the United States. In the closing months of World War I, Anderson was appointed head of reconstruction aid in Europe. After the war she served for a year in Serbia. She returned to the Newark schools in 1920 to become director of the city's comprehensive special education program. She received her PhD from New York University in 1922. She served as president of the American Association on Mental Deficiency in 1941.

REFERENCES

Anderson, M. L. (1917). *Education of defectives in the public schools.* Yonkers, NY: World Book.

Whitney, E. A. (1953). Some stalwarts of the past. *American Journal of Mental Deficiency, 57,* 345–360.

PAUL IRVINE
Katonah, New York

ANENCEPHALY

Anencephaly is a congenital disorder marked by the absence of the cerebral cortices. It belongs to a class of disorders that are termed neural tube defects (NTD) and results from the failure of the neural tube to close during embryogenesis. The neural tube, which is the precursor to the brain and spinal cord, usually closes by the 28th day after conception (Kloza, 1985). If this does not occur completely, various defects to the central nervous system (CNS) become manifest. If this occurs "lower" on the neural tube, spina bifida will be present. However, if the "top" of the neural tube remains open, anencephaly results. Anencephaly with spina bifida, rarely occurs (Swaiman & Wright, 1973).

As anencephaly is ostensibly marked by the absence of the cerebral cortices, the centers of higher cognitive functioning are absent. Therefore, while certain subcortical structures may remain intact (producing the reflex patterns and responses often indicative of neonates), higher cerebral activity is precluded by the absence of structures subserving those functions. Many anencephalics are stillborn, as they lack the brain structures necessary to maintain respiration and other functions vital to survival. On the occasion that the newborn is physiologically viable, it should be remembered that associative processes, reasoning, and cognitive and language development are not possible. Therefore, educational services are not a practical consideration and absolute custodial supervision and care are indicated. Ethical considerations pertaining to care must also come into play.

The development of anencephaly and other NTDs is believed to be multifactorial. The second most common group of congenital anomalies, with environment, intrauterine environment, and genetic factors implicated in their development are NTDs. Kandel, Schwartz, and Jessell (1991) provide a detailed review of the development of NTDs, including anencephaly. Geographically, anencephaly appears to be a more common occurrence on the East Coast of the United States and in the Rio Grande Valley of Texas. It is found more frequently in female births than male (2:1). It has been suggested that a higher prevalence of anencephaly is found in lower socioeconomic class families (James, Nevin, Johnston, & Merrett, 1981; Nevin, Johnston, & Merrett, 1981).

While treatment of anencephaly is not feasible, prenatal screening has been effective in identifying anencephaly prior to birth. With NTDs, a substance called alpha fetoprotein (AFP) occurs in higher concentration in the amniotic fluid surrounding the fetus (Adinolfi, 1985; Kloza, 1985). The AFP enters the mother's circulation either by the amniotic fluid or the placenta; it can then be measured in the mother's blood. Higher levels of AFP in the mother's blood at certain times in fetal gestation indicate NTDs. This method of identifying anencephaly has been shown to be 99 percent reliable, with a reliability of similar magnitude for other NTDs such as spina bifida.

REFERENCES

Adinolfi, M. (1985). The development of the human blood-csf-brain barrier. *Developmental Medicine and Child Neurology, 27*(4), 532–537.

James, W. H., Nevin, N. C., Johnston, W. P., & Merrett, J. D. (1981). Influence of social class on the risk of recurrence of anencephaly and spina bifida. *Developmental Medicine and Child Neurology, 23*(5), 661–662.

Kandel, S., Schwartz, J., & Jessell, T. (1991). *Principles of neural sciences* (3rd ed.). New York: Elsevier.

Kloza, E. M. (1985). Prenatal screening: Neural tube defects. *Disorders of Brain Development and Cognition.* Boston: Eunice Kennedy Shriver Center and Harvard Medical School.

Nevin, N. C., Johnston, W. P., & Merrett, J. D. (1981). Influence of social class on the risk of recurrence of anencephaly and spina bifida. *Developmental Medicine and Child Neurology, 23*(2), 151–154.

Swaiman, K. F., & Wright, F. S. (1973). Neurologic diseases due to developmental and metabolic defects. In A. B. Baker & L. H. Baker (Eds.), *Clinical neurology.* New York: Harper & Row.

ELLIS I. BAROWSKY
*Hunter College, City University
of New York*

BABY DOE
CONGENITAL DISORDERS

ANGELMAN SYNDROME

Angelman syndrome (formally Happy Puppet syndrome) is an emerging disorder, little studied, with no good population studies completed to allow proper prevalence or incidence estimates. However, it is roughly estimated to be 1 in 10,000 to 1 in 20,000 (Steinman, 2003). Many, but not all, Angelman syndrome individuals have deletions on chromosome 15 in maternally related regions (q11–q12) while others are of unknown pathogenic origin. The disorder is characterized by physical, motoric, and behavioral features. Physical features include a wide mouth, prominent lower jaw, and microbrachycephalia. Motor problems are related to diverse, jerky, sometimes rhythmic movements. Some children experience particular difficulties with inadequate control of chewing and swallowing which creates feeding problems. However, these problems abate after infancy in most cases. Acquisition of walking is delayed, and mild to severe ataxia after learning to walk is common.

A variety of behavioral and cognitive problems are evident. Most children with Angelman syndrome have severe to profound levels of mental retardation, although some patients may reach moderate and, rarely, mild levels of mental retardation. Spoken language is absent in 75–80 percent of children with Angelman syndrome, but receptive language is typically superior to expressive language. Some do develop skills in sign language but normal levels of communication have not been seen in any published case. Behavioral presentation of Angelman syndrome often includes hyperactivity, impulsivity, episodic pica, random

bursts of laughter (in nearly all cases), jerky nighttime movements, and a generally happy disposition.

Diagnosis is sometimes very difficult, as Angelman has similarities of presentation to Rett syndrome and to Prader-Willi syndrome in a number of cases. Detailed cytogenic studies are often necessary for proper diagnosis and even then the diagnosis may still be only inferred rather than confirmed. EEG is helpful as a common pattern with posterior slow wave activity used as a marker variable. CT and MRI are normal in 30–35 percent of cases, and others show mixed results with diffuse atrophy, deep white matter lesions (periventricular leukomalacia), and cerebellar growth retardation all having been documented in various cases.

At present 100 percent of children with Angelman syndrome are believed to require special education services, typically as children with mental retardation, although numerous related services may be required (Steinman, 2003). Intervention is largely related to symptom management and the teaching of fundamental adaptive behavior and communication skills. Sheltered employment is possible in many but not all cases. However, more and better longitudinal studies of Angelman syndrome individuals are needed to document the long-term effects of interventions and general life outcomes.

REFERENCE

Steinman, D. R. (2003). Angelman syndrome. In E. Fletcher-Janzen & C. R. Reynolds (Eds.), *Childhood disorders diagnostic desk reference* (pp. 41–42). New York: Wiley.

CECIL R. REYNOLDS
Texas A&M University

PRADER-WILLI SYNDROME
RETT SYNDROME

ANIMALS FOR INDIVIDUALS WITH DISABILITIES

Today, animals are being used to assist individuals with disabilities with daily living. For centuries, the blind have used dogs to assist them in ambulation. Recently, pilot programs using domesticated monkeys to assist moderately to severely disabled persons in the home to perform rote chores has been a successful innovation. Horseback riding has emerged as a leisure-time pursuit for many types of disabled persons.

The benefits of human/animal interaction are now being realized, especially for special education purposes. Lowered blood pressure has been documented in studies where the participants had regular contact with dogs. In another study, Friedman (1980) found that the survival rate of hypertensive persons increased dramatically with pet ownership. Pets have been considered effective agents in the reduction of everyday stress. They provide a sense of relaxation (Kidd, 1981). They also provide a chance to exercise, and for many a sense of security (White & Watson, 1983).

Animals provide the opportunity to communicate. This is probably the most valuable attribute of the human/animal relationship. Levinson (1969) states that an animal can have a "very positive effect on a family and that they have the potential to bridge the gap between children and adults by providing a common object of responsibility."

According to Levinson (1969), the introduction of animals into a residential setting for the disabled indicates that the staff believes that anything of possible treatment value to the disabled can and should be used. It reveals an awareness of the potential healing properties of pet ownership, even if those benefits have not been scientifically documented in the laboratory.

A child with disabilities is not constantly reminded of his or her disability in the interaction with a pet. A deaf child can care for a dog competently and receive all of the rewards that a hearing child would for the same efforts. The same is true for a variety of handicaps; only the type of pet might have to be changed. A child confined to a wheelchair may interact well with a rabbit or an aquarium and achieve a sense of purpose and responsibility previously unrealized.

The teaching of the emotionally disturbed child provides a setting in which the use of animals may be especially beneficial. Typically, motivating this student to participate in class can be a difficult task for the teacher. Often, these students have never learned to care for or share with others. The animal in the class may provide both the subject matter and the motivation to learn. The child who had previously trusted no one can begin to trust the teacher for the first time when he or she sees the teacher's concern in dealing with the classroom pet. This could be the first step by the child in accepting the structure of the class (Levinson, 1969).

REFERENCES

Friedman, E. (1980, July/August). Animal companions and one year survival of patients after discharge from a coronary care unit. *Public Health Reports, 44*(4), 37–42.

Kidd, A. (1981). Dogs, cats and people. *Mills Quarterly, 23*(8), 23–28.

Levinson, B. (1969). *Pet oriented child psychotherapy.* Springfield, IL: Thomas.

White, B., & Watson, T. (1983). *Pet love, how pets take care of us.* New York: Pinnacle.

THOMAS R. BURKE
*Hunter College, City University
of New York*

**EQUINE THERAPY
THERAPEUTIC RECREATION**

ANNALS OF DYSLEXIA

Originating in 1950 as the *Bulletin of the Orton Society* under the editorial leadership of June Lyday Orton, the annual periodical of the Orton Dyslexia Society was renamed the *Annals of Dyslexia* in 1981. It was designed as a means to enhance communication among the members of the Orton Dyslexia Society, an organization founded in 1949 to further research and work with children with specific language disabilities.

The journal was aimed at a professional multidisciplinary membership, consisting of neurologists, psychologists, pathologists, psychiatrists, educators, and social workers. Through concrete illustration of the practical applications of new knowledge, *Annals* served as a bridge between the researcher and the field worker.

The *Annals of Dyslexia* ceased publication in 1988.

ELIZABETH DANE
*Hunter College, City University
of New York*
First edition

KAY E. KETZENBERGER
*The University of Texas of the
Permian Basin*
Second edition

ANNUAL DIRECTORY OF EDUCATIONAL FACILITIES FOR THE LEARNING DISABLED

See BIENNIAL DIRECTORY OF EDUCATIONAL FACILITIES FOR THE LEARNING DISABLED.

ANNUAL GOALS

Annual goals describe expected student performance, are an important part of an individual education plan (IEP), and are in compliance with the Individuals with Disabilities Education Improvement Act of 2004. Each IEP must contain a statement of annual educational goals consisting of specific objectives indicating the condition under which desired performance should occur, a description of the desired performance, and a listing of the criteria for adequate performance. The proportion of IEP objectives achieved by each student at the end of the term divided by the total number written at the start of the term has been used as a measure of educational progress (Brinker & Thorpe, 1984).

Public Law 94-142 was first to mandate that pupils' rates of progress be continuously monitored so that educational programs can be reassessed and improved as students move toward goals. A common method used in instruction is the pretest, teach, posttest design. In assessing pupils, teachers in special education commonly rely on informal observation and develop curriculum-based measurement systems matched to annual goals.

Findings indicate that the use of more systematic measurement and evaluation systems than those currently in use result in better student achievement toward goals (Fuchs, Deno, & Mirkin, 1984). Another finding is that public goal setting between student and teacher is more effective than private goal setting in increasing on-task behavior in the classroom (Lyman, 1984). One suggested system is the Goal Attainment Scale (GAS), a method that can help special educators to become more accountable and effective and increase the likelihood that curricula will become student centered rather than method centered.

The method involves devising a set of goals with the involved persons, developing a set of expected outcomes for each goal, scoring the outcomes on a five-point continuum from worse than expected to better than expected, and calculating a summary score of outcomes across the goals. Mutual determination of goals and their importance by the persons involved ensures relevance and meaning to parents, students, and educators. This mutual determination also helps students to learn about alternative behaviors and helps to clarify expectations for both students and teachers. GAS is independent of theoretical predispositions and can be used by teachers to clarify specific problems, sharpen goal setting, and point out directions for action (Carr, 1979). Setting objective, observable goals and evaluating outcomes is crucial to student progress (Martens et al., 1999), and this position continues in the latest reauthorization of the Individuals with Disabilities Education Improvement Act (IDEIA) of 2004. While benchmarks and objectives for annual goals have been eliminated from the latest legislation, it remains to be seen how progress towards annual goals will be determined.

REFERENCES

Brinker, R. P., & Thorpe, M. E. (1984). Integration of severely handicapped students and the proportion of IEP objectives achieved. *Exceptional Children, 51,* 168–175.

Carr, R. A. (1979). Goal Attainment Scaling as a useful tool for evaluating progress in special education. *Exceptional Children, 46,* 88–95.

Fuchs, L. S., Deno, S. L., & Mirkin, P. K. (1984). The effects and frequent curriculum-based measurement and evaluation on pedagogy, student achievement and student awareness of learning. *American Education Research Journal, 21,* 449–460.

Gerardi, R. J., Grohe, B., Benedict, G. C., & Collidge, P. G. (1984). IEP—more paperwork and wasted time. *Contemporary Education, 56,* 39–42.

Jaffe, M. J., & Snelbecker, G. E. (1982). Evaluating independent education programs: A recommendation and some programmatic implications. *Urban Review, 14*(2), 73–81.

Lyman, R. D. (1984). The effect of private and public goal setting on classroom on-task behavior of emotionally disturbed children. *Behavior Therapy, 15,* 395–402.

Martens, B., Witt, J., Daly, E., & Vollmer, T. (1999). Behavior analysis: Theory and practice in educational settings. In C. R. Reynolds & T. B. Gutkin (Eds.), *The handbook of school psychology* (3rd ed., pp. 638–663). New York: Wiley.

CATHERINE O. BRUCE
*Hunter College, City University
of New York*

INDIVIDUAL EDUCATION PLAN
INDIVIDUALS WITH DISABILITIES EDUCATION IMPROVEMENT ACT OF 2004 (IDEIA)

ANNUAL REPORT TO CONGRESS ON THE IMPLEMENTATION OF THE INDIVIDUALS WITH DISABILITIES EDUCATION ACT, TWENTY-FIFTH EXECUTIVE SUMMARY OF THE

The 25th Annual Report to Congress has been designed to showcase the data collected from states and the national studies that make up the Office of Special Education Programs's (OSEP) National Assessment of the Implementation of the Individuals with Disabilities Education Act (IDEA). Annual reports are provided every year, the latest report is for the year 2003. To this end, OSEP proposed questions about the characteristics of children and students receiving services under Parts B and C, the settings in which they receive services, their transition from Part C to Part B and from school to adult life, and their disabilities. Answers to the questions are shown through graphs, charts, and tables complemented by short explanatory text. The report is divided into three sections: a national picture of children and students with disabilities served under Parts C and B, individual profiles of states that summarize selected aspects of special education in each state, and data tables that show states' ranking regarding exiting and educational environments for Part B and early childhood intervention and settings for Part C. Some key findings from the report are presented in the following.

Infants and Toddlers Served under IDEA, Part C

- Both the number and the percentage of infants and toddlers served under Part C have increased steadily from 1998 to 2001. In all years, 2-year-olds were the largest proportion (53 percent) of children served under Part C (p. 4).

- The racial or ethnic composition of these children is quite similar to that of the general infant and toddler population—the majority are White, followed by Hispanic, and then Black children (p. 7).

- Most infants and toddlers served under Part C in 2000 received services at home; the percentage of this population served in programs for children with developmental delay or other disabilities decreased substantially between 1996 and 2000 (p. 10).

- The majority of Part C infants and toddlers (62.6 percent) are eligible to transition to Part B services when they turn age 3 (p. 12).

Children Ages 3 through 5 Served under IDEA, Part B

- Since 1991, the number of children ages 3 through 5 who receive services under Part B of IDEA has increased steadily (p. 18). As of December 1, 2001, 5.2 percent of the total population of 3- through 5-year-olds living in the 50 states and the District of Columbia were estimated to be receiving services (p. 18).

- The majority of children ages 3 through 5 receiving special education services are White; White children also make up the majority of the general preschool population (p. 23).

- In 2000, 51 percent of preschoolers received special education services in either early childhood settings or part-time early childhood or part-time early childhood special education settings (p. 25).

- Special education teachers serving children ages 3 through 5 with disabilities are primarily White and female. Six and a half percent of these preschool special teachers also report having a disability themselves (p. 29).

Students Ages 6 through 21 Served under IDEA, Part B

- On December 1, 2001, 8.9 percent of 6- through 21-year-olds were receiving special education services under IDEA. The number of students with disabilities receiving services has increased slowly since 1992 (p. 32).

- In contrast, the number of students receiving services for autism has increased markedly, from a little less than 10,000 in 1992 to approximately 65,000 in 2001 (p. 36).

- According to findings from two of OSEP's National Assessment studies, the Special Education Elementary Longitudinal Study (SEELS) and National Longitudinal Transition Study–2 (NLTS2), students with disabilities are more likely to be poor than students in the general population (pp. 46–47).

- Parent reports as shown in SEELS and NLTS2 data indicate that more Black students with disabilities are suspended or expelled from school than are White or Hispanic students. Overall, parents report that about one-third of students ages 13 through 17 with disabilities have been suspended or expelled (pp. 57–58).

- Most students with disabilities (around 96 percent) are being educated in regular school buildings, and almost half are in regular classrooms for most of the day (p. 61). However, 26 percent of students ages 6 through 12 with disabilities and 36 percent of students ages 13 through 17 with disabilities have been retained in grade at least once (p. 77). Even so, the proportion of high school students being educated at the typical grade level for their age has increased from 32 percent in 1987 to 53 percent in 2001 (p. 80).

- In 2000 to 2001, 47.6 percent of students ages 14 and older with disabilities exited school with a regular high school diploma. A total of 41.1 percent of students ages 14 and older with disabilities dropped out (pp. 69–70).

State Profiles

State profiles include number of school districts, public school enrollment, per-pupil expenditures, and percentage of children living below the poverty level. For Part B, the profiles include number of children served under IDEA, percentage exiting with a diploma, percentage dropping out, number of special education teachers, and percentage of fully certified teachers. Race or ethnicity and education environments data are provided in charts.

For Part C, the profiles list the lead agency for early intervention services, number of infants and toddlers receiving early intervention services, percentage of infants and toddlers served in the home, and percentage of infants and toddlers served in programs for typically developing children. Race or ethnicity and reasons for exiting early intervention are provided in charts.

All reports about IDEA are available for review and download on the OSEP web site at http://www.ed.gov/about/reports/annual/osep/2003/index.html.

Staff

ANOMALIES, PHYSICAL

See PHYSICAL ANOMALIES.

ANOREXIA NERVOSA

Anorexia nervosa (starvation due to nerves) is a condition in which an individual eats little or no food for prolonged periods. No physical basis for the abnormal eating can be found. This disorder can be life-threatening, is increasing in incidence, and is a serious problem for medical and psychological professionals.

Although famous and tragic cases such as that of singer Karen Carpenter have made anorexia familiar, little can confidently be said about specific etiology or overall effective treatment. Anorexics share certain personality characteristics and frequently have families with a particular complex of unhealthy attitudes and behaviors. The physical appearance of anorexics is emaciated.

Anorexia is largely a disorder of middle- and upper-class adolescent females. It occurs approximately nine times more often in women than in men, and may affect one in one hundred white women between the ages of 12 and 18 years (Newman & Halvorson, 1983). The most common age of onset for anorexia is early adolescence (Newman & Halvorson, 1983).

Diagnostic criteria for anorexia nervosa may be summarized as involving intense fear of becoming obese, which does not diminish as weight loss progresses; disturbed body image (e.g., feeling fat even when emaciated); refusal to maintain normal body weight; and in postmenarcheal females, amenorrhea (i.e., the absence of at least three consecutive menstrual cycles; American Psychiatric Association, 1994).

Anorexics are subject to numerous additional complications, including malnutrition, edema, loss of hair, hyperactivity, hypoglycemia, vitamin deficiencies, constipation, weakness, and fatigue. In extreme cases, death may result from starvation, electrolyte depletion, or cardiac arrhythmia (Newman & Halvorson, 1983).

Anorexic sufferers share many behaviors and concerns among each other. They are terrified of becoming obese and measure their worth and self-esteem by how much they weigh and how much their stomachs protrude. They tend to be perfectionists, overdemanding of themselves, and very success-oriented. Low self-esteem and fear of rejection, especially by the opposite sex, are common. They have difficulty allowing anyone to become emotionally close to them.

Many anorexics were model children who were "people pleasers." They tend to be introverted, well-behaved, compulsive, self-critical, and very conscientious. As the disorder progresses, anorexics frequently become suspicious, indecisive, stubborn, unsociable, and disliking of any change. Phobic, depressive, or hysterical features are also common. Perceptions of events often become very distorted.

Studies indicate that children as young as 8 to 10 years old may be likely to be concerned with weight and body esteem. Shapiro, Newcomb, and Loeb (1997) found that 8- to 10-year-old children admitted to concern with their body weight and dieting. The investigators concluded that eating disorders or disregulated-restrained eating in vulnerable children and adolescents might be both expressed and internalized at an extremely early age. Brumberg (1997) report that studies have demonstrated that as many as 53 percent of 13-year-olds and 78 percent of 17-year-olds are dissatisfied with their bodies. *Seventeen* magazine in 1995 ran a headline in the July 1995 issue which asked: "Do You Hate Your Body? How to Stop." Although the article offered adolescents ways to stop hating their bodies, the author confessed that it is very difficult to do so in a culture where your body is very important. Wolf (1994) stated that the world never gives girls the message that their bodies are valuable simply because they themselves are inside them. Until our culture tells young girls that they are welcome in any shape—that women are valuable with or without the excuse of beauty—girls will continue to starve.

The specific etiologies of anorexia nervosa are not known, but are thought to be biopsychosocial diseases. Unknown biological predispositions may interact with both individual psychological states and needs and our culture's emphasis, especially for females, on thinness as a worthy or desirable characteristic (Wooley & Wooley, 1985). Several etiological factors can be described:

1. According to Bruch (1985), in the past 20 years the average female under 30 years of age has become heavier; at the same time, the ideal shape for women has been in the direction of being thinner. To be thin is to increase women's desirability both in their eyes and the eyes of others. The result is demonstrated in the mushrooming of the weight reduction industry and the numerous books and magazine articles that have appeared on losing weight and dieting.

2. Wooley and Wooley (1985) quote from Ambrose Bierce's Devil's Dictionary: "To men a man is but a mind, who cares what face he carries? Or what form he wears? But woman's body is the woman." For many centuries females' cultural conditioning has tied self-esteem to physical attractiveness. Many therapists think that recent cultural emphasis on "thinness is beautiful and good" has contributed to the increased incidence of eating disorders (Wooley & Wooley, 1985). The message to woman in particular is that in order to be popular, attractive, accepted, sexy, healthy, and desired in the world of work, they must be thin. The ideal of feminine beauty increasingly conforms each year to the adolescent male physique, implying emulation of men both behaviorally and physically (Wooley & Wooley, 1985). This change may be due to broader social changes involving competition between women and men for prestige and power. Also involved for many young women is the resolution of intense identification conflicts with their parents. Young women today are the first generation raised by extremely weight-conscious mothers who additionally view themselves as failures by current social standards of beauty.

3. Bruch (1985) says that cultural emphasis for slimness as determining factor does not explain the more severe disturbance of "frantic preoccupation with excessive slenderness of the anorexic." She believes that the changing status of expectations for women is important in understanding the etiology. Females, says Bruch, who have been raised as "clinging vines" and future wives, and who find themselves during their teens with the expectation to demonstrate that they are women of achievement, may find that they are filled with self-doubt and uncertainty. By bowing to the dictum to be thin, they are validating that they deserve respect.

Anorexia can begin with a stressful life situation for which the young woman does not possess appropriate coping skills. Real or perceived perfection, sexual engagements, or loss of some kind frequently precedes development of the disorder. Any change can be catastrophic for an anorexic. Worrying about performing perfectly and being socially accepted often results in situations in which anorexics find themselves out of control. Magical thinking is common.

According to Bemis and colleagues, who have studied hypothalamic functions in anorexics, starvation may actually damage the hypothalamus, and emotional stress may interfere with hypothalamic functioning. Further, psychological aberrations associated with anorexia may be relatively independent expressions of a primary hypothalamic deficiency that is of unknown origin (Bemis, 1978).

Women may be biologically more susceptible to eating disorders than men because women tend to demonstrate greater appetite fluctuations when confronted by stress. Also, through socialization, women are more likely than men to inhibit expression of negative feelings, leading to internal stress. This internal stress may exacerbate a biological predisposition.

Certain family factors facilitate the development of anorexia. If a parent has had the disorder or is either extremely thin or obese, the chances of a young woman becoming anorexic increase (Neuman & Halvorson, 1983). In families of anorexics, food is usually a primary issue. The family may use food for other than nutritional purposes. For example, eating may be a way of dealing with personal problems or negative or positive feelings, or it may be a method of presenting the appearance of a happy family. Power struggles over eating are extremely common.

Families of anorexics show certain personality patterns, although no one pattern appears consistently. Mothers are frequently intrusive and dominating and have experienced clinical depressions, whereas fathers appear passive and aloof from the family. Less frequently, these patterns may be reversed (Newman & Halvorson, 1983).

Family interpersonal dynamics are a significant contributing factor. Features that appear to be correlated with the development of the disorder are rigidity, lack of conflict resolution, overprotectiveness, and enmeshment (appearing to be a very close family). Keeping the peace at any cost is a high priority in these families; conflicts are not dealt with openly. In many families of anorexics, the anorexic generally feels powerless and ineffective, and behaves primarily on the basis of what other people want or need. Often the family has not encouraged or allowed the young woman to develop her autonomy or individuality. Only compliance is tolerated. Anorexia may develop as a result of a young woman's attempt to take control of her own life and achieve her own sense of identity. She learns that one thing she can control is her weight. Families must realize that this is an emotionally based disorder with the attempt to control, hide, avoid, and forget emotional pain. Nobody can make these anorexics eat, therefore it is important not to immediately focus on the food (Something Fishy Website).

In some cases the family unconsciously does not want the child to grow up. This message is received by the child, who in turn exhibits anorexic behavior, which then leads to failure to develop secondary sexual characteristics. Some anorexics enjoy being viewed as special by their families. Thus being anorexic can bring a great deal of attention, leading to self-perpetuation of the disorder.

Adolescent peer memberships are viewed as being critical in making the transition from childhood to adulthood. Some investigators have noted that anorexics have few if any close peer friendships (Neuman & Halvorson, 1983). Adolescent anorexics' overdependence and involvement with their families may prevent the formation of normal adolescent peer relationships. Thus, these youngsters may be at great disadvantage in making the essential developmental transition to adulthood.

Fifty percent of women diagnosed and treated for anorexia nervosa can be expected to recover completely within 2 to 5 years. Nutritional improvement or recovery can be expected in approximately two thirds of treated cases. Usually, after adequate body weight has been attained, menstruation will resume within a year.

As many as half of all anorexics experience a relapse. Approximately 38 percent may be re-hospitalized at some point during the next 2 years. Three to 25 percent of anorexia nervosa cases end in death from medical complications or suicide. This disorder has the highest death rate in psychiatry.

No consensus exists regarding the most effective form of treatment for anorexia nervosa (Vandereycken & Meermann, 1984). The course of treatment typically begins with stabilizing the patient's health, and then it is important that a course of therapy takes place (Something Fishy Website). Current treatment is aimed at first normalizing body weight, correcting the irrational thinking about weight loss, and finally preventing relapse. To obtain these goals, one must be admitted to a hospital or a day treatment program where the disorder can be monitored (Walsh & Devlin, 1998).

Many forms of treatment for anorexia are used. Therapists have used behavioral therapy, diet counseling, cognitive therapy, cognitive-behavioral treatment, drug treatment, and family therapy with varying degrees of success (Garner & Garfinkel, 1985). Whatever the treatment approach, the usual goals are aimed at increasing confidence and self-esteem, challenging irrational or "anorexic" thinking, developing autonomy, and teaching coping skills. Further, Vandereycken and Meermann (1984, p. 219) suggest that the "best guarantees of success in therapy are a constructive patient/therapist working relationship and an explicit but consistent treatment plan/contract." In the case of drug treatment, the therapist is not trying to treat the eating disorder with medication, but the emotional disorder that they are suffering from that causes the eating disorder (Something Fishy Website).

Hospitalization becomes necessary when outpatient therapy fails to reverse an impasse or a deteriorating physical or psychological course. The therapist assumes considerable physical and psychological control and responsibility for the care of the hospitalized anorexic. A weight restoration program is usually initiated in which the anorexic is expected to gain at least 1 pound a week until she achieves a target weight consisting of 95 percent of her ideal weight (Anderson, Morse, & Santmyer, 1985).

Psychotherapy combined with the restoration of weight through direct management of the anorexic's eating is effective in varying degrees. The anorexic has, through her disorder, avoided dealing with several important issues that need to be addressed in psychotherapy. These include individuation, assuming responsibility, separation, becoming an adult, making career and other decisions, and dealing with the loss of one's own life. A key factor in treating eating disorders is to develop a framework for intervention. One should begin prevention of eating disorders to help control the problem. Prevention should be aimed at the students who are susceptible to develop this disorder (Schwitzer, Bergholz, Dore, & Salimi, 1998). Prevention relies on educating individuals about anorexia nervosa. Educating these individuals by giving them facts increases knowledge, and that will likely change their attitude toward anorexia. If the individual continues to develop anorexia, it is assumed that this education will intrigue them to seek help for their existing problem.

Certain beliefs and values seem very important in the maintenance of these conditions. One of these is the belief that weight and shape are extremely important and need to be closely controlled at all cost. A change in these psychopathological beliefs and values concerning body weight and shape may be necessary for complete recovery. Self-help and support groups may be valuable. According to Garrett (1997), anorexics claim that events, people, and processes outside therapy were the most relevant things towards their recovery.

Because eating-disordered individuals are usually perfectionists, teachers can help by advising and encouraging them to take fewer courses and to balance academic loads by combining difficult classes with classes that are less demanding. If hospitalization becomes necessary, and the anorexic student expresses fear that she will be unable to maintain her academic standing, the teacher can point out that usually hospital personnel are more than willing to assist the patient by insuring that the patient will be provided the opportunity to continue uninterrupted with academic requirements. Major treatment centers as well as many hospitals have educational components and academic teachers on their staff.

REFERENCES

American Psychiatric Association. (1994). *Diagnostic and statistical manual of mental disorders* (4th ed.). Washington, DC: Author.

Anderson, A. E., Morse, C., & Santmyer, K. (1985). Inpatient treatment for anorexia nervosa. In D. M. Garner & P. E. Garfinkel (Eds.), *Handbook of psychotherapy for anorexia nervosa and bulimia* (pp. 311–343). New York: Guilford.

Bemis, K. M. (1978). Current approaches to the etiology and treatment of anorexia nervosa. *Psychological Bulletin, 35,* 395–617.

Bruch, H. (1985). Four decades of eating disorders. In D. M. Garner & P. E. Garfinkel (Eds.), *Handbook of psychotherapy for anorexia and bulimia* (pp. 7–18). New York: Guilford.

Brumberg, J. J. (1977). *The body project: An intimate history of American girls.* New York: Vintage.

Garner, D. M., & Garfinkel, P. E. (Eds.). (1985). *Handbook of psychotherapy for anorexia nervosa and bulimia.* New York: Guilford.

Garrett, C. J. (1998). Recovery from anorexia nervosa: A sociological perspective. *International Journal of Eating Disorders, 21,* 261–272.

Halmi, K. A. (1983). Advances in anorexia nervosa. In M. Wolrich & D. K. Routh (Eds.), *Advances in development and behavioral pediatrics* (Vol. 4, pp. 1–23). Greenwich, CT: Jai Press.

Hart, K. J., & Ollendick, T. H. (1985). Prevalence of bulimia in working and university women. *American Journal of Psychiatry, 142,* 851–854.

Johnson, C., & Flach, A. (1985). Family characteristics of 105 patients with bulimia. *American Journal of Psychiatry, 142,* 1321–1324.

Mitchell, J. E., Halsukami, D., Eckert, E. D., & Pyle, R. L. (1985). Characteristics of 275 patients with bulimia. *American Journal of Psychiatry, 142,* 251–255.

Newman, P. A., & Halvorson, P. S. (1983). *Anorexia nervosa and bulimia: A handbook for counselors and therapist.* New York: Van Nostrand Reinhold.

Schwitzer, A. M., Bergholz, K., Dore, T., & Salimi, L. (1998). Eating disorders among college women: Prevention, education, and treatment responses. *College Health, 45,* 199–207.

Shapiro, S., Newcomb, M., & Loeb, T. B. (1997). Fear of fat, disregulated-restrained eating, and body-esteem: Prevalence and gender differences among eight- to ten-year-old children. *Journal of Clinical Psychology, 26*(4).

Vandereycken, W., & Meermann, R. (1984). *Anorexia nervosa: A clinician's guide to treatment.* Berlin: de Gruyter.

Walsh, B. T., & Devlin, M. (1998). Eating disorders: Progress and problems. *Science, 280,* 1387–1391.

Wooley, S. C., & Wooley, O. W. (1985). Intensive outpatient and residential treatment for bulimia. In D. M. Garner & P. E. Garfinkel (Eds.), *Handbook of psychotherapy for anorexia nervosa and bulimia* (pp. 391–430). New York: Guilford.

C. SUE LAMB
University of North Carolina at Wilmington

WENDY L. FLYNN
Staffordshire University

BULIMIA NERVOSA
EATING DISORDERS
OBSESSIVE-COMPULSIVE DISORDERS

ANOSMIA

The term *anosmia* derives from the Greek *an* (without) and *osme* (odor); it refers to the absence or impairment of the sense of smell. Hyposmia refers to diminished olfactory functioning (Mannella, 1999). Synonyms for this condition include anodmia, anosphrasia, and olfactory anesthesia (*Dorland's*, 1981). Organic forms of anosmia are categorized as afferent (related to impaired conductivity of the olfactory nerve), central (due to cerebral disease), obstructive (related to obstruction of the nasal fossae), and peripheral (due to diseases of peripheral olfactory nerves; *Blakiston's*, 1979).

The most common cause of anosmia is a severe head cold or respiratory infection, which intranasal swelling blocks the nasal passages, preventing odors from reaching the olfactory region. This type of anosmia is temporary. Other organic causes of this condition include neoplasms (tumors), head injuries, or chronic rhinitis associated with granulomatous diseases (Levin, Benton, & Grossman, 1982; Mennella, 1999; *Mosby's*, 1983; Thomson, 1979). Anosmia also is a characteristic of olfactogenital dysplasia, also known as *Kallman's syndrome* or anosmia-eunuchoidism. This condition, more prevalent in males, is associated with lack of development of secondary sexual characteristics and anosmia. The apparently *X*-linked autosomal dominant or recessive inheritable condition is associated with dysfunction of the hypothalamus and the pituitary (Magalini, 1971). Anosmia with these etiologies typically is a permanent condition. Decreased sense of smell, microsmia, is also common with aging and among smokers.

Psychological forms of anosmia, while less common, may occur. Phobias or fears have been identified as precipitating such forms of anosmia (*Mosby's*, 1983). Specific types of anosmia include anosmia gustatoria (loss of the ability to smell foods) and preferential anosmia (loss of the ability to smell certain odors; *Dorland's*, 1981). Mennella (1999) provides a detailed description of conditions associated with a disturbance of olfaction and excellent clinical analyses with children.

REFERENCES

Blakiston's Gould medical dictionary (4th ed.). (1979). New York: McGraw-Hill.

Dorland's illustrated medical dictionary (26th ed.). (1981). Philadelphia: Saunders.

Levin, H. A., Benton, A. L. M., & Grossman, R. G. (1982). *Neurobehavioral consequences of closed head injury*. New York: Oxford University Press.

Magalini, S. (1971). *Dictionary of medical syndromes*. Philadelphia: Lippincott.

Mennella, J. A. (1999). Taste and smell. In K. F. Swaiman & S. Ashwal (Eds.), *Pediatric neurology* (pp. 105–113). St. Louis, MO: Mosby.

Mosby's medical and nursing dictionary. (1983). St. Louis, MO: Mosby.

Thomson, W. A. R. (1979). *Black's medical dictionary* (32nd ed.). New York: Barnes & Noble.

CATHY F. TELZROW
Kent State University

TRAUMATIC BRAIN INJURY

ANOXIA

Anoxia literally means an absence of oxygen, a condition that is incompatible with life. Recent terminology more correctly uses the term hypoxia to refer to a condition of lowered oxygen intake. Although hypoxia is compatible with life, long-term sequelae may result depending on the degree and duration of the condition.

Anoxia may be a rare cause of mortality in individuals experiencing status epilepticus (Pellock, 1999) carbon monoxide poisoning, placental insufficiency, microcephaly, or micrencephaly (De Meyer, 1999).

REFERENCES

De Meyer, W. (1999). Microcephaly, micrencephaly, megalocephaly and megalencephaly. In K. F. Swaiman & S. Ashwal (Eds.), *Pediatric neurology* (pp. 301–311). St. Louis, MO: Mosby.

Pellock, J. M. (1999). Status epilepticus. In K. F. Swaiman & S. Ashwal (Eds.), *Pediatric neurology* (pp. 683–691). St. Louis, MO: Mosby.

BRENDA M. POPE
New Hanover Memorial Hospital

ASPHYXIA
HYPOXIA

ANTECEDENT

An antecedent is an event, or predictor, that occurs prior to a specific behavior that leads to or triggers the occurrence of that behavior (Haager & Klinger, 2005; McLoughlin & Lewis, 2005; Scott, Liaupsin, Nelson, & Jolivette, 2003; Taylor, 2006). Antecedents are monitored to help teachers and researchers determine the function of a particular behavior and how to control the frequency, intensity, duration, or latency of that specific behavior (Heward, 2006; McLoughlin

& Lewis, 2005). Isolating a specific behavior and defining it in observable and measurable terms allows the antecedents and consequences to be identified. The behavior that is being analyzed is often referred to as the *target behavior* (Alvero & Austin, 2004; Pierangelo & Giuliani, 2006). By manipulating either an antecedent that leads to the target behavior or a consequence of the behavior, modifications can be made to the target behavior. In this way, the teacher or researcher may increase a desired behavior or decrease an undesirable behavior (Scott et al., 2003).

Following the preceding procedure, if there is a student that is engaging in disruptive behaviors, the first step is to define those behaviors. For example, a student's disruptive behaviors may be operationally defined as repeatedly tapping his pencil on his desk hard enough to produce noise. We then monitor these behaviors recording not only their frequency but also the events that occur before (antecedents) and after (consequences) the behaviors.

Antecedents can be divided into three categories: (1) antecedents that occur in the environment of the target behavior, sometimes called *fast triggers,* (2) antecedents that occur outside of the environment of the target behavior, sometimes called *setting events* or *slow triggers,* and (3) conditions that increase or decrease the likelihood of the behavior occurring, sometimes called *establishing operations.* An antecedent that occurs immediately before the specific, or target, behavior are the easiest to identify and manipulate. When this occurs, the link from antecedent to behavior may become obvious if systematic observation of the target behavior is implemented (Magg, 1999; Scott et al., 2003; Taylor, 2006; Heward, 2006).

We may find that the tapping behavior described previously increases after the teacher has asked for a volunteer or when instructions are given to read silently. By knowing these events trigger the target behaviors, they can be manipulated to reduce the occurrence of the target behaviors. The teacher may ask that the students to put all materials away, including pencils, before asking the class to get out silent reading books.

When an antecedent is removed from the specific environment (occurring before the behavior, but not in the same environment) it is referred to as a *setting event,* as it sets the stage for the event (target behavior) to occur (Heward, 2006; McLoughlin & Lewis, 2005; Taylor, 2006). Because of the separation in time from the antecedent to the target behavior, this form of antecedent is more difficult to connect to the target behavior. However, this form of antecedent is important to identify in order to understand why the behavior is occurring. It is therefore necessary to monitor and accurately record the events that occur regarding a student in all environments so that accurate information can be used to analyze a behavior.

Using the example of the pencil tapping behavior, a teacher may discover that the behavior increases whenever the student has missed the bus that day or on the days that the student goes to speech therapy. These events are outside of the immediate classroom environment but are affecting the behavior. Knowing this, the teacher may choose to have silent reading on a different day instead of one of the days the student has speech therapy.

The final form of antecedent that may affect the target behavior is an establishing operation or ecological event. This type of antecedent is a condition that affects the likelihood that the student or subject will perform the target behavior (Heward, 2006; Taylor 2006). Some examples of such conditions include the student or subject being tired, rested, full, hungry, cold, or hot. Because these conditions are intangible, this form of antecedent is the most difficult to monitor; however, once they are identified, they can be controlled.

Continuing to use the example of the student that taps his pencil, by examining all the factors that could be contributing to the tapping behavior, it is possible that intangible patterns may be discovered. It is possible that the teacher, using systematic monitoring of the behavior, discovers that the behavior escalates as the day goes on and then drops again in the afternoon. In this example, it is possible that hunger is adding to the frequency of the tapping. Decreasing the level of hunger in the student may decrease the behavior.

REFERENCES

Alvero, A. M., & Austin, J. (2004). The effects of conducting behavioral observations on the behavior of the observer. *Journal of Applied Behavior Analysis, 37,* 457–468.

Haager, D., & Klinger, J. K. (2005). *Differentiating instruction in inclusive classrooms: The special educator's guide.* New York: Allyn & Bacon.

Heward, W. L. (2006). *Exceptional children: An introduction to special education* (8th ed.). Upper Saddle River, NJ: Pearson Prentice Hall.

Magg, J. (1999). *Behavior management: From theoretical implications to practical applications.* San Diego: Singular.

McLoughlin, J. A., & Lewis, R. B. (2005). *Assessing students with special needs* (6th ed.). Upper Saddle River, NJ: Pearson Prentice Hall.

Pierangelo, R., & Giuliani, G. A. (2006). *Assessment in special education: A practical approach* (2nd ed.). New York: Allyn & Bacon.

Scott, T. M., Liaupsin, C. J., Nelson, C. M., & Jolivette, K. (2003). Ensuring student success through team-based functional behavioral assessment. *Teaching Exceptional Children, 35,* 16–21.

Taylor, R. L. (2006). *Assessment of exceptional students: Educational and psychological procedures* (7th ed.). New York: Allyn & Bacon.

WALTER A. ZILZ
Bloomsburg University

ANTECEDENT TEACHING

Antecedent stimuli are those events that occur before a desired response that affect the probability of the occurrence of that response. In *Science and Human Behavior,* Skinner (1953) describes the response sequence as having three parts: the antecedent events, the response, and the consequences. Although much of operant conditioning focuses on the use of consequences to shape learning, antecedent events are equally important in this process. Antecedent teaching involves the use of both antecedent stimuli and antecedent responses in order to increase the frequency of the desired response (Ormrod, 2003). Examples of antecedent stimuli include cueing (or prompting), setting events, generalization, and discrimination. An example of an antecedent response is behavioral momentum.

Cueing involves verbal and nonverbal signals that remind students of expected behaviors. Directing a class to put away their reading materials before lining up to get a drink is an example of a verbal form of cueing. Placing a finger over one's lips in order to quiet a class is an illustration of nonverbal cueing. Setting events involve creating environments whereby the desired response is more likely to occur. An example of a setting event is increasing students' social interaction by having them complete projects in small groups.

Generalization occurs when a learner recognizes that certain responses are expected in similar types of settings. After learning that one must speak quietly in a school library, one recognizes that similar behavior is expected in public libraries. The final component, discrimination, occurs when one recognizes the conditions or circumstances when certain behaviors are expected and when they are not. One raises a hand to ask a question during school but not at home during dinner.

Behavioral momentum, an antecedent response, is the phenomenon of continuing to make appropriate responses based on prior responses. This is more likely to occur if tasks are arranged from least difficult to most difficult. Adding a column of four-digit numbers is more likely to occur after successfully adding a series of two- and three-digit number columns.

Researching the effects of antecedent stimuli on student behavior has been particularly helpful in assisting students with special needs in inclusive settings (Flood & Wilder, 2002; Harrell, 1996; Scott, Liaupin, Nelson & Jolivette, 2003). Scott et al. (2003) analyzed teachers' directives that triggered inappropriate verbal outbursts in a middle school student. By examining patterns in verbal antecedent stimuli, student responses, and resulting consequences, the team was able to identify the types of antecedents that worked effectively in facilitating appropriate student behavior. Whereas directions that required extensive peer interaction resulted in disrespectful comments, instructions that allowed for individually completed assignments resulted in compliance and significant achievement. By subsequently allowing the student to complete all group assignments independently, teachers were able to interact effectively with the student, and the student was able to remain in the general education setting.

Research involving antecedent stimuli has also focused on increasing student achievement and teacher effectiveness. Comparing various types of antecedent stimuli enables educators to determine more effective methods when working with students with special needs. Singleton, Schuster, Morse, and Collins (1999) found that students with Mental Retardation mastered grocery vocabulary more rapidly when utilizing an antecedent prompt and testing approach. However, students retained the information longer and were able to make generalizations more effectively when utilizing simultaneous prompting procedures.

Research of antecedent stimuli has also focused on teacher effectiveness. Wolfe (1990) found that utilizing visual prompts enhanced teacher questioning strategies and directives when teaching music. Britton, Raizen, Kaser, and Porter (2002), in seeking to close the current achievement gap that exists in mathematics between White and urban minority schools, call for more ethnographic studies that focus on the antecedent instructional conditions that facilitate or frustrate the development of proficiency in quantitative problem solving.

Teachers exert tremendous control over the antecedents to which their students are exposed. These include not only methodological approaches but also curriculum, materials, and classroom atmosphere. The area of antecedent teaching is both broad and important. For more information on how this strategy blends with the area of behavioral teaching, the reader is referred to Skinner (1953, 1968) and Repp (1983).

REFERENCES

Britton, E., Raizen, S., Kaser, J., & Porter, A. (2002). *Open questions in mathematics education.* (ERIC Digest ED 478719)

Flood, W. A., & Wilder, D. A. (2002). Antecedent assessment and assessment based treatment of off-task behavior in a child diagnosed with Attention-Deficit/Hyperactivity Disorder. *Education and Treatment of Children, 25,* 331–338.

Harrell, C. (1996). *General classroom structural interventions for teaching students with Attention-Deficit/Hyperactivity Disorder.* (ERIC Document Reproduction Service No. ED399699)

Ormrod, J. E. (2003). *Educational psychology: Developing learners* (4th ed.). Upper Saddle River, NJ: Merrill Prentice Hall.

Repp, A. C. (1983). *Teaching the mentally retarded.* Englewood Cliffs, NJ: Prentice Hall.

Scott, T. M., Liaupsin, C. J., Nelson, C. M., & Jolivette, K. (2003). Ensuring student success through team-based functional behavior assessment. *Teaching Exceptional Children, 35*(5), 16–21.

Singleton, D. K., Schuster, J. W., Morse, T. E., & Collins, B. C. (1999). A comparison of antecedent prompt and test and simultaneous prompting procedures in teaching grocery words to adolescents with Mental Retardation. *Education and Training in Mental Retardation and Developmental Disability, 34,* 182–199.

Skinner, B. F. (1953). *Science and human behavior.* New York: Macmillan.

Skinner, B. F. (1968). *The technology of teaching.* New York: Appleton-Century-Crofts.

Wolfe, D. E. (1990). Effect of a visual prompt on changes in antecedents and consequents of teaching behavior. *Music Education, 44*(1), 9–13.

ANDREW R. BRULLE
JILLIAN N. LEDERHOUSE
Wheaton College

ADVANCE ORGANIZERS
APPLIED BEHAVIOR ANALYSIS

ANTHROPOSOPHIC MOVEMENT

The anthroposophic movement was founded by Rudolf Steiner (1861–1925). Steiner defined anthroposophy as knowledge produced by the higher self in man, and a way of knowledge that undertakes to guide man's spirit to communion with the spirit of the cosmos (Wannamaker, 1965). Anthroposophy postulates a spiritual world beyond man's sensory experiences. Steiner proposed that, through proper training, each person could develop an enhanced consciousness that would restore values and morality to materialistic society.

Steiner became involved in the education of both adults and children. Anthroposophic education for adults took place at the Goetheanum, a school for physical science, near Basal, Switzerland. The Waldorf School, founded in Stuttgart, Germany, in 1919, was the first of several schools for children that sought to reach the inner nature of the child and provide guidance to maturity. By 1965, 80 Waldorf Schools had been attended by more than 25,000 children in the United States and Europe (Wannamaker, 1965). Eurythmy (movement of speech and music) was used to develop concentration, attention, imitation, and an awareness of position in space (Zeigler, 1979). The schools included programming for the emotionally disturbed, socially maladjusted, and other exceptional children.

During a residential tutorship, Steiner began to apply anthroposophic training to the mentally handicapped. Karl Konig, a student of Steiner's, continued the application of Steiner's techniques in an approach known as curative education (Payne & Patton, 1981). In 1939 Konig founded the first integrated community for the mentally retarded, based on the anthroposophic philosophy in Aberdeen, Scotland (Payne & Patton, 1981). This "Camphill movement" formulated anthroposophy into the following four bases of curative education:

A right to education for all children

A humanistic/developmental perspective

An accepting milieu, providing the retarded with stability and support

Group and individual instruction, providing the retarded with a sense of integration with mankind

Camphill communities are comprised of approximately equal numbers of retarded and normal citizens. These self-sufficient, monasticlike communes are comprised of "families" of no more than 15 persons, about half of whom are retarded. Criteria for admission include the ability to care for personal needs and adequate physical health (Zipperlen, 1975). Presently, there are communities in 21 countries in the world (Camphill, 2005).

REFERENCES

Camphill. (2005). *Global directory.* Retrieved June 19, 2005, from http://www.camphill.org.uk/directory/index/.

Payne, J. S., & Patton, J. R. (1981). *Mental retardation.* Columbus, OH: Merrill.

Steiner, R. (1972). *Outline of occult science.* New York: Anthroposophical Society.

Wannamaker, O. D. (1965). *The anthroposophical society: The nature of its objectives.* New York: Anthroposophical Society.

Ziegler, E. F. (1979). *A history of physical education and sport.* Englewood Cliffs, NJ: Prentice Hall.

Zipperlan, H. R. (1975). Normalization. In J. Wortis (Ed.), *Mental retardation and developmental disabilities. Volume VII.* New York: Brunner/Mazel.

ANNE M. BAUER
University of Cincinnati

CAMPHILL COMMUNITY MOVEMENT
HUMANISM AND SPECIAL EDUCATION

ANTICONVULSANTS

Anticonvulsants are medications used to control seizure activity. The appropriate anticonvulsant is chosen on the basis of its safety record, side effects, and the type of seizures that need treatment (Kutscher, 2005). Investigation of the possible effects of anticonvulsant medications on a person's ability to function has been complicated by certain methodological difficulties, including the use of only normal controls, the interaction of a placebo with an active agent, and the use of a limited number of performance measures. Studies tend to fall into three different groups: those that have not distinguished among different drugs, those examining the effects of specific drugs, and those that have included the measurement of serum (blood) anticonvulsant levels (Corbett & Trimble, 1983).

Phenobarbital is perhaps one of the most widely investigated anticonvulsants with regard to effects on cognitive functioning. Lennox (1940) assessed the causes of mental deterioration in 1,245 individuals with epilepsy and determined that in 15 percent of the cases, the anticonvulsant medication was the cause. In a later publication, Lennox and Lennox (1960) reduced this number to 5 percent. Relatively few studies on the effects of multiple drugs on children have been carried out. Of the investigations reported, the results have been conflicting. Chaudhry and Pond (1961) examined the causes of intellectual deterioration in 28 children with epilepsy and found no evidence to suggest that anticonvulsant medications were responsible for the noted declines in functioning. Rather, these authors suggested that such declines were related to seizure frequency. In a study of 117 children with seizures in regular public school classes, Holdsworth and Whitmore (1976) reported no differences in academic achievement depending on whether or not phenobarbital had been prescribed. These findings lend support to an earlier study that assessed the psychological performance of 26 epileptic patients over a three-month period and found little effect on total environmental adjustment caused by the use of anticonvulsants (Loveland, Smith, & Forster, 1957). There were, however, no controls in the study and the majority of patients had been receiving anticonvulsant medication for several years prior to the study.

Conversely, a number of studies of multiple drug effects have reported learning impairments with specific deficits noted in visual-spatial perception and performance (Cepeda, 1997; Rayo & Martin, 1959; Tchicaloff & Gaillard, 1970). In a study by Hutt, Jackson, Belsham, and Higgins (1968), phenobarbital was administered to normal subjects with serum level control. Decreases in abilities were noted that were related to phenobarbital blood serum levels. These effects were seen most prominently on tasks requiring sustained attention, psychomotor performance, and spontaneous speech. The drug effects became more prominent as the tasks became longer and more difficult and as the degree of external constraint (having the examiner in the room) was decreased. It was concluded that phenobarbital has effects maximally evident on tasks requiring attention and concentration, but that it also may have pronounced effects on motor coordination.

Unfavorable behavioral changes have been estimated to occur in 20 to 75 percent of children receiving phenobarbital as prophylaxis for febrile convulsions in infancy (Bennett & Ho, 1997; Heckmatt, Houston, & Dodds, 1976; Thorn, 1975; Wolf & Forsythe, 1978). Although no significant IQ differences were reported for groups of toddlers receiving

an 8- to 12-month period of phenobarbital or placebo, there were effects on memory that were related to blood serum levels and effects on comprehension that were related to the duration of treatment (Camfield et al., 1979). There was no evidence of hyperactivity, although 15 of the 315 children on phenobarbital in the study did demonstrate an increase in "daytime fussiness and irritability."

Phenytoin (Dilantin) is the most widely used anticonvulsant in the world (Bennett & Ho, 1997; Dodrill, 1981; Hartlage & Hartlage, 1997). It has been shown to be effective with a broad range of attacks including generalized tonic-clonic seizures, most types of partial seizures, and some other less frequently observed seizure types. Acute intoxication with phenytoin leads to a confusional state, occasionally referred to as encephalopathy, which is associated with neurological symptoms of toxicity, especially ataxia and nystagmus (Corbett & Trimble, 1983). It also has been demonstrated that prolonged use of this medication, even in low doses (Logan & Freeman, 1969; Vallarta, Bell, & Reichert, 1974), may result in a clinical picture of a progressive degenerative disorder that may occur without the classic signs of such a disorder. Rosen (1968) and Stores (1975) have both reported impaired intellectual performance on long-term treatment with phenytoin. Dodrill (1975) reports that phenytoin has behavioral effects specifically related to motor performance decrements.

Ethosuximide (Zarontin), an anticonvulsant used with children for control of absence (petit mal) seizures, has been shown to impair memory and speech as well as result in affective disturbances (Guey et al., 1967). Soulayrol and Roger (1970) reported intellectual impairment in children treated with this medication; however, other studies have not confirmed this (e.g., Brown et al., 1975).

Carbamazepine (Tegretol) has been reported to have psychotropic effects. About half of 40 studies cited by Dalby (1975), in a major review of the literature, reported a beneficial psychologic effect. Typically, improvements in mood and behavior have been noted, as manifested by greater cooperativeness, reduced irritability, and a possible decrease in aggression. Increases in cognitive skill levels have been reported as well (Bennett & Ho, 1997). There have been no reported studies of the effects of primidone (Mysoline) on behavior in children, although adults occasionally have been reported to develop a florid confusional state on doses within the normal therapeutic range (Booker, 1972). It is well recognized that the drug initially may cause drowsiness and have effects similar to phenobarbital in causing restlessness in some children.

Trimble and Corbett (1980a, 1980b) studied the relationship between anticonvulsant drug levels and the behavior and cognitive performance of 312 children with seizures. The drug most commonly prescribed was phenytoin, followed by carbamazepine, valproic acid, primidone, and phenobarbital. A decrease in IQ was noted in 15 percent of the 204 children studied; these children had significantly higher mean phenytoin and primidone levels than other subjects. A distinct relationship between an increase in serum drug levels and a decline in nonverbal skills was reported.

Newer anticonvulsants such as gabapentin (neurontin), topiramate (Topamax), tiagabine (Gabatril), and lamotrigine (Lamictal) are generally used as add-on therapy for partial seizures in children under the age of 12 (Kutscher, 2005). Despite these side effects associated with anticonvulsants, they are recognized as essential in the management of epilepsy. According to Dodrill (1981), when anticonvulsant blood serum levels fall within therapeutic ranges and when there are no overt signs of toxicity, the chances of deleterious effects are minimal if detectable at all. Furthermore, the deleterious effects are distinctly offset by decreased seizure frequency, which has known effects on the deterioration of mental functions. It is far preferable to have modest drug side effects than seizures. Other, low incidence drugs used as anticonvulsants are reviewed in detail by Bennett and Ho (1997).

REFERENCES

Bennett, T., & Ho, M. (1997). The neuropsychology of pediatric epilepsy and antiepileptic drugs. In C. R. Reynolds & E. Fletcher-Janzen (Eds.), *Handbook of clinical child neuropsychology* (2nd ed., pp. 517–538). New York: Plenum.

Booker, H. E. (1972). Primidone toxicity. In D. M. Woodbury, J. K. Penry, & R. P. Schmidt (Eds.), *Antiepileptic drugs* (pp. 169–204). New York: Raven.

Brown, T. R., Dreifuss, F. E., Dyken, P. R., Goode, D. J., Penry, J. K., Porter, R. J., White, B. J., & White, P. T. (1975). Ethosuccimide in the treatment of absence (petit mal) seizures. *Neurology, 25,* 515–525.

Camfield, C. S., Chaplin, S., Doyle, A. B., Shapiro, S. H., Cummings, C., & Camfield, P. R. (1979). Side effects of phenobarbitone in toddlers: Behavioral and cognitive effects. *Journal of Pediatrics, 95,* 361–365.

Cepeda, M. (1997). Nonstimulant psychotropic medication: Desired effects and cognitive/behavioral adverse effects. In C. R. Reynolds & E. Fletcher-Janzen (Eds.), *Handbook of clinical child neuropsychology* (2nd ed., pp. 573–586). New York: Plenum.

Chaudhry, M. R., & Pond, D. A. (1961). Mental deterioration in epileptic children. *Journal of Neurology, Neurosurgery, & Psychiatry, 24,* 213–219.

Corbett, J. A., & Trimble, M. R. (1983). Epilepsy and anticonvulsant medication. In M. Rutter (Eds.), *Developmental neuropsychiatry* (pp. 112–129). New York: Guilford.

Dalby, M. A. (1975). Behavioral effects of carbamazepine. In J. K. Penry & D. D. Daley (Eds.), *Advances in neurology* (Vol. 11, pp. 130–149). New York: Raven.

Dodrill, C. B. (1975). Diphenylhydantoin serum levels, toxicity, and neuropsychological performance in patients with epilepsy. *Epilepsia, 16,* 593–600.

Dodrill, C. B. (1981). Neuropsychology of epilepsy. In S. B. Filskov & T. J. Boll (Eds.), *Handbook of clinical neuropsychology* (pp. 366–395). New York: Wiley.

Guey, J., Charles, C., Coquery, C., Roger, J., & Soulayrol, R. (1967). Study of the psychological effects of ethosuccimide on 25 children suffering from petit mal epilepsy. *Epilepsia, 8,* 129–141.

Hartlage, R. L., & Hartlage, L. C. (1997). The neuropsychology of epilepsy: Overview and psychosocial aspects. In C. R. Reynolds & E. Fletcher-Janzen (Eds.), *Handbook of clinical child neuropsychology* (2nd ed., pp. 506–516). New York: Plenum.

Heckmatt, J., Houston, A., & Dodds, K. (1976). Failure of phenobarbitone to prevent febrile convulsions. *British Medical Journal, 1,* 559–561.

Holdsworth, L., & Whitmore, K. (1976). A study of children with epilepsy attending ordinary schools. *Developmental Medicine & Child Neurology, 16,* 746–758.

Hutt, S. J., Jackson, P. M., Belsham, A., & Higgins, G. (1968). Perceptual motor behavior in relation to blood phenobartitone levels: A preliminary report. *Development Medicine & Child Neurology, 10,* 626–632.

Kutscher, M. L. (2005). *Diagnostic tests and treatment.* Retrieved June 19, 2005, from http://www.pediatricneurology.com/treatment.htm

Lennox, W. G. (1940). Brain injury, drugs, and environment as a cause of mental decay in epilepsy. *American Journal of Psychiatry, 99,* 174–180.

Lennox, W. G., & Lennox, M. A. (1960). *Epilepsy and related disorders.* Boston: Little, Brown.

Logan, W. J., & Freeman, J. M. (1969). Pseudodegenerative diseases due to diphenylhydantoin intoxication. *Archives of Neurology, 21,* 631–637.

Loveland, N., Smith, B., & Forster, F. (1957). Mental and emotional changes in epileptic patients on continuous anticonvulsant medication. *Neurology, 7,* 856–865.

Rayo, D., & Martin, F. (1959). Standardized psychometric tests applied to the analysis of the effects of anticonvulsant medication on the proficiency of young epileptics. *Epilepsia, 1,* 189–207.

Rosen, J. A. (1968). Dilantin dementia. *Transactions of the American Neurological Association, 93,* 273–277.

Soulayrol, R., & Roger, J. (1970). Effects psychiatriques defovorables des medications antiepileptiques. *Revue de Neuropsychiatrie Infantile* (English abstract), *18,* 599–603.

Stores, G. (1975). Behavioral effects of anticonvulsant drugs. *Developmental Medication & Child Neurology, 17,* 547–658.

Tchicaloff, M., & Gaillard, F. (1970). Quelques effets indesirables des medicaments antiepileptiques sur les rendements intellectuels. *Revue de Neuropsychiatrie Infantile* (English abstract), *18,* 599–603.

Thorn, I. (1975). A controlled study of prophylactic longterm treatment of febrile convulsions with phenobarbital. *Acta Neurologica Scandinavica, 60,* 67–70.

Trimble, M. R., & Corbett, J. A. (1980a). Anticonvulsant drugs and cognitive function. In J. A. Wada & J. K. Penry (Eds.), *Advances in epileptology: The X International Symposium.* New York: Raven.

Trimble, M. R., & Corbett, J. A. (1980b). Behavioral and cognitive disturbances in epileptic children. *Irish Medical Journal, 73,* 21–28.

Vallarta, J. M., Bell, D. B., & Reichert, A. (1974). Progressive encephalopathy due to chronic hydantoin intoxication. *American Journal of Diseases of Children, 128,* 27–34.

Wolf, S. M., & Forsythe, A. (1978). Behavior disturbance, phenobarbital, and febrile seizures. *Pediatrics, 61,* 728–730.

RICHARD A. BERG
West Virginia University
Medical Center

DILANTIN
MEDICATION
PHENOBARBITAL
SEIZURE DISORDERS
TEGRETOL

ANTIHISTAMINES

Antihistamines are a class of pharmaceutical agents that block the effect of histamine. Histamine is a naturally occurring body substance that is released in certain allergic reactions. Typically, antihistamines are more effective in preventing rather than in reversing the action of histamine. Unfortunately, antihistamines have not been found to have any dramatic effects in children with asthma or other severe disease of an allergic nature (Markowitz, 1983). For pediatric populations, antihistamines may be effective in the treatment of hay fever or mild recurrent hives of unknown etiology. Some antihistamines, particularly Atarax and Vistaril, are used as safe, alternative antianxiety medications without withdrawal (Cepeda, 1997). Some research also has suggested the potential efficacy of antihistamines in the prevention of motion sickness in children (Macnair, 1983).

Typically, antihistamines are found in cold preparations prescribed for children (Pruitt, 1985). Children who are treated with antihistamines are likely to have less severe runny noses, yet the other features of the common cold are not significantly affected by this class of drugs. Antihistamines have atropine like effects that diminish the amount of secretions produced by the irritated lining of the nose or bronchial passages. Although some antihistamines have been marketed as cough suppressants, a number of studies have shown that antihistamines are no better than placebos in relieving children of the symptoms of the common cold (Markowitz, 1983).

Because the use of minor and major tranquilizers carries significant disadvantages in the treatment of behavioral and anxiety disorders in children (Popper, 1985), it has been suggested that antihistamines be used short term for calming acutely anxious children (Cepeda, 1997) and for controlling agitation in severely psychotic children (Popper, 1985). Risks of recreational abuse, management abuse, tolerance, and dependence are also lower than for anti-anxiety agents and major tranquilizers (Cepeda, 1997; Popper, 1985), making this class of drugs more appealing for use by the practicing physician. The enduring cognitive effects of antihistamines are not well documented in the empirical literature, although some recent research has suggested an amelioration of behavioral difficulties and improved academic performance in response to antihistamine therapy (McLoughlin et al., 1983). Further, some investigators (Mattes, 1979; Millichap, 1973) have found antihistamines to be efficacious in the treatment and management of hyperactivity. While the effects of antihistamines on cognitive and learning outcome appear to be somewhat promising, more research must be mounted before any definitive conclusions can be made in this area. Moreover, while the use of antihistamines in the treatment of psychiatric disorders of children may provide a safer alternative than the use of other psychotropic agents, including neuroleptic agents and antianxiety drugs, it still entails some of the same risks and the physician must carefully weigh the potential benefits against any possible risks.

Although the long-term effects of antihistamines have received little systematic study, the use of these agents appears to provide primarily short-term benefits. They are typically safe and consequently are often sold without a prescription. They may have adverse effects, although these usually occur with higher doses. Sedation is the most common side effect in children, but some tolerance may develop. These negative side effects are associated mostly with the first-generation oral antihistamines. Second-generation antihistamines cause little or no sedation effect due to their low lipophilicity, their large molecular size, their greater affinity for peripheral H_1 receptors and their relative lack of affinity for neuroreceptors (NIAID, 2003).

Combinations of antihistamines with other central nervous system depressants (e.g., alcohol) should be avoided. In high doses, or for children who are particularly sensitive to these agents, antihistamines may cause undesirable side effects. These may include excitation, nervousness, palpitations, rapid heartbeat, dryness of the mouth, urinary retention, and constipation. In rare instances, red blood cells can burst (hemolytic anemia) or bone marrow can be depleted of blood-forming cells (arganulocytosis; Markowitz, 1983). Sustained antihistamine usage with pediatric populations may be associated with persistent daytime drowsiness, "hangover," or mild enduring effects on cognition (Popper, 1985). Although such side effects are better tolerated by younger children than by adolescents, the occurrence of these effects should result in the prompt cessation of antihistamine therapy.

REFERENCES

Cepeda, M. (1997). Nonstimulant psychotropic medication: Desired effects and cognitive/behavioral adverse effects. In C. R. Reynolds & E. Fletcher-Janzen (Eds.), *Handbook of clinical child neuropsychology* (2nd ed., pp. 573–586). New York: Plenum Press.

Macnair, A. L. (1983). Cinnarizine in the prophylaxis of car sickness in children. *Current Medical Research Opinion, 8,* 451–455.

Markowitz, M. (1983). Immunity, allergy, and related diseases. In R. E. Behrman & V. C. Vaughn (Eds.), *Nelson textbook of pediatrics* (pp. 497–594). Philadelphia: Saunders.

Mattes, J. (1979). Trial of diphenpyraline in hyperactive children (letter). *Psychopharmacology Bulletin, 15,* 5–6.

McLoughlin, J., Nall, M., Isaacs, P., Petrosko, J., Karibo, J., & Lindsey, B. (1983). The relationship of allergies and allergy treatment to school performance and student behavior. *Annals of Allergy, 51,* 506–510.

Millichap, J. G. (1973). Drugs in management of minimal brain dysfunction. *Annals of the New York Academy of Science, 205,* 321–334.

National Institute of Allergy and Infectious Diseases (NIAID). (2005). *Current trends.* Retrieved June 19, 2005, from http://www.nih.gov/research/Allergic_Reactions.pdf

Popper, C. W. (1985). Child and adolescent psychopharmacology. In R. Michels & J. O. Cavenar (Eds.), *Psychiatry* (Vol. 2, pp. 1–23). New York: Lippincott.

Pruitt, A. W. (1985). Rational use of cold and cough preparations. *Pediatric Annals, 14,* 289–291.

RONALD T. BROWN
Emory University School of Medicine

TRANQUILIZERS

ANTISOCIAL BEHAVIOR

A study by Peterson (1961) considered a sampling of many behaviors of children that could be considered as antisocial. More than 400 representative case folders from files of a child-guidance clinic were inspected and the referral problems of each child noted. Peterson's results indicated that the interrelationship among 58 items could be reduced to two independent clusters: conduct problems and personality problems. The two dimensions of problems most frequently reported among the public school students in these two major clusters were aggression and withdrawal. Each child could be placed somewhere in these two dimensions regardless of the number of problem behaviors or other dimensions the child manifested. Children's behaviors differ quantitatively not qualitatively. The degree of quantitative difference between normal and abnormal is usually slight.

Definitions are particularly difficult to generate when context is general and critical, as is the case when the word "social" is used. While there is a need to convey with words what is meant by antisocial behavior, the intensity, timeliness, and impact of a behavior on others in the culture/society/group where the behavior is experienced determines the definition; therefore, a static meaning is not effective. Antisocial behaviors or misbehaving (disliked performances) are accepted daily by society. A behavior is labeled antisocial when the tolerance level of an observer is exceeded with respect to that observer's interpretation of societal rules.

For example, aggressive antisocial behavior is manifested when a student stands and yells a phrase of profanity during a school assembly. The consequences of such behavior could be removal from the audience (peer group), immediate verbal reprimand by adult authorities, a quick trip to the administrator's office, or dismissal from a school. In contrast, if the same pupil were to stand during a professional ball game and yell the same phrase of profanity, not only might the audience approve of the behavior, it might even reward the verbal expressiveness.

Variables in the environment that define the tolerance level of observers when a behavior is judged antisocial are many: time, social status, money, event, location, age, reputation, intensity, duration, frequency, and group expectations. When the cumulative effect of these variables is negative, exceeding the dynamic acceptable definition of the moment, a person's behavioral performance is judged antisocial. For example, when a behavior is poorly timed, appropriate social status is not recognized, intensity is high and loud, the behavior is against school rules, reputation is known, duration is long, frequency is perceived as too often, and other students are conforming to rules of the environment, an antisocial behavior is said to exist. To identify specific factors related to perceptions of antisocial behavior, recent investigation has emphasized those behaviors that teachers and students find most disturbing. Aggressive behavior is most often primary, but withdrawal behaviors such as fear, anxiety, and tension are also defined as antisocial.

This second type of antisocial behavior is reported to be more tolerable to society. The child suffering from withdrawal may be in deeper pain, despair, or depression than an aggressive individual; however, such a child is less aversive to adults and peers, and less likely to excite the environment into action. These children have too little behavior rather than too much. Characteristics accompanying withdrawal are feelings of inferiority and self-consciousness, social withdrawal, shyness, anxiety, weeping, hypersensitivity, infrequent social smiles, nail chewing, depression and chronic sadness, drowsiness, sluggishness, daydreaming, passivity, short attention span, preoccupation, and somber quietness. These children are also picked on by others.

The term antisocial behavior is often applied when behaviors remain inflexible, or frozen, and the person performing the behaviors continues to react to the environment in a manner judged by the group to be displeasing, inappropriate and uncomfortable. The label antisocial behavior is attached to the person displaying the behavior and the definition itself magnifies the individual's differences. Not only does the behavior classify a person, but the antisocial definition itself accentuates differences. Only if classification leads to positive action through school programs on the behalf of the child is this definition constructive.

Characteristics

Patterns, for example, of antisocial behavior have received a variety of labels, for example, unsocialized aggressive, conduct disorder, aggressive, unsocialized psychopathic, psychopathic delinquent, antisocially aggressive, and sadistically aggressive. Children exhibiting antisocial behaviors apparent to school officials and teachers may demonstrate one or more of the following characteristics.

1. An inability to learn that cannot be explained by conventional intellectual, sensory, or health factors. A learning-disabled child seldom escapes recognition. He or she is frequently labeled learning disabled, thus lowering self-esteem. The inability to learn is perhaps the single most significant characteristic of antisocial children, with the learning disability manifested as the inability to profit from social experiences and/or academic instruction.

2. An inability to build and maintain satisfactory interpersonal relationships with peers and teachers; to demonstrate sympathy and warmth toward others; to stand alone when necessary; to have close friends; to be aggressively constructive; to enjoy working and playing with others as well as working and playing alone. Children who are unable to build and maintain satisfactory interpersonal relationships are easily defined as different by teachers and peers.

3. "Inappropriate" behaviors or feelings that occur under normal conditions. What is appropriate is judged by the teacher and the student's peers. This judgment is sensed by children because of their ability to profit from school experiences and relate to their teachers. Children classified as antisocial often cannot learn what is appropriate because of their inability to relate to and profit from cultural experiences. This amplifies the daily failures of children who fail to conform to social/cultural rules and exacerbates their lack of socialization.

4. Lack of flexibility. When behaviors become frozen into patterns of inappropriateness of such intensity, duration, and frequency that they interfere with social activities of a group, those behaviors are identified as antisocial.

5. Depression and general moods of unhappiness, characteristics of withdrawal. When children seldom smile and express unhappiness in play, art work, group discussions, and language arts, the observer should watch for antisocial expression.

6. A tendency to develop physical symptoms, pains, or fears, especially in reaction to school situations or authority figures. These symptoms may indicate potential antisocial behaviors.

7. Disobedience, disruptiveness, fighting, temper tantrums, irresponsibility, impertinence, jealousy, anger, bossiness, the use of profanity, attention-seeking behavior, boisterousness, defiance of authority, feelings of guilt and inadequacy, irritability, and quarrelsomeness. These descriptors are often associated with antisocial phenomena.

Behaviors described by these characteristics may formulate a pattern of active antisocial behavior that results in conflict with parents, peers, and social institutions. Children and adolescents who represent extreme patterns of antisocial behaviors are likely to have difficulty with law-enforcement agencies. Extreme antisocial behavior will be defined as criminal conduct and result in arrest, incarceration, recidivism, and failure to become a good citizen.

Acquisition

The possibility of hereditary or predispositional factors cannot be ignored, neither can the contributions of organic factors be ruled out. Prematurity (birth weight less than 5 pounds), is regarded as an important cause of brain damage in children. Epilepsy and cerebral palsy studies report higher prevalances of antisocial behaviors among those with known brain lesions. Situations where trait patterns of deviant behavior can be studied along with the mechanisms by which the acquisition of the traits occurs is very revealing. Sociological literature has emphasized social class, deviant social organization, and social inequalities as influential. The family is also a setting where deviant behavior has been studied. It is obvious in making the acquisition of principal behavioral patterns of antisocial behavior more probable. Psychiatric illness in parents reflects an increased rate of behavior problems in children. Antisocial parents tend to rear antisocial children. Childhood behavior problems are more common among lower socioeconomic classes. To what extent the influence of parents' disturbances on the child's behavior is genetic and to what extent it is environmental, is speculative.

Children with antisocial behaviors are most visible when required to pay strict attention, follow directions, demonstrate control, exhibit socially acceptable behavior, and master academic skills. School, the primary socializing agency for society, emphasizes conformity and educational achievement. These expectations are basic to the order of formal training. When children are unable to meet these expectations, concerns frequently arise among teachers. Questions educators pose may include: How many children are there? How do they behave? How can they be controlled and managed in the classroom? How should they be classified to reduce effects created by labels? What support systems can provide these children with needed programs?

Terms used in educational settings to describe children with antisocial behaviors are emotionally disturbed, socially maladjusted, minimally neurologically impaired, culturally disadvantaged, behavior disordered, educationally handicapped, and conduct disturbed. Such labels represent different orientations that exist among educators confronted with the task of providing educational programs for children with antisocial behaviors. All these labels could be used collectively for a single child experiencing difficulty in school. For qualification for programs, labels and treatments should be closely related to how the antisocial child (in classroom, community, or at home) is perceived (by educators, social groups, or family). Educational offerings frequently depend on how a child is perceived and the attitude of the referring school toward the child.

Treatment

When an individual has appropriate behavioral responses in his or her repertoire and exhibits these responses under appropriate circumstances, antisocial behavior is interpreted. Through systematic and explicit application of the principles of learning, behavior management can be applied in educational settings to treat antisocial behaviors.

The individual can be helped to change deficient or maladaptive behavior by receiving assistance to modify his or her responses to specific sound cues. In the case of maladaptive behavior, for example, aggression could be modified to be elicited or emitted under appropriate circumstances only. This type of behavioral learning, unlearning, or relearning is known as behavior management. The teacher or behaviorist operates on the assumption that the behavior can be modified without understanding why the behavior is antisocial. The antecedents to the behavior need not be reconstructed to initiate corrective action. Teaching the child to react more appropriately is the only relevant issue, not finding out how the child came to behave antisocially. The focus during behavior therapy is on teaching new behaviors and eliminating old ones. The first task of the therapist (teacher) is to decide which behavior should be modified. Once a target behavior is defined, the treatment goal can be specified. Treatments are based on principles of learning: respondent learning, operant conditioning, interrelationships of operation and respondent factors, social reinforcement, desensitization, and aversive and contingency control. The treatment goal is assessed when the antisocial behavior has become adapted. If in the process of identifying target behaviors the teacher discovers antecedents as causes, the organization of the classroom environment, stimuli, and consequences can be arranged so that the learning situation supports the child's development. An engineered, structured classroom with clear-cut expectations and rewarding consequences for appropriate behavior and academic accomplishment can result in definite academic and behavioral gains. Primary or tangible rewards, teacher attention, "game" approaches, and high-interest activities can become successful interventions for adapting antisocial behaviors. Precision teaching involves selecting a behavior, charting it on a graph, recording changes and occurrences, analyzing the child's performance, and changing the program according to program effects. Some schools use a resource room concept, in which the child participates part time in a special program and part time in a regular class program.

Completely self-contained classrooms for children with more severe learning and behavioral problems can be successful. The engineered classroom directs attention to the establishment of specific goals or develops a sequence of behavioral objectives, for example, attention, response, order, exploration, social activity, mastery, and achievement. This engineering translates behavior modification strategy into realistic use in the classroom. There is constant manipulation of stimuli and intervention in the class to assure a child's continued success.

There are limitless behaviors that can disturb, interfere, or interrupt. There are as many interventions to attempt to modify disturbing behaviors. The range of children's behaviors that are judged negatively is extensive, especially in the complex social system called school. Our tendency is to cause a child to internalize his or her problematic characteristics through inadvertent reinforcement.

Reactors classify, define, program, analyze, label, and provide some services to those identified as aggressive when threatening behaviors become a serious concern. Seldom do educators recognize the responder as a contributor to the disturbances. The child judged as antisocial is the one who violates a large number of behavioral codes, yet some of the most seriously troubled go unrecognized and untreated as passive aggressors.

The intensity of observer reaction may be related to the observer's own social tolerance and his or her difficulty in controlling comparable tendencies. Certainly, the observer's tolerance plays a significant role in determining the services to be received by the antisocial performer.

If a tree crashes in the forest but there is no human ear to hear it, is there a noise? When an individual behaves in an antisocial fashion, does the disturbance exist without a reactor to register the event? Does the disturbance reside in the child or the reactor, or is it a product of both?

REFERENCE

Quay, H. C., & Werry, J. S. (1972). *Psychopathological disorders of childhood*. New York: Wiley.

ANNE SABATINO
Hudson, Wisconsin

CONDUCT DISORDER
EMOTIONAL DISORDERS
SERIOUSLY EMOTIONALLY DISTURBED

ANTISOCIAL PERSONALITY

The antisocial personality is characterized by a recurring pattern of antisocial behaviors and a general disregard for the rights of others. This pattern of behavior has, in the past, been referred to as psychopathy or sociopathy. It emerges during childhood in the form of truancy and other school-related academic and behavior problems such as delinquency, lying, fighting, sexual promiscuity, substance abuse, and running away from home. The *DSM-IV* (American Psychiatric Association, 1994) requires at least four of the following nine manifestations of the disorder be present before a diagnosis of antisocial personality disorder (APD) is made: inability to sustain consistent work behavior; lack of ability to function as a responsible parent; failure to accept social norms with respect to lawful behavior; inability to maintain enduring attachment to a sexual partner; irritability or aggressiveness; failure to honor financial obligations; failure to plan ahead, or impulsivity; disregard for the truth; and recklessness. Cleckley (1976) has identified other characteristics such as lack of remorse or shame, failure to learn from experience, poor judgment, and absence of anxiety.

The diagnosis of APD is typically reserved for individuals age 18 and over. Younger children and adolescents who manifest signs of APD are diagnosed as conduct disorder. There are four subtypes of conduct disorder depending on the presence or absence of normal social attachments and aggressive behavior. Many, but not all, children who manifest conduct disorder go on to develop an antisocial personality disorder (Loeber, 1982). Research has identified five factors that appear to play a role in the etiology of APD including heredity, brain abnormalities, autonomic nervous system underarousal, and family and environmental influences.

REFERENCES

American Psychiatric Association. (1994). *Diagnostic and statistical manual of mental disorders* (4th ed.). Washington, DC.

Cleckley, H. M. (1976). *The mask of sanity* (5th ed.). St. Louis, MO: Mosby.

Loeber, R. (1982). The stability of antisocial and delinquent behavior: A review. *Child Development, 53,* 1431–1446.

ROBERT G. BRUBAKER
Eastern Kentucky University

AGGRESSION
CONDUCT DISORDER

ANTISOCIAL PERSONALITY DISORDER

Antisocial Personality Disorder (ASPD) falls under the broadband heading of *Personality Disorders* found in the *Diagnostic and Statistical Manual of Mental Disorders,* fourth edition (*DSM-IV;* American Psychiatric Association, 1994). According to the *DSM-IV,* to be diagnosed with ASPD an individual must demonstrate a pervasive pattern of disregard for and violation of the rights of others occurring since age 15, as evidenced by three or more of the following characteristics: (1) a failure to conform to social norms with respect to lawful behaviors such as by repeatedly engaging in acts that are grounds for arrest; (2) a pattern of deceitfulness exhibited by the use of aliases, repeated lying, or surreptitiously depriving others out of personal profit or pleasure; (3) impulsivity or failure to plan ahead; (4) behaving in an irritable and aggressive manner, as documented by repeated physical fights or assaults; (5) showing reckless disregard for the safety of others or one's self; (6) consistent irresponsibility, as documented by a failure to honor financial obligations or being unable to maintain consistent work or employment over time; and (7) demonstrating an aloofness or lack of remorse toward having hurt, mistreated, or stolen from someone.

In addition, the individual must be at least 18 years of age at the time of ASPD diagnosis; there must be evidence of a diagnosis of Conduct Disorder (CD) with onset before age 15 years; and the individual's antisocial behavior cannot occur exclusively during the course of Schizophrenia or a Manic Episode. As the *DSM-IV* points out, the core feature of ASPD is the pervasive pattern of disregard for and violation of the rights of others that often begins in childhood or early adolescence. The use of deceit and manipulation are constant themes in the life and behavior of such individuals (American Psychiatric Association, 1994).

Educational practitioners need to be aware that just as there is a developmental progression or link between Oppositional Defiant Disorder (ODD) and CD, there is also a developmental progress, or strong link, between CD in childhood or adolescence and ASPD in adulthood (Hinshaw & Lee, 2003; for a broader understanding of developmental issues related to ODD or CD, child psychopathology, and antisocial behavior, the reader is directed to the work of Cicchetti & Nurcombe, 1993; Dishion, French, & Patterson, 1995; Mash & Dozois, 2003). Adults diagnosed with ASPD have almost always been diagnosed with CD earlier in life, with the predicted poor outcome of ASPD being increased significantly if Substance Abuse is involved (Hinshaw & Lee, 2003). Moreover, official court record evidence shows that 50 percent to 70 percent of youths with CD, or youths who have been arrested for delinquent acts during childhood or adolescence, are arrested in adulthood (Lahey & Loeber, 1997). Longitudinal sample studies have documented that 40 percent to 43 percent of children or youth with CD who had either been reared in institutional or group home settings or who had been receiving treatment in psychiatric clinics for severe Antisocial Behavior met criteria for ASPD in adulthood (Harrington, Fudge, Rutter, Pickles, & Hill, 1991; Zoccolillo, Pickles, Quinton, & Rutter, 1992). Kratzer and Hodgins (1997) study also supports these findings in which a large birth cohort of over 12,700 males and females were followed up at age 30. By age 30, 76 percent of the males and 30 percent of the females who met criteria for childhood CD had either a criminal record, a mental disorder (i.e., severe Substance Abuse), or both.

Although, as the preceding data suggests, not all children or youth with CD end up with a diagnosis of ASPD, it still begs the question of what predicts whether a child with CD will be diagnosed with later adult ASPD. To date, relatively few predictive studies have been carried out; however, some researchers have found that (1) children with CD with a biological parent with ASPD are more likely to meet the criteria of ASPD than children with CD who do not have a biological parent with ASPD, (2) lower intelligence is associated with the persistence of juvenile delinquency and CD into adulthood, and (3) a history of ASPD in a biological parent is the most powerful predictor of *persistence* of CD from childhood into adolescence, but this predictive relationship is affected by whether youths have strong verbal abilities (i.e., verbal IQ score above 100), such that if a child or youth with CD possesses a verbal IQ score of above 100 and does not have a biological parent with ASPD, then there is a substantially lower risk of persistent CD than for all other children or youth with CD (Lahey & Loeber, 1997).

The preceding data and information make it clear that adults who meet criteria for ASPD will have started their antisocial lifestyle earlier in life, before age 15, in fact, as the diagnosis of ASPD requires an individual to have previously met criteria for CD (Hinshaw & Lee, 2003; Kratzer & Hodgins, 1997). Interestingly, and while rare, there are small subgroups of adults who engage in antisocial activities without any noteworthy childhood patterns of behavior indicative of CD (Hinshaw & Lee, 2003). Children and youth who display CD are highly likely to become substance abusers, juvenile delinquents, and adult criminals; as adults with ASPD, these poor and negative outcomes continue to exacerbate, leading to further troubles such as marital discord or divorce; mental health or psychiatric difficulties of all types; premature death; holding multiple jobs over a short time span; unemployment; having no confiding relationships; persistent friction with friends, workmates, and neighbors; domestic violence; inept parenting; drug and alcohol addiction; and so on (Dishion et al., 1995; Kratzer & Hodgins, 1997). These poor adult outcomes have their genesis in childhood, making it abundantly clear that in order to prevent such outcomes, early intervention and treatment at home and school is critical and may be the best and only opportunity these children have to lead successful lives as adults (Farmer, Compton, Burns, & Robertson, 2002; Walker, Colvin, & Ramsey, 1995).

REFERENCES

American Psychiatric Association. (1994). *Diagnostic and statistical manual of mental disorders* (4th ed.). Washington, DC: Author.

Cicchetti, D., & Nurcombe, B. (Eds.). (1993). Towards a developmental perspective on Conduct Disorder [special issue]. *Developmental Psychopathology, 5,* 518–537.

Dishion, T. J., French, D. C., & Patterson, G. R. (1995). The development and ecology of Antisocial Behavior. In D. Cicchetti & D. J. Cohen (Eds.), *Developmental psychopathology* (Vol. 2, pp. 421–471). New York: Wiley.

Farmer, M. Z., Compton, S. N., Burns, B. J., & Robertson, E. (2002). Review of the evidence base for treatment of childhood psychopathology: Externalizing disorders. *Journal of Consulting and Clinical Psychology, 70,* 1267–1302.

Harrington, R., Fudge, H., Rutter, M., Pickles, A., & Hill, J. (1991). Adult outcome of childhood and adolescent depression: I. Links with Antisocial Disorder. *Journal of the American Academy of Child and Adolescent Psychiatry, 30,* 434–439.

Hinshaw, S. P., & Lee, S. S. (2003). Conduct and Oppositional Defiant Disorders. In E. J. Mash & R. A. Barkley (Eds.), *Child psychopathology* (2nd ed., pp. 144–198). New York: Guilford.

Kratzer, L., & Hodgins, S. (1997). Adult outcomes of child conduct problems: A cohort study. *Journal of Abnormal Child Psychology, 25,* 65–81.

Lahey, B. B., & Loeber, R. (1997). Attention-Deficit/Hyperactivity Disorder, Oppositional Defiant Disorder, Conduct Disorder, and Adult Antisocial Behavior: A life span perspective. In D. M. Stoff, J. Breiling, & J. D. Maser (Eds.), *Handbook of Antisocial Behavior* (pp. 51–59). New York: Wiley.

Mash, E. J., & Dozois, D. J. A. (2003). Child psychopathology: A developmental-systems perspective. In E. J. Mash & R. A. Barkley (Eds.), *Child psychopathology* (2nd ed., pp. 3–71). New York: Guilford.

Walker, H. M., Colvin, G., & Ramsey, E. (1995). *Antisocial Behavior in school: Strategies and best practices.* Pacific Grove, CA: Brooks/Cole.

Zoccolillo, M., Pickles, A., Quinton, D., & Rutter, M. (1992). The outcome of Childhood Conduct Disorder: Implications for defining adult Personality Disorder and Conduct Disorder. *Psychological Medicine, 22,* 971–986.

Rollen C. Fowler
Eugene 4J School District,
Eugene, Oregon

ANXIETY

We live in an "age of anxiety" (Spielberger & Rickman, 1990, p. 69). People have become more anxious and worried than ever before (Twenge, 2000). In recent years, children and adolescents have reported higher levels of anxiety than individuals in decades past (Twenge, 2000). Twenge suggests that a decrease in social connectedness and an increase in environmental threat may be responsible for the increased levels of anxiety reported among our nation's youth.

Anxiety is a basic emotion that humans have experienced since the beginning of mankind (McReynolds, 1985).

Anxiety is a unique emotion as it may be viewed in both a positive and negative light. From a positive perspective, anxiety occurs normally in a child's development, and its presence indicates that one's development is progressing at an expected rate (Huberty, 1997). For example, toddlers typically show signs of anxiety in the presence of strangers, preschoolers and elementary school–age children usually become anxious in the presence of animals, children in middle school typically show signs of anxiety when they visit a dentist's or principal's office, and adolescents usually become anxious when they are required to give a speech in front of a class (Barrios & Hartmann, 1997). Anxiety may also be adaptive and alert a child to a real threat or potentially dangerous situation (Huberty, 1997). The child may react to the real threat or potentially dangerous situation with a fight-or-flight response. Besides being a normative indicator of development or an adaptive response to a potentially threatening environmental event or cue, anxiety may motivate and facilitate a child's performance so that the child performs optimally on a task or an activity (Huberty, 1997). Research has suggested that a moderate level of anxiety (i.e., not too much or not too little) may boost a child's performance. In contrast, very low and very high levels of anxiety are more likely to be associated with poorer performance (Yerkes & Dodson, 1908). Most researchers in the field of anxiety believe a curvilinear relationship (i.e., an inverted U-shaped relationship) exists between anxiety and performance. From a negative perspective, anxiety may be "a destructive and debilitating force in human behavior" (Richmond, 2000, p. 124). At extremely high levels, anxiety may interfere with a child's academic, behavioral, emotional, and social functioning. As a result, clinic- or school-based interventions may be required to treat the devastating effects of anxiety.

Anxiety is somewhat portentous and may manifest itself in many different ways. As mentioned earlier, anxiety may be a simple reaction to an environmental event, or it may represent a symptom in and of itself. Anxiety may be a symptom in another disorder, or it may represent a disorder of various types (American Psychiatric Association, 2000; Lowe & Reynolds, 2000; Reynolds, 1998).

Defining the boundary between normal and pathological anxiety has been a struggle within the field. Wakefield (1992) proposed that normal and pathological anxiety can be distinguished from each other based on a harmful dysfunction account of the disorder. According to Wakefield, two interrelated criteria must be met in order for pathological anxiety to exist: (1) a psychobiological mechanism must malfunction, and (2) the malfunctioning of the psychobiological mechanism must result in suffering, maladaptation, or both (Evans et al., 2005). In contrast, Evans and colleagues proposed that normal and pathological anxiety can be distinguished from each other based on three clinical features: distress, dysfunction, and symptom inflexibility. Although Wakefield (1992) and Evans and colleagues (2005) have suggested criteria for distinguishing normal

and pathological anxiety, it is not known at the present time whether their criteria represent the ideal criteria in making this distinction.

Anxiety is viewed as a multidimensional construct and consists of three dimensions—cognitive, behavioral, and physiological. These three components may be manifested by a child in varying degrees. The cognitive component may consist of ruminative thoughts, excessive worries, and attention and memory difficulties. Behavioral manifestations may include fidgety behaviors, motor restlessness, and avoidance or escape behaviors in the presence of anxiety-provoking stimuli. The physiological component may consist of rapid heartbeat, perspiration, muscle tension, headaches, and stomachaches (Huberty, 1997).

One of the most prevalent conceptualizations of anxiety is provided by the state-trait model of anxiety. Spielberger (1972) viewed state anxiety as a transitory condition that varied across individuals and situations, whereas trait anxiety was viewed as a more permanent condition. Spielberger (1972) defined *state anxiety* as "feelings of tension, apprehension, nervousness, and worry, with associated activation or arousal of the autonomic nervous system" (p. 29). State anxiety occurs when a child perceives a situation as threatening, resulting in a complex set of emotional reactions that may vary in degree and intensity to a real or imagined threat (Reynolds & Richmond, 1985). In contrast, trait anxiety is viewed as a stable personality characteristic. A child with a high level of trait anxiety has a propensity to feel anxious (Spielberger, 1972). The child frequently experiences anxiety even when anxiety-provoking stimuli are relatively weak (Reynolds & Richmond, 1985).

Prevalence rates of various anxiety symptoms in community samples of children have been difficult to estimate. Kashani and Orvaschel (1990) reported that the prevalence of anxiety symptoms in community samples of children and adolescents have ranged as high as 67 percent. In contrast, Puskar, Sereika, and Haller (2003) examined anxiety symptoms in a community sample of 466 adolescents and found that 20 percent of their sample reported elevated levels of anxiety. Puskar and colleagues also found that females reported more anxiety than males. This finding of a gender difference in anxiety symptoms reported is consistent with the literature. However, it is unclear at the present time whether females experience more anxiety symptoms than males or whether females recognize more readily their anxieties than males (Reynolds, 1998). Additional research is needed to explore this issue. Few studies have examined racial or ethnic differences in anxiety symptoms among children. Of the few studies conducted to date, findings suggest that ethnic majority and minority children may have more similarities than differences in the levels and types of anxieties reported (Ginsburg & Silverman, 1996; Neal, Lilly, & Zakis, 1993). Although additional studies need to be conducted to obtain a better understanding of the relationship between anxiety and different demographic variables, it is clear, based on the prevalence rates reported, that anxiety is a major problem experienced by many children and that early detection is needed to reduce anxiety and its negative effects in the child population.

Early detection of anxiety in children typically involves the use of different assessment techniques. A multimethod approach is strongly advocated in the assessment of anxiety in children. In the multimethod approach, a variety of measures are used, including clinical interviews, direct observations, behavior rating scales, personality measures, and possibly psychophysiological measures (Lowe & Reynolds, in press). Behavior rating scales, including self-report measures, are popular and effective techniques used in the early detection of anxiety in children.

Because other emotional, behavioral, and social concerns often accompany anxiety problems in children, it is useful to use both broadband and narrowband behavioral rating scales. Broadband instruments allow a more global assessment of a child's behavior. With broadband measures, different dimensions of personality may be assessed, such as depression and withdrawn behavior, in addition to anxiety. Broadband instruments may include different forms for different raters such as parents, teachers, and the child. This allows information to be collected from multiple sources in multiple settings in which a child's behavior is observed. One of the most widely used broadband measures is the Achenbach System of Empirically Based Assessment (ASEBA; Achenbach & Rescorla, 2001). The ASEBA consists of three scales: a parent rating scale, a teacher rating scale, and a self-report scale. The ASEBA is used to assess social competencies, adaptive functioning, and problematic behaviors, including anxiety, in children and adolescents, ages 1.5 to 18. Another widely used broadband instrument is the Behavior Assessment System for Children, Second Edition (BASC-2; Reynolds & Kamphaus, 2004). The BASC-2 assesses behavioral and emotional difficulties, including anxiety, in children and adolescents, ages 2 to 25. Like the ASEBA, the BASC-2 consists of multiple forms that are completed by multiple raters. The BASC-2 includes a parent rating scale, a teacher rating scale, and a self-report scale. Finally, the Beck Youth Inventories, Second Edition (BYI-II; Beck, Beck, Jolly, & Steer, 2005) measures emotional and social difficulties in children and adolescents, ages 7 to 18. The BYI-II is a self-report measure and consists of five scales assessing symptoms across several domains, including anxiety.

When assessing anxiety in children, it is also useful to include one or more narrowband measures of anxiety. Whereas broadband instruments measure a wide array of psychological dimensions, narrowband measures focus on a specific domain such as anxiety. One of the most widely used narrowband instruments is the State-Trait Anxiety Inventory (STAI; Spielberger, Gorsuch, & Lushene, 1970). This scale provides a measure of both state and trait anxiety and can be used with high school students and adults. A children's version of the STAI, the State-Trait Anxiety

Inventory for Children (STAI-C; Spielberger, Edwards, Lushene, Montuori, & Platzek, 1973), is also available for individuals in Grades 4 through 6. Another popular measure used to assess anxiety in children and adolescents is the Revised Children's Manifest Anxiety Scale (RCMAS; Reynolds & Richmond, 1978). The RCMAS is a self-report measure designed to assess the level and nature of anxiety in children and adolescents, ages 6 to 19. The RCMAS consists of a Total Anxiety scale, which provides a global measure of chronic manifest anxiety, and three anxiety subscales (Worry/Oversensitivity, Social Concerns, and Physiological Anxiety). The Multidimensional Anxiety Scale for Children (MASC; March, 1997) is another self-report measure used to assess anxiety in individuals between the ages of 8 and 19. The MASC consists of four scales: Physical Symptoms, Harm Avoidance, Social Anxiety, and Separation/Panic. Several MASC scales also include subscales. The Fear Survey Schedule for Children–Revised (FSSC-R; Ollendick, 1983) is a narrowband instrument used to measure the number of fears and the overall level of fearfulness in children, ages 7 to 18. The Social Anxiety Scale for Children, Revised (SASC-R; LaGreca & Stone, 1993) and the Social Anxiety Scale for Adolescents (SAS-A; LaGreca & Lopez, 1998) are self-report measures used to assess a child or adolescent's anxiety in social situations. Both the SASC-R and the SAS-A include a Total Social Anxiety scale as well as three subscales: Fear of Negative Evaluation (FNE), Social Avoidance and Distress of New Situations or People (SAD-New), and Social Avoidance and Distress of General Situations or People (SAD-General). Finally, the Social Phobia Anxiety Inventory for Children (SPAIC; Beidel, Turner, & Morris, 1998) and the Social Phobia Anxiety Inventory (SPAI; Turner, Dancu, & Beidel, 1996) are measures used to assess anxiety and fears related to social situations in individuals, ages 8 to 14 and 15 and older, respectively. These broadband and narrowband measures are widely used in the schools and clinical settings by mental health professionals to specify the nature of anxiety along with other concerns. Results obtained with these assessment tools are then directly linked to intervention strategies when needed in an attempt to reduce a child's anxiety and collateral concerns.

RFERENCES

Achenbach, T. M., & Rescorla, L. A. (2001). *Achenbach System of Empirically Based Assessment.* Burlington, VT: University of Vermont, Research Center for Children, Youth, and Families.

American Psychiatric Association. (2000). *Diagnostic and statistical manual of mental disorders* (4th ed., text revision). Washington, DC: Author.

Barrios, B. A., & Hartmann, D. P. (1997). Fears and anxieties. In E. J. Mash & R. A. Barkley (Eds.), *Treatment of childhood disorders* (pp. 249–337). New York: Guilford.

Beck, J. S., Beck, A. T., Jolly, J. B., & Steer, R. A. (2005). *The Beck Youth Inventories* (2nd ed.). San Antonio, TX: Psychological Corporation.

Beidel, D. B., Turner, S. M., & Morris, T. L. (1998). *The Social Phobia and Anxiety Inventory for Children*. North Tonawanda, NY: Multi-Health Systems.

Evans, D. L., Foa, E. B., Gur, R. E., Hendin, H., O'Brien, C. P., Seligman, M. E. P., et al. (2005). *Treating and preventing adolescent mental health disorders: What we know and what we don't know*. New York: Oxford Press.

Ginsburg, G. S., & Silverman, W. K. (1996). Phobic and anxiety disorders in Hispanic and Caucasian youth. *Journal of Anxiety Disorders, 10,* 517–528.

Huberty, T. J. (1997). Anxiety. In G. Bear, K. Minke, & A. Thomas (Eds.), *Children's needs II: Development, problems and alternatives* (pp. 305–314). Bethesda, MD: National Association of School Psychologists.

Kashani, J. H., & Orvaschel, H. (1990). A community study of anxiety in children and adolescents. *American Journal of Psychiatry, 147,* 313–318.

LaGreca, A. M., & Lopez, N. (1998). Social anxiety among adolescents: Linkages with peer relations and friendships. *Journal of Abnormal Child Psychology, 26,* 83–94.

LaGreca, A. M., & Stone, W. L. (1993). Social Anxiety Scale for Children–Revised: Factor structure and concurrent validity. *Journal of Clinical Child Psychology, 22,* 17–27.

Lowe, P. A., & Reynolds, C. R. (2000). Exploratory analysis of the latent structure of anxiety among older adults. *Educational and Psychological Measurement, 60,* 100–116.

Lowe, P. A., & Reynolds, C. R. (in press). Examination of the psychometric properties of the Adult Manifest Anxiety Scale–Elderly scores. *Educational and Psychological Measurement.*

March, J. S. (1997). *Multidimensional Anxiety Scale for Children.* North Tonawanda, NY: Multi-Health Systems.

McReynolds, P. (1985). Changing conceptions of anxiety: A historical review and a proposed integration. *Issues in Mental Health Nursing, 7,* 131–158.

Neal, A. M., Lilly, R. S., & Zakis, S. (1993). What are African American children afraid of? A preliminary study. *Journal of Anxiety Disorders, 7,* 129–139.

Ollendick, T. H. (1983). The reliability and validity of the Revised Fear Survey Schedule for Children (FSSC-R). *Behaviour Research and Therapy, 21,* 685–692.

Puskar, K., Sereika, B., & Haller, L. (2003). Anxiety, somatic complaints, and depressive symptoms in rural adolescents. *Journal of Child and Adolescent Psychiatry, 2,* 265–273.

Reynolds, C. R. (1998). Need we measure anxiety differently for males and females? *Journal of Personality Assessment, 70,* 212–221.

Reynolds, C. R., & Kamphaus, R. W. (2004). *Behavior Assessment Scale for Children* (2nd ed.). Circle Pines, MN: American Guidance Services.

Reynolds, C. R., & Richmond, B. O. (1978). What I think and feel: A revised measure of children's manifest anxiety. *Journal of Abnormal Child Psychology, 6,* 271–280.

Reynolds, C. R., & Richmond, B. O. (1985). *Revised Children's Manifest Anxiety Scale manual.* Los Angeles: Western Psychological Services.

Richmond, B. O. (2000). Anxiety. In C. R. Reynolds & E. Fletcher-Janzen (Eds.), *Encyclopedia of special education* (2nd ed., pp. 124–125). New York: Wiley.

Spielberger, C. D. (1972). Anxiety as an emotional state. In C. D. Spielberger (Ed.), *Anxiety: Current trends in theory and research* (pp. 24–49). New York: Academic Press.

Spielberger, C. D., Edwards, C. D., Lushene, R. E., Montuori, I., & Platzek, D. (1973). *The State-Trait Anxiety Inventory for Children.* Palo Alto, CA: Consulting Psychologists Press.

Spielberger, C. D., Gorsuch, R. L., & Lushene, R. E. (1970). *The State-Trait Anxiety Inventory.* Palo Alto, CA: Consulting Psychologists Press.

Spielberger, C. D., & Rickman, R. L. (1990). Assessment of state and trait anxiety. In N. Sartorius, V. Andreoli, G. Cassano, L. Eisenberg, P. Kielholz, P. Pancheri, et al. (Eds.), *Anxiety: Psychobiological and clinical perspectives* (pp. 69–83). New York: Hemisphere.

Turner, S. M., Dancu, C. V., & Beidel, D. B. (1996). *The Social Phobia and Anxiety Inventory.* North Tonawanda, NY: Multi-Health Systems.

Twenge, J. M. (2000). The age of anxiety? Birth cohort change in anxiety and neuroticism, 1952–1993. *Journal of Personality and Social Psychology, 79,* 1007–1021.

Wakefield, J. C. (1992). The component of mental disorder: On the boundary between biological facts and social values. *American Psychologist, 47,* 373–388.

Yerkes, R. M., & Dodson, J. D. (1908). The relation of strength of stimulus to rapidity of habit-formation. *Journal of Comparative and Neurological Psychology, 18,* 459–482.

PATRICIA A. LOWE
JENNIFER M. RAAD
University of Kansas

ANXIETY DISORDERS

Anxiety is a common mental health concern found among many children. *Anxiety* is defined as "an unpleasant emotional state or reaction that is distinguished from other states by a unique combination of experiential qualities and physiological changes" (Spielberger & Rickman, 1990, p. 69). Anxiety consists of multiple cognitive, physiological, and behavioral phenomena. The cognitive component may include worry, concentration difficulties, and memory and attention problems. Physiological manifestations may consist of muscle tension, perspiration, heart palpitations, headaches, and stomachaches, whereas the behavioral patterns may include motor restlessness and fidgety behaviors (Huberty, 1997). Mild anxiety problems found in children are typically short-lived. However, severe anxiety problems experienced by some children are typically chronic, interfere with their adaptive functioning, and persist into adulthood (Keller et al., 1992; Ollendick & King, 1994; Vasey & Ollendick, 2000).

Pathological anxiety in children is determined by three clinical features: degree of distress and dysfunction and symptomatic inflexibility. Degree of distress and dysfunction varies in importance as a function of an individual's age, whereas symptomatic inflexibility is relevant, regardless of a person's age (Evans et al., 2005). Children with Anxiety Disorders experience a high degree of distress, severe dysfunction, and symptomatic inflexibility.

There are 15 types of Anxiety Disorders specified in the *Diagnostic and Statistical Manual of Mental Disorders-Fourth Edition-Text Revision* (*DSM-IV-TR;* American Psychiatric Association, 2000). These disorders include Generalized Anxiety Disorder, Separation Anxiety Disorder, Specific Phobia, Social Anxiety Disorder, Obsessive-Compulsive Disorder, Posttraumatic Stress Disorder, Acute Stress Disorder, Anxiety Disorder Not Otherwise Specified, Panic Attack, Panic Disorder with and without Agoraphobia, Agoraphobia without a History of Panic Disorder, Anxiety Disorder Due to a General Medical Condition, and Substance-Induced Anxiety Disorder. Of these 15 types of Anxiety Disorders, the most common Anxiety Disorders found among children are Separation Anxiety Disorder, Generalized Anxiety Disorder, and Specific Phobia (Silverman & Kurtines, 2001).

Although there are different types of Anxiety Disorders, these disorders share several common features. These features include sympathetic activation, faulty threat perception, attentional hypervigilance, chronic worry, and escape and avoidance behaviors. Activation of the sympathetic nervous system is an adaptive response to a potential threat. Most anxiety states result in the activation of the sympathetic nervous system, producing physiologic changes in the body such as increased muscle tension, respiration, cardiac output, and sweating. However, in the case of Anxiety Disorders, the system is activated in the absence of a real or potential threat. Faulty threat perception is another common feature found among individuals with Anxiety Disorders. Individuals with Anxiety Disorders erroneously perceive situations as threatening when, in fact, they are not. The third common feature is attentional hypervigilance. Individuals with Anxiety Disorders attend excessively to what they perceive as threat cues. The excessive attention to these perceived threat cues reduces attentional resources to process corrective threat disconfirming information. As a result, attentional hypervigilance may exacerbate anxiety because these individuals continue to perceive the cues as threatening when in reality they are not. A fourth feature is chronic worry. Individuals with Anxiety Disorders worry about current and future events. Avoidance and escape behaviors are additional features shared among individuals with Anxiety Disorders. Escape or avoidance behaviors are likely to be demonstrated when a perceived threat cue is present (Telch, Smits, Brown, & Beckner, 2002).

Prevalence rates for any Anxiety Disorder found in children range from 5.78 percent to 17.7 percent (Silverman & Kurtines, 2001). According to Merrell (2001), Anxiety Disorders may be the largest group of internalizing disorders found among children. Gender differences have been reported among children, with girls more likely than boys to have an Anxiety Disorder (Costello, Egger, & Angold, 2004). Of the few studies conducted to date, there is little evidence to suggest differences in the pattern of childhood Anxiety Disorders across different racial groups (Safren et al., 2000). In contrast, age differences have been noted in Anxiety Disorders across the child and adolescent life span, with an increase in the prevalence of Anxiety Disorders reported with an increase in age. However, Separation Anxiety Disorders do not follow this age trend (Silverman & Kurtines, 2001).

Examination of Anxiety Disorders from a developmental perspective reveals that Specific Phobias and Separation Anxiety Disorders have the earliest onset. Both disorders have an onset in early childhood. Generalized Anxiety Disorders are likely to appear slightly later, around the age of 8 to 10. In contrast, the onset for Social Anxiety Disorders, Panic Disorders with and without Agoraphobia, and Obsessive-Compulsive Disorders typically occurs in adolescence (Saavedra & Silverman, 2002).

Children diagnosed with an Anxiety Disorder are likely to have another comorbid condition (American Psychiatric Association, 2000). High rates of comorbidity exist between Anxiety Disorders and depression. The rate of comorbidity reported between these two internalizing disorders is as high as 60 to 70 percent (Wilmshurst, 2005). There is much discussion in the field as to whether anxiety and depression are separate disorders. Some researchers believe that the two disorders are distinct, whereas other researchers believe that the two disorders are related. Watson and Clark (1984) proposed a tripartite model to explain the relationship between anxiety and depression. According to the tripartite model, negative affectivity (emotional distress) is the underlying trait shared by both disorders, whereas low positive affectivity (anhedonia) is unique to depression, and physiologic arousal is unique to anxiety (Watson & Clark, 1984). Other researchers have suggested a sequential link between the two disorders, with anxiety serving as an early precursor to a Depressive Disorder (Costello, Mustillo, Erkanli, Keeler, & Angold, 2003). Comorbidity rates between different types of Anxiety Disorders are also high. Children who have been diagnosed with an Anxiety Disorder as their primary diagnosis often present with another Anxiety Disorder (Wilmshurst, 2005). Besides depression and Anxiety Disorders, other common comorbid disorders include Attention-Deficit/Hyperactivity Disorder, Oppositional Defiant Disorder, and Conduct Disorder (Costello et al., 2004).

The costs of Anxiety Disorders are high (Greenberg et al., 1999). Greenberg and colleagues conducted one of the most comprehensive studies of the monetary costs of Anxiety Disorders. Greenberg et al. reported the total costs of Anxiety Disorders were 63.1 billion dollars. This figure is based on the monetary value of the dollar in 1998. Non-psychiatric and psychiatric treatment were identified as the major costs.

Many children with Anxiety Disorders experience difficulty in the school setting. Impairments in social (Beidel, Turner, & Morris, 2000; Caster, Inderbitzen, & Hope, 1999) and academic functioning (Ialongo, Edelsohn, Werthamer-Larsson, Crockett, & Kellam, 1994, 1995; Woodward & Fergusson, 2001) have been reported. Ialongo et al. (1994) assessed 1,197 children in the first grade and found an inverse relationship between anxiety and academic performance. Ialongo and colleagues reported that children with higher levels of anxiety were 2.4 times more likely than their same-age peers to perform in the lowest quartile of reading achievement. These same children were 7.7 times more likely to perform in the lowest quartile of math achievement in comparison to their peers. Four years later, these children with higher levels of anxiety were 10 times more likely than their same-age peers to be in the lower one-third of their class academically.

Besides academic difficulties, many children with Anxiety Disorders experience poor peer relationships. These children are more likely than their peers to have negative perceptions about themselves and their relationships with others (Huberty, 1997). These negative perceptions about their relationships with others reduce the likelihood of these children's interactions with others and may result in social isolation.

Most schools are cognizant of the negative effects anxiety has on the socioemotional and academic functioning of children (Cohen, 1999). Children with an Anxiety Disorder may qualify for special education and related services under the emotional disturbance (ED) category of the *Individuals with Disabilities Education Improvement Act of 2004* (IDEIA). To meet the eligibility criteria, a child must exhibit one or more of the following conditions, and the condition(s) must have occurred over a long period of time and to a marked degree and must adversely affect the child's educational performance:

1. An inability to learn that cannot be explained by intellectual, sensory, or health factors.
2. An inability to build or maintain satisfactory interpersonal relationships with peers and teachers.
3. Inappropriate types of behavior or feelings under normal circumstances.
4. A general pervasive mood of unhappiness or depression.
5. A tendency to develop physical symptoms or fears associated with personal or school problems (34 C.F.R. § 300.8).

Different theories exist about the origin of an Anxiety Disorder. According to the psychoanalytic approach, anxiety results from the conflict between a child's ego and impulses unacceptable to it. The child's ego defends itself by forcing the impulses out of consciousness. In the conflict, anxiety is displaced or transferred to some other form or idea, giving rise to one of the Anxiety Disorders (Freud, 1924). Learning theories suggest that anxiety is acquired through and maintained by classical and operant conditioning or possibly modeling. In classical conditioning, a neutral stimulus becomes associated with an aversive stimulus (an unconditioned stimulus) and acquires the properties of the unconditioned stimulus. The neutral stimulus is designated the conditioned stimulus. The conditioned stimulus then produces fear, which may generalize to other neutral stimuli. In operant conditioning, fear of an object or a situation is maintained by a negative reinforcement contingency. The feared object or situation is avoided or attempts are made to escape from the situation. Escape or avoidance behavior is maintained because it reduces a child's anxiety. In modeling, the child observes other's reactions to aversive stimuli and situations. The child then models the behavior of others in response to similar aversive stimuli and situations (Vasey & Ollendick, 2000). The cognitive approach to Anxiety Disorders assumes aberrant cognitions underlie symptom expression. Cognitive researchers suggest that a child who is anxious exhibits threat-related attentional and interpretive biases. That is, the child selectively attends to threat-related stimuli and interprets ambiguous stimuli in a threatening manner (Evans et al., 2005). Biological explanations of Anxiety Disorders have focused on structural regions of the brain, genetic transmission, neurotransmitter functions, immunology, and autonomic nervous system activity. Abnormalities of autonomic regulation, with greater activation in the right frontal area of the brain (Gorman & Sloan, 2000), perturbations in the hypothalamic-pituitary-adrenal axis (Essex, Klein, Cho, & Kalin, 2002), and abnormalities in the immune system (Kagan, Snidman, McManis, & Woodward, 2001) have been reported in individuals with Anxiety Disorders or the offspring of individuals with Anxiety Disorders. Recent studies in behavioral genetics have suggested that childhood anxiety symptoms are moderately inheritable, accounting for about one-third of the variance in most cases (Eley, 1999; Silverman & Kurtines, 2001). Examination of epidemiological findings and genetic data strongly imply distinct biological profiles for the different types of Anxiety Disorders. Many of these biological profiles suggest neurochemical processes are the underlying factor in many of these disorders (Evans et al., 2005). Behavioral inhibition, another biological factor, has received attention as a risk factor in the development of childhood Anxiety Disorders (Vasey & Ollendick, 2000). Emotional factors and family factors may also predispose a child to an Anxiety Disorder. Deficits in emotional regulation and overcontrolling parents low in affection who demonstrate inconsistent parenting styles are believed to put a child at risk for an Anxiety Disorder (Vasey & Ollendick, 2000).

A multimethod, multisetting, multitrait approach has been recommended in the assessment of children with an Anxiety Disorder (Huberty, 1997). A multimethod, multisetting, multitrait approach involves obtaining information from multiple sources (parent, teacher, and child) and settings (home and school) and assessing multiple traits or characteristics (internalizing, externalizing, and social behaviors) to pinpoint problematic areas of concern. As part of the assessment process, behavior observations are performed; parent, teacher, and child interviews are conducted; rating scales are completed by the parent, teacher, and child if applicable; and multidimensional personality scales are administered. If cognitive or academic difficulties exist, standardized measures of intelligence and academic achievement as well as informal measures such as curriculum-based measures may be administered. Other areas that may need to be assessed include a child's self-esteem, coping skills, and peer relationships. Family functioning may be another area to examine as well as a child's thoughts, beliefs, and attributions about anxiety (Huberty, 1997).

Once an evaluation has been conducted, the results of the assessment are linked to intervention strategies to address the areas of concern. For children with Anxiety Disorders, pharmacotherapy, cognitive-behavior therapy, or a combination of the two are effective strategies to treat Anxiety Disorders in children (Evans et al., 2005). Other treatment strategies may be needed to address related concerns and comorbid conditions.

Specific information about the common Anxiety Disorders (Generalized Anxiety Disorder, Obsessive-Compulsive Disorder, Panic Disorder, Posttraumatic Stress Disorder, Separation Anxiety Disorder, Specific Phobia, and Social Anxiety Disorder) found in children follows. Although not listed as a separate disorder in the *DSM-IV-TR,* School Phobia is also included because of its prevalence among children. Controversy exists as to whether School Phobia is a Specific Phobia, Social Anxiety Disorder, Separation Anxiety Disorder, or a behavioral outcome, resulting from one of the Anxiety Disorders. A description, prevalence, comorbidity, etiology, and treatment of each Anxiety Disorder are discussed.

Generalized Anxiety Disorder

Generalized Anxiety Disorder, which now includes Overanxious Disorder of Childhood, is characterized by an excessive and chronic state of worry about a variety of events, circumstances, or situations such as friends, family, health, schoolwork, appearance, money, or one's future. Another central characteristic of a Generalized Anxiety Disorder is a child's inability to control his or her worry. Children with a Generalized Anxiety Disorder may experience restlessness, fatigue, irritability, concentration difficulties, muscle tension, or sleep problems. These symptoms must be present for

at least 6 months (American Psychiatric Association, 2000). Lifetime prevalence of a Generalized Anxiety Disorder is between 2 and 5 percent (Wilmshurst, 2005). Prevalence estimates reported for an Overanxious Disorder in children range from .5 percent to 7.1 percent (Evans et al., 2005). Comorbid disorders found among children with a Generalized Anxiety Disorder include Separation Anxiety Disorder, depression, Specific Phobia, and Social Anxiety Disorder (Evans et al., 2005). Genetics may play an important role in the development of a Generalized Anxiety Disorder in children. Cognitive factors may also explain the development of Generalized Anxiety Disorder as children may attend to and interpret ambiguous stimuli negatively. Finally, familial factors such as parenting and behavior modeling may increase the risk for a Generalized Anxiety Disorder in children (Wilmshurst, 2005). Cognitive-behavioral therapy can help children cope with and reduce their levels of anxiety. For children of anxious parents, it is most effective to involve the entire family in cognitive-behavioral therapy as reinforcement and modeling of appropriate behavior at home is important. Medication has also been shown to be effective in the treatment of a Generalized Anxiety Disorder in children (Evans et al., 2005).

Obsessive-Compulsive Disorder

Obsessive-Compulsive Disorder usually develops during adolescence and consists of obsessions or compulsions. Obsessions are recurrent thoughts or worries that cause distress or interfere with one's ability to function normally. These obsessions then may lead to compulsions, which are repetitive behaviors or rituals that the individual performs in order to relieve the distress caused by obsessions or prevent dreaded events or situations from occurring (American Psychiatric Association, 2000). Obsessions and compulsions in children often center on four primary areas: contamination (hand washing), safety (checking), preoccupations with orderliness and symmetry (aligning), and counting or touching rituals. An Obsessive-Compulsive Disorder may cause severe difficulties in children's lives, as they may feel embarrassed by their rituals or the need to follow rigid routines. In addition, many children experience problems in school because of concentration problems, preoccupations, or perfectionist tendencies (Wilmshurst, 2005). Prevalence estimates for an Obsessive-Compulsive Disorder in children have ranged from 1 percent to 4 percent (Evans et al., 2005; Wilmshurst, 2005). Co-occurring disorders include depression (Evans et al., 2005), behavior disorders (Geller et al., 2001). and Tic Disorders (Evans et al., 2005). A number of etiologies have been offered to explain an Obsessive-Compulsive Disorder, including genetics, neurotransmitters (i.e., low levels of serotonin), highly critical and overinvolved parents, and maladaptive thinking patterns (Wilmshurst, 2005). Treatment strategies to address an Obsessive-Compulsive Disorder in children include medication and cognitive-behavior therapy involving repeated exposure and response prevention (Evans et al., 2005).

Panic Disorder

A Panic Disorder consists of recurrent, unexpected Panic Attacks. Each attack is followed by a concern about having another attack, worry about the consequences of an attack, or change in behavior related to the attack. The concern, worry, or change in behavior lasts at least 1 month (American Psychiatric Association, 2000). These attacks consist of an extreme fear of imminent danger along with associated somatic symptoms such as heart palpitations, difficulty breathing, sweating, and choking (Evans et al., 2005). Cognitive symptoms include feelings of depersonalization, urge to leave the situation, and feelings of losing control or going crazy. To meet the diagnostic criteria for a Panic Attack, at least four somatic or cognitive symptoms must be present (Wilmshurst, 2005). Attacks have an acute onset and often last for approximately 10 minutes. This disorder is relatively rare in children before puberty. When a Panic Disorder follows a progressive pattern, it often develops in puberty with attacks becoming more frequent and often evolving into Agoraphobia (fear of public places) in adulthood. Community samples have reported lifetime prevalence rates as high as 3.5 percent, with onset typically occurring in later adolescence to early adulthood. Panic Disorders occur more frequently in females (Wilmshurst, 2005). This disorder is often comorbid with Agoraphobia, other Anxiety Disorders, and depression. The etiology of Panic Disorders suggests that genetics plays a role as well as the neurotransmitter norepinephrine. One treatment option is the use of antidepressant medication. Many antidepressant medications increase the level of norepinephrine in the brain. Another treatment option is the use of cognitive-behavioral techniques, with an emphasis on increasing coping skills, reevaluating cognitive appraisals, and systematic desensitization (Wilmshurst, 2005). Studies conducted using cognitive and cognitive-behavioral strategies appear promising (Evans et al., 2005).

Posttraumatic Stress Disorder

Posttraumatic Stress Disorder is a disorder in which an individual reexperiences a traumatic event along with a state of heightened physiological arousal and the avoidance of stimuli associated with the event. The traumatic event may involve the experience of a serious injury or witnessing a serious injury or a death. The response to the traumatic event consists of fear or helplessness and, in children, agitation or disorganized behavior. The symptoms must last for at least 1 month; if less than 1 month, an Acute Stress Disorder may be present. There must also be significant distress or impairment in social, school, or other important areas of functioning (American Psychiatric Association, 2000). Reexperiencing the trauma is another central characteristic and may manifest itself in several ways, including flashbacks, nightmares, or images (Evans et al., 2005). Young children may also reenact the trauma through play (Wilmshurst, 2005). High comorbidity rates with Social Anxiety Disorder, Disruptive Behavior Disorders, depression, and Panic Disorder have been reported (Evans et al., 2005). A common reaction to trauma in adolescents is to increase risk-taking behaviors, which can lead to additional stress (Wilmshurst, 2005). Community-based studies suggest that the lifetime prevalence rate for a Posttraumatic Stress Disorder is approximately 8 percent (American Psychiatric Association, 2000). Community violence is a variable that is strongly correlated with a Posttraumatic Stress Disorder, and there is a high rate of Posttraumatic Stress Disorder in those that have experienced Sexual Abuse (Wilmshurst, 2005). Factors which can influence a person's vulnerability for a Posttraumatic Stress Disorder include gender (i.e., being female), history of Physical or Sexual Abuse, exposure to violence, separation from parents before the age of 10, and existence of an Anxiety Disorder, Depressive Disorder, or another psychiatric disorder. Evidence indicates that stressful events can lead to physiological changes in the body. Abnormal levels of the neurotransmitter norepinephrine and increases in the hormone cortisol have been found in children with a Posttraumatic Stress Disorder as well as alternations in the hippocampus's ability to regulate stress hormones (Wilmshurst, 2005). Limited use of medication has been reported in the treatment of a Posttraumatic Stress Disorder in children (Evans et al., 2005). Studies conducted using cognitive-behavioral strategies have found significant increases in adaptive functioning and a decrease in Posttraumatic Stress Disorder symptoms in groups of children who have experienced Sexual Abuse, war, earthquakes, and exposure to community violence and crime (Evans et al., 2005).

School Phobia

School Phobia is generally described as frequent absences from school, which are not due to an actual illness or truancy. Several other terms such as *school avoidance* and *school refusal* have also been used to describe the same behavior (Paige, 1993). Common symptoms of a School Phobia are somatic complaints and excessive fears, although the fears do not have to be excessive in a child. The somatic complaints disappear once school has been avoided for the day (Paige, 1993). Research on the prevalence rate of School Phobia varies from 1.7 percent to 5 percent, with a similar prevalence rate for males and females (Paige, 1997). Typical age of onset for a School Phobia is between 6 and 10 years of age. Theories about the etiology of a School Phobia vary and include anxious mothers who want to keep their child at home, separation anxiety, school factors such as bullying, or the occurrence of a significant event such as an accident or a death. A School Phobia is maintained by the positive reinforcement and reduction of fear a child receives for staying home (Paige, 1993). Children with a School Phobia are also more likely to exhibit another Specific Phobia, Social Anxiety Disorder, Separation Anxiety Disorder, or depression (Paige, 1997). One of the key components of treatment of a School Phobia is that it must occur quickly before a pattern of school avoidance becomes ingrained and reinforced. Research indicates that behavioral techniques such as systematic desensitization, contingency management programs, and behavioral contracting have been successful in the treatment of a School Phobia. Medications which help children to relax or reduce depression might be helpful as an adjunct to a behavioral approach. A team approach involving parents and school personnel working together is recommended (Paige, 1993).

Separation Anxiety Disorder

Separation Anxiety Disorder involves unrealistic worry or anxiety that accompanies separation from home or a caretaker to such a degree that it interferes with appropriate behavior. The unrealistic worry or distress must be present for at least 4 weeks. A Separation Anxiety Disorder usually develops before adolescence, and is one of the earliest-occurring Anxiety Disorders (Evans et al., 2005). Children may experience nightmares involving the theme of separation as well as physical symptoms such as headaches, stomachaches, nausea, or vomiting. The excessive worry may stem from a child's fear of harm coming to the caregiver or fear of being separated from or losing the caregiver. Children with a Separation Anxiety Disorder may refuse to be separated from the caregiver, to be alone without the caregiver, or even to sleep separately from the caregiver (American Psychiatric Association, 2000). Children with a Separation Anxiety Disorder are often described by parents as being demanding and intrusive (Wilmshurst, 2005). A Separation Anxiety Disorder affects approximately 4 percent of the general population (Wilmshurst, 2005). Comorbid disorders found among children with a Separation Anxiety Disorder include a Generalized Anxiety Disorder, Specific Phobia, Social Anxiety, and possibly Panic Disorder (Evans et al., 2005). Many children with a Separation Anxiety Disorder also have a mother with a history of an Anxiety Disorder, suggesting either a genetic link or other familial factors, such as overprotectiveness, modeling of avoidant behavior, or reinforcement of the child's avoidant behavior. Other familial factors that play an important role are maternal depression and family dysfunction. In these situations, the child may be reluctant to leave the home for fear that he or she will not be able to care for or protect the primary caregiver (Wilmshurst, 2005). Finally, from a cognitive perspective, children with a Separation Anxiety Disorder may experience distorted, maladaptive, catastrophic, and ruminative thoughts, which lead them to misinterpret am-

biguous stimuli as threatening. Treatment of a Separation Anxiety Disorder includes cognitive-behavior techniques and behavioral strategies such as contingency management programs or behavioral contracts. Additionally, if familial factors are involved, it is often most effective to involve the entire family with the chosen intervention (Wilmshurst, 2005).

Specific Phobia

Specific Phobia is one of the earliest occurring Anxiety Disorders (Wilmshurst, 2005). Symptoms of a Specific Phobia include an extreme or irrational fear or anxiety that is associated with specific animals or insects, aspects of the natural environment (e.g., storms, heights, or water), blood (e.g., seeing an injury or receiving an injection), situations (e.g., crossing bridges or being in enclosed places), or other stimuli (e.g., loud sounds or costumed characters). This fear causes extreme distress and significant impairment in normal functioning and may be expressed in children by crying, tantrumming, freezing, clinging, or experiencing physiological reactions such as dizziness, shortness of breath, increased heart rate, and fainting (American Psychological Association, 2000; Wilmshurst, 2005). Children may often feel a strong desire to escape from or avoid the fear-inducing object or situation, which may result in even more intense feelings of anxiety and panic when they are unable to escape or avoid the feared object or situation. Prevalence rates for a Specific Phobia among children are estimated to be around 15 percent (Silverman & Nelles, 2001). Comorbid conditions associated with a Specific Phobia include another phobia, Depressive Disorder, Generalized Anxiety Disorder, Separation Anxiety Disorder, and Social Anxiety Disorder (Evans et al., 2005; Wilmshurst, 2005). The development of a Specific Phobia is best understood as an interaction between the child's temperament, characteristics of the child's family, and the child's exposure to traumatic or frightening experiences. Most commonly, a Specific Phobia is linked to conditioning experiences, wherein a child develops anxious or fearful reactions in response to a frightening or stressful experience (i.e., classical conditioning). Other theories suggest that a Specific Phobia may result from family characteristics. For example, children may learn to react in certain ways by observing a parent's fearful behavior (Wilmshurst, 2005). Behavioral and cognitive-behavioral techniques such as participant modeling, reinforced practice, systematic desensitization, and self-instructional training have been suggested as useful techniques in the treatment of a Specific Phobia in children (Ollendick & King, 1998).

Social Anxiety Disorder

Social Anxiety Disorder, also known as *Social Phobia*, is characterized by an extreme worry over ridicule, humiliation, or embarrassment in social situations, which may include speaking in class, talking to authority figures, conversing with peers, eating, drinking, or writing in public (American Psychiatric Association, 2000). Children with a Social Anxiety Disorder tend to respond to social or performance situations with avoidant or escape behavior and increased physiological arousal (Wilmshurst, 2005). These individuals often have poor social skills. A Social Anxiety Disorder usually develops during adolescence (American Psychiatric Association, 2000). Prevalence estimates of 1 to 2 percent have been reported for children with a Social Anxiety Disorder (Wilmshurst, 2005). Children with a Social Anxiety Disorder are at an increased risk for depression, Substance Abuse, Specific Phobia, Separation Anxiety Disorder (Evans et al., 2005), and Generalized Anxiety Disorder (Wilmshurst, 2005). A Social Anxiety Disorder is strongly linked with children's temperament styles (Biederman et al., 1993). Biederman and colleagues found that children with behavioral inhibition were at an increased risk for a Social Anxiety Disorder. Children who are at a higher risk of developing a Social Anxiety Disorder are more likely to have a first-degree biological relative with the disorder, suggesting a genetic component (American Psychiatric Association, 2000). Treatment for a Social Anxiety Disorder includes social skills training (Wilmshurst, 2005), cognitive-behavior therapy, family therapy, and medication (Evans et al., 2005).

Anxiety Disorders are chronic and debilitating conditions that impact a large number of children with mental health disorders. The costs associated with Anxiety Disorders are exorbitant to the child, family, and society. After 2 decades of research, medication, cognitive-behavior therapy (CBT), and a combination of the two strategies have been shown to be effective in treating most Anxiety Disorders in children (Evans et al., 2005). However, it is unclear at the present time whether the combination of CBT and medication is more effective in treating Anxiety Disorders in children than either treatment alone (Evans et al., 2005). Empirically supported treatments (ESTs) are available to treat Anxiety Disorders. Empirically supported treatments consist of education, cognitive restructuring, relaxation training, and exposure. Future research is still needed to identify the most essential components of these multitreatment packages.

REFERENCES

American Psychiatric Association. (2000). *Diagnostic and statistical manual of mental disorders* (4th ed., text revision). Washington, DC: Author.

Beidel, D. C., Turner, S. M., & Morris, T. L. (2000). Behavioral treatment of childhood Social Phobia. *Journal of Consulting and Clinical Psychology, 68,* 1072–1080.

Biederman, J., Rosenbaum, J. F., Boldue-Murphy, E. A., Faraone, S. V., Chaloff, J., Hirshfeld, D. R., & Kagan, J. (1993). A 3-year follow-up of children with and without behavioral inhibition. *Journal of the American Academy of Child and Adolescent Psychiatry, 32,* 814–821.

Caster, J. B., Inderbitzen, H. M., & Hope, D. (1999). Relationship between youth and parent perceptions of family environment and social anxiety. *Journal of Anxiety Disorders, 13,* 237–251.

Cohen, J. (1999). *Educating the minds and hearts: Social emotional learning and the passage into adolescence.* New York: Teachers College Press.

Costello, E. J., Egger, H. L., & Angold, A. (2004). The developmental epidemiology of Anxiety Disorders. In T. Ollendick & J. March (Eds.), *Phobic and Anxiety Disorders in children and adolescents* (pp. 61–91). New York: Oxford University Press.

Costello, E. J., Mustillo, S., Erkanli, A., Keeler, G., & Angold, A. (2003). Prevalence and development of psychiatric disorders in childhood and adolescence. *Archives of General Psychiatry, 60,* 837–844.

Eley, T. C. (1999). Behavioral genetics as a tool for developmental psychology: Anxiety and depression in children and adolescents. *Clinical Child and Family Psychology Review, 2,* 21–36.

Essex, M. J., Klein, M. H., Cho, E., & Kalin, N. H. (2002). Maternal stress beginning in infancy may sensitize children to later stress exposure: Effects on cortisol and behavior. *Biological Psychiatry, 52,* 776–784.

Evans, D. L., Foa, E. B., Gur, R. E., Hendin, H., O'Brien, C. P., Seligman, M. E. P., et al. (2005). *Treatment and preventing adolescent mental health disorders: What we know and what we don't know.* New York: Oxford Press.

Freud, S. (1924). *Collected papers* (Vol. 1). London: Hogarth Press.

Geller, D. A., Biederman, J., Farapme, S., Agranat, A., Cradlock, K., Hagermoser, L., et al. (2001). Disentangling chronological age from age of onset in children and adolescents with Obsessive-Compulsive Disorder. *International Journal of Neuropsychopharmacology, 4,* 69–178.

Gorman, J. M., & Sloan, R. P. (2000). Heart rate variability in Depressive and Anxiety Disorders. *American Heart Journal, 140,* 77–83.

Greenberg, P. E., Sisitsky, T., Kessler, R. C., Finkelstein, S. N., Berndt, E. R., Davidson, J. R. T., et al. (1999). The economic burden of Anxiety Disorders in the 1990s. *Journal of Clinical Psychiatry, 60,* 427–235.

Huberty, T. J. (1997). Anxiety. In G. Bear, K. Minke, & A. Thomas (Eds.), *Children's needs II: Development, problems and alternatives* (pp. 305–314). Bethesda, MD: National Association of School Psychologists.

Ialongo, N., Edelsohn, G., Werthamer-Larsson, L., Crockett, L., & Kellam, S. (1994). The significance of self-reported anxious symptoms in first grade children. *Journal of Abnormal Child Psychology, 22,* 441–455.

Ialongo, N., Edelsohn, G., Werthamer-Larsson, L., Crockett, L., & Kellam, S. (1995). The significance of self-reported symptoms in the first grade children: Prediction to anxious symptoms and adaptive functioning in fifth grade. *Journal of Child Psychology Psychiatry, 36,* 427–437.

Individuals with Disabilities Education Improvement Act of 2004 (Public Law 108-446). (2004). *Federal Register, 70*(118). Retrieved June 28, 2005, from http://www.ed.gov/policy/speced/guid/idea/idea2004.html

Kagan, J., Snidman, N., McManis, M., & Woodward, S. (2001). Temperamental contributions to the affect family of anxiety. *Psychiatric Clinics of North America, 24,* 677–688.

Keller, M. B., Lavori, P. W., Wunder, J., Beardslee, W. R., Schwartz, C. E., & Roth, J. (1992). Chronic course of Anxiety Disorders in children and adolescents. *Journal of the American Academy of Child and Adolescent Psychiatry, 31,* 595–599.

Merrell, K. W. (2001). *Helping students overcome depression and anxiety: A practical guide.* New York: Guilford.

Ollendick, T. J., & King, N. J. (1991). Origins of childhood fears: An evaluation of Rachman's theory of fear acquisition. *Behaviour Research and Therapy, 29,* 117–123.

Ollendick, T. J., & King, N. J. (1994). Diagnosis, assessment, and treatment of internalizing problems in children. *Journal of Consulting and Clinical Psychology, 6,* 918–927.

Ollendick, T. J., & King, N. J. (1998). Empirically supported treatment for children with Phobic and Anxiety Disorders: Current status. *Journal of Clinical Child Psychology, 27,* 156–167.

Paige, L. Z. (1993). *The identification and treatment of School Phobia.* Silver Spring, MD: National Association of School Psychologists.

Paige, L. Z. (1997). School Phobia, school refusal, and school avoidance. In G. G. Bear, K. M. Minke, & A. Thomas (Eds.), *Children's needs II: Development, problems and alternatives* (pp. 339–347). Bethesda, MD: National Association of School Psychologists.

Saavedra, L. M., & Silverman, W. K. (2002). Classification of Anxiety Disorders in children: What a difference two decades make. *International Review of Psychiatry, 14,* 87–101.

Safren, S. A., Gonzalez, R. E., Horner, K. J., Leung, A. W., Heimberg, R. G., & Juster, H. R. (2000). Anxiety in ethnic minority youth: Methodological and conceptual issues and review of the literature. *Behavior Modification, 24*(2), 147–183.

Silverman, W. K., & Kurtines, W. M. (2001). Anxiety Disorders. In J. N. Hughes, A. M. LaGreca, & J. C. Conoley (Eds.), *Handbook of psychological services for children and adolescents* (pp. 225–244). New York: Oxford University Press.

Silverman, W. K., & Nelles, W. B. (2001). The influence of gender on children's ratings of fear and self and same-aged peers. *The Journal of Genetic Psychology, 148,* 17–21.

Spielberger, C. D., & Rickman, R. L. (1990). Assessment of state and trait anxiety. In N. Sartorius, V. Andreoli, G. Cassano, L. Eisenberg, P. Kielholz, P. Pancheri, et al. (Eds.), *Anxiety: Psychobiological and clinical perspectives* (pp. 69–83). New York: Hemisphere.

Telch, M. J., Smits, J. A., Brown, M., & Beckner, V. (2002). Treatment of Anxiety Disorders: Implications for medical cost offset. In N. Cummings, W. T. O'Donohue, K. E. Ferguson (Eds.), *The impact of medical cost offset on practice and research: Making it work for you* (pp. 167–200). Reno, NV: Context Press.

Vasey, M. W., & Ollendick, T. H. (2000). Anxiety. In A. J. Sameroff, M. Lewis, & S. M. Miller (Eds.), *Handbook of developmental psychopathology* (2nd ed., pp. 511–529). New York: Kluwer Academic/Plenum Press.

Watson, D., & Clark, L. A. (1984). Negative affectivity: The disposition to experience aversive emotional states. *Psychological Bulletin, 96*(3), 465–490.

Wilmshurst, L. (2005). *Essentials of child psychopathology.* New York: Wiley.

Woodward, L. J., & Fergusson, D. A. (2001). Life course outcomes of young people with Anxiety Disorders in adolescence. *Journal of the American Academy of Child and Adolescent Psychiatry, 40,* 1086–1093.

PATRICIA A. LOWE
JENNIFER M. RAAD
JACQUELINE S. SCHON
University of Kansas

APGAR RATING SCALE

The Apgar Rating Scale was specifically designed to assess medical distress in newborns. Ratings are made by attending nurses or physicians at 1 minute after birth, with possible further ratings at 3, 5, and 10 minutes. Five vital signs, heart rate, respiratory effort, reflex irritability, muscle tone, and color, are rated on a 3-point scale: 2 if present, 1 if not fully present, and 0 if absent. Thus the range of possible scores is 0–10, with scores greater than 7 (about 70 percent of all newborns) indicating excellent condition, 3–7 (24 percent of all newborns) indicating a moderately depressed condition, and less than 3 (6 percent of all newborns) indicating a severely depressed condition (Apgar, 1953; Apgar, Holaday, James, & Weisbrott, 1958; NCEMI, 2005).

The Apgar Scale has been used extensively in research in anesthesiology, obstetrics, pediatric neurology, and developmental psychology. Apgar scores are predictive of infant mortality: 15 percent of neonates with severely depressed scores die within 7 months, compared with 0.13 percent of those receiving scores of 10 (Apgar et al., 1958). There is also a moderate relationship between Apgar scores and intellectual and motor development: Edwards (1968), for example, found an Apgar correlation of 0.251 with Stanford-Binet IQ, 0.456 with a battery of fine-motor tasks, and 0.480 with gross-motor tasks at age 4. The 5-minute postnatal Apgar scores were more predictive than 1-minute scores in Edwards' study.

REFERENCES

Apgar, V. (1953). A proposal for a new method of evaluation of the newborn infant. *Current Researches in Anesthesia and Analgesia, 32,* 260–267.

Apgar, V., Holaday, D., James, L., Weisbrott, I., & Berrien, C. (1958). Evaluation of the newborn infant—second report. *Journal of the American Medical Association, 168,* 1985–1988.

Edwards, N. (1968). The relationship between physical condition immediately after birth and mental and motor performance at age four. *Genetic Psychology Monographs, 78,* 257–289.

NCEMI. (2005). *National Center for Emergency Medicine Apgar Score.* Retrieved June 19, 2005, from http://www.ncemi.org

JOHN MACDONALD
Eastern Kentucky University

LOW BIRTH WEIGHT INFANTS
NEONATAL BEHAVIORAL ASSESSMENT SCALE
PREMATURITY/PRETERM

APHASIA

Everyone with the diagnosis of aphasia has an acquired language disorder, but the type of language disorder (problems understanding talking, problems talking, problems reading, problems writing) and the severity of these difficulties vary, reflecting the different locations and the extent of the damage to the brain. For most people, damage to the left side (hemisphere) is responsible for the aphasia. Aphasia usually has a sudden onset such as a result from a brain injury or stroke, but some individuals have a slower onset as with the development of a brain tumor (NIDCD, 2005).

There also are similarities in the type of problems using language among persons whose brains have been damaged in the same location. Aphasiologists are persons who study aphasia and attempt to provide a structure for understanding and diagnosing this language disorder upon the basis of these variations and similarities. As a result of their studies, there are many different definitions of aphasia and many different classification systems offering a means of subdividing aphasia (Chapey, 1994; Davis, 1993).

Literature within the last decade reflects a general agreement on the following: The term aphasia (acquired language disorder due to brain damage) applies to persons who formerly had intact, developed language functioning and, therefore, the term aphasia does not apply to language disorders experienced by children (Davis, 1993). Some aphasiologists (Darley, 1982; Schuell, 1972) set forth arguments against subdividing or classifying aphasia according to differences or similarities of symptoms. In the opinion of these experts, the variations in symptoms reflect degrees of problems in the total, integrated brain function.

However, if classification is considered, one common basis is nonfluent versus fluent. In this case, separation is made on the basis of whether the symptoms of a person's language disorder result in a disruption of fluency (Hegde, 1994). Rosenbek, Wertz, and LaPointe (1989) define being fluent as producing five or more connected words. Obviously, persons who have aphasia and who cannot produce five or more connected words have nonfluent aphasia. Further common subdivision types within nonfluent aphasia include Broca's, global, isolation, and transcortical motor. Subdivisions of fluent aphasia include Wernicke's transcortical sensory and conduction.

Other common perspectives seen in the literature for defining symptoms of aphasia are those in terms of cognitive impairments (Chapey, 1981; Davis, 1993) and linguistic analysis of the disordered language (Jakobsen, 1971; Caplan, 1991). Cognitive definitions of aphasia are based on the idea that cognition underlies language and that if language is impaired, some aspects of cognition also must be impaired. Descriptions of symptoms are reported as impairments in long- and short-term memory for words, phrases, and sentences and as impairments in processing linguistic information (Hegde, 1994). Research done from the linguistic point of view is called "neurolinguistic," and it analyzes the symptoms from a perspective of whether a patient shows difficulties in linguistic units if they are shorter or longer, simple or complex, active or passive, embedded or unembedded, and so forth (Hegde, 1994).

The types of language disorders encountered by persons with aphasia include difficulties in comprehending spoken language (for example, the patient cannot point to a picture or object named, or the person may not know the meaning of ordinary words) and difficulties in talking (the patient may substitute sounds or words and create new words that do not mean anything to the listener, or the person may omit sounds within words or whole words). Persons with aphasia may struggle to get out any words and speak very little, or they may talk a great deal with ease, but the words and grammar do not have meaning for the listener. Persons with aphasia may also experience difficulties in reading or writing and doing number calculations (Hegde, 1994). In addition, there are often many related disorders that occur from the damage to the overall neurological network, such as motor speech problems or paresis of the oral structure and/or arm and leg.

Over one million people in the United States suffer from aphasia and each day almost 300 new cases occur. Rehabilitation requires commitment and support from professionals and family. In an effort to provide a better understanding of this disorder, a national organization, the National Aphasia Association has been formed (LaPointe, 1997). This organization can be reached at 29 John Street, Suite 1103 New York, NY 10038. Telephone: (800) 922-4622, e-mail: naa@aphasia.org, Internet: www.aphasia.org

REFERENCES

Caplan, D. (1991). Agrammatism is a theoretically coherent aphasic category. *Brain and Language, 40,* 274–281.

Chapey, R. (1981). Assessment of language disorders in adults. In R. Chapey (Ed.), *Language intervention strategies in adult aphasia* (pp. 31–84). Baltimore: Williams & Wilkins.

Chapey, R. (1994). *Language intervention strategies in adult aphasia* (3rd ed.). Baltimore: Williams & Wilkins.

Darley, F. (1982). *Aphasia.* Philadelphia: W. B. Saunders.

Davis, G. (1993). *A survey of adult aphasia and related language disorders* (2nd ed.). Englewood Cliffs, NJ: Prentice Hall.

Hegde, M. (1994). *A coursebook on aphasia and other neurogenic language disorders.* San Diego: Singular.

Jakobsen, R. (1971). Two aspects of language and two types of aphasic disturbances. In R. Jakobson & M. Halle (Eds.), *Fundamentals of language* (2nd ed.). The Hague, Netherlands: Mouton.

LaPointe, L. (1997). *Aphasia and related neurogenic language disorders* (2nd ed.). New York: Thieme.

National Institute on Deafness and Other Communication Disorders (NIDCD). (2005). *Aphasia.* Retrieved June 19, 2005, from http://www.nidcd.nih.gov/health/voice/aphasia.asp

Rosenbek, J., LaPointe, L., & Wertz, R. (1989). *Aphasia: A clinical approach.* Austin, TX: PRO-ED.

Schuell, H. (1972). *The Minnesota Test of Differential Diagnosis of Aphasia.* Minneapolis: University of Minnesota Press.

SHEELA STUART
George Washington University

CHILDHOOD APHASIA
DEVELOPMENTAL APHASIA
LANGUAGE DISORDERS

APHASIA, DEVELOPMENTAL

See CHILDHOOD APHASIA; LANGUAGE DISORDERS.

APNEA, INFANTILE

Apnea is defined as a lack of respiration for a period of 20 to 30 seconds with or without an accompanied decrease in heart rate to ≤80 beats per minute with resultant cyanosis. Twenty-five percent of infants in premature nurseries, but only a small percentage of full-term infants, exhibit apnea (Nemours Foundation, 2005). Apnea, therefore, appears in most cases to stem from actual immaturity of the neural mechanism responsible for regulation of respiration. When immature, this mechanism is vulnerable to metabolic disturbances in calcium and blood-sugar levels, changes in body temperature, or disturbances in brain-wave patterns that occur during seizures or normal REM (rapid eye movement) sleep. The association between apnea and sleep is significant because premature sleep up to 80 percent of the time and REM sleep are the predominant sleep states of these infants (Parry, Baldy, & Gardner, 1985). Apnea is less frequently caused by actual obstruction of the airway itself either from excessive mucus or improper body positioning, as premature infants have very flexible tracheas.

Apnea owed to immaturity or genetic influences appears to be a possible cause of sudden infant death syndrome (SIDS). The fact that SIDS occurs most frequently in children less than 1 year of age supports this theory. Treatment focuses on prevention and involves general measures to promote adequate respiration until the infant "outgrows" the condition. Correction of existing chemical imbalances may be all that is required. Theophylline, a respiratory stimulant drug, decreases apnea and is widely used. Most infants reinstitute breathing with gentle tactile stimulation such as stroking or jostling, but at times they require manual ventilation to prevent prolonged anoxia and to restore breathing. Occasionally apnea becomes so severe that the child has to be temporarily placed on a respirator (Volpe & Koenigsberger, 1981). Generally, the heart and respiratory rates of premature infants should be closely monitored for signs of apnea. A home monitor may be necessary for infants with persistent apnea. Full-term infants who are at high risk for SIDS should also be monitored for apnea (Spitzer & Fox, 1984).

Prognosis is generally good for infants who do not experience prolonged apnea and who are otherwise healthy. It becomes less favorable with increased frequency and duration of apneic episodes (Parry et al., 1984). However, at least one study suggests that infantile apnea may be associated with deficiencies in later gross motor, and perhaps some cognitive, functions and behavior (Deykin, Bauman, Kelly, Hsieh, & Shannon, 1984). Since apnea produces transient hypoxia, it can, when extensive, cause many of the problems associated with that disorder.

Patients and family members may find assistance with the American Sleep Apnea Association located at 1424 K Street NW, Suite 302, Washington, DC 20005. Telephone: (202) 293-3650, Internet: www.sleepapnea.org

REFERENCES

Deykin, E., Bauman, M., Kelly, D., Hsieh, C., & Shannon, D. (1984). Apnea of infancy and subsequent neurologic, cognitive and behavioral status. *Pediatrics, 73,* 638–645.

Nemours Foundation. (2005). *Apnea of prematurity.* Retrieved June 19, 2005, from http://www.nemours.org

Parry, W., Baldy, M., & Gardner, S. (1985). Respiratory diseases. In G. B. Merenstein, & S. L. Gardner (Eds.), *Handbook of neonatal intensive care.* St. Louis, MO: Mosby.

Spitzer, A., & Fox, W. (1984). Infant apnea, an approach to management. *Clinical Pediatrics, 23,* 374–380.

Volpe, J., & Koenigsberger, R. (1981). Neurologic disorders. In G. B. Avery (Ed.), *Neonatology: Pathophysiology and management of the newborn* (2nd ed., pp. 920–923). Philadelphia: Lippincott.

BRENDA M. POPE
*New Hanover Memorial
Hospital*

ANOXIA
INFANT STIMULATION

APPLIED BEHAVIOR ANALYSIS

Applied behavior analysis is an approach for changing behavior that involves the systematic application of a set of principles derived from psychological theories of learning. Applied behavior analysis has been demonstrated to be a highly effective management system in both school (Alberto & Troutman, 1982; Martens et al., 1999) and home situations (Becker, 1971). Its principles have been successfully applied to a wide range of children's problems, including academic problems such as reading, handwriting, and task completion, and social and behavioral problems such as aggression, shyness, and school avoidance.

Applied behavior analysis and behavior modification are closely related terms. Both involve the application of principles of learning to the changing of behavior. Technically, behavior modification is the broader term, including behavior change strategies that are not based on learning principles (e.g., chemotherapy, the use of physical restraints, and brain surgery). Behavior modification in schools has become synonymous with reinforcement programs derived from operant conditioning principles. Operant conditioning procedures change behavior through changing the events that follow behaviors (i.e., consequences of behavior). Applied behavior analysis applies principles derived from operant conditioning, social learning theory, and respondent conditioning. The applied behavior analyst assesses and treats behavior in terms of both consequences and antecedents (i.e., events that precede behavior). These antecedent events may be environmental events or cognitive events (i.e., thoughts, attitudes, or perceptions) that are thought to influence behavior.

The principles of learning that are applied to problem behaviors include positive reinforcement, negative reinforcement, shaping, prompting, fading, extinction, punishment, modeling, discrimination learning, task analysis, and self-instructional talk. Most of these terms are described in more detail in separate entries in this encyclopedia but they are summarized here. Then the steps in behavior analysis are outlined. Finally, applied behavior analysis is illustrated with a case study.

Positive reinforcement involves presenting a reward to a child after the child performs a specific desired behavior. If that behavior occurs more frequently after the reward, positive reinforcement has occurred. A reinforcer, or reward, is defined in terms of its effect on the behavior it follows. If something (a stimulus) follows a specific behavior and the rate of that behavior increases, that stimulus is a reinforcer. There are no universal reinforcers; children can react differently to such potential reinforcers as adult praise and bubble gum. Allowing a child 5 extra minutes of free time when he or she completes an arithmetic assignment with 80 percent accuracy is an example of positive reinforcement. It is important that the positive reinforcer be contingent on the specific desired behavior. If the behavior occurs, then the reinforcer is given. If the behavior does not occur, or does not occur at the specified frequency, then the reinforcer is not given. Sometimes teachers and parents will inadvertently follow an undesired behavior with a positive reinforcer. For example, when a child gets out of his or her seat, the teacher calls out that child's name. If the out-of-seat behavior occurs

more frequently, the teacher calling out the child's name is a reinforcer. When reinforcement is used, the reinforcement can follow every appropriate behavior (continuous reinforcement schedule) or only a portion of the appropriate behaviors (intermittent reinforcement). Continuous reinforcement results in a quick increase in the rate of the reinforced behavior, and intermittent reinforcement results in maintenance of the behavior change when the behavior is no longer being reinforced.

When a behavior that has been followed by a reinforcer in the past no longer is reinforced, *extinction* has occurred. Often the immediate result of extinction is a temporary increase in the previously reinforced behavior. If a teacher who has attended to a child's temper tantrums begins to ignore the temper tantrums, the child is likely to increase the frequency and duration of tantrum behavior; however, if the teacher continues to ignore the tantrums (and there are no other reinforcers that follow the tantrums, like peer attention), the tantrums should decrease in frequency.

Negative reinforcement, like *positive reinforcement,* is a procedure for increasing the rate of a desired behavior. In negative reinforcement, some unpleasant event (stimulus) is terminated following the desired behavior. For example, a teacher tells students that children who complete their assignments at 85 percent accuracy will be relieved of their homework assignment.

Punishment is a process in which the consequences of a behavior reduce the future rate of that behavior. There are three types of punishment procedures. In the application of an unpleasant consequence, a behavior is followed by some unpleasant stimulus, such as extra work, a verbal reprimand, or physical punishment. In response cost, a teacher removes a reinforcer contingent on a specified behavior. Children may lose 3 minutes of recess each time they receive a check next to their names on the board. In *time out,* the child is denied the opportunity to participate in positive reinforcement for a specified period of time, contingent on a specified undesired behavior. Requiring a child to sit on a bench at recess when playing roughly or to sit on a mat during art are examples of time out.

When a child has learned to say "red" only to colors in the red spectrum, the response of saying "red" is under the *stimulus control* of the color red. This control is established by reinforcing the correct response and/or punishing the incorrect response. The reinforcer may be praise or a star. The punisher may be "no" or an X on the paper. When the child learns to respond differently to red and not red, this shows *discrimination learning.* The child who goes to the cookie box when Mother is occupied on the telephone has also mastered a discrimination learning task. Going to the cookie box is reinforced with a cookie when Mother is on the phone. When Mother is not on the phone, she either prevents the child from getting a cookie or reprimands the child.

Shaping involves reinforcing improvement in behavior. For example, a child may work only three math problems during a 30-minute period. The teacher would like the child to work 15 problems. (It is assumed the teacher has determined that the problems are at the appropriate level of difficulty for the child.) If reinforcement were contingent on the child working 15 problems, reinforcement would not occur. The teacher establishes a series of steps between the current level of performance and the goal behavior and applies differential reinforcement at each step. Only if the child performs the behavior at or above the behavioral criterion at the operative step in the hierarchy does the child receive the reinforcer. When the child is consistently successful at one step, the next step is operative, and the child's behavior must meet or exceed the criterion for reinforcement at that step. A related procedure is *task analysis,* which involves specifying the prerequisite behaviors to successful performance of a given behavior. Many instructional tasks are composed of several smaller steps that occur in a specific order. Often the difficulty of the task is the reason a child is having difficulty mastering the task. A *skill hierarchy* breaks a complex skill, such as two-digit multiplication, into sequential steps in which each step is a prerequisite for the next higher step in the hierarchy. Skill hierarchies exist in all areas of human learning, including reading, penmanship, dressing, and eating. Task analysis is a useful tool for selecting what skill to teach. Shaping procedures involve the application of reinforcement and extinction to teaching the selected skill.

Prompting involves the use of additional cues to increase the probability the child will respond appropriately to the discriminative stimulus. These extra cues increase the saliency of the discriminative stimuli and are phased out as soon as the behavior is under control of the discriminative stimulus. Prompts may be visual, verbal, or physical. The first-grade teacher who places pictures with letters of the alphabet is using visual prompts to increase the probability that the child will make the correct letter-sound association. The phasing out of prompts involves gradually decreasing the saliency of the prompt.

Modeling involves having a teacher or peer demonstrate the desired behavior to a child. Models can be live or filmed. When models are present at the time the child imitates the modeled behavior, the model serves as a special type of visual prompt. The effects of modeling extend beyond the direct and immediate imitation of specific behaviors. Children can learn complex sequences of behavior (e.g., participating in a game or ordering a meal in a restaurant) through observation. Furthermore, modeling effects do not depend on the child or the model receiving reinforcement for the imitated behaviors. An impulsive child who is paired with a more reflective child to work on puzzles and games may later adopt a more reflective problem-solving approach.

In recent years behavior analysts have attempted to modify cognitions (i.e., thoughts, attitudes, and perceptions) that are thought to influence overt behavior (Meyers & Craighead, 1985). For example, an impulsive child may be instructed to imitate a model who talks out loud while solving a problem. The model provides the child with an example of helpful *self-instructional talk* (Hughes, 1999; Meichenbaum & Goodman, 1971).

Steps in Behavior Analysis

In applying the preceding principles, the behavior analyst follows a six step process.

1. Identify the target behaviors. Rather than being satisfied with the problem definition "Lucy is lazy," the analyst states the behavior in specific, observable, behavioral terms. Lazy does not tell us what Lucy does or does not do, and two people might have different ideas about what lazy means. Is Lucy daydreaming or is she turning in messy work? Unless the target behaviors are defined specifically and behaviorally, the existing antecedents and consequences of the behavior cannot be determined, and reinforcement and punishment cannot be administered consistently.

Once the problem, or undesired behavior, is stated in behavioral terms, the desired replacement behavior is stated. If the problem behavior is daydreaming, the desired behavior might be working on the task. The replacement behavior is incompatible with the undesired behavior. That is, Lucy cannot be daydreaming and working on the task at the same time.

2. Count the target behaviors. Since the undesired and replacement behaviors are incompatible, only one needs to be counted. Counting behaviors is necessary to evaluate the effectiveness of the behavior change intervention. This preintervention count is referred to as the baseline. It is preferable to count the target behavior continuously from the baseline until the intervention has been in effect for long enough to determine its effectiveness. A follow-up count following the intervention determines the durability of the behavior change. There are several different ways to count behavior. In a frequency count, each incidence of the target behavior is counted or tallied. The count may occur during a part of the day only. Frequency counts are appropriate for discrete behaviors that either occur infrequently (e.g., hitting) or for a short duration (e.g., calling out answers in class). In a duration count, the percentage of time that a behavior occurs is estimated. Duration counts are best suited for behaviors that occur infrequently and have a duration of more than a few seconds. Owing to the difficulty of actually timing the amount of time a child is engaged in a behavior such as being off-task, a time sampling procedure is usually used to estimate the percentage of time the behavior occurs. The teacher may set a timer to go off at five randomly set intervals during a 30-minute work period or record whether the child was on-task or off-task each time the timer rang. If the child was on task at four out of five rings, the teacher estimates that the child was on task 80 percent of the time.

The results of the count are charted on a graph similar to the one in the following figure.

3. Assess the antecedents and consequences of both the desired and undesired behaviors. The purpose of this step is to determine the consequences and antecedents that may be maintaining the undesired behavior and to identify possible reinforcers for increasing the desired behavior and conditions under which the desired behavior is more likely to occur. The analyst determines what happens after the child engages in the undesirable behavior. How does the teacher respond? What is the reaction of peers? What is the effect of the undesirable behavior on the child's assignment? The analyst determines the conditions under which the undesired behavior is most likely to occur (antecedents). Are there certain task characteristics (i.e., presentation of materials, subject matter, amount of structure, length or difficulty of the assignment, response requirements), setting characteristics (i.e., independent seatwork, group discussion, certain persons nearby), or other conditions (i.e., time of day, medication levels) that are associated with the undesired behavior? The same investigation of consequences and antecedents surrounding the desired behavior is accomplished at this step. This assessment of antecedent and consequent events may uncover unintended reinforcers that are contingent on the undesired behavior (e.g., the child gets the play materials when pushing a peer, the teacher attends to whining behavior, or the child avoids the task by turning in incomplete work) as well as insufficient reinforcers or even punishers following the desired behavior (e.g., the child gets extra work after completing in-class assignments or the child receives no positive peer attention when he or she asks politely to play).

4. Based on the analysis at step 3, create a plan for changing antecedent and consequent events to result in an increase in the desired behavior and a decrease in the undesired behavior. Any of the learning principles previously discussed may be applied at this step. Prompts may be added, reinforcement and punishment contingencies changed, shaping and extinction procedures implemented.

5. Implement the planned intervention. During implementation, counting of the target behaviors continues.

6. Evaluate the effectiveness of the intervention. Using the data obtained from the counting to compare the baseline performance with performance during the intervention, the intervention may be continued as is, modified, or terminated. If the intervention is having the desired outcome, the analyst will want to plan to gradually withdraw teacher-administered reinforcers (going from continuous to intermittent schedules), gradually phase out prompts, and select the next most important target behavior to improve or increase the difficulty of the reinforced behavior. To increase the probability the desired behavior will generalize to other settings, the intervention may be applied in different settings. If the intervention is not having the desired outcome, the analyst

will reexamine hypotheses created at stage 3, resulting in a modified intervention plan at stages 4 and 5.

Illustrative case study. The hypothetical case of Andy illustrates the six steps of behavior analysis. Andy, a seven-year-old second grader, was aggressive on the playground, and his teacher asked the consultant for assistance in reducing Andy's aggressiveness.

1. Identify the target behaviors. The consultant helped the teacher state the problem behavior in behavioral terms by asking questions like "What would Andy be doing if I saw him act aggressively?" The specific undesired behaviors were hitting, pushing, grabbing, kicking, and threatening to hurt a child. Using questions like, "What would you like Andy to do instead of hitting, grabbing, etc.?", the consultant helped the teacher define the desired behavior as participating nonaggressively.

2. Count the target behaviors. Because Andy's aggressive behavior tended to occur during outdoor play, the counting occurred during outdoor play. Because the aggressive behaviors occurred frequently and did not last over time, a frequency count was used. Aggressive behaviors were counted for five consecutive days to obtain a baseline (Figure 1).

3. Assess antecedents and consequences. Informal and formal observations of Andy indicated that aggressive behaviors were associated with the following antecedent events: unstructured play and teacher far away. Andy was more likely to participate when play was structured and the teacher was nearby. When Andy was aggressive, the following consequences were likely to occur: the teacher talked with him, he was sent to the principal's office (about one-third of the time), and he got to play with the equipment of his choice (the children he bullied gave in to him). When Andy participated without being aggressive, he received no teacher or principal attention and the other children rejected him.

4. As a result of the assessment at step 3, the following plan was selected. Andy was encouraged to play more

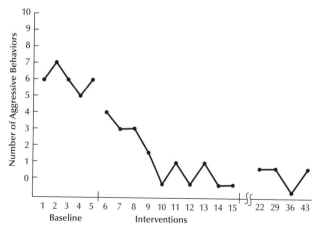

Figure 1 Frequency of aggressive behavior during approximately 30 minutes of outdoor play

structured games and the teacher stayed close to Andy during outdoor play. When Andy behaved aggressively, he was given one warning signal, a whistle. If he continued to play aggressively, he was given a second signal to go sit on a bench for 5 minutes. He received no verbal attention from the teacher or principal when he played aggressively. When Andy participated nonaggressively, he earned the privilege of being equipment monitor, responsible for bringing and returning all playground equipment. The teacher and principal praised Andy for participating nonaggressively, and his classmates were primed to react positively to Andy by the promise of a group reward, contingent on Andy's meeting the weekly goal for playing nonaggressively. The group reward was 10 extra minutes of recess time.

5. Implement the planned intervention. The intervention plan was explained to Andy and to the class before it was implemented.

6. Evaluate the effectiveness of the intervention. Figure 1 shows the results of the frequency count of aggressive behaviors during baseline and intervention. Owing to the decrease in aggressive behaviors, the plan was continued for 2 weeks. After the 2 weeks, the teacher gradually introduced less structure, supervised play less closely, and offered praise less frequently. The teacher counted the aggressive behaviors again on four occasions after the initial intervention was terminated. Based on results at these follow-up counts, the teacher removed the group contingency (day 22) and Andy was only occasionally permitted to be equipment monitor (day 26).

REFERENCES

Alberto, P. A., & Troutman, A. C. (1982). *Applied behavior analysis for teachers.* Columbus, OH: Merrill.

Becker, W. C. (1971). *Parents are teachers.* Champaign, IL: Research Press.

Hughes, J. N. (1999). *Child psychotherapy.* In C. R. Reynolds & T. B. Gutkin (Eds.), *The handbook of school psychology* (3rd ed., pp. 745–763). New York: Wiley.

Martens, B., Witt, J., Daly, E., & Vollmer, T. (1999). Behavior analysis: Theory and practice in educational settings. In C. R. Reynolds & T. B. Gutkin (Eds.), *The handbook of school psychology* (3rd ed., pp. 638–663). New York: Wiley.

Meichenbaum, D. N., & Goodman, J. (1971). Training impulsive children to talk to themselves: A means of developing self-control. *Journal of Abnormal Psychology, 77,* 115–126.

Meyers, A. W., & Craighead, W. E. (1985). *Cognitive behavior therapy with children.* New York: Plenum.

JAN N. HUGHES
Texas A&M University

BEHAVIOR MODIFICATION
BEHAVIORAL ASSESSMENT
BEHAVIORAL OBJECTIVES
TASK ANALYSIS

APPLIED PSYCHOLINGUISTICS

Applied Psycholinguistics publishes original articles on the psychological processes involved in language. Articles address the development, use, and impairment of language in all its modalities, including spoken, signed, and written. *Applied Psycholinguistics* is of interest to professionals in a variety of fields, including linguistics, psychology, speech and hearing, reading, language teaching, special education, and neurology. Specific topics featured in the journal include language development (the development of speech perception and production, the acquisition and use of sign language, studies of discourse development, second language learning); language disorders in children and adults (including those associated with brain damage, retardation and autism, specific learning disabilities, hearing impairment, and emotional disturbance); literacy development (early literacy skills, dyslexia and other reading disorders, writing development and disorders, spelling development and disorders); and psycholinguistic processing (bilingualism, sentence processing, lexical access).

In addition to research reports, theoretical reviews will be considered for publication, as will short notes, discussions of previously published papers, and book reviews. The journal will occasionally publish issues devoted to special topics within its purview. *Applied Psycholinguistics* is published by Cambridge University Press, The Edinburgh Building, Shaftesbury Road, Cambridge CB2 2RU UK.

PHILIP M. PRINZ
Pennsylvania State University
First edition

RACHEL M. TOPLIS
Falcon School District 49
Colorado Springs, Colorado
Third edition

APRAXIA

See DEVELOPMENTAL APRAXIA.

APTITUDE TESTING

The term *aptitude test* has been traditionally employed to refer to tests designed to assess the level of development attained by an individual on relatively homogenous and clearly defined segments of ability, such as spatial visualization, numerical aptitude, or perceptual speed. Aptitude tests measure the effects of learning under the relatively uncontrolled and unknown conditions of daily living. In this sense, they differ from achievement tests that measure the effects of a relatively standardized set of experiences encountered in an educational program. The two types of tests differ in use as well. Achievement tests generally represent a terminal evaluation of an individual's status on the completion of training. Aptitude tests serve to predict subsequent performance. They are employed to estimate the extent to which an individual will profit from a specific course of training, or to predict the quality of achievement in a new situation.

The term *special aptitude* originated at a time when the major emphasis in testing was placed on general intelligence. Traditional intelligence tests were designed primarily to yield a single global measure of an individual's general level of cognitive development such as an IQ. Although they were comprised of a heterogeneous grouping of subtests, both practical and theoretical analysis soon revealed that intelligence tests were limited in their coverage of abilities, and that more precise measures were required. This development led to the construction of separate tests for measuring areas of ability that were not included in the intelligence batteries. Traditional intelligence tests oversampled abstract functions involving the use of verbal or numerical symbols; therefore, a particular need was felt for tests covering the more concrete or practical abilities. The earliest aptitude tests were those measuring mechanical aptitude, but soon tests to measure clerical, musical, and artistic aptitude were developed. These special aptitudes were regarded as supplementary to the IQ in a description of an individual, and were usually administered in conjunction with a standard intelligence battery.

A strong impetus to the construction of special aptitude tests was provided by the problems of matching job requirements with the specific pattern of abilities that characterize each individual, a task commonly faced by psychologists in career counseling or in the classification of industrial and military personnel. Intelligence tests were not designed for this purpose. Aside from the limited representation of certain aptitudes discussed earlier, their subtests or item groups were often too unreliable to justify the sort of intra-individual analysis required for classification purposes. To respond to this need, the testing field turned to the development of multiple aptitude batteries.

Like intelligence tests, multiple aptitude batteries measure a number of abilities, but instead of a total score, they yield a profile of scores, one for each aptitude; thus they provide a suitable instrument for making intra-individual analysis (Anastasi, 1997). In addition, the abilities measured by multiple aptitude batteries are often different than those measured by intelligence batteries. Aptitude batteries tend to measure more concrete skills, such as arithmetic reasoning, numerical aptitude, perceptual speed, and spatial visualization, thereby placing less emphasis on verbal skills than intelligence tests.

Nearly all multiple aptitude batteries have appeared since 1945. Much of the test research and development began in the armed forces during World War II, when the Air Force designed special batteries to select training candidates to be pilots, bombardiers, radio operators, and range finders. The armed services still sponsor a considerable amount of research in this area, but a number of multiple aptitude batteries have been developed for civilian use in educational and vocational counseling and in personnel selection and classification (Murphy, 1994).

The application of factor analysis to the study of trait organization provided the theoretical basis for the construction of multiple aptitude batteries. Factor analysis identified, sorted, and defined the abilities that were loosely grouped under the definition of intelligence. The tests that best measured the factors identified in the analysis were then included in the multiple aptitude battery. The Chicago Test of Primary Mental Abilities (1941) represents the first attempt to construct a battery based on factor analysis using the pioneer factor analytic work of Thurstone (1938). Most multiple aptitude batteries developed since that time have employed the use of factor analysis in construction.

About a dozen multiple aptitude batteries have been developed for use in a number of fields. These instruments vary widely in approach, technical quality, and the amount of available validation data. In business and industry, data gained from the administration of multiple aptitude test batteries may be used for institutional decisions regarding the assignment of personnel to different jobs. In education, multiple aptitude batteries such as the SRA Primary Mental Abilities Test (Hanna, 1992) are used to guide the admission of students to different educational curricula (Schutz, 1972). The armed services use aptitude data to assign specific job classifications to personnel after screening with a more general instrument (Weitzman, 1985). The Air Force pioneered this practice, but all branches of the armed services now use the Armed Services Vocational Aptitude Battery (ASVAB; Bayroff, 1968).

A number of multiple aptitude batteries have been designed for use with high school students to aid in the transition from high school to work or postsecondary training (e.g., Ball Foundation, 2002). The most widely used of these tests is the Differential Aptitude Test (DAT; Bennett, Seashore, & Wesman, 1990). Based on the factor analytic work of Thurstone (1938), the DAT is used in the educational and vocational counseling of students. It provides a profile of scores on eight subtests: Verbal Reasoning, Numerical Ability, Abstract Reasoning, Clerical Speed and Accuracy, Mechanical Reasoning, Spatial Relations, Spelling, and Language Usage. In the most recent fifth edition of the DAT, significant changes have occurred in the battery of tests. The fifth edition is divided into two parallel forms for grades 7–9 and 10–12. New items have been added, old items have been revised and updated, and the overall testing time has been shortened by reducing the length of some tests. Using the student's profile in conjunction with an interest inventory, a counselor can use a computer or casebook to predict the student's success in postsecondary education, or generate a list of potential careers. A vast amount of validity data is available for the DAT. The predictive validity coefficients are high, indicating that the DAT serves as a good predictor of high school achievement in academic and vocational programs (Schmitt, 1995). However, the differential validity of the separate tests is quite poor. The DAT should therefore be used cautiously for classification purposes (such as to identify possible fields of educational or occupational specialization; Hattrup, 1995; Wise, 1995).

In 1987 the Computerized Adaptive Testing (CAT) edition of the DAT was developed, which allowed the test to be administered via Apple II or DOS-based IBM-compatible systems. However, the CAT has not been revised in light of recent technological innovations, and has therefore become somewhat obsolete (White, 1985). The Comprehensive Ability Battery (Hakstian & Cattell, 1977) and the Guilford-Zimmerman Aptitude Survey (Guilford & Zimmerman, 1956) are other multiple aptitude batteries that are often used in transition and vocational education (Biskin, 1995).

Many aptitude tests have been designed explicitly for counseling purposes in which classification decisions are preeminent. In a counseling situation, the profile of test scores is used to aid the counselor in choosing among several possible fields of educational or occupational specialization. The General Aptitude Test Battery (GATB; U.S. Department of Labor, 1980) was developed by the U.S. Employment Services (USES) for use by employment counselors in state employment services offices. The GATB is comprised of 12 tests that combine to yield nine factor scores: Intelligence, Verbal Aptitude, Numerical Aptitude, Spatial Aptitude, Form Perception, Clerical Perception, Motor Coordination, Finger Dexterity, and Manual Dexterity. The profile of these subtest scores can then be compared with profiles corresponding to a huge number of job categories. An alternative form is available for non-reading adults and there is also an addition for use with individuals who are deaf. A host of studies have been conducted on the GATB, which have consistently shown that the test is a reasonable predictor of performance across a range of jobs (Bemis, 1968).

Unlike the multiple aptitude batteries, special aptitude tests typically measure a single aptitude. Certain areas such as vision, hearing, motor dexterity, and artistic talents are often judged to be too specialized to justify inclusion in standard aptitude batteries, yet often these abilities are vital to a certain task. Special aptitude tests were designed to measure such abilities. They are often administered in conjunction with an aptitude battery, either to assess a skill not included in the battery or to further probe a skill or interest. Special aptitude tests may also be custom-made for a particular job, and be constructed using a simulation of the requisites of the job, such as the Minnesota Clerical Test (The Psychological Corporation, 1992), the Meier Art Judgment Test (Meier, 1942), or the Seashore Measure of Musical Talents (Seashore, 1938). Despite wide use in education, counseling, and industry, the development of aptitude tests has been slow (Murphy, 1994). Many of the aptitude tests currently in use were developed in the 1940s and 1950s and have been revised and reissued in subsequent years.

REFERENCES

Anastasi, A. (1997). *Psychological testing* (7th ed.). Saddle River, NJ: Prentice Hall.

Ball Foundation. (2002). *Ball Career System technical manual.* Glen Ellyn, IL: Author.

Bayroff, A. G., & Fuchs, E. F. (1968). The armed forces vocational aptitude battery. *Proceedings of the 76th annual convention of the American Psychological Association, 3,* 635–636.

Bemis, S. E. (1968). Occupational validity of the General Aptitude Test Battery. *Journal of Applied Psychology, 52,* 240–244.

Bennett, G. K., Seashore, H. G., & Wesman, A. G. (1990). *Fifth edition manual for Differential Aptitude Tests, Forms S and T.* New York: Psychological Corporation.

Biskin, B. H. (1995). Review of the Guilford-Zimmerman Interest Inventory. In J. C. Conoley & J. C. Impara (Eds.), *The twelfth mental measurements yearbook* (pp. 442–443). Lincoln, NE: Buros Institute of Mental Measurements.

Guilford, J. P., & Zimmerman, W. S. (1956). *The Guilford-Zimmerman Aptitude Survey.* New York: McGraw-Hill.

Hakstian, A. R., & Cattell, R. B. (1977). *The Comprehensive Ability Battery.* Champaign, IL: Institute for Personality and Ability Testing.

Hanna, G. S. (1992). Review of the SRA Achievement Series Forms 1 & 2 and survey of Basic Skills Form P & Q. In J. J. Kramer & J. C. Conoley (Eds.), *The eleventh mental measurements yearbook* (pp. 859–861). Lincoln, NE: Buros Institute of Mental Measurements.

Hattrup, D. (1995). Review of Differential Aptitude Tests: Fifth Edition. In J. C. Conoley & J. C. Impara (Eds.), *The twelfth mental measurements yearbook* (pp. 302–304). Lincoln, NE: Buros Institute of Mental Measurements.

Meier, N. C. (1942). *Art in human affairs.* New York: McGraw-Hill.

Murphy, K. R. (1994). Aptitude interest measurement. In D. J. Keyser & R. C. Sweetland (Eds.), *Test critiques: Volume 10* (pp. 31–38). Austin, TX: PRO-ED.

The Psychological Corporation. (1992). *Minnesota Clerical Test.* New York: Author.

Schmitt, N. (1995). Review of Differential Aptitude Tests: Fifth Edition. In J. C. Conoley & J. C. Impara (Eds.), *The twelfth mental measurements yearbook* (pp. 304–305). Lincoln, NE: Buros Institute of Mental Measurements.

Schutz, R. E. (1972). S.R.A. primary mental abilities. *Seventh mental measurements yearbook* (Vol. 11, pp. 1066–1068). Highland Park, NJ: Gryphon.

Seashore, C. E. (1938). *Psychology of music.* New York: McGraw-Hill.

Thurstone, L. L. (1938). Primary mental abilities. *Psychometric Monographs.* No. 1.

U.S. Department of Labor, Employment, and Training Administration. (1980). *Manual, USES General Aptitude Test Battery.* Washington, DC: U.S. Government Printing Office.

Weitzman, R. A. (1985). Review of the Armed Services Vocational Battery. In J. V. Mitchel (Ed.), *The ninth mental measurements yearbook* (Vol. 1, pp. 83–84). Lincoln, NE: Buros Institute of Mental Measurements.

White, K. R. (1985). Review of the Comprehensive Ability Battery. In J. V. Mitchel (Ed.), *The ninth mental measurements yearbook* (Vol. 1, pp. 377–379). Lincoln, NE: Buros Institute of Mental Measurements.

Wise, S. L. (1995). Review of Differential Aptitude Tests: Computerized Adaptive Edition. In J. C. Conoley & J. C. Impara (Eds.), *The twelfth mental measurements yearbook* (pp. 300–301). Lincoln, NE: Buros Institute of Mental Measurements.

LIZANNE DESTEFANO
University of Illinois

ACHIEVEMENT TESTS
ASSESSMENT, CURRICULUM BASED
CRITERION-REFERENCED TESTING
VOCATIONAL EDUCATION

APTITUDE-TREATMENT INTERACTION

Aptitude-treatment interaction refers to an educational phenomenon in which students who are dissimilar with regard to a particular aptitude perform differently under alternate instructional conditions. The alternate instructional conditions are specifically designed to reflect the students' aptitude differences. Thus, if a significant performance difference between the groups results under alternate instructional conditions, an aptitude by treatment interaction has occurred.

Aptitude-treatment interactions have been discussed at length by Bracht (1970), who defines an aptitude-treatment interaction as "a significant disordinal interaction between alternate treatments and personological variables" (p. 627). A personological variable is any measure of an individual characteristic such as learning style, intelligence, achievement anxiety, or locus of control. Disordinal interactions refer to performance differences between groups that denote the significantly better performance of one group under one set of conditions and the significantly better performance of the second group under alternate conditions. Figure 1 graphically displays a disordinal aptitude-treatment interaction.

Figure 1 depicts hypothetical data for two groups of students who differ on a particular aptitude, one group being high and the other being low. Alternate treatments, matched to the students' aptitude, were provided. Students with

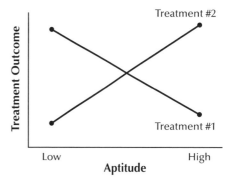

Figure 1 Disordinal aptitude-treatment interaction

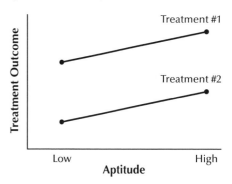

Figure 2 Hypothetical experimental outcome that is not indicative of an aptitude-treatment interaction

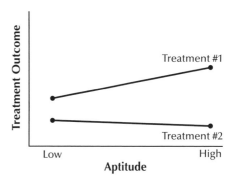

Figure 3 Hypothetical experimental outcome that is not indicative of an aptitude-treatment interaction

low aptitude performed better under treatment number 1. Students with high aptitude performed better under treatment number 2. The data confirm the occurrence of an aptitude-treatment interaction and support the use of different instructional approaches for these two groups of students.

Figures 2 and 3, respectively, display hypothetical experimental outcomes that are not indicative of an aptitude-treatment interaction. In Figure 2, both groups of students, despite the aptitude difference, performed better under treatment number 1. In Figure 3, treatment number 1 was again superior for both groups of students. However, the differences for the low-aptitude students under treatment conditions number 1 and number 2 were not significant. The aptitude difference does not suggest the use of different treatments for the two groups; other factors may dictate the use of one or the other treatment for both groups. In this instance, the aptitude dimension did not clarify the choice between treatments.

Interest in aptitude-treatment interactions is fueled by the widely espoused commitment to individualization of instruction and the quest for teaching adaptations that enhance individual student performance. Appreciation for individual differences is a relatively recent development (Snow, 1977). Snow believes that the "recognition that individual differences in aptitude not only predict learning outcomes but also often interact with instructional treatment variations" (p. 11). This concept makes adaptive instruction a possibility. Teachers have long recognized individual differences and have accommodated such differences in a myriad of ways. Nowhere is the concern for individual differences greater than in special education. The Individual Educational Program requirement of PL 94-142 and its revisions has mandated individualized educational planning for all exceptional children. Adaptation and accommodation to individual learner needs and characteristics is at the heart of the special education instructional process. Corno and Snow (1986), in a discussion of adapted teaching, view adaptations as involving either direct aptitude development or circumvention of inaptitude. In special education, the adage "teach to the strengths and remediate the weaknesses" prevails. Teachers generally seek intact or relatively strong abilities as avenues for instruction. Accompanying remediation is most often focused on specific skill or knowledge deficits that impede academic performance or independent functioning. Unfortunately, the commitment among educators, particularly teachers of the exceptional, to individualized instruction in practice is not matched by a strong commitment to educational research. "While it is clear that teachers adapt their behavior to students' individual differences at virtually all levels of education, what is less clear is the underlying logic and intentionality that governs these adaptations" (Corno & Snow, 1986, p. 614).

The systematic experimental investigation of teaching adaptations in relation to student characteristics is the focus of aptitude-treatment interaction research. However, the research to date underscores the difficulties associated with investigations of this kind. Bracht's review of 90 aptitude-treatment interaction studies yielded only five in which disordinal interactions were found. However, Bracht's review did help to clarify the nature of the aptitude and treatment variables and to identify the variables that increase the probability of significant aptitude-treatment interactions. Bracht's review included five studies that involved handicapped learners; none of the studies yielded significant interactions. Bracht notes that the subjects in these five studies bore categorical labels such as mentally retarded and emotionally disturbed. Such broad categories tend to mask the considerable heterogeneity that exists within the groups—a factor that works against the prob-

ability of aptitude-treatment interactions. In another review, Ysseldyke (1973) discussed five aptitude-treatment interaction studies involving handicapped learners grouped for instruction according to modality differences. Auditory and/or visual functioning were the modalities under consideration. Instruction matched to modality strengths or preferences failed to yield evidence of significant interactions across a variety of academic outcome measures (e.g., reading achievement and word recognition skills) in any of these studies.

Another review of research specifically involving modality-instructional matching was reported by Arter and Jenkins (1977). Preset criteria limited the number of studies reviewed in depth to 14. In all of the studies, the students were assigned to a modality group based on a statistical difference in modality functioning (modality assessments had adequate test-retest reliability and validity). Alternate instructional methods had a clear modality emphasis and outcome measures were constant across the groups. Only one study (Bursuk, 1971) demonstrated a significant modality-instruction interaction. This study involved tenth-grade below-average readers who were given instruction in listening and reading comprehension (reading comprehension lessons were given to the visual modality preference group only) over an entire school semester. The authors point out the specificity and control of subjects, treatments, and outcome measures that distinguish the Bursuk study from the remaining 13 research reports.

The results from studies specifically designed to demonstrate the interaction between modalities and instruction have not been a deterrent to practitioners. Despite the lack of supportive research, instruction based on the modality concept has been used for many years. The modality model of instruction is founded on aptitude-treatment interaction theory, but the applicability of aptitude-treatment interaction theory to modality-based instruction has yet to be demonstrated and validated to this day.

Aptitude-treatment interaction research is by no means confined to special education or to investigations of modality-based instruction. Aptitude-treatment interaction research has been conducted in other academic areas such as math (Holton, 1982) and reading (Blanton, 1971). The results generally have been disappointing.

The number of research studies that have successfully demonstrated aptitude-treatment interactions is limited, but the research has provided considerable insight into the complexities of the interaction phenomenon and the conditions that favor the occurrence of aptitude-treatment interactions (Veeman & Elshout, 1994). Bracht (1970) found that disordinal interactions were related to the degree of control over treatment tasks, the factorial makeup of the specific personological variables, and the nature of the dependent outcome variables. Controlled treatments, factorially simple personological variables, and specific, rather than complex, outcome variables favor aptitude-treatment interaction (Mills, Dale, Cole, & Jenkins, 1995). Snow (1977) stresses the "essential importance of detailed description of specific instructional variables and specific groups of people" (p. 12) to aptitude-treatment interaction research. In retrospect, the research reports that documented significant aptitude by treatment interactions displayed the prerequisite degree of control and specificity of critical variables that seem essential for aptitude-treatment interactions to occur.

The research findings to date suggest that each aptitude-treatment interaction, when found, will be valid only in a specific context. Each finding will pertain to a particular group of students under particular instructional conditions. Generalizations, if made at all, will be limited. Educators should not anticipate general educational theories with potential for broad application to emerge from aptitude-treatment interaction research. Rather, aptitude-treatment interaction theory implies ongoing evaluation of student and instructional variables and a constant readiness to adjust to meet changing conditions.

REFERENCES

Arter, J. A., & Jenkins, J. R. (1977). Examining the benefits of modality considerations in special education. *Journal of Special Education, 11*(3), 281–298.

Berliner, C. D., & Cohen, L. S. (1973). Trait-treatment interaction and learning. In F. N. Kerlinger (Ed.), *Review of research in education* (Vol. 1). Ithasca, IL: Peacock.

Blanton, B. (1971). Modalities and reading. *Reading Teacher, 25*(2), 210–212.

Bracht, G. H. (1970). Experimental factors related to aptitude-treatment interactions. *Review of Educational Research, 40*(50), 627–645.

Bursuk, L. A. (1971). Sensory mode of lesson presentation as a factor in the reading comprehension improvement of adolescent retarded readers. (ERIC Document Reproduction Service No. ED 047 435)

Corno, L., & Snow, R. E. (1986). Adapting teaching to individual differences among learners. In M. C. Wittrock (Ed.), *Handbook of research on teaching* (3rd ed.). New York: Macmillan.

Holton, B. (1982). Attribute-treatment-interaction research in mathematics education. *School Science & Mathematics, 82*(7), 593–601.

Mills, P. E., Dale, P. S., Cole, K. N., & Jenkins, J. R. (1995). Follow-up of children from academic and cognitive preschool criteria at age 9. *Exceptional Children, 61,* 378–393.

Snow, R. E. (1977). Individual differences and instructional theory. *Educational Researcher, 6*(10), 11–15.

Snow, R. E. (1984). Placing children in special education: Some comments. *Educational Researchers 13*(3), 12–14.

Veeman, M. V., & Elshout, J. J. (1994). Differential effects of instructional support on learning in simulation environments. *Instructional Science, 22,* 363–383.

Ysseldyke, J. E. (1973). Diagnostic-prescriptive teaching: The search for aptitude-treatment interactions. In L. Mann & D. A. Sabatino (Eds.), *The first review of special education.* Philadelphia: JSE.

LIBBY GOODMAN
Pennsylvania State University

DIAGNOSTIC PRESCRIPTIVE TEACHING
DIRECT INSTRUCTION
REMEDIATION, DEFICIT-CENTERED MODELS OF
TEACHER EFFECTIVENESS

ARC, THE

The Arc was founded in 1950 as the National Association of Parents and Friends of Mentally Retarded Children. The organization has undergone several name changes, but its mission has remained constant: to improve the quality of life for children and adults with mental retardation, as well as their families, through education, research, and advocacy.

From 1952 to 1974, the organization was known as the Association for Retarded Children. The name was then changed to the National Association for Retarded Citizens (NARC) in order to reflect a growing service to adults as well as children. In 1980, NARC became the Association for Retarded Citizens of the United States. In 1991, the word "retarded" was removed, and the organization changed its name to The Arc.

Throughout its nearly 50-year history, The Arc has taken a leadership role in encouraging research into the causes and prevention of mental retardation, and in educating the public in the results of that research. Some of the research projects and developments funded by The Arc include a new screening test for phenylketonuria (PKU) in 1961, the Bioengineering Program launched in 1982, and ongoing research on fetal alcohol syndrome. The Arc has also spearheaded efforts to influence federal policy toward children and adults with mental retardation. Some of its successes include the expansion of Medicaid to finance residential programs, Supplemental Security Income, the passage of Public Law 94-142, the passage of the "Baby Doe" Amendments to the Child Abuse Act protecting newborns with disabilities from the withdrawal of medical care, and the Fair Housing Act Amendment of 1988, which prohibits housing discrimination based on disability. The Arc also serves as a clearinghouse for information on subjects important in the field of mental retardation, from medical advances to education to setting up financial trusts. It also funds numerous publications, many of which can be downloaded from its website.

Among the association's goals are

- increasing the availability of health care for people with mental retardation

- helping people understand and comply with the public accommodations requirements of the Americans with Disabilities Act
- ensuring the legal rights of criminal offenders with mental retardation
- reducing the incidence of fetal alcohol syndrome
- providing all children, regardless of disability, with a free and appropriate public education
- protecting the rights of people with mental retardation to enjoy community living, obtain employment, vote, and be protected from abuse and neglect.

The Arc has 1100 state and local chapters, with over 140,000 members. Information on membership, publications, and topics of interest can be obtained from The Arc National Headquarters, 1010 Wayne Avenue, Suite 650, Silver Spring, MD 20910. Telephone: (301) 565-3842.

REFERENCE

The Arc of the United States. [Organization Website]. Retrieved November 4, 1998, from http://thearc.org/

DONNA WALLACE
*The University of Texas of the
Permian Basin*

**AAMR, AMERICAN ASSOCIATION ON MENTAL RETARDATION
MENTAL RETARDATION**

ARCHITECTURAL BARRIERS

Efforts to fully integrate individuals with disabilities into the societal mainstream have demanded the elimination of physical barriers that impede access to facilities, work (Stark, 2004), and the surrounding environment. Common barriers to facility or service accessibility confronted by handicapped citizens include constricted entranceways, ill-equipped public facilities (e.g., restrooms and parking areas), limited passageways, poor room spacing and layout, inadequate lighting, and limitations in the availability of supplementary mediums for providing public information (e.g., braille directions, visual warning or evacuation alarms).

Prior to the 1960s, the vast majority of buildings and thoroughfares were designed for the "ideal user" (i.e., an able-bodied young adult). However, with the passage of the Architectural Barriers Act of 1968 which mandated all buildings being accessible, the National Center for Law and the Handicapped (1978) and the U.S. Department of Housing and Urban Development (1983) the confluence of federal and state legislation, judicial pronouncements, and

publicly accepted standards of accessibility brought about significant and permanent changes in the architectural design of structures and thoroughfares. These changes prompted the removal of barriers that inhibited the accessibility (e.g., mobility and orientation) of physically and sensorily impaired citizens.

The American National Standards Institute (ANSI) specifications, originally adopted in 1961 and updated in the 1970s, establish barrier-free criteria for buildings, entranceways, and thoroughfares. These standards are designed to eliminate all architectural barriers that have historically impeded the access of the following populations:

Nonambulatory Disabled. People with physical impairments that confine them to wheelchairs.

Semiambulatory Disabled. People with physical impairments that cause them to walk with insecurity or difficulty and require the assistance of crutches, walkers, or braces.

Coordination Disabled. Those with impairments of muscle control that result in faulty coordination and that create an increased potential for personal injury.

Sight Disabled. Those with impairments that affect vision, either totally or partially, to the extent that an individual functioning in the environment is insecure or liable to injury.

Hearing Disabled. People with impairments that affect hearing, either totally or partially, to the extent that an individual functioning in the environment is insecure or liable to injury.

Modifications that may be required to eliminate architectural barriers in facilities and along public accessways include, but are not limited to, the construction of ramps, wheelchair lifts, and curbing cutouts; the improvement of transfer areas and enlarged spaces for parking facilities; the enhancement of public facilities such as restrooms, telephones, physical education facilities, and dining areas; and the improvement of passageways, entrances (e.g., doors, doorways), room designs (e.g., spacing and layout), facility lighting, and public/user information systems.

The Americans with Disabilities Act of 1990 extended all of the architectural barrier-free activities of state and local governments and businesses whether they were receiving federal funding or not. Regularly updated guidelines are published and the minimal requirements for accessibility include guidelines for new construction, additions, alteration, and historic buildings. The full guidelines can be seen at the ADA website: http://www.access-board.gov/adaag/html. The guidelines are extensive in breadth and depth and include subjects such as platform lifts, sinks, signage, telephones, and drinking fountains. The last update was in 2002. Direct inquiries can be answered by e-mail ta@access-board.gov or telephone (800) 872-2253 or (800) 993-2822 (TTY).

REFERENCES

National Center for Law and the Handicapped. (1978, July/August). *Moving toward a barrier free society: Amicus.* South Bend, IN: Amicus.

Stark, S. (2004). Removing environmental barriers in the homes of older adults with disabilities improves occupational performance. *Occupation, Participation, & Health, 24,* 32–39.

U.S. Department of Housing and Urban Development. (1983). *Access to the environment.* Washington, DC: U.S. Government Printing Office.

GEORGE JAMES HAGERTY
Stonehill College

ACCESSIBILITY OF BUILDINGS
AMERICANS WITH DISABILITIES ACT
ARCHITECTURE AND INDIVIDUALS WITH DISABILITIES

ARCHITECTURE AND INDIVIDUALS WITH DISABILITIES

The 2000 National Census results state that 77,429,844 individuals have a sensory, physical, mental or self-care disability in the United States (U.S. Census Bureau, 2003). Just over 6.8 million Americans living outside of institutions use assistive devices to help them with mobility. The use of wheelchairs, canes and other devices is influenced by age, ethnicity and gender (Kaye, Kang, & LaPlante, 2000).

Apart from the visually handicapped/blind, hearing impaired/deaf, and physically/orthopedically impaired, are those individuals who have health impairments involving cardiopulmonary disorders or neuromuscular diseases. These disorders may permit some mobility but may result in diminished stamina, poor coordination, or limited grasping and manipulative capacity.

Architectural considerations vary and are dependent on whether the handicap is physical, visual, or aural. In fact, such considerations can involve competing requirements that necessitate the establishment of unique environments for the physically handicapped in comparison with the visually handicapped. For example, a physically handicapped person confined to a wheelchair may function best in spaces that are open and large. In contrast, individuals who are blind may do better in smaller spaces where key elements of the sensory environment are within close range. Similarly, an environment that reflects noises may be advantageous for the blind but a disadvantage to the hearing impaired, who have difficulty in attenuating to multiple acoustical cues.

There are a number of general factors to be considered in designing or adapting environments:

1. Many handicapped persons may be smaller or weaker than average; therefore, slopes, reach distances, and forces necessary to open and close objects should be reduced.

2. A number of individuals who use mobility-assist devices (e.g., wheelchairs) may have secondary disabilities that involve difficulty in strength, grasping, etc.

3. Most persons blind at birth, or shortly after birth, know braille, while those adventitiously blind often do not know braille.

4. Tactile signals and signs should be few in number and their location carefully considered to ensure uniformity of placement throughout a building.

5. Audible signals should be in the lower frequencies, because persons lose the capacity to hear higher frequencies with increasing age.

6. Many deaf and blind persons can hear and see in favorable environments such as acoustically "dead" surroundings for the deaf and well-lit and magnified print environments for the blind.

7. Visual and aural signals are best to provide redundancy of cues and to accommodate deaf or blind persons (Sorensen, 1979, p. 2).

Through the use of mobility training programs provided through special education classes or rehabilitation efforts, the blind are able to go virtually anywhere. While guide dogs are used by a small proportion of the blind population, most blind people are initially guided through a building and later follow a memorized route. As might be expected, the primary impediments for the blind are unanticipated hazards such as people or objects moving across their paths or objects placed temporarily in a familiar area. Some specific building modifications that can be of assistance to the blind include:

Providing steps and stairs that are not open and do not have square, extended nosings on each step.

Using sound-reflecting walls since such walls allow the blind to better use their sense of hearing as a guide (moreover, sounds reflected from surfaces assist in orienting the blind to their position in an area).

Changing the construction materials in walking surfaces to denote entrances, restrooms, stairs, and other potentially hazardous areas.

Identifying doors leading to dangerous areas by door knobs that are distinctive from that of hardware used throughout the remainder of a building.

Placing all signs and letters/numbers at a consistent height, usually between 5 feet and 5 feet, 6 inches from the floor, so that the blind will know where to find them.

Of all those having auditory deficits, few are totally deaf. Even with a large hearing loss, many of those who are legally deaf can hear and comprehend if the environment is devoid of ambient noises. Modifications that can be of assistance to the deaf include:

Warning and direction devices equipped with visual indicators, as well as audible signals.

Telephones equipped with amplifiers for the hard of hearing and telephone typewriters for those who cannot use a standard phone even with amplification.

Clear signs so the deaf do not have to ask for directions since some deaf individuals have a difficult time talking and being understood.

Those individuals who have physical disabilities can be divided into those who are ambulant (able to walk with canes, crutches, or braces) and the chair-bound. The architectural requirements for those two groups, while similar, differ in some respects.

The ambulant disabled frequently have difficulty in stooping or bending. Consequently, modifications may include:

Placing handles, controls, switches, etc., within the reach of a standing person so stooping is unnecessary.

Placing ramps with a maximum gradient of slope of 1:12.

Using steps and stairs with nonprotruding nosings so individuals with restricted joint movement or braces will not catch their toes as they climb.

Placing hand rails on both sides of steps and stairs that extend beyond the first and last steps.

Chairbound individuals evidencing high degrees of independence use collapsible adult-size wheelchairs. Apart from the greater space needed for wheelchair movement, the chair-bound individual may need:

Grab bars to transfer via the front of the wheelchair to the shower, bed, and so on.

Space alongside a chair or bed.

The placement of countertops, control devices, and so on within the low to middle range of a standing person's areas of reach.

Much of the impetus for the modification of buildings and facilities for the physically handicapped began with the Architectural Barriers Act of 1968 (PL 90-480) and its subsequent amendments. The act specifies that buildings financed with federal funds must be designed and constructed to be accessible to the physically handicapped. In addition, the Rehabilitation Act of 1973 (PL 93-112 and its amendments) created the Architectural and Transportation Barriers Compliance Board, which has as its mission, in part, to:

Ensure compliance with the Architectural Barriers Act, as amended.

Examine alternative approaches to barriers that confront handicapped individuals in public settings.

Determine the measures that federal, state, and local governments should take to eliminate barriers.

Many states, by state statute, require that accessibility for the physically handicapped be provided in newly constructed, privately funded buildings that are open to the public. All states require that publicly funded buildings be accessible to the handicapped. A number of states require that when extensive remodeling is undertaken, such remodeling will include making the building accessible.

The Americans with Disabilities Act of 1990 requires accessibility, and its subsequent revisions have provided up-to-date and consistently revised guidelines for removing and preventing architectural barriers for individuals with disabilities. An ADA technical assistance center can be found at http://www.adaportal.org. This center has an extensive list of resources.

REFERENCES

Americans with Disabilities Act of 1990 42 U.S.C. §§ 12101 et seq.

Harkness, S. P., & Groom, J. N. (1976). *Building without barriers for the disabled.* New York: Whitney Library of Design.

Kaye, H. S., Kang, T., & LaPlante, M. P. (2000). *Mobility device use in the United States.* San Francisco: University of California, San Francisco, Disability Statistics Center.

Moe, C. (1977). *Planning for the removal of architectural barriers for the handicapped.* Monticello, IL: Council of Planning Librarians.

Sorensen, R. J. (1979). *Design for accessibility.* New York: McGraw-Hill.

U.S. Census Bureau. (2003). *American community survey summary tables.* Retrieved June 22, 2005, from http://www.factfinder.census.gov

PATRICIA ANN ABRAMSON
Hudson Public Schools, Hudson, Wisconsin

ACCESSIBILITY OF BUILDINGS
AMERICANS WITH DISABILITIES ACT
MOBILITY INSTRUCTION
MOBILITY TRAINERS

ARCHIVES OF CLINICAL NEUROPSYCHOLOGY

Archives of Clinical Neuropsychology (*ACN*) is the official journal of the National Academy of Neuropsychology (NAN), a 4000+ member organization composed primarily of practicing clinical neuropsychologists. The journal was founded in 1985 under the NAN Presidency of Raymond Dean, who became its first editor. Originally a quarterly, the journal increased to 8 times a year in 1996, and also enlarged its page format to accommodate more articles. It is free as a benefit of membership in the Academy and available by subscription to nonmembers. The present editor is W. D. Gouvier of Louisiana State University. The journal is owned by the Academy and published by Elsevier Science, the largest scientific publisher in the world today.

The journal publishes original research dealing with psychological aspects of the etiology, diagnosis, and treatment of disorders arising out of dysfunction of the central nervous system. Manuscripts that provide new and insightful reviews of existing literature or raise professional issues are also accepted on occasion. The journal reviews books and tests of interest to the field, and publishes the abstracts of the annual meeting of the Academy. A Grand Rounds section is also included that provides in-depth information about individual or small groups of patients with unique, unusual, or low incidence disorders. According to impact factors calculated by the Social Science Citation Index, the journal is one of the most influential in the field of clinical neuropsychology.

CECIL R. REYNOLDS
Texas A&M University

ARGENTINA, SPECIAL EDUCATION SERVICES FOR YOUNG CHILDREN IN

Among the countries of Latin America, Argentina has a well-established record of providing educational services to its citizens. Mandatory school attendance was established in 1884 and Argentina has the highest literacy rate (84 percent) in Latin America (UNESCO, 1984). The National Directorate of Special Education is responsible for the special instruction of mentally, physically, and socially handicapped students. Services are provided from preschool through adulthood.

Early intervention services for children from birth to age 3 were scarce in Argentina and poorly organized (UNESCO, 1981). There was a need for early educational intervention services for children and their families prior to enrolling a child in a nursery school or special center. As a result, services were developed for early stimulation and education. These services are divided by handicapping condition and are provided in infant consultation units. For children with slight to moderate mental handicaps, services focus on sensory and motor stimulation, socialization skills, and speech development. Parents are involved in these activities

so that follow through can be done at home. For children with physical handicaps (blind, partially sighted, deaf or hard of hearing), the education is divided into two stages. The first stage is early neurological and sensory stimulation; it is continued until the child has reached a developmental level of 18 months (UNESCO, 1981). The next stage involves stimulation of sensorimotor activities, language development, and the development of self-care and socialization skills. Guidance and educational services also are given to the families.

The primary goal of these intervention programs is to raise the child's level of developmental functioning so that he or she can enter a prenursery special education program. Along with outreach to parents is the involvement and continuing education of special education teachers. There is a central registry of handicapped children so that they may be referred to the appropriate resources. Primary prevention programs are initiated via the media, with special programs for or articles on handicapped children. Public meetings on issues relating to handicapped students constitute an ongoing effort at general education as to the needs of handicapped children.

REFERENCES

UNESCO. (1981). *Handicapped children: Early detection, intervention and education in selected case studies from Argentina, Canada, Denmark, Jamaica, Jordan, Nigeria, Sri Lanka, Thailand, and the United Kingdom* (Report No. ED/MD/63). Paris: Author.

UNESCO. (1984). Wastage in primary education from 1970 to 1980. *Prospects, 14,* 348–367.

KAREN F. WYCHE
Hunter College, City University of New York

PERU, SPECIAL EDUCATION IN

ARITHMETIC REMEDIATION

Remediation in arithmetic has evolved into an instructional system comprised of goals and objectives; tests at various levels and of kinds that assess the objectives; instructional activities that represent curriculum at the concrete, pictorial, and abstract levels; and summative evaluations. Instructional goals are based on the general mathematics goals of a school district or similar educational agency. These goals usually emerge from curriculum groups of teachers, supervisors, administrators, and content specialists from outside the school district. In some cases, goals are determined by available textbooks. Objectives are translations of the goals into observable performance statements.

According to the National Council of Supervisors of Mathematics (NCSM, 1979), the goal of the mathematics curriculum that was determined in 1977 (NCSM, 1977) should be to ensure that each student is able to

1. Solve problems
2. Apply mathematics to everyday situations
3. Determine if results are reasonable
4. Estimate
5. Compute
6. Use geometry
7. Measure
8. Read, interpret, and construct tables, charts, and graphs
9. Use mathematics to predict
10. Understand the role of computers

Objectives used to assess each of the NCSM goals might be to

1. Generate a list of possible solutions for finding the difference between two integers
2. Purchase items from a store and use the correct amount of money
3. State whether a series of answers make sense
4. State whether a quantity is reasonable for a specified purpose
5. Add with renaming
6. Find the circumference of a circle
7. Find the volume of a container
8. Interpret a graph showing income of teachers compared to inflation rates over time
9. Use a graph to predict direction of a group of stocks over time
10. Describe the use of the computer as a mathematics tutor

Diagnostic assessments may include survey tests, concept tests, interviews, attitude scales, and learning style inventories. Survey tests tap broad ranges of mathematics competence and serve to present an overview of students' strengths and weaknesses. Survey tests also are referred to as screening tests, where there are relatively few items for each of a great number of objectives. Survey tests have the following characteristics:

1. They may be group or individually administered
2. Test items are usually sequenced from easy to difficult
3. They are usually not timed
4. They may be machine scored

5. Test results indicate further areas of investigation in terms of student strengths and weaknesses

Concept tests may be used for diagnosing in more depth weaknesses identified in the survey test. Concept tests tap objectives with a greater number of items than survey tests. There may be five items on the concept test as compared with two on the survey test for each objective. Furthermore, a greater number of objectives are assessed on achievement or concept tests.

Interviews are crucial to diagnostic assessment, which is the foundation for designing, developing, implementing, and evaluating remedial programs in mathematics. Interviews occur after the paper-pencil assessments and may accompany additional diagnosis at concrete and pictorial levels. Interviews provide a structure for probing how and what a student is thinking. The following types of data may emerge from interviews: (1) what the student is thinking; (2) the student's thought processes, for example, whether the thinking is concrete or simplistic, whether cause-effect relations are apparent; (3) the problem-solving strategies being used by the student; (4) the mode of representation that appears most comfortable for the student: concrete, pictorial, or abstract; (5) how the student's performance compares with age peers as well as with other things that the student can do, for example, science, writing, art, music, sports, and social interaction. Interviews may be organized around topics such as whole numbers, fractions, geometry, measurement, and mathematical applications. The purpose of the interview is to collect data in a manner that is more thorough than from written tests. It is important to probe during an interview and to avoid correcting errors and instructing. If the student gets stuck, rephrase questions and move to a lower but related objective. The interview should allow the diagnostic teacher to identify error patterns, understand the student's thinking in regard to isolated errors, and observe whether the student's performance differs on the same objective with concrete models, or pictorial and abstract representations. Data from interviews should clarify performance on written assessments. The following matrix serves as a structure for selecting interview activities in terms of mode of representation of probe items:

The following are guidelines for conducting an interview:

1. Establish rapport to get to know the student and allow the student to relax.
2. Explain the purpose of the meeting as well as what you wish to learn. Ask the student whether he or she has any questions about the meeting.
3. Probe and learn about the student's strengths and weaknesses; do not teach.
4. Check to determine whether the student can perform prerequisite as well as corequisite skills. Prerequisites

are subskills or components of a task; corequisites are parallel tasks. Multiplication and division may be considered corequisites by the time the student is in grade five; addition is prerequisite to multiplication, while subtraction is prerequisite to division.

5. Look for generic patterns of performance that may be trouble spots. Most errors in arithmetic are not random but represent patterns of misunderstanding.

6. Ask questions that serve different purposes to help identify different styles of thinking. Include divergent and convergent types such as "How many different ways can you use these materials to help you find an answer?" or "What is your favorite color?"

Attitude scales provide information about the student's interest in, fear of, or enjoyment of arithmetic. Often those students who do not do well in mathematics have high anxiety toward the subject and do not like mathematics. Thus because attitude often interacts with performance, it is necessary to gather information about the student's attitude as part of the diagnostic process. The following are some instruments that assess attitude toward mathematics: (1) Aiken Mathematics Attitude Scale (Aiken, 1972); (2) Dutton Mathematics Attitude Scale (Dutton, 1956); and (3) Mott Mathematics Student Survey (Mott, 1984).

Learning style inventories provide another view of how the student learns best. This type of inventory may assess preferences by the student such as grouping (e.g., small group, large group, or individual), or preferences concerning instruction (e.g., teacher explanations, peer tutoring, or self-instruction).

Cawley (1985), Reisman and Kauffman (1980), and Reisman (1981), presented a number of remedial instructional strategies. These include the following:

1. Present small amounts of a sequence to be learned in an organized format
2. Use visual or auditory cues that highlight what is to be learned
3. Use separating and underlining as cues
4. Emphasize patterns
5. Teach rehearsal strategies such as repetition, verbal elaboration, systematic scanning, and grouping material to be remembered
6. Reinforce attention to a relevant dimension
7. Point out relevant relationship
8. Emphasize differences in distinctive features of stimuli
9. Control irrelevant stimuli
10. Replace incidental learning tasks with structured intentional learning tasks
11. Reduce complexity of task
12. Use consistent vocabulary
13. Use a model whose competency in the task has been established
14. Encourage deferred judgment during problem solving
15. Use peer-team learning
16. Provide immediate knowledge of results
17. Plan for transfer in learning
18. Use short, simple sentences when giving directions
19. Use concrete examples of spatial and quantitative relationships
20. Use prompting

Summative evaluation should include broad objectives that allow students to demonstrate their ability to compare, summarize, classify, interpret, judge, imagine, hypothesize, and engage in decision making. Remediation is an integrated system of assessment and instruction. The concept of remediation described here goes beyond the diagnose-prescribe model that focuses on fixing with a remedy, to the preventive model that implies doing it right the first time.

The NCSM has called for schools to have designated mathematics program leaders to help meet the current challenges in mathematics education (NCSM, 1998).

REFERENCES

Aiken, L. R. (1972, March). Research on attitudes toward mathematics. *Arithmetic Teacher, 19*(3), 229–234.

Brown, J. S., & Burton, R. R. (1978). Diagnostic models for procedural bugs in basic mathematical skills. *Cognitive Science, 2,* 155–192.

Cawley, J. F. (1985). *Cognitive strategies and mathematics for the learning disabled.* Rockville, MD: Aspen.

Dutton, W. H. (1956). Attitudes of junior high school pupils toward arithmetic. *School Review, 64,* 18–22.

Mott, T. (1984). *Mott mathematics student survey.* Unpublished doctoral dissertation, University of Pittsburgh.

NCSM. (1977). *NCSM position paper on basic mathematical skills.* Retrieved June 22, 2005, from http://www.ncsmonline.org

NCSM. (1998). *The case for designated mathematics program leaders.* Retrieved June 22, 2005, from http://www.ncsmonline.org

Reisman, F. K. (1981). *Teaching mathematics: Methods and content.* Boston: Houghton Mifflin.

Reisman, F. K. (1982). *A guide to the diagnostic teaching of arithmetic.* Columbus, OH: Merrill.

Reisman, F. K., & Kauffman, S. H. (1980). *Teaching mathematics to children with special needs.* Columbus, OH: Merrill.

Suydam, M. N. (1979, February). The case for a comprehensive mathematics curriculum. *Arithmetic Teacher, 26,* 10–13.

FREDRICKA K. REISMAN
Drexel University

ACALCULIA
MATHEMATICS, LEARNING DISABILITIES IN

ARMITAGE, THOMAS RHODES (1824–1890)

Thomas Rhodes Armitage, an English physician forced by failing sight to leave the practice of medicine, founded the British and Foreign Blind Association in 1868. This organization, which became the Royal National Institute for the Blind, had as its major purposes the establishment of an effective educational program for the blind and the elimination of the existing confusion over printing systems for the blind.

Armitage established the Royal Normal College and Academy of Music to provide vocational preparation for blind students. Eighty percent of its graduates became self-supporting, a unique accomplishment in that time. After conducting an extensive study of printing systems for the blind, Armitage and his association became the leading English proponents of braille. They were instrumental in the ultimate adoption of that system throughout Britain.

REFERENCES

Armitage, T. R. (1886). *Education and employment for the blind* (2nd ed.). London: Harrison.

Ross, I. (1951). *Journey into light.* New York: Appleton-Century-Crofts.

PAUL IRVINE
Katonah, New York

ARMSTRONG V. KLINE (1979)

Armstrong v. Kline was filed on behalf of children with disabilities seeking special education services during the summer term. The plaintiffs argued that handicapped children needed continuous, year-round programming in order to receive an appropriate education. The state countered that summer school was beyond the needs of these children and was not made available to nonhandicapped children free of charge and therefore was not required. In finding that some handicapped children are in need of year-round services, the court used the reasoning that "the normal child, if he or she has had a loss, regains lost skills in a few weeks, but for some handicapped children, the interruption in schooling by the summer recess may result in substantial loss of skills previously learned."

The court was referring principally to the severely handicapped, concluding that they would most likely require summer sessions. Of particular importance is that the court's finding seems to shift the burden of proof from the parents (to show need) to the school district (to show a lack of necessity for year-round programming). This ruling has been upheld in the appeals process and subsequent court cases (e.g., *Battle v. Commonwealth of Pennsylvania*, 1980). The court did not issue a blanket requirement for summer sessions for all handicapped children but, rather, required a determination to be made on the basis of the needs of the individual child. This ruling ultimately forced the development of better techniques for assessing retention and regression among disabled students and helped pave the way for later federal regulations relating to extended school year services.

REFERENCES

Armstrong v. Kline, 476 F. Supp. 583 (E.D. Pa. 1979), aff'd CA78-0172 (3rd Cir. 1980).

Battle v. Commonwealth of Pennsylvania, 629 F. 2d 269 (3rd Cir. 1980).

CECIL R. REYNOLDS
Texas A&M University
Second edition

KIMBERLY F. APPLEQUIST
*University of Colorado at
Colorado Springs*
Third edition

EXTENDED SCHOOL YEAR FOR STUDENTS WITH DISABILITIES

ARMY GROUP EXAMINATIONS

The Group Examination Alpha, better known as the Army Alpha, was the first group test of intelligence for adults. The examination was one of a battery of tests developed as a result of the armed forces's need during World War I to have an objective means of classifying vast numbers of recruits for military service.

The original examination, consisting of 13 subtests, was developed between June and September 1917 by the Committee on the Psychological Examining of Recruits. The committee was chaired by R. M. Yerkes and included W. V. Bingham, H. H. Goddard, A. S. Otis, T. H. Haines, L. M. Terman, F. L. Wells, and G. M. Whipple. Although experience among measurement experts with group examination procedures was rare, the committee relied heavily on A. S. Otis's group adaptation to the Binet scales for content and standards for administration (Yoakum & Yerkes, 1920). The committee worked continuously for almost a month developing, selecting, and adapting methods for the test content, and another month thoroughly testing the efficacy methods in military stations across the United States. The resulting version of the test consisted of eight subtests: (1) oral directions, (2) disarranged sentences, (3) arithmetic reasoning, (4) information, (5) Otis synonyms and antonyms, (6) practical judgment, (7) number series complete, and (8) analogies. There were five alternative forms provided and the average administration time was 40 to 50 minutes for groups of up to 500 recruits (Linden & Linden, 1968).

Between April 1 and December 1, 1918, Army Alpha was administered to approximately 1,250,000 military recruits. Contributing to its reliability and concurrent validity, the Army Alpha correlated with other ability measures as follows:

0.50 to 0.70 with officer ratings

0.80 to 0.90 with Stanford-Binet

0.72 with Trabue B and LC completion test combined

0.80 with Beta

0.94 with composite of Alpha, Beta, and Stanford-Binet.

Army Beta

The Army Alpha had more than adequately addressed the need for an instrument with which large numbers of individuals could be evaluated in a short period of time, but another problem quickly emerged. Army psychologists did not know what to do about the approximately 30 percent of the draftees who either could not read English or read so slowly that they could not perform on the Army Alpha. The Army Group Examination Beta, or Army Beta, was prepared to meet this need. The development of an instrument that could be group-administered without a heavy emphasis on reading or understanding verbal language presented special problems. These problems were mainly eliminated through the use of demonstration charts and pantomime to convey instructions (Yoakum & Yerkes, 1920).

The final version of the examination consisted of seven subtests: (1) maze test, (2) cube analysis, (3) X-O series, (4) digit symbol, (5) number checking, (6) pictorial completion, and (7) geometrical completion. The Beta also took approximately 50 minutes to administer and yielded the same type of numerical scores as the Alpha. Although the ability scores obtained on the Beta were somewhat less accurate than on the Alpha for the higher range of intelligence, the data obtained revealed the following correlations:

0.80 with the Alpha

0.73 with the Stanford-Binet

0.91 with the Stanford-Binet, Alpha, and Beta

The general administration procedure for the Army examinations soon became routine. Groups of draftees (100 to 500) reported to a special building to take the mental test(s). Based on whether the draftees could speak and/or write English, they were assigned to take either the Army Alpha for literates or Army Beta for illiterates or foreign-born recruits. Depending on the individual's performance on one of these tests, a decision was made regarding classification in the military or on the need for further testing to ascertain mental capacity for military service. Individuals failing the Alpha exam were automatically administered the Beta exam to factor out the possible role of reading and oral language in their poor performance. Anyone failing the Alpha exam and the Beta exam initially was given one of three individual performance examinations. Thus, no individual was designated as mentally incompetent solely based on performance on the group examinations.

The Army Alpha and the Army Beta yielded numerical scores of ability ranging from 0 to 212, which for military classification purposes were translated into the letter grades A, B, C, D, or E. Classifications were assigned as in the following examples:

Intelligence Grade	Probable Classification	Definition	Score (Alpha)
A	High officer type	Very superior	135–212
B	Commissioned/ Noncommissioned officer	Superior	105–134
⋮			
D–	Considered fit for regular duty; rarely suited for tasks requiring special skill or alertness	Very inferior	0–14

The scores on the Alpha showed a high correlation with the individual's social status. The data also seemed to indicate a high correlation between an individual's Alpha score and level of occupational responsibility (Yoakum & Yerkes, 1920). These data were at least partially responsible for the soon to be widespread use of tests to predict vocational success, but as Matarazzo (1972) points out in reporting this data, there was a failure to highlight the considerable overlap in the scores obtained by individuals in the various occupational groups. More important, the vast amounts of data generated from the Army Alpha exams provided glimpses of the full range of adult abilities, confirming Galton's assumption that intelligence test scores are normally distributed in the population at large. Additionally, these data were largely responsible for the practice of using a fixed mental age for calculating adult intelligence.

The practical utility of the entire battery is expounded in terms of the number of men discharged from military service before the country wasted vast amounts of money, effort, and time training them. Yoakum and Yerkes (1920) reported that between April and November 1918, 45,653 draftees were found deficient to serve in the military. From a measurement or psychometric perspective, the subtests and techniques developed and used for the army group examinations paved the way for the tremendous growth of group and individual testing in education and industry. Subtests developed for the army examinations are very much in evidence on most current tests of intelligence. For example, the Wechsler scales are composed of subtests that are in many respects identical to the subtests on the Army Alpha and Beta. This is not surprising: the author of these scales, David Wechsler, participated in the army testing program during World War I.

The influence of the army group examinations is not all positive. Anastasi (1976) reminds us that often tests modeled after the army examinations failed to acknowledge and account for the limitations of the technical properties of the group examination methods. This failure resulted in much of the negative sentiment toward ability testing in the United States. That sentiment threatened the demise of psychological testing. Thus the army examinations may have done as much to retard as to advance the progress of psychological tests. The ease and efficiency of these group techniques also created a preference for impersonal testing as opposed to the more clinical, individual testing methods promoted by pioneers such as Binet (Matarazzo, 1972).

REFERENCES

Anastasi, A. (1976). *Psychological testing* (4th ed.). New York: Mac-Millan.

Linden, K. W., & Linden, J. D. (1968). *Modern mental measurement: A historical perspective.* Boston: Houghton-Mifflin.

Matarazzo, J. D. (1972). *Wechsler's measurement and appraisal of adult intelligence* (5th ed.). Baltimore: Williams & Wilkins.

Yoakum, C. S., & Yerkes, R. M. (1920). *Army mental tests.* New York: Holt.

JULIA A. HICKMAN
Bastrop Mental Health Association

INTELLIGENCE TESTING
MEASUREMENT

ARTHRITIS, JUVENILE

Juvenile rheumatoid arthritis (JRA) is a systemic disease that causes inflammation of one and usually more joints. The manifestations of JRA vary considerably among patients. The most common symptoms include joint swelling, warmth, tenderness, and pain, which may lead to stiffness, contractures, and retardation of growth. This disease is usually accompanied by fever bursts, rash, and visceral symptoms.

This form of arthritis is the most common connective tissue disease in children and is the most prevalent of the arthritic diseases. It has been estimated that around 250,000 Americans have JRA with an incidence of 1.1 cases per year in 1,000 school-age children (Varni & Jay, 1984). The disease affects more girls than boys. It is similar to adult rheumatoid arthritis except that it typically appears before puberty and is more likely to stay in remission.

The causes of JRA are only recently known. Infection, autoimmune disorders, trauma, psychological stress, and heredity all have been considered, but evidence now supports the ideas that JRA is primarily an autoimmune disorder (Rennebohm, 1994). As there are no known causes, there are also no known cures. The most common treatment is the administration of nonsteroidal anti-inflammatory drugs such as aspirin. Other common drug treatments include gold salts, antimalarial drugs, corticosteroids, and penicillamine. Immune system medications such as methotrexate and azathiprine may also be employed (Arthritis Foundation, 2005). Special exercises and sometimes periods of rest may also be employed. Different kinds of heat may be applied to reduce stiffness and pain, and a variety of other pain-control measures have been tried. Splints are often used to prevent deformity and enhance function. Surgery, including total joint replacement, may sometimes be necessary and can be beneficial.

There are basically three forms of JRA: systemic, polyarticular, and pauciarticular. The systemic form accounts for approximately 20 percent of the population with JRA. High fevers, rashes, stomach pains, and severe anemia are usually present in this type. Pauciarticular accounts for 30 to 40 percent of the cases. It begins by affecting only a few joints, usually the large ones (knees, ankles, or elbows). Polyarticular is the most common type, accounting for 40–50 percent of children with JRA. This type affects several joints (five or more), usually small joints of the fingers and hands (Arthritis Foundation, 1983).

The long-term effects of JRA vary greatly depending on the type as well as the individual. There is no way to know the outcome of the disease in its early stages. However, the overall prognosis for children with JRA is good. Most will be able to go through adulthood without any severe physical limitations. Only about 25 percent will suffer any significant disability (Jay, Helm, & Wray, 1982). In most cases the disease will go into permanent remission but structural damages and functional limitations will remain. In other cases the disease may continue to be active throughout the individual's life (Rennebohm, 1994).

In addition to physical considerations, certain psychological aspects of JRA are also important. McAnarney, Pless, Satterwhite, and Friedman (1974) found that children who have JRA but no disabilities have more emotional problems than disabled arthritics. They also found that parents of the nondisabled children had a poorer understanding of the disease and were less likely to acknowledge its impact on the child's behavior, schooling, and social relations. Litt, Cuskey, and Rosenburg (1982) found that good self-image and greater autonomy coincided with higher compliance in treatment.

Wilkinson (1981) studied the emotional and social behavior of adolescents with chronic rheumatoid arthritis. She found that one of the major complaints among these adolescents was people's tendency to treat them as younger than their age because of their smaller size. She also reported a high anxiety level because of restricted mobility and fears about an uncertain future. Children with JRA are at increased risk of emotional and behavioral problems but there is considerable variability in the response to the disorder psychologically (Varni, Rapoff, & Waldrov, 1994).

Schaller (1982) stressed the need to avoid an image of chronic invalidism. It is important to account for the limitations experienced by individuals with JRA; however, when not specifically restricted by the disease, they should be expected to perform as well as their peers.

The way children are treated by others affects their self-image; therefore, those working with these children should help them to avoid feelings of inferiority. Wilkinson (1981) reported that the adolescents in her study expressed a desire for more social contacts with able-bodied individuals and a desire to be in regular rather than special classes.

In the classroom as well as at home, children should not be unnecessarily restricted from activities. They should be encouraged to find alternatives when they cannot participate in regular play. Periodically calling on the child to do an activity requiring movement may help relieve stiffness whenever the child is not in pain. Beales, Keen, and Holt (1983) stressed the importance of being aware of the child's perception of pain. Children may be less likely to interpret internal sensations as pain and therefore may fail to recognize it as a warning sign. Often, even when children know they are in pain they may not complain and may even try to conceal it. Some visible signs that may help determine the presence of pain are walking with a stiff gait, taking short steps, tense muscles, and inability to perform certain tasks. Cognitive behavior therapies may be useful in controlling chronic pain in JRA (see Arthritis Foundation, 2005; Varni et al., 1994).

REFERENCES

Arthritis Foundation. (1983). *Arthritis in children and when your student has childhood arthritis.* Atlanta, GA: Patient Services Department.

Arthritis Foundation. (2005). *Medications.* Retrieved June 22, 2005, from http://www.nim.nih.gov

Beales, J. G., Keen, J. H., & Holt, P. L. (1983). The child's perception of the disease and the experience of pain in juvenile arthritis. *Journal of Rheumatology, 10*(1), 61–65.

Jay, S., Helm, S., & Wray, B. B. (1982). Juvenile rheumatoid arthritis. *American Family Physician, 26*(2), 139–147.

Litt, I. F., Cuskey, W. R., & Rosenberg, A. (1982). Role of self-esteem and autonomy in determining medication compliance among adolescents with juvenile rheumatoid arthritis. *Pediatrics, 69*(1), 15–17.

McAnarney, E. R., Pless, I. B., Satterwhite, B., & Friedman, S. B. (1974). Psychological problems of children with chronic juvenile arthritis. *Pediatrics, 53,* 523–528.

Rennebohm, R. M. (1994). Juvenile rheumatoid arthritis: Medical issues. In R. Olson, L. Mullins, J. Gillman, & J. Chang (Eds.), *The sourcebook of pediatric psychology* (pp. 70–74). Boston: Allyn & Bacon.

Schaller, J. G. (1982). Juvenile rheumatoid arthritis. *Pediatric Annals, 11*(4), 375–382.

Varni, J., Rapoff, M., & Waldron, S. (1994). Juvenile rheumatoid arthritis: Psychological issues. In R. Olson, L. Mullins, J. Gillman, & J. Chang (Eds.), *The sourcebook of pediatric psychology* (pp. 75–89). Boston: Allyn & Bacon.

Varni, J. W., & Jay, S. M. (1984). Biobehavioral factors in juvenile rheumatoid arthritis: Implications for research and practice. *Clinical Psychology Review, 4,* 543–560.

Wilkinson, V. A. (1981). Juvenile chronic arthritis in adolescence: Facing the reality. *International Rehabilitation Medicine, 3,* 11–176.

DAN HATT
NURI PUIG
LOGAN WRIGHT
University of Oklahoma

PHYSICAL DISABILITIES

ARTICULATION DISORDERS

Articulation involves the study of (1) the phonemes in a given language, (2) the manner in which they are produced, (3) the order in which they are acquired by the members of a culture, and (4) the disorders which may occur. There are forty phonemes in the English language, consisting of twenty-six consonants and fourteen vowels (Bernthal & Bankson, 1998). A phoneme is defined as the smallest difference conveying a change of meaning. This is in contrast to an allophone which includes all of the acceptable productions of a given phoneme. Allophonic variations do not impact meaning.

The consonant sounds may be differentiated on the basis of three distinctive features: place, manner, and voicing. A vowel varies according to tongue height, placement, and whether the tongue is tense or lax. There are also other characteristics of phonemes, known as suprasegmentals, that cause variations in sounds but do not signal a difference of meaning in English. Suprasegmentals are distinctive in some languages. For example, in tonal languages, the pitch of a phoneme signals a change in meaning.

If a traditional view of articulation development is taken, the age of emergence of specific phonemes may be identified. For example, /p/, /b/, and /m/ are early developmental phonemes and are typically in a child's repertoire by age 3. In contrast, the /s/ phoneme may not emerge until a child is 8 years of age or older. Numerous studies, including one by Sander (1972), have examined the age of emergence of various phonemes. All children have articulation errors when they are young and are moving through the normal developmental process. The errors decrease in number as the child matures. Generally, articulation development is thought to be complete by age 8, although some children continue to develop articulation skills beyond this age.

When a child or adult has an articulation disorder, it is characterized by sound production errors, usually involving less than 10 phonemes. The individual's underlying rule system for combining sounds into words is thought to be intact. That is, the speaker understands how sounds are put together to make words which convey meaning, but the speaker is having trouble making individual sounds. The errors can further be classified as phonetic or phonemic in nature.

A listener will generally understand a person with articulation errors, although speech production will attract the listener's attention. The misarticulations may vary in severity from a mild distortion to omission. The least noticeable error is a mild distortion. The listener will recognize the sound as an /s/, for example, but its production will be just outside of the acceptable allophonic range. Only the skilled listener is likely to note this error. As the degree of distortion increases into the more severe range, the average listener will become aware of the error in production. Even though the phoneme is recognizable as a particular phoneme, it will call attention to itself. Further on the continuum of severity is substitution, in which another phoneme is used in place of the one that is intended. For example, a person may substitute a /t/ for a /k/. The most severe error is an omission, in which the sound is left out.

The order of progression of severity is based on the impact the error has on intelligibility and the knowledge the speaker has about the phoneme. In regard to intelligibility, a distortion of a phoneme in a word generally does not impair the listener's understanding of a word. A substitution or omission may make it difficult for the listener to identify the word being used. The knowledge a speaker has about the phoneme is also reflected in the type of error used. When the phoneme is distorted, the speaker knows that for example, it is an /s/ but they are unable to correctly execute the production. When the error is a substitution, for example /p/ for /s/, the speaker knows a sound is required in a particular location in a word but isn't sure which sound belongs there. In contrast, when a phoneme is omitted, the speaker doesn't realize a phoneme is needed. Thus, omission is the most severe type of error, followed by substitution and distortion.

The more common sources of articulation errors are (1) inaccurate learning, (2) incorrect speech models, (3) structural deficits of the speech and hearing mechanism, and (4) imprecise and/or poor coordination of motor movements. In the first instance, inaccurate learning, something interferes with the process as the child is acquiring a sound. For example, if a child has fluid in his or her ears or brain injury at a critical point in the acquisition of a phoneme, the child may not hear the sound or its replication accurately. It is thought that children rely heavily on the auditory modality when sounds are being learned, but later shift their focus to the proprioceptive/kinesthetic aspects for monitoring the accuracy of their productions. Thus, initially they focus on how their sound matches up auditorily to that produced by others, but later, once the phoneme is learned, they pay less attention to the auditory aspects and focus on how it feels both proprioceptively and kinesthetically. They then are thought to make the assumption that if the phoneme felt like last time, it must be correct. An erroneously learned production is thus maintained. Second, a child may have a family member or significant other who has an articulation error and is providing incorrect models for the child. Learning of faulty articulation is likely to occur because the child will imitate the errored phoneme and incorporate it into his or her repertoire. Third, structural abnormalities of the speech and hearing mechanism may be a contributing factor to articulation errors. Examples are teeth that do not occlude properly or inadequate velopharyngeal closure. The structure may interfere with the ability to produce acceptable phonemes. Fourth, imprecise motor movements and/or the coordination of these movements may cause articulation errors. Correct articulation requires precise placement, timing, and accurate movement of the articulators. Persons with cerebral palsy, dysarthria, or apraxia, for example, have difficulty in these domains, and their speech production is affected to varying degrees.

The treatment for articulation errors generally consists of teaching the phoneme in isolation, and then assisting the client in generalizing the new sound throughout their sound system. Traditional strategies, such as those suggested by Van Riper (1978) or Bankson and Bernthal (1998), may be used. Minimal pairs and co-articulation strategies may also be utilized. Typically, the prognosis for resolving the errors is good. The American Speech-Language-Hearing Association (2005) has an excellent website with current and helpful resources for articulation problems.

REFERENCES

American Speech and Language Association. (2005). *Articulation problems.* Retrieved June 22, 2005, from http://www.kidsource .com/ASHA/index.html

Bernthal, J., & Bankson, N. (1998). *Articulation and phonological disorders* (4th ed.). Boston: Allyn & Bacon.

Sander, E. (1972). When are speech sounds learned? *Journal of Speech and Hearing Disorders, 37,* 55–63.

Van Riper, C. (1978). *Speech correction: Principles and methods* (6th ed.). Englewood Cliffs, NJ: Prentice Hall.

SUSANN DOWLING
University of Houston

COMMUNICATION DISORDERS
SPEECH AND LANGUAGE DISABILITIES
LANGUAGE DISORDERS

ART THERAPY

The use of clients' artwork by psychiatrists and psychologists to understand their psychopathology has been around for many years. There have been instances as early as the 1900s, where psychiatrists used drawings to observe and understand the psychopathology of their clients. Despite this practice, the actual practice of art therapy has only existed since the mid-twentieth century (Malchiodi, 2005).

There have been two pioneers for art therapy in the United States: Margaret Naumburg and Edith Kramer (Ulman, 2001). Naumburg based her concept of art therapy on the psychoanalytic approach by Freud and Jung. Naumburg believed that artwork could be used as symbolic speech for the unconscious, uncovering deep emotions. Expressions of these unconscious emotions using artwork have been based on psychoanalytic and analytic techniques such as free association, transference between the client and therapist, and spontaneous art expression. About the same time Naumburg began to make advances in the area of art therapy, there was a second pioneer, Kramer, in the United States who brought her ideas and concepts to the area of art therapy (Ulman, 2001).

Kramer comprised her concept of art therapy using an emphasis on art in psychotherapy. Kramer believed that art is a means by which therapists can create human experiences. These experiences allowed the individuals to relive particular experiences in therapy as a way to resolve any conflicts that have arisen (Ulman, 2001). Both Naumburg and Kramer's concepts were used to help adults and children deal with depression and traumatic events.

Art therapy has been used to help juvenile offenders. Venable (2005) found that engaging juvenile offenders in artwork afforded them opportunities that gave them a better insight on life. For example, through a mural project the juvenile offenders were able to maintain positive relationships with teachers as well as learn various techniques pertaining to art.

Another population that art therapy has been used with is children with emotional disturbances. Graham (1994) believed that art could be a successful way for children with emotional problems to deal with the traumas or negative experiences in their lives. For example, through their paintings and drawings, children can express their feelings and thoughts that they may feel are hard to express to others. Although advances have been made in art therapy, there is still little research on outcome studies addressing the effectiveness of art therapy; however, the techniques and concepts of art therapy are still used by many in diverse professions.

REFERENCES

Graham, J. (1994). The art of emotionally disturbed adolescents: Designing a drawing program to address violent imagery. *American Journal of Art Therapy, 34,* 115–121.

Malchiodi, C. (2005). Expressive therapies. In C. Malchiodi (Ed.), *Art therapy* (pp. 16–45). New York: Guilford.

Ulman, E. (2001). Art therapy: Problems of definition. *American Journal of Art Therapy, 40,* 16–26.

Venable, B. (2005). At risk and in need: Reaching juvenile offenders through art. *Art Education, 58,* 48–53.

TIA BILLY
Texas A&M University

BEHAVIOR DISORDERS
EMOTIONAL DISORDERS
RECREATIONAL THERAPY

ASPERGER SYNDROME

Asperger syndrome (AS) is associated with Hans Asperger, a Viennese physician who, in 1944, wrote a paper to the psychiatric community about a behavior pattern he had observed in his work with children with significant and chronic neurodevelopment social disorders, calling the disorder "autistic psychopathy" (Myles & Simpson, 2001; Safran, Safran, & Ellis, 2003). Because Asperger's paper was written in German and not widely known or read in English-speaking countries, the syndrome was lost and not heard of again until 1981 when Lorna Wing wrote about his work and when Uta Frith translated his paper in 1991 (Frith, 1991; Wing & Potter, 2002). According to Safran (2001), despite increased attention of AS in American psychiatry, there has been comparably less attention and interest regarding AS in the American special education literature. In 1994, the American Psychiatric Association included AS in the *Diagnostic and Statistical Manual of Mental Disorders,* fourth edition (*DSM-IV*) as a Pervasive Developmental Disorder of Childhood along with Autistic Disorder, Rett's Disorder, Childhood Disintegrative Disorder, and Pervasive Developmental Disorder Not Otherwise Specified. Asperger Syndrome was finally included in the 1997 Individuals with Disabilities Education Act (IDEA) disability category under Autistic Spectrum Disorder (ASD) to reflect the wide-ranging variability in how autism is manifested from more severe forms to AS but also because of core, overlapping similarities in how their behaviors affect or impact major life activities and functioning. Like with autism, AS is a disorder that is now seen as genetically-based, affecting brain development and impairing social interaction, communication, and imagination; it is not a condition caused by poor parenting (Klin, Volkmar, & Sparrow, 2000; Wing & Potter, 2001).

There is concern that since ASD is now one of the IDEA disability categories, there will be a sharp rise in the number of special education referrals made for individuals exhibiting symptoms of AS. The concern is not just because AS is now a part of the *DSM-IV* and IDEA classification systems, but because of the concern associated with reported AS or ASD prevalence rates (Safran, 2001). Safran (2001) reports on a study showing prevalence rates as high as .71 percent of the general population in Sweden (.44 percent of girls; .91 percent of boys), suggesting that this may indicate a large underserved population of individuals in the United States. Myles and Simpson (2001) report that prevalence rates for AS are estimated to be as many as 48 per 10,000 children; however, these data are regarded as *guestimates* because definitive tracking data on the incidence or prevalence of AS is sorely lacking. Investigating this issue, Wing and Potter (2002) conducted an extensive review of studies reporting an annual rise in the incidence and prevalence rates of ASD (which includes children with autism) and found that, whereas prevalence rates for autism before the 1990s were thought to be between 2 to 4 per 10,000 children, reported rates had skyrocketed to as high as 60 per 10,000 (and even higher when considering the whole ASD range itself). After examining the research, Wing and Potter (2002) noted that the majority of the evidence reporting an increase in prevalence was due to changes in diagnostic criteria and an increased public awareness and recognition of ASD. Other minor reasons for this seemingly spurious spike in prevalence is due to (1) differences in methods used in studies, (2) recognition that ASD can be associated with Severe or Profound Mental Retardation, average or high intellectual ability, and psychiatric disorders of any type, (3) the development of specialist services for ASD and genetic factors as evidenced from twin studies, and (4) a possibility of a true increase (but which is still an open question). Of particular interest regarding environmental causes, the media and public in the 1990s were focused on a possible link between autism and vaccination with mumps, measles, and rubella (MMR) vaccine or with other vaccines containing mercury in a preservative. Empirical evidence to date has not supported this hypothesis, however (Wing & Potter, 2002).

The *DSM-IV* definition or diagnostic criteria of AS (American Psychiatric Association, 1994, p. 77) requires evidence of (1) qualitative impairments in social interaction and (2) restricted areas of interest, and stereotyped behaviors and activities. Within the social impairment domain, at least

two of the following must be documented: (1) marked impairment in the use of multiple nonverbal behaviors such as eye-to-eye gaze, facial expression, body postures, and gestures to regulate social interaction, (2) failure to develop peer relationships appropriate to developmental level, (3) lack of spontaneous seeking to share enjoyment, interests, or achievements with other people (e.g., by a lack of showing, bringing, or pointing out objects of interest to other people), and (4) lack of social or emotional reciprocity.

Within the restricted areas of interest domain at least one of the following must be present: (1) encompassing preoccupation with one or more stereotyped and restricted patterns of interest that is abnormal either in intensity or focus, (2) apparently inflexible adherence to specific, nonfunctional routines or rituals, (3) stereotyped and repetitive motor mannerisms (e.g., hand or finger flapping or twisting or complex whole-body movements), and (4) persistent preoccupation with parts of objects. Asperger Syndrome must cause significant impairment in major life areas or functioning (e.g., social, vocational), no general or significant delay in language and cognitive development is present, and criteria cannot also be met for another specific Pervasive Developmental Disorder (PDD) or Schizophrenia (American Psychiatric Association, 1994).

Characteristics of Asperger Syndrome

The lack of delays in language skills, self-help skills, cognitive development, and curiosity about the environment are what sets AS apart from other PDD categories in the *DSM-IV,* and yet their peculiar language behavior (e.g., misperception of social language or cues, odd vocal prosody), motor clumsiness, and nonverbal communication problems (e.g., limited gestures, inappropriate facial expressions) can confound straightforward identification (Safran, 2001). Individuals with AS present unique characteristics across at least six areas of functioning: (1) social, (2) behavioral/ emotional, (3) intellectual/cognitive, (4) academic, (5) sensory, and (6) motor.

First and foremost, AS is considered a social disorder (Frith, 1991; Klin, Volkmar, et al., 2000; Myles & Andreon, 2001; Myles & Simpson, 2001). Individuals with AS are noted for their lack of motivation to interact with others; while they may be able to engage in routine social interactions, the quality of their social behavior may range from being withdrawn or detached to being very socially unskilled. Because of these social difficulties, individuals with AS may display emotional vulnerability and stress over not understanding social situations and how to apply social rules when social situations are so variable and seemingly inconsistent (e.g., out on the playground), especially when individuals with AS tend to demand sameness and strict application of rules (Williams, 2001). Related to these issues involving social interaction is what is referred to as *theory of mind,* where it is believed that individuals with AS possess limited understanding of the internal thoughts, feelings, and beliefs of other people (i.e., poor empathy skills) and often lack self-awareness of their place in the world (Safran, 2001; cf. Frith, 1991; Klin, Volkmar, et al., 2000).

Behavioral or emotional challenges occur most often in relation to social deficits or ineptness. In their inability to predict or control outcomes in social situations, individuals with AS may react in anger, frustration, aggression, or with panic. Interestingly, in a study reported by Myles and Simpson (2001), while teachers viewed students with AS as being at-risk for anxiety, depression, attention problems, and withdrawal, students with AS did not perceive themselves to have any significant problems at all.

Although students or individuals with AS generally experience normal intellectual and language development, relatively little is really known about their cognitive abilities. What little research has been conducted suggests that while IQ scores range from deficient to superior, scores generally fell in the average range. Their performance on IQ measures suggests also that individuals with AS generally have strong nonverbal reasoning abilities and visual-motor spatial integration skills. Difficulties were noted on tasks involving visual-motor coordination; during testing they were distractible, had little interest in school-related tasks, showed weak visual-memory ability, and limited understanding of social judgment or comprehension (Myles & Simpson, 2001). Both Myles and Simpson and Klin, Volkmar, et al. (2000) express caution that studies have generally failed to generate a specific cognitive profile for individuals with AS, and because of test scatter (variable subtest scores), global indices of verbal and performance functioning may misrepresent actual cognitive abilities.

Academically, students with AS benefit from general classroom experiences. They are intellectually capable, possess good rote memory skills, and are motivated to be with peers. Social and communication deficits connected with AS, however, often lead to academic problems, especially when they become obsessed with issues and engage in their literal and concrete thinking styles (Williams, 2001). When academic problems do occur, it tends to be with comprehending abstract materials, comprehending verbally presented information, written language, mathematical equation solving, and language-based critical thinking. Strengths have been noted in their understanding of factual material, oral expression, and reading recognition. The difficulty for students with AS is that many teachers fail to recognize their special education needs because these individuals, with their pedantic speech, advanced vocabulary, and little professor style of interaction often come across as knowing or understanding more than they really do (Myles & Simpson, 2001; Safran, 2001; Safran et al., 2003).

Teachers and parents of students with AS observe that these students experience atypical responses to sensory input. Students with AS may be hypersensitive to light, sounds, or physical proximity or touch. As a result, this hypersensitivity to certain stimuli may lead to increased behavior problems (Myles & Simpson, 2001). Other behaviors related to sensory issues include reports of high tolerance for pain and self-stimulatory activity and other unusual stereotypical behavior patterns (e.g., light filtering with hands or fingers). Stereotypic, self-stimulatory behavior may occur more often when the student with AS is fatigued or under stress (Myles & Simpson, 2001).

One of the other characteristics common to individuals with AS is poor motor skills, balancing, and coordination. These problems make it difficult for students to engage in a variety of games requiring gross motor abilities and may further exacerbate their social integration and interaction with other peers (Klin, Volkmar, et al., 2000; Myles & Simpson, 2001). Fine motor skill deficits will interfere with writing, art, and other industrial arts opportunities at school. Klin, Volkmar, et al. (2000) note that it is quite common for school-based occupational therapists to provide sensory integration therapy related to motor deficits. Empirical evidence for the effects of sensory integration are lacking, but as reported in Klin, Volkmar, et al. (2000), such methods could provide strategies for increasing the comfort level for students with a particular sensory issue and provide a means for engaging the student socially with enjoyable motor activities.

Screening and Assessment

Firm protocols for identifying individuals with AS do not exist at this time, primarily because most instruments and procedures were developed with the intent of diagnosing autism instead (Klin, Sparrow, Marans, Carter, & Volkmar, 2000; Safran et al., 2003). More recently, however, several AS screening measures were developed and are available for professionals to use, such as the Australian Scale for Asperger's Syndrome, the Autism Spectrum Disorders Screening Questionnaire (ASDSQ), the Asperger Syndrome Diagnostic Scale (ASDS), and the Gilliam Asperger's Disorder Scale (GADS). Presently, only the ASDSQ has been field-tested and validated (Safran, 2001). Reviews of the research on the other screening measures indicate a need for further empirical validation and norming in the United States (Safran et al., 2003). A diagnostic interview instrument that is available is the Asperger Syndrome Diagnostic Interview (ASDI), which Safran et al. (2003) state is useful as a guide for further assessment but should not be used as the sole instrument for basing a diagnosis of AS.

In public education, the use of screening instruments would be just one part of the overall diagnostic process in identifying students with possible AS. The diagnostic or evaluation process would consist of a comprehensive interdisciplinary assessment where information or data are gathered by such professionals as speech or language pathologists, school psychologists, family members, general education teachers, occupational therapists, school social workers, and school nurses. The information gathered would include, but not be limited to, developmental history, psychiatric or health history of the family, direct observations in a variety of settings, academic and social-behavioral skills, functional communication language skills, motor skills, and occupational or sensory profile information (cf. Klin, Sparrow, et al., 2000; Safran et al., 2003). Asperger Syndrome is a heterogeneous population bringing with it unique combinations or patterns of skills and behaviors expressed in varying degrees of severity. Given the complexity of AS, Klin, Sparrow, et al. (2000) stress that (1) it is important that parents observe and participate in the evaluation to help demystify the assessment process for them, clarify shared observations, and help foster understanding of the disorder, (2) evaluation findings should be translated into a single coherent picture of the child and stress the implications of the findings in terms of the child's day-to-day adaptations, learning, psychological well-being, and vocational training, and (3) because of the lack of understanding or awareness of educators and mental health professionals about the disorder, its features, and other associated conditions (e.g., poor motor planning or control), there needs to be consistent and clear communication among agencies to secure and implement intervention with fidelity.

Treatment and Intervention

A great deal of effective programming strategies and resources exist to aid in supporting students with AS in schools (cf. Klin, Volkmar, et al., 2000; Myles & Andreon, 2001; Myles & Simpson, 2003; Safran, 2001; Safran et al., 2003; Williams, 2001). For example, for effective social interventions or supports, educators might try teaching the hidden curriculum (i.e., social skills not directly taught but which children are assumed to know), using social autopsies to help develop an understanding of the social mistakes they made; or employing a buddy system to help with social interactions. For issues related to academics, use the student's special interests (e.g., *Star Wars*) as a positive reinforcer to help strengthen classroom behavior; if fluorescent lighting is affecting learning, provide sunglasses; teach metacognitive skills such as self-interrogation to help with organizational skills. For students with AS who have behavioral challenges related to changes in routines, providing posted schedules and lists of routines helps their environment become more predictable. Other classroom or academically related strategies might include a peer note-taker to help the student with AS who has fine-motor challenges or using the priming technique to help children with AS become familiar with academic material prior to its use in school, thereby reducing potential stress and anxiety and increasing the potential for success. These and many more strategies and interventions are available to the educator and mental health practitioner from the sources listed in the reference section as well as in these sources' own reference list. Because AS has only shown up recently, educational practitioners must understand that the field is still struggling to understand the nature and

unique facets of AS; AS still lacks a clear definitive definition of what specific methods and strategies to employ that have the greatest effect and cost benefit. However, researchers are encouraged that the instructional and behavioral strategies that are currently available to educators do have a positive impact in helping students with AS succeed at school and prepare for adulthood (Myles & Simpson, 2001; Safran, 2001; Williams, 2001).

REFERENCES

American Psychiatric Association. (1994). *Diagnostic and statistical manual of mental disorders* (4th ed.). Washington, DC: Author.

Frith, U. (Ed.). (1991). *Autism and Asperger Syndrome.* Cambridge: Cambridge University Press.

Klin, A., Sparrow, S. S., Marans, W. D., Carter, A., & Volkmar, F. R. (2000). Assessment issues in children and adolescents with Asperger Syndrome. In A. Klin, F. R. Volkmar, & S. S. Sparrow (Eds.), *Asperger Syndrome* (pp. 309–339). New York: Guilford.

Klin, A., Volkmar, F. R., & Sparrow, S. S. (Eds.). (2000). *Asperger Syndrome.* New York: Guilford.

Myles, B. S., & Andreon, D. (2001). *Asperger Syndrome and adolescence: Practical solutions for school success.* Shawnee Mission, KS: AAPC.

Myles, B. S., & Simpson, R. L. (2001). Effective practices for students with Asperger Syndrome. *Focus on Exceptional Children, 34*(3), 1–14.

Safran, S. P. (2001). Asperger Syndrome: The emerging challenge to special education. *Exceptional Children, 67,* 151–160.

Safran, S. P., Safran, J. S., & Ellis, K. (2003). Intervention ABCs for children with Asperger Syndrome. *Topics in Language Disorders, 23,* 154–165.

Williams, K. (2001). Understanding the student with Asperger Syndrome: Guidelines for teachers. *Intervention in School and Clinic, 36,* 287–292.

Wing, L., & Potter, D. (2002). The epidemiology of Autistic Spectrum Disorders: Is the prevalence rising? *Mental Retardation and Developmental Disabilities Research Reviews, 8,* 151–161.

ROLLEN C. FOWLER
*Eugene 4J School District,
Eugene, Oregon*

AUTISM
AUTISM TREATMENT OPTIONS
CHRONIC ILLNESS IN CHILDREN

ASPERGER SYNDROME DIAGNOSTIC SCALE

The Asperger Syndrome Diagnostic Scale (ASDS; Myles, Jones-Bock, & Simpson, 2000) is an individually administered measure used to identify children or adolescents ages 5 through 18 who manifest the characteristics of Asperger's

Disorder. The scale contains 50 yes or no items that are divided into five subscales of behavior including Language, Social, Maladaptive, Cognitive, and Sensorimotor. These items are summed to produce an Asperger Syndrome Quotient (ASQ), which indicates the likelihood that an individual has this disorder. Administration usually takes between 10 and 15 minutes, and the measure should be completed by an individual who has had direct, sustained contact with the child or adolescent for at least 2 weeks (e.g., parents, teachers). The record form provides the rater with instructions and contains a score summary section, a profile of scores, and an ASQ interpretation guide. There is an additional section that provides the examiner with questions that may be used to obtain further diagnostic information.

This measure was normed on a sample of 115 children and adolescents between 5 and 18 years of age who had been diagnosed with Asperger's Disorder. The sample was representative of the 1997 U.S. Census data with respect to race and geographic region. There was a significantly larger percentage of males in the sample compared with females as it has been reported in research that males are four times more likely to be diagnosed with Asperger's Disorder than females (Kadesjo, Gillberg, & Hagberg, 1999). The ASDS yields percentile ranks and standard scores ($M = 10$, $SD = 3$) for the subtests and a percentile rank and quotient score ($M = 100$, $SD = 15$) derived from the sum of the subscale scores.

The internal consistency of the items on the ASDS was determined to be .83 using Cronbach's coefficient alpha, suggesting that the items are quite consistent. Despite the criticism that some behavior rating scales have received regarding their lack of established interrater reliability (Reid, Maag, & Vasa, 1993), the ASDS has demonstrated an interrater reliability coefficient of .93. Item analysis of the ASQ has shown that the items have strong discriminating power, and the ASDS has demonstrated an 85 percent accuracy rate in the identification of individuals with Asperger's Disorder. Research has shown that this measure can effectively discriminate individuals with Asperger's Disorder from other diagnostic groups such as autism, behavior disorders, Attention-Deficit/Hyperactivity Disorder, and learning disabilities.

Goldstein's review of the scale (2002) raised concerns about the validity of the ASDS, the population upon which it was normed, and the ability of the ASDS to provide accurate differential diagnoses. Goldstein noted that the scale may hold promise as a research tool, but there appeared to be little evidence that it could distinguish among the various types of Pervasive Developmental Disorders or diagnose Asperger syndrome specifically.

REFERENCES

Goldstein, S. (2002). Review of the Asperger Syndrome Diagnostic Scale. *Journal of Autism & Developmental Disorders, 32,* 611–614.

Kadesjo, B., Gillberg, C., & Hagberg, B. (1999). Brief report: Autism and AS in seven-year-old children: A total population study. *Journal of Autism and Developmental Disorders, 29,* 327–331.

Myles, B., Jones-Bock, S., & Simpson, R. (2000). *Asperger Syndrome Diagnostic Scale: Examiner's manual.* Austin, TX: PRO-ED.

Plake, B. S., Impara, J. C., & Spies, R. A. (Eds.). (2003). *The fifteenth mental measurements yearbook.* Lincoln, NE: Buros Institute of Mental Measurements.

Reid, R., Maag, J. W., & Vasa, S. F. (1993). Attention deficit hyperactivity disorder as a disability category: A critique. *Exceptional Children, 60,* 198–214.

RON DUMONT
Fairleigh Dickinson University

JOHN O. WILLIS
Rivier College

ASPHYXIA

Asphyxia is a medical emergency requiring immediate intervention to prevent infant mortality and morbidity (Golden & Peters, 1985). Asphyxia occurs with inadequate oxygenation and cellular perfusion. This article deals specifically with asphyxia that occurs during the time of birth or shortly thereafter. Many terms are associated with oxygen deprivation during this period; pertinent information can be found in different sources under the headings of neonatal asphyxia, asphyxia neonatorium, perinatal asphyxia, intrapartum asphyxia, and hypoxic ischemic encephalopathy (HIE). Asphyxia has been hard to define accurately, which has caused difficulty in research on its effects and prognosis for recovery. The classical definition of asphyxia has been a low Apgar score with more emphasis on the 5- or even 10-minute scores than on the 1-minute (Fitzhardinge & Pape, 1981). As low Apgar scores are not necessarily associated with asphyxia, however, this definition is not always accurate and is a poor predictor for neurological outcome. Predicting outcome is very difficult. Even infants with 0 Apgar scores at birth have survived after efficient intervention with no serious handicaps (Rosen, 1985). Incidence of damage is generally overestimated when compared with actual findings (Brann, 1985). HIE, whose description follows, is predictive of later deficits.

Four basic mechanisms underlie asphyxia during the immediate perinatal period: (1) interruption of umbilical blood flow; (2) failure of placental exchange because of premature separation of the placenta from the uterus; (3) inadequate perfusion or oxygenation of the maternal side of the placenta as in severe hypotension; and (4) infant failure to inflate the lungs and complete transition to extrauterine life. In early stages, asphyxia may reverse spontaneously if the cause is removed, but later stages require varying degrees of medical intervention because of circulatory and neurological changes (Fitzhardinge & Pape, 1981).

Asphyxia is a progressive yet potentially reversible process with severity and duration of the insult affecting later outcome. Severe asphyxia can result in death within 10 minutes without proper intervention (Fitzhardinge & Pape, 1981). Delayed intervention may exacerbate cellular injury in all organ systems, contributing to a poor outcome. The brain is the most vulnerable system and mediates the most pronounced effects on later life. Asphyxia not only affects the brain directly, but also impairs the autoregulation centers controlling cerebral blood flow, which may cause intraventricular hemorrhage with resultant complications (Golden & Peters, 1985). Premature infants appear to be particularly susceptible to this complication.

Cerebral palsy (CP) is the most frequent complication of asphyxia (Swaiman & Russman, 2006). Even then, risk is high only when the Apgar score is low (<3) for prolonged periods (>10 to 15 minutes; Freeman, 1985). The incidence of CP may be as high as 38 percent in infants with Apgar scores of 0 to 3 at 20 minutes, and often occurs in conjunction with mental retardation and seizures. Asphyxia does not seem to be associated with severe mental retardation in the absence of CP (Paneth & Stark, 1983).

HIE may result from severe asphyxia. Children diagnosed with HIE show signs of neurologic dysfunction within 1 week, and often within 12 hours, after birth. The major signs of dysfunction include seizures, altered states of consciousness, and abnormalities in tone, posture, reflexes, and respiration. Infants who exhibit seizures have a 30 to 75 percent likelihood of long-term sequelae. Mortality is high among infants who had definite neurologic abnormality at discharge. Full-term infants with a history of asphyxia and an abnormal neurologic exam during the first week of life show a 7 percent incidence of early death and a 28 percent incidence of neurological handicaps. The most common deficits seen in severely affected children include spastic quadriplegia (a form of CP), severe mental retardation, seizures, hearing deficits, and microcephaly. Treatment for HIE is improving but research is difficult. Identification of infants at risk for neurological handicaps is becoming increasingly important as early intervention techniques improve (Brann, 1985).

Overall, the majority of asphyxiated infants suffer no detectable neurologic or intellectual sequelae. Prognosis is good even in relatively serious cases if neurologic examination is normal by 1 week of age. As would be expected, prognosis is poor when the asphyxia is long and severe or subsequent abnormal clinical features appear (Paneth & Stark, 1983). Much about asphyxia and its sequelae is still not well understood. However, adequate prenatal care, careful monitoring during labor and delivery with prompt obstetrical intervention, and immediate intervention after delivery by professionals skilled in resuscitation all contribute to lowering the incidence of asphyxia and lessening its long-term effects (Hill & Volpe, 2006; Phibbs, 1981).

REFERENCES

Brann, A., Jr. (1985). Factors during neonatal life that influence brain disorders. In J. Freeman (Ed.), *Prenatal and perinatal factors associated with brain disorders* (NIH Pub #85-1149, pp. 263–358). Bethesda, MD: National Institutes of Health.

Fitzhardinge, P. M., & Pape, K. E. (1981). Follow-up studies of the high risk newborn. In G. Avery (Ed.), *Neonatology: Pathophysiology and management of the newborn* (2nd ed., pp. 350–367). Philadelphia: Lippincott.

Freeman, J. (1985). Summary. In J. Freeman (Ed.), *Prenatal and perinatal factors associated with brain disorders* (NIH Pub #85-1149, pp. 13–32). Bethesda, MD: National Institutes of Health.

Golden, S., & Peters, D. (1985). Delivery room care. In G. Merenstein & S. Gardner (Eds.), *Handbook of neonatal intensive care* (pp. 31–54). St. Louis, MO: Mosby.

Hill, A., & Volpe, J. J. (2006). Hypoxic-ischemic cerebral injury in the newborn. In K. F. Swaiman & S. Ashwal (Eds.), *Pediatric neurology* (4th ed., pp. 191–202). St. Louis, MO: Mosby.

Paneth, N., & Stark, R. I. (1983). Cerebral palsy and mental retardation in relation to indicators of perinatal asphyxia. *American Journal of Obstetrics & Gynecology, 146,* 960–966.

Phibbs, R. H. (1981). Delivery room management of the newborn. In G. Avery (Ed.), *Neonatology: Pathophysiology and management of the newborn* (2nd ed., pp. 350–367). Philadelphia: Lippincott.

Rosen, M. G. (1985). Factors during labor and delivery that influence brain disorders. In J. Freeman (Ed.), *Prenatal and perinatal factors associated with brain disorders* (NIH Pub #85-1149, pp. 13–32). Bethesda, MD: National Institutes of Health.

Swaiman, K. F., & Russman, B. S. (2006). Cerebral palsy. In K. F. Swaiman & S. Ashwal (Eds.), *Pediatric neurology* (4th ed., pp. 312–324). St. Louis, MO: Mosby.

BRENDA M. POPE
*New Hanover Memorial
Hospital*

ANOXIA
APGAR RATING SCALE
CEREBRAL PALSY
LOW BIRTH WEIGHT INFANTS
PREMATURITY

ASSESSMENT, CURRICULUM BASED

See CURRICULUM-BASED ASSESSMENT.

ASSESSMENTS, ALTERNATE

Alternate assessments provide a vehicle for students to demonstrate their knowledge and skills through an alternative format to traditional testing. With the passage of the No Child Left Behind (NCLB) Act of 2001 (2002) and the reauthorization of the Individuals with Disabilities Education Improvement Act (2004), alternate assessments are most frequently defined in the context of statewide assessment programs. In a statewide test program, alternate assessments are used to evaluate the performance and progress of students with significant cognitive disabilities who are deemed unable to validly participate in a state's traditional assessment system. They are designed to capture a student's performance and progress toward grade-level content standards and are judged against a state's alternate achievement standards.

Typical statewide assessments are designed to allow educators to make broad inferences about what a student knows and can do in various settings and under various conditions; statewide alternate assessments do not allow for similar inferences. Because alternate assessments usually narrow the depth, breadth, or complexity of the content being assessed, inferences based on a student's score are restricted. In most cases, the data derived from alternate assessments will have limited generalizability to other contexts. Educators who interpret and use scores on alternate assessments should be aware of the limited generalizability of the data they provide.

Federal regulations make it clear that *all* students are to be assessed on a state's academic content standards (U.S. Department of Education, 2003). For example, a student who is expected to demonstrate knowledge of the critical features of biographies in the 10th grade may demonstrate their knowledge through a traditional statewide assessment or through an alternate assessment. The content remains the same regardless of assessment format. However, in an alternate assessment, the depth, breadth, or complexity of behaviors required on the test will be different from those expected of students on the traditional test. Differences between alternate assessments and traditional assessments, therefore, do not lie in their content standards but instead in the achievement standards associated with each type of assessment.

The format of alternate assessments varies from state to state. The majority of states use portfolio systems (Thompson & Thurlow, 2003), while a smaller number employ checklists or rating scales to measure the performance and progress of students with significant cognitive disabilities. A student's individualized education program (IEP) should not be used as an alternate assessment (U.S. Department of Education, 2003). Although the data obtained from an IEP is valuable and should be used to drive instructional programs for students with disabilities, it should not be used in a state accountability system. Empirical research into the effects of various formats on the technical adequacy of the test or the quality of inferences derived from test scores is limited. As states continue to refine their alternate assessments, the focus needs to be on creating assessments that accurately measure students' performance on grade-level

content standards as well as contribute valid data to a state's accountability system (Johnson & Arnold, 2004).

Each student's IEP team decides how he or she will participate in a state's assessment system, and decisions are made on an individual basis. The federal government places only one parameter around this decision: Only those students with significant cognitive disabilities may participate (U.S. Department of Education, 2005). Once it is established that a student has a significant cognitive disability, his or her IEP team relies on various sources of information to inform their decision about the appropriateness of that student participating in an alternate assessment. Only if the student is unable to validly participate in a state's traditional assessment (with or without accommodations) is participation in an alternate assessment considered. The decision is not based on the student's disability per se but instead based on the student's ability to validly participate in a state's traditional assessment.

The percentage of students participating in an alternate assessment differs by state (Wiley, Thurlow, & Klein, 2005). No limits exist related to the number of students who may participate in an alternate assessment. However, according to NCLB, a school district may only include 1 percent of the total number of scores rated "proficient" or higher (on the alternate assessment) in their adequate yearly progress (AYP) calculations. All of the scores beyond the 1-percent cap are scored as "not proficient" regardless of the actual score.

In May 2005, the U.S. Department of Education released initial guidelines allowing states to include up to 2 percent of students measured against modified achievement standards. Unlike alternate achievement standards developed to measure students with significant cognitive disabilities, modified achievement standards are developed to measure progress and performance of students with persistent academic difficulties that challenge their ability to reach grade-level achievement standards even with research-based instruction. Release of these guidelines on the inclusion of an additional 2 percent of students in alternate assessments measured against modified achievement standards was due in part to research demonstrating that some students display persistent cognitive challenges that impede their ability to meaningfully participate in a state's traditional assessment. The decision was also in response to the concerns of many educators that including only 1 percent of students in an alternate assessment program leaves many students with no options for validly participating in a statewide test system. For these students, the alternate assessment has been shown to be too easy, while the traditional assessment is too hard. Other educators, however, are concerned that increasing the percentages allowable for AYP will result in lower expectations for those students with disabilities who are currently making progress toward passing the traditional assessment. This concern may be addressed at the level of the state department, as participation in an alternate assessment judged against modified achievement standards will not be mandated but instead will provide another option for educators as they strive for valid inclusion of all students in statewide accountability programs.

REFERENCES

Individuals with Disabilities Education Improvement Act of 2004, 20 U.S.C. § 1400, H.R. 1350.

Johnson, E., & Arnold, N. (2004, September). Validating an alternate assessment. *Remedial and Special Education, 25,* 266–275.

No Child Left Behind Act of 2001, Pub. L. No. 107-110, 115 Stat. 1425 (2002).

Thompson, S., & Thurlow, M. (2003). 2003 *State special education outcomes: Marching on.* Minneapolis: University of Minnesota, National Center on Educational Outcomes. Retrieved January 18, 2005, from http://education.umn.edu/NCEO/OnlinePubs/ 2003StateReport.htm

U.S. Department of Education. (2003). *Title I—Improving the academic achievement of the disadvantaged; Final Rule, 68 Fed. Reg. 236* (December 9, 2003).

U.S. Department of Education. (2005). *Alternate achievement standards for students with the most significant cognitive disabilities: Non-Regulatory guidance* (August, 2005).

Wiley, H. I., Thurlow, M. L., & Klein, J. A. (2005). *Steady progress: State public reporting practices for students with disabilities after the first year of NCLB (2002–2003)* (Technical Report 40). Minneapolis: University of Minnesota, National Center on Educational Outcomes. Retrieved September 8, 2005, from http:// education.umn.edu/NCEO/OnlinePubs/Technical40.htm

LINDY CRAWFORD
*University of Colorado at
Colorado Springs*

ACHIEVEMENT TESTS
BEHAVIOR ASSESSMENT SYSTEM FOR CHILDREN–
  SECOND EDITION
"g" FACTOR THEORY
INDIVIDUALS WITH DISABILITIES EDUCATION
  IMPROVEMENT ACT OF 2004 (IDEIA)
INTELLIGENCE TESTING
INTELLIGENT TESTING
KAUFMAN ASSESSMENT BATTERY FOR CHILDREN–
  SECOND EDITION
NO CHILD LEFT BEHIND ACT
VINELAND ADAPTIVE BEHAVIOR SCALES–SECOND
  EDITION
WECHSLER ADULT INTELLIGENCE SCALE–THIRD EDITION
WECHSLER INTELLIGENCE SCALE FOR CHILDREN–
  FOURTH EDITION

ASSIMILATION

Assimilation is one of two complementary processes of adaptation to the environment in Jean Piaget's theory of intellectual development; its counterpart is accommodation. Assimilation involves incorporating external elements (objects or events) into existing cognitive or sensorimotor schemes; incoming information is interpreted or adjusted in a manner consistent with current cognitive structures. In contrast, accommodation involves changing the structures that assimilate information (Brainerd, 1978).

The distinction between assimilation and accommodation can be illustrated by a physiological example: digestion of food (Ginsburg & Opper, 1969). Acids (or the body's current schemes or structures) transform the food into a form that can be used; thus elements of the external world are assimilated. Accommodation occurs in this example when, in order to deal with a foreign substance, stomach muscles contract, acids are released by certain organs, and so forth. Physical structures (the stomach and other organs) accommodate to an external element (food).

Assimilation involves both constraints on the nature and range of a child's interactions with the environment and the seeking out of new stimuli that can be assimilated into existing schemes (Gelman & Baillargeon, 1983). Piaget discusses three forms of assimilation: functional assimilation, which involves a basic tendency to use an existing structure such as a sucking reflex; recognitory assimilation, which involves recognizing particular situations in which the scheme should be applied; and generalizing assimilation, which involves a tendency to generalize a scheme to new objects and situations (Ginsburg & Opper, 1969).

REFERENCES

Brainerd, C. J. (1978). *Piaget's theory of intelligence.* Englewood Cliffs, NJ: Prentice Hall.

Gelman, R., & Baillargeon, R. (1983). A review of some Piagetian concepts. In P. H. Mussen (Ed.), *Handbook of child psychology: Vol. III. Cognitive development* (pp. 167–230). New York: Wiley.

Ginsburg, H., & Opper, S. (1969). *Piaget's theory of intellectual development: An introduction.* Englewood Cliffs, NJ: Prentice Hall.

LINDA J. STEVENS
University of Minnesota

ACCOMMODATION
PIAGET, JEAN

ASSISTIVE DEVICES

Assistive devices, or aids, are intended to enhance the daily functioning of people with disabilities. As such, such devices may be specifically created for this application, or they may consist of adaptations to existing devices. The intent of these devices is to replace, compensate for, or improve the individual's specific abilities or task performances. Assistive devices can be classified in three general categories based on the functions they are intended to enhance: medical, mobility, and sensory. Examples of devices specifically created for such purposes related to general mobility or performance include canes, walkers, wheelchairs, and shower chairs (MedicineNet, 2005). Amplified telephones, computer screen magnification, ramps, and automatic door openers would be examples of adaptations to existing devices that improve accessibility or quality of utilization.

Assistive devices can be as simple as modified eating utensils, adapted books, pencil holders, bathing accessories, and grab bars. Assistive devices can also be complex and incorporate various combinations of mechanical, electronic, and computer resources. The creation of microcomputer components with specialized control devices, electronic communication devices, and other sophisticated electronic components has greatly increased the quantity and quality of resources available to individuals with disabilities. In addition, there has been a blending of devices across categories, such as intelligent electronic controls for wheelchairs and computer-based devices that control lights, doors, appliances and telephone access. Voice recognition systems integrated with mechanical systems that allow the individual to act on any aspect of the environment are also becoming readily available. Such systems provide the ability to open windows, turn on lights, lock doors, and so on. Additional computer-based assistive technologies include alternative keyboards and mice, head pointing devices, voice recognition software, and screen magnification software. Such components not only allow the individual to gain access and control of the computer for accomplishing tasks such as Internet browsing, word processing, and e-mail, but also they can then be used to have the computer control external devices. Both expressive and receptive communications abilities have become greatly enhanced by applications such as synthesized speech technologies that provide text-to-speech screen readers for individuals with visual disabilities and similar text readers for individuals who are unable to speak. Thus, the various computer mechanical input devices, telecommunications interfaces, and specialized software all combine to provide computer-based assistive systems that can provide benefits to the full range of disabilities and performance. The following web sites provide additional information and definitions:

Augmentative Communication Glossary, 1999, http://www.cs.wright.edu/bie/rehabengr/AAC/ glossary.htm

BMC Remedy Service Management, 2005, http://www.remedy.com/customers/dev_community/ UserExperience/glossary.htm

Children's Hospital at Montefiore, 2004, http://montekids.org/healthlibrary/peds/growth/ glossary.htm

London Health Sciences Centre, 2005, http://www.lhsc.on.ca/programs/msclinic/define/ a.htm

MedicineNet, 2005, *Definition of assistive device* Retrieved May 20, 2006, from http://www.medterms.com/script/main/art .asp?articlekey=2372

RONALD ZELLNER
Texas A&M University

ASSISTIVE TECHNOLOGY ACT

ASSISTIVE TECHNOLOGY ACT

In 1998 Congress enacted the Assistive Technology Act (P.L. 105-394), commonly known as the *Tech Act*. Today, funding authorized by the Tech Act supports three general types of programs, which vary from state to state:

- Assistive technology (AT) state grant programs, which provide a variety of services including demonstration centers to allow people to see different types of assistive technology, equipment loan and recycling programs, and information and referral services
- Protection and advocacy services for persons needing legal assistance in obtaining services
- Federal or state partnership alternative financing programs that provide low-interest loans to persons with disabilities to purchase assistive technology.

On June 14, 2004, the House passed H.R. 4278, the Improving Access to Assistive Technology for Individuals with Disabilities Act of 2004, introduced on May 5, 2004. The bill amends the Assistive Technology Act of 1998 to support programs of grants to states to address the assistive technology needs of individuals with disabilities. The House and the Senate passed H.R. 4278, and it was signed into law by President Bush on October 25, 2004. To read the bill as signed into law, go to http://thomas.loc.gov/cgi-bin/ query/z?108:H.R.4278.ENR:

STAFF

ASSISTIVE TECHNOLOGY FOR HEARING IMPAIRMENTS

Telecommunication Device for the Deaf (TDD)/ Text Telephone (TTY)

This is a device that enables people who are deaf to communicate by phone via a typewriter that converts typed letters into electric signals through a modem. These signals are sent through the phone lines and then translated into typed messages and printed on a typewriter connected to a phone on the other end.

Assistive Listening Device (ALD)

The intelligibility of the human voice is degraded by poor room acoustics as well as hearing loss. Most assistive listening devices (ALDs) use a microphone or transmitter positioned close to the instructor's mouth to send the instructor's voice through the air or by cable to the receiver worn by the student. By placing the microphone close to the instructor's mouth, ALDs can provide clear sound over distances, eliminate echoes, and reduce surrounding noises. This is a distinct acoustic advantage of ALDs compared to personal hearing aids. The microphone location allows the level of the speaker's voice to stay constant to the listener regardless of the distance between the two.

There are different types of ALDs (FM, Soundfield Amplification, and Induction Loop Systems), each system having special features, capabilities, advantages, and disadvantages. No single technology is without limitations or can be expected to fulfill all the essential auditory needs of all users. It is important to find the one that is right for the individual with a hearing loss.

ANNE REBER

Texas A&M University

ASSISTIVE DEVICES
ASSISTIVE TECHNOLOGY ACT

ASSISTIVE TECHNOLOGY IN HIGHER EDUCATION

Assistive technology is used extensively in higher education. Although the laws and statutes that govern the provision of services in higher education are somewhat different, the types of technologies used are very similar. As in the lower grades, alternative format production is a big issue. But unlike them, higher education has additional issues, especially with the textbook adoption process. Alternative format production is often the first step in the service provision process for a disability service office and therefore warrants some attention.

Textbook Adoptions and Alternative Format Production

Differences between the textbook adoption models of elementary and higher education contribute to major differences in the service provision model of the two systems. In the kindergarten through twelfth grade (K–12) environment, it is typical for the textbook adoption process to take 2 to 3 years. Books are submitted by publishers to the state board of education for review. To even be considered, most publishers have to sign assurances that the book will be provided in accessible formats by the time of purchase. Publishers agree to this because they know that they will have sufficient time to produce such resources when and if the book is adopted. They further know that the quantities ordered will justify the time and expense of creating accessible formats. After a lengthy period of time, the book is officially adopted by the state, purchased in quantity, and shipped to the school districts for use. The average lifespan of a typical K–12 textbook is 2 to 3 years, but some states use books much longer.

In contrast to the K–12 model, textbook adoptions in higher education proceed much quicker as they are, in many cases, determined solely by the instructor. The instructors choose their course books, in many cases, independently of other instructors or departments. To keep current with this selection process, publishers focus more on variety and currency. Consequently, textbooks must be constantly updated in order for the publisher to keep competitive and make money. In general, institutional adoption policies in the higher education environment are loosely enforced, even if they exist. Many instructors feel strongly that institutional adoption policies is a blow to academic freedom, while others see utility in having some policies to insure consistency across the institution. The net result is a system of textbook adoption that has far more current textbooks than the K–12 system, but sacrifices process, consistency, and accessibility.

Given this model, there are three issues that affect format production in higher education when compared to that of K–12. The first issue relates to publishers. In most states, publishers have no legal responsibility to provide alternative formats to institutions of higher education. Some exceptions to this are California and Illinois. Moreover, publishers' infrastructures have been optimized to produce a final product that is physically printed on paper and distributed. Any other product format (such as a hypertext markup language [HTML] version of a textbook) must be produced from the print-optimized version. This leads to accessibility barriers. The bottom line is that publishers have little or no responsibility to provide accessible text materials in the higher education environment.

At this point in time, publishers cannot produce an accessible format without significant time and money. Recently, publishers have examined a change in process to produce digital formats of textbooks that transform gracefully into other formats. Slowly, publishers are moving in the digital direction. As more and more states approve statutes requiring accessible texts and national pressure mounts to address the issue in a legal manner, publishers are beginning to put the necessary changes into place.

This illustration is not meant to infer that publishers don't care about accessibility. On the contrary, they see accessibility as a means not only of assisting students with disabilities but also as a competitive advantage. After all, the same techniques that make information accessible to students with disabilities also make the information accessible to nondisabled students who may access the information using other means.

The second issue is related to the manner of provision of higher education. Higher education has evolved more and more into a customer-driven model of consumerism. This has led to a wide variety of classes and courses of study to meet the needs of the diverse student population. As a result, students can register for any course they are qualified to take at virtually any time. Because very few textbooks are available in an accessible format, accessible formats must be created ad hoc by the institution. This problem gives the disability services office little or no time to prepare.

The third issue is related to the selection of textbooks by instructors. It is not uncommon for the more populous courses to change textbooks annually or even each semester. Because staffing for courses is often delayed, instructors are sometimes assigned late to courses. In the absence of a textbook adoption policy, instructors may choose textbooks just before or even after a course begins. A recent survey of a major 4-year university revealed that 15 percent of textbook adoptions were given to the bookstores after the first day of class. This selection process provides little time for the disability services office to produce alternative formats.

Types of Assistive Technology in Higher Education

All of the major classes of assistive technology are represented in higher education, but some are less common than others. For example, augmentative communication technology, which is common in K–12, is generally not provided in higher education. Devices such as communication boards and speech synthesis microphones are generally provided by the student, not by the institution. Under the higher education model, augmentative communication in most cases would be considered a personal device and therefore not legally mandated to be provided, whereas in K–12, these devices were provided by the school district (under the Individuals with Disabilities Education Act [IDEA]). Once the student moves out of the K–12 system, their personal technology needs are handled in many cases by state vocational rehabilitation (VR) agencies. Thus assistive technology is split between VR and the college, with the college providing access to learning materials and VR supporting personal technology needs.

Many colleges offer alternative format production services to include recording text materials onto tape and textbook scanning. In some cases, Braille and tactile graphic production services are provided. Modern Braille printers are capable of combining tactile graphics with Braille text and in some cases can even produce multiheight graphic embossing (see http://viewplustech.com/). Scanners are common and are usually equipped with optical character recognition software that is used to produce electronic versions of printed materials.

Getting the material converted into an accessible format is only the first step in giving the student access via assistive technology. Technologies commonly used to deliver the accessible material once it is converted include text-to-speech, print Braille, refreshable Braille, and screen magnification. Some student populations such as those with visual impairments may use a combination of technologies, such as text-to-speech and screen magnification. Increasingly, students with learning disabilities are using assistive technologies such as text-to-speech to listen to their text materials while reading them.

The advent of ubiquitous digital players such as MP3 players has given rise to a new alternative format process. Recently, some colleges have begun using textbook scanning combined with text-to-speech to output audio of scanned materials to digital files, such as MP3 files. These files can be burned to CD and played on a computer or downloaded to a portable digital audio player. The new technologies available greatly automate and speed this process to help disability services meet the tight turnaround requirements associated with higher education structures. For example, there is equipment readily available that removes a textbook's binding, and the pages are then scanned via an automatic feeder to provide an electronic version of the contents. The electronic text content is then converted to audio files for use in a digital audio player or integrated into special instructional resources.

Voice recognition software has been used in higher education for a number of years although it is not as common as other technologies. In the opinion of this reviewer, the technology is just now coming into its own, and it will be several years before voice recognition is as common as other assistive technologies. Currently, voice control over regular computer operations (e.g., open, close, send, print) is readily available on standard operating systems. Affordable dictation software is also available but requires extensive training for efficient use.

For students with hearing impairments, the use of wireless amplification systems (often termed *FM systems*) is a fairly common accommodation. Because this device offers access to the material presented in class, many colleges consider this device within their purview and will provide them. Computer-assisted captioning systems are also becoming more common. This accommodation consists of software usually used with a portable computer in the classroom that is used to record the audio portion of a class. Most systems do not produce a word-for-word transcript but rather an approximation or summary of what is said. Computer-assisted captioning requires a trained captionist in most cases. Although word-for-word, real-time captioning (e.g., courtroom type captioning) is sometimes used, it is less common than approximate dialog systems. As faculty more commonly use electronic formats for creation of their lecture materials, these materials may be made available to disability services offices for conversion to alternative formats. In keeping with the concept of universal design, such multiple formats are beginning to appear as part of the delivery format of many courses and will benefit all students, whether or not they have a disability.

REFERENCE

ViewPlus Technologies. (2005). *Braille printers and Braille embossing hardware.* Retrieved October 20, 2005, from http:// viewplustech.com/

DAVID SWEENEY
RONALD ZELLNER
Texas A&M University

ASSISTIVE TECHNOLOGY ACT
LEARNING DISABLED COLLEGE STUDENTS

ASSOCIATION FOR CHILDHOOD EDUCATION INTERNATIONAL

Founded in 1892, the Association for Childhood Education International (ACEI) is a not-for-profit professional education association of educators, parents, and other caregivers interested in promoting quality education practices for children. The organization was originally conceived to provide a formal organization to promote the interest and professionalism of the kindergarten movement throughout the world. With over 11,000 members in the United States and Canada, ACEI is the oldest organization of its kind. Members participate in local and state group activities, including meetings, workshops, and regional conferences. Annual Study Conferences have been held each year since 1896 to share ideas and contribute to the standard of excellence in teaching in all arenas, such as public and private day care centers, kindergartens, elementary schools, middle schools, high schools, and university-level teacher education programs.

The mission of ACEI is to promote the inherent rights, education, and well-being of all children, from infancy through early adolescence, in the home, school, and community. The organization is member-driven and is guided by a dynamic philosophy of education that is flexible and responsive to human needs in a changing society. Members are dedicated to a holistic, child-centered approach to education that considers the child's experiences in the home, school, community, and world.

ACEI is interested in promoting good educational practices for children. By acting as a facilitator for the sharing and dissemination of information through publications and conferences, the organization provides a service to its members and to the education community as a whole. This is accomplished through the regular publication of two refereed professional journals, *Childhood Education* and *Journal of Research in Childhood Education.* Additionally, the Association publishes books, newsletters, pamphlets, position papers, and position statements that relate to the welfare of children; recommend sound, developmentally appropriate educational practice; and include practical application guidelines for educators.

Other contributions of the organization include the publication of *Childhood Education,* a professional journal of theory and practice in the field. The journal has consistently sought to make a thoughtful, multifaceted contribution to the growing body of knowledge concerning children and the learning process. In 1986 an additional publication, *Journal of Research in Childhood Education,* was created as a vehicle for sharing research knowledge as it is acquired. A catalog containing information regarding ACEI publications is available free upon request.

Improved standards for teacher preparation and others involved with the care and development of children are among the association's goals. ACEI was appointed to serve as the organization responsible for overseeing the folio review process of elementary teacher preparation programs offered at U.S. colleges and universities seeking accreditation through the National Council for Accreditation of Teacher Education.

A library, including volumes on childhood and elementary education, is maintained at association headquarters. Association offices are located at 17904 Georgia Avenue, Suite 215, Olney, MD 20832. Telephone: (800) 423-3563 and (301) 570-2111.

TAMARA J. MARTIN
*The University of Texas of the
Permian Basin*

ASSOCIATION FOR CHILDREN AND ADULTS WITH LEARNING DISABILITIES

See LEARNING DISABILITIES ASSOCIATION.

ASSOCIATION FOR PERSONS WITH SEVERE HANDICAPS

See TASH.

ASSOCIATION FOR POSITIVE BEHAVIOR SUPPORT

The mission of the Association for Positive Behavior Support (APBS) is to help individuals improve their quality of life and reduce problem behaviors by advancing the development and use of positive behavior support. Positive behavior support (PBS) is an approach derived from social, behavioral, and biomedical science that is applied at the individual or systems level to achieve reduction in problem behaviors and improved quality of life. Problem behaviors such as aggression, self-injury, bullying, insubordination, disruption, vandalism, withdrawal, nonresponsivity and truancy continue to be among the most common reasons why people with and without disabilities are excluded from typical home, school, work, and community contexts. Problem behaviors function as barriers to the development of social relationships, employment, academic achievement, functional life skills, self-determination, health, and safety. Public policy in the areas of prevention, early intervention, education, adult services, and family support has moved to emphasize the active inclusion of all individuals in typical social and cultural contexts as well as the direct guidance of support options by self-advocates and their families. Problem behaviors remain a major barrier to achieving these public policy goals and to achieving the personal visions of individuals with and without disabilities and their families.

Positive behavior support is a practical and effective response to the challenges posed by problem behaviors. The vision of the APBS is to develop, disseminate, and continuously evaluate PBS practices, systems, and outcomes. The APBS's activities are based on the belief that PBS is an effective approach that is applicable across contexts with all people and is of specific value for advocates (including self-advocates), families, and all professionals who work with individuals with problem behavior. Further, the APBS believes that if PBS practices and systems are made more readily available, the result will not simply be reduction in problem behaviors but a dramatic improvement in the quality of the lives led by individuals receiving support.

The APBS is an active body, focusing its attention on dissemination, education, and public policy efforts. Specifically, the APBS does the following:

- Serves as an international forum for individuals interested in PBS
- Hosts an annual international conference
- Supports and promotes the *Journal of Positive Behavior Interventions*
- Publishes a quarterly newsletter
- Manages and links web sites on PBS practices, systems, and examples
- Engages in policy development around the provision of behavior support
- Maintains a directory of members to facilitate interaction among individuals interested in PBS practices
- Is working toward establishing national standards that define competency in the application of PBS
- Encourages the training of professionals skilled in PBS practices through the development of training materials and the embedding of PBS content in relevant professional certificate and degree programs
- Promotes access to state-of-the-art books and literature pertaining to PBS

Membership

All members of the organization (regular and student members) vote on business matters and elect members of the board. In addition, members also receive a subscription to the *Journal on Positive Behavior Interventions,* subscription to the quarterly *APBS Newsletter,* and discounted registration for the annual APBS Conference. The APBS hosts an annual international conference at locations around the United States. For additional information on APBS, go to http://www.APBS.org.

TIM KNOSTER
*Bloomsburg University of
Pennsylvania*

BEHAVIOR THERAPY
POSITIVE BEHAVIORAL SUPPORT

ASSOCIATION FOR SPECIAL EDUCATION TECHNOLOGY

See CENTER FOR APPLIED TECHNOLOGY.

ASSOCIATION FOR THE ADVANCEMENT OF BEHAVIOR THERAPY

The Association for Advancement of the Behavioral Therapies was founded in 1966 and renamed the Association for the Advancement of Behavior Therapy (AABT) in 1968. Headquartered in New York City, the AABT is a not-for-profit organization of over 4,500 mental health professionals and students who utilize and/or are interested in empirically based behavior therapy and cognitive behavior therapy. Membership is interdisciplinary and consists of psychologists, psychiatrists, social workers, physicians, nurses, and other mental health professionals who treat over 90 mental health problems. AABT does not certify its members.

Among its activities, the AABT sponsors training programs and lectures aimed at professionals and semiprofessionals, provides communication accessibility among behavior therapists interested in similar areas of research or specific problems, and maintains a speaker's bureau. Affiliates of the Association conduct training meetings, workshops, seminars, case demonstrations, and discussion groups. In addition, the AABT holds committees on continuing and public education and provides referrals to the general public upon request (a $5 postage and handling fee is required). A Fact Sheet regarding the problem for which help is being sought and the pamphlet, *Guidelines for Choosing a Behavior Therapist,* are included with mailed referrals. Referrals can be obtained by visiting AABT's web site at www.aabt.org/aabt.

The Association's Media & Community Connection Program assists the media with background information and news of the latest developments in the behavioral therapies. The program also helps locate suitable experts in the field for interviews or speaking engagements. Providing membership services to mental health professionals and students seeking to network with like-minded colleagues and to remain current in the behavioral therapies is another activity of the AABT.

AABT offers Full and Associate professional memberships and sponsors an Annual Convention every November, attracting approximately 2,000 participants. One to three smaller educational seminars are held each year as well. Two peer-reviewed journals, *Behavior Therapy* and *Cognitive & Behavioral Practice,* are published by the organization in addition to its newsletter, *The Behavior Therapist.* For a list of AABT publications or for information regarding upcoming educational programs, please call (212) 647-1890 or visit the AABT web site at www.aabt.org/aabt.

MARY LEON PEERY
Texas A&M University
First edition

TAMARA J. MARTIN
*The University of Texas of the
    Permian Basin*
Second edition

ASSOCIATION FOR THE GIFTED, THE

Founded in 1958, The Association for the Gifted is one of the 17 divisions of The Council for Exceptional Children. The purposes of this association are to (1) promote the welfare and education of children and youth with gifts, talents, and/or high potential; (2) improve educational opportunities for individuals from all diverse groups with gifts, talents, and/or high potential; (3) sponsor and foster activities to develop the field of gifted education, such as the dissemination of information, the conduct of research, and other scholarly investigations; (4) support and encourage specialized professional preparation for educators of individuals with gifts, talents, and/or high potential, as well as for professional persons in related fields; and (5) work with organizations, agencies, families, or individuals whose purposes are consistent with those of The Association for the Gifted.

The Association distributes two publications to its membership. One, the *Journal for the Education of the Gifted,* is a forum for theoretical, descriptive, and research articles that analyze and communicate information about the needs of children and youth with gifts, talents, and/or high potential. The *Journal* also serves as a forum for the exchange of diverse ideas and points of view on the education of the gifted and talented. The second publication, *TAG Update,* is the Association's newsletter, containing brief, timely information on the Association's activities, upcoming events, workshops and institutes, reports on legislation, and relevant news from other organizations.

Membership inquiries should be made to The Association for the Gifted, The Council for Exceptional Children, 1110 N. Glebe Road, Suite 300, Arlington, VA 22201. Only members of The Council for Exceptional Children are eligible to join The Association for the Gifted. Special membership categories for students and parents and professionals are available for those who qualify for these discounted membership rates.

STAFF

ASSOCIATION OF BLACK PSYCHOLOGISTS

The Association of Black Psychologists (ABPsi) was founded in San Francisco in 1968 when a number of black psychologists from across the country met to discuss the serious problems facing black psychologists and the larger black community. The founding members began building an organization through which they could confront the long-neglected needs of black professionals. They also hoped to have a positive impact on the mental health of the black community through programs, services, training, and advocacy. The Association is organized into four regions as well as a student division. From the original group, the membership of ABPsi has grown into an international organization of over 1,300 psychologists and mental health professionals, committed to addressing the mental health issues of individuals throughout the African diaspora.

The main offices of the Association of Black Psychologists can be reached at P.O. Box 55999, Washington, DC 20040-5999, or by telephone at (202) 722-0808.

NADINE M. LAMBERT
University of California, Berkeley
First edition

KAY E. KETZENBERGER
*The University of Texas of the
    Permian Basin*
Second edition

ASSOCIATIVE LEARNING

Associative learning, as demonstrated in the classical conditioning experiments of Pavlov (1927), is based on the concept that events or ideas that are experienced at the same time tend to become associated with each other. When a new (conditioned) stimulus is presented with an old (unconditioned) stimulus, the conditioned stimulus assumes the capability of eliciting a (conditioned) response almost identical to the original (unconditioned) response. The conditioned stimulus should be presented about half a second before the unconditioned stimulus for maximum effectiveness.

Associative learning is routinely applied when students recognize words, spell, and recall math facts. A number of remedial techniques are also based on the associative principle. Multisensory approaches to reading, which presume the formation of associative bonds across sensory modalities, have been successful in remediating deficits in mildly and severely reading-disabled children and in retarded students (Sutaria, 1982). Visual imagery training, in which children learn to associate mental pictures with printed text, has been shown to improve learning-disabled students' reading comprehension (Clark, Warner, Alley, Deshler, & Shumaker, 1981).

Children with mental retardation, for whom associative skills are often an area of relative strength, have improved their memory performance when taught to pair words according to their conceptual similarity (Lathey & Tobias, 1981). Associative learning is a fundamental principle of teaching, and children's associative learning skills can be corrected and compensated for by using a variety of techniques (Woolfolk, 1995).

REFERENCES

Clark, F., Warner, M., Alley, G., Deshler, D., Shumaker, J., Vetter, A., & Nolan, R. (1981). *Visual imagery and self questioning.* Washington, DC: Bureau of Education for the Handicapped. (ERIC Document Reproduction Service No. ED 217 655)

Lathey, J. W., & Tobias, S. (1981, April). *Associative and conceptual training of retarded and normal children.* Paper presented at the annual meeting of the American Educational Research Association, Los Angeles. (ERIC Document Reproduction Service No. ED 206 139)

Pavlov, I. P. (1927). *Conditioned reflexes.* London: Oxford University Press.

Sutaria, S. (1982). *Multisensory approach to teaching of reading to learning disabled students.* Paper presented at the annual meeting of the World Congress on Reading, Dublin, Ireland. (ERIC Document Reproduction Service No. ED 246 600)

Woolfolk, A. E. (1995). *Educational psychology* (6th ed.). Boston: Allyn & Bacon.

GARY BERKOWITZ
Temple University

CONDITIONING
REVISUALIZATION

ASTHMA

Asthma is the most prevalent chronic health problem among children (American Lung Association, 2005). In 2002, asthma was the third leading cause of hospitalizations among children under 15 years of age. An asthmatic episode is characterized by a series of events that conclude in narrowed airways within the lungs. Initially, the lining of the lungs swells, the muscle surrounding the bronchial tubes tightens, and mucus secretion is increased in the airway. As a consequence, wheezing, coughing, shortness of breath, and tightness in the chest is evident during an asthmatic episode and results from this narrowing of airways.

There are two types of asthma: extrinsic and intrinsic (Asthma and Allergy Foundation of America, 2005). Extrinsic (or allergic) asthma symptoms are related to a specific allergen. Extrinsic asthma is the most common form of asthma and can be triggered by the inhalation of dust mites, animal dander, pollen, mold, chemicals, and so on. Intrinsic (or nonallergic) asthma symptoms are not related to a specific allergic reaction. Triggers for intrinsic asthma include anxiety, stress, vigorous exercise, cold or dry air, smoke, environmental pollution, and other irritants.

Medical treatments in the form of prescription drugs for childhood asthma are separated into five groups: inhaled bronchodilator medications, anti-inflammatory medications, systemic bronchodilator medications, systemic corticosteroid medications, and leukotriene modifiers (American Lung Association, 2005). Inhaled bronchodilators are the most effective treatment for opening of airways constricted by asthma and are commonly used by children with mild asthma. This type of medication is only used when necessary, while anti-inflammatory medication is used on a daily basis. Anti-inflammatory medications are used for children with moderate to severe asthma to control airway inflammation. Neither inhaled bronchodilators nor anti-inflammatory medications have severe side effects. Systemic bronchodilators, on the other hand, can have unpleasant side effects that are rarely life threatening. This type of medication is available in a slow release form, which can be especially helpful for nocturnal asthmatics. Systemic corticosteroid medication is prescribed for children who have severe asthma attacks that are not effectively helped by the aforementioned medication groups. Systemic corticosteroids are used only for severe episodes and are not recommended for long-term use. However, because severe uncontrolled asthma is a potentially life-threatening illness, use of a corticosteroid may be the better option. Leukotriene modifiers are a new type of medication for long-term, everyday usage. They open the airways by preventing inflammation and swelling, and decreasing mucus in the lungs.

Children using medications containing corticosteroids decrease serotonin levels (Pretorius, 2005). There are researchers that argue that lower free serotonin levels in the plasma are advisable to reduce asthmatic symptoms. However, reduced serotonin levels in the brain can be linked to depressive symptoms, impulse control problems, and aggression. It is therefore plausible for a child prescribed with antidepressants, or medication for Attention-Deficit/Hyperactivity Disorder (ADHD) to display asthmatic symptoms, while, conversely, children utilizing corticosteroid medications may show depressive symptoms, behavior problems, or aggression.

Research aimed at pinpointing possible interventions to reduce asthma symptoms are commonly related to diet (Nafstad, Nystad, Magnus, & Jaakkola, 2003; Oddy, Klerk, Kendall, Mihrshahi, & Peat, 2004). Studies have shown increasing food rich in omega-3 fatty acids (e.g., fresh or oily fish, whole grains) while decreasing intake of omega-6 fatty acids (e.g., margarines, processed food) can help with children's asthma symptoms (Oddy et al., 2004). Researchers hypothesize this phenomenon may be related to the anti-inflammatory effects of omega-3 fatty acids. In a related study research showed that fish consumption in the first year of life reduced the likelihood of asthma in children at risk for developing the disease (Nafstad et al., 2003).

Children with asthma should have an asthma-management plan on record in the administrative office (Madden, 2000). This plan is developed by the child's physician and should include such information as routine and emergency medications, symptoms of attack, emergency contact information, and whether the child should have an inhaler at all times. This point may conflict with certain schools' zero-tolerance drug policies and decrease a child's self-confidence to manage his or her chronic illness. Indoor air quality should be monitored on a regular basis to help avoid potential asthmatic reactions (DePaepe, Garrison-Kane, & Doelling, 2002). The Environmental Protection Agency (EPA) has published a guide to managing asthma in schools that includes such suggestions as controlling animal and cockroach allergens, controlling moisture and cleaning up any mold, eliminating secondhand smoke, reducing dust, developing asthma management plans, and providing school-based education (2000).

School teachers can easily be taught to recognize symptoms of respiratory distress in children with asthma (Sapien, Fullerton-Gleason, & Allen, 2004). In one study, after a 1-hour informational video, teachers were more accurate in identifying asthma symptoms. Teachers also expressed an increase in their comfort level in regard to general asthma knowledge and medication information. A greater improvement in asthma-related knowledge was related to the video intervention when compared to didactic intervention.

Approximation 20 to 25 percent of all school absences are from children with asthma (Sapien, Fullerton-Gleason, & Allen, 2004). The effects of absenteeism can commonly be seen in the child's academic performance. Asthmatic children may also display concentration problems, inattentiveness, problems with short-term memory, and decreased psychomotor functioning (Naudé & Pretorius, 2003).

REFERENCES

American Lung Association. (2005). *Asthma and children*. Retrieved September 3, 2005, from http://www.lungsusa.org

Asthma and Allergy Foundation of America. (2005). *Asthma overview*. Retrieved September 3, 2005, from http://www.aafa.org

DePaepe, P., Garrison-Kane, L., & Doelling, J. (2002). Supporting students with health needs in schools: An overview of selected health conditions. *Focus on Exceptional Children, 35,* 1–14.

Environmental Protection Agency. (2000). *IAQ tools for schools: Managing asthma in the school environment,* EPA #402-K-00-003, 2–23.

Madden, J. (2000). Managing asthma at school. *Educational Leadership, 57*(6), 50–52.

Nafstad, P., Nystad, W., Magnus, P., & Jaakkola, J. (2003). Asthma and allergic rhinitis at 4 years of age in relation to fish consumption. *Journal of Asthma, 40*(4), 343–348.

Naudé, H., & Pretorius, E. (2003). Investigating the effects of asthma medication on the cognitive and psychosocial functioning of primary school children with asthma. *Early Child Development and Care, 173*(6), 699–709.

Oddy, W. H., Klerk, N. H., Kendall, G. E., Mihrshahi, S., & Peat, J. K. (2004). Ratio of omega-6 to omega-3 fatty acids and childhood asthma. *Journal of Asthma, 41*(3), 319–326.

Pretorius, E. (2005). Asthma medication and the role of serotonin in the development of cognitive and psychological difficulties. *Early Child Development and Care, 175*(2), 139–151.

Sapien, R. E., Fullerton-Gleason, L., & Allen, N. (2004). Teaching school teachers to recognize respiratory distress in asthmatic children. *Journal of Asthma, 41,* 739–743.

MIRANDA KUCERA
*University of Colorado at
Colorado Springs*

CHRONIC ILLNESS

ASTIGMATISM

Astigmatism is a refractive error that causes reduced visual acuity and a lack of sharply focused, clear vision. In astigmatism, the curve of the cornea is irregular. Because of this irregularity, some light rays may come to focus in front of the retina, some on the retina, and some at the theoretical point behind it. The result is distorted or blurred vision and headache or eye fatigue after intensive close work.

Astigmatism does not seem to be clearly related to difficulties in learning to read. However, astigmatism can be a component of amblyopia (lazy eye) which does have a serious effect on reading and near work in general (NEI, 2005).

The special educator should be aware of the symptoms of astigmatism (Rouse & Ryan, 1984): headaches; discomfort in tasks that demand visual interpretation; problems seeing far as well as near; red eyes; distortion in size, shape, or inclination of objects; frowning and squinting at desk tasks; and nausea in younger or lower-functioning students. Astigmatism is generally correctable with eyeglasses or contact lenses, which should be worn full-time by affected students. These students may be helped in the classroom by being moved closer to the front of the room and by a reduction in the amount of time spent on near tasks.

REFERENCES

NEI. (2005). *National Eye Institute: Childhood's most common eye disorder.* Retrieved June 22, 2005, from http://www.nei.nih.gov/news/pressreleases/041105.asp

Rouse, M. W., & Ryan, J. B. (1984). Teacher's guide to vision problems. *Reading Teacher, 38*(3), 306–317.

ANNE M. BAUER
University of Cincinnati

VISUAL ACUITY
VISION TRAINING

ASYMMETRICAL TONIC NECK REFLEX

Asymmetric tonic neck reflex (ATNR) is one of a group of postural central nervous system reflexes that in the normal child is inhibited and incorporated into more sophisticated motor skills. The ATNR can be demonstrated easily in normal infants to about 40 weeks by placing the child on the back and turning the head to the left or right. As the face is turned to the left, the left arm extends and the right arm flexes, bringing the right hand flexed to the skull side of the head simultaneous with flexion of the leg on that and the opposite side. In the normal child with no pathology, this reflex is gradually inhibited; thus, children of 24 to 36 months can reach for toys in front of them; look to the side and still bring a cracker or spoon to the mouth when the head is in midposition; and cross the midline. Later on, the child can sustain weight on the arms and knees, and rotation of the head will not result in collapse or support on the skull side arm.

The child who has central nervous system damage above the level of the midbrain (usually considered to be in the basal ganglia, cerebral cortex, or both) will demonstrate a persistent ATNR well beyond the age of 1 year, with ac-companying profound damage into adult life. The child with severe ATNR finds self-feeding impossible. Persistence of ATNR can interfere with sitting and standing balance and dressing and writing, and make voluntary motion difficult or impossible.

Some help can be provided to children with delayed inhibition of ATNR by positioning and adaptive motor responses in physical and occupational therapy. Proper classroom seating can help moderately to severely involved children learn to diminish uninhibited reflexive responses when they are relaxed and listening. Excitement, anxiety, and stress may override the child's ability to inhibit the reflexive movement, making controlled, purposeful movement difficult or impossible for the more severely involved young adult with persistent uninhibited ATNR.

RACHEL J. STEVENSON
Bedford, Ohio

CENTRAL NERVOUS SYSTEM

ATARAX

Atarax (hydroxyzine hydrochloride) may be used for short-term symptomatic relief of anxiety and tension and as an adjunct in organic disease states in which anxiety is manifested. It also may be used as a sedative; the most common manifestation of overdosage is extreme sedation. Other uses include treatment of pruritis owed to allergic conditions such as chronic urticaria and dermatoses. Although not a cortical depressant, its action may be due to suppression of activity in certain key regions of the subcortical area of the central nervous system with the effect of relaxing skeletal muscles (Konopasek, 2004). Adverse reactions may include dryness of mouth and drowsiness, with the possibility of tremor, involuntary motor activity, and convulsions reported in cases where higher than recommended doses have been used.

A brand name of Roeris Pharmaceuticals, it is available in tablets of 10, 25, 50, and 100 milligrams, and as a syrup. The recommended dosage for children under 6 years of age is 50 mg daily in divided doses, and for children over 6 years of age 50 to 100 mg daily in divided doses. When used as a sedative, dosage is recommended to be 0.6 mg/kg (milligram per kilogram of body weight) at all childhood ages, and 50 to 100 mg for adults.

REFERENCE

Konopasek, D. E. (2004). *Medication fact sheets.* Longmont, CO: Sopris West.

LAWRENCE C. HARTLAGE
Evans, Georgia

ATAXIA

Ataxia is a type of cerebral palsy caused by the loss of cerebellar control. It is characterized by an unbalanced gait. An ataxic gait is often referred to as a drunken gait, as it resembles the walk of someone who is intoxicated.

According to Batshaw and Perret (1981), "The cerebellum coordinates the action of the voluntary muscles and times their contractions so that movements are performed smoothly and accurately" (p. 163). That is, the cerebellum senses where the limb is in space (based on input to the cerebellum), estimates where the target is, integrates the information, and then carries out the infinitesimal corrections necessary to compensate for inaccuracies in motor output, thereby maintaining fluid movement.

A child whose primary diagnosis is ataxia has poor righting and equilibrium reactions, and a staggering, lurching, irregular, and broad-based gait (Brown, 1973). According to Connor, Williamson, and Siepp (1978), the child has difficulty sustaining posture, as well as shifting posture in a coordinated manner. He or she often stumbles and falls. This postural instability may make the child overly cautious. The child may stiffen his or her trunk abnormally in order to increase stability. When walking, the child may visually fix on an object in the environment in an effort to maintain postural control. According to Walsch (1963), when an older child attempts purposeful reaching, he or she often overshoots the mark because of the presence of a distal, wavering tremor. Nystagmus is often present. The causes of ataxia are many. Extensive pediatric neurology texts such as Swaiman and Ashwal (2006) note ataxia in many common and rare disorders and diseases.

It is important that physical therapy begin as early as possible. According to Connor et al. (1978), early intervention should concentrate on the development of proximal control and stability. Repetition and reinforcement of movement is necessary so that responses become reliable. Activities that increase tremors or stiffening must be avoided. However, because children with ataxia demonstrate variations in their movement behavior, individual program planning is necessary.

REFERENCES

Batshaw, M. L., & Perret, Y. M. (1981). *Children with handicaps: A medical primer.* Baltimore: Brookes.

Bobath, B., & Bobath, K. (1976). *Motor development in the different types of cerebral palsy.* London: Heinemann Medical.

Brown, J. E. (1973). Disease of the cerebellum. In A. B. Baker & L. H. Baker (Eds.), *Clinical neurology, Vol. II.* New York: Harper & Row.

Connor, F. P., Williamson, G. G., & Siepp, J. M. (1978). *Program guide for infants and toddlers with neuromotor and other developmental disabilities.* New York: Teachers College Press.

Swaiman, K. F., & Right, F. S. (Eds.). (1982). *The practice of pediatric neurology* (2nd ed.). St. Louis, MO: Mosby.

Swaiman, K. F., & Ashwal, S. (2006). *Pediatric neurology* (4th ed.). St. Louis, MO: Mosby.

Walsch, G. (1963). *Cerebellum, posture, and cerebral palsy* (Clinics in Developmental Medicine, No. 8). London: Heinemann Medical Books.

CAROLE REITER GOTHELF
Hunter College, City University of New York

CEREBRAL PALSY
CEREBELLAR DISORDERS

ATHETOSIS

Athetosis is a central nervous system disorder characterized by slow, writhing movements, most notable in the extremities. These involuntary muscle movements have been described also as wormlike or snakelike. The actual movements consist of alternating flexion–extension and supination–pronation of the limbs, and are usually associated with increased, though variable, muscle tone (Chow, Durard, Feldman, & Mills, 1979).

Athetosis is most commonly a form of cerebral palsy (CP) in childhood accounting for approximately 15 to 30 percent of children with that diagnosis; however, the overall incidence rate is declining, probably because of improved neonatal intensive care (Batshaw & Perret, 1981). The condition, also known as choreo-athetoid CP, often occurs in conjunction with other forms of CP, especially spasticity. As a form of cerebral palsy, athetosis is one of a group of nonprogressive neuromotor disorders caused by earlier brain damage. Unlike other common forms of CP, the athetoid type presents a problem of controlling movement and posture rather than a difficulty in initiating voluntary movement. The uncontrolled, purposeless, involuntary movements associated with athetosis are not evidenced during sleep. Although the precise nature of the central nervous system insult is often indeterminable, among known causes may be various prenatal factors (e.g., anoxia, blood group incompatibilities, excessive radiation dosage during gestation, physical injuries, various maternal infections); perinatal factors (e.g., prematurity, head trauma, asphyxia, kernicterus); and postnatal factors (e.g., head trauma, hemorrhage, infections of the brain or cranial linings). In the United States, one to two children per thousand may be affected by CP, including athetosis or mixed cerebral palsy with athetosis. It is believed that in the more pure athetoid type of CP, the site of lesion is generally in the basal ganglia or extrapyramidal track (Kandel, Schwartz, & Jessell, 1991; Vaughan, McKay, & Behrman, 1979).

Secondary problems important to the special educator frequently accompany athetosis. Early difficulties may be observed in sucking, feeding, chewing, and swallowing. Special techniques to deal with these problems may come from speech/language pathologists, occupational therapists, physical therapists, or physicians. Speech articulation is often impaired and drooling may be present. In addition, hearing loss, epilepsy, and mental retardation may exist simultaneously. However, careful assessment of cognitive functioning is essential because both speech and motor skills are affected.

Little, if any, in the way of curative action is successful with cerebral palsy. Early intervention, special education, and vocational rehabilitation will be important, but the exact nature of the treatment approach will depend largely on the presence, nature, and degree of concomitant disorders. As many as 70 percent of children with the athetoid type of CP may function in the mentally retarded range, so educational and habilitative services must take into account the child's developmental limitations. Because facial muscles are involved in athetosis, vision disorders, especially of the eye-muscle imbalance type, may be present in more than 40 percent of the affected group (Black, 1980). Hearing loss is also common, though less so than vision problems, necessitating early and continuous audiometric evaluations and the possible provision of amplification devices. Physical therapy, including bracing and splinting to help maintain balance and to control involuntary movements, may be indicated in many cases. Orthopedic surgery and neurosurgery, though sometimes helpful with other forms of CP, have not yet shown promise for children with athetosis (Kutz & Semrud-Clikeman, 2003).

REFERENCES

Batshaw, M. L., & Perret, Y. M. (1981). *Children with handicaps: A medical primer*. Baltimore: Brookes.

Black, P. D. (1980). Ocular defects in children with cerebral palsy. *British Medical Journal, 281,* 487.

Chow, M. P., Durand, B. A., Feldman, M. N., & Mills, M. A. (1979). *Handbook of pediatric primary care*. New York: Wiley.

Kandel, E., Schwartz, J., & Jessell, T. (1991). *Principles of neural science* (3rd ed.). New York: Elsevier.

Kutz, A. S., & Semrud-Clikeman, M. (2003). Atheosis. In E. Fletcher-Janzen & C. R. Reynolds (Eds.), *Childhood disorders diagnostic desk reference* (pp. 71–73). New York: Wiley.

Vaughan, V. C., McKay, R. J., & Behrman, R. E. (1979). *Nelson textbook of pediatrics*. Philadelphia: Saunders.

JOHN D. WILSON
Elwyn Institutes

CENTRAL NERVOUS SYSTEM
CEREBRAL PALSY

ATTACHMENT DISORDER

Attachment disorder derives from Bowlby's theoretical and process theory of attachment to caregivers or significant others in the course of normal development, a theory that also provides psychologists and special educators a framework for investigating atypical patterns of attachment in life (cf. Bowlby, 1982). Bowlby proposed that *attachments* (1) referred to a *pattern* of organized behavior within a relationship, not a static trait infants and children simply possessed. Attachments were not immutable and not independent of experience; (2) are framed by early experience, but are also transformed by later experience in life. This proposition is now referred to as a *dynamic systems theory of psychopathology,* based on the complex interactions experienced over life development; and (3) in early life (i.e., infancy or toddlerhood) often play a role in the developmental dynamic that produces pathology; however, this complex role depends on a surrounding context of sustaining environmental supports. Early experience influences later life outcomes, but the quality of those later life relationships also depends on the sustaining or supporting context in which those relationships are expressed (Carlson & Sroufe, 1995; Sroufe, Carlson, Levy, & Egeland, 1999).

If the developmental pathway model of attachment theory is conceptualized as a tree, then (1) there are more branches in the broad center of the large array of overall branches (i.e., owing to considerable diversity of experiences); (2) starting on any major trunk allows a large number of possible outcomes due to the complex number and diversity of subsequent branchings (i.e., due to circumstances, one can potentially and probabilistically deviate to the outward smaller branchings or continue along the main, normally developing branch); and (3) the longer the deviating offshoot branches are followed from the main branch, the more unlikely will there be a return to the main or central branch. Change or adaptations in attachments are more likely during infancy and toddlerhood, but if development continues to go awry well into adolescence, a return to a more healthy and organized form of attachment in relationships is viewed as quite difficult (Bowlby, 1973; Speltz, DeKlyen, & Greenburg, 1999; Stroufe et al., 1999). It must be kept in mind that Bowlby and his (and others') research does not support or suggest a linear pathway from early disruptions in attachment to later psychopathology; rather, (developmental) psychopathology will be the product of ongoing difficult challenges in life and the cumulative maladaptations to those challenges (Sroufe et al., 1999).

Assessment and Individual Differences in Quality of Attachment

Assessment of early dyadic relational patterns between infant and caregiver are drawn from (1) Ainsworth's Strange Situation procedure, developed from cross-cultural field research and home observations and used with most 12- to 18-month-old infants or toddlers; (2) the Attachment Q-Set; and (3) direct observations and perceptions of teacher-child relationships (Ainsworth, Blehar, Waters, & Wall, 1978; Carlson & Sroufe, 1995; Howes & Ritchie, 1999).

In the Strange Situation procedure, eight increasingly stressful analog episodes are presented: (1) caregiver and infant are introduced to an unfamiliar, sparsely furnished room containing a variety of attractive, age-appropriate toys; (2) the infant is allowed to explore with the caregiver present, seated in a chair; (3) a stranger enters, sits quietly, converses with the caregiver, then initiates interaction with the infant, taking cues from the baby; (4) the caregiver leaves; (5) the caregiver returns, and the stranger leaves unobtrusively; (6) the caregiver leaves the infant alone; (7) the stranger enters, attempts to comfort the infant if needed; and (8) the caregiver returns. The coder or observer seeks to classify behavioral organization during reunion episodes, those of proximity seeking, contact making, contact resistance, and avoidance (Ainsworth et al., 1978; Main & Solomon, 1990).

Based upon the outcome of the Strange Situation procedure, patterns of behavior are classified as either (1) *secure attachment,* where infants readily separate from caregivers and easily become absorbed in exploration. When wary of a stranger, threatened, or distressed by separation, the infant seeks contact and consolation until he or she is calm again. The infant's emotional regulation is considered to be smooth and well integrated; (2) *anxious / avoidant attachment,* which occurs when the caregiver's presence does not reduce distress or promote exploration. Such infants show little affective interaction with caregivers, show little suspicion of strangers, and are generally upset only if left alone. When the caregiver returns, such infants do not actively initiate interaction and are unresponsive to the caregiver's interactive attempts. As stress increases, so does avoidance of the caregiver. Emotional regulation for this type of infant is considered to be overly rigid; (3) *anxious / resistant attachment,* where infants show impoverished exploration and play and are wary of strangers and novel situations. They may cry even before being separated from the caregiver (i.e., are clingy), and upon reunion with the caregiver, they have tremendous difficulty settling down as if not reassured by their mother's presence or comforting. The emotional regulation of such infants is thought to come from intermittent caregiver responses to stress, producing a constant state of arousal in them. In their constant vigilant state, these infants may actually heighten their distress in order to elicit caregiver responses; and (4) *disorganized / disoriented attachment,* seen when infants and caregivers have no coherent relational strategies. There may be inconsistent or unusual behaviors such a hand-flapping, freezing, and other stereotypies that indicate seemingly undirected (disorganized) behavioral patterns to strange situations. It is hypothesized that incomprehensible or frightening caregiver behavior has interfered with the formation of coherent attachment strategies. For such infants, the caregiver serves as both a source of fear and a biologically based source of reassurance. No effective emotional regulation is thought to occur among these infants (Bowlby, 1973, 1980, 1982; Carlson & Sroufe, 1995).

The Strange Situation procedure used to arrive at these attachment classifications has been criticized for its lack of discriminant validity due to limited assessment ecology and restricted use with infant- or toddler-age children (Howes & Ritchie, 1999). The Attachment Q-Set (AQS; Waters & Deane, 1985), which has good validity with the Strange Situation procedure, is a viable alternative (Howe & Ritchie, 1999) because it can be used with a broader age range and is based on direct observations in the child's natural home environment. The AQS yields a continuous score, representing the degree of attachment security and now has subscales aimed at capturing the attachment organizations of insecure (avoidant or ambivalent or resistant) or secure (seeking comfort, proximity, and harmonious interactions). Speltz et al. (1999) also describe an observation coding system called the Preschool Attachment Assessment System (PAAS) for evaluating brief separation and reunion episodes between children and parents. The PAAS measures approach and avoidance behaviors as well as codes the content and affectivity of the child's verbal and nonverbal communication to the parent.

There is growing research support for the use of observations of teacher-child relationships in child care settings as well as gathering elementary school teacher perceptions of the teacher-child relationship. Research findings from both of these literature bases suggest that teachers can be successful in developing teacher-child relationships that are wholly different in quality than what they experience at home (Howes & Ritchie, 1999).

Bowlby's (1973, 1980, 1982) theory suggests that for individuals with impaired attachments, their stressful style of responding to others, themselves, and the environment might provide the basis for developing specific disorders. Expanding on these theoretical claims, Carlson and Sroufe (1995) explain that for individuals adopting an *avoidant / dismissing* strategy (because of insensitive or unpredictable parents), symptomatic behavior might include attempts to minimize attachment behavior and feelings. They might not only mask their own emotional expressions to avoid being hurt, but they may also view others as untrustworthy and overidealize attachment relationships to the point that when these ideals go unrealized, anger, resentment, and aggression are displayed.

Conduct Disorders and antisocial personality styles are often associated with this pattern of emotional regulation and behavior (cf. Speltz et al., 1999), sometimes leading to depression because of continual failed relationships. Concerning individuals with *resistant / preoccupied* strategies of attachment, relational anxiety reduces exploration and increased attachment behavior (e.g., enmeshed, clingy relations). Such individuals have difficulty managing anxiety, manifest phobias and Conversion Disorders, and are preoccupied with personal suffering (Bowlby, 1973; Carlson & Sroufe, 1995) to the point of exaggerating their emotions and negative beliefs about themselves, which keep them confused about relationships. Bowlby (1973) further notes that a child's school refusal, psychosomatic symptoms, or phobias are often connected to family attachment patterns where the child is anxious about the availability or well-being of the parent(s). For individuals with *avoidant / dismissing* and *resistant / preoccupied* relationship strategies, death or major separations only serve to confirm their worst nightmare about the psychological availability of the attachment figure, leading to intense despair and anxiety (Bowlby, 1980). As a result, if one has a history of avoidant attachment behavior, mourning may be delayed for months or years, irritability and strain will be exhibited, and depression may occur long after the loss or separation was experienced. Resistant attachment issues may lead individuals to express intense anger or self-reproach with depression that lasts much longer than normal (Carlson & Sroufe, 1985).

Attachment disorders are best viewed as relational problems triggered as a result of dysfunctional or impaired parent-child transactions, which then become absorbed as part of the individual's unique psychological identity and functioning (Carlson & Sroufe, 1995; Sroufe et al., 1999). Considerable research has been conducted to examine the circumstances that affect or strain attachment relationships in infancy and toddlerhood as well as to investigate conditions in which maladaptive attachment patterns impact or effect psychological adjustment later in life. Such research issues related to attachment are commonly found in investigations of infant colic, infant failure to thrive, Feeding Disorders (e.g., Pica, Rumination Disorder, posttraumatic feeding problems), sleep disorders, Posttraumatic Stress Disorder, and Reactive Attachment Disorder. In addition, direct and collateral research on later psychiatric functioning has covered issues related to autism, Oppositional Defiant Disorder, Conduct Disorder, depression or anxiety, maltreatment, borderline and Dissociative Disorders, and adult pathology (cf. Carlson & Sroufe, 1995; Lyons-Ruth, Zeanah, & Benoit, 2003; Sroufe et al., 1999). As Carlson and Sroufe (1985) point out, a careful analysis of the current and longitudinal research on attachment in early care and later pathology supports a transactional multidetermined view of the development of psychopathology. What is less clear is the exact relationship between attachment and stressful life experiences, most likely due to variations in research design and methodology.

REFERENCES

Ainsworth, M. D. S., Blehar, M., Waters, E., & Wall, S. (1978). *Patterns of attachment.* Hillsdale, NJ: Erlbaum.

Bowlby, J. (1973). *Attachment and loss: Vol. 2. Separation.* New York: Basic Books.

Bowlby, J. (1980). *Attachment and loss: Vol. 3. Loss.* New York: Basic Books.

Bowlby, J. (1982). *Attachment and loss: Vol. 1. Attachment* (2nd ed.). New York: Basic Books.

Carlson, E. A., & Sroufe, L. A. (1995). Contribution of attachment theory to developmental psychopathology. In D. Cicchetti & D. J. Cohen (Eds.), *Developmental psychopathology: Vol. 1. Theory and methods* (pp. 517–528). New York: Wiley.

Howes, C., & Ritchie, S. (1999). Attachment organizations in children with difficult life circumstances. *Development and Psychopathology, 11,* 251–268.

Lyons-Ruth, K., Zeanah, C. H., & Benoit, D. (2003). Disorder and risk for disorder during infancy and toddlerhood. In E. J. Mash & R. A. Barkley (Eds.), *Child psychopathology* (2nd ed., pp. 589–631). New York: Guilford.

Main, M., & Solomon, J. (1990). Procedures for identifying infants as disorganized/disoriented during the Ainsworth strange situation. In M. T. Greenburg, D. Cicchetti, & E. M. Cummings (Eds.), *Attachment in the preschool years* (pp. 121–160). Chicago: University of Chicago Press.

Speltz, M. L., DeKlyen, M., & Greenburg, M. T. (1999). Attachment in boys with early onset conduct problems. *Development and Psychopathology, 11,* 269–285.

Sroufe, L. A., Carlson, E. A., Levy, A. K., & Egeland, B. (1999). Implications of attachment theory for developmental psychopathology. *Development and Psychopathology, 11,* 1–13.

Waters, E., & Deane, K. (1985). Defining and assessing individual differences in attachment relationships: Q-methodology and the organization of behavior in infancy and early childhood. In I. Brotherhood & E. Waters (Eds.), *Growing points of attachment theory and research* (pp. 41–65). *Monographs of the Society for Research in Child Development, 50*(1–2, Serial No. 209).

ROLLEN C. FOWLER
*Eugene 4J School District,
Eugene, Oregon*

EMOTIONAL DISORDERS
EMOTIONAL LABILITY

ATTENTION-DEFICIT/ HYPERACTIVITY DISORDER

Attention-Deficit/Hyperactivity Disorder (ADHD) is one of the most common disorders found among children. Children with ADHD exhibit more attention difficulties or hyperactive-impulsive behaviors than their same-age peers (American Psychiatric Association, 2000). Individuals with ADHD experience problems with sustained attention (i.e., maintaining attention to tasks with little intrinsic value) or selective attention (i.e., filtering essential from nonessential details), exhibit excessive motor movement, and demonstrate behavioral disinhibition (i.e., difficulty adjusting behavior to situational demands; Barkley, 1998). According to Barkley, behavioral disinhibition, overactivity, and inattention are the primary characteristics of ADHD.

Prevalence rates of ADHD among the school-age population have varied widely from about 1 percent to 9 percent (Bird, 1996), with 3 percent to 7 percent being the most common prevalence estimates reported among experts in the field (American Psychiatric Association, 2000). Attention-Deficit/Hyperactivity Disorder is reported to be more prevalent in males than in females, with the proportion of males to females manifesting the disorder ranging from 2:1 to 9:1 (American Psychiatric Association, 2000).

From a historical perspective, the conceptualization of ADHD and the terms used to describe the disorder have undergone a series of revisions. In the 1940s and 1950s, restless, impulsive, distractible, and inattentive behaviors currently associated with children with ADHD were attributed to brain damage. The term *Minimal Brain Damage* (MBD) was used during this period of time to describe these children whose greatest difficulty was their excessive activity levels (Strauss & Lehtinen, 1955). A lack of clear evidence supporting the link between organic impairment and excessive activity levels resulted in a change in terminology in the early 1960s. The term *Minimal Brain Damage* was replaced with a new label, *Minimal Brain Dysfunction*. Several years later, the term *minimal brain dysfunction* was replaced with a new label, *Hyperkinetic Reaction of Childhood*. The term *Hyperkinetic Reaction of Childhood* first appeared in the revised nomenclature of the American Psychiatric Association's *Diagnostic and Statistical Manual of Mental Disorders,* second edition (*DSM-II;* American Psychiatric Association, 1968). The primary feature of this disorder in the *DSM-II* was hyperactivity. Controversy surrounded the use of the *Hyperkinetic Reaction of Childhood* label in the late 1960s and 1970s because of the seemingly incompatible symptom presentation of this disorder. Some children with the disorder exhibited hyperactivity-impulsive behaviors, while other children with the disorder experienced attention difficulties (Wilmshurst, 2005). Along with the controversy, a shift in focus occurred during this period of time as inattentiveness was viewed as the most salient feature of this disorder (Douglas & Peters, 1979). As a result, the term and the description of the disorder changed from *Hyperkinetic Reaction of Childhood* to *Attention Deficit Disorder* (ADD) in the third revision of the *DSM,* the *DSM-III* (American Psychiatric Association, 1980). The *DSM-III* also recognized two distinct subtypes of ADD, Attention Deficit Disorder with Hyperactivity and Attention Deficit Disorder without

Hyperactivity. Children with Attention Deficit Disorder with Hyperactivity exhibited inattention and hyperactive behavior, whereas children with Attention Deficit Disorder without Hyperactivity experienced only attention problems. Later in the 1980s, the *DSM* was revised again. In the *Diagnostic and Statistical Manual of Mental Disorders,* third edition, revised (*DSM-III-R;* American Psychiatric Association, 1987), the subtyping was eliminated and Attention Deficit Disorder with Hyperactivity became known as Attention-Deficit Hyperactivity Disorder. In contrast, Attention Deficit Disorder without Hyperactivity was removed as a subtype.

The current conceptualization of ADHD and terms used to describe the disorder appear in the *Diagnostic and Statistical Manual of Mental Disorders,* fourth edition, text revision (*DSM-IV-TR;* American Psychiatric Association, 2000). In the *DSM-IV-TR,* three subtypes of ADHD are recognized, Attention-Deficit/Hyperactivity Disorder, Combined Type, Attention-Deficit/Hyperactivity Disorder, Predominately Inattentive Type, and Attention-Deficit/Hyperactivity Disorder, Predominately Hyperactive-Impulsive Type. These three subtypes are identified based on the degree to which a child exhibits the core features of ADHD (Wilmshurst, 2005). The three core features of the disorder include hyperactivity, impulsivity, and inattentiveness. The commonly seen, especially in lay publications, but unfortunately, also in some professional publications, designation of ADD is archaic and no longer considered a valid diagnosis.

Children who meet the criteria for the most common subtype of ADHD, Attention-Deficit/Hyperactivity Disorder, Combined Type, display both inattentive and hyperactive-impulsive behaviors. Children with the Combined Type exhibit at least six of nine symptoms in the inattentive category (makes careless mistakes or does not attend to details in work, has problems sustaining attention, does not seem to listen, does not follow through on instructions or does not complete work, has problems organizing tasks, forgets things, is easily distracted, loses things, and is reluctant to engage in activities requiring mental effort) and at least six of nine symptoms in the hyperactive-impulsive category (fidgets with hands or feet or squirms in seat, has difficulty remaining seated, runs and climbs excessively in inappropriate places, has difficulty playing quietly, is extremely active, talks excessively, blurts out answers, has difficulty taking turns, and interrupts others; American Psychiatric Association, 2000). In contrast, children with Attention-Deficit/Hyperactivity Disorder, Predominately Inattentive Type exhibit at least six of nine symptoms in the inattentive category and less than six of nine symptoms in the hyperactive-impulsive category (American Psychiatric Association, 2000). These children experience attention difficulties, but they do not meet the diagnostic criteria for hyperactivity-impulsivity. Many children with the Predominately Inattentive type have concentration and academic difficulties and suffer from internalizing disorders such as depression or anxiety (Weiss, Worling, & Wasdell, 2003). Children with Attention-Deficit/Hyperactivity Disorder, Predominately Hyperactive-Impulsive Type exhibit at least six of nine symptoms in the hyperactive-impulsive category and less than six of nine symptoms in the inattentive category. Children with the Predominately Hyperactive-Impulsive Type demonstrate hyperactive-impulsive behaviors, but they do not meet the diagnostic criteria for inattentiveness (American Psychiatric Association, 2000). Many children who are diagnosed with this subtype experience social and academic problems due to their impulsive nature (Wilmshurst, 2005). The symptoms associated with the three subtypes of ADHD must (1) be present for at least 6 months, (2) cause significant impairment in social or academic functioning, and (3) occur across two or more settings (e.g., home and school). In addition, some of the symptoms associated with the different subtypes of ADHD must have been present before age 7 (American Psychiatric Association, 2000).

Most children with ADHD begin to exhibit symptoms of the disorder in early childhood. Around the age of 3 or 4, hyperactive-impulsive behaviors are first observed in children with ADHD. Hyperactive-impulsive behaviors are thought to come before inattention (Green, Loeber, & Lahey, 1991). Attention difficulties among children with ADHD are typically not detected until these individuals begin school (Wilmshurst, 2005) and experience learning difficulties (Applegate et al., 1997). When children with ADHD reach adolescence, many of these individuals display fewer hyperactive-impulsive behaviors and show improvement in their attention span (Hart, Lahey, Loeber, Applegate, & Frick, 1995). However, behavioral problems and cognitive difficulties persist with some of these individuals. In adulthood, many individuals with ADHD have reported an overall reduction in both hyperactive-impulsive and inattention symptoms (Shaffer, 1994), but for many, the disorder lasts a lifetime (Weiss & Hechtman, 1993).

Comorbid disorders are common among children with ADHD. According to Barkley (1998), more than 50 percent of children with ADHD have one or more co-occurring disorders. The most prevalent comorbid disorders are Conduct Disorders and Oppositional Defiant Disorders. Approximately 50 percent of children with ADHD have a Conduct Disorder, and 35 percent to 60 percent have an Oppositional Defiant Disorder (Szatmari, Boyle, & Offord, 1989). Other common, but less prevalent, comorbid disorders include Bipolar Disorders, Major Depressive Disorders, Anxiety Disorders, Learning Disorders, and Communication Disorders. Some children with ADHD have a Tic Disorder. However, the co-occurrence of a Tic Disorder occurs less frequently in children with ADHD (American Psychiatric Association, 2000).

Many children with ADHD have poor interpersonal relationships. Approximately 50 percent of children with ADHD experience peer rejection and have difficulty establishing and maintaining friendships (Landau, Milich, & Diener, 1998) due to their bossy, impulsive, intrusive, and argumentative nature. Some of these children demonstrate aggressive behavior toward peers because they misinterpret social cues from their environment (Barkley, 1998), which, in turn, leads to peer rejection. Few or no friends put these individuals at risk for future socioemotional problems. Relationships with adults are also problematic for many of these children. Children with ADHD are less compliant to teacher and parent requests and receive more reprimands and punishment from significant adults in their lives (Barkley, 1998).

Besides poor interpersonal relationships, many children with ADHD experience academic and cognitive problems. Evidence suggests that children with ADHD score on average nine points below their peers on standardized measures of intelligence (Frazier, Demaree, & Youngstrom, 2004). Frazier and colleagues meta-analyzed 137 studies and found a statistically significant difference in overall cognitive ability between individuals with ADHD and controls. The weighted mean effect size was .61. According to the authors, this finding suggests that individuals with ADHD may have mild global cognitive inefficiencies or multiple specific deficits. Children with ADHD may also experience academic problems, with 30 percent of these children retained at least once in their academic careers (Barkley, 1998). Because many of these children struggle in the academic arena, approximately 30 percent will not finish high school (Barkley, 1998). Many students with ADHD struggle in a number of academic areas, including reading, mathematics, spelling, and writing (Barkley, 1998). Students who experience academic difficulties may qualify for special education and related services under the learning disability (LD) or other health impairment (OHI) category of the Individuals with Disabilities Education Act (IDEA) or for accommodations in the regular education classroom under Section 504 of the Rehabilitation Act. Approximately 30 percent of children with ADHD participate in special education programs (Barkley, 1998).

Significant controversy exists regarding the exact cause of ADHD (Wilmshurst, 2005), with a number of different etiologies offered to explain the disorder. However, neurobiological factors have received substantial empirical support in recent years as the greatest contributors to ADHD (Barkley, 1998). With modern technology, functional resonance imaging (FMRI) and single photon emission computed topography (SPECT) scans have revealed different activity levels in different regions of the brain of children with ADHD in comparison to children without ADHD. Children with ADHD have less activity in the frontal region of the brain and more activity in the cingulate gyrus than children without ADHD. The frontal region of the brain and the cingulate gyrus are responsible for executive functioning and focused attention, respectively (Wilmshurst, 2005). Another plausible explanation for the disorder is heredity

(Edelbrock, Rende, Plomin, & Thompson, 1995). ADHD runs in families, with 50 percent of children with ADHD having a parent who also has the disorder (Biederman et al., 1995). Low levels of neurotransmitters have also been identified as a possible cause of ADHD. Research has shown that children with ADHD have lower levels of dopamine, epinephrine, and norepinephrine than children without ADHD and that these neurotransmitters are associated with attention and motor activity (Wilmshurst, 2005). Barkley (1997) cogently argued that deficits in the behavioral inhibition system provide an explanation for the disorder and the cognitive, behavioral, and social deficits observed in children with ADHD. Other possible neurological etiologies include prenatal and perinatal complications, exposure to environmental toxins, and infections. Environmental factors such as poor parenting, parental characteristics, chaotic home environment, and lower socioeconomic background have also been suggested as possible etiologies for the disorder. However, these factors have received little empirical support as causes of ADHD (Anastopoulos, Klinger, & Temple, 2001).

A multimethod approach in the assessment of children with ADHD has been recommended (Bradley & DuPaul, 1997). A multimethod assessment approach involves obtaining information from multiple informants (e.g., parent, teacher, child), measures, and settings (home, school) to pinpoint problematic areas of concern. Once the problematic areas are identified, intervention strategies are developed based on the assessment results to address these areas of concern.

A comprehensive evaluation of a child with ADHD in a clinical setting includes clinical interviews with the parent, teacher, and child; a medical examination consisting of a medical interview and a physical examination; and completion of behavioral rating scales by the parent, teacher, and child if applicable (Barkley & Edwards, 1998). Popular behavioral rating scales used in the assessment of children with ADHD includes the *Achenbach System of Empirically-Based Assessment* (ASEBA; Achenbach & Rescorla, 2001), the *Behavior Assessment System for Children–Second Edition* (BASC-2; Reynolds & Kamphaus, 2004), the *Brown Attention-Deficit Disorder Scales* (Brown ADD Scales; 2001), the *Conners' Rating Scale–Revised* (CRS-R; Conners, 1997), and the *Behavior Rating Inventory of Executive Function* (BRIEF; Gioia, Isquith, Guy, & Kenworthy, 2000). Additional behavior rating scales may be included to address other areas of concern. Behavioral observations, intelligence and academic achievement measures, neuropsychological tests, personality measures, and projectives may also be included to assess cognitive impairments or to aid in differential diagnosis (Gordon & Barkley, 1998).

Assessment of children with ADHD in a school setting may be conducted within a problem-solving model (see Hoff, Doepke, & Landau, 2002 for a discussion on the use of a problem-solving model in the assessment of children with ADHD). As part of the prereferral process, interviews with the parent, teacher, and child are conducted; behavior observations are performed; and behavior rating scales are completed by the parent, teacher, and child if applicable. A functional behavior assessment may also be performed to address behavioral concerns and curriculum-based measures may also be administered to assess academic problems. Based on these assessment results, intervention strategies are selected and implemented to address the issues of concern. If the intervention strategies prove to be ineffective, a comprehensive evaluation may be conducted and include standardized measures of intelligence and academic achievement and other measures, depending on the referral and information obtained in the assessment process. Based on the results of this comprehensive evaluation and a discussion among members of a multidisciplinary team consisting of school personnel, parents, and possibly the child, a child may be eligible for special education and related services under IDEA or for accommodations in the regular education classroom under Section 504 of the Rehabilitation Act (Lowe, 2005).

Many factors must be considered when providing treatment to children with ADHD. Because of the cross-situational pervasiveness of the disorder, comorbid and associative features, and symptoms, a multimodal approach has been used with many of these children (Anastopoulos et al., 2001). Medication, behavior modification techniques, counseling, and parent training have received empirical support (Pelham, Wheeler, & Chronis, 1998).

Stimulant medication has been reported to be the most effective single treatment in reducing the core symptoms of ADHD (MTA Cooperative Group, 1999). The rationale for the use of medication in the treatment of ADHD rests on the assumption that low levels of catecholamines (i.e., dopamine, epinephrine, and norepinephrine) are the cause of the disorder. Stimulant medication in current use to treat ADHD includes Ritalin, Concerta, Focalin, Metadate, Methylin Adderall, Dexedrine, Dextrostat, and Cylert (Wilmshurst, 2005). Antidepressant medication has also been used to treat ADHD, including Imipramine and Wellbutrin. Antidepressant medication has been prescribed in many cases to reduce or eliminate motor tics, which can be a side effect associated with the ingestion of stimulant medication or to elevate a child's mood. A new nonstimulant medication, Strattera, received Food and Drug Administration (FDA) approval for use in the treatment of children with ADHD in 2003 (Wilmshurst, 2005). Collaboration among medical professionals, school personnel, and parents is needed to ensure thorough monitoring of the medication that an optimal dose is prescribed to children with ADHD.

Although medication has been effective in reducing hyperactive-impulsive behaviors and increasing attention in children with ADHD, there are side effects associated with the use of medication. Short-term side effects of stimulant medications include stomachaches; weight, height, and appetite suppression; and sleeping difficulties. Long-term side effects of stimulant medications include dysphoria, insomnia, increase in heart rate and blood pressure, and loss of appetite. The side effects associated with the long-term use of these medications across the life span are not known at the present time.

Nonpharmacological interventions have also been used in the treatment of children with ADHD. Parent training has been shown to be effective in reducing children's noncompliant behavior and increasing adults' parenting skills (Sonuga-Barke, Daley, Thompson, Laver-Bredbury, & Weeks, 2001). Parent training involves training adults in behavior modification techniques. Through training, parents learn ways to reduce their child's inappropriate behavior and to increase their child's appropriate behavior. A positive side effect of this training has been reduced levels of stress among parents (Sonuga-Barke et al., 2001).

Behavior modification techniques are effective intervention strategies to increase appropriate behavior and decrease inappropriate behavior among children with ADHD (Pfiffner & Barkley, 1998; Wilmshurst, 2005). Behavior modification strategies involve the manipulation of antecedents to modify the environment or task characteristics associated with a child's difficulties or the delivery of positive or negative consequences contingent upon the type of behavior demonstrated by the child. Modifications in the environment may include reducing the noise level in the classroom or moving a child's desk closer to the teacher and away from distractors to increase a child's attention. Praising or giving a child a tangible reward after the child sits quietly and completes his or her class work or taking away a privilege after a child runs around the classroom are examples of behavior modification strategies in which appropriate behavior is rewarded and inappropriate behavior results in negative consequences.

Home-school contingencies represent another group of behavioral strategies effective with children with ADHD (Pelham et al., 1998). Home-school contingencies represent one of the most widely used strategies with these children (Pfiffner & Barkley, 1998). The effectiveness of home-school contingencies is dependent upon collaboration between the home and school. An example of a home-school contingency is a daily report card that goes back and forth between the home and the school. Consequences are delivered in the home environment based on the child's behavior or academic performance in the school setting. Ratings of the child's behavior or academic performance are recorded on the report card, and the child carries the report to and from school on a daily basis. With home-school contingencies, generalization and maintenance of desired behavior are more likely to occur because the behavior is being addressed in two settings.

Peer strategies are a fourth group of strategies effective with children with ADHD. Peer tutoring and classwide peer tutoring have been effective in improving academic performance and classroom behavior of children with ADHD (DuPaul & Henningson, 1993). Peer tutoring strategies are most effective when children with ADHD are paired with peers who serve as good role models (Pfiffner & Barkley, 1998).

Social skills training is another popular strategy used with children with ADHD. Many children with ADHD experience poor interpersonal relationships. The purpose of social skills training is to promote social competence. However, research has suggested that social skills training has not been extremely effective with high incidence populations, including children with ADHD (Gresham, Sugai, & Horner, 2001). Gresham and colleagues' meta-analysis revealed a weak effect for social skills training in improving the social competence of high incidence populations and problems with skill maintenance and generalization.

Self-management strategies have also been used with children with ADHD. Self-management strategies emphasize the development of self-control. Self-management strategies include self-instruction, self-monitoring, self-reinforcement, and problem-solving strategies. Overall, these strategies have fallen short of initial expectations (Braswell et al., 1997).

REFERENCES

Achenbach, T. M., & Rescorla, L. A. (2001). *Achenbach System of Empirically-Based Assessment.* Burlington: University of Vermont, Research Center for Children, Youth, and Families.

American Psychiatric Association. (1968). *Diagnostic and statistical manual of mental disorders* (2nd ed.). Washington, DC: Author.

American Psychiatric Association. (1980). *Diagnostic and statistical manual of mental disorders* (3rd ed.). Washington, DC: Author.

American Psychiatric Association. (1987). *Diagnostic and statistical manual of mental disorders* (3rd ed., rev. ed.). Washington, DC: Author.

American Psychiatric Association. (2000). *Diagnostic and statistical manual of mental disorders* (4th ed., text revision). Washington, DC: Author.

Anastopoulos, A. D., Klinger, E. E., & Temple, E. P. (2001). Treating children and adolescents with Attention-Deficit/Hyperactivity Disorder. In J. N. Hughes, A. M. LaGreca, & J. C. Conoley (Eds.), *Handbook of psychological services for children and adolescents* (pp. 245–265). New York: Oxford University Press.

Applegate, B., Lahey, B. B., Hart, E. L., Biederman, T., Hynd, G. W., Barkley, R. A., et al. (1997). Validity of the age-of-onset criterion for ADHD: A report from the DSM-IV field trials. *Journal of the American Academy of Child and Adolescent Psychiatry, 36,* 1211–1221.

Barkley, R. A. (1997). *ADHD and the nature of self-control.* New York: Guilford.

Barkley, R. A. (1998). *Attention-Deficit Hyperactivity Disorder.* New York: Guilford.

Barkley, R. A., & Edwards, G. (1998). Diagnostic interview, behavior rating scales, and the medical examination. In R. A. Barkley

(Ed.), *Attention-deficit hyperactivity disorder* (pp. 263–293). New York: Guilford.

Biederman, J., Wozniak, J., Kiely, K., Ablon, S., Faraone, S., Mick, E., et al. (1995). CBCL clinical scales discriminate prepubertal children with structured interview-derived diagnosis of mania from those with ADHD. *Journal of the American Academy of Child and Adolescent Psychiatry, 34,* 464–471.

Bird, H. (1996). Epidemiology of childhood disorders in a cross-cultural context. *Journal of Child and Adolescent Psychiatry, 35,* 1440–1448.

Bradley, K. L., & DuPaul, G. J. (1997). Attention-Deficit/Hyperactivity Disorder. In G. G. Bear, K. M. Minke, & A. Thomas (Eds.), *Children's needs II: Development, problems and alternatives* (pp. 109–117). Bethesda, MD: National Association of School Psychologists.

Braswell, L., August, G. J., Bloomquist, M. L., Realmuto, G. M., Skare, S. S., & Crosby, R. D. (1997). School-based secondary prevention for children with disruptive behavior. *Journal of Abnormal Child Psychology, 25,* 197–205.

Brown, T. K. (2001). *Brown Attention-Deficit Disorder Scale.* San Antonio, TX: Harcourt Assessment.

Conners, C. K. (1997). *Conners Rating Scale* (rev. ed.). Toronto: Multi-Health Systems.

Douglas, V. I., & Peters, K. G. (1979). Toward a clearer definition of the attentional deficit in hyperactive children. In G. A. Hale & M. Lewis (Eds.), *Attention and the development of cognitive skills* (pp. 173–247). New York: Plenum.

DuPaul, G. J., & Henningson, P. N. (1993). Peer tutoring effects on the classroom performance of children with Attention Deficit Hyperactivity Disorder. *School Psychology Review, 22,* 134–143.

Edelbrock, C. S., Rende, R., Plomin, R., & Thompson, L. (1995). A twin study of competence and problem behavior in childhood and early adolescence. *Journal of Child Psychology and Psychiatry, 36,* 775–786.

Frazier, T. W., Demaree, H. A., & Youngstrom, E. A. (2004). Meta-analysis of intellectual and neuropsychological test performance in Attention-Deficit/Hyperactivity Disorder. *Neuropsychology, 18,* 543–555.

Gioia, G. A., Isquith, P. K., Guy, S. C., & Kenworthy, L. (2000). *Behavior Rating Inventory of Executive Function.* Odessa, FL: Psychological Assessment Resources.

Gordon, M., & Barkley, R. A. (1998). Test and observational measures. In R. A. Barkley (Ed.), *Attention-Deficit Hyperactivity Disorder* (pp. 345–372). New York: Guilford.

Green, S. M., Loeber, R., & Lahey, B. B. (1991). Stability of mothers' recall of the age of onset of their child's attention and hyperactivity problems. *Journal of the American Academy of Child and Adolescent Psychiatry, 38,* 503–512.

Gresham, F. M., Sugai, G., & Horner, R. H. (2001). Interpreting outcomes of social skills training for students with high incidence disabilities. *Exceptional Children, 67,* 331–334.

Hart, E. L., Lahey, B. B., Loeber, R., Applegate, B., & Frick, P. J. (1995). Developmental change in Attention-Deficit Hyperactivity Disorder in boys: A four-year longitudinal study. *Journal of Abnormal Child Psychology, 23,* 729–750.

Hoff, K. E., Doepka, K., & Landau, S. (2002). *Best practice in the assessment of children with Attention-Deficit/Hyperactivity Disorder.* In A. Thomas & J. Grimes (Eds.), *Best practices in school psychology* (Vol. 4, pp. 1129–1146). Washington, DC: National Association of School Psychologists.

Landau, S., Milich, R., & Diener, M. B. (1998). Peer relations of children with attention-deficit-disordered boys. *Journal of Abnormal Child Psychology, 16,* 69–81.

Lowe, P. A. (2005). Attention-Deficit/Hyperactivity Disorder. In S. W. Lee & P. A. Lowe (Eds.), *The encyclopedia of school psychology* (pp. 32–35). Thousand Oaks, CA: Sage.

MTA Cooperative Group. (1999). A 14-month randomized clinical trial of treatment strategies for Attention-Deficit/Hyperactivity Disorder. *Archives of General Psychiatry, 56,* 1073–1086.

Pelham, W. E., Jr., Wheeler, T., & Chronis, A. (1998). Empirically supported psychosocial treatments for Attention-Deficit/Hyperactivity Disorder. *Journal of Clinical Child Psychology, 27,* 190–205.

Pfiffner, L. J., & Barkley, R. A. (1998). Treatment of ADHD in school settings. In R. A. Barkley (Ed.), *Attention-Deficit Hyperactivity Disorder* (pp. 458–490). New York: Guilford.

Reynolds, C. R., & Kamphaus, R. W. (2004). *Behavior Assessment System for Children* (2nd ed.). Circle Pines, MN: American Guidance Services.

Shaffer, D. (1994). Attention Deficit Hyperactivity Disorder in adults. *American Journal of Psychiatry, 151,* 633–638.

Sonuga-Barke, E. J., Daley, D., Thompson, M., Laver-Bredbury, C., & Weeks, A. (2001). Parent-based therapies for preschool Attention-Deficit/Hyperactivity Disorder: A randomized controlled trial with a community sample. *Journal of the American Academy of Child and Adolescent Psychiatry, 40,* 402–408.

Strauss, A. A., & Lehtinen, L. E. (1955). *Psychopathology and education of the brain-injured child.* New York: Grune & Stone.

Szatmari, P., Boyle, M., & Offord, D. R. (1989). ADHD and Conduct Disorder: Degree of diagnostic overlap and differences among correlates. *Journal of the American Academy of Child and Adolescent Psychiatry, 28,* 865–872.

Weiss, G., & Hechtman, L. R. (1993). *Hyperactive children grown up* (2nd ed.). New York: Guilford.

Weiss, M. D., Worling, D. E., & Wasdell, M. B. (2003). A chart review study of the inattentive and combined types of ADHD. *Journal of Attention Disorders, 7,* 1–9.

Wilmshurst, L. (2005). *Essentials of child psychopathology.* New York: Wiley.

PATRICIA A. LOWE
University of Kansas

CECIL R. REYNOLDS
Texas A&M University

ATTENTION SPAN
HYPERACTIVITY
RITALIN
STIMULANT DRUGS
TRAUMATIC BRAIN INJURY

ATTENTION SPAN

Adequate attention span requires optimal arousal, selection of task-relevant information, maintenance of attention long enough to get a task done, and central processing of the task (Cohen, 1993; Posner & Boies, 1971). Arousal is assessed by heart rate, respiration, or other indicators of autonomic arousal, and there is a level that is optimal for learning. At very low levels of arousal, learning is inefficient and attention to environmental stimuli is diffuse; at very high levels, attention is narrowed but learning becomes inefficient, particularly for complex tasks. Teachers can increase arousal by increasing the novelty of classroom activities, by asking students questions to generate curiosity (Berlyne, 1960), by rotating students in and out of the "action zone" (the T-shaped front-row-and-center region of the classroom; Piontrowski & Calfee, 1979), or by directing questions to students outside the action zone.

Attention span in children can be negatively affected by sleep deprivation, attention-deficit disorder, depression, and many other disorders. Selective attention is assessed most frequently by use of incidental learning tasks. The child is instructed to recall a specific set of items (e.g., pictures of animals), but other incidental items (e.g., household items) are actually paired with the target (central) items during presentation. After being given tests of recall for central items, the child is tested for recall of the central-incidental pairs. The assumption is that only items that are attended to will be recalled. Recall for central items increases steadily from preschool age through adolescence, while memory for incidental items remains stable. The correlation between central and incidental recall becomes increasingly negative between ages 6 and 13 in normal children, indicating an increasing ability to screen out distractions with age. Adolescents and adults appear to screen out distractors by rehearsing central stimuli (Hagen & Stanovich, 1977). Hallahan et al. have found selective attention deficits to be common in children with learning problems. They also found that these children can be trained to improve their attention to central stimuli by using task-relevant self-talk and by being reinforced for recall of central items (Hallahan & Reeve, 1980).

Maintenance of attention can be assessed by observation, by interviewing, by self-monitoring, or through formal testing (see Reynolds & Bigler, 1997, 1994; Rossman, 2006). In observational methods, eye contact with assigned task materials, with the teacher during instruction, or during task-relevant interaction with peers, is scored as engaged (on-task); other activities are scored as nonengaged (Piontrowski & Calfee, 1979). Observed engaged time is related to achievement; for example, Leach reports that 58 percent of the variance in primary mathematics achievement is accounted for by academic engaged time (Leach & Dolan, 1985). Observed on-task attention increases from ages 5 to 11 (Higgins & Turnure, 1984), although students may become more adept at appearing to maintain attention with development (Hudgins, 1967). Self-monitoring of "paying attention" improved observed engaged time among second graders, and reinforcement for self-monitoring accuracy improved engaged time more than self-monitoring alone (Rooney, Hallahan, & Lloyd, 1984).

REFERENCES

Berlyne, D. (1960). *Conflict, arousal, and curiosity*. New York: McGraw-Hill.

Cohen, R. A. (1993). *The neuropsychology of attention*. New York: Plenum Press.

Hagen, J. W., & Stanovich, K. E. (1977). Memory: Strategies of acquisition. In R. V. Kail & J. W. Hagen (Eds.), *Perspectives on the development of memory and cognition*. Hillsdale, NJ: Erlbaum.

Hallahan, D. P., & Reeve, R. E. (1980). Selective attention and distractibility. In B. K. Keogh (Ed.), *Advances in special education, Vol. 1*. Greenwich, CT: JAI Press.

Higgins, A. T., & Turnure, J. E. (1984). Distractibility and concentration of attention in children's development. *Child Development, 55*, 1799–1810.

Hudgins, B. B. (1967). Attending and thinking in the classroom. *Psychology in the Schools, 66*, 29–32.

Leach, D. J., & Dolan, N. K. (1985). Helping teachers increase student academic engagement rate: The evaluation of a minimal feedback procedure. *Behavior Modification, 9*, 55–71.

Piontrowski, D., & Calfee, R. (1979). Attention in the classroom. In G. A. Hale & M. Lewis (Eds.), *Attention and cognitive development* (pp. 297–329). New York: Plenum.

Posner, M. I., & Boies, S. J. (1971). Components of attention. *Psychological Review, 78*, 391–408.

Reynolds, C. R., & Bigler, E. D. (1994). *Test of memory and learning*. Austin, TX: PRO-ED.

Reynolds, C. R., & Bigler, E. D. (1997). Clinical neuropsychological assessment of child and adolescent memory with the Test of Memory and Learning. In C. R. Reynolds & E. Fletcher-Janzen (Eds.), *The handbook of clinical child neuropsychology* (3rd ed., pp. 296–319). New York: Plenum.

Rooney, K. J., Hallahan, D. P., & Lloyd, J. W. (1984). Self-recording of attention by learning disabled students in the regular classroom. *Journal of Learning Disabilities, 17*, 360–364.

Rossman, N. P. (2006). Traumatic brain injury in children. In K. F. Swaiman & S. Ashwal (Eds.), *Pediatric neurology* (4th ed., pp. 873–895). St. Louis, MO: Mosby.

JOHN MACDONALD
Eastern Kentucky University

ATTENTION-DEFICIT/HYPERACTIVITY DISORDER
HYPERACTIVITY
HYPERKINESIS
TEST OF MEMORY AND LEARNING

ATTRIBUTIONAL RETRAINING

Many pupils with disabilities perceive themselves to be incompetent in a variety of school-related activities. While these self-perceptions may accurately reflect limited skills in these areas, they may also affect youngsters' willingness to engage in learning tasks. When presented with school tasks, even tasks in which they have evidenced recent success, many pupils will state that they cannot do the work and as a consequence will not even try. To address the learning needs of their students, special education teachers need to focus on their students' cognitive and motivational characteristics. An intervention procedure entitled attributional retraining has been used to influence pupils' self-perceptions and their subsequent motivation to learn.

Attribution retraining may be defined as a systematic set of procedures designed to influence individuals' perceptions concerning the causes of their performance on tasks. Many of the procedures are derived from research in the area of cognitive behavior modification. In attributional retraining the focus is on modifying learners' thoughts concerning why they have succeeded or failed on a task. Although attributional retraining procedures have been used in treatment programs for a variety of problems including alcoholism, anxiety, depression, and diet management, the focus, here, will be on the use of these procedures with youngsters who evidence severe learning problems.

Most of the attributional retraining programs focus on the role of effort on student achievement. This emphasis is due, in part, to the fact that pupils can choose to change their levels of effort. In addition, high achieving students tend to attribute successes to their ability and effort and ascribe their failures to lack of effort. When students perceive that increased effort will result in success, they persist; this, in turn, enhances their performance. In contrast, children who have learning problems frequently attribute their failures to lack of ability, and fail to persist on academic tasks.

One of the first attributional retraining studies was conducted by Dweck (1975). In this investigation, children identified as learned helpless were asked to solve arithmetic problems. One group of pupils was given math tasks in which they continually succeeded; another group was given tasks that they occasionally failed at. When pupils did not correctly respond on an arithmetic task, they were given attributional feedback indicating that they should have tried harder. All the youngsters in the study were subsequently given difficult math problems. Pupils who received the attributional feedback maintained or improved their performances after failure, whereas the performances of children who continually succeeded deteriorated if they failed on a math problem. Chapin and Dyck (1976) and Fowler and Peterson (1981) subsequently reported that persistence on academic tasks was jointly affected by reinforcement procedures and attribution retraining. Fowler and Peterson also reported that reinforcement/attribution retraining

that involved direct attributional feedback to pupils was more effective in increasing reading persistence than other treatment procedures. Recently, educational researchers have reported that attribution training procedures may influence students' use of learning strategies (Johnson & Winograd, 1985; Palmer & Goetz, 1984). Attribution training may affect both pupils' achievement outcomes and how they learn.

Related to the attributional retraining research, Decharms (1976) developed a two-part program to help teachers enhance personal causation of elementary-aged children. The project was designed to influence pupils' goal planning and ultimately produce a person who is in control of his or her achievements. The experiment involved two groups: one consisted of motivation-trained teachers using an experimental curriculum; a control group had untrained teachers and the regular curriculum. The first step involved a personal causation training course for all teachers in the experimental group, followed by a year-long implementation of a number of classroom exercises. Personal causation training did appear to affect pupil's self-confidence and their academic achievement scores. Four years later, a semistructured interview revealed higher personal goals and responsibility orientation for those children in the trained group over those in the untrained group. Five years later, it was found that more pupils from the trained group had graduated. While there were a variety of components to the training program, one of the crucial elements was teaching the pupils that they had control over their achievement outcomes.

Although additional research is needed to determine how and when to most effectively use attributional retraining procedures, it appears that teachers' direct attributional feedback to children does influence students' willingness to learn and their school achievement. Teachers' systematic feedback to their pupils that effort is important in determining their successes or failures may affect youngsters' persistence on school tasks and ultimately their achievement.

Teachers who influence the class climate for assisting peers giving positive feedback to children with disabilities can positively affect attributions about self efficacy (Altermatt & Pomerantz, 2003). Siblings can also be utilized in this manner (Gnaulati, 2002). Praise from others (teachers, siblings, or peers) can have significant positive effects as long as it is directed to controllable causes and is perceived as sincere (Henderlong & Lepper, 2002).

REFERENCES

Altermatt, E. R., & Pomerantz, E. V. (2003). The development of competence-related motivational beliefs: An investigation of similarity and influence among friends. *Journal of Educational Psychology, 95,* 111–123.

Chapin, M., & Dyck, D. G. (1976). Persistence in children's reading behavior as a function of N length and attribution retraining. *Journal of Abnormal Psychology, 85,* 511–515.

Decharms, R. (1976). *Enhancing motivation: Change in the class-room.* New York: Irvington.

Dweck, C. S. (1975). The role of expectations and attributions in the alleviation of learned helplessness. *Journal of Personality and Social Psychology, 31,* 674–685.

Fowler, J. W., & Peterson, P. L. (1981). Increasing reading persistence and altering attributional style of learned helpless children. *Journal of Educational Psychology, 73,* 251–260.

Gnaulati, E. (2002). Extending the uses of sibling therapy with children and adolescents. *Psychotherapy: Theory, Research, Practice, Training, 39,* 76–87.

Henderlong, J., & Lepper, M. R. (2002). The effects of praise on children's intrinsic motivation: A review and synthesis. *Psychological Bulletin, 128,* 774–795.

Johnson, P. H., & Winograd, P. N. (1985). Passive failure in reading. Unpublished manuscript.

Palmer, D. J., & Goetz, E. T. (1988). Selection and use of study strategies: The role of the studier's beliefs about self and strategies. In C. Weinstein, E. Goetz, & P. Alexander (Eds.), *Learning and study strategies: Issues and assessments, instructions and evaluations.* New York: Academic.

Douglas J. Palmer
Norma Guerra
Texas A&M University

LEARNED HELPLESSNESS
MOTIVATION

ATTRIBUTIONS

By definition, many special education pupils experience a history of failure prior to being referred and ultimately placed in special education classes. It is this background of failure, current achievement problems, and the recognition that other pupils are doing well on classroom assignments that leads to perceptions of lack of competence. In turn, these perceptions concerning lack of ability influence pupils' expectancy for future performance and their willingness to try new tasks and persist on difficult ones.

Recently there has been considerable interest generated concerning the consequences of repeated academic failure and its effect on the motivation and achievement of special education children. The repeated academic failure experienced by these students may cause them to doubt their abilities and reduce their persistence and effort when exposed to novel or familiar tasks. Researchers have found that learning-disabled (LD) children are less likely than nondisabled children to attribute their failures to insufficient effort and more likely to attribute their failures to their own inabilities. LD pupils also have exhibited less persistence on achievement tasks than nondisabled pupils. Investigators have found that LD pupils' tendency to attribute failure to ability is negatively related to persistence.

It has also been reported that when LD children succeed at a task, they are less likely to attribute the success of their abilities and more likely to attribute the success to luck or ease of the task. These children appear to blame themselves when they fail and not give themselves credit when they succeed. Low levels of persistence and effort often result in additional failures, and the special education student, more frequently subjected to these difficulties, is caught in a vicious downward spiral of motivation and performance (Licht & Kistner, 1986). Measures of children's attributional styles are now included on several widely used assessment devices (Reynolds & Kamphaus, 1992).

REFERENCES

Heider, F. (1958). *The psychology of interpersonal relations.* New York: Wiley.

Licht, B. G., & Kistner, J. A. (1986). Motivational problems of learning disabled children: Individual differences and their implications for treatment. In J. K. Torgesen & B. W. L. Wong (Eds.), *Learning disabilities: Some new perspectives.* Orlando, FL: Academic.

Reynolds, C. R., & Kamphaus, R. W. (1992). *Behavior assessment system for children.* Circle Pines, MN: American Guidance Service.

Weiner, B. (1972). *Theories of motivation: From mechanism to cognition.* Chicago: Rand McNally.

Weiner, B. (1974). *Achievement motivation and attribution theory.* Morristown, NJ: General Learning.

Weiner, B. (1979). A theory of motivation for some classroom experiences. *Journal of Educational Psychology, 71,* 3–25.

Douglas J. Palmer
Michael L. Stowe
Texas A&M University

LOCUS OF CONTROL

ATYPICAL CHILD SYNDROME

Atypical child syndrome is a term borrowed from the medical profession and is no longer in common usage. The current term referring to this group is exceptional children. An exceptional child is one who deviates from the norm and could be categorized on the basis of a set of physical and/or behavioral characteristics. There are a variety of specific disorders in the area of special education that use the term syndrome as a part of the classification. Hunter syndrome, Down syndrome, Turner syndrome, Lesch-Neyhan syndrome, Cornelin deLange syndrome, Sturge-Weber syndrome, and Klinefelter's syndrome are but a few that are discussed in the special education literature.

A wide range of disabilities contribute to the atypical

child's condition. That condition may range from mild to severe, physical to mental, educational to social, or any combination of those conditions. What is difficult is to fit an individual into a category, as each individual has a different combination and severity of disability. Disability classifications are set up according to the characteristics of the children that deviate from the average or normal child and should be used to help educational programs meet the individual's needs. Kirk (1972) describes five categories: (1) communication disorders (learning disabilities and speech handicaps); (2) mental deviations (gifted and retarded); (3) sensory handicaps (auditory and visual); (4) neurological, orthopedic, or other health problems; and (5) behavior disorders. Although these categories have been used by psychology, sociology, physiology, and the medical profession, they will be briefly addressed from the educational standpoint.

Learning disabilities is a classification for those individuals that have language difficulties, visual or auditory-perceptual problems, and memory or other cognitive disabilities. Many times the learning problems contribute to behavior problems resulting from academic failure, unobtainable expectations, frustrations, etc. Although definitions have related these dysfunctions to the central nervous system (Clements, 1966), remediation is dealt with through educational intervention with a focus on academic, social, and emotional adjustment.

Mental retardation involves below average intellectual functioning with social and behavioral deficits. Grossman (1973) describes five levels of individuals with retardation, all of whom have IQs below 85 and engage in behaviors inappropriate for their age group. Individuals with borderline retardation (from 85 to 70 IQ) are frequently referred to as slow learners. Individuals with mild retardation (the educable mentally retarded) range from 69 to 55 IQs and have some potential to master basic academic skills. These individuals can live as independent or semiindependent adults. Moderately or trainable mentally retarded individuals with IQs of 54 to 40 have potential for learning self-help, social, and communication skills and simple occupational tasks. Severely mentally retarded individuals range from 39 to 25 IQs and need continual monitoring. They may be taught simple self-help skills, work tasks, and some type of communication system. The profoundly retarded, with IQs below 25, are totally dependent and require close supervision. Some may be able to perform self-help skills. Educational programs for the mentally retarded have made great gains. Depending on severity, educational programs range from self-contained classrooms to special schools and employ a great many management and instructional techniques (Snell, 1978). The goal is to teach these individuals skills to help them become as independent as possible.

Sensory handicaps range greatly from minimal visual defects and hard of hearing to blindness and deafness. Education can range from no special programming, to special part-time instruction from an itinerant teacher, to special schools. Focus in the public schools is on auditory and visual perception training.

Bleck and Nagel (1975) offer an excellent handbook for teachers of the physically handicapped. Basically, these individuals are disabled in motor abilities that do not affect educational achievement, although there may be some difficulties in social and emotional adjustment. The school needs to adapt the physical environment to accommodate wheelchairs, braces, etc. Teachers with neurologically impaired students need to be aware of complications, such as seizures.

Behavior disorders interfere with a child's growth and the development of relationships with others. Hewett and Jenkins (1945) define three types of behavior disorders involving those having unsocialized aggression (participating with peers in misdemeanors and crime) or overinhibition (overdependent and withdrawn). All involve social maladjustments and emotional disturbances. Although they are dealt with through the mental health fields, education has taken on prevention and treatment. The intervention, whether through resource rooms, itinerant teachers, special classes, special or residential schools, or hospitals, includes psychodynamics, behavior modification, and developmental, ecological, or psychoeducational strategies (Kirk, 1972).

REFERENCES

Bleck, E. G., & Nagel, D. A. (1975). *Physically handicapped children: A medical atlas for teachers.* New York: Grune & Stratton.

Clements, D. D. (1966). *Minimal brain dysfunction in children* (Public Health Service Publication No. 415). Washington, DC: Department of Health, Education, and Welfare.

Fliegler, I. A., & Bish, C. E. (1959, December). Summary of research on the academically talented student. *Review of Educational Research, 29,* 408–450.

Hewett, L. E., & Jenkins, R. L. (1945). *Fundamental patterns of maladjustment: The dynamics of their origin.* Springfield: State of Illinois.

Gloss, G. H., & Jones, R. L. (1968). *Correlates of school district provisions for gifted children: A statewide study.* Paper presented at the annual meeting of the Council for Exceptional Children, New York.

Grossman, H. J. (Ed.). (1973). Manual on terminology and classification in mental retardation. *American Journal of Mental Deficiency* (Special issue. Series No. 2).

Kirk, S. A. (1972). *Educational exceptional children.* Boston: Houghton Mifflin.

Snell, M. E. (1978). *Systematic instruction of the moderately and severely handicapped.* Columbus, OH: Merrill.

Donna Filips
Steger, Illinois

EVALUATION
LEARNING DISABILITIES
MENTAL RETARDATION

AUDIOGRAM

An audiogram is a standardized graphic representation of hearing thresholds to discrete pure tones (American National Standards Institute [ANSI], 1996). The abscissa of the audiogram shows frequency in Hertz (Hz) from 25 to 8000 Hz. The ordinate shows hearing level (HL) in decibels (dB) from −10 to 120 dB. Audiometric zero was derived by taking an average of 100 healthy youths over a frequency range from 20 Hz to 10 KHz from 1971 to 1973 under the laboratory conditions (International Standards Organization [ISO], 1988). Air conduction thresholds are represented by a circle for the right ear and an *X* for the left ear. Air conduction thresholds reflect the integrity of the whole of the auditory system. Brackets represent bone conduction thresholds. Traditionally, the right ear was also represented by the color red and the left by the color blue, but this is less common now due to black-and-white copies, scanner and printers (Katz, 2000).

Bone conduction bypasses the middle ear system and reveals the integrity of the auditory system at its most basic level. Sound presented at high enough intensity will cross over to the other ear, and another sound must be used to mask that ear. The level of 40 dB is the lowest signal known to cross, and this is the level where masking is to be implemented, for air conduction and masking should always be used for bone conduction (ANSI, 1996). In practice, it is not necessary to mask bone conduction thresholds if there is no difference in air conduction thresholds and the bone conduction scores and there is no air-bone gap (Katz, 2001). There are seven categories of hearing levels that are usually used: normal or no impairment, −10 to 15 dB; slight or minimal loss, 16 to 25 dB; mild loss, 26 to 30 dB; moderate loss, 31 to 50 dB; moderate or severe loss, 51 to 70 dB; severe loss, 71 to 90 dB; and profound loss, 91 dB or greater (VA National Center for Health Promotion and Disease Prevention, 2004).

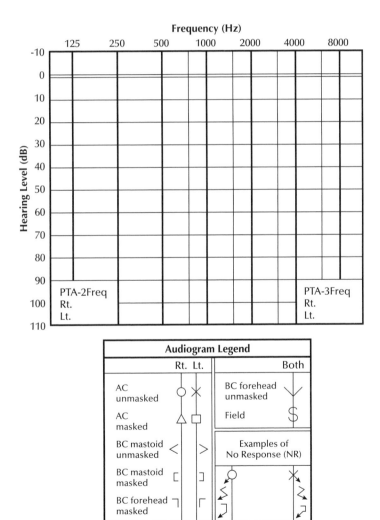

Figure 1 Audiogram form and symbols

REFERENCES

American National Standards Institute (ANSI). (1972). *Title of standard S3.13-1972. Catalogue of ANSI standards.* Retrieved May 20, 2006, from http://www.ansi.org/ansidocstore/product.asp?sku=ANSI+Catalog

American National Standards Institute (ANSI). (1996). *Title of standard s3.6-1996. Catalogue of ANSI standards.* Retrieved May 20, 2006, from http://www.ansi.org/ansidocstore/product.asp?sku=ANSI+Catalog

International Standards Organization (ISO). (1998). *Title of standard: 389-1:1988.*

Katz, J. (2001). *Handbook of clinical audiology.* Baltimore: Williams & Wilkins.

VA National Center for Health Promotion and Disease Prevention. (2004). *Audiogram.* Retrieved September 13, 2005, from http://www.nchpdp.med.va.gov/MonthlyPreventionTopics/2004_08/DegreeOfHearingLoss.doc

THOMAS A. FRANK
Pennsylvania State University
First edition

LISA WILDMO
Bryan, Texas

AUDITORY DISCRIMINATION
AUDITORY PERCEPTION
DEAF

AUDIOLOGY

Raymond Carhart (1947, as cited in Rintlemann, 1985) is credited with coining the term *audiology* for the new profession of hearing science. Soldiers returning from World War II with service-connected hearing losses caused the rapid development of the field of audiology. Originally intended just to provide rehabilitation services, the scope of practice has increased to include the nonmedical management of hearing and balance disorders in children as well as adults such as tinnitus management, hearing aids, cochlear implants, assistive devices, hearing conservation programs, ototoxic drug management, interoperative monitoring, central auditory processing assessment, and cerumen removal.

Entry-level educational requirements for professionals in audiology include a master or doctoral degree. Licensure to practice audiology is required in all 50 states. The practice of audiology encompasses a comprehensive array of professional services related to the prevention of hearing loss and the audiological identification, assessment, diagnosis, and treatment of persons with impairment of auditory and vestibular function and to the prevention of impairments associated with them (American Academy of Audiology,

n.d.). Audiologists serve in a number of roles, including clinician, therapist, teacher, consultant, researcher, and administrator (Martin & Greer, 1999).

Audiologists serve populations ranging from neonates to the geriatric populations. Audiologists can be found in diverse settings from private practice, schools, hospitals, universities, medical centers, and rehabilitation centers to government health care facilities (Martin & Greer, 1999).

REFERENCES

American Academy of Audiology. (n.d.). *What is an audiologist?* Retrieved September 13, 2005, from http://www.audiology.org/about/

Martin, F. N., & Greer, J. C. (1999). *Introduction to audiology* (7th ed.). Boston: Allyn & Bacon.

Rintlemann, W. F. (Ed.). (1985). *Hearing assessment.* Baltimore: University Park Press.

LISA WILDMO
Bryan, Texas

AUDITORY PROCESSING
DEAF

AUDIOMETRY

Audiometry encompasses several techniques and procedures that effectively assess hearing. Routine and accurate calibration of the audiometer, a device used in the assessment of hearing, is critical in identifying hearing impairment. An audiological evaluation typically entails the use of pure-tone and speech audiometry in addition to acoustic immittance measurements, which assess the function of the middle ear, and otoacoustic emissions, which assess outer hair cell functioning.

Pure-tone audiometry requires an individual to respond to tones that are presented at various frequencies in order to determine threshold levels. There are two types of pure-tone measures: air conduction and bone conduction. Classification regarding the degree and type of hearing loss for each ear is possible by integrating the results of both measures. Air-conduction testing involves delivering a tone through the entire auditory pathway (outer, middle, and inner ear) by means of a headphone or insert transducer. Bone-conduction testing requires the use of a bone-conduction transducer, a vibrating device placed on the skull in order to stimulate fluids of the inner ear. Therefore, bone-conduction testing bypasses the outer and middle ear. The specific procedures for pure-tone audiometry have been specified by the American National Standards Institute (1997).

There are two types of speech audiometry: those that assess threshold and those that determine speech discrimination ability. Speech detection threshold is determined by measuring the lowest level at which an individual can detect speech sounds, while speech recognition threshold is determined by measuring the lowest level at which the individual can both hear and correctly identify the speech stimulus. Speech recognition tests use spondaic words, two syllable words that contain equal stress on each syllable (i.e., baseball). Speech discrimination tests present phonetically balanced speech stimuli at a comfortable listening level in order to assess speech comprehension. The aforementioned tests are applicable for populations capable of responding behaviorally (middle childhood and older).

Acoustic immittance measurements, a battery of techniques that may be performed on individuals of all ages, requires the use of a specific device termed an *immittance bridge*. This device is not capable of measuring hearing and instead allows for measuring the physical volume of the external auditory canal and the compliance of the tympanic membranes (ear drums) by recording a tympanogram. In addition, most immittance devices allow for measurement of the acoustic reflex contraction, a stapedial reflex that is elicited in response to loud stimuli.

Otoacoustic emissions is a relatively new and noninvasive technology that has been adopted into the general audiometric test battery. Similar to acoustic immittance, otoacoustic emissions are not a measure of hearing. Instead, they objectively assess the functioning of outer hair cells that reside on the cochlea. Otoacoustic emissions are particularly useful for individuals who are unable to respond behaviorally to air-conduction, bone-conduction, or speech audiometry tests, including newborns, malingerers, and individuals with physical or cognitive disabilities. Adequate identification and assessment of hearing impairments can be achieved through the application of various audiological techniques.

REFERENCES

American National Standards Institute. (1997). *Method for manual pure-tone threshold audiometry.* New York: Author.

Hall, J. W. (2000). *Handbook of otoacoustic emissions.* Gainesville, FL: Singular.

Jacobson, J., & Jacobson, C. (2004). Evaluation of hearing loss in infants and young children. *Pediatric Annals, 33*(12), 811–821.

NICOLE NASEWICZ
CASSIE EIFFERT
University of Florida

AUDITORY ABNORMALITIES

Auditory abnormalities or abnormalities that manifest as hearing loss may be sensory, neural, or both and may arise from differing causes. Although half of all auditory abnormalities are considered to be genetic in origin, 90 percent of all people with a congenital hearing loss have normal hearing parents, suggesting that this is a recessive trait (Toriellos, Reardon, & Gorlin, 2004). Karlsson, Harris, and Svartengen (1997) also found that 50 percent of all late onset hearing loss, or hearing loss in people over the age of 65, has a genetic component. Further, genetic conditions seem to have equal prevalence in all types of hearing loss.

Although hearing loss is usually associated with only the ear, auditory abnormalities can occur in any location through the entire auditory system. Hearing losses in the past have been classified using the interchangeable terms as *sensory-neural, sensorineural,* or *neurosensory.* Advances in clinical equipment and testing technique is allowing a more precise diagnosis and allow for the terms to be split. Otoacoustic emissions give us an indication of how the cochlea is functioning. Auditory brainstem response testing allows us to check the neural pathways to the auditory cortex. Acoustic reflexes check the auditory pathways to the level of the superior olivary complex. Impedance measures check the integrity of the middle ear system. Pure-tone testing checks the integrity of the whole of the system. Central auditory tests give us a glimpse of how the processing centers are working. With these advances, four main types of hearing loss can occur depending on location of the lesion. These types are conductive, sensory, neural, and vestibular.

Conductive hearing losses are caused by structural abnormalities such as atresia, otosclerosis, middle ear effusion, and eustachian tube dysfunction. This type of auditory abnormality accounts for the most common problem in children, with three out of four children having experienced an ear infection by the time they are 3 years old, and has the most educational significance (National Institute on Deafness and Communication Disorders [NIDCD], n.d.). Frequent ear infections put the child at risk for not only speech and language deficits but also for central auditory processing difficulties. Conductive hearing losses can be remediated medically and surgically.

Sensory auditory abnormalities are those caused by problems in the cochlea or auditory sense organ. Inner and outer hair cells can be damaged by ototoxic medications, excessive noise, obesity, and vascular problems that deprive the cochlea of blood supply and oxygen as well as by genetic conditions. Treatment options for this type of auditory abnormality include hearing aids and cochlear implants (NIDCD, n.d.).

Neural abnormalities are those that occur above the level of the cochlea in the auditory system. Acoustic neuromas, auditory neuropathy, and central auditory processing disorders are examples of neural abnormalities. Hearing aids are not usually the first choice of remediation for these types of difficulties but can be helpful in some instances. Remediation is dependent on the site of lesion and may include surgical options in the case of a tumor or auditory rehabilitation in the case of auditory processing difficulties (NIDCD, n.d.).

Vestibular disorders often are overlooked when thinking of auditory impairments. The vestibular system is located in the inner ear. Approximately 42 percent of the population will seek medical treatment for dizziness in their lifetime, and the majority of the causes will lie within the inner ear (Vestibular Disorders Association, n.d.). Causes of vestibular disorders include blows to the head; ototoxic medications, such as high-dose or long-term antibiotics; ear infections; or stroke. In many cases, however, cause of damage to the vestibular system cannot be determined. Treatment options include vestibular rehabilitation, mediation, and surgery (Vestibular Disorders Association, n.d.).

REFERENCES

Karlsson, K. K., Harris, J. R., & Svartengren, M. (1997). Description and preliminary results from an audiometric study of male twins. *Ear and Hearing, 18,* 114–120.

National Institute on Deafness and Communication Disorders (NIDCD). (n.d.). *Statistics and human communication.* Retrieved September 13, 2005, from www.nidcd.nih.gov/health/statistics/hearing.asp

Toriellos, H., Reardon, W., & Gorlin, R. (2004). *Hereditary hearing loss and its syndromes* (2nd ed.). Oxford: Oxford University Press.

Vestibular Disorders Association. (n.d.). *Vestibular disorders.* Retrieved September 13, 2005, from www.vestibular.org

LISA WILDMO
Bryan, Texas

AUDITORY DISCRIMINATION
AUDITORY PERCEPTION
DEAF

AUDITORY DISCRIMINATION

Auditory discrimination is the ability to determine the differences between the speech sounds and sequencing. Auditory discrimination is the middle rung in the processing of sound. An acoustic signal must first be perceived, then discriminated, and, finally, processed. These three terms (*perception, discrimination, processing*) often are used interchangeably.

It has been demonstrated that speech discrimination scores cannot be predicted from pure-tone thresholds alone (Rintlemann, 1985). Speech discrimination scores give us an understanding of a higher level of processing than pure

tones alone. Meaning can be attached to the different signals. Temporal processing or frequency, duration, and ordering must take place in order to understand the speech signal. In addition, auditory closure must take place in order to integrate the preceding information.

Discrimination tests conducted as part of a comprehensive audiological evaluation usually refer to speech discrimination testing. Generally, this is performed by presenting a standardized monosyllable word list like the NU6 or the CID W22 through headphones. Individuals may be asked to repeat words or may be asked if two words are the same or different. Monosyllabic words are used as they offer the least redundancy. The percentage correct is given as the speech discrimination scores. Difficulties at the discrimination level will lead to difficulties recognizing and using the prosodic aspects of speech, reading, and subtle changes in meaning as a result of prosodic changes (Bellis, 1996). Auditory discrimination of phonemes (single speech sounds) and tones has been linked to reading ability and disability (Lachmann, Berti, Kujala, & Schröger, 2005). Similarly, discrimination training has been found to result in better phonological processing in children (Moore, Rosenberg, & Coleman, 2005).

Auditory discrimination is a neural response and current research is looking into electroacoustic testing to help diagnose problems with discrimination. Electroacoustic testing is currently being used to calculate hearing thresholds in the infant and hard-to-test population, but it has been very difficult to determine discrimination abilities within this group as traditional testing has involved language and reasoning requirements. The Mismatched Negativity Test is one such electrophysiological test being studied (Cheour, Lappaenen, & Kraus, 2000).

REFERENCES

Bellis, T. J. (1996). *Assessment and management of central auditory processing disorders in the educational setting.* San Diego: Singular.

Cheour, M., Leppaenen, P., & Kraus, N. (2000). Mismatched negativity (MMN) as a tool for investigating auditory discrimination and sensory memory in infants and children. *Clinical Neurophysiology, 111,* 4–16.

Lachmann, T., Berti, S., Kujala, T., & Schröger, E. (2005). Diagnostic subgroups of developmental dyslexic have different deficits in neural processing of tones and phonemes. *International Journal of Psychophysiology, 56,* 105–120.

Moore, D. R., Rosenberg, J. F., & Coleman, J. S. (2005). Discrimination training of phonemic contrasts enhances phonological processing in mainstream school children. *Brain and Language, 94,* 72–85.

Rintlemann, W. F. (1985). *Hearing assessment.* Baltimore: University Park Press.

Lisa Wildmo
Bryan, Texas

AUDITORY PERCEPTION
DEVELOPMENTAL DYSLEXIA
DYSLEXIA
READING DISORDERS

AUDITORY PERCEPTION

Auditory perception is the ability to identify, interpret, and attach meaning to sound to make it meaningful phenomena (Garstecki & Erber, 1997). These abilities rely on several intact neurological processes such that sound must be heard and transmitted to appropriate structures within the brain. When these processes are not intact, difficulties in auditory perception occur.

Auditory perception follows a developmental trajectory (Moore, 2002; Boothroyd, 1997). Children at 6 months of age demonstrate the beginnings of auditory perception by contrasting phonemes, phoneme recognition, recognition of speech in noise, selective attention, and the use of linguistic content (Boothroyd, 1997). Complete maturation of the auditory system is not complete until later childhood—ages 5 to 12 years (Moore, 2002).

The terms *auditory perception* and *auditory processing* often are used interchangeably in the literature. Children with auditory perceptual problems and auditory processing disorders often exhibit language and learning disabilities (Garstecki & Erber, 1997). Auditory perception problems are found concomitantly with or misdiagnosed as Learning Disorders. Standard pure-tone and speech-discrimination evaluations are not sufficient to rule out an auditory perceptional problem (Katz & Wilde, 1985).

Fisher (1976) developed a checklist of 25 warning signs for which a child should be evaluated for an auditory perceptual problem. These included saying "what" in the absence of a hearing loss, inattentiveness, frequent middle ear infections, asking for repetitions, poor fine-motor coordination, difficulty following directions, poorer verbal than performance scores on intelligence tests, and inconsistencies in academic subjects.

REFERENCES

Boothroyd, A. (1997). Auditory development of the hearing child. *Scandinavian Audiology, 46*(Suppl.), 9–16.

Fisher, L. I. (1976). *Fisher auditory problems checklist.* Cedar Rapid, IA: Grant Wood Area Educational Agency.

Garstecki, D. C., & Erber, S. F. (1997). Hearing loss management in children and adults. In G. T. Menchers, S. E. Gerber, & A. McComve (Eds.), *Audiology and auditory dysfunction* (pp. 220–232). Needham Heights, MA: Allyn & Bacon.

Katz, J., & Wilde, L. (1985). Auditory perceptional disorders in children. In J. Katz (Ed.), *Handbook of clinical audiology* (3rd ed., pp. 664–668). Baltimore: Williams & Wilkins.

Moore, J. K. (2002). Maturation of human auditory cortex: Implications for speech perception. *Annals Oto-Rhino-Larngology, 189*(Suppl.), 7–10.

Lisa Wildmo
Bryan, Texas

AUDITORY DISCRIMINATION
AUDITORY PROCESSING

AUDITORY PROCESSING

Although the terms *auditory perception* and *auditory processing* often are used interchangeably in the literature, auditory processing (or central auditory processing [CAP]) is the area we are most concerned about when we are dealing with children who are experiencing language and reading problems. In this context, *auditory processing* is an umbrella term used for the complex task of taking in all the auditory information and making it salient to the task at hand. According the American Speech-Language-Hearing Association (ASHA; 1996) auditory processing involves mechanisms responsible for sound localization, lateralization, auditory discrimination, auditory pattern recognition, temporal aspects of audition, and auditory performance with competing acoustic signals. Given the multiple components, there is no wonder that Phillips (2002) concluded that "Central Auditory Processing Disorders (CAPD) are probably as idiosyncratic as the individuals they affect" (p. 256).

Due to the complexity of auditory processing, a multidisciplinary approach is recommended for assessment and management of auditory processing disorders (APDs). The team should include, but is not limited to, a speech language pathologist, audiologist, psychologist, parents, physicians, and classroom and special education teachers (Bellis & Ferre, 1996). Management of APD should focus on the range of listening and learning deficits experienced by the individual child. Recommended intervention is a combination of "auditory training, metalinguistic and metacognitive strategies designed to increase the scope and use of the auditory and central resources" (Wertz, Hall, & Davis, 2002, p. 282). Management also is focused on improving signal-to-noise ratios, improving listening skills, and the auditory behaviors of difficult listening situations for those with APD.

REFERENCES

American Speech-Language-Hearing Association (ASHA). (1996). Central auditory processing: Current status of research and implications for clinical practice. *American Journal of Audiology, 5,* 41–45.

Bellis, T., & Ferre, J. (1996). Assessment and management of central auditory processing disorders in children. *Educational Audiology Monograph, 6,* 23–27.

Phillips, D. (2002). Central auditory system and central auditory processing disorders: Some conceptual issues. *Seminars in hearing, 23,* 251–261.

Wertz, D., Hall, J. W., & Davis, W. (2002). Auditory processing disorders: Management approaches past to present. *Seminars in Hearing, 23,* 277–285.

LISA WILDMO
Bryan, Texas

AUDITORY DISCRIMINATION
AUDITORY PERCEPTION
CENTRAL AUDITORY DYSFUNCTION
LEARNING DISABILITIES

AUDITORY–VISUAL INTEGRATION

Auditory–visual perceptual integration is poorly understood; therefore, it is seldom measured and described in the psychoeducational diagnostic process. Instead, beginning in the 1920s with German psychology, and later (1930s) in clinical work, the focus fell almost solely on visual–motor perceptual development. Indeed, psychology in general, and Gestalt psychology in particular, drew heavily from the easily administered, easily scored visual motor tests. Bender's (1938) *Visual-Motor Gestalt Test,* an extension of Wertheimer's (1923) laboratory instrument, soon became the most commonly administered psychological test. Early on, these easily administered tests showed substantial correlations with intelligence (Armstrong & Hauck, 1960) as a diagnostic test for brain damage (Shaw & Cruickshank, 1956), academic achievement (Koppitz, 1958), emotional difficulties (Clawson, 1959), and perceptual development (Koppitz, 1962).

Auditory perception, which in many respects appears to be a sensory–perceptual corollary of visual perception, remains relatively unexplored. The reason may be that the auditory perceptual structures are less well understood than visual perception, and more difficult to ascertain. For example, it is difficult to identify precisely where auditory sensorial function stops, perception begins, auditory perception ends, and receptive language begins.

The result has been that psychologists and special educators have generally limited the theoretical scope to an explanation of auditory–visual perceptual integration as an operational construct important to human learning. However, that fact also conveys a certain ambience, as remedial educators have been tenacious about the importance of auditory–visual integration within the reading process. They believe that reading would be a slow, awkward instructional process in the absence of integrating perceptual symbolic information from the primary sensory channels. Many reading experts are convinced that perceptual integration is critical to early learning of letters and letter phonemic symbolism.

For example, the visual perceptual system may neurally code a "B" and a "D" as distinct symbols based on luminancy differences. A "B" uses a different neuronal subsystem than a "D" because it draws on lateral inhibition and activation associated with on-center neurons; "D" draws on off-center neurons. Symbolic clarity in the visual perceptual realm may be influenced by these factors, all of which have been well investigated: extent and organization of retinal area activities; transformation of receptive-field organization; and estimates of size of receptive field.

In reading, as in most visual tasks, the eye gathers information during the pauses between saccadic movements. Ultimately, stimulus letters are recognized; that is, an appropriate subvocal or auditory response (saying a letter) occurs. The recognition (perceptual) memory can hold at least three letters for a period of about 1 second, until they have been rehearsed.

A scan component is needed to transform the visual information in very short-term visual perceptual memory into motoric information, and then auditory information. Actually, the visual scan component has at least three distinguishable functions: deciding which areas of the visual field contain information; directing processing capacity to the locations selected by the prescan ("attention"); and converting the visual input from the selected locations into the forms of motor memory units and ultimately auditory information.

In principle, although not in detail, the auditory scan is exactly analogous to the visual scan. The auditory scan selects some contents of auditory memory (e.g., the sound representation of one letter) and converts them into motor information. A street address is remembered by placing it into auditory–perceptual memory. By means of this short-term loop, information can be retained in auditory short-term memory. Subvocal rehearsal, the subvocal output of the rehearsal component, is entered into the auditory short-term memory just as though it had been a vocal output. Once that occurs, visual imagery results. The importance of visual–auditory or auditory–visual perceptual integration becomes paramount when confronting remedial reading difficulties. Critchley (1964) noted that children with so-called congenital word blindness failed to develop visual perceptual memory, while their auditory perceptual memory was unaffected.

A great deal of literature from the mid and late 1960s suggested a close interrelationship between the short-term storage mechanisms of vision and audition. Conrad (1959) showed that subjects frequently make substitution errors when recalling lists of visually presented letters in which the letter substituted (e.g., ANQT) sounds similar to the correct letter (e.g., ANQE). Although these letters are highly dissimilar in appearance, they sound similar when spoken aloud. Thus, visual material, Conrad suggests, must have been translated and encoded in auditory storage.

Murray (1968) reported extensive studies of short-term

storage for visual and auditory items. His results showed how the similarity of sounds affected recall of the list (acoustic similarity). In Murray's experiment, conditions enabling the auditory system to assist in the coding and storing of incoming information tend to produce superior performances; this may indicate that the auditory mechanism is generally superior to the visual mechanism in this respect. Such a superiority has also been demonstrated by Murdock (1968).

Wickelgren (1965) has demonstrated that the presence of acoustic elements in visually presented material can influence the accuracy of recall. Subjects listened to four random letters. Next, eight letters were visually presented and copied by the subject. Finally, a test of the first four aural letters was administered. Even though the interpolated material had to be copied rather than spoken, if the eight letters were similar in sound to the aural letters, performance on auditory recall was poorer than when the visual letters were quite dissimilar in sound.

Ross (1969) developed a logical test of the audio–visual interaction in short-term storage by measuring the retention of simple symbols (+ and −) either organized in patterns (e.g., − + + − + − +) or unpatterned (e.g., + − + + − + − − +). Blanton and Odom (1968) found a superiority in seeing and hearing children over deaf children in terms of the span of digits that could be recalled. However, this result may reflect greater experience with numbers on the part of the normal children.

In short, an integration of information from the visual and auditory perceptual channel seems to be occurring. How else, in fact, could a person read graphics, or listen to others read, and write the graphic symbol being received aurally? Reading is a dual process that, except for the learner with disabilities who may be missing one of the sensory channels or have perceptual deficits, is an integrated function. Current research is going towards a dual model of working memory that includes separate visual and auditory channels. On some tasks learners can integrate words and pictures more easily if the words are presented auditorily rather than visually (Mayer & Romano, 1998). With infants, for example, the synchronicity of visual and auditory stimuli are not as important as with older children and adults indicating developmental trends in integrating auditory and visual information presented at the same time (Lewkowicz, 1996).

In summary, auditory–visual integration would appear to be the internal stimulation of the opposite modality, for instance, visual perceptual information is received and a signal system translates the meaning to the auditory perceptual modality in reading. Information on the assumed trait is limited, and awaits much research. It does seem likely that this function holds promise as a predictor of what modality may be used as a unisensory or multisensory receiving mechanism in planning an intervention (Movellan & McClelland, 2001).

REFERENCES

Armstrong, R. G., & Hauck, P. A. (1960). Correlates of the Bender-Gestalt scores in children. *Journal of Psychological Studies, 11,* 153–158.

Bender, L. (1938). *Visual Motor Gestalt Test and its clinical use.* American Ortho Psychiatry Association Research Monograph 3.

Birch, H. G., & Belmont, L. (1965). Auditory-visual integration in brain damaged and normal children. *Journal of Developmental Medicine and Child Neurology, 7,* 135–144.

Blanton, R. L., & Odom, P. B. (1968). Some possible interferences and facilitation effects of pronounciability. *Journal of Verbal Learning Behavior, 7,* 844–846.

Clawson, A. (1959). The Bender-Gestalt Visual Motor Gestalt Test as an index of emotional disturbance in children. *Journal of Project Technology, 23,* 198–206.

Conrad, R. (1959). Errors of immediate memory. *British Journal of Psychology, 50,* 349–359.

Critchley, M. (1965). *The dyslexic child.* London: Heineman.

Koppitz, E. M. (1958). The Bender Gestalt Test and learning disturbances in young children. *Journal of Clinical Psychology, 14,* 292–295.

Koppitz, E. M. (1962). Diagnosing brain damage in young children with the Bender Gestalt Test. *Journal of Consultative Psychology, 26,* 541–546.

Lewkowicz, D. J. (1996). Perception of auditory visual temporal synchrony in human infants. *Journal of Experimental Psychology: Human Perception & Performance, 22,* 1094–1106.

Mayer, R. E., & Romano, R. (1998). A split-attention effect in multimedia learning: Evidence for dual processing systems in working memory. *Journal of Educational Psychology, 90,* 312–320.

Movellan, J. R., & McClelland, J. L. (2001). The Morton-Massaro law of information integration: Implications for models of perception. *Psychological Review, 108,* 113–148.

Murdock, B. B., Jr. (1968). Modality effects in short-term memory: Storage or retrieval? *Journal of Experimental Psychology, 78,* 70–86.

Murray, D. J. (1968). Articulation and acoustic confusability in short-term memory. *Journal of Experimental Psychology, 78,* 679–684.

Ross, B. M. (1969). Sequential visual memory and the limited magic of the number seven. *Journal of Experimental Psychology, 80,* 339–347.

Shaw, M. C., & Cruickshank, W. M. (1956). The use of the Bender-Gestalt Test with epileptic children. *Journal of Clinical Psychology, 12,* 192–193.

Wertheimer, M. (1923). Untersuchanger zur Lehre von der Gestalt. II. *Psychol. forsch, 5,* 301–350.

Wickelgren, W. A. (1965). Acoustic similarity and intrusion errors in short-term memory. *Journal of Experimental Psychology, 70,* 102–108.

DAVID A. SABATINO
*West Virginia College of
Graduate Studies*

AUDITORY PERCEPTION
AUDITORY PROCESSING
VISUAL PERCEPTION AND DISCRIMINATION

AUSTRALIA, SPECIAL EDUCATION IN

Background and Context

Like many western countries, Australia's early provisions for children with special education needs were through institutions and schools established by charitable organizations for people with disabilities in vision or hearing. For example, in Sydney, New South Wales (NSW), a school for deaf children was opened by the Institution for Deaf, Dumb, and Blind in 1860 (Drummond, 1978; Snow, 1990). That organization continues today as the Royal NSW Institute for Deaf and Blind Children, providing a range of on-site and community-based services for deaf, blind, deaf-blind, and other multiply-handicapped children. Similar developments took place in other states, such as Victoria, where a school for the blind was established in 1866 by the Victorian Royal Blind Society, and in South Australia where a school for deaf children was established in 1874 (Drummond, 1978).

The separate development of Australia's states from beginnings as English colonies meant that each developed its own set of governmental powers and responsibilities, gradually emerging as sovereign states and agreeing to form the federation of states which became known as the Commonwealth of Australia in 1901. While the advent of federation meant that some governmental powers became the province of the new federal government, many, such as the responsibility for universal public education, remained within the jurisdiction of individual states. As a result, the states' public education systems, which were established independently in the late nineteenth century, continued to grow under their own administrations. Services for children with disabilities were slow to be introduced by these state governments, until influences such as the reorganization of schooling into primary and secondary levels and an age-grade placement model identified particular problems for schools in providing for students with intellectual disabilities. Not surprisingly for that time, a segregated special education model was widely adopted for those students (see Snow, 1990, for a fuller discussion of these events in one Australian state between 1880 and 1940).

Early Provisions

From these beginnings it has been possible to see the emergence in all Australian states and territories of a range of government-supported special education services. These included a rapid increase in the number of self-contained classes in regular schools, especially for children with mild intellectual difficulties (in the IQ range of 50/55 to 75/80 points); an initially small number of separate special schools along with limited support to voluntary organizations establishing their own special schools for children with moderate and severe disabilities. However, by the late 1970s, state governments moved to take over the ownership and running of voluntary association schools, under an initiative funded by the federal government (Karmel, 1973).

More recently, special education service provision has changed dramatically, to include mainly regular school-based or itinerant services to support those children and their teachers in regular classes. This applies for children with emotional or behaviour disorders (Conway, 1994), though some difficulty is often experienced in identifying the extent to which this problem should be seen as a concern of special education, or as part of the general student welfare/support services of the regular school system. Indeed, the very notion of special education as a separate parallel school system has also been questioned in a growing number of Australian states, as detailed below (Peach, 1991) and also as questioned in the United States (Will, 1986). Associated with this is increasing uncertainty in defining and diagnosing children as having a behavior problem or as being emotionally disturbed. While problems of definition are one issue, more important for schools is the matter of deciding on best educational provisions.

Varying forms of support have been offered to children with learning difficulties, a term used to describe children with deficits in skills of literacy and/or numeracy, in the absence of apparent causes associated with physical, intellectual, or sensory impairment. Support for these children over the years has included the special class, the resource room with a specially trained teacher for withdrawal lessons one or two times a week, and more recently, the support teacher (learning difficulties) who works in the classroom of the regular teacher on a team-teaching basis for a short period (Department of Education, Queensland, 1993; Directorate of School Education, Victoria, 1993; Northern Territory Board of Studies, 1994; NSW Department of School Education, 1992; Ministry of Education, Western Australia, 1993; Special Education Consultative Committee [South Australia], 1994).

Many children with severe intellectual and/or multiple difficulties had been confined to residential institutional settings, often with no access to identified educational programs until this situation was addressed through federal government initiatives in the late 1980s. As a result, the Children in Institutions program saw the introduction of teachers to institutional settings, caring for children with severe intellectual and multiple disabilities. More recently, many of those children have been moved to community-based residential settings, with their education taking place in either a special school or special class in a regular school.

A development in Australia from the early 1970s has been the growth of early intervention services for children with developmental disabilities and their families. Although such services had been in place for many years through the institution-based programs offering services for the deaf or for the physically handicapped (Drummond, 1978), more widespread generic services commenced at university-affiliated research programs (Pieterse, Bochner, & Bettison, 1988), often based on models such as those of Hayden and Dmitriev (1975) at the University of Washington in the United States. These were gradually adopted by community-based groups across the country, often supported by other universities, or by government departments involved in early childhood matters (e.g., community services, health, education; Linfoot, 1992, 1997).

Commonwealth or Federal Government Initiatives

This overview of the development of special education in Australia must acknowledge the significant influence of federal government initiatives introduced in the Australian parliament in the early 1970s. Initiatives were then taken nationally for the first time on school education in Australia, university education being already funded by the Australian government. From 1972 onward, following recommendations of a Commonwealth Parliament Standing Committee on the needs of physically and mentally handicapped persons in Australia, the national government undertook a program to provide supplementary funding to states to assist handicapped persons through initiatives involving preschool education, improved education for handicapped children and adolescents, special education teacher training, and the provision of vocational services (Drummond, 1978). Those activities resulted from a significant injection of funds for special education services across Australia, and made the most significant contribution of government support for special education services in government and nongovernment schools to that time. Those initiatives were first presented in recommendations of the Interim Committee of the Australian Schools Commission (Karmel, 1973). More recent statements of Australian government level support for special education can be found in an Australian government paper to the Organization for Economic Cooperation and Development (OECD; Department of Education, Training & Development, 1992) and in the Australian government's current guidelines on Commonwealth Programs for Schools (Department of Employment, Education, & Youth Affairs, 1997).

Current State of Special Education and Emerging Trends

Special education services in Australia have been broadly influenced by developments in countries such as the United Kingdom, where the Warnock report publicized debate on special education services (Committee of Enquiry into the Education of Handicapped Children and Young People, 1978) and the United States, whose series of public laws prescribing educational provisions for students with disabilities are well-known (Ysseldyke, Algozzine, & Thurlow, 1992). In Australia, there has been no equivalent national legislation on special education, nor a Bill of Rights-style document guaranteeing similar individual expectations of their society. In 1992, however, the Australian federal parliament passed the Disability Discrimination Act, making unlawful discrimination against people with disabilities in access to employment, housing, and education. While offering some protection to the access rights of students with disabilities to education in regular schools, the legislation also provides for *exemption* from its provisions to educational institutions which might suffer an unjustifiable hardship in providing the special services needed to sustain a particular student's enrollment (Commonwealth of Australia, 1992). Most Australian states have developed their own legislation in support of the Commonwealth's Disability Discrimination Act (for example, the Disability Services Act, 1993, in NSW) and these have been influenced by the principles and language of normalization (Wolfensberger, 1972). In most Australian states, the principle of the continuum of special education services is supported, involving the placement of each student in a setting best suited to individual needs but as close as possible to a least restrictive or regular class setting. Nevertheless, there is considerable variation between the states in the extent to which this principle is applied. This is most clearly seen in changing trends in special school enrollments as shown below.

Particularly Australian issues in special education services relate to the needs of indigenous Australians with special education needs and the problems of providing special education services in remote and rural areas, where a sparsely distributed population is scattered over an area the size of western Europe. The compounded disadvantage of disability, geographic isolation, and membership of marginalized groups including women and those of different ethnic and cultural backgrounds have been well described by Germanis-Koutsounadis (1990). The national government initiatives include the English as a Second Language Program; the Special Education Program (e.g., recurrent grants including integration support; pre-school special education; children in residential institutions; children with severe disabilities; other training services); the Disadvantaged Schools program (special projects in literacy, numeracy, money management, initiatives to improve retention rates) for schools meeting criteria in relation to socioeconomic disadvantage; and the Country Area program, designed to provide resources to attempt to "minimize the imbalance between rural and urban education" (Australian Education Council, 1989, pp. 156–158).

Towards Inclusion

Probably the most significant change to special education services in recent years, both in Australia as in other countries, has been the effect of the so-called inclusion movement (Foreman, 1996; Ysseldyke et al., 1992). A trend has emerged by which many more children with special needs are placed in regular classes, with greater expectations on the regular school to be responsible for the educational program. This has been accompanied by a trend to eliminate separate Directorates of Special Education from within Australia's state education departments but to attach special education school support responsibility to school district level administrators and consultancy services. An account of this process of administrative change was set out by Peach (1991), a Deputy Director General of Education in the Australian state of Queensland, in a paper to Australia's special education professional organization (Australian Association of Special Education). Citing support in the literature for the merger of regular and special education, Peach described the end of the

> dual state system of education . . . with separate schools for students with severe intellectual and multiple disabilities and separate special classes for students categorized as hearing impaired, visually impaired and mildly intellectually handicapped. (p. 358).

The closing of separate Directorates of Special Education has also been effected in other states. In NSW, this was accomplished at the end of 1997, with responsibility for special education statewide policy development subsumed within a division within the bureaucracy responsible for all student welfare issues in schools. Unlike Queensland, the state of NSW has disbanded its regional administration layer within the bureaucracy. Instead, administration of schools is supervised by small district offices headed by superintendents across the state. These, in turn, are closely directed by the central Head Office bureaucracy. Although the administrative reform process of education services was still underway in this state in 1998, it is apparent that more centralized control of schools and schooling is one overall result of the reforms.

Associated with these changes in NSW are trends towards the increasing use of inclusive education practices in the delivery of support services outlined in a recently commissioned report, *The Integration / Inclusion Feasibility Study* (McRae, 1996). Also interesting is that the data presented in that report show that changes have already occurred towards inclusion. For example, in the period 1985–98, there was a fall of 30 percent in NSW in the number of students enrolled in special schools, although the school population as a whole has remained static in that period. This is in line with the position nationally, where data cited from a study of DeLemos (1994) show a fall in special *school* enrollments of 37 percent nationally (p. 24). While some increase in the proportion of special *class* enrollments is noted in

the data over that period, by far the greater increase is noted in enrollments of students with disabilities in *regular classes*. Some of these regular class enrollments would have been supported by state or federal government integration funds to schools to support those students in regular classes. However, many of those placements are likely to reflect the changing expectations of many parents that they wish their children with disabilities to be educated in regular classes irrespective of government policy changes.

Considerable differences exist between the various states' special education enrollment data for 1992. These show that special class provisions were rarely used at all (just 2 percent) by students in government schools in Victoria, with most students placed in special schools (44 percent), or in regular classes with support (54 percent). By contrast, in NSW, around 46 percent were in special classes, 21 percent in special schools, and 33 percent in regular classes. Most other Australian states fell between these two positions, although South Australia reported 68 percent of its students with disabilities in regular schools, with special classes and special schools used for 19 percent and 13 percent respectively (McRae, 1996, p. 25). Non-government schools across Australia accounted in 1992 for 28 percent of the school population generally but under 17 percent of those students identified with disabilities. Of these, most were provided for in regular classes (Catholic schools) though 40 percent of the small number enrolled in independent schools (2,377 nationally) were in special schools (DeLemos, 1994, cited in McRae, 1996).

These data show, then, that there has been quite some disparity between Australian states. The wish of state governments to maintain their responsibilities for public education administration suggests that these differences will continue as each tries to reflect its own community's attitude to issues such as special education services, while the national government role remains restricted to special initiative funding to extend state services to areas considered to have been overlooked by states. The extent to which national governments may continue such a role may well be limited in future years as current constraints on domestic public expenditure continue.

REFERENCES

Australian Education Council. (1989). *National report on schooling in Australia.* Canberra: Author.

Committee of Enquiry into the Education of Handicapped Children and Young People. (1978). *Special education needs.* London: HMSO.

Conway, R. N. F. (1994). Students with behavioural and emotional problems. In A. F. Ashman & J. Elkins (Eds.), *Educating children with special needs* (2nd ed.). Sydney: Prentice Hall.

DeLemos, M. (1994). *Schooling for students with disabilities.* Melbourne: Australian Council for Educational Research.

Department of Education, Queensland. (1993). *Educational provision for students with disabilities: Policy statement and management plan.* Brisbane: Author.

Department of Employment, Education, & Training. (1991). *Country paper by Australia, on the project Active Life for Disabled Youth-Integration in the School.* Prepared for the Organization for Economic Co-operation and Development, Centre for Educational Research and Innovation. Canberra: Author.

Department of Employment, Education, Training and Youth Affairs. (1997). Special learning needs. *Commonwealth programmes for schools quadrennial administrative guidelines, 1997–2000.* Canberra: Author.

Directorate of School Education, Victoria. (1993). *Educational opportunities for students with disabilities and impairments.* Melbourne: Author.

Disability Discrimination Act. (1992). Section 22, Division 2-Discrimination in other areas. Canberra: Commonwealth of Australia. (Internet: http://www/austlii.edu.au/au/legis/cth/consol_act/dda1992264/s22.html)

Drummond, N. W. (1978). *Special education in Australia.* Sydney: Royal Far West Children's Health Scheme.

Foreman, P. (Ed.). (1996). *Integration and inclusion in action.* Sydney: Harcourt Brace.

Germanos-Koutsounadis, V. (1990). "Fair Go" access and equity issues for Australians with disabilities who are from non-English speaking backgrounds (NESB), aboriginal, Torres Strait Islanders, women and from remote areas. *Australian Disability Review, 3*(90), 3–10.

Hayden, A. H., & Dmitriev, V. (1975). The multidisciplinary preschool program for Down syndrome children at the University of Washington model preschool center. In B. Z. Friedlander, G. M. Sterritt, & G. E. Kirk (Eds.), *Exceptional infant: Assessment and intervention* (Vol. 3). New York: Brunner/Mazel.

Karmel, P. (1973). *Schools in Australia: Report of the interim committee for the Australian Schools Commission.* Canberra: Australian Government Publishing Service.

Linfoot, K. W. (1992). The delivery of early intervention services for infants and preschool children: A ten year retrospective. *The Australasian Journal of Special Education, 16*(1), 42–47.

Linfoot, K. W. (1997). *Access to early intervention for families of children with disabilities in rural areas of New South Wales: A research report.* Penrith, NSW: University of Western Sydney, Nepean.

McRae, D. (1996). *The integration / inclusion feasibility study.* Sydney: NSW Department of School Education.

Ministry of Education, Western Australia. (1993). *Social justice in education: Policy and guidelines for the education of students with disabilities.* Perth: Author.

NSW Department of School Education. (1992). *Special Education.* Sydney: Author.

Northern Territory Board of Studies. (1994). *Provision for students with disabilities in Northern Territory Schools.* Darwin: Author.

Peach, F. (1991). Crossing boundaries—Present realities and future possibilities. Opening address to the 15th National Conference of the Australian Association of Special Education. *Proceedings of the 15th National Conference of the Australian Association of Special Education.* Brisbane: AASE.

Pieterse, M., Bochner, S., & Bettison, S. (Eds.). (1988). *Early intervention for children with disabilities: The Australian experience.* Sydney: Macquarie University.

Snow, D. (1990). Historicising the integration debate. *Australasian Journal of Special Education, 13*(2), 28–38.

Special Education Consultative Committee (South Australia). (1994). *Schools for all.* Adelaide: Author.

Wolfensberger, W. (1972). *The principle of normalization in human services.* Toronto: National Institute on Mental Retardation.

Ysseldyke, J. E., Algozzine, B., & Thurlow, M. L. (1992). *Critical issues in special education* (2nd ed.). Boston: Houghton Mifflin.

KEN LINFOOT
University of Western Sydney

NEW ZEALAND, SPECIAL EDUCATION IN

AUTISM

Leo Kanner's 1943 paper, "Autistic Disturbances of Affective Contact," made autism a medical entity. It took twenty more years for autism to become a cultural entity—an intriguing (to outsiders) and devastating (to families) aberration of child development whose incidence, causes, and treatment were mysteries demanding solutions. Prevalence estimates for autism have ranged from the earlier figure of approximately 4 or 5 per 10,000 children to more recent findings of about 1 per 1,000 children (Bryson, 1996), with a ratio of 3 or 4 males to each female. Differences in rates over time may reflect expansion of the list of criteria that define autism, increased reporting (Coleman & Gillberg, 1985), environmental pollution, and iatrogenic (illness-producing) effects of antibiotics (Rimland, 1997). The onset of autism (the beginning of a child's atypical trajectory of psychosocial development) often occurs in the first months of the child's life (Coleman & Gillberg, 1985). Early abnormalities of development crystallize into autism around two and a half years (Folstein & Rutter, 1987).

The lives of many individuals with autism are characterized by marginality with respect to ordinary adolescent and adult activities. Several decades ago, for example, Rutter et al. (1967) stated that a minority of persons with autism reached a good level of social adjustment by adolescence, and even fewer entered paid employment. Recent research is more encouraging. As an autistic child grows through adolescence and adulthood, activity level decreases, ease at managing undesirable behavior increases, and language, sociability, and activities of daily living improve (Mesibov, 1983). Good outcomes (e.g., social relatedness and independent living) appear to be predicted by reactions to sound, less problem behavior at earlier ages, language, schooling, and higher IQ in early childhood (Coleman & Gillberg, 1985).

Characteristics of Autism

As indicated by the name itself, the most striking and pervasive feature of autism is a child's difficulty participating in the social world. Even with his or her parents, an autistic child may seem alone; in social relationships generally, he or she may be unattached or have a difficult time sustaining attachment. In particular, a child may (1) pay little attention to other persons; (2) avoid physical contact and even the gaze of other persons (Lord, 1993); (3) fail to initiate interaction with others, or initiate interaction in ritualized ways (Hauck, Fein, Waterhouse, & Feinstein, 1995); (4) fail to imitate simple routine actions, for example, waving bye-bye (Coleman & Gillberg, 1985); (5) fail to follow simple instructions (Coleman & Gillberg, 1985); and (6) have much difficulty taking the role or standpoint of the other person (Schopler & Mesibov, 1995), as indicated by not sharing attention with others to the same task at hand, not displaying empathy, and seemingly not understanding emotions displayed by other persons (Lord, 1993). In summary, the child with autism, perhaps from infancy, is not geared into the patterns of interaction—the various forms of turn-taking during meals, play, and other social activities—which are the vehicle that brings children into the already organized social world.

Second features of autism are overselectivity and overreactivity in attention and attachment. For example, a child with autism may (1) pay attention to stimuli that are irrelevant to a task (e.g., a shiny bolt on a refrigerator door, rather than the handle); (2) stare fixedly and for long periods at spinning objects and flapping hands; (3) have "bizarre attachments to certain objects, such as stones, curls of hair, pins, pieces of plastic toys, or metals," apparently on the basis of color or texture (Coleman & Gillberg, 1985, p. 21); and (4) pay little attention and underreact to relevant events (e.g., verbal, facial, and postural cues signifying intentions, expectations, and feelings of other persons; Green, Fein, Joy, & Waterhouse, 1995).

Third, individuals with autism show uneven levels of competence across functional domains (Dawson, 1996; Rutter, 1983). Approximately 75 percent of autistic children are mentally retarded (Rutter, 1983). For example, autistic children may have much skill with spatial relations and memory, along with severe impairments in the following areas:

1. *Language.* Autistic children generally acquire speech sounds in typical fashion and learn to form words, but are impaired with respect to comprehension and language use; e.g., sharing or requesting information and initiating or reciprocating in conversation (Green, Fein, Joy, & Waterhouse, 1995; Prizant, 1996; Rimland, 1964).
2. *Social Skills.* For example, greetings and goodbyes, understanding and following requests, jointly working at tasks, taking the role of another person.
3. *Abstract Reasoning.* For example, figuring out sequences and abstracting general principles from specific events; imagination.
4. *Typical or Appropriate Play.* For example, imaginative and cooperative play (Lewis & Boucher, 1995; Lord, 1993). For example, a child with autism may sit for hours rocking back and forth, staring intently at his or her fingers or at shiny objects, or make hundreds of ritualistic gestures during the day, like moving his or her hands and fingers in a fixed pattern, pulling at his or her hair, or twisting his or her face into strange expressions.

Fourth, a child with autism may engage in self-injury or even self-mutilation, especially if he or she is nonverbal (Shodell & Reiter, 1968). Examples include pinching, scratching, biting or striking himself, raising callouses and welts, and sometimes tearing his or her flesh (Schopler, 1995).

Finally, as described below, substantial evidence indicates neurological abnormalities or differences in individuals with autism (Dawson, 1996). For example, Reichler and Lee (1987) comment that autism is generally seen as "the expression of some underlying brain dysfunction" that is "associated with multiple etiologies, any one of which could potentially cause central nervous systems dysfunction" (p. 15).

Approaches to Cause and Treatment

Until the mid-1960s, the psychodynamic or psychogenic approach provided the predominant explanation and treatment of autism (Rimland, 1964). Autism was presumed to be caused by early interactions with the parents. Kanner (1943) originally observed that the parents, particularly the mothers, appeared cold and hostile towards their children. Mothers were characterized with the phrase "refrigerator mothers." Bettelheim (1967) in particular adopted the position that autism owed to poor parenting and that therapy required removing autistic children from their hostile home environment. However, no basis for parental, or any other early social, cause of autism has been found. Unfortunately, therapists blamed parents for their children's autism for decades, itself an iatrogenic effect (e.g., Torrey, 1977).

Pharmacological/Medical

Suggested pathogenic agents underlying autism are many and varied, ranging from genetic factors to infectious processes during prenatal (e.g., rubella and possibly cytomegalovirus), perinatal, early postnatal (e.g., herpes simplex infection), and later occurring conditions (Coleman, 1987; Reichler & Lee, 1987). Evidence for a genetic component in autism is strong (Bailey, Phillips, & Rutter, 1996): Identical twins have a higher probability than fraternal twins of both being diagnosed with autism, and the probability of autism in siblings is 50 times higher than in the general population (Silliman, Campbell, & Mitchell, 1989). However, the specific role of genetic factors in autism is not yet clear (Folstein & Rutter, 1987), although some children with autism test positive for Fragile X. In addition, recent medical research has found additional factors that may start a trajectory towards the diagnosis of autism and may help explain certain behavioral excesses and developmental deficits identified earlier. These factors include:

1. Elevated levels of serotonin and dopamine in the blood, immature patterns of circadian rhythms for corticosteroids, and abnormalities in brain-stem auditory evoked responses (Coleman & Gillberg, 1985; Volkmar & Anderson, 1989).

2. Abnormalities (e.g., reduced size, or hypoplasia) of the brain's cerebellar vermis, which may help explain difficulties in arousal, attention, speech, and motor output (Hashimoto et al., 1995).

3. Possible overactivation of the right hemisphere of the brain, which may help explain chronic high levels of arousal and therefore overselectivity to novelty and underattention to speech and social cues (e.g., facial expressions).

A variety of medications, vitamins, dietary changes, and psychiatric treatments have been used over the years—not as remedies for autism, but for specific symptoms and associated problems, such as seizures, destructive behavior, and stimulus overreactivity (Gualtieri, Evans, & Patterson, 1987). These include vitamin B6, Deanol, chlorpromazine, clozapine, gluten-free diets, lithium, haloperidol, fenfluramine, L-dopa, D amphetamine, Naltrexone, electroconvulsive therapy, insulin coma therapy, opiate antagonists, and leucotomy. Results have ranged from poor to good. The current situation with respect to medical explanations and treatments is perhaps best summarized by Waterhouse, Wing, and Fein (1989): "Despite clinical impressions of a unity among typically autistic children, investigations of the group, regardless of which set of diagnostic criteria has been used, have found no shared etiology, no shared uniquely pathognomic neural deficit, no shared cognitive deficit, no distinct shared behavioral pattern, no shared specific life course, and no shared response to drug treatment."

Behavioral Approaches

Currently, the behavioral approach (including applied behavior analysis and precision teaching) is the best choice for educating children with autism. The behavioral approach rests on about 75 years of behavioral science research, particularly social learning and the experimental analysis of behavior. For practitioners of the behavioral approach, a child's maladaptive behavior and development are the most pressing problems. Moreover, the most verifiable and reliable remedies to date are environmental operations, events of instruction, and patterns of communication in the child's environments, as described by Engelmann and Carnine (1991); Mattaini (1996); Schlinger and Blakely (1994); and Gagne, Briggs, and Wager (1992).

A sample of reportedly effective behavioral-educational programs for children with autism includes those described by Anderson, Avery, DiPietro, Edwards, and Christian (1987); Fenske, Zalenski, Krantz, and McClannahan (1985); Fox, Dunlap, and Philbrick (1997); Hamblin et al. (1971); Harris, Handleman, Kristoff, Bass, and Gordon (1990); Harris, Handleman, Gordon, Kristoff, and Fuentes (1991); Holmes (1998); Howlin and Rutter (1987); Hoyson, Jamieson, and Strain (1984); Koegel and Johnson (1989); Koegel and Koegel (1996); Koegel, Rincover, and Egel (1982); Kozloff (1994a, 1994b, 1998); Lord, Bristol, and Schopler (1993); Lovaas (1977, 1987); Maurice, Green, and Luce (1996); McClannahan and Krantz (1997); McEachlin, Smith, and Lovaas (1993); Prizant and Wetherby (1989, 1993); Rogers (1996); Rogers and DiLalla (1991); Rogers and Lewis (1989); Schopler, Lansing, and Waters (1983); Smith, Eikseth, and Lovaas (1997); and Watson, Lord, Schaffer, and Schopler (1989).

The best educational programs seem to have the following features:

1. Programs for autistic children based on principles of learning are designed to foster competencies that will enable children to participate in family, peer group, church, school, and other environments. In general, child-teacher interaction is structured so that inappropriate behaviors are weakened (usually with combinations of extinction and time out) while developmentally feasible and socially functional behaviors (attention, cooperation, imitation, play, speech, activities of daily living) are strengthened via the systematic use of compliance training, modeling, prompting, errorless learning, response chaining, and differential reinforcement of desirable behavior.

   Learning appropriate behavior (e.g., speech) as a substitute for inappropriate behavior (e.g., pulling and pushing) is a slow process consisting of numerous steps. The teacher might first reinforce a mute child for making any sounds. Then when the child's rate of vocalizing has increased and she is emitting many different sounds, the teacher will reinforce the child only when the child repeats a particular sound after the teacher, that is, when the child imitates the teacher. In this way, words, sentences, and conversation are shaped up as closer and closer approximations to functional speech are prompted and reinforced. The same shaping process is used to teach a child to name objects, to read and write, to play, and to cooperate. In other words, the teacher attempts to build up the child's repertoire of appropriate behavior as a substitute for autistic behavior.

2. Curricula in the better schools are a synthesis of contributions of many bodies of knowledge regarding psychosocial development. In particular, excellent programs pay attention to:

   a. *Respondent learning*—how movements are assembled into reflexive emotional and attention responses.

   b. *Operant learning*—how contingencies of reinforcement teach individuals to perform actions with more or less skill, frequency, intensity, generality, and duration.

   c. *Applied behavior analysis*—using principles of respondent and operant learning to assess an individual's behavioral repertoire and environments, and suggest how to foster beneficial change either in the context of "discrete-trials" (highly structured turn taking) or in more naturalistic ("free operant") environments.

   d. *Forms and processes of child-caregiver and child-peer interaction.*

   e. *Cognitive developmental psychology and ecological psychology*—on how routine tasks and activities in a person's round of daily life (akin to scripts, frames, templates, or scaffolds) help a person organize actions into larger classes and sequences (Barker, 1968; Fogel, 1992).

   f. *The personalization process* in families, schools, and neighborhoods, by which valued versus degraded social positions, roles, and identities are bestowed on children (Henry, 1966; Kozloff, 1994a).

3. Excellent educational programs work on all eight phases of learning. These phases are as follows.

   a. *Acquisition* is the early phase when a child learns concepts, propositions, and operations (tool skills, learning channels), and strategies for assembling these elements into more complex and successful or accurate composite sequences (e.g., solving problems).

   b. *Fluency* means behavior is performed accurately, smoothly, and at effective and/or culturally desirable speeds, durations, and intensities (Binder, 1996; Dougherty & Johnson, 1996; Lindsley, 1996). For example, a child not only knows how to read words accurately (acquisition), but reads quickly and almost automatically.

   c. *Endurance* means a person fluently (rapidly and accurately) performs a task for an extended period. Endurance is fostered by practicing and improving concepts and tool skills; increasing the duration of practice sessions; and shifting performances from practice environments to naturalistic environments.

   d. *Behavioral momentum* (Plaud & Gaither, 1996) means a person fluently (rapidly and accurately) performs a task despite distractions; e.g., other students' talking. Momentum is fostered by practice to the point of fluency and beyond; practice in the presence of increasingly obtrusive distractors; and by introducing events that have been associated with reinforcement (e.g., music or a teacher's presence).

   e. *Generalization* (sometimes called *application*) means a person learns to transfer concepts, propositions, strategies, and operations acquired in one environment to other environments. For example, generalization of reading would involve reading at home and in class; reading newspapers, posters, graffiti, TV screens, and computers as well as school books; reading different type faces; and reading for various purposes (e.g., pleasure, following recipes, and crossing streets; Mundschenk & Sasso, 1995).

   f. *Adaptation,* not to be confused with generalization, involves altering (not simply transferring) concepts, propositions, strategies, and operations to suit the circumstances. This could mean using different movements, tools, or sequences, or adding a side-sequence.

   g. *Retention* means a performance is fluent despite time between practice or performance. Retention is a function of past fluency and endurance.

   h. *Maintenance* means a person performs competently in the absence of instructional scaffolding or assistance, i.e., the person is a more independent learner.

4. The better programs have strong collaborative relationships with parents and offer training programs and support. Important activities include assessing children's competencies, impairments, and preferences; translating assessment information into program plans; conducting complementary home programs; and evaluating and revising children's programs (Anderson, Avery, DiPietro, Edwards, & Christian, 1987; Holmes, 1998; Huynen, Lutzker, Bigelow, Touchette, & Campbell, 1996; Koegel, Bimbela, & Schreibman, 1996; Kozloff, 1998; Kozloff, Helm, Cutler, Douglas-Steele, Wells, & Scampini, 1988; Marcus & Schopler, 1989).

REFERENCES

Anderson, S. R., Avery, D. L., DiPietro, E. K., Edwards, G. L., & Christian, W. P. (1987). Intensive home-based early intervention with autistic children. *Education and Treatment of Children, 10,* 352–366.

Bailey, A., Phillips, W., & Rutter, M. (1996). Autism: Towards an integration of clinical, genetic, neuropsychological, and neurological perspectives. *Journal of Child Psychology and Psychiatry, 37,* 89–126.

Barker, R. (1968). *Ecological psychology.* Stanford, CA: Stanford University Press.

Bettelheim, B. (1967). *The empty fortress: Infantile autism and the birth of the self.* New York: Free Press.

Binder, C. (1996). Behavioral fluency: Evolution of a new paradigm. *The Behavior Analyst, 19,* 163–197.

Bryson, S. E. (1996). Brief report: Epidemiology of autism. *Journal of Autism and Developmental Disorders, 26,* 165–167.

Coleman, M. (1987). The search for neurological subgroups in autism. In E. Schopler & G. Mesibov (Eds.), *Neurobiological issues in autism* (pp. 163–178). New York: Plenum.

Coleman, M., & Gillberg, C. (1985). *The biology of the autistic syndromes.* New York: Praeger.

Courchesne, E. (1989). Neuroanatomical systems involved in infantile autism. In G. Dawson (Ed.), *Autism: Nature, diagnosis, and treatment* (pp. 119–143). New York: Guilford.

Engelmann, S., & Carnine, D. (1991). *Theory of instruction: Principles and applications* (Rev. ed.). Eugene, OR: ADI.

Fenske, E. C., Zalenski, S., Krantz, P. J., & McClannahan, L. E. (1985). Age at intervention and treatment outcome for autistic children in a comprehensive intervention program. *Analysis and Intervention in Developmental Disabilities, 7,* 7–31.

Fogel, A. (1992). Movement and communication in infancy: The social dynamics of development. *Human Movement Science, 11,* 387–423.

Folstein, S. E., & Rutter, M. (1987). Familial aggregation and genetic implication. In E. Schopler & G. Mesibov (Eds.), *Neurobiological issues in autism* (pp. 83–105). New York: Plenum.

Fox, L., Dunlap, G., & Philbrick, L. A. (1997). Providing individual supports to young children with autism and their families. *Journal of Early Intervention, 21,* 1–14.

Gagné, R. M., Briggs, L. J., & Wager, W. W. (1992). *Principles of instructional design* (4th ed.). Fort Worth, TX: Harcourt Brace Jovanovich.

Gaultieri, T., Evans, R. W., & Patterson, D. R. (1987). The medical treatment of autistic people. In E. Schopler & G. Mesibov (Eds.), *Neurobiological issues in autism* (pp. 373–388). New York: Plenum.

Green, L., Fein, D., Joy, S., & Waterhouse, L. (1995). Cognitive functioning in autism. In E. Schopler & G. Mesibov (Eds.), *Learning and cognition in autism* (pp. 13–31). New York: Plenum.

Hamblin, R. L., Buckholdt, D., Ferritor, D., Kozloff, M., & Blackwell, L. (1971). *The humanization processes.* New York: Wiley.

Harris, S., Handleman, J. S., Kristoff, B., Bass, L., & Gordon, R. (1990). Changes in language development among autistic and peer children in segregated and integrated preschool settings. *Journal of Autism and Developmental Disorders, 20,* 23–32.

Hashimoto, T., Tayama, M., Murakawa, K., Yoshimoto, T., Miyazaki, M., Harada, M., & Kurado, Y. (1995). Development of the brain stem and cerebellum in autistic patients. *Journal of Autism and Developmental Disorders, 25,* 1–18.

Hauck, M., Fein, D., Waterhouse, L., & Feinstein, C. (1995). Social initiations by autistic children to adults and other children. *Journal of Autism and Developmental Disorders, 25,* 579–595.

Henry, J. (1966). Personality and aging—with special reference to hospitals for the aged poor. In J. C. McKinney & F. T. DeVyver (Eds.), *Aging and social policy* (pp. 281–301). New York: Meredith.

Holmes, D. L. (1998). *Autism through the lifespan: The Eden model.* Bethesda, MD: Woodbine House.

Howlin, P., & Rutter, M. (1987). *Treatment of autistic children.* Chichester, England: Wiley.

Hoyson, M., Jamieson, B., and Strain, P. S. (1984). Individualized group instruction of normally developing and autistic-like children: A description and evaluation of the LEAP curriculum model. *Journal of the Division of Early Childhood, 8,* 157–171.

Huynen, K. B., Lutzker, J. R., Bigelow, K. M., Touchette, P. E., & Campbell, R. V. (1996). Planned activity training for mothers of children with developmental disabilities. *Behavior Modification, 20,* 406–427.

Kanner, L. (1943). Autistic disturbances of affective contact. *Nervous Child, 2,* 217–250.

Koegel, R. L., Bimbela, A., & Schreibman, L. (1996). Collateral effects of parent training on family interactions. *Journal of Autism and Developmental Disorders, 26,* 347–359.

Koegel, R. L., & Johnson, J. (1989). Motivating language use in autistic children. In G. Dawson (Ed.), *Autism: Nature, diagnosis, and treatment* (pp. 310–325). New York: Guilford.

Koegel, R. L., & Koegel, L. K. (1996). *Teaching children with autism: Strategies for initiating positive interactions and improving learning opportunities.* Baltimore: Paul H. Brookes.

Koegel, R. L., Rincover, A., & Egel, A. L. (1982). *Educating and understanding autistic children.* San Diego, CA: College Hill Press.

Kozloff, M. A. (1998). *Reaching the autistic child* (Rev. ed.). Cambridge, MA: Brookline Books.

Kozloff, M. A. (1994a). *Improving educational outcomes for children with disabilities: Guidelines and protocols for practice.* Baltimore: Paul H. Brookes.

Kozloff, M. A. (1994b). *Improving educational outcomes for children with disabilities: Principles of assessment, program planning and evaluation.* Baltimore: Paul H. Brookes.

Laski, K. E., Charlop, M. H., & Schreibman, L. (1988). Training parents to use the Natural Language Paradigm to increase their autistic children's speech. *Journal of Applied Behavior Analysis, 21,* 391–400.

Lewis, V., & Boucher, J. (1995). Generativity in the play of young people with autism. *Journal of Autism and Developmental Disorders, 25,* 105–121.

Lichstein, K. L., & Schreibman, L. (1976). Employing electric shock with autistic children: A review of the side effects. *Journal of Autism and Childhood Schizophrenia, 6,* 163–173.

Lindsley, O. R. (1996). The four operant freedoms. *The Behavior Analyst, 19,* 199–210.

Lord, C. (1993). Early social development in autism. In E. Schopler, M. E. Van Bourgondien, & M. M. Bristol (Eds.), *Pre-school issues in autism* (pp. 61–94). New York: Plenum.

Lord, C., Bristol, M., and Schopler, E. (1993). Early intervention for children with autism and related developmental disorders. In E. Schopler, M. E. Van Bourgondien, & M. M. Bristol (Eds.), *Preschool issues in autism* (pp. 199–221). New York: Plenum.

Lovaas, O. I. (1977). *The autistic child: Language development through behavior modification.* New York: Irvington.

Lovaas, O. I. (1987). Behavioral treatment and normal educational and intellectual functional of young autistic children. *Journal of Consulting and Clinical Psychology, 55,* 3–9.

Marcus, L. M., & Schopler, E. (1989). Parents as co-therapists with autistic children. In C. E. Schaefer & J. M. Briesmeister (Eds.), *Handbook of parent training: Parents as co-therapists for children's behavior problems* (pp. 337–360). New York: Wiley.

Maurice, C., Green, G., & Luce, S. C. (1996). *Behavioral intervention for young children with autism.* Austin, TX: PRO-ED.

Mattaini, M. A. (1996). Envisioning cultural practices. *The Behavior Analyst, 19,* 257–272.

McClannahan, L. E., & Krantz, P. J. (1997). In search of solutions to prompt dependence: Teaching children with autism to use photographic activity schedules. In D. M. Baer & E. M. Pinkston (Eds.), *Environment and behavior* (pp. 271–278). Westview Press.

McEachlin, J. J., Smith, T., & Lovaas, O. I. (1993). Long-term outcome for children with autism who received early intensive behavioral treatment. *American Journal on Mental Retardation, 97,* 359–372.

Mesibov, G. B. (1983). Current perspectives and issues in autism and adolescence. In E. Schopler & G. B. Mesibov (Eds.), *Autism in adolescents and adults* (pp. 37–53). New York: Plenum.

Mundschenk, N. A., & Sasso, G. M. (1995). Assessing sufficient social exemplars for students with autism. *Behavioral Disorders, 21,* 62–78.

Plaud, J. J., & Gaither, G. A. (1996). Behavioral momentum: Implications and development from reinforcement theories. *Behavior Modification, 2,* 183–201.

Prizant, B. M. (1996). Brief report: Communication, language, social, and emotional development. *Journal of Autism and Developmental Disorders, 26,* 173–178.

Prizant, B. M., & Wetherby, A. M. (1989). Enhancing language and communication in autism. In G. Dawson (Ed.), *Autism: Nature, diagnosis, and treatment* (pp. 282–309). New York: Guilford.

Prizant, B. M., & Wetherby, A. M. (1993). Communication in preschool autistic children. In E. Schopler, M. E. Van Bourgondien, & M. M. Bristol (Eds.), *Preschool issues in autism* (pp. 95–128). New York: Plenum.

Reichler, R. J., & Lee, E. M. C. (1987). Overview of biomedical issues in autism. In E. Schopler & G. Mesibov (Eds.), *Neurobiological issues in autism* (pp. 13–41). New York: Plenum.

Rimland, B. (1964). *Infantile autism.* New York: Appleton-Century-Crofts.

Rimland, B. (1997, October). Historical perspectives and techniques that work. Paper presented at the International Symposium on Autism, Illinois Center for Autism, McKendry College, Lebanon, IL.

Rogers, S. L. (1996). Brief report: Early intervention in autism. *Journal of Autism and Developmental Disorders, 26,* 243–246.

Rogers, S. J., & DiLalla, D. L. (1991). A comparative study of the effects of a developmentally based preschool curriculum on young children with autism and young children with other disorders of behavior development. *Topics in Early Childhood Special Education, 11,* 29–47.

Rogers, S. J., & Lewis, H. C. (1989). An effective day treatment model for young children with pervasive developmental disorders. *Journal of the American Academy of Child and Adolescent Psychiatry, 28,* 207–214.

Rutter, M. (1983). Cognitive deficits in the pathogenesis of autism. *Journal of Child Psychology and Psychiatry, 24,* 513–531.

Rutter, M., Greenfield, D., & Lockyer, L. (1967). A five to fifteen year follow-up study of infantile psychosis. *British Journal of Psychiatry, 113,* 1183–1199.

Schlinger, H. D., & Blakely, E. (1994). A descriptive taxonomy of environmental operations and its implications for behavior analysis. *The Behavior Analyst, 17,* 43–57.

Schopler, E. (1995). *Parent survival manual.* New York: Plenum.

Schopler, E., Lansing, M., & Waters, L. (1983). *Individualized assessment and treatment for autistic and developmentally disabled children: Volume 3. Teaching activities for autistic children.* Austin, TX: PRO-ED.

Schopler, E., & Mesibov, G. (1995). Introduction to learning and cognition in autism. In E. Schopler & G. Mesibov (Eds.), *Learning and cognition in autism* (pp. 3–11). New York: Plenum.

Silliman, E. R., Campbell, M., & Mitchell, R. S. (1989). Genetic influences in autism and assessment of metalinguistic performance in siblings of autistic children. In G. Dawson (Ed.), *Autism: Nature, diagnosis, and treatment* (pp. 225–259). New York: Guilford.

Stahmer, A. C. (1995). Teaching symbolic play skills to children with autism using pivotal response training. *Journal of Autism and Developmental Disorders, 25,* 123–141.

Tager-Flusberg, H. (1989). A psycholinguistic perspective on language development in the autistic child. In G. Dawson (Ed.), *Autism: Nature, diagnosis, and treatment* (pp. 92–115). New York: Guilford.

Tobias, M. (1959). The disturbed child—A concept: Usefulness of Deanol in management. *American Practitioner's Digest of Treatment, 10,* 1759–1766.

Torrey, E. F. (1977). A fantasy trial about a real issue. *Psychology Today, 10*(10), 24.

Volkmar, F. R., & Anderson, G. M. (1989). Neurochemical perspectives on infantile autism. In G. Dawson (Ed.), *Autism: Nature, diagnosis, and treatment* (pp. 208–224). New York: Guilford.

Vollmer, T. R., Northup, J., Ringdalh, J. E., LeBlanc, L. A., & Chauvin, T. M. (1996). Functional analysis of severe tantrums displayed by children with language delays. *Behavior Modification, 20,* 97–115.

Waterhouse, L., Wing, L., & Fein, D. (1989). Re-evaluating the syndrome of autism in the light of empirical research. In G. Dawson (Ed.), *Autism: Nature, diagnosis, and treatment* (pp. 263–281). New York: Guilford.

Watson, L., Lord, C., Schaffer, B., & Schopler, E. (1989). *Teaching spontaneous communication to autistic and developmentally handicapped children.* Austin, TX: PRO-ED.

Wing, L., & Gould, L. (1979). Severe impairments of social interaction and associated abnormalities in children: Epidemiology and classification. *Journal of Autism and Developmental Disorders, 9,* 11–29.

MARTIN A. KOZLOFF
University of North Carolina at Wilmington

ASPERGER SYNDROME
AUTISTIC BEHAVIOR
NATIONAL SOCIETY FOR CHILDREN AND ADULTS WITH AUTISM

AUTISM DIAGNOSTIC INTERVIEW–REVISED

The Autism Diagnostic Interview–Revised (ADI-R; LeCouteur, Lord, & Rutter, 2003) is a structured interview for use in the diagnosis of autism spectrum disorders. It is referred to as the gold standard for a clinical interview related to autism for individuals with a mental age of 18 months or higher (Constantino et al., 2003). The comprehensive interview provides information related to language and communication, reciprocal social interactions, and restricted or repetitive or stereotyped behaviors and interests. Depending on the individual being assessed and the caregiver, the interview takes about 2 hours to complete (LeCouteur et al., 2003). Use of the ADI-R requires not only experience with the population and basic interviewing skills but also training specific to the ADI-R. Responses are scored and interpreted based on either a diagnostic algorithm or current behavior algorithm or both depending on the purpose of the assessment (Lord, Rutter, & LeCouteur, 1994). The ADI-R does not have prescribed descriptive classifications; results are intended to provide information that would support the diagnosis of autism spectrum disorders and to identify needs of children and adults for intervention planning. The ADI-R is available in 11 languages and is used worldwide (Lord & Corsello, 2005).

Psychometric properties of the ADI-R are adequate; with appropriate training, interrater reliability for the scoring of the interview has been reported to be good to excellent (.90 or higher; Constantino et al., 2003; de Bildt et al., 2004). Statistical analysis was used in setting cut scores for the ADI-R (Lord et al., 1997). Discriminant evidence is provided in the manual. Bishop and Norbury (2002) concluded that results of the ADI-R were most consistent with the child's actual diagnosis. Additional support for discriminant validity from the research literature was found for the ADI-R (e.g., Noterdaeme, Mildenberger, Sitter, & Amorosa, 2002). At the same time, Bishop and Norbury (2002) found a low level of agreement for the ADI-R and other parent interview information with the other specific measures of autistic tendencies. They concluded that this was in part because of the extent to which pragmatic language issues and age confound diagnosis. In a study comparing the ADI-R with diagnostic decisions, de Bildt et al. (2004) found adequate agreement, but noted age effects.

REFERENCES

Bishop, D. V. M., & Norbury, C. F. (2002). Exploring the borderlands of Autistic Disorder and specific language impairment: A study using standardized diagnostic instruments. *Journal of Child Psychology and Psychiatry, 43,* 917–929.

Constantino, J. N., Davis, S. A., Todd, R. D., Schindler, M. K., Gross, M. M., Brophy, S. L., et al. (2003). Validation of a brief quantitative measure of autistic traits: Comparison of the Social Responsiveness Scale with the Autism Diagnostic Interview–Revised. *Journal of Autism and Developmental Disorders, 33,* 427–433.

de Bildt, A., Sytema, S., Ketelaars, C., Kraijer, D., Mulder, E., Volkmar, F., & Minderaa, R. (2004). Interrelationship between Autism Diagnostic Observation Schedule–Generic (ADOS-G), Autism Diagnostic Interview-Revised (ADI-R), and the *Diagnostic and Statistical Manual of Mental Disorders (DSM-IV-TR)* classification of children and adolescents with Mental Retardation. *Journal of Autism and Developmental Disorders, 34,* 129–137.

LeCouteur, A., Lord, C., & Rutter, M. (2003). *The autism diagnostic interview: Revised.* Los Angeles: Western Psychological Services.

Lord, C., & Corsello, C. (2005). Diagnostic instruments in autistic spectrum disorders. In F. R. Volmar, R. Paul, A. Klin, & D. Cohen (Eds.), *Handbook of autism and pervasive developmental disorders* (Vol. 2, 3rd ed., pp. 730–771). New York: Wiley.

Lord, C., Pickles, A., McLennan, J., Rutter, M., Bregman, J., Folstein, S., et al. (1997). Diagnosing autism: Analyses of data from the Autism Diagnostic Interview. *Journal of Autism and Developmental Disorders, 27,* 501–517.

Lord, C., Rutter, M., & LeCouteur, A. (1994). Autism Diagnostic Interview Revised: A revised version of a diagnostic interview for caregivers of individuals with possible Pervasive Developmental Disorders. *Journal of Autism and Developmental Disorders, 24,* 659–685.

Noterdaeme, M., Mildenberger, K., Sitter, S., & Amorosa, H. (2002). Parent information and direct observation in the diagnosis of Pervasive and specific Developmental Disorders. *Autism, 6,* 159–168.

CYNTHIA A. RICCIO
Texas A&M University

AUTISM
AUTISM DIAGNOSTIC OBSERVATION SYSTEM

AUTISM DIAGNOSTIC OBSERVATION SYSTEM

The Autism Diagnostic Observation System (ADOS; Lord, Rutter, DiLavore, & Risi, 1999) is a measure used in the assessment of autism spectrum disorders that combines direct observation in contrived situations or presses with information obtained from parent interview. The assessment is semistructured, and the activities provide opportunities to observe a range of social and communication behaviors. The ADOS consists of four modules; the child is administered the module that is best aligned with his or her overall language functioning from nonverbal to fluent. Each of the modules is estimated to take 35 to 40 minutes; only one module is administered to each child. The activities and skills covered by the ADOS are intended to have direct implications for intervention (Lord et al., 1999). Although not appropriate for nonverbal adolescents or adults with autism, the ADOS is intended for use with all others who may have autism. Use of the ADOS requires experience, skills, and practice (Lord & Corsello, 2005); workshops are available on a regular basis to learn appropriate administration.

Following the observations, the results are considered in relation to cut scores for autism, Pervasive Developmental Disorders, atypical autism, and the general category of autism spectrum disorders (Lord et al., 1997). Psychometric properties (e.g., interrater reliability, internal consistency, temporal stability) are good (e.g., Lord et al., 2000). Content is appropriate for diagnosis with coverage of three domains essential for diagnosis of autism spectrum disorders—communication, social behavior, and repetitive motor or stereotypy—included in each module. Discriminant evidence is provided in the manual. Additional support for discriminant validity from the research literature was found as well (e.g., Noterdaeme, Mildenberger, Sitter, & Amorosa, 2002). In a study comparing the ADOS results with diagnostic decisions, de Bildt et al. (2004) found adequate agreement, but noted age effects. The ADOS is gradually gaining acceptance worldwide as the gold standard for assessment of autism spectrum disorders (Lord & Corsello, 2005).

REFERENCES

de Bildt, A., Sytema, S., Ketelaars, C., Kraijer, D., Mulder, E., Volkmar, F., et al. (2004). Interrelationship between Autism Diagnostic Observation Schedule–Generic (ADOS-G), Autism Diagnostic Interview–Revised (ADI-R), and the *Diagnostic and Statistical Manual of Mental Disorders (DSM-IV-TR)* classification of children and adolescents with Mental Retardation. *Journal of Autism and Developmental Disorders, 34,* 129–137.

Lord, C., & Corsello, C. (2005). Diagnostic instruments in autistic spectrum disorders. In F. R. Volmar, R. Paul, A. Klin, & D. Cohen (Eds.), *Handbook of autism and Pervasive Developmental Disorders* (Vol. 2, 3rd ed., pp. 730–771). New York: Wiley.

Lord, C., Pickles, A., McLennan, J., Rutter, M., Bregman, J., Folstein, S., et al. (1997). Diagnosing autism: Analyses of data from the Autism Diagnostic Interview. *Journal of Autism and Developmental Disorders, 27,* 501–517.

Lord, C., Risi, S., Lambrecht, L., Cook, E. H., Jr., Leventhal, B. L., DiLavore, P. C., et al. (2000). The Autism Diagnostic Observation Schedule–Generic: A standard measure of social and communication deficits associated with the spectrum of autism. *Journal of Autism and Developmental Disorders, 30,* 205–223.

Lord, C., Rutter, M., DiLavore, P. C., & Risi, S. (1999). *Autism Diagnostic Observation System.* Los Angeles: Western Psychological Services.

Noterdaeme, M., Mildenberger, K., Sitter, S., & Amorosa, H. (2002). Parent information and direct observation in the diagnosis of Pervasive and specific Developmental Disorders. *Autism, 6,* 159–168.

CYNTHIA A. RICCIO
Texas A&M University

AUTISM
AUTISM DIAGNOSTIC INTERVIEW–REVISED

AUTISM SOCIETY OF AMERICA

The Autism Society of America (ASA) was founded in 1965 to help parents, family members, professionals, and caregivers learn about autism and how to effectively deal with the disability. ASA has over 24,000 members joined through a network of 225 chapters in 46 states across the country. The mission of ASA is to promote lifelong access and opportunities for persons within the autism spectrum and their families to be fully included, participating members of their communities through advocacy, public awareness, education, and research related to autism. ASA believes that each person with autism is a unique individual, and its policies promote the active and informed involvement of family members and those with autism in the planning of individualized, appropriate services and supports.

The ASA provides current information about autism through distribution of free packets of materials on a variety of topics; a comprehensive, bimonthly newsletter, the *Advocate;* and an annual national conference each July. An extensive library of information on issues affecting children and adults with autism, Pervasive Developmental/Disorder-not otherwise specified (PDD-NOS), Asperger's, or other related disorders is maintained by the Society. In addition, ASA furnishes national legislators and government agencies with information about the needs of people with autism and their families and promotes medical research in the field.

Local chapters help families find trained professionals and service providers in their communities and organize parent support groups. Some chapters also host presentations by autism experts and advocate at the state level for improvements in programs and services specific to the disability.

A variety of information packets are available from the ASA national office, including materials dealing with general information about autism, facilitated communication, insurance, medications, education, and adult issues. Information provided assists families in appropriately matching the unique needs and potential of individuals with autism to treatments or strategies likely to be effective in moving the person closer to normal functioning. The Society promotes treatments supported by research while asserting that no one treatment exists which is equally effective for all persons. In doing so, they focus on important areas to consider when formulating a treatment plan, including social skill development, communication, behavior, and sensory integration.

Headquarters of the Autism Society of America are located at 7910 Woodmont Avenue, Suite 650, Bethesda, MD 20814-3015. ASA may be reached by phoning 1-800-3AUTISM or on the internet at http://www.autism-society.org/.

TAMARA J. MARTIN
The University of Texas of the Permian Basin

AUTISM TREATMENT OPTIONS

Autism Treatment Options (ATO) is a nonprofit organization that was established in 1994 by parents of autistic children. The main objective of ATO is to provide parents and others interested in the field of autism with information on different types of treatments. ATO publishes the *Autism Options Guide—Resource Handbook,* a book that provides readers with a great deal of information on available autism resources.

ATO seeks to increase the awareness of available options for parents and professionals, and also to provide support for family members of autistic persons. Members of ATO are continually updated on current research and new treatments and findings in the field. Membership is open to parents, relatives, and professionals with an interest in autism. For further information about ATO, contact them at Autism Treatment Options Inc., P.O. Box 10772, Goldsboro, NC 27532-0772.

JENNIFER MIGHT
University of North Carolina at Wilmington

AUTISTIC BEHAVIOR

Autistic behavior is the name for those activities and characteristics frequently associated with the developmental disorder known various as autism, early infantile autism, or Kanner's (1943) syndrome. Although autism spectrum disorders have well-defined diagnostic criteria, a wide variety of behaviors are said to be autistic. Further, many of the behaviors are occasionally exhibited by children with other developmental syndromes and disorders such as mental retardation, cerebral palsy, and serious disorders of receptive and/or expressive language. A particular pattern of symptoms, including an early age of onset as well as social and language peculiarities, characterizes the syndrome known as autism and distinguishes it from all other childhood psychotic disorders. Thus, the mere presence of behaviors called autistic in a child's repertoire does not guarantee that autism is the appropriate diagnosis for that child. Further, it is very unusual for any child diagnosed as autistic to show all of the behaviors that have been associated with autism.

One of the first attempts to compile the range of behaviors observed among autistic children was made by Creak (1964) and her colleagues in Great Britain. Similar sets of observations have been reported since that time by others. The observations may be summarized as follows:

1. Unusual and/or self-stimulatory behaviors such as rocking to and fro, flicking fingers in front of the eyes, flapping arms or hands rapidly at particular frequencies, adopting unusual postures, or toe walking.

2. Reluctance to use the distance receptors of vision and hearing. This translates into an avoidance of eye contact and inattention to auditory and visual cues and information. By contrast there is often an excessive and age-inappropriate reliance on near receptors such as taste, touch, and smell for exploration. The threshold for pain may also be unusually high.

3. A preoccupation with certain objects or the operations of objects, often without respect to their intended function. For example, a child may be fascinated by an empty record turntable spinning or may play with a toy truck only by turning it on its side to spin its wheels.

4. The absence of speech or, where speech exists, delays and/or peculiarities such as the use of jargon, the repetition of phrases or whole passages (echolalia), the reversal or misuse of personal pronouns, and idiosyncratic use of words (neologisms).

5. Unusual anxieties, often unrelated to actual environmental circumstances. For instance, a child may become unusually upset if furniture is rearranged in a room, but may remain calm and seemingly unconcerned while involved in an auto accident or while performing dangerous activities such as climbing or balancing at great heights.

6. An unwillingness to have familiar routines changed or delayed and a reluctance to participate in new activities or to process unexpected events. Thus a child may insist on walking exactly the same route to school daily, may wish to constantly possess a particular toy, or consume only certain foods. Any changes or interruptions of these routines produce extreme anxiety.

7. A pattern of uneven intellectual development characterized by general mental retardation with "islands" of near normal, normal, or even supranormal functioning. A child may not be able to answer simple questions (why, when, where, etc.), but the same child may perform complex mathematical calculations or read large and unfamiliar words, though this skill is usually not accompanied by adequate comprehension.

Many authors have attempted to provide rating scales as an aid in formulating a diagnosis to quantify the types and amounts of autistic behavior a child shows while being observed. Three scales in fairly widespread use are the Behavior Rating Instrument for Autism and Other Atypical Children, second edition (Ruttenberg et al., 1991), the Childhood Autism Rating Scale (CARS; Schopler et al., 1985), and the Vineland Adaptive Scales, second edition (Sparrow, Cicchetti, & Balla, 2005). Such scales may be useful in planning educational or behavioral intervention programs because they focus on particular problem behaviors and they usually reliably discriminate among samples of normal, retarded, and people with autism. However, they are less useful in establishing individual diagnoses because they only tap behaviors observed within the relatively brief observation period. They tend to be of greatest use in the most severe cases of autism, where mental retardation is also likely to be quite marked. Nevertheless, the scales are very useful in the overall process of diagnosis and intervention.

REFERENCES

Creak, M. (1964). Schizophrenic syndrome in childhood: Further progress report of a working party. *Developmental Medicine and Child Neurology, 6,* 530–535.

Freeman, B., Ritvo, E., & Schroth, P. (1984). Behavior assessment of the syndrome of autism: Behavior Observation System. *Journal of the American Academy of Child Psychiatry, 23,* 588–594.

Kanner, L. (1943). Autistic disturbances of affective contact. *Nervous Child, 2,* 217–250.

Ruttenberg, B. A., Wenar, C., & Wolf, E. G. (1991). *Behavior Rating Instrument for Autistic and Other Atypical Children* (2nd ed.). Wood Dale, IL: Stoelting.

Schopler, E., Reichler, R., & Renner, B. (1985). *Childhood Autism Rating Scale (CARS).* Wood Dale, IL: Stoelting.

Sparrow, S., Cicchetti, D. V., & Bala, D. A. (2005). *Vineland Adaptive Scales* (2nd ed.). Circle Pines, MN: AGS.

JERRY L. SLOAN
*Wilmington Psychiatric
Associates*

ASPERGER SYNDROME
AUTISM
NATIONAL SOCIETY FOR CHILDREN AND ADULTS WITH
   AUTISM

AUTOMATICITY

Automaticity is an aspect of perceptual and motor processing that occurs outside of conscious awareness. Factors such as stimulus novelty and response practice have been found to be related to automaticity in cognitive functioning (Neiser, 1976). When aroused by a novel or difficult stimulus, extensive cognitive processing occurs, forcing the event into conscious awareness. However, a habitual response elicited by an expected stimulus may be performed at an automatic level requiring little or no attention.

Humans have a limited attention capacity, therefore automatic functions add to the efficiency of the information processing system (Kutas & Hillyard, 1980). Many simple perceptual processes are innately automatic, while even complex activities such as reading can become automatic with sufficient practice. In fact, Hancock and Byrd (1984) state that reading efficiency is dependent on the extent to which decoding skills become automatized, and Garnett and Fleischner (1980) have related automatization to basic math facts acquisition.

Learning disabilities and mental retardation have been discussed in terms of deficient automatization processes. Learning-disabled children have been found to take longer to produce acquired math facts than their non-disabled peers (Garnett & Fleischner, 1980). Their inability to perform this well-drilled task at an automatic level suggests that learning-disabled children's thinking processes are more circuitous and attention demanding. Severely disabled readers have been found to have difficulty processing letters within words, while less impaired readers, who have automatized letter recognition, read whole words in a controlled, attention-demanding manner (Hancock & Byrd, 1984). Other research (Hurks et al., 2005) suggests that children with ADHD have no impairments in automatic preparations for visuomotor tasks but have great difficulty in visuomotor tasks that require planning and preparation.

Other researchers have suggested that automatic functions may be available to learning-disabled and retarded students, but that other factors impede their effects. Thus, children with retardation have been found to perform as well as their nonretarded peers on a measure of perceptual memory automatization (Stein, Laskowski, & Trancone, 1982). The children with retardation, however, had more difficulty organizing new skills, thereby preventing the automatization of more complex processes. In another study, learning-disabled children were found to produce the correct definitions of familiar words at a rate equal to that of nondisabled children, but showed a rapid decline in rate and accuracy when unfamiliar words were introduced (Ceci, 1983). As more purposeful processing was required, the learning-disabled students failed to decode the words, and instead substituted words that could be processed at an automatic level. Other skills must also become automatic and can be assessed in kindergarten (Schatschneider, Fletcher, Francis, Carlson, & Foorman, 2004).

REFERENCES

Ceci, S. J. (1983). Automatic and purposeful semantic processing characteristics of normal and language/learning disabled children. *Developmental Psychology, 19*(3), 427–439.

Garnett, K., & Fleischner, J. (1980). *Automatization and basic fact performance of normal and learning disabled children* (Technical Report No. 10). Washington, DC: Office of Special Education. (ERIC Document Reproduction Service No. ED 210 839)

Hancock, A. C., & Byrd, D. (1984, April). *Automatic processing in normal and learning disabled children.* Paper presented at the annual meeting of the Southwestern Psychological Association, New Orleans. (ERIC Document Reproduction Service No. ED 246 414)

Hurks, P. P., Adam, J. J., Hendrickson, J. G. M., Vles, J. S. H., Feron, F. J. M., Kaiff, A. C., Kroes, M., Crolla, I. F. A., van Zeben, T. M. C. B., & Bolles, J. (2005). Controlled visuomotor preparation deficits in attention-deficit/hyperactivity disorder. *Neuropsychology, 19,* 66–76.

Kutas, M., & Hillyard, S. A. (1980). Reading senseless sentences: Brain potentials reflect semantic incongruity. *Science, 207,* 203–204.

Neiser, U. (1976). *Cognition and reality.* San Francisco: Freeman.

Schatschneider, C., Fletcher, J. M., Francis, D. J., Carlson, C. D., & Foorman, B. R. (2004). Kindergarten prediction of reading skills: A longitudinal comparative analysis. *Journal of Educational Psychology, 96,* 265–282.

Stein, D. K., Laskowski, M. A., & Trancone, J. (1982). *Automatic memory processes in mentally retarded persons.* Paper presented at the annual meeting of the American Psychological Association, Washington, DC. (ERIC Document Reproduction Service No. ED 227 604)

GARY BERKOWITZ
Temple University

COGNITIVE STRATEGIES
CONDITIONING
TRANSFER OF TRAINING

AUTOMUTISM

See ELECTIVE MUTISM.

AUTONOMIC REACTIVITY

The autonomic nervous system consists of the sympathetic nervous system and the parasympathetic nervous system. The sympathetic nervous system increases heart rate, adrenal secretions, sweating, and other responses that prepare the body for vigorous activity. The parasympathetic nervous system increases salivation, digestion, and other vegetative responses while antagonizing many effects of the sympathetic nervous system.

The sympathetic system can be activated by sudden sensory stimuli or by emotional experiences. The response to a stimulus depends on one's interpretation of the stimulus and not on just the stimulus itself. Shock believed to be escapable increases heart rate; shock believed to be inescapable decreases it (Malcuit, 1973). A task given to fifth-grade boys as a test increased heart rate; a similar task given to them as a game decreased it (Darley & Katz, 1973).

The sympathetic nervous system is apparently most reactive in early childhood, when gauged by variability of heart rate (Shields, 1983). Sympathetic reactivity is fairly stable over time and may be related to personality traits. Many people with an antisocial personality have a weak sympathetic response to frightening stimuli.

REFERENCES

Darley, S. A., & Katz, K. (1973). Heart rate changes in children as a function of test versus game instructions and test anxiety. *Child Development, 44,* 784–789.

Malcuit, G. (1973). Cardiac responses in aversive situation with and without avoidance possibility. *Psychophysiology, 10,* 295–306.

Shields, S. A. (1983). Development of autonomic nervous system responsivity in children: A review of the literature. *International Journal of Behavioral Development, 6,* 291–319.

JAMES W. KALAT
North Carolina State University

CENTRAL NERVOUS SYSTEM
LEARNED HELPLESSNESS

AVERSIVE CONTROL

The use of aversive stimuli to control behavior is one of the most controversial techniques employed by teachers, researchers, psychologists, therapists, and others. The effectiveness of this procedure is defined by its effect on behavior: It suppresses the behavior that it follows. This definition is similar to that for punishment. Indeed, aversive control is one form of punishment.

The controversy surrounding the use of aversive control is illustrated by Wood and Lakin (1982). They indicate that, although most states approve of the use of moderate corporal punishment, it is specifically forbidden by statutes in others (e.g., Maine and Massachusetts).

The use of aversive consequences for behavior control generally is viewed as a technique to be used only when other techniques have not been successful. Snell (1983) indicates that:

> Aversive conditioning using strong primary aversion (such as electric shock and slapping) to eliminate behavior is very defensible in two general instances: when the behavior is so dangerous or self-destructive that positive reinforcement and extinction are not feasible and when all other intervention methods (reinforce competing response, extinction, milder punishment forms) have been applied competently and have been documented as unsuccessful. (p. 140)

Despite the reservations that have been expressed regarding the use of aversives, aversives have been used to control behavior, particularly self-injurious behavior (SIB). Lemon juice (Sajwaj, Libet, & Agras, 1974), noxious odors (Baumeister & Baumeister, 1978), and electric shock are examples of aversive methods that have been used.

At times and under certain conditions, aversive procedures have been found to be the treatment of choice. However, aversive control should be reduced or eliminated when the desired behavior change has occurred or when the target behavior responds to less severe techniques. Suppression, and not elimination, of targeted behavior may result from using this technique. Unexpected and unintended results often occur whenever a punishment procedure is used; it is possible that similar side effects may occur when aversive control is used.

The use of aversives to control behavior raises many ethical questions. The basic rationale for the use of aversives is that other methods have failed, the child is at risk, and the aversive to be used is not as harmful as the behavior that is targeted for change.

REFERENCES

Baumeister, A., & Baumeister, A. (1978). Suppression of repetitive self-injurious behavior by contingent inhalation of aromatic ammonia. *Journal of Autism & Childhood Schizophrenia, 8,* 71–77.

Sajwaj, T., Libet, J., & Agras, S. (1974). Lemon juice therapy: The control of life threatening rumination in a six-month old infant. *Journal of Applied Behavior Analysis, 1,* 557–566.

Snell, M. (Ed.). (1983). *Systematic instruction of the moderately and severely handicapped* (2nd ed.). Columbus, OH: Merrill.

Wood, F. H., & Lakin, K. C. (Eds.). (1982). *Punishment and aversive stimulation in special education: Legal, theoretical and practical issues in their use with emotionally disturbed children and youth.* Reston, VA: Council for Exceptional Children.

PHILIP E. LYON
College of St. Rose

BEHAVIOR MODIFICATION
OPERANT CONDITIONING
PUNISHMENT

AVERSIVE STIMULUS

An aversive stimulus whether unconditioned (e.g., bright lights) or conditioned (e.g., a frown or gesture) is "an unpleasant object or event" (Sulzer-Azaroff & Mayer, 1986) that can be used to decrease or increase a behavior. When presented as a consequence of, or contingent on, a specific behavior, it may be used to reduce or eliminate the rate of that behavior. However, when an aversive stimulus is removed contingent on the emission of a behavior, it may increase the rate of that behavior. In any case, an aversive stimulus is typically referred to as a punisher.

The application of aversive stimuli to effectively reduce or eliminate severe self-destructive behaviors and/or severe chronic behaviors has been demonstrated by several researchers including Lovaas and Simmons (1969) and Risley (1968). However, the many disadvantages of applying aversive stimuli to reduce behaviors (e.g., withdrawal, aggression, generalization, imitation, negative self-statements; Sulzer-Azaroff & Mayer, 1986) seem to outweigh the advantages. Aversive stimuli to reduce behaviors should be reserved for serious destructive behaviors and employed only when other less aversive procedures have been tried. A more detailed presentation of the use of aversive stimuli may be found in Sulzer-Azaroff and Mayer (1986).

REFERENCES

Lovaas, O. I., Simmons, J. O. (1969). Manipulation of self destruction in three retarded children. *Journal of Applied Behavior Analysis, 2,* 143–157.

Risley, T. (1968). The effects and side effects of punishing the autistic behaviors of a deviant child. *Journal of Applied Behavior Analysis, 1,* 21–35.

Sulzer-Azaroff, B., & Mayer, G. R. (1986). *Achieving educational excellence using behavior strategies.* New York: Holt, Rinehart, & Winston.

ALLISON LEWIS
LOUIS J. LANUNZIATA
University of North Carolina at Wilmington

BEHAVIOR MODIFICATION
PUNISHMENT

AVEYRON, WILD BOY OF

See WILD BOY OF AVEYRON.

AYLLON, TEODORO (1929–   )

Teodoro Ayllon obtained his PhD in clinical psychology in 1959 at the University of Houston. His special areas of interest are in behavior and condition therapy and applied behavior analysis. His major field of interest is in clinical psychology. He has done extensive research in behavioral analysis and management and has published articles and books concerning this subject. He is currently working on a book on children and their families.

Some of his principal contributions include "Eliminating Discipline Problems by Strengthening Academic Performance," "The Elimination of Discipline Problems Through a Combined School-Home Motivational System," and "Behavioral Management of School Phobias." In these articles, Ayllon discusses a procedure in which discipline problems and school phobias can be remedied by having parents support the child with positive reinforcement to increase motivation to go to school and improve performance.

He continues his research in clinical psychology and behavioral management and remains involved in the field of psychology. Ayllon's work has been recognized with honors. He retired as a professor of psychology and special education in the psychology department at Georgia State University in 1997.

He is currently Professor Emeritus at Georgia State University and maintains offices in Atlanta and Duluth. Dr. Ayllon's current interests include problem-orientated, solution-focused and time limited behavioral family therapy for children and adolescents.

REFERENCES

Ayllon, T. (1974). Eliminating discipline problems by strengthening academic performance. *Journal of Applied Behavior Analysis, 7,* 71–76.

Ayllon, T. (1999). *How to use token economy and point systems* (2nd ed.). Texas: PRO-ED.

Ayllon, T., & Freed, M. (1989). *Stopping baby's colic.* New York: Putnam.

Ayllon, T., Garber, S., & Pisor, K. (1975). The elimination of discipline problems through a combined school-home motivational system. *Journal of Behavior Therapy, 6,* 616–626.

Ayllon, T., Smith, D., & Rogers, M. (1970). Behavioral management of school phobia. *Journal of Behavioral Therapy & Experimental Psychiatry, 1,* 125–138.

Rebecca Bailey
Texas A&M University

Rachel M. Toplis
*Falcon School District 49,
Colorado Springs, Colorado*

AYRES, A. JEAN (1920–1988)

A. Jean Ayres died on December 16, 1988 at the age of 68. Ayres obtained her BS in 1945 and MS in 1954 in Occupational Therapy, and went on to earn her PhD in 1961 in Educational Psychology from the University of Southern California. She worked as an occupational therapist in several California rehabilitation centers, and between 1955 and 1985, she taught and conducted research at the University of Southern California in the Departments of Occupational Therapy and Special Education, achieving the rank of emeritus professor after her retirement in 1985. Ayres was also in private practice in occupational therapy from 1977 to 1984.

Occupational therapy, particularly as related to perceptual and sensory integrative dysfunction and neuromuscular integration, was the focus of her work. From 1964 to 1966, she was a postdoctoral trainee at the University of California, Los Angeles Brain Research Institute, which led to her discovery of sensory integration dysfunction, a neurological disorder of the senses characterized by learning and behavioral problems as well as pain associated with the performance of even simple daily tasks. Ayres had struggled with learning problems similar to those caused by the disease, ultimately identifying an inefficient organization of sensory information received by the nervous system as its cause. Perhaps her greatest contribution was the development of sensory-integrative therapy, a neurologically-based treatment for learning disorders widely used among occupational therapists. She is also credited with devising the Southern California Sensory Integration Tests and the Sensory Integration and Praxis Tests, tools used for identifying the disorder.

Distinguishing her work from others, Ayres (1972) used a neurological as opposed to an educational or psychodynamic approach to learning and behavior disorders, emphasizing the normalization of the sensory integration process

A. Jean Ayres

in the brain stem while not excluding cortical integrative processes. Her research found that students with certain identifiable types of sensory integrative dysfunctions who received occupational therapy specifically for the integrative dysfunction, showed greater gains in academic scores than those who received an equal amount of time in academic work.

During her distinguished career, Ayres published over 50 tests, articles, and films. She was the recipient of the Eleanor Clarke Slagle Lectureship and the Award of Merit, the highest honors conferred by the American Occupational Therapy Association, and she was named to the 1971 edition of *Outstanding Educators of America.* Ayres was a charter member of the honorary Academy of Research of the American Occupational Therapy Association.

REFERENCE

Ayres, A. J. (1972). Improving academic scores through sensory integration. *Journal of Learning Disabilities, 5,* 338–343.

E. Valerie Hewitt
Texas A&M University
First edition

Tamara J. Martin
*The University of Texas of the
   Permian Basin*
Second edition

**OCCUPATIONAL THERAPY
SENSORY INTEGRATIVE THERAPY**

B

BABINSKI REFLEX

The Babinski reflex was first recognized in 1896 by a French neurologist of Polish descent, Joseph Francois Felix Babinski. Babinski was a pupil of Charcot and was the first to differentiate between a normal and pathologic response of the toes. The Babinski sign, or extensor plantar response, is a phenomenon observed when the sole of the foot is stroked from below the heel toward the toes on the lateral (outside) side. The big toe turns upward or toward the head with the other toes fanned out and extended and the leg is withdrawn.

As the nervous system matures and the pyramidal tract gains more control over spinal motorneurons, the Babinski reflex will not be observed. Indeed, scratching the sole of the foot of a normal person with a dull object will produce a downward flexion of all toes. The presence of Babinski's reflex after the first year of life is an indication of damage to cortical motor neurons and a dysfunction of the pyramidal tract, and further neurological evaluation is required.

There has been controversy over the pathophysiologic interpretation of the Babinski sign or reflex; however, it is considered the single most important sign in clinical neurology because of its reliability. The clinical utility of the Babinski reflex has remained unchanged for over 100 years after its initial description.

REFERENCES

Bassetti, C. (1995). Babinski and Babinski sign. *Spine, 20*(23), 2591–2594.

Estanol, V. B., Huerta, D. E., & Garcia, R. G. (1997). 100 years of the Babinski sign. *Review Invest Clinical, 49*(2), 141–144.

van Gijn, J. (1995). The Babinski reflex. *Postgraduate Medical Journal, 171*(841), 645–648.

Rothenberg, M. A., & Chapman, C. F. (1994). *Dictionary of medical terms* (3rd ed.). Hauppauge, NY: Barron's.

ELAINE FLETCHER-JANZEN
*University of Colorado at
Colorado Springs*

APGAR RATING SCALE
DEVELOPMENTAL MILESTONES
PLANTAR REFLEX

BABY DOE

The term *Baby Doe,* traditionally used in legal pleadings and court proceedings to represent an infant the privacy and anonymity of whom the parties or the court wish to protect, has come to signify the issue of denying life-sustaining treatment to infants born with permanent handicaps combined with life-threatening but surgically correctible conditions. These infants are the focus of a debate that tests the limits of medical certainty in diagnosis and raises profound legal and ethical issues.

A major stimulus to the ethical and legal debate on foregoing life-sustaining treatment for newborns was provided by Duff and Campbell (1973). Their article describes how and why nontreatment was chosen for 43 out of 299 infants during a 30-month period in the intensive care nursery at Yale New Haven Hospital.

The term *Infant Doe* was first used on April 9, 1982, when a baby boy born with Down syndrome and esophageal atresia (a defect that prevents normal feeding) was born in Bloomington, Indiana. His parents refused to give consent for surgery to correct the tracheoesophageal defect. The courts refused to intervene, and Infant Doe died 6 days later. The Reagan administration responded by informing hospitals that Section 504 of the Rehabilitation Act of 1973, which prevents discrimination against individuals with handicaps in programs receiving federal funds, protects imperiled newborns. The administration issued an Interim Final Regulation in March 1983 that articulated this policy of nondiscrimination and established procedures to implement it. This regulation was overturned by a federal court because of the administration's failure to follow established notice and comment procedures in promulgating it.

In July 1983 the Reagan administration issued a second similar proposed rule. It stated that treatment of an infant with a handicap was mandatory unless treatment was medically contraindicated. It provided that the denial of treatment on the basis of a potentially disabling or handicapping condition constituted unlawful discrimination. It was also specified that this regulation was not intended to mandate futile therapies that would only prolong an infant's process of dying.

On October 11, 1983, Baby Jane Doe was born in Port

Jefferson, New York. She was born with myelomeningocele, hydrocephaly, microcephaly, bilateral upper extremity spasticity, a prolapsed rectum, and a malformed brain stem. Her parents chose a course of conservative treatment as an alternative to surgery. Based on anonymous information, the Department of Health and Human Services filed a complaint with the state Child Protection Agency. The July, 1983 ruling made it clear that the federal government was ready to step in if the decision of a state agency was considered insufficient. This case focused attention on the question of the federal government's right to intrude into the private realm of family decision making.

In 1983, the President's Commission for the Study of Ethical Problems in Medicine and Biomedical Research issued, as part of its report, a statement on the decision to forgo life-sustaining treatment in critically ill newborns. It contrasted the presumption that parents are the appropriate decision makers for their infants with the *parens patriae* (literally, "parent of the country") power of the state. That is, while laws concerning the family protect a substantial range of discretion for parents, the state may supervise parental decisions before they become operative to ensure that the choices made are not neglectful or abusive to the child. It concluded that public policy should resist state intervention into family decisions unless serious issues are at stake and the intervention is likely to achieve better outcomes. Additionally, the commission suggested that infants with handicaps be treated no less vigorously than their nonhandicapped peers. However, it also suggested that futile therapies that merely delay death without offering a reasonable probability of saving a baby's life should be avoided. Finally, in ambiguous cases, where the course of action that would benefit the infant is not chosen by the parents, authorized persons acting for the state as *parens patriae* must step in.

On April 15, 1985, the Department of Health and Human Services issued the final rule and model guidelines that encouraged hospitals to establish infant care review committees (ICRCs). This was part of the child abuse and neglect prevention and treatment program included in the Child Abuse Amendments of 1984 (PL 98-457). This legislation attempted to protect the rights of infants with disabilities and limit governmental intervention into the practice of medicine and parental responsibilities. The purpose of the ICRCs was to educate hospital personnel and families of infants with disabilities and life-threatening conditions, to recommend guidelines concerning the withholding from infants of medically indicated treatment (including appropriate hydration, nutrition, and medication), and to offer counsel and review in cases involving infants with disabling and life-threatening conditions.

Later research (Carter, 1993) surveying military and civilian neonatologists found that, despite frequency of po-tential cases for review, ICRCs were seldom consulted. In fact, 67 percent of neonatologists surveyed indicated that the Baby Doe regulations has affected neither their thinking about ethical issues nor their practice.

The practice of decision making continues to be primarily led by the parents and neonatologist or by multidisciplinary conferences that typically do not include the nurses who deliver care (Martin, 1989). The use of multidisciplinary conferences predates the Baby Doe regulations.

The Child Abuse Amendments of 1984 (PL 98-45) state three circumstances under which treatment is not considered medically indicated: the infant is chronically and irreversibly comatose, the treatment would prolong dying but not be effective in ameliorating life-threatening conditions, and the treatment itself would be futile and inhumane. However, when even one of these three circumstances exists (and therefore failure to provide treatment would not be considered withholding medically indicated treatment), the infant must be provided with appropriate hydration, nutrition, and medication. Additionally, the law states that the withholding of treatment must not be based on subjective opinions about the future quality of life of such person but is to be based on the treating physicians' "reasonable medical judgment." These guidelines are advisory and not mandatory in any way because Congress did not make the rules binding on the states. Rather, it conditioned the receipt of federal funds upon incorporation of the rule into each state's law. Most states have accepted the condition, largely through rulemaking by state child abuse agencies. The rules continue to be vigorously debated (Newman, 1989).

REFERENCES

Carter, B. S. (1993). Neonatologists and bioethics after Baby Doe. *Perinatol, 13*(2), 144–150.

Duff, R. S., & Campbell, A. G. M. (1973). Moral and ethical dilemmas in the special-care nursery. *New England Journal of Medicine, 289,* 890–894.

Federal Register. (1985, April 15). Child abuse and neglect prevention and treatment program; final rule. Model guidelines for health care providers to establish infant care review committees. *50,* 14878–14901.

Martin, D. A. (1989). Nurse's involvement in ethical decision-making with severely ill newborns. *Issues in Pediatric Nursing, 12*(6), 463–473.

Newman, S. A. (1989). Baby Doe, Congress and the states: Challenging the federal treatment standard for impaired infants. *American Journal of Law and Medicine, 15*(1), 1–60.

President's Commission for the Study of Ethical Problems in Medicine and Biomedical and Behavioral Research. (1983). *A report on the ethical, medical and legal issues in treatment decisions.* Washington, DC: Author.

Rhoden, N. K., & Arras, J. D. (1985). Withholding treatment from Baby Doe: From discrimination to child abuse. *Milbank Memorial Fund Quarterly / Health and Society, 63,* 27–50.

Vitiello, M. (1984). The Baby Jane Doe litigation and Section 504: An exercise in raw executive power. *Connecticut Law Review, 17*, 95–164.

CAROLE REITER GOTHELF
Hunter College, City University of New York
First edition

ELAINE FLETCHER-JANZEN
University of Colorado at Colorado Springs
Second edition

KIMBERLY F. APPLEQUIST
University of Colorado at Colorado Springs
Third edition

BAER, DONALD M. (1931–2002)

Donald M. Baer received his BA degree in liberal arts from the University of Chicago in 1950 and his PhD in experimental psychology in 1957. At the time of his death he worked at the Department of Human Development of the University of Kansas at Lawrence.

He was most noted for his work with retarded children and reinforcement of appropriate behavioral imitativeness. He has explored environmental situations in which retarded individuals can be taught imitation and language through the use of behavioral reinforcement and shaping techniques. He found that after reinforcement for appropriate imitation, generalization to similar situations was enhanced. Much of Baer's research focused on the learning process as it relates to social and personal adaptation in young children.

He published over two hundred articles, chapters, and books, and made many more presentations. His published work addressed a variety of topics such as experimental methods and design, research in early childhood education, developmental disabilities and mental retardation, language development, self-regulation, and social development amongst other things. He also served as an expert witness, testifying on behalf of parents who sought the best possible education for their autistic children.

Between 1957 and 1965, with his colleague, Sidney W. Bijou, Dr. Baer established the "behavior analysis" approach to child development at the University of Washington (e.g., Bijou & Baer, 1961) where Don also contributed fundamentally to the experimental analysis of child behavior. In the late 1960s Dr. Baer, with Montrose Wolf and Todd Risley, founded the discipline of applied behavior analysis at the University of Kansas.

Don received many awards during his lifetime, among them the 1987 Don Hake Award from Division 25 (Behavior Analysis) of the American Psychological Association (APA)

for work that bridges basic and applied research, APA's 1996 Division 33 (Mental Retardation and Developmental Disabilities) Edgar A. Doll Award for his contributions to people with developmental disabilities, and the 1997 award for Distinguished Service to Behavior Analysis from the Society for the Advancement of Behavior Therapy. He also served as president of the Society for the Experimental Analysis of Behavior (1983–1984) and the Association for Behavior Analysis (1980–1981), as the editor of the *Journal of Applied Behavior Analysis* (1970–1971) and the associate editor of this and other journals (e.g., *American Journal of Mental Deficiency*), and as a reviewer of federal grants and for numerous additional scientific journals. Don was also widely invited to give colloquia, and was often an international distinguished visiting professor (e.g., in Australia, Brazil, Japan, New Zealand, Norway, Spain).

REFERENCES

Baer, D. M., & Pinkston, E. M. (Eds.). (1997). *Environment and behavior.* Boulder, CO: Westview.

Baer, D. M. et al. (1967). The development of imitation by reinforcing behavioral similarity to a model. *Journal of the Experimental Analysis of Behavior, 10*, 405–416.

Bijou, S. W., & Baer, D. M. (1961). *Child development, Vol. 1: A systematic and empirical theory.* New York: Appleton-Century-Crofts.

Bijou, S. W., & Baer, D. M. (1978). *Behavior analysis of child development.* Englewood Cliffs, NJ: Prentice Hall.

RICK GONZALES
Texas A&M University
First edition

DEBORAH B. GUILLEN
The University of Texas of the Permian Basin
Second edition

RACHEL M. TOPLIS
Falcon School District 49, Colorado Springs, Colorado
Third edition

BANDURA, ALBERT (1925–   )

Albert Bandura is a David Starr Jordan Professor of Social Science in Psychology at Stanford University. He received his bachelor's degree from the University of British Columbia in 1949 and his PhD degree from the University of Iowa in 1952. After completing his doctorate, Bandura joined the faculty at Stanford University where he has remained throughout his career. He has served as the school's chairman of the Department of Psychology, and was honored by Stanford as the recipient of an endowed chair.

Influenced by K. L. Spence and the Hullian research tra-

Albert Bandura

dition, Bandura is recognized as one of the founders of social learning theory. He proposes that human thought, affect, and behavior are strongly influenced by vicarious learning, and he is a proponent of social cognitive theory. This theory accords a central role to cognitive, vicarious, self-regulatory, and self-reflective processes in sociocognitive functioning. According to Bandura, psychology, through its research, bears an obligation to society for the betterment of humanity.

Bandura has authored nine books and countless articles on a wide range of issues in psychology. In addition, he serves on numerous editorial boards of journals and serials. His recent book, *Social Foundations of Thought and Action: A Social Cognitive Theory,* provides the conceptual framework for and analyzes the large body of knowledge bearing on social cognitive theory. *Self-Efficacy: The Exercise of Control,* his latest book, presents efficacy belief as the foundation of action, and in it Bandura asserts that unless people believe they can produce desired effects by their actions, they have little incentive to act. Other publications include *Social Learning and Personality Development, Social Learning Theory, Aggression: A Social Learning Analysis, Principles of Behavior Modification,* and *Psychological Modeling, Conflicting Theories.*

Bandura's contributions to psychology have been recognized in the honors and awards he has received. He was elected to the presidency of the American Psychological Association (APA) in 1974 and the Western Psychological Association in 1980. His numerous awards included the Distinguished Scientific Contributions Award of the American Psychological Association; the Distinguished Scientist Award, Division 12 of the APA; the William James Award for outstanding achievements in psychological science of the American Psychological Society; the Distinguished Contribution Award of the International Society for Research on Aggression; and a Guggenheim Fellowship.

Bandura has been elected to the American Academy of Arts and Sciences and the Institute of Medicine of the National Academy of Sciences, and is the recipient of 11 honorary degrees. He has also served as chairman of the

Board of Directors for the APA, trustee for the American Psychological Foundation, and chairman of the Western Psychological Association.

In 2001, he received the Lifetime Achievement Award from the Association for the Advancement of Behavior Therapy. In April of 2004, he received an honorary degree from the University of Athens. In October 2004, he received an award from the University of Catama. In May 2004 he received the Lifetime Achievement Award from the Western Psychological Association as well as the coveted James McKeen Cattell Award from the American Psychological Society. In August of 2004, Professor Bandura received the outstanding lifetime contribution to psychology award from the American Psychological Association.

Bandura's research interests include investigating the power of psychological modeling in shaping human thought, emotion, and action. He is currently investigating "the mechanisms of human agency: how people exercise influence over their own motivation and behavior," and how an individual's perceptions of their ability to influence events affects their lives. Bandura is also researching how stress reactions and depressions are caused.

REFERENCES

Bandura, A. (1969). *Principles of behavior modification.* New York: Holt, Rinehart, & Winston.

Bandura, A. (1971). *Psychological modeling, conflicting theories.* Chicago: Aldine-Atherton.

Bandura, A. (1973). *Aggression: A social learning analysis.* Englewood Cliffs, NJ: Prentice Hall.

Bandura, A. (1977). *Social learning theory.* Englewood Cliffs, NJ: Prentice Hall.

Bandura, A. (1986). *Social foundations of thought and action: A social cognitive theory.* Englewood Cliffs, NJ: Prentice Hall.

Bandura, A., & Walters, R. H. (1963). *Social learning and personality development.* New York: Holt, Rinehart, & Winston.

Bandura, A. (1997). *Self-efficacy: The exercise of control.* New York: Freeman & Company.

Pajares, F. (2004). *Albert Bandura: Biographical sketch.* Retrieved February 18, 2005, from http://www.emory.edu/EDUCATION/mfp/bandurabio.html

MARY LEON PERRY
Texas A&M University
First edition

TAMARA J. MARTIN
The University of Texas of the Permian Basin
Second edition

RACHEL M. TOPLIS
Falcon School District 49, Colorado Springs, Colorado
Third edition

SOCIAL LEARNING THEORY

BANNATYNE, ALEXANDER D. (1925–   )

Alexander Bannatyne received his BA in education and philosophy at Auckland University in New Zealand in 1949. He obtained his PhD in psychology at the institute of Psychiatry at the University of London in 1953. As a professor, he taught on learning disabilities to doctoral students at the University of Illinois, 1966 to 1969.

Bannatyne's major areas of work are in dealing with learning-disabled children and their reading, writing, and spelling abilities. Bannatyne believes that to understand abnormal, one must be knowledgeable about what is normal. Only through presentation of the abnormal in conjunction with a knowledge of the normal can we work out what has gone wrong; only then do we have standards against which to measure degrees and types of abnormalities (Bannatyne, 1971). Bannatyne did studies on the relationships among learned and unlearned handedness, spelling ability, mirror imaging, motor functioning, balance, memory for designs, and auditory vocal sequencing in terms of hemispheric activity and dominance. He found that three types of brain functions may exist: (1) an efficient balanced brain associated with unlearned handedness, balance ability, and competent spelling; (2) a less verbally efficient right hemisphere dominant brain that seems to give mirror imaging, spatial competence, and left-handedness; and (3) a brain that is visuospatially inept even though it is not given to the drawing of mirror images.

Dr. Bannatyne was an associate professor at the Children's Research Center at the University of Illinois. He has authored many books. Some of his major works include *Language, Reading, and Learning Disabilities, Bannatyne System: Reading, Writing and Spelling, Body Image,* and *How Children Can Learn to Live Rewarding Lives.*

REFERENCES

Bannatyne, A. D. (1971). *Language, reading, and learning disabilities.* Springfield, IL: Thomas.

Bannatyne, A. D. (1973a). *Body image: Communication program.* Lafayette, LA: Learning System.

Bannatyne, A. D. (1973b). *How children can learn to live rewarding lives.* Springfield, IL: Thomas.

Bannatyne, A. D. (1973c). *Reading: An auditory-vocal process.* San Rafael, CA: Academic Therapy.

Bannatyne, A. D. (1975). *Bannatyne system: Reading, writing, and spelling.* Lafayette, LA: Learning System.

ELIZABETH JONES
Texas A&M University

BARDON, JACK I. (1925–1993)

Jack I. Bardon earned his BA in psychology at Cleveland College of Western Reserve University in 1949, with a minor in education. He continued his professional education at the University of Pennsylvania, earning the MA in psychology in 1951 and a PhD in clinical psychology in 1956. From 1952 until 1958, Bardon was a school psychologist in the Princeton, New Jersey schools and served as coordinator of special education services from 1958 to 1960. In 1960 he became director of the Rutgers University doctoral program in school psychology with the academic rank of associate professor. He was promoted to professor in 1963 and became head of the department in 1968.

During his tenure at Rutgers, Bardon began to have an impact nationally on the delivery of school psychological services to handicapped children. His program in school psychology at Rutgers was one of the early pioneering programs in the field and, along with the University of Texas program, had a major influence on the development of doctoral schools of psychology. The Rutgers program reflected Bardon's own prominent, driving interest: to determine how the body of knowledge and the methods and techniques of psychology can be applied to the improvement of schooling generally, and to meeting the special needs of exceptional children in schools specifically. Bardon was instrumental in developing the primary role definitions of school psychologists (Bardon, 1982; Bardon & Bennett, 1974). Bardon was involved in work to help differentiate school psychology from other disciplines (Bardon, 1983). His work has benefited special education and regular education by improving the ability of school psychologists to provide services to children at all levels. In Bardon's most recent work (1992), he discussed the rationale for successes and failures in educational undertakings and how they relate to the field of school psychology.

Bardon left Rutgers in 1976 to accept a professorship at

Jack I. Bardon

the University of North Carolina at Greensboro, where he became an Excellence Foundation Professor in 1983. Bardon was editor of the *Journal of School Psychology* from 1968 to 1971, was president of the Division of School Psychology of the American Psychological Association in 1969, and served on the board of directors of the American Orthopsychiatric Association from 1981 to 1984.

Jack Bardon retired from the University of North Carolina at Greensboro in 1991, and died in November, 1993. He worked hard throughout his career to apply psychological theory, principles, and practice to the field of education, and is credited by his colleagues with having made a substantial impact in the definition of school psychology, professional organizational issues, and in the debate over levels of training in school psychology.

REFERENCES

Bardon, J. I. (1982). The psychology of school psychology. In C. R. Reynolds & T. B. Gutkin (Eds.), *The handbook of school psychology.* New York: Wiley.

Bardon, J. I. (1983). Psychology applied to education: A specialty in search of an identity. *American Psychologist, 38,* 185–196.

Bardon, J. I. (1992). Solving educational problems: Working across institutional, cultural and political differences. *School of Psychology Quarterly, 7,* 137–147.

Bardon, J. I., & Bennett, V. C. (1974). *School psychology.* Englewood Cliffs, NJ: Prentice Hall.

CECIL R. REYNOLDS
Texas A&M University
First edition

DEBORAH B. GUILLEN
The University of Texas of the Permian Basin
Second edition

BARRAGA, NATALIE C. (1915–   )

Natalie C. Barraga obtained her BA in home economics from North Texas State University in 1938; her MEd from the University of Texas, Austin, in 1957; and her EdD in special education for the visually impaired from George Peabody College for Teachers in 1963. Barraga's entry into the study of the visually impaired originated from a prior interest in child development and a concern for her daughter, who had a severe visual impairment. Years of teaching focused her objectives on those learners who had low vision. She experimented with ways to help students learn and read visually when they had a desire to do so.

Barraga's research documented that the use of vision (when impairment is present) is learned and not determined by acuity measurements, and that functional academic

Natalie C. Barraga

visual tasks could be taught with a sequential progressive learning program. She developed visual assessment tools and published a systematic instructional program, *Development of Efficiency in Visual Functioning.*

Professor emerita at the University of Texas at Austin, Barraga has published several books, monographs, assessment instruments, and articles. She has lectured extensively overseas, and maintains an interest in promoting interdisciplinary communication and an international exchange of information, especially with Third World countries.

Her publications include "Innovations in Teacher Education" (1981), reviewing trends associated with visually impaired children; "Perspectives on Working with Visually Impaired Persons Worldwide" (1989), examining differences in philosophies of education; and "Infusion of Research and Practice into Personnel Preparation" (1990), discussing challenges related to personal preparation for the field of vision disabilities.

REFERENCES

Barraga, N. C. (1981). Innovations in teacher testing. *Journal of Visual Impairment & Blindness, 75,* 96–100.

Barraga, N. C. (1989). Perspectives on working with visually impaired persons worldwide: Looking forward. *Journal of Visual Impairment & Blindness, 83,* 84–87.

Barraga, N. C. (1990). Infusion of research and practice into personnel preparation. *Peabody Journal of Education, 67,* 10–21.

ELAINE FLETCHER-JANZEN
University of Colorado at Colorado Springs
First edition

TAMARA J. MARTIN
The University of Texas of the Permian Basin
Second edition

BARRIER-FREE EDUCATION

The delivery of special education services to all children with disabilities in the least restrictive environment, as required by the Individuals with Disabilities Act and related state and federal laws and regulations, means that school buildings and facilities must be designed or altered to make those services accessible. Barrier-free design standards typically give technical specifications that cover building entrances and exits, parking, curbs, stairs, elevators, lavatories, drinking fountains, hazard warnings, and building elements and fixtures. In both new construction and modifications of existing facilities, buildings may be subject to a variety of definitions and design standards (Redden, 1979). In 1973, the American National Standards Institute (ANSI) criteria were cited in the regulations for Section 504 of the Rehabilitation Act of 1973 as the minimum access standard to assure compliance with nondiscrimination provisions. The design standards set forth in the Uniform Federal Accessibility Standards (UFAS; 1984) generally were consistent with federal standards in effect, major model building codes, and most state and local codes; they were based on ANSI A117.1-1980. The 1984 UFAS criteria were geared to adult dimensions and anthropometrics. Some states, however, developed design guidelines for special education facilities that considered the total learning environment for children with all types of disabilities (Abend, Bedner, Froehlinger, & Stenzler, 1979). A barrier-free environment requires the removal of all architectural barriers to accessibility (Redden, 1979). It should be noted that the regulations for Section 504 (which were applicable to recipients of funds from the U.S. Department of Education or Health and Human Services) did not require barrier-free environments. Section 504 required *program accessibility*—that is, a recipient's program or activity, when viewed in its entirety, was to be readily accessible to and usable by disabled persons. Access to each facility was not required. While the program accessibility standards could be achieved by a number of effective methods, including structural changes, priority was to be given to methods that provide the most integrated setting appropriate. Under Section 504, it was not permissible to isolate disabled students in a single accessible building.

The passage of the Americans with Disabilities Act of 1990 (ADA) substantially supported the intent of accessibility spelled out in Section 504. Title II of the ADA did not impose any major new requirements on school districts because school districts received federal funds and were required to provide accessibility under Section 504 as far back as 1973. However, as the ADA expanded nondiscriminatory protection to school students, it also took precedent over any lesser stringent rules in Section 504, the ADA reiterated that

A school district must ensure that students with disabilities are not excluded from participation in, or denied the benefits of, its services, programs, and activities. It must also ensure that they are not subjected to discrimination by the school system. (U.S. Department of Education, p. 45)

The ADA provided new guidelines and self-evaluation surveys based on the Americans with Disabilities Act Accessibility Guidelines for Buildings and Facilities (ADDAG; U.S. Department of Education, 1996).

The Office for Civil Rights (OCR) enforces Title II of the ADA and Section 504 of the Rehabilitation Act of 1973. The OCR investigates complaints filed by individuals or their representatives, who believe that they have been discriminated against because of a disability. The OCR can be reached at U.S. Department of Education, Office for Civil Rights, 330 550 12th Street, S.W., Washington, D.C. 20202-1100. Their toll-free telephone number is (800) 421-3481 and TDD number is (877) 521-2172. The OCR can also be reached via e-mail at OCR@ed.gov, or through the Department of Education's web site (http://www.ed.gov).

In addition, one can find numerous Internet web sites designed to provide information about the accommodation of specific disabilities, which can help teachers, parents, and students overcome educational obstacles.

REFERENCES

Abend, A. C., Bedner, M. J., Froehlinger, V. J., & Stenzler, Y. (1979). *Facilities for special educational services: A guide for planning new and renovated schools.* Reston, VA: Council for Exceptional Children.

Redden, M. R. (Ed.). (1979). *Assuring access for the handicapped.* San Francisco: Jossey-Bass.

Uniform Federal Accessibility Standards (UFAS). (1984, August 7). 49 F.R. 31528-31621.

U.S. Department of Education, Office for Civil Rights. (1996). *Compliance with the Americans with Disabilities Act: A self-evaluation guide for public elementary and secondary schools.* Washington, DC: U.S. Government Printing Office.

SHIRLEY A. JONES
Virginia Polytechnic Institute and State University
First edition

ELAINE FLETCHER-JANZEN
University of Colorado at Colorado Springs
Second edition

KIMBERLY F. APPLEQUIST
University of Colorado at Colorado Springs
Third edition

ACCESSIBILITY OF BUILDINGS
ACCESSIBILITY OF PROGRAMS
AMERICANS WITH DISABILITIES ACT
REHABILITATION ACT OF 1973, SECTION 504

BARRIERS, ARCHITECTURAL

See ARCHITECTURAL BARRIERS.

BARSCH, RAY H. (1917–)

Ray H. Barsch earned his BA in special education in 1950 and MEd in school psychology in 1952 from the University of Wisconsin, Milwaukee. He went on to receive his PhD in educational psychology from Northwestern University in 1959 under the direction of Claude Mathis, Paul Witty, and Helmer Myklebust.

Barsch is principally known for his development of a curriculum called movigenics, a theory of movement developed from "the study of origin and development of patterns of movement in man and the relationship of those movements to his learning efficiency." He regards movigenics as "orientation—a cognitive map to guide practitioners toward a goal of practical synthesis" (Barsch, 1976).

As an ardent supporter of interdisciplinary approaches to assessment and teaching in special education, Barsch defines learning disabilities as a concept that focuses on learning rather than "a frantic but seldom fruitful effort to delineate a uniform and specific set of characteristics" (Barsch, 1976).

Barsch became a professor in the department of special education at California State University, Northridge in 1970, and in the division for continuing education at the University of Santa Clara. Among other positions and consultantships, Barsch directed teacher preparation programs in the department of counseling and behavioral studies at the University of Wisconsin (1963–1966) and the Easter Seal Development Center in Milwaukee, Wisconsin (1950–1964).

From the early 1970s to the early 1980s, Barsch was a professor in the School of Education at the California State University, Northridge. He also directed the Ray Barsch Center for Learning, where he specialized in one-on-one therapy for children with specific learning problems and counseled parents. In addition, he has supervised the development of the Special Education Teacher Program in Ventura, California, as well as the training of graduate students in various evaluation and therapy techniques.

His (1995) book, *Fine Tuning: An Auditory-Visual Training Program,* describes exercises for developing students' listening skills, and a 1992 reprint in the *Journal of Learning Disabilities* of Barsch's article, "Perspectives on Learning Disabilities," has generated substantial debate, highlighting the absence of progress in defining, classifying, and providing appropriate interventions for learning disabilities. This piece, originally published in 1968, examines learning dis-

abilities from the perspective of history, viewing them as a concept rather than a category, promoting interdisciplinary convergence, evaluating various delivery systems, and noting a new recognition of human divergence.

Of his many awards, in 1974 Barsch received the International Milestone Award of the International Federation of Learning Disabilities at its world congress in the Netherlands.

REFERENCES

Barsch, R. H. (1976). *Achieving perceptual motor efficiency: A space oriented approach to learning* (Vol. 1). Seattle, WA: Special Child.

Barsch, R. H. (1992). Perspectives on learning disabilities: The vectors of a new convergence. *Journal of Learning Disabilities, 25,* 6–16.

Barsch, R. H. (1995). *Fine tuning: An auditory-visual training program.* Novato, California: Academic Therapy.

ELAINE FLETCHER-JANZEN
University of Colorado at Colorado Springs
First edition

TAMARA J. MARTIN
The University of Texas of the Permian Basin
Second edition

BASC

See BEHAVIOR ASSESSMENT SYSTEM FOR CHILDREN–2.

BASAL READERS

Basal reader programs are comprehensive, meaningfully sequenced collections of stories, frequently arranged in groups according to a central theme or topic. Smith and Johnson (1980) described these programs as being based on the belief that a controlled vocabulary of high-frequency words, coupled with the presentation of easily decodable pattern words, facilitates learning to read and the improvement of reading skills.

Basal reader programs are intended to be used to instruct children from the stage of nonreading, through the acquisition of developing skills, to the level of mature, flexible reading. Typically, these programs include various correlated and supplementary materials including teachers' manuals, workbooks, skills sheets, activity boxes, criterion-referenced monitoring systems, and even computer software management programs. This self-contained aspect of basal reader programs is intended to provide all that is necessary for a core reading program. Teachers are carefully guided through instructional directed reading activities as outlined in the accompanying manuals. The structure of these lesson plans, explained by both Stauffer (1969) and Harris (1970), follows the sequence of prereading preparation, guided silent reading, oral rereading and comprehension assessment, skill development activities, and enrichment. In addition, teachers are usually provided with suggestions for choosing related books and other materials to use in conjunction with the basal reader. A survey of 500 educators by Bauman and Heubach in 1996 found that teachers believed that these materials have an empowering effect by providing additional instructional ideas to draw from, adapt, or extend (Bauman & Heubach, 1996).

Of course, the reading books themselves constitute the essential materials in any basal program. Usually there is a set of readiness materials for use with children at the beginning stages of reading instruction. These are followed by readers considered to be at the preprimer and primer levels of difficulty. The readers contain a limited number of frequently repeated words that assist in the development of a basic sight vocabulary. These basic reading books are followed by progressively more difficult readers extending through all the elementary grades and frequently into the middle and junior high grades as well. Many of these higher level basal readers consist of comprehensive literary anthologies and, according to Ringler and Weber (1984), may include a variety of narrative types such as realistic fiction, fantasy, science fiction, folklore, poetry, and plays.

In recent years basal readers have been analyzed in terms of cultural competence. Foley and Boulware (1996) found that gender equity reflected in basal readers has not essentially changed since the 1960s. In addition, analyses of basal readers regarding race and ethnicity indicate that these aspects of culture are omitted from the majority of basal texts. The omission of race and/or ethnicity from basal selections and teacher manuals may not meet the needs of many children (McDermott, 1997). Other criticisms of basal readers suggest that publisher censorship still exists and essential components of literary works are being eliminated by widespread anthologization (Reutzel & Larsen, 1995). However, others (Risner & Nicholson, 1996) applaud the addition of questions to the readers that support higher levels of comprehension than previously found. Therefore, research still suggests that basal readers support the development of additional teacher materials and engaging activities that, in turn, elevate student reading comprehension. Basal readers are currently being challenged by other approaches such as the workshop approach, which appears to be more flexible (Turner, 2004).

REFERENCES

Bauman, J. F., & Heubach, K. M. (1996). Do basal readers deskill teachers? A national survey of educator's use and opinions of basals. *Elementary School Journal, 96,* 511–526.

Foley, C. L., & Boulware, B. J. (1996). Gender equity in 1990 middle school basal readers. *Reading Improvement, 33,* 220–223.

Harris, A. J. (1970). *How to increase reading ability* (5th ed.). New York: McKay.

McDermott, P. (1997). The illusion of racial diversity in contemporary basal readers: An analysis of teacher manuals. Evaluative/feasibility report: speech/conference paper. Abstract from: ERIC Item No. ED407473.

Reutzel, D. R., & Larsen, N. S. (1995). Look what they've done to real children's books in the new basal readers. *Language Arts, 72,* 495–507.

Ringler, L. H., & Weber, C. K. (1984). *A language-thinking approach to reading.* New York: Harcourt Brace Jovanovich.

Risner, G. P., & Nicholson, J. I. (1996). *The new basal readers: What levels of comprehension do they promote? Evaluative / feasibility report.* (ERIC Item No. ED403546)

Smith, R. J., & Johnson, D. D. (1980). *Teaching children to read* (2nd ed.). Reading, MA: Addison-Wesley.

Stauffer, R. G. (1969). *Directing reading maturity as a cognitive process.* New York: Harper & Row.

Turner, J. S. (2004). When teachers are readers. *National Association of Elementary School Principals Newsletter, 83,* 5.

JOHN M. EELLS
Souderton Area School District,
Souderton, Pennsylvania
First edition

ELAINE FLETCHER-JANZEN
University of Colorado at
Colorado Springs
Second edition

HIGH INTEREST–LOW VOCABULARY READING DISORDERS READING REMEDIATION

BASELINE DATA

A baseline measurement occurs prior to the beginning of an intervention. It involves precise counting of the target behavior (i.e., dependent variable) during whatever current conditions exist. A common misconception is that baseline data can only be gathered in the absence of any intervention. This is not true. Baselines are measures of behavior under current conditions. If these conditions are not ones in which there is no intervention, then this information should be stated in the program outline. If there is an informal intervention that currently is ongoing (e.g., telling a child to "stop"), then this response should continue. If one were to attempt to stop intervening with a behavior and then take baseline data, that person would be defeating the purpose of the baseline procedure because removing the intervention procedure acts as an intervention itself. Data gathered during this time would be intervention data and different from those that were representative of the behavior during the condition in which the behavior became important enough to the practitioner to attempt intervention aided by data collection.

Baselines are meant to be representative measures of the target behavior. As such they should also be reliable and valid. Reliability should be scored by having two persons simultaneously record the data and by comparing those data records using different calculation procedures (e.g., Kappa), dependent on which recording technique was used (e.g., momentary time sampling) and the properties of the data. Validity, in its simplest form, requires that a measure be that which was purported. If after writing the behavioral definition of the target behavior the definition was compared to the behavior to determine whether the behavior written was that which the student exhibited, the primary form of validation would be completed. If the definition is given to another person and he or she is asked whether the written definition was observable in the student's behavior, and if that person found it to be so, the second form of validation would be completed.

Baseline data should be stable prior to the initiation of intervention. Stability is said to have occurred when there is an absence of directionality or trend in the data and when there is restricted variation in the pattern of the data. Trend is said to occur when there are three or more data points patterned in a specific direction. This is also referred to as celeration and is illustrated by data that accelerated or decelerated. Baseline data that are either accelerating or decelerating are generally not useful as preintervention data. The trend in the data suggests that there is already something that is influencing the target behavior. However, when the trend is countertherapeutic (i.e., moving in the undesired direction), the need for protracted baseline data collection is negated. Therefore, if the trend of the baseline data is therapeutic, continuation of the baseline is indicated until such time as the behavior becomes acceptable or until it levels off and becomes stable. If the data are countertherapeutic, this is not necessary and intervention can be begun in 5 to 10 sessions or days.

Variability in the data during baseline in the absence of a significant trend must be measured by examining its degree to determine its effect on the baseline. Baseline data should be stable so that the practitioner can say with reasonable certainty that the target behavior occurred in a specific condition prior to intervention. Stability is measured as the degree of variability about the mean. In research and teaching with humans we would look for ±50 percent variability

about the baseline mean (Alberto & Troutman, 1982). For example, if we gathered 10 days of baseline data and then summed each day's score and divided by 10 we would have the mean of the baseline. If this mean were 40 percent, then all data should fall between 60 and 20 percent during the baseline as that is the range established by the ±50 percent rule. A single (or perhaps 2) data point(s) falling outside this range could be judged to be an oddity; it should not hamper the identification of these data as stable. However, more than this number would indicate a lack of stability and a longer baseline would be required. Baseline stability or countertherapeutic trend is a basic requirement prior to the initiation of intervention programming.

REFERENCE

Alberto, P. A., & Troutman, A. C. (1982). *Applied behavior analysis for teachers.* Columbus, OH: Merrill.

LYLE E. BARTON
Kent State University

APPLIED BEHAVIOR ANALYSIS
BEHAVIOR MODIFICATION

BASE RATE

A base rate is a baseline measurement of a target behavior's rate of responding. This measurement is useful when the student's behavior of interest is one for which frequency recording is the appropriate recording strategy and for which rate of responding is the appropriate datum. The latter case is true when the response frequency dependent on duration of observation is important. For example, should the target behavior be either units of "X" assembled in a workshop or incidences of aggressive behavior, frequency would be an appropriate recording strategy. If, in addition, the issue of importance is this number within a specified time frame, then rate of response becomes the appropriate datum. If this period of observation tends to vary, then rate of response is the only appropriate datum. Therefore, the special education practitioner would record the frequency of student response and then divide the frequency by the number of minutes (or hours) of observation. The resultant figure (e.g., 1.56, 0.75, 0.05) would be indicative of the relative frequency of responding per unit of measurement (e.g., minutes, hours) and would be reported as rate per minute (rpm) or rate per hour (rph).

To determine the base rate, these data would be gathered over a period of days or sessions and would be examined to meet the criterion for stability for any baseline data; that is, the data must be stable (have limited variability) or countertherapeutic. Stability is said to occur when the data vary no more than ± 50 percent of the baseline mean (Alberto & Troutman, 1982). A countertherapeutic trend is said to occur when the data are not stable but moving in the opposite direction. Base-rate data are usually reported as a mean figure (e.g., "the mean base rate was . . ."), however, these data may be reported as including the range and the usual data display via a graph.

REFERENCE

Alberto, P. A., & Troutman, A. C. (1982). *Applied behavior analysis for teachers*. Columbus, OH: Merrill.

LYLE E. BARTON
Kent State University

APPLIED BEHAVIOR ANALYSIS
BEHAVIOR MODIFICATION

BASIC SKILLS TRAINING

Historically, the term "basic skills" refers to the traditional disciplines of reading, writing, and arithmetic that are stressed in the early years of formal education. These areas of study are those that are seen as necessary for an individual to become a contributing member of society. Without at least a rudimentary proficiency in these basic areas, individuals experience difficulty in developing independence and self-esteem.

The exceptional child or adult, however, may require a completely different type of basic skill training than the traditional disciplines deemed necessary for normal functioning within society. Depending on the severity of the handicapping condition, basic skills for special education may vary little or greatly from those of regular students and adults. Basic skills training for exceptional children could best be termed those activities and subject areas that provide for each child's individual learning abilities (allowing for his or her weaknesses) in such a way that deviation from the norm is as limited as possible. This training allows children to accomplish what Blake (1981) refers to as "cultural tasks," in which needs are met through means that are acceptable to society.

Specifically, basic skills for the exceptional child might include those skills noted by Berdine and Blackhurst (1981): training in attention skills, increased memory capacity, the ability to transfer and generalize recently learned skills, and language. In addition, study skills, self-management skills and computer competence are needed as basic skills. Therefore, for the special education student, the basic skills required for academic success are more process-orientated than for regular education students.

In recent years, inclusive programming has sought to as-

sist the special education student in the acquisition of basic skills. Instead of pulling special education students out of the content classes, they have remained with specialized assistance (McCollum & Tindal, 1996). Unfortunately, little data exists to support the effectiveness of this programming for basic content skills at this time.

There is some evidence that computer assisted learning takes place by online computer services. These services assist high school special education students enter career-focused activities that require basic processing skills that reflect organization, problem-solving, and attention. Also, basic skills training can be melded with goals for appropriate behavior (Russell, 2005).

REFERENCES

Berdine, W. H., & Blackhurst, A. E. (1981). *An introduction to special education*. Boston: Little, Brown.

Blake, K. A. (1981). *Educating exceptional pupils: An introduction to contemporary practices*. Reading, MA: Addison-Wesley.

McCollum, S., & Tindal, G. (1996). Supporting students in content areas classes using an outcome-based system of collaboration. *Special Services in the Schools, 12,* 1–17.

353 Project (1996). *Advancing basic skills through the use of online services 1995–1996 special 353 project*. (ERIC Item No. ED402488)

Russell, S. E. (2005). Information skills and the special needs student. *Academic Exchange Quarterly, 33,* 4–5.

JAMES H. MILLER
University of New Orleans
First edition

ELAINE FLETCHER-JANZEN
*University of Colorado at
Colorado Springs*
Second edition

FUNCTIONAL DOMAINS
FUNCTIONAL INSTRUCTION

BATEMAN, BARBARA (1933–   )

Barbara Bateman received her BA (1954) in psychology from the University of Washington, her MA (1958) from San Francisco State College, and her PhD in special education (1962) from the University of Illinois. In the early years of her professional career, she taught mentally retarded and emotionally disturbed blind children at Washington State Hospital and a variety of exceptional children in the Oregon public schools. Bateman continued in the field teaching at the university level and became professor of education at the University of Oregon in 1969.

Barbara Bateman

She retired from the University of Oregon in 1994 and is currently Professor Emeritus. Bateman maintains a private practice as a legal consultant in special education. Her interests currently include legally correct and educationally useful implementation of IDEA and other special education law. Dr. Bateman has received many honors including *Who's Who of American Women, 6th Edition, Who's Who in the West, 12th Edition,* and *Community Leaders of America.* She was one of 53 individuals named as "Influential Person in the Development of the Field of Special Education" in *Remedial and Special Education 21* (Nov./Dec. 2000).

She has always been a strong advocate of direct instruction, and has urged the field of education to accept the direct instructional philosophy, methods, and materials in publications such as *Essentials of Teaching* (1971) and *Teaching Reading to Learning Disabled and Other Hard-to-Teach Children* (1979). In the 1970s, Bateman's interests broadened to the legal aspects of special education; she received her JD from the University of Oregon Law School in 1976, and has published on law and special education including her influential publication, *Better IEPs.*

REFERENCES

Bateman, B. (1971). *Essentials of teaching.* Sioux Falls, SD: Adapt Press.

Bateman, B. (1979). Teaching reading to learning disabled and other hard-to-teach children. In L. Resnick & P. Weaver (Eds.), *Theory and practice of early reading.* Hillsdale, NJ: Erlbaum.

Bateman, B. D. (1996). *Better IEPs.* Longmont, CO: Sopris West.

Bateman, B. D., & Linden, M. A. (in press). *Better IEPs: How to develop legally correct and educationally useful programs* (4th ed.). Verona, WI: Attainment.

Bateman, B. D., & Herr, C. M. (2003). *Writing measurable IEP goals and objectives.* Verona, WI: Attainment.

Herr, C. M., & Bateman, B. D. (2005). *Better IEP meetings.* Verona, WI: Attainment.

STAFF
First edition

RACHEL M.TOPLIS
Falcon School District 49,
Colorado Springs, Colorado
Third edition

BATTERED CHILD SYNDROME

In 1962, pediatrician C. Henry Kempe published an article entitled "The Battered Child Syndrome." This marked the first official recognition by the medical establishment of the problem of child abuse. Kempe's article focused on abuse as a deliberate, violent attack on a child by a malicious adult and criticized the medical profession for failing to diagnose and report such cases. Child abuse is a broad term currently used to describe incidents of violent attack, neglect, or sexual abuse that may result in psychological and behavioral disturbances as well as physical or even life-threatening injury. Ellerstein (1981) states that between 1 and 3 percent of children in the United States are abused. Figures vary depending on laws governing reporting and definitions of child abuse. Indeed, the incidence of severe violence against children declined in the mid- to late 1980s. Possible reasons cited for the lower rate were an increased reluctance to report, differences in the methods of study, years of prevention and treatment efforts, and effects of changes in American society and family patterns that produce lower rates of violence towards children. However, regardless of decline, about 4,000 children die each year as a result of abuse.

Researchers have investigated several factors associated with child abuse. Various models, each emphasizing the importance of particular factors, have been formulated to explain the phenomenon. The psychopathological model focuses on the personality characteristics of the perpetrator. Attributes such as personal history of abuse, low self-esteem, and inability to cope with frustration are seen as important contributing factors (Gil, 1975). In the sociological model, environmental factors such as poverty, acceptance of corporal punishment, and overcrowding in the home receive emphasis (Gil). The cognitive-behavioral model takes into account style of responding to stress and the belief systems of abusive parents (Green, 1984). A broader model encompassing the preceding elements and accounting for the significance of interactions between parents and children is referred to as the ecological model (Roscoe et al., 1985).

Investigators have found that some children are more likely than others to become victims of child abuse. Children at increased risk for abuse often come from larger than average families, have low birth weights or were premature as infants, and fail to form attachment bonds with a caregiver. A comparison of incidence rates suggests that age, family income, and ethnicity were risk factors for both sexual and physical abuse. Gender was a risk factor for sexual abuse but not physical abuse (Cappelleri, Echenrode, & Powers, 1993). Males are more likely to be abused, as are disabled, retarded, and otherwise different or difficult children (Newberger, 1982).

Kempe's early article on the battered child syndrome achieved considerable public notoriety and drew the attention of legislators, resulting in the passage of mandatory reporting of child abuse in all 50 states. Physicians and other health professionals are legally required to report suspected child abuse. Additionally, most states require other professionals having contact with children to report suspected cases of abuse. These professionals include teachers, social workers, and child-care workers.

In 1997, child protection professionals were surveyed regarding their opinions about the best papers and chapters on child abuse available. Kempe's 1962 article was cited as one of the best resources on child abuse and a seminal work (Oates & Donnelly, 1997).

REFERENCES

Cappelleri, J. C., Echenrode, J., & Powers, J. L. (1993). The epidemiology of child abuse: Findings from the second national incidence and prevalence study of child abuse and neglect. *American Journal of Public Health, 83,* 1622–1624.

Ellerstein, N. S. (Ed.). (1981). *Child abuse and neglect: A medical reference.* New York: Wiley.

Gil, D. (1975). Unraveling child abuse. *American Journal of Orthopsychiatry, 45,* 345–356.

Green, A. (1984). Child maltreatment: Recent studies and future directions. *Journal of the American Academy of Child Psychiatry, 23,* 675–678.

Kempe, C. H. (1962). The battered child syndrome. *Journal of the American Medical Association, 181,* 17–24.

Newberger, E. H. (Ed.). (1982). *Child abuse.* Boston: Little, Brown.

Oates, R. K., & Donnelly, A. C. (1997). Influential papers in child abuse. *Child Abuse and Neglect, 21,* 319–326.

Roscoe, B., Callahan, J., & Peterson, K. (1985). Who is responsible? Adolescents' acceptance of theoretical child abuse models. *Adolescence, 20,* 188–197.

BERNICE ARRICALE
*Hunter College, City University
of New York*
First edition

ELAINE FLETCHER-JANZEN
*University of Colorado at
Colorado Springs*
Second and Third editions

CHILD ABUSE
CHILD CARE AGENCIES
CHILD CARETAKER

BAUMEISTER, ALFRED A. (1934–   )

Born in Fairbanks, Alaska, Alfred A. Baumeister received his BA from the University of Alaska (1957) and his MA (1959) and PhD (1961) in psychology from George Peabody College. He is presently a professor at Vanderbilt University and George Peabody College, and directed the John F. Kennedy Center for Research on Education and Human Development at Vanderbilt University from 1983–1990.

Baumeister has presented over 150 papers and published over 200 original investigations, literature reviews, and theoretical reports, many of which are concerned with learning and memory processes among mentally retarded children. He found that there are quantitative and structural differences in the short-term information processing capabilities of retarded and nonretarded subjects (Baumeister, Runcie, & Gardepe, 1984). Another major effort has been directed at understanding the treatment of aberrant behavior such as stereotyped movements and self-injurious actions.

Baumeister has been active in the improvement of psychological services to the mentally retarded. He has written about the role of the psychologist in public institutions (Baumeister & Hillsinger, 1984) and has served as a consultant to several state and federal agencies. He is a member of the Psychology Review Committee for the Joint Committee of the Accreditation of Hospitals.

Baumeister has been president of both the American Academy on Mental Retardation and the Division of Mental

Alfred A. Baumeister

Retardation of the American Psychological Association. For several years, he served as a witness before the U.S. House and Senate appropriations subcommittees. He has received awards for research contributions from the American Association on Mental Deficiency (1979) and the American Academy on Mental Retardation (1986). He continues to publish on a variety of special education topics (Baumeister & Bacharach, 1996; Baumeister, Bacharach, & Baumeister, 1997).

REFERENCES

Baumeister, A. A., & Bacharach, V. R. (1996). A critical analysis of the infant health and development program. *Intelligence, 23*(2), 79–104.

Baumeister, A. A., Bacharach, V. R., Baumeister, Alan A. (1997). "Big" versus "little" science: Comparative analysis of program projects and individual research grants. *American Journal on Mental Retardation, 102*(3), 211–227.

Baumeister, A. A., & Hillsinger, L. B. (1984). The role of psychologists in public institutions for the mentally retarded revisited. *Professional Psychology, 15,* 134–141.

Baumeister, A. A., Runcie, D., & Gardepe, J. (1984). Processing of information in iconic memory: Differences between normal and retarded subjects. *Journal of Abnormal Psychology, 93,* 433–447.

E. VALERIE HEWITT
Texas A&M University

BAYLEY SCALE FOR INFANT DEVELOPMENT–SECOND EDITION

The Bayley Scale for Infant Development–Second Edition (BSID-II; Bayley, 1993) is an individually administered measure of developmental functioning of infants and children between 1 and 42 months of age that includes three scales: Mental, Motor, and Behavior Rating. It was designed to (1) produce observable behavioral responses in infants; (2) assess children's level of cognitive, language, personal-social, and gross-motor development; (3) identify areas of impairment or delay; (4) develop curricula for interventions; and (5) assess interventions. The BSID-II presents infants with situations and tasks designed to produce an observable set of behavioral responses. The observed responses are scored on complementary development scales—Mental Scale, Motor Scale, and Behavior Rating Scale.

The test takes 15 to 35 minutes to administer to children less than 15 months of age and up to 60 minutes for children older than 15 months of age. The Mental Scale assesses cognitive, language, and personal-social developments, and the Motor Scale assesses fine- and gross-motor development. The Behavior Rating Scale is completed by the assessor throughout the testing situation and allows for greater interpretation of the Mental and Motor Scales. Typical areas of assessment within the Behavior Rating Scale are attention, arousal, orientation, engagement, emotional regulation, and motor quality. The manual provides scoring instructions for each item as well as information for interpretation of the results using case studies as examples. The Bayley Infant Neurodevelopmental Screener, which contains 11 to 13 items selected from the BSID-II, allows programs with high caseloads to screen infants 3 to 24 months for neurological impairment or developmental delay in 10 to 20 minutes.

The BSID-II was standardized on a stratified random sample of 1,700 children (850 boys and 850 girls). The sample was stratified in terms of age, sex, region, race or ethnicity, and parent education. Seventeen age groups were created, ranging in age from 1 month to 42 months, each with 100 children. Internal consistency has been shown to be .88 for the Mental Scale, .84 for the Motor Scale, and .88 for the Behavior Rating Scale using Cronbach's alpha. Test-retest reliability has shown coefficients for children aged 1 to 12 months of .83 for the Mental Scale and .77 for the Motor Scale. On the Behavior Rating Scale, for children aged 1 month, the test-retest reliability was .55, and at 12 months of age it was .90. For children aged 24 and 42 months, test-retest reliability was seen to be .91 for the Mental Scale, .79 for the Motor Scale, and .60 for the Behavior Rating Scale. The overall test-retest reliability coefficients were .78 for the Motor Scale and .87 for the Mental Scale. Original interrater reliability coefficients for the BSID-II were .96 for the Mental Scale, .75 for the Motor Scale, and between .47 and 1.00 for the Behavior Rating Scale. Chandlee, Heathfield, Salganik, Damokosh, and Radcliffe (2002) found similar interscorer reliability when 60 items from the BSID-II Mental Scale were administered to 29 children between the ages of 12 and 39 months. Agreement between scorers was generally 90 percent or above, but 23 percent of the items showed reliability below 90 percent.

Concurrent validity studies have been performed on the BSID-II and the BSID. For the Mental Development Index, the correlation was .62, and for the Psychomotor Development Index, the correlation was .63. Goldstein, Fogle, Wieber, and O'Shea (1995) compared administrations of the BSID and BSID-II to high-risk preterm infants and found that the two tests correlated very highly. Mean scores from the BSID-II were lower than those from the BSID, as was expected.

The Mental Development Index has been correlated with the McCarthy Scales of Children Abilities (MSCA) and the Wechsler Preschool and Primary Scale of Intelligence–Revised (WPPSI-R) Full Scale IQ, Verbal IQ, and Performance IQ. Results showed correlations of .79, .73, .73, and .63, respectively. The Psychomotor Development Index has also been correlated with the same instruments, and correlations were .45, .41, .39, and .37, respectively. Tests have shown the BSID-II as a whole to be in 80 percent agreement with the Denver Developmental Screening Test–II when classifying children.

REFERENCES

Bayley, N. (1993). *Bayley Scales of Infant Development* (2nd ed.). San Antonio, TX: Psychological Corporation.

Black, M. M., & Matula, K. (1999). *Essentials of Bayley Scales of Infant Development–II assessment.* New York: Wiley.

Chandlee, J., Heathfield, L. T., Salganik, M., Damokosh, A., & Radcliffe, J. (2002). Are we consistent in administering and scoring the Bayley Scales of Infant Development–II? *Journal of Psychoeducational Assessment, 20,* 183–200.

Glenn, S. M., Cunningham, C. C., & Dayus, B. (2001). Comparison of the 1969 and 1993 standardizations of the Bayley Mental Scales of Infant Development for infants with Down's syndrome. *Journal of Intellectual Disability Research, 45,* 56–62.

Goldstein, D. J., Fogle, E. E., Wieber, J. L., & O'Shea, T. M. (1995). Comparison of the Bayley Scales of Infant Development–Second edition and the Bayley Scales of Infant Development with premature infants. *Journal of Psychoeducational Assessment, 13,* 391–396.

Impara, J. C., & Plake, B. S. (Eds.). (1998). *The thirteenth mental measurements yearbook* (pp. 612–614). Lincoln, NE: Buros Institute of Mental Measurements.

Niccols, A., & Latchman, A. (2002). Stability of the Bayley Mental Scale of Infant Development with high risk infants. *British Journal of Developmental Disabilities, 48,* 3–13.

RON DUMONT
Fairleigh Dickinson University

JOHN O. WILLIS
Rivier College

EARLY EXPERIENCE AND CRITICAL PERIODS
EARLY IDENTIFICATION OF CHILDREN WITH DISABILITIES

BECHTEREV (BEKHTIAREV) VLADIMIR M. (1857–1927)

Vladimir M. Bechterev was born in Viatka province, Russia. He was a noted physiologist and neuropathologist and the founder of the School of Reflexology. He was also the founder of the first Russian experimental psychological laboratory at the University of Kazan. Bechterev obtained his PhD at the Military Medical Academy in St. Petersburg (Petrograd, now Leningrad) in 1881. He continued postgraduate studies at the universities of Leipzig, Berlin, and Paris. At Leipzig he became familiar with the work of Wilhelm Wundt, considered to be the founder of experimental psychology. In 1885 Bechterev became professor at the University of Kazan and in 1893, professor at the Military Medical Academy.

The same year he began to publish a journal, *Neurological Review.* Bechterev was also interested in the education of exceptional children. His work in this area is referred to as pedagogical reflexology. In 1911 he addressed the International Congress of Pedology in Brussels, Belgium. His pioneering work contributed immensely toward the future development of Soviet defectology.

Bechterev made an important contribution to the knowledge of anatomy and physiology of the nervous system. He conducted research on localization function of the brain and became famous for his work on nerve currents. He also identified the layer of fibers in the cerebral cortex known as Bechterev's fibers.

Bechterev was a prolific writer who produced over 135 publications and papers, including *General Principles of Reflexology* (1918) and *Objective Psychology* (1913).

REFERENCES

Bechterev, V. M. (1913). *Objective psychologie oder psychoreflexologia.* Leipzig/Berlin: Verlag Teubner.

Bechterev, V. M. (1918). *Obshtchie osnovi reflexologii* (General principles of reflexology). St. Petersburg.

Debus, A. G. (Ed.). (1968). *World who's who in science.* Chicago: Marquis.

Prokhorov, A. M. (Ed.). (1970). *Bolshaya Sovetskay Entsyklopedia* (Major Soviet encyclopedia) (3rd ed.). Moscow: Soviet Encyclopedia Publishing.

IVAN Z. HOLOWINSKY
Rutgers University

BECKER, WESLEY C. (1928–   )

A native of Rochester, New York, Wesley C. Becker received his BA (1951), MA (1953), and PhD (1955) from Stanford University in psychology, statistics, and learning theory, respectively. Originally a child clinical psychologist, Becker's initial research interest was in how behavior problems and personality characteristics develop as a function of parental child-rearing practices. This developed into an interest in applications of behavior analysis to changing parent and child behaviors. His book, *Parents Are Teachers,* has been published in German, Portuguese, and Spanish. Becker's interest shifted to applications of behavior analysis to teachers and problem students (Becker, 1986; Becker, Engelmann & Thomas, 1975). In the late 1960s, he became interested in effective instructional practices, especially as they applied to hard-to-teach children. This is still his major interest, but he has become more active in disseminating research findings on effective instructional practices, such as the direct instruction (DI) follow-through model and its long-term effects on students (Becker, 1984; Gersten, Keating, & Becker, 1991).

Becker has been a member of Phi Beta Kappa and a consultant to the Australian Association for Direct Instruction and has been included in *Who's Who in America*.

REFERENCES

Becker, W. C. (1971). *Parents are teachers.* Champaign, IL: Research.

Becker, W. C. (1984, March 18–23). *Direct instruction—A twenty year review.* Paper presented at the 16th Annual Banff International Conference on Behavioral Science Honoring B. F. Skinner's 80th birthday, Banff, Canada.

Becker, W. C. (1986). *Applied psychology for teachers: A behavioral cognitive approach.* Chicago: Science Research Associates.

Becker, W. C., Engelmann, S., & Thomas, D. R. (1975). *Teaching 1: Classroom management.* Palo Alto, CA: Science Research Associates.

Gersten, R., Keating, T., & Becker, W. C. (1991). The continued impact of the direct instructional model: Longitudinal studies of follow through students. *Education & Treatment of Children, 11*(4), 318–327.

E. VALERIE HEWITT
Texas A&M University
First edition

DEBORAH B. GUILLEN
The University of Texas of the Permian Basin
Second edition

BEERS, CLIFFORD W. (1876–1943)

Clifford W. Beers founded the mental hygiene movement following 3 years as a patient in mental hospitals in Connecticut in the early part of the twentieth century. Because of the abuses that he suffered, he left the hospital determined to reform the system, to see harsh custodial care replaced with medical treatment. His book, *A Mind That Found Itself*, published in 1908, gives a vivid account of his experiences, and at the time created a public outcry against inhumane treatment of mental patients.

A gifted speaker and organizer, Beers obtained the support of eminent psychiatrists and other prominent people to form the Connecticut Society for Mental Hygiene in 1908, the National Committee for Mental Hygiene in 1909, and the International Committee for Mental Hygiene in 1930.

Beers's influence on the mental hygiene movement has been a lasting one, both through the work of the outstanding people he enlisted in the movement, and the continued popularity of *A Mind That Found Itself*, still in print after more than three-quarters of a century.

REFERENCE

Beers, C. W. (1981). *A mind that found itself* (5th ed.). Pittsburgh: University of Pittsburgh Press.

PAUL IRVINE
Katonah, New York

BEERY-BUKTENICA DEVELOPMENTAL TEST OF VISUAL-MOTOR INTEGRATION–FIFTH EDITION

The Beery-Buktenica Developmental Test of Visual-Motor Integration (Beery VMI; Beery, Buktenica, & Beery, 2004) is a measure of visual and motor integration for ages 2 through 18. The Short Format and Full Format tests present individuals with drawings of geometric forms arranged in order of increasing difficulty, which they are asked to copy on the record form. The Beery VMI includes supplemental tests of visual perception and motor coordination that are generally administered when results show that further testing is necessary. With these supplemental tests, a comparison of the individual's test results with relatively pure visual and motor performances can be obtained. The test can be administered individually or to groups, although individual administration is recommended for the supplemental tests. The authors suggest that these tests should be given in the following order in which they were normed: VMI, Visual Perception, and Motor Coordination. Administration time varies from 10 to 15 minutes for the Short Form and Full Form tests and is approximately 5 minutes for the supplemental tests. The record form provides the examinee with instructions, and the manual contains administration guidelines and examples of correct and incorrect responses for each item.

This measure was normed in 2003 on a national sample of 2,512 individuals between 2 and 18 years of age. The sample was representative of the 2000 U.S. Census data with respect to gender, ethnicity, and geographic location. Results are reported as standard scores (M = 100, SD = 15), scaled scores (M = 10, SD = 3), percentiles, or other equivalents. In the newest edition of the VMI, the manual also provides approximately 600 Stepping Stones, or milestones, derived from age-specific norms from birth through 6 years of age.

The internal consistency of the items on the Beery VMI was determined to be .96, and interrater reliability coefficients ranged from .92 to .98 for the VMI and its supplemental Visual Perception and Motor Coordination tests. Test-retest reliability ranges from .85 to .89 for a mean time interval of 10 days. Past versions of the test have been frequently correlated with the original Bender-Gestalt, with a median correlation of .56. In particular, significant correlations have been demonstrated for the Bender Visual

Motor Gestalt Test and the VMI with a sample of gifted elementary school students (Knoff & Sperling, 1986), and the VMI showed more developmental sensitivity than the Bender-Gestalt Test when used in a sample of emotionally and behaviorally disturbed adolescents (Shapiro & Simpson, 1994). The Beery VMI has also demonstrated correlations ranging from .62 to .75 with the Copying, Position in Space, and Eye-Hand Coordination subtests of the Developmental Test of Visual Perception (DTVP-2), whereas the correlation between the Beery VMI and the Drawing subtest of the Wide Range Assessment of Visual Motor Abilities (WRAVMA) was only .52. Past editions of the VMI have been found to be a good predictor of academic or other problems when used in combination with other measures, though correlations decline as children progress through grade levels.

Although no review of the Beery VMI–Fifth Edition was available at the time of this writing, the fourth edition was reviewed in Plake and Impara (2001).

REFERENCES

Beery, K. E., Buktenica, N. A., & Beery, N. A. (2004). *The Beery-Buktenica Developmental Test of Visual-Motor Integration: Administration, scoring and teaching manual.* Minneapolis, MN: NCS Pearson.

Knoff, H. M., & Sperling, B. L. (1986). Gifted children and visual-motor development: A comparison of Bender-Gestalt and VMI test performance. *Psychology in the Schools, 23,* 247–251.

Marr, D., & Cermak, S. (2002). Predicting handwriting performance of early elementary students with the Developmental Test of Visual-Motor Integration. *Perceptual & Motor Skills, 95,* 661–669.

Plake, B. S., & Impara, J. C. (Eds.). (2001). *The fourteenth mental measurements yearbook* (pp. 621–630). Lincoln, NE: Buros Institute of Mental Measurements.

Shapiro, S. K., & Simpson, R. G. (1994). Patterns and predictors of performance on the Bender-Gestalt and the Developmental Test of Visual Motor Integration in a sample of behaviorally and emotionally disturbed adolescents. *Journal of Psychoeducational Assessment, 12,* 254–263.

RON DUMONT
Fairleigh Dickinson University

JOHN O. WILLIS
Rivier College

VISUAL-MOTOR INTEGRATION
VISUAL PERCEPTION AND DISCRIMINATION

BEHAVIOR

A behavior is a person's action or a reaction under specified conditions. Behaviors are monitored in order for teachers and researchers to determine their function, and how to control their frequency, intensity, duration or latency. The behavior that is being analyzed is often referred to as the *target behavior*. Isolating a specific behavior and defining it in observable and measurable terms allows its antecedents and consequences to be identified. By manipulating either the antecedent that leads to the target behavior or the consequences of the behavior modifications can be made to the target behavior. A teacher or researcher may increase a desired behavior or decrease an undesirable behavior (Alvero & Austin, 2004; Haager & Klinger, 2005; Heward, 2006; McLoughlin & Lewis, 2005; Pierangelo & Giuliani, 2006; Taylor, 2006).

It is first necessary to define the target behavior in terms that are both observable and measurable. This definition needs to be specific enough so that consistency can be maintained both over time and between observers. Based on this definition, accurate measures of frequency, intensity, duration, or latency can be acquired as well as the antecedents and consequences of the behavior (Scott, Liaupsin, Nelson & Jolivette, 2003).

The teacher or researcher must first decide what the behavior is that will be examined. It is not enough to say that the student is engaging in disruptive behaviors. The specific behavior must be described in such a way that all who are involved are using the same definition. For example, a behavior may be repetitively tapping a pencil against a desk or book with enough force to make a noise heard by the teacher at the front of the room. It may be necessary to further define the term repetitively, that is, three or more taps within 5 seconds. A clear definition of the behavior allows every person that is observing the student to focus on the same behavior. In addition, a clear definition maintains a consistency within the teacher or researcher's observation.

Behaviors can be divided into two broad categories, desirable and undesirable. Behaviors that are undesirable are those that should be decreased. In order to decrease undesirable behaviors, it should be arranged that antecedents that lead to the least likelihood of the behavior occurring are present and that after the behavior occurs those consequences that lead to the least likelihood of the behavior reoccurring should be presented. A person's use of a particular behavior has developed over time, therefore, to modify that behavior requires consistent and deliberate measures over time (Haager & Klinger, 2005; Heward, 2006; McLoughlin & Lewis, 2005; Pierangelo & Giuliani, 2006; Scott et al., 2003; Taylor, 2006).

The example used earlier of the pencil tapping student is an example of an undesired behavior. As described previously, a teacher or researcher that wished to reduce this behavior would first observe the student in the environment in which the behavior was occurring to identify the antecedents and consequences of the behavior. If, for example, the student pencil tapped more often during math class, the consequences for the tapping is to be told that he must put his pencil away. The function of the behavior may be to avoid the math work. By understanding how the antecedent—asking the student to do math increases the behavior—and the consequences of removing the pencil allows the student to avoid work, the teacher can manipulate these variables to reduce the frequency of the behavior.

Desirable behaviors are those that should be increased. In order to increase desirable behaviors, it should be arranged that antecedents that lead to the greatest likelihood of the behavior occurring are present and that after the behavior occurs those consequences that lead to the greatest likelihood of the behavior reoccurring should be presented (Haager & Klinger, 2005; Heward, 2006; McLoughlin & Lewis, 2005; Pierangelo & Giuliani, 2006; Scott et al., 2003; Taylor, 2006).

The example used earlier of a student's pencil tapping is an example of an undesired behavior. What we would like to see is the student using his pencil to solve the math problems. So the teacher or researcher observes when the desired behavior occurs, what antecedents trigger this behavior, and what consequences follow when the student performs the desired behavior. If, for example, when the student is given basic addition problems he uses his pencil to solve the problems without tapping (the desired behavior), the current consequences are that the teacher ignores the behavior and continues with the lesson. A teacher that is systematically observing and monitoring the student could identify that the antecedent of basic addition leads to the desired behavior and by manipulating the consequences to include reinforcement, the desired behavior could be increased. In addition, through systematically manipulating the antecedent, the desired behavior could be shaped to occur more frequently across settings.

REFERENCES

Alvero, A. M., & Austin, J. (2004). The effects of conducting behavioral observations on the behavior of the observer. *Journal of Applied Behavior Analysis, 37*, 457–468.

Haager, D., & Klinger, J. K. (2005). *Differentiating instruction in inclusive classrooms: The special educator's guide.* New York: Allyn & Bacon.

Heward, W. L. (2006). *Exceptional children: An introduction to special education* (8th ed.). Upper Saddle River, NJ: Pearson Prentice Hall.

McLoughlin, J. A., & Lewis, R. B. (2005). *Assessing students with special needs* (6th ed.). Upper Saddle River, NJ: Pearson Prentice Hall.

Pierangelo, R., & Giuliani, G. A. (2006). *Assessment in special education: A practical approach* (2nd ed.). New York: Allyn & Bacon.

Scott, T. M., Liaupsin, C. J., Nelson, C. M., & Jolivette, K. (2003). Ensuring student success through team-based functional behavioral assessment. *Teaching Exceptional Children, 35*(5), 16–21.

Taylor, R. L. (2006). *Assessment of exceptional students: Educational and psychological procedures* (7th ed.). New York: Allyn & Bacon.

WALTER A. ZILZ
Bloomsburg University

ADAPTIVE BEHAVIOR
EMOTIONAL DISORDERS

BEHAVIOR ANALYSIS

See APPLIED BEHAVIOR ANALYSIS.

BEHAVIOR ANALYST™, BOARD CERTIFIED ASSOCIATE

Board certified associate behavior analysts (BCABA®s) are certified by the Behavior Analyst Certification Board® (BACB®). Individuals who wish to be board certified associate behavior analysts (BCABAs) must have at least a bachelor's degree, have 135 classroom hours of specific coursework, meet supervised experience requirements, and pass the Associate Behavior Analyst Certification Examination. Once certified, BCBAs must accumulate 24 hours of continuing education credit in behavior analysis over a 3-year period to maintain their credential.

The BCABA conducts descriptive behavioral assessments and is able to interpret the results and design ethical and effective behavior analytic interventions for clients. The BCABA designs and oversees interventions in familiar cases (e.g., similar to those encountered during their training) that are consistent with the dimensions of applied behavior analysis. The BCABA obtains technical direction from a Board Certified Behavior Analyst (BCBA) for unfamiliar situations. The BCABA is able to teach others to carry out interventions once the BCABA has demonstrated competency with the procedures involved under the direct supervision of a BCBA. The BCABA may assist a BCBA with the design and delivery of introductory level instruction in behavior analysis. It is strongly recommended that the BCABA practice under the supervision of a BCBA, and that those governmental entities regulating BCABAs require this supervision. Additional information may be obtained at www.BACB.com.

REFERENCES

Johnston, J. M., & Shook, G. L. (2001). A national certification program for behavior analysts. *Behavioral Interventions, 16*(2), 77–85.

Moore, J., & Shook, G. L. (2001). Certification, accreditation and quality control in behavior analysis. *The Behavior Analyst, 24,* 45–55.

Shook, G. L. (2005). An examination of the integrity and future of Behavior Analyst Certification Board credentials. *Behavior Modification, 29*(0), 562–574.

Shook, G. L., & Favell, J. E. (1996). Identifying qualified professionals in behavior analysis. In C. Maurice, G. Green, & S. C. Luce (Eds.), *Behavioral intervention for young children with autism: A manual for parents and professionals* (pp. 221–229). Austin: PRO-ED.

Shook, G. L., Johnston, J. M., & Mellichamp, F. (2004). Determining essential content for applied behavior analyst practitioners. *The Behavior Analyst, 27*(1), 67–94.

Shook, G. L., & Neisworth, J. (2005). Ensuring appropriate qualifications for applied behavior analyst professionals: The Behavior Analyst Certification Board. *Exceptionality, 13*(1), 3–10.

Shook, G. L., Rosales, S. A., & Glenn, S. (2002). Certification and training of behavior analyst professionals. *Behavior Modification, 26*(1), 27–48.

STAFF

BEHAVIOR ANALYST CERTIFICATION BOARD®, INC.

The Behavior Analyst Certification Board® (BACB®) is a nonprofit 501(c)(3) corporation established to meet professional credentialing needs identified by behavior analysts, government, and consumers of behavior analysis services. The BACB's mission is to develop, promote, and implement a national and international certification program for behavior analyst practitioners. The BACB has established uniform content, standards, and criteria for the credentialing process that are designed to meet the following:

1. The legal standards established through state, federal, and case law.
2. The accepted standards for national certification programs.
3. The best-practice and ethical standards of the behavior analysis profession. The BACB enjoys the support of the Association for Behavior Analysis International.

The BACB program is based on the successful Behavior Analysis Certification Program developed by the state of Florida. Similar programs were established in California, Texas, Pennsylvania, New York, and Oklahoma. All of these programs transferred their certificants and credentialing responsibilities to the BACB and closed. The Behavior Analyst Certification Board credentials practitioners at two levels. Individuals who wish to become Board Certified Behavior Analysts™ (BCBA®s) must possess at least a master's degree, have 225 classroom hours of specific graduate-level coursework, meet supervised experience requirements, and pass the Behavior Analyst Certification Examination. Persons wishing to be Board Certified Associate Behavior Analysts (BCABA®s) must have at least a bachelor's degree, have 135 classroom hours of specific coursework, meet supervised experience requirements, and pass the Associate Behavior Analyst Certification Examination. The BACB certificants must accumulate continuing education credit to maintain their credentials.

The Behavior Analyst Certification Board has developed the following:

1. Eligibility standards to take the BACB certification examinations.
2. Renewal and recertification standards to maintain certification.
3. Guidelines for responsible conduct for behavior analysts.
4. Professional disciplinary standards with review committee appeal procedures.
5. A certificant registry.
6. A process to approve university course sequences and university practica.
7. Procedures to approve continuing education providers.
8. Professionally developed and maintained certification examinations.

The Behavior Analyst Certification Board generally administers the examinations three times per year in over 200 sites within the United States and over 150 sites outside the United States. Additional information on the Behavior Analyst Certification Board may be obtained at www.BACB.com.

REFERENCES

Johnston, J. M., & Shook, G. L. (2001). A national certification program for behavior analysts. *Behavioral Interventions, 16*(2), 77–85.

Moore, J., & Shook, G. L. (2001). Certification, accreditation and quality control in behavior analysis. *The Behavior Analyst, 24,* 45–55.

Shook, G. L. (2005). An examination of the integrity and future of Behavior Analyst Certification Board credentials. *Behavior Modification, 29*(0), 562–574.

Shook, G. L., & Favell, J. E. (1996). Identifying qualified professionals in behavior analysis. In C. Maurice, G. Green, & S. C. Luce (Eds.), *Behavioral intervention for young children with autism: A manual for parents and professionals* (pp. 221–229). Austin: PRO-ED.

Shook, G. L., Johnston, J. M., & Mellichamp, F. (2004). Determining essential content for applied behavior analyst practitioners. *The Behavior Analyst, 27*(1), 67–94.

Shook, G. L., & Neisworth, J. (2005). Ensuring appropriate qualifications for applied behavior analyst professionals: The Behavior Analyst Certification Board. *Exceptionality, 13*(1), 3–10.

Shook, G. L., Rosales, S. A., & Glenn, S. (2002). Certification and training of behavior analyst professionals. *Behavior Modification, 26*(1), 27–48.

STAFF

BEHAVIOR ANALYST™, BOARD CERTIFIED

Board Certified Behavior Analysts (BCBA®s) are certified by the Behavior Analyst Certification Board®. Individuals who wish to become BCBAs must possess at least a master's degree, have 225 classroom hours of specific graduate-level coursework, meet supervised experience requirements, and pass the Behavior Analyst Certification Examination. Once certified, BCBAs must accumulate 36 hours of continuing education credit in behavior analysis over a 3-year period to maintain their credential.

The board certified behavior analyst is an independent practitioner who also may work as an employee or independent contractor for an organization. The BCBA conducts descriptive and systematic (e.g., analogue) behavioral assessments, including functional analyses, and provides behavior analytic interpretations of the results. The BCBA designs and supervises behavior analytic interventions. The BCBA is able to effectively develop and implement appropriate assessment and intervention methods for use in unfamiliar situations and for a range of cases. The BCBA seeks the consultation of more experienced practitioners when necessary. The BCBA teaches others to carry out ethical and effective behavior analytic interventions based on published research and designs and delivers instruction in behavior analysis. It is strongly recommended that the BCBA supervise the work of board certified associate behavior analysts and others who implement behavior analytic interventions. Additional information may be obtained at www.BACB.com.

REFERENCES

Johnston, J. M., & Shook, G. L. (2001). A national certification program for behavior analysts. *Behavioral Interventions, 16*(2), 77–85.

Moore, J., & Shook, G. L. (2001). Certification, accreditation and quality control in behavior analysis. *The Behavior Analyst, 24*, 45–55.

Shook, G. L. (2005). An examination of the integrity and future of Behavior Analyst Certification Board credentials. *Behavior Modification, 29*(0), 562–574.

Shook, G. L., & Favell, J. E. (1996). Identifying qualified professionals in behavior analysis. In C. Maurice, G. Green, & S. C.

Luce (Eds.), *Behavioral intervention for young children with autism: A manual for parents and professionals* (pp. 221–229). Austin: PRO-ED.

Shook, G. L., Johnston, J. M., & Mellichamp, F. (2004). Determining essential content for applied behavior analyst practitioners. *The Behavior Analyst, 27*(1), 67–94.

Shook, G. L., & Neisworth, J. (2005). Ensuring appropriate qualifications for applied behavior analyst professionals: The Behavior Analyst Certification Board. *Exceptionality, 13*(1), 3–10.

Shook, G. L., Rosales, S. A., & Glenn, S. (2002). Certification and training of behavior analyst professionals. *Behavior Modification, 26*(1), 27–48.

STAFF

BEHAVIOR ASSESSMENT SYSTEM FOR CHILDREN–2

The Behavior Assessment System for Children–2 (BASC-2; Reynolds & Kamphaus, 2004) is a multimethod, multidimensional system that is used to evaluate the behavior and self-perceptions of children of ages 2 years, 6 months to 21 years, 11 months. It is made up of five components, each of which may be used individually or in any combination.

The Teacher Rating Scales (TRS) are a comprehensive measure of both adaptive and problem behaviors in the school setting that is intended to be filled out by teachers or others who fill a similar role. The respondent rates descriptors of behaviors on a four-point scale of frequency, ranging from Never to Almost Always. It takes 10 to 20 minutes to complete and has three forms with items targeted at three age levels: preschool (2.5–5), child (6–11), and adolescent (12–21). The composite scores include Externalizing Problems, Internalizing Problems, School Problem (6–21), Adaptive Skills, and a broad composite, the Behavioral Symptoms Index (BSI). The TRS has various optional content scales that assist in the interpretation of the primary BASC-2 scales and also broaden the assessment to include recent concerns in behavioral assessment (e.g., Bullying, Anger Control, evaluation of Bipolar Disorder, etc.). The TRS includes a validity check to detect a negative response set on the part of the teacher doing the rating.

The Parent Rating Scales (PRS) are a comprehensive measure of a child's adaptive and problem behaviors in community and home settings. The PRS uses the same four-choice response format as the TRS and also takes 10 to 20 minutes to complete. The PRS assesses the same clinical problems and adaptive behavior domains as the TRS; however, it does not include the School Problems composite or the Learning Problems and Study Skills scales, and it includes an additional adaptive scale (Activities of Daily Living). The PRS also includes the same validity scales as the TRS.

The Self-Report of Personality (SRP) is a personality inventory that consists of true or false statements. It takes about 20 to 30 minutes to complete and has three forms: child (8–11), adolescent (12–21), and college (18–25). The composite scores include School Maladjustment, Clinical Maladjustment, Personal Adjustment, and on overall composite score, the Emotional Symptoms Index (ESI), which is composed of both negative (clinical) scales and positive (adaptive) scales. Multiple indexes are incorporated to assess the validity of the child's responses. The SRP has various optional content scales to assist in the interpretation of the primary BASC-2 scales and also broaden the assessment to include recent concerns in behavioral assessment (e.g., Anger Control, Ego Strength). A version of the SRP normed in an interview format for ages 6 through 7 is scheduled for release in spring of 2005 (SRP-I) as is a version designed for college students (SRP-CS).

The Structured Development History (SDH) is an extensive survey of a child's social and medical information. The SDH, completed by a clinician during an interview with parent or guardian, is useful in the diagnostic and treatment process. It may also be completed by a parent or other knowledgeable caregiver independently as a questionnaire.

The Student Observation System (SOS) is a form for recording a direct observation of the classroom behavior of a child. Children's positive and negative behaviors are recorded using the technique of momentary time sampling during 3-second intervals spaced 30 seconds apart over a 15-minute period. It can be used when initially assessing the child as part of the diagnostic process and also repetitively to evaluate the effectiveness of treatment programs. An electronic version of the SOS, known as the *BASC Portable Observation Program* (POP), is available in Portable Data Acquisition (PDA) format.

Parent Feedback Forms are provided for each form of the PRS, TRS, and the SRP. These explain the purpose and use of the instrument in lay language and provide a parent-oriented summary and explanation of the child's or adolescent's score along with directions for obtaining additional information.

The BASC-2 Parent Ratings Scales, Self-Report of Personality, and Structured Developmental History are available in Spanish as well as English. Audio CDs are provided in English and Spanish for the PRS and the SRP as well.

The BASC-2 composite scores are converted to *t* scores that have a mean of 50 and a standard deviation of 10. The manual that accompanies the BASC-2 contains instructions for administering and scoring the TRS, PRS, and SRP and provides information for using the SDH and SOS. It also has information on the development, appropriate uses, validity, reliability, and interpretation of all components

of the BASC-2. There are three formats available for the TRS, PRS, and SRP: hand scoring, computer entry, and scannable forms. The hand scoring forms allow the teacher, parent, or child to record their responses next to the items rather than on a separate answer sheet. These forms are printed in a convenient self-scoring format, which allows them to be scored rapidly without using templates or keys. The computer-entry forms are designed to allow users to key item responses into a personal computer in about 2 to 5 minutes. The scannable forms are designed for use with mark-read (bubble) scanners. There is also a Spanish edition of the PRS that is available in hand-scoring or computer-entry format.

The standardization sample was collected from over 375 testing sites that were selected to provide diversity in geographic region, socioeconomic status, and culture and ethnicity. The sample included 4,650 TRS ratings, 4,800 PRS ratings, and 3,400 SRP ratings. These samples were representative of the 2001 Current Population Survey. General education classrooms in public and private schools were targeted for data collection. Parental permission was obtained for each form collected. The PRS ratings included in the norm samples were obtained from only one of the child's parents or guardians. Teachers were each assigned up to four TRS ratings per classroom. This data-gathering technique resulted in substantial overlap between the norm samples for the TRS, PRS, and SRP.

The internal consistency reliability for the PRS and SRP averaged in the low to mid .80s for all three levels—preschool (P), child (C), and adolescent (A). The internal consistency was in the middle to upper .80s for the PRS. The test-retest reliability of the TRS had median values of .82, .86, and .81, and the PRS had median values of .77, .84, and .81 for the scales at the three age levels, respectively. The test-retest reliability for the SRP had median values of .71, .75, and .84 at each level.

Impressive evidence of convergent validity of the BASC-2 is based on its correlations with several other measures, including the Achenbach System of Empirically based Assessment (ASEBA) Youth Self-Report (ABEBA; Achenbach & Rescorla, 2001), the Conners-Wells Adolescent Self-Report (CASS; Conners & Wells, 1997), the Childrens Depression Inventory (CDI; Kovacs, 2001), the Revised Children's Manifest Anxiety Scale (RCMAS; Reynolds & Richmond, 2001), the Brief Symptoms Inventory (BSI; Derogatis, 1993), the Beck Depression Inventory–II (BDI-II; Beck, Steer, & Brown, 1996), and the Minnesota Multiphasic Personality Inventory–2 (MMPI-2; Butcher et al., 2001).

To aid evaluators with the interpretation of the BASC-2 results, the manual provides information regarding the profiles of the following groups: Attention-Deficit/Hyperactivity Disorder, Bipolar Disorder, depression disorders, emotional behavioral disorders, hearing impairments, Pervasive Developmental Disorders (including Asperger and autism), and Speech and Language Disorders.

REFERENCES

Achenbach, T., & Rescorla, S. D. (2001). *Achenbach System of Empirically-based Assessment.* Burlington, VT: ASEBA.

Adams, C. D., & Drabman, R. S. (1994). BASC: A critical review. *Child Assessment News, 4,* 1–5.

Beck, A., Steer, R. A., & Brown, G. (1996). *Beck Depression Inventory.* San Antonio, TX: Harcourt.

Butcher, J. N., Dahlstrom, W. G., Graham, J., Tellegen, A., & Kaemmer, B. (2001). *Minnesota Multiphasic Personality Inventory* (2nd ed.). Minneapolis, MN: Pearson.

Clausen, H. H. (2003). The clinician's guide to the Behavior Assessment System for Children. *Child Neuropsychology, 9,* 234–236.

Conners, C. K., & Wells, K. C. (1997). A new self-report scale for assessment of adolescent psychopathology: Factor structure, reliability, validity and diagnostic sensitivity. *Journal of Abnormal Child Psychology, 25,* 487–497.

Derogatis, L. R. (1993). *Brief Symptoms Inventory.* Minneapolis, MN: Pearson.

Doyle, A., Ostrander, R., Skare, S., Crosby, R. D., & August, G. (1997). Convergent and criterion-related validity of the Behavior Assessment System for Children-Parent Rating Scales. *Journal of Clinical Child Psychology, 26,* 276–284.

Flanagan, D. P., Alfonso, V. C., Primavera, L. H., Povall, L., & Higgins, D. (1996). Convergent validity of the BASC and SSRS: Implications for social skills assessment. *Psychology in the Schools, 33,* 13–23.

Flanagan, R. (1995). A review of the Behavior Assessment System for Children (BASC): Assessment consistent with the requirements of the Individuals with Disabilities Education Act (IDEA). *Journal of School Psychology, 33,* 177–186.

Gladman, M., & Lancaster, S. (2003). A review of the Behavior Assessment System for Children. *School Psychology International, 24,* 276–291.

Kline, R. B. (1994). Test review: New objective rating scales for child assessment, I. Parent- and teacher-informant inventories of the Behavior Assessment System for Children, the Child Behavior Checklist, and the Teacher Report Form. *Journal of Psychoeducational Assessment, 12,* 289–306.

Kline, R. B. (1995). Test review: New objective rating scales for child assessment, II. Self-report scales for children and adolescents: Self-Report of Personality of the Behavior Assessment System for Children, the Youth Self-Report, and the Personality Inventory for Youth. *Journal of Psychoeducational Assessment, 13,* 169–193.

Kovacs, M. (2001). *Child Depression Inventory.* North Towanda, NY: MHS.

McCloskey, D. M., Hess, R. S., & D'Amato, R. C. (2003). Evaluating the utility of the Spanish version of the Behavior Assessment System for Children-Parent Report System. *Journal of Psychoeducational Assessment, 21,* 325–337.

Reynolds, C. R., & Richmond, B. O. (2001). *The Revised Children's Manifest Anxiety Scale.* Austin, TX: PRO-ED.

Reynolds, C. R., & Kamphaus, R. (2004). *Behavior Assessment System for Children* (2nd ed.). Circle Pines, MN: AGS.

Sandoval, J. (1998). Review of the Behavior Assessment System for Children. In J. C. Impara & B. S. Plake (Eds.), *The thirteenth mental measurements yearbook* (pp. 128–131). Lincoln, NE: Buros Institute of Mental Measurements.

Wilder, L. K., & Sudweeks, R. R. (2003). Reliability of ratings across studies of the BASC. *Education & Treatment of Children, 26,* 382–399.

Witt, J. C., & Jones, K. M. (1998). Review of the Behavior Assessment System for Children. In J. C. Impara & B. S. Plake (Eds.), *The thirteenth mental measurements yearbook* (pp. 131–133). Lincoln, NE: Buros Institute of Mental Measurements.

RON DUMONT
Fairleigh Dickinson University

JOHN O. WILLIS
Rivier College

BEHAVIOR CHARTING

Behavior charting is a term commonly used as an equivalent to describe a graphic representation of behavioral data. Graphing behavioral data allows the special educator to see changes easily in target behaviors (behaviors that are to be increased or decreased in frequency or duration). The ordinate, or vertical line, of the graph is labeled with the behavioral measurement scale. This could be the number of occurrences of off-task behavior, the number of fights a child has, or the percentage of time that a child follows instructions. The abscissa, or horizontal line, is labeled with the unit of time. This could be treatment sessions, days, weeks, minutes, or other intervals over which changes in behavior can be measured (Sulzer-Azaroff & Mayer, 1977).

REFERENCE

Sulzer-Azaroff, B., & Mayer, G. R. (1977). *Applying behavior-analysis procedures with children and youth.* New York: Holt, Rinehart and Winston.

RANDY W. KAMPHAUS
University of Georgia

APPLIED BEHAVIOR ANALYSIS

BEHAVIOR, DESTRUCTIVE

See DESTRUCTIVE BEHAVIORS.

BEHAVIOR DISORDERS

Students with behavior disorders demonstrate a prolonged pattern of behavior that is considered maladaptive or problematic relative to age and cultural and ethnic norms and across settings and interventions, to an extent that interferes with their ability to function in their environment (e.g., Kauffman, 2005). Students with behavior disorders may exhibit (1) *externalizing* behaviors (i.e., behaviors that are focused outward, including physical aggression, property destruction, self-injurious behavior, and verbal aggression), (2) *internalizing* behaviors (i.e., behaviors that are focused inward including social withdrawal), or (3) a *combination* of externalizing and internalizing behaviors. Although the label *behaviorally disordered* or BD is preferred by some school professionals, as it may be "more accurate" and "less stigmatizing" (Kauffman, 2005, p. 6), federal legislation uses the label *emotionally disturbed* or ED.

Federal Definition

The 1997 regulations for the Individuals with Disabilities Education Act provide the federal definition for *emotional disturbance.*

> (i) The term means a condition exhibiting one or more of the following characteristics over a long period of time and to a marked degree that adversely affects a child's educational performance: (A) An inability to learn that cannot be explained by intellectual, sensory, or health factors. (B) An inability to build or maintain satisfactory interpersonal relationships with peers and teachers. (C) Inappropriate types of behavior or feelings under normal circumstances. (D) A general pervasive mood of unhappiness or depression. (E) A tendency to develop physical symptoms or fears associated with personal or school problems. (ii) The term includes schizophrenia. The term does not apply to children who are socially maladjusted, unless it is determined that they have an emotional disturbance (34 CFR Part 300.7(c)(4). (Office of Special Education and Rehabilitative Services, 1997)

This definition has been greatly criticized; as Cullinan (2004) discusses, arriving at an agreed upon definition ED or BD is a complicated and currently unfinished process.

Varying Labels

Various combinations of adjectives (e.g., *emotionally, behaviorally, socially,* and *personally*) and terms (*disturbed, disordered, maladjusted, handicapped, conflicted, impaired*) are found in the research literature, legislation, and other materials (Kauffman, 2005). As a general rule, educators should use the federally accepted label (ED) when discussing eligibility for special education services and the preferred label (BD) when conversing with other professionals.

Etiology and Diagnosis of BD

Although the specific cause(s) have not been determined, most researchers suggest that BD results from interplay of biological and environmental factors (Kauffman, 2005). Behavior disorders are typically identified through a multistage assessment process (e.g., *Systematic Screening for Behavior Disorders;* Walker & Severson, 1990), and screening should begin as early as possible (Kauffman, 2005). In general, this process should involve multiple methods (e.g., interviews, observations, norm and criterion referenced assessments, etc.) and multiple informants (parents, school professionals, the child when appropriate) across multiple settings and time. Additionally, students must meet federal, state, and district eligibility criteria to receive special education services under the category of ED.

Evidence-Based Strategies for Intervention

Research shows that students with behavior disorders, like many students, benefit from a consistent, predictable, and positive environment. Schoolwide and setting-specific positive behavior interventions have produced positive effects (e.g., decreases in inappropriate and increases in appropriate behavior) for students in general and students with behavior disorders in particular (e.g., Safran & Oswald, 2003).

When individualized supports are necessary, students with behavior disorders benefit from function-based behavior intervention plans (e.g., Ingram, Lewis-Palmer, & Sugai, in press). That is, plans that take into account (1) why the student is engaging in inappropriate behavior (e.g., to get access to or to escape from something), (2) teach the student new skills that meet the same function, and (3) ensure that the student is more successful in meeting their needs through appropriate skills than inappropriate behavior (Crone & Horner, 2003).

REFERENCES

Crone, D. A., & Horner, R. H. (2003). *Building positive behavior support systems in schools: Functional behavioral assessment.* New York: Guilford.

Cullinan, D. (2004). Classification and definition of emotional and behavioral disorders. In R. B. Rutherford, M. M. Quinn, & S. R. Mathur (Eds.), *Handbook of research in emotional and behavioral disorders* (pp. 94–110). New York: Guilford.

Ingram, K., Lewis-Palmer, T., & Sugai, G. (in press). Function-based intervention planning: Comparing the effectiveness of FBA indicated and contra-indicated intervention plans. *Journal of Positive Behavior Interventions.*

Kauffman, J. M. (2005). *Characteristics of emotional and behavioral disorders of children and youth* (8th ed.). Upper Saddle River, NJ: Pearson.

Office of Special Education and Rehabilitative Services. (1997). *IDEA '97 Final Regulations: 34 CFR Part 300, Assistance to*

States for the Education of Children with Disabilities: Part B of the Individuals with Disabilities Education Act. Retrieved May 21, 2006, from http://www.cec.sped.org/law_res/doc/law/regulations/index.php

Safran, S. P., & Oswald, K. (2003). Positive behavior supports: Can schools reshape disciplinary practices? *Exceptional Children, 6,* 361–373.

Walker, H., & Severson, H. (1990). *Systematic Screening for Behavior Disorders (SSBD).* Longmont, CO: Sopris West.

BRANDI SIMONSEN
University of Connecticut

BEHAVIOR ASSESSMENT SYSTEM FOR CHILDREN–2
EMOTIONAL DISORDERS
EMOTIONAL LABILITY

BEHAVIOR INTERVENTION PLANS

Behavior intervention plans consist of multiple intervention and support strategies. Strategies are identified and built into an individual's program based on hypotheses that summarize the results of a functional behavior assessment. Intervention plans are far more likely to yield positive results when based on a functional behavior assessment (Carr et al., 2002). It is highly unlikely that any single intervention or support can address the comprehensive needs of a person (student) who has a history of serious problem behavior. Additionally, when the reason for problem behaviors varies depending on the situation, a different set of strategies may be needed to address each unique situation.

Comprehensive intervention plans are hypothesis driven, person-centered and uniquely tailored to an individual's typical daily routines across home, school and community settings (Bambara & Knoster, 1998). Effective intervention plans are personalized and, therefore, there is no one behavior intervention plan that fits everyone or all situations.

The four component parts of behavior intervention plans include (1) short-term prevention, (2) teaching of socially acceptable alternative skills, (3) consequence strategies, and (4) long-term prevention. In addition, it is important for intervention teams to identify support needs for each team member to increase the likelihood of adequate fidelity in implementation of the intervention plan.

Short-Term Prevention

Effective teachers understand that the most successful classroom management procedures are proactive (e.g., establishing clear behavioral expectations and establishing rapport with the students). In a similar sense, short-term prevention emphasizes (proactive) antecedent and setting event interventions that address both the fast and slow triggers that set the stage for problem behavior with the student of concern. Specifically, interventions are put in place to eliminate or modify the fast and slow triggers to problem behavior as identified in the hypotheses formulated through the functional behavior assessment process. Short-term prevention is powerful in that it (1) provides immediate relief from frustrating and problematic situations and (2) expands opportunities to teach socially acceptable alternative skills. Short-term prevention typically involves combinations of the following techniques: (1) removing a problem event (e.g., not asking a student to read aloud), (2) modifying a problem event (e.g., reducing the number of math problems on an independent worksheet), (3) interspersing difficult or unpleasant events with easy or pleasant events (e.g., having two mastery level problems for each instructional level problem on a worksheet), (4) adding events that promote desired behavior (e.g., building into activities things of interest to the student such as selecting reading on a topic of interest), and (5) blocking or neutralizing the impact of negative events (e.g., allowing for opportunities for the student to get up and get a drink on hot days).

Teaching Socially Acceptable Alternative Skills

Effective behavior intervention plans teach socially acceptable alternative skills that enable the student to achieve desired outcomes. Typically individuals (students) engage in serious problem behavior because (1) they do not have the skills to meet their needs in a socially acceptable manner (i.e., skill deficit) or (2) they have learned that the problem behavior brings about the desired results more efficiently than socially acceptable alternatives. In either case, behavior intervention plans focus on teaching socially acceptable alternative skills that will enable the student to achieve the desired outcome (function). There are three types of alternative skills that should be targeted in behavior intervention plans: (1) functional equivalents that serve the exact same function as the problem behavior (e.g., raising hand in class to gain attention as opposed to yelling and jumping up and down out of seat), (2) general skills that help to alter problem situations and prevent the need for problem behavior (e.g., improve general reading skills so that when reading tasks are assigned they create less stress for the student), and (3) coping skills that teach students to cope or tolerate difficult situations (e.g., teach the student to take a cleansing breath and close his eyes to calm down when stressed). Each of these types of alternative skills should be a part of teaching strategies in a behavior intervention plan.

Consequence Strategies

Consequence strategies are used to reinforce the acquisition and use of socially acceptable alternative skills as well as reduce the effectiveness of problem behavior. Reinforcement for the student's use of the functional equivalent is best delivered by providing access to the function (e.g., providing attention when appropriately requested as opposed to problem behavior). Reinforcement for general and coping skills may take many forms including verbal praise combined with stickers or points. When redirection for problem behavior occurs, the student of concern should be redirected to use his or her targeted alternative skills (e.g., saying "stop grabbing my arm; I want you to say help to get my attention"). Practitioners should strive to reinforce the student of concern for appropriate behavior four times for every one time that redirection for problem behavior occurs.

Long-Term Prevention

Long-term prevention focuses on the typical rhythm and routines of daily life for the student of concern. Dissatisfaction with daily events may contribute directly to student problem behavior (e.g., the student does not want to work in a sheltered workshop but rather at the local supermarket). Further, students are more likely to learn and use socially acceptable alternative skills in environments that are perceived as enjoyable and of interest.

Long-term prevention is most concerned with quality of life factors (e.g., personal satisfaction with the status of relationships and opportunities to engage in activities and events of interest). Behavior intervention plans should systematically design procedures to increase the likelihood of both maintenance (over time) and generalization (to new situations) of socially acceptable alternative skills (e.g., reinforcement procedures continue to be used in the classroom for the student's use of the communication board as well as in the hallway, on the playground, and in the lunch room). These types of interventions contribute to long-term prevention through general improvement of the student's quality of life (as viewed from that student's perspective).

Supports for Team Members

It is important to implement the behavior intervention plan with a sufficient degree of fidelity. One common inhibitor to implementation of behavior intervention plans is that team members may have needs themselves that go unaddressed (Knoster, 2003). The effectiveness of any behavior intervention plan is adversely affected when this occurs. As such, it is important that the design team that comprises relevant stakeholders in the process identify and take steps to address specific needs that they may have in order to implement the behavior intervention plan. Supports for team members may include training in regard to the interventions and supports to be implemented, assistance in altering the student's daily schedule, or establishing a series of scheduled meetings to review student progress and problem solve situations that may arise.

REFERENCES

Bambara, L. M., & Knoster, T. (1998). *Designing positive behavior support plans.* Washington, DC: American Association on Mental Retardation.

Carr, E. G., Dunlap, G., Horner, R. H., Koegel, R. L., Turnbull, A. P., Sailor, W., et al. (2002). Positive behavior support: Evolution of an applied science. *Journal of Positive Behavior Interventions, 4,* 4–16.

Knoster, T. (2003). Practical application of functional behavioral assessment in schools. In G. Dunlap & L. Bambara (Eds.), *Positive behavior support: Critical articles on improving practice for individuals with severe disabilities* (pp. 81–91). Austin, TX: PRO-ED.

TIM KNOSTER
Bloomsburg University

INDIVIDUAL EDUCATION PLAN
POSITIVE BEHAVIORAL SUPPORT

BEHAVIOR MODELING

Modeling is a training intervention that was popularized by social learning theory and the works of Albert Bandura (Bandura, 1971). When using this procedure, the practitioner physically demonstrates or shows a visual representation (e.g., photo sequence, videotape, movie) of the production of the behavior. In essence, the practitioner shows the student the appropriate way to respond. The demonstration often includes secondary informational sources such as feedback about the model's success and the environmental and contextual cues that led the model to behave in the particular fashion demonstrated.

The effectiveness of this procedure can be enhanced through attention to several variables. Of primary consideration are the characteristics of the person providing the model. In some cases the person who demonstrates the behavior could be another student. This would be appropriate when the other student is (1) competent to do the behavior; (2) someone the student can identify with (i.e., someone similar to himself or herself); (3) someone held in high esteem by the target student; (4) able to demonstrate the appropriate behavior clearly; (5) able to demonstrate novel responses that the target student has not yet learned to do; and (6) reinforced for the performance of the target behavior.

Student factors are also important to the modeling process. First, the student must be sufficiently motivated to become an active participant in the modeling process. An absence of sufficient motivation will negate the qualities of the model and the modeling event. Second, the attention of the student must be keyed to the relevant properties of the modeled behavior. Third, the student must have sufficient motor abilities to replicate the modeled behavior. Finally, the ability of the student to remember and recall the modeled act will greatly affect the general and functional utility of the modeled behavior. This retention is based on two processes: imagination and verbalization. In the first case, when stimuli are consistently paired, the occurrence of one of the paired stimuli will signal the other. In the second case, labeling of an event (a verbal process whether vocalized or not) lends saliency to the event.

Factors related to the instructional variables can also affect the effectiveness of modeling. Reinforcement for the modeled behavior must be sufficient in quantity and quality to bring about student participation. For example, Lovaas (1967) has shown that children imitate precisely when they are rewarded for precise replication of modeled behaviors. However, when children are reinforced nondifferentially (i.e., for approximations of the response), they produce poorly matched responses. Modeled behavior is most effectively acquired and maintained when the modeled behaviors are familiar and functional to the target student. Overt rehearsals of the modeled response can considerably enhance the acquisition and maintenance of the modeled behavior.

Modeling, therefore, is a useful instructional procedure. As a technology for instruction, it requires that its users follow specific procedures to produce maximum results. These procedures are neither esoteric nor difficult to follow. Because modeling is thought to be a "least restrictive" instructional prompting procedure, and because it is usable in most environments, it should be considered to be an instructional procedure of choice under most circumstances.

REFERENCES

Bandura, A. (1971). Analysis of modeling processes. In A. Bandura (Ed.), *Psychological modeling: Conflicting theories.* Chicago: Aldine-Atherton.

Lovaas, O. I. (1967). A behavior therapy approach to the treatment of childhood schizophrenia. In J. P. Hill (Ed.), *Minnesota symposia on child psychology* (Vol. 1). Minneapolis: University of Minnesota Press.

LYLE E. BARTON
Kent State University

COGNITIVE BEHAVIOR THERAPY
SOCIAL LEARNING THEORY
THEORY OF ACTIVITY

BEHAVIOR MODIFICATION

Behavior modification is generally regarded as a term that encompasses the various methods derived from learning theory that are used to alter the response patterns of humans and other animals. The term has been used in this way by Bandura (1969); he and other behaviorists such as Skinner (1965) have enumerated a wide variety of learning principles that have been translated into methods for learning or changing behavior.

Although behavior modification is sometimes considered as a unitary position in discussions of certain issues in psychology, the techniques involved are derived from several different theoretical approaches to learning. Each approach tends to emphasize environmental determinants, as opposed to person-based determinants, of individual differences among organisms in the way in which they learn behavior. On the other hand, each approach also emphasizes the importance of determining the specific environmental variables that influence the behavior of an individual.

One such approach (Wolpe, 1982) is based on classical or respondent conditioning, which was studied extensively early in the twentieth century by Ivan Pavlov, the Russian psychologist, and John Watson, the American sometimes known as the father of behaviorism. In this type of learning, a neutral stimulus is paired in time with another stimulus (called the unconditioned stimulus) already able to elicit a particular response, usually unlearned, from an organism's repertoire. Through repeated pairings, this neutral stimulus also acquires the capability of eliciting the original (or unconditioned) response; this neutral stimulus is called the conditioned stimulus. For example, Watson and Rayner (1920) performed a classic study in which a neutral stimulus (a white rat) took on fear-inducing properties for a young boy when it was presented to the child paired with a sudden loud noise (an unconditioned stimulus) that startled and frightened the child (the unconditioned response). Soon the child began attempting to avoid the white rat because of its newly acquired association with the loud noise. Classical conditioning is apparently important in establishing subtle types of learning such as attitudes, basic emotional states such as love, fear and trust, and other similar behaviors acquired over long periods of time.

A second major approach to behavior modification (Skinner, 1965) is based on operant or instrumental conditioning. The basis of this approach is the so-called law of effect articulated by Thorndike (1935). He proposed that responses followed by pleasurable consequences would be strengthened, whereas responses followed by unpleasant consequences would be weakened. This formulation was refined and greatly expanded by others, notably Skinner, who had demonstrated that consequences (Thorndike would have called them effects) are important in learning a wide variety of behaviors. Most of these behaviors involve some activity or operation (hence the term operant conditioning) in the form of a skill the organism learns. An important derivative of operant conditioning has been described by Premack (1965). He showed that the opportunity to perform a desirable activity may be used as a consequence to reinforce or strengthen the performance of a less preferred activity. Thus a person may be willing to do something relatively unpleasant (perhaps balancing a checkbook or reading a boring book) if this activity is followed soon thereafter by a pleasurable activity (perhaps a movie or a golf outing).

The modification of behavior using the outlined principles of operant conditioning is sometimes called applied behavior analysis. Usually this involves detailed empirical specification of the behavior to be changed (or to be learned), careful observation of the contributing conditioning elements, and the development of a strategy (changing antecedent stimulus conditions, response consequences, or both) to achieve the desired results. It is important to note that the use of behavior modification techniques does not require the use of terms such as normal or abnormal to describe the behavior being examined. In fact, the learning theorists who have contributed to the development of behavior modification techniques assume that behavior is learned according to principles that operate nearly identically in all situations, even though a given observer may have a higher or lower value to place on a particular learned behavior. As a result, descriptive terms such as abnormal are frequently rejected because their use tempts us to infer that different laws of learning have governed the behavior so described.

REFERENCES

Bandura, A. (1969). *Principles of behavior modification*. New York: Holt, Rinehart, & Winston.

Premack, D. (1965). Reinforcement therapy. In D. Levine (Ed.), *Nebraska symposium on motivation*. Lincoln: University of Nebraska Press.

Skinner, B. F. (1965). *Science and human behavior*. New York: Free Press.

Thorndike, E. L. (1935). *The psychology of wants, interests and attitudes*. New York: Appleton, Century.

Watson, J., & Rayner, R. (1920). Conditioning emotional response. *Journal of Experimental Psychology, 3,* 1–14.

Wolpe, J. (1982). *The practice of behavior therapy* (3rd ed.). New York: Pergamon.

JERRY L. SLOAN
*Wilmington Psychiatric
Associates*

APPLIED BEHAVIOR ANALYSIS
OPERANT CONDITIONING

BEHAVIOR PROBLEM CHECKLIST, REVISED

The Revised Behavior Problem Checklist (RBPC; Quay & Peterson, 1983) is a widely researched rating scale for the clinical evaluation of deviant behavior. The original Behavior Problem Checklist (BPC) was developed in 1967 and the RBPC is the revised version of this scale. The RBPC consists of four major scales and two minor scales. The major scales include: Conduct Disorder (22 items), Socialized Aggression (17 items), Attention Problems–Immaturity (16 items), and Anxiety–Withdrawal (11 items). The two minor scales are Psychotic Behavior (6 items) and Motor Tension–Excess (5 items). In addition, twelve items are included for research purposes, and do not contribute to the overall score.

The revised version uses a weighted scoring system (2 = severe problem; 1 = mild problem; 0 = not a problem, no opportunity to observe, don't know). One problem associated with this scoring system is the failure to discriminate between the three possible zero responses (Roberts, 1986). Thus a score of zero does not necessarily indicate the absence of a behavior problem. Checklists and scoring templates are included with the manual. The checklists can be completed in approximately 15 minutes by any observer who is familiar with the subject. Scoring templates provide raw scores for each of the four major and two minor scales, and can be completed in 5–10 minutes.

Estimates of internal consistency reliability range from .68 to .95. Interrator reliabilities range from .52 to .85. Test-retest reliabilities (two-month interval) range from .49 to .83 ($N = 149$). Support for validity includes a substantial relationship between the RBPC and the BPC, discrimination between normal children and clinical groups, and support from numerous studies for many facets of validity (Dezolt, 1992; Hinshaw et al., 1987; Lahay & Piacentini, 1985). The authors do not provide representative norms based on U.S. Census data, but recommend developing local norms. However, the use of local norms without reference to a normative sample may be complicated by such things as cultural variation within communities and transient populations. The manual provides means and standard deviations for scale scores from clinical and nonclinical samples, and from parent and teacher ratings. However, little demographic information is included; thus, it is unclear whether these samples are representative.

The RBPC is a useful screening instrument for assessing behavior problems along four independent dimensions commonly associated with emotional disturbance (Quay, 1983). However, the absence of a well-defined normative sample is cause for some concern (Shapiro, 1992).

REFERENCES

Dezolt, D. M. (1992). Review of the Revised Behavior Problem Checklist. In J. J. Kramer & J. C. Conoley (Eds.), *The eleventh mental measurements yearbook* (pp. 764–765). Lincoln, NE: Buros Institute of Mental Measurements.

Hinshaw, S. P., Morrison, D. C., Carte, E. T., & Cornsweet, C. (1987). Factorial dimensions of the Revised Behavior Problem Checklist: Replication and validation within a kindergarten sample. *Journal of Abnormal Child Psychology, 15,* 309–327.

Lahay, B. B., & Piacentini, J. C. (1985). An evaluation of the Quay-Peterson Revised Behavior Problem Checklist. *Journal of School Psychology, 23,* 285–289.

Quay, H. C. (1983). A dimensional approach to behavior disorder: The Revised Behavior Problem Checklist. *School Psychology Review, 12,* 244–249.

Quay, H. C., & Peterson, D. R. (1983). *Interim manual for the Revised Behavior Problem Checklist.* Coral Gables, FL: University of Miami.

Roberts, T. (1986). Revised Behavior Problem Checklist. In D. L. Keyser & R. C. Sweetland (Eds.), *Test critiques: Volume 5* (pp. 371–377). Kansas City, MO: Test Corporation of America.

Shapiro, E. S. (1992). Review of the Revised Behavior Problem Checklist. In J. J. Kramer & J. C. Conoley (Eds.), *The eleventh mental measurements yearbook* (pp. 765–766). Lincoln, NE: Buros Institute of Mental Measurements.

LIZANNE DESTEFANO
University of Illinois

BEHAVIOR THERAPY

Behavior therapy encompasses a broad range of philosophical, theoretical, and procedural approaches to the "alleviation of human suffering and the enhancement of human functioning" (Davison & Stuart, 1975, p. 755). An approach to assessment, therapy, ethics, and professional issues, it has been used successfully with a variety of populations (adults, children, adolescents, mentally retarded, etc.) in diverse settings (schools, hospitals, psychiatric facilities, mental health centers, etc.) and for various problems (anxiety, depression, addictive disorders, social skills deficits, psychotic behaviors, marital dysfunction, academic skills, parent-child problems, etc.). There are probably few human behaviors that have not been addressed by behavior therapists.

A number of terms with somewhat different origins and connotations have been used almost interchangeably to denote the field. These terms include behavior therapy, behavior modification, applied behavior analysis, social learning theory, cognitive-behavior therapy, clinical behavior therapy, and multimodal behavior therapy. Attempts to clarify or standardize the meaning of the various terms based on the populations served (e.g., individual or group), techniques used (e.g., systematic desensitization, contingency management), methodologies (e.g., single-subject designs), or theoretical bases (e.g., classical conditioning, operant conditioning) have failed to gain wide acceptance (Franzini & Tilker, 1972; Wilson, 1978).

Several formal definitions of behavior therapy have been proposed. For example, Wolpe (1982) defined behavior therapy as "the use of experimentally established principles and paradigms of learning to overcome unadaptive habits" (p. 1).

Whereas Wolpe's definition emphasizes a theoretical basis of behavior therapy, other definitions stress the methods of inquiry used by behavior therapists. For example, Ross, in his presidential address to the Association for Advancement of Behavior Therapy, defined behavior therapy as "the empirically controlled application of the science of human behavior to the alleviation of psychological distress and the modification of maladaptive behavior" (Ross, 1985, p. 196). This definition reflects the growing acceptance of methodological behaviorism, which focuses on the methods used in obtaining psychological information. Such a definition, however, does not delineate behavior therapy from other construct systems that might also use empirical methods of inquiry.

The difficulty of arriving at a single definition of behavior therapy was well summarized by Kazdin and Wilson (1978):

> Contemporary behavior therapy is marked by a diversity of views, a broad range of heterogeneous procedures with different theoretical rationales, and open debate about conceptual bases, methodological requirements, and evidence of efficacy. In short, there is no clearly agreed upon or commonly accepted definition of behavior therapy. (p. 1)

This lack of consensus reflects both the continuous development of behavior therapy and the various models within the behavioral construct system.

At least four major models within behavior therapy can be identified: (1) applied behavior analysis, (2) neobehavioristic mediational model, (3) social learning theory, and (4) cognitive-behavior therapy (Agras, Kazdin, & Wilson, 1979). The models differ on the bases of historical tradition, fundamental principles, and therapeutic procedures.

Applied behavior analysis draws heavily from the Skinner tradition of operant conditioning. Behavior is assumed to be under the control of environmental stimuli. These controlling stimuli include the consequences of behavior as well as the antecedent events that are associated with differential consequences. Intervention involves the manipulation of the controlling environmental stimuli in order to modify overt behavior. Therapeutic procedures are based on principles derived from operant conditioning such as reinforcement, punishment, extinction, and stimulus control. The token economy, in which appropriate behaviors earn tokens that later can be exchanged for desired activities, consumable goods, and privileges, is a procedure representative of applied behavior analysis.

The neobehavioristic mediational model is based primarily on the principles of classical conditioning derived from the learning theories of Pavlov, Hull, and Mowrer (Wolpe, 1982). The model emphasizes the role of anxiety as a conditioned emotional response. For example, the anxiety response can be elicited by previously neutral stimuli as a result of pairing those neutral stimuli with noxious stimuli.

Therapeutic procedures such as systematic desensitization and flooding are designed to reduce the anxiety underlying behavioral disorders by exposing the individual to the conditioned, feared stimulus in the absence of the noxious stimulus.

According to the third model, social learning theory (Bandura, 1977), three interacting systems regulate behavior. The first system is external stimulus control, which regulates behavior either through the association of stimuli, as in classical conditioning, or through antecedent stimuli reliably predicting differential consequences of behavior. Response feedback, primarily in the form of reinforcing consequences, provides a second regulatory system. Finally, cognitive processes mediate the effect of external events by influencing which events are attended to and how those events are perceived and interpreted. An important cognitive mediator of behavior change is self-efficacy, the expectation that the behavior required to produce an outcome can be performed. Social learning theory further posits that human functioning is a result of the reciprocal interaction among behavior, the environment, and a person's cognitions (Bandura, 1981). That is, not only does the environment influence behavior, but a person's behavior also influences the environment. Modeling of the desired behavior by the therapist, either with or without the client's subsequent performance, is a therapeutic procedure derived from social learning theory's emphasis on cognitive processes such as the capacity to learn through observation.

The most recent development in behavior therapy is the emergence of cognitive-behavior therapy (Beck, 1976; Mahoney, 1974). According to this model, it is the perception of events rather than the events themselves that most influence behavior. Further, adaptive and maladaptive patterns are acquired through cognitive processes. Thus irrational beliefs, errors of logic, faulty self-talk, dysfunctional attributions, and mental representations of one's self and one's world contribute to behavioral and emotional disorders. Cognitive restructuring, in which clients are taught to examine and change faulty cognitions, is a representative procedure used in cognitive-behavior therapy. Cognitive behavior therapy has become the treatment of choice for several adult and childhood disorders, including panic, phobic, and obsessive-compulsive disorders. It has also dominated outcome research on psychological therapy (Wilson, 1997).

Despite the diversity of models in the behavioral construct system and the inability to provide a single definition of behavior therapy, a number of characteristics and assumptions of behavior therapy can be delineated (Agras et al., 1979; Haynes, 1984; Kazdin & Hersen, 1980). No one of these characteristics is definitive of the field, nor does any one necessarily differentiate behavior therapy from other systems. Nevertheless, taken together, they represent the common core of behavior therapy.

One set of characteristics concern methods of inquiry:

1. There is a commitment to empiricism and scientific methodology as the primary basis for developing and evaluating concepts and therapeutic techniques.
2. There is a commitment to an explicit, testable, and falsifiable conceptual foundation.
3. Therapeutic procedures and hypotheses with sufficient precision to make evaluation, replication, and generalization possible are specified.
4. There are close ties to the experimental findings of the science of psychology.
5. There is a low level of inference about data so as to minimize biases.

These epistemological principles imply that behavior therapy will continue to evolve as new knowledge is gained from empirical findings.

A second set of characteristics concerns the assumptions about behavior and behavioral disorders.

1. There is a deterministic model of behavior in which environmental antecedents and consequences are assumed to have the greatest impact on behavior. Recently, interactional models have been introduced in which behavior, the environment, and the person (most notably cognitive events and physiological conditions) are all presumed to influence one another.
2. There is an emphasis on current determinants of behavior as opposed to historical determinants (i.e., early childhood experiences).
3. The same principles that govern normal behavior also govern abnormal behavior. That is, no qualitative difference separates normal from abnormal behavior.
4. There are multiple determinants of behavior. The determinants of behavioral disorders may vary from individual to individual, and from one disorder to another.
5. Both the disease model of abnormal behavior and the implication that dysfunctional behavior is a sign or symptom of an underlying illness are rejected. Instead, dysfunctional behavior is construed as a "problem in living" or as learned, maladaptive behavior. Thus the dysfunctional behavior itself is targeted for behavior change.
6. Psychological disorders can be expressed in behavioral, cognitive, and affective modes. These modes can covary to differing degrees owing to situational factors and individual differences.
7. There is the relative specificity of behavior to the situation in which it occurs as opposed to the belief that behavior is consistent across situations.

A third set of characteristics concerns the methods of behavior change:

1. Therapeutic procedures are derived from experimental-clinical psychology.

2. Therapy is conceptualized as an opportunity to unlearn maladaptive behaviors and to learn adaptive behaviors.

3. The importance of tailoring therapy to the individual based on an assessment of the idiosyncratic determinants of the individual's dysfunctional behavior is emphasized.

4. The importance of the therapist-client interaction as one source of behavior change is emphasized.

5. There is an ongoing evaluation of intervention results in order to modify procedures as needed.

6. Intervention results are generalized from the intervention setting to the client's natural environment.

In conclusion, behavior therapy is a multifaceted and diverse system linked by a common core of assumptions. It is a viable system that has withstood numerous criticisms to emerge as a major approach within the psychological treatment field.

REFERENCES

Agras, W. S., Kazdin, A. E., & Wilson, G. T. (1979). *Behavior therapy: Toward an applied clinical science.* San Francisco: Freeman.

Bandura, A. (1977). *Social learning theory.* Englewood Cliffs, NJ: Prentice Hall.

Bandura, A. (1981). In search of pure unidirectional determinants. *Behavior Therapy, 12,* 30–40.

Beck, A. T. (1976). *Cognitive therapy and the emotional disorders.* New York: International Universities Press.

Davison, G. C., & Stuart, R. B. (1975). Behavior therapy and civil liberties. *American Psychologist, 30,* 755–763.

Franzini, L. R., & Tilker, H. A. (1972). On the terminological confusion between behavior therapy and behavior modification. *Behavior Therapy, 3,* 279–282.

Haynes, S. N. (1984). Behavioral assessment of adults. In M. Hersen & G. Goldstein (Eds.), *Handbook of psychological assessment.* New York: Pergamon.

Kazdin, A. E., & Hersen, M. (1980). The current status of behavior therapy. *Behavior Modification, 4,* 283–302.

Kazdin, A. E., & Wilson, G. T. (1978). *Evaluation of behavior therapy: Issues, evidence, and research strategies.* Cambridge, MA: Ballinger.

Mahoney, M. J. (1974). *Cognition and behavior modification.* Cambridge, MA: Ballinger.

Ross, A. O. (1985). To form a more perfect union: It is time to stop standing still. *Behavior Therapy, 16,* 195–204.

Wilson, G. T. (1978). On the much discussed nature of the term "behavior therapy." *Behavior Therapy, 9,* 89–98.

Wilson, G. T. (1997). Behavior therapy at century close. *Behavior Therapy, 28*(3), 449–457.

Wolpe, J. (1982). *The practice of behavior therapy* (3rd ed.). New York: Pergamon.

JEFFREY L. PHILLIPS
University of North Carolina at Wilmington

APPLIED BEHAVIOR ANALYSIS
BEHAVIOR MODIFICATION
DESENSITIZATION
SOCIAL LEARNING THEORY

BEHAVIOR THERAPY

Behavior Therapy is the official publication of the Association for the Advancement of Behavior Therapy (AABT). As an international journal, *Behavior Therapy* is "devoted to the application of the behavioral and cognitive sciences to the conceptualization, assessment and treatment of psychopathology and related clinical problems." The journal publishes empirical research, theoretical reviews, literature reviews, and case studies. *Behavior Therapy* is available to all members of AABT. For additional information on AABT, including access to abstracts from *Behavior Therapy,* go to http://aabt.org/.

RANDALL L. DE PRY
University of Colorado at Colorado Springs

BEHAVIOR RATING INVENTORY OF EXECUTIVE FUNCTION

The Behavior Rating Inventory of Executive Function (BRIEF; Gioia, Isquith, & Kenworthy, 2000) is a Likert-type questionnaire developed to assess a wide range of developmental and acquired neurological conditions in children ages 5 to 18 years. There are two rating forms, one for parents and one for teachers. Each form takes 10 to 15 minutes to complete and 15 to 20 minutes to score. The questionnaires consist of 86 items although each form uses different questions. Both forms measure eight different aspects of executive functioning: inhibit, shift, emotional control, plan/organize, initiate, monitor, organization of materials, and working memory. In addition to the eight clinical scales, the BRIEF also measures two validity scales and forms two broader indexes: Behavioral Regulation (3 scales) and Metacognition (5 scales) as well as a Global Executive Composite score. The BRIEF provides separate normative tables for both the parent and teacher forms with *t* scores, percentiles, and 90 percent confidence intervals for four developmental age groups by gender.

Normative data was collected from 1,419 parents and 720 teachers from rural, suburban, and urban areas in Maryland consistent with the 1999 U.S. Census estimates of socioeconomic status, ethnicity, and gender distribution. Internal consistency is good, ranging from .80 to .98. Reliabilities were similar across teacher and parents forms. All of the clinical scales and composites have high reliability except the initiate and shift scales, which tend to be the least reliable. Test-retest reliabilities were conducted on the parent form clinical and normative samples and the teacher normative sample and were reported in the mid to upper .80s. Interrater reliabilities for the parent and teacher raters were moderate ($r = .50$ or below). Divergent validity is reported as adequate; however, convergent validity was difficult to assess as there are few available measures that examine metacognitive functioning.

Reviewers found the materials easy to use for parents, teachers, and test administrators. The protocols are arranged in an efficient manner and are attractive. The rating scales are easy to score by hand, and examiners have the option of purchasing a computer-scoring program. The manual also includes six case illustrations that are helpful guides to interpretation. One problem is the lack of information regarding interpretation of the BRIEF. Three levels of interpretation are possible: Global Executive Composite (child's executive dysfunction level), Behavioral Regulation Index (child's ability to switch set), and Metacognition Index (initiate, plan, organize, and sustain future oriented problem solving). It is important to note that the manual does not note how the sites and participants in the pilot were chosen, why more fathers were not solicited to participate, and why the sample was not larger. Additionally, the fact that the sample was only drawn from Maryland may affect the normative data.

REFERENCES

Gioia, G. A., & Isquith, P. K. (2004). Ecological assessment of executive function in traumatic brain injury. *Developmental Neuropsychology, 25,* 135–158.

Gioia, G. A., Isquith, P. K., Guy, S. C., & Kenworthy, L. (2000). Test review: Behavior Rating Inventory of Executive Function. *Child Neuropsychology, 3,* 235–238.

Gioia, G. A., Isquith, P. K., & Kenworthy, L. (2000). *BRIEF: Behavior Rating Inventory of Executive Functions.* Lutz, FL: PAR.

Gioia, G. A., Isquith, P. K., Retzlaff, P. D., & Espy, K. A. (2004). Confirmatory factor analysis of the Behavior Rating Inventory of Executive Function (BRIEF) in a clinical sample. *Child Neuropsychology, 8,* 249–57.

Mahone, E. M., Cirino, P. T., Cutting, L. E., Cerrone, P. M., Hagelthorn, K. M., Hiemenz, J. R., et al. (2002). Validity of the behavior rating inventory of executive function in children with ADHD and/or Tourette's Syndrome. *Archives Clinical Neuropsychology, 17,* 643–662.

Plake, B. S., Impara, J. C., & Spies, R. A. (Eds.). (2003). *The fifteenth mental measurements yearbook* (pp. 1412–1415). Lincoln, NE: Buros Institute of Mental Measurements.

RON DUMONT
Fairleigh Dickinson University

JOHN O. WILLIS
Rivier College

BEHAVIORAL ASSESSMENT

Behavioral assessment is an important component of evaluation and intervention planning by addressing a wide range of referral questions. Behavioral data can measure numerous actions that directly impede learning, such as withdrawal, defiance, or aggression. However, even when the referral concern is primarily academic rather than behavioral, behavioral components can indirectly effect learning ability (e.g., frustration tolerance, test anxiety, study habits). In fact, the Individuals with Disabilities Education Improvement Act of 2004 recommends classroom behavioral observations as a component of an assessment.

Various behavioral assessment methods may be used, including record reviews, interviewing, observations, rating scales, and adaptive behavior measures. Record reviews can yield insight on past trauma (e.g., abuse), major life-changing events (e.g., custody issues), school discipline actions, criminal history (e.g., adjudicated youth programs), and school attendance or achievement patterns. Interviewing parents, teachers, other caregivers, and students can provide information on medical concerns, family interaction patterns, events that precipitated behaviors, support networks, and student strengths outside of academics (e.g., altruistic deeds). An emphasis on identifying student strengths and positive behaviors can aid in designing strength-based interventions. When deriving hypotheses from interview information, one should consider the broader context of ethnic, cultural, and socioeconomic factors. Awareness of diversity issues can aid school personnel in better understanding children's behaviors and response styles (Kamphaus & Frick, 2000). Strengths of record review and interviewing techniques include information on past behavior patterns, perceptions, feelings, and home interaction styles. Limitations include lack of context for recorded events and possible weaknesses in children's self-perceptions or parental reporting bias.

Behavioral difficulties can be the result of complex interactions between risk factors, personality, academic frustrations, and environmental variables that reinforce behaviors (Evans et al., 2005; Frick, 1998; Mash & Barkley, 2003). Therefore, observational data often are crucial in behavioral assessments. The first step in behavioral observation is defining the behaviors to be monitored (e.g., withdrawn behaviors include diverting eye contact, self-isolation, not responding to direct questions). Observational data may be quantified to provide frequency, duration, latency, intensity, and time-of-day information. These data can be used to measure intervention efficacy by providing a baseline comparison for pre- and postintervention behavior frequency.

Observational data in the form of narrative recordings and anecdotal notes can be used to document children's verbal interactions and surrounding events in an effort to identify antecedent and consequent conditions that may impact behaviors. Knowledge of preceding events and outcomes for behaviors can provide data for functional analysis procedures that include changing antecedents or consequences to test hypotheses about their role in sustaining particular behaviors (Kaplan & Carter, 1995). An ecological approach to observation reviews physical, instructional, and interaction elements (e.g., noisy equipment, unclear rule expectations) in the classroom (Sattler, 2002). Based on ecological data, interventions may focus on implementing environment changes or providing positive behavioral supports rather than academic remediation. Strengths of observational methods include their providing insights on antecedents and consequences of behaviors, revealing environmental variables, and frequency and duration data. Their limitations include providing no information on internal thoughts or moods, observer bias, and reactivity if the person is aware of being observed.

Behavior rating scales can provide an additional measure that incorporates teachers, parents, and student self-report data on the same behaviors (e.g., Behavior Assessment System for Children–II, Child Behavior Checklist). Rating scales may measure behaviors across a continuum, from internalizing to externalizing, and provide national norms that indicate at-risk and clinically maladaptive ranges. When omnibus rating scales indicate areas of significant concern, practitioners also may administer single construct rating scales that offer more in-depth information on specific symptoms (e.g., for depression, use the Children's Depression Inventory). Strengths of rating scales include cross-reference comparisons of multiple opinions and well-established national norms. Limitations include forms of rater bias and only modest correlations between various informant ratings (Kamphaus & Frick, 2000).

Adaptive scales also can provide additional objective measures of children's behavior in domains not typically addressed by behavior ratings scales. These skills include one's ability to function independently and to meet personal and social responsibility competencies (Sattler, 2002). Some instruments (e.g., Adaptive Behavior Assessment System–

II) include norm references for skill areas recommended from the American Association of Mental Retardation such as communication, home or school daily living, self-care, social interaction, health and safety, and work behaviors (Harrison & Oakland, 2003; Rust & Wallace, 2004). Other instruments (e.g., Battelle Developmental Inventory) can provide criterion-referenced information on skill hierarchies (Sattler, 2002). Adaptive behavior evaluation is required when diagnosing Mental Retardation. Additionally, these data can provide valuable insight as part of behavioral assessment batteries for children without cognitive deficits (e.g., lack of communication skills in aggressive children). Strengths of adaptive scales include insight for behavioral functioning at home and in the community as well as objective norm comparison of skills with other children the same age. Limitations include possible informant response distortions or limited ability to provide accurate answers and estimations of some behaviors not directly observed (Kamphaus & Frick, 2000; Sattler, 2002).

Because each assessment method has both strengths and limitations, best-practices in assessment warrant including multiple sources of data when making decisions for children with consideration for the validity and reliability of each measure (American Educational Research Association, 1999). Behavioral assessment that includes a broad spectrum of both quantitative and qualitative data can provide valuable insight to school personnel and students. Successful intervention for more extensive and serious behavioral difficulties can require a comprehensive behavioral assessment that requires a collaborative effort of teachers, parents, students, school psychologists, counselors, and social workers (Mash & Barkley, 2003).

REFERENCES

American Educational Research Association. (1999). *Standards for educational and psychological testing.* Washington, DC: Author.

Evans, D. L., Foa, E. B., Gur, R. E., Hendin, H., O'Brien, C. P., Seligman, M. E., et al. (Eds.). (2005). *Treating and preventing adolescent mental health disorders: What we know and what we don't know.* New York: Oxford Press.

Frick, P. J. (1998). *Conduct Disorders and severe antisocial behavior.* New York: Plenum Press.

Harrison, P. L., & Oakland, T. (2003). *Adaptive Behavior Assessment System* (2nd ed.). San Antonio, TX: Harcourt Assessment.

Individuals with Disabilities Education Improvement Act of 2004. 20 U.S.C. § 1400 et seq.

Kamphaus, R. W., & Frick, P. J. (2000). *Clinical assessment of child and adolescent personality and behavior.* Needham Heights, MA: Allyn & Bacon.

Kaplan, J. S., & Carter, J. (1995). *Beyond behavior modification: A cognitive-behavioral approach to behavior management in the school.* Austin, TX: PRO-ED.

Mash, E. J., & Barkley, R. A. (Eds.). (2003). *Child psychopathology* (2nd ed.). New York: Guilford.

Rust, J. O., & Wallace, M. A. (2004). Test review: Adaptive Behavior Assessment System (2nd ed.). *Journal of Psychoeducational Assessment, 22,* 367–373.

Sattler, J. M. (2002). *Assessment of children: Behavioral and clinical applications* (4th ed.). La Mesa, CA: Author.

DIANA JOYCE
University of Florida

BEHAVIOR ASSESSMENT SYSTEM FOR CHILDREN–2

BEHAVIOR DISORDERS

BEHAVIORAL CONSULTATION

Over the last three decades, consultation has become an increasingly important tool in the provision of psychological services to children and youths in educational settings (Meacham & Peckham, 1978; Ramage, 1979). School-based consultation may be rendered from a variety of theoretical perspectives. These include mental health consultation, which is linked to psychodynamic theories of personality (Caplan, 1970), organization development consultation (Schmuck, 1982), which has its origins in social psychological theory strongly influenced by the Lewinian perspective, and behavioral consultation, which is linked to behavioral theory (Bandura, 1977; Skinner, 1953). The following discussion describes the behavioral approach to consultation services.

There are no characteristics that uniquely define consultation. Consequently, there are no features that uniquely characterize behavioral consultation. Nonetheless, there are features that tend to be associated with consultation services. Perhaps the most widely shared attribute of consultation activities is that they generally involve indirect service (Bergan, 1977). Typically, service is rendered by a consultant (e.g., psychologist) to a consultee (e.g., teacher), who in turn provides services to one or more clients (e.g., students). The indirect approach to service characteristic of consultation is generally regarded as a major advantage of this form of service delivery. A consultant providing services to a number of consultees can bring expertise to many more clients than could be served by a direct-service approach. There is a multiplier effect in which the skills of the consultant can be brought to bear on client problems without the extensive time commitment required when the consultant provides direct services to the client.

A second attribute of consultation is that it is generally a problem-solving venture in which the consultant provides expert advice related to a problem presented by the consultee (Bergan, 1977). The consultant usually elicits a description of the problem from the consultee, assists in the development of a plan to solve the problem, and participates in an evaluation to determine the extent to which the problem has been solved.

A third feature of consultation is that it is typically assumed to involve a collegial relationship between the consultant and the consultee (Bergan, 1977). This means that the consultant has no direct authority over the consultee and the consultee has no direct authority over the consultant. Rather, each has an area of professional responsibility with respect to the services provided to the client. The consultant serves as an adviser. The consultee uses consultant advice in making and implementing decisions aimed at solving the problem(s) presented in consultation.

The three attributes discussed in the preceding paragraphs are not unique to behavioral consultation. Yet, they are a part of consultation rendered from a behavioral perspective. What distinguishes behavioral consultation from other varieties of consultation is the use of a behavioral perspective in providing consultation services (Bergan, 1977; Feld, Bergan, & Stone, 1984). The behavioral viewpoint affects consultation in three important ways. First, it dictates that problems presented in consultation be conceptualized from a behavioral perspective. Second, it calls for the use of behavioral principles in designing interventions to solve problems. Third, it assumes an empirical approach to determining the effectiveness of consultation interventions.

Consultation services are generally rendered in a series of stages, each of which is designed to address a particular aspect of the problem-solving endeavor. Four stages are generally recognized in consultation (Bergan, 1977; Dorr, 1979; Goodwin & Coates, 1976; Tombari & Davis, 1979). They are (1) problem identification, (2) problem analysis, (3) plan implementation, and (4) problem evaluation.

Problem identification sets the direction that consultation will take. Within the behavioral perspective, a problem is defined in terms of a discrepancy between observed behavior and desired behavior. The problem is to eliminate the discrepancy. Determining the existence of a discrepancy between observed and desired behavior requires that the concerns communicated by the consultee be expressed in behavioral terms. During problem identification, the consultant assists the consultee to describe current client functioning and desired functioning in terms of current behaviors and desired behaviors. Data are generally collected to document the status of current behavior. A problem exists if the data reveal a difference between current and desired behavior that the consultee regards as a significant discrepancy.

Problem analysis follows problem identification. During this stage of consultation, the factors that may be influencing client behaviors of concern are identified and a plan is formulated to effect desired changes in behaviors. Behavioral principles are heavily relied on in determining influences on behavior. Problem analysis generally begins with the specification of antecedent and consequent environmental conditions that may be affecting behavior. However, client skills and behavioral patterns may also be the subject of analysis (Piersel, 1985). After hypothesized influences on client behavior have been identified, a plan is formulated to change client behavior. The consultant is generally responsible for specifying the strategies that may be used to achieve behavior change. However, the consultee often plays a major role in identifying specific tactics that may be useful in implementing a plan. For example, a consultant may determine that positive reinforcement may be useful in increasing a particular behavior of concern to the consultee. The consultee may then identify the type of reinforcement to be used with the behavior.

After a suitable plan has been formulated, it is implemented. Implementation is generally the responsibility of the consultee. However, the consultee may direct an implementation effort in which others actually carry out the plan. For instance, a teacher may direct a peer tutoring program designed to increase the reading skills of a group of children. The principal role of the consultant during implementation is one of monitoring what is occurring and of assisting the consultee to make minor revisions in the plan in those instances in which the plan is not working as expected.

The final stage in consultation is problem evaluation. During this phase of consultation, the consultant and the consultee determine the extent to which the goals of consultation have been achieved and the extent to which the plan implemented to attain goals has been effective. Evaluation data guide the course of consultation. If the goals of consultation have been achieved, a new problem may be identified or services may terminate. If the goals of consultation have not been achieved, consultation generally returns to problem analysis.

Behavioral consultation has been most widely applied in solving learning and/or adjustment problems manifested by children and youths in educational settings (Bergan, 1977). In the typical case, services are directed toward one client (e.g., a student). However, there have been many applications involving groups. For example, consultation may be used to modify the behavior of all of the children in a class (Bergan, 1977). It has also been suggested that behavioral consultation could be useful for organization development including all of the individuals associated with an educational setting (Piersel, 1985). However, applications of behavioral consultation for this purpose are lacking.

Piersel (1985) has outlined procedures for using behavioral consultation in special education programs. He points out that consultation is ideally suited to meeting the goal of providing students eligible for special services with a program that reflects the least restrictive alternative environment for rendering services. Piersel indicates that consultation should begin with an attempt to solve problems manifested by the child in the regular classroom environment. When evidence is gathered indicating that a solution cannot be achieved in the classroom, placement in a special program is considered. It is at this point that assessment and case conferences with the family and other professionals occur.

There is a large body of research documenting the effectiveness of behavioral consultation (Feld et al., 1984). Research on the effectiveness of behavioral consultation is of two types. The first involves studies of the application of behavioral principles in consultation to achieve changes in behavior. Research of this kind has shown the behavioral approach to be effective in remediating a large variety of behavioral and academic problems (Bergan & Tombari, 1976; Conoley & Conoley, 1982; Medway, 1979; Medway & Forman, 1980).

The second body of research on the effectiveness of the behavioral approach compares the effectiveness of behavioral consultation with that of other forms of service. Many of the comparative studies have methodological flaws (Medway, 1979) and therefore results and generalization are inconclusive.

Recent developments in behavioral consultation focus on collaborative arrangements between parents of special education students and educators. Specific emphasis has been placed on the cultural-ethnic lifestyle considerations (Fine & Gardner, 1994).

REFERENCES

Bandura, A. (1977). *Social learning.* Englewood Cliffs, NJ: Prentice Hall.

Bergan, J. R. (1977). *Behavioral consultation.* Columbus, OH: Merrill.

Bergan, J. R., & Tombari, M. L. (1976). Consultant skill and efficiency and the implementation of outcomes of consultation. *Journal of School Psychology, 14,* 3–13.

Caplan, G. (1970). *The theory and practice of mental health consultation.* New York: Basic Books.

Conoley, J. C., & Conoley, C. W. (1982). The effects of two conditions of client-centered consultation on student teacher problem descriptions and remedial plans. *Journal of School Psychology, 20,* 323–328.

Dorr, D. (1979). Psychological consulting in the schools. In J. J. Platt & R. J. Wicks (Eds.), *The psychological consultant.* New York: Grune & Stratton.

Feld, J. D., Bergan, J. R., & Stone, C. A. (1984). Behavioral approaches to school based consultation: Current status and future directions. In C. A. Maher (Ed.), *Behavioral approaches to providing educational services in schools.* Hillsdale, NJ: Erlbaum.

Fine, M. J., & Gardner, A. (1994). Collaborative consultation with families of children with special needs: Why bother? *Journal of Educational and Psychological Consultation, 5,* 283–308.

Goodwin, D. L., & Coates, T. J. (1976). *Helping students help themselves.* Englewood Cliffs, NJ: Prentice Hall.

Meacham, M. L., & Peckham, P. D. (1978). School psychologists at three-quarters century: Congruence between training, practice, preferred role and competence. *Journal of School Psychology, 16,* 195–206.

Medway, F. J. (1979). How effective is school consultation: A review of recent research. *Journal of School Psychology, 17,* 275–282.

Medway, F. J., & Forman, S. G. (1980). Psychologists' and teachers' reactions to mental health and behavioral school consultation. *Journal of School Psychology, 18,* 338–348.

Piersel, W. C. (1985). Behavioral consultation: An approach to problem solving in educational settings. In J. R. Bergan (Ed.), *School psychology in contemporary society.* Columbus, OH: Merrill.

Ramage, J. C. (1979). National survey of school psychologists: Update. *School Psychology Digest, 8,* 153–161.

Schmuck, R. A. (1982). Organizational development in the schools. In C. R. Reynolds & T. B. Gutkin (Eds.), *The handbook of school psychology.* New York: Wiley.

Skinner, B. F. (1953). *Science and human behavior.* New York: Macmillan.

Tombari, M. L., & Davis, R. A. (1979). Behavioral consultation. In G. D. Phye & D. J. Reschly (Eds.), *School psychology: Perspectives and issues.* New York: Academic.

JOHN R. BERGAN
University of Arizona

BEHAVIORAL ASSESSMENT
CONSULTATION
CONSULTATION, MENTAL HEALTH

BEHAVIORAL DEFICIT

The terminology associated with behavioral deficit has become confused as a result of various incomplete usages. The original usage was associated with the 1961 American Association on Mental Retardation inclusion of adaptive behavior in their definition of mental retardation. Adaptive behavior implies that many educational, psychological, sociological, and biological influences interact on the child, affecting function and performance. Principally, it is a term designed to offset the dependence the public schools, mental health agencies, and social welfare institutions had placed on measured intelligence.

The original concept was closely associated with developmental disabilities. Work in the late 1950s, and early 1960s with children with disabilities resulted in a description of developmental lag, placing the emphasis for the disability on irregular test protocols and subtest patterns clinically thought to reflect possible neurological insult. The search had begun by psychoeducational researchers to specify the nature of these so-called behavioral deficits through the use of test and subtest patterns. In 1966, S. D. Clements placed into motion, through the committee he chaired on minimal neurological impairment, the search for neurological damage as an explanation of specific learning disabilities.

Tests designed to measure visual and auditory perceptual, perceptual-motor, and other cognitive abilities began to flood the market. The term specific added to learning disabilities accentuated that a deficit in one or more of the psychological processes was accountable for the condition.

In 1974, Gleason and Haring provided the first general behavioral definition of learning disabilities and in so doing used the term behavioral deficit as the principal construct associated with the concept learning disabilities: "We define a learning disability as a behavioral deficit almost always associated with academic performance and that can be remediated by precise, individualized instructional programming" (p. 226).

There are two major issues that surround the construct of behavioral deficits. The first is the possibility or utility of cognitive skills being broken into specific component parts. It should be remembered that all assumed cognitive behaviors are named, usually after a test or subtest designed to measure them. They are not occurrences in nature that are directly observable. The second issue is the reliability of most tests designed to ascertain or describe a basic behavior and therefore illustrate a behavioral deficit. As the reliability decreases, so does the validity.

A behavioral deficit then is a concept suggesting that human abilities are not all the same, and in some cases fall to a deficit level. Operationally defining a deficit has not been well done through the use of tests or subtests in terms of when a deficit statistically or clinically exists. Therefore, while the concept itself has driven several major thrusts (both diagnostic and treatment), including the term developmental disability to some degree, and theoretically is responsible for describing learning disability, it remains an incomplete term, less than fully developed by those who use it on a clinical basis.

REFERENCES

Clements, S. D. (1966). *Task force I: Minimal brain dysfunction in children. Monograph No. 3.* Washington, DC: U.S. Government Printing Office.

Gleason, C., & Haring, N. (1974). Learning disabilities. In N. G. Haring (Ed.), *Behavior of exceptional children* (pp. 245–295). Columbus, OH: Merrill.

DAVID A. SABATINO
*West Virginia College of
Graduate Studies*

ABILITY TRAINING, EARLY EFFORTS IN
BEHAVIORAL OBJECTIVES

BEHAVIORAL DISORDERS, JOURNAL OF

The *Journal of Behavioral Disorders* is the official journal of the Council for Children with Behavioral Disorders

(CCBD) of the Council for Exceptional Children. Founded in 1975, *Behavioral Disorders* serves as a resource for those professionals interested in the education and treatment of behaviorally disordered children and youth.

The journal, with a quarterly distribution to the 8,400 members of CCBD and hundreds of individual and institutional subscribers, was developed under the editorships of Albert Fink of Indiana University (1975–1978), Denzil Edge of the University of Louisville (1978–1981), and Robert B. Rutherford, Jr., of Arizona State University (1981–1987) into a forum for the publication of manuscripts derived from documented thought and empirical evidence. These data-based articles are presented in several forms: experimental research (either original or replications), research and practice reviews and analyses, program or procedure descriptions, and scholarly reviews of texts, films, and other media. The editorial process of the journal is designed to thoroughly and professionally analyze submitted manuscripts in terms of originality, relevance of topic, importance of the findings or concepts, content organization, and documentation.

Historically, *Behavioral Disorders* evolved from an early dependence on cosponsored thematic issues and reliance on solicited manuscripts to an open journal relying on unsolicited manuscripts submitted by professionals in the field. *Behavioral Disorders* has contributed significantly to the professional literature on behavioral disorders of children and youths.

ROBERT B. RUTHERFORD, JR.
Arizona State University

BEHAVIORAL AND EMOTIONAL RATING SCALE

The Behavioral and Emotional Rating Scale: A Strength-Based Approach to Assessment (BERS; Epstein & Sharma, 1998) is an individually administered 52-item scale that assesses children's (ages 5:0 through 18:11) emotional and behavioral strengths in five factor-analytically derived subscales. The first subscale, Interpersonal Strengths (e.g., "uses anger management skills," 15 items), assesses a child's ability to control emotions or behavior in a social situation. The second subscale, Family Involvement (e.g., "participates in family activities," 10 items), focuses on a child's participation and relationship with his or her family. The third subscale, Intrapersonal Strengths (e.g., "demonstrates a sense of humor," 11 items), assesses a child's outlook on his or her competence and accomplishments. Subscale four, School Functioning (e.g., "completes homework regularly," 9 items), focuses on a child's competence in school and classroom tasks. The fifth subscale, Affective Strengths (e.g., "asks for help," 7 items), addresses a child's ability to express feelings toward others and to accept affection from others.

A teacher, caregiver, or any adult knowledgeable about the child can complete the BERS although there is only one form. The adult reads a statement (e.g., "participates in family activities") and chooses the number on a Likert-type scale from 0 to 3 (0 = not at all like the child; 1 = not much like the child; 2 = like the child; 3 = very much like the child) that best represents the child's emotions or behaviors in the past 3 months. Respondents are also asked to complete eight open-ended questions about the child's personal and situational resiliencies and protective factors (e.g., "What are the child's favorite hobbies or activities?" "Who is this child's favorite teacher?"). Information obtained from the BERS is useful in the development of individualized education programs (IEPs), treatment or intervention planning, and evaluation of a program or treatment plan.

Raw scores from the five subscales can be converted to percentile ranks and to standard scores with a mean of 10 and a standard deviation of 3. Summing the standard scores of the five subscales and converting the sum into a quotient derives an overall "Strength Quotient" with a mean of 100 and a standard deviation of 15.

The BERS was normed on students between the ages of 5:0 and 18:11 using data collected from February to November 1996. Separate norms were produced for 2,176 students without disabilities and 861 students with emotional and behavioral disorders. The manual reports demographics of this standardization sample based on age, gender, geographic location, race, ethnicity, and socioeconomic status. Based on these data, separate male and female norms for children without disabilities and separate male and female norms for children with emotional and behavioral disorders were calculated. Although the BERS covers the age range of 5 to 18, there are no separate age-based norm tables in the manual.

The interrater reliability of the BERS was tested on pairs of teachers and classroom aides who were asked to complete the BERS on 96 students previously diagnosed with emotional or behavioral disorders. Correlations between the two raters on the subscale and overall BERS scores were between .83 and .98. Content sampling revealed that items on the BERS correlate above .80, making it a highly reliable scale. The test-retest reliability was tested on special education teachers who were asked to complete the BERS on 10 of their students and then, approximately 2 weeks later, again asked to complete the BERS on the same students. Correlations between the two sets of ratings on the subscale and overall BERS scores were between .85 and .99. Evidence for criterion validity is moderate to high based on the relationship between the BERS and the Teacher Report Form (Achenbach, 1991), the Self-Perception Profile for Children (Harter, 1985), and the Walker-McConnell Scale of Social Competence and School Adjustment (Walker & McConnell, 1988). Construct validity was confirmed through statistically different scores on the mean scores of the nondisordered and disordered children used to norm the scale.

REFERENCES

Achenbach, T. M. (1991). *Manual for the Teacher Report Form and 1991 profile.* Burlington: University of Vermont, Department of Psychiatry.

Dumont, R., & Rauch, M. (2003). Test review: Behavioral and Emotional Rating Scale by M. Epstein & J. Sharma (PRO-ED, 1998). *NASP Communiqué, 28,* article 7. Retrieved May 22, 2004, from www.nasponline.org/publications/cq287Test.html

Epstein, M. H. (1998). Assessing the emotional and behavioral strengths of children. *Reclaiming Children and Youth, 6,* 250–252.

Epstein, M. H., Harniss, M. K., Pearson, N., & Ryder, G. (1999). The Behavioral and Emotional Rating Scale: Test-retest and inter-rater reliability. *Journal of Child and Family Studies, 8,* 319–327.

Epstein, M. H., & Sharma, J. (1998). *Behavioral and Emotional Rating Scale: A strength based approach to assessment.* Austin, TX: PRO-ED.

Friedman, P., Friedman, K. A., & Weaver, V. (2003). Strength-based assessment of African-American adolescents with behavioral disorders. *Perceptual & Motor Skills, 96,* 667–673.

Harter, S. (1985). *Manual for the Self-Perception Profile for Children.* Denver, CO: University of Denver.

Quay, H., & Peterson, D. R. (1996). *Revised Behavior Problem Checklist: Professional manual.* Odessa, FL: Psychological Assessment Resources.

Trout, A. L., Ryan, J. B., & La Vigne, S. P. (2003). Behavioral and Emotional Rating Scale: Two studies of convergent validity. *Journal of Child and Family Studies, 12,* 399–410.

Walker, H. M., & McConnell, S. R. (1988). *Manual for the Walker-McConnell Scale of Social Competence and School Adjustment.* Austin, TX: PRO-ED.

RON DUMONT
Fairleigh Dickinson University

JOHN O. WILLIS
Rivier College

BEHAVIORAL MOMENTUM

Behavioral momentum is a metaphor applied to the observation that human (and animal) free-operant behavior possesses *momentum* under steady-state conditions of reinforcement and is resistant to change when the behavior experiences a change in the interval- or ratio-schedule of reinforcement (Mace et al., 1988; Nevin, 1988; Nevin, Mandell, & Atak, 1983). Steady-state conditions are synonymous with free-operant reinforcement where the individual is free to complete one response, receive reinforcement from the environment, and then go on to freely emit another response with the goal of receiving additional reinforcement. This is in contrast to more restricted discrete-trial learning situations where response emission is controlled by someone (or something) else other than the individual (e.g., a special education teacher teaching math to students in the learning center).

Nevin's observation that persistent, free-operant behavior possesses momentum was borne out of his experimental resistance-to-change research in the laboratory with pigeons, rats, and monkeys. In order to better communicate these observations, Newtonian mechanics was used as an analogy to help explain and understand the phenomenon, especially as it relates to human behavior in applied settings (Nevin et al., 1983). The Newtonian model describes momentum as the product of the velocity and mass of a moving body. The greater the mass of that moving body, the less impact any external force will have in altering its velocity. In relation to human learning, behavioral momentum can be thought of as the product of resistance to change (mass) and baseline response rate (velocity; Nevin, 1988). Behavioral *mass* is shaped by Pavlovian stimulus-reinforcer contingencies, while *velocity* of behavior is shaped by response-reinforcer contingencies (Plaud & Gaither, 1996). In theory, then, newly learned behavior moving at a particularly high velocity and mass will persist, or resist change, in the face of obstacles or interventions such as when reinforcement is no longer delivered for an emitted response (i.e., extinction procedures) or perhaps when a more demanding response is required of the person. Embedded within the behavioral momentum paradigm are issues related to the partial reinforcement effect, continuous reinforcement, establishing operations, and Herrnstein's matching law; however, due to space limitations, the reader is directed to the work of Brandon and Houlihan (1997), Houlihan and Brandon (1996), Nevin (1988), Nevin (1996), Plaud and Gaither (1996), and Strand (2000), for further independent study and analysis.

The first applied behavioral momentum research study with human subjects began with Mace and colleagues (1988) in which a series of three to five high-probability compliance requests (i.e., high-*p* requests) were issued to subjects with Mental Retardation just prior to the delivery of a low-probability compliance request (i.e., low-*p* request) the subject(s) rarely complied with. Mace et al. (1988) demonstrated that when a series of high-*p* requests are presented to these subjects, dramatic increases in compliance to low-*p* requests occur. Mace et al.'s (1988) initial study spawned a program of research in the field of applied behavior analysis aimed at using the behavioral momentum strategy to increase the frequency of compliance with individuals in clinical or applied contexts. Successful replications of behavioral momentum have since occurred across a variety of populations including children with autism, individuals with self-injurious behavior, children with social skills deficits, individuals noncompliant with their medical regimens, and adult undergraduate students (Brandon & Houlihan, 1997; Plaud & Gaither, 1996). Behavioral momentum techniques have improved a variety of problematic behaviors such as decreasing vomiting, aggression, and stereotypic touching and increasing attempts to do difficult tasks and initiating social contacts (Strand, 2000). The apparent success of behavioral momentum techniques led Davis and Brady (1993) to suggest that the intervention should be utilized to improve language skills, motor skills, academic skills, and self-help skills. Strand (2000) also comments that behavioral momentum is a relevant heuristic for behavioral family therapy involving conduct disordered children, especially for increasing highly reinforcing reciprocal interactions between parents and their children and for helping to explain the effectiveness of parental *scaffolding* techniques designed to increase child social and cognitive skills beyond their present level of performance.

Although behavioral momentum research has enjoyed popularity and success, it has not been without its limitations and controversies. For example, while behavioral momentum is an interesting use of a metaphor to help explain and predict behavioral compliance, the procedures found in the high-*p* technique are not new to the experimental analysis of behavior. In fact, Houlihan and Brandon (1996), and Brandon and Houlihan (1997) trace functionally similar procedures in the behavioral compliance literature as far back as Weiss's (1934) study of factors affecting preschool children's compliance to commands and are concerned by the current tendency of researchers to cite pre-Nevin (i.e., before 1983) studies as evidence for behavioral momentum. Disquieting, according to Houlihan and Brandon (1996), is the fact that behavioral momentum bears a formal resemblance to Hull and Spence's *habit strength* concept that explained the strength of behavior as being based upon frequent stimulus-response pairings (i.e., drive) and motivation to engage in behavior based upon reinforcement (i.e., incentive).

Houlihan and Brandon (1997) maintain that there has been an overextension of the behavioral momentum metaphor from the experimental animal literature to compliance research with human subjects, promoting the idea that the high-*p* sequence itself is the source of reinforcement responsible for behavioral change. What Houlihan and Brandon have pointed out (among other things) is that the high-*p* process may in fact be applying stimulus control and manipulating an establishing condition in which the person presenting the high-*p* prompts becomes the critical source of reinforcement, not the high-*p* prompt procedure itself. Such a possibility weakens the argument that what is in operation is *behavioral momentum,* but rather a *concurrent chain* schedule of reinforcement where two (or more) concurrently available sources of reinforcement exist for the subject to choose from. When using a high-*p* prompt strategy as one of the concurrent chains to increase the likelihood of compliance, the procedure functions as an *establishing operation* whereby all compliance behaviors reinforced by a therapist or teacher potentially compete against other concurrently available chains of reinforcement (see Brandon & Houlihan, 1997, for a fuller explanation).

Although Houlihan and Brandon (1996) and Brandon and Houlihan (1997) are concerned about researchers borrowing a metaphor from physics and applying it beyond its applicable boundaries with human behavior in applied settings, they acknowledge that behavioral momentum strategies are effective in increasing the frequency of behavior that are resistant to other conventional behavioral approaches. As such, the high-*p* procedure has demonstrated its utility and social validity. Research still needs to continue on its application and generalization beyond problems of noncompliance as well as investigate whether practitioners can effectively implement the strategy on their own in school or clinic settings; this would help determine if the efficacy of the high-*p* strategy is due to researcher effects or the potency and simplicity of the high-*p* strategy itself. Finally, behavioral momentum should be involved in analyzing more highly persistent free-operant behaviors such as gambling, smoking, or other health-related problem behaviors that are difficult to bring under stimulus control and decrease in incidence and prevalence (Brandon & Houlihan, 1997).

REFERENCES

Brandon, P. K., & Houlihan, D. (1997). Applying behavioral theory to practice: An examination of the behavioral momentum metaphor. *Behavioral Interventions, 12,* 113–131.

Davis, C. A., & Brady, M. P. (1993). Expanding the utility of behavioral momentum with young children: Where we've been, where we need to go. *Journal of Early Intervention, 17,* 211–223.

Houlihan, D., & Brandon, P. K. (1996). Compliant in a moment: A commentary on Nevin. *Journal of Applied Behavior Analysis, 29,* 549–555.

Mace, F. C., Hock, M. L., Lalli, J. S., West, B. J., Belfiore, P., Pinter, E., et al. (1988). Behavioral momentum in the treatment of noncompliance. *Journal of Applied Behavior Analysis, 21,* 123–141.

Nevin, J. A. (1988). Behavioral momentum and the partial reinforcement effect. *Psychological Bulletin, 103,* 44–56.

Nevin, J. A. (1996). The momentum of compliance. *Journal of Applied Behavior Analysis, 29,* 535–547.

Nevin, J. A., Mandell, C., & Atak, J. R. (1983). The analysis of behavioral momentum. *Journal of the Experimental Analysis of Behavior, 39,* 49–59.

Plaud, J. J., & Gaither, G. A. (1996). Human behavioral momentum: Implications for applied behavior analysis and therapy. *Journal of Behavior Therapy and Experimental Psychiatry, 27,* 139–148.

Strand, P. S. (2000). A modern behavioral perspective on child Conduct Disorder: Integrating behavioral momentum and matching theory. *Clinical Psychology Review, 20,* 593–615.

Weiss, L. A. (1934). An experimental investigation of certain factors involved in the preschool child's compliance with commands. *Journal of Child Welfare, 9,* 127–157.

Rollen C. Fowler
*Eugene 4J School District,
Eugene, Oregon*

APPLIED BEHAVIOR ANALYSIS
BEHAVIORAL ASSESSMENT

BEHAVIORAL OBJECTIVES

In the broadest sense, an objective is a statement of an aim or desired outcome. In an educational sense, an instructional objective may be a quantifiable and/or an observable academic or social achievement that specifies the enabling steps necessary to accomplish the objective in a stated period of time. All instructional or behavioral objectives must have observable or measurable outcomes. The difference between an instructional and a behavioral objective is the result to be achieved. The latter may be broader in scope and not confined to an educational effort; it may rather include a wide range of specified behavioral outcomes, for example, speech, language, perceptual development, motor training, and social skill development.

Behavioral objectives and instructional (teaching) objectives are frequently used interchangeably. While each impacts on the other, these two sets of objectives address two different performances. A behavioral objective focuses on any visible activity displayed by a learner (student). It has at its core the terminal behavior, or what the learner can demonstrate has been learned. An instructional objective may include the desired learner outcomes; it will specify the criteria acceptable for success in attaining that outcome, but it focuses on what will be taught and how it will be taught.

The purpose for developing behavioral objectives is to increase teaching efficiency by having educators and behavioral scientists determine what it is that will be learned, how it will be taught, what materials will be used, and the length of time within which it should be learned against a predetermined criteria or standard. Behavioral objectives become targets to which teachers can direct their instruction. In the process of instruction, their use requires educators to determine whether outcomes or observations of performance are being effectively and efficiently provided and creating an exactness for what is learned and how it is taught. Thus, a teaching methodology may be used for a specified amount of time under conditions that will permit the educator to judge the amount of progress being made. Mager (1962) notes, "An instructor will function in a fog of his own making until he knows what he wants his students to be able to do at the end of the instruction" (p. 2).

One of the most common points of confusion is between a course description (or what a course is about) and behavioral objectives (those specific, measurable, or observable performances a student will demonstrate at the completion of a course). Behavioral objectives must contain statements of concrete, measurable, or observable performances. In contrast, nonbehavioral goals are broad, abstract statements; they are not derived from previous observations or performance test data. They do not consider the skills necessary to enter into a next level of work. Nonbehavioral objectives are based on philosophy, ideology, and attitude, not the proficiency of task to be taught.

Popham and Baker (1970) note five different considerations necessary in the preparation and use of behavioral objectives. They are

1. *Systematic instructional decision making.* The use of behavioral objectives and the measured outcome to determine the most efficient method of instruction and how effective a specified method was in achieving an objective.

2. *Behavioral and/or educational objectives.* Determine what is to be accomplished, in what time period, and how it is to be accomplished.

3. *Selection of appropriate educational objectives.* Selecting significant and meaningful objectives is not easy; indeed, the task tends to be elusive and difficult. Educators must choose between the content (e.g., a math score, reading score from a formal or informal test, new words to be learned) and behaviors that are reasoned to influence the process of learning (e.g., time on task). Many times the two intersect and both become important elements in achieving a goal.

4. *Establishing performance standards.* One of the most difficult tasks is to set the criteria that denote whether a behavioral objective has been achieved successfully. There are no absolutes or clear rules for achieving that purpose. Some guidelines exist, such as the 80/80 criterion, which states that 80 percent of what has been taught must be demonstrated as a successfully learned outcome at an 80 percent minimal level of performance. Thus, if 10 words were taught, on measurement eight words must be learned before the next list of words is taught. Many educators use the 80 percent criterion as a minimal standard for instructional or subject matter content objectives. A large percentage of these same practitioners believe that a 90 percent criterion is useful with behavioral objectives. The establishment of performance standards addresses the sophistication or precision of the objective. While performance standards may largely be intuitive, a performance standard frequently addresses the knowledge the educator has of the learner.

5. *The curriculum rationale.* Educators spend their professional lives developing and implementing the curriculum. Countless hours are spent discussing curriculum questions each school year through school-district, building-level, and grade-level curriculum committees; in addition, thousands of curriculum guides exist in the United States. Combine those teacher-made curricula and guides with the innumerable commercially printed materials, and it would appear the curricular-planning process is complete. It is not. Despite all these efforts, 20 to 30 percent of schoolchildren fail academically or socially each year. Why?

A simple and very clear explanation is that most curricula are targeted at theoretical learners who are ready to learn and have no disabilities. An educator using a general curricular guide or commercial material is exclusively concerned with determining the objectives for the educational system, and not any one typical or atypical youth in that system. There are basically two kinds of decisions that educators must make. First, they must decide what the objectives (the ends) of the instructional system should be; second, they must decide on the procedures (the means) for accomplishing those objectives. This is, the curricular rationale for using behavioral or instructional objectives. This point becomes critical when individualization of instruction is sought. The use of behavioral objectives suggests the teacher is selecting and evaluating instructional procedures to accomplish those objectives. Thus teachers are engaged in instructional decision making. Herein resides the critical difference between using a curriculum and an instructional objectives process. Instructional objectives require stated levels of success, and measured and/or observable outcomes. In short, they are empirical solutions requiring data. Curricular structures are generally value-based.

How then are behavioral objectives established? Usually by determining a behavioral characteristic such as inattentiveness, or a score on a test, or a set of facts or things to be learned, for example, words or numbers. Behavioral objectives specify what it is to be learned and place a comfortable floor beneath the learner by dropping below what the learner can do initially and ending with what the learner can comfortably learn in a given period of time. A sound behavioral objective does not test the learner's limit, unless designed to do so for good reason.

A behavioral objective is one activity in a series of, or sequence of, activities to be learned. That sequence can become the curriculum. The principal reason for having many small, tightly sequenced steps in the curriculum is that learner performance is examined frequently. More important, the learner is provided with corrective feedback after every trial. That point is critical. What the learner knows does not fall to an assumption that cannot be proven. Behavioral or instructional objectives, once sequenced, become important interlocking steps. Because the ability of children to learn varies widely, particularly when materials change, each objective permits the individual student the necessary time on tasks.

The three major advantages of a behavioral objective are:

1. Students are not compared with others, but with themselves and the speed with which they may learn a given task comfortably.

2. Each tightly sequenced step is validated in the curricular process; all assumptions about learning rate or about what has been learned are rejected.

3. There is a starting point, something the student knows, and a stopping point, a task within the comfort level to be learned.

REFERENCES

Mager, R. F. (1962). *Preparing instructional objectives*. Palo Alto, CA: Fearon.

Popham, W. J., & Baker, E. (1970). *Establishing instructional goals*. Englewood Cliffs, NJ: Prentice Hall.

DAVID A. SABATINO
*West Virginia College of
Graduate Studies*

AGE-APPROPRIATE CURRICULUM
POSITIVE BEHAVIORAL SUPPORT
TEACHING STRATEGIES

BEHAVIORAL OBSERVATION

Behavior observation is at the core of behavioral assessment. Behavior observation is a procedure for categorizing motor and verbal behavior into an organized permanent record. A behavior observation system meets three criteria (Jones, Reid, & Patterson, 1974). These include "recording of behavioral events in their natural settings at the time they occur, not retrospectively; the use of trained impartial observer-coders, and descriptions of behaviors which (sic) require little if any inference by observers to code the events" (p. 46). Excluded from this definition are narrative recordings, anecdotal records, checklists and rating scales, and procedures that require a person to observe and record his or her own behavior.

Behavior observations occur in diverse settings and for numerous purposes. In educational settings, behavior observations are used for purposes of diagnosing individual students, planning an intervention to modify a pupil's behavior, evaluating interventions, consulting with teachers, and conducting research.

Although specific observational procedures and instruments vary in many important ways, they all require selectivity. The observation instrument structures the observer's attention to those selected aspects of behavior and the setting that are presumed to be most relevant to the purposes of the observation. Behavior occurs in a continuous stream, yet the observer must categorize behavior into objectively defined behavioral codes and encode it into an organized, permanent record. Care in defining what is to be observed is critical to measurable results. Narrative recordings and checklists can assist in selecting the most significant behavioral codes as well as the contextual, or environmental, events thought to be associated with the selected behaviors. Data on these antecedent and consequent events are useful in designing a plan for modifying the behaviors of concern.

To minimize observer subjectivity, the selected behaviors

are defined as objectively as possible. "Aggressive behavior" is not as objective a definition as "hits, shoves, grabs, and tackles." Although "aggressive behavior" can serve as useful shorthand in coding behavior, the clear specification of the behaviors encompassed by this term gives the observer an objective definition of aggression. When the behavioral codes are objectively defined, any two trained observers should agree on the presence or absence of a behavior. Behavior observations can occur in natural settings (e.g., classroom, peer group, or home) or in simulated or role playing settings.

Observational instruments vary in their degree of formality from homemade teacher-used instruments to published instruments requiring highly trained observers. Three major types of observational procedures are frequency recordings, duration recordings, and interval recordings (Barton & Ascione, 1984). In frequency recordings, the number of times a behavior occurs within the observational period is recorded. Frequency recordings are best suited to behaviors that have a discrete beginning and end, that last approximately the same amount of time each time they occur, and that do not occur so frequently that separating each occurrence becomes difficult. Hand raises, inappropriate noises, bed-wetting, and hitting are examples of frequency target behaviors. Figure 1 shows the results of a frequency recording of a disruptive student's behavior. Each block represents 1 minute, and each observational period lasts 15 minutes. The totals at the end of each row are the frequencies of that target behavior in a 15-minute period. Observations should continue over several days to obtain a reliable measure.

A duration recording is a direct measure of the amount of time an individual engages in the target behavior. Duration recordings are most appropriate for behaviors that have a clear beginning and ending and that last for more than a few seconds. If a child gets out of his or her seat and stays out

of the seat for periods of time ranging from 1 to 6 minutes, a duration count would indicate the percentage of time the child was out of the seat during the observational period.

In interval recordings, the occurrence or nonoccurrence of selected behaviors during a series of equal time intervals is recorded. Interval recording is recommended when several behaviors need to be observed, when behaviors occur at a high rate, or when behaviors do not have clear-cut beginnings and ends. There are several variations of interval recording procedures. Typically, some sort of signaling device (e.g., an audio timer or beeps on a prerecorded cassette) cues the observer to make a recording. The observer records which target behavior occurred during the preceding interval (usually 10 seconds).

Frequency, duration, and interval recordings can be adapted to a format that allows recording of selected antecedents and consequences of the behavioral codes. At the same time the observed child's behavior is coded, the antecedent and consequent circumstances are coded. Barton and Ascione (1984) provide examples of these different observational instruments.

Observational procedures are measurement procedures, and their reliability and validity need to be established. An important part of establishing reliability is determining the extent to which two observers agree in their use of the instrument while observing the same behavior and context. Recent advances in computer technology have supported reliable data collection by the use of software such as the Direct Observation Data System (DODS). This program saves time, standardizes input, and is preferred by educators over other methods (Johnson, Brady, & Larson, 1996). Validity issues include the relationship of the behavioral code to the referral problem (face validity) and the normality of the observed behavior. One way of determining whether a child's behavior in particular settings (e.g., a classroom) is atypical is to observe other children in the same settings. If the observer alternates between observing the target child and observing other children in a classroom, the observer will have a composite observation of the typical child to

Observer: Cathy Snow (consultant)
Date: November 5, 1985
Student: Julie
Circumstance: Math seatwork

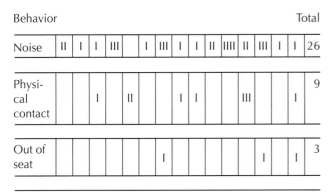

Figure 1 Frequency recording sheet

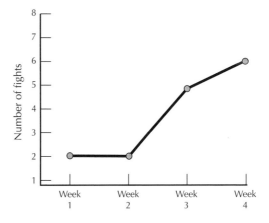

Figure 2 Behavioral chart

compare with the referred child. The observer must also be culturally competent so as to include the sociocultural context to the observation process.

REFERENCES

Barton, C. J., & Ascione, F. R. (1984). Direct observation. In T. H. Ollendick & M. Hersen (Eds.), *Child behavioral assessment* (pp. 166–194). New York: Pergamon.

Johnson, H., Brady, S., & Larson, E. (1996). A microcomputer-based system to facilitate direct observation data collection and assessment in inclusive settings. *Journal of Computing in Childhood Education, 7*, 3–4.

Jones, R. R., Reid, J. B., & Patterson, G. B. (1974). Naturalistic observation in clinical assessment. In P. McReynolds (Ed.), *Advances in psychological assessment.* San Francisco: Jossey-Bass.

JAN N. HUGHES
Texas A&M University

APPLIED BEHAVIOR ANALYSIS
BEHAVIOR THERAPY

BEHAVIORAL SUPPORT

See SUPPORT, BEHAVIORAL.

BEHAVIOR ANALYSIS, APPLIED

See APPLIED BEHAVIOR ANALYSIS.

BEHAVIORISM

The root of behaviorism is the term behavior, which may be defined as the set or universe of things an organism can do, or more simply, what an organism does. Typically, behavior is a term used in the fields of psychology or sociology to describe human or animal activity, but it is important to note that the term can be, and is, applied to a wide range of other things, including plants, simple microorganisms, machines, and even subatomic particles. The critical attribute is that the activities or functions of the organism must be observable and therefore capable of being measured. Just as it is possible to speak of the behavior of single organisms of varying complexity and composition, it is also possible to examine the behavior of organisms in groups. The empirical emphasis of the term behavior is especially prominent in the United States, where the term is associated with a particular school of psychology known as behaviorism. Behaviorism has its philosophical

roots in the radical empiricist traditions of early thinkers such as John Locke and David Hume in Europe and in the twentieth-century movement known as logical positivism. The common thread philosophically is that behavior may be (and, for some, must be) understood purely as a lawful phenomenon in itself, without reference to intervening variables such as will, mind, volition, or motivation, which purport to explain why behavior occurs.

Early in the twentieth century, the young discipline of psychology was quite concerned with such concepts as will and mind, notably in the work of introspectionists such as Titchner. However, when Pavlov and his colleagues demonstrated that learning was a process whose parameters could be empirically specified and whose results could be reliably predicted, psychologists such as John Watson saw that human behavior could be studied in a simpler, more elegant way, as other sciences were being studied. Watson articulated his position as follows: "Psychology, as the behaviorist views it, is a purely objective, experimental branch of science which needs introspection as little as do the sciences of chemistry and physics. . . ." (1913, p. 176). Watson's fervent rejection of the idea of introspection, mental states, or any other nonempirical behavior analysis has earned him general recognition as the founder of behaviorism.

It remained for later thinkers, notably Edward L. Thorndike and B. F. Skinner, to refine and clearly articulate behaviorism. Watson had emphasized stimulus conditions (following Pavlov's respondent conditioning principles) in his work; the most famous example was his introduction of the fear of a white rat in a young boy (Watson & Rayner, 1920). Thorndike (1935), through his Law of Effect, and Skinner (1953), through his Principle of Reinforcement, argued that the consequences of response determine much of what we learn. Skinner in particular has written extensively of the many ways in which this operant conditioning can be observed and applied in our daily affairs. Like Watson before him, Skinner adamantly rejects the need for a psychology of the mind or any other attempt to understand behavior in subjective terms. For Skinner, behavior is conditioned by external events, and as such it can be controlled, predicted, and studied by empirical methods. The wide range of studies of both human and animal learning (Kazdin, 1975; Kimble, 1961) as a function of behavioral methods demonstrate how powerful the principles of behaviorism can be when effectively applied.

More recently, behaviorists cautiously have begun to reexamine the role of mental processes in determining behavior. Members of this new school of thought, sometimes called cognitive behaviorism, include psychologists such as Albert Bandura (1977) and Donald Meichenbaum (1977). Reconsideration of the role of mental process in behavior has come about for two reasons. First, certain kinds of learning, such as modeling, occur in the absence of typical observable consequences. It is thought that in some cases a form of self-reinforcement (or perhaps self-punishment) through language is responsible for strengthening the behavior (Bandura, 1977). Others (e.g., Meichenbaum, 1977) have noted that traditional behavioral learning paradigms have been too simplistic to account for the wide array of individual differences in behavior, especially among humans. Even unyielding behavioral analyses such as Skinner's make use of variables such as reinforcement history, which imply some sort of cognitive process in mediating across gaps in time.

The influence of behavioristic thought in psychology is undeniable. The emphasis on empirical research conditions that seemed so strident and incongruous in Watson's time is now taught as the basis of good research, and the importance of both Pavlovian and Skinnerian conditioning has been observed even in popular literature. Behavioristic methods of treatment occupy a prominent place in the study of psychopathology, and behavioral principles are being applied in industrial/organizational settings. As the school of thought broadens its consideration of variables involved in behavior, it holds even brighter promise as a tool for understanding what we do and why we do it.

REFERENCES

Bandura, A. (1977). Self-efficacy: Toward a unifying theory of behavioral change. *Psychological Review, 84,* 191–215.

Kazdin, A. (1975). *Behavior modification in applied settings.* Homewood, IL: Dorsey.

Kimble, G. A. (1961). *Hilgard and Marquis' conditioning and learning* (2nd ed.). New York: Appleton-Century-Crofts.

Meichenbaum, D. (1977). *Cognitive behavior modification: An integrative approach.* New York: Plenum.

Skinner, B. F. (1953). *Science and human behavior.* New York: Free Press.

Thorndike, E. L. (1935). *The psychology of wants, interests and attitudes.* New York: Appleton-Century.

Watson, J. (1913). Psychology as the behaviorist views it. *Psychological Review, 20,* 1958–1977.

Watson, J., & Rayner, R. (1920). Conditioning emotional responses. *Journal of Experimental Psychology, 3,* 1–14.

Jerry L. Sloan
Wilmington Psychiatric
Associates

BEHAVIOR MODIFICATION
PSYCHOANALYSIS AND SPECIAL EDUCATION
SOCIAL LEARNING THEORY

BELGIUM, SPECIAL EDUCATION IN

Belgium is composed of three regions (Flanders, Wallonia, and Brussels) and includes two linguistic communities (one French speaking and one Flemish speaking). Belgium's federal form of government recognizes and respects regional differences. For example, each linguistic community is responsible for education and health policies. Nevertheless, special education policies and organizational structures are somewhat similar in both linguistic communities. This discussion focuses only on the nature of special education services provided under laws and regulations enacted by the federal state and the French speaking community of Belgium in order to avoid needless complexity.

Special education services are provided in self-contained schools, those specifically devoted to these programs. Special education students generally are not educated in regular education schools or mainstream classes. Special education programs are organized in reference to the following eight diagnostic categories (Conseil de la Communauté Française de Belgique, 2004). Type 1 addresses the needs of elementary and secondary level students with Mild Mental Retardation. The following six categories address the needs of nursery-, elementary-, and secondary-level students who have Moderate Mental Retardation (type 2), behavioral or Personality Disorders (type 3), physical disabilities (type 4), diseases (type 5), visual disorders (type 6), and hearing disorders (type 7). Type 8 is for elementary students who display instrumental disabilities. They include speech, perceptual, and spatial disorders that are assumed to underlie a learning disability. Students who display two or more disability types typically are placed in a program best suited to serve their most dominant disability type. At the secondary-school level, each of the seven types of special education programs is organized in four different forms that correspond to four disability levels. At one extreme, form 1 is for the most severely disabled children; its goal is to develop adaptive skills. At the other extreme, form 4 is for the least severely disabled children; its goal is to develop the abilities required for higher education.

During the 2002 to 2003 school year in the French speaking region of Belgium, 0.6 percent of nursery school students, 4.6 percent of elementary school students, and 3.8 percent of secondary school students were enrolled in a special education program (Ministère de la Communauté Française, 2003). Among them, at the elementary school, 24.7 percent were enrolled in type 1, 12.4 percent in type 2, 11.2 percent in type 3, 4.3 percent in type 4, 2.9 percent in type 5, 0.5 percent in type 6, 2.0 percent in type 7, and 42.0 percent in type 8. Thus, students with an instrumental disability constitute the largest number of students served in special education at the elementary school. At the secondary school, 52.8 percent were enrolled in type 1, 17.8 percent in type 2, 19.9 percent in type 3, 5.8 percent in type 4, 1.3 percent in type 5, 1.0 percent in type 6, and 1.4 percent in type 7. The type 8 program being no longer organized at the secondary school, a part of the students are directed to type 1, type 2 or type 3 programs, while the others are directed to an ordinary educational program. Thus, at the secondary school, students with Mild Mental Retardation constitute, by far, the largest number of students served in special education.

Three services offer educational support to families with

children who display severe levels of a disability: early assistance services, integration services, and housing services. Early assistance services are intended to help the child with disabilities and his or her family from birth to age 7. They provide educational, social, and psychological support, including educational counseling, coordination of care, and assessment of progress. Integration services provide similar services for children ages 6 through 20, including family guidance, collaborative support between them and special education schools, and other services designed to promote the child's autonomy and social integration. Housing services provide accommodation and educational support for children 24 hours a day when their families are unable to care for them for whatever the reason (e.g., the severity of the disability, distance between home and special education school, parent incompetence).

Special education programs are organized to meet children's special educational needs and to help them to reach their highest level of development. The rights of children and families to access special education resources are guaranteed by law. However, parents are not obligated to access them. Placement in a special education program always requires parental consent. The parents, a teacher, or a physician typically are the first persons to identify physical, behavioral, or learning problems. The children are then referred to a Centre Psycho-Medico-Social (Psychological Medical and Social Center), or a Service de Santé Mentale (Mental Health Service). Psychological Medical and Social Centers are independent bodies, subsidized by the education administration, and collaborate with schools to provide school-based guidance and counseling services. The Psychological Medical and Social Center director always is a psychologist and leads a team composed of several psychologists, social workers, and a nurse. The Mental Health Services comprise independent teams, subsidized by the health administration, who work to prevent mental disorders and provide ambulatory treatment for those with these disorders. The Mental Health Service director always is a psychiatrist and leads a team composed of several psychiatrists, psychologists, and social workers. The Psychological Medical and Social Centers and Mental Health Services are the only services that can authorize the enrollment of a child in a special education program. Authorization for Types 1, 2, 3, 4, and 8 special education programs require a multidisciplinary assessment that culminates in a report that includes medical, psychological, and social information that provides support for the enrollment.

Authorization for types 5, 6, and 7 special education programs requires only a medical assessment. Policies governing this work discuss the child's personal characteristics to be assessed and diagnostic criteria; preferred methods and tests to be used are not specified (Ministère de l'Education de la Recherche et de la Formation, 1995). Consistent with the need for reports from the Psychological Medical and Social Centers and Mental Health Services, a certificate recommending a special education program must be issued. Parents then may select the school in which the desired program is provided.

A school can provide programs for one or more of the eight diagnostic types. A school's educational team always includes teachers trained in special education, paramedical professionals (e.g., speech-therapists, physical therapists, and nurses), psychologists, and social workers. This team and the associated Psychological Medical and Social Center form the classroom council, the goal of which is to specify an individualized educational program for each student and to appraise a student's development and achievement during the school year. This council also determines the child's specialized treatments (e.g., language, physical, or psychological services). The social workers ensure a relation between school and families, including linking them to their child's educational program.

The development of special education programs can be flexible, with each educational team able to define the program most suited to a child's needs. These programs are not restricted to the traditional school subjects (e.g., mathematics, reading) and may include the development of autonomy, communication skills, and social relationships. The main goal of all the special education programs is to help promote the best adaptation of a child to society.

Issues pertaining to the integration of students with special needs in the ordinary school system have been discussed for some time. Progress has been limited and not likely to increase soon. Only children enrolled in types 4, 6, or 7 special education programs (and form 3 or 4 in secondary schools) can be integrated either part time or full time in an ordinary school (Conseil de la Commuauté Française de Belgique, 2004) and will receive support from professionals working in the special school where they are coenrolled. Only a limited number of students with special needs are in integrated programs.

REFERENCES

Conseil de la Communauté Française de Belgique. (2004). *Décret organisant l'enseignement spécial.* Brussels, Belgium: Author.

Ministère de l'Education de la Recherche et de la Formation. (1995). *Circulaire ministérielle fixant la modèle de protocole justificatif à délivrer par les centres psycho-médico-sociaux et les organismes habilités à délivrer le rapport d'inscription dans un des types d'enseignement spécial.* Brussels, Belgium: Communauté Française de Belgique.

Ministère de la Communauté Française. (2003). *Statistique des établissements, des élèves et des diplômes de l'enseignement de plein exercice. Annuaire 2001–2002.* Brussels, Belgium: Author.

JACQUES GRÉGOIRE
*Catholic University of Louvain,
Belgium*

INTERNATIONAL ETHICS AND SPECIAL EDUCATION

BELL, ALEXANDER GRAHAM (1847–1922)

Alexander Graham Bell, inventor of the telephone, educator, and spokesperson for the deaf, was born and educated in Scotland. Emigrating first to Canada and then to the United States, Bell, whose father and grandfather were authorities in the field of speech, and who had himself specialized in the anatomy of the vocal apparatus, opened a school in Boston for the training of teachers of the deaf in 1872; he became a professor at Boston University and married one of his students, Mabel Hubbard, who was deaf, as was his mother.

Widely acclaimed for his numerous inventions, Bell used his vast influence to foster his major interest, the teaching of the deaf. An avid proponent of oral methods of teaching the deaf, Bell became the acknowledged leader of the oral movement in the United States. He also campaigned tirelessly for the establishment of day schools for the deaf to provide an alternative to residential school placement. Bell was a founder of the American Association to Promote the Teaching of Speech to the Deaf, later renamed the Alexander Graham Bell Association for the Deaf, and of the *Volta Bureau,* which he established for the dissemination of knowledge about the deaf.

REFERENCE

Bruce, R. V. (1973). *Alexander Graham Bell and the conquest of solitude.* Boston: Little, Brown.

PAUL IRVINE
Katonah, New York

BELL, TERREL H. (1921–1996)

Terrel H. Bell died at his home in Salt Lake City on June 23, 1996 at the age of 74. Bell was born in Lava Hot Springs, Idaho, and received a master's degree from the University of Idaho in 1954 and a PhD in Educational Administration from the University of Utah in 1961. He was the recipient of 21 honorary doctorates conferred by various colleges and universities throughout the United States during his lifetime.

After serving in World War II as a U.S. Marine, Bell was a superintendent of schools in Idaho, Wyoming, and Utah. He was U.S. Commissioner of Education from 1974 to 1976 and secretary of the U.S. Department of Education from 1981 to 1984. He appointed members, wrote the national charter, and provided support and leadership for the work of the National Commission on Excellence in Education. The commission report, "A Nation At Risk," found serious flaws in the education system and concluded that schools were mired in mediocrity. Twelve national forums were sponsored to disseminate the commission report, which is credited with prompting a movement to overhaul education. Over 12 million copies of the report have been printed, reprinted, and widely distributed.

Bell's numerous honors and awards include the Department of Defense Distinguished Public Service Medal awarded by Secretary of Defense Casper Weinberger in 1984. He authored numerous books and publications, and remained active in promoting education and learning after leaving the government. He subsequently taught Educational Administration at the University of Utah, and founded the educational consulting firm of T. H. Bell and Associates. In 1991, he wrote *How to Shape Up Our Nation's Schools: Three Crucial Steps for Renewing American Education.*

REFERENCES

Bell, T. H. (1956). *The prodigal pedagogue.* New York: Exposition.

Bell, T. H. (1960). *A philosophy of education for the space age.* New York: Exposition.

Bell, T. H. (1972). *Your child's intellect: A parent's guide to home based preschool education.* Salt Lake City, UT: Olympus.

Bell, T. H. (1974). *Active parent concern.* Englewood Cliffs, NJ: Prentice Hall.

Bell, T. H. (1984). *Excellence.* Salt Lake City, UT: Deseret.

ROBERTA C. STOKES
Texas A&M University
First edition

TAMARA J. MARTIN
The University of Texas of the Permian Basin
Second edition

BELLEVUE PSYCHIATRIC HOSPITAL

The history of psychiatric care at Bellevue Hospital Center and the history of psychiatric care in the United States are closely interwoven. Bellevue has been at the vanguard of treatment for the mentally ill since the eighteenth century, pioneering methods of identifying and categorizing patients, training psychiatrists and psychiatric nurses, and developing out-patient as well as in-patient courses of treatment.

The Public Workhouse and House of Correction, which opened in 1736, ultimately became Bellevue Hospital. It contained a six-bed unit designed to provide care for "the infirm, the aged, the unruly, and the maniac." By 1826, a total of 82 of the 184 patients were listed as insane. In 1879 a pavilion for the insane was erected within hospital grounds. The concept of including the care and treatment of psychiatric patients in a general hospital rather than entirely apart from the treatment of the physically ailing was revolutionary.

In 1902 the Department of Bellevue and Allied Hospitals appointed a resident physician, two assistants, and trained nurses to provide medical attention for psychiatric patients, thereby providing the framework for the development of a modern psychiatric service. During the early 1900s, the primary function of the department of psychiatry at Bellevue was to "afford temporary care and treatment for those patients who are to be transferred to the state hospital for mental diseases within 10 days." Perhaps a more important function than maintaining patients on remand was to "provide care for another group of patients which had hitherto been neglected, patients whose psychoses are of such a character that they are not suitable for commitment to a hospital for the insane nor are they acceptable in a general hospital, e.g., cases of mild mental disorders, psychoneuroses, epilepsy, deliria, transitory attacks of confusion or excitement." Simultaneously, in an effort to discourage long-term hospitalization, the department of psychiatry at Bellevue established mental health clinics and the practice of ongoing contact with patients' families.

The Children's Inpatient Psychiatric Service began at Bellevue in 1920. Separate male and female adolescent wards were maintained providing for 30 patients each. In 1935 the New York City Board of Education established a special school for emotionally disturbed children at Bellevue. Now designated as P.S. 106, the school continues to function at Bellevue.

In establishing itself as a psychiatric prison ward, Bellevue has contributed to forensic medicine via the Psychiatric Clinic of the Court of General Sessions, established in 1931. This psychiatric prison ward encouraged the development of rigid safeguards for the rights of all psychiatric patients, including prisoners.

Among many firsts at Bellevue, in 1936 Karl Murdock Bowman was the first physician in the country to use insulin shock therapy for treatment of mental illness. In 1939 David Wechsler developed the Wechsler-Bellevue Scale of Intelligence, later called the Wechsler Adult Intelligence Scale, a test still widely used today. Wechsler went on to develop a number of intelligence tests often used with handicapped children including the Wechsler Intelligence Scale for Children and the Wechsler Pre-School Scale of Intelligence. Loretta Bender, a pioneer in work with autistic children and youths, worked at Bellevue during the 1950s and 1960s. In 1984, when its facilities in the New Bellevue Hospital at 27th Street and East River Drive in New York City were completed, Bellevue's psychiatric department was united for the first time with the rest of Bellevue. Psychiatry was truly integrated into a full-service hospital setting.

In recent years, Bellevue has continued to lead the field of psychiatric treatment. In the 1990s Bellevue was innovative in developing treatment modalities for individuals with substance abuse and mental illness with peer-led milieu therapy. In addition, "social marketing" was promoted by developing educational print materials for immigrant, low-literate, and other hard-to-reach groups (Dooley, 1996). The institution also developed a model for hospital-based alcoholism outpatient treatment services for homeless alcoholics (Miescher & Galanter, 1996). A vivid portrait of the everyday life of the staff and patients at Bellevue is portrayed in the 1995 book by the chief psychologist at Bellevue, Frederick Covan, and is entitled *Crazy All the Time: Life, Lessons, and Insanity on the Psych Ward of Bellevue Hospital.*

REFERENCES

Bellevue Hospital Center. (n.d.). *Bellevue hospital center.* New York: Author.

Covan, F. L., & Kahn, C. (1995). *Crazy all the time: Life, lessons, and insanity on the psych ward of Bellevue Hospital.* New York: Simon & Schuster.

Dooley, A. R. (1996). A collaborative model for creating patient education resources. *American Journal of Health Behavior, 20,* 15–19.

Miescher, A., & Galanter, M. (1996). Shelter-based treatment of the homeless alcoholic. *Journal of Substance Abuse Treatment, 13,* 135–140.

New York City Health and Hospitals Corporation. (1984). *The nation's largest municipal health care system: Directory of services.* New York: Author.

Walsh, J. (Ed.). (1982). *Bellevue.* New York: Bellevue Hospital Center.

Catherine Hall Rikhye
Hunter College, City University of New York
First edition

Elaine Fletcher-Janzen
University of Colorado at Colorado Springs
Second and Third editions

BENADRYL

Benadryl (diphenhydramine hydrochloride) is used for perennial or seasonal (hay fever) allergic rhinitis, motion sickness, and allergic conjunctivitis owed to inhalant allergens and foods. An antihistamine, it has anticholinergic (drying) and sedative side effects. In isolated cases, it has been used as a sedative for treatment of hyperactivity, and as a treatment for Parkinsonian symptoms associated with the side effects of antipsychotic medications (Konopasek, 2004). Adverse reactions include diminished mental alertness in both adults and children, with occasional excitation in the young child. A 1993 study (Vuurman, van Veggel,

Uiterwijk, Leutner, & O'Hanlon, 1993) found that allergic reaction reduces learning ability in children. In addition, this effect is aggravated by diphenhydramine. Therefore, parents and educators should be aware that while Benadryl relieves some of the uncomfortable symptoms of allergies it increases problems in learning. Accommodations for the child with allergies should be specifically targeted to sedation if the child is taking Benadryl. These accommodations could include decreasing workload, increasing time for rehearsal of learning material and communications with parents on a daily basis to assist in the monitoring of side effects and learning retention.

A brand name of Parke-Davis Company, it is available in capsules of 25 and 50 mg; as an elixir for oral use; and in injectable syringes. Dosage for children (over 20 pounds) is 12.5 to 25 mg three to four times daily, with maximum daily dosage not in excess of 300 mg. For adults, dosage is 25 to 50 mg three to four times daily. Overdose with this or other antihistamines may cause hallucinations, convulsions, and death.

REFERENCES

Konopasek, D. E. (2004). *Benadryl.* Longmont, CO: Sopris West.

Physician's desk reference. (1997). Oradell, NJ: Medical Economics.

Vuurman, E. F., van Veggel, L. M., Uiterwijk, M. M., Leutner, D., & O'Hanlon, J. F. (1993). Seasonal allergic rhinitis and antihistamine effects on children's learning. *Annals of Allergy, 71*(2), 121–126.

LAWRENCE HARTLAGE
Evans, Georgia
First edition

ELAINE FLETCHER-JANZEN
*University of Colorado at
Colorado Springs*
Second and Third editions

BENDER, LAURETTA (1897–1987)

Born in Butte, Montana, in 1897, Lauretta Bender obtained her BS and MA degrees from the University of Chicago in 1922 and 1923, respectively. She obtained her MD degree at the State University of Iowa in 1926 and returned to Chicago (Billings Hospital) for her internship (1927–1928) and residency in neurology (1928). A residency in psychiatry at Boston's Psychopathic Hospital preceded another psychiatric residency, in 1929–1930, at Johns Hopkins' Phipps Clinic. She also received postgraduate training in neuroanatomy, physiology, and pathology at the University of Amsterdam on a Rockefeller grant in 1926–1927.

Bender held numerous appointments, including assis-

tant instructor of neuropathology at Iowa (1923–1926) and several psychiatric positions in the New York City area. These include senior psychiatrist at Bellevue Hospital (1930–1956), director of the Child Guidance Clinic at the New York City Infirmary (1954–1960), principal research scientist of Child Psychiatry at New York State Department of Mental Hygiene (1956–1960), director of Psychiatric Research at the Children's Unit of Creedmor State Hospital (1960–1969), and attending psychiatrist at the New York Psychiatric Institute (1969–1973). She held teaching positions at New York University, Adelphi College Graduate School, and Columbia University. She retired in 1973 and moved to Annapolis, MD, where she remained until her death on January 4, 1987, at the age of 89.

Bender received numerous awards during her career, among them the Adolph Meyer Award in 1953 for her contributions to the profession's knowledge base on schizophrenic children, and was named Medicine's Woman of the Year for New York in 1958. She was a fellow of the American Medical Association, American Psychiatric Association, American Neurological Association, and American Orthopsychiatric Association.

With over 100 chapters and articles, Bender is widely published in the fields of child psychiatry, neurology, and psychology. She is best known for her Visual Motor Gestalt Test (1937), several books, including *Psychopathological Disorders of Children with Organic Brain Disease* (1956), and studies of learning disabilities (1970). Her theory of the role of brain pathology in the development of childhood schizophrenia is less known but also important. In addition, she developed the Face-Hand Test, which examines double simultaneous tactile sensation (face and hand). A variation of this test, the Fink-Green-Bender Test, has been used to discriminate between children with neurologic and schizophrenic disorders.

REFERENCES

Bender, L. (1937). *A visual motor gestalt test and its clinical use.* New York: American Orthopsychiatric Association.

Bender, L. (1956). *Psychopathological disorders of children with organic brain disease.* Springfield, IL: C. Thomas.

Bender, L. (1970). Use of the visual motor gestalt test in diagnosing learning disability. *Journal of Special Education, 4,* 29–39.

ANTONIO E. PUENTE
*University of North Carolina at
Wilmington*
First edition

KAY E. KETZENBERGER
*The University of Texas of the
Permian Basin*
Second edition

BENDER VISUAL-MOTOR GESTALT TEST–SECOND EDITION

BENDER VISUAL-MOTOR GESTALT TEST–SECOND EDITION

The original Bender-Gestalt test was a frequently administered and thoroughly researched drawing test. Originally developed as a measure of visual-motor maturity in children, the test has come to be used as a projective personality technique as well as being used with children as an indicator of school readiness, emotional problems, and learning difficulties. It has also become widely used as screening measure for neurological impairment in both adults and children. The Bender-Gestalt II (Brannigan & Decker, 2003) is an individually administered assessment used to evaluate visual-motor integration skills in children and adults ages 4 to 85. It consists of 16 geometric designs, printed on stimulus cards. These designs include the original nine designs from the Bender-Gestalt Test and seven new designs that have been included to enhance its utility in educational, psychological, and neuropsychological assessment. The Bender-Gestalt II also includes an Observation Form as well as two supplemental tests, the Motor Test and the Perception Test, which aid in evaluating the examinee's performance on the Bender-Gestalt II. Administration involves two phases: the Copy phase and the Recall phase. In the Copy phase, the examinee is asked to copy each of the designs onto a blank sheet of paper. In the Recall phase, the examinee is asked to redraw the designs from memory. Although the test has no time limits, the examiner records how long it takes the examinee to reproduce the designs. The Bender-Gestalt II examiner's manual contains administration and scoring guidelines; information on the standardization and norming process; normative tables; reliability and validity test data; and a new, easy-to-use global scoring system.

The standardization sample of the Bender-Gestalt II was based on a stratified, random sampling plan of 4,000 individuals, ages 4 to 85, devised to match the percentages of the stratification variables from the U.S. 2000 Census. The normative sample was designed to be nationally representative and matched to percentages of the U.S. population for demographic variables, including age, sex, race or ethnicity, geographic region, and socioeconomic level (educational attainment). In addition, large numbers of individuals from clinical or special populations were collected to study the differential effects of group inclusion on test performance. These populations included individuals with Mental Retardation, specific learning disabilities, Attention-Deficit/Hyperactivity Disorder, serious emotional disturbances, autism, Alzheimer's disease, and giftedness. After all normative data were collected, z-scores were transformed into a standard score scale (M = 100, SD = 15). Scores were rounded and truncated to limit the standard score range to 4 standard deviations above and below the mean, providing a range of standard scores from 40 to 160.

A variety of methods was used to estimate the reliability of the Bender-Gestalt II Copy and Recall phases. When using the Global Scoring System, the average interrater reliability was .90 for the Copy phase and .96 for the Recall

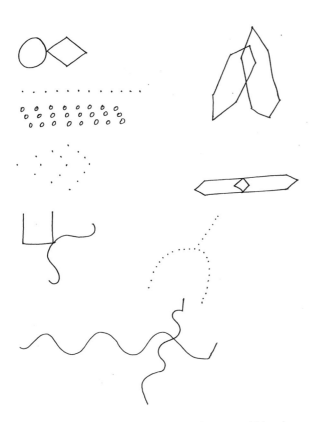

Figure 1   Bender drawings of a normal ten year old female

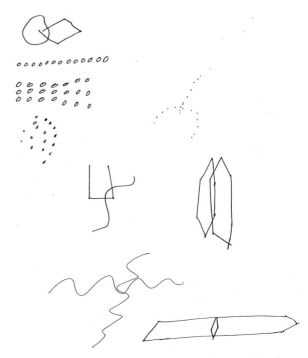

Figure 2 Bender drawings indicating some impulsivity and visual motor/ perceptual problems

phase, both impressive given its ease of use and diverse applications. Using the split-half procedure to measure internal consistency, the overall reliability for the standardization group was .91 with an average standard error of measurement of 4.55, indicating consistent and stable measurement. In test-retest reliability studies, the average corrected coefficient was .85 for the Copy phase and .83 for the Recall phase. These coefficients were well within the acceptable range. Evidence also suggests high validity. Several studies demonstrated a high correlation between the Bender-Gestalt II and intelligence, achievement, and visual-motor ability measures, which are often used in comprehensive psychoeducational assessment. The results also suggest that the Bender-Gestalt II is related to, yet distinct from, other constructs. The Bender-Gestalt II measures a single underlying construct that is sensitive to maturation or development, and scores are highly influenced by and sensitive to clinical conditions. This dimensionality provides added utility to the test.

REFERENCE

Brannigan, G. G., & Decker, S. L. (2003). *Bender Visual-Motor Gestalt Test—Second Edition: Examiner's manual.* Itasca, IL: Riverside Publishing.

RON DUMONT
Fairleigh Dickinson University

JOHN O. WILLIS
Rivier College

**VISUAL-MOTOR AND VISUAL-PERCEPTUAL PROBLEMS
VISUAL PERCEPTION AND DISCRIMINATION**

BENNETT, VIRGINIA C. (1916–1998)

Virginia C. Bennett, a former nurse, studied elementary education at Rutgers University, earning a BA in this field in 1956. She subsequently was awarded an MEd in educational psychology (1961) and the EdD in school psychology (1963), both from Rutgers University, where she was on the faculty from 1963 until her retirement in 1983. During the years 1960 to 1963, Bennett was a W. S. Grant Foundation fellow.

Bennett worked in school psychology as both a practitioner and a trainer of school psychologists. Her primary interest was identification of children with learning problems, with emphasis on the remediation process, for those identified, through planning programs for teachers to implement within the regular classroom setting. She pioneered the mainstreaming of children identified for special educational resources in her practice in the New Jersey schools. With her doctoral students, she planned and implemented a program for the early identification (screening) of kindergarten children in the public schools of Trenton, New Jersey, a school district with a high proportion of minority group and Hispanic children.

Although always interested in the problems of schoolchildren, and always convinced that the public schools are the most effective milieu for dealing with those problems, Bennett's interests throughout 25 years as a school psychologist and a trainer in a highly urban state focused in later years on the problems of poor African American children and youths, as well as on those of the increasing numbers of Hispanic children in the schools. These latter interests are exemplified in her publication of work with school-age parents and in the development of a doctoral program geared to the application of psychological knowledge and skills to the solution of educational problems.

Bennett was recognized for her leadership in school psychology, where she was perhaps best known for her work with Bardon (Bardon & Bennett, 1974; Bennett & Bardon, 1976). With Bardon, she pioneered the development of professional preparation programs for school psychologists. In 1977 the Division of School Psychology of the American Psychological Association recognized her with the Distinguished Service Award.

REFERENCES

Bardon, J. I., & Bennett, V. C. (1974). *School psychology.* Englewood Cliffs, NJ: Prentice Hall.

Bennett, V. C., & Bardon, J. I. (1976). Applied research can be useful. *Journal of School Psychology, 14,* 67–73.

CECIL R. REYNOLDS
Texas A&M University

BENZEDRINE

Benzedrine is a psychostimulant that acts on the central nervous system. It was the subject of widespread abuse and distribution under the slang term "bennies" until the 1970s. Its previous legitimate uses included, at times, the treatment of hyperactivity and obesity. Recent study indicates some evidence to support the judicious use of psychostimulants in "selected clinical instances of several adult psychiatric syndromes." It is no longer in use in the treatment of childhood or adolescent disorders.

REFERENCE

Chiarello, R. J., & Cole, J. O. (1987). The use of psychostimulants in general psychiatry: A reconsideration. *Archives of General Psychiatry, 44,* 286–295.

STAFF

**ATTENTION-DEFICIT/HYPERACTIVITY DISORDER
DEXEDRINE**

BEREITER, CARL (1930–   )

Carl Bereiter received his BA (1951) and MA (1952) in comparative literature and his PhD (1959) in education from the University of Wisconsin. He was a research associate at Vassar College (1959–1961) and then joined the faculty at the University of Illinois (1961–1967). Since 1967, Bereiter has been a professor at the Ontario Institute for Studies in Education.

In the early 1960s, Bereiter and Siefried Engelmann taught reading, mathematics, and logical skills to young disadvantaged children. Out of this effort came the method they called direct instruction, an approach that was often misperceived as behavioristic rather than rational analysis of difficulties of understanding.

Most of Bereiter's work has been in collaboration with Marlene Scardamalia. Through research on composing and comprehension processes, they have identified an immature strategy that seems to reflect a general way of coping superficially with academic tasks. This discovery led to Bereiter's broadening his studies to intentional learning: how it develops, how it is influenced by school practices, and how a higher level of intentional control over learning can be fostered in students. His most recent work, in this area, has been in using Computer Supported Intentional Learning Environment (CSILE) software. CSILE is intended to create a knowledge-building society by linking diverse participants, including school children and parents, teacher education and medical students, project researchers, and software developers.

REFERENCES

Bereiter, C., & Engelmann, S. (1966). *Teaching disadvantaged children in the preschool*. Englewood Cliffs, NJ: Prentice Hall.

Bereiter, C., & Scardamalia, M. (1985). Cognitive coping strategies and the problem of "inert" knowledge. In S. S. Chipman, J. W. Segal, & R. Glaser (Eds.), *Thinking and learning skills: Research and open questions* (Vol. 2, pp. 65–80). Hillsdale, NJ: Erlbaum.

Scardamalia, M., & Bereiter, C. (1996). Engaging students in a knowledge society. *Educational Leadership, 54*(3), 6–10.

DEBORAH B. GUILLEN
*The University of Texas of the
Permian Basin*

BETA III

The Beta III (Kellog & Morton, 1999) provides a quick assessment of adults' (aged 16 to 89), nonverbal intellectual capabilities, including visual information processing, spatial and nonverbal reasoning, processing speed, and aspects of fluid intelligence. It is easily administered and hand scored either individually or in a group and requires only 30 minutes to complete. It is useful for screening large populations of people for whom administering comprehensive test batteries would be difficult, including low-functioning or low-skilled individuals, and is ideal for use in prison systems, companies, and schools. Administration instructions for the Beta III are available in English or Spanish, making it one of the most comprehensive of language-free and culture-fair tests.

Beta III is the updated version of the Revised Beta Examination, Second Edition, which was published in 1974. It features new norms, contemporary and larger artwork, new items, a new subtest (Matrix Reasoning), extended age range, low floors for individuals with average and lower cognitive abilities, and higher ceiling with more challenging items. Five subtests make up the Beta III: Coding, which contains code symbols with numbers that are assigned to the symbols at the top of the page; Picture Completion, which requires the subject to draw in what is missing to complete the picture; Clerical Checking, which entails circling an *equal* or a *not equal* symbol depending on whether pairs of pictures, symbols, or numbers are the same or different; Picture Absurdities, where the subject is asked to place an *X* on the one picture out of four that shows something wrong or foolish; and Matrix Reasoning, which requires the subject to choose the missing symbol or picture that best completes a set of symbols or pictures.

Extensive reliability and validity studies have been conducted with Beta III. The test was normed on a sample of 1,260 adults, including people with Mental Retardation and more than 400 prison inmates. The sample was representative of the 1997 U.S. Census data with respect to age, gender, race or ethnicity, educational level, and geographic region. The Beta III was validated using other well-known tests, including the WAIS-III, ABLE-II, Raven's Standard Progressive Matrices, the Revised Minnesota Paper Form Board Test (RMPFBT), Personnel Tests for Industry—Oral Direction Test (PTI-ODT), Bennett Mechanical Comprehensive Test (BMCT), and Revised Beta Examination, Second Edition (Beta II).

REFERENCES

Kellog, C. E., & Morton, N. W. (1999). *Beta III*. San Antonio, TX: Psychological Corporation.

McCallum, S., Bracken, B., & Wasserman, J. (2000). *Essentials of nonverbal assessment*. New York: Wiley.

RON DUMONT
Fairleigh Dickinson University

JOHN O. WILLIS
Rivier College

BETTELHEIM, BRUNO (1903–1990)

Bruno Bettelheim received his doctoral degree from the University of Vienna in 1938. He was strongly influenced by Freudian thought. Bettelheim was a psychiatrist who gained his fame from work with emotionally disturbed children, particularly those with autism.

During his long association with the University of Chicago, Bettelheim acted as principal of the University of Chicago's Sonia Shankman Orthogeneic School, a residential treatment center for severely emotionally disturbed children. The philosophy and operation of the Shankman School are described in Bettelheim's book *Love Is Not Enough* (1950), and four case studies of the treatment there are covered in his *Truants from Life* (1955).

Bettelheim sought in his treatment of severely disturbed children to create a particular social environment, a society with its own definite set of mores, closely paralleling those of society at large. He believed that social norms and standards are important to the treatment of emotionally disturbed children just as they are important in normal populations.

Bettelheim published many books, including *Children of the Dream* (1969) and *The Empty Fortress* (1967). He died in 1990 at the age of 87.

REFERENCES

Bettelheim, B. (1950). *Love is not enough: The treatment of emotionally disturbed children.* Glencoe, IL: Free Press.

Bettelheim, B. (1955). *Truants from life: The rehabilitation of emotionally disturbed children.* Glencoe, IL: Free Press.

Bettelheim, B. (1967). *The empty fortress: Infantile autism and the birth of the self.* London: Collier-Macmillan.

Bettelheim, B. (1969). *Children of the dream.* New York: Macmillan.

REBECCA BAILEY
Texas A&M University

BIALER, IRVING (1919–2000)

Irving Bialer received his BA (1943) from Brooklyn College and his PhD (1960) in clinical psychology from George Peabody College, with a minor in education of exceptional children. His major field of interest was in clinical psychology; mental retardation and clinical child psychology were two special areas of interest.

His publications dealt with issues of assessment and diagnosis in the areas of mental retardation and neurological impairment, personality and motivational development in retarded individuals, and drug-related treatments for behavior problems in neuropsychiatrically impaired children.

He had over 30 publications to his credit, including books, articles, and book chapters. Some of his most significant publications include a chapter in *Social-Cultural Aspects of Mental Retardation,* discussing the relationship of mental retardation to emotional disturbance and physical disability, and *The Psychology of Mental Retardation: Issues and Approaches* (coedited with Manny Sternlicht), which focuses on the theoretical, practical issues and approaches to dealing with the psychology of mentally retarded people. Bialer and R. L. Cromwell (1965) wrote an article entitled "Failure as Motivation with Mentally Retarded Children," which was published in the *American Journal of Mental Deficiency.*

Bialer has held many academic positions in psychology and special education and was a consulting editor to the *American Journal of Mental Deficiency* as well as the journal's book review editor from 1971 to 1981.

REFERENCES

Bialer, I. (1970). Relationship of mental retardation to emotional disturbance and physical disability. In H. C. Haywood (Ed.), *Social-cultural aspects of mental retardation* (pp. 607–660). New York: Appleton-Century-Crofts.

Bialer, I., & Cromwell, R. L. (1965). Failure as motivation with mentally retarded children. *American Journal of Mental Deficiency, 69,* 680–684.

Bialer, I., & Sternlicht, M. (Eds.). (1970). *The psychology of mental retardation: Issues and approaches.* New York: Psychological Dimensions.

REBECCA BAILEY
Texas A&M University

BIBLIOTHERAPY

The bibliotherapy process is frequently summed into the three stages of identification, catharsis, and insight (Sridhar & Vaughn, 2000). *Bibliotherapy* is defined as "the use of reading materials for help in solving personal problems or for psychiatric therapy" (Merriam-Webster Online Dictionary, 2005). This description is broad, thus allowing for different interpretations and diverse application. Bibliotherapy can be used to explore and develop an individual's self-concept, increase understanding of human behavior, foster honest self-appraisal, relieve emotional or mental pressure, demonstrate that people encounter the same difficulties in life, provide various solutions to a problem, and assist in planning a constructive course of action (Aiex, 1993).

The bibliotherapy process as described by some practitioners (Orton, 1997; Pardeck, 1993) begins with identifying a person's needs. The second component involves matching these needs with appropriate reading materials. This process may entail consideration of the person's age, sex, race, reading level, and the nature of the themes. The next step is to establish the setting and time to engage in therapy. Other integral components include designing follow-up activities for the reading and motivating the client(s). The next step involves engaging the person in the reading, viewing, or listening phase. Time for reflection and discussion is necessary to allow the individual to process the story and determine how it relates to his or her experiences. The final steps include the introduction of follow-up activities related to the story and assisting the person in achieving closure to the personal problems addressed in the story (Orton, 1997; Pardeck, 1993). Follow-up activities to reading the story may consist of retelling the story, an in-depth discussion of the book, engaging in art activities, creative writing, or dramatic activities, including the use of role playing and puppets.

Books are selected with themes that closely match the student's identified needs and have a desired therapeutic content. The books should be at the student's reading ability and interest level. The characters and themes should be believable to promote student empathy. The themes must be realistic and entail creativity in problem solving (Jackson, 2001; Pardeck & Pardeck, 1993). Books utilized in bibliotherapy include short stories of fiction, self-help, fairy tales, picture books, and nonfiction biographies (Orton, 1997).

The effectiveness of bibliotherapy is somewhat mixed. Bibliotherapy can be effective for cultivating assertiveness, changing attitudes, promoting self-development, and achieving therapeutic benefits (Sridhar & Vaughn, 2000). In addition, bibliotherapy seems to have success in promoting self-esteem, problem-solving skills, interpersonal relationships, as well as improving academic achievement and reading comprehension (Borders & Paisley, 1992; Pardeck, 1993; Sridhar & Vaughn, 2000).

REFERENCES

Aiex, N. (1993). *Bibliotherapy. ERIC Digest.* (ERIC Document Reproduction Service No. ED357333)

Borders, S., & Paisley, P. O. (1992). Children's literature as a resource for classroom guidance. *Elementary School Guidance and Counseling, 27*(2), 131–140.

Jackson, S. A. (2001). Using bibliotherapy with clients. *Journal of Individual Psychology, 57*(3), 289–297.

Merriam-Webster Online Dictionary. (2005). *Bibliotherapy.* Retrieved May 21, 2006, from http://www.m-w.com/cgi-bin/dictionary?book=Dictionary&va=bibliotherapy&x=26&y=16

Orton, G. L. (1997). *Strategies for counseling children and their parents.* Pacific Grove, CA: Brooks/Cole.

Pardeck, J. T. (1993). *Using bibliotherapy in clinical practice: A guide to self-help books.* Westport, CT: Greenwood Press.

Pardeck, J. T., & Pardeck, J. A. (Eds.). (1993). *Bibliotherapy: A clinical approach to helping children.* Langhorne, PA: Gordon and Breach Science Publishers.

Sridhar, D., & Vaughn, S. (2000). Bibliotherapy for all: Enhancing reading comprehension, self-concept, and behavior. *Teaching Exceptional Children, 33*(2), 74–82.

LINDA RADBILL
University of Florida

BASAL READERS
HIGH INTEREST–LOW VOCABULARY
RECORDING FOR THE BLIND

BIELSCHOLWSKY SYNDROME

See JUVENILE CEREBROMACULAR DEGENERATION.

BIENNIAL DIRECTORY OF EDUCATIONAL FACILITIES FOR THE LEARNING DISABLED

The *Biennial Directory of Educational Facilities for the Learning Disabled* is published by Academic Therapy Publications. It contains a listing of nonpublic educational facilities that specialize in programs for the learning disabled. The directory lists facilities in alphabetical order by state. Following the name, location, director, and number of staff members is coded information describing the following: type of facility—educational, related professional service (diagnostic, optometric, etc.), or summer camp; age ranges accepted; boys only, girls only, or coeducational; full day, part day, or residential; and fee information. A copy of the directory can be obtained from Academic Therapy Publications for a small fee to cover postage and handling (currently $5.00), at 20 Commercial Boulevard, Novato, CA 94949.

DANIEL R. PAULSON
University of Wisconsin at Stout

BIJOU, SIDNEY W. (1908–   )

Born in Baltimore, Maryland, Sidney W. Bijou received his BS in business administration from the University of Florida in 1933. He received his MS (1937) from Columbia University and his PhD (1941), both in psychology, from the University of Iowa. Professor emeritus at the University of Illinois, Bijou has been an adjunct professor of special education and psychology at the University of Arizona, and more recently the University of Nevada.

Although he was the coauthor of the *Wide Range Achievement Test* (Bijou & Jastak, 1941), his major interest is in the behavioral analysis of child development (Bijou, 1978; Bijou & Baer, 1965, 1978). He also coauthored a book on the behavior analysis and modification of children (Bijou & Ruiz, 1981). One of his major contentions is that the child and the environment are always interacting and maintaining a symbiotic relationship. He emphasizes the commonality of a general goal for children, normal and retarded, in early childhood education, regardless of age or degree of handicapping condition, while stressing individualization of education and treatment.

Bijou has been a National Institute of Mental Health senior fellow, a Fullbright-Hays fellow, president of the Midwestern Association of Behavior Analysis, and president of the American Psychological Association's Division of Developmental Psychology. He has also received the Research Award from the American Association of Mental Deficiency, and the G. Stanley Hall Award in child development from the American Psychological Association. The sum of Bijou's vast experience in the field is reflected in his 1996 article, "Reflections on Some Early Events Related to Behavior Analysis of Child Development."

REFERENCES

Bijou, S. W. (1976). *Child development: The basic stage of early childhood.* Englewood Cliffs, NJ: Prentice Hall.

Bijou, S. W. (1996). Reflections on some early events related to behavior analysis of child development. *Behavior Analyst, 19*(1), 49–60.

Bijou, S. W., & Baer, D. M. (1965). *Child development: Universal stage of infancy* (Vol. 2). New York: Appleton-Century-Crofts.

Bijou, S. W., & Baer, D. M. (1978). *Behavior analysis of child development.* Englewood Cliffs, NJ: Prentice Hall.

Bijou, S. W., & Jastak, J. F. (1941). *Wide range achievement test.* New York: Psychological Corporation.

Bijou, S. W., & Ruiz, R. (Eds.). (1981). *Behavior modification: Contributions to education.* Hillsdale, NJ: Erlbaum.

E. Valerie Hewitt
Texas A&M University

BILINGUAL ASSESSMENT AND SPECIAL EDUCATION

The assessment of children who are culturally and linguistically diverse for special education services has been a controversial issue for nearly thirty years. This controversy first received national attention via the case of Diana *v.* California in 1970 involving the identification of Spanish-speaking children as mentally retarded on the basis of being assessed in English. The safeguards decreed in this case had an impact on both legal requirements and professional ethical standards. Public Law 94-142 mandated that children be assessed in their primary language. Chapter 13 of the American Psychological Association's *Standards for Edu-cational and Psychological Testing* (1985) acknowledges the need for assessing the native language of children.

Legal requirements and ethical standards, however, have not resolved the issue of disproportionate representation of culturally and linguistically diverse children in special education. The problem of disproportionate representation across different special education categories pertains both to overrepresentation (Artiles & Trent, 1994; Chinn & Hughes, 1987; Ortiz & Yates, 1983; Robertson, Kushner, Starks, & Drescher, 1994; Tucker, 1980; Wright & Cruz, 1980) and underrepresentation (Chinn & Hughes, 1987; Gersten & Woodward, 1994; Ortiz & Yates, 1983; Robertson et al., 1994).

There are many possible factors that contribute to the disproportionate representation of linguistically diverse students in special education. Ochoa, Powell and Robles-Pina (1996) state that the following are among some of the reasons why this problem continues today: "(a) socioeconomic status of minorities students, (b) test bias associated with cultural differences, (c) factors associated with second language acquisition, and (d) inappropriate referrals" (p. 251).

In addition to these four aforementioned variables, the role of the school psychologist with respect to appropriately conducting and interpreting test results is a critical factor that can reduce the probability of misdiagnosing bilingual and/or limited-English-proficient (LEP) children. While experts (Barona & Santos de Barona, 1987; Caterino, 1990; Esquivel, 1988; Figueroa, 1990; Hamayan & Damico, 1991; Wilen & Sweeting, 1986) have provided the field of school psychology with recommended procedures and factors to consider when conducting bilingual assessment, recent research indicates that practitioners have not been exposed to this information. Ochoa, Rivera, and Ford (1997) found that 83 percent of the school psychologists who conducted bilingual assessment self-reported that they had not received adequate training in this area by their university training program. "Moreover, 56 percent stated that they [school psychologists] had received no or very little training on interpreting results of bilingual assessments" (Ochoa, Rivera, & Ford, 1997, p. 341).

Given this lack of training, it is critical that the assessment practices school psychologists use with bilingual and/or LEP children be reviewed. These include the following: (a) use of interpreters, (b) the extent to which and how language proficiency is assessed, (c) methods used to assess intellectual functioning, academic achievement, and adaptive behavior, and (d) compliance with Section Four of the exclusionary clause of Public Law 94-142.

Use of Interpreters

The use of interpreters is common practice in bilingual assessment. This is not surprising due to the many different low-incidence language groups school psychologists have to assess (Ochoa, Gonzalez, Galarza, & Guillemard, 1996). Ochoa, Gonzalez et al. (1996) reported that 53 percent of school psychologists use interpreters. They found that 77 percent of school psychologists who use interpreters self-reported that they were clearly not trained by their university training program on how to do so. Moreover, approximately two-thirds of the interpreters used by the school psychologists did not have training to work in this capacity. Ochoa, Gonzalez et al. (1996) and Nuttall (1987) state the need for interpreter training. When school psychologists must resort to using interpreters, they should review the literature pertaining to the skills they should acquire in this situation (Figueroa, Sandoval, & Merino, 1984) as well as the skills that the interpreter should possess (Chamberlain & Medeiros-Landurand, 1991; Medina, 1982; Miller & Abudarham, 1984; Scribner, 1993; Wilen & Sweeting, 1986).

Language Proficiency Assessment

Language proficiency assessment is an essential component of bilingual assessment because it provides the school psychologist with information about (a) the appropriateness of the child's current educational placement with respect to his/her language development (Ochoa, Galarza, & Gonzalez, 1996) and (b) the child's native and second language development with respect to whether the student has achieved Cognitive Academic Language Proficiency (CALP). Cummins (1984) states that it is important to differentiate between CALP, which takes 5 to 7 years to acquire and is the type of proficiency which one needs to be successful in an academic context, and Basic Interpersonal Communication Skills (BICS), which is the proficiency one needs in social settings and only takes about two years to acquire. If a bilingual student does not have CALP in English, he or she will find the linguistic demands of his instructional arrangement to be difficult, which could result in academic failure. Ochoa, Galarza, and Gonzalez (1996) concluded from their study of the language proficiency assessment practices of school psychologists when conducting bilingual assessment that they " . . . are not implementing the following recommended language proficiency practices: (a) conducting their own testing rather than relying on external data, (b) obtaining information about the LEP child's CALP level, and (c) utilizing informal language assessment methods . . . " (p. 33).

Intellectual Functioning, Academic and Adaptive Behavior Assessment

With respect to intellectual functioning, Ochoa, Powell, and Robles-Pina's (1996) study noted the following assessment trends used with bilingual and LEP students: (a) multiple measures are utilized; (b) nonverbal measures are commonly used; and (c) formally, informally translated tests and alternative/dynamic methods (i.e., Learning Potential Assessment Device and System of Multicultural Pluralistic Assessment)

are often not used. In the area of academic assessment of second language learners, approximately 75 percent of school psychologists reported that they used the Woodcock instruments in both English and Spanish (Ochoa, Powell, & Robles-Pina, 1996). Moreover, the use of curriculum-based measurement (66 percent of school psychologists) and criterion reference testing (49 percent of school psychologists) in Spanish are also common practice to assess achievement (Ochoa, Powell, & Robles-Pina, 1996). With respect to adaptive behavior, the most commonly used measure with bilingual students is the Vineland Adaptive Behavior Scales–Survey Edition (Ochoa, Powell, & Robles-Pina, 1996).

Section Four of the Exclusionary Clause

Section Four of the exclusionary clause of Public Law 94-142 states that a student should not be identified as learning disabled if the "discrepancy between ability and achievement is primarily the result of environmental, cultural, or economic disadvantage" (U.S. Office of Education, 1977). Ochoa, Rivera, and Powell's (1997) study examined how school psychologists complied with this legal requirement. They identified 36 factors that school psychologists used which could be summarized by the following six major themes: "(a) family and home factors, (b) language instruction and language-related factors, (c) assessment instrument and procedural safeguards, (d) educational history factors, (e) general educational factors, and (f) other" (p. 163). Ochoa, Rivera, and Powell (1997) conclude that "the extent to which many of these factors are used, however, appears to be low. Moreover, many additional important factors are completely overlooked by school psychologists" (p. 163).

Conclusion

A review of the aforementioned research concerning the assessment practices used with bilingual and/or LEP students suggests that this area will continue to be controversial. Perhaps the words of Chinn and Hughes (1987) best summarize this situation: "The assessment of minority children for educational placement continues to be one of the more volatile issues in special education" (p. 45).

REFERENCES

American Psychological Association. (1985). *Standards for educational and psychological testing.* Washington, DC: American Psychological Association.

Artiles, A. J., & Trent, S. C. (1994). Overrepresentation of minority students in special education: A continuing debate. *The Journal of Special Education, 27*(4), 410–437.

Barona, A., & Santos de Barona, M. (1987). A model for assessment of limited English proficiency students referred for special education services. In S. H. Fradd & W. J. Tikunoff (Eds.), *Bilingual education and bilingual special education* (pp. 183–209). San Diego: College Hill Press.

Caterino, L. C. (1990). Step-by-step procedure for the assessment of language minority children. In A. Barona & E. E. Garcia (Eds.), *Children at risk: Poverty, minority status, and other issues in educational equity* (pp. 269–282). Washington, DC: National Association of School Psychologists.

Chamberlain, P., & Medeiros-Landurand, P. (1991). Practical considerations in the assessment of LEP students with special needs. In E. V. Hamayan & J. S. Damico (Eds.), *Limiting bias in the assessment of bilingual students* (pp. 111–156). Austin, TX: PRO-ED.

Chinn, P. C., & Hughes, S. (1987). Representation of minority students in special classes. *Remedial and Special Education, 8,* 41–46.

Cummins, J. (1984). *Bilingual special education issues in assessment and pedagogy.* San Diego: College-Hill.

Cummins, J. (1992). Bilingual education and English immersion: The Ramirez report in theoretical perspective. *Bilingual Research Journal, 16,* 91–104.

Esquivel, G. B. (1988). Best practices in the assessment of limited English proficient and bilingual children. In A. Thomas & J. Grimes (Eds.), *Best practices in school psychology* (pp. 113–123). Washington, DC: National Association of School Psychologists.

Figueroa, R. A. (1990). Best practices in the assessment of bilingual children. In A. Thomas & J. Grimes (Eds.), *Best practices in school psychology II* (pp. 93–106). Washington, DC: National Association of School Psychologists.

Figueroa, R. A., Sandoval, J., & Merino, B. (1984). School psychology and limited-English-proficient (LEP) children: New competencies. *Journal of School Psychology, 22,* 131–143.

Gersten, R., & Woodward, J. (1994). The language-minority student and special education: Issues, trends, and paradoxes. *Exceptional Children, 60*(4), 310–322.

Hamayan, E. V., & Damico, J. S. (Eds.). (1991). *Limiting bias in the assessment of bilingual students.* Austin, TX: PRO-ED.

Medina, V. (1982). *Issues regarding the use of interpreters and translators in a school setting.* (ERIC Reproduction No. ED 161191)

Miller, N., & Abudarham, S. (1984). Management of communication problems in bilingual children. In N. Miller (Ed.), *Bilingualism and language disability: Assessment and remediation* (pp. 177–198). San Diego: College-Hill.

Nuttall, E. V. (1987). Survey of current practices in the psychological assessment of limited-English-proficiency handicapped children. *Journal of School Psychology, 25,* 53–61.

Ochoa, S. H., Galarza, A., & Gonzalez, D. (1996). An investigation of school psychologists' assessment practices of language proficiency with bilingual and limited-English-proficient students. *Diagnostique, 21*(4), 17–36.

Ochoa, S. H., Gonzalez, D., Galarza, A., & Guillemard, L. (1996). The training and use of interpreters in bilingual psychoeducational assessment: An alternative in need of study. *Diagnostique, 21*(3), 19–40.

Ochoa, S. H., Powell, M. P., & Robles-Pina, R. (1996). School psychologists' assessment practices with bilingual and limited-English-proficient students. *Journal of Psychoeducational Assessment, 14,* 250–275.

Ochoa, S. H., Rivera, B., & Ford, L. (1997). An investigation of school psychology training pertaining to bilingual psychoeducational assessment of primarily Hispanic students: Twenty-five years after Diana *v.* California. *Journal of School Psychology, 35,* 329–349.

Ochoa, S. H., Rivera, B., & Powell, M. P. (1997). Factors used to comply with the exclusionary clause with bilingual and limited-English-proficient pupils: Initial guidelines. *Learning Disabilities Research & Practice, 12,* 161–167.

Ortiz, A., & Yates, J. (1983). Incidence of exceptionality among Hispanics: Implications for manpower planning. *National Association of Bilingual Education Journal, 7,* 41–54.

Robertson, P., Kushner, M. I., Starks, J., & Drescher, C. (1994). An update of participation rates of culturally and linguistically diverse students in special education: The need for a research and policy agenda. *The Bilingual Special Education Perspective, 14*(1), 3–9.

Scribner, A. P. (1993). The use of interpreters in the assessment of language minority students. *The Bilingual Special Education Perspective, 12*(1), 2–6.

Tucker, J. A. (1980). Ethnic proportions in classes for the learning disabled: Issues in nonbiased assessment. *Journal of Special Education, 14,* 93–105.

U.S. Office of Education. (1977). Assistance to states for education of handicapped children: Procedures for evaluating specific learning disabilities. *Federal Register, 42,* 65083.

Wilen, D. K., & Sweeting, C. V. M. (1986). Assessment of limited English proficient Hispanic students. *School Psychology Review, 15,* 59–75.

Wright, P., & Cruz, R. S. (1983). Ethnic composition of special education programs in California. *Learning Disability Quarterly, 6,* 387–394.

HECTOR SALVIA OCHOA
Texas A&M University

BILINGUAL SPECIAL EDUCATION CULTURALLY/LINGUISTICALLY DIVERSE GIFTED STUDENTS

BILINGUAL SPECIAL EDUCATION

By the year 2025, approximately 40 percent of the total United States population will be African American, Hispanic, or Asian American (Townsend, 1995) and by 2080, non-Hispanic Whites will be a minority. Every region of the country has experienced significant increases in the number of individuals from minority backgrounds, and schools are reporting dramatic increases in the number of language minority students they serve. "Language minority" refers to students who come from homes or communities where a language other than English is spoken. A subset of this population are limited English proficient (LEP) students, whose English skills are so limited they cannot profit from instruction delivered entirely in English and thus require the support of special language programs such as bilingual education or English as a second language instruction. LEP students represent some 200 language groups with Spanish being the most common language spoken (approximately 75 percent), followed by Vietnamese, Hmong, Cantonese, Cambodian, and Korean.

There is substantial evidence that educational services currently being provided to language minority students are not sufficient to meet their needs. These students experience higher rates of retention and school attrition, score poorly on standardized tests, are underrepresented in colleges and universities, and complete post-secondary studies at low rates. They are also disproportionately represented in special education.

Disproportionate Representation in Special Education

The prevalence of disabilities among language minority students is difficult to determine because local, state, and federal education agencies do not usually report disabilities by language proficiency level. Representation is affected by such factors as definitions, eligibility criteria, geographic location, percentage of minority enrollment, district size, and available program options. Consequently, in some states, LEP students are underrepresented, while in others they are seriously overrepresented in programs for students with special needs (Harry, 1992). Patterns of over- and under-identification suggest that some students are inappropriately placed in special education, but that others are neither being identified nor receiving the services they need and to which they are entitled. Because bilingual special education is a new field, research on second language learners with disabilities is limited and, consequently, when LEP students are identified as being eligible for special education, school districts struggle with how to best address disability- and language-related needs simultaneously.

Prevention and Prereferral

With increasing frequency, service delivery models such as the Assessment and Intervention Model for the Bilingual Exceptional Student (Ortiz & Wilkinson, 1991) emphasize proactive steps to ensure that all students are academically successful by creating school climates which reflect awareness and acceptance of diversity, high expectations for all students, a challenging curriculum, quality bilingual education and ESL programs, and involvement of parents and communities. Prereferral interventions are designed to strengthen teachers' abilities to provide appropriate educational opportunities to a diverse student population. This is accomplished through professional development, which focuses on helping teachers understand the characteristics of language minority students, instructional practices known to be effective for these learners, and by giving teachers access to consultants or problem solving teams which help them design interventions to address students learning difficulties. If LEP students are ultimately referred for a comprehensive individual assessment, prereferral data help document that external factors such as limited English proficiency or lack of appropriate instruction have already been eliminated as possible causes of problems.

Assessment

Although inappropriate assessment is one of the primary causes of disproportionate representation of language minority students in special education, research on best practices in assessment of these students is still limited (Ortiz, 1997). Adaptation of standardized procedures is quite common (e.g., translations, use of interpreters, modification of test content). However, such adaptations invalidate the test, making scoring and interpretation of outcomes difficult and error-prone (Damico, 1991). Only those instruments which include appropriate samples of language minority students in the norming sample should be used in making eligibility decisions. If test norms are not appropriate, or if standardized administration procedures are violated, it is recommended that patterns of performance be described and used diagnostically to support eligibility decisions rather than reporting test scores. If performance on the formal and informal measures are positively correlated, multidisciplinary teams can be more confident that the student has a disability.

Students with disabilities demonstrate skills and abilities significantly deviant from those of students from similar language and cultural backgrounds. In the case of LEP students assessed only in English, assessments should document that the student's performance is discrepant with that of other LEP students who have had similar exposure to native language and/or English as a second language instruction. Behaviors are not deviant unless they are significantly different from the student's reference group.

Instruction

Individualized education programs (IEPs) for language minority students specify goals and objectives for native language and ESL instruction and include instructional recommendations that reflect understanding of cultural differences, socioeconomic background, preferred modalities, learning styles, and appropriate reinforcements (Yates & Ortiz, 1998). Because of the need to accommodate students' limited English proficiency, a combination of "reciprocal interaction" teaching approaches and basic skills instruction seem to be most beneficial for LEP students with disabilities (Cummins, 1984; Robertson-Courtney, Wilkinson, & Ortiz, 1991; Willig, Swedo, & Ortiz, 1987). Approaches which focus solely on teaching discrete skills in English are problematic for LEP students because activities that are simplified to focus on specific skills are frequently stripped of context and lose their meaning and purpose, becoming incomprehensible to the second language learner. Lessons which focus on specific skills (e.g., phonology or grammar) and accuracy may actually interfere with the second language acquisition process, since instruction attempts to correct "errors" which are, in reality, developmental. Reciprocal interaction approaches, on the other hand, are characterized by genuine dialogue between students and teacher, in both oral and written communication, opportunities for meaningful language use, collaborative learning groups, the teaching of basic skills in the context of lessons which focus on higher order thinking, and the incorporation of language use and development across the curriculum.

Service delivery models and alternative instructional arrangements are being explored in an effort to ensure that language minority students are served by special educators who have expertise in how language and culture influence learning (Yates & Ortiz, 1998). For example, students who are limited English proficient can be served by: (a) bilingual special educators (i.e., teachers whose certification program focused specifically on the education of language minority students with disabilities); (b) special education teachers with dual certification in special education and bilingual education or English as a second language; or (c) by bilingual education teachers with the support and consultation of the special education teacher. For effective service delivery, linkages between special education, special language programs, and general education must be established, instructional and related services must be coordinated, and the roles and responsibilities of all personnel who work with these students must be defined. Additionally, teacher education programs must prepare both monolingual and bilingual special educators to serve linguistically and culturally diverse learners. The content of pre-service teacher education which leads to licensure and certification, and perhaps even more importantly, professional development and graduate teacher training programs, must reflect competencies that promote the interface between linguistic and culturally diversity and disabilities.

REFERENCES

Cummins, J. (1984). *Bilingualism and special education: Issues in assessment and pedagogy.* Clevedon, Avon, England: Multilingual Matters Ltd.

Damico, J. S. (1991). Descriptive assessment of communicative ability in limited English proficient students. In E. V. Hamayan & J. S. Damico (Eds.), *Limiting bias in the assessment of bilingual students* (pp. 157–217). Austin, TX: PRO-ED.

Harry, B. (1992). *Cultural diversity, families, and the special education system: Communication and empowerment.* New York: Teachers College Press.

Ortiz, A. A. (1997). Learning disabilities occurring concomitantly with linguistic differences. *Journal of Learning Disabilities, 30*(3), 321–332.

Ortiz, A. A., & Wilkinson, C. Y. (1991). Assessment and intervention model for the exceptional bilingual student (AIM for the BESt). *Teacher Education and Special Education, 14*(1), 11–18.

Robertson-Courtney, P., Wilkinson, C. Y., & Ortiz, A. A. (1991). Reciprocal interaction-oriented strategies for literacy development: Teacher training outcomes. *Journal of the New York State Association for Bilingual Education, 7*(1), 95–109.

Townsend, W. A. (1995). *Pocket digest: Digest of education statistics for limited English proficient students.* Washington, DC: Office of Bilingual Education and Minority Languages Affairs.

Willig, A. C., Swedo, J. J., & Ortiz, A. A. (1987). *Characteristics of teaching strategies which result in high task engagement for exceptional limited English proficient Hispanic students.* Austin: The University of Texas, Handicapped Minority Research Institute on Language Proficiency.

Yates, J. R., & Ortiz, A. A. (1998). Developing individualized educational programs for the exceptional bilingual student. In L. Baca & H. Cervantes (Eds.), *The Bilingual Special Education Interface* (3rd ed., pp. 188–212). Columbus, OH: Merrill.

HECTOR SALVIA OCHOA
Texas A&M University

ALBA ORTIZ
SHERNAZ B. GARCIA
University of Texas

BILINGUAL ASSESSMENT AND SPECIAL EDUCATION CULTURALLY/LINGUISTICALLY DIVERSE STUDENTS AND LEARNING DISABILITIES

BILINGUAL SPEECH LANGUAGE PATHOLOGY

Bilingual speech language pathology is an emerging field within the profession of speech language pathology. It is recognized as an area of the field that serves individuals who are bilingual and have a communication disorder. There are graduate programs in the United States that train bilingual clinicians and adhere to the profession's position statement on academic and clinical competencies. The American Speech-Language Hearing Association approved a position statement that defines who can be a bilingual speech language pathologist and/or audiologist. This position statement includes the language proficiency required in the minority language and also the academic competencies necessary to provide services (Kayser, 1995). The definition states (ASHA, 1989): "Speech-language pathologists or audiologists who present themselves as bilingual for the purposes of providing clinical services must be able to speak their primary language and to speak (or sign) at least one other language with native or near-native proficiency in lexicon (vocabulary), semantics (meaning), phonology (pronunciation), morphology/syntax (grammar), and pragmatics (uses) during clinical management" (p. 93). The academic requirements (ASHA, 1995) include the following: (1) language proficiency: native or near native fluency in both the minority language and the English language; (2) normative processes: the ability to describe the process of normal speech and language acquisition for both bilingual and monolingual individuals and how those processes are manifested in oral and written language; (3) assessment: the ability to administer and interpret formal and informal assessment procedures to distinguish between communication difference and communication disorders; (4) intervention: the ability to apply intervention strategies for treatment of communicative disorders in the minority language; and (5) cultural sensitivity: the ability to recognize cultural factors that affect the delivery of speech-language pathology and audiology services to the minority language speaking community.

REFERENCES

American Speech-Language-Hearing Association (ASHA). (1989). Definition: Bilingual speech-language pathologists and audiologists. *ASHA, 31*(3), 93.

American Speech-Language-Hearing Association (ASHA). (1995). Clinical management of communicatively handicapped minority language populations. *ASHA, 27*(6), 29–32.

Kayser, H. (1995). An emerging specialist: The bilingual speech-language pathologist. In H. Kayser (Ed.), *Bilingual speech-language pathology: An Hispanic focus* (pp. 1–14). San Diego: Singular.

HORTENCIA KAYSER
New Mexico State University

BILINGUAL VERBAL ABILITY TESTS

The Bilingual Verbal Ability Tests (BVAT; Munoz-Sandoval, Cummins, Alvarado, & Ruef, 2000) are designed to provide a measure of overall verbal ability and a unique combination of cognitive and academic language abilities for bilingual individuals.

The BVAT comprises three individually administered subtests: (1) Picture Vocabulary, in which the subject is required to name a pictured object with gradually increasing degrees of difficulty; (2) Oral Vocabulary, which is broken into two tasks: Synonyms, where the subject is required to make a synonymous word association with gradually increasing difficulty; and Antonyms, where the subject is required to make an opposite word association with gradually increasing degrees of difficulty; and (3) Verbal Analogies, where the subject is required to recognize the analogous relationships between two words and to find a third word that bears the same relationship.

All the subtests are administered first in the English language. Each item failed in English is readministered in the native language. If the child answers correctly in his or her native language, that score is added to the score for that subtest. The overall subtest score is based on the child's knowledge or reasoning skills using both languages, thus reflecting the nature of the bilingual ability.

These tests are drawn from the Woodcock Johnson–Revised (WJ-R) Cognitive (COG) Battery and translated into 15 different languages, presumably the most widely used languages in the United States: Arabic, Chinese (simplified and traditional), English, French, German, Haitian-Creole, Hindi, Hmong, Italian, Japanese, Korean, Navajo, Polish, Portuguese, Russian, Spanish, Turkish, and Vietnamese. These three subtests have been translated from English into 18 languages.

There are two basic options for the BVAT interpretation: age based or grade based. In addition to standard scores, the Relative Proficiency Index (the same indicator as the Relative Mastery Index in the WJ-R), and percentile ranks, the BVAT offers an instructional-zones index, five levels of English-language proficiency (Negligible, Very Limited, Limited, Fluent, and Advanced), and aptitude or achievement discrepancies in relation to the WJ-R Achievement Tests. All scoring is automated through the Scoring and Reporting Program software, which is a standard feature of the BVAT kit. The BVAT Comprehensive Manual contains the Examiner Training and Practice Exercises. A training videotape, prepared by the publisher, accompanies the test.

The BVAT provides an overall score (BVA) that can be used to determine an individual's overall level of verbal ability. Raw scores are converted to standard scores, percentile ranks, age and grade equivalents, relative proficiency index, instructional ranges, and cognitive-academic language proficiency (CALP) levels.

The U.S. normative data for the BVAT on 5,602 subjects was obtained during WJ-R COG standardization (1988–1989). Reliability was calculated through a split-half procedure corrected for length by the Spearman-Brown formula and resulted in reliability coefficients in the high .80s for the subtests and in the mid .90s for the clusters. Construct validity was reported within the .7 to .9 range.

Some of the 15 languages have deleted items (sometimes up to four items) because of the untranslatable nature of these items (see Table 8-5, p. 71, in the test manual). It is not clear what effect it may have on the scores obtained if they are based on norms that include all items. Another aspect of the content validity is the issue of uneven complexity (from a relatively easy naming task in Picture Vocabulary to a much more difficult verbal reasoning task in Verbal Analogies).

REFERENCES

Munoz-Sandoval, A. F., Cummins, J., Alvarado, C. G., & Ruef, M. L. (2000). *Bilingual Verbal Ability Tests (BVAT)*. Itasca, IL: Riverside.

Reviewed in Plake, B. S., & Impara, J. C. (Eds.). (2001). *The four-teenth mental measurements yearbook* (pp. 119–121). Lincoln, NE: Buros Institute of Mental Measurements.

Woodcock, R. W., McGrew, K., & Mather, N. (2001). *Woodcock-Johnson III Tests of Cognitive Abilities.* Itasca, IL: Riverside.

RON DUMONT
Fairleigh Dickinson University

JOHN O. WILLIS
Rivier College

BILL OF RIGHTS FOR THE DISABLED

The Bill of Rights for the Disabled is a codification by the United Cerebral Palsy Association of rights that have been won for individuals with disabilities in court cases and before legislatures during the 1960s and 1970s. These rights are as follows:

1. The right to prevention, early diagnosis, and proper care.
2. The right to a barrier-free environment and accessible transportation.
3. The right to an appropriate public education.
4. The right to necessary assistance, given in a way that promotes independence.
5. The right to a choice of lifestyles and residential alternatives.
6. The right to an income for a lifestyle comparable to that of the able-bodied.
7. The right to training and employment as qualified.
8. The right to petition social institutions for just and humane treatment.
9. The right to self-esteem.

STAFF

BINET, ALFRED (1857–1911)

Alfred Binet, the founder of French experimental psychology, became director of the Laboratory of Physiological Psychology at the Sorbonne in Paris in 1895. In the same year, he and a colleague founded the first French journal of psychology, *Année psychologique*. He was cofounder of the Société Libre pour l'Étude Psychologique de l'Enfant, which after his death became the Société Alfred Binet.

Binet's investigations took him outside the laboratory. He observed children in schools and camps and used questionnaires and interviews to collect data. In 1904, the minister of public instruction appointed him to a commission created to formulate methods for identifying mentally retarded children in the public schools so that these children could be given a special school program. Out of Binet's work with this commission came the first scale for measuring intelligence, based on the idea of classifying children according to individual differences in performance of tasks requiring thinking and reasoning. On the assumption that intelligence increases with age, he employed the concept of mental age. Results were expressed both as mental age and by a score obtained by subtracting mental age from chronological age. The German psychologist William Stern proposed an improved way of expressing the test results: dividing mental age by chronological age, yielding an intelligence quotient.

The scale was first published by Binet and Theodore Simon in 1905 and was revised in 1908 and 1911. It was translated into English by H. H. Goddard in the United States. In 1916, L. M. Terman at Stanford University published his *Stanford Revision of the Binet Scales.* For half a century dozens of translations and revisions of Binet's scales dominated the field of intelligence testing; they are still extensively used.

Alfred Binet had a variety of other interests in the field of psychology. One of his earliest works was a book on hypnosis. In addition, he developed, with Simon, a classification of mental disorders. He also used pictures and inkblots to study thought processes, foreshadowing later projective techniques.

REFERENCES

Varon, E. J. (1935). The development of Alfred Binet's psychology. *Psychological Monographs* (No. 207). Princeton, NJ: Psychological Review.

Watson, R. I. (1963). *The great psychologists.* New York: Lippincott.

PAUL IRVINE
Katonah, New York

BIOCHEMICAL IRREGULARITIES

It has been long recognized that a large number of metabolic diseases have characteristic clinical, pathological, and biochemical irregularities that can be attributed to the congenital deficiency of a specific enzyme. This inadequacy is in turn owed to the presence of a particular abnormal gene. The identification and consequent understanding of such biochemical problems began in the early part of the twentieth century with the first demonstration of Mendelian inheritance in humans. A. E. Garrod (Roberts, 1967) derived the basic concept of these disorders through studies on the rare condition known as alcaptonuria (Garrod, 1909). His classical investigation of this abnormality has provided an elegant and simple model for the interpretation of a great variety of different inherited diseases subsequently discovered.

Alcaptonuria is a condition in which large quantities of homogentisic acid are excreted into the urine, which turns black on standing. Under normal conditions, the amino acid tyrosine is converted through a series of enzymatic reactions to fumarate and acetoacetate (La Du, 1966). Garrod noted that when homogentisic acid, a normal intermediary metabolite of tyrosine, was fed to alcaptonuric subjects, it was excreted quantitatively in urine, whereas when given to normal subjects it appeared to be readily metabolized. Additionally, the administration of tyrosine or proteins containing it to alcaptonurics augmented the excretion of homogentisic acid.

The other striking feature of alcaptonuria to which Garrod drew attention was its familial distribution. After studying the characteristic pedigrees of these subjects, he concluded that they implied a hereditary or genetic basis for the condition. Garrod pointed out that the homogentisic acid must be derived from tyrosine and that the essential feature of alcaptonuria was a block in the metabolism of this substance, whereby breakdown could proceed only as far as homogentisic acid.

Eventually Garrod described a number of metabolic peculiarities of this kind and called them inborn errors of metabolism. He viewed the inborn errors as conditions in which the specific enzyme deficiency effectively blocked at a particular point a sequence of reactions that form part of the normal course of metabolism. As a result, metabolites

immediately preceding the block would accumulate and metabolites subsequent to the block would not be formed (Harris, 1975). The various biochemical, clinical, and pathological manifestations of the condition could be regarded as secondary consequences of this primary metabolic defect. These secondary changes might be complex and widespread and would depend in general on the nature and the biochemical effects of the metabolites that tended to accumulate or whose formation was restricted (Harper, Rodwell, & Mayes, 1977).

It is now understood that the end products of gene action are proteins, either structural cell components, elements of extracellular matrices, or enzymes. Since genes are potentially mutable units, a change in a gene will disturb the synthesis of the specific protein for which it is responsible. This results in the formation of a different protein (or no protein at all), which alters the process or processes that depend on it. When the protein is absent or deficient, the normal process is impaired. The expression of such a mutation is a phenotypic effect of more or less consequence to the individual. Such defects in cellular enzyme formation are most often characterized by abnormal protein, carbohydrate, or fat metabolism.

All biochemical processes are under genetic control and each consists of a complex sequence of reactions. Part (a) of Figure 1 schematically represents a portion of a normal metabolic pathway. A substrate, the substance on which an enzyme acts, is converted into a product through the activity of a specific enzyme. A metabolic pathway consists of many such reactions or steps, each being dependent on the previous reaction and each catalyzed by a specific enzyme (Jenkins, 1983). Part (b) of the figure illustrates how

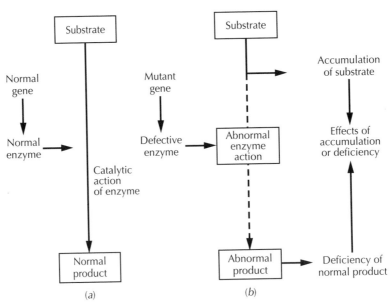

Figure 1 Alternative metabolic pathways. (a) formation of a normal product. (b) accumulation of substrate or deficiency of product as a result of an abnormal metabolic pathway (adapted from Whaley and Wong, 1983)

a change in a gene that interferes with the synthesis of an essential enzyme interrupts this process. A block in the normal pathway may produce an accumulation of the substances preceding the block, such as the monosaccharide (simple sugar) galactose in classic galactosemia (Brown, 2003) or the amino acid phenylalanine in phenylketonuria (La Conte, 2003). In other cases, the block may create a deficiency in the normal product, such as the pigment melanin in albinism or the hormone thyroxine in familial cretinism. Sometimes alternative metabolic pathways are used that result in an increase in the products of these processes such as phenylketones in phenylketonuria. The effects of defective gene action are often observable in the individual as diseases.

There are many inherited disorders caused by an inborn error of metabolism that involves either the accumulation or degradation of metabolic processes. For the most part, they are rare diseases (NORD, 2005), and the mode of transmission is almost always autosomal recessive genes. This may be best understood by considering the double-dose effect as it relates to the concept that one gene is responsible for one enzyme. If a specific gene controls the formation of an essential enzyme, and each individual has two such genes (the normal homozygote), then the enzyme is produced in normal amounts. The heterozygote, who has only one gene with a normal effect, is still capable of producing the enzyme in sufficient amounts to carry out the metabolic function under normal circumstances. However, the abnormal homozygote, who inherits a defective gene from each parent, has no functional enzyme and is, thus, clinically affected. It is becoming increasingly possible to detect and, therefore, to screen for a large variety of such inborn errors of metabolism. This should lead to the detection of the presence of the disease in the heterozygote (who is a carrier), the newborn, and the fetus before birth, thus allowing for proper genetic counseling of the parents and successful treatment of affected individuals (Goodenough, 1978).

REFERENCES

Brown, R. T. (2003). Galactosemia. In E. Fletcher-Janzen & C. R. Reynolds (Eds.), *Childhood disorders diagnostic desk reference.* New York: Wiley.

Garrod, A. E. (1909). *Inborn errors of metabolism.* New York: Oxford University Press.

Goodenough, U. (1978). *Genetics* (2nd ed.). New York: Holt, Rinehart, & Winston.

Harper, H. A., Rodwell, V. W., & Mayes, P. A. (1977). *Review of physiological chemistry* (16th ed.). Los Altos, CA: Lange Medical.

Harris, H. (1975). *The principles of human biochemical genetics* (2nd ed.). New York: American Elsevier.

Jenkins, J. B. (1983). *Human genetics.* New York: Benjamin/Cummings.

La Conte, M. (2003). Phenylketonuria. In E. Fletcher-Janzen & C. R. Reynolds (Eds.), *Childhood disorders diagnostic desk reference.* New York: Wiley.

La Du, B. N. (1966). Alcaptonuria. In J. B. Stanbury, J. B. Wyngaarden, & D. S. Fredickson (Eds.), *The metabolic basis of inherited diseases.* New York: McGraw-Hill.

NORD. (2005). *National Organization of Rare Disorders.* Retrieved June 30, 2005, from http://www.nord.org

Roberts, J. A. F. (1967). *An introduction to medical genetics* (4th ed.). New York: Oxford University Press.

Whaley, L. F., & Wong, D. L. (1983). *Nursing care of infants and children* (2nd ed.). St. Louis, MO: Mosby.

Timothy A. Ballard
University of North Carolina at Wilmington

CONGENITAL DISORDERS
CRETINISM
INBORN ERRORS OF METABOLISM
PHENYLKETONURIA

BIOFEEDBACK

Biofeedback is a treatment technique in which people are trained to change bodily functions such as temperature or muscle tension based on signals from their own bodies. The word *biofeedback* was first used in the late 1960s to describe laboratory procedures being used to train experimental research subjects to alter brain activity, blood pressure, heart rate, and other bodily functions that normally are not controlled voluntarily. Measuring a temperature with a thermometer or weight on a scale are both devices that provide feedback about the body's condition. Typically, however, biofeedback measurements used to enhance treatment are more complex and measure internal bodily function with sensitivity and precision. For example, machines designed to assess muscle tension translate electrical signals up the skin, converting them to something as simple as a flashing light that increases in intensity as muscles grow more tense to something more complex, such as a visual array on a computer screen.

At first, researchers believed that properly developed biofeedback techniques would make it possible to do away with drug treatments that often cause uncomfortable side effects in patients with serious conditions such as high blood pressure or even cancer. Today, most researchers and scientists agree that such hopes were not realistic. Biofeedback can help in the treatment of many diseases and painful conditions, but it is not a panacea. Biofeedback has shown that human beings have more control over so-called involuntary bodily functions than once thought possible. However, it has also been demonstrated that nature limits the extent of such control.

As with learning any skill, the person receiving biofeedback attempts to monitor his or her performance and thus improve their ability to relax. With muscular feedback, when a light flashes or the screen demonstrates increased tension, the individual attempts to make internal adjustments that then alter the signals or feedback. Clinical biofeedback techniques used today include treatment of many conditions, including headache, disorders of the digestive system, blood pressure problems, cardiac arrhythmias, circulatory conditions, paralysis, and even epilepsy.

Scientific method has yet to completely explain the means by which biofeedback is effective. Individuals who benefit from biofeedback are trained to relax and modify their behavior. Most scientists believe that relaxation is a key component if biofeedback is to be effective. It is thought that stressful events produce strong emotions that arouse certain physical responses. Many of these responses are controlled by the sympathetic nervous system, the network of nerves that help prepare the body to meet emergencies. When an individual faces any type of physical threat or illness, this system is likely to be innervated. Pupils dilate to let in more light. Blood vessels near the skin contract to reduce bleeding. Those in the brain and muscles dilate to increase oxygen supply. The gastrointestinal tract, including the stomach and intestine, slows down to reduce the energy expended in digestion. The heart beats faster and blood pressure rises. As the stressful event passes, the body returns to normal. Researchers believe that when this system is innervated on a regular basis, relaxation becomes habitual. When the body is repeatedly aroused, one or more bodily functions may become permanently overactive. Biofeedback is aimed at changing habitual reactions to stress that cause pain or disease.

Biofeedback is not a passive process. Individuals must examine their behavior and the activities that contribute to distress and problems. They must recognize that they can, through their own efforts, remedy some physical ailments. They often have to practice relaxation exercises on a daily basis between biofeedback sessions. Biofeedback specialists include physicians, psychologists, dentists, and even physical therapists. The Association for Applied Psychophysiology and Biofeedback (formerly the Biofeedback Society of America) is a national membership association for professionals using biofeedback. The organization produces a journal, news magazine, and other biofeedback-related publications.

SAM GOLDSTEIN
University of Utah

BIOGENIC MODELS
MAGNETIC RESONANCE IMAGING
SPECT, SINGLE PHOTON EMISSION COMPUTED
TOMOGRAPHY

BIOGENIC MODELS

Biogenic, or organic, models present causes of human actions in terms of the biological substrate that underlies behavior. Thus to predict, explain, and control behavior, the various activities of the nervous system and other bodily organs must be understood and manipulated. Implicit in this model is the notion that effective therapies will primarily involve biological manipulations such as drugs or surgery. This approach can be contrasted with psychogenic models that emphasize psychological constructs as explanatory mechanisms of behavior (Bootzin, 1984; Franzblau, Kanadanian, & Rettig, 1995).

Contemporary models of behavior are rarely in absolutely biological or psychological terms, but when a model is primarily biogenic in nature there are important implications for the user's conceptual framework in understanding behavior and implementing behavioral change programs. Biogenic models place the locus of the cause of problem behavior squarely within the individual's biological status and give only minimal roles to other parts of the ecosystem such as family or school. Most contemporary biogenic models are reductionistic and pin their ultimate hopes on an understanding of the relationships among biological, biochemical, and behavioral phenomena. Alterations, which are observed in cognitions or social relations, can be viewed as symptoms of physiological actions. Although our current understanding of biological factors may not allow for biochemical cures for all behavioral problems, the ultimate direction of the biogenic approach lies in biomedical interventions (Engel, 1977).

Critics of the biogenic model have difficulty denying that in a physical sense all behavior can ultimately be traced to biological processes. They do contend, however, that reductionist approaches may not always be the most fruitful guides to practice in education. Biogenic models tend to blame the victim by emphasizing changing the organism and not the environment or situation in which the individual exists (Albee, 1980; Millon & Davis, 1995). It is often the case that concepts of the biogenic model are confused with those of the medical or disease model. Engel (1977), however, proposed a disease model that replaced a biomedical with a biopsychosocial approach to the understanding of disordered behavior. This is now the norm (Suls & Rothman, 2004).

The organic (biogenic) model represents one of the major historical threads in the understanding of the etiology of abnormal behavior. This model has been advanced at least since the time of the Greek physician Hippocrates (Brown, 1986), and is still seen in such concepts as minimal brain dysfunction (Bootzin, 1984). Indeed, for thousands of years, it was the only viable alternative to magical or supernatural explanations of exceptional behavior. It should be noted, however, that biogenic models have not always resulted in more humane treatment or exacting scientific research into the nature of behavior disorders. For example, the warehousing of patients in the late nineteenth- and early twentieth-century psychiatric hospitals was the result in part of a belief that dealing with mental disease was hopeless until science found a biological cure (Erickson & Hyerstay, 1980).

Biogenic models may be of value to the classroom special education teacher as the basis for planning interventions. Reed (1979) noted the role of neuropsychological diagnoses in developing educational techniques that take into account deficits in brain function. In addition the biopsychosocial model takes into account aspects of chronic illness which are common to children in special education.

REFERENCES

Albee, G. (1980). A competency model to replace the deficit model. In M. Gibbs, J. Lachenmeyer, & J. Sigal (Eds.), *Community psychology: Theoretical and empirical approaches* (pp. 213–238). New York: Gardner.

Bootzin, R. (1984). *Abnormal psychology: Current perspectives* (4th ed.). New York: Random House.

Brown, R. T. (1986). Etiology and development of exceptionality. In R. T. Brown & C. R. Reynolds (Eds.), *Psychological perspectives on childhood exceptionality: A handbook* (pp. 181–229). New York: Wiley.

Engel, G. (1977). A need for a new medical model: A challenge for biomedicine. *Science, 96,* 129–136.

Erickson, R., & Hyerstay, B. (1980). Historical perspectives on treatment of the mentally ill. In M. Gibbs, J. Lachenmeyer, & J. Sigal (Eds.), *Community psychology: Theoretical and empirical approaches* (pp. 29–64). New York: Gardner.

Franzblau, S. H., Kanadanian, M., & Rettig, E. (1995). Critique of reductionistic models of obsessive compulsive disorder. *Social Science and Medicine, 41,* 99–112.

Millon, T., & Davis, R. D. (1995). The development of personality disorders. In *Developmental psychopathology, Vol. 2.* New York: Wiley.

Reed, H. (1979). Biological defects in special education: An issue in personnel preparation. *Journal of Special Education, 13,* 9–33.

Suls, J., & Rothman, A. (2004). Evolution of biopsychosocial model: Prospects and challenges for health psychology. *Health Psychology, 23,* 119–125.

LEE ANDERSON JACKSON, JR.
University of North Carolina at Wilmington

BIOLOGICAL BASIS OF EMOTIONAL DISORDERS
BIOLOGICAL BASIS OF LEARNING AND MEMORY
MEDICAL MODEL, DEFENSE OF

BIOLOGICAL BASIS OF EMOTIONAL DISORDERS

Biological factors contribute to emotional disorders in various ways. A genetic predisposition has been strongly implicated for schizophrenia, depression, and manic-depressive illness. There is at least moderate evidence of a genetic contribution to childhood autism, obsessive-compulsive disorder (Franzblau, Kanadanian, & Rettig, 1995), panic disorder, disability (Heubner & Thomas, 1995), and other conditions.

Whether because of genetics, improper nutrition, or other sources, certain areas of the nervous system can misfunction in ways that lead to behavioral abnormalities. For example, individuals who are subject to panic disorder have an overresponsive sympathetic nervous system. Even at rest, they have an elevated heart rate and blood epinephrine level compared with controls (Nesse et al., 1984). They may respond with anxiety, agitation, and palpitations to injections that produce only mild signs of arousal in other people (Charney, Heninger, & Breier, 1984; Liebowitz et al., 1984). On the other hand, studies have documented a relationship between low physiological arousal and antisocial behavior (Susman, 2001).

Many types of emotional disorders have been linked to abnormalities affecting one or more synaptic transmitter systems in the brain. One example is depression. Most antidepressant drugs prolong the activity of the monoamine transmitters (dopamine, norepinephrine, and serotonin) in the brain. One interpretation of the effect of antidepressant drugs has been that they counteract an initial deficiency in the activity at monoamine synapses. That interpretation may be incorrect, however; a prolonged increase in the abundance of synaptic transmitter molecules at a synapse leads to a compensatory decline in the later release of that transmitter and to a decline in the number of receptors sensitive to that transmitter. Because of the multitude of effects, it is uncertain whether the antidepressant drugs help to repair an initial overactivity or underactivity of the monoamine synapses. Nevertheless, it is likely that some disorder of those synapses is responsible for many manifestations of depression.

Another probable example of a behavioral disorder linked to abnormalities at synapses is Gilles de la Tourette's syndrome. This uncommon condition affects mostly boys and has its onset in childhood. The symptoms include tics, repetitive movements, repetitive sounds, and learning disabilities (Golden, 1977). Although the cause is not known, the usual treatment is haloperidol and other drugs that block dopamine synapses in the brain.

The biological basis of an emotional disorder need not be a permanent chemical disorder of the brain, however, and drugs are not always the best remedy for a biological disorder. Many cases of depression have been linked to inadequate or poorly timed sleep. Occasionally, individuals suffer from winter depressions as a result of inadequate sunlight. Uncorrected visual problems may lead to headaches. Many adolescents experience moodiness and aggressive outbursts that may be triggered by hormonal changes. A lack of exercise may predispose the body to overreact to stress. Malnutrition can aggravate psychological disorders as well. In certain cases, emotional disorders can be alleviated by reducing stress, altering sleep, diet, exercise, and other habits without resorting to tranquilizers, antidepressant drugs, or other medical interventions (Kalat, 1984; Wickramasekera, Davies, & Davies, 1996).

REFERENCES

Charney, D. S., Heninger, G. R., & Breier, A. (1984). Noradrenergic function in panic anxiety. *Archives of General Psychiatry, 41,* 751–763.

Franzblau, S. H., Kanadanian, M., & Rettig, E. (1995). Critique of the reductionist models of obsessive compulsive disorder. *Social Science and Medicine, 41,* 99–112.

Golden, G. S. (1977). Tourette syndrome. *American Journal of Diseases of Children, 131,* 531–534.

Heubner, R. A., & Thomas, R. (1995). The relationship between attachment, psychopathology, and childhood disability. *Rehabilitation Psychology, 40,* 111–124.

Kalat, J. W. (1984). *Biological psychology* (2nd ed.). Belmont, CA: Wadsworth.

Liebowitz, M. R., Fyer, A. J., Gorman, J. M., Dillon, D., Appleby, I. L., Levy, G., Anderson, S., Levitt, M., Palij, M., Davies, S. O., & Klein, D. F. (1984). Lactate provocation of panic attacks: Vol. I. Clinical and behavioral findings. *Archives of General Psychiatry, 41,* 764–770.

Nesse, R. M., Cameron, O. G., Curtis, G. C., McCann, D. S., & Huber-Smith, M. J. (1984). Adrenergic function in patients with panic anxiety. *Archives of General Psychiatry, 41,* 771–776.

Susman, E. J. (2001). Mind-body interaction and development: Biology, behavior, and context. *European Psychologist, 6,* 163–171.

Wickramasekera, I., Davies, T. E., & Davies, S. M. (1996). Applied psychophysiology: A bridge between the biomedical model and the biopsychosocial model in family medicine. *Professional Psychology: Research & Practice, 27,* 221–233.

JAMES W. KALAT
North Carolina State University

DIAGNOSTIC AND STATISTICAL MANUAL OF MENTAL DISORDERS (DSM-IV-TR)
EMOTIONAL DISORDERS

BIOLOGICAL BASIS OF LEARNING AND MEMORY

To understand the biological basis of learning and memory, two largely independent questions must be dealt with: (1) How does a pattern of experience alter the future properties of cells and synapses in the nervous system? (2) How do populations of altered cells work together to produce adaptive behavior?

Striking progress has been made toward answering the first question. According to studies of invertebrates, short-term increases in behavior can be induced by chemical changes that block the flow of potassium across the pre-synaptic membrane of certain neurons. Longer lasting changes in behavior require the synthesis of proteins in the neurons to be changed (Kandel & Schwartz, 1982). Protein synthesis also appears to be necessary for learning by vertebrates, especially for long-term retention (Davis & Squire, 1984).

Certain of the brain changes associated with learning or the ability to learn are large enough to be visible under a light microscope. Enhanced learning ability is associated with a proliferation of glial cells and increased branching of dendrites (Uphouse, 1980). Impaired learning associated with the opposite anatomical changes. The extent of branching of dendrites is highly correlated with the number of synapses found in the brain.

Memory, on the other hand, is "attention" that leaves tracks or traces in the brain. Biologically, memory functions at two broad levels, one at the cellular level and one at a systems level. The creation of memories changes individual cell membranes and synaptic physiology (Reynolds & Bigler, 1997).

Investigators have not determined how the changed neurons operate together to produce the overall changes in behavior identified as learning. They have, however, identified areas of the mammalian brain that are necessary for certain aspects of learning. The famous neurological patient H. M. had most of his hippocampus removed as a treatment for severe epilepsy. He can recall very few events that have occurred since that operation, although he has been able to learn new skills such as reading material written in mirror fashion and working the Tower of Hanoi puzzle (Cohen & Squire, 1980; Milner, Corkin, & Teuber, 1968). Experiments with animals have indicated that amnesia is most severe if damage to the hippocampus is combined with damage to the amygdala. Damage to those two areas impairs animals' ability to store sensory information and respond to it a few minutes later (Zola-Morgan & Squire, 1985). Various other patterns of learning and memory loss occur after damage to the frontal lobes of the cerebral cortex and to numerous subcortical structures.

Majovski (1997) has suggested that:

> Data collected from studies of heredity and environment show that morphogenetic development of the brain's intellectual nature is attributable to both genetic and social environmental influences, the former having slightly greater effect than the latter. What this suggests is that several different cortical and cortical-subcortical systems are operative during the process of learning and information storage. What the infant senses, then, may be in part the result of what is neurally "set" to sense or competent to sense via a selective attention process. (p. 83)

The interactive process of learning and memory with the environmental and physical factors in childhood suggests a highly interactive biological set.

Impaired learning and memory among children and adolescents are not generally caused by discretely localized brain damage. Exposure to alcohol and other toxins in utero can greatly impair brain development, as can severe malnutrition, or a chronic lack of social stimulation in early childhood. Head injury leading to a temporary loss of consciousness is a commonly overlooked source of minor, diffuse brain damage (Bruce & Echemendia, 2003). These factors coupled with the process of brain development and acculturation (Uomoto & Wong, 2000) makes the diagnosis of learning and memory problems very difficult.

REFERENCES

Bruce, J. M., & Echemendia, R. J. (2003). Delayed-onset deficits in verbal encoding strategies among patients with mild traumatic brain injury. *Neuropsychology, 17,* 622–629.

Cohen, N. J., & Squire, L. R. (1980). Preserved learning and retention of pattern-analyzing skill in amnesia: Dissociation of knowing how and knowing that. *Science, 210,* 207–211.

Davis, H. P., & Squire, L. R. (1984). Protein synthesis and memory: A review. *Psychological Bulletin, 96,* 518–559.

Kandel, E. R., & Schwartz, J. H. (1982). Molecular biology of learning: Modulation of transmitter release. *Science, 218,* 433–443.

Majovski, L. V. (1997). Development of higher brain functions in children: Neural, cognitive, and behavioral perspectives. In C. R. Reynolds & E. Fletcher-Janzen (Eds.), *Handbook of clinical child neuropsychology* (2nd ed., pp. 63–101). New York: Plenum.

Milner, B., Corkin, S., & Teuber, H. L. (1968). Further analysis of the hippocampal amnesic syndrome: 14-year follow-up study of H. M. *Neuropsychologia, 6,* 215–234.

Moscovitch, M. (1985). Memory from infancy to old age: Implications for theories of normal and pathological memory. *Annals of the New York Academy of Sciences, 444,* 78–96.

Reynolds, C. R., & Bigler, E. D. (1997). Clinical neuropsychological assessment of child and adolescent memory with the Test of Learning & Memory. In C. R. Reynolds & E. Fletcher-Janzen (Eds.), *Handbook of clinical child neuropsychology* (2nd ed., pp. 296–329). New York: Plenum.

Uphouse, L. (1980). Reevaluation of mechanisms that mediate brain differences between enriched and impoverished animals. *Psychological Bulletin, 88,* 215–232.

Uomoto, J. M., & Wong, T. M. (2000). Multicultural perspectives on the neuropsychology of brain injury assessment and rehabilitation. In E. Fletcher-Janzen, T. L. Strickland, & C. R. Reynolds (Eds.), *Handbook of cross cultural neuropsychology* (pp. 169–184). New York: Springer.

Zola-Morgan, S., & Squire, L. R. (1985). Medial temporal lesions in monkeys impair memory on a variety of tasks sensitive to human amnesia. *Behavioral Neuroscience, 99,* 22–34.

JAMES W. KALAT
North Carolina State University
First edition

ELAINE FLETCHER-JANZEN
*University of Colorado at
Colorado Springs*
Second and Third editions

BIOLOGICAL FACTORS AND SOCIAL CLASS

See SOCIAL CLASS AND BIOLOGICAL FACTORS.

BIRCH, HERBERT G. (1918–1973)

Herbert G. Birch was born in New York City on April 21, 1918. He graduated from New York University (NYU) in 1939, and received the PhD degree in psychology in 1944. In 1960 Birch received the MD degree from the New York College of Medicine. He served as a research associate at the Yerkes Laboratories for Primate Biology from 1944 to 1946, as an instructor in psychology at NYU the next year, and as an assistant and associate professor at the City College of New York from 1947 to 1955. For the following 2 years, Birch was research associate at Bellevue Medical Center in New York City. From the time he received the MD degree in 1960 until his death, he was a member of the faculty of the Albert Einstein College of Medicine in New York City, first as an associate research professor and then as a full professor of pediatrics and director of the Center for Normal and Aberrant Behavioral Development. Concurrently, he was professor of psychology and education at the Ferkauf Graduate School of Humanities and Social Sciences, Yeshiva University.

An internationally known researcher in child development and brain injury, Birch was the author of 200 articles and coauthor of six books, the latter including *Brain Damage in Children* (1964), *Disadvantaged Children: Health, Nutrition, and School Failure* (1970), and *Children with Cerebral Dysfunction* (1971). He served in an editorial capacity for a number of journals, including the *Journal of Special Educa-*

Herbert G. Birch

tion, the *American Journal of Mental Deficiency,* the *American Journal of Child Psychology and Human Development,* and the *International Journal of Mental Health.* In 1971 he received the Kennedy International Award for Scientific Research for outstanding scientific research contributing to the understanding and alleviation of mental retardation.

Birch died at his home in Suffern, New York, on February 4, 1973. In his eulogy, Dr. Leon Eisenberg said of Birch, "Those who knew Herbert Birch recognized that they were in the presence of authentic genius. His knowledge was encyclopedic; his intellect, prodigious; his productivity, unmatched." In May 1973, Birch was posthumously granted the Research Award of the American Association on Mental Deficiency.

REFERENCES

Birch, H. G. (Ed.). (1964). *Brain damage in children.* Baltimore: Williams & Wilkins.

Birch, H. G., & Diller, K. (1971). *Children with cerebral dysfunction.* New York: Grune & Stratton.

Birch, H. G., & Gussow, J. D. (1970). *Disadvantaged children: Health, nutrition and school failure.* New York: Grune & Stratton.

Eisenberg, L. (1971). Herbert Birch 1918–1973. *International Journal of Mental Health, 1,* 80–81.

PAUL IRVINE
Katonah, New York

BIRCH, JACK W. (1915–1998)

A native of Glassport, Pennsylvania, Jack W. Birch began his career as an elementary education teacher after receiving a BS (1937) with majors in English and science and a minor in special education from California University of Pennsylvania. He later went on to earn his MEd from Pennsylvania State University (1941) and a PhD in Psychology from the University of Pittsburgh (1951).

Birch taught classes for educable mentally retarded children, and was a psychologist and supervisor of special education. From 1948 to 1958 he was director of special education for the Pittsburgh Public Schools, and spent the remainder of his career at the University of Pittsburgh as a professor of psychology and education, chairman of the Department of Special Education, and an associate dean in the School of Education. He was among the initial faculty organizers of the University Senate and served as its vice president. Birch became an emeritus professor in 1985 at the age of 70. He was active in the field of education and community service until his death on April 1, 1998.

As a young teacher in Eastern Pennsylvania in the 1930s, Birch was aghast at the ineptitude of a book about reme-

dial reading he had purchased. He wrote the publisher, complaining of the money he had wasted buying the book and indicating that he could do a better job himself. The response from the publisher encouraged him to go ahead and try, so he did. His first book was published by that same company, beginning a long career combining his interests in research, writing, and special education. He published over 120 articles and books on topics including gifted and talented persons and individuals with mental retardation, speech handicaps, blindness, deafness, and physical handicaps. *Teaching Exceptional Children in All America's Schools* and *Reports on the Implementation and Effects of the Adaptive Learning Environments Model in General and Special Education Settings* are two of his major books. His writings also included books related to aspects of academia, including writing better dissertations and how to make the best use of retired professors.

Believing that students with handicaps should have an opportunity to display skills society assumed they were incapable of developing, Birch was among early advocates of mainstreaming students with handicaps. In 1978 he reviewed the process of mainstreaming in a national sample of school systems, concluding that expansion of individualized education was a necessity and recommending ways to effectively implement mainstreaming. Four essential conditions were cited for successful mainstreaming: (1) regular educators must be oriented to the adaptation requirements for the inclusion of pupils with handicaps; (2) teachers must learn to use the specialized instructional materials exceptional children may need; (3) regular classroom teachers must be able, through an overt arrangement, to obtain help for pupils from special education teachers; and (4) regular classroom teachers must receive immediate assistance (with no loss of face) if a crisis in class or individual management occurs. Birch's research also indicated that many young people who were believed to have mental disabilities actually suffered from hearing problems, and that their ability to learn would be enhanced by first addressing the hearing problem.

During his lifetime, Birch traveled to numerous countries, frequently as a consultant in special education to various foreign governments and schools, and from 1985 to 1986, he was the Belle van Zuijlen professor of clinical child psychology and pedagogy at the University Utrecht, Netherlands. Among his memberships, he was a fellow of the American Psychological Association; regional chairman of the Commission on Psychology, Education, Nomenclature, and Standards of the American Association of Mental Deficiency; and president of both the Council for Exceptional Children and the Foundation for Exceptional Children. For his contributions to special education and rehabilitation, Birch received an award from the Pennsylvania Federation of the Council for Exceptional Children, and he was also honored for his service with an award from The National Accreditation Council of Services to the Blind and Visually Handicapped.

REFERENCES

Birch, J. W. (1978). Mainstreaming that works in elementary and secondary schools. *Journal of Teacher Education, 29,* 18–21.

Reynolds, M. C., & Birch, J. W. (1982). *Teaching exceptional children in all America's schools.* Reston, VA: Council for Exceptional Children.

Wang, M. C., & Birch, J. W. (1985). *Reports on the implementation and effects of the adaptive learning environments model in general and special education settings.* Pittsburgh, PA: University of Pittsburgh.

E. Valerie Hewitt
Texas A&M University
First edition

Tamara J. Martin
The University of Texas of the Permian Basin
Second edition

BIRTH INJURIES

Birth injuries are the traumatic injuries to the brain, skull, spinal cord, peripheral nerves, and muscle of the newborn that occasionally occur during the birth process. These injuries include cephalohematoma, skull fracture, central nervous system hemorrhage, spinal cord injury, peripheral nerve injury, bony injury, abdominal injury, cerebral palsy, and seizure disorders. The frequency of these birth injuries has greatly decreased with the declining use of high and midforceps, better monitoring during labor, and decreased vaginal breech deliveries (Brann, 1985). However the frequency of birth injuries may vary depending on the introduction of new techniques to assist delivery such as vacuum extraction (Hes, de Jong, Paz, & Avezaat, 1997).

Cephalohematoma usually refers to a benign traumatic lesion to the skull in which blood pools under the periosteum and is confined by suture boundaries. But 10 to 25 percent of all cephalohematomas are associated with an underlying skull fracture. These fractures rarely pose major problems but if depressed can result in compression of the skull (Menkes, 1984).

Central nervous system hemorrhage may be caused by mechanical trauma to the infant's brain during the birth process. The hemorrhage may occur in the subarachnoid space, the subdural space, or the dural space, or it may be intracerebral. The most common type of traumatic central nervous system hemorrhage is the subarachnoid hemorrhage resulting from tears in the meninges. Usually this is a benign condition unless it is associated with perinatal hypoxia or meningitis (Oxorn, 1986).

Subdural hemorrhage, now uncommon, may result in hydrocephalus and seizures. Intracerebral hemorrhage, one of the rarest types of traumatic central nervous system hemorrhage in the newborn, may result in increased intracranial pressure, hemiparesis, and convulsions. Hemorrhage into the dural space is also rare, but it usually results in massive hemorrhage and early neonatal death (Brann, 1985).

Traumatic spinal cord injuries are unusual. The most common sites of damage are the lower cervical and upper thoracic regions. These injuries can lead to stillbirth, respiratory failure, paralysis, or spasticity (Oxorn, 1986).

Peripheral nerve injuries can involve trauma to the brachial plexus, the phrenic nerve, the facial nerve, or the radial nerves. The nerve injuries are usually caused by traction or direct compression of the nerve itself. Trauma to the brachial plexus may cause muscle atrophy, contractures, and impaired limb growth (Menkes, 1984). The most common brachial plexus injury is Erb's palsy which involves extension and paralysis of the arm, wrist and fingers. Although quick recovery may be observed, complete recovery can take months (Smith & Ouvrier, 2006).

Trauma to the phrenic nerve may cause diaphragm paralysis and mimic congenital pulmonary or heart disease, resulting in long-term ventilatory support. Damage to the facial nerve results in weakness of the muscles to the affected side of the face, causing failure on the affected side of the mouth to move and the eyelid to close. Radial nerve injury may result in wrist drop and the inability to extend the fingers and the thumb (Menkes, 1984).

Traumatic bony injuries include fractures of the clavicle, humerus, and femur. Fracture of the clavicle is the most common bony injury; it usually occurs in association with shoulder dystocia. Fractures of the humerus and femur are rare and result from traumatic delivery (Oxorn, 1986).

Traumatic abdominal injuries are uncommon but they can have serious consequences. The traumatic abdominal injuries include hepatic or splenic rupture; they result from traumatic delivery. These injuries are usually life-threatening conditions (Oxorn, 1986).

Cerebral palsy is a chronic nonprogressive disorder of the pyramidal motor system resulting in lack of voluntary muscle control and coordination. The cause is uncertain but cerebral anoxia during the perinatal period has been associated with the resulting cerebral damage (Rosen, 1985).

There are several types of cerebral palsy: spastic, dyskinetic, ataxic, and mixed-type. Spastic cerebral palsy, the most common clinical type, is characterized by hypertonicity, uneven muscle tone, persistent primitive reflexes, lack of normal postural control, and incomplete spastic paralysis (Whaley & Wong, 1983).

Dyskinetic cerebral palsy is characterized by slow, writhing movements that involve the entire body. There is also high-frequency deafness associated with this type of cerebral palsy. Ataxic cerebral palsy is manifested by irregular muscle action and failure of muscle coordination. Mixed-type cerebral palsy is manifested by a combination of spasticity and atethosis, the slow writhing movements (Whaley & Wong, 1983).

Disabilities associated with cerebral palsy include mental retardation, seizure disorders, impaired behavioral and interpersonal relationships, and impairment of other senses. Approximately two-thirds of those diagnosed with cerebral palsy are also mentally retarded. About 50 percent of those with cerebral palsy have some type of seizure disorder. Those with impaired behavioral relationships usually have poor attention spans and hyperactive behavior. Impairment of the other senses include both visual and hearing defects (Batshaw & Perret, 1981). Cerebral palsy is a lifelong affliction. Most of those with the disorder live to adulthood but only 10 percent become self-supporting. The other 90 percent need support both medically and socially (Batshaw & Perret).

Seizure disorders may result from many causes, including perinatal asphyxia, intracranial hemorrhage, infection, congenital defects, metabolic disorders, drug withdrawal, inherited defects, and kernicterus. Perinatal asphyxia is the most frequent cause of seizures in the pre- and full-term infant. Perinatal asphyxia as the cause of neonatal seizures has the poorest prognosis. Approximately 60 percent of those infants with seizures caused by perinatal asphyxia have permanent neurologic sequelae and lifelong seizure disorders (Brann, 1985; Hill & Volpe, 2006).

REFERENCES

Batshaw, R. L., & Perret, Y. M. (1981). *Children with handicaps: A medical primer.* Baltimore: Brookes.

Brann, A. W. (1985). Factors during neonatal life that influence brain disorders. In J. M. Freeman (Ed.), *Prenatal and perinatal factors associated with brain disorders* (NIH Publication No. 85-1149, pp. 263–358). Bethesda, MD: U.S. Department of Health and Human Services.

Hes, R., de Jong, T. H., Paz, D. H., & Avezaat, C. J. (1997). Rapid evolution of a growing skull fracture after vacuum extraction. *Pediatric Neurosurgery, 26,* 269–274.

Hill, A., & Volpe, J. J. (2006). Hypoxic-ischemic cerebral injury in the newborn. In K. F. Swaiman & S. Ashwal (Eds.), *Pediatric neurology* (4th ed., pp. 191–204). St. Louis, MO: Mosby.

Menkes, J. H. (1984). Neurologic evaluation of the newborn infant. In M. E. Avery & H. W. Taeusch (Eds.), *Schaffer's diseases of the newborn* (5th ed., pp. 652–661). Philadelphia: Saunders.

Oxorn, H. (1986). *Human labor and birth* (5th ed.). Norwalk, CT: Appleton-Century-Crofts.

Rosen, M. G. (1985). Factors during labor and delivery that influence brain disorders. In J. M. Freeman (Ed.), *Prenatal and perinatal factors associated with brain disorders* (NIH Publication No. 85-1149, pp. 359–440). Bethesda, MD: U.S. Department of Health and Human Services.

Smith, S. A., & Ouvrier, R. (2006). Peripheral neuropathies in children. In K. F. Swaiman & S. Ashwal (Eds.), *Pediatric neurology* (4th ed., pp. 1178–1201). St. Louis, MO: Mosby.

Whaley, L. F., & Wong, D. L. (1983). *Nursing care of infants and children* (2nd ed.). St. Louis, MO: Mosby.

ELIZABETH R. BAUERSCHMIDT
University of North Carolina at Wilmington

ABSENCE SEIZURES
BRAIN DAMAGE/INJURY
CEREBRAL PALSY
GRAND MAL SEIZURES

BIRTH ORDER

Birth order, or sibling status, refers to a child's ordinal position in the family. There has been much speculation about the effects of birth order on important variables such as personality characteristics, mental illness, intelligence, achievement, and occupational status; but consistent relationships have been difficult to establish unequivocally. The study of birth order can be traced at least as far back as *English Men of Science* (1874), in which Galton reported that firstborns were considerably overrepresented among the scientists of his day. Alfred Adler (1958) was also convinced of the influence of family position on development, and stated that "... position in the family leaves an indelible stamp upon the style of life." (p. 154) In contrast, Craig (1996) concludes that there are no consistent personality characteristics associated with birth order.

There is an intuitive appeal to the view that each ordinal position is accompanied by unique family environments and patterns of family interactions. It is congruent with a social theory of personality development, one that emphasizes the interpersonal relationships that stem from the dynamics of a child's ordinal position. Over the course of childhood, any consistent differences in social learning experiences might well produce varied personality and achievement profiles or distinctive behavioral traits for children within the same family (Forer, 1976). For example, the amount of time that parents have available for a particular child is a function of birth order. Parents spend almost twice as much time in direct contact with firstborns as they do with succeeding children (White, Kaban, & Attanucci, 1979). Further, the older child in a typical American family is accorded more opportunities to practice language skills and take responsibility for and teach younger siblings (Harris, 1973; Smith, 1984).

Harris (1973) describes the firstborn as being adult-civilized; parents are more actively involved in nurturing and guiding their firstborn child. Younger children in the family are more likely to be peer-civilized. Therefore, the firstborn or only child would be expected to identify more closely with the parents and hold more traditional values than laterborn children (Schacter, 1959; Sutton-Smith & Rosenburg, 1970). As subsequent children are added to the family, parents spend less and less time in direct care, and older siblings assume more responsibility for child care. The opportunity to teach younger siblings and assignment of more responsible roles within the family may enhance firstborns' intellectual development. It is also possible that firstborns receive more intellectual stimulation during infancy and more direct achievement training during the preschool years than laterborns do (Bradley & Caldwell, 1984; Rothbart, 1971).

Various personality profiles, though sometimes overlapping and inconsistent, have been suggested for prominent ordinal positions. The proposed profiles follow:

Firstborn. Firstborns are said to exhibit higher standards of moral honesty, have higher need for achievement, earlier social maturation, better work habits, and higher need for recognition and approval (Forer, 1976; Harris, 1973). Firstborns are also considered to rate higher in leadership, independence, and sensitivity to stress (Sutton-Smith & Rosenberg, 1970), and tend to be dominant, more aggressive, ambitious and conservative (Koch, 1955).

Secondborn. Secondborns are believed to have good social skills, seek out group activities, and maintain better relationships in life than do firstborns. They also show more dependency behavior and seek more adult help and approval (Forer, 1976; McGurk & Lewis, 1972).

Middleborn. Middleborns, like secondborns, show better interpersonal skills and tend to express greater sensitivity to the feelings and needs of others (Falbo, 1981; Miller & Maruyama, 1976). Middle children generally have the fewest behavior problems, enjoy a healthier adjustment to life and as adults experience less anxiety in new or threatening situations (Touliatos & Lindholm, 1980; Yannakis, 1976). They also show more concern for peer norms and consequently accept peer advice more readily (Harris, 1973).

Lastborn. The youngest child is more likely to exhibit dependency and be peer oriented (Schacter, 1959). This birth order also has been associated with higher propensity to use alcohol and cigarettes (Ernst & Angst, 1983).

Onlyborn. Only children have a tendency to be leaders rather than joiners and show considerable affinity for independent behavior (Falbo, 1981). Schacter (1959) reports that only children experience more fear and anxiety during adolescence and adulthood than laterborn children. Conventional wisdom that singletons are selfish, lonely, and uncooperative is unsupported (Falbo, 1984).

Many factors affect a child's perception of ordinal position and associated family dynamics. Sex of siblings and spacing are important, as is the status of adopted children and stepchildren. For example, Adler (1958) has suggested that the male child with all female siblings may place more emphasis on his masculinity. A secondborn might assume the responsibilities of a firstborn who is developmentally delayed. With adopted children or stepchildren, previous family interactional patterns may have consequences for adjustment to new ordinal positions.

Several large-scale studies have found relationships between birth order and intelligence and achievement (Belmont & Marolla, 1973; Berbaum & Moreland, 1980; Zajonc & Markus, 1975). On the average, oldest children have higher IQs and have higher achievement in school and in careers. Only children also tend to be high achievers (Zajonc & Markus, 1975). However, a more recent study using a large data set from 1973 found that birth-order effects, when measured by educational attainment (i.e., total years of education), are negligible for small sib sizes, such as one to four children. For large families, it was found that lastborns and next-to-lastborns did considerably better than firstborns (Blake, 1990). Birth order and SAT data showed virtually no correlation. When these data were collected, presumably more resources were available for the lastborn child and more educational opportunities were afforded them.

Zajonc and Markus (1976) developed a model to make predictions concerning the relationship of birth order and intellectual ability. The confluence model uses an estimate of the average intellectual environment (AIE) of the family to predict the intelligence of each child, where AIE is equal to the total intellectual level of the family divided by the number of family members. According to the model, in a family with two children spaced only a few years apart, the second child is expected to have a lower IQ. In a family where the spacing between first and secondborn exceeds 7 years, the prediction would be reversed. The model also predicts that children from father-absent families and twins should have lowered IQs, as will laterborns from larger families.

There is no support in the literature for the confluence model. Reported birth order effects appear to be artifacts of sibship size or socioeconomic status; birth order is essentially random (Steelman, 1985). Furthermore, children raised in single-parent families do not show the poor intellectual performances that confluence theory predicts (Entwistle & Alexander, 1990).

Page and Grandon (1979) proposed the admixture theory as an alternative interpretation of the reported correlation of birth order with intellectual functioning. In their view, social class, race, and family size interact to determine birth order effects. Furthermore, their analysis indicates that social class and race are the dominant factors, while family size and birth order are actually negligible in their effects.

It must also be remembered that even the reported differences in IQ correlated with birth order are quite small and have been obtained only when large numbers of families are compared. It is therefore unwise to make predictions for individuals on the basis of birth order. Family size, family structure, and income have far greater effects on IQ than birth order. Wide spacing of siblings also tends to eliminate any evidence of birth order effects (Shaffer, 1993). To the degree that birth order may have consequences for achievement, it should not be assumed that such effects occur cross-culturally (LeVine, 1990).

As for personality, some research has found that firstborn infants, preschoolers, and adults are more socially outgoing and more interested in peer contacts than laterborns (Schachter, 1959; Snow, Jacklin, & Maccoby, 1981; Vandell, Wilson, & Whalen, 1981). There is some evidence that laterborn children tend to be somewhat more popular on average than firstborn children (Miller & Maruyama, 1976). And birth order may be a factor that contributes to children's acceptance by peers. One rationale offered is that laterborn children must learn to negotiate with older, more powerful siblings, and hence learn how to cooperate. Acquiring and using more conciliatory interpersonal skills may enable laterborns to be more popular than firstborns, who may use their greater power to dominate their younger siblings and use coercive ways with peers (Berndt & Bulleit, 1985).

However, as with correlations reported between birth order and measures of intelligence, ordinal position effects reported for sociability are quite small. Thus, one must conclude that birth order plays at best only a minor role in determining how sociable a child is likely to become. The same is true for effects on peer popularity. More research is needed before we can understand how children's experiences in their families are translated into patterns of behavior and social standing outside the family.

There is by no means unanimity of thinking about the value of birth order for understanding personality (Dunn & Plomin, 1990; Ernst & Angst, 1983; Schooler, 1972). That birth order may be significant for some individuals is not in dispute. Rather, the contention of critics of the birth order variable is that its significance is wholly unpredictable and certainly far less important than other social or genetic variables. Ernst and Angst concluded their extensive analysis of birth order and personality by saying:

> Birth order and sibship size do not have a strong impact on personality. The present investigation points instead to a broken home, an unfriendly educational style, and a premature disruption of relations with parents as concomitants of neuroticism and to higher income and social class . . . and an undisturbed home as concomitants of higher achievement. . . . Birth order influences on personality and IQ have been widely overrated. (p. 242)

And Dunn and Plomin (1990) assert that birth order "plays only a bit-part in the drama of sibling differences" (p. 85).

However, Frank Sulloway (1996), in his book *Born to Rebel*, marshals persuasive evidence for the contributions of birth order to personality development. His meta-analysis leads him to conclude that for the personality dimension of openness to experience, laterborns are more nonconforming, adventurous, and unconventional. And firstborns tend to be more responsible, achievement-oriented, and organized. They also tend to be more emotionally unstable, anxious, and fearful. In short, "firstborns tend to be dominant, aggressive, ambitious, jealous, and conservative" (p. 79). He also claims that birth order effects are 5 to 10 times greater for the key personality dimensions of openness to experience, conscientiousness, agreeableness, and neuroticism than they are for academic achievement and IQ.

It does appear that birth order, at certain times and in some cultures, has been a significant developmental variable. In societies where primogeniture has been important, the life experiences of firstborn males were vastly different from those of other siblings and were no doubt instrumental in promoting their success. There is also some evidence to support the influence of birth order, as mediated through the complex dynamics of family experience, on certain dimensions of human personality. Although birth order can affect developmental outcomes, its importance cannot be systematically predicted, and thus should be considered with reasonable caution as a potential contributor to personality development.

REFERENCES

Adler, A. (1958). *What life should mean to you.* New York: Capricorn.

Belmont, L., & Marolla, F. A. (1973). Birth order, family size, and intelligence. *Science, 182,* 1096–1101.

Berbaum, M. L., & Moreland, R. I. (1980). Intellectual development within the family: A new application of the confluence model. *Developmental Psychology, 16,* 506–518.

Berndt, T. J., & Bulleit, T. N. (1985). Effects of sibling relationships on preschoolers' behavior at home and at school. *Developmental Psychology, 21,* 761–767.

Blake, J. (1989). *Family size and achievement.* Berkeley: University of California.

Bradley, R. H., & Caldwell, B. M. (1984). 174 children: A study of the relationship between home environment and cognitive development during the first 5 years. In A. W. Gottfried (Ed.), *Home environment and early cognitive development. Longitudinal research.* Orlando, FL: Academic.

Craig, G. J. (1996). *Human development.* Upper Saddle River, NJ: Prentice Hall.

Dunn, J., & Plomin, R. (1990). *Separate lives: Why siblings are so different.* New York: Basic Books.

Entwistle, D. R., & Alexander, K. L. (1990). Beginning school math competence: Minority and majority comparisons. *Child Development, 61,* 454–471.

Ernst, C., & Angst, J. (1983). *Birth order: Its influence on personality.* Berlin: Springer-Verlag.

Falbo, T. (1981). Relationship between birth category, achievement, and interpersonal orientation. *Journal of Personality and Social Psychology, 41,* 121–131.

Forer, L. K. (1976). *The birth order factor.* New York: McKay.

Galton, F. (1874). *English men of science.* London: McMillan.

Harris, I. D. (1973). Differences in cognitive style and birth order. In J. C. Westman (Ed.), *Individual differences in children* (pp. 199–210). New York: Wiley.

Koch, H. L. (1955). Some personality correlates of sex, sibling position, and sex of sibling among five- and six-year old children. *Genetic Psychology Monographs, 52,* 3–50.

LeVine, R. A. (1990). Enculturation: A biosocial perspective on the development of self. In D. Cicchetti & M. Beeghly (Eds.), *The self in transition: Infancy to childhood* (pp. 99–117). Chicago: University of Chicago.

McGurk, H., & Grandon, G. M. (1979). Birth order: A phenomenon in search of an explanation. *Developmental Psychology, 7,* 33, 366.

Miller, N., & Maruyama, G. (1976). Ordinal position and peer popularity. *Journal of Personality and Social Psychology, 33,* 123–131.

Page, E. B., & Grandon, G. M. (1979). Family configuration and mental ability: Two theories contrasted with U.S. data. *American Educational Research Journal, 16,* 257–272.

Rogers, J. L. (1984). Confluence effects: Not here, not now! *Developmental Psychology, 20,* 321–331.

Rothbart, M. K. (1971). Birth order and mother-child interaction in an achievement situation. *Journal of Personality and Social Psychology, 17,* 113–120.

Schacter, S. (1959). *The psychology of affiliation.* Stanford, CA: Stanford University.

Schooler, C. (1972). Birth order effects: Not here, not now. *Psychological Bulletin, 78,* 161–175.

Shaffer, D. R. (1993). *Developmental psychology: Childhood and adolescence* (3rd ed.). Pacific Grove, CA: Brooks/Cole.

Smith, T. (1984). School grades and responsibility for younger siblings: An empirical study of the teaching function. *American Sociological Review, 49,* 248–261.

Snow, M. E., Jacklin, C. N., & Maccoby, E. E. (1981). Birth-order differences in peer sociability at thirty-three months. *Child Development, 52,* 589–595.

Stagner, R., & Katzoff, E. T. (1936). Personality as related to birth order and family size. *Journal of Applied Psychology, 20,* 340–346.

Steelman, L. C. (1985). A tale of two variables: A review of the intellectual consequences of sibship size and birth order. *Review of Educational Research, 55,* 353–386.

Sulloway, F. J. (1996). *Born to rebel: Birth order, family dynamics, and creative lives.* New York: Pantheon.

Sutton-Smith, B., & Rosenberg, B. G. (1970). *The sibling.* New York: Holt, Rinehart, & Winston.

Touliatos, J., & Lindholm, B. W. (1980). Birth order, family size, and children's mental health. *Psychological Reports, 46,* 1097–1098.

Vandell, D. L., Wilson, K. S., & Whalen, W. T. (1981). Birth-order and social experience differences in infant-peer interaction. *Developmental Psychology, 17,* 438–445.

White, B. L., Kaban, B. T., & Attanucci, J. S. (1979). *The origins of human competence.* Lexington, MA: Heath.

Yiannakis, A. (1976). Birth order and preference for dangerous sports among males. *Quarterly Research, 47,* 42–67.

Zajonc, R. B., & Markus, G. B. (1975). Birth order and intellectual development. *Psychological Review, 82,* 74–88.

JAMES M. APPLEFIELD
University of North Carolina at Wilmington

PERSONALITY ASSESSMENT
SOCIOECONOMIC STATUS
TEMPERAMENT

BIRTH TRAUMA

According to Freudian psychodynamic theory, early traumatic and painful events produce memories that, when repressed into the unconscious, may affect later life. Otto Rank (1929) elaborated on the proposition that birth is itself traumatic: It suddenly and painfully thrusts the infant from the warm, secure womb into a cold, hostile, and frustrating world. When frustrated later in life, people may in some ways behave as though they wished to return to the womb.

More recently, Leboyer (1975) has argued that birth should be as gentle as possible for both mother and infant. In his birthing technique, the shock of birth is reduced by, among other things, keeping light and noise levels in the delivery room low. At birth, the newborn is placed on the mother's breast, massaged to decrease initial crying, and placed in a warm bath. The father attends and assists in handling the newborn.

Although some physicians initially suggested that Leboyer's method put both newborn and mother at risk, research indicates that the procedure is safe. Relative to those conventionally delivered, Leboyer infants evidence normal physiological functioning (Kliot & Silverstein, 1984) and no differences in either maternal or infant morbidity or infant behavior (Nelson et al.). At present, with the exception of shorter active labors among mothers expecting a Leboyer delivery (Nelson et al., 1980), advantages of the method appear more psychological than physiological (Grover, 1984). Indeed, evidence of long-term consequences of both conventional and Leboyer births are notably lacking, and the concept of birth trauma, particularly the Rankian version, is largely in disrepute.

Considering the other side of the issue, Handley et al. (1997) asked whether infants who had endured traumatic near-death births showed any later adverse effects. They longitudinally compared the development from 4 to 8 years of age of a group who had nearly suffocated during birth with a group who had experienced a normal birth. The two groups had comparable familial characteristics. The group that suffered the traumatic birth experience did not show meaningful deficits in cognitive and motor development, health, or general behavior.

Evidence of long-term effects of birth experiences, varying from Leboyer's gentle technique through traumatic ones, is notably lacking. Although it still has adherents, the concept of birth trauma, particularly the Rankian version, is largely in disrepute.

REFERENCES

Grover, J. W. (1984). Leboyer and obstetric practice. *New York State Journal of Medicine, 84,* 158–159.

Handley, D. M., Low, J. A., Burke, S. O., Wuarick, M., Killen, H., & Derrick, E. J. (1997). Intrapartum fetal asphyxia and the occurrence of minor deficits in 4 to 8 year old children. *Developmental Medicine and Child Neurology, 39,* 508–514.

Kliot, D., & Silverstein, L. (1984). Changing maternal and newborn care. *New York State Journal of Medicine, 84,* 169–174.

Leboyer, F. (1975). *Birth without violence.* New York: Knopf.

Nelson, N. M., Enkin, M. W., Saigal, S., Bennett, K. J., Milner, R., & Sackett, D. L. (1980). A randomized clinical trial of the Leboyer approach to childbirth. *New England Journal of Medicine, 302,* 655–60.

Rank, O. (1929). *The trauma of birth.* New York: Harcourt, Brace.

ROBERT T. BROWN
SHIRLEY PARKER WELLS
University of North Carolina at Wilmington
First edition

AIMEE R. HUNTER
University of North Carolina at Wilmington
Second edition

ATTACHMENT DISORDER
CHILD ABUSE

BLATT, BURTON (1927–1985)

Burton Blatt, widely known as a leader in the movement for deinstitutionalization of people with mental retardation, began his professional career as a special class teacher in the public schools of New York City. After earning the doctorate in special education at Pennsylvania State University in 1956, he served on the faculties of Southern Connecticut State College and Boston University before joining the faculty of Syracuse University in 1969, where he served as dean of the School of Education from 1976 until his death in 1985.

In 1971 he formed the Center on Human Policy at Syracuse University, devoted to the study and promotion of open settings for people with mental retardation and other disabilities. His work was characterized by an inspirational humanism that contributed greatly to his effectiveness as a leader.

REFERENCES

Blatt, B. (1984). Biography in autobiography. In B. Blatt & R. J. Morris (Eds.), *Perspectives in special education: Personal orientations* (pp. 263–307). Glenview, IL: Scott, Foresman.

Blatt, B., & Kaplan, F. (1966). *Christmas in purgatory: A photographic essay on mental retardation* (2nd ed.). Boston: Allyn & Bacon.

Semmel, M. I. (1985). In memoriam: Burton Blatt, 1927–1985. *Exceptional Children, 52,* 102.

PAUL IRVINE
Katonah, New York

BLIND

Blind is a term used to refer to those students who have either no vision or, at most, light perception (the ability to tell light from dark) but no light projection (the ability to identify the direction from which light comes; Colenbrander, 1977; Faye, 1970; NICHCY, 1998). Educationally, one who is blind learns primarily through tactual, auditory, and kinesthetic experiences, without the use of vision. The legal term for blindness is corrected visual acuity of 20/200 or less in the better eye and/or field of vision of 20 degrees or less (Goble, 1984; NICHCY, 1998). Severe visual impairments (legally or totally blind) occur at a rate of .06 per 1,000 (NICHCY, 1998). Individuals classified as blind under this legal definition receive certain benefits such as special educational materials and an extra income tax deduction.

The degree to which blindness or any type of visual impairment affects development depends on the type of visual loss, the severity of the loss, the age of onset, intellectual abilities, and environmental experiences. Lack of vision results in delays or limitations in motor, cognitive, and social development.

Blind children are limited in their ability to get about. Without visual input, the blind infant is not motivated to reach and move toward interesting objects in the environment. As soon as the blind infant finds it exciting to hear sounds, he or she will begin to reach and move toward the objects in the environment that produce sound. This does not occur for several months, because hearing sound does not motivate movement toward objects as soon as seeing objects (Fraiberg, 1977). As a result of the limitation in mobility, an older blind student cannot change his or her surroundings and activities as freely as a sighted one. Blind students, therefore, are dependent on assistance from others; this affects their attitudes and social relationships (Gourgey, 1998; Lowenfeld, 1981).

Cognitively, blind children are restricted in their range and variety of experiences. They cannot perceive objects in the environment that are beyond their grasp, including those that are too large or too small, or those that are moving. Blind children who use their tactual sense cannot directly observe such objects as the sun, the moon, and the clouds. Large buildings, mountains, and rivers cannot be observed as a whole. Other examples of objects that are inaccessible are flies, ants, butterflies, and spider webs: they are too fragile. Other objects such as burning wood or boiling water, cannot be touched under certain circumstances. Hearing, while it gives clues such as distance and direction, does not give a concrete idea of an object. If a blind child hears a bird, he or she can learn its sound and identify its location, but cannot perceive its shape, size, or other physical characteristics (Lowenfeld, 1981).

Socially, blind children are limited in interaction with the environment. They cannot see facial expressions of parents, teachers, and peers; they cannot model appropriate social behavior through imitation; and sometimes they are unaware of the presence of others unless a sound is made. While touch provides direct information, it is often socially unacceptable (Division for the Visually Handicapped, Council for Exceptional Children, 1982).

Historically, academically oriented blind and low-vision students have been mainstreamed successfully into regular classes. They obtain their specialized skills in a variety of placement options. These include:

1. *Itinerant Program.* The blind or low-vision student is enrolled in the regular class in the neighborhood school and an itinerant teacher who travels from school to school provides direct instruction and serves as a consultant to the regular teachers several times a week.

2. *Resource Room Program.* The blind or low-vision student is enrolled in the regular class in a school within the district or town and a resource room teacher is housed in the school and is readily available to work with the student on a daily basis at regularly scheduled times and when needed.

3. *Special Class.* The blind or low-vision student is enrolled in a self-contained class in a public or private school setting for most of the day. Usually, those students with multiple impairments in addition to a visual handicap are placed in this type of setting.

4. *Residential School.* The blind or low-vision student enrolled in this placement usually has additional disabilities and/or cannot be cared for adequately at home. Sometimes blind students attend residential schools for short periods of time to develop intensive skills in such areas as orientation and mobility, vocational training, and technology (Cartwright, Cartwright, & Ward, 1981).

The unique curriculum for blind students includes reading and writing braille; typing; listening skills using human and synthetic speech; map and chart reading; domestic skills; orientation and mobility; career education; and instruction in the use of special aids and equipment such as the Cranmer abacus, talking calculators, cassette tape recorders, electronic reading machines, and other hardware and software adaptations that access computers (Heward & Orlansky, 1984).

The National Federation of the Blind (NFB) has an excellent website devoted to technology for the blind. It displays recent assistive devices, includes news on special issues such as voting machine accessibility, and represents individuals who are blind in accessibility issues with large companies and agencies (NFB, 2005). Major resources relevant to blind students cited by the National Information Center for Children and Youth with Disabilities (1998) are:

American Council of the Blind Parents
c/o American Council of the Blind
1155 15th Street N.W., Suite 720
Washington, D.C. 20005
(202) 467-5081; 1-800-424-8666
Web Address: http://www.acb.org

American Foundation for the Blind
11 Penn Plaza, Suite 300
New York, NY 10001
1-800-AFBLIND (Toll Free)
To order publications, call: 1-800-232-3044
E-mail: afbinfo@afb.org
Web Address: http://www.afb.org/afb

Blind Children's Center
4120 Marathon Street
Los Angeles, CA 90029-0159
(213) 664-2153; 1-800-222-3566
E-mail: info@blindcntr.org
Web Address: http://www.blindcntr.org/bcc

Division for the Visually Handicapped
c/o Council for Exceptional Children
1920 Association Drive
Reston, VA 22091-1589
(703) 620-3660

National Association for Parents of the Visually Impaired, Inc.
P.O. Box 317
Watertown, MA 02272
(817) 972-7441
800-562-6265

National Association for Visually Handicapped
22 West 21st Street, 6th Floor
New York, NY 10010
(212) 889-3141
E-mail: staffnavh@org
Web Address: http://www.navh.org

National Braille Association, Inc. (NBA)
3 Townline Circle
Rochester, NY 14623
(716) 427-8260

National Braille Press
88 St. Stephen Street
Boston, MA 02115
(617) 266-6160; 1-800-548-7323

National Eye Institute
National Institutes of Health
U.S. Department of Health & Human Services
Building 31, Center Drive, MSC2510
Bethesda, MD 20892-2510
(301) 496-5248
Web Address: http://www.nei.nih.gov

National Federation of the Blind, Parents Division
c/o National Federation of the Blind
1800 Johnson Street
Baltimore, MD 21230
(410) 659-9314
E-mail: epc@roudley.com
Web Address: http://www.nfb.org

National Library Services for the Blind and Physically Handicapped
Library of Congress
1291 Taylor Street, N.W.
Washington, D.C. 20542
(202) 707-5100; 1-800-424-8567
E-mail: nls@loc.gov
Web Address: http://www.loc.gov./nls

Prevent Blindness America
500 E. Remington Road
Schaumburg, IL 60173
(708) 843-2020; 1-800-221-3004 (Toll Free)
E-mail: info@preventblindness.org
Web Address: http://www.prevent-blindness.org

The Foundation Fighting Blindness
(formerly National Retinitis Pigmentosa Foundation)
Executive Plaza One, Suite 800
11350 McCormick Road
Hunt Valley, MD 21031-1014
1-800-683-5555 (Toll Free)
(410) 785-1414; (410) 785-9687 (TT)
Web Address: http://www.blindness.org

REFERENCES

Cartwright, G. P., Cartwright, C. A., & Ward, M. (1981). *Educating special learners.* Belmont, CA: Wadsworth.

Colenbrander, A. (1977). Dimensions of visual performance. *Archives of American Academy of Ophthalmology, 83,* 332–337.

Division for the Visually Handicapped, Council for Exceptional Children. (1982). *Visual impairments fact sheet.* Reston, VA: ERIC Clearinghouse on Handicapped and Gifted Children.

Faye, E. E. (1970). *The low vision patient.* New York: Grune & Stratton.

Fraiberg, S. (1977). *Insights from the blind.* New York: Basic Books.

Goble, J. L. (1984). *Visual disorders in the handicapped child.* New York: Marcel Dekker.

Gourgey, C. (1998). Music therapy in the treatment of social isolation in visually impaired children. *RE:view, 29,* 157–162.

Heward, W. L., Orlansky, M. D. (1984). *Exceptional children.* Columbus, OH: Merrill.

Lowenfeld, B. (1981). *Berthold Lowenfeld on blindness and blind people.* New York: American Foundation for the Blind.

National Federation of the Blind (NFB). (2005). *Technology for the blind.* Retrieved July 1, 2005, from http://www.nfb.org/tech.htm

National Information Center for Children and Youth with Disabilities (NICHCY). (1998). *General information about visual impairments Fact Sheet Number 13.* Washington, DC: Author.

ROSANNE K. SILBERMAN
Hunter College, City University of New York

AMERICAN PRINTING HOUSE FOR THE BLIND
BLINDISMS
BRAILLE
ELECTRONIC TRAVEL AIDS

BLIND INFANTS

An increase in the birth of blind infants can be related to four major factors: (1) prematurity; (2) family history of a visual defect; (3) infection during pregnancy; and (4) difficult or assisted labor (Ellingham et al., 1976). With increasing medical advances in saving premature infants, the incidence of retinopathy of prematurity (previously termed retrolental fibroplasia) is rising (Morse & Trief, 1985).

The increase of visually impaired infants demands focused attention toward early intervention efforts. Unfortunately, many of the infants born prematurely are also born with deafness, mental retardation, and blindness (Morse & Trief, 1985). Programs for both normally developing blind infants and multiply disabled infants require intervention in areas including motor, sensory, communication, and conceptual development. Parent involvement is a critical component in the early intervention of blind infants (CEC, 1987; Moore, 1984). As an example, Ferrell (1985) developed a training handbook for parents of visually impaired and multiply disabled children, describing several intervention strategies. Current research is mostly focused on early social and emotional development in terms of interactions between babies and their caregivers. A list of references that may be helpful to the reader are below. Online resources can be found at the Blind Babies Foundation website at http://www.blindbabies.org/index.htm.

REFERENCES

Aitken, K., & Trevarthen, C. (1997). Self/other organization in human psychological development. *Development and Psychopathology, 9*(4), 653–677.

Bigelow, A. (1995). The effect of blindness on the early development of the self. In P. Rochat et al. (Eds.), *The self in infancy: Theory and research* (Vol. 112, pp. 327–347). Amsterdam, Netherlands: North Holland/Elsevier Science.

Chen, D. (1996). Parent-infant communication: Early intervention for very young children with visual impairment or hearing loss. *Infants and Young Children, 9,* 1–12.

Chen, D. (1999). Interactions between infants and caregivers: The context for early intervention. In D. Chen (Ed.), *Essential elements in early intervention: Visual impairment and multiple disabilities* (pp. 22–48). New York: American Foundation for the Blind.

Council for Exceptional Children (CEC). (1992). *Visual impairments.* (ERIC Digest No. E511)

Dote-Kwan, J. (1995). Impact of mothers' interactions on the development of their young visually impaired children. *Journal of Visual Impairment & Blindness, 89,* 47–58.

Ellingham, T., Silva, P., Buckfield, P., & Clarkson, J. (1976). Neonatal at risk factors, visual defects and the preschool child: A report from the Queen Mary Hospital multidisciplinary child development study. *New Zealand Medical Journal, 83,* 74–77.

Erwin, E. J. (1994). Social competence in young children with visual impairments. *Infants and Young Children, 6,* 26–33.

Erwin, E. J., & Hill, E. W. (1993). Social participation of young children with visual impairments in specialized and integrated environments. *Journal of Visual Impairment & Blindness, 87*(5), 138–142.

Ferrell, K. (1985). *Reach out and teach: Meeting the training needs of parents of visually and multiply handicapped young children.* New York: American Foundation for the Blind.

Hughes, M., Dote-Kwan, J., & Dolendo, J. (1998). A closer look at the cognitive play of preschoolers with visual impairments in the home. *Exceptional Children, 64,* 451–462.

Kekelis, L. (1992). A field study of a blind preschooler. In S. L. Sacks, L. Kekelis, & R. Gaylord-Ross (Eds.), *The development of social skills by blind and visually impaired students.* New York: American Foundation for the Blind.

Kekelis, L. (1996). Blind and sighted children with their mothers: The development of discourse skills. *Journal of Visual Impairment & Blindness, 90*(5), 423–436.

Moore, S. (1984). The need for programs and services for visually handicapped infants. *Education of the Visually Handicapped, 16,* 48–57.

Morse, A., & Trief, E. (1985). Diagnosis and evaluation of visual dysfunction in premature infants with low birth weight. *Journal of Visual Impairment & Blindness, 79,* 248–251.

Preisler, G. M. (1997). Social and emotional development of blind children: A longitudinal study. In V. Lewis & G. Collis (Eds.), *Blindness and psychological development in young children.* Leicester, England: British Psychological Society.

Sacks, S. Z., & Silberman, R. K. (2000). Social skills. In A. J. Koenig & M. C. Holbrook (Eds.), *Foundations of education: Instructional strategies for teaching children and youths with visual impairments* (Vol. 2, pp. 616–652). New York: American Foundation for the Blind.

VIVIAN I. CORREA
University of Florida

BLIND
VISUAL IMPAIRMENT

BLINDISMS

Blindisms is a term used to describe a group of simple or complex repetitive behaviors that involve both small movements of various parts of the body, such as eye rubbing, head turning, and hand flapping, and large body movements such as rocking or swaying (Warren, 1984). This term is actually a misnomer, since these behaviors occur in other types of children as well, including those who are autistic, retarded, and even normal. More appropriate terms that do not single out blind children are stereotypic behaviors or mannerisms.

One of the most common mannerisms in blind children is pressing on one or both eyes. Pressure on the eyeball results in a pleasurable sensation to the child, that is, the child may find it entertaining and relaxing. The most active eye pressers are children with retinal disorders (Scott, Jan, & Freeman, 1985). Children who are continual eye pressers tend to have deeply depressed eyes and black circles around their eyes; this detracts from their overall appearance. Another common mannerism, not considered by parents to be unusual when it first develops, is rocking. Whereas sighted children find other pleasurable activities to replace rocking, blind children tend to persevere in this activity.

Mannerisms frequently occurring in children with low

vision, particularly those with rubella, are light gazing at the sun or fluorescent lights and waving of fingers in front of their eyes against the lights. Many become so involved in these behaviors that it is extremely difficult to direct their attention to more appropriate activities within the environment (Scott et al., 1985).

There are several theories regarding the causes of stereotypic behaviors in blind children. One of them is that these behaviors are efforts to increase the level of sensory stimulation (Burlingham, 1967; Curson, 1979; Scott et al., 1985). It has also been suggested that stereotypic repetitive behaviors are pleasurable because of the motor discharge (Burlingham, 1965). Another theory related to cause of stereotypic behaviors is that the behaviors are a result of social rather than sensory deprivation (Warren, 1984). However, according to Webster (1983), one cannot separate the sensory stimulation factor from the social stimulation factor in the case of blind infants. Williams (1978) has indicated that mobility plays a role in inhibiting stereotypic behavior patterns, and that lack of early mobility causes these behaviors to perpetuate.

Stereotypic behaviors tend to increase in both sighted and blind children when they are under stress. However, these repetitive patterns are fewer, and more intensely practiced, in blind children (Warren, 1984). They continue because they become self-reinforcing and therefore self-sustaining (Eichel, 1979). Research studies have shown that behavior modification approaches can reduce or eliminate some stereotypic behaviors in visually impaired children (Brame, Martin, & Martin, 1998; Caetano & Kaufman, 1975; Miller & Miller, 1976; Williams, 1978).

Parents and teachers are advised to work together to help blind and low-vision children develop positive exploratory and mobile behaviors. These efforts will enable this population to become more socially accepted by their peers, and to attend more to the outside environment.

REFERENCES

Brame, C. M., Martin, D., & Martin, P. (1998). Counseling the blind or visually impaired child: An examination of behavioral techniques. *Professional School Counseling, 1,* 60–62.

Burlingham, D. (1965). Some problems of ego development in blind children. *Psychoanalytic Study of the Child, 20,* 194–208.

Burlingham, D. (1967). Developmental considerations in the occupations of the blind. *Psychoanalytic Study of the Child, 22,* 187–198.

Caetano, A. P., & Kaufman, J. M. (1975). Reduction of rocking mannerisms in two blind children. *Education of the Visually Handicapped, 7,* 101–105.

Curson, A. (1979). The blind nursery school child. *Psychoanalytic Study of the Child, 34,* 51–83.

Eichel, V. J. (1979). A taxonomy for mannerisms of blind children. *Journal of Visual Impairment and Blindness, 72,* 125–130.

Jan, J. E., Freeman, R. D., & Scott, E. P. (1977). *Visual impairment in children and adolescents.* New York: Grune & Stratton.

Miller, B. S., & Miller, W. H. (1976). Extinguishing "blindisms": A paradigm for intervention. *Education of the Visually Handicapped, 8,* 6–15.

Scott, E. P., Jan, J. E., & Freeman, R. D. (1985). *Can't your child see?* Austin, TX: PRO-ED.

Smith, M. A., Chethik, M., & Adelson, E. (1969). Differential assessments of "blindisms." *American Journal of Orthopsychiatry, 39,* 807–817.

Warren, D. H. (1984). *Blindness and early childhood development.* New York: American Foundation for the Blind.

Webster, R. (1983). What—no blindisms in African blind children? *Imfama, 7,* 16–18.

Williams, C. E. (1978). Strategies of intervention with the profoundly retarded visually-handicapped child: A brief report of a study of stereotypy. *Occasional Papers of the British Psychological Society, 2,* 68–72.

Rosanne K. Silberman
Hunter College, City University of New York

BLIND
SELF-STIMULATION
VISION TRAINING
VISUAL IMPAIRMENT

BLIND LEARNING APTITUDE TEST

The Blind Learning Aptitude Test (BLAT) was developed in 1969 by T. Ernest Newland as a nonverbal, individually administered multiple aptitude battery for use with blind and partially sighted children and adolescents. The age range of BLAT is from 6 to 20 years, but it is most often recommended for use between the ages of 6 and 12. The test was designed to objectively measure learning process rather than learning product in blind children by minimizing the influence of experiences to which the sighted child is subjected. In fact, the majority of the items were taken from tests designed to minimize cultural bias. The BLAT items are presented in an embossed format involving dots and lines similar to those used in braille; however, no knowledge of braille is required to complete the test. The test consists of 61 tactile stimulus items, and 49 of those are scored while 12 are used for training purposes. The items measure abilities such as discrimination, generalization, and sequencing (Buros, 1978).

The BLAT manual (Newland, 1971) provides detailed directions for administering the test, including techniques for introducing the examinee to the test, guiding the examinee's fingers across stimulus items, and dealing with special situations that may arise. No formal time limits are provided, though the manual states that examinees typically respond to individual items within two minutes (Herman, 1985). The scoring procedure is deceptively simple. Items are scored right or wrong, and the number of correct items serves as the total raw score. Complications may arise, however, as the response sheet is laid out in such a way that training items are not clearly differentiated from actual test items. The BLAT yields a learning aptitude test quotient with a mean of 100 and a standard deviation of 15 points, making it similar to the IQ. The BLAT also yields a learning aptitude age, which is defined as the midpoint of an age range for a given score.

Standardized on a sample of 961 blind students in a number of residential and day schools for the blind across the United States, the author reports reliability coefficients ranging from 0.86 to 0.93. However, much of the reliability data is indeterminate, as many tables lack information such as Ns, means, and standard deviations. Data on the validity of the BLAT is also incomplete. Factor analysis indicated some tendency for the items to fall into groups that relate to the six different items used in the test. However, information is not provided on the nature or size of the sample, nor how the factors were extracted or rotated.

Although it was welcomed as an alternative to traditional tests for the blind on its development in 1969, the BLAT is not widely used in education or research today.

REFERENCES

Buros, O. K. (1978). *The eighth mental measurements yearbook.* Highland Park, NJ: Buros Foundation.

Herman, D. O. (1985). Blind Learning Aptitude Test. In D. L. Keyser & R. C. Sweetland (Eds.), *Test critiques* (Vol. 3, pp. 32–36). Kansas City, MO: Test Corporation of America.

Newland, T. E. (1971). *Manual for the Blind Learning Aptitude Test: Experimental edition.* Urbana, IL: Author.

LIZANNE DeSTEFANO
University of Illinois

BLIND
VISUAL IMPAIRMENT
VISUAL PERCEPTION AND DISCRIMINATION

BLISSYMBOLS

Blissymbols, or Blissymbolics, is a graphic symbol system that was originally created by Charles K. Bliss in 1942 (Bliss, 1965). Blissymbols consist of 100 meaningful picture symbols that are combined in a logical manner for communication. Not simply a set of symbols, Blissymbolics is a language that has its own linguistic rule system. Blissymbolics was originally developed to be a language that could be easily learned and understood for international communication. In 1971, Blissymbols were first used as an augmentative communication symbol system for nonspeaking handicapped persons at the Ontario Crippled Children's Center in Toronto, Canada (Silverman, McNaughton, & Kates, 1978). Currently, Blissymbolics is one of many picture graphic symbol systems that have been developed for use with augmentative communication systems and is comprised of over 3,000 symbols (BCI, 2005).

In Blissymbolics, the symbols are designed to depict the semantic concepts they represent. The meaning of the symbol can be pictographic, ideographic, or arbitrary (Figure 1). Pictographic symbols physically look like the concept they represent. Ideographic symbols represent feelings or ideas about a concept. Arbitrary symbols are usually used only as semantic grammatical markers. Some symbols are mixed, with one or more categories of meaning combined.

Figure 1 Categories of Blissymbol concept representation

By combining the basic 100 symbols together, many word concepts can be communicated. For example, the symbols for *happy* and *thing* are combined to create *toy,* a thing that can make someone happy (Figure 2).

Figure 2 Combining Blissymbols to create new word concepts

Blissymbolics uses semantic indicators to convey complex linguistic concepts such as plurality, action, number, and tense. In addition, the meaning of a symbol can change through changes in symbol size, orientation, position, or by adding pointers. The Blissymbolics Communication Institute (BCI), in Toronto, Canada, has developed an international standardized vocabulary of Blissymbols that is published in a user's dictionary (Hehner, 1980). New symbols are added after they are approved by BCI. Symbols that are newly created but are not approved should be designated with the combined symbol until they are approved (Figure 3).

Spaceship
(combine) flying plane to (the) stars (combine)

Figure 3 Use of the combined symbol to create new words

There are many methods of teaching the symbols. Shepard and Haaf (1995) distinguished that teaching the composite meaning of a symbol as well as the meaning of the elements from which it was comprised was superior to a paired association method.

Many studies have documented the effectiveness of using Blissymbols with individuals who are nonspeaking and who have physical disabilities (Silverman et al., 1978). In addition, they have been used with individuals who are mentally retarded, autistic (Kozleski, 1991), hearing impaired, and adults with aphasia. Blissymbols are best suited for persons who are unable to use traditional written language as an alternative communication method but are capable of learning large vocabularies. Blissymbols Communication International is a non-profit, charitable organization that has the worldwide license for the use and publication of Blissymbols (BCI, 2005).

REFERENCES

BCI. (2005). *Blissymbols Communication International.* Retrieved July 1, 2005, from http://www.blissymbolics.org

Bliss, C. K. (1965). *Semantography-Blissymbolics.* Sydney, Australia: Semantography.

Hehner, B. (1980). *Blissymbols for use.* Toronto, Canada: Blissymbolics Communication Institute.

Kozleski, E. B. (1991). Visual symbol acquisition by students with autism. *Exceptionality, 24*(4), 173–194.

Shepard, T. A., & Haaf, R. B. (1995). Comparison of two training methods in the learning and generalization of Blissymbolics. *Augmentative and Alternative Communication, 11*(3), 154–164.

Silverman, F., McNaughton, S., & Kates, B. (1978). *Handbook of Blissymbolics.* Toronto, Canada: Blissymbolics Communications Institute.

SHARON L. GLENNEN
Pennsylvania State University

ALTERNATIVE COMMUNICATION METHODS IN SPECIAL EDUCATION

BLOOM, BENJAMIN S. (1913–1999)

Bloom obtained his BA and MS degrees from Pennsylvania State University, and went on to earn his PhD from the University of Chicago in 1942. He was noted for his work with taxonomies of educational objectives, the impact of environment and heredity on intelligence, and mastery learning.

Bloom's *Taxonomy of Educational Objectives* (1956) classifies cognitive behaviors according to a hierarchy of domains, providing a framework for viewing the educational process, classifying goals of the educational system, and specifying objectives for learning experiences. The hierarchy includes knowledge, comprehension, application, analysis, synthesis, and evaluation.

Bloom's (1964) book, *Stability and Change in Human Characteristics,* refuted the commonly held assumption that learning occurs in a regular, ascending line, demonstrating the developing function of intelligence as well as the increased stability of measured intelligence with age. In terms of intelligence measured at the age of 17, his correlational data and absolute scale of intelligence development indicated that approximately 50 percent of IQ development occurs before age 4, with 80 percent of the development of adult IQ taking place by 8 years of age. His findings also demonstrated that changes in relevant environmental factors have the greatest effect on a specific characteristic during its most rapid period of change. Bloom's research in this area resulted in an educational shift, with increased focus on the early years of development.

His interest also included the identification and availability of highly favorable learning conditions. In his research, he found that mastery learning, including detailed trial tests and a variety of feedback correctives, can be used to improve levels of learning of groups of students, with trial test/feedback correctives helping students discover and correct learning errors (Brandt, 1979).

Bloom's career included positions as the Charles Swift Distinguished Service professor emeritus at the University of Chicago from 1970 and professor of education at Northwestern University, Evanston, Illinois from 1983 to 1989. He served as an education advisor to the governments of India and Israel and as vice-chairman of the Meeting of Experts on Curriculum of General Education in Moscow in 1968. He was the recipient of the John Dewey award of the John Dewey Society (1968), the Teachers College medal for distinguished service of Columbia University (1970), and the award for distinguished contributions to education of the American Educational Research Association (1970). Bloom's numerous writings include *All Our Children Learning: A Primer for Parents, Teachers, and other Educators* (1980), *The State of Research on Selected Alterable Variables in Education* (1980), and *Developing Talent in Young People* (1985).

REFERENCES

Bloom, B. S. (Ed.). (1956). *Taxonomy of educational objectives. The classification of educational goals-Handbook I, cognitive domain.* New York: McKay.

Bloom, B. S. (1964). *Stability and change in human characteristics.* New York: Wiley.

Bloom, B. S. (1980). *The state of research on selected alterable variables in education.* Chicago: University of Chicago.

Bloom, B. S., & Sosniak, L. A. (1985). *Developing talent in young people.* New York: Ballantine.

Brandt, R. (1979). A conversation with Benjamin Bloom. *Educational Leadership, 37*(2), 157–161.

ANN E. LUPKOWSKI
Texas A&M University
First edition

TAMARA J. MARTIN
*The University of Texas of the
Permian Basin*
Second edition

BOBATH METHOD

Karel Bobath, a neuropsychiatrist, and Berta Bobath, a physiotherapist, developed an assessment and treatment program in England based on central nervous system (CNS) functioning. Their approach focuses on the whole child and is referred to as neurodevelopmental treatment (NDT).

Central nervous system functioning is regarded as the basis of all motor functioning. It provides the individual with the ability to perform all posture and movement tasks, from the most simple to the most highly integrated complex ones. The individual is able to maintain the head and trunk in a mid-line or balanced position while pursuing a motor task because of the working of the CNS.

If for some reason—as in cerebral palsy, other developmentally delaying conditions of childhood, or stroke—the working of the CNS is impaired, a therapist trained to use the NDT method would work with the person to improve the quality of tone and movement. Problems related to tone, posture, and fluidity of movement are the focus of the therapy.

Treatment has two basic goals: (1) the inhibition of primitive and postural reflexes that are abnormally present, and (2) the facilitation of insufficiently developed normal postural reactions. All therapy is developmentally oriented and is determined by the unique, specific needs of the individual.

Through therapy the individual experiences the feeling of more normal movement patterns and works to maintain these new, more efficient motor patterns. The treatment is dynamic in that there is interaction as the therapist makes constant changes in handling to match the individual's postural and movement responses.

It is the normal postural reflex mechanism that provides the basis for the individual to exhibit normal postural tone and variety in movement patterns. Through the process of co-contraction, the trunk and head (proximal parts) are stabilized, thus allowing for more finitely graded motor activity to be performed by the arms, hands, legs, and feet (distal parts). It is important for the individual to develop a more normal postural reflex mechanism so that efficient,

purposeful actions can increase. The righting and equilibrium reactions are the bases of the normal postural reflex mechanism.

A major emphasis of NDT when employed with children is that parents and teachers be taught appropriate handling techniques by the therapist with the physician's approval. For carryover and integration of new skills to occur, the same handling procedures used by the therapist should be used at home and in the classroom. The Bobath method has been criticized as being "insufficient in meeting the special cognitive, social, and emotional problems and integrating these variables into patient examination and physical rehabilitation" (Rasmussen, 1994). In addition, the National Center on Physical Activity and Disability (NCPAD; 2005) reports that there is no scientific evidence to support this form of therapy over any other or no therapy at all.

REFERENCES

Bobath, K. (1980). *A neurophysiological basis for the treatment of cerebral palsy.* Philadelphia: Lippincott.

Levitt, S. (1982). *Treatment of cerebral palsy and motor delay.* Oxford, England: Blackwell Scientific.

Morrison, D., Pothier, P., & Horr, K. (1978). *Sensory-motor dysfunction and therapy in infancy and early childhood.* Springfield, IL: Thomas.

National Center on Physical Activity and Disability (NCPAD). (2005). *A brief history of therapy in the treatment of cerebral palsy.* Retrieved from http://www.ncpad.org/disability/fact_sheet.php?sheet=119&section=954

Rasmussen, G. (1994). A new approach to physical rehabilitation. In A. L. Christensen & B. Uzzell (Eds.), *Brain injury and physical rehabilitation.* Hillsdale, NJ: Erlbaum.

Scherzer, A., & Tscharnuter, I. (1990). *Early diagnosis and therapy in cerebral palsy.* New York: Marcel Dekker.

MARY K. DYKES
University of Florida

CEREBRAL PALSY
OCCUPATIONAL THERAPY
PHYSICAL THERAPY

BODER TEST OF READING-SPELLING PATTERNS

The Boder Test of Reading-Spelling Patterns (the Boder Test) is subtitled "A diagnostic test for subtypes of reading disability," a designation that reflects the medical orientation of the test's senior author and the need for a typology of dyslexia. Boder and Jarrico (1982), in devising the Boder Test, relied on several assumptions about children and about reading.

The first assumption is that each dyslexic reader has a distinctive pattern of cognitive strengths and weaknesses across the two primary factors of the reading process: the visual gestalt and the auditory analytic functions. In Boder's scheme, the former underlies the development of a sight vocabulary and the latter the development of phonic word analysis or word attack. The Boder Test thus gives the following as its operational definition of developmental dyslexia:

> A reading disability in which the reading and spelling performance gives evidence of cognitive deficits in either the visual gestalt function or auditory analytic function, or both. A corollary of this definition is that when the reading-spelling pattern of poor readers gives no evidence of such cognitive deficits, the reading disability is regarded as nonspecific rather than dyslexic. (Boder & Jarrico, 1982, p. 5)

Accordingly, the Boder Test is intended to allow for differential diagnosis of developmental dyslexia by analyzing together a child's reading and spelling performances as interdependent functions. The manual describes what is offered as "a systematic sequence of simple reading and spelling tasks . . ." giving "an essentially qualitative analysis of the ability to learn to read and spell, for which quantitative criteria are provided" (Boder & Jarrico, 1982, p. 5).

Four subgroups of reading disability are then identified: (1) *dysphonetic dyslexics,* children with strong visual-gestalt reading functions and weak phonic analysis; (2) *dyseidetic dyslexics,* children with strong phonic analysis functions and weak visual gestalt areas; (3) *mixed dysphonetic-dyseidetic,* children who are weak in visual gestalt and phonic analysis; and (4) *nonspecific reading disability,* children strong in visual gestalt and phonic analysis function but not reading well. According to Boder and Jarrico (1982, p. 6), these patterns exist only among reading-disabled children, for "strengths and deficits in the gestalt and analytic functions of dyslexic children are manifested in three characteristic reading-spelling patterns not found among good readers who are at or above grade level in both reading and spelling." Significant reading retardation is defined in the Boder Test as reading two or more years below normal expectancy for grade level or mental age, although it is noted that performance one year below may be diagnostically significant. The authors further assert (p. 9) that the "test can make a reliable early diagnosis of a reading disability and identify the child's preferred modality, either visual or auditory, in learning how to read."

The test proper consists of an oral reading test (word recognition) and a written spelling test. The spelling words are determined from the results of the reading test. The test is individually administered in not more than about 30 minutes. According to the manual, the test may be administered by teachers, reading specialists, psychologists, physicians, and speech therapists.

The reading test consists of 13 "graded" word lists of 20 words each; half of each list contains words that are phonetically regular and half words that are not phonetic. Word lists are presented twice, in timed (1 second) and untimed (10 seconds) conditions. Reading level is determined to be the grade level corresponding to the highest graded word list at which the students read 50 percent or more of the words correctly. A more precise reading level is obtained by giving 2 months of additional credit for each word read correctly from the flash presentation above this basal level. Two other scores are yielded by the Boder Test, reading age (reading level −5) and reading quotient (RA/CA) × 100; if the child's overall mental ability is substantially above or below average, this quotient is to be corrected for MA by use of the following formula: RQ = (2RA/(MA + CA)) × 100 or, by using RQ = (3RA/(MA + CA + Grade Age)) × 100. A set of rules is provided based on the RQ and the pattern of spelling errors to allow classification of each child as normal, dysphonetic, dyseidetic, mixed, or nonspecific in reading skill.

Although the Boder Test is the product of much clinical experience with children and reflects great insight into abnormal reading processes, the technical development of the Boder Test was inadequate to support its use in other than research settings. The use of antiquated quotients for scaling, the failure to collect normative data, and significant problems with the development of reliability and validity data (Flynn, 1992) all argue strongly against use of the scale. Boder's model of reading disabilities may still be useful in the conceptualization and treatment of children's reading difficulties, particularly in learning disabilities placements where differentiated instruction is possible, although the visual learner-auditory learner aspects of the approach are antiquated and have not been supported over the years (Reynolds, 1981). The use of the Boder Test in the diagnosis or evaluation of dyslexia or other reading difficulties is unsupportable at this time and other means of implementing Boder's model of dyslexia should be pursued.

REFERENCES

Boder, E., & Jarrico, S. (1982). *Boder Test of Reading-Spelling Patterns.* New York: Grune & Stratton.

Flynn, J. M. (1992). Electrophysiological correlates of dyslexic subtypes. *Journal of Learning Disabilities, 25*(2), 133–141.

Reynolds, C. R. (1981). Neuropsychological basis of intelligence. In G. Hynd & J. Obrzunt (Eds.), *Neuropsychological assessment and the school aged child: Issues and procedures.* New York: Grune & Stratton.

CECIL R. REYNOLDS
Texas A&M University

GRADE EQUIVALENTS
RATIO IQ
READING DISORDERS

BODY IMAGE

Body image refers to a person's conceptions of their body type and physical features. A person can hold either a positive body image or a negative body image (body dissatisfaction). People who possess a negative body image are at increased risk for low self-esteem, depression, and impaired social and sexual functioning (Davison & McCabe, 2005). Furthermore, body image dissatisfaction and Eating Disorder symptomatology, especially in females, are strongly linked (Lokken, Worthy, & Trautmann, 2004; McGee, Hewitt, Sherry, Parkin, & Flett, 2005).

A review of the literature on gender differences in body image dissatisfaction across the life span revealed specific developmental trends and several consistent patterns (McCabe & Ricciardelli, 2004). First, during childhood, males and females report similar levels of body dissatisfaction. Whereas females tend to report a desire for thinness, males tend to be split among a desire either to gain or lose weight. By adolescence, the gender gap among body dissatisfaction appears to increase as males report less body dissatisfaction than girls. As was reported for prepubescent males, adolescent males are divided in their desire either to gain or to lose weight. This decrease in body dissatisfaction among adolescent males may be because puberty brings males closer to the ideal body type, with the broadening of the chest and shoulders, whereas puberty often carries females further away from the ideal body type with the widening of the hips and increased fat deposits (McCabe, Ricciardelli, & Finemore, 2002).

The ideal body types presented in the media can create decreased body image satisfaction in females and males. An examination of male body types presented by the media to children (e.g., muscular models, movie stars, action figures) reveals that presented body types frequently have more muscular body types than can be achieved without the use of anabolic steroids (Labre, 2002). This impossible-to-reach ideal body type is presented to even very young children (Pope, Phillips, & Olivardia, 2000). For example, the G.I. Joe doll, a popular toy among young boys, has a physique more muscular than that of any known human. Males who possess a predisposition to internalize the ideal images presented in the media reported increased body dissatisfaction due to repeated exposure to such images of the ideal male body type presented by the media (Humphreys & Paxton, 2004). In contrast, the media often portrays the female ideal body type as an extremely emaciated ectomorph type, one that cannot be healthily achieved by most females. The presentation of an extremely thin ideal body type has been linked to the formation of Eating Disorders in female children, adolescents, and adults (Lokken et al., 2004). Other conditions, including feedback from parents, also can contribute to the development of a positive or negative body image (McCabe & Ricciardelli, 2003).

Few studies have been conducted to determine factors that promote resilience to body image dissatisfaction, especially in males. However, Choate (2005) proposed a theoretical model of body image resilience in females. In her model she attributes feelings of holistic balance, which in turn encourage females to develop body image resilience, to supportive family relationships in which parents emphasize the importance of achievement in numerous domains, including satisfaction with gender role, confidence in physical and athletic abilities, and possession of effective skills to cope with the stress associated with development and transitions, instead of focusing only on appearance.

REFERENCES

Choate, L. H. (2005). Toward a theoretical model of women's body image resilience. *Journal of Counseling and Development, 83,* 320–330.

Davison, T. E., & McCabe, M. P. (2005). Relationship between men's and women's body image and their psychological, social, and sexual functioning. *Sex Roles, 52,* 463–475.

Humphreys, P., & Paxton, S. J. (2004). Impact of exposure to idealized male images of adolescent boys' body image. *Body Image, 1,* 253–266.

Labre, M. P. (2002). Adolescent boys and the muscular male body ideal. *Journal of Adolescent Health, 30,* 233–242.

Lokken, K. L., Worthy, S. L., & Trautmann, J. (2004). Examining the links among magazine preference, levels of awareness and internalization of sociocultural appearance standards, and presence of eating-disordered symptoms in college women. *Family and Consumer Sciences Research Journal, 32,* 361–381.

McCabe, M. P., & Ricciardelli, L. A. (2003). Sociocultural influences on body image and body changes among adolescent boys and girls. *Journal of Social Psychology, 40,* 209–224.

McCabe, M. P., & Ricciardelli, L. A. (2004). Body image dissatisfaction among males across the life span: A review of past literature. *Journal of Psychosomatic Research, 56,* 675–685.

McCabe, M. P., Ricciardelli, L. A., & Finemore, J. (2002). The role of puberty, media and popularity with peers on strategies to increase weight, decrease weight and increase muscle tone among adolescent boys and girls. *Journal of Psychosomatic Research, 52,* 145–153.

McGee, B. J., Hewitt, P. L., Sherry, S. B., Parkin, M., & Flett, G. L. (2005). Perfectionist self-presentation, body image, and Eating Disorder symptoms. *Body Image, 2,* 29–40.

Pope, H. G., Phillips, K. A., & Olivardia, R. (2000). *The Adonis Complex: The secret crisis of male body obsession.* New York: Free Press.

ALLISON G. DEMPSEY
University of Florida

ANOREXIA NERVOSA
EATING DISORDERS

BODY TYPE

Body type refers to a person's overall body shape. Although body type is largely determined by one's genetic disposition, other conditions, including diet, exercise, and use of medications, may influence the body's appearance.

There are three different categories of body types: endomorph, ectomorph, and mesomorph. Rarely does a person embody one distinct body type; instead, most people display some combination of all three types, with one type being more dominant.

The endomorph body type is characterized by big bones, slow metabolism, and a high percentage of body fat. People who have a predominantly endomorph body type may experience greater difficulties controlling their weight through exercise and diet than do people with predominance for the ectomorph or mesomorph body types. The ectomorph body type is characterized by a linear physique, low percentage of body fat, and a high metabolism. The mesomorph body type is characterized by broad shoulders and a narrow waist, high metabolism, and large muscles.

Preference for specific body types varies by gender and ethnicity (Greenberg & LaPorte, 1996). However, many studies have found that the media frequently portrays an extreme mesomorph body type as the ideal body type for men, sometimes so extreme that it cannot be achieved without the use of anabolic steroids (Labre, 2002). In contrast, the media often portrays the female ideal body type as an extremely emaciated ectomorph body type, which cannot be healthily achieved by most females. This presentation of an extremely thin ideal body type has been linked to the formation of Eating Disorders in female adolescents and adults (Lokken, Worthy, & Trautmann, 2004).

William Sheldon (Sheldon & Stevens, 1942) devised his somatotype theory, which designated that the same genes that determine a person's body type also affect the formation of a personality. Thus, he proposed that each body type was associated with a specific set of personality variables. For example, Sheldon postulated that endomorphs tend to be tolerant, extroverted, and extravagant. Ectomorphs tend to be shy and introspective. Mesomorphs tend to be assertive and energetic. However, this theory has been discredited due to a lack of findings that support a link between temperament and body type (Catell & Metzner, 1993).

REFERENCES

Catell, P., & Metzner, R. (1993). The body type/temperament mismatch and self-actualization. *Psychological Reports, 72,* 1165–1166.

Greenberg, D. R., & LaPorte, D. J. (1996). Racial differences in body type preferences of men for women. *International Journal of Eating Disorders, 19,* 275–278.

Labre, M. P. (2002). Adolescent boys and the muscular male body ideal. *Journal of Adolescent Health, 30,* 233–242.

Lokken, K. L., Worthy, S. L., & Trautmann, J. (2004). Examining the links among magazine preference, levels of awareness and internalization of sociocultural appearance standards, and presence of eating-disordered symptoms in college women. *Family and Consumer Sciences Research Journal, 32,* 361–381.

Sheldon, W. H., & Stevens, S. S. (1942). *The varieties of temperament.* New York: Harper & Row.

ALLISON G. DEMPSEY
University of Florida

BOEHM TEST OF BASIC CONCEPTS–THIRD EDITION

The Boehm Test of Basic Concepts–Third Edition (BTBC-3; Boehm, 2000a) was developed to assess the understanding of basic concepts in young children. The test can be administered individually or in group format in kindergarten, Grade 1, and Grade 2. Children are asked to correctly identify a picture from among several choices when presented with verbal cues incorporating such terms as *over, least, left,* and so on. Based on these results, children can be identified as deficient in conceptual development and assessed for school readiness.

The BTBC-3 assesses 50 basic concepts most frequently occurring in kindergarten and first- and second-grade curricula. These include size (e.g., medium sized), direction (away), quantity (as many), time (first), classification (all), and general (other).

Two parallel forms, E and F, allow for pre- and posttesting to help determine whether the student's comprehension of the concept is consistent across multiple contexts. The results can be used to demonstrate progress as a result of teaching or intervention. The manual includes directions for administration in English and Spanish.

The BTBC-3 gives raw scores and percentile ranks. It was normed on two samples in the fall of 1999 (Form E, $N = 2,866$; Form F, $N = 3,189$) and in the spring of 2000 (Form E, $N = 2,348$; Form F, $N = 2,196$). Reliability studies yielded coefficients alpha between .80 to .91. An alternate-forms reliability study showed that nearly 94 percent of students had a difference of 4 or fewer raw score points from one form to the other.

REFERENCES

Boehm, A. E. (2000a). *Boehm Test of Basic Concepts, Third Edition.* San Antonio, TX: Psychological Corporation.

Boehm, A. E. (2000b). Assessment of basic relational concepts. In B. A. Bracken (Ed.), *Psychoeducational assessment of preschool children* (3rd ed., pp. 186–203). Needham Heights, MA: Allyn & Bacon.

RON DUMONT
Fairleigh Dickinson University

JOHN O. WILLIS
Rivier College

BONET, JUAN P. (1579–1629)

Juan Pablo Bonet, a Spanish philologist, instructed deaf students in language and articulation, and taught them a manual alphabet and system of signs that he had developed. He wrote the first book on the education of the deaf, *Simplification of the Letters of the Alphabet and Method of Teaching Deaf-Mutes to Speak.* This work, which appeared in 1620, provided a basis for the developments relating to the education of the deaf in Europe and Great Britain during the eighteenth century (Lane, 1984).

REFERENCE

Lane, H. (1984). *When the mind hears.* New York: Random House.

PAUL IRVINE
Katonah, New York

BORDERLINE PERSONALITY DISORDER

Borderline personality disorder is a diagnostic classification included in the *Diagnostic and Statistical Manual of Mental Disorders,* fourth edition (*DSM-IV;* American Psychiatric Association, 1994). In the past, various borderline disorders were described in ambiguous terms as mild (or latent) forms of schizophrenia (falling somewhere between psychosis and neurosis). With the publication of the *DSM-III,* the disorder received official recognition as a distinct diagnostic entity, closer in form to the affective disorders than schizophrenia (Archer, Ball, & Hunter, 1985; NIMH, 2005).

The diagnosis of borderline personality disorder requires the presence of at least five of the following: impulsive or unpredictable behavior, unstable interpersonal relationships, difficulty in controlling anger or inappropriate anger, identity disturbance, unstable mood (including depression, anxiety, and irritability), physically self-damaging acts, chronic feelings of boredom, and intolerance of being alone. As is the case with other personality disorders, the borderline disorder represents a chronic, pervasive pattern of behavior that emerges during late childhood/adolescence and interferes with social and occupational functioning for much of the individual's adult life. Despite the presence of symptoms during adolescence, the *DSM-IV* recommends that this diagnosis be reserved for individuals 18 years of age and older. For those under 18, the diagnosis of identity disorder, characterized by a similar clinical picture (e.g., mild depression, anxiety, self-doubt, negative/oppositional behavior), is preferred. Identity disorder reflects an inability to establish an acceptable sense of self and includes uncertainty about such issues as career goals, sexual orientation or behavior, moral values, friends, and long-term goals. Contrary to DSM-IV recommendations, however, the borderline diagnosis is often used with children and adolescents (Bradley, 1981), a practice that has recently received some empirical support (Archer et al., 1985).

The advent of managed care companies has severely restricted the ability of the helping professions to give significant and long-term care to individuals with this condition. Consequently many individuals with borderline personality disorder are left to fend for themselves after short-term treatment. There is some research to support dialectic behavior therapy as a psychotherapeutic method for this disorder. In addition, frequent psychopharmacological treatment is used with BPD to reduce impulsivity, mood instability and aggression (NIMH, 2005).

REFERENCES

American Psychiatric Association. (1994). *Diagnostic and statistical manual of mental disorders* (4th ed.). Washington, DC: Author.

Archer, R. P., Ball, J. D., & Hunter, J. A. (1985). MMPI characteristics of borderline psychopathology in adolescent inpatients. *Journal of Personality Assessment, 49,* 47–55.

Bradley, S. J. (1981). The borderline diagnosis in children and adolescents. *Child Psychiatry & Human Development, 12*(2), 121–127.

Gabbard, G. O. (1997). Borderline personality disorder and rational managed care policy. *Psychoanalytic Inquiry, 10,* 17–28.

NIMH. (2005). *National Institute of Mental Health: Borderline personality disorder.* Retrieved July 1, 2005, from http://www.nimh.nih.gov/publicat/bpd.cfm

Widiger, T. A. (1982). Psychological tests and the borderline diagnosis. *Journal of Personality Assessment, 46,* 227–238.

ROBERT G. BRUBAKER
Eastern Kentucky University

CHILDHOOD PSYCHOSIS
CHILDHOOD SCHIZOPHRENIA
DIAGNOSTIC AND STATISTICAL MANUAL OF MENTAL DISORDERS (DSM-IV-TR)

BOWER, ELI M. (1917–1991)

Eli M. Bower obtained a BS degree from New York University in 1937 and an MA from Columbia University in 1947. He continued his education at Stanford University, receiving his EdD in counseling psychology in 1954. He was Professor Emeritus and president of the American Orthopsychiatry Association at the University of California, Berkeley. Bower was a pioneer in the field of early childhood education of handicapped children. Serving as a member of the California Governor's Advisory Committee on Children and Youth, he assumed an important role in the development of state policy on the education of emotionally handicapped and gifted children. He also held the position of deputy director of the California Department of Mental Hygiene in the early 1960s.

His major areas of study included orthopsychiatry, enhancing growth and learning for the disabled, and engaging children in the school setting with games. By bringing together mental health professionals and parents of disabled children, orthopsychiatry was founded in 1924. Orthopsychiatry is defined as the science of the study and treatment of behavior disorders, particularly those involving young people.

Bower's interest in this area was focused on behavioral and social problems and their daily resolution (Bower, 1971). He also believed that games should be encouraged as teaching devices, allowing children the freedom to be involved while learning to relate to the real world. Bower looked at the question of whether children with learning disabilities could be helped in an economical, effective, and institutionally acceptable manner early enough to change their course of school development.

Bower wrote several books and more than 100 articles. Some of his major works include *Games in Education and Development, Early Identification of Emotionally Handicapped Children in School,* and *Orthopsychiatry and Education.* Eli Bower died at his home in Alameda, California, on December 20, 1991 at the age of 74.

Eli M. Bower

REFERENCES

Bower, E. M. (1971). *Orthopsychiatry and education.* Detroit: Wayne State University Press.

Bower, E. M. (1974). *Early identification of emotionally handicapped children in school.* Springfield, IL: Thomas.

Bower, E. M., & Shears, L. M. (1974). *Games in education and development.* Springfield, IL: Thomas.

ELIZABETH JONES
Texas A&M University
First edition

TAMARA J. MARTIN
The University of Texas of the Permian Basin
Second edition

BRACKEN BASIC CONCEPT SCALE–REVISED

The Bracken Basic Concept Scale–Revised (BBCS-R; Bracken, 1998) is a developmentally sensitive measure of children's basic concept acquisition and receptive language skills. It can be used as a language measure, a school readiness screener, and an intelligence screener, although its primary purpose is to measure basic concept acquisition. This latest version contains colorful artwork, new items and improved norms. The BBCS-R measures basic concept acquisition and receptive language skills. It comprises items relating to 301 basic concepts in 11 distinct conceptual categories: Colors, Numbers/Counting, Comparisons, Quantity, Direction/Position, Textiles/Materials, Time/Sequence, Letters, Sizes, Shapes, and Self/Social Awareness.

The BBCS-R was normed on a nationally representative sample of 1,100 children, 200 at each age group. Included in the sample were proportionate samples of children with disabilities (e.g., developmentally delayed, learning disabled). Separate samples of Spanish speaking children (e.g., Caribbean, Mexican, Puerto Rican) were also tested to provide technical data for using the BBCS-R with Hispanic youth. For English speaking children, the average subtest reliability coefficient ranged from .73 to .98, while the total test reliabilities ranged from .96 to .99 across age spans. Reliability for the Spanish speaking children were very similar. The technical manual for the BBCS-R provides several sources of validity data, including content, construct, and criterion-related validity. The BBCS-R is linked directly to remedial and instructional interventions through the Bracken Concept development program.

REFERENCES

Bracken, B. A. (1998). *Examiner's manual for the Bracken Basic Concept Scale–Revised.* San Antonio, TX: Psychological Corporation.

Panter, J. E. (2000). Validity of the Bracken Basic Concept Scale–Revised for predicting performance on the Metropolitan Readiness Test–Sixth Edition. *Journal of Psychoeducational Assessment, 18,* 104–110.

Plake, B. S., & Impara, J. C. (Eds.). (2001). *The fourteenth mental measurements yearbook* (pp. 210–212). Lincoln, NE: Buros Institute of Mental Measurements.

Wilson, P. (2004). A preliminary investigation of an early intervention program: Examining the intervention effectiveness of the Bracken Concept Development Program and the Bracken Basic Concept Scale–Revised with Head Start students. *Psychology in the Schools, 41,* 301–311.

RON DUMONT
Fairleigh Dickinson University

JOHN O. WILLIS
Rivier College

BRAIDWOOD, THOMAS (1715–1806)

Thomas Braidwood, a Scottish teacher, established Great Britain's first school for the deaf in Edinburgh in 1760. Unaware of the methods of teaching the deaf that had been developed on Europe by Heinicke, Epée, and others, Braidwood developed his own techniques, through which his students learned to speak and lip read, and to read and write. Once he had established the effectiveness of his methods, Braidwood published a proposal for the provision of public funds for the education of those deaf students whose families could not afford to pay for schooling, and for the training of teachers in his methods. When public funding was not granted, Braidwood declared that the system would remain his property, and swore to secrecy the family members and others at the school who had learned his techniques (Bender, 1970).

Braidwood moved his school to Hackney, near London, in 1783. Because of his obsession with secrecy, it was not until after Braidwood's death that the details of his methods became known. The writings of his nephew, Joseph Watson, who assisted him at Hackney and later established England's first school for the indigent deaf, showed that Braidwood had developed an elaborate oral method of instruction that generally paralleled the development of the oral approach elsewhere. Braidwood's great contribution was the initiation of education for the deaf in Great Britain (Bender, 1970).

REFERENCE

Bender, R. (1970). *The conquest of deafness.* Cleveland: Case Western Reserve University.

PAUL IRVINE
Katonah, New York

BRAILLE

Braille is a tactile system that individuals who are blind use to read and write. The basis of braille is a rectangular "cell" consisting of six raised dots, two vertical rows of three dots each. The official code, Standard English Braille (Grade 2), consists of alphabet letters, numbers, punctuation, composition signs, and 189 contractions and short-form words, both of which are abbreviations of whole words to increase the speed of reading and writing braille. The Nemeth Braille code is used to transcribe mathematics and science; other codes are used to transcribe foreign languages and musical notation.

The first tactually perceptible code was developed in the early nineteenth century by Charles Barbier, a French army officer; its purpose was to send and receive messages at night. Louis Braille modified Barbier's code and published his system in 1829, while he was a professor at the Paris School for the Blind. Although Braille was permitted to teach his system outside of school hours, it was not officially accepted by the school until 1854, two years after he died. In the United States, the first school to adopt Braille's code was the Missouri School for the Blind, in 1869.

Reading and writing braille is taught to blind students by educators specifically trained to teach these skills to visually handicapped pupils placed in a variety of settings, including resource room or itinerant programs within the public school, or a residential school for the blind. The majority of experienced braille readers use two hands. A skilled two-handed reader usually begins reading a line of braille by placing both hands at the beginning of the line; when the middle of the line is reached, the right hand continues across the line, while the left hand moves in the opposite direction and locates the beginning of the next line. After the entire first line has been read by the right hand, the left hand reads the first several words on the next line, while the right hand moves quickly back to meet the left hand (Mangold, 1982). Important mechanical skills needed by braille readers include light finger touch, finger curvature, smooth independent hand movements, and page turning.

A major disadvantage of braille reading is that its average speed is two to three times slower than that of print reading. An average speed of 90 words per minute has been reported as typical for readers in the upper elementary grades (Harley, Henderson, & Truan, 1979). Braille books are also large and cumbersome, and they require large amounts of storage space. However, Mellor (1979) reports that braille as a medium for reading and recording information is superior to other mediums for providing random access to a page; skimming a page; labeling; filing; writing memorandums; reading tables and diagrams; reading technical or difficult material; allowing the reader to be an active participant in reading; and providing deaf-blind individuals with their only means of reading.

Young blind children learn to write braille using a Perkins

Brailler, a six-keyed device that has similarities to a typewriter. Once blind students become proficient in reading braille and in using the Brailler, they are taught to use the slate and stylus, a more complex procedure in which braille dots are punched out one at a time by hand, from right to left. While the Brailler is easier to use, the slate and stylus is smaller, easier to carry, and more useful for taking short notes.

Braille historically has not been well suited to mathematics or physics studies and a new system called "Better Braille" was introduced by John Goodnae, a physicist who lost his sight. There have also been calls for a certified braille system that would eradicate problems with international use (International Braille Research Center, 2005). In addition, braille-reading students have been found to be significantly ahead of their sighted peers in spelling; braille students make less than half the spelling mistakes of their sighted peers (Grenier & Giroux, 1997).

There have been several innovations in braille reading, writing, and production. One of them is an electronic braille device that can send and retrieve information to and from a computer. This device can store information on audio cassette tapes and present it in a braille display of 20 or more characters in a single line of movable pins representing braille dots. The blind individual presses on a keyboard similar to the Brailler and the information is converted to a digital code that is recorded on the tape in a cassette. The encoded information moves the six pins up and down so that the reader can read the configurations on the one-line display. When the reader gets to the end of the line, he or she touches a switch, which then presents the next line of braille stored on the cassette. Blind students can write and edit their papers with ease using one of these machines (Olson, 1981; Ruconich, 1984). The electronic braille device reduces considerably the storage space needed for braille materials since an ordinary 60-minute audio cassette tape can store the equivalent of 400 pages of bulky paper braille. It is marketed by several commercial companies.

Another invention is an electronic braille printer that enables a person to produce hard-copy braille in either six- or eight-dot computer code. It also provides an onboard Grade 1 translator. Using translation software, the user can produce Grade 2, Nemeth, or music braille codes in six-dot computer braille code mode.

Another innovation is a paperless braille device that provides access to the screen of a computer by directly reading the computer's memory. It enables the blind person to access information on a full screen in increments of up to 20 characters while maintaining orientation to screen format through the use of auditory and tactile cues.

While the cost of such electronic braille devices is currently high, their benefits are overwhelmingly positive in enabling blind individuals to access the available technology and the internet. As a result, more and more of this equipment will become available for use by blind students in special education programs yearly.

REFERENCES

Grenier, D., & Giroux, N. (1997). A comparative study of spelling performance of sighted and blind students in senior high school. *Journal of Visual Impairment and Blindness, 91,* 393–400.

Harley, R. K., Henderson, F. M., & Truan, M. B. (1979). *The teaching of braille reading.* Springfield, IL: Thomas.

International Braille Research Center. (2005). *Promoting literacy for the blind.* Retrieved July 1, 2005, from http://www.braille.org/

Mangold, S. (1982). Teaching reading via braille. In S. Mangold (Ed.), *A teachers' guide to the special educational needs of blind and visually handicapped children.* New York: American Foundation for the Blind.

Mellor, C. M. (1979). Technical innovations for braille reading, writing, and production. *Journal of Visual Impairment and Blindness, 73,* 339–341.

Olson, M. R. (1981). *Guidelines and games for teaching efficient braille reading.* New York: American Foundation for the Blind.

Ruconich, S. (1984). Evaluating microcomputer access technology for use by visually impaired students. *Education of the Visually Handicapped, 15,* 119–125.

ROSANNE K. SILBERMAN
*Hunter College, City University
of New York*

BLIND
VERSABRAILLE

BRAILLE, LOUIS (1809–1852)

Louis Braille, blinded in an accident at the age of three, developed his system of reading and writing for the blind while serving as a teacher at the Institution National des Jeunes Aveugles, the school for the blind in Paris. Dissatisfied with earlier approaches that were cumbersome and difficult to read, Braille developed a code employing one or more raised dots in a cell three dots high and two wide. An accomplished musician, he also worked out an application of his system to musical notation. Ironically, his school did not accept his system and actually forbade its use. Braille feared that his invention would die with him, but it survived, although it did not immediately flourish. It was not until 1916 that braille was officially adopted by the schools for the blind in the United States. A universal braille code for the English-speaking world was adopted in 1932.

REFERENCE

Kugelmass, J. (1951). *Louis Braille: Windows for the blind.* New York: Messner.

PAUL IRVINE
Katonah, New York

BRAILLE
RECORDINGS FOR THE BLIND

BRAIN DAMAGE/INJURY

The expression brain injury denotes a condition where extragenetic influences arrest or impair the normal structure, growth, development, and functioning of brain tissue (Cruickshank, 1980). Damage to the brain can be either congenital or acquired after birth, with acquired damage resulting most frequently from trauma (Rourke, Bakker, Fisk, & Strang, 1983). The severity of dysfunction and prognosis for recovery following trauma depend on many variables, including the nature, location, and extent of the injury, the developmental level, and demographic factors such as age and sex (Rourke et al., 1983).

Brain damage is but one of many important variables that influence behavior. To understand a child's learning problems, nonneurological factors must be investigated carefully. Even in a case of documented brain injury, learning impairment may reflect an impoverished home environment, problems in emotional adjustment, poor motivation, systemic health problems, developmental lags, and genetic predispositions (Figure 1).

Brain damage may be the most important factor in a given case, but the label brain injury offers no clarification unless the nature, location, and extent of the damage are understood. There is also considerable danger in labeling a child brain damaged. To do so implies permanence, encourages drug treatment, minimizes the importance of education or remediation, and shifts responsibility to physicians (Gaddes, 1980). Given such a label, important and remediable strengths may be ignored. However, the label of traumatic brain injury entered the official handicapping conditions list in 1990 with the advent of the Individuals with Disabilities Act (IDEA), a revision of Public Law 94-142 and subsequent revisions. The official label mandated that school personnel resist old nosology of "damage" and look more towards recovery and rehabilitation.

Clinical neuropsychological assessment of a child involves the elucidation of brain-behavior relationships in a

Organic	Genetic
	Neurological
	Systemic
Individual	Cognitive
	Emotional
	Cultural
	Achievement
Social/Situational	Family
	Social
	Academic

Figure 1 Factors that influence behavior

developing human organism; consequently, this is a unique area of inquiry with problems quite different from those encountered in investigating the mature brain (Rourke et al., 1983). The developing brain undergoes rapid changes, and brain damage during childhood may impair future development of certain cognitive and behavioral capacities.

The brain of a child shows a capacity for development and recovery of function following brain injury. It has been argued (the Kennard principle) that early brain damage produces less dramatic behavioral effects and better prospects for recovery than damage in later life. This claim is only partially correct. The prognosis of early brain damage depends on many variables, including the type, location, and extent of the injury (Rourke et al., 1983). Most brain-injured children show some capacity for development of functions or recovery of functions, although it is difficult to predict the extent, rate, and degree of improvement because it depends on a number of neurological and psychological factors (Chronin, 2001; Kolb & Fantie, 1997; Rourke et al., 1983).

Early brain damage may produce permanent dysfunction, delayed onset of dysfunction, or no dysfunction, depending on the maturational status of the system (Teuber & Rudel, 1962). For example, the effect of brain damage initially may be mild until functions subserved by damaged tissue become crucial for behavioral performance during development.

The term growing into a deficit has been used to emphasize the importance of the maturational status of the brain area at the time of damage (Rourke et al., 1983). Rourke (1983) argues that attentional deficits are a special problem for the young brain-damaged child, while older brain-damaged children show cognitive deficits. Rourke contends the young brain-injured child also has cognitive deficits, but they may not be apparent because of the generalized effects of attentional deficits. As attentional deficits resolve, the previously masked cognitive deficits become evident. Part of the process of recovery may involve the brain-injured child's learning to solve old problems in new ways by reorganizing functional elements of the behavioral repertoire (Luria, 1973). Thus one important premise of neuropsychology is that if the nature and extent of the deficit can be identified early in life, effective remediation can be instituted to minimize the consequences of brain damage on future learning.

In summary, consequences of brain lesions must be assessed in light of the dynamic nature of the developing brain and its emerging anatomical and functional asymmetries. Only by looking at these factors can we hope to understand the apparent paradox that the immature brain is simultaneously characterized by both a greater vulnerability to cerebral impairment and an apparently enhanced potential for recovery of function (Chelune & Edwards, 1981).

There are few common behavior patterns characterizing brain damage. However, most changes suggest a loss of the normal inhibitory influence of the cortex on behavior

(Rutter, 1983). There is also frequently a deficit in attention that can lead to perseveration, hyperactivity, and impaired sensory processing (Cruickshank, Bentzen, Ratzeburg, & Tannhauser, 1961; Gordon, White, & Diller, 1972; Haskell, Barrett, & Taylor, 1977).

Attention deficit disorders or hyperactivity represent early and common consequences of brain injury. Such behaviors may reflect a deficit in planning and regulation of behavior, a deficit in memory, or loss of inhibitory control on the brain stem reticular system. In cases where a major behavioral component of the dysfunction is attention deficits, other deficits may not be observable or may not be easily measured.

Deficits affecting primarily the diencephalon often produce impaired memory consolidation. Individuals with such deficits may be able to attend to a task but they do not benefit from their experiences. As with attentional deficits, memory deficits can be pervasive and lead to more generalized deficits unless effectively remediated.

Higher level functions involve more complex cortical processing of information. The left hemisphere processes verbal material and deals with material in a discrete manner. The right hemisphere deals with nonverbal and new material in a more global manner. Functions can be divided further in each hemisphere; thus cortical damage can have dramatically different effects on behavior and learning depending on the brain area damaged. Cognitive functions relate primarily to cortical processing and include a broad range of behaviors. Early deficits in acquired brain damage may be generalized, but most pronounced recovery is noted in sensory and motor function and speech comprehension. Often recovery of language is given precedence and other functions may suffer. Left hemisphere damage is likely to impair syntactical functions, although with increasing severity, more general language processing may be involved. Furthermore, right-sided sensory and motor deficits may be observed as well as processing of verbally labeled material. Right hemisphere impairment results in deficits in visuospatial functions and spatial memory. Recovery of these functions is likely to lag behind language. Developmental changes appear to shift from right hemisphere global functions to left hemisphere linguistic functions. Rourke (1983) postulates that the left hemisphere functions in an automated manner, thus freeing the right hemisphere to deal with novelty, complexity, and intermodal integration.

Brain damage not only attenuates intellectual functions but also increases the chance of problems in emotional adjustment (Rutter, 1981). While brain damage can cause emotional lability, emotional problems are usually secondary or reactive to intellectual impairment, physical handicaps, or altered peer relations. The emotional consequences of brain injury are substantially influenced by the child's level of preinjury functioning as well as post-injury social support systems. Social learning is a complex cognitive function that involves learning social cues and gestures and modifying social behavior. Head-injured children are most likely to retain characterological deficits that limit full remediation (Lezak, 1976).

Neuropsychological assessment in the schools is a topic that has received much support during the last decade. Literature in the fields of special education, school psychology, and, recently, child neuropsychology has espoused understanding neuropsychological principles when assessing and planning educational intervention for children who are experiencing significant learning or behavioral problems in school (D'Amato, Fletcher-Janzen & Reynolds, 2005; Hynd & Obrzut, 1981; Rourke et al., 1983).

Impaired learning may reflect the influence of multiple factors; therefore, an initial step in understanding the nature of learning impairment is to explore carefully the various potential contributing factors in each case. Once these factors are identified they can be prioritized in terms of their assumed significance (Long, 1985). In this way a framework is established for diagnosing the significance of brain-damage effects in each individual case.

An adequate evaluation involves assessing intelligence (verbal and nonverbal), memory, academic achievement, and emotional adjustment. In some cases more specific neuropsychological functions also must be tested (Figure 2). In addition, consideration must be given to social/environmental factors and their contribution to overall performance. The assessment must produce a valid and reliable picture of the individual's strengths and weaknesses, and allow inferences about underlying brain functions to be made. It is important to differentiate between behavioral problems that reflect structural lesions and behaviors having no direct relationship to the brain's continuity.

Determining the nature (e.g., acute vs. chronic) and extent of brain damage of the child presents a much more difficult task for the neuropsychologist than the diagnosis of adult brain injury. The major difficulty concerns the role of age and development in children. Children change quickly in the kinds of skills we can expect them to acquire, and all children with the same chronological age are not at the same developmental level. It is necessary to take developmental factors into account. A basic rule in assessing children is to use multiple tests so that patterns and changes can be seen. The resulting profile then can be used to determine whether the hypothesis of delayed development is tenable (D'Amato et al., 2005; Golden & Anderson, 1979).

Assessment of intellectual and academic strengths and

Basic sensory and motor functions
Perceptual and perceptual-motor functions
Attention
Language abilities
Intelligence
Problem-solving and abstract reasoning
Memory
Emotional adjustment

Figure 2 Essential areas of neuropsychological assessment

weaknesses for remedial or rehabilitative purposes, such as constructing an individual educational program (IEP), is maximally useful only when certain requirements are met (Hartlage, 1981). First, a majority of the child's educationally related cognitive abilities and methods of higher order information processing skills must be assessed in a quantifiable, replicable, and valid manner. Second, the assessment should be translated into a relevant and valid educational plan. Third, the assessment procedures should be reasonably efficient in terms of time and effort needed to administer and interpret them. In essence, the neuropsychological assessment process should be designed to test the specific referral problem and to provide the information needed to devise an appropriate program for the child in question (Fletcher-Janzen, 2005; Hartlage, 1981).

Comprehensive neuropsychological batteries developed for use with children such as the Reitan-Indiana Neuropsychological Battery and the Luria-Nebraska Neuropsychological Battery-Children's Revision add significantly to the evaluation and remedial planning process (Berg et al., 1984; Lezak, 1976). The major drawback to the use of these and similar batteries is the great deal of time and training required for administration and interpretation (Hartlage, 1981; Reynolds, 1981).

Hartlage (1981) suggests an alternative approach in the application of neuropsychological principles to the interpretation of developmental, behavioral, and test data that can provide a systematic framework for understanding patterns of learning strengths and weaknesses and for making direct translations of the findings into intervention strategies that are uniquely relevant to the child's cerebral organization. By knowing the neuropsychological implications of common psychoeducational tests, such as the Wechsler Intelligence Scale for Children–IV (WISC-IV), and Bender-Gestalt, the neuropsychologist can determine which additional tests, if any, are needed to complete an adequate neuropsychological diagnostic profile (Hartlage, 1981). Detection with an accurate description of dysfunction leads to a remediation program to enhance the child's acquisition of skills using the child's intact areas and capitalizing on the child's neuropsychological strengths.

There are basically two approaches to the development of educational intervention based on psychoeducational test data: the strength model and the deficit model (Clark & Reynolds, 1984; Hartlage & Telzrow, 1984; Reynolds, 1981). The deficit model is the one most familiar to educators. This model is based on the premise that greater use of an impaired function will increase competency in that area (Hartlage & Telzrow, 1984) or restore dysfunctional neurological systems to their normal capacity (Clark & Reynolds, 1984). When neurological or genetic bases exist for the child's problem, the deficit approach to remediation is doomed to failure because it attempts to identify damaged or dysfunctional areas of the brain and focuses training specifically on those areas.

An academic intervention plan that focuses on deficits is not only ineffective, it is also more frustrating for the child, teacher, and parents (Hartlage & Telzrow, 1984). According to Reynolds (1981), this approach could be harmful to the child in that there is a high likelihood for failure and subsequent loss of self-esteem. To date there is limited empirical evidence to suggest any significant gains in academic or general behavioral functioning as a result of these efforts (Clark & Reynolds, 1984).

Remediation based on strengths has received little emphasis in educational settings primarily because eligibility for special education services is tied directly to the identification of deficits and treatments to restore those deficits (Hartlage & Telzrow, 1984). Reynolds (1981) has proposed the adoption of a habilitative or a strength model for the remediation of learning or behavioral problems. This approach involves designing instructional strategies that are based on or capitalize on the cognitive and neuropsychological strengths that are sufficiently intact so as to enable the child to successfully complete steps in an educational program (Clark & Reynolds, 1984; Reynolds, 1981). The strength model has been found to be effective in rehabilitation programs for adults, and preliminary research (Reynolds, 1981) shows great promise in its application with children.

To develop an individualized remediation strategy, careful attention must be given to the level of functioning and the role that various brain systems play in such functions. Luria's model of hierarchical systems is a convenient conceptual framework. The foundation for learning is based, at the lowest level, on attention. While the whole brain is involved in attention, in most cases the brain stem is of primary importance and brain-stem lesions can disrupt attention significantly. The child must be able to select salient cues and attend to them in order to learn effectively. When attention deficits are present, other intervention strategies may be ineffective. Attention deficits can be managed to some extent by (1) restricting distractors in the environment, (2) presenting more potent stimuli, and (3) dividing study into shorter periods of time. If these strategies are unsuccessful, consideration should be given to referral to pediatric neurology for psychopharmacological treatment.

Like attention, memory is related to total brain function and memory stores are located throughout the central cerebrum. However, the diencephalon and limbic system are particularly important for memory consolidation (storage of information). Deficits in memory obviously impair learning and severely limit acquisition of information. Intervention can be enhanced by (1) aiding the child in strategies for processing information by presenting it in discrete units, (2) increasing incentives, as most are strongly linked to memory consolidation, (3) sustaining practice, and (4) using multimodal sensory input. In memory rehabilitation in children, it is important to understand areas of weakness and assist in resorting to alternative methods of input and storage.

Remediation strategies must take into account strengths

and deficits in higher level or cortical processing. With a comprehensive assessment, including neuropsychological assessment, not only modality but material specific weaknesses can be identified and remediation can be established to bypass such weaknesses.

Intervention and remediation in brain-impaired children involve standard procedures with adjustment in manner or mode of presentation. These children need sustained study on material where they receive effective feedback, and where material is interesting and presented on their level. Computer systems are an ideal tool for special education with such children, as they can provide individualized courses of study. Such systems should be viewed as an adjunct rather than a replacement for the educator.

REFERENCES

Berg, R. A., Bolter, J. F., Chien, L. T., Williams, S. J., Lancster, W., & Cummins, J. (1984). Comparative diagnostic accuracy of the Halstead-Reitan and Luria-Nebraska neuropsychology adult and children's batteries. *International Journal of Clinical Neuropsychology, 6,* 200–204.

Chelune, G. J., & Edwards, P. (1981). Early brain lesions: Ontogenetic-environmental consideration. *Journal of Consulting & Clinical Psychology, 49,* 777–790.

Clark, J. H., & Reynolds, C. R. (1984, August). *Habilitation or rehabilitation: Strength versus deficit.* Paper presented at the meeting of the American Psychological Association, Toronto, Canada.

Chronin, A. F. (2001). Traumatic brain injury in children: Issues in community function. *American Journal of Occupational Therapy, 55,* 377–384.

Cruickshank, W. M. (Ed.). (1980). *Psychology of exceptional children and youth.* Englewood Cliffs, NJ: Prentice Hall.

Cruickshank, W. E., Bentzen, F. A., Ratzeburg, E. H., & Tannhauser, M. T. (1961). *A teaching method for brain-injured and hyperactive children: A demonstration-pilot study.* Syracuse, NY: Syracuse University Press.

D'Amato, R., Fletcher-Janzen, E., & Reynolds, C. R. (2005). *School neuropsychology.* New York: Wiley.

Fletcher-Janzen, E. (2005). School neuropsychological assessment. In R. D'Amato, E. Fletcher-Janzen, & C. R. Reynolds (Eds.), *School neuropsychology.* New York: Wiley.

Gaddes, W. H. (1980). *Learning disabilities and brain function: A neuropsychological approach.* New York: Springer-Verlag.

Golden, C. J., & Anderson, S. (1979). *Learning disabilities and brain dysfunction: An introduction for educators and parents.* Springfield, IL: Thomas.

Gordon, R., White, D., & Diller, L. (1972). Performance of neurologically impaired preschool children with educational material. *Exceptional Child, 38,* 428–437.

Hartlage, L. C. (1981). Neuropsychological assessment techniques. In C. R. Reynolds & T. Gutkin (Eds.), *Handbook of school psychology* (pp. 296–320). New York: Wiley.

Hartlage, L. C., & Telzrow, C. F. (1984). Neuropsychological basis of educational assessment and programming. In P. E. Logue & J. M. Schear (Eds.), *Clinical neuropsychology: A multidisciplinary approach* (pp. 297–313). Springfield, IL: Thomas.

Haskell, S. H., Barrett, E. K., & Taylor, H. (1977). *The education of motor and neurologically handicapped children.* New York: Wiley.

Hynd, G. W., & Obrzut, J. E. (1981). *Neuropsychological assessment and the school-age child.* New York: Grune & Stratton.

Kolb, B., & Fantie, B. (1997). Development of the child's brain and behavior. In C. R. Reynolds & E. Fletcher-Janzen (Eds.), *Handbook of clinical child neuropsychology.* New York: Plenum.

Lezak, M. D. (1976). *Neuropsychological assessment.* New York: Oxford University Press.

Long, C. J. (1985). Neuropsychology in private practice: Its changing focus. *Psychotherapy in Private Practice, 3,* 45–55.

Luria, A. R. (1973). *The working brain: An introduction to neuropsychology.* New York: Basic Books.

Otto, W., McMenemy, R. A., & Smith, R. (1973). *Corrective and remedial teaching.* Boston: Houghton Mifflin.

Reitan, R. M., & Davison, L. A. (1974). *Clinical neuropsychology: Current status and applications.* New York: Wiley.

Reynolds, C. R. (1981). Neuropsychological assessment and the habilitation of learning: Considerations in the search for the aptitude × treatment interaction. *School Psychology Review, 10,* 343–349.

Rourke, B. P. (1983). Reading and spelling disabilities: A developmental neuropsychological perspective. In U. Kirk (Ed.), *Neuropsychology of language, reading and spelling* (pp. 209–234). New York: Academic.

Rourke, B. P., Bakker, D. J., Fisk, J. L., & Strang, J. D. (1983). *Child neuropsychology: An introduction to theory, research, and clinical practice.* New York: Guilford.

Rutter, M. (1981). Psychological sequelae of brain damage in children. *American Journal of Psychiatry, 138,* 1533–1544.

Rutter, M. (1983). *Developmental neuropsychiatry.* New York: Guilford.

Stevens, M. M. (1982). Post concussion syndrome. *Journal of Neurosurgical Nursing, 14,* 239–244.

Teuber, H. L., & Rudel, R. (1962). Behavior after cerebral lesions in children and adults. *Developmental Medicine & Child Neurology, 4,* 3–20.

CHARLES J. LONG
University of Memphis

TINA L. BROWN
Memphis State University

NEUROPSYCHOLOGY
TRAUMATIC BRAIN INJURY

BRAIN DISORDERS (DEGENERATIVE MOTOR DYSFUNCTION)

Degenerative disorders of the central nervous system are a group of diseases of unspecified etiology leading to progressive deterioration and, eventually, death. Many of these disorders demonstrate a familial pattern and for some there is evidence of heritability (Gelbard, Boustany, & Shor, 1997; Slager, 1970). Recent studies that began with attempts to understand cell loss during normal development have now began to contribute to the understanding of the process of pathological cell loss (Gelbard et al., 1997). Specific degenerative disorders are characterized by their unique clinical and pathological features associated with age of onset and type and progression of symptoms (Alpers & Mancoll, 1971; Fletcher-Janzen & Reynolds, 2003; Slager, 1970).

Major degenerative brain disorders such as Alzheimer's disease, Pick's disease, and Creutzfeldt-Jakob disease have their onset during the middle to late adult years. The same is typically true of the major motor neuron disease, amyotrophic lateral sclerosis, and Huntington's chorea, a major, degenerative disease of the basal ganglia. The remainder of this chapter will describe briefly several degenerative disorders that affect children and hence have relevance for special education.

Several genetically determined disorders are associated with progressive cerebral degeneration in children. Major types are the lipid storage disease, the leukodystrophies, and progressive degeneration of the gray matter (Fletcher-Janzen & Reynolds, 2003; Sandifer, 1967). Tay-Sachs disease, a major example of cerebral lipidosis that is confined to children of Jewish descent, is an infantile variety of cerebromacular degeneration (Walton, 1971; Wilson, 2003). Symptoms, which emerge during early infancy and result in death during the second or third year of life, include spastic paralysis, epilepsy, dementia, and optic atrophy leading to blindness (Sandifer, 1967). Alper's disease is an example of a disorder characterized by gray matter degeneration. Onset of symptoms occurs during infancy or early childhood. Symptoms include mental deficiency, cerebral palsy, ataxia, blindness, and epilepsy (Hargrave, 2003; Slager, 1970). Death typically occurs within a few months to several years (Sandifer, 1967). Hallervorden-Spatz disease encompasses a group of degenerative disorders that affect boys more than girls (Halliday, 1995; Plotts, 2003; Sandifer, 1967). Symptoms occur between the ages of 8 and 10 and include spastic paralysis, choreo-athetosis, and slowly developing dementia (Sandifer, 1967). The development of magnetic resonance imaging has increased the number of reports of this disease and the case-to-case variability is considerable. Demyelinating leukodystrophies are disorders associated with progressive paralysis and increased mental impairment (Conway, 1977). One example in metachromatic leukodystrophy, inherited as an autosomal recessive trait. Apparently normal development up until about 2 years is followed by onset of symptoms that include ataxia, impairment in swallowing and speaking, tonic seizures, and mental regression (Conway, 1977). Other examples of the demyelinating leukodystrophies include Krabbe's disease, Grienfield's disease, and Alexander's disease (Conway, 1977; Rollins, 2003).

Spinocerebellar ataxias are a group of degenerative disorders involving the cerebellum and associated pathways. Friedreich's ataxia is an autosomal recessive disorder with symptoms developing between ages 7 and 15 (Conway, 1977). Early symptoms include ataxia, gait disturbances, and poor coordination, including frequent falling (Rosenberg, 1979). Other cerebellar signs, including nystagmus, dysarthria, and sensory impairments distally may be evident. Other forms of progressive ataxia affecting children include Ramsay Hunt syndrome, hereditary cerebellar ataxia, and Louis-Bar syndrome (Conway, 1977).

Demyelinating encephalopathies are a group of progressive degenerative disorders resulting in death. One example is Leigh's disease (subacute necrotizing encephalopathy), an autosomal recessive condition with onset occurring during infancy. Characteristics of this disorder include hypotonia, ataxia, and spasticity. Respiratory or feeding problems may be associated with this condition, resulting in failure to thrive (Conway, 1977; Schnoebelen & Semrud-Clikeman, 2003; Slager, 1970). Schilder's disease is another example of the demeylinating encephalopathies. The progressive deterioration associated with this condition may result in significant behavioral disturbance in children during the middle years of childhood (Conway, 1977; Lahroud, 2003). More advanced symptoms of Schilder's disease include ataxia, cortical blindness, seizures, and deafness.

Some authors include among the degenerative diseases of the nervous systems neurocutaneous syndromes such as neurofibromatosis and tuberous sclerosis (Rosenberg, 1979; Walton, 1971). Such disorders may be expressed with wide degrees of severity, hence individual monitoring is essential. In summary, degenerative disorders of the nervous system are progressive, frequently hereditary conditions that produce significant mental, motor, and behavioral impairments that frequently result in death. Because of the genetic component associated with the transmission of many of these conditions, genetic counseling may be advisable for parents who have one affected child. Special education and related services may be required for children with degenerative disorders who survive to school age. The assistance of a variety of social service agencies may be of value to the families of afflicted children for counseling and group and individual support.

REFERENCES

Alpers, B. J., & Mancoll, E. L. (1971). *Clinical neurology* (6th ed.). Philadelphia: Davis.

Conway, B. L. (1977). *Pediatric neurologic nursing.* (2003). St. Louis, MO: Mosby.

Fletcher-Janzen, E., & Reynolds, C. R. (Eds.). (2003). *Childhood diagnostic desk reference.* New York: Wiley.

Gelbard, H. A., Boustany, R. M., & Shor, N. F. (1997). Apoptosis in childhood neurologic disease. *Pediatric Neurology, 16,* 93–97.

Halliday, W. (1995). The nosology of Hallervorden-Spatz disease. *Journal of the Neurological Sciences, 134,* 84–91.

Hargrave, J. (2003). Alper's disease. In E. Fletcher-Janzen & C. R. Reynolds (Eds.), *Childhood disorders diagnostic desk reference* (p. 29). New York: Wiley.

Lahroud, I. T. (2003). Schilder disease. In E. Fletcher-Janzen & C. R. Reynolds (Eds.), *Childhood disorders diagnostic desk reference* (p. 556). New York: Wiley.

Plotts, C. (2003). Hallervodern-Spatz. In E. Fletcher-Janzen & C. R. Reynolds (Eds.), *Childhood disorders diagnostic desk reference* (p. 277). New York: Wiley.

Rollins, D. A. (2003). Krabbe's disease. In E. Fletcher-Janzen & C. R. Reynolds (Eds.), *Childhood disorders diagnostic desk reference* (p. 353). New York: Wiley.

Rosenberg, R. N. (1979). Inherited degenerative diseases of the nervous system. In P. B. Beeson, W. McDermott, & J. B. Wyngaarden (Eds.), *Cecil textbook of medicine* (15th ed., pp. 764–772). Philadelphia: Saunders.

Sandifer, P. H. (1967). *Neurology in orthopaedics*. London: Butterworths.

Schnoebelen, S., & Semrud-Clikeman, M. (2003). Leigh's disease. In E. Fletcher-Janzen & C. R. Reynolds (Eds.), *Childhood disorders diagnostic desk reference* (p. 365). New York: Wiley.

Slager, U. T. (1970). *Basic neuropathology*. Baltimore: Williams & Wilkins.

Walton, J. N. (1971). *Essentials of neurology* (3rd ed.). Philadelphia: Lippincott.

CATHY F. TELZROW
Kent State University

CONGENITAL DISORDERS
GAIT DISTURBANCES
NEUROPSYCHOLOGY
PHYSICAL ANOMALIES

BRAIN GROWTH PERIODIZATION

Brain growth periodization refers to the rapid unequal development of the central nervous system (CNS) in general and the brain in particular. Following the moment of conception, neuronal cells begin an accelerated developmental course of division and reorganization (Gardner, 1969). This process involves the sequence of neuronal cell proliferation, migration, differentiation, axonal growth, formation of synapses, process of elimination, and, finally, myelination. Complexity of this emerging system is immense, and it grows within the context of plasticity and modifiability that exists throughout prenatal, perinatal, and early postnatal development (Moore, 1985).

The formation of the neural plate, which is marked by rapid neuronal cell proliferation, is evident within 16 days following conception. This plate then folds over into a tube shape. After a month, it closes toward the front and rear. The majority of cells attach themselves to the front of the tube and eventually form the brain.

Cell differentiation occurs at variable rates, as dictated by the location of cells within the CNS, where the cortical areas change rapidly and other areas mature more slowly. Next, the axonal growth and dendritic formations of the cells expand to make synaptic connections to one another. This highly ordered circuitry, which links up the brain electrochemically, is controlled by genetic programming and is largely influenced by the environment. One function of the synapses is related to specificity of action, which changes relative to location in the CNS (Sidman & Rakic, 1982). The primary sensory and motor structures are examples of highly specific functioning areas.

Genetic programming initiates the processes of brain growth, but environmental influences modify its form and function. Myelination can be thought of as insulating the neuronal cells to increase the conductivity of sending or receiving electrochemical messages. Early influences of nutrition and mother's health and lifestyle impinge on prenatal development; social, cultural, and economic factors further refine brain growth through postnatal life (Avery, 1985; Freeman, 1985; Shore, 2002).

Epstein (1978) has postulated that periodic growth spurts of the brain occur at predictable ages, and that rapid growth periods are associated with increases in mental age. Further, complementary curricula employed during rapid growth periods would maximize the individual's biological capacities to facilitate learning. Although the theory appears logical, research has not yet decided its empirical efficacy. Indeed, studies challenging pace of growth (McCall, 1988), continuity as opposed to "spurts of growth" (Thornburg, Adey, & Finnis, 1986) and practicality of the concept to everyday academics (McCall, 1990) have been presented.

The observation of a growing and changing system that is adapting to environmental influences before and after birth complicates the prediction of any pathological outcome (i.e., early insult resulting in later specific learning disorders). Indeed, psychopathology and stressful environments can lead to enduring changes in brain structure and functioning (Carrey, 2001). Special educators should be aware of the periodic growth of the brain in the framework of a dynamic interaction between genetics and environment. Recognition of this complex process promotes understanding of students' individual differences and necessitates the development of unique perspectives for intervention.

REFERENCES

Avery, G. (1985). Effects of social, cultural and economic factors on brain development. In J. M. Freeman (Ed.), *Prenatal and perinatal factors associated with brain damage* (Publication No. 85-1149, pp. 163–176). Washington, DC: National Institutes of Health.

Carrey, N. (2001). Developmental neurobiology: Implications for pediatric psychopharmacology. *Canadian Journal of Psychiatry, 46,* 810–818.

Epstein, H. T. (1978). Growth spurts during brain development: Implications for educational policy and practice. In J. S. Chall

& A. F. Mirsky (Eds.), *Education & the brain* (pp. 343–370). Chicago: University of Chicago Press.

Freeman, J. M. (1985). *Prenatal and perinatal factors associated with brain damage* (Publication No. 85-1149). Washington, DC: National Institutes of Health.

Gardner, E. (1968). *Fundamentals of neurology.* Philadelphia: Saunders.

McCall, B. (1988). Growth periodization in mental test performance. *Journal of Educational Psychology, 80,* 217–233.

McCall, B. (1990). The neuroscience of education: More research is needed before Application. *Journal of Educational Psychology, 82,* 885–888.

Moore, R. Y. (1985). Normal development of the nervous system. In J. M. Freeman (Ed.), *Prenatal and perinatal factors associated with brain damage* (Publication No. 85-1149, pp. 33–51). Washington, DC: National Institutes of Health.

Shore, A. N. (2002). The neurobiology of attachment and early personality organization. *Journal of Prenatal and Perinatal Psychology and Health, 16,* 249–263.

Sidman, R. L., & Rakic, P. (1982). Development of the human central nervous system. In W. Haymaker & R. D. Adams (Eds.), *Histology and histopathology of the nervous system* (pp. 3–145). Springfield, MA: Thomas.

Thornburg, H. D., Adey, K. L., & Finnis, E. (1986). A comparison of gifted and nongifted early adolescents' movement toward abstract thinking. *Journal of Early Adolescence, 6,* 231–245.

Scott W. Sautter
Peabody College, Vanderbilt University

BRAIN DAMAGE/INJURY
BRAIN DISORDERS (DEGENERATIVE MOTOR DYSFUNCTION)
NEUROLOGICAL ORGANIZATION

BRAIN INJURY ASSOCIATION

The Brain Injury Association (BIA), formerly the National Head Injury Foundation, was founded in 1980 by concerned parents and professionals as the first national organization to advocate for persons with head injuries and their families. Today its mission is "to promote awareness, understanding, and prevention of brain injury through education, advocacy, research grants, and community support services that lead toward reduced incidence and improved outcomes for children and adults with brain injury." The BIA is the only national nonprofit organization working on behalf of those with brain injury, maintaining 42 state affiliates and several hundred local support groups nationwide (BIA, 1998).

With 5.3 million persons living with brain injury, the physical and emotional effects on individuals, their families, and communities are overwhelming. Brain injury is the single most prevalent cause of death and disability of our youth, with one infant, child, or adult sustaining this type of injury every 15 seconds as a result of motor vehicle accidents, falls, sports and recreational activities, abuse, or violence (BIA, 1998).

Increasing awareness, education, and prevention of brain injury is accomplished through the organization's work in conjunction with a diverse group of individuals, including persons with brain injury and their families, rehabilitation providers, physicians, attorneys, educators, therapists, case managers, counselors, government organizations, corporate partners, and citizens. Prevention and education is attained through public awareness initiatives, training seminars, and publications, while advocacy results from work with government entities at all levels. BIA efforts in these areas have resulted in such important measures as safety belt and car seat legislation and heightened awareness of the dangers of drinking and driving. Also in the area of education, the Violence and Brain Injury Institute, founded by the BIA in conjunction with other institutions, is currently developing the Headsmart® Schools Program, a brain injury and violence prevention program for elementary and preschools focusing on brain development and both intentional and unintentional injuries (BIA, 1998).

Veterans and military personnel are assisted by the recent adoption of the Defense and Veterans Head Injury Program (DVHIP), a program established in 1992 representing a collaborative effort among the Department of Defense, the Department of Veterans Affairs, and the Brain Injury Association. The program ensures that veterans and military personnel with brain injury receive the best medical services, collecting and compiling outcome data on the effectiveness and cost of various treatments and rehabilitation regimens in furtherance of this goal (BIA, 1998).

Information on brain injuries is provided by the organization's interactive multimedia software program, the Brain Injury Resource Center, available in certain emergency and trauma centers as well as state association offices throughout the nation. The BIA also publishes *Brain Injury Source,* a magazine devoted to professionals in the field, and a catalog of current educational resources. The organization annually confers several prestigious awards to those who have made outstanding contributions to the field of brain injury. The Brain Injury Association headquarters are located at 8201 Greensboro Dr., Suite 611, Mclean, VA 22102. Telephone: (703) 761-0750.

REFERENCE

The Brain Injury Association (BIA). (1998, October 1). *Welcome to the Brain Injury Association, Inc.* Retrieved December 29, 1998, from http://www.biausa.org/

Tamara J. Martin
The University of Texas of the Permian Basin

TRAUMATIC BRAIN INJURY

BRAIN ORGANIZATION

See NEUROLOGICAL ORGANIZATION.

BRAIN STEM AUDIOMETRY

Brain stem audiometry is an electrophysiologic measurement of hearing function currently known as auditory brain stem response (ABR) audiometry. As a diagnostic procedure, brain stem audiometry is used for the assessment of a peripheral hearing function (especially for high-risk infants; Durieux-Smith, Picton, Edwards, & MacMurray, 1987; Kaga, Yasui, & Yuge, 2002; individuals who are retarded, and those individuals who are unable to respond appropriately to traditional tests) and to determine the neurological integrity of the auditory nerve and brain stem (especially for adults suspected of having an auditory nerve or brain stem tumor or other neural pathology). Brain stem audiometry can be done when the patient is lightly sedated, asleep, or awake.

Brain stem audiometry is possible because the neural reaction of the brain stem is time-locked to an acoustic stimulus while higher level ongoing brain stem neural activity is random. Consequently, with the use of an averaging computer, the time-locked brain stem neural response to an acoustic stimulus can be extracted from the random ongoing higher level brain stem neural activity.

A brain stem audiometer contains an averaging computer that triggers stimulus-generating instrumentation that transduces an acoustic stimulus through an earphone, loudspeaker, or bone vibrator. The patient is fitted with an active surface electrode along the midline of the head (usually at the vertex) and reference surface electrodes (usually on each mastoid or earlobe). The output of the electrodes are amplified, filtered, and directed to the averaging computer, which is programmed to present many repetitions of the same stimulus and average the response of the neural activity for each stimulus for a period of about 10 milliseconds following the onset of the stimulus. The resultant pattern, known as the ABR waveform, is characterized by six to seven identifiable peaks having different latencies and amplitudes. Each peak is thought to originate from a neural generator starting with the auditory nerve through the brain stem. Peak I and especially Peak V are the most robust in reference to stimulus level and procedural variables.

If brain stem audiometry is done to determine the existence of a peripheral hearing impairment, an ABR waveform is obtained to high level auditory stimuli and to the same stimuli at lower levels until an ABR waveform cannot be determined for each ear. Then the latency of Peaks I and V at each stimulus level (intensity) are usually plotted on an intensity-latency graph referenced to age-appropriate norms. This procedure allows for determining the degree and type of peripheral hearing loss. When used to determine neurological integrity, an ABR waveform is usually obtained for one or two high-level auditory stimuli for each ear. The amplitude and latency of the ABR peaks are analyzed individually and compared across ear and to norms to determine whether a pathologic condition exists.

REFERENCES

Davis, H. (1976). Principles of electric response audiometry. *Annals of Otology, Rhinology, & Laryngology, 85*(28), 1–96.

Durieux-Smith, A., Picton, T., Edwards, C. G., & MacMurray, B. (1987). Brainstem electric-response audiometry in infants of a neonatal intensive care unit. *Audiology, 26,* 284–297.

Fria, T. (1980). The auditory brain stem response: Background and clinical applications. *Maico Monographs in Contemporary Audiology, 2,* 1–44.

Glasscock, M. E., Jackson, G. G., & Josey, A. F. (1981). *Brainstem electric response audiometry.* New York: Thieme-Stratton.

Kaga, K., Yasui, T., & Yuge, T. (2002). Auditory behaviors and auditory brainstem responses of infants with hypogenesis of cerebral hemispheres. *Acta Oto-Laryngologica, 12,* 16–20.

Jacobson, J. T. (1983). Auditory evoked potentials. In *Seminars in hearing* (Vol. 4). New York: Thieme-Stratton.

THOMAS A. FRANK
Pennsylvania State University

AUDIOLOGY
AUDIOMETRY

BRAIN TUMORS

Brain tumors are the most frequent type of childhood cancer, after leukemia. Over half of the brain tumors in childhood occur in the area of the cerebellum and brain stem; the rest occur higher in the brain, primarily in the cerebrum. Presenting symptoms for children with cerebellar tumors include early morning headaches, nausea and vomiting, vision problems, and loss of balance. Children with tumors located higher in the brain may experience more focal symptoms such as weakness on one side of the body or vision problems. For any child with a brain tumor, these symptoms are often accompanied by changes in mood and academic performance. These findings can easily lead parents or teachers to assume that the child is developing a school phobia or behavioral problems.

Many brain tumors are treated successfully with various combinations of surgery, radiation, and chemotherapy. Depending on the type and location of the tumor, and the treatment, most children are able to resume schooling (at least on a limited basis) within a few months following treatment. Teachers need to be aware of the treatment regimen and possible side effects for a child recovering from a brain tumor. For a period of 2 to 4 months following surgery, mood and behavior changes are frequently observed, presumably a result of cranial irradiation and the psychological impact of having been diagnosed with a severe illness (Katz, 1980; Mulhern, Crisco, & Kun, 1983; Richards & Clark, 2003). Some of these children will receive chemotherapy for 1 to 3 years following surgery. Most children experience at least one of the following side effects: hair loss (usually reversible), nausea, behavioral changes, and painful mouth sores. Cortisone, taken to reduce the traumatic effects of surgery, also may cause changes in mood and physical appearance.

A decline in academic performance following surgery (compared with their previous performance) can be expected for most of these children (Hirsch et al., 1979; Radcliffe, Bunin, Sutton, & Goldwein, 1994; Walther & Gutjahr, 1982). There is some evidence to suggest that survivors also experience non-verbal learning disabilities (Carey, Barakat, Foley, Gyato, & Phillips, 2001). After returning to school, children may improve gradually in school performance. Other children experience a continued decline in academic performance as a result of the various treatment side effects. A continued decline also could signal a recurrence of the tumor. Regular communication with the child's primary physician is important to obtain information regarding the medical treatment and, in turn, to inform the physician about the child's functioning at school.

As these children resume school, they need regular, detailed assessment of their abilities and deficits. A complete neuropsychological assessment should be obtained every few years. There have not been enough studies to predict what specific deficits will occur; however, available data suggest that most children recovering from brain tumors suffer from at least one of the following: (1) poor coordination, (2) poor memory, (3) difficulty in acquiring and integrating new concepts, (4) a decline in overall IQ (ranging from only a few to 20 or more points), (5) emotional problems, especially somatic worries and low self-esteem (Mulhern et al., 1983). Most of these children will require either special education placement and a learning program that emphasizes gradual acquisition and practice of basic skills or placement in a regular classroom with the ready availability of additional resources. Parents can play a significant role in helping the child to perform at a maximal level.

Students who had previously done well in school often are frustrated by their inability to work as quickly and efficiently as before (Paviour, 1988). Teachers need to offer reassurance and encouragement, as well as extra time to learn and practice new material. Some students with impaired efficiency can continue to learn and use new information, but they may require more time than usually allowed on a timed exam to demonstrate their true levels of ability.

REFERENCES

Carey, M. E., Barakat, L. P., Foley, B., Gyato, K., & Phillips, P. C. (2001). Neuropsychological functioning and social functioning of survivors of pediatric brain tumors: Evidence of nonverbal learning disability. *Child Neuropsychology, 7,* 265–272.

Hirsch, J. F., Renier, D., Czernichow, R., Benveniste, L., & Pierre-Kahn, A. (1979). Medulloblastoma in childhood. Survival and functional results. *Acta Neurochirurgica, 48,* 1–15.

Katz, E. R. (1980). Illness impact and social reintegration. In J. Kellerman (Ed.), *Psychological aspects of childhood cancer* (pp. 14–46). Springfield, IL: Thomas.

Mulhern, R. K., Crisco, J. J., & Kun, L. E. (1983). Neuropsychological sequelae of childhood brain tumors: A review. *Journal of Clinical Child Psychology, 12*(1), 66–73.

Paviour, R. (1988). Walking in the valley of death: The impact of brain tumors on children. *Child & Adolescent Social Work Journal, 5,* 315–324.

Radcliffe, J., Bunin, G. R., Sutton, L. N., & Goldwein, J. (1994). Cognitive deficits in long term survivors of childhood medulloblastoma and other noncortical tumors age dependent effects of whole brain radiation. *International Journal of Developmental Neuroscience, 12,* 327–334.

Richards, L., & Clark, E. (2003). Brain tumor. In E. Fletcher-Janzen & C. R. Reynolds (Eds.), *Childhood disorders diagnostic desk reference* (pp. 94–95). New York: Wiley.

Walther, B., & Gutjahr, P. (1982). Development after treatment of cerebellar medulloblastoma in childhood. In D. Voth, P. Gutjahr, & C. Langmaid (Eds.), *Tumours of the central nervous system in infancy and childhood* (pp. 389–398). Berlin: Springer-Verlag.

SAMUEL LeBARON
PAUL M. ZELTZER
*University of Texas Health
Science Center*

BRAIN DISORDERS (DEGENERATIVE MOTOR DYSFUNCTIONS)
CHEMOTHERAPY

BRAZELTON, THOMAS B. (1918–   )

A native of Waco, Texas, Thomas B. Brazelton received his BA in 1940 from Princeton University and his MD from Columbia College of Physicians and Surgeons in 1943. He served his internship in 1944 at Roosevelt Hospital in New York City, and completed his residency (1947–1950) in child psychiatry at Putnam Children's Center, Roxbury, Massachusetts. Brazelton was an instructor in pediatrics (1951–1972) and clinical professor of pediatrics (1972–1986) at Harvard University Medical School, and served as director of the Child Development Unit, Children's Hospital Medical Center, Boston, Massachusetts from 1972 to 1992. Brazelton is currently Professor Emeritus at Harvard Medical School and President of Brazelton Touchpoints Center, Children's Hospital, Boston.

Brazelton's research has focused on early attachment of infants to their primary caregivers as well as cross-cultural research on child-rearing practices in Kenya, Guatemala, Mexico, and Greece. His comparison of interactional behaviors of African and American mothers' age-appropriate teaching tasks indicated that while techniques differed, both groups demonstrated positive interactions (Dixon et al., 1984). Brazelton views these findings as important in terms of culture-specific values, expectations for children, and goals and assumptions of the teaching process.

Brazelton (1973) developed the Brazelton Behavioral Assessment Scale, a tool for behavioral evaluation of newborn infants that measures interactions between the infant and social or potentially social stimuli, the infant's various reflexes, and physiologic responses to stress. Additional research led to his finding that term infants are more likely than preterm infants to lead interactions with their mothers, thus offering a possible explanation for later reported differences in children's development (Lester, Hoffman, & Brazelton, 1985).

For his work with infants, Brazelton received an award from the Child Study Association of America, and *Parent's Magazine* has awarded him a medal for outstanding service to children. He is the recipient of an Emmy award for Daytime Host (1994) for his cable television program, "What Every Baby Knows." Brazelton has served as president of the National Center for Clinical Infant Programs (1988–1991), president of Zero to Three (1989–1991), and member of the National Commission on Children (1989–1992). He has authored numerous books and articles, including *The Earliest Relationship* (1991), *Touchpoints: Your Child's Emotional and Behavioral Development* (1995), and *Going to the Doctor* (1996).

REFERENCES

Brazelton, T. B. (1973). *Neonatal behavioral assessment scale.* Philadelphia: Lippincott.

Brazelton, T. B. (1995). *Touchpoints: Your child's emotional and behavioral development.* London: Penguin.

Brazelton, T. B. (1996). *Going to the doctor.* Reading, MA: Addison-Wesley.

Brazelton, T. B., & Cramer, B. G. (1991). *The earliest relationship: Parents, infants, and the drama of early attachment.* London: Karnac.

Dixon, S. D., LeVine, R. A., Richman, A., & Brazelton, T. B. (1984). Mother-child interaction around a teaching task: An African-American comparison. *Child Development, 55*(4), 1252–1264.

Lester, B. M., Hoffman, J., & Brazelton, T. B. (1985). The rhythmic structures of mother-infant interaction in term and preterm infants. *Child Development, 56*(1), 15–27.

E. Valerie Hewitt
Texas A&M University
First edition

Tamara J. Martin
The University of Texas of the Permian Basin
Second edition

Laura Dewey Bridgman

BRIDGMAN, LAURA DEWEY (1829–1899)

Laura Dewey Bridgman, deaf and blind from the age of 2, entered the Perkins Institution and Massachusetts School for the Blind at the age of 7. The director of the institution, Samuel Gridley Howe, developed an educational program for Bridgman and she quickly learned to read from raised letters and to communicate with manual signs. She related well to people and developed into a cheerful, intelligent woman who used her talents to teach other deaf-blind students at Perkins.

Bridgman was the first deaf-blind person to become well educated, and her achievement received wide attention. Charles Dickens visited her and published an account of their meeting. That publication led Helen Keller's mother to appeal to Howe to find a teacher for Helen; the teacher he recommended was Anne Sullivan Macy, who, as a student at Perkins had lived in the same house as Bridgman. What Bridgman accomplished was later repeated by Helen Keller and other similarly handicapped persons. But Bridgman was the first to demonstrate that proper education could enable a deaf-blind person to lead a happy and productive life.

REFERENCE

Ross, I. (1951). *Journey into light.* New York: Appleton-Century-Crofts.

Paul Irvine
Katonah, New York

BRIGANCE DIAGNOSTIC INVENTORIES

The Brigance Inventories are a comprehensive set of individually administered criterion-referenced tests. There are several inventories, each covering a specific age range, that are used for assessment, diagnosis, record keeping, and instructional planning. The following paragraphs briefly describe the intended use of each of the inventories.

The Brigance Diagnostic Inventory of Early Development, Revised (Brigance, 1991) is designed to assess infants and children under age seven. In addition to being an assessment instrument, an instructional guide, a record keeping tracking system, and a tool for developing individualized education programs, it can also serve as a resource for training parents and professionals. The Inventory of Early Development-Revised offers a variety of possible assessment methods: parent interview, teacher observation, group administration, or informal appraisal of the child's performance in the school setting. The goal of the assessment of the child under age seven is to identify those segments of the curriculum objectives that have been mastered. The following skill areas are assessed: Preambulatory Motor Skills and Behaviors, Gross-Motor Skills and Behaviors, Fine-Motor Skills and Behaviors, Self-Help Skills, Speech and Language Skills, General Knowledge and Comprehension, Social and Emotional Development, Readiness, Basic Reading Skills, Manuscript Writing, and Basic Math.

There are two Brigance measures that assess only kindergarteners and first graders. The Brigance Diagnostic Inventory of Basic Skills (Brigance, 1977) is designed for students in kindergarten and the first grade and assesses basic readiness and academic skills with the following subtests: Readiness, Reading, Language Arts, and Math. The Brigance K and 1 Screen-Revised (Brigance, 1992) is designed for students in kindergarten and first grade and assesses pupils' basic skills in order to identify special service referrals, determine appropriate pupil placement, and assist in planning individual pupil programs. The following basic skills are evaluated with the K and 1 Screen–Revised: personal data response, color recognition, picture vocabulary, visual discrimination, visual motor skills, standing gross motor skills, ability to draw a person (body image), rate counting, identification of body parts, ability to recite alphabet, comprehension of verbal directions, numeral comprehension, recognition of lower and upper case letters, auditory discrimination, print personal data, syntax and fluency, and numerals in sequence.

The Brigance Diagnostic Comprehensive Inventory of Basic Skills (Brigance, 1983) is designed to assess students in kindergarten through the ninth grade. The Comprehensive Inventory of Basic Skills contains 203 skill sequences to be assessed in the areas of reading, listening, research and study skills, spelling, language, and mathematics. The Brigance Diagnostic Inventory of Essential Skills (Brigance, 1981) is designed for students with special needs in fourth through twelfth grade and assesses basic academic (Reading, Language Arts, and Mathematics) and applied skills relevant to functioning as citizen, consumer, worker, and family member. Ten rating scales cover traits, behaviors, attitudes, and skills.

Reviewers of the Brigance Diagnostic Inventories consistently have noted that the lack of reliability or validity data for these measures is troubling (Berk, 1995; Carpenter, 1995; Watson, 1995). Also questioned by one reviewer was the appropriateness of the instruments for students who do not speak English as a first language (Berk, 1995). The instruments are generally viewed as viable tool because of their flexibility and planning utility (Carpenter, 1995). One reviewer viewed the Brigance Inventories as positive methods for identifying a child's strengths and weaknesses (Penfield, 1995). Because of the lack of validity data, these inventories are perhaps best used as informal screening measures to provide assistance to teachers in planning curriculum objectives. Also because of the lack of data, placement decisions based on the inventories are inappropriate (Watson, 1995).

REFERENCES

Berk, R. (1995). Review of the Revised Brigance K & 1 Screen for Kindergarten and First Grade Children–Revised. In J. C. Conoley & J. C. Impara (Eds.), *The twelfth mental measurements yearbook* (pp. 133–134). Lincoln, NE: Buros Institute of Mental Measurements.

Brigance, A. H. (1977). *Brigance Diagnostic Inventory of Basic Skills.* North Billerica, MA: Curriculum Associates.

Brigance, A. H. (1981). *Brigance Diagnostic Inventory of Essential Skills.* North Billerica, MA: Curriculum Associates.

Brigance, A. H. (1983). *Brigance Diagnostic Comprehensive Inventory of Basic Skills.* North Billerica, MA: Curriculum Associates.

Brigance, A. H. (1991). *Brigance Diagnostic Inventory of Early Development, Revised.* North Billerica, MA: Curriculum Associates.

Brigance, A. H. (1992). *Brigance K and 1 Screen–Revised.* North Billerica, MA: Curriculum Associates.

Carpenter, C. D. (1995). Review of the Revised Brigance Diagnostic Inventory of Early Development. In J. C. Conoley & J. C. Impara (Eds.), *The twelfth mental measurements yearbook* (pp. 852–853). Lincoln, NE: Buros Institute of Mental Measurements.

Penfield, D. A. (1995). Review of the Revised Brigance Diagnostic Inventory of Early Development. In J. C. Conoley & J. C. Impara (Eds.), *The twelfth mental measurements yearbook* (pp. 853–854). Lincoln, NE: Buros Institute of Mental Measurements.

Watson, T. S. (1995). Review of the Revised Brigance K & 1 Screen for Kindergarten and First Grade Children–Revised. In J. C. Conoley & J. C. Impara (Eds.), *The twelfth mental measurements yearbook* (pp. 134–135). Lincoln, NE: Buros Institute of Mental Measurements.

ELIZABETH O. LICHTENBERGER
The Salk Institute

CRITERION-REFERENCED TESTING

GRADE EQUIVALENTS

Minnis, H., Ramsay, R., Ewije, P., & Kumar, C. (1995). Osteogenesis imperfecta and non-accidental injury. *British Journal of Psychiatry, 166,* 824–825.

JOHN E. PORCELLA
Rhinebeck Country School

BRITTLE BONE DISEASE (OSTEOGENESIS IMPERFECTA)

Osteogenesis imperfecta appears in several forms, one that is nearly always fatal to the neonate (osteogenesis imperfecta congenita), and a later appearing variation (osteogenesis imperfecta tarda) in which the affected individual may live a normal life (Behrman & Vaughan, 1983). The congenital variety results from an autosomal recessive gene; the later appearing from an autosomal dominant gene.

The later appearing type (OI Type I) is present in 1 out of 30,000 births. Bone fractures are present at birth about 10 percent of the time and scoliosis is seen in about 20 percent of affected adults. There is a distinct blue coloring and bulging appearance of the white portion of the eyes (sclera). One-third of this group will show hearing impairment after age 10; earlier onset is uncommon. "Occurrence of neonatal fractures does not predict more deformity or more handicap" (Behrman & Vaughan, 1983).

In the second type (OI Type II), the condition is generally fatal. Half of the infants survive the birth process but expire soon afterward, usually to respiratory difficulties associated with the skeletal anomalies. The limbs are usually severely deformed. There is no effective treatment for Type II.

Management of the disorder centers around proper support of skeletal growth. Parents must learn first aid for fractures. The youngster must learn to engage in activities that minimize the risk of fracture without becoming inactive. Nutrition and genetic counseling are essential, as is a careful monitoring of the hearing loss (Bennett, 1981).

Studies have suggested that early diagnosis is very important to prevent families from being suspected of child abuse (Brodin, 1990). A 30-year-old Nigerian woman in England had her 3-week-old infant removed from her care when the infant was presented at a hospital with multiple fractures of the femurs and ribs. It was only several months later that osteogenesis imperfecta was diagnosed. The disruption in the mother-child bonding was not measurable (Minnis, Ramsay, Ewije, & Kumar, 1995).

REFERENCES

Behrman, R., & Vaughan, V. (1983). *Nelson textbook of pediatrics* (12th ed.). Philadelphia: Saunders.

Bennett, P. (1981). *Diseases, The nurse's reference library series.* Philadelphia: Informed Communications Book Division.

Brodin, J. (1990). Children with osteogenesis imperfecta and their daily living. *Handicap Research Group Report, 4,* 2.

CHRONIC ILLNESS IN CHILDREN

OSTEOPOROSIS

BROCA, PIERRE PAUL (1824–1880)

Pierre Paul Broca, a French surgeon and physical anthropologist noted for his studies of the brain and skull, was a member of the Academy of Medicine in Paris and professor of surgical pathology and clinical surgery. Through postmortem examinations he learned that damage to the third convolution of the left frontal lobe of the brain (Broca's convolution) was associated with loss of the ability to speak; this was the first demonstration of a connection between a specific bodily activity and a specific area of the brain. His announcement of this finding in 1861 led to a vast amount of research on cerebral localization.

Broca was a key figure in the development of physical anthropology in France. He founded a laboratory, a school, a journal, and a society for the study of anthropology. He originated techniques and invented instruments for studying the skull, and helped to establish that the Neanderthal man discovered in his time was a primitive ancestor of modern man.

REFERENCE

Talbott, J. H. (1970). *A biographical history of medicine: Excerpts and essays on the men and their work.* New York: Grune & Stratton.

PAUL IRVINE
Katonah, New York

BROCA'S APHASIA

Broca's aphasia is one of several subdivisions of nonfluent aphasia. Originally the symptoms associated with this acquired language disorder were believed to occur as a result of damage to Broca's Area, the posterior-inferior (third) frontal gyrus of the left hemisphere, also known as Broadman's area 44 (Hegde, 1994). Kearns (1997) reports that as modern neuroradiographic techniques obtain sophisticated data related to symptoms characteristic of damage to this area, it is often evident that many different parts of the brain may be damaged while still resulting in the type of symptoms classified as Broca's. Obviously, as our knowledge base expands, the model of brain function from a purely localized perspective is yielding to an overall view of brain function as a total system with localized areas and a myriad of vital pathways.

The major language characteristics most often associated with this diagnosis are: nonfluent and effortful speech, many inappropriate pauses, short mean length of utterance, telegraphic speech limited to nouns and verbs, omission of grammatical function words (articles, pronouns, auxiliary verbs, and some prepositions), impaired repetition of words and sentences, and impaired confrontation naming. Although these persons may have some problems in the area of auditory comprehension, silent reading comprehension, and writing, these persons most often have better skills in these areas than in their expressive communication (Hegde, 1994; Kearns, 1997). Other types of nonfluent aphasia include the following.

Transcortical Motor Aphasia

Originally the symptoms associated with this acquired language disorder were believed to occur as a result of damage to the watershed regions between the middle cerebral and anterior arteries and in the premotor area in front of the motor cortex. However, as Kearns reports (1997), as modern neuroradiographic techniques obtain sophisticated data related to symptoms characteristic of damage to this area, it is often evident that many different parts of the brain may be damaged while still resulting in the type of symptoms classified as transcortical motor aphasia.

The major language characteristics most often associated with this diagnosis are nonfluency, paraphasia, agrammaticisms, telegraphic (similar to those described in Broca's aphasia) and intact repetition (differing from Broca's aphasia), and echolalia. Comprehension may be impaired for complex speech but is generally good for simple conversation (Chapey, 1994; Hegde, 1994), with the individual focusing more on prearticulatory monitoring than post articulatory monitoring of speech (Oomen, Postma, & Kolk, 2001).

Global Aphasia

Originally, the symptoms associated with this acquired language disorder were believed to occur as a result of damage to the entire perisylvian region. All the so-called language centers are believed to be affected with destruction of the left fronto-temporoparietal regions. This disorder reflects a depth of neural destruction to the point that damage to cortical white matter was assumed even prior to the new view of systemic brain function (pathways vs. localization; Hegde, 1994).

Persons with this diagnosis have profoundly impaired language skills in all ways, and fluency is greatly reduced (naming, repetition, auditory comprehension, reading, and writing are impaired). Language is limited to a few words, exclamations or automatic speech (Chapey, 1994; Hegde, 1994).

Isolation Aphasia

This is a rare type of nonfluent aphasia with severe impairment to all language functions except preservation of the skill to repeat words. It is this characteristic that discriminates between global aphasia and isolation aphasia. This subdivision is not acknowledged by all aphasiologists (Hegde, 1994).

REFERENCES

Chapey, R. (1994). *Language intervention strategies in adult aphasia* (3rd ed.). Baltimore: Williams & Wilkins.

Hegde, M. (1994). *A coursebook on aphasia and other neurogenic language disorders.* San Diego: Singular.

Kearns, K. P. (1997). Broca's aphasia. In L. L. LaPointe (Ed.), *Aphasia and related neurogenic language disorders* (pp. 1–41). New York: Thieme.

Oomen, C. E., Postma, A., & Kolk, H. H. J. (2001). Prearticulatory and post-articulatory self-monitoring in Broca's aphasia. *Cortex, 37,* 627–641.

SHEELA STUART
George Washington University

BRONFENBRENNER, URI (1917–   )

Uri Bronfenbrenner was born in Moscow, Russia in 1917, and came to the United States at an early age. He received his BA degree from Cornell University in 1938, his EdM from Harvard in 1940, and his PhD in developmental psychology from the University of Michigan in 1942. After World War II, Bronfenbrenner returned to the University of Michigan as assistant professor. In 1948, he joined the faculty of Cornell as professor of psychology, child development, and family relationships, and currently holds the position of Jacob Gould Schurman Professor Emeritus of Human Development and Family Studies and Professor Emeritus of Psychology.

Bronfenbrenner has written extensively in the field of developmental psychology. He is perhaps best known for his ecological approach to developmental psychology. The ecological environment, according to Bronfenbrenner, is like a set of nested Russian dolls in which one doll contains another which contains another and so forth. He recognizes three levels of ecological environment in psychological development. "At the innermost level is the immediate setting containing the developing person. This can be the home, the classroom, or . . . the laboratory" (Bronfenbrenner, 1979).

Involving influences beyond the immediate setting and the relationships among them, the school and peer group exemplify the next level. Bronfenbrenner (1979) contends that a "child's ability to learn to read . . . may depend no less on how he is taught than on the existence and nature of ties between the school and the home." The third level consists of influences from events that occur in settings in which the child is not directly involved. According to Bronfenbrenner, our industrialized society, in which both parents are employed, has a direct influence on how children develop.

Bronfenbrenner is also well-known for his comparison of education in the United States and the former Soviet Union. He has authored 15 books and countless articles. His most recent book, *The State of Americans: This Generation and the Next,* was published in 1996. Other publications include *The Ecology of Human Development: Experiments by Nature and Design and Two Worlds of Childhood: U.S. and USSR.*

Bronfenbrenner's writing interests range from developmental behavioral genetics to practical aspects of memory. His numerous awards include six honorary doctorates from various colleges and universities, the Lifetime Contribution to Developmental Psychology in the Service of Science and Society Award of the American Psychological Association, Division 7; the James McKeen Cattell Award for Distinguished Scientific Contribution of the American Psychological Society; the Award for Distinguished Scientific Contributions in Child Development of the Society for Research in Child Development, and the Camille Cosby "World of Children" Award.

REFERENCES

Bronfenbrenner, U. (1972). *Two worlds of childhood: U.S. and USSR.* New York: Simon & Schuster.

Bronfenbrenner, U. (1979). *The ecology of human development: Experiments by nature and design.* Cambridge, MA: Harvard University Press.

Bronfenbrenner, U., McClelland, P., Wethington, E., Moen, P., & Ceci, S. J. (1996). *The state of Americans: This generation and the next.* New York: Free Press.

Tamara J. Martin
*The University of Texas of the
Permian Basin*

BROWN, ANN L. (1943–1999)

Ann Brown received a BA in psychology with first-class honors in 1964 from Bedford College of the University of London, and her PhD in psychology in 1967, also from the University of London. She was a Professor of Cognition and Development in the Graduate School of Education at the University of California, Berkeley, and was previously on the faculty at the University of Illinois.

Brown's research focused in the area of cognitive psychology, including cognition, metacognition, cognitive development, intentional learning, and transfer of learning. She distinguished between knowledge, or *cognition,* and how that knowledge is understood, or *metacognition,* and is an acknowledged leader in the field of metacognition. Major works include *Knowing When, Where, and How to Remember* (1978) and *Metacognition Reconsidered* (Reeve & Brown, 1984), the latter describing modifications Brown views as necessary for successful interventions based on metacognitive principles, including increased attention to pertinent developmental issues, and understanding transition from other-regulated to self-regulated thought. She was one of the founders and principal researchers of the Learning and Development Program, a research center within the Graduate School of Education at UC Berkeley. Her most recent articles focused on the integration of psychological theory and the design of innovative learning environments, and guided discovery.

Brown was highly active within the profession throughout her career. She was president of the National Academy of Education (1998), and a past president of the American Educational Research Association (1993–94). Between 1976 and 1979, she was associate editor for the journal *Child Development,* and later a member of the Harvard University Press *Cognitive Science Series* and the MIT Press *Learning and Development and Conceptual Change Series.* Other editorial activities include serving as consulting editor for numerous scholarly journals, including the *Journal of Experimental Psychology, Developmental Psychology, American Journal of Mental Deficiency,* and the *American Journal of Psychology.* She also served as a member of the governing board of the Cognitive Science Society.

In 1997, Brown received the American Psychological Society James McKeen Catell Fellow Award for Distinguished Service to Applied Psychology, and was the recipient of AERA's Distinguished Research Award in 1991.

REFERENCES

Brown, A. L. (1978). Knowing when, where and how to remember: A problem in metacognition. In R. Glasser (Ed.), *Advances in instructional psychology.* Hillsdale, NJ: Erlbaum.

Reeve, R. A., & Brown, A. L. (1984). *Metacognition reconsidered: Implications for intervention research.* Champaign, IL: University of Illinois.

Tamara J. Martin
*The University of Texas of the
Permian Basin*

BROWN, LOU (1939–   )

Lou Brown received BA and MA degrees in Social Studies Education and Clinical Psychology from East Carolina University and a PhD degree in Special Education from Florida State University in 1969. Since 1969 he has been a professor in the Department of Rehabilitation Psychology and Special Education at the University of Wisconsin.

His efforts in the field of education have focused on the development of service delivery models, curricula, and values that prepare individuals with disabilities to live, work, and play in integrated society. His dream is that some day in the near future all such persons will live in decent family-style settings that contain no more than two unrelated persons with disabilities, perform real work in the real world next to nondisabled coworkers, enjoy rich and varied recreation and leisure lives with their nondisabled friends and neighbors, and have access to and use all community environments.

Brown's strong belief that individuals with disabilities can become productive members of integrated society, as well as his call for the termination of institutions, special schools and classes, sheltered workshops, activity centers, enclaves, group homes, and other manifestations of segregation, caused many in the past to consider his views radical and extreme. Such views are common today. He believes that many educational and vocational training programs do not adequately prepare persons with and without disabilities to function in integrated society. Thus, he contends that massive changes are needed in the ways we serve and prepare others to serve those with disabilities.

Brown has lectured, consulted, and served as a technical advisor for various organizations, school districts, colleges, and universities throughout the United States and abroad. He has written countless books and articles, and has been as a member of several editorial boards of publications including *The Journal of Special Education*, the *Encyclopedia of Special Education* (First Edition), *The Journal of the Association for Persons With Severe Handicaps, Journal of Applied Behavior Analysis, Exceptional Children, Teaching Exceptional Children, Education and Training of the Mentally Retarded*, and *Career Development for Exceptional Individuals*.

Recent publications by Brown include *Serving formerly excluded or rejected students with disabilities in regular education classrooms in home elementary schools: Three options* (Brown et al., 2002), *The buyout option for students with significant disabilities during the transition years* (Owens et al., 2002), and *Factors affecting the social experiences of students in elementary physical education classes* (Suomi et al., 2003).

REFERENCES

Brown, L., Kluth, P., Suomi, J., Jorgensen, J., & Houghton, L. (2002). Serving formerly excluded or rejected students with disabilities in regular education classrooms in home elementary schools: Three options. In W. Sailor (Ed.), *Whole school success and inclusive education: Building partnerships for learning, achievement and accountability* (pp. 182–194). New York: Teachers College Press.

Owens Johnson, L., Brown, L., Temple, J., McKeown, B., Ross, C., & Jorgensen, J. (2002). The buyout option for students with significant disabilities during the transition years. In W. Sailor (Ed.), *Whole school success and inclusive education: Building partnerships for learning, achievement and accountability* (pp. 106–120). New York: Teachers College Press.

Suomi, J., Collier, D., & Brown, L. (2003). Factors affecting the social experiences of students in elementary physical education classes. *Journal of Teaching in Physical Education, 22*(2), 186–202.

TAMARA J. MARTIN
*The University of Texas of the
Permian Basin*

RACHEL M. TOPLIS
*Falcon School District 49,
Colorado Springs, Colorado*

BROWN, ROBERT T. (1940–   )

Born in 1940 in Greenwich, Connecticut, Robert T. Brown obtained his BA degree from Hamilton College in 1961 and his PhD in experimental psychology from Yale University in 1966. At Yale he worked with Allan R. Wagner and Frank A. Logan before conducting his dissertation research under the supervision of William Kessen. After a USPHS postdoctoral fellowship at the University of Sussex, he was on the faculty of William and Mary and then the University of North Carolina, Chapel Hill. He is now professor of psychology at the University of North Carolina, Wilmington.

Robert T. Brown

His research on the effects of rearing environments on problem solving in rats and on imprinting in chicks and ducklings has influenced theories of early experience and critical periods. In addition to being a consulting editor of the *Encyclopedia of Special Education,* he coedited two books of relevance to special education, *Perspectives on Bias in Mental Testing* (Reynolds & Brown, 1984) and *Psychological Perspectives on Childhood Exceptionality: A Handbook* (Brown & Reynolds, 1986). He coedits, with Cecil R. Reynolds the Plenum Perspectives on Individual Differences, a series of professional books.

More publications include "Exercise Demonstrating a Genetic-Environment Interaction" (Brown, 1989), providing instruction for introducing and conducting an interaction between genetics and environment, and "Ex-huming an Old Issue" (Brown & Jackson, 1992), an article reviewing research on inductive reasoning errors.

REFERENCES

Brown, R. T., & Reynolds, C. R. (Eds.). (1986). *Psychological perspectives on childhood exceptionality: A handbook.* New York: Wiley.

Brown, R. T. (1989). Exercise demonstrating a genetic-environment interaction. *Teaching Psychology, 16.*

Brown, R. T., & Jackson, L. A. (1992). Ex-huming an old issue. *Journal of School Psychology, 30,* 215–221.

Reynolds, C. R., & Brown, R. T. (Eds.). (1984). *Perspectives on bias in mental testing.* New York: Plenum.

CECIL R. REYNOLDS
Texas A&M University
First edition

TAMARA J. MARTIN
*The University of Texas of the
Permian Basin*
Second edition

BROWN v. BOARD OF EDUCATION

The landmark 1954 Supreme Court decision in *Brown v. Board of Education* (347 U.S. 483, 1954) reversed racially discriminatory segregation in public schools throughout the country and laid the groundwork for subsequent litigation and legislation that has had a tremendous impact on the field of education in general and special education in particular. The case, actually a consolidation of cases from four separate states, was brought to the Supreme Court by a Kansas African-American family, the Browns, along with African-American students from South Carolina, Delaware, and Virginia who sought admission to public schools that were at that time restricted to Anglo-American students. The African-American students had been denied admission to these schools under the "separate but equal" doctrine

outlined nearly 60 years earlier in the Supreme Court case *Plessy v. Ferguson* (1896), which held that the Fourteenth Amendment's requirement for equal treatment of all citizens was fulfilled if different races were provided with facilities that were "substantially equal" though separate. The plaintiffs did not argue that the schools that they were attending were not of the same quality that other students attended, rather, they argued that, in fact, the "separate but equal" doctrine was inherently unequal and that by being denied access to the same educational facilities that Anglo-American students attended, they were being deprived of their right to an equal education.

Relying in part on behavioral science evidence, the Supreme Court ruled unanimously in favor of the plaintiffs, stating that the segregated schools violated the students' rights to an equal education under the Fourteenth Amendment to the U.S. Constitution. The justices found that segregated schools created irreparable harm to minority students, noting that state-sanctioned segregation created the impression that the segregated minority group was inferior to Anglo Americans. Justice Warren's opinion notes:

> Today . . . [education] is a principal instrument in awakening the child to cultural values, in preparing him for later professional training, and in helping him to adjust normally to his environment. In these days, it is doubtful that any child may reasonably be expected to succeed in life if he is denied the opportunity of an education. Such an opportunity, where the state has undertaken to provide it, is a right which must be made available to all on equal terms. (347 U.S. 483)

Ultimately, the *Brown* decision was important not only for outlawing school segregation, opening the door to a more open, less discriminatory educational system for all students, but also for opening the door to later cases relating to the provision of a free appropriate public education to students with disabilities. Almost 20 years later, attorneys cited the *Brown* decision in arguments in two important special education cases: *Pennsylvania Association for Retarded Citizens* (1972), and *Mills v. Board of Education of the District of Columbia* (1972). These court decisions played a major role in the enactment of the Education for All Handicapped Children Act of 1975 (P.L. 94-142), which in turn served as the predecessor for the Individuals with Disabilities Education Act (IDEA).

The Department of Education has stated that the "Brown decision was a crowbar for change, and we are all the better for it" (Riley, 1994). However others (Ruiz, 1994) suggested that although 500 school districts were ordered to desegregate, 40 years after the *Brown* decision, very few of those schools were found by the courts to have completed the process. Ruiz (1994) suggested that the central tenet of *Brown* is in danger of being lost amidst "voluminous paperwork and clever legal arguments." Race discrimination issues are still prominent; however, the issues have evolved into conflicts about ability grouping, bilingual education, harassment, educational services for undocumented immigrants, and different kinds of educational remedies in school desegregation cases (Heubert, 1994).

REFERENCES

Heubert, J. P. (1994). *"Brown" at 40: The tasks that remain for educators and lawyers.* (ERIC Clearinghouse No. EA026514)

Riley, R. W. (1994). *Fulfilling the promise of Brown.* Washington, DC: Department of Education.

Ruiz, C. M. (1994). *Equity, excellence and school reform: A new paradigm for desegregation.* (ERIC Clearinghouse No. 026648)

EMILIA C. LOPEZ
Fordham University
Second edition

KIMBERLY F. APPLEQUIST
*University of Colorado at
Colorado Springs*
Third edition

CONSTITUTIONAL LAW (IN SPECIAL EDUCATION)
CULTURE FAIR TEST
DISPROPORTIONALITY
**MILLS v. BOARD OF EDUCATION OF THE DISTRICT OF
COLUMBIA**
**PENNSYLVANIA ASSOCIATION FOR RETARDED CITIZENS
v. PENNSYLVANIA**
SOCIOECONOMIC STATUS

BRUININKS-OSERETSKY TEST OF MOTOR PROFICIENCY

The Bruininks-Oseretsky Test of Motor Proficiency (Bruininks, 1978) is an individually administered test of gross and fine motor functioning of children from 4 1/2 to 14 1/2 years of age. It is the latest revision of the Oseretsky tests of motor proficiency published in Russia in 1903 (later translated into English by Edgar Doll in 1946). The complete battery comprises 46 items subdivided into 8 subtests: Running Speed and Agility (1 item), Balance (8 items), Bilateral Coordination (8 items), Strength (3 items), Upper-Limb Coordination (9 items), Response Speed (1 item), Visual-Motor Control (8 items), and Upper Limb Speed and Dexterity (8 items). In addition to subtest scores, composite scores are available for the gross motor subtest scores, the fine motor subtests, and the total battery. The complete form takes from 45 to 60 minutes to administer. There is also a 14-item short form, requiring 15 to 20 minutes, which provides a single index of general motor proficiency.

Subtest and composite scores can be expressed in terms of age-based standard scores, percentile ranks, and stanines. Age equivalents are available for each subtest. The battery was standardized on a sample of 765 children, and was distributed across ten age groups from 4–6 to 14–15 years. The sample was stratified by age, sex, race, community size, and geographic region according to the 1970 U.S. Census. Test-retest reliability coefficients for the separate subtests range from .58 to .89 for Grade 2, and from .29 to .89 for Grade 6. The lower reliability scores for Grade 6 are probably a result of the maximum point scores achieved by many older children (Anastasi, 1997). Validity was investigated using factor analysis of items, age differentiation, and comparative studies with retarded and learning-disabled children.

The Bruininks-Oseretsky Test is a useful tool for measuring gross and fine motor skills, developing and evaluating motor training programs, and screening for special purposes (Sabatino, 1985). It should be noted, however, that the test is a product measure of motor development as opposed to a process measure. Product measures focus on the outcome of movement, while process measures emphasize the movement of the body when performing particular motor tasks or skills (Harrington, 1985). Thus the Bruininks-Oseretsky is best combined with other measures of sensory and motor development in order to provide an appropriate indication of motor development.

REFERENCES

Anastasi, A. (1997). *Psychological testing* (7th ed.). Saddle River, NJ: Prentice Hall.

Bruininks, R. H. (1978). *Bruininks-Oseretsky Test of Motor Proficiency.* Circle Pines, MN: American Guidance Services.

Doll, E. A. (1946). *The Oseretsky Tests of Motor Proficiency.* Minneapolis, MN: American Guidance Service.

Harrington, R. G. (1985). Bruininks-Oseretsky Test of Motor Proficiency. In D. L. Keyser & R. C. Sweetland (Eds.), *Test critiques* (Vol. 3, pp. 99–110). Kansas City, MO: Test Corporation of America.

Sabatino, D. (1985). Review of the Bruininks-Oseretsky Test of Motor Proficiency. In J. V. Mitchel (Ed.), *The ninth mental measurements yearbook* (Vol. 1, pp. 235–236). Lincoln, NE: Buros Institute of Mental Measurements.

LIZANNE DESTEFANO
University of Illinois

VISUAL-MOTOR INTEGRATION
VISUAL PERCEPTION AND DISCRIMINATION

BRUNER, JEROME (1915–   )

Bruner obtained his BA from Duke University in 1937 and his PhD in Psychology from Harvard University in 1941. For almost three decades he was Professor of Psychology at Harvard University (1945–1972), and also served as Director of the Center for Cognitive Studies there, founded by him in the 1960s. He was professor at both Oxford and Cambridge Universities in England, and has held the positions of George Herbert Mead Professor at the New School for Social Research and fellow of the Institute for the Humanities at New York University. In 1991 Bruner was visiting professor at the New York University Law School and presently he continues at NYU as a University Professor and Research Professor of Psychology. Bruner's area of interest appears to be the application of narrative principles to an understanding of legal processes.

Known by some as the only real intellectual in modern cognitive psychology, in his long career as a psychologist and teacher, Bruner has frequently rejected prevailing views, becoming a major influence in moving American psychology towards a more cognitive approach in the process. His principal areas of research have focused on the knowledge acquisition processes, including perception, memory, learning, thought, language, and literary and scientific creation.

In the 1950s Bruner demonstrated that perceptions are not merely mental photographs, but are actively shaped by the meaning to the individual of what is perceived. This research gave rise to the widely criticized "New Look" movement in psychology, which focused on factors such as how perception is affected by individual intentions or emotions. This movement was the precursor of cognitive psychology, a theory that continues to thrive today. Bruner's research in this area was later expanded to include studies conducted in Senegal in the 1960s of cultural influences on individual perception, an element he concluded was missing from Jean Piaget's child development model.

Another of Bruner's major contributions involved infant learning and the formerly prevalent notion that children's learning occurs entirely as a result of what they experience. This "blank slate" theory was challenged by his study indicating that infants could control whether slides of a woman's face were in or out of focus via their sucking patterns, suggesting a sense of intention as a factor in their intellectual development. These findings were the beginning of his conception for the development of the Head Start programs for preschool children in the United States.

Bruner's effort to bridge the gap between psychology and the humanities is reflected throughout his work. Believing that psychology, particularly cognitive psychology, has become excessively narrow, he has attempted to expand the discipline into the realms of philosophy, the arts, and literature, thus providing a broader perspective of the human mind. Some have criticized Bruner's (1990) call for a "renewed cognitive revolution," arguing that he fails to specify the direction of the movement as well as the obstacles that must be overcome for its success (Shanker, 1992).

His more recent work has focused on the study of narrative modes of thought, analyzing the words and construction used by individuals as they relate the story of their lives. Bruner argues that how the stories are told "becomes so habitual that they finally become recipes for structuring experience itself, for laying down routes into memory," therefore shaping the way people experience life itself.

His numerous publications include *A Study of Thinking* (1956), centering on problem-solving and thinking; *The Process of Education* (1960), a controversial study of the underlying structure of science curriculum; *Actual Minds, Possible Worlds* (1986), dealing with narrative modes of thought; and *Child's Talk* (1985), a summation of his findings and arguments regarding language learning. Bruner has served on two presidential commissions and received numerous awards and honorary degrees. In 1987 in Bern, Switzerland, he was awarded the prestigious Balzan Prize, previously given to Jean Piaget and Jorge Luis Borges, and only rarely presented to an American.

REFERENCES

Bruner, J. S. (1961). *The process of education*. Cambridge, MA: Harvard University Press.

Bruner, J. S. (1986). *Actual minds, possible worlds*. Cambridge, MA: Harvard University Press.

Bruner, J. S. (1990). *Acts of meaning*. Cambridge, MA: Harvard University Press.

Bruner, J. S., Goodnow, J. J., & Austin, G. A. (1956). *A study of thinking*. New York: Wiley.

Bruner, J. S., & Watson, R. (1985). *Child's talk: Learning to use language*. New York: Norton.

Shanker, S. (1992). In search of Bruner. *Language and Communications, 12,* 53–74.

TAMARA J. MARTIN
*The University of Texas of the
Permian Basin*
Second edition

RACHEL M. TOPLIS
*Falcon School District 49,
Colorado Springs, Colorado*

BRUXISM AND THE STUDENT WITH DISABILITIES

Bruxism can be defined as the nonfunctional gnashing and grinding of teeth occurring during the day or night. The adverse effects of bruxism include severe dental wear, damage to the alveolar bone, temporomandibular joint disorders, and hypertrophy of masticatory muscles, as well as occasional infection. It can also result in significant pain, permanent damage to the structures of the mouth and jaw, and lost teeth

(Rugh & Robbins, 1982). Dental wear is the most commonly used measure to determine the extent of bruxism.

Estimates of the frequency of bruxism in the nonretarded population have ranged between 5 percent (Reding et al., 1966) to a high of 21 percent (Wigdorowicz-Makowerowa et al., 1977), with no significant differences between sexes (Bober, 1982) or age groups (Lindqvist, 1971).

Investigators have reported more dental wear as a consequence of bruxism in severely mentally retarded children than in nonretarded children (Lindqvist & Heijbel, 1974). An informal survey by Blount et al. (1982) indicated that 21.5 percent of a profoundly retarded group engaged in bruxism. The study of Richmond et al. of some 433 mentally retarded individuals in a state institution revealed a rate of 41 to 59 percent in this group based on a questionnaire used with direct-care staff who were asked to observe the residents. Higher rates were reported for deaf retarded individuals. Older patients were more likely to grind teeth and wear into the dentin than younger patients.

A variety of explanations for bruxism have been advanced. The etiology of bruxism has been approached along lines of local, psychological, neurophysiological and systemic causes (Glaros & Melamed, 1992). An example of a local cause is occlusive abnormalities. Glaros and Rao (1977) believe that stress is a major cause. Systemic explanations include heredity factors and endocrinal or neurological dysfunction. It has been suggested (Lindqvist & Heijbel, 1974) that bruxism may be a form of stereotypy among retarded populations. It has also been suggested that bruxism can be the result of negative side effects of certain medications such as SSRIs (Bostwick & Jaffee, 1999).

While such methods as deep muscle relaxation and massed practice have been found to assist individuals of normal intelligence, these methods require a certain level of cognitive ability to be successfully deployed and may not be suited for bruxists who have cognitive difficulties or retardation. Behavioral methods to reduce bruxism have been favored in recent years (Rugh & Robbins, 1982). Thus positive reinforcement has been used to reduce its incidence in retarded individuals (i.e., to reinforce nonbruxist behaviors) and to encourage incompatible behaviors such as keeping the mouth open. Problems with positive reinforcers include the fact that social and tactile reinforcers usually do not have strong effects with severely retarded individuals. Edibles result in further chewing, thus reinforcing behaviors that are not compatible with efforts to reduce bruxism.

Hence behavioral treatment has sometimes been of an aversive nature (e.g., using a contingent sound blast). Such treatment, however, involves expensive equipment. Blount et al. (1982) were able to use a much simpler method, known as icing, with two profoundly retarded women. They greatly reduced their bruxism and successfully generalized their improvements beyond the training sessions. In icing there is a brief contingent application of ice to cheeks or chin as an aversive stimulus. Another, similar method of aversive control of bruxism in a mentally retarded nonverbal child in a class for trainable mentally retarded children was accomplished by Kramer (1981). The method involved the use of a contingent verbal "no" accompanied by the teacher's finger to the child's jaw. Unfortunately, the treatment ideology and modalities has been haphazard for bruxism; therefore, most treatment effects are short-lived (Glaros & Melamed, 1992).

REFERENCES

Blount, R. L., Drabman, R. S., Wilson, N., & Stewart, D. (1982). Reducing severe diurnal bruxism in two profoundly retarded females. *Journal of Applied Behavior Analysis, 15,* 565–571.

Bober, H. (1982). Cause and treatment of bruxism and bruxomania. *Dental Abstracts, 3,* 658–659.

Bostwick, J. M., & Jaffee, M. S. (1999). Buspirone as an antidote to SSRI-induced bruxism. *Journal of Clinical Psychiatry, 60,* 857–860.

Glaros, A. G., & Melamed, B. G. (1992). Bruxism in children, Etiology and treatment. *Applied and Preventive Psychology, 1,* 191–199.

Glaros, A. G., & Rao, S. M. (1977). Bruxism: A critical review. *Psychological Bulletin, 84,* 767–781.

Heller, R. F., & Strang, H. R. (1973). Controlling bruxism through automated aversive conditioning. *Behavior Research & Therapy, 11,* 327–328.

Kramer, J. J. (1981). Aversive control of bruxism in a mentally retarded child: A case study. *Psychological Reports, 49,* 815–818.

Lindqvist, B. (1971). Bruxism in children. *Odontologisk Revy, 22,* 413–424.

Lindqvist, B., & Heijbel, J. (1974). Bruxism in children with brain damage. *Acta Odontologica Scandinavica, 32,* 313–319.

Reding, G. R., Rubright, W. C., & Zimmerman, S. O. (1966). Incidence of bruxism. *Journal of Dental Research, 45,* 1198–1204.

Rugh, J. D., & Robbins, W. J. (1982). Oral habit disorders. In B. Ingersoll (Ed.), *Behavioral aspects in dentistry* (pp. 179–202). New York: Appleton-Century-Crofts.

Wigdorowicsz-Makowerowa, N., Grodzki, C., & Maslanka, T. (1977). Frequency and etiopathogenes of bruxism (on the basis of prophylactic examinations of 1000 middle-aged men). *Czaopismo-Stomatologiczne, 25,* 1109–1112.

DAVID C. MANN
St. Francis Hospital

DENTISTRY AND THE EXCEPTIONAL CHILD
SELF-INJURIOUS BEHAVIOR

BUCKLEY AMENDMENT

See FAMILY EDUCATIONAL RIGHTS AND PRIVACY ACT.

BULIMIA NERVOSA

Bulimia nervosa (a term of Greek origin meaning "ox hunger") is an eating disorder that is also referred to as the binge-purge syndrome. It is a condition in which an individual alternately binges (grossly overeats) and purges (rids the body of food or fluids). Although difficult to comprehend, bulimics apparently may ingest as many as 20,000 calories in one binge episode. Bulimics commonly chew and spit out food (Mitchell, Halsukami, Eckert, & Pyle, 1985). Bingeing is mainly on foods rich in carbohydrates; purging may be through vomiting, abuse of laxatives or diet tablets, or excessive exercise, regardless of fatigue (Garner & Garfinkel, 1985). No physical basis for the abnormal eating can be found. This disorder can be life-threatening, is increasing in occurrence, and is a serious problem for medical and psychological professionals who are attempting to treat it. Unlike anorexia, which has been known for centuries, bulimia is of relatively recent origin. Indeed, professional journals have commonly reported on bulimia only since the 1970s. This recency is partly responsible for the relatively little firm knowledge about bulimia and the absence of generally effective treatments. Incidence rates that vary with age, race, job status, and ethnic background further hamper general understanding of the disorder.

Bulimia characteristically is largely a disorder of women, with 9–17 times more women than men hospitalized for an eating disorder (Goetestan, Erikson, Heggestad, & Neilson, 1998). It is largely restricted to white women from middle- and upper-class social classes, although it is becoming more common among women from lower social economic status. Further, incidence is increasing among African American women as they become acculturated into the dominant White society. Although mainly a western cultural problem, eating disorders do occur in other cultures. For example, Srinivasan, Suresh, and Jayaram (1998) found that eating disorders occur in India but in milder form without the severe escalation found in Western countries. Onset of bulimia is generally between 18 and 20 years of age, with a peak onset at about the age of 18 years of age (Neuman & Halvorson, 1983). Bulimia is more common than anorexia nervosa and may affect 5 percent of college women and 1 percent of young employed women (Hart & Ollendick, 1985). Twenty to 30 percent of college women may occasionally engage in bulimic behavior.

Although primarily affecting women, bulimia also is seen, and in some areas increasingly, in men. Reasons for the disorder appear to be quite different in men and women except in sports (e.g., gymnastics) or vocations (e.g., modeling or dancing) that impose comparable demands on members of both sexes. Those engaged in high-powered sports such as running and wrestling or vocations are particularly at risk. One study (McNulty, 1997) reported that Navy servicemen showed prevalence rates of 2.5 percent for anorexia and 6.8 percent for bulimia. In men, bulimia may be driven by individual competition where weight or appearance and goals of "perfection" are important. Male bulimics may need a high calorie intake for energy but at the same time fear not being able to burn off the fat. If a Naval officer wants high scores on body measurements and fitness tests, then he may find purging an effective means, in the short term.

Although bulimia is more common than anorexia, it is harder to recognize because affected individuals do not show severe weight loss and are usually of normal or slightly above normal weight. The stereotypical bulimic's physical appearance may not be apparent to anyone else, possibly not even the sufferer's spouse, as was the case of Princess of Wales, Diana.

However, some general etiological factors and occasionally effective treatments have been described. Bulimics share personality characteristics and have families with a particular complex of unhealthy attitudes and behaviors. Bulimics can suffer from gastrointestinal problems and serious potassium depletion and damage to their teeth due to the acid nature of the regurgitated food. In extreme cases, death may result. As is the case with anorexia, bulimia is viewed as a biopsychosocial disorder.

DSM-IV (American Psychiatric Association, 1994) criteria for bulimia include: (a) recurrent episodes of secretive binge eating (rapid consumption of a large amount of food in a short period of time); (b) termination of bingeing because of abdominal pain, sleep, or social interruptions; and (c) recurrent episodes of purging as an attempt to lose weight or avoid gaining weight through self-induced vomiting, severe diets, abuse of laxatives, cathartics, or diuretics, or excessive exercise. The bulimic suffers frequent weight fluctuations owing to alternating binges and fasts, awareness that the eating pattern is abnormal, and fear of not being able to stop eating voluntarily. Depression and self-deprecating thoughts may follow eating binges (American Psychiatric Association, 1994). *DSM-IV* distinguishes between purging and non-purging types of bulimia. A purging type periodically engages in the act of self-induced vomiting or the use of laxatives, whereas a non-purging type uses diets, exercise, and fasting instead of regular self-induced vomiting.

Considering biological aspects, bulimia leads to a variety of physiological complications, including cardiac irregularities, kidney dysfunction, neurological abnormalities, gastrointestinal pain, salivary gland enlargement (appearance of a chipmunk), edema and bloating, electrolyte imbalance, amenorrhea, dermatological disorders, and finger clubbing or swelling. Finger abnormalities result from the pressure against the mouth during self-induced vomiting. Abuse of laxatives can lead to permanent nerve damage in the colon, chronic stomach overloading, and potential of stomach rupture. Several of these complications can result in death.

Psychologically, bulimics share many behaviors and concerns. They are terrified of becoming obese, and measure their worth and self-esteem by how much they weigh and how little their stomachs protrude. They tend to be perfectionists, overdemanding of themselves, and very success-oriented. Low self-esteem and fear of rejection, especially by the opposite sex, are common. They are typically helpless, ineffective, nonassertive, have maturity fears, tension management problems, and difficulty in identifying or describing internal states (Johnson & Flach, 1985). Their relationships tend to be superficial and lack genuineness, as they have difficulty allowing others to become emotionally close to them. They are very good at distancing themselves from people while seeming to be friendly and sociable. A common underlying fear is, "If this person really gets to know me, he or she won't like me." They frequently fear sexual rejection or not being good enough to please a sexual partner. Bulimics may additionally overidentify with femininity. Drug abuse among bulimics and their families occurs at a high rate (Herzog, 1982). Motivation for change is extremely difficult to maintain, making therapy difficult.

Bulimics commonly report that their disorder originated out of possible "comfort eating" stemming from loneliness, stress, or some other self-induced inadequacy, such as low self-esteem. Suicide can also be a fatal result of either lack of observation from family and friends, lack of support (as interpreted by the bulimia), or the lack of help from themselves or possibly from the therapist (Hsu, 1990). Not surprisingly, both depression and anxiety are comorbid conditions (Cooper & Fairburn, 1986).

The third aspect of the biopsychosocial triad model of bulimia is social factors. Many bulimics spend so much time in their eating rituals that they do not have time for a normal social life. In one study (Mitchell et al., 1985) 70 percent had interpersonal relations difficulties, 53 percent had family problems, and 50 percent had work-related interpersonal difficulties. Bulimics can also use their eating habits to shut out the world. They can avoid engaging with others or becoming involved in a situation that could potentially be out of their control. Eating rituals are one thing that bulimics (and anorexics as well) believe they can continue to control, even though it is evident to those who know them that they have actually lost control. The specific etiology of bulimia is not known.

The biopsychosocial model suggests that unknown biological predispositions may interact with both individual psychological states and needs and society's emphasis, especially for women, on thinness as a desirable characteristic (Wooley & Wooley, 1985). Families of bulimics are characterized by a paradoxical combination of enmeshment and disengagement, showing high family conflict with little emphasis on self-expression, especially over conflict. Intellectual achievement is emphasized at the expense of social activities (Johnson & Flach, 1985).

Much of the bulimic's perceived control simply does not exist. The social world exposes vulnerable people to things that, depending on their perception, can exploit their fears. Mass communication can intensify people's low self-esteem and fear of rejection. Consider, for example, size 6 models

in fashion shows; Sarah Ferguson, the Duchess of York, saying how easy it is to lose weight; and advertisements for weight-loss programs such as Weight Watchers. Supermodels or representatives of diet programs frequently suffer from serious eating disorders themselves. Numerous media messages instill an unrealistic view of the human form that may enhance fear of "fatness." At the same time, of course, the average weight of American children and adults continues to increase—the average dress size of American adult women is size 12–14.

Treatment can be very difficult. Usually, the longer the bulimic has been ill, the more difficulty she will have in overcoming the disorder. Also, as mentioned previously, lack of motivation for change makes working with bulimics on an outpatient basis difficult. The drive for a weight loss or the perfect body may outweigh the drive for being cured. Numerous difficulties in addition to the motivation problem interfere with recovery. Bulimia nervosa seems to have an addictive quality that is usually not seen in anorexia nervosa. Many therapists believe that treatment is likely to fail if this addictive quality is not addressed. Unfortunately, both bingeing and purging behaviors may have strong and immediate reinforcement qualities. Finally, continual dieting often results in compensatory overeating which appears to have a physiological component. Whether or not inpatient treatment is necessary depends on factors as weight, self-harm tendencies, and other comorbid symptoms.

Cognitive behavior therapy has at least short-term success, although dropout rates vary from 0 to 34 percent (Robin, Gilroy, & Dennis, 1998). Long-term follow-up studies indicate that approximately 33 percent of patients remain symptom-free (Robin et al., 1998). Cognitive behavior therapy has the further advantage of being demonstrably effective in dealing with comorbid factors such as anxiety and depression. Family therapy has been discussed as another way of assisting patients with bulimia nervosa, but little research supports its effectiveness. As a recurring theme, no matter what kind of therapy is offered, whether cognitive behavioral, interpersonal, psychodynamic, or pharmacological, without sufficient and persistent motivation, bulimics will probably find treatment unsuccessful.

No consensus exists regarding the most effective form of treatment for eating disorders (Vandereycken & Meermann, 1984). Therapists have used behavioral therapy, diet counseling, cognitive therapy, cognitive-behavioral treatment, drug treatment, and family therapy with varying degrees of success (Garner & Garfinkel, 1985). Whatever the treatment approach, the usual goals are aimed at increasing confidence and self-esteem, challenging irrational or anorectic thinking, developing autonomy, and teaching coping skills. Unfortunately, group therapy sessions may provide an environment in which bulimics can feed on each other's effective purging techniques and become essentially schools for training better bulimics. Further, Vandereycken and Meermann (1984, p. 21) suggest that the "best guarantees of success in therapy are a constructive patient/therapist working relationship and an explicit but consistent treatment plan/contract."

Certain beliefs and values seem to be very important in the maintenance of these conditions. One of these is the belief that weight and shape are extremely important and need to be closely controlled at all costs. A change in these psychopathological beliefs and values concerning body weight and shape may be necessary for complete recovery. Self-help and support groups such as Overeaters Anonymous may be valuable.

Because eating-disordered individuals are usually perfectionists, teachers can help by advising and encouraging them to take fewer courses and to balance academic loads by combining difficult classes with classes that are less demanding. If hospitalization becomes necessary and the student expresses fear that she will be unable to maintain her academic standing, the teacher can point out that hospital personnel are usually more than willing to assist the patient by administering academic tests and by making arrangements to assist meeting other academic requirements. Major treatment centers, as well as many hospitals, have educational components and academic teachers on their staff.

REFERENCES

American Psychiatric Association. (1994). *Diagnostic and statistical manual of mental disorders* (4th ed.). Washington, DC: Author.

Anderson, A. E., Morse, C., & Santmyer, K. (1985). Inpatient treatment for anorexia nervosa. In D. M. Garner & P. E. Garfinkel (Eds.), *Handbook of psychotherapy for anorexia nervosa and bulimia* (pp. 311–343). New York: Guilford.

Bemis, K. M. (1978). Current approaches to the etiology and treatment of anorexia nervosa. *Psychological Bulletin, 35,* 593–617.

Bruch, H. (1985). Four decades of eating disorders. In D. M. Garner & P. E. Garfinkel (Eds.), *Handbook of psychotherapy for anorexia and bulimia* (pp. 7–18). New York: Guilford.

Cooper, P. J., & Fairburn, C. G. (1986). The depressive symptoms of bulimia nervosa. *British Journal of Psychiatry, 148,* 234–246.

Garner, D. M., & Garfinkel, P. E. (Eds.). (1985). *Handbook of psychotherapy for anorexia nervosa and bulimia.* New York: Guilford.

Goetestan, K. G., Erikson, L., Heggestad, T., & Neilson, S. (1998). Prevalence of eating disorders in Norwegian general hospitals 1990–1994: Admissions per year and seasonality. *International Journal of Eating Disorders, 23,* 57–64.

Halmi, K. A. (1983). Advances in anorexia nervosa. In M. Wolraich & D. K. Routh (Eds.), *Advances in development and behavioral pediatrics* (Vol. 4, pp. 1–23). Greenwich, CT: JAI Press.

Hart, K. J., & Ollendick, T. H. (1985). Prevalence of bulimia in working and university women. *American Journal of Psychiatry, 142,* 851–854.

Herzog, D. B. (1982). Bulimia: The secretive syndrome. *Psychosomatics, 23,* 481–487.

Hsu, T. (1990). *Eating disorders.* New York: Guilford.

Johnson, C., & Flach, A. (1985). Family characteristics of 105 patients with bulimia. *American Journal of Psychiatry, 142,* 1321–1324.

Mitchell, J. E., Halsukami, D., Eckert, E. D., & Pyle, R. L. (1985). Characteristics of 275 patients with bulimia. *American Journal of Psychiatry, 142,* 251–255.

Neuman, P. A., & Halvorson, P. S. (1983). *Anorexia nervosa and bulimia: A handbook for counselors and therapists.* New York: Van Nostrand Reinhold.

Robin, A. L., Gilroy, M., & Dennis, A. B. (1998). Treatment of eating disorders in children and adolescents. *Clinical Psychology Review, 18,* 421–446.

Srinivasan, T. N., Suresh, T. R., & Jayaram, V. (1998). Emergence of eating disorders in India: Study of eating distress syndrome and development of a screening questionnaire. *International Journal of Social Psychiatry, 44,* 189–198.

Vandereycken, W., & Meermann, R. (1984). *Anorexia nervosa: A clinician's guide to treatment.* Berlin: de Gruyter.

Wooley, S. C., & Wooley, O. W. (1985). Intensive outpatient and residential treatment for bulimia. In D. M. Garner & P. E. Garfinkel (Eds.), *Handbook of psychotherapy for anorexia nervosa and bulimia* (pp. 391–430). New York: Guilford.

C. Sue Lamb
University of North Carolina at Wilmington

Wendy L. Flynn
Staffordshire University

ANOREXIA NERVOSA
EATING DISORDERS

BUREAU OF EDUCATION FOR THE HANDICAPPED

The Bureau of Education for the Handicapped (BEH) was created in 1966 to administer all U.S. Office of Education programs designed for individuals with disabilities. During the late 1960s and early 1970s, BEH administered newly created federal programs for individuals with disabilities, including regional resource centers that provided testing to determine the special education needs of disabled children. It also administered service centers for the deaf-blind; offered technical assistance on programs for the gifted and talented; provided funds for recruiting and training special education personnel; created experimental preschool and early education programs that could serve as models for school districts; and mounted research projects concerning individuals with disabilities. Eventually, BEH's responsibility was extended to include the provision of technical assistance, compliance monitoring, and evaluation of state education agency and local school district implementation of PL 93-380, the Education Amendments of 1974, and PL 94-142, the Education of All Handicapped Children Act of 1975. The BEH was succeeded in name but not in authority and responsibility by the Office of Special Education when the U.S. Department of Education was created in 1980. For a more detailed description of federal legislation and the role of BEH, see Weintraub, Abeson, Ballard, and LaVor (1976).

REFERENCE

Weintraub, F. J., Abeson, A., Ballard, J., & LaVor, M. L. (1976). *Public policy and the education of exceptional children.* Reston, VA: Council for Exceptional Children.

ROLAND K. YOSHIDA
Fordham University

BUREAU OF INDIAN AFFAIRS: OFFICE OF INDIAN EDUCATION PROGRAMS

The mission of the Office of Indian Education Programs (OIEP) is to:

provide quality education opportunities from early childhood throughout life in accordance with the Tribe's needs for cultural and economic well-being in keeping with the wide diversity of Indian Tribes and Alaska Native villages as distinct cultural and governmental entities. OIEP manifests consideration of the whole person, taking into account the spiritual, mental, physical, and cultural aspects of the person within a family and Tribal of Alaska Native village contexts. (OIEP, 1998)

The OIEP has developed an extensive list of goals and benchmarks. These goals do not address exceptional children per se, but do include goals that pertain to areas that overlap with special education programs such as behavioral management, alcohol and drug abuse, culturally appropriate assessment instrument for reading and language arts, attendance issues, and staff development (OIEP, 1998).

The OIEP fulfills its mission through its organization located in Washington, D.C. as well as in twenty-five offices throughout the United States. The 185 elementary and secondary schools funded by the federal government provide an education program to 50,000 students from birth through grade twelve. The OIEP also operates two colleges and funds twenty-five colleges operated by tribes and tribal organizations.

The Bureau of Indian Affairs Office of Indian Education Programs maintains an informative webpage at http://www.oiep.bia.edu/. An extensive newsletter *American Indian Education News* is available from this web site. The information in this entry was taken from the OIEP webpage with gracious permission from the BIA.

ELAINE FLETCHER-JANZEN
University of Colorado at Colorado Springs

CULTURAL BIAS IN TESTING

BURKS' BEHAVIOR RATING SCALES

The Burks' Behavior Rating Scales (BBRS), Preschool and Kindergarten Form and Grades One–Nine Form, are rating inventories used to identify the type and severity of problem behaviors exhibited by referred children ages 2 to 15. The scales may be completed by parents, teachers, or any responsible person who knows the rated child well. Raters use a five-point scale ranging from 1 ("You have not noticed this behavior at all") to 5 ("You have noticed this behavior to a very large degree") to render quantitative judgments about the severity of observed negative behaviors.

Individual items are clustered together to form 19 (18 for the Preschool and Kindergarten Form) factor-analytically derived behavior categories bearing diagnostic labels such as excessive withdrawal, excessive dependency, poor coordination, poor academics, poor impulse control, poor reality contact, or excessive aggressiveness. Items are summed for each behavior category (usually by someone other than the rater) and transferred to a profile sheet. The profile sheet orders each category score along a continuum indicating the degree of significance of the presence of each negative behavior. Significance ratings can be used in differential diagnosis and in prioritizing intervention needs. Comparison of score profiles obtained from various raters can help broaden the scope of understanding and interpretation of the child's behavior patterns. The BBRS manual includes a lengthy discussion of the possible meanings of category scores and intervention suggestions for each problem behavior area. The BBRS has received favorable reviews as a clinical tool to aid in behavior assessment (Lerner, 1985).

REFERENCES

Burks, H. F. (1977). *Burks' Behavior Rating Scales.* Los Angeles: Western Psychological Services.
Lerner, J. V. (1985). Review of the Burks' Behavior Rating Scales. In D. J. Keyser & R. C. Sweetland (Eds.), *Test critiques* (Vol. 2, pp. 108–112). Kansas City, MO: Test Corporation of America.

George McCloskey
Philadelphia College of Osteopathic Medicine

BEHAVIOR PROBLEM CHECKLIST, REVISED

BUROS MENTAL MEASUREMENTS YEARBOOK

There are sixteen *Mental Measurements Yearbooks* (*MMYs*). The yearbooks, which originated in 1938 (Buros, 1938), provide test users with factual information on all known tests published separately in the English-speaking countries of the world. In addition, the books contain test reviews written by professional people representing a variety of viewpoints. The volumes are also sources of comprehensive bibliographies for specific tests, and references relevant to the tests.

The purpose of all the *MMYs* is to provide a forum in which tests can be reviewed candidly to facilitate intelligent consumer choice and use of tests. The most recent *MMY* (Spies & Plake, 2005) contains descriptive information on new or revised tests, test reviews, extensive listings of test references and reviewer references, several indexes including indexes of test titles, classified subject areas, publishers, scores, and names of test authors and reviewers. In addition, the Buros Library of Mental Measurements provides qualitative reviews on computer-based test interpretation systems (Plake, Conoley, Kramer, & Murphy, 1989).

The books are published by the Buros Institute of Mental Measurements, located since 1979 at the University of Nebraska, Lincoln, Department of Educational Psychology. The institute, established originally by Oscar K. Buros, has published over 20 volumes (edited by Buros) relating to test description and review. Online access to the *MMY* can be found at www.unl.edu/buros.

REFERENCES

Buros, O. K. (1938). *The 1938 mental measurements yearbook.* Highland Park, NJ: Gryphon.

Plake, B. S., Conoley, J. C., Kramer, J. J., & Murphy, L. L. (1989). Buros bulletin. *Educational Measurement: Issues & Practices, 8,* 20–21.

Spies, R. A., & Plake, B. S. (2005). *The sixteenth mental measurements yearbook.* Lincoln, NE: Buros Institute.

JANE CLOSE CONOLEY
University of Nebraska
First edition

ELAINE FLETCHER-JANZEN
University of Colorado at
Colorado Springs
Third edition

BUROS, OSCAR K.
TESTS IN PRINT

BUROS, OSCAR K. (1905–1978)

Oscar K. Buros is remembered internationally as the foremost proponent of critical analyses of educational and psychological tests. Buros attended the State Normal School in Superior, Wisconsin, from 1922 to 1924 and completed his undergraduate education at the University of Minnesota in 1925. Buros received his graduate degree from the Teachers College, Columbia University. He accepted a faculty appointment at Rutgers University in 1932 and was a member of that faculty until his retirement in 1965. During World War II, he was in charge of testing for the U.S. Army's specialized training program, and later an adviser on the assessment of leadership at West Point.

He married Luella Gubrud who, an accomplished artist in her own right, later shared with him the responsibilities for the famous *Buros Mental Measurements Yearbook* (*MMY*) series. It was she who saw the last edition through to its completion following his death on March 19, 1978. Buros published the first *MMY* in 1938. Seven other *Yearbooks* followed, as well as the *Mental Measurements Yearbook* monographs series (1968, 1970, and 1975a–i) and the *Tests in Print* series (1961, 1974).

He was the recipient of many professional honors and awards. Some of these were citations in 1953 from both the American Educational Research Association and the American Psychological Association for excellence in contributions to measurement; a senior Fulbright lectureship in statistics at Makerere University College, Uganda, 1956–1957; the 1965 Phi Delta Kappa research award; and in 1973 both an honorary Doctor of Science degree from Upsala College and the Distinguished Service to Measurement Award from the Educational Testing Service. Buros was a fellow of the American Statistical Association and the American Psychological Association. Rutgers University's Graduate School of Applied and Professional Psychology established a professorship in Buros's honor in 1985.

In 1979, the Buros Institute of Mental Measurements was moved to the University of Nebraska-Lincoln. The institute has continued the Buros tradition by publishing *Tests in Print III* (Mitchell, 1983) and up to twelve *Mental Measurements Yearbooks* (Conoley, Impara, & Murphy, 1995).

REFERENCES

Buros, O. K. (1938). *The 1938 mental measurements yearbook.* Highland Park, NJ: Gryphon.

Buros, O. K. (1961). *Tests in print.* Highland Park, NJ: Gryphon.

Buros, O. K. (1968). *Reading tests and reviews I.* Highland Park, NJ: Gryphon.

Buros, O. K. (1970). *Personality tests and reviews I.* Highland Park, NJ: Gryphon.

Buros, O. K. (1974). *Tests in print II*. Highland Park, NJ: Gryphon.

Buros, O. K. (1975a). *Personality tests and reviews II*. Highland Park, NJ: Gryphon.

Buros, O. K. (1975b). *Reading tests and reviews II*. Highland Park, NJ: Gryphon.

Buros, O. K. (1975c). *Intelligence tests and reviews II*. Highland Park, NJ: Gryphon.

Buros, O. K. (1975d). *English tests and reviews*. Highland Park, NJ: Gryphon.

Buros, O. K. (1975e). *Foreign language tests and reviews*. Highland Park, NJ: Gryphon.

Buros, O. K. (1975f). *Mathematics tests and reviews*. Highland Park, NJ: Gryphon.

Buros, O. K. (1975g). *Science tests and reviews*. Highland Park, NJ: Gryphon.

Buros, O. K. (1975h). *Social studies tests reviews*. Highland Park, NJ: Gryphon.

Buros, O. K. (1975i). *Vocational tests and reviews*. Highland Park, NJ: Gryphon.

Conoley, J. C., Impara, J. C., & Murphy, L. L. (Eds.). (1995). *The twelfth mental measurements yearbook*. Lincoln, NE: Buros Institute of Mental Measurements.

Mitchell, J. V., Jr. (1983). *Tests in print III*. Lincoln, NE: Buros Institute of Mental Measurements.

Mitchell, J. V., Jr. (1985). *The ninth mental measurements yearbook*. Lincoln, NE: Buros Institute of Mental Measurements.

JANE CLOSE CONOLEY
University of Nebraska

TESTS IN PRINT

BURT, SIR CYRIL (1883–1971)

Sir Cyril Burt became the first psychologist in the world to be employed by a school system when he was appointed to the position of psychologist with the London County Council in 1913. Burt's career centered around the application of psychology to the study and education of children. He made pioneering investigations in the areas of mental retardation, delinquency, and the genetics of intelligence, and conducted studies that served as models of the application of the scientific method to the study of human characteristics. Burt developed numerous tests for use by school psychologists and published his influential *Factors of the Mind* in 1941. He was co-editor of the *British Journal of Statistical Psychology*.

From 1931 until his retirement in 1950, Burt was professor of psychology at University College, London, where he devoted most of his attention to the training of psychologists and the continuation of his research and writing. He was knighted in 1946.

Sadly, Burt's work and reputation are marred by findings that he deliberately fabricated data in some of his best known studies. These acts of fraud cast doubt on his research findings, but do not erase his great contributions to psychology as a clinician, theoretician, and teacher (Hearnshaw, 1979).

REFERENCES

Burt, C. (1941). *The factors of the mind: An introduction to factor analysis in psychology*. New York: Macmillan.

Hearnshaw, L. S. (1979). *Cyril Burt, psychologist*. Ithaca, NY: Cornell University Press.

PAUL IRVINE
Katonah, New York

C

CAFÉ AU LAIT SPOTS

Café au lait spots are areas of patchy pigmentation of skin, usually light brown in color. They are so-named because of their resemblance in color to coffee with cream. They are of diagnostic significance because they may indicate the presence of serious disease such as neurofibromatosis, polyostotic fibrous dysplasia, or tuberous sclerosis (*Blakiston's*, 1979; Johnson, 1979). Café au lait spots may be found in normal individuals.

When six or more café au lait spots are present and they are larger than 1.5 cm in diameter, neurofibromatosis is suspected (Johnson, 1979; Steinman & Nussbaum, 2003). Neurofibromatosis, also known as Von Recklinghausen's disease, is a genetic disorder inherited as an autosomal dominant trait (Batshaw & Perret, 1981). In addition to the presence of café au lait spots, which exist at birth and hence aid in the diagnosis of this condition, other symptoms include multiple skin-colored tumors or nodules and freckles of the axillae (armpits), which represent the Crowe's sign of neurofibromatosis.

Neurofibromatosis may have numerous neurological, psychological, and educational implications. Tumors or neurofibromas typically develop prior to puberty. These tumors may be associated with the spinal or cranial nerves and hence may result in sensory deficits such as visual or hearing impairment. Enlargement and deformation of the bones and scoliosis (curvature of the spine) may occur. Hypertension may be present in young victims of this condition. There is reported to be an increased incidence of mental retardation (Johnson, 1979) and school problems associated with neurofibromatosis (Batshaw & Perret, 1981). In severe cases, the presence of multiple contiguous tumors produces elephantiasis neuromatosa, a cosmetically disfiguring condition. While skin tumors may be removed, there is some evidence these may recur and multiply (*Fact Sheet*, 1983).

In addition to neurofibromatosis, café au lait spots also have been observed in other neurocutaneous syndromes such as tuberous sclerosis (Bourneville's disease; Rosenberg, 1979). Also inherited as an autosomal dominant trait, tuberous sclerosis is characterized by nevi or moles on the face, epilepsy, and mental retardation (Rosenberg). The course of tuberous sclerosis begins with the onset of epilepsy and declining mental ability during the first decade, with development of facial lesions around the cheeks and nose several years later (Rosenberg).

Café au lait spots occurring in the size and number as noted previously are considered diagnostically significant in neurofibromatosis. Ninety percent of afflicted individuals are reported to exhibit them at birth (Johnson, 1979). Because their presence is associated with serious medical conditions such as neurofibromatosis and tuberous sclerosis, identification of numerous café au lait spots in children without medical diagnoses warrants referral to a physician. Educational management of children who have been diagnosed as having neurofibromatosis or tuberous sclerosis should be conducted on an individual basis because the severity and expression of symptoms vary widely.

REFERENCES

Batshaw, M. L., & Perret, Y. M. (1981). *Children with handicaps: A medical primer*. Baltimore: Brookes.

Blakiston's Gould medical dictionary (4th ed.). (1979). New York: McGraw-Hill.

Fact sheet: Neurofibromatosis. (1983). Bethesda, MD: National Institute of Neurological and Communicative Disorders and Stroke.

Johnson, M. (1979). Certain cutaneous diseases with significant systemic manifestations. In P. B. Beeson, W. McDermott, & J. B. Wyngaarden (Eds.), *Cecil textbook of medicine* (15th ed., pp. 2266–2312). Philadelphia: Saunders.

Rosenberg, R. N. (1979). Inherited degenerative diseases of the nervous system. In P. B. Beeson, W. McDermott, & J. B. Wyngaarden (Eds.), *Cecil textbook of medicine* (15th ed., pp. 764–772). Philadelphia: Saunders.

Steinman, D. R., & Nussbaum, N. (2003). In E. Fletcher-Janzen & C. R. Reynolds (Eds.), *Childhood disorders diagnostic desk reference* (p. 101). New York: Wiley.

CATHY F. TELZROW
Kent State University

MINOR PHYSICAL ANOMALIES
NEUROFIBROMATOSIS

CALDWELL, BETTYE M. (1924–   )

Bettye M. Caldwell received her BA (1945) from Baylor University, her MA (1946) from the University of Iowa, and her PhD (1951) in psychology from Washington University. Caldwell's career, which has spanned more than 30 years, reflects her interest in early childhood education and development. Currently, she is a Donaghey Distinguished Professor of Education at the University of Arkansas at Little Rock.

Since the late 1960s, when Caldwell was a member of the National Advisory Committee for Research and Evaluation for Project Head Start, she has maintained an interest in the impact of research on social policy. She has devoted her efforts to early intervention programs for very young handicapped children, demonstration daycare centers, and training parents and others who work with young children. By studying the impact of day care on factors such as intellectual and social development and mother-child attachment, Caldwell has shown that day care can have a significant, positive impact on children, especially those from disadvantaged backgrounds (Caldwell, 1977).

One of Caldwell's major research interests has been the measurement of the quality of a child's home environment. The HOME (Home Observation for Measurement of the Environment) Inventory, which resulted from this work, is used worldwide as a measure of the learning environment within the home. Having such information available is vital both for the determination of the extent to which atypical development is due to inadequate or inappropriate environmental stimulation, and for the design of intervention programs (Bradley & Caldwell, 1984).

Caldwell has been involved as one of the major investigators in a large, 10-site study concerned with the effects of different patterns of child care during early infancy. She has also developed a unique training program for caregivers in educare settings that integrates knowledge and skills from both nursing and education. The training is based on contemporary research on brain development and early experience. Caregivers are taught to introduce learning activities that will meet the needs of the developing brain at each chronological age period and thereby facilitate emotional and cognitive advances in the children.

A leader in her field, Caldwell has been president of the National Association for the Education of Young Children (1982–1984) and editor of the journal *Child Development* (1968–1971). She has served on the editorial board and the board of directors for other journals and organizations. She also has earned international notice, serving as a U.S. delegate to the U.S.S.R. and the People's Republic of China to study early education programs in those countries.

Dr. Caldwell has published over 200 articles and books dating back to 1951. She has also written many articles for magazines and has written and produced several educational films and videos.

REFERENCES

Bradley, R. H., & Caldwell, B. M. (1984). 174 children: A study of the relation between home environment and mental development in the first five years. In A. Gottfried (Ed.), *Home environment and early cognitive development* (pp. 5–56). New York: Academic.

Caldwell, B. M. (1977). Child development and social policy. In M. Scott & S. Grimmett (Eds.), *Current issues in child development*. Washington, DC: National Association for the Education of Young Children.

ANN E. LUPKOWSKI
Texas A&M University
First edition

TAMARA J. MARTIN
*The University of Texas of the
   Permian Basin*
Second edition

Bettye M. Caldwell

CALIFORNIA VERBAL LEARNING TEST–SECOND EDITION

The California Verbal Learning Test–Second Edition (CVLT-II; Delis, Kramer, Kaplan, & Ober, 2000) is an individually administered measure used to assess verbal learning and memory in adults ages 16 through 89. The Standard and Alternate Forms of the test contain 16 items to recall from two lists. The Short Form of the test contains two lists of 9 words. Administration time for the Standard and Alternate Forms is 30 minutes and a 30-minute time delay used to assess delayed recall. The Short Form takes 15 minutes to administer, plus a 15-minute delay interval.

The CVLT-II uses two hypothetical shopping lists, the "Monday List" and the "Tuesday List." In the first five trials, the examinee is presented the "Monday List" and is asked to recall all 16 words from the list. The "Tuesday List," which contains 16 new words to be recalled, is then presented as an interference task. The Tuesday trial is followed by a short-delay free-recall trial and short-delay cued-recall trial of the Monday list. After a 30-minute delay in which non-verbal intelligence can be assessed, a long-delay free-recall trial, long-delay cued-recall trial, and a recognition trial of the "Monday List" are administered. An addition to the CVLT-II from the original version is a forced-choice recognition trial, which is designed to detect malingering. The Short Form can be used when administration time is limited and the Alternate Form can be used when it is necessary to re-test an examinee. The CVLT-II contains an administration manual with verbal prompts for the instructor, and three versions of the record form to record the examinee's responses. The record forms contain the items from both lists and gives space to record responses from each trial.

The CVLT-II was co-normed with the Wechsler Abbreviated Scale of Intelligence (WASI) and the Delis-Kaplan Executive Function System (DKEFS). The test was standardized using a sample composed of 1,087 adults matched to population data from the March 1999 U.S. Census. The data from the sample was stratified along the categories of age, gender, race/ethnicity, geographic region and education level. The CVLT-II yields raw scores that are then transformed to standardized scores. Recall trials 1–5 were scaled using a normalized T-metric with a mean of 50 and a standard deviation of 10. All other scores on the test were normed on a linear z-score metric, with a mean of 0 and a standard deviation of 1.0. Norms were established for seven unique age groups ranging from 16 through 89 years of age.

Reliability for the CVLT-II was evaluated using three separate indices. The first index assessed consistency of performance across trials. Split-half reliability for the total sample was .94. The second reliability index evaluated consistency of performance in the four categories of words on the list across all five trials. The overall reliability for the total sample was .82. The third reliability index examined the number of times each of the words was recalled across the five initial trials. The split-half reliability for the total sample was .78. These figures indicate that overall, the trials show a high degree of internal consistency. The reliability of the Alternate Form based on administration of both the Standard and Alternate Forms was evaluated by administering both forms to a sample of 288 adults with an average 21 days between administrations. Reliability coefficients for the key CVLT-II variables ranged from .72 to .79. Test-retest stability was assessed by retesting a group of 78 adults ranging in age from 16 to 88 years, with a median retest interval of 21 days. The correlation of scores between the two test administrations was .82. The validity of the CVLT-II was based on the validity information for the original CVLT. Construct validity for the original CVLT was examined in over 200 research studies. Because there is a great deal of concurrent validity between the CVLT and the CVLT-II,

this is an indication of a comparable level of validity in the second version of the CVLT. Construct validity was evaluated using methods such as factor analysis to test the relationship between the test and variables known to account for variability in learning and memory and by correlating performance on the CVLT-II to verbal intelligence.

REFERENCES

Delis, D., Kramer, J., Kaplan, E., & Ober, B. (2000). *California Verbal Learning Test–Second edition manual.* Harcourt Brace and Company.

Impara, J. C., & Plake, B. S. (Eds.). (1998). *The thirteenth mental measurements yearbook.* Lincoln, NE: Buros Institute of Mental Measurements.

Stricker, J. L., Brown, G. G., Wixted, J., Baldo, J. V., & Delis, D. C. (2002). New semantic and serial clustering indices for the California Verbal Learning Test–Second Edition: Background, rationale, and formulae. *Journal of the International Neuropsychological Society, 8,* 425–35.

RON DUMONT
Fairleigh Dickinson University

JOHN O. WILLIS
Rivier College

CALIFORNIA VERBAL LEARNING TEST–CHILDREN'S VERSION

The California Verbal Learning Test–Children's Version (CVLT-C; Delis, Kramer, Kaplan, & Ober, 1994) is an individually administered measure used to assess verbal learning and memory in children and adolescents ages 5 through 16.11 years. The test contains 30 items to recall from two lists. Administration time is 15 to 20 minutes, and a 20-minute time delay used to assess delayed recall. The CVLT-C uses two hypothetical shopping lists, the "Monday List" and the "Tuesday List." In the first five trials, the child is presented the "Monday List" and is asked to recall all 15 words from the list. The "Tuesday List," which contains 15 new words to be recalled, is then presented as an interference task. The Tuesday trial is followed by a short-delay free-recall trial and short-delay cued-recall trial of the Monday list. After a 20-minute delay in which non-verbal intelligence can be assessed, a long-delay free-recall trial, long-delay cued-recall trial, and a recognition trial of the "Monday List" are administered. The CVLT-C requires an administration manual with verbal prompts for the instructor, and a record form to record the child's responses. The record form contains the items from both lists and gives space to record responses from each trial.

The CVLT-C was co-normed with the Children's Category Test (CCT). The standardization sample consisted of 920 children in 12 age groups ranging from 5 through 16 years of age. The test was standardized using a stratified random sample of children based on data from the March 1988 U.S. Census. The data from the sample was stratified along the categories of age, gender, race/ethnicity, geographic region and parent education level. For the stratification variables selected, the CVLT-C standardization sample strongly approximated the population of school-age children represented in the 1988 U.S. Census data.

Reliability for the CVLT-C was evaluated using three separate indices. The first index assessed consistency of performance across trials. Odd-even reliability had an average coefficient of .88; the coefficient alpha was an average of .85. The second reliability index evaluated consistency of performance across semantically unrelated item sets. The average reliability coefficient was .72. The third reliability index measured across-word consistency. The average odd-even correlation was .83 and the average alpha coefficient was .81. These figures indicate that overall, the trials show a high degree of internal consistency. Test-retest stability was assessed by retesting a group of 106 children. The median retest interval was 28 days. The correlations ranged from .38 to .90 for the 8 year-old group, .17 to .77 for the 12 year-old group, and .31 to .85 for the 16 year-old group. Although these are modest levels of reliability, they are within the expected limits given the kind of test. The CVLT-C was developed based on research in cognitive science research and is therefore considered both content and criterion valid. Construct validity was evaluated using factor analysis. For the CVLT-C, factors whose eigenvalues were 1 or greater were retained, and loadings on a factor greater than .40 were considered significant. The factor analysis revealed that the CVLT-C corresponds to the Adult CVLT in terms of factor loading.

REFERENCES

Delis, D., Kramer, J., Kaplan, E., & Ober, B. (1994). *California Verbal Learning Test–Children's Version manual.* Harcourt Brace and Company.

Impara, J. C., & Plake, B. S. (Eds.). (1998). *The thirteenth mental measurements yearbook.* Lincoln, NE: Buros Institute of Mental Measurements.

Levin, H. S., Song, J., & Scheibel, R. S. (2000). Dissociation of frequency and recency processing from list recall after severe closed head injury in children and adolescents. *Journal of Clinical & Experimental Neuropsychology, 22,* 1–15.

Yeates, K. O., Blumenstein, E., & Patterson, C. M. (1995). Verbal learning and memory following pediatric closed-head injury. *Journal of the International Neuropsychological Society, 1,* 78–87.

RON DUMONT
Fairleigh Dickinson University

JOHN O. WILLIS
Rivier College

CAMP, BONNIE W. (1931–   )

Bonnie Camp received her BA from Mississippi State College for Women in 1948, and her MA and PhD in clinical psychology from Indiana University in 1954. She went on to receive her MD in 1965 from the University of Colorado School of Medicine and pediatric training from the University of Colorado Health Sciences Center. In 1972, she received a Research Career Award from NIMH for her studies on learning disabilities. She also served on the faculty of Pediatrics and Psychiatry at the University of Colorado School of Medicine, and was director of the JFK Child Development Center at the University of Colorado Health Sciences Center before retiring in 1993.

While employed as a pediatrician in the Denver Health and Hospitals Neighborhood Health Center, Camp organized a tutorial reading program for children with severe reading delay in the center's catchment area using community aides, older students, and volunteers. The program was eventually extended to schools throughout the Denver School District.

Camp is best known for her development of the Think Aloud Program (Bash & Camp 1985a, 1985b, 1986; Camp & Bash, 1981, 1985). Think Aloud is a cognitive behavior modification program designed to improve social and cognitive problem-solving skills in young children. It was conceived as a training program to decrease impulsivity, encourage consideration of alternatives and plan a course of action. It emphasizes the use of cognitive modeling as a teaching tool whereby teachers model their own strategies for thinking through problems. Camp is currently professor emeritus of pediatrics and psychiatry at the University of Colorado School of Medicine.

REFERENCES

Bash, M. A. S., & Camp, B. W. (1985a). *The Think Aloud Classroom Program for grades 3 and 4.* Champaign, IL: Research Press.

Bash, M. A. S., & Camp, B. W. (1985b). *The Think Aloud Classroom Program for grades 5 and 6.* Champaign, IL: Research Press.

Bash, M. A. S., & Camp, B. A. (1986). Training teachers in the Think Aloud Classroom Program. In G. Cartledge & J. Milburn (Eds.), *Teaching social skills to children: Innovative approaches.* New York: Pergamon Press.

Camp, B. W., & Bash, M. A. S. (1981). *Think Aloud: Increasing social and cognitive skills—A problem-solving program for children.* Champaign, IL: Research Press.

Camp, B. W., & Bash, M. A. S. (1985). *The Think Aloud Classroom Program for grades 1 and 2.* Champaign, IL: Research Press.

STAFF

CAMPBELL, SIR FRANCIS JOSEPH (1832–1914)

Francis J. Campbell was born on a farm in Tennessee on October 9, 1832. Blinded in an accident at the age of 3, he was

Sir Francis Joseph Campbell

educated at the newly opened Tennessee State Institution for the Blind, where he later served as a teacher of music while studying at the University of Tennessee. Following a period as a student at Harvard University and then as a teacher of the blind in Wisconsin, he became an instructor at Perkins Institution and Massachusetts Asylum for the Blind, where he served for 11 years as head of the music department.

A talented pianist, Campbell left Perkins to continue his music education in Europe and to study methods of teaching the blind. While in London he met Thomas Rhodes Armitage, a blind physician who had just completed joining together Britain's numerous organizations for the blind into a federation that ultimately became known as the Royal National Institute for the Blind.

Campbell's account of the large number of students at Perkins whom he had helped prepare for successful careers as professional musicians led Armitage to establish a music school to train blind children, with Campbell as headmaster. Starting in 1872 with two students, the school ultimately became the Royal Normal College and Academy of Music, with an enrollment, by 1885, of 170 students. Campbell's original faculty included a number of teachers from Perkins, and through the years he maintained a continuing exchange of teachers with Perkins and other schools in the United States. As a result, the Royal Normal College and Academy of Music probably had more influence on American teaching methods than any other foreign school. The institution, under Campbell, combined general education and physical training with careful vocational preparation, job placement, and follow-up after graduation. Between 80 and 90 percent of the graduates became self-supporting, mostly as musicians, teachers, and technicians trained in piano tuning and repair. This unprecedented achievement stimulated an emphasis on vocational preparation in schools for the blind throughout the world.

Campbell believed strongly in the value of physical exercise, and took great pride in his own physical prowess—he once scaled the formidable Mont Blanc, a feat that he considered one of the crowning achievements of his life. He viewed physical training as an essential ingredient in any educational program preparing the blind for active and productive lives and developed an extensive physical education program that greatly influenced other schools for the blind.

In recognition of his work on behalf of the blind, Campbell was knighted by King Edward VII in 1909. Campbell retired as headmaster in 1912. He died on June 30, 1914.

REFERENCES

Koestler, F. A. (1976). *The unseen minority: A social history of blindness in America.* New York: McKay.

Ross, I. (1951). *Journey into light.* New York: Appleton-Century-Crofts.

PAUL IRVINE
Katonah, New York

CAMPHILL COMMUNITY MOVEMENT

The Camphill Community (movement) was founded by Karl Koenig a respected Viennese pediatrician (1902–1966) after he fled the Nazi powers of central Europe in 1939. The name Camphill refers to the group's first house in Aberdeen, Scotland (Baron & Haldane, 1991).

The Camphill Community is based on the writings of Rudolph Steiner (1861–1925). It works for a full understanding of people's spiritual being, eternal purpose, and earthly tasks. The goals of Steiner's work (known as anthroposophy) include allowing all human beings, disabled or not, to develop to their potential and to find a productive place in society. The fostering and development of individual human dignity is of paramount importance.

Camphill villages (there are 80) are currently found in countries worldwide, with 7 in the United States. Despite minor differences, village life centers around the family, community, and productive, meaningful work. The family typically consists of parents, children, and a number of mentally disabled individuals living and working together, free from labels and distinctions. Mutual responsibility is stressed; no salaries are paid but individuals have their needs met by the community.

The Camphill Special School, Glenmoore, Pennsylvania, serves 72 children from elementary through high school age. Its program complements the philosophies of the larger Camphill Community and provides the "structure, rhythm, regularity, and consistency" needed for curative education. Each child works from an individual education program based on an adaptation of the Waldorf School movement. The education of the whole child is stressed; specific therapies (painting, speech, medicine, music) are provided depending on need. Older students are prepared vocationally for life after graduation through training in groundskeeping, woodwork, and household activities.

A 4-year training seminar is offered in the Beaver Run, Pennsylvania school. It is designed to train the individual in curative education using the Waldorf curriculum, as well as in all aspects of community living in the Camphill tradition.

Persons interested in joining or learning more about the Camphill communities are encouraged to contact them directly at http://www.camphill.org.

REFERENCE

Baron, S., & Haldane, D. (1991). Approaching Camphill: From the boundary. *British Journal of Special Education, 18*(2), 75–78.

JOHN E. PORCELLA
Rhinebeck Country School

CAMPING FOR CHILDREN WITH DISABILITIES

Camping for children with disabilities is divided into two types—individual and organized camping. The camping areas used for individualized camping are either in developed or wilderness states. Developed campsites are usually near conveniences that facilitate their use by special needs campers (e.g., they offer amenities such as tent pads, electrical and water outlets, and restroom facilities). Their nature paths are wide and smooth to facilitate travel for children and youths who are wheelchair-bound or impaired in motor functioning (Gerstein, 1992; Sessoms, 1984).

Wilderness campgrounds have cruder facilities and fewer activity programs for the handicapped than developed camping areas. Most are designed for a low level of human use. They lack conveniences such as smooth paths and picnic facilities. As a rule, they are considered closed to the physically handicapped, though there are no limitations to other persons.

Organized camping has been defined as the merging of outdoor recreation and education in a campsite setting (Sessoms, 1984). Organized camping is carried out on day and residential bases. Activities at organized camps for disabled individuals range from general activities (such as sports and games, hobbies, arts and crafts, and drama) to special-purpose activities such as computer training and weight control. These camps are also likely to emphasize education and rehabilitation (Wiseman, 1982). Major emphases in organized camps are to foster socialization skills, the acceptance of responsibilities, and the learning of leisure skills, and to facilitate living in communal atmospheres.

Organized camping programs for children with disabilities are sponsored by the following types of agencies: (1) private or commercial campers agencies, whose fees come from their clients; (2) quasipublic agencies, some of whose funds come from donations and endowments, while the balance is paid by the participants (e.g., Easter Seals and American Red Cross camps); and (3) public-camping programs supported and sponsored by either local or municipal parks and recreation systems, or by organizations serving the disabled and parent groups.

Four different types of organized camping programs may be distinguished. One type is camps that are located within communities where campers participate on a daily basis; these have accessible toilets, play, and eating areas. Another type is resident camps for children with special needs. These have cabins, dining halls, staff quarters, and indoor and outdoor recreation facilities. Their sessions last from 1 to 8 weeks. A third type is combination resident and daycamping opportunities that permit some campers to attend daily while others remain overnight. Finally, there are special purpose camps that promote a single concept or activity such as a specific sport or religion (Wiseman, 1982).

Since 1975, some programs have adopted noncategorical approaches (i.e., involving all campers with disabilities in a normalized integrated camp program). Campers are evaluated for an integrated camping program on the basis of their level of functioning in camp activities. The camper with a disability is placed in integrative, halfway, or special groups in such integrated camps depending on his or her capabilities.

In integrative camping, campers with disabilities participate in all activities together with able-bodied campers. Handicapped campers in the halfway group may have the potential for regular group participation but still lack some ability to fully engage in activities. Usually, they engage in the same activities as the regular group and share the same facilities, but they do so separately (Sessoms, 1984).

Disabled campers in the special group require a segregated and supervised program because of the severity and complexity of their condition. All camping activities are modified to the capabilities and interests of this group. The American Camp Association (ACA) provides a very helpful web site for persons searching for specific needs camps at www.acacamps.org. This web site creates a specific profile of the needs of the camper and possible opportunities. There are twenty-three types of special needs identified such as diabetes, spina bifida, and substance abuse (ACA, 2005).

REFERENCES

American Camp Association (ACA). (2005). *Search for camps for those with special needs.* Retrieved July 13, 2005, from http://www.acacamps.org

American Camping Association standards for persons with special needs (Part IIC). (1980). Martinsville, IN: Bradford Woods.

Choosing a summer camp. (1985). *Exceptional Children, 14*(3), 37–39.

Gerstein, J. (1992). *Direction of experiential therapy and adventure-based counseling programs.* (ERIC Clearinghouse No. ED39 80 21)

Physical Education for the Handicapped. (1982). *Involving impaired and handicapped persons in regular camp programs.* Washington, DC: IRUC.

Sessoms, H. (1984). *Leisure services* (3rd ed.). Englewood Cliffs, NJ: Prentice Hall.

Wiseman, D. (1982). *A practical approach to adapted physical education.* Reading, MA: Addison-Wesley.

THOMAS R. BURKE
Hunter College, City University of New York

EQUINE THERAPY
RECREATIONAL THERAPY

CANADA, SPECIAL EDUCATION IN

Canada is one of the few countries in the world that does not have a national education system; education is the exclusive jurisdiction of the 10 provinces and 2 territories[1] that make up the country. The only common vehicle that exists to discuss educational policy at the national level is the Council of Ministers of Education, Canada,[2] however, this body serves only as a mechanism to discuss issues of concern to the provinces and territories as it has no regulatory power over special education. The lack of a Canadian office of education results in considerable diversity in the organization and governance of special education across the country.

Within each province and territory, there is, in most cases, a provincial or territorial act designed to regulate education. This legislation is broad in scope and typically includes such things as the definitions of responsibilities for personnel associated with educational delivery, the organization and structure of schools and their governing bodies, and policies regarding fiscal matters. The result is that education differs from province/territory to province/territory. Special education is subsumed under the various political jurisdictions, and its profile in each province/territory varies as a function of the current legislation and policies that are in place, the financial resources committed to service provision, and regional priorities. In sum, there is no Canadian picture of special education; rather, there is a kaleidoscope of legislation, policy, and practice that varies across the country.

A combination of geographical and language factors continue to influence special education in Canada (Hutchinson & Wong, 1987). The majority of Canada's population is concentrated in the southern portion of the country, which results in a reasonably efficient pool of services for the majority of the population, which tends to be clustered in urban areas. Using geography as a framework, however, providing special education services for the minority of the population is both costly and inefficient. For example, there are several areas of the country where school authorities serve a sparse population spread over several hundred miles. Within such a service area there may be only a few people who require special education support service; however, they may be located in opposite ends of the catchment area. This geographic spread might be further complicated by the language(s) spoken and by an increasing cultural diversity. In addition to the two official national languages (English and French), a growing number of individuals have another native language and speak English or French only secondly or thirdly. There also are areas of the country where the majority cultural group is, for example, Indo-Canadian or Inuit. The change in cultural diversity is not limited to the sparsely populated regions of the country; because of immigration, English has now been reduced to a minority language status in Vancouver and Richmond, British Columbia ("English," 1998). The end result of this amalgamation is that service providers must be aware of diverse cultural values and be sensitive to the possibility that different languages are spoken at home, at school, and in the community, while providing the required services at a reasonable cost in an era of diminished fiscal resources.

The history of special education in Canada was described as follows by Hutchinson and Wong (1987):

1. Until 1969, special education developed more rapidly in larger cities than in rural communities; however, there was considerable interprovincial/interterroritial variation in service provision.

2. As of 1969, there were offices of special education in half of the provincial Ministries or Departments of Education, with approximately 3 percent of school-aged students receiving special education services.

3. From 1969 to 1972, special education developed rapidly, with seven provinces (British Columbia, Alberta, Saskatchewan, Manitoba, Ontario, Quebec, and Newfoundland) advancing new or revised legislation or policy and the remainder committing to change their special education legislation or policy.

4. An important trend during 1969 to 1972 was increasing concern over finding alternatives to special

class placement and the beginning of service provision, through integration, in regular classrooms.

5. During the early to mid-1970s, two key reports were issued. First came the Standards for Educators of Exceptional Children (Hardy, McLeod, Minto, Perkins, & Quance, 1971), in which both a set of minimum standards and a model of training for teachers of exceptional children were advanced, which were translated in provincial and territorial guidelines. Second, a committee of the Council for Exceptional Children in Canada (Treherne, Dice, Grigg, & Sanche, 1974) prepared a report that advanced principles to govern legislation for children with special needs, which had a variable degree influence over the legislation proposed in different provinces/territories.

6. During the mid-1980s, it was estimated that 12 percent of the school population required special education; however, the accuracy of this estimation was questioned since there was no national office of education in Canada and provinces reported incidence data differently. By this time, every province had published legislation, regulations, policies, and/or guidelines for special education. The predominant models of service delivery were adapted from the United States and ranged from segregation to integration.

During the mid to late 1980s, the trends established during the middle of the decade continued; however, some new significant Canadian developments occurred as well. One of the most significant influences on Canadian special education was introduced in 1982. The full impact of the Canadian Charter of Rights and Freedoms (1982), however, was not felt by special educators until Section 15 was implemented in 1985 (MacKay, 1987). Section 15 of the Charter contained this key clause: "Every individual is equal before and under the law and has the right to the equal protection and equal benefit of the law with discrimination and, in particular, without discrimination based on race, national or ethnic origin, colour, religion, sex, age, or mental or physical disability." MacKay noted that Section 15 could provide the legal grounds on which to request the provision of well-funded special education programs and to challenge the segregation of children. Provinces/territories, however, can sidestep the implications of the Charter by invoking the "notwithstanding" clause, declaring that the education statute operates notwithstanding the Charter. There were also shifts in the preparation of materials to prepare special educators that had a Canadian flavor. For the first time, Canadian special educators introduced professional texts that initially were adaptations of work published in the United States (for example, Hammill, Bartel, & Bunch, 1984) but subsequently were written specifically for Canadian audiences (for example, Bachor & Crealock, 1986). This trend has continued with both adapted (Friend, Bursuck, &

Hutchinson, 1998) and unique texts (for example, Andrews & Lupart, 1993; Crealock & Bachor, 1995) continuing to be published.

During this period, policies and practices established in the United States and (to a lesser extent) Europe, continued to influence service delivery models adopted in Canada as well. One notable example was the regular education initiative which led to the introduction of the full-service school (school-based service provision). Further, partly as a result of a British influence, Canadian schools have changed to school-based management, which has resulted in increased parental advocacy for all children and, in some provinces, the establishment of parent advisory councils. Deinstitutionalization gained momentum with the closure of provincial schools for the deaf and/or blind, with services being shifted to local school jurisdictions and of provincial institutions for the mentally disabled, and with accommodation and services being provided in the local community through group homes.

During the 1990s, the dominant theme in special education at the school level has been the evolution of services known as inclusion, in which most students remain in the regular classroom. Current policies across the country have been designed to support inclusion. For example, the policy of the Northwest Territories includes the following statement: "Inclusive schooling is both a philosophy and a practice. However, including all students in regular classrooms with their age peers, and responding to individual needs and strengths, requires a number of conditions and practices. . . ." A listing of territorial, regional, and school-based requirements for inclusion is given in the policy (Northwest Territories, Department of Education, Culture, and Employment, 1998). As a consequence, the regular classroom has become the home base of most children and adolescents with special needs, and curriculum adaptations are made if required. Given this trend, it is not possible to estimate realistically the percentage of individuals with special educational needs being served in total; however, about 1 to 3 percent of students are still being provided services within non-graded special education classrooms.

Within the community, an important change that has been taking place is an increase in transportation options and environmental accessibility. Notable examples are the emergence of a paratransit systems such as minibuses that are wheelchair accessible; modifications in sidewalk curbs by rounding them so that they are accessible to wheelchairs, and the introduction of sound-signal cues at traffic lights for the visually impaired. Finally, increasingly sophisticated assistive technology—such as high-speed computers with voice input, adapted keyboards allowing individuals to attain full employment, and specialized telephone systems to facilitate communication—has become available, which has resulted in increased accessibility for individuals with special needs. Each of these shifts at the school and community levels needs to be tempered by the emergence of conservative budget policies by provincial/territorial governments. This fiscal policy has meant that the major priority has been on balanced budgets, and all service provision within the school system and the community has been judged against this budgetary standard.

The scope and substance of special education in Canada has changed substantially, and likely will continue to reform in at least two ways. First, special education no longer applies to school-aged children exclusively. It has been expanded to include services for younger children and to respond to meeting the needs of adults. Second, the substance of special education is being expanded to address a wider mandate of social and economic issues that affect the quality of life of both children and adults with special needs. As noted above, however, this expanded mandate comes in a period of fiscal conservatism and the impact on social services generally and on service provision for people with various challenges is unknown.

NOTES

[1]The provinces in Canada from east to west are Newfoundland and Labrador, Prince Edward Island, Nova Scotia, New Brunswick, Quebec, Ontario, Manitoba, Saskatchewan, Alberta, and British Columbia. Currently there are two Canadian territories, from west to east the Yukon and the Northwest Territories. It should be noted, however, that in 1993, there was an agreement passed to separate the Northwest Territories (NWT) into two independent jurisdictions. This agreement came into effect on April 1, 1999. The new territories are Nunavut and an as yet unnamed western section of NWT, now the Mackenize Delta area.

[2]This Canadian federal agency has its own web page and can be found at http://www.cmec.ca/in both English and French.

REFERENCES

Andrews, J., & Lupart, J. (Eds.). (1993). *The inclusive classroom: Educating exceptional children* (pp. 293–329). Toronto: Nelson Canada.

Bachor, D., & Crealock, C. (1986). *Instructional strategies for students with special needs.* Scarborough, Ontario: Prentice Hall, Canada.

Canadian Charter of Rights and Freedoms. (1982). Schedule B of *Canada Act, 1982* (U.K.) c. 11 (1982).

Crealock, C., & Bachor, D. (1995). *Instructional strategies for students with special needs* (2nd ed.). Scarborough, Ontario: Allyn & Bacon.

English now minority tongue. (1998, March 3). *The Globe and Mail,* p. A3.

Friend, M., Bursuck, W., & Hutchinson, N. (1998). *Including exceptional students: A practical guide for classroom teachers* (Canadian ed.). Scarborough, Ontario: Prentice Hall, Canada.

Hardy, M., McLeod, J., Minto, H., Perkins, S., & Quance, W. (1971). *Standards for educators of exceptional children.* Toronto: Crainford.

Hammill, D. D., Bartel, N. R., & Bunch, G. O. (Eds.). (1984). *Teaching children with learning and behavior problems* (Canadian ed.). Toronto: Allyn & Bacon.

Hutchinson, N. L., & Wong, B. (1987). Special education in Canada. In C. R. Reynolds & L. Mann (Eds.), *Encyclopedia of special education: A reference for the education of the handicapped and other exceptional children and adults.* New York: Wiley.

MacKay, A. W. (1987). The charter of rights and special education: Blessing or curse? *Canadian Journal for Exceptional Children, 3,* 118–127.

Northwest Territories, Department of Education, Culture, and Employment. Inclusive schooling. Retrieved March 11, 1998, from http://siksik.learnnet.nt.ca/DOCS/juniorHandbook/Inclusive Schooling.html

Treherne, D., Dice, T. L., Grigg, E. E., & Sanche, R. P. (1974). *A matter of principle: Standards governing legislation for services for children with special needs.* Regina, Saskatchewan: Council for Exceptional Children.

DAN G. BACHOR
University of Victoria

HUMANISM AND SPECIAL EDUCATION
POLITICS AND SPECIAL EDUCATION

CANCER, CHILDHOOD

Cancer is distinguished from other diseases by the rapid growth of abnormal cells in the body. When cancer cells travel to other parts of the body and invade tissues and organs, the process is referred to as metastasis. Many types of cancers form tumors, however the most common type of childhood cancer, leukemia, does not form tumors. Leukemia is rather a disease of the blood-forming tissues in which immature lymphocytes and white blood cells proliferate while red blood cells decrease (Brown & Madan-Swain, 1993).

Cancer is the leading cause of death from disease in children under the age of 15. Fortunately, due to medical advances in childhood cancer research, death rates from childhood cancer have declined about 49 percent since 1975 (American Cancer Society, 2005). The treatment of cancer involves radiation, surgery, and/or chemotherapy. Children undergoing cancer treatment will often suffer from fatigue, weight loss, nausea, and irritability. Chemotherapy and radiation treatments have shown to negatively affect children's cognitive abilities such as attention, memory, distractibility, visual-spatial function, visual-motor function, and executive functions (Kaemingk et al., 2004). Such deficits are sometimes not evident until up to two years post diagnosis.

Children survivors of leukemia may have academic difficulties in reading, spelling, and more commonly, math (Kaemingk et al., 2004). Math difficulties related to mathematical operations, mental calculations, and math applications have been found when compared to healthy peers or normative levels. Deficiencies have also been evident in the areas of verbal memory, auditory attention, basic reading skills, and psychomotor speed. Math performance among leukemia survivors has been shown to improve with individual tutoring; however, it is unknown whether this type of intervention will also aid in attention, memory, or other cognitive tasks.

Children who survive cancer may be at an increased risk of psychosocial difficulties related to the stress of disease and treatment as well as their isolation from peers (Shelby et al., 1998). Peer relations and participation in school-related activities tend to decline, potentially leading to difficulties in specific developmental milestones (Stam, Grootenhuis, & Last, 2005). Recent research examining the course of life with survivors of childhood cancer shows significant differences between survivors and their peers in regard to developmental milestones. Young adult survivors tend to achieve fewer milestones than their healthy peers in areas such as autonomy development, psychosexual development, and social development. Fulfilling developmental milestones is important for adjustment in adult life; therefore, certain steps can be taken for the childhood survivor to aid in their development. For example, encouraging the child to be involved in peer activities, as well as encouraging independence, may aid the child's journey toward healthy development.

Recovering from cancer can be a lengthy process. For some children, referral to special education services may be an option when they are unable to cope with the demands of school. Under the guidelines of IDEA, cancer survivors are guaranteed appropriate educational services (Spinelli, 2002).

REFERENCES

American Cancer Society. (2005). *Children and cancer: Information and resources.* Retrieved September 2, 2005, from http://www.cancer.org

Brown, R., & Madan-Swain, A. (1993). Cognitive, neuropsychological, and academic sequelae in children with leukemia. *Journal of Learning Disabilities, 26*(2), 74–90.

Kaemingk, K., Carey, M., Moore, I., Herzer, M., & Hutter, J. (2004). Math weaknesses in survivors of acute lymphoblastic leukemia compared to healthy children. *Child Neuropsychology, 10*(1), 14–23.

Stam, H., Grootenhuis, M. A., & Last, B. F. (2005). The course of life of survivors of childhood cancer. *Psycho-Oncology, 14,* 227–238.

Shelby, M., Nagle, R., Barnett-Quenn, L., Quattlebaum, P., & Wuori, D. (1998). Parental reports of psychosocial adjustment and social competence in child survivors of acute lymphocytic leukemia. *Children's Health Care, 27*(2), 113–129.

Spinelli, C. (2002). Educational and psychosocial implications affecting childhood cancer survivors: what educators needs to know. *Journal of the Council for Exceptional Children, 11*(1), 49–64.

MIRANDA KUCERA
*University of Colorado at
Colorado Springs*

BRAIN DISORDERS
CHEMOTHERAPY
CHRONIC ILLNESS IN CHILDREN

CANTRELL, ROBERT P. (1938–)

Robert P. Cantrell received his BA in 1960 and MA in 1962 in psychology from Baylor University. He received his PhD in 1969 from George Peabody College for Teachers with a major in experimental child psychology and a minor in special education. Since 1980, he has been an adjunct professor in the department of special education, Kent State University, an adjunct professor in the department of specialized instructional programs, Cleveland State University, the codirector of the Institute for Ecological Study of Children and Youth, and the director of research, Positive Education Program, Cleveland, Ohio. He has remained at the Positive Education Program, and is currently a Research Fellow with them.

Early experiences as a psychologist on a special education diagnostic team taught him that teachers of special children demand practical solutions to their special teaching problems. Partly from these experiences, he became an advocate of a heuristic, ecological system of problem solving (Cantrell & Cantrell, 1977). Although many professionals learn over time to develop solutions to these practical problems, he recognized that there are inadequate means by which we

Robert P. Cantrell

transmit this knowledge of effective intervention strategies to the next generation of professionals.

Cantrell has worked towards the identification of intervention strategies that produce the most efficient and effective changes in the ecologies of behavior-disordered children (Cantrell & Cantrell, 1980) and continues to focus much of his research on the analysis of and interventions with troubled behavioral ecologies. His most recent published works describe an ecological treatment program for emotionally or behaviorally disordered children, with the goal of creating "a single, coordinated system of care of each child and family" (Cantrell, Cantrell, & Smith, 1998); and underlying assumptions and implications for education; treatment with an ecological perspective (Cantrell, Cantrell, Valore, Jones, & Fecser, 1999).

REFERENCES

Cantrell, M. L., Cantrell, R. P., & Smith, D. A. (1998). Coordinating care through connections' liaison staff: Services, costs, and outcomes. In M. Epstein & K. Kutash (Eds.), *Outcomes for children and youth with emotional and behavioral disorders and their families: Programs and evaluation best practices* (pp. 205–229). Austin, TX: Pro-Ed.

Cantrell, M. P., Cantrell, R. P., Valore, T. G., Jones, J. M., & Fecser, F. A. (1999). *A revisitation of the ecological perspective on emotional and behavioral disorders: Underlying assumptions and implications for education and treatment.* Retrieved December 10, 2005, from http://www.ccbd.net

Cantrell, R. P., & Cantrell, M. L. (1977). Evaluation of a heuristic approach to solving children's problems. *Peabody Journal of Education, 54*(3), 168–173.

Cantrell, R. P., & Cantrell, M. L. (1980). Ecological problem solving: A decision-making heuristic for prevention-intervention education strategies. In J. Hogg & P. Mittler (Eds.), *Advances in mental handicap research* (Vol. 1). New York: Wiley.

E. Valerie Hewitt
Texas A&M University
First edition

Kay E. Ketzenberger
The University of Texas of the Permian Basin
Second edition

CARDIAC DISORDERS

Congenital cardiac disorders, with their subsequent physical impairments, constitute some of the most common and serious childhood illnesses. Congenital cardiac disorders are those in which defects in the structure of the heart and/or great vessels alter the normal flow of blood through the cardiorespiratory system. Whaley and Wong (1983) report the incidence of congenital heart disease to occur in approximately 8/1000 to 10/1000 live births which amounts to approximately 40,000 children a year (American Heart Association [AHA], 2005). They also report that congenital anomalies are the major cause of death outside of prematurity. However, with the evolution of palliative and varied surgical techniques, the percentage of those infants who survive cardiac malformations/lesions in the neonatal period has dramatically increased; therefore, serious complex defects currently account for a large number of individuals passing through infancy and childhood into full maturity (AHA, 2005; Nelson, Behrman, & Vaughn, 1983). Surgically corrected congenital defects constitute the largest group of those surviving until adulthood.

There are two types of heart disease in children, acquired and congenital. Acquired cardiac disorders develop sometime during childhood and include Kawasaki disease, rheumatic fever, and infectious endocarditis (AHA, 2005). The cause of congenital cardiac anomalies is still relatively unknown at this time; however multifactorial patterns have been associated with an increased incidence of the disease. The following prenatal factors have been identified as having causal relationships of varying degrees: maternal rubella infection and other viruses such as cytomegalovirus, coxsackle virus B, and nerpesvirus nomines B (Nelson et al., 1983; Nora, 1971); poor maternal nutrition (Reeder, Mastroianni, & Martin, 1983); alcohol, dextroamphelamine, lithium chloride, progesterine/estrogen, and warafin, which are suspected teratogenic agents, as well as maternal overexposure to radiation (Taybi, 1971).

Genetic factors have also been associated with an increased incidence of cardiac disorders. Those parents who already have a child with a cardiac defect have a higher incidence of a second child with a cardiac malformation than parents with an unaffected child (King, 1975). Although this incidence is higher than the general population, it is still quite low (2 to 5 percent; King, 1975, p. 87; Nelson et al., 1983, p. 1121). Other factors predisposing children to congenital heart disease are parents who have congenital cardiac disease themselves or chromosomal aberrations such as Down's syndrome and/or other noncardiac anomalies. Between 30 and 40 percent of all children with Down syndrome have heart defects of some kind (Fletcher-Janzen & Reynolds, 2003; Rowe & Uchida, 1961).

The general signs and symptoms associated with congenital cardiac defects in children have been outlined by Miller (1985): (1) dyspnea, especially on exertion; (2) feeding difficulties or a general failure to thrive; (3) stridor or choking spells; (4) increased heart and respiratory rate (tachypnea) with retractions when the ribs show with each breath; (5) numerous respiratory tract infections; (6) in older children, delayed or poor physical and/or mental development with a decreased exercise tolerance; (7) cyanosis, posturing (particularly a squatting position and clubbing of fingers and toes); (8) heart murmurs; and (9) dyaphoresis.

Cardiac lesions have been classified into two broad categories: acyanotic and cyanotic. "Acyanotic defects are those in which the blood flows from the arterial (left, oxygenated) side of the heart to the venous (right, deoxygenated) side as a result of a connection between the two sides and/or from a pressure gradient (left-to-right shunt)" (Carroll-Johnson & Neal, 1985, p. 605). Most acyanotic disorders are asymptomatic. There are six acyanotic defects demonstrating the left to right shunting of blood. The blood flows from the left ventricle to the right ventricle, where it mixes with venous blood with ventricular-septal defects (VSD). Watson (1968) has cited ventricular-septal defects as the most common cause of cardiac mortality. Atrial-septal defects (ASD) have blood flowing from the left atrium to the right atrium, then through the right ventricle before moving into the pulmonary artery and pulmonary circulation. Patent ductus arteriosus (PDA) is signified when the ductus arteriosus, which normally closes after birth, remains patent, thus recirculating blood repeatedly through the lungs, and, in essence, overoxygenating the blood. The fourth acyanotic lesion is a coarctation of the aorta. Narrowing of the aorta in this lesion manifests itself with an increased blood pressure in the upper extremities with a reciprocal decrease in pressure in the systemic circulation. Aortic stenosis is the narrowing or general inflexibility of the aortic valve, which increases the workload of the left ventricle with subsequent left ventricular hypertrophy resulting. Pulmonary stenosis in a like manner is the narrowing of the pulmonary valve. However, this narrowing results in decreased blood flow to the lungs and an increase in right ventricular pressure.

There are four cyanotic defects, with the outstanding clinical feature being cyanosis. The tetralogy of Fallot, with its four associated defects, has been described by Sacksteder, Gildea, and Dassy (1978, p. 267) as "(1) a large membranous ventricular septal defect; (2) right ventricular outflow obstruction; (3) right ventricular hypertrophy; and (4) dextroposition or overriding of the aorta." The outstanding clinical feature is cyanosis, along with associated features such as clubbing of nailbeds and squatting posture.

In addition to the tetralogy of Fallot, transposition of the great arteries is another cyanotic disorder. In this instance, the aorta arises from the right ventricle and the pulmonary artery from the left ventricle. Hence, two parallel and separate circulatory systems exist, one pulmonary and one systemic. This condition is incompatible with life unless coexisting lesions allow a mixture of blood to sustain life until the heart can be surgically repaired (Sacksteder et al., 1978, p. 266).

The type of medical intervention or surgical treatment required for congenital heart disease depends on the type or severity of the cardiac lesion. The majority of children with mild congenital heart disease require no treatment. Children with severe heart defects may develop congestive heart failure, which is frequently treated with a cardiac glycoside (digoxin) and furesmide (lasix). Selective palliative surgical procedures may be done to improve oxygenation temporarily until the child grows. Total correction of the heart defect is usually postponed until the benefits of surgery outweigh the risks, or until the child is between the ages of 3 and 5 years (Rowe, 1978).

Parents of children with congenital heart defects are encouraged to treat their children normally. In all but the most severe cases (Morris 1993), a normal life can be expected. Restriction of the child's activities is rarely suggested, but it is often implemented as a control measure by parents. Discipline problems are common, and sibling rivalry is seen frequently because of the attention given the child with the cardiac disorder by parents, health care workers, and educators. The best means of avoiding overprotection of the child is to have a functional knowledge of the child's unique disorder. Overprotection frequently results in increased anxiety in the child and interferes with a normal lifestyle. Parents are recommended to manage their child's heart condition by providing a well-balanced diet, prevention of anemia, and the usual childhood immunizations.

Those children whose lesions are moderate to severe need not severely restrict their activities. Nelson et al. (1983, p. 1167) suggest merely tailoring the child's activities to his or her ability to participate; however, rough competitive contact sports should be avoided. Generally, the child will establish his or her own limits. Nelson et al. (1983) also suggests that transportation to and from school may help school performance by eliminating excessive fatigue.

Additional, but imperative, guidelines for all children with cardiac lesions include treating bacterial infections vigorously but not prophylactically to prevent infective endocarditis. Specifically, cyanotic children should be alert for dehydration and iron deficiencies, which may interfere with activity tolerance. As maturity is achieved, women should be counseled regarding the risks of childbearing and the use of contraceptives.

The American Heart Association has an informative web site for children with cardiac disorders. It can be found at www.americanheart.org. In addition, the Health Resources and Services Administration of the federal government has online guidelines for health safety in the public schools that specifically mentions cardiac disorders. The guidelines can be downloaded in printable form from www.nationalguidelines.org.

REFERENCES

American Heart Association (AHA) for parents. (2005).

Carroll-Johnson, R. M., & Neal, M. C. (Eds.). (1985). *American Journal of Nursing, 1985 nursing boards review* (pp. 605–607). Pacific Palisades, CA: Nurseco.

Fletcher-Janzen, E., & Reynolds, C. R. (2003). *Childhood disorders diagnostic desk reference.* New York: Wiley.

King, O. M. (Ed.). (1975). *Care of the cardiac surgical patient.* St. Louis, MO: Mosby.

Miller, A. (Ed.). (1985). *Mosby's comprehensive review of nursing* (11th ed., pp. 400–405). St. Louis, MO: Mosby.

Morris, R. D. (1993). Neuropsychological, academic, and adoptive functioning in children who survive in-hospital cardiac arrest and resuscitation. *Journal of Hearing Disabilities, 26*(1), 46–51.

Nelson, W. E., Behrman, R. E., & Vaughn, V. C. (Eds.). (1983). *Textbook of pediatrics* (12th ed., pp. 1121–1167). Philadelphia: Saunders.

Nora, J. J. (1971). Etiologic factors in congenital heart diseases. In S. Kaplin (Ed.), *Pediatric clinics of North America* (Vol. 18, pp. 1059–1074). Philadelphia: Saunders.

Reeder, S. J., Mastroianni, L., & Martin, L. (Eds.). (1983). *Maternity nursing* (15th ed.). Philadelphia: Lippincott.

Rowe, R. D. (1978). Patent ductus arteriosus. In J. Keith, R. Rowe, & R. Vlad (Eds.), *Heart disease in infancy and children* (3rd ed.). New York: Macmillan.

Rowe, R. D., & Uchida, I. A. (1961). Cardiac malformation in mongolism: A prospective study of 184 mongoloid children. *American Journal of Medicine, 31,* 726–735.

Sacksteder, S., Gildea, J. H., & Dassy, C. (1978, February). Common congenital cardiac defects. *American Journal of Nursing,* 266–272.

Taybi, H. (1971). Roentgen evaluation of cardiomegaly in the newborn period and early infancy. In S. Kaplin (Ed.), *Pediatric clinics of North America, 18*(4), 1031–1058. Philadelphia: Saunders.

Watson, H. (Ed.). (1968). *Pediatric cardiology.* London: Lloyd-Luke.

Whaley, L. F., & Wong, D. L. (1983). The child with heart disease. In L. F. Whaley & D. L. Wong (Eds.), *Nursing care of infants and children* (2nd ed., pp. 1279–1337). St. Louis, MO: Mosby.

MARY CLARE WILLIAMS
Ramey, Pennsylvania

PHYSICAL EDUCATION FOR STUDENTS WITH DISABILITIES
PHYSICAL DISABILITIES

CAREER EDUCATION FOR STUDENTS RECEIVING SPECIAL EDUCATION SERVICES

Career education is an essential component of transition planning which moves the student from school to the working world. Career education is particularly important for those students receiving special education services. Although definitions vary, career education has two levels. The first level of career education is the general orientation to the working world. The next step in career education is personalization of knowledge and skill development for the individual. Career education generally includes three components: identifying interests and aptitudes; developing or increasing awareness and knowledge of occupational alternatives; and developing and supporting attitudes and habits related to work.

Attention to career education is part of the changes made to IDEIA 2004 (PL 108-446). In particular, the principles of career education are evident in the changes made to the definition of transitional services. Specifically, the law requires that transition services be based on the individual child's strengths, preferences, and interests (NICHCY, 2005). This is essentially career education, although the term is not used in the law's language. "Transition services" is the most recent terminology.

While career education might be thought of as something that occurs in the later school years, in reality, the foundation for aptitude and interest, knowledge, and attitudes about the working world occur throughout the child's school year. Identifying interests and aptitudes is an ongoing process, with looking at what the young student can do and expanding on potential. Developing awareness and knowledge of occupational alternatives can be initiated through activities such as career days and field trips in the community. Development of attitudes toward work begin in the earliest years of education, where children can learn about the value of working hard and having pride in their efforts. Identifying interests and aptitudes; developing or increasing awareness and knowledge of occupational alternatives; and developing and supporting attitudes and habits related to work must be purposely taught, trained, and observed. Having career- or transition-oriented curriculum infused in the early school years can help students' knowledge and skill foundations for later training and may help decrease at-risk behaviors, such as dropping out later (Razeghi, 1998).

As the student gets older, career education knowledge and skill sets may be part of the general curriculum available to all students. The Individualized Educational Plan (IEP) will set out specific goals and objectives that are linked to the student's working future. The student in special education may take classes that are in the general curriculum (e.g., industrial arts or agriculture science) that are related to future goals or interests. The student may be involved in activities such as work study that specially relate to career development. Paid employment for students in special education during high school can also be considered and may be one key predictor of future success (Eisenman, 2003). Other options, particularly for students with higher incidence special education needs, may be school-wide activities such as career fairs, specific courses such as cooking, activities such as college nights, and outside employment. For students with more diverse learning needs, career education may be infused in the Life Skills curriculum or may be individualized to meet the needs of each student. This may include activities such as sheltered employment or work activities, where the work and support is tailored to the individual student.

For most students, formal career counseling will generally include three components: assessment, counseling, and planning (Roessler, Shearing, & Williams, 2000). Assessment can include standardized tests of interests and aptitude as well as interviews with the student, teachers, and parents about strengths, interests, and preferences. For students with greater cognitive or other challenges, the assessment process will also include careful assessment of overall life skills.

The assessment process will be followed with individualized counseling, which includes the student and parents. Parent involvement and support appears to be crucial (Eisenman, 2003). Assessment results are shared, and they can become the foundation of the counseling. Counseling includes understanding and sharing student and parent perspectives on the future, including career goals and living arrangements.

At this point, planning for the desired outcomes occurs. This includes involvement of community and/or state agencies, determining and following through on changes in legal standing such as managing conservator for the parents, and determination of future living arrangements. For all students, the goal of career education is to maximize their potential in the working world.

REFERENCES

Eisenman, L. T. (2003). Theories in practice: School-to-work-transitions-for-youth with mild disabilities. *Exceptionalities, 11*(2), 89–102.

NICHCY. (2005). *NICHCY Connections to Resources on IDEA 2004*. Retrieved September 8, 2005, from http://www.nichcy.org/resources/IDEA2004resources.asp

PL 108-446 The Individuals With Disabilities Education Improvement Act of 2004.

Razeghi, J. A. (1998). A first step toward solving the problem of special education dropouts: Infusing career education into the curriculum. *Intervention in School & Clinic, 33*(3), 148–157.

Roessler, R., Shearing, A., & Williams, E. (2000). Three recommendations to improve transition planning in the IEP. *Journal for Vocational Special Needs, 22*(2), 31–36.

Constance J. Fournier
Texas A&M University

LEARNING DISABLED COLLEGE STUDENTS
REHABILITATION
VOCATIONAL EVALUATION

CARIBBEAN, SPECIAL EDUCATION IN

Recognition of special education is a relatively recent phenomenon in the Caribbean. Although services for persons with special needs were evident in the first half of the twentieth century, increased government involvement began in the second half of the century. Nongovernmental organizations and individuals with humanitarian concerns were the architects of special education services in the region,

and these groups are still involved. Consequently, national associations for the deaf and local chapters of the Salvation Army, for example, continue to play indispensable roles in educating persons with hearing and visual impairments. Activities relating to physical disabilities, mental retardation, learning disabilities, and multiple disabilities have gained prominence over the years.

There is no island with a legislated policy exclusively for special education. However, interest groups use existing legislation relating to general education, as well as statements made by governments relating to "education for all," as fuel in their quest for appropriate support. Governments are committed, therefore, to the concept of equal educational opportunities for children with special needs in the school system. This commitment is displayed in special education units (departments responsible for national special education affairs) in the Education Ministries of the Republic of Trinidad and Tobago and Jamaica, and at least one special education officer in some of the other islands. Education officers work in close collaboration with special and mainstream schools and other relevant institutions. Most of the special education schools and institutions are incorporated into the public system; therefore, governments are responsible for recurrent expenditure including the payment of salaries. There are, however, some institutions operating independently by private sector and nongovernmental organizations.

In the Caribbean, most of the children with special needs are in mainstream schools without adequate support. For example, in the Republic of Trinidad and Tobago, the Ministry of Education (1993) reports that approximately "13.1 percent of special needs children are not in school; 5.8 percent are in preschool; 5.1 percent are attending special schools; 6.7 percent are in other facilities, while 67.2 percent are in mainstream schools in which there are no provisions for them." The implications is that only 2.1 percent of children with special needs are in the mainstream with adequate support.

A similar situation is also evident in Jamaica, where persons attending either government-aided special schools or enrolled in facilities operated by nongovernmental agencies comprise 0.64 percent of the 680,700 individuals in the mainstream preschool to secondary population (Planning Institute of Jamaica, 1996). However, using census data for four of fourteen parishes, obtained from the Statistical Institute of Jamaica, Hall and Figueroa 1998: note that persons with disabilities comprised 4.8 percent of the population in these parishes, and that approximately 1.8 percent or 4,364 were in the 10–19 age group. From this group, 1000 were attending secondary schools. A survey of secondary schools in the four parishes mentioned indicate that both students with special needs and their teachers believed that support was either absent or inadequate (Hall & Figueroa, 1998).

Overall, the support provided in the region is at varying levels of quality and organization, both within schools and institutions. In Jamaica, for example, there is a national braille and large print service, and over 400 texts have been printed and distributed to schools. Furthermore, at the Mona Campus of the University of the West Indies (UWI), there is a very active committee for students with special needs comprised of students and staff. Over the years, the committee has been acquiring resource materials to enhance the learning environment of the students. In January 1998, a member of the committee, who is blind and also a graduate student, created history when he was appointed Senator by the Jamaican Prime Minister.

Throughout the region, the current decade has witnessed intense efforts by persons with and without disabilities to pass local legislation relating to special needs. For example, in Jamaica, the Combined Disabilities Association finalized a draft of a policy for disabled persons in Jamaica for submission to the government. The basic tenets are grounded in the "Standard Rules on the Equalization of Opportunities," published by the United Nations. Education is one of the eleven policy issues addressed in the draft (Combined Disabilities of Jamaica, 1997).

The training of special education teachers began in 1971 with the introduction of a one-year certificate program at UWI Mona Campus for teachers of the deaf. In 1976, Mico Teachers College began offering a 3-year program in mental retardation, learning disabilities, hearing impairment, and physical disabilities. These initial training program are still available, and recently visual impairment was included. In 1986, Mico, in collaboration with UWI, began a Bachelor in Education program in special education. Each of the programs mentioned has had large financial support from the Government of the Netherlands and regional governments, and is accessed by students throughout the region. In 1994, a B.Ed. in "Managing Learning Difficulties" began at Mona, UWI. The program focuses on learners in mainstream classes. Graduate level courses in special education are offered at Mona, and Cave Campus in Barbados introduced a Master in Education in special education during the 1997–98 academic year. In Trinidad and Tobago the local teachers' association, working in collaboration with a university in the United Kingdom, offers graduate level training to its teachers.

There are other training programs throughout the region. For example, the Caribbean Association for the Mental Retarded or Developmental Disabilities (CAMRODD), a regional association, has a 3-year Parent Empowerment Program. Pairs of parents and professionals from several islands including Antigua, Saba, St. Lucia, Barbados, St. Vincent, and Trinidad and Tobago were involved (CAMRODD, 1997). The general plan is for participants involved in training to implement parent training workshops in their communities.

The major challenge in the region is economic constraint, and this manifests itself in part in limited resources including personnel. Identifying persons without overt disabilities continues to be a challenge in the absence of appropriate assessment measures and in the inability of educators to employ nontraditional or alternative measures. There is also the need for general education for parents and professionals as well as urging agencies to collaborate so that limited resources can be maximized.

Future directions in the field must encompass aspects of early identification of special needs, more community involvement, inclusion, giftedness, and public education. In Barbados, for example, there are plans to assess annually children in the 3 to 7 year age group for visual, hearing, and speech impairments (Ministry of Education, Youth Affairs, & Culture, 1995). The Republic of Trinidad and Tobago has plans to establish regional diagnostic prescriptive centers. The Mico College Centre for Child Assessment and Research, a diagnostic and therapeutic center, is committed to intensify its efforts in the area of research and its dissemination. The UWI, working with both governmental and nongovernmental agencies, is continuing to set standards and respond to needs with the delivery of relevant research and pedagogy. Finally, if work in progress in the area of special needs continues unabated, and plans articulated are implemented, interest groups within the region can greet the end of the millennium with optimism.

REFERENCES

Caribbean Association for the Mentally Retarded or Developmental Disabilities (CAMRODD). (1997). *CAMRODD's parent empowerment programme*. Jamaica: 3D's Documentation Unit.

Combined Disabilities of Jamaica. (1997). *Draft national policy for persons with disabilities*. Jamaica: Author.

Hall, W. M., & Figueroa M. (1998). Jamaican children with special needs: Concerns, realities and possibilities. *Disability and Society, 13*(2).

Ministry of Education. (1993). *Education Policy Paper: 1993–2003*. Trinidad and Tobago: Author.

Ministry of Education, Youth Affairs, & Culture. (1995). *White Paper on education reform: Preparing for the 21st century*. Barbados: Government of Barbados.

Planning Institute of Jamaica. (1996). *Economic and social survey of Jamaica*. Jamaica: Author.

WINNIFRED M. HALL
University of the West Indies, Jamaica

COLLETTE LEYVA
KIMBERLY M. RENNIE
Texas A&M University

INTERNATIONAL ETHICS AND SPECIAL EDUCATION

CARNINE, DOUGLAS W. (1947–   )

A native of Sullivan, Illinois, Douglas Carnine obtained his BS (1969), in psychology from the University of Illinois, Urbana, his MA (1971) in special education from the University of Oregon, Eugene, and PhD (1974) in educational psychology from the University of Utah, Salt Lake City. In 1975 Carnine became an assistant professor in the Department of Education at the University of Oregon, Eugene, where he achieved the rank of full professor in 1987. Dr. Carnine is the director of the National Center to Improve Tools in Education (NCITE) which has focused on state literacy initiatives and also works with legislative and state groups to support research-based educational tools for at-risk students.

As an undergraduate student, Carnine began working with Wesley Becker to conduct research on classroom management, and later assisted Siegfried Englemann in the development of DISTAR arithmetic as well as the implementation, in 10 school districts in eight states, of the direct instruction model of teaching (Silbert, Carnine, & Stein, 1981). These experiences led to his belief that curriculum, staff development, and administrative leadership must be addressed in any program intended to improve schools.

Carnine's focus shifted from the notion that administrators should take the lead in introducing school effectiveness programs to an emphasis on teaching variables (Engelmann & Carnine, 1982). Discouraged about excessive demands on teacher's time, he has also investigated the effects of technology on the quality of instructional programs and improving teacher effectiveness (Carnine, 1983).

Writing extensively on school-improvement programs, his publications include *Theory of Instruction* (1982) and *Learning Pascal* (1988) as well as chapters in *School Improvement Programs: A Handbook for Educational Leaders* (1995) and *Changing School Reading Programs* (1988). His most recent book is called *Teaching Struggling and At-Risk Readers* by Prentice Hall (Carnine & Silbert, 2005). He was a featured speaker at the 1994 Summit on Learning Disabilities of the National Center for Learning Disabilities, Inc., and is recognized in *Who's Who in American Education,* third edition.

REFERENCES

Carnine, D. (1983). Direct institutional: In search of instructional solutions for educational problems. In D. Carnine & D. Elkind (Eds.), *Interdisciplinary voices in learning disabilities and remedial education* (pp. 1–66). Austin, TX: PRO-ED.

Carnine, D. (1988). How to overcome barriers to student achievement. In S. J. Samuels & P. D. Pearson (Eds.), *Changing school reading programs: Principles and case studies.* Newark, DE: International Reading Association.

Carnine, D. W., Grossen, B., & Silbert, J. (1995). Direct instruction to accelerate cognitive growth. In J. H. Block, S. T. Everson, & T. R. Guskey (Eds.), *School improvement programs: A handbook for educational leaders.* New York: Scholastic.

Carnine, D. W., & Silbert, J. (2005). *Teaching struggling and at-risk readers: A direct instruction approach.* New York: Prentice Hall.

Englemann, S., & Carnine, D. W. (1982). *Theory of instruction.* New York: Irvington.

Niedelman, M. S., & Carnine, D. (1988). *Learning Pascal.* Glenview, IL: Scott-Foresman.

Silbert, J., Carnine, D., & Stein, M. (1981). *Direct instruction mathematics.* Columbus, OH: Merrill.

E. Valerie Hewitt
Texas A&M University
First edition

Tamara J. Martin
The University of Texas of the Permian Basin
Second edition

Douglas W. Carnine

CARROW ELICITED LANGUAGE INVENTORY

The Carrow Elicited Language Inventory (CELI; Carrow, 1974) is a diagnostic test of expressive language, containing 51 sentences and one phrase that the child is required to repeat. The mean sentence length is 6 words. The sentences were selected to include basic sentence types, specific grammatical morphemes, and select transformational rules. The grammatical morphemes include nouns, plurals, verbs, adjectives, adverbs, pronouns, articles, negatives, prepositions, demonstratives, conjunctions, and contractions. The child's responses are audio taped to assist the examiner in scoring errors on substitutions, omissions, additions, transpositions, and reversal. The manual provides mean total error scores and mean subcategory error scores for children between the ages of 3 years and 7 years 11 months at one year intervals. Percentile and stanine scores are also available.

The CELI was normed in 1973 on 475 White middle-class Texans between 3 years and 7 years 11 months. Children who were identified with speech or language disorders were excluded from the normative sample. Validity of the CELI has been established by its ability to discriminate between children with and without language disorders and to identify children at high risk for learning disorders (Blau, Lahey, & Oleksiuk-Velez 1984; Swift, 1984). Test-retest reliability at 2 week intervals is reported at .98, but this should be interpreted with caution because of the small sample size employed.

A major assumption underlying the CELI is that a child's imitations of model sentences will closely resemble his or her proficiency in spontaneous speech. However, numerous studies question the validity of the sentence imitation tasks as a valid measure of spontaneous language (Connell & Myles-Zitzer, 1982; Haniff & Seigel, 1975; Kuczaj & Maratsos, 1975; McDale & Simpson, 1983; Prutting, Gallagher, & Mulac, 1975). A weakness of this test is that the normative data is limited (small sample size, restricted geographic region, and limited SES) and out of date.

REFERENCES

Blau, A. F., & Lahey, M., Oleksiuk-Velez, A. (1984). Planning goals for intervention: Language testing or language sampling? *Exceptional Children, 1,* 78–79.

Carrow, E. (1974). *Carrow Elicited Language Inventory.* Boston: Teaching Resources Corporation.

Connell, P. J., & Myles-Zitzer, C. (1982). An analysis of elicited imitation as a language evaluation procedure. *Journal of Speech and Hearing Disability, 47,* 390–396.

Haniff, M. H., & Seigel, G. M. (1981). The effect of context on verbal elicited imitation. *Journal of Speech and Hearing Disability, 46,* 27–30.

Kuczaj, S., & Maratsos, M. (1975). What children can say before they will. *Merrill-Palmer Quarterly, 21,* 89–112.

McDade, H. L., & Simpson, M. A. (1983). Reply to Carrow-Woolfolk. *Journal of Speech and Hearing Disorders, 3,* 334–335.

Prutting, C. A., Gallagher, T. M., & Mulac, A. (1975). The expressive portion of the NSST compared to a spontaneous language sample. *Journal of Speech and Hearing Disabilities, 40,* 40–48.

Swift, C. (1984). Sentence imitation in kindergarten children at risk for learning disability: A comparative study. *Language, Speech, & Hearing Services in Schools, 1,* 10–15.

MARGO E. WILSON
Lexington, Kentucky
First edition

ROSEANN BISIGHINI
The Salk Institute
Second edition

LANGUAGE DELAYS
LANGUAGE DISORDERS

CARTWRIGHT, G. PHILLIP (1937–   )

G. Phillip Cartwright received his BS in 1960 in psychology and MS in 1962 in special education from the University of Illinois. He received his PhD in 1966 in special education and educational research from the University of Pittsburgh. Currently, he is professor and head of the Division of Special Education and Communication Disorders, Pennsylvania State University.

In the 1960s, Cartwright became convinced that the American education system was not providing an adequate education for children with disabilities. He attempted to implement the then heretical idea of training regular educators to identify youngsters with disabilities in their early years and to help those youngsters to succeed in a regular classroom. Cartwright also proposed that the training of both regular and special education teachers be modified to include learning the use of alternative training approaches (Cartwright, 1977). One such approach is the use of computer technology in the process of training teachers. With this philosophy, Cartwright developed a series of computer-assisted instruction (CAI) courses.

Cartwright continues his work in the field of computer-assisted instruction, writing pieces for *Change* promoting an increase in expertise and technology through partnerships between business and higher education (Barton & Cartwright, 1997) and outlining a technology program using a computer program to deliver courses at universities (Sedlak, 1997).

G. Phillip Cartwright

Cartwright has been recognized in *American Men and Women in Science, Who's Who in the East,* and *Leaders in Education.*

REFERENCES

Barton, L., & Cartwright, G. P. (1997). Reciprocal technology transfer: Changing partnerships. *Change, 29,* 44–47.

Cartwright, G. P. (1977). Educational technology. In S. Tarver & R. Kneedler (Eds.), *Changing perspectives in education.* Columbus, OH: Merrill.

Cartwright, G. P. (1984). Computer applications in special education. In D. F. Walker & R. D. Hess (Eds.), *Instructional software for design and use.* Belmont, CA: Wadsworth.

Cartwright, G. P., Cartwright, C. A., & Robine, G. C. (1972). CAI course in the early identification of handicapped children. *Exceptional Children, 38,* 453–459.

Sedlak, R. A. (1997). Two approaches to distance education: Lessons learned. *Change, 29,* 54–56.

E. Valerie Hewitt
Texas A&M University

CASCADE MODEL OF SPECIAL EDUCATION SERVICES

The Cascade Model of Special Education Services is a conceptualization of the range of placement and service options that used to be available for children with disabilities. The placement options were presented in hierarchical form and ranged from the least restrictive placement in the regular education classroom to the most restrictive placement in hospital or institutional settings. The Cascade Model was first proposed by Reynolds in 1962 and an amended version was proposed by Deno in 1970. Both proposals predated the passage of the Education of All Handicapped Children Act of 1975 (PL 94-142), a time when placement and service options for the handicapped were scarce. Reynolds and Birch (1977) characterized the pre-PL 94-142 administrative arrangements as a two-box system in which parallel but separate educational programs for regular and special education were in operation within school buildings. Interaction and movement of children between the two systems was difficult at best, and more often, nonexistent. The Cascade Model helped create understanding of and support for a better system that "facilitates tailoring of treatment to individual needs rather than a system for sorting out children so they will fit conditions designed according to group standards not necessarily suitable for the particular case" (Deno, 1970, p. 235).

The Cascade Model visually appeared as a triangular form that contained two essential elements: the degree of placement specialization and the relative number of children in the various placement options. The base of the triangle coincided with regular classroom placement, the preferred

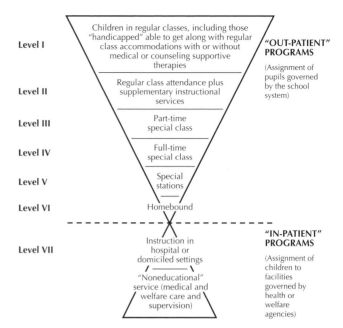

Figure 1 The cascade system of special education service. The tapered design indicates the considerable difference in the numbers involved at the different levels and calls attention to the fact that the system serves as a diagnostic filter. The most specialized facilities are likely to be needed by the fewest children on a long-term basis. This organizational model can be applied to the development of special education services for all types of disabilities.

placement for the largest number of students with disabilities. Progressively more specialized placements were included as the triangle extended toward the apex. The decreasing width of the triangle reflected the decreasing numbers of children to be placed in progressively more restrictive environments. Deno's Cascade Model was widely cited and reproduced; it has become a fundamental concept for the field of special education. (See Figure 1 for an example of the Cascade Model.)

The basic concepts of specialization embodied in the Cascade Model were subsequently incorporated into federal and state laws as the least restrictive environment principle (Peterson, Zabel, Smith, & White, 1983). Variations of the Cascade Model have been presented by other authors (Cartwright, Cartwright, & Ward, 1985). However, the basic elements of degree of restrictiveness and relative numbers of children in the different placement options were retained.

Despite its popularity and utility, the Cascade Model was criticized. Reynolds and Birch (1977) viewed the original Cascade Model as "too place oriented" because of its "clearest focus on administrative structures and places." They offered an alternative conceptualization of the Cascade Model in which instructional diversity was emphasized. (See Figure 2.)

The Instructional Cascade envisioned the regular education classroom as the primary and optimal setting for the delivery of specialized services to children with disabilities. Children were seen as moving among the levels of the cascade for educational purposes. Ideally, a child would be

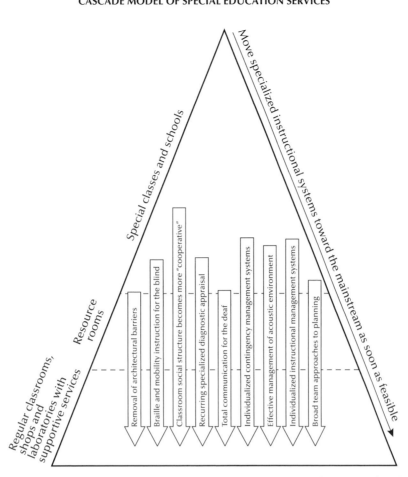

Figure 2 Changes occurrng in the cascade (fewer specialized places; more diverse "regular" places)

moved to a more restrictive setting only for compelling educational reasons and was moved back as quickly as possible. The introduction of inclusive programming in the past few years has created a debate as to whether special education should abolish the Cascade Model. On one hand are conservative educators who believe in the original model that provided integration on a case by case method. On the other hand are abolitionists who believe in full inclusion for all special education students. At this time, federal law still supports individualization and many follow its lead (Fuchs, 1994). Retrospective studies in the next few years will probably determine the debate and also determine how the cascade of services will change. For example, Wolfe and Hall (2003) have devised a "cascade of integration options" for students with severe disabilities to receive full inclusion. This cascade includes options from unadapted participation in the general curriculum to functional curriculum outside the general education classroom. Regardless of names or labels, however, the determination of placement will always depend on the best interests of the student.

REFERENCES

Cartwright, G. P., Cartwright, C. A., & Ward, M. E. (1985). *Educating special learners* (2nd ed.). Belmont, CA: Wadsworth.

Deno, E. (1970). Special education as developmental capital. *Exceptional Children, 37*(3), 229–237.

Fuchs, D. (1994). *Best practices in school psychology: Peabody reintegration project.* (ERIC document No. ED378774)

Peterson, R. L., Zabel, R. H., Smith, C. R., & White, M. A. (1983). Cascade of services model and emotionally disabled students. *Exceptional Children, 49*(5), 404–408.

Reynolds, M. C. (1962). A framework for considering some issues in special education. *Exceptional Children, 28*(7), 367–370.

Reynolds, M. C., & Birch, J. W. (1977). *Teaching exceptional children in all America's schools.* Reston, VA: Council for Exceptional Children.

Woffe, P. S., & Hall, T. E. (2003). Making inclusion a reality for students with severe disabilities. *Teaching Exceptional Children, 3,* 56–60.

LIBBY GOODMAN
Pennsylvania State University

INCLUSION
LEAST RESTRICTIVE ENVIRONMENT
PHILOSOPHY OF EDUCATION FOR INDIVIDUALS WITH DISABILITIES
SPECIAL CLASS

CASE HISTORY

Case histories serve several purposes: to provide information about rare disorders, individual differences in treatment responsiveness, or the natural course for a disorder (Kratochwill, 1985); to provide information necessary to plan and monitor appropriate treatment; to provide data needed by external agencies; to illuminate pitfalls to be avoided; and to provide information for scientific, administrative, and instructional purposes.

Identification information in a complete case history should include client's name, date of birth, sex, ethnicity, dominant language, marital status, guardians' names if a minor, residence, phone number, persons to notify in an emergency, medical status, and current program status (e.g., grade or placement if an educational setting); this information should be in an easily located part of the record. Historical data, as determined relevant for client welfare by a multidisciplinary committee, should include developmental, health, and educational history; work history if an adult; and significant family events.

Specific statements of the concerns of the referral agent should be included. The client's status at the time of referral should include information about current health, including current medications; sensory or perceptual abilities; motor abilities; language skills; current adaptive behavior; intellectual abilities and academic skills; other cognitive data, such as current belief systems or attributions as may be pertinent to the referral problem; emotional behavior; social skills and behavior; family status; and vocational aptitudes, skills, and interests. A description of the client's current status with respect to the referring problem should always be included. The preintervention frequency of the problem behavior should be recorded to establish treatment effectiveness at a later time.

The case history should contain not only the treatment goals for a client, but the process by which those goals were determined, including dates of meetings for discussing goals, those who were present, alternative plans discussed, costs and benefits of alternative plans, and the final treatment plan agreed on. Records should also be maintained of the course of treatment implementation, including the goal to which the treatment session was directed, what was done during the session, and the clinician's notes about difficulties or unexpected results.

To establish intervention effectiveness, a record must be maintained of changes in the client's behavior or level of skill. Data from observations, self-monitoring, or other methods can be collected and recorded and effectiveness assessed by means of single-subject designs (Barlow & Hersen, 1984). These techniques have the advantage of demonstrating that specific treatments have been tried and have been effective or noneffective; of being sensitive to subtle changes in behavior; and of allowing the comparison of several alternative treatments.

REFERENCES

Barlow, D. H., & Hersen, M. (1984). *Single-case experimental designs: Strategies for studying behavior change* (2nd ed.). New York: Pergamon.

Kratochwill, T. R. (1985). Case study research in school psychology. *School Psychology Review, 14,* 204–215.

JOHN MACDONALD
Eastern Kentucky University

MEDICAL HISTORY
MENTAL STATUS EXAMS

CATALOG OF FEDERAL DOMESTIC ASSISTANCE

The *Catalog of Federal Domestic Assistance* (CFDA) is a compendium of over 1,300 programs, projects, and activities of the federal government that provide benefits or assistance to the public. The catalog provides basic descriptive information on each program or activity, such as the purposes of the program, eligible applicants, total funds available, examples and dollar range of prior awards, and person to contact. The catalog covers programs providing both financial and nonfinancial forms of assistance (e.g., information, technical assistance, transfer of real property). It is updated and published twice a year by the General Services Administration (1998), an agency of the federal government.

Programs are organized by sponsoring agency, but are also indexed across all agencies by subject area, by the type of entity or individual eligible to apply for assistance, and even by application deadline. The indexes make the catalog a useful reference guide for someone trying to locate potential sources of assistance for a particular project or in a specific subject area (e.g., mental retardation, early childhood education).

The catalog is distributed free of charge on a limited basis to state and local officials. It can be purchased on machine readable tape, diskettes, and/or CD ROM from the General Services Administration, Ground Floor, Reporters Building, 300 7th Street, SW, Washington, DC 20407. Their telephone number is 202-708-5126. The web site for the CFDA allows full free access to the catalog along with a user guide, search function and additional resources. It can be found at http://www.12.46.245.173/cfda/cfda.html.

REFERENCE

General Services Administration. (1998). *Catalog of federal domestic assistance.* Washington, DC: Author.

JAMES R. RICCIUTI
United States Office of
Management and Budget

CATARACTS

A cataract is an imperfection in the clarity or a clouding of the lens of the eye. It will be experienced by a majority of people who live to an old age (Eden, 1978). In children, some cataracts are present at birth and other develop with metabolic or systemic abnormalities. In older children, cataracts are related to injuries or ocular inflammation due to juvenile arthritis (University of Minnesota, 2005).

Eden (1978) defines three types of cataracts. Senile cataracts are those that occur as part of the normal aging process. Cell layers form around the lens as people grow older; this is similar to rings forming in the trunks of trees. The lens becomes opaque and loses its resiliency. Secondary cataracts are those that result from some other trauma or disease. For example, persons with diabetes often develop cataracts. Secondary cataracts can also result from excessive radiation, electrical shock, and the side effects of some drugs. Excessive use of cortisone, for example, has been related to the development of lens opacity. Congenital cataracts are those that are present from birth. This type of cataract is very rare. Illnesses during pregnancy such as German measles (rubella) can cause congenital cataracts (Harley & Lawrence, 1977).

It was once thought that cataracts had to be "ripe" before the lens could be removed. For example, *Melloni's Illustrated Medical Dictionary* (Dox, Melloni, & Eisner, 1979) defines a mature cataract as one in which the entire lens substance has become opaque and thus easy to separate from its capsule. However, Eden (1978) reports that such ripening is not necessary before surgery is possible.

Some cataracts get progressively worse; others do not. Some cataracts involve only the periphery of the lens; others may be more centrally located (Harley & Lawrence, 1977). Therefore, the symptoms can vary a great deal from patient to patient, and, although surgery is the only cure, it is often not necessary.

Post operative treatment of cataract removal involves the use of regular glasses or contact lenses, or the insertion of artificial plastic lenses in the eye itself. Such treatments are effective in restoring vision to the affected eye.

REFERENCES

Dox, I., Melloni, B. J., & Eisner, G. (1979). *Melloni's illustrated medical dictionary*. Baltimore: Williams & Wilkins.

Eden, J. (1978). *The eye book*. New York: Viking.

Harley, R. K., & Lawrence, G. A. (1977). *Visual impairment in the schools*. Springfield, IL: Thomas.

University of Minnesota. (2005). *Cataracts in children*. Retrieved July 21, 2005, from http://www.tc.umn.edu/~chris196/cataracts.htm

THOMAS E. ALLEN
Gallaudet College

AMBLYOPIA
BLIND

CATEGORICAL EDUCATION

Categorical education was the practice of separating handicapped children into subgroups representing different types of disability. Each subgroup had a specific categorical designation and its members were reviewed as a cohesive group for instructional purposes. The traditional categorical group structure presumed that there were significant homogeneity of student characteristics within each subgroup and that there was significant heterogeneity among the groups. That is, the members of one group shared common qualities that distinguished them from the members of all other groups. The assumptions of homogeneity within categories and heterogeneity among categories were not well founded (Hallahan & Kauffman, 1977; Iano, 1972; Kirk & Elkins, 1975; Leland, 1977), particularly for the mildly disabled.

Various categorical labels have been used to designate the separate subgroups of children with disabilities. Different labels were frequently used to apply to essentially the same children (e.g., perceptually impaired, minimally brain damaged, and minimal cerebral dysfunction were terms that have been subsumed under the term learning disabilities). Dementia, feeblemindedness, and idiot were terms that originally, gave way to the general label of mental retardation. The Education for All Handicapped Children Act of 1975 (PL 94-142) stipulated 11 handicapping conditions: mentally retarded, hard of hearing, deaf, speech impaired, deaf-blind, learning disabled, visually handicapped, seriously emotionally disturbed, orthopedically handicapped, other health impaired, and multihandicapped. These categories became the prototype for the nation and were reflected in state and local plans for the education of handicapped children. They also continue to grow and change such as with the inclusion of traumatic brain injury (TBI).

Although the categories of disabilities recognized by states and school districts was more consistent as a result of PL 94-142, the specific criteria actually used to identify handicapped children varied greatly from state to state and among local school districts. The variability in identification and placement criteria created the phenomenon that the same child could be placed in different categories in different states or school systems. Under a categorical system, the child invariably was, and still is labeled with a disability designation. The process of labeling has been studied and the negative consequences of labeling for the child, family, and school community have been discussed at length. Discussions of the pros and cons of categorical labels are available in numerous works (Hewitt & Forness, 1977; Kirk & Gallagher, 1979; Lilly, 1979; Reschley, 1996).

A long-term disaffection with traditional categorical education has led to the development of alternative practices. Critics of traditional categorical labels such as mentally retarded, learning disabled, or socially emotionally disturbed emphasize that such labels are of little use to the teacher who must plan appropriate instructional programs. Therefore the shift to inclusive practices of placement has placed emphasis on outcome rather than diagnosis or label. Alternate assessments (such as curriculum-based assessment) has also de-emphasized labels and classification, and have attempted to individualize instructions to learner needs as opposed to label.

REFERENCES

Hallahan, D. P., & Kauffman, J. M. (1977). Labels, categories, behaviors: ED, LD, and EMR reconsidered. *Journal of Special Education, 11*(2), 139–149.

Hewitt, F. M., & Forness, S. R. (1977). *Education of exceptional learners.* Boston: Allyn & Bacon.

Iano, R. P. (1972). Shall we disband special classes? *Journal of Special Education, 6*(2), 167–177.

Kirk, S. A., & Gallagher, J. J. (1979). *Educating exceptional children.* Boston: Houghton Mifflin.

Kirk, S. A., & Elkins, J. (1975). Characteristics of children enrolled in the child service demonstration centers. *Journal of Learning Disabilities, 8*(10), 630–637.

Leland, H. (1977). Mental retardation and adaptive behavior. *Journal of Special Education, 6*(1), 71–80.

Lilly, M. S. (1979). *Children with exceptional needs.* New York: Holt, Rinehart & Winston.

Reschley, D. J. (1996). Identification and assessment of students with disabilities. *Future of Children, 6,* 1, 40–43.

LIBBY GOODMAN
Pennsylvania State University

CASCADE MODEL OF SPECIAL EDUCATION SERVICES
LEAST RESTRICTIVE ENVIRONMENT

CATECHOLAMINES

Epinephrine (adrenaline) and norepinephrine (noradrenaline) are hormones of the sympathetic division of the autonomic nervous system. Epinephrine was the first hormone to be isolated, and by 1897 Abel had separated it from the adrenal gland and found it to be represented by the formula $C17\ H15\ No4$. By 1905, the Japanese chemist Takamine treated Abel's abstract and named the product adrenaline, with the formula $C9\ H13\ No3$ (Krantz & Carr, 1961). Norepinephrine was not identified until 1942; it derives its name from the German expression Nitrogen ohne radikal, referring to the fact that the molecule is identical to that of epinephrine except for missing the methyl group on the nitrogen atom.

Epinephrine produces a variety of metabolic effects useful in an emergency: increased epinephrine levels result in what is often called the "fight, flight, or fright" reaction (West & Todd, 1963). Epinephrine stimulates the effector cells of the pilomotor nerves to cause hair erection, and also causes pupillary dilation, giving rise to the picture of a fright reaction. By also causing a rapid rise in blood pressure and an increase in the rate and amplitude of respiration, it prepares for more effective fright or flight from danger. The metabolic behavioral effects of epinephrine and norepinephrine are in some ways opposite, in that while epinephrine is associated with tachycardia (rapid heartbeat), norepinephrine is associated with brachycardia (slow heart action; Eranko, 1955). In children, normal levels in plasma are 3–6 m/l for norepinephrine, and >1 m/l for epinephrine (Cone, 1968).

REFERENCES

Cone, T. E. (1968). The adrenal medulla. In R. Cooke & S. Levin (Eds.), *The biologic basis of pediatric practice* (pp. 1171–1177). New York: McGraw-Hill.

Eranko, O. (1955). Distribution of adrenaline and noradrenaline in the adrenal medulla. *Nature, 88,* 175.

Krantz, R. C., & Carr, C. J. (1961). The *pharmacologic principles of medical practice* (5th ed.). Baltimore: Williams & Wilkins.

West, E. S., & Todd, W. R. (1963). *Textbook of biochemistry* (3rd ed.). New York: Macmillan.

LAWRENCE C. HARTLAGE
Evans, Georgia

EPINEPHRINE
PHOBIAS AND FEARS

CAT SCAN

Computerized axial tomography (CAT) scanning is an imaging technique (Binder, Haughton, & Ho, 1979) that permits visualization of many of the important landmarks and structures of the brain (see Figure 1). This is a recent technique that did not become commercially available until 1973 (Hounsfield, 1973). The importance of this breakthrough in diagnostic neuroradiology is exemplified by the fact that the 1979 Nobel Prize in Medicine was awarded to the scientists G. N. Hounsfield and A. M. Cormack, who established the theoretical physics and radiographic basis for CAT scanning. The fascinating history behind these monumental breakthroughs is reviewed in the text by Oldendorf (1980).

CAT scanning is accomplished by passing a narrow X-ray beam directed toward a detector on the other side through the patient's head (or body). The detector is sensitive to the number of X-ray beam particles that pass through the tissue; this in turn is related to the density of the tissue (e.g.,

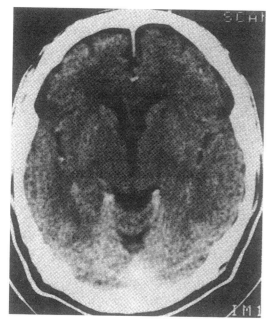

Figure 1 CAT scan image of the brain in horizontal plane. The two upside down L-shaped dark areas represent the anterior horns of the lateral ventricles. The light area just adjacent and lateral to these structures is the caudate nucleus. The centrally located dark area just below the anterior horns in this figure represents the third ventricle. On either side of the third ventricle is the thalamus. The angular slightly darker area that runs from the outside top of the candate nucleus down and adjacent to the outside of the thalamus is the internal capsule. Lateral to the internal capsule is the putamen-globus pallidus complex.

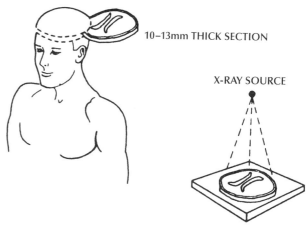

Figure 2 Diagrammatic representation of the position of the view of the CAT image

the greater the density the fewer the X-ray particles that pass through). The X-ray beam is passed through the head (or body) in numerous planes so as to examine the same point from multiple directions, thus allowing a specification of density for any given point on the surface of a plane.

Next, each density point is color-coded depending on the degree of density; these various density points are used to computer generate an "image" of the tissue being examined (see Figure 2).

CAT scanning has numerous useful applications. The CAT image approximates an actual anatomic specimen taken in a similar plane; thus significant structural abnormalities can be detected. This is particularly true in cases of cerebral trauma, vascular infarctions, congenital and neoplastic disorders, and degenerative brain diseases (see Figure 3). For children with developmental disorders, CAT scanning may reveal any major structural anomalies of the brain, but it has not been found to be routinely diagnostic in children in which the only problem is a learning disability (Denkla, LeMay, & Chapman, 1985). These observations suggest that, in general, there is no gross anatomic derangement associated with learning disorders.

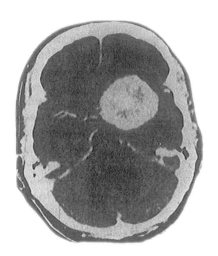 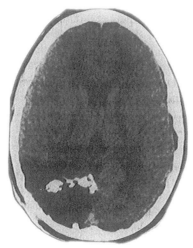 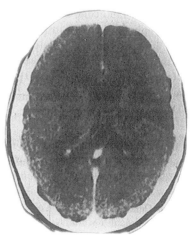

Figure 3 Representative CAT scan depicting different types of organic pathology. Left: tumor (meningioma). Middle: gunshot wound. Right: stroke dark area on right side).

REFERENCES

Binder, G. A., Haughton, V. M., & Ho, K-C. (1979). *Computed tomography of the brain in axial, coronal and sagittal planes* Boston: Little, Brown.

Denkla, M. B., LeMay, M., & Chapman, C. A. (1985). Few Ct scan abnormalities found ever in neurologically impaired learning disabled children. *Journal of Learning Disabilities, 18,* 132–135.

Hounsfield, G. N. (1973). Computerized transverse axial scanning (tomography). I. Description of system. *British Journal of Radiology, 46,* 1016–1022.

Oldendorf, W. H. (1980). *The quest for an image of brain.* New York: Raven Press.

ERIN D. BIGLER
Brigham Young University

DIFFUSION TENSOR IMAGING
NUCLEAR MAGNETIC RESONANCE
X-RAY SCANNING TECHNIQUES

THE CATTELL-HORN-CARROLL THEORY OF COGNITIVE ABILITIES

The Cattell-Horn-Carroll (CHC) theory of cognitive abilities is the most comprehensive and empirically supported psychometric theory of the structure of cognitive abilities to date. It represents the integrated works of Raymond Cattell, John Horn, and John Carroll (Alfonso, Flanagan, & Radwan, 2005; Horn & Blankson, 2005; McGrew, 2005; Neisser et al., 1996). Because it has an impressive body of empirical support in the research literature (e.g., developmental, neurocognitive, outcome-criterion) it is used extensively as the foundation for selecting, organizing, and interpreting tests of intelligence and cognitive abilities (e.g., Flanagan & Ortiz, 2001; McGrew & Flanagan, 1998). Most recently, it has been used for classifying both intelligence and achievement tests to: (a) facilitate interpretation of abilities; and (b) provide a foundation for organizing assessments for individuals suspected of having a learning disability (Flanagan, Ortiz, & Alfonso, 2006; Flanagan, Ortiz, Alfonso, & Mascolo, in press). Additionally, CHC theory is the foundation on which most new and recently revised intelligence batteries were based (see Kaufman, Kaufman, Kaufman, & Kaufman, 2005; Roid & Pomplum, 2005; Schrank, 2005). A brief overview of the evolution of CHC theory follows.

Fluid-Crystallized (*Gf-Gc*) Theory

The original *Gf-Gc* theory was a dichotomous conceptualization of human cognitive ability put forth by Raymond Cattell in the early 1940s. Cattell based his theory on the factor-analytic work of Thurstone conducted in the 1930s.

Cattell believed that Fluid Intelligence (*Gf*) included inductive and deductive reasoning abilities that were influenced by biological and neurological factors as well as incidental learning through interaction with the environment. He postulated further that Crystallized Intelligence (*Gc*) consisted primarily of acquired knowledge abilities that reflected, to a large extent, the influences of acculturation (Cattell, 1957, 1971).

In 1965, John Horn expanded the dichotomous *Gf-Gc* model to include four additional abilities, including visual perception or processing (*Gv*), short-term memory (Short-term Acquisition and Retrieval—SAR or *Gsm*), long-term storage and retrieval (Tertiary Storage and Retrieval—TSR or *Glr*), and speed of processing (*Gs*). Later he added auditory processing ability (*Ga*) to the theoretical model and refined the definitions of *Gv, Gs,* and *Glr* (Horn, 1968; Horn & Stankov, 1982).

In the early 1990s, Horn added a factor representing an individual's quickness in reacting (reaction time) and making decisions (decision speed). The acronym or code for this factor is *Gt* (Horn, 1991). Finally, quantitative (*Gq*) and broad reading-writing (*Grw*) factors were added to the model based on the research of Horn (e.g., 1991) and Woodcock (1994), respectively. Based largely on the results of Horn's thinking and research, *Gf-Gc* theory expanded into an eight-factor model that became known as the Cattell-Horn *Gf-Gc* theory (Horn, 1991; see Horn and Blankson, 2005, for a comprehensive review of Horn's contribution to *Gf-Gc* theory).

Carroll's Three-Stratum Theory

In his review of the extant factor-analytic research literature, Carroll differentiated factors or abilities into three strata that varied according to the "relative variety and diversity of variables" (Carroll, 1997, p. 124) included at each level. The various *G* abilities are the most prominent and recognized abilities of the model. They are classified as broad or stratum II abilities and include abilities such as *Gf* and *Gc,* the two original factors. According to Carroll (1993), *broad* abilities represent "basic constitutional and long standing characteristics of individuals that can govern or influence a great variety of behaviors in a given domain" and they vary in their emphasis on process, content, and manner of response (p. 634). Broad abilities, like *Gf* and *Gc,* subsume a large number of narrow or stratum I abilities of which approximately 70 have been identified (Carroll, 1993, 1997). *Narrow* abilities "represent greater specializations of abilities, often in quite specific ways that reflect the effects of experience and learning, or the adoption of particular strategies of performance" (Carroll, 1993, p. 634). The hierarchical structure of *Gf-Gc* theory is demonstrated for the domain of Visual Processing (*Gv*) in Figure 1.

In the *Gf-Gc* taxonomy, *Gv* is classified as a broad stratum II cognitive ability. The 11 narrow or stratum I visual

Broad
(Stratum II) Ability

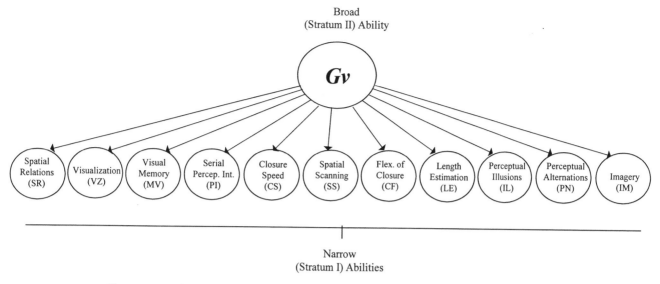

Narrow
(Stratum I) Abilities

Figure 1 A visual processing (*Gv*) example demonstrating the hierarchical structure of *Gf-Gc* Theory

processing abilities that comprise *Gv* demonstrate the "broadness" or breadth of this factor. Figure 1 shows that 11 different narrow or specialized visual abilities have been identified in the literature. The broad *Gv* ability and the narrow abilities it encompasses are defined later, as are the remaining *Gf-Gc* broad and narrow abilities that comprise CHC theory. The significant, moderate to high intercorrelations displayed by the narrow (*Gv*) abilities suggest the presence of a broader factor or construct that accounts for this shared and (as depicted in Figure 1) supposed "Visual Processing" variance. The broad *Gv* factor is hypothesized to represent this higher-order explanatory construct and is believed to exert a significant common effect (reflected by the direction of the arrows in Figure 1) on the narrow abilities. When this concept is extended to the 9 other broad ability domains, each of which also subsumes a number of narrow abilities, it is clear that *Gf-Gc* theory is quite comprehensive. The broadest or most general level of ability in the *Gf-Gc* model is represented by stratum III, located at the apex of Carroll's (1993) hierarchy. This single cognitive ability, which subsumes both broad (stratum II) and narrow (stratum I) abilities, is interpreted as representing a general factor (i.e., *g*) that is involved in complex higher-order cognitive processes (Gustaffson & Undheim, 1996; Jensen, 1997; McGrew & Woodcock, 2001).

It is important to note that the abilities within each level of the hierarchical *Gf-Gc* model typically display non-zero positive intercorrelations (Carroll, 1993; Gustafsson & Undheim, 1996). For example, similar to the previous *Gv* discussion, the different stratum I (narrow) abilities that define the various *Gf-Gc* domains are correlated positively and to varying degrees. These intercorrelations give rise to and allow for the estimation of the stratum II (broad) ability factors. Likewise, the positive nonzero correlations among the stratum II (broad) *Gf-Gc* abilities allows for the

estimation of the stratum III (general) *g* factor. The positive factor intercorrelations within each level of the *Gf-Gc* hierarchy indicate that the different *Gf-Gc* abilities do not reflect completely independent (uncorrelated or orthogonal) traits. However, they can, as is evident from the vast body of literature that supports their existence, be reliably distinguished from one another and therefore represent unique, albeit related, abilities (see Keith, 2005).

Similarities and Differences between the Cattell-Horn Model and the Carroll Model

Simplified versions of the Cattell-Horn and Carroll models of the structure of abilities (i.e., where the narrow abilities are omitted) are presented together in Figure 2. A review of Figure 2 shows a number of important similarities and differences between the two models. In general, these models are similar in that they both include some form of fluid intelligence (*Gf*), crystallized intelligence (*Gc*), short-term memory and learning (*Gsm* or *Gy*), visual perception or processing (*Gv*), auditory perception or processing (*Ga* or *Gu*), long-term retrieval (*Glr* or *Gr*), processing speed (*Gs*), and decision and reaction time speed (*CDS* or *Gt*) abilities. Although there are some differences in the broad ability definitions, as well as in the specific narrow abilities that are subsumed by the respective broad *Gf-Gc* abilities, the major structural differences between the two models are primarily fourfold (McGrew, 1997, 2005).

First, the Cattell-Horn and the Carroll models differ in their inclusion of *g* (global or general ability) at stratum III. According to Carroll (1993, 1997, 2005), the general intelligence factor at the apex of his three-stratum theory is analogous to Spearman's *g*. The off-center placement of *g* (to the left side of Figure 2) in the Carroll model is intended to reflect the strength of the relations between *g* and the

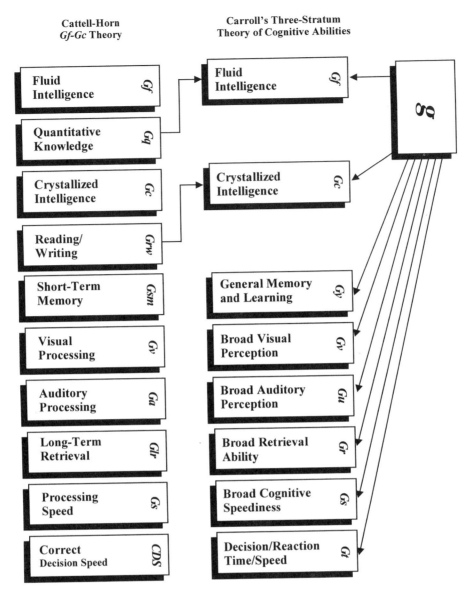

Figure 2 Comparison of Cattell-Horn *Gf-Gc* and Carroll Three-Stratum theories

Note. Narrow abilities are omitted from this figure. From Flanagan, Ortiz, Alfonso, and Mascolo (2002). Published by Allyn & Bacon, Boston, MA. Copyright © 2002 by Pearson Education. Reprinted by permission.

respective broad *Gf-Gc* abilities. As represented in Carroll's model in Figure 4 (i.e., the top half of the figure), *Gf* has the strongest association with *g*, followed by *Gc*, and continuing on through the remaining abilities to the two broad abilities that are weakest in association with *g* (i.e., *Gs* and *Gt*).

Although Carroll (1997) has stated that the evidence for *g* is "overwhelming," Horn disagrees strongly, believing *g* to be primarily a statistical artifact (see Horn, 1991; Horn & Blankson, 2005; Horn & Noll, 1997). Accordingly, Horn posits a *truncated hierarchical model*—that is, a model that does not contain a single *g* factor at the apex (Jensen, 1998). Debates about the nature and existence of *g* have waxed and waned for decades and have been some of the liveliest

debates in differential psychology (Gustafsson & Undheim, 1996; Jensen, 1997). Much of the debate has been theoretical in nature, with definitions of *g* ranging from an index of neural cognitive efficiency, general reasoning ability, or mental energy to a mere statistical irregularity (Neisser et al., 1996). After being "more or less banned from the scientific scene" (Gustafsson & Undheim, 1996), the prominent position of *g* in contemporary psychometric models of the structure of abilities (e.g., Carroll's three-stratum model and Jensen's [1998] "*g* factor" treatise) has helped it to take center stage once again in intelligence research and dialogue. Interested readers are directed to the writings of Carroll (1993, 1997), Horn (1991), Horn and Blankson

(2005), Horn and Noll (1997), and Jensen (1997, 1998) for further discussion of *g*-related issues and research.

Second, in the Cattell-Horn model, quantitative knowledge and quantitative reasoning abilities together represent a distinct broad ability, as depicted by the *Gq* rectangle in the bottom half of Figure 2. Carroll (1993), however, views quantitative ability as "an inexact, unanalyzed popular concept that has no scientific meaning unless it is referred to the structure of abilities that compose it. It cannot be expected to constitute a higher-level ability" (p. 627). As such, Carroll classified quantitative reasoning as a narrow ability subsumed by *Gf,* as indicated by the arrow leading from the *Gq* rectangle in the Cattell-Horn model to the *Gf* rectangle in the Carroll model in Figure 2. Furthermore, Carroll included mathematics achievement and mathematics knowledge factors in a separate chapter in his book, which described a variety of knowledge and achievement abilities (e.g., technical and mechanical knowledge, knowledge of behavioral content) that are not included in his theoretical model.

Third, recent versions of the Cattell-Horn model have included a broad English-language reading and writing ability (*Grw*) that is depicted in the bottom half of Figure 2 (Flanagan, McGrew, & Ortiz, 2000; McGrew, 1997; Woodcock, 1993). Carroll, however, considers reading and writing to be narrow abilities subsumed under the broad ability of *Gc*, as reflected by the arrow leading from the *Grw* rectangle in the Cattell-Horn model to the *Gc* rectangle in the Carroll model in Figure 2.

Fourth, the Cattell-Horn and the Carroll models differ in their treatment of certain narrow memory abilities. Carroll combined both short-term memory and the narrow abilities of associative, meaningful, and free-recall memory (defined later in this chapter) with learning abilities under his General Memory and Learning factor (*Gy*). Horn (1991) made a distinction between immediate apprehension (e.g., short-term memory span) and storage and retrieval abilities. The reader is referred to McGrew (1997, 2005) for a more complete discussion of these differences.

Notwithstanding the important differences between the Cattell-Horn and the Carroll models, in order to realize the practical benefits of using theory to guide test selection, organization, and interpretation, it is necessary to define a single taxonomy—one that can be used to classify the individual tests of psychoeducational batteries, including tests of cognitive abilities and processes as well as tests of academic achievement. A first effort to create a single taxonomy for this purpose was an integrated Cattell-Horn and Carroll model proposed by McGrew (1997). McGrew and Flanagan (1998) subsequently presented a slightly revised integrated model, which was further refined by Flanagan, et al. (2000). The integrated model presented by Flanagan and colleagues was accepted by both John Horn and John Carroll and thus became known as the Cattell-Horn-Carroll

(CHC) theory, reflecting the order in which these theorists made their contributions.

CHC Theory

The integration of the Cattell-Horn *Gf-Gc* theory and Carroll's three-stratum theory, or simply CHC theory, is presented in Figure 3. This figure depicts the current structure of contemporary CHC theory and reflects the manner in which the Cattell-Horn and Carroll models have been integrated (i.e., based mainly on the work of McGrew, 1997; see also Flanagan, et al., 2000). In this figure, CHC theory includes 10 broad cognitive abilities, which are subsumed by over 70 narrow abilities. The abilities printed in italic in Figure 3 are those that were not included in Carroll's three-stratum model but that were included by Carroll in his definitions of *knowledge* and *achievement* (Carroll, 1993). The abilities printed in bold in Figure 5 are those that were placed under CHC broad abilities in a differing manner than that proposed by Carroll (1993). These changes (or otherwise integrations of the Cattell-Horn and the Carroll models) are based on the most recent developments of and refinements to the Cattell-Horn model (e.g., Horn & Noll, 1997) and recent factor-analysis research (e.g., Woodcock, McGrew, & Mather, 2001). The interested reader is referred to McGrew (2005) for a more comprehensive description of the specific ways in which CHC theory represents an integration of the Cattell-Horn and Carroll models.

The exclusion of *g* in Figure 5 does not mean that the integrated model does not contain a separate general human ability or that *g* does not exist. Rather, *g* was omitted by McGrew (1997) and Flanagan et al. (2000) because it was judged to have little practical relevance to the selection and organization of tests around referral concerns—particularly those involving suspected learning disability (LD)—and the interpretation of cognitive and academic capabilities via cross-battery principles and procedures (Flanagan & Ortiz, 2001; Flanagan et al., 2006).

CHC theory represents the culmination of more than 60 years of factor-analysis research in the psychometric tradition. However, in addition to structural evidence, there are other sources of validity evidence, some quite substantial, that support CHC theory. Prior to defining the broad and narrow abilities that comprise CHC theory, a brief overview of the validity evidence in support of this structure of cognitive abilities is presented.

A Network of Validity Evidence in Support of CHC Theory

It is beyond the scope of this article to provide a fully detailed account and review of all the validity evidence currently available in support of the CHC structural model as well as the broad and narrow ability constructs it encompasses.

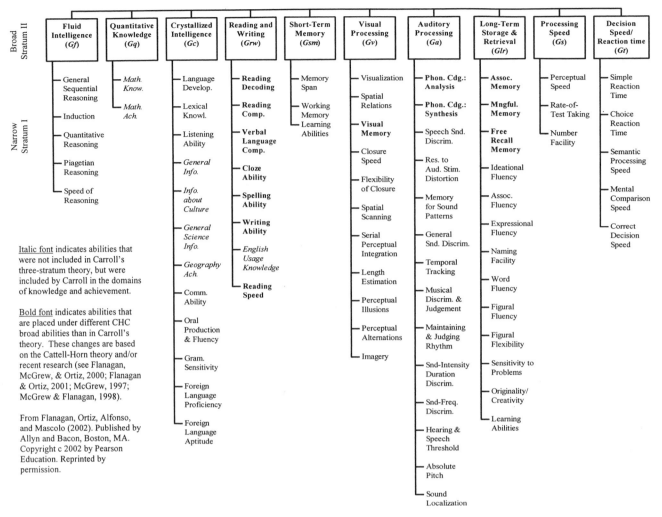

Figure 3 The Cattell-Horn-Carroll Theory of Cognitive Abilities (CHC Theory)

The interested reader is referred to Carroll (1993, 2005), Flanagan et al., (2000), Horn and Blankson (2005), Horn and Noll (1997), and McGrew (1997, 2005) for a more thorough discussion.

Briefly, the CHC structure of abilities is supported by factor-analytic (i.e., structural) evidence as well as developmental, neurocognitive, and heritability evidence (see Horn & Blankson, 2005; Horn & Noll, 1997, and McGrew, 2005, for a summary). Additionally, there is a mounting body of research available on the relations between the broad cognitive CHC abilities and many academic outcomes (summarized in Flanagan, et al., 2002, in press) as well as occupational outcomes (Ackerman & Heggestad, 1997; McGrew & Flanagan, 1998). Furthermore, studies have shown that the factor structure of CHC theory is invariant across the lifespan (Bickley, Keith, & Wolfe, 1995; Keith, 2005; Woodcock et al., 2001) and across gender, ethnic, and cultural groups (e.g., Carroll, 1993; Gustafsson & Balke, 1993; Keith, 1997, 1999). In general, CHC theory is based on a more extensive network of validity evidence than other contemporary multidimensional ability models (see Daniel,

1997; Kranzler & Keith, 1999; McGrew, 2005; McGrew & Flanagan, 1998; Messick, 1992; Sternberg & Kaufman, 1998).

Given the breadth of empirical support for the CHC structure of intelligence, it provides one of the most useful frameworks for designing and evaluating psychoeducational batteries, including intelligence and achievement tests (Flanagan, 2000; Flanagan & McGrew, 1997; Kaufman, 2000; Keith & Kranzler, 1999; Keith, Kranzler, & Flanagan, 2001; Keith & Witta, 1997; Kranzler, Keith, & Flanagan, 2000; McGrew, 1997; Woodcock, 1990; Ysseldyke, 1990). Moreover, in light of the well-established structural validity of CHC theory, external validity support for the various CHC constructs, derived through sound research methodology, can be used confidently to guide test interpretation (see Bensen, 1998; Evans, Floyd, McGrew, & Leforgee, 2002; Floyd, Evans, & McGrew, 2003; Flanagan, 2000; Vanderwood, McGrew, Flanagan, & Keith, 2002).

It is important to recognize that research related to CHC theory is not static. Rather, research on the hierarchical structure of abilities (within the *Gf-Gc* and now CHC framework) has been systematic, steady, and mounting for decades. Definitions of the broad and narrow abilities comprising CHC theory are presented in the next section.

Broad and Narrow CHC Ability Definitions

These definitions presented here were derived from an integration of the writings of Carroll (1993), Gustafsson and Undheim (1996), Horn (1991), McGrew (1997), McGrew, Werder, and Woodcock (1991), and Woodcock (1994). The narrow ability definitions are presented in Tables 1 through 10.

Fluid Intelligence (Gf)

Fluid intelligence refers to mental operations that an individual uses when faced with a relatively novel task that cannot be performed automatically. These mental operations may include forming and recognizing concepts, perceiving relationships among patterns, drawing inferences, comprehending implications, problem solving, extrapolating, and reorganizing or transforming information. Inductive and deductive reasoning are generally considered to be the hallmark narrow-ability indicators of *Gf*. Although most practitioners would agree that this ability is typically not measured directly by individually administered achievement batteries, some tests of achievement clearly involve the use of specific *Gf* abilities. For example, many tests of reading comprehension require individuals to draw inferences from the text.

Aside from general inductive and deductive reasoning abilities, *Gf* also subsumes more specific types of reasoning, most notably Quantitative Reasoning (RQ). Unlike the other narrow *Gf* abilities, RQ is more directly related to formal instruction and classroom related experiences. Definitions of the narrow abilities subsumed by *Gf* are presented in Table 1.

Crystallized Intelligence (Gc)

Crystallized intelligence refers to the breadth and depth of a person's acquired knowledge of a culture and the effective application of this knowledge. This store of primarily verbal or language-based knowledge represents those abilities that have been developed largely through the "investment" of other abilities during educational and general life experiences (Horn & Blankson, 2005; Horn & Noll, 1997).

Gc includes both declarative (static) and procedural (dynamic) knowledge. Declarative knowledge is held in long-term memory and is activated when related information is in working memory (*Gsm*). Declarative knowledge includes factual information, comprehension, concepts, rules, and relationships, especially when the information is verbal in nature. *Declarative knowledge* refers to knowledge "that something is the case, whereas procedural knowledge is knowledge of how to do something" (Gagne, 1985, p. 48). *Procedural knowledge* refers to the process of reasoning with previously learned procedures in order to transform knowledge. For example, a child's knowledge of his or her street address would reflect declarative knowledge, whereas a child's ability to find his or her way home from school would require procedural knowledge (Gagne, 1985). The breadth of *Gc* is apparent from the number of narrow abilities (12) it subsumes (see Table 2).

A rather unique aspect of *Gc* not seen in the other broad abilities is that it appears to be both a store of acquired knowledge (e.g., lexical knowledge, general information, information about culture) as well as a collection of processing abilities (e.g., oral production and fluency, listening ability). Although *Gc* is most often conceptualized much like *Gq* and *Grw* as an ability that is highly dependent on learning experiences (especially formal, classroom-type experiences), it also seems to encompass abilities that are more process oriented. The narrow ability of General Information (K0) for example, is clearly a repository of learned information, whereas the narrow Listening Ability (LS) appears to represent the ability to effectively comprehend and process information presented orally. Although comprehension is of course dependent on knowledge of the words being presented, the nature of these two *Gc* abilities is clearly not identical. Although research is needed to discern the nature of acquired knowledge versus processing abilities within the *Gc* domain, assessment of *Gc* should pay close atten-

Table 1 Narrow *Gf* stratum I ability definitions

Narrow stratum I name (code)	Definition
Fluid intelligence (Gf)	
General Sequential Reasoning (RG)	Ability to start with stated rules, premises, or conditions, and to engage in one or more steps to reach a solution to a novel problem (also called "deduction").
Induction (I)	Ability to discover the underlying characteristic (e.g., rule, concept, process, trend, class membership) that governs a problem or a set of materials.
Quantitative Reasoning (RQ)	Ability to inductively and deductively reason with concepts involving mathematical relations and properties.
Piagetian Reasoning (RP)	Seriation, conservation, classification, and other cognitive abilities as defined by Piaget's developmental theory.
Speed of Reasoning (RE)	(Not clearly defined by existing research.)

Table 2 Narrow *Gc* stratum I ability definitions

Narrow stratum I name (code)	Definition
Crystallized intelligence (Gc)	
Language Development (LD)	General development, or the understanding of words, sentences, and paragraphs (*not* requiring reading), in spoken native language skills.
Lexical Knowledge (VL)	Extent of vocabulary that can be understood in terms of correct word meaning.
Listening Ability (LS)	Ability to listen and comprehend oral communications.
General (verbal) Information (K0)	Range of general knowledge.
Information about Culture (K2)	Range of cultural knowledge (e.g., music, art).
General Science Information (K1)	Range of scientific knowledge (e.g., biology, physics, engineering, mechanics, electronics).
Geography Achievement (A5)	Range of geographic knowledge.
Communication Ability (CM)	Ability to speak in "real life" situations (e.g., lecture, group participation) in an adult-like manner.
Oral Production and Fluency (OP)	More specific or narrow oral communication skills than reflected by Communication Ability (CM).
Grammatical Sensitivity (MY)	Knowledge or awareness of the grammatical features of the native language.
Foreign Language Proficiency (KL)	Similar to Language Development (LD), but for a foreign language.
Foreign Language Aptitude (LA)	Rate and ease of learning a new language.

Table 3 Narrow *Gq* stratum I ability definitions

Narrow stratum I name (code)	Definition
Quantitative knowledge (Gq)	
Mathematical Knowledge (KM)	Range of general knowledge about mathematics.
Mathematical Achievement (A3)	Measured mathematics achievement.
Quantitative Reasoning (RQ)[a]	Ability to inductively and deductively reason with concepts involving mathematical relations and properties.

[a]Although RQ is a narrow *Gf* ability, it is included here because its measurement is relevant to the comprehensive assessment of overall mathematics ability.

tion to the nature of the narrow abilities that define this broad domain. Despite the interrelatedness of all narrow abilities under *Gc,* there may well be times when focus on the abilities that are more process oriented, as opposed to those that are knowledge oriented, is most important, and vice versa.

Quantitative Knowledge (Gq)

Quantitative knowledge represents an individual's store of acquired quantitative-declarative and procedural knowledge. The *Gq* store of acquired knowledge represents the ability to use quantitative information and manipulate numeric symbols. *Gq* abilities are typically measured by achievement tests. For example, most comprehensive tests of achievement include measures of math calculation, applied problems (or math problem solving), and general math knowledge. Although some intelligence batteries measure aspects of *Gq* (e.g., Arithmetic on the Wechsler Scales, Quantitative Reasoning on the SB5), they typically do not measure this ability comprehensively.

It is important to understand the difference between *Gq* and the Quantitative Reasoning (RQ) ability that is subsumed by *Gf*. On the whole, *Gq* represents an individual's store of acquired mathematical knowledge, including the ability to perform mathematical calculations (i.e., procedural knowledge). Quantitative Reasoning represents only the ability to reason inductively and deductively when solving quantitative problems. *Gq* is most evident when a task requires mathematical skills (e.g., addition, subtraction, multiplication, division) and general mathematical knowledge (e.g., knowing what the square-root symbol means). RQ, on the other hand, would be required to solve for a missing number in a number series task (e.g., 3, 6, 9, ___), for example. Three narrow abilities are listed and defined under *Gq* in Table 3.

Reading/Writing Ability (Grw)

Reading / Writing ability is an acquired store of knowledge that includes basic reading, reading fluency, and writing skills required for the comprehension of written language

Table 4 Narrow *Grw* stratum I ability definitions

Narrow stratum I name (code)	Definition
Reading / Writing (Grw)	
Reading Decoding (RD)	Ability to recognize and decode words or pseudowords in reading.
Reading Comprehension (RC)	Ability to comprehend connected discourse during reading.
Verbal (printed) Language Comprehension (V)	General development, or the understanding of words, sentences, and paragraphs in native language, as measured by *reading* vocabulary and *reading* comprehension tests.
Close Ability (CZ)	Ability to supply words deleted from prose passages that must be read.
Spelling Ability (SG)	Ability to spell.
Writing Ability (WA)	Ability to write with clarify of thought, organization, and good sentence structure.
English Usage Knowledge (EU)	Knowledge of writing in the English Language with respect to capitalization, punctuation, usage, and spelling.
Reading Speed (RS)	Time required to silently read a passage or series of sentences as quickly as possible.

and the expression of thought via writing. It includes both basic abilities (e.g., reading decoding and fluency, spelling) and complex abilities (e.g., comprehending written discourse, writing a story). Like *Gq, Grw* is considered to be an "achievement" domain, and therefore, has been measured traditionally (and almost exclusively) by tests of academic achievement. In Carroll's (1993) three-stratum model, eight narrow reading and writing abilities are subsumed by *Gc* in addition to other abilities. In the CHC model, these eight narrow abilities define the broad *Grw* ability. These *Grw* narrow abilities are defined in Table 4.

A closer review of the nature of *Grw* presents a rather curious finding. Although reading and writing are often thought of as distinct academic abilities, the research underlying the classification of these narrow abilities suggests that they are very closely related abilities (Woodcock, 1994). The strong relationship seems to imply that a measure of reading is an accurate measure of writing ability, just as a measure of writing ability is an accurate measure of reading ability. Without question, reading and writing go hand in hand, and for good reason—they are the basic elements of proficiency with the symbolic aspect of language. Language abilities are clearly present in the various narrow abilities found under the broad *Gc* ability described previously, but generally are limited to those involving the receptive and expressive aspects of language. *Grw,* however, seems to represent skill in the symbolic aspect of language where facility with the written form of speech and communication are required. Reading, therefore, is the ability to decode the symbols automatically in order to derive linguistic meaning, and writing is the automatic production of symbols to express linguistic meaning. In this sense, reading and writing are seen to be highly interrelated components of the same fundamental construct. It is likely only a semantic issue that creates a sense of reading and writing as being more distinct than they actually are. Use of the label "*Grw*—reading and writing" reflects this semantic separation, whereas another label, reflecting a broad *literacy* factor, for example,

may better capture the true essence of this variable (Flanagan et al., in press). Because of its basis in both reading and writing skills, the term *literacy* seems to provide a better umbrella for covering the types of abilities that are currently found under the label of *Grw*. This presumes, of course, that reading and writing are indeed quite interchangeable as measures of symbolic-language processing (i.e., literacy). Although current research suggests that this is true (Woodcock, 1994), it is rather preliminary and largely unreplicated. Thus, if future research reveals that reading and writing abilities are relatively distinct constructs, then the label itself may need to be split accordingly (i.e., *Gr*—reading and *Gw*—writing).

Short-Term Memory (Gsm)

Short-term memory is the ability to apprehend and hold information in immediate awareness and then use it within a few seconds. *Gsm* is a limited-capacity system, as most individuals can retain only seven "chunks" of information (plus or minus two chunks) in this system at one time. An example of *Gsm* is the ability to remember a telephone number long enough to dial it, or the ability to retain a sequence of spoken directions long enough to complete the tasks specified in the directions. Given the limited amount of information that can be held in short-term memory, information is typically retained for only a few seconds before it is lost. As most individuals have experienced, it is difficult to remember an unfamiliar telephone number for more than a few seconds unless one consciously uses a cognitive learning strategy (e.g., continually repeating or rehearsing the numbers) or other mnemonic device. When a new task requires an individual to use his or her *Gsm* abilities to store new information, the previous information held in short-term memory is either lost or must be stored in the acquired stores of knowledge (i.e., *Gc, Gq, Grw*) through the use of *Glr*.

In the CHC model, *Gsm* subsumes the narrow ability

of working memory, which has received considerable attention recently in the cognitive psychology literature (see Kane, Bleckley, Conway, & Engle, 2001). Working memory is considered to be the "mechanism responsible for the temporary storage and processing of information" (Richardson, 1996, p. 23). It has been referred to as the "mind's scratchpad" (Jensen, 1998, p. 220) and most models of working memory postulate a number of subsystems or temporary "buffers." The phonological or articulatory loop processes auditory-linguistic information, whereas the visuospatial sketch/scratchpad (Baddeley, 1986, 1992; Logie, 1996) is the temporary buffer for visually processed information. Most working-memory models also posit a central executive or processor mechanism that coordinates and manages the activities and subsystems in working memory.

Carroll (1993) is skeptical of the working-memory construct, as reflected in his conclusion that "although some evidence supports such a speculation, one must be cautious in accepting it because as yet there has not been sufficient work on measuring working memory, and the validity and generality of the concept have not yet been well established in the individual differences research" (p. 647). Notwithstanding, the working-memory construct has been related empirically to a variety of different outcomes, including many specific reading and math skills (see Flanagan et al., 2002, in press). Therefore, despite the questions that have been raised regarding its validity as a measurable construct, Flanagan et al. (2000) and Woodcock et al. (2001) included working memory in the CHC taxonomy in light of the current literature that argues strongly for its predictive utility (e.g., Ackerman, Beier, & Boyle, 2002; Hitch, Towse, & Hutton, 2001). Nevertheless, given that Carroll has raised questions about the validity of the construct of working memory, it is important to remember that this construct was included in current CHC theory primarily for practical application and ease of communication. Additional research is necessary before definitive decisions can be reached about the inclusion or exclusion of working memory in CHC theory. The narrow *Gsm* abilities are defined in Table 5.

Visual Processing (Gv)

Visual processing (*Gv*) is the ability to generate, perceive, analyze, synthesize, store, retrieve, manipulate, transform, and think with visual patterns and stimuli (Lohman, 1994). These abilities are measured frequently by tasks that require the perception and manipulation of visual shapes and forms, usually of a figural or geometric nature (e.g., a standard block design task). An individual who can mentally reverse and rotate objects effectively, interpret how objects change as they move through space, perceive and manipulate spatial configurations, and maintain spatial orientation would be regarded as having a strength in *Gv* abilities. *Gv* abilities have been found to be related significantly to higher-level mathematics achievement (e.g., geometry and trigonometry; Casey, Nuttall, & Pezaris, 1997; Hegarty & Kozhevnikov, 1999). The various narrow abilities subsumed by *Gv* are listed and defined in Table 6.

Auditory Processing (Ga)

In the broadest sense, auditory abilities "are cognitive abilities that depend on sound as input and on the functioning of our hearing apparatus" (Stankov, 1994, p. 157) and reflect "the degree to which the individual can cognitively control the perception of auditory stimulus inputs" (Gustafsson & Undheim, 1996, p. 192). *Auditory processing* is the ability to perceive, analyze, and synthesize patterns among auditory stimuli, and to discriminate subtle nuances in patterns of sound (e.g., complex musical structure) and speech when presented under distorted conditions. Although *Ga* abilities do not require the comprehension of language (*Gc*) per se, they are important in the development of language skills (Liberman, Shankweiler, Fischer, & Carter, 1974; Wagner & Torgesen, 1987). *Ga* subsumes most of those abilities referred to as "phonological awareness/processing." Tests that measure these abilities (e.g., phonetic coding tests) are found typically on achievement batteries. In fact, the number of tests specifically designed to measure phonological processing has increased significantly in recent years, presumably as a result of the consistent finding that phonological awareness/processing appears to be the core deficit in individuals with reading difficulties (e.g., Morris et al., 1998; Vellutino, Scanlon, & Lyon, 2000; Velluntino & Scanlon 2002). However, as can be seen from the list of narrow abilities subsumed by *Ga* (Table 7), this domain is very broad, extending far beyond phonetic coding ability.

In CHC theory, Carroll's Phonetic Coding (PC) narrow

Table 5　Narrow *Gsm* stratum I ability definitions

Narrow stratum I name (code)	Definition
Short-term memory (Gsm)	
Memory Span (MS)	Ability to attend to and immediately recall temporally ordered elements in the correct order after a single presentation.
Working Memory (MW)	Ability to temporarily store and perform a set of cognitive operations on information that requires divided attention and the management of the limited capacity of short-term memory.
Learning Abilities (L1)	Ability to apprehend newly presented information and to demonstrate subsequent acquisition of such information (e.g., via controlled learning tasks).

Table 6 Narrow *Gv* stratum I ability definitions

Narrow stratum I name (code)	Definition
Visual processing (Gv)	
Spatial Relations (SR)	Ability to rapidly and manipulate relatively simple visual patterns or to maintain orientation with respect to objects in space.
Visual Memory (MV)	Ability to form and store a mental representation or image of a visual stimulus and then recognize or recall it later.
Closure Speed (CS)	Ability to quickly combine disconnected, vague, or partially obscured visual stimuli or patterns into a meaningful whole, *without knowing in advance* what the pattern is.
Flexibility of Closure (CF)	Ability to find, apprehend, and identify a visual figure or pattern embedded in a complex visual array, *when knowing in advance* what the pattern is.
Spatial Scanning (SS)	Ability to accurately and quickly survey a spatial field or pattern and identify a path through the visual field or pattern.
Serial Perceptual Integration (PI)	Ability to apprehend and identify a pictorial or visual pattern when parts of the pattern are presented rapidly in serially or successive order.
Length Estimation (LE)	Ability to accurately estimate or compare visual lengths and distances without using measurement instruments.
Perceptual Illusions (IL)	Ability to resist being affected by perceptual illusions involving geometric figures.
Perceptual Alternations (PN)	Consistency in the rate of alternating between different visual perceptions.
Visualization (Vz)	Ability to mentally manipulate objects or visual patterns and to "see" how they would appear under altered conditions.
Imagery (IM)	Ability to vividly mentally manipulate abstract spatial forms. (Not clearly defined by existing research.)

Table 7 Narrow *Ga* stratum I ability definitions

Narrow stratum I name (code)	Definition
Auditory processing (Ga)	
Phonetic Coding: Analysis (PC:A)	Ability to segment units of speech sounds into smaller units of speech sounds.
Phonetic Coding: Synthesis (PC:S)	Ability to blend smaller units of speech together into larger units of speech.
Speech Sound Discrimination (US)	Ability to detect differences in speech sounds under conditions of little distraction or distortion.
Resistance to Auditory Stimulus Distortion (UR)	Ability to understand speech and language that has been distorted or masked in one or more ways.
Memory for Sound Patterns (UM)	Ability to retain on a short-term basis auditory events such as tones, tonal patterns, and voices.
General Sound Discrimination (U3)	Ability to discriminate tones, tone patterns, or musical materials with regard to pitch, intensity, duration, and rhythm.
Temporal Tracking (UK)	Ability to track auditory temporal events so as to be able to count, rearrange, or anticipate them.
Musical Discrimination and Judgment (U1, U9)	Ability to discriminate and judge tonal patterns in music with respect to melodic, harmonic, and expressive aspects (e.g., phrasing, tempo, and intensity variations).
Maintaining and Judging Rhythm (U8)	Ability to recognize and maintain a musical or equal time beat.
Sound-Intensity/Duration Discrimination (U6)	Ability to discriminate sound intensities and to be sensitive to the temporal/rhythmic aspects of tonal patterns.
Sound-Frequency Discrimination (U5)	Ability to discriminate frequency attributes (pitch and timbre) of tones.
Hearing and Speech Threshold factors (UA, UT, UU)	Ability to hear pitch and varying sounds over a range of audible frequencies.
Absolute Pitch (UP)	Ability to perfectly name or identify the pitch of tones.
Sound Localization (UL)	Ability to localize heard sounds in space.

ability was split into separate analysis (PC:A) and synthesis (PC:S) abilities. Support for two different PC abilities comes from a growing number of sources. First, in a sample of kindergarten students, Yopp (1988) reported evidence in favor of two phonemic awareness factors: simple phonemic awareness (required one operation to be performed on sounds) and compound phonemic awareness (required holding sounds in memory while performing another operation on them). Second, in what appears to be the most comprehensive *Ga* factor-analytic study to date, Stankov and Horn (1980) presented evidence for seven different auditory abilities, two of which had tests of sound blending (synthesis) and incomplete words (analysis) as factor markers. Third, the WJ Sound Blending and Incomplete Words tests (which are almost identical in format to the tests used by Stankov and Horn) correlated only moderately (.37 and .46 and 13.7 percent and 21 percent shared variance) across the kindergarten to adult WJ-R and WJ III norm samples, respectively—a correlation range that suggests that these tests are measuring different aspects of PC. Fourth, using confirmatory factor-analytic methods, Wagner, Torgesen, Laughton, Simmons, and Rashotte (1993) presented a model of phonological processing that included separate auditory analysis and synthesis factors.

Although the features of these different auditory factors across respective studies are not entirely consistent, there are many similarities. For example, Yopp's (1988) simple phonemic factor appears to be analogous to Wagner and colleagues' (1993) synthesis factor and the factor Stankov and Horn (1980) identified with the aid of sound blending tasks. Also, Yopp's (1988) compound phonemic factor bears similarities to Wagner and colleagues' analysis factor and the Stankov and Horn factor identified, in part, by an incomplete words task. Presently, it appears that Wagner and colleagues' analysis-synthesis distinction is likely the most useful. According to Wagner and associates, analysis and synthesis can be defined as "the ability to segment larger units of speech into smaller units" and "the ability to blend smaller units of speech to form larger units" (p. 87), respectively. The analysis-synthesis distinction continues to be empirically supported as demonstrated by the separate Phonetic Coding: Analysis and Phonetic Coding: Synthesis tests included in the new WJ III (Woodcock et al., 2001).

Long-Term Storage and Retrieval (Glr)

Long-term storage and retrieval is the ability to store information in and fluently retrieve new or previously acquired information (e.g., concepts, ideas, items, names) from long-term memory. *Glr* abilities have been prominent in creativity research, where they have been referred to as idea production, ideational fluency, or associative fluency. It is important not to confuse *Glr* with *Gc*, *Gq*, and *Grw*, which represent to a large extent an individual's stores of acquired knowledge. Specifically, *Gc*, *Gq*, and *Grw* represent

what is stored in long-term memory, whereas *Glr* is the *efficiency* by which this information is initially stored in and later retrieved from long-term memory.

It is also important to note that different processes are involved in *Glr* and *Gsm*. Although the word *long-term* frequently carries with it the connotation of days, weeks, months, and years in the clinical literature, long-term storage processes can begin within a few minutes or hours of performing a task. Therefore, the time lapse between the initial task performance and the recall of information related to that task is not necessarily of critical importance in defining *Glr*. More important is the occurrence of an intervening task that engages short-term memory during the interim before the attempted recall of the stored information (e.g., *Gc*; Woodcock, 1993). In the present CHC model, 13 narrow memory and fluency abilities are included under *Glr* (see Table 8).

Processing Speed (Gs)

Processing speed or mental quickness is often mentioned when talking about intelligent behavior (Nettelbeck, 1994). Processing speed is the ability to fluently and automatically perform cognitive tasks, especially when under pressure to maintain focused attention and concentration. "Attentive speediness" encapsulates the essence of *Gs*. *Gs* is measured typically by fixed-interval timed tasks that require little in the way of complex thinking or mental processing (e.g., the Wechsler Animal Pegs, Symbol Search, Cancellation, and Digit Symbol/Coding tests).

Recent interest in information-processing models of cognitive functioning has resulted in a renewed focus on *Gs* (Kail, 1991; Lohman, 1989, McGrew, 2005). A central construct in information-processing models is the idea of limited processing resources (e.g., the limited capacities of short-term and working memory): "Many cognitive activities require a person's deliberate efforts and people are limited in the amount of effort they can allocate. In the face of limited processing resources, the speed of processing is critical because it determines in part how rapidly limited resources can be reallocated to other cognitive tasks" (Kail, 1991, p. 492). Woodcock (1993) likens *Gs* to a valve in a water pipe. The rate in which water flows in the pipe (i.e., *Gs*) increases when the valve is opened wide and it decreases when the valve is partially closed. Four different narrow speed of processing abilities are subsumed by *Gs* in the present CHC model (see Table 9).

Decision Speed/Reaction Time (Gt)

In addition to *Gs*, both Carroll and Horn included a second broad speed ability in their respective models of the structure of abilities. Processing Speed or Decision Speed/Reaction Time (*Gt*), as proposed by Carroll, subsumes narrow abilities that reflect an individual's quickness in reacting

Table 8 Narrow *Glr* stratum I ability definitions

Narrow stratum I name (code)	Definition
Long-term storage and retrieval (Glr)	
Associative Memory (MA)	Ability to recall one part of a previously learned but unrelated pair of items when the other part is presented (i.e., paired-associative learning).
Meaningful Memory (MM)	Ability to recall a set of items where there is a meaningful relation between items or the items comprise a meaningful story or connected discourse.
Free Recall Memory (M6)	Ability to recall as many unrelated items as possible, in any order, after a large collection of items is presented.
Associational Fluency (FA)	Ability to rapidly produce words or phrases associated in meaning (semantically associated) with a given word or concept.
Expressional Fluency (FE)	Ability to rapidly think of and organize words or phrases into meaningful complex ideas under highly general or more specific cueing conditions.
Ideational Fluency (FI)	Ability to rapidly produce a series of ideas, words, or phrases related to a specific condition or object. (Quantity not quality is emphasized.)
Naming Facility (NA)	Ability to rapidly produce names for concepts when presented with a pictorial or verbal cue (sometimes called Rapid Automatic Naming [RAN] in the literature).
Word Fluency (FW)	Ability to rapidly produce words that have specific phonemic, structural, or orthographic characteristics (independent of word meanings).
Figural Fluency (FF)	Ability to rapidly draw or sketch several examples or elaborations when given a starting visual or descriptive stimulus.
Figural Flexibility (FX)	Ability to quickly change set in order to generate new and different solutions to figural problems.
Sensitivity to Problems	Ability to identify and state practical problems in a given situation and/or rapidly think of and state various solutions to, and/or consequences of, such problems.
Originality/Creativity (FO)	Ability to rapidly produce original, clever, or uncommon verbal or ideational responses to specified tasks.
Learning Abilities (L1)	Ability to apprehend newly presented information and to demonstrate subsequent acquisition of such information (e.g., via controlled learning tasks).

Table 9 Narrow *Gs* stratum I ability definitions

Narrow stratum I name (code)	Definition
Processing speed (Gs)	
Perceptual Speed (P)	Ability to rapidly search for and compare known visual symbols or patterns presented side-by-side or separated in a visual field.
Rate-of-Test-Taking (R9)	Ability to rapidly perform tests that are relatively easy or that require very simple decisions.
Number Facility (N)	Ability to rapidly and accurately manipulate and deal with numbers, from elementary skills of coming and recognizing numbers to advanced skills of adding, subtracting, multiplying and dividing numbers.
Semantic Processing Speed (R4)	Ability to rapidly make decisions that require some encoding and mental manipulation of stimulus content.

(reaction time) and making decisions (decision speed). Correct Decision Speed (CDS), proposed by Horn as a second speed ability (*Gs* being the first), is typically measured by recording the time an individual requires to provide an answer to problems on a variety of tests (e.g., letter series, classifications, vocabulary; Horn, 1988, 1991). Because Correct Decision Speed appeared to be a much narrower ability than *Gt,* it is subsumed by *Gt* in CHC theory.

It is important not to confuse *Gt* with *Gs*. *Gt* abilities reflect the immediacy with which an individual can react to stimuli or a task (*typically* measured in seconds or parts of seconds), whereas *Gs* abilities reflect the ability to work quickly over a longer period of time (typically measured in intervals of 2 to 3 minutes). Being asked to read a passage (on a self-paced scrolling video screen) as quickly as possible and, in the process, touch the word *the* with a stylus pen each time it appears on the screen, is an example of *Gs*. The individual's *Gs* score would reflect the number of correct re-

Table 10 Narrow *Gt* stratum I ability definitions

Narrow stratum I name (code)	Definition
Decision speed / Reaction time (Gt)	
Simple Reaction Time (R1)	Reaction time to the presentation of a single visual or auditory stimulus.
Choice Reaction Time (R2)	Reaction time to one of two or more alternative stimuli, depending on which alternative is signaled.
Mental Comparison Speed (R7)	Reaction time where the stimuli must be compared for a particular attribute.

sponses (taking into account errors of omission and commission). In contrast, *Gt* may be measured by requiring a person to read the same text at his or her normal rate of reading and press the space bar as quickly as possible whenever a light is flashed on the screen. In this latter paradigm, the individual's score is based on the average response latency or the time interval between the onset of the stimulus and the individual's response. Table 10 includes descriptions of the narrow abilities subsumed by *Gt*.

Conclusion

The Cattell-Horn-Carroll theory is the most researched, empirically supported, and comprehensive hierarchical psychometric framework of the structure of cognitive abilities. It reflects a major review and reanalysis of the world's literature on individual differences in cognitive abilities, collected over most of a century (Carroll, 1993). The culmination of the monumental contributions of Raymond Cattell, John Horn, and John Carroll, know as CHC theory, will define the taxonomy of cognitive differential psychology for decades to come.

REFERENCES

Ackerman, P. L., Beier, M. E., & Boyle, M. B. (2002). Individual differences in working memory within a nomological network of cognitive and perceptual speed abilities. *Journal of Experimental Psychology: General, 131,* 567–605.

Ackerman, P. L., & Heggestad, E. D. (1997). Intelligence, personality, and interests: Evidence for overlapping traits. *Psychological Bulletin, 121*(2), 219–45.

Alfonso, V. C., Flanagan, D. P., & Radwan, S. (2005). The impact of the Cattell-Horn-Carroll theory on test development and interpretation of cognitive and academic abilities. In D. P. Flanagan & P. L. Harrison (Eds.), *Contemporary intellectual assessment: Theories, tests, and issues* (2nd ed., pp. 185–202). New York: Guilford.

Baddeley, A. (1986). *Working memory.* Oxford: Oxford University Press.

Baddeley, A. (1992). Is working memory working? The fifteenth Bartlett Lecture. *Quarterly Journal of Experimental Psychology, 44A,* 1–31.

Bensen, J. (1998). Developing a strong program of construct validation: A test anxiety example. *Educational Measurement: Issues and Practice, 17*(1), 10–22.

Bickley, P. G., Keith, T. Z., & Wolfe, L. M. (1995). The three-stratum theory of cognitive abilities: Test of the structure of intelligence across the life span. *Intelligence, 20,* 309–328.

Carroll, J. B. (1993). *Human cognitive abilities: A survey of factor-analytic studies.* Cambridge, England: Cambridge University Press.

Carroll, J. B. (1997). The three-stratum theory of cognitive abilities. In D. P. Flanagan, J. L. Genshaft, & P. L. Harrison (Eds.), *Contemporary intellectual assessment: Theories, tests, and issues* (pp. 122–130). New York: Guilford.

Carroll, J. B. (2005). The three-stratum theory of cognitive abilities. In D. P. Flanagan & P. L. Harrison (Eds.), *Contemporary intellectual assessment: Theories, tests, and issues* (2nd ed., pp. 69–76). New York: Guilford.

Casey, M. B., Nuttall, R. L., & Pezaris, E. (1997). Mediators of gender differences in mathematics college entrance test scores: A comparison of spatial skills with internalized beliefs and anxieties. *Developmental Psychology, 33*(4), 669–680.

Cattell, R. B. (1957). *Personality and motivation structure and measurement.* New York: World Book.

Cattell, R. B. (1971). *Abilities: Their structure, growth, and action.* Boston: Houghton Mifflin.

Daniel, M. H. (1997). Intelligence testing: Status and trends. *American Psychologist, 52*(10), 1038–1045.

Evans, J., Floyd, R., McGrew, K. S., & Leforgee, M. 2002. The relations between measures of Cattell-Horn-Carroll (CHC) cognitive abilities and reading achievement during childhood and adolescence. *School Psychology Review, 3,* 2, 246.

Flanagan, D. P. (2000). Wechsler-based CHC cross-battery assessment and reading achievement: Strengthening the validity of interpretations drawn from Wechsler test scores. *School Psychology Quarterly, 15*(3), 295–329.

Flanagan, D. P., & McGrew, K. S. (1997). A cross-battery approach to assessing and interpreting cognitive abilities: Narrowing the gap between practice and cognitive science. In D. P. Flanagan, J. L. Genshaft, & P. L. Harrison (Eds.), *Contemporary intellectual assessment: Theories, tests, and issues* (pp. 314–325). New York: Guilford.

Flanagan, D. P., McGrew, K. S., & Ortiz, S. O. (2000). *The Wechsler intelligence scales and CHC theory: A contemporary approach to interpretation.* Boston: Allyn & Bacon.

Flanagan, D. P., & Ortiz, S. O. (2001). *Essentials of cross-battery assessment.* New York: Wiley.

Flanagan, D. P., Ortiz, S. O., & Alfonso, V. C. (2006). *Essentials of cross-battery assessment* (2nd ed.). Hoboken, NJ: Wiley. Manuscript in preparation.

Flanagan, D. P., Ortiz, S. O., Alfonso, V. C., & Mascolo, J. T. (2002). *The achievement test desk reference (ATDR): Comprehensive assessment of learning disabilities.* Boston: Allyn & Bacon.

Flanagan, D. P., Ortiz, S. O., Alfonso, V. C., & Mascolo, J. T. (in press). *The achievement test desk reference (ATDR), 2nd edition: A guide to learning disability identification.* Hoboken, NJ: Wiley.

Floyd, R. G., Evans, J. J., & McGrew, K. S. (2003). Relations between measures of Cattell-Horn-Carroll (CHC) cognitive abilities and mathematics achievement across the school-age years. *Psychology in the Schools, 40*(2), 155–171.

Gustaffson, J. E., & Undheim, J. O. (1996). Individual differences in cognitive functions. In D. C. Berliner & R. C. Calfee (Eds.), *Handbook of Educational Psychology* (pp. 186–242). New York: Macmillan.

Gustafsson, J. E., & Balke, G. (1993). General and specific abilities as predictors of school achievement. *Multivariate Behavioral Research, 28*(4), 407–434.

Hegarty, M., & Kozhevnikov, M. (1999). Types of visual-spatial representations and mathematical problem solving. *Journal of Educational Psychology, 91*(4), 684–689.

Hitch, G. J., Towse, J. N., & Hutton, U. M. Z. (2001). What limits working memory span? Theoretical accounts and applications for scholastic development. *Journal of Experimental Psychology: General, 130*(2), 184–198.

Horn, J. L. (1968). Organization of abilities and the development of intelligence. *Psychological Review, 75,* 242–259.

Horn, J. L. (1988). Thinking about human abilities. In J. R. Nesselroade & R. B. Cattell (Eds.), *Handbook of multivariate psychology* (Rev. ed., pp. 645–685). New York: Academic Press.

Horn, J. L. (1991). Measurement of intellectual capabilities: A review of theory. In K. S. McGrew, J. K. Werder, & R. W. Woodcock (Eds.), *Woodcock-Johnson technical manual* (pp. 197–232). Chicago: Riverside.

Horn, J. L., & Blankson, N. (2005) Foundations for better understanding of cognitive abilities. In D. P. Flanagan & P. L. Harrison (Eds.), *Contemporary intellectual assessment: Theories, tests, and issues* (2nd ed., pp. 41–68). New York: Guilford.

Horn, J. L., & Noll, J. (1997). Human cognitive capabilities: *Gf-Gc* theory. In D. P. Flanagan, J. L. Genshaft, & P. L. Harrison (Eds.), *Contemporary intellectual assessment: Theories, tests, and issues* (pp. 53–91). New York: Guilford.

Horn, J. L., & Stankov, L. (1982). Auditory and visual factors of intelligence. *Intelligence, 6,* 165–185.

Jensen, A. R. (1997, July). *What we know and don't know about the g factor.* Keynote address delivered at the bi-annual convention of the International Society for the Study of Individual Differences. Aarhus, Denmark.

Jensen, A. R. (1998). *The g factor: The science of mental ability.* Westport, CT: Praeger Publishers.

Kail, R. (1991). Developmental changes in speed of processing during childhood and adolescence. *Psychological Bulletin, 109,* 490–501.

Kane, M. J., Bleckley, M. K., Conway, A. R. A., & Engle, R. W. (2001). A controlled-attention view of working-memory capacity. *Journal of Experimental Psychology General, 130*(2), 169–183.

Kaufman, A. S. (2000). Foreword. In D. P. Flanagan, K. S. McGrew, & S. O. Ortiz (Eds.), *The Wechsler intelligence scales and CHC theory: A contemporary approach to interpretation* (p. iv). Boston: Allyn & Bacon.

Kaufman, J. C., Kaufman, A. S., Kaufman, J., & Kaufman, N. L. (2005). The Kaufman Assessment Battery for Children—second edition, and the Kaufman Adolescent and Adult Intelligence Test. In D. P. Flanagan & P. L. Harrison (Eds.), *Contemporary intellectual assessment: Theories, tests, and issues* (2nd ed., pp. 344–370). New York: Guilford.

Keith, T. Z. (1997). Using confirmatory factor analysis to aid in understanding the constructs measured by intelligence tests. In D. P. Flanagan, J. L. Genshaft, & P. L. Harrison (Eds.), *Contemporary intellectual assessment: Theories, tests, and issues* (pp. 373–402). New York: Guilford.

Keith, T. Z. (1999). Effects of general and specific abilities on student achievement: Similarities and differences across ethnic groups. *School Psychology Quarterly, 14*(3), 239–262.

Keith, T. Z. (2005). Using confirmatory factor analysis to aid in understanding the constructs measured by intelligence tests. In D. P. Flanagan & P. L. Harrison (Eds.), *Contemporary intellectual assessment: Theories, tests, and issues* (2nd ed., pp. 581–614). New York: Guilford.

Keith, T. Z., & Kranzler, J. H. (1999). The absence of structural fidelity precludes construct validity: Rejoinder to Naglieri on what the cognitive assessment system does and does not measure. *School Psychology Review, 28*(2), 303–321.

Keith, T. Z., Kranzler, J. H., & Flanagan, D. P. (2001). What does the Cognitive Assessment System (CAS) measure? Joint confirmatory factor analysis of the CAS and the Woodcock-Johnson Tests of Cognitive Ability (3rd ed.). *School Psychology Review, 30,* 89–119.

Keith, T. Z., & Witta, E. L. (1997). Hierarchical and cross-age confirmatory factor analysis of the WISC-III: What does it measure? *School Psychology Quarterly, 12,* 89–107.

Kranzler, J. H., & Keith, T. Z. (1999). Independent confirmatory factor analysis of the Cognitive Assessment System (CAS): What does the CAS measure? *School Psychology Review, 28,* 117–44.

Kranzler, J. H., Keith, T. Z., & Flanagan, D. P. (2000). Independent examination of the factor structure of the Cognitive Assessment System (CAS): Future evidence challenging the construct validity of the CAS. *Journal of Psychoeducational Assessment, 18,* 143–159.

Liberman, I., Shankweiler, D., Fischer, F. W. and Carter, B. (1974). Explicit syllable and phoneme segmentation in the young child. *Journal of Experimental Child Psychology, 18,* 201–212.

Logie, R. (1996). The seven ages of working memory. In J. Richardson, R. Engle, L. Hasher, R. Logie, E. Stoltzfus, & R. Zacks (Eds.), *Working memory and human cognition* (pp. 31–65). New York: Oxford.

Lohman, D. F. (1989). Human intelligence: An introduction to advances in theory and research. *Review of Educational Research, 59*(4), 333–373.

Lohman, D. F. (1994). Spatial ability. In R. J. Sternberg (Ed.), *Encyclopedia of human intelligence* (pp. 1000–1007). New York: Macmillan.

McGrew, K. S. (1997). Analysis of the major intelligence batteries according to a proposed comprehensive *Gf-Gc* framework. In D. P. Flanagan, J. L. Genshaft, & P. L. Harrison (Eds.), *Contemporary intellectual assessment: Theories, tests, and issues* (pp. 151–180). New York: Guilford.

McGrew, K. S. (2005). The Cattell-Horn-Carroll theory of cognitive abilities: Past, present, and future. In D. P. Flanagan & P. L. Harrison (Eds.), *Contemporary intellectual assessment: Theories, tests, and issues* (2nd ed., pp. 136–182). New York: Guilford.

McGrew, K. S., & Flanagan, D. P. (1998). *The Intelligence Test Desk Reference (ITDR): Gf-Gc cross-battery assessment*. Boston: Allyn & Bacon.

McGrew, K. S., Werder, J. K., & Woodcock, R. W. (1991). *Woodcock-Johnson Psycho-Educational Battery—revised technical manual*. Chicago: Riverside.

McGrew, K. S., & Woodcock, R. W. (2001). Technical manual. *Woodcock-Johnson III*. Itasca, IL: Riverside.

Messick, S. (1992). Multiple intelligences or multilevel intelligence? Selective emphasis on distinctive properties of hierarchy: On Gardner's *Frames of Mind* and Sternberg's *Beyond IQ* in the context of theory and research on the structure of human abilities. *Psychological Inquiry, 3*(4), 365–384.

Morris, R. D., Stuebing, K. K., Fletcher, J. M., Shaywitz, S. E., Lyon, G. R., Shankweiler, D. P., & Katz, L., et al. (1998). Subtypes of reading disability: Variability around a phonological core. *Journal of Educational Psychology, 90*(3), 347–373.

Neisser, U., Boodoo, G., Bouchard, T. J., Boykin, A. W., Brody, N., Ceci, S. J., et al. (1996). Intelligence: Knowns and unknowns. *American Psychologist, 51*, 77–101.

Nettelbeck, T. (1994). Speediness. In R. J. Sternberg (Ed.), *Encyclopedia of human intelligence* (pp. 1014–1019). New York: Macmillan.

Richardson, J. (1996). Evolving concepts of working memory. In J. Richardson, R. Engle, L. Hasher, R. Logie, E. Stoltzfus, & R. Zacks (Eds.), *Working memory and human cognition* (pp. 3–30). New York: Oxford.

Roid, G. H., & Pomplun, M. (2005). Interpreting the Stanford-Binet Intelligence Scales, fifth edition. In D. P. Flanagan, & P. L. Harrison (Eds.), *Contemporary intellectual assessment: Theories, tests, and issues* (2nd ed., pp. 325–343). New York: Guilford.

Schrank, F. A. (2005). Woodcock-Johnson III tests of cognitive abilities. In D. P. Flanagan & P. L. Harrison (Eds.), *Contemporary intellectual assessment: Theories, tests, and issues* (2nd ed., pp. 371–401). New York: Guilford.

Stankov, L. (1994). Auditory abilities. In R. J. Sternberg (Ed.), *Encyclopedia of human intelligence* (pp. 157–162). New York: Macmillan.

Stankov, L., & Horn, J. L. (1980). Human abilities revealed through auditory tests. *Journal of Educational Psychology, 72*(1), 21–44.

Sternberg, R. J., & Kaufman, J. C. (1998). Human abilities. *Annual Review of Psychology, 49*, 479–502.

Vanderwood, M. L., McGrew, K. S., Flanagan, D. P., & Keith, T. Z. (2002). The contribution of general and specific cognitive abilities to reading achievement. *Learning and Individual Differences, 13*, 159–188.

Vellutino, F. R., & Scanlon, D. M. (2002). The interactive strategies approach to reading intervention. *Contemporary Educational Psychology, 27*, 573–635.

Vellutino, F. R., Scanlon, D. M., & Lyon, G. R. (2000). Differentiating between difficult-to-remediate and readily remediated poor readers: More evidence against the IQ-achievement discrepancy definition of reading disability. *Journal of Learning Disabilities, 33*(3), 223–238.

Wagner, R. K., & Torgesen, J. K. (1987). The nature of phonological processing and its causal role in the acquisition of reading skills. *Psychological Bulletins, 101*(2), 192–212.

Wagner, R. K., Torgesen, J. K., Laughton, P., Simmons, K., & Rashotte, C. A. (1993). Development of young readers' phonological processing abilities. *Journal of Educational Psychology, 85*(1), 83–103.

Woodcock, R. W. (1990). Theoretical foundations of the WJ-R measures of cognitive ability. *Journal of Psychoeducational Assessment, 8*, 231–258.

Woodcock, R. W. (1993). An information processing view of *Gf-Gc* theory. *Journal of Psychoeducational Assessment Monograph Series, 11*, 80–102.

Woodcock, R. W. (1994). Measures of fluid and crystallized intelligence. In R. J. Sternberg (Ed.), *The encyclopedia of human intelligence* (pp. 452–456). New York: Macmillan.

Woodcock, R. W., McGrew, K. S., & Mather, N. (2001). *Woodcock-Johnson III tests of achievement*. Itasca, IL: Riverside.

Yopp, H. K. (1988). The validity and reliability of phonemic awareness tests. *Reading Research Quarterly, 23*(2), 159–177.

Ysseldyke, J. (1990). Goodness of fit of the Woodcock-Johnson Psycho-Educational Battery—revised to the Horn-Cattell *Gf-Gc* theory. *Journal of Psychoeducational Assessment, 8*, 268–275.

DAWN P. FLANAGAN
St. John's University

INTELLIGENCE TESTING
INTELLIGENCE TESTING, HISTORY OF
INTELLIGENT TESTING

CATTELL, JAMES MCKEEN (1860–1944)

James McKeen Cattell was educated at Lafayette College in Pennsylvania and the University of Leipzig in Germany. He worked under Wilhelm Wundt at Leipzig and at Sir Francis Galton's psychological laboratory in London. He held the world's first professorship in psychology, at the University of Pennsylvania, and later was professor of psychology and head of the department of psychology at Columbia University (Woodworth, 1944).

A devoted researcher, Cattell conducted significant investigations in areas such as reaction time, perception, association, and individual differences. He developed numerous tests and coined the term mental tests. He studied the backgrounds and characteristics of eminent scientists, and published the widely used directory *Biographical Dictionary of American Men of Science.* To promote the practical application of psychology, he founded the Psychological Corporation and served as its president for many years. He also edited a number of influential journals, including the *American Journal of Psychology, Psychological Review,* and *Science.* Cattell, through his students, research, and writing and editing, was a major figure in the development of psychology as a profession in the United States (Watson, 1968).

REFERENCES

Watson, R. I. (1968). *The great psychologists.* New York: Lippincott.

Woodworth, R. S. (1944). James McKeen Cattell, 1860–1944. *Psychological Review, 51,* 201–209.

PAUL IRVINE
Katonah, New York

CAWLEY'S PROJECT MATH

Project MATH (Mathematics Activities for Teaching the Handicapped) is a comprehensive developmental mathematics program for children with special needs. The program was developed by Dr. John Cawley and his associates at the University of Connecticut under a federal grant operated from 1970 to 1975. The project was entitled "A Program Project Research and Demonstration Effort in Arithmetic Among the Mentally Handicapped"; it is available commercially.

The teaching model used in the curriculum is called the *Interactive Unit* (IU). This teaching model allows for the presentation of information to the learner in four different ways and also allows the learner to respond to questions or information in four different ways. There are 16 possible interactions that can take place between the teacher and the learner for any concept being taught. No interaction is considered to be cognitively superior to another. The interactive unit teaching model offers several advantages for the instructor. Chief among these advantages is that the model allows an instructor to teach around a disability. Learners who have difficulty in reading or writing may be taught by any of the remaining nine interaction possibilities. The instructor components of the IU are state, construct, present, and graphically symbolize. The learner components are state, construct, identify, and graphically symbolize.

The goal of the curriculum is to give a balanced emphasis to the development of skills, concepts, and social growth. The content of the math strands addressed are patterns, numbers, operations, measurements, fractions, and geom-

etry. There are multiple lessons and support materials for concepts taught in each strand. A math concept inventory accompanies each level of the curriculum. This inventory is essentially a criterion-referenced test used to make initial placement decisions in the curriculum and to measure growth.

The verbal problem solving component of the curriculum is unique in that problem solving is introduced at the lowest level of the curriculum (Level I) and is carried out in an increasingly complex manner in the remaining levels. Problem solving is viewed as the ultimate objective of the mathematics curriculum. Unlike most mathematics programs, reading is not an essential prerequisite for entry into the verbal problem-solving exercises; the need for computational skills is also minimized. The focus of the verbal problem-solving component is on the processing of information necessary for the solution, not on the practice of computational skills. Levels I and II use sets of pictures, cards, and prepared scripts to guide a teacher and learner through the problem-solving activities. In Level III, reading is required for the first time. The use of extraneous information and language plays a major role in the problem-solving activities.

The final component of the Cawley's Project MATH curriculum consists of *Social Utilization Units.* These units are real-life extensions of the verbal problem-solving exercises; they require teams of learners to use mathematics to solve real-life problems. The units also stress social responsibility in that each member of the team is responsible for performing a task or gathering information so that the team's problem can be solved.

Two years of field testing, from 1972 to 1974, was undertaken. It involved 1,917 children instructed by 116 teachers in seven states. In addition to the curricular development thrust of the project, a large number of research studies were undertaken and published, primarily in the area of verbal problem solving. Cawley has continued to build on the Project MATH materials and to expand the basic model so that it can be used by a wide variety of special educators (Thornton, 1995). Cawley continues to develop ways to reduce the inconvenience between special and general education mathematics instruction (Palmer & Cawley, 1995), and examines the MATH performance of students from different economic backgrounds (Pacer Center, 2005).

REFERENCES

Cawley, J. F. (Ed.). (1984). *Developmental teaching of mathematics for the learning disabled.* Rockville, MD: Aspen Systems.

Cawley, J. F. (Ed.). (1985). *Secondary school mathematics for the learning disabled.* Rockville, MD: Aspen Systems.

Cawley, J. F., Goodstein, H. A., Fitzmaurice, A. M., Lepore, A., Sedlak, R. A., & Althaus, V. (1976, 1977). *Project MATH: Mathematics activities for teaching the handicapped: Levels I–V.* Tulsa, OK: Educational Progress Corporation.

Goodstein, H. A. (1981). Are the errors we see the true errors? Error analysis in verbal problem solving. *Topics in Learning and Learning Disabilities, 1*(3), 31–45.

Pacer Center. (2005). *Standards-based reform.* Retrieved from http://www.pacer.org/text/legislation/idea/sbReform.htm

Palmer, R. S., & Cawley, J. F. (1995). Mathematics curricula frameworks: Goals for general and special education. *Focus on Learning Problems in Mathematics, 17,* 2, 50–66.

Thornton, C. A. (1995). Promising research, programs, and projects. *Teaching Children Mathematics, 2,* 2, 134–135.

ROBERT A. SEDLAK
University of Wisconsin at Stout

MATHEMATICS, LEARNING DISABILITIES IN
MATHEMATICS, REMEDIAL

CENTER FOR APPLIED SPECIAL TECHNOLOGY

The Center for Applied Special Technology (CAST) is a nonprofit organization founded in 1984, with the mission of expanding opportunities for people with disabilities through the development of and innovative uses of technology. Center activities include research, product development, and work with educational settings in the service of furthering universal design for learning. In its early years, CAST sought to help people with disabilities through the development and provision of assistive technology on the individual level; however, they realized that this approach by itself kept the burden of adapting to a disability on each individual, and failed to address systemically the many barriers that the vast majority of learners with disabilities encounter.

As a result, CAST now works from the premise that the most effective way to expand educational opportunities is " . . . through universal design for learning. The phrase 'universal design' refers to the creation of computer software and learning models that are usable by everyone, including individuals of all ages, whether they are gifted, are typical learners, or have special needs" (CAST, 1998).

The CAST offices are located at 39 Cross Street, Suite 201, Peabody, MA 01960, and may be reached at (978) 531-8555, or (978) 538-3110 (TTY).

REFERENCE

Center for Applied Special Technology. (1998). *About CAST—Mission and history.*

KAY E. KETZENBERGER
*The University of Texas of the
Permian Basin*

CENTILE SCORES

See PERCENTILE SCORES.

CENTRAL AUDITORY DYSFUNCTION

Central auditory dysfunction is a term used to describe a broad spectrum of difficulties that may arise when an individual attempts to process an auditory signal. This disorder occurs even in people without measurable hearing loss. The term implies that when an individual has normal hearing status, but exhibits certain difficulties in correctly interpreting an auditory signal, there is some type of damage in the brain.

During the past three decades, a number of tests were devised to evaluate the integrity of the central auditory processing mechanism. These measures were used to evaluate the auditory processing of adults with anatomical lesions. Generally, these tests presented speech signals that reduced redundancy and made listening more difficult. It was found in a series of correlational studies that the performance of adults with known lesions was poorer than that of normal adults (Berlin & Lowe, 1972). It was then assumed that children who also performed poorly on similar tests suffered from some type of central auditory dysfunction (Keith, 1988). In the past 30 years, there have been attempts to determine whether children with language disorders also have a central auditory dysfunction. If they did, the question pertains to the relationship between the two and what remedial strategies could be used successfully. Language acquisition, language disorders of various types, and learning disabilities have all been considered to be directly related to various types of central auditory dysfunction (Cherry, 1992; Garstecki & Erler, 1997).

Two basic types of tests are given to evaluate the central auditory functioning of an individual. The first type is designed to evaluate the auditory neuromaturational level of the individual. Keith (1981) suggests that these tests should (1) not be loaded with language comprehension items; (2) not require linguistic manipulation of the signal; (3) not require, or least minimize, cross-modal input or response; (4) use nonlinguistic signal; and (5) be primarily a speech imitative task using nonmeaningful material or speech material so familiar that comprehension plays no role in the process. To that end, Keith (1986) developed a Central Auditory Processing Disorder (CAPD) assessment instrument called the SCAN: A Screening Test for Auditory Processing Disorders. The SCAN includes three subtests: a filtered word test, an auditory figure-ground test, and a competing word test. The SCAN was originally normed on children ages 3 to 11 (Cherry, 1992). Another CAPD test, the Selective Auditory Attention Test (SAAT) was developed by Cherry (1980). The SAAT is used to assess auditory distractibility and Attention Deficit Hyperactivity Disorder. The SAAT includes two subtests, a monosyllabic word test given in quiet and a similar monosyllabic word list with a semantic distractor. Keith (1988) also suggested that tests of CAPD include:

1. *Auditory localization.* Generally children are able to localize at a very early age so any normal child past infancy should be able to localize without difficulty.

2. *Binaural synthesis.* An example of this test is the Rapidly Alternating Speech Perception Test, where sentences are switched rapidly from one ear to the other. If the child has difficulty with this test, there may be a lesion located in the brainstem.

3. *Binaural separation.* The Staggered Spondaic Word Test is used to determine whether the child shows ear dominance or whether the left ear score increases with age. Dichotic listening tests are also included in this category to determine whether children are establishing hemispheric dominance. A failure to do so may imply a neurological basis for a learning, reading, or language problem.

4. *Resistance to distortion.* Three types of tests are generally used in this category: speech in noise, filtered speech, and time-compressed speech. Individuals with normal central auditory functioning generally have no difficulty with these tasks, but when there is a specific lesion or other auditory abnormality, the individual will have difficulty in understanding speech with reduced redundancy.

Keith (1988) notes that these tests are only to be used after language has emerged. He also notes that the tests have substantial maturational effects up until about age of 12. Research has indicated that there are children with no apparent language or learning difficulties who perform poorly on these tests. Likewise, there are children with such difficulties who have no problems with the tests. Keith cautions that while these tests might find some indication of the neurologic status of a child, they do not indicate specific language, learning, or reading deficits. Further, they do not in themselves suggest any particular remediation strategy.

The second type of test can be categorized as auditory-language tests. These tests are heavily loaded both cognitively and linguistically. Examples are tests in which the child must point to a series of pictures in the order in which the words are heard. It should be noted that this task is not simply a single-factor auditory-perceptual test, but requires memory and comprehension. Another example of an auditory-language test is one that asks the child to listen to a word with a phoneme missing, and then identify the missing phoneme. This is a complex language-mediated task requiring the child to analyze a distorted signal. Another frequently administered test, the Goldman-Fristoe-Woodcock Test of Auditory Discrimination Noise Subtest, contains a similarly difficult task. The child must use visual perception, auditory-visual association, and an auditory-visual-motor response with a vocabulary that may not be familiar.

While noting that a number of children with language problems do poorly on tests of central auditory functioning, Rees (1981) observes that it is not at all clear whether the deficits actually produce the language disorders or whether they are simply behavioral correlates of these and other disabilities. She further criticizes these tests, stating that "no one has developed an intelligible account of how these central auditory processing skills, or the lack of them, relate to language acquisition or academic learning" (p. 118). She considers the tests that are heavily loaded with linguistic and cognitive material to be tests designed more to evaluate an individual child's metalinguistic ability (the ability to analyze and talk about language) than to measure directly the child's ability to learn language. While these tasks may be good indicators of the individual child's ability to function successfully in school, she questions whether they have a fundamental relationship with central auditory processing. Rees notes that in some ways all the phenomena that have been clustered under the rubric of central auditory functioning have only one thing in common. They all involve data taken in through the ear.

In summary, central auditory dysfunction refers to problems individuals may exhibit in processing an auditory signal even when they have no specific hearing loss. When adults with known brain lesions were asked to perform specific tasks, related to auditory functioning, it was found that they exhibited specific problems. Some children with learning problems performed similarly on tests of auditory processing. It was presumed they also might have some kind of brain damage. Two types of tests are given to test auditory functioning. The first evaluates auditory maturational level. The second tests language-related auditory functions. It is not clear whether there is a cause-and-effect relationship between auditory functioning and learning disorders.

REFERENCES

Berlin, C., & Lowe, S. S. (1972). Temporary and dichotic factors in central auditory testing. In J. Katz (Ed.), *Handbook of clinical audiology, 4th edition.* Baltimore: Williams and Wilkins.

Cherry, R. (1980). *Selective Auditory Attention Test (SAAT).* St. Louis, MO: Auditec of St. Louis.

Cherry, R. (1992). Screening and evaluation of central auditory processing disorders in young children. In J. Katz, N. Steckler, & D. Henderson (Eds.), *Central auditory processing: A transdisciplinary view* (pp. 129–140). St. Louis, MO: Mosby.

Garstecki, D. C., & Erler, S. F. (1997). Hearing loss management in children and adults. In G. T. Mencher, S. E. Gerber, & A. McCombe (Eds.), *Audiology and auditory dysfunction* (pp. 220–232). Needham Heights, MA: Allyn & Bacon.

Keith, R. W. (1981). *Central auditory and language disorders in children.* San Diego: College Hill.

Keith, R. W. (1986). *SCAN: A screening test for auditory processing disorders.* San Diego: The Psychology Corp.

Keith, R. W. (1988). Central auditory tests. In L. N. McReynolds & D. Yoder (Eds.), *Handbook of speech language pathology and audiology* (pp. 1215–1236). Toronto: BC Decker.

Rees, N. S. (1981). Saying more than we know: Is auditory processing a meaningful concept? In R. W. Keith (Ed.), *Central auditory and language disorders in children* (pp. 94–120). San Diego: College Hill.

CAROLYN L. BULLARD
Lewis & Clark College
First edition

KATHLEEN M. CHINN
New Mexico State University
Second edition

AUDITORY ABNORMALITIES
AUDITORY DISCRIMINATION
AUDITORY PERCEPTION
AUDITORY-VISUAL INTEGRATION

CENTRAL NERVOUS SYSTEM

The central nervous system (CNS) refers to the brain, including the cerebral cortex, cranial nerves, cerebellum, spinal cord, and other subcortical structures contained within the cranial vault. It consists of more than 100 billion neurons and approximately 10 times that number of glial cells. The cerebral cortex represents the CNS structure underlying most adaptive behavior, including sensation, perception, judgment, intellective functioning, and purposeful movement. Divided into two cerebral hemispheres, the respective cerebral cortices tend to be differentiated in terms of functions. As with other CNS structures that develop embryologically from the prosencephalon, the cerebral hemispheres have contralateral representation (i.e., the left side of the cortex controls the right side of the body, and vice versa). Each cerebral hemisphere is divided into anterior and posterior regions by the central sulcus or fissure of Rolando. Those cortical areas just anterior to the Rolandic fissure are specialized for motor functions, with motor enervation proceeding from superior areas of the motor strip, which control lower extremity movement, downward to more inferior areas, which control movement of the face. Just posterior to the Rolandic fissure is the sensory area, which controls such phenomena as sensitivity to stimulation for body areas corresponding to those enervated by the motor strip.

In addition to lateralized representation of motor and sensory functions, the cerebral cortex areas are also specialized for processing given types of information, and for processing information in given ways. In essentially all right-handed and in most left-handed individuals, the left cerebral hemisphere is more efficient in processing verbal or linguistic types of information, with the right hemisphere more specialized for the processing of spatial types of information. This specialization of function can be demonstrated in normal individuals by injecting fast-acting barbiturate types of drugs such as sodium amytal into a selected cerebral hemisphere. Following such an injection to the left cerebral hemisphere, for example, individuals will normally experience a brief period of aphasia, during which they are both unable to comprehend spoken language and to formulate verbalizations. Within a few minutes, all verbal functions return to preinjection levels. Similar temporary impairment of spatial function is demonstrated on right hemisphere injection (Hartlage & Flanigin, 1982).

In addition to specialization for type and process of cognitive information processing, the cerebral hemispheres also mediate differentiated emotional functions. Damage, deprivation of blood supply, unilateral electroconvulsive treatment, and depressant medication all have been shown to result in different emotional responses for each cerebral hemisphere. Insult to the right cerebral hemisphere produces what has been called the "la belle indifference syndrome," characterized by poor monitoring of behavior and euphoria. Insult to the left hemisphere produces the "catastrophic reaction," characterized by depression (Robertson & Inglis, 1973; Schwartz, Davidson, & Maer, 1975; Tucker, 1981).

Anatomically, the cerebral hemispheres are divided into four lobes. The frontal lobes are separated posteriorly from the parietal lobes by the central sulcus, and from the temporal lobes by the Sylvan fissure, which also separates the superiorly located parietal lobes from the temporal lobes. The occipital notch, at the posterior end of the parietal lobes, divides the parietal lobes from the occipital lobes. An approach to further subclassification of the cerebral hemispheres is the cytoarchitectural system of Brodmann, in which discrete areas of the cerebral cortices are divided into 52 Brodmann areas (Krieg, 1957) and are referred to and identified by numbers corresponding to those locations. For example, "Brodmann's area 8" corresponds to the frontal eye fields.

There is good evidence that in most individuals the cerebral hemispheres are not symmetrical (Geschwind & Levitsky, 1968; Von Bonin, 1962). This asymmetry has been related to differences in facility with processing certain types of information and other psychological characteristics (Lansdell & Smith, 1975; Levy, 1974; Reynolds, 1981; Reynolds, Kamphaus, Rosenthal, & Hiemenz, 1997). This hemispheric asymmetry has been postulated as being etiologic in certain mental disorders such as schizophrenia (Gruzelier, 1984; Newlin, Carpenter, & Golden, 1981), autism (Colby & Parkinson, 1977; Dawson, Warrenburg, & Fuller, 1982), and a number of other maladaptive behaviors (Sandel & Alcorn, 1980).

Separating the right and left cerebral hemispheres is the corpus callosum, which contains many fibers that convey impulses between the hemispheres. Right-handed individuals have a somewhat smaller corpus callosum than do individuals who are left handed or with mixed hand dominance. This phenomenon may be related to greater hemispheric specialization in strongly right-handed individuals (Witelson, 1985).

Although much adaptive behavior is attributed to the cerebral hemispheres, other portions of the central nervous system mediate behaviors of crucial importance to the individual. The 12 cranial nerves (olfactory, optic, oculomotor, trochlear, trigeminal, abducens, facial, acoustic, glossopharyngeal, vagus, accessory, and hypoglossal) control such functions as smell, visual acuity, eye movement, facial sensation and movement, and hearing.

The cerebellum, located posteriorly and partially under the occipital lobe, with connections to many portions of the cerebral cortex, is involved with balance and with coordination of some motor activities (because some areas of the cerebellum are uniquely sensitive to the effects of alcohol, law enforcement officers often check some aspects of cerebellar function when screening drivers suspected of intoxication). A number of brain areas often referred to as subcortical (e.g., amygdala, hippocampus, thalamus) because of their location under the cortex, have been identified as playing important roles in such behaviors as emotion, memory, movement, and the integration of information from diverse cortical areas (Riklan & Levita, 1965). The medulla, that portion of the central nervous system that bridges with the spinal cord, is more involved with lower sensory and motor functions than with higher cognitive abilities.

Although some areas of the CNS have been shown to be crucial for the performance of given tasks, the CNS functions in an interrelated way for the execution of most complex tasks. Damage to the CNS will almost always result in a complex disorder requiring special educational services.

REFERENCES

Colby, K. M., & Parkinson, C. (1977). Handedness in autistic children. *Journal of Autism and Childhood Schizophrenia, 7,* 3–9.

Dawson, G., Warrenburg, S., & Fuller, D. (1982). Cerebral lateralization in individuals diagnosed as autistic in early childhood. *Brain and Language, 15,* 353–368.

Geschwind, N., & Levitsky, W. (1968). Human brain: Left-right asymmetries in temporal speech region. *Science, 161,* 186–187.

Gruzelier, J. H. (1984). Hemispheric imbalances in schizophrenia. *International Journal of Psychophysiology, 1,* 227–240.

Hartlage, L. C., & Flanigin, H. (1982, October). *An abbreviated intracarotical amytal testing procedure.* Paper presented at the annual meeting of the National Academy of Neuropsychologists, Atlanta, GA.

Krieg, W. J. S. (1957). *Brain mechanisms in diachrome* (2nd ed.). Evanston, IL: Brain Books.

Lansdell, H., & Smith, F. J. (1975). Asymmetrical cerebral function for two WAIS factors and their recovery after brain injury. *Journal of Consulting and Clinical Psychology, 43,* 931.

Levy, H. (1974). Psychological implications of bilateral asymmetry. In S. J. Dimond & J. G. Beaumont (Eds.), *Hemispheric function in the human brain.* London: Elek Science.

Newlin, D. B., Carpenter, B., & Golden, C. (1981). Hemispheric asymmetries in schizophrenia. *Biological Psychiatry, 16,* 561–581.

Reynolds, C. R. (1981). The neuropsychological basis of intelligence. In G. Hynd & J. Obrzut (Eds.), *Neuropsychological assessment of the school aged child: Issues and procedures.* New York: Grune & Stratton.

Reynolds, C. R., Kamphaus, R. W., Rosenthal, B. L., & Hiemenz, J. R. (1997). Applications of the Kaufman Assessment Battery for Children (K-ABC) in neuropsychological assessment. In C. R. Reynolds & E. Fletcher-Janzen (Eds.), *Handbook of clinical child neuropsychology* (2nd ed.). New York: Plenum.

Riklan, M., & Levita, E. (1965). Laterality of subcortical involvement and psychological functions. *Psychological Bulletin, 64,* 217–224.

Robertson, A. D., & Inglis, J. (1973). Cerebral asymmetry and electroconvulsive therapy. *Proceedings of the 81st Annual Convention of the American Psychological Association, 8,* 431–432.

Sandel, A., & Alcorn, J. (1980). Individual hemispherity and maladaptive behaviors. *Journal of Abnormal Psychology, 9,* 514–517.

Schwartz, G. E., Davidson, R. J., & Maer, F. (1975). Right hemisphere lateralization for emotion in the human brain: Interactions with cognition. *Science, 190,* 286–288.

Tucker, D. M. (1981). Lateral brain function emotion, and conceptualization. *Psychological Bulletin, 89,* 19–46.

Von Bonin, G. (1962). Anatomical asymmetries of the cerebral hemispheres. In V. B. Mountcastle (Ed.), *Interhemispheric relations and cerebral dominance* (pp. 1–6). Baltimore: Johns Hopkins Press.

Witelson, S. F. (1985). The brain connection: The corpus callosum is larger in left handers. *Science, 229,* 665–668.

LAWRENCE C. HARTLAGE
Evans, Georgia

APHASIA
BRAIN ORGANIZATION
CEREBRAL DOMINANCE
CEREBRAL FUNCTION, LATERALIZATION OF
LEFT BRAIN/RIGHT BRAIN

CENTRAL PROCESSING DYSFUNCTIONS IN CHILDREN

The world is a colorful, noisy, and interesting place. To learn and respond to the world around them, infants, children, adolescents, and adults receive information about their world through the senses of vision, hearing, smell, touch, and bodily movement.

The brain serves as a center for: (1) receiving incoming sensations from the eyes, ears, skin, muscles, and internal organs; (2) analyzing and organizing sensory information; (3) interpreting or giving meaning to the sensory information that is being received; (4) generating messages to send to all parts of the body for purposes of responding; and (5) storing information for later use (Chalfant & Scheffelin, 1969).

When the brain does not function properly in receiving, analyzing, and storing sensory information or sending messages to the bodily parts, a dysfunction is said to exist. Because the brain is part of the central nervous system, which processes sensory information, a breakdown in this system is often referred to as a central processing dysfunction.

Central processing dysfunctions can be caused by damage to the brain, but brain damage is not always the cause. There are many cases in which individuals behave as if they had a central processing dysfunction, but show no evidence of brain damage. All of the causes of central processing dysfunctions are not yet known.

There are three major systems in which a central processing dysfunction might occur: the visual processing system, the auditory processing system, and the haptic processing system. Symptoms of dysfunctions in these systems follow.

With visual processing dysfunctions, a student may have normal visual acuity but have difficulty processing and obtaining meaning from visual information. Some of the major characteristics of visual processing dysfunctions are difficulty in (1) attending to or focusing on what is seen; (2) seeing the difference between printed numbers, letters, and words; (3) learning spatial relationships such as left-right, up-down, far-near; (4) distinguishing a figure or object from the background within which it is embedded; (5) reorganizing a whole when one or more of its parts are missing, as in constructing a puzzle; (6) remembering what has been seen; and (7) responding quickly to visual stimuli. Visual processing dysfunctions may result in academic learning disabilities in reading, writing, and arithmetic (Kirk & Chalfant, 1984).

In auditory processing dysfunctions, a student may have normal hearing, but have difficulty in processing what is heard. Auditory processing dysfunctions are characterized by difficulty in (1) listening or attending to sound; (2) locating the origin or source of sound; (3) hearing the differences or similarities between pitch, loudness, rhythm, melody, rate, or duration of sounds; (4) listening to a teacher's instructions (figure) through the interferences of classroom noises (background); (5) reorganizing a spoken word when only part of the word is heard, e.g., telepho—; (6) remembering what has been heard; and (7) associating sounds to experiences such as "ding-dong" to a bell. Dysfunctions in auditory processing may result in learning disabilities in understanding spoken language, expressing oneself through oral language, forming concepts, and developing abstract thinking skills (Kirk & Chalfant, 1984).

In the haptic processing system, the term haptic processing refers to the information received from both touch and movement. Dysfunctions in the haptic system will result in difficulty in performing fine motor tasks such as writing, manipulating tools and equipment, or learning motor performance skills. There are two subsystems for haptic processing (Gibson, 1965). The first subsystem is the tactile or cutaneous one. If a dysfunction exists in the tactile system, difficulties may be experienced in (1) being sensitive to the presence of pressure or textures on the skin; (2) reorganizing objects through the sense of touch; (3) perceiving information about surface areas, sizes, shapes, boundaries, angles, etc.; and (4) being sensitive to pressure or aware of pain. Children with difficulties in the tactile system will have difficulty performing any task that requires the coordinated use of fingers such as learning to button or use a knife, fork, or spoon, or writing.

The second subsystem is the kinesthetic one. Bodily movement such as the movement of fingers, toes, arms, legs, head, lower jaw, tongue, and trunk, provides information about the body itself. Movement also provides information about direction and the location of objects in the environment in relation to the body itself. Muscular efforts such as lifting, pulling, and pushing objects give information about the weight of objects and gravity. Dysfunctions in the kinesthetic system result in difficulty in learning movement patterns such as crawling, walking, eating, dressing, undressing, writing, and riding a bicycle, or those needed for competing in sports activities (Kirk & Chalfant, 1984).

In summary, central processing dysfunctions can have a wide range of impact on a child or student. Young children often will be delayed in developing an understanding of and the use of oral language, visual-motor coordination, and/or cognitive abilities such as attention, discrimination, memory, conceptualization, and problem-solving skills. Students of school age may present academic disabilities in reading, writing, spelling, or arithmetic.

REFERENCES

Chalfant, J. C., & Scheffelin, M. A. (1969). *Central processing dysfunction in children: A review of research* (NINDS Monograph No. 9). Washington, DC: U.S. Department of Health, Education, and Welfare.

Gibson, J. J. (1965). *The senses considered as perceptual systems.* Boston: Houghton Mifflin.

Kirk, S. A., & Chalfant, J. C. (1984). *Academic and developmental learning disabilities*. Denver: Love.

JAMES C. CHALFANT
University of Arizona

BRAIN DAMAGE/INJURY
LEARNING DISABILITIES
LEARNING DISABILITIES, PROBLEMS IN DEFINITION OF
LEARNING STYLES

CENTRAL TENDENCY

Measures of central tendency are used to describe the typical or average score in a sample or population of scores. Many measures of central tendency exist, but the three most popularly used in the behavioral sciences are the mean, the median, and the mode.

The mean is the most widely used measure of central tendency. It is the arithmetic average of a given set of scores. For example, given the set of scores 87, 96, 98, 110, 113, 114, 119, the mean is 105.29, the sum of the seven scores divided by the number of scores, seven.

The median of a set of scores is the score that divides the set into two groups with each group containing the same number of scores. To compute the median, first rank the set of scores from smallest to largest. When the number of scores is odd and there are no ties, the median is the middle score. For example, the median of the above scores is 110. When the number of scores is even, with no ties, the median is the average of the two middle scores. Thus, the median score of 87, 96, 98, 110, 113, 114, 119, 120 is 110 + 113/2 = 111.50.

The mode is the score that occurs most frequently in a set of scores. For the scores 87, 96, 98, 98, 98, 110, 113, 114, 119, the mode is 98. When there are two modes, the distribution of scores is said to be bimodal. All three measures may be used when the data are quantitative. The median and mode are used with ranked data, whereas only the mode is applicable to nominal data.

The mean is the preferred measure of central tendency when the variable measured is quantitative and the distribution is relatively symmetric. It is relatively stable and reflects the value of every score in the distribution and, unlike the median and the mode, it is amenable to arithmetic and algebraic manipulations. These qualities make the mean useful not only for describing the average of a set of scores, but also for making inferences about population means. We can infer the value of the population mean from the sample mean, and also make inferences about the differences between population means for the same or different groups of individuals on one or more variables. When the distribution of scores is skewed, or the variable being measured is qualitative, the mean is not the preferred measure of central tendency.

For skewed distributions, the median is used. This is because the median is not affected by the scores falling above and below it. For example, the median of the scores 109, 108, 107, 106, 60 is 107; it more accurately reflects the typical score than the mean of 98. Inferences about the population median may also be concluded (see Marascuilo & McSweeney, 1977).

When the distribution is symmetric and unimodal, the median, mean, and mode are the same. When the distribution is skewed, however, the median and mean are unequal with median > mean in negatively skewed distributions and mean > median in positively skewed distributions.

REFERENCES

Glass, G. V., & Hopkins, K. D. (1984). *Statistical methods in education and psychology* (2nd ed.). Englewood Cliffs, NJ: Prentice Hall.

Hays, W. L. (1981). *Statistics* (3rd ed.). New York: Holt, Rinehart and Winston.

Kirk, R. E. (1984). *Elementary statistics* (2nd ed.). Monterey, CA: Brooks/Cole.

MacGillivray, H. L. (1985). Mean, median, mode, and skewness. In S. Kotz, N. L. Johnson, & C. B. Read (Eds.), *Encyclopedia of the statistical sciences* (Vol. 5). New York: Wiley.

Marascuilo, L. A., & McSweeney, M. (1977). *Nonparametric and distribution-free methods for the social sciences*. Monterey, CA: Brooks/Cole.

GWYNETH M. BOODOO
Texas A&M University

STANDARD DEVIATION

CEREBELLAR DISORDERS

The cerebellum is an oval-shaped portion of the brain under the occipital lobe of the cerebrum and behind the brain stem. It has a right and left hemisphere and a central section. The cerebellum integrates information vital to the control of posture and voluntary movement. The cerebellum is responsible for maintaining equilibrium and trunk balance; regulating muscle tension, spinal nerve reflexes, posture, and balance of the limbs; and regulating fine movements initiated by the frontal lobes.

Persons with cerebellar dysfunction may show any or all of the following deficits: wide-based clumsy gait; tremor on attempted motion; clumsy, rapid alternating movements; inability to control the range of voluntary movements with overshooting the goal most common; low muscle tone; and scanning speech with inappropriate accenting of syllables. Rapid alternating eye movements (nystagmus) may be observed as a component of closely associated vestibular involvement.

Tumors of the cerebellum, heavy metal poisoning, repeated high fever or head trauma, and hypothyroidism can affect the cerebellum directly. The cerebellum receives postural and movement information from many parts of the brain, integrates them, and sends information out to motor coordinating areas, therefore the function of the cerebellum may be impaired by a wide range of neurological conditions. Multiple sclerosis, blood clots, and congenital anomalies of other parts of the brain can influence the cerebellum via input/output tracts as well. The spinocerebellar diseases are a family of degenerative hereditary diseases that affect (to varying degrees) the cerebellum, spinal cord, brain stem, and other parts of the nervous system. Most of these diseases have their onset in childhood, are slowly progressive, and have no known specific inheritance patterns, cause, or treatment, although in some individual family studies clinical findings and inheritance patterns are consistent. It is believed that inherited biochemical abnormalities are causal, and some have been identified. Some diseases in this category with early onset, rapid progression, and strong familial tendencies are Marie's ataxia, Roussy-Levy syndrome, and Friedreich's ataxia. Although progression results in clumsiness, poor balance, later use of a wheelchair for safety, slurred speech, and loss of skilled hand function, there is usually no related impairment to intelligence.

Friedreich's ataxia is a hereditary disease of unknown origin with symptoms of frequent falling, clumsiness, and incoordination (ataxia) beginning between age 5 and 25. Slurred speech, swallowing difficulty, contractures, deformities, and weakness typically result in the need to use a wheelchair within 5 to 10 years. The lack of intellectual impairment is often in considerable contrast to the severity of the physical impairments, a circumstance that represents a challenge to educators to provide stimulating instruction within the limitations presented by the child's deteriorating physical condition. Occupational, physical, and speech therapists can provide useful adaptive support techniques to the child's teachers and family so that optimal function can continue as long as possible. Clinical experience has shown that these children are vulnerable because of their insight into the progressive nature of their disease. Anxiety, anger, and depression may occur, and such feelings may be exacerbated by observing the struggles and deaths of elder siblings. The impact on family life when several siblings have Friedreich's ataxia is profound. Since the average onset age is 13 years, a family may have a number of children before the eldest has symptoms and is diagnosed. Clinical experience suggests that early admission of all symptomatic family members to special education programs where supportive related services are available can help normalize adaptive responses and provide maximum comfort, safety, deformity prevention, and learning opportunities while prolonging activity. Estimates suggest that with proper management there may be 10 to 20 years of productivity following onset (Clark, 2003). Death frequently is due to progressive heart failure, medical complications, or effects of inactivity rather than the disease itself.

Dr. John C. Eccles (1973), a recognized authority on the cerebellum, believes that the relative simplicity of neuronal design, together with its well-defined action in control of movement, will result in the cerebellum becoming one of the first parts of the brain where linkage between structure and function can be documented. The rapid growth of specific knowledge about cerebellar diseases suggests that differential diagnosis by a skilled neurologist together with genetic studies when indicated are imperative in children with cerebellar disorders, as there are treatable conditions that may present symptoms similar to the degenerative disorders.

REFERENCES

Berkow, R. (Ed.). (1982). *The Merck manual of diagnosis and therapy* (14th ed.). Rahway, NJ: Merck, Sharp & Dohme.

Clark, E. (2003). Brain disorders & degenerative motor diseases. In E. Fletcher-Janzen & C. R. Reynolds (Eds.), *Childhood disorders diagnostic desk reference* (pp. 91–92). New York: Wiley.

Eccles, J. C. (1973). *The understanding of the brain.* New York: McGraw-Hill.

Stolov, W. C., & Clowers, M. R. (Eds.). (1981). *Handbook of severe disability* (stock #017-090-00054-2). Washington, DC: U.S. Government Printing Office.

RACHAEL J. STEVENSON
Bedford, Ohio

ATAXIA
BRAIN ORGANIZATION
FRIEDREICH'S ATAXIA

CEREBRAL DOMINANCE

Cerebral dominance refers to the asymmetrical lateralization of language and perceptual functions in the human brain. Cerebral dominance, or hemispheric specialization, was initially applied to language functions that are served by the left hemisphere in most individuals. However, the term was later expanded to include cognitive functions of nonverbal reasoning and visual-spatial information processing that are associated with the right hemisphere. In short, functions associated with the left hemisphere involve processing linguistic, analytical, and sequential information while the right hemisphere is responsible for processing nonlinguistic or spatial information in a holistic fashion (see Witelson, 1976).

Early reference to cerebral dominance can be traced back to Dax in 1836 and Broca in 1861; they found that damage to the left hemisphere results in disorders of speech and language. They believed that the left hemisphere is the dominant side for most people in that it controls the functions of language (Gaddes, 1980). The notion of cerebral dominance was further delineated by the writings of Jackson, who postulated that the left hemisphere is the dominant or the leading side and right hemisphere is the automatic and minor side (Dean, 1984). The emphasis in determining cerebral dominance for language was also noted by Orton (1937). He speculated that delayed or incomplete lateralization for linguistic functions by the left hemisphere results in the types of language disorders often seen in children.

Methods for assessing specializations of each hemisphere have employed invasive techniques such as direct electrical stimulation of the brain, hemispheric anesthetization, and split-brain studies. *Noninvasive procedures* have involved dichotic listening and split-visual field research.

Research using direct electric stimulation of the brain was pioneered by Penfield (Penfield & Roberts, 1959). This technique was developed to map the centers of the brain that controlled specific functions prior to surgical procedures. Since the brain does not contain pain receptors, the patient was conscious when a small electrical current was applied to the surface of the brain to determine areas of the brain associated with such functions as vision, hearing, olfaction, or haptic sensations. Applications of electrical stimulation to areas believed to control speech would be verified by the patient's inability to talk. These "aphasic arrests" would occur only when areas of the brain associated with speech were electrically stimulated. In this way, hypotheses about other functions of the brain could also be verified if responses associated with those functions were absent during stimulation.

Another invasive technique to study brain functioning has been to anesthetize one hemisphere by injecting sodium amytal in the carotid artery located on either the right or left side of the patient's neck. This procedure, known as the Wada test, quickly anesthetized that side of the brain. For example, if the left side or the side dominant for language was infused, the individual would become speechless while the drug was in effect, while the functions of the right hemisphere would remain intact. Wada and Rasmussen (1960) hypothesized that the left hemisphere is dominant for processing verbal information and the right hemisphere for nonverbal information. To demonstrate this, Wada and his associate injected sodium amytal into the left hemisphere and asked the patient to sing "Happy Birthday"; the patient was able to hum the tune without producing the words. When the right hemisphere was anesthetized and the patient was required to perform the same task, the patient was only able to recite the words of "Happy Birthday" in a monotone without producing a tune. Using this procedure, Milner (1974) found that 95 percent of right-handed and 70 percent of left-handed individuals are left hemisphere dominant for language.

Split-brain surgery or commissurotomy is another invasive technique used to study cerebral dominance. A commissurotomy is a surgical procedure used to stop the spread of seizure activity from a focal point in one hemisphere to the other hemisphere via the corpus callosum. This procedure involves the severing of the corpus callosum, a large band of nerve fibers that connects the left and right hemispheres, thereby preventing any communication between the hemispheres.

Much research was conducted by Speery in the 1950s. Researchers were able to localize functions of language, motoric control of the same or opposite sides of the body, and visual discrimination (Hacaen, 1981). In one study that examined visual perception, Levy and her associates (Levy, Trevarthen, & Speery, 1972) used stimulus figures in which the left half of one face was joined with the right half of another. The patient was required to gaze at a dot on the center of the screen before a figure was flashed on the screen. The presentation was such that each half of the face would be projected to only one hemisphere. When the patient was asked to respond by pointing to the correct picture from available alternatives, the left sides of faces, which are processed by the right hemisphere, were correctly chosen more often than the right sides regardless of the hand used for pointing. However, when the patient was required to verbally identify the picture, the face on the right side (left hemisphere) was chosen, although the number of errors made by this response mode was much higher. These results were subsequently replicated using other stimuli, suggesting that the right hemisphere is superior in processing nonverbal visual stimuli.

A noninvasive technique in the study of brain-behavior relationships has been dichotic listening. This procedure involves the simultaneous presentation of verbal or nonverbal information to each ear. Similar but different information is presented to each ear and the subject's task is to identify or recall what was heard. This technique was initially developed by Broadbent (1954) to study auditory attention and later adapted by Kimura (1961) to study cerebral lateralization. Studying normal individuals, Kimura found that subjects were more able to identify correctly verbal information when it was presented to the right ear (left hemisphere). If the information was nonverbal, however, a left-ear advantage (right hemisphere) was found. Kimura also showed that if patients having neurological disorders were found to be left hemisphere dominant for language (via the Wada test), a right-ear advantage was noted for verbal information. Similarly, if the patient was right hemisphere dominant for language, a left-ear advantage (right hemisphere) was found for verbal information. These findings suggested that superiority for each ear varies with the specialization in function for the opposite hemisphere.

Studies that have examined language lateralization for dyslexic children using a dichotic listening paradigm have found mixed results. Dyslexic or reading-disabled children are usually characterized by a significant lag in reading achievement despite average intelligence and an absence of any sensory-motor, neurological or emotional difficulties (Hynd & Cohen, 1983). Some studies (e.g., Witelson & Rabinovitch, 1972) have reported that children with dyslexia show a left-ear advantage for verbal information. Other researchers (e.g., Leong, 1976) have demonstrated a right-ear advantage for verbal information for both dyslexic and normal readers. Differential findings may be partially due to differences in methodology, criteria of subject selection, and age and attention effects (Hugdahl, Carlsson & Eichele, 2001).

Another noninvasive technique in studying cerebral dominance has been split-visual field research. This involves a tachistoscopic presentation of verbal or spatial information to either the right-half or left-half visual fields. The visual pathways are such that information perceived in the left-visual field is processed by the right hemisphere while right-visual field information is processed by the left hemisphere. Studies have demonstrated that while word recognition levels were lower for the dyslexic children when compared with normal readers, both readers showed a right-visual field superiority for words (Marcel & Rajan, 1975). However, when pictures were presented to either visual field, Witelson (1976) reported that while normal readers had a significant left visual-field advantage, this difference was not significant for a dyslexic group. These results suggest that while dyslexic readers, like normal readers, have a left-hemisphere representation for language, the dyslexic group appears to lack right-hemisphere specialization for visual-spatial information.

In sum, invasive and noninvasive techniques have made significant contributions in mapping functions of the brain. However, our knowledge of hemispheric specializations is far from complete. Given the inter-individual differences in cognitive processing, the brain's ability to compensate for damage, and developmental factors, the assessment of hemispheric specializations remains a complex and sometimes chaotic (Reynolds, Kamphaus, Rosenthal, & Hiemenz, 1997) endeavor.

REFERENCES

Broadbent, D. E. (1954). The role of auditory localization in attention and memory. *Journal of Experimental Psychology, 47,* 191–196.

Dean, R. S. (1984). Functional lateralization of the brain. *Journal of Special Education, 18,* 239–256.

Gaddes, W. H. (1980). *Learning disabilities and brain function: A neuropsychological approach.* New York: Springer-Verlag.

Hacaen, H. (1981). Apraxias. In S. B. Filskov & T. J. Boll (Eds.), *Handbook of clinical neuropsychology.* New York: Wiley.

Hugdahl, K., Carlsson, G., & Eichele, T. (2002). Age effects in dichotic listening to consonant-vowel syllables: Interactions with attention. *Developmental Neuropsychology, 20,* 445–457.

Hynd, G., & Cohen, M. (1983). *Dyslexia: Neuropsychological theory, research, and clinical differentiation.* New York: Grune & Stratton.

Jackson, J. H. (1874). On the duality of the brain. *Medical Press Circulator, 1,* 19, 41, 63.

Kimura, D. (1961). Cerebral dominance and the perception of verbal stimuli. *Canadian Journal of Psychology, 15,* 166–171.

Leong, C. K. (1976). Lateralization in severely disabled readers in relation to functional cerebral development and synthesis of information. In R. M. Knights & D. J. Bakker (Eds.), *Neuropsychology of learning disorders: Theoretical approaches.* Baltimore: University Park Press.

Levy, J., Trevarthen, C., & Speery, R. W. (1972). Perception of bilateral chimeric figures following hemispheric disconnection. *Brain, 95,* 61–78.

Marcel, T., & Rajan, P. (1975). Lateral specialization of recognition of words and faces in good and poor readers. *Neuropsychologia, 13,* 489–497.

Milner, B. (1974). Hemispheric specialization scope and limits. In F. O. Schmitt & F. G. Warden (Eds.), *The neurosciences: Third study programme.* Cambridge, MA: MIT Press.

Orton, S. T. (1937). *Reading, writing, and speech problems in children.* New York: Norton.

Penfield, W., & Roberts, L. (1959). *Speech and brain mechanisms.* Princeton, NJ: Princeton University Press.

Reynolds, C. R., Kamphaus, K. W., Rosenthal, B. L., & Hiemenz, J. R. (1997). Applications of the Kaufman Assessment Battery for Children in neuropsychological assessment. In C. R. Reynolds & E. Fletcher-Janzen (Eds.), *Handbook of clinical child neuropsychology* (2nd ed.). New York: Plenum.

Wada, J. A., & Rasmussen, T. (1960). Intracarotid injection of sodium amytal for lateralization of cerebral speech dominance: Experimental and clinical observations. *Journal of Neurosurgery, 17,* 266–282.

Witelson, S. F. (1976). Abnormal right hemisphere specialization in developmental dyslexia. In R. M. Knights & D. F. Bakker (Eds.), *Neuropsychology of learning disorders: Theoretical approaches.* Baltimore: University Park Press.

Witelson, S. F. & Rabinovitch, M. S. (1972). Hemispheric speech lateralization in children with auditory-linguistic deficits. *Cortex 8,* 412–426.

GURMAL RATTAN
Indiana University of Pennsylvania

RAYMOND S. DEAN
Ball State University
Indiana University School of Medicine

CEREBRAL FUNCTION, LATERALIZATION OF

The human brain is divided longitudinally into two distinct hemispheres. Research over the past century has confirmed early speculations (Broca, 1861; Dax, 1865) that each of these cerebral hemispheres serve specialized functions (Dean, 1984). Although anatomical differences have been identified between hemispheres at birth, more complex patterns of functional specialization may well continue to develop throughout childhood (Dean, 1985).

Our present understanding of the lateralization of functions in the cerebral cortex owes much to the early efforts of investigations of the late nineteenth century (e.g., Broca, 1861; Dax, 1865; Jackson, 1874). Based on case studies of patients with confirmed brain damage, a number of researchers (e.g., Broca, 1861) argued in favor of the localization of individual functions (e.g., speech) to specific structures of the brain. Moreover, it was generally reported during this time that with damage to the left cerebral hemisphere, one could expect impaired language functions (Broca, 1861; Dax, 1865). These early underpinnings of the notion of lateralization were further extended by Jackson (1874), who suggested that a lateralization of functions corresponds to the two hemispheres of the brain. Jackson (1874) argued that the left cerebral hemisphere is responsible for language-related functions, while the right hemisphere is the more automatic side, responsible for sensation and perception. The notion of hemispheric dominance grew out of such early arguments, which equated language lateralization in the left hemisphere with control functions. Although rather naive some hundred years later, the idea of hemispheric dominance continues in the literature. Clearly, these early case studies, which attempted to draw conclusions concerning the neuropsychology of normal individuals based on observations of patients with brain damage, were limited. However, the scientific interest stimulated by these reports in tandem with increasingly sophisticated approaches in research is responsible for the wealth of our present knowledge about the functioning of the brain.

While the differences in hemispheric functioning are acknowledged by most neuroscientists, the specific mechanism underlying these differences continues to be debated. At this point, it is not clear whether functional lateralization is related to differences in processing (e.g., Geschwind & Levitsky, 1968), storage (e.g., Dean, 1984), or attention (e.g., Kinsbourne, 1975). However, most researchers have found the arguments attributing observed differences to processing predisposition for the individual hemispheres compelling. From this point of view, the differences in functioning for the sides of the brain are due to biological differences in processing information that implicate the left hemisphere in language-related tasks and the right side in nonverbal elements.

Although communication between hemispheres is acknowledged, specific functional differences may be attributed to the individual hemispheres. Indeed, it is rather well established that the left hemisphere of the brain best processes information in a sequential, temporal, and analytic fashion. This may be likened to a verbal-sequential mode of thought in which information is represented, processed, and encoded with the aid of linguistic units (Dean, 1983; Paivio, 1971).

A second mode of thought may be seen to correspond to the functions of the right hemisphere. This mode is most clearly oriented toward processing visual information in a concrete, simultaneous, or holistic fashion (e.g., Sperry, 1974). Rather primitive when compared with the left, the right hemisphere seems predisposed to represent, reorganize, and encode visual-spatial elements (e.g., Dimond & Beaumont, 1974). Indeed, the use of imagery seems to be the most idiosyncratic expression of its processing (Seamon & Gazzaniga, 1973).

Hemispheric lateralization has been argued to be an interactive process in which the mode is dependent on the degree of cognitive reformulation, constraints of attention, and actual hemispheric differences in function (Dean, 1984; Gordon, 1974; Kinsbourne, 1997; Paivio, 1971). It has been suggested that normal individuals can employ different strategies that make differential use of one hemisphere or the other regardless of the form of the original stimulus (Dean, 1984). Clearly, information presented in a visual fashion may be encoded almost entirely in semantic terms (Conrad, 1964). So, too, it has been shown that verbal stimuli may be encoded and recalled as visual memory traces (Bower, 1970; Dean, 1983). As Dean (1984) points out, "even young learners can generate visual or verbal encoding strategies which correspond to hemispheric specific abilities regardless of the form of the original stimulus array" (p. 249). This point of view acknowledges independent cognitive processes served by each hemisphere while it stresses the importance of interhemispheric communication. It seems, therefore, that the verbal-nonverbal or left-right hemispheric differences may well be an exaggeration of reality. That is, cerebral lateralization may be more heuristically attributed to modes of processing information than to lateralization for specific stimuli. Therefore, the total task demands for the process of a given bit of information are necessary prior to assuming hemispheric lateralization.

The lateralization of functions is dependent in part on the degree to which cognitive processing is necessary for interpretation and encoding (e.g., Gordon, 1974). Indeed, few differences have been found between hemispheres for lower level information processing. For example, in the discrimination of sensory elements such as brightness, color, pressure, sharpness, pitch, and contour, little lateralization exists in processing (e.g., Dean, 1984; Rabinowicz, 1976). However, when learners are required to form generalizations, categorize, reorder, or integrate, or when they are called on to abstract common elements, clear hemispheric differences emerge. As would be expected, cerebral lateralization is dependent on the amount of interpretation or prior knowledge that the subject must draw on in dealing with the incoming information. Such cognitive processing enhances the degree to which functionally lateralized abilities are relied on (e.g., Moscovitch, 1979).

Although less than complete agreement exists among neuroscientists, it would seem that functional lateralization of cerebral hemispheres of the brain corresponds to the developmental pattern of consolidation that occurs from birth and progresses through adolescence (Dean, 1985). Dean (1984) argues that the rate of lateralization in the child varies with the specific function being examined. In keeping with this hypothesis, Krashen (1973) has offered data favoring a progressive decrease in the role played by the right cerebral hemisphere in verbal-analytic tasks with the child's increasing neurological development. The progressive lateralization of cerebral functions seems concomitant with the rate and variable progression in the maturation of the commissure-association cortex (Sperry, 1969).

Gender differences have been reported for the lateralization of cerebral functions. The force of the data in this area suggests less secure hemispheric specialization for females than for males (e.g., Witelson, 1976). Although anatomical gender differences exist (e.g., MacLusky & Naftolin, 1981), the functional differences found for males and females seem more heuristically attributed to organizational factors than differences in structure (e.g., Kolata, 1979). However, language lateralization develops and is localized similarly in males and females and does not seem to address cognitive differences usually found (Sommer, Aleman, Bouma, & Kahn, 2004). A convincing argument may be made for a genetic-hormonal cultural locus for observed gender differences (Dean, 1984).

In sum, the functioning of the left hemisphere seems predisposed to process information in a sequential, temporal, or analytic fashion; as such, language is an excellent tool for such forms of cognition. The right hemisphere, in contrast, is best prepared to function in a more simultaneous, holistic, or nonverbal fashion, with spatial reasoning and imagery being the most consistently reported mode of thought. This pattern corresponds with a large body of research in both cognitive psychology and the neurosciences. A good deal of interhemispheric communication should be recognized and functional lateralization is exhibited only as the individual must employ higher order cognitive skills in an attempt to comprehend or learn the incoming information.

REFERENCES

Bower, G. H. (1970). Analysis of a mnemonic device. *American Scientist, 58,* 496–510.

Broca, P. (1861). Nouvelle observation d'aphemie produite par une lesion de la moite posterieure des deuxieme et troiseme circonvolutions frontales. *Bulletin de la Society Anatomique de Paris, 36,* 398–407.

Conrad, R. (1964). Acoustic confusions in immediate memory. *British Journal of Psychology, 55,* 75–83.

Dax, G. (1865). Lesions de la moitie gauche de l'encephale coincident avec l'oubli des signes de la pensee. *Gazette Hebdomadaire de Medicine et de Chirurgie, 2,* 259–262.

Dean, R. S. (1983, February). *Dual processing of prose and cerebral laterality.* Paper presented at the annual meeting of the International Neuropsychological Society, Mexico City, Mexico.

Dean, R. S. (1984). Functional lateralization of the brain. *Journal of Special Education, 18*(3), 239–256.

Dean, R. S. (1985). Foundation and rationale for neuropsychological bases of individual differences. In L. C. Hartlage & C. F. Telzrow (Eds.), *The neuropsychology of individual differences: A developmental perspective.* New York: Plenum.

Dimond, S., & Beaumont, J. (1974). *Hemisphere function in the human brain.* London: Elek Scientific Books.

Geschwind, N., & Levitsky, W. (1968). Human brain: Left-right asymmetries in temporal speech region. *Science, 161,* 186–187.

Gordon, H. W. (1974). Auditory specialization of the right and left hemispheres. In M. Kinsbourne & W. L. Smith (Eds.), *Hemispheric disconnection and cerebral function.* Springfield, IL: Thomas.

Jackson, J. H. (1874). On the duality of the brain. In J. Taylor (Ed.), *Selected writings of John Hughlings Jackson, Vol. 2.* London: Hodder & Stoughton.

Kinsbourne, M. (1975). Cerebral dominance, learning, and cognition. In H. R. Myklebust (Ed.), *Progress in learning disabilities.* New York: Grune & Stratton.

Kinsbourne, M. (1997). Mechanisms and development of cerebral lateralization in children. In C. R. Reynolds & E. Fletcher-Janzen (Eds.), *Handbook of clinical child neuropsychology* (2nd ed.) New York: Plenum.

Kolata, G. B. (1979). Sex hormones and brain development. *Science, 205,* 985–987.

Krashen, S. D. (1973). Lateralization, language learning, and the critical period: Some new evidence. *Language Learning, 23,* 63–74.

MacLusky, N. J., & Naftolin, F. (1981). Sexual differentiation of the central nervous system. *Science, 211,* 1294–1302.

Moscovitch, M. (1979). Information processing and the cerebral hemispheres. In M. S. Gazzaniga (Ed.), *Handbook of behavioral neurobiology, Vol. 2: Neuropsychology.* New York: Plenum.

Paivio, A. (1971). *Imagery and verbal processes.* New York: Holt, Rinehart, & Winston.

Rabinowicz, B. H. (1976). *A non-lateralized auditory process in speech perception.* Unpublished master's thesis, University of Toronto.

Seamon, J. G., & Gazzaniga, M. D. (1973). Coding strategies and cerebral laterality effects. *Cognitive Psychology, 5,* 249–256.

Sommer, E. C., Aleman, A., Bouma, A., & Kahn, R. S. (2004). Do women really have more bilateral language representation than men? A meta-analysis of functional imaging studies. *Brain, 8,* 1845–1852.

Sperry, R. W. (1969). A modified concept of consciousness. *Psychological Review, 76,* 532–536.

Sperry, R. W. (1974). Lateral specialization in the surgically separated hemispheres. In F. O. Schmitt & F. G. Worden (Eds.), *The neurosciences: Third study program.* New York: Wiley.

Witelson, S. F. (1976). Early hemisphere specialization and interhemisphere plasticity: An empirical and theoretical review. In

S. Segalowitz & F. Gruber (Eds.), *Language and development and neurologic theory.* New York: Academic.

RAYMOND S. DEAN
*Ball State University
Indiana University School of
Medicine*

HEMISHERIC FUNCTIONS
LATERALITY
LEFT BRAIN/RIGHT BRAIN
NEUROPSYCHOLOGY

CEREBRAL INFARCTION

Cerebral infarction refers to the death of brain tissues resulting from a sudden onset of a circulation disorder that often leads to a neurological deficit. Infarction is caused by conditions of anoxia, hypoglycemia, or ischemia (Toole, 1984; Toole & Patel, 1974). Anoxic infarction results from a lack of oxygen to the brain, whereas hypoglycemic infarction occurs when an insufficient level of blood glucose exists for a prolonged period of time despite normal circulation. The most prevalent of the infarctions, however, is ischemic infarction, which results from a sudden interruption of blood supply owed to an obstruction in an artery. Cerebral infarction can occur in any of the cerebral blood vessels of the carotid (anterior portion of the brain) or vertebral basilar (posterior portion of the brain) systems. It may be confused with symptomology resulting from cerebral hemorrhage, tumor, or other space-occupying lesions. Because ischemic infarctions are the most common, they will be the focus of the remaining discussion.

Transient ischemic attack (TIA) refers to a temporary obstruction of blood vessels; this is frequently caused by platelet-fibrin emboli or blood clots (de Veber, 1999). An embolus is an aggregate of blood particles and tissue overgrowth (thrombus), fatty deposits, clumps of bacteria, or obstructive gas bubbles that block the blood vessels. Other causes of TIAs are acute high blood pressure and vasospasm or spasmodic constriction of blood vessels.

Transient ischemic attacks always have a sudden onset and peak in intensity within 2 to 5 minutes. Symptoms quickly disappear, within 30 minutes, but if symptoms persist past 24 hours, the diagnosis changes to a complete stroke or a cardiac vascular accident. Causes of TIAs are numerous and can be from intravascular disorders of the metabolic, hematologic or prothrombotic states; trauma, vasculitis, and heart disease (de Veber, 1999). The extent to which TIAs result in temporary or permanent neurological damage in unclear. Symptoms of carotid TIA include monocular blindness or blurring of vision in a previously normal eye; aphasic reactions such as difficulty with writing, reading, arithmetic, receptive and expressive language; and contralateral weakness and numbness of the face, arm, and leg, which may occur either simultaneously or separately. Weakness is characterized by heaviness or clumsiness of the extremities, while numbness can be described as a numbing sensation or a pins or needles sensation. These sensations do not spread or "march" to the various anatomical parts, but occur simultaneously. Vertebral basilar TIAs, however, have the following symptomology: vertigo (spinning movement of the environment); intermittent diplopia (double vision); visual blurring of both eyes; espisodic ataxia (gait problems); and spells in which sudden loss of strength in the lower extremities causes the patient to fall to the ground without loss of consciousness.

Transient ischemic attacks may occur sporadically or regularly, either in a short time span or over several months or years. More than one-third of the patients with diagnosed TIAs sustain a complete stroke within one year, while more than one-half of these patients eventually sustain a major stroke during their lifetime. Patients with TIAs may suffer mild cognitive impairments, especially on delayed recall tasks (Lezak, 1983). Patients suspected of having a TIA can have the diagnosis confirmed by an angiography, which enables a radiological visualization of the blood vessels.

Medical therapy usually involves a regimen of drugs that have the properties of inhibiting the formation or aggregation of red blood cells and the narrowing of arteries. Such drugs consist of aspirin, Anturane, Persantine, and Conmadin (Lubic & Palkovitz, 1979).

REFERENCES

de Veber, G. (1999). Cerebrovascular disease in children. In K. F. Swaiman & S. Ashwal (Eds.), *Pediatric neurology* (3rd ed., pp. 1101). St. Louis, MO: Mosby.

Lezak, M. D. (1983). *Neuropsychological assessment* (2nd ed.). New York: Oxford University Press.

Lubic, L. G., & Palkovitz, H. P. (1979). *Discussions in patient management: Stroke.* New York: Medical Examination.

Toole, J. F. (1984). *Cerebrovascular disorders* (3rd ed.). New York: Raven.

Toole, J. F., & Patel, A. N. (1974). *Cerebrovascular disorders* (2nd ed.). New York: McGraw-Hill.

GURMAL RATTAN
*Indiana University of
Pennsylvania*

RAYMOND S. DEAN
*Ball State University
Indiana University School of
Medicine*

ANOXIA

CEREBRAL LESION, CHRONIC

A chronic cerebral lesion is one that has been in existence beyond what might be considered to be the amount of time required for recovery of lost function.

Chronic cerebral lesions, much like acute cerebral lesions, are likely to influence behavior in ways related to their location and extent or size. Unlike acute cerebral lesions, however, chronic cerebral lesions may have greater effects on behavior than effects related to their location and extent. Increased effects on behavior can result from two conditions. The primary behavioral loss can be due to the interruption of developmental schemata, whereby a child who sustains a chronic cerebral lesion at an early age may be precluded from development of the normal repertoire of behaviors dependent on the integrity of the area of lesion. The normal sequence of ontogenetic recapitulation of phylogenetic phenomena is interrupted. Therefore, not only is there limitation of the behavior dependent on the specific area of cerebral tissue that sustains a lesion, but also of the subsequent behaviors dependent on the development of that initial behavior. The secondary loss from a chronic cerebral lesion results from a disuse atrophy phenomenon, whereby deterioration of muscle tissue or degeneration of neurotransmitter receptor sites, resulting secondary to the lesion, inhibits the development, performance, or acquisition of given behavioral skills.

Chronic cerebral lesions, especially those acquired after the developmental sequence is completed, may have lesser behavioral effects than those of acute lesions, in that the individual over time may acquire compensatory skills that help overcome some of the behavioral limitations imposed by the lesion.

Although chronic cerebral lesions can have onset at any age, many such lesions of congenital or prenatal onset result in death or profound developmental handicap. Onset age appears to be related to the severity of the handicap imposed by the lesion. Although it has been traditional to believe that the effects of chronic brain lesions are less severe in children because of presumed greater plasticity in the organization of their central nervous systems (Lyons & Matheny, 1984), there is accumulating evidence that a chronic cerebral lesion acquired early in childhood may have more severely debilitating effects (Cermak, 1985; Levin, Benton, & Grossman, 1982). There is also evidence that such lesions limit the development of memory and intellectual ability to a greater extent with early age onset than with later age onset (Levin, Eisenberg, Wigg, & Kobayashi, 1982). Further, there is evidence to suggest a greater likelihood of emotional problems resulting from chronic cerebral lesions at an early age (Rutter, 1981). These problems may interact with cognitive problems, depending on the age at which the lesion was acquired (Lyons & Matheny, 1984). The selective results of unilateral cerebral lesions on such specific aspects of behavior as language development, previously thought to be less specific when acquired at an early age, have been found to be similar in early childhood onset to those of later age onset (Aram et al., 1985). Even for those children who appear to show good recovery from early onset chronic cerebral lesions, there is a strong likelihood that special educational placement may be necessary (Lehr, 1984). The etiology of the chronic cerebral lesion, whether from head injury, brain tumor, or radiation therapy, appears to be unrelated to the neuropsychological outcome (Bruce, 1982).

Although developments in neurochemistry suggest that neurochemical adaptations at surviving synapses may mediate behavioral changes over time, which would account for frequent observations that behavioral consequences of chronic cerebral lesions change as time following the injury increases (Marshall, 1984), there is no generally accepted explanation for why this change over time should occur.

REFERENCES

Aram, D. M., Ekelman, B. L., Rose, D. F., & Whitaker, H. A. (1985). Verbal and cognitive sequelae following unilateral lesions acquired in early childhood. *Journal of Clinical and Experimental Neuropsychology, 7,* 55–78.

Bruce, D. A. (1982). Comment. *Neurosurgery, 11,* 672–673.

Cermak, L. A. (1985, February). The effects of age at onset and causal agent of brain injury on later adaptive functioning in children. Paper presented at the International Neuropsychological Society, San Diego. Abstract in *Proceedings* (p. 10).

Lehr, E. (1984, August). Good recovery from severe head injury in children and adolescents. Paper presented at American Psychological Association meeting, Toronto, Ontario.

Levin, H. S., Benton, A. L., & Grossman, R. G. (1982). *Neurobehavioral consequences of closed head injury.* New York: Oxford University Press.

Levin, H. S., Eisenberg, H. M., Wigg, N. R., & Kobayashi, K. (1982). Memory and intellectual ability after head injury in children and adolescents. *Neurosurgery, 11,* 668–672.

Lyons, M. J., & Matheny, A. P. (1984). Cognitive and personality differences between identical twins following skull fracture. *Journal of Pediatric Psychology, 9,* 485–494.

Marshall, J. F. (1984). Brain function: Neural adaptations and recovery from injury. *Annual Review of Psychology, 35,* 277–308.

Rutter, M. (1981). Psychological sequelae of brain damage in children. *American Journal of Psychiatry, 138,* 1533–1544.

LAWRENCE C. HARTLAGE
Evans, Georgia

BIRTH INJURIES
BRAIN DAMAGE/INJURY
CEREBRAL INFARCTION
TRAUMATIC BRAIN INJURY

CEREBRAL PALSY

Cerebral palsy (CP), sometimes called congenital spastic paralysis, is characterized by varying degrees of disturbance of voluntary movements caused by damage to the brain. Cerebral refers to the brain and palsy refers to weakness or lack of control. Cerebral palsy was originally called Little's disease after the English surgeon William John Little, who first described it. Later, Winthrop Phelps, an orthopedic surgeon, coined the term cerebral palsy and brought it into common usage as a result of his extensive work with this population in the United States.

There is agreement among experts in the field that cerebral palsy is a complex of characteristics attributed to brain injury. It has been defined by the United Cerebral Palsy Research and Educational Foundation as having the following elements: (1) being caused by injury to the brain; (2) causing motor disturbance, including paralysis, weakness, and uncoordination; (3) consisting of a cluster of symptoms; (4) usually originating in childhood; and (5) perhaps including learning difficulties, psychological problems, sensory defects, convulsions, and behavioral disorders of organic origin. In addition to these elements, cerebral palsy is nonprogressive, static, and unamenable to treatment.

There are two major types of CP: spastic, characterized by sudden, violent, involuntary muscular contractions, and athetosic, characterized by ceaseless, involuntary, slow, sinuous, writhing movements. The physical symptoms of CP can be so mild that they are detected only with difficulty, or they can be so profound that the affected individual is almost complete physically incapacitated. It is not unusual for a cerebral palsied individual to function normally intellectually. However, this intelligence is often masked (at least to the lay person) by uncontrolled physical characteristics, involuntary movements of the body and extremities, speech disorders, and drooling. Cerebral palsy is not a disease, and it is not curable.

The incidence of cerebral palsy varies; a conservative estimate of its occurrence is 1.5 to 2.0 cases per 1000 live births. It has been estimated that the incidence may be higher in areas where there is inadequate prenatal care and accompanying prematurity. It is estimated that there are 750,000 individuals with cerebral palsy in the United States (UCP, 1998, 2005). While CP occurs at every socioeconomic level, it is more prevalent among lower socioeconomic groups. Children born in poverty situations have a greater chance of incurring brain damage from factors such as malnutrition, poor prenatal and postnatal care, and environmental hazards during infancy. Cerebral palsy occurs slightly more frequently in males than in females, and more white than black children are affected. Cerebral palsy makes up the largest category of physical disabilities, representing 30 to 40 percent of all children in programs for the physically disabled.

In most cases, cerebral palsy is congenital (approximately 90 percent of all cases; UCP, 2005), meaning damage to the brain occurs during pregnancy or at birth. However, infectious diseases or severe head injuries can cause cerebral palsy at any time in life. Postnatal causes are said to be acquired, whereas those present at birth are congenital. It is generally agreed that CP cannot be inherited.

Prenatal causes of CP include German measles in the mother, pH incompatibility, maternal anoxia, use of drugs, and metabolic disorders such as maternal diabetes. Faulty growth of the fetal brain may occur if the mother is malnourished during pregnancy. In addition, maternal exposure to the toxic substances in X-rays may also damage the brain of the fetus. Perinatal (birth process) causes include prolonged labor, breech delivery, anoxia, and prematurity. High fever, poisonings, and other related factors may cause harm immediately following birth. After birth (postnatal) causes include anoxia, direct trauma to the brain, and infection. Poisonings also may contribute to brain damage during the postnatal period. In some cases, severe and consistent child beating has caused CP.

It is estimated that as many as three-quarters of all persons with CP have additional disabilities such as retardation, seizures, auditory and visual impairments, or communication disorders (UCP, 1998, 2005). Approximately 50 to 60 percent of CP children are retarded. Mental retardation has been difficult to diagnose in the population since intelligence tests were standardized on children with adequate speech, language, and motor abilities. Seizures are associated with approximately 25 to 35 percent of individuals with cerebral palsy and are much more prevalent with spastic CP persons. Strabismus (squinting) occurs in approximately 30 to 35 percent of cerebral-palsied individuals. Some athetotic CPs experience farsightedness while spastic CPs are nearsighted. Visual field reduction also can occur in some types of CP (Caputo, 1975).

Speech and/or language problems can range from normal speech and reception processing and expression to that which is nonfunctional. Speech in the two major types of CP has been characterized by Berry and Eisenson (1956) as (1) spastic speech, e.g., "slow, labored rate, lack of vocal inflection, gutteral or breathy quality of voice, uncontrolled volume, and, most important, grave articulatory problems which reflect the inability to secure graded, synchronous movement of the tongue, lips, and jaw"; and (2) athetoid speech, for example, "varying gradations of a pattern of irregular, shallow, and noisy breathing; whispered or hoarse phonation, and articulatory problems varying from the extremes of complete mutism of extreme dysarthria (impaired articulation) to a slight awkwardness in lingual movement."

Speech disorders are found in 70 percent of cerebral-palsied children. It has been reported that speech defects are found in 88 percent of persons with athetosis, 85 percent of those with ataxia, and 52 percent of those who are spastic.

Most of the speech problems are caused by problems controlling the muscles used to make speech sounds.

Minear (1965) developed a classification scheme for cerebral-palsied individuals based on motor characteristics as well as the area of the body where the problem is located. The six types within the motor component were adopted by the American Academy for Cerebral Palsy and have been described by others (Bleck, 1975; Denhoff, 1976; Healy, 1983). The six types include spasticity, athetosis, ataxia, rigidity, tremor, and mixed.

Spasticity is the most common type of CP, occurring in approximately 40 to 60 percent of the total. Stiffness of the muscles in spastic children occurs when the injury is on the brain surface or when it involves those nerves leading from the surface through the substance of the brain and onto the spinal cord. The spastic type is characterized by a loss of voluntary motor control. When the child initiates voluntary movement, it is likely to be jerky, with lack of control in the body extremities. This disability may affect any or all limbs. Involvement in the upper extremities may include varying degrees of flexing of the arms and fingers, depending on the severity of the disability. When lower extremities are involved, there may be a scissoring movement of the legs, caused by muscle contractions.

Athetosis is the second largest group in the CP population, occurring in approximately 15 to 20 percent of the total. This type is caused by injury to the brain's motor switchboard. Athetoid children are characterized by involuntary jerky, writhing movements, especially in the fingers and wrists. The head is often drawn back with the neck extended and mouth open. There are generally two types of athetosis: tension and nontension. The tension athetoid's muscles are always tense; this reduces contorted movement of limbs. The nontension athetoid has contorted movements without muscle tightness. Unlike the spastic child, all movements cease during sleep. The movements occur only in a conscious state; when emotionality increases, athetosis movements become intensified. Athetoids are usually higher in intelligence than spastic CP victims.

Ataxia is less prevalent than spasticity and athetosis. Together with tremor and rigidity, it makes up approximately 8 percent of the total CP population. The injury is in the cerebellum. Ataxic children are characterized by a lack of coordination and sense of balance. The eyes are often uncoordinated and the child may stumble and fall frequently.

Rigidity and tremor types of CP are extremely rare. Rigidity is unlike the other types in that the lower level of muscles stiffen and a rigid posture is maintained. The rigid type is usually severely retarded with a high incidence of convulsions. In tremor, there is involuntary movement in one extremity, usually one hand or arm. The motion may vary in its consistency and pattern. In intention tremor, the involuntary movement happens only when the child attempts an activity while in constant tremor. The involuntary movement is continuous.

Mixed in another variation of CP. It is a combination of the other five types with one type predominating. Approximately 30 percent of individuals with CP have more than one type.

The movement or motor component of the clinical classification system is composed of two types, pyramidal and extrapyramidal. The pyramidal type refers to the spastic cerebral-palsied group because the usual nerve cell involved in this disorder is shaped like a pyramid. Extrapyramidal refers to all other types of CP, athetosis, rigidity, tremor, ataxia, and mixed, in which the area of the brain affected is composed of conglomerates of nerve cells (Capute, 1975).

In addition to describing CP by type of neuromuscular or motor involvement, Denhoff (1976) also characterized this multihandicapped population by the body parts that are affected. This is also known as topographical classification, with (generally) seven types. With hemiplegia, one half, either the right side or left side, of the body is involved. Of cerebral-palsied individuals 30 to 40 percent fall into this category. The legs are involved to a greater extent than the arms with diplegia. Of all cerebral-palsied children 10 to 20 percent are diplegic. Quadriplegia involves all four limbs accounts for 15 to 20 percent of the total CP population. With paraplegia, occurring in 10 to 20 percent of all cerebral cases, only the legs are involved. Monoplegia involves only one limb and triplegia involves three limbs. These two types rarely occur. With double hemiplegia, both halves of the body are involved, but unlike quadriplegia, the two sides are affected differently. This type, too, rarely occurs.

Also CP can be classified by the severity of the motor involvement. Deaver (1966) described the CP child based on the mild, moderate, and severe classification scheme. Even though the descriptions were formulated several years ago, they are still useful today because of the explicitness of the activity level included in each category. In the mild category, no treatment is needed. The individual has no speech problem, is able to care for himself or herself, and can walk without the aid of appliances. In the moderate category, treatment is needed for speech problems and/or difficulties in ambulation and self-care. Braces and other equipment are needed. In the severe category, treatment is needed, but the degree of involvement is at a level wherein the prognosis for speech, self-care, and ambulation is poor.

Educational programs for children with cerebral palsy in the public schools gained momentum in the early 1970s with the emphasis on deinstitutionalization and normalization. Prior to this, many of these children, with multiple handicaps and not adequately diagnosed, remained in institutions for the mentally retarded.

It is generally agreed by experts in the field that treatment and educational considerations are extremely important and more complicated because cerebral-palsied children are multihandicapped. Not only must special equipment and facilities be provided to accommodate their physical disabilities, but additional special education techniques are needed to accommodate other handicaps (mental retardation, learning disabilities, auditory and visual disabilities).

When planning and implementing educational programs for cerebral-palsied individuals, a cadre of persons working in a multidisciplinary approach must be used. Many educators and physicians (Capute, 1975; Gearheart, 1980; Healy, 1983) have delineated the specific roles of the individuals who must work together in the education of cerebral-palsied children. The degree of CP and physical characteristics will determine the extent of participation by the physician. The physician may prescribe drugs for the patient to relax and to control the convulsions as well as treat overall health problems. Braces and other mechanical devices that provide support and allow children to walk are usually prescribed by medical doctors. The physical therapist works to facilitate motor development, to prevent or slow orthopedic problems, and to improve posture and positioning so that the child may benefit from other intervention activities. The occupational therapist uses creative, educational, and recreational activities to enhance self-help skills and teach parents to handle the child's daily living activities. The speech pathologist will monitor the child's progress in speech and language and provide therapy if the child is able to benefit from it. The speech therapist also may work with parents and other educational personnel on how to stimulate language development. An audiologist, learning disabilities specialist, and teacher of the mentally retarded may be needed to provide some direct and indirect services to the primary teacher when required. Biofeedback clinicians may be useful in teaching the individual what muscle groups are voluntarily effected (UCP, 1998, 2005).

A variety of specialized equipment is available to teachers, including adapted typewriters, pencil holders, book holders, page turners, and special desks to make cerebral-palsied individuals more self-sufficient.

The success achieved by the cerebral-palsied child depends largely on the extent of his or her physical and mental disability. While some cerebral-palsied people will need constant care in a protected environment, many can lead relatively normal lives and become productive citizens if given the opportunity.

REFERENCES

Berry, M. F., & Eisenson, P. (1956). *Speech disorders.* New York: Appleton-Century-Crofts.

Bleck, E. E. (1975). Cerebral palsy. In E. E. Bleck & D. A. Nagel (Eds.), *Physically handicapped children: A medical atlas for teachers.* New York: Grune & Stratton.

Capute, A. J. (1978). Cerebral palsy and associated dysfunctions. In R. H. Haslam & P. G. Valletutti (Eds.), *Medical problems in the classroom.* Baltimore: University Park Press.

Cruickshank, W. M. (1976). *Cerebral palsy: A developmental disability.* Syracuse, NY: Syracuse University Press.

Deaver, G. G. (1955). Cerebral palsy: Methods of evaluation and treatment. *Institute of Physical Medicine & Rehabilitation, 9.*

Denhoff, E. (1978). Medical aspects. In W. M. Cruickshank (Ed.), *Cerebral palsy: A developmental disability* (3rd ed.). Syracuse, NY: Syracuse University Press.

Gearheart, B. R. (1980). *Special education for the 80s.* St Louis, MO: Mosby.

Healy, A. (1983). Cerebral palsy. In J. A. Blackman (Ed.), *Medical aspects of developmental disabilities in children—birth to three.* Iowa City: University of Iowa Press.

Minear, W. L. (1956). A classification of cerebral palsy. *Pediatrics, 18,* 841–852.

United Cerebral Palsy (UCP). (1998). *Comments on biofeedback.* Retrieved from www.ucpa.org

United Cerebral Palsy (UCP). (2005). *Cerebral Palsy facts and figures.* Retrieved July 19, 2005, from http://www.ucp.org

CECELIA STEPPE-JONES
North Carolina Central University

HABILITATION OF INDIVIDUALS WITH DISABILITIES
HIGH-INCIDENCE DISABILITIES
MULTIPLE HANDICAPPING CONDITIONS
PHYSICAL DISABILITIES
UNITED CEREBRAL PALSY

CERTIFICATION/LICENSURE ISSUES

With only a few exceptions, the issues and standards involving special education programs do not differ from those that apply to teacher education programs nationwide. These issues include teacher testing, the use of teaching personnel having college degrees but lacking teacher preparation courses, standards used to approve teacher education programs, and state certification requirements. These issues are now magnified with the concept of "highly qualified special education teacher" mandates put forth in the revision of IDEA, Individuals with Disabilities Education Improvement Act of 2004 (IDEIA).

A number of states have moved toward, or implemented, the use of tests as part of the certification process. Some states require a test of basic skills prior to entering a teacher education program (e.g., California, Missouri), while other states require teachers to achieve a passing score on a content area test. It has been suggested that such tests will have a significant impact on the qualifications of individuals desiring to become teachers, particularly minority populations (Feistritzer, 1983). Feistritzer (1983) has suggested that the number of minority candidates entering teacher preparation programs has declined considerably in recent years. The Center for Minority Research in Special Education (COMRISE; 1998, 2005) is attempting to increase the number and research capacity of minority scholars in institutions of higher education with high minority enrollments and is trying to improve the quality and effectiveness of these programs.

An issue that has importance to special education is that of appropriate certification in the actual field of teaching. While most teachers are certified to teach in some field, not all teachers have been trained and certified to teach in the field to which they are assigned. For example, large numbers of special education teachers are not certified in special education or are not teaching the types of disabled children and youths for which they hold a special education certificate. Thus teachers who are qualified to teach nondisabled children in elementary schools may be teaching learning-disabled, emotionally disturbed, or some other type of disabled children. While emergency, temporary, or provisional certificates permit regular education teachers to teach disabled learners, there is some question as to whether this constitutes the most appropriate and effective instruction for these students. An analysis of the changes made in the past 25 years to special education coursework for regular educators seeking recertification shows dramatic advances (Patton & Braithwaite, 1990).

Many teacher-training programs are competency-based and result in program graduates receiving generic teaching licenses or endorsements. While this affords local school districts considerable flexibility for serving students, there is concern that distinct differences exist among differing handicapping conditions that cannot be met through the preparation of a generic teacher. While the needs of some students with disabilities can be served using generic teaching personnel, the use of resource rooms for some learners (learning disabled, etc.) often results in placement with a noncategorically certified teacher rather than a teacher who holds a categorical (learning disabled, etc.) certificate.

Certification and licensure are also affected by supply and demand. In the past, special education teachers have been in short supply and the use of temporary or provisional certificates, as noted earlier, became common. This led to the development of teacher preparation programs that prepare teachers to meet temporary endorsement requirements as well as to meet full certification requirements. In many respects, programs become defined by the certification standards they parallel and are not being designed to promote excellence. Teachers, or prospective teachers, tend to enroll in programs that most expeditiously meet the minimum standards necessary for them to maintain or gain employment. For this reason, preparation programs in competitive situations (i.e., with other institutions of higher education) may feel compelled to meet minimum training requirements, which, in turn, become maximum training requirements.

The development of inclusionary education has changed the requirements of teacher preparation from a focus of individual mastery to a consultation/collaboration format. The inclusion of special education students in the regular classroom has mandated teacher preparation to prepare students for collaborative teaching arrangements (Campbell & Fyfe, 1995). Programs that involve students in practicum supervision involving regular-education cooperating teachers, special-education cooperating teachers, and university supervisors are growing in number (Ludlow, Wienke, Henderson, & Klein, 1998). The reflection of educational service delivery trends such as inclusion in teacher preparation, however, is not uniform and assessing competency is difficult at best.

Current issues now remain with the fulfillment of IDEIA requirements that require a bachelor's degree, a state special education license non-waived licensure (not temporary or provisional), responsibility to provide consultative services to a care content highly qualified teacher, and passing of a state test in subjects of the basic school curriculum (NEA, 2005).

REFERENCES

Campbell, D. M., & Fyfe, B. (1995). *Reforming teacher education: The challenge of inclusive education.* Paper presented at the Annual Meeting of the Association of Independent Liberal Arts Colleges for Teacher Education (Washington, DC, February 12, 1995).

COMRISE. (1998). *Center of Minority Research in Special Education.* Charlottesville: University of Virginia, Curry School of Education.

COMRISE. (2005). *Center of Minority Research in Special Education.* Retrieved July 19, 2005, from http://www.curry.edschool .virginia.edu/go/comrise/home.html

Council for Exceptional Children. (1983). Code of ethics and standards for professional practice. *Exceptional Children, 50,* 205–218.

Feistritzer, C. E. (1983). *The condition of teaching.* Lawrenceville, NJ: Princeton University Press.

Ludlow, B. L., Wienke, W. D., Henderson, J., & Klein, H. (1998). A collaborative program to prepare mainstream teachers: Using peer supervision by general and special educators. In American Council on Rural Special Education Conference Proceedings *Coming together: Preparing for Rural Special Education in the 21st Century.* March 25–28.

Maple, C. C. (1983). Is special education certification a guarantee of teaching excellence? *Exceptional Children, 49,* 308–313.

National Education Association (NEA). (2005). *What constitutes a highly qualified special education teacher.* Retrieved July 19, 2005, from http://www.nasde.org/documents/IDEA

Patton, J. M., & Braithwaite, R. (1990). Special education certification/recertification for regular educators. *Journal of Special Education, 24,* 117–124.

PATRICIA ANN ABRAMSON
Hudson Public Schools, Hudson, Wisconsin

PROFESSIONAL STANDARDS FOR SPECIAL EDUCATORS
PERSONNEL TRAINING IN SPECIAL EDUCATION

CHALFANT, JAMES C. (1932–   )

A native of Fremont, Ohio, James Chalfant obtained his BS in 1954, MS in 1958, and EdD in 1965 from the University of Illinois. Early in his career, Chalfant's interest focused on an integrated training program for children with Down syndrome. Made available by the state of Illinois to all teachers of children with Down syndrome, the program involved intensive behavior shaping of self-help skills and the development of language, motor, and social skills (Chalfant, Silikovitz, & Tawney, 1977).

Chalfant is also noted for his extensive work on the development of teacher assistance teams, a team problem-solving model designed to assist and support individual teachers in managing situations for which the teacher needed additional help that was otherwise unavailable. This work is detailed in a chapter written by Chalfant in *Critical Issues in Gifted Education: Programs for the Gifted in Regular Classrooms* (1993).

During his distinguished career, Chalfant has been head of the Division of Special Education, Rehabilitation, and School Psychology at the University of Arizona, where he remains an active researcher and teacher with the rank of full professor. His most current research involves the study of self-concept in the visually impaired, and he teaches courses in learning disabilities, program development/service delivery, self-esteem, and cognitive abilities.

Chalfant was a member of a U.S. Department of Education task force focusing on issues and practices related to the identification of students with learning disabilities, and he was honored with a Presidential Citation for Outstanding Services for his work with the U.S. Office of Education's Division of Handicapped Children and Youth. Chalfant is also the recipient of the Award of Honor of the South African Association for Children with Learning Disabilities as "the international educator who has most influenced the field of learning disabilities in South Africa."

REFERENCES

Chalfant, J. C. (1993). Teacher assistance teams: Implications for the gifted. In C. J. Maker (Ed.), *Critical issues in gifted education: Programs for the gifted in regular classrooms*. Austin, TX: PRO-ED.

Chalfant, J. C., & Pysh, M. V. (1982). *Teacher assistance teams: A procedure for supporting classroom teachers* (filmstrip; audiocassette; handout). New Rochelle, NY: Pem Press/Pathescope Educational Media.

Chalfant, J. C., Silikovitz, R. G., & Tawney, J. W. (1977). *Systematic instruction for retarded children: The Illinois program.* Danville, IL: Interstate.

E. VALERIE HEWITT
Texas A&M University
First edition

TAMARA J. MARTIN
The University of Texas of the Permian Basin
Second edition

CHALL, JEANNE S. (1921–1999)

Jeanne S. Chall earned her BBA from the City College of New York in 1941. She went on to do her graduate work at Ohio State University, receiving her PhD in 1952. Chall taught at the City College of the City University of New York for 15 years. She joined the faculty at Harvard in 1965.

Chall became a leading expert in reading research and instruction during her time there. Dr. Chall was professor emerita at the Graduate School of Education (GSE) when she died on November 27, 1999. At Harvard, she founded the Harvard Reading Laboratory in 1966 and directed the lab for more than 20 years. She trained legions of researchers, reading teachers, and policy experts. Chall was called upon by a succession of U.S. presidents and secretaries of education to bring her wisdom to national literacy efforts.

Chall served on numerous national committees and

Jeanne S. Chall

acted in a consulting capacity to various government education agencies. In addition, she was a member of the editorial boards of several journals in the fields of reading, education, and educational psychology, including *Reading Research Quarterly* and the *Journal of Educational Psychology*. Three major books on reading have been authored by Chall, one currently in its third edition (1967, 1983a, 1983b, 1996a, 1996b). In earlier work, she authored two columns on the readability of instructional materials. She also published diagnostic instruments to aid in the diagnosis of reading and other language-related disorders. The *Roswell-Chall Diagnostic Reading Test of Word Analysis Skills* (1997) is the most notable of these instruments.

Chall published widely on readability of instructional materials and other texts, coauthoring the Dale-Chall formula in 1948 and the New Dale-Chall formula in 1996. In 1996, she wrote a book entitled *Qualitative Assessment of Text Difficulty: A Practical Guide for Teachers and Writers*.

In addition to her diagnostic instruments, Chall's major contributions to the field of special education were her research in reading and learning disabilities and in teacher training in these closely related areas. She received many honors for her outstanding achievements. In 1979, Chall was elected to the Reading Hall of Fame and the National Academy of Education. In 1982, Chall received both the American Educational Research Association Award for Distinguished Contributions to Research in Education and the American Psychological Association Edward L. Thorndike Award for Educational Psychology. In 1996, she received the Samuel T. Orton Award from the Orton Dyslexia Society. In the weeks before passing away, Chall completed her final volume, *The Academic Achievement Challenge: What Really Works in the Classroom?*, which was published in 2000 by Guilford Press.

REFERENCES

Chall, J. S. (1967, 1983a, 1966a). *Learning to read: The great debate* (3rd ed.). Fort Worth, TX: Harcourt Brace.

Chall, J. S. (1983b, 1996b). *Stages of reading development* (2nd ed.). Fort Worth, TX: Harcourt Brace.

Chall, J. S., Jacobs, V. A., & Baldwin, L. E. (1990). *The reading crisis: Why poor children fall behind*. Cambridge, MA: Harvard University Press.

Chall, J. S. & Dale, E. (1995). *Readability revisited and the New Dale-Chall Readability Formula*. Cambridge, MA: Brookline Books.

Chall, J. S., Bixxes, G., Conard, S., & Harris-Sharples, S. (1996). *Qualitative assessment of text difficulty: A practical guide for teachers and writers*. Cambridge, MA: Brookline Books.

Chall, J. S. (2000). *The academic achievement challenge: What really works in the classroom?* New York: Guilford.

Jeanne Chall, Reading Expert And Psychologist, Dies At Age 78. *Harvard Gazette* Archives. Retrieved August 4, 2005, from http://www.news.harvard.edu/gazette/1999/12.02/chall.html

Roswell, F. G., & Chall, J. S. (1997). *Roswell-Chall Diagnostic Test of Word Analysis Skills* (4th ed.). Cambridge, MA: Educators Publishing Company.

KATHRYN A. SULLIVAN
Texas A&M University
First edition

TAMARA J. MARTIN
*The University of Texas of the
    Permian Basin*
Second edition

RACHEL M. TOPLIS
*Falcon School District 49,
    Colorado Springs, Colorado*
Third edition

CHANGING CRITERION DESIGN

The changing criterion design allows the researcher to examine the effect of a behavior change program in a stepwise fashion. This single-subject design was described by Hartmann and Hall (1976) as "applicable to a wide range of treatment problems that can be modified in a stepwise manner and where reasonably prompt changes to a new, stable level are expected in response to changes in the criterion" (p. 531).

This research design is useful for evaluating the effect of instructional programs (e.g., increases in reading rate and increases in correct responding), shaping and fading programs (e.g., increasing academic engagement and decreasing talk-outs), and the measurement of reinforcement contingencies (e.g., increasing homework completion and increasing demonstrations of specified behavioral expectations) in a manner that strategically increases or decreases the target behavior so that the instructional objective can be met. For example, the changing criterion design has been used to evaluate the effect of a reinforcement contingency on the number of correct math problems for a student with emotional and/or behavioral disorders (Hartmann & Hall, 1976); the effect of a smoking reduction program (Hartmann & Hall); and the effect of an instructional program for increasing the number of math problems attempted by a student with minor problem behavior and low levels of work completion (Schloss & Sedlak, 1982).

The changing criterion design requires that the baseline phase is longer than the subsequent treatment phases. Once data has been demonstrated to be stable and/or trending in a counter-therapeutic direction, the criterion steps are chosen using the average of the baseline data as a guide in either an accelerating or decelerating direction, depending on what is being measured (see Figure 1). Each criterion step should provide a convincing demonstration of the behavior change and data stability prior to changing to the

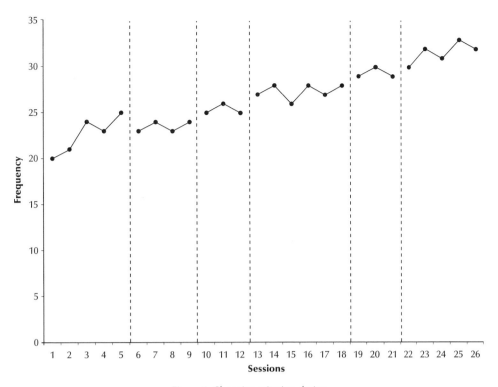

Figure 1 Changing criterion design

next criterion level (Schloss & Sedlak, 1982). Cooper, Heron, and Heward (1987) write that "proper implementation of the changing criterion design requires the careful manipulation of three design factors: length of phases, magnitude of criterion changes, and number of criterion changes. Since each phase in the changing criterion design serves as a baseline for comparing changes in responding measured in the next phase, each phase must be long enough to achieve stable responding" (p. 220). Additional considerations for use of this design include replicating the effect by providing at least four changes in criterion level, varying the magnitude of criterion changes, and varying the length of time for responding at each criterion step (Tawney & Gast, 1984).

REFERENCES

Cooper, J. O., Heron, T. E., & Heward, W. L. (1987). *Applied behavior analysis.* New York: Macmillan.

Hartmann, D. P., & Hall, R. V. (1976). The changing criterion design. *Journal of Applied Behavior Analysis, 9,* 527–532.

Schloss, P. J., & Sedlak, R. A. (1982). Application of the changing-criterion design in special education. *Journal of Special Education, 16,* 359–367.

Tawney, J. W., & Gast, D. L. (1984). *Single subject research in special education.* New York: Merrill.

RANDALL L. DE PRY
*University of Colorado at
Colorado Springs*

BEHAVIOR ASSESSMENT
RESEARCH IN SPECIAL EDUCATION

THE CHC CROSS-BATTERY APPROACH

The Cattell-Horn-Carroll (CHC) Cross-Battery approach (hereafter referred to as the XBA approach) was introduced by Flanagan and her colleagues in the late 1990s (Flanagan & McGrew, 1997; Flanagan, McGrew, & Ortiz, 2000; McGrew & Flanagan, 1998; Ortiz & Flanagan, 2002). The XBA approach provides practitioners with the means to make systematic, valid, and *up-to-date* interpretations of intelligence batteries and to augment them with other tests in a way that is consistent with the empirically supported CHC theory of cognitive abilities. Moving beyond the boundaries of a single intelligence *test kit* by adopting the psychometrically and theoretically defensible XBA principles and procedures represents a significantly improved method of measuring cognitive abilities (Carroll, 1998; Kaufman, 2000).

According to Carroll (1997), the CHC taxonomy of human cognitive abilities "appears to prescribe that individuals should be assessed with respect to the *total range* of abilities the theory specifies" (p. 129). However, because Carroll recognized that "any such prescription would of course create enormous problems," he indicated that "[r]esearch is needed to spell out how the assessor can select what abilities need to be tested in particular cases" (p. 129). Flanagan and colleagues' XBA approach was developed specifically to "spell out" how practitioners can conduct assessments that approximate the total range of broad cognitive abilities more adequately than what is possible with most single intelligence batteries. In a review of the XBA approach, Carroll (1998) stated that it "can be used to develop the most appropriate information about an individual in a given testing situation" (p. xi). In Kaufman's (2000) review of the XBA, he stated that the approach is based on sound assessment principles, adds theory to psychometrics, and improves the quality of the assessment and interpretation of cognitive abilities and processes.

Noteworthy is the fact that the "crossing" of batteries is not a new method of intellectual assessment. Neuropsychological assessment has long adopted the practice of crossing various standardized tests in an attempt to measure a broader range of brain functions than that offered by any single instrument (Lezak, 1976, 1995). Nevertheless, several problems with crossing batteries have plagued assessment-related fields for years. Many of these problems have been circumvented by Flanagan and colleagues' XBA approach (see Table 1 for examples). But unlike the XBA model, the various so-called "cross-battery" techniques applied within the field of neuropsychological assessment, for example, are not grounded in a systematic approach that is both psychometrically and theoretically defensible. Thus, as Wilson (1992) cogently pointed out, the field of neuropsychological assessment is in need of an approach that would guide practitioners through the selection of measures that would result in more specific and delineated patterns of function and dysfunction—an approach that provides more clinically useful information than one that is "wedded to the utilization of subscale scores and IQs" (p. 382). Indeed, all fields involved in the assessment of cognitive functioning have some need for an approach that would aid practitioners in their attempt to "touch all of the major cognitive areas, with emphasis on those most suspect on the basis of history, observation, and on-going test findings" (Wilson, 1992, p. 382). The XBA approach represents a quantum leap in this direction. The definition of XBA assessment as well as the *foundation* and *rationale* for and *application* of this approach are depicted in Figure 1 and are described briefly in the following paragraphs.

Definition

The XBA approach is a time-efficient method of cognitive assessment that is grounded in CHC theory and research. It allows practitioners to reliably measure a wider range (or a more in-depth but selective range) of cognitive abilities than that represented by most single intelligence batteries. The XBA approach is based on three foundational sources of information, or three pillars (Flanagan & McGrew, 1997; Flanagan, Ortiz, & Alfonso, 2006; Flanagan & Ortiz, 2001; McGrew & Flanagan, 1998). Together, these pillars provide the knowledge base necessary to organize theory-driven, comprehensive, reliable and valid assessment of cognitive abilities and processes.

Foundations of the XBA Approach

The first pillar of the XBA approach is CHC theory. This theory was selected to guide assessment and interpretation because it is based on a more thorough network of validity evidence than other contemporary multidimensional ability models of intelligence (see McGrew & Flanagan, 1998; Messick, 1992; Sternberg & Kaufman, 1998). According to Daniel (1997), the strength of the multiple (CHC) cognitive abilities model is that it was arrived at "by synthesizing hundreds of factor analyses conducted over decades by independent researchers using many different collections of tests. Never before has a psychometric ability model been so firmly grounded in data" (pp. 1042–1043). Because the broad and narrow abilities that comprise CHC theory have been defined elsewhere in this book (see Flanagan, this volume), these definitions will not be reiterated here.

The second pillar of the XBA approach is the CHC broad (stratum II) classifications of cognitive and academic ability tests. Specifically, based on the results of a series of cross-battery (or joint) confirmatory factor-analysis studies of the major intelligence batteries and task analyses conducted by many test experts, Flanagan and colleagues classified all the subtests of the major cognitive and achievement batteries according to the particular CHC broad abilities they measured. To date, over 500 CHC broad ability classifications have been made based on the results of these studies. These classifications of cognitive and academic ability tests assist practitioners in identifying measures that assess various aspects of the *broad* abilities represented in CHC theory, such as Fluid Intelligence (*Gf*), Crystallized Intelligence (*Gc*), Short-Term Memory (*Gsm*), and Quantitative Knowledge (*Gq*). Classification of tests at the broad ability level is necessary to improve upon the validity of cognitive assessment and interpretation. Specifically, broad ability classifications ensure that the CHC constructs that underlie assessments are minimally affected by *construct irrelevant variance* (Messick, 1989, 1995). In other words, knowing what tests measure what abilities enables clinicians to organize tests into *construct relevant* clusters—clusters that are less "contaminated" by other constructs because they contain only measures that are *relevant* to the construct or ability of interest.

The third pillar of the XBA approach is the CHC narrow (stratum I) classifications of cognitive and academic ability tests. These classifications were originally reported in McGrew (1997). Subsequently, Flanagan and colleagues provided content validity evidence for the narrow ability classifications underlying the major intelligence and achievement batteries (Flanagan & Ortiz, 2001; Flanagan, Ortiz, & Alfonso, 2006; Flanagan, Ortiz, Alfonso & Mascolo, 2002, 2006). Use of narrow ability classifications were necessary to ensure that the CHC constructs that underlie assessments are well represented. That is, the narrow abil-

Table 1 Parallel needs in cognitive assessment-related fields addressed by the CHC cross-battery approach

Need within assessment-related fields[1]	Need addressed by the XBA approach
School Psychology, Clinical Psychology, and Neuropsychology have lagged in the development of conceptual models of the assessment of individuals. There is a need for the development of contemporary models.	The XBA approach meets this need.
It is likely that there is a need for events external to a field of endeavor to give impetus to new developments and real advances in that field.	Carroll and Horn's *Fluid-Crystallized* theoretical models and systematic programs of research in cognitive psychology provided the impetus for the XBA approach and led to the development of better assessment instruments and procedures.
There is a need for truly unidimensional assessment instruments for children and adults. Without them, valid interpretation of test scores are problematic at best.	Many scale and composite measures or intelligence batteries are mixed, containing excess reliable variance associated with a construct irrelevant to the one interpreted. The XBA approach ensures that assessments include clusters that are relatively pure measures of CHC broad and narrow abilities, allowing for valid interpretation of multiple unidimensional abilities.
There is a need to utilize a conceptual framework to direct any approach to assessment. This would aid in both the selection of instruments and methods, and in the interpretation of test findings.	The XBA approach to assessment is based on CHC theory. Since this approach links all the major intelligence batteries (and a variety of supplemental tests) to this theory, both selection of tests and interpretation of test findings is made easy.
It is necessary that the conceptual framework or model underlying assessment incorporates various aspects of neuropsychological and cognitive ability function that can be described in terms of constructs that are recognized in the neuropsychological and cognitive psychology literature.	The XBA approach incorporates various aspects of neuropsychological and cognitive ability function that are described in terms of constructs that are recognized in the related literature.
There is a need to adopt a conceptual framework that allows for the measurement of the full range of behavioral functions subserved by the brain. Unfortunately, in neuropsychological assessment there is no inclusive set of measures that is standardized on a single normative population.	XBA assessment allows for the measurement of a wide range of broad and narrow cognitive abilities specified in contemporary CHC theory. Although a XBA norm group does not exist, the characteristics of the normal probability curve are used to interpret XBA assessment data effectively.
Because there are no truly unidimensional measures in psychological assessment, there is a need to select subtests from standardized instruments that appear to reflect the neurocognitive function of interest. In neuropsychological assessment, the aim, therefore, is to select those measures that, on the basis of careful task analysis, appear mainly to tap a given construct.	The XBA approach is defined by a CHC classification system. Subtests from the major intelligence batteries (and various supplemental instruments) were classified empirically as measures of broad and narrow CHC constructs. Use of these classifications allows practitioners to be reasonably confident that a given test taps a given construct.
It is clear that an eclectic approach is needed in the selection of measures, preferably subtests rather than the omnibus IQs, in order to gain more specificity in the delineation of patterns of function and dysfunction.	The XBA approach ensures that two or more relatively pure, but qualitatively different, indicators of each *broad* cognitive ability are represented in a complete assessment. Two or more qualitatively similar indicators are necessary to make inferences about specific or *narrow* CHC abilities. This process is eclectic in its selection of measures, but attempts to represent all broad and narrow abilities by using a subset of measures from only two batteries (that were normed within a few years of one another). Additional iterations of assessment that may be necessary to delineate patterns of cognitive strengths and weaknesses may require the introduction of subtests from other batteries.
There is a need to solve the potential problems that can arise from crossing normative groups as well as sets of measures that vary in reliability.	In XBA assessment, one can typically achieve baseline data in cognitive functioning across seven or eight CHC broad abilities through the use of only two well-standardized batteries, which minimizes the effects of error due to norming differences. Also, since interpretation of both broad and narrow CHC abilities is made at the cluster (rather than subtest) level, issues related to low reliability are less problematic in this approach. Finally, because confidence intervals are used for all broad and narrow ability clusters, the effects of measurement error are reduced further.

[a]Information obtained, in part, from Wilson (1992).

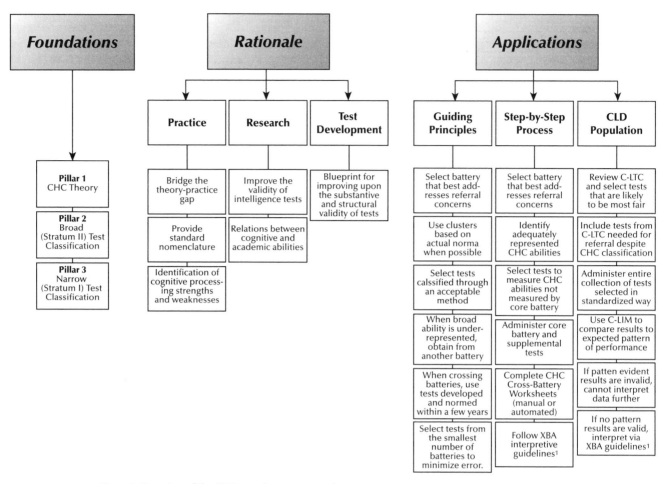

Figure 1 Overview of the CHC cross-battery approach

[1]Flanagan, D. P., Ortiz, S. O., Alfonso, V. C., & Mascolo, J. P. (2006). *Achievement Test Desk Reference (ATDR): A Guide to Learning Disability Identification–2nd Edition (ATDR-II)*. New York: Wiley & Sons.

Flanagan, D. P., Ortiz, S. O., Alfonso, V. C. (2006) *Essentials of Cross-Battery Assessment–2nd Edition*. New York: John Wiley & Sons.

Note: CHC = Cattell-Horn-Carroll; C-LTC = Culture-Language Test Classifications; C-LIM = Culture-Language Interpretive matrix.

ity classifications of tests assist practitioners in combining qualitatively different narrow ability indicators (or tests) of a given broad ability into clusters so that appropriate inferences can be made from test performance. Taken together, the three pillars underlying the XBA approach provide the necessary foundation from which to organize assessments of cognitive and academic abilities that are theoretically driven, comprehensive, and valid.

Rationale for the CHC Cross-Battery Approach

The XBA approach has significant implications for practice, research, and test development. A brief discussion of these implications follows.

Practice

The XBA approach provides "a much needed and updated bridge between current intellectual theory and research and

practice" (Flanagan & McGrew, 1997, p. 322). The results of several joint factor analyses conducted over the past 10+ years demonstrated that none of our intelligence batteries contained measures that sufficiently approximated the full range of *broad* abilities that define the structure of intelligence specified in contemporary psychometric theory (e.g., Carroll, 1993; Horn, 1991; Keith, Kranzler, & Flanagan, 2001; McGrew, 1997; Phelps, McGrew, Knopik, & Ford, 2005; Woodcock, 1990). Indeed, the joint factor analyses conducted by Woodcock (1990) suggested that it may be necessary to "cross" batteries to measure a broader range of cognitive abilities than that provided by a single intelligence battery.

The findings of these joint factor analyses of intelligence batteries that were published before 1998 are presented in Table 2. As may be seen in this table, most batteries fall far short of measuring all seven of the broad cognitive abilities listed. Of the major intelligence batteries in use prior to 1998, most failed to measure three or more broad

Table 2 Representation of broad CHC abilities on nine intelligence batteries published prior to 1998

	Gf	Gc	Gv	Gsm	Glr	Ga	Gs
WISC-III	—	Vocabulary Information Similarities Comprehension	Block Design Object Assembly Picture Arrangement Picture Completion Mazes	Digit Span	—	—	Symbol Search Coding
WAIS-R	—	Vocabulary Information Similarities Comprehension	Block Design Object Assembly Picture Completion Picture Arrangement	Digit Span	—	—	Digit-Symbol
WPPSI-R	—	Vocabulary Information Similarities Comprehension	Block Design Object Assembly Picture Completion Mazes Geometric Design	Sentences	—	—	Animal Pegs
KAIT	Mystery Codes Logical Steps	Definitions Famous Faces Auditory Comprehension Double Meanings	Memory for Block Designs	—	Rebus Learning Rebus Delayed Recall Auditory Delayed Recall	—	—
K-ABC	Matrix Analogies	—	Triangles Face Recognition Gestalt Closure Magic Window Hand Movements Spatial Memory Photo Series	Number Recall Word Order	—	—	—
CAS	—	—	Figure Memory Verbal Spatial Relations Nonverbal Matrices	Word Series Sentence Repetition Sentence Questions	—	—	Matching Numbers Receptive Attention Planned Codes Number Detection Planned Connection Expressive Attention
DAS	Matrices Picture Similarities Sequential and Quantitative Reasoning	Similarities Verbal Comprehension Word Definitions Naming Vocabulary	Pattern Construction Block Building Copying Matching Letter-Like Forms Recall of Designs Recognition of Pictures	Recall of Digits	Recall of Objects	—	Speed of Information Processing
WJ-R	Concept Formation Analysis-Synthesis	Oral Vocabulary Picture Vocabulary Listening Comprehension Verbal Analogies	Spatial Relations Picture Recognition Visual Closure	Memory for Words Memory for Sentences Numbers Reversed	Memory for Names Visual-Auditory Learning Delayed Recall: Memory for Names Delayed Recall: Visual-Auditory Learning	Incomplete Words Sound Blending Sound Patterns	Visual Matching Cross Out
SB:FE	Matrices Equation Building Number Series	Verbal Relations Verbal Relations Absurdities Vocabulary	Pattern Analysis Bead Memory Copying Memory for Objects Paper Folding & Cutting	Memory for Sentences Memory for Digits	—	—	—

Note: CHC classifications are based on the literature and primary sources as Carroll (1993), Horn (1991), McGrew (1997), McGrew and Flanagan (1998), and Woodcock (1990), WISC-III = Wechsler Intelligence Scale for Children–Third Edition (Wechsler, 1991); WAIS-R = Wechsler Adult Intelligence Scale–Revised; WPPSI-R = Wechsler Preschool and Primary Scale of Intelligence–Revised; KAIT = Kaufman Adolescent and Adult Intelligence Test; K-ABC = Kaufman Assessment Battery for Children (Kaufman & Kaufman, 1983); CAS = Cognitive Assessment System; DAS = Differential Ability Scales; WJ-R = Woodcock-Johnson Psycho-Educational Battery–Revised; SB:FE = Stanford-Binet Intelligence Scale–Fourth Edition.

CHC abilities (viz., *Ga, Glr, Gf, Gs*) that were (and are) considered important in understanding and predicting school achievement. In fact, *Gf,* often considered to be the *essence* of intelligence, was either not measured or not measured adequately by most of the intelligence batteries included in Table 2 (i.e., WISC-III, WAIS-R, WPPSI-R, K-ABC, and CAS).

The finding that the abilities *not measured* by the intelligence batteries listed in Table 2 are *important in understanding children's learning difficulties* provided the impetus for developing the XBA approach. In effect, the XBA approach was developed to systematically replace the dashes in Table 2 with tests from another battery. As such, this approach guides practitioners in the selection of tests, both core and supplemental, that together provides measurement of abilities that is considered sufficient in both breadth and depth for the purpose of addressing referral concerns.

Another benefit of the XBA approach is that it facilitates communication among professionals. Most scientific disciplines have a standard nomenclature (i.e., a common set of terms and definitions) that facilitates communication and guards against misinterpretation. For example, the standard nomenclature in chemistry is reflected in the *Periodic Table;* in biology, it is reflected in the classification of animals according to phyla; in psychology and psychiatry, it is reflected in the *Diagnostic and Statistical Manual of Mental Disorders;* and in medicine, it is reflected in the *International Classification of Diseases.* Underlying the XBA approach is a standard nomenclature or *Table of Human Cognitive Abilities* that includes classifications of over 500 tests according to the broad and narrow CHC abilities they measure (see also Flanagan & Ortiz, 2001; Flanagan, Ortiz, & Alfonso, 2006; Flanagan et al., 2006). The XBA classification system has had a positive impact on communication among practitioners, has improved research on the relations between cognitive and academic abilities, and has resulted in substantial improvements in the measurement of cognitive constructs, as may be seen in the design and structure of current intelligence tests.

Finally, the XBA approach offers practitioners a psychometrically defensible means to identifying population-relative (or normative) strengths and weaknesses. According to Brackett and McPherson (1996) "the limited capacity of standardized instruments to assess isolated cognitive processes creates a major weakness in intracognitive discrepancy models. Although analysis of [Wechsler] subtests typically report measures of distinct cognitive abilities, such abilities may not emerge by individual subtests but rather in combination with other subtests" (p. 79). The XBA approach addresses this limitation. By focusing interpretations on cognitive ability clusters (i.e., combination of subtests) that contain qualitatively different indicators of each broad CHC cognitive ability (or process), the identification of normative processing strengths and weaknesses

via XBA procedures is both psychometrically defensible and theoretically sound. In sum, the XBA approach addresses the longstanding need within the entire field of assessment, from learning disabilities to neuropsychological assessment, for methods that "provide a greater range of information about the ways individuals learn—the ways individuals receive, store, integrate, and express information" (Brackett & McPherson, 1996, p. 80).

Research

The XBA approach was also developed to promote a greater understanding of the relationship between cognitive abilities and important outcome criteria. Because XBA assessments are based on the empirically supported CHC theory and constructed in a psychometrically defensible manner, they represent a valid means of measuring cognitive constructs (Flanagan, 2000; Phelps et al., 2005). It is noteworthy that when second-order constructs are composed of (moderately) correlated but qualitatively distinct measures, they will tend to have higher correlations with complex criteria (e.g., academic achievement), as compared to lower-order constructs, because they are broader in what they measure (Comrey, 1988). Predictive statements about different achievements (i.e., criterion-related inferences) that are made from XBA clusters are based on a more solid foundation than individual subtests (and perhaps some global scores from single intelligence batteries) because the predictor constructs are represented by relatively pure and qualitatively distinct measures of broad CHC abilities. Thus, improving the validity of CHC ability measures has further elucidated the relations between CHC cognitive abilities and processes and different achievement and vocational/occupational outcomes (e.g., Flanagan, 2000; McGrew et al., 1997).

Test Development

Although there was substantial evidence of at least eight or nine broad cognitive CHC abilities by the late 1980s, the tests of the time did not reflect this diversity in measurement. For example, Table 2 shows that the WPPSI-R, K-ABC, KAIT, WAIS-R, and CAS batteries only measured 2–3 broad CHC abilities adequately. The WPPSI-R primarily measured *Gv* and *Gc.* The K-ABC primarily measured *Gv* and *Gsm,* and to a much lesser extent *Gf,* while the KAIT primarily measured *Gc* and *Glr,* and to a much lesser extent *Gf* and *Gv.* The CAS measured *Gs, Gsm,* and *Gv.* Finally, while the DAS, SB:IV, and WISC-III did not provide sufficient coverage of abilities to narrow the gap between contemporary theory and practice, their comprehensive measurement of approximately four CHC abilities was nonetheless an improvement over the aforementioned batteries. Table 2 shows that only the WJ-R included measures of all broad cognitive abilities listed in the table. Nevertheless, most of the broad abilities were not measured adequately by the WJ-R (Alfonso, Flanagan, & Radwan, 2005; McGrew & Flanagan, 1998).

In general, Table 2 shows that *Gf, Gsm, Glr, Ga,* and *Gs* were not measured well by the majority of intelligence tests published prior to 1998. Therefore, it is clear that most test authors did not use contemporary psychometric theories of the structure of cognitive abilities to guide the development of their intelligence tests. As such, a substantial theory-practice gap existed—that is, theories of the structure of cognitive abilities were far in advance of the instruments used to operationalize them. In fact, prior to the mid-1980s, theory seldom played a role in intelligence-test development. The numerous dashes in Table 2 exemplify the "theory-practice gap" that existed in the field of intellectual assessment at that time (Alfonso et al., 2005).

In the past decade, *Gf-Gc* theory, and more recently CHC theory, has had a significant impact on the revision of old and development of new intelligence batteries. For example, a wider range of broad and narrow abilities is represented on current intelligence batteries than that represented on previous editions of these tests. Table 3 provides several salient examples of the impact that CHC theory and XBA classifications has had on intelligence-test development over the past 2 decades. This table lists the major intelligence tests in the order in which they were revised, beginning with those tests with the greatest number of years between revisions (i.e., KABC) and ending with newly developed tests and tests that have yet to be revised (e.g., WRIT and DAS, respectively). As is obvious from a review of Table 3, CHC theory and XBA classifications have had a significant impact on recent test development.

Of the seven intelligence batteries (including both comprehensive and brief measures) that were published since 1998, the test authors of three clearly used CHC theory and XBA classifications as a blueprint for test development (i.e., WJ III, SB5, KABC-II); and the test authors of two were obviously influenced by CHC theory (i.e., RIAS and WRIT). Only the authors of the Wechsler Scales (i.e., WPPSI-III, WISC-IV, and WAIS-III) did not state explicitly that CHC theory was used as a guide for revision. Nevertheless, these authors acknowledged the research of Cattell, Horn, and Carroll in their most recent manuals (Wechsler, 2002, 2003). Presently, as Table 3 shows, nearly all intelligence batteries that are used with some regularity subscribe either explicitly or implicitly to CHC theory.

Convergence toward the incorporation of CHC theory is also seen clearly in Table 4. This table is identical to Table 2 except it also includes the subtests from the most recent revisions of the tests from Table 3. A review of Table 4, which includes all intelligence batteries that were published after 1998, shows that many of the gaps in measurement of broad cognitive abilities have been filled. Specifically, the majority of tests published after 1998 now measure 4–5 broad cognitive abilities adequately (see Table 4), as compared

to 2–3 (see Table 2). For example, Table 4 shows that the WISC-IV, WAIS-III, WPPSI-III, KABC-II, and SB5 measure 4–5 broad CHC abilities. The WISC-IV measures *Gf, Gc, Gv, Gsm,* and *Gs,* while the KABC-II measures *Gf, Gc, Gv, Gsm,* and *Glr.* The WAIS-III measures *Gc, Gv, Gsm,* and *Gs* adequately, and to a lesser extent *Gf,* while the WPPSI-III measures *Gf, Gc, Gv,* and *Gs* adequately. Finally, the SB5 measures four CHC broad abilities (i.e., *Gf, Gc, Gv, Gsm;* cf. Alfonso et al., 2005).

Table 4 shows that the WJ III continues to include measures of all the major broad cognitive abilities and now measures these abilities well, particularly when it is used in conjunction with the Diagnostic Supplement (DS; Woodcock, McGrew, & Schrank, 2003). Third, a comparison of Tables 2 and 4 indicates that two broad abilities not measured by many intelligence batteries prior to 1998 are now measured by the majority of intelligence batteries available today: that is, *Gf* and *Gsm.* These broad abilities may be better represented on revised and new intelligence batteries because of the accumulating research evidence regarding their importance in overall academic success (see Flanagan, et al., 2006, for a review). Finally, Table 4 reveals that intelligence batteries continue to fall short in their measurement of three CHC broad abilities: specifically, *Glr, Ga,* and *Gs.* Thus, although there is greater coverage of CHC broad abilities now than there was just a few years ago, the need for the XBA approach to assessment remains (Alfonso, et al., 2005).

Application of the XBA Approach

Guiding Principles

In order to ensure that XBA procedures are psychometrically and theoretically sound, it is recommended that practitioners adhere to several guiding principles. These principles were listed previously in Figure 1 and are defined briefly in the following paragraphs.

First, select a comprehensive intelligence battery as your core battery in assessment. It is expected that the battery of choice will be one that is deemed most responsive to referral concerns. These batteries may include, but are certainly not limited to the Wechsler Scales, WJ III, SB5, and KABC-II. It is important to note that the use of co-normed tests, such as the WJ III tests of cognitive ability and tests of achievement and the KABC-II and KTEA-II, may allow for the widest coverage of broad and narrow CHC abilities and processes.

Second, use subtests and *clusters / composites* from a single battery whenever possible to represent broad CHC abilities. In other words, best practices involve using actual norms whenever they are available in lieu of arithmetic averages of scaled scores from different batteries. In the past, it was necessary to convert subtest scaled scores from different batteries to a common metric and then average them (after

Table 3 Impact of the CHC theory on intelligence test development

Test (year of publication) CHC Impact	Revision (year of publication) CHC Impact
K-ABC (1983) No obvious impact.	**KABC-II (2004)** Provided a second global score that include fluid and crystallized abilities; included several new subtests measuring reasoning; interpretation of test performance may be based on CHC theory or Luria's theory; provided assessment of five CHC broad abilities (Kaufman, Kaufman, Kaufman, & Kaufman, 2005).
SB:FE (1986) Used a three-level hierarchical model of the structure of cognitive abilities to guide construction of the test: the top level included general reasoning factor or *g*; the middle level included three broad factors called crystallized abilities, fluid-analytic abilities, and short-term memory; the third level included more specific factors including verbal reasoning, quantitative reasoning, and abstract/visual reasoning.	**SB5 (2003)** Used CHC theory to guide test development; increased the number of broad factors from 4 to 5; included a Working Memory Factor based on research indicating its importance for academic success (Roid & Pomplum, 2005).
WAIS-R (1981) No obvious impact.	**WAIS-III (1997)** Enhanced the measurement of fluid reasoning by adding the Matrix Reasoning subtest; included four index scores that measure specific abilities more purely than the traditional IQs provided in the various Wechsler Scales; included a Working Memory Index based on recent research indicating its importance for academic success.
WPPSI-R (1989) No obvious impact.	**WPPSI-III (2002)** Incorporated measures of Processing Speed that yielded a Processing Speed Quotient based on recent research indicating the importance of processing speed for early academic success; enhanced the measurement of fluid reasoning by adding the Matrix Reasoning and Picture Concepts subtests.
WJ-R (1989) Used modern *Gf-Gc* theory as the cognitive model for test development; included two measures of each of eight broad abilities.	**WJ III (2001)** Used CHC theory as a "blueprint" for test development; included two or three qualitatively different narrow abilities for each broad ability; the combined cognitive and achievement batteries of the WJ III include 9 of the 10 broad abilities subsumed in CHC theory.
WISC-III (1991) No obvious impact.	**WISC-IV (2003)** Eliminated Verbal and Performance IQs; replaced the Freedom from Distractibility Index with the Working Memory Index; replaced the Perceptual Organization Index with the Perceptual Reasoning Index; enhanced the measurement of fluid reasoning by adding the Matrix Reasoning and Picture Concepts subtests; enhanced the measurement of Processing Speed with the addition of the Cancellation subtest.
RAIS (2003) Included indicators of fluid and crystallized abilities.	
WRIT (2002) Developed to be consistent with current theories of intelligence; evaluated multiple abilities; provided Crystallized and Fluid IQs based on the Cattell-Horn theory.	
CAS (1997) No obvious impact.	
KAIT (1993) Included subtests organized according to the work of Horn and Cattell; provided Fluid and Crystallized IQs.	
DAS (1990) No obvious impact.	

Note: K-ABC = Kaufman Assessment Battery for Children (Kaufman & Kaufman, 1983); KABC-II = Kaufman Assessment Battery for Children–Second Edition (Kaufman & Kaufman, 2004); SB:FE = Stanford-Binet Intelligence Scale–Fourth Edition (Thorndike, Hagen, & Sattler, 1986); SB5 = Stanford-Binet Intelligence Scales–Fifth Edition (Roid, 2003); WAIS-R = Wechsler Adult Intelligence Scale–Revised (Wechsler, 1981); WAIS-III = Wechsler Adult Intelligence Scale–Third Edition (Wechsler, 1997); WPPSI-R = Wechsler Preschool and Primary Scale of Intelligence–Revised (Wechsler, 1989); WPPSI-III = Wechsler Preschool and Primary Scale of Intelligence–Third Edition (Wechsler, 2002); WJ-R = Woodcock-Johnson Psycho-Educational Battery–Revised (Woodcock & Johnson, 1989); WJ III = Woodcock-Johnson III Tests of Cognitive Abilities (Woodcock, McGrew, & Mather, 2001); WISC-III = Wechsler Intelligence Scale for Children–Third Edition (Wechsler, 1991); WISC-IV = Wechsler Intelligence Scale for Children–Fourth Edition (Wechsler, 2003); RAIS = Reynolds Intellectual Assessment Scales (Reynolds & Kamphaus, 2003); WRIT = Wide Range Intelligence Test (Glutting, Adams, & Sheslow, 2002); CAS = Cognitive Assessment System (Das & Naglieri, 1997); KAIT = Kaufman Adolescent and Adult Intelligence Test (Kaufman & Kaufman 1993); DAS = Differential Ability Scales (Elliott, 1990).

Table 4 Representation of broad CHC abilities on eight intelligence batteries published after 1998

	Gf	Gc	Gv	Gsm	Glr	Ga	Gs
WISC-IV	Matrix Reasoning Picture Concepts	Vocabulary Information Similarities Comprehension Word Reasoning	Block Design Picture Completion	Digit Span Letter-Number Sequencing	—	—	Symbol Search Coding Cancellation
WAIS-III[a]	Matrix Reasoning	Vocabulary Information Similarities Comprehension	Block Design Object Assembly Picture Arrangement Picture Completion	Digit Span Letter-Number Sequencing	—	—	Symbol Search Digit-Symbol Coding
WPPSI-III	Matrix Reasoning Picture Concepts	Vocabulary Information Similarities Comprehension Receptive Vocabulary Picture Naming Word Reasoning	Block Design Object Assembly Picture Completion	—	—	—	Coding Symbol Search
KABC-II	Conceptual Thinking Block Counting Pattern Reasoning Story Completion Riddles	Expressive Vocabulary Verbal Vocabulary	Triangles Gestalt Closure Hand Movements Rover	Number Recall Word Order	Face Recognition Atlantis Rebus Atlantis—Delayed Rebus—Delayed	—	—
WJ III/DS	Concept Formation Analysis-Synthesis Number Series Number Matrices	Verbal Comprehension General Information Bilingual Verbal Comprehension	Spatial Relations Picture Recognition Planning Visual Closure Block Rotation	Memory for Words Numbers Reversed Auditory Working Memory Memory for Sentences	Visual-Auditory Learning Retrieval Fluency Visual-Auditory Learning—Delayed Rapid Picture Naming Memory for Names Memory for Names—Delayed	Sound Blend Auditory Attention Incomplete Words Sound Pattern—Voice Sound Pattern—Music	Visual Matching Decision Speed Pair Cancellation Cross Out
SB5	Nonverbal Fluid Reasoning Verbal Fluid Reasoning Nonverbal Quantitative Reasoning Verbal Quantitative Reasoning	Nonverbal Knowledge Verbal Knowledge	Nonverbal Visual-Spatial Processing Verbal Visual-Spatial Processing	Nonverbal Working Memory Verbal Working Memory	—	—	—
RIAS	Odd-Item Out	Guess What Verbal Reasoning	What's Missing	Verbal Memory Nonverbal Memory	—	—	—
WRIT	Matrices	Verbal Analogies Vocabulary	Diamonds	—	—	—	—

Note: CHC classifications are based on the literature and primary sources such as Carroll (1993); Flanagan and Ortiz (2001); Flanagan, Ortiz, and Alfonso (2006); Horn (1991); McGrew (1997); and McGrew and Flanagan (1998). WISC-IV = Wechsler Intelligence Scale for Children–Fourth Edition (Wechsler, 2003); WAIS-III = Wechsler Adult Intelligence Scale–Third Edition; WPPSI-III = Wechsler Preschool and Primary Scale of Intelligence–Third Edition (Wechsler, 2002); KABC-II = Kaufman Assessment Battery for Children–Second Edition; WJ III = Woodcock-Johnson III Tests of Cognitive Abilities; WJ III/DS = Diagnostic Supplement to the Woodcock-Johnson III Tests of Cognitive Abilities (Woodcock, McGrew, & Mather, 2003); SB5 = Stanford-Binet Intelligence Scales–Fifth Edition; RIAS = Reynolds Intellectual Assessment Scales; WRIT = Wide Range Intelligence Test.

[a]Although the WAIS-III was published in 1997, it is included in this table because its predecessor, the Wechsler Adult Intelligence Scale–Revised, was included in Table 2, and in order to present all revised Wechsler Scales in one table.

determining that there was a nonsignificant difference between the scores) in order to build construct-relevant broad CHC ability clusters. Because the development of current intelligence batteries benefited greatly from current theory and research, this practice is seldom necessary at the broad ability level. It continues to be necessary at the narrow ability level and when testing hypotheses about aberrant performance within broad ability domains (see Flanagan, Ortiz, & Alfonso, 2006; Flanagan et al., 2006 for details).

Third, when constructing CHC broad and narrow ability clusters, select tests that have been classified through an acceptable method, such as through CHC theory-driven factor analyses or expert consensus content-validity studies. All test classifications included in the works of Flanagan and colleagues have been classified through these acceptable methods (Flanagan & Ortiz, 2001; Flanagan, Ortiz, & Alfonso, 2006; Flanagan et al., 2006). For example, when constructing broad (stratum II) ability composites or clusters, *relatively pure CHC indicators* should be included (i.e., tests that had either *strong* or *moderate* [but not mixed] loadings on their respective factors in theory-driven within- or cross-battery factor analyses). Furthermore, to ensure appropriate construct representation when constructing broad (stratum II) ability composites, *two or more qualitatively different* narrow (stratum I) ability indicators should be included to represent each domain. Without empirical classifications of tests, constructs may not be adequately represented and, therefore, inferences about an individual's broad (stratum II) ability cannot be made. Of course, the more broadly an ability is represented (i.e., through the derivation of composites based on *multiple* qualitatively different narrow ability indicators), the more confidence one has in drawing inferences about that broad ability underlying a composite. A minimum of two qualitatively different indicators per CHC composite is recommended in the XBA approach for practical reasons (viz., time efficient assessment).

Fourth, when at least two qualitatively different indicators of a broad ability of interest are not available on the core battery, then supplement the core battery with at least two qualitatively different indicators of that broad ability from another battery. In other words, if an evaluator is interested in measuring Auditory Processing (*Ga*), and the core battery includes only one or no *Ga* subtests, then select a *Ga cluster* from another battery to supplement the core battery.

Fifth, when crossing batteries (e.g., augmenting a core battery with relevant CHC clusters from another battery) or when constructing CHC broad or narrow ability clusters using tests from different batteries (e.g., averaging scores when the broad ability cluster of interest is not available), select tests that were developed and normed within a few years of one another to minimize the effect of spurious differences between test scores that may be attributable to the "Flynn effect" (Flynn, 1984). The XBA worksheets developed by Flanagan and colleagues include only those tests that were normed within 10 years of one another.

Sixth, select tests from the smallest number of batteries to minimize the effect of spurious differences between test scores that may be attributable to differences in the characteristics of independent norm samples (McGrew, 1994). In most cases, using select tests from a single battery to augment the constructs measured by any other major intelligence battery is sufficient to represent the breadth of broad cognitive abilities adequately, as well as to allow for at least three qualitatively different narrow ability indicators of most broad abilities.

Noteworthy is the fact that when the XBA guiding principles are implemented systematically and the recommendations for development, use, and interpretation of clusters are adhered to, the potential error introduced through the crossing of norm groups is negligible (Flanagan & Ortiz, 2001; McGrew & Flanagan, 1998). Furthermore, although there are other limitations to crossing batteries, this systematic approach to the assessment and interpretation of cognitive abilities has far *fewer* implications with regard to the potential for error than those associated with the improper use and interpretation of cognitive performance inherent in traditional assessment approaches (e.g., subtest analysis, discrepancy analysis, atheoretical approaches to assessment and interpretation; see Flanagan, Ortiz, & Alfonso, 2006).

Step-by-Step Process

The XBA approach can be carried out, using any intelligence battery as the core instrument in assessment, following six simple steps (see Figure 1). These steps are described in detail in Flanagan and Ortiz (2001); Flanagan, Ortiz, and Alfonso (2006); and Flanagan et al. (2002, 2006), and, therefore, will only be highlighted here.

The first step of the XBA approach involves selecting a battery that is most conducive to a number of variables, including the age of the child, his or her developmental level and proficiency in English, the specific referral concerns, and so forth. As such, while a test like the WJ III may be appropriate for a relatively bright and articulate seventh-grader who is struggling in math and science, it may not be the best instrument of choice for a third-grader who is an English Language Learner and who is significantly behind her classmates in all academic areas, despite the fact that the WJ III provides the most comprehensive coverage of CHC abilities. This is because many of the WJ III tests have relatively high and particularly receptive language demands. In the case of this third-grader, an intelligence battery such as the KABC-II may be more appropriate because its language demands and cultural loadings are generally quite low.

The second step of the XBA approach required that the

examiner identify the CHC broad abilities that are adequately measured by the core battery. Table 4 may be useful in this regard. If the battery does not allow for adequate measurement of the broad and narrow abilities considered most germane in light of the referral, then it will be necessary to supplement the core battery.

The third step requires that the examiner select a supplemental battery that includes measurement of all or nearly all of the abilities that are deemed necessary to assess vis-a-vis the referral but are not measured by the core battery. Several examples of how to supplement each of the major intelligence tests to gain a better or more in-depth understanding of CHC broad and narrow abilities can be found in Flanagan, Ortiz, and Alfonso (2006) and Flanagan and colleagues (2002, 2006).

Step four requires that the examiner administer and score the core and supplemental tests. Step five involves completing the XBA worksheets. While these worksheets may be completed manually, most users prefer the automated versions. Therefore, after administering and scoring the cross-battery assessment, the examiner need only enter scaled scores into an automated worksheet. The many benefits of such a worksheet are described in detail in Flanagan, Ortiz, and Alfonso (2006). The final step, step six, requires that the examiner follow the XBA interpretive guidelines outlined by Flanagan and her colleagues.

Although a step-by-step approach to XBA assessment is available, it is important to understand that the XBA approach is not a "cookbook" method for assessment. The XBA principles, procedures, and steps, as well as the XBA automated worksheets, are intended to guide practitioners *systematically* through the process of test selection and test interpretation in order to maximize the implementation of psychometrically and theoretically defensible evaluations. Thus, clinical ingenuity, judgment, and experience remain important and necessary components of competent, defensible, and sound assessment and interpretation practices.

Extending the XBA Approach to Culturally and Linguistically Diverse Populations

As a natural result from efforts to classify tests according to the broad and narrow ability constructs they measure, XBA assessment was extended along additional dimensions that provide applicability to culturally and linguistically diverse populations (Flanagan & Ortiz, 2001; Flanagan, Ortiz, & Alfonso, 2006; Ortiz & Flanagan, 2002).

These dimensions, now known as the Culture-Language Test Classifications (C-LTC) and Culture-Language Interpretive Matrix (C-LIM) center around additional classification of intelligence and special-purpose (i.e., supplemental) tests according to two important variables—cultural loading and linguistic demand. *Cultural loading* refers to the degree or extent to which any given test requires culture-specific knowledge that is inherently embedded in tests. Tests vary widely on this basis ranging from those that have high cultural loadings (e.g., Wechsler Information) to those that have relatively low cultural loadings (e.g., KABC-II Triangles).

Similar to cultural loading, *linguistic demand* represents a classification based on the degree or extent to which language or communication is required in order for a given test to be administered to, comprehended by, or responded to by the examinee. Some tests have high language demands (e.g., Wechsler Vocabulary), whereas others have low language demands (e.g., UNIT Cube Design). Note that although some tests can be administered in a completely nonverbal manner (e.g., pantomime, gestures), some degree of communication is required in order for the examinee to comprehend what is expected (e.g., the nature of the task, when to start, when to stop, when to work quickly) and in what manner an acceptable response is to be given. Thus, all tests have some degree of language (or communication) demands and all tests are culturally loaded to some extent (Sattler, 1992).

Note that test performance is not adversely influenced or biased merely because tests are culturally loaded or make particular language demands. Rather, test performance may reflect bias only when children are tested who do not meet particular assumptions that accompany psychometric testing. Chief among these is the assumption of comparability, which specifies that "the students we test are similar to those on whom the test was standardized" (Salvia & Ysseldyke, 1991; p. 18). In other words, we assume that the level of acculturation and linguistic history of the students we test are comparable to the students included in the test's normative sample. Differences in experiential histories, particularly those related to level of acculturation and English-language proficiency, represent the greatest threats to the validity of this assumption and thus the validity that may be ascribed to any inferences drawn from test data. For example, because a growing number of school-age children in the United States are frequently raised in culturally different or bicultural environments and because they are frequently bilingual (nonnative English speakers), they cannot be presumed to be "comparable" to the individuals on whom any current tests have been normed. When norms are used that do not control for the effect of cultural and linguistic differences, test performance may be more of a reflection of an individual's level of acculturation or English-language proficiency than the constructs of interest (e.g., auditory processing, intelligence) for individuals who are English-language learners and who are not fully acculturated. Thus, careful attention must be paid to these inherent qualities of tests that directly affect performance, and thereby threaten the validity of findings, for individuals whose cultural and linguistic backgrounds differ from the mainstream (Valdés & Figueroa, 1994).

Classifying tests according to degree of cultural loading and degree of linguistic demand and providing a matrix to assist in interpretation of test findings have three fundamental benefits. First, the C-LTC provides a systematic method for the deliberate and careful selection of tests that are low on these dimensions (i.e., cultural loading and linguistic demand), allowing for a better approximation of the true performance of diverse children. In other words, practitioners can use the classifications to select tests that are likely to result in fairer and more accurate estimates of the ability being measured in an individual from a diverse background. Second, the C-LIM organizes obtained data in a way that makes use of the known "pattern" of performance for diverse individuals established over many decades of research. Historically, a pattern of attenuated performance as a function of a test's cultural loading and linguistic demand has been observed (Valdes & Figueroa, 1994). The C-LIM is designed to evaluate the degree to which an individual's test performance follows this historical pattern. When it does, it can be presumed that cultural and linguistic factors were the primary influences on performance and thus the results are not valid and cannot be interpreted as reflections of true intellectual capabilities. When the pattern is absent, it can be presumed that cultural or linguistic factors did not influence test performance adversely and that the findings represent reliable and valid estimates of performance. Thus, the basic question in assessment of diverse individuals (i.e., is low performance due to differences in culture/language or to a disorder of cognitive deficiency?) can be addressed directly. And third, when it is deemed that culture or language were not the primary factors that affected test performance, subsequent test interpretation continues to be based on current science and modern conceptualizations of intelligence. We do not propose, however, that these extensions of the XBA approach by themselves are sufficient to evaluate the performance of diverse children fairly. On the contrary, we view these extensions as supplemental to the broader assessment process, guiding test selection and interpretation in a manner that may more appropriately meet the needs of diverse populations within the context of a comprehensive, defensible system of nondiscriminatory assessment.

The XBA Approach in Perspective

Although not without its limitations, since its formal introduction to the field, the XBA approach has been well received (e.g., Borgas, 1999; Carroll, 1998; Daniel, 1997; Esters, Ittenbach, & Han, 1997; Genshaft & Gerner, 1998; Kaufman, 2000), and has grown in popularity because of the need for such an approach, particularly in the evaluation of suspected learning disability (e.g., Kavale & Mostert, 2005). However, like any new approach, especially one that differs markedly from traditional methods, there are often a variety of questions and misconceptions (e.g., practical, psychometric, theoretical, logistical) that arise with re-

spect to its implementation. Table 5 includes a sampling of a few misconceptions about XBA assessment that have emerged within the past few years along with corresponding clarifications. After reviewing Table 5 and the many commentaries and articles that have been written about this approach, it should be clear that the XBA approach is a viable and time-efficient method of measuring and interpreting cognitive and academic abilities and processes. More recently, the XBA approach has been used within the context of an operational definition of learning disability that is consistent with current federal and legal mandates (Flanagan et al., 2006).

Conclusions

The XBA approach is a method that allows practitioners to augment or supplement any major intelligence battery to ensure measurement of a wider range of broad cognitive abilities in a manner consistent with contemporary theory and research. The foundational sources of information upon which the XBA approach was built (i.e., the classifications of the major intelligence batteries according to CHC theory) provide a way to systematically construct a more theoretically driven, comprehensive, and valid assessment of cognitive abilities. When the XBA approach is applied to the Wechsler Intelligence Scales, for example, it is possible to measure important abilities that would otherwise go unassessed (e.g., *Ga, Glr*)—abilities that are important in understanding school learning and a variety of vocational and occupational outcomes (e.g., Flanagan et al., 2006; Flanagan & Kaufman, 2004).

The XBA approach allows for the measurement of the major cognitive areas specified in CHC theory with emphasis on those considered most critical on the basis of history, observation, and available test data. The CHC classifications of a multitude of cognitive ability tests bring stronger content and construct-validity evidence to the evaluation and interpretation process. As test development continues to evolve and becomes increasingly more sophisticated (psychometrically and theoretically), batteries of the future will undoubtedly possess stronger content and construct validity. (A comparison of Tables 2 and 4 illustrates this point.) Notwithstanding, it is unrealistic from an economic and practical standpoint to develop a battery that operationalizes contemporary CHC theory fully (Carroll, 1998). Therefore, it is likely that the XBA approach will become increasingly important as the empirical support for CHC theory mounts.

With a strong research base and a multiplicity of CHC measures available, XBA procedures can aid practitioners in the selective measurement of cognitive abilities that are important with regard to the examinee's presenting problem(s). In particular, because the XBA approach was developed following important psychometric and validity principles, practitioners are able to address the "disorder

Table 5 Misconceptions about the CHC cross-battery approach and corresponding clarifications

Misconceptions	Clarifications
In order to conduct cross-battery assessments, I will need access to all the major intelligence batteries or at least most of them.	Only two intelligence batteries are needed to conduct most comprehensive cross-battery assessments. Access to additional batteries or tests may be required if more in-depth assessment in a given domain is necessary.
The XBA approach takes more time than single-battery assessment.	When compared to a single intelligence battery, there is no appreciable increase in time involved in conducting a cross-battery assessment. In fact, when conducting *selective* cross-battery assessments, the time required is often less than administering any one of the major intelligence batteries.
The XBA approach to assessment is complicated.	This method of assessment is characterized by an easy to follow set of six steps that guides the practitioner through designing, scoring, and interpreting cross-battery assessments.
The CHC theory underlying the XBA approach is supported by only factor-analytic evidence and, therefore, is limited.	CHC theory is supported by a network of validity evidence (developmental, neuro-cognitive, etc.) that exceeds that in support of any other psychometric theory of multiple cognitive abilities. Therefore, within the psychometric tradition, it is the theory around which cognitive functioning should be interpreted.
Some abilities do not correlate highly with g (or general intelligence), such as Gs, and therefore are not important to measure.	The importance of assessing certain CHC abilities should be guided by referral concerns as well as their established relations to outcome criteria (e.g., academic achievement). It is incorrect to assume that an ability is unimportant solely on the basis of its relation to g (see Flanagan, Ortiz, Alfonso, & Mascolo, 2006).
Combining tests from different intelligence batteries is an inappropriate and invalid use of intelligence tests.	The cluster scores derived from XBA are more reliable and valid than individual tests (i.e., subtests) because they are based on the aggregate of two qualitatively different and empirically strong narrow ability indicators of a particular broad ability construct.
Because most current intelligence tests are grounded in CHC theory, there is not as great a need to combine tests from different batteries to form broad ability clusters.	Most intelligence tests yield broad ability clusters that are derived from qualitatively different aspects of the contracts presumed to underlie the clusters. Crossing batteries therefore may simply involve administering a core battery and supplementing it with broad ability clusters from another battery—clusters that represent abilities not measured by the core battery. However, there remains a need to cross batteries to follow up on aberrant findings as well as to measure specific narrow abilities well.
Because the XBA approach involves using two or more measures that were normed at different times and on different populations, a cross-battery norm group does not exist. This leads to potential errors in interpretation.	Ideally, a comprehensive CHC assessment should be based on a single battery of tests normed on a single sample. However, currently this option neither exists, nor is it practical. To fully operationalize CHC theory using at least two subtests to represent every broad and narrow ability, well over 100 subtests would be needed. The potential error that results from conducting an incomplete assessment of cognitive abilities through conventional (and atheoretical) methods is deemed greater than the error associated with the "crossing" of norm samples, especially when the XBA principles, procedures and interpretive guidelines are followed.
Traditional assessment data are easily interpreted through the plotting of test scores and well established intra- and inter-individual discrepancy procedures. XBA data are not as easily interpreted.	XBA data may be interpreted in much the same way as traditional assessment data. However, the XBA integrated intra- and inter-cognitive analysis procedures are far in advance of those associated with traditional batteries (e.g., ipsative) because they are psychometrically and theoretically defensible and are conducted as part of a *systematic* approach to assessment. Also, XBA results can be plotted on a profile (manually or using automated XBA worksheets) that allows for a graphic depiction of performance.
The language of XBA approach is not user friendly.	The language used in XBA reports is no more confusing or difficult than that used in a standard or traditional Wechsler report. Although the former uses CHC terminology (as opposed to verbal/nonverbal and simultaneous/successive terminology), it is the responsibility of the practitioner to communicate the meaning of any psychological term. It is no more difficult to describe Visual Processing (a broad ability within the CHC framework) than it is to describe Simultaneous Processing or "Nonverbal" ability. Moreover, because nearly all current intelligence tests are based on CHC theory and detailed CHC interpretive approaches have been developed for those that are not (e.g., WISC-IV; Flanagan & Kaufman, 2004), all professionals engaged in the assessment of cognitive abilities and processes should be well-versed in CHC terminology.

in a basic psychological process" component of learning disability more reliably and validly.

In the past, the lack of theoretical clarity of widely used intelligence tests (e.g., the Wechsler Scales) confounded interpretation and adversely affected the examiner's ability to draw clear and useful conclusions from the data. The XBA approach has changed the direction of intellectual assessment in several ways. It has aided test authors and publishers in clarifying the theoretical underpinnings of their instruments. It has influenced the interpretation approaches of several commonly used intelligence batteries (e.g., KABC-II, WISC-IV). It has provided a means for understanding the relations between specific cognitive and academic abilities, thereby aiding significantly in the design and interpretation of assessments of individuals suspected of having a learning disability. And, it has assisted in narrowing the gap between theory and practice in assessment-related fields. As a result, measurement and interpretation of human cognitive abilities is guided more by science than clinical acumen.

REFERENCES

Alfonso, V. C., Flanagan, D. P., & Radwan, S. (2005). The impact of the Cattell-Horn-Carroll theory on test development and interpretation of cognitive and academic abilities. In D. P. Flanagan & P. L. Harrison (Eds.), *Contemporary intellectual assessment: Theories, tests, and issues* (2nd ed., pp. 185–202). New York: Guilford.

Borgas, K. (1999). Intelligence theories and psychological assessment: Which theory of intelligence guides your interpretation of intelligence test profiles? *The School Psychologist, 53,* 24–25.

Carroll, J. B. (1993). *Human cognitive abilities: A survey of factor-analytic studies.* Cambridge, England: Cambridge University Press.

Carroll, J. B. (1997). The three-stratum theory of cognitive abilities. In D. P. Flanagan, J. L., Genshaft, & P. L. Harrison (Eds.), *Contemporary intellectual assessment: Theories, tests, and issues* (pp. 122–130). New York: Guilford.

Carroll, J. B. (1998). Foreword. In K. S. McGrew & D. P. Flanagan, *The intelligence test desk reference: Gf-Gc cross-battery assessment* (pp. xi–xii). Boston: Allyn & Bacon.

Comrey, A. L. (1988). Factor-analytic methods of scale development in personality and clinical psychology. *Journal of Consulting and Clinical Psychology, 56,* 754–761.

Daniel, M. H. (1997). Intelligence testing: Status and trends. *American Psychologist, 52,* 1038–1045.

Esters, E. G., Ittenbach, R. F., & Han, K. (1997). Today's IQ tests: Are they really better than their historical predecessors? *School Psychology Review, 26,* 211–223.

Flanagan, D. P. (2000). Wechsler-based CHC cross-battery assessment and reading achievement: Strengthening the validity of interpretations drawn from Wechsler test scores. *School Psychology Quarterly, 15,* 295–329.

Flanagan, D. L., & Kaufman, A. S. (2004). *Essentials of the WISC-IV.* New York: Wiley.

Flanagan, D. P., & McGrew, K. S. (1997). A cross-battery approach to assessing and interpreting cognitive abilities: Narrowing the gap between practice and cognitive science. In D. P. Flanagan, J. L. Genshaft, & P. L. Harrison (Eds.), *Contemporary intellectual assessment: Theories, tests, and issues* (pp. 314–325). New York: Guilford.

Flanagan, D. P., McGrew, K. S., & Ortiz, S. O. (2000). *The Wechsler intelligence scales and Gf-Gc theory: A contemporary approach to interpretation.* Needham Heights, MA: Allyn & Bacon.

Flanagan, D. P., & Ortiz, S. O. (2001). *Essentials of cross-battery assessment.* New York: Wiley.

Flanagan, D. P., Ortiz, S. O., & Alfonso, V. C. (2006). *Essentials of cross-battery Assessment* (2nd ed.). New York: Wiley.

Flanagan, D. P., Ortiz, S. O., Alfonso, V. C., & Mascolo, J. T. (2002). *The achievement test desk reference (ADTR): Comprehensive assessment and learning disabilities.* Boston: Allyn & Bacon.

Flanagan, D. P., Ortiz, S. O., Alfonso, V. C., & Mascolo, J. T. (2006). *The achievement test desk reference (ADTR): A guide to learning disability identification.* Boston: Allyn & Bacon.

Floyd, R. G., Keith, T. Z., Taub, G., & McGrew, K. S. (in press). Cattell-Horn-Carroll cognitive abilities and their effects on reading decoding skills: *g* has indirect effects, more specific abilities have direct effects. *School Psychology Quarterly.*

Flynn, J. R. (1984). The mean IQ of Americans: Massive gains 1932 to 1978. *Psychological Bulletin, 95,* 29–51.

Genshaft, J. L., & Gerner, M. (1998). CHC cross-battery assessment: Implications for school psychologists. *Communique, 26*(8), 24–27.

Horn, J. L. (1991). Measurement of intellectual capabilities: A review of theory. In K. S. McGrew, J. K. Werder, & R. W. Woodcock (Eds.), *Woodcock-Johnson technical manual* (pp. 197–232). Chicago: Riverside Publishing.

Kaufman, A. S. (2000). Forward. In Flanagan, D. P., McGrew, K. S., & Ortiz, S. O. (Eds.), *The Wechsler intelligence scales and Gf-Gc theory: A contemporary approach to interpretation.* Needham Heights, MA: Allyn & Bacon.

Keith, T. Z., Kranzler, J. H., & Flanagan, D. P. (2001). Independent confirmatory factor analysis of the Cognitive Assessment System (CAS): What does the CAS measure? *School Psychology Review, 28,* 117–144.

Lezak, M. D. (1976). *Neuropsychological assessment.* New York: Oxford University Press.

Lezak, M. D. (1995). *Neuropsychological assessment* (3rd ed.). New York: Oxford University Press.

McGrew, K. S. (1994). *Clinical interpretation of the Woodcock-Johnson Tests of Cognitive Ability* (Rev. ed.). Boston: Allyn & Bacon.

McGrew, K. S. (1997). Analysis of the major intelligence batteries according to a proposed comprehensive CHC framework. In D. P. Flanagan, J. L. Genshaft, & P. L. Harrison (Eds.), *Contemporary intellectual assessment: Theories, tests, and issues* (pp. 151–180). New York: Guilford.

McGrew, K. S., & Flanagan, D. P. (1998). *The intelligence test desk reference (ITDR): CHC cross-battery assessment.* Boston: Allyn & Bacon.

McGrew, K. S., Flanagan, D. P., Keith, T. Z. & Vanderwood, M. (1997). Beyond g: The impact of CHC specific cognitive abilities research on the future use and interpretation of intelligence tests in the schools. *School Psychology Review, 26,* 189–210.

Messick, S. (1989). Validity. In R. Linn (Ed.), *Educational measurement* (3rd ed., pp. 104–131). Washington, DC: American Council on Education.

Messick, S. (1992). Multiple intelligences or multilevel intelligence? Selective emphasis on distinctive properties of hierarchy: On Gardner's *Frames of Mind* and Sternberg's *Beyond IQ* in the context of theory and research on the structure of human abilities. *Psychological Inquiry, 3,* 365–384.

Messick, S. (1995). Validity of psychological assessment: Validation of inferences from persons' responses and performances as scientific inquiry into score meaning. *American Psychologist, 50,* 741–749.

Ortiz, S. O., & Flanagan, D. P. (2002). Best practices in working with culturally and diverse families. In A. Thomas & J. Grimes (Eds.), *Best practices in school psychology IV* (pp. 337–352). Washington, DC: National Association of School Psychologists.

Phelps, L., McGrew, K. S., Knopik, S. N., & Ford, L. (2005). The general (g) broad and narrow CHC stratum characteristics of the WJ III and WISC-III tests: A confirmatory cross-battery investigation. *Journal of School Psychology, 320,* 66–58.

Salvia, J., & Ysseldyke, J. E. (1991). *Assessment* (5th ed.). New York: Houghton Mifflin.

Sattler, J. M. (1992). *Assessment of children* (3rd ed.). San Diego, CA: Author.

Sternberg, R. J., & Kaufman, J. C. (1998). Human abilities. *Annual Review of Psychology, 49,* 479–502.

Valdés, G., & Figueroa, R. A. (1994). *Bilingualism and testing: A special case of bias.* Norwood, NJ: Ablex Publishing.

Vanderwood, M., McGrew, K. S., & Flanagan, D. P. (2001). Examination of the contribution of general and specific cognitive abilities to reading achievement. *Learning and Individual Differences, 13,* 159–188.

Wechsler, D. (2002). *Wechsler Preschool and Primary Scale of Intelligence* (3rd. ed.). San Antonio, TX: The Psychological Corporation.

Wechsler, D. (2003). *Wechsler Intelligence Scale for Children* (4th ed.). San Antonio, TX: The Psychological Corporation.

Wilson, B. C. (1992). The neuropsychological assessment of the preschool child: A branching model. In I. Rapin & S. I. Segalowitz (Vol. Eds.), *Handbook of neuropsychology: Vol. 6. Child neuropsychology* (pp. 377–94). San Diego, CA: Elsevier.

Woodcock, R. W. (1990). Theoretical foundations of the WJ-R measures of cognitive ability. *Journal of Psychoeducational Assessment, 8,* 231–58.

Woodcock, R. W., McGrew, K. S., & Schrank, F. A. (2003). *Diagnostic supplement to the Woodcock-Johnson III Tests of Cognitive Abilities.* Itasca, IL: Riverside.

Dawn P. Flanagan
St. John's University

Vincent C. Alfonso
Fordham University

Samuel O. Ortiz
St. John's University

CHEMICALLY DEPENDENT YOUTHS

Chemically dependent youths are children and adolescents who want and need continued use of a psychoactive substance to sustain or maintain a chronic state of euphoria or intoxication. Alcohol and drug use by young people must be viewed not in isolation but in concert with that period of life known as adolescence. Substance use and addiction have profound effects on development and have serious implications for the future functioning of the abuser (Cohen, 1983).

The period of life commonly referred to as adolescence generally runs from 12 to 22 years of age. Adolescents are often described by age groupings: early (12 to 15), middle (15 to 18), and late (18 to 22). Although these divisions are convenient, they do not adequately describe the complex period of adolescence. More important are the biological, emotional, social, academic, and intellectual changes that young people undergo as they move from childhood to adulthood. Because these phases vary widely across adolescents and even within the same adolescent, no one variable, including age, is sufficient. The complex interplay of these dynamic phases in youth and the distinct stages of movement from drug use to chemical dependency best explain chemical dependency. Newman and Newman (1975) note that the physical development that accompanies puberty leads to a heightened awareness of body sensations. Drugs, especially marijuana and the hallucinogens, accentuate pleasurable bodily sensations and may be used by adolescents in an attempt to increase the sense of physical arousal. Cohen (1984) warns that adolescence, a period of critical psychosocial development when adaptive responses are being learned, is much more vulnerable to the loss of learning time than is adulthood.

Two types of chemical dependency occur, physical and psychological. Some substances induce tolerance and create a physical craving and addiction cycle, whereas others create a psychological dependency in which the user experiences changes in mood. Further, some compounds create both a physical and psychological dependency. In the latter case, chemically dependent youths may undergo detoxification to treat the physical craving and resultant withdrawal symptoms, but may continue to experience a craving or felt need to use again. This process sets up a cycle of dependency, detoxification, and return to use that accounts for the recidivism rate among addicted youths.

Psychological dependence is characterized by a drive to continue taking a drug when the user feels the effects of the drug are needed to maintain his or her sense of well being at an optimal level. The complex interaction of drug effects, personality, and stage of development constitute the degree of psychic craving or compulsion the user may experience. Drug-seeking behavior or compulsive drug use develops when the user comes to believe that the drug can produce pleasure and deter discomfort such that continuous or periodic administration of the drug is required. This mental state is the most powerful of all the factors involved in chronic intoxication with psychoactive drugs (Adesso, 1985).

Physiological dependence is characterized by reliance of body tissue on the continued presence of a drug within the user's system. Its presence is unknown to the user as long as the drug continues to be taken and is of no immediate consequence until the drug is withdrawn or no longer available. The magnitude of the dependence and the severity of the withdrawal symptoms vary directly with the type, amount, frequency, and duration of the drug use. Physiological dependence manifests itself as severe and immediate physical pain and discomfort, commonly referred to as withdrawal symptoms or abstinence syndrome. Symptoms may include fever, chills, gastrointestinal cramps, watery eyes, runny nose, and muscle cramping or spasms. They are frequently accompanied by psychological dependence. For drugs like alcohol, barbiturates, narcotic analgesics (morphine, Percodan, heroin) and cocaine, withdrawal symptoms and accompanying psychological dependence are so uncomfortable and threatening that they motivate young drug users to continue to seek and administer the drug. For drugs like stimulants (speed), and to a lesser degree marijuana and hallucinogenics (LSD, mescaline, psilocybin, peyote), the primary disturbance is psychological rather than physiological. But it should be noted that although the symptoms are not as severe as with physiological withdrawal, the user does experience discomfort of a mental or emotional nature (Bardo & Risner, 1985).

Different drug compounds act on different youths in different ways, both psychologically and physiologically. A 13-year-old pubescent male who is smoking two to three joints of high-grade (THC potent) marijuana daily over a 5- to 6-month period is likely to develop a psychological compulsion while not experiencing physical withdrawal symptoms on cessation. However, evidence suggests that THC lowers levels of the male hormone testosterone in the young male's system, retarding development of secondary sexual characteristics. Additionally, an amotivational syndrome from chronic cannabis intoxication results in lethargy, restlessness, and increased irritability (Cohen, 1984). Conversely, the same male drinking 1 to 3 ounces of alcohol (beer, wine, or hard liquor) over the same period of time will most likely experience both psychological and physiological withdrawal symptoms. Although medical complications may be more severe in the latter case, emotional, social, and intellectual complications occur in both.

Kandel (1984) proposes that culturally determined developmental stages of drug behavior are observed in adolescents. Initiation, progression, and regression in drug behavior are related to factors like prior delinquent behavior, high levels of drug-using peer affiliations, and parental models who use or abuse alcohol and drugs. The role of genetics in the development of substance abuse is also a major area of concern (Crabbe et al., 1985). Extensive research, primarily using animal models, indicates a strong predisposition to addiction in the offspring of addicted parents, particularly those using alcohol and sedative compounds. In sum, environment, psychosocial variables, and genetics are important concepts for consideration in adolescent substance abuse.

A single episode of intoxication does not produce either physical or psychological dependency. Several stages occur in the move from no use to dependency. The initial reason to try any drug depends more on the value the youth places on its use than on its pharmacological properties. Curiosity and availability, key factors at this stage, are influenced by the social factors of peer pressure and acceptance, adult role models, and family norms or values. Adolescents with learning disabilities are at particularly high risk for chemical dependency (Karacostas & Fisher, 1993) as are those with a history of physical and emotional abuse (Grella & Joshi, 2003). The majority of youthful experimenters do not proceed through all stages to dependence because of the drug effects themselves not being valued and the fact that most peer-group norms do not support continued use (Kandel et al., 1978).

Experimental use may proceed to casual or occasional use, frequently referred to as socio-recreational use. This pattern usually involves imitation of adult role models who drink during social gatherings or use other drugs as mood enhancers. The youthful user may use drugs while at a party once or twice a month, or while attending a movie or listening to music with friends. Such use tends to be spontaneous and in a social context where drugs are readily available. Reasons for use are primarily social in that friends use and approve of use. Also, the drugs enhance self-confidence and social interaction during the identity phase of adolescence. The youthful user does not avidly seek drugs at this stage but will participate with a group if drugs are available.

The third stage, regular use, is distinguished from socio-recreational use by several features. The user at this stage actively seeks drugs, and is rarely seen in a social context without being intoxicated. Psychological dependence occurs. The user perceives that he or she functions better in social gatherings while intoxicated. Regular use also may involve physiological dependence if the user develops tolerance to a drug and experiences physical discomfort with cessation. The pharmacological properties of the drug become critical at this point. Whether the user proceeds into the final stage, dependency, is partly a function of what the drug does for the user's personality and the user's stage in adolescence.

The final stage is physical and/or psychological reliance on the drug to produce the user's desired effect. Heavy or compulsive use implies daily intoxication, although the user may indulge in binge-type use. Although only a minority of users become chemically dependent youths, the central factor is the degree to which use dominates the life of the adolescent. Intoxication may avoid other critical issues of adolescence (e.g., responsibilities of school and family, stress, lack of self-confidence) or mask the pain and discomfort of other pathological personality or mental disorders. Psychological and physical dependence are critical at this stage because regardless of reasons for continued use, the youthful user will have to continue to take the drug in order to avoid the newly acquired set of symptoms and difficulties associated with chemical dependency (Kandel, 1984). Although chemical dependency is not an official handicapping condition under federal legislation, it has been considered (Williams, 1990), and specialized programs for individuals with disabilities have been developed (Campbell, 1994), such as the Mental Health/Chemical Dependency/Mental Retardation Certificate at the Columbus State Community College (CSCC; 2005).

REFERENCES

Adesso, V. J. (1985). Cognitive factors in alcohol and drug use. In M. Galizio & S. A. Maisto (Eds.), *Determinants of substance abuse* (pp. 179–208). New York: Plenum.

Bardo, M. T., & Risner, M. E. (1985). Biochemical substrates of drug abuse. In M. Galizio & S. A. Maisto (Eds.), *Determinants of substance abuse* (pp. 65–99). New York: Plenum.

Campbell, J. (1994). Issues in chemical dependency treatment and aftercare for people with learning differences. *Health and Social Work, 19,* 1, 63–70.

Cohen, S. (1983). *The alcoholism problems.* New York: Haworth.

Cohen, S. (1984). Adolescence and drug abuse: Biological consequences. In D. J. Lettieri & J. P. Ludford (Eds.), *Drug abuse and the American adolescent* (pp. 104–109). Rockville, MD: National Institute on Drug Abuse.

Crabbe, J. C., McSwigan, J. D., & Belknap, J. K. (1985). The role of genetics in substance abuse. In M. Galizio & S. A. Maisto (Eds.), *Determinants of substance abuse* (pp. 13–54). New York: Plenum.

Columbus State Community College (CSCC). (2005). *MH / CD / MR Program.* Retrieved July 19, 2005, from http://www.cscc.edu/DOCS/mhcd/mh/cdmr.htm

Grella, C. E., & Joshi, V. (2003). Treatment processes and outcomes among adolescents with a history of abuse who are in drug treatment. *Child Maltreatment, 8,* 7–18.

Kandel, D. B. (1980). Developmental stages in adolescent drug involvement. In D. J. Lettieri, M. Sayers, & H. W. Pearson (Eds.), *Drug abuse and the American adolescent* (pp. 120–127). Rockville, MD: National Institute on Drug Abuse.

Kandel, D. B. (1984). Drug use by youth: An overview. In D. J. Lettieri & J. P. Ludford (Eds.), *Drug abuse and the American adolescent* (pp. 1–24). Rockville, MD: National Institute on Drug Abuse.

Kandel, D. B., Kessler, R. C., & Margulies, R. (1978). Adolescent initiation into stages of drug use: A developmental analysis. In D. B. Kandel (Ed.), *Longitudinal research in drug use: Empirical findings and methodological issues* (pp. 73–99). Washington, DC: Hemisphere.

Karacostas, D. D., & Fisher, G. L. (1993). Chemical dependency in students with and without hearing disabilities. *Journal of Hearing Disabilities, 26,* 491–495.

Newman, B. M., & Newman, P. R. (1975). *Development through life: A psychosocial approach.* Homewood, IL: Dorsey.

Williams, R. W. (1990). Adolescent chemical dependency as a handicapping condition: An analysis of state regulations. *Journal of Chemical Dependency, 1,* 1, 69–82.

L. Worth Bolton
*Cape Fear Substance Abuse
Center*

**ALCOHOL AND DRUG ABUSE PATTERNS
DRUG ABUSE
SUBSTANCE ABUSE**

CHEMOTHERAPY

The treatment of cancer in children usually includes chemotherapy, which consists of drugs that are administered to the child intravenously, intramuscularly, or orally on a repeated schedule (e.g., every 10 days or every month). The purpose of chemotherapy is to poison the cancer cells. Unfortunately, it also is toxic to healthy cells of the body. As a result, many children receiving chemotherapy experience unpleasant side effects.

Two common side effects of chemotherapy are nausea and vomiting. Children differ in the extent to which they have these symptoms. Furthermore, the degree of nausea and vomiting for a given child may vary widely from one course of chemotherapy to the next, even when there are no changes in chemotherapy. Many children feel intensely ill during the days they receive chemotherapy and for a few days afterward. Other children are able to carry on with play and other normal activities to varying degrees (Kidshealth, 2005; Zeltzer, LeBaron & Zeltzer, 1984).

Another possible side effect is a temporary susceptibility to bacterial infection or excessive bleeding. During such a period, physicians usually will advise the child not to participate in any contact sports or activities (e.g., gymnastics) that might increase the risk of bleeding. Because children on chemotherapy also are sometimes at risk for severe illness with certain viral infections, doctors often advise these children to stay home from school for a period of time if there is an outbreak of chicken pox. However, for the majority of time the child is receiving chemotherapy, the doctor usually will permit the child to engage in all normal school activities, including sports.

Another problem related to chemotherapy is that total hair loss may occur. Baldness is the most troublesome side effect of chemotherapy for many children. Bald children may feel so embarrassed that they refuse to go to school. Many children cope with this problem by wearing a cap, kerchief, or wig; others explain to their friends the reason for the baldness. Fortunately, in almost all cases, the hair grows back once chemotherapy is completed.

What are the effects of chemotherapy on the child's behavior and academic performance? Many of these children are absent from school at regular intervals because of medical appointments and chemotherapy side effects. Some children also stay home because of embarrassment over hair loss and fear of being rejected by peers. A further reason for school absence is a fear of failure because of the large amount of school material missed (Deasy-Spinetta, 1981; Deasy-Spinetta & Spinetta, 1980; Katz, Kellerman, Rigler, Williams, & Siegle, 1977; Kidshealth, 2005).

For some children, radiation to the head produces cognitive deficits, especially when combined with injections of chemotherapy into the spinal canal. Many children with cancer show little or no evidence of cognitive deficits, but these are problems that can occur gradually and may be long-lasting. During the acute phase of radiation therapy, there often is transient swelling of the brain, which could produce additional temporary cognitive deficits.

There are several ways educators can be helpful to the student who is receiving chemotherapy. A teacher or counselor needs to contact the student's parents to discuss ways in which the student's educational needs can be met. For example, if the student is in the hospital, a few books and short assignments could be sent. If the child is likely to be at home for some time, homebound education may be indicated. A student who would not otherwise qualify for special education can qualify on the basis of the illness and can benefit greatly from both home and hospital teacher visits combined with regular school attendance.

With the permission of the child's parents, it usually is helpful to contact the student's physician to learn about the doctor's expectations regarding the student's capabilities during the period of treatment. The teacher also can ask the student how he or she feels about returning to school. A discussion of the student's needs and feelings with classmates can give the class an opportunity to discuss their misconceptions and worries about the student, as well as to ask questions. Children who are unable to return to school for a period of time usually appreciate receiving cards, drawings, or letters from classmates at school.

Educators need to be aware that hospitalization or confinement to bed at home because of nausea and vomiting does not necessarily preclude school work. On the contrary, involvement in school work, at least at a minimal level, can have therapeutic value. By attending school a few hours a day, having a homebound teacher, or doing some school work in the hospital, children can be distracted from unpleasant physical symptoms or worries. Some adolescents who receive chemotherapy in the morning prefer to come to school in the afternoon rather than to spend the rest of the day at home feeling sick. If the student experiences some nausea, he or she may need to leave the class abruptly. If these considerations are discussed in advance, then involvement in school can be therapeutic for many children and may reduce the severity of nausea and vomiting.

Teachers can be most helpful to children receiving chemotherapy by maintaining a flexible attitude and realistic expectations. Most children receiving chemotherapy can maintain a normal educational load. However, specific expectations regarding homework and exams need to be flexible because of the intermittent nature of treatment-related problems. Frequent consultation with the student and parent will help to define reasonable and appropriate education goals. An excellent web site for teachers is provided by Kidshealth.org. The information on this web site explains the use of chemotherapy and its effects (Kidshealth, 2005).

REFERENCES

Deasy-Spinetta, P. (1981). The school and the child with cancer. In J. J. Spinetta & P. Deasy-Spinetta (Eds.), *Living with childhood cancer* (pp. 153–168). St. Louis, MO: Mosby.

Deasy-Spinetta, P. M., & Spinetta, J. J. (1980). The child with cancer in school: Teachers' appraisal. *American Journal of Pediatric Hematology / Oncology, 2,* 89–94.

Katz, E. R., Kellerman, J., Rigler, D., Williams, K., & Siegle, S. E. (1977). School intervention with pediatric cancer patients. *Journal of Pediatric Psychology, 2,* 72–76.

Kidshealth. (2005). *Chemotherapy.* Retrieved July 19, 2005, from http://www.kidshealth.org/kid/health_problems/cancer/chemo.html

Zeltzer, L. K., LeBaron, S., & Zeltzer, P. M. (1984). The adolescent with cancer. In R. Blum (Ed.), *Chronic illness and disabilities in childhood and adolescence* (pp. 375–395). Orlando, FL: Grune & Stratton.

SAMUEL LEBARON
LONNIE K. ZELTZER
*University of Texas Health
Science Center*

CANCER, CHILDHOOD
HOMEBOUND INSTRUCTION

CHESS, STELLA (1914–   )

Stella Chess was born and educated in New York City. She received her BA from Smith College in 1935 and MD from New York University School of Medicine in 1939. She served several internships, including psychoanalytic training, and became a diplomate of the American Board of Psychiatry and Neurology in Child Psychiatry in 1959. A member of the staff at New York Medical College from 1945, she became Professor and Director of the Division of Child Psychiatry in 1964. In 1966 Chess moved to a full professorship at New York University.

Stella Chess

Chess is best known for her collaboration (1956–present) with her husband, Alexander Thomas, and Herbert Birch (deceased) on a longitudinal study of the individual characteristics of children. This study found early differentiable temperament factors that persist and strongly influence child-environment interaction and later behavior. Additional longitudinal studies by Chess include behavioral patterns and child care practices of Puerto Rican families in New York City (1956–1970), children with multiple handicaps and congenital rubella (1970–1981), and children with mild mental retardation (1963–1968).

For her book, *How to Help Your Child Get the Most Out of School* (1974), Chess was awarded the Family Life Book Award of the Child Study Association of America. Her many awards and honors include the Honors Award from the Society for Research in Child Development for Distinguished Contributions to Psychiatric Theory (1993), the Adolph Myers Award of the American Psychiatric Association for Scientific Contributions to Psychiatric Theory and Practice (1996), and the George Tarjan Award from the American Academy of Child and Adolescent Psychiatry for Significant Contributions to Mental and Developmental Disabilities.

Chess and Thomas were editors of the series *Annual Progress in Child Psychiatry and Child Development* from 1968 to 1970. Other books include *Origins and Evolution of Behavior Disorders: From Infancy to Early Adult Life* (1984/1987) and *Temperament: Theory and Practice* (1996). With well over 50 publications spanning 25 years, including journal articles, authored books, and edited books, Chess remains highly active and productive in her fields of interest.

REFERENCES

Chess, S., & Thomas, A. (1974). *Annual progress in child psychiatry and child development.* New York: Brunner/Mazel.

Chess, S., & Thomas, A. (1987). *Origins and evolution of behavior disorders: Infancy to early adult life.* Cambridge, MA: Harvard University Press.

Chess, S., & Thomas, A. (1996). *Temperament: Theory and practice.* New York: Brunner/Mazel.

Chess, S., & Whitbread, J. (1974). *How to help your child get the most out of school.* Garden City, NY: Doubleday.

ELAINE FLETCHER-JANZEN
*University of Colorado at
Colorado Springs*
First edition

TAMARA J. MARTIN
*The University of Texas of the
Permian Basin*
Second edition

CHILD ABUSE

The age-old phenomenon of child maltreatment only formally attracted the attention of mental health professionals in the 1960s. Psychiatric and psychological exploration of child battering has lagged two decades behind the pioneering efforts of pediatricians and radiologists in establishing medical diagnostic criteria for physical abuse in children. Between 1963 and 1965, the passage of laws by all 50 states requiring medical reporting of child abuse ultimately subjected the abusing parents to legal process; these laws were also the catalyst for the formation of child protective services throughout the nation. The first psychological studies of abusing parents were carried out during this period.

Child abuse is currently regarded as the leading cause of death in children and a major public health problem. The National Child Abuse and Neglect Data System (NCANDS) reported an estimated 1,400 child fatalities in 2002, and many believe this figure to be an underrepresentation. Young children are the most frequent targets of child abuse and approximately one third of their deaths are a result of neglect alone (NCANDS, 2005). The proliferation of child abuse and neglect might bear some relationship to the alarming general increase of violence in our society demonstrated by the rising incidence of violent crimes, delinquency, suicide, and lethal accidents. In the last 30 years, child abuse has become a major focus of research and clinical study. A concerted effort is being made by federal, state, and local governments to develop programs for the study, prevention, and treatment of child abuse.

Owing to its complexity and far-reaching consequences, the problem of child abuse has attracted the attention of professionals from widely divergent backgrounds. Contributions to this area have come from the fields of pediatrics, psychiatry, psychology, social work, sociology, nursing, education, law, and law enforcement. Such multidisciplinary involvement has been essential in tracking down cases, locating medical treatment, and arranging for protective intervention and long-term planning with families. At the same time, it has become a source of confusion as a result of the differing roles, frames of reference, and terminology of each specialty. Exclusively cultural, socioeconomic, psychodynamic, and behavioral interpretations of the child abuse syndrome have failed to present the full picture.

The definition of child abuse has been continually expanding in recent years. In a classic paper, "The Battered Child Syndrome" (Kempe et al., 1962), described child abuse as the infliction of serious injury on young children by parents or caretakers. The injuries, which included fractures, subdural hematoma, and multiple soft tissue injuries, often resulted in permanent disability and death. Fontana's (1964) concept of the "maltreatment syndrome" viewed child abuse as one end of a spectrum of maltreatment that also included emotional deprivation, neglect, and malnutrition. Helfer (1975) recognized the prevalence of minor injuries resulting from abuse and suspected that abuse might be implicated in 10 percent of all childhood accidents treated in emergency rooms. Gil (1974) extended the concept of child abuse to include any action that prevents a child from achieving his physical and psychological potential.

Child protective services are specialized agencies existing under public welfare auspices; they are responsible for receiving and investigating all reports of child abuse or maltreatment for the purpose of preventing further abuse, providing services necessary to safeguard the child's well-being, and strengthening the family unit. These agencies are responsible for maintaining service until the conditions of maltreatment are remedied. They also have the mandate to invoke the authority of the juvenile or family court to secure the protection and treatment of children whose parents are unable or unwilling to use their services.

The wide variety of behavior and personality traits observed in abusing parents suggests that a specific abusive personality does not exist. Rather, individuals with a certain psychological makeup operating in combination with the burden of a painfully perceived childhood and immediate environmental stress might be likely to abuse the offspring who most readily elicits the unhappy childhood imagery of the past. Frequently the perpetrator is a young adult in his or her mid 20s, without a high school diploma, living at the poverty level, with depression (NCANDS, 2005).

While environmental stress has often been suggested as a prominent etiological factor in child abuse, the precise definition of this relationship has eluded most investigators. One author has attributed child abuse almost exclusively to socioeconomic determinants (Gil, 1968, 1970), but most researchers agree that environmental stress is only the catalyst, in many instances, for an abuse-prone personality.

The stress argument has at least in part been predicated on the high percentage of low socioeconomic status (SES), multiple problem families in child abuse registers through-

out the country. It is probable that reporting procedures themselves have led to the greater emphasis on socioeconomic determinants. Any controlled study that matches for SES is compelled to look beyond such variables as family income for the origins of child abuse. The conclusion that Spinetta and Rigler (1972) reach in their review of the literature is far more likely—that environmental stress is neither necessary nor sufficient for child abuse but that it does, in some instances, interact with other factors such as parent personality variables and child behaviors to potentiate child battering.

Environmental stress includes current events that widen the discrepancy between the limited capacity of the parents and increased child-rearing pressures. The stress may consist of a diminution of child-rearing resources owing to a spouse's illness or desertion, or to the unavailability of an earlier caretaker such as a neighbor or some other family member.

Environmental stress also includes the actual or threatened loss of a key relationship that provides the parent with emotional security and dependency gratification. This may occur when the spouse becomes physically or emotionally unavailable or when ties with parents or important relatives are severed owing to estrangement, illness, or death. Additional child-rearing pressures such as the birth or illness of another child, or the assumption of temporary care of other children, create environmental stress that may also lead to child abuse.

Justice and Duncan (1975) described the contribution of work-related pressures to environmental stress in situations of child abuse. They cited four types of work-related situations: unemployed fathers caring for children at home; working mothers with domestic obligations; overworked husbands who neglect their wives; and traumatic job experiences resulting in undischarged tension. Justice and Justice (1979) were able to document the importance of stress in terms of excessive life changes in child-abusing families by means of the *Social Readjustment Rating Scale* developed by Holmes and Rahe (1967).

The greatest area of agreement in the field of child abuse has pertained to the history and background of the abusive parents themselves. These individuals have usually experienced abuse, deprivation, rejection, and inadequate mothering during childhood. As children they were subjected to unrealistic expectations and premature demands by their parents. Parents with these characteristics are said to have "abuse-prone" personality traits.

The psychodynamics in a given case of child abuse are largely determined by the abuse-prone personality traits of the parent. The relationship between the abusing parent and his or her child is distorted by the cumulative impact of the parent's own traumatic experiences as a child reared in a punitive, unloving environment. Individuals who abuse their children cannot envision any parent-child relationship as a mutually gratifying experience. The task of parenting mobilizes identifications with the parent-aggressor, child-victim dyad of the past. The key psychodynamic elements in child abuse are role reversal, excessive use of denial and projection as defenses, rapidly shifting identifications, and displacement of aggression from frustrating objects onto the child.

Role reversal occurs when the unfulfilled abusing parent seeks dependency gratification, which is unavailable from his or her spouse or family, from the "parentified" child. It is based on an identification with the child-victim. The child's inability to gratify the father or mother causes the youngster to be unconsciously perceived as the rejecting mother. This intensifies the parent's feelings of rejection and worthlessness, which further threaten his or her narcissistic equilibrium. These painful feelings are denied and projected onto the child, who then becomes the recipient of the parent's self-directed aggression.

Any plan for the prevention or treatment of child abuse must be designed to create a safe environment for the child and to modify the potentiating factors underlying abuse. Therefore, an effective treatment program must deal specifically with the parental abuse proneness, those characteristics of the child that make him or her vulnerable for scapegoating, and the environmental stresses that trigger the abusive interaction.

A wide range of psychotherapeutic and educational techniques have proven successful in reducing the symptoms and problems of abused children. In general, these children present with ego deficits and cognitive impairment to such a degree that an emphasis on ego integration, reality testing, containment of drives and impulses, and strengthening of higher level defenses (similar to those techniques applied to borderline and psychotic children) proves necessary.

The ideal objective in studying and treating child abuse on a nationwide scale is, as with any major public health problem, the development of a strategy for prevention. Thus far, early case findings and protective intervention in abusing families have been the primary areas of interest for workers in this field. As more basic knowledge is accumulated about the child-abuse syndrome, through clinical experience and research, one can envision a logical shift in focus from treatment and rehabilitation (secondary prevention) to primary intervention. The National Clearinghouse on Child Abuse and Neglect (NCANDS; 2005) has an extensive web site with multiple topics, resources and links.

REFERENCES

Fontana, V. (1964). *The maltreated child*. Springfield, IL: Thomas.

Gil, D. (1968). Incidence of child abuse and demographic characteristics of persons involved. In R. E. Helfer & C. H. Kempe (Eds.), *The battered child*. Chicago: University of Chicago Press.

Gil, D. (1970). *Violence against children*. Cambridge, MA: Harvard University Press.

Gil, D. (1974). *A holistic perspective on child abuse and its prevention*. Paper presented at the Conference on Research on Child Abuse, National Institute of Child Health and Human Development, Washington, DC.

Helfer, R. E. (1975). *The diagnostic process and treatment programs*. Washington, DC: U.S. Department of Health, Education and Welfare, National Center for Child Abuse and Neglect.

Holmes, T., & Rahe, R. (1967). The social readjustment rating scale. *Journal of Psychosomatic Medicine, 11,* 213–218.

Justice, B., & Duncan, D. (1975). *Child abuse as a work-related problem*. Paper presented at American Public Health Association, Chicago.

Justice, B., & Justice, R. (1979). *The broken taboo: Sex in the family*. New York: Human Science Press.

Kempe, C. H., Silverman, F., Steele, B., Droegemueller, W., & Silver, H. (1962). The battered child syndrome. *Journal of the American Medical Association, 181,* 17–24.

NCANDS. (2005). *National Clearinghouse on Child Abuse and Neglect Information*. Retrieved July 19, 2005, from http://www.nccanch.acf.hhs.gov/pubs/factsheets/fatality.pdf

Spinetta, J., & Rigler, D. (1972). The child abusing parent: A psychological review. *Psychological Bulletin, 77,* 296–304.

CHARLES P. BARNARD
University of Wisconsin at Stout

ABUSED CHILDREN, PSYCHOTHERAPY WITH

See **BATTERED CHILD SYNDROME**

CHILD DEVELOPMENT

Since its inception in 1930, *Child Development* was published six times a year by the University of Chicago Press. It is a professional journal sponsored by the Society for Research in Child Development. As an interdisciplinary group, the Society for Research in Child Development uses the *Child Development* journal to publish manuscripts from all academic and professional disciplines that study developmental processes. The articles range from empirical and theoretical to reviews of previous research. The scholarly papers that appear in *Child Development* focus on the growth and development of children from conception through adolescence, including the development of language, thinking and reasoning, moral judgment, social skills, and family relationships.

The distribution of the journal, while primarily North American, is international. The editorial board is made of world renowned scholars. *Child Development,* clearly the most comprehensive journal in this field, is read by psychologists, pediatricians, anthropologists, social workers, and others who wish to obtain information related to research in child development.

The editor of *Child Development* is Lynn S. Liben and subscription information can be obtained online from Blackwell Publishing at http://www.blackwellpublishing .com/cservices/single.asp or by calling Blackwell Publishing Customer Service Center at (800) 835-6770.

Michael J. Ash
Jose Luis Torres
Texas A&M University

CHILD FIND

Child find is a federal requirement for states to identify, locate, and evaluate all children, from birth to age 21, in need of special education services as mandated through Part C of the Individuals with Disabilities Education Act (IDEA) of 1997 and the Individuals with Disabilities Education Improvement Act (IDEIA) of 2004. The term *child find* has been in use since 1974. In 1986, Congress authorized support for the Infants and Toddlers with Disabilities Program under Part H of the Education for All Handicapped Children Act, which is now known as "child find" through the IDEA. This legislation represents an effort to promote the importance of early intervention for children with disabilities and to provide services for their family's functioning abilities. In addition, the federal definition of *child find* includes a requirement for states to find nontraditional or highly mobile children (such as migrant and homeless children). There are two programs providing services to children who are eligible under the IDEA guidelines, the Early Intervention Program (Part C) and the Preschool Special Education Program (Part B/619). Through these programs, each state is required to have a comprehensive child find system. A comprehensive system includes a definition of the target population, public awareness, referral and intake, screening and identification of young children who may be eligible for IDEA services, eligibility determination, tracking, and interagency coordination. Unfortunately, the states differ on their systems for identifying children (U.S. Office of Special Education Programs, 1997; The Dynamic Community Connections Project, 2005).

The research supports early intervention as the best way to help children with disabilities. The number of children served under Part C of IDEA has increased by 25 percent from 1994–1999 (The Dynamic Community Connections Project, 2005). However, the National Early Intervention Longitudinal Study (Hebbeler et al., 2004) estimated the average age of identifying children with a developmental delay is 15.5 months. Furthermore, children of color represented 44 percent of the early intervention population, which is greater than their representation in the general population (37 percent).

Due to health disparities and unequal access to health care, there is an effort to improve access to services for children. Therefore, states coordinate a variety of child find strategies to notify the public and improve program participation, especially among diverse groups. Methods such as door-to-door visits, brochures, and contacting pediatricians were useful in notifying the public (Karnes & Shaunessy, 2004). Pavri (2001) proposed several guidelines in an attempt to develop culturally sensitive programs. A study conducted in Hawaii examined equity of access to referrals and enrollment and found promising results with low-income and immigrant households, but improvements for access to resources were needed for military families and families whose children lacked health insurance (Shapiro & Derrington, 2004). One of the few nationwide studies examined families' experiences with determining their child's eligibility, interaction with professionals, and satisfaction with services (Bailey, Hebbeler, Scarborough, Spiker, & Mallik, 2004). Interestingly, some states, including Kansas, Louisiana, Pennsylvania, Tennessee, and West Virginia incorporate "gifted" in their child find eligibility definitions and further initiatives to develop a national child find plan to identify this group are occurring (Shapiro & Derrington, 2004).

The U.S. Office of Special Education Programs is funding studies from six states for the early childhood child find demonstration projects. These feasibility projects are the *Interagency Collaboration for Colorado Part C Child Find*, Denver, CO. *Enhanced Child Find through Newborn Hearing Screening*, Farmington, CT; *Strategies for Effective and Efficient "Keiki" (Child) Find (Project SEEK)*, Honolulu, HI; *Dynamic Community Connections: A Process Model for Enhancing Child Find in Rural Areas*, Missoula, MT; *Promoting Early Identification and Support for Families of Young Children: The Early Connections Project*, Durham, NH; and *Creating Partnerships between Pediatric Practitioners and Early Developmental Interventionists for Child Find (PEDI-Link)*, Burlington, VT (The Dynamic Community Connections Project, 2005). Furthermore, there are national reports on the success of child find. The Office of Special Education collects annual data and provides data fact sheets on Part C of IDEA (U.S. Office of Special Education Programs, 2005). In addition, there are annual reports to Congress about the effectiveness of IDEA (Twenty-fifth Annual Report, 2003).

REFERENCES

Bailey, D., Hebbeler, K., Scarborough, A., Spiker, D., & Mallik, S. (2004). First experiences with early intervention: A national perspective. *Pediatrics, 113,* 887–897.

The Dynamic Community Connections Project. (2005). *Child find.* Retrieved July 29, 2005, from www.childfindidea.org

Hebbeler, K., Wagner, M., Spiker, D., Scarborough, A., Simeonsson, R., & Collier, M. (2004). A national look at children and families entering early intervention. *Exceptional Children, 70,* 469–484.

Individuals with Disabilities Education Act (IDEA) P.L. 105-17. (1997). [Electronic version]. Retrieved July 28, 2005, from http://www.cec.sped.org/law_res/doc/law/law/index.php

Individuals with Disabilities Education Improvement Act (IDEIA) P.L. 108-446. (2004). [Electronic version]. Retrieved September 6, 2005, from http://www.ed.gov/policy/speced/guid/idea/idea2004.html

Karnes, F. A., & Shaunessy, E. (2004). A plan for child find in gifted education. *Roeper Review, 26,* 229–233.

Pavri, S. (2001). Developmental delay or cultural difference? Developing effective child find practices for young children from culturally and linguistically diverse families. *Exceptional Children, 4,* 2–9.

Shapiro, B. J., & Derrington, T. M. (2004). Equity and disparity in access to services: An outcome-based evaluation of early intervention child find in Hawai'i. *Topics in Early Childhood Special Education, 24,* 199–213.

Twenty-fifth annual report to Congress on the implementation of the IDEA. (2003). Washington, DC: U.S. Department of Education.

U.S. Office of Special Education Programs. (2005). *Individuals with disabilities education act (IDEA) data: Part C annual report tables.* Retrieved July 29, 2005, from http://www.ideadata.org/PartCReport.asp

Krystal T. Cook
Texas A&M University

**DEVELOPMENTAL DELAY
EARLY IDENTIFICATION OF CHILDREN WITH
DISABILITIES**

CHILD GUIDANCE CLINIC

Child guidance clinics are the result of the blending of several historical forces. The feminist movement was instrumental in opening the way for the *Century of the Child* (Key, 1909). This was precipitated by a new interest in child psychology that occurred at the turn of the century. Concern for children was also evidenced at this time in the passage of child labor laws. Also, as compulsory education gained momentum, problem children could no longer be hidden away at home and school-related problems became more prominent. In fact, the first clinic created for children (Lightner Witmer, at the University of Pennsylvania in 1896) was primarily concerned with the adaptation of children to the school situation. In 1891, America's earliest child psychologist of renown, G. Stanley Hall, designed the first journal devoted to child psychology; it served as a record of educational literature, institutions, and progress.

A second major force in the development of child clinics was the mental hygiene movement that was stimulated by the publication of *The Mind That Found Itself* (Beers, 1908). Beers and his associates set out to disprove the age-old dictum that suggested once insane, insane forever. This proved

to be a significant step in the direction of acknowledging that if mental hygiene held value for adults, the same must hold true for children.

Another significant force was the influence of the psychiatrists that came to be known as the Boston Group. They viewed mental disorders as maladjustments of the personality rather than as diseases of the nervous system. Adolf Meyer (1928), a member of this group, believed that all possible factors should be considered, including original endowment, personality traits, home influences, habits, bodily ailments, and environmental stresses. Meyer is also believed to be the initiator of psychiatric social work as his wife visited the homes of his patients to determine emotional histories and information about their personalities and other illnesses. Meyer's wife was also concerned with preparing families for the return of the patient to the home setting. This interest in families and the childhood experiences of adult patients established a precedent for similar interest in the families and experiences of child patients.

By 1921 there were a number of clinics for children that were attached to mental hospitals, social agencies, schools, and colleges. Child guidance clinics were formally organized under that name in 1922 by the National Committee for Mental Hygiene and the Commonwealth Fund. These early clinics emphasized a team approach to the diagnosis and treatment of children's problems. A social worker and psychologist (under the supervision of a psychiatrist) constituted the treatment team. Thus, the interdisciplinary team concept was initiated, and it was revolutionary for its time. While interdisciplinary teams today have considerable overlap in role and function, the early teams were regimented so that the psychologist did the necessary testing, the social worker dealt with the parents (typically just the mother), and the psychiatrist worked with the child.

The Philadelphia Child Guidance Clinic was one of these early clinics; it has survived the years and seems reflective of the changes that have evolved. This is the clinic that is identified strongly with one of the major orientations to working with families: primarily structural family therapy as developed by Salvador Minuchin (1974). As Minuchin was an employee of the Philadelphia-based clinic, so were other influential persons in the development of family therapy such as Jay Haley, Harry Aponte, and Braulio Montalvo. This clinic also demonstrates the great overlap of functioning by various disciplines; social workers, psychologists, and psychiatrists all share equally in the delivery of services. In fact, a project supervised by Haley and Minuchin in the early 1970s focused on the training of lay people as significant helpers with troubled families. The Philadelphia Child Guidance Clinic, with its emphasis on one-way mirrors live supervision, and video taping has also distinguished itself as a significant training institution. While not on the same scale as the Philadelphia clinic many other clinics have followed the lead and developed themselves as centers of treatment and training (Chandra, Srinath & Kinshore,

1993). Certainly, the early child guidance clinics initiated the development of a far more elaborate treatment delivery system, but their influence still seems easily distinguishable as one considers the many community mental health centers that feature the multidisciplinary treatment teams that are now considered standard practice.

REFERENCES

Beers, C. (1908). *The mind that found itself.* New York: Longmans, Green.

Chandra, P. S., Srinath, S., & Kinshore, A. (1993). Disturbed children grown up: Follow up of a child guidance clinic population into adulthood. *NIMHANS Journal, 11,* 1, 43–47.

Key, E. (1909). *The century of the child.* New York: Putnam.

Meyer, A. (1928). Presidential address: 35 years of psychiatry in the United States and our present outlook. *American Journal of Psychiatry,* LXXXV, 1–32.

Minuchin, S. (1974). *Families and family therapy.* Cambridge, MA: Harvard University Press.

CHARLES P. BARNARD
University of Wisconsin at Stout

CHILD PSYCHIATRY
CHILD PSYCHOLOGY

CHILD MALTREATMENT AND DISABILITIES

Child maltreatment is the general term used to describe all forms of child abuse and neglect. The federal government defines child abuse and neglect in the Child Abuse Prevention and Treatment Act as "the physical and mental injury, sexual abuse, negligent treatment, or maltreatment of a child under the age of 18 by a person who is responsible for the child's welfare under circumstances which indicate that the child's health or welfare is harmed or threatened." Each state elaborates on the federal definition of child maltreatment and specifically defines what constitutes each type of abuse for residents of that state.

Relationships between disabilities and child maltreatment have been known for several decades. Children diagnosed with disabilities are several times more likely than their nondisabled peers to have a confirmed history of maltreatment. In addition, children with a history of maltreatment are more likely to be diagnosed with a disability. While researchers have determined this strong link exists, the nature of this relationship is not clear.

In 1962, the importance of child maltreatment was heightened when Kempe introduced the termed *battered child syndrome.* His scholarship and that of others helped raise awareness and spearheaded legislation in the fight against child abuse and neglect (Kempe, Silverman, Steele, Droegemueller, & Silver, 1962). One of the first studies directly exploring relationships between child maltreatment and children with disabilities analyzed the maltreatment histories of 3,881 hospitalized children using records from child protection services, foster care, and law enforcement to determine if there was a history of maltreatment (Sullivan & Knutson, 2000). Children with disabilities were found to be at risk for maltreatment.

A follow-up study (Sullivan & Knutson, 2002) dispelled any doubts of the previous findings. A review of records from 50,278 students enrolled in public and Archdiocese schools in Omaha, Nebraska, found that children placed in special education were 3.4 times more likely to be maltreated than their classmates without disabilities. In addition, 22 percent of children with a history of maltreatment were receiving special education services.

Most children suffered from more than one form of maltreatment. Neglect was the most common form of abuse. Compared to their classmates without disabilities, children with disabilities were 3.88 times more likely to be emotionally abused, 3.79 times more likely to be physically abused, 3.76 times more likely to be neglected, and 3.14 times more likely to be sexually abused. Among children who had confirmed histories of abuse, 50 percent were diagnosed with a behavioral disorder, 30 percent as having speech and language disorders, and 25 percent with mental retardation or health impairments. Thus, there is no question that a strong relationship exists between child maltreatment and disability.

Instances in which child abuse directly causes the disability were examined. The shaken baby syndrome (SBS) was one of the most common. Among children who survive this type of attack, approximately 60 percent suffer from severe disabilities. A study tracing the histories of 25 shaken baby syndrome infants found only 10 survived and only one was discharged without a diagnosed disability (Fischer & Allasio, 1994). In addition to shaken baby syndrome in infants, approximately one-fourth of serious brain injury in young children results from child abuse. For example, Reece and Sege (2000) found that child abuse was the cause of 19 percent of the cases where children under the age of 6.5 were admitted to the hospital with brain injury. Cases of brain injury suffered as a result of physical abuse are the clearest link that abuse causes disability.

Child maltreatment can have adverse behavioral and psychological effects. Learning and behavior problems may be one of the most common effects of child maltreatment (Mansell & Sobsey, 2001). Children who suffer horrific forms of child maltreatment may develop Posttraumatic Stress Disorder (PTSD) for which the more common forms of complications are withdrawal, aggression, sexually inappropriate behavior, depression, and low self-esteem (Mansell & Sobsey). Regression in learning also is common because children become preoccupied with the traumatic events they experienced. Given these conditions, children can respond to stress with intense neurological and neuropsychological reactions that can block their ability to learn in the classroom.

Current research is focusing on neurological effects and brain development during the first years of life. Children who experience severe and ongoing trauma are more likely to develop a host of neurological deficits, including mental illness, vulnerability to addictions, damage to the structure of the hippocampus, seizures, attention deficits (Brownlee, 1996) as well as the limbic system, one essential to attention in young children (Teicher, Glod, Surrey, & Swett, 1993).

Various conditions may increase the risk for children to develop disabilities along with becoming victims of child maltreatment. Substance abuse during pregnancy is one of the most common forms. Approximately 2 percent of women reportedly consumed more than five drinks in one day during their pregnancy (Batshaw & Conlon, 1997). Approximately 2 babies out of 1,000 are born with fetal alcohol syndrome, and 4 out of 1,000 are born with a milder condition. These children account for nearly 10 to 20 percent of the population with mental retardation (Batshaw & Conlon).

Drug abuse also plays a major role in contributing to disabilities in prenatal children. Approximately 1 percent of pregnant women report using cocaine at some time during their pregnancy (Sobsey, 2002). These babies are more likely to be born premature, display developmental problems, and numerous other complications. Parental drug use is highly correlated with the occurrence of child abuse within the home (Thyen, Leventhal, Yazdgerdi, & Perrin, 1997).

Spousal abuse and domestic violence also increases the risk for children to develop disabilities along with becoming victims of child maltreatment. Approximately 10 percent of women report violence during pregnancy. Mothers experiencing both physical and nonphysical abuse are more than twice as likely to deliver premature and low birth weight babies. Their higher level of anxiety increases the risk of decreased blood flow to the uterus (Fernandez & Krueger, 1999), thus increasing the likelihood of the fetus being born with a disability. A child who witnesses domestic violence also becomes more likely to develop a disability or suffer from violence-invoked injury. High levels of stress in children may result in such medical problems as asthma, diarrhea, ulcers, and intestinal problems (Horton & Cruise, 2001). Children also run the risk of regressing in their development in such areas as toileting, language, eating, and sleeping patterns (Margolin, 1998).

Educators can expect 10 percent of their students to display both a history of maltreatment and a diagnosed disability (Sullivan and Knutson, 2000). These students are likely to display various learning, behavioral, and academic challenges. Teachers, school psychologists, and other early interventionists constitute a large faction of frontline professionals who should become engaged in preventing, intervening, and providing treatment for this population. Regardless of the dangers their home environment presents, most children attend on a daily basis a public school system that is committed to serving the needs of all children. Thus, educators and other school personnel should be vigilant in identifying and serving this large and vulnerable population.

REFERENCES

Batshaw, M. L., & Conlon, C. J. (1997). Substance abuse: A preventable threat to development. In M. L. Batshaw (Ed.), *Children with disabilities* (4th ed., pp. 143–162). Baltimore: Brookes.

Brownlee, S. (1996, November 11). Fear can harm a child's brain, is it reversible? *U.S. News and World Report.*

Child Abuse Prevention and Treatment Act (CAPTA) as amended by Keeping Children and Families Safe Act of 2003, 42 U.S.C. § 5106(g) (2003).

Fernandez, F. M., & Krueger, P. M. (1999). Domestic violence: Effect on pregnancy outcome. *Journal of the American Osteopathic Association, 99,* 254–256.

Fischer H, & Allasio D. (1994). Permanently damaged: long-term follow-up of shaken babies. *Pediatrics, 33,* 696–698.

Horton, C., & Cruise, T. (2001). *Child abuse & neglect: The school's response.* New York: Guilford.

Kempe, C. H., Silverman, F. N., Steele, B. F., Droegemueller, W., & Silver, H. K. (1962). The battered child syndrome. *Journal of the American Medical Association, 181,* 17–24.

Mansell, S., & Sobsey, D. (2001). *Counseling people with developmental disabilities who have been sexually abused.* Kingston, NY: NADD Press.

Margolin, G. (1998). *Effects of domestic violence on children. In Violence against Children in the Family and the Community* (pp. 57–102). Washington, DC: American Psychological Association.

Reece, R. M., & Sege, R. (2000). Childhood head injuries: Accidental or inflicted? *Archives of Pediatric and Adolescent Medicine, 154,* 11–15.

Sobsey, D. (2002). Exceptionality, education, and maltreatment. *Exceptionality, 10*(1), 29–46.

Sullivan, P. M., & Knutson, J. F. (1998). The association between child maltreatment and disabilities in a hospital-based epidemiological study. *Child Abuse & Neglect, 22,* 271–278.

Sullivan, P. M., & Knutson, J. F. (2000). Maltreatment and disabilities: A population-based epidemiological study. *Child Abuse & Neglect, 24,* 1257–1273.

Teicher, M., Glod, C., Surrey, J., & Swett, C. (1993). Early childhood abuse and limbic system ratings in adult psychiatric outpatients. *Journal of Neuropsychiatry and Clinical Neurosciences, 5,* 301–306.

Thyen, U., Leventhal, J. M., Yazdgerdi, S. R., & Perrin, J. M. (1997). Concerns about child maltreatment in hospitalized children. *Child Abuse & Neglect, 21,* 187–198.

DANIELLE MADERA
University of Florida

BATTERED CHILD SYNDROME
CHILD ABUSE

CHILD WITH A DISABILITY, DEFINITION OF

The Education for All Handicapped Children Act of 1975 (P.L. 94-142) originally defined the disability conditions that are eligible for services that are reimbursable by the federal government. Early versions of the Individuals with Disabilities Education Act (IDEA) maintained essentially the same wording in the definition of "handicapped". More recent iterations of the IDEA and its implementing regulations have adopted the now preferred term "child with a disability" when referring to children eligible for certain types of assistance under the IDEA. The regulations currently in effect to implement the IDEA define a child with a disability as a child evaluated in accordance with the regulations who is found as "having mental retardation, a hearing impairment including deafness, a speech or language impairment, a visual impairment including blindness, serious emotional disturbance, an orthopedic impairment, autism, traumatic brain injury, an other health impairment, a specific learning disability, deaf-blindness or multiple disabilities, and who, by reason thereof, needs special education and related services" (34 C.F.R. 300.7(a)(1). Children requiring only "related services" under the IDEA who do not need special education services are not included in this definition, although if the service that is considered a related service under federal law is considered a special education service under applicable state standards, the child is still considered a child with a disability (34 C.F.R. 300.7(a)(2)). Proposed regulations issued June 21, 2005, to implement the most recent version of the IDEA, which was passed in 2004, make only minor, non-substantive changes to this definition.

The terms used in the definition of "child with a disability" are further defined by the current regulations as follows:

(1)(i) *Autism* means a developmental disability significantly affecting verbal and nonverbal communication and social interaction, generally evident before age 3, that adversely affects a child's educational performance. Other characteristics often associated with autism are engagement in repetitive activities and stereotyped movements, resistance to environmental change or change in daily routines, and unusual responses to sensory experiences. The term does not apply if a child's educational performance is adversely affected primarily because the child has an emotional disturbance, as defined in paragraph (b)(4) of this section.

   (ii) A child who manifests the characteristics of "autism" after age 3 could be diagnosed as having "autism" if the criteria in paragraph (c)(1)(i) of this section are satisfied.

(2) *Deaf-blindness* means concomitant hearing and visual impairments, the combination of which causes such severe communication and other developmental and educational needs that they cannot be accommodated in special education programs solely for children with deafness or children with blindness.

(3) *Deafness* means a hearing impairment that is so severe that the child is impaired in processing linguistic information through hearing, with or without amplification, that adversely affects a child's educational performance.

(4) *Emotional disturbance* is defined as follows:

   (i) The term means a condition exhibiting one or more of the following characteristics over a long period of time and to a marked degree that adversely affects a child's educational performance:

     (A) An inability to learn that cannot be explained by intellectual, sensory, or health factors.

     (B) An inability to build or maintain satisfactory interpersonal relationships with peers and teachers.

     (C) Inappropriate types of behavior or feelings under normal circumstances.

     (D) A general pervasive mood of unhappiness or depression.

     (E) A tendency to develop physical symptoms or fears associated with personal or school problems.

   (ii) The term includes schizophrenia. The term does not apply to children who are socially maladjusted, unless it is determined that they have an emotional disturbance.

(5) *Hearing impairment* means an impairment in hearing, whether permanent or fluctuating, that adversely affects a child's educational performance but that is not included under the definition of deafness in this section.

(6) *Mental retardation* means significantly subaverage general intellectual functioning, existing concurrently with deficits in adaptive behavior and manifested during the developmental period, that adversely affects a child's educational performance.

(7) *Multiple disabilities* means concomitant impairments (such as mental retardation-blindness, mental retardation-orthopedic impairment, etc.), the combination of which causes such severe educational needs that they cannot be accommodated in special education programs solely for one of the impairments. The term does not include deaf-blindness.

(8) *Orthopedic impairment* means a severe orthopedic impairment that adversely affects a child's educational performance. The term includes impairments caused by congenital anomaly (e.g., clubfoot, absence of some member, etc.), impairments caused by disease (e.g., poliomyelitis, bone tuberculosis, etc.), and impairments from other causes (e.g., cerebral palsy, amputations, and fractures or burns that cause contractures).

(9) *Other health impairment* means having limited strength, vitality or alertness, including a height-

ened alertness to environmental stimuli, that results in limited alertness with respect to the educational environment, that—

(i) Is due to chronic or acute health problems such as asthma, attention deficit disorder or attention deficit hyperactivity disorder, diabetes, epilepsy, a heart condition, hemophilia, lead poisoning, leukemia, nephritis, rheumatic fever, and sickle cell anemia; and

(ii) Adversely affects a child's educational performance.

(10) *Specific learning disability* is defined as follows:

(i) *General.* The term means a disorder in one or more of the basic psychological processes involved in understanding or in using language, spoken or written, that may manifest itself in an imperfect ability to listen, think, speak, read, write, spell, or to do mathematical calculations, including conditions such as perceptual disabilities, brain injury, minimal brain dysfunction, dyslexia, and developmental aphasia.

(ii) *Disorders not included.* The term does not include learning problems that are primarily the result of visual, hearing, or motor disabilities, of mental retardation, of emotional disturbance, or of environmental, cultural, or economic disadvantage.

(11) *Speech or language impairment* means a communication disorder, such as stuttering, impaired articulation, a language impairment, or a voice impairment, that adversely affects a child's educational performance.

(12) *Traumatic brain injury* means an acquired injury to the brain caused by an external physical force, resulting in total or partial functional disability or psychosocial impairment, or both, that adversely affects a child's educational performance. The term applies to open or closed head injuries resulting in impairments in one or more areas, such as cognition; language; memory; attention; reasoning; abstract thinking; judgment; problem-solving; sensory, perceptual, and motor abilities; psychosocial behavior; physical functions; information processing; and speech. The term does not apply to brain injuries that are congenital or degenerative, or to brain injuries induced by birth trauma.

(13) *Visual impairment including blindness* means an impairment in vision that, even with correction, adversely affects a child's educational performance. The term includes both partial sight and blindness.

34 C.F.R. 300.7(c). The proposed regulations issued in June 2005 make only minor, non-substantive changes to these definitions.

KIMBERLY F. APPLEQUIST
*University of Colorado at
Colorado Springs*

DISABILITY
DISABILITY ETIQUETTE
INDIVIDUALS WITH DISABILITIES EDUCATION
    IMPROVEMENT ACT OF 2004 (IDEIA)

CHILDHOOD APHASIA

Childhood aphasia, a label used in the pediatric and neurologic literature to describe disorders of speech and language in children, covers various disorders of communication. It is applied to children who have impairment of previously normal language and to children who failed in the normal acquisition of language.

The term aphasia derives from adult pathology in which an acute or progressive lesion produces a characteristic language disorder; it is "a clinical term that denotes the loss or impairment of language following brain damage and therefore, by definition, aphasia is a neurologic disorder" (Benson, 1979). When the brain has reached maturity, all the cerebral areas have their specialized activities. The language function is localized in the left hemisphere in right-handed people but also in the majority of left-handed persons. The cerebral hemispheres are not symmetrical anatomically or functionally. The asymmetry is already present in the fetus, but it becomes more marked in adult life. The planum temporale (superior temporal cortex) is larger on the left side of the brain and corresponds to an auditory association area which, in the adult, is included in the receptive area for language, called Wernicke's area. The left hemisphere is preponderant for language but its activities result from relations with different areas of the same hemisphere and also with the right hemisphere, which participates in language function.

An exhaustive study of cerebral lateralization, cerebral dominance, and asymmetrical functions in the nervous system was reviewed by Geschwind and Galaburda (1985). Many classifications of the adult aphasias are known. Benson (1979) describes in detail eight different types of acquired aphasia that are based on the possibility of the patient expressing himself or herself in a fluent way or not, of understanding spoken language or not, of repeating, reading, and writing. In the adult there are mainly two groups of aphasia. The first, in which the patient is more affected in the comprehension of oral language, is called receptive, sensory, or Wernicke's aphasia. The patient is able to speak fluently but speech may have no connection with the questions asked. The pathology involves the posterior-superior portion of the first temporal gyrus (Wernicke's area). In the second group, the aphasic patient has great difficulties with speech but is able to write or to show the answers indicating that comprehension is correct. This is expressive, motor, or Broca's aphasia. The underlying pathology affects mainly the prerolandic region of the brain (frontal operculum or Broca's area).

Acquired aphasia in children is defined as impairment of previously normal language. Even in similar pathologic processes, as in adults, the clinical symptoms of aphasia in children depend on the degree of language development prior to cerebral insult. Childhood aphasia is characterized by an absence of spontaneous expressive language (oral, written, and gestural), producing a clinical syndrome of nonfluent speech or mutism (Wright, 1982). In all cases, the lexicon is reduced and the syntax is simplified; there is no logorrhea and even the lesion is temporal. Recovery is more frequent and rapid than in the adult, but when children regain language they rarely return to the premorbid level. Guttmann (1942) showed that disorders of language are mainly a reduction of the verbal expression of speech (thus, mainly a motor disorder). The prognosis is good unless there are simultaneous expressive and comprehension disorders.

Basser (1962) supported hemispheric equipotentiality because pre- or perinatal hemiplegia does not produce language impairment if the lesion is left or right; there is a possible transfer to the other hemisphere of the processes responsible for language when the damage is early, before language development. But if language is already acquired at the time of the hemiplegia, there is a persistent language deficit. Alajouanine and Lhermitte (1965) studied acquired aphasia in 32 children ages 6 to 15 years. The lesion was always in the left hemisphere, either traumatic or vascular. In all cases, they observed a reduction in expression in oral language, written language, or gestures; spontaneous language was nearly absent. Lenneberg (1967) suggested that up to age 11, language function could be assumed by the right hemisphere. However, Hecaen (1976) showed that 88 percent of acquired aphasias in children are due to left hemisphere lesions, while only 33 percent have right hemisphere lesions. Woods and Teuber (1978) confirmed that less than 10 percent of acquired aphasia results from right hemisphere lesions; if left-handedness is excluded, only 5 percent are due to right hemispheric lesions. Recovery, more frequent than in adults, is less evident if there are bilateral lesions. Recovery is better and more likely to occur with early lesions, before age 8. The recovery is never complete in comparison with normal controls, even when the child is no longer aphasic. In children with an injury prior to 12 months, there is no deficit in language, but the verbal IQ is significantly lower than that of sibling controls, showing that hemispheric specialization for language is very early. If the injury to the left hemisphere is made after 1 year, there is a persistent aphasic deficit as well as impaired cognitive function (Woods & Carey, 1979).

A syndrome of aphasia with convulsive disorders has been described in childhood by Landau and Kleffner (1957; GAPS, 2005). This syndrome occurs in children who have had normal language development. It may begin between 18 months of age and 13 years, but the peak is reached between 3 and 7 years. The affected children may develop acutely or progressively (over days to months) a severe impairment of verbal comprehension as well as a loss of expressive language. At times, they appear deaf. The deficit has been ascribed to a verbal auditory agnosia (Rapin et al., 1977) or autism, developmental disorder, hearing impairment, childhood schizophrenia, attention deficit hyperactivity disorder, mental retardation, or emotional/behavioral disorders (GAPS, 2005). The aphasic disorder may fluctuate with complete recovery and relapse. Intelligence remains normal. Outcome is variable with complete recovery or persistence of a mild or moderate deficit. Epileptic fits usually precede the language disorder, but they are not always present even though the electroencephalogram (EEG) always shows paroxysmal epileptic activity. The clinical fits usually disappear before 15 years and the EEG also becomes normal. No organic lesion has been shown in this syndrome.

Developmental language disorders or dysphasias are seen in children who have never acquired normal language function. They have been described under various terms: congenital or developmental aphasias, specific language disorders, and dysphasias. From the literature it appears that the capability for human language is partially an innate cognitive skill (Mayeux & Kandel, 1985). The process of acquisition of normal language function (Rapin, 1982; Wright, 1982) starts at birth. Infants with normal hearing are sensitive to sounds and react to them; they progressively become able to discriminate the acoustically subtle phonetic cues crucial for the comprehension of human language. This sensitivity is lost as language is acquired. Children learn to associate meaningful visual precepts (visual memory) with discriminable auditory ones (auditory memory), and to demonstrate this by pointing to objects on verbal command. Therefore, language acquisition is not a passive operation based on imitation. The child will only start to repeat syllables and words when he or she is able to segment speech sounds and elemental units of meaningful language extracted from the casual conversation all around. Auditory comprehension precedes speaking. An infant understands the meaning of a word before vocalizing it and initially learns to comprehend the spoken symbol of a word (decoding). When the child comprehends the word, he or she is able to express the language symbol (encoding; Wright, 1982). Children progressively acquire the rules of grammar and form sentences by age 4. It will take a child much longer to perfect articulatory skills and to learn to produce highly complex sentences. The addition of new words throughout the vocabulary continues throughout life. The process of acquisition follows a progression related to the overall maturation and development of the infant, but it also requires normal functioning and control of the structures involved in sound production.

The acquisition of language by children in all cultures follows a similar series of stages. Some children progress through these stages faster than others, but the average age for each stage is the same for all cultures, with peaks of development at certain age. At 3 to 6 months, an infant is able to do cooing, then babbling at 6 to 9 months. At 9 to 12 months, the baby imitates sounds and says the first intelligible words. By 14 months, the first word is given in a specific sense, usually "mommy" and "daddy." By 18 months, the vocabulary has 10 to 15 words. At 2 years, the child is able to make some sentences containing two or three words. At 3 years, speech contains questions and statements, as well as some emotional tone. Questions are of importance as they show the interest of the child in the surrounding world. At 4 years, complex sentences of a few words are used and the child knows his or her first and last names.

Developmental language disorders traditionally have been divided into two groups. The first is disorders of receptive language, in which impaired comprehension is the essential feature; however, one may find some degree of verbal language and articulation dysfunction. The second group is expressive language disorders, characterized by delayed talking; poverty of words (especially in naming); and agrammatical spontaneous speech but normal comprehension, provided the child has no deafness, no mental retardation, no cerebral palsy and is not psychiatrically disturbed and did not suffer from environmental deprivation. As this type of classification has not satisfied clinicians or linguists, other subgroups have been proposed (Aram & Nation, 1975; Bishop & Rosenbloom, in 1987; Rapin, 1982, 1985). The classification presented by Rapin (1985) takes into account the input-central processing-output stages of language operation as well as the level of language most severely affected; it is based on the various levels of acquisition of language. The levels are phonology (concerned with sounds used as linguistic symbols), grammar (syntax and morphology, or the arrangement of words into meaningful sentences), semantics (the representation of meaning in language), pragmatics (how language is used).

In verbal auditory agnosia (word deafness), one is incapable of decoding the sounds around him or her (phonologic level, first necessary step to comprehension of language). The child does not understand phonemes or verbal words; therefore, he or she cannot reproduce them, is mute, or utters single words with phonologic distortion. The syntax is poor. These children learn gestural language and can express themselves through drawings. Their comprehension of symbols and cognitive functions is good and is expressed through games. They will benefit from teaching techniques for deaf children.

In semantic-pragmatic syndrome, the child has an impaired comprehension of the meaning and intent of communication but has good phonology and syntax. The child has a fluent language and often reproduces what is said, but is echolalic for even well-constructed sentences. As the deficit affects comprehension and use of language, the syndrome will be mainly observed with sophisticated questions. If these are put in a simply way, the child can answer yes or no, showing the deficit is not a cognitive one. These children have good auditory memory and are able to repeat long sentences, but their spontaneous speech often lacks precision. As pragmatics is affected in this syndrome, the subject cannot read facial expression or recognize tone of voice, so speech can be unadapted to the situation, creating difficulties in social contacts and behavioral problems. These children also can learn to read, but they do not totally understand what they read.

In semantic-syntactic-organizing syndrome, the deficit lies at two levels: syntax, necessary to organize words into meaningful sentences, and semantics, which is concerned with the meaning of sentences. Therefore, children are dysfluent using incorrect words in an inadequate order. The repetition of words is better than spontaneous speech.

Mixed receptive-expressive (phonologic-syntactic) syndrome is the most frequently seen syndrome of the developmental dysphasias. Comprehension is always better than expression, and can even be normal. The children are dysfluent, have a reduced vocabulary, and an elementary syntax. The phonology is also impaired, producing some distortions of poorly articulated words. Speech may be telegraphic.

In severe expressive syndrome (verbal apraxial), children with normal comprehension have a deficiency in coding language symbols into words. Their speech is extremely poor; often the children are mute. They learn to read and sign.

Phonological programming deficit syndrome is a subgroup of severe expressive syndrome. Children have a good comprehension, are fluent, and are able to speak in sentences. Phonologic disorder produces distorted pronunciation with substitutions or omissions in words; speech is uncomprehensible to other than family members. This can be further confounded when bilingualism is present (Paradis, 1995).

The classifications used in developmental language disorders are still descriptive and the anatomic clinical correlations are less well understood than in adult or childhood acquired language disorders. The mechanisms involved are not only dependent on the left hemisphere, they have still to be elucidated.

REFERENCES

Alajouanine, T., & Lhermitte, F. (1965). Acquired aphasia in children. *Brain, 88,* 653–662.

Aram, D. M., & Nation, J. E. (1975). Patterns of language behavior in children with developmental language disorders. *Journal of Speech & Hearing Research, 18,* 229–241.

Basser, L. S. (1962). Hemiplegia of early onset and the faculty of speech with special reference to the effects of hemispherectomy. *Brain, 85,* 427–460.

Benson, D. F. (1979). Aphasia. In K. M. Heilman & E. Valenstein (Eds.), *Clinical neuropsychology* (pp. 22–58). New York: Oxford University Press.

Bishop, D. V. M., & Rosenbloom, L. (1987). Childhood language disorders: Classification and overview. In W. Yule, M. Rutter, & M. Bax (Eds.), *Language development and disorders. Clinics in developmental medicine.* Blackwell Scientific & Lippincott.

Genetic Information and Patient Services (GAPS). (2005). *Landau-Kleffner syndrome.* Retrieved July 20, 2005, from http://www.icomm.ca/geneinfo/index.html

Geshwind, N., & Galaburda, A. M. (1985). Cerebral lateralization. Biological mechanisms, associations and pathology. *Archives of Neurology, 42-I,* 428–459; 42-II, 521–552; 42-III, 634–654.

Guttmann, E., (1942). Aphasia in children. *Brain, 65,* 205.

Hecaen, H. (1976). Acquired aphasia in children and the ontogenesis of hemispheric functional specialization. *Brain & Language, 3,* 114–134.

Landau, W. M., & Kleffner, F. R. (1957). Syndrome of acquired aphasia with convulsive disorder in children. *Neurology, 7,* 523–530.

Lenneberg, E. H. (1967). *Biological foundations of language.* New York: Wiley.

Mayeux, R., & Kandel, E. R. (1985). Natural language, disorders of language, and other localizable disorders of cognitive functioning. In E. R. Kandel & J. H. Schwartz (Eds.), *Principles of Neural Science.* New York: Elsevier.

Paradis, M. (1995). *Aspects of bilingual aphasia.* New York: Pergammon.

Rapin, I. (1982). *Children with brain dysfunction: Neurology, cognition, language and behavior.* New York: Raven.

Rapin, I. (1985). Communication disorders in children. In H. Szliwowski & J. Bormans (Eds.), *Progrès en neurologie pédiatrique.* Brussels: Prodim.

Rapin, I., Mattis, S., Rowan, A. J., & Golden, G. G. (1977). Verbal auditory agnosia in children. *Developmental Medicine & Child Neurology, 19,* 192–207.

Woods, B. T., & Carey, S. (1979). Language deficits after apparent clinical recovery from childhood aphasia. *Annals of Neurology, 6,* 405–409.

Woods, B. T., & Teuber, H. L. (1978). Changing patterns of childhood aphasia. *Annals of Neurology, 3,* 273–280.

Wright, F. S. (1982). Disorders of speech and language. In K. F. Swaiman & F. S. Wright (Eds.), *The practice of pediatric neurology.* St. Louis, MO: Mosby.

HENRI B. SZLIWOWSKI
CATHERINE WETZBURGER
*Hôpital Erasme, Université
Libre de Bruxelles, Belgium*

APHASIA
LANGUAGE DISORDERS
LEFT BRAIN/RIGHT BRAIN
MUTISM

CHILDHOOD NEUROSIS

See PSYCHONEUROTIC DISORDERS.

CHILDHOOD PSYCHOSIS

Researchers in child psychology and psychiatry agree that there exist identifiable-clinical syndromes where children are out of touch with reality, withdraw from the social world around them, and show unusual and bizarre behaviors. These psychotic children present great challenges to their caretakers: parents who try to provide for the psychotic child's needs and integration into the family system; teachers who try to educate the child and provide basic social skills training; and mental health professionals who try to treat the child clinically.

Consider the following case that the author supervised at a community mental health center. A 9-year-old boy was referred by foster parents following a sudden onset of bizarre destructive behavior and hallucinations. He thought monsters lurked behind doors, heard voices, and displayed bizarre speech during psychotic episodes. This child had been placed in several different foster homes since being abused and neglected as an infant. Two of his siblings were being legally adopted by one set of foster parents, but this child's behavior had led them to decide not to adopt him. He showed poor social skills, was intrusive with others (i.e., did not keep his hands to himself), and had a short attention span. He tolerated stress poorly and would sometimes lash out at others in a violent manner when frustrated. Several psychiatric hospitalizations had only temporarily stabilized self-control and reality orientation. This child was psychotic.

Other clinical cases make the important point that highly unusual and even bizarre behavior does not necessarily imply that a child is psychotic. During the clinical evaluation, for example, one 8-year-old boy freely launched into colorful descriptions of monsters and secret fantasy worlds. His conversation was marked by bizarre verbalizations with little distinction between reality and illusion. He mixed grandiose and paranoid ideas with characters of fantasy and real significant others from his life. Taken out of context, these verbalizations might be construed to reflect an active psychotic delusional state. However, on other occasions, the child was able to perceive reality accurately and to describe his delusions as a fantasy game. This child was not psychotic, but used fantasy as a retreat from high conflict and turmoil in his life. His family history did suggest that he was at risk for developing a psychotic state under stress since his mother had been diagnosed as schizophrenic.

Incidence of childhood psychosis is estimated to be approximately .01 to .05 per 1,000 children and increasing with age (Dekeyzer & Clark, 2003). Unfortunately, methodological difficulties impede accurate estimates of incidence. However, research consistently shows that more boys than girls are diagnosed for each of the psychotic disorders. Estimated differences vary considerably, but it appears that at least twice as many boys are diagnosed as psychotic (Wing, 1968).

Early interest in psychotic states in children appeared

near the turn of the twentieth century in the writings of Kraepelin and Bleuler, who introduced the terms dementia Praecox (early insanity) and schizophrenia (split mind), respectively. Both of these pioneers felt that the onset of many of their adult patients' psychotic disorders had been in their childhood. Thus childhood psychosis was seen as essentially identical symptomatically to adult schizophrenia. The concept of childhood psychoses gained greater acceptance as a result of articles by Potter (1933), Bender (1942), and Bradley and Bowen (1941) on childhood schizophrenia; Kanner (1943) on early infantile autism; Rank (1949) on atypical child psychosis; Mahler (1952) on symbiotic psychosis. These early writings were uniformly based on medical model or disease conception of mental abnormality and were marked by conceptual ambiguity and a lack of specific diagnostic criteria (Wing, 1968).

The evolution of theoretical syndromes points to three general types of childhood psychosis: (1) childhood schizophrenia, (2) early infantile autism, and (3) atypical or symbiotic psychosis.

Interest in childhood schizophrenia followed Potter's (1933) paper. The schizophrenic child was seen as someone who was disinterested in the environment, manifested disturbed thought processes and frequently poor verbal skills, had difficulty in forming emotional attachments to others, and showed bizarre behaviors with a tendency to perseverate in various activities. This view of childhood schizophrenia was modeled after adult schizophrenia.

Research on childhood autism was pioneered by Kanner (1943), who described autistic children as generally having a limited ability to relate to other people beginning in infancy, a language disturbance making it difficult to communicate with others, and conspicuous and obsessive behavior for repetition and maintaining sameness.

Symbiotic psychosis is a rare subtype described by Mahler (1952) as a disturbance owed to intense resistance by the child to becoming psychologically independent of the mother. The number of cases reported is small. The syndrome may be due to repeated early traumatic events and also may stem from a constitutional predisposition to fail to see the mother as a separate object (Mahler, 1965). The onset of this syndrome occurs between 2½ and 5 years of age, preceded by fairly normal development during the first 2 years of life. The onset of symptoms can be set off by such events as illness of a mother, birth of a sibling, or the beginning of school. Figure 1 shows the general distribution of cases (not necessarily according to Mahler's theory) of childhood psychoses given on age of onset.

The child manifests the behaviors of extreme separation anxiety, emotional withdrawal, and distortions of reality similar to autism. Threats of separation create panic. Frustration tolerance is low, and even minor disruptions in routine create panic. There is a craving for sameness. This type of environmental disinterestedness diminishes contact with reality. This syndrome produces hypoactivity or hyperactivity, peculiar thoughts and abnormal speech,

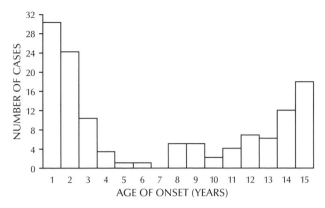

Figure 1 Distribution of cases of childhood psychosis given by age of onset (first detection)

and aggressive behavior such as biting and hitting. The central symptom is profound anxiety to the point of panic over the possibility of separation from the mother. When this bond is threatened, the symbiotic child may show excessive screaming and temper tantrums. These episodes may be followed by disturbed thinking and the expression of bizarre ideas. Following the onset of the psychotic state, the child may show regression in previously acquired habits such as toilet training and disturbances in other behaviors such as eating and sleeping.

The *Diagnostic and Statistical Manual of Mental Disorders Fourth Edition Text Revision* (*DSM-IV-R;* American Psychiatric Association, 2000) attempted to integrate the various approaches to childhood psychosis. This was not an easy task because of the complexity of the subject matter and the distinct points of view on such disorders as childhood schizophrenia. The resulting classification system is organized under the concept of pervasive developmental disorders, with separate subcategories for infantile autism and childhood onset pervasive developmental disorder. This latter category is very general and appears to reflect early research on childhood schizophrenia represented by the work of Lauretta Bender; it excludes work on symbiotic psychosis by Mahler. A separate less specifically defined category, atypical pervasive developmental disorder, allows the clinician to use diagnostic flexibility in describing the individual case, including a symbiotic psychotic child. The clinician can draw on the diagnostic criteria for adult schizophrenia in determining the appropriateness of this category for a child. The *DSM-IV* represents the most current thinking of the mental health profession on these disorders, and contains specific criteria for each psychotic disorder.

Treatment Approaches

Psychotherapy. Individual psychotherapy has been widely used in the treatment of childhood psychosis. Treatment approaches differ depending on the clinician's theory of the causes of the disorder, but they have in common an attempt to resolve psychic turmoil. Psychoanalytic-based approaches focus on the individual child and the presumed intrapsychic conflicts created by a fractured mother-child relationship (Mahler, 1965). Other approaches focus more on interpersonal skills and involve other family members in the treatment (Reiser, 1963).

Research on the effectiveness of psychotherapy with psychotic children has produced differing estimates of improvement. Most writers agree that it often helps to improve symptoms, but there is disagreement on how much it contributes beyond an untreated recovery rate. Some reported recovery rates have been astoundingly high, but the research is difficult to evaluate because of differing criteria used to measure success and lack of untreated control groups.

Milieu and Educational Therapy. This approach manipulates the total environment in a residential setting. It addresses impairments to all areas of functioning and employs multiple treatments (individual, educational, and group therapy). Children referred for these programs are usually the most disturbed; this may partly explain why clinical improvement occurs in a high percentage of cases. Milieu therapy often focuses on improving adaptive self-care skills and improving reality orientation to facilitate better relatedness to others (Zimmerman, 1994). Research on the effectiveness of such programs is difficult to evaluate owing to lack of experimental controls, diverse groups of psychotic children, and small sample sizes. However, more structured programs appear to be more effective (Schopler, 1974).

Behavior Therapy. Principles of learning theory have been successfully applied to treating the symptoms of psychotic children, especially autism (Fester, 1961). The application of behavioral contingencies has helped child care workers and parents to shape the behavior of disturbed children in positive ways, but research suggests that the effects are not easily generalizable across settings.

Organic Treatments. A wide variety of physical treatments have been attempted. Electroconvulsive shock therapy, sensory deprivation, vitamin therapy, hallucinogenic drugs (LSD), and antipsychotic drugs all have been used. Campbell (1973) concluded that little success can be attributed to any of these treatments though antipsychotic drugs are effective in alleviating the worst of some symptoms such as aggressiveness and hallucinations.

In summary, biological, genetic (Crow, Done & Sacker, 1995), and family factors combine to produce psychotic disturbance in children. A small percentage of children appear to be at risk of developing psychotic symptoms owed to these etiological factors when exposed to extreme environmental stress. Although a variety of treatments may produce some positive changes, long-term prognosis is generally poor for psychotic children. A high percentage continue to show psychotic symptoms or minimal social adjustment over time. With onset before age 10, the prognosis appears to be particularly poor. When a therapist and/or parent demonstrates a high degree of emotional involvement over time, the prognosis improves.

REFERENCES

American Psychiatric Association. (2000). *Diagnostic and statistical manual of mental disorders* (4th ed., Text Revision). Washington, DC: Author.

Bender, L. (1942). Schizophrenia in childhood. *Nervous Child, 1,* 138–140.

Bradley, C., & Bowen, M. (1941). Behavior characteristics of schizophrenic children. *Psychiatric Quarterly, 15,* 296–315.

Campbell, M. (1973). Biological interventions in psychoses of childhood. *Journal of Autism & Childhood Schizophrenia, 3,* 347–373.

Crow, T. J., Done, D. J., & Sacker, A. (1995). Childhood precursors of psychosis as clues to its evolutionary origins. *European Archives of Psychiatry & Clinical Neuroscience, 245,* 2, 61–69.

Dekeyzer, L., & Clark, E. (2003). Childhood psychosis. In E. Fletcher-Janzen & C. R. Reynolds (Eds.) *Childhood disorders diagnostic desk reference* (pp. 123–124). New York: Wiley.

Ferster, C. (1961). Positive reinforcement and behavioral deficits of autistic children. *Child Development, 32,* 437–456.

Kanner, L. (1943). Autistic disturbances of affective contact. *Nervous Child, 2,* 217–250.

Mahler, M. (1952). On child psychosis in schizophrenia: Autistic and symbiotic infantile psychosis. *Psychoanalytic Study of the Child, 7,* 286–305.

Mahler, M. (1965). On early infantile psychosis: The symbiotic and autistic syndromes. *Journal of the American Academy of Psychiatry, 4,* 554–568.

Potter, H. W. (1933). Schizophrenia in children. *American Journal of Psychiatry, 12,* 1253–1270.

Quay, H. C., & Werry, J. S. (1979). *Psychopathological disorders of childhood* (2nd ed.). New York: Wiley.

Rank, B. (1949). Adaptation of the psychoanalytic technique in the treatment of young children with atypical development. *American Journal of Orthopsychiatry, 19,* 130–139.

Reiser, D. (1963). Psychosis of infancy and early childhood. *New England Journal of Medicine, 269,* 790–798, 844–850.

Schopler, E. (1974). Changes of direction with psychotic children. In A. Davids (Ed.), *Child personality and psychopathology: Current topics* (Vol. 1). New York: Wiley.

Werry, J. S. (1972). Childhood psychosis. In H. D. Quay & J. S. Werry (Eds.), *Psychopathological disorders of childhood.* New York: Wiley.

Wing, J. (1968). Review of B. Bettelheim, *The empty fortress. British Journal of Psychiatry, 114,* 788–791.

Zimmerman, P. D. (1994). Bruno Bettelheim: The mysterious other: Historical reflect on the treatment of childhood psychosis. *Psychoanalytic Review, 81,* 3, 411–413.

WILLIAM G. AUSTIN
*Cape Fear Psychological
Services*

AUTISM
BORDERLINE PERSONALITY DISORDER
DEPRESSION, CHILDHOOD AND ADOLESCENT
EMOTIONAL DISORDERS
MENTAL STATUS EXAMS
PSYCHONEUROTIC DISORDERS

CHILDHOOD SCHIZOPHRENIA

The term *childhood schizophrenia* is one that is the subject of considerable dispute among authorities in the fields of child psychiatry and psychology. The dispute has mainly to do with the boundaries of this term and the validity of the concept of a childhood onset schizophrenic disorder. As a result of the uncertainty and differences of opinion, firm conclusions have not been reached, and the variation in interpretation of the term childhood schizophrenia has made compilation of a data base problematic.

A large part of the current confusion about childhood schizophrenia results from changes in the definition of the term itself. As Walk (1964) has noted, most authors prior to 1930 tended to diagnose schizophreniclike disorders in children much as they would have diagnosed them in adults. Typical of this literature is De Sanctis's (1906) use of the term *dementia precocissimia*, which apparently was a variant of Kraepelin's concept of *dementia praecox* in adults.

By about 1935, several major clinics had been established in the United States for the study and treatment of severe children's disorders. The directors of these clinics (Bender, 1947; Kanner, 1943; Potter, 1933) all published descriptions of their samples of children and follow-up studies delineating the children's progress. Throughout the period 1930 to 1960, the terms infantile psychosis, autism, and childhood schizophrenia tended to be used interchangeably, although Kanner and his colleagues (Kanner, 1949; Kanner & Eisenberg, 1955) tended to define autism as a separate category that was seen as the earliest form of schizophrenia. Most of these early authors also agreed that schizophrenic disorders closely resembling the adult disorder could occur in childhood, although adult symptoms such as delusions and hallucinations did not occur before about age six. Creak (1961) provided a working definition of childhood schizophrenia that included nine basic characteristics. However, this definition included a substantial overlap into both the autistic and schizophrenic syndromes. Early analytic writers such as Bettelheim (1950) and Szurek (1956) also tended to lump a wide variety of disorders under the rubric of childhood psychosis. In contrast to earlier authorities who were uncertain about etiology, psychoanalytic writers felt that the etiology of the disorder was always psychogenic.

By the end of the period 1965 to 1980, it became clear that some important and distinct subpopulations were emerging. Barbara Fish and her colleagues (Fish et al., 1968) developed a classification system based on language and the ability to integrate basic functions in infancy, and Rutter (1978) presented his findings from long-term studies at Maudsley Hospital in London. In addition, Kolvin (1971), Vrono (1974), and others had published epidemiological data that demonstrated that two major peaks occurred in the distribution of cases across age. The first, at about 2 to 3 years consisted of cases of autism and autisticlike disorders. The second, occurring in early adolescence, consisted of cases resembling adult schizophrenia with delusions, hallucinations, and a thought disorder of form or content. It was also clear that a mixed or residual group with unclear symptoms existed, and most writers clearly acknowledged that some crossover cases existed that did not follow the age of onset distinction. This tripartite division of severe childhood disorders is the basis of the third edition of the *Diagnostic and Statistical Manual of Mental Disorders,* Fourth Edition, Text Revision (*DSM-IV-TR;* American Psychiatric Association, 2000) classification of pervasive developmental disorders.

In *DSM-IV,* childhood schizophrenia is not set apart as a separate category, but is diagnosed using the adult criteria for schizophrenia. These include

A. *Characteristic symptoms:* Two (or more) of the following, each present for a significant portion of time during a 1-month period (or less if successfully treated):
   (1) delusions
   (2) hallucinations
   (3) disorganized speech (e.g., frequent derailment or incoherence)
   (4) grossly disorganized or catatonic behavior
   (5) negative symptoms (i.e., affective flattening, alogia, or avolition)
B. *Social / occupational dysfunction:* For a significant portion of the time since the onset of the disturbance, one or more major areas of functioning such as work, interpersonal relations, or self-care are markedly below the level achieved prior to the onset (or when the onset is in childhood or adolescence, failure to achieve expected level of interpersonal, academic, or occupational achievement).
C. *Duration:* Continuous signs of the disturbance persist for at least 6 months. This 6-month period must include at least 1 month of symptoms (or less if successfully treated) that meet Criterion A (i.e., active phase symptoms) and may include periods of prodromal or residual symptoms. During these prodomal or residual periods, the signs of the disturbance may be manifested by only negative symptoms or two or more symptoms listed in Criterion A present in an attenuated form (e.g., odd beliefs, unusual perceptual experiences).
D. *Schizoaffective and Mood Disorder exclusion:* Schizoaffective Disorder and Mood Disorder with Psychotic

Features have been ruled out because either (1) no Major Depressive, Manic, or Mixed Episodes have occurred concurrently with the active-phase symptoms; or (2) if mood episodes have occurred during active-phase symptoms, their total duration has been brief relative to the duration of the active and residual periods.

E. *Substance / general medical condition exclusion:* The disturbance is not due to the direct physiological effects of a substance (e.g., a drug of abuse, a medication, or a general medical condition.

F. *Relationship to a Pervasive Developmental Disorder:* If there is a history of autistic disorder or another pervasive developmental disorder, the additional diagnosis of Schizophrenia is made only if prominent delusions or hallucinations are also present for at least a month (or less if successfully treated).

DSM-IV suggests that this approach is controversial. Part of the problem involves the inherent difficulty in identifying delusions, hallucinations, and thought disorders in children whose language abilities are very limited. Another shortcoming involves the inability to diagnose organic disorders in children, especially at an early age. Finally, a number of authors (e.g., Fish & Ritvo, 1979) have noted the crossover of children from one category to another. This crossover does not occur often in samples of more retarded children, who tend to show more autistic symptoms, but it occurs often enough among samples with average intelligence to prompt concern about the diagnostic criteria.

Demographic data using the *DSM-IV* criteria for schizophrenia in children are virtually nonexistent except insofar as they may be inferred from data obtained for adults. The overall incidence of schizophrenia is thought to range between 15 and about 1 percent of the population, with an equal sex distribution and a higher incidence rate in lower socioeconomic classes. It also appears to have a higher incidence in some families, but the concordance rate, even in monozygotic twins, is not perfect, implying intervening environmental and/or biological factors. The lower limit for the age of onset using the *DSM-IV* criteria appears to be 8 or 9 years, but there are isolated reports of much earlier onset. As Rutter (1974) notes, the differences in age of onset between autism and schizophrenia and the low incidence of any severe disorder between ages three and early adolescence suggest that both autism and schizophrenia are etiologically distinct and valid syndromes. Unfortunately, little of substance can be said regarding the prognosis or etiology of schizophrenia in children or adults. Whereas autism has been linked to a number of organic and/or genetic conditions, the changing definition of childhood schizophrenia has prevented the compilation of a large enough data base to permit inferences about etiology. The same general state of affairs exists concerning prognosis, although in adults, schizophrenia is thought

to have a very poor outcome and a high relapse rate, as noted in *DSM-IV*.

As noted previously, early in the last century it was common to lump all severe childhood disorders together diagnostically; it was assumed that these were earlier forms of adult schizophrenia. In the last 30 years, however, it has become clear that distinctions should be made among these disorders. The most important differential diagnoses are between schizophrenia and disorders such as autism, mental retardation, and pervasive developmental disorders or disintegrative diseases of organic origin such as Heller's syndrome. Some of these disorders are documented in *DSM-IV* and some are not, but delineation of the differences among them may illuminate the nature of schizophrenia in children.

Both schizophrenia and mental retardation may coexist in the same individual, and *DSM-IV* is careful to point out that some of the social isolation and odd behavior seen in retarded children, especially at a very early age, may be mistaken for symptoms of schizophrenia. In general, however, among the retarded one may expect to find a steady, unremitting course to the disorder, whereas schizophrenics will usually show a prolonged period of normal development. In addition, many retarded persons have physical (particularly facial) stigmata that permit their identification into basic syndromes, but the presence of such stigmata is rare in child schizophrenia of later onset. Goldfarb (1967) has noted stigmata present in early onset psychoses and Bender (1947) also noted their presence among psychotic children, but it is not clear how their samples correspond to current *DSM-IV* categories. Hallmarks of schizophrenia such as delusions and hallucinations are rarely found in individuals who are diagnosed only as retarded. It is generally possible to distinguish between retardation and schizophrenia when careful psychological testing is done to establish the subject's mental age as a baseline for judging the appropriateness of language and social behavior.

By far the most effort has been expended to differentiate schizophrenia from infantile autism. Kanner (1943) initially described autism as the earliest form of schizophrenia, but it has become clear that there are marked differences between the two disorders. First, Rutter (1974) points out that there is a great difference in the distribution of the age of onset between the two disorders, with a peak at 2 to 3 years for the onset of autism and a much later peak in adolescence for schizophrenia. In addition, the course of the two disorders differs sharply, with schizophrenic children having a period of normal development followed by an uneven course, whereas autistic children show deviant development from birth and a consistent course. The symptoms themselves differ: schizophrenic symptoms such as delusions and hallucinations are rare in autism, whereas the autistic child's need for sameness and frequent seizures (in about 25% of cases) are not usual features of schizophrenia. Although most major studies of schizophrenia show a familial loading for schizophrenia and an equal sex distribution, schizophrenia is rare in the families of autistic children and autism occurs more frequently in boys than girls by a ratio of about 4:1 (Rutter, 1985). In most cases (a few exceptions have been reported) children who are diagnosed as autistic do not resemble schizophrenics as adults (Kanner & Eisenberg, 1955).

Some authorities have noted that distinguishing between autism and other disorders is particularly difficult when the child is of average intelligence and does not show many of the characteristic language and behavior peculiarities of the younger and/or more limited autistic child. Asperger (1944) proposed that these children constitute a separate diagnostic group characterized by normal intellect, restricted and obsessive interests in certain subjects or activities, and constricted emotional and social responses. However, this description also applies to many children who have been diagnosed as autistic at an earlier age, especially those with better intelligence and/or language skills.

Schopler (1985) has pointed out that until some behavior distinction between higher level autism and so-called Asperger's syndrome can be demonstrated, confusion might be reduced if Asperger's syndrome were not regarded as a distinct diagnostic category. Most cases could adequately be classified as autistic or as schizoid disorders of adolescence (Rutter & Schopler, 1985). Both high-level autism and the adolescent schizoid disorder differ from schizophrenia, however, because the former disorders do not have hallucinations as a major feature and have an earlier age of onset with a fairly even course marked by the failure to develop normal social relationships.

Heller (1930) described a disorder in which an initial period of 3 to 4 years of apparently normal development is followed by a gradual and widespread disintegration of behavior involving areas as diverse as receptive and expressive language and bowel and bladder training. Social impairment and a general loss of interest in the outside world follow. Other disorders such as tuberous sclerosis may, in the early stages, show some features similar to schizophrenia. However, the early onset age of these latter disorders and the broad deterioration (including social skill areas such as toileting), accompanied in some cases by seizures and other physical problems, are the distinguishing features for differential diagnosis. The etiology is thought to be organic.

Because of the heterogeneity of the cases that have been labeled as schizophrenia, a wide variety of treatments have been employed, as has been the case with autism. Insofar as schizophrenic children may have more intact intellectual/language skills than children with other severe disorders, the traditional play, insight-oriented, and "talking" therapies might be expected to be more effective. Unfortunately, no good studies documenting the utility of this approach are available, again owing in part to differences in diagnostic terminology over the years. The most common form of treatment today involves parental support, counseling, and special psychoeducational strategies, much as with autistic children. In fact, many classes for severely disturbed or psychotic children contain a mix of autistic, schizophrenic, and other types of children. The prognosis for children with schizophrenia is one of a life-long course and the need for supportive structures (George, 2003). Treatment often includes psychoactive medications and research has supported the use of clozapine (George, 2003).

REFERENCES

American Psychiatric Association. (2000). *Diagnostic and Statistical Manual of Mental Disorders* (4th ed., text revision). Washington, DC: author.

Asperger, H. (1944). Die autistischen psychopathen im kindersalter. *Archives Fur Psychiatrie und Nervenkrankheiten, 117,* 76–136.

Bender, L. (1947). Childhood schizophrenia. Clinical study of one hundred schizophrenic children. *American Journal of Orthopsychiatry, 17,* 40–56.

Bettelheim, B. (1950). *Love is not enough.* Glencoe, IL: Free Press.

Campbell, M. (1975). Pharmacotherapy in early infantile autism. *Biological Psychiatry, 10,* 399–423.

Creak, M. (1961). Schizophrenia syndrome in childhood: Progress report of a working party. *Cerebral Palsy Bulletin, 3,* 501–504.

DeSanctis, S. (1906). On some varieties of dementia praecox. Translated and reprinted in J. G. Howells, *Modern perspectives in international child psychiatry.*

Fish, B., & Ritvo, E. (1979). Psychoses of childhood. In J. Noshpitz (Ed.), *Basic handbook of child psychiatry.* New York: Basic Books.

Fish, B., Shapiro, T., & Campbell, M. (1968). A classification of schizophrenic children under five years. *American Journal of Psychiatry, 124,* 1415–1423.

George, C. (2003). Childhood Schizophrenia. In E. Fletcher-Janzen & C. R. Reynolds (Eds.), *Childhood disorders diagnostic desk reference* (pp. 125–126). New York: Wiley.

Goldfarb, W. (1967). Factors in the development of schizophrenic children: An approach to subclassification. In J. Romano (Ed.), *The origins of schizophrenia.* New York: Excerpta Media Foundation.

Heller, T. (1930). About dementia infantilis. Reprinted in J. Howells (Ed.), *Modern perspectives in international child psychiatry.* Edinburgh: Oliver & Boyd.

Kanner, L. (1943). Autistic disturbances of affective contact. *Nervous Child, 2,* 219–230.

Kanner, L. (1949). Problems of nosology and psychodynamics of early infantile autism. *American Journal of Orthopsychiatry, 19,* 416–426.

Kanner, L., & Eisenberg, L. (1955). Notes on the follow-up studies of autistic children. In P. Hoch & J. Zubin (Eds.), *Psychopathology of childhood.* New York: Grune & Stratton.

Kolvin, I. (1971). Psychoses in childhood—A comparative study. In M. Rutter (Ed.), *Infantile autism: Concepts, characteristics and treatment.* London: Churchill-Livingstone.

Potter, H. (1933). Schizophrenia in children. *American Journal of Psychiatry, 12,* 1253–1270.

Rutter, M. (1974). The development of infantile autism. *Psychological Medicine, 4,* 147–163.

Rutter, M. (1978). Diagnosis and definition. In M. Rutter & E. Schopler (Eds.), *Autism: A reappraisal of concepts and treatment.* New York: Plenum.

Rutter, M. (1985). Infantile autism and other pervasive developmental disorders. In M. Rutter & L. Hersov (Eds.), *Child and adolescent psychiatry: Modern approaches.* Oxford: Blackwell Scientific.

Rutter, M., & Schopler, E. (1985). Autism and pervasive developmental disorders: Concepts and diagnostic issues. Paper prepared for National Institute of Mental Health Research Workshop, Washington, DC.

Schopler, E. (1985). Convergence of learning disability, higher-level autism, and Asperger's syndrome. *Journal of Autism and Developmental Disabilities, 15*(4), 359.

Szurek, S. (1956). Childhood schizophrenia symposium 1955: Psychotic episodes and psychotic maldevelopment. *American Journal of Orthopsychiatry, 25,* 519–543.

Vrono, M. (1974). Schizophrenia in childhood and adolescence. *International Journal of Mental Health, 2,* 7–116.

Walk, A. (1964). The pre-history of child psychiatry. *British Journal of Psychiatry, 110,* 754–767.

ERIC SCHOPLER
University of North Carolina at Chapel Hill

JERRY L. SLOAN
Wilmington Psychiatric Associates

AUTISM
CHILDHOOD PSYCHOSIS
PSYCHONEUROTIC DISORDERS

CHILD PSYCHIATRY

Child psychiatry is a subdiscipline of psychiatry, a branch of medicine focusing on human emotional development and pathology. As a subspeciality, child psychiatry is approximately 75 years old, with Freud's treatment of a young boy in 1909 marking its genesis (Jones, 1959). The practitioner of child psychiatry must have comprehensive training both in general psychiatry and child development. This includes a firm understanding of trends in cognitive, language, and motor development. Training in neurology is also essential in understanding which developmental delays may be attributed to organic as opposed to psychogenic etiology (AACAP, 2005).

Initial involvement of the child psychiatrist is focused on the mentally retarded and an assessment of them for the purpose of deciding on entrance to state schools and hospitals for the mentally retarded. This may have been influenced by European trends in determining which children were able to benefit from a public education and which were ineligible as a result of deficient mental abilities (Wolman, 1972). This focus has been greatly expanded to areas of treatment and prevention, with assessment being regarded as the role of a multidisciplinary team.

While the earliest child psychiatrists often acted in a unitary fashion, more contemporary approaches have included psychiatrists as team members. This has also been reflected in their involvement in a larger variety of agencies than traditionally noted. Earlier trends in child psychiatry have placed the psychiatrist in medically oriented facilities such as hospitals, state homes for the retarded, and pediatric services. Recent trends have included child psychiatric services in child-guidance clinics, community mental health facilities, and, with the introduction of PL 94-142, in community-based schools.

Along with this shift in orientation, child psychiatrists have attained more of a consultant status (Knapp & Harris, 1998); they are no longer seen as the sole practitioner for the young child. Their presence is observed throughout the progression from the mainstream classroom to the residential facility. For example, if the child with special needs is educated within the mainstream class, resource room, or special education class, the child psychiatrist may consult to assist in determining developmental needs requiring medical attention. This assessment is made in conjunction with other members of the multidisciplinary team. As the placement shifts to a more restrictive milieu, as with residential placement, the multidisciplinary team remains the functional unit for developing the individual education plan (IEP), with the child psychiatrist maintaining a consultant and team-member status and contributing from his or her area of expertise.

Another domain of child psychiatry includes participation on recommendations of Committees for the Handicapped (COH) and school-based guidance and support teams. Within his or her area of expertise, this new consultant to the educational system contributes in a unique manner, evaluating the child for possible psychopharmacological intervention to assist in the learning process. With the advent of medications focusing on attentional deficit disorders, disruptive behaviors, and childhood depression syndromes, new tools interface the educational and the medical approaches with child development and treatment. This required the special knowledge that the child psychiatrist is trained to possess. Transcending traditional training in dynamic psychotherapy, the knowledge of more contemporary behavioral management techniques has also become part of the armamentarium of this profession, thus allowing for additional assistance in structuring the child's environment for facilitating growth. In conjunction with significant school personnel and the family, the child psychiatrist may assist in developing treatment plans geared to maximize the child's educational experience. To carry out this role, the practitioner must have a sound foundation of knowledge about child development, assessment of personality and its pathology, child neurology, therapeutic intervention, and prevention (AACAP, 2005; Noshpitz, 1979).

REFERENCES

AACAP. (2005). *Facts for families.* Retrieved July 20, 2005, from http://www.aacp.org/publications/factsfam/

Jones, E. (Ed.). (1959). *Sigmund Freud: Collected papers* (5 vols). New York: Basic Books.

Knapp, P. K., & Harris, E. S. (1998). Consultation—liaison in child psychiatry: A review of the past 10 years. *Journal of the American Academy of Child and Adolescent Psychiatry, 37,* 2, 139–146.

Noshpitz, J. D. (1979). *Basic handbook of child psychiatry* (4 vols). New York: Basic Books.

Wolman, B. B. (Ed.). (1972). *Manual of child psychopathology.* New York: McGraw-Hill.

ELLIS I. BAROWSKY
*Hunter College, City University
of New York*

CASCADE MODEL OF SPECIAL EDUCATION SERVICES
MENTAL STATUS EXAMS
MULTIDISCIPLINARY TEAM

CHILD PSYCHOLOGY

Child psychology is concerned with answering two basic questions: How do children change as they develop, and what are the determinants of these developmental changes? (Hetherington & Parke, 1979). Modern child psychology is particularly concerned with understanding the processes that produce and account for age-related changes in children. Child psychology is concerned with development from conception to adolescence.

Historically, child psychology can be traced to the work of G. Stanley Hall, president of Clark University and one of the founders of the American Psychological Association (Kessen, 1965). In 1893 Hall published *The Contents of Children's Minds,* the first systematic study of large groups of children using a questionnaire method to obtain information about children's and adolescents' behaviors, attitudes, and interests. During the early years of this century, research in child psychology was primarily atheoretical and focused on the description of age changes in physical, psychological, and behavioral characteristics. Child psychologists in the past several decades, however, have been primarily interested in studying the basic processes underlying development.

Some of the earliest researchers and theorists who had great impact on the expansion of the field of child psychology were Binet, who developed the first test of intelligence, Gesell, who investigated perceptual-motor abilities in young children, Freud, who proposed a theory of personality development, and Piaget, who published an influential theory of children's cognitive development.

Biologists and geneticists have made important contributions to an understanding of some of the processes and mechanisms related to development (Mash & Dozois, 2003). Behavior geneticists have been concerned with the mechanisms by which genetic factors contribute to a wide range of individual differences observed in human behavior across the entire life span. Research suggests that genetic factors play a role in the development of many physical and physiological characteristics, in intelligence, sociability, emotional responsiveness, and in some types of psychopathology.

Developmental changes in sensory capacities, visual-perceptual abilities, and fine and gross motor skills are major areas of study by child psychologists during the period of infancy. Among the specific areas studied are sound discrimination, visual stimulus preferences, and depth perception. Another important focus of child psychologists during infancy has been the effects of early experiences on their cognitive, motor, and social-emotional development. Among the issues addressed are the timing of experiences (i.e., early versus later experiences; the existence of critical periods) and concerns with the plasticity of development (i.e., will previously acquired behavior patterns be modified by later experience?; Bower, 1977).

Child psychologists recognize the influence of heredity on setting the foundation for the course of development. These genetic factors interact with the child's learning experiences to determine actual developmental outcomes. Learning processes (e.g., conditioning mechanisms, imitation), are therefore an important area of study by child psychologists.

During the past three decades, five areas of development have received considerable attention by child psychologists. These areas are emotional development, language development, cognitive development, moral development, and the development of sex role behaviors (Mussen, 1970).

In the area of emotional development, research has focused on the manner in which positive and negative emotions originate and how the expression of emotions changes with age (Yarrow, 1979). Another area that has attracted considerable interest is the development of attachment, in which infants show a specific desire to be near particular caretakers in their environment. Related to this issue is the study of the development of fears in the young child, particularly the fear of strangers. Child psychologists also have been interested in the ways that children learn to label and recognize their own and other people's emotions. Resiliency is also a new area of interest in child development. Researchers are examining the positive attributes of children that allow them to withstand negative experiences and thrive (Goldstein, & Brooks, 2005).

Language development represents one of the most significant achievements of childhood because of its importance in communication, thinking, and learning. Child psychologists differ on their views of the mechanisms underlying the development of language. Some argue that language is innate while others contend that language can be accounted for by traditional principles. A third view, which is held by most current theorists, is that both genetic and learning factors play a role in language development (Dale, 1976; Lyon, Fletcher, & Barnes, 2003).

Research in children's cognitive development has dominated the field of child psychology. The area of cognition pertains to the mental activity and behavior through which knowledge is acquired and processed, including learning, perception, memory, and thinking. The psychological processes that underlie cognitive development are of particular interest to the child psychologist, including the operations involved in receiving, attending to, discriminating, transforming, storing, and recalling information.

Piaget (1952) developed the most comprehensive and influential theory of cognitive development. His theory emphasized developmental changes in the organization and structure of intelligence, and how differences in those structures are reflected in the learning of children at different ages. Another component of Piaget's theory involved his approach to the development of social cognition, i.e., the way in which children perceive, understand, and think about themselves, other people, and social interactions. Piaget's provocative theory probably has stimulated more research by contemporary child psychologists than any other theory.

In addition to investigating the basic processes by which children learn, researchers also have investigated how children retain information and recognize, recall, and use it when needed. A distinction is made between two types of memory: short term and long term. Developmental changes in various strategies used by children to facilitate memory such as rehearsal, mental imagery, and organization, also have been investigated by child psychologists.

Child psychologists have noted individual differences in the cognitive styles that children use to process information. One of the most frequently studied dimensions of cognitive style is reflectivity-impulsivity. Reflectivity-impulsivity is associated with a number of intellectual, social, and personality factors.

Cognitive problem-solving abilities, as reflected in the concept of intelligence, have attracted the attention of psychologists for nearly a century. Child psychologists have addressed such issues as whether intelligence is a unitary, generalized ability, or a group of relatively separate abilities. There have been debates between those groups who argue that intelligence is genetically determined and, therefore,

not alterable, and those who suggest that intelligence is more dependent on learning experiences. Similarly, the development and use of intelligence tests has generated considerable controversy within the field, with some investigators arguing that such tests are culturally biased toward white middle-class experiences. Intelligence tests, based on the concept of global intelligence, yield a single IQ score and continue to be widely used by practicing psychologists in clinical and academic settings.

The development of sex roles also has been an area of study in child psychology. Sex-role typing is the process by which children acquire the values and behaviors that are regarded as appropriate to either males or females in a specific culture. Characteristics of masculinity and femininity appear to be developed very early in life and are stable over time. Research indicates that the development of sex roles and sex differences in behavior is a complex phenomenon that involves the interaction of biological, social, and cognitive factors (Maccoby & Jacklin, 1974).

One component of the socialization process of children that has been of particular interest to child psychologists is the development of moral values and moral behaviors. Psychological research has focused on three basic aspects of morality: (1) cognitive factors including knowledge of ethical rules and judgments about whether various acts are right or wrong; (2) behavioral factors involving negative acts such as cheating, lying, resisting temptation, and controlling aggression, and behaviors involved in prosocial acts such as sharing, cooperation, altruism, and helping; and (3) emotional factors of morality such as feelings of guilt following a transgression (Hoffman, 1979).

Children are intimately involved in a number of social systems including the family, peer group, and school. Child psychologists have investigated the influence of these social systems on various aspects of the development of children (Hartup, 1979).

There is a long history of interest by child psychologists in the family's role in the socialization process. Of particular interest has been the relationship between child-rearing attitudes and practices and children's cognitive, personality, and social development. Contemporary issues pertaining to the family that have been investigated by child psychologists include the effects of child abuse, divorce, single-parent families, and maternal employment on the child's development.

Relationships with age mates are another important influence on the development of children. Age-related changes in peer interactions and the role of play behaviors have been the focus of much research. The influence of peers as models for negative and prosocial behaviors, and factors affecting peer group acceptance, also have been investigated.

Finally, child psychologists have studied the influence of the school as a socializing agent with children. In particular, the effects of teachers on children's academic achievement as well as social and emotional development has been examined. One area of interest has been an investigation of the impact of teacher expectations on children's performance in the classroom.

The major research interests in child psychology have changed over the course of time, often in response to social and historical pressures. Much of the knowledge that has accumulated in this field has been used to meet the needs of children in today's society and improve their well being through the implementation of various programs and services. In recent years, child psychologists have become increasingly interested and influential in the formulation of social policies affecting children (Seitz, 1979). A review of development in child psychology from the 1960s to 1990s can be found in Reese (1993).

REFERENCES

Bower, T. G. R. (1977). *A primer of infant development.* San Francisco: Freeman.

Dale, P. S. (1977). *Language development: Structure and function* (2nd ed.). New York: Holt, Rinehart, & Winston.

Goldstein, S., & Brooks, R. B. (2005). *Resilience in children.* New York: Springer.

Hartup, W. W. (1979). The social worlds of childhood. *American Psychologist, 34,* 944–950.

Hetherington, E. M., & Parke, R. D. (1979). *Child psychology: A contemporary viewpoint* (2nd ed.). New York: McGraw-Hill.

Hoffman, M. L. (1979). Development of moral thought, feeling, and behavior. *American Psychologist, 34,* 958–966.

Kessen, W. (1965). *The child.* New York: Wiley.

Lewis, M. (Ed.). (1976). *Origins of intelligence.* New York: Plenum.

Lyon, G. R., Fletcher, J. M., & Barnes, M. C. (2003). Learning disabilities. In E. J. Mash & R. A. Barkley (Eds.), *Child psychopathology* (pp. 520–574). New York: Guilford.

Maccoby, E. E., & Jacklin, C. N. (1974). *The psychology of sex differences.* Stanford: Stanford University Press.

Mash, E. J., & Dozois, D. J. A. (2003). Child psychopathology. In E. J. Mash & R. A. Barkley (Eds.), *Child psychopathology* (pp. 3–74). New York: Guilford.

Mussen, P. H. (Ed.). (1970). *Carmichael's handbook of child psychology.* New York: Wiley.

Piaget, J. (1952). *The origins of intelligence in children.* New York: International Universities Press.

Reese, H. W. (1993). Developments in child psychology from the 1960s to the 1990s. *Developmental Review, 13,* 4, 503–524.

Rosenthal, D. (1970). *Genetic theory and abnormal behavior.* New York: McGraw-Hill.

Seitz, V. (1979). Psychology and social policy for children. *American Psychologist, 34,* 1007–1008.

Yarrow, L. J. (1979). Emotional development. *American Psychologist, 34,* 951–957.

LAWRENCE J. SIEGEL
*University of Texas Medical
Branch, Galveston*

CHILD PSYCHIATRY
CLINICAL PSYCHOLOGY
PEDIATRIC PSYCHOLOGIST

CHILD SERVICE DEMONSTRATION CENTERS

Child Service Demonstration Centers (CSDCs) (1971–1980) were federally funded operations that, in their totality, represented the largest single national commitment specifically made to the education of the learning disabled (Mann et al., 1984).

Their beginnings are to be found in several pieces of legislation. PL 88-164, passed in 1963, which predated the introduction of the modern term learning disabilities (LD), provided assistance to learning-disabled children in a bill directed at the educational needs of handicapped children under the rubric of "crippled and other health impaired." Then, under PL 91-230, passed in 1969, the U.S. commissioner of education was enjoined by Congress "to seek to make equitable geographic distribution of training programs, and train personnel throughout the nation, and . . . to encourage the establishment of a model training center in each of the states." This was to be done by making grants or contracts available to public schools, state educational agencies, nonprofit organizations, and colleges and universities. Such model centers for the learning disabled were then authorized, and ultimately created, under PL 91-230, Title VI-G.

This law made possible Child Service Demonstration Centers to serve learning-disabled students. Under the law, the to-be-created centers were to; (1) provide testing and educational evaluation to identify learning-disabled students; (2) develop and conduct model programs designed to meet their special educational needs; (3) assist appropriate educational agencies, organizations, and institutions "in making such model programs available to other children with learning disabilities"; and (4) disseminate new methods or techniques for overcoming learning disabilities and evaluate their effectiveness.

From 1971 to 1980, 97 CSDCs were created in all, with each of the 50 states being served by at least one during that time. The majority operated under the auspices of state educational agencies (SEAs). A good number also operated out of universities, and sometimes out of local educational agencies (LEAs), often on the basis of their serving as agencies of the states. The private sector was only minimally represented.

Many of the CSDCs were to carry out state as well as federal mandates. Often they were supported by state and local funds and resources that allowed them to augment their efforts far beyond the limits allowed by their relatively meager funds. Thus the hopes of the federal government that state and local education agencies would contribute to the support of the CSDCs with their own funds were realized.

The federal government had high hopes for the CSDCs. They were expected to assume major responsibility for trailblazing in the creation of service models, programs, and technologies; the identification, diagnosis, and remediation of learning disabilities; and the training of regular as well as special education teachers, specialists, and administrators. They were also expected to play a major role in research on the learning disabled. Furthermore, they were cast as both transformation instigators and partners for state educational agencies. In these roles they were expected to help the state agencies to plan and implement statewide learning disabilities programs and services; indeed, the initial CSDCs were granted to state educational agencies to further this expectation.

While every state had at least one project, as did the Commonwealth of Puerto Rico, some states had multiple centers operating at the same time under their state educational departments (e.g., California, New York). Most centers operated for 3 years; reapplication and competition for further funding was needed for subsequent years. The strategy was that the first year would involve planning, the second year the actual operation of the center, and the third year replication and dissemination. Some states, however, put projects together to create longitudinal efforts of some duration.

During their tenure, the CSDCs served a mix of urban, suburban, and rural areas. Most of the services were rendered, however, to rural children. This was in large part the result of the federal government's insistence that unserved and underserved learning-disabled students, who were in greatest abundance in rural areas at the time, be given priority in the provision of services.

For much the same reason, the racial composition of the learning-disabled students served by the CSDCs included a disproportionate number of minority students. Two projects were directed to American Indians and two to Puerto Rican students, while many of the urban and rural centers were oriented to the needs of black students. This is an interesting point in light of the fact that some advocacy groups at the time were claiming that learning disabilities were a white middle-class syndrome, with minority students being consigned to classes for the mentally retarded or having their academic problems neglected.

The CSDCs emphasized elementary school-aged children since the LD movement is generally oriented to this stage of education. There were some preschool and secondary efforts as well. Interest and efforts in the latter accelerated during the later years of funding as the federal government increased its emphasis on secondary school programming.

The CSDCs were in the vanguard of mainstreaming and the provision of special education services in the least restrictive environment. They also did much to relate special education services for learning-disabled pupils to those of general education. In these respects they clearly fulfilled the federal government's expectations. Their major service delivery models were those of resource rooms, consulting teachers, and regular classrooms.

The assessment and diagnostic efforts of the CSDCs were traditional. They were strictly secondary to the service and training functions assumed by the centers. Furthermore, they eventually resulted in controversies that still percolate in education. Although the CSDCs were expected to identify appropriately handicapped children who had specific learning disabilities, as per federal definitions, their screening and identification efforts were such as to assign children to their services on the basis of academic failure and other school problems rather than on the basis of any precise learning disability criteria. It was on such bases that a position was taken by some critics that the concept of learning disabilities, as a defensible independent diagnostic entity apart from and different from school failure, could not be sustained.

The intervention models stressed by the CSDCs were strongly academic, as might be expected since students receiving services from the CSDCs usually had been referred because of academic problems. Remedial reading was the treatment of choice, on similar grounds. Perceptual motor training, including ITPA-based interventions, held the second highest priority, particularly in the early projects, when perceptual motor training was still the vogue. Surprisingly, the behavioral movement that so dominated special education during much of the CSDCs' sway does not appear to have greatly influenced most of the CSDCs, though some had strong behavioral emphases. While only several projects have averred ecological orientations, there was an ecological shift over the course of CSDC operations. Earlier projects were committed to overcoming learning disabilities through direct intervention, while later ones were more likely to emphasize helping learning-disabled students to adjust to academic and school environments and assisting schools in their accommodations to the special needs of learning-disabled students.

One of the major efforts made by CSDCs was in respect to training. Some of this was at the college and university level. Most, often representing an introduction to LD concepts and practices, was of an in-service nature directed at regular as well as special education teachers, administrators, paraprofessionals, and parents.

The CSDCs' efforts at replication were considerable. Most of the replications were at the local level, with far fewer at the state level. Impressive is the fact that there were 16 national replications. The CSDCs generated an extraordinary number of screening, remedial, and curricular materials and training manuals for teachers and parents. Because these were in the public domain, many were adapted by schools subsequent to the CSDCs' close, though often without awareness of their origins.

While there were some exemplary research efforts, the CSDCs remained essentially service agencies and, generally speaking, did not assume the research leadership originally expected of them. This was not surprising since neither their funding, personnel capabilities, nor the nature of local conditions were such as to encourage earnest research. The Learning Disability Institutes, funded in 1977, were created in response the federal government's recognition of these facts and a desire to seek wider research efforts from other sources.

Public Law 91-239 also authorized the creation of the Leadership Training Institute (LTI) at the University of Arizona (1971–1974). The institute was supposed to assist the CSDCs in addition to carrying out its own research and training missions. It was later replaced by the National Learning Disabilities Assistance Project (1975–1979), which was entirely devoted to providing support functions for the CSDCs.

The federal government clearly expected the CSDCs to have a major national impact on LD practices. That they did not fulfill such expectations can be attributed to a variety of causes. One was the fact that their allocation of funds was far below original authorizations. Another was that individual centers came on line too slowly and irregularly, thus any collaborative thrust on their part was weakened. Still another reason was that they did not affect state educational policies as had been hoped, the states usually pursuing their own LD agendas rather than those of the federal government or of the CSDCs. Furthermore, the demands made on the CSDCs regularly changed as a consequence of changes in federal direction and because of disagreements among recognized LD specialists as to the nature of learning disabilities and the goals of intervention. Finally, most of the projects were funded for only 3 years, and several were funded for 2 or less, hardly time to create forceful and enduring efforts. Nevertheless, they did sensitize many areas of the nation and its schools to the needs of learning-disabled children and provided them with guidance, training, programs, materials, and direct services during a period when the field of learning disabilities was still emerging as an area of educational concern in the United States. Undoubtedly, they also shaped current concepts and services.

The CSDCs were subject to a number of external evaluations. A study of the CSDCs' intervention efforts was carried out by Kirk and Elkin in 1975. In 1976 a major yearlong effort was made by the American Institute of Research to examine the operations of the CSDCs. In 1979 Ysseldyke et al. began their studies of the CSDCs' assessment approaches (Thurlow & Ysseldyke, 1979). At the final closing of the CSDCs, Mann et al. published several summative articles reviewing the status and contributions of the CSDCs (Boyer et al., 1982; Mann et al., 1983; Mann et al., 1984).

REFERENCES

Boyer, C. W., Mann, L., Davis, C. H., Metz, C. M., & Wolford, B. (1982). The Child Service Demonstration Centers: Retrospect of an age. *Academic Therapy, 18,* 171–177.

Kirk, S. A., & Elkin, V. (1975). Characteristics of children enrolled in the Child Service Demonstration Centers. *Journal of Learning Disabilities, 16,* 63–68.

Mann, L., Davis, C. H., Boyer, C. W., Metz, C. M., & Wolford, B. (1983). LD or not LD, that was the question: A retrospective analysis of the Child Service Demonstration Centers' compliance with the federal definition of learning disabilities. *Journal of Learning Disabilities, 16,* 14–17.

Mann, L., Cartwright, G. P., Kenowitz, L. A., Boyer, C. W., Metz, C. M., & Wolford, B. (1984). The Child Service Demonstration Centers: A summary report. *Exceptional Children, 50,* 532–540.

Thurlow, M. L., & Ysseldyke, J. E. (1979). Current assessment and decision making practices in model LD programs. *Learning Disability Quarterly, 4,* 15–24.

JONI J. GLEASON
University of West Florida

DIAGNOSIS IN SPECIAL EDUCATION LEARNING DISABILITIES

CHILD VARIANCE PROJECT

The Conceptual Project in Child Variance was undertaken from 1970 to 1972 at the University of Michigan under the direction of William C. Rhodes. It was funded as a special project by the (then) Bureau of Education for the Handicapped to "order and organize the vast but scattered literature on emotional disturbance and other types of variance in children" and to "serve as a prototype for combining the functions of graduate training and professional research" (Rhodes & Tracy, 1974, p. 1). The product of this prodigious undertaking is a series of five volumes in which the literature on explanations of variance, intervention with variant children, and service provision are integrated and synthesized.

The first volume, *Conceptual Models,* has had a significant impact on subsequent treatments of childhood emotional disturbance and the education of disturbed children. The volume is comprised of papers in which explanatory models from five perspectives are presented. These models include biological, behavioral, psychodynamic, sociological, and ecological accounts of deviance. A paper on counter-theoretical perspectives is included, as is a paper by Rhodes establishing a framework for understanding and synthesizing these diverse accounts.

The organization of the second volume, *Interventions,* derives from the first. In it, intervention with variant children is considered from biophysical, behavioral, psychodynamic, environmental, and countertheoretical perspectives. (The paper on environmental intervention explores approaches derived from both the sociological and ecological perspectives.) Of course, the rapid and multifaceted advance in the treatment of disturbed children in the decade since the publication of this volume has limited its usefulness. Nonetheless, the logic of its organization has endured. The idea that intervention must be understood in the context of the explanatory system has influenced scholars and teacher trainers to this day.

In the third volume, *Service Delivery Systems,* the development of contemporary services for deviant children provided by educational, correctional, mental health, and social welfare systems and religious institutions is analyzed from a historical perspective. The current services provided by these systems in a representative American community are examined and evaluated through a series of case studies. The fourth volume, *The Future,* is a treatise by Rhodes on the somewhat profound cultural and philosophical changes that must be realized for our society to fulfill its caretaking role. The fifth volume, *Exercise Book,* presents a series of exercises through which the sometimes complex and abstract content of the previous volumes may be brought to life for students.

Although the project has not yet realized the ultimate and far-reaching goals set forth by Rhodes in *The Future,* its impact on our thinking about emotional disturbance, the education of emotionally disturbed children, and the training of teachers of the emotionally disturbed has been significant and enduring. The organization of explanatory theory and its application to the understanding of intervention approaches are legacies of the Child Variance Project. Furthermore, its emphasis on the understanding of problems in their broadest context provided impetus to the subsequent development of ecological theory and intervention approaches.

REFERENCES

Rhodes, W. C. (1975). *A study of child variance: Vol. 5. Exercise book.* Ann Arbor: University of Michigan Press.

Rhodes, W. C., & Tracy, M. L. (1974). Preface. In W. C. Rhodes & M. L. Tracy (Eds.), *A study of child variance: Vol. 2. Interventions* (pp. 1–15). Ann Arbor: University of Michigan Press.

Rhodes, W. C., & Tracy, M. W. (Eds.). (1974). *A study of child variance: Vol. 1. Conceptual models.* Ann Arbor: University of Michigan Press.

Rhodes, W. C., & Tracy, M. L. (1974). *A study of child variance: Vol. 2. Interventions.* Ann Arbor: University of Michigan Press.

Rhodes, W. C., & Tracy, M. W. (Eds.). (1974). *A study of child variance: Vol. 3. Service delivery systems.* Ann Arbor: University of Michigan Press.

Rhodes, W. C., & Tracy, M. L. (1974). *A study of child variance: Vol. 4. The future.* Ann Arbor: University of Michigan Press.

PAUL T. SINDELAR
Florida State University

AFFECTIVE EDUCATION
EMOTIONAL DISORDERS

CHILDREN OF A LESSER GOD

Children of a Lesser God is a play by Mark Medoff that was a hit on the Broadway stage in 1980. It is about the meeting, courtship, and marriage of James Leeds, a speech teacher at a state school for the deaf, and Sarah Norman, a maid at the school who has been deaf from birth and who refuses to lip read or speak. Sarah wishes to be left alone in her silent world. James insists that she learn to lip read and speak if she is to achieve first-class citizenship in the hearing, speaking world. He repeats aloud everything he and Sarah sign in an attempt to teach Sarah to lip read. The two cannot reconcile their differences, and, in the end, they separate. James asks Sarah to return, but it is left unclear whether or not the marriage will be successful.

Mark Medoff, the author of *Children of a Lesser God,* found sign language an interesting theatrical device, and used deafness as a symbol for the problems inherent in all human communication. He wrote the play for Phyllis Frelich, a founding member of the National Theater of the Deaf, in response to her difficulty in finding roles. The play was developed based on situations suggested by Medoff and improvised by Frelich and her husband Robert Steinberg, who originally played the role of James in workshop and regional productions of the play.

REFERENCES

Guernsey, O. L., Jr. (Ed.). (1980). *The best plays of 1979–1980.* New York: Dodd, Mead.

Kakutani, M. (1980, April 1). Deaf since birth, Phyllis Frelich became an actress and now a star. *New York Times, III,* 7:1.

Medoff, M. (1980). *Children of a lesser god.* New York: Dramatists Play Service.

CATHERINE O. BRUCE
*Hunter College, City University
of New York*

DEAF
DEAF EDUCATION
SIGN LANGUAGE

CHILDREN'S DEFENSE FUND

The Children's Defense Fund (CDF) is an advocacy organization for poor, minority, and handicapped children. The mission of the CDF is to "Leave No Child Behind" (CDF, 1999). Efforts are undertaken on behalf of large numbers of children as opposed to individual children. Relevant to special education, the organization has addressed exclusion of children from school as well as the labeling and treatment of children with special needs (Staff, 1974). The CDF maintains a lobbying organization, pursuing an annual legislative agenda in the U.S. Congress; works with state and local child advocates, providing information, technical assistance, and support; monitors the development and implementation of federal and state policies; and litigates selected cases (CDF, n.d.).

The CDF also develops information on key issues affecting children. It has published books and handbooks of interest to special education, including *94-142 and 504: Numbers that Add Up to Educational Rights for Handicapped Children, How to Help Handicapped Children Get an Education.* A monthly newsletter, *CDF Reports,* is also published.

The CDF was founded in 1973. Until 1978 CDF was known as the Children's Defense Fund of the Washington Research Project. It is a private organization, with its main office in Washington DC at 25 E. Street NW, Washington DC 20001. The CDF has a very informative web site at www.childrensdefense.org.

REFERENCES

Children's Defense Fund (CDF). (1999). *About the Children's Defense Fund.* Washington, DC: Author.

Staff. (1974). An interview with Marian Edelman Wright. *Harvard Educational Review, 44,* 53–73.

DOUGLAS L. FRIEDMAN
Fordham University

CHILDREN'S MANIFEST ANXIETY SCALE

Originally published in 1956 by Castaneda, McCandless, and Palermo as a downward extension of Taylor's Manifest Anxiety Scale for adults (Taylor, 1951), the Children's Manifest Anxiety Scale (CMAS) was substantively revised in 1978 (Reynolds & Richmond). The *Revised Children's Anxiety Scale* (RCMAS) was published in 1985 (Reynolds & Richmond). Since its first publication, more than one hundred fifty articles using the CMAS or the RCMAS have been published in various scholarly journals. These scales have been used in studies of the effects of anxiety on children's learning, behavior in the classroom, and response to a variety of treatment programs, and in descriptive studies of anxiety and its relationship to behavior, gender, ethnicity, age, socioeconomic status, and other variables.

Designed to measure anxiety of long-standing duration (i.e., trait as opposed to state or situational anxiety), the RCMAS has four empirically derived subscales titled: Concentration/Social, Worry and Oversensitivity, Physiological Anxiety, and Lie or Social Desirability. Standard scores are provided for a total anxiety score and for each subscale. Reliability data are good with most studies reporting internal consistency estimates in the .80s across age (5 to 19 years), gender, and race (Black, White, and Hispanic). Extensive validity data are provided in the test manual (Reynolds & Richmond, 1985).

The RCMAS is used principally by school, child clinical, and pediatric psychologists in the screening and diagnosis of various anxiety-related emotional disorders in children, and by researchers interested in children's anxiety. Learning-disabled and other groups of children in special education programs have been shown to display higher than normal levels of anxiety on the RCMAS (Paget & Reynolds, 1984), while students in programs for the intellectually gifted demonstrate lower than average anxiety levels when compared with the normal population (Scholwinski & Reynolds, 1985). The RCMAS is currently being revised.

REFERENCES

Castaneda, A., McCandless, B., & Palermo, D. (1956). The children's form of the Manifest Anxiety Scale. *Child Development, 27,* 327–332.

Paget, K. D., & Reynolds, C. R. (1984). Dimensions, levels, and reliabilities on the Revised Children's Anxiety Scale with learning disabled children. *Journal of Learning Disabilities, 17,* 137–141.

Reynolds, C. R., & Richmond, B. O. (1978). What I think and feel: A revised measure of children's manifest anxiety. *Journal of Abnormal Psychology, 43,* 281–283.

Reynolds, C. R., & Richmond, B. O. (1985). *Revised Children's Manifest Anxiety Scale.* Los Angeles: Western Psychological Services.

Scholwinski, E., & Reynolds, C. R. (1985). Dimensions of anxiety among high IQ children. *Gifted Child Quarterly, 29,* 125–130.

Taylor, J. A. (1951). The relationship of anxiety to the conditioned eyelid response. *Journal of Experimental Psychology, 41,* 18–92.

CECIL R. REYNOLDS
Texas A&M University

ANXIETY
ANXIETY DISORDERS

CHILDREN'S RIGHTS INTERNATIONALLY

The concept of children's rights evolved from being minimally and unevenly valued to near universally recognized by governments at the end of the twentieth century. During the nineteenth and twentieth centuries, societal concern for children moved from long-standing consideration of them as the property of parents, without protection, genuine personal identity, or rights (Aries, 1962; de Mause, 1975), to being viewed as potential resources to present and future societies and progressively, although as yet incompletely, to being valued as rights-bearing persons with individual personalities. This evolution of thinking increasingly recognizes children's *being* and *becoming* states. Although they are vulnerable, malleable, and en route to higher levels of development, they also are fully human at each point in their lives and with views and capacities deserving respect and support (Verhellen, 1994).

The formalization of international rights standards and requirements occurs through legal instruments, known as treaties, that are legally binding, specify implementation mechanisms, hold ratifying states parties (i.e., officially committed national governments) accountable, and contain non-binding declarations, standards, and rules.

Knowledge of the history of attempts to establish international legal instruments relevant to children provides some clarification of progress in conceptualizing and respecting children's rights. Among non-binding instruments are the 1924 Declaration of Geneva, which is protection and development oriented; the Universal Declaration of Human Rights, a comprehensive document applying to the child indirectly by implication (United Nations General Assembly, 1948); the 1959 U.N. Declaration of the Rights of the Child, including ten principles on the right to care, protection, and development. Other instruments dealing with children in conflict with the law, including the United Nations Rules for the Protection of Juveniles Deprived of their Liberty, the United Nations Standard Minimum Rules for Administration of Juvenile Justice, and the United Nations Guidelines for the Prevention of Juvenile Delinquency, were adopted in the 1980s and 1990s.

The rights of persons with disabilities have been the topic of two U.N. declarations and one set of rules: the 1971 Declaration on the Rights of Mentally Retarded and the 1975 Declaration on the Rights of Disabled Persons, both of which should be applicable to children but neither of which contains language making this clear; and the 1993 Standard Rules on the Equalization of Opportunities for Persons with Disabilities, covering preconditions, target areas, and implementation measures for equal participation, and affirming its relevance to children by citing the Convention on the Rights of the Child (described below) in its preamble.

Among the treaties or binding instruments, some in-directly and/or directly focus on children. Treaties that are more indirect, yet applicable to children, include four U.N. treaties: the International Covenant on Economic, Social, and Cultural Rights (adopted 1996, in force 1976) that protects against economic and social discrimination and exploitation; the International Covenant on Civil and Political Rights (adopted 1996, in force 1976) that protects children even more directly and prohibits a sentence of death for those under 18 years of age; the International Convention on the Protection of the Rights of All Migrant Workers and Members of their Families (adopted 1990, in force 2003) that prohibits discrimination, protects identity, and encourages education; and the International Labor Organization Convention (No. 169) on Indigenous and Tribal Peoples in Independent Countries (adopted 1989, in force 1991) that refers to children as it outlines fair and secure working conditions and the need for indigenous education.

Treaties directly focused on children include international labor conventions, which are child protection treaties. Among them are the 1919 International Labor Organization Conventions Nos. 5 and 6, which is the earliest of child rights treaties dealing with age minimums for work and protection from dangerous work; the United Nations Convention on the Rights of the Child (Convention on the Rights of the Child; United Nations General Assembly, 1989), the first comprehensive treaty on children's rights (discussed in upcoming sections); the 1990 Charter on the Rights and Welfare of the African Child, a comprehensive treaty strongly influenced by the Convention on the Rights of the Child; the European Convention on the Exercise of Children's Rights, adopted by the Council of Europe in 1996, basically dealing with enabling procedures; and treaties of the Hague Conference on Private International Law, harmonizing conflicts between differing national family laws, such as the 1980 Convention on the Civil Aspects of International Child Abduction and the Convention on Protection of Children and Co-Operation in Respect of Intercountry Adoption (concluded 1993, in force 1995).

The Convention on the Rights of the Child represents the hallmark in the ascendance of recognition and support for children's rights. In conjunction with the 1979 International Year of the Child, the Polish government proposed a treaty be drafted that would give legally binding rights to children. Representatives of the U.N.'s member nations deliberated 10 years on the development of this Convention (Detrick, 1992). It was adopted by the United Nations General Assembly without dissent in 1989, entered into force in 1990, and ratified by 191 of the 193 recognized nations by 1997, making it, in these terms, the most successful human rights treaty in history.

The Convention on the Rights of the Child has 3 parts: Part 1 includes 41 articles on substantive rights themes (clarified below), and parts 2 and 3 include 13 articles discussing implementation mechanism (reports to the Committee on the Rights of the Child by States Parties; Articles 43–45) and procedural matters (e.g. ratification, entry into force, amending procedures; United Nations General Assembly, 1989).

The Convention on the Rights of the Child has become the pre-eminent international guiding framework and set of standards for children's rights. Its importance as the central rallying point for child advocacy work internationally can be argued at least six reasons: a high level of international participation occurred in the drafting of the treaty; its comprehensive range, including both minimum standards and aspirational goals; it ratification by nearly all nations has raised it to the height of universal standards; states parties (nations that have ratified) are required to periodically and publicly report their progress in achieving its standards to the United Nations Committee of the Child (the official monitoring mechanism for the Convention, hereafter referred to as the Committee) and are expected to pursue further improvements; opinions and expertise of non-governmental bodies and experts are welcomed and applied by the Committee in its processes to support effective implementation; and progress is promoted primarily through public accountability, guidance, and moral persuasion.

Human rights generally are categorized as civil, political, economic, social and cultural for adults. For children, and particularly in the Convention, human rights more often are organized under themes of survival, protection, development, and participation. The following are illustrative examples: Article 6 acknowledges the right to life, survival and development; Article 19 acknowledges the right to protection from all forms of physical and mental violence, injury, abuse, neglect, or exploitation; Articles 28 and 29 acknowledge the rights to education on the basis of equal opportunity and to education directed to full development of personality, talents, and mental and physical abilities; and Articles 12, 13, 14, 15, and 17 acknowledge the rights to express one's views and have them given due weight, access to and exchange of information, freedom of belief, and freedom of association.

Some of the Convention's rights and imperatives are particularly relevant to children with disabilities, including the expectation that the child's maturity and evolving capacities will be considered in the exercise of rights, as specifically supported in Articles 5, 12, and 14. Two articles have been drawn out for special consideration regarding persons with disabilities by the Committee in its guidelines for the development of reports to it by states parties (Committee on the Rights of the Child, 1996): Article 2 requires non-discrimination in application of rights and in which disability is a specifically identified category for which discrimination is prohibited, and Article 23 states the special measures needed to ensure the rights of children with disabilities (Hodgkin & Newell, 1998), as follows:

Article 23

1. States Parties recognize that a mentally or physically disabled child should enjoy a full and decent life, in conditions which ensure dignity, promote self-reliance and facilitate the child's active participation in the community.

2. States Parties recognize the right of the disabled child to special care and shall encourage and ensure the extension, subject to available resources, to the eligible child and those responsible for his or her care, of assistance for which application is made and which is appropriate to the child's condition and to the circumstances of the parents or others caring for the child.

3. Recognizing the special needs of a disabled child, assistance extended in accordance with paragraph 2 of the present article shall be provided free of charge, whenever possible, taking into account the financial resources of the parents or others caring for the child, and shall be designed to ensure that the disabled child has effective access to and receives education, training, health care services, rehabilitation services, preparation for employment and recreation opportunities in a manner conducive to the child's achieving the fullest possible social integration and individual development, including his or her cultural and spiritual development

4. States Parties shall promote, in the spirit of international cooperation, the exchange of appropriate information in the field of preventive health care and of medical, psychological and functional treatment of disabled children, including dissemination of and access to information concerning methods of rehabilitation, education and vocational services, with the aim of enabling States Parties to improve their capabilities and skills and to widen their experience in these areas. In this regard, particular account shall be taken of the needs of developing countries.

Work to further address the international rights of children with disabilities continues internationally. In 1997 the Committee on the Rights of the Child devoted its annual Day of General Discussion to Children with Disabilities. It focused specifically on the right to life, development, self-representation, full participation, and full participation in education. The Committee's recommendations are available on its web site (http://www.ohchr.org/english/bodies/crc/discussion.htm). Strong support was expressed for the right to inclusion in everyday life, including education, which the Committee has continued to support in its communications with governments.

The first International Conference on Children's Rights in Education (Hart, Cohen, Erickson, & Flekkoy, 2001; Prospects, 1999) gave specific attention to the rights of children with disabilities (Saleh, 2001). The Committee currently is drafting another of its General Comments (an expanded commentary and guideline for the Convention on the Rights of the Child commissioned by the Committee) that will address the rights of children with disabilities. This General Comments was to be considered at the September 2005 meeting of the Committee and made available following its adoption. Related developments can be found on the Committee's web site (http://www.ohchr.org/english/bodies/crc/index.htm). In addition, an international review of human rights standards for children with disabilities has been developed that assists in assessing progress in implementing the Convention on the Rights of the Child internationally. This document is found in a report to the United Nations General Assembly Session on Children in 2001 (see Lansdown, 2001; http://www.daa.org.uk/ItisOurWorldToo.htm).

As promulgated in the Convention, children's rights primarily address issues for which governments are responsible. However, this emphasis does not usurp the rights and responsibilities of parents. They are specifically considered in 19 articles of the Convention. Nor does this emphasis suggest that governments and laws alone can achieve the full intentions of the spirit of the rights it embodies. The Convention both explicitly and implicitly refers at numerous points to the responsibilities of private as well as public institutions and bodies, and, in so doing, recognizes that children's rights must become a part of the fabric of everyday living if they are to be realized. The Committee has appreciated the importance of going beyond law in implementing children's rights, as exhibited in its repeated encouragement for child rights education for professionals serving children so that their practices will be duly influenced and influencing. At its 37th Session held September 2004, the Committee endorsed the international program Child Rights Education for Professionals, coordinated by the International Institute for Child Rights and Development (www.iicrd.org).

State party implementation reports to the Committee on the Rights of the Child, alternative non-governmental reports, together with critiques, responses, and recommendations of the Committee itself can be found on the web site of the Office of the United Nations High Commissioner for Human Rights (http://www.ohchr.org/english/bodies/crc/index.htm).

REFERENCES

Aries, P. (1962). *Centuries of childhood.* New York: Vintage Books.

Committee on the Rights of the Child (1996). *Reporting guidelines to governments: General guidelines regarding the form and contents of periodic reports to be submitted by States Parties under Article 44, Paragraph 1(b), of the Convention.* Geneva, Switzerland: Office of the United Nations High Commissioner of Human Rights (http://www.unhchr.ch/tbs/doc.nsf/(Symbol)/CRC.C.58.En?Opendocument).

De Mause, L. (1975). *The history of childhood.* New York: Harper & Row.

Detrick, S., Doek, J., & Cantwell, N. (Eds.). (1992). *The United Nations Convention on the Rights of the Child: A Guide to the "Travaux Preparatoires."* Dordrecht: Martinus Nijhoff.

Hart, S. N., Cohen, C. P., Erickson, M. F., & Flekkoy, M. (Eds.). (2001). *Children's rights in education.* London: Jessica Kingsley.

Hodgkin, R., & Newell, P. (1998). *Implementation handbook for the Convention on the Rights of the Child.* New York: UNICEF.

Lansdown, G. (2001). *It's our world too! A report on the lives of disabled children.* London, UK: Disability Awareness in Action.

Prospects. (1999, June). 110 Open File: Children's rights in education. *Prospects,* 110, 29, 2 (Brussels), pp. 181–266.

Saleh, L. (2001). The rights of children with special needs: From rights to obligations and responsibilities. In S. N. Hart, C. P. Cohen, M. F. Erickson, M. F., & M. Flekkoy (Eds.), *Children's rights in education* (pp. 110–135). London: Jessica Kingsley.

United Nations (U.N.) General Assembly. December 10, 1948. *Adoption of a universal declaration of human rights.* New York: Author.

United Nations (U.N.) General Assembly. November 20, 1989. *Adoption of a Convention on the rights of the child.* New York: Author.

Verhellen, E. (1994). *Convention on the Rights of the Child; Background, motivation, strategies, and main themes.* Garant, Netherlands: Leuven-Apeldoorn, Grarant Publishers.

STUART N. HART
*University of Victoria, Victoria,
British Columbia*

CYNTHIA PRICE COHEN
*Child Rights International
Research Institute*

INTERNATIONAL ETHICS AND SPECIAL EDUCATION
INTERNATIONAL SCHOOL PSYCHOLOGY ASSOCIATION

CHINA, SPECIAL EDUCATION IN

History of Special Education Services

China has a history of civilization exceeding five thousand years. The description of disabled people (deaf and blind) was first documented in the fourth century BC in Zuo. The progressive thought that all people with disabilities should be well taken care of was explicitly stated in the Book of Rites, in the second century BC. In 1859, Hong Rengan proposed that institutions for disabled people be established. However, the first school for the blind was founded by a British missionary named William Murray in Beijing, in 1874. Thirteen years later (1887), an American, C. R. Mills, became the founder of the first school for the deaf in Shandong. It was not until 1916 when the first Chinese, Zhang Jian, opened Nantong School for the Deaf in Jiangsu, which is still in operation. By 1948, there were a total of 42 special schools for the deaf and blind, with an enrollment of 2,380 students and 360 faculty/staff members. Among these schools, eight were funded by the public. At that time, special education was categorized as social education.

After the People's Republic of China was founded in 1949, the government integrated special education into the general educational system and new special education programs were created in the Department of Education. The number of schools for the deaf and blind increased significantly from 64 to 253 between 1953 and 1963. According to statistics in 1984, the enrollment of deaf and blind students was 33,055, served by 8,000 faculty and staff. Meanwhile, four schools for students with other disabilities came into existence. In 1997, there were a total of 1,440 special education schools—27 higher education institutions, 845 schools for the deaf, 143 schools for the deaf and blind, and 425 schools for children with disabilities. The number of disabled students enrolled also increased to 340,621, along with 43,296 faculty and staff members.

In 1987, the survey results showed that there were 52 million disabled people in China, 4.9 percent of the national population. It was estimated that 60 million people were handicapped out of 1.2 billion Chinese; among them 12.3 million were under 18, which was 2.58 percent of the total population. The enrollment rate of school-age children with visual, hearing, speech, and mental disabilities increased from 20 percent (1991) to nearly 60 percent (1995).

Legal Rights and Public Policy

A legal regulation system regarding special education has been developing since 1980. Provision No. 45 of the Constitution of People's Republic of China (1982) states that all disabled persons have the right to be educated. In response to the Constitution, provincial governments support special education through various ways to meet their local needs. Special education is also touched upon in specific legal regulations. It is stipulated in Provision No. 9 of the Law of Compulsory Education (1986) that the government is obligated to set up and support special education schools or classes for disabled children, and any individuals are encouraged to found schools. Special law—Law of the PRC on the Protection of Disabled Persons—was constituted in 1990. This law declares that the educational rights of the disabled are protected, and classifies special education as one of the components of general education. Nine provisions in Regulation No. 3 of the 1990 law stipulate the responsibilities, policies, funding, approaches, adult education, training of faculty/staff, and so on in special education. Rules and regulations were also established for various departments in the government, specifying how they comply with the laws. Fifty-two provisions in Educational Regulations for the Disabled Persons specifically define the education of the disabled at different stages. In addition, other relevant laws such as Law of Teachers and Law of Vocational Education also relate to special education.

The following aspects are highlighted in the laws and regulations. It is clearly stated that teaching disabled children is one of the important components in compulsory education, which must be insured and enforced by the government. The educational policy regarding disabled people observes the principle of keeping a balance of popularization and advancement, with the former as the focus. While the priority is to improve compulsory and vocational education, preschool education should be strengthened and secondary and higher education should gradually be developed. It is stipulated that multiple methods should be applied in the education of disabled children. The guiding principle in special education is that general education schools function as the backbone, and learning in regular classrooms and special education classes/programs constitute the main body. The training of faculty and staff should be emphasized and the supply for special education should be assured.

Present Structure

Special education can be defined in the following two ways: (1) in a broad sense, it may indicate the education of all children who have special needs including the gifted and talented and juvenile criminals, or (2) in a narrow sense, it may imply the education of all kinds of mentally and physically disabled people. Currently, the emphasis in special education is placed on the training of people, especially children, with various disabilities, though the study of all who need special care in education is being conducted simultaneously.

China is developing a special education system with its own characteristics, responding to the situation of a large number of disabled children, a developing economy, and a developing educational foundation. This system is neither complete segregation nor mainstreaming and inclusiveness; it is a combination of general education and special education—each is independent but also integrated. Special education is in one of three forms: special education schools, special education programs, and learning in regular class. However, the majority of the students are enrolled in either special programs or regular classes in general education schools.

The focus of special education is within the nine-year compulsory education. Early childhood education is considered critical and the early intervention and training of deaf and mentally disabled children have received a great deal of attention. Meanwhile, disabled adult vocational education also grows rapidly. In 1997, 610 adult vocational education institutions were registered and 1.5 million disabled people were trained. In addition to advancing their education in regular higher educational institutions, disabled people also enjoy the privilege of attending two universities founded exclusively for them. Although the national educational department established standard curriculum and instruction materials in special education, local educational institutions are encouraged to make any changes to accommodate their specific needs.

Financing

As is the general nine-year compulsory primary and secondary education, special education is run and supported by local governments. On the other hand, noncompulsory early childhood and higher education is supported by the central government and by individuals. The central government has increased its budget to improve and further develop special education in the past decade. In 1994, the national financial budget for special education reached ¥28 million, a 142 percent increase of the budget in 1990. A special allowance was provided by relevant central government departments for the purpose of enhancing special education in 1989—¥14 million were allocated between 1989 and 1995. Consequently, local governments followed the example, creating their special allowance for special education. Another financial source for special education is donations and fund raising. Economically disadvantaged students are supported with assistantship and scholarship awarded by the government.

Education and Training of Educators

There was no special institution where faculty and staff were trained for special education in P.R. China until 1980. Special education majors received their training at secondary normal schools in several provinces in the early 1980s. The special education program was created at Beijing Normal University in 1986. At present, there are 34 secondary special education normal schools in operation. Special education programs are offered in five nationally and two provincially affiliated normal universities, where teacher candidates pursue bachelor's degrees. Graduate programs are also available at institutions such as Beijing Normal University. Bachelor's degrees can be completed in four years, and master's degrees in three years. Special education classes are opened in general secondary normal schools to train special education candidates in a regular classroom setting. Various workshops and long distance learning also are part of the overall training system. In addition, the National Educational Committee often entrusts relevant institutions with seminars for different types of education professionals, such as principals and special education administrators. Experts from home and abroad are invited to lecture and teach at these seminars. Moreover, professional special education research institutions and mass research organizations have been developed. Journals such as *Modern Special Education* and *Special Education in*

China are published periodically. Lastly, special educators are entitled to a special allowance which equals to 15–25 percent of their base salary.

Relationship to Other Social Services

Special education touches all walks of life. In 1993, the State Council Coordinating Committee on Disability was organized, with chief officers from 34 departments as its members. The central government issued *Work Program for Disabled Persons During the 9th Five-Year Plan Period, 1996–2000*. Specific requirements and implementation plans have been proposed in early intervention community services, compulsory education, vocational education, employment, culture, appliances for the handicapped, immunization, legality, reduction of expenses, and organization. A series of special regulations are also included in laws and policies. For instance, Electoral Law states that disabled people have equal rights to vote, Inheritance Law stipulates that the disabled have equal property and civil rights, and Criminal Law and Civil Law insure that the disabled are protected in human rights and lawsuits. In employment, a quota of 1.5–2 percent is assigned for any institution to hire the disabled. Nontax or tax deduction is applicable to any enterprise whose employees are handicapped. The blind enjoy free reading materials and free urban transportation. It is also regulated that the third Sunday of May each year is the national Individuals with Disabilities' Day.

Trends and Goals for the Present and Near Future

A Chinese-style special education system is being established on the basis of adapting models from other countries to serve the needs of China. The national government has set the following five priorities in developing special education for the near future.

1. The expansion of special education in rural areas will be emphasized. For those places where special education has been available, the focus will be placed on educational improvement and reform. The goal is to increase the enrollment rate of disabled children to that of regular children. Approximately 80 percent of all blind, deaf, and mentally handicapped children are expected to attend schools.
2. Early childhood special education will be improved considerably, and families and communities are encouraged to participate in early intervention.
3. Vocational training for the disabled will be strengthened, with short-term training as the primary means.

4. Promotions systems will be established for special education teachers to improve their benefits.

5. Further research will be conducted on the education of children with learning disability, autism, and other disabilities.

Due to historical reasons, special education in Taiwan, Hong Kong, and Macao shares similar cultural tradition and background with that in P.R. China. However, each has formed its own characteristics in classification, standards, and educational methods in their process of development. In December of 1997, a symposium was held at Taibei Normal University to discuss special education in mainland China and Taiwan. The theme of the conference was to create a brand new world of special education with love and wisdom. The interaction among Chinese and international special education professionals has increased significantly in recent years. These educators' interactions enhance mutual understanding and advance the knowledge of special education by all nations.

REFERENCES

Law of the People's Republic of China on the Protection of Disabled Persons. (1991). Beijing, China: Hua Xia.

Mao, Y. (1993). Viewpoints gleaned from participating early intervention in China. *Early Child Development and Care, 84,* 59–74.

Piao, Y. (Ed.). (1995). *Special pedagogy.* Fuzhou: Fujian Education Press.

Piao, Y. (1987). China, People's Republic of. In J. Van Cleve (Ed.), *Gallaudet encyclopedia of deaf people and deafness* (Vol. 1, pp. 181–184). New York: McGraw-Hill.

Piao, Y., Gargiulo, R., & Yun, X. (1995). Special education in the People's Republic of China: Characteristics and practices. *International Journal of Special Education, 10*(1), 52–65.

State Council. (1994). The provisions on the education of disabled persons. *People's Daily,* August 27.

State Education Commission. (1995). *Documents of special education,* 1990–1995. Beijing: Author.

State Statistics Bureau. (1987). *First national sampling of the handicapped.* Beijing, China: Author.

Work Program for Disabled Persons During the 9th Five-Year National Development Plan (1996–2000). (1992). Beijing, China: Hua Xia.

Yang, H., & Wang, H. (1994). Special education in China. *Journal of Special Education, 28*(1), 93–105.

Yun, X. (1994), China. In K. Mazurek & M. Winzer (Eds.), *Comparative studies in special education* (pp. 163–178). Washington, DC: Gallaudet University Press.

YONGXIN PIAO
Beijing Normal University

PING LIN
Elmhurst College

HONG KONG, SPECIAL EDUCATION IN
JAPAN, SPECIAL EDUCATION IN

CHLAMYDIA TRACHOMATIS INFECTIONS

Chlamydia trachomatis is the most prevalent sexually transmitted infection in the United States today. The annual incidence is estimated to be as high as 3 million (CDC, 2005; Washington, Gove, Schachter, & Sweet, 1985). Of sexually active adolescents who were examined, about 22 percent had a chlamydia infection (Fraser, Rettig, & Kaplan, 1983).

Chlamydia is spread by intimate and/or sexual contact, and affects both women and homosexual/heterosexual men in all socioeconomic classes. The disease is especially alarming because it is often silent, having no symptoms. Up to 70 percent of women and 25 percent of men with chlamydia may be relatively asymptomatic (CDC, 2005; Washington et al., 1985).

The bacteria can cause painful urination and pelvic urinary, eye, and respiratory infections in both sexes. Additional symptoms in women may include vaginal discharge, lower abdominal pain or sensitivity, abnormal Pap smear (often described as heavy or moderate inflammation), vaginal bleeding between periods even when taking birth-control pills regularly, and uterine infection. Symptoms in men may include penile discomfort and/or discharge.

If silent or not correctly diagnosed and treated, the disease can lead to such serious complications as pelvic inflammatory disease, ectopic (tubal) pregnancy, infertility, and, possibly, cervical cancer in women and urethritis and sterility in men. Though common, the disease may not be recognized among individuals with mental retardation, often thought of as asexual by many medical or social work personnel. Mentally retarded adolescents, and young adults in particular, should receive education in the recognition of chlamydia and other venereal diseases.

There is some evidence that in pregnant women chlamydia infections may lead to prematurity. It is the leading cause of early infant pneumonia and conjunctivitis (CDC, 2005). Chlamydia infections are curable with a full 21-day treatment with tetracycline. A 7-day treatment may be effective for men, but not for women. Sulfisoxazole and erythromycin are also effective, but penicillin is not.

REFERENCES

Centers for Disease Control and Prevention (CDC). (2005). *What is Chlamydia?* Retrieved June 9, 2006, from http://www.cdc.gov/std/chlamydia/STDFact-Chlamydia.htm#What is

Fraser, J., Rettig, P., & Kaplan, D. (1983). Prevalence of cervical chlamydia trachomatis and Neisseria gonorrheae in female adolescents. *Pediatrics, 71,* 333–336.

Washington, E., Gove, S., Schachter, J., & Sweet, R. (1985). Oral contraceptives, chlamydia trachomatis infection, and pelvic inflammatory disease. *Journal of the American Medical Association, 253,* 2246–2250.

C. Sue Lamb
Ginga L. Colcough
University of North Carolina at
Wilmington

HERPES SIMPLEX I AND II

CHLORPROMAZINE

Chlorpromazine (CPZ) is the generic name for Thorazine, a phenothiazine used in the treatment of psychoses and other psychiatric disorders (Conley et al., 1998). Though CPZ was synthesized by Charpentier in 1950 during research intended to produce an antipsychotic medication, the endeavor began in 1949 with a French surgeon Laborit, who was seeking a medication to reduce shock during surgery (Leavitt, 1982). Chlorpromazine is used primarily in the treatment of schizophrenia, but also has been used at low dosages to treat nausea and seasickness.

Though the actions of CPZ on the central nervous system (CNS) are not completely understood, it tends to produce the following behavioral changes: decreases apparent agitation, decreases perceptions of anxiety, decreases reports of hallucinatory experiences, produces mild to moderate sedating effects that appear to be both dosage and clinical condition dependent, and decreases spontaneous motor activity.

Because CPZ and all phenothiazines appear to block dopamine receptors in the CNS, a number of motor-related adverse effects are noted, especially during initial usage, chronic usage, or at high dosages. Three general reactions may be observed: dystonic reactions (most often with children, especially during acute infections or while dehydrated; these include spasms of neck muscles, rigidity with extension of back muscles, jaw tics, difficulty in swallowing or talking, and facial spasms with tongue protrusion, and may be accompanied by sweating or pallor); feelings of motor restlessness (e.g., agitation, inability to sit still, tapping of feet, insomnia, strong desire to move about without reported anxiety; often occurs within 2 to 3 days of initiating treatment); parkinsonlike symptoms (most frequent with elderly persons; include masked facial appearance, increased salivation/drooling, motor slowing, including slowed speech, swallowing difficulties, and cogwheel rigidity; McEvoy, 1985). In addition, blurred vision and dry mouth are reported during early stages of treatment. A persistent motor syndrome called tardive dyskinesia, characterized by rhythmic involuntary movements of facial and oral musculature and occasionally the limbs, may develop in conjunction with CPZ administration (Konopasek, 2004). The elderly,

especially females, on high dosages are reported as most at risk for this condition.

REFERENCES

Conley, R. R., Tamminga, C. A., Bartro, J. J., Richardson, C., Peske, M. Lingle, J., Hegerty, J., Love, R., Gounaris, C., & Zaremba, S. (1998). Olanzapine compared with chlorpromazine in treatment-resistant schizophrenia. *American Journal of Psychiatry, 155,* 7, 914–920.

Konopasek, D. E. (2004). *Medication fact sheets.* Longmont, CO: SoprisWest.

Leavitt, F. (1982). *Drugs and behavior.* New York: Wiley.

McEvoy, G. K. (1985). *American hospital formulary service: Drug information 85.* Bethesda, MD: American Society of Hospital Pharmacists.

Robert F. Sawicki
Lake Erie Institute of
Rehabilitation

PHENOTHIAZINES

CHOLINESTERASE

Neurons are the basic information processing and transmitting elements of the central nervous system. The transmission of impulses across these nerve cells is a biochemical process. As such, a neurochemical process is the foundation of all human behavior.

Impulses travel from one neuron to another across a biochemical junction (synapse). Specifically, when an impulse reaches the terminal button of a neuron, it releases a transmitter substance called acetylcholine (ACh), which causes a temporary change in the membrane of the receiving neuron. If there is sufficient chemical stimulation, the second neuron will subsequently fire. Following the alteration of the membrane potential, the enzyme *cholinesterase* (ChE) neutralizes (destroys) the transmitter substance and thus restores the synapse to a resting state. In this way a single impulse is transmitted through the nervous system.

Neuroscientists have long hypothesized that this biochemical process underlies learning and memory functioning in the brain (Hillgard & Bower, 1975). While a clear relationship has not been established between cholinesterase activity and memory functioning, a number of investigators have consistently found a cholinergic deficit in dementia patients (e.g., Giacobini, Gracon, Smith, & Hoover, 1997; Perry et al., 1978). Based on postmortem examination, these investigators found reduced cholinesterase levels in those areas of the brain typically associated with memory (e.g., the hippocampus). Thus, it appears that a reduction in cholinesterase activity may be related to memory dysfunctions.

Research efforts are presently under way that examine the relationship between increased cholinergic activity and memory and learning functions, and the role of cholinesterase in obsessive-compulsive disorder (Erzegovesi, Bellodi & Smeraldi, 1995). Interestingly, cholinesterase inhibitors are being used to treat mild to moderate symptoms of Alzheimer's disease as they increase levels of acetylcholine in the brain (Alzheimer's Association, 2005).

REFERENCES

Alzheimer's Association. (2005). *Fact sheet: About FDA-approved cholinesterase inhibitors.* Retrieved July 20, 2005, from http://www.alz.org/Resources/Topicindex/cholinesteraseinhibitors.asp

Erzegovesi, S., Bellodi, L., & Smeraldi, E. (1995). Serum cholinesterase in obsessive-compulsive disorder. *Psychiatry Research, 58,* 3, 265–268.

Giacobini, E., Gracon, S., Smith, F., & Hoover, T. (1997). Cholinesterase inhibitors in Alzheimer disease treatment. In R. E. Becker & E. Giacobini (Eds.), *Alzheimer Disease: From molecular biology to therapy.* Boston, MA: Birkhauser.

Hillgard, E. R., & Bower, G. H. (1975). *Theories of learning.* Englewood Cliffs, NJ: Prentice Hall.

Perry, E. K., Tomlinson, B. E., Blessed, G., Bergmann, K., Gibson, P. H., & Perry, R. H. (1978). Correlation of cholinergic abnormalities with senile plaques and mental test scores in senile dementia. *British Medical Journal, 2,* 1457–1459.

JEFFREY W. GRAY
Ball State University

RAYMOND S. DEAN
*Ball State University
Indiana University School of
Medicine*

NEUROLOGICAL ORGANIZATION
SYNAPSES

CHOMSKY, NOAM (1928–   )

Noam Chomsky was born on December 7, 1928 in Philadelphia, Pennsylvania. His undergraduate and graduate years were spent at the University of Pennsylvania, where he received his BA in 1949 and his PhD in Linguistics in 1955. From 1951 to 1955, Chomsky was a Junior Fellow of the Harvard University Society of Fellows. It was during this time that he completed his doctoral dissertation entitled *Transformational Analysis.* The major theoretical viewpoints of the dissertation were published in the monograph *Syntactic Structure* in 1957, which was later expanded in a more extensive work published in 1975, *The Logical Structure of Linguistic Theory.*

Noam Chomsky

Chomsky joined the staff of the Massachusetts Institute of Technology (MIT) in 1955, and in 1961 was appointed full professor in the Department of Modern Languages and Linguistics, currently the Department of Linguistics and Philosophy. From 1966 to 1976, he was the Ferrai P. Ward Professor of Modern Languages and Linguistics, and he was appointed Institute professor in 1975.

Chomsky is famous for the construction of a system of generative programs developed out of his interest in modern logic and mathematics. His theory proposes that the grammatical rules for any given language are, in general, similar in all languages. He is best known for his work on the "Chomsky hierarchy," which classifies language groups according to the different types of grammars that generate them. In particular, he was the first linguist to identify what are today thought of as "context-free" grammars. Among his earlier works are *Cartesian Linguistics* (1966) and *Language and Mind* (1968).

Chomsky became interested in politics and the dynamics of governmental power during the Vietnam War, and has subsequently written much on language, politics, philosophy, and the media. Among the best known are *Manufacturing Consent* (1988), *Necessary Illusions* (1989), and *Deterring Democracy* (1992). He has also written and lectured widely on contemporary issues, international affairs, intellectual issues, and U.S. foreign policy.

From 1958 to 1959, Chomsky was in residence at the Institute for Advanced Study at Princeton, New Jersey. He delivered the John Locke Lectures at Oxford in 1969, the Bertrand Russell Memorial Lecture at Cambridge University in 1970, the Nehru Memorial Lecture in New Delhi in 1972, and the Huizinga Lecture in Leiden in 1977. His numerous honors include honorary degrees from the University of London, University of Pennsylvania, Georgetown University, and Cambridge University. He is a Fellow of the American Academy of Arts and Sciences as well as a member of other professional and learned societies including the National Academy of Science. In addition, he is a recipient of the Distinguished Scientific Contribution Award of the American Psychological Association (APA). Chomsky remains on the faculty at MIT, and continues to be actively involved in the wide variety of interests that have marked his career as a highly productive scholar and citizen.

REFERENCES

Chomsky, A. N. (1957). *Syntactic structures*. 'S-Gravenhage: Mouton.

Chomsky, A. N. (1966). *Cartesian linguistics: A chapter in the history of rationalist thought*. New York: Harper & Row.

Chomsky, A. N. (1968). *Language and mind*. New York: Harcourt, Brace and World.

Chomsky, A. N. (1975). *Logical structure of linguistic theory*. New York: Plenum.

Chomsky, N. (1992). *Deterring Democracy*. New York: Hill & Wang.

Ivan Z. Holowinsky
Rutgers University
First edition

Kay E. Ketzenberger
Tamara J. Martin
The University of Texas of the Permian Basin
Second edition

CHOREA

Choreiform movement is a term used to describe a disorder characterized by quick, sudden, random, purposeless, jerky, irregular, spasmodic movement. Choreiform movement can occur in any body part and often is observed in shoulders, arms, and hands, or in the tongue and face as grimaces. Chorea often occurs with writhing and twisting movements that are called atheosis. Chorea can be induced by drugs, metabolic and endocrine disorders, and vascular incidents (NINDS, 2005).

Two major kinds of chorea are of primary interest to school personnel because of their possible school-age onsets and their markedly different outlook for recovery or prognosis. Sydenham's chorea (also known as chorea minor, rheumatic chorea, or St. Vitus's dance) is a disease of the central nervous system that usually occurs following streptococcal inflammation. Its slow start, often several months after the initial infection, begins with choreiform movements after the initial infection, begins with choreiform movements involving all muscles except those of the eyes, and may involve obsessive-compulsive symptoms (Swedo & Leonard, 1994). There are seldom any specific laboratory findings. There is no specific treatment except for sedation and protection from injury, together with prophylactic follow-up for identified residual infection. Recovery is slow and spontaneous, usually within 3 to 6 months, with no permanent damage to the central nervous system. Medical follow-up is recommended, and return to regular school is encouraged as soon as the transitory motor symptoms permit. The disease is reported to be more common in girls, with onset most frequent in summer and early fall (Berkow, 1982).

The second major type of chorea is Huntington's chorea (also known as chorea degenerative, progressive, or hereditary). The age of insidious onset of Huntington's chorea is reported by most sources to be between 30 and 50 years (Barr, 1979; Chusid, 1976; Clark, 1975; NINDS, 2005). However, a subtype of this disease has been described with onset in childhood, with initial symptoms of stiffness (rigidity), slowed movement (bradykinesia), and later choreiform movement (Berkow, 1982). The disease is characterized by progressive choreiform movement, progressive mental deterioration, and marked personality changes. Swallowing becomes difficult, walking impossible, and dementia profound with progression. Death usually follows within 10 to 15 years. Treatment is symptomatic for motor symptoms. There is no known treatment for the dementia.

Huntington's chorea is transmitted as an autosomal dominant trait, which means that half of the children of an affected parent are at risk for developing the disease. Those who do not have the disease do not transmit it. In cases where the family history is not known, affected individuals with onset after childbearing years may transmit the disease to offspring before their own onset. Research has been directed toward a chemical identification of those with the disease, but at present the only conclusive evidence is family history, and *all* potential known carriers are advised not to have children. Chusid (1976) suggests that most American cases have been traced to two brothers who emigrated from England.

Clinical experience suggests that the subtypes with early childhood onset appears to progress more rapidly to early death. The presence of several children with the disorder in one family is a devastating experience. The serious implications of Huntington's chorea should serve to reinforce the importance of differential diagnosis of choreiform movement disorders by a skilled neurologist with appropriate medical follow-up. Supportive special education services should be provided.

REFERENCES

Barr, M. L. (1979). *The human nervous system* (3rd ed.). Hagerstown, MD: Harper & Row.

Berkow, R. (Ed.). (1982). *The Merck manual of diagnosis and therapy* (14th ed.). Rahway, NJ: Merck, Sharp & Dohme.

Chusid, J. G. (1976). *Correlative neuroanatomy and functional neurology* (16th ed.). Los Angeles: Lang Medical.

Clark, R. G. (1975). *Manter and Gatz's essentials of clinical neuroanatomy and neurophysiology* (5th ed.). Philadelphia: Davis.

National Institute of Neurological Disorders and Stroke (NINDS). (2005). *NINDS chorea information page.* Retrieved July 20, 2005, from http://www.ninds.nih.gov/disorders/chorea/chorea.htm

Stolov, W. C., & Clowers, M. R. (Eds.). (1981). *Handbook of severe disability* (stock #017-090-00054-2). Washington, DC: U.S. Government Printing Office.

Swedo, S. E., & Leonard, H. (1994). Childhood movement disorders and obsessive compulsive disorder. *Journal of Clinical Psychiatry, 55,* 3, 32–37.

RACHAEL J. STEVENSON
Bedford, Ohio

GENETIC COUNSELING
HUNTINGTON'S CHOREA

CHORIONIC VILLUS SAMPLING

Chorionic villus sampling (CVS), sometimes called chorionvillus biopsy, is a relatively new technique that allows diagnosis of chromosomal abnormalities, many inborn errors of metabolism, and other disorders, in the first trimester of pregnancy. Most women who have CVS are over 35 years of age (CDC, 2005). Conducted before organogenesis is complete, it cannot detect reliably disorders such as neural tube defects; they may be assessed with later maternal serum alpha-fetoprotein (AFP) screening.

CVS has clear advantages over amniocentesis as a technique for antenatal (prenatal) diagnosis. It can be performed optimally at 9 weeks of pregnancy as opposed to 16 to 18 weeks, and results, including chromosomal analyses, are available about a week after testing, as opposed to the 2 to 4 weeks for amniocentesis (*Lancet,* 1986). Thus genetic counseling can be provided early in pregnancy in cases where disorders are identified, avoiding some of the ethical and emotional concomitants of later abortion.

In CVS, 10–50 mg of placental tissue are removed. Enzyme assay and DNA analysis are performed directly on this tissue; chromosomal analysis is generally done on cultures of the CVS tissue. Most CVS assays are done transcervically, with a small percentage conducted abdominally (*Lancet,* 1986).

Risk of CVS is not established, although the likelihood of it infecting the embryo appears low. Of particular concern is the suggestion of greater risk of test-induced abortion following CVS than following amniocentesis (Clarke, 1985), although at least one study has found no difference between the two techniques (Jahoda, Vosters, Sacks, & Galjaard, 1985). A number of questions, particularly regarding safety, remain unanswered (*Lancet,* 1986) but risk factors appear to be relatively low at 0.5 percent to 1.0 percent (CDC, 2005). Widespread availability of CVS will depend on the outcome of large-sample controlled studies of risk and accuracy. Research reports are appearing frequently, and coordinated evaluation studies in Europe, Canada, and the United States began in 1985 (Clarke, 1985). In 1990, more than 200,000 procedures were performed in the United States (CDC, 2005).

REFERENCES

Centers for Disease Control and Prevention (CDC). (2005). *Chorionic villus sampling: Recommendations for prenatal counseling.* Retrieved July 20, 2005, from http://www.cdc.gov/mmwr/preview/mmwrhtm/00038393.htm

Clarke, M. (1985). Fetal diagnosis trial. *Nature, 315,* 269.

Jahoda, M. G., Vosters, R. P. L., Sacks, E. S., & Galjaard, H. (1985). Safety of chorionic villus sampling. *Lancet, 2,* 941–942.

Staff. (1986). The potential of chorionic villus sampling. *Lancet, 1,* 76.

ROBERT T. BROWN
University of North Carolina at Wilmington

BRENDA M. POPE
New Hanover Memorial Hospital

AMNIOCENTESIS
CHROMOSOMES, HUMAN ANOMALIES, AND CYTOGENETIC ABNORMALITIES
MATERNAL SERUM ALPHA-FETOPROTEIN (AFP) SCREENING

CHROMOSOMES, HUMAN ANOMALIES, AND CYTOGENETIC ABNORMALITIES

Chromosomal (cytogenetic) abnormalities are the most frequent cause of congenital (present at birth) malformations, affecting some 1 in 200 newborns (Moore, 1982). Their importance is reflected in the fact that they account for at least 10 to 15 percent of individuals with mental retardation severe enough to require institutionalization (Moore, 1982; Pueschel, 1983) and for about 8 to 10 percent of newborn and early infant deaths (Sperling, 1984). Further, some 30 percent of spontaneously aborted embryos/fetuses had a chromosomal abnormality, an incidence 50 times higher than that in live births, meaning that incidence in all pregnancies must be about 5 percent (Sperling, 1984).

Because chromosomal abnormalities involve disruption in the action of many genes, most are associated with severe and varied effects (Brown, 1986). These frequently, but not always, involve general and specific intellectual deficits, particular facial anomalies and cardiovascular, digestive, and pulmonary defects. Further, people with a chromosomal abnormalities usually have such characteristic phenotypes (physical appearance and physiological and behavioral functioning) that they frequently look more like unrelated persons with the same chromosomal abnormality than like their own siblings (Dobyns, 1999; Moore, 1982). The common characteristics that differentiate individuals with one abnormality from normal people or those with a different abnormality are called syndromes. Some two dozen chromosomally based syndromes have been identified. Although some, particularly the familiar Down, Klinefelter, and Turner syndromes are relatively common, others are so rare that only 50 or so cases have been reported (Smith, 1982).

This entry will address general issues about abnormalities, provide background information for more specialized reading, and address similarities and differences among currently identified syndromes. As is the case with other genetically based disorders and congenital and perinatal abnormalities, new research routinely leads to significant changes in knowledge.

Vogel and Motulsky (1979, p. 18) elegantly describe human cytogenetics as "a successful late arrival." Although the chromosome theory of inheritance had been proposed in 1902, cytogenetics really began in 1956 with the discovery that the diploid number of human chromosomes was 46 instead of the commonly accepted 48. To give an idea of past attitudes toward the handicapped and their behavior, the diploid number 48 had been found by Painter (1923) in studies of spermatogenesis in testes of three inmates of the Texas State Insane Asylum who had been castrated because of, among other things, their excessive masturbation. When in 1959 researchers discovered chromosomal bases for three common and well-established human syndromes (Down, Klinefelter, and Turner), human cytogenetics really came into its own. Since then, a variety of chromosomally based syndromes have been discovered on the basis of now routine cytogenic analysis of spontaneously aborted fetuses, early death newborns and infants, and individuals with physical and behavioral abnormalities. A number of children traditionally labeled by diagnosticians as "syndromish in appearance" (something looks wrong but no etiology is known) now are identified as having a chromosomal abnormality. In most cases, the description of the physical and behavioral characteristics of the syndrome has followed, rather than preceded, chromosomal analysis. Further, subsequent studies have identified multiple chromosomal bases for syndromes such as Down, Klinefelter, and Turner that help to account for high variability among and even within affected individuals. A variety of technical advances account for much of our knowledge about these abnormalities (Dobyns, 1999; Sperling, 1984; Vogel & Motulsky, 1979).

Normal and Abnormal Karyotypes

Normal humans have 23 pairs of chromosomes in all body cells, 22 pairs of autosomes, and one pair of sex chromosomes. Females normally have two long X sex chromosomes and males one long X and one shorter Y sex chromosomes. Chromosomes (colored bodies) are visible only early in mitosis, when cell samples are subjected to certain stains. A karyotype is a picture of chromosomes arranged by pair. The 22 autosomal pairs are arranged from the longest (1) to the shortest (22), followed by the sex chromosomes. A karyotype, showing chromosomal bands, of a normal human male is shown in Figure 1. Figure 2 shows a typical chromosome pair; the short arm is termed "p" and the long arm, "q"; the two arms are held together at the centromere, or primary constriction. Cohen and Nadler (1983) suggest the useful mnemonic of associating "p" with petite. Chromosomes are grouped into three types: metacentric (e.g., numbers 1 and 3), where the arms are nearly equal in length; submetacentric (e.g., numbers 4 and 5), where the "p" arm is distinctly shorter than the "q"; and acrocentric (e.g., numbers 14 and 21), which have a secondary constriction and abbreviated and apparently genetically inactive satellite "p" arms.

Normal Cell Division. During mitosis, the process of duplication of body cells, each of the 46 chromosomes divides and one member of each migrates to a pole of the cells. When the cell divides, each offspring cell contains the same 23 pairs of chromosomes. Thus mitosis is a process of chromosome duplication. In meiosis, the process of production of germ cells (sperm and eggs), each of the 23 chromosome pairs divides and one member of each pair migrates to a pole of the cell. When the cell divides, each offspring has 23 chromosomes. Thus each germ cell has 23 chromosomes. Meiosis is a process of chromosome reduction. Women's eggs will all have 22 autosomes and an X chromosome; men's sperm all have 22 autosomes and can have either an X or Y. In sexual recombination, when a sperm penetrates an egg, the resulting zygote normally has the appropriate 46 chromosomes. Thus gender of offspring is determined by the father's sperm.

Abnormal Karyotypes. Abnormalities can be: (1) an abnormal total number of chromosomes in an individual's body cells; (2) structural aberrations resulting from breakage in one or more chromosomes; or (3) populations of cells of different chromosome numbers in the same individual (mosaicism).

Aneuploidies refers to deviations, greater or fewer, in number of chromosomes from the normal 46. The most common aneuploidy is trisomy 21, which accounts for the greatest number of chromosomal abnormalities in spontaneous abortions as well as in live births. Trisomies on most pairs are prenatally lethal. Similarly, monosomy, absence of one of

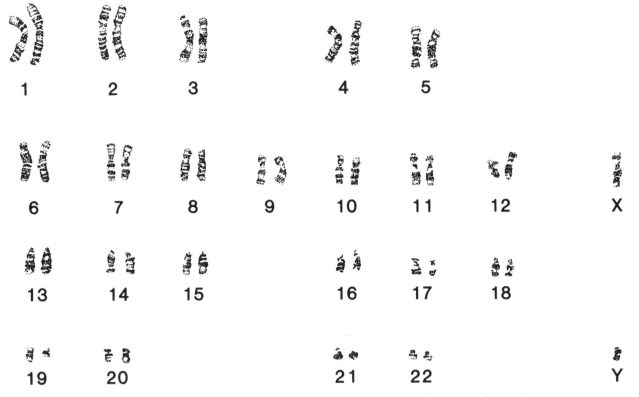

Figure 1 Karyotype for a normal human male. Twenty-two pairs of autosomes have been ordered and numbered according to convention from largest to smallest. Sex chromosomes are labeled X and Y.

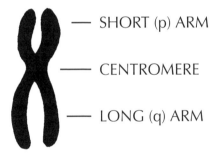

— SHORT (p) ARM

— CENTROMERE

— LONG (q) ARM

Figure 2 Standard nomenclature for describing parts of a chromosome, after Cohen and Nadler (1983)

a pair, resulting in fewer that 46 chromosomes, is virtually always prenatally lethal, except for Turner's syndrome, in which one X chromosome is missing (45,X). Even then, only one in 150 to 200 45,X embryos survives to full-term birth. The most common cause of aneuploidy is nondisjunction, the failure of a chromosome pair to split during formation of germ cells in meiosis. Thus one offspring germ cell will have a "double dose" of one chromosome and the other will have none. Anaphase lag can also produce monosomy.

Mosaicism results from nondisjunction occurring mitotically in a cell in an embryo in an early stage of development. As a result, if the embryo survives and continues to develop, it will have both normal and abnormal, generally trisomic, cell populations. Because of the presence of normal cells,

individuals with mosaicism will generally show less severe symptoms than those with the pure syndrome.

The basis for nondisjunction is not known, but is presumed to be manifested biochemically. In nondisjunction Down's syndrome, approximately 80 percent of the cases result from maternal and 20 percent from paternal nondisjunction (Sperling, 1984). Since all autosomal trisomies (not just Down syndrome) increase dramatically with maternal age, research focuses on factors that correlate with aging, including potential problems with aging oocytes themselves. Hypothesized links with irradiation, chemical agents, methods of birth control, and endocrine factors have not been fully confirmed, but some evidence suggests they play a role (Hassold & Jacobs, 1984).

Chromosomes may break, with material being either lost or attached to another chromosome. The most common structural aberrations are translocations, which result when two chromosomes break and parts of one are transferred to another. A reciprocal translocation occurs when two nonhomologous chromosomes exchange pieces. Individuals with such translocation chromosomes themselves have an appropriate balance of chromosomes and are phenotypically normal. Since they are carriers of a translocation chromosome, their offspring may suffer from duplication-deficiency syndromes, notably partial trisomies.

Important because of clinical implications are centric

fusions, or Robertsonian translocations. Centric fusion occurs when two acrocentric chromosomes each break near the centromere and rejoin. Generally, the short arms of both and the centromere of one are lost. Again, individuals may be unaffected, although they have one fewer than normal chromosome, but they are carriers. Their offspring may have a trisomy syndrome. Monosomies are also possible, but appear to be prenatally lethal. The best known translocation is Down's syndrome, resulting from centric fusion of chromosome 21 with chromosome 14 or, less frequently, 15.

Several other structural aberrations also may occur. Simple loss of part of a chromosome may result in a deletion syndrome. Isochromosomes occur when instead of a chromosome pair dividing longitudinally through the centromere, it divides horizontally, producing two chromosomes with identical arms. Fertilization will produce a cell with three "p" or "q" arms and only one of the other. When the segment between two breaks in a chromosome becomes inverted, reversing the gene order, an inversion results. Ring chromosomes occur when both ends of a chromosome break off and the tips of the centric segment rejoin. The resulting circular chromosome is unstable and has material from both ends deleted.

Standard Nomenclature. Normal and abnormal human karyotypes are described using a standard system, general aspects and examples of which are given here. More detailed descriptions are in Cohen and Nadler (1983), Smith (1982), Vogel and Motulsky (1979), and most human genetics textbooks.

As shown in Table 1, the order of information is (1) total number of chromosomes; (2) sex chromosomes; and (3) any abnormalities. Extra or missing chromosomes are indicated by "+" and "−", respectively, before the affected chromosome's number; extra or missing parts are indicated by "+" and "−", respectively, after the affected part. Structural aberrations are indicated by a standard abbreviation followed, parenthetically, by the number of the affected chromosome(s). Then, also parenthetically, the affected arm(s) and, if known, the chromosomal band numbers, are stated. Mosaics are indicated by a (/) mark separating descriptions of the two cell populations.

Abnormalities and Their Characteristics

Although chromosomal syndromes vary widely in their effects, the various types share some characteristics. Because much genetic material has been either added or is missing, many are lethal and most of the rest involve multiple and severe complications. However, as normal individuals vary in their physical and behavioral characteristics, so do those affected by chromosomal abnormalities. Not all will show even all of the major effects.

The description and characteristics of major cytogenic abnormalities occurring in live births are in Tables 2 and 3. It is important that different sources vary in their estimates of incidence and specification of major characteristics. In a number of cases, subsequent cases have led to changes in what were initially thought to be defining characteristics. For example, Cat-eye syndrome (trisomy 22p) was named for the striking coloboma of the iris seen originally. However, it has occurred only in a minority of the 40 cases that had been reported at the time of Smith's summary (1982).

Chromosomal Aneuploidies. The most common abnormalities are aneuploidies, involving an added or missing chromosome (Table 2). Multiple forms of some may occur. By far the most common is Down syndrome (trisomy 21), but several others have been reported. Early death is common in all, and in some types virtually all die in early infancy. Although each has individual characteristics, all involve brain damage generally resulting in moderate to severe mental retardation, congenital heart disease, and malformed ears. Specific facial, limb, and digit abnormalities are also common. All increase dramatically in incidence with maternal age (Vogel & Motulsky, 1979).

Turner and Klinefelter syndromes have clear phenotypic characteristics and were described before the development of modern cytogenic techniques. Both are associated with absence of puberty and sterility. Unfortunately, as pointed out by Brown (1986), textbook authors have frequently described sex-chromosome aneuploidies in chapters on mental retardation. However, standard forms are associated with low average intelligence (IQ ≈ 90), not mental retardation, although incidence of mental retardation is higher than among the normal population. Many affected individuals will complete high school and college. Mosaic Turner females and Klinefelter males will be less affected. Klinefelter males and Poly-X females with extra X chromosomes above trisomy for sex chromosomes are much more adversely affected and likely to be retarded (Korf, 1999).

Table 1 Examples of karyotype nomenclature

Karyotype	Description
46,XX; 46,XY	Normal female and male
47,XX,+21	Female with trisomy 21 (Down's syndrome)
46,XY/47,XY+21	Male with mosaic trisomy 21 (Down's syndrome)
46XY,+t(14q21q)	Male with Down's syndrome owed to centric-fusion type translocation between chromosomes 14 and 21
46,XX,del(5p) or 46,XX,5p−	Female with cri du chat owed to deletion of part of short arm of chromosome 5
46,XY,fra X(q27)	Male with fragile X syndrome, involving constriction at distal end of long arm of chromosome

Table 2 Chromosomal aneuploidies and characteristics

Syndrome	Incidence (live births)	Source	Characteristics
Autosomal Trisomies			
Trisomy 8	Very Rare	Mosaicism (mainly)	Variable height; MR (M → S); CHD; poor coordination; prominent forehead; deep-set eyes; digital abnormalities
Trisomy 9	Very rare	Mosaicism (mainly)	LBW; MR (S); CHD; low-set malformed ears; joint contractures; majority die in infancy
Trisomy 13 (Patau syndrome)	1:7000 to 20,000	Nondisjunction	LBW; MR (S); CHD; apnea; seizures; bilateral cleft lip and/or palette; failure to thrive; majority die in infancy
Trisomy 18 (Edwards syndrome)	1:8000	Nondisjunction	Three times more frequent in females; LBW; MR (S); failure to thrive; CHD; prominent occiput, majority die in infancy
Trisomy 21 (Down syndrome)	1:650–800	Nondisjunction—94% Mosaicism—2.4% Translocation—3.3%	MR (M → Mod); CHD; hypotonia; flat occiput; epicanthic fold; large tongue; above average infant death rate
Trisomy 22	Very rare	Nondisjunction (?)	MR; growth retardation; microcephaly; CHD; cleft palate; digit abnormalities; majority die in infancy
Sex Chromosome Aneuiploidies			
Turner syndrome	1:10,000	Various	Short stature; sterility; short webbed neck; broad, flat chest; IQ ≈ 90
(45,X)	57% of cases	Missing paternal X	
(45,X/46,XX, others)	12% of cases	Mosaicism	
(45,X/46,XY)	4% of cases	Mosaicism	
(Other)	27% of cases	Inversion and deletion	
Klinefelter syndrome	1:1000	Various	Sterility; hypogonadism; decreased facial and pubic hair; IQ ≈ 90; behavior problems
(47,XXY)	82% of cases	Nondisjunction	
(48,XXXY)`	3% of cases	Nondisjunction	More problems with added X chromosomes
(49,XXXXY)	<1% of cases	Nondisjunction	
(47,XXY/46,XY)	8% of cases	Mosaicism	
(Others)	6% of cases		
Poly X Syndrome	1:1000	Nondisjunction	No characteristic features; some delayed speech and motor development; more problems with added X chromosomes
(47,XXX)	98+% of cases		
(48,XXXX)	Rare		
47,XYY syndrome	1:1000	Nondisjunction	Variable features; tall; impulsive behavior; IQ ≈ 90

Source: Information from Cohen and Nadler (1983), Gerald and Meryash (1983), and Smith (1982).

Note: MR = mental retardation (S = severe; Mod = moderate, M = mild); CHD = congenital heart disease; LBW = low birth weight.

Table 3 Syndromes involving abnormal part of chromosomes

Syndrome	Incidence	Source	Characteristics
Autosomal Partial Trisomies			
Trisomy 9p	Rare	Translocation (?)	MR (S); delayed growth and puberty; delayed language; digital abnormalities
Partial trisomy 10q	Rare	Translocation (?)	LBW; MR (S); flat occiput; digital abnormalities; CHD; 50% die in infancy
Trisomy 20p	Rare	Translocation (?)	MR (M → Mod); hypotonia; facial abnormalities; digital deformities
Cat-eye syndrome (trisomy 22p)	Rare	Translocation (?)	MR (M); emotional retardation; normal growth; CHD; coloboma of iris; other eye defects
Autosomal Partial Deletion			
4p–	Rare(?)	Partial deletion	LBW; MR (S); beaked nose; microcephaly; cleft palate; hypotonia; seizures; early death
Cri du chat (5p–)	Rare	Partial deletion	LBW; MR (S); catlike cry; hypotonia; epicanthal folds; microcephaly
9p–	Rare	Partial deletion	Normal growth; MR (S); micronathia; trignocephaly; wide-spaced nipples
11p– (Andiria-Wilms Tumor Association)	Rare	Partial deletion	MR (Mod → S); growth deficiency; microcephaly; eye defects: micronathia; andiria; Wilms tumor
13p–	Rare	Partial deletion	LBW; MR (S); failure to thrive; microcephaly; CHD; facial and digital abnormalities
18p–	Rare	Partial deletion	Variability in effect; LBW; MR (variable); epicanthal folds; large, floppy ears
18q–	Rare	Partial deletion	LBW; MR (S); seizures; CHD; microcephaly; limb, digital, and genital abnormalities
21q–	Rare	Partial deletion	MR; hypertonia; growth retardation; microcephaly; micrognathia; large ears
22q–	Rare	Partial deletion	MR; hypotonia; microcephaly; epicanthal folds; digital abnormalities
Constriction Syndrome			
Fragile X	1:1000 males	Constriction at distal end of long arm of X chromosome	Long face; prominent chin; MR (M → S); developmental delay; language problems; specific learning problems

Source: Information from Cohen and Nadler (1983), Gerald and Meryash (1983), and Smith (1982).

Note: MR = mental retardation (S = severe; Mod = moderate, M = mild); CHD = congenital heart disease; LBW = low birth weight.

Klinefelter and Poly-X syndromes increase with maternal age (Hassold & Jacobs, 1984). However, incidence of neither Turner nor XYY syndrome correlates with maternal age, consistent with largely paternal origin (Hassold & Jacobs, 1984; Simpson, 1982).

Abnormal Parts of Chromosomes. Several partial trisomy syndromes, involving extra chromosomal material, and deletion syndromes are known, as shown in Table 3. Mental retardation of some degree is common to all. Low birth weight and specific facial and digital anomalies are also frequent.

Of particular current interest is Fragile X syndrome, resulting from a constriction in the X chromosome, which cytogenic studies reveal to be relatively common. Associated with mental retardation in affected males, it appears to be second only to Down syndrome as a cytogenic cause of mental retardation.

Human Genome Project

The Human Genome Project (HGP) was the international, collaborative research program whose goal was the complete mapping and understanding of all the genes of human beings. All our genes together are known as our "genome." The HGP was the natural culmination of the history of genetics research.

The HGP has revealed that there are probably somewhere between 30,000 and 40,000 human genes. The completed human sequence can now identify their locations. This ultimate product of the HGP has given the world a resource of detailed information about the structure, organization and function of the complete set of human genes. This information can be thought of as the basic set of inheritable "instructions" for the development and function of a human being.

The International Human Genome Sequencing Consortium published the first draft of the human genome in the journal *Nature* in February 2001 with the sequence of the entire genome's three billion base pairs some 90 percent complete. A startling finding of this first draft was that the number of human genes appeared to be significantly fewer than previous estimates, which ranged from 50,000 genes to as many as 140,000. The full sequence was completed and published in April 2003.

Upon publication of the majority of the genome in February 2001, Francis Collins, the director of the National Human Genome Research Institute noted that the genome could be thought of in terms of a book with multiple uses: "It's a history book—a narrative of the journey of our species through time. It's a shop manual, with an incredibly detailed blueprint for building every human cell. And it's a transformative textbook of medicine, with insights that will give health care providers immense new powers to treat, prevent and cure disease."

The tools created through the HGP also continue to inform efforts to characterize the entire genomes of several other organisms used extensively in biological research, such as mice, fruit flies and flatworms. These efforts support each other, because most organisms have many similar, or "homologous," genes with similar functions. Therefore, the identification of the sequence or function of a gene in a model organism, for example, the roundworm C. elegans, has the potential to explain a homologous gene in human beings, or in one of the other model organisms.

This ambitious project required a variety of new technologies that made it possible to construct a first draft of the human genome relatively rapidly. These techniques included: DNA Sequencing, the Employment of Restriction Fragment-Length Polymorphisms (RFLP), Yeast Artificial Chromosomes (YAC), Bacterial Artificial Chromosomes (BAC), the Polymerase Chain Reaction (PCR), and Electrophoresis.

Of course, information is only as good as the ability to use it. Therefore, advanced methods for widely disseminating the information generated by the HGP to scientists, physicians, and others is necessary to ensure the most rapid application of research results for the benefit of humanity.

Biomedical technology and research are particular beneficiaries of the HGP.

However, the momentous implications to individuals and society from possessing the detailed genetic information made possible by the HGP were recognized from the outset. Another major component of the HGP—and an ongoing component of NHGRI—is, therefore, devoted to the analysis of the ethical, legal, and social implications of the newfound genetic knowledge and the subsequent development of policy options for public consideration (National Human Genome Research Institute, 2005).

Implications for Special Educators

As cytogenic analyses become more standard, increasing numbers of children will be identified as having some chromosomal disorder. Many minor ones will have few implications for teachers. Others will be associated with general and specific intellectual deficits, coordination problems, and emotional disorders. Special educators and others in education generally may need to become familiar with the syndrome and standard nomenclature. Further, research will doubtless render some current knowledge incorrect and we must be ready to accept new information. It should be kept in mind that syndromes can induce stereotypes, and that affected children should be treated on the basis of their individual characteristics, not the general ones of a syndrome.

REFERENCES

Brown, R. T. (1986). Etiology and development of exceptionality. In R. T. Brown & C. R. Reynolds (Eds.), *Psychological perspectives on childhood exceptionality: A handbook* (pp. 181–229). New York: Wiley.

Cohen, M. M., & Nadler, H. L. (1983). Chromosomes and their abnormalities. In R. E. Behrman & V. C. Vaughn, III (Eds.), *Nelson textbook of pediatrics* (12th ed., pp. 288–310). Philadelphia: Saunders.

Dobyns, W. B. (1999). Introduction to genetics. In K. F. Swaiman, & S. Ashwal (Eds.), *Pediatric neurology* (pp. 325–353). St. Louis, MO: Mosby.

Gerald, P. S., & Meryash, D. L. (1983). Chromosomal disorders other than Down syndrome. In M. D. Levine, W. B. Carey, A. C. Crocker, & R. T. Gross (Eds.), *Developmental-behavioral pediatrics* (pp. 346–353). Philadelphia: Saunders.

Hassold, T. J., & Jacobs, P. A. (1984). Trisomy in man. *Annual Review of Genetics, 18,* 69–97.

Korf, B. R. (1999). Chromosomes and chromosomal abnormalities. In K. F. Swaiman & S. Ashwal (Eds.), *Pediatric neurology* (pp. 354–376). St. Louis, MO: Mosby.

Moore, K. L. (1982). *The developing human* (3rd ed.). Philadelphia: Saunders.

Painter, T. S. (1923). Studies in mammalian spermatogenesis. II. The spermatogenesis of man. *Journal of Experimental Zoology, 37,* 291–321.

Pueschel, S. M. (1983). The child with Down syndrome. In M. D. Levine, W. B. Carey, A. C. Crocker, & R. T. Gross (Eds.), *Developmental-behavioral pediatrics* (pp. 353–362). Philadelphia: Saunders.

National Human Genome Research Institute. (2005). Retrieved December 14, 2005, at http://www.genome.gov/12011238

Scarr, S., & Kidd, K. K. (1983). Developmental behavior genetics. In P. W. Mussen, M. M. Haith, & J. J. Campos (Eds.), *Handbook of child psychology: Infancy and developmental psychobiology* (4th ed., Vol. 2, pp. 345–433). New York: Wiley.

Simpson, J. L. (1982). Abnormal sexual differentiation in humans. *Annual Review of Genetics, 16,* 193–224.

Smith, D. W. (1982). *Recognizable patterns of human malformation* (2nd ed.). Philadelphia: Saunders.

Sperling, K. (1984). Frequency and origin of chromosome abnormalities in man. In G. Obe (Ed.), *Mutations in man* (pp. 128–146). Berlin and New York: Springer-Verlag.

Vogel, F., & Motulsky, A. G. (1979). *Human genetics.* Berlin and New York: Springer-Verlag.

ROBERT T. BROWN
University of North Carolina at Wilmington
First and Second editions

STAFF
Third edition

CRI DU CHAT SYNDROME
DOWN SYNDROME
ETIOLOGY
FRAGILE X SYNDROME
KLINEFELTER'S SYNDROME
TURNER SYNDROME
XYY SYNDROME

CHRONIC ILLNESS IN CHILDREN

Approximately 6 to 15 percent of children and adolescents live with a chronic illness such as diabetes, asthma, cancer, cystic fibrosis, epilepsy, muscular dystrophy, sickle cell anemia, migraines, and many others (Powers et al., 2003; Thies & McAllister, 2001). Special education programs were designed with developmentally disabled children in mind; therefore, children with chronic illness do not have a special program designed around their educational and health needs.

Children with chronic illness have multiple professionals involved in supporting their well being in the health care setting as well as the academic setting. Professionals such as teachers, doctors, school nurses, school administrators, medical consultants, therapists, and learning support staff all have important roles in the child's life. Collaboration and communication among the professionals involved is imperative to the child's well being. However, research has indicated that this communication is lacking, especially between health care providers and school staff (Lightfoot, Muckherjee, & Sloper, 2001). School teachers are often cognizant of specific children in their school or class who have a chronic health condition; however, educators commonly lack the information necessary to adequately aid the child (Clay et al., 2004). Issues surrounding confidentiality on the part of the health care staff contributes to the educators' lack of knowledge surrounding the health condition of the child, which leads to inadequate educational support. Educators, administrators, and support staff may benefit from educational programs to assist in recognition of certain chronic health conditions, such as asthma (Sapien, Fullerton-Gleason, & Allen, 2004).

Children born with extremely low birth weight have three times the chance of developing chronic health conditions compared to normal birth weight children (Mayor, 2005). Chronic health conditions linked to low birth weight include asthma, cerebral palsy, and visual difficulties. In addition, these children are at a higher risk for certain cognitive and social difficulties, such as decreased cognitive ability and school achievement as well as poor motor skills and social adaptive functioning.

Cognitive effects have been researched among specific chronic health conditions such as diabetes and cancer. Ferguson et al. (2005) examined neurodevelopment among early onset type 1 diabetes with results indicating lower nonverbal intelligence and slower psychomotor speed in adults who developed diabetes before the age of seven. The researchers also found structural brain abnormalities among the same population, possibly supporting the hypothesis that early onset of type 1 diabetes could be harmful to normal brain development. Similarly, cancer survivors often show declines in memory, attention, reading skills, and psychomotor speed (Kaemingk et al., 2004). Cognitive deficits and problems in school functioning have also been shown in children with sickle cell disease (Schatz, Finke, & Kellett, 2002), Lyme disease (Tager et al., 2001), chronic migraines (Powers et al., 2003), and epilepsy (Sanyal & Rajagopalan, 2005).

School absenteeism is common among children with chronic health conditions. Frequent and/or chronic absence can potentially affect the child's schoolwork and learning process. The majority of students will be able to catch up on their work with minimal help; however, some children will experience anxiety as a result of the workload which will thereby drain their already exhausted bodies further interfering with their cognitive abilities (Shiu, 2001).

A minority of students will have significant impairments

related to the illness or subsequent medical treatment. These students would benefit from an individualized educational program to assist in their academic endeavors. The challenges the student will face on return to school can be lessened to a certain degree with school programs designed to ease the transition, thereby alleviating anxiety and positively affecting performance and attendance. Children with chronic illness are served under the "other health impaired" category in the Individuals with Disabilities Education Act.

REFERENCES

Clay, D. L., McCarthy, A., Kelly, M. W., Johnson, S., Roman, J. & Zimmerman, M. (2004). Changes in medications administered in schools. *Journal of School Nursing, 22,* 102–107.

Ferguson, S., Blane, A., Wardlaw, J., Frier, B., Perros, P., McCrimmon, J. et al. (2005). Influence of an early-onset age of type 1 diabetes on cerebral structure and cognitive function. *Diabetes Care, 28,* 1431–1438.

Kaemingk, K., Carey, M., Moore, I., Herzer, M., & Hutter, J. (2004). Math weaknesses in survivors of acute lymphoblastic leukemia compared to healthy children. *Child Neuropsychology, 10*(1), 14–23.

Lightfoot, J., Muckherjee, S. & Sloper, P. (2001). Supporting pupils with special health needs in mainstream schools: Policy and practice. *Children & Society, 15,* 57–69.

Mayor, S. (2005). Extremely low birth weight is linked to risk of chronic illness. *British Medical Journal, 331,* 180.

Powers, S., Patton, S., Hommel, K., & Hershey, A. (2003). Quality of life in childhood migraines: clinical impact and comparison to other chronic illness. *Pediatrics, 112*(1), 1–5.

Sanyal, N. & Rajagopalan, N. (2005). A comparative cognitive profile of epileptic and non-epileptic normal preadolescents. *Journal of Projective Psychology & Mental Health, 12*(2), 129–140.

Sapien, R., Fullerton-Gleason, L., & Allen, N. (2004). Teaching school teachers to recognize respiratory distress in asthmatic children. *Journal of Asthma, 41*(7), 739–743.

Schatz, J., Finke, R., & Kellett, J. (2002). Cognitive functioning in children with sickle cell disease: A meta-analysis. *Journal of Pediatric Psychology, 27*(8), 739–748.

Shiu, S. (2001). Issues in the education of students with chronic illness. *International Journal of Disability, Development, and Education, 48*(3), 269–281.

Tager, F., Fallon, B., Keilp, J., Rissenberg, M., Jones, C., & Liebowitz, M. (2001). A controlled study of cognitive deficits in children with chronic Lyme disease. *Journal of Neuropsychiatry & Clinical Neuroscience, 13*(4), 500–507.

Thies, K., & McAllister, J. (2001). The health and education leadership project: a school initiative for children and adolescents with chronic health conditions. *Journal of School Health, 71*(5), 167–172.

MIRANDA KUCERA
*University of Colorado at
Colorado Springs*

CITIZEN ADVOCACY GROUPS

See ADVOCACY GROUPS, CITIZEN.

CIVIL RIGHTS OF INDIVIDUALS WITH DISABILITIES

A person with a disability has certain rights guaranteed by law that relate to education, employment, health care, senior citizen activities, welfare, and any other private services, programs, or activities that receive federal assistance.

Diamond (1979) has summarized the need for services and the specific rights of individuals with disabilities from a personal perspective. She reports that persons with disabilities have a right to private and public education at the elementary, secondary, and postsecondary levels. In addition to the education curriculum, supportive or rehabilitative services should be made available. When requiring a service (e.g., when dining out or shopping) the same courtesies should be extended to individuals with disabilities as to others.

People with disabilities have the right to travel assisted or unassisted on airplanes, trains, buses, and taxi cabs. Persons with disabilities have a right to gain entrance to public facilities without being inconvenienced, and buildings should be free of architectural barriers. Individuals with disabilities have a right to receive equal treatment by doctors and hospitals. This will require that medical personnel acquire understanding and knowledge of disabilities. Individuals with disabilities have a right to apply for any license (e.g., marriage, fishing) made available to nondisabled individuals without additional requirements or embarrassment. It is unlawful to discriminate against individuals with disabilities regarding employment practices. It is also unlawful for the owner of commercial property to refuse to sell, rent, or lease, or in any way discriminate because of a disability. As important as the services needed is the right to feel assured that the members of society will look on individuals with disabilities as responsible people capable of making a contribution to society.

It is the responsibility of the Office of Civil Rights in the Department of Education and the Office of Civil Rights in the Department of Health and Human Services to enforce federal laws prohibiting discrimination against persons on the basis of race, color, national origin, sex, age, or disability in federally assisted programs or activities, and to investigate discrimination complaints brought by individuals under a variety of statutes guaranteeing the rights of individuals with disabilities, including in particular the Americans with Disabilities Act (Office of Civil Rights, 1998).

REFERENCES

Diamond, S. (1979). Developmentally disabled persons: Their rights and their needs for services. In R. Weigerink & J. Pelosi (Eds.), *Developmental disabilities: The DD movement* (pp. 15–25). Baltimore: Brookes.

Office of Civil Rights. (1998). *Mission statement.* Washington, DC: U.S. Department of Education.

CECILIA STEPPE-JONES
*North Carolina Central
University*
Second edition

KIMBERLY F. APPLEQUIST
*University of Colorado at
Colorado Springs*
Third edition

ACCESSIBILITY OF BUILDINGS
ACCESSIBILITY OF PROGRAMS
AMERICANS WITH DISABILITIES ACT
INDIVIDUALS WITH DISABILITIES EDUCATION
IMPROVEMENT ACT OF 2004 (IDEIA)
REHABILITATION ACT OF 1973, SECTION 504
SOCIAL BEHAVIOR OF INDIVIDUALS WITH DISABILITIES

CLASS-ACTION LAWSUITS

Class actions are lawsuits in which a class of persons is represented by one or more of its members. In federal and in most state courts, groups of persons who have similar interests in the law and fact of the lawsuit can sue or be sued through a representative who acts on their behalf. A class action offers the following: the benefits of a clear resolution of a specific issue; the convenience of a useful method to assert legal rights in cases that have common interest where small individual claims might otherwise preclude judicial relief; and the saving of time, money, and effort by eliminating repetitious lawsuits (Redden & Vernon, 1980).

General requirements of a class action are as follows: the representative class must be large, although no specific number has been determined, so that it would be impractical to name each individual as a party to be brought before the court; the court must be able to clearly recognize the group as a class by virtue of its well-defined interests; and members of the class must raise the same questions of law and fact. The existence of an ascertainable class is evidenced by its certification by the court, which is necessary for the maintenance of a class action. All persons who will be affected by a judgment in a class action must be notified that such an action has commenced; each is provided an opportunity to present his or her side of the case. The court's ruling in a class-action suit applies to all members of that class unless a member has requested an option indicating that he or she does not wish to be bound by the specified court action (Payne & Patton, 1980; Redden & Vernon, 1980).

Court rulings in class-action suits have stimulated both litigation and legislation on behalf of individuals with disabilities. During the 1950s courts were confronted with class actions concerning the civil rights of handicapped children and adults. The majority of the actions were focused on the public's responsibility to provide education and treatment for handicapped citizens. The legal doctrines which courts have relied upon to substantiate the right to an education for the handicapped stem, in part, from the Supreme Court ruling in *Brown v. Board of Education.* The Supreme Court ruled in this landmark decision that all children are constitutionally entitled to an equal educational opportunity (Abeson & Bolick, 1974; Kirp, 1976). Subsequent class-action suits addressed the enforcement of the ruling in *Brown v. Board of Education* (Martin, 1980). Handicapped children were no longer denied a public education; however, many issues remained unresolved, and new issues surfaced in the courts, as well. For example, several state laws still regarded the severely handicapped as uneducable and thereby excluded this group from public schools. Questions regarding racial overrepresentation in special programs were also subjects of extensive litigation (Kirp, 1976).

The major legislation that governs our present delivery of services to exceptional children, the Individuals with Disabilities Education Act (IDEA), precipitated litigation that was more diverse and more individualized, thereby decreasing the numbers of representative classes. With the advent of the earlier version of IDEA, the Education for All Handicapped Children Act of 1975 (PL 94-142), class-action suits declined and individual legal claims were filed in matters of due process, Individualized Education Plan (IEP) challenges, placement, and related services.

REFERENCES

Abeson, A., & Bolick, N. (1974). *A continuing summary of pending and completed litigation regarding the education of handicapped children.* Reston, VA: Council for Exceptional Children.

Kirp, D. (1976). *Trends in education: The special child goes to court.* Columbus, OH: University Council for Educational Administration.

Martin, R. (1980). *Educating handicapped children the legal mandate.* Champaign, IL: Research Press.

Patten, J., & Patton, J. (1981). *Mental retardation.* Columbus, OH: Merrill.

Redden, K., & Vernon, E. (1980). *Modern legal glossary.* Charlottesville, VA: Michie.

FRANCES T. HARRINGTON
Radford University
Second edition

KIMBERLY F. APPLEQUIST
*University of Colorado at
Colorado Springs*
Third edition

BROWN V. BOARD OF EDUCATION
INDIVIDUALS WITH DISABILITIES EDUCATION
    IMPROVEMENT ACT
LARRY P.

CLASSROOM MANAGEMENT

Broadly conceived, classroom management refers to the orderly organization of materials and activities and the development of acceptable student behavior within the school learning environment. Although a deceptively simple concept, any consideration of the purposes and techniques of classroom management suggests numerous other educational concerns. Classroom management techniques must be in harmony with the school's perception of the nature and purpose of instruction and must satisfy a significant number of ethical and legal concerns. Similarly, the school's organizational structure must be constructed in a manner that will allow meeting the psychoeducational assumptions implicit in any selected alternative especially for students in special education. For these reasons, classroom management techniques must be selected with regard to many considerations. Few authors advocate a single approach as optimal for all settings.

Although classroom management can be broadly conceived, the usual topic of interest is the behavior of students and, specifically, discipline in the classroom. Clearly, the control of student behavior receives far more emphasis than other potential events that could be associated with classroom management. Public opinion consistently notes school discipline, often described as student control, to be a major problem in schools. In addition, a 1981 survey of teachers conducted by the National Education Association found 90 percent of the respondents indicating negative instructional outcomes as a result of student misbehavior. Cruickshank (1981) found similar results in that the control of students was seen to be one of the five most important issues identified by teachers throughout the course of a 15-year longitudinal study. Clearly then, classroom management is now virtually synonymous with discipline.

Given the widespread concern for discipline in the schools, it is not surprising that many models of classroom management have emerged. Since most of the efforts of classroom management techniques are devoted to redirecting atypical behavior, most currently advocated procedures were derived from intervention strategies used in laboratory or clinical settings. In past times, relatively few of the available procedures were initially developed within the classroom (Gunter & Denny, 1996), although there are exceptions (e.g., Cantor & Cantor, 1976; Kounin, 1977). In conceptualizing variations in individuals, Rhodes and Tracy (1972) enumerated several general models that emphasize

a perspective on the causes and alteration of behavior that continue today.

Almost all current approaches to classroom management are derived from one of the following perceptions. The *biophysical model* emphasizes the role of biology as a determinant of behavior. Interventions drawn from this model emphasize the control of environmental stimuli to a limited extent, and tend to rely more on the effects of diets, the elimination of environmental hazards to biological processes, genetic counseling, and the use of psychotropic drugs. The *sociological model* emphasizes the context of the school in society. This approach stresses the role of society in determining the nature of behaviors in need of control and the social forces operating to promote or inhibit specific behaviors (Tierno, 1991). Classroom management techniques drawn from this viewpoint tend to emphasize the influence of, for example, community and peer group on individual behavior. The *behavioral model* emphasizes, in particular, the immediate consequences of behavior for its role in the subsequent occurrence or lack of occurrence of behavior. Classroom management strategies drawn from this influence generally emphasize the role of the teacher (or other significant individuals) in the provision of consequences to particular behaviors. Control is sought by the careful manipulation of consequences. The *ecological model* emphasizes the context of behavior, noting that behavior never occurs in isolation and that naturally occurring events coerce specific types of behavior, e.g., a chair promotes sitting behavior, close proximity may promote speaking behavior. Finally, *the psychodynamic model* represents many alternative viewpoints that conceptualize the individual as possessing a dynamic intrapsychic life. The personality emerging from these inner forces becomes the basis for behavior. Personality formation and its ultimate effect on behavior is interpreted differently across the many models. However, virtually all psychodynamic models see the basis for behavioral change as the personal realization of the causes of one's behavior.

All of the above models have had significant influence on the development of techniques for classroom management. The sociological and ecological models, though theoretically suggesting great promise, have generally not spawned specific procedures widely placed into practice. The biophysical model has largely remained the purview of physicians. Both the psychodynamic and the behavioral models have, however, demonstrated immense appeal to educators and have generated many variations in approach. Of the two, the behavioral model is now the more dominant in the special education literature, but is taking into account social constructivist classrooms (Brophy, 1998). Early conceptualizations that relied on the teacher's control of contingencies have been augmented in recent years through the widespread use of modeling techniques (e.g., Bandura, 1969), cognitive behavior modification (e.g., Meichenbaum, 1977), group contingency programs (e.g., Litow & Pumroy, 1975), use of different modalities and other advances (NEA, 2005). Of course, current trends are for the use of evidence-based techniques of classroom management (Marzano, Marzano, & Pickering, 2003).

Significant problems in transfer of training and generalization of learned behaviors remain obstacles to the use of the approach. An excellent overview of representative classroom management techniques can be found in Charles (1985), Walker and Shea (1984), and the National Education Association web site at http://www.nea.org.

REFERENCES

Bandura, A. (1969). *Principles of behavior modification.* New York: Holt.

Brophy, J. (1998). Classroom management as socializing students into clearly articulated roles. *Journal of Classroom Interaction, 33,* 1, 1–4.

Cantor, L., & Cantor, M. (1976). *Assertive discipline. A take charge approach for today's educator.* Seal Beach, CA: Cantor and Associates.

Charles, C. M. (1985). *Building classroom discipline: From models to practice* (2nd ed.). New York: Longman.

Cruickshank, D. (1981). What we know about teachers' problems. *Educational Leadership, 38,* 402–405.

Gunter, P. L., & Denny, R. K. (1996). Research issues and needs regarding teacher use of classroom management strategies. *Behavior Disorders, 22,* 1, 15–20.

Kounin, J. (1977). *Discipline and group management in classrooms.* New York: Holt.

Litow, L., & Pumroy, D. K. (1975). A brief review of classroom group-oriented contingencies. *Journal of Applied Behavior Analysis, 8,* 341–347.

Marzano, R. J., Marzano, D. J., & Pickering, D. J. (2003). *Classroom management that works: Research-based strategies for every teacher.* Washington, DC: ASCD.

Meichenbaum, D. (1977). *Cognitive-behavior modification: An integrative approach.* New York: Plenum.

National Education Association (NEA). (2005). *Classroom management.* Retrieved July 21, 2005, from http://www.nea.org/classroom management/visual cues 050720.html

Rhodes, W. L., & Tracy, M. L. (Eds.). (1972). *A study of child variance: Conceptual models.* Ann Arbor: University of Michigan.

Tierno, M. J. (1991). Responding to the socially motivated behaviors of early adolescents: Recommendations for Classroom Management. *Adolescence, 26,* 103, 569–577.

Walker, J. E., & Shea, T. M. (1984). *Behavior management: A practical approach for educators* (3rd ed.). St. Louis, MO: Times Mirror/Mosby.

TED L. MILLER
University of Tennessee

APPLIED BEHAVIOR ANALYSIS
BEHAVIORAL ASSESSMENT
DISCIPLINE

CLAUSEN, JOHS (1913–   )

Johs Clausen was born in Bergen, Norway. He is a psychophysiologist and researcher in mental retardation. In 1939 he obtained his MA at the University of Oslo and in 1956 his PhD at the Faculty of Medicine, University of Oslo. Between 1949 and 1951, Clausen was a research fellow at Columbia University. He participated in the Columbia Greystone Project and the New York State Brain Research Project. He was also a research fellow with the Norwegian Research Council from 1953 to 1955; an associate scientist at the New York Psychiatric Institute from 1955 to 1966; and research psychologist, chief of psychological research, and research administrator at the Training School at Vineland (American Institute of Mental Studies). Clausen conducted research on ability structures and autonomic nervous functions in mentally retarded individuals. From 1966 to 1984, Clausen was chief research scientist, department of psychology, New York State Institute for Basic Research in Mental Retardation.

Among his numerous professional affiliations, Clausen has been a member of the American Psychological Association, Eastern Psychological Association, American Association for the Advancement of Science, American Association on Mental Deficiency, and the American Academy on Mental Retardation. He is the author of *Ability Structure and Subgroups in Mental Retardation* as well as more than 55 scientific studies.

REFERENCE

Clausen, J. (1966). *Ability structure and subgroups in mental retardation.* Washington, DC: Spartan.

IVAN Z. HOLOWINSKY
Rutgers University

CLEFT LIP/PALATE

The phenomenon of cleft lip and palate is a rather frequent one all over the world: 0.1 percent of all neonates are born with a more or less severe cleft, ranging from a cleft uvula or a partly cleft upper lip to a two-sided complete cleft of upper lip, jaw, and hard and soft palate. Normally, three main groups are discerned: cleft lip only (CL), cleft palate only (CP), and cleft lip and palate combined (CLP). Cleft lip and palate malformations are congenital and originate in the fourth to seventh week (CL) and in the seventh to twelfth week (CP) of embryonic development. Although in some cases viral, medical, and X-ray influences may play a role in causing these malformations, they are generally believed to have a hereditary basis. The chance of cleft lip and palate increases accordingly as the occurrence of clefts in a family are more frequent and more severe, and with the closeness of the relationship (mother or father). The occurrence of clefts is more frequent in boys than in girls, and, moreover, types of clefts are not equally divided between the sexes. There are also ethnic differences in incidence of cleft lip/palate. It occurs more often in Asians (approx. 1.7 per 1,000 births) and among certain Native American tribes (3.7 per 1,000 births) and less frequently in African Americans (1 per 2,500 births; March of Dimes, 2005).

Problems arising from being born with a cleft lip and palate are highly dependent on the part of the world in which the baby is born. In Third World countries, where no surgery is done on cleft lip and palate children, the main problem is survival and nourishment. In highly developed countries, the problems for cleft lip and palate children mainly concern communication and socialization. But even in these countries, a large differentiation can be found in the treatment of children with cleft lip and palate depending on the scientific ideas and theories of the treating medical team. However, for all newborn babies with cleft lip and palate, the first problem encountered is the feeding, because of the difficulties in sucking and swallowing. In Third World countries, infants depend entirely on breast feeding; if the baby is kept in a somewhat deviant feeding position (almost vertically sitting on the mother's lap or nearly horizontally held against the body of the mother), breast feeding is generally considered to be successful. Breast feeding is advisable in highly developed countries as well, because apart from other advantages, it is highly beneficial to the mother-child bond. In case of insurmountable breast feeding problems, feeding by means of special spoons and cups is preferred to bottles with long nipples (so-called lamb's nipples). Sometimes the infant will be provided with an obturator, a small plastic plate covering the cleft in the palate. This may help normal sucking, but it must be frequently renewed and readjusted because of the growing of the infant's mouth.

In most countries where surgery is applied, the child passes through a whole program of treatment and rehabilitation during the first years of life, often starting with healing of the lip followed by closure of the soft palate some months later, and sometimes the hard palate as well. The schedule and type of treatment depends to a large extent on the philosophy of the medical team. For example, the plastic surgeon will stress the aesthetic and visible aspects, the orthodontist the dental aspects, the speech pathologist the importance of the development of language and speech, and so on. Nevertheless, it will be clear that the best results are achieved by an interdisciplinary team of experts in close cooperation, all aiming to establish normal appearance, normal dental function, and good language and communication skills. The whole rehabilitation program is normally spread over more than 15 years (March of Dimes, 2005).

As for the intellectual abilities of cleft lip and palate children, many prejudices have to be disproved. Visible congenital deformations, especially of the head, are often wrongly associated with poor intellectual capacities. In recent research, children with cleft lip and palate were found to have at least average general intelligence, with no intellectual differences between boys and girls. The lowest scoring group are children with cleft palate only (CP), the group with no visible abnormalities.

As for the speech and language development and related verbal expression abilities of children with cleft lip and palate, a clear delay is found compared with the average population. One of the causes might be hearing problems, since children with cleft lip and palate have increased chances of inflammation of the middle ear combined with hearing impairment. Nevertheless, these possible hearing losses are not considered to be the main cause of the speech and language delays. Nor are the pronunciation problems that result from the abnormalities of the speech production mechanism, although a thorough speech training program will nearly always be necessary. No one-to-one relationship can be found between the severity of the malformation or the proportions of the cleft and the degree of delay in language and speech development. More and more, the psychosocial development of the child is believed to be a ground for speech and language problems.

Because interaction between parent and child is the cradle of the development of communication, it is clear that acceptance of the infant and his or her difficulties is a must. The birth of a child with a cleft lip and palate will undoubtedly cause the parents a degree of concern. The questions of the parents, their anxieties and concerns, require immediate professional counseling to create safe and adjusted surroundings for the child. Well-balanced interaction between parents and infant provides the possibility for the cleft palate child to develop normal linguistic, communicative, and social skills.

REFERENCES

Brookshire, B. L., Lynch, J. I., & Fox, D. R. (1984). *A parent-child cleft palate curriculum.* Tigard, OR: C. C. Publications.

Heineman-de Boer, J. A. (1985). *Cleft palate children and intelligence.* Lisse, Netherlands: Sweets & Zeitlinger.

March of Dimes. (2005). *Cleft lip and cleft palate.* Retrieved July 22, 2005, from http://www.marchofdimes.com/professionals/681_1210.asp

McWilliams, B., Morris, H., & Shelton, R. (1990). *Cleft palate speech* (2nd ed.). Philadelphia, PA: B. C. Decker.

Moller, K. & Starr, C. (1993). *Cleft palate: Interdisciplinary issues and treatment: For clinicians by clinicians.* Austin, TX: PRO-ED.

F. J. Koopmans-Van Beinum
Amsterdam, The Netherlands
First edition

Robert L. Rhodes
New Mexico State University
Second edition

LANGUAGE DISORDERS
LANGUAGE DISORDERS, EXPRESSIVE
PHYSICAL ANOMALIES

CLELAND, CHARLES C. (1924–   )

Charles Cleland received his BS in political science in 1950, and his MS in educational psychology in 1951, from Southern Illinois University. Cleland's doctoral work in educational psychology and general and industrial management at the University of Texas, Austin (1957), presented a theme that has been reflected in most of his work.

After a year as chief psychologist at the Lincoln State School (Illinois), Cleland returned to Texas to the Austin State School. In 1959 he was promoted to superintendent of the Abilene State School, where he stayed for four years until joining the faculty in the educational psychology department at the University of Texas, Austin.

Since that time, Cleland has been a professor of special education and educational psychology, teaching courses primarily in the areas of mental retardation, residential care, and management of service facilities. Although Cleland does not view himself as researcher (personal communication, June 26, 1985), his 250 articles, chapters in books, monographs, and books on a wide variety of subjects may prove otherwise. His principal publications include *Mental Retardation: Developmental Approach, Exceptionalities Through the Lifespan, Mental Retardation Approaches to Institutional Change,* and *Mental Retardation.*

Dr. Cleland is Professor Emeritus in the department of special education at the University of Texas at Austin.

Charles C. Cleland

REFERENCES

Cleland, C. C. (1978). *Mental retardation: A developmental approach.* Englewood Cliffs, NJ: Prentice Hall.

Cleland, C. C. (1992). *Mental retardation.* New York: Wiley.

Cleland, C. C., & Schwartz, J. D. (1969). *Mental retardation approaches to institutional change.* New York: Grune & Stratton.

Cleland, C. C., & Schwartz, J. D. (1982). *Exceptionalities through the lifespan.* New York: Macmillan.

ELAINE FLETCHER-JANZEN
*University of Colorado at
Colorado Springs*

CLERC, LAURENT (1785–1869)

Laurent Clerc, deaf from the age of one, was educated at the Institution Nationale des Sourdes Muets in Paris and following graduation served as a teacher there. He traveled to the United States with Thomas Hopkins Gallaudet to open the nation's first school for the deaf, now the American School for the Deaf, at Hartford, Connecticut, in 1817. Schooled in the teaching methods of Epée and Sicard, Clerc was the school's first teacher and was responsible for the training of new teachers.

Clerc was the first educated deaf person to be seen in the United States. He exemplified the potential of education for the deaf, and was influential in the movement to establish public responsibility for the education of the deaf.

REFERENCES

Lane, H. (1984). *When the mind hears.* New York: Random House.

Turner, W. W. (1871). Laurent Clerc. *American Annals of the Deaf, 15,* 14–25.

PAUL IRVINE
Katonah, New York

CLINICAL EVALUATION OF LANGUAGE FUNDAMENTALS, THIRD EDITION

The Clinical Evaluation of Language Fundamentals, Third Edition (CELF-3; Semel, Wiig, & Secord, 1995) is an individually administered battery of tests that can be used to diagnose language disorders. The battery is designed to be administered to individuals ages 6 through 21 and takes approximately 45 to 60 minutes to administer. There are two stimulus easels that contain visual stimuli. Examinee responses are recorded on the record form.

The CELF-3 consists of subtests that are categorized into either Expressive or Receptive domains. Subtests include Formulated Sentences (subject is given target word and picture stimulus and asked to form sentence), Sentence Assembly (subject produces 2 semantically and syntactically intact sentences from visually and orally presented words or word clusters), Word Structure (subject completes orally presented sentences with picture stimuli), Word Associations (subject lists as many words within given category as possible in 1 minute), Recalling Sentences (subject imitates orally presented sentences), Sentence Structure (subject points to one of four pictures in response to an orally presented stimulus), Semantic Relationships (subject listen to four facts, then selects two of four visually presented options), Word Classes (subject picks 2 out of 3 or 4 orally presented words that go together), and Concepts and Directions (subject identifies pictures of geometric shapes in response to orally presented direction). The scores in each domain produce Receptive and Expressive Language Composites that together are used to obtain the Total Language Score. Each provides standard scores, percentile ranks, and age equivalents.

The norms are based on a sample of 2,450 students that ranged in age from 6 to 21 years. The standardization sample consisted of normally achieving students; however, a number of cases of individuals with language disorders were collected to add to the battery's clinical validity. The sample was representative of U.S. children with respect to sex, race, geographic region family income, and highest education achieved by primary caregiver.

Internal consistency tests for the Standard Scores ranged from .83 to .95 and from .54 to .95 for the subtests (Semel et al., 1995). Test-retest reliability was calculated using 152 individuals from the norming sample. Semel et al. reported that reliability results for the Receptive Language Scores, and that Expressive Language Scores were .80 and .86 respectively and the mean correlation for the Total Language Score was .91. Reliability scores on the subtests ranged from .52 to .90. Semel et al. performed a discriminant analysis to determine the extent to which the CELF-3 would discriminate between individuals who did and did not have a learning disorder. Results indicated a 71.3 percent concurrence between the CELF-3 and school system classification requirements. Validity was further examined by comparing the CELF-3 to the Wechsler Intelligence Scale for Children (WISC-III). Correlations ranging from .56 to .75 were found. Research is supportive of the CELF-3 as a measure of verbal ability, but its role as an effective predictive instrument or as one legitimate for the language disabled population is questionable due to the normative sample used.

REFERENCES

Biddle, A., Watson, L., Hooper, C., et al. (2002). *Criteria for determining disability in speech-language disorders: Evidence report / technology assessment no. 52.* Rockville, MD: Agency for Healthcare Research and Quality.

Impara, J. C., & Plake, B. S. (Eds.). (1998). *The thirteenth mental measurements yearbook.* Lincoln, NE: Buros Institute of Mental Measurements.

Semel, E. M., Wiig, E. H., & Secord, W. A. (1995). *Clinical Evaluation of Language Fundamentals, Third Edition.* San Antonio, TX: The Psychological Corporation.

RON DUMONT
Fairleigh Dickinson University

JOHN O. WILLIS
Rivier College

CLINICAL INTERVIEW

Assessment interviews are conducted to identify and define current problems, to collect information concerning why current problems exist, or to make a diagnostic decision. The focus can be on information the client provides directly (content interviews), or on information that the client's behavior provides (process interviews, also known as mental status exams), or both. Manuals for conducting process interviews with children include Beiser's (1962), Goodman and Sours' (1967), and Greenspan's (1981). Content interviews have been emphasized in the literature on behavioral assessment of adult disorders (e.g., Haynes, 1978); prior to 1975, however, there were few references to content interviews with children. Since then, a number of studies have demonstrated that children can directly provide reliable information (e.g., Abu-Saad & Holzemer, 1981; Herjanic & Campbell, 1977), particularly when describing publicly observable events.

As with any assessment instrument, the quality of an interview depends on getting accurate information with the least amount of error. Three major sources of error are present in the interview: the interviewer, the interviewee, and the interview setting. One obvious interviewer error is the failure to ask for necessary information. It is unlikely that information that is not specifically asked for will be obtained; thus the information needed from an interview should be well planned. Some interviews are highly structured (e.g., the Vineland Adaptive Behavior Scales); others use rough organizing frameworks such as BASIC ID (Lazarus, 1973) or S-O-R-K-C (Kanfer & Saslow, 1969). The interview also may be organized ad hoc by the clinician. Several structured interviews for the assessment of child psychopathology exist (e.g., Edelbrock & Costello, 1984;

Orvaschel, Sholomskas, & Weissman, 1980; The Structured Clinical Interview for the *DSM-IV-TR,* 2004 by First Gibbon, Spitzer & Williams, 2005). The specific plan an interviewer uses will depend on the interviewer's purpose and theoretical model (Ventura, Lieberman, Green, Shaner & Mintz, 1998). The interviewer, however, must be careful not to lead the client's responses; only information to which the client has access should be asked for, and it should be clear to the client that no one response is favored by the interviewer. A second information-gathering error is the failure to recognize and clarify ambiguous responses. This source of error can be reduced by asking questions that clarify contradictory information.

A great deal of information can be given during interviews; thus, the storage and retrieval system used by the clinician is a third potential source of error. Audio or video recording ensures that all information given is stored, but recordings are cumbersome to review, may have adverse effects on rapport, and are not readily available in some settings. Notetaking is more efficient and can be more easily organized, but notetaking can also detract from rapport with some clients. Notetaking also has the effect of implicitly reinforcing clients for giving specific types of information, an advantage if this is information that the clinician needs. The interviewer may decide to neither record nor take notes; but the interviewer then needs to rely more heavily on specific memory strategies (e.g., making frequent summary statements of known information), and later writing notes.

An interviewer may use tactics that initially result in accurate information, but the information quality will deteriorate throughout the interview if the interviewer does not maintain a relationship in which the client continues to want to give accurate information. Maintaining warmth, empathy, genuineness, and person reinforcement may help maintain rapport. The interviewer must remain alert to changes in affect and change tactics to maintain an appropriate and culturally competent (Lesser, 1997) relationship.

Sources of interviewee error fall into categories of effects of developmental deficits, client perceptions of the nature and consequences of the interview, and fatigue. To the extent that the effects of these sources of error are under some control by the interviewer, they represent interviewer errors of control. Clinicians should be alert to signs of fatigue and other physiological effects. Interview sessions should be as short as possible and conducted at times when the client is rested and least distractible. Children and developmentally delayed adults have deficits in their knowledge of vocabulary and conversational conventions (Conti & Camras, 1984; Dickson, 1981), in their understanding of what a listener needs to know (Flavell et al., 1968), and in the facility with which they can meet the cognitive demands of answering questions (Shatz, 1977). These sources of error can be partly controlled by ensuring that vocabulary used by the interviewer is familiar to the client, by keeping cognitive demands low (e.g., by asking for single bits of information

at once rather than multiple bits), and by clearly explaining what information the interviewer knows and what information is needed. There is evidence that closed-ended or multiple-response format questions (e.g., "When the other kids call you that name, do you feel angry, sad, or something else?") obtain more reliable responses from developmentally younger persons than open-ended questions (e.g., "How do you feel when they call you that name?"), and some evidence that open-ended questions produce more refusals and less complete information than closed-ended ones (Ammons, 1950; Miller & Bigi, 1979). However, there is a tendency for developmentally delayed adults and children to give acquiescent responses to yes-no questions, and to give the last choice in multiple-response formats (Sigelman et al., 1981). There is a also a tendency for normal children under six to assume that they understand ambiguous questions and not ask clarifying questions (Robinson & Robinson, 1984). These deficits imply that when interviewing young children and developmentally delayed older persons, clinicians need to ask closed-ended questions, but avoid yes-no formats; clinicians should also be alert to a possible response bias. Sigelman et al. (1981) found a picture-choice format to be the most reliable, but nonverbal formats for interviewing may not always be available.

The interviewee's expectations about the interview and about what will be done with the information obtained is also likely to affect validity. Clinicians should ensure that clients understand what will happen during the interview, why the interview is being conducted, and how the information will be used, and should elicit any concerns the client has about the interview. In interpreting data, the clinician should consider the likelihood that the client may have been giving biased responses because of the demands of the setting; for example, when interviewing a client in a dormitory about involvement in an incident of stealing, it is likely that the client will give biased information, particularly if the client believes such information will be shared with houseparents. Bias owed to ecological demand characteristics can be reduced if the interview is designed so that the client believes the interview will be ecologically helpful. If the clinician begins the interview by asking whether there are problems in the setting that the client would like to have ameliorated, the client is more likely to be cooperative in sharing information.

The interview setting influences the interview, and can therefore be a source of error. Interviewer and interviewee should generally be alone unless the presence of other persons is expected to enhance the quality of the interview (e.g., a young child may be very fearful unless mother is present). The clinician needs to consider how the presence of other persons may affect the demand characteristics of the interview when interpreting the results. The client's prior experience with the clinician may also bias results; this problem is minimal in situations in which interviewer and interviewee have never met. The location of the interview may also affect the information that is elicited; interviewing a child in a classroom, for example, may generate a client expectation that the interviewer is a teacher; on the other hand, the setting can be used to prompt information that may not be normally accessible. It's possible, for example, that a child will give more reliable information about what has occurred in a classroom when the child is interviewed alone in the classroom. The setting for the interview should be carefully planned by the clinician.

The building blocks of a good clinical interview have been described as respect, curiosity, listening, searching for patterns and hypotheses, and supporting competence (Pennsylvania Public Welfare, 2005). These building blocks appear to summarize the goals of a competent clinical interview that compliments special education objectives and goals.

REFERENCES

Abu-Saad, H., & Holzemer, W. L. (1981). Measuring children's self-assessment of pain. *Issues in Comprehensive Pediatric Nursing, 5,* 337–349.

Ammons, R. B. (1950). Reactions in a projective doll-play interview of white males two to six years of age to differences in skin color and facial features. *Journal of Genetic Psychology, 76,* 323–341.

Beiser, H. R. (1962). Psychiatric diagnostic interviews with children. *Journal of the American Academy of Child Psychiatry, 1,* 656–670.

Conti, D. J., & Camras, L. A. (1984). Children's understanding of conversational principles. *Journal of Experimental Child Psychology, 38,* 456–463.

Dickson, W. P. (1981). Introduction: Toward an interdisciplinary conception of children's communication abilities. In W. P. Dickson (Ed.), *Children's oral communication abilities* (pp. 1–10). New York: Academic.

Edelbrock, C., & Costello, A. J. (1984). *A review of structured psychiatric interviews for children.* Unpublished manuscript.

First, M. B., Gibbon, M., Spitzer, R. L., & Williams, J. B. W. (2005). *SCID web page.* Retrieved July 22, 2005, from http://www.scid4.org/

Flavell, J. H., Botkin, P. T., Fry, C. L., Wright, J. W., & Jarvis, P. E. (1968). *The development of role-taking and communication skills in children.* New York: Wiley.

Goodman, J., & Sours, J. (1967). *The child mental status examination.* New York: Basic Books.

Greenspan, S. I. (1981). *The clinical interview of the child.* New York: McGraw-Hill.

Haynes, S. N. (1978). The behavioral interview. In S. N. Haynes (Ed.), *Principles of behavioral assessment.* New York: Gardner Press.

Herjanic, B., & Campbell, W. (1977). Differentiating psychiatrically disturbed children on the basis of a structured interview. *Journal of Abnormal Child Psychology, 5,* 127–134.

Kanfer, F. H., & Saslow, G. (1969). Behavioral diagnosis. In C. M. Franks (Ed.), *Behavior theory: Appraisal and status.* New York: McGraw-Hill.

Lazarus, A. (1973). Multimodal behavior therapy: Treating the BASIC ID. *Journal of Nervous and Mental Disease, 156,* 404–411.

Lesser, I. M. (1997). Cultural considerations using The Structured Clinical Interview for *DSM-III* for mood and anxiety disorder assessment. *Journal of Psychopathology & Behavioral Assessment, 19,* 149–160.

Miller, P. H., & Bigi, L. (1979). The development of children's understanding of attention. *Merrill-Palmer Quarterly, 25,* 235–250.

Orvaschel, H., Sholomskas, D., & Weissman, M. M. (1980). *The assessment of psychopathology and behavioral problems in children: A review of epidemiological and clinical research (1967–1979).* Rockville, MD: National Institute of Mental Health, Division of Biometry and Epidemiology (DHHS Publication No. (ADM)80-1037).

Pennsylvania Public Welfare. (2005). *Building blocks of the clinical interview.* Retrieved July 22, 2005, from http://www.dpw.state.pa.us

Robinson, E. J., & Robinson, W. P. (1984). Realizing you don't understand: A further study. *Journal of Child Psychology and Psychiatry, 25,* 621–627.

Shatz, M. (1977). The relationship between cognitive processes and the development of communication skills. *Nebraska Symposium on Motivation, 25,* 1–42.

Sigelman, C. K., Schoenrock, C. J., Winer, J. L., Spanhel, C. L., Hromas, S. G., Martin, P. W., Budd, E. C., & Bensberg, G. J. (1981). In R. H. Bruininks, C. E. Meyers, B. B. Sigford, & K. C. Lakin (Eds.), *Deinstitutionalization and community adjustment of mentally retarded people.* Washington, DC: American Association of Mental Deficiency.

Ventura, J., Liberman, R. P., Green, M. F., Shaner, A., & Mintz, J. (1998). Training and quality assurance with Structured Clinical Interview for *DSM-IV* (SC ID-I/P). *Psychiatry Research, 19,* 2, 16–17.

JOHN MACDONALD
Eastern Kentucky University

ASSESSMENTS, ALTERNATIVE MENTAL STATUS EXAMS

CLINICAL PSYCHOLOGY

Clinical psychology is the branch of psychology devoted to the scientific study, assessment, diagnosis, and treatment of mental disorders. Clinical psychology has its origins in 1896 with the construction of the first psychological clinic by Lightner Witmer at the University of Pennsylvania (Benjamin, 1997). In 1907, Witmer founded and served as editor of *The Psychological Clinic,* a journal describing the types of problems and work performed at the clinic. Witmer wrote the initial article in the new journal and described his work with a child referred for treatment of bad spelling in school (Witmer, 1907). The article was titled "Clinical

Psychology," wherein Witmer applied this name to his work, and became known as the founder of clinical psychology (Benjamin, 1997).

Initially, clinical psychology was most interested in the development and assessment of human abilities, and provided the government the means to test intelligence, achievement, vocational interests, and personality characteristics of recruits during both world wars. After World War II, the Veterans Administration hired large numbers of clinical psychologists to work with disabled veterans, and the psychologists' roles expanded beyond assessment to psychotherapy (Phares, 1979). During this time, clinical psychology gained professional status by obtaining licensure in most states, and establishing independent practice activities.

Training for clinical psychology is normally four years of graduate coursework followed by a full-time year of internship. Courses taken for the degree include basic psychological areas such as social, learning, methodology, and biological with advanced coursework in assessment and psychopathology (Matthews & Walker, 1997). The PhD (Doctor of Philosophy) degree is the traditional degree for clinical psychology and usually involves a scientist-practitioner model of training. The PsyD (Doctor of Psychology) is a newer degree focusing more on practitioner training with less emphasis on research productivity. Current requirements for licensure usually involves both a written and oral examination followed by a year of post-doctoral supervision. Additionally, the American Psychological Association provides accreditation for clinical psychology programs, allowing for common goals and training among diverse graduate programs.

At the present time, clinical psychologists are in everexpanding positions committed to the advancement and promotion of mental health and human well-being. They serve in the traditional roles of providing diagnosis and assessment functions and psychotherapy, but are increasingly called upon to provide consultation, supervision, or assume administrative positions (Matthews & Walker, 1997). Current theoretical perspectives include psychodynamic, behavioral, cognitive, humanistic, and systemic. Clinical psychologists work with all age groups from infants to the elderly; and they are also developing specialty areas such as forensic psychology, health psychology, children, the aging, scientific research, psychology of women, child health problems and ethnic minority issues. Finally, clinical psychologists work in a wide range of settings such as individual practice, mental health clinics, hospitals, schools, universities, counseling centers, legal systems, government organizations, and the military services.

REFERENCES

Benjamin, L. T., Jr. (1997). *A history of psychology: Original sources and contemporary research* (2nd ed.). New York: McGraw-Hill.

Matthews, J. R., & Walker, C. E. (1997). *Basic skills and professional issues in clinical psychology.* Boston: Allyn & Bacon.

Phares, E. J. (1979). *Clinical psychology: Concepts, methods, and profession* (Vols. 1–2). Homewood, IL: Dorsey Press.

Witmer, L. (1907). Clinical psychology. *The Psychological Clinic, 1,* 1–9.

LINDA M. MONTGOMERY
The University of Texas of the Permian Basin

CLINICAL INTERVIEW
DIAGNOSTIC AND STATISTICAL MANUAL OF MENTAL DISORDERS (DSM-IV)
MENTAL STATUS EXAMS

CLINICAL TEACHING

Clinical teaching is teaching prescriptive (diagnosis → prescription → remediation), with the intent of matching the student's strengths and weaknesses to a specific type of instruction. Clinical teaching is therefore often called diagnostic-prescriptive teaching. It is a continuous testteach-test process. This process was influenced by Johnson and Myklebust (1967), Smith (1968, 1974), Learner (1985), and many others. Teaching strategies in clinical teaching include task analysis and applied behavior analysis.

Learner (1985) views the clinical teaching process as a five-stage repetitive cycle of decision making that consists of assessment, planning, implementation, evaluation, and modification of the assessment. She further adds that the clinical teacher considers the student's ecological, home, social, and cultural environments.

Smith (1983) offers eight steps in the clinical teaching process: (1) the clinical teacher should objectively observe and analyze the student's classroom abilities; (2) the teacher should objectively observe and analyze the nature of the student's successes and difficulties on different types of tasks; (3) the teacher should scrutinize the characteristics of alternative tasks and settings; (4) compare and contrast how information gained from step (3) might interact with the observations in steps (2) and (1) so as to result in more favorable achievement; (5) the teacher should consult with the student whenever possible, present the choices for modification, and together decide which ones to try; (6) the teacher should set short-term goals, make the modifications; (7) teach; and (8) evaluate progress after a reasonable time interval; if successful, continue teaching similar but higher level objectives; if unsuccessful retrace steps 1–7 (p. 361).

Recently there has been a shift away from clinical teaching toward educational design that includes variables associated move with potential and diversity (Duke, 2000).

REFERENCES

Duke, D. L. *A design for Alana: Creating The next generation of American Schools.* Bloomington IN: Phi Delta Kappa International.

Johnson, D., & Mykelbust, H. (1967). *Learning disabilities: Educational principles and practices.* New York: Grune & Stratton.

Learner, J. (1985). *Learning disabilities: Theories, diagnosis, and teaching strategies* (4th ed.). Boston: Houghton Mifflin.

Smith, C. R. (1983). *Learning disabilities: The intervention of learner, task and setting.* Boston: Little, Brown.

Smith, R. M. (1968, 1974). *Clinical teaching: Methods of instruction for the retarded.* New York: McGraw-Hill.

MARIBETH MONTGOMERY KASIK
Governors State University

DIAGNOSTIC PRESCRIPTIVE TEACHING

CLOSED CIRCUIT TELEVISION

Closed Circuit Televisions (CCTVs) are assistive devices used by people with low vision to magnify print media. Similar to microfiche readers, CCTVs consist of a camera, viewing screen, and movable media platform. Conventional CCTVs utilize these three components in an integrated device, usually designed to fit on a desktop. Print media is placed on the movable platform, which is located directly below the camera and viewing screen, and can be moved two-dimensionally along the X and Y axes. Clutches on both axes allow the media to be maneuvered smoothly in one axis without jitter in the second axis, thus making the task of reading text easier. Viewing screens, or monitors, are large (usually 21″ or bigger) and, in modern devices, display color images more often than black and white. Integrated circuitry provides convenience features, such as automatic focus, zoom, reverse video, color filtering, and masking controls to display only one line of text at a time.

Hybrid devices have been developed, which provide a mobile solution. For example, a small handheld camera may be paired with a battery-operated viewing screen for easy portability. The technology has even paired handheld cameras with tiny display screens placed in goggles or visors. The user points the mobile camera at the object to be viewed and the image is displayed inside the wearable visor. Lens systems can be used in conjunction with CCTV visors to create a custom solution for the user.

DAVID SWEENEY
Texas A&M University

ASSISTIVE DEVICES
ASSISTIVE TECHNOLOGY ACT

CLOZE TECHNIQUE

The cloze technique is a procedure that is used for both the assessment and instruction of reading comprehension skills. Based on the psychological construct of closure, the technique was first developed by Taylor (1953), who believed that a person reading a narrative or expository selection psychologically endeavors to complete a pattern of thought and language that is left incomplete. With the cloze technique, such a language pattern is typically a reading passage from which words have been deleted. Typically, in a reading selection of approximately 250 words, every tenth lexical word would be deleted and it would be the reader's task to fill in the missing words.

According to Rye (1982), the cloze technique may be more appropriately considered a construction procedure, whereby the reader uses both linguistic knowledge and past experience to complete sentences in appropriate ways. Experience and language are used to choose the correct grammatical class of words.

Cloze exercises may be developed from basal reader texts, trade books, content area materials, and any other reading selections that are appropriate for a given population of readers. Often, the cloze procedure has been used as a device for the assessment of reading comprehension. As described by Smith and Johnson (1980), it may involve the use of a variety of cloze passages taken from the same reading material. For example, three different passages of approximately 100 words in length may be taken from the beginning, middle, and end of a selection. Then, certain words are deleted (e.g., every fifth or tenth lexical word). The reader's task is to read the passage and write in the missing word on a blank. Ekwall (1985) elaborated on this procedure by stating that the first and last sentences of the selection should be left intact, with every fifth word omitted to be replaced with a blank of 10 spaces in length. Again, the reader is required to read the selection and fill in blank spaces with a word that would seem to fit.

Cloze exercises can be used with either individual students or groups of students. As an assessment tool, there is usually no time limit for the completion of a cloze exercise. The evaluation or scoring of a cloze passage is usually based on a percentage of blank spaces that have been completed correctly. Furthermore, according to Smith and Johnson (1980), only the exact deleted word should be counted as correct. If a student is able to complete approximately 45 to 50 percent of the omitted spaces correctly, the reading material is judged to be at the reader's instructional level. If 60 percent or more of the blanks have been filled in correctly, the selection is probably at the reader's independent reading level. If fewer than 45 percent of the blanks are completed correctly, the material is at the reader's frustration reading level.

In addition to being used as a diagnostic measure, the cloze technique can also be used to improve reading comprehension in an instructional setting. In this manner, the technique can be used as a prereading activity to determine the reader's ability to deal with certain material, and as a postreading activity to develop certain comprehension skills and to practice various comprehension strategies (e.g., the use of context clues in understanding what has been read).

The cloze technique, therefore, based on the construct of perception and closure as defined by the gestalt psychologists, assumes the ability of a fluent reader to predict or anticipate what is coming next in a reading passage. This requires the use of various reading skills, including context clues, knowledge of linguistic patterns, and the ability to comprehend in general what is being read. As Rye (1982) describes, the activity involves a sampling of information from a contextual setting and the formation of hypotheses, a prediction of what will appear subsequently in the selection both linguistically and conceptually. The value of the cloze technique as both a diagnostic and instructional device lies in its demand on the reader's comprehension abilities and a variety of language skills.

REFERENCES

Ekwall, E. E. (1985). *Locating and correcting reading difficulties* (4th ed.). Columbus, OH: Merrill.

Miller, W. H. (1974). *Reading diagnosis kit.* New York: Center for Applied Research in Education.

Rye, J. (1982). *Cloze procedure and the teaching of reading.* Exeter, NH: Heinemann.

Smith, R. J., & Johnson, D. D. (1980). *Teaching children to read* (2nd ed.). Reading, MA: Addison-Wesley.

Taylor, W. L. (1953). Cloze procedure: A new tool for measuring readability. *Journalism Quarterly, 30,* 415–433.

JOHN M. EELLS
Souderton Area School District,
Souderton, Pennsylvania

READING DISORDERS
READING REMEDIATION

CLUTTERING

Cluttering is a speech disorder—or, more specifically, a fluency disorder—related to stuttering. Importantly, the two disorders are not the same. Cluttering is characterized by excessive breaks in the normal flow of speech that result from disorganized speech planning, talking too fast or in a jerky fashion, or simply being unsure of what one wants to say. By contrast, the person who stutters typically knows exactly what he or she wants to say but is temporarily unable to say it, thus repeating or prolonging sounds or syllables, blocking, and/or using accessory (secondary) devices

(e.g., eye-blinks, synonyms for difficult words, or abnormal facial postures; Daly, 1996; St. Louis & Myers, 1997). Because cluttering is not well-known, there is much ambiguity about the disorder. For example, the speech of many people who clutter is often described by themselves or others as stuttering. Moreover, cluttering frequently coexists with stuttering and some authorities question whether or not a reliable definition of cluttering has been established (e.g., Curlee, 1996).

The definition of cluttering recently adopted by the fluency disorders division of the American Speech-Language-Hearing Association is "a fluency disorder characterized by a rapid and/or irregular speaking rate, excessive disfluencies, and often other symptoms such as language or phonological errors and attention deficits" (St. Louis, Hanley, & Hood, 1998). Clutterers' speech does not sound fluent; in other words, they do not appear to be clear about either what they want to say or how to say it. They manifest excessive levels of normal disfluencies, such as interjections (e.g., "um," or "you know") and revisions (e.g., "We went over . . . we started to go to grandma's."; St. Louis, Hinzman, & Hull, 1985). They manifest little or no physical struggle in speaking and they have a few, if any, accessory behaviors. A rapid and/or irregular speaking rate would be present in a speaker who shows symptoms of speaking too fast, whether based on actual syllable-per-minute counts or simply an overall impression; sounding jerky; or using pauses during speech that are too short, too long, or improperly placed.

These fluency and rate deviations are often considered to be the essential symptoms of cluttering (St. Louis, 1992). Other characteristics may also be present but are not mandatory. These include confusing, disorganized language or conversational skills, often with word-finding difficulties; limited awareness of fluency or rate problems; temporary improvement when asked to slow down or to pay attention to speech (or when being tape recorded); specific sound misarticulations, slurred speech, or deleting nonstressed syllables in longer words (e.g., "ferchly" for "fortunately"); speech that is difficult to understand; a family history of stuttering and/or cluttering; social or vocational problems; learning disabilities; attention deficit/hyperactivity disorder; sloppy handwriting; difficulty with organizational skills for daily activities; and/or auditory perceptual difficulties (Daly, 1992; St. Louis & Myers, 1995, 1997; Weiss, 1964).

A team approach to assessment and diagnosis with cluttering is often necessary. In addition to a standard speech evaluation by a speech-language pathologist (SLP), contributions or reports from classroom teachers, special educators, psychologists, or (possibly) neuropsychologists may also be warranted. The SLP evaluation will carefully assess the fluency problem, but also any coexisting oral-motor, language, or articulation problems. If the suspected clutterer is in school, special education personnel may be asked to provide information on learning, social problems, and attention or behavioral problems, and psychologists could be requested to provide test information on academic achievement or intelligence. The eventual diagnosis should specify whether or not cluttering is present and also what other problems are present, such as stuttering, a language disorder, or a learning disability (St. Louis & Myers, 1997).

Therapy for clutterers generally addresses the contributing problems before focusing directly on fluency. Ordinarily, one of the first goals of therapy is to reduce the speaking rate, although this may not be easy for the clutterer to achieve. Some clutterers respond well to "timing" their speech to a delayed auditory feedback (DAF) device; some do not. Another technique that has been found helpful with younger clutterers is to use the analogy of a speedometer wherein rapid speech is above the speed limit, and "speeding tickets" are given for exceeding the limit (St. Louis & Myers, 1995, 1997).

Articulation and language symptoms are often reduced if the clutterer can achieve a slower rate. Sometimes, however, these problems need to be addressed directly. One technique involves practice first in using short, highly structured utterances. It may also be helpful for clutterers to learn to exaggerate stressed syllables in longer words while being sure to include all the unstressed syllables (e.g., "par-tic′-u-lar," "con-di′-tion-al," or "gen-er-o′-si-ty"; St. Louis & Myers, 1997).

Some clutterers benefit from planning both the content (the "what") of a message as well as the delivery (the "how"). For example, the "what" can be taught as formulating a telegram (e.g., "Car won't start. I pump accelerator. Carburetor gets flooded."). The "how" then focuses on filling in the appropriate small words (e.g., "My car often won't start after it sits for a few minutes. I pump the accelerator a few times before trying again. Often, the carburetor gets flooded."; Myers & Bradley, 1992).

As noted, many clutterers also stutter, and often the cluttering is masked by the stuttering. In some of these individuals, the cluttering emerges as the individual gets control of the stuttering or begins to stutter less (Van Riper, 1992). Yet, whether or not the clutterer also stutters (or previously stuttered), any therapy techniques that focus attention on fluency targets, such as easy onset of the voice, more prolonged syllables, or correct breathing, can also help the person to manage many of the cluttering symptoms. The important thing is that the clutterer learn to pay attention to—or monitor—his or her speech and do anything that makes it easier to remember to do so (Craig, 1996; Langevin & Boberg, 1996).

Lack of awareness is a particularly difficult clinical problem, for many clutterers are genuinely unaware of the extent of their cluttering behaviors. They must be taught to be careful observers of listener feedback. Some older clutterers are better able to monitor if they listen daily to a tape with a short sample of their disorganized cluttered speech and, immediately following, a sample of their clear, monitored speech (Daly, 1992).

It is currently impossible to predict with accuracy whether or not a clutterer will benefit from speech therapy. Most who benefit have become convinced from friends, family, or employers (or on their own) that they do have a significant speech problem. Also, motivation is a key element; successful clients typically have good reason for working hard to change, such as the likelihood of a job promotion. On the other hand, clutterers who are not sure that they have a problem, or are relatively unconcerned about it, tend not to improve as much or as easily from therapy (Daly, 1992; St. Louis & Myers, 1997).

REFERENCES

Craig, A. (1996). Long-term effects of intensive treatment for a client with both a cluttering and stuttering disorder. In K. O. St. Louis (Ed.), *Research and opinion on cluttering: State of the art and science,* Special issue of the *Journal of Fluency Disorders, 21,* 329–335.

Curlee, R. F. (1996). Cluttering: Data in search of understanding. In K. O. St. Louis (Ed.), *Research and opinion on cluttering: State of the art and science,* Special issue of the *Journal of Fluency Disorders, 21,* 315–327.

Daly, D. A. (1992). Helping the clutterer: Therapy considerations. In F. L. Myers & K. O. St. Louis. *Cluttering: A clinical perspective* (pp. 107–124). Kibworth, Great Britain: Far Communications. (Reissued in 1996 by Singular Press, San Diego, California)

Langevin, M., & Boberg, E. (1996). Results of intensive stuttering therapy with adults who clutter and stutter. In K. O. St. Louis (Ed.), *Research and opinion on cluttering: State of the art and science,* Special issue of the *Journal of Fluency Disorders, 21,* 315–327.

Myers, F. L., & Bradley, C. L. (1992). Clinical management of cluttering from a synergistic framework. In F. L. Myers & K. O. St. Louis (Eds.), *Cluttering: A clinical perspective* (pp. 85–105). Kibworth, Great Britain: Far Communications. (Reissued in 1996 by Singular Press, San Diego, California)

St. Louis, K. O. (1992). On defining cluttering. In F. L. Myers & K. O. St. Louis (Eds.), *Cluttering: A clinical perspective* (pp. 37–53). Kibworth, Great Britain: Far Communications. (Reissued in 1996 by Singular Press, San Diego, California)

St. Louis, K. O., Hanley, J. M., & Hood, S. B. (1998). *Terminology pertaining to fluency and fluency disorders.* Final report of the Terminology Task Force of the Special Interest Division on Fluency and Fluency Disorders of the American Speech-Language-Hearing Association.

St. Louis, K. O., Hinzman, A. R., & Hull, F. M. (1985). Studies of cluttering: Disfluency and language measures in young possible clutterers and stutterers. *Journal of Fluency Disorders, 10,* 151–172.

St. Louis, K. O., & Myers, F. L. (1995). Clinical management of cluttering. *Language, Speech, and Hearing Services in Schools, 25,* 187–195.

St. Louis, K. O., & Myers, F. L. (1997). Management of cluttering and related fluency disorders. In R. Curlee & G. Siegel (Eds.), *Nature and treatment of stuttering: New directions* (pp. 313–332). New York: Allyn & Bacon.

Van Riper, C. (1992). Foreword. In F. L. Myers, & K. O. St. Louis, *Cluttering: A clinical perspective* (pp. vii–ix). Kibworth, Great Britain: Far Communications. (Reissued in 1996 by Singular Press, San Diego, California)

Weiss, D. (1964). *Cluttering.* Englewood Cliff, NJ: Prentice Hall.

KENNETH O. ST. LOUIS
West Virginia University

COCKAYNE SYNDROME

Cockayne syndrome (CS) is rare genetic disorder, autosomally recessive, of unknown prevalence. Males and females are equally affected. In CS, growth and development are normal for at least the first year followed by neurodevelopmental retardation that may not become especially prominent in many cases until 4 or 5 years of age.

In the early stages of CS, these children are often misdiagnosed with ADHD or with various coordination disorders. Typically, mental retardation develops in the childhood years and may be mild to severe. Photosensitivity is common and peripheral neuropathy develops. Small stature with large ears occurs routinely. Leukodystrophy occurs in all cases along with premature death. There is no cure, and the only treatment is symptom management. Diagnosis is by physical examination and CT or MRI (Gillberg, 1995). Symptoms are usually well-expressed by age 10 years.

Special education will typically be required for intellectual impairment and externalizing behavior problems. Dwarfism and emotional symptoms may occur as well, and may require special assistance. Thorough psychoeducational evaluations on a yearly basis are required due to the severity of the disorder and the rapid changes that may occur in behavior, intellect, and motor skills.

REFERENCE

Gillberg, C. (1995). *Clinical child neuropsychiatry.* Cambridge: Cambridge University Press.

CECIL R. REYNOLDS
Texas A&M University

CODE OF FAIR TESTING PRACTICES IN EDUCATION

The Code of Fair Testing Practices in Education (Code) is a guide for professionals in fulfilling their obligation to provide and use tests that are fair to all test takers regardless of age, gender, disability, race, ethnicity, national origin, religion, sexual orientation, linguistic background, or other personal characteristics. Fairness is a primary consideration in all aspects of testing. Careful standardization of tests and administration conditions helps to ensure that all test takers are given a comparable opportunity to demonstrate what they know and how they can perform in the area being tested. Fairness implies that every test taker has the opportunity to prepare for the test and is informed about the general nature and content of the test, as appropriate to the purpose of the test. Fairness also extends to the accurate reporting of individual and group test results. Fairness is not an isolated concept, but must be considered in all aspects of the testing process.

The Code applies broadly to testing in education (admissions, educational assessment, educational diagnosis, and student placement) regardless of the mode of presentation, so it is relevant to conventional paper-and-pencil tests, computer-based tests, and performance tests. It is not designed to cover employment testing, licensure or certification testing, or other types of testing outside the field of education. The Code is directed primarily at professionally developed tests used in formally administered testing programs. Although the Code is not intended to cover tests made by teachers for use in their own classrooms, teachers are encouraged to use the guidelines to help improve their testing practices.

The Code addresses the roles of test developers and test users separately. Test developers are people and organizations that construct tests, as well as those that set policies for testing programs. Test users are people and agencies that select tests, administer tests, commission test development services, or make decisions on the basis of test scores. Test-developer and test-user roles may overlap, for example, when a state or local education agency commissions test development services, sets policies that control the test development process, and makes decisions on the basis of the test scores.

Many of the statements in the Code refer to the selection and use of existing tests. When a new test is developed, when an existing test is modified, or when the administration of a test is modified, the Code is intended to provide guidance for this process.

The Code is not intended to be mandatory, exhaustive, or definitive, and it may not be applicable to every situation. Instead, the Code is intended to be aspirational and is not intended to take precedence over the judgment of those who have competence in the subjects addressed.

The Code provides guidance separately for test developers and test users in four critical area:

A. Developing and Selecting Appropriate Tests

B. Administering and Scoring Tests

C. Reporting and Interpreting Test Results

D. Informing Test Takers

The Code is intended to be consistent with the relevant parts of the Standards for Educational and Psychological Testing (American Educational Research Association [AERA], American Psychological Association [APA], and National Council on Measurement in Education [NCME], 1999). The Code is not meant to add new principles over and above those in the Standards or to change their meaning. Rather, the Code is intended to represent the spirit of selected portions of the Standards in a way that is relevant and meaningful to developers and users of tests, as well as to test takers and/or their parents or guardians. States, districts, schools, organizations, and individual professionals are encouraged to commit themselves to fairness in testing and safeguarding the rights of test takers. The Code is intended to assist in carrying out such commitments.

The Code has been prepared by the Joint Committee on Testing Practices, a cooperative effort among several professional organizations. The aim of the Joint Committee is to act, in the public interest, to advance the quality of testing practices. Members of the Joint Committee include the American Counseling Association (ACA), the American Educational Research Association (AERA), the American Psychological Association (APA), the American Speech-Language-Hearing Association (ASHA), the National Association of School Psychologists (NASP), the National Association of Test Directors (NATD), and the National Council on Measurement in Education (NCME).

Copyright 2004 by the Joint Committee on Testing Practices. This material may be reproduced in whole or in part without fees or permission, provided that acknowledgment is made to the Joint Committee on Testing Practices. Reproduction and dissemination of this document are encouraged. This edition replaces the first edition of the Code, which was published in 1988. Please cite this document as follows: Code of Fair Testing Practices in Education. (2004). Washington, DC: Joint Committee on Testing Practices. (Mailing Address: Joint Committee on Testing Practices, Science Directorate, American Psychological Association, 750 First Street, NE, Washington, DC 20002-4242; http://www.apa.org/science/jctpweb.html). Contact APA for additional copies.

A. Developing and Selecting Appropriate Tests

TEST DEVELOPERS	TEST USERS
Test developers should provide the information and supporting evidence that test users need to select appropriate tests.	Test users should select tests that meet the intended purpose and that are appropriate for the intended test takers.
A-1. Provide evidence of what the test measures, the recommended uses, the intended test takers, and the strengths and limitations of the test, including the level of precision of the test scores.	A-1. Define the purpose for testing, the content and skills to be tested, and the intended test takers. Select and use the most appropriate test based on a thorough review of available information.
A-2. Describe how the content and skills to be tested were selected and how the tests were developed.	A-2. Review and select tests based on the appropriateness of test content, skills tested, and content coverage for the intended purpose of testing.
A-3. Communicate information about a test's characteristics at a level of detail appropriate to the intended test users.	A-3. Review materials provided by test developers and select tests for which clear, accurate, and complete information is provided.
A-4. Provide guidance on the levels of skills, knowledge, and training necessary for appropriate review, selection, and administration of tests.	A-4. Select tests through a process that includes persons with appropriate knowledge, skills, and training.
A-5. Provide evidence that the technical quality, including reliability and validity, of the test meets its intended purposes.	A-5. Evaluate evidence of the technical quality of the test provided by the test developer and any independent reviewers.
A-6. Provide to qualified test users representative samples of test questions or practice tests, directions, answer sheets, manuals, and score reports.	A-6. Evaluate representative samples of test questions or practice tests, directions, answer sheets, manuals, and score reports before selecting a test.
A-7. Avoid potentially offensive content or language when developing test questions and related materials.	A-7. Evaluate procedures and materials used by test developers, as well as the resulting test, to ensure that potentially offensive content or language is avoided.
A-8. Make appropriately modified forms of tests or administration procedures available for test takers with disabilities who need special accommodations.	A-8. Select tests with appropriately modified forms or administration procedures for test takers with disabilities who need special accommodations.
A-9. Obtain and provide evidence on the performance of test takers of diverse subgroups, making significant efforts to obtain sample sizes that are adequate for subgroup analyses. Evaluate the evidence to ensure that differences in performance are related to the skills being assessed.	A-9. Evaluate the available evidence on the performance of test takers of diverse subgroups. Determine to the extent feasible which performance differences may have been caused by factors unrelated to the skills being assessed.

B. Administering and Scoring Tests

TEST DEVELOPERS	TEST USERS
Test developers should explain how to administer and score tests correctly and fairly.	Test users should administer and score tests correctly and fairly.
B-1. Provide clear descriptions of detailed procedures for administering tests in a standardized manner.	B-1. Follow established procedures for administering tests in a standardized manner.
B-2. Provide guidelines on reasonable procedures for assessing persons with disabilities who need special accommodations or those with diverse linguistic backgrounds.	B-2. Provide and document appropriate procedures for test takers with disabilities who need special accommodations or those with diverse linguistic backgrounds. Some accommodations may be required by law or regulation.
B-3. Provide information to test takers or test users on test question formats and procedures for answering test questions, including information on the use of any needed materials and equipment.	B-3. Provide test takers with an opportunity to become familiar with test question formats and any materials or equipment that may be used during testing.
B-4. Establish and implement procedures to ensure the security of testing materials during all phases of test development, administration, scoring, and reporting.	B-4. Protect the security of test materials, including respecting copyrights and eliminating opportunities for test takers to obtain scores by fraudulent means.
B-5. Provide procedures, materials and guidelines for scoring the tests, and for monitoring the accuracy of the scoring process. If scoring the test is the responsibility of the test developer, provide adequate training for scorers.	B-5. If test scoring is the responsibility of the test user, provide adequate training to scorers and ensure and monitor the accuracy of the scoring process.
B-6. Correct errors that affect the interpretation of the scores and communicate the corrected results promptly.	B-6. Correct errors that affect the interpretation of the scores and communicate the corrected results promptly.
B-7. Develop and implement procedures for ensuring the confidentiality of scores.	B-7. Develop and implement procedures for ensuring the confidentiality of scores.

C. Reporting and Interpreting Test Results

TEST DEVELOPERS	TEST USERS
Test developers should report test results accurately and provide information to help test users interpret test results correctly.	Test users should report and interpret test results accurately and clearly.
C-1. Provide information to support recommended interpretations of the results, including the nature of the content, norms or comparison groups, and other technical evidence. Advise test users of the benefits and limitations of test results and their interpretation. Warn against assigning greater precision than is warranted.	C-1. Interpret the meaning of the test results, taking into account the nature of the content, norms or comparison groups, other technical evidence, and benefits and limitations of test results.
C-2. Provide guidance regarding the interpretations of results for tests administered with modifications. Inform test users of potential problems in interpreting test results when tests or test administration procedures are modified.	C-2. Interpret test results from modified test or test administration procedures in view of the impact those modifications may have had on test results.
C-3. Specify appropriate uses of test results and warn test users of potential misuses.	C-3. Avoid using tests for purposes other than those recommended by the test developer unless there is evidence to support the intended use or interpretation.
C-4. When test developers set standards, provide the rationale, procedures, and evidence for setting performance standards or passing scores. Avoid using stigmatizing labels.	C-4. Review the procedures for setting performance standards or passing scores. Avoid using stigmatizing labels.
C-5. Encourage test users to base decisions about test takers on multiple sources of appropriate information, not on a single test score.	C-5. Avoid using a single test score as the sole determinant of decisions about test takers. Interpret test scores in conjunction with other information about individuals.
C-6. Provide information to enable test users to accurately interpret and report test results for groups of test takers, including information about who were and who were not included in the different groups being compared, and information about factors that might influence the interpretation of results.	C-6. State the intended interpretation and use of test results for groups of test takers. Avoid grouping test results for purposes not specifically recommended by the test developer unless evidence is obtained to support the intended use. Report procedures that were followed in determining who were and who were not included in the groups being compared and describe factors that might influence the interpretation of results.

TEST DEVELOPERS	TEST USERS
C-7. Provide test results in a timely fashion and in a manner that is understood by the test taker.	C-7. Communicate test results in a timely fashion and in a manner that is understood by the test taker.
C-8. Provide guidance to test users about how to monitor the extent to which the test is fulfilling its intended purposes.	C-8. Develop and implement procedures for monitoring test use, including consistency with the intended purposes of the test.

D. Informing Test Takers

Under some circumstances, test developers have direct communication with the test takers and/or control of the tests, testing process, and test results. In other circumstances the test users have these responsibilities.

Test developers or test users should inform test takers about the nature of the test, test taker rights and responsibilities, the appropriate use of scores, and procedures for resolving challenges to scores.
D-1. Inform test takers in advance of the test administration about the coverage of the test, the types of question formats, the directions, and appropriate test-taking strategies. Make such information available to all test takers.
D-2. When a test is optional, provide test takers or their parents/guardians with information to help them judge whether a test should be taken—including indications of any consequences that may result from not taking the test (e.g., not being eligible to compete for a particular scholarship) —and whether there is an available alternative to the test.
D-3. Provide test takers or their parents/guardians with information about rights test takers may have to obtain copies of tests and completed answer sheets, to retake tests, to have tests rescored, or to have scores declared invalid.
D-4. Provide test takers or their parents/guardians with information about responsibilities test takers have, such as being aware of the intended purpose and uses of the test, performing at capacity, following directions, and not disclosing test items or interfering with other test takers.
D-5. Inform test takers or their parents/guardians how long scores will be kept on file and indicate to whom, under what circumstances, and in what manner test scores and related information will or will not be released. Protect test scores from unauthorized release and access.
D-6. Describe procedures for investigating and resolving circumstances that might result in canceling or withholding scores, such as failure to adhere to specified testing procedures.
D-7. Describe procedures that test takers, parents/guardians, and other interested parties may use to obtain more information about the test, register complaints, and have problems resolved.

JOINT COMMITTEE ON TESTING PRACTICES

COGENTIN

Cogentin is the proprietary name of benztropine mesylate, a skeletal muscle relaxant used in the treatment of Parkinson's disease (Modell, 1985). Cogentin acts on the basal ganglia of the brain. By restoring more normal chemical balance in the basal ganglia, specific movement disorders associated with parkinsonism are relieved. Cogentin reduces tremors, gait disturbances, and rigidity in afflicted individuals (Ellis & Speed, 1998; Long, 1982). Common side effects, especially during initial drug use, include blurred vision, nervousness, constipation, and dryness of the mouth. On rare occasions more serious side effects may occur, including confusion, hallucinations, nausea, and vomiting (Long, 1982). Common cold and cough remedies may interact unfavorably with Cogentin. The drug is not recommended for use in children under 3 years of age, and should be used with caution in older children (Konopasek, 2003; Long, 1982; *Physician's Desk Reference*, 1983).

REFERENCES

Ellis, K. L., & Speed, J. (1998). Pharmacologic management of movement disorder after midbrain haemorrhage *Brain Injury, 12,* 7, 623–628.

Konopasek, D. E. (2003). Medication fact sheets. Longmont, CO: Sopris West.

Long, J. W. (1982). *The essential guide to prescription drugs.* New York: Harper & Row.

Modell, W. (Ed.). (1985). *Drugs in current use and new drugs* (31st ed.). New York: Springer.

Physician's desk reference (37th ed.). (1983). Oradell, NJ: Medical Economics.

CATHY F. TELZROW
Kent State University

MEDICATION

COGNITIVE ASSESSMENT SYSTEM

The Cognitive Assessment System (CAS; Naglieri & Das, 1997a) is a test of cognitive ability. It is administered individually and was created for children ages 5 years through 17 years and 11 months. The test comprises a total of 12 subtests and can be administered in two forms. The Standard battery consists of all 12 subtests, while the Basic battery is made up of 8 subtests. Administration time is 60 minutes and 45 minutes, respectively.

The CAS was created as a tool for professionals to complete clinical, psychoeducational, and neuropsychological evaluations and is based on the PASS model. The PASS theory is represented by four scales on the CAS, specifically Planning, Attention, Simultaneous, and Successive cognitive processes (PASS). The first process, Planning, is an individual's ability to conceptualize and then apply the proper strategies to successfully complete a novel task. Essentially, the individual must be able to determine, select, and then use a strategy to efficiently solve a problem. Attention is a cognitive process by which an individual focuses on one cognitive process while excluding extraneous competing stimuli. The third process, Simultaneous processing, is the integration of stimuli into a coherent whole. Fourth is Successive processing, which involves organizing various things into a specific sequential order. A Full Scale score can also be obtained from the data.

Standard scores are provided for all subtests, with a mean of 10 and a standard deviation of 3. The four scales, along with the Full Scale score, are also reported as standard scores, and have a mean of 100 and a standard deviation of 15.

The CAS was standardized on a stratified random sample of 2,200 American children and adolescents aged 5 years 0 months to 17 years 11 months, using the 1990 U.S. Census data. Strata included race, gender, region, community setting, educational classification, classroom placement, and parent education. A total of 240 examiners were utilized for standardization, along with 68 sites.

Reliability data are impressive. Median internal consistency reliabilities for the Full Scale are .96 on the Standard battery and .87 on the Basic battery. Internal consistency for the scales is also very good; reliability coefficients range from .88 to .93. Median test-retest reliability coefficients for the Basic and Standard batteries are .82. Studies investigating the criterion validity of the CAS have generally shown that the CAS does not sufficiently correlate with other measures of cognitive ability. Because many of these measures are based on the Cattell-Horn-Carroll theory, these results are seen by some as lending evidence to the assertion that the CAS is an alternative way of validly conceptualizing intelligence.

Overall, the CAS is a well-standardized instrument. Because the test is based on the PASS theory and differs from other assessment tools, it may offer a different context through which measures of intelligence can be measured and thought of. It has also been suggested that the CAS has implications that are important in the learning environment. Although the CAS demonstrates assets, it does have limitations. In particular, caution must be exercised when using the data for interpretation. There is much overlap within the Attention scale and the Planning scale, so it may be difficult to separately interpret their results. Despite the fact that Naglieri and Das provide factor analytic evidence to support the CAS and the PASS model, further validation is needed.

REFERENCES AND ADDITIONAL INFORMATION

Hildebrand, D. K., & Sattler, J. M. (2001). Cognitive Assessment System. In J. M. Sattler (Ed.), *Assessment of children: Cognitive applications* (4th ed., pp. 548–550). San Diego: Jerome M. Sattler.

Keith, T. Z., Kranzler, J. H., & Flanagan, D. P. (2001). What does the Cognitive Assessment System (CAS) measure? Joint confirmatory factor analysis of the CAS and the Woodcock-Johnson Tests of Cognitive Ability (3rd ed.). *School Psychology Review, 30,* 89–119.

Kranzler, J. H., & Keith, T. Z. (1999). Independent confirmatory factor analysis of the Cognitive Assessment System (CAS): What does CAS measure? *School Psychology Review, 28,* 117.

Naglieri, J. A. (1999). How valid is the PASS theory and CAS? *School Psychology Review, 28,* 145.

Naglieri, J. A., & Das, J. P. (1997a). *Cognitive Assessment System.* Chicago: Riverside Publishing.

Naglieri, J. A., & Das, J. P. (1997b). *Cognitive Assessment System: Interpretive handbook.* Chicago: Riverside Publishing.

Plake, B. S., & Impara, J. C. (Eds.). (2001). *The fourteenth mental measurements yearbook.* Lincoln, NE: Buros Institute of Mental Measurements.

RON DUMONT
Fairleigh Dickinson University

JOHN O. WILLIS
Rivier College

INTELLIGENCE
INTELLIGENT TESTING
KAUFMAN ASSESSMENT BATTERY FOR CHILDREN–II

COGNITIVE BEHAVIOR THERAPY

The term cognitive behavior therapy refers to a diverse assemblage of theoretical and applied orientations that share three underlying assumptions. First, a person's behavior is mediated by cognitive events (i.e., thoughts, images, expectancies, and beliefs). Second is a corollary to the first; it states that a change in mediating events results in a change in behavior. Third, a person is an active participant in his or her own learning. The third assumption recognizes the reciprocal relationships among a person's thoughts, behavior, and environment and runs counter to the behaviorist's unidirectional view of the individual as a passive recipient of environmental influences.

During the reign of behaviorism in American psychology, cognitions were banned from investigation because the earlier methods used in their investigation were methodologically unsound and because cognitions, which are not directly observable, were considered inappropriate subject matter for the scientific study of psychology. During the 1960s, an explosion of research into such cognitive processes as attention, memory, problem solving, imagery, self-referent speech, beliefs, attributions, and motivation heralded a cognitive revolution in American psychology. Behaviorists impressed with the rigor of experimental cognitive psychologists and alert to the limitations of traditional behaviorism increasingly considered the role of cognitive variables in the development of behavior and in the treatment of maladaptive behavior. Because Bandura's research in observational learning was couched in a learning theory framework, it provided a timely bridge between the cognitivists and behaviorists. Bandura's explanations for modeling became more cognitive as he introduced such cognitive constructs as attention, retention, and expectancies to explain observational learning. Bandura's view of the reciprocal relationships among cognitions, behavior, and environment remains a basic tenet of cognitive behavior therapy. The widely discussed *controversy* between the cognitivists and the behaviorists that was prevalent in the 1960s and early 1970s quieted. The compatibility of the two perspectives has been recognized and the advantages of the joint consideration of cognitions and behaviors in modifying behaviors has been demonstrated.

A variety of therapies derived from research in cognitive psychology and taking advantage of the broadened behavioral perspective were developed and subjected to empirical test. These therapies attempt to modify thinking processes as a mechanism for effecting cognitive and behavioral changes. Particular therapeutic approaches that are closely identified with cognitive behavior therapy include modeling, self-instructional training, problem-solving training, rational emotive therapy, cognitive therapy, self-control training, and cognitive skills training. Because self-instructional training and problem-solving training illustrate the dual focus on cognitions and behavior, have been researched in schools, and are particularly well suited to classroom application, they will be briefly described in this entry.

In self-instructional training, the child is taught to regulate his or her behavior through self-talk. The child is taught to ask and to answer covertly questions that guide his or her own performance. The questions are of four types:

1. Questions about the nature of the problem ("OK. Now what is it I have to do? I have to find the two cars that are twins.")
2. Plans, or self-instructions for solving the task ("How can I do it? I could look at each car carefully, looking at the hood first, and then the front wheels, until I get to the end.")
3. Self-monitoring ("Am I using my plan?")
4. Self-evaluation. ("How did I do? I did fine because I looked at each car carefully and I found the twins.")

The particular self-statements vary according to the type of task.

The steps in teaching children to use self-speech to guide problem-solving behavior are derived from research in the developmental sequence by which language regulates one's behavior. First, an adult talks out loud while solving a task, and the child observes (modeling). Next, the child performs the same task while the adult verbally instructs the child. Next, the child performs the task while instructing himself or herself out loud. Then the child performs the task while whispering. Finally, the child performs the task while talking silently to himself or herself, with no lip movements.

Research in self-instructional talk has demonstrated that it helps impulsive children to think before acting (Meichenbaum & Goodman, 1971). While treated children have improved on novel problem-solving tasks and academic performance (Camp, Blom, Hebert, & Van Doorninck, 1977; Douglas, Parry, Marton, & Garson, 1976; Meichenbaum & Goodman, 1971), results of treatment on classroom behavior have been inconclusive (Camp, 1980; Camp et al., 1977).

Problem-solving training is similar to self-instructional training in that the child is taught to think through problems following a systematic problem-solving process. In a series of studies, Spivack and Shure (1974; Spivack, Platt, & Shure, 1976) taught preschool children the following interpersonal cognitive problem-solving skills: problem identification, means-end thinking, alternative thinking, and consequential thinking. Means-end thinking includes the ability to plan, step-by-step, ways to reach an interpersonal goal. Alternative thinking includes the ability to generate different plans for solving a given interpersonal problem. Consequential thinking is the ability to anticipate and evaluate consequences of a given interpersonal solution. These skills are taught in game-type interactions involving pictures, puppets, and stories depicting interpersonal problem situations. Research on problem-solving training has demonstrated improvement on teacher ratings, academic performance, and behavior observations (Shure, 1981).

In terms of psychotherapeutic intervention, cognitive behavior therapy has been shown to be very helpful with pain control (Tan & Leucht, 1997), depression (Murphy, Carney, Kreserich, & Wetzel, 1995), body dysmorphic disorder (Neziroglu, McKay, Todaro, & Yaryura-Tobias, 1996), and eating disorders (Eldredge et al., 1997). However, there are two caveats for using cognitive behavior therapy with school-aged populations. The first is including both the assessment of logical/analytical thought structures *and* social perspective-taking abilities of the child when planning a course of cognitive behavior therapy (Kinney, 1991). The second, which pertains to any age of client/subject, is that multicultural influences and diversity must be taken into account and formally addressed if the course of treatment is to be successful (Hays, 1995).

REFERENCES

Camp, B. W. (1980). Two psychoeducational treatment programs for young aggressive boys. In C. K. Walen & B. Henker (Eds.), *Hyperactive children—The social psychology of identification and treatment.* New York: Academic.

Camp, B. W., Blom, G. E., Hebert, F., & Van Doorninck, W. J. (1977). "Think Aloud": A program for developing self-control in young aggressive boys. *Journal of Abnormal Child Psychology, 5,* 157–169.

Douglas, V. I., Parry, P., Marton, P., & Garson, C. (1976). *Journal of Abnormal Child Psychology, 4,* 389–410.

Eldredge, K. L., Agras, W. S., Arnow, B., Telch, C. F., Bell, S., Castonguay, L., & Marnell, M. (1997). The effects of extending cognitive-behavior therapy for binge eating disorder among initial treatment nonresponders. *International Journal of Eating Disorders, 21,* 4, 347–352.

Hays, P. A. (1997). Multicultural applications of cognitive behavior therapy. *Professional Psychology: Research & Practice, 26,* 3, 309–315.

Kinney, A. (1991). Cognitive-behavior therapy with children: Developmental considerations. *Journal of Rational-Emotive & Cognitive Behavior Therapy, 9,* 1, 51–61.

Meichenbaum, D. H., & Goodman, J. (1971). Training impulsive children to talk to themselves: A means of developing self-control. *Journal of Abnormal Psychology, 77,* 115–126.

Neziroglu, F., McKay, D., Todaro, J., & Yaryura-Tobias, J. A. (1996). Effect of cognitive behavior therapy on persons with body dysmorphic disorder and comorbid Axis II diagnosis. *Behavior Therapy, 27,* 1, 67–77.

Shure, M. B. (1981). Social competence as a problem-solving skill. In J. D. Wine & M. D. Smyne (Eds.), *Social competence* (pp. 158–185). New York: Guilford.

Spivack, G., Platt, J. J., & Shure, M. B. (1976). *The problem-solving approach to adjustment.* San Francisco: Jossey-Bass.

Spivack, G., & Shure, M. B. (1974). *Social adjustment of young children: A cognitive approach to solving real-life problems.* San Francisco: Jossey-Bass.

Tan, Siang-Yang, & Leucht, C. A., (1997). Cognitive-behavioral therapy for clinical pain control: A 15-year update and its relationship to hypnosis. *International Journal of Clinical & Experimental Hypnosis, 45,* 4, 396–416.

JAN N. HUGHES
Texas A&M University

COGNITIVE RETRAINING
COGNITIVE STRATEGIES
SELF-CONTROL CURRICULUM

COGNITIVE DEVELOPMENT

Cognitive development consists of numerous overlapping conceptual and theoretical processes involving changes that occur in mental capacity and facility between birth and death. Cognition, the product of cognitive development, refers to mental processes by which individuals acquire knowledge. Moreover, cognition is the process of acquiring a conscious awareness that helps us to "know" and "understand" in a wide spectrum of activities such as remembering, learning, thinking, and attending. As a human phenomenon, cognition is comprised of unobservable events, their subsequent comprehension, and resultant response (Flavell, 1982). These covert behaviors characterize the activities of human thought processes.

In an effort to present general parameters of childhood cognitive development as it pertains to special education, several cognitive perspectives must be addressed. The human is an active problem solver who attempts to discriminate, extract, and analyze information; subsequently, directed planful action undergoes developmental change. Three contemporary theoretical orientations are consistent with the theme of the child as an active problem solver: Piaget's theory of cognitive development, information-processing approaches, and social learning theory.

One of the most influential descriptors of how development occurs is Piaget's theory of cognitive development (Piaget, 1970). In his work, cognitive structures are represented in the symbolic medium of formal logic, where each structure is regarded as a broad system of logical operations that mediates and unites a whole range of more specific intellectual behaviors and characteristics. Even though research with large samples of infants have confirmed Piaget's theories, certain aspects of his developmental accounts have come under scrutiny (Flavell, 1980; Gelman, 1978) and warrant revision or reinterpretation. Nevertheless, the Piagetian approach remains an important scientific paradigm on human intellectual development. The formative phases of the domain of study known as cognitive development are rooted in Piaget's theoretical formulations.

Piaget defines intelligence as a basic life function through which an individual adapts to the environment. In Piaget's view, children do not simply receive information from the environment, they actively seek and achieve knowledge through their own efforts. This interaction, from Piaget's biological perspective, is viewed as adaptation. Organisms adapt by using their newly acquired information by processing and gaining understanding of the environment. Thus adaptation and construction of reality depend on a child's level of cognitive development.

Piaget views cognitive development as a process of the development of cognitive structures and intellectual functions. He uses the term schema to describe mental structures used by the individual to represent, organize, and interpret experience. Therefore, a schema is defined as a pattern of thought or action by which an individual constructs an "understanding" of some aspect of the environment. Three types of intellectual structures have been defined by Piaget: sensorimotor (organized behavior patterns used to represent or respond to objects or experiences), symbolic (internal cognitive images used to represent past experiences), and operational (internal cognitive images that organize thoughts logically).

According to Piaget's theory, cognitive development depends on maturation (genetically transmitted) and the child's interactions with the environment. Contingent on normal maturation are the organism's ability to adapt to environmental changes and demands. Thus, with maturation, assimilation, and accommodation (Piaget, 1970), the human organism tries to interpret new experiences in terms of existing information.

Analogously, through accommodation, the child modifies an existing schema to suit a novel experience. Hence, Piaget describes intellectual growth as an active process whereby children are repeatedly assimilating new experiences and accommodating their cognitive structures to their new experiences. The cognitive operations of adaptation and organization facilitate children's ability to construct a progressively better understanding of the world. A child's formulation of self and external world depend on the knowledge base acquired up to the particular point in time at which a response is necessary. Consequently, the greater immaturity of the child's cognitive system, the more limited the interpretation of environmental events.

Age ranges designated for each of Piaget's four stages are average estimates; nonetheless, the sequential emergence of hierarchical "stages" are believed to be absolutely constant or invariant. Piaget felt that earlier developmental stages are not skipped en route to later stages. Accomplishments for each stage are said to accumulate (i.e., skills achieved in earlier stages are not lost with the advent of latent stages).

Sensorimotor Stage

During the sensorimotor stage of development, birth to about 2 years of age, cognitive development originates with ability to organize and coordinate bodily sensations and perceptions with the child's own physical movements and actions. Throughout sensorimotor development, an infant progresses from instinctual reflexive actions at birth to symbolic reflexive actions toward the end of the second year.

Initial means of coordinating sensation and action are accomplished through instinctual reflexive behaviors such as sucking and rooting. These behaviors are exhibited during substage 1 simple reflexes (ages birth to 1 month).

Substage 2, first habits and primary circular reactions, is comprised of first acquired adaptations. For example, when orally stimulated by a bottle during the first substage (simple reflexes), an infant might suck; conversely, during the second substage, repetitions of sucking may commence when no bottle is present.

During substage 3 (4 to 8 months), secondary circular reactions, behaviors are also repetitious and pleasurable; however, they focus on events and objects in the external environment that occur by chance.

Throughout substage 4 (8 to 12 months), coordination of secondary schemata, cognitive thought is comprised of intentional combining previously unrelated stimuli, producing simple feats, solving simple problems, and imitating the behavior of others. Piaget suggests that throughout substage 4, an infant is applying known cognitive structures to new situations to produce coordinated, goal-directed, and independent imitative actions with his or her own body or environment.

Substage 5 (12 to 18 months), tertiary circular reactions, is evidenced by exploratory trial and error schematas in which the infant purposely discovers new procedures to solve problems or reproduce interesting outcomes. Piaget refers to this period as the developmental starting point for human curiosity and interest in novelty.

Finally, during the last sensorimotor substage (18 to 24 months), internalization of cognitive structures begins to develop. Mental functioning shifts from a purely sensorimotor plane to a symbolic plane in which infants develop the ability to use primitive symbols.

Object Permanence

Object permanence, considered one of the infant's most significant cognitive development achievements during the sensorimotor stage, is the idea that people, places, and things continue to exist when they are no longer visible or detectable through the senses. According to Piaget, the object concept first appears during substage 4, coordination of secondary schemata. During substage 5, tertiary circular reactions, an infant searches for and locates hidden objects in novel and familiar locations; nonetheless, this occurs only if movement of the objects is visible. In the final sensorimotor substage, object permanence is complete; invisible movement of objects can be followed in the imagination by means of mental representations. Thus the infant searches for and finds objects that have been hidden through visible displacements.

Contrary to Piaget, Bower's (1982) research suggests that infants understand object permanence earlier, during primary circular reactions, even though they will not search for objects during this substage. Evidence of object permanence in Bower's research is indicated by the infant's surprise or anticipation of perceived object location. Bower suggests that errors in spatial reasoning, rather than absence of the object concept, account for younger infants' failure to search in Piagetian tasks.

Preoperational Stage

In the preoperational stage (ages 2 to 7 years), a period when symbolic schemata predominates, a young child's symbolic system expands such that use of language and perceptual images moves well beyond abilities at the end of the sensorimotor period. The preoperational stage consists of two phases: the preconceptual period (ages 2 to 4 years) and the intuitive period (ages 5 to 7 years).

According to Piaget, deficits in logical reasoning are evident throughout the preconceptual period. For example, egocentrism, the most salient feature of preconceptual thought, is evidenced by an inability to distinguish easily between a child's own perspective and that of someone else. Another deficit exhibited during the preconceptual period is animism; the young child believes that inanimate objects have human qualities and are capable of human action. During the preconceptual period, pretend play develops to a level in which children are capable of creating fantasy worlds, inventing imaginary playmates, participating in role playing, and using play as a vehicle for coping with emotional crises.

The second phase of the preoperational stage, the intuitive period, is an extension of preconceptual thought where the use of symbolic thought improves. Perceptually based logic appears in class inclusion problems such as "a string of beads that has both blocks and beads," whereby the child focuses on one feature only. According to Piaget, the child has a hard time thinking about the subset.

To aid in the use of symbolic thought, two main systematic capabilities are necessary during the preoperational period: centration and irreversibility. Fundamentally, centration is a child's tendency to focus on a single aspect of a problem while ignoring other information that helps the child to answer correctly. Irreversibility is the inability to reverse or to undo an action mentally.

Research (Flavell, Everett, Croft, & Flavell, 1981; Mossler, Marvin, & Greenberg, 1976) suggests that preoperational children are less egocentric, take another's point of view, and can conserve, contrary to what Piaget found. Gelman (1978) found that preschoolers are capable of causal reasoning. Additional research (Beilin, 1980) indicates that conservation problems can be taught to preoperational children by methods such as identity training (i.e., objects or substances transformed in a conservation task are still the same regardless of their new appearance). Finally, the work of Acredolo and Acredolo (1979) suggests that reversibility and compensation are not absolutely necessary for conservation.

Concrete Operations Stage

Piaget's concrete operations stage, a period between ages 7 and 11 years, is a stage during which the child's thinking crystallizes into a coherent organization of cognitive operations. Cognitive deficits most evident in the preoperational stage completely fade during the concrete operations stage.

Cognitive operations shift to a more refined system of thought that leads to levels that facilitate previously unattainable competencies. During concrete operations development, children often display horizontal decalage meaning the child can solve some conservation problems but not others. For example, conservation skills such as reversibility develop such that the child can mentally reverse flow of action and thereby realize that a column of water can look the same when poured back into its original container. Ability to classify and reverse enables linguistic humor to develop. Another shift is the move from egocentrism to relativism. The child can now decenter, or operate with two or more aspects of a problem simultaneously.

Formal Operations Stage

The formal operations stage, the final stage of Piaget's cognitive development theory, is characterized by the ability to reason abstractly and hypothetically. Abstract quality of thought can be seen primarily in the adolescent's use of verbal propositions in problem solving. For example, the concrete thinker (sensorimotor stage) needs to see concrete elements A, B, and C to be able to make the logical inference that if A>B and B>C, then A>C. Conversely, formal thinkers can solve the previous problem merely by having it presented as a verbal puzzle.

Although the transition to formal operations takes place gradually over several years, systematic and abstract thinking builds a foundation for considering morality, justice, beliefs, and values. Socially, the formal thinker no longer need rely on concrete experiences with people to form complex judgments about them.

Formal Thought in Adolescence

Since Piaget's classic experiments, many researchers have delved into the nature of adolescent thought. Their objective has been to specify the characteristics that distinguish this form of reasoning and problem solving from other more primitive forms.

One important characteristic of formal thought involves seeking explanations rather than mere descriptions of what has been observed. Another characteristic of formal thought involves the ability to remove oneself from the immediate context of a problem in order to get an additional perspective. One of the most socially significant characteristics of formal thought is the metacognitive ability to thinking about thinking (i.e., the ability to reflect on the thought process itself). In sum, formal thought is characterized by a relative freedom from the immediate constraints of a problem, which results in flexibility.

Late Adolescence and Adulthood

During this stage the most pronounced changes in cognitive development have taken place. Nonetheless, small but observable changes are still evident later in life. Young adults, from Erikson's (1963) theory of psychosocial development, experience a crisis of identity versus role confusion. Moreover, sex and romance influence the role of young adults.

Cognitive development continues to refine in its development as the young adult attempts to conceptualize a life-long role in society by selecting an occupation. This mature realism about one's occupation is seen as a process that remains throughout one's life, sometimes leading to midlife career changes.

Information-Processing Approach to Cognitive Development

As a model of human cognitive development, information processing explains decision making, knowing, and remembering as processes. In this approach to the study of cognitive development, the mind is conceived of as a complex cognitive system, analogous in some ways to a computer. In essence, human cognition becomes what the computer must know in order to produce behavior y. Information from the environment is abstracted from sensory systems and "flows" through a variety of proposed information-processing components. Information is transformed and analyzed at each step; feedback and feedforward loops among the components influence these transformations and analyses. Planning and purposeful thinking are derived by executive functions. The executive system contains sets of elementary information-processing rules that construct, execute, and monitor the flow of information to achieve objectives.

Most of the information-processing research builds directly on Piaget's contributions to the understanding of cognitive development. Contrary to Piaget's structural explanation underlying the thought structure of logic in thought processes and operational reversibility, information processing accounts for and identifies specific mental processes by which cognition is processed. Some researchers, such as Pascual-Leone (1980) and Case (1978), have modified Piagetian theory to take into account information-processing considerations (also called neo-Piagetian theories). One such approach is Siegler's (1981) rule-assessment approach. In essence, Siegler's work examines a child's problem-solving skills within a domain at different ages. A child's pattern of responses across problems helps to determine which of information-processing rules the child is using.

Several other information-processing perspectives have examined cognitive development. For example, researchers have found that young children have limited attention and persistence at tasks (Wellman, Ritter, & Flavell, 1975) and that their curiosity interferes with systematic problem solving. Thus, contrary to Piagetian theory, very young children may fail to solve many problems because they are unable to sustain their attention long enough to gather the necessary information. By about age 5 children become more persistent in their attempts to solve problems. Hence younger children may know to look first at relevant stimuli and label them; whereas, older children are better at selectively attending without special training.

Social Learning Theory

Social learning theorists (Bandura, 1977b) suggest that cognitive development is much more than a result of some combination of individual characteristics and environmental influences. They view all three as existing within a mutually interdependent network; they exist as a set of reciprocal determinants. Thus cognitions, beliefs, and expectations influence behavior and vice versa. Behavior partially determines the nature of the environment, whereas cognitions determine the psychological definitions of the environment.

Learning takes place either directly (through association of behaviors and consequences) or through modeling. The direct consequences of behavior, or reinforcements, are not conceptualized in the more traditional fashion that ignores awareness of the contingencies on the part of the child. Hence consequences of behavior explicitly carry information and function to provoke the individual into formulating and testing hypotheses. Thus reinforcement influences whether or not a response will elicit cognitions or thoughts about stimulus associations.

Learning is thought to be acquired through modeling. All new behaviors are observed along with their consequences. Inherent symbolic abilities facilitate abstraction and representation of information and provide an efficient means for retaining that information. From a social learning perspective, the anticipation of reinforcement may serve as a stimulus to direct attention to a model's behavior; hence, reinforcement may facilitate learning.

In summary, social learning theory places a great deal of emphasis on symbolic and self-regulatory processes. Cognitive development is important to the extent that changes in cognitive functioning influence changes in those processes. In children, development becomes more refined with experience and actual manipulation and consequently, children are better able to represent efficiently and retain observational experiences. Additionally, symbolic processes, attentional processes, and motivational processes change with observational learning.

Implications for Special Education

Traditional stages of cognitive development apply to individuals with and without disabilities alike. Handicapping conditions, however, may result in irregularities or delays in cognitive development, particularly in profoundly mentally retarded or multiply impaired persons. Some profoundly mentally retarded individuals never progress into the higher stages of cognitive development such as preoperational or operational thought. Other children acquire skills by rote or through carefully structured instruction, but have difficulty in applying them to new situations (Brown, Campione, & Murphy, 1977).

Most mildly and moderately retarded children do progress through Piaget's lower stages of cognitive development; however, their rate of skill acquisition is much slower. As the child gets older, the gap between the age at which specific skills are expected to be learned and the age at which they are actually learned increases. The retarded child also performs cognitive tasks with less efficiency than the nonretarded child (Campione & Brown, 1978).

Individuals with learning disabilities (LD) represent the largest percentage of the disabled population (U.S. Office of Special Education, 1996); they evidence a broad array of cognitive dysfunctions. These deficits emerge when academic learning lags with age. Children who are learning disabled may not exhibit specific cognitive problems early in development; however, skills acquired during Piaget's preoperational stage (intuitive thinking) are learned at a slower pace. Thus, problems in areas such as mathematics, reading, and memory are more prevalent.

During the primary years, children with LD have problems with seriation and classification tasks that are essential for mathematics. They cannot sort objects by size, match objects, or grasp the concept of counting and addition. In reading, LD children evidence word recognition errors (omissions, insertions, substitutions, reversals, and transpositions) and comprehension errors (inability to recall facts, sequences, or main ideas).

Word recognition difficulties suggest that LD children are unable to make a word or a letter stand for or represent something else. These are preconceptual skills (ages 2 to 7) of cognitive development in which symbolic thought develops. Problems with centration may inhibit reading comprehension.

Students with learning disabilities generally have problems with recalling auditory and visual stimuli. They also have problems with tasks requiring production or generation of specific learning or memorization strategies that influence the efficient organization of input for retrieval and recall. Bauer (1979) found that poor readers perform poorly on memory tasks that require complex organizational and retrieval strategies. Kauffman and Hallahan (1979) suggest that LD students fail to engage in strategies that enhance

attention and recall. These deficits are evident when applied to academic tasks.

Cognitive development may be viewed from numerous perspectives and subsequently applied to academic problems encountered in the field of special education. The information-processing approach to cognitive development is still in the early stage. It is best described as a complement to, rather than a replacement for, Piaget's earlier framework. However, recent research suggests that infants and young children are more competent and adults less competent that once thought (Flavell, 1992). Growth and extension of the cognitive development literature continues and quite often fills in some of the gaps in Piaget's model (Siegler & Crowley, 1991); hence, advances in empirical findings will eventually aid in the development of successful school-based interventions.

REFERENCES

Acredolo, L., & Acredolo, L. T. (1979). Identity, compensation, and conservation. *Child Development, 50,* 524–535.

Bauer, R. H. (1979). Memory, acquisition, and category clustering in learning disabled children. *Journal of Experimental Child Psychology, 217,* 365–383.

Beilin, H. (1980). Piaget's theory: Refinement, revision, or rejection? In R. Kluwe & H. Spada (Eds.), *Developmental models of thinking.* New York: Academic.

Bower, T. G. R. (1982). *Development in infancy.* San Francisco: Freeman.

Brown, A., Campione, J., & Murphy, M. (1977). Maintenance and generalization of training meta-mnemonic awareness of educable retarded children. *Journal of Experimental Child Psychology, 24,* 191–211.

Campione, J. C., & Brown, A. (1978). Toward a theory of intelligence: Contributions from research with retarded children. *Intelligence, 2,* 279–304.

Case, R. S. (1978). Intellectual development from birth to adulthood: A neo-Piagetian interpretation. In R. W. Siegler (Ed.), *Children's thinking: What develops?* Hillsdale, NJ: Erlbaum.

Erikson, E. H. (1963). *Childhood and society* (2nd ed.). New York: Norton.

Flavell, J. (1980, Fall). A tribute to Piaget. *Society for Research in Child Development Newsletter.*

Flavell, J. (1982). On cognitive development. *Child Development, 53,* 1–10.

Flavell, J. (1992). Cognitive development. *Developmental Psychology, 28,* 998–1005.

Flavell, J., Everett, B. A., Croft, K., & Flavell, E. R. (1981). Young children's knowledge about visual perception: Further evidence for the Level 1-Level 2 distinction. *Developmental Psychology, 15,* 95–120.

Gelman, R. (1978). Cognitive development. *Annual Review of Psychology, 29,* 297–332.

Kauffman, J. M., & Hallahan, D. P. (1979). Learning disabled and hyperactivity. In B. B. Lahey & A. E. Kazdin (Eds.), *Advances in clinical child psychology* (Vol. 2). New York: Plenum.

Mossler, D. G., Marvin, R. S., & Greenberg, M. T. (1976). Conceptual perspective taking in 2- to 6-year-old children. *Developmental Psychology, 12,* 85–86.

Moynahan, E. D. (1973). The development of knowledge concerning the effect of categorization upon free recall. *Child Development, 44,* 238–246.

Pascual-Leone, J. (1980). Constructive problems for constructive theories: The current relevance of Piaget's work and a critique of information-processing simulation psychology. In R. H. Kluwe & H. Spada (Eds.), *Developmental models of thinking.* New York: Academic.

Piaget, J. (1970). Piaget's theory. In P. H. Mussen (Ed.), *Carmichael's manual of child psychology* (Vol. 1). New York: Wiley.

Siegler, R. S. (1981). Developmental sequences within and between concepts. *Monographs for the Society for Research in Child Development, 46* (Serial No. 189).

Siegler, R. S., & Crowley, K. (1991). The microgenetic method. *American Psychologist, 46,* 6, 606–620.

U.S. Office of Special Education. (1996). *Eighteenth annual report to Congress on the implementation of Public Law 94-142: The Education for All Handicapped Children Act.* Washington, DC: U.S. Department of Education.

Wellman, H. M., Ritter, K., & Flavell, J. (1975). Deliberate memory in the delayed reactions of very young children. *Developmental Psychology, 11,* 780–787.

JOSE LUIS TORRES
MICHAEL J. ASH
Texas A&M University

COGNITIVE STRATEGIES
COGNITIVE STYLES
INFORMATION PROCESSING
INTELLIGENCE
PIAGET, JEAN
SOCIAL LEARNING THEORY

COGNITIVE IMPAIRMENT AND METAL POLLUTANTS

It is well known that children who are exposed to high doses of lead and other metal pollutants may suffer permanent neurological sequelae and cognitive impairments (Hartman 1995; Moon, Marlow, Stellern, & Errera, 1985). The causes of metal pollution are often associated with substandard living conditions (e.g., living in dilapidated substandard housing with peeling lead-based paints or plaster, living with household dust carrying metal pollutants, and living in proximity to heavy traffic or factories with noxious emissions). Inadequate nutrition also contributes to the effects of metal pollution.

Some of the physical difficulties associated with metal pollution are loss of appetite, chronic abdominal pain, headache, and anemia. Reported behavior difficulties associated with high levels of such poisoning are decreased learning performance, deficient attention, irritability, and clumsiness. Investigators have implicated metal toxicity in nonadaptive behavior as manifested in classroom situations (Marlowe, Moon, Errera, Cossairt, McNeil, & Peak, 1985), associated with learning-disabled children (Marlowe, Errera, Cossairt, & Welch, 1985) and with emotional disturbances in children (Marlowe, Errera, & Jacoby, 1983).

The assessment of metal concentrations in humans is easily carried out through various bodily analyses (e.g., of blood, teeth, and hair). The study of hair is both easy and noninvasive: Samples are subjected to the study of atomic absorption spectroscopy (Laker, 1982). Trace elements such as metals accumulate in hair at concentrations that are usually higher than in the blood serum. Hair thus can provide a record of a child's nutrient and mineral status. A method appropriate to classroom use to help teachers identify children who are potentially suffering from metal pollution is the Metal Exposure Questionnaire (Marlowe et al., 1983). This provides quantitative information about the possibility that a schoolchild is suffering significantly from metal pollutants.

Many of studies of metal pollutant effects suffer from methodological errors. One of the more significant of these is that while investigators study the effects of one toxic metal, they often fail to take into account the effects of other toxic metals on a child's behavior (Hartman, 1995; Moon et al., 1985).

While there is clear evidence indicating that high doses of metal pollution are physically and cognitively deleterious, there is less certainty as to whether low doses of such metals have significant effects. A number of studies have suggested that they do. Low levels of arsenic, cadmium, mercury, aluminum, and lead have been implicated in cognitive, perceptual, and behavioral childhood developmental deficits (Winneke et al., 1983). Some investigators also have hypothesized that metal combinations have interactive effects, thereby increasing the total toxicity in a child (Moon et al., 1985).

Among the more comprehensive reviews of literature concerning the behavioral effects of metal pollutants is that of Rimland and Larson (1983), who summarized studies of the relationship between incidence of learning disabilities and long-term, low-level metal exposure as measured through hair analysis. They found a total of nine studies. In five of the studies, learning-disabled subjects were found to have significantly more lead and/or cadmium than their controls. In the four remaining studies, the learning-disabled students were found to be somewhat higher in lead, cadmium, and/or aluminum concentrations.

The potential widespread nature of metal pollutants' toxic effects has been demonstrated by Moon et al. (1985). These investigators, studying a randomly selected sample of elementary school children, found significant relationships between low metal concentrations and diminished performance on a variety of cognitive and academic tasks. They also discovered interactive effects. Thus, both increases in arsenic and its interaction with lead were significantly related to decreased reading and spelling achievement. Increases in aluminum and the interaction of aluminum with lead were associated with decreased visual motor performance. An excellent review of the neuropsychological segnelae of toxic substance exposure can be found by Hartman (1995). Readers may also wish to access the National Institute of Neurological Disorders and Stroke for resources on neurotoxicology at http://www.ninds.nih.gov/disorders/neurotoxicity.

REFERENCES

Hartman, D. E. (1995). *Neuropsychological toxicology* (2nd ed.). New York: Plenum.

Laker, M. (1982). On determining trace element levels in man: The uses of blood and hair. *Lancet, 12,* 260–263.

Marlowe, M., Errera, J., Cossairt, A., & Welch, K. (1985). Hair mineral content as a predictor of learning disabilities. *Journal of Learning Disabilities, 40,* 221–225.

Marlowe, M., Errera, J., & Jacoby, J. (1983). Increased lead and cadmium levels in emotionally disturbed children. *Journal of Orthomollecular Psychiatry, 12,* 260–267.

Marlowe, M., Moon, C., Errera, J., Cossairt, A., McNeil, A., & Peak, R. (1985). Main and interaction effects of metallic toxins on classroom behavior. *Journal of Abnormal Child Psychology, 13,* 185–198.

Moon, C., Marlowe, M., Stellern, J., & Errera, J. (1985). Main and interaction effects of metallic pollutants on cognitive functioning. *Journal of Learning Disabilities, 18,* 217–220.

Rimland, B., & Larson, G. E. (1983). Hair mineral analysis and behavior: An analysis of 51 studies. *Journal of Learning Disabilities, 16,* 279–285.

Winneke, G., Kramer, U., Brockhaus, U., Evers, U., Kujanek, G., Lechner, H., & Janke, W. (1983). Neuropsychological studies in children with elevated tooth-lead concentrations. *International Archives of Occupational Environmental Health, 51,* 231–252.

LESTER MANN
*Hunter College, City University
of New York*

LEAD POISONING
POVERTY, RELATIONSHIP TO SPECIAL EDUCATION

COGNITIVE MAPPING SOFTWARE

Cognitive mapping software refers to a computer program that can visually map compositional ideas, thoughts and concepts using symbols and graphics rather than text. Cognitive mapping has its roots, and is very similar to, flowcharting. However, unlike flowcharts, cognitive mapping software has evolved with robust sets of symbols and

graphics encompassing more than just procedural symbols. Furthermore, the software can convert a cognitive map into a linear textual document similar to an outline. For example, consider the following cognitive map:

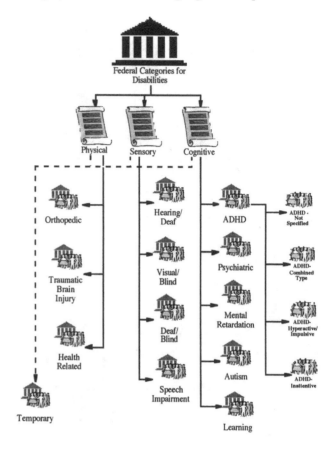

Cognitive mapping software may render this map into the following outline:

Federal Categories for Disabilities
  I. Physical
      A. Orthopedic
      B. Traumatic Brain Injury
      C. Health Related
      D. Temporary
 II. Sensory
      A. Hearing/Deaf
      B. Visual/Blind
      C. Deaf/Blind
      D. Speech Impairment
      E. Temporary
III. Cognitive
      A. ADHD
          1. ADHD—Not Specified
          2. ADHD—Combined Type

   3. ADHD—Hyperactive/Impulsive

   4. ADHD—Inattentive

 B. Learning

 C. Psychiatric

 D. Mental Retardation

 E. Autism

 D. Temporary

This process has been found to be useful for some students with learning disabilities and ADHD as it provides a visual-spatial method of composition which some students find easier to do. Because the software can create a linear outline of the symbol map, a student may use this to jump-start a composition. An example of cognitive mapping software is Inspiration. This software comes in different versions, some targeted for early childhood, while others are targeted with specific symbol sets at later grades and even professional endeavors such as engineering.

REFERENCE

Inspiration Software. (2005). Retrieved October 8, 2005, from http://www.inspiration.com/

STAFF

COGNITIVE RETRAINING

Cognitive retraining, or cognitive training, is used to describe various intervention or treatment efforts that are intended to promote positive adaptive functioning in individuals with neurologically based cognitive deficits (Barrett & Gonzalez-Rothi, 2002). Historically, cognitive retraining has been considered in the context of intense program development in head injury rehabilitation. In this context, cognitive retraining is associated with restoration of function through process-specific interventions. The objectives of cognitive approaches involve restoration, or development of, specific skills and abilities, or compensatory training with the ultimate goal of optimizing adjustment and outcome (Eslinger & Oliveri, 2002). Research specific to cognitive retraining is done within the fields of pediatric neuropsychology, rehabilitation psychology, or cognitive psychology as opposed to school psychology. Cognitive training programs have received the most attention in the context of rehabilitation for individuals who have sustained traumatic brain injury (TBI; Mateer & Mapou, 1996; Park & Ingles, 2000; Sbordone, 1986). The underlying rationale is that behavior results from the action and interaction of neurons and the related presumption that this action and interaction can be altered (or bypassed) by changing the associated neurological processes (for additional detail see Barrett & Gonzalez-Rothi, 2002).

Rehabilitation approaches generally either target underlying impairments as in deficit models or use intact processes or external means to address those functional areas affected (Glisky & Glisky, 2002). The exclusive emphasis on the underlying impairment ignores those intact functions of the individual, and, as suggested by the aptitude by treatment interaction studies, there is no evidence of progress with a focus on remediation of deficits. As such, a preferred approach focuses on optimizing the remaining function in the area of the deficit. Although there is a continued goal of restoring or developing that functional ability to the extent feasible, there is more of a focus on refining how the functional capacities that remain can be used (Anderson, 2002). Instead of drill and practice, the emphasis is on strategy instruction and metacognitive training. These methods may be most appropriate for individuals with mild to moderate impairments, who have sufficient intact abilities to master the strategies. Compensation approaches identify ways to bypass deficit skills through the use of intact functions or external aids or substitute methods of reaching the same goal (Anderson, 2002).

Ylvisaker and Szerekes (1996) identified goals of cognitive approaches to intervention as follows: (1) the restoration or development of cognitive processes or systems that were delayed or impaired by the injury or disorder; (2) acquisition of new knowledge that increasingly facilitates effective information processing; (3) increasing the strategic approaches of individuals and equipping them with strategic procedures that enable them to accomplish goals; (4) identification of ways in which academic, social, and vocational environments can be modified to promote success despite ongoing cognitive challenges; (5) identification of instructional strategies that are consistent with the child's profile of cognitive strengths and weaknesses that can be used with greatest effectiveness in school; and (6) heightening children's understanding of their needs so that they are increasingly active participants in the process of solving the many problems caused by their cognitive deficits. Regardless of whether the child has sustained a head injury, has a learning disability, or has some other neurological disorder, these goals would be appropriate and would improve the overall adjustment and functioning of the child.

With cognitive retraining, intervention involves implementation of environmental manipulations, training in compensatory activities, and use of activities designed to restore or improve underlying abilities (Mateer, 1999). The major methods used in cognitive retraining include: (1) metacognitive interventions; (2) strategy instruction; (3) computer-assisted training; (4) biofeedback; (5) use of external aids and environmental supports; and (6) domain-specific learning. When impairments or disabilities are viewed in the context of cognitive deficits, cognitive approaches seem like a logical approach (Mateer, Kerns, &

Eso, 1996). Further, cognitive mechanisms such as working memory capacity, inhibition, and strategic problem solving are important for a broad range of intellectual and social behaviors (Welsh, 2002).

Unfortunately, critical evaluation of cognitive retraining or training programs is limited to general reviews and discussions of methodological problems specific to a given population (e.g., see McCaffrey & Gansler, 1992, for strategies with traumatic brain injuries). Park and Ingles' (2000) meta-analysis indicated that the majority of studies yielded small effect sizes (-0.01 to $0.41; X = 0.15$). Suslow, Schonauer, and Arolt (2001) concurred with regard to small effect sizes and also pointed to the low power and contradictory results of available studies. More extensive research is needed to determine the extent of generalizability, maintenance, and efficacy of the varying cognitive approaches for specific populations and neurocognitive profiles.

REFERENCES

Anderson, S. W. (2002). Visuospatial impairments. In P. J. Eslinger (Ed.), *Neuropsychological interventions: Clinical research and practice* (pp. 163–181). New York: Guilford.

Barrett, A. M., & Gonzalez-Rothi, L. J. (2002). Theoretical bases for neuropsychological interventions. In P. J. Eslinger (Ed.), *Neuropsychological interventions: Clinical research and practice* (pp. 16–37). New York: Guilford.

Eslinger, P. J., & Oliveri, M. V. (2002). Approaching interventions clinically and scientifically. In P. J. Eslinger (Ed.), *Neuropsychological interventions: Clinical research and practice* (pp. 3–15). New York: Guilford.

Glisky, E. L., & Glisky, M. L. (2002). Learning and memory impairments. In P. J. Eslinger (Ed.), *Neuropsychological interventions: Clinical research and practice* (pp. 137–162). New York: Guilford.

Mateer, C. A. (1999). The rehabilitation of executive disorders. In D. T. Stuss, G. Winocur, & I. H. Robertson (Eds.), *Cognitive rehabilitation* (pp. 314–322). Cambridge, England: Cambridge University Press.

Mateer, C. A., Kerns, K. A., & Eso, K. L. (1996). Management of attention and memory disorders following traumatic brain injury. *Journal of Learning Disabilities, 29,* 618–632.

Mateer, C. A., & Mapou, R. L. (1996). Understanding, evaluation, and managing attention disorders following traumatic brain injury. *Journal of Head Trauma Rehabilitation, 11,* 1–16.

McCaffrey, R. J., & Gansler, D. A. (1992). The efficacy of attention-remediation programs for traumatically brain-injured survivors. In C. J. Long & L. K. Ross (Eds.), *Handbook of head trauma: Acute care to recovery* (pp. 203–217). New York: Plenum Press.

Park, N. W., & Ingles, J. L. (2000). Effectiveness of attention training after an acquired-brain injury: A meta-analysis of rehabilitation studies. *Brain Cognition, 44,* 5–9.

Sbordonne, R. (1986). Does computer assisted cognitive rehabilitation work? A case study. *Psychotherapy in Private Practice, 4*(4), 51–61.

Suslow, T., Schonauer, K., & Arolt, V. (2001). Attention training in the cognitive rehabilitation of schizophrenic patients: A review of efficacy studies. *Acta Psychiatrica Scandinavica, 103,* 15–23.

Welsh, M. C. (2002). Developmental and clinical variations in executive functions. In D. L. Molfese & V. J. Molfese (Eds.), *Developmental variations in learning: Applications to social, executive function, language and reading skills* (pp. 139–185). Mahwah, NJ: Erlbaum.

Ylvisaker, M., & Szekeres, S. F. (1996). Cognitive rehabilitation for children with traumatic brain injury. In P. W. Corrigan & S. C. Yudkfsky (Eds.), *Cognitive rehabilitation for neuropsychiatric disorders.* Washington, DC: American Psychiatric Press.

CYNTHIA A. RICCIO
Texas A&M University

BIOFEEDBACK
COGNITIVE STRATEGIES
METACOGNITION
TRAUMATIC BRAIN INJURY

COGNITIVE STRATEGIES

Cognitive strategies are cognitive processes that we use to monitor, control, and manage our cognitive functioning. They mediate both learning and performance. While cognitive strategies have been studied under various names for a long time, credit should probably go to Bruner, Goodnow, and Austin (1956) for first using the construct in the modern-day sense of the term. During recent years, there has been considerable interest in the training and remediation of such strategies.

All of us, whether child, adult, gifted, or mentally retarded, constantly use cognitive strategies to control and direct our thinking and behavior. Word attack skills are strategic in nature, as are the carrying processes used in arithmetic. The ways students take notes or check test responses for accuracy are determined strategically. The manner in which an individual deports himself or herself during a job interview is strategically controlled.

While a variety of cognitive theories have influenced work on cognitive strategies, information processing theories have been the most influential of all. Defining cognitive strategies from an information processing point of view, Young has pointed out that most tasks and problems can be carried out and solved in a variety of different ways and that individuals "have at their command a number of different strategies from which to choose for these purposes . . . there is an analogy between strategies and the subroutines used by computer programmers to organize [their programs]" (1978, pp. 357–358).

Cognitive strategies are theoretically distinguished from

cognitive capacities (abilities) and knowledge information). They are regarded as cognitive techniques that guide the ways our capacities are exercised and our knowledge is used. Strategies are learned both informally and formally. Most important from the standpoint of special education is that they are susceptible to training and improvement.

Apropos of this susceptibility is the distinction that has been made between fixed and modifiable cognitive characteristics (Baron, 1978). Fixed cognitive characteristics (i.e., cognitive capacities or abilities such as intelligence and memory) are difficult to influence environmentally or to change to any significant degree. Modifiable cognitive characteristics, such as cognitive strategies, however, are usually amenable to change and may be significantly improved by education and remediation. While fixed cognitive characteristics ultimately set limits on the development and expression of all cognitive processes, including cognitive strategy, some cognitive researchers believe that effective use of cognitive strategies can overcome "hard wired" cognitive limitations to a great degree: that students with mental retardation, for example, can approach normal cognitive achievement in certain areas if they are taught how to use strategies properly. One of the most important of intervention studies with the mentally retarded was carried out in the area of strategic training by Belmont and Butterfield (1975). These investigators found that with strategic training, mentally retarded learners were able to function on levels equivalent to those of non-retarded individuals in particular tasks.

Some cognitive strategies are general and can be applied across a broad spectrum of activities (e.g., checking one's work for accuracy on completion is a general strategy that is useful in most tasks). Other strategies are only applicable to specific situations (e.g., applying the processes of single-column addition).

There are short-term cognitive strategies and there are long-term ones. A student will apply certain strategies when taking a particular multiple choice quiz and these strategies serve a short-term purpose. The same student may develop a plan for gaining entry to professional school and in such a case, long-term strategies will be involved.

Cognitive strategies are sometimes used with full awareness of their application. At other times they operate automatically and with little or no consciousness of their use. We are usually most conscious of using them and laborious in their application when we are first learning them or when we attempt to correct or improve on them. As a rule, the more automatically cognitive strategies operate, and the less aware we are of their operations, the smoother and more effortless they will be. They are also likely to be more effective from the standpoint of freeing up our cognitive apparatuses to work on other aspects of a task or problem. Thus a concert pianist's efforts at interpreting music is at first consciously strategic in nature. The pianist plays with conscious intent to give the music certain nuances while practicing it. During the concert, however, such strategies, while still directing the pianist's playing, work at lower levels of awareness or entirely in an automatic fashion. Indeed, a high degree of awareness of any strategic intentions on the pianist's part would make it impossible to sustain smooth playing, particularly during passages of high velocity.

The particular cognitive strategies that an individual acquires and uses depend on that individual's experiences and instruction. They also depend on the individual's abilities and maturity. An adult will usually use more sophisticated and effective strategies than a 10-year-old child. A gifted child uses more complex strategies and has access to a wider range of strategies than does a retarded child. A deaf child will be limited in the use of certain strategies because of limited language capabilities but may learn to use still others more effectively than hearing children (Mann & Sabatino, 1985).

Not all cognitive strategies have the same degree of effectiveness. Some are effective for an appropriate age level or handicap but not for others (e.g., a first grader uses counting strategies that are effective for that age but may actually have negative effects if used in later grades). A child with learning disabilities may be ineffective at strategies that a good learner uses with ease.

Some strategies may even be harmful. A child who is a social isolate may use strategic approaches to other children that are intended to make friends but instead result in rejection. A child who is having trouble with advanced mathematics keeps using calculation strategies that are cumbersome and that interfere with understanding. If remedial cognitive strategy training is to succeed with such children, it will often require the unlearning of "bad" strategies prior to the acquisition of good ones.

Furthermore, it is not enough to know how to use a particular strategy well. It also is required that the user be skilled in its application and know when the strategy is appropriate or when another strategy should be used instead. Regular practice under varied conditions appears essential for most new strategies to become effective. Mentally retarded students will almost always be found to be deficient in their use of cognitive strategies and to require a great deal of rehearsal to master new strategies (Baron, 1978).

Success in school may ultimately depend on the number of effective strategies that a student can appropriately employ. Children with good abilities may fail academically because they do not know enough effective strategies to deal with their school work, or because they rely on inadequate or inappropriate strategies, or because they fail to effectively use the good strategies at their disposal. On the other hand, children with limited abilities may succeed academically because they have learned to use cognitive strategies to compensate for and minimize the impact of their deficiencies.

A number of classification systems have been suggested for cognitive strategies. Baron (1978) has suggested that we categorize them in three ways: (1) central strategies that are basic to the development of others strategies; (2) general strategies applicable to a variety of situations; and (3) specific strategies pertaining to particular types of applications.

Newell (1979) has addressed the classification of strategies using an analogy of an inverted cone of strategic skills. At the bottom of the cone are a large number of strategies that apply only to certain problems or situations (e.g., a carrying strategy for two-column addition). Such narrow strategies may be powerful and, if properly used, should effectively solve the problems to which they are applied. They are, however, limited to specific types of problems or work only under particular conditions.

As we move up Newell's inverted cone to its tip we find more generalizable but less effective strategies; there is a tradeoff between generalizability and effectiveness. At the very tip of the cone we find a few highly general strategies that are applicable to almost any problem or situation but that are weak and by themselves unable to solve any specific problem. Checking one's school work to see that it is accurate is an example of a general beneficial cognitive strategy, but it has weak effects and by itself can solve no specific problem. In between lie a variety of intermediate-level strategies that vary in specificity and power. It has been suggested that the most useful approach to cognitive strategy training from a general remedial standpoint might be to address such intermediate level strategies (Brown & Palincsar, 1982). Thus scanning written pages in a systematic left to right fashion is a strategy that has some specificity (i.e., it applies to reading); it also has some generality in that it applies to a wide range of reading.

In determining what type of strategies to use with special education students, the cognitive trainer is confronted with decisions as to optimal training programs. Teachers engaged in the cognitive training of learning-disabled children might well stick to specific and intermediate-level strategies that are directly applicable to particular types of school work. Psychologists might be interested in more general types of cognitive strategic training such as is involved in problem solving, test taking, etc.

A distinction has been made between blind and informed cognitive strategy training. Blind training programs are ones in which the subjects do not know the purpose of the training they are receiving. Informed cognitive strategy training not only trains the pupils strategically but helps them to understand the purpose of the training and the benefits to be derived from it. There is evidence that both types of training programs can be effective. However, students trained under informed conditions are likely to use their strategies more effectively and to continue to use them after their formal training is over (Kendall, Borkowski, & Cavanaugh, 1980).

A number of researchers have offered recommendations to guide cognitive strategy training with handicapped students (Belmont & Butterfield, 1979; Brown & Palinscar, 1982; Borkowski & Cavanaugh, 1980; Kreiner, 1992). Some investigators have advised that teachers of handicapped students may wish to use cognitive strategy curricula (Borkowski & Cavanaugh, 1979; Winschel & Lawrence, 1975).

The most active interest in cognitive strategies currently is in metacognition, which represents a supraordinate realm of executive cognitive strategies that monitor and regulate lower level strategies, and in cognitive behavioral interventions, which involve strategic training.

REFERENCES

Baron, J. (1978). Intelligence and general strategies. In G. Underwood (Ed.), *Strategies of information processing* (pp. 403–450). London: Academic.

Belmont, J. M., & Butterfield, E. C. (1979). Learning strategies as determinants of memory deficiencies. *Cognitive Psychology, 2,* 411–420.

Borkowski, J. G., & Cavanaugh, J. C. (1979). Maintenance and generalization of skills and strategies by the retarded. In W. R. Ellis (Ed.), *Handbook of mental deficiency* (2nd ed.). Hillsdale, NJ: Erlbaum.

Borkowski, J. G., & Kornarski, E. A. (1981). Educational implications of efforts to change intelligence. *Journal of Special Education, 15,* 289–306.

Brown, A. C., & Palincsar, A. S. (1982). Inducing strategic learning from texts by means of informed, self control training. *Topics in Learning & Learning Disabilities, 2,* 1–17.

Bruner, J. S., Goodnow, J. J., & Austin, G. A. (1956). *A study of thinking.* New York: Wiley.

Kendall, C. R., Borkowski, J. G., & Cavanaugh, J. C. (1980). Metamemory and the transfer of an interrogative strategy by EMR children. *Intelligence, 4,* 255–270.

Kreiner, D. S. (1992). Reaction times measures of spelling. *Journal of Experimental Psychology: Learning, Memory, & Cognition, 18,* 4, 765–776.

Mann, L., & Sabatino, D. A. (1985). *Foundations of cognitive processes in remedial and special education.* Rockville, MD: Aspen.

Newell, A. (1979). One final word. In D. T. Tuma & F. Reid (Eds.), *Problem solving and education: Issues in teaching and research.* Hillsdale, NJ: Erlbaum.

Winschel, J. F., & Lawrence, E. A. (1975). Short-term memory: Curricular implications for the mentally retarded. *Journal of Special Education, 9,* 395–408.

Young, R. M. (1978). Strategies and the structure of a cognitive skill. In G. Underwood (Ed.), *Strategies of information processing* (pp. 357–401). London: Academic.

Zigler, E., & Balla, D. (1971). Luria's verbal deficiency theory of mental retardation and performance on sameness, symmetry and opposition tasks: A critique. *American Journal of Mental Deficiency, 74,* 400–416.

JONI J. GLEASON
University of West Florida

COGNITIVE STYLES
INFORMATION PROCESSING
METACOGNITION

COGNITIVE STYLES

Cognitive styles are constructs that help to explain the ways that personality variables affect cognition. Kogan has defined them as reflecting "individual variations in *modes* of attending, perceiving, remembering and thinking" (1980, p. 64). Two individuals who score identically on intelligence and other cognitive aptitude or achievement tests and are the same in information processing capabilities may nevertheless differ significantly in school work, success on the job, and other behaviors because they differ in their cognitive styles (Mann & Sabatino, 1985).

The study of cognitive styles began in earnest following World War II, urged on by concern about the psychiatric casualties of that war and postwar interest in personal self-development and psychotherapy. Personality assessment had become exceedingly popular. Thus interest developed respecting the ways that personality variables affect cognitive variables. Studies of what came to be known as cognitive styles emerged.

Interest in cognitive styles first appeared most prominently in the work of George Klein and associates at the Menninger clinic. While the original work was conceptualized in terms of perceptual attitudes (perceptual types of tests being used as the most prominent way of assessing cognitive styles), later research emphasized the cognitive aspects of the research and the term cognitive controls became the dominant descriptor applied to work seeking to determine how personality factors interact with and influence cognitive skills.

Many definitions of cognitive styles have been offered. They generally agree that cognitive styles should be thought of as personality characteristics or traits that are related to other personality characteristics. Furthermore, while cognitive styles cannot always be distinguished or separated from cognitive skills, they are distinct from cognitive contents.

A considerable number of different types of cognitive styles have been distinguished through research. Some are similar, but others are clearly different in their implications for cognitive functioning. It is not unusual to study children and adults from the standpoint of several different cognitive styles.

While the assessment of cognitive styles of schoolchildren is usually done through paper and pencil questionnaires and tests, problem-solving tasks and perceptual types of apparatus are also used. Among the most ingenious of the latter has been the tilting-room chair test (Goldstein & Blackman, 1977). In this test, the subjects sit in a chair that is suspended in a small room. Both the chair and the room may be tilted either left or right in varying degrees. In one version, the Room-Adjustment Test (RAT), the room is tilted 56 degrees and chair 22 degrees. There are eight trials; in four of these trials the room and chair are tilted in the same direction; in the other four they are tilted in opposite directions. The object of the test is to determine the degree of effectiveness with which the subject can direct the examiner to reorient the room to an upright position under these circumstances. In the Body Adjustment Test (BAT), the room remains tilted and the subject directs the examiner to move him or her to an up-right position. The degree to which the subjects succeed on these orientation tasks was originally used to assess an individual's ability at field articulation and later to assess an individual's degree of field independence-dependence.

The scores assigned an individual on the basis of performance on cognitive-style assessments are usually used to place the subject somewhere on a bipolar continuum whose poles represent opposing stylistic types (e.g., leveling-sharpening, scanning-focusing). The more the individual's score is oriented toward one pole or another, the more he or she is characterized as being typified by the particular cognitive style associated with that pole. In the case of some cognitive styles, however, an individual will be characterized as belonging to one of several cognitive style categories, according to the means by which questions were answered or problems solved. This category is presumed to identify the way that an individual characteristically perceives, thinks, solves problems, etc. An example of this is provided by conceptual styles tasks that categorize children as to whether they tend to be analytic, categorical, or relational in their thinking.

Though there has been disagreement on the issue, Kogan has suggested that cognitive styles can be classified on the basis of whether the results obtained are judgmental (i.e., have positive or negative implications attached to particular styles and their scores). Thus certain cognitive styles clearly suggest good or poor cognitive performance (e.g., Witkin's field dependence-independence continuum). Other cognitive styles, however, only indirectly imply cognitive strength or weakness, while still others appear to be truly stylistic (i.e., inputing neither cognitive strength nor weakness but rather suggesting different ways of thinking. Still other cognitive styles can be interpreted either in terms of cognitive strengths and weaknesses or in purely stylistic terms, depending on the circumstances of usage and interpretation.

While the study of cognitive styles began with adult populations, it gradually moved over to juvenile populations as well, including those of children with learning problems and disabilities. This has been more for research rather than diagnostic purposes. The two most popular of cognitive-style study approaches to schoolchildren and special education students are those of field independence dependence and conceptual tempo. Blackman and Goldstein (1982) have suggested that a major reason for their popularity is the easy availability of instruments to assess them. Another reason seems to be that they appear to be cognitive styles that may have particular relevance to school work.

There have been many studies suggesting that field-independent students are better and more self-dependent learners than field-dependent ones; that they are better decoders in reading than field-dependent students; and that they are better at math and science as well. Field-independent students have been found to do better in "discovery" types of learning situations, while field-dependent students are benefited by structured learning situations. Gifted children are more likely to be field independent than mentally retarded ones (Mann & Sabatino, 1985). Learning-disabled pupils are more likely to be field dependent than normal readers.

In respect to conceptual tempo, this cognitive-style dimension characterizes children on the basis of their placement on a reflection-impulsivity dimension, according to their performance on problem-solving tests, etc. As might be expected, reflective children are usually better students, while impulsive ones are more likely to read inaccurately and to manifest behavior problems.

While the research into cognitive styles has been very active, and results are regularly found indicating that cognitive styles are significantly related to school and academic variables that are important to both disabled and nondisabled children, the sum and substance of this research does not appear to support a position that knowledge of a disabled child's particular cognitive style, in and of itself, is particularly helpful in respect to predicting school achievement (Swanson, 1980) or in guiding day-to-day instruction or management. Socioeconomic and general cognitive factors play roles of far greater importance in the school lives of special education students. Indeed, many of the significant differences found in the school performances of special education students who differ in cognitive style appear to be the result of consequences of investigators confounding their variables.

The most popular variant or offshoot of cognitive styles currently are identified as learning styles based on objective imaging and EEG examinations (Riding, Glass, Butler, Pleydell-Pearce, 1997). Since learning styles tend to be educationally oriented, they have received a great deal of attention in educational circles. Learning style constructs, which emphasize learning preferences rather than personality characteristics, have taken much of the attention away from other types of cognitive styles among researchers concerned with school and academic achievement.

REFERENCES

Blackman, S., & Goldstein, K. M. (1982). Cognitive styles and learning disabilities. *Journal of Learning Disabilities, 15,* 106–113.

Goldstein, K. M., & Blackman, S. (1977). *Cognitive styles: Five approaches to theory and research.* New York: Wiley.

Kane, M. (1984). Cognitive styles of thinking and learning. Part one. *Academic Therapy, 19,* 527–536.

Klein, G. S., & Schlesinger, H. J. (1949). Where is the perceiver in perceptual theory? *Journal of Personality, 18,* 32–47.

Kogan, N. (1980). Cognitive styles and reading performance. *Bulletin of the Orton Society, 39,* 63–77.

Mann, L., & Sabatino, D. A. (1985). *Foundations of cognitive processes in remedial and special education.* Rockville, MD: Aspen.

Riding, R. J., Glass, A., Butler, S. R., & Pleydell-Pearce, C. W. (1997). Cognitive style and individual differences in EEG alpha during information processing. *Educational Psychology, 17,* 219–234.

Swanson, L. (1980). Cognitive style, locus of control, and school achievement in learning disabled females. *Journal of Clinical Psychology, 36,* 964–967.

EMILY WAHLEN
LESTER MANN
Hunter College, City University of New York

LEARNING STYLES
SPERRY, R.
SPLIT-BRAIN RESEARCH
TEMPERAMENT

COLITIS

Ulcerative colitis is a chronic inflammatory disease of the colon (large intestine). It is a progressive disease, spreading to include part or all of the colon and rectum. It is characterized by alternating remissions and relapses. The disease is usually more severe in children than adults, carrying an increased risk of malignancy because of the greater severity and duration of the disease (Dixon & Walker, 1984). A disease closely related to ulcerative colitis is Crohn's disease, which involves the small intestine as well as the large. Symptomatology and progression in Crohn's closely resembles that in ulcerative colitis.

The cause of ulcerative colitis is unknown. Symptoms of the disease include diarrhea with blood and mucous, abdominal pain preceding defecation, anemia, and rectal urgency. Weight loss is apparent in some children owing to reduced caloric intake or to limitation of food eaten to avoid discomforts of the disease (Dixon & Walker, 1984).

Treatment of colitis varies with severity and extent of the disease. The goal of treatment for children is to bring about remission to allow normal growth and development. Medical therapy includes use of corticosteroids to control inflammation and sulfasalazine to control flare-ups. Undesirable side effects of the two precipitate cautious use with children. Corticosteroids interfere with growth, increase susceptibility to infection, and cause temporary alterations in physical appearance. Sulfasalazine can cause headaches, nausea, vomiting, anorexia, and rash.

If the disease does not respond to medical therapy, or if it involves complications, surgery is required. Part or all of the colon is removed and then resected together or attached to the abdominal wall. If attached to the abdominal wall, a stoma is formed to allow excretion of waste products into an external collecting apparatus. With surgery, the effects of the disease disappear.

Children and their families need a great deal of emotional support and understanding in dealing with the manifestations of the disease and the effects of treatment (Burke, Neigut, Kocoshis, & Chandra, 1994; Melvin, 2003). Children need special understanding and encouragement when dealing with side effects of steroid treatment or adjusting to the use of an external collecting apparatus. Advances in development of collection apparatus now make it possible for most children to participate in many activities and sports. Most individuals with colitis live a normal life under prolonged medical care.

REFERENCES

Bokey, E. L., & Shell, R. (1985). *Stomal therapy: A guide for nurses, practitioners and patients.* Sydney, Australia: Pergamon.

Burke, P. M., Neigut, D., Kocoshis, P. R., & Chandra, R. (1994). Correlates of depress in new onset pediatric bowel disease. *Child Psychiatry and Human Development, 24,* 4, 275–283.

Dixon, M. L., & Walker, W. A. (1984). Ulcerative colitis and Crohn's disease. In S. S. Gellis & B. M. Kagan (Eds.), *Current pediatric therapy* (pp. 195–198). Philadelphia: Saunders.

Goodman, M. J., & Sparberg, M. (1978). *Ulcerative colitis.* New York: Wiley.

Goulston, S. J., & McGovern, V. J. (1981). *Fundamentals of colitis.* Oxford, England: Pergamon.

Hanauer, S. B. (1984). Ulcerative colitis. In R. E. Rakel (Ed.), *Conn's current therapy* (pp. 410–415). Philadelphia: Saunders.

Melvin, B. (2003). Crohn's Disease. In E. Fletcher-Janzen & C. R. Reynolds (Eds). *Childhood disorders diagnostic desk reference* (pp. 156–157). New York: Wiley.

CHRISTINE A. ESPIN
University of Minnesota

FAMILY RESPONSE TO A CHILD WITH DISABILITIES
PHYSICAL DISABILITIES

COLLABORATION

See INCLUSION.

COLLABORATIVE PERINATAL PROJECT

The main purpose of the Collaborative Perinatal Project was to evaluate factors in pregnancy that may relate to cerebral palsy and other abnormalities of the central nervous system. The project was sponsored by the National Institute of Neurological and Communicative Disorders and Strokes. Over 50,000 pregnant women were recruited (from January 1959 to December 1965) for the largest prospective study of its kind. Although readers of the study are urged to regard conclusions as tentative, it is generally agreed that this massive undertaking adds substantially to what is known about the general epidemiology of birth defects.

Data collected at the 14 university-affiliated hospitals included information on the mother's social and medical background; coexisting diseases; complications of pregnancy; current drug/medication use; and previous use of drugs (extending beyond the mother's last menstrual period). Each participant was interviewed at least monthly throughout pregnancy, at scheduled intervals during the infant's first 2 years, and annually until the child reached 8 years. Records on each child until the age of 8 years include birth and developmental history, diseases, noted congenital defects, and information on siblings and father. Infants received daily examinations for the first 7 days of life (and weekly for prolonged postnatal hospitalizations), with an extensive, standard pediatric exam at age one. Of the mortality rate (4.4 percent or 2,227 stillborn or died before age 4), 81 percent came to autopsy.

A tangential purpose of this project was the epidemiological investigation of the possible teratogenic role of drugs (or those drugs that cause malformations): In other words, the relationship between drugs taken during pregnancy and malformations in offspring. Although frequent hypotheses are suggested, only a few such relationships are accepted universally as causal. Potent teratogens (e.g., thalidomide) are identified relatively easily. Less potent drugs with less dramatic outcomes are equally important but more difficult to isolate and detect. The Collaborative Perinatal Project provided the opportunity to use a battery of epidemiological and statistical method to screen a variety of drugs against a variety of malformation outcomes.

The study (1) provided quantitative information, much not previously available, on relationships among birth defects; (2) confirmed and elaborated on, in quantitative terms, factors such as single umbilical artery and birth defects; (3) raised, in quantitative terms, hypotheses concerning risk factors, some previously suspected but without quantitative information and some not previously suspected; and (4) concluded that birth defects are rarely attributable to a single cause and that many malformation outcomes appear to have multiple risk factors that are interrelated.

Heinonen et al. (1977) were commissioned by the National Institutes of Health to document all findings. Their text contains detailed information on methods, malformations, drugs used, etc. The data from the project continue to be analyzed (Friedman, Granick, Bransfield & Kreisher, 1995), and debated (Hardy, 2003; James, 1996).

REFERENCES

Friedman, H. S., Granick, S., Bransfield, S., & Kreisher, C. (1995). Gender difference in early life risk factors for substance use/abuse: A Study of an African-American Sample. *American Journal of Drug & Alcohol Abuse, 21,* 4, 511–531.

Hardy, J. B. (2003). The collaborative perinatal project: Lessons and legacy. *Annuals of Epidemiology, 13*(5), pp. 303–311.

Heinonen, O. P., Slone, D., & Shapiro, J. (1977). *Birth defects and drugs in pregnancy.* Littleton, MA: Publishing Sciences Group.

James, W. H. (1996). Debate and argument: The sex ratio of the sibs of neurodevelopmentally disordered children. *Journal of Child Psychology & Psychiatry & Allied Disciplines, 37,* 5, 619.

C. MILDRED TASHMAN
College of St. Rose

CONGENITAL DISORDERS
LOW BIRTH WEIGHT INFANTS
PREMATURITY

COLLEGE PROGRAMS FOR DISABLED COLLEGE STUDENTS

Following the end of World War II, the majority of colleges and universities in the United States became more sensitive to the needs of students who would have been financially disabled without the original G.I. bill. This same sensitivity, however, on the part of colleges and universities for those who were physically, socially, and/or academically disabled did not manifest itself to any major degree until the 1970s.

In April 1978 the Association on Handicapped Student Service Programs in Post-Secondary Education (AHSSPPE) came into existence. This organization, along with others, provided professional support for full implementation of the Architectural Barriers Act of 1968 as upgraded and expanded on by Section 504 of the Vocational Rehabilitation Act of 1973, which became operational in April of 1977. The net effect of this act and its revisions was to ensure the access and use of public schools (elementary through college) by the physically disabled through assurance that the schools would be constructed to accommodate the handicapped person.

Similarly, by the late 1970s a few colleges and universities began formal programs to serve college-bound students who had academic deficits resulting from either some innate and formal learning (language) disability and/or environmentally induced one. Those higher education institutions having programs for this population were identified in part by research projects sponsored by the National Association of College Admission Counselors (NACAC; Mangrum, 1984). Two agencies that contributed to the development of the NACAC directory of college programs were the Post Secondary School Committee of the Association for Children with Learning Disabilities (ACLD) and the Loyola Academy of Wilmette, Illinois. Other references that identify colleges and universities having academic support services are Liscio's *A Guide to Colleges for Learning Disabled Students;* Mangrum and Strichart's *College and the Learning Disabled Student;* the *FCLD's Guide for Parents of Children with Learning Disabilities;* and *Peterson's Guide to Colleges with Programs for Learning Disabled Students.* These references suggest that the prospective user ask certain questions, as identified by Liscio (1984):

1. Is there a special program for learning-disabled students?
2. How many full-time learning-disabled students are enrolled in the program?
3. Is there a brochure or written description of the program available?
4. Do learning-disabled students in special programs take regular college courses?
5. Are special courses required of learning-disabled students? Do they carry college credit? Can credit be used toward graduation?
6. Are there additional tuition or fee requirements for learning-disabled students? (p. 12)

Additionally, the prospective users of these references and others like them, following a personal onsite examination of the institution and its services as listed, will probably determine that the primary thrust or intent of the institution's services falls into one of two categories: (1) assistance and support that is not necessarily remedial, and (2) assistance and support that is intended to be remedial. The former is specifically characterized by the use of books on tape (the same service used by blind students); oral presentations instead of written exams; cassette tapes in lieu of written papers; readers for reading textbooks and exams; and notetakers. These services allow the language-handicapped student to cope and to graduate in spite of unremediated reading and spelling deficits.

The college-aged learning-disabled student who is looking for a school to attend will find that the majority of two- and four-year higher education institutions (both public and private) that offer support services will be of the type just depicted; for example, those that provide assistance and support that is not necessarily intended to be remedial. The student who wishes to become language independent, academically as well as socially, might want to consider the other major type of service.

Those institutions that intend to remediate the student's language handicap and his or her accompanying social and psychological deficits, will be characterized by instruction that is designed to remediate the student's reading, spelling, written expression, and arithmetic deficits. The kind of instruction that would be most commonly used would directly reteach the basic or requisite information that must be known to read, spell, write, and carry out mathematical operations. Other probable aspects of this second service posture would be the use of tutors who have been trained to carry out direct remediation of the students academic deficits and formal support programs that deal directly with the student's social habilitation and psychological needs. Both types of schools offer their learning-disabled students the opportunity to take exams in a private setting without time constraints, use tape recorders to record lectures, take a reduced load as necessary, and partake in the institution's traditional student support services. Beyond the traditional academic assistance and/or remediation, most institutions of higher learning also offer counseling and testing support services. The University of Washington provides some helpful resources for college funding strategies for students with disabilities at http://www.washington.edu/doit/Brochures/Academics/financial-aid.html.

REFERENCES

The FCLD guide for parents of children with learning disabilities. (1984). New York: Foundation for Children with Learning Disabilities.

Kavale, K., & Forness, S. (1985). *The science of learning disabilities.* San Diego, CA: College Hill.

Liscio, M. A. (1984). *A guide to colleges for learning disabled students.* Orlando, FL: Academic.

Mangrum, C. T., & Strichart, S. S. (1984). *College and the learning disabled student.* Orlando, FL: Grune & Stratton.

Nash, R. T. (1985). Remediation courses, Project Success, University of Wisconsin-Oshkosh. Unpublished raw data.

Peterson's guide to colleges with programs for learning disabled students. (1985). Princeton, NJ: Peterson's Guide.

ROBERT T. NASH
University of Wisconsin Oshkosh

COLOR BLINDNESS

The inability to perceive or discriminate colors is known as color blindness. There are four main types of color blindness, each containing a number of subtypes. The most rare type is known as *achromotopsia*. In this condition, the subject sees no color; everything is perceived as black, white, or shades of gray. This condition can result from a degenerative process. In the absence of such pathology, the condition is due to an autosomal recessive gene and is extremely rare.

The more common types of color vision disturbances are closely related to retinal physiology, specifically, to the structure and function of the cones. Since the cones are not evenly distributed in the retina, color vision in the visual field is somewhat variable. Color perception is not possible in the periphery of the visual field and diminishes as the object moves away from the point of fixation (Wald, 1968). The perception of color is dependent on not only the presence of different types of cone cells, but of complex chemical pigments thought to respond selectively to the different wavelengths of light.

Protanopia refers to the condition in which the individual has difficulty in distinguishing red. *Deuteranopia* is the condition in which the individual has difficulty in distinguishing green. *Tritanopia* is the condition in which the individual cannot distinguish blue; it is a severe and rare form of colorblindness, affecting less than .1 percent of the population. Tritanopia is considered to be an autosomal dominant trait.

Red-green color disturbances occur in both protanopia and deuteranopia. The former is more severe and less common than the latter. Both are sex-linked (X) recessive, traits, explaining their nearly exclusive presence in males. The prevalence of protanopia is about 1:100; deuteranopia about 1:20 (Linksz, 1964).

Determination of the condition is easily made using pseudoisochromatic plates (Isihara test) that present colored patterns or numbers to the individual. The normal person sees one pattern or number and those with color disturbances see the stimulus differently (Thuline, 1972). Color perception can be diminished by papillitis, a condition where the optic disk becomes inflamed. The causes of papillitis are numerous and can include toxins, tumors, or syphillis (Riccio, 2003).

Color blindness is not generally considered to be a significant handicap. Some authors (Cooley, 1977) feel that the tests are far too sensitive and that some persons have been needlessly denied employment. The classroom teacher, especially in the early grades, should expect to find at least one color-blind male in the classroom. Tasks involving color discrimination must be eliminated. The literature is replete with retinal changes owed to phenothiazine (Mellaril, Thorazine) administration (Apt, 1960; Weekly et al., 1960). Color vision anomalies may occur if a youngster is under phenothiazine therapy.

REFERENCES

Apt, R. (1960). Complications of phenothiazine tranquilizers ocular side effects. *Survey Ophthalmology, 5,* 550.

Cooley, D. (Ed.). (1977). *Family medical guide.* New York: Better Homes and Gardens.

Linksz, A. (1964). *An essay on color vision and clinical color vision tests.* New York: Grune & Stratton.

Riccio, C. (2003). Papillitis. In E. F. Janzen, & C. R. Reynolds (Eds), *Childhood disorders diagnostic desk reference* (pp. 448–449). New York: Wiley.

Thuline, H. (1972). Color blindness in children: The importance and feasibility of early recognition. *Clinical Pediatrics, 11*(5), 295–299.

Wald, G. (1968). The receptors of human color vision. *Science Magazine, 145,* 1007.

Weekly, R., Potts, A., Rebotem, J., & May, R. (1960). Pigmentary retinopathy in patients receiving high doses of a new phenothiazene. *Archives of Ophthalmology, 64,* 65.

JOHN E. PORCELLA
Rhinebeck Country School

MELLARIL
THORAZINE
VISUAL PERCEPTION AND DISCRIMINATION
VISUAL IMPAIRMENT

COMMUNICATION AIDS, ELECTRONIC

See ELECTRONIC COMMUNICATION AIDS.

COMMUNICATION BOARDS

Communication boards are simple, nonelectronic, augmentative communication systems used by nonspeaking persons. They are usually made individually according to the skills and needs of the nonspeaking user. The advantages of communication boards are their flexibility and low cost. Any symbol system ranging from objects and pictures to written alphabet letters can be used as message symbols. The communication board can be accessed by direct selection, through scanning, or by an encoding process. As the nonspeaking person's skills change over time, the communication board can be easily adapted to reflect those changes.

The major disadvantage of communication boards is the lack of spoken or written output from the system. The listener who interacts with a nonspeaking communication board user must be able to physically see the communication board to receive a message. For long messages, the listener must remember each symbol selected and mentally sequence the symbols back together to understand the message. Communication boards are used frequently with children and adults who have limited vocabularies. In addition, they are often used as a secondary backup communication device for nonspeaking persons who rely primarily on sophisticated electronic augmentative systems.

REFERENCES

Goossens, C., Crain, S. S., & Elder, P. S. (1995). *Engineering the preschool environment for interactive symbolic communication.* Birmingham, AL: Southeast Augmentative Communication Conference Publications.

Musselwhite, C. R., & St. Louis, K. O. (1982). *Communication programming for the severely handicapped: Vocal and non-vocal strategies.* Houston, TX: College-Hill.

SHARON GLENNEN
Pennsylvania State University
First edition

SHEELA STUART
George Washington University
Second edition

AUGMENTATIVE COMMUNICATION DEVICES
COMPUTER USE WITH STUDENTS WITH DISABILITIES
ROBOTICS

COMMUNICATION DISORDERS

Communication disorders are defined as an observed disturbance in the normal speech, language, or hearing processes as determined by (1) objective signs (i.e., measurable characteristics that can be observed by other persons), (2) social signs (i.e., failing to understand a speaker's meaning and responding inappropriately resulting in mutual embarrassment), and (3) personal signs (i.e., a person's reactions to a self-perceived disorder; Plante & Beeson, 1999). Communication disorders may involve the processes of listening, speaking, reading, writing, and thinking. The American Speech-Language-Hearing Association (ASHA) estimates that about 10 percent of the population in the United States (approximately 25 million individuals of all ages) has some form of communication disorder involving speech, language, and/or hearing (Shames, Wiig, & Secord, 1994). Severity of communication disorders ranges from mild to severe/profound across different levels of communication (prelinguistic, sounds and letters, words, phrases and sentences, oral and literate discourse [conversation, narration, exposition] and discourse plus [nonliteral language, mathlanguage (including time and money), computer language, foreign language, and career or employment language]). Communication disorders are categorized as impairment (abnormality of structure or function at the organ level), disability (functional consequences of an impairment), or handicap (social consequences of impairment or disability; Gelfer, 1996).

Communication disorders may be caused by: (1) physical

conditions (e.g., oral facial anomalies, cerebral palsy), (2) physiological conditions (e.g., neurological impairment), (3) psychological conditions (e.g., emotional/behavioral disorders such as neuroses and psychoses; learning, motivation), or (4) social conditions (e.g., lack of stimulation or communicative interaction with other humans; Boone & Plante, 1993; Pressley & McCormick, 1995). Communication disorders affect not only the individuals who have the disorder, but others (family, peers, caregivers, colleagues) with whom the individuals need to communicate.

Because the purposes of communication are to regulate social interactions or interpersonal functions, as well as to transmit scientific or logically based knowledge and skills, communication disorders have a far-reaching effect on society. Communication rules and use vary from culture to culture and, therefore, differentiation is made among communication differences, communication delays, and communication disorders. It is generally recognized that to progress through life, humans must be able to understand and use, with some degree of competence, the cognitive, linguistic, and contextual conventions associated with oral, literate, and manually coded communication systems.

Speech Disorders

Speech disorders are variations from commonly used acoustic characteristics of the utterances one makes, rather than of the meaning of the utterances (Hegde, 1995; Silverman, 1995). Speech disorders include articulation (the process of producing vowels and consonants that result in meaningful language morphemes, words, phrases, sentences, and discourse), stuttering (the interruption of the flow of speech, characterized by sound or word repetitions, prolongations, and blocking of sound), and voice (production of the frequency and intensity of speech sounds that is atypical of sex, physical maturity, and age resulting in disorders of phonation and resonance). Associated features of speech disorders may be rate of speaking (too fast or too slow for communicative purposes) and dysphagia (disordered swallowing because of inflammation, compression, paralysis, weakness, or hypertonicity of the esophagus).

Language Disorders

Language disorders involve the impaired ability to receive, process, and use auditory, visual, and haptic (touch and movement) symbols in order to negotiate meaning for social interaction and/or academic/professional communication learning. Language disorders may involve nonverbal symbols or verbal language (phonologic, semantic, syntactic, morphologic, and pragmatic linguistic rule systems). Language disorders are often classified as receptive (watching, listening, reading), expressive (moving/gesturing, speaking, writing), or a combination of receptive and expressive

(Palmer & Yantis, 1990). Language disorders include the problems associated with understanding and use of oral-aural language, braille, and manually coded communication systems (Nelson, 1998).

Auditory language disorders include problems making sense of speech sounds, single words, phrases, sentences, thoughts, concepts, and ideas. Visual language disorders include problems making sense of the nonverbal dimensions of communication that are critical in the pragmatic dimensions of communication (i.e., who can communicate what, with whom, how, when, where, and why), as well as decoding and encoding the graphemic and geometric visual symbols used for Augmentative/Alternative Communication (AAC) systems, reading, writing, mathematics, and the physical and technological sciences. Haptic language disorders include problems receiving, interpreting, and using nonverbal symbols involved in pragmatics, the linguistic symbols and motor acts associated with cursive and manuscript writing, and with specialized systems such as braille and manually-coded communication.

Language disorders and learning disabilities are integrally related. Preschool-aged children with a diagnosed language disorder (learning to communicate) will likely encounter problems with academic language (communicating to learn) when they enter a formal education system. Although the underlying problem is the encoding and decoding of symbols (language disorder), the disorder may be termed a learning disability because of the problems encountered learning academic material. The preferred term is language-learning disorder (Gelfer, 1996; Nelson, 1998; Plante & Beeson, 1999). Because individuals do not outgrow language-learning disorders, they continue to encounter social or academic problems as adults. The communication-learning deficits that are evident at the adult level are referred to as adaptive communication-learning disorders (Weller, Crelly, Watteyne, & Herbert, 1992).

Hearing Disorders

Hearing disorders stem from problems within the auditory system. Although this is usually associated with the ear, it may also be located in the areas of the peripheral and central nervous system where the perception of word meanings and associations occur. Individuals with ear infections or allergy/cold related symptoms may have temporary or chronic problems with hearing. Hearing impairments may slowly develop with advancing age. Irreversible impairment can occur following unusual levels of noise exposure, or from ototoxic drugs. Hearing impairments can easily lead to serious difficulties in the ability to perceive and understand the speech and language of others, resulting in speech and/or language disorders (Gelfer, 1996; Minifie, 1994; Plante & Beeson, 1999).

Early identification and intervention are important to maximize the successful management of both individuals with communication disorders and their families. Communication disorders should be assessed and treated by speech-language pathologists and audiologists who hold state licensure or who hold the certificate of clinical competence in speech-language pathology (CCC-SLP) or audiology (CCC-A) from ASHA. Speech-language pathologists and audiologists work in schools, hospitals, rehabilitation centers, long-term care facilities, through contract health care companies, and in private practice (Boone & Plante, 1993; Gelfer, 1996; Hegde, 1995; Minifie, 1994; Palmer & Yantis, 1990; Shames et al., 1994; Silverman, 1995).

ASHA promotes aggressive prevention practices: primary (e.g., prenatal care to prevent a disorder from occurring), secondary (e.g., early identification and intervention to eliminate or minimize the effects of a disorder) and tertiary (decrease the possibility of further problems occurring because of an existing disorder, such as aspiration pneumonia related to dysphagia; Plante & Beeson, 1999). The American Speech-Language-Hearing Association provides information through print and broadcast media. Contact can be made at: 10801 Rockville Pike, Rockville, MD 20852; (301) 897-5700 voice or TTY; fax (301) 571-0481; or on the internet at http://www.asha.org/.

REFERENCES

Boone, D. R., & Plante, E. (1993). *Human communication and its disorders* (2nd ed.). Englewood Cliffs, NJ: Prentice Hall.

Gelfer, M. P. (1996). *Survey of communication disorders: A social and behavioral perspective.* New York: McGraw-Hill.

Hegde, M. N. (1995). *Introduction to communicative disorders* (2nd ed.). Austin, TX: PRO-ED.

Minifie, F. D. (Ed.). (1994). *Introduction to communication sciences and disorders.* San Diego: Singular Publishing Group.

Nelson, N. W. (1998). *Childhood language disorders in context: Infancy through adolescence* (2nd ed.). Boston: Allyn & Bacon.

Palmer, J. M., & Yantis, P. A. (1990). *Survey of communication disorders.* Baltimore: Williams & Wilkins.

Plante, E., & Beeson, P. M. (1999). *Communication and communication disorders: A clinical introduction.* Boston: Allyn & Bacon.

Pressley, M., & McCormick, C. B. (1995). *Advanced educational psychology: For educators, researchers, and policymakers.* New York: HarperCollins.

Shames, G. H., Wiig, E. H., & Secord, W. A. (1994). *Human communication disorders: An introduction* (4th ed.). New York: Merrill/Macmillan.

Silverman, F. H. (1995). *Speech, language, & hearing disorders.* Boston: Allyn & Bacon.

Weller, C., Crelly, C., Watteyne, L., & Herbert, M. (1992). *Adaptive language disorders of young adults with learning disabilities.* San Diego: Singular Publishing Group.

STEPHEN S. FARMER
New Mexico State University

APHASIA
AUDIOLOGY
AUDITORY ABNORMALITIES
LANGUAGE DEFICIENCIES AND DEFICITS
LANGUAGE DISORDERS
LANGUAGE DISORDERS, EXPRESSIVE

COMMUNICATION METHODS IN SPECIAL EDUCATION, ALTERNATIVE

See ALTERNATIVE COMMUNICATION METHODS IN SPECIAL EDUCATION.

COMMUNICATION SPECIALIST

A communication specialist is any one of a number of professionals who deal with aspects of both normal and disordered human communication. Such an individual may have expertise in communication theory, small group communication, organizational communication, or rhetoric. This individual may call himself or herself a linguist, a psycholinguist, a sociolinguist, a cultural linguist, or a rhetorician. The specialist is concerned with the influence of such diverse disciplines as linguistics, psychology, and sociology on human communication in general and language and speech in particular. In addition, these professionals study the development of normal communication theories and processes.

The study of disordered communication can also be considered in the realm of the communication specialist. The individual typically has expertise in communication disorders, education of the hearing impaired, or neurolinguistics. Speech and language disorders in children and adults can be studied from an organic (anatomic and physiologic) or functional (psychological, learning) perspective. The specialist in disordered communication may be concerned with such problems as language delay in children from multiple articulation errors or delay in (or loss of) the acquisition of morphologic, syntactic, or semantic rules of language. The communication specialist will also be concerned with language disorders owed to neurologic factors (e.g., brain damage).

HARVEY R. GILBERT
Pennsylvania State University

COMMUNICATION DISORDERS
SPEECH AND LANGUAGE DISABILITIES
SPEECH-LANGUAGE PATHOLOGIST

COMMUNITY-BASED INSTRUCTION

Community-based instruction refers to the opportunity for students to have direct interaction with resources in the community while participating in educational programs. With the current emphasis on education in the least restrictive environment for all students with disabilities, community-based instruction has been implemented in many special education programs, especially in those that serve students with moderate to severe handicaps. For students with moderate and severe disabilities to perform adequately in normalized postschool environments, skills must be taught in locations where they will naturally occur (Brown et al., 1983). Indeed, community-based instruction is a more powerful predictor of education/adaptive gains than intelligence quotient, level of ambulation, or presence of behavior problems (McDonnell, 1993).

Community-based instruction may be implemented using a number of models (Brown et al., 1983). These include consecutive instruction, whereby skills are taught in a simulated setting within the school facility until a certain skill level is reached; instruction in nonschool settings then follows. Concurrent instruction can occur where instruction takes place in both school and nonschool settings at daily or weekly intervals. Nonschool instruction can be implemented with direct training in nonschool (community) settings only students must have current access or have contact with the setting in the future.

Community-based instruction may involve training in a number of areas. Ordering, purchasing, and eating food in a restaurant may be taught. Use of consumer services such as public transportation, banks, and laundromats may be emphasized during training. Recreation skills may be taught in natural community sites including parks, community gymnasiums, aerobics/fitness centers, and video arcades. Students may be taught to use stores and shops such as grocery stores, pharmacies, and department stores. Vocational skills may be taught in community vocational sites. Selection of community-based training sites can be determined by examining the current and future needs of particular students in community-referenced activities (Wehman, Renzaglia, & Bates, 1985). Certain skills such as street crossing, appropriate social interaction with nondisabled peers and adults, and nonvocal or vocal communication may be taught in more than one community-based training activity.

A number of advantages in using community-based instruction with students who have moderate to severe disabilities have been cited by professionals in the field of special education. If training takes place in heterogeneous, nonschool environments, student adaptive functioning will be more likely in current and subsequent community settings. Transfer and generalization of community skills will be more likely to occur when taught in natural rather than simulated settings (Brown et al., 1979; Brown et al., 1976; Council for Exceptional Children, 1990; Wehmeyer, 2002). In addition, students with disabilities participating in community-based instruction will have frequent access to nondisabled peers who may serve as role models. In turn, the awareness by nondisabled people of their peers with disabilities will be enhanced. This will enable the nondisabled peers to be cognizant of the abilities of individuals with disabilities, thus promoting a smoother transition to postschool environments on the part of disabled individuals. Parent and teacher expectations of student abilities may be increased when community-based instruction occurs. Finally, the opportunity for students to sample the reinforcing aspects of activities in the community can be an advantage in achieving acquisition of functional skills (Wehman & Hill, 1982; Wehman et al., 1985).

A number of factors need to be taken into account when considering community-based instruction. These include staffing, transportation, scheduling, costs, necessary curriculum changes, and modifications for severely physical disabled students (Hamre-Nietupski et al., 1982). Considerations such as these require careful planning on the part of teachers and administrators to facilitate adequate community-based programming.

REFERENCES

Brown, L., Branston, M. B., Hamre-Nietupski, S., Pumpian, I., Certo, N., & Gruenwald, L. (1979). A strategy for developing chronological age-appropriate and functional curricular content for severely handicapped adolescents and young adults. *Journal of Special Education, 13,* 81–90.

Brown, L., Nietupski, M., & Hamre-Nietupski, S. (1976). Criterion of ultimate functioning. In M. A. Thomas (Ed.), *Hey, don't forget me!* Reston, VA: Council for Exceptional Children.

Brown, L., Nisbet, J., Ford, A., Sweet, M., Shiraga, B., York, J., & Loomis, R. (1983). The critical need for nonschool instruction in educational programs for severely handicapped students. *Journal of the Association for Persons with Severe Handicaps, 8*(3), 71–77.

Council for Exceptional Children. (1990). *Designing community-based instruction.* Research brief for teachers. Reston, VA: Author.

Hamre-Nietupski, S., Nietupski, J., Bates, P., & Maurer, S. (1982). Implementing a community-based educational model for moderately and severely handicapped students: Common problems and suggested solutions. *Journal of the Association for Persons with Severe Handicaps, 7*(4), 38–43.

McDonnell, J. (1993). Impact of community-based instruction on the development of adaptive behavior of secondary-level students with mental retardation. *American Journal on Mental Retardation, 97,* 5, 575–584.

Wehman, P., & Hill, J. (1982). Preparing severely handicapped youth for less restrictive environments. *Journal of the Association for Persons with Severe Handicaps, 7*(1), 33–39.

Wehman, P., Renzaglia, A., & Bates, P. (1985). *Functional living skills for moderately and severely handicapped individuals.* Austin, TX: Pro-Ed.

Wehmeyer, M. L. (2002). *Teaching students with mental retardation.* Baltimore: Paul H. Brookes.

CORNELIA LIVELY
University of Illinois, Urbana-Champaign

COMPENSATORY EDUCATION
NONSHELTERED EMPLOYMENT
SHELTERED WORKSHOPS
VOCATIONAL EDUCATION

COMMUNITY-BASED JOB TRAINING FOR STUDENTS WITH AUTISM AND DEVELOPMENTAL DISABILITIES

The need to better prepare persons with disabilities for life after high school has become recognized by federal and local agencies and has been well documented in the professional literature. Now the development of programs to facilitate the transition from school to adult living has received substantial funding and attention. A major component of this transition movement involves vocational preparation of students with disabilities.

The purpose of community-based job training is to prepare students for employment through the provision of instruction in actual job tasks at work sites within the local community. Research has shown that, because students with developmental disabilities often have difficulty transferring skills learned in one situation to another (Division TEACHH Administration and Research, 2005; Koegel, Rincover, & Egel, 1982), it is advantageous to assess and to teach job skills in the settings in which they will ultimately have to be performed (Berkell, 1985; Black & Langone, 1995). Through the provision of vocational training in job sites within the community, teachers can facilitate student mastery of specific job skills, as well as the development of interpersonal job-related skills required to maintain various employment positions.

There are five major phases involved in community-based job training: (1) student evaluation, (2) job development, (3) instruction at the work site, (4) supervision reduction, and (5) client follow-up. Each of these phases must be addressed by the vocational trainer regardless of the student's ability level.

Vocational training should begin with an assessment of a person's interests and aptitudes for different jobs. This involves the realistic assessment of learner needs and characteristics. Many of the vocational evaluation instruments commonly used by special educators and vocational rehabilitation counselors are useful for assessing mildly and moderately handicapped youths, but they provide less useful information when used with individuals with severe learning problems. For persons with developmental disabilities, assessment is most appropriately conducted through on-the-job evaluation, work samples, and interview techniques.

Vocational evaluation is both a student-centered and work-related assessment process. Prior to beginning a community-based job training program, the teacher must survey the local job market to become aware of the types of jobs available and plan the curriculum to prepare students for these types of work.

In order to match the student to a particular job, the evaluator requires information not only about student preferences, abilities, and behaviors, but also about the demands of the job and the behavioral characteristics required of workers on the job. Job analysis is the systematic study of an occupation in terms of what the worker does in relation to data, people, and things; the methodology and techniques employed; the machines, tools, equipment, and work aids used; the materials, products, subject matter, or services that result; and the traits required of the worker (Grandin, 1999; McCray, 1982). This procedure is especially useful as a means of identifying essential job tasks; it provides much instructionally relevant information.

A comprehensive approach to vocational preparation involves both job skill development and the development of work-related skills. Job skills training generally focuses on use of equipment, production rate, and quality of the product produced. Work-related behaviors include self-care and grooming, communication skills, interpersonal social skills, leisure skills for break times, and travel skills.

Direct skill training and ongoing assessment are the major instructional requirements of a community-based job training program (Rusch & Mithaug, 1980). Instruction that is systematic and behavioral in nature tends to be most effective in vocational training.

The type and amount of supervision required by a student at a work site is often contingent on the nature of the handicapping condition and the complexity of the job task. Some autistic and developmentally disabled students may need ongoing supervision for an indefinite period of time, while others will require only a minimum of supervision following their initial training.

One key to increasing independence on the job is to fade, or reduce, supervision and assistance to the student as soon as possible in order to avoid the development of dependency on the teacher. Rotating supervisors during the training sessions is also beneficial in reducing such dependency, as well as in increasing generalization from the teacher to an actual job supervisor.

In contrast to job training programs for mildly disabled persons, students with autism and developmental disabilities may require systematically planned job retention and follow-up services for many years following graduation from school. Methods of determining follow-up intervention strategies include periodic employee evaluations and progress reports, parent/guardian questionnaires, on-site visits, and telephone contacts with employers and family members or group home staff (Moon, Goodall, Barcus, & Brooke, 1985).

A problem or potential problem may be discovered through the use of such ongoing follow-up assessment procedures. When the client is in a new job situation, it is also helpful to request that the employer contact the job trainer with any concerns as soon as they arise. As the client and the employer become more comfortable with each other, the need for contact with the job trainer will become less frequent.

Preparation of students with developmental disabilities for productive employment has become a major educational concern. Issues regarding the selection of instructional locations and the types of assessment and training methods used in vocational preparation programs have received increased attention in the past decade. Research has shown that, because students with autism and developmental disabilities often have difficulty in transferring skills learned from one situation to another, it is advantageous to teach job skills in community-based settings rather than in the classroom even though inclusive educational settings may support generalization (Bang & Lamb, 1997). By providing vocational training in the job sites within the community, teachers can help students to master the necessary competencies for specific jobs and to learn job-related skills necessary to maintain various employment positions.

REFERENCES

Bang, Myong-Ye, & Lamb, P. (1997). *Impacts of an inclusive school-to-work program.* Paper presented at the Annual Convention of the Council for Exceptional Children, Salt Lake City, UT, April 9–13.

Black, R. S., & Langone, J. (1995). *Generalization of work-related social behavior for persons with mental retardation.* Paper presented at the Annual International Conference of the Division on Cancer Development and Transition. Raleigh, NC, October 19–21.

Division TEACHH Administration and Research. (2005). *Autism primer.* Retrieved December 15, 2005, from http://www.teachh.com/20ques.htm#JobSkill

Grandin, T. (1999). *Choosing the right job for people with Autism.* Retrieved December 15, 2005, from http://www.autism.about.com

Koegel, R. L., Rincover, A., & Egel, A. I. (1982). *Educating and understanding autistic children.* San Diego, CA: College Hill.

Moon, S., Goodall, P., Barcus, M., & Brooke, V. (Eds.). (1985). *The supported work model of competitive employment for citizens with severe handicaps: A guide for job trainers.* Richmond: Rehabilitation and Training Center, Virginia Commonwealth University.

Rusch, F. R., & Mithaug, D. E. (1980). *Vocational training for mentally retarded adults: A behavior analytic approach.* Champaign, IL: Research.

Schutz, R. P., & Rusch, F. R. (1982). Competitive employment: Toward employment integration for mentally retarded persons. In K. P. Lynch, W. E. Kiernan, & J. A. Stark (Eds.), *Prevocational and vocational education for special needs youth: A blue-print for the 1980's* (pp. 133–160). Baltimore: Brookes.

Stodden, R. A., Casale, J., & Schwartz, S. E. (1977). Work evaluation and the mentally retarded: Review and recommendations. *Mental Retardation, 15,* 25–27.

DIANNE E. BERKELL
C.W. Post Campus, Long Island University

SHELTERED WORKSHOPS
VOCATIONAL REHABILITATION COUNSELING

COMMUNITY-BASED SERVICES

The concept of normalization has led to the current trend of serving individuals who might have been institutionalized in the community. These individuals must be provided with support services to help them successfully adjust to community life. To achieve the goal of normalization, the disabled should be involved in developmental activities that are closely associated with those of nondisabled individuals. These activities should center around integration into the normal life of the community. To the maximum extent possible, each individual's developmental activities should focus on the following life cycle. During infancy and early childhood, skill development should be related to sensorimotor skills, communication, self-help, and socialization. During the stages of childhood and early adolescence, there should be application of basic academic skills in daily life activities; application of appropriate reasoning and judgment in mastery of the environment; and participation in interpersonal relationships. During late adolescence and adulthood, vocational and social activities should be the major areas of focus (Grossman, 1977). Intagliata, Kraus, and Willer (1980) conducted a study to determine the impact of deinstitutionalization on the community-based service system. Basic observations reported in this study include the following:

Agencies served a large portion of formerly institutionalized individuals.

Agencies served individuals with low intellectual levels.

Formerly institutionalized individuals required needed services to be more intensive.

Special programs were needed to provide appropriate services for the lower functioning individuals.

Pollard, Hall, and Kiernan (1979) state that there are many services available to the disabled from various separate systems such as health, education, rehabilitation, recreation, employment, and housing. However, when these systems are working separately, there is little chance for them to solve the varied problems of the disabled. There is a great need for these human services to work together to provide comprehensive community services (Pires, 1992).

On June 22, 1999, the U.S. Supreme Court affirmed that policy by ruling in Olmstead v. L.C. that under the Americans With Disabilities Act (ADA) unjustifiable institutionalization of a person with a disability who, with proper support, can live in the community is discrimination. In its ruling, the Court said that institutionalization severely limits the person's ability to interact with family and friends, to work and to make a life for him or herself.

The Olmstead case was brought by two Georgia women whose disabilities include mental retardation and mental illness. At the time the suit was filed, both plaintiffs were receiving mental health services in state-run institutions, despite the fact that their treatment professionals believed they could be appropriately served in a community-based setting. In accordance with that Court ruling, the U.S. Department of Health and Human Services (HHS) issued guidance to state Medicaid directors on how to make state programs responsive to the desires of disabled persons to live in appropriate community-based settings. The Administration's goal was to integrate people with disabilities into the social mainstream with equal opportunities and the chance to make choices.

The Court based its ruling in Olmstead on sections of the ADA and federal regulations that require states to administer their services, programs and activities in the most integrated setting appropriate to the needs of qualified individuals with disabilities.

Under the Court's ruling, certain principles have emerged:

1) unjustified institutionalization of people with disabilities is discrimination and violates the ADA;

2) states are required to provide community-based services for persons with disabilities who are otherwise entitled to institutional services when the state's treatment professionals reasonably determine that community placement is appropriate; the person does not oppose such placement; and the placement can reasonably be accommodated, taking into account resources available to the state and the needs of others receiving state-supported disability services;

3) a person cannot be denied community services just to keep an institution at its full capacity; and,

4) there is no requirement under the ADA that community-based services be imposed on people with disabilities who do not desire it.

The Court also said that states are obliged to make reasonable modifications in policies, practices, or procedures when the modifications are necessary to avoid discrimination on the basis of disability, unless the public entity can demonstrate that making the modifications would fundamentally alter the nature of the service, program or activity. Meeting the fundamental alteration test takes into account three factors: the cost of providing services in the most integrated setting; the resources available to the state; and how the provision of services affects the ability of the state to meet the needs of others with disabilities.

Over the past few years, HHS has focused on expanding and promoting home- and community-based services, offering support and technical assistance to states and using the flexibility of the Medicaid program. To help states comply with the Court ruling, Health Care Financing Administration and the HHS Office for Civil Rights have begun working with states and the disability community toward the goals of promoting home- and community-based services; honoring individual choice in service provision; and acknowledging that resources available to a state are limited by the need to serve both community-based and institutionalized persons.

In addition to continued technical assistance to states, HHS will review relevant federal Medicaid regulations, policies and previous guidance to assure that they are compatible with requirements of the ADA and Olmstead decision and that they facilitate states' efforts to comply with the law (CMS, 1999).

According to Schalock (1985), comprehensive community-based services for the disabled include community living alternatives, habilitation programs, and support programs. Community living alternatives range from the highest level of independence, independent living, to congregate living, home care, supervised living, staffed apartments, and group homes, to the lowest level of independence, community institutional facilities. The habilitation programs in education range from the highest level of community integration, mainstreamed classes in public schools, to resource rooms, day training programs, and residential programs, to the lowest level of community integration, homebound instruction. The habilitation programs in employment range from the highest level of productivity, competitive employment, to transitional employment, sheltered workshop, and work activity, to the lowest level of activity, day training programs. The last category of comprehensive community services, support services, includes health and mental health care, legal services, home assistance (respite care), early identification/intervention, and transportation. In addition, the importance of the following points in designing and providing community living and habilitation alternatives are crucial:

Natural environments are the preferred service settings.

Generic services should be used as much as possible.

Assistance to the client should be provided only at the level actually needed to promote independence and self-sufficiency.

Training should focus on increasing the client's independence, productivity, and community integration.

Everyone has potential for growth regardless of his or her current functioning level (Schalock, 1985 p. 38).

Scheerenberger (1981) conducted a study of all superintendents of public residential facilities throughout the United States. All superintendents completed the questionnaire. The results indicated that the community variables that resulted in problems causing community placement failures included inadequacies in appropriate living settings, behavioral management programs, specialized services, and adult programs. Community services for the mildly and moderately retarded that were considered to be effective were transportation, medical services, educational opportunities, and advocacy. On the other hand, these same services for the severely and profoundly retarded were found to be less than adequate.

REFERENCES

Centers for Medicare and Medicaid Services (CMS). (2000). *Assuring access to community living for the disabled.* Retrieved December 15, 2005, from http://www.cms.hhs.gov/apps/media/press

Grossman, H. J. (Ed.). (1977). *Manual on terminology and classification in mental retardation* (Special Publication No. 2). Washington, DC: American Association on Mental Deficiency.

Intagliata, J., Kraus, S., & Willer, B. (1980). The impact of deinstitutionalization on a community-based service system. *Mental Retardation, 18,* 302–308.

Pires, S. (1992). *Issues related to community-based service delivery for children and adolescents with mental illness and their families.* Washington, DC: Georgetown University Child Development Center.

Pollard, A., Hall, H., & Kiernan, C. (1979). Community services planning. In P. R. Magrab & J. O. Elder (Eds.), *Planning services to handicapped persons: Community, education, health.* Baltimore: Brookes.

Schalock, R. L. (1985). Comprehensive community services: A plea for interagency collaboration. In R. H. Bruininks & K. C. Lakin (Eds.), *Living and learning in the least restrictive environment.* Baltimore: Brookes.

Scheerenberger, R. C. (1981). Deinstitutionalization: Trends and difficulties. In R. H. Bruininks, C. E. Meyers, B. B. Sigford, & K. C. Lakin (Eds.), *Deinstitutionalization and community adjustment of mentally retarded people.* Washington, DC: American Association on Mental Deficiency.

JANICE HARPER
*North Carolina Central
University*

DEINSTITUTIONALIZATION
NORMALIZATION
REHABILITATION

COMMUNITY RESIDENTIAL PROGRAMS

There is an array of community residential options available. Foster homes, also known as personal care homes or family care homes (McCoin, 1983), are private homes rented or owned by a family with one or more persons with disabilities living as family members (Hill & Lakin, 1984). The number of residents rarely exceeds six (Miller & Intagliata, 1984). These residences are licensed by a state agency or a local facility (e.g., a hospital). Foster homes are available for both children and adults. They tend to be homelike, with the person with the disability being "one of the family."

Group homes are residences with staff to provide care and supervision of one or more persons with disabilities (Hill & Lakin, 1984). Financial support comes from a variety of sources, including churches, states, private nonprofit organizations, and private for-profit organizations (Miller & Intagliata, 1984). It is not uncommon to find group homes staffed with house parents (a man and a woman who live in the residence, with one having an additional outside job) and one or two additional staff members for the hours when the majority of residents are home. The number of residents living in groups varies from home to home. Most of the research conducted has involved group homes serving under 20 residents (Miller & Intagliata).

Semiindependent living facilities are facilities having separate units or apartments with staff members living in one unit or apartment; however, staff members live in the same building to provide support services to those in need. Services might include assistance with budgeting or managing money, housework, or laundry. Currently, these facilities are mainly supported by nonprofit organizations (Hill, Lakin, & Bruininks, 1984).

Domicilary care facilities are community-based facilities whose primary function is to provide shelter and protection to the residents. There are no training or rehabilitation activities conducted (Miller & Intagliata, 1984). Since there is a lack of emphasis on training or rehabilitation, these types of facilities are deemed most appropriate for persons with high levels of independent living skills who need little or no additional training, or for those persons who, because of severe medical or physical needs or age, would not benefit from additional skill training (Miller & Intagliata). The number of residents in these facilities ranges from 5 to 200. Most of these facilities are operated by individual proprietors (Hill et al., 1984).

Although there are a variety of names given to domiciliary care facilities, there are generally two broad categories. Board and care facilities are also known as boarding homes and adult homes. As a general rule, these facilities provide a room and meals to the residents. Some also provide limited supervision. The major source of support for most residents is Social Security (Miller & Intagliata, 1984). Health care facilities are also known as convalescent care homes, nursing homes, skilled nursing facilities, intermediate care facilities, and health-related facilities (Miller & Intagliata). In addition to providing a room and meals, these facilities also provide some level of nursing care to the residents. Generally, these facilities are funded through Medicare and Medicaid.

Halfway houses are short-term residential options available to persons leaving institutional settings (Katz, 1968). The setting is supervised with emphasis on facilitating the person's reentry into the community. The number of residents ranges from 12 to 25. An extensive report on residential services can be found by Prouty and Lakin (1997).

REFERENCES

Hill, B. K., & Lakin, K. C. (1984). *Classification of residential facilities for mentally retarded people* (Brief No. 24). Minneapolis: Center for Residential and Community Services, University of Minnesota, Department of Educational Psychology.

Hill, B. K., Lakin, K. C., & Bruininks, R. H. (1984). Trends in residential services for people who are mentally retarded 1977–1982. *Journal of the Association for Persons with Severe Handicaps, 9*(4), 243–251.

Katz, E. (1968). *The retarded adult in the community.* Springfield, IL: Thomas.

McCoin, J. M. (1983). *Adult foster homes: Their managers and residents.* New York: Human Sciences.

Miller, B., & Intagliata, T. (1984). *Promises and realities for mentally retarded citizens: Life in the community.* Baltimore: University Park Press.

Prouty, R., & Lakin, K. (1997). *Residential Services for Persons with Development Disabilities: Status and Trends through 1996, Report #49.* Minneapolis: University of Minnesota.

SUE ANN MORROW
EDGE, Inc.

LONNY W. MORROW
Northeast Missouri State University

INDEPENDENT LIVING CENTERS
RESIDENTIAL FACILITIES

COMPAZINE

Compazine (prochlorperazine) is used for the short-term treatment of generalized nonpsychotic anxiety, the control of severe nausea and vomiting (Konopasek, 2004) and the management of the manifestations of psychotic disorders (Servis & Miller, 1997). Compazine may impair mental or physical abilities, especially during the first few days of therapy. Adverse reactions can include drowsiness, dizziness, blurred vision, restlessness, agitation, jitteriness, insomnia, and motor dysfunctions such as muscle spasms, pseudoparkinsonism, and tardive dyskinesia. Overdose can produce coma.

A brand name of Smith Kline and French, Compazine is available in tablets of 5, 10, and 25 mg, in sustained release capsules of 10, 15, and 30 mg in injectible ampuls, and in suppositories of 2 1/2, 5, and 25 mg. Dosage may vary, ranging from 2 1/2 mg, according to the symptom being treated. It is given one or two times per day for severe nausea and vomiting in young children to a maximum of 25 mg per day in children 6 to 12 years of age being treated for psychosis.

REFERENCES

Konopasek, D. E. (2004). *Medication fact sheets.* Longmont, CO: Sopris West.

Physician's desk reference. (1984). (pp. 1874–1877). Oradell, NJ: Medical Economics.

Servis, M., & Miller, B. (1997). Treatment of psychosis with prochlorperazine in the ICU setting. *Psychosomatics, 38,* 6, 589–590.

LAWRENCE C. HARTLAGE
Evans, Georgia

ATARAX
BENADRYL
NAVANE

COMPENSATORY EDUCATION

Compensatory education usually refers to supplemental educational services provided through federal, state, or local programs to educationally disadvantaged children in schools with concentrations of children from low-income families. The largest such program is that authorized by Chapter 1 of the Education Consolidation and Improvement Act, formerly known as Title I of the Elementary and Secondary Education Act (ESEA). Federal grants are made through state education agencies to local school districts based on the number of children from families in poverty. About 90 percent of all districts receive Chapter 1 funds. Local educational agencies then allocate funds to schools based on poverty and educational criteria. Schools provide services to children based not on family income, but on extent of educational deprivation. This determination is made at the local level within broad federal guidelines. In general, schools with the greatest concentrations of children from poor families and children most in need of services receive priority in program delivery.

Additional children receive services from state and local compensatory education programs, and some Chapter 1 participants receive additional services from such programs. Participants are concentrated in lower achievement quartiles; as the achievement quartile increases, percent participation in Chapter 1 decreases (White, 1984).

The law allows for a wide range of services to be provided: instructional services, purchase of materials and equipment, teacher training, construction, and social and health services. Historically, about 80 percent of funds were spent on instructional services (White, 1984), with particular emphasis on reading and math. About three-fourths of participants receive compensatory reading and almost one-half receive compensatory math, with language arts the next most common service (Carpenter & Hopper, 1985). Almost two-thirds of districts pull students out of regular classrooms to provide services in classes that are likely to be smaller and more personnel-intensive than regular classes. Title I average class size was about 10 children, with a student-to-instructor ratio of 4.5 to 1 (White, 1984).

Compensatory education programs resemble special education programs for learning-disabled children in several ways. They attempt to address a similar symptom: low or lower-than-expected achievement. There is a special concentration on attacking difficulties with reading and mathematics skills. Children are often removed from regular classrooms for part of the school day for more personnel-intensive services in smaller classes. That is not to suggest that children served, educational needs, or instructional content of programs for learning-disabled children and compensatory education are identical, or that learning-disabled children are interchangeable with children receiving compensatory education. They are not. But in terms of difficulty addressed, administrative design, or general approach to service delivery, there are important similarities.

Given the Chapter 1 eligibility criterion of educational disadvantagement, nothing prohibits a child with a disability who receives special education and related services from also being served as an educationally deprived child through compensatory education. Anecdotal evidence suggests this may not be common.

It is important to note that the No Child Left Behind Act (NCLB), passed in 2001, introduced sweeping changes to the ESEA, and in particular to Chapter 1 programs. Under the NCLB, the focus has shifted from the income levels of families of students at a school to the performance of the school, as measured by statewide academic requirements for adequate yearly progress, without regard to the socioeconomic status of the students attending it. Although funding for older Chapter 1 programs was authorized under NCLB through 2007, the ultimate fate of such programs remains unclear, as does the ultimate impact on the children who are in such programs. The true consequences, in terms of educational outcomes, will probably not be known for many years.

It is also important to remember that many compensatory education programs run by state and local educational agencies complement and extend Chapter 1. Information on children served, services provided, and evaluation results of these programs is available from state and local education agencies.

REFERENCES

Carpenter, M., & Hopper, P. (1985). *Synthesis of state Chapter 1 data: Draft summary report*. Washington, DC: Advanced Technology.

White, B. F. (1984). *Compensatory education*. Washington, DC: Office of Management and Budget.

JAMES R. RICCIUTI
*United State Office of
Management and Budget*
Second edition

KIMBERLY F. APPLEQUIST
*University of Colorado at
Colorado Springs*
Third edition

NO CHILD LEFT BEHIND ACT

COMPETENCY TESTING FOR TEACHERS

See HIGHLY QUALIFIED TEACHERS.

COMPETING BEHAVIOR PATH ANALYSIS

Competing behavior path analysis and its related principles and procedures has typically been used in the context of situations in which students are exhibiting problem behaviors, including aggression toward others, self-injurious behavior (e.g., head-hitting), destruction of materials, and other disruptive behaviors (e.g., talking out in the classroom). Completing a *competing behavior path analysis* (CBA) is a step in the process of developing a *behavior support plan* (BSP) for a student engaging in such behaviors (O'Neill et al., 1997).

The conceptual foundation for this type of analysis was presented by Billingsley and Neel (1985) and Horner and Billingsley (1988). They discussed how, in various situations, desired appropriate student behaviors can be thought of as being in competition with problem behaviors. That is, in a given situation a student may be able to exhibit a variety of problematic or appropriate behaviors. For example, in a situation in which a student is asked to complete an academic task or activity, s/he could either begin working on the task or could exhibit disruptive or aggressive behavior. Horner and Billingsley outlined a number of factors that may influence which types of behaviors might occur, including the presence or absence of stimuli which influence the different behaviors, and the likelihood of reinforcing consequences for them. For example, a student may learn through experience that a certain teacher or staff person is very likely to allow the student to escape from non-preferred academic tasks if disruptive or aggressive behavior occurs. Thereafter, the presence of that teacher or staff person may substantially increase the likelihood that such problem behavior will occur versus more appropriate work activity. In such a case, the problem behavior "won the competition" in relation to the desired appropriate behavior (i.e., work completion).

A practical process for applying these concepts to analyze problem situations was presented by O'Neill et al. (1997). They discussed a competing behavior analysis as a transitional step between a functional behavioral assessment (FBA) and the development of a behavior support plan for an individual student. The FBA should produce a variety of information, including: (1) description of the full range of problem behaviors of concern, (2) identification of the setting and antecedent events which predict the occurrence of the behaviors, and (3) identification of the reinforcing outcomes that are maintaining the behaviors (i.e., the functions they are serving for the student). This information is used to generate hypotheses or summary statements that succinctly pull together the information. An example of a summary statement would be: "When Mario has had little sleep, and he is asked to do difficult academic activities, he will curse, throw materials, and/or spit at the teacher in order to escape the task demands." Such a statement identifies a setting event (lack of sleep), a more immediate antecedent (difficult task demands), the behaviors which might occur, and the apparent function of the behaviors, or the reinforcing outcome maintaining them (escape from difficult/aversive tasks). A FBA may result in multiple such statements for

a given student, depending on the range of behaviors they exhibit and the functions they may be serving.

According to O'Neill et al. (1997), competing behavior analysis (CBA) provides a framework for a three-step process in moving from the results of a FBA to the details of developing a behavior support plan. First, the summary statement or hypothesis is diagrammed on a Competing Behavior Analysis Form. Figure 1 presents a version of this form. The components of the summary statement presented above for Mario are laid out on the middle line of the form (setting event, antecedent, behavior, maintaining consequence). The second step involves identifying two things; (a) the general desired behavior appropriate for that situation, and (b) an appropriate alternative or replacement behavior that will produce the same outcome which the problem behaviors currently produce. In the example of Mario in Figure 1, the general desired behavior was for Mario to complete his assigned work, which would lead to a grade or other evaluation, and presumably some kind of positive recognition from the teacher. An alternative replacement behavior would be for Mario to request assistance with the difficult work. This would be functionally equivalent to the problem behaviors in allowing him to escape the aversive aspects of the difficult tasks. (Note: This diagram/format illustrates the different possible behavior "paths" which might be followed in particular situations; hence the term *competing behavior path analysis*.)

Once the competing behavior path analysis is completed, the third main step in the process is to identify behavioral support strategies that will increase the probability of the desired and replacement behaviors, and decrease the likelihood of the problem behaviors. One function of the CBA format is to encourage consideration of a comprehensive range of strategies to influence problem behavior situations. That is, it is important to consider potential changes which could be made in each component of the framework (i.e., setting events, antecedents, teaching alternative behaviors, and consequences for appropriate and problem behaviors). It is beyond the scope of this entry to provide more detail on intervention strategies. However, there are an increas-

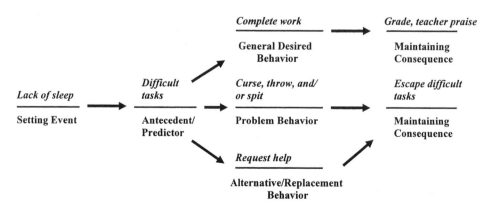

Figure 1 An example of a competing behavior analysis diagram

ing number of resources available for teachers and other practitioners which provide more detail in this area (e.g., Bambara & Kern, 2005). In addition, there are indications that the competing behavior analysis logic and format is being adopted and used by practitioners in the field (e.g., Chandler & Dahlquist, 2002; Condon & Tobin, 2000; Scott & Nelson, 1999). Finally, it is worth noting that the CBA method is frequently a component of a more comprehensive general approach known as *positive behavior support* (PBS; Bambara, Dunlap, & Schwartz, 2004).

REFERENCES

Bambara, L. M., Dunlap, G., & Schwartz, I. (Eds.). (2004). *Positive behavior support: Critical articles on improving practice for individuals with severe disabilities.* Austin, TX: PRO-ED.

Bambara, L. M., & Kern, L. (2005). *Individualized supports for students with problem behaviors: Designing positive behavior plans.* New York: Guilford.

Billingsley, F. F., & Neel, R. S. (1985). Competing behaviors and their effects on skill generalization and maintenance. *Analysis and Intervention in Developmental Disabilities, 5,* 357–372.

Chandler, L. K., & Dahlquist, C. M. (2002). *Functional assessment: Strategies to prevent and remediate challenging behavior in school settings.* Columbus, OH: Merrill.

Condon, K. A., & Tobin, T. J. (2001). Functional behavioral assessment at work. *Teaching Exceptional Children, 33,* 44–51.

Horner, R. H., & Billingsley, F. F. (1988). The effect of competing behavior on the generalization and maintenance of adaptive behavior in applied settings. In R. H. Horner, G. Dunlap, & R. L. Koegel (Eds.), *Generalization and maintenance: Life-style changes in applied settings* (pp. 197–220). Baltimore: Paul H. Brookes.

O'Neill, R. E., Horner, R. H., Albin, R. W., Storey, K., Sprague, J. R., & Newton, J. S. (1997). *Functional assessment and program development for problem behavior: A practical handbook* (2nd ed.). Belmont, CA: Wadsworth.

Scott, T. M., & Nelson, C. M. (1999). Using functional behavioral assessment to develop effective intervention plans: Practical classroom applications. *Journal of Positive Behavior Interventions, 1,* 242–251.

ROB O'NEILL
University of Utah

BEHAVIORAL ASSESSMENT
POSITIVE BEHAVIORAL SUPPORT

COMPREHENSIVE ASSESSMENT OF SPOKEN LANGUAGE

The Comprehensive Assessment of Spoken Language (CASL; Cardow-Woolfolk, 1999) is an individually admin-istered, norm-referenced test that provides an assessment of the oral language skills of children and young adults. Only a verbal or nonverbal (pointing) response is required of the examinee, and reading or writing ability is not needed to respond to test items. Each of the 15 CASL tests is a highly reliable, stand-alone test. The clinician is free to give one test or several and can report the score(s) with confidence. Subtest must be given in conjunction with other subtests to form a composite score.

The CASL provides an in-depth assessment of four language categories:

- *Lexical / Semantic Language,* assessed using the following tests

  Basic Concepts: Examiner reads a sentence aloud while examinee looks at four pictures and points to the picture or part of the picture that represents the correct response.

  Antonyms: Examiner says a stimulus word, and the examinee must respond orally with a single word that means the opposite of the stimulus word.

  Synonyms: Examiner says a stimulus word and four synonym options, then repeats the stimulus word. The examinee chooses the option that means the same as the stimulus.

  Sentence Completion: Examiner reads the stimulus sentence, which is missing the last word, and the examinee must respond with a single word that meaningfully completes the sentence.

  Idiomatic Language: Examiner reads the stimulus idiom, which is missing its final part, and the examinee must complete the phrase with an acceptable form of the idiom.

- *Syntactic Language,* assessed using the following tests

  Syntax Construction: Examiner reads the stimulus item while the examinee looks at a picture. The examinee must respond with a word, phrase, or sentence that is grammatically and semantically appropriate.

  Paragraph Comprehension: Examiner reads a stimulus paragraph twice, then reads a series of items relating to the paragraph while the examinee looks at a set of pictures for each item and responds by pointing to or giving the number of the correct response.

  Grammatical Morphemes: Examiner reads one pair of words or phrases that demonstrates an analogy, then reads the first word or phrase of a second pair. The examinee must complete the analogy of the second pair.

  Sentence Comprehension: For each item, examiner reads two pairs of stimulus sentences, one pair at a time. The examinee must determine whether both sentences in each pair mean the same thing.

Grammaticality Judgment: Examiner reads a stimulus sentence that is grammatically either correct or incorrect. The examinee must judge the correctness of the sentence and, if it is incorrect, must correct it by changing only one word.

- *Supralinguistic Language,* assessed using the following tests

  Nonliteral Language: Examiner reads the stimulus item and the accompanying question, and the examinee must answer by explaining the nonliteral meaning of the item.

  Meaning from Context: Each item contains a very uncommon word. The examiner reads the item, and the examinee must explain the meaning of the uncommon word by using context clues.

  Inference: Examiner describes a situation in which part of the information is omitted, then asks an accompanying question. The examinee must answer the question using world knowledge to infer the missing information.

  Ambiguous Sentences: Examiner reads the stimulus item, and examinee must respond with two possible meanings for the item.

- *Pragmatic Language,* assessed using the following test

  Pragmatic Judgment: Examiner reads a situation that represents some aspect of everyday life that requires communication or a pragmatic judgment on the part of the examinee. The examinee responds with the appropriate thing to say or do in the situation.

The CASL was standardized on 1,700 persons between the ages of 3.0 and 21.11 years who were selected to match the 1994 U.S. Census data. The manual provides evidence for strong reliability. Internal reliability ranged from .64 to .94 depending on the subtest. Core composites and indexes also showed high reliability, with most being in the low to mid .90s. Test-retest reliability is reported as ranging from .92 to .93 for core composites and .88 to .96 for indexes. The manual also provides adequate evidence for content, construct, and criterion-related validity. Intercorrelations among the test components ranged from .30 to .79 and provide evidence to suggest that each test is measuring something unique but high enough to support their combination to produce the core composite and index scores. Age-based and grade-based standard scores (M = 100, SD = 15), grade and test-age equivalents, percentiles, normal curve equivalents (NCEs), and stanines are available.

ADDITIONAL INFORMATION

Plake, B. S., Impara, J. C., & Spies, R. A. (Eds.). (2003). *The fifteenth mental measurements yearbook.* Lincoln, NE: Buros Institute of Mental Measurements.

RON DUMONT
Fairleigh Dickinson University

JOHN O. WILLIS
Rivier College

COMPREHENSIVE RECEPTIVE AND EXPRESSIVE VOCABULARY TEST–SECOND EDITION

The Comprehensive Receptive and Expressive Vocabulary Test–Second Edition (CREVT-2; Wallace & Hammill, 1994) provides an efficient measure of both receptive and expressive oral vocabulary. It is used predominantly to identify students who fall significantly below their age group in oral vocabulary proficiency and to note discrepancies between levels of receptive and expressive skill.

Administration time for the CREVT-2 takes about 20–30 minutes. All words in the CREVT-2 are appropriate for children and adults and were found to be unbiased. The Receptive Vocabulary Subtest requires the examinee to point to a picture of a word said by the examiner. The 61 items are thematic, full-color photographs representing concepts with which most people are familiar, such as animals, transportation, household appliances, recreation, and clerical materials. The Expressive Vocabulary Subtest asks the examinee to define words said by the examiner, encouraging the individual to discuss in detail each stimulus word. The 25 items of this subtest relate to the same 10 common themes used in the Receptive Vocabulary Subtest (animals, transportation, occupations, etc.), allowing for easy transition from subtest to subtest. The applications of basals and ceilings allow this test to be given quickly and make it appropriate for a wide age range.

To quantitatively measure performance, the raw scores obtained on each subtest are converted to standard scores and percentile ranks. Age equivalents are also given.

The CREVT-2 was normed on a representative sample of 2,545 persons, ages 4.0 through 89.11. Norms were stratified by age according to gender, socioeconomic standing, disability, ethnicity, and other critical variables. This sample reflected the 2000 U.S. Census data.

Reliability coefficients are provided for subgroups of the normative sample. New validity studies have been conducted paying close attention to how the CREVT-2 would generalize to the population.

REFERENCES

Plake, B. S., Impara, J. C., & Spies, R. A. (Eds.). (2003). *The fifteenth mental measurements yearbook.* Lincoln, NE: Buros Institute of Mental Measurements.

Smith, T., Smith, B. L., & Eichler, J. B. (2002). Validity of the Comprehensive Receptive and Expressive Vocabulary Test in assessment of children with speech and learning problems. *Psychology in the Schools, 39,* 613–619.

Wallace, G., & Hammill, D. D. (1994). *Comprehensive Receptive and Expressive Vocabulary Test.* Austin, TX: Pro-Ed.

RON DUMONT
Fairleigh Dickinson University

JOHN O. WILLIS
Rivier College

COMPREHENSIVE TEST OF NONVERBAL INTELLIGENCE

The Comprehensive Test of Nonverbal Intelligence (CTONI; Bradley-Johnson, 1997) measures nonverbal reasoning abilities of individuals aged 6 through 90 for whom other tests may be inappropriate or biased. Because CTONI contains no oral responses, reading, writing, or object manipulation it is particularly appropriate for students who are bilingual, speak a language other than English, or are socially or economically disadvantaged, deaf, language disordered, motor impaired, or neurologically impaired. The CTONI should not be administered to people with vision problems. It is easy to administer and score and requires only 1 hour to complete. The CTONI instructions can be administered orally to students who speak English or in pantomime for those who speak languages other than English or who are deaf, aphasic, or neurologically impaired. One criticism has been that the CTONI manual does not provide information about whether the test was standardized using pantomime, oral, or computerized administration.

The CTONI measures analogical reasoning, categorical classifications, and sequential reasoning in two different contexts: pictures of familiar objects (people, toys, and animals) and geometric designs (unfamiliar sketches, patterns, and drawings). There are six subtests in total. Three subtests use pictured objects while three use geometric designs. Each subtest contains 25 items. Examinees indicate their answers by pointing to alternative choices. In addition to raw scores, standard scores, percentiles, and age equivalents, CTONI also provides three composite IQ scores; Nonverbal Intelligence Quotient, Pictorial Nonverbal Intelligence Quotient, and Geometric Nonverbal Intelligence Quotient. Items have been carefully reviewed to protect against bias in regard to race, gender, ethnicity, and language.

The CTONI was normed on a sample of over 2,901 individuals from America in two samples (2,129 in 1995 and 772 in 1996) and is representative of the 1990 *Statistical Abstract of the United States* with respect to age, gender, race/ethnicity, educational level, and geographic region. Reliability studies of the CTONI provide evidence for content sampling, time sampling, and interscorer reliability and have yielded reliability coefficients of .80 or greater. Studies have reported content, criterion-related, and construct validity as well.

This nonverbal intelligence test is also available in a computer-administered format, the CTONI-CA. It is an interactive multimedia test that can easily be completed on a computer. Instructions are given in a clear human voice, and the examinee simply points the mouse and clicks on the answer. When the test is completed, the examinee can see comprehensive results on the screen or print up a report.

REFERENCES

Athanasiou, M. S. (2000). Current nonverbal assessment instruments: A comparison of psychometric integrity and test fairness. *Journal of Psychoeducational Assessment, 18,* 211–229.

Bradley-Johnson, S. (1997). Test review: Comprehensive Test of Nonverbal Intelligence. *Psychology in the Schools, 34,* 289–292.

Drossman, E. R., Maller, S. J., & McDermott, P. A. (2001). Core profiles of school-aged examinees from the national standardization sample of the Comprehensive Test of Nonverbal Intelligence. *School Psychology Review, 30,* 586–598.

Impara, J. C., & Plake, B. S. (Eds.). (1998). *The thirteenth mental measurements yearbook.* Lincoln, NE: Buros Institute of Mental Measurements.

Lassiter, K. S., Harrison, T. K., & Matthews, T. D. (2001). The validity of the Comprehensive Test of Nonverbal Intelligence as a measure of fluid intelligence. *Assessment, 8,* 95–103.

RON DUMONT
Fairleigh Dickinson University

JOHN O. WILLIS
Rivier College

COMPREHENSIVE TEST OF PHONOLOGICAL PROCESSING

The Comprehensive Test of Phonological Processing (CTOPP; 1999) assesses phonological awareness, phonological memory, and rapid naming. The CTOPP's principle uses are to identify individuals who are significantly below their peers in important phonological abilities, to determine strengths and weaknesses among developed phonological processes, and to document an individual's progress in phonological processing as a result of special intervention programs.

Because the test spans such a wide range of ages and abilities, it was necessary to develop two versions of the test. Version 1 is designed primarily for kindergartners and first graders (ages 5–6) and contains seven core subtests and one supplemental test. Version 2 is designed for persons in second grade through college (ages 7–24) and contains six core subtests and eight supplemental tests.

The CTOPP contains the three composites: Phonological Awareness Quotient (PAQ), which measures awareness of and access to phonological structure of oral language; Phonological Memory Quotient (PMQ), which measures the ability to code information phonologically for temporary storage in working or short-term memory; and Rapid Naming Quotient (RNQ), which measures efficient retrieval of phonological information from long-term or permanent memory, as well as the examinee's ability to execute a sequence of operations quickly and repeatedly.

The test contains the following subtests: Elision, Blending Words, Sound Matching, Memory for Digits, Nonword Repetition, Rapid Color Naming, Rapid Digit Naming, Rapid Letter Naming, Rapid Object Naming, Blending Nonwords, Phoneme Reversal, Segmenting Words, and Segmenting Nonwords.

Composite scores are reported by combining scores from the following tasks for each construct listed:

- Ages 5 and 6:

  Phonological Awareness: Elision, Blending Words, and Sound Matching

  Phonological Memory: Memory for Digits and Nonword Repetition

  Rapid naming: Rapid Color Naming and Rapid Object Naming

- Ages 7–24:

  Phonological Awareness: Elision and Blending Words

  Phonological Memory: Memory for Digits and Nonword Repetition

  Rapid naming: Rapid Digit Naming and Rapid Letter Naming

All subtests begin with item 1. The ceilings are uniform on all subtests—three missed items in a row, except for the sound matching (four out of seven items are missed) and the rapid naming tasks (measure time; if names more than four items incorrectly, no score for the subtest). If items are given above the ceiling and any of these items are passes, they are scored as incorrect.

Scores provided include percentiles, standard scores, and age and grade equivalents. Subtest standard scores have a mean of 10 and a standard deviation of 3. The composite quotients have a mean of 100 and a standard deviation of 15. The manual also provides information relating the

CTOPP standard scores to NCE scores, T scores, Z-scores, and stanines.

The CTOPP was normed on 1,656 individuals ranging in age from 5 through 24 and residing in 30 states. The total school-age population was 1,544. Over half of the norming sample came from children in elementary school (through grade 5), where the CTOPP is expected to have its widest use. The demographic characteristics of the normative sample are representative of the U.S. population as a whole with regard to gender, race, ethnicity, residence, family income, educational attainment of parents, and geographic regions. The sample characteristics were stratified by age and keyed to the demographic characteristics reported in the 1997 *Statistical Abstract of the United States*.

Most of the average internal consistency or alternate forms reliability coefficients exceed .80. The test-retest coefficients range from .70 to .92.

REFERENCES AND ADDITIONAL INFORMATION

Bhat, P., Griffin, C. C., & Sindelar, P. T. (2003). Phonological awareness instruction for middle school students with learning disabilities. *Learning Disability Quarterly, 26,* 73–87.

Havey, J. M., Story, N., & Buker, K. (2002). Convergent and concurrent validity of two measures of phonological processing. *Psychology in the Schools, 39,* 507–514.

Hintze, J. M., Ryan, A. L., & Stoner, G. (2003). Concurrent validity and diagnostic accuracy of the Dynamic Indicators of Basic Early Literacy Skills and the Comprehensive Test of Phonological Processing. *School Psychology Review, 32,* 541–556.

Lennon, J. E., & Slesinski C. (2001). Comprehensive Test of Phonological Processing (CTOPP): Cognitive-Linguistic assessment of severe reading problems.

Wagner, R., Torgesen, J. & Rashotte, C. (1999). *Comprehensive Test of Phonological Processing.* Austin, TX: PRO-ED.

CECIL R. REYNOLDS
Texas A&M University

COMPREHENSIVE TRAIL MAKING TEST

The Comprehensive Trail Making Test (CTMT, 2002) is a standardized set of five visual search and sequencing tasks that are heavily influenced by attention, concentration, resistance to distraction, and cognitive flexibility (or set-shifting). Its may be especially useful in the detection of brain compromise and in tracking progress in rehabilitation. It may also be used to detect frontal lobe deficits; problems with psychomotor speed, visual search and sequencing, and attention; and impairments in set-shifting.

The basic task of the CTMT is to connect a series of stimuli (numbers, expressed as numerals or in word form, and letters) in a specified order as fast as possible. The test includes five trails, each administered in numerical order. These include:

Trail 1—The examinee draws a line to connect the numbers 1 through 25 (each contained in a plain circle) in order.

Trail 2—The examinee draws a line to connect the numbers 1 through 25 in order. Each numeral is contained in a plain circle and twenty-nine empty distractor circles also appear on the page.

Trail 3—The examinee draws a line to connect the numbers 1 through 25 in order. Each numeral is contained in a plain circle. On the same page there are also thirteen empty distractor circles and 19 distractor circles containing irrelevant line drawings.

Trail 4—The examinee draws a line to connect the numbers 1 through 21 in order. Twelve of the numbers are presented as Arabic numerals (e.g., 1, 7), and each is contained in a plain circle; nine numbers are spelled out (e.g., Ten, Four) and contained in rectangular boxes.

Trail 5—The examinee draws a line to connect in alternating sequence the numbers 1 through 13 and the letters A through L. The examinee begins with 1 and then draws a line to A, then proceeds to 2, then B, and so on until all the numbers and letters are connected. Each of the numbers and letters is contained in a plain circle. Fifteen empty distractor circles appear on the same page.

The score derived for each trail is the number of seconds required to complete the task. Errors made by the examinee are not counted or scored, but they are corrected by the examiner and thus add to the completion time. Normative scores are provided in the form of *T*-scores, having a mean of 50 and a standard deviation of 10, along with their accompanying percentile ranks. *Z* scores and stanines are also available. The composite score is obtained by summing the *T*-scores from the individual trails and looking up that sum in the manual.

The CTMT is standardized on a nationwide sample of 1,664 persons from 19 states. Demographic characteristics of the sample included geographic area, gender, race, ethnicity, family income, parent education, and disability, and each matched 1998 U.S. Census data fairly closely (within 0 to 7 percentage points). Norms were collected for 13 age groups: full year from ages 11 to 16, combined ages 17 through 19, 10-year groupings for ages 20 through 69 (e.g., 20 through 29), and a 5-year groupings for 70 through 75. For the full year age groups (11 through 16) the number of participants in each group ranged from 79 to 106. For the remaining combined age groups, the number ranged from 104 to 205. Internal reliability coefficients for each individual trail ranged from .67 to .83 across all ages while the composite score has a reliability coefficient of .90 or higher at all ages. Test-retest reliabilities for a sample of 30 individuals tested one week apart ranged from .70 to .78 for the five trails and .84 for the composite. Validity evidence provided in the manual shows strong, consistent evidence for the CTMT.

REFERENCES

Plake, B. S., Impara, J. C., & Spies, R. A. (Eds.). (2003). *The fifteenth mental measurements yearbook.* Lincoln, NE: Buros Institute of Mental Measurements.

Reynold, C. R. R. (2002). *Comprehensive Trail Making Test.* Austin, TX: PRO-ED.

RON DUMONT
Fairleigh Dickinson University

JOHN O. WILLIS
Rivier College

COMPULSORY ATTENDANCE (AND STUDENTS WITH DISABILITIES)

Compulsory school attendance laws have been in effect in nearly every state and in most other parts of the western world for the bulk of the twentieth century. These laws require the parents or legal guardians of all children to send them to school or to provide an equivalent education. The ages of children for whom school attendance is compulsory varies as well, but includes children between the ages of 7 and 16 years in the vast majority of states. The courts have exempted some religious groups from the enforcement of compulsory attendance laws, notably the Amish nationwide and in some states the Mennonites. The states differ greatly in what constitutes a legal school under their compulsory attendance laws. Some states recognize only state-certified and supervised schools (public or private), while some allow children to attend noncertified church-supported schools. Others are even more liberal and allow home schooling accomplished by lay parents. Compulsory attendance laws have been the subject of much litigation since their initial enactment.

Many consider compulsory attendance laws to be an infringement on various rights granted to the general population in the first 10 amendments to the U.S. Constitution (the Bill of Rights). However, the courts have held, with minor religious exceptions, that the state has a compelling interest in the welfare of all children within its jurisdiction and that the provision for education under compulsory circumstances is an acceptable part of this compelling interest and is a legal extension of the police powers of the state. The full extent of the state's compelling interest in education has yet to be defined in adequate detail by the courts, but it is related to the provision of an education that allows individuals to become contributing members of society, preventing them from becoming burdens on the state.

Prior to the passage of the Education for All Handicapped Children Act of 1975 (PL 94-142), which required the states to make available to all disabled children a free, appropriate, public education, few states enforced their compulsory attendance laws where disabled children were involved. Many school districts throughout the country would not allow many children with disabilities to attend, and in many such instances, encouraged parents to keep these children at home. Many states remain lax in the enforcement of compulsory attendance statutes with regard to the handicapped. With the growing problem of delinquency in the United States, there has been a recent trend away from strict enforcement of truancy laws.

In most states, children with disabilities are included in the compulsory attendance laws and the failure (or refusal) of the parents or legal guardians to present these children for school attendance is likely actionable on civil and/or criminal bases in most states. However, school officials or child welfare workers will, in the typical case, have to take the lead in seeking the enforcement of compulsory attendance laws for children with disabilities. It is clear, however, that unless specifically exempted by the wording of the state statute, disabled children are required to attend school. What constitutes a school or an equivalent educational program may be different for the disabled than the nondisabled given the broad authority granted to multidisciplinary teams to diagnose and prescribe educational plans.

CECIL R. REYNOLDS
Texas A&M University
Second edition

KIMBERLY APPLEQUIST
*University of Colorado at
Colorado Springs*
Third edition

INDIVIDUALS WITH DISABILITIES EDUCATION IMPROVEMENT ACT OF 2004 (IDEIA)

COMPUTER-ASSISTED INSTRUCTION

Introduction

Not so long ago, the computer was a rare and exotic sight in American classrooms. Then, during the 1970s, many schools began acquiring computers and putting them to use for instruction, drill and practice, recordkeeping, and other applications.

The use of computers expanded rapidly during the 1980s. Between 1981 and the end of the decade:

- American schools acquired over two million computers.
- The number of schools owning computers increased from approximately 25 percent to virtually 100 percent.
- More than half the states began requiring—or at least recommending—preservice technology programs for all prospective teachers (Kinnaman, 1990).

Many educators, legislators, parents, and researchers have expressed concern about the educational effectiveness of using computers in schools. Because the acquisition of computer hardware and educational software programs involves a considerable monetary investment, these groups want assurance that computers in the schools are more than expensive and entertaining toys; they desire evidence that educational computer use truly enhances learning in demonstrable ways.

Fortunately, a great deal of research has been conducted during the 1970s, 1980s, and early 1990s on the effects of computer use on student achievement, attitudes, and other variables, such as learning rate. This research covers a wide range of topics, from computerized learning activities that supplement conventional instruction, to computer programming, to computerized recordkeeping, to the development of databases, to writing using word processors, and other applications.

The main focus of this report is the most commonly used and most frequently researched kind of educational computer use—computer-assisted instruction (CAI). Findings about other educational computer applications are presented as they relate to this main focus.

Definitions

It will be helpful, before discussing the research findings, to offer some definitions of CAI and other kinds of learning activities involving computers. As Kulik, Kulik, and Bangert-Drowns point out in their 1985 research summary, "the terminology in the area is open to dispute" (p. 59). This is putting it mildly. Those seeking to make sense of the array of terms used by educators and researchers— computer-assisted instruction, computer-based education, computer-based instruction, computer-enriched instruction, computer-managed instruction—can easily become confused. The following definitions are a synthesis of those offered by Bangert-Drowns et al. (1985), Batey (1986), Grimes (1977), and represent commonly accepted (though certainly not the only) definitions of these terms:

- Computer-based education (CBE) and computer-based instruction (CBI) are the broadest terms and can refer to virtually any kind of computer use in educational settings, including drill and practice, tutorials, simulations, instructional management, supplementary exercises, programming, database development, writing using word processors, and other applications. These terms may refer either to stand-alone computer learning activities or to computer activities that reinforce material introduced and taught by teachers.

- Computer-assisted instruction (CAI) is a narrower term and most often refers to drill-and-practice, tutorial, or simulation activities offered either by themselves or as supplements to traditional, teacher-directed instruction.

- Computer-managed instruction (CMI) can refer either to the use of computers by school staff to organize student data and make instructional decisions or to activities in which the computer evaluates students' test performance, guides them to appropriate instructional resources, and keeps records of their progress.

- Computer-enriched instruction (CEI) is defined as learning activities in which computers (1) generate data at the students' request to illustrate relationships in models of social or physical reality, (2) execute programs developed by the students, or (3) provide general enrichment in relatively unstructured exercises designed to stimulate and motivate students.

The CAI Research Base

The findings offered in this summary emerge from an analysis of the 59 research reports cited in the Key References section of the bibliography. Each of these reports documents some relationship(s) between computer-based learning and student outcomes. Twenty-eight are research studies, 22 are reviews, and 9 are meta-analyses of research studies. Twelve of the documents focus on elementary students, 19 are concerned with secondary students, 7 cover the elementary-secondary range, 5 involve subjects spanning the elementary-postsecondary range, and the age/grade levels of subjects are not specified in 16 of the reports.

Most of the studies involved American students, but Israeli and Canadian subjects are also represented. Other specific populations serving as subjects in the documents include economically disadvantaged students (4), special education students (5), remedial students (2), and Hispanic students (2). The rest of the documents either concerned general student populations or did not specify characteristics of their subjects.

The 59 reports were concerned with the effects of one or more of the following types of educational computer use on student outcomes: CAI (35), CBE in general (15), the use of word processors for written composition (5), computer-managed instruction (3), programming (2), and simulations (4).

The effects of computer use on a large number of outcome areas were examined, including academic achievement in general (30), mathematics (13), language arts (8), reading

(3), science (2), problem-solving skills (2), and health and social studies (1 each). Studies also focused on students' attitudes toward the content of courses in which computers were used (21), computers themselves (19), school in general (6), the quality of instruction in courses with computer activities (4), and themselves as learners (4). Other outcome areas include learning rate (10), learning retention (9), locus of control and motivation, computer literacy, and cooperation/helping (4 each).

Research Findings

Computer Use and Student Achievement

The single best-supported finding in the research literature is that the use of CAI as a supplement to traditional, teacher-directed instruction produces achievement effects superior to those obtained with traditional instruction alone. Generally speaking, this finding holds true for students of different ages and abilities and for learning in different curricular areas. As summarized in Stennett's 1985 review of reviews, "well-designed and implemented D&P [drill-and-practice] or tutorial CAI, used as a supplement to traditional instruction, produces an educationally significant improvement in students' final examination achievement" (p. 7).

(Research support: Bahr and Rieth, 1989; Bangert-Drowns, 1985; Bangert-Drowns et al., 1985; Batey, 1986; Bracey, 1987; Braun, 1990; Burns & Bozeman, 1981; Capper & Copple, 1985; Edwards et al., 1975; Ehman & Glen, 1987; Gore et al., 1989; Grimes, 1977; Hawley, Fletcher, & Piele, 1986; Horton, Lovitt, & Slocum, 1988; Kann, 1987; Kulik, Kulik, & Bangert-Drowns, 1985; Martin, 1973; Mevarech & Rich, 1985; Mokros & Tinker, 1987; Okey, 1985; Ragosta, Holland, & Jamison, 1982; Rapaport & Savard, 1980; Rupe, 1986.

Some writers also reported on research that compared the effects of CAI alone with those produced by conventional instruction alone. Here, results are too mixed to permit any firm conclusion. Some inquires have found CAI superior, some have found conventional instruction superior, and still others have found no difference between them (Capper & Copple, 1985; Edwards et al., 1975; Rapaport & Savard, 1980).

Other researchers and reviewers compared the achievement effects produced by all forms of computer-based instruction (sometimes alone and sometimes as a supplement to traditional instruction) as compared with the effects of traditional instruction alone. While the research support is not as strong as that indicating the superiority of CAI, the evidence nevertheless indicates that CBE approaches as a whole produce higher achievement than traditional instruction by itself (Bangert-Drowns, 1985; Bangert-Drowns, et al., 1985; Braun, 1990; Hasselbring, 1984; Kulik, 1983, 1985; Kulik, Bangert, & Williams, 1983; Kulik & Kulik, 1987; Roblyer et al., 1988).

This group of findings supports the conclusion drawn by Dalton and Hannafin in their 1988 study to the effect that "while both traditional and computer-based delivery systems have valuable roles in supporting instruction, they are of greatest value when complementing one another" (p. 32).

Researchers concerned with student writing outcomes have determined that writing performance is superior when the teaching approach emphasizes "writing as a process," rather than focusing only on the end product—the finished composition. The writing-as-a-process approach encourages students to engage in prewriting activities, followed by drafting, revising, editing, and final publication, with each step receiving considerable attention and often feedback from teachers or peer editors.

Word processing programs, with their capability to add, delete, and rearrange text, are seen as being far more congruent with the writing process than more laborious pencil-and-paper approaches. And indeed, most research in this area indicates that the use of word processors in writing programs leads to better writing outcomes than the use of paper-and-pencil or conventional typewriters. Specific positive outcomes associated with the use of word processors in writing include:

- Longer written samples
- Greater variety of word usage
- More variety of sentence structure
- More accurate mechanics and spelling
- More substantial revision
- Greater responsiveness to teacher and peer feedback
- Better understanding of the writing process
- Better attitudes toward writing
- Freedom from the problem of illegible handwriting (Batey, 1986; Bialo & Sivin, 1990; Collins & Sommers, 1984; Dickinson, 1986; Kinnaman, 1990; MacGregor, 1986; Rodriguez & Rodriguez, 1986).

Researchers are careful to point out that these desirable outcomes are obtained when computers are used as part of a holistic, writing-as-a-process approach. Only using computers for drill and practice on isolated subskills, such as grammar and mechanics, is not associated with improved writing achievement.

Learning Rate

As well as enabling students to achieve at higher levels, researchers have also found that CAI enhances learning rate. Student learning rate is faster with CAI than with conventional instruction. In some research studies, the students learned the same amount of material in less time than the traditionally instructed students; in others, they learned more material in the same time. While most researchers don't specify how much faster CAI students learn, the work of Capper and Copple (1985) led them to the conclusion that CAI users sometimes learn as much as 40 percent faster than those receiving traditional, teacher-directed instruction (Batey, 1986; Capper & Copple, 1985; Edwards et al., 1975; Grimes, 1977; Hasselbring, 1984; Kulik, 1983, 1985; Kulik et al., 1983; Kulik & Kulik, 1987; Rapaport & Savard, 1980; Rupe, 1986; Stennett, 1985).

Retention of Learning

If students receiving CAI learn better and faster than students receiving conventional instruction alone, do they also retain their learning better? The answer, according to researchers who have conducted comparative studies of learning retention, is yes. In this research, student scores on delayed tests indicate that the retention of content learned using CAI is superior to retention following traditional instruction alone (Capper & Copple, 1985; Grimes, 1977; Kulik, 1985; Kulik et al., 1983; Kulik et al., 1985; Rupe, 1986; Stennett, 1985).

Attitudes

Much of the research that examines the effects of CAI and other computer applications on student learning outcomes also investigates effects upon student attitudes. This line of inquiry has brought most researchers to the conclusion that the use of CAI leads to more positive student attitudes than the use of conventional instruction. This general finding has emerged from studies of the effects of CAI on student attitudes toward:

- Computers and the use of computers in education (Batey, 1986; Ehman & Glen, 1987; Hasselbring, 1984; Hess & Tenezakis, 1971; Kulik, 1983, 1985; Kulik et al., 1983; Roblyer, 1988)
- Course content/subject matter (Batey, 1986; Braun, 1990; Dalton & Hannafin, 1988; Ehman & Glen, 1987; Hounshell & Hill, 1989; Rapaport & Savard, 1980; Roblyer et al., 1988; Rodriguez & Rodriguez, 1986; Stennett, 1985)
- Quality of instruction (Kulik et al., 1983; Kulik & Kulik, 1987; Rupe, 1986)
- School in general (Batey, 1986; Bialo & Sivin, 1990; Ehman & Glen, 1987; Roblyer et al., 1988)
- Self-as-learner (Mevarech & Rich, 1985; Robertson et al., 1987; Rupe, 1986).

Other Beneficial Effects

The effects of CAI on other student outcomes have not been as extensively researched as CAI's effects on achievement, learning rate, retention, and attitudes. Some researchers have, however, investigated CAI's influence on other variables and found it to confer benefits on:

- *Locus of control.* Capper and Copple (1985), Kinnaman (1990), and Louie (1985) found that CAI students have more of an internal locus of control/sense of self-efficacy than conventionally instructed students.
- *Attendance.* CAI students had better attendance in Capper and Copple's 1985 study, Rupe's 1986 review.
- *Motivation / time-on-task.* Capper and Copple (1985) found that CAI students had higher rates of time-on-task than traditionally instructed controls.
- *Cooperation / collaboration.* Cooperative, prosocial behavior was greater with CAI in the work of Dickinson (1986); Mevarech, Stern, and Levita (1987); and Rupe (1986).

CAI and Different Student Populations

Is CAI more effective with some student populations than others? Many researchers have conducted comparative analyses to answer this question and have produced findings in several areas.

Younger versus older students. Most comparative studies have shown that CAI is more beneficial for younger students than for older ones. While research shows CAI to be beneficial to students in general, the degree of impact decreases from the elementary to secondary to postsecondary levels (Bangert-Drowns, 1985; Bangert-Drowns et al., 1985; Becker, 1990; Bracey, 1987; Ehman & Glen, 1987; Hasselbring, 1984; Kulik et al., 1985; Okey, 1985; Stennett, 1985).

Lower-achieving versus higher-achieving students. These comparisons show that CAI is more effective with lower-achieving students than with higher-achieving ones. Again, both lower- and higher-achieving students benefit from CAI. However, the comparatively greater benefits experienced by lower-achieving students, like those experienced by younger students, are largely due to the need these groups have for elements common to the majority of CAI programs—extensive drill and practice, privacy, and immediate feedback and reinforcement (Bangert-Drowns, 1985; Bangert-Drowns et al., 1985; Edwards et al., 1975; Kinnaman, 1990; Kulik et al., 1985; Martin, 1973; Okey, 1985; Roblyer, 1988).

Economically disadvantaged versus higher-SES students. Researchers note that CAI confers greater benefits on economically disadvantaged students than those from more privileged backgrounds. Lower SES students, too, benefit greatly from opportunities to interact privately with CAI drill-and-practice and tutorial programs (Bangert-Drowns et al., 1985; Becker, 1990; Mevarech & Rich, 1985; Ragosta, Holland, & Jamison, 1982; Stennett, 1985).

Lower-versus higher-cognitive outcomes. Closely related to the previous is the finding that CAI is more effective for teaching lower-cognitive material than higher-cognitive material. This research makes essentially the same point— that CAI is particularly effective for reinforcing the basic, fact-oriented learning most often engaged in by younger, lowerachieving, and/or lower SES students (Ehman & Glen, 1987; Hasselbring, 1984)

Disabled learners. Research conducted with learning disabled, mentally retarded, hearing impaired, emotionally disturbed, and language-disordered students indicates that their achievement levels are greater with CAI than with conventional instruction alone. In some of this research, disabled CAI students even outperformed conventionally taught, nondisabled students (Bahr & Rieth, 1989; Bialo & Sivin, 1980; Hall, McLoughlin, & Bialozor, 1989; Horton, Lovitt, & Slocum, 1988; Schmidt et al., 1985–86)

Males versus females. This comparison was not addressed by enough researchers to draw firm conclusions. The 1988 meta-analysis of 82 studies of CBE conducted by Roblyer and colleagues concluded that effect differences slightly favor boys over girls, with differences falling short of statistical significance.

CAI and Different Curricular Areas

A few researchers undertook to compare the effectiveness of CAI in different curricular areas. Their findings, though not conclusive, indicate that CAI activities are most effective in the areas of science and foreign languages, followed, in descending order of effectiveness, by activities in mathematics, reading, language arts, and English as a Second Language (ESL), with CAI activities in ESL found to be largely ineffective (Capper & Copple, 1985; Kulik et al., 1985, Roblyer et al., 1988; Rodriguez & Rodriguez, 1986).

Why Students like CAI

An earlier section of this report offers research evidence showing that CAI enhances student attitudes toward several aspects of schooling. Some researchers took these investigations a step further by asking students what it is about CAI that they like. The following is a list of reasons given by students for liking CAI activities and/or favoring them over traditional learning. These student preferences also contribute to our understanding of why CAI enhances achievement.

Students say they like working with computers because computers:

- Are infinitely patient
- Never get tired
- Never get frustrated or angry
- Allow students to work privately
- Never forget to correct or praise
- Are fun and entertaining
- Individualize learning
- Are self-paced
- Do not embarrass students who make mistakes
- Make it possible to experiment with different options
- Give immediate feedback
- Are more objective than teachers
- Free teachers for more meaningful contact with students
- Are impartial to race or ethnicity
- Are great motivators
- Give a sense of control over learning
- Are excellent for drill and practice
- Call for using sight, hearing, and touch
- Teach in small increments
- Help students improve their spelling
- Build proficiency in computer use, which will be valuable later in life
- Eliminate the drudgery of doing certain learning activities by hand (e.g., drawing graphs)
- Work rapidly—closer to the rate of human thought (Bialo & Sivin, 1980; Braun, 1990; Lawton & Gerschner, 1982; Mokros & Tinker, 1987; Robertson et al., 1987; Rupe, 1986).

Many of these items point to students' appreciation of the immediate, objective, and positive feedback provided by computer learning activities by comparison with teacher-directed activities. As Robertson and colleagues (1987) point out:

> This reduction in negative reinforcement allows the student to learn through trial and error at his or her own pace. Therefore, positive attitudes can be protected and enhanced. (p. 314)

Cost-Effectiveness

While cost considerations are not a major focus of this report, it is worth noting that some of the research on effectiveness also addressed the cost-effectiveness of CAI and other computer applications. Ragosta, Holland, and Jamison (1982) concluded that equal amounts of time of CAI reinforcement and the more-expensive one-to-one tutoring produced equal achievement effects. Niemiec, Sikorski, and Walberg (1989) also found CAI activities significantly more cost-effective than tutoring and suggested that computers be used more extensively in schools. And in their 1986 study of costs, effects, and utility of CAI, Hawley, Fletcher, and Piele noted that the cost differences between CAI and traditional instruction were insignificant and concluded that "the microcomputer-assisted instruction was the cost-effective alternative of choice" for both grades addressed in the study (p. 22).

Summary

The research base reviewed in preparation for this report indicates that:

- The use of CAI as a supplement to conventional instruction produces higher achievement than the use of conventional instruction alone.
- Research is inconclusive regarding the comparative effectiveness of conventional instruction alone and CAI alone.
- Computer-based education (CAI and other computer applications) produce higher achievement than conventional instruction alone.
- Student use of word processors to develop writing skills leads to higher-quality written work than other writing methods (paper and pencil, conventional typewriters).
- Students learn material faster with CAI than with conventional instruction alone.
- Students retain what they have learned better with CAI than with conventional instruction alone.
- The use of CAI leads to more positive attitudes toward computers, course content, quality of instruction, school in general, and self-as-learner than the use of conventional instruction alone.
- The use of CAI is associated with other beneficial outcomes, including greater internal locus of control, school attendance, motivation/time-on-task, and student-student cooperation and collaboration than the use of conventional instruction alone.
- CAI is more beneficial for younger students than older ones.
- CAI is more beneficial with lower-achieving students than with higher-achieving ones.
- Economically disadvantaged students benefit more from CAI than students from higher socioeconomic backgrounds.
- CAI is more effective for teaching lower-cognitive material than higher-cognitive material.

- Most handicapped students, including learning disabled, mentally retarded, hearing impaired, emotionally disturbed, and language disordered, achieve at higher levels with CAI than with conventional instruction alone.

- There are no significant differences in the effectiveness of CAI with male and female students.

- Students' fondness for CAI activities centers around the immediate, objective, and positive feedback provided by these activities.

- CAI activities appear to be at least as cost-effective as—and sometimes more cost-effective than—other instructional methods, such as teacher-directed instruction and tutoring.

"Most programs of computer-based instruction evaluated in the past," wrote Kulik and Kulik in 1987, "have produced positive effects on student learning and attitudes. Further programs for developing and implementing computer-based instruction should therefore be encouraged." Based on review of the research evidence published both before and after Kulik and Kulik's paper, the present report strongly supports this conclusion.

REFERENCES

Bahr, C. M., & Rieth, H. J. (1989). The effects of instructional computer games and drill and practice software on learning disabled students' mathematics achievement. *Computers in the Schools, 6*(3/4), 87–101.

Bangert-Drowns, R. L. (1985, March–April). *Meta-analysis of findings on computer-based education with precollege students.* Paper presented at the Annual Meeting of the American Educational Research Association, Chicago, IL.

Bangert-Drowns, R. L., Kulik, J. A., & Kulik, C. C. (1985). Effectiveness of computer-based education in secondary schools. *Journal of Computer-Based Instruction, 12*(3), 59–68.

Batey, A. (1986, December). *Building a case for computers in elementary classrooms: A summary of what the researchers and the practitioners are saying.* Paper presented at the Second Leadership in Computer Education Seminar, Seattle, WA.

Becker, H. J. (1987). *The impact of computer use on children's learning: What research has shown and what it has not.* Paper presented at the Annual Meeting of the American Educational Research Association, Washington, DC.

Becker, H. J. (1990). *When powerful tools meet conventional beliefs and institutional constraints: National survey findings on computer use by American teachers.* Baltimore: Johns Hopkins University, Center for Social Organization of Schools.

Bialo, E., & Sivin, J. (1980). *Report on the effectiveness of microcomputers in schools.* Washington, DC: Software Publishers Association.

Bracey, G. W. (1987). Computer-assisted instruction: What the research shows. *Electronic Learning, 7*(3), 22–23.

Braun, L. (1990). *Vision: TEST (technologically enriched schools of tomorrow) final report: Recommendations for American educational decision makers.* Eugene, OR: The International Society for Technology in Education.

Burns, P. K., & Bozeman, W. C. (1981). Computer-assisted instruction and mathematics achievement: Is there a relationship? *Educational Technology, 21*(10), 32–39.

Campbell, D. L., Peck, D. L., Horn, C. J., and Leigh, R. K. (1987). Comparison of computer-assisted instruction and print drill performance: A research note. *Educational Communication and Technology Journal, 35*(2), 95–103.

Capper, J., & Copple, C. (1985). *Computer use in education: Research review and instructional implications.* Washington, DC: Center for Research into Practice.

Collins, J. L., & Sommers, E. A. (Eds.). (1984). *Writing online: Using computers in the teaching of writing.* Montclair, NJ: Boynton/Cook.

Dalton, D. W., & Hannafin, M. J. (1988). The effects of computer-assisted and traditional mastery methods on computation accuracy and attitudes. *Journal of Educational Research, 82*(1), 27–33.

Dickinson, D. K. (1986). Cooperation, collaboration and a computer: Integrating a computer into a first–second grade writing program. *Research in the Teaching of English, 20*(4), 357–78.

Edwards, J., Norton, S., Taylor, S., Weiss, M., & Dusseldorp, R. (1975). How effective is CAI? A review of the research. *Educational Leadership, 33*(2), 147–53.

Ehman, L. H., & Glen, A. D. (1987). *Computer-based education in the social studies.* Bloomington: Indiana University.

Gore, D. A., Morrison, G. N., Maas, M. L., and Anderson, E. A. (1989). A study of teaching reading skills to the young child using microcomputer-assisted instruction. *Journal of Educational Computing Research, 5*(2), 179–85.

Grimes, D. M. (1977). *Computers for learning: The uses of computer assisted instruction (CAI) in California public schools.* Sacramento: California State Department of Education.

Hall, E. R., McLaughlin, T. F., & Bialozor, R. C. (1989). The effects of computer-assisted drill and practice on spelling performance with mildly handicapped students. *Reading Improvement, 26*(1), 43–49.

Hasselbring, T. (1984). *Research on the effectiveness of computer-based instruction: A review* (Technical Report No. 84.1.3). Nashville, TN: George Peabody College for Teachers, Learning Technology Center.

Hawley, D. E., Fletcher, J. D., & Piele, P. K. (1986). *Costs, effects, and utility of microcomputer-assisted instruction.* Eugene: University of Oregon.

Hess, R. D., & Tenezakis, M. D. (1971). *Selected findings from the computer as a socializing agent: Some socioaffective outcomes of CAI.* Stanford, CA: Stanford University School of Education.

Horton, S. V., Lovitt, T. C., & Slocum, T. (1988). Teaching geography to high school students with academic deficits: Effects of a computerized map tutorial. *Learning Disability Quarterly, 11*(4), 371–79.

Hounshell, P. B., & Hill, S. R., Jr. (1989). The microcomputer and achievement and attitudes in high school biology. *Journal of Research in Science Teaching, 26*(6), 543–549.

Kann, L. K. (1987). Effects of computer-assisted instruction on selected interaction skills related to responsible sexuality. *Journal of School Health, 57*(7), 282–287.

Kinnaman, D. E. (1990). What's the research telling us? *Classroom Computer Learning, 10*(6), 31–35; 38–39.

Kinzie, M. B., Sullivan, H. J., & Berdel, R. L. (1988). Learner control and achievement in science computer assisted instruction. *Journal of Educational Psychology, 80*(3), 299–303.

Kulik, J. (1985, April). *Consistencies in findings on computer-based education.* Paper presented at the Annual Meeting of the American Educational Research Association.

Kulik, J. A. (1983). Synthesis of research on computer-based instruction. *Educational Leadership, 41*(1), 19–21.

Kulik, J. A., Bangert, R. L., & Williams, G. W. (1983). Effects of computer-based teaching on secondary school students. *Journal of Educational Psychology, 75*(1), 19–26.

Kulik, J. A., & Kulik, C. C. (1987, February–March). *Computer-based instruction: What 200 evaluations say.* Paper presented at the Annual Convention of the Association for Educational Communications and Technology, Atlanta, GA.

Kulik, J. A., Kulik, C. C., & Bangert-Drowns, R. L. (1985). Effectiveness of computer-based education in elementary schools. *Computers in Human Behavior, 1*(1), 59–74.

Lawton, J., & Gerschner, V. T. (1982). A review of the literature on attitudes towards computers and computerized instruction. *Journal of Research and Development in Education, 16*(1), 50–55.

Lopez, C. L., & Harper, M. (1989). The relationship between learner control of CAI and locus of control among hispanic students. *Educational Technology Research and Development, 37*(4), 19–28.

Louie, S. (1985) *Locus of control among computer-using school children. A report of a pilot study.* Tucson, AZ: National Advisory Council for Computer Implementation in Schools.

MacGregor, S. K. (1986). Computer-assisted writing environments for elementary students. *Proceedings of the National Educational Computing Conference.* Eugene, OR: International Council for Computers in Education.

Martin, G. R. (1973). *The 1972–73 Drill and Practice Study* (TIES Research Project Report) St. Paul: Minnesota School District Data Processing Joint Board.

Mevarech, A. R., & Rich, Y. (1985). Effects of computer assisted mathematics instruction on disadvantaged pupils' cognitive and affective development. *Journal of Educational Research, 79*(1), 5–11.

Mevarech, Z. R., Stern, D., & Levita, I. (1987). To cooperate or not to cooperate in CAI: That is the question. *Journal of Educational Research, 80*(3), 164–167.

Mikkelsen, V. P., Gerlach, G., & Robinson, L. (1989). Can elementary school students be taught touchtyping in unsupervised environments? *Reading Improvement, 26*(1), 58–63.

Mokros, J. R., & Tinker, R. F. (1987). The impact of microcomputer-based labs on children's ability to interpret graphs. *Journal of Research in Science Teaching, 24*(4), 369–383.

Okey, J. R. (1985, April). *The effectiveness of computer-based education: A review.* Paper presented at the Annual Meeting of the National Association for Research in Science Teaching.

Ragosta, M., Holland, P. W., & Jamison, D. T. (1982). *Computer-assisted instruction and compensatory education: The ETS/LAUSD study. The executive summary and policy implications.* Princeton, NJ: Educational Testing Service.

Rapaport, P., & Savard, W. G. (1980). *Computer-assisted instruction* (Topic Summary Report). Portland, OR: Northwest Regional Educational Laboratory.

Robertson, E. B., Ladewig, B. H., Strickland, M. P., & Boschung, M. D. (1987). Enhancement of self-esteem through the use of computer-assisted instruction. *Journal of Educational Research, 80*(5), 314–316.

Roblyer, M. D. (1988). The effectiveness of microcomputers in education: A review of the research from 1980–1987. *Technological Horizons in Education Journal, 16*(2), 85–89.

Roblyer, M. D. (1989). *The impact of microcomputer-based instruction on teaching and learning: A review of recent research.* Syracuse, NY: ERIC Clearinghouse on Information Resources.

Roblyer, M. D., Castine, W. H., & King, F. J. (1988). *Assessing the impact of computer-based instruction: A review of recent research.* New York: Haworth Press.

Rodriguez, D., & Rodriguez, J. J. (1986). *Teaching writing with a word processor, grades 7–13.* Urbana, IL: ERIC Clearinghouse on Reading and Communication Skills and National Council of Teachers of English.

Rupe, V. S. (1986). *A study of computer-assisted instruction: Its uses, effects, advantages, and limitations.* South Bend: Indiana University.

Stennett, R. G. (1985). *Computer assisted instruction: A review of the reviews.* London: The Board of Education for the City of London. (ERIC Document Reproductive Service No. ED 260687)

KATHLEEN COTTON
*Northwestern Regional
Education Laboratory,
Portland, Oregon*

COMPUTERIZED AXIAL TOMOGRAPHY

See CAT SCAN.

COMPUTER LITERACY

Because state of the art of computer technology and the Internet is constantly changing, so too is the definition of computer literacy. In the past, computer literacy was virtually synonymous with learning to write computer programs. Typically, computer novices gained an understanding of the machines by writing programs in BASIC (Beginner's All-Purpose Symbolic Instructional Code). The major thrust in computer literacy today has shifted away from programming and toward the applications of computer technology in various settings, particularly the home, school, and office. The primary reason for this shift has been the increased availability of good software, inexpensive hardware, and access to the internet.

The problem of defining computer literacy is compounded by the fact that individuals with different educational levels have differing computer needs. Meeting these needs requires varying levels of expertise. For example, for the high-school student, computer literacy encompasses the following areas: basic knowledge of how to operate a computer; an understanding of how computers are used in work and for leisure; an appreciation of the ethical, social, and economic ramifications of computer usage; and an ability to use computers and the Internet for instruction, information collection and retrieval, word processing, decision making, and problem solving.

For teachers, computer literacy means being knowledgeable about the capabilities of hardware and software and understanding how computers and the Internet can enhance students' educational experiences. For those who work with disabled students, computer literacy also implies an understanding of the ways in which technology can be used to improve services to special needs learners. Specifically, to be computer literate, special educators should acquire the following competencies:

1. Understand the fundamental operation and care of computers and software.

2. Become fluent in the basic terminology of computer technology.

3. Be able to apply computer technology to improve instruction.

4. Be able to use computers for management of instruction.

5. Understand how microprocessor-based technology can compensate for motoric, sensory, and cognitive disabilities.

6. Become proficient in evaluating software and hardware.

7. Be able to use an authoring system or language to develop instructional programs.

8. Understand the principles of telecommunication, especially as they apply to the improvement of instruction and learning.

9. Be able to access and utilize information retrieved from the Internet.

Educators continue to debate the inclusion of computer programming as a component of computer literacy. Many educators, particularly those who work with young children and/or gifted and talented children, believe that teaching students to write programs can help them to develop problem-solving skills that can be applied to real-life experiences. For example, Papert (1980) mentions that the language Logo was designed by Piagetian psychologists to help children "think about thinking" (i.e., to understand the steps they go through in solving a problem).

For teachers and teacher educators, however, the development of authoring systems and languages has reduced the need for learning an all-purpose language such as BASIC. An authoring system is a highly structured template that allows computer users with a minimal understanding of computer technology to develop computer-assisted tutorials and drill and practice routines. Proficiency in high-level languages such as PASCAL or "C" would be left to educators who are interested in designing state-of-the-art instructional and management software (Cartwright, 1984).

REFERENCES

Cartwright, G. P. (1984). Technology competencies for special education doctoral students. *Teacher Education and Special Education, 7,* 82–87.

Computer competency. (1983, May). *Chronicle of higher education,* p. 5.

Papert, S. (1980). *Mindstorms.* New York: Basic Books.

Schery, T., & Spaw, L. (1993, December 14). *Computer talk: Helping young handicapped children communicate.* Paper presented at the CEC Conference, San Diego, CA.

ELIZABETH MCCLELLAN
*Council for Exceptional
Children*

COMPUTER-ASSISTED INSTRUCTION

COMPUTERS AND EDUCATION, AN INTERNATIONAL JOURNAL

Computers and Education is a scholarly journal published by the Pergamon division of Elsevier Publishing. Since 1977, the journal has provided a forum for communication in the use of all forms of computing. *Computers and Education* publishes papers in the language of the academic computer user on educational and training system development using techniques from and applications in many knowledge domains including: graphics, simulation, computer-aided design, computer integrated manufacture, and artificial intelligence and its applications. The journal is published 8 times a year and subscriptions can be ordered online from www.elsevier.nl/inca/publications/store/.

COMPUTERS IN HUMAN BEHAVIOR

Computers in Human Behavior is a scholarly journal devoted to research that attempts to articulate the relationship between psychology, the science of human behavior, and technological advances in computer science. Articles are concerned with advances in research design and the technology of research, but also with the effects of computers on the topics chosen for study by psychologists, such as the use of health promotion programs to promote behavioral change, and use of virtual reality programs. Changes in clinical practice, ethics, and standards related to computers are also examined. Articles appearing in the journal have also included studies of the equivalence of testing conditions (computerized vs. standard administration), computerized interpretation of tests. The latter two areas are of interest to special educators as several articles have addressed placement decisions and educational diagnosis using computer programs to interpret tests. *Computers in Human Behavior* is a Pergamon Press journal; it began publication in 1985.

REFERENCES

Bosworth, K., Gustafson, D. H., & Hawkins, R. P. (1994). The BARN system and impact of adolescent health promotion via computer. *Computers in Human Behavior, 10,* 4, 467–482.

Riva, G. (1998). Virtual environment for body image modification: Virtual reality system for the treatment of body image disturbances. *Computers in Human Behavior, 14,* 3, 477–490.

CECIL R. REYNOLDS
Texas A&M University

COMPUTER USE WITH STUDENTS WITH DISABILITIES

For disabled persons, computers have three main functions: compensation for disabilities, management, and instructional delivery.

In terms of compensation for disabilities, one of the most exciting aspects of computer technology is the use of augmentative devices for communication and control. Computers help users overcome communication problems associated with limited mobility and sensory impairment. To increase the speed and accuracy of using computers, engineers and educators have developed special input and output devices. Innovative input devices include voice recognition, speech synthesizers (Schery & Spaw, 1993), the mouse, joysticks and game paddles, mechanical keyboard aids such as guards, mouths, headsticks, and splints. Examples of computer output devices are synthetic speech, Blissymbols, tactile display (Opticon), braille, and portable computer printers (Brady, 1982).

For individuals with cerebral palsy, amyotrophic lateral sclerosis, or severe paralysis, one of the biggest problems of computer usage is the multiple simultaneous key strokes required to run many pieces of standard software. To take advantage of a computer's capacity to control the environment, a person with limited mobility must have an adaptive firmware card. The card is a device that enables a person with limited mobility to run software by activating a single switch (Schwedja & Vanderheiden, 1982). Single switches and expanded keyboards require only slight movement, such as the blinking of an eye.

Access to standard software allows disabled individuals to use computers for information management. The four primary areas of information management are word processing, data base management, financial management, and telecommunication. Word processing programs allow users to draft, edit, and print text with relative ease. Changing margins and moving sentences or paragraphs are a matter of a few key strokes. Learning-disabled students can use word processing programs to overcome some of the problems associated with writing and spelling (Arms, 1984). Database management programs are used to store, sort, and retrieve large amounts of information. In special education, administrators and teachers use database management programs to file information such as students' names, addresses, birth dates, disabilities, and test scores. Financial management programs such as spreadsheets allow users to create, monitor, and change budgets. Other programs help with checkbook balancing and income tax preparation.

With the use of the Internet, computer users have access to virtually limitless sources of information. Subscribers can access stock market reports, make travel reservations, obtain up-to-the-minute weather reports, or search through large bibliographic databases and web sites for information on a given topic.

Word processing, data base management, financial management, and telecommunications packages have reached a high level of sophistication. Users can now take the information from one program and load it into another. If, for example, a user wanted to include a budget in a manuscript, he or she could load the information from a spreadsheet program into the text of a word processing program. Or, for example, a homebound individual could compose text on the word processor and send it to a teacher or other interested party by email.

In addition to the functions that allow computers to aid in communication and information management, computers have certain characteristics that enhance the delivery of instruction. Interaction means that computers can perform many of the functions that are typically performed by the teacher such as providing immediate feedback. Software can be designed so that rates of response and level of difficulty can be varied according to the student. One of the characteristics that tends to motivate students is branching capability (i.e., the capability of moving from one part of a program to another). Branching allows learners to decide whether they need to repeat material or move on to new material. Moreover, computers are tireless; they do not become irritated when asked to repeat information or activities.

REFERENCES

Arms, V. M. (1984). A dyslexic can compose a computer. *Educational Technology, 24,* 39–41.

Brady, M. (1982). The Trace Center International Hardware/Software Registry: Programs for handicapped students. *Journal of Special Education Technology, 5,* 16–21.

Gibbons, A. S. (1993). The future of computer-managed instruction (CMI). *Educational Technology, 33,* 5, 7–11.

McClellan, E. (1984). Introduction to microcomputers. In E. McClellan (Ed.), *Microcomputer applications in special education* (pp. 1–21). Reston, VA: Council for Exceptional Children.

Schery, T., & Spaw, L. (1993, December 14). *Computer talk: Helping young handicapped children communicate.* Paper presented at the Council for Exceptional Children Conference, San Diego, CA.

Schwejda, P., & Vanderheiden, G. (1982). Adaptive-firmware card for the Apple II. *Byte, 7,* 276–314.

ELIZABETH MCCLELLAN
*Council for Exceptional
Children*

COMPUTER LITERACY

CONCEPT FORMATION

The term concept is used to describe one of the ways the human mind organizes the tremendous amounts of data with which it is bombarded. As Ausubel (1968) points out:

> Anyone who pauses long enough to give the problem some serious thought cannot escape the conclusion that man lives in a world of concepts, rather than a world of objects, events, and situations. . . . Reality, figuratively speaking, is experienced through a conceptual or categorical filter. (p. 505)

A concept would appear to be a mental construct that serves to group together similar entities. Having knowledge of a concept means having at least knowledge of the common elements that define inclusion or exclusion of an entity from a category. The presence of a concept is tested by observing which objects are placed in the same category or are acted on similarly. The individual carrying out such an activity may or may not have any idea what the concept is that he or she is using for categorization, nor what the common elements may be.

There are often confusions between the ideas of concept and language. It is not an uncommon approach to define a concept as "something about an idea expressed in words of our language" (Platt, 1963, p. 21). However, it is clear that animals as well as humans have concepts (Humphrey, 1984). A dog does not react to an unfamiliar cat each time it sees one as if it were a unique object. Rather, it behaves toward the cat based on its past experiences with other cats. The dog, then, must have some concept of cats.

The relationship between a concept and language is a culturally contextual and problematical one, however. Gagne (1970), for example, has argued that there are two types of concepts, concrete ones such as "dog," which are based on direct empirical experience, and those such as "uncle" or "democracy" which cannot exist without language. It is further argued by some that the way language organizes and categorizes information actually effects the way one perceives incoming data. For example, different languages break up the color spectrum differently. A number of studies have been conducted to determine whether individuals from different cultures actually perceive colors differently, based on their language.

Two general approaches for concept formation have been described (Martorella, 1972). The first is inductive, the second deductive. Concepts learned inductively start with a group of facts, data, or concepts that are already understood. Through the use of certain intellectual skills, new, more abstract concepts are developed. For example, to assist a child in learning the rule that "e" in a VCVe word usually makes the vowel long, the child could compare two lists of similar words, one containing the final "e," the other not. The deductive approach, on the other hand, begins by presenting the more abstract principle. The learner develops an understanding of the principle through repeated mental operations on examples pertinent to the concept. In this case, a child would be presented with the rule about the final "e" first, and then would be shown a number of examples. Research has not yet determined that teaching using either type of model is clearly superior. There is, in fact, some indication in cognitive style research that the success of one method over the other is at least to some degree dependent on a person's individual learning style (Witkin, Moore, Goodenough, & Cox, 1977).

Vygotsky (1962) made a similar distinction between two types of conceptual learning. He described two methods for learning concepts depending on whether the concept is spontaneous or scientific. Spontaneous concepts are learned from day-to-day concrete exposure to specific examples of the concept. An example of this type of concept would be that of "dog." The individual learns what a dog is by living with a dog and by seeing pictures of many different kinds of dogs. However, a term like exploitation is probably learned through a mediated situation in a formal learning environment. The individual is presented with only the beginning schematics of the term's meaning. A fuller understanding is gained over time with examples not directly experienced by the learner, but learned through discussion and reading.

In a sense, the development of spontaneous concepts is an upward process, the development of scientific ones a downward one. Concepts learned through an upward process start with a number of concrete examples, with the learner developing a general notion of the essence of "dogginess." Concepts learned through a downward process tend to start with definitions, with the learner gradually determining which specific instances are examples of the general notion.

Behaviorists have attempted to explain the development of concepts in strict stimulus-response terms. Vygotsky and others have objected to this explanation on the grounds that while the mental processes described by behaviorists are necessary, they are not sufficient for explaining how external phenomena become categorized into conceptual frameworks. These thinkers find the stimulus-response paradigm an inadequate explanation for how the brain arrives at the essence of concepts such as dogginess or exploitation.

Festinger (1957), in describing the process of concept formation, borrowed from the Piagetian notion of equilibrium. Festinger stated that if an organism has two cognitions that are perceived as being dissonant with one another, there is a tendency to attempt a modification of the cognitive structures to reduce the dissonance. This process, he states, creates new concepts. For example, if a child calls all animals doggie but notices others call some of those cats, the child will in time modify his or her notion of what characteristics identify members of the class of dogs.

DeCecco (1968) has proposed the following general model for teaching concepts:

1. Describe what performance is expected after the concept is taught.
2. For complex concepts, reduce the number of attributes to be taught; emphasize dominant attributes.
3. Provide clear verbal associations.
4. Give positive and negative examples of the concept.
5. Present the examples either in close succession or simultaneously.
6. Present a new positive example, asking the student to identify it.
7. Verify the student's understanding of the concept.
8. Ask the student to define the concept.
9. Provide opportunities for the student to practice the concept with appropriate reinforcement (p. 58).

There was considerable interest in the process of concept formation during the late 1960s and early 1970s, when new mathematics and social studies curricula were being developed. The back-to-basics movement led to a declining interest in this field of inquiry. Recently, with the introduction of problem solving into the curriculum, a renewed interest in concept formation has developed. The hope is that, particularly for students with special needs, understanding how concept formation occurs in a culturally competent Context (Gonzales & Schallert, 1993) will guide teachers in helping their students become more effective learners.

REFERENCES

Ausubel, D. P. (1968). *Educational psychology: A cognitive view.* New York: Holt, Rinehart, & Winston.

DeCecco, J. P. (1968). *The psychology of learning and instruction.* Englewood Cliffs, NJ: Prentice Hall.

Festinger, L. (1964). The motivating factor of cognitive dissonance. In R. C. Harper et al. (Eds.), *The cognitive processes.* Englewood Cliffs, NJ: Prentice Hall.

Gagne, R. M. (1970). *The conditions of learning* (2nd ed.). New York: Holt, Rinehart, & Winston.

Gonzales, V., & Schallert, D. (1993, April 12–16). *Influence of linguistic, and cultural variables on conceptual learning in second language situations.* Paper presented at the Annual Meeting of the American Educational Research Association, Atlanta, GA.

Humphrey, N. (1984). *Consciousness regained: Chapters in the development of the mind.* Oxford, England: Oxford University Press.

Martorella, P. H. (1972). *Concept learning: Designs for instruction.* Scranton, PA: Intext Educational.

Platt, M. M. (1963). Concepts and the curriculum. *Social Education, 27,* 21.

Vygotsky, L. S. (1962). *Thought and language.* Cambridge, MA: MIT Press.

Witkin, H. A., Moore, C. A., Goodenough, D. R., & Cox, P. W. (1977). Field-dependent and field-independent cognitive styles and their educational implications. *Review of Educational Research, 47,* 1–64.

CAROLYN L. BULLARD
Lewis & Clark College

ABSTRACT THINKING, IMPAIRMENT IN THOUGHT DISORDERS
VYGOTSKY, LEV S.

CONCEPT OF ACTIVITY

See THEORY OF ACTIVITY; VYGOTSKY, L. S.

CONCRETE OPERATIONS

Concrete operations is the third of four invariant stages of Piaget's theory of cognitive development. According to Piaget, the distinctive features of children's thought occurring during the period of concrete operations are logic and objectivity that includes the ability to perform mental manipulations directly related to objects and events. These manipulations, which emerge between the ages of approximately 7 to 11 years, are termed operations by Piaget. To qualify as an operation, an action must be internalizable, reversible, and part of an overall system of actions. By internalizable Piaget meant that a child can think about the action "without losing their original character of actions" (1953, p. 8). An example of internalization during the concrete operations stage is the performance of mental arithmetic. Essential to understanding number and size relationships are transitivity and associativity. Transitivity, the basis for seriation, is the ability to arrange a series of events or objects in a continuum such as "less than," "greater than," "fewer than," or "more than." Associativity is demonstrated by understanding that parts of a whole may be combined in different ways without effecting a change on the whole.

Reversibility is another ability that characterizes a child's thought during the concrete operations stage. The child is able to reverse actions mentally (e.g., the child learns that the number of fingers on a hand counted sequentially from thumb to little finger is the same as counted from little finger to thumb, or the child imagines the effect weights will have when placed on or taken off a scale). Actions cannot be isolated manipulations. Instead, they are part of a coherent system of thinking. Concrete operational children develop a capacity to think about concept classes in equivalent and hierarchic forms; for example, oranges and bananas are both fruit, fruit is food, but all food is not fruit.

The classic measure of whether a particular child is capable of concrete operational thinking is provided by the task of conservation. There are more than 1000 published studies on conservation (Yussen & Santrock, 1982). In a classic study, a child is seated before two same size beakers equally filled with water and a taller empty beaker. The experimenter pours one of the beakers into the tall empty one and asks the child if the amounts in the tall beaker and the unpoured beaker are the same or different. The conserver (i.e., the concrete operational thinker), knows that the amount of liquid has not changed and that if it were poured back into the original container (internalization of a reversible action) it would be the same.

In recent years, several aspects of Piaget's theory of cognitive development have been challenged (Flavell, 1992). As early as 1964, Jerome Bruner showed that children who should not be able to conserve, according to Piaget, could do so if the transformation of the object (pouring the beaker of water) were hidden from view. Since then, there has been considerable debate as to the accuracy of Piaget's four-stage model. It now seems clear that many specifics of Piaget's theory such as the age of onset of concrete operations, are in doubt. Nonetheless, the elegance and insight that Piaget brought to the study of children's thinking was immense.

REFERENCES

Bruner, J. S. (1964). The course of cognitive growth. *American Psychologists, 19,* 1–15.

Flavell, J. H. (1992). Cognitive development: Past, present, and future. *Developmental Psychology, 28,* 6, 998–1005.

Piaget, J. (1953). *Logic and psychology.* Manchester, England: Manchester University.

Yussen, S. R., & Santrock, J. W. (1982). *Child development: An introduction.* Dubuque, IA: Brown.

MICHAEL ASH
JOSE LUIS TORRES
Texas A&M University

COGNITIVE DEVELOPMENT

CONDITIONED REINFORCER

A *conditioned reinforcer* is a concept found and used primarily within the field of Applied Behavior Analysis. In essence, this concept relates to when a reinforcing event has acquired its efficacy because of an individual's life history or strong association with certain environmental stimuli (Pierce & Epling, 1995). Conditioned, or secondary, reinforcers are not related to any biological need or desire; rather, they are a result of each individual's unique social history, and as a result, these conditioned reinforcers are always changing or evolving. When a neutral stimulus is "conditioned," it implies that a learning process has occurred between the presentation or withdrawal of a stimulus and the consequences on behavior. The end result of this process is that it strengthens a target behavior; that is, there will be concomitant increases in the desired behavior when the conditioned reinforcer is presented to, or withdrawn from, the person. This process of developing a conditioned reinforcer occurs by repeatedly and contingently pairing a neutral consequence with another stimulus that is already reinforcing to the individual (Skinner, 1953). Social attention and approval (and disapproval) are powerful human conditioned reinforcers because of how much control they have in manipulating or effecting behavioral change in people.

Perhaps the best example of a conditioned reinforcer is money. Money is inherently neutral, either just a slip of colorful paper or small piece of metal. However, when a person learns that money can purchase many highly valuable things or events, it quite quickly becomes a powerful tool for increasing behavior in people. In school settings, many things can take on conditioned reinforcer status if such repeated and contingent pairing is made (e.g., computer time, recess, peer relations, social praise from adults, etc.); however, a conditioned reinforcer is only "reinforcing" if increases in target behaviors are associated with it. Whether by presenting or withdrawing a conditioned reinforcer, concomitant increases in behavior must occur. If the target behavior decreases when the reinforcer is presented or withdrawn then it is quite likely that the stimulus being presented or withdrawn was actually a punisher (i.e., an aversive) and involves the process called "punishment" which is a behavioral technique designed to weaken the occurrence of a particular behavior (Bijou, 1993).

Conditioned reinforcers can be subcategorized as either tangible, activity-oriented, social, or generalized reinforcers (Cooper, Heron, & Heward, 1987). *Tangibles* could include trinkets, stickers, toys, gel-pens; *activity* reinforcers might include board games, computer games, going to the movies or a baseball game; *social* reinforcers might include hugs, kisses, positive statements/comments, proximity to a person. A *generalized* reinforcer, on the other hand, provides individuals with access to a wide variety/range of primary or secondary (conditioned) reinforcers. Token economy systems are a good example of how conditioned reinforcers can be used to increase target behaviors, a behavioral system that is well established in the research literature (e.g., Kazdin, 1977; Kazdin & Bootzin, 1972). Basically, when a consequence is successfully paired with several unconditioned or conditioned reinforcers, it is called a generalized conditioned reinforcer. Due to the fact that a generalized conditioned reinforcer is tied to many different reinforcing events or stimuli, it is useful for avoiding satiation because a menu of reinforcing possibilities is available instead of just one (Wolery, Bailey, & Sugai, 1988).

When a stimulus is paired with a reinforcer to become a conditioned reinforcer, the stimulus is not what has changed, but the person, because it is their behavior that has been modified. It must be kept in mind that while it is convenient to speak of a conditioned reinforcer as a real "thing" that has an assumed reinforcing effect on a person, the person's behavioral response to the conditioned reinforcer is not arbitrary. A conditioned reinforcer may lead to a reinforcing event, but the reinforcing effect of an event is not the specific property of the event itself. Rather, it belongs to the actual changes in ongoing behavior. The defining characteristic of a conditioned (secondary) reinforcer is how it changes behavior (Morse & Kelleher, 1977).

REFERENCES

Bijou, S. W. (1993). *Behavior analysis of child development* (2nd rev. ed.). Reno, NV: Context Press.

Cooper, J. O., Heron, T. E., & Heward, W. L. (1987). *Applied behavior analysis*. New York: Macmillan.

Kazdin, A. E. (1977). *The token economy: A review and evaluation*. New York: Plenum Press.

Kazdin, A. E., & Bootzin, R. R. (1972). The token economy: An evaluative review. *Journal of Applied Behavior Analysis, 5,* 343–372.

Morse, W. H., & Kelleher, R. T. (1977). Determinants of reinforcement and punishment. In W. K. Honig & J. E. R. Staddon (Eds.), *Handbook of operant behavior* (pp. 174–200). Englewood Cliffs, NJ: Prentice Hall.

Pierce, W. D., & Epling, W. F. (1995). *Behavior analysis and learning*. Englewood Cliffs, NJ: Prentice Hall.

Skinner, B. F. (1953). *Science and human behavior*. New York: Macmillan.

Wolery, M., Bailey, D. B. Jr., & Sugai, G. M. (1988). *Effective teaching: Principles and procedures of applied behavior analysis with exceptional students*. Boston, MA: Allyn & Bacon.

ROLLEN C. FOWLER
Eugene 4J School District,
Eugene, Oregon

BEHAVIORAL ASSESSMENT
BEHAVIOR DISORDERS

CONDITIONING

Conditioning is a general term that describes a strengthening (through a predictive relationship) of an association between a stimulus and a response or between two stimuli. With conditioning, responses become increasingly likely to occur under appropriate circumstances. In operant conditioning, the probability of a response that has been followed by reinforcement increases. In Pavlovian (or respondent or classical) conditioning, the probability of a response to an initially neutral stimulus increases when that neutral stimulus is followed by one that reliably elicits a response in reflex fashion. Pavlovian conditioning is named after the great Russian physiologist Ivan Pavlov (1927), whose research established the basic phenomena associated with this type of conditioning. However, the phenomenon itself had been discovered and described some years earlier by an American psychologist, E. B. Twitmeyer.

Basic Aspects for Pavlovian Conditioning

The paradigm for Pavlovian conditioning is:

CS → UCS → UCR   (before conditioning)
CS → CR   (after conditioning)

Pairing of an initially neutral conditional stimulus (CS) with an unconditional stimulus (UCS) that reliably elicits a response (UCR) leads to a conditional response (CR) occurring to the CS. Frequently, but not always, the CR is similar to the UCR in form. For example, Pavlov would sound a bell (CS) and then give a dog food (UCS) that elicited salivation (UCR). After several pairings of the bell with food, the bell itself elicited salivation. Using the paradigm:

CS → UCS → UCR   (before conditioning)
(bell) (food) (salivation)

CS → CR   (after conditioning)
(bell) (salivation)

we can see that through pairing, a response can occur to a stimulus that never occurred to it before.

Watson (1916) made Pavlovian conditioning the basic form of learning in his formulation of behaviorism. In 1920 Watson and Rayner published a classic article on conditioning of an emotional response in a human infant. While one experimenter held a white rat (CS) toward 11-month-old Albert, the other experimenter hit a bar with a hammer, making a very loud noise (UCR) that elicited crying (UCS) from Albert. After only five pairings, the rat itself elicited crying (CR).

The basic aspects of conditioning can be briefly described:

Acquisition. With repeated trials, strength of the CR increases to some maximum level.

Extinction. Presentation of the CS without the UCS leads to a decrease in intensity of the CR until no response is observed.

Spontaneous Recovery. Presenting the CS after some delay following extinction may revoke a CR, although it will be of relatively low intensity.

Reacquisition. Repairing of the CS and UCS generally leads to more rapid reconditioning than original conditioning.

Generalization. After conditioning, a CR will tend to occur, but at lower intensity, to similar stimuli.

Discrimination. Presentation of one CS (CS^1) followed by a UCS and of another (CS^2) not followed by a UCS will generally result in the subject developing a discrimination such that it produces a CR to CS^1 but not CS^2.

Some Important Issues

The nature of the CR. Pavlov proposed that the CS came to take the place of the UCS—stimulus substitution—in a mechanical process. Thus, the CR should be similar in form to the UCR. However, although dogs salivate to both bells and food, they do not try to eat the bell. Indeed, they look at and move toward the food dish, behaviors that suggest that conditioning produces a CR that anticipates the UCS (Zener, 1937). Research (Rescorla, 1966; Siegel, 1975) sug-

gests that in at least some cases, conditioning indeed leads to the CS eliciting a CR that reflects expectancy of the UCS. For example, Siegel gave rats a series of insulin injections in which the hypodermic needle was the CS, the insulin was the UCS, and insulin-elicited hypoglycemia was the UCS. In response to a CS-only test, the rats showed hyperglycemia, as though they were compensating for the anticipated UCS, insulin. The influential Rescorla and Wagner (1972) model proposes that conditioning will occur only when the CS provides information ("expectancy") about the UCS.

Biological constraints on learning. Although early theorists felt that all stimuli and responses should be equally conditionable, research shows that they are not. In their now classic study, Garcia and Koelling (1966) gave rats either "sweet water" or "bright-noisy water" (water paired with flashing lights and noise) and then either shocked them or made them ill. Of rats given sweet water, only those made ill subsequently avoided drinking the water; of rats given bright-noisy water, only those shocked subsequently avoided drinking. Similar results appear to hold in humans (Seligman, 1970). The specificity of "cue-consequence relations" is a topic of current interest. The implication is that some types of associations have particularly important adaptive value, and have been selected through evolution.

Consideration of biological factors helps to resolve the controversial question of whether or not young infants demonstrate classical conditioning. Although the existence of such conditioning had been generally accepted, Sameroff (1971) concluded that positive studies either could not be replicated or suffered from methodological problems, and that conditioning in newborns had not clearly been demonstrated. Sameroff and Cavenaugh (1979) later suggested that studies published since the initial review, which successfully demonstrated conditioning, had used CS and UCS pairings of biological relevance to the newborn. Indeed, by pairing biologically relevant stimuli, Blass, Ganchrow, and Steiner (1984) have obtained conditioning in infants of 2 to 48 hours of age. Tactile stimulation (CS) was followed by presentation of sucrose solution (UCS) that elicited sucking (UCR). Newborns sucked during CS in conditioning and showed extinction of sucking during subsequent CS-only trials. Further, seven of eight experimental infants cried during extinction trials at a time when the sucrose had been presented, suggesting an affective component of the conditioning.

Long-delay learning. Initially, research indicated that the CS and UCS had to be closely linked in time for conditioning to occur. However, in some circumstances, particularly where the UCS elicits illness, an association may be formed with a novel taste or olfactory CS encountered over 12 hours earlier (Revusky & Garcia, 1970). Thus, under circumstances such as food poisoning, a CR can occur to a stimulus removed in time from the UCS. Some have suggested that aversions to food that develop in cancer patients undergoing chemotherapy may be classically conditioned since most chemotherapeutic agents induce intense symptoms of food poisoning (Braveman & Bronstein, 1985).

Higher-order conditioning. The potential role of Pavlovian conditioning is greatly extended by higher-order conditioning, originally described by Pavlov and studied in detail by Rescorla (1980). In such conditioning, a first CS (CS1) is paired with a UCS to establish a CR to CS1. Then, a second CS (CS2) is paired only with CS1, leading to the response conditioned to CS1 now occurring to CS2. Thus, once a response has been conditioned to a CS, other CSs may be tied to it that are not themselves directly associated with the UCS but are remote from it. If the original link between CS1 and the UCS is broken, as in extinction, the higher-order CRs also diminish.

Applications to Children's Development

Development of emotions. Since the time of Watson, Pavlovian conditioning has played an important role in accounting for the association of positive and negative emotional reactions with particular stimuli. Watson and Rayner demonstrated how conditioning could lead to negative emotions such as fear. Indeed, conditioning is viewed as a major process underlying the development of severe fears or phobias.

As conditioning may induce phobias, so it may be used to reduce them. As early as 1924, Jones "counterconditioned" a severe fear of rabbits in a child, Peter, by pairing a rabbit with pleasurable stimuli such as peer play and ice cream cones. By the end of the process, Peter no longer feared rabbits and, indeed, was petting them. This procedure, now called desensitization, is one of the most effective means of treating phobias in children and adults. Conditioning may also produce positive emotional responses, as shown, for example, in children's excitement at the sight of a favored food, person, or toy.

Development of meaning. Conditioning is one process thought to underlie the attachment of meaning to words (Mowrer, 1954). Pairing a word (CS) with the object (UCS) signified by the word will result in responses elicited by the object becoming attached to the word as a CR. Thus, pairing the word *doll* with an actual doll leads to responses elicited by the doll becoming associated with *doll*. Although a conditioning model cannot deal with all meaning, particularly that involving abstract concepts, it does provide a framework for understanding how reactions to stimuli can become attached to symbols for them. If an object comes to elicit an emotional response, then the word for the object may also elicit that response. If a child who has been painfully knocked to the ground by a large dog now fears all large dogs, he or she may show fear at the phrase *large dog*. On the other hand, a child who likes ice cream cones might well show positive anticipation to the phrase *ice cream cone*.

Also important is the related concept of mediated or semantic generalization. Once a CR occurs to a word, it will occur to words similar in meaning if the individual has developed a concept involving that word. Thus, if conditioned to respond to the word *shoe,* an individual will respond more to *boot,* or other words similar in meaning, than to *shoot,* a word similar in physical characteristics. Already apparent by at least age eight semantic generalization becomes stronger with age (Osgood, 1953).

Implications for Educators

Those dealing with children need to be sensitive to the fact that they and the situation they are in are paired with what they say and do to the children. So is the situation paired with peers' reactions to children. Thus, teachers who use aversive means of classroom management may condition children to be anxious about them and their classrooms. Similarly, children who are ridiculed in class or on the playground or who experience much failure and little success may become conditioned to fear school itself and teachers generally. In extreme, a school phobia may result.

We should also be aware that children will arrive at school with conditioned likes and dislikes and emotional responses. Some may have been specifically food poisoned or have had gastric distress after eating and may have strong aversions to certain foods. Others may have strong fears. However controversial it may be, those in special education should consider the roles of conditioning when predicting the effects of inclusion on children with disabilities. Those children who succeed socially and academically will have a positive conditioning experience, whereas those who are not accepted and/or fail academically may suffer from negative conditioning and develop conditioned responses associated with anxiety and fear of failure.

REFERENCES

Blass, E. M., Ganchrow, J. R., & Steiner, J. E. (1984). Classical conditioning in new born humans 2–48 hours of age. *Infant Behavior and Development, 7,* 223–235.

Braveman, N. S., & Bronstein, P. (Eds.). (1985). Experimental assessments and clinical applications of conditioned food aversions. *Annals of the New York Academy of Sciences, 443.*

Garcia, J., & Koelling, R. A. (1966). Relation of cue to consequence in avoidance learning. *Psychonomic Science, 4,* 123–124.

Jones, M. C. (1924). A laboratory study of fear: The case of Peter. *Pedagogical Seminary and Journal of Genetic Psychology, 31,* 308–315.

Mowrer, O. H. (1954). The psychologist looks at language. *American Psychologist, 9,* 660–694.

Osgood, C. E. (1953). *Method and theory in experimental psychology.* New York: Oxford University Press.

Pavlov, I. P. (1927). *Conditioned reflexes* (translated by G. V. Anrep). New York: Oxford University Press.

Rescorla, R. A. (1966). Predictability and number of pairings in Pavlovian fear conditioning. *Psychonomic Science, 4,* 383–384.

Rescorla, R. A. (1980). *Pavlovian second-order conditioning.* Hillsdale, NJ: Erlbaum.

Rescorla, R. A., & Wagner, A. R. (1972). A theory of Pavlovian conditioning: Variations in the effectiveness of reinforcement and nonreinforcement. In A. H. Black & W. F. Prokasy (Eds.), *Classical conditioning II: Current research and theory.* New York: Appleton-Century-Crofts.

Revusky, S. H., & Garcia, J. (1970). Learned associations over long delays. In G. H. Bower & J. T. Spence (Eds.), *The psychology of learning and motivation* (Vol. 4). New York: Academic.

Sameroff, A. J. (1971). Can conditioned responses be established in the newborn infant? *Developmental Psychology, 5,* 1–12.

Sameroff, A. J., & Cavenaugh, P. J. (1979). Learning in infancy: A developmental perspective. In J. D. Osofsky (Ed.), *Handbook of infant development* (pp. 344–392). New York: Wiley.

Seligman, M. E. P. (1970). On the generality of the laws of learning. *Psychological Review, 77,* 406–418.

Siegel, S. (1975). Conditioning insulin effects. *Journal of Comparative and Physiological Psychology, 89,* 189–199.

Watson, J. B. (1916). The place of the conditioned reflex in psychology. *Psychological Review, 23,* 89–116.

Watson, J. B., & Rayner, R. (1920). Conditioned emotional reactions. *Journal of Experimental Psychology, 3,* 1–14.

Zener, K. (1937). The significance of behavior accompanying conditioned salivary secretion for theories of the conditioned reflex. *American Journal of Psychology, 50,* 384–403.

ROBERT T. BROWN
University of North Carolina at Wilmington

BEHAVIOR MODIFICATION
OPERANT CONDITIONING

CONDUCT DISORDER

Conduct disorder is a behavioral disorder in youth characterized by a "repetitive and persistent pattern of behavior in which the basic rights of others or major age-appropriate societal norms or rules are violated" (American Psychiatric Association, 1994, p. 85). The behaviors fall into four basic groups: (1) aggressive behaviors that cause or threaten physical harm to people or animals; (2) nonaggressive behaviors that cause harm to property; (3) deceitfulness or theft; and (4) serious violations of rules. Three or more of the characteristics must have been present for 12 months or more, and at least one of the characteristics for 6 months for a diagnosis to be made. Overall, the disturbance in conduct must significantly impair the youth's social, academic, or oc-

cupational functioning. The prevalence of conduct disorder has increased over the past few decades: For males under the age of 18, rates changed from 6 percent to 16 percent, and females from 2 percent to 9 percent (American Psychiatric Association, 1994).

Individuals with conduct disorder may not be the best informants about their own behavior; therefore, it is important that diagnosticians conduct assessments that are multi-setting, multi-modal, and multi-method to accurately assess functioning (Sommers-Flanagan & Sommers-Flanagan, 1998). Many individuals with conduct disorder have little empathy for the feelings of others, and may negatively distort the positive intentions of others. The disorder is also highly correlated with early and risky sexual behavior, substance abuse, recklessness, and illegal acts. The onset of conduct disorder may occur as early as age 5, but it usually begins in late childhood or early adolescence. Many youth diagnosed with this disorder continue to show similar behaviors in adulthood (Storm-Mathisen & Valglum, 1994) and meet the criteria for Antisocial Personality Disorder (American Psychiatric Association, 1994). There is a significant overlap of other psychiatric disorders (such as depression) with conduct disorders (Offord, Boyle, & Racine, 1991), especially in incarcerated juvenile populations (Eppright, Kashani, Robison, & Reid, 1993). Substance abuse is a significant precursor for disorders of conduct (Storm-Mathisen & Valglum 1994), especially in Hispanic populations (Steward, Brown, & Myers, 1997).

There is a great deal of research activity devoted to the treatment of youth with conduct disorders, and there are constant calls citing the need for new models of treatment delivery (Kazdin, 1997). Treatments include problem-solving skills training, parent management training, functional family therapy, and multisystemic therapy (Kazdin, 1997). The treatments are usually delivered in residential facilities and are subject to the common criticism of not being amenable to demonstrating clinically significant change that generalizes to every patient's situation. In addition, research about the treatments are not longitudinal in nature (Kazdin, 1993, 1997), which compromises the certainty of results. There have been some promising psychopharmacological treatments that are being researched (Shah, Seese, Abikoff, & Klein, 1994), but no conclusive results are available because of the multiple etiologies of conduct disorder (Stoewe, Kruesi, & Lelio, 1995). An exciting line of research stems from the field of neuropsychiatry where organic etiologists, such as early traumatic brain injury, are being studied with reasonable treatment success (Wood & Singh, 1994). Some researchers of conduct disorders, after reviewing treatment effectiveness, suggest that prevention is a far more an effective and economical use of resources (Dodge, 1993; Offord, 1994.)

Special education services may be available to students with conduct disorders usually because of the comorbidity with handicapping conditions such as serious emotional disturbance, attention-deficit hyperactivity disorder, and learning disabilities. However, far too many of these students are underidentified and they subsequently enter the juvenile justice system where specific treatments that are linked to the etiology of the disorder are seldom available. School psychologists and support personnel can best serve these students by using multiple sources of information and assessment, not only for diagnosis, but also for treatment. Success in the demands of everyday living for these students requires that the school, community, and home work in unison.

REFERENCES

American Psychiatric Association. (1994). *Diagnostic and statistical manual of mental disorders* (4th ed.). Washington DC: Author.

Dodge, K. A. (1993). The future of research on the treatment of conduct disorder. *Development and Psychopathology, 5,* 1–2, 311–319.

Eppright, T. D., Kashani, J. H., Robison, B. D., & Reid, J. C. (1993). Comorbidity of conduct disorder and personality disorders in an incarcerated juvenile population. *American Journal of Psychiatry, 150,* 8, 1233–1236.

Kazdin, A. E. (1993). Treatment of conduct disorder: Progress and directions in psychotherapy research. *Development & Psychopathology, 5,* 1–2, 277–310.

Kazdin, A. E. (1997). Practitioner review: Psychosocial treatments for conduct disorder in children. *Journal of Child Psychology & Psychiatry & Allied Disciplines, 38,* 2, 161–178.

Offord, D. R., Boyle, M. H., & Racine, Y. A. (1991). *The epidemiology of antisocial behavior in childhood and adolescence.* Hillsdale, NJ: Erlbaum.

Offord, D. R., & Bennett, K. J. (1994). Conduct disorder: Long-term outcomes and intervention effectiveness. *Journal of the American Academy of Child & Adolescent Psychiatry, 33,* 8, 1069–1078.

Shah, M. R., Seese, L. M., Abikoff, H., & Klein, R. G. (1994). Pemoline for children and adolescents with conduct disorder: A pilot investigation. *Journal of Child & Adolescent Psychopharmacology, 4,* 4, 255–261.

Sommers-Flanagan, J., & Sommers-Flanagan, R. (1998). Assessment and diagnosis of conduct disorder. *Journal of Counseling & Development, 76,* 2, 189–197.

Stewart, D. G., Brown, S. A., & Myers, M. G. (1997). Antisocial behavior and psychoactive substance involvement among Hispanic and non-Hispanic Caucasian adolescents in substance abuse treatment. *Journal of Child and Adolescent Substance Abuse, 6,* 4, 1–22.

Storm-Mathisen, A., & Vaglum, P. (1994). Conduct disorder patients 20 years later: A personal follow-up study. *Acta Psychiatrica Scandinavica, 89,* 6, 416–420.

Stoewe, J. K., Kruesi, M. J. P., & Lelio, D. F. (1995). Psychopharmacology of aggressive states and features of conduct disorder. *Child & Adolescent Psychiatric Clinics of North America, 4,* 2, 359–379.

Wood, I. K., & Singh, N. N. (1994). The impact of neuropsychiatry upon forensic issues related to children and adolescents. In L. F. Koziol & C. E. Stout (Eds.), *The neuropsychology of mental disorders: A practical guide.* Springfield, IL: Charles C. Thomas.

ELAINE FLETCHER-JANZEN
*University of Colorado at
Colorado Springs*

ANTISOCIAL PERSONALITY
EMOTIONAL DISORDERS
SUBSTANCE ABUSE

CONDUCTIVE HEARING LOSS

Auditory functioning can be altered at several levels: the ear, the auditory nerve, or the brain. In the ear, there are two types of anatomical structures—those concerned with the mechanical transmission of sound (a physical process) and those concerned with the transformation of the sound waves into nervous impulses (a biological process). Conductive hearing loss (CHL) applies to the condition resulting from an alteration of the former in opposition to sensory-neural hearing loss, which results from pathology of the latter. The combination of CHL with sensory-neural hearing loss is called mixed hearing loss. For more details about terms and causes of the different types, see Davis and Silverman (1960).

The mechanical transmission of the sound vibrations obeys the laws of acoustics. It is effected by the external and middle ear, the fluids of the inner ear, and the combined displacements of the cochlea's basilar and tectorial membranes. These bring the vibrations to bear on the sensory cells of the organ of Corti, the hair cells. There the conduction process ends; the hair cells are the transducers that transform the acoustic phenomenon into a biochemical and bioelectrical event. The CHL alone is never greater than 60 dB hearing loss, for higher intensity sounds reach the inner ear directly through the skull (von Békésy, 1948). In small children, it is often superimposed on sensoryneural hearing loss, thereby producing an additional deficiency.

Interference with the conduction process most commonly occurs at the level of external or middle ear structures.

One of the most frequent causes of temporary CHL is the external obstruction of the external ear canal (the auditory meatus) by cerumen, a waxlike secretion, especially in individuals with mental retardation (Crandell & Roesner, 1993). Obstruction by foreign bodies is also relatively frequent, especially in children. Various malformations of the external ear can affect hearing, the most serious being nondevelopment of the external auditory meatus.

The tympanic membrane, or eardrum, located between the external and middle ear, is linked with the malleus, incus, and stapes. With these ossicles it constitutes the tympano-ossicular chain, which transmits the sound arriving through the external ear to the oval window, an orifice in the bony wall separating middle and inner ear. Numerous pathological processes can affect these structures and thus produce conductive hearing loss. The eardrum can be swollen by inflammation, stiffened by sclerosis, or perforated (Nicholls & Pelletier, 2003). The ossicles may be partly or totally absent or malformed. The mobility of the chain may be reduced by fixation of the stapes in the oval window owing to abnormal bone proliferation at that level. This occurs in otosclerosis (otospongiosis), a frequent condition in adults and a rare one in children.

The accumulation of fluid in the ear occurs in several different forms of otitis media. One of them, serous otitis media, is a frequent chronic or semichronic disease of small children up to 5 or 6 years of age. It is often associated with obstruction of the eustachian tube. These conditions can usually be alleviated or cured relatively easily by medical and/or surgical treatment. However, since the CHL caused by them is mild or moderate, it is often ignored or neglected. This could have serious consequences in later life. Animal studies by Webster and Webster (1979) have shown that temporary moderate auditory restriction in the rat produces changes in the auditory brain stem nuclei. Studies reviewed by Ruben (1984) indicate that language-related skills may be durably impaired, even after restoration of normal hearing, in children who had prolonged CHL during the early years of life. This is because the early years are a particularly sensitive period for language development.

Because CHL affects only the mechanical part of the auditory channel, it produces a decrease in the sound pressure level reaching the inner ear, but no qualitative deformation of that sound. Therefore, a hearing aid that amplifies the sound waves, inasmuch as it does not itself introduce distortions, is capable of restoring a practically normal hearing sensation. While most causes of CHL can be efficiently corrected by medical and/or surgical treatment, the latter may have to be delayed, especially in children where plastic reconstruction surgery can only be done at a certain age level. For these patients, as well as for those where medico-surgical therapy has failed, is contraindicated, is impossible for practical reasons, or is refused by the patient, a well-adapted hearing aid is an excellent solution.

While CHL alone does not prevent spoken language development, it may severely slow down its progression and affect speech skills if undiagnosed or inadequately treated. In the latter case, speech and hearing therapy, following the appropriate medical and/or surgical treatment and/or hearing aid fitting, may be required. Special education may also be necessary as a temporary measure for those children whose speech and language deficiencies prevent them from holding their own in a school for those who hear normally. The great majority of children with CHL, however, can follow their whole curriculum in a mainstream situation, for instance, in ordinary schools with hearing children.

REFERENCES

Crandell, C. C., & Roesner, R. J. (1993). Incidence of Excessive/Impacted Cerumen in individuals with mental retardation: A longitudinal study. *American Journal on Mental Retardation, 97,* 5, 568–574.

Davis, H., & Silverman, S. R. (1960). *Hearing and deafness.* New York: Holt, Rinehart and Winston.

Nicholls, J., & Pelletier, S. (2003). Conductive hearing loss. In E. Fletcher-Janzen & C. R. Reynolds (Eds.), *Childhood disorders diagnostic desk reference* (pp. 146–147). New York Wiley.

Ruben, R. J. (1984). An inquiry into the minimal amount of auditory deprivation which results in a cognitive effect in man. *Acta Oto-Laryngological* (Suppl. 414), 157–164.

von G. Békésy (1948). Vibration of the head in a sound field and its role in hearing by bone conduction. *Journal of the Acoustical Society of America, 20,* 749–760.

Webster, D. B., & Webster, M. (1979). Effects of neonatal conductive hearing loss on brain stem auditory nuclei. *Annals of Otology, Rhinology and Laryngology, 88,* 684–688.

OLIVIER PÉRIER
*Université Libre de Bruxelles
Centre Comprendre et Parler,
Belgium*

DEAF
DEAF EDUCATION
DEPRIVATION, BIONEURAL RESULTS OF

CONFIDENTIALITY OF INFORMATION

See BUCKLEY AMENDMENT; INDIVIDUALS WITH DISABILITIES EDUCATION IMPROVEMENT ACT OF 2004 (IDEIA).

CONGENITAL DISORDERS

Two concepts are joined together in the expression congenital disorders, making it pertinent to begin this entry with a short comment on each. Congenital stands for present at birth. This definition does not imply any causal relationship. Nevertheless, for a long time, the terms congenital and hereditary have been confused. Indeed, some congenital disorders may be hereditary, but in many others heredity is not involved. Thus the clear recognition of the absence of any familial factor allows many couples to be reassured concerning the possible recurrence of congenital disorders.

Disorder (malformation or anomaly are also used) means any defect when compared with the normal. Earlier, mainly visible anomalies were detected; today, disorders are described at any level, on the surface or inside the organism, with the aid of sophisticated technical procedures. Therefore, according to Warkany (1971), "Congenital malformations are structural defects present at birth. They may be gross or microscopic, on the surface of the body or within it, familial or sporadic, hereditary or nonhereditary, single or multiple." Only the molecular level must be added to this definition to include all congenital disorders.

Estimations of the incidence of congenital disorders vary from report to report, depending heavily on the mode of ascertainment: external examination only at birth, X-rays, microscopic analyses of tissues, functional tests, inclusion or exclusion of stillbirths, distinction between major and minor defects, and even the personal interest of the examiner in charge at the birth of the child. Thus in a Belgian study, significantly more congenital heart anomalies were observed in two maternity wards participating in a concerted action project of the European Economic Community, probably because the neonatologist pediatricians had special training in cardiology (Borlée-Grimée, De Wals, & Vinçotte-Mols, 1985). Nevertheless, a mean figure could be 2 to 3 percent. This may seem very high, but it is well established that stillbirths show more congenital anomalies than live births, and that at least 50 percent of abortions of the first trimester show severe chromosome defects that are likely linked with expulsion (Boué & Boué, 1975). Therefore, the figure of 2 to 3 percent represents only a small proportion of all malformed embryos. Moreover, all disorders are included, from severe congenital heart malformations incompatible with life, to the partial fusion of two small toes. On the other hand, it is important to point out that congenital disorders are not so exceptional in our species and fortunately, not all are associated with a severe handicap. To our knowledge, there is no particular definition of major and minor anomalies; the interpretation is usually left to reporting authors.

There are many causes of congenital disorders. It is possible to distinguish three broad categories: (1) disorders genetically transmitted following classical Mendelian modes (McKusick, 1983), (2) disorders owed to anomalies of the genetic material but usually not transmitted (e.g., chromosome anomalies), and (3) disorders owed to environmental factors. Many can be recognized at birth by at least one characteristic symptom and some others are detected only later in life.

Dominant heredity is most frequently observed in the case of minor anomalies that do not impair normal life (e.g., supernumerary or fused fingers or toes). A dominant congenital defect is theoretically transmitted to half the offspring, and may be followed through many generations. Sometimes, one generation seems skipped over, or, on the contrary, more severely affected: this is due to variations in penetration or expressivity of the gene. However, severe congenital disorders can be transmitted through a dominant mode. This is the case in Huntington's chorea, a disease of the nervous system (for a recent review, see Robert, 1985). Strictly speaking, Huntington's chorea is a congenital disorder, the gene responsible for it being present at birth. However, carriers of the mutation enjoy a normal life until 30 or 40 years of age and in reproduction transmit the gene to half their offspring. The onset of the disease is observed with a progressive neurological symptomatology (involuntary movements), and often a psychiatric component (depression sometimes ending in suicide). Death usually follows 10 to 15 years after the onset of symptoms.

Recessive heredity is characterized by the birth of affected children to normal parents. Indeed, the father and the mother are heterozygous for a common mutant gene, and 25 percent of their offspring are homozygous and affected. Hundreds of examples are found in McKusick's catalog of Mendelian diseases in man (1983). When the disorder is severe, people with the disease usually do not reproduce and the genes are eliminated: the reservoir of the disease is thus found in the heterozygous carriers. Many recessive disorders are rare: consanguineous marriages are a well-known favoring factor, as is a common ethnic background (e.g., Tay-Sachs disease is more frequent in Ashkenazi Jews, sickle-cell anemia in blacks, thalassemia in Mediterranean populations). However, this is not a general rule, and unrelated parents from different ethnic backgrounds may be heterozygous for a common recessive gene (a well-known example is mucoviscidosis). When a recessive disorder is suspected, the diagnosis must first be firmly established with the use of appropriate techniques: X-rays, laboratory tests, pathologic and molecular studies. Genetic counseling then becomes possible.

Congenital disorders may be sex-linked, either dominant or recessive. In the first case, females and males are affected, in the second only males. Some common congenital malformations such as cleft lip and palate, clubfoot, spina bifida cystica, anencephaly, and pyloric stenosis are not transmitted through simple Mendelian inheritance, but nevertheless show a clear familial aggregation (Carter, 1976). In these cases, a particular genetic mechanism, called polygenism, is involved. In short, the anomaly is determined by more than one gene, all acting in the same direction and possibly interacting with environmental factors. Beyond a given threshold, the malformation is present. For instance, let us suppose a birth defect associated with the presence of five specific genes acting together in a specific environment. The intact father may possess four of them and the intact mother three. Unpredictably, they can transmit to one of their children five or more deleterious genes. Of course, they may also have non-affected children. The risk is not of the monogenic type (i.e., 50 percent, 25 percent), or sex-linked. Empirical tables have been proposed after tabulating direct observations. For example, in a determined population, the risk of having a child with a cleft lip is 1 in 1000 births. A couple who already has one affected child will have a risk increase of 40 times (4 percent; Carter, 1976). If one of the two parents is affected, the risk before any pregnancy is around 3 percent. If one of the parents is affected and one child is also affected, the risk is 11 percent. A major cause of congenital anomalies, usually associated with mental retardation, is chromosome anomalies. The malformations are undoubtedly of genetic origin, owed to anomalies of genetic material, but even if they are genetic and congenital, they are usually not hereditary.

A number of congenital disorders are due to environmental factors. The term environmental must, however, be understood in a broad sense: everything that alters the normal parameters of the body, the body being considered a conglomerate of cells. Clearly, this means that environmental factors can originate from the surrounding area in which the patient lives (e.g., radiation, viruses, drugs), or inside his or her own body (e.g., diabetes, hypothyroidism). This creates abnormal environmental conditions for the cells and, if the patient is a pregnant woman, for the fetus.

In experiments with animals, many agents are known to cause congenital disorders when they are administered to pregnant females (Warkany, 1971). The systematic study of these effects is called teratology. A catalog of teratogenic agents is regularly published and kept up to date (Shepard, 1983). Many drugs are known to be associated with fetal malformations. Pregnant women are usually warned to seek medical advice before taking any medication. Nevertheless, some compounds, although carefully tested before marketing, escape detection and are responsible for the birth of malformed babies. The case of thalidomide is well known. This sedative drug, used also by pregnant women for nausea and vomiting, was found to induce severe anomalies in the human fetus when ingested between the 35th and the 50th day after the last menstrual period (the 23rd to 38th day after conception). Rat and mouse embryos did not seem to suffer from thalidomide administered to pregnant females. However, when the relationship between human malformations and thalidomide was established, the effect of the drug was studied again on macaques. They showed the same sensibility as man. Rabbits also suffered, but to a lesser degree. This demonstrates the importance of selecting a good experimental model. All teratogenic agents cannot be reviewed here; only a few will be discussed.

Ionizing radiations have a well-known teratogenic effect. However fear of congenital malformations in the fetus must not stop pregnant women from having examinations needed for their health (and thus for their baby's health). The teratogenic effect is dose-dependent; it also depends on the site of irradiation and the advancement of the pregnancy. As all this has been extensively demonstrated, it is best to advise the radiologist about a pregnancy or to perform a pregnancy test in case of doubt. Some viruses, but not all, also present with teratogenic activity. The example of rubella is well known; however, the risk is not the same throughout pregnancy. The maximum fetal sensitivity is during the first trimester. Alcohol ingestion may be harmful and cause fetal alcohol syndrome. Heavy smoking is also responsible for fetal damage and low birth weight. Diseases of the mother may affect the fetus if not corrected. Diabetes causes the birth of large infants, higher mortality at birth, and a tendency to hypoglycemia and respiratory distress after delivery (Delaney & Ptacek, 1970). Moreover, some authors are convinced that congenital malformations are more frequent in children of diabetic mothers or at least that some diabetic mothers are more at risk than others. However, if the ingestion of some drugs is known to be teratogenic, the absence of other elements, like vitamins, is harmful. Nutritional deficiencies as a cause of congenital malformations in experimental animals are well documented (Warkany, 1971). These situations are seldom encountered under normal human living conditions, but they explain why a vitamin supplement is advised for pregnant women.

The prevention of congenital malformations has many aspects. An important and simple means of prevention is regular medical surveillance during pregnancy. Another mode of prevention is to avoid any known teratogenic agent and to have balanced nutritional intake. If the birth of a child with severe congenital disorder is followed by death, necropsy is of paramount importance to determine the recurrence risk for the parents. However, sophisticated means of surveillance have been developed for the at-risk mother to be. Prenatal diagnosis is offered, including chromosome analysis of the fetus, research on abnormal genes at the molecular level with recombinant DNA techniques, blood sampling or biopsy of the fetus, follow-up of the anatomical growth of the fetus with ultrasound, various biochemical dosages in the amniotic fluid, and direct viral research on fetal tissues. For some defects, no known treatment is possible, and interruption of pregnancy may appear as the most appropriate solution. For others, treatment is possible either directly with the fetus or just after birth. Thus if a curable congenital heart malformation is diagnosed before birth, the mother can be delivered in a hospital specializing in the correction of such an anomaly.

Neonatal screening is important in some metabolic or endocrine disorders. For instance, hypothyroidism at birth is responsible for future mental retardation of the child, known as cretinism. Nevertheless, after delivery, hypothyroidic children are potentially normal, the maternal thyroid having supplemented the fetus. Immediate substitution treatment allows normal intellectual development. Hypothyroidism can be diagnosed just after birth by the increase of the hormone stimulating the thyroid activity (the thyreostimulating hormone [TSH]) in the blood. Testing is possible on a few drops of blood taken in the perinatal period, and the affected babies, duly treated, enjoy normal development (Delange et al., 1979). Many other disorders can be detected by neonatal screening (Bickel et al., 1980), and progress in this area is promising. This compensates for the high incidence of congenital disorders at birth.

REFERENCES

Bickel, H., Guthrie, R., & Hammersen, G. (1980). *Neonatal screening for inborn errors of metabolism* (Vol. 1). Berlin: Springer-Verlag.

Borlée-Grimée, I., De Wals, P., & Vinçotte-Mols, M. (1985). Problems in the ascertainment of congenital heart disease. Review of 308 cases registered in Hainaut from 1979 to 1982. In P. De Wals, J. A. C. Weatherall, & M. F. Lechat (Eds.), *Registration of congenital anomalies in Eurocat Centers 1979–1983.* Louvain-la-Neuve, Cabay.

Boué, J., Boué, A., & Lazar, P. (1975). The epidemiology of human spontaneous abortions with chromosome anomalies. In R. J. Blondau (Ed.), *Aging gametes.* Basel, Switzerland: Karger.

Carter, C. O. (1976). Genetics of common single malformations. *British Medical Bulletin, 32,* 21–26.

Delange, F., Beckers, C., Höfer, R., König, M. P., Monaco, F., & Varrone, S. (1979). Neonatal screening for congenital hypothyroidism in Europe. *Acta Endocrinologica, 90*(Suppl. 223), 1–27.

Delaney, J. J., & Ptacek, J. (1970). Three decades of experience with diabetic pregnancies. *American Journal of Obstetrics & Gynecology, 106,* 550.

McKusick, V. (1983). *Mendelian inheritance in man* (6th ed.). Baltimore: Johns Hopkins University Press.

Robert, J. M. (1985). La chorée de Huntington: Histoire naturelle de la maladie. *Journal de Genetique Humaine, 33,* 83–90.

Shepard, T. H. (1983). *Catalog of teratogenic agents* (4th ed.). Baltimore: Johns Hopkins University Press.

Warkany, J. (1971). *Congenital malformations* (Vol. 1). Chicago: Year Book Medical.

L. KOULISCHER
*Institut de Morphologie
Pathologique, Belgium*

GENETIC COUNSELING
GENETIC VARIATIONS

CONGENITAL WORD BLINDNESS, HISTORY OF

This term refers to "a condition in which, with normal vision and therefore seeing the letters and words distinctly, an individual is no longer able to interpret written or printed language" (Hinshelwood, 1917, p. 2). The term was the title of a book written by Hinshelwood (1917) in which he described case studies and intervention techniques with individuals who evidenced word blindness. Hinshelwood's clients showed such disability subsequent to strokes or brain damage induced by chronic alcoholism. He extended the use of this term to children who showed the same reading disability. However, "congenital word blindness" was originally used by Morgan (1896), whose paper was one of the first to document a clear case of severe reading disability in a 14-year-old boy of apparent brightness. The boy knew all his letters and could write and read them singly. However, except for some common sight words such as the, and, of, and that, he could not read any word, even words that he encountered daily, such as the name of his father's house. The boy's parents provided him with tutors and sent him to schools to teach him to read, but despite concerted teaching efforts, the boy's reading disability persisted.

Morgan and Hinshelwood were opthalmologists. They were intrigued by their clients and observed and recorded the details of severe reading disabilities. They both used the term congenital word blindness to describe adults and children with clear, pronounced reading disabilities. Specifically, Hinshelwood (1917) hypothesized that children with congenital word blindness sustained a brain defect in the left hemisphere, where he thought visual word and letter memories were stored. According to Hinshelwood, the inability to read was attributed to deficient visual memory, for he believed good readers recognize or remember words by activating a visual picture rather than by analyzing individual letters in the words. Additionally, both he and Morgan considered such a brain defect to be congenital (Smith, 1983).

Hinshelwood believed that intensive practice and the development of the brain's visual memory would enable individuals with congenital word blindness to reach reading proficiency (Mercer, 1983). Specifically, he suggested a three-stage approach to the remediation of deficits: teaching the individual letters for storage in the supposed visual-memory center of the brain; teaching word recognition by spelling the printed words aloud so as to use the individual's good auditory memory for letter sounds; and enabling storage of the reading words using oral and written practice. It has been suggested that Hinshelwood's emphasis on visual memory and generally visual interpretations of reading disability had a significant impact on subsequent visual-perceptual theories of learning disabilities (Smith, 1983).

REFERENCES

Hinshelwood, J. (1917). *Congenital word blindness.* London: Lewis.

Mercer, C. D. (1983). *Students with learning disabilities* (2nd ed.). Columbus, OH: Charles E. Merrill.

Morgan, W. P. (1896). A case of congenital word blindness. *British Medical Journal, 2,* 1378.

Smith, C. R. (1983). *Learning disabilities: The interaction of learner, task and setting.* Boston: Little, Brown.

BERNICE Y. L. WONG
Simon Fraser University

DYSLEXIA
READING DISORDERS

CONNERS' PARENT RATING SCALES–REVISED, CONNERS' TEACHER RATING SCALES–REVISED, CONNERS-WELLS ADOLESCENT SELF-REPORT SCALE

The revised Conners rating scale follows the original aims of the earlier version in assessing Attention-Deficit/Hyperactivity Disorder (ADHD; Conners, 1997). Both the Conners Parent Rating Scales Revised (CPRS-R:L and CPRS-R:S) and the Conners Teacher Rating Scales Revised (CTRS-R:L and CTRS-R:S) are designed to assess ADHD and related behavioral problems, including cognitive problems, family problems, emotional problems, anger control problems, and anxiety problems for children aged 3 to 17. These measures should be used as an ancillary source of information rather than the sole means of diagnosing ADHD. Because ADHD treatments have differential efficacy depending on the *Diagnostic and Statistical Manual of Mental Disorders,* fourth edition (*DSM-IV*) subtype (Inattentive, Hyperactive, or Combined), the ability of the Conners scales to assist in this differential is important. They have been shown to be useful as screening tools but not as the primary methods of diagnosis or distinguishing between ADHD subtypes (Hale, How, Dewitt, & Coury, 2001).

Both the parent and teacher measures are available as a long form and a short form. The long forms for both parent (CPRS-R:L) and teacher (CTRS-R:L) scales include Oppositional, Cognitive Problems, Hyperactivity, Anxious-Shy, Perfectionism, Social Problems, the Conners Global Index, Restless-Impulsive, Emotional Liability, *DSM-IV* symptom subscales including *DSM-IV* Inattentive and *DSM-IV* Hyperactive-Impulsive. For the parent scale, there is an additional Psychosomatic scale. The CPRS-R:L contains 80 items and the CTRS-R:L contains 80 items and the CTRS-R:L contains 59 items. Each takes approximately 20 minutes to complete.

The short forms of the parent (CPRS-R:S) and teacher (CTRS-R:S) scales include Oppositional, Cognitive Problems, and Hyperactivity scales and the ADHD Index. The CPRS-R:S contains 27 items, and the CTRS-R:S contains 28 items. Each takes under 10 minutes to complete. Both the short and long forms have questions in a Likert 4-point scale (from "never" to "very often").

The CPRS-R:L was normed on parents or guardians of 2,482 children ages 3 to 17. Eighty-three percent of the children were Caucasian, but the normative sample also included African Americans, Hispanics, Asian Americans, Native Americans, and others. Gender distribution was approximately equal. Internal reliability (Cronbach's alpha coefficient) is reported for each scale by gender and ranged from .73 to .94. Test-retest intervals between 6 and 8 weeks were studied for each subscale using 49 children (average age 11.8) and ranged from .47 to .85.

The CTRS-R:L was normed on teachers of 1,973 children ages 3 to 17. Seventy-eight percent of the adolescents were identified by teachers as Caucasian. Test-retest intervals between 6 and 8 weeks were studied for each subscale using 50 children (average age 11.2) and ranged from .47 to .88. CTRS-R:L internal reliability (Cronbach's alpha coefficient) is reported for each scale, divided by gender, and ranged from .77 to .96. Test-retest reliability ranged from .62 to .87 (Danforth & DuPaul, 1996).

The validity of this measure was determined by its ability to discriminate between clinically referred and nonreferred children. (Miller, Kolewiccz, & Klien, 1997). Correlations (concurrent validity) between parent and teacher ratings for individual subscales ranged from .12 to .47 for males and .21 and .55 for females, indicating that teacher and parent raters often perceived the same children quite differently.

The Conners-Wells Adolescent Self-report Scales (CASS-L and CASS-S) are new additions to the parent and teacher rating scales. The long form (CASS-L) contains 10 subscales, including Family Problems, Emotional Problems, Conduct Problems, Cognitive Problems, Anger Control Problems, Hyperactivity, ADHD Index, and *DSM-IV* subscales including *DSM-IV* Inattentive and *DSM-IV* Hyperactive-Impulsive, and takes approximately 20 minutes to complete.

The CASS-L contains 87 items that are rated using an adapted Likert 4-point scale (from "never" to "very often") by adolescents between 12 and 17 years of age. The CASS-L was normed on 3,394 adolescents between the ages of 12 and 17 (1,558 males and 1,846 females). Sixty-two percent of this sample was Caucasian. Internal reliability (Cronbach's alpha coefficient) is reported for each scale by gender and ranged from .75 to .92. Test-retest intervals between 6 and 8 weeks were studied for each subscale using 50 children (mean age 14.8) and ranged from .73 to .89.

The CASS-S contains 27 items and takes under 10 minutes. It contains subscales that closely follow the short forms for parents and teachers and include Conduct Problems, Cognitive Problems, Hyperactive-Impulsive, and an ADHD Index.

REFERENCES

Conners, C. K. (1997). *Conners Rating Scales–Revised Technical Manual.* North Tonawanda, NY: Multi-Health Systems.

Conners, C. K. (1999). Conners Rating Scales–Revised. In M. E. Maruish (Eds.), *Use of psychological testing for treatment planning and outcomes assessment* (2nd ed., pp. 467–495). Mahwah, NJ: Erlbaum.

Danforth, J. S., & DuPaul, G. J. (1996). Interrater reliability of teacher rating scales for children with Attention-Deficit/Hyperactivity Disorder. *Journal of Psychopathology & Behavioral Assessment, 3,* 227–237.

Hale, J. B., How, S. K., Dewitt, M. B., & Coury, Daniel, L. (2001). Discriminant validity of the Conners Scales for ADHD Subtypes. *Current Psychology, 20,* 231–250.

Miller, L. S., Koplewiccz, H. S., & Klein, R. G. (1997). Teachers' ratings of hyperactivity, inattention, and conduct problems in preschoolers. *Journal of Abnormal Child Psychology, 2,* 113–119.

Plake, B. S., & Impara, J. C. (Eds.). (2001). *The fourteenth mental measurements yearbook.* Lincoln, NE: Buros Institute of Mental Measurements.

RON DUMONT
Fairleigh Dickinson University

JOHN O. WILLIS
Rivier College

CONSCIENCE, LACK OF IN INDIVIDUALS WITH DISABILITIES

Society is particularly concerned that children develop the skills to regulate their own behavior or, stated differently, internalize moral principles. Situations often arise that pose a conflict between the individual desires of the person and the requirements of society. These circumstances call for the exercise of self-control as the person suppresses self-interested behavior in favor of actions that serve the needs of others. Two areas of research bear directly on this problem—altruism and resistance to temptation.

Altruism

Altruism refers to behavior that is carried out to benefit another in the absence of threat or expected reward. Altruism entails self-control since the helper must weigh the costs of helping (e.g., material loss or physical danger) against the benefits (e.g., self-satisfaction) of helping (Kanfer, 1979). Research with children has relied on several measures of altruism, including donating possessions to a charity or another child, willingness to rescue someone in trouble, peer ratings, and naturalistic observations of helping and sharing.

Most children show an increase in sharing during the period of middle childhood. This change parallels children's decreasing egocentrism and increasingly sophisticated moral reasoning abilities. However, the relationship among these variables is not clearly understood. At least with children of average IQ, general level of cognitive development is unrelated to various measures of altruism (Rushton & Wiener, 1975). There does appear to be a weak relationship between generosity and level of moral reasoning among 7- to 11-year-old children, but it is not known if moral reasoning directly affects moral behavior (Rushton, 1975). Most studies fail to find a relationship between sex and altruism, but when differences are noted they tend to show females as more altruistic (Krebs, 1970). Finally, investigators have found a substantial degree of behavioral specificity across situations that offer an opportunity for altruistic behavior. For example, a child may donate a toy to a needy stranger but fail to volunteer time to help a peer. The correlation across measures is about .30 and may reflect the weak effect of an underlying personality variable or experimental or psychometric artifacts (Rushton, 1976).

One research finding that is unequivocal is that the altruistic behavior of children can be modified. Numerous studies have shown that children will imitate an altruistic model (Harris, 1971). In fact, the influence of a model was shown in one study to extend up to 4 months, even though posttesting was conducted under very different circumstances (Rushton, 1975). These results have obvious implications for child-rearing practices.

Resistance to Temptation

Resistance to temptation is another example of self-control. Here the child is required to exercise self-restraint in the absence of immediate surveillance. Several studies have examined variables that promote this form of self-control. From a developmental perspective, the emergence of language is important in that it allows the child to regulate his or her behavior by stating rules of conduct (Kanfer & Phillips, 1970). The ability to verbalize rules may be necessary but usually is not sufficient for resisting temptation.

Children who score high on resistance to temptation often make use of cognitive strategies (i.e., self-control techniques). A body of work by Kanfer (Hartig & Kanfer, 1973; Kanfer & Zich, 1974) and Mischel (Mischel, Ebbesen, & Zeiss, 1972; Mischel & Patterson, 1978) has shown that resistance to temptation is enhanced when children distract themselves (e.g., sing songs or thinking of a "fun activity"), repeatedly state a rule (e.g., "I'm a good girl if I don't look at the hampster"), or engage in mental transformations (e.g., "The pretzel is really just a log of wood"). The fact that older children are more successful in such situations is in part attributed to a greater facility in the use of language and a larger repertoire of cognitive strategies.

Researchers have just recently begun to extend these findings to retarded individuals. It has been noted that mildly retarded adolescents prefer immediate rewards even though by waiting they could receive twice as many of those rewards (Franzini, Litrownik, & Magy, 1978). In one study with moderately retarded adolescents, training in self-instruction ("I am gonna get more money if I wait to get paid . . . I sure am a good worker") reinforced practice and the provision of successful models led to a fivefold increase in the delay of gratification (Franzini, Litrownik, & Magy, 1980).

The importance of verbal controlling strategies in resistance to temptation is underscored by a study comparing Down's syndrome children to nonretarded children matched for level of cognitive development. On the average, the retarded children were less able to resist temptation than were the nonretarded children, a finding consistent with the Franzini et al. (1980) study. Interestingly, those Down's syndrome children that were most successful were observed to spontaneously engage in verbal and nonverbal behaviors that served to distract them from the desired object (Kopp, Krakow, & Johnson, 1983).

In considering the research in both the areas of altruism and resistance to temptation, a clear directive for teachers and parents is evident. In order to enhance self-control one should not think in terms of building the child's character. Instead, the child should be taught specific verbal and non-verbal behavioral skills that can be used for self-regulation in tempting situations.

REFERENCES

Franzini, L. R., Litrownik, A. J., & Magy, M. A. (1978). Immediate and delayed reward preferences of TMR adolescents. *American Journal of Mental Deficiency, 82,* 406–409.

Franzini, L. R., Litrownik, A. J., & Magy, M. A. (1980). Training trainable mentally retarded adolescents in delay behavior. *Mental Retardation, 18,* 45–47.

Harris, M. (1971). Models, norms and sharing. *Psychological Reports, 29,* 147–153.

Hartig, M., & Kanfer, F. H. (1973). The role of verbal self-instructions in children's resistance to temptation. *Journal of Personality & Social Psychology, 25,* 259–267.

Kanfer, F. H. (1979). Personal control, social control, and altruism: Can society survive the age of individualism? *American Psychologist, 34,* 231–239.

Kanfer, F. H., & Phillips, J. S. (1970). *Learning foundations of behavior therapy.* New York: Wiley.

Kanfer, F. H., & Zich, J. (1974). Self-control training: The effects of external control on children's resistance to temptation. *Developmental Psychology, 10,* 108–115.

Kopp, C. B., Krakow, J. B., & Johnson, K. L. (1983). Strategy production by young Down syndrome children. *American Journal of Mental Deficiency, 88,* 164–169.

Krebs, D. L. (1970). Altruism: An examination of the concept and a review of the literature. *Psychological Bulletin, 73,* 258–302.

Mischel, W., Ebbesen, E. B., & Zeiss, A. R. (1972). Cognitive and attentional mechanisms in delay of gratification. *Journal of Personality & Social Psychology, 21,* 204–218.

Mischel, W., & Patterson, C. J. (1978). Effective plans for self-control. In W. A. Collins (Ed.), *Minnesota symposia on child psychology* (Vol. 2). Hillsdale, NJ: Erlbaum.

Rushton, J. P. (1975). Generosity in children: Immediate and long term effects of modeling, preaching, and moral judgment. *Journal of Personality & Social Psychology, 31,* 459–466.

Rushton, J. P. (1976). Socialization and the altruistic behavior of children. *Psychological Bulletin, 83,* 898–913.

Rushton, J. P., & Wiener, J. (1975). Altruism and cognitive development in children. *British Journal of Social & Clinical Psychology, 14,* 341–349.

LAURENCE C. GRIMM
University of Illinois

ATTACHMENT DISORDER
IMPULSE CONTROL
MORAL REASONING
SELF-CONTROL CURRICULUM

CONSENT, INFORMED

Informed consent is founded on the ethical responsibility of researchers and diagnosticians to disclose the potential risks and benefits associated with participation in a research study or in educational and psychological testing (American Educational Research Association, American Psychological Association, & National Council on Measurement in Education, 1985; Schloss & Smith, 1999). Informed consent, as public policy, is linked to historical human rights violations in medical, social, and psychological research. The National Commission (1979) describes two important examples of human rights violations in the twentieth century, " . . . the exploitation of unwilling prisoners as research subjects in Nazi concentration camps was condemned as a particularly flagrant injustice. In this country, in the 1940s, the Tuskegee syphilis study used disadvantaged, rural black men to study the untreated course of a disease that is by no means confined to that population. These subjects were deprived of demonstrably effective treatment in order not to interrupt the project, long after such treatment became generally available" (p. 7). A number of other high profile examples, including the infection of children with disabilities with hepatitis, introduction of cancer cells into chronically ill patients with dementia, secret radiation experiments with human subjects, and intentionally deceiving research subjects as part of psychological research (see Brody, Gluck, & Aragon, 1997; Jacobs & Zonnenberg, 2004) led to the passage of the *National Research Act* in 1974 (PL 93-348).

The National Commission for the Protection of Human Subjects of Biomedical and Behavioral Research was created as a result of the passage of PL 93-348. The National Commission was tasked with developing guidelines and principles for research involving human participants. The dissemination of *The Belmont Report* (National Commission, 1979) was the result of this work and serves as a seminal document in guiding the practice of researchers nationally. Specific guidelines for ethical research practice, as outlined in *The Belmont Report,* include respect for persons, beneficence, and justice, and are discussed below.

Respect for persons includes two important principles: the principle of the autonomy of individuals and the principle of protection for those with "diminished autonomy" (National Commission, 1979, p. 5). The acknowledgement of personal autonomy suggests that most persons are capable of making choices and decisions regarding their lives, including participation in research. Brody et al. (1997) write "*Personal autonomy* refers to a respect for the integrity of the individual. It is recognized legally as the right of self-determination and constitutionally as the right of privacy. In the research context, autonomy is honored and preserved through the participant's right to consent or refuse participation" (p. 286). Protection of those with diminished autonomy suggests that additional protections and safeguards are needed for those who might not be in a position to provide informed consent to participate in research. Examples of persons who may need additional safeguards include children, persons with cognitive disabilities, persons with chronic illnesses, and prisoners. *The Belmont Report* concludes that "the extent of protection afforded should depend upon the risk of harm and the likelihood of benefit. The judgment that any individual lacks autonomy should be periodically reevaluated and will vary in different situations" (p. 5).

Beneficence refers to an obligation of researchers to make every effort to "maximize possible benefits" (National Commission, 1979, p. 6) by not engaging in research activities that could potentially cause physical or psychological harm. Beneficence is a principle that receives careful scrutiny when a researcher presents a proposal to his or her Institutional Review Board (IRB). The IRB is typically charged with reviewing all research proposals that involve human participants and determining if the proposals comply with federal regulations (Gall, Borg, & Gall, 1996). In terms of beneficence, the IRB is obligated to determine if the risk-to-benefit ratio is reasonable given the nature of the study.

The principle of justice suggests that all persons should be treated equally, including how potential participants are selected to participate in a research study, the availability of treatment, and the provision of informed consent. This principle is rooted in the history of marginalized populations (e.g., the disabled, prisoners, economically disadvantaged) that have been the subject of research abuses. In other words, "the selection of research subjects needs to be scrutinized in order to determine whether some classes" (e.g., welfare patients, particular racial and ethnic minorities, or person confined to institutions) are being systematically selected simply because of their easy availability, their compromised position, or their manipulability, rather than for reasons directly related to the problem being studied (National Commission, 1979, p. 7). In addition to outlining ethnical principles, *The Belmont Report* provides specific standards for the application of these principles within the context of conducting biomedical and behavioral research, including standards for providing informed consent, standards for the assessment of risk and benefits, and standards for the selection of potential participants.

Informed consent, by definition, "ensures that research participants enter the research of their free will and with understanding of the nature of the study and any possible dangers that may arise. It is intended to reduce the likelihood that participants will be exploited by a researcher persuading them to participate without fully knowing what the study's requirements are" (Gay & Airasian, 2003, p.

81). *The Belmont Report* (National Commission, 1979) uses the following benchmarks to guide how informed consent should be obtained, including how and what information is communicated, comprehension of that information by the potential participant, and the provision of voluntariness and choice of participation throughout the research study. Information refers to a complete disclosure of what the researcher intends to do and stating (verbally and in writing) any anticipated risks and benefits associated with the study. The standard of comprehension suggests that the researcher has taken into account the potential subject's capabilities and has presented all information in a manner that is easily understood. Voluntariness refers to the exercise of a person's free will to participate or not participate in the absence of coercion or undue influence. This standard also suggests that a person can withdraw from a research study at any time without penalty.

Fisher (2004) outlines important considerations for obtaining informed consent as part of the Revised American Psychological Association's Ethics Code and the Health Insurance Portability and Accountability Act (HIPAA). These standards provide guidelines for obtaining informed consent from adolescents with adult legal status; standards for working with persons who are English Language Learners, including the appropriate use of interpreters; standards for obtaining assent from minors who are potential participants in a research project; and standards for working with legal guardians, in particular, guardians of foster children and juvenile detainees.

According to the National Commission (1979), the IRB must determine if the risks, as stated in the proposal, are justified, thereby giving the potential participant(s) the opportunity to carefully determine if they would like to participate in the proposed study. In describing what constitutes a risk, *The Belmont Report* writes "Many kinds of possible harms and benefits need to be taken into account. There are, for example, risks of psychological harm, physical harm, legal harm, social harm and economic harm and the corresponding benefits. While the most likely types of harms to research subjects are those of psychological or physical pain or injury, other possible kinds should not be overlooked" (p. 10).

Finally, procedures for subject selection must be carefully reviewed. All efforts should be maintained that will protect against bias and knowingly providing an undue burden on potential classes of participants. Moreover, vulnerable populations that may need additional safeguards should be carefully reviewed following the principles of informed consent, beneficence, and justice as described above (National Commission, 1979).

Informed consent as public policy has been well defined and articulated. However, informed consent is also part of a larger research ethic that is intended to fully disclose the risks and benefits associated with participation in a research study and eliminate the potential for physical, social, and psychological harm that may occur from participation in biomedical and behavioral research. *The Belmont Report* (National Commission, 1979) provides principles for ethical research, including demonstrating respect for all potential participants, beneficence, and social justice. Application of these principles is found in the standards of informed consent, assessment of risk and benefits, and the selection of participants.

REFERENCES

American Educational Research Association, American Psychological Association, & National Council on Measurement in Education. (1985). *Standards for educational and psychological testing.* Washington, DC: Author.

Brody, J. L., Gluck, J. P., & Aragon, A. S. (1997). Participants' understanding of the process of psychological research: Informed consent. *Ethics and Behavior, 7,* 285–298.

Fisher, C. B. (2004). Informed consent and clinical research involving children and adolescents: Implications for the revised APA ethics code and HIPAA. *Journal of Clinical Child and Adolescent Psychology, 33,* 832–839.

Gall, M. D., Borg, W. R., & Gall, J. P. (1996). *Educational research: An introduction* (6th ed.). White Plains, NY: Longman.

Gay, L. R., & Airasian, P. (2003). *Educational research: Competencies for analysis and applications* (7th ed.). Upper Saddle River, NJ: Prentice Hall.

Jacobs, F., & Zonnenberg, A. (2004). Tangible and intangible cost of "protecting human subjects": The impact of the National Research Act of 1974 on university research activities. *Education Policy Analysis Archives, 12,* 1–12.

National Commission for the Protection of Human Subjects of Biomedical and Behavioral Research (National Commission). (1979). *Belmont report: Ethical principles and guidelines for the protection of human subjects of research.* Washington DC: U.S. Department of Health, Education, and Welfare.

Schloss, P. J., & Smith, M. A. (1999). *Conducting research.* Upper Saddle River, NJ: Prentice Hall.

RANDALL L. DE PRY
University of Colorado at Colorado Springs

RESEARCH IN SPECIAL EDUCATION

CONSENT DECREE

A consent decree is a legal mandate or court order issued by a judiciary authority that has jurisdiction over the particular civil matter resolved in the decree. It is a legally enforceable order of that court. Consent decrees derive from the agreement of the adversarial parties to a civil lawsuit to end their disagreement provided that certain acts are performed by one or both parties and agreed to in order to avoid continuing litigation. The agreement is drawn up by the two parties,

signed by the appropriate legal representatives, and submitted to the court for review. If the court decides the agreement is fair and entered into with appropriate understanding and representation by both parties, the court will then mandate and enforce the decree by court order.

Many special education cases are decided by consent agreements that become enforceable court decrees. Among the best known and most influential are *Diana v. State Board of Education* (1970) and *Guadalupe v. Tempe Elementary School District* (1972). Consent decrees are binding only on the parties to the decree, and do not constitute case law that may be cited as true legal precedent. However, they can influence policymakers in the legislative process, prompting new laws that address the substantive issues underlying the consent decrees.

CECIL R. REYNOLDS
Texas A&M University
Second edition

KIMBERLY F. APPLEQUIST
University of Colorado at Colorado Springs
Third edition

DIANA V. STATE BOARD OF EDUCATION

CONSEQUENCES

Consequences are the events that occur as a result of a particular behavior. Consequences are monitored to help teachers and researchers determine the function of a particular behavior, and how to control the frequency, intensity, duration or latency of that specific behavior. The behavior that is being analyzed is often referred to as the target behavior (Pierangelo & Giuliani, 2006; Taylor, 2006). Isolating a specific behavior and defining it in observable and measurable terms allows the antecedent and consequences to be identified (Scott, Liaupsin, Nelson, & Jolivette, 2003). Manipulating either an antecedent that leads to the target behavior or a consequence of the behavior, modifications can be made to the target behavior. In this way the teacher or researcher may increase a desired behavior or decrease an undesirable behavior (Haager & Klinger, 2005; Heward, 2006; McLoughlin & Lewis, 2005; Pierangelo & Giuliani, 2006; Scott et al., 2003; Taylor, 2006).

If a teacher or researcher wishes to modify a student's behavior, they must define the behavior in specific terms so that it is recognized by all people who will observe the student, and to insure that consistency is maintained. For example, a student may engage in disruptive behaviors, defined as striking his hand against the desk with enough force to create a noise that is heard in all areas of the classroom. Systematic observations of not only the behavior, but the events preceding the behavior (antecedents) and the events that occur as a result of the behavior (consequences) are then recorded.

Consequences should be recorded using measurable and observable terms. It is important to separate what you believe or feel is happening from what is physically happening. Everything that occurs as a result of the target behavior is a consequence; use of class time to resolve the issue, giving of a reward, attention of peers, attention of the teacher, loss of these attentions, or any other change that occurs in the environment due to the target behavior are consequences (Friend, 2005; Scott et al., 2003). These consequences can be divided into two categories, punishment and reinforcement (Heward, 2006; Haager & Klinger, 2005).

Punishment reduces the likelihood that the behavior will occur again. The intent of the teacher or researcher does not determine if a consequence is a punishment. If the frequency, intensity, duration, or latency of the target behavior is reduced after the consequence occurs then that consequence is by definition a punisher for that behavior (Alberto & Troutman, 1990).

If the student in the aforementioned example strikes his hand against the desk and the teacher takes time out of class to tell him to stop, but the overall frequency of the behavior is not reduced, then telling him to stop is not a punisher. In fact, if the behavior increases (perhaps the student is seeking attention) the behavior is actually being reinforced.

Reinforcement increases the likelihood that the behavior will occur again. By carefully monitoring the consequences that are occurring and the patterns of future behaviors, researchers and teachers can manipulate the consequences that occur as a result of a behavior and thus influence the likelihood that that behavior will occur again (Alberto & Troutman, 1990; Haager & Klinger, 2005; Heward, 2006; McLoughlin & Lewis, 2005; Pierangelo & Giuliani, 2006; Scott et al., 2003; Taylor, 2006). The teacher or researcher can arrange for reinforcing consequences to occur for desirable behaviors and punishing consequences to occur for undesirable behaviors.

In the example used so far, the teacher or researcher would need to determine the behavior they would like to have the student perform instead of striking the desk. This is often referred to as a replacement behavior (Alberto & Troutman, 1990; Taylor, 2006). The researcher would then manipulate the antecedents to generate the desired behavior, such as asking the student to lace his fingers together and rest them on the desk. Immediately after the student complies (performing the desired target behavior), the teacher could praise, reward, or in any other way create a reinforcing consequence for the student. Through the use of reinforcement (manipulating the consequences), the frequency of the student demonstrating the desired behavior can be increased.

REFERENCES

Alberto, P. A., & Troutman, A. C. (1990). *Applied behavior analysis for teachers* (3rd ed.). Columbus, OH: Merrill.

Friend, M. (2005). *Special education: Contemporary perspectives for school professionals.* New York: Pearson Education.

Haager, D., & Klinger, J. K. (2005). *Differentiating instruction in inclusive classrooms: The special educator's guide.* New York: Allyn & Bacon.

Heward, W. L. (2006). *Exceptional children: An introduction to special education* (8th ed.). Upper Saddle River, NJ: Prentice Hall.

McLoughlin, J. A., & Lewis, R. B. (2005). *Assessing students with special needs* (6th ed.). Upper Saddle River, NJ: Prentice Hall.

Pierangelo, R., & Giuliani, G. A. (2006). *Assessment in special education: A practical approach* (2nd ed.). New York: Allyn & Bacon.

Scott, T. M., Liaupsin, C. J., Nelson, C. M., & Jolivette, K. (2003). Ensuring student success through team-based functional behavioral assessment. *Teaching Exceptional Children, 35*(5), 16–21.

Taylor, R. L. (2006). *Assessment of exceptional students: Educational and psychological procedures* (7th ed.). New York: Allyn & Bacon.

Walter A. Zilz
Bloomsburg University

BEHAVIORAL ASSESSMENT
BEHAVIOR DISORDERS

CONSORTIUM FOR CITIZENS WITH DISABILITIES

The Consortium for Citizens with Disabilities (CCD) is a coalition of approximately 100 national disability organizations working together to advocate for national public policy on behalf of the 54 million children and adults with disabilities and their families living in the United States. CCD's Chairman is currently Curt Decker of National Disability Rights Network (NDRN).

The CCD's goal is to achieve federal legislation that ensures that all Americans with disabilities are fully integrated into the mainstream of society. To achieve this goal CCD engages in advocacy efforts that:

- Ensure the self-determination, independence, empowerment, integration, and inclusion of children and adults with disabilities in all aspects of society
- Enhance the civil rights and quality of life of all people with disabilities and their families
- Reflect the values of the Americans with Disabilities Act

CCD was originally formulated in the late 1960s and early 1970s on an ad hoc basis to advocate support for the Developmental Disabilities Act, legislation to provide grants to states to coordinate and plan services for people with developmental disabilities, and grants to train professionals in various developmental disabilities service fields. In 1975, the coalition became more formalized and officially became the Consortium Concerned with the Developmentally Disabled. Over time, the coalition grew and the focus expanded to federal legislation and legal issues affecting people with disabilities, including education, employment, rights, housing, and long term services and supports. CCD played a significant role in the enactment of the 1990 Americans with Disabilities Act. The coalition voted in the mid 1980s to change its name to the Consortium for Citizens with Disabilities to reflect the reality of its membership and focus. Today CCD has almost 100 member organizations working through 15 task forces. CCD achieves its goals by:

- Identifying and researching public policy issues, developing testimony and policy recommendations and encouraging innovative solutions to public policy concerns
- Educating members of Congress in an effort to improve public policies and programs on behalf of individuals with disabilities
- Encouraging people with disabilities and their families to advocate for themselves and coordinating grass roots efforts to support them

CCD envisions an American society in which all individuals, aided by an enabling government, have the freedom and opportunity to exercise individual decisions concerning their own lives, welfare, and personal dignity. This society would be fully accessible to all individuals with disabilities and their families, and they would be included and able to fully participate in all aspects of community life. The consortium has been formulated to make this vision a reality for all Americans.

The organization is based in Washington, DC, at: The Consortium for Citizens with Disabilities, 1331 H Street, NW, Suite 301, Washington, DC 20005, (202) 783-2229 phone; (202) 783-8250 fax; email: Info@c-c-d.org. The web site address is http://www.c-c-d.org.

STAFF

CONSTITUTIONAL LAW (IN SPECIAL EDUCATION)

Judicial interpretations of the Constitution and its amendments have played a major role in the comparatively re-

cent efforts to obtain and maintain appropriate special education programs and services for children and youth with disabilities and their families. The groundwork for this role was laid in the 1954 Supreme Court decision in *Brown* v. *Board of Education;* the decision made clear that separate education facilities for children of different races are inherently not equal (Lippman & Goldberg, 1973). This decision affirmed that, because of the importance of education today, education "is a right which must be available to all on equal terms" (*Brown* v. *Board of Education,* 347 U.S. 483). Citing this decision almost 20 years later, attorneys in two class-action suits built their arguments for landmark special education cases that were resolved in federal district courts (*Pennsylvania Association for Retarded Citizens* v. *Commonwealth of Pennsylvania,* 334 F. Supp. 1257, E.D. Pa., 1971), which made clear that mentally retarded children in Pennsylvania are entitled to free education programs appropriate for their needs; and *Mills* v. *Board* (*Mills* v. *Board of Education, District of Columbia,* 348 F. Supp. 866, 1972), which extended free and appropriate education to all children with disabilities in the District of Columbia.

Both the *PARC* and *Mills* cases have been cited in subsequent litigation involving similar and related principles that eventually were incorporated into federal legislation. Of particular importance to special education are the Rehabilitation Act of 1973, which requires access to programs and facilities, and more recently the Individuals with Disabilities Education Act (IDEA) and subsequent amendments, the latest being in 2004. They embody the principles of zero project, nondiscriminatory testing, individualized and appropriate education planning and programming, least restrictive alternative as preferred educational placement, and procedural due process. All of these principles can be found in the guarantees of the Fifth and Fourteenth amendments to the Constitution (Turnbull & Fiedler, 1984) which state:

- No person shall . . . be deprived of life, liberty, or property, without due process of law (Constitution of the United States, Amendment V, 1791).
- No State shall make or enforce any law which shall abridge the privileges or immunities of citizens of the United States; nor shall any State deprive any person of life, liberty or property without due process of law, nor deny to any person within its jurisdiction the equal protection of the laws (Constitution of the United States, Amendment XIV, 1868).

For a detailed discussion of litigation in special education and its reliance on constitutional guarantees and interpretations of the Supreme Court, see Turnbull and Fiedler (1984). Recent litigation has focused on the constitutionality of state financing systems (Verstegen, 1998).

REFERENCES

Lippman, L., & Goldberg, I. (1973). *Right to education: Anatomy of the Pennsylvania case and its implications for exceptional children.* New York: Teachers College Press.

Turnbull, J. R., III, & Fiedler, C. R. (1984). *Judicial interpretation of the Education for All Handicapped Children Act.* Reston, VA: Council for Exceptional Children.

Verstegen, D. A. (1998). *Landmark court decisions challenge state special education funding. Center for Special Education Brief.* Palo Alto, CA: American Institutes for Research.

MARJORIE E. WARD
The Ohio State University
Second edition

KIMBERLY F. APPLEQUIST
University of Colorado at
Colorado Springs
Third edition

BROWN v. BOARD OF EDUCATION
LARRY P.
MILLS v. BOARD OF EDUCATION OF THE DISTRICT OF COLUMBIA
PASE v. HANNON
PENNSYLVANIA ASSOCIATION FOR RETARDED CITIZENS v. PENNSYLVANIA

CONSULTATION

Consultation refers to a professional relationship in which a specialist attempts to improve the functioning of another professional. Although there are many models of school consultation, each with different sets of assumptions, techniques, and goals, Bergan and Tombari's definition (1976) is general enough to encompass the idiosyncrasies of these various models. "Consultation refers to services rendered by a consultant (e.g., school psychologist) to a consultee (e.g., teacher) who functions as a change agent with respect to the learning or adjustment of a client (e.g., a child) or a group of clients" (p. 4).

Consultation in school settings is an indirect model of providing broadly defined mental health services to children. The consultant attempts to effect a change in children's behavior and learning by attempting to change the teacher's (or administrator's) attitudes, perceptions, and behaviors. One of the rationales for consultation is the economy of resources it offers. By improving teacher and administrator functioning, the psychologist can affect many more children than possible in the traditional counseling and testing models of service delivery.

Certain key elements distinguish consultation from other professional activities. First, consultation is a professional-to-professional relationship that is focused on helping the consultee to do a job. Consultation is a voluntary relationship; thus the consultee is free to accept or reject the consultant's help and recommendations. In turn, the consultee is expected to contribute to the problem-solving process and is responsible for implementing action plans that result from the consultation. Finally, the consultant respects the confidential nature of the relationship.

One professional activity that shares similarities with consultation is supervision; however, consultation differs from supervision in several important ways. Because the supervisor is administratively responsible for the supervisee's work, the supervisee is obligated to accept the supervisor's advice. A supervisor is usually a senior professional in the same discipline as the supervisee, whereas the consultant is usually trained in a discipline different from that of the consultee. Thus supervision involves a hierarchical obligatory relationship, while consultation involves a egalatarian voluntary relationship.

Consultation has both remedial and preventive goals, but different consultation models emphasize one or the other goals. Thus when consulting with a teacher, the consultant attempts to improve both the learning and adjustment of the child about whom the teacher is concerned and the teacher's ability to cope effectively with similar children in the future. This latter, preventive goal of consultation allows psychologists to broaden their impact beyond the target child.

The goals of consultation listed by Conoley and Conoley (1982) are relevant to several consultation models and include: (1) providing an objective point of view; (2) increasing problem-solving skills; (3) increasing coping skills; (4) increasing freedom of choice; (5) increasing commitment to choices made; and (6) increasing available resources.

The different models of school consultation do not have identical conceptual bases. For example, behavioral consultation is based on social learning theory, and the technology of applied behavioral analysis is used to change students' and teachers' behaviors. Process consultation is based on social, psychological, and general systems theory and assumes interpersonal and group processes affect educational outcomes. There are certain assumptions, or concepts, that are common to the various models. Two shared assumptions are that children's classroom behaviors and learning are determined by variables in the child and in the classroom setting and that the consultant must work jointly with the consultee to solve problems.

Considerable attention in the consultation literature is given to the task of entry as a consultant into an organization. Entry tasks include: (1) obtaining approval for consultation from administrators; (2) establishing a shared set of expectations with administrators and teachers regarding consultation's purposes, the roles and responsibilities of the consultant and consultees, confidentiality, and the types of problems to be discussed in consultation; and (3) establishing the consultant as a credible and trustworthy resource person. If teachers are accustomed to receiving recommendations from psychologists, and the psychologist-consultant does not carefully lay the groundwork for the consultative relationship, the teacher and the psychologist will find themselves working at cross purposes, based on their differing expectations for the interaction.

Consultation involves two jobs: working on the content, or specific problem brought to consultation, and working on the process of helping the consultee improve his or her job-related performance. It is important for the consultant to have specialized knowledge that is relevant to the consultation content (e.g., the particular behavior, learning, or programmatic concern). Indeed, the reason the consultee asked for the consultant's help is that the consultee believes the consultant has such relevant knowledge. Knowledge bases the psychologist-consultant might draw from in teacher consultation include child development, theories of learning, childhood psychopathology, tests and measurements, diagnosis of learning and behavior, group processes, individual instructional programming, and treatment of childhood learning and behavioral disorders.

In addition to content skills, the consultant must have skills necessary for establishing and maintaining rapport with the consultee and for facilitating the consultee's professional growth. Thus the consultant: (1) seeks clarification, encouraging consultees to see problems from new or broader perspectives; (2) supports the consultee while he or she is grappling with the problem, boosting consultee motivation and self-confidence; (3) asks questions that require consultees to validate information; (4) probes for feelings to help consultees accept their emotional reactions to children; (5) provides choices to increase consultee freedom to choose and commitment to choices made; and (6) confronts consultees either directly or indirectly to increase consultee objectivity. An example of an indirect confrontation is telling a female teacher who is inappropriately "mothering" a young girl that the girl is expecting the teacher to do too much for her and the girl needs to learn that the teacher cannot be her mother. An example of a direct confrontation is telling a male teacher that he seems to be apologizing to his students when he assumes an authoritative role, and that perhaps students are misbehaving because they are picking up on his discomfort in the authoritarian role.

Five models of school consultation are described with respect to their primary purpose and the roles and skills required of the consultant. Psychoeducational consultation is the type of consultation most frequently practiced in schools. After the psychologist has evaluated a child, the psychologist interprets the evaluation results to the teacher, presents recommendations to the teacher, and engages the teacher in a discussion of these recommendations so that the teacher will be able to choose and implement one or more recommendations. The primary purpose is remedial. The consultant's primary role is to diagnose the problem and recommend treatment.

Behavioral consultation is based on social learning theory. The behavioral consultant applies the technology of applied behavior analysis to the task of changing student and teacher behavior. The consultant observes the child as well as the teacher in the classroom to identify and count target behaviors, determine antecedents and consequences of those target behaviors, and recommend changes expected to result in a change in target behaviors. Because the teacher is ultimately responsible for making any changes that are recommended by the consultant, the consultant needs to establish a collaborative working relationship with the teacher. The primary goal in behavioral consultation is remedial; however, the consultant expects consultees will improve their skills in applied behavior analysis and will apply their new skills to similar problems in the future.

In educational consultation, the consultant presents new information or teaches new skills to consultees by conducting in-service workshops. The effective consultant-trainer carefully assesses educational needs of the workshop audience as well as the expectations of the administrators, and provides training that matches those needs and expectations. It is important, in cases of individual student consultation, that the question of needing informed consent from the parents is considered (Heron, 1996).

The mental health consultant's primary purpose is to improve the consultee's ability to effectively cope with similar problems in the future without the consultant's continued help. The particular problem discussed in consultation acts as leverage for changing the consultee's behavior. A secondary goal is to change the child's behavior. Because the focus is on the consultee, the consultant's process skills are especially important. The mental health consultant uses clinical interviewing skills to determine the reason a teacher is experiencing difficulty and employs different consultation approaches depending on the presumed reason for the consultee's difficulty. When the consultee's problem is presumed to be a lack of objectivity, the consultant uses specialized skills that require specialized training in consultation techniques. The consultant attempts to minimize the teacher's displacement of personal problems onto the work setting.

In program consultation, the consultant is requested by the administration to design or to evaluate a specific program such as a gifted education program, a race relations program, or a truancy program. The consultant must have experience and skills relevant to the particular program. The consultant issues a written report that contains recommendations for the school to implement.

Process consultation, like program consultation, is initiated by an administrator. It attempts to effect a change in the system rather than in the individual teacher or child. Process consultation is based on social psychological and general systems theory. The process consultant attempts to improve interpersonal and group processes used by administrators, teachers, parents, and students to reach educational objectives. Thus the consultant will involve the administrators and teachers in a mutual problem-solving effort aimed at diagnosing and changing such human processes as communication, leadership, decision making, and trust. The process consultant does not deal directly with the subject matter of the interactions of an organization. Rather, the consultant provides help with the methods of communication, problem solving, planning, and decision making (Schmuck, 1976).

Consultation is a term that encompasses a diverse set of models for delivering psychological services to a school (or other organization). The common thread is that the psychologist attempts to affect change in clients of the organization (e.g., students) by influencing the behaviors of persons who have a responsibility for client care.

REFERENCES

Bergan, J. R., & Tombari, M. L. (1976). Consultant skill and efficiency and the implementation and outcomes of consultation. *Journal of School Psychology, 14*(1), 3–14.

Conoley, J. C., & Conoley, C. W. (1982). *School consultation: A guide to practice and training.* New York: Pergamon.

Heron, T. E. (1996). Ethical and legal issues in consultation. *Remedial and Special Education, 17,* 6, 377–385.

Schmuck, R. A. (1976). *Process consultation and organization development.* Reading, MA: Addison-Wesley.

JAN N. HUGHES
Texas A&M University

**CONSULTATION, MENTAL HEALTH
MULTIDISCIPLINARY TEAM
PREREFERRAL INTERVENTIONS
PRESCHOOL SCREENING
PROFESSIONAL SCHOOL PSYCHOLOGY**

CONSULTATION, INCLUSION AND

See INCLUSION.

CONSULTATION, MENTAL HEALTH

Mental health consultation is an indirect mode of providing mental health services to clients served by some agency. The mental health consultant attempts to improve the psychological adjustment of persons in the community (i.e., students, parishioners, probationers, or patients) by consulting with professional caregivers in the community (i.e., teachers, clergymen, probation officers, or doctors). Gerald Caplan's seminal book, *The Theory and Practice of Mental Health Consultation* (1970), summarized his most important writings on the subject and offered the first comprehensive coverage of this mode of providing mental health services. Caplan defined mental health consultation as "a process of interaction between two professional persons—the consultant, who is a specialist, and the consultee, who invokes the consultant's help in regard to a current work problem with which he is having some difficulty and which he has decided is within the other's area of specialized competence" (p. 19). Other persons have broadened this definition to include consultation with more than one consultee and consultation with nonprofessionals (Altrocchi, 1972).

The mental health consultant may be a psychiatrist, psychologist, or social worker, and the consultee may be any person whose ministrations to lay persons in the community have mental health implications. Mental health consultation is more prevalent in schools than in other settings. Reasons for its prevalence in schools include the opportunity provided in schools to affect the mental health of large numbers of children through consultation with a small number of teachers, the recognition of the importance of schooling on children's mental health, the presence of psychologists in schools, and the demonstrated relevance of psychological theories and knowledge to educational goals and practices. Consistent with the focus of this work, the following discussion of consultation will be specific to mental health consultation in schools.

There are several key elements in the previous definition of consultation that distinguish consultation from other professional activities. First, the consultee (teacher, principal, other administrator) invokes the consultant's help. Because consultation is a professional-to-professional interaction, the consultee is responsible for determining whether the assistance of the consultant would be helpful.

Second, the consultee retains responsibility for the problem. Thus, when teachers or administrators ask for a consultant's help, they do not diminish their responsibility for instructing the child or administering the program. Because the consultee retains responsibility for the problem and its handling, the consultee is an active participant in a joint problem-solving process. Responsibility for problem formulation and solution is shared between the consultant and consultee. Thus, consultation is different from referral of a child to a psychologist who then assumes sole responsibility for diagnosing the problem and prescribing treatment. In the referral model, the treatment may or may not be the teacher's responsibility to implement. By contrast, any recommendations that result from the consultation process are the responsibility of the consultee to implement. Moreover, the consultee is free to accept or to reject the consultant's advice, and the consultee may terminate the relationship at any point. The consultant has no authority over the consultee except the authority of the consultant's good ideas.

Consultation is a confidential relationship. By the time

a teacher seeks a consultant's help, he or she may feel discouraged. Teachers would be reluctant to reveal their perceived failures in consultation if the relationship were not confidential. The active role of the teacher-consultee requires the teacher to communicate openly and honestly, with no fear that the consultant will disclose aspects of the communication to third parties. The active role is necessary because the consultant depends on the teacher's wealth of information regarding the problem, including past efforts to solve it. Furthermore, the teacher's values, beliefs, role constraints, resources for solving the problem, instructional methods, interactional style, knowledge base, and skills are important variables for the consultant to consider in jointly designing a plan for solving the problem brought to consultation. If the consultation plan is not compatible with the unique characteristics of the teacher's work situation, either it will not be implemented as intended or it will result in a disruption of the teacher's functioning. The confidential nature of the consultation relationship enables the consultee to play the active role required in consultation.

Consultation is a collaborative relationship. The consultant's role is that of a facilitator. Although consultation includes giving expert advice, the consultant's primary method of assisting teachers includes offering observations, asking questions that clarify the problem or place the problem in a new perspective, suggesting information that needs to be obtained in order to understand the problem, serving as a springboard for the teacher's own ideas, and sharing pertinent knowledge from such fields as child development, learning theory, group processes, behavior analysis, child psychopathology, tests and measurements, or family systems theory.

The problems discussed in consultation are work-related problems. The consultant does not help the consultee solve personal problems. Although personal problems influence work performance, the professional-to-professional nature of consultation requires a focus on work-related concerns. When personal problems are brought up by the teacher, the consultant conveys an accepting attitude but refocuses the discussion on the teacher's professional functioning.

Caplan categorized mental health consultation as to the kind of problem dealt with (a case or an administrative problem) and as to the focus (the client or program on the one hand or the consultee on the other). This resulted in four categories of consultation.

In *client-centered case* consultation, the focus is on a child's problems. The goal of change in the teacher is secondary to the goal of formulating the problem. A written report to the teacher summarizes the diagnostic findings and recommendations for the teacher's handling of the problem.

In *consultee-centered case* consultation, the focus is on the student; however, the consultant's primary goal is change in the teacher's knowledge, skills, self-confidence, or objectivity. The problem case is a leverage point for effecting a change in the teacher that will enable the teacher to work more effectively, not only with the particular child who is the focus of consultation, but also with similar children in the future. This expected ripple effect in consultation extends the impact of consultation to an indefinite number of children. Because a change in the teacher is the primary goal, the consultant spends considerable time with the teacher, helping the teacher gain new perspectives, insights, knowledge, and skills that will generalize to similar problems in the future. Rather than offering an expert formulation of the problem and strategy for change, the consultant engages the teacher as a peer professional in a problem-solving process, facilitating the teacher's ability to solve the problem independently. As assumption in consultee-centered case consultation is that the teacher will generalize new learnings to future cases if the teacher accepts responsibility for the problem formulation and action plans in consultation. In this type of consultation, the task of assessing the child's problem is secondary to the task of assessing the nature of the teacher's work difficulty, which may involve a lack of knowledge, skills, self-confidence, or professional objectivity. The consultant's expertise is directed primarily to the task of helping the teacher remedy whichever of these shortcomings is present. It is this type of consultation about which the most has been written, and it is this type of consultation that has become nearly synonymous with the term mental health consultation.

In *program-centered administrative* consultation, the focus is on a particular program for which the administrator-consultee has responsibility. The primary goal is the assessment of obstacles to achieving goals of a particular program. After a site visit and interviews with persons in the school, a written report summarizing the consultant's findings and recommendations is prepared. As in client-centered case consultation, the goal of educating administrators to handle similar problems in the future is secondary.

In *consultee-centered administrative* consultation, the focus is on the administrator's skills in areas such as group processes, leadership, and interpersonal relationships. This model of consultation is frequently referred to as organizational development consultation. It assumes that change in social structures and human processes within a school will result in the greatest positive impact on the mental health of students and teachers.

Typically, the consultant has no line authority over consultees. Two sources of influence over consultees available to consultants are expert and referent power (Meyers, Parsons, & Martin, 1979). Expert power is the influence the consultant has with a consultee based on the consultee's attribution of expertise to the consultant. Teachers seek out a consultant's help because they believe the consultant has special expert knowledge relevant to the problem for which consultation is sought. Referent power is influence the consultant has with consultees based on the consultee's identification with the consultant. When a consultee admires the consultant and identifies with the consultant's values, attitudes, and behaviors, the consultant is attributed referent power. Much of the consultation literature focuses on methods of building rapport, or referent power. While not using the term referent power, Caplan recommends such identification techniques as emphasizing the peer-professional relationship, "onedownsmanship," empathic listening, conveying respect for the consultee, accepting the consultee, emphasizing commonalities, being approachable, and engaging in informal social contacts with consultees.

Although consultation is different from teaching, the consultant has an educational role. As teacher, the consultant instructs, shares information, translates psychological theories into educationally relevant practices, models approaches, offers ideas, and interprets data. As facilitator, the consultant provides a model of professional objectivity, guides teachers in problem solving, encourages, helps consultees deal with affect that may decrease their ability to deal effectively with a problem, and helps consultees avoid displacement of personal problems in the work setting. The consultant also facilitates communication among different organizational units within the school (i.e., regular and special education teachers, grade level teachers, and administrators).

Empirical evidence derived from over 60 studies on the effectiveness of consultation services in alleviating special problems brought to consultation is positive (Mannino & Shore, 1975; Medway, 1979). Fewer studies on the preventive goals of consultation have been published; however, the results of these studies are positive (Gutkin & Curtis, 1982).

REFERENCES

Altrocchi, J. (1972). Mental health consultation. In S. Golann & C. Eisdorfer (Eds.), *Handbook of community mental health* (pp. 477–507). New York: Appleton-Century-Crofts.

Caplan, G. (1970). *The theory and practice of mental health consultation.* New York: Basic Books.

Gutkin, T. B., & Curtis, M. J. (1982). School-based consultation: Theory and techniques. In C. R. Reynolds & T. B. Gutkin (Eds.), *The handbook of school psychology* (pp. 796–828). New York: Wiley.

Mannino, F. V., & Shore, M. F. (1975). Effecting change through consultation. In F. V. Mannino, B. W. MacLennan, & M. F. Shore (Eds.), *The practice of mental health consultation.* New York: Gardner.

Medway, F. J. (1979). How effective is school consultation: A review of recent research. *Journal of School Psychology, 17,* 275–282.

Meyers, J., Parsons, R. D., & Martin R. (1979). *Mental health consultation in the schools.* San Francisco: Jossey-Bass.

JAN N. HUGHES
Texas A&M University

CONSULTATION
PSYCHOLOGY IN THE SCHOOLS
SCHOOL PSYCHOLOGY

CONTINGENCY CONTRACTING

A contingency contract is a behavior management technique designed to decrease unwanted behaviors or increase desired behaviors. These specific behaviors may be academic or social in nature. The contract is a written agreement signed by all parties that details the expected behaviors and the various consequences associated with the degree of compliance with its terms. Although contingency contracts have been used extensively in the special education environment, they have become increasingly popular management alternatives in inclusive settings for both students with disabilities and gifted students who require individualized programs.

Contingency contracts have been demonstrated to decrease unwanted behaviors such as school tardiness (Din, Isaac, & Rietveld, 2003), disruptive behavior in the general education classroom (Wilkinson, 2003) and suspensions among middle school students (Novell, 1994). Examples of using this technique to develop desired academic behaviors include increasing assignment completion in sixth grade students (Poston, 1991) and increasing proper capitalization and punctuation (Newstrom, McLaughlin, & Sweeney, 1999).

Stuart (1971) recommends incorporating five components into an ideal contract. First, a precise explanation of the behaviors, penalties, rewards, and privileges must be provided. For example, if a teacher wanted a student to remain in his/her seat in exchange for extra time at the computer, the time of in-seat behavior that must be exhibited before earning a specified amount of computer time needs to be detailed. Closely related, the second component necessitates that all behaviors are observable and measurable and all terms are specified. For example, once computer time has been earned, one should be able to refer to the contract to learn when this time may be claimed. While "in-seat behavior" can be operationally defined and accurately measured, behaviors such as "attending" or "listening" are more nebulous and would be difficult (though not impossible) to measure reliably enough for use in a contract. Third, contingencies for failure to meet the terms of the contract should be specified for both parties. Just as the child must experience the consequences if he/she does not perform as required, the teacher must also be willing to experience consequences (e.g., double reinforcement for the student) if his/her part of the agreement is not fulfilled. Fourth, a bonus clause for consistent performance may be included if the student or teacher feels it may be beneficial. This addition would emphasize the positive aspects of the contract. Finally, either the contract or the teacher should provide a means of monitoring the contract's effectiveness. By providing for this feedback, the contract can help to induce more positive comments on the part of the involved parties when each is in compliance with the contract terms.

Contingency contracts have also been used to increase

both academic skills and autonomous learning behaviors in gifted students by describing independent projects and structuring working conditions for such students in the regular classroom. By offering optional assignments at varying degrees of challenge and clearly articulating the expected behaviors during completion of a project, such agreements enable highly capable learners to receive appropriate support without disrupting regular classroom activity (Hishinuma, 1996). Winebrenner (2000) not only incorporates these two components of the contract but also recommends that it detail the level of participation expected in the regular educational program. By including these provisions, gifted students will know when they are expected to work without their teacher's assistance, when they can receive help, and when they are expected to join their classmates.

One of the major features of contingency contracts is that they tend to develop a more collaborative relationship between student and teacher, since the student generally has an active role in formulating the plan. Kohn (1993) supports the use of contracts if the agreement is jointly constructed and recommends that the student be an integral part of the process.

Contingency contracting has demonstrated great promise as a useful management tool for both special and regular educators. Because contracts enhance communication by specifying expectations on the part of both parties, compliance with the terms and performance can be measured easily and contingencies can be enforced. As with any behavioral strategy, however, the procedure is only as effective as its consistent application. For information on implementation and examples of contracts, see Winebrenner (1996, 2000) and Downing (1990).

REFERENCES

Din, F. S., Isaak, L. R., & Rietveld, J. (2003). *Effects of contingency contracting on decreasing student tardiness.* (ERIC DRS No. 474642)

Downing, J. A. (1990). Contingency contracts: A step-by-step format. *Intervention in School and Clinic, 26,* 111–113.

Hishinuma, E. S. (1996). Motivating the gifted underachiever: Implementing reward menus and behavioral contracts within an integrated approach. *Gifted Child Today Magazine, 19,* 30–35, 43–48.

Kohn, A. (1993). *Punished by rewards.* New York: Houghton Mifflin.

Newstrom, J., McLaughlin, T. F., & Sweeney, W. J. (1999). The effects of contingency contracting to improve the mechanics of written language with a middle school student with behavior disorders. *Child and Family Behavior Therapy, 2,* 39–48.

Novell, I. (1994). *Decreasing school suspensions among middle school children by implementing a rehabilitation in-room suspension.* (ERIC DRS No. ED371833)

Poston, R. (1991). *Increasing assignment completion of sixth grade students through behavior modification.* (ERIC DRS No. ED339455)

Stuart, R. B. (1971). Behavioral contracting within the families of delinquents. *Journal of Behavior Therapy and Experimental Psychiatry, 2,* 1–11.

Wilkinson, L. (2003). Using behavioral consultation to reduce challenging behavior in the classroom. *Preventing School Failure, 47,* 100–105.

Winebrenner, S. (1996). *Teaching kids with learning difficulties in the regular classroom: Strategies and techniques every teacher can use to challenge and motivate struggling students.* Minneapolis, MN: Free Spirit Publishing.

Winebrenner, S. (2000). *Teaching gifted kids in the regular classroom: Strategies and techniques every teacher can use to meet the academic needs of the gifted and talented.* Minneapolis, MN: Free Spirit Publishing.

ANDREW R. BRULLE
JILLIAN N. LEDERHOUSE
Wheaton College

BEHAVIORAL ASSESSMENT
BEHAVIOR DISORDERS

CONTINUOUS REINFORCEMENT

Positive reinforcement is the increase in the frequency of a response following the presentation of something pleasant or desirable. For example, teachers often praise and provide points for work completion to increase the likelihood that students will engage in this behavior in the future. A reinforcement schedule refers to how frequently a reinforcer will be delivered and there are two basic schedules of reinforcement: continuous and intermittent. Continuous reinforcement involves reinforcing an individual's behavior or response each time it occurs whereas intermittent reinforcement involves reinforcing the behavior or response on some occasions but not others (Chance, 1999). In schools and in the community, the majority of behavior is reinforced on intermittent schedules as it is typically impossible to reinforce each appropriate academic or social behavior that an individual exhibits.

The use of continuous reinforcement schedules is important to establish the association between engaging in a certain behavior and receiving a reinforcer (Alberto & Troutman, 2003). For example, students learn that each time their teacher points to a letter and they identify the letter name correctly, they receive verbal praise. Often, once the association between engaging in a certain behavior and receiving a reinforcer has been established, it is important to switch to a more intermittent schedule of reinforcement to effectively maintain behavior over time. In some cases, continuous schedules of reinforcement will always be appropriate such as when solving crossword puzzles, using vending machines, or ordering food at a restaurant (Pryor,

1999). If we did not obtain the food we wanted when ordering at a restaurant, this behavior (i.e., food ordering) would cease very quickly.

In general, continuous schedules of reinforcement should be used when individuals are learning new behaviors or responses (Kazdin, 2000). When an individual is learning a new behavior, such as riding a bike, the final behavior as well as the responses that are close to the final behavior (e.g., putting feet on the pedals, keeping hands positioned correctly on the handlebars) should be reinforced on a continuous basis. Once the behavior is learned, it no longer needs to be reinforced on a continuous schedule. There are often reinforcers in the natural environment that take over and reinforcement from teachers and/or caregivers is no longer needed to maintain the behavior. In the example of riding a bike, a child receives reinforcement from caregivers during the learning process, but once he or she has learned the behavior other reinforcers, such as being able to get to the park quickly via bike riding, help maintain the behavior over time.

There are several problems associated with the use of continuous reinforcement schedules (Alberto & Troutman, 2003). To begin with, when using this type of schedule, once the reinforcer is withdrawn or no longer provided, the desired behavior will rapidly decline and cease to occur (i.e., extinguish). Secondly, an individual who is reinforced on a continuous basis may become satiated or tired of the reinforcer, especially when food is used as a reinforcer. Finally, individuals may begin to expect a reinforcer for every appropriate behavior exhibited or may only engage in an appropriate behavior when a reinforcer is desired. For these reasons, it is important to switch to intermittent schedules of reinforcement as soon as the individual has learned the desired behavior.

REFERENCES

Alberto, P. A., & Troutman, A. C. (2003). *Applied behavior analysis for teachers* (6th ed.). Upper Saddle River, NJ: Pearson Education.

Chance, P. (1999). *Learning and behavior.* Pacific Grove: Brooks/Cole.

Kazdin, A. E. (2000). *Behavior modification in applied settings.* Belmont: Wadsworth.

Pryor, K. (1999). *Don't shoot the dog.* New York: Bantam Books.

LEANNE S. HAWKEN
University of Utah

BEHAVIORAL ASSESSMENT
BEHAVIOR DISORDERS

CONTINUUM OF SPECIAL EDUCATION SERVICES

See INCLUSION.

CONTINUUM OF SUPPORT

See POSITIVE BEHAVIORAL SUPPORT, SCHOOL-WIDE

CONTRACT PROCUREMENT

Contract procurement is a term used in vocational rehabilitation facilities, sheltered workshops, and work activities centers. The term is simply defined; however, the concept and process are more complex. The word contract refers to jobs that are used in the cited facilities to teach work habit skills or trade skills, or provide activities that result in reimbursement to persons with disabilities. The term procurement refers to the act of attaining contracts. The term contract procurement, as it relates to programs for the disabled, refers to the process of attaining work from businesses to be done by persons with disabilities. Subcontracts and prime manufacturing are two categories of contracts.

Subcontracts are jobs that are attained from businesses and that involve no purchases of materials or equipment. An example would be assembling circuit boards for microcomputers. Company A manufactures the parts to be assembled on the circuit boards. They purchase the boards and the boxes for shipping, and send a truck once a week to pick up the assembled and packaged product. The contract involves only labor; on completion of the contract, all surplus parts are returned to Company A.

Prime manufacturing contracts necessitate the purchase and inventory of materials to create a product. Attaining work is a sales function. In the process of selling the abilities of a work program, not only the equipment available but the manpower require legal protection. For example, Company A subcontracts the assembly of circuit boards to Work Program B. All assembly and packaging is done at Work Program B's site. However, Company A gets a special order for microcomputers with an additional resistor on the circuit boards that are already assembled into the microcomputers and boxed. The deadline is such that delivery and pickup of changes is too costly between Company A and Work Program B. Consequently, a labor force must be procured and attained by Company A if their business is to complete the work. They must open the boxes and add the resistor to each microcomputer circuit board, then repackage the unit.

Understanding that sales is a key concept in contract procurement is important. Often work programs fail to understand that attaining work is a process of identifying, attaining, working, and delivering. Some programs still use nonsales people to attain work and deliver a product, thus causing contract procurement for persons with disabilities to be thought of as cheap, subsidized labor.

The process of attaining work is subdivided into time and motion studies, and submitting a bid for subcontract or setting a price for prime manufacturing. Time and motion refers to setting up the work in the most efficient manner and then timing the steps in completing the work. The federal Department of Labor publications explain the rules for time and motion studies. A bid should include the following information: labor rate, overhead, materials, handling and waste, freight, and profit.

The bid also should include any conditions that may need to be included in the subcontract that concern the workshop regulations.

JEFF HEINZEN
Indianhead Enterprise

HABILITATION OF INDIVIDUALS WITH DISABILITIES
REHABILITATION

CONTROL GROUPS

Control groups are aggregates of subjects who do not receive the treatment of interest in an experimental or quasi-experimental intervention. They are used in research and program evaluation to provide baselines against which to measure the impact of an experimental manipulation and as a means to rule out alternative explanations of "treatment" effects. Control groups are useful particularly in field settings, where there may be a number of plausible rival accounts for the meaning of the researcher's observations. Whether the study is an elaborate investigation or the simple introduction of classroom innovation, control groups are often crucial to the interpretation of results.

The logic of the use of control groups centers around the ability to equate subjects in the "treatment" (experimental) and control groups on all factors except the treatment of interest. Many studies are limited because the assignment of subjects to experimental and control groups is such that the assumption of equivalence is not tenable. In addition, the nature of the research setting may result in the contamination of the control groups by such factors as rivalries with the experimental group or imitation of the treatment by the control group (Cook & Campbell, 1979).

Control groups often involve a no-treatment control, where members engage in their activities with no intervention by the experimenter. Cook, Leviton, and Shadish (1985) note that rather than a no-treatment control group, it might be preferable to use a control that allows for comparison between the treatment of interest and another intervention. This might particularly be the case where practitioners are concerned with the relative efficacy of approaches or where ethical constraints prohibit withdrawal or denial of treatment.

Particularly in the case of quasiexperimental designs,

where random assignment of subjects is not possible, a number of control groups are often used to rule out different competing interpretations. For example, members of a placebo control group receive an irrelevant treatment that gives an amount of time and attention similar to that of the experimental group (Cook & Campbell, 1979).

It is commonplace to introduce innovative programs in special education. By following proper control group design, one can judge the effectiveness of "reforms as experiments" and make policy decisions on a more rational basis (Campbell, 1969).

REFERENCES

Campbell, D. T. (1969). Reforms as experiments. *American Psychologist, 24,* 409–429.

Cook, T. D., & Campbell, D. T. (1979). *Quasiexperimentation: Design and analysis issues for field settings.* Chicago: Rand McNally.

Cook, T. D., Leviton, L. C., & Shadish, W. R. (1985). Program evaluation. In G. Lindzey & E. Aronson (Eds.), *Handbook of social psychology* (3rd ed., Vol. 1, pp. 699–777). New York: Random House.

LEE ANDERSON JACKSON, JR.
*University of North Carolina at
Wilmington*

MEASUREMENT
RESEARCH IN SPECIAL EDUCATION

CONVERGENT AND DIVERGENT THINKING

Emerging from Guilford's structure of intellect model of human intelligence, the concepts of convergent and divergent thinking are often applied to the education of gifted children. Both are viewed as high-level cognitive operations that individuals use when making decisions (Guilford, 1966, 1984).

Convergent thinking requires a narrowing process by which an individual develops classification rules that explain the relationships among objects and concepts. Essential to this process is the invocation of recall and recognition strategies. As such, the products of convergent thinking tend to be in the form of single "correct" answers. Critics have argued that typical school instruction demands an inappropriate proportion of convergent thinking at the expense of more creative (divergent) processes (Steffin, 1983).

Divergent thinking involves a broad scanning operation, enabling an individual to generate multiple possible solutions. It has received a major share of research attention in creativity, problem solving, and critical thinking (Steffin, 1983).

Guilford (1984) has discussed three aspects of divergent thinking. One aspect, fluency, relates to the breadth of associations available to an individual regarding a particular stimulus. A second, flexibility, is defined as the simultaneous consideration of multiple classes of information. In contrast to convergent processes, flexibility allows the individual to develop novel combinations. The third aspect, elaboration, is an integrative process that results in the formation of a broad theory. Here the thinker, demonstrating insight, is able to make predictions based on incomplete information.

Several studies have shown that young children's divergent productions can be increased by the use of open-ended questions in class discussions (Pucket-Cliatt, Shaw, & Sherwood, 1980; Thomas & Holcomb, 1981). These studies have also suggested that teachers can become increasingly comfortable using open-ended questions and that they can decrease their reliance on rote memory activities.

Steffin (1983) suggests that computers offer new opportunities for fostering divergent thinking. Increasingly sophisticated computer simulations, with their capacity for user-controlled interaction and variability in presentation, can teach students to develop algorithms that can be generalized across learning situations.

While learning-disabled (Jaben, 1983) and language-deficient (Burrows & Wolf, 1983) children have shown gains in creativity following training in divergent thinking, the observation and development of creative thinking in gifted students continues to dominate the research literature at the present time (Hildebrand, 1991; Kaufman, 2005.).

REFERENCES

Burrows, D., & Wolf, B. (1983). Creativity and the dyslexic child: A classroom view. *Annals of Dyslexia, 33,* 269–274.

Guilford, J. P. (1966). Basic problems in teaching for creativity. In C. W. Taylor & F. E. Williams (Eds.), *Instructional media and creativity.* New York: Wiley.

Guilford, J. P. (1984). Varieties of divergent production. *Journal of Creative Behavior, 18,* 1–10.

Hildebrand, V. (1991). Young children's care and education: Creative teaching and management. *Early Child Development and Care, 71,* 63–72.

Kaufman, J. (2005). Creativity and the special education student. In E. Fletcher-Janzen & C. R. Reynolds (Eds.), *The special education almanac* (pp. 369–390). New York: Wiley.

Jaben, T. H. (1983). The effects of creativity training on learning disabled students' creative written expression. *Journal of Learning Disabilities, 16,* 264–265.

Pucket-Cliatt, M. J., Shaw, J. M., & Sherwood, J. M. (1980). Effects of training on the divergent thinking abilities of kindergarten children. *Child Development, 51,* 1061–1064.

Steffin, S. A. (1983). Fighting against convergent thinking. *Childhood Education, 59,* 255–258.

Thomas, E., & Holcomb, C. (1981). Nurturing productive thinking in able students. *Journal of General Psychology, 104,* 67–79.

GARY BERKOWITZ
Temple University

CREATIVE PROBLEM SOLVING
TEACHER EXPECTANCIES
TEACHING STRATEGIES

CONVULSIONS, FEBRILE

See FEBRILE CONVULSIONS.

CONVULSIVE DISORDERS

See SEIZURE DISORDERS.

COOPERATIVE TEACHING

See INCLUSION.

COPROLALIA

Coprolalia is a condition characterized by an irresistible urge to utter obscene words and phrases and uncontrollable performance of obscene gestures (Singer, 1997), which are frequently observed together. Obscenities are interspersed randomly within a dialogue, interrupting the normal flow of conversation. The cursing is usually uttered during a break between sentences and in a loud, sharp tone in contrast to normal voice. The frequency of obscene utterances has a tendency to vary from low to high frequencies for extended periods of time. Coprolalic episodes are positively associated with periods of anxiety and anticipation.

Coprolalia is most often associated with Gilles de la Tourette's syndrome (TS) and is evident in some patients following a stroke (Slappey & Brown, 2003). As with other tics associated with TS, coprolalia can be controlled by TS patients for brief intervals. Lees, Robertson, Trimble, and Murray (1984) report that TS patients exhibiting coprolalia attempt to substitute euphemisms or somewhat disguised neologisms for obscenities. Early estimates of the prevalence of coprolalia in Tourette syndrome patients were approximately 60 percent, but have been revised to approximately 33 percent (Lees et al., 1984). Coprolalia tends to peak in adolescence and to wane in adulthood (Singer, 1997).

Both medical and behavioral treatments have been used successfully to control coprolalic expressions. Erenberg, Cruse, and Rothner (1985) report that the preferred medical treatment is the use of dopamine-blocking agents such as haloperidol, a drug used in treating hyperkinetic and manic disorders. Comings and Comings (1985) recommend starting with low doses of haloperidol (.05 mg daily for 1 week) and increasing the dosage by .05 mg at weekly intervals until a 70 to 90 percent reduction of symptoms occurs. Because of the sedative side effects of haloperidol, stimulant drugs may be given simultaneously. Price, Lockman, Pauls, Cohen, and Kidd (1986) report, however, that stimulant drugs appear to be associated positively with increases in the frequency of tics.

Behavioral treatments have included the use of self-management and negative practice techniques. Friedman (1980), for instance, had a patient substitute socially acceptable utterances for obscenities whenever she had the urge to curse. Evans and Evans (1983) decreased the rate of utterances of an expletive using a self-counting procedure. The patient simply recorded each frequency of his use of the target expletive. Storms (1985) had patients practice their tics until they were tired, had them rest, and then repeated the practice.

Medical and behavioral treatments of coprolalia have been used in combination with each other as well as in isolation. Storms (1985), for instance, used doses of haloperidol in combination with negative practice to reduce the frequency of tics. Medical marijuana is also being researched and preliminary results at the reduction and overall symptom relief is good (Slappey & Brown, 2003).

REFERENCES

Comings, D. E., & Comings, B. G. (1985). Tourette syndrome: Clinical and psychological aspects. *Human Genetics, 37*, 435–450.

Erenberg, G., Cruse, R. P., & Rothner, A. D. (1985). Gilles de la Tourette's syndrome: Effects of stimulant drugs. *Neurology, 35,* 1346–1348.

Evans, W. H., & Evans, S. S. (1983). Self-counting in the treatment of Gilles de la Tourette syndrome. *Journal of Precision Teaching, 4,* 14–17.

Friedman, S. (1980). Self-control in the treatment of Gilles de la Tourette's syndrome: Case study with 18-month follow-up. *Journal of Consulting & Clinical Psychology, 48,* 400–402.

Lees, A. J., Robertson, M., Trimble, M. R., & Murray, N. M. F. (1984). A clinical study of Gilles de la Tourette syndrome in the United Kingdom. *Journal of Neurology, Neurosurgery, & Psychiatry, 47,* 1–8.

Price, R. A., Leckman, J. F., Pauls, D. L., Cohen, D. J., & Kidd, K. K. (1986). Gilles de la Tourette syndrome: Tics and central nervous system stimulants in twins and non-twins. *Neurology, 36,* 232–237.

Singer, C. (1997). Coprolalia and other coprophenomena. *Neurologic Clinics, 15,* 2, 299–308.

Slappey, J., & Brown, R. T. (2003). Coprolalia. In E. F. Janzen & C. R. Reynolds (Eds.), *Childhood disorders diagnostic desk reference* (pp. 150–151). New York: Wiley.

Storms, L. (1985). Massed negative practice as a behavioral treatment for Gilles de la Tourette's syndrome. *American Journal of Psychotherapy, 39,* 277–281.

LAWRENCE J. O'SHEA
University of Florida

STIMULANT DRUGS
TICS
TOURETTE SYNDROME

COPROPRAXIA

See COPROLALIA.

CORE SCHOOL

The term core refers to an educational concept that first emerged in the United States in the 1930s and 1940s. The core school tries to provide a common background for all students and engineer a course of study that combines basic topics from school subjects that are usually taught separately. The intention of this concept was to make education more meaningful for students. Most popular in the 1950s, its popularity has declined in recent years, but it is still operational (Manning, 1971).

The core concept has two basic components: time and philosophy (Oliver, 1965). Time is usually administered through a "block time class," for example, two or more class periods are joined together in order to study a wide range of related subjects. The philosophy of core involves the breaking down of strict boundaries between disciplines. Thus, students may study a topic from literary, historical, mathematical, and artistic viewpoints concurrently rather than as separate topics in isolated classes (Manning, 1971; Oliver, 1965).

Beyond these two basic components, cores are identified as having the following characteristics (Hass, 1970; Manning, 1971; Oliver, 1965):

1. They are problem centered.
2. Learning is done through firsthand experiences by the learner.
3. Students are involved in the planning, teaching, and evaluation processes.
4. Students are provided with opportunities for total growth by way of lifelike environments.
5. The instruction is more personal, allowing for individual guidance.
6. There are opportunities for integrated knowledge across subject lines.

The core concept, when practiced, will probably be more student-oriented than may occur in other settings. The organization and overlapping of classes can be especially beneficial to the special education student needing structure and concentrated study. Student-oriented classes provide motivation for paying attention and becoming an active participant in the learning process.

REFERENCES

Hass, G., Wiles, K., & Bondi, J. (1970). *Reading in curriculum* (2nd ed.). Boston: Allyn & Bacon.

Manning, D. (1971). *Toward a humanistic curriculum.* New York: Harper & Row.

Oliver, A. I. (1965). *Curriculum improvement: A guide to problems, principles, and procedures.* New York: Dodd, Mead.

ROBERT T. NASH
University of Wisconsin Oshkosh

ECOLOGICAL EDUCATION FOR CHILDREN WITH DISABILITIES
HOLISTIC APPROACH AND LEARNING DISABILITIES
TEST-TEACH-TEST PARADIGM

CORNELIA DE LANGE SYNDROME

Cornelia De Lange syndrome is a developmental disability first reported by Brachman in 1916 and further investigated by De Lange in 1933 (Goodman & Gorlin, 1977). It may also be referred to as *Amsterdam dwarfism* (Clarke & Clarke, 1975). Currently, no definitive test or genetic analysis to confirm the diagnosis exists. However, it is suspected of being an autosomal dominant disorder associated with mutations on chromosome 3 (Gillberg, 1995). Diagnosis rests on the presenceor absence of a number of physical, cognitive, and behavioral characteristics.

Cornelia De Lange infants show a lower than normal birth weight and length, and can be described as failing to thrive. The majority are found to be functioning in the lower reaches of the moderately retarded range. A few reported cases have shown functioning levels approaching the low average range. Motor problems are pronounced.

These children appear remarkably similar in appearance, substantiating the probability of a genetic etiology as well as a syndrome. Nearly all of the children show thick curly eyebrows, long eyelashes, and increased facial hair. They have thin lips forming a downward slanting mouth, with smaller than normal-sized limbs, hands, feet, and head. Many exhibit a characteristic low-pitched gravelly voice early in infancy (Smith & Jones, 1982).

Behaviorally, these children may demonstrate autistic-like behaviors as well as the potential for self-abusive behaviors. They may be stubborn and difficult to manage and may bruise easily, an observation that may be of particular interest to the special educator. The syndrome tends to be relatively uncommon, with reported incidence rates varying from 1:30,000 to 1:50,000 live births (Goodman, 1977), and appears to affect males and females equally (Corlett, 2003). There is no syndrome-specific treatment and outcome is poor in many respects. However, there is hope that the Human Genome Project may shed light on why genes sometimes malfunction (Corlett, 2003).

REFERENCES

Clarke, A., & Clarke, D. B. (1975). *Mental deficiency, the changing perspectives* (3rd ed.). New York: Free Press.

Corlett, M. (2003). Cornelia De Lange syndrome. In E. Fletcher-Janzen & C. R. Reynolds (Eds.). *Childhood disorders diagnostic desk reference* (pp. 152–153). New York: Wiley.

Gillberg, C. (1995). *Clinical child neuropsychiatry.* Cambridge: Cambridge University Press.

Goodman, R., & Gorlin, R. (1977). *Atlas of the face of genetic disorders.* St. Louis, MO: Mosby.

Smith, D., & Jones, R. (1982). *Recognizable patterns of human malformation* (3rd ed.). Philadelphia: Saunders.

JOHN E. PORCELLA
Rhinebeck Country School

AUTISM

CORRECTIONAL EDUCATION

The Correctional Education Association (1983) defined correctional education as a coordinated system of individualized learning services and activities conducted within the walls of a correctional facility. Services are provided by certified educational staff and are designed to meet the identified needs of the inmate population in the areas of basic education leading to a high-school credential; vocational training geared toward obtaining entry-level skills and maintaining competitive employment; and development of attitudes, skills, and abilities in the context of sociopersonal development.

It is difficult to summarize the types of correctional education programs available in institutions because services vary among and within states. Few states provide comprehensive educational services to meet the identified educational needs. Usually, a state will focus on just a few program areas such as higher education or adult education.

Estimates indicate that 85 to 95 percent of the incarcerated adults do not have high-school diplomas. Many of them can neither read nor write after completing their sentences (Loeffler & Martin, 1982). From a survey conducted by Bell (1979), it was found that 50 percent of the adults in federal and state institutions were illiterate. Researchers such as Roberts (1973) state that the average inmate is unable to complete a job application, read and understand newspapers, or apply for an automobile operator's license (Day & McCane, 1982). In addition, 70 percent of the inmates have had no vocational training prior to sentencing. The National Advisory Council on Vocational Education found that the typical inmate is male, poor, and with less than 10 years of schooling. Gehring (1980) described correctional students as frequently afflicted by special learning and/or drug-related problems, accustomed to violence, and lacking in academic skills.

According to the U.S. Department of Justice (1983), the incarceration rate for individuals not completing elementary school is 259 per 1,000 for males between the ages of 20 to 29 years; for elementary school graduates, it is 83 per 1,000; for those completing 9 to 11 years in school, it is 70 per 1,000; for high-school graduates, it decreased to 11 per 1,000; and for persons with 16 years of schooling, the rate drops to 1 per 1,000.

Numerous research studies on correctional education programs have documented the effectiveness of both juvenile and adult correctional programs (Correctional Education Association, 1983). Correctional education programs have resulted in increased employment and improved quality of life for released inmates.

A major difficulty facing correctional educational administrators stems from the fact that the quantity of existing correctional education programs is insufficient to meet the needs of the hundreds of thousands of men, women, and children who are incarcerated in correctional institutions throughout the United States. The lack of public support and financial resources for correctional education programs severely limit the extent of correctional program effectiveness.

REFERENCES

Bell, R. (1979, June). *Correctional education program for inmates* (National Evaluation Programs, Phase I). Washington, DC: U.S. Department of Justice.

Correctional Education Association. (1983). *Lobbying for correctional education: A guide to action.* (Available from Correctional Education Association, 1400 20th Street, NW, Washington, DC 20009)

Day, S. R., & McCane, M. R. (1982). *Vocational education in corrections* (Information Series 237, 11–12). Columbus, OH: State University, National Center for Research in Vocational Education.

Gehring, T. (1980, September). Correctional education and the U.S. Department of Education. *Journal of Correctional Education, 35*(4), 137–141.

Loeffler, C. A., & Martin, T. C. (1982, April). *The functional illiterate: Is correctional education doing its job?* Huntsville, TX: Marloe Research.

Roberts, A. R. (1973). *Readings in prison education.* Springfield, IL: Thomas.

U.S. Department of Justice. (1983, October). *Report to the nation on crime and justice. The data* (NCJ-87060, p. 37). Rockville, MD: Bureau of Justice Statistics.

STAN A. KARCZ
University of Wisconsin at Stout

CORRECTIONAL SPECIAL EDUCATION
JUVENILE DELINQUENCY
RIGHT TO EDUCATION

CORRECTIONAL SPECIAL EDUCATION

Over 500,000 criminal offenders are currently housed in the nation's 559 state and federal prisons and 3493 local jails. Of this population, approximately 72,000 are incarcerated in state juvenile correctional facilities, jails, and group homes. In addition, almost 3 million persons are under community supervision instead of in confinement (Bureau of Justice Statistics, 1998). This rate of incarceration is among the highest in the world.

A large portion of the incarcerated population have educational disabilities. For example, Morgan's (1979) survey indicated that 42 percent of incarcerated juveniles met IDEA definitional criteria as handicapped. Surveys of adult correctional facilities in Oregon (Hurtz & Heintz, 1979) and Louisiana (Klinger, Marshall, Price, & Ward, 1983) suggest similar proportions of persons with disabilities in adult prisons, for example, between 30 and 50 percent.

Correctional education, which consists of formal educational programs ranging from basic literacy training to postsecondary vocational and university education, is offered in the vast majority of correctional facilities in the United States. Such programs typically are voluntary in adult facilities, but mandatory for juveniles. The administrative regulations for IDEA specifically include correctional education programs in the mandate for a free and appropriate public education for persons with disabilities 21 years of age and under; however, less than 10 percent of the state departments of juvenile and adult corrections are in compliance (Coffey, 1983). States not in compliance are experiencing heightened pressure through litigation (Wood, 1984) and administrative sanction to provide special education programs. Increased interest in correctional special education is reflected in federally funded demonstration and training projects, receipt of PL 94-142 state flow-through monies by correctional education programs, and the development of training programs for correctional special educators.

In 1984 the Correctional/Special Education Training (C/SET) Project staff (Rutherford, Nelson, & Wolford, 1985) surveyed the 85 state departments of juvenile and/or adult corrections and the 50 state departments of education to determine the number of offenders in juvenile and adult correctional facilities with disabilities.

There are 33,190 individuals incarcerated in state juvenile correctional facilities. Of this number, 30,681 or 92 percent, are in correctional education programs. The estimated number of juvenile offenders with disabilities is 9,443, or 28 percent of the total incarcerated population. The number of juveniles receiving special education services is 7,750, or 23 percent of the number of juveniles in corrections. Thus, according to state administrators' estimates, approximately 80 percent of juvenile offenders with disabilities are being served.

In addition to the data collected concerning offenders with disabilities in juvenile corrections, data were also collected relative to services for inmates with disabilities in state adult correctional facilities. An estimated 117,000 of those in adult corrections are under the age of 22 (Gerry, 1985) and thus potentially eligible for special education services under IDEA.

Of the 399,636 adults in state corrections programs, approximately 118,158 or 30 percent are receiving correctional education services. Based on data reported by 31 states, the estimated number of offenders with disabilities in adult corrections is 41,590 or 10 percent, 4,313 of whom, or less than 1 percent, are receiving special education services.

Currently a need exists for correctional special education services in juvenile and adult correctional institutions, raising the question of what constitutes an effective correctional special education program. Some researchers (e.g., Gerry, 1985; Smith & Hockenberry, 1980; Smith, Ramirez, & Rutherford, 1983) have delineated essential compliance issues with regard to implementation of IDEA in correctional education programs. There are six factors that are important to the implementation of meaningful correctional special education programs. These are (1) procedures for conducting functional assessments of the skills and learning needs of handicapped offenders; (2) the existence of a curriculum that teaches functional academic and daily living skills; (3) the inclusion of vocational special education in the curriculum; (4) the existence of transitional programs and procedures between correctional programs and the public schools or the world of work; (5) the presence of a comprehensive system for providing institutional and community services to handicapped offenders; and (6) the provision of in-service and preservice training for correctional educators in special education.

REFERENCES

Bureau of Justice Statistics. (1998). *Justice statistics*. Washington, DC: U.S. Department of Justice.

Coffey, O. D. (1983). Meeting the needs of youth from a corrections viewpoint. In S. Braaten, R. B. Rutherford, & C. A. Kardash (Eds.), *Programming for adolescents with behavioral disorders* (pp. 79–84). Reston, VA: Council for Children with Behavioral Disorders.

Gerry, M. H. (1985). *Monitoring the special education programs of correctional institutions*. Washington, DC: U.S. Department of Education.

Hurzt, R., & Heintz, E. I. (1979). *Incidence of specific learning disabilities at Oregon State Correctional Institution*. Paper presented at the National Institute of Corrections Conference, Portland, OR.

Klinger, J. H., Marshall, G. M., Price, A. W., & Ward, K. D. (1983). A pupil appraisal for adults in the Louisiana Department of Corrections. *Journal of Correctional Education, 34*(2), 46–48.

Morgan, D. J. (1979). Prevalence and types of handicapping conditions found in juvenile correctional institutions: A national survey. *Journal of Special Education, 13*, 283–295.

Rutherford, R. B., Nelson, C. M., & Wolford, B. I. (1985). Special education in the most restrictive environment: Correctional/special education. *Journal of Special Education, 19*, 60–71.

Smith, B. J., & Hockenberry, C. M. (1980). Implementing the Education for All Handicapped Children Act, P.L. 94-142, in youth corrections facilities: Selected issues. In F. J. Weintraub, A. Abeson, J. Ballard, & M. L. LaVor (Eds.), *Public policy and the education of exceptional children* (pp. 1–36). Reston, VA: Council for Exceptional Children.

Smith, B. J., Ramirez, B., & Rutherford, R. B. (1983). Special education in youth correctional facilities. *Journal of Correctional Education, 34*, 108–112.

Wood, F. J. (1984). *The law and correctional education*. Tempe, AZ: Correctional Special Education Training Project.

Robert B. Rutherford, Jr.
Arizona State University

CORRECTIONAL EDUCATION
JUVENILE DELINQUENCY

COSTA RICA, SPECIAL EDUCATION IN

Costa Rica has the strongest public education system in Central America. The 1869 constitution mandated a free, obligatory, and state-supported educational system—making Costa Rica one of the first countries in the world to pass such legislation (Biesanz, Biesanz, & Biesanz, 1982; Creedman, 1991). Approximately 25 percent of the national budget is dedicated to education (United Nations Educational and Scientific Organization [UNESCO], 1997) and elementary schools can be found even in the most isolated regions of the country. As a result, Costa Rica's literacy rate of 93 percent is one of highest in all of Latin America (Economic Commission for Latin America and the Caribbean [ECLAC], 1996; UNESCO, 1997).

Costa Rica is equally progressive in the area of special education. Special education services were formally established in 1939 when the Fernando Centeno Güell School for children with mental retardation was created near the capital city of San José (Asesoría General de Educación Especial, 1992). Public special education services were first ensured through the Fundamental Law of Education of 1957, which declared that students had the right to a special education, if so needed, and the right to special didactic techniques and materials; and that parents had the right to information on how to care for their child. Costa Rica has continued to pass progressive legislation for individuals with disabilities. The recently enacted Equal Opportunity Law for Persons with Disabilities (1996) includes antidiscriminatory clauses and guarantees equal rights for individuals with disabilities across all sectors of public life. Special education has been redefined in this law as "the combination of assistance and services at the disposal of students with special educational needs, whether they be temporary or permanent" (Sección VI, Artículo 27). The Equal Opportunity Law also strongly suggests that students with disabilities should be integrated into regular education classrooms that are "preferentially in the educational center closest to their home" (Capítulo I, Artículo 18).

Special education services in Costa Rica have rapidly expanded in the last 35 years. Until the early 1970s, students with disabilities received instruction at one of 20 segregated special education campuses (Bulgarelli, 1971). However, in 1978, the Ministry of Education began to place special education classrooms on regular education campuses through a national integration program (Castillo & Stough, 1988). By 1984, 11 special education schools, 103 self-contained classrooms, and 15 resource rooms were in existence, most located in the heavily populated Central Valley (Castillo & Stough, 1988). In the late 1980's, the Ministry of Education was able to rapidly expand the number of resource rooms in the country by hiring teachers to instruct *recargo*, or an extra shift, each day (Stough & Aguirre-Roy, 1997). By 1988, the *recargo* model had become the predominate special education delivery model in elementary schools. There are now over 600 classrooms that are taught by recargo teachers (A. R. Aguirre-Roy, pers. comm., February, 1998).

Approximately 20,000 students with disabilities receive services through the public education system in Costa Rica (Asesoría General de Educación Especial, 1993). The Department of Special Education uses the diagnostic categories of learning disabilities, mental retardation, emotional disturbance, speech impaired, auditory impaired, visually impaired, physically disabled, psychosocially disordered, and multiply handicapped. Eligibility for services is determined through a psychological and educational assessment conducted by a diagnostic team consisting of a psychologist, social worker, educator, and psychiatrist (Mainieri Hidalgo & Méndez Barrantes, 1992). Children with disabilities are eligible to receive educational services beginning at birth and these services continue through age 18, when most Costa Ricans finish high school.

Early stimulation classes for children five and under are located in elementary schools in most large towns and in the Central Valley region surrounding San José. In rural areas, parents often take their children to the nearest town on a weekly or biweekly basis to attend class. At the elementary level, students with learning disabilities or mild mental retardation receive services in resource rooms. These are typically "pull-out" programs in which

students receive instruction in small groups from a *recargo* teacher. These teachers usually deliver 20 hours of instruction a week, using one hour each day for planning and consulting with general education teachers (González Trejos, 1992). Students who are labeled as emotionally disturbed, who have sensory impairments, or who have moderate to severe disabilities are placed in self-contained classrooms or on separate school campuses. In rural areas, such as the Guanacaste region, several itinerant teachers have been hired to travel intermittently to schools that have small numbers of students with special needs. At the high-school level, students with mild disabilities usually attend a vocational, rather than academic, high school. There are also several special education high schools that serve students with more severe disabilities and focus on the development of vocational skills. The number of special education programs drops drastically at the high school level, however, and the great majority of students with disabilities, particularly moderate to severe disabilities, do not graduate from high school.

While the Ministry of Education promotes programs which are "integrated into the community, always using the least restrictive methods" (Asesoría General de Educación Especial, 1993), the reality is that the delivery of special education services usually segregates students with disabilities from their same-age peers. The Ministry is piloting a co-teaching model in which special educators teach in collaboration with general educators (Nieto, pers. comm., June 2, 1997); however, it is too early to speculate on how this new model might change the current special education practices.

Special education in Costa Rica suffers from the same obstacles that have been described in other developing countries: limited material resources, geographic isolation of large segments of the population, and insufficient training programs (see González-Vega & Céspedes, 1993; Marfo, Walker, & Charles, 1986). The greatest national need is for trained professionals. Few special education teacher training programs exist outside of the capital city and teachers in rural areas usually have had no formal training with students with disabilities (Stough, 1989; Villarreal, 1989). Physical therapists, speech therapists, and psychologists are also scarce and often have limited experience in the area of disabilities.

Recent educational initiatives have exponentially increased the number of students receiving special education in Costa Rica and the Ministry of Education is making a focused effort to coordinate these services. Undeniably progressive legislation now supports the rights of individuals with disabilities to work, receive public health services, and to be educated. While special education continues to expand in Costa Rica, untrained personnel limit the effectiveness of this instruction. The current challenge for Costa Rica is to ensure the quality of these special services, as well as the accessibility to them.

REFERENCES

Asesoría General de Educación Especial. (1992). *Estructura, principios, normas y procedimientos de la educación especial en Costa Rica* [Structure, principles, norms and procedures of special education in Costa Rica]. San José, Costa Rica: Ministerio de Educación Pública.

Asesoría General de Educación Especial. (1993, March). *La educación especial en Costa Rica* [Special education in Costa Rica]. Paper presented at the meeting of the Conferencia Hemisférica sobre Discapacidad, Washington, DC.

Biesanz, R., Biesanz, K. Z., & Biesanz, M. H. (1982). *The Costa Ricans.* Englewood Cliffs, NJ: Prentice Hall.

Bulgarelli, O. A. (Ed.). (1971). *El desarrollo nacional en 150 años de vida independiente* [National development in 150 years of independent life]. San José, Costa Rica: Publicaciones de la Universidad de Costa Rica.

Castillo, G., & Stough, L. M. (1988, May). *Informe a visita a Tegulcigalpa* [Report on a visit to Tegulcigalpa]. Unpublished manuscript.

Creedman, T. S. (1991). *Historical dictionary of Costa Rica* (2nd ed.). Metuchen, NJ: The Scarecrow Press.

Economic Commission for Latin America and the Caribbean (ECLAC). (1996). *Statistical yearbook for Latin America and the Caribbean.* Chile: United Nations Publication.

González Trejos, F. (1992). *Información sobre el funcionamiento de las aulas recurso de problemas de aprendizaje* [Information on the functioning of resource rooms for learning disabilities]. San José, Costa Rica: Ministerio de Educación Pública.

González-Vega, C., & Céspedes, V. H. (1993). Costa Rica. In S. Rottenberg (Ed.), *A World Bank comparative study. The political economy of poverty, equity, and growth. Costa Rica and Uruguay.* New York: Oxford University Press.

Lara, S., Barry, T., & Simonson, P. (1995). *Inside Costa Rica.* Albuquerque, NM: Interhemispheric Resource Center.

Ley de Igualdad de Oportunidades para las Personas con Discapacidad [Law of Equal Opportunity Law for Persons with Disabilities]. (1996).

Ley Fundamental de Educación de Costa Rica, Capítulo IV, Artículos 27, 28, y 29 [Costa Rican Fundamental Law of Education, Chapter IV, Articles 27, 28, and 29]. (1957).

Mainieri Hidalgo, A., & Méndez Barrantes, Z. (1992). *Detección de problemas de aprendizaje: Antología* [Detection of learning disabilities: Anthology]. San José, Costa Rica: Editorial Universidad Estatal a Distancia.

Marfo, K., Walker, S., & Charles, B. (1986). *Childhood disability in developing countries: Issues in habilitation and special education.* New York: Praeger.

Stough, L. M. (1990, January). *Special education and teacher training in the third world: Costa Rican and Honduran rural education programs.* Paper presented at the annual meeting of the Southwest Educational Research Association, Austin, TX.

Stough, L. M., & Aguirre-Roy, A. R. (1996). Learning disabilities in Costa Rica: Challenges for an "army of teachers." *Journal of Learning Disabilities, 30,* 566–571.

United Nations Educational and Scientific Organization (UNESCO). *UNESCO Statistical Yearbook.* (1997). Lanham, MD: Bernan.

Villarreal, B. (1989). *An analysis of the special education services for children and youth in Costa Rica.* Unpublished doctoral dissertation, University of San Diego, CA.

LAURA M. STOUGH
Texas A&M University

COUNCIL FOR CHILDREN WITH BEHAVIORAL DISORDERS

The Council for Children with Behavioral Disorders (CCBD) is the division of the Council for Exceptional Children (CEC) that is dedicated "to supporting the professional development and enhancing the expertise of those who work on behalf of children with challenging behavior and their families. CCBD is committed to students who are identified as having emotional and behavioral disorders and those whose behavior puts them at risk for failure in school, home, and/or community. CCBD supports prevention of problem behavior and enhancement of social, emotional, and educational well-being of all children and youth." The division works to promote educational services, advocate for children and youth with emotional and behavioral disorders, and disseminate research, practice, and policy information through journals, professional conferences, publications, and its web site.

CCBD is open to all members of CEC. The division provides the research journal, *Behavioral Disorders,* practitioner-oriented publication *Beyond Behavior,* and the *CCBD Newsletter* to all members. In addition, members can access position papers, policy recommendations, and online articles from the CCBD web site. CCBD sponsors an international conference and has strands and networking opportunities at the CEC Convention & Expo each year. For additional information on the programs and services that CCBD offers to its members, go to the division's web site at http://www.ccbd.net/or http://www.cec.sped.org.

RANDALL L. DE PRY
*University of Colorado at
Colorado Springs*

COUNCIL FOR EDUCATIONAL DIAGNOSTIC SERVICES

The Council for Educational Diagnostic Services (CEDS) is the division of the Council for Exceptional Children (CEC) that focuses on the promotion of "the most appropriate education of children and youth through appraisal, diagnosis, educational intervention, implementation, and continuous evaluation of a prescribed educational program." The association seeks to integrate diagnostic and prescriptive services across disciplines to support exceptional children, promote research on the use and application of psychoeducational assessment, and support research that will directly benefit members in applied settings.

CEDS is open to all members of CEC. The association provides the journal *Assessment for Effective Intervention,* which publishes research that has direct implications for educational diagnosticians, such as special educators, school psychologists, and others who use assessment data to support exceptional children. In addition, the association has a listserv that serves as a forum for electronic discussion of issues that are of interest to members. Additional information on the services that CEDS provides to its members can be found at http://www.unr.edu/educ/ceds/index.html and http://www.cec.sped.org.

RANDALL L. DE PRY
*University of Colorado at
Colorado Springs*

COUNCIL FOR EXCEPTIONAL CHILDREN

The Council for Exceptional Children (CEC) is the world's largest professional organization dedicated to the welfare of exceptional children. The CEC was founded in 1922 at Teachers' College, Columbia University. Today, its United States and Canadian membership includes approximately 50,000 persons, including over 9,000 members of the organization's 288 student chapters. There are also 269 state, local, and provincial chapters in the United States and Canada. The organization is further divided into special interest groups, including divisions on the physically handicapped, behavior disorders, mental retardation, communication disorders, learning disabilities, visually handicapped, talented and gifted, early childhood education, special education administration, career development, technology and media, educational diagnostic services, teacher education, international special education, cultural and linguistic diversity, research, and pioneers of the CEC.

CEC members include educators, parents, students, and others concerned with the education of children with disabilities and gifted and talented children and youth. The CEC's membership is dedicated to increasing educational opportunities for all exceptional children and youth and to improving conditions for the professionals who work with them. The CEC advocates for appropriate governmental policies, sets professional standards, provides continual professional development, advocates for newly and historically underserved individuals with exceptionalities, and helps professionals obtain conditions and resources necessary for effective professional practice.

CEC has been highly visible as an advocate for federal legislation and funding for the gifted and the disabled.

The organization issues two respected periodicals, *Exceptional Children* and *Teaching Exceptional Children.* The former is more research and policy oriented, while the latter is geared more toward practitioners' needs. In addition, several hundred books, multimedia packages, bibliographies, and fact sheets are available from CEC. Access to nearly one half a million references on handicapped and gifted children can be obtained from ERIC (Educational Resources Information Center) and CEC Information Services. Each year, a national convention sponsored by CEC attracts thousands of professionals, paraprofessionals, and parents. In the past few years, CEC has sponsored successful topical workshops devoted to areas such as microcomputer use in special education, black exceptional children, and early childhood special education. Periodic international conferences are also sponsored by CEC.

The CEC's founding in 1922 was predated by other organizations concerned with the disabled; Convention of American Instructors of the Deaf, 1850; American Association of Instructors of the Blind, 1853; Conference of Executives of American Schools for the Deaf, 1863; American Association on Mental Deficiency, 1876; American Association to Promote the Teaching of Speech to the Deaf, 1890; and National Education Association's Department of Special Education, 1897. The CEC was founded the same year that a related organization, the National Association for the Study and Education of Exceptional Children, was disbanded. Four years earlier, the National Education Association (NEA) discontinued its Department of Special Education.

Elizabeth E. Farrell, who had been active in NEA's special education activities earlier, other Teachers' College faculty, and advanced students in the 1922 summer session at Columbia, formed CEC at a meeting on August 10 in a downtown New York restaurant. The early years found an organization without a true central office, limited funds, and a heavy reliance on volunteers for its existence. Various internal and external problems nearly ended CEC in its first two decades.

Wooden (1980) claims that one of the organization's strength was its system of local chapters. Grass-roots leadership was developed through planning and carrying out of professional activities at the local level. A sense of the *whole child* developed among members: since CEC's interests were broader than early groups with single-category interests. After the 1930s depression, CEC began to stabilize with the nation. Reorganization of the council's internal structure and a better financial situation allowed for expansion of CEC's role and activities. Today, despite some decline in membership from its peak in the 1970s, CEC is respected as a leader and advocate in its field. It works cooperatively with other organizations to promote the education and welfare of all exceptional children and youth. The Council for Exceptional Children's headquarters are now located at 1920 Association Drive, Reston, VA 20191, and may be reached by phone at (703) 620-3660.

REFERENCE

Wooden, H. Z. (1980). Growth of a social concept. *Exceptional Children, 47*(1), 40–46.

JOHN D. WILSON
Elwyn Institutes

COUNCIL FOR EXCEPTIONAL CHILDREN, DIVISION ON CAREER DEVELOPMENT AND TRANSITION

The Division on Career Development and Transition (DCDT) is the division of the Council for Exceptional Children (CEC) that promotes "efforts to improve the quality of and access to career/vocational and transition services, increase the participation of education in career development and transition goals and to influence policies affecting career development and transition services for persons with disabilities." The division believes that transition services are critically important for exceptional students as they transition from school to meaningful post-school outcomes. In addition, DCDT believes that these services should promote self-determination, be learner- and community-based, be culturally competent, be interdisciplinary, and take into account the full lifespan of the student.

DCDT is open to all members of CEC. The division provides the journal *Career Development of Exceptional Individuals,* which publishes research articles and highlights programs that focus on the mission of DCDT, for all members. In addition, the division posts position papers, which are available on its web site, that address critical issues that apply to career development and transition services for persons with disabilities. DCDT also hosts an annual international conference, which focuses on research and issues related to career and transition services at the national, state, and local levels. Additional information on DCDT can be found on its web site at http://www.dcdt.org/and http://www.cec.sped.org.

RANDALL L. DE PRY
*University of Colorado at
Colorado Springs*

COUNCIL FOR EXCEPTIONAL CHILDREN, DIVISION FOR COMMUNICATIVE DISABILITIES AND DEAFNESS

The Division for Communicative Disabilities and Deafness (DCDD) is one of 17 divisions of the Council for Exceptional Children (CEC). The primary mission of the Division for Communicative Disabilities and Deafness is to promote the welfare, development, and education of infants, toddlers, children, and youth with communicative disabilities or who are deaf and hard of hearing. In addition, DCDD seeks to promote growth in professionals and families as a means to better understand the development of communicative abilities and the prevention of communicative disabilities.

DCDD plans a large segment of the annual CEC Convention & Expo each year to provide professional development for its members and others who attend the convention. The annual meeting is held at the convention within a social gathering called the MemberFest. The division maintains a membership of at least 700 paid members who meet the membership qualifications established by CEC.

All members of the division must hold concurrent membership in the CEC. Although membership varies from year to year, the division maintains approximately 1,500 members. Membership in the division consists of regular and student members. Regular membership is open to professional personnel engaged in the education or provision of services for infants, toddlers, children, and youth with developmental communication needs or communication disorders and to other individuals interested in the purpose of the division. Student membership is available for pre-service students and students continuing their education who are in full-time attendance during the academic year at a regionally accredited college or university. All members must pay annual dues to both the division and the CEC.

Officers of the division include president, president elect, past president, secretary, financial officer, and chairs of six constituent committees. The president appoints other executive board members for three-year terms, including chairs of the Knowledge and Skills committee, Professional Development committee, and the Newsletter Editor. Ad hoc committees are appointed for special topics and projects.

DCDD's Publication Board oversees its many publications. The past president chairs the Publication Board. *Communication Disorders Quarterly* (CDQ) is the division's journal, published by Pro-ED in Austin, Texas. Prior to 1999, the journal was called *Journal of Communication Disorders and Deafness* (JCCD). To review these articles go to http://pegasus.cc.ucf.edu/~abrice/jccd.html. The *DCDD New Times* is the division's newsletter, with copies available online on the DCDD web site four times a year. The newsletter is distributed to the membership inside the journal, *Communication Disorders Quarterly.* The listserv is an interactive feature of the organization's web site and enables members to exchange valuable information about communication disability, evidence-based assessment and intervention, and special education programs and services in all fifty states and Canada. DCDD has representation on the Council of Educators of the Deaf,

National Joint Committee on Learning Disabilities, and the National Joint Committee for the Communication Needs of Persons with Severe Disabilities. For additional information, go to DCDD's web site at http://education .gsu.edu/dcdd.

JUDY K. MONTGOMERY
Chapman University

COUNCIL FOR EXCEPTIONAL CHILDREN, DIVISION FOR CULTURALLY AND LINGUISTICALLY DIVERSE EXCEPTIONAL LEARNERS

The Division for Culturally and Linguistically Diverse Exceptional Learners (DDEL) is a division of the Council for Exceptional Children (CEC) that "promotes the advancement and improvement of educational opportunities for culturally and linguistically diverse learners with disabilities and/or gifts and talents, their families, and the professional who serve them." The association advocates for policies and procedures that support the needs of diverse learners; promotes collaboration across disciplines; dissemination of research and ideas to members and other interested parties; technical assistance at the preservice and inservice levels; and recruitment and retention of personnel from diverse populations.

DDEL is open to all members of CEC. The association provides the journal *Multiple Voices for Ethnically Diverse Exceptional Learners,* which publishes research on preferred practices, assessment, and other topics of interest to DDEL members. The association also publishes the *DDEL Newsletter* that provides recent developments, training opportunities, information on political action, and information on conferences for members. DDEL sponsors sessions for members at the annual CEC Convention & Expo and provides ongoing networking opportunities at the conference. For additional information on DDEL, go to its web site at http://www.cec.sped.org/Content/NavigationMenu/AboutCEC/Communities/Divisions/#9.

RANDALL L. DE PRY
*University of Colorado at
Colorado Springs*

COUNCIL FOR EXCEPTIONAL CHILDREN, DIVISION ON DEVELOPMENTAL DISABILITIES

The Division on Developmental Disabilities (DDD) is the division of the Council for Exceptional Children (CEC) that is "committed to enhancing the quality of life of individuals, especially children and youth, with developmental disabilities, including those with cognitive disabilities/mental retardation, autism, and related disabilities." The division goals include increasing the competence of persons who work with children and youth with developmental disabilities, to address critical issues that face professionals, to advocate for persons with developmental disabilities, and to grow and enhance membership.

DDD is open to all CEC members. The association provides numerous publications, including many in electronic formats. DDD publishes the journals *Education and Training in Developmental Disabilities* and *Focus on Autism and Other Developmental Disabilities.* Each journal publishes research on effective practice for professionals, parents, and other interested parties. An archive has been created on the web site that allows users to search past issues of the journal and locate articles of interest. The division also publishes a newsletter titled *DDD Express* four times per year, which includes important division information and features such as the "Teacher's Corner" and a message from the current president. DDD also makes available a video, book, and monograph series for members who would like access to evidenced-based strategies and implementation ideas that are presented in a user friendly format. Current topics include social behavior, literacy, differentiated instruction, assessment, inclusion, and best practices. Additional information on DDD can be found at http://www. dddcec.org and http://www.cec.sped.org.

RANDALL L. DE PRY
*University of Colorado at
Colorado Springs*

COUNCIL FOR EXCEPTIONAL CHILDREN, DIVISION FOR EARLY CHILDHOOD

The Division for Early Childhood (DEC) is one of 17 divisions of the Council for Exceptional Children (CEC), the largest international professional organization dedicated to improving educational outcomes for individuals with exceptionalities, students with disabilities, and/or the gifted. DEC is especially for individuals who work with or on behalf of children with special needs and their families. Founded in 1973, the division is dedicated to promoting policies and practices that support families and enhance the optimal development of children from birth to age eight. Children with special needs include those who have disabilities, developmental delays, are gifted/talented, or are at risk of future developmental problems.

DEC is committed to promoting parent-professional collaboration in all facets of planning, designing, and implementing early childhood intervention services and is devoted to advocating for policy, planning and best practice in prevention and intervention. DEC supports full access for young children with special needs and their families to natural settings and service delivery options, respect for family values, diverse cultural and linguistic backgrounds, and family circumstance, and supporting those who work with or on behalf of infants and young children with special needs and their families.

DEC provides specific services to its members through collaboration and communication among organizations, practitioners and family members; innovations in research and the development of new knowledge; dissemination and use of information about research, resources, best practices and current issues; and professional development through an array of activities and strategies. More information can be obtained by visiting DEC's web site at http://www.decsped .org/and http://www.cec.sped.org.

BETH ROUS
University of Kentucky

COUNCIL FOR EXCEPTIONAL CHILDREN, DIVISION FOR LEARNING DISABILITIES

The Division for Learning Disabilities (DLD) is the division of the Council for Exceptional Children (CEC) that "works to improve services, research and legislation for individuals with learning disabilities." Members of DLD can access numerous services and resources on the *TeachingLD* web site, including membership information, resources and research on the causes of learning disabilities, specialized support and services offered to students with learning disabilities, strategies for teaching students with learning disabilities, resources for finding colleagues, discussion groups, and information on upcoming conferences.

DLD is open to members of CEC. The division publishes the journal *Learning Disabilities Research & Practice*. This journal presents current research about working with children and youth with learning disabilities. In addition, members receive *Current Practice Alerts* that provide a synopsis of evidence-based instructional practices. The alerts are co-sponsored by DLD and the CEC Division for Research. Additional resources for members include teacher's guides, lesson plans that can be downloaded, listings of professional organizations and technical assistance centers, and general information about learning disabilities. DLD also sponsors a conference titled "Bridging the Gap between Research and Practice" for educators and researchers annually. Additional

information on DLD can be found at http://www.teachingld .org/and http://www.cec.sped.org.

RANDALL L. DE PRY
*University of Colorado at
Colorado Springs*

COUNCIL FOR EXCEPTIONAL CHILDREN, DIVISION FOR PHYSICAL AND HEALTH DISABILITIES

The Division for Physical and Health Disabilities (DPHD) is the division of the Council for Exceptional Children (CEC) that "advocates for quality education for all individuals with physical disabilities, multiple disabilities, and special health cares needs served in schools, hospitals, or home settings." DPHD seeks to advocate for resources at the local, state, and national levels that benefit exceptional learners with physical and health disabilities, disseminate research, and provide technical assistance to professionals at the preservice and inservice levels.

DPHD is open to all members of CEC. The division provides the journal *Physical Disabilities-Education and Related Services* to all members. This journal is published twice a year and provides up-to-date information on research, practice, and services for children and youth with physical and health disabilities. In addition, members receive *The DPHD Newsletter* which provides current division information, including information on conferences and political action. The division also sponsors sessions and activities for members at the annual CEC Convention & Expo. Additional information on DPHD can be found at http://www.cec.sped .org/Content/NavigationMenu/AboutCEC/Communities/ Divisions/Division_for_Physical_and_Health_Disabilities_ DPHD_.htm.

RANDALL L. DE PRY
*University of Colorado at
Colorado Springs*

COUNCIL FOR EXCEPTIONAL CHILDREN PIONEERS DIVISION

The Council for Exceptional Children's Pioneers Division (CEC-PD) is available for CEC members who have maintained 20 or more years of membership. Membership is also open to life members of CEC, retired members, and past presidents of CEC. The goals of CEC-PD are to provide community awareness of the educational needs of children and youth with disabilities and those who are gifted, volunteer time and expertise toward activities that promote programs and policies that support exceptional children, and to provide ongoing support for the activities of CEC. Members of CEC-PD receive *The Pioneers Press* newsletter which is published three times per year. In addition, the division sponsors sessions, activities, and a dinner at the CEC Convention & Expo each year. For additional information, go to CEC-PD's web site at http://www.cec.sped.org/Content/Navigationmenu/AboutCEC/Communities/Divisions/CEC_Pioneers _Division_CEC_PD_.htm

RANDALL L. DE PRY
*University of Colorado at
Colorado Springs*

COUNCIL FOR EXCEPTIONAL CHILDREN, DIVISION FOR RESEARCH

The Division for Research (CEC-DR) is the division of the Council for Exceptional Children (CEC) that "supports and encourages useful and sound research about children, youth, and adults with disabilities, their families, and the people who work with them." The division seeks to advance the use of evidence-based strategies as it relates to programs and practices for children and youth with disabilities and those who are gifted.

CEC-DR is open to all CEC members. Members of CEC-DR receive the *Journal of Special Education* and *Focus on Research*. These publications provide current research and important information for members on projects, funding, and include discussion forums and member opinions on current issues facing the field. In addition, the division collaborates with the U.S. Department of Education on the development and dissemination of a publication titled *Research Connections,* which highlights evidence-based strategies for use in educational settings that serve students with disabilities. Additional information on CEC-DR can be found at http://www.cecdr.org and http://www.cec.sped.org.

RANDALL L. DE PRY
*University of Colorado at
Colorado Springs*

COUNCIL FOR EXCEPTIONAL CHILDREN, DIVISION OF INTERNATIONAL SPECIAL EDUCATION AND SERVICES

In June, 1978, the Council for Exceptional Children held the first World Congress on Future Special Education in Stirling, Scotland (Fink, 1978). Following that meeting in order to preserve the momentum created by this Congress, some university faculty members organized a special interest group within the CEC's Teacher Education Division. This group was concerned primarily with the international aspects of delivery of special education services to children with disabilities. Since the scope of interest went beyond teacher education, a separate division of the CEC, known as the Division of International Special Education and Services (DISES), was formed in 1990 with the mission of assisting in the improvement of the quality of special education and services to individuals with disabilities throughout the world.

With the breakup of the USSR and the movement away from communism in the former Soviet republics, DISES established relations with several organizations serving children with disabilities, especially in St. Petersburg and Moscow, Russia; Latvia; Lithuania; and Kazakhstan. In 1993, working with Project Concern International, DISES identified special educators to assist adolescents who had been institutionalized in Romania to function independently. Also during 1993, DISES served as the international portion of a COSMOS Corporation project to identify trends in the delivery of special education services, and to anticipate how educational technology could be used effectively for students with disabilities throughout the world. In 1995, DISES, working with the Citizen Ambassador Program of People to People International, led a special education delegation visiting programs in China.

DISES has also been active in disseminating information about special education programs worldwide through its newsletter and special publications. Four monographs have been published, and a professional journal, *The Journal of International Special Needs Education* (*JISNE*) began publication in 1998. The editors of the DISES newsletter are Bob Henderson of the University of Illinois (bob-h@uiuc.edu), Lisa Dieker of the University of Wisconsin-Milwaukee (dieker@csd.uwm.edu), and Yash Bhagwanj (bhagwanj@students.uiuc.edu); and the editor of *JISNE* is Robert Michael (michaelr@npvm.newpaltz.edu).

Another major activity of DISES has been the organization of the Special Education World Congress 2000 (SEWC 2000), held in Vancouver, British Columbia during April 2–5, 2000. Building on previous conferences, SEWC 2000 involves partnerships with the other CEC divisions; professional organizations dealing with various disabilities, such as the American Association on Mental Retardation and the American Foundation for the Blind; international groups such as UNESCO, the World Health Organization, the International Association of Special Education, and Rehabilitation International; and special education offices in various Ministries of Education. A unique feature of SEWC 2000 has been the use of the Internet to conduct "cyber seminars," in which participants read and commented on professional papers that were published on the SEWC 2000 web page (http://cid.unomaha.edu/wwwsped/wc/2000.html).

REFERENCE

Fink, A. H. (1978). *International perspectives on future special education*. Reston, VA: Council for Exceptional Children.

COUNCIL FOR EXCEPTIONAL CHILDREN, DIVISION OF TEACHER EDUCATION

The Teacher Education Division (TED) is the division of the Council for Exceptional Children (CEC) that "supports and stimulates continued improvements in practices in order for all individuals with diverse abilities and disabilities to achieve optimal educational outcomes." The division is made up of persons who are interested in the professional development of teacher educators—and others who train and support educators—who serve children and youth with exceptional learning needs and their families.

TED is open to all CEC members. Members of TED receive *Teacher Education and Special Education* and the *TED Newsletter*. These publications provide members with information on research, practice, and general information on current initiatives, division news, and conferences. The division holds an annual conference where teacher educators, researchers, and other interested professionals meet to discuss issues such as teacher preparation, research, technology, and service delivery. Additional information on TED can be found at http://www.tedcec.org and http://www.cec.sped.org.

Randall L. De Pry
*University of Colorado at
Colorado Springs*

COUNCIL FOR EXCEPTIONAL CHILDREN, DIVISION OF TECHNOLOGY AND MEDIA

The Technology and Media Division (TAM) is the division of the Council for Exceptional Children (CEC) that provides "services to members, divisions, subdivisions, federations, to federal, state and local education agencies, and to business and industry regarding the current and future uses of technology and media with individuals with exceptionalities." The division seeks to promote collaboration, encourage development of technology and media, disseminate research and information, advance technical standards, provide technical assistance, and advocate for policies, procedures, and funding for individuals with exceptional learning needs.

TAM is open to all CEC members. Members of TAM receive *The Journal of Special Education Technology* and the *TAM Connector*. These publications provide research, practice, legislative updates, and division information for members. In addition, members have access to *TAM Tech in Action* and *TAM Reports*, which are available on the TAM web site. The division holds an annual conference for its members and other interested professionals. Conference presentations focus on the practical application of assistive technology across disciplines and persons with exceptional learning needs. Additional information on TAM can be found at http://www.tamcec.org and http://www.cec.sped.org.

Randall L. De Pry
*University of Colorado at
Colorado Springs*

COUNCIL FOR EXCEPTIONAL CHILDREN, DIVISION ON VISUAL IMPAIRMENT

The Division for Visual Impairment (DVI) is the division for the Council for Exceptional Children (CEC) that "advances the education of children and youth who have visual impairments that impede their educational progress." The division engages in a wide range of activities including advocating for federal, state, and local policies that support the education of children and youth with visual impairments, curriculum and resource development, connecting research to practice at the preservice and inservice levels, and career and transition planning.

DVI is open to all CEC members. Members receive the *DVI Quarterly* newsletter as part of their membership. In addition, members have access to position papers that address issues in the areas of professional practice, curriculum development, and adaptations. Additional information on DVI can be found at http://www.ed.arizona.edu/dvi/welcome.htm and http://www.cec.sped.org/.

Randall L. De Pry
*University of Colorado at
Colorado Springs*

COUNCIL FOR LEARNING DISABILITIES

In 1968 educators formed the Division for Children with Learning Disabilities (DCLD) within the Council for Exceptional Children (CEC; Hallahan, Kauffman, & Lloyd, 1985). Both groups believed that without a name to identify a group of children who did not fit into any other handicapping condition, there would be difficulty in obtaining needed funds for special services.

During the early 1980s emerged the realization that not only did children have learning disabilities but so did adults. Consequently, the Division for Children with Learning Disabilities became the Council for Learning Disabilities (CLD). Besides this change of name, CLD changed its affiliation as it seceded from the Council for Exceptional Children (Lerner, 1985). The majority of CLD's membership voted to become a separate and independent organization.

Conferences and newsletters sponsored by CLD provide a valuable means of sharing information and serve as a stimulus for research, program development, and advocacy. In addition, CLD formed a strong national lobbying group to promote legislative recognition of learning disabilities.

REFERENCES

Hallahan, D. P., Kauffman, J. M., & Lloyd, J. W. (1985). *Introduction to learning disabilities*. Englewood Cliffs, NJ: Prentice Hall.

Learner, J. W. (1985). *Learning disabilities*. Dallas: Houghton Mifflin.

JOSEPH M. RUSSO
*Hunter College, City University
of New York*

COUNCIL OF ADMINISTRATORS OF SPECIAL EDUCATION

The Council of Administrators of Special Education (CASE) was founded in 1952 as a division of the Council for Exceptional Children (CEC). The CASE membership of 5,200 includes administrators, directors, supervisors, and coordinators of local private and public special education programs, schools, or classes serving children and youth with special needs. There are also a number of members who are state department personnel as well as those who are university faculty engaged in the preparation of special education administrators. The purpose of CASE is to promote professional leadership, provide opportunity for the study of problems common to its members and to provide information for developing improved services to exceptional children. CASE has 41 Subdivisions in the U.S. and Canada.

CASE provides six newsletters and two issues of its refereed journal *CASE in POINT* to its members annually. Through its publications program the Council also offers publications of interest to administrators. CASE provides professional development opportunities to its members. Among those are an annual institute devoted to the study of a specific topic and an annual conference offering a wide range of topics for discussion and study. CASE maintains a web site at http://www.members.aol.com/casecec/index.htm where members may obtain current information on a variety of topics and activities of the Council.

The office may be contacted at Fort Valley State University, 1005 State University Drive, Fort Valley, GA 31030 or via e-mail through its web site.

JO THOMASON
Executive Director, CASE

COUNSELING INDIVIDUALS WITH DISABILITIES

With so much emphasis placed on disabled individuals' educational, adaptive behavior, and social skill needs, their emotional needs are often forgotten. Indeed, disabled individuals often have issues that affect their lives that could be addressed and resolved through the counseling process. For example, some mentally retarded individuals experience feelings of frustration because of their disability and its limitations and could benefit from counseling support. Learning-disabled students, given the peer rejection sometimes associated with their academic difficulties, also might benefit from therapeutic attention. And clearly, counseling should be a central intervention for behaviorally and emotionally disturbed persons.

While the need for counseling with the disabled is apparent, the specific counseling techniques, or approaches that are most effective under defined circumstances are not empirically evident. From a comprehensive diagnostic and treatment perspective, the multimodal approach of Lazarus (1976) has been used with disabled children. Using Lazarus's *BASIC ID* modalities (behavior, affect, sensation, images, cognition, interpersonal relationships, and drugs/biological functioning), disabled children's comprehensive social-emotional needs are analyzed and a counseling and psychotherapy program is developed to address the modalities most critical to the identified issues. Keat (1979) has also proposed a multimodal therapy approach, which he has used with learning-disabled children, summarized by the acronym HELPING (health, emotions-feelings, learning-school, personal relationships, imagination-interests, need to know-think, guidance of antecedents-behaviors-consequences). Again, primary concerns in the modality areas are identified and then targeted for counseling support.

From a purely counseling perspective, a number of therapeutic approaches are available. Prout and Brown (1983) identified six major theoretical approaches to counseling and psychotherapy that can be adopted when handicapped individuals are the primary clients: behavior therapy, reality therapy, person-centered therapy, rational-emotive therapy, Adlerian therapy, and psychoanalytic/psychodynamic therapy. Behavior therapy has been especially useful with behaviorally disturbed individuals. Using operant or classical conditioning, cognitive, or social learning behavioral approaches, positive behaviors are taught and/or reinforced while disruptive or disturbing behaviors are altered or extinguished. The other psychotherapeutic approaches have been used, in addition to the behavioral, for emotionally disturbed individuals who manifest an assortment of affectively based difficulties and issues. Additionally, all of these approaches can be applied to the emotional issues that often coexist or result from other handicapping conditions.

Besides the psychotherapeutic approaches, a number of more specialized approaches are available when counseling disabled individuals. Briefly reviewed in Reynolds and Gutkin (1982), these include family therapy approaches, sociodrama, developmental therapy, art therapy, music therapy, and holistic or milieu therapy. Again, these approaches often become part of a comprehensive program that addresses disabled children's educational, social-emotional, affective, family, and adaptive needs. In many cases, the use of counseling occurs only as an afterthought to what is otherwise a comprehensive program. Clearly, the possibility that disabled children have related or separate counseling needs must be emphasized in research programs and in applied settings.

REFERENCES

Keat, D. B. (1979). *Multimodal therapy with children.* New York: Pergamon.

Lazarus, A. A. (1976). *Multimodal behavior therapy.* New York: McGraw-Hill.

Prout, H. T., & Brown, D. T. (1983). *Counseling and psychotherapy with children and adolescents.* Tampa, FL: Mariner

Reynolds, C. R., & Gutkin, T. B. (1982). *The handbook of school psychology.* New York: Wiley.

HOWARD M. KNOFF
University of South Florida

BEHAVIOR MODIFICATION
FAMILY THERAPY
PSYCHOTHERAPY

CRATTY, BRYANT J. (1929–   )

As an assistant, associate, and full professor of kinesiology at the University of Southern California since 1961, Bryant Cratty has done research on perceptual and motor development and its relationship to the human personality. He developed programs for the neurologically impaired in the early 1960s that expanded to research of learning games to aid slow learners to acquire academic skills.

In 1970, Cratty published *Perceptual and Motor Development in Infants and Children,* which traced motor development from infancy to adolescence and gave specific

Bryant J. Cratty

teaching suggestions. In *Motor Activity and the Education of Retardates,* Cratty offered detailed curriculum guides, including relaxation and motor activities that would assist a child in gaining self-confidence. In 1991, Cratty, with Iranide Deoliveira, examined and assessed infants who had been exposed to cocaine prenatally: measurable delays were noted.

Cratty has published over 55 books and monographs (many translated into 15 languages and braille) that range from graduate texts in motor development and learning to applied sports psychology. He has also published over 100 articles in domestic and foreign journals and lectured in 20 countries. Presently Dr. Cratty is Professor Emeritus at the Physiological Sciences Department of the University of California Los Angeles.

REFERENCES

Cratty, B. J. (1975). *Motor activity and the education of retardates* (2nd ed.). Philadelphia, PA: Lea and Febiger.

Cratty, B. J. (1980). *Adapted physical education for handicapped children and youth.* Denver, CO: Love.

Cratty, B. J. (1985). *Active learning* (2nd ed.). Englewood Cliffs, NJ: Prentice Hall.

Cratty, B. J. (1986). *Perceptual and motor development in infants and children* (3rd ed.). Englewood Cliffs, NJ: Prentice Hall.

Deoliveira, I. J., & Cratty, B. J. (1991) Survey of ten infants exposed prenatally to maternal cocaine use. *International Journal of Rehabilitation Research, 14,* 3, 265–274.

ELAINE FLETCHER-JANZEN
*University of Colorado at
Colorado Springs*

CREATIVE PROBLEM SOLVING

Creative problem solving (CPS) is a structured model for using knowledge and imagination to arrive at a creative, innovative, or effective solution to a problem. CPS occurs when one of several conditions is satisfied: the product is novel or has value, the thinking used is unconventional and requires rejection or modification of previous ideas, thinking requires motivation or perseverance over a length of time, or the initial problem is vague or poorly defined, so problem formulation is part of the solution (Kletke, Mackay, Barr, & Jones, 2001).

Developed by Alex F. Osborn (1953), the original process consisted of three steps: fact finding, including problem definition and preparation; idea finding, including idea production and idea development; and solution finding, including evaluation and adoption. This process was refined by Parnes in 1967 and evolved into a five-step comprehensive model that incorporated findings from applied and theoretical research on creative thinking and behavior. The five steps are fact finding, problem finding, idea finding, solution finding, and acceptance finding.

CPS, also known as the Osborn-Parnes Model, is the most widely used method to encourage the application of creative thinking skills in the solving of problems. Deferred judgment is fundamental to the CPS process. This principle is based on Osborn's original notion that when judgment is withheld during ideation, at least 70 percent more good ideas are produced (1953). Throughout the process both divergent and convergent thinking constantly occur as the problem solver moves from one step to the next. Prior to the first step of CPS, there is the "mess" or preparation stage in which the identification or recognition of a situation of personal importance is determined. In fact finding, the emphasis is on gathering all possible background information that may help to define the real problem. Data is collected, facts about the situation are explored, and what is known about the situation is sought out and analyzed. Judgment is withheld until all alternatives have been exhausted. The next step focuses on the problem.

In problem finding, the emphasis is on restating the problem for solution. The problem is examined from a wide variety of perspectives and is redefined, narrowed, and analyzed. As the problem is being defined, it is recommended that the phrase "In what ways might I . . ." (IWWMI) be used to encourage more ideas and further elaborations. Again, it is important that judgment be deferred so that thoughts about the problem may flow freely. Sometimes new facts or data will cause a return to step one for more fact finding.

Once the problem has been satisfactorily defined, the third step, called idea finding, occurs. The intent is to generate ideas and possible solutions. Deferred judgment is important for idea finding as well. Many techniques may be used to generate ideas. The most popular is brainstorming, to generate new and frequently innovative ideas. Application of the four cardinal rules of brainstorming are a must to ensure that ideas flow freely before they are judged for their merits. The rules of brainstorming are (1) rule out criticism; (2) welcome freewheeling or wild ideas; (3) seek quantity; and (4) seek combination and improvement. Other techniques that may be used here and throughout the five steps to encourage the production of ideas are idea spurring questions, morphological analyses, synectics, attribute listing, scampering, and free association.

In step four, solution finding, the goal is to choose those alternatives that seem to provide the greatest potential for solving the problem. Criteria for evaluating solutions are developed and applied to each possible solution. The best idea, or combination of ideas to solve the problem is chosen. Those ideas not chosen should not be discarded for they may be used later.

The final step, acceptance finding, involves preparations to put the idea into use. The challenge is to make it acceptable. This involves developing a plan for carrying out an idea and to sell and promote it. Considerations must be given to all factors that may aid or hinder the implementation of the plan.

Parnes (1967) has emphasized the importance of knowledge and imagination in creative productivity. Through the Creative Problem Solving Institute, in university classes, and other settings, he has successfully demonstrated that the process is easy to learn and applicable to many situations. College students, government officials, business persons, artists, educators, parents, and children are among those who have learned to apply the set of skills in CPS to the solution of practical problems.

Brophy (1998) constructed a matching theory regarding CPS. This theory maintains that creatively solvable problems differ in levels of complexity, levels of knowledge needed, and amounts of convergent and divergent thought needed. Thus, problem solvers best match the needs of particular problems based on their preferences, abilities, knowledge, and work plans.

The literature on CPS is extensive. Reviews of the CPS process have been completed by Parnes (1981) and Noller (1977), among others. Edwards (1986) has provided an extensive review of information on approaches to enhance creative thinking and ideation during the CPS process. Researchers have taken an interest in the link between CPS and computers. It has been postulated that incorporating creativity enhancing techniques into computer systems may improve some outcomes of CPS (Kletke et. al, 2001). These systems have come to be known as Computerized Creativity Support Systems (CCSS). Another topic of interest for CPS researchers is individual vs. group performance. Mumford, Feldmen, Hein, and Nagao (2001) indicated that more available ideas led to better individual performance, and in group settings, providing information about the problem content lead to more elaboration and refinement of solutions to problems.

REFERENCES

Brophy, D. R. (1998). Understanding, measuring, and enhancing individual creative problem solving effects. *Creativity Research Journal, 11*(2), 123–150.

Edwards, M. O. (1986). *Idea power: Time tested methods to stimulate your imagination.* Buffalo, NY: Bearly.

Kletke, M. G., Mackay, J. M., Barr, S. H., & Jones, B. (2001). Creativity in the organization: The role of individual creative problem solving and computer support. *International Journal of Human-Computer Studies, 55*(3), 217–237.

Noller, R. B. (1977). *Scratching the surface of creative problem solving.* Buffalo, NY: D.O.K.

Mumford, M. D., Feldmen, J. M., Hein, M. B., & Nagao, D. J. (2001). Tradeoffs between ideas and structure: Individuals vs. group performance in creative problem solving. *Journal of Creative Behavior, 35*(1), 1–23.

Mumford, M. D., & Gustafson, S. B. (1988). Creativity syndrome: integration, application, and innovation. *Psychological Bulletin, 103,* 27–43.

Osborn, A. F. (1953). *Applied imagination.* New York: Scribner.

Parnes, S. J. (1967). *Creative behavior guidebook.* New York: Scribner.

Parnes, S. J. (1981). *The magic of your mind.* Buffalo, NY: Bearly.

Kristiana Powers
California State University, San Bernadino

CREATIVITY
CREATIVITY TESTS

CREATIVE PROBLEM SOLVING INSTITUTE

The Creative Problem Solving Institute (CPSI) is a multidisciplinary, multilevel program designed to familiarize participants with the principles and techniques of creative problem solving (CPS). Founded in 1955 by Alex Osborn, the institute is sponsored by the Creative Education Foundation. In its first years, the institute's program was based on brainstorming, a procedure introduced by Osborn to facilitate creative thinking in a group. Osborn's (1953) notion was that "most of us can work better creatively when teamed up with the right partner because collaboration tends to induce effort, and also to spur our automatic power of association" (p.72). His conceptualization of the creative problem-solving process included three steps: (1) fact finding, (2) idea finding, and (3) solution finding (Osborn, 1953).

Sidney J. Parnes, who succeeded Osborn as the director of the institute, retained the basic principles of the original model while extending the process to encompass a more eclectic approach. Kitano and Kirby (1986) summarized Parnes's approach as follows: "The Model consists of six steps and incorporates a variety of research-supported techniques for stimulating creativity, including brainstorming, synectics, incubation, imaging, deferred judgment, forced relationships and practice" (p. 205). The six steps as outlined by Parnes (1977) are objective finding, fact finding, problem finding, idea finding, solution finding, and acceptance finding. Each step can be thought of as having two phases, a divergent phase (coming up with many ideas) and an evalu-

DIVERGENT PHASE	CPS STAGE	EVALUATIVE PHASE
• Opportunities are explored • Situations are searched for possible opportunities	**OBJECTIVE FINDING**	• Challenge is accepted • Systematic effort is taken to respond to challenge
• Data are gathered • Situation is examined from many viewpoints • Info, impressions, feelings are collected	**FACT FINDING**	• Most important data are identified and analyzed
• Many possible problem statements are generated in the form "In what ways might I (we) . . . ?"	**PROBLEM FINDING**	• A working problem statement is chosen
• Many different ways of responding to the problem statement are developed and listed	**IDEA FINDING**	• Ideas that seem most promising or interesting are selected for further examination
• Many possible criteria are formulated for use in reviewing and evaluating ideas	**SOLUTION FINDING**	• The most important criteria are selected • These criteria are used to evaluate, refine, and strengthen ideas
• Possible sources of assistance and implementation steps are identified	**ACCEPTANCE FINDING**	• Specific plans are formulated • Roles are assigned • Timeline is set

Figure 1 The CPS model of creative problem solving

ative phase (selecting best candidate ideas). A model of the process is shown in Figure 1 (adapted from Baer, 1997).

The annual summer institute has a range of programs, including ones for participants new to CPS training and extension programs for participants who have experience working with the CPS model. In addition to annual summer institutes, regional Creative Problem Solving institutes, symposiums, and workshops are held throughout the year. The CPSI attracts people from business, education, and government to its summer institutes and other programs. Participants receive training from specialists with varied experiences in fields associated with creativity.

REFERENCES

Baer, J. (1997). *Creative teachers, creative students.* Boston: Allyn & Bacon.

Kitano, M. K., & Kirby, D. F. (1986). *Gifted education: A comprehensive review.* Boston: Little, Brown.

Osborn, A. F. (1953). *Applied imagination: Principles and procedures of creative problem-solving* (Rev. ed.). New York: Scribner.

Parnes, S. J. (1977). Guiding creative action. *Gifted Child Quarterly, 21*(4), 460–476.

JOHN BAER
Rider University

CREATIVITY, THEORIES OF
CREATIVITY TESTS

CREATIVE STUDIES PROGRAM

The Creative Studies Program was started with graduate-level courses in 1967 by Stanley J. Parnes at Buffalo State College in New York to enhance various aspects of college students' present and future behaviors both in college and the general community (Parnes & Noller, 1972a). Parnes and his colleagues developed the Creative Studies Program curriculum based on an earlier project, Creative Problem Solving.

The Creative Problem Solving curriculum is a five-step process: (1) fact finding, (2) problem finding, (3) idea finding, (4) solution finding, and (5) acceptance finding that emphasizes the generation of a variety of alternatives prior to selecting or implementing a solution (Maher, 1982). The general purposes of the Creative Problem Solving Model are, first, to provide a sequential process that will enable an individual to work from an accumulation of information to arrive at a creative, innovative, or effective solution, and, second, to improve students' overall creative behavior (Maher, 1982).

In implementing the Creative Studies Project curriculum at Buffalo State College, Noller and Parnes (1972) developed a two-year, four-semester curriculum. The first year of the curriculum provided the students with hands-on experience in creativity. Such experiences were provided through a variety of instructional procedures, including the use of discussions, creative media (e.g., sculpture, art, dance), films, and guest leaders (Noller & Parnes, 1972). The second year of the project provided the students an opportunity to lead others through the project's curriculum.

The Creative Studies Program appears to be a successful method to increase the creative performance of college students (Maher, 1982; Parnes & Noller, 1972b). These students do better in school, perform better on three out of five mental operations (cognition, divergent production, and convergent production) in Guilford's Structure of Intellect Model (Guilford, 1967), and are more productive in nonacademic settings calling for creative performance. Torrance (1972) notes that the Creative Problem Solving curriculum or its modifications (e.g., the Creative Studies Program) is successful in teaching children to think creatively 91–92 percent of the time.

Buffalo State College was the first college to establish such a program; there are now at least 39 different programs and course that have similar missions. Buffalo State College has five full-time professors in the program, led by Gerald Puccio (Xu, McDonnell, & Nash, 2005).

REFERENCES

Guilford, J. P. (1967). *The nature of human intelligence.* New York: McGraw-Hill.

Maher, C. J. (1982). *Teaching models in the education of the gifted.* Rockville, MD: Aspen.

Noller, R. B., & Parnes, S. J. (1972). Applied creativity: The Creative Studies Project: Part III—The curriculum. *Journal of Creative Behavior, 6,* 275–294.

Parnes, S. J., & Noller, R. B. (1972a). Applied creativity: The Creative Studies Project: Part I—The development. *Journal of Creative Behavior, 6,* 11–22.

Parnes, S. J., & Noller, R. B. (1972b). Applied creativity: The Creative Studies Project: Part II—Results of the two-year program. *Journal of Creative Behavior, 6,* 164–186.

Torrance, E. P. (1972). Can we teach children to think creatively? *Journal of Creative Behavior, 6,* 114–143.

Xu, F., McDonnell, G., & Nash, W. R. (2005). A survey of creativity courses at universities in principal countries. *Journal of Creative Behavior, 39,* 75–88.

ROJA DILMORE-RIOS
California State University, San Bernardino

CREATIVITY
CREATIVITY TESTS

CREATIVITY

Creativity is a complex and multifaceted phenomenon of human behavior. Early philosophers conceptualized creativity as a mystical characteristic, resulting from divine intervention. The psychodynamic approach viewed creativity as an "unconscious process through which libidinal or aggressive energies are converted into culturally sanctioned behaviors" (Freud, 1924).

Today, the creative *person, process, product,* and *environment* are the vantage points from which creativity is most often discussed. Psychologists taking the person-centered view focus on individual differences in people's creativity, as well as the distinctive attributes of creative people. The psychometric approach has made a significant contribution to the measurement of creativity in individuals. This approach originated with Guilford (1950) when he urged psychologists to open up research on creativity, which he saw as a long-neglected but important attribute of humans. Psychometric researchers developed various measures to assess creativity, but have traditionally focused on divergent thinking ability. The most frequently used measure of creativity is the Torrance Tests of Creative Thinking (1974), which measures divergent thinking by scoring along the dimensions of originality, fluency, flexibility, and elaboration. Other measures of creativity that focus on divergent thinking are batteries developed by Guilford (1959), Getzels and Jackson (1962), and Wallach and Kogan (1965). Critics have emphasized the need to measure processes of creativity other than divergent thinking, such as evaluative thinking and problem identification.

The distinctive characteristics of creative individuals have also been investigated. Consistent among the many descriptions of creative persons are traits and behaviors such as unusual sensitivity to their environment, independence in thinking, nonconforming in their behaviors, and persistence at tasks. Creative people also tend to be open to new ideas and experiences and less accepting of traditional points of view. Exploring ideas for their own sake, a marked sense of humor, a high tolerance for ambiguity, and strong self-confidence in their own work are other common traits of highly creative people.

What happens in the creative process? Wallas (1926) described the process as consisting of four stages: preparation, incubation, illumination, and verification. Torrance defined the process as "one of becoming sensitive to or aware of problems . . . bringing together available information . . . searching for solutions . . . and communicating the results" (Torrance & Myers, 1970, p. 22).

Other psychologists have used experimental and computer-simulation methodologies to investigate the creative process. Such approaches usually take place in controlled laboratory environments, rely on quantitative measurement, and seek to determine causality by manipulating variables and measuring its effects on creativity.

Some of the earliest experimental studies focused on the nature of insight (Sternberg & Davidson, 1995). Today, an active area of research is based on the Creative Cognition approach (Smith, Ward, & Fink, 1995), which adopted the experimental methodologies of cognitive psychology to elucidate the creative thinking process. Creative Cognition researchers have identified two main phases of creative invention that occur in a cyclical fashion in ordinary individuals. During the *generative phase,* the individual generates numerous candidate ideas or solutions and forms a mental representation (referred to as a preinventive structure). Then during the *exploratory* stage, the individual examines the candidate mental representations and ideas and works out their implications. A number of mental processes enter into the generative phase, including retrieval, association, synthesis, transformation, analogical transfer, and categorical reduction. Computer simulations have been conducted to simulate the creative problem-solving process, using heuristics derived from the cognitive task analysis of people solving creative problems (Langley et al., 1987).

Leading proponents of the search for methods to teach creative cognitive processing have been Parnes (1967) and Torrance (1979). Parnes developed the Creative Problem Solving Process, a five-step method combining knowledge and imagination in problem solving. Torrance (1979) created a three-stage instructional model—the Incubation Model—that integrates creativity objectives with content objectives. More recently, Sternberg has viewed creativity as a decision and has proposed strategies to develop creativity (Sternberg & Grigorenko, 2000). Nickerson (1999) provides further information on different methods to enhance creativity.

Creative products may be ideas, works of art, or scientific theories, provided certain criteria are met. There is a general consensus that creative products must be novel and relevant to a problem, situation, or goal. A relatively recent product assessment method is the Consensual Assessment Technique (CAT) developed by Amabile (1982). According to the CAT, participants are asked to complete some task in a specific domain (such as poetry), and experts in that domain (such as poets) independently rate the creativity of the products. If the interrater agreement is high, then the mean rating of the judges is used as a dependent measure of creativity (Hennessey & Amabile, 1988).

Psychologists taking the biographical approach to studying creativity have tended to focus on famous real-world creators and the personal and environmental factors that affect the quality and quantity of their products. The biographical approach has its roots in Galton (1869), Terman (1925), and Cox (1926). Current biographical researchers apply both qualitative case-study methodologies (Gardner, 1993; Wallace & Gruber, 1989) as well as historiometric quantitative measurement (Simonton, 1999).

An environment or situation that is open and accepting is critical for the release and development of creative potential. Csikszentmihalyi (1999) argues for a systems model of creativity that focuses on the interrelation of the *domain, field,* and *individual.* The domain consists of a set of rules, procedures, and instructions for action. The field includes all the individuals who act as gatekeepers to the domain. According to the systems model, creativity occurs when an individual makes a change in the information contained in a domain, and that change is selected by the field for inclusion in the domain. Torrance (1962) has suggested that other important variables are those that encourage unusual questions and ideas and those that allow performance to occur without constant threat of evaluation.

The debate regarding the nature of the relationship between creativity and intelligence has not been conclusively resolved. Kitano and Kirby (1986) contend that creativity is distinguishable from general intelligence. That is, "an individual can be extremely bright but uncreative, or highly creative but not necessarily intellectually gifted" (Kitano & Kirby, 1986, p. 192). Other researchers view intelligence as a subset of creativity. According to the Investment Theory of Creativity (Lubart & Sternberg, 1995), creativity requires a combination of six distinct but interrelated resources: intellectual abilities, knowledge, styles of thinking, personality, motivation, and environment. It has been estimated that an IQ of at least 120 is generally necessary for high creativity. IQ levels may vary according to the nature of the creative act.

REFERENCES

Amabile, T. M. (1982). Social psychology of creativity: A consensual assessment technique. *Journal of Personality and Social Psychology, 43,* 997–1013.

Csikszentmihalyi, M. (1999). Implications of a systems perspective for the study of creativity. In R. J. Sternberg (Ed.), *Handbook of creativity* (pp. 313–339). New York: Cambridge University Press.

Cox, C. (1926). *The early mental traits of three hundred geniuses.* Stanford, CA: Stanford University Press.

Freud, S. (1924). *The relations of the poet to day-dreaming.* In collected papers (Vol. 2). London: Hogarth. (Original work published 1908)

Galton, F. (1869). *Hereditary genius: An inquiry into its laws and consequences.* London: Macmillan.

Gardner, H. (1993). *Multiple intelligences: The theory in practice.* New York: Basic Books.

Getzels, J. W., & Jackson, P. W. (1962). *Creativity and intelligence: Explorations with gifted students.* New York: Wiley.

Guilford, J. P. (1950). Creativity. *American Psychologist, 5,* 444–454.

Guilford, J. P. (1959). Three faces of intellect. *American Psychology, 14,* 469–479.

Hennessey, B. A., & Amabile, T. M. (1988). The conditions of creativity. In R. J. Sternberg (Ed.), *The nature of creativity: Contemporary psychological perspectives* (pp. 11–38). Cambridge, UK: Cambridge University Press.

Kitano, M. K., & Kirby, D. F. (1986). *Gifted education: A comprehensive view.* Boston: Little, Brown.

Langley, P., Simon, H. A., Bradshaw, G. L., & Zytkow, J. M. (1987). *Scientific discovery: Computational explorations of the creative process.* Cambridge, MA: MIT Press.

Lubart, T. J., & Sternberg, R. J. (1995). An investment approach to creativity: Theory and data. In S. M. Smith, T. B. Ward, & R. A. Finke (Eds.), *The creative cognition approach* (pp. 269–302). Cambridge, MA: MIT Press.

Nickerson, R. S. (1999). Enhancing creativity. In R. J. Sternberg (Ed.), *Handbook of creativity* (pp. 392–431). New York: Cambridge University Press.

Parnes, S. J. (1967). *Creative behavior guidebook.* New York: Scribner.

Simonton, D. K. (1999). Creativity from a historiometric perspective. In R. J. Sternberg (Ed.), *Handbook of creativity* (pp. 116–137). New York: Cambridge University Press.

Smith, S. M., Ward, T. B., & Finke, R. A. (Eds.). (1995). *The creative cognition approach.* Cambridge, MA: MIT Press.

Sternberg, R. J., & Davidson, J. E. (Eds.). (1995). *The nature of insight.* Cambridge, MA: MIT Press.

Sternberg, R. J., & Grigorenko, J. L. (2000). *Teaching for successful intelligence.* Arlington Heights, IL: Skylight Training and Publishing.

Terman, L. M. (1925). *Mental and physical traits of a thousand gifted children.* Stanford, CA: Stanford University Press.

Torrance, E. P. (1962). *Guiding creative talent.* Englewood Cliffs, NJ: Prentice Hall.

Torrance, E. P. (1974). *Torrance Tests of Creative Thinking.* Bensonville, IL: Scholastic.

Torrance, E. P., & Myers, R. E. (1970). *Creative learning and teaching.* New York: Dodd, Mead.

Wallace, D. B., & Gruber, H. E. (Eds.). (1989). *Creative people at work: Twelve cognitive case studies.* New York: Oxford University Press.

Wallach, M. A., & Kogan, N. (1965). *Modes of thinking in young children.* New York: Holt, Rinehart, & Winston.

Wallas, G. (1926). *The art of thought.* New York: Harcourt Brace Jovanovich.

SCOTT BARRY KAUFMAN
Yale University

CREATIVITY, THEORIES OF
CREATIVITY TESTS

CREATIVITY, AMUSEMENT PARK THEORY (APT MODEL) OF

The APT model uses the metaphor of an amusement park to explore the process of creativity (Baer & Kaufman, 2005; Kaufman & Baer, 2004a, 2005a). First there are *initial requirements* (intelligence, motivation, and environment) that must be present at some level for all creative work—much as you need certain basic requirements in order to go to an amusement park (e.g., transportation, a ticket). Next, there are *general thematic areas* in which someone could be creative (e.g., the arts, science); this level is like deciding which type of amusement park to visit (e.g., a water park, a zoo). The next level focuses on more specific *domains*—within the general thematic area of "the arts," for example, could be such varied domains as dance, music, visual art, and so on. Similarly, once you have selected the type of amusement park you want to visit, you must then choose a particular park. Finally, once you have settled on a domain, there are *micro-domains* that represent specific tasks associated with each domain—much as there are many individual rides to select from once you are at an amusement park.

The APT model attempts to integrate both domain-general and domain-specific views of creativity. The first level (initial requirements) is very general, and each subsequent level gets more and more domain specific. By the final level (micro-domains), the theory is very domain specific.

Initial requirements are things that are necessary, but are not by themselves sufficient, for any type of creative production. They include such things as intelligence, motivation, and suitable environments. Each of these factors is a prerequisite to creative achievement in any domain, and if someone lacks the requisite level of any of these initial requirements, then creative performance is at best unlikely.

Every field of creative endeavor is part of a large general thematic area, all of whose component fields share an underlying unity. General thematic areas are similar in nature to what some people call domains (Feist, 2004) or intelligences (Gardner, 1999).

Within each of the general thematic areas are several more narrowly defined creativity domains. Knowledge plays a large role at the domain level. For example, although psychology, sociology, criminal justice, and political science all may require many skills in the general thematic area of Empathy/Communication, the knowledge bases for these four social science subjects are strikingly different, with only modest overlap, as are the knowledge bases that are foundational for work in the life sciences, chemistry, and physics, even though all will require skill in the Math/Science general thematic area.

Although there are many commonalities among all the tasks that are part of a domain, there are still big differences in what one needs to know, and what one needs to know how to do, in order to be creative when undertaking different tasks in that domain. This is rather like the transition from undergraduate to graduate education. Everyone in a graduate program in psychology, for example, may be preparing for a career as a psychologist, but future clinical psychologists, social psychologists, and cognitive psychologists likely take very few of the same courses. Similarly, studying fruit flies intensively for 5 years may help one develop creative theories in one of biology's micro-domains but be of little use in another, and practicing on a 12-string guitar may help one perform creatively in some micro-domains of the music world but not others.

The APT model provides a hierarchical model that makes it possible to accommodate both the domain-general aspects of creativity and the many levels of domain specificity of creativity that research (Baer, 1993; Kaufman & Baer, 2004b, 2004c, 2005b) has demonstrated.

REFERENCES

Baer, J. (1993). *Divergent thinking and creativity: A task-specific approach.* Hillsdale, NJ: Erlbaum.

Baer, J., & Kaufman, J. C. (2005). Bridging generality and specificity: The Amusement Park Theoretical (APT) model of creativity. *Roeper Review, 27,* 158–163.

Feist, G. J. (2004). The evolved fluid specificity of human creative talent. In R. J. Sternberg, E. L. Grigorenko, & J. L. Singer (Eds.), *Creativity: From potential to realization* (pp. 57–82). Washington, DC: American Psychological Association.

Gardner, H. (1999). *Intelligence reframed: Multiple intelligences for the 21st century.* New York: Basic Books.

Kaufman, J. C., & Baer, J. (2004a). The Amusement Park Theoretical (APT) model of creativity. *The Korean Journal of Thinking & Problem Solving, 14*(2), 15–25.

Kaufman, J. C., & Baer, J. (2004b). Hawking's haiku, Madonna's math: Why it's hard to be creative in every room of the house. In R. J. Sternberg, E. L. Grigorenko, & J. L. Singer (Eds.), *Creativity: From potential to realization* (pp. 3–19). Washington, DC: American Psychological Association.

Kaufman, J. C., & Baer, J. (2004c). Sure, I'm creative—but not in math!: Self-reported creativity in diverse domains. *Empirical Studies of the Arts, 22*(2), 143–155.

Kaufman, J. C., & Baer, J. (2005a). The Amusement Park Theory of Creativity. In J. C. Kaufman & J. Baer (Eds.), *Creativity across domains: Faces of the muse* (pp. 321–328). Hillsdale, NJ: Erlbaum.

Kaufman, J. C., & Baer, J. (Eds.). (2005b). *Creativity across domains: Faces of the muse.* Hillsdale, NJ: Erlbaum.

JOHN BAER
Rider University

CREATIVITY, THEORIES OF
GIFTED CHILDREN

CREATIVITY, CONSENSUAL ASSESSMENT OF

The Consensual Assessment Technique (CAT; Amabile, 1982, 1996; Baer, Kaufman, & Gentile, 2004) is widely used in creativity research. In the CAT, subjects are asked to create something, and experts are then asked to evaluate the creativity of those products. Poems, collages, and stories have been widely used in CAT studies, and the potential range of creative products that might work using the CAT is quite wide. In the CAT, rather than trying to measure some skill that is theoretically linked to creativity, it is the actual creativity of things subjects have produced that is assessed.

The basic procedure when using the CAT is to provide subjects with some instruction for creating some kind of product and then have experts independently assess the creativity of those artifacts. For example, in one study "students were given a line drawing of a girl and a boy . . . [and] asked to write an original story in which the boy and the girl played some part" (Baer, 1994a, p. 39). Experts in the area of children's writing were then asked to rate the creativity of the stories on a scale of 1.0 to 5.0. These expert judges were not asked to explain or defend their ratings in any way. They were simply asked to use their expert sense of what is creative in the domain in question to rate the creativity of the products in relation to one another. Interrater reliabilities among expert judges are generally quite good, typically in the .70-to-.90 range (Amabile, 1996; Baer, 1993, 1998; Hennessey & Amabile, 1999; Runco, 1989).

The key issue regarding the validity of any test is whether the test is measuring what it's supposed to measure, and one of the great strengths of the CAT is how clearly and directly it can respond to this question. The CAT assesses the creativity of a variety of products (poems, collages, etc.) of psychological studies the same way creativity is assessed at the genius level—by experts in that field. While it is true that experts don't always agree and expert opinion may change over time, at a given point in time there is no more objective or valid measure of the creativity of a work of art than the collective judgments of artists and art critics, just as there is no more valid measure of the creativity of a scientific theory than the collective opinions of scientists working in that field.

CAT ratings of poems, stories, and collages have been shown to be valid measures of poetry-writing, story-writing, and collage-making creativity. It is less clear whether these measures also assess more general creativity-relevant skills, a topic about which there has been much debate (Amabile, 1982, 1996; Baer, 1993, 1994a, 1996; Conti, Coon, & Amabile, 1996); but for experimental studies designed to determine the impact of a wide variety of interventions, training, or experimental constraints, CAT ratings have been shown to work quite well. The CAT is not tied to any one theory of creativity, and so its validity does not rise or fall with one's opinion of any particular theory. Unlike most creativity-assessment techniques, the CAT is totally uncommitted (and therefore unbiased) regarding most of the big questions in creativity research. For example, it can be used equally well by those who believe that creativity has a significant domain-transcending, general component (e.g., Amabile, 1982, 1996), those who argue for a more domain-specific understanding of creativity (e.g., Baer, 1994a, 1996), or even

those who wish to separate domain-general and domain-specific variance in creativity (e.g., Baer, 1993; Conti et al., 1996). This would be impossible with most creativity tests (such as the widely used divergent-thinking tests) because such tests assume a high level of generality of creativity. CAT ratings are also generally stable across time (Baer, 1994b), but they respond quite well to real within-subject changes in motivation (e.g., Amabile, 1996) or skill (e.g., Baer, 1994a).

CAT ratings can also be used within a classroom to assess creativity, but to a very limited degree. CAT ratings can be used to compare one student's creativity on a particular task to the creativity of other students on the same task, but because creativity varies a great deal from domain to domain (and even on tasks in the same domain; Baer, 1993), CAT ratings cannot be used to compare students' creativity more generally. It is also not possible to devise any meaningful norms for CAT-based assessments, and therefore the use of the CAT has been primarily in creativity research, not in classroom applications.

REFERENCES

Amabile, T. M. (1982). Social psychology of creativity: A consensual assessment technique. *Journal of Personality and Social Psychology, 43,* 997–1013.

Amabile, T. M. (1996). *Creativity in context: Update to the social psychology of creativity.* Boulder, CO: Westview.

Baer, J. (1993). *Creativity and divergent thinking: A task-specific approach.* Hillsdale, NJ: Erlbaum.

Baer, J. (1994a). Divergent thinking is not a general trait: A multi-domain training experiment. *Creativity Research Journal, 7,* 35–46.

Baer, J. (1994b). Performance assessments of creativity: Do they have long-term stability? *Roeper Review, 7*(1), 7–11.

Baer, J. (1996). The effects of task-specific divergent-thinking training. *Journal of Creative Behavior, 30,* 183–187.

Baer, J. (1998). The case for domain specificity in creativity. *Creativity Research Journal, 11,* 173–177.

Baer, J., Kaufman, J. C., & Gentile, C. A. (2004). Extension of the consensual assessment technique to nonparallel creative products. *Creativity Research Journal, 16,* 113–117.

Conti, R., Coon, H., & Amabile, T. M. (1996). Evidence to support the componential model of creativity: Secondary analyses of three studies. *Creativity Research Journal, 9,* 385–389.

Hennessey, B. A., & Amabile, T. M. (1999). Consensual assessment. In M. A. Runco & S. R. Pritzker (Eds.), *Encyclopedia of creativity* (Vol. 1, pp. 346–359). San Diego, CA: Academic Press.

Runco, M. A. (1989). The creativity of children's art. *Child Study Journal, 19,* 177–190.

JOHN BAER
Rider University

CREATIVITY TESTS
CREATIVITY, THEORIES OF

CREATIVITY, FAIRNESS AND

Standardized tests are often criticized as being biased, and these criticisms can come in two main forms. A common lay approach to criticizing tests as biased is to point to significant differences that occur between males and females and among ethnic groups on various tests of aptitude or ability. Indeed, a wide variety of measures of intelligence and ability have shown lower scores for African Americans and Latinos (see Loehlin, 1999, for an overview).

Psychometric approaches to bias in testing take a more sophisticated view of the problem and do not accept the view that just because two groups may perform differently on a mental test, the test itself must be in error or biased. Current approaches evaluate content statistically that may be inappropriate because it unfairly favors one group over another. Methods are commonly applied as well to determine whether different constructs may be measured across nominal groups by the same test (e.g., a test may measure verbal ability in Caucasians, but may be measuring something quite different in Latino/a population; Reynolds, Lowe, & Saenz, 1999).

One approach to seeking out nonbiased assessment is to supplement traditional assessment with additional measures of constructs that may be influencing a score on a traditional test of ability or achievement. Creativity is a prime candidate to be such a supplement. One reason is that creativity is related to intelligence and academic ability, yet not so closely related as to not account for additional variance. Indeed, creativity is an important, if not essential, part of most major theories of intelligences (see Kaufman, 2005, for an overview). Another promising reason is the reduction in gender and ethnicity differences.

There are several studies that show a lack of race and ethnic differences in measures of creativity. African Americans and Caucasians did not show significant differences on the Torrance Test of Creative Thinking (TTCT) at the elementary school level (Glover, 1976b) and the college level (Glover, 1976a), while one study found African Americans having higher Fluency and Originality scores on the Figural subtest of the TTCT (Kaltsounis, 1974). In addition, the poems, stories, and personal narratives by African Americans and Caucasians did not show any significant difference in their creativity ratings by expert judges (Kaufman, Baer, & Gentile, 2004).

Comparisons of Caucasians and Latinos also provide evidence that some measures of creativity show few differences. While three of four TTCT-Verbal forms showed Caucasians scoring significantly higher than Latinos, there were no significant differences on the Figural forms (Argulewicz & Kush, 1984). In addition, the Creativity scale of the Scales for Rating the Behavioral Characteristics of Superior Students (SRBCSS) showed no significant differences (Argulewicz, Elliott, & Hall, 1982).

There are many additional constructs that may be used as part of such a supplemental approach to nonbiased testing (e.g., emotional intelligence, motivation, thinking styles), but creativity serves as a good exemplar of this approach. There are multiple ways of measuring creativity, extensive studies have examined creativity across many different possible groups, the relationship between intelligence and creativity has been well explored, and the field is still actively studied. An examiner who adds a creativity measure—or a measure of other alternative cognitive constructs—may be able to minimize possible testing bias (Kaufman, in press).

REFERENCES

Argulewicz, E. N., Elliott, S. N., & Hall, R. (1982). Comparison of behavioral ratings of Anglo-American and Mexican-American gifted children. *Psychology in the Schools, 19*, 469–472.

Argulewicz, E. N., & Kush, J. C. (1984). Concurrent validity of the SRBCSS Creativity Scale for Anglo-American and Mexican-American gifted students. *Educational and Psychological Research, 4*, 81–89.

Glover, J. A. (1976a). Comparative levels of creative ability in Black and White college students. *Journal of Genetic Psychology, 128*, 95–99.

Glover, J. A. (1976b). Comparative levels of creative ability among elementary school children. *Journal of Genetic Psychology, 129*, 131–135.

Kaltsounis, B. (1974). Race, socioeconomic status and creativity. *Psychological Reports, 35*, 164–166.

Kaufman, J. C. (2005). Non-biased assessment: A supplemental approach. In C. L. Frisby & C. R. Reynolds (Eds.), *Children's Handbook of Multicultural School Psychology* (pp. 824–840). New York: Wiley.

Kaufman, J. C., Baer, J., & Gentile, C. A. (2004). Differences in gender and ethnicity as measured by ratings of three writing tasks, *Journal of Creative Behavior, 38*(1), 56–69.

Loehlin, J. C. (1999). Group differences in intelligence. In R. J. Sternberg (Ed.), *Handbook of intelligence* (pp. 176–193). Cambridge: Cambridge University Press.

Reynolds, C. R., Lowe, P. A., & Saenz, A. L. (1999). The problem of bias psychological assessment. In C. R. Reynolds & T. B. Gutkin (Eds.), *The handbook of school psychology* (pp. 549–596). New York: Wiley.

JAMES C. KAUFMAN
California State University, San Bernardino

CREATIVITY
CULTURALLY/LINGUISTICALLY DIVERSE GIFTED STUDENTS

CREATIVITY TESTS

Creativity tests have been in widespread application for more than 50 years in both research on cognitive skills and in the identification of gifted and talented children for participation in special education programs. However, it was the tremendous increase of interest in giftedness and creativity and concomitant funding of such research from about 1953 to 1963 that fueled research in the area. Major conceptual advances occurred during this period as E. Paul Torrance began studying creativity in earnest and such classic and influential works as Guilford's (1959) "Three Faces of Intellect" and Getzels and Jackson's (1962) *Intelligence and Creativity* were published. Guilford was most influential in proposing the concept of convergent and divergent thinking, the latter being closely associated with creative thinking. Getzels and Jackson changed the dominant views of the relationship between IQ and creativity by postulating, based on their extensive study, that creativity was far more independent of IQ than previously believed, especially at the upper-IQ levels. This work paved the way for the development of modern creativity tests.

In the 1960s, Guilford and Torrance developed and employed measures of divergent thinking used in the early study of creativity. Guilford's battery of tests, based on his Structure of the Intellect model (Guilford, 1962) makes a distinction among different thinking abilities most relevant for creativity, which are said to be the divergent production abilities that allow information to be generated from information; and transformation abilities, which involve modification of what one experiences thus producing new patterns. Although Guilford's work has earned support over the decades, his battery of tests does not have the extensive validity research as compared with the Torrance tests, a series of tests for predicting the ability of an individual to behave creatively. These tests have been developed over a period of 25 years by J. P. Torrance and his associates and are incorporated into the Torrance Tests of Creative Thinking or the TTCT (Torrance & Ball, 1984).

Though these creativity tests and many others are commercially available and often used in the assessment of creativity, many psychometricians consider such tests to be experimental due to the many deficiencies inherent within them (Anastasi, 1982). One deficiency in particular is in the lack of construct validity. The major creativity tests attempt to measure multiple dimensions of creativity, including such variables as fluency, originality, unusual responses, flexibility, resistance to premature closure, and so on. It remains unclear though whether these dimensions are sufficiently independent to warrant differentiation in the measurement process (Heausler & Thompson, 1988). The measurement of creativity has also been found to be relatively task specific (i.e., performance on creativity measures does not generalize well to tasks outside of the test and the test setting giving psychometricians concern over the shortage of content validity). Even with the large body of research on creativity tests, the relationship between one's score for creativity with existing tests and major variables of personality and intelligence is uncertain. Furthermore, creativity tests lack

standardization. The items in creativity tests with very few exceptions (such as the Welsh Figure Preference Test), are open-ended and thus on the subjective side of the scoring continuum and induce the necessity for highly trained assessors to all agree on the relevant criteria. For this reason it is particularly important to assess the interscorer reliability of creativity tests before placing them into practice.

Creativity tests are probably better than most psychometricians believe (Bennett, 1972; Wallach, 1968). The relatively weak results of research on this genre of tests, compared with the outcome of research on tests of intelligence and academic achievement, are more reflective of the difficult nature of the concept than of any intrinsic flaw in the major scales in use today (Parkhurst, 1999). Creativity has proven a difficult concept to master and the state of the psychometric data regarding creativity tests generally reflects the nature of the concept. Despite these problems, the use of creativity tests continues to be an accepted activity in programs for the gifted and talented and has been defended by Torrance (1984), through the demonstration that tests for creativity can identify the gifted individuals as consistently as IQ tests, hence suggesting that they can be useful in recognizing the bright child who is highly creative but not necessarily above average in intelligence.

REFERENCES

Anastasi, A. (1982). *Psychological testing* (5th ed.). New York: Macmillan.

Bennett, G. K. (1972). Review of the Remote Associates Test. In O. K. Euros (Ed.), *Seventh mental measurements yearbook*. Highland Park, NJ: Gryphon.

Guilford, J. P. (1959). Three faces of intellect. *American Psychologist, 14,* 469–479.

Guilford, J. P. (1962). Potentiality for creativity. *Gifted Child Quarterly, 6,* 87–90

Getzels, J. W., & Jackson, P. W. (1962). *Creativity and intelligence.* New York: Wiley.

Heausler, N. L., & Thompson, B. (1988). Structure of the Torrance Tests of creative Thinking. *Educational and Psychological Measurement, 48,* 463–468.

Parkhurst, H. B. (1999). Confusion, lack of consensus, and the definition of creativity as a construct. *Journal of Creative Behavior, 33,* 1–21.

Torrance, E. P. (1984). The role of creativity in identification of the gifted and talented. *Gifted Child Quarterly, 28,* 153–156.

Torrance, E. P., & Ball, O. E. (1984). *Torrance tests of creative thinking. Streamlined.* Bensonville, IL: Scholastic.

Wallach, M. A. (1968). Review of the Torrance Test of Creative Thinking. *American Educational Research Journal, 5,* 272–281.

MELANIE L. BROMLEY
California State University, San Bernardino

CREATIVE PROBLEM SOLVING
TORRANCE, E. PAUL
TORRANCE TESTS OF CREATIVE THINKING
WELSH FIGURE PREFERENCE TEST

CREATIVITY, THEORIES OF

Creativity is a complex phenomenon that involves a combination of individual and social factors. Earlier theories of creativity examined the role of the subconscious, thinking processes, such as creative problem solving and traits and behaviors of the creative individual. Recent theories of creativity situate creativity in a social context to emphasize the interaction among individuals' systems (family and workplace) and sociocultural constructions (e.g., knowledge domains).

Early theories of individual creativity examined the artist and artwork, rooted in artistic essays (Mozart, 1878) and psychoanalytic theories of mind. Freud (1970) suggested that the concepts of the imagination and aesthetic pleasure, sublimated fantasy originating in childhood play, were integral to the artistic process. Jung (1952), however, emphasized analysis of the creative work of art, attempting to steer away from individual pathologies associated with creativity. Maslow's (1971) work on self-actualization helped to broaden the meaning of creativity beyond an artistic capacity toward an orientation to novelty and change, theorizing creativity as a latent feature of all humans.

The study of creativity continued to branch out to personality studies, psychometric approaches, and empirical studies of exemplary scientists with the underlying idea that once one could identify features of creative individuals, one could teach practical creative strategies in schools and in workplaces to advance society. Dewey (1910) suggested that creative problem solving is a basic cycle of perceiving and defining a problem, devising solutions, weighing consequences, and accepting a solution. Wallas (1926) offered four steps to creative problem solving: preparation, incubation, inspiration, and evaluation. Building on these conceptions, Parnes (1962) introduced brainstorming as a commonsensical individual and group approach based on deferred judgment to produce a range of ideas. Guilford's (1959) work on the structure of the intellect identified divergent thinking, the ability to produce associative concepts, as a cornerstone of creativity. Additional creativity traits in the literature include fluency of ideas, flexibility, toleration of ambiguity, independent thinking, nonconformist behavior, and persistence. Torrance (1962) studied developmental aspects of creativity, focusing on developing imagination and fostering a sense of individuality among gifted and talented children. Together, this body of creativity research helped to launch interest in creativity-oriented classroom instruction and programs.

Expanding upon these individual theories of creativity, researchers increasingly focused on the interaction between the creative individual and his or her environment. Robert Sternberg and his colleagues, for example, developed two prominent theories. The investment theory of creativity (Sternberg & Lubart, 1995) suggests that creativity involves conscious decision-making on the part of the creative individual. Similar to conceptions of creative problem solving, this model emphasizes redefining problems, questioning assumptions, idea generation, taking sensible risks, and tolerating ambiguity. The propulsion model (Sternberg, 1999, 2003; Sternberg, Kaufman, & Pretz, 2002) provides a framework for considering whether a given creative contribution replicates prior contributions or represents a breakthrough that actually propels a domain. Gardner's (1988) holistic model of creativity considers four areas: the sub-personal (genetic), the personal (cognition, motivation, personality), extrapersonal (knowledge domain), and multi-personal (the field). Amabile's (1996) componential model also posits that creativity results from individual skill and domain knowledge, but stresses the task motivation and the influence of extrinsic motivation, whether rewards or constraints. Amabile's model has been used to study creativity in social systems (e.g., parenting, schooling, families, teams, and organizations). Similarly, Csikszentmihalyi (1999) proposed a systems model that views creativity as an interaction among individual talent, traits, and ability (person); formal training in a particular area (domain); and external acceptance of a contribution (field). Taken together, these individual theories and system models provide a set of useful frameworks for considering creativity processes and outcomes in schooling and organizations.

REFERENCES

Amabile, T. M. (1996). *Creativity in context: Update to the social psychology of creativity.* Boulder, CO: Westview.

Csikszentmihalyi, M. (1999). Implications of a systems perspective for the study of creativity. In R. J. Sternberg (Ed.), *Handbook of human creativity* (pp. 313–338). New York: Cambridge University Press.

Dewey, J. (1910). *How we think.* Boston: D. C. Heath.

Freud, S. (1970). Creative writers and day-dreaming. In P. E. Vernon (Ed.), *Creativity* (pp. 126–134). Baltimore: Penguin Books. (Original work published 1908)

Gardner, H. (1988). Creative lives and creative works: A synthetic scientific approach. In R. J. Sternberg (Ed.), *The nature of creativity: Contemporary psychological perspectives* (pp. 125–147). New York: Cambridge University Press.

Guilford, J. P. (1959). Traits of creativity. In P. E. Vernon (Ed.), *Creativity* (pp. 167–188). Baltimore: Penguin Books.

Jung, C. G. (1952). Psychology and literature. In B. Ghiselin (Ed.), *The creative process* (pp. 208–223). New York: Madision Books.

Maslow, A. H. (1971). *The farther reaches of human nature.* An Esalen Book. New York: Viking Press.

Mozart, W. A. (1970). A letter. In P. E. Vernon (Ed.), *Creativity* (pp. 55). Baltimore: Penguin Books. (Original work published 1878)

Parnes, S. J. (1962). Do you really understand brainstorming? In S. J. Parnes & H. F. Harding (Eds.), *A source book for creative thinking* (pp. 283–290). New York: Charles Scribner's Sons.

Sternberg, R. J. (1999). A propulsion model of creative contributions. *Review of General Psychology, 3,* 83–100.

Sternberg, R. J. (2003). *Wisdom, intelligence and creativity synthesized.* New York: Cambridge University Press.

Sternberg, R. J., Kaufman, J. C., & Pretz, J. E. (2002). *The creativity conundrum.* New York: Psychology Press.

Sternberg, R. J., & Lubart, T. I. (1995). *Defying the crowd.* New York: Free Press.

Torrance, E. P. (1962). Ten ways of helping young children gifted in creative writing and speech. *Gifted Child Quarterly, 6,* 121–127.

Wallas, G. (1926). *The art of thought.* London: C. A. Watts.

JEN KATZ-BUONINCONTRO
University of Oregon

CREATIVITY TESTS
CREATIVITY, FAIRNESS AND

CRETINISM

Cretinism is a metabolic endocrine abnormality that is caused by a thyroid gland disorder (Singleton & D'Amato, 2003). It exists in many forms. Athyrotic hypothyroidism is the congenital absence or partial absence of the thyroid gland. Endemic cretinism is a dietary deficiency of iodine. Familial hypothyroidism is an inborn error of thyroid metabolism and iodine transport. Intrauterine hypothyroidism occurs in infants whose mothers were on antithyroid therapy during pregnancy. Prior to the advent of diets containing iodine and the addition of iodine to table salt within the last hundred years, the endemic form was most common in areas where iodine-rich seafoods were difficult to obtain, for example, the mountainous regions of western Europe and the mid-western United States.

Individuals with untreated congenital hypothyroidism have characteristic features: wide-set eyes, broad nose bridge, and protruding tongue. The head appears to be oversized. The abdomen is large and protrudes with frequent umbilical hernia. Extremities look as though they are shortened and there is general low muscle tone. mental retardation is a frequent result of the untreated condition.

Felix Platter (1536–1614), a Swiss physician, was one of the first to note the existence of endemic cretinism. In the early part of the sixteenth century, a Swiss physician, Aureolus Theophrastus Bombastus Von Hohenheim, better known as Paracelsus (1493–1541), observed that cretinism was associated with mental retardation. Wolfgang Hoefer (1614–1681), a court physician in Vienna, offered the first extensive description of cretinism. He contended that cretinism could be attributed primarily to food and a poor education.

Throughout the nineteenth century, governments in central Europe expended resources and attention on the investigation and treatment of cretinism. Johann Jacob Guggenbuhl (1816–1863), a Swiss physician, devoted his life to the "cure and prophylaxis" of cretinism. During this time cretinism was viewed as typifying all forms of mental deficiency. The first journal on mental deficiency, which was published in 1850, was entitled *Beobachtungen tuber den Cretinismus (Observations of Cretinism).*

Owing to the work of Thomas Curling in 1860 and Charles Fogge in 1870, cretinism was identified as related to hypothyroidism. The English physician George Murray developed the first thyroid treatment in 1891. However, etiological and pathological subtleties remained unknown and unappreciated until the twentieth century. In 1975, Dr. Jean H. Dussault from Quebec developed the screening test for neonatal hypothyroidism that is used in the United States today.

Treatment consists of replacement of the thyroid hormone, thyroxin, with synthetic preparations. The results of treatment depend not only on the length of time before treatment is begun but on the severity and type of hypothyroidism. Occurring in one in every 6,000 children, hypothyroidism is one of the most common inborn errors of metabolism (Singleton & D'Amato, 2003). The direct result of early identification is the opportunity for early treatment. This, in turn, allows children born with hypothyroidism to develop normally, obviating the need for special education.

REFERENCES

Dussault, J. H., Coulombe, P., Laberge, C., Letarte, J., Guyda, H., & Khoury, K., (1975). Preliminary report on a mass screening program for neonatal hypothyroidism. *Journal of Pediatrics, 86,* 670–674.

Gearheart, B. R., & Litton, F. W. (1975). *The trainable retarded: A foundations approach.* St. Louis, MO: Mosby.

Kanner, L. (1967). Historical review of mental retardation (1800–1965). *American Journal of Mental Deficiency, 72,* 165–189.

Klein, A. H., Meltzer, S., & Kenny, F. M. (1972). Improved prognosis in congenital hypothyroidism treated before age 3 months. *Journal of Pediatrics, 81,* 912–915.

Prehem, H. J., & Cegelka, P. T. (1982). *Mental retardation: From categories to people.* Columbus, OH: Merrill.

Scheerenberger, R. C. (1983). *A history of mental retardation.* Baltimore: Brookes.

Singleton, J. L., & D'Amato, R. C. (2003). Cretinism In E. Fletcher-Janzen & C. R. Reynolds (Eds.) *Childhood disorders diagnostic desk reference* (pp. 154–155). New York: Wiley.

CAROLE REITER GOTHELF
*Hunter College, City University
of New York*

HYPOTHYROIDISM
INBORN ERRORS OF METABOLISM

CRI DU CHAT SYNDROME (CAT CRY SYNDROME)

Discovered by Jerome Lejeune, director of the department of genetics at the University of Paris, and his coworkers, Gautier and Turpin, in 1963, cri du chat syndrome is associated with a partial deletion of one of the chromosomes in the B group; specifically, there is a deletion of the short arm of chromosome 5 (5p–). Cri du chat syndrome is the most frequently reported of the autosomal deletion syndromes. The name was derived from the characteristic high-pitched, mewing cry, closely resembling the cry of a kitten, that is heard in the immediate newborn period, lasts several weeks, and then disappears with the exception of some cases, in which the catlike cry persists into adulthood. Incidence is estimated at 1:50,000 births (Hynd & Willis, 1987).

Affected infants show low birth weight, failure to thrive, hypotonia, microcephaly, a round or moon-faced appearance with hypertelorism (wide-set eyes), antimongoloid or downward sloping palpebral fissures with or without epicanthal folds, strabismus, and a broad-based nose. Ears are low-set and abnormally shaped with malformations, including narrow external canals and preauricular tags. Micrognathia, a short neck, and varying degrees of syndactyly are present. Various types of congenital heart defects and abnormal dermatoglyphics are frequently noted. Major diagnostic features include severe mental retardation and markedly delayed motor development.

A significant number of cri du chat infants survive to adulthood and continue to demonstrate microcephaly. They also have short stature, facial asymmetry, dental malocclusions, skeletal problems such as scoliosis, eye defects, and a waddling gait. These individuals are at or below the trainable level. As school-aged children, they are found in classes for the moderately and severely retarded. According to Gearheart and Litton (1975), the incidence of cri du chat is not known. Berg et al. (1970) found that 7 of the 744 patients with IQs below 35 had this defect. Goodman and Gorlin (1970) reported that a preponderance of patients were female.

No treatment is presently available for this syndrome. As with other chromosome defects, prevention is associated with amniocentesis and genetic counseling. The possibility of a recurrence of the syndrome in another member of the family is rare unless the condition is due to a translocation chromosome. Most cases of cri du chat syndrome are sporadic, with about 13 percent originating from a balanced carrier parent who is phenotypically normal.

Future research will focus on earlier identification of the syndrome and effective intervention strategies (Guy & Nussbaum, 2003).

REFERENCES

Berg, J. M., McCreary, B. D., Ridler, M. A., & Smith, G. F. (1970). *The deLange syndrome.* Oxford, England: Pergamon.

Berkow, R. (Ed.). (1982). *The Merck manual of diagnosis and therapy* (14th ed.). Rahway, NJ: Merck Sharp & Dohme Research Laboratories.

Cegelka, P. T., & Prehn, H. J. (1982). *Mental retardation: From categories to people.* Columbus, OH: Merrill.

Gearheart, B. R., & Litton, F. W. (1975). *The trainable retarded: A foundations approach.* St. Louis, MO: Mosby.

Goodman, R. M., & Gorlin, R. J. (1970). *The face in genetic disorders.* St. Louis, MO: Mosby.

Guy, K. L., & Nussbaum, N. L. (2003). Cri du Chat Syndrome. In E. Fletcher-Janzen & C. R. Reynolds (Eds.), *Childhood disorders diagnostic desk reference* (pp. 156–157). New York: Wiley.

Holmes, L. B., Moses, H. W., Halldorsson, S., Mack, C., Pavt, S. S., & Matzilevich, B. (1972). *Mental retardation: An atlas of diseases with associated physical abnormalities.* New York: Macmillan.

Hynd, G., & Willis, G. (1987). *Pediatric neuropsychology.* Boston: Allyn & Bacon.

Lejeune, J., Gautier, M., & Turpin, R. (1959). *Les chromosomes humains en culture des tissues: Competes rendus hebdomadaires des seances de l'Academie des Sciences* (pp. 248–602). Paris: l'Academie des Sciences.

Zellweger, H., & Ionasescu, V. (1978). Genetics of mental retardation. In C. H. Carter (Ed.), *Medical aspects of mental retardation* (2nd ed.). Springfield, IL: Thomas.

CATHERINE HALL RIKHYE
*Hunter College, City University
of New York*

CHROMOSOMES, HUMAN ANOMALIES, AND
   CYTOGENETIC ABNORMALITIES
MENTAL RETARDATION

CRIME AND INDIVIDUALS WITH DISABILITIES

Public Law 94-142 first mandated that educational services be provided to all youths with disabilities no matter where they reside, a mandate continued by its successor, the Individuals with Disabilities Education Act (IDEA). Johnson (1979) indicates that about one third of incarcerated youths are thought to have serious learning disabilities, in contrast to only 16 percent of the unincarcerated population.

Morgan (1979) conducted a study to produce a national profile of disability conditions. He sent questionnaires to administrators of juvenile correctional facilities in 50 states and 5 U.S. territories. Among the respondents, only 6 did not provide most of the requested information; 204 institutions responded. Among the findings, Morgan reports that:

1. Compared to the national incidence of children with disabilities (12.3 percent), 42.4 percent of delinquent children committed to correctional institutions were found to have some type of disability.

2. The disabilities with the highest incident rates in correctional facilities were emotional disturbance (16.23 percent), learning disabilities (10.59 percent), and educable Mental Retardation (7.69 percent).

Morgan (1979) indicates that the figure 42 percent is inflated, while other studies put the figure between 28 and 43 percent (Fink, 1991; Rutherford, 1985). Keilitz and Miller (1980) combined results of several studies, including Morgan's (1979), and concluded that those studies suggest that (a) prevalence estimates of the major categories of emotional disorders, learning disabilities, and Mental Retardation are of greater magnitude than expected on the basis of estimates of prevalence among the general student population; and (b) the great difference in prevalence of disabilities between those youths outside and inside the justice system remains even when study design problems and bias are minimized.

Much speculation exists as to the relationship between criminal behavior and disability. Siegel and Senna (1981) assign theories that attempt to determine the cause of delinquency into four categories: individualized, social structure, social process, and social reaction. Unfortunately, the variables and factors that impact on these theories are the same that are used to describe the educable mentally retarded and emotionally disabled.

Keilitz and Miller (1980) present three rationales as the most prominent explanations of the disproportionate prevalence of disabilities among youths in the justice system. The three are school failure, susceptibility, and differential treatment.

Despite these attempts to account for unexpectedly high prevalence, there is no definitive explanation for the disproportionate number of youths with disabilities in the justice system. There is clear evidence that services (Johnson, 1979) mandated under PL 94-142 and the IDEA must be provided and that these services have not been fully implemented. The problem of disabilities as they relate to crime is serious and needs much more attention, especially in the areas of research, programs, and prevention (Brown & Robbins, 1979).

REFERENCES

Brown, S., & Robbins, M. (1979). Serving the special education needs of students in correctional facilities. *Exceptional Children, 45,* 574–579.

Fink, C. M. (1991). Special education in service for correctional education. *Journal of Correctional Education, 41*(4), 186–190.

Johnson, J. (1979). An essay on incarcerated youth: An oppressed group. *Exceptional Children, 45,* 566–571.

Keilitz, I., & Miller, S. L. (1980). Handicapped adolescents and young adults in the justice system. *Exceptional Education Quarterly, 1*(2), 117–126.

Morgan, D. I. (1979). Prevalence and type of handicapping conditions found in juvenile correctional institutions: A national survey. *Journal of Special Education, 13,* 283–295.

Rutherford, R. B., Jr. (1985). Special education in the most restrictive environment: Correctional/special education. *Journal of Special Education, 19,* 59–71.

Siegel, L. J., & Senna, J. J. (1981). *Juvenile delinquency: Theory, practice, and law.* St. Paul, MN: West.

Philip E. Lyon
College of St. Rose
First edition

Kimberly F. Applequist
University of Colorado at Colorado Springs
Third edition

EDUCATIONALLY DISADVANTAGED

See JUVENILE DELINQUENCY

CRISIS INTERVENTION

Crisis intervention is a service spontaneously available to individuals and students who are in need of immediate assistance (Kelly & Vergason, 1978). Caplan defines a crisis as a sudden onset of behavioral imbalance in a child where previous function was stable (Caplan, 1963). The intent of intervention in a crisis is to provide knowledge of coping behaviors of enduring value. According to Swanson and Reinert (1976), a child in conflict is one "whose manifested behavior has a deleterious effect on his/her personal or educational development and/or the personal or educational development of his peers" (p. 5).

Intervention at the point of disruption or crisis is not new. Traditionally, the crisis was handled by an administrator or teacher. According to Long, Morse, and Newman (1976):

> the problem is these are usually of a reflexive and haphazard type. From our analysis of acts and reactions in the school setting it appears that a good many leave much to be desired. Since they usually lack an awareness of the underlying conditions, they are reactions to symptoms, often with a curbing intention [p. 232]. Also these crisis situations may be only "a crisis to the teacher who is the consumer of the behavior." (p. 325)

The crisis concept has changed in four ways. The first is in consultation, which has gone from supervisory to strategic planning. In other words, clinicians and teachers work together toward resolution. The second is in the use of the helping teacher, who becomes responsible for the disturbed child. The third change is in the style of interviewing proposed by Redl called life space interviewing (LSI). The fourth change occurs in a system to manage the confrontation situations that are found in secondary education.

The holding of crisis meetings is one way to develop a positive, success-oriented classroom. When disruptions such as fights, serious arguments, misunderstandings, and expressions of angry feelings (verbal or physical) occur, impromptu crisis meetings help students understand and resolve serious conflicts (Redl, 1959). These meetings, which involve only those students who were actually involved in the problem situation, can take place in the classroom, lunchroom, or playground. To conduct a crisis meeting, the following steps are usually taken:

1. *Cooling off.* Students should be given a few minutes to cool off if they are very upset and not ready to engage in thoughtful discussion. If necessary, students can be sent to their desks, a quiet area, or the principal's office.

2. *Setting rules.* The meeting is initiated by speaking in a calm manner. Ground rules for the discussion are set. These may include avoiding arguing and listening to what each person has to say.

3. *Listening actively.* The student is asked to describe the incident, what led up to the incident, and how he or she feels. After listening carefully, the listener rephrases what the student has said to show understanding. Other students may be asked to summarize or repeat what the first student said. Then the second student is asked to give his or her recollection of the incident. During the active listening phase, the main goal is to obtain a clarification of what happened and how the participants are feeling. Helping students clarify their feelings may also serve to drain off some anger or frustration.

4. *Exploring the problem.* At this step, the problem is considered at length. Questions such as how the problem could have been avoided, what can be done the next time the problem begins, and what consequences should be expected (Glass et al., 1982) can be addressed.

Another resource is the crisis or helping teacher. Gearheart and Weishahn find that this teacher

provides temporary support and control to troubled students when they are unable or unwilling to cope with the demands of the regular classroom. The type of service the Crisis Teacher provides requires that he/she be available at the time of the crisis. Working closely with the regular classroom teachers, he/she provides support, reassurance, and behavioral management strategies. Troubled students come and go on either a regular or an episodic basis, depending on the needs of the students. When the teacher is not dealing with a crisis, he/she can be helping less troubled students academically and behaviorally. He/she can make referrals to supportive services, provide the needed intensive assistance for the more severely troubled students, and follow up on specific recommendations. The crisis teacher becomes an active partner with the teacher, mental health personnel, and parents in helping this student. (p. 223)

Another form of crisis intervention is the LSI method which was developed to help teachers become effective in talking to children and to help teachers use these skills as a specific management tool (L'Abate & Curtis, 1975). There are two main goals: clinical exploitation of life events and immediate emotional first aid. There are both long-range and immediate goals. This kind of therapy may help the student to express hostility, frustration, or aggression; provide support while helping the student to avoid panic or guilt; help the student to maintain relationships; allow teachers to supervise behavior and ensure conformity to rules; and help teachers in settling complex situations (L'Abate & Curtis, 1975). Bernstein (1963) in L'Abate and Curtis (1975) provides some guidelines for LSI:

1. Be polite.
2. Do not tower above a child; bend down to him.
3. Be sure of yourself.
4. Use "why" sparingly.
5. Encourage talk about the actual situation.
6. Help the child to avoid being overwhelmed by shame or guilt by minimizing the problem.
7. Help the child to express his or her feelings about the situation.
8. Be aware of the kind of thinking demanded by a particular situation.
9. Work with the child to make the situation better.
10. Allow the child time to ask questions.

L'Abate and Curtis (1975) list some limitations of LSI:

1. It requires the teacher to have an ability to understand human behavior in more of an art than a science form.
2. It often requires more time than a regular classroom teacher with 30 students has to spare; this is where the helping teacher could assist.
3. It requires education and cooperation among all members of the school staff.

The resource classroom is yet another way to help exceptional children. Here the child is provided with instruction and emotional support by the resource teacher for part of the day. The child may move between the classrooms and receive instruction from both teachers. It is even possible that the child can be placed on a limited day schedule in cases where he or she cannot handle either the resource or regular classroom. In summary, crisis intervention can be the most appropriate kind of action if all psychological, sociological, and educational knowledge is applied at the correct moment in time.

REFERENCES

Caplan, G. (1963). Opportunities for school psychologists in the primary prevention. *Mental Hygiene, 47*(4), 525–539.

Gearheart, B. R., & Weishahn, M. W. (1980). *The handicapped student in the regular classroom.* St. Louis, MO: Mosby.

Glass, R., Christiansen, J., & Christiansen, J. L. (1982). *Teaching exceptional students in the regular classroom.* Boston: Little, Brown.

Kelly, L. J., & Vergason, G. A. (1978). *Dictionary for special education and rehabilitation.* Denver, CO: Love.

L'Abate, L., & Curtis, L. T. (1975). *Teaching the exceptional child.* Philadelphia: Saunders.

Long, H. J., Morse, W. C., & Newman, R. G. (1976). *Conflict in the classroom: The education of emotionally disturbed children.* Belmont, CA: Wadsworth.

Redl, F. (1959). Concept of the life space interview. *American Journal of Orthopsychiatry, 29*(1), 1–18.

Swanson, L. H., & Reinert, H. R. (1979). *Teaching strategies for children in conflict curriculum methods, and materials.* St. Louis, MO: Mosby.

RICHARD E. HALMSTAD
University of Wisconsin at Stout

LIFE SPACE INTERVIEWING
REDL, FRITZ

CRISIS TEACHER

The concept of the crisis teacher/helping teacher was initiated, according to Long, Morse, and Newman (1976), as the result of the efforts of a staff of elementary teachers in a high problematic school. The crisis teacher was first an educator trained in psychoeducational theory and practice who provided direct assistance to regular classroom teachers and students that might exhibit disruptive (crisis) behaviors. Ultimately, this educator would enhance the learning environment by providing a liaison between the crisis teacher and the regular classroom teacher. This brought to the classroom teacher immediate peer help as opposed to the consultants, such as the school psychologist, school counselor, or principal, ordinarily sought out.

Historically, crises had been met by sending the students involved to the principal's office. Frequently, this procedure would yield less than adequate results for various reasons. First, the principal was often uninformed of the events leading up to the classroom crisis. Second, the principal's administrative responsibilities may make him or her unavailable when needed most. Third, the repressive nature

of being sent to the principal's office could have, in some instances, exacerbated the problem. In addition, resorting to this method of crisis resolution in some instances resulted in an inadvertent reinforcer being applied to the situation.

Regular classroom teachers were cognizant of the needs expressed by all students in their classrooms and as such understood that not all children manifested disruptive behaviors at all times. However, teachers were aware that every child in the classroom had the right to an equal share of his or her time. Since disruptive children could not always be physically removed from the classroom and other students had educational needs to be met, the crisis teacher concept seemed to meet the purpose of addressing the one who needed help, while keeping the classroom teacher in continuing interaction with other students.

Immediate help from a crisis teacher was also seen as an effort to interject a process that would promote a more expedient method of handling psychoeducational problems manifested by the disruptive student. Prior to such a process being developed, regular classroom teachers resorted to punishment and then waited until a staffing could be arranged to receive advice from a psychologist, nurse, counselor, special education teacher, or other team member. Again, the regular classroom teacher was faced with receiving well-meaning but delayed corrective suggestions that proved inappropriate to their needs. As cited by Reynolds and Birch (1977), such advice was often impractical. Teachers knew what to do but did not have the resources to implement the course of action advocated by a team to which the teacher was not always a contributing member.

Due to changes in special education over the years, the crisis teacher model is no longer popular.

REFERENCES

Long, N. J., Morse, W. C., & Newman, R. G. (1976). *Conflict in the classroom: The education of emotionally disturbed children* (3rd ed.). Belmont, CA: Wadsworth.

Reynolds, M. C., & Birch, J. W. (1977). *Teaching exceptional children in all America's schools.* Reston, VA: Council for Exceptional Children.

RICHARD E. HALMSTAD
University of Wisconsin at Stout

CRISIS INTERVENTION
RESOURCE ROOM
SPECIAL CLASS

CRISSEY, MARIE SKODAK (1910–2000)

Born in Lorain, Ohio, Marie Skodak Crissey obtained her BS and MA degrees from Ohio State University in 1931. She was an Institute of International Education fellow at the

University of Budapest in 1931–1932. Crissey became interested in factors influencing development of intelligence and school achievement partly through the influence of Henry H. Goddard and Sidney Pressey. Her PhD was in developmental psychology from the University of Iowa in 1938.

She was well known for her still frequently cited classic research (Skodak, 1939; Skodak & Skeels, 1949) on the heredity-environment issue, which countered the then widely held concept of genetically determined and fixed IQ. She found that the IQs of adopted children correlated more highly with the estimated intelligence of their biological rather than their adoptive parents, but that their actual level of intelligence was closer to that of their adoptive parents. Thus her research showed both hereditary and environmental influences on intelligence, and demonstrated that favorable home environment could raise levels of intelligence. From an applied standpoint, she emphasized the potential effectiveness of environmental intervention programs to stimulate the development of children from deprived backgrounds.

During her professional career, Crissey developed special education programs, intervention programs for disabled and deprived children, vocational guidance programs for high school students, and vocational rehabilitation services for the disabled. She was at the Child Guidance Center at Flint, Michigan, from 1938 to 1946 and was director of school psychology and special education at Dearborn, Michigan, from 1949 to 1969. She had a private practice in psychology (Anonymous, 1984). She was a fellow of the American Association of Mental Deficiency and of five divisions of the American Psychological Association. Among her numerous awards were the Joseph P. Kennedy International Award for research in mental retardation in 1968 and a citation for distinguished service from the American Psychological Association in 1972.

REFERENCES

Anonymous. (1984). Crissey, Marie Skodak. In R. Corsini (Ed.), *Encyclopedia of psychology* (Vol. 2). New York: Wiley.

Skodak, M. (1939). Children in foster homes: A study of mental development. *University of Iowa Studies in Child Welfare, 16*(1).

Skodak, M., & Skeels, H. M. (1949). A final follow-up study of one hundred adopted children. *Journal of Genetic Psychology, 75*, 85–125.

ROBERT T. BROWN
University of North Carolina at Wilmington

CRITERION-REFERENCED TESTING

Criterion-referenced testing is a method for examining a person's performance with respect to a standard or criterion. It is commonly contrasted with norm-referenced testing, in which a person's performance is compared with that of other persons who make up a norm group. While this concept has been used in pedagogy for millennia, it was formalized by Glaser and Klaus (1962). In their conception, a criterion is a level of performance achieved only when the person being examined is able to perform certain tasks. These tasks have been determined to be necessary for learning. During the course of study there may be many criteria, which may be viewed as stages or intermediate steps. The assessment of the performance on the tasks necessary to achieve criteria is commonly called criterion referenced testing (CRT). A criterion referenced test is thus a test constructed to assess the performance level of examinees in relation to a well-defined domain of content (Hambleton, 1999).

In the late 1960s criterion-referencing became commonly associated with mastery (Glass, 1978; Popham & Husek, 1969), especially with minimum-competency testing. In this variant, CRT is intended to classify persons into those who can and those who cannot perform at some minimally acceptable level. Nearly all states in the United States require some form of minimum-competency testing (Hambleton, 1999). Purposes for the testing include issuing of high-school diplomas, passage to high school from junior high, and comparison of classes and schools for various political purposes. While the latter reason is almost never formally stated, it is common practice in many states to publish building- or district-level average test performance. These are then compared with state "competitors." There have been numerous proposals to link teacher salaries to their classrooms' performance on such tests. In only a few isolated school districts have such procedures been established.

The major issues in CRT are definition of the content, development of the tests, evaluation of test characteristics, standard setting and test results use (National Education Association [NEA], 2006). A useful text on these issues has been compiled by Berk (1984a); more current thinking by researchers in the CRT field is reviewed by Hambleton (1999).

Definition of the content for criterion-referenced tests is closely tied to instruction. If one uses the Glaser and Husek concept of CRT, a careful analysis of the tasks being required of the students forms the basis for the test. Those tasks are separated either hierarchically or organizationally into stages or steps. Tests are constructed that sample the behaviors the student must exhibit to demonstrate knowledge or mastery for each step. In hierarchical content, the student must know certain content or be able to perform certain tasks before the next content or task can be attempted. Many courses in mathematics exhibit such structure. Other content may have an organizational sequence that is not inherent to it such as English literature. It may be studied historically, thematically, or by type such as poetry, novel, and essay. Criterion-referenced testing may be used to indicate level of achievement for each part. Nitko (1984) refers to ordering and definition for domains.

A domain may be ordered or unordered and well-defined or ill-defined. He asserts that CRT should be used only with well-defined content domains.

There has been relatively little research on developing items or questions for CRTs, and most test developers have used item-writing technology developed for norm-referenced achievement tests. Roid and Haladyna (1980) have attempted to develop an item-writing technology using algorithms for sentence writing. Other proposed approaches are based on mapping and on factor analysis (Roid, 1984). Future efforts are certain to use computers in the generation of items for CRTs.

Analysis of item and test characteristics has received considerable attention from psychometricians. Both classical reliability theory and item characteristic curve theory have been applied to the analysis of items and of the entire test. Reliability of CRT tests has been derived for test scores (Berk, 1984b) and for the classification decision (Hambleton, 1999; Subkoviak, 1984).

A major debate erupted in the latter 1970s over the issue of standards setting: Can standards be set and who sets them? Glass (1978) argued that the arbitrariness of standard setting results in poor educational practice and that test scores should be interpreted in other, unspecified ways. Numerous authors argued for standard setting, and several techniques, notably owed to Nedelsky, Angoff, and Ebel, have been developed. Hambleton (1999), Shepard (1984), and the NEA (2006) give overviews of the issues and the techniques.

REFERENCES

Berk, R. A. (Ed.). (1984a). *A guide to criterion-referenced test construction*. Baltimore: Johns Hopkins University Press.

Berk, R. A. (1984b). Conducting the item analysis. In R. A. Berk (Ed.), *A guide to criterion-referenced test construction* (pp. 97–143). Baltimore: Johns Hopkins University Press.

Glaser, R. (1963). Instructional technology and the measurement of learning outcomes. Some questions. *American Psychologist, 18*, 519–521.

Glaser, R., & Klaus, D. J. (1962). Proficiency measurement: Assessing human performance. In R. M. Gagne (Ed.), *Psychological principles in systems development* (pp. 419–474) New York: Holt, Reinhart & Winston.

Glass, G. V. (1978). Standards and criteria. *Journal of Educational Measurement, 59*, 602–605.

Hambleton, R. (1999). Criterion-referenced testing: Principles, technical advances, and evaluation guidelines. In C. R. Reynolds & T. B. Gutkin (Eds.), *The handbook of school psychology* (3rd ed., pp. 409–433). New York: Wiley.

National Education Association (NEA). (2006). *Standardized testing*. Retrieved January 14, 2005, from http://www.nea.org/accountability/standardization.html

Nitko, A. J. (1984). Defining "Criterion-Referenced Test." In R. A. Berk (Ed.), *A guide to criterion-referenced test construction* (pp. 8–28). Baltimore: Johns Hopkins University Press.

Popham, W. J., & Husek, T. R. (1969). Implications of criterion-referenced measurement. *Journal of Educational Measurement, 6*, 1–9.

Roid, G. H. (1984). Generating the test items. In R. A. Berk (Ed.), *A guide to criterion-referenced test construction* (pp. 49–77). Baltimore: Johns Hopkins University Press.

Roid, G. H., & Haladyna, T. M. (1980). The emergence of an item-writing technology. *Review of Educational Research, 50*, 293–314.

Shepard, L. A. (1984). Setting performance standards. In R. A. Berk (Ed.), *A guide to criterion-referenced test construction* (pp. 169–198). Baltimore: Johns Hopkins University Press.

Subkoviak, M. J. (1984). Estimating the reliability of mastery non-mastery classifications. In R. A. Berk (Ed.), *A guide to criterion referenced test construction* (pp. 267–291). Baltimore: Johns Hopkins University Press.

Victor L. Willson
Texas A&M University

MINIMUM COMPETENCY TESTING
NORM-REFERENCED TESTING

CRONBACH, LEE J. (1916–2001)

Lee J. Cronbach attended Fresno College, gaining his BA degree in 1934. After completing his MA degree at the University of California, Berkeley, in 1937, he attended the educational psychology program at the University of Chicago, gaining his PhD in 1940.

In 1940 Cronbach went to the State College of Washington as instructor in the department of psychology. He stayed there until 1946, advancing to the rank of assistant professor. During World War II, he was involved with the University of California division of War Research at San Diego, serving as research psychologist. After the war, Cronbach spent three years (1946–1948) as assistant professor of education at the University of Chicago. In 1948 Cronbach went to the University of Illinois, where he remained until 1964. Cronbach was also a professor of education at Stanford University for 16 years. He served the American Psychological Association as chairman of its Committee on Test Standards (1950–1953) and served on the Committee on Psychological Tests. His book, *Essentials of Psychological Testing,* is considered a classic in the field.

Cronbach is well known for his work as coinvestigator on the Terman Study of Children of High Ability, a project he joined in 1963. That study was a long-term longitudinal study of intellectually gifted students. The study has demonstrated much of what we know of the lives and productivity of the intellectually gifted. It has dispelled many of the common stereotypes surrounding the intellectually gifted. Cronbach is also well known for his work on measurement theory, program evaluation, and instruction. He developed the most frequently used measure of reliability for psychological and educational assessments known as "Cronbach's alpha." At the time of his death, Cronbach was working on a paper commemorating the fiftieth anniversary of the publication of the alpha paper. Lee Cronbach died of congestive heart failure in his Palo Alto home on October 1, 2001.

REFERENCES

Cronbach, L. J. (1951). Coefficient Alpha and the internal structure of tests. *Psychometrika, 16,* 297–334.

Cronbach, L. J. (1960). *Essentials of psychological testing* (2nd ed.). New York: Harper & Brothers.

Cronbach, L. J., & Gleser, G. C. (1965). *Psychological test and personnel decisions* (2nd ed.). Champaign: University of Illinois Press.

RAND B. EVANS
Texas A&M University

JESSI K. WHEATLEY
Falcon School District 49,
Colorado Springs, Colorado

CROSS-CULTURAL ADAPTABILITY INVENTORY

The Cross-Cultural Adaptability Inventory (CCAI; Kelly & Meyers, 1992) is a 50-item self-scored inventory that measures the ability of an individual to live and work in a cross-cultural environment. The CCAI is a self-assessment inventory. The instrument was first developed in 1987 by Dr. Colleen Kelly, a human resource specialist, and Dr. Judith Meyers, a clinical psychologist with a specialty in diagnostics. The instrument met the needs of cross-cultural specialists who needed a training tool to promote cross-cultural understanding and insight. The CCAI focuses on four skill areas which research has shown to be critical in adapting to other-cultures. The CCAI is based on a cultural general approach, which purports that there are certain commonalities to all areas across cultural transitions, regardless of the culture of origin. It provides a frame of reference for evaluating individuals adapting from one culture to another or working in a multicultural setting.

The inventory is a self-report instrument that requires individuals to respond along a six-point Likert scale. Because of its high face validity, the questions can be transparent: Individuals who want to place themselves in a favorable light can slant their answers. However, respondents are encouraged to be honest about their responding style, so that the information will be useful. The instrument stanine scores on four dimensions associated with cross-cultural adaption. Scores are plotted on a circle graph, and the individual compares their four scores to one another. Follow-up training focuses on skill development in needed areas.

The Emotional Resilience scale is the largest of the four, with 18 items. The content focus involves coping with stress and ambiguity, rebounding from imperfections and mistakes, trying new things and experiences, and interacting with people in new or similar situations. People who are emotionally resilient tend to have a positive attitude, resourcefulness, and the ability to modulate negative emotions.

The next dimension, Flexibility/Openness, has 17 items and assesses the extent to which a person enjoys the different ways of thinking and behaving that are usually encountered in a cross-cultural experience. The items deal with openness toward those who are different from oneself, tolerance of others, and flexibility with regard to new experiences. It involves a nonjudgmental approach and flexibility in behavior.

The Perceptual Acuity scale has ten items and deals with attention to communication cues and the accurate perception of cues across cultures. It assesses behaviors as well as perceptions. Perceptual acuity is synonymous with cultural empathy. It is the ability to distinguish the logic and coherence of other cultures, and involves the ability to interpret nonverbal and social cues.

The final scale is Personal Autonomy, which has seven items. It deals with personal identity, confidence in one's values and beliefs, and a sense of empowerment in the context of an unfamiliar environment with different values. It measures a person's sense of identity and adherence to a strong set of cultural values, as well as respecting the values and traditions of another culture.

The CCAI is a popular instrument among trainers and cross-cultural specialists because it is research-based, easy to understand and administer, self-scoring, inexpensive, and easily available. It was normed on a population of 653 cross-cultural specialists, foreign students, educators, missionaries, and business people. The test underwent two revisions where factor analysis, principle components analysis, and item analysis were performed. The final version was published by NCS in 1992. The instrument has excellent alpha reliability, face validity, and construct validity. Predictive validity has not been established, and it is not recommended that the CCAI be used for selection purposes.

The CCAI is used to develop insight into the adaption process, increase awareness of cross-cultural issues, and provide training for individuals living and working in other cultures. It also has application for multicultural work groups. The CCAI has been used to train foreign students and to prepare business people and their families for relocation abroad. The CCAI has trained volunteer groups working abroad (such as missionaries) and has assisted social service groups working with immigrant populations. The CCAI is also an excellent tool for training counselors, teachers, and principals in the issues of cross-cultural competency. Psychotherapists have found the CCAI useful in working with foreign-born patients as a feedback tool.

The CCAI has a manual that provides thorough information on the development of the instrument, the theories underlying the instrument, and the statistical data supporting it. Training tools are available that provide a full-day training design, as well as follow-up materials in the form of action planning. A feedback form is also available.

REFERENCE

Kelly, C., & Meyers, J. (1992). *The Cross-Cultural Adaptability Inventory* (CCAI). Minneapolis, MN: National Computer Systems.

JUDITH MEYERS
San Diego, California

CROSS-CULTURAL SPECIAL EDUCATION

See CULTURALLY/LINGUISTICALLY DIVERSE STUDENTS AND LEARNING DISABILITIES.

CROSS MODALITY TRAINING

Cross modality training refers to teaching the neurological process of converting information received through one input modality to another system within the brain. The process is also referred to as intersensory integration, intermodal transfer, and transducing. Cross modality integration problems have been linked historically to learning disabilities. It has been hypothesized that certain learners may process visual and auditory information accurately when each type of information is presented distinctly, but that those students may be deficient in tasks requiring them to shift or cross information between sensory systems (Chalfant & Scheffelin, 1969).

Reading, where the learner must relate visual symbols to auditory equivalents, is one academic domain for which cross modal integration is required. Johnson and Myklebust (1978) proposed that some reading disorders are due to an inability to make such conversions within the neurosensory system. It also has been proposed that disabilities such as apraxia, or the inability to plan and execute appropriate motor action, are related to inadequate cross modality integration because the child must convert an auditory memory of a word into motor output (Lerner, 1985).

Cross modality training programs have been devised to address intersensory integration problems. For example, Frostig (1965, 1968) advocated cross modality exercises, including activities such as describing a picture (visual to auditory), following spoken directions (auditory to motor), and feeling objects through a curtain and drawing their shapes on paper (tactile to visual-motor). Scant research is available to support the use of cross modality training as a strategy to improve students' academic skills. Additionally, few, if any, tests are designed to assess cross-modal perception. However, cross modality training a speaking, writing connection has recently became popular but lacks a theoretical base (Weissburg, 2006).

REFERENCES

Chalfant, J., & Scheffelin, M. (1969). *Central processing dysfunction in children* (NINDS Monograph NO. 9). Bethesda, MD: U.S. Department of Health, Education, and Welfare.

Frostig, M. (1965). Corrective reading in the classroom. *Reading Teacher, 18,* 573–580.

Frostig, M. (1968). Education for children with learning disabilities. In H. Myklebust (Ed.), *Progress in learning disabilities.* New York: Grune & Stratton.

Johnson, D., & Myklebust, H. (1967). *Learning disabilities: Educational principles and practices.* New York: Grune & Stratton.

Lerner, J. W. (1985). *Learning disabilities: Theories, diagnosis, and teaching strategies.* Boston: Houghton Mifflin.

Weissburg, R. (2006). *What cross-modality studies (don't) tell us about L2 writing.* Retrieved January 14, 2006, from http://www.symposium:)slw.org/2006/

DOUGLAS FUCHS
LYNN S. FUCHS
Peabody College, Vanderbilt University

DEVELOPMENTAL TEST OF VISUAL PERCEPTION–SECOND EDITION
FROSTIG REMEDIAL PROGRAM
MULTISENSORY INSTRUCTION

CROUZON'S SYNDROME (CRANIOFACIAL DYSOSTOSIS)

Crouzon's syndrome (CS) is believed to be a congenital disability that follows a pattern of autosomal dominance. The major physical characteristics are a result of premature closing of the skull, which causes cranial deformity, widely spaced eyes (which may protrude), and a misshapened face. The nasal bridge may be flat and the nose beaked with underdeveloped nasal sinuses. Malformation of the ear canals and eyes as a result of hypertension and orbital deformity is said to occur in 70 to 80 percent of the cases (along with optic atrophy); this may cause visual and hearing problems. The upper jaw and bones of the midface may be underdeveloped and the lower jaw may be prominent. Crowding, misalignment of upper teeth, and an enlarged tongue may cause some problems with eating and speech development. Higher incidence of infections also may occur, and in some cases congenital heart disease has been reported. Mental retardation may be noted in some children, but most have average mental abilities. In rare instances, spina bifida may be present (Carter, 1978).

Some related services may be necessary if visual, aural, and motor problems exist. Speech therapy will probably be required. In addition, psychological and guidance counseling may be required because of the physical appearance of the child. Mainstreamed placement with support services is often the proper educational approach for CS children (Fasnacht-Hill, 2003).

REFERENCES

Carter, C. (Ed.). (1978). *Medical aspects of mental retardation* (2nd ed.). Springfield, IL: Thomas.

Fasnacht-Hill, L. (2003). Crouzon syndrome. In E. Fletcher-Janzen & C. R. Reynolds (Eds.), *Childhood disorders diagnostic desk reference* (pp. 157–158). New York: Wiley.

Goodman, R., & Gorlin, R. (1977). *Atlas of the face in genetic disorders* (2nd ed.). St. Louis, MO: Mosby.

SALLY L. FLAGLER
University of Oklahoma

CRUICKSHANK, WILLIAM M. (1915–1992)

William M. Cruickshank received his BA in 1937 from Eastern Michigan University, his MA in 1938 from the University of Chicago, and his PhD in 1945 from the University of Michigan.

Cruickshank was the founder and director of the Division of Special Education and Rehabilitation and distinguished professor at Syracuse University from 1946 to 1967. He subsequently became director of the Institute for the Study of Mental Health and Related Disabilities

William M. Cruickshank

and professor of child and family health, psychology, and education at the University of Michigan from 1967 until his retirement.

Since 1937 Cruickshank's main interests were in the area of brain-injured children, neurologically handicapped children, and the neurophysiological characteristics of accurately defined learning-disabled children. Author of over 200 books, articles, and edited books (some of which are translated in several languages), Cruickshank's major publications include *Teaching Methods for Brain-Injured and Hyperactive Children* (1961), *Learning Disabilities in Home, School, and Community* (1977), and *Psychoeducational Foundations of Learning Disabilities* (1973).

Holder of six honorary degrees, he taught in many countries and remained active as a visiting professor and lecturer for a number of years following his retirement from the University of Michigan. As the founder, first president (1975–1985), and executive director of the International Academy for Research in Learning Disabilities, he was an international authority on the problems of learning-disabled children and youths. Dr. William Cruickshank passed away in 1992, after a long and productive career.

REFERENCES

Cruickshank, W. M. (1977). *Learning disabilities in home, school, and community* (Rev. ed.). Syracuse, NY: Syracuse University.

Cruickshank, W. M., et al. (1961). *Teaching methods for brain-injured and hyperactive children*. Syracuse, NY: Syracuse University.

KAY E. KETZENBERGER
*The University of Texas of the
Permian Basin*

CRYPTOPHASIA

Cryptophasia is a language disorder characteristic of twins. It occurs in 40–47 percent of all twin pairs in early childhood (Caldwell, 2003). Twins often have delayed language development accompanied by what appears to be a jargon that only the twins understand. This jargon is a form of imitation of adult language with its own syntax, a type of "pidgin." The language may become elaborate and complex but remains, for the most part, understandable only to the twins. The language develops as they attempt to imitate the speech sounds of adults. Since twins spend an inordinate amount of time together, they begin to understand approximations of mature language and reinforce each other for use of this lesser form of communication. Cryptophasia retards normal language development and therefore twins may need speech/language services in special education (Caldwell, 2003).

REFERENCE

Caldwell, C. M. (2003). Cryptophasia. In E. Fletcher-Janzen & C. R. Reynolds (Eds.). *Childhood disorders diagnostic desk reference* (pp. 158–159). New York: Wiley.

CECIL R. REYNOLDS
Texas A&M University

LANGUAGE DELAYS
LANGUAGE DISORDERS
TWINS

CRYSTALLIZED V. FLUID INTELLIGENCE

See CATTELL-HORN-CARROLL THEORY OF COGNITIVE ABILITIES.

CUED SPEECH

Cued speech was developed in 1967 by R. Orin Cornett at Gallaudet College in Washington, DC. It was designed to clarify ambiguity experienced by severely and profoundly hearing-impaired individuals relying on lipreading as a means of comprehending speech (Evans, 1982; NCSA, 2006). During speechreading, hearing-impaired individuals may confuse many sounds such as /p/, /m/, and /b/, because they are visually similar. Users of cued speech attempt to overcome this confusion by providing a visual supplement to information presented through speechreading.

This system includes 12 hand signals or cues (presented in Figure 1). Four cues are hand positions that differentiate between groups of vowel sounds. A hand can be placed at the side of the face, the throat, the chin, or the corner of the mouth. Eight cues, based on America Sign Language (ASL) hand shapes, are hand configurations used to visually differentiate between groups of consonants (Wilbur, 1979; NCSA, 2006). For example, a full hand represents the /m/, /f/, and /t/ sounds, whereas the extension of only the index finger represents the /d/, /p/, and /zh/ sounds. An auditory signal is visually supplemented by superimposing a consonant hand configuration on a vowel hand position. For example, the words *mitt* and *bit* may appear similar to the hearing-impaired speech reader; however, these words are cued differently. *Mitt* is cued with a full hand positioned at the throat, whereas *bit* is cued by placing a "b" hand shape at the throat.

Use of cued speech requires training for both the sender and the hearing-impaired individual. Cornett (1967) reports that an average of approximately 12 to 20 hours is required to develop proficient use of cued speech. Actually, time will vary with the individual learner and fluency comes with practice.

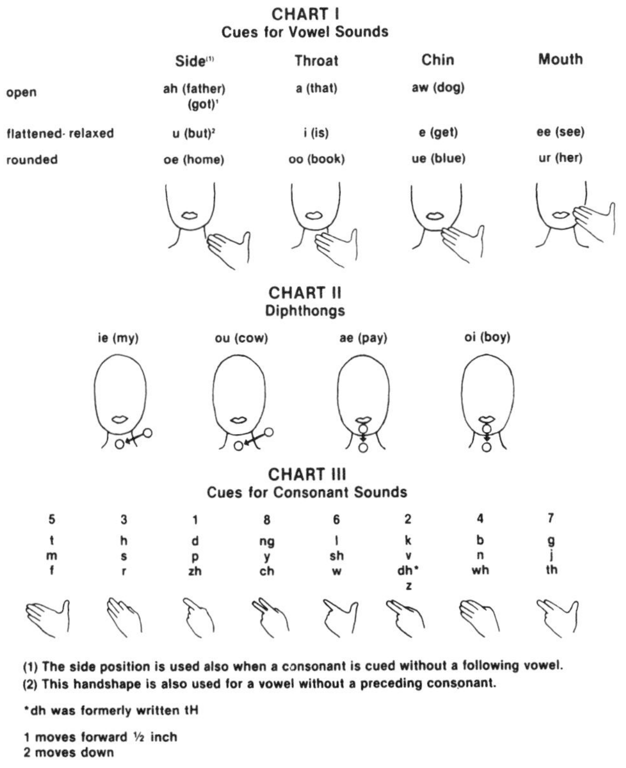

Figure 1 Cued speech—English

There are advantages and disadvantages associated with the use of cued speech. Its advantages include an adherence to the philosophy of oralism. Cued speech supplements information presented through speechreading; however, it cannot be used and understood in the absence of speech. In addition, use of cued speech has been associated with increases in speechreading accuracy (Clarke & Ling, 1976; Ling & Clarke, 1975; NCSA, 2006), vocabulary, and intelligibility (Rupert, 1969). Disadvantages include the questionable phonetic competence of users, lack of transfer potential to reading (Wilbur, 1979), and an overdependence on cues (Clarke & Ling, 1976). The National Cued Speech Association (NCSA) can be found online at http://www.cuedspeech.org.

REFERENCES

Clarke, B. R., & Ling, D. (1976). The effects of using cued speech: A follow-up study. *Volta Review, 78,* 23–34.

Cornett, R. O. (1967). Cued speech. *American Annals of the Deaf, 112,* 3–13.

Evans, L. (1982). *Total communication: Structure and strategy.* Washington, DC: Gallaudet College Press.

Ling, D., & Clarke, B. R. (1975). Cued speech: An evaluative study. *American Annals of the Deaf, 120,* 480–488.

National Cued Speech Association (NCSA). (2006). *Cued speech index.* Retrieved January 19, 2006, from http://www.cuedspeech.org

Rupert, J. (1969). Kindergarten program using cued speech at the Idaho School for the Deaf. *Proceedings of the 44th Meeting of American Instructors of the Deaf.* Berkeley, CA.

Wilbur, R. B. (1979). *American Sign Language and sign systems.* Baltimore: University Park Press.

MAUREEN A. SMITH
Pennsylvania State University

SIGN LANGUAGE
TOTAL COMMUNICATION

CUISENAIRE RODS

Cuisenaire rods, named for the Belgian mathematician who designed them, consist of a set of small colored wooden rods of varying lengths. Gattegno, a British psychologist, popularized their use for both mathematics and language instruction through combinations of size and color (Itaurian, 2006). Karambelas (1971) described how the rods are used in language instruction.

There have been many studies of the use of Cuisenaire rods in mathematics instruction. Hawkins (1984) introduced the relationship in the Pythagorean theorem to low-ability seventh graders using Cuisenaire rods. Sweetland (1984) used the rods in teaching multiplication of fractions. LeBlanc (1976) designed a teacher preparation program in elementary school mathematics using Cuisenaire rods as the vehicle for actively engaging prospective teachers in mathematics with the goal of applying that mathematics in the elementary school. McDonald (1981) incorporated the rods in teaching binomial expressions and Ginther (1970) designed applications of the rods in advanced mathematics. Urion (1979) developed a Cuisenaire rod activity for generating approximations of pi. Knowles (1979) described the use of the rods and the calculator in examining decimals that result from division of whole numbers. Ewbank (1978) and Hater (1970) drew attention to the use of color in mathematics instruction including Cuisenaire rods, number lines, magic squares, and combinatorial problems. Davidson (1977) suggested uses for the rods in teaching mathematics from basic arithmetic through algebra.

Brooks (1977) described a game for two teams that uses dice, meter sticks, and Cuisenaire rods. The games provide practice in number facts, regrouping, and use of the rods in relation to the metric system. Shively and Holz (1975) used the rods to illustrate finite mathematical systems. Steiner (1975) designed activities with Cuisenaire rods, Dienes Blocks, and Papy's minicomputer. Sheffelin and Seltzer (1974) described a workshop for 300 participants on the use of Cuisenaire rods with learning-disabled children. Kamps (1970) tested portions of Piaget's model for the development of operational conservation and measurement of length with 102 second-grade students from three different cities. One group had participated in the American Association for the Advancement of Science—A Process Approach science program in grades Kindergarten through 2, one group had received limited experience in linear measurement, and one group had used Cuisenaire rods in grades 1 and 2. A Kruskal-Wallis one-way analysis of variance revealed no significant difference at the .05 level among the three groups of students.

REFERENCES

Brooks, M. J. (1977). The one-meter dash. *Arithmetic Teacher, 24*(4), 327–328.

Davidson, P. S. (1977). Rods can help children learn at all grade levels. *Learning, 6*(3), 86–88.

Ewbank, W. A. (1978). The use of color for teaching mathematics. *Arithmetic Teacher, 26*(1), 53–57.

Ginther, J. L. (1970). An application of Cuisenaire rods in advanced mathematics. *School Science & Mathematics, 70*(3), 250–253.

Hater, M. A. (1970). Investigation of color in the Cuisenaire rods. *Perceptual & Motor Skills, 31*(2), 441–442.

Hawkins, V. J. (1984). The Pythagorean theorem revisited: Weighing the results. *Arithmetic Teacher, 32*(4), 36–37.

Itaurian, M. (2006). *Cuisenaire rods in the language classroom.* Retrieved January 19, 2006, from http://www.teachingenglish .org.uk/think/resources/rods.shtml/

Kamps, K. G. (1970). An investigation of portions of a model for acquisition of conservation and measurement of length based on performance of selected second grade children on six Piaget-type tasks. *Research in Education.* (Ann Arbor, MI: University Microfilms, SEO15002)

Karambelas, J. (1971). Teaching foreign languages "the silent way." *Association of Departments of Foreign Languages Bulletin, 3*(1), 41.

Knowles, F. (1979). Coloured rods, a calculator, and decimals. *Mathematics Teaching, 86,* 28–29.

LeBlanc, J. F. (1976). *Addition and subtraction Mathematics-methods program unit.* Bloomington, IN: Mathematics Education Development Center, Indiana University.

McDonald, J. R. (1981). Sharing teaching ideas: Factor cards: A device for GFC; A model of 3-space; Discovery in advanced algebra with concrete models. *Mathematics Teacher, 74*(5), 349–358.

Sheffelin, M. A., & Seltzer, C. (1974). Math manipulatives for learning disabilities. *Academic Therapy, 9*(5), 357–362.

Shively, J. E., & Holz, A. W. (1975). Finite operational systems for elementary students. *School Science & Mathematics, 75*(2), 191–196.

Steiner, H. G. (1975). Mathematical analysis of Piaget's grouping concept. Papy's minicomputer as a grouping. *International Journal of Mathematical Education in Science & Technology, 5*(2), 241–250.

Sweetland, R. D. (1984). Understanding multiplication of fractions. *Arithmetic Teacher, 32*(1), 48–52.

Urion, D. K. (1979). Using the Cuisenaire rods to discover approximations of pi. *Arithmetic Teacher, 27*(4), 17.

FREDRICKA K. REISMAN
Drexel University

CULTURAL ATTITUDES TOWARDS SPECIAL EDUCATION

The children and youth of the United States represent an increasingly diverse variety of cultural and linguistic groups. Between 1995 and 2050 the overall U.S. population is forecast to grow by almost 50 percent, with the Anglo (White, Not of Hispanic Origin) population experiencing the smallest proportional increase (approximately 7 percent; U.S. Bureau of the Census, 1994). This is in sharp contrast to the proportional increase forecast for the African American population (70 percent), Native American population (83 percent), Hispanic population (258 percent), and the Asian/Pacific Islander population (269 percent) during the same time period.

In order to provide appropriate educational services for such a heterogeneous population, an understanding of cultural affiliation and corresponding cultural attitudes as related to special education is necessary. A cultural group, for the purpose of this entry, is defined as a group set apart from others because of its national origin or distinctive cultural patterns (Schaefer, 1990). It is furthermore recognized that although members of a cultural group may have common values, beliefs, and behaviors, no individual member exemplifies all of the groups modal practices (Wehrly, 1995). The following sections include a discussion of the literature related to cultural attitudes toward special education, a summary of common attitudes reported for various cultural groups, and an analysis of the benefits and limitations of our current knowledge base.

The present body of literature related to cultural attitudes towards special education is largely focused on suggestions for practice in the special education arena and can be generally categorized as either (a) theory-based (e.g., "best practice" papers in which general knowledge of specific cultural groups is applied to the school setting), or (b) research-based (i.e., the presentation of data to demonstrate specific relationships between cultural attitudes and educational strategies). Thus, cultural attitudes towards special education are presented within the framework of these two categories.

Theory-Based Literature

Throughout the last century two main theoretical perspectives have been employed when working with culturally and linguistically diverse children within the school setting (Bowman, 1994). These two perspectives may be simplistically categorized as uniformity and diversity. The theoretical perspective of uniformity, labeled by Kohlberg and Mayer (1972) as "cultural transmission," places an emphasis on socializing children into a uniform culture through standardized curricula, educational experiences, and achievement expectations. In contrast, the theoretical perspective of diversity emphasizes the uniquely individual nature of education and the need for schools to address the cultural, linguistic, and intellectual heterogeneity of children.

Special education service delivery as mandated by public law (e.g., PL 94-142, IDEA, IDEIA) is based upon the theoretical perspective of diversity. In order to effectively meet the legal requirements set forth within the public law, it is necessary for school personnel to have a basic understanding of the attitudes and beliefs common to the different culturally and linguistically diverse groups which they serve. Numerous special education theorists have attempted to provide such an understanding through the application of specific cultural knowledge to the interpersonal interactions which take place within a school setting (e.g., Banks, 1994; Harry, 1992; Lynch & Hansen, 1992). The following is a synopsis of theory-based literature regarding the attitudes of culturally and linguistically diverse parents towards special education.

Parental Attitudes

The topic of parental attitudes towards special education as discussed in theory-based literature is typically focused on specific cultural groups.

Parents of African American origin. Literature regarding the attitudes of African American parents is limited and thus far suggests that parents may emphasize the role of immediate and extended family members (Seligman & Darling, 1989) and that attitudes towards severe disability may be often be related to a traditionally fatalistic interpretation of events (Harry, 1992). Common to many cultural groups, this fatalistic perception is described by Seligman and Darling (1989) as a seemingly passive acceptance of life circumstances which may in turn assist in the acceptance of a child's disability. African American parents of children with more mild forms of disability may display attitudes of caution and skepticism due to a well-documented history of group misdiagnosis and inappropriate special education service delivery (Harry, 1992).

Parents of Hispanic origin. Hispanic parents may also emphasize the role of immediate and extended family members and may be strongly tied to familism. This traditional view of the child as a reflection of the family unit may make acceptance of a severe disability more difficult for many Hispanic parents (Harry, 1992). A common cultural perception, in which developmental and intellectual disabilities are indistinguishable from mental disorders and mental illness, may add to the difficulty of acceptance (Adkins & Young, 1976). As a result of these two factors, the stigma associated with severe disabilities may be quite personal and significant for many Hispanic parents. On the other hand, a cultural emphasis on family relations and social interactions may assist parents in the acceptance of more mild forms of disability (Seligman & Darling, 1989). The mildly disabled child's ability to maintain their social role with immediate and extended family members may be a source of encouragement for parents and may even serve as a foundation for questioning the validity of the schools classification of their child. Common cultural attitudes of deference towards and respect for teachers and other school personnel may inhibit parental communication of concerns and expectations related to the special education process (Harry, 1992).

Parents of Asian/Pacific Island origin. Severe disabilities within the Asian/Pacific Islander culture have typically been viewed as the result of previous actions of parents or ancestors, the influence of spiritual forces (as in the case of some Southeast Asian groups), specific behaviors of the mother during pregnancy, or the imbalance of physiological functions (Chan, 1986). The potential cause of a disability may therefore be a source of shame for parents in that it is thought to reflect on the past or present behavior of family members. In addition, the inability of a child with a severe disability to represent the family through academic or occupational success may serve as a secondary source of embarrassment for some parents (Yano, 1986, as cited in Harry, 1992). A traditional Asian social structure which places the needs of the group before the needs of the individual may help influence acceptance of the situation and parental attitude towards special education service delivery (Dao, 1991). Asian/Pacific Islander parents of children with more mild forms of disability may tend to interpret the source of difficulty as "laziness" or ineffective training at home (Chan, 1986).

Parents of Native American origin. In accordance with traditional beliefs, many Native American parents view disabilities as having both a spiritual and physical etiology. The singular biological/psychoeducational viewpoint of the public schools in regard to disabilities may limit the course of action preferred by many Native American parents (Harry, 1992). Likewise, the public school procedure of interacting directly with parents may bypass the complex system of extended family communication shared by many Native Americans (Huang & Gibbs, 1992). The attitude of parents towards special education may also be influenced by the emphasis placed on childhood independence and the use of extended family members as caregivers. The extended support system available to the child and their freedom to find their own place in community relations

is exemplified by the absence of words such as "disabled" and "handicapped" from most Native American languages (Harry, 1992).

Benefits and Limitations

The benefit of theory-based literature within this area is the increased awareness and improved communication which results from a basic understanding of a groups common beliefs and practices. Flanagan and Miranda (1995) note that the specific information generated about a given culture through theory-based literature aids in understanding the values, beliefs, and behaviors that are expressed in cross-cultural interactions. Unfortunately, the tendency to generalize cultural attitudes to all members of a particular group to the exclusion of individual traits and preferences may serve as its greatest limitation. This concern sparked Lynch and Hanson (1992) to caution against the use of theory-based literature as a cross-cultural "recipe book" which stereotypes individuals rather than providing a foundation for better understanding.

Research-Based Literature

There is a limited number of research-based studies addressing the attitudes of culturally and linguistically diverse groups within the United States towards special education. The few studies which are available tend to be ethnographic in nature and are focused on parental and teacher attitudes regarding (a) meanings attached to disabilities or special education labels, (b) the role of language and culture in special education placements, (c) special education instruction format, and (d) parental participation in the special education process. The majority of researchers within this area employed naturalistic research methodologies such as interviews, surveys, or both, with not all studies including a quantitative analysis of results. The results from a sample of exemplary research-based studies are included in this section.

Parental Attitudes

Research-based studies regarding culturally and linguistically diverse parental attitudes towards special education have addressed various topics.

Meanings attached to labels. Studies on the meanings attached to special education labels by culturally and linguistically diverse parents reveal that (a) their concept and boundaries of "normal" may be different from that of the educational system (Bennett, 1988; Danseco, 1997; Harry, 1992; Rodriguez, 1995; Zetlin, Padron, & Wilson, 1996); (b) they are often confused by the specific terminology or labels common to special education (e.g., handicapped, disabled, impaired, retarded) and may associate these labels with more severe, as opposed to mild, manifestations of impairments (Danseco, 1997; Harry, 1992); (c) they may perceive the label as somehow reflective of family inadequacies (Harry, 1992); and (d) may attach biomedical and sociocultural (e.g., spiritual) causes to the labels (Danseco, 1997; Rodriguez, 1995).

Perceived role of language and culture. Several studies (e.g., Harry, 1992; Rodriguez, 1995; Zetlin et al., 1996) revealed parental perceptions that their child was placed in special education as a result of a language and cultural difference and not because of a true handicapping condition. This sentiment was reported by parents from various cultural and linguistic backgrounds (e.g., Hispanic and Southeast Asian).

Instructional format concerns. While parents tend to report positive feelings regarding the smaller group size for instruction found in special education, they also expressed concern that the slower pace, and lack of actual individualization of instruction might hinder, rather than help, their children (Harry, 1992; Zetlin et al., 1996). Confusion seems to exist among some parents as to how native language and culture should be utilized in their child's instruction (Zetlin et al., 1996), while others felt that instruction should focus on English and reading (Harry, 1992; Rodriguez, 1995).

Factors affecting parental participation. Parental opportunities for participation in the special education process was often reported by parents as (a) impersonal and one-sided (e.g., during meetings), with school personnel underestimating parental capabilities and limiting parental voice and power in decision-making; (b) overwhelming with regard to the number of letters and forms involved; (c) constrained by the parents' limited knowledge of the special education process (e.g., legal rights and necessity of attendance at meetings; Bennett, 1988; Danseco, 1997; Harry, 1992; Rodriguez, 1995); and (d) permeated with distrust (Bennett, 1988; Harry, 1992).

School Personnel Attitudes

Research-based studies within this area are generally focused on the attitudes of culturally and linguistically diverse school personnel, primarily teachers, towards special education. Two recent studies provide an example of this type of research. Rodriguez (1995) and Paez, Flores, and Trujillo (in press) surveyed culturally and linguistically diverse teachers employed in bilingual education programs. Both studies revealed that the teachers' knowledge of special education services and processes were limited and that the older the age group (Rodriguez, 1995) or the longer the time since college graduation (Paez, in press) the less informed they generally were.

According to Rodriguez (1995), there was significant variation among 100 teachers of Southeast Asian origin with regard to the belief that spiritual forces or destiny cause a child's disability with approximately one third agreeing, over one third disagreeing, and the rest being ambivalent on this point. Many of these teachers felt that children were often misplaced in special education and were discriminated against because of lower English proficiency. Moreover, they reported that lower levels of English proficiency among some students of Southeast Asian origin resulted in lower expectations for these students on the part of other school personnel.

Benefits and Limitations

The benefits of research-based literature in this area are that it provides for data-based decision making, often validates best practices literature, and supports a naturalistic or personalized approach to research. However, the current methodological approach in which surveys, interviews, or a combination of both are utilized is limited by subjectivity (e.g., in the generation of questions and consolidation of results) and the possible intrusion of the interviewer in the process. In addition, when the attitudes surveyed are those of culturally and linguistically diverse groups, the studies are ethnographic and have additional constraints, such as language and sociocultural barriers which are encountered whether the researcher is or is not a member of the cultural group.

Conclusion

It is clear that cultural attitudes play an important role in a family's adjustment to a child with a disability and the impact the situation has on the family's responsiveness and receptivity to sources of help (Fine & Gardner, 1994). The work of Harry (1992) serves as an example of the use of theory-based knowledge to construct data-based research. It is this type of application which will allow accurate and pertinent knowledge regarding cultural attitudes to be applied to the special education setting. Regardless of the informational source, whether it be theory- or research-based literature, the attitudes of culturally and linguistically diverse parents towards special education must be viewed within the context of the current life situation of the individual caregiver (Fracasso & Busch-Rossnagel, 1992). Dennis and Giangreco (1996) expand on this sentiment by noting that contextual considerations which should be considered include the emotional climate of racial or ethnic discrimination experienced by the individual, the implications of poverty, the neighborhood and living environment, and the degree and duration of acculturation into the dominant cultural group. Added to this list is the universal and very individual experience of caring for a child with special needs (Lynch & Hansen, 1992).

REFERENCES

Adkins, P. G., & Young, R. G. (1976). Cultural perceptions on the treatment of handicapped school children of Mexican-American parentage. *Journal of Research and Development in Education, 9*(4), 83–90.

Banks, J. A. (1994). *An introduction to multicultural education.* Boston: Allyn & Bacon.

Bennett, A. T. (1988). Gateways to powerlessness: Incorporating Hispanic deaf children and families into formal schooling. *Disability, Handicap, and Society, 3*(2), 119–151.

Bowman, B. T. (1994). The challenge of diversity. *Phi Delta Kappan, 76,* 218–224.

Chan, S. Q. (1986). Parents of exceptional Asian children. In M. K. Kitano & P. C. Chinn (Eds.), *Exceptional Asian children and youth* (pp. 36–53). Reston, VA: Council for Exceptional Children.

Danseco, E. R. (1997). Parental beliefs on childhood disability: Insights on culture, children development, and intervention. *International Journal of Disability, Development and Education, 44,* 41–52.

Dao, M. (1991). Designing assessment procedures for educationally at-risk Southeast Asian-American students. *Journal of Learning Disabilities, 24,* 594–601.

Dennis, R. E., & Giangreco, M. F. (1996). Creating conversation: Reflections on cultural sensitivity in family interviewing. *Exceptional Children, 63*(1), 103–113.

Fine, M. J., & Gardner, A. (1994). Collaborative consultation with families of children with special needs-why bother? *Journal of Educational and Psychological Consultation, 5,* 283–308.

Flanagan, D. P., & Miranda, A. H. (1995). Best practices in working with culturally different families. In A. Thomas & J. Grimes (Eds.), *Best practices in school psychology III* (pp. 1049–1060). Washington, DC: NASP.

Fracasso, M., & Busch-Rossnagel, N. (1992). Parents and children of Hispanic origin. In M. Procidano & C. Fisher (Eds.), *Contemporary families: A handbook for school professionals* (pp. 83–98). New York: Teachers College Press.

Harry, B. (1992). *Cultural diversity, families and the education system: Communication and empowerment.* New York: Teachers College Press.

Huang, L. N., & Gibbs, J. T. (1992). Partners or adversaries? Home-school collaboration across culture, race, and ethnicity. In S. L. Christenson & J. C. Conoley (Eds.), *Home-school collaboration* (pp. 81–109). Silver Spring, MD: National Association of School Psychologists.

Kohlberg, L., & Mayer, R. (1972). Development as the aim of education. *Harvard Educational Review, 42,* 449–469.

Lynch, E. W., & Hansen, M. J. (1992). *Developing cross-cultural competence: A guide for working with young children and their families.* Baltimore: Paul H. Brookes.

Paez, D., Flores, J., & Trujillo, T. (in press). Rural school personnel's conceptions of issues of diversity. *Rural Special Education Quarterly, 17.*

Rodriguez, J. (1995). *Southeast Asian's conception of disabilities and special education intervention in American schools.* Lowell: University of Massachusetts, College of Education. (ERIC Document Reproduction Service No. 388 740)

Schaefer, R. T. (1990). *Racial and ethnic groups* (4th ed.). Glenview: Scott Foresman.

Seligman, M., & Darling, R. B. (1989). *Ordinary families, special children.* New York: Guilford.

U.S. Bureau of the Census. (1990). *1990 United States census.* Washington, DC: U.S. Department of Commerce, Economics and Statistics Administration.

U.S. Bureau of the Census. (1994). *Population projections of the United States by age, sex, race, and Hispanic origin: 1995–2050.* Washington, DC: U.S. Department of Commerce, Economics and Statistics Administration.

Wehrly, B. (1995). *Pathways to multicultural counseling competence: A developmental journey.* Pacific Grove, CA: Brookes/Cole.

Zetlin, A., Padron, M., & Wilson, S. (1996). The experience of five Latin American families with the special education system. *Education and Training in Mental Retardation and Developmental Disabilities, 31,* 22–28.

ROBERT L. RHODES
DORIS PAEZ
New Mexico State University

CULTURAL BIAS IN TESTING

The cultural test bias hypothesis is the contention that racial and ethnic group differences in mental test scores are the result of inherent flaws in the tests themselves. These flaws bias, or cause systematic error, in a manner that causes ethnic minorities to earn low scores. Mean differences in scores among groups are then interpreted as artifacts of the test and not as reflecting any real differences in mental abilities or skills.

Mean differences in mental test scores across race are some of the most well-established phenomena in psychological research on individual differences. One of the primary explanations of these differences is that they are produced by people who are reared in very different environments, with lower scoring groups having been relatively deprived of the quantity and quality of stimulation received in the formative years by higher scoring groups. Another explanation is that lower scoring groups reflect a difference in the genetic potential for intellectual performance. Most contemporary views take an environment X genetic interaction approach.

Cultural bias in testing has existed as a potential explanation at least since it was raised by Sir Cyril Burt (1921), with occasional papers on the issue appearing over the years. It was not widely accepted as a serious hypothesis until the late 1960s, when the Association of Black Psychologists (ABP) called for a moratorium on the use of psychological tests with minorities and disadvantaged students, particularly with regard to placement in special education programs. In 1969 the ABP issued an official policy statement encouraging parents of black children to refuse to allow their children or themselves to be evaluated on any achievement, intelligence, aptitude, or performance test.

The primary objections to the testing of minorities on the basis of race or cultural bias in the tests have been classified by Reynolds (1982a) into six categories as follows:

1. *Inappropriate content.* Black or other minority children have not been exposed to the material on the test questions or other stimulus materials. The tests are geared toward white middle-class homes and values.

2. *Inappropriate standardization samples.* Ethnic minorities are underrepresented in the collection of normative reference group data. In the early years, it was not unusual for standardization samples of major tests to be all white.

3. *Examiner and language bias.* Since most psychologists are white and primarily speak only standard English, they intimidate blacks and other minorities. They are also unable to communicate accurately with minority children. Lower test scores for minorities, then, are said to reflect this intimidation and difficulty in the communication process, not lower ability levels.

4. *Inequitable social consequences.* As a result of bias in educational and psychological tests, minority group members, who are already at a disadvantage in the educational and vocational markets because of past discrimination, are disproportionately relegated to dead-end educational tracks and thought unable to learn. Labeling effects also fall into this category.

5. *Measurement of different constructs.* Related to item (1), this position asserts that the tests are measuring significantly different attributes when used with children from other than the white middle-class culture.

6. *Differential predictive validity.* While tests may accurately predict a variety of outcomes for white middle-class children, they fail to predict at an acceptable level any relevant criteria for minority group members. Corollary to this objection is a variety of competing positions regarding the selection of an appropriate, common criterion against which to validate tests across cultural groupings. Scholastic or academic attainment levels are considered by a variety of black psychologists to be biased as to criteria.

Additionally, it has been argued (see Reynolds, Lowe, & Saenz, 1999, for a discussion) that minority and majority groups have qualitatively distinct forms of intelligence and personality and thus cannot be assessed with the same methods, negating any attempt to compare groups or test performance.

The actions by the ABP had several positive effects. Prior to the call for a moratorium on testing of minorities, little actual research existed in the area. Much research was prompted by the ABP position as it brought the race bias hypothesis to the forefront of explanations of race differences in intelligence. Also in response to this call for a moratorium, the American Psychological Association Board of Scientific Affairs had a committee appointed to study the use of tests with disadvantaged students. The committee, headed by T. Anne Cleary, gave its official report in the form of an article in *American Psychologist* (Cleary, Humphreys, Kendrick, & Wesman, 1975).

Research on race bias in testing was, and continues to be, of major importance to psychology as well as to society. The cultural test bias hypothesis is probably one of the most crucial scientific questions facing psychology (Reynolds, 1981). If this hypothesis ultimately is accepted as correct, then the past 100 years or so of research into the psychology of individual differences (or differential psychology, the basic psychological science underlying all fields of applied psychology) must be dismissed as artifactual, or at least as confounded, since such research is based on standard psychometric methodology. Race bias in testing is being tested in the judicial courts as well as in the scholarly court of open inquiry. Two major court decisions, known as *Larry P.* (1979) and *PASE* (1980), have given conflicting opinions regarding the issues. Of two federal district courts, one decided that intelligence tests are racially biased and the other decided they are not biased.

Contrary to the position of the late 1960s, considerable research is now available regarding race bias in testing. For the most part, this research has failed to support the test bias hypothesis, revealing that (1) well-constructed, well-standardized educational and psychological tests predict future performance in an essentially equivalent manner across race for U.S.-born ethnic minorities; (2) the internal psychometric structure of the tests is essentially invariant with regard to race; and (3) the content of these tests is about equally appropriate across these groups (Reynolds, 1982a; Reynolds et al., 1999; Reynolds & Carson, 2005).

Race bias in testing is one of the most controversial and violently emotional issues in psychology. It will not be resolved entirely on the basis of research and data, as tests have unquestionably been abused in their past use with minority groups. Much of the controversy centers around the placement of minority children in special education programs. Thus, special consideration must be given to ensure that the misuses and abuses of the past are thwarted by "intelligent testing" (Kaufman, 1979). A general review of race bias in testing can be found in Jensen (1980). Specialty reviews of race bias in employment testing have been done by Hunter et al., 1979), and of bias in the testing of children by Reynolds (1982a; Reynolds et al., 1999; Reynolds & Carson, 2005). A book length debate of the issues can be found in Reynolds and Brown (1984). Methodology for investigating most aspects of cultural bias in testing relevant to special education is reviewed in Reynolds (1982b) and Reynolds et al. (1999).

REFERENCES

Burt, C. (1921). *Mental and scholastic tests.* London. In P. S. Kiy. Cleary, T. A., Humphreys, L. G., Kendrick, S. A., & Wesman, A. (1975). Educational uses of tests with disadvantaged students. *American Psychologist, 30,* 15–41.

Hunter, J. E., Schmidt, F. L., & Hunter, R. (1979). Differential validity of employment tests by race: A comprehensive review and analysis. *Psychological Bulletin, 86,* 721–735.

Jensen, A. R. (1980). *Bias in mental testing.* New York: Free Press.

Kaufman, A. S. (1979). Intelligence testing with the WISC-R. New York: Wiley.

Reynolds, C. R. (1981). In support of bias in mental testing and scientific inquiry. *Behavioral & Brain Sciences, 3,* 352.

Reynolds, C. R. (1982a). The problem of bias in psychological assessment. In C. R. Reynolds & T. B. Gutkin (Eds.), *The handbook of school psychology.* New York: Wiley.

Reynolds, C. R. (1982b). Methods for detecting construct and predictive bias. In R. A. Berk (Ed.), *Handbook of methods for detecting test bias.* Baltimore: Johns Hopkins University Press.

Reynolds, C. R., & Brown, R. T. (1984). *Perspectives on bias in mental testing.* New York: Wiley.

Reynolds, C. R., & Carson, A. D. (2005). Methods for assessing cultural bias in testing. In C. L. Frisby & C. R. Reynolds (Eds.), *Comprehensive handbook of multicultural school psychology* (pp. 795–823). New York: Wiley.

Reynolds, C. R., Lowe, P., & Saenz, A. (1999). The problem of bias in psychological assessment. In C. R. Reynolds & T. B. Gutkin (Eds.), *The handbook of school psychology* (3rd ed., pp. 549–595). New York: Wiley.

CECIL R. REYNOLDS
Texas A&M University

LARRY P.
MARSHALL v. GEORGIA
PASE v. HANNON

CULTURAL DEPRIVATION

See EARLY EXPERIENCE AND CRITICAL PERIODS; SOCIOECONOMIC STATUS.

CULTURAL-FAMILIAL RETARDATION

The term cultural-familial retardation has long been used to indicate mild retardation of unknown etiology that is associated with a family history of mild retardation, and a home environment that provides adverse experiences that are believed to inhibit mental development. The word cultural suggests an environmental basis; familial implies a genetic origin. Synonyms include sociocultural or psychosocial, intrinsic, subcultural, endogenous, familial retardation and psychosocial (Schroeder, Gerry, Gertz & Velasquez, 2002). Individuals in this population usually have IQs in the range of mild retardation (about 55 to 70), have no demonstrable biological pathology to account for the retardation, usually have a parent or sibling who is retarded, and come from low socioeconomic status homes (Gillberg, 1995; Wrestling, 1986).

The specific cause of cultural-familial retardation is uncertain, but it probably involves interactive factors; each factor alone is not sufficient to explain the intellectual and behavioral deficits. The present consensus is that the interactions among psychosocial, environmental, and genetic factors are so great and begin so early in life that one cannot place responsibility on any single cause in individual cases (Grossman, 1983). A few decades ago it was believed that this type of retardation was inherited, and environmental factors were discounted. Polygenic inheritance is suggested because this type of retardation is not randomly distributed among the poverty stricken, but most often found in families where the mother is retarded.

Mild retardation is less common in children born to healthy, mature women than in children born to adolescent mothers, women who are malnourished, or women who get poor prenatal care and are thus especially vulnerable to infections, trauma, and prenatal intoxications. Children born to such mothers have a relatively high incidence of prematurity and/or low birth weight, factors that are related to problems in physical and intellectual development. However, most children born to such women, or born prematurely, are not retarded.

Specific environmental factors include extreme malnourishment during early infancy, severe early social isolation, very large families with closely spaced births, very harsh or abusive discipline, severe neglect, marked parental ignorance about health care, chaotic or highly disorganized family life, and extremely inadequate educational opportunities. However, the severe malnutrition during late pregnancy and early infancy that causes retardation in underdeveloped countries is virtually unknown in America and the other factors listed are found in families where there is no retardation.

Educable or mildly retarded (EMR) children without known biological cause for the retardation follow the normal sequence of physical and intellectual development. Retarded children go through the usual Piaget sequences of cognitive development, but more slowly. Very few reach the formal operations stage that normal children reach around age 12 (Inhelder, 1968; Zigler & Balla, 1982). Usually EMR students master basic academic skills. On intelligence and academic achievement tests they tend to have low scores on most subtests of the scales, in contrast to learning-disabled children, who may score low on one or two subtests (and who are more likely to come from middle-class families). The EMR students require more trials to learn new skills than normal children, perhaps because of attentional and short-term memory difficulties or failure to develop effective strategies for learning and problem solving (Warren & Taylor, 1984).

In the past, many dropped out of school early, but now most complete high school, usually in special education programs that focus on occupational skills during adolescence. It has been estimated that although poor children make up about 80 percent of the educable mentally retarded students in schools, only about 10 percent of American children living in poverty will be classified as mildly retarded (Haywood, Burns, Arbitman-Smith, & Delclos, 1984). Children from such families may also contribute to normal, slow-learning, and gifted populations (Richardson, 1968). Cultural–familial retardation accounts for about 29 percent of all cases of mild mental retardation but only 4 percent of moderate to severe cases of mental retardation (Gillberg, 1995).

Some psychologists and educators have proposed that much of the responsibility for retardation in culturally disadvantaged families is with the environment outside the home, particularly the educational system. Mildly retarded students have been called "six-hour retarded children," implying that they are retarded only during school hours; however, there is little evidence for assuming that those children cope as well as others outside of school. Criticism of schools is partially based on the fact that prevalence studies have shown a higher percentage of identified cases during school years than before or after those years (Richardson, 1968). School demands may tax the abilities of mildly retarded individuals more than some activities of later life; for example, good reading comprehension and high mathematics are important, but they are not essential for some occupations. If we classify as retarded any adults who are competitive and consistently employed full-time, many former EMR students would not be considered retarded as adults, whatever an earlier classification, and whatever their IQs as adults. Levine (1985) reported a high correlation between stress and anxiety, especially for unemployed mildly retarded adults; therefore, personality factors as well as job skills and IQ may be relevant in the classification of adults.

Some sociologists and educators have argued that children in this group are not really retarded, but that intelligence tests are biased against poor children, especially minority ones. This argument seems to ignore the fact that some children from the same families and communities are successful with the same test items that others fail. Careful empirical evaluations of tests and test items offer little support for claims of test bias in well-constructed, properly standardized tests (Reynolds, 1983; Reynolds, Lowe, & Saenz, 1999). Modifying (raising) scores because of economic disadvantages would merely make it more difficult for low-scoring and disadvantaged students to meet eligibility criteria for services they need.

Many misconceptions about cultural-familial retardation stem from interpretations and misinterpretations of the work of Henry Herbert Goddard. Publicity after the publication of The Kallikaks (Goddard, 1912) led to fear and prejudice toward retarded persons, especially those from poor families. The Kallikak study was part of a large study of over 300 families in which feeblemindedness was reported in two or more members of the same primary family for several generations. Goddard described an attractive young Caucasian woman to whom he gave the pseudonym of Deborah Kallikak (adapted from Greek words meaning good and bad) and her relatives in two lines of descent traced from Martin Kallikak, a Revolutionary War soldier. One line, from Martin's marriage to a prominent woman, was filled with outstanding citizens. Deborah's line, said to be from Martin's mating with a barmaid, had feeblemindedness, poverty, shiftlessness, illegitimacy, and alcoholism in each generation. Descriptions of Deborah's mental development and her skills as an adult make it clear that she functioned at a retarded level; she could do embroidery and simple carpentry, and manage second-grade academic work. Broad media coverage of Goddard's conclusion that retardation was hereditary was overgeneralized and assumed to apply to all persons from low-income families. Interpretations of Goddard's work influenced state sterilization laws and the placement of state schools for the retarded in remote areas as protection for the schools and for society. By 1950 practices and law had changed. Goddard's work was reevaluated by modern research criteria, and was sharply criticized (Smith, 1985). During the 1960s and 1970s, some psychologists took a strong environmentalist position.

Children in the cultural-familial group look much like other children and are usually not recognized as retarded by their families during preschool years. They are more likely than others to need eyeglasses and to have frequent illnesses or other health problems (perhaps related to inadequate health care and habits).

Follow-up studies of former students in EMR classes indicate that as adults, many meet the demands of society more easily than they did school demands. From 40 to 80 percent are employed as adults, but employment is likely to be in unskilled or semiskilled work and incomes may be at or below the poverty level. Whether similar adults who received no special education fare as well is uncertain, but the evidence suggests that they may not.

Edgerton et al. studied the community life of retarded adults. They used repeated interviews and direct observations in 1960–1961, 1972–1973, and 1983 (Edgerton, Bollinger, & Herr, 1984). Case histories and descriptions of the original 48 persons described in The Cloak of Competence (Edgerton, 1967) indicate that those studied belong to the cultural-familial group. Edgerton found them to be on the lower end of the continuum on almost every index of economic and social functioning. They lived in slum areas, under deplorable conditions, had very little job security and few marketable skills. Almost all had found a "benefactor" (spouse, relative, or friend) to help them cope with the stresses of everyday life such as losing jobs or friends, having illnesses and financial problems. Life was not easy for them, but many of the 15 adults (mean age 56) remaining in 1983 reported at least moderate satisfaction with life.

Since mid-century, extensive efforts have been made to interrupt the vicious cycle of poverty, social incompetence, and prejudice associated with cultural-familial retardation. The establishment of the federal Office of Economic Opportunity (OEO) in the 1960s illustrates a massive effort to provide health, educational, and social intervention. The OEO's most visible and enduring program is Project Head Start, a preschool program for young children. Federal and state programs have had impact, but have not even approached the goal of reducing mental retardation by half, as was predicted in 1962 by the President's Panel on Mental Retardation. Project Head Start is now one of the largest health service providers for young children in America. It has been very successful in health areas, but its effects on intellectual functioning and academic achievement are less certain. However, there have been positive results in federally funded research in rigorously controlled experimental preschool programs. In addition, a collaborative study of the pooled data from 11 major studies on the long-term effects of early educational intervention projects designed to prevent the progressive decline in cognitive skills of children from low-income families (primarily minorities) suggests that carefully planned early intervention may have a positive effect on school competence. The competence was measured by assignment to special education programs or repeated grades, the development of abilities as measured by standardized tests, and the effect of attitudes and values of children and on families, both measured by questionnaires (Lazar & Darlington, 1982).

Experimental educational interventions designed to reverse retardation and other severe learning problems in school-age students are exemplified by studies using the Instrumental Enrichment "mediated learning experience" approach developed in Israel (Feuerstein, Rand, Hoffman, & Miller, 1980) and used at several North American sites by Haywood of Vanderbilt University (Haywood & Arbitman-Smith, 1981). Both the American and the Israeli investigators reported positive effects from the use of Instrumental Enrichment, particularly for adolescents with severe educational disadvantages, but initial gains may not be sustainable.

Studies of socially competent children who are at high risk for retardation may provide especially useful information. Werner and Smith (1982) described the "resilient" children in a 20-year study of 698 multiracial children in Hawaii. The resilient children grew to successful, competent adulthood despite poverty, parents with little formal education, and a good deal of stress. Factors associated with resilience were fewer serious childhood illnesses, development of more internal locus of control, well-spaced families of less than five children, and high-achievement motivation.

Das (1973), who has lived in several cultures, has suggested that the technology and cultural demands of society may be important factors in determining whether individuals are classified as mildly retarded. He noted that "biases" in the West emphasize verbal abilities and reasoning, and that the educational systems selectively refer children showing deficiencies in these areas for special education. School experiences are an integral part of a child's growth and development; they transmit the values of the majority culture. Cultural-familial children generally are less adept in language and reasoning than those from higher socioeconomic status families; thus, they start school at a disadvantage. In a technological society in which high-level verbal and reasoning skills are needed and valued, these children begin at a disadvantage that might not be such a problem in a simpler society. It is unlikely that we will soon prevent cultural-familial retardation in America, but progress is being made in reducing associated medical problems and perhaps ameliorating some of the severe learning and educational problems of children from families in which the risk of cultural-familial retardation is high.

REFERENCES

Das, J. P. (1973). Cultural deprivation and cognitive competence. In N. R. Ellis (Ed.), *International review of research in mental retardation* (Vol. 6). New York: Academic.

Edgerton, R. B. (1967). *The cloak of competence: Stigma in the lives of the mentally retarded.* Berkeley: University of California Press.

Edgerton, R. B., Bollinger, M., & Herr, B. (1984). The cloak of competence: After two decades. *American Journal of Mental Deficiency, 88,* 345–351.

Feurerstein, R., Rand, Y., Hoffman, M. B., & Miller, R. (1980). *Instrumental enrichment.* Baltimore: University Park Press.

Gillberg, C. (1995). *Clinical child neuropsychiatry.* Cambridge: Cambridge University Press.

Goddard, H. H. (1912). *The Kallikak family: A study in the heredity of feeble-mindedness.* New York: Macmillan.

Grossman, H. J. (Ed.). (1983). *Classification in mental retardation.* Washington, DC: American Association on Mental Deficiency.

Haywood, H. C., & Arbitman-Smith, R. (1981). Modification of cognitive functions in slow learning adolescents. In P. Mittler (Ed.), *Frontiers of knowledge in mental retardation: Social, educational, and behavioral aspects.* Baltimore: University Park Press.

Haywood, H. C., Burns, S., Arbitman-Smith, R., & Delclos, V. R. (1984). Forward to fundamentals; Learning and the 4th R. *Peabody Journal of Education, 61*(3), 6–35.

Inhelder, B. (1968). *The diagnosis of reasoning in the mentally retarded* (translated by W. B. Stephens). New York: Day.

Lazar, I., & Darlington, R. (1982). Lasting effects of early education: A report from the consortium for longitudinal studies. *Monographs of the Society for Research in Child Development, 47*(serial nos. 2–3).

Levine, H. G. (1985). Situational anxiety and everyday life experiences of mildly mentally retarded adults. *American Journal of Mental Deficiency, 90,* 27–83.

Reynolds, C. R. (1983). Test bias: In God we trust; all others must have data. *Journal of Special Education, 17,* 241–260.

Reynolds, C. R., Lowe, P., & Saenz, A. (1999). The problem of bias in psychological assessment. In C. R. Reynolds & T. B. Gutkin (Eds.), *The handbook of school psychology* (3rd ed., pp. 549–595). New York: Wiley.

Richardson, S. A. (1968). The influence of social-environmental and nutritional factors on mental ability. In N. S. Scrimshaw & J. E. Gordon (Eds.), *Malnutrition, learning, and behavior.* Cambridge, MA: MIT Press.

Schroeder, S. R., Gerry, M., Gertz, G., & Velasquez, F. (2002). *Usage of the term "mental retardation": Language, Image, & Public education.* Retrieved January 19, 2006, from http://www.ssa.gov/disability/MentalRetardationReport.pdf

Smith, J. D. (1985). *Minds made feeble: The myth and legacy of the Kallikaks.* Rockville, MD: Aspen.

Warren, S. A., & Taylor, R. L. (1984). Education of children with learning problems. *Symposium on learning disorders, pediatric clinics of North America.* Philadelphia: Saunders.

Werner, E. E., & Smith, R. S. (1982). *Vulnerable but invincible: A longitudinal study of resilient children and youth.* New York: McGraw-Hill.

Westling, D. L. (1986). *Introduction to mental retardation.* Englewood Cliffs, NJ: Prentice Hall.

Zigler, E., & Balla, D. (1982). Introduction: The developmental approach to mental retardation. In E. Zigler & D. Balla (Eds.), *Mental retardation: The development-difference controversy.* Hillside, NJ: Erlbaum.

SUE ALLEN WARREN
Boston University

ABCEDARIAN PROJECT
EDGERTON, R.
EDUCABLE MENTALLY RETARDED
GODDARD, H. H.
MENTAL RETARDATION

CULTURALLY/LINGUISTICALLY DIVERSE ISSUES IN EARLY CHILDHOOD

See EARLY CHILDHOOD, CULTURALLY/LINGUISTICALLY DIVERSE ISSUES IN.

CULTURALLY/LINGUISTICALLY DIVERSE STUDENTS AND LEARNING DISABILITIES

Students who are culturally and linguistically diverse (CLD) who experience academic difficulties are often misidentified, misplaced, and misinstructed. Historically, these students been overrepresented in special education (Mercer & Rueda, 1991), although for many, their academic problems were more a result of limited English proficiency than a learning disability. More recently, some CLD students have been denied special education services as a reaction to the previous trend of misidentification, resulting in an underrepresentation of CLD students (Frisby & Reynolds, 2005; Gersten & Woodward, 1994).

One critical issue for providing appropriate services for CLD students with learning disabilities is first determining if a student's academic difficulties are the result of a specific learning disability or other causal factors. Has the student had sufficient educational opportunity? Is the student literate in his or her native language? Does the student have the requisite English proficiency to successfully complete academic tasks in English? Is the student familiar with the content presented in academic subject areas? Is the student's behavior significantly different from peers from the same language and/or cultural group?

If the answer to any of these questions is no, then prereferral interventions are in order. Prereferral interventions are systematic, documented modifications suggested by a site based team, often called a Student Study Team, to ensure student success. Such interventions may include adapting assignments in ways that capitalize on the student's strengths, involving parents in the teaching and learning process, and using teaching approaches known to be effective with CLD learners.

If difficulties persist after appropriate interventions have been exhausted, a referral for special education services may be in order. Assessment of CLD students includes testing in the student's native language as well as English, to ensure the problem is evident in both languages. Also, informal measures should be used to support or refute the findings of standardized measures.

Once a learning disability has been diagnosed, a linguistically appropriate Individualized Education Plan (IEP) is developed to reflect the student's cultural and language needs. The IEP addresses areas (such as language support options) that meet students' cultural and linguistic needs, including primary language support, ESL, and/or sheltered instruction. The IEP should also specify the language of instruction for each instructional goal, the specifics of the systematic development of English language skills, and how progress in these language-related areas will be measured.

Primary language support is best provided by the special education teacher who is proficient in the student's native language; however, shortage of bilingual special education teachers is critical. Other options for primary language support include a bilingual paraprofessional, community volunteer, or a peer from the same cultural group. Sheltered instruction is an effective instructional approach for students who have intermediate proficiency in English, or when primary language support is not available.

Sheltered instruction takes into linguistic needs of CLD learners by modifying the curriculum and delivery of instruction to make it understandable for them. CLD students with learning disabilities need extra support in acquiring content area concepts as well as developing English language skills (Echevarria & Graves, 1998).

The following issues in the education of CLD students with learning disabilities should be considered:

- Special educators must address the cognitive and language needs of English language learners who have learning disabilities.
- Instruction, including ESL teaching, may need to be more explicit for students with learning disabilities since they tend not to learn incidentally.
- Instruction must be meaningful and relevant to students' cultural and educational experiences.
- Learning environments must be culturally responsive, accommodating the learning needs of culturally diverse learners.
- Assessing whether students acquired the academic concepts and language development objectives of lessons is essential. This can be done by establishing relevant goals, carefully analyzing and documenting the student's progress, or reteaching the lesson, based on the needs of the student.
- Modifications may include adapting the curriculum, using visuals to accompany oral presentation of information, and embedding activities in meaningful experiences that are linguistically and educationally rich.

Finally, special educators and paraprofessionals working with students with learning disabilities often are overlooked or excluded from general education professional development sessions that deal with culturally and linguistically diverse students. Special educators and paraprofessionals must be trained in current instructional practices in working with CLD students. Moreover, little interface occurs between special educators and those professionals who have expertise in working with CLD students (Gersten & Woodward, 1994). The focus needs to be on meeting the individual student's needs, not on purview. Increased communication and collaboration between programs and service providers, as well as support from administrators, would alleviate some of the issues relative to educating CLD students with learning disabilities.

REFERENCES

Echevarria, J., & Graves, A. (1998). *Sheltered content instruction: Teaching English-language learners with diverse abilities.* Boston: Allyn & Bacon.

Frisby, C., & Reynolds, C. R. (2005). *Comprehensive handbook of multicultural school psychology.* New York: Wiley.

Gersten, R., & Woodward, J. (1974). The language minority student and special education: Issues, trends and paradoxes. *Exceptional Children, 60*(4), 310–322.

Mercer, J., & Rueda, R. (1991, November). *The impact of changing paradigms of disabilities on assessment of special education.* Paper presented at the Council for Exceptional Children Topical Conference on At-Risk Children & Youth, New Orleans.

JANA ECHEVARRIA
AMITA EDRAN
*California State University,
Long Beach*

DISPROPORTIONALITY

See

LEARNING DISABILITIES

CULTURALLY/LINGUISTICALLY DIVERSE GIFTED STUDENTS

The immortal words of Harry Passow (1986) express concerns for the exclusion of various cultural and linguistic populations in gifted education programs:

> . . . these populations constitute the largest reservoir of untapped and underdeveloped talent available in our society. There is clear evidence that talent is not the prerogative of any racial or ethnic group, any social class, or any residential area. It may lie untapped in some situations under some conditions, but no population has either a monopoly or an absence of giftedness. (p. 27)

The fact is that students with special gifts and talents come from all populations, and as society becomes increasingly diverse, educators are faced with a challenge in meeting the needs of students who have special gifts from all populations represented in society. However, government and media reports indicate that educators are not effectively identifying and serving minority students, particularly those who are either considered limited English proficient, or those who are from low socioeconomic status (SES) backgrounds and/or from other cultures out of the mainstream middle-class Anglo American culture. In fact, these groups are not fairly represented in programs for the gifted and talented (Irby, 1993; Ortiz & González, 1989; USDE, 1993).

In the early 1970s, the term culturally different was used to refer to children who were from low SES backgrounds and/or who were not members of the hegemonous society;

however, in the later part of that decade, the term culturally diverse began to be used (Frasier, 1977). Zuke (1983) defined culturally diverse gifted children as those "who by reason of cultural identification and socioeconomic status have not been able to assimilate themselves into the dominant culture"; assimilation was a key term used in this definition. Later, Sheehy (1986) and Goffin (1988) suggested that cultural diversity is evidenced through any of an individual's traditional customs and sex-role behaviors that are different from those observed in the mainstream culture. Additionally, cultural differences may be found in learning styles, listening behaviors (Trueba, 1983) and response patterns (Cohen, 1988; Harris, 1988) that are typically associated with mainstream giftedness.

Because cultural diversity, it has been defined, is closely associated with the language(s) one speaks, (García, 1994; Lara-Alecio & Irby, 1996), it is difficult to view cultural diversity apart from linguistic diversity when identifying and serving the gifted student. Linguistically and culturally diverse gifted students must then be defined within their own socio-linguistic-cultural context. Typically, school district personnel base definitions on the mainstream, Anglo middle-class gifted student, without taking into consideration cultural and linguistic diversity (Bermúdez & Rakow, 1990; Cohen, 1988). Borrowing from Renzulli's (1986) original definition of giftedness, a simple definition of the linguistically and culturally diverse gifted could be individuals who possess above average intelligence, task commitment, and creativity, with these three components being viewed solely within the individual's socio-linguistic-cultural context (Lara-Alecio & Irby, 1993). Other definitions, such as the multiple intelligence model promoted by Gardner (1983) may be applied, but all must be set within the same socio-linguistic-cultural context. Definitions of giftedness must be far more inclusive than they currently are, and far more adapted to a society defined by cultural and linguistic diversity.

There are a number of reasons that have been posed for the inequities in services provided to culturally and linguistically diverse gifted student populations. The challenge of providing appropriate services is particularly complex when native language and culture are conflicting with the child's new cultural and language environment. The exclusion of the culturally and linguistically diverse groups of underidentified and underserved children in programs for the gifted has at least three main implications. First, such exclusion sends a negative message to underrepresented populations and implies that they are somehow less able than those in mainstream populations. Many teachers hold opinions that there are just no gifted minorities, or that minority children are in need of academic, remediation, particularly those who are limited English proficient (Davis & Rimm, 1989). Additionally, when teachers equate giftedness with an IQ score of 130 (García, 1994), it further denigrates the diverse child's true abilities. Being fluent in English

does not mean that the child has the same cultural experiences as the mainstream child; thus, identifying a limited English proficient child with standardized test scores based on majority culture may not be valid (González, Bauerie, & Félix-Holt, 1994).

Because of the misunderstandings among educators regarding this population (García, 1994), and furthermore, because Borland and Wright (1994) suggested that the potential for giftedness is present in roughly equal proportions in all groups of our society, there is a need to develop valid and reliable methods of screening and identifying culturally and linguistically diverse potentially gifted students (Irby, Hernandez, Torres, & González, 1997). Additionally, with increasing reliance on nominations from teachers who are guided by a checklist of behaviors commonly attributed to exceptional children (Strom, Johnson, Strom, & Strom, 1992), it becomes important for teachers to have valid, defining characteristics with which to screen culturally and linguistically diverse populations.

Several formal instruments or techniques for identifying potentially gifted individuals who are culturally and linguistically diverse have surfaced over the past three decades and include the child's cultural context. Among those are the Baldwin Matrix (Baldwin, 1977), the System of Multicultural Pluralistic Assessment (SOMPA; Mercer & Lewis, 1978), Kranz Talent Identification Instrument (KTII; Kranz, 1981), the Structure of the Intellect Test (Meeker, 1985), Torrance Tests of Creative Thinking (TTCT; Solomon, 1974; Torrance, 1970, 1977), Group Inventory for Finding Talent (Rimm, 1976), and Fraiser's Talent Assessment Profile (1990). For screening purposes, the Hispanic Bilingual Gifted Screening Instrument (Irby & Lara-Alecio, 1996) is under development and has been specifically designed for Hispanic linguistically and culturally diverse students (Irby et al., 1997). Eleven characteristic aspects of gifted students have been determined to be significant for identifying potential within the population of diverse students: Motivation for Learning, Social and Academic Language, Cultural Sensitivity, Familial, Collaboration, Imagery, Achievement, Creative Performance, Support, Problem Solving, and Locus of Control (Lara-Alecio, Irby, & Walker, 1997).

A second implication for the culturally and linguistically diverse populations' underrepresentation in gifted programs is that the very exclusion of these groups is contradictory to the American principles of egalitarianism (Gintis, 1988). The task of providing equitable services for the gifted is made more difficult by the lack of uniformity in objective identification procedures and in appropriate needs-based curriculum services (Kaufman, 2005). Uniformity does not preclude the use of a multi-dimensional approach to identification of giftedness (Frasier, 1992; Irby & Lara-Alecio, 1997; Kitano, 1991; Maker & Schiever, 1989; Zappia, 1989). Furthermore, a study conducted by Irby, Henderson, and Berry (1992) determined that in many cases there was little or no match between the programmatic services being provided and a district's plan of gifted identification.

The third implication is that practitioners must learn how to change the programmatic services and/or the identification plans that merge at a point that respond to their particular populations within their communities. Curriculum cannot be discussed or developed in isolation to the definition of giftedness and identification of the particular cultural and language minority group. There is a sufficient amount of theoretical claims regarding who these children are and what type of curricular programming they need, but there is little empirical data to support these claims (Frasier, 1978; Irby & Lara-Alecio, 1993; Zappia, 1989), and few teachers are trained at a level to make data-based decisions regarding the program structure for the culturally and linguistically diverse gifted child (Ford & Harris, 1990).

In summary, there are several principles that may be followed to improve the numbers of culturally and linguistically diverse students served in gifted education programs.

1. The definition used in the school district should be inclusive Renzulli (1986) noted that the definition of giftedness must be based on research about characteristics of gifted individuals; in this case, those individuals would be representative the diverse group to be served. Furthermore, researchers should identify ecological characteristics of the diverse group.

2. Definitions should be connected to the identification procedures and those identification procedures should be diverse (Frasier, 1990). Look for the diversity.

3. Identification procedures should be multifaceted or multidimensional, including objective and subjective data. Data should also be gathered from those who know the child on a personal/cultural level (Frasier, 1990). Additionally, the instruments used should be based on sociocultural and linguistic characteristics of the referent population; seek out valid and reliable instruments in the child's native language or use nonverbal measures.

4. Implement an identification program early that includes a screening phase, an evaluation phase, and a recommendation phase (Frasier, 1990).

5. Make sure that all relevant information on a student has been reviewed prior to making a decision (Frasier, 1990).

6. Train teachers in general and specific diverse population characteristics of giftedness (Lara-Alecio & Irby, 1993; Rogers, 1986). Use a send-in model with the teacher of the gifted—send them into the classrooms and have them observe functional levels of children within the classrooms on various types of activities. When observing, have them focus on products and performance. Additionally, have the teacher solicit products and performances demonstrated away from school.

7. Program options must match district definitions and identification procedures (Frasier, 1990; Lara-Alecio & Irby, 1993). The best learning environment should be provided for the student (Frasier, 1990).

8. Bilingual/bicultural instruction should be provided in early programming, in particular, which suggests a two-way bilingual campus program. Trained bilingual, biliterate, and bicultural teachers are needed for the gifted program (Lara-Alecio & Irby, 1993). Curriculum for the general education program should have a multicultural perspective, which would urge educators to modify their opinions regarding cultural diversity (Kitano, 1991).

9. Include staff development for mainstream and gifted education teachers with a suggested model that includes workshops on research in this field, exploration of negative myths about the culturally and linguistically diverse, how to develop supportive environments, how to help alter attitudes about specific diverse populations, and how to utilize bilingualism in the classroom.

10. Come to a point of viewing cultural and linguistic diversity as an asset, not as a liability or as a need for remediation. Educators need to celebrate differences and develop a secure communicative environment in which the diverse gifted can thrive.

REFERENCES

Baldwin, A. Y. (1977). *Baldwin identification matrix inservice kit for the identification of gifted and talented students.* East Aurora, NY: Trillium.

Bermúdez, A., & Rakow, S. (1993). Analyzing teachers' perception of identification procedures for gifted and talented Hispanic limited English proficient students at risk. *Journal of Educational Issues of Language Minority Students, 7,* 21–31.

Borland, J. H., & Wright, L. (1994). Identifying young, potentially gifted, economically disadvantaged students. *Gifted Child Quarterly, 38,* 164–171.

Cohen, M. (1988). Immigrant children need aid, study says. *The Boston Globe,* p. 25.

Davis, G., & Rimm, S. (1989). *Education of the gifted and talented* (2nd ed.). Englewood Clifs, NJ: Prentice Hall.

Ford, D. Y., & Harris, J. J. (1990). On discovering the hidden treasure of gifted and talented African American children. *Roeper Review, 13*(1), 27–37.

Frasier, M. (1977). Help for organizing productive experience (HOPE) for the culturally diverse gifted and talented. Reston,

VA: Council for Exceptional Children. (ERIC Document Repro-duction Service No. ED 141 981 & EC 101 227)

Frasier, M. (1978). Culturally different gifted/talented: Educa-tional implications: Cognitive. In H. N. Rivlin (Ed.), *Advantage: Disadvantaged gifted.* Presentations from the Third National Conference on Disadvantaged Gifted (53–57). Ventura, CA: Ventura County Superintendent of Schools Office.

Frasier, M. (1990). *Frasier's Talent Assessment Profile.* Athens, GA: University of Georgia.

Frasier, M. (1992). Ethnic/minority children: Reflections and direc-tions. In *Challenges in gifted education: Developing potential and investing in knowledge for the 21st century.* Columbus: Ohio State Department of Education (ED 344 402)

Gardner, H. (1983). *Frames of mind: The theory of multiple intel-ligences.* New York: Basic.

García, J. H. (1994). Nonstandardized instruments for the assess-ment of Mexican-American children for gifted/talented pro-grams. In S. H. García (Ed.), *Addressing cultural and linguistic diversity in special education: Issues and trends.* Reston, VA: Council for Exceptional Children.

García, E. (1994). *Understanding and meeting the challenge of student cultural diversity.* Boston: Houghton Mifflin.

Gintis, H. (1988). Education, personal development, and the human dignity. In H. Holtz et al. (Eds.), *Education and the American dream: Conservatives, liberals and radicals debate the future education.* Greenwood: Berging & Garrey.

Goffin, G. (1988). Putting our advocacy efforts into a new context. *Journal of the National Association for the Education of Young Children, 43*(3), 52–56.

González V., Bauerie, P., & Félix-Holt, M. (1994). A qualitative assessment method for accurately diagnosing bilingual gifted children. In L. M. Malave (Ed.), *National Association for Bilin-gual Education.* San Jose, CA.

Harris, R. (1988). *Cultural conflict and patterns of achievement in gifted Asian-Pacific children.* Paper presented at the meet-ing of the National Association for Asian and Pacific American Education.

Irby, B. "Hispanic LEP Gifted Students." *Education Week.* (1993, May).

Irby, B., Hernández, L., Torres, D., & González, C. (1985). *The corre-lation between teacher perceptions of giftedness and the Hispanic bilingual screening instrument.* Unpublished manuscript, Sam Houston State University, Huntsville, TX.

Irby, B., Henderson, D., & Berry, K. (1992). *State of gifted education in Texas.* An unpublished manuscript submitted to the Texas Association of Gifted and Talented for a Grants in Excellence project. Huntsville, TX: Sam Houston State University.

Irby, B. & Lara-Alecio, R. (1997). Attributes of Hispanic gifted bi-lingual students as perceived by bilingual educators in Texas. *NYSABE Journal, 11,* 120–142.

Kaufman, J. (2005). Nonbiased assessment: A supplemental approach. In C. L. Frisby & C. R. Reynolds (Eds.), *Comprehensive handbook of multicultural school psychology* (pp. 825–840). New York: Wiley.

Kitano, M. K. (1991). A multicultural education perspective on serving the culturally diverse gifted. *Journal for the Education of the Gifted, 15*(1), 4–19.

Kranz, B. (1981). *Kranz talent identification instrument.* Moorhead, MN: Moorhead State College.

Lara-Alecio, R., & Irby, B. (1993). *Reforming identification procedures for the bilingual gifted child.* Paper presented at BEAM, The Ninth Annual Bilingual/ESL Spring Conference, Denton, TX.

Lara-Alecio, R., & Irby, B. (1996). Bilingual education & multicul-tural education: An inclusively oriented educational delivery system. *Journal of Educational Issues of Language Minority Students, 17,* 11–24.

Maker, C. J., & Scheiver, S. W. (Eds.). (1989). *Critical issues in gifted education: Defensible programs for cultural and ethnic minorities.* Austin, TX: PRO-ED.

Mercer, J. R., & Lewis, J. F. (1978). Using the system of multicul-tural pluralistic assessment (SOMPA) to identify the gifted minority child. In A. Y. Baldwin, G. H. Gear, & L. J. Lucito (Eds.), *Educational planning for the gifted* (pp. 7–14). Reston, VA: Council for Exceptional Children.

Meeker, M. N., Meeker, R., & Roid, G. (1985). Structure-of-intellect learning abilities test (SOI-LA). Los Angeles: Western Psycho-logical Services.

Ortíz, V., & González, A. (1989). Validation of a short form of the WISC-R with accelerated and gifted Hispanic students. *Gifted Child Quarterly, 33,* 152–155.

Passow, H. *Educational programs for minority/disadvantaged gifted students.* (1986, February 6). Paper prepared for pre-sentation in the Distinguished Lecture Series of the San Diego Unified School District, California.

Renzulli, J. S. (1986). The three-ring conception of giftedness: A de-velopmental model for creative productivity. In R. J. Sternberg & J. E. Davidson (Eds.), *Conception of giftedness.* Cambridge, MA: Cambridge University Press.

Rimm, S. B. (1976). *GIFT: Group Inventory for Finding Creative Talent.* Watertown, WI: Educational Assessment Service.

Rogers, K. (1986). *Review of research on the education of intellectu-ally and academically gifted students.* St. Paul: Minnesota State Department of Education.

Strom, R., Johnson, A., Strom, S., & Strom, P. (1992). *Educating gifted children: Genetic studies of genius* (Vol. 1). Stanford CA: Stanford University Press.

Sheehy, G. (1986). *Spirit of survival.* New York: Bantam.

Torrance, E. P. (1970). *Encouraging creativity in the classroom.* Dubuque, IA: William C. Brown.

Torrance, E. P. (1997). *Discovery & nurturance of giftedness in the culturally different.* Reston, VA: Council for Exceptional Children.

Trueba, H. (1983). Adjustment problems of Mexican and Mexican-American students. An anthropological study. *Learning Dis-ability Quarterly, 6*(4), 395–415.

U.S. Department of Education, Office of Educational Research and Improvement. (1993). *National excellence: A case for developing America's talented.* Washington, DC: U.S. Government Print-ing Office.

Zappia, I. A. (1989). Identification of gifted Hispanic students: A multidimensional view. In C. J. Maker & S. W. Schiever (Eds.), *Critical issues in gifted education, Vol. 2: Defensible programs for cultural and ethnic minorities* (pp. 19–26). Austin, TX: PRO-ED.

Zuke, M. (1983). *Building bridges for culturally diverse gifted students.* (ERIC Document Reproduction Service No. ED 234570)

RAFAEL LARA-ALECIO
Texas A&M University

BEVERLY J. IRBY
Sam Houston State University

CREATIVITY
DISPROPORTIONALITY
GIFTED AND TALENTED CHILDREN
GIFTED AND LEARNING DISABILITIES

CULTURALLY AND LINGUISTICALLY DIVERSE STUDENTS IN SPECIAL EDUCATION, FAMILIES OF

School involvement by culturally and linguistically diverse families of children with disabilities should be seen in the context of the way parental roles have been conceptualized by professionals over the past four decades (for a comprehensive review, see Turnbull & Turnbull, 1996). Prior to the 1970s, the emphasis was on psychoanalytic approaches that (a) promoted a pathological view of families of children with disabilities, presenting the mother as victim or patient in severe psychological crisis, and (b) completely omitted the impact of differential cultural beliefs and practices on family reactions. The early 1970s saw the advent of the "parent as teacher" approach, which sought to promote positive parental involvement through behavioral training programs, based predominantly on the childrearing practices and personal interaction styles prevalent among white, middle-class families. While some professionals failed to recognize or give credence to non-mainstream family patterns and practices, others interpreted parenting patterns that deviated from the mainstream as evidence of "deprivation" of culture.

The advent of PL 99-142 in 1975 brought into focus the ideal of the parent as collaborator with professionals. This concept of parent participation was based on the model of the middle-class advocate who would participate in formal conference and, if necessary, draw on the availability of due process of law. Early studies of parent participation revealed that the advocacy role expected of parents was an ideal very difficult to achieve, even for middle-class parents. For low-income and minority parents, the challenge has been even more difficult.

The first direct attention to adaptations that might be needed for particular minority groups to participate effec-

tively in the IEP process came from Marion (1979). Marion advocated adaptations that ought to have been considered basic requirements for interactions with all families, such as a personalized approach, respectful verbal and nonverbal interactions, simplification of educational jargon, and full, comprehensible explanation of rights, procedures, and test results. Overall, Marion's main point was that poor and minority parents stood at a disadvantage in terms of the stigma that had traditionally been attached to their ethnicity, culture, and social status, and that careless, even disrespectful, treatment of such parents was common. Marion's concerns have been echoed by researchers who studied the perceptions and experiences of families from various cultural backgrounds, such as American Indians (Connery, 1987), Chinese Americans (Smith & Ryan, 1987; Tran, 1982; Trueba, Jacobs, & Kirton, 1990), Mexican Americans (Lynch & Stein, 1987), African Americans (Harry, Allen, & McLaughlin, 1995; Patton & Braithwaite, 1984; Redding & Arrigo, 2005; Tomlinson, Acker, Canter, & Lindborg, 1977), Puerto Rican Americans (Harry, 1992), and a mixed nationality Hispanic group (Bennett, 1988). Other researchers have pointed to culturally based differences in interaction styles and levels of information, which tend to serve as barriers to effective parent-professional communication (Chan, 1986; Correa, 1989; Cunningham, Cunningham, & O'Connell, 1987; Harry, 1992; Leung, 1988; Sontag & Schact, 1994; Tran, 1982; Zetlin, Padron, & Wilson, 1996). Studies show that low levels of parental awareness of available services and their perceptions of their eligibility for such services are highly correlated with low income and geographic location (Huang & Van Horne, 1995; Sontag & Schact, 1994). Further, school personnel's strong identification with the culture of professionalism tends to dominate their interactions with parents (Bailey et al., 1992; Katz & Scarpatti, 1995) contributing to a "we-they posture by which parents are seen as adversaries rather than allies" (Harry, Allen, & McLaughlin, 1995, p. 374). Parental participation may also be negatively affected by differing cultural constructions of disability and developmental norms (Barnwell & Day, 1996; Harry & Kalyanpur, 1994). These differences often affect parental understanding of the assessment and diagnosis process as well as the setting of educational goals for students (Linan-Thompson & Jean, 1997). With regard to more severe disabilities, cross-cultural studies indicate unequivocally that while all groups recognize gross developmental, behavioral, or sensory impairments, the attributions for their etiology or importance differ widely, as do the extent of the stigma or value attached to the condition (Fadiman, 1997; Scheer & Groce, 1988;). For children with milder disabilities, research reveals that culture and acculturation are strong predictors of parental expectations of children's cognitive and social development (Goodnow, Cashmore, Cotton, & Knight, 1984; Hess, Kashigawi, Azuma, Price, & Dickson, 1980; Quirk et al., 1986; Rosenthal, 1985). These variances in parental beliefs on children's development have implications for the classification of children as "mildly retarded," "behavior disordered," or "learning disabled." Studies show that many culturally diverse parents hold broader parameters of normalcy than allowed by the school-based evaluations by which children are classified (Harry, 1992; Harry et al., 1995).

In summary, attempts to examine parent participation among ethnic minorities reveal the following patterns: (a) lower levels of involvement than White counterparts, (b) lower awareness of procedures, rights, and services, (c) expressed sense of isolation and low self-confidence in dealing with professionals, (d) stressful life circumstances and lack of logistical supports such as transportation, child care, and respite, (e) culturally-based assumptions of deference to, and/or mistrust of school personnel, (f) professionals' implicit or explicit discouragement of parents' participation in the special education process, and (g) culturally-based dissonance between parental and professional understandings of the meanings and importance of disabilities.

Since the mid-1980s, because of PL 99-457, the ideal of parent participation has evolved into a vision of family-centered practice with issues of diverse family beliefs and practices becoming a crucial focus in the effort to address the problems listed above. Family-centered practice revolves around the concept of family empowerment, or the process of helping families increase control over their lives and take action to get what they want. Empowerment occurs when professionals (a) give families information about services and their rights; (b) facilitate their participation; for instance, by arranging transportation and/or childcare and scheduling meetings at times convenient to parents; and (c) develop collaborative relationships with families by affirming and building on family strengths, honoring cultural diversity, creative and cooperative problem-solving, and establishing trust and respect (Dunst & Trivette, 1987; Lynch & Hanson, 1992; Salend & Taylor, 1993; Turnbull & Turnbull, 1996). Evidence for the continuing centrality of this ideal is the 1997 re-authorization of IDEA. This current focus has generated the need for reconceptualizing culture—whether it is perceived as a static or discrete phenomenon—in order to prevent families from being presented in stereotypic ways. The original notion of culture as a process of stages (for instance, from traditional to bicultural to assimilation) through which individuals from minority groups might move, has gradually been superceded by a less discrete view of culture where boundaries are variable according to different dimensions of individual identity, thus acknowledging that an individual may assume multiple group memberships simultaneously (Banks & Banks, 1992).

This definition has also provided a need for context, which brings the focus of study to the precise realm of the individual family, rather than assuming that a generalized concept of the family's cultural tradition will be adequate. By applying Bronfenbrenner's theory of nested systems and Vygotsky's concept of the zone of proximal development,

all development is seen as being based in participation in specific social and cultural settings or an individual's "ecocultural niche" (Tharp & Gallimore, 1988), combining the family's ecology and culture. This perspective takes into account more than just the ethnic status of the family by including contextual variables, such as education, acculturation, socioeconomic status, or geographic location, and the effects of these on the daily routines of families to describe a family in all its individuality, as opposed to generalizations about what a family from "this" or "that" cultural group would be expected to look like. The importance of examining contextual influences to avoid cultural stereotypes is well-illustrated, for instance, by Mardiros' (1989) study of Mexican-American parents which demonstrated that parents from a relatively homogenous cultural group, who held similar beliefs regarding the causation of a disability, still displayed a range of responses, some very proactive and creative, others passive and resigned. Similarly, Harry et al. (1995) offer evidence of effective single parenting when they note that the six "living alone" mothers were the most proactive advocates in a sample of 24 African American families of preschoolers with mild disabilities.

Several writers have identified strategies that specifically accommodate this new concept of contextualized culture toward increasing the participation of culturally and linguistically diverse parents in the special education process.

1. Developing self-awareness as a first step towards understanding one's personal and professional values (Caple, Salsido, & di Cecco, 1995). This can involve examining genealogical records and asking oneself questions like "When I was growing up, what did my family say about people from different cultures?" (Hyun & Fowler, 1995), or "Why do I want 21-year-old Husain to move into a group home?" to recognize the cultural value that underlies one's professional recommendation (Kalyanpur & Harry, 1997).

2. Engaging in conversations with families to learn about their culture and values. This involves using naturalistic means for collecting information about families' situations, including open-ended interviewing (Harry, 1992), and identifying and involving key and/or extended members of the family (Linan-Thompson & Jean, 1997). Professionals should identify and accommodate the family's preferred method of communication, whether written or verbal, English or native language (Barnwell & Day, 1996); make time to listen to parents' stories (Caple, Salsido, & di Cecco, 1995; Kalyanpur & Rao, 1991; Thorp, 1997); and respect their input in the decision-making process (Correa, 1987; Harry, 1992).

3. Making available services and professional recommendations that are compatible with families' values. This involves working with the family to identify their

resources and supports and modifying service options or developing creative, individualized alternatives (Correa, 1989; Harry, 1992; Rueda & Martinez, 1994). Comer and Haynes (1991) describe the successful efforts of the Yale Child Study Center Team to "change the ecology of a school" and empower low-income parents by improving parental status and meaningful collaboration between parents and professionals in special education. The program contained three mechanisms for change: (1) a governance mechanism, the school planning and management team, that represented all the adult stakeholders in the school to develop a plan for restructuring the school; (2) a mental health team to address the developmental and behavioral needs of students; and (3) a parent program which focused on supporting the social program of the school restructuring plan and on the academic program as needed. The parent program created social occasions for families and professionals to meet, developing a sense of community, and encouraged parent volunteers to participate in a broad range of school activities from helping in classrooms to participation on the school planning and management team. The authors attribute the success of the entire program to allowing parents to participate in the way they were comfortable and effective and to play meaningful roles, with staff support, with a clear direction and purpose. Unfortunately, efforts to replicate this model have not been as successful in involving special education teachers and parents (Ware, 1994).

In conclusion, school involvement by families from culturally and linguistically diverse backgrounds continues to be problematic. However, parental participation can be enhanced when professionals use naturalistic collection of information about families' situations in order to find out where a family stands on a given issue, are aware of their own cultural influence in the decision-making process, and are committed to flexibility and responsiveness to the need for change.

REFERENCES

Bailey, D. B., Jr., Buysse, V., Edmondson, R., & Smith, T. (1992). Creating family-centered services in early intervention: Perceptions of professionals in four states. *Exceptional Children, 58,* 298–309.

Banks, J., & Banks, C. A. (1992). *Multicultural education: Issues and perspectives* (2nd ed.). Boston: Allyn & Bacon.

Barnwell, D. A., & Day, M. (1996). Providing support to diverse families. In P. J. Beckman (Ed.), *Strategies for working with families of young children with disabilities* (pp. 47–68). Baltimore: Brookes.

Bennett, A. T. (1988). Gateways to powerlessness: Incorporating Hispanic deaf children and families into formal schooling. *Disability, Handicap & Society, 3,* 119–151.

Caple, F. S., Salsido, R. M., & di Cecco, J. (1995). Engaging effectively with culturally diverse families and children. *Social Work in Education, 17*(3), 159–170.

Chan, S. (1986). Parents of exceptional Asian children. In M. K. Kitano & P. C. Chinn (Eds.), *Exceptional Asian children and youth* (pp. 36–53). Reston, VA: Council for Exceptional Children.

Comer, J. P. & Haynes, N. M. (1991). Parent involvement in schools: An ecological approach. *The Elementary School Journal, 91*(3), 271–277.

Connery, A. R. (1987). *A description and comparison of Native American and Anglo parents' knowledge of their handicapped children's rights.* Doctoral dissertation, Northern Arizona University.

Correa, V. I. (1989). Involving culturally diverse families in the educational process. In S. H. Fradd & M. J. Weismantel (Eds.), *Meeting the needs of culturally and linguistically different students: A handbook for educators* (pp. 130–144). Boston: College-Hill.

Cunningham, K., Cunningham, K., & O'Connell, J. C. (1987). Impact of differing cultural perceptions on special education service delivery. *Rural Special Education Quarterly, 8*(1), 2–8.

Dunst, C. J., & Trivette, C. M. (1987). Enabling and empowering families: Conceptual and intervention issues. *School Psychology Review, 16,* 443–456.

Fadiman, A. (1997). *The spirit catches you and you fall down: A Hmong child, her American doctors, and the collision of two cultures.* New York: Farrar, Strauss and Giroux.

Goodnow, J. J., Cashmore, J., Cotton, S., & Knight, R. (1984). Mothers' developmental timetables in two cultural groups. *International Journal of Psychology, 19,* 193–205.

Harry, B. (1992). *Cultural diversity, families, and the special education system: Communication and empowerment.* New York: Teachers College.

Harry, B., & Kalyanpur, M. (1994). The cultural underpinnings of special education: Implications for professional interactions with culturally diverse families. *Disability & Society, 9*(2), 145–165.

Harry, B., Allen, N., & McLaughlin, M. (1995). Communication versus compliance: African American parents' involvement in special education. *Exceptional Children, 61*(4), 364–377.

Hess, R. D., Kashigawi, K., Azuma, H., Price, G. G. & Dickson, W. P. (1980). Maternal expectations for the mastery of developmental tasks in Japan and the United States. *International Journal of Psychology, 15,* 259–271.

Huang, G. G., & Van Horn, P. (1995). Using child care services: Families with disabled children in nonmetropolitan areas. *Rural Special Education Quarterly, 14*(4), 27–36.

Hyun, J. K., & Fowler, S. A. (1995). Respect, cultural sensitivity, and communication: Promoting participation by Asian families in the Individualized Family Service Plan. *Teaching Exceptional Children, 28*(1), 25–28.

Kalyanpur, M., & Harry, B. (1997). A posture of reciprocity: A practical approach to collaboration between professionals and parents of culturally diverse backgrounds. *Journal of Child and Family Studies, 6*(4), 485–509.

Kalyanpur, M., & Rao, S. S. (1991). Empowering low-income, black families of handicapped children. *American Journal of Orthopsychiatry, 61,* 523–532.

Katz, L., & Scarpati, S. (1995). A cultural interpretation of early intervention teams and the IFSP: Parent and professional perceptions of roles and responsibilities. *The Transdisciplinary Journal, 5*(2), 177–192.

Leung, E. K. (1988). Cultural and acculturational commonalties and diversities among Asian Americans: Identification and programming considerations. In A. A. Ortiz & B. A. Ramirez (Eds.), *Schools and the culturally diverse student* (pp. 86–95). Reston, VA: ERIC.

Linan-Thompson, S., & Jean, R. E. (1997). Completing the parent participation puzzle: Accepting diversity. *Teaching Exceptional Children, 52*(6), 46–50.

Lynch, E. W., & Hanson, M. J. (1992). *Developing cross-cultural competence: A guide for working with young children and their families.* Baltimore: Brookes.

Lynch, E. W., & Stein, R. (1987). Parent participation by ethnicity: A comparison of Hispanic, Black, and Anglo families. *Exceptional Children, 54,* 105–11.

Mardiros, M. (1989). Conception of childhood disability among Mexican-American parents. *Medical Anthropology, 12,* 55–68.

Marion, R. (1979). Minority parent involvement in the IEP process: A systematic model approach. *Focus on Exceptional Children, 10*(8), 1–16.

Patton, J. M., & Braithwaite, R. L. (1984, August). Obstacles to the participation of Black parents in the educational programs of their handicapped children. *Centering Teacher Education,* 34–37.

Quirk, M., Ciottone, R., Minami, J., Wapner, S., Yamamoto, S., Ishii, S., Lucca-Irizarry, C., & Pacheco, A. (1986). Values mothers hold for handicapped and nonhandicapped preschool children in Japan, Puerto Rico, and the United States Mainland. *International Journal of Psychology, 21,* 463–485.

Redding, R. E., & Arrigo, B. (2005). Multicultural perspectives on delinquency among African-American youth: Etiology and intervention. In C. L. Frisby & C. R. Reynolds (Eds.), *Comprehensive handbook of multicultural school psychology* (pp. 710–743). New York: Wiley.

Rosenthal, D. (1985, July). *Child-rearing and cultural values: A study of Greek and Australian mothers.* Paper presented at the meeting of the International Society for the Study of Behavioural Development, Tours, France.

Rueda, R., & Martinez, I. (1994). Fiesta educativa: One community's approach to parent training in developmental disabilities for Latino families. *JASH, 17*(2), 95–103.

Salend, S. J., & Taylor, L. (1993). Working with families: A cross-cultural perspective. *Remedial and Special Education, 14*(5), 25–32.

Scheer, J., & Groce, N. (1988). Impairment as a human constant: Cross-cultural and historical perspectives on variation. *Journal of Social Issues, 44*(1), 23–37.

Smith, M. J., & Ryan, A. S. (1987). Chinese-American families of children with developmental disabilities: An exploratory study of reactions to service providers. *Mental Retardation, 25*(6), 345–350.

Sontag, J. C., & Schacht, R. (1994). An ethnic comparison of parent participation and information needs in early intervention. *Exceptional Children, 60*(5), 422–433.

Tharp, R. G., & Gallimore, R. (1988). *Rousing minds to life: Teaching, learning and schooling in social context.* Cambridge, MA: Cambridge University Press.

Thorp, E. K. (1997). Increasing opportunities for partnership with culturally and linguistically diverse families. *Intervention in School and Clinic, 32*(5), 261–269.

Tomlinson, J. R., Acker, N., Canter, A., & Lindborg, S. (1977). Minority status, sex and school psychological services. *Psychology in the Schools, 14*(4), 456–460.

Tran, X. C. (1982). *The factors hindering Indochinese parent participation in school activities.* San Diego, CA: San Diego State University, Institute for Cultural Pluralism. (ERIC Document Reproduction Service No. ED 245-018)

Trueba, H., Jacobs, L. & Kirton, E. (1990). *Cultural conflict and adaptation: The case of Hmong children in American society.* New York: Falmer Press.

Turnbull, A. P., & Turnbull, H. R. (1997). *Families, professionals, and exceptionality: A special partnership* (3rd ed.). Upper Saddle River, NJ: Merrill.

Ware, L. P. (1994). Contextual barriers to collaboration. *Journal of Educational and Psychological Consultation, 5*(4), 339–357.

Zetlin, A., Padron, M., & Wilson, S. (1996). The experience of five Latin American families with the special education system. *Education and Training in Mental Retardation and Developmental Disabilities, 31,* 22–28.

BETH HARRY
University of Miami

MAYA KALYANPUR
Towson University

FAMILY COUNSELING

CULTURALLY/LINGUISTICALLY DIVERSE STUDENTS, REPRESENTATION OF

Special educators have debated for decades about the disproportionate representation of ethnic and linguistic minority students in special and gifted education programs. This phenomenon refers to unequal proportions of culturally diverse students in these special programs. Two patterns are associated with disproportionality, namely over- and underrepresentation of minority students. The former tends to occur in special education; specifically, in the mild disability categories—such as, mild mental retardation (MMR), specific learning disabilities (SLD), and serious emotional disturbances (SED). Underrepresentation is generally observed in programs for students with gifts and talents (G&T). Historically, certain ethnic minority groups (particularly African American) and poor and male students have been most affected by disproportionality.

Litigation (particularly placement bias cases) has been at the center of disproportionality discussions. For instance, some of the most important rulings in *Diana* v. *California Board of Education* (1970) and *Larry P.* v. *Riles* (1979) (which involved Latino and African American students respectively) included (a) intelligence tests were culturally and linguistically biased, (b) biased assessment resulted in the overrepresentation of Latino and African American students in MMR programs, (c) alternative procedures were needed to assess students' abilities (e.g., nonverbal tests, assessment in native language), and (d) many students needed to be retested and reclassified. These cases were very influential in the passage of federal legislation designed to protect the rights of individuals with disabilities, specifically in the inclusion of a requirement that identification and assessment procedures must be nondiscriminatory.

Although disproportionality patterns persisted throughout the 1970s and 1980s (Artiles & Trent, 1994), it was not until the 14th Report that the U.S. Department of Education (USDOE) provided enrollment data in disability programs by ethnic group. Interestingly, disproportionate representation has received more attention in the 1990s. For instance, the USDOE authorized the National Academy of Sciences to conduct a study on disproportionality (B. Ford, pers. comm., November 1997). It is ironic that this interest has emerged at a time when societal attitudes toward culturally diverse people are hostile and intolerant; two compelling examples being the anti-immigrant and the anti-Affirmative Action discourse, litigation, and policymaking.

Causes of Disproportionate Representation

The most widely used explanation of this problem is based on the deficit thinking that has characterized theories about minority students' educational performance (Trent, Artiles, & Englert, 1998). It has been concluded that many of these students lack the abilities and skills needed to succeed in the general educational system; hence, they need to receive specialized services. The most favored argument to explain minority students' deficits is the nefarious effects of poverty which is rampant among these groups. Because of their higher levels of poverty, the argument follows, we should expect a higher incidence of negative developmental outcomes (e.g., disabilities) among these groups. In this vein, research has linked poverty to placement in special education; however, we need more inquiries to understand (a) the complex nature of this association, (b) minorities' resilience to the negative effects of poverty, and (c) the role of structural factors in the production of higher rates of poverty among minority groups.

An alternative position posits that deficit explanations oversimplify this complex problem by blaming the student and disregarding the significant impact of contextual, technical, structural, and ideological factors. For example, a critical technical factor is related to the procedures used in the special education field. Also, such patterns seem to vary according to school location. For example, it has been found that the psychometric profiles of students with LD in urban and suburban schools differ to the point that many identified students in urban schools did not fit the established eligibility criteria for LD (e.g., in terms of ability levels; Gottlieb, Alter, Gottlieb, & Wishner, 1994).

Furthermore, we must be mindful of the nature of the disproportionality data. Many of these analyses draw from the Office for Civil Rights (OCR) survey data, which purportedly have several methodological limitations. For instance, the data are not based on a nationally representative sample, different surveys have sampled school districts with distinct demographic profiles, and distinct sampling procedures have been used over the different surveys, which complicates longitudinal and comparative analyses (Reschly, 1997). Hence, the question arises as to how we can assess the magnitude and causes of disproportionality given the potential confounding effect of the aforementioned technical aspects.

Another factor that complicates disproportionality analyses is our limited understanding of the role of culture in human development. For instance, an analysis of 22 years of research in four major special education journals showed a paucity of studies on ethnic minority students, a narrow scope of research topics, and a disregard for potential interactions between sociocultural variables (e.g., ethnicity and language, gender, or social class; Artiles, Trent, & Kuan, 1997; Oakland & Gallegos, 2005). How, then, can educators discern the influence of language, cognitions, social class, and ethnicity on students' competence and performance? How can educators make decisions about students' competence based on culturally-insensitive criteria? Indeed, this paucity of knowledge has enormous implications for the identification of students' needs and the provision of adequate educational services.

Other factors could impinge upon this predicament, though they have received scant attention by the research community. For instance, we need to investigate how disproportionality can be exacerbated, masked, or reduced in distinct contexts by (a) the quality of the instructional context, (b) the role of racism and discrimination, (c) the dismissal of alternative ways of knowing in the design and implementation of school rules, curricula, assessment practices, and expectations, (d) the inattention to the influence of sociocultural variables in researchers' labor (e.g., investigators' beliefs or values about cultural diversity), (e) the disregard for within-cultural-group variability, (f) the failure to include minority students' perspectives in investigations, and (g) the availability of alternative services (e.g., prereferral, bilingual education, and Chapter 1 programs).

Looking Ahead: Risks and Possibilities

We must transcend oversimplification of this problem so that we do not debate endlessly whether special education is harmful to minority students, whether disabilities exist or are social constructions, or whether minority students' poverty is the cause of the problem. By focusing on these oversimplifications we run the risk of losing generations of culturally diverse students, the future of our nation. At the same time, this multidimensional problem affords us the possibility to rethink the meaning and place of special education in our increasingly diverse society. For this purpose, we must acknowledge that implicit in this predicament are assumptions about human difference and about the role of education in a heterogeneous society. Hence, we must undertake two crucial tasks in the immediate future. First, we must conduct more and better studies that address the limitations of past research. Second, we must strengthen the theoretical grounding of the disproportionality discourse to begin grappling with equity issues in the education of culturally diverse students and with how our educational system meets the needs of an increasingly diverse society.

REFERENCES

Artiles, A. J., & Trent, S. C. (1994). Overrepresentation of minority students in special education: A continuing debate. *Journal of Special Education, 27,* 410–437.

Artiles, A. J., Trent, S. C., & Kuan, L. A. (1997). Learning disabilities research on ethnic minority students: An analysis of 22 years of studies published in selected refereed journals. *Learning Disabilities Research & Practice, 12,* 82–91.

Gottlieb, J., Alter, M., Gottlieb, B. W., & Wishner, J. (1994). Special education in urban America: It's not justifiable for many. *Journal of Special Education, 27,* 453–465.

Oakland, T., & Gallegos, E. M. (2005). Selected legal issues affecting students from multicultural backgrounds. In C. R. Frisby & C. R. Reynolds (Eds.), *Comprehensive handbook of multicultural school psychology* (pp. 1048–1078). New York: Wiley.

Reschly, D. J. (1997). *Disproportionate minority representation in general and special education: Patterns, issues, and alternatives.* Des Moines: Iowa Department of Education.

Trent, S. C., Artiles, A. J., & Englert, C. S. (1998). From deficit thinking to social constructivism: A review of special education theory, research and practice. *Review of Research in Education.*

ALFREDO J. ARTILES
University of California, Los Angeles

STANLEY O. TRENT
University of Virginia

CULTURAL PERSPECTIVES ON BEHAVIORAL DISORDERS

Children with behavioral disorders constitute one of the major national issues confronting the schools and society.

There is increasing concern about the academic failure and school dropout rate of U.S. children and adolescents identified with behavioral disorders (BD). Observation, diagnosis, and intervention strategies for these students are poorly defined nationally (Sabatino, 1987). The current definition of BD may encourage the underidentification of students with behavioral disorders from the entire school-age population, while promoting an overrepresentation of students identified as BD from culturally diverse groups (Algozzine, Ruhl, & Ramsey, 1991). The rates of identification, placement, and achievement of children and adolescents with BD are strongly correlated with gender, race, and other cultural dimensions. However, these issues are often neglected in our educational system (Singh, Oswald, Wechsler, & Curtis, 1997).

In 1990, about one-third of school age children in the United States were children from nondominant cultures (Maag & Howell, 1992). The growing diversity in student population has increased the potential and practice for inappropriate educational placement of students. For example, in 1987, African Americans were 16 percent of the total enrollment in the nation's school system. However, in the same year, African Americans made up 27 percent of the students identified as having a behavioral/emotional disorder in the public schools. There is concern by many in this country that this 11 percent discrepancy is based on faulty thinking, biases, and inappropriate identification of culturally diverse students (Harry, 1992). Anglo American students are less likely to be identified as BD or placed in restrictive settings than are students from other cultures, particularly African American students. Hispanic American students are underrepresented in BD across most of the nation.

Overrepresentation of Culturally Diverse Students

Unfortunately, many culturally diverse groups of students are being misidentified as behaviorally disordered. This phenomenon is causing a misuse of services for other students who may need them but are not yet identified. Minority groups, other than ethnic minority children, are also affected by this situation. Students with limited English proficiency (LEP) are frequently misplaced in programs for students with BD. Students from nondominant cultural backgrounds should not be at risk for being labeled as BD simply for displaying traits reflecting their cultural upbringing.

The mismatch between schools and culturally diverse homes is a factor influencing the misidentification of students as BD. A home culture exists for all students, and this culture may be discrepant with the traditional Anglo middle-class public school culture. This discrepancy is often viewed by school personnel as a problem within the individual student instead of a cultural mismatch. The student may then be identified as having a behavioral problem and assigned a label, with a resulting loss of self-esteem (Algozzine et al., 1991).

Children of immigrant families and children from wartorn and politically repressive countries are vulnerable to being mislabeled as BD, yet often do not have their needs recognized by school personnel. Additionally, many students who are lesbian, gay, or bisexual are at risk for being identified as BD when they have no disability. The same scenario holds true for children raised in families with same-sex partners (McIntyre, 1996).

Preservice Training and Recruitment

Improved preservice training for future educators and improved recruitment of teachers of students with behavioral disorders may help solve the problem of inadequate education of culturally diverse students.

Preservice training. Most teachers do not have a solid grounding in multicultural education. Those that did receive multicultural training in college were trained about "culture within a cultural literacy model." This model teaches cultural diversity within the limited framework of race and ethnicity. Preservice teachers are often taught general characteristics and stereotypes regarding different minority groups. Research demonstrates that teacher sensitivity and general knowledge about a student's culture is correlated to student achievement; therefore, reevaluation of instructing preservice teachers needs to occur (Harry, 1992). In addition to preservice training, continued training inservice in the profession should also be provided on this topic.

Recruiting preservice teachers. Recruitment and retention of culturally diverse preservice teachers also needs to be addressed by colleges and universities. In special education classrooms, a disparity often exists between cultural background of students and teachers. This difference is even greater in programs involving students with BD. Gender issues are also important to consider. Female teachers refer students, particularly boys, for behavioral problems more often than male teachers. This problem will continue to increase as fewer males and culturally diverse individuals choose teaching as a career. This shortage of professionals from culturally diverse backgrounds leads to problems of isolation of majority students from teachers of culturally diverse backgrounds, reduces role models for culturally diverse students, and yields inadequate expertise in recommending multicultural changes and training to other school colleagues.

Aggressive recruitment of culturally diverse preservice teachers is necessary. While it is recognized that one's cultural background does not guarantee the ability to relate and work effectively with students exhibiting BD, the need for the recruitment of professionals from culturally diverse backgrounds is evident (McIntyre, 1996). Unfortunately,

states such as California, Texas, and Michigan have been court-ordered to reduce or stop opportunities that would recruit underrepresented groups to meet a particular professional need. Practices such as these are hurting attempts to increase the cultural diversity of educators to serve students with BD.

Inadequately prepared professionals. To ensure that students with BD have access to a free appropriate public education, there must be an adequate supply of teachers and other instructional and noninstructional staff with appropriate training or certification (USDOE, 1996). There are 331,392 special education teachers in the United States, yet many of these teachers are not professionally certified (6.3 percent). In addition, there are inadequate numbers of teachers of special education, with a reported 3,643 special education teachers needed. These problems increase when we look at instructing students with BD. Many of the teachers ($n = 30,151$) who work with students with BD are not certified or not adequately trained to work with students with BD (Katsiyannis, Landrum, Bullock, & Vinton, 1997).

Cultural Mismatch of Teachers and Students

Behavioral patterns and values are often defined by and vary by culture. Also, behaviors and actions viewed as aberrant often vary by culture. Teachers who are unaware of cultural differences often misinterpret and judge culturally-determined behavior as being evidence of BD. In such a subjective climate, culturally diverse students identified as BD are set up for failure (Harry, 1992). Far too few educators realize that many culturally different youth view the school environment as alienating. Also, many African American, Mexican American, Native American, and Native Hawaiian students feel great pressure from their peers not to achieve (Ogbu, 1992). Due to numerous factors, such as historical oppression and an emphasis on cultural cohesion and cooperation rather than competition, individual success in schooling is often viewed as rejection of one's cultural group.

Cultural diversity misidentified as a behavioral disorder. The cultural mismatch between the teacher and the student often results in students from some cultures being misidentified as BD by teachers who are not aware or culturally competent. Educators generally have a more negative attitude towards students with BD, as a group, than towards students with other disabilities such as learning disabilities (Algozzine et al., 1991). By adding cultural diversity along with BD, the bias against these students by many teachers is exaggerated (Algozzine et al., 1991). Because some teachers discriminate against students because of their racial, ethnic, political, or socioeconomic backgrounds, it is obvious that the coupling of BD with any of these traits has the potential for heightening the imbalance (Singh et al., 1997).

A continuation of this practice is present in the data collected in the area of student discipline. Some teachers' differential use of disciplinary practices with Anglo American students and those from other cultures is well-documented (Harry, 1992). African American students experience the most severe forms of discipline. The educational system is in the unfortunate position of having culturally inexperienced teachers from the dominant culture (over 80 percent European American females) teaching students of increasing diversity.

Cultural competence. Culturally competent teachers acknowledge, accept, and value cultural differences in their students. Teachers must be aware of their own culture as well as the culture of others and must acknowledge how it could bias their service towards students (Singh et al., 1997). A teacher should assess students with BD through their students' cultural backgrounds while acknowledging the expectations of the dominant culture.

Educators teach students prosocial norms for the public school setting usually from a middle class European-American perspective. Educators need to also incorporate values and behavioral standards from other cultural groups. Teachers must ensure that students have pride in their original culture as well as observing the determined norms for a particular setting. Modification of classroom practices can promote self-esteem and motivation for all students. (McIntyre, 1996).

Biased Assessment Practices

Most individuals truly understand only their own culture and frequently find it difficult to appreciate behavior that is different from their own. This fact influences not only the way educators teach, but also the way students are assessed. Culturally-based behavioral patterns often differ from what is considered normative on assessment instruments (Harry, 1992). Cultural biases and prejudices are often acknowledged to exist in many standardized instruments, particularly those measuring self-concept (McIntyre, 1996).

Complexity of cultural diversity and BD. The assessment of students for the possible presence of BD is a complex process that becomes more difficult when students are from a culturally diverse background. It has been demonstrated that assessment tools reflect cultural as well as school learning, but the invisible quality of many central aspects of culture makes the identification of cultural bias a challenging task (Harry, 1992). For example, it is easy to see that testing an LEP student in English would be unfair, but it is less obvious to many that standard English testing can be unfair to speakers of nonstandard varieties of the language. There is a pressing need for the development and implementation of more appropriate and accurate methods of assessment

for culturally diverse students. This need is particularly noticeable in the area of behavioral disorders, since students who display culturally different behaviors are particularly susceptible to this diagnosis.

Assessment changes. The entire approach to assessment may need to change for students with BD who are culturally diverse. A more holistic method of assessment could be incorporated and framed within the context of a student's culture. The practice of using norm-referenced tests is problematic because these tests have often been shown to be based on middle-class Anglo American values and experiences (Singh et al., 1997). Assessment procedures should help to differentiate BD from cultural differences in behavior. Also, a diverse multidisciplinary team reviewing students' assessments can help increase cultural awareness and decrease misidentification of students as BD.

The public school system needs to continue to move away from a cultural deficit model to a cultural difference model. A cultural difference model accepts that the cognitive, learning, and motivational styles of students are different from those often expected by the teacher, who is usually from the dominant culture (Singh et al., 1997) while a cultural deficit model uses the culture as the explanation for school failures. The idea that all students should assimilate and fit into the majority culture has been successfully challenged by the concept of cultural pluralism.

The United States is becoming a country where minority groups are becoming the majority (Robinson & Bradley, 1997). These demographic changes require adaptations in assessment and teaching in our public schools. Current trends lead to an overrepresentation of culturally diverse students being misidentified as emotionally or behaviorally disordered. In most cases, culturally divergent behaviors can be respected (McIntyre, 1996). Acknowledging culture as a predominant factor in shaping behaviors and values and respecting culturally defined traits will yield a more productive learning and teaching environment for culturally diverse students, students with BD, and teachers. This change also should result in more accurate identification of all students and more appropriate support for students who have BD, and it potentially will decrease the misdiagnosis of culturally diverse students (Singh et al., 1997).

REFERENCES

Algozzine, B., Ruhl, K., & Ramsey, R. (1991). *Behaviorally disordered? Assessment for identification and instruction.* Reston, VA: Council for Exceptional Children.

Harry, B. (1992). *Cultural diversity, families, and the special education system: Communication and empowerment.* New York: Teachers College.

Katsiyannis, A., Landrum, T. J., Bullock, L., & Vinton, L. (1997). Certification requirements for teachers of students with emotional or behavioral disorders: A national survey. *Behavioral Disorders, 22*(3), 131–140.

Maag, J. W., & Howell, K. W. (1992). Special education and the exclusion of youth with social maladjustments: A cultural-organizational perspective. *Remedial and Special Education, 13*(1), 47–54, 59.

McIntyre, T. (1996). Guidelines for providing appropriate services to culturally diverse students with emotional and/or behavioral disorders. *Behavioral Disorders, 21*(2), 137–144.

Ogbu, J. U. (1992). Understanding cultural diversity and learning. *Educational Researcher, 21*(8), 5–14.

Robinson, B., & Bradley, L. J. (1997). Multicultural training for undergraduates: Developing knowledge and awareness. *Journal of Multicultural Counseling and Development, 25*(4), 281–289.

Sabatino, D. A. (1987). Behavior disorders. In C. R. Reynolds & Lester Mann (Eds.), *The encyclopedia of special education* (Vol. 1). New York: Wiley.

Singh, N. N., Ellis, C. R., Oswald, D. P., Wechsler, H. A., & Curtis, W. J. (1997). Value and address diversity. *Journal of Emotional and Behavioral Disorders, 5*(1), 24–35.

U.S. Department of Education. (1996). *Eighteenth annual report to Congress on the implementation of the Individuals with Disabilities Education Act.* Washington, DC.

NANCY E. ALGERT
LINDA H. PARRISH
Texas A&M University

CULTURE FAIR TEST

Education and processes of socialization teach individuals cultural knowledge. Many standardized tests measure how well one has learned the information specific to a particular culture. The development of culture fair tests was begun to neutralize the culturally loaded information found in standardized tests (Lewis, 1998). A test used to assess diverse cultural groups cannot contain items specific to any one particular culture; otherwise, it would not be considered to have content validity.

The Culture Fair Intelligence Test (Cattell, 1973) is a measure virtually devoid of verbal content (the test uses a paper and pencil format). It consists of novel problem-solving items that do not occur in any particular culture. The test format is multiple choice and includes four subtests: Series Completion, Classification, Matrices, and Conditions. Different levels are administered depending on the subject's age: 4 to 8 years, 8 to 14 years, or 14 to adult. Similar to other standardized tests, the results of the Culture Fair Intelligence Test are expressed as deviation IQs with a mean of 100 and a standard deviation of 16.

Lewis (1998) notes that there are some weaknesses of the Culture Fair Intelligence Test. One is that it uses fairly extensive verbal instructions during administration of the test. This causes difficulty for linguistically different clients. Therefore, although the test does not have culturally loaded information items or verbal components, the verbal nature

of the directions themselves are problematic. Also, the subtests emphasize speed. This emphasis on speed can differ cross-culturally, and thereby reduces the cultural fairness of the instrument. These potential problems should be taken into account when assessing clients of different cultural backgrounds. Anastasi (1988) has noted that the interpretation of test scores are "by far the most important considerations in the assessment of culturally diverse groups" (p. 66). Misinterpretation of scores with these groups is a serious concern.

REFERENCES

Anastasi, A. A. (1988). *Psychological testing* (6th ed.). New York: Macmillan.

Cattell, R. B. (1973). *Technical supplement for the Culture Fair Intelligence Tests Scales 2 and 3.* Champaign, IL: Institute for Personality and Ability Testing.

Lewis, J. E. (1998). Nontraditional uses of traditional aptitude tests. In R. J. Samuda, R. Feurerstein, A. S. Kaufman, J. E. Lewis, & R. J. Sternberg (Eds.), *Advances in cross cultural assessment.* Thousand Oaks, CA: Sage.

ELIZABETH O. LICHTENBERGER
The Salk Institute

CULTURAL BIAS IN TESTING

CULTURE FREE SELF-ESTEEM INVENTORIES–THIRD EDITION

The Culture Free Self-Esteem Inventories–Third Edition (CFSEI-3) is a set of self-report inventories used to measure self-esteem in a culturally fair manner. It is to be administered individually or in groups to children and adolescents between the ages of 6:0 and 18:11. Administration takes approximately 15 to 20 minutes, and requires individuals to write or respond verbally to a series of "yes or no" items. It is composed of three age-appropriate forms: Primary, Intermediate, and Adolescent. All three forms provide a Global Self-Esteem Quotient and a defensive measure to assess the degree to which an individual's response may be guarded. In addition, the Intermediate and Adolescent forms provide self-esteem scores in the following categories: Academic, General, Parental/Home, and Social. The Adolescent Form also includes a score for Personal Self-Esteem. An Examiner's Manual and easy-to-use Profile and Scoring Forms are provided. The CFSEI-3 is easy to administer and score. Responses (simple yes-or-no answers) can be either written or spoken. Conversion tables provide subscale standard scores based on a mean of 10 and a standard deviation of 3, and quotient scores based on a mean of 100 and a standard deviation of 15.

The CFSEI-3 was standardized on a sample of 1,727

school-age individuals from 17 states. The sample was representative of the 2000 U.S. census with respect to geographic region, gender, race, rural or urban residence, ethnicity, family income, parent education, and disability. Content, criterion prediction, and construct identification were used to investigate validity. The CFSEI-3 correlates strongly with other self-esteem and self-concept measures. Information regarding differential item functioning analyses and separate reliability and validity information for seven subgroups (male, female, European-American, African-American, Hispanic-American, gifted and talented, and learning disabled) is provided with the test kit. In addition, a full chapter in the Examiner's Manual is devoted to the CFSEI-3's absence of bias.

Content sampling and time sampling estimates were used to assess reliability. For the Global Self-Esteem Quotient scores, the average internal consistency coefficients range from .81 to .93, while the average time sampling coefficients range from .72 to .98.

REFERENCES

Plake, B. S., Impara, J. C., & Spies, R. A. (Eds.). (2003). *The fifteenth mental measurements yearbook.* Lincoln, NE: Buros Institute of Mental Measurements.

Web site of test's author: http://www.jamesbattle.com/cfsei.htm.

RON DUMONT
Fairleigh Dickinson University

JOHN O. WILLIS
Rivier College

CURRICULUM

Educational curriculum is what students learn, or the content of instruction. Historically, the curriculum of U.S. public education was specified in broad, global terms, addressing abstract notions such as Americanization and instilling of democratic values in youths (Mulhern, 1959). In the twentieth century, however, developments in learning theory such as Thorndike's demonstration of the specificity of transfer promoted a reconceptualization of learning from concurrent strengthening of global faculties to sequential mastery of numerous, definite, and particularized skills and knowledge (Fuchs & Deno, 1982). This reconceptualization has led to alternative ways of specifying school curricula for distinct behavioral outcomes (Bloom, Hastings, & Madaus, 1971). Current curriculum statements typically represent carefully sequenced, calibrated, and organized sets of tasks, regularly called objectives (Johnson, 1967).

In special education, as in regular education, curriculum is derived from an analysis of the needs of society. This anal-

ysis, however, renders considerably different instructional focuses for mildly and severely disabled students. For the mildly disabled, analysis of the needs of society results in a curriculum similar, if not identical, to that of normally developing pupils; it includes curricular tasks such as reading, writing, and mathematics. For the more severely disabled, this analysis results in a curriculum that addresses basic survival skill requirements. These alternative educational focuses often are referred to as developmental curriculum (which identifies tasks for normally performing children; Snell, 1983) and functional curriculum (which addresses skills necessary for ultimate attainment of self-sufficiency; Holvoet, Guess, Mulligan, & Brown, 1980).

For the mildly disabled student, the curriculum may be resequenced, broken down into smaller tasks, reorganized, or taught via dramatically different instructional strategies. Two alternative ways of addressing curriculum for the mildly disabled have been referred to as the task analytic approach and the ability training model (Ysseldyke & Salvia, 1974). With the task analytic approach, the curriculum is approached by breaking down terminal tasks into sets of subskills, which are addressed separately and sequentially and ultimately synthesized into final tasks of the curriculum (Howell, 1986). With the ability training model, hierarchies of abilities that are prerequisite to mastery of basic reading, writing, and mathematics skills such as perceptual-motor or psycholinguistic abilities are hypothesized. These abilities are addressed before the standard school curriculum is taught. In both cases, however, the ultimate curriculum, or the final educational objective, remains constant and is consonant with the curricular goals of the mainstream educational environment.

In contradistinction, the functional curriculum of the more severely disabled population is determined more individually. It addresses objectives that (1) represent the practical or functional skills most likely to be needed currently or in the near future; (2) span the four instructional domains of domestic, leisure/recreational, community, and vocational skills; (3) are suitable for the student's chronological age; and (4) address the pupil's current performance levels and are reasonably thought to be attainable (Snell, 1983). The basic assumptions of a functional curriculum for individuals with severe disabilities are that the school's responsibility is to teach skills that optimize a person's independent and responsible functioning in society (Hawkins & Hawkins, 1981). For the individuals with severe disabilities, these skills must be chosen from a group of tasks and activities that have a high probability of being required and that increase self-sufficiency (Brown et al., 1979).

REFERENCES

Bloom, B. S., Hastings, J. T., & Mandaus, G. F. (1981). *Handbook on formative and summative evaluation of student learning.* New York: McGraw-Hill.

Brown, L., Branston, M. B., Hamre-Nietupski, S., Pumpian, I., Certo, N., & Gruenewald, L. (1979). A strategy for developing chronological age appropriate and functional curricular content for severely handicapped adolescents and young adults. *Journal of Special Education, 13,* 81–90.

Fuchs, L. S., & Deno, S. L. (1982). *Developing goals and objectives for educational programs.* Washington, DC: American Association of Colleges for Teacher Education.

Hawkins, R. P., & Hawkins, K. K. (1981). Parental observation on the education of severely retarded children: Can it be done in the classroom? *Analysis & Intervention in Developmental Disabilities, 1,* 13–22.

Holvoet, J., Guess, D., Mulligan, M., & Brown, F. (1980). The Individualized Curriculum Sequencing model (II): A teaching strategy for severely handicapped students. *Journal of the Association for the Severely Handicapped, 5,* 337–351.

Howell, K. W. (1986). Direct assessment of academic performance. *School Psychology Review, 15,* 324–335.

Johnson, M. (1967). Definitions and models in curriculum theory. *Educational Theory, 7,* 127–140.

Mulhern, J. (1959). *A history of education* (2nd ed.). New York: Ronald.

Snell, M. E. (1983). *Systematic instruction of the moderately and severely handicapped* (2nd ed.). Columbus, OH: Merrill.

Ysseldyke, J. E., & Salvia, J. (1974). Diagnostic prescriptive teaching: Two models. *Exceptional Children, 41,* 181–185.

LYNN S. FUCHS
Peabody College, Vanderbilt University

ANNUAL GOALS

CURRICULUM, AGE-APPROPRIATE

An age-appropriate curriculum is a special-educational curriculum that consists of activities that are matched to both the students' chronological ages and their developmental or skill levels. This match has been difficult to achieve, especially for older trainable and severely disabled students who continue to function on preschool levels. The older students with severe disabilities often need continued training in fine motor, cognitive, and language skills, but also need to acquire skills that can be used immediately and will transfer to later community and vocational placements (Drew, Logan, & Hardman, 1984).

The Education for All Handicapped Children Act (PL 94-142), and its successor, the Individuals with Disabilities Education Act, has mandated an appropriate education for all students with disabilities, but wide differences remain when defining this term. The justification for using an age-appropriate education lies in the principle of normalization, which Nirje (1979) has defined as follows: "Making available to all mentally retarded people patterns of life and conditions of everyday living which are as close as possible to the regular circumstances of society" (p. 73). Although it may appear unrealistic to teach age-appropriate behaviors to students with severe developmental delays, Larsen and Jackson (1981) argue that this is the mission of special education: "No, we will not be completely successful (but) . . . our goals for students will stress skills relevant to the general culture, rather than skills that have a proven value only in special-education classrooms" (p. 1).

Our current knowledge of developmental milestones, task analysis procedures, and behavior modification principles can be used in adopting this approach if we also examine the "age-appropriateness" of the materials, skills, activities, environments, and reinforcers used during instruction. For example, in learning visual discrimination of shapes, elementary-age students may use form boards and shape sorters, while older students use community signs and mosaic art activities. For other skills, calculators may be used instead of number lines; colored clothing can be sorted rather than colored cubes; and the assembly of vocational products may replace peg boards and beads (Bates, Renzaglia, & Wehman, 1981).

Because there are many skills that older severely disabled youths will never acquire (e.g., reading a newspaper, buying groceries), the curriculum focuses on those abilities that can be learned (e.g., reading survival signs, following directions). To identify these skills for each group of students, Brown et al. (1979) employ an ecological inventory approach listing the environments and subenvironments where the students currently (or will eventually) function. An inventory of the activities in each environment and a listing of skills needed to participate in those activities provide the framework for selecting curriculum goals. In this approach, for example, the basic skill of matching pictures leads to finding grooming items in a drugstore, and identifying different foods leads to ordering in a fast-food restaurant.

Classroom design and décor also should reflect the chronological age of the students. For older youths, pictures of teen activities and movie celebrities are more age-appropriate decorations than cartoon characters. Many special-education classrooms have moved into secondary buildings, opening up opportunities to use age-appropriate training sites such as home economics rooms.

Severely handicapped students may have extremely slow learning rates and much difficulty in generalizing learning skills to new situations. Therefore, their education must include the teaching of critical skill clusters and opportunities to practice functional skills in natural settings, such as sheltered workshops, supermarkets, and public transportation. For a more detailed description of curricular approaches to teaching functional skill clusters see Guess and Noonan (1982).

REFERENCES

Bates, P., Renzaglia, A., & Wehman, P. (1981). Characteristics of an appropriate education for severely and profoundly handicapped students. *Education & Training of the Mentally Retarded, 16,* 142–149.

Brown, L., Branston, M. B., Homre-Nietupski, S., Pumpian, I., Certo, N., & Grunewald, L. (1979). A strategy for developing chronological age appropriate and functional curriculum content for severely handicapped adolescents and young adults. *Journal of Special Education, 13,* 81–90.

Drew, C. J., Logan, D. R., & Hardman, M. L. (1984). *Mental retardation: A life cycle approach* (3rd ed.). St. Louis, MO: Times Mirror/Mosby.

Guess, D., & Noonan, M. J. (1982). Curricula and instructional procedures for severely handicapped students. *Focus on Exceptional Children, 14,* 9–10.

Larsen, L. A., & Jackson, L. B. (1981). Chronological age in the design of educational programs for severely and profoundly impaired students. *PRISE Reporter, 13,* 1–2.

Nirje, B. (1979). Changing patterns in residential services for the mentally retarded. In E. L. Meyen (Ed.), *Basic readings in the study of exceptional children and youth.* Denver, CO: Love.

KATHERINE D. COUTURIER
Pennsylvania State University

KIMBERLY F. APPLEQUIST
*University of Colorado at
Colorado Springs*

CURRICULUM-BASED ASSESSMENT

Curriculum-based assessment (CBA), defined as a procedure for determining the instructional needs of a student based on the student's ongoing performance with existing course content, comprises a broad category of assessment procedures that are tied to curriculum (Tucker, 1985). CBA includes a range of testing procedures that may or may not be standardized. These procedures are intended to directly assess a student's performance on the curriculum that is being taught so as to evaluate student progress on specific as well as general goals and provide an analysis of the skills a student has and has not mastered. Knowledge of the skills and objectives a student has attained facilitate the placement of the student at a proper instructional level and the teachers' and parents' ability to make decisions about the suitable instructional goal (Salvia & Ysseldyke, 2004).

Within an instructional decision-making model, CBA is though to improve instruction by providing corrective feedback (Thomas & Grimes, 2002). CBA seeks to answer the following five questions: (1) What does the student know? (2) What can the student do? (3) How does the student think? (4) How does the student approach difficult tasks? (5) What does the teacher do next? (See Gickling, 1998.) CBA provides direct measurement of student performance on the curriculum and evaluates student progress on specific as well as general goals. Frequent administrations (e.g., three to four times per year) are thought to provide sensitive information about discreet yet important changes in student performance (Salvia & Hughes, 1990).

CBA may involve administering tests in each academic subject that was, is, and will be taught. A student's performance generally is compared to that of his or her peers or the expected level of attainment based on the student's curriculum. For example, when assessing reading of a student beyond grade two, CBA may involve administering short (150 to 200 words) oral reading passages taken from the reading series in which the student is being taught. Reading fluency is measured as the number of words read correctly per minute, and comprehension is measured by the number of questions passed. CBA in mathematics may involve administering approximately 30 math problems per grade level. Probes assess single skills (e.g., single digit addition or subtraction) or multiple skills (e.g., adding two and three digit numbers). When assessing writing, CBA may use a "story starter" that provides a student with an initial idea on which to write. After some time period (e.g., 3 minutes), the number of words correctly written is counted. When assessing spelling, CBA may require the student to write three sets of 20 words from successive grade level probes taken randomly from the text used in the spelling curriculum (Shapiro, 1996).

The CBA process is based on established research and helps educational professionals, students, and parents gain an accurate picture of a student's current knowledge and skills. CBA's advantages over norm-referenced achievement tests include a more direct examination of student performance on current curricula, improved content validity by examining student performance on products related to the curriculum, and directly linking assessment and instruction. Its disadvantages include an inability to compare a student's performance with the performances of a large, national sample of same-age peers and an inability to describe performance in reference to a normal distribution. Also, short test sessions prohibit professionals from making observations that facilitate adjustments to match student learning style and temperament.

REFERENCES

Gickling, E. E. (1998). *Instructional assessment training manual.* Unpublished manuscript.

Salvia, J., & Hughes, C. (1990). *Curriculum-based assessment: Testing what's taught.* New York: Macmillan.

Salvia, J., & Ysseldyke, J. E. (2004). *Assessment in special and inclusive education* (9th ed.). Boston: Houghton Mifflin.

Shapiro, E. S. (1996). *Academic skills problems: Direct assessment and intervention* (2nd ed.). New York: Guilford.

Thomas, A., & Grimes, J. (Eds.). (2002). *Best practices in school psychology IV.* Betheseda, MD: National Association of School Psychologists.

Tucker, J. (1985). Curriculum-based assessment: An introduction. *Exceptional Children, 52,* 199–204.

JEFFREY DITTERLINE
University of Florida

ASSESSMENT, CURRICULUM BASED
CURRICULUM, AGE-APPROPRIATE
NORM-REFERENCED TESTING
RESPONSE TO INTERVENTION

CURRICULUM FOR STUDENTS WITH MILD DISABILITIES IN SPECIAL EDUCATION

The definition of curriculum varies in the literature but in the broadest sense, it is used in the field in two ways: (1) to indicate a plan for the education of learners, and (2) to identify a field of study. The word curriculum comes from a Latin root meaning race course; it can be regarded as the standardized ground covered by students in their race for a diploma (Zais, 1976).

Special education curriculum for the mildly disabled learner consists of learning tasks, activities, or assignments that are directed toward increasing a student's knowledge or skills in a specific content or subject area. It is the special educator's task to identify the differences between the regular and special education curriculum and to make educational decisions based on available assessment data.

The decision to provide variation in content may be less significant in educating learners with mild disabilities than the decision to provide variation in the conditions under which learning can be best facilitated. A critical issue involves the determination of the need for compensatory versus remedial curricula (Case, 1975). Many of the strategies and techniques used with mildly handicapped learners in special education overlap with Chapter I, other remedial programs, and regular education.

Mainstreaming and inclusion has encouraged efforts to help the over 70 percent of special education students who spend at least part of the day in regular classrooms to master the regular curriculum or "face curricular isolationism" (O'Connell-Mason & Raison, 1982).

This special education curriculum must be coordinated with regular education curriculum, which in turn must be modified or changed at times to accommodate students with different learning styles. The curricula must be designed to meet the particular needs and characteristics of the individuals who are to learn various contents.

Howell, Kaplan, and O'Connell (1979) indicate that to date, the research has not demonstrated the superiority of one type of curriculum modification over another. However, there are a number of general types of modifications that have been found useful: (1) eliminate or reduce the subjects in the student's curriculum; (2) develop or identify an alternative curriculum; (3) alter expectations for the quantity or quality of work; (4) teach subject matter more slowly; (5) teach only the most essential subject matter; (6) develop a parallel curriculum; (7) provide a supplemented curriculum; or (8) adjust materials and/or response modes.

Growth in the field of special education curricula for mild disabilities has become an integral part of regular education. It is clear that the similarities are greater than the differences. The same principles and procedures, with some modifications, can be used to instruct all children. All children can reach their potential given the opportunity, effective teaching, and proper resources (Berdine & Blackhurst, 1985).

REFERENCES

Berdine, W. H., & Blackhurst, A. E. (1985). *An introduction to special education.* Boston: Little, Brown.

Case, R. (1975). Gearing the demands of instruction to the developmental capacities of the learner. *Review of Educational Research, 45,* 3–9.

Howell, K. W., Kaplan, J. S., & O'Connell, C. Y. (1979). *Evaluating exceptional children: A task analysis approach.* Columbus, OH: Merrill.

O'Connell-Mason, C., & Raison, S. B. (1982). *Curriculum assessment and modification.* Washington, DC: American Association of Colleges for Teacher Education.

Zais, R. S. (1976). *Curriculum: Principles and foundations.* New York: Harper & Row.

DEBORAH A. SHANLEY
*Medgar Evers College, City
University of New York*

CURRICULUM, AGE-APPROPRIATE
MAINSTREAMING
TASK ANALYSIS

CURRICULUM FOR STUDENTS WITH SEVERE DISABILITIES

Educational curriculum is what students learn, or the content of instruction. Historically, the curricula of U.S. public education was specified in broad, global terms, addressing abstract notions such as Americanization and instilling of democratic values in youths (Mulhern, 1959). In the twentieth century, however, developments in learning theory such as Thorndike's demonstration of the specificity of transfer promoted a reconceptualization of learning from concurrent strengthening of global faculties to sequential mastery of numerous, definite, and particularized skills and knowledge (Fuchs & Deno, 1982). This reconceptualization led to alternative ways of specifying school curricula for distinct behavioral outcomes (Bloom, Hastings, & Madaus, 1971). Current curriculum statements typically represent carefully sequenced, calibrated, and organized sets of tasks, regularly called objectives (Johnson, 1967).

In special education, as in regular education, curriculum is derived from an analysis of the needs of society. For the severely disabled individual, this analysis results in curriculum that addresses basic survival skill requirements. This educational focus, which represents an alternative to the normal or developmental educational curriculum (Snell, 1983), is referred to as a functional curriculum. The basic assumptions of a functional curriculum for the severely disabled are that the school's responsibility is to teach skills that optimize a person's independent and responsible functioning in society (Hawkins & Hawkins, 1981) and that, for children with severe disabilities, these skills must be chosen from a group of tasks and activities that have a high probability of being required and that increase self-sufficiency (Brown et al., 1979).

This functional curriculum is determined individually and addresses objectives that (1) represent practical or functional skills most likely to be needed currently or in the near future; (2) are suitable for the student's chronological age; (3) address the pupil's current performance levels and are reasonably thought to be attainable; and (4) span four instructional domains (Snell, 1983).

The four domains of instructional content are domestic, leisure/recreational, community, and vocational. The domestic domain includes skills performed in and around the home, including self-care, clothing care, housekeeping, cooking, and yard work. In the leisure-recreational domain are skills needed to engage in spectator or participant activities performed for self-pleasure. Skills required in the community domain include street crossing, using public transportation, shopping, eating in restaurants, and using other public facilities such as parks. The vocational domain addresses skills necessary for employment such as appropriate work dress and demeanor, assembly line behavior, interviewing for jobs, completing work applications, and punctuality.

The process of determining appropriate functional curricula on an individual basis has been conceptualized as comprising five steps (Brown et al., 1979): (1) selecting curriculum domains; (2) identifying and surveying current and future natural environments; (3) dividing the relevant environments into subenvironments; (4) inventorying these subenvironments for the relevant activities performed there; and (5) examining the activities to isolate the skills required for their performance.

To address the functional curriculum for individuals with severe disabilities, instructional strategies typically have been based on behavioral methodology. The instructional process begins with a descriptive analysis of the environmental events subsequent to, antecedent to, or during recurring behavioral events, with the purpose of identifying possible discriminative and reinforcing stimuli. Then, a task analysis of terminal objectives is conducted; in it subskills necessary for successful mastery of the final objectives are identified. Next, subskill instructional objectives are established and initial teaching strategies are specified. Then ongoing assessments of pupils' progress toward goals are collected as the instructional hypothesis is implemented. Finally, ongoing assessment data are evaluated and employed formatively to redesign instructional procedures in order to increase the probability of goal attainment.

REFERENCES

Bloom, B. S., Hastings, J. T., & Madaus, G. F. (1981). *Handbook on formative and summative evaluation of student learning.* New York: McGraw-Hill.

Brown, L., Branston, M. B., Hamre-Nietupski, S., Pumpian, I., Certo, N., & Gruenewald, L. (1979). A strategy for developing chronological age appropriate and functional curricular content for severely handicapped adolescents and young adults. *Journal of Special Education, 13,* 81–90.

Fuchs, L. S., & Deno, S. L. (1982). *Developing goals and objectives for educational programs.* Washington, DC: American Association of Colleges for Teacher Education.

Hawkins, R. P., & Hawkins, K. K. (1981). Parental observation on the education of severely retarded children: Can it be done in the classroom? *Analysis & Intervention in Developmental Disabilities, 1,* 13–22.

Holvoet, J., Guess, D., Mulligan, M., & Brown, F. (1980). The Individualized Curriculum Sequencing model (II): A teaching strategy for severely handicapped students. *Journal of the Association for the Severely Handicapped, 5,* 337–351.

Johnson, M. (1967). Definitions and models in curriculum theory. *Educational Theory, 7,* 127–140.

Mulhern, J. (1959). *A history of education* (2nd ed.). New York: Ronald.

Snell, M. E. (1983). *Systematic instruction of the moderately and severely handicapped* (2nd ed.). Columbus, OH: Merrill.

LYNN S. FUCHS
Peabody College, Vanderbilt University

CURRICULUM
FUNCTIONAL INSTRUCTION
FUNCTIONAL SKILLS TRAINING

CURRICULUM IN EARLY CHILDHOOD INTERVENTION

The curricula used in early intervention vary depending on the needs of the children served. Generally, however, they address developmental areas critical to the child's psychological/behavioral maturation and later school success (Bailey & Wolery, 1984). Early intervention curricula are likely to emphasize motor, cognitive, language, social, and self-help skill development. Early intervention instructors will likely address the development of gross and fine motor skills, eating and self-help skills, toileting, dressing, and undressing. A distinction has been made between developmental and functional approaches in early childhood curricula. The first emphasizes developmental progress; the second is more concerned with training for independent functioning (Bailey & Wolery, 1984).

The purposes of early intervention curricula are to develop, habilitate, or accelerate young children's development. In the case of disabled children, the intent is to minimize the effects of children's disabilities on later development and learning and academic performance. With mildly to moderately disabled children, early curriculum is more likely to emphasize developmental training. With more severely disabled children, the emphasis is likely to be on functional training, for example, facilitating independent functioning.

There is considerable interaction between the various curriculum areas in any particular instructional approach. For example, eating training involves fine motor, social, and communication skill development as well as self-help training. A variety of curricula for early intervention are currently available. Few of them are distinguished by validation efforts. Bailey, Jens, and Johnson (1983) have published a recent review of infant curricula.

REFERENCES

Bailey, D. B., Jens, K. G., & Johnson, N. (1983). Curricula for handicapped infants. In F. Fewell & S. G. Garwood (Eds.), *Educating handicapped infants.* Rockville, MD: Aspen.

Bailey, D. B., Jr., & Wolery, M. (1984). *Teaching infants and preschoolers with handicaps.* Columbus, OH: Merrill.

MARY MURRAY
Journal of Special Education

EARLY IDENTIFICATION OF CHILDREN WITH DISABILITIES
PRESCHOOL ASSESSMENT
PRESCHOOL SPECIAL EDUCATION

CUSTODIAL CARE OF INDIVIDUALS WITH DISABILITIES, HISTORY OF

Organized care for individuals with disabilities goes back no more than 150 years. If we consider the disabled to include the insane, mentally infirm, orphans, the poor, and those found to be criminal in nature, then we can easily locate the second American Revolution as during the Jackson presidency (Rothman, 1971). Prior to this period, care of individuals with disabilities was managed primarily by families, neighbors, and friends of the disabled. In the case of criminals, the offenders were put to death.

During the Jacksonian period large institutions were constructed in Boston, New York, and Philadelphia. Almshouses for the poor were constructed in smaller communities. Governmental agencies and the wealthy provided funds for the erection of insane asylums. Soon the medical profession was actively using the asylums as an integral part of care for the insane. It was also during this time that penitentiaries proliferated throughout the East Coast states. In addition, homes built with public funds and other types of asylums were constructed for orphans and delinquent children. In Rothman's (1971) *Discovery of the Asylum,* we find ample documentation of reform during the Jacksonian period. As Rothman has stated, this period could appropriately be referred to as "the age of the asylum."

Interested investigators have claimed that the growth of institutions in America for the insane, orphans, poor, criminals, and, one could hypothesize, the mentally retarded, paralleled the growth of psychiatry. It was 300 years prior to the advent of the first U.S. institutions that we find King Henry VIII taking the old monastery of St. Mary of Bethlehem in London, England, and reserving it solely for the care of the mentally ill. One can assume that at that time little was known about any differentiation of diagnosis between the mentally disturbed and the mentally retarded. Thus, the idiot and the insane were probably treated much the same. St. Mary's provided deplorable conditions and inadequate care for the infirm. Other asylums soon appeared in Mexico (1566), France (1641), Moscow (1764), and Vienna (the famous Lunatics' Tower, 1784). All of these institutions were the forerunners of similar edifices in America. Many of the first institutions were nothing more than a modification of a penal institution. An example of such early primitive care can be seen in the description of Lunatics' Tower:

> It was an ornately decorated tower within which were square rooms. The doctors and keepers lived in the square rooms, while the patients were confined in the spaces between the walls of the square rooms and the outside of the tower. The patients were put on exhibit to the public for a small fee. (Coleman, 1984)

An account (Coleman, 1984) of the LaBicetre Hospital in Paris is said to be representative of most institutions for the insane throughout the eighteenth century.

The patients were ordinarily shackled to the walls of their dark, unlighted cells by iron collars which held them flat against the wall and permitting little movement. Oftimes, there were also iron hoops around the waists of the patients and both their hands and feet were chained. Although these chains usually permitted enough movement that the patients could feed themselves out of bowls, they often kept them from being able to lie down at night. Since little was known about dietetics, and the patients were presumed to be animals anyway, little attention was paid to whether they were adequately fed or to whether the food was good or bad. The cells were furnished only with straw and were never swept or cleaned; the patient remained in the midst of all the accumulated ordure. No one visited the cells except at feeding time, no provision was made for warmth, and even the most elementary gestures of humanity were lacking. (modified from Selling, 1943)

What is striking to the reader is the never ending stream of trends in the care of the disabled, often instituted in the name of progress. In fact, care was generally for profit, coercion, incarceration, or medical validation. Historical accounts indicate that while benevolence was the primary motivation for the creation of institutional care, society also needed to seek stability from social disruption.

Humanitarian reform of institutions both in Europe and America occurred on a small scale during the eighteenth century. Pinel's experiments at LaBicetre included removing the chains, adding sunlit rooms, extending kindness, and including freedom to exercise. Reactions by patients were recorded as overwhelmingly positive by even the most seriously disturbed (Zilboorg & Henry, 1941, p. 3232). William Tuke, an English Quaker, also provided a humane environment, at the York Retreat in England, while in America Benjamin Rush, the founder of American psychiatry, provided care in a more benevolent manner. Such examples of humane treatment, however, are isolated, as most institutions continued to treat their residents much like animals and such labels as "snake pits" and "schools for unimprovable or unteachable idiots" were not uncommon.

Notable among Americans who created a moral cognizance of existing deplorable conditions was Dorothea Dix (1802–1887). In her famous *Memorial,* submitted to the U.S. Congress in 1848, she remarked that she had observed

more than 9000 idiots, epileptics, and insane in the United States, destitute of appropriate care and protection . . . bound with galling chains; bowed beneath fetters and heavy iron balls attached to drag chains, lacerated with ropes, scourged with rods, and terrified beneath storms of execration and cruel blows; now subject to jibes and scorn and torturing tricks; now abandoned to the most outrageous violations. (Zilboorg & Henry, 1941, pp. 583–584)

This message was repeated often as Dix and her followers became instrumental in improving conditions throughout the United States, Canada, and Scotland. She is credited with establishing 32 hospitals. Unfortunately, most asylums continued to be unfit for humans.

It was not until the late 1800s that the mentally retarded were beginning to be seen as a group separate, at least in name, from other of society's deviant groups. There is reason to suspect that the mentally retarded had often been punished severely and in some instances hanged for criminal activities beyond their comprehension. The first institutions constructed solely for the mentally retarded seem to have been built for educational purposes. These temporary boarding school-type facilities were established primarily for the "improvables." The schools rejected admittance to those who could not be cured and returned to their families. Even the famed Fernald State School sought to create an institution that would not serve uncurables. When the effort to educate the mentally retarded and return them to society failed, retarded individuals' care deteriorated. The retarded were viewed as subhuman and unable to be taught productive skills. The failure was probably due to the unrealistically high expectations of complete recovery.

The perception of failure and disappointment prevailed after these early attempts at cure failed. Along with this perception came a dramatic change in the care of retarded individuals. People that had the potential to be developmentally changed were treated accordingly, while those thought of as having subhuman qualities were treated as animals.

State schools and institutions soon gave way to asylums. In 1893 the Custodial Asylum for Unteachable Idiots was founded in Rome, New York. Governor Butler of Massachusetts said:

A well-fed, well-cared for idiot is a happy creature. An idiot awakened to his condition is a miserable one. . . . It is earnestly urged that the best disposal to be made of this large class of the permanently disabled is to place it in custodial departments of institutions for the feebleminded persons . . . under the same merciful system that inspires hope and help for the lowest of humanity. (Kerlin, 1888, quoted in Kugel & Shearer, 1976)

It was also during this time (1885) that Illinois built a facility to provide for custodial care; the states of Iowa and Connecticut followed. Intentions were noble. There was an implied protectiveness associated with each state's appropriation for an asylum (Kugel & Shearer, 1976, p. 52). History, however, has recorded the opposite to have been the case.

In the early 1900s perceptions of the mentally retarded again changed and custodial care was said to have deteriorated. The moron and imbecile were soon made the source of all social ills. Leaders in the field such as M. W. Barr, a past president of the American Association for Mental Retardation (AAMR), issued indictments of imbeciles as a threat to home and community. Calling for action, Johnson (1901) spoke bluntly when he stated that in order to prevent the propagation of idiocy and imbecility it might be "necessary to kill them or to resort to the knife" (Kugel & Shearer, 1976, p. 57). With attitudes such as these, it is little wonder that retarded individuals received deplorable care for the next 50 years.

The severely retarded were gradually dehumanized and moved to the back wards. These wards as well as other asylum cells were filthy and overcrowded. Such facilities were often referred to as the land of the living dead. In the fall of 1965 Senator Robert Kennedy visited several of his state's institutions; he was appalled at the conditions he encountered. Additional investigations by Blatt (1970) further delineated the horrors: "in toilets, I frequently saw urinals ripped out, sinks broken and toilet bowls backed up . . . I found incredible overcrowding" (p. 13). The national average cost of caring for the mentally retarded in 1962 was less than $5 per day per patient. Some states managed to lower that to less than $2.50 per day.

Blatt (1970) further described conditions in several institutions. He saw 7 foot by 7 foot isolation cells that seldom included beds, washstands, or toilets. Restraints were common. There were alarming shortages of staff and one supervisor for each 100 severely retarded individuals was not uncommon. It is small wonder that patients were locked up, restrained, or sedated. The odors of the wards and dayrooms were overpowering even though rooms were hosed down daily to move the human excretions to sewers located in the center of the rooms.

Blatt's (1966) photographic essay, "Christmas in Purgatory" did much to alert professionals and the general public to the deplorable conditions existing for the institutionalized retarded. Those pictures of the stark gray, high walls, barred windows, beds pushed head to head, patients lying unclothed in feces, and rooms full of young children, left their mark. The ensuing years have seen a movement away from those custodial conditions. Even in the 1960s, many institutions such as the Seaside, also chronicled by Blatt, were providing residential treatment that encouraged more and better trained staff, family participation, fewer closed wards, sunlit areas, medical and dental attention, and daily hygienic care. Within the last 30 years, the mentally retarded have been part of a deinstitutionalization movement unlike that of any era in U.S. history. Residential homes for individuals with disabilities are commonplace and the U.S. educational system now provides especially designed curricula to teach basic independent living skills. In addition, government-supported projects have proliferated throughout the United States and now include not only programs for assessment and training but opportunities in employment that were nonexistent only a few years ago.

REFERENCES

Blatt, B., & Kaplan, F. (1966). *Christmas in purgatory*. Boston: Allyn & Bacon.

Blatt, B. (1970). *Exodus from pandemonium*. Boston: Allyn & Bacon.

Coleman, J. C., Butcher, J. N., & Carson, R. C. (1984). *Abnormal psychology and modern life* (7th ed.). Glenview, IL: Scott, Foresman.

Kugel, R. B., & Shearer, A. (Eds.). (1976). *Changing patterns in residential services for the mentally retarded*. Washington, DC: President's Committee on Mental Retardation.

Rothman, D. J. (1971). *The discovery of the asylum*. Boston: Little, Brown.

Selling, L. S. (1943). *Men against madness*. New York: Garden City Books.

Zilboorg, G., & Henry, G. W. (1941). *A history of medical psychology*. New York: Norton.

RICHARD E. HALMSTAD
University of Wisconsin at Stout

DEINSTITUTIONALIZATION
INSTITUTIONALIZATION

CYLERT

Cylert (Pemoline) is a mild central nervous system stimulant medication that is used in the management of hyperactive children. While the onset of effectiveness of Cylert has been found to be slower than that of some other central nervous system stimulants, it also has been found to have a longer half-life, 12 hours compared with 4 hours for other stimulants (Ross & Ross, 1982). Because of this longer half-life, Cylert need be administered only on a once-daily basis. For hyperactive children, this eliminates the social stigma associated with taking medication at school. In addition, parents are better able to supervise drug administration, thereby reducing the possibility of drug abuse and increasing the probability of compliance. Another advantage of Cylert therapy over other psychostimulants in pediatric populations is its long duration of therapeutic action without sympathomimetic cardiovascular effects. In fact, therapeutic effects of Cylert have been found to be similar to those of amphetamines and methylphenidate (Ross & Ross, 1982). Clinical trials have yielded data to indicate that Cylert enhances short-term memory, attentiveness to cognitive and academic tasks, and social functioning (Ross & Ross, 1982).

As with other psychostimulants, one concern with Cylert administration has been the occurrence of side effects. While mild side effects, including insomnia, headaches, anorexia, abdominal pains, dizziness, and nausea have been reported, of greater concern is the elevation of liver enzymes, which often necessitates the withdrawal of medication. Severe dysphoric effects following the cessation of Cylert also have been reported in some isolated cases (Brown, Borden, Spunt, & Medenis, 1985).

REFERENCES

Brown, R. T., Borden, K. A., Spunt, A. L., & Medenis, R. (1985). Depression following Pemoline withdrawal in a hyperactive child. *Clinical Pediatrics, 24,* 174.

Ross, D. M., & Ross, S. A. (1982). *Hyperactivity: Current issues, research and theory* (2nd ed.). New York: Wiley-Interscience.

RONALD T. BROWN
*Emory University School of
Medicine*

**HYPERACTIVITY
MEDICAL MANAGEMENT**

CYSTIC FIBROSIS

Cystic fibrosis (CF) is one of the most common genetic diseases to effect Caucasian populations, affecting approximately 1 in 3,400 live births. CF rarely affects other ethnic populations. For example, the incidence in the African-American population is only 1 in 17,000 live births. CF is an autosomal recessive disease—thus, both parents must be carriers of the defective gene to produce an affected child (FitzSimmons, 1993).

CF is primarily a disease of the respiratory and digestive systems, resulting from a genetic defect that disrupts the way salt and water move in and out of the body's cells. In CF patients, the body develops thick, sticky mucus secretions that clog airways in the lungs, leading to frequent infections and inflammation (Quittner, Modi, & Roux, 2004). Lung disease in patients with CF is progressive; respiratory failure accounts for more than 85 percent of mortality (FitzSimmons, 1993). The respiratory effects of CF often result in a chronic cough. Because CF has such a profound impact on respiratory function, treatment for CF generally attempts to keep the lungs cleared of mucus and minimize lung infection and inflammation. This is accomplished through a variety of means, including airway clearance to help physically loosen the secretions, medications to help thin the sticky mucus, and antibiotics (oral or inhaled). Many of these treatments are managed on a daily basis by the child's parents at home. Sometimes, a child with CF will need to be hospitalized to receive intravenous antibiotics and other more intensive treatments. The frequency of these hospitalizations varies from child to child, and each hospitalization may last 2 or more weeks (Quittner et al., 2004).

In addition to respiratory complications, the digestive system also is affected by the thick, sticky secretions, which block the pancreas during the prenatal developmental period. This blockage prevents the release of enzymes needed to digest food, resulting in malabsorption of nutrients and fat, digestive difficulties, and diminished growth. As a result, children with CF must consume more calories than their typical peers (125 to 150 percent of the Recommended Daily Allowance) and also must take pancreatic enzyme replacements (in pill or powder form) with every meal and snack. Despite these treatments, children with CF are often shorter and thinner than their peers (Quittner et al., 2004).

Recent scientific advances in the treatment of CF include more powerful antibiotics, new methods of delivering antibiotics to the lungs, and earlier diagnosis. Thus, the life span of children with CF has increased. In the 1960s most individuals with CF died during childhood. Today, children born with CF can expect to reach adulthood; the median survival age is approximately 31 (FitzSimmons, 1993).

Aggressive treatment of CF has enabled most children with CF to attend school regularly. Children and adolescents with CF are not at increased risk for cognitive or academic problems (Thompson et al., 1992). However, other challenges at school may arise. School problems for children with CF are more likely to concern management of CF symptoms and treatments, absenteeism, and interaction with peers (DiGirolamo, Quittner, Ackerman, & Stevens, 1997). For example, children with CF may resist taking medication at school because they are worried about looking different in front of their peers. Children with CF may be absent from school more often because of hospitalizations or clinic visits and may fall behind in their schoolwork if plans are not set up ahead of time to deal with absences (Quittner et al., 2004). Thus, professionals involved in the education of a child with CF should be well-informed about the child's medical condition and maintain frequent communication with the child's parents in order to facilitate adjustment in the school setting.

REFERENCES

DiGirolamo, A. M., Quittner, A. L., Ackerman, V., & Stevens, J. (1997). Identification and assessment of ongoing stressors in adolescents with chronic illness: An application of the behavior-analytic model. *Journal of Clinical Child Psychology, 26,* 53–66.

FitzSimmons, S. C. (1993). The changing epidemiology of cystic fibrosis. *Journal of Pediatrics, 122,* 1–9.

Quittner, A. L., Modi, A. C., & Roux, A. L. (2004). Psychosocial challenges and clinical interventions for children and adolescents with cystic fibrosis: A developmental approach. In R. Brown (Ed.), *Handbook of pediatric psychology in school settings* (pp. 333–61). Mahwah, NJ: Erlbaum.

Thompson, R. J., Gustafson, K. E., Meghdadpour, S., Harrell, E., Johndrow, D. A., & Spock, A. (1992). The role of biomedical and psychosocial processes in the intellectual and academic functioning of children and adolescents with cystic fibrosis. *Journal of Clinical Psychology, 48*(1), 3–10.

AMY LOOMIS ROUX
University of Florida

ADAPTED PHYSICAL EDUCATION
CYSTIC FIBROSIS FOUNDATION
HEALTH MAINTENANCE PROCEDURES

CYSTIC FIBROSIS FOUNDATION

The Cystic Fibrosis Foundation is a voluntary, nonprofit health organization that actively supports research and treatment for cystic fibrosis. Founded in 1955 by a small group of parents of children with cystic fibrosis, it was originally conceived to raise money for research to find a cure and improve the quality of life for individuals with the disease. With the help of more than 250,000 volunteers operating in 65 chapters and branch offices across the United States, the organization depends on public support to implement its programs.

The Foundation actively supports the advancement of medical science by funding research centers at leading universities and medical centers throughout the United States and providing a variety of grants to scientists for research on the disease. It also offers comprehensive diagnosis and treatment for people with cystic fibrosis through a nationwide network of 113 cystic fibrosis care centers. In addition to the research, diagnostic, and treatment services provided, the centers also offer professional medical education and training and conduct clinical trials testing new drug therapies. The Therapeutic Development Program, which provides matching funds to biotechnology companies to stimulate development of new therapies, furnishes the infrastructure needed to conduct these clinical trials in the early phases.

The Cystic Fibrosis Foundation influences public policy related to the disease by working closely with the U.S. Congress, the Food and Drug Administration, and pharmaceutical companies to speed the development of drugs to treat the disorder. The organization's efforts in this area also include advocating for increased funding for the National Institutes of Health and testifying before Congress to encourage more money for research.

Information on a variety of subjects related to cystic fibrosis, including updates on research, clinical trials, public policy issues and ways to become involved with the Cystic Fibrosis Foundation may be obtained through its web site at www.cff.org. The Foundation may be contacted at its national offices at 6931 Arlington Road, Bethesda, MD 20814, by telephone at (800) FIGHTCF, (301) 951-4422, or fax at (301) 951-6378.

CYTOMEGALOVIRUS

The cytomegalovirus is a filterable DNA virus in the family of herpes viruses. It is responsible for the infectious disease known as cytomegalic inclusion disease. The virus is not easily eliminated and persists in host tissues for months, years, or even a lifetime. It produces a chronic infection with a variable incubation period, outcome, and course. The infection may be a significant form of congenital disease in newborns whose immune system is incompletely developed or in adults who are immunosuppressed such as individuals with AIDS (Sessoms, & Brown, 2003).

There are two patterns of infection: localized and generalized. In the localized form, inclusion bodies are found only in the salivary glands; this clinical entity sometimes is referred to as generalized salivary gland disease. The second, generalized, form is represented in two principal types: that accompanied by necrotizing and calcifying encephalitis and that associated with enlargement of the spleen and the liver, lymphadenopathy, and blood dyscrasias. There is increasing recognition of the association of this infection with acquired immune deficiency syndrome (AIDS). Where there is significant cerebral damage, there is often ocular involvement.

It is generally agreed that the virus is widespread; the localized form of the disease is both frequent in occurrence and asymptomatic. Ten to thirty-two percent of autopsied infants show evidence of localized disease. Although the generalized form of the disease may occur in adults, it is characteristically seen in infants and children, occurring in up to 1 percent of children. Cytomegalovirus has been detected in up to 90 percent of immunosuppressed kidney transplant patients; active infection may predispose these patients to bacterial superinfection and transplant rejection. The virus also alters the immune system, although apparently only during the acute phase of infection; the mechanism for immunosuppression is not fully understood.

Because many organs may be affected in generalized disease, the clinical features are variable. Usually there is an acute or subacute febrile illness, and infants are likely to have been premature. There may be severe jaundice and bleeding tendencies, and enlargement of the spleen and liver is frequent. Pneumonia and renal involvement often are present. In the encephalitic form, hydrocephalus and chorioretinitis occur. Most infected infants succumb to encephalitic disease. Among those who survive, mental or motor retardation, microcephaly, seizures, and ocular involvement are common. Ocular lesions include microcornea, chorioretinitis, pseudocolobomas of the retina, retinal hemorrhage, pale optic discs, uveitis, keratoconjunctivitis, and dacryoadenitis.

The diagnosis is best established by recovery of the virus from the urine, saliva, or aqueous humor of the eye. Congenital toxoplasmosis is difficult to differentiate, but radiologic evidence of periventricular calcification suggests cytomegalic inclusion disease. Other diseases to be differentiated include generalized bacterial infection, herpes simplex encephalitis, congenital liver deformities, and diseases of the reticuloendothelial system. No treatment has been effective in controlling this disease. Several antiviral medications used to control the herpes virus have been tried with minimal success.

REFERENCES

Friedlaender, M. H. (1963). Immunology of infections systemic diseases that affect the eye. In T. D. Duane & E. A. Jaeger (Eds.), *Biomedical foundations of ophthalmology*. Hagerstown, MD: Harper & Row.

Sessoms, A., & Brown, R. T. (2003). Cytomegalovirus, Congenital. In E. Fletcher-Janzen & C. R. Reynolds (Eds.), *Childhood disorders diagnostic desk reference* (pp. 164–165). New York: Wiley.

Walsh, F. B., & Hoyt, W. F. (1969). *Clinical neuro-ophthalmology*. Baltimore: Williams & Wilkins.

GEORGE R. BEAUCHAMP
Cleveland Clinic Foundation

**CHRONIC ILLNESS IN CHILDREN
HERPES SIMPLEX I AND II**

D

DAILY LIVING SKILLS

The term daily living skills refers to those skills that individuals use in their personal self-care and occasionally in their interactions with others. A wide range of specific behaviors may be included under each of these headings. The skills might appear to be very straightforward (e.g., grasping a brush handle) or extremely complex (e.g., developing healthy eating habits). The range of skills and behaviors that are often included under the rubric of daily living skills is best conceptualized as points along a continuum. At one end of the continuum essential daily living skills might include toileting, feeding, and dressing. Moving along the continuum toward increasing independence, a second level of skills could include hand washing, toothbrushing, etc. Daily living skills that might be taught at a higher level of independence include menstrual hygiene, shaving, and other more complex tasks.

As the student masters behaviors that are taught at fundamental levels, these newly acquired behaviors become the building material for future skill development. The end result of effective instruction in the skills that students use day to day is seen in the student's mastery of more complex conceptually oriented skills (e.g., sexual awareness, diet planning) that frequently subsume previously mastered skills. The goal in teaching these skills is to assist the exceptional needs learner in the development of more normative abilities. As these skills are taught and mastered, the student is more likely to gain access to more normative age-appropriate environments and interactions with others.

Nonexceptional children typically learn these skills (as a matter of course) through the instruction and modeling of parents, siblings, and peers, and through their own natural exploration of their environment. The exceptional child, however, often has disabilities that impair his or her ability to observe, explore, internalize, and use the skills that might otherwise be acquired. Physical disabilities may prevent the exceptional child from making use of information that he or she is able to absorb. The emotionally disordered child may exhibit problem behaviors that actively interfere with the learning of daily living skills. In addition, some exceptional children, notably those in institutions and segregated classrooms; may lack role models and/or access to the type of environments that allow the sort of exploration and ex-perimentation necessary for the acquisition of daily living skills. Indeed, some environments actually discourage the development of such skills by prohibiting, in the interest of efficiency, neatness, etc., the exceptional individual from becoming involved in any aspect of his or her own care. Thus, the exceptional child often requires systematic instruction and/or various forms of environmental adaptation to enable him or her to reach the full development of potential in the area of daily living skills. As Bigge and O'Donnell (1976) have pointed out, not only is it necessary to teach exceptional children daily living skills in order to enable them to cope effectively with their present day-to-day experiences, but it is also necessary to provide them with the chance to survive in society and contribute to it. Failure to assist exceptional children in learning these skills can only result in their becoming unnecessarily dependent adults.

The following skills have been identified as essential to meet the demands of everyday adult living (Brolin, 1989):

> MANAGING PERSONAL FINANCES
> Count money and make correct change.
> Manage a savings and checking account.
> Maintain a personal budget and keep records.
> Demonstrate personal finance decision-making skills.
> Make responsible expenditures.
> Calculate and pay taxes.
> Use credit responsibly.
> Pay bills.
> Deal with renting or leasing.
> SELECTING AND MANAGING A HOUSEHOLD
> Perform or arrange for home maintenance.
> Perform housekeeping tasks.
> Plan and prepare meals.
> Fill out warranty cards for new appliances and mail them.
> CARING FOR PERSONAL NEEDS
> Exhibit proper grooming and hygiene.
> Dress appropriately.
> Obtain health care.
> Avoid substance abuse.
> Demonstrate knowledge of common illnesses, prevention and treatment.
> Maintain physical fitness, nutrition and weight.
> SAFETY AWARENESS
> Identify safety signs.

Identify unfamiliar odors.

Identify unfamiliar sounds.

Demonstrate knowledge and ability to evacuate a building in an emergency.

Read and understand basic safety procedures.

Obey safety rules when walking during the day or at night.

RAISING, PREPARING, AND CONSUMING FOOD

Purchase food and plan meals.

Clean food preparation areas.

Store food properly.

Prepare meals, read labels, and follow recipes.

Demonstrate appropriate eating habits.

Plan and eat balanced meals.

BUYING AND CARING FOR CLOTHING

Wash clothing.

Purchase clothing.

Demonstrate knowledge of prices and sales.

Iron, mend, and store clothing.

Demonstrate use of dry cleaner and laundromat.

EXHIBITING RESPONSIBLE CITIZENSHIP

Demonstrate knowledge of civil rights and responsibilities.

Get legal aid.

Report a crime.

Register with Selective Service at age 18.

Demonstrate knowledge of local, state, and federal governments.

Demonstrate knowledge of the law and ability to follow the law.

Demonstrate knowledge of citizen rights and responsibilities.

Vote.

USING RECREATIONAL FACILITIES AND ENGAGING IN LEISURE ACTIVITIES

Demonstrate knowledge of available community resources.

Choose and plan activities.

Demonstrate knowledge of the value of recreation.

Engage in group and individual activities.

Plan vacation time.

Plan a social event.

Engage in hobbies, sports, music, arts and crafts.

GETTING AROUND THE COMMUNITY

Differentiate between right side and left side, front and back, to demonstrate location.

Demonstrate knowledge of traffic rules and safety.

Demonstrate knowledge and use of many means of transportation including carpools.

Understand and use a map.

Drive a car; obtain a learner's permit, then a driver's license.

Obtain car insurance.

Accept and give criticism.

Develop confidence in self.

Identify and distinguish the proper way to answer and use the telephone.

Wear appropriate apparel, using clothes or uniforms to fit social and work situations.

ACHIEVING SOCIALLY RESPONSIBLE BEHAVIOR

Develop respect for the rights and properties of others.

Recognize authority and follow instructions.

Demonstrate appropriate behavior and social etiquette in public places and when dating or eating out.

Demonstrate knowledge of important character traits.

Recognize personal roles.

MAINTAINING GOOD INTERPERSONAL SKILLS

Demonstrate listening and responding skills.

Establish and keep close relationships.

Make and keep friendships.

ACHIEVING INDEPENDENCE

Do things without help.

Accept responsibility for actions.

Get around the community and be able to travel.

Cope with changes in travel schedule.

Cope with being lost.

Follow travel safety procedures.

Choose friends.

Get to school on time.

Decide what to wear.

ACHIEVING PROBLEM-SOLVING SKILLS

Seek assistance when needed.

Recognize problems.

Anticipate consequences.

Develop and evaluate alternatives.

Develop goals, solutions, and plans.

COMMUNICATING WITH OTHERS

Recognize and respond to emergency situations.

Communicate with understanding.

Demonstrate knowledge of social cues and the subtleties of conversation, both verbal and nonverbal.

Listen to others.

Owing to the complexity, the uniqueness of mental and physical conditions and limitations, and the variety of skills to be taught, a wide range of goals exists in the area of daily living skills. Some children may become self-reliant; others may be able to accomplish only the most basic of daily living tasks (Bigge & O'Donnell, 1976). In addition, the techniques used in teaching these skills will vary widely in accordance with the child's abilities, attention motor imitation, and verbal comprehension (Snell, 1978).

Prior to beginning training in daily living skills, there must be an initial period of assessment. At times it will be more efficient to first strengthen verbal skills, attending, and imitation. Likewise, behaviors such as those that are disruptive, aggressive, or nonresponsive may not only interfere with the teaching process but may lead to inaccurate test results and confused training methods. Thus, these behaviors are best decreased or eliminated before assessment begins. The assessment itself should produce not only a detailed analysis of existing daily living skills and needs, but also an estimate of additional factors that might affect training—current level of development and functioning in relevant areas, physical limitations, problem behaviors, and practical considerations such as accessibility of needed facilities and specialized equipment. An excellent source of objective assessment that can be used is the Vineland Adaptive Behavior Skills, 2nd edition (Sparrow, Cicchetti, & Balla, 2005).

Once the assessment is complete, the child's individual needs can be clearly defined and appropriate goals set. A task analysis of the skill(s) to be taught can then be completed and any necessary adaptive equipment (e.g., a special spoon handle or clothing with velcro fastenings) can be obtained. Following this, the child is guided through the successive steps, with assistance being gradually cut back until the child is able to perform the task independently and across settings. The issues of generalization and maintenance are of utmost importance in the teaching of daily living skills. Teachers of exceptional students should consider, at all times, the learning characteristics of the students in conjunction with the potential for new behavior.

REFERENCES

Bigge, J. L., & O'Donnell, J. G. (1976). *Teaching individuals with physical and multiple disabilities.* Columbus, OH: Merrill.

Brolin, D. E. (1989). *Life centered career education: A competency based approach* (3rd ed.). Reston, VA: Council for Exceptional Children.

Snell, M. E. (1978). *Systemic instruction of the moderately and severely handicapped.* Columbus, OH: Merrill.

ELAINE FLETCHER-JANZEN
*University of Colorado at
Colorado Springs*

ECOLOGICAL ASSESSMENT
FUNCTIONAL DOMAINS
FUNCTIONAL SKILLS TRAINING

DANCE THERAPY

Dance therapy is a method by which movement is incorporated into a therapeutic or educational program. As a therapy approach, dance has been used to enhance traditional methods of medical and verbal group therapies with numerous populations, including the aged, the mentally ill, and the mentally retarded. Dance is especially useful with the retarded because it does not require verbal abilities (Rogers, 1977). Benefits noted through informal observations of dance therapy programs have included improvements in general motility, speech patterns, locomotion, and

social ability (Barteneiff & Lewis, 1980). Dance therapy has also resulted in reduction of muscle tension and trait anxiety (Kline et al., 1978).

Dance has also been used in a broader context to promote physical and social development. Crain, Eisenhart, and McLaughlin (1984) implemented a dance program with mildly retarded adolescent students that included movement orientation, movement exploration, dance foundations, rhythms, and traditional dances. They noted improvements for 11 of 13 participants in areas of physical and social development.

Dance therapy is useful with special populations both as an adjunct to normal group verbal therapies and as a method to enhance physical, social, and educational development (Gladding, 1992).

REFERENCES

Barteneiff, I., & Lewis, D. (1980). *Body movement: Coping with the environment.* New York: Gordon & Breach.

Crain, C., Eisenhart, M., & McLaughlin, J. (1984). The application of a multiple measurement approach to investigate the effects of a dance program on educable mentally retarded adolescents. *Research Quarterly for Exercise & Sport, 55,* 231–236.

Gladding, S. T. (1992). *Counseling as an art: The creative arts in counseling.* Alexandria, VA: American Counseling Association.

Kline, F., Burgoyne, R. W., Staples, F., Moredock, P., Snyder, V., & Ioerger, M. (1978). A report on the use of movement therapy for chronic, severely disabled outpatients. *Art Psychotherapy, 5,* 181–183.

Rogers, S. B. (1977). Contributions of dance therapy in a treatment program for retarded adolescents and adults. *Art Psychotherapy, 4,* 195–197.

Sparrow, S. S., Cicchetti, D. V., & Barrow, D. A. (2005). *The Vineland Adaptive Behavior Scales* (2nd ed.). Circle Pines, MN: AGS.

CHRISTINE A. ESPIN
University of Minnesota

RECREATION FOR INDIVIDUALS WITH DISABILITIES
RECREATIONAL THERAPY

DANDY-WALKER SYNDROME

Dandy-Walker syndrome (DWS) is a congenital anomaly that involves the formation of a large cyst in the posterior region of the brain (known as a Dandy-Walker Formation) that results in hydrocephalus and agenesis of the central region or vermis of the cerebellum (Greenspan, 1998). It is similar to Joubert syndrome in the latter respect and has some overlapping symptoms. Etiology is unknown, but DWS is thought to be, not genetic, but related to some invasive organism, possibly cytomegalovirus. It is sometimes diagnosable via ultrasound in utero but is more likely to be detected in infancy and early childhood.

There are significant impairments associated with most cases of DWS including mental retardation of varying degrees (in about 50 percent of cases), nonverbal learning disabilities in higher functioning DWS patients, sporadic cases including agenesis of the corpus callosum (Tucker & Vaurio, 2003), and many social and behavioral problems.

Specific psychoeducational recommendations cannot be made for all DWS patients due to the degree of variability in outcome. Most will require special education services, often as Other Health Impaired, but consistent assessment and modification of programming are typically necessary. The successfulness of the shunt for the hydrocephalus is crucial to a positive outcome, and the earlier the shunting takes place, the better the prognosis.

REFERENCES

Greenspan, S. (1998). Dandy-Walker syndrome. In L. Phelps (Ed.), *Health-related disorders in children and adolescents* (pp. 219–223). Washington, DC: American Psychological Association.

Tucker, D. M., & Vaurio, R. (2003). Agenesis of the corpus callosum. In E. Fletcher-Janzen & C. R. Reynolds (Eds.), *Childhood disorders diagnostic desk reference* (pp. 15–16). New York: Wiley.

STAFF

DATA-BASED INSTRUCTION

Data-based instruction is a way of describing, measuring, and assessing behavior for instructional purposes. The system is based on the behavioral theories of B. F. Skinner (1938). Data-based instruction emerged from the concept of precision teaching. Precision teaching involves operationally defining behavior and measuring, recording, and assessing behavior to determine the success of an instructional program (Idol-Maestas, 1983).

Lilly (1979) listed the eight basic steps of data-based instruction. The first step is to define the instructional problem in behavioral terms. The use of behavioral terms allows the teacher to pinpoint specific descriptions of behaviors that need addressing. The behavior should be defined in such a manner that anyone observing the child would be able to determine what the behavior is and when it occurs.

The second step involves assessing the problem so the teacher will have some idea of the student's present level of performance before intervention. There must be a pattern of behavior established during baseline. Therefore, one to five instances of baseline data of each behavior is required. Baseline data collected before intervention will serve as a measure of the student's progress after intervention has been implemented.

Once the behavior has been defined and baseline data collected, the next step is to state the objectives of the instructional program. What are the teacher's expectations as a result of the educational intervention? These objectives should be clear and specific. In breaking down instructional objectives into teachable components, instructional objectives may become simple and clear or complex and detailed. Therefore, some objectives may need to be broken down into small teachable steps. This process is called task analysis. In the determination of teaching-learning procedures, the teacher should determine the instructional strategies that will be used. In data-based instruction there are no specific instructional strategies that must be used. Any strategy that produces good results is acceptable. The emphasis is placed on determining the instructional objectives first; then instructional strategies and materials are selected based on the objectives.

Once the instructional program is implemented, it is very important to collect data on a continuous basis. This information is used to assess the effectiveness of the instructional program. The more often the data are collected, the more reliable and consistent the information. These data should be collected in the same manner as the baseline data to ensure appropriateness and the accuracy of the conclusions. Lilly (1977) states that it is important for the teacher to record the data so that it can be used for instructional decisions. Recording the data is done by charting the information on a graph. There are many formats used to chart data, however, the most important consideration is that the data display a visual presentation of the student's behavior for a specific amount of time.

The data that has been collected over time is used to make decisions concerning the effectiveness of the instructional program. The following guidelines are suggested by Lilly (1979), and have not essentially changed since they were published:

1. Allow enough time for an instructional procedure to have an effect (at least 1 week).
2. Do not allow a student to continue more than 2 or 3 weeks without making progress.
3. When progress does not occur, blame the instruction program, not the child.
4. When progress does occur, celebrate with everyone involved.
5. Use progress charts in discussing school programs with parents.

In addition, Lilly (1977) states that it is essential to ask the following questions during instructional decision time.

1. Is progress sufficient to justify continuation of the present instructional procedures?
2. Do progress data indicate that the instructional objectives and/or methodology is appropriate or inappropriate for the student?

3. Is the criterion level appropriate for the instructional objective?

4. If the objective is reached, what is the appropriate next step?

At all times, precision teaching and data-based instruction involves "being aware of the relationship between teaching and learning, measuring student performance regularly and frequently, and analyzing the measurements to develop instructional and motivational strategies" (West, 1990). Data-based instruction continues to be the most efficient method of remediating behavior (Lewis, Heflin, & Di Gangi, 1991).

REFERENCES

Idol-Maestas, L. (1983). *Special educator's consultation handbook.* Rockville, MD: Aspen.

Lewis, T. J., Heflin, J., & Di Gangi, S. A. (1991). *Teaching students with behavior disorders: Basic questions and answers.* Reston, VA: Council for Exceptional Children. (ED No. 333659). Stock No. P337.

Lilly, M. S. (1977). Evaluating individual education programs. In S. Torres (Ed.), *A primer on individualized education programs for handicapped children* (pp. 26–30). Reston VA: Council for Exceptional Children.

Lilly, M. S. (1979). Learning and behavior problems, current trends. In M. S. Lilly (Ed.), *Children with exceptional needs: A survey of special education.* New York: Holt, Rinehart & Winston.

Skinner, B. F. (1938). *The behavior of organisms.* New York: Appleton Century.

West, R. (1990). Precision teaching: An introduction. *Teaching Exceptional Children, 22,* 4–9.

JANICE HARPER
North Carolina Central University

DIAGNOSTIC PRESCRIPTIVE TEACHING
PRECISION TEACHING

DAY-CARE CENTERS

Formal day-care programs originated during the Industrial Revolution with custodial care in factory rooms for young children of working mothers. Early in this century, the Salvation Army in Baltimore and Hull House in Chicago began day-care programs for infants and children of working mothers. Beginning in 1933, the Federal Work Relief Project supported Emergency Nursery Schools (ENS) as a way of providing jobs for unemployed teachers. The ENS programs were similar to the later Head Start programs in that they were for preschool children, offered medical services, emphasized nutrition, and provided in-service staff training; however, ENS emphasized nurturing care while Head Start emphasizes more formal education. When the ENS program ended, day care for mothers working in war industries was funded under the Lanham Act until 1946. Other day-care programs were supported by industry during World War II. None of those early programs were intended for children with disabilities, but probably some with mild problems were admitted.

Programs exclusively for disabled children excluded from school began in the 1950s. Sponsored and conducted by parent groups, most were for moderately retarded children. In the 1960s the Massachusetts Department of Mental Health added a day-care program to its preschool program because many severely retarded children were excluded from schools. Very few private preschools, kindergartens, or public schools accepted children with severe disabilities until the late 1970s. Most blind, deaf, severely retarded, and severely physically impaired children could stay at home without day-care services or go to a state-supported residential facility. After implementation of PL 94-142 in 1977, school systems supported educational programs that replaced (and were often similar to) the private day-care facilities for school-age children. Then day-care services were developed for preschool- and postschool-age disabled groups. This is noted in the American Association on Mental Deficiency's definition of day care: "extended care services provided on an ongoing basis for individuals residing in the community and not eligible for school programs or workshops; involves social, physical, recreational, and personal-care training and activity" (Grossman, 1983, p. 167).

Efforts at integrating disabled and nondisabled preschool day-care programs have increased in recent years (Branca, 1988; Guralnick, 1978, 1994, 1995; Templeman, 1989). A national survey of day-care facilities for young children and infants showed that some children with disabilities were eligible for integrated services. About 21 percent of the centers reported accepting children with physical and emotional problems; about 14 percent would accept retarded children (Coelen, Galantz, & Calore, 1979). The tendency for separation of disabled from nondisabled children is still reflected in professional literature, with almost no mention of disabilities in day-care journals and books. A few booklets (e.g., Granato, 1972) offer common-sense suggestions for day-care providers working with children with disabilities.

Empirical studies evaluating the effects of day-care programs for children with disabilities and adults are rare, but comments on scientific and social policy issues in a book by Zigler and Gordon (1982) suggest that the research trend is toward identifying factors associated with different outcomes rather than simply attempting to determine whether day care is good for children. Guralnick (1994, 1995) studied the parent's perception of early integration of exceptional preschoolers. Notwithstanding the parental concerns of peer rejection, most parents perceived positive gains for their children.

In addition, Zigler (1991, 1995) cites the 1990 Child Care

and Development Act as a step towards the solutions of day/child care problems. Indeed, Zigler predicted the inclusion of integrated child care provided by the public schools and supported by parents and family. Community placements also give services for young children with severe disabilities that are successful (Branca, 1988). Best practices for the inclusion of preschoolers with moderate to profound disabilities can be found in Templeman (1989).

REFERENCES

Branca, R. A. (1988). *Implementing a program of supportive services to severely handicapped preschool age children in community programs.* (Eric Clearinghouse No. EC212115)

Coelen, C., Galantz, F., & Calore, D. (1979). *Day care centers in the United States: A national profile.* Cambridge, MA: Abt Associates.

Granato, S. (1972). *Day care: Serving children with special needs.* Washington, DC: U.S. Government Printing Office.

Grossman, H. J. (1983). *Classification in mental retardation.* Washington, DC: American Association on Mental Deficiency.

Guralnick, M. J. (1978). *Early intervention and the integration of handicapped and nonhandicapped children.* Baltimore: University Park Press.

Guralnick, M. J. (1994). Mother's perceptions of the benefits and drawbacks of early childhood mainstreaming. *Journal of Early Intervention, 18*(2), 168–38.

Guralnick, M. J. (1995). Parent perspectives of peer relationships and friendships in integrated and specialized programs. *American Journal on Mental Retardation, 99*(5), 457–476.

Templeman, T. P. (1989). Integration of children with moderate and severe handicaps into a daycare center. *Journal of Early Intervention, 13*(4), 315–328.

Zigler, E. F., & Finn-Stevenson, M. (1995). The child care crisis: Implications for the growth and development of the nation's children. *Journal of Social Issues, 51*(3), 215–231.

Zigler, E. F., & Gilman, E. (1991). Beyond academic instruction: The twenty-first century school model for preschoolers. *New Directions for Child Development, 53,* 75–82.

Zigler, E. F., & Gordon, E. W. (Eds.). (1982). *Day care: Scientific and social issues.* Boston: Auburn House.

SUE ALLEN WARREN
Boston University
First edition

HEAD START
LEAST RESTRICTIVE ENVIRONMENT
MAINSTREAMING
RESPITE CARE

DAYDREAMING

The literature on daydreaming from the special educator's perspective tends to fall into three categories. In the first, daydreaming is seen as a symptom of disability. In the second, it is associated with creativity and giftedness. In the third, it is reported to be an effective therapeutic device. As a symptom of disability, daydreaming is associated with both physical and cognitive disorders. It has been suggested that a central nervous system dysfunction may cause a lag in brain structure development leading to behavior such as daydreaming that inhibits learning. Petite mal epileptic seizures are also often mistaken for daydreaming. As a result, medical screening might be appropriate for chronic daydreamers. Cognitively, Blanton (1983) and others classify daydreaming as an immature behavior—along with hyperactivity, distractibility, impulsivity, procrastination, messiness, and sloppiness—that becomes a problem in educational situations. Besides possible physiological causes, inordinate daydreaming may be due to shyness (Sheridan, Kratochwill, & Elliot, 1990), deep emotional problems, or to a student's inability to focus attention on a task for any length of time.

Suggested treatments for problem daydreaming vary as widely as suggested causes. Mock, Swanson, and Kinsbourne (1982) found that among hyperactive students with distractible cognitive styles (characterized by daydreaming, slow response time, and high error rates), the use of ritalin improved performance on some school-related tasks, decreasing both decision time and error rates. Practical suggestions for teachers include calling the student's attention to the task at hand in some inconspicuous way such as placing a hand on the student's paper or using physical proximity to convey expectations. Operant conditioning can be effective as well, using reward points or some other positive reinforcement when students finish tasks. Allowing students to choose activities that are inherently interesting to them also fosters prolonged attention.

If daydreaming needs to be overcome in some students, it seems that it should be fostered in others. The connection between fantasy and creativity is widely recognized. Daydreaming seems to accompany the period of incubation that precedes creative production. Fred Kekule's discovery of the molecular structure of benzene is a common example of the power of relaxed, unguided fantasy. Guides for parents of gifted children consistently recommend allowing their children time to daydream, even though, like the learning disabled, gifted children must often be encouraged to stay on task. These two views of daydreaming—as a creative tool for gifted children and as an obstacle for the learning disabled—may be understood in light of findings by Kanter (1982). After controlling for IQ, Kanter found that frequent daydreamers are slow in response production and weak in verbal creativity, but gifted in visual creative abilities. Treatments vary as educators try to overcome the former with the learning disabled and foster the latter in the gifted.

Daydreaming itself has been used in a variety of ways as a clinical device. Programmed imaging, as McQueen (1983) describes it, is often used to develop skills in the psycho motor domain. Subjects practice basketball free throws in their mind's eye, for example, before going onto the court. Controlled experiments have shown this to be highly effective. Guided daydreaming, which until recently was a more common technique in Europe than in the United States, is controlled by someone who stays outside the activities of the participants. The leader, usually a teacher or therapist, talks the subjects through an experience. This is often useful for relaxation and as an aid to memory, self-awareness, and clarifying goals or realizing internal conflicts. Once a subject becomes adept at disciplined daydreaming, it can be used as a powerful tool. Therapists have reported decreased incidence of depression, phobias, and psychosomatic disorders in patients trained to use their imaginations. It has also aided those who have trouble making decisions. Subjects are encouraged to imagine possible scenarios that might occur in consequence of a variety of decisions and then choose the most desirable. Neurotic or otherwise undesirable behaviors have also been modified with clinical use of imagery. One technique is to have the subjects practice substitute behaviors mentally before incorporating them into their daily activities. A more extreme method is the use of aversive imagery techniques, in which highly negative mental pictures are evoked to discourage maladaptive behaviors such as compulsive stealing (Singer, 1974).

REFERENCES

Blanton, G. H. (1983, February). *Social and emotional development of learning disabled children.* Paper presented at the annual convention of the Association for Children and Adults with Learning Disabilities, Washington, DC. (ERIC Document Reproduction Service No. ED 232 336)

Kanter, S. (1982). Divergent thinking abilities as a function of daydreaming frequency. *Journal for the Education of the Gifted, 5*(1), 12–23.

McQueen, D. (1983, March). *Imaging as a heuristic.* Paper presented at the annual meeting of the Conference on College Composition and Communication, Detroit, MI. (ERIC Document Reproduction Service No. ED 234 429)

Mock, K. R., Swanson, J. M., & Kinsbourne, M. (1978, March). *Stimulant effect on matching familiar figures: Changes in impulsive and distractible cognitive styles.* Paper presented at the annual meeting of the American Educational Research Association, Toronto, Canada. (ERIC Document Reproduction Service No. ED 160 189)

Sheridan, S. T., Kratochwill, T., & Elliott, S. (1990). Behavioral consultation with parents and teachers. *School Psychology Review, 19,* 33–52.

Singer, J. L. (1974). *Imagery and daydream methods in psychotherapy and behavior modification.* New York: Academic.

JANET S. BRAND
Hunter College, City University of New York

HYPNOSIS
IMAGERY

DEAF

The word deaf is applied to persons who cannot hear or have a major hearing impairment. In classical writings as well as in common talk, until only a few years ago, the word deaf frequently had a strongly pejorative connotation, either in its figurative sense of deaf to the word of God or in locutions such as deaf and dumb. The latter clearly indicated a belief that those who are deaf from birth also have an intellectual defect. The term deaf-mute (used either as an adjective or as a noun), carried the notion of a double infirmity, until it was realized that the absence of speech, in those born deaf, was not related to a deficiency of the vocal organs and was only the consequence of the lack of hearing. Deaf now is used alone mostly since a majority of deaf persons have no other infirmity aside from possibly an oral language deficiency.

There is as yet no universally accepted definition of the different categories of hearing impairment. All the existing classifications are based on the mean speech range frequency thresholds obtained for the best ear by pure tone. The classification of the Bureau International d'Audiophonologie (BIAP; International Office for Audiophonology) is based on the mean hearing loss for 500, 1000, and 2000 Hz (International Standards Organization [ISO]). It uses the terms recommended by the World Health Organization for the grading of all types of impairments: mild (20–40 dB), moderate (40–70 dB), severe (70–90 dB), and profound (more than 90 dB). The last category is itself divided in three subgroups, because there are large differences in the possibilities of residual hearing use among those whose average loss is only slightly superior to 90 dB and those who have a more than 100 dB hearing loss. Other classifications use different gradings and terms for the less than 70 dB categories, but there is fair agreement concerning the definition of the severe and profound groups.

Pure-tone audiometry, however, provides only a partial picture of the residual hearing capacity. It does not reflect the variable potential gain that can be brought by adequate hearing aid fitting. Several authors such as Pollack (1964), advocate the aided audiogram as a more meaningful measure of functional hearing capacity. Even this, however, does not reflect the qualitative aspects of residual hearing, which may vary extensively among individuals with the same pure-tone audiometric thresholds. Some insight about the quality of hearing may be gained by investigation of psychoacoustic tuning curves (Harrison, 1984), but these measures cannot presently be applied to small children because they require the subjects' active and informed cooperation.

These difficulties in establishing a well-founded functional classification have led several authors to adopt simpler general definitions for educational purposes. According to the Conference of Executives of American Schools for the Deaf (Frisina, 1974), a deaf person is one whose hearing is disabled to an extent (usually 70 dB International Standards Organization or greater) that precludes the understanding of speech through the ear alone, without or with the use of a hearing aid; a hard-of-hearing person is one whose hearing is disabled to an extent (usually 35 to 69 dB International Standards Organization) that makes difficult, but does not preclude, the understanding of speech through the ear alone, without or with a hearing aid.

It is necessary to stress the importance in both of these definitions of the word usually because there is a large overlap in the degree of pure-tone hearing loss of people who functionally correspond to one or the other category. Recently, Quigley and Kretschmer (1982) stated that for educational purposes, "a deaf child or adult is one who sustained a profound (91 dB or greater) primarily sensori-neural hearing impairment prelingually" (p. 2). This trend toward considering as deaf only those with a larger than 90 dB hearing impairment is probably related to development of early intervention programs and improvement of hearing aids, resulting in earlier and better spoken language acquisition for an increasing number of the less profoundly hearing impaired.

In addition to the former definitions, the definition that was adopted by a UNESCO experts' committee (1985) introduces the notion of relativity of deafness to prevalent socioeconomic conditions:

> To be considered as *deaf* those children whose spontaneous speech and language development have been very much retarded or is completely absent due to their severe hearing impairment or a hearing impairment combined with a lack of training and/or technical amplification. In countries with adequate resources for diagnosis, training, and provision of hearing aids, some children with hearing impairment would not be included in the above-mentioned group, whereas they would be regarded as functionally deaf in countries lacking these resources. (p. 5)

Other terms such as auditorially impaired or deficient, acoustically impaired, hypoacoustic, or, in French, demi-sourd (half deaf), are used either as synonyms for deaf and hearing impaired or to designate a category of the latter. The word cophotic, limited to the medical profession, is applied to those ears that have completely lost their auditory function.

The World Health Organization recommends that a distinction be made in all physical or mental defects, among impairment, disability, and handicap. Deaf children and adults are impaired in having a pathological auditory system. They are consequently disabled by difficulty in perceiving speech and environmental sounds. This disability can make them more or less severely handicapped by limiting their overall personal and social functioning. Some types of impairment, those owed to conductive hearing loss, can be alleviated or cured by medical and/or surgical therapy. For most deaf persons, as defined by the Conference of Executives of American Schools for the deaf, the physical impairment is due to inner ear or nervous system damage and is irreversible. The disability can, however, be reduced by appropriate hearing aid fitting, training, and, in the case of children, education. The handicap can be lessened or even eliminated in two ways: through the reduction of the disability or through the functioning in a sociocultural group where hearing is not necessary.

Among deaf and hard-of-hearing children and adults, it is important to distinguish between those who were affected from birth or shortly thereafter (before language was established) and those who became hearing impaired later on. These groups are commonly called prelingually and postlingually deaf, respectively. The prelingually deaf child cannot acquire language by the same natural process as the normally hearing. Their auditory pathways in the brain, as well as those parts of the cerebral cortex concerned with the processing of spoken language, are not adequately stimulated in the early years most favorable for language development. This lack of adequate stimulation during the sensitive period not only results in great difficulties in the acquisition of spoken language skills, but may also produce permanent structural changes in the central nervous system. These changes could diminish the capacity of the brain to efficiently process speech-linked information later on, even if normal hearing could be restored, or artificial hearing produced (Périer et al., 1984).

Because of the interference of deafness with language acquisition, prelingually deaf children and adults markedly differ from the postlingually deafened. The latter have a sensory impairment that interferes with their ability to perceive speech and other sounds, but they have a normally and completely developed language function. Although the quality of their speech may become distorted after some time because of the lack of auditory feedback, they usually remain intelligible. Their reading and writing capacities remain intact. By contrast, prelingually deaf children have such difficulties in acquiring spoken language that most of them, when they leave school as adolescents or young adults, have a linguistic insufficiency in addition to their sensory impairment (Conrad, 1979). Not only are they deficient in oral language skills, but also in reading and writing capacities. This linguistic insufficiency constitutes a serious handicap for their integration within the society of the normally hearing. It can, however, be attenuated and largely prevented by early and adequate education. When this includes sign language, a normal linguistic function may be developed in that modality, allowing full participation in the sociocultural life of the deaf community.

Deafness is related to a physical impairment, like other disabilities requiring rehabilitative and educational measures. It differs, however, from all these by a unique feature: the fact that this disability has given birth to a specific language, sign language (Bellugi, 1972). Just as a wide variety of spoken languages have evolved among the normally hearing world population, different sign languages have originated among the scattered communities of deaf people (Stokoe, 1972). However, many western world sign languages have a partly common trunk because of the important influence of the Abbé de l'Epée, the first educator of the deaf to recognize, in the late eighteenth century in France, the sign language of the deaf. There are, therefore, more common or similar signs among western sign languages than there are common or similar words in spoken languages. This facilitates communication among deaf people of different nationalities.

The use of sign language eliminates all handicaps for those who are proficient in it. Indeed, it is the normally hearing individual who becomes handicapped when he or she tries to participate in a group where sign language is the principal or only mode of communication. The common language is a powerful bond that largely contributes to the creation of a group identity. This tendency is strengthened when the group is a minority subjected to strong social pressure. This is particularly true for the deaf, because sign language was not recognized as a proper language until several linguists such as William Stokoe (1972), Ursula Bellugi (1972), and others brought forward the convincing results of their research. They demonstrated that sign languages of the deaf are as worthy of esteem and respect as vocal languages, possessing all the attributes of the latter except oral realization. Among these attributes are not only grammatical correctness, arbitrariness, and double articulation, but also more affective qualities such as the capacity to express humor and poetry.

In the past, many deaf individuals did not themselves realize the value of their manual language (Meadow, 1980). They were influenced by the hearing society's contempt for what was regarded as a primitive and crude mode of communication, incapable of expressing abstraction and therefore unsuitable for high-level intellectual processes. The new status of sign language has done much not only to promote its diffusion and enrichment, but also to upgrade its users' self-confidence and self-esteem. This has given new impetus to deaf organizations and prompted the birth of such movements as Deaf Pride. This movement promulgates the notion that the deaf are equal but different and want this difference to be recognized and taken into account in the organization of society as a whole. Sign language supports deaf culture, mainly characterized by social and artistic events. It is, however, more appropriate to speak of cultural values rather than of a complete culture because the deaf share many ingredients of the hearing majorities' cultures such as their literature and their religions.

While some of the deaf reject spoken language and refuse to make any efforts at participation in sociocultural activities with the hearing, most of them aspire to bilingualism (i.e., the use of both sign and spoken languages) and biculturalism. Individuals who are deaf are considered bilingual if they are able to communicate effectively in both American Sign Language (ASL) and English or the spoken language of their country. They are considered bicultural if they are capable of functioning in both the deaf community and the majority culture (Baker & Baker, 1997). Bilingual-bicultural programs in the schools differ

from other programs most notably by the approach to first language acquisition. These programs advocate for ASL to be the first language of children who are deaf because cognitive research indicates that "effective language has to be fast and clear. ASL is an efficient language for visual learning and is easier for deaf children to acquire as a first language than any form of English" (Finnegan, 1992, in Baker & Baker, 1997).

Bilingual-bicultural programs are generally found outside mainstream education and are relatively new. The gain in popularity may well be hampered or supported by achievement outcome studies. Baker and Baker (1997) suggest that students in rural areas may not have access to this approach, and classes for caregivers (especially in rural areas) are necessary for success.

Better information for society at large and sensitization to the rightful demands of the deaf have contributed to strengthening biculturalism. An important event in bringing the deaf to the attention of the hearing world was the success of Mark Medoff's play *Children of a Lesser God,* in which a deaf actress held the principal part. The play was awarded the Tony Award for best play of the year in 1980. In addition, the "Deaf Prez Now" or Gallaudet University protest in 1988 galvanized individuals who are deaf in ways that have not impacted the hearing community. In 1988 students at Gallaudet University protested the hiring of a hearing University President. They were successful in removing the President from office. The students removed hearing members of the board of trustees as well (McIntosh, 1996).

According to many psychologists and sociolinguists, it is important for the personality structure of severely and profoundly hearing-impaired individuals that they identify themselves as deaf. The realization that they are different, but not inferior, allows them to direct all their energies in a positive direction, rather than striving toward the unattainable goal of trying to be like the hearing. According to this view, deaf children of hearing parents (who represent more than 90 percent of deaf children) should be given the opportunity at an early age for social intercourse with deaf adults who can serve as realistic models. For many deaf adults, sign language is essential for the full expression of their personality. As a consequence, they deeply feel their belonging to the deaf community and cherish the values of deaf culture. The concept of "identity formation" is starting to be realized in the deaf and hearing communities. Professionals are being invited to take a more "ethical and positive view of sign language and the deaf community" (Carver, 1999). It is clearly felt that deaf culture adds to, and does not detract from, a child's education and identity formation (Carver, 1999).

REFERENCES

Baker, S., & Baker, K. (1997). *Educating children who are deaf or hard-of-hearing: Bilingual-bicultural education.* Reston, VA:

ERIC Clearinghouse on Disabilities and Gifted Education. (ERIC Digest No. E 553)

Bellugi, U. (1972). Studies in sign language. In T. J. O'Rourke (Ed.), *Psycholinguistics and total communication: The state of the art. American Annals of the Deaf* (pp. 68–74).

Carver, R. (1999). Identity and deafness: Who am I? *Deaf World web:* dww.org

Conrad, R. (1979). *The deaf school child.* London: Harper & Row.

Finnegan, M. (1992). Bilingual-bicultural education. *The Endeavor, 3,* 1–8.

Frisina, R. (1974). *Report of the committee to redefine deaf and hard of hearing for educational purposes.* (Mimeo).

Harrison, R. V. (1984). Objective measures of cochlear frequency selectivity in animals and in man. A review. *Acta Neurological Belgica, 84,* 213–232.

Meadow, K. P. (1980). *Deafness and child development.* London: Arnold.

Périer, O., Alegria, J., Buyse, M., D'Alimonte, G., Gilson, D., & Serniclaes, W. (1984). Consequences of auditory deprivation in animals and humans. *Acta Oto-Laryngologica* (Suppl. 411), 60–70.

Pollack, D. (1964). Acoupedics: A uni-sensory approach to auditory training. *Volta Review, 66,* 400–409.

Quigley, S. P., & Kretschmer, R. E. (1982). *The education of deaf children: Issues, theory and practice.* London: Arnold.

Stokoe, W. C. (1972). *Semiotics and human sign language.* Paris: Mouton.

UNESCO. (1985). *Consultation on alternative approaches for the education of the deaf.* Paris: UNESCO Headquarters.

OLIVIER PÉRIER
*Université Libre de Bruxelles
Centre Comprendre et Parler,
   Belgium*
First edition

ELAINE FLETCHER-JANZEN
*University of Colorado at
   Colorado Springs*
Second edition

**CONDUCTIVE HEARING LOSS
DEAF EDUCATION**

DEAF, INTERPRETERS FOR

See INTERPRETERS FOR THE DEAF.

DEAF-BLIND

There exists a broad range of visual and auditory impairments among deaf-blind persons, indicating an enormous diversity in the severity of disabilities within this population. The term deaf-blind (also called dual sensory impairment) covers persons with severe visual and hearing disabilities who are unable to profit from special programs designed solely for deaf or blind children and youths (*Federal Register,* 1975).

It is estimated that there are over 5,000 children and youth who are deaf-blind in the United States (Arizona Deaf-Blind Project, 1998). Maternal rubella, CHARGE Association, Usher's syndrome, and meningitis are among the top four causes of deaf-blindness in the United States. Additionally, deaf-blind persons often are afflicted with congenital heart disease, mental retardation (Vernon, Grieve, & Shaver, 1980), physical handicaps, social/emotional issues, and communication delays (Arizona Deaf-Blind Project, 1998).

Deaf-blindness has often been associated with Helen Keller and her teacher Anne Sullivan (Lash, 1980). Although some deaf-blind people function within or above normal intelligence, many require extraordinary educational training. The separate disabilities are not additive but multiplicative in nature (Warren, 1984), and often cause severe learning problems. Deaf-blind children have often been referred to as the most difficult group of children to educate (Sims-Tucker & Jensema, 1984). They frequently engage in stereotypic behaviors that interfere with learning and communication. In an attempt to meet the special needs of this population, Regional Centers for Services for Deaf-Blind Children was established in 1967 (Sims-Tucker & Jensema, 1984).

Educational programming for deaf-blind children, including assessment and evaluation, continues to be a difficult task. The trend in educating children with severe disabilities has emphasized a more functional curriculum (Brown et al., 1979). Similarly, educators of deaf-blind children are turning to these curricular approaches for developing intervention programs in such areas as self-help, prevocational and vocational skills, communication, and sensory development (Vadasy & Fewell, 1984). Programming developed by Van Dijk (1971) has provided teachers, parents, and therapists with an invaluable communication curriculum that incorporates movement theory, which is often associated with the coactive movement. In addition, the emphasis on visual as well as auditory training can be seen in educational programs developed by Goetz and Utley (undated) and Efron and DuBoff (1979).

The Arizona Deaf-Blind Program was established as a federally-funded free resource for professionals and families working with deaf-blind individuals. It is housed at the Arizona School for the Deaf and Blind. The program provides consultation services for families of deaf-blind children, provides a lending library, and maintains an online interactive web page. The project can be contacted at P.O. Box 87010, Tucson, AZ, 85754 or at www.azdb.org. Their telephone is 520-770-3680. Other resources are:

American Association of the Deaf-Blind, Inc.
Silver Spring, Maryland 20901
Telephone: 301-588-6545
TTY: 301-523-1265

Helen Keller National Center for Deaf-Blind
111 Middle Neck Road
Sands Point, New York 11050
Telephone: 516-944-8900
TTY: 516-944-8637

REFERENCES

Arizona Deaf-Blind Program. (1998). *Deaf-blindness fact sheet.* Retrieved from www.azdb.org

Brown, L., Branston, M., Hamre-Nietupski, S., Pumpian, I., Certo, N., & Gruenewald, L. (1979). A strategy for developing chronological age appropriate and functional curricular content for severely handicapped adolescents and young adults. *Journal of Special Education, 13,* 81–90.

Efron, M., & DuBoff, B. (1979). *A vision guide for teachers of deaf-blind children.* Raleigh, NC: South Atlantic Regional Center for Services to Deaf-Blind Children.

Goetz, L., & Utley, B. (undated). *Auditory assessment and program manual for severely handicapped deaf-blind students.* Parsons, KS: Words & Pictures.

Lash, J. P. (1980). *Helen and teacher: The story of Helen Keller and Anne Sullivan Macy.* New York: Delacorte.

Lockett, T., & Rudolph, J. (1980). Deaf-blind children with maternal rubella: Implications for adult services. *American Annals of the Deaf, 125,* 1000–1006.

Sims-Tucker, B., & Jensema, C. (1984). Severely and profoundly auditorially/visually impaired students: The deaf-blind population. In P. Valletutti & B. Sims-Tucker (Eds.), *Severely and profoundly handicapped students: Their nature and needs* (pp. 269–317). Baltimore: Brookes.

Vadasy, P., & Fewell, R. (1984). Predicting the futures of deaf-blind adolescents: Their living and vocational options. *Education of the Visually Handicapped, 16,* 12–19.

Van Dijk, J. (1971). Learning difficulties and deaf-blind children. *Proceedings of the Fourth International Conference on Deaf-Blind Children.* Watertown, MA: Perkins School for the Blind.

Vernon, M., Grieve, B., & Shaver, K. (1980). Handicapping conditions associated with the congenital rubella syndrome. *American Annals of the Deaf, 125*(8), 993–997.

Warren, D. (1984). *Blindness and early childhood development.* New York: American Foundation for the Blind.

VIVIAN I. CORREA
University of Florida
First edition

ELAINE FLETCHER-JANZEN
University of Colorado at Colorado Springs
Second edition

DEAF
KELLER, HELEN
MOVEMENT THERAPY
VISUAL IMPAIRMENT

DEAF EDUCATION

The history of deaf education is relatively short because no records exist of organized teaching in prehistoric times or in the ancient civilizations of Egypt, Greece, and Rome. Although a few records exist of previous isolated examples of deaf individuals reaching some degree of education, Pedro Ponce de Leon (1520–1584) is generally considered to be the first teacher of the deaf. A Benedictine monk, he was entrusted with the education of several deaf children of Spanish nobility, and received wide publicity as a result of his successes. The records concerning the first teachers of the deaf are full of information showing that many of the techniques used today find their roots in the work of those pioneers. The reader is referred to the excellent survey by Moores (1978) for a review. However, it is necessary to mention the Abbott de l'Epée and Samuel Heinicke, because confrontation between their methods was at the heart of the oral versus manual controversy that has profoundly divided deaf educators for two centuries.

De l'Epée established the first public school for the deaf in the world, in 1755, in his Paris home. He started it when he was asked to give religious instruction to deaf twin sisters who used signs to communicate between them. De l'Epée understood that gestures could express human thought as much as spoken language and believed sign language to be the natural language of the deaf. He, therefore, set out to learn it from his pupils, but felt compelled to supplement their natural signs by newly formed "methodical" signs in order to obtain a complete sign counterpart of French syntax and morphology. The teaching of articulation was regarded by him as of lesser importance than that of signs and written language.

Samuel Heinicke taught several deaf children as a private tutor in different parts of Germany and established a school in Leipzig in 1778. He prided himself on being able to teach his pupils to speak clearly, and was strongly opposed to the teaching of written before spoken language, which he considered the only appropriate vehicle of thought. Heinicke and his followers Graser and Hill bitterly criticized de l'Epée's method, considering speech to be the first priority of teaching and sign language detrimental to that cause.

Controversy between the advocates of oralism and manualism, which started with de l'Epée and Heinicke, was lively during most of the nineteenth century, not only in Europe, but also in the United States. The first school for the deaf in the United States was founded by Thomas Hopkins Gallaudet, in 1847, with Laurent Clerc, a deaf teacher trained in Paris by de l'Epée's successor, Sicard. Other manual schools were created along the same lines, most of them paying little or no attention to the teaching of speech and articulation. Other U.S. educators responded with the creation of strictly oral schools. The controversy between manual and oral methods was later embodied by two exceptional personalities: Edward Miner Gallaudet (Thomas's son) and Alexander

Graham Bell. The former was convinced of the importance of spoken as well as sign language and was instrumental in establishing an oral-manual combined method in most American schools. Bell observed that education of the deaf in residential schools isolated them from the hearing society, and claimed that sign language was detrimental to the acquisition of English. He advocated the elimination of both sign language and the deaf teachers who used it.

In 1880 an international congress of educators of the deaf convened in Milan, Italy. It adopted two resolutions:

1. Considering the unquestionable superiority of speech over signs for the most perfect knowledge of language, the oral method must be preferred to the gestual method.

2. Considering that the simultaneous use of signs and speech has the disadvantage of being noxious to speech, to lip reading, and to the precision of ideas, the purely oral method must be preferred.

These resolutions were enforced in all European countries, but in the United States Edward Gallaudet opposed Bell and managed to restrict their application. Not only did he maintain a school system using the combined oral-manual method, but he was also able to educate teachers of the deaf in this method at the National Deaf Mute College in Washington, DC; that school was to become the present Gallaudet College. From that time on, the opposition between Bell and Gallaudet increased. It led to the formation of two rival groups of schools and teachers: the exclusively oral and the combined oral-manual.

In Europe, oral education continued to prevail, unchallenged, during more than half of the twentieth century. After World War II, progress in electroacoustic technology gave new impetus to oralism. Hopes arose that auditory training with sophisticated apparatus and efficient individual hearing aids combined with lip reading would enable hearing-impaired children to develop their speech skills, both receptively and expressively, to a much larger extent then previously. Whetnall and Fry in London (1964) and the John Tracy Clinic in Los Angeles (Thielman, 1970), among many others, considered that early intervention would allow most deaf children to attend ordinary schools for the normally hearing or special units attached to those schools. The integration—or mainstreaming—movement that they initiated progressively gathered more and more strength in Great Britain than in the United States and continental Europe.

It is generally accepted today that many hearing-impaired children, with early education, proper hearing aid fitting, and continued support, can successfully be educated with the normally hearing (Nix, 1976; Webster & Ellwood, 1985). While the degree of hearing loss is an important factor in determining which hearing-impaired children can be mainstreamed, it is generally recognized that this factor is by no means decisive in itself. Some profoundly deaf children can succeed in ordinary schools, while others with more residual hearing may not be able to do so (Périer et al., 1980). There is, therefore, no consensus concerning the proportion of deaf and hard-of-hearing children that should be integrated. The present situation varies greatly among nations. In some such as Italy, the official policy is that all handicapped children should be mainstreamed. Other countries, like West Germany, maintain separate special school systems for the profoundly deaf and the hard of hearing, so that even the majority of the latter are not educated with the normally hearing. Several developing countries where special education has yet to be organized view mainstreaming as a tempting alternative to the building and maintaining of special schools. Caution against the excesses of such a trend is voiced by numerous educators of the deaf, who argue that most of the profoundly deaf will continue to need special education. The pros and cons of mainstreaming have been aptly described by Meadow (1980), who argues that the options should carefully be weighed for each child.

Sign language interpretation services for the deaf have been developed primarily in the United States to assist the deaf in all circumstances in which they may benefit from them. Legal provisions ensuring that a deaf child has the right to the best possible education has made it possible in some cases to provide support services in schools or universities, allowing more deaf children and students to be mainstreamed than was formerly possible. In addition to sign language interpretation, other forms of interpretation are beginning to be developed in some countries: oral interpretation and oral interpretation with cued speech.

While the trend toward mainstream education has steadily increased over the years, the hope that early speech and hearing training would solve the language and education difficulties of most hearing-impaired children has proved overly optimistic. Several studies, among them Conrad's (1979), demonstrated that whatever method was used, whether oral or manual, the majority of deaf school graduates reached a mean reading age equivalent only to that of 9- to 10-year-old hearing children. Thus, the existing methods had not prevented relative failure to develop good command of the societal language (English in this case), even in its written form. Other studies reviewed by Quigley & Kretschmer (1982) showed that deaf children of deaf parents who had had signs as their first language were not disadvantaged in the oral skills and had slightly but significantly better gradings in overall language evaluation when compared with deaf children of hearing parents.

These results, together with the rehabilitation of sign language, were largely instrumental in the birth and development of the total communication (TC) philosophy. This, as defined by Denton (1970), is the right of a deaf child to learn to use all forms of communication available to develop language competence. This includes the full spectrum: child-devised gestures, speech, formal sign language, finger spelling, speech reading, reading, writing, as well as any other methods that may be developed in the future. Every deaf child should also be provided with the opportunity to learn to use any remnant of residual hearing he or she may have by employing the best possible electronic equipment for amplifying sound. Many schools in the United States, and a growing number throughout the world, have adhered to the principle of TC, although there are various interpretations of its meaning. More and more infant programs throughout the world are using it from the earliest age; many are urging parents to learn to communicate with their children through signs in addition to speech. Such combination of signs and speech has been termed bimodal communication by Schlesinger (1978).

Several types of manual aids other than signs are used to facilitate the reception or the production of spoken language. While many educators are using these or some form of bimodal communication for the profoundly deaf, others continue to use exclusively oral methods.

Table 1 is an attempt at classification of the methods currently used. It must be borne in mind, however, that various combinations are possible; some techniques developed within the framework of a given method are applicable in other contexts. For instance, in some Belgian centers, cued speech (3.1) is used in combination with bimodal communication (4.1) and with the verbo-tonal method (1). Five groups can be distinguished: auditory, oral, oral plus manual aids, combined, and manual.

1. *Auditory unisensory or acoupedic* methods rely on auditory training to develop spoken language. Speech reading is either not encouraged or suppressed during training periods (Pollack, 1964). In the verbo-tonal method (Guberina, Skaric, & Zaga, 1972), perception of acoustic features through the tactile sense is used in addition to hearing. The auditory global approach of Calvert and Silverman (1975) stands at the margin between the acoupedic and the oral-aural, since

"the primary, although not always the exclusive, channel for speech development is auditory."

2. *Oral also called oral-aural* (Simmons-Martin, 1972). Auditory perception and speech reading are used as well as other modalities, but signs are excluded. Ling (1976) describes systematic speech development procedure primarily based on audition though not neglecting tactile and visual support, as in Calvert and Silverman's multisensory approach, used when the auditory global is not sufficient. Van Uden's maternal reflective method (1970) insists on the necessity of active oral-aural dialogue and natural prosody.

3.1 *Oral-aural plus lip-reading complements.* In cued speech (Cornett, 1967) and related systems, the oral-aural approach is combined with a system of hand shapes executed near the mouth, synchronously with speech. The hand brings only that part of the information that is not supplied by lip reading. The combination of this information allows the deaf child to unequivocally identify by sight the speech sounds and syllables that the hearing identify through the ear (Nicholls & Ling, 1982; Périer et al., 1986).

3.2 *Oral-aural plus manual representation of phonemes.* In the French Borel-Maisonny method (1979), and in the German Phonembestimmte Manual System (PMS) of Schulte (1974), the oral-aural methodology is aided by contrived gestures that correspond to some of the characteristics of speech sounds and thus help in their identification and production. The gestures bring independent information that is not linked to lip reading.

3.3 *Oral-aural plus finger spelling.* These are the U.S. Rochester (Scouten, 1942) and U.S.S.R. neo-oralism (Morkovin, 1960) methods. Finger spelling is executed by the teacher simultaneously with speech; the child is asked to accompany his or her own speech by finger spelling. Since the latter is a representation of written language, reading and writing are strongly emphasized.

4.1 *Unilingual bimodal communication or simultaneous method.* One language, that of the hearing society and of most deaf children's parents, is simultaneously expressed in speech and signs. There are numerous varieties of signed representations of spoken language. Some are close to the regional sign language of the deaf, differing mostly in word order; others use additional signs to convey syntactical and morphological information; still others are wholly contrived (Crystal & Craig, 1978).

4.2 *Bilingual bimodal communication.* Spoken language in an oral-aural approach is used in certain situations by hearing persons, while sign language is used in other situations by deaf and hearing persons. In early education, it is often considered acceptable for hearing parents who have not yet mastered sign language to use those signs they have learned in combination with their spoken language (Bouvet, 1981; Erting, 1978).

5. *Visual unisensory communication by sign language alone.* While no educators advocate that deaf children should not learn the major societal language, a few favor the ex-

Table 1 Classifications of methods used in deaf education

1. Auditory		Auditory unisensory or acoupedic
2. Oral		Oral-aural, multisensory
3. Oral + Manual Aids	3.1	Oral-aural + lip-reading complements
	3.2	Oral-aural + manual representation of phonemes
	3.3	Oral-aural + finger spelling
4. Combined	4.1	Unilingual bimodal communication or simultaneous method
	4.2	Bilingual bimodal communication
5. Manual		Visual unisensory communication by sign language alone

clusive use of sign language for early education. Only when sign language is firmly established as a first language is the majority's societal language taught as a second language (Ahlgren, 1980). In some programs, teaching is first done in the written form, spoken language being delayed (Mali & Rickli, 1983).

The status of deaf education in 1985 was characterized by a great vitality and a large diversity, although the antagonism between methods has somewhat abated. The oral-manual controversy is not as bitter as before, with most people on each side now recognizing the merits of the other (Tervoort, 1982a, 1982b). The question is not so much of a choice between exclusively oral and combined oral-manual methods as of deciding for whom, when, how, and how much each modality should be used. General agreement exists on the paramount importance of early detection, assessment, and intervention, including proper hearing aid fitting and maintenance. The role of parents as the first educators of their deaf children, already stressed by Whetnall and Fry and the John Tracy Clinic, is widely recognized (UNESCO, 1985). Their full participation is essential for the success of any method. Parents should, therefore, be thoroughly informed about the different programs available so that they can make their own choices. The fact that more than 90 percent of deaf children's parents are normally hearing must be taken into account in any decision about education policy. Whichever method is adopted, and whether priority is given to speech or sign, educators of today all have common goals: to enable deaf children to acquire the mastery of language needed to assert their personalities and attain full accomplishment; to bring deaf children to complete literacy, through which they will be able to reach the degree of academic achievement corresponding to their intellectual capacities and personal motivation.

REFERENCES

Ahlgren, E. (1980). *The sign language group in Stockholm*. In E. Ahlgren & Bengman (Eds.), Papers from the first international symposium on the sign language research (pp. 3–7). Leksand.

Borel-Maisonny, S. (1979). *Absence d'expression verbale*. Paris: A.R.P.L.O.E.

Bouvet, D. (1981). *La Parole de l'enfant sourd*. Paris: Presses Universitaires de France, Collection Le Fil Rouge.

Calvert, D. R., & Silverman, S. R. (1975). *Speech and deafness: A text for learning and teaching*. Washington, DC: A. G. Bell Association.

Conrad, R. (1979). *The deaf school child*. London: Harper & Row.

Cornett, R. O. (1967). Cued speech. *American Annals of the Deaf, 112,* 3–13.

Crystal, D., & Craig, E. (1978). Contrived sign language. In I. M. Schlesinger & L. Namir (Eds.), *Sign language of the deaf* (pp. 141–168). New York: Academic.

Denton, D. (1970). *Remarks in support of a system of total communication for deaf children*. Communication Symposium. Frederick, MD: Maryland School for the Deaf.

Erting, C. (1978). Language policy and deaf ethnicity in the United States. *Sign Language Studies, 19,* 139–152.

Guberina, P., Skaric, I., & Zaga, B. (1972). *Case studies in the use of restricted bands of frequencies in auditory rehabilitation of the deaf*. Zagreb, Yugoslavia: Institute of Phonetics Faculty of Arts.

Ling, D. (1976). *Speech and the hearing-impaired child: Theory and practice*. Washington, DC: A. G. Bell Association.

Malé, A., & Rickli, F. (1983). *Introduction au bilinguisme: Langue des signes française—français oral, à l'école de Montbrillant*. Geneva, Switzerland: Départment de l'Instruction Publique.

Moores, D. F. (1978). *Educating the deaf: Psychology, principles, and practices*. Boston: Houghton Mifflin.

Morkovin, B. (1960). Experiment in teaching deaf preschool children in the Soviet Union. *Volta Review, 62,* 260–268.

Nicholls, G. H., & Ling, D. (1982). Cued speech and the reception of spoken language. *Journal of Speech and Hearing Research, 25,* 262–269.

Nix, G. (1976). *Mainstream education for hearing impaired children and youth*. New York: Grune & Stratton.

Périer, O., Capouillez, J. M., & Paulissen, D. (1980). The relationship between the degree of auditory deficiency and the possibility of successful mainstreaming in schools for hearing children. In H. Hartmann (Ed.), *1st International Congress of the Hard of Hearing* (pp. 348–353). Hamburg: Deutscher Schwerhorigenbund.

Périer, O., Charlier, B., Hage, C., & Alegria, J. (1986). Evaluation of the effects of prolonged cued speech practice upon the reception and internal processing of spoken language. *Proceedings of the 1985 International Congress of Educators of the Deaf*. Manchester, England.

Pollack, D. (1964). Acoupedics: An unisensory approach to auditory training. *Volta Review, 66,* 400–409.

Quigley, S. P., & Kretschmer, R. F. (1982). *The education of deaf children: Issues, theory and practice*. London: Arnold.

Schlesinger, H. S. (1978). The acquisition of bimodal language. In I. M. Schlesinger & L. Namir (Eds.), *Sign language of the deaf*. New York: Academic.

Schulte, K. (1974). *The phonemetransmitting manual system* (PMS). Heidelberg: Julius Verlag.

Scouten, E. (1942). *A revaluation of the Rochester method*. Rochester, NY: Rochester School for the Deaf.

Simmons-Martin, A. (1972). The oral/aural procedure: Theoretical basis and rationale. *Volta Review, 74,* 541–551.

Tervoort, B. T. (1982a). Communication and the deaf. *Proceedings of the International Congress on Education of the Deaf* (pp. 219–229). Heidelberg: Julius Verlag.

Tervoort, B. T. (1982b). The future: Oralism versus manualism? *Proceedings of the International Congress on Education of the Deaf* (pp. 544–547). Heidelberg: Julius Verlag.

Thielman, V. (1970). John Tracy Clinic correspondence course for parents of preschool deaf children. *Proceedings of the International Congress on Education of the Deaf* (pp. 156–158). Stockholm.

UNESCO. (1985). *Consultation on alternative approaches for the education of the deaf*. Paris: UNESCO.

Van Uden, A. (1970). New realizations in the light of the pure oral method. *Volta Review, 72,* 524–536.

Webster, A., & Ellwood, J. (1985). *The hearing-impaired child in the ordinary school.* London: Croom Helm.

Whetnall, E., & Fry, D. (1964). *The deaf child.* Springfield, IL: Thomas.

Olivier Périer
*Université Libre de Bruxelles
Centre Comprendre et Parler,
Belgium*

AMERICAN SIGN LANGUAGE
DEAF
FINGERSPELLING
TOTAL COMMUNICATION

DEAF, INTERPRETERS FOR

See INTERPRETERS FOR THE DEAF.

DEAN-WOODCOCK NEUROPSYCHOLOGICAL BATTERY

The Dean-Woodcock Neuropsychological Battery (DWNB; Dean & Woodcock, 2003) is a comprehensive battery that assesses individuals' emotional, sensory, and motor functioning. The DWNB consists of the Dean-Woodcock Sensory-Motor Battery, the Dean-Woodcock Structured Neuropsychological Interview, and the Dean-Woodcock Emotional Status Examination. The DWNB is designed to be administered to individuals ages 4 through 80 (and older). The entire DWNB takes approximately 1 hour and 45 minutes to administer. The Dean-Woodcock Sensory-Motor Battery takes 30 to 45 minutes to administer, and the Structured Neuropsychological Interview and Emotional Status Examination each take 30 minutes. The latter two may be given before or after the Sensory-Motor Battery.

During the Structured Neuropsychological Interview, the examinee is asked questions about his or her medical and family background. The Emotional Status Examination includes signs and symptoms of major disorders. The Sensory-Motor Battery is composed of 18 subtests divided into four major areas: Sensory Tests, Tactile Tests, Subcortical Motor Tests, and Cortical Motor Tests. The DWNB contains an Examiners Manual, Stimulus Book, and Manipulatives Kit. The DWNB is easily transported, including Record Forms in its carrying case.

Norms for the Dean-Woodcock Sensory Motor Battery are based on a sample of 1,011 individuals that ranged in age from 4 to 80 years. The sample was representative of the U.S. population with respect to sex, race, age, and handedness according to the 2000 Census. Individuals with a history of psychiatric, neurological, or orthopedic disorders were excluded, as were those with a history of sensory motor impairment and/or head injury. Studies indicated that the Sensory Motor Battery was both reliable and valid.

Many of the tests and procedures are not new; rather the battery is a compilation of neuropsychological measures that have been demonstrated as having high clinical utility. What sets this battery apart is the standard administration procedures and normative sample base (Dean & Woodcock, 2003).

REFERENCES

Dean, R. S., & Woodcock, R. W. (2003). *Examiner's manual: Dean-Woodcock Neuropsychological Battery.* Itasca, IL: Riverside Publishing.

Dean, R. S., & Woodcock, R. W. (2003). *Dean-Woodcock Neuropsychological Battery.* Itasca, IL: Riverside Publishing.

Ron Dumont
Fairleigh Dickinson University

John O. Willis
Rivier College

NEUROPSYCHOLOGY

DEBORAH P. v. TURLINGTON

Deborah P. v. Turlington (1979) is the federal district court case that struck down the competency testing program requirements for high-school graduation in the state of Florida. Deborah P. represented the class of all students in the state who were in danger of failing the test, including students of all ethnic backgrounds. The federal district court found that the competency testing program was unconstitutional for two reasons. The program had failed to provide students with adequate notice of the changes in requirements for a diploma, and the program was held to be racially discriminatory under the Fourteenth Amendment. According to the court, the competency testing program tended to perpetuate preexisting patterns of racial discrimination within the Florida school system. Children in special education programs were not specifically addressed in *Deborah P.,* however, similar issues may be raised if special education students are required to pass competency tests or denied diplomas on the basis of testing programs that discriminate on the basis of race or handicapping condition.

REFERENCE

Deborah P. v. Turlington. (1979). #78-892-CIV-T-C, U.S. District Court, Middle District, Tampa Division, July 12 (slip opinion).

CECIL R. REYNOLDS
Texas A&M University
First edition

KIMBERLEY APPLEQUIST
*University of Colorado at
Colorado Springs*
Third edition

DECROLY, OVIDE (1871–1932)

Ovide Decroly, a Belgian physician whose hospital work brought him into contact with many handicapped children, reasoned that the best treatment for such children would be a sound educational program. He established a special school for "the retarded and abnormal" in 1901. A few years later, he founded a school for normal children, where he demonstrated that the methods he was using successfully with handicapped children were equally effective with the nonhandicapped.

Decroly's educational methods were unique. The cornerstone of his method was what he called the "center of interest." Centers of interest were developed around four basic needs: food, protection from the elements, defense against common dangers, and work. Emphasis was placed on learning through activities that grow out of the interests and needs of the students. As much as a year's study could grow out of one topic or theme.

Decroly's work profoundly influenced the European concept of education for both normal and handicapped children. Many of his ideas were similar to those of John Dewey, but Decroly was more a practitioner than a philosopher and his foremost contribution was the establishment of schools that served as models of education based on the needs of children.

REFERENCES

Hamaide, A. (1924). *The Decroly class.* New York: Dutton.

Kajava, K. (1951). *The traditional European school and some recent experiments in the new education.* Doctoral dissertation. New York: Columbia University.

PAUL IRVINE
Katonah, New York

DEINSTITUTIONALIZATION

Deinstitutionalization has been a movement based on the principles of normalization. Individuals with disabilities, mostly the retarded and emotionally disabled, have been moved out of institutions into alternative community living arrangements. Wolfensberger (1972), one of the most outspoken advocates of both deinstitutionalization and normalization, maintained that normalization referred not to treatment but to services, situations, and attitudes that would bring about humane care for the disabled. The practice called for small, community-based group homes that permitted residents to participate in local activities and be closer to their families as opposed to long-term, total life care in institutions. Community residential facilities were small in size, house an equally small number of persons, and were meant to be either a permanent residence or a transitional training residence for retarded adults. These facilities ranged in design from loosely supervised apartments to group homes with live-in house parents (Baker, Seltzer, & Seltzer, 1977).

The trend toward deinstitutionalization of retarded persons began approximately 45 years ago when President Kennedy remarked that the practice of institutionalized segregation from the rest of society was immoral. In 1974 President Nixon announced the goal of returning half of all institutionalized retarded individuals to community settings (Braddock, 1977). The basic construct for the deinstitutionalization movement included: (1) the creation and maintenance of environments that did not impose excessive restrictions on disabled persons; (2) the creation of arrangements that brought persons as close as possible to the social and cultural mainstream; and (3) guaranteed that the human and legal rights of disabled citizens were protected (Neufeld, 1979, p. 115).

Numerous studies have been conducted over the past 45 years to assess outcomes for individuals who were a part of deinstitutionalization. The results of these studies are mixed. Many studies cite improvement in quality of life, adaptive behavior skills, and self-care skills (Fine, 1990; Larsen & Lakin, 1989; Lord & Pedlar, 1991).

Other studies present a more negative outcome, with deinstitutionalized mentally retarded individuals being overrepresented in the homeless (Roleff, 1996). Indeed, Craig and Paterson (1988) cited lack of long-term support for mentally ill individuals, and estimated that there are 300,000 mentally ill homeless persons in the United States. Perhaps the most disturbing of studies regarding deinstitutionalization is by Strauss and Kastner. In 1996 they compared risk-adjusted odds of mortality of people with mental retardation living in institutions or the community from 1980 to 1992 in California. It was estimated that the mortality was 72 percent higher in the community. It was suggested that the reason for the difference was the availability and adherence to health care (Strauss & Kastner, 1996).

For children, deinstitutionalization has had mixed results. Many children return to their families and research suggests that one-third will return to state schools. However, daily living skills training and vocational training are widely available, and many children who were origi-nally placed in contained classrooms are included in the mainstream in less than a year (Laconia State School, 1987).

In summary, outcome studies for deinstitutionalization indicate that many individuals with mental retardation achieve much better self-help and daily living skills when living in the community. However, many do not receive the community support or health care that is necessary for day-to-day living. Indeed, many individuals who are psychiatri-cally disabled may live in homeless conditions.

For deinstitutionalization to produce effective results, several issues should be considered. Adequate alternatives that are properly designed, properly maintained, and prop-erly supervised should be developed. In addition, compre-hensive evaluations of the individual's ability to succeed in a community-based facility should be made.

REFERENCES

Baker, B. L., Seltzer, G. B., & Seltzer, M. M. (1977). *As close as possible. Community residences for retarded adults.* Boston: Little, Brown.

Braddock, D. (1977). *Opening closed doors: The deinstitutionaliza-tion of disabled individuals.* Reston, VA: Council of Exceptional Children.

Craig, R. T., & Paterson, A. (1988). The homeless mentally ill; No longer out of sight and out of mind. *State Legislative Report, 13,* 30. National Conference of State Legislatures, Denver, CO.

Fine, M. (1990). Changes in adaptive behavior of older adults with mental retardation following deinstitutionalization. *American Journal on Mental Retardation, 94,* 6, 661–668.

Laconia State School. (1987). Deinstitutionalization of minors with mental retardation. *Abstract X: Research & Resources on Special Education.* Reston, VA: ERIC Clearinghouse on Handicapped and Gifted Children.

Larson, S. A., & Lakin, C. (1989). Deinstitutionalization of persons with mental retardation; The impact on daily living skills. *Policy Research Brief, 1,* 1.

Lord, J., & Pedlar, A. (1991). Life in the community: Four years after closure of an institution. *Mental Retardation, 29*(4), 213–221.

Roleff, T. L. (1996). *The homeless: Opposing viewpoints.* San Diego, CA: Greenhaven Press.

Strauss, D., & Kastner, T. A. (1996). Comparative mortality of peo-ple with mental retardation in institutions and the community. *American Journal on Mental Retardation, 101*(1), 26–40.

Neufeld, G. R. (1979). Deinstitutionalization procedures. In R. Wiegerink & J. W. Pelosi (Eds.), *Developmental disabilities: The DD movement* (pp. 115–126). Baltimore: Brookes.

Wolfensberger, W. (1972). *The principle of normalization in hu-man services.* Toronto, Ontario: National Institute on Mental Retardation.

CECELIA STEPPE-JONES
*North Carolina Central
University*
First edition

ELAINE FLETCHER-JANZEN
*University of Colorado at
Colorado Springs*
Second edition

COMMUNITY-BASED SERVICES
NORMALIZATION
REHABILITATION

DELACATO, CARL H. (1923–   )

Carl H. Delacato earned his BS in Education from West Chester State College in 1945. He continued his education, obtaining the MS in 1948 and EdD in 1952 from the Univer-sity of Pennsylvania. From 1945 to 1964, he was assistant headmaster at Chestnut Hill Academy in Philadelphia, and in 1948, he founded and directed the Chestnut Hill Reading Clinic. During his distinguished career, he has served as associate director and instructor at the Institutes for the Achievement of Human Potential, Philadelphia, Pennsylva-nia (1953–1973); professor and chairman of the Department of Developmental Education, University of Plano, Plano, Texas; and director of the Institute for Rehabilitation of the Brain Injured, Morton, Pennsylvania (1974–1989).

Delacato (1968) has focused his study on neurological or-ganization and patterning. The Doman-Delacato Treatment Method for children with neurological disabilities, developed by Delacato and Glenn Doman, is a remedy based on the neurological organization of the individual. Neurological organization is defined by Delacato as a physiologically optimum condition existing uniquely and most completely in man, resulting from total, uninterrupted ontogenetic development. Delacato discovered that learning, behav-ioral, and motor disorders were disabilities that occurred along a continuum of severity as a result of brain injury or

Carl H. Delacato

incomplete neural development. Delacato contends that assessment and modification of neurological organization can be utilized for the diagnosis, treatment, and prevention of language problems.

Delacato's numerous awards include the Distinguished Alumnus award of West Chester College (1978), the Gold Medal Honor of Brazil (1960), and the first Trailblazer award of the University of Plano (1966). His major publications include *The Diagnosis and Treatment of Speech* (1968), *Neurological Organization and Reading* (1966), *A New Start for the Child with Reading Problems* (1970), and *The Ultimate Stranger: The Autistic Child* (1974). In addition, Delacato has contributed numerous articles on rehabilitation and education to professional journals, and has served as editor of *American Lectures in Education and Learning*.

REFERENCES

Delacato, C. H. (1966). *Neurological organization and reading.* Springfield, IL: Thomas.

Delacato, C. H. (1968). *The diagnosis and treatment of speech and reading problems.* Springfield, IL: Thomas.

Delacato, C. H. (1982). *A new start for the child with reading problems: A manual for parents* (Rev. ed.). Morton, PA: Morton.

Delacato, C. H. (1984). *The ultimate stranger: The autistic child.* Novato, CA: Arena.

ELIZABETH JONES
Texas A&M University
First edition

TAMARA J. MARTIN
*The University of Texas of the
   Permian Basin*
Second edition

JESSI K. WHEATLEY
*Falcon School District 49,
   Colorado Springs, Colorado*
Third edition

DELAYED LANGUAGE

See LANGUAGE DELAYS.

DE LEON, PEDRO

See PONCE DE LEON, PEDRO DE.

DE L'EPÉE, ABBÉ CHARLES MICHEL (1712–1789)

Abbé Charles Michel de l'Epée founded in Paris in 1755 the first public school for the deaf, the *Institution Natio-*

Abbé Charles Michel De l'Epée

nale des Sourds Muets. The Abeé developed a systematic language of signs based on the earlier work of Jacob Rodrigues Pereire. His system of signs was the basis of the instructional system in the United States' first school for the deaf, the American School for the Deaf. It is still in use today in modified form.

REFERENCE

Lane, H. (1984). *When the mind hears.* New York: Random House.

PAUL IRVINE
Katonah, New York

DELINQUENCY, HANDICAPPING CONDITIONS AND

It has been estimated that between 30 percent and 70 percent of juvenile offenders have handicapping conditions that require special education services (EDJJ, 2006; OJJDP, 1998). This number may be low because many youths are identified with a handicapping condition before their incarceration (Perryman, DiGangi, & Rutherford, 1989). In addition, it is estimated that 22 percent of incarcerated youth have significant mental health problems (OJJDP, 1998). Estimates of prevalence of handicapping conditions among juvenile delinquents vary dramatically (Crawford, 1982; Murphy, 1986; Nelson & Rutherford, 1989; OJJDP, 1998). These disparities largely can be attributed to methodological inconsistencies in identification of the major handicapping conditions. Further methodological inconsistencies exist in the defining of juvenile delinquency. The criteria for identifying juvenile delinquents are not uniform across state departments of correction (Murphy, 1986). Indeed, differential diagnosis of handicapping conditions as well as juvenile delinquency appear, in part, to be a state phenomenon.

Though tenuous, the accumulated body of research indicates that the prevalence of handicapping conditions among juvenile delinquents is disproportionate to that reported in nondelinquent populations (Crawford, 1982; Keiltz & Dunivant, 1986; Murphy, 1986; OJJDP, 1998). However, the actual prevalence of the major handicaps among juvenile delinquents is difficult to establish. This difficulty can be attributed to the lack of uniform procedures in identifying handicapping conditions and juvenile delinquency. These findings have important implications concerning the identification and servicing of delinquents with disabilities under the provision of the Individuals with Disabilities Education Improvement Act (IDEIA; 2004) and its predecessor in 1975. Many states were slow to provide special education services to incarcerated youth, which resulted in more than 20 class action lawsuits involving special education over the years. Unfortunately, few of the cases went to court; therefore, very few published judicial opinions exist (OJJDP, 1998). The Office of Juvenile Justice and Delinquency Prevention (OJJDP) has advocated for stronger links between correctional facilities and school districts, fiscal autonomy for cost-per-pupil budgeting, adherence to the standards for correctional education programs put out by the Correctional Education Association, and avoidance of litigation.

Leone (1991) suggests that the social disadvantages and characteristics associated with juvenile delinquents may lead to increased likelihood of contact with the criminal justice system. Although there is a correlation between poor social and conflict resolution skills and delinquent behavior, no causality can be inferred. Several studies are available that address the effectiveness of special education programs in corrections. Bachara and Zaba (1978) found that the juvenile offenders who were offered remediation in the form of special education, tutoring, or perceptual-motor training exhibited a significantly lower recidivism rate than those who were not offered these programs (Karcz, 1987). Other researchers of the juvenile delinquent population have found that there exists an overall impoverishment of adaptive skill behaviors for this population (Baerman & Siegal, 1976). Other studies (Forbes, 1991; Grande & Koorland, 1988) suggest that the uniqueness of the correctional setting realizes special problems with staff training, special educator training for correctional settings, curriculum design, and interagency cooperation.

Several successful approaches to assisting special education students who are incarcerated utilize research-based reading instruction (Brunner, 1993), cite cooperative learning techniques as being successful with this population (Ragan, 1993), and have found support for Team-Assisted Individualization (TAI; Salend & Washin, 1988).

OJJDP (1998) has suggested the following recommendations to parents or guardians of incarcerated youth who have handicapping conditions:

Discuss the need for appropriate services at the facility with:
Teachers and tutors at the facility
A facility administrator
A special education attorney in the area or a law school clinical program
A professor of education
Parents
Obtain the Correctional Education Association standards on correctional education programs.
Review the facility's educational standards.
Establish a committee of educators, advocates, and administrators to:
Ensure that IEPs are conducted in a timely fashion by qualified personnel.
Revise the educational standards of the facility.
Simplify the eligibility determination for special education services.
Ensure that the facility has qualified teachers.
Involve local advocacy groups that support children and persons with disabilities.
Contact an attorney who can assist you in bringing litigation against the facility if education services not improve.

The National Center on Education, Disability, and Juvenile Justice (EDJJ) is funded by the Office of Special Education Programs. EDJJ has produced a readily available CD-ROM, *Meeting the Educational Needs of Students with Disabilities in Short-Term Detention Facilities,* which provides an overview of the issues and strategies involved in the delivery of special education and related services in jails and detention centers. The CD will be most useful to educators, administrators, and policymakers who work with this population of students, and is designed as a guide for the implementation of basic components of special education programs and practices in short-term detention facilities. The procedures and practices described on the CD are based on available research, best practice, and the experiences of the authors. It can be obtained from the EDJJ web site at http://www.edjj.org.

REFERENCES

Bachara, G. H., & Zaba, J. N. (1978). Learning disabilities and juvenile delinquency. *Journal of Learning Disabilities, 11,* 58–62.

Berman, A., & Siegal, A. (1976). Adaptive and learning skills in juvenile delinquents: A neuropsychological analysis. *Journal of Learning Disabilities, 9,* 51–53.

Brunner, M. (1993). *Reduced recidivism and increased employment opportunity through research-based reading instruction.* Clearinghouse No. CS011379. Washington, DC: U.S. Department of Justice.

Crawford, D. (1982). *Prevalence of handicapped juveniles in the justice system: A study of the literature.* Phoenix, AZ: Research & Development Training Institutes.

Forbes, M. A. (1991). Special education in juvenile correctional facilities: A literature review. *Journal of Correctional Education, 42*(1), 31–35.

Grande, C. G., & Koorland, M. A. (1988). A complex issue: Special education in corrections. *Children and Youth Services Review, 10*(4), 345–350.

Karcz, S. A. (1987). Delinquency and special education. In C. R. Reynolds & Lester Mann (Eds.), *Encyclopedia of special education* (1st ed.). New York: Wiley.

Keiltz, I., & Duvinant, N. (1986). The relationship between learning disability and juvenile delinquency: Current state of knowledge. *Remedial & Special Education, 7*(3), 18–26.

Leone, P. E. (1991). *Juvenile corrections and the exceptional student.* (ERIC Digest No. E509)

Murphy, D. A. (1986). The prevalence of handicapping conditions among juvenile delinquents. *Remedial and Special Education, 7*, 7–17.

National Center on Education, Disability, and Juvenile Justice (EDJJ). (2006). Retrieved January 19, 2006, from http://www.edjj.org

Nelson, C. M., & Rutherford, R. B. (1989). *Impact of the correctional special education training (C / SET) project on correctional special education.* Paper presented at the CEC/CCBD National Topical Conference on Behavior Disorders, Charlotte, NC.

Office of Juvenile Justice and Delinquency Prevention (OJJDP). (1998). *Educational advocacy for youth with disabilities. Beyond the walls: Improving conditions of confinement for youth in custody.* Rockville, MD: Juvenile Justice Clearing House.

Perryman, P., DiGangi, S. A., & Rutherford, R. B. (1989). *Recidivism of handicapped and nonhandicapped juvenile offenders: An exploratory analysis.* Paper presented at the Learning Handicapped Offender Conference, Pittsburgh, PA.

Ragan, P. E. (1993). Cooperative learning can work in residential care settings. *Teaching Exceptional Children, 25*(2), 48–51.

Salend, S. J., & Washin, B. (1988). Team-assisted individualization with handicapped adjudicated youth. *Exceptional Children, 55*(2), 174–180.

HARRISON C. STANTON
Las Vegas, Nevada
First edition

ELAINE FLETCHER-JANZEN
*University of Colorado at
Colorado Springs*
Second edition

**JUVENILE DELINQUENCY
LEARNING DISABILITIES**

DELIS-KAPLAN EXECUTIVE FUNCTION SYSTEM

The Delis-Kaplan Executive Function System (D-KEFS; Delis, Kaplan, & Kramer, 2001) is a comprehensive assessment of higher-level thinking and cognitive flexibility, key components of executive functions believed to be mediated primarily by the frontal lobe. It is the first nationally standardized set of tests to evaluate higher-level cognitive functions in both children and adults, ages 8 through 89 years. There are two forms available: The Standard Record Forms include nine D-KEFS tests.

Sorting Test assesses problem-solving, verbal and spatial concept formation, and flexibility of thinking on a conceptual task.

Trail Making Test assesses flexibility of thinking on a visual-motor task.

Verbal Fluency Test assesses fluent productivity in the verbal domain.

Design Fluency Test assesses fluent productivity in the spatial domain.

Color-World Interference Test assesses verbal inhibition.

Tower Test assesses planning and reasoning in the spatial modality as well as impulsivity.

20 Questions Test assesses hypothesis testing, verbal and abstract thinking, and impulsivity.

Word Context Test assesses deductive reasoning and verbal abstract thinking.

Proverb Test assesses metaphorical thinking and the ability to generate versus comprehend abstract thought.

The Alternate Record Forms include alternate versions of the Sorting, Verbal Fluency, and 20 Questions Tests, the three tests most susceptible to practice effects. An alternate set of Sorting Cards is also available.

The D-KEFS is individually administered, and its game-like format is designed to be interesting and engaging for examinees, encouraging optimal performance without providing "right/wrong" feedback that can create frustration for some examinees. It can be administered as a complete set in 90 minutes, or individual tests can be administered in varying time frames. The complete testing kit includes an examiner's manual that provides clear instructions for administration and interpretation, as well as guidance for choosing appropriate subtests if the entire battery is not being administered. The D-KEFS can either be hand scored or scored using the D-KEFS Scoring Assistant, which is convenient and dramatically reduces scoring time. The nine D-KEFS subtests can either be recorded and scored as a complete battery or as individual subtests. With this software, the score reports can be produced, viewed, and printed on a PC in either tabular or graphic format.

The national standardization of the D-KEFS (1998–2000) included over 1,700 children and adults, from ages 8 to 89 years, demographically and regionally matched with the U.S. population. D-KEFS is correlated with the Wechsler Abbreviated Scale of Intelligence (WASI) and the California

Verbal Learning Tests–Second Edition (CVL T-II), providing information concerning the role of intellectual ability and memory on D-KEFS performance. No factor analyses were done.

Reliability scores for the D-KEFS are generally below .80, the minimum value that has been suggested for both internal consistency and test-retest reliability. Only 53 of the 316 reliability values presented (17 percent) met this standard. The reliability may be lowered by constricted ranges of scores among normal participants. Alternatively, several of the tests are fairly short, which may adversely affect reliability and sensitivity. Evidence regarding validity is not strong. Data are presented for two small clinical groups that are of questionable usefulness in demonstrating specific deficits in executive functions.

REFERENCES AND ADDITIONAL INFORMATION

Delis, D. C., Kaplan, E., & Kramer, J. H. (2001). *Delis-Kaplan Executive Function System: Examiner's manual.* San Antonio, TX: Psychological Corporation.

Delis, D. C., Kramer, J. H., & Kaplan, E. (2004 Reliability and validity of the Delis-Kaplan Executive Function System: An update. *Journal of the International Neuropsychological Society, 10,* 301–303.

Plake, B. S., Impara, J. C., & Spies, R. A. (Eds.). (2003). *The fifteenth mental measurements yearbook.* Lincoln, NE: Buros Institute of Mental Measurements.

Schmidt, M. (2003). Hit or miss? Insight into executive functions: Review of Delis-Kaplan Executive Function System—2001. *Journal of International Neuropsychological Society, 9,* 960–965.

RON DUMONT
Fairleigh-Dickinson University

JOHN O. WILLIS
Rivier College

DE LORENZO, MARIA E. G. E. (1927–   )

Maria E. De Lorenzo is a noted Uruguayan special educator. She obtained her BA in education at Teacher's College, Montevideo, Uruguay (1941), and her MA in clinical psychology at the University of Michigan, Ann Arbor (1948). She served as director of School N.1 for mentally retarded children (1949–1967) and as a member of the National Board of Elementary Education in Uruguay from 1967 to 1972. From 1966 to the present, De Lorenzo has been chief of the Mental Retardation Unit of the Inter-American Children's Institute, a specialized agency of the Organization of American States.

She frequently acts as a consultant for numerous international organizations such as the United Nations, the Organization of American States, Partners of the Americas, the President's Committee on Mental Retardation (U.S.), and the International League of Societies for Persons with Mental Handicaps. Since 1967, De Lorenzo has been a member of various U.N. organizations, among them the World Health Organization, U.N. Educational, Scientific, and Cultural Organization, and U.N. International Children's Emergency Fund. She is a member of numerous professional associations and of the editorial boards of the *International Journal of Rehabilitation Research,* the *Journal of Learning, Disabilities,* and the *Infant Mental Health Journal.*

De Lorenzo received numerous honors and special appointments, such as, the Joseph P. Kennedy Award (1966), the Leadership Award for Achievements in Mental Deficiency (1976), and the Award of Merit granted by the President's Committee on Mental Retardation (1977). She also received the associate researcher *honoris causa* at the Research Department of the Bureau of Child Research, University of Kansas (1972). In 1978, De Lorenzo was invited to be the main speaker at the opening session of the World Congress on Future Social Education, organized by the Council for Exceptional Children in Sterling, Scotland. Her work was featured in the 1994 publication, *Comparative Studies in Special Education,* an examination of special education provisions throughout the world.

REFERENCE

Mazurek, K., & Winzer, M. A. (Eds.). (1994). *Comparative studies in special education.* Washington, DC: Gallaudet University.

IVAN Z. HOLOWINSKY
Rutgers University
First edition

TAMARA J. MARTIN
The University of Texas of the Permian Basin
Second edition

DELUSIONS

Delusions are false or erroneous ideas that people believe wholeheartedly but that have no basis in fact and may involve a misinterpretation of perceptions or experiences (American Psychiatric Association, 1994; Barlow & Durand, 2005). Making a professional distinction between a delusion and a strongly held belief is not easy, and may come down to the person's degree of conviction for holding on to the idea despite compelling, contradictory evidence; the tenacity of which Jaspers (1963) thought of as a basic characteristic of "madness."

Delusions are most often associated with the psychotic mental disorder of Schizophrenia, but can occur in other disorders such as Dementia of Alzheimer's Type or Major Depressive Disorder with Psychotic Features (American Psychiatric Association, 1994; Barlow & Durand, 2005). Mack, Franklin, and Frances (2003) describe, too, how delusions can also occur in substance use disorders. For example, amphetamine use stimulates the nervous system by enhancing activity of norepinephrine and dopamine, making them more available throughout the brain, which can lead to hallucinations and paranoid delusions.

Concerning Schizophrenia, delusions are regarded as one of four major "Characteristic" symptoms (i.e., criterion A) associated with the disorder; the other symptoms being hallucinations, disorganized speech, grossly disorganized or catatonic behavior, and negative symptoms (i.e., affective flattening, alogia, avolition). If delusions are considered so bizarre, that is, they are implausible and not understandable and do not seem to come from ordinary life experiences, then only this single symptom is needed to satisfy criterion A instead of the required two of the four listed (criteria B, C, D, E, and F, still must be considered before making a formal diagnosis).

In addition to being considered one of the major characteristic symptoms, delusions are also referred to as one of the "positive symptoms," along with hallucinations, disorganized speech (i.e., frequent derailment or incoherence), and grossly disorganized or catatonic behavior, because of the observed excess or distortion of normal functions (Barlow & Durand, 2005). "Negative" symptoms are regarded as those in which a dimunition or loss of normal functions has occurred, such as is the case with symptoms like flattening of affect or loss of personal volition (American Psychiatric Association, 1994). Moreover, delusions are included in the top ten "first rank" symptoms list psychiatry uses for diagnosing Schizophrenia—a diagnostic list that is meant to strike an optimal balance between efficient classification and comprehensive description of the disorder (Andersen & Flaum, 1991).

A variety of delusional types exist but perhaps the more well known are delusions of grandeur, delusions of persecution, delusions of reference, and delusions of control. *Delusions of grandeur* are marked by the belief that one is a great inventor, religious savior, or other specially empowered person. *Delusions of persecution* are probably the most common form of delusion among individuals with Schizophrenia (Barlow & Durand, 2005) and center on the belief that they are being plotted or discriminated against, spied on, slandered, threatened, attacked, or deliberately victimized. *Delusions of reference* occur when individuals with Schizophrenia attach special and personal meaning to the actions of others or to various objects or events. When individuals with Schizophrenia believe their feelings, thoughts, and actions are being controlled by other people, then *delusions of control* are in operation (American Psychiatric Association, 1994; Barlow & Durand, 2005; Ho, Black, & Andreasen, 2003).

Other unique forms of delusions known as *Capgras syndrome* and *Cotard's syndrome* are also described in the literature (cf. Black & Andreasen, 1999). Capgras syndrome is the belief that someone a person knows has been replaced by a double. Cotard's syndrome is the belief that a part of one's body has been changed in some impossible way. More recently in the literature, *erotomanic delusions* have been the topic of discussion due to their association with criminal stalking behavior. This particular delusion describes the individual's belief that, without any basis whatsoever, he or she is loved by someone who may actually be a casual acquaintance or even a complete stranger. These individuals develop far-fetched fantasies that drive them to protect, harm, or even kill the person they desire (Silva, Derecho, Leong, & Ferrari, 2000).

Assessing and classifying delusions is no simple task; in fact, they are seen as a multidimensional and varied phenomenon. Individuals with Schizophrenia, for example, are often full of conviction and convinced of the reality of their beliefs; their delusions often extend into various areas of their lives, such as only at work with the boss versus being convinced that everyone in the world is persecuting them. Delusions are often bizarre and depart from culturally determined consensual reality, such as believing they are the Creator of the universe or hear "strange buzzing" sounds in their head: proof positive of alien brain-washing activity. Delusions can be very logical, consistent, and systematic; or the converse. Delusions can exert low or extreme pressure on a person, keeping a person only occasionally distracted by fleeting thoughts of being a famous movie star versus being totally obsessed and energized by a delusion, devoting themselves day and night to figuring out how the CIA has recruited them into their organization without their consent and knowledge. Suffice it to say, delusions are not static experiences, but are extremely dynamic in nature and come in a full range of expression.

In an intriguing discussion by Roberts (1991), the idea is posited that delusions may give purpose for people with Schizophrenia who are otherwise quite upset by the strange changes taking place within themselves. The emerging idea has little support, but in Roberts's (1991) study, "deluded" individuals expressed a much stronger sense of purpose and meaning in life, and less depression than compared to matched individuals who previously had delusions but were recovering. This suggests that delusions might serve as an adaptive function for individuals with Schizophrenia.

For further investigation into the phenomenon of delusions, the reader is directed to the classic "three Christs" study of Rokeach (1964) where the author spent a great deal of time at a mental hospital interviewing three individuals with Schizophrenia who all held the same delusion that they were Jesus Christ. Also, Fleschner (1995) presents a fascinating, first-person account of the insights of a patient with Schizophrenia.

REFERENCES

American Psychiatric Association. (1994). *Diagnostic and statistical manual of mental disorders* (4th ed.). Washington, DC: Author.

Andreasen, N. C., & Flaum, M. (1991). Schizophrenia: The characteristic symptoms. *Schizophrenia Bulletin, 17,* 27–49.

Black, D. W., & Andreasen, N. C. (1999). Schizophrenia, schizophreniform disorder and delusional (paranoid) disorders. In R. E. Hales, S. C. Yudofsky, & J. A. Talbott (Eds.), *Textbook of clinical psychiatry* (3rd ed., pp. 425–477). Washington, DC: American Psychiatric Press.

Barlow, D. H., & Durand, V. M. (2005). *Abnormal psychology: An integrative approach* (4th ed.). Belmont, CA: Wadsworth.

Fleschner, C. L. (1995). First person account: Insight from a schizophrenia patient with depression. *Schizophrenia Bulletin, 21,* 703–7.

Ho, B-C., Black, D. W., & Andreasen, N. C. (2003). Schizophrenia and other psychotic disorders. In R. E. Hales & S. C. Yudofsky (Eds.), *Textbook of clinical psychiatry* (4th ed., pp. 379–438). Washington, DC: American Psychiatric Press.

Jaspers, K. (1963). *General psychopathology* (J. Hoeing & M. W. Hamilton, Trans.). Manchester, England: Manchester University Press.

Mack, A. H., Franklin, J. E., & Frances, R. J. (2003). Substance use disorders. In R. E. Hales & S. C. Yudofsky (Eds.), *Textbook of clinical psychiatry* (4th ed., pp. 309–377). Washington, DC: American Psychiatric Press.

Roberts, G. A. (1991). Delusional belief and meaning in life: A preferred reality? *British Journal of Psychiatry, 159,* 20–29.

Rokeach, M. (1964). *The three christs of Ypsilanti.* New York: Random House.

Silva, J. A., Derecho, D. V., Leong, G. B., & Ferrari, M. M. (2000). Stalking behavior in delusional jealousy. *Journal of Forensic Science, 45,* 77–82.

ROLLEN C. FOWLER
Eugene 4J School District,
Eugene, Oregon

CHILDHOOD PSYCHOSIS
CHILDHOOD SCHIZOPHRENIA

DEMENTIA

Dementia is a generic term applied to a pattern of observable abnormalities in mental abilities, with impairment in at least three of the following five functions: memory, visuospatial skills, emotion or personality, language, and cognition. Combinations of symptoms are caused by many different etiologies (Hegde, 1994). Some literature agrees that irreversible dementia can be subdivided into three major areas: primary degenerative dementia, multi-infarct dementia, and all other dementia diagnoses of terminal diseases collectively (Shekim, 1997). Dementia of the Alzheimer's type is the most common, and it is caused by structural and chemical changes in the brain. The second most common, multi-infarct dementia, is caused by repeated focal lesions from strokes. Dementia is associated with acquired immunodeficiency syndrome (AIDS), Pick's disease, Parkinson's disease, supranuclear palsy, Binswanger's disease, Creutzfeldt-Jakob disease, Huntington's disease, and Korsakoff's disease (Payne, 1997). In addition, reversible dementias arise from adverse drug interactions or toxicity, metabolic and endocrine disorders, infections, intracranial masses, normal-pressure hydrocephalus, alcohol abuse, vitamin deficiencies, neurosyphilis, arteriosclerotic complications, and epilepsy (Tonkovich, 1988).

Assessment and diagnosis of dementia is a team effort involving physicians, speech-language pathologists, psychologists, and other specialists. The final determination is made on the basis of case history, clinical examination, neurological tests, brain imaging, laboratory tests, communication assessment, and assessment of intellectual functions. Analysis of higher intellectual and language functions include verbal description of common objects, immediate and delayed story retelling, and verbal fluency ("Tell me all the words you can think of beginning with T"; Hegde, 1994).

Language problems frequently observed in early stages of dementia are mild naming problems, verbal paraphasia (saying words that are similar to the target word), subtle problems in comprehending abstract meanings, impaired picture description, difficulty in topic maintenance, and repetitive speech. As the disease progresses, symptoms include severe memory problems in all forms of memory; generalized intellectual deterioration; profound disorientation to place, person, and time; speech at a rapid rate with echolalia (repeating what was said to them); pallilalia (repeating one's own utterances); jargon; and inattention to social conventions (Hegde, 1994).

REFERENCES

Hegde, M. N. (1994). *A coursebook on aphasia and other neurogenic language disorders.* San Diego: Singular.

Payne, J. C. (1997). *Adult neurogenic language disorders: Assessment and treatment.* San Diego: Singular.

Shekim, L. (1997). Dementia. In L. L. LaPointe (Ed.), *Aphasia and related neurogenic language disorders* (2nd ed., pp. 238–249). New York: Thieme.

Tonkovich, J. L. (1988). Communication disorders in the elderly. In B. B. Shadden (Ed.), *Communication behavior and aging: A sourcebook for clinicians* (pp. 197–218). Baltimore: Williams & Wilkins.

SHEELA STUART
George Washington University

DEMENTIAS OF CHILDHOOD

Dementia refers to a global cognitive decline that impacts more than one component of cognitive functioning and involves a memory impairment. The term *decline* indicates deterioration in cognitive functioning from a previous higher level of functioning (American Psychiatric Association, 2000). The etiology of dementia may be traced to a general medical condition, persistent effects of a substance, or multiple causes. The acquired nature of dementia suggests that it results in decreased mental functioning over time, as compared to an acute or sudden onset. Dementia describes conditions that are usually "both progressive and irreversible" (Lezak, 1995, p. 204).

Characteristics are:

1. Clinically significant deterioration in cognitive functioning that gets progressively worse over time.
2. Memory deficits including difficulties with registration, retention, recall, or recognition of new information.
3. Slowed reaction time.
4. Deficits in cognitive processes possibly including aphasia (language disturbance), apraxia (impaired motor functioning), agnosia (inability to recognize or identify objects), or impaired executive abilities.
5. Typically dementia presents as a gradual onset of symptoms and continued cognitive decline.
6. No evidence of impaired consciousness or awareness (not the result of delirium or amnesia).

While degenerative disorders affect less than 1 percent of people under 65 year of age, many conditions that occur during childhood can produce dementia (Gurland & Crass, 1986). Dementia in children can be classified similar to how they are identified in adults. They are the result of general medical conditions, persistent substance exposure, or a mixture of the two. Medical conditions that may cause dementia include brain tumors or neoplasms, which can lead to changes in cognitive functioning. The impact of a medical condition on declining mental abilities in dementia depends on the size, location, and rate of growth of the tumor or neoplasm (Lezak, 1995). Children treated with chemotherapy for acute lymphocytic leukemia or childhood leukemia have also been known to suffer from neuropsychological impairments (Teeter & Semrud-Clikeman, 1997). Dementia resulting from kidney dialysis affects less than 1 percent of individuals undergoing dialysis (Lezak, 1995).

Cerebrovascular disease, or strokes, can produce impairments in cognitive ability and are referred to as vascular dementia. Dementia may also be associated with traumatic brain injuries. The juvenile type of Huntington's disease can cause cognitive impairments, memory retrieval deficits, and difficulties with planning and attention (American Psychiatric Association, 2000). Lastly, medical conditions such as brain lesions (hydrocephalus), endocrine disorders (hypothyroidism), nutritional deficiencies (Vitamin B_{12} deficiency), immune conditions, and metabolic diseases can produce symptoms of dementia (American Psychiatric Association, 2000).

Children infected with HIV may develop symptoms of progressive neurodevelopment degeneration termed HIV encephalopathy, neuroaids, or AIDS dementia complex (Aylward, 1997). This condition initially consists of mild symptoms such as depression, forgetfulness, or difficulty sustaining attention but can develop into complete dementia (Lezak, 1995). There is no known treatment for AIDS dementia.

There is evidence that individuals with Trisomy 21, commonly referred to as Down syndrome, may experience aspects of dementia by the time they are adolescents. One possible explanation for this occurrence is an accelerated rate of aging and reduced temporal lobe functioning in this population (Miezejeski, Devenny, Krinsky-Mchale, Zigman, & Silverman, 2000). Research suggests that some individuals with Trisomy 21 experience brain atrophy and metabolic deficits similar to those associated with Alzheimer's disease (Nadel, 1999).

Acute or chronic exposure to substances can produce symptoms of dementia in children. Contact with neurotoxins, such as lead, mercury, certain insecticides, solvents, or carbon monoxide can lead to significant cognitive impairments. Ingestion of alcohol, inhalants, sedatives, hypnotics, anxiolytics, or medications such as anticonvulsants or intrathecal methotrexate can also produce indications of dementia (American Psychiatric Association, 2000).

Although it can be difficult to assess the degree of cognitive deterioration in young children, worsening school performance, significant developmental delays, or divergence from normal development can be early signs of dementia (American Psychiatric Association, 2000). Mental status examinations and neuropsychological assessment can be useful for identifying cognitive assets and deficits. Assessment of memory functioning including short-term memory, long-term retrieval, and recognition can also provide valuable information. Deficits in expressive and receptive language abilities and executive functioning are often present.

For special education purposes, children with dementias may be eligible to receive services under the classification Other Health Impairment. If they are eligible to receive special education services, academic support could be beneficial. Treatment typically consists of cognitive rehabilitation techniques to compensate for memory impairment (e.g., the use of visual imagery and verbal encoding strategies). External memory aids, such as tape recorders and notebooks, also can be helpful. Pharmacological interventions such as cholinergically active drugs that are known to impact memory and cognition positively may also be useful.

REFERENCES

American Psychiatric Association. (2000). *Diagnostic and statistical manual of mental disorders* (4th ed., Text Revision). Washington, DC: Author.

Aylward, G. P. (1997). *Infant and early childhood neuropsychology.* New York: Plenum Press.

Gurland, B. J., & Crass, P. S. (1986). Public health perspectives on clinical memory testing of Alzheimer's disease and related disorders. In L. W. Poon (Ed.), *Clinical memory assessment of older adults.* Washington, DC: American Psychological Association.

Lezak, M. D. (1995). *Neurological assessment* (3rd ed.). New York: Oxford University Press.

Miezejeski, C. M., Devenny, D. A., Krinsky-Mchale, S., Zigman, W., & Silverman, W. (2000). Aging in persons with Down syndrome and mental retardation: Receptive language, visual motor integration, and fluency [Abstract]. *Archives of Clinical Neuropsychology, 15.*

Nadel, L. (1999). Down syndrome in cognitive neuroscience perspective. In H. Tager-Flusberg (Ed.), *Neurodevelopmental disorders.* Cambridge, MA: MIT Press.

Teeter, P. A., & Semrud-Clikeman, M. (1997). *Child neuropsychology: Assessment and interventions for neurodevelopmental disorders.* Boston: Allyn & Bacon.

BOB KIRCHNER
University of Northern Colorado

SHAWN POWELL
*United States Air Force
Academy*

DEMOGRAPHY OF SPECIAL EDUCATION

This article is a summary and text of the *25th Annual Report to Congress on the Implementation of the Individuals with Disabilities Education Act.* It has been provided in this volume so that readers may reference the document in its entirety and with objectivity. The original document can be found online at the Office of Special Education Programs at http://www.ed.gov/about/reports/annual/osep/2003/index.html.

The 25th Annual Report to Congress has been designed to showcase the data collected from states and the national studies that make up the Office of Special Education Programs' (OSEP) National Assessment of the Implementation of the Individuals with Disabilities Education Act (IDEA). To this end, OSEP proposed questions about the characteristics of children and students receiving services under Parts B and C, the settings in which they receive services, their transition from Part C to Part B and from school to adult life, and their disabilities. Answers to the questions are shown through graphs, charts, and tables complemented by short explanatory text. The report is divided into three sections: a national picture of children and students with disabilities served under Parts C and B; individual profiles of states that summarize selected aspects of special education in each state; and data tables that show states' ranking regarding exiting and educational environments for Part B and early

childhood intervention and settings for Part C. Some key findings from the report are presented below.

Infants and Toddlers Served Under IDEA, Part C

- Both the number and the percentage of infants and toddlers served under Part C have increased steadily from 1998 to 2001. In all years, 2-year-olds were the largest proportion (53 percent) of children served under Part C.

- The racial/ethnic composition of these children is quite similar to that of the general infant and toddler population—the majority are white, followed by Hispanic, and then black children. Most infants and toddlers served under Part C in 2000 received services at home; the percentage of this population served in programs for children with developmental delay or other disabilities decreased substantially between 1996–2000.

- The majority of Part C infants and toddlers (62.6 percent) are eligible to transition to Part B services when they turn age 3.

- Since 1991, the number of children ages 3 through 5 who receive services under Part B of IDEA has increased steadily. As of December 1, 2001, 5.2 percent of the total population of 3- through 5-year-olds living in the 50 states and the District of Columbia were estimated to be receiving services.

- The majority of children ages 3 through 5 receiving special education services are white; white children also make up the majority of the general preschool population.

- In 2000, 51 percent of preschoolers received special education services in either early childhood settings or part-time early childhood/part-time early childhood special education settings.

- Special education teachers serving children ages 3 through 5 with disabilities are primarily white and female. Six and a half percent of these preschool special teachers also report having a disability themselves.

Students Ages 6 Through 21 Served Under IDEA, Part B

- On December 1, 2001, 8.9 percent of 6- through 21-year-olds were receiving special education services under IDEA. The number of students with disabilities receiving services has increased slowly since 1992. In contrast, the number of students receiving services for autism has increased markedly, from a little less than 10,000 in 1992 to approximately 65,000 in 2001.

- According to findings from two of OSEP's National Assessment studies, the Special Education Elementary Longitudinal Study (SEELS) and National Longitudinal Transition Study–2 (NLTS2), students with disabilities are more likely to be poor than students in the general population.

- Parent reports as shown in SEELS and NLTS2 data indicate that more black students with disabilities are suspended or expelled from school than are white or Hispanic students. Overall, parents report that about one third of students ages 13 through 17 with disabilities have been suspended or expelled.

- Most students with disabilities (around 96 percent) are being educated in regular school buildings, and almost half are in regular classrooms for most the day. However, 26 percent of students ages 6 through 12 with disabilities and 36 percent of students ages 13 through 17 with disabilities have been retained in grade at least once. Even so, the proportion of high school students being educated at the typical grade level for their age has increased from 32 percent in 1987 to 53 percent in 2001.

- In 2000–01, 47.6 percent of students ages 14 and older with disabilities exited school with a regular high school diploma. A total of 41.1 percent of students ages 14 and older with disabilities dropped out.

State Profiles

State profiles include number of school districts, public school enrollment, per-pupil expenditures, and percentage of children living below the poverty level. For Part B, the profiles include number of children served under IDEA, percentage exiting with a diploma, percentage dropping out, number of special education teachers, and percentage of fully certified teachers. Race/ethnicity and education environments data are provided in charts.

For Part C, the profiles list the lead agency for early intervention services, number of infants and toddlers receiving early intervention services, percentage of infants and toddlers served in the home, and percentage of infants and toddlers served in programs for typically developing children. Race/ethnicity and reasons for exiting early intervention are provided in charts.

Section I.
The National Picture

Infants and Toddlers Served Under IDEA, Part C

The Education of the Handicapped Act Amendments of 1986 established the Early Intervention Program for Infants and Toddlers with Disabilities under Part H (now Part C) of the Individuals with Disabilities Education Act (IDEA). The program assists states in developing and implementing a statewide, comprehensive, coordinated, multidisciplinary, interagency system to make early intervention services

available to all children with disabilities from birth through age 2.

This program is based on the premise that early intervention in the lives of children with disabilities and their families provides greater opportunities for improving developmental outcomes.

Trends in Numbers and Percentages of Infants and Toddlers Served

How many infants and toddlers receive early intervention services?

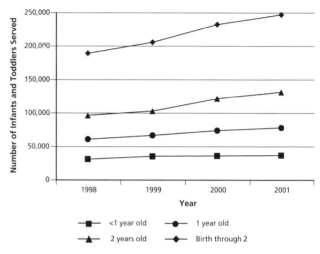

Figure 1 Number of infants and toddlers served under Part C of IDEA: 1998 through 2001

Source: U.S. Department of Education, Office of Special Education Programs, Data Analysis System (DANS), Table AH1 in vol. 2 of this report. Data are for the 50 states, D.C., Puerto Rico, and the outlying areas.

- On December 1, 2001, IDEA, Part C was serving 247,433 infants and toddlers.

- The number of children served under IDEA, Part C increased 31 percent between 1998 and 2001—from 189,462 to 247,433.

- The largest single-year increase in the number of infants and toddlers served was 13 percent. The number of children served increased from 206,111 in 1999 to 232,815 in 2000.
  [Data for 2000 were revised since the 24th Annual Report. Twelve states or outlying areas revised their child count for 2000.]

- In all years, 2-year-olds were the largest proportion (53 percent in 2001) of children served under Part C. Infants less than 1 year old comprised 15 percent of all infants and toddlers served in 2001.

- From 1998 to 2001, the growth in the number of infants and toddlers served was slowest for the infants less than 1 year old (18 percent). The growth in the number of infants and toddlers who were 1 and 2 years old was 28 percent and 36 percent, respectively.

What percentage of the birth-through-2-year-old population is served by Part C?

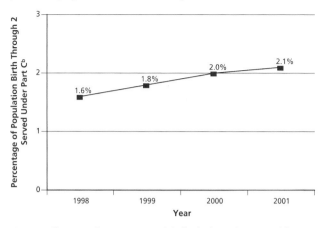

Figure 2 Change in the percentage of the birth-through-2-year-old population served under Part C: 1998 through 2001[a]

Source: U.S. Department of Education, Office of Special Education Programs, Data Analysis System (DANS), Table AH7 in vol. 2 of this report. Population data for 1998 through 1999 are July estimates as of the date of the first release. These estimates are based on the 1990 decennial Census. For 2000 and 2001, population data are July 1 estimates, released October 2003. These data are based on the 2000 decennial Census. The population estimates are from the Population Estimates Program, U.S. Census Bureau, Population Division.

[a]Percentage of population is calculated by dividing the count of children served by the total general population estimates for children in this age range for that year.

[b]Data from 50 states and the District of Columbia.

- The percentage of infants and toddlers served under Part C increased from 1.6 percent in 1998 to 2.1 percent in 2001.

The Race/Ethnicity of Children Served

[The race/ethnicity categories presented here are those used by the Office of Special Education Programs to collect the IDEA, Section 618 data. Other racial/ethnic categories or combinations of racial/ethnic categories are used in other data included in this report.]

What is the race/ethnicity of the infants and toddlers receiving early intervention services?

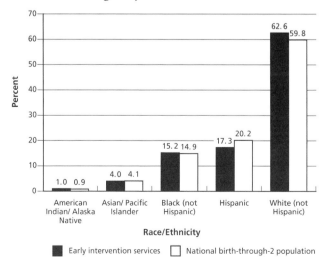

Figure 3 Racial/ethnic composition of children served under IDEA in 2001 and the national birth-through-2 population[a]

Source: U.S. Department of Education, Office of Special Education Programs, Data Analysis System (DANS), Table AH7 in vol. 2. The population data are July 1 estimates for 2001 released in October 2003. The Census' multiracial category was apportioned into each of the five single race/ethnicity categories in proportion to each category's relative size. These estimates are based on the 2000 decennial Census and come from the Population Estimates Program, U.S. Census Bureau, Population Division.

[a]Data are for the 50 states and the District of Columbia.

- The racial/ethnic composition of infants and toddlers receiving early intervention services is similar to the racial/ethnic composition of the general population of infants and toddlers.
- Most infants and toddlers receiving early intervention services are white.
- Hispanic children are the next largest racial/ethnic group who are served under Part C, followed by black children.

Age at Entry to Early Intervention Services

Does the age of entry into early intervention services differ by disability?

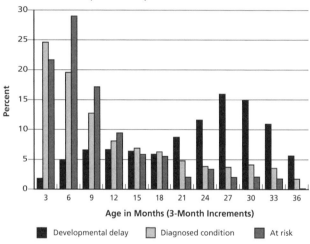

Figure 4 Average age of entry into early intervention by disability-related condition: 1997–98

Source: NEILS Initial Program Data.

- It appears that younger infants and toddlers are more likely to have either a diagnosed condition or are at risk compared to older infants and toddlers, who are more likely to have a developmental delay. Three-month-olds are the most likely to have a diagnosed condition, while 6-month-olds are most likely to be at risk.
- The majority of infants and toddlers who enter with a developmental delay are 27 months old or greater.
- Children begin receiving early intervention most often in the first 9 months after birth, when they are approximately 28 months of age.

NEILS, part of OSEP's National Assessment, is a longitudinal study that is following more than 3,300 infants and toddlers with disabilities or at risk for disabilities and their families through their experiences in early intervention and into early elementary school. The study is providing information about the characteristics of children and families, the services they receive, and the outcomes they experience.

Trends in Early Intervention Service Settings

Does the primary early intervention setting differ by race/ethnicity?

Table 1 Percentage of children by early intervention setting and race/ethnicity: 2000

Setting	All	American Indian/ Alaska Native	Asian/ Pacific Islander	Black (not Hispanic)	Hispanic	White (not Hispanic)
Home	71.8	76.0	76.1	65.5	68.1	74.3
Hospital (inpatient)	0.5	0.4	0.2	1.3	0.2	0.4
Programs for children with developmental delays or disabilities	10.9	7.9	10.8	11.7	12.9	9.5
Programs for typically developing children	4.3	7.9	2.8	7.0	3.1	4.2
Residential facility	0.1	0.2	0.1	0.1	0.1	0.1
Service provider location	10.0	6.0	8.8	11.3	13.6	9.2
Other settings	2.4	1.6	1.1	3.0	2.1	2.2
Total	100.0%	100.0%	100.0%	100.0%	100.0%	100.0%

Source: U.S. Department of Education, Office of Special Education Programs, Data Analysis System (DANS), Tables AH3 and AH10 in vol. 2. Data are for the 50 states, D.C., Puerto Rico, and the outlying areas.

- Most children in all racial/ethnic groups receive early intervention services primarily in the home or in programs for typically developing children. American Indian/Alaska Native children are most often served in these settings (83.9 percent), followed by Asian/Pacific Islander (78.9 percent) and white children (78.5 percent). Hispanic (71.2 percent) and black (72.5 percent) infants and toddlers are somewhat less likely to be served in these settings.

What is the primary service setting of infants and toddlers receiving early intervention services?

2000

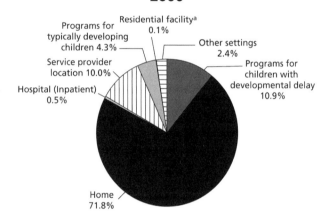

1996

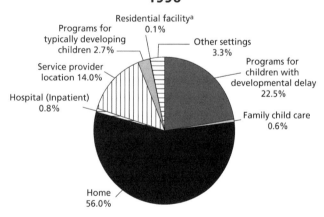

Figure 5 Percentage of infants and toddlers with disabilities served in various settings: 1996 and 2000

Figure 5 (cont.)

Source: U.S. Department of Education, Office of Special Education Programs, Data Analysis System (DANS), Table AH3 in vol. 2. Data are for the 50 states, D.C., Puerto Rico, and the outlying areas.

[a]The percentage of children being served in residential facilities is too small to register on the chart.

- In 2000, most (71.8 percent) infants and toddlers were being served primarily in the home, followed by 10.9 percent being served in a program for children with developmental delays or disabilities, and 10.0 percent in a service provider location.
- Between 1996 and 2000, the percentage of infants and toddlers being served primarily in a program for children with developmental delays or disabilities decreased by more than 50 percent, while the percentage of those being served primarily in the home increased by more than 15 percent. All other settings differed by a maximum of 3 percent between 1996 and 2000.

Infants and Toddlers Exiting Part C

[Under Part C of IDEA, states must ". . . ensure a smooth transition for toddlers receiving early intervention services . . . to preschool or other appropriate services" (IDEA, §637(a)(8)).]

What happens when children reach age 3 and no longer receive early intervention services?

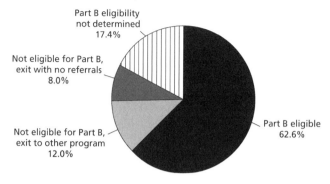

Figure 6 Percentage of children transitioning from Part C at age 3, by exiting category: 2000ᵃ

Source: U.S. Department of Education, Office of Special Education Programs, Data Analysis System (DANS), Table AH4 in vol. 2. Data are for the 50 states, D.C., Puerto Rico, and the outlying areas.

ᵃDoes not include information on children who complete their individualized family services plan (IFSP), no longer require services, and exit before age 3.

- The majority (62.6 percent) of Part C children are eligible for Part B services when they turn age 3. Some children exit Part C at age 3 without determination of their eligibility for Part B (17.4 percent). Children specifically deemed ineligible for Part B services either exit to another program (12.0 percent) or leave with no referral to another program (8.0 percent).

What are the differences in exiting categories for children in different racial/ethnic groups who are exiting Part C at age 3?

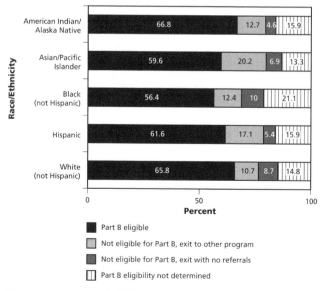

Figure 7 Percentage of children transitioning from Part C at age 3, by exiting category and race/ethnicity: 2000–01

Source: U.S. Department of Education, Office of Special Education Programs, Data Analysis System (DANS), Table AH11 in vol. 2. Data are for the 50 states, D.C., Puerto Rico, and the outlying areas.

- American Indian/Alaska Native (66.8 percent) and white infants and toddlers (65.8 percent) were somewhat more likely to be determined Part B eligible than were Hispanic (61.6 percent), Asian/Pacific Islander (59.6 percent), and black (56.4 percent) infants and toddlers.

- Black infants and toddlers were more likely than other racial/ethnic groups to have their Part B eligibility undetermined (21.1 percent), followed by Native American/Alaska Native (15.9 percent) and Hispanic (15.9 percent).

The Impact of Early Intervention Services on Infants and Toddlers Served

[The data presented here are exemplary of the type of information collected by NEILS on the impact of early intervention services on infants and toddlers receiving these services. Additional data on the impact of early intervention services can be found on the NEILS Web site, www.sri.com/neils/.]

What progress do infants and toddlers make in their communications skills while receiving early intervention services?

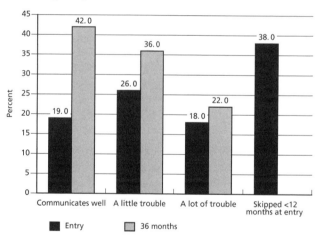

Figure 8 How well child makes needs known at entry and at 36 monthsᵃ: 1997–98

Source: NEILS Parent Survey.

ᵃOnly children 12 months of age or older were evaluated for communication.

- According to these data, children are twice as likely to communicate well at 36 months than at time of entry.

- At time of entry, about a fourth of the children (26.1 percent) had little trouble communicating, and 18 percent had a lot of trouble.

- At 36 months, almost half (42 percent) communicated well, followed by over a third (36 percent) who had little trouble, and one in five (22 percent) who had a lot of trouble.

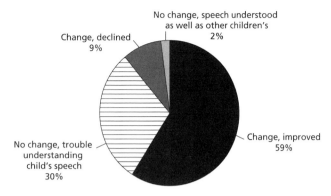

Figure 9 Change in others' understanding of child's speech between time of entry and at 36 months[a]: 1997–98

Source: NEILS Parent Survey.

[a]Only children 12 months of age or older were evaluated for speech.

- More than two-thirds of children (59 percent) who were 12 months old at entry had a positive change in their speech.

- About a third of infants and toddlers (32 percent) experienced no change in their speech, and 9 percent experienced a decline in their ability to be verbally understood.

Children Ages 3 Through 21 Served Under Idea, Part B

[Data from individual states impact these national data; in particular, data from one large state show many more 4-year-olds served than 5-year-olds served in 2001. No explanation was provided by the state for the pattern observed.]

Part B of IDEA provides funds to states to assist them in providing a free appropriate public education (FAPE) to children with disabilities who are in need of special education and related services. To be eligible for funding under this program, a state must make FAPE available to all disabled children residing in the state, ages 3 through 21, except that they are not required to serve children ages 3 through 5 and ages 18 through 21 if serving such children is inconsistent with state law or practice or the order of any court. The act has four primary purposes: to ensure that all children with disabilities have FAPE available to them with special education and related services designed to meet their individual needs, to ensure that the rights of children with disabilities and their families are protected, to assist states and localities in providing education for all children with disabilities, and to assess and ensure the effectiveness of efforts to educate children with disabilities.

In 1997 Congress made significant changes to IDEA, going beyond ensuring educational equity for children with disabilities. With access to public schools already guaranteed for 6.4 million children with disabilities, the 1997 reauthorization of IDEA set educators' and policymakers' sights on setting higher expectations and improving achievement for

these students, as well as on ensuring positive transitions to work or postsecondary education after graduation.

Children Ages 3 Through 5 Served Under IDEA, Part B

IDEA requires states to have policies and procedures in effect to ensure the provision of FAPE to all 3- through 5-year-olds with disabilities in order to be eligible for funds under the Preschool Grants Program and other IDEA funds targeted to children ages 3 through 5 with disabilities. States may also, at their discretion, serve 2-year-olds who will turn 3 during the school year.

How many preschoolers are served under IDEA, Part B?

[Source: U.S. Department of Education, Office of Special Education Programs, Data Analysis System (DANS). Tables AA1, AA8, and AF7 in vol. 2. Data are for the 50 states, D.C., Puerto Rico, and the outlying areas.]

- On December 1, 2001, a total of 620,195 children ages 3 through 5 were served under Part B. Of these, 612,084 were served in the 50 states and the District of Columbia. This number represents 5.2 percent of the total population of 3- through 5-year-olds living in the states and the District of Columbia.
  [The percentage of general population was calculated using the July 1 population estimates for 2001 released October 2003. The number served in the 50 states and the District of Columbia was divided by the general U.S. population estimate for children in this age range.]

- Of the total number of preschoolers receiving special education services, 21.9 percent were 3 years old, 35.8 percent were 4 years old, and 42.3 percent were 5 years old.

How has the number of preschoolers served under Part B changed over the past 10 years?

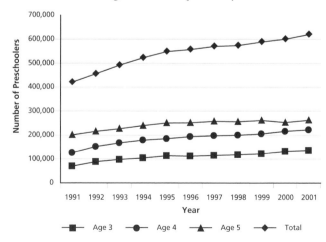

Figure 10 Number of preschoolers served under IDEA, Part B: 1991 through 2001[a]

Source: U.S. Department of Education, Office of Special Education Programs, Data Analysis System (DANS), Tables AA8 and AA9 in vol. 2. Data are for the 50 states, D.C., Puerto Rico, and the outlying areas.

ᵃFor 1991 through 1994, the counts include children served under Chapter 1 of ESEA (SOP). For 1991 only, children served under Chapter 1 of ESEA (SOP) are only included in the total count because the data were not disaggregated by age year. Beginning in 1994–95, all services to children and youth with disabilities were provided only through IDEA, Part B. Data for 2000 were revised since the 24th Annual Report to Congress on Implementation of IDEA. Twelve states revised their child count for 2000.

- Since 1991, the number of preschoolers served under Part B grew from 422,217 to 620,195. This is an increase of 197,978 preschoolers or a 46.9 percent growth in the number of children served.
- The number of preschoolers served under Part B increased for each age year. From 1991 to 2001, the number of 3-year-olds served increased 93.6 percent, the number of 4-year-olds served increased 75.9 percent, and the number of 5-year-olds served increased 30.7 percent.

As part of its National Assessment, OSEP is funding the Pre-elementary Early Education Longitudinal Study (PEELS). The study focuses on the characteristics of children receiving preschool special education; the programs and services they receive; their experiences in transitioning from early intervention programs to preschool and from preschool to elementary school; the results they achieve in preschool, kindergarten, and early elementary school; and the factors that contribute to better results.

The Race/Ethnicity of Preschoolers Served

[The race/ethnicity categories presented here are those used by the Office of Special Education Programs to collect the IDEA, Section 618 data. Other racial/ethnic categories or combinations of racial/ethnic categories are used in other data included in this report.]

What is the racial/ethnic composition of the preschool IDEA population?

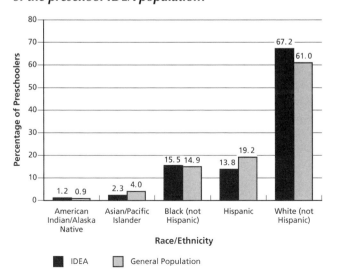

Figure 11 Racial/Ethnic composition of children ages 3 through 5 served under IDEA and the national preschool population, Part B: 2001–02ᵃ

Source: U.S. Department of Education, Office of Special Education Programs, Data Analysis System (DANS), Tables AA14 and AF7 in vol. 2. The population data are July 1 estimates for 2001 released October 2003. The Census' multi-racial category was apportioned into each of the five single race/ethnicity categories in proportion to each category's relative size. These estimates are based on the 2000 decennial Census and come from the Population Estimates Program, U.S. Census Bureau, Population Division.

ᵃData are for the 50 states and the District of Columbia.

- In the 50 states and the District of Columbia, the largest percentage of preschoolers served under Part B were white (67.2 percent). White children also composed the largest percentage of the preschool population (61.0 percent).
- The percentage of Hispanic preschoolers served under Part B (13.8 percent) is somewhat smaller than the percentage of Hispanic preschoolers in the general population (19.2 percent). This was also true for Asian/Pacific Islanders; the percentage of Asian/Pacific Islander preschoolers served under Part B (2.3 percent) was smaller than the percentage of Asian/Pacific Islander preschoolers in the population (4.0 percent).
- The percentages of American Indian/Alaska Native and black preschoolers served under Part B were slightly larger (1.2 percent and 15.5 percent, respectively) than in the general population (0.9 percent and 14.9 percent, respectively).

States report race/ethnicity data in five categories: American Indian/Alaska Native, Asian/Pacific Islander, black (not Hispanic), Hispanic, and white (not Hispanic).

What is the likelihood of children ages 3 through 5 in each racial/ethnic group being served under IDEA, Part B, as compared to that of all other children ages 3 through 5?

Risk ratios compare the proportion of a particular racial/ethnic group served under Part B to the proportion of all other racial/ethnic groups combined. A risk ratio of 1.0 indicates no difference between the racial/ethnic groups.

Table 2 Risk ratios by race/ethnicity for children ages 3 through 5 served under IDEA, Part B: 2001–02 for the 50 states and the District of Columbia

Race/ethnicity	Child count	3–5 population	Risk index[a]	Risk ratio[b] vs. all other children
American Indian/Alaska Native	7,445	108,371	6.87	1.30
Asian/Pacific Islander	13,825	465,807	2.97	0.55
Black (not Hispanic)	94,880	1,722,543	5.51	1.05
Hispanic	84,570	2,222,419	3.81	0.67
White (not Hispanic)	411,364	7,056,878	5.83	1.31
Race/ethnicity total[c]	612,084	11,576,018	5.29	N/A

Source: U.S. Department of Education, Office of Special Education Programs, Data Analysis System (DANS), Tables A14 and AF7 in vol. 2. Population data are July 1 estimates for 2001 released October 2003. The Census' multiracial category was apportioned into each of the five single race/ethnicity categories in proportion to each category's relative size. These estimates are based on the 2000 decennial Census and come from the Population Estimates Program, Census Bureau, Population Division.

[a]Risk was calculated by dividing the number of children with disabilities in the racial/ethnic group by the total number of children in the racial/ethnic group.

[b]Overall risk ratios were calculated by dividing the risk index for the racial/ethnic group by the risk index for all other students.

[c]The race/ethnicity total may not equal Part B total for the 50 states and D.C. because not all children were reported by race/ethnicity.

- American Indian/Alaska Native children ages 3 through 5 were 1.3 times more likely to be served under Part B than all other groups combined.

- White children ages 3 through 5 were 1.3 times more likely to be served under Part B than all other groups combined.

- Asian/Pacific Islander children ages 3 through 5 were just over half as likely to be served under Part B than all other groups combined.

- In 2000, 51 percent of preschoolers received special education services in either early childhood settings or part-time early childhood/part-time special education settings.

- Only 3 percent of preschoolers were served primarily at home.

- A total of 14.6 percent of preschoolers were served in other settings, including residential facilities, separate schools, itinerant services outside the home, or reverse mainstream settings.

Trends in Preschool Service Settings

What is the primary service setting for preschoolers with disabilities?

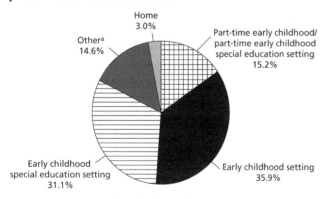

Figure 12 Percentage of preschoolers with disabilities served in various settings: 2000–01

Source: U.S. Department of Education, Office of Special Education Programs, Data Analysis System (DANS), Table AB1. Data are for the 50 states, D.C., Puerto Rico, and the outlying areas.

[a]Other includes residential facilities, separate schools, itinerant services outside the home, and reverse mainstream preschool environment. (The reverse mainstream setting is an educational program designed primarily for children with disabilities that includes 50 percent or more children without disabilities.)

Do service settings for preschoolers differ by racial/ethnic group?

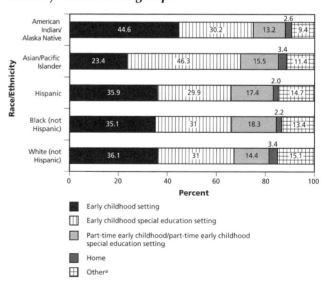

Figure 13 Preschool service setting by racial/ethnic group: 2000–01

Source: U.S. Department of Education, Office of Special Education Programs, Data Analysis System (DANS), Table AB9 in vol. 2. Data are for the 50 states, D.C., Puerto Rico, and the outlying areas.

- American Indian/Alaska Native preschoolers with disabilities are more likely to receive special education and related services in early childhood settings than are children from any other group (44.6 percent).
- Asian/Pacific Islander preschoolers with disabilities are most likely to receive special education and related services in early childhood special education settings than are children from any other group (46.3 percent).
- Black preschoolers with disabilities are more likely than other preschool children to receive special education and related services in a part-time early childhood/part-time early childhood special education setting (18.3 percent).
- Hispanic and white preschoolers with disabilities are more likely than other preschool children to receive special education and related services in "other" settings (14.7 percent and 15.1 percent, respectively).

Workforce

What are the characteristics of teachers who serve preschoolers with special needs?

During the 2000–01 school year, there were 34,342 special education teachers serving preschoolers with disabilities in the United States and outlying areas. About 88.8 percent of them were fully certified for their positions. According to the Study of Personnel Needs in Special Education (SPeNSE):
[These figures are from DANS, Table AC1 in vol. 2; other data are from SPeNSE. See http://ferdig.coe.ufl.edu/spense/for more information on preschool teachers and other special education personnel.]

- 98.6 percent were female;
- 90.0 percent were white;
- 6.4 percent were Hispanic; and
- 6.5 percent have a disability.

The average preschool special education teacher serves 14 children, and 72 percent of preschool special education teachers serve children ages birth to 5 exclusively.

SPeNSE, another component of OSEP's National Assessment studies, described the quality of the workforce serving children and youth with disabilities and factors affecting workforce quality.

How do preschool special education teachers spend their time?

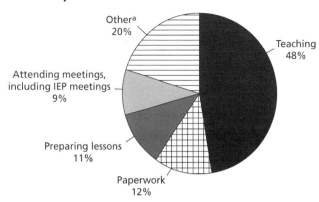

Figure 14 How preschool special education teachers spend their time: 2000
Source: SPeNSE Service Provider Survey. The percentages above are based on the mean number of hours spent per week on each activity. Preschool teachers worked 49.9 hours per week on average.

How long do preschool special education teachers intend to stay in the field?

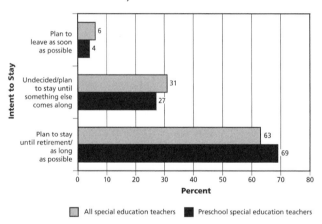

Figure 15 How long preschool special education teachers intend to stay in the field, as compared to all special education teachers: 2000
Source: SPeNSE Service Provider Survey.

- Almost 70 percent of preschool special education teachers are planning to remain in the field until they retire or as long as possible.

Students Ages 6 Through 21 Served Under Idea, Part B

Since the 1975 passage of the Education for All Handicapped Children Act (EHA, PL 94-142), the Department of Education has collected data on the number of children served under the law. Early collections of data on the number of children with disabilities served under Part B of IDEA used nine disability categories. Through the subsequent years and multiple reauthorizations of the act, the disability categories have been expanded to 13 and revised, and new data collections have been required.

In 1997, the law was reauthorized with several major revisions (IDEA Amendments of 1997; PL 105-17). One revision was the requirement that race/ethnicity data be collected on the number of children served. The reauthorization also allowed states the option of reporting children ages 6 through 9 under the developmental delay category.

How many 6- through 21-year-olds are served under IDEA?

[Source: U.S. Department of Education, Office of Special Education Programs, Data Analysis System (DANS), Tables AA1, AA3, and AF7 in vol. 2. Data are for the 50 states, D.C., Puerto Rico, and the outlying areas.]

- On December 1, 2001, a total of 5,867,234 students with disabilities in the 6-through-21 age group were served under IDEA. Of these 5,795,334 were served in the 50 states and the District of Columbia. This number represented 8.9 percent of the general 6- through 21-year-old population living in the United States.
  [The percentage of population was calculated using the July 1 population estimates for 2001 released October 2003. The number served in the 50 states and the District of Columbia was divided by the general U.S. population estimate for this age range.]

- Based on public school enrollment, 12.1 percent of students were receiving special education and related services in 2001.
  [The percentage of public school enrollment was calculated using 2001–02 data from the Common Core of Data. The total number served was divided by the total student enrollment for the 50 states, D.C. Puerto Rico, and the outlying areas.]

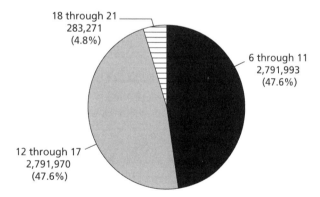

Figure 16 Number and percentage of students ages 6 through 21, served under IDEA, by age group, during the 2001–02 school year

Source: U.S. Department of Education, Office of Special Education Programs, Data Analysis System (DANS), Table AA1 in vol. 2. Data are for the 50 states, D.C., Puerto Rico, and the outlying areas.

- Almost equal numbers of 6- through 11- and 12- through 17-year-olds received special education services in 2001.

- For the 2001–02 school year, 6- through 11-year-olds with disabilities made up 48 percent of the total served under IDEA; 12- through 17-year-olds made up 48 percent, and 18- through 21-year-olds made up the remainder.

How has the number of 6- through 21-year-olds served under IDEA, Part B, changed over time?

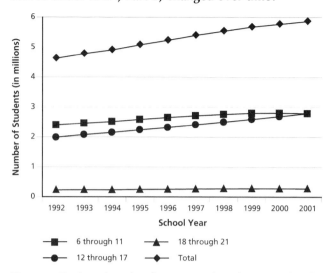

Figure 17 Total number of students ages 6 through 21 served under IDEA, by age group: 1992–93 to 2001–02

Source: U.S. Department of Education, Office of Special Education Programs, Data Analysis System (DANS), Table AA9 in vol. 2. Data are for the 50 states, D.C., Puerto Rico, and the outlying areas.

- Since 1992–93, the number of students ages 18 through 21 served under IDEA has remained fairly constant.

- The number of 6- through 11-year-olds served under IDEA grew until 1999–2000 and has since shown small declines in the number of children served. The number of 12- through 17-year-olds served under IDEA has grown each year.

Has the disability distribution of children receiving services for specific learning disabilities and autism under Part B changed over time?

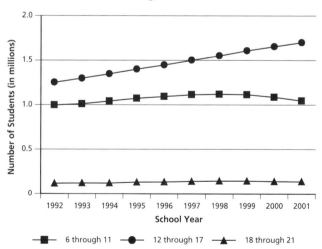

Figure 18 Number of students with specific learning disabilities served under IDEA, by age group: 1992–93 to 2001–02

Source: U.S. Department of Education, Office of Special Education Programs, Data Analysis System (DANS), Table AA9 in vol. 2. Data are for the 50 states, D.C., Puerto Rico, and the outlying areas.

• While the number of students receiving services for specific learning disabilities in the 12-through-17 age group has increased over the past 10 years, the number of 6- through 11-year-olds and 18- through 21-year-olds has remained steady.

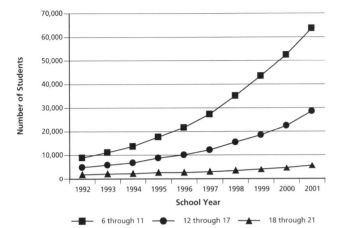

Figure 19 Number of students with autism served under IDEA, by age group: 1992–93 to 2001–02

Source: U.S. Department of Education, Office of Special Education Programs, Data Analysis System (DANS), Table AA9 in vol. 2. Data are for the 50 states, D.C., Puerto Rico, and the outlying areas.

• Autism was added as an optional reporting category in 1991 and was a required category beginning in 1992.

• Although autism makes up a small percentage of children served under IDEA, the number of students receiving services for autism in the 6-through-11 and 12-through-17 age groups grew markedly over the past 10 years.

How many students have co-occurring disabilities?

Table 3 Percentage of students with co-occurring disabilities: 2000–01

	Children (ages 6 through 12)	Youth (ages 13 through 17)
One disability	56.9	42.9
Two disabilities	28.6	19.2
Three disabilities	10.0	28.0
Four or more disabilities	4.5	9.0

Sources: SEELS Parent Survey and NLTS2 Parent Survey.

• Nearly 15 percent of students with disabilities ages 6 through 12 have three or more disabilities; almost 30 percent have two disabilities; and more than half have only one disability.

• About 28 percent of students with disabilities ages 13 through 17 have three disabilities; 19 percent have two disabilities and about 43 percent have only one disability.

These data come from National Assessment studies sponsored by OSEP. The Special Education Elementary Longitudinal Study (SEELS) and the National Longitudinal Transition Study-2 (NLTS2) examine the characteristics, experiences, and achievements of a nationally representative sample of elementary, middle, and secondary students receiving special education and related services.

In which categories are students with attention deficit disorder/attention deficit hyperactivity disorder (ADD/ADHD) served?

Table 4 Distribution of parent-reported student ADD/ADHD by primary disability category[a]: 2000–01

Primary IDEA category[b]	Percentage of ADD/ADHD students served[c]
Specific learning disabilities	41
Speech/language impairments	15
Mental retardation	11
Emotional disturbance	14
Hearing impairments	1
Visual impairments	0
Orthopedic impairments	1
Other health impairments	12
Autism	2
Traumatic brain injury	0
Multiple disabilities	2
Deaf-blindness	0
Total	99

Source: SEELS Parent Survey.

[a]SEELS uses the acronym AD/HD for these students.]

[b]SEELS did not sample students with developmental delay.

[c]Total does not equal 100 due to rounding.

• SEELS data indicate that, overall, 27 percent of students with disabilities have ADD/ADHD, according to parent reports.

• Although students with ADD/ADHD are served under IDEA, it is not a discrete disability category. Forty-one percent of all elementary and middle school-aged students with disabilities whose parents report that their children have ADD/ADHD are served under the specific learning disabilities category, while each of four other disability categories contains more than 10 percent of these students.

Gender

What is the gender distribution for students ages 6 through 12 with disabilities?

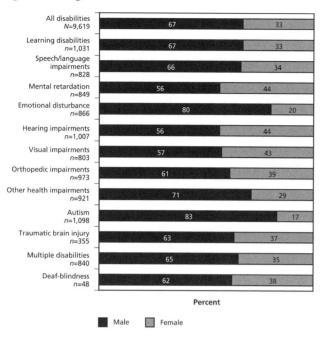

Figure 20 Disability category[a] by gender for students ages 6 through 12: 2000–01

Source: SEELS Parent Survey.

[a]SEELS did not sample students classified as developmentally delayed.

What is the gender distribution for students ages 13 through 17 with disabilities?

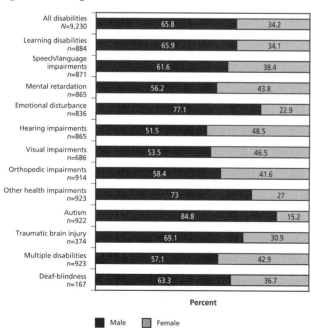

Figure 21 Disability category by gender for students ages 13 through 17: 2000

Source: NLTS2 Parent Survey.

- According to SEELS and NLTS2, males account for almost two-thirds of students ages 6 through 17 served under IDEA. In children ages 6 through 12, males represent 80 percent of students with emotional disturbance and 83 percent of students with autism. In those ages 13 through 17, they represent 77 percent of students with emotional disturbance and 85 percent of students with autism.

Race/Ethnicity

[The race/ethnicity categories presented here are those used by the Office of Special Education Programs to collect the IDEA, Section 618 data. Other racial/ethnic categories or combinations of racial/ethnic categories are used in other data included in this report.]

What is the racial/ethnic composition of the 6- through 21-year-old IDEA population?

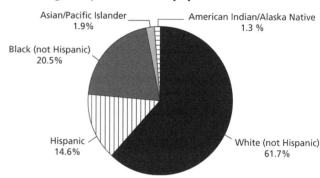

Figure 22 Racial/ethnic composition of students ages 6 through 21 served under IDEA, Part B: 2001[a]

Source: U.S. Department of Education, Office of Special Education Programs, Data Analysis System (DANS), Table AA15 in vol. 2.

[a]Data are for 50 states and District of Columbia.

- While 16.6 percent of children between the ages of 6 and 21 in the general population are Hispanic and 15.1 percent are black, according to 2001 population estimates, black students make up a larger proportion of students served under IDEA than do Hispanic students.

[Population data are July 1 estimates for 2001, based on the 2000 decennial Census. The estimates were released by the Population Estimates Program, U.S. Census Bureau, Population Division in October 2003.]

What disabilities do students ages 6 through 21 have who receive special education services?

Table 5 Disability distribution, by race/ethnicity, of students ages 6 through 21 served under IDEA: 2001

Disability	American Indian/Alaska Native	Asian/Pacific Islander	Black (not Hispanic)	Hispanic	White (not Hispanic)	All students served
Specific learning disabilities	56.0	42.1	45.4	58.9	48.1	49.2
Speech or language impairments	16.8	25.1	14.6	17.7	20.0	18.6
Mental retardation	8.2	9.4	17.4	8.1	8.6	10.3
Emotional disturbance	7.7	5.0	11.3	5.0	8.0	8.1
Multiple disabilities	2.3	2.7	2.1	2.0	2.2	2.2
Hearing impairments	1.1	3.0	1.0	1.6	1.1	1.2
Orthopedic impairments	0.8	1.8	0.9	1.3	1.4	1.3
Other health impairments	4.4	4.4	4.3	3.2	7.0	5.8
Visual impairments	0.4	0.8	0.4	0.5	0.4	0.4
Autism	0.8	4.1	1.4	1.1	1.8	1.7
Deaf-blindness	0.0	0.1	0.0	0.0	0.0	0.0
Traumatic brain injury	0.3	0.4	0.3	0.3	0.4	0.4
Developmental delay	1.2	1.0	0.9	0.4	0.8	0.8
All disabilities	100.0	100.0	100.0	100.0	100.0	100.0

Source: U.S. Department of Education, Office of Special Education Programs, Data Analysis System (DANS), Table AA15 in vol. 2. Data are for the 50 states, D.C., Puerto Rico, and the outlying areas.

- For all racial/ethnic groups, more students with specific learning disabilities were served than students with any other disability in 2001.

- The percentages of white students in most disability categories are very similar to the percentages for the IDEA student population as a whole.

- The order of the five largest disability categories is the same for four of the five race/ethnicity groups: specific learning disabilities, speech or language impairments, mental retardation, emotional disturbance, and other health impairments. For black students, however, mental retardation is the second most frequently reported disability category.

- The percentages of American Indian/Alaska Native and Hispanic students with disabilities who received special education for specific learning disabilities are relatively higher when compared with the percentage for all students with disabilities (56.0 percent and 58.9 percent v. 49.2 percent). The percentage of Asian/Pacific Islander students with disabilities who have specific learning disabilities is lower than the percentage for all students with disabilities (42.1 percent v. 49.2 percent).

- The percentage of black students with specific learning disabilities is lower than the percentage of all students with specific learning disabilities served under Part B (45.4 percent v. 49.2 percent).

- The percentage of black students with disabilities who received special education services for mental retardation is substantially higher than the percentage for any other racial/ethnic group (17.4 percent compared with 8.2 percent for American Indian/Alaska Native students with disabilities, 9.4 percent for Asian/Pacific Islander students with disabilities, 8.1 percent for Hispanic students with disabilities, and 8.6 percent for white students with disabilities).

- The percentage of black students with disabilities who received special education services for emotional disturbance is considerably higher than the percentage for any other racial/ethnic group (11.3 percent compared with 7.7 percent for American Indian/Alaska Native students with disabilities, 5.0 percent for Asian/Pacific Islander students with disabilities, 5.0 percent for Hispanic students with disabilities, and 8.0 percent for white students with disabilities).

- The percentage of white students with disabilities who received special education services for other health impairments is nearly twice the percentage for the nearest racial/ethnic group (7.0 percent v. 4.4 percent).

What is the likelihood of students ages 6 through 21 in each racial/ethnic group being identified with a given disability as compared to that of all other students ages 6 through 21?

Risk ratios compare the proportion of a particular racial/ethnic group served under Part B to the proportion of all other racial/ethnic groups combined. A risk ratio of 1.0 indicates no difference between the racial/ethnic groups.

Table 6 Overall risk ratios[a] for students ages 6 through 21, by race/ethnicity for selected disability categories: 2001–02

Disability	American Indian/ Alaska Native	Asian/Pacific Islander	Black (not Hispanic)	Hispanic	White (not Hispanic)
Specific learning disabilities	1.50	0.39	1.31	1.07	0.88
Speech or language impairments	1.21	0.65	1.07	0.82	1.13
Mental retardation	1.09	0.44	2.99	0.58	0.63
Emotional disturbance	1.25	0.29	2.21	0.52	0.87
Multiple disabilities	1.33	0.57	1.40	0.76	1.00
Hearing impairments	1.25	1.20	1.11	1.19	0.81
Orthopedic impairments	0.89	0.70	0.96	0.90	1.15
Other health impairments	1.07	0.36	0.99	0.44	1.69
Visual impairments	1.19	0.94	1.21	0.89	0.96
Autism	0.64	1.22	1.17	0.52	1.22
Deaf-blindness	1.94	0.93	0.90	0.96	1.05
Traumatic brain injury	1.25	0.56	1.27	0.62	1.18
Developmental delay	1.98	0.64	1.65	0.44	1.06
All Disabilities	1.33	0.47	1.45	0.86	0.93

Source: U.S. Department of Education, Office of Special Education Programs, Data Analysis System (DANS), Tables AA15 in vol. 2. Data are for the 50 states, D.C., Puerto Rico, and the outlying areas. Population data are July 1 estimates for 2001 released October 2003. The Census' multiracial category was apportioned into each of the five single race/ethnicity categories in proportion to each category's relative size. The estimates are based on the 2000 decennial Census and come from the Population Estimates Program, Census Bureau, Population Division.

[a]Overall risk ratios were calculated by dividing the risk index for the racial/ethnic group by the risk index for all other students. Risk was calculated by dividing the number of children with disabilities in the racial/ethnic group by the total number of children in the racial/ethnic group.

- Black students are 2.99 times more likely to be classified as having mental retardation and 2.21 times more likely to be classified as having emotional disturbance than all other groups combined.

- American Indian/Alaska Native students are 1.50 times more likely to be served for specific learning disabilities than all other groups combined.

- Asian/Pacific Islander students are less than half as likely to be served for specific learning disabilities, mental retardation, emotional disturbance, or other health impairments than all other groups combined.

- Hispanic students are less than half as likely to be served for other health impairments and developmental delay than all other groups combined.

Household Income

What is the household income of families with students ages 6 through 17 who receive special education?

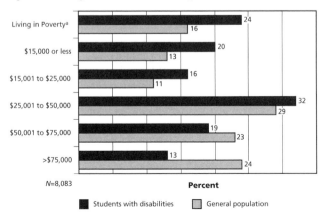

Figure 23 Families of students ages 6 through 12, by household income level and by disability status: 2000–01

Sources: Income in 1999 for households of 6- to 13-year-olds with disabilities, SEELS Parent Survey, 2002; Income in 1997 for households with children ages 6 to 17, U.S. Census, 2001. Population income data from the National Household Education Survey (NHES), 1999.

[a]SEELS uses the federal Orshansky index to define poverty. This is adjusted for family size, and it is computed as the estimated cash to minimally meet food needs x 3. It is based on income rather than resources and ignores many non-cash benefits (food stamps, school lunches, Medicaid, housing subsidies, educational grants, and loans). It ignores wealth (i.e., owning a farm is not counted). For SEELS, the parents of students with disabilities reported their household income in categories (e.g., $25,001–$50,000) rather than a specific dollar value; thus, the poverty rates for SEELS data are estimated.

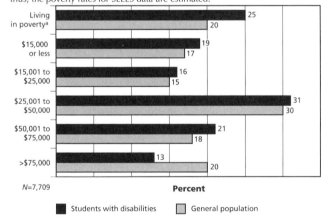

N=7,709

Figure 24 Families of students ages 13 through 17, by household income level and by disability status: 2001

Sources: NLTS2 Parent Survey. Population income data are from the National Household Education Survey (NHES), 1999.

[a]A dichotomous variable indicating that a student's household was in poverty was constructed using parents' reports of household income and household size and federal poverty thresholds for 2000. These thresholds indicate the income level; however, NLTS2 respondents reported household income in categories (e.g., $25,501 to $30,000) rather than a specific dollar amount. Estimates of poverty status were calculated by assigning each household to the mean value of the category of income reported by the parent and comparing that value to the household's size to determine poverty status.

- As reported by parents, students with disabilities are more likely to be poor than students in the general population. According to SEELS and NLTS2 data, almost one-fourth (24 percent) of elementary and middle school students and 25 percent of high school students with disabilities live in poverty compared with 20 percent of the general population. In 1987, 38 percent of high school students with disabilities lived in poverty.

Use of Medications

How many school-age children with disabilities are taking medications?

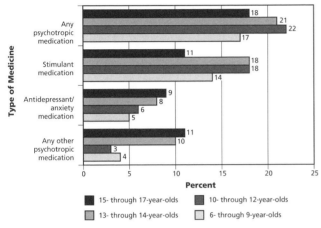

Figure 25 Medication use of children with disabilities, by age group and type of medicine: 2000–01

Sources: SEELS Parent Survey; NLTS2 Parent Survey.

- The use of psychotropic medications is highest among middle-school-age students. Parents report that 17 percent of 6- through 9-year-olds take these medications compared with 22 percent of those who were 10 through 12 years old and 21 percent of 13- through

14-year-olds. The rate declines to 18 percent among older high school students.

- Stimulants are the most commonly reported psychotropic medications; 14 percent of early elementary students take them. The rate of use rises to 18 percent for middle schoolers and declines to 11 percent of youth ages 15 through 17.

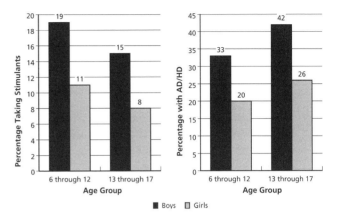

Figure 26 Percentage of students with disabilities ages 6 through 17 taking stimulant medication and classified as ADD/ADHD, by gender: 2000–01

Sources: SEELS Parent Survey; NLTS2 Parent Survey.

- Boys are much more likely than girls to take stimulants. Among boys, 19 percent of 6- through 12-year-olds and 15 percent of 13- through 17-year-olds take stimulants. This compares with 11 percent and 8 percent of girls in the two age groups.
- The high rate of taking stimulant medications among boys is consistent with the high rate of parent-reported ADD/ADHD among boys. Almost one-third of 6- through 12-year-old boys and 42 percent of 13- through 17-year-old boys are reported by parents to have ADD/ADHD. Rates for girls are 20 percent and 26 percent for the two age groups.

Table 7 Percentage of students with disabilities using medications, by disability category and age: 2000–01

Disability	Any psychotropic medication		Antidepressant or antianxiety medication		Antipsychotic medication		Any other psychotropic medication	
	Ages 6–12	Ages 13–17	Ages 6–12	Ages 13–17	Ages 6–12	Ages 13–17	Ages 6–12	Ages 13–17
Learning disability	8	13	15	9	4	5	2	6
Speech/language impairment	8	10	7	6	2	5	1	5
Mental retardation	24	19	18	12	7	8	6	12
Emotional disturbance	52	42	40	29	24	29	16	34
Hearing impairment	13	10	11	6	4	5	1	6
Visual impairment	12	13	6	4	5	7	4	9
Orthopedic impairment	24	16	19	11	6	7	4	9
Other health impairment	52	44	47	38	13	21	7	25
Autism	3	43	20	22	19	32	14	38
Traumatic brain Injury	25	23	15	12	11	15	10	19
Multiple disabilities	27	25	19	15	8	14	8	20
Deaf-blindness	17	20	4	8	7	12	12	15

Sources: SEELS Parent Survey; NLTS2 Parent Survey.

- Some students in each disability category take psychotropic medication. This is due, in part, to some students in each disability category also having ADD/ADHD and emotional disturbance, according to parental reports.

- The number of students with disabilities taking psychotropic medications ranges from 10 percent or fewer of those with speech impairments to about half of children and youth with emotional disturbance or other health impairments. According to SEELS and NLTS2, among elementary and middle school students whose parents report they have ADD/ADHD, 65 percent take some kind of psychotropic medication, with 55 percent taking stimulants specifically.

- Taking stimulants is highest among those with emotional disturbance or other health impairments, according to SEELS and NLTS2.

- Use of other kinds of psychotropic medications increases with age for all disability categories.

Social Activities and Outcomes

How often do children with disabilities socialize outside the classroom?

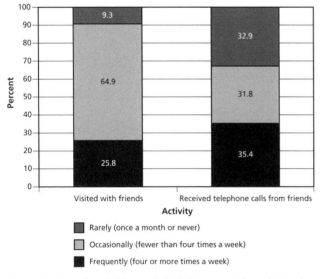

Figure 27 How often children with disabilities ages 6 through 12 either visit with or receive telephone calls from friends: 2000–01

Source: SEELS Parent Survey.

- According to parent reports, more than 90 percent of students with disabilities ages 6 through 12 visit with friends outside of school occasionally or frequently.

- According to the SEELS Parent Survey, the correlations between children with disabilities who received phone calls and visits from friends and other social interactions ranged from .27 to .32 ($p < .001$ and $p < .001$ across the relationships).

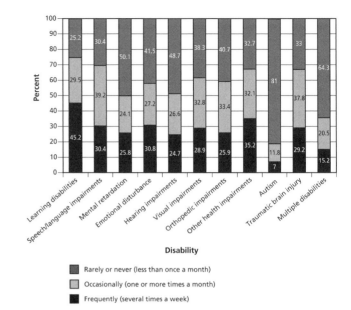

Figure 28 How often children with disabilities ages 6 through 12 received calls from friends, by disability category[a,b]: 2000–01

Source: SEELS Parent Survey.

[a]SEELS did not sample students with developmental delay.

[b]There were too few students with deaf/blindness to report.

- As reported by parents, students with autism, multiple disabilities, mental retardation, or hearing impairments are less likely to receive telephone calls from friends.

- Students with learning disabilities receive calls from friends most frequently.

How many elementary and middle school students with disabilities participate in extracurricular activities, compared to students without disabilities?

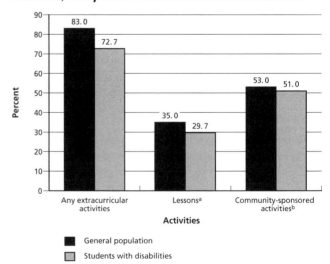

Figure 29 Participation in extracurricular activities, by disability status and activity: 2000–01

Sources: SEELS Parent Survey; National Survey of America's Families, 1999.

- Almost three-fourths of elementary and middle school children with disabilities are reported by their parents to have participated in extracurricular activities during the 1999–2000 school year. This is slightly less than the general population, according to the National Survey of America's Families.

- Slightly over 50 percent of elementary and middle school children with disabilities, according to their parents, participate in community-sponsored activities. This appears to be about as often as their counterparts in the general population.

How do secondary school-age students with disabilities spend their time outside of school?

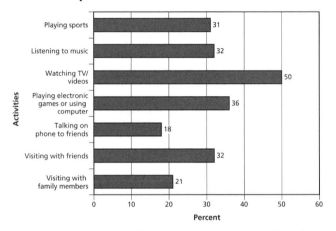

Figure 30 Activities reported by parents as most common for students with disabilities ages 13 through 17: 2001
Source: NLTS2 Parent Survey.

- Television and video watching is the activity most commonly reported by parents.

- According to the NLTS2 Parent Survey, parents report that youth with disabilities spend an average of almost 16 hours per week watching TV and videos. About 25 percent of youth with disabilities are relatively infrequent TV and video watchers, spending 6 hours or fewer per week watching them. A similar percentage spend more than 20 hours a week in front of the television set.

- The survey also showed that girls are significantly more likely than boys to spend time with family members (girls: 26.0 percent, boys: 17.7 percent) and on the phone with friends (girls: 22.7 percent; boys: 15.0 percent). They also are more likely than boys to spend time listening to music (girls: 37.2 percent; boys: 28.8 percent). In contrast, boys are more likely than girls to spend time playing sports or in other physical or outdoor activities (boys: 48.0 percent; girls: 29.2 percent), and more boys than girls spend most of their time using the computer for electronic games, communication, or other purposes (boys: 38.6 percent; girls: 30.6 percent).

Discipline and Social Problems at School

Do suspension and expulsion rates differ by race/ethnicity?

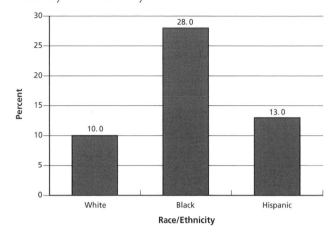

Figure 31 Elementary and middle school-age students with disabilities ages 6 through 12, suspended/expelled from school, by race/ethnicity[a]: 2000–01
Source: SEELS Parent Survey.

[a]SEELS data yielded too few observations for other races/ethnicities to report.

- Parents report more suspensions and expulsions for black students (28 percent) than for Hispanic students (13 percent) or white students (10 percent).

How often are secondary school-age students with disabilities suspended or expelled?

Table 8 Suspension and expulsions of students with disabilities by age: 2001

Suspended or expelled	Age 13 through 14	Age 15	Age 16	Age 17	Total
No	72.7	65.9	64.5	64.3	67.3
Yes	27.3	34.1	35.5	35.7	32.7
No. of students in sample	3,021	2,194	2,215	1,410	8,840

Source: NLTS2 Parent Survey.

- About one-third of all students ages 13 through 17 with disabilities have been suspended or expelled.

- More older students with disabilities were expelled than were 13- through 14-year-olds.

What is the percentage of 6- through 12-year-old students with disabilities who have been suspended or expelled?

- According to 2000–01 SEELS data, parents reported that 8.7 percent of 6- through 9-year-olds have been suspended or expelled. For 10- through 12-year-olds, the percentage is 18.9 percent.
  [These data differ from the data reported by states on discipline actions because NLTS2 and SEELS data are based

on parent reports of whether a student with a disability was ever suspended or expelled. States report counts of students with disabilities who were suspended or expelled for more than 10 days during a given school year only, and the source of these data is school administrative records.]

Do suspensions and expulsions for secondary school-age students differ by race/ethnicity?

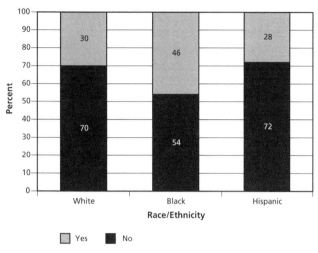

Figure 32 Youths with disabilities ages 13 through 17 ever suspended or expelled from school, by race/ethnicity: 2001

Source: NLTS2 Parent Survey.

- When asked whether their child had ever been suspended or expelled, 46 percent of parents of black students responded "Yes." White and Hispanic parents responded to this question in the affirmative less often; 30 percent and 28 percent, respectively, indicating that their child had ever been suspended or expelled (NLTS2 Parent Survey).

What percentage of students with disabilities experience other social problems at school?

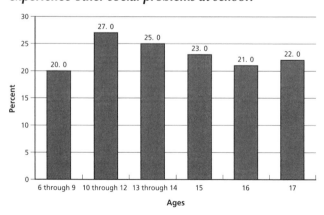

Figure 33 Percentage of students with disabilities who have been physically attacked or involved in fights at school, by age: 2000–01

Sources: SEELS Parent Survey, NLTS2 Parent Survey.

- According to parental reports in the SEELS study, 20 percent of students ages 6 through 9 with disabilities have been physically attacked or involved in fights at school, and more than a quarter of 10- through 12-year-olds with disabilities have been physically attacked or involved in fights at school (27 percent).

- Approximately one-quarter of students ages 13 through 17 were physically attacked or involved in fights at school.

Educational Environments

To what extent are students with disabilities educated with their nondisabled peers?

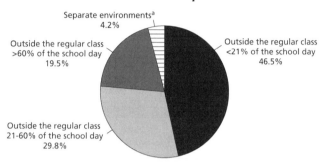

Figure 34 Educational environments of students ages 6 through 21 with disabilities: 2000

Source: U.S. Department of Education, Office of Special Education Programs, Data Analysis System (DANS), Table AB2 in vol. 2. Data are for the 50 states, D.C., Puerto Rico, and the outlying areas.

[a]Separate environments include public and private residential facilities, public and private separate facilities, and homebound/hospital environments.

- Most students (about 96 percent) with disabilities are being educated in regular school buildings.

- Almost half of all students with disabilities (46.5 percent) are being educated in the regular classroom for most of the school day. That is, they are outside the regular classroom for less than 21 percent of the school day.

Are students with different disabilities served in different educational environments?

Table 9 Percentage of students ages 6 through 21 with disabilities receiving services in different educational environments: December 1, 2000

Disabilities	Served outside the regular class			Separate environments[a]
	<21 percent of the day	21–60 percent of the day	>60 percent of the day	
Specific learning disabilities	44.3	40.3	14.4	1.0
Speech or language impairments	85.6	8.4	5.1	0.9
Mental retardation	13.2	29.1	51.7	6.1
Emotional disturbance	26.8	23.4	31.8	18.1
Multiple disabilities	12.1	16.0	45.5	26.4
Hearing impairments	42.3	20.0	22.5	15.3
Orthopedic impairments	46.4	23.4	24.3	6.0
Other health impairments	45.1	33.9	16.7	4.4
Visual impairments	50.5	20.1	16.0	13.4
Autism	24.3	15.3	46.4	14.0
Deaf-blindness	18.1	9.9	34.2	37.8
Traumatic brain injury	32.3	27.9	29.4	10.4
Developmental delay	46.4	29.9	22.3	1.3

Source: U.S. Department of Education, Office of Special Education Programs, Data Analysis System (DANS), Table AB2 in vol. 2. Data are for the 50 states, D.C., Puerto Rico, and the outlying areas.

[a]Separate environments (public and private residential facilities, public and private separate facilities, and homebound/hospital environments)

- The percentage of students in each educational environment varies by disability category:
  - Students with speech or language impairments are most likely to be educated with their nondisabled peers. They are also the least likely to be educated in the most restrictive, separate environments.
  - Students with multiple disabilities, mental retardation, or deaf-blindness are the least likely to be educated in the most inclusive environments, that is, outside the regular classroom less than 21 percent of the day.
  - Students with deaf-blindness or multiple disabilities are most likely to be educated in separate environments.

- Overall, 28 percent of students with disabilities ages 6 through 12 are served in the regular education classroom 100 percent of the time (SEELS School Survey).
- Students with speech/language impairments are most commonly served in the regular education classroom 100 percent of the time (55 percent).
- Students with mental retardation and multiple disabilities are most rarely served in the regular education classroom 100 percent of the time (7 percent and 5 percent, respectively).

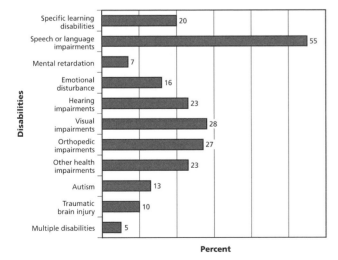

Figure 35 Percentage of students ages 6 through 12 included in the regular classroom 100 percent of the time, by disability category[a,b]: 2001

Source: SEELS School Survey.

[a]SEELS did not sample students with developmental delay.

[b]There were too few students with deaf-blindness to report.

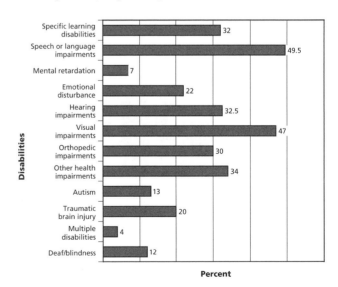

Figure 36 Percentage of students with disabilities ages 13 through 17 included in the regular classroom 100 percent of the time, by disability: 2002

Source: NLTS2 School Survey.

- Overall, 28.2 percent of students with disabilities ages 13 through 17 are served in the regular classroom 100 percent of the time (NLTS2 School Survey).

- In a comparison of school data collected in 1987 (NLTS) and 2002 (NLTS2), students ages 15 through 19 with disabilities were about equally likely to receive some instruction in general education classes (83 percent vs. 88 percent); however, they were much less likely to spend any time in a special education class (90 percent vs. 70 percent). This suggests that a larger proportion of the school day was spent in general education in 1987 than in 2002.

- In 2002, students with disabilities were more likely to be attending regular public schools (94 percent in NLTS2 vs. 90 percent in NLTS) than in 1987.

- Students with disabilities were much more likely in 2002 than in 1987 to be taking courses that prepared them for postsecondary education, including mathematics (92 percent vs. 72 percent), science (83 percent vs. 50 percent), social studies (88 percent vs. 74 percent), and foreign language (21 percent vs. 5 percent). They were less likely to take vocational education (61 percent vs. 76 percent) (2002 data are from the NLTS2 School Survey; 1987 data are from NLTS).

- According to the NLTS2 School Survey and the SEELS School Survey, students in seven disability categories ages 13 through 17 were included in the regular classroom 100 percent of the time more often than students in those categories ages 6 through 12 (see Figure 35). The largest percentage difference was for those with visual impairment at 19 percent.

Source: U.S. Department of Education, Office of Special Education Programs, Data Analysis System (DANS), Table AB2 in vol. 2. Data are for the 50 states, D.C., Puerto Rico, and the outlying areas.

- As might be expected, students with severe disabilities are more likely to be educated outside the regular classroom for longer periods of the day. Less than one-quarter of students with mental retardation, multiple disabilities, autism, or deaf-blindness spend less than 21 percent of the school day being educated outside the regular classroom.

- Students with speech or language impairments are most likely to be educated in the regular classroom for longer periods of the day. A total of 85.6 percent of students with this type of disability spend less than 21 percent of the school day being educated outside the regular classroom.

- Students with the most severe types of disabilities are more likely to be educated in separate environments. A total of 37.8 percent of students with deaf-blindness, 26.4 percent of students with multiple disabilities, and 18.1 percent of students with emotional disturbance are educated principally in separate environments.

- Very small percentages of students with specific learning disabilities, speech or language impairments, or developmental delay are educated in separate environments (approximately 1.0 percent of students within each of these disabilities).

Where are students of different ages served?

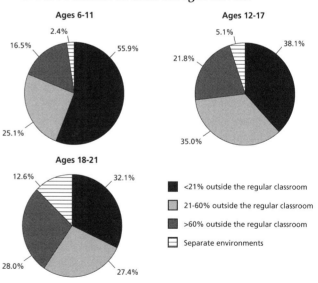

Figure 38 Percentage of students with disabilities educated in various environments, by age group: 2000[a]

Source: U.S. Department of Education, Office of Special Education Programs, Data Analysis System (DANS). Tables AB3, AB4, AB5 in vol. 2. Data are for the 50 states, D.C., Puerto Rico, and the outlying areas.

[a]Separate environments include public and private residential facilities, public and private separate facilities, and homebound/hospital environments.

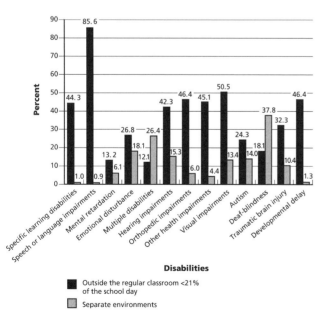

Figure 37 Percentage of students with disabilities ages 6 through 21 educated outside the regular classroom less than 21 percent of the school day and in separate environments: 2000

- Younger students with disabilities are more likely to be educated for more of the school day in the regular classroom. Fifty-six percent of students ages 6 through 11 with disabilities are educated less than 21 percent of the time outside the regular classroom, while 38 percent of those ages 12 through 17 and 32 percent of those ages 18 through 21 are educated less than 21 percent of the time outside the regular classroom.

- A much higher percentage of older students with disabilities are being educated in separate environments (13 percent of those in the 18-through-21 age groups as opposed to 2 percent of those in the 6-through-11 age group and 5 percent of those in the 12-through-17 age group).

To what extent are students with disabilities of different racial/ethnic groups being educated with their nondisabled peers?

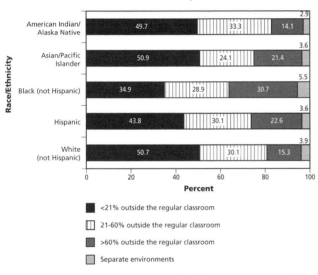

Figure 39 Percentage of students with disabilities ages 6 through 21 being educated in different educational environments, by race/ethnicity: 2000–01

Source: U.S. Department of Education, Office of Special Education Programs, Data Analysis System (DANS), Table AB10 in vol. 2. Data are for the 50 states, D.C., Puerto Rico, and the outlying areas.

- Educational environments differ by race/ethnicity. Black students with disabilities are the least likely of any racial/ethnic group to be educated inside the regular classroom. Fifty-one percent of Asian/Pacific Islander and white students with disabilities are educated outside the regular class less than 21 percent of the day compared to 35 percent of black students with disabilities.

- Black students with disabilities are more likely than American Indian/Alaska Native or white students to be educated outside the regular classroom more than

60 percent of the school day. Thirty-one percent of black students with disabilities are educated outside the regular classroom more than 60 percent of the day compared to 14 percent of American Indian/Alaska Native students with disabilities and 15 percent of white students with disabilities.

- Less than one-half of Hispanic students and approximately one-third of black students with disabilities are being educated less than 21 percent outside the regular classroom.

Have educational environments for students with disabilities changed in the past 10 years?

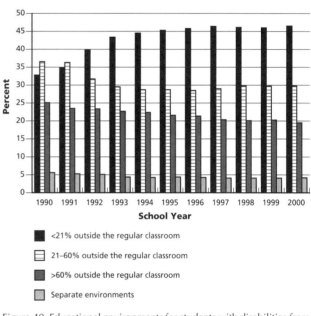

Figure 40 Educational environments for students with disabilities from 1990 to 2000

Source: U.S. Department of Education, Office of Special Education Programs, Data Analysis System (DANS), Table AB7 I in vol. 2. Data are for the 50 states, D.C., Puerto Rico, and the outlying areas.

The trend over the past 10 years has been to serve more children in less restrictive environments. From 1990 to 2000:

- The percentage of students being educated outside the regular class less than 21 percent of the day increased from 33 percent to 46 percent.

- In comparison, the percentage of students being educated in all other environments decreased. The percentage served outside the regular classroom 21 percent to 60 percent of the school day decreased from 36 percent to 30 percent, the percentage served outside the classroom more than 60 percent of the school day decreased from 25 percent to 20 percent, and the percentage of students educated in separate environments decreased from 6 percent to 4 percent.

What supports are available to students with disabilities so they can access the general education curriculum?

Table 10 Percentage of schools reporting teachers' strategies used to support special education students' access to the general education curriculum: 1999–2000

Strategies	Large extent	Moderate extent	Small extent	Not at all
Curriculum modification	51	34	13	3
Instructional modification and adaptation	51	38	11	1
Alternative grouping strategy	30	39	23	8
Cooperative learning	28	46	20	6
Peer tutoring	21	36	38	5
Multiage classrooms	9	14	19	56
Student(s) followed for multiple years	8	10	20	62
Cross-grade grouping	8	16	32	44

Source: SLIIDEA School Survey.

- According to principals, teachers in their school use a variety of teaching strategies to support special education students' access to the general curriculum. More than 80 percent of all schools use modification and adaptation of curriculum and instruction to a moderate or large extent.

- Teachers may also modify the structure of the class to support special education students' access to the general education curriculum. About 70 percent of schools use alternative grouping and cooperative learning strategies, and 57 percent use peer tutoring strategies to a moderate or large extent. Less than 25 percent of schools use multiage classrooms, curriculum looping, or cross-grade grouping to facilitate access to the general education curriculum.

Table 11 Percentage of schools reporting use of support services by one or more students with disabilities: 1999–2000

Support system	One or more students with disabilities used service
Speech or language therapy	89
Occupational therapy	71
Family training, counseling, and other support	56
Nursing service/health service	52
Psychological service	51
Physical therapy	51
Special transportation	50
Social work services	49
One-to-one paraeducator/assistant	49
Assistive technology service/device	45
Tutoring	43
Adaptive physical education	42
Service coordination/case management	41
Audiology/hearing service	37
Vision services	26
Communication service	17

Source: SLIIDEA School Survey.

- Schools use a variety of related services and accommodations to support students with disabilities' access to the general education curriculum. The most commonly reported supports are speech or language therapy (89 percent) and occupational therapy (71 percent).

- A little over half of the schools provided family training and counseling services (56 percent), nursing services (52 percent), psychological services (51 percent), physical therapy (51 percent), and special transportation services (50 percent) to support students with disabilities.

Educational Outcomes for Students with Disabilities

What are the household income and race/ethnicity of students with disabilities retained in grade by percentage?

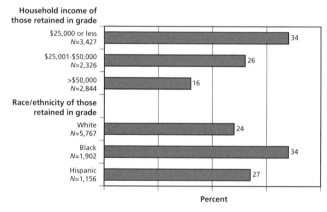

Figure 41 Parents' reports of students ever being retained in grade by household income and race/ethnicity: 2000–01

Source: SEELS Parent Survey.

- Thirty-four percent of students with disabilities with a household income of $25,000 or less had ever been retained in grade, while only 16 percent of students with disabilities with a household income of more than $50,000 ever had been retained in grade.

- A lower percentage of white and Hispanic students had ever been retained in grade (24 percent and 27 percent, respectively), while 34 percent of black students with disabilities had been retained in grade.

How often are students with disabilities retained in grade?

Table 12 Percentage of elementary and middle school students with disabilities, by age and grade level: 2001

	Age								
Grade	6	7	8	9	10	11	12	13	14
Ungraded	12	3	3	2	2	2	1	1	
1st	88	86	32	2					
2nd		10	60	31	2				
3rd			4	61	35	5	1		
4th				4	58	38	6		
5th					2	50	34	4	1
6th						5	53	45	14
7th							5	45	83
8th								4	3
Multigrade		1							
Total	100	100	100	100	100	100	100	100	100

Source: SEELS School Survey.

Note: Details may not add to 100 because of rounding.

- Elementary and middle school students with disabilities often do not move from grade level to grade level with their nondisabled peers; that is, they are held back a grade at least once or start school later than nondisabled students. For example, the average 9-year-old is in the fourth grade; however, only about 4 percent of 9-year-old students with disabilities are in the fourth grade.

- Especially in their early elementary careers, students with disabilities tend to be classified as "ungraded."

- Parents report that 26 percent of elementary and middle school students with disabilities have been retained in grade (SEELS School Survey).

Table 13 Percentage of students with disabilities, ages 13–17, by age and grade level: 2002

	Age			
Grade	13 to 14	15	16	17
Ungraded	1	1	1	3
1st–6th	1			
7th	34	2		
8th	53	27	3	
9th	11	57	26	7
10th	1	14	54	35
11th			14	49
12th or 13th			2	5
Multigrade				1
Total	100	100	100	100

Source: NLTS2 School Survey.

Note: Details may not add to 100 because of rounding.

- According to NLTS2, secondary students with disabilities are frequently retained in grade at least once. While the typical 15-year-old is in 10th grade, only 14.1 percent of 15-year-old students with disabilities who are age 15 are in 10th grade.

- Parents of secondary students with disabilities report that 36 percent of these students have repeated a grade some time in their school enrollment (NLTS2 Parent Survey).

- In 1987, 32 percent of high school students with disabilities were at the typical grade level for their age while in 2001 this proportion was 53 percent (NLTS2 School Survey).

How do students with disabilities perform academically?

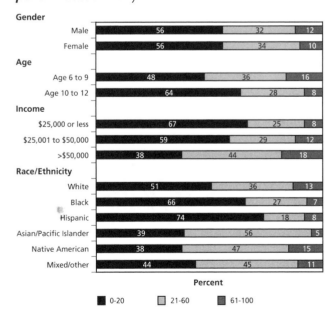

Figure 42 Performance of students with disabilities ages 6 to 12 on standardized assessments of letter-word identification skills (percentage in each percentile rank range), by gender, age income, and race/ethnicity[a,b]: 2001

Source: SEELS Direct Assessment.

[a]For the standardized assessments, each student's performance is associated with a percentile score that reflects the proportion of individuals of that student's age

in the general population who received a lower score on that assessment. The bar segments in the graph indicate the proportion of SEELS students whose percentile rank on the assessment fell within the percentile range (e.g., 0 to 20, 21 to 60, etc.) specified by the segment pattern. For example, 56 percent of the SEELS male students performed similarly to the bottom 20 percent of students in the general population. If students with disabilities were performing on the level of students in the general population, then only about 20 percent of the SEELS students would receive scores similar to their general population age peers in the 0 to 20th percentile range.

[b]Letter-Word Identification—Measures the student's reading skills in identifying isolated letters and words. It is not necessary that the student knows the meaning of any words correctly identified.

How do students with disabilities perform academically?

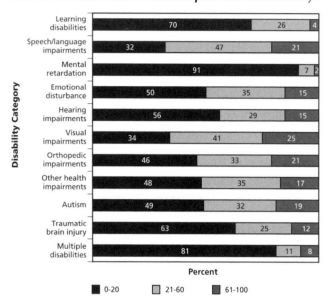

Figure 43 Letter-word identification (percentage in each percentile rank range), by disability category[a,b] for elementary and middle school students with disabilities, ages 6 through 12[c,d]: 2001

Source: SEELS Direct Assessment.

[a]SEELS did not sample students with developmental delay.

[b]There were too few cases of deaf/blindness to report.

[c]For the standardized assessments, each student's performance is associated with a percentile-score that reflects the proportion of individuals of that student's age in the general population who received a lower score on that assessment. The bar segments in the graph indicate the proportion of SEELS students whose percentile rank on the assessment fell within the percentile range (e.g., 0 to 20, 21 to 60, etc.) specified by the segment pattern. For example, 56 percent of the SEELS male students performed similarly to the bottom 20 percent of students in the general population. If students with disabilities were performing on the level of students in the general population, then only about 20 percent of the SEELS students would receive scores similar to their general population age peers in the 0 to 20th percentile range.

[d]Letter-Word Identification—Measures the student's reading skills in identifying isolated letters and words. It is not necessary that the student knows the meaning of any words correctly identified.

How do students with disabilities perform academically?

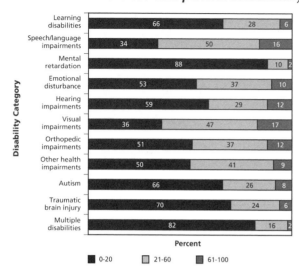

Figure 44 Passage comprehension (percentage in each percentile rank range), by disability category[a,b] for elementary and middle school students with disabilities, ages 6 through 12[c,d]: 2001

Source: SEELS Direct Assessment.

[a]SEELS did not sample students with developmental delay.

[b]There were too few students with deaf/blindness to report.

[c]For the standardized assessments, each student's performance is associated with a percentile score that reflects the proportion of individuals of that student's age in the general population who received a lower score on that assessment. The bar segments in the graph indicate the proportion of SEELS students whose percentile rank on the assessment fell within the percentile range (e.g., 0 to 20, 21 to 60, etc.) specified by the segment pattern. For example, 56 percent of the SEELS male students performed similarly to the bottom 20 percent of students in the general population. If students with disabilities were performing on the level of students in the general population, then only about 20 percent of the SEELS students would receive scores similar to their general population age peers in the 0 to 20th percentile range.

[d]Passage Comprehension—Measures the student's skill in reading a short passage and identifying a missing key word (i.e., a fill in the blank procedure); student must exercise a variety of comprehension and vocabulary skills.

How do students with disabilities perform academically?

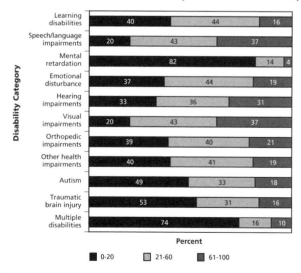

Figure 45 Calculation (percentage in each percentile rank range), by disability category[a,b] for elementary and middle school students with disabilities, ages 6 through 12[c,d]: 2001

Source: SEELS Direct Assessment.

[a]SEELS did not sample students with developmental delay.

[b]There were too few students with deaf/blindness to report.

[c]For the standardized assessments, each student's performance is associated with a percentile score that reflects the proportion of individuals of that student's age in the general population who received a lower score on that assessment. The bar segments in the graph indicate the proportion of SEELS students whose percentile rank on the assessment fell within the percentile range (e.g., 0 to 20, 21 to 60, etc.) specified by the segment pattern. For example, 56 percent of the SEELS male students performed similarly to the bottom 20 percent of students in the general population. If students with disabilities were performing on the level of students in the general population, then only about 20 percent of the SEELS students would receive scores similar to their general population age peers in the 0 to 20th percentile range.

[d]Calculation—Measures the student's ability to perform mathematical calculations ranging from simple addition to calculus; student is not required to make any decisions about what operations to use or what data to include.

How do students with disabilities perform academically?

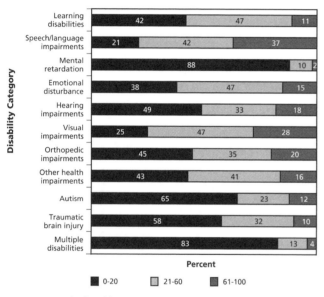

Figure 46 Applied problems (percentage in each percentile rank range), by disability category[a,b] for elementary and middle school students with disabilities, ages 6 through 12[c,d]: 2001

Source: SEELS Direct Assessment.

[a]SEELS did not sample students with developmental delay.

[b]There were too few students with deaf/blindness to report.

[c]For the standardized assessments, each student's performance is associated with a percentile score that reflects the proportion of individuals of that student's age in the general population who received a lower score on that assessment. The bar segments in the graph indicate the proportion of SEELS students whose percentile rank on the assessment fell within the percentile range (e.g., 0 to 20, 21 to 60, etc.) specified by the segment pattern. For example, 56 percent of the SEELS male students performed similarly to the bottom 20 percent of students in the general population. If students with disabilities were performing on the level of students in the general population, then only about 20 percent of the SEELS students would receive scores similar to their general population age peers in the 0 to 20th percentile range.

[d]Problem Solving—Measures the ability to analyze and solve problems in mathematics; student must decide not only the appropriate mathematical operations to use but also which of the data to include in the calculation.

- According to SEELS, among students ages 6 through 12 from the various disability categories, there is great diversity in standardized scores for both reading and mathematics. Some students in each disability category achieve reading and/or math scores at, or close to, those of their same-age peers without disabilities. However, many have not yet become proficient. With the exception of the speech/language impairments and visual impairment categories, nearly 50 percent or more of students in the other disability categories scored at or below the 20th percentile on measures of reading (decoding and comprehension). Overall, students with disabilities receive higher scores on standardized tests of mathematics than reading skills.

- Sixty-seven percent of students with disabilities from low-income households ($25,000 or less) had scores at or below the 20th percentile for letter/word identification. Thirty-eight percent of the students from households with over $50,000 income had scores at/or below the 20th percentile.

- Nearly three-fourths or more of students in the mental retardation or multiple disabilities categories scored in the lowest performance range (below the 21st percentile) on the passage comprehension, letter/word identification, mathematical calculation, and applied problem assessments.

Table 14 Average scores and performance levels of fourth- and eighth-grade students on NAEP 2000 and 2002 reading assessments, by disability status

2000 and 2002 Grade 4 average scale scores and percent at or above basic and at or above proficient[a]								
	N		Mean		% at or above basic[b]		% at or above proficient	
	2000	2002	2000	2002	2000	2002	2000	2002
Students with disabilities[b]	317	11,984	167	187	22	30	8	9
Students without disabilities	7,757	128,593	217	221	62	67	31	33

2002[c] Grade 8 average scale scores and percent at or above basic and at or above proficient[a]				
	N	Mean	% at or above basic[b]	% at or above proficient
Students with disabilities	10,220	228	36	6
Students without disabilities	104,956	268	79	35

Source: NAEP, June 2003.

Note: NCES defines students with disabilities as those who have IEPs.

[a]Scores on the NAEP reading assessment fall on a 0–500 point scale delineated by three skill levels: Basic, Proficient, and Advanced.

[b]The NAEP reading assessment was not administered to eighth-grade students in 2000.

[c]Results for the sample of students with IEPs cannot be generalized to the total population of students with IEPs.

- Students with IEPs appear to have scored lower than did students without IEPs on the NAEP fourth-grade reading assessment in both 2000 and 2002.
- The scores of IEP students on the NAEP fourth-grade reading assessment appear to have improved between 2000 and 2002; that is, it appears that more students with IEPs scored at or above basic and at or above proficient.
- On the eighth-grade NAEP reading assessment, the proportion of students with IEPs who scored at or above basic appears to be less than half of the proportion of students without IEPs who scored at or above basic. When the proportions of both groups scoring at or above proficient are compared, the differences are greater with only 6 percent of students with IEPs scoring at this level compared to 35 percent of students without IEPs.

The National Assessment of Educational Progress (NAEP), also known as the Nation's Report Card, is the only nationally representative and continuing assessment of what America's students know and can do in various subject areas. Since 1969, assessments have been conducted periodically in reading, mathematics, science, writing, U.S. history, civics, geography, and the arts.

Expenditures for Special Education

What are the total expenditures to provide services to students with disabilities ages 6 through 21?

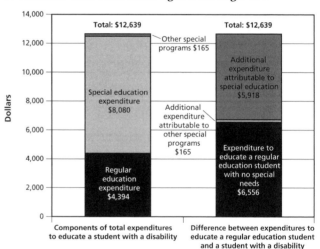

Figure 47 Calculation of additional expenditures for a student with a disability: 1999–2000

Sources: SEEP District and School Surveys.

- In per pupil terms, the total spending used to educate the average student with a disability is $12,639. This amount includes $8,080 per pupil on special education services, $4,394 per pupil on regular education services, and $165 per pupil on services from other special needs programs (e.g., Title I, English language learners, or gifted and talented education).
- The data derived from SEEP indicate that the base expenditure on a regular education student is $6,556 per pupil. Comparing this figure to the average expen-

diture for a student eligible to receive special education services, the additional expenditure attributable to special education is $5,918 per pupil.

During the 1999–2000 school year, the United States spent about $50 billion on special education services. Another $27.3 billion was expended on regular education services for students with disabilities eligible for special education, and an additional $1 billion was spent on other special needs programs (e.g., Title I, English language learners, or gifted and talented education). Thus, total spending to educate all students with disabilities found eligible for special education programs was $78.3 billion.

How are special education expenditures allocated?

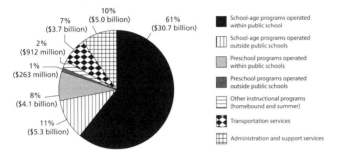

Figure 48 Allocation of special education expenditures: 1999–2000
Sources: SEEP District and School Surveys.

- Focusing on the $50 billion of special education spending, it is useful to see how funds are allocated among different spending components. Special education spending includes central office administration and support of the program, direct instruction and related services for preschool (ages 3 through 5) and school-aged (ages 6 through 21) students, special education summer school, programs for students who are home-bound or hospitalized, and special transportation services. The preceding figure shows the percentage and dollar amount of special education spending on each of these components.

How does spending on special education students vary across districts?

- According to the SEEP District Survey, the smallest districts reported a level of actual expenditure that is 14 percent higher than the actual expenditure in the districts with enrollment of 25,000 or more students ($14,062 vs. $12,309), and a cost-adjusted level of expenditure that is 22 percent higher ($14,815 vs. $12,138). While the differences based on actual expenditures are not statistically significant, the differences based on cost-adjusted expenditures are both economically and statistically significantly different

from each other (economic significance indicates a difference large enough to have an effect on the levels of services being offered).

[This adjustment compensates for differences in the prices paid for comparable resources used in providing special education services in different geographic locations throughout the United States.]

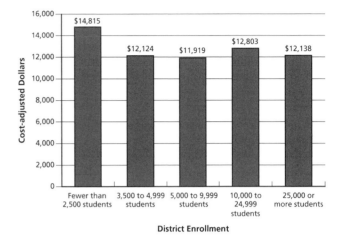

Figure 49 Total expenditure (cost-adjusted) across districts to educate a student with a disability, classified by size of district enrollment: 1999–2000
Sources: SEEP District and School Surveys.

- The spending ratio (relative spending on a special education student vs. regular education student) for the smallest districts is estimated to be 2.19, compared to a national average spending ratio of 1.90 (see Figure 47) (SEEP District and School Surveys).

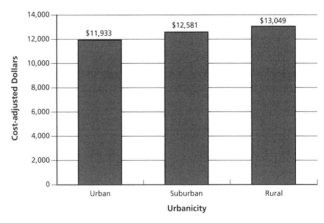

Figure 50 Total expenditure (cost-adjusted) across districts to educate a student with a disability, classified by degree of urbanicity[a]: 1999–2000
Sources: SEEP District and School Surveys; NCES, 1999–2000.

[a]The three categories represent a consolidated version for the locale type variable included with the Common Core of Data published by NCES, 1999–2000.

- Rural districts spend the most in cost-adjusted dollars, and urban districts spend the least, with suburban districts in between.

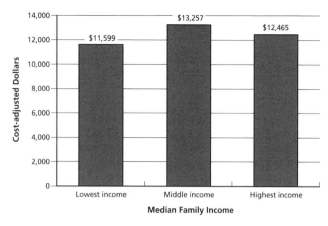

Figure 51 Total expenditure (cost-adjusted) across districts to educate a student with a disability, classified by median family income[a]: 1999–2000

Sources: SEEP District and School Surveys; U.S. Census Bureau, 1990.

[a]This family income variable uses data from the 1990 U.S. Census organized by school district.

- The third of districts with the lowest median family income spend the least to educate a student with disabilities. Districts with middle-income families spend $1,658 more per student than districts with the lowest income families.

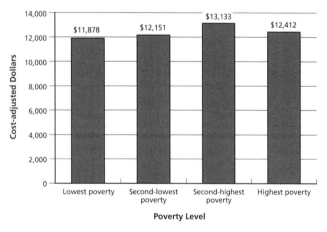

Figure 52 Total expenditure (cost-adjusted) across districts to educate a student with a disability, classified by student poverty level[a]: 1999–2000

Sources: SEEP District and School Surveys.

[a]Poverty is defined in terms of the percentage of students eligible for free or reduced-price lunch.

- Low-poverty districts have the lowest spending ratios. No consistent positive or negative relationship is found for expenditures and districts' student poverty levels. However, low-poverty districts have the lowest spending ratios, 1.72, compared to 1.86 for the second lowest quartile, and 1.97 and 1.98 for the two highest poverty quartiles (relative spending on a special education student vs. regular education student).

- The spending ratio (relative spending on a special education student vs. regular education student) for the smallest districts is estimated to be 2.19, compared to a national average spending ratio of 1.90 (SEEP District and School Surveys).

What is being expended for special education transportation?

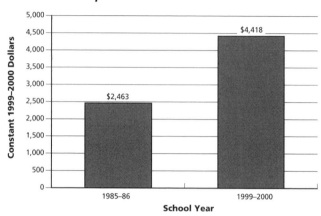

Figure 53 Changes in expenditure per pupil on special transportation services from 1985–86 to 1999–2000 (expressed in constant 1999–2000 dollars)

Sources: SEEP District and School Surveys.

- Special education transportation expenditure per pupil in constant dollars (i.e., actual spending adjusted by the Consumer Price Index) has increased since the 1985–86 school year from $2,463 to $4,418 during the 1999–2000 school year, an increase of 80 percent. The per pupil spending on regular transportation rose from $365 to $442, an increase of 21 percent (SEEP District and School Surveys).

- Special transportation spending per pupil is nearly 10 times greater than spending on regular transportation. This represents an increase since 1985–86 when per pupil special transportation spending was around seven times more than that of regular transportation (SEEP District and School Surveys).

- During the 1999–2000 school year, the nation's school districts spent around $13.1 billion on home-to-school and school-to-school transportation services for all K-12 students in public schools (SEEP District and School Surveys).

- The total expenditure on special transportation services is estimated to be about $3.7 billion. This represents about 28 percent of the total school transportation expenditures in the United States and approximately 7 percent of the total spending on special education services (SEEP District and School Surveys).

Trends in School Exiting and Transition

How has the graduation rate changed over time for students with different disabilities?

Table 15 Percentage[a] of students age 14 and older with disabilities who graduated with a standard diploma: 1993–94 through 2000–01

Disability	1993–94	1994–95	1995–96	1996–97	1997–98	1998–99[a]	1999–2000	2000–01
Specific learning disabilities	49.1	47.7	48.2	48.8	51.0	51.9	51.6	53.6
Speech/language impairments	42.9	41.7	42.2	44.8	48.1	51.2	53.2	52.3
Mental retardation	35.0	33.8	34.0	33.0	34.3	36.0	34.3	35.0
Emotional disturbance	27.0	26.0	25.1	25.9	27.4	29.2	28.6	28.9
Multiple disabilities	36.1	31.4	35.3	35.4	39.0	41.0	42.1	41.6
Hearing impairments	61.9	58.2	58.8	61.8	62.3	60.9	61.8	60.3
Orthopedic impairments	56.7	54.1	53.6	54.9	57.9	53.9	51.2	57.4
Other health impairments	54.6	52.6	53.0	53.1	56.8	55.0	56.4	56.1
Visual impairments	63.5	63.7	65.0	64.3	65.1	67.6	66.5	65.9
Autism	33.7	35.5	36.4	35.9	38.7	40.5	40.7	42.1
Deaf-blindness[c]	34.7	30.0	39.5	39.4	67.7	48.3	39.5	41.2
Traumatic brain injury	54.6	51.7	54.0	57.3	58.2	60.6	56.7	57.5
All disabilities	43.5	42.1	42.4	43.0	45.3	46.5	46.1	47.6

Source: U.S. Department of Education, Office of Special Education Programs, Data Analysis System (DANS), Table AD1 in vol. 2. These data are for the 50 states, D.C., Puerto Rico, and the outlying areas.

[a]The percentage of students with disabilities who exit school with a regular high school diploma and the percentage who exit school by dropping out are performance indicators used by OSEP to measures progress in improving results for students with disabilities. The appropriate method for calculating graduation and dropout rates depends on the question to be answered and is limited by the data available. For reporting under the Government Performance and Results Act (GPRA), OSEP calculates the graduation rate by dividing the number of students age 14 and older who graduated with a regular high school diploma by the number of students in the same age group who are known to have left school (i.e., graduated with a regular high school diploma, received a certificate of completion, reached the maximum age for services, died, moved and are not known to be continuing in an education program, or dropped out). These calculations are presented here. Not all states award a certificate of completion. In all years presented, Kansas, Massachusetts, New Jersey, Oklahoma, Texas, and Guam did not report any students receiving a certificate of completion. Since 1997, Minnesota has not reported any students receiving a certificate of completion. Since 1998, Arizona and Ohio have not reported any students receiving a certificate of completion. Prior to 1999, Pennsylvania did not report any students receiving a certificate of completion.

[b]Two large states appear to have underreported dropouts in 1998–99. As a result, the graduation rate is somewhat inflated that year.

[c]Percentages are based on fewer than 150 students exiting school.

- In 2000–01, 47.6 percent of the students ages 14 and older with disabilities exited school with a regular high school diploma.
- From 1993–94 through 2000–01, there was little change in the relative standing of graduation rates for the various disability categories.
  - Students with visual impairments or hearing impairments consistently had the highest graduation rates.
  - Students with mental retardation or emotional disturbance consistently had the lowest graduation rates.

- From 1993–94 through 2000–01, the graduation rate improved for most disability categories.
  - The largest gains were made by students with autism and speech/language impairments. Notable gains were also made by students with deaf-blindness and multiple disabilities.
  - No meaningful change occurred in the graduation rate for students with mental retardation, orthopedic impairments, or other health impairments.

How has the dropout rate changed over time for students with different disabilities?

Table 16 Percentage[a] of students age 14 and older with disabilities who dropped out of school: 1993–94 through 2000–01

Disability	1993–94	1994–95	1995–96	1996–97	1997–98	1998–99[b]	1999–2000	2000–01
Specific learning disabilities	43.1	44.7	44.4	43.4	41.3	40.2	39.9	38.7
Speech/language impairments	49.3	51.4	50.4	48.0	44.5	40.9	39.3	39.7
Mental retardation	35.4	37.9	38.0	38.2	36.3	34.9	35.7	34.3
Emotional disturbance	67.8	69.2	69.9	69.2	67.2	65.5	65.2	65.1
Multiple disabilities	24.6	35.1	27.4	27.7	26.3	28.1	25.7	26.7
Hearing impairments	24.3	28.0	28.3	25.6	23.5	24.8	23.2	24.5
Orthopedic impairments	25.1	27.9	28.9	27.3	24.3	27.4	30.4	27.0
Other health impairments	37.4	38.1	36.8	37.8	34.9	36.3	35.2	36.2
Visual impairments	24.5	24.4	22.3	21.4	21.7	20.6	20.2	21.1
Autism	25.9	29.5	23.8	24.0	19.2	22.8	23.4	20.8
Deaf-blindness[c]	24.5	25.5	12.8	27.3	11.8	25.0	25.4	22.9
Traumatic brain injury	28.2	32.9	30.7	29.6	26.1	27.2	28.8	28.9
All disabilities	45.1	47.0	46.8	45.9	43.7	42.3	42.1	41.1

Source: U.S. Department of Education, Office of Special Education Programs, Data Analysis System (DANS), Table AD1 in vol. 2. These data are for the 50 states, D.C., Puerto Rico, and the outlying areas.

[a]See note on previous table as to how percentage was calculated. The dropout rate is calculated in the same manner, but with the number of dropouts in the numerator. Students who moved and are not known to be continuing in an education program are treated as dropouts.

[b]Two large states appear to have underreported dropouts in 1998–99. As a result, the dropout rate is somewhat understated that year.

[c]Percentages are based on fewer than 150 students exiting school.

- In 2000–01, 41.1 percent of the students ages 14 and older with disabilities exited school by dropping out.
- From 1993–94 through 2000–01, the percentage of students with disabilities dropping out decreased from 45.1 percent to 41.1 percent.
  - Students with visual impairments consistently had the lowest dropout rates.
  - Students with emotional disturbance consistently had the highest dropout rates.
  - In every year, students with emotional disturbance had a dropout rate that was substantially higher than the dropout rate for the next highest disability category.
- From 1993–94 through 2000–01, the dropout rate declined for students in most categories.
  - The improvement was most notable for students with autism and speech/language impairments.
  - The dropout rate also notably declined for students with visual impairments and specific learning disabilities.
  - No meaningful change occurred in the dropout rate for students with hearing impairments.

Are the graduation and dropout rates the same for students with disabilities in different racial/ethnic groups?

Table 17 Percentage[a] of students age 14 and older with disabilities who graduated with a standard diploma or dropped out, by race/ethnicity: 2000–01

Race/ethnicity	Graduated with a standard diploma		Dropped out	
	Number	Percentage	Number	Percentage
American Indian/Alaska Native	2,533	41.9	3,157	52.2
Asian/Pacific Islander	3,583	60.6	1,652	28.0
Black (not Hispanic)	27,999	36.5	34,085	44.5
Hispanic	24,087	47.5	22,073	43.5
White (not Hispanic)	132,714	56.8	79,220	33.9

Source: U.S. Department of Education, Office of Special Education Programs, Data Analysis System (DANS), Table AD4 in vol. 2. These data are for the 50 states, D.C., Puerto Rico, and the outlying areas.

[a]Percentage is calculated by dividing the number of students age 14 and older in each racial/ethnic group who graduated with a regular high school diploma (or dropped out) by the number of students age 14 and older in that racial/ethnic group who are known to have left school (i.e., graduated with a regular high school diploma, received a certificate of completion, reached the maximum age for services, died, moved and are not known to be continuing, or dropped out.) Students who moved and are not known to be continuing in an education program are treated as dropouts. Not all states award a certificate of completion. In 2000–01, Arizona, Kansas, Massachusetts, Minnesota, New Jersey, Ohio, Oklahoma, Texas, and Guam did not report any students receiving a certificate of completion.

- The graduation rate is highest for Asian/Pacific Islander (60.6 percent) and white (56.8 percent) students with disabilities. Both rates are above the graduation rate for all students with disabilities (47.6 percent) (see Table 15).

- The graduation rate is lowest for black students with disabilities (36.5 percent).

- The dropout rate is lowest for Asian/Pacific Islander (28.0 percent) and white students with disabilities (33.9 percent). Both rates are below the dropout rate for all students with disabilities (41.1 percent) (see Table 16).

- The dropout rate is highest for American Indian/Alaska Native (52.2 percent) students with disabilities.

- Black (44.5 percent) and Hispanic (43.5 percent) students with disabilities had similar dropout rates.

What procedures are used by states, local education agencies, and schools to prevent students with disabilities from dropping out of school?

Table 18 Percentage of states reporting on individual schools' dropout rates for students with and without disabilities: 1999–2000 school year

Practice		Percent
State included dropout rates in school reports and . . .		71
Students with disabilities were included in calculation but not separately reported	51	
Rates were reported separately for students with disabilities	18	
Students with disabilities were not included in calculations and were not separately reported	2	
State did not include dropout rates in its school reports		16
State did not issue school reports		12

Source: SLIIDEA State Survey.

- Almost three-fourths of the states (71 percent) issued individual school reports that included dropout rates.

- Of the 35 states that issued dropout reports, 25 states combined the dropout rates for general education students and students with disabilities; nine states reported rates separately for students with disabilities, and one state did not report the rates of students with disabilities.

Table 19 Percentage of districts that tracked dropout risk factors for students with disabilities: 1999–2000

Risk Factors	Percent
Tracked any of the following factors	60
Tracked the following risk factors:	
Excessive absences	58
Significant discipline problems	53
One or more suspensions from school	48
Juvenile justice involvement	35
Previously retained in grade	32
Limited English proficiency	29
Older than norm for grade	28
Family or economic problems	26

Source: SLIIDEA District Survey.

- Sixty percent of districts track dropout risk factors for students with disabilities.

- The most commonly tracked risk factors are excessive absences (58 percent), significant discipline problems (53 percent), and suspensions (48 percent).

Table 20 Percentage of schools reporting factors used to select students for participation in the school's dropout prevention program—middle and high schools: 1999–2000

Factors	Percent
Academic performance	22
Absentee record	21
Counselor's referral	21
Teacher referral	19
Disciplinary problem	17
Student previously retained in grade	17
Parental request	16
Student older than norm for grade	16
Student request	13
Disability category	4

Source: SLIIDEA School Survey.

- Academic performance (22 percent), absentee record (21 percent), and counselor's referral (21 percent) are the most common factors used to select students for participation in a middle or high school dropout prevention program.

- A student's disability category is the least likely reported factor (4 percent) used to select students for participation in a school's dropout prevention program.

What do we know about the employment of older students with disabilities?

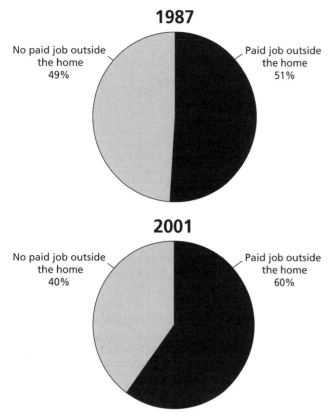

1987

No paid job outside
the home
49%

Paid job outside
the home
51%

2001

No paid job outside
the home
40%

Paid job outside
the home
60%

Figure 54 Employment of students ages 15 through 17 with disabilities in 1987 and 2001

Sources: NLTS Parent Survey; NLTS2 Parent Survey.

- According to NLTS2, among 15- to 17-year-olds in 2001, 60 percent had worked in 2000, a rate similar to the general population and up from 51 percent ($p < .01$) in 1987.
- The percentage of employed youth ages 15 through 17 making at least minimum wage is equal to the percentage not making minimum wage (NLTS2).
- The percentage of employed youth ages 15 through 17 making above minimum wage increased from 41 percent in 1987 to 68 percent in 2001 ($p < .001$) (NLTS2).

What transition services are available to help students with disabilities move from secondary school to adult life?

Table 21 Percentage of high schools that offered various services to help students with disabilities transition from school to adult life: 1999–2000

Transition services	Percent of high schools
Formal assessment of career skills or interests	99
Career counseling	98
Job applications instruction	97
Job search instruction	97
Job readiness or prevocational training	96
Interviewing instruction	96
Postsecondary education/training applications assistance	95
Postsecondary and training institutions counseling	95
Counseling about support services for students with disabilities	94
Counseling about financial aid	92
Community work experience	89
Community work exploration	87
Referrals to potential employers	85
Specific job skills training	85
Job coaches to monitor job performance	78
Job coaches/staff who work with employers to modify jobs	67
Self-advocacy curriculum	55

Source: SLIIDEA School Survey.

- Most districts offer a range of services to assist the transition of students with disabilities to adult life. More than 90 percent of all high schools offer a formal assessment of career skills or interests, career counseling, job readiness or prevocational training, instructions in job searching and other similar services, as well as counseling and support regarding postsecondary institutions.
- Between 80 percent and 90 percent of high schools offer community work experience, community work exploration, referrals to potential employers, and specific job skills training.
- Fewer than 80 percent of high schools provide job coaches who work with employers, job coaches who monitor performance, or a self-advocacy curriculum.

Workforce

Who provides services to 6- through 21-year-olds with disabilities?

Table 22 Characteristics of service providers for students with disabilities

Demographics	Special education teacher	General education teacher	Paraprofessional	Speech-language pathologist
Sex: female	85	76	94	96
Race/ethnicity: white	86	88	78	94
Identifying themselves as having a disability	14	6	5	5
Mean age	43	43	44	43

Source: SPeNSE Service Provider Survey.

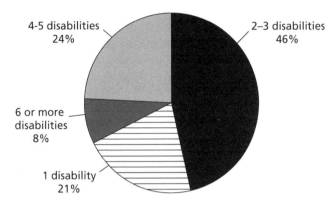

Figure 55 Number of different disabilities on special educators' caseloads: 2000

Source: SPeNSE Service Provider Survey.

- Today's special educators must be innovative, adaptive, and prepared to use an array of instructional approaches that suit students with a wide variety of needs.

- Almost 80 percent of special education teachers serve students with two or more primary disabilities, and 32 percent teach students with four or more different primary disabilities.

- On average, almost one-fourth of their students are from a cultural or linguistic group different from their own, and 7 percent of their students are English language learners (SPeNSE Provider Survey).

REFERENCES FOR SECTION I

U.S. Bureau of the Census. Population data for 2000 and 2001 retrieved October 2003, from www.census.gov/popest/data/states/files/STCH-6R.CSV. This file is now archived at census .gov/popest/archives/2000s/vintage_2002/ST-EST2002/STCH-6R .txt/

U.S. Bureau of the Census. Population data for 1999 retrieved October 2000, from hwww.census.gov/popest/archives/1990s/stats/st-99-10.txt

U.S. Bureau of the Census. Population data for 1998 retrieved October 1999. This file is no longer available on the Web site.

Shackelford, J. (2002). *State and jurisdictional eligibility definitions for infants and toddlers with disabilities under IDEA* (NECTAC Notes No. 11). Chapel Hill: The University of North Carolina,

FPG Child Development Institute, National Early Childhood Technical Assistance Center.

Subcommittee on Attention-Deficit/Hyperactivity Disorder and Committee on Quality Improvement. (2001). *Pediatrics, 108*(4), 1033.

U.S. Department of Education, National Center for Education Statistics. (1999). National Household Education Survey, [Computer file]. ICPSR version, Washington, DC: U.S. Department of Education, Office of Educational Research and Improvement [Producer], 2000. Ann Arbor, MI: Inter-university Consortium for Political and Social Research [Distributor], 2003.

It is clear that the disproportionality of ethnic minorities and inner-city youth in special education continues to be a source of investigation. Issues such as socioeconomic status and assessment bias are ongoing even after being subject to close scrutiny by researchers in the field and the U.S. Department of Education.

The demography of special education allows us to examine our advances in the understanding of handicapping conditions (such as the addition of Traumatic Brain Injury as a handicapping condition); it allows us to examine how we define disability from year to year; it allows us to track the impact of shifts in paradigms (such as inclusion); and it allows us to hold the field accountable for culturally competent services.

The Annual Report to Congress, written by Office of Special Education of the U.S. Department of Education, is published every year and is available online for inspection at www.ed.gov/pubs. The facts and table in this entry were taken verbatim from *Twenty fifth Annual Report to Congress* (2003).

REFERENCE

U.S. Department of Education. (2003). *Twenty fifth annual report to Congress: To assure the free appropriate public education of all children with disabilities: Implementation of the Individuals with Disabilities Education Act (IDEA).* Washington, DC: Author.

ELAINE FLETCHER-JANZEN
*University of Colorado at
Colorado Springs*

POLITICS AND SPECIAL EDUCATION
SPECIAL EDUCATION, FEDERAL IMPACT ON

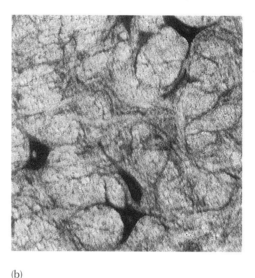

(b)

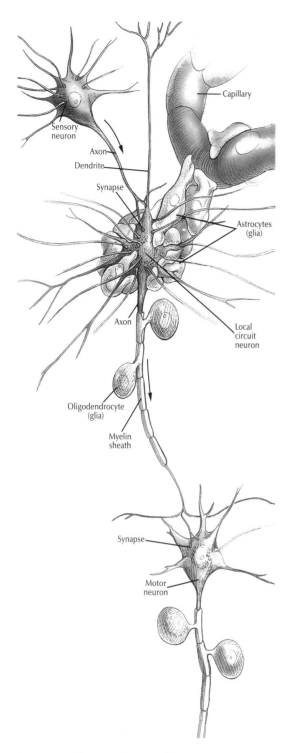

Figure 1 (a) Left, a neural circuit. A large neuron with multiple dendrites receives synaptic contact from another neuron at upper left. It sends its myelinated axon into a synaptic connection with a third neuron at bottom. These neural surfaces are shown without the extensive investment of glia that envelop the branch extending toward the capillary at upper right. (b) Two views of synapses at different magnifications, as seen through the electron microscope.

DENDRITES

A typical neuron is depicted in Figure 1. The nucleus of the cell, called the soma or perikaryon, has various protruding elements. The main protruding element is the axon.

Typically surrounding the soma, except where the axon exits, are a variety of smaller protruding elements that form the dendritic network of the neuron. The dendrites have an appearance somewhat akin to branches of a leafless tree and *dendron* is the Greek stem meaning tree. The dendrites serve as the neurotransmitter receptacle sites, as does the soma itself, from neurotransmitter release from the axon of a different neuron. The synaptic termination actually occurs on little spines that arise from the dendrite. These spines are numerous. For example, a single motor neuron may have as many as 4,000 spines on its dendrites. Although it was originally assumed that the dendrite served a rather passive role in neuronal transmission, it is now speculated that the dendritic processes play a much more dynamic and active role in neurotransmission (Cooper, Bloom, & Roth, 1978; Cotman & McGaugh, 1980) and neurobehavioral (i.e., learning) functions.

REFERENCES

Cooper, J. R., Bloom, F. E., & Roth, R. H. (1978). *The biochemical basis of neuropharmacology* (3rd ed.). New York: Oxford University Press.

Cotman, C. W., & McGaugh, J. L. (1980). *Behavioral neuroscience.* New York: Academic.

ERIN D. BIGLER
Austin Neurological Clinic
University of Texas

CENTRAL NERVOUS SYSTEM
GLIAL CELLS

DENMARK, SPECIAL EDUCATION IN THE FOLKESKOLE IN

The term *Folkeskole* refers to the Danish municipal primary and lower secondary school system. All children of compulsory education age, despite the nature of their special needs, have a right to free education in the Folkeskole. Education, not schooling, is compulsory. Whether education is received in the publicly provided municipal school, in a private school, or at home, is a matter of parental choice provided certain standards are met.

In Denmark pupils with special needs that attend a private school are offered special education for free provided their special educational needs are assessed by a local pedagogical-psychological counseling center. Under Danish laws, its so-called welfare system offers persons full compensation for services that address needs persons have not personally caused. As noted in the following, achieving this status has taken years.

Since the founding of the Folkeskole in 1814, children were guaranteed the right to seven years of education in religion, reading, writing, and arithmetic. Special education services initially were not provided.

During the early twentieth century, teachers began to focus more on individual pupils. After 1924, children with severe sensory, motor, and mental handicaps received training in schools administrated by the Ministry of Social Affairs. This ministry provided free educational services independent of the Folkeskole. Around 1930, some more wealthy municipalities established special education services for children

with minor special educational needs even though they had no legal duty to do so. The School Act of 1937 established the first national services for children who were unable to benefit from ordinary teaching, if conditions allowed.

World War II delayed the development of special education to some degree. However, following a report from the Commission for Special Education, special training services were introduced in the School Act of 1958. From that time, municipalities have provided special education services for the most chronic disabilities.

At first, care for the handicapped was guided by the desire to provide mutual protection to those with and without handicaps by separating them. This lead to the construction of residential institutions in rural areas in which the handicapped could receive various forms of care and live throughout one's life. Teaching cognitive skills was not emphasized in that cognitive abilities were not seen as important. Parents of children with handicaps began to protest the nature of these services. They wanted their child to remain in their home during childhood and to be prepared to lead an ordinary life as much as possible by receiving adequate training, including the acquisition of academic skills. These desires challenged local public school. With support from some politicians and school officials, some children with quite severe handicaps became integrated in some mainstream local schools.

Since the 1960s, children who are blind and visually impaired have been integrated in local school. Later, those with other disabilities increasingly were integrated in the local school, most often in special classes. Children with the most severe sensory, motor, and mental handicaps continued to receive their teaching and training in institutions run by the Ministry of Social Affairs.

The School Act of 1975 required all municipalities to provide special education services for every pupil who could not benefit from the ordinary education. The Act made education compulsory for ages 7 through 16, with 10th grade optional. Moreover, municipal Folkeskoles were required to provide a one-year preschool program. Although voluntary, 98 percent of Danish children attend these classes. In 1980, the Ministry of Social Affairs' responsibilities for providing educational services to children from birth to 18 were transferred to the Ministry of Education. Special education assistance to infants is provided only to those with speech and/or language difficulties. However, municipalities often interpret this policy broadly by providing services to young children with various needs.

Consistent with Danish traditions, the development of integrated social and school services for special needs children has been initiated by a group of dedicated persons (e.g., parents, politicians, teachers) who eventually prevailed by convincing the Danish Parliament to enact laws favoring a more inclusive policy. Thus, since 1980, the Folkeskole has provided educational services to all children in a manner consistent with the Act.

In accord with this change favoring a more inclusive tone in education, municipalities modified social programs to provide support that enabled parents of special needs children to have them live at home.

Responsibility for educating pupils of the most severe handicaps (approximately 1.35 percent of all children) was placed in counties that developed a special school system and a consultant service. In addition, over time, municipal governments assumed more responsibility for providing special education services, resulting in significant developments in these services at the local municipal level.

New models of special education were introduced, including the provision of intensive training to a child the entire school day (e.g., intensive reading for 3 or more weeks) in a clinic setting. The term *clinic* in the Folkeskole refers to special rooms in a school well equipped for special training of children by well-trained teachers. These services generally provide part-time training in one or two subjects (e.g., reading, arithmetic). Children with attention problems or other behavior disorders also may receive training in a specific subject. If approved by parents, pupils may receive training in their free time in a clinic in addition to their fully integrated program in an ordinary class. A two-teacher model for use in mainstream classrooms also has been introduced.

Parents are centrally involved in decisions regarding their special needs children. Part 9 of the Folkeskole Act addresses parent complaints. Complaints about decisions taken by school officials may be brought before municipal authorities (Section 51 [1]). In addition, municipal council's decisions regarding referral or refusal to refer to special education can be brought before a Complaints Commission for Extensive Special Education (Section 51 a [1] and [3]).

In 2007, a new reform is scheduled to be implemented, resulting in reducing the current 275 municipalities to 99. These municipalities will assume total responsibility for the education of all children, including special needs children. This change is triggered by knowledge that the current system that divides responsibilities between municipalities and counties is inefficient. At this time, neither of these two government bodies accepts responsibility for needed services, believing the other is responsible. This change will help ensure needed services are delivered.

Municipal governments will assume administrative responsibility for special schools that currently are the responsibility of counties. In 2007 the current 14 counties will be reduced to 5 regions. These will offer consultative service to municipalities and the parents limited on issues important to the care and teaching of a child with very severe and special needs. Moreover these regions will be responsible for a few schools for pupils with low incidence and complicated handicaps (e.g., blind-deaf children, children with multiple and severe handicaps that demands very special care). The municipal council will refer pupils whose development requires extensive care to these regional schools and may refer pupils to a school in another municipality if it is thought to be more appropriate.

Each municipality must establish a pedagogical-psychological counseling service. The Danish Folkeskole is centrally regulated by the Act on the Folkeskole, which establishes the framework for a school's services and activities. Although all municipal schools have common aims, individual municipalities are responsible for deciding how its schools are to function within the framework of the Act on the Folkeskole (Part 1 of the Folkeskole Act).

The use of diagnostic categories has been discussed lively in Denmark. Diagnoses by medical personnel generally have become less common. Decisions as to whether a child requires special support are dependent on an individual assessment (The Act on the Danish Folkeskole).

Referral to special education shall be made upon pedagogical and psychological counseling and upon consultation with the pupil and his/her parents (Part 2 of The Folkeskole Act, Section 12 [2]). These and other legal provisions underscore the need for school officials and the pedagogical-psychological counseling service to closely cooperate when providing special education services to students in mainstream schools. Pedagogical-psychological professionals provide advisory services that examine the nature of needs and, if required, propose remedies for them. These professionals also are responsible for follow-up evaluations and, if and when needed, for proposing adjustments in services.

Due to the decentralization of the educational system, the pedagogical-psychological counseling centers have developed unevenly. Staff normally consists of some psychologists trained in different areas (e.g., learning difficulties, social-emotional problems). Special education instructional assistance may include teaching pupils all subjects specified by the Folkeskole and providing training and preparation for later work, special educational assistance to parents and teachers, special educational materials and technical aids, and personal assistance through counseling and other sources. Moreover, a child with a severe motor handicap may have his/her own helper to assist as needed.

During the 2004–5 school year, 688,000 pupils attended primary and lower education, 88 percent of whom attended the Danish Folkeskole. The remaining 12 percent received their education in private schools, and a few were taught by their parents. These figures seem to be stable from year to year (http://pub.uvm.dk).

About 12 percent of Danish pupils receive special education services in various degrees according to their individual needs. During the 2003–4 school year, about 1.5 percent (9,868) received extensive special education services, some in municipal folkeskole and most in special schools. The percent of pupils between ages 6 and 16 who received extensive special education services by disability categories follows: Mental Retardation 45 percent; behavior disorders and emotional problems (inclusive Autism) 27 percent; reading, language, and speech learning difficulties 9 percent;

motor difficulties (e.g., spastic children) 4 percent; blindness or severe reduction of sight 1 percent; deafness or severe hearing problems 5 percent; and other reasons 8 percent (http://www.uvm.dk/05/vidtg.htm?menuid=6410).

Pupils with special needs may receive instruction in one or more subjects in the ordinary class or special instruction as a supplement to that received in the ordinary class. Some pupils do not attend an ordinary class and instead receive instruction in a special class that may be placed within the municipal school or in a special school in the county.

New initiatives on special education in the Folkeskole outline the importance of inclusiveness and differentiated teaching to all pupils. Those providing educational-psychological advisory services play an important role in promoting inclusiveness in mainstream schools, in that they are involved with all three types of education: ordinary education, education of pupils with ordinary special educational needs, and pupils with profound special educational needs. The counseling and guidance services provided to schools and parents greatly influence local attitudes and decisions regarding educational and organizational action programs (http://www.european-agency.org; European Agency: National Overview in the Field of Special Needs Education).

In 2000, a 3-year program was launched with the goal to improve and maintain the quality of special needs education in Denmark. Both politicians and professionals have emphasized that local schools should be able to meet the educational needs of the majority of pupils. The belief that children deserved the right to interact socially with peers and adults in a local environment is strongly held. Although efforts to mainstream pupils are strong, educators also recognize that the needs for all children will not be met in the ordinary mainstream school classes. Special classes and special schools are needed.

Thus, the term *quality* must be seen from a number of different angles in order to influence attitudes, to question traditions in the school, and to provide quality teaching to all pupils (http://www.uvm.dk/cgi/printpage/pf.cgi).

Teachers traditionally were trained in special education in teachers' colleges. They now receive most of their training in special education after being certificated as a teacher. Teachers responsible for the total teaching of one or more pupils with special needs often will have completed a program of education that qualifies them for their responsibilities. However, this is not a legal responsibility. Thus, those who teach pupils with special educational needs first complete their initial training as teachers and then complete a special 1-year course in special education.

REFERENCES

The Folkeskole Act no. 509, 199

Consolidation Act no. 730, 2000

Consolidation Act no. 896, 2000

Directions on PPR 2002, regarding Pedagogical Psychological Advisory Center

Directions on the Folkeskole's efforts to students, whose development demands special considerations and support.

The homepage address of the Ministry of the Education: http://www.uvm.dk/

Online literature: http://eng.uvm.dk/publications/engonline.htm and http://www.uvm.dk/cgi/printpage/pf.cgi

The homepage address of the European Agency: National Overview in the Field of Special Needs Education: http://www.european-agency.org

ELISABETH JACOBSON
Copenhagen, Denmark

BELGIUM, SPECIAL EDUCATION IN
FRANCE, SPECIAL EDUCATION IN

DENO, EVELYN N. (1911–2005)

As a developmental psychologist, Evelyn Deno specialized in the design and delivery of helping services for handicapped children and their parents. As a preschool, elementary, and college teacher of 17 years, Deno earned her MA in 1950, and PhD in 1958, in child development and clinical psychology from the University of Minnesota, where she taught graduate-level classes in child development. She then went on to become director of special education and rehabilitation for the Minneapolis public schools. She returned to the University of Minnesota in 1967 as professor of educational psychology and director of the Psycho-Educational Center. She was also codirector of the Leadership Training Institute for the USOE Bureau of Professional Development.

Best known for her "cascade of special education services" concept and diagram, Deno always saw the need for "helping service systems and political agents to promote a more compatible match between individual aspirations and the constraining social and physical environmental realities" (pers. comm., August 27, 1985). She applied developmental theory to see

> how people with special adjustment problems can be helped to survive in a culture and society inclined to regard deviance from the "norm" (or what is expected) as a problem of the deviant one, not a challenge to society's ability and obligation to respect individual differences." (pers. comm., August 27, 1985)

Deno's interests were with the adjustment problems of older persons and the design and implementation of programs for them to serve as counselors to their peers, tutors, and as "special friends" to learning-disabled and emotionally disturbed children. She received a number of awards for outstanding contributions in her field. Service delivery models designed and tested under her direction have been designated as national service prototypes. Her ideas on merging special and general education, labeling, and blaming students' failure to learn solely on teachers were analyzed in an article in the *Journal of Special Education* (Hallahan & Kauffman, 1994).

Deno retired from the University of Minnesota in the mid-1970s, and lived in the Twin Cities area of Minnesota. She edited an anthology of personal experiences of those involved in the major paradigm shift in 1955 in special education, when Minnesota passed into law the requirement that individual school systems provide educational services to all handicapped children, rather than placing them in residential state institutions.

Deno received numerous local, state, and national awards for her many contributions to the education and habilitation of people with disabilities. She lived a well and full life, passing away June 4th, 2005.

REFERENCE

Hallahan, D. P., & Kauffman, J. M. (1994). Toward a culture of disability in the aftermath of Deno and Dunn. *Journal of Special Education, 27*, 496–508.

ELAINE FLETCHER-JANZEN
*University of Colorado at
Colorado Springs*
First edition

KAY E. KETZENBERGER
*The University of Texas of the
Permian Basin*
Second edition

JESSI K. WHEATLEY
*Falcon School District 49,
Colorado Springs, Colorado*
Third edition

DENTISTRY AND THE EXCEPTIONAL CHILD

The physical consequences and personal discomfort of dental disorders and untreated oral diseases for disabled individuals are obvious; they include pain, oral abscesses, and loss of teeth (DECOD, 2006). The educational and social implications are, perhaps, just as important. Bad teeth, gum disorders, etc. can cause bad breath and cosmetic disabilities and thus make the social acceptance of disabled children and adults more difficult. The cosmetic implications of good dental health for the disabled have been recognized by many states that provide dental care to vocational rehabilitation clients, though the need for services usually outstrips the resources available to meet them.

A number of diverse physiological social and economic factors have been identified as being responsible for the greater degree of dental and oral disorders in disabled populations. Malformations and abnormal development of certain teeth are thus coincidental with certain types of handicapping conditions. Particular dental difficulties have been found to be associated with various types of handicapping conditions. Individuals with Down syndrome have been found to experience a relatively low incidence of tooth decay but a high incidence of periodontal or gum disease (Pugliese, 1978), while the gums of many epileptic individuals have been found to overgrow as a consequence of dilantin use (Nowaka, 1976). Neurological seizures or motor disabilities may result in head injuries that cause serious damage to oral structures. Motor impairments, limited cognitive understanding of the importance of good dental habits, and poor motivation often limit the carrying out of oral hygiene practices by children with disabilities and frustrate parents' training and monitoring efforts.

The strained economic conditions of many disabled children is another reason for the high incidence of oral disease in special education populations. Many disabled children come from socioeconomically disadvantaged families that are not likely to emphasize the precepts of oral hygiene in their daily living or to afford dental care. Furthermore, there has been a reduction of dental support for such families in Medicaid programs. Indeed, the federal government, under Title XIX, does not require that states provide any dental services to adult Medicaid recipients.

Additionally, until recently, barrier restrictions, difficulties in patient management, and negative attitudes have limited receptivity in dental professionals with regard to the provision of services to difficult patients. Difficulties in patient management and negative attitudes on the part of dental health professionals negatively affect the provision of dental care to difficult to treat patients with disabilities. Beyond such problems, even when willing and proficient service providers are available, parents of exceptional children and agencies serving them are often unaware of their availability.

Specific difficulties with respect to preventing or ameliorating dental problems and oral disease in students with disabilities are attributable to the attitudes of school personnel generally and special education personnel in particular. There is very little attention paid to the dental/oral needs and problems of exceptional children in our schools currently. This is in part a consequence of changing conditions of service provision to disabled children. Increasingly, as that provision has moved from segregated circumstances such as institutions in which health care considerations are predominant over educational ones, to the less restrictive environments of day and public school programs, there has been a decided shift from concern with the physical (care) needs of disabled schoolchildren to their specific instructional needs. While the health professionals and special education teachers serving special education populations undoubtedly recognize the needs of disabled children for good oral training and dental health care, they are not likely to emphasize these in their day to day individualized education plan practices. Present-day special education requires the provision of so many mandated educational services that the laborious training of children in instructionally peripheral areas of brushing, flossing, etc. is likely to be neglected.

The 1970s were a particularly active period with respect to comprehensive investments of time and effort in improving dental care for individuals with disabilities. One of the most important efforts in this respect was the funding by the Robert Wood Johnson Foundation during 1974–1978 of 11 dental schools across the country. This funding was to support the development of comprehensive dental school training programs relative to the provision of services to disabled individuals (i.e., to develop specialized skills and technology, to create positive attitude change in dental professionals, to develop referral and service delivery capabilities at dental schools, and to institutionalize aspects of these programs at dental schools following funding).

Evaluation of these projects revealed decreased anxiety in faculty, staff, and students in working with exceptional students, increased ability to communicate with individuals with disabilities regarding their dental problems, and improved dental care practices. Positive attitude changes were reported in persons affected by the program (e.g., decreased fear and anxiety), as well as a better understanding of handicapped dental patients. A comprehensive report on the Robert Wood Johnson Foundation's program, the most ambitious privately funded one to date, is available from the Educational Testing Service (Campbell, Esser, & Flaugher, 1982).

Apropos of the Robert Wood Johnson Foundation's work, Stiefel and Truelove (1985) reported on the 5-year postgraduate program at the University of Washington that resulted in significant cognitive changes and gains in confidence respecting the treatment of individuals with disabilities by dentists, dental hygienists, and assistants who participated in a postgraduate program. Curricula guidelines are also available (DECOD, 2006; Jolly, 1990).

While there has been a steady if meager stream of publications concerning the dental management of children with disabilities, of interest is the work of such investigators as Price (1978) and Pugliese (1978). Much of this interest, as might be expected, has been in the direction of preventive dentistry, and in the participation of home, school, and community in the dental management of individuals with disabilities. The Association for Retarded Citizens' position is that dental treatment should "be of the same quality as received by other people, preserve or enhance the individual's health and be administered only with the *informed consent* of the person or his or her surrogate decision maker" (ARC, 1992, p. 1). Callahan (1983a, 1983b), among others, has emphasized that effective dental care for individuals with disabilities must go beyond the improvement of dental services per se and improved technology to improving the willingness of dental practitioners to engage school and other service providers in the dental care of exceptional students. Callahan emphasizes the value of preventive services that will improve the dental status of individuals with disabilities and reduce the costs of their dental care. For those individuals with disabilities who will remain school and community based (this means most disabled children and adults), programs of comprehensive preventive dental care should be emphasized over those of costly treatment.

What can be accomplished through preventive programs has been demonstrated through model outreach programs implemented by the National Foundation of Dentistry for the Handicapped (NFDH; 2006; Callahan, 1983b). These programs have incorporated daily oral hygiene programs into the practices at a variety of special education schools, sheltered workshops, and group homes at relatively modest costs. They rely on periodic screening to detect dental disorders while they are still easily manageable. They use referral networks to coordinate the delivery of dental treatment to those disabled individuals who require it. Most important, they use teachers, counselors, vocational rehabilitation personnel, houseparents, and other service personnel, in addition to those from the dental professions, on their service delivery teams. Similar concerted efforts might be valuable in bringing special education and special educators fully into the teaching and training of oral hygiene methods and precepts.

Interest in applying dental and oral hygiene principles in work with more severely disabled populations is evidenced by the work of Feldman and Elliot (1981). Finally, because the vast majority of special education students these days reside at home, it is encouraging to observe recent efforts directed toward parents as oral hygiene trainers and monitors. Thus an article by Stark, Markel, Black, & Greenbaum (1985) provides guidelines to parents respecting their children's dental needs with regard to nutrition, medication, visits to the dentist, and the inculcation of proper dental care habits. In addition the American Academy of Pediatric Dentistry (AAPD; 2006) has developed a video for parents of exceptional children.

REFERENCES

American Academy of Pediatric Dentistry (AAPD). (2006). *Dental care for a special child.* Retrieved January 20, 2006, from http://www.aapd.org/publications/brochures/specialcare.asp

Association for Retarded Citizens (ARC). (1992). *Position paper on medical and dental treatment.* Arlington, TX: Author.

Callahan, W. P. (1983a). Dental disease: A continuing education problem for the disabled individual. *Journal of Special Education, 17,* 355–359.

Callahan, W. P. (1983b). The effectiveness of instructional programming on the reduction of dental diseases in mentally retarded individuals. *Mental Retardation, 21,* 260–262.

Campbell, J. Y., Esser, B. F., & Flaugher, R. L. (1982). *Evaluation of a program for training dentists in the care of handicapped patients* (Report No. QAT24225). Princeton, NJ: Educational Testing Service.

DECOD. (2006). *Dental education in the care of persons with disabilities.* Retrieved January 20, 2006, from http://www.dental.washington.edu/departments/oralmed/decod

Dentistry and the handicapped. (1981). (Videotape). Denver: LA-DOCA.

Feldman, D., & Elliot, T. A. (1981). A multidimensional oral hygiene curriculum for the severely and profoundly handicapped. *Journal of Special Education Technology, 4,* 33–45.

Jolly, D. E. (1990). Curriculum guidelines for training general practice residents to treat the person with a handicap. *Journal of Dental Education, 54*(5), 293–297.

NFDH. (2006). *National foundation of dentistry for the handicapped.* Retrieved January 20, 2006, from http://www.nfdh.org

Nowak, A. J. (1976). *Dentistry for the handicapped patient.* St. Louis, MO: Mosby.

Price, J. H. (1978). Dental health education for the mentally and physically handicapped. *Journal of School Health, 48,* 171–173.

Pugliese, R. (1978). Oral health status in a group of mentally retarded patients. *Rhode Island Dental Journal, 11,* 6–9.

Stark, J., Markel, G., Black, C. M., & Greenbaum, J. (1985). Day to day dental care: A parents' guide. *Exceptional Parent, 15,* 15–17.

Stiefel, D. J. (1980). Dental care for the handicapped at the University of Washington. *Journal of Dental Medicine, 44,* 141–145.

Stiefel, D. J., & Truelove, E. L. (1985). A postgraduate dental training program for treatment of persons with disabilities. *Journal of Dental Education, 49,* 85–90.

U.S. Department of Health, Education, and Welfare, Public Health Service. (1979). *Basic data on dental examination findings of persons.* Hyattesville, MD: National Center for Health Statistics

U.S. Public Health Service. (1980). *Special report on dental care for handicapped people.* Arlington, VA: Rehabilitation Services Administration, U.S. Department of Health, Education, and Welfare.

DAVID C. MANN
St. Francis Hospital

**BRUXISM AND THE STUDENT WITH DISABILITIES
INDIVIDUAL EDUCATION PLAN
SELF-HELP TRAINING**

DEPAKENE

Depakene is an antiepileptic agent known generically as valproic acid. Depakene is the most recently introduced anticonvulsant medication. It differs both chemically and in clinical action from most other anticonvulsants (Goldensohn, Glaser, & Goldberg, 1984). Generally this medication is used either as the sole or adjunctive treatment for simple (petit mal) and complex absence seizures as well as generalized seizure disorders. The precise mechanism by which Depakene works is unknown; however, some research has suggested that its activity is related to increased brain levels of gamma-aminobutyric acid.

While there is little research on the behavioral effects of Depakene, uncontrolled trials suggest that it may improve visual-motor coordination (Schlack, 1974), alertness, and school performance (Barnes & Bower, 1975). Nausea and gastrointestinal irritation are common side effects of Depakene, but these can be controlled through dosage or by giving the drug with food. If Depakene is given with other medications, particularly phenobarbital, there can be extreme, temporary sedation as well as awkward motor movements. Some of the more extreme side effects include a disruption of platelet functioning, liver damage, and pancreas failure, all of which have the potential to be fatal. For these reasons, Depakene typically is held in reserve as a medication of final resort for those individuals with seizures that cannot be controlled by other medication. For those who are using the ketogenic diet there may also be possible interactions (Ballaban-Gil, O'Dell, Pappo, Moshe, & Shinnar, 1998).

REFERENCES

Ballaban-Gil, K., Callahan, C., O'Dell, C., Pappo, M., Moshe, S., & Shinnar, S. (1998). Complications of the ketogenic diet. *Epilepsia, 39*(7), 744–748.

Barnes, S. E., & Bower, B. D. (1975). Sodium valproate in the treatment of intractible childhood epilepsy. *Developmental Medicine and Child Neurology, 17,* 175–181.

Goldensohn, E. S., Glaser, G. H., & Goldberg, M. A. (1984). Epilepsy. In L. P. Rowland (Ed.), *Merritt's textbook of neurology* (7th ed., pp. 629–650). Philadelphia: Lea & Febiger.

Schlack, H. G. (1974). Ergenye in the treatment of epilepsy. *Therapiewoche, 24,* 39–42.

RICHARD A. BERG
West Virginia University Medical Center, Charleston Division

**ANTICONVULSANTS
SEIZURE DISORDERS**

DEPENDENT VARIABLE

Dependent variable is a term that is used to indicate the variable that you wish to measure and change as part of an experimental study (Alberto & Troutman, 2006). Bailey and Burch (2002) write that the word "*dependent* refers to the fact that this variable *depends upon* some experimental manipulations that you will make in the course of the experiment" (p. 64). Examples of dependent variables include

(a) number of times a student raises her hand following a teacher's question, (b) the percent of time a student is academically engaged during a defined instructional period, (c) the reading rates of a small group of students who are at risk for reading failure, (d) the amount of time a student participates in nonstructured activities during recess, and (e) the percent correct on weekly spelling tests for a student during baseline and intervention phases.

Each of the dependent variables listed previously can be both measured and changed as part of an experiment. For example, a teacher reported that her student rarely raises her hand and often blurts out answers to the teacher's question. After reviewing the baseline data, the teacher learns that this student only raises her hand on the average of 1 time per instructional period, but blurts out answers nearly 10 times per instructional period. The teacher implements an intervention in which prior to the beginning of class she verbally precorrects the student to remember to raise her hand and wait to be called on by the teacher. This antecedent-based instructional strategy (i.e., "precorrection"; see De Pry & Sugai, 2002) is implemented and the observer continues to collect data on hand raising in exactly the same manner as she did during the baseline phase. Following the procedures for the ABAB design, the teacher withdrew the intervention and reinstated it one more time to examine the effect of the precorrection intervention on the frequency of hand raising. The data suggested that the student increased hand raising to nearly 8 times per instructional period in both intervention phases. By measuring the dependent variable in baseline and intervention conditions the teacher was able to demonstrate that hand raising increased in the presences of the intervention strategy.

The dependent variable should always be operationally defined. An operational definition is a written statement that precisely defines the behavior you wish to measure in terms that are observable, measurable, and replicable (Fletcher-Janzen & De Pry, 2003). Operational definitions require that the teacher or researcher consider the relevant behavioral dimensions of the behavior of concern prior to writing the definition. Behavioral dimensions include consideration for how often a behavior occurs (frequency), how long the behavior occurs (duration), where the behavior occurs (locus), how hard or damaging the behavior is (magnitude), and the amount of time that it takes for the person to engage in the behavior following the antecedent stimulus (latency; Wolery, Bailey, & Sugai, 1988).

Bailey and Burch (2002) suggest that the following factors be considered when defining the dependent variable. First, the teacher or researcher should consider the face validity of the definition, that is, how it agrees with the standard usage of the proposed dependent variable. Next, the teacher or researcher should determine if the dependent variable has been previously defined as part of his or her review of the extant research literature and to what degree the same definition can be used (replicated) as part of the

proposed study. If an existing definition is not available or appropriate for the study, then creating and pilot testing a new definition is appropriate. This process includes carefully defining the dependent variable as previously described and testing for reliability prior to implementing data collection on the dependent variable.

Once defined, the dependent variable informs the teacher or researcher on the appropriate data-collection strategy. For example, if you want to count the frequency of a discrete behavior, then event recording is the most effective method. If you are interested in examining how long a person engages in a behavior, then duration recording is the best choice. And if you are interested in the amount of time it takes from the time a teacher gives a request until the student engages in behavior, then latency recording is the appropriate data-collection method. Data collected on the dependent variable is always plotted along the ordinate or Y-axis of a graph and interobserver reliability data is collected (approximately 20 percent of the total sample) to document consistency between the primary observer and an independent observer.

REFERENCES

Alberto, P. A., & Troutman, A. C. (2006). *Applied behavior analysis for teachers* (7th ed.). Upper Saddle River, NJ: Prentice Hall.

Bailey, J. S., & Burch, M. R. (2002). *Research methods in applied behavior analysis*. Thousand Oaks, CA: Sage.

De Pry, R. L., & Sugai, G. (2002). The effect of active supervision and precorrection on minor behavioral incidents in a sixth grade general education classroom. *Journal of Behavioral Education, 11,* 255–267.

Fletcher-Janzen, E., & De Pry, R. L. (2003). *Teaching social competence and character: An IEP planner with goals, objectives, and interventions.* Longmont, CO: Sopris West Educational Services.

Wolery, M., Bailey, D. B., Jr., & Sugai, G. M. (1988). *Effective teaching: Principles and procedures of applied behavior analysis for exceptional students.* Boston: Allyn & Bacon.

RANDALL L. DE PRY
*University of Colorado at
Colorado Springs*

RESEARCH IN SPECIAL EDUCATION

DEPRESSION, CHILDHOOD AND ADOLESCENT

Depression is a mood (affective) disorder that affects approximately 2 percent of children and adolescents in the general population (Kashani et al., 1983). Once considered exclusively the domain of psychiatry, depressive disorders can and should be considered by school personnel in identification, assessment, and treatment (Reynolds & Stark,

1987). Students with emotional or behavioral disorders (EBD) and learning disabilities (LD) may be particularly at risk for developing depression. For example, Maag and Behrens (1989a) found that about 21 percent of EBD and LD students experienced significant depressive symptomatology. However, an important distinction should be made between depressive symptomatology and the clinical disorder:

> As a symptom, depression refers to sad affect and as such is a common experience of everyday life. As a syndrome or disorder, depression refers to a group of symptoms that go together. Sadness may be part of a larger set of problems that include the loss of interest in activities, feelings of worthlessness, sleep disturbances, changes in appetite, and others. (Kazdin, 1990, p. 121)

These distinctions may explain part of the discrepancy and debate over the actual prevalence of depression among students with EBD and LD. For example, Maag and Reid (1994) found that 10 percent of students with LD experienced significant depressive symptomatology. However, only 2 percent of them obtained Beck Depression Inventory (BDI) scores that corresponded to levels of clinical depression. This prevalence estimate is the same that exists in the general population of youngsters. In their meta-analytic review, Maag and Reid (2006) concluded that, although students with LD have statistically greater depressive symptomatology than their nondisabled peers, the magnitude was most likely not great enough to place them in the clinical range for a depressive disorder.

Much less is know about depression in students with EBD than those with LD. This lack of data is anomalous because one of the five federal criteria for students being identified and served under the emotional disturbance category is "a general pervasive mood of unhappiness or depression (U.S. Department of Education, 1999, p. 12422). On the other hand, it may be a fate accompli that students with EBD experience depression because it is one of the defining criteria.

One of the first studies examining depression among students with EBD was conducted by Cullinan, Schloss, and Epstein (1987). They found that students with EBD displayed greater depression scores than their nondisabled peers. However, depression was measured using a subscale of the Behavior Problem Checklist (BPC), which was not designed to specifically assess depression. Several years later, Maag and his colleagues examined depression among this population using instruments specific to depression in correctional settings and public schools using a variety of constructs and analyses including gender, age, and extreme scores (DiGangi, Behrens, & Maag, 1989; Maag & Behrens, 1989a, 1989b; Maag, Behrens, & DiGangi, 1992). They concluded that students with EBD obtained statistically higher depression and negative cognition scores than their nondisabled peers. Since that time, a smattering of studies have been conducted with results indicating students with EBD

displayed mild but insignificant differences in depression as compared to their nondisabled peers (Allen-Meares, 1991; Stanley, Dai, & Nolan, 1997), the presence of depressive subtypes (Carmanico et al., 1998), and a greater number of externalizing versus internalizing comorbid disorders (Pellegrino, Singh, & Carmanico, 1999).

Characteristics of Childhood and Adolescent Depression

There are a variety of characteristics associated with childhood and adolescent depression including, but not limited to, low-self esteem, cognitive disturbances, deficient social skills, locus of control, substance abuse, familial stressors, and poor academic skills (e.g., Maag & Forness, 1991; Maag & Rutherford, 1987, 1988; Reynolds, 1985). Kazdin (1990) stated that three specific characteristics have received the most research: prevalence, gender, and age.

Prevalence

Most prevalence estimates address the severity of depressive symptoms as reported from rating scales. In the general population, estimates range from 1.3 percent to 7.3 percent with an acknowledged prevalence around 2 percent (Kazdin, 1990). In clinic samples (i.e., youngsters receiving inpatient or outpatient treatment for a psychiatric disorder), estimates of depressive disorders range between 10 percent to 20 percent (Kashani et al., 1983). Perhaps the greatest disparity in prevalence estimates involves samples of students with EBD and LD. Researchers have consistently found that students with EBD and LD obtained statistically significant higher depression scores than their nonhandicapped peers with prevalence estimates topping off at 21 percent (e.g., Maag & Behrens, 1989a; Maag et al., 1992; Maag & Reid, 2006). However, there is a difference between statistical and clinical significance. The prevalence of depression among students with EBD and LD when using cutoff scores reflecting clinical depression mirrors the general population at 2 percent. Some of the discrepancies in prevalence estimates result, in part, from the impact of gender and age.

Gender and Age Differences

Gender and age are related variables that are difficult to separate. Depression tends to be more prevalent among women than men (Kazdin, 1990). Gender differences typically do not surface until adolescence, when more females than males experience severe depressive symptomatology (Angold, Weissman, John, Wickramaratne, & Drusoff, 1991; Mezzich & Mezzich, 1979; Teri, 1982). Similar results were obtained by Maag and Behrens (1989a) with adolescent females three times more likely to report severe depressive symptomatology than their male counterparts. In general, except for very young children (aged 1–6), who have low rates of depression (Kashani, Cantwell, Shekim, & Reid, 1982; Kashani, Ray, & Carlson, 1984), age differences in both youngsters with and without disabilities tend to be mediated by gender (e.g., Fleming & Offord, 1990; Maag & Behrens, 1989a; Rutter, 1986).

Smucker, Craighead, Craighead, and Green (1986) found several age- and gender-related differences with respect to specific characteristics of depression. For adolescent males, acting-out behaviors were more highly correlated with overall depression scores than for adolescent females. These gender differences were not observed in children (grades 3–6). They also found that a generally dysphoric mood and a negative view of self correlated more highly with total depression scores for both preadolescent and adolescent females (grades 3–9) than for same-aged males.

Assessment of Depression

There are generally four ways to assess depression. The most robust method is for a licensed child psychologist or psychiatrist to render a diagnosis based on a clinical interview. Self-report rating scales such as the *Beck Depression Inventory* (BDI), *Children's Depression Inventory* (CDI), and *Reynolds Adolescent Depression Scale* (RADS) may be used in conjunction with a clinical interview but are also sometimes used in isolation to estimate prevalence (Maag & Forness, 1991; Maag & Reid, 2006). Rating scales completed by others (i.e., parents or teachers), such as the *Children's Depression Rating Scale* (CDRS) and *Depression and Anxiety in Youth Scale* (DAYS), are also commonly used. Less frequently used are peer report measures such as the *Peer Nomination Inventory for Depression* (PNID). These scales have been the subject of extensive reviews (e.g., Kazdin, 1987, 1990; Maag & Forness, 1991; Reynolds, 1985) and, therefore, are not reviewed again here. Rather, issues related to the use of ratings scales and the role of school personnel in early identification of depression are presented.

Issues in the Use of Rating Scales

Many prevalence estimates of depression (using general, clinical, and special education samples), including conclusions reached regarding gender and age differences, are based on scores obtained from rating scales either completed by the child or others that have flawed or inadequate psychometric properties. For example, high scores on the BDI may nevertheless only represent a normal scattering of depressive symptoms among nonclinical populations (Beck, Steer, & Garbin, 1988). CDI scores of children diagnosed as depressed by DSM criteria have not always differed from those of nonclinically diagnosed children (Saylor, Finch, Spirito, & Bennett, 1984). The DAYS has been touted as a good measure for depression among children because it is completed by children, teachers, and parents (New-

comer, Berenbaum, & Bryant, 1994). However, it is fairly new—compared to the BDI and CDI—and less is known about its psychometric properties and normative sample sizes have been small.

Another key methodological consideration is that empirically derived cutoff scores typically yield a high percentage of false positives and false negatives (Kazdin, 1987). False positives and negatives will be influenced by the sensitivity and specificity of an instrument (Reid & Maag, 1994). Sensitivity refers to the percentage of students who receive a statistically significant cutoff score on a depression measure and have also been diagnosed as depressed by a clinician (true positives). Specificity refers to the percentage of students that have not obtained a statistically significant cutoff score and also have not been diagnosed as depressed by a clinician (true negatives). Although youngsters who have been diagnosed as clinically depressed have scored higher on self-report measures than those without a diagnosis, results have not always been clinically or statistically significant (Kazdin, 1987; Maag & Reid, 1994). Furthermore, Saylor et al. (1984) found that the breadth of CDI scores for students diagnosed as clinically depressed were quite broad—ranging from 4 to 32.

Role of School Personnel in Early Identification

Educators should play a strategic role in the early identification of depression. Youngsters spend more time in school than in most other structured settings outside the home, and their most consistent and extensive contact is with educators. Furthermore, students' behaviors, interpersonal relationships, and academic performance—all important indicators of mood and the ability to cope—are subject to ongoing scrutiny in the classroom. Consequently, school personnel may be the first professionals to notice developing problems. Unfortunately, school personnel have not always possessed specific and accurate information about childhood and adolescent depression (Clarizio & Payette, 1990; Maag, Rutherford, & Parks, 1988; Peterson, Wonderlich, Reaven, & Mullins, 1987).

Reynolds (1986) developed a three-stage screening program to identify depression in students: (1) conducting large-group screening with self-report depression measures, (2) retesting children 3 to 6 weeks later who met cutoff score criteria for depression during Stage 1 screening, and (3) conducting individual clinical interviews with students who manifest clinical levels of depression at both Stage 1 and Stage 2 evaluations. The easy part of this process is conducting activities during Stages 1 and 2 that can be undertaken by classroom teachers. Retesting children during Stage 2 is important to weed out students who experience a transient depressed mood during the initial screening or exaggerated their depressive symptomatology. Stage 3 is more problematic because it requires conducting individual clinical interviews by a licensed psychologist or psychiatrist.

School psychologists who are state licensed may conduct these interviews. Otherwise, the school can only recommend to parents that they take their child to see a child psychologist or psychiatrist for further evaluation.

School-Based Interventions

Over 15 years ago, Reynolds and Stark (1987) began describing school-based intervention strategies to treat depression in children and adolescents and described difficulties in implementing them. First, treating depression should not be approached in a cavalier fashion. Depression is a serious mental disorder that may have life-threatening consequences. Second, clinically trained individuals, such as school psychologists, counselors, and social workers, should work collaboratively with teachers to provide consultation in the development and implementation of interventions. Third, prevention may be the best approach for treating depression in schools.

A variety of school-based interventions have been used to treat depression in children and adolescents. Behaviorally oriented social-skills training interventions emerged in the 1980s (e.g., Schloss, Schloss, & Harris, 1984). Activity scheduling—a process that involves the systematic planning of a child's daily activities—has been recommended to increase activity level and reduce time spent in negative ideation (Reynolds & Stark, 1987; Stark et al., 1996). Three components of self-control training have been used to successfully treat depression in youths: self-monitoring, self-evaluation, and self-reinforcement (e.g., Reynolds & Coats, 1986; Stark, Reynolds, & Kaslow, 1987). Finally, cognitive-behavioral interventions have received the most attention and offer the greatest nonpharmaceutical promise for treating childhood and adolescent depression (Maag & Swearer, in press). In this section, the roles of school psychologists, school counselors, and special educators in treating depression is described.

Primary Role of School Psychologists and Counselors

School psychological and counseling services have evolved to the point of considerable compatibility (Murphy, DeEsch, & Strein, 1998). Training accreditation standards for both professions include skill development in the areas of assessment, consultation, and counseling and in facilitating the delivery of comprehensive services within a multidisciplinary team concept (Council for Accreditation of Counseling and Related Educational Programs, 1994; National Association of School Psychologists, 1994). In addition, school psychologists and counselors alike obtain licenses in their respective areas that permit them to conduct psychotherapy and receive third party reimbursement. They also have unique training and expertise that compliment each other—especially when it comes to addressing the needs of students who display depressive symptomatology. School counselors have

skills in small group counseling, large group developmental interventions, and vocational and career development. School psychologists possess expertise in applied behavior analysis, cognitive and personality assessment, individual therapy, and organizational consultation. Although there are some administrative, professional, and personal barriers, the partnership between both professionals greatly enhance outcomes for students with depression.

Nastasi, Varjas, Bernstein, and Pluymert (1997) described four levels of services across which school psychologists can be involved either directly or indirectly in developing mental health programs in schools:

1. *Prevention:* helping a school choose a program for students to manage their feelings.
2. *Risk reduction:* helping counselors target students whose parents suffer from depressive disorders and work with these students in a support group.
3. *Early intervention:* helping preschool and elementary teachers recognize the signs and symptoms of depressive disorders.
4. *Treatment:* delivering direct treatment to students experiencing a depressive disorder.

School counselors have been assuming an increased role as mental health therapists in schools (Lockhart & Keys, 1998). Nowhere is this role as important as it is in providing services for students who are depressed or experiencing depressive symptomatology. Evans, Van Velsor, and Schumacher (2002) described the role of school counselors in using cognitive behavioral interventions as that of active collaboration with the student. They described three classic levels of prevention using cognitive-behavioral interventions (CBI) that school counselors can undertake: primary, secondary, and tertiary.

Ancillary Role of Special Educators

Special educators are not trained, nor do they hold licenses, to provide counseling services to students with disabilities. That is not to say, however, that they cannot play an important ancillary role because many have received training in various techniques associated with cognitive-behavioral interventions such as self-monitoring, cognitive strategy instruction, social skills training, and problem-solving training (Maag & Katsiyannis, 1996). It would be a relatively simple matter for school psychologists or counselors to modify these approaches and consult with special educators who would implement these techniques for treating students who are depressed (Maag & Swearer, 2006).

Conclusion

Clinical depression affects about 2 percent of children in the general population, including those identified by schools as EBD and LD. The prevalence of depression is similar for boys and girls, but increases for females when they reach adolescence. Boys typically display externalizing behaviors while girls manifest depression with internalizing symptoms. A variety of self and other report rating scales have been developed to assess depression. However, a diagnosis of depression should be made by a licensed child psychologist or psychiatrist using a clinical interview and perhaps including scores from depression rating scales. School-based treatments for depression have appeared in the literature for the past 15 years. The most common approaches are social skills training, self-management, and cognitive-behavioral interventions. School psychologists and counselors can coordinate and implement treatment with special educators providing ancillary support.

REFERENCES

Allen-Meares, P. (1991). A study of depressive characteristics in behaviorally disordered children and adolescents. *Children and Youth Services Review, 13,* 271–286.

Angold, A., Weissman, M. M., John, K., Wickramaratne, P., & Drusoff, B. (1991). The effects of age and sex on depression ratings in children and adolescents. *Journal of the American Academy of Child and Adolescent Psychiatry, 30,* 67–74.

Beck, A. T., Steer, R. A., & Garbin, M. G. (1988). Psychometric properties of the Beck Depression Inventory: Twenty-five years of evaluation. *Clinical Psychology Review, 8,* 77–100.

Carmanico, S. J., Erickson, M. T., Sing, N. N., Best, A. M., Sood, A. A., & Oswald, D. P. (1998). Diagnostic subgroups of depression in adolescents with emotional and behavioral disorders. *Journal of Emotional and Behavioral Disorders, 6,* 222–232.

Clarizio, H. F., & Payette, K. (1990). A survey of school psychologists' perspectives and practices with childhood depression. *Psychology in the Schools, 27,* 57–63.

Council for the Accreditation of Counseling and Related Educational Programs. (1994). *Accreditation procedures manual and application.* Alexandria, VA: Author.

Cullinan, D., Schloss, P. M., & Epstein, M. H. (1987). Relative prevalence and correlates of depressive characteristics among seriously emotionally disturbed and nonhandicapped students. *Behavioral Disorders, 12,* 90–98.

DiGangi, S. A., Behrens, J. T., & Maag, J. W. (1989). Dimensions of depression: Factors associated with hopelessness and suicidal intent among special populations. *Monograph in Behavioral Disorders, 12,* 47–53.

Evans, J. R., Van Velsor, P., & Schumacher, J. E. (2002). Addressing adolescent depression: A role for school counselors. *Professional School Counseling, 5,* 211–219.

Fleming, J. E., & Offord, D. R. (1990). Epidemiology of childhood depressive disorders: A critical review. *Journal of the American Academy of Child and Adolescent Psychiatry, 29,* 571–80.

Kashani, J. H., Cantwell, D. P., Shekim, W. O., & Reid, J. C. (1982). Major depressive disorder in children admitted to an inpatient community mental health center. *American Journal of Psychiatry, 139,* 671–672.

Kashani, J. H., McGee, R. O., Clarkson, S. E., Anderson, J. C., Walton, L. A., Williams, S., et al. (1983). Depression in a sample of 9-year old children. *Archives of General Psychiatry, 40,* 1217–1233.

Kashani, J. H., Ray, J. S., & Carlson, G. A. (1984). Depression and depression-like states in preschool-age children in a child development unit. *American Journal of Psychiatry, 141,* 1397–1402.

Kazdin, A. E. (1987). Assessment of childhood depression: Current issues and strategies. *Behavioral Assessment, 9,* 291–319.

Kazdin, A. E. (1990). Childhood depression. *Journal of Child Psychology and Psychiatry, 31,* 121–160.

Lockhart, E. J., & Keys, S. G. (1998). The mental health counseling role of school counselors. *Professional School Counseling, 1,* 3–6.

Maag, J. W., & Behrens, J. T. (1989a). Depression and cognitive self-statements of learning disabled and seriously emotionally disturbed adolescents. *Journal of Special Education, 23,* 17–27.

Maag, J. W., & Behrens, J. T. (1989b). Epidemiologic data on SED and LD adolescents reporting extreme depressive symptomatology. *Behavioral Disorders, 15,* 21–27.

Maag, J. W., Behrens, J. T., & DiGangi, S. A. (1992). Dysfunctional cognitions associated with adolescent depression: Findings across special populations. *Exceptionality, 3,* 31–47.

Maag, J. W., & Forness, S. R. (1991). Depression in children and adolescents: Identification, assessment, and treatment. *Focus on Exceptional Children, 24*(1), 1–19.

Maag, J. W., & Katsiyannis, A. (1996). Counseling as a related service for students with emotional or behavioral disorders: Issues and recommendations. *Behavioral Disorders, 21,* 293–305.

Maag, J. W., & Reid, R. (1994). The phenomenology of depression among students with and without learning disabilities: More similar than different. *Learning Disabilities Research and Practice, 9,* 91–103.

Maag, J. W., & Reid, R. (2006). Depression among students with learning disabilities: Assessing the risk. *Journal of Learning Disabilities, 39,* 3–10.

Maag, J. W., & Rutherford, R. B., Jr. (1987). Behavioral and learning characteristics of childhood and adolescent depression: Implications for special educators. In S. Braaten, R. B. Rutherford, Jr., & J. W. Maag (Eds.), *Programming for adolescents with behavioral disorders* (Vol. 3, pp. 55–70). Reston, VA: Council for Children with Behavioral Disorders.

Maag, J. W., & Rutherford, R. B., Jr. (1988). Review and synthesis of three components for identifying depressed students. In R. B. Rutherford, Jr., C. M. Nelson, & S. R. Forness (Eds.), *Bases of severe behavioral disorders in children and youth* (pp. 205–230). San Diego, CA: College-Hill.

Maag, J. W., Rutherford, R. B., Jr., & Parks, B. T. (1988). Secondary school professionals' ability to identify depression in adolescents. *Adolescence, 23,* 73–82.

Maag, J. W., & Swearer, S. M. (2006). Cognitive-behavioral interventions for depression: Review and implications for school personnel. *Behavioral Disorders, 30,* 116–119.

Mezzich, A. C., & Mezzich, J. E. (1979). Symptomatology of depression in adolescence. *Journal of Personality Assessment, 43,* 267–275.

Murphy, J. P., DeEsch, J. B., & Strein, W. O. (1998). School counselors and school psychologists: Partners in student services. *Professional School Counseling, 2,* 85–87.

Nastasi, B. K., Varjas, K., Bernstein, R., & Pluymert, K. (1997). *Exemplary mental health programs: School psychologists as mental health service providers.* Bethesda, MD: National Association of School Psychologists.

National Association of School Psychologists. (1994). *Standards for training and credentialing in school psychology.* Washington, DC: Author.

Newcomer, P. L., Berenbaum, E. M., & Bryant, B. R. (1994). *Depression and anxiety in youth scale: Examiner's manual.* Austin, TX: PRO-ED.

Pellegrino, J. F., Singh, N. N., & Carmanico, S. J. (1999). Concordance among three diagnostic procedures for identifying depression in children and adolescence with EBD. *Journal of Emotional and Behavioral Disorders, 7,* 118–127.

Peterson, L., Wonderlich, S. A., Reaven, N. M., & Mullins, L. L. (1987). Adult educators' response to depression and stress in children. *Journal of Social and Clinical Psychology, 5,* 51–58.

Reid, R., & Maag, J. W. (1994). How many fidgets in a pretty much: A critique of behavior rating scales for identifying students with ADHD. *Journal of School Psychology, 32,* 339–354.

Reynolds, W. M. (1985). Depression in children and adolescence: Diagnosis, assessment, intervention strategies, and research. In T. R. Kratochwill (Ed.), *Advances in school psychology* (Vol. 4, pp. 133–189). Hillsdale, NJ: Erlbaum.

Reynolds, W. M. (1996). A model for screening and identification of depressed children and adolescents in school settings. *Professional School Psychology, 1,* 117–129.

Reynolds, W. M., & Coats, K. I. (1986). A comparison of cognitive-behavioral therapy and relaxation training for the treatment of depression in adolescents. *Journal of Consulting and Clinical Psychology, 54,* 653–660.

Reynolds, W. M., & Stark, K. D. (1987). School-based intervention strategies for the treatment of depression in children and adolescents. In S. G. Forman (Ed.), *School-based affective and social interventions* (pp. 69–88). New York: Haworth.

Rutter, M. R. (1986). The developmental psychopathology of depression: Issues and perspectives. In M. R. Rutter, C. E. Izard, & P. B. Read (Eds.), *Depression in young people: Developmental and clinical perspectives* (pp. 3–30). New York: Guilford.

Saylor, C. F., Finch, A. J., Jr., Spirito, A., & Bennett, B. (1984). The Children's Depression Inventory: A systematic evaluation of psychometric properties. *Journal of Consulting and Clinical Psychology, 52,* 955–967.

Schloss, P. J., Schloss, C. N., & Harris, L. (1984). A multiple baseline analysis of an interpersonal skills training program for depressed youth. *Behavioral Disorders, 9,* 182–188.

Smucker, M. R., Craighead, W. E., Craighead, L. W., & Green, J. J. (1986). Normative and reliability data for the Children's Depression Inventory. *Journal of Abnormal Child Psychology, 14,* 25–39.

Stanley, P. D., Dia, Y., & Nolan, R. F. (1997). Differences in depression and self-esteem reported by learning disabled and behavior disordered middle school students. *Journal of Adolescence, 20,* 219–222.

Stark, K. D., Kendall, P. C., McCarthy, M., Staford, M., Barron, R., & Thomeer, M. (1996). *ACTION: A workbook for overcoming depression.* Ardmore, PA: Workbook Publishing.

Stark, K. D., Reynolds, W. M., & Kaslow, N. J. (1987). A comparison of the relative efficacy of self-control and behavior therapy for the reduction of depression in children. *Journal of Abnormal Child Psychology, 15,* 91–113.

Teri, L. (1982). The use of the Beck Depression Inventory with adolescents. *Journal of Abnormal Child Psychology, 10,* 277–282.

U.S. Department of Education. (1999). Assistance to states for the education of children with disabilities and the early intervention program for infants and toddlers. *Federal Register, 64*(48), CFR Parts 300 and 303.

JOHN W. MAAG
University of Nebraska–Lincoln

EMOTIONAL DISORDERS
EMOTIONAL LABILITY

DEPRIVATION

See POST-INSTITUTIONALIZED CHILD.

DEPRIVATION, BIONEURAL RESULTS OF

The term deprivation is usually used to mean the absence or reduction of normal sensory input to the nervous system. Its meaning is sometimes extended to include restriction or suppression of opportunities for normal motoric activities associated with exploration, play, and social intercourse. The bioneural results of deprivation have mostly been investigated through animal experiments.

The visual system has been studied extensively. Various changes reviewed by Vrensen and De Groot (1974) have been observed in the visual cortex of animals reared in the dark. Monocular deprivation has been shown to produce more salient changes than binocular; competition between the two sides seems to be a more important factor than deprivation per se. The changes are particularly marked, and largely irreversible, when deprivation occurs during a critical period of early life. The best known examples are the protracted loss of vision through one eye in kittens (Wiesel & Hubel, 1965) and monkeys (Hubel, Wiesel, & LeVay, 1976), resulting from a brief period of interference with that eye's function shortly after birth. Stimulation of the deprived eye no longer elicits normal activity in the visual area of the brain because this has become reorganized in favor of the other eye.

In the auditory system, complete suppression of input is impossible without destruction of both inner ears, since otherwise there is always some perception of the sounds produced in the animal's own body. Temporary restriction of auditory stimuli can be achieved by rearing in a sound-attenuated environment or by interfering with the external or middle ear structures that transmit sound to the inner ear. Both methods produce perturbations of the auditory function and neuronal alterations of brain stem auditory nuclei (Webster & Webster, 1979). Significant changes in the microscopic structure of the auditory cortex have been observed in mutant mice with hereditary deafness owed to inner ear degeneration (Périer et al., 1984). As in the visual system, there are critical or sensitive periods of development during which plasticity is greatest and the results of deprivation most evident (Eggermont, 1986).

Nonspecific reduction of sensory stimulation is achieved by rearing animals in standard or isolated laboratory conditions as opposed to environmental complexity. In these experiments, there is a reduction of the normal span of sensory experiences, motor activities, and social exchanges. Behavioral differences as well as differences in cerebral structures are observed. Both have been extensively reviewed by Walsch (1980, 1981a, 1981b).

In man, the counterpart of animal experiments on the visual system is functional amblyopia, a condition observed in some children who have suffered from unattended squinting or other conditions interfering with the vision of one eye. Even after correction of the pathological condition, the deprived eye may remain largely nonfunctional. Partial auditory deprivation is a frequent occurrence in small children as a result of serous otitis media. It seems to cause long-lasting learning difficulties, even after normal hearing has been restored. All degrees of hearing loss, from mild to profound, might affect the human auditory pathways and cortex, as shown in animals. These possible effects in man have been discussed by Ruben and Rapin (1980). Studies in language development indicate that infants possess a capacity for making phonetic distinctions which must, to persist, be confirmed by the corresponding sounds of language spoken in their environment. Some studies indicate that children with congenital or early acquired hearing loss might lose this early competence (Serniclaes, D'Alimonte, & Alegria, 1984).

Examples of extreme multisensory and social deprivation in man are afforded by "wolf" children and exceptional cases such as that of Genie, a girl maintained in isolation for years by psychotic parents (Curtiss, 1977). The complexity of such cases as well as the lack of sufficient information about their early life make their interpretation difficult. Less severe but more frequent deprivation situations occur in hospitalism (Spitz, 1945) and in poorly stimulating familial background. It is probable, though yet unproven, that these have bioneural consequences in addition to the well-known psychological ones.

REFERENCES

Curtiss, S. (1977). *Genie, a psycholinguistic study of a modern day "wild child."* New York: Academic.

Eggermont, J. (1986). Critical periods in auditory development. Proceedings of the Nijmegen Workshop. *Acta Otolaryngologica* (Stockholm) (Supplement 491), 153–160.

Hubel, D. H., Wiesel, T. N., & LeVay, S. (1976). Functional architecture of area 17 in normal and monocularly deprived Macaque monkeys. *Cold Spring Harbor Symposium on Quantitative Biology, 40,* 581–589.

Périer, O., Alegria, J., Buyse, M., D'Alimonte, G., Gilson, D., & Serniclaes, W. (1984). Consequences of auditory deprivation in animals and humans. *Acta Otolaryngologica* (Stockholm), *411,* 60–70.

Ruben, R. J., & Rapin, I. (1980). Plasticity of the developing auditory system. *Annals of Otology Rhinology and Laryngology, 89,* 303–311.

Serniclaes, W., D'Alimonte, G., & Alegria, J. (1984). Production and perception of French stops by moderately deaf subjects. *Speech Communication, 3,* 185–198.

Spitz, R. A. (1945). Hospitalism—An inquiry into the genesis of psychiatric conditions in early childhood. *Psychoanalytic Study of the Child, 1,* 53–74.

Vrensen, G., & De Groot, D. (1974). The effect of dark rearing and its recovery on synaptic terminals in the visual cortex of rabbits. A quantitative electron microscopic study. *Brain Research, 78,* 263–278.

Walsch, R. (1980). Effects of environmental complexity and deprivation on brain chemistry and physiology: A review. *International Journal of Neuroscience, 11,* 77–89.

Walsch, R. (1981a). Effects of environmental complexity and deprivation on brain anatomy and histology: A review. *International Journal of Neuroscience, 12,* 33–51.

Walsch, R. (1981b). Sensory environments, brain damage, and drugs: A review of interactions and mediating mechanisms. *International Journal of Neuroscience, 14,* 129–137.

Webster, D. B., & Webster, M. (1979). Effects of neonatal conductive hearing loss on brain stem auditory nuclei. *Annals of Otology Rhinology, & Laryngoly, 88,* 684–688.

OLIVIER PÉRIER
*Université Libre de Bruxelles
Centre Comprendre et Parler,
Belgium*

**EARLY EXPERIENCE AND CRITICAL PERIODS
GENIE
LANGUAGE, ABSENCE OF
LANGUAGE DELAYS**

DESENSITIZATION

Desensitization is a behavioral-based procedure developed by psychiatrist Joseph Wolpe, in 1958 (Gerald, 2001). Wolpe based his desensitization procedure on the classical conditioning methods developed in the 1920s by John Watson and Mary Cover Jones. The use of desensitization peaked in the 1960s and 1970s; nevertheless, it is still widely used.

The decline has been attributed to more rapidly moving techniques, such as flooding and implosive therapy. Also, the shift toward cognitive-behavioral therapy is seen as a factor, however, less direct (McGlynn, Smitherman, & Gothard, 2004).

With desensitization, the therapist begins by asking the client questions regarding his or her anxieties or phobias. The client is then asked to self-monitor himself or herself to see how and when his or her anxieties or phobias are provoked. The therapist begins with relaxation techniques to allow the client to feel safe and calm. Once the client is relaxed the therapist asks the client to imagine neutral scenes that do not provoke anxiety and eventually to imagine scenes related to his or her anxiety or phobia. The client is relaxed again, and this process evolves in a hierarchy of anxiety-eliciting scenes. Throughout sessions, the therapist may model for the client and respond to the client with prompts or reinforcements to eventually fade out the anxiety-producing response. When the client can imagine the anxiety- or phobia-eliciting scene and remain calm, treatment ends. This form of treatment is efficient because it only requires the use of imagery of the anxiety-producing situation. The client in pure desensitization therapy is never brought face to face with the stimulus. However, the therapist may introduce the stimulus by way of in vivo desensitization or flooding (Gerald, 2001).

Desensitization is currently used for test anxiety (Powell, 2004), performance anxiety (Lazarus & Abramovitz, 2004), and has proven to be effective. Although these are its primary uses it has also been used effectively in treating Anorexia Nervosa, obsessions, compulsions, stuttering, body image disturbances, nightmares, and depression (Gerald, 2001).

REFERENCES

Gerald, C. (2001). Behavior therapy. In J. Martinez & A. Berterretche (Eds.), *Theory and practice of counseling and psychotherapy* (pp. 266–269). Belmont, CA: Wadsworth/Thomson Learning.

Lazarus, A. A., & Abramovitz, A. (2004). A multimodal behavioral approach to performance anxiety. *Journal of Clinical Psychology, 60,* 831–840.

McGlynn, F. D., Smitherman, T. A., & Gothard, K. D. (2004). Comment on the status of systematic desensitization. *Behavior Modification, 28,* 194–205.

Powell, D. H. (2004). Behavioral treatment of debilitating test anxiety among medical students. *Journal of Clinical Psychology, 60,* 853–865.

SELINA RIVERA-LONGORIA
Texas A&M University

BEHAVIOR THERAPY
COGNITIVE BEHAVIOR THERAPY
INTERVENTION

DES LAURIERS, AUSTIN M. (1917–1983)

Austin Des Lauriers earned his PhD in 1942 from the University of Montreal. From 1967 to 1970, he was professor and director of research and training at the University of Missouri Medical Center in Kansas City. He also served as professor and director of the Child Study Center at Ottawa, where he maintained a private practice.

Des Lauriers' work primarily centered on school psychology, autism, and schizophrenia. However, his views on functional literacy in business were featured in the quarterly publication *Learning in the Workplace* (Des Lauriers, 1990); and at the Working Conference on Vermont's Heritage for Teachers, his work contributed to the proceeding devoted to the development of teaching materials to be used in Vermont's classrooms (True, 1984).

Des Lauriers' research interests have focused on topics of childhood schizophrenia (Des Lauriers, 1962) and autism. He held that the autistic child's condition and behavior (in an arrested form) involve the same conflicts that a normal child experiences. His book, *Your Child Is Asleep* (1969), is considered a classic in the field.

REFERENCES

Des Lauriers, A. M. (1962). *The experience of reality in childhood schizophrenia.* New York: I.V.P.

Des Lauriers, A. M., & Carlson, C. F. (1969). *Your child is asleep: Early infantile autism.* Homewood, IL: Dorsey.

Learning in the workplace. (1990). Toronto Frontier College.

True, M. (1984). Teaching Vermont's heritage. *Proceedings of the Working Conference on Vermont's Heritage for Teachers.* Burlington: Vermont University.

RICK GONZALES
Texas A&M University
First edition

TAMARA J. MARTIN
The University of Texas of the Permian Basin
Second edition

DES LAURIERS–CARLSON HYPOTHESIS

In 1969 Austin Des Lauriers and Carole Carlson found that the reticular activating system was involved in the cause of early infantile autism. They proposed an imbalance in the relationship between the reticular activating system and the limbic system. The limbic system, which is involved in emotion, motivation, and reinforcement, is inhibited by the reticular activating system, rendering the autistic child unable to make associations between behavior and positive or negative consequences. The work of Des Lauriers and

Carlson came after Kanner (1943) identified the behavioral characteristics of children who were qualitatively different from other childhood clinical populations. These symptoms included the inability to develop relationships, a delay in speech acquisition, echolalia, and repetitive play activities. These have become identifying characteristics of early infantile autism.

The etiology of early infantile autism was once thought to be based on abnormal family relationships and early parenting experiences (Kanner, 1943). There have since been many theories that attempt to understand the complicated disorder. Findings are mixed and tentative. The focus has included abnormal parenting and family relationships (a theory that has been recently eliminated; this act is seen as the most important improvement in treatment of autistic children (Schopler, 1990), the social environment, and biochemical and organic deficits as contributing factors.

Although much of the early research focused on family and environmental causes, some research identifies possible involvement with neurochemistry, developmental biology, neurophysiology, and neuroanatomy (Hanson & Gottesman, 1976). In 1983 Gillberg and Gillberg reported an increase in pre- and perinatal hazards that are suggestive of brain dysfunction in infantile autism. Recent advances in cytogenetics have resulted in the identification of a specific biological marker or fragile site on the X chromosome. These are indicators that there is a coexistence of autism with the fragile X chromosome, suggesting an etiological link (August & Lockhart, 1984). Sherman, Nass, and Shapiro (1984) researched cerebral blood flow in autistic children. Their research suggested depressed gray matter cerebral blood flow in autistic subjects; this may reflect their mental retardation. These findings lend support to the hypothesis of Damasio and Maurer (1978), who suggested that autism is the result of abnormalities of the mesolimbic dopaminergic system.

Currently, it is generally accepted that early infantile autism is a behavioral syndrome reflecting abnormal brain functioning (Sherman et al., 1984) and multiple causes (Schopler, 1990). These findings present a challenge for special educators who are involved in the education and treatment of autistic persons. McDonald and Sheperd (1976) reported that teachers play a major role in educating autistic children using criterion-referenced assessment and behavior teaching practices in a comprehensive program. This work has led to involvement of special education in the treatment of autism.

REFERENCES

August, J. A., & Lockhart, H. L. (1984). Familial autism and the fragile X chromosome. *Journal of Autism & Developmental Disorders, 14,* 197–203.

Damasio, A. R., & Maurer, R. G. (1978). A neurological model for children with autism. *Archives of Neurology, 35,* 771–776.

Des Lauriers, A. M., & Carlson, C. F. (1969). *Your child is asleep: Early infantile autism.* Homewood, IL: Dorsey.

Gillberg, C., & Gillberg, C. I. (1983). Infantile autism: A total population study of reduce optimality in the pre-peri and neonatal period. *Journal of Autism & Developmental Disorders, 13,* 153–166.

Hanson, D. R., & Gottesman, I. I. (1976). The genetics, if any, of infantile autism and childhood schizophrenia. *Journal of Autism & Developmental Disorders, 6,* 209, 231.

Kanner, L. (1943). Autistic disturbances of affective contact. *Nervous Child, 2,* 217–250.

McDonald, J. E., & Sheperd, G. (1976). The autistic child, a challenge for educators. *Psychology in the Schools, 13,* 248–256.

Schopler, E. (1990). *Neurobiological correlates of autism.* Reston, VA: ERIC Publications. (ERIC Clearinghouse No. EC300540)

Sherman, M., & Nass, R., & Shapiro, T. (1984). Brief report: Regional cerebral blood flow in autism. *Journal of Autistic & Developmental Disorders, 14,* 439–446.

STEVEN GUMERMAN
Temple University

AUTISM
RETICULAR ACTIVATING SYSTEM

DESPERT, JULIETTE L. (1892–1982)

Juliette L. Despert, MD, child psychiatrist and researcher, received her education in her native France and in the United States. During her many years as a practicing psychiatrist, she contributed numerous articles to professional journals and published over half a dozen books, including *The Emotionally Disturbed Child: An Inquiry into Family Patterns, Schizophrenia in Childhood,* and *Children of Divorce,* and developed the Despert Fables.

REFERENCES

Despert, J. L. (1953). *Children of divorce.* New York: Doubleday.

Despert, J. L. (1968). *Schizophrenia in childhood.* New York: Brunner.

Despert, J. L. (1970). *The emotionally disturbed child: An inquiry into family patterns.* New York: Doubleday.

PAUL IRVINE
Katonah, New York

DESTRUCTIVE BEHAVIORS

To specify all acts in which persons engage that could be considered destructive is impossible; the topography of various destructive behaviors is at least as diverse as the people who exhibit them. A number of factors mitigate against a universally acceptable definition of destructive behaviors and are generally accounted for in operational definitions of such acts. There are at least three elements that should be implicitly or explicitly incorporated into operational definitions of destructive behaviors. One element is that of intentionality. For example, a child who accidentally breaks a dish is not generally considered destructive, but one who deliberately breaks a dish is considered destructive. Second, characteristics of the behavior itself (e.g., intensity, frequency) play a definitional role. For instance, children who occasionally bite their fingernails are not considered to be self-destructive, while those who often bite their hands until they bleed generally are considered self-destructive. Third, situational factors influence definitions. Persons who intentionally break a glass in a restaurant are considered destructive; in contrast, in some wedding ceremonies the intentional breaking of a glass is a socially sanctioned event. Much has been asserted in recent years that society has redefined destructive behavior in a more innocuous fashion: a statement about society's increasing tolerance for deviant behaviors (Moynihan, 1994).

A multitude of treatment programs that have successfully reduced various types of destructive behaviors have been reported. These programs have ranged in scope from large district-wide programs to reduce vandalism to interventions that have reduced the destructive behavior of a single individual. Likewise, the programs have varied a great deal according to the procedures used. As in the case with selecting any procedure to reduce behavior, a host of ethical, moral, legal, empirical, and practical issues must be attended to (see Foxx, 1982; Polsgrove, 1983; Repp, 1983). In the following paragraphs, effective programs for reducing various destructive behaviors are briefly discussed in approximate order of increasing intrusiveness. It should be stressed, however, that ineffective programs, regardless of their level of intrusiveness, should never be perpetuated.

There have been many examples of positively-based programs to reduce destructive behaviors. An interesting large-scale program to reduce acts of vandalism was reported by Mayer, Butterworth, Nefpaktitis, and Sulzer-Azaroff (1983). Selected teachers in 18 schools participated in workshops and consultation sessions. Over the three-year study, the teachers significantly increased their rates of praise. Acts of vandalism were significantly reduced and decreases in other disruptive and destructive student behaviors were also observed. Russo, Cataldo, and Cushing (1981) reported that positively reinforcing compliance resulted in decreased acts of self-destruction among three children, although no contingencies were in effect for the self-destructive behaviors. Using a DRO procedure (reinforcement delivered for nonoccurrence of behavior), Frankel, Moss, Schofield, and Simmons (1976) eliminated aggressive and self-destructive acts.

Extinction combined with positive reinforcement was used by Martin and Treffry (1970) to eliminate poor posture and self-destructive behaviors in a 16-year-old partially paralyzed mentally retarded girl with cerebral palsy. She was positioned in such a manner that if she slouched she was not visible to the persons administering the reinforcers. If she was engaging in self-destructive behaviors, she was also not reinforced.

A variety of destructive behaviors exhibited by five mentally retarded boys were reduced by a nonexclusionary timeout procedure (Foxx & Shapiro, 1978). A number of advantages are associated with this technique compared with other forms of timeout procedures.

An overcorrection procedure (a punishment technique involving the correction of the undesirable behavior followed by practicing the desirable behavior) was used by Foxx and Azrin (1972) to eliminate the destructive behavior of a profoundly retarded adult female. Other punishment procedures (e.g., contingent electric shock, aromatic ammonia, citric acid, etc.) have also been used to decrease destructive behaviors.

Irrespective of the particular type of destructive behavior, these responses merit our best professional interventions. A variety of treatments (in addition to the ones mentioned here) have proven successful, but careful attention to aspects of individual cases is essential.

REFERENCES

Foxx, R. M. (1982). *Decreasing behaviors of severely retarded and autistic persons.* Champaign, IL: Research Press.

Foxx, R. M., & Azrin, N. H. (1972). Restitution: A method of eliminating aggressive-disruptive behavior of retarded and brain damaged patients. *Behavior Research and Therapy, 10,* 15–27.

Foxx, R. M., & Shapiro, S. T. (1978). The timeout ribbon: A nonexclusionary timeout procedure. *Journal of Applied Behavior Analysis, 11,* 125–136.

Frankel, F., Moss, D., Schofield, S., & Simmons, J. Q. (1976). Use of differential reinforcement to suppress self-injurious and aggressive behavior. *Psychological Reports, 39,* 843–849.

Martin, G. L., & Treffry, D. (1970). Treating self-destruction and developing self-care skills with a severely retarded girl: A case study. *Psychological Aspects of Disability, 17,* 125–131.

Mayer, G. R., Butterworth, T., Nafpaktitis, M., & Sulzer-Azaroff, B. (1983). Preventing school vandalism and improving discipline: A three-year study. *Journal of Applied Behavior Analysis, 16,* 355–369.

Moynihan, P. (1994). Defining deviancy down: How we've become accustomed to alarming levels of crime and destructive behavior. *American Educator, 17,* 10–18.

Polsgrove, L. (Ed.). (1983). Aversive control in the classroom. *Exceptional Education Quarterly, 3*(4).

Repp, A. C. (1983). *Teaching the mentally retarded.* Englewood Cliffs, NJ: Prentice Hall.

Russo, D. C., Cataldo, M. F., & Cushing, P. J. (1981). Compliance training and behavioral covariation in the treatment of multiple behavior problems. *Journal of Applied Behavior Analysis, 14,* 209–222.

JAMES P. KROUSE
*Clarion University of
Pennsylvania*

ACTING OUT
APPLIED BEHAVIOR ANALYSIS
EMOTIONAL DISORDERS
REALITY THERAPY

DETROIT TESTS OF LEARNING APTITUDE–FOURTH EDITION

The Detroit Tests of Learning Aptitude–Fourth Edition (DTLA-4; Hammill, 1998) are intended for use with children and adolescents ages 6:0 to 17:0. There is also an adult version for ages 16:0 through 79:0 and a primary version for children aged 3:0 to 9:11. It was designed to (1) measure both general intelligence and discrete ability areas; (2) show the effects of language, attention, and motor abilities on test performance; and (3) allow interpretation in light of current theories of intellect.

The DTLA-4 consists of 10 subtests that take between 40 minutes and 2 hours to administer. Administration time varies by individual as none of the subtests are timed. To administer the test, an examiner's manual, two color picture books for the subtests, profile and summary forms, examiner's record booklets, response forms, story sequence chips, and design sequence cubes are needed. Percentiles, standard scores, and age equivalents can be derived from this test. A computerized scoring program is available to convert raw scores to the three types of scores, as well as to calculate intra-ability differences.

The 10 subtests of the DTLA-4 include Word Opposites, Design Sequences, Sentence Imitation, Reversed Letters, Story Construction, Design Reproduction, Basic Information, Symbolic Relations, Word Sequences, and Story Sequences. The Picture Fragments subtest found in previous editions has been removed to shorten the length of administration. These subtests measure a variety of specific cognitive abilities, including vocabulary, auditory and visual memory, and visual problem solving. Scoring of the subtests results in scaled scores (M = 10; SD = 3), which are then compiled into 16 composite scores (M = 100; SD = 15), including the Overall Composite, Optimal Level Composite, Domain Composites, and Theoretical Composites. The Overall Composite is formed from the scaled scores of all of the subtests in the battery. The Optimal Level Composite is calculated from the four highest subtest scores, giving an estimate of the individual's potential, or highest level of performance possible when any inhibiting influences are disregarded.

Domain Composites are given for language, attention, and manual dexterity, while Theoretical Composites allow for interpretation in terms of major theories proposed by Horn and Cattell, Jensen, Das, and Wechsler.

The DTLA-4 was standardized on 1,350 students in 37 states, stratified by age. This sample was representative of the 1996 U.S. census with respect to gender, race, ethnicity, residence (urban or rural), family income, educational attainment of parents, and geographic distribution. With respect to reliability, test-retest studies range from .71 to .96 for the subtests, while coefficients for the composites exceed .90. Internal consistency was shown to exceed .80 for the subtests and .90 for the composites. Scorer reliability coefficients were in the .90s for all tests. Several factor analyses have been completed regarding the validity of the DTLA-4 showing intercorrelation between the subtests, chronological age, and tests of academic achievement. Criterion prediction validity has been examined through the comparison of the DTLA-4 with various aptitude tests, including the TONI3, WISC, KABC, PPVT, and WJPEB.

Test bias was considered throughout test construction. The effects of bias in terms of culture, race, and gender were controlled and minimized by the inclusion of minority and disabled groups within the normative sample. Internal consistency was seen throughout these subgroups. Differential item functioning analysis was used to reduce item bias, and delta score values were used to identify potential bias.

REFERENCES AND ADDITIONAL INFORMATION

Hammill, D. (1998). *Detroit Tests of Learning Aptitude–4.* Austin, TX: PRO-ED.

Plake, B. S., & Impara, J. C. (Eds.). (2001). *The fourteenth mental measurements yearbook.* Lincoln, NE: Buros Institute of Mental Measurements.

RON DUMONT
Fairleigh Dickinson University

JOHN O. WILLIS
Rivier College

DEVELOPMENTAL APHASIA

See CHILDHOOD APHASIA; LANGUAGE DISORDERS.

DEVELOPMENTAL APRAXIA

Developmental apraxia is a childhood disorder of sensory integration interfering with ability to plan and execute skilled or nonhabitual motor tasks in the absence of muscle weakness or paralysis (Davis, Jakielski, & Marquardt, 1998; Hall, Jordan, & Robin, 1993). Voluntary or purposeful motor acts are inconsistently produced while involuntary movements remain intact. The condition is characterized by difficulty in articulation of speech (oral, speech, or verbal apraxia); formation of letters in writing; difficulty with visual-spatial tasks such as drawing, block arrangements, assembling stick designs or shapes in drawing; or problems in sequential movements of gesture, pantomime, dressing, grooming, or eating (Hall et al., 1993; Shriberg, Aram, & Kwiatkowski, 1997). In less severe forms, apraxia may be referred to as dyspraxia (Dewey, 1995; Missiuna & Polatajko, 1995).

Developmental apraxia of speech (DAS) is a nonlinguistic sensorimotor disorder of articulation characterized by impaired capacity to program and position the speech musculature and the sequencing of muscle movements (respiratory, laryngeal, and oral) for the volitional production and sequencing of phonemes. Children with developmental apraxia of speech have more addition errors (producing extra phonemes), prolongation errors, repetitions of sounds and syllables, and nonphonemic productions such as glottal plosives, bilabial fricatives, nasal assimilation and distortions such as subtle voicing and devoicing errors that are not overt substitution errors (Davis et al., 1998; Hall et al., 1993; Shriberg et al., 1997).

Whereas speech-language pathologists may be more familiar with the term developmental apraxia of speech, occupational and physical therapists may use the term Developmental Coordination Disorders (DCD; David, 1995; Willoughby & Polatajko, 1995). This condition is also referred to as clumsy child syndrome, mild motor problems, incoordination, developmental apraxia or dyspraxia, perceptual motor dysfunction, visual-motor problems and sensory-integrative dysfunction. The *Diagnostic and Statistical Manual of Mental Disorders (DSM-IV;* American Psychiatric Association, 1994) description of DCD implicitly excludes the coordination disturbances affecting speech motor skill development, even though phonological awareness deficits are frequently found in children diagnosed with DCD. A consensus does not exist for etiology of the condition (Davis et al., 1998; Dewey, 1995; Hall et al., 1993; Shriberg et al., 1997). Developmental apraxia of speech and developmental coordination disorders can impact on the social and academic dimensions of the communication-learning process across the life course, but particularly do so in childhood.

REFERENCES

American Psychiatric Association. (1994). *Diagnostic and statistical manual of mental disorders* (4th ed.). Washington, DC: Author.

David, K. S. (1995). Developmental coordination disorders. In S. Campbell (Ed.), *Physical therapy for children* (pp. 425–456). Philadelphia: W. B. Saunders.

Davis, B. L., Jakielski, K. J., & Marquardt, T. P. (1998). Developmental apraxia of speech: Determiners of differential diagnosis. *Clinical Linguistics and Phonetics, 12,* 25–45.

Dewey, D. (1995). What is developmental dyspraxia? *Brain and Cognition, 29,* 254–274.

Hall, P. K., Jordan, L. S., & Robin, D. A. (1993). *Developmental apraxia of speech: Theory and clinical practice.* Austin, TX: PRO-ED.

Missiuna, C., & Polatajko, H. (1995). Developmental dyspraxia by any other name: Are they all just clumsy children? *The American Journal of Occupational Therapy, 49,* 619–627.

Shriberg, L., Aram, D., & Kwiatkowski, J. (1997). Developmental apraxia of speech: I. Descriptive and theoretical perspectives. *Journal of Speech, Language and Hearing Research, 40,* 273–285.

Willoughby, C., & Polatajko, H. (1995). Motor problems in children with developmental coordination disorder: Review of the literature. *The American Journal of Occupational Therapy, 49,* 787–793.

STEPHEN S. FARMER
New Mexico State University

DEVELOPMENTAL ASSESSMENT OF YOUNG CHILDREN

The Developmental Assessment of Young Children (DAYC; Vorress & Maddox, 1998) is designed for children between birth and 5 years 11 months. It is an individually administered test of developmental abilities in the adaptive, cognitive, communication, physical, and social-emotional domains. Each of the five domains reflects areas that are required for assessment and intervention for young children according to Individuals with Disabilities Education Act (IDEA). This particular measure can be tailored to the specific assessment needs of each child, or all domains may be administered. The DAYC has four uses: the identification of children with developmental delays, recognition of strengths and weaknesses, documentation of a child's progress, and measurement of children's developmental abilities for research purposes.

The Cognitive subtest consists of 78 items that assess concept development. The Communication subtest consists of 78 items measuring receptive/expressive language and verbal/nonverbal abilities. The Social-Emotional subtest consists of 58 items that assess social awareness in relationships and social competence. The Physical Development subtest consists of 87 items measuring motor development. The last subtest, Adaptive Behavior, consists of 62 items that assess independent functioning in self-help.

Administration time is approximately 1 hour and 40 minutes for the comprehensive battery. Each subtest requires about 20 minutes to complete. Testing may occur over more than one session; however, it should be completed as soon as possible. Administration is fairly straightforward. Items passed receive 1 point and those failed receive 0 points. Basal and ceilings are utilized for each subtest. Data are recorded on the subtest scoring forms. The DAYC provides standard scores, percentile scores, and age equivalents as well as a General Development Quotient (GDQ) if all five subtests are completed.

Normative data were collected on a national sample of 1,269 individuals consistent with the 1996 U.S. Census. The sample also includes an "at-risk" category of children with no present disability but an identified risk factor. Internal consistency reliability coefficients range from .90 to .99, and test-retest reliability was good ($r = .90$). Three types of validity were reported in the manual. Content-description validity correlations range from .94 to .99. Criterion-related validity was examined through comparison with the Battelle Developmental Inventory Screening Test and the Revised Gesell and Amatruda Developmental and Neurologic Examination. Coefficients were significant at the .01 level with the Batelle (range from .47 to .61) and at the .05 level with the Gesell (range from .41 to .53). Construct validity was assessed, but statistical data were not reported in the available reviews.

Reviews state that the DAYC is well organized, easy to understand, and simple to use. One limitation of the DAYC is the lack of research regarding treatment effects. It is suggested that the DAYC is not appropriate for evaluating change after a program intervention.

REFERENCES

Plake, B. S., & Impara, J. C. (Eds.). (2001). *The fourteenth mental measurements yearbook*. Lincoln, NE: Buros Institute of Mental Measurements.

Vomess J. K., & Maddox, T. (1998). *Developmental Assessment of Young Children (DAYC)*. Austin, TX: PRO-ED.

RON DUMONT
Fairleigh Dickinson University

JOHN O. WILLIS
Rivier College

DEVELOPMENTAL DELAY

Arnold Gessell (1925, 1946), in his pioneering research at the Yale Institute for Child Development, established a sequence of developmental norms, or milestones, through which individuals progress on their way toward normal development. Under his maturational conceptualization, individuals achieve certain developmental milestones that represent indicators of both current and future development and adjustment. Most infants and children reach these critical milestones within expected time frames. Such milestones

include the abilities to make eye contact, exhibit fine and gross motor skills, develop language, achieve continence, reciprocate during play, and read independently. In some cases, however, developmental delays can occur, which portend possible developmental disabilities. The early pioneering work on developmental milestones has made it possible for the early identification of delays to occur (Baron-Cohen, 1989; Passey & Feldman, 2004).

Developmental delay is a term used to denote when babies or children *fail* to reach certain developmental milestones, or do so at a *markedly slow* rate (First & Palfrey, 1994). It is well understood that infants and children develop at varying rates. Some sit at 6 months, others at 4 months, and still others at 8 months. Given the fact that slight variations in normal development unequivocally exist, the term *developmental delay* is generally reserved for instances when infants or children have more than one delay or exhibit significant maturational lag in a critical, functional skill (Squires, Nickel, & Eisert, 1996). For example, the inability to develop adequate verbal skills by the age of 5 would represent a developmental delay of notable concern. The defining feature of developmental delays is the relationship with untoward outcomes. For example, recent research has suggested that 3-year-old children with developmental delays present significantly greater behavior problems than typically developing same-age peers (Baker, Blacher, & Olsson, 2005; Baker, Blacher, Crnic, & Edelbrock, 2002). The phenomena of developmental delays have also been referred to as a young child's "failure to thrive," and is typically characterized by slow weight gain (Corbett & Drewett, 2004). However, while some studies suggest a specific linkage between failure to thrive in infancy and its adverse effects on cognitive development (e.g., cognitive delay), to date there is no clear consensus in the literature as to the relation between an infant's failure to thrive and developmental delay (Batchelor, 1999; Boddy, Skuse, & Andrews, 2000; Wright, 2000).

Developmental delays are capable of being measured on both quantitative (i.e., by degree or extent of delay) and qualitative (i.e., by kind or type of delay) dimensions. A delay, for example, in developing ambulation until the age of 4 is quantitatively more severe than a delay in walking until age 3. Moreover, a noticeable maturational lag in developing language skills has qualitatively different implications than a delay in responding adequately to visual stimuli. A diagnosis of developmental delays is best performed using a multimethod, multi-informant, and multisetting approach to determine whether target pupils can or cannot perform certain behavioral markers or do so at a rate that is significantly below that observed in normal children the same age (Salvia & Ysseldyke, 2003).

Developmental delays can have many different causes, such as genetics (i.e., Down syndrome) or complications during pregnancy and birth (i.e., prematurity, infection). Recent studies have focused on the most common known cause of developmental delay, Fragile X syndrome. Specifically, investigators have found that the silencing of the FMR-1 gene is singly involved in the pathogenesis of Fragile X syndrome at the molecular level, leading to a lack of production of the FMR-1 protein (FMRP) synthesis. There is increasing evidence that suggests a correlation between higher FMRP levels and greater phenotypic expression (e.g., developmental delays). Often, however, the specific cause is unknown, although some causes can be reversed if caught early enough, such as hearing loss from chronic ear infections, or lead poisoning. In any case, whether the causes can be reversed or whether the delay suggests an unalterable, lifelong condition, it is important to identify developmental delays so that families can seek appropriate treatment for their child or begin to cope and adjust to the difficulties that lie ahead.

Early diagnosis in infants and children depends upon early identification of features associated with particular developmental disabilities. As a result, early screening for developmental delays has become the gold standard of clinical practice when assessing for the early warning signs of developmental disabilities (Gray & Tonge, 2005). The use of developmental screening questionnaires by primary care physicians and early childhood professionals is the best and most frequently employed method to identify developmental disorders (Fenton et al., 2003; Filipek et al., 1999). The theoretical importance of identifying infants and young children with developmental problems through the use of developmental screening measures and linking the data to services has been recognized by a number of professional organizations including the American Academy of Pediatrics, the Child Welfare League of America, and the American Academy of Child and Adolescent Psychiatry.

Contemporaneously, the notion of developmental delay is used in a variety of contexts to guide important professional practices: education, clinical, and legal/political. Indeed, developmental delays play a vital role in the clinical diagnosis of several *DSM-IV* disorders including, but not limited to, Pervasive Developmental Disorder, Autistic Disorder, Mental Retardation, Specific Learning Disability, and Asperger Syndrome. To receive a diagnosis of Autistic Disorder, for instance, individuals must have pronounced delays in acquiring language skills and in responding appropriately to social cues, both of which should occur regularly by the age of 3—a point at which most children are identified with Autistic Disorder (*DSM-IV-TR*, 2000; Howlin & Moore, 1997).

Children with developmental delay are eligible to receive services as mandated under federal law. They are also the subject of early "child find" and intervention efforts. The category "developmental delay" was first incorporated into the 1986 revision of the Individuals with Disabilities Education Act (IDEA), and more recently has been retained in the 2004 Individuals with Disabilities Education Improvement Act (IDEIA). The description of developmental delay in IDEIA (2004) is as follows:

> (i) experiencing developmental delays, as defined by the State and as measured by appropriate diagnostic instruments and procedures, in 1 or more of the following areas: physical development; cognitive development; communication development; social or emotional development; or adaptive development;
>
> (1) A rigorous definition of the term "developmental delay" that will be used by the State in carrying out programs under this part in order to appropriately identify infants and toddlers with disabilities that are in need of services under this part. (p. 2739)

In sum, the development of norms pertaining to child development helped in the identification of children who were delayed in meeting developmental milestones. Early screening efforts aimed at identifying children at risk of, or having, developmental delays are now part of state mandated child find efforts. Many developmental delays can lead to developmental, educational, or social problems for the child. Fortunately, early intervention efforts can ameliorate or even prevent subsequent delays.

REFERENCES

American Psychiatric Association. (2000). *Diagnostic and statistical manual of mental disorders* (4th ed., text revision). Washington, DC: Author.

Baker, B. L., Blacher, J., Crnic, K. A., & Edelbrock, C. (2002). Behavior problems and parenting stress in families of three-year-old children with and without developmental delays. *American Journal on Mental Retardation, 107,* 433–444.

Baker, B. L., Blacher, J., & Olsson, M. B. (2005). Preschool children with and without developmental delay: Behavior problems, parents' optimism and well-being. *Journal of Intellectual Disability Research, 49,* 575–590.

Batchelor, J. (1999). *Failure to thrive in young children: Research and practice evaluated.* London: The Children's Society.

Baron-Cohen, S. (1989). The autistic child's theory of mind: A case of specific developmental delay. *Journal of Child Psychology and Psychiatry, 30*(2), 285–297.

Boddy, J., Skuse, D., & Andrews, B. (2000). The developmental sequelae of non-organic failure to thrive. *Journal of Child Psychology and Psychiatry, 41,* 1003–1014.

Corbett, S. S., & Drewett, R. F. (2004). To what extent is failure to thrive in infancy associated with poorer cognitive development? A review and meta-analysis. *Journal of Child Psychology and Psychiatry, 45,* 641–654.

Fenton, G., D'Ardia, C., Valente, D., Del Vecchio, I., Fabrizi, A., & Bernabei, P. (2003). Vineland adaptive behavior profiles in children with autism and moderate to severe developmental delay. *Autism, 7,* 269–287.

Filipek, P. A., Accardo, P. J., Baranek, G. T., et al. (1999). The screening and diagnosis of autism spectrum disorders. *Journal of Autism and Developmental Disorders, 29,* 439–484.

First, L. R., & Palfrey, J. S. (1994). The infant or young child with developmental delay. *New England Journal of Medicine, 330,* 478–483.

Gessel, A. (1925). *The mental growth of the pre-school child.* New York: MacMillan.

Gessel, A., & Ilg, F. L. (1946). *The child from five to ten.* New York: Harper & Brothers.

Gray, K. M., & Tonge, B. J. (2005). Screening for autism in infants and preschool children with developmental delay. *Australian & New Zealand Journal of Psychiatry, 39*(5), 378–386.

Howlin, P., & Moore, A. (1997). Diagnosis in autism: A survey of over 1,200 patients in the UK. *Autism: The International Journal of Research and Practice, 1,* 135–162.

Individuals with Disabilities Education Act Amendments of 1986, 20. U.S.C. § 1400 *et seq.*

Passey, J., & Feldman, M. (2004). Descriptive analysis of parent-child interactions in young children with or at risk for developmental delay. *Behavioral Interventions, 19*(4), 233–246.

Salvia, J., & Ysseldyke, J. (2003). *Assessment in special and inclusive education* (9th ed.). New York: Houghton Mifflin.

Squires, J., Nickel, R. E., & Eisert, D. (1996). Early detection of developmental problems: Strategies for monitoring young children in the practice setting. *Journal of Developmental and Behavioral Pediatrics, 17,* 420–427.

Wright, C. M. (2000). Identification and management of failure to thrive: A community perspective. *Archives of Disease in Childhood, 82,* 5–9.

CLAYTON R. COOK
JAMES LYONS
JAN BLACHER
*University of California,
Riverside*

DEPRIVATION
INDIVIDUALS WITH DISABILITIES IMPROVEMENT
EDUCATION ACT OF 2004 (IDEIA)
EARLY EXPERIENCES

DEVELOPMENTAL DISABILITIES

Developmental disabilities is a term representing an umbrella category referring to a diverse group of physical, cognitive, psychological, sensory, and speech impairments that begin anytime during an individual's development up to 22 years of age. According to the Developmental Disabilities Assistance and Bill of Rights Act of 2000 (Public Law 106-402), a developmental disability results in substantial functional limitations in three or more of the following areas of major life activity: (1) self-care, (2) receptive and expressive language, (3) learning, (4) mobility, (5) self-direction, (6) capacity for independent living, and (7) economic self-sufficiency. Individuals from birth to age 9, who have a substantial developmental delay or a specific

congenital or acquired condition, may be considered to have a developmental disability without meeting three or more of the criteria described *if* there is a high probability of the individual meeting those criteria later in life. Additionally, the term developmental disabilities reflects the individual's need for support services or other forms of assistance requiring individual planning or coordination, and that are lifelong or of extended duration.

In the past 4 decades, the field of developmental disabilities has undergone a series of social, political, and scientific changes. These changes have resulted in many modifications to the definition of developmental disabilities and societal responses to individuals with these disabilities. The Developmental Disabilities Services and Facilities and Construction Act of 1970 (Public Law 91-517) defined the term developmental disabilities as follows:

> Disabilities attributable to mental retardation, cerebral palsy, epilepsy or another neurological condition of an individual found by the Secretary [Health, Education, and Welfare] to be closely related to mental retardation or to require treatment similar to that required for a mentally retarded individual, which disability originates before such an individual attains age 18, which has continued or can be expected to continue indefinitely, and constitutes a substantial handicap to the individual. (sec. 6001)

Public Law 91-517 came from the efforts of a national coalition to minimize categories of exceptionality and to make services more available to people who did not meet the criteria for Mental Retardation but still showed evidence of multiple handicaps and adaptive delays. The Act brought under a single federal legislative umbrella three major disorders: Mental Retardation, cerebral palsy, and epilepsy. It also included all other neurological conditions occurring before age 18 that produce consequences similar to those of the main three. The intent of the legislation was to bring together under one law disability groups that have comparable service needs. The goal was to improve services and increase coordination among the many public and private agencies that provide such services.

Following the 1970 legislation, the term developmental disabilities was altered to include autism and a few specific learning disabilities (e.g., dyslexia) in the Developmentally Disabled Assistance and Bill of Rights Act of 1975 (Public Law 94-103). However, these pieces of federal legislation still reflected a categorical definition of developmental disabilities, where the needs and services of people were classified under disparate descriptions that focused on etiological and medical origins. The original intent of coining the term developmental disabilities was to reflect a functional definition that focused on common adaptive problems. This was finally accomplished with the enactment of the Rehabilitation Comprehensive Services and Developmental Disabilities Amendments of 1978 (Public Law 95-602). All other legislation following the 1978 Act have used a functional definition of developmental disabilities, replacing the terminology of specific conditions (e.g., Mental Retardation, cerebral palsy) and focusing solely on the effects of the disabilities, especially when they are severe and chronic in nature.

These modifications to the definition of developmental disabilities were significant in that they were ultimately translated into guidelines for the delivery of special education services and related support services in community-based rehabilitation and treatment settings. Currently, there are approximately 4.5 million individuals with developmental disabilities in the United States. Without appropriate services and supports, options (e.g., education, employment, housing) for these individuals are minimal. The most recent piece of legislation pertaining to developmental disabilities is the Developmental Disabilities Assistance and Bill of Rights Act of 2000 (Public Law 106-402). This Act ensures that people with developmental disabilities and their families receive the services and supports they need to participate in the planning and designing of those services. The Administration on Developmental Disabilities (ADD), the federal agency responsible for implementation and administration of Public Law 106-402, focuses on eight areas for services and programs: Employment, Education, Child Care, Health, Housing, Transportation, Recreation, and Quality Assurance.

Currently, the field of developmental disabilities has become more progressive. There has been an expansion of inclusive community options and the number of people in large congregate facilities continues to decline. Furthermore, research, policy, and practice now emphasize quality-of-life issues, self-determination, and services required by individuals with dual-diagnoses or other psychopathologies. A robust self-advocacy movement has also emerged and person-centered planning is an aspiration in virtually every state. It is also likely that with the burgeoning emphasis on the genetic origins of behavior and disability, the developmental disabilities concept may broaden. Roles for family members of persons with developmental disabilities continue to expand.

In summary, the term developmental disability means a severe, chronic disability of an individual that is attributable to a mental or physical impairment or combination of mental and physical impairments. The impairment must manifest before the individual attains age 22 and must be likely to continue indefinitely. Former definitions involved the removal of explicit references to the specific categories of developmental disabilities. The current definition emphasizes considerable functional limitations and identifies individuals whose disabilities will create needs in particular activities.

REFERENCES

Blacher, J., & Baker, B. L. (2002). *The best of AAMR. Families and mental retardation: A collection of notable AAMR journal articles across the 20th century*. Washington, DC: American Association on Mental Retardation.

Kazdin, A. E. (2000). *Encyclopedia of psychology* (Vol. 3). Washington, DC: Oxford University Press.

Luckasson, R., Borthwick-Duffy, S., Buntinx, W. H. E., Coulter, D. L., Craig, E. M., & Reeve, A., et al. (2002). *Mental retardation: Definition, classification, and systems of supports* (10th ed.). Washington, DC: American Association on Mental Retardation.

McLaughlin, P. J., & Wehman, P. (1996). *Mental retardation and developmental disabilities* (2nd ed.). Austin, TX: PRO-ED.

Schalock, R. L. (2004). The emerging disability paradigm and its implications for policy and practice. *Journal of Disability Policy Studies, 14*(4), 204–215.

Thompson, R. J., & O'Quinn, A. N. (1979). *Developmental disabilities*. New York: Oxford University Press.

ARAKSIA KALADJIAN
University of California, Riverside

CAMERON L. NEECE
University of California, Los Angeles

CEREBRAL PALSY
MENTAL RETARDATION

DEVELOPMENTAL DISABILITIES ASSISTANCE ACT AND BILL OF RIGHTS

The Developmental Disabilities Assistance and Bill of Rights Act Amendments of 1994 was originally enacted as Title 1 of the Mental Retardation Facilities and Construction Act of 1963, Public Law, 88-164 and was amended in 1981, 1987, 1990, and 1994. The purpose of the Act is to:

> assure that individuals with developmental disabilities and their families participate in the design of and have access to needed community services, individualized supports, and other forms of assistance that promote self-determination, independence, productivity, and integration and inclusion in all facets of community life, through culturally competent programs authorized under this title. (42 U.S.C. §15001[b])

This is carried out through the participation of State Councils on Developmental Disabilities, the development of state protection and advocacy systems, the support of university-affiliated programs, and the support of national initiatives to collect data and provide technical assistance to state Councils.

The Act also states Congress's findings with respect to the rights of individuals with developmental disabilities as follows:

1. Individuals with developmental disabilities have a right to appropriate treatment, services, and habilitation for such disabilities.

2. The treatment, services, and habitation [sic] for an individual with developmental disabilities should be designed to maximize the potential of the individual and should be provided the setting that is least restrictive of the individual's personal liberty.

3. The Federal Government and the States both have an obligation to ensure that public funds are provided only to institutional programs, programs, and other community programs, including educational programs in which individuals with developmental disabilities participate, that

   a. provide treatment, services, and habilitation that are appropriate to the needs of such individuals, and
   b. meet minimum standards relating to:
      i. provision of care that is free of abuse, neglect, sexual and financial exploitation, and violations of legal and human rights and that subjects individuals with developmental disabilities to no greater risk of harm than others in the general population;
      ii. provision to such individuals of appropriate and sufficient medical and dental services;
      iii. prohibition of the use of physical restraint and seclusion for such an individual unless absolutely necessary to ensure the immediate physical safety of the individual or others, and prohibition of the use of such restraint and seclusion as a punishment or as a substitute for a habilitation program;
      iv. prohibition on the excessive use of chemical restraints on such individuals and the use of such restraints as punishments or as a substitute for a habilitation program or in quantities that interfere with services, treatment, or habilitation for such individuals; and
      v. provision for close relatives or guardians of such individuals to visit the individuals without prior notice.

4. All programs for individuals with developmental disabilities should meet standards:

   a. that are designed to assure the most favorable possible outcome for those served; and
   b.i. in the case of residential programs serving individuals in need of comprehensive health-related, habilitative, assistive technology or rehabilitative services, that are at least the equivalent to those standards applicable to intermediate care facilities for the mentally retarded, promulgated in regulations of the Secretary on June 3, 1988, as appropriate, taking into account the size of the institutions and the service delivery arrangements of the facilities of the programs;
   ii. in the case of other residential programs for individuals with developmental disabilities, that assure that

   I. care is appropriate to the needs of the individuals being served by such programs;
   II. the individuals admitted to facilities of such programs are individuals whose needs can be met through services provided by such facilities; and
   III. the facilities of such programs provide for the humane care of the residents of the facilities, are sanitary, and protect their rights; and
   iii. in the case of nonresidential programs, that assure that the care provided by such programs is appropriate to the individuals served by the programs. (42 U.S.C. §15009[a])

Congress specifically indicated within the statute that these rights are "in addition to any constitutional or other rights otherwise afforded to all individuals" (42 U.S.C. §15009[b]).

Under Part B of the Act, the State Developmental Disabilities Council program provides financial assistance to each state to support the activities of State Councils on Developmental Disabilities. The councils are made up of individuals who have developmental disabilities, family members, and representatives of state agencies that provide services to individuals with developmental disabilities. The council develops and implements a statewide plan to address employment (which is a federally mandated priority) and case management, child development, and community living. Fiscal year 2004 funding for the Act was $149,861,569, according to the Administration on Developmental Disabilities web site.

The Administration on Developmental Disabilities receives annual reports from states and provides its own annual report on the implementation of the Act. The Administration is located at Administration on Developmental Disabilities Administration for Children and Families, U.S. Department of Health and Human Services, Mail Stop: HHH 405-D, 370 L'Enfant Promenade, S.W., Washington, DC 20447. The telephone is (202) 690-6590 (voice) and (202) 245-2890 (TDD). The Administration on Developmental Disabilities also maintains an extensive webpage on the internet: http://www.acf.dhhs.gov/programs/add//.

ELAINE FLETCHER-JANZEN
*University of Colorado at
Colorado Springs*
Second edition

KIMBERLY F. APPLEQUIST
*University of Colorado at
Colorado Springs*
Third edition

INDIVIDUALS WITH DISABILITIES EDUCATION IMPROVEMENT ACT OF 2004 (IDEIA) OFFICE OF CIVIL RIGHTS

DEVELOPMENTAL DISABILITIES LEGAL RESOURCE CENTER

See PROTECTION AND ADVOCACY SYSTEM—DEVELOPMENTALLY DISABLED.

DEVELOPMENTAL DYSLEXIA, HISTORY OF

Developmental dyslexia is typically perceived as a complex heterogeneous reading disorder. It appears to stem from a selective disturbance of the maturation of neurological functions thought to be responsible for the acquisition of reading and writing skills. It is genetically determined and thus distinct from acquired alexia from traumatic brain injury (Gaddes, 1976). Critical components of the disorder that are relative to the individual's unique patterns of intrinsic abilities and extrinsic assets dictate that the dyslexic must have at least average intelligence; sufficient cultural and linguistic opportunity; emotional stability; access to appropriate instruction; and approximately normal sensory acuity (Rourke & Gates, 1981). Prognosis of relative success in compensating for the disorder's consequences is based on early identification, delineation of the individual's unique pattern of strengths and weaknesses, capitalization on unique educational strategies, and concomitant appropriate sociocultural/familial support systems.

More than 90 years worth of published material (Benton, 1980) has been generated by the disorder; its history has been rich with conflicting information. To state that developmental dyslexia has been a confusing disorder would be diplomatic at best; however, continued research in the differentiation of subtypes, longitudinal studies on developmental changes, technological advances related to etiology, and empirical results from promising intervention programs continue to refine conceptualizations of dyslexia.

The origin of the term dyslexia has been attributed to Kausmaul, who in 1877 defined the word *alexia* as word blindness. In 1891 Dejerine provided autopsy data on individuals who had suffered cerebrovascular injury and were left with reading disabilities. In 1896 Morgan described a famous dyslexic case study concerning an intelligent 14-year-old male who could not read or write but could perform algebra. These studies indicated specific deficits or abnormal development of the angular gyrus region in the dominant hemisphere (Dalby, 1979).

In 1900 Hinshelwood reported that the disorder caused partial or complete loss of visual memory for letters and words. In 1901 Nettleship observed that a disproportionate number of males had dyslexia, the disorder tended to run in families, and there was the presence of a linguistic factor. Four years later, Fisher recommended implementation of a "look and say" method of instruction for individuals who

had a phonemic analysis deficit. This remediation used global word recognition. Interestingly, he also advocated teaching children to write with their left hands, based on the assumption that the right hemisphere subserved the learning process in children with faulty left hemispheres. Marie, in 1906, disagreed with the localizationalist theories of brain functioning, then the prevalent school of thought, which assumed specific behaviors were attributed to specific brain areas. He argued that there could not be specific centers for reading because reading was a new development in humans (Pirozzolo, 1981).

Educational and clinical psychologists' interest in dyslexia gained momentum during the first two decades of the twentieth century. Research focused on the basic underlying factors that presumably caused failure in learning to read, and two schools of thought emerged. The first emphasized the relation of perceptual and cognitive disabilities and the second concentrated on environmental factors (Benton, 1980). A new perspective on dyslexia was formulated by Orton toward the end of the second decade.

Orton related reading disability to a defective interhemispheric organization of cerebral function. It was assumed to be the result of a faulty maturational process of establishing specialization of function in a single hemisphere. The consequences of incomplete hemispheric dominance were said to lead to confusion and failure to read effectively (Johnson & Myklebust, 1967).

Behavioral and personality disorders in dyslexics were investigated in the 1930s. It was assumed that psychotherapy should be the primary mode of intervention before and during educational remediation. In the early 1940s, Werner and Strauss (Dalby, 1979) stated that brain damage was present, whether detectable by neurological means, as long as similar behavior patterns were exhibited. They initiated the term minimal brain damage (MBD), which, unfortunately, was embraced by zealous individuals who then attributed MBD to the entire population of persons with learning disorders. Without substantial evidence to support the conclusion that brain damage existed minimally, dissimilar disorders were erroneously lumped together (e.g., attention deficit disorders, developmental dyslexia). The devastating impact of these erroneous labels was unfortunately incurred by the child (Hobbs, 1975).

To complicate this picture further, incidence rates for dyslexics in the general population ranged from 10 to 30 percent, as reported in the voluminous post-World War II research on dyslexia. It became clear, however, that many researchers had failed to differentiate specific reading disability from failure to read owing to other factors (e.g., lack of normal intelligence, primary sensory impairments, lack of adequate educational and cultural opportunities, and emotional instability). The field of developmental dyslexia became clouded, and, as Benton and Pearl (1978) note, this large volume of research did little to differentiate distinct subtypes of dyslexia. The concept of dyslexia appeared to mean different things to different people. Adams (1967) found 23 definitions of dyslexia in the literature and he argued for abandonment of the term. It has been observed that the particular way in which research in developmental dyslexia is conducted stems directly from its definition, and if that definition is not one that is commonly accepted, researchers' results will differ accordingly (Rourke, 1976; Sawyer, 1992). It is currently estimated that 15 percent of the school population is dyslexic, as are over 85 percent of adult illiterates (Griesbach, 1993; Orton-Gillingham Practitioners and Educators, 1998).

From the 1960s to the present, research proceeded by varied means. Renewed interest in Orton's work followed advances in asymmetrical hemispheric specialization research (e.g., dichotic listening, dichaptic discrimination, and tachistoscopic methods). Medical technology has furthered investigations in the neurological basis of dyslexia by means of electroencephalography, computerized tomography scanning, cerebral blood flow studies, positron emission tomography, and autopsies on dyslexic and normal brains. Current research in the educational/neuropsychological literature (Hynd & Obrzut, 1981; Knights & Bakker, 1976; Lyon, Fletcher, & Barnes, 2003) has supported the involvement of higher cortical impairment in developmental dyslexia.

Evidence from research on pre- and perinatal events in relation to dyslexia has demonstrated the importance of this period on the child's development. However, there is no strong evidence to substantiate that abnormalities in this period lead directly to specific reading disability. Extensive data from twin research (Herschel, 1978) showed a genetic basis to developmental dyslexia, although there is little evidence to support particular biochemical, physiological, or behavioral attributes linked specifically to dyslexia.

Sex differences are apparent in that males are disproportionately represented in reading-disabled populations. Data exist that indicate even normal girls are more adept at the learning-to-read process than normal boys. Anatomical data further substantiate those claims, since myelination occurred more rapidly in the left hemisphere for girls and the right hemisphere for boys (Dalby, 1979). Other sex differences have been hypothesized to be maturational lags in hemispheric specialization shifts in the learning-to-read process (Rourke, 1982), where girls pass through the stages faster than boys (Gaddes, 1976). These hypotheses suggest that the right hemisphere-mediated functions may have a critical role in the initial stages of the acquisition of the reading process, whereas the left hemisphere-mediated functions may be more efficient in using a routinized mode that stems from that acquisition. This right-to-left shift in hemispheric specialization may be a function of increased competence with the learning-to-read process.

The current perspective on developmental dyslexia has focused on more stringent methods of research in the identification of distinct subtypes (Rourke & Gates, 1981). Converging data from this body of research suggested a need for a multidimensional definition; it was clear that appropriate identification of dyslexics could not be made solely on the basis of poor reading achievement with approximately average intelligence (Yule & Rutter, 1976). The presence of differences in the types of dyslexia necessitates different strategies of educational interventions. Recognition of these differences became more pronounced following multivariate analyses of clinical neuropsychological methods (Lyon et al., 2003; Petrauskas & Rourke, 1979) and important developmental changes, described in longitudinal research (Satz, Taylor, Friel, & Fletcher, 1978).

The neuropsychological evidence has suggested the presence of several subtypes of dyslexic readers, two of which are fairly distinct in older children and adults: auditory-linguistic deficient (dysphonetic) readers and visual-spatial deficient (dyseidetic) readers, as described by Pirozzolo (1981). Others have described a mixed dyslexic group (both dysphonetic and dyseidetic); an unspecified group (of which subcortical impairment cannot be completely ruled out), and a normal group; or linguistic, perceptual, and mixed groups (Masutto, 1994); and phonological and surface types (Lyon et al., 2003; Murphy & Pollatsek, 1994).

REFERENCES

Adams, R. B. (1967). *Dyslexia: A discussion of its definition.* Paper prepared for the second meeting of the Federal Government's Attack on Dyslexia. Washington, DC: Bureau of Research, U.S. Office of Education.

Benton, A. L. (1980). Dyslexia: Evolution of a concept. *Bulletin of the Orton Society, 30,* 10–26.

Benton, A. L., & Pearl, D. (1978). *Dyslexia: An appraisal of current knowledge.* New York: Oxford University Press.

Dalby, J. T. (1979). Deficit or delay: Neuropsychological models of developmental dyslexia. *Journal of Special Education, 3,* 239–264.

Frank, J., & Levinson, H. (1973). Dysmetric dyslexia and dyspraxia: Hypothesis and study. *Journal of the American Academy of Child Psychiatry, 12,* 690–701.

Gaddes, W. H. (1976). Prevalence estimates and the need for definition of learning disabilities. In R. Knights & D. Bakker (Eds.), *The neuropsychology of learning disorders: Theoretical approaches* (pp. 3–24). Baltimore: University Park Press.

Griesbach, G. (1993). *Dyslexia: It's history, etiology, and treatment.* (ERIC Clearinghouse No. CS011300)

Hartlage, L. C., & Telzrow, C. F. (1983). The neuropsychological basis of educational intervention. *Journal of Learning Disabilities, 16,* 521–523.

Herschel, M. (1978). Dyslexia revisted: A review. *Human Genetics, 40,* 115–134.

Hobbs, N. (1975). *The futures of children: Categories, labels, and their consequences.* San Francisco: Jossey-Bass.

Hynd, G. W., & Obrzut, J. E. (1981). *Neuropsychological assessment and the school-age child: Issues and procedures.* New York: Grune & Stratton.

Johnson, D. J., & Myklebust, H. R. (1967). *Learning disabilities: Educational principles and practices.* New York: Grune & Stratton.

Knights, R., & Bakker, D. (1976). *The neuropsychology of learning disorders: Theoretical approaches.* Baltimore: University Park Press.

Lyon, G. R., Fletcher, J. M., & Barnes, M. C. (2003). Learning disabilities. In E. J. Mash & R. A. Barkley (Eds.), *Child Psychopathology* (2nd ed., pp. 520–586). New York: Guilford.

Masutto, C. (1994). Neurolinguistic differentiation of children with subtypes of dyslexia. *Journal of Learning Disabilities, 27*(8), 520–526.

Murphy, L., & Pollatsek, A. (1994). Developmental dyslexia: Heterogeneity without discrete subgroups. *Annals of Dyslexia, 44,* 120–146.

Orton-Gillingham Practitioners and Educators. (1998). *Dyslexia.* Retrieved from www.ols.net./users/orton/index.htm

Petrauskas, R. J., & Rourke, B. P. (1979). Identification of subtypes of retarded readers: A neuropsychological multivariate approach. *Journal of Clinical Neuropsychology, 1,* 17–37.

Pirozzolo, F. J. (1981). Language and brain: Neuropsychological aspects of developmental reading disability. *School Psychology Review, 3,* 350–355.

Rourke, B. P. (1976). Reading retardation in children: Developmental lag or deficit? In R. Knights & D. Bakker (Eds.), *The neuropsychology of learning disorders: Theoretical approaches* (pp. 125–137). Baltimore: University Park Press.

Rourke, B. P. (1982). Central processing deficiencies in children: Toward a developmental neuropsychological model. *Journal of Clinical Neuropsychology, 4,* 1–18.

Rourke, B. P., & Gates, R. D. (1981). Neuropsychological research and school psychology. In G. W. Hynd & J. E. Obrzut (Eds.), *Neuropsychological assessment and the school-age child: Issue and procedures* (pp. 3–25). New York: Grune & Stratton.

Satz, P., Taylor, H. G., Friel, J., & Fletcher, J. M. (1978). Some developmental and predictive precursors of reading disabilities: A six year follow-up. In A. L. Benton & D. Pearl (Eds.), *Dyslexia: An appraisal of current knowledge* (pp. 313–347). New York: Oxford University Press.

Sawyer, D. J. (1992). Dyslexia: Introduction to Special Series. *Journal of Learning Disabilities, 25,* 1, 38.

Yule, W., & Rutter, M. (1976). Epidemiological and social implications of specific reading retardation. In R. Knights & D. Bakker (Eds.), *The neuropsychology of learning disorders: Theoretical approaches* (pp. 25–39). Baltimore: University Park Press.

SCOTT W. SAUTTER
Peabody College, Vanderbilt University

DEVELOPMENTAL MILESTONES

Childhood development is marked by a number of developmental milestones. While brain maturation and physical development are continuous throughout childhood, the resulting acquisitions of and improvements in abilities can cause the sudden emergence of behaviors or ways of thinking that were not possible previously. For example, the infant's first smile, first unaided steps, and first words that bring joy to parents represent milestones resulting from continuous and interrelated developmental processes and interaction with the environment. Relatively obvious physiological developments together with less obvious brain maturation, cognitive development, and stimulation from the environment result in the apparently sudden emergence of new skills and abilities. While the first responsive smile, those first wobbly steps, and the first recognizable words are three of the most obvious milestones of early childhood, there are a host of physical, biological, cognitive, emotional, and social milestones that, taken together, allow us to form a normative picture of childhood development.

Physical Milestones

In infancy, milestones in motor development tend to be the most noticeable. Most parents will eagerly announce their child's first success at standing unaided or his or her first steps. Developmentalists distinguish between gross and fine motor skills, gross motor skills being those that involve large muscle groups (crawling, walking, running, etc.) and fine motor skills being those involving smaller muscles such as the fingers and including grasping objects and manipulating tools. Both gross and fine motor skills develop out of innate reflexes present at birth and follow a predictable series of developmental milestones with each skill built on the previous one. As infants' brains develop and they gain muscle strength and coordination, their reflexes begin to come under conscious control. As gross motor skills develop, they become able to coordinate arm and leg movements and by about 7 months many are able to coordinate their limbs sufficiently well to move by crawling on their stomach. Crawling then develops into creeping, or moving on hands and knees with the stomach raised off the ground. As balance, strength, and coordination continue to develop infants become able to pull themselves to a sitting position and to support themselves in a sitting position. As balance continues to improve, they are able to take tentative steps with support, to stand unaided, and ultimately to walk unaided (Bayley, 1969).

The development of fine motor skills follows a parallel sequence. Newborns have a reflexive grasp and will close their palms around any object their hand contacts. In the first few months of life, infants bat at objects in their environment. As fluid eye-hand coordination develops, infants become able to direct their hands effectively to objects in their environment (White, 1971). They can open their fist en route and, once contact is made, grasp the object with their palms. This *palmar grasp* works well for handling wooden blocks and rattles, but is not effective for picking up smaller objects. As muscle development and eye-hand

Table 1 Gross and fine motor skill development (approximate ages in months)

Gross motor skills	Age for mastery		Fine motor skills	Age for mastery	
	Median	Range[a]		Median	Range[a]
Able to lift head to 45°	0.9	0–1.8	Holds onto ring	.8	.3–3[b]
Able to lift head to 90°	2.1	1.4–2.9	Able to grasp rattle	3.2	2.7–3.6
Bear weight on legs	2.6	1.8–3.5	Partially opposes thumb	4.9	4–8[b]
Able to roll over	3.2	2.0–4.2	Reaches for pellet	5.6	4–8[b]
Pull self to sitting position	3.4	2.9–4.0	Thumb opposed to fingers	6.9	5–9[b]
Pull self to standing position	8.3	7.8–9.0	Bang 2 cubes held in hands	7.7	6.7–10.6
Stand unaided	11.5	10.2–12.5	Thumb-finger grasp	8.0	7.4–9.0
Walk well	12.2	10.9–13.6	Able to place block in cup	9.9	11.0–12.3
Kick ball forward	18	16–21	Scribbling	13.1	12.0–14.3
Hopping	42	39–45	Able to build a tower of 4 cubes	19.2	16.1–22.4

[a]Lower limit of range = 25th percentile and upper limit = 75th percentile unless otherwise noted.

[b]Lower limit of range = 5th percentile and upper limit = 95th percentile.

coordination improves, the palmar grasp is replaced by the *pincer grasp,* in which the thumb and fingers and then the thumb and forefinger are opposed (Bayley, 1969).

Typical ages for the emergence of various motor skills among healthy children have been determined and some examples are given in the Table 1 (Bayley, 1969; Frankenberg, Dodds, Archer, Shapiro, & Bresnick, 2001).

It is important to note that, while the developmental sequence is the same for all normal children, there is a great deal of individual variation in the age at which specific abilities emerge. Most of the range data in Table 1 are for the 25th to 75th percentiles, and they give a misleadingly small picture of the amount of variation among the majority of children. For example, as the table indicates, the average age for children to pull themselves to a standing position was 8.3 months and the range for the 25th and 75th percentiles was 7.8 to 9.0 months (Frankenberg et al., 2001). However, the range for the 5th and 95th percentiles for the same skill was 5 to 12 months. (Bayley, 1969). Thus, there was a full 7-month spread between the ages at which most children first demonstrated the ability to pull themselves to a standing position.

While physical milestones occur in rapid succession during the infant and toddler years, as the child enters the play years, physical milestones become less apparent as growth slows and the child masters and integrates existing physical abilities. Things remain relatively calm until the hypothalamus in the brain triggers the period of rapid physical growth and sexual maturation known as puberty (Berger, 2005). As with other developmental domains, the *sequence* of events experienced in puberty is more or less constant, although there is some variation to the sequence among normal adolescents (Rogol, Roemmich, & Clark, 2002). However, as in other domains, there is great variation in the ages at which individuals experience specific milestones. For example, for the majority of girls, the appearance of breast buds can occur anywhere between the

ages of 8 and 13 years. The typical developmental sequence is also different for girls and boys, and girls generally experience earlier onset of puberty than do boys. Table 2 shows the typical sequence of pubertal development for girls and boys (Berger, 2005).

Among boys, the most noticeable signs of puberty are the growth spurt, the deepening of the voice, and the appearance of secondary sex characteristics, such as facial hair. In females, menstruation is the primary indication of the change from girlhood to womanhood, although girls also go through a growth spurt at the beginning of puberty.

Cognitive Milestones

Physical and motor developmental milestones are relatively easy to identify because they are characterized by discrete changes. Cognitive development also results in various developmental milestones, but these are more difficult to identify because they are subtle and they appear gradually. To developmentalists, however, these milestones are just as significant as a child's first step or the growth spurt of puberty. In the 1950s, Piaget described a stage theory of cognitive development in children and adolescents that has been supported, with some modifications, by a large body of research data. Piaget proposed four major stages in cognitive development: the sensorimotor, preoperational, concrete-operational, and formal-operational stages.

According to Piaget, during the first 2 years of life, infants are in the sensorimotor stage. During this stage the child changes dramatically, from a wordless newborn, whose behaviors are primarily reflexive, to a talking 2-year-old who has developed an impressive mastery of his or her immediate environment. Two major accomplishments during the sensorimotor stage are the development of the concept of object permanence and the beginnings of symbolic thought (Piaget, 1954).

In the first few months of life, the infant's world is largely

Table 2 Typical developmental sequence of puberty

Girls	Approximate average age (years)	Boys
Ovaries increase production of estrogen and progesterone	9	
Uterus and vagina enlarge	9.5	Testes increase production of testosterone
Breast bud stage	10	Testes and scrotum enlarge
Appearance of pubic hair	11	
Weight spurt begins		
Peak height spurt	11.5	Appearance of pubic hair
Peak muscle and organ growth	12	Penis growth begins
Hips noticeably widen		
First menstrual period	12.5	First ejaculation
		Weight spurt begins
First ovulation	13	Peak height spurt
Voice lowers	14	Peak muscle and organ growth
		Shoulders noticeably broaden
Final pubic hair pattern	15	Voice lowers
		Facial hair appears
Full breast growth	16	
	18	Final pubic hair pattern

restricted to the immediate environment. "Out of sight, out of mind" is an appropriate description for the infant's understanding of objects. Until about 6 months of age, infants typically lose interest in objects or people when they are removed from the sensory field. Beginning at about 6 months, infants will stare at the doorway and may cry when their caregivers "disappear." This change in behavior seems to indicate an awareness, on the infant's part, that the caregiver is a separate entity that has somehow exited from the world.

Piaget investigated the development of object permanence in his own children, using an infant version of hide-and-seek, in which he hid a toy, in full view of the child, under a cloth or pillow and this technique has been used innumerable times since then to investigate children's understanding of object permanence. Children under about 8 months of age will often reach for the cloth, but then soon abandon the search. However, children over 10 months old will pull the cloth away to reveal the toy. Piaget interpreted this difference as indicating that the older children had developed the ability to hold an image of an object in memory long enough to search for it. That is, they understood that an object still existed even when it had disappeared from view. The development of object permanence represents a milestone in memory development. Once infants can represent objects in their minds they are no longer limited to reacting to the immediate environment and they become more effective at acting on their environment. This development combined with infants' developing gross and fine motor skills sets the stage for active exploration of the environment.

The second major accomplishment of the sensorimotor stage is the development of symbolic thought, or the ability to think using symbols, which is the foundation of language. However, the roots of language development actually begin

much earlier than this. Bloom (1998) noted that the turn-taking behavior seen in conversation is evident in the behavior of 3-month-old infants and their caregivers. Physical and cognitive development allows infants to vocalize certain syllables by age 6- to 9-months. Deaf infants born to signing parents begin to babble with their hands and fingers at the same age (Bloom, 1998). As with the development of motor skills, children's language development follows an invariant sequence of stages, although the ages at which individual children reach specific milestones vary significantly. An infant's random vocalizations evolve into babbling, which, in turn, evolves into the first recognizable words, typically soon after the infant's first birthday. There follows a period of relatively slow acquisition of additional words until, by about 18 months old, the typical infant knows about 50 words. Around the 19th month, the pace of word acquisition increases dramatically, beginning a period known as the *vocabulary spurt*. During this period children learn new words at rates of between 5 and 13 words per day, such that by the time the child reaches first grade he or she has an impressive vocabulary of about 10,000 words (Bloom, 1998). However, language acquisition is not just about vocabulary. Children have to learn how to put words together to make meaningful sentences. The first words are followed by holophrases, in which a single word is used to express a complete thought, additional information being supplied through the tone, loudness, and cadence with which the word is spoken (Berger, 2005). Then come two-word phrases and eventually simple sentences at about 24 months. As with all areas of development, it is important to note that there is significant interindividual variation in achievement of these milestones, as Table 3 indicates (Bloom, 1998).

The development of effective symbolic thought marks the transition to the preoperational stage of cognitive develop-

Table 3 Language milestones

	Age of emergence (months)	
	Mean	Range
First words	13	10–17
Vocabulary spurt	19	13–25
First complete sentences	24	18–32

ment, usually at about age 2 years. In this stage, children are able to represent objects in their environment, but cannot yet use logical operations in their thinking, which is egocentric and illogical, and is often referred to as *magical thinking*. The primary obstacles to logical thought in this stage are *centration*, or the tendency to focus on only one aspect of the situation; *irreversibility*, or the inability to understand that some operations can be reversed to produce the initial state; and focusing too much on appearances. Egocentrism prevents a child from viewing a situation from another person's perspective. For example, when asked if his brother has a brother, the preoperational child is likely to answer "no," unable to comprehend that he is his brother's brother. (Obviously this does not work if there is a third brother in the picture!) Centration, irreversibility, and a focus on appearances lead to an ability to understand the principle of conservation. This is usually demonstrated by pouring an equal amount of liquid into a tall and a short glass. The preoperational child will believe that the tall glass now contains more liquid than the short glass, because he or she is influenced by the appearances and focuses on only one aspect of the situation—the height of the liquid in the glass (Lefrancois, 1995)

Around the age of 5 or 7, children become less focused on appearances and are more able to think about more than one aspect of a situation simultaneously. As they begin to understand the concepts of conservation and reversibility, they move into Piaget's third stage, concrete operations. Children are now able to think logically and to use logical operations. However, they are able to apply these to concrete, or real-world, situations only. They are not yet able to think in the abstract or to contemplate things that do not exist. However, they are now able to understand that actions and relationships follow logical rules (Lefrancois, 1995). A major hallmark of the concrete operational stage is the understanding of classification, the ability to organize items into groups based on some attribute, and children in this stage become avid collectors of all sorts of things such as baseball cards and coins. Related to classification is seriation, another skill that becomes apparent in the concrete operational stage. Children in this stage are able to rank order numbers of items accurately, based on some variable (e.g., height, length), a task that generally stumps children in the preoperational stage. The ability of children in the concrete operational stage to consider more than one aspect of a situation allows them to view situations from more than one perspective. Now the child who is asked if his brother has a brother can answer that he is his brother's brother.

Other observable abilities include the concept of *identity*, or the awareness that certain characteristics of an object can remain the same even when others change (such as the volume of liquid remaining the same even though the height increases when it is poured into a tall thin glass) and *reciprocity*, or the concept that a change in one attribute can compensate for a change in another (e.g., the increased height of liquid in a tall thin glass is compensated by the reduced width).

The transition to Piaget's fourth stage, formal operational thought, occurs when brain maturation has progressed to the point where abstract thought is possible, usually in mid to late adolescence (Berger, 2005; Inhelder & Piaget, 1958). Piaget viewed this stage as the culmination of cognitive development, but more recent researchers have provided evidence for additional development and the emergence of postformal thinking in early adulthood. With the attainment of formal operational thought, thinking becomes independent of the constraints of the real world. Adolescents become able to think about how things could be. They develop *counterfactual thinking*, or the ability to reason logically about situations that do not or could not exist in reality. Often this results in them becoming highly critical of the way things are. They become much more adept at solving logical problems as the trial-and-error approach of concrete operations is replaced by hypothetico-deductive thought in which hypotheses are developed and tested in a logical and systematic fashion (Lefrancois, 1995).

Although Piaget's descriptions of the stages of cognitive development have generally held up well, his predictions of the ages of transition have not. Research has shown that evidence of specific abilities is dependent on the technique used to assess children's thinking and that specific abilities can often be detected at significantly earlier ages than Piaget originally proposed. Also, children's development does not occur in a vacuum and social, cultural, and environmental factors have been shown to exert significant influences on the emergence of specific abilities. In addition, it appears that achievement of formal operations is not as universal as Piaget believed. In one study, only about 50 percent of adults were estimated to have achieved formal operational thought (REF). Nevertheless, Piaget's stage theory of cognitive development remains a useful description of the development of cognition among children and it has served as the foundation for a number of other developmental theories including Kohlberg's stages of moral development (Reimer, Paolito, & Hersh, 1980) and Selman's stages of social-perspective taking (Selman & Schulz, 1990).

Social Milestones

Human infants rely on parental care and protection to survive. It has been proposed that this need may have resulted in the development of the specific signs and signals that infants use to keep their caregivers nearby (Bowlby, 1980). The first social smile, noticed by all parents, is part of a larger system known as the *attachment behavioral system.* This system appears to operate to ensure the infant is kept safe and protected. By using different attachment behaviors, infants signal their need for attention, express preferences for particular people, object angrily if they are separated from an attachment figure, and seek comfort from their attachment object when the environment is threatening (Main, 1981). Smiling is one example of an attachment behavior. Infants' smiles strengthen when their caregiver is nearby, encouraging social interaction between caregiver and infant. Bowlby proposed four developmental phases in the attachment behavioral system. In Phase I, which under ideal conditions lasts for 8 to 12 weeks after birth, the infant responds reflexively to human contact in ways that tend to prolong contact, but is unable to discriminate self from other or between other people. During Phase II, which lasts until age 6 to 9 months, the reflexive behaviors of Phase I come under conscious control and the infant is able to integrate attachment behaviors into more complex chains of behavior. Also, the infant becomes able to discriminate between significant caregivers and other people and is likely to direct attachment behaviors at one or two principal caregivers. In addition, infants begin to initiate attachment behaviors instead of simply responding to contact with the caregiver (Marvin & Britner, 1999).

With the development of locomotion and the consequent ability to control the proximity to the caregiver, the infant transitions to Phase III. According to Bowlby, the infant now has an internal image of the goal state (contact with the caregiver) and is able to select behaviors that will realize the goal. At the same time, the infant begins to use communicative signals as means to achieve the goal state. During Phase III wariness of unfamiliar people increases markedly, and, in the presence of unfamiliar others, the infant will retreat to the caregiver for safety. In Phase IV, which develops sometime between the ages of 3 and 4 years, the child becomes less dependent on physical proximity with the caregiver, and attachment is perceived more as an ongoing relationship with the caregiver. Beyond the preschool years, Bowlby believed that the attachment behavioral system continues to develop, but that this development does not represent any qualitative change to a new stage (Marvin & Britner, 1999).

It should be clear from this very brief description of Bowlby's ideas that each developmental phase in attachment behaviors depends on the successful resolution of the previous stage. The formation of adequate caregiver-infant attachments during the first year of life appears to be a requirement for healthy development during the toddler, preschool, and later years. Once formed, the benefits of secure attachment appear to continue into the toddler, preschool, and school years (Bretherton & Waters, 1985).

Securely attached toddlers seem competent and self-assured as they explore their environments and are likely to become preschoolers who are regarded as leaders and sought by other children as playmates (Bronson, 1981). In addition, a positive relationship with a caregiver seems to set the stage for the development of successful friendships, which provide social and cognitive support, ease the normative transitions of childhood, and are crucial to successful social development (Berndt, 2004; Hartup, 1996; Rubin, Bukowski, & Parker, 1998).

Closing Thoughts

While it is convenient to divide human development into specific domains, it is important to remember that all developmental domains are interlinked and that none occurs in isolation. Brain maturation affords improvements in cognition that allow the emergence of language, but the emergence of language, in turn, influences cognition. Developing motor skills eventually lead to independent locomotion that opens up multiple opportunities for exploration of the environment and for cognitive stimulation. Each domain of development affects and is affected by all others. In addition, social, biological, cultural, and environmental factors exert significant influences on development and should never be ignored. Skills and abilities tend to emerge earlier among cultures that value and encourage them, while genetic and racial differences result in differences in the ages at which milestones are reached among different groups. As an example, in the United States, African-American girls tend to mature earlier than Caucasian girls, with mean ages for menstruation of 12.0 years for African-Americans and 12.7 years for Caucasians (Biro et al., 2001). The impact of environmental factors is evidenced by the fact that in contemporary western cultures the average age of the onset of menstruation is now 3 years lower than it was in European countries during the late 1800s (Tanner & Eveleth, 1975). This shift is believed to be due to better nutrition, more favorable socioeconomic conditions, and improvements in general health.

Developmental milestones take many forms. The rapid physical changes that occur during infancy and the physical milestones that herald a new period of life are readily identified because they represent an abrupt break with the past. Similar milestones characterize cognitive and social development, but they tend to emerge gradually and to be subtler. Object permanence, the first words, and the attainment of concrete-operational thinking are each noticeable milestones in a continuously unfolding developmental process. Each milestone represents both the culmination of previous processes and the foundation for further development. Social and emotional milestones include attachment behaviors and the establishment of supportive friendships. In assessing the achievement of any milestone, but a social milestone in particular, it is essential that it be investigated and assessed in a culturally competent fashion, because family and social relationships are contextually and culturally loaded concepts (Nissani, 1993; Rocco, 1993; Winborne & Randolf, 1991). Examined together, the succession of physical, mental, and social milestones chart an individual's progress on the journey of life, but it must be remembered that, for each of us, that journey is unique, and that difference does not necessarily imply deficit.

REFERENCES

Bayley, N. (1969). *Manual for the Bayley scales of infant development.* New York: Psychological Corporation.

Berger, K. (2005). *The developing person through the life span.* New York: Worth.

Berndt, T. J. (2004, July). Children's friendships: Shifts over a half-century in perspectives on their development and their effects. *Merrill-Palmer Quarterly, 50*(3), 206–223.

Biro, F. M., MacMahon, R. P., Striegel-Moore, R., Crawford, P. B., Obarzanek, E., & Morrison, J. A. (2001). Impact of timing of pubertal maturation on growth in black and white female adolescents: The National Heart, Lung, and Blood Institute Growth and Health Study. *The Journal of Pediatrics, 138*(5), 636–643.

Bloom, L. (1998). Language acquisition in its developmental context. In W. Damon & N. Eisenberg (Eds.), *Handbook of child psychology: Vol 2. Cognition, perception, and language* (5th ed., pp. 309–370). New York: Wiley.

Bowlby, J. (1980). *Attachment and loss: Loss, sadness, and depression* (Vol. 3). New York: Basic Books.

Bretherton, I., & Waters, E. (1985). Growing points of attachment theory and research. *Monographs for the Society for Research in Child Development, 50,* 209.

Bronson, W. C. (1981). *Toddlers' behavior with agemates: Issues of interaction, cognition, and affect.* Norwood, NJ: Ablex.

Frankenberg, W. K., Dodds, J., Archer, P., Shapiro, H., & Bresnick, B. (2001). The Denver II: A major revision and restandardization of the Denver Developmental Screening Test. *Pediatrics, 89*(1), 91–97.

Hartup, W. W. (1996). The company they keep: Friendships and their developmental significance. *Child Development, 67,* 1–13.

Inhelder, B., & Piaget, J. (1958). *The growth of logical thinking from childhood to adolescence.* New York: Basic Books.

LeFrancois, G. R. (1995). *Theories of human learning.* Pacific Grove, CA: Brooks/Cole.

Main, M. (1981). Avoidance in the service of attachment. In K. Immelmann, G. W. Barlow, L. Petrinovich, & M. Main (Eds.), *Behavioral development: The Bielefeld Interdisciplinary Project.* London: Cambridge University Press.

Marvin, R. S., & Britner, P. A. (1998). Normative development. In J. Cassidy & P. R. Shaver (Eds.), *Handbook of attachment* (pp. 44–67). New York: Guilford.

Piaget, J. (1954). *The construction of reality in the child.* New York: Ballantine.

Reimer, J., Paolitto, D. P. & Hersh, R. (1983). *Promoting moral growth: From Piaget to Kohlberg* (2nd ed.). New York: Longman.

Rocco, S. (1993). *New visions for the developmental assessment of infants and young children.* (ERIC Clearinghouse No. EC302834)

Rogol, A. D., Roemmich, J. N., & Clark, P. A. (2002). Growth at puberty. *Journal of Adolescent Health, 31,* 192–200.

Rubin, K. H., Bukowski, W., & Parker, J. G. (1998). Peer interactions, relationships, and groups. In W. Damon & N. Eisenberg (Eds.), *Handbook of child psychology: Vol 3. Social, emotional, and personality development* (5th ed., pp. 619–700). New York: Wiley.

Selman, R. L. & Schulz, L. H. (1990). *Making a friend in youth.* Chicago: University of Chicago Press.

Tanner, J. M., & Eveleth, P. B. (1975). Variability between populations in growth and development at puberty. In S. R. Berenberg (Ed.), *Puberty: Biologic and psychosocial components.* Leiden, Netherlands: Stenfert Kroese.

White, B. L. (1971). *Human infants: Experience and psychological development.* Englewood Cliffs, NJ: Prentice Hall.

Winborne, D. G., & Randolf, S. M. (1991). *Developmental expectations and outcomes for African-American infants.* (ERIC Clearinghouse No. PS019880)

JOHN CRUMLIN
*University of Colorado at
Colorado Springs*

DEVELOPMENTAL DELAY
DEVELOPMENTAL NORMS

DEVELOPMENTAL NORMS

Developmental norms describe the position of an individual along a continuum of development. Two fundamental types of developmental norms are age equivalents and grade equivalents. They are obtained by administering a test to several successive age or grade groups; the average, or typical, performance of each age or grade group is subsequently determined and becomes the norm for a particular age or grade group (Anastasi, 1982).

A number of human traits demonstrate growth with increasing age, including abstract intelligence, vocabulary or language acquisition, and motor skill development. Age equivalents have frequently been used to interpret performance for age-related traits. The average test score obtained by successive age or grade groups is determined based on the performance of a carefully selected sample of individuals. The age (in years and months) for which a particular test score was the average becomes the age equivalent for that particular test score (e.g., a child who answered 35 questions correctly on a receptive language test received an age equivalent of 4–6, meaning that 35 was the average, or typical, score for children aged 4 years, 6 months tested in the norming program). The term mental age refers to an age equivalent obtained from an intelligence test. A child with a mental age of 6 years, 3 months, for example, performed as well as the average child aged 6 years, 3 months.

Skills that develop as a direct result of school instruction such as reading or mathematics have frequently been assessed with tests that yield grade equivalents. The typical, or average, performance of successive grade groups is determined for a carefully selected sample of pupils. The grade for which a certain test score was the average becomes the grade equivalent for that particular test score (e.g., a pupil who answered 40 questions correctly on a mathematics concepts test received a grade equivalent of 6.2, meaning that 40 was the average score for pupils in the second month of grade 6; Thorndike & Hagen, 1977).

Age and grade equivalents have come into disfavor for a number of reasons:

1. They represent scales having unequal units because human traits typically develop faster in the earlier years and slow down in adolescence and adulthood. Thus, the difference in performance between ages 3 and 4 (e.g., may be much greater than the difference in performance between ages 14 and 15 for a particular trait). Similarly, the difference in performance between grade equivalents 1.0 and 2.0 may be much greater than that between 8.0 and 9.0. This characteristic makes interpretation difficult.

2. They are not as rich in meaning as within-group norms (standard scores and percentile ranks) because they "match" the individual's performance to the age or grade group for which that performance was just average.

3. They can imply a level of functioning or skill development that is misleading. A fifth-grade pupil who receives a reading comprehension grade equivalent of 10.8 is not necessarily reading at the same level as a student in the eighth month of the tenth grade. The grade equivalent of 10.8 is to some extent a contrivance of the grade equivalent score scale and simply means the pupil is reading very well for a fifth grader (Cronbach, 1984). Grade equivalents are especially difficult to interpret when obtained from group achievement tests. Mental ages for adolescence and adulthood likewise do not describe actual performance at those ages and often represent an arbitrary and artificial extension of the mental age scale.

In summary, age and grade equivalents are developmental norms that, when interpreted cautiously, can sometimes provide useful information; however, within group norms such as standard scores and percentile ranks they are the preferred method of test interpretation.

REFERENCES

Anastasi, A. (1982). *Psychological testing* (5th ed.). New York: Macmillan.

Cronbach, L. J. (1984). *Essentials of psychological testing* (4th ed.). New York: Harper & Row.

Thorndike, R. L., & Hagen, E. P. (1977). *Measurement and evaluation in psychology and education.* New York: Wiley.

GARY J. ROBERTSON
American Guidance Service

GRADE EQUIVALENTS
NORM-REFERENCED TESTING

DEVELOPMENTAL OPTOMETRY

The relationship between vision, sight, and learning took on a new meaning in 1922 when A. M. Skeffington, an optometrist who help found the Postgraduate Optometric Extension Program, lectured on the concept that Snellen visual acuity (sight) and visual effectiveness (vision) were not one in the same. In the 1930s George Crow and Margaret Eberl expanded this concept by instituting the use of preventive lenses and visual training to enhance visual abilities, promote visual efficiency, and reduce or eliminate visual anomalies such as amblyopia, strabismus, and binocular dysfunction. At the same time, the American Optometric Association published a pamphlet, "It is a Cruel Test," stating that "Optometry is not interested in merely whether the child sees well—it is interested in whether he sees efficiently."

Clinical studies in the visual development of the school-age child took a dramatic step forward in the 1940s at the Clinic of Child Development at Yale University. Gesell, Ilg, and Bullis (1949) established that the eye and the other sensory modalities take turns in the development of the mind. They stated that vision is so fundamental in the growth of the mind that the body takes hold of the physical world with his eyes long before he takes hold with his hands. The eyes lead in the patterning of behavior.

The team at the Clinic of Child Development Center observed visual behavior from the earliest stages. It was noted, for example, that the newborn eyes wander without a stimulus. However, after a few hours, the child can often fixate briefly. By 16 weeks the eyes are leading the other senses, but they also begin to team with the hands. Through these observations, it was established that visual development began at birth despite the fact that vision appeared to be a "fleeting, discontinuous performance."

At the Child Development Center, Getman also developed, applied, and modified optometric techniques to test the visual development of the child from 21 to 48 months. These new tests and modifications were necessitated by the fact that adult testing procedures were of little value in the testing of children.

Getman found that monocular and binocular fixation,

near and far point shifting of attention, and depth perception and spatial awareness develop and increase throughout childhood at varying rates. The studies revealed the importance of how the visual mechanism is involved in the total performance of the child. The concept of developmental vision that Getman and Kephart elaborated on also established a causal relationship between early motor patterns and the development of binocularity. Therefore, any delay or omission in development could result not only in binocular defects but in amblyopias and anisometropias. According to Solan (1979) any deviation from the normal ontogeny of motor and sensory maturation is considered to be significant.

Renshaw, Getman, and Skeffington studied the retinoscopic reflex during reading in conjunction with the lie detector test. They noted that when reading, stress could be revealed by the blood pressure, respiration, galvanic skin response, and retinoscopic reflex. These studies, along with the work of Huebal, Wiesel, and others, established that vision is not just genetically endowed; it develops. The concept of function altering structure rather than structure altering function became embodied in developmental vision theory. Solan (1979) states that by integrating the concepts of Myklebust, Strauss, Werner, Birch, Kephart, Piaget, Jensen, and others, the developmental optometrist is able to construct a diagnostic and therapeutic regimen. Developmental and perceptual therapy provides a child experiencing a learning disability with those characteristics normally associated with good students who are efficient learners.

The optometrist specializing in the field of developmental vision includes in the basic vision examination a careful case history that covers any significant information on the prenatal, perinatal, and postnatal disorders and any delays in the developmental milestones. The visual examination includes the standard testing procedures such as visual acuity, ocular health status of the eyes, binocular status, refractive status, and accommodative facility. Additional tests may probe the child's concept of laterality, directionality, dominance, eye-hand coordination, and visual perception.

Training of the child with developmental vision problems encompasses the standard visual training procedures. These include enhancement of ocular motility, stereopsis, eye-hand coordination, and accommodation. Additional techniques may emphasize bilateral and binocular integration. It is also important for the optometrist to collaborate with special services personnel to assist in the psychological conditions that sometimes exist with vision difficulties (Biaggo & Bittner, 1990).

The optometrist, as Solan (1979) states, blends professional and intellectual skills to develop in the learning-disabled child a suitable level of visual functional readiness for learning, the sensory-motor skills necessary for a child to respond to classroom instruction, and cognitive skills and conceptual tempo required for assimilation and generalization in learning reasoning and problem solving.

REFERENCES

Barsch, R. H. (1964, January). The role of cognition in movement. *Optometric Child Vision Care & Guidance, 8*(4), 17–23.

Biaggio, M. K., & Bittner, E. (1990). Psychology and optometry: Interaction and collaboration. *American Psychologist, 45*(12), 1313–1315.

Gesell, A., Halverson, A. Z., & Amstruda, C. (1940). *The first five years of life.* New York: Harper & Brothers.

Gesell, A., Ilg, F. L., & Bullis, G. E. (1949). *Vision: Its development in infant and child.* New York: Harper & Brothers.

Getman, G. (1960). *Techniques and diagnostic criteria for the optometric care of children's vision,* Duncan, OK: Occupational Education Programs.

Getman, G. (1962). *How to develop your child's intelligence.* Luverne, MI: Author.

Getman, G., & Bullis, G. (1950). *Developmental vision* (Vol. 1). Duncan, OK: Occupational Education Programs.

Getman, G., & Kephart, N. (1957). *Developmental vision* (Vol. 2). Duncan, OK: Occupational Education Programs.

Kephart, N. C. (1960). *The slow learner in the classroom.* Columbus, OH: Charles E. Merril.

Lavatelli, C. (1973). *Piaget's theory applied to an early childhood curriculum.* Boston: Center for Media Development.

Piaget, J., & Inhelder, B. (1956). *The child's conception of space.* London: Routledge & Kegan Paul.

Skeffington, A. (1957). *Developmental vision* (Vol. 1). Duncan, OK: Occupational Education Programs.

Solan, H. (1979). *Learning disabilities: The role of the developmental optometrist, 50*(11), 1265. St. Louis, MO: American Optometric Association.

Bruce P. Rosenthal
State University of New York

DEVELOPMENTAL PSYCHOLOGY

Developmental Psychology is a publication of the American Psychological Association. Founded in 1968, its first editor was Boyd R. McCandless of Emory University.

The journal's primary purpose is to publish reports of empirical research on topics pertaining to developmental psychology. Developmental psychology is defined as including variables pertaining to growth and development broadly cast. Not only chronological age and physical growth variables are included, but also other factors, such as sex and socioeconomic status.

Developmental Psychology is published bimonthly. Manuscripts may be sent to *Developmental Psychology,* American Psychological Association, 1200 Seventeenth Street, NW, Washington, DC 20036.

Elizabeth Jones
Texas A&M University

DEVELOPMENTAL TEST OF VISUAL PERCEPTION: SECOND EDITION

The Developmental Test of Visual Perception: Second Edition (DTVP-2; 1993) 1993 is a revision of The Marianne Frostig Developmental Test of Visual Perception originally authored by Frostig, Maslow, Lefever, & Whittlesey (1963). The new edition includes numerous improvements, is suitable for children ages 4 to 10, measures both visual perception and visual-motor integration skills, has eight subtests, is based on updated theories of visual perception development, and can be administered to individuals in 35 minutes. The DTVP-2 subtests are Eye-Hand Coordination, Copying, Spatial Relations, Position in Space, Figure-Ground, Visual Closure, Visual-Motor Speed, and Form Constancy.

The DTVP-2 is unique among other tests of visual perception and visual-motor integration because (1) its subtests are reliable at the .8 or .9 levels for all age groups; (2) its scores are validated by many studies; (3) its norms are based on a large representative sample keyed to the 1990 census data; (4) it yields scores for both pure visual perception (no motor response) and visual-motor integration ability; and (5) it has been proven to be unbiased relative to race, gender, and handedness.

The DTVP-2 was standardized on 1,972 children from 12 states. Characteristics of the normative sample approximate those provided in the 1990 *Statistical Abstract of the United States* with regard to gender, geographical region, ethnicity, race, and urban/rural residence. Standard scores, normal curve equivalents (NCEs), percentiles, and age equivalents are provided in the Examiner's Manual.

This test was reviewed in *The Twelfth Mental Measurements Yearbook* by Bologna (1995) and Tindal (1995). Bologna stated that the revised test was an impressive revision of a previously weak instrument; Tindal described the test as useful in determining General Visual Perception, Motor Reduced Visual Perception, and Visual-Motor Integration.

REFERENCES

Bologna, N. B. (1985). Review of the Developmental Test of Visual Perception: Second Edition. In J. C. Conoley & J. C. Impara (Eds.), *The twelfth mental measurements yearbook* (pp. 289–292). Lincoln: Buros Institute of Mental Measurements, University of Nebraska Press.

Frostig, M., Maslow, P., Lefever, D. W., & Whittlesey, J. R. B. (1963). *The Marianne Frostig Developmental Test of Visual Perception.* Palo Alto, CA: Consulting Psychologists Press.

Hammill, D. D., Pearson, N. A., & Voress, J. K. (1993). *Developmental Test of Visual Perception–Second Edition.* Austin, TX: PRO-ED.

Tindal, G. (1985). Review of the Developmental Test of Visual Perception: Second Edition. In J. C. Conoley & J. C. Impara (Eds.), *The twelfth mental measurements yearbook* (pp. 289–292). Lincoln: Buros Institute of Mental Measurements, University of Nebraska Press.

Nils A. Pearson
PRO-ED, Inc.

DEVELOPMENTAL THERAPY

Developmental therapy is a method of educating severely socially, emotionally, and behaviorally disabled children. It has normal social-emotional development as its goal. Developmental sequences in behavior, social communication, socialization, and cognition provide the framework for the curriculum. Devised by Mary M. Wood and associates (1979, 1986), developmental therapy links theory and research about normal social-emotional development to classroom practices. It was first demonstrated in 1970 at the Rutland Psychoeducational Center in Athens, Georgia, in a collaborative effort between the public school system, the mental health system, the University of Georgia, and the U.S. Department of Education.

Developmental therapy has been used successfully with severely emotionally disturbed and autistic children from age 2 to 16 years in preschool, elementary, middle school, and high-school classes. It also has been used effectively in day-treatment settings and residential facilities. Educators have adapted aspects of developmental therapy to resource rooms, self-contained classrooms, and regular education classes. It has extensive applications in the therapeutic arts, including art, music, and recreation therapies. It has also been adapted for use in camp settings and leisure programs, and for parents in home programs with autistic children. It was approved by the U.S. Office of Education, National Institute of Education Joint Dissemination Review Panel in 1975 as an exemplary educational program with documented effectiveness. It received validation again in 1981 from the same panel as an exemplary training model for teachers.

The foundation for developmental therapy is based on theory and research about social, emotional, cognitive, communication, and behavioral development. There is agreement that social knowledge, language, and judgment play important roles in governing behavior and that these are acquired through social experience. There also is agreement that the quality of interactions with others influences the form behavior will take. In addition, developmental theorists provide the concept of ordered, sequential processes in thinking, feeling, behaving, and relating from infancy through adolescence. Their work provides a reference for understanding the extent to which social and affective skills can be taught and the limitations that can be expected at any particular stage (Erikson, 1977; Flavell, 1977; Kohlberg, 1983; Piaget, 1977). Social learning and behavioral theorists provide knowledge about the impact of others on the development of self-control and self-regulated behavior. Studies of modeling, imitation, punishment, discipline, aggression by adults toward children, and the role of reasoning in behavioral management provide understanding about how social behavior emerges (Bandura, 1977; Selman, 1980; Turiel, 1983). Psychoanalytic theorists focus on feelings, anxieties, defense mechanisms, ego functions, and relationships with adults (Freud, 1965; Loevinger, 1976; Maccoby, 1980). These major constructs from different theoretical orientations have been integrated into the practices of developmental therapy.

Students are grouped for developmental therapy according to their stage of social-emotional development. Groups range in size from 4 to 12 students, with the smaller groups used for students at lower developmental stages and those with severe psychopathology. Each group is conducted by a lead teacher-therapist and a support teacher aide. The goals and specific program (treatment) objectives and procedures for each stage are based on individual assessment of each student's social-emotional development. Characteristic roles for adults and the activities, materials, schedules, and behavior management strategies are specified by the stage.

The instrument used to assess each student's social-emotional development is the Developmental Therapy Objectives Rating Form (DTORF). This instrument provides specific individual education plan (IEP) short-term objectives and long-range program goals. Since the first field testing, the DTORF has been used with several thousand students ages 2 to 16 with a range of handicapping conditions, including children who are autistic, mentally retarded, severely multihandicapped, deaf, schizophrenic, nonhandicapped, and gifted. Several studies provide adequate support for the effectiveness of developmental therapy (Kaufman, Paget, & Wood, 1981; Wood, 1997; Wood & Swan, 1978).

Developmental therapy has received contextual endorsement because of the directives for Part H of the Individuals with Disabilities Education Act (IDEA) and its amendments. Professionals working with young children with behavioral disorders and their families have adopted developmental therapy because it is based on the child's current level of performance rather than chronological age. This concept is conducive to the practicalities of working within the family system as mandated by IDEA (Hanft & Striffler, 1995; Zabel, 1991).

REFERENCES

Bandura, A. (1977). *Social learning theory.* Englewood Cliffs, NJ: Prentice Hall.

Erikson, E. H. (1977). *Toys and reasons.* New York: Norton.

Flavell, J. H. (1977). *Cognitive development.* Englewood Cliffs, NJ: Prentice Hall.

Freud, A. (1965). *Normality and pathology in childhood: Assessment of development.* New York: International Universities Press.

Hanft, B., & Striffler, N. (1995). Incorporating developmental therapy in early childhood programs: Challenges and promising practices. *Infants and Young Children, 8*(2), 37–47.

Kaufman, A., Paget, C., & Wood, M. M. (1981). Effectiveness of developmental therapy for severely emotionally disturbed children. In F. H. Wood (Ed.), *Perspectives for a new decade: Education's responsibility for seriously emotionally disturbed and behaviorally disordered children and youth.* Reston, VA: Council for Exceptional Children.

Kohlberg, L. (1983). *Essays on moral development* (Vol. 2). San Francisco: Harper & Row.

Loevinger, J. (1976). *Ego development.* San Francisco: Jossey-Bass.

Maccoby, E. E. (1980). *Social development.* New York: Harcourt, Brace & Jovanovich.

Piaget, J. (1977). *The development of thought.* New York: Viking.

Selman, R. (1980). *The growth of interpersonal understanding.* New York: Holt, Rinehart & Winston.

Turiel, E. (1983). *The development of social knowledge.* Cambridge, MA: Cambridge University Press.

Wood, M. M. (1979). *The developmental therapy objectives: A self-instructional workbook.* Austin, TX: PRO-ED.

Wood, M. M. (1986). *Developmental therapy in the classroom.* Austin, TX: PRO-ED.

Wood, M. M. (1997). *Social competence for young children: An outreach project for inservice training.* (ERIC Clearinghouse No. EC305787)

Wood, M. M., & Swan, W. W. (1978). A developmental approach to educating the disturbed young child. *Behavioral Disorders 3,* 197–209.

Zabel, M. K. (1991). Teaching young children with behavior disorders: Working with behavior disorders. *ERIC Clearinghouse on Handicapped and Gifted Children.* Reston, VA: Council for Exceptional Children. (ERIC Document No. EC300413)

MARY M. WOOD
University of Georgia
First edition

EMOTIONAL DISORDERS
SOCIAL LEARNING THEORY

DEVEREUX BEHAVIOR RATING SCALE–SCHOOL FORM

The Devereux Behavior Rating Scale–School Form (DSF; Naglieri, LeBuffe, & Pfeiffer, 1993) is based on federal criteria and is designed to evaluate behaviors of children and adolescents that may be indicative of moderate to severe emotional disturbances. This instrument is also useful for providing normative comparisons of behavior and for comparative results from different informants (e.g., parents, teachers). It is used for assessing a child or adolescent in a variety of settings. The information derived from the DSF can be used for treatment planning and for the evaluation of pre/post measures of treatment. It is effective in evaluating progress during educational interventions and can be helpful in determining whether a child or adolescent should be placed in a special education program due to a serious emotional disturbance. The DSF has two forms that include separate sets of items appropriate for children ages 5 to 12 and for adolescents ages 13 to 18. The scale includes 40 items consisting of four subscales that address areas identified in the federal definition of Serious Emotional Disturbance. The areas are Interpersonal Problems, Inappropriate Behaviors/Feelings, Depression, and Physical Symptoms/Fears. It takes approximately 5 minutes to administer.

The DSF results are compared to a nationally standardized sample of more than 3,000 cases that are approximated closely to the 1990 census data on all demographic variables. There are separate norms for age and sex for both parent and teacher raters. The form is easy to administer and score with items and directions written at the sixth-grade reading level. There is multilevel analysis and interpretation, with the Total Scale Score and Subscale Scores assisting the evaluator in eligibility determination. The Subscale Scores help facilitate IEP planning and the design of preferred intervention. The Problem Item Scores help to identify specific behavioral problems for treatment.

The DSF internal consistency estimates are calculated according to age and gender; age and rater; and age, rater, and gender. The DSF Total Scale internal reliability coefficients range from .92 (parent ratings for females aged 13–18) to .97 (teacher ratings for males and females aged 5–12). The median Total Scale reliability coefficients by age are .96 (ages 5–12) and .94 (ages 13–18); by gender, .95 (males) and .94 (females); and by rater, .93 (parents) and .96 (teachers). The median internal reliability coefficients for the four subscales across rater, gender, and age are .85 (Interpersonal Problems), .84 (Inappropriate Behaviors/Feelings), .84 (Depression), and .82 (Physical Symptoms/Fears). The median reliability coefficient across all subscales, age, rater, and gender is .84. The DSF has very good test-retest reliability (24 hours, 2 weeks, and 4 weeks) and interrater reliability.

The construct-related validity of the DSF indicates that all item total correlations are significant ($p < .01$) and clearly indicates that the items are highly correlated to the total score. A considerable amount of data was collected and evaluated by the authors to determine the criterion-related validity of the DSF. The examination included ratings of regular education children and adolescents compared to seriously emotionally disturbed children and adolescents from a number of different settings. In addition, another study examined whether the criterion-related validity of the DSF could be generalized to racial or ethnic subpopulations. Results based on this study support the DSF's usefulness in screening for serious emotional disturbances and suggest that the criterion-related validity is generalized to Caucasian, African-American, and Hispanic children (Goh, 1997).

REFERENCES AND ADDITIONAL INFORMATION

Floyd, R. G., & Bose, J. E. (2003). Behavior rating scales for assessment of emotional disturbance: A critical review of measurement characteristics. *Journal of Psychoeducational Assessment, 21,* 43–78.

Gimpel, G. A., & Nagle, R. J. (1996). Factorial validity of the Devereux Behavior Rating Scale–School Form. *Journal of Psychoeducational Assessment, 14,* 334–348.

Goh, D. S. (1997). Clinical utility of the Devereux Behavior Rating Scale–School Form among culturally diverse children. *Psychology in the Schools, 34,* 301–308.

Impara, J. C., & Plake, B. S. (Eds.). (1998). *The thirteenth mental measurements yearbook.* Lincoln, NE: Buros Institute of Mental Measurements.

Naglieri, J. A., LeBuffe, P. A., & Pfeiffer, S. I. (1993). *Devereux Behavior Rating Scale–School Form test manual.* San Antonio, TX: Psychological Corporation.

Naglieri, J. A., & Gottling, S. H. (1995). Use of the Teacher Report Form and the Devereux Behavior Rating Scale–School Form with learning disordered/emotionally disordered students. *Journal of Clinical Child Psychology, 24,* 71–76.

Nickerson, A. B., & Nagle, R. J. (2001). Interrater reliability of the Devereux Behavior Rating Scale–School Form: The influence of teacher frame of reference. *Journal of Psychoeducational Assessment, 19,* 299–316.

RON DUMONT
Fairleigh Dickinson University

JOHN O. WILLIS
Rivier College

DEVEREUX SCALES OF MENTAL DISORDERS

The Devereux Scales of Mental Disorders (DSMD; Naglieri, LeBuffe, & Pfeiffer, 1994) are designed to assess whether a child or adolescent is experiencing, or is at risk for, psychopathology, including externalizing disorders (attention/delinquency and conduct scales), internalizing disorders (anxiety and depression scales), and critical pathology disorders (acute problems and autism scales). It is useful for evaluating treatment effectiveness and in analyzing information for treatment planning. The DSMD has two levels: a 111-item child form for ages 5 to 12 and a 110-item adolescent form for ages 13 to 18. The content of the items is based on the diagnostic criteria of the *Diagnostic and Statistical Manual of Mental Disorders,* fourth edition (*DSM-IV*). The DSMD takes 15 minutes to complete and the rater can be any adult who has known the child for at least 4 weeks. Parent and teacher raters use the same form, with separate norms provided for each. The scales are easily completed, scored, and interpreted and are written at the sixth-grade reading level. Items are rated on a 5-point Likert-type scale ranging from 0 ("never") to 4 ("very frequently").

The DSMD can be hand scored or computer scored, and it helps professionals assess behavior in a variety of settings. The results are compared to a national standardized sample of more than 3,000 cases approximated closely to the 1990 census. There are separate norms for females and males. The DSMD scoring method allows professionals to compare DSMD scores of the same child or adolescent at different points in time during treatment.

The DSMD Total Score internal consistency coefficients were .98 by age, .98 by gender, and .97 (parents) and .98 (teachers) by rater. The median reliability coefficients for the composite scales on the child form are .97 (Externalizing), .94 (Internalizing), and .90 (Critical Pathology). For the six scale scores on the child form, the median reliability coefficients are .96 (Conduct), .84 (Attention), .88 (Anxiety), .89 (Depression), .90 (Autism), and .78 (Acute Problems). The median reliability coefficients for the composite scales on the adolescent form are .94 (Externalizing), .96 (Internalizing), and .92 (Critical Pathology). For the six scale scores on the adolescent form, the median reliability coefficients are .96 (Conduct), .75 (Delinquency), .84 (Anxiety), .93 (Depression), .88 (Autism), and .90 (Acute Problems). The DSMD has good test-retest (24-hour and 1-week intervals) and interrater reliability.

The DSMD authors have cited in the test manual numerous studies that provide support for the DSMD's differential validity including adolescents diagnosed with anxiety disorders, conduct disorders, and depressive disorders. In addition, the DSMD *T*-scores are distinguished between children and adolescents with psychiatric diagnoses and nonclinical children and adolescents. Other studies have found the DSMD to be able to differentiate between inpatient children and adolescents diagnosed with ADHD and those with a Conduct Disorder diagnosis and the DSMD Composite and Subscales Scales accurately differentiate between inpatient children and adolescents diagnosed with depressive disorders, disruptive disorders, and psychotic disorders. The DSMD has been reported to produce greater classification accuracy than the REIS Scales and the Teacher Report Form (TRF) in finding behavioral and emotional disturbances in children and adolescents with Mental Retardation. The DSMD also has been found to have higher specificity and positive predictive power that the TRF when evaluating serious emotional problems in children and adolescents (Smith & Reddy, 2000). The DSMD was also compared to the Child Behavior Checklist (CBCL) for diagnostic classification accuracy in adolescents. The DSMD and CBCL were comparable in classifying oppositional or conduct disorder, the CBCL was superior for classifying major depression, and the DSMD was superior for classification of substance abuse (Curry & Ilardi, 2000).

REFERENCES AND ADDITIONAL INFORMATION

Curry, J. F., & Ilardi, S. S. (2000). Validity of the Devereux Scales of Mental Disorders with adolescent psychiatric inpatients. *Journal of Clinical Child Psychology, 29,* 578–588.

Gimpel, G. A., & Nagle, R. J. (1999). Psychometric properties of the Devereux Scales of Mental Disorders. *Journal of Psychoeducational Assessment, 17,* 127–144.

Naglieri, J. A., LeBuffe, P. A., & Pfeiffer, S. I. (1994). *The Devereux Scales of Mental Disorders test manual.* San Antonio, TX: Psychological Corporation.

Plake, B. S., & Impara, J. C. (Eds.). (2001). *The fourteenth mental measurements yearbook.* Lincoln, NE: Buros Institute of Mental Measurements.

Smith, S. R., & Reddy, L. A. (2000). A test review of the Devereux Scales of Mental Disorders. *Canadian Journal of School Psychology, 15,* 85–91.

Smith, S. R., & Reddy, L. A. (2002). The concurrent validity of the Devereux Scales of Mental Disorders. *Journal of Psychoeducational Assessment, 20,* 112–127.

Smith, S. R., Reddy, L. A., & Wingenfeld, S. A. (2002). Assessment of psychotic disorders in inpatient children and adolescents: Use of the Devereux Scales of Mental Disorders. *Journal of Psychopathology & Behavioral Assessment, 24,* 269–273.

Smith, S. R., Wingenfeld, S. A., & Hilsenroth, M. J. (2002). The use of the Devereux Scales of Mental Disorders in the assessment of Attention-Deficit/Hyperactivity Disorder and conduct disorder. *Journal of Psychopathology & Behavioral Assessment, 22,* 237–255.

RON DUMONT
Fairleigh Dickinson University

JOHN O. WILLIS
Rivier College

DEVIATION IQ

A standard score, known as a deviation IQ, was introduced to overcome the technical problems inherent in the ratio IQ. A standard score is obtained by converting raw test scores from a standardization sample to a normalized score distribution with a fixed mean and standard deviation. Deviation IQs typically have a mean of 100 and a standard deviation of the authors' choosing such as 15 for Wechsler tests and 16 for the Stanford-Binet. There is no difference between Wechsler and Binet IQs in the 90 to 110 range, but the further the score from average, the greater the difference, as illustrated in Table 1. Standard scores are used to convert ordinal to interval data. Standard (normalized) scores provide equal variability at each age level and standard scores

Table 1 Percentile rank equivalents for deviation IQs with standard deviations of 15, 16, and 20[a]

Percentile rank	Wechsler 15z + 100	Stanford-Binet 16z + 100	ASVAB 20z + 100
0.1	55	52	40
0.9	65	62	53
2.0	69	67	59
2.9	72	70	62
5.0	75	74	67
9.7	81	79	74
14.7	84	83	79
25.8	90	90	87
40.1	96	96	95
50.0	100	100	100
59.9	104	104	105
74.2	110	110	113
84.1	115	116	120
90.3	120	121	126
95.0	125	126	133
97.1	129	130	138
98.0	131	133	141
98.9	135	137	146
99.9	145	148	160

[a]Wechsler refers to Wechsler Preschool and Primary Scale of Intelligence, Wechsler Intelligence Scale for Children–Revised, and the Wechsler Adult Intelligence Scale–Revised. Stanford-Binet refers to the 1972 and 1985 editions only. ASVAB is the common abbreviation for the Armed Services Vocational Assessment Battery.

from one test can be directly compared with standard scores from another. In individual assessment, David Wechsler introduced the deviation IQ with his Wechsler-Bellevue scale in 1939. (The deviation IQ had been used with some group tests earlier.) Wechsler chose to use a standard score with a standard deviation of 15 (instead of 16, the median standard deviation of the contemporary Binet) because most people are more familiar with units of 5 (i.e., 5, 10, 15) than of 4 (i.e., 4, 8, 12, 16). Today most test authors use a deviation IQ with a standard deviation of either 15 or 16, but some use 20 and even 24.

Because of the popularity among professionals of the concept of the standard score with a mean of 100 and a standard deviation of 15 or 16, and because of the lack of popularity of the letters I and Q, some contemporary test authors have changed the name of the score from IQ to Learning Quotient (LQ), General Cognitive Index (GCI), Mental Processing Composite, etc. Whatever standard scores may be called, when they are derived from a test of mental ability, they are interpreted in the same way as deviation IQs, that is, as indicating where the individual stands in relation to others of his or her age on the content of the test.

It should be noted that the Wechsler-Bellevue (predecessor of the Wechsler Adult Intelligence Scale) was developed for adults rather than children/adolescents and that mental test raw scores for average adults are very little higher than those of adolescents. Since the average raw score at age 50 is actually a little lower than of age 20, it makes no sense to refer to someone as having reached a mental age of 50 or to divide such a score by chronological age. With adults, as with children, a deviation IQ is a convenient index for indicating the current level of intellectual development and functioning (as later qualified). By mid-adolescence and for many predictions, tests with norms based on educational status may be better than those based on age.

Since an IQ is a score from a test and since the content of tests of mental ability differ not only from each other but also within a test from childhood to adolescence, the term IQ should be preceded by the name of the test from which it was derived and accompanied by the age at which it was obtained. As a score, an IQ indicates both an individual's ability level at a given point in time and the relationship of the individual's score to those obtained by others of his or her age. As such, an IQ should be considered as a descriptive rather than an explanatory term. An IQ can be used to help understand a person's current level of cognitive functioning associated with learning in the mainstream culture. Scores from mental ability scales are to some extent reflections of previous learning within the culture in which the test was standardized, and they are predictors of subsequent educational performance in that culture over the next few years.

IQs are often thought of as indicators of scholastic or educational aptitude. However, they do not reflect important variables such as mechanical, motor, musical, and artistic aptitudes. IQs do not reflect skills in building or maintaining inter- or intrapersonal relationships. Only to a limited extent do IQs reflect such catalytic variables as persistence, enthusiasm for a particular kind of effort, or divergent thinking. Decisions about an individual need to be based on more than scores from one test of cognitive ability.

JOSEPH L. FRENCH
Pennsylvania State University

INTELLIGENCE QUOTIENT
RATIO IQ

DEXEDRINE

(Dextroamphetamine sulfate), an amphetamine, is used in the treatment of attention deficit disorder with hyperactivity (RxList, 1997), narcolepsy, and as short-term therapy for exogenous obesity. Although amphetamines are known to work as central nervous stimulants, the mechanism whereby they produce mental and behavioral effects in children is not known. Adverse reactions can include palpitations and rapid heartbeat; euphoria, restlessness, and insomnia; and exacerbation of motor and vocal tics and

Tourette's syndrome. Overdose may result in assaultiveness, confusion, hallucinations, and panic states usually followed by fatigue and depression.

A brand name of Smith Kline and French, Dexedrine is available in 5 mg tablets; 5, 10, and 15 mg sustained released capsules, and elixir. Recommended dosage for attention deficit disorder with hyperactivity in children 6 years of age and older is to start with 5 mg once or twice daily, with daily dosage to be raised, if needed, in increments of 5 mg at weekly intervals, typically not to exceed a total of 40 mg per day.

REFERENCE

Physicians' desk reference. (1984). (pp. 1878–1880). Oradell, NJ: Medical Economics.

RxList. (1997). *Internet drug index.* Retrieved from www.rxlist .com/

LAWRENCE C. HARTLAGE
Evans, Georgia

ATTENTION DEFICIT/HYPERACTIVITY DISORDER
RITALIN

DIABETES

Diabetes is a chronic metabolic disease affecting approximately 18 million Americans. Common symptoms of diabetes include extreme hunger and thirst, frequent urination, irritability, weakness, fatigue, nausea, and high blood and urine sugar levels. Two major types of diabetes have been identified. Type I, or insulin dependent diabetes, was formerly called juvenile-onset because it usually occurred in children and adolescents. Type II, or noninsulin dependent, was formerly called maturity-onset. In Type I diabetes, the pancreas does not function properly, resulting in little to no insulin production and a build-up of sugar in the bloodstream. Treatment involves insulin injections, diet, and regular exercise. Approximately 1.5 million Americans are Type I diabetics. It is thought that there is a genetic predisposition for diabetes. At present there is no known cure. Obesity and stress can contribute to the onset of diabetes.

Hypoglycemia (low blood sugar) and hyperglycemia (high blood sugar) are the two most common emergencies encountered by diabetics. Hypoglycemia occurs when the blood sugar drops too low because of too much insulin, not enough food, or too much exercise. Symptoms include anger or bad temper, sudden staggering and poor coordination, pale color, disorientation, confusion, and sweating, eventually leading to stupor or unconsciousness, also called insulin shock. This condition is treated by administering some form of sugar such as fruit juice or candy. If unconsciousness occurs, a child should receive emergency medical care.

Hyperglycemia occurs when there is too little insulin, when infection or illness is present, or when too much food or drink is consumed. Symptoms of hyperglycemia include drowsiness, extreme thirst and frequent urination, fruity or wine-smelling breath, heavy breathing, flushed skin, vomiting, and eventually stupor or unconsciousness, called a diabetic coma. Treatment of this condition is usually the administration of insulin with the supervision of a healthcare professional.

Some diabetics develop complications such as retinopathy, that sometimes result in blindness, diabetic neuropathy or nerve disease, diabetic nephropathy or kidney disease, cardiovascular disease, or respiratory failure. Diabetes and its complications is the number three cause of nonaccidental death among children in the United States (Wright, Schafer, & Solomons, 1979).

It has been suggested by researchers that by the time a child reaches the developmental age of 12, he or she should be able to take the lead by doing his or her own urine or blood sugar tests and administration of insulin. Keep in mind that children in special education classes may reach these developmental ages at slower rates and thus may be more reliant on teachers and parents for assistance in complying with their diabetic regimen. In such cases teachers must be aware of the regimen. Parents should inform teachers about their child's needs, which may include a special diet, especially at lunch and snack time, time to run tests and take insulin injections, exercise, and signs of emergency, especially hyperglycemia and hypoglycemia. However, teachers should make every effort not to separate the child from the peer group. The diabetic child has the same needs for support, encouragement, and understanding as other children and should be encouraged to participate in all activities.

Compliance with the diabetic treatment regimen is usually difficult for a child and it may be more difficult for a child in special education who does not understand all of the rules of diabetes. It is important in this case that the teacher and school staff work with the child's parents to understand the special needs and restrictions diabetes places on the child. Teachers need to be aware of the diabetic child's developmental age and work with the child to develop responsibility, independence, and self-reliance compatible with his or her age of development. Should parents prove either unsophisticated or unresponsive, direct teacher-physician contact becomes essential. Indeed, school districts have been found in violation of the Americans with Disabilities Act (1990) with respect to their treatment of students with diabetes (Vennum, 1995). In addition, most parents surveyed by the American Diabetes Association (1996) indicate dissatisfaction with their child's diabetes management in school. Certainly, higher expectations for school involvement are the current trend.

REFERENCES

American Diabetes Association. (1984). *A word to . . . teachers and school staff.* Alexandria, VA: Author.

American Diabetes Association. (1984). *Your child has diabetes: What you should know.* Alexandria, VA: Author.

American Diabetes Association. (1984). *An Introduction: What you need to know about diabetes.* Alexandria, VA: Author.

American Diabetes Association. (1996). This can't be happening in our schools! *Diabetes Forecast, 49*(2), 61–66.

Carpenter, J. (1976). *Diabetes: A handicap.* Unpublished manuscript.

Vennum, M. K. (1995). Students with diabetes: Is there legal protection? *Journal of Law and Education, 24*(1), 33–69.

Wright, L., Schafer, A., & Solomons, G. (1979). *Encyclopedia of pediatric psychology.* Baltimore: University Park Press.

JANET CARPENTER
LOGAN WRIGHT
University of Oklahoma

FAMILY RESPONSE TO A CHILD WITH DISABILITIES HEALTH IMPAIRMENTS

DIAGNOSIS IN SPECIAL EDUCATION

Diagnosis or evaluation is an essential step in the process of identifying those children in need of special education services. Matarazzo and Pankratz (1984) define psychological diagnosis as: "(1) the process of classifying information relevant to an individual's emotional and behavioral state, and (2) the name assigned the state, taken generally from a commonly accepted classification system" (p. 369). Based on this definition, diagnosis in special education involves taking the information obtained through the assessment of a student's emotional, behavioral, academic, and intellectual functioning and classifying that information based on some accepted diagnostic system. The specific diagnostic system used determines the specific classification or name given to that student's level of functioning or condition.

The diagnostic procedure traditionally employed in special education has been one based on a medical model (Reynolds, 1984; Ysseldyke & Algozzine, 1982). This model is one borrowed from psychological diagnostic systems. It consists of preparing catalogs of systems of various special and remedial conditions and determining the extent to which an individual has characteristics similar to those of the known condition (Ysseldyke & Algozzine, 1982). According to Reynolds (1984), the focus has been on "intrapsychic causes of psychological dysfunction to the exclusion of extrapersonal factors, and on the deficiencies and weaknesses of individuals rather than on their strengths" (p. 453).

There have been many problems associated with the use of this type of a diagnostic model in special education. One problem centers on the fact that a wide variety of diagnostic systems have been developed. This has resulted in a situation in which the assessment of one student can produce very different diagnoses depending on the diagnostic system being referred to. There also tends to be considerable variations among the diagnoses of individuals classified under the same diagnostic system (Edgar & Hayden, 1985; Reynolds, 1984). These inconsistencies have made the process of special education diagnosis complicated and controversial.

The passage of PL 94-142, the Education for All Handicapped Children Act of 1975, began the formal process of diagnosis in special education. Subsequent amendments defined and redefined the different handicapping conditions; and as the Act changed its name in 1990 to the Individuals with Disabilities Education Act (IDEA), so did the idea of "handicaps" change to "disabilities."

The emphasis on cultural competency in diagnosis is not new, but it is much more emphasized in the scientific literature and in current law. Cultural competence also refers to the individual who is conducting the evaluation. The individual must have professional training in multicultural issues and demonstrate competence in assessment and diagnosis of children and adolescents of different socioeconomic status, gender, ethnicity, handicapping condition, and acculturation.

School psychologists traditionally have been the gatekeeper in the diagnosis/eligibility process. School psychology emphasized classification. Rosenfield and Nelson (1995) state:

> But as the current ethical, political, legal and educational context has evolved, there has been a re-examination of the purposes and applications of data gathered during assessment process (Taylor et al., 1993). In a position paper on the Role of the School Psychologist in Assessment (1994), the National Association of School Psychologists endorsed the proposition that assessment practices must be linked to prevention and intervention to provide positive outcomes for students. Thus, there is an increasing emphasis on information that is "useful in designing, implementing, monitoring, and evaluating interventions." (Reschly, Kicklighter, & McKee, 1988, pp. 9–50)

Diagnosis in special education, therefore, has taken on a broader definition and is linked much more to intervention than ever before. Rosenfield and Nelson (1995) suggest that there are three purposes of school psychological assessment: (1) informing/entitlement/classification decisions, (2) planning interventions, and (3) evaluating outcomes. Diagnosis and outcome are on the same continuum as opposed to being discrete entities. This shift in paradigm has also changed assessment instrument usage. The use of more natural and dynamic forms of assessment that directly impact instructional delivery and behavior management are common (Rosenfield & Nelson, 1995).

It is obvious that there is much diversity in the diagnosis of the mildly mentally retarded, learning disabled, and emotionally disturbed. According to Edgar and Hayden (1985), these handicapping conditions belong to a large percent of the total handicapped population and are the ones that are most difficult to quantify. These categories are basically indistinguishable from one another, and the population of children within these categories is indistinguishable from the larger group of children with general learning problems (e.g., disadvantaged, slow learner, etc.).

Each of these nonquantifiable categories has a history of problems in terms of the criteria used in their identification. For example, mild retardation is defined based on an IQ; there has been continual criticism of the use of IQ tests with minority population (Edgar & Hayden, 1985). The high percentage of minority students diagnosed as mentally retarded has brought charges from some that the traditional IQ tests cannot be reliably used to diagnose mental retardation. It has also been virtually impossible to define the distinction between seriously emotionally disturbed and socially maladjusted. There are no quantitative measures available for determining who is seriously emotionally disturbed. Emotional disturbance tends to be a socially defined condition, as does mild mental retardation and learning disabilities. Many of the problems associated with the diagnosis of learning disabilities have already been discussed. Edgar and Hayden (1985) feel that the only quantifiable aspect of the learning disabled definition is low achievement, which could classify 20 to 30 percent of all school-age children. Reynolds (1984) concludes that a large segment of children being served as learning disabled may not, in fact, be learning disabled. These are usually the intellectually borderline and low average children. According to Reynolds (1984), this is due, in part, to the diversity of models of severe discrepancy as well as to biases in the referral process favoring low IQ, low-achieving children. It will be interesting to see if the demise of the discrepancy model will alter the amount of children identified as needing special education.

Diagnosis in special education has attempted and failed to follow the traditional model of psychological diagnosis. This model has not been proven to be an effective one for special education. One of the main criticisms of this diagnostic system has been its inability to provide reliable and valid classifications of the conditions involved in special education diagnosis. Conditions such as mental retardation, emotional disturbance, and learning disabilities have not been quantifiably defined and are therefore difficult to classify. Despite these serious flaws, the concept of formal diagnosis is still considered to be of vital importance, and has changed to fit the current demands of Individuals with Disabilities Education Improvement Act (IDEIA) and intervention and outcome-focused needs of special education.

REFERENCES

Edgar, E., & Hayden, A. H. (1985). Who are the children special education should serve? And how many children are there? *Journal of Special Education, 18,* 523–539.

Grossman, H. J. (Ed.). (1983). *Classification in mental retardation.* Washington, DC: American Association on Mental Deficiencies.

Hammill, D. D., Larsen, S. C., Leigh, J., & McNult, G. (1981). A new definition of learning disabilities. *Learning Disabilities Quarterly, 4,* 336–342.

Matarazzo, J. D., & Pankratz, L. D. (1984). Diagnosis. In R. J. Corsini (Ed.), *Encyclopedia of psychology* (pp. 369–372). New York: Wiley.

Mercer, C. D., Hughes, C., & Mercer, A. R. (1985). Learning disabilities definitions used by state education departments. *Learning Disabilities Quarterly, 8,* 45–55.

National Information Center for Children and Youth with Disabilities. (1998). *Evaluation and Testing Guidelines.* Washington, DC: Author.

Reynolds, C. R. (1984). Critical measurement issues in learning disabilities. *Journal of Special Education, 18,* 451–475.

Reynolds, C. R., Gutkin, T. B., Elliot, S. N., & Witt, J. C. (1984). *School psychology: Essentials of theory and practice.* New York: Wiley.

Rosenfield, S., & Nelson, D. (1995). *The school psychologist's role in school assessment.* (ERIC Digest No. ED391985)

Ysseldyke, J. E., & Algozzine, B. (1982). *Critical issues in special and remedial education.* Boston: Houghton Mifflin.

LORI E. UNRUH
Eastern Kentucky University

AAMR, AMERICAN ASSOCIATION ON MENTAL RETARDATION
DIAGNOSTIC AND STATISTICAL MANUAL OF MENTAL DISORDERS
LEARNING DISABILITIES, SEVERE DISCREPANCY ANALYSIS IN MENTAL STATUS EXAMS

DIAGNOSTIC ACHIEVEMENT BATTERY–SECOND EDITION

The Diagnostic Achievement Battery–Second Edition (DAB-2; Newcomer, 1990) uses 12 subtests divided into five areas: listening (Story Comprehension, Characteristics), speaking (Synonyms, Grammatic Completion), reading (Alphabet/Word Knowledge, Reading Comprehension), writing (Capitalization, Punctuation, Spelling, Writing Composition), and mathematics (Mathematics Calculation, Mathematics Reasoning) for children between the ages of 6 and 14. Subtest raw scores convert to standard scores (M = 10, SD = 3) and percentile ranks. By combining subtests, composite scores (M = 100, SD = 15) are generated that reliably assess global strengths and weaknesses. The composites are Listening, Speaking, Reading, Writing, Mathematics, Spoken Language, Written Language, and Total Achievement.

The test was normed on 2,623 students residing in 40 states. The sample is representative of the nation as a whole with regard to gender, race, ethnicity, geographic region, and urban/rural residence. Reliability coefficients are high. Evidence of content, concurrent, and construct validity also is provided.

Compton (1996) reports that the DAB-2 measures a wide variety of skills that are directly related to classroom performance. Bernier and Hebert (1995) find that the DAB-2 is a well-designed individual diagnostic test. Brown (1995) reports that the subtests seem to measure common constructs.

REFERENCES

Bernier, J., & Hebert, M. (1995). Review of the Diagnostic Achievement Battery, Second Edition. In J. C. Conoley & J. C. Impara (Eds.), *The twelfth mental measurements yearbook* (pp. 294–295). Lincoln: Buros Institute of Mental Measurements, University of Nebraska Press.

Brown, R. (1995). Review of the Diagnostic Achievement Battery, Second Edition. In J. C. Conoley & J. C. Impara (Eds.), *The twelfth mental measurements yearbook* (pp. 295–296). Lincoln: Buros Institute of Mental Measurements, University of Nebraska Press.

Compton, C. (1996). *A guide to 100 tests for special education.* Upper Saddle River, NJ: Globe Fearon.

Newcomer, P. L. (1990). *Diagnostic Achievement Battery: Second Edition.* Austin, TX: PRO-ED.

TADDY MADDOX
PRO-ED, Inc.

DIAGNOSTIC AND STATISTICAL MANUAL OF MENTAL DISORDERS

The most widely used system for psychiatric diagnosis and classification in the United States is the fourth edition of the *Diagnostic and Statistical Manual of Mental Disorders* (*DSM-IV;* American Psychiatric Association, 1994). The current version of the *DSM,* called the *DSM-IV-TR* was published in July 2000. It is considered to be a minor revision confined to the descriptive text that accompanies each disorder (American Psychiatric Association, 2000). The first edition of the *DSM* was published in 1952, with the first revision appearing in 1968. All revisions of the *DSM* were developed for use with children, adolescents, and adults. The revision process included literature reviews, data reanalyses, and field trials. The American Psychiatric Association also publishes the *DSM-IV* Sourcebook, which provides a comprehensive and convenient reference record of the clinical and research support for the various revision decisions.

The purpose of the *DSM* "is to provide clear descriptions of diagnostic categories in order to enable clinicians and investigators to diagnose, communicate about, study,

and treat people with various mental disorders" (American Psychiatric Association, 1994). The *DSM* uses a multiaxial classification system. Each axis refers to a different domain of information that may help the professional plan treatment plans and advice, and predict outcomes for the patient or student.

Axis I: Clinical Disorders
           Other Conditions that May Be a Focus of
           Clinical Attention
Axis II: Personality Disorders
           Mental Retardation
Axis III: General Medical Conditions
Axis IV: Psychosocial and Environmental Problems
Axis V: Global Assessment of Functioning

The multiaxial system assists the clinician in making a diagnosis that is biopsychosocial in nature. In other words, the information given is holistic and takes the mental, physical, and social aspects of the individual's life into consideration. This is particularly appropriate for the 1990s, where the field of psychology has recognized the need for cultural competence in diagnosis.

The *DSM-IV* includes a section on "Disorders Usually First Diagnosed in Infancy, Childhood, or Adolescence." The diagnoses included in this section are: Mental Retardation, Learning Disorders, Motor Skills Disorder, Communication Disorders, Pervasive Developmental Disorders, Attention-Deficit and Disruptive Behavior Disorders, Feeding and Eating Disorders of Infancy or Early Childhood, Tic Disorders, Elimination Disorders, and a category of Other Disorders of Infancy Childhood or Adolescence. The latter diagnoses include Separation Anxiety Disorder, Selective Mutism, Reactive Attachment Disorder of Infancy or Early Childhood, Stereotypic Movement Disorder and Disorder of Infancy, Childhood, or Adolescence NOS.

The *DSM-IV* defines "mental disorder" in much the same way as its predecessors:

> a clinically significant behavioral or psychological syndrome or pattern that occurs in an individual and that is associated with present distress (e.g., a painful symptom) or disability (i.e., impairment in one or more important areas of functioning) or with a significantly increased risk of suffering death, pain, disability, or an important loss of freedom. In addition, this syndrome or pattern must not be merely an expectable and culturally sanctioned response to a particular event, for example, the death of a loved one. Whatever its cause, it must currently be considered a manifestation of a behavioral, psychological, or biological dysfunction in the individual." (American Psychiatric Association, 1984, p. xxi)

A criticism of this definition of mental disorder that is particularly relevant to children is that it includes areas not typically regarded as mental disorders such as developmental disorders and learning disabilities. Concerns have been expressed that children diagnosed with specific developmental or learning problems will be diagnosed and stigmatized as having a mental disorder (Rutter & Schaffer, 1980). The issue of labeling children for special education placement decisions has been controversial over the years, and it continues to be a source of frustration for many students, professionals, and parents. Therefore, the *DSM-IV* is probably best used in clinical settings where specific psychiatric treatment plans follow the specific psychiatric diagnoses. The *DSM-IV* provides at best only, a basis for diagnosis and treatment for learning problems. In educational settings, special education professionals have the expertise to specify learning strengths and weaknesses and develop individual academic treatment plans that are carried out in the most appropriate learning environment.

A *DSM-IV* for primary care physicians has been developed, *DSM-IV* Primary Care Version (American Psychiatric Association, 1995), which is a volume devised to assist the primary care physician during routine patient visits. This version focuses on common conditions such as anxiety, depression, and substance abuse, diagnoses that the primary care physician is likely to encounter and to need specialized knowledge. The volume also assists in communication between primary care physicians and psychiatrists. Children and adolescents presenting with the more common mental disorders may be identified by their primary physicians, and this may help in prevention and the availability of treatment.

REFERENCES

American Psychiatric Association. (2006). *Frequently asked questions: Diagnostic and statistical manual of mental disorders.* Retrieved January, 2006, from http://www.apa@psych.org

American Psychiatric Association. (1994). *Diagnostic and statistical manual of mental disorders* (4th ed.). Washington, DC: Author.

American Psychiatric Association. (1995). *Diagnostic and statistical manual of mental disorders, fourth edition, primary care version.* Washington, DC: Author.

LAWRENCE J. SIEGEL
University of Texas Medical Branch, Galveston
First edition

ELAINE FLETCHER-JANZEN
University of Colorado at Colorado Springs
Second edition

CLINICAL PSYCHOLOGY
MENTAL ILLNESS
MENTAL STATUS EXAMS

DIAGNOSTIC ASSESSMENTS OF READING WITH TRIAL TEACHING STRATEGIES

The Diagnostic Assessments of Reading with Trial Teaching Strategies (DARTTS) program is a two-component program comprising the Diagnostic Assessment of Reading (DAR) and Trial Teaching Strategies (TTS) and is designed for reading teachers, classroom teachers, special education and Title I teachers, and other professionals.

The DAR component is an individually administered criterion-referenced assessment of reading. The six subtests that make up the scale are Word Recognition (reading words from graded word lists), Word Analysis (letter knowledge, matching letters and words, and letter-sound correspondence knowledge), Oral Reading (graded reading passages), Silent Reading Comprehension (graded reading passages with comprehension assessed with multiple choice questions), Spelling (writing dictated words), and Word Meaning (providing a definition for each word from graded word lists presented orally). For the DAR, the examiner simultaneously administers and scores the tests, marking students' responses as correct, incorrect, or omitted. A mastery criterion has been established for each test, and the student continues with each test until the highest mastery level has been established.

The TTS component identifies how each student learns best through microteaching sessions. The TTS procedures are suitable for all teaching approaches and are used flexibly to aid any student reading at any level.

Raw scores can be converted to national percentile ranks. This assessment was standardized nationally on 1,664 students, and validity measures were determined using the Gates-MacGinitie Vocabulary Test. During the 1990–91 school year, a validation study was conducted with about 4,000 students on the DARTTS program. Participating students were tested with a nationally standardized reading test immediately before and then again after the use of the DARTTS materials to measure short-term gains. Then they were retested at the end of the school year to assess long-term stability of gains. Data from the validation study are included in the DARTTS technical manual.

REFERENCE

Conoley, J. C., & Impara, J. C. (Eds.). (1995). *The twelfth mental measurements yearbook.* Lincoln, NE: Buros Institute of Mental Measurements.

RON DUMONT
Fairleigh Dickinson University

JOHN O. WILLIS
Rivier College

DIAGNOSTIC PRESCRIPTIVE TEACHING

Diagnostic prescriptive teaching "refers to the practice of formulating instructional prescriptions on the basis of differential diagnostic results" (Arter & Jenkins, 1979, p. 518). Although any educational plan for an individual learner should spring from assessment, diagnostic prescriptive teaching has had a more specific meaning. The key idea underlying diagnostic prescriptive teaching is that a given diagnostic pattern is linked differentially to a specific instructional strategy (methods, materials, techniques, etc.). That a given set of assessment findings implies an accompanying set of instructional strategies is assumed.

In the early 1970s, when ability training began to receive criticism from within the field of learning disabilities (Hammill, 1972; Hammill, Goodman, & Wiederholt, 1974), Ysseldyke and Salvia (1974) suggested that diagnostic prescriptive teaching should be based on one of two theoretical models. The first model is the ability training model. From this perspective, the diagnosed strengths and weaknesses are conceptualized primarily as perceptual or psycholinguistic in nature and understood to be the basis for academic skills. Training programs are then differentially prescribed to improve the underlying abilities demonstrating weaknesses. For example, if a student is diagnosed as expressing figure-ground errors, the prescribed educational plan would include remedial figure-ground activities, without any "advice" from the diagnostic pattern to suggest how teaching the ability will or should relate to the level of academic skill. The second model is the task analysis model. From this perspective, the diagnosis or assessment targets are the specific academic skills for the purpose of identifying the skills within the learner's repertoire. The goal of instruction is then the attainment of those new or missing skills. For example, if assessment identifies a student knows only 75 percent of the addition facts through 10, the prescription is that the student should be taught the remaining 25 percent without any "advice" from the assessment results of how those skills should be taught.

Since the early 1970s, diagnostic prescriptive teaching has taken on a meaning broader than the two theoretical models. Smead and Schwartz (1982) developed a model that is integrative in nature. Moving beyond the ability training model with its focus nearly completely on perceptual or psycholinguistic processes. They identified three learner-focused areas from which diagnostic information has relevance for instruction: motivational-emotional, cognitive-perceptual, and neurological-physical. In a similar manner, they focused on a greater variety of dimensions than did those previously concerned solely with the application of task analysis to special education. In addition, they suggested that a third set of factors must be considered: the environmental characteristics of the learning situation, which include sociological, emotional, pedagogical, contingency, standing patterns of behavior, and physical fac-

tors. Finally, they suggested that the interactions among these three sets of factors—learner focused, task focused, and environmental focused—must also be diagnosed and related to the instructional prescription.

Thus, diagnostic prescriptive teaching has become better understood with the realization that a series of diagnostic patterns with related prescribed activities is simplistic given the complexity and variety of learners, tasks, and environments—and how they interact. Prescribed instructional goals must flow from assessment, addressing the learner and his/her style of learning, the skills or abilities that must be learned, and the situation and contingencies under which learning will be best facilitated. More recent studies (Covey, 1991; Fox & Thompson, 1994) suggest that diagnostic-prescriptive teaching techniques such as multisensory approaches, mapping strategies, peer learning, and process writing have achieved good outcomes with learning disabled students.

REFERENCES

Arter, J. A., & Jenkins, J. R. (1979). Differential diagnosis-prescriptive teaching: A critical appraisal. *Review of Educational Research, 49,* 517–555.

Covey, D. G. (1991). *The influence of teaching the main idea, drawing conclusions, and making inferences on the improvement of writing skills.* (ERIC Clearinghouse No. CS213114)

Fox, L. H., & Thompson, D. L. (1994). *Bringing the lab school method to an inner-city school.* (ERIC Clearinghouse No. EC304266)

Hammill, D. (1972). Training visual perceptual processes. *Journal of Learning Disabilities, 5,* 39–44.

Hammill, D., Goodman, L., & Wiederholt, J. L. (1974). Visual-motor processes: Can we train them? *Exceptional Children, 41,* 5–14.

Smead, V. S., & Schwartz, N. H. (1982, August). *An integrative model for instructional planning.* Paper presented at the 19th Annual Meeting of the American Psychological Association, Washington, DC.

Ysseldyke, J. E., & Salvia, J. (1974). Diagnostic-prescriptive teaching: Two models. *Exceptional Children, 41,* 17–32.

STEVEN R. TIMMERMANS
*Mary Free Bed Hospital and
Rehabilitation Center*

DIAGNOSTIC TEACHING
DIRECT INSTRUCTION

DIAGNOSTIC TEACHING

Diagnostic teaching is the name given an instructional process used to discover the instructional and environmental conditions under which student learning is most productive.

Diagnostic teaching is also referred to as clinical teaching and data-based instructional decision making.

Diagnostic teaching differs from a diagnostic-prescriptive model of instruction. In a diagnostic-prescriptive approach, a student's achievement and learning characteristics are assessed. Subsequently, recommendations for instructional delivery are drawn from this information. This model relies on inference from a static data base (e.g., test information) for prediction of optimal instructional arrangements. In common use, such a model often fails to make use of information gained during the instructional process.

Diagnostic teaching, although sometimes included as a step in a diagnostic-prescriptive model of instruction (Reynolds & Birch, 1977), is more commonly viewed as an alternative assessment system. Like a diagnostic-prescriptive approach, diagnostic teaching makes use of test information about a student's achievement and learning characteristics, but it differs from a diagnostic-prescriptive model in a number of significant ways.

Diagnostic teaching is a process of systematic discovery rather than prediction. Reisman (1982), in discussing application of diagnostic teaching to mathematics, describes a process with five steps: (1) identify strengths and weaknesses in mathematics; (2) hypothesize reasons for achievement and nonachievement; (3) formulate instructional objectives; (4) teach to the objectives; and (5) evaluate student learning.

Zigmond, Vallecorsa, and Silverman (1983) propose a model of diagnostic teaching that is similar to that of Reisman but that is more detailed; it contains 12 discrete steps. Other and different models of diagnostic teaching are available (Walker, 1988). Differences tend to be in the thoroughness of description. Most have a set of common characteristics.

Diagnostic teaching is a cyclical process that is continued throughout the duration of student instruction. It involves planning, executing, and evaluating teaching hypotheses (Wixson, 1991). It is used to find the most effective match of learner characteristics and instructionally relevant variables. However, there is a recognition that because the difficulty of material and the demands of schooling change over time, the most appropriate combinations of instructional variables will change over time as well.

Since diagnostic teaching is an ongoing process, the diagnostician is most properly a skilled teacher rather than a diagnostic specialist who does not have continual contact with the student. The child's teacher is also in the best position to judge whether student performance or a particular instructional interchange is typical and of significance or merely an exception to the norm. The teacher's ability to note student habits and learning strategies, likes and dislikes, reactions to grouping arrangements, etc., provides the basis on which trial modifications in instruction can be made.

Diagnostic teaching requires the diagnostician to be familiar with a variety of different curricular approaches. For any given approach, the diagnostician must be able to determine where the student might encounter difficulty. This allows the teacher to provide instruction at an appropriate level of difficulty using curricula that require different student behaviors, capacities, and experiences. Howell and Kaplan (1980) demonstrate how basic skills can be analyzed for use in diagnostic teaching.

Diagnostic teaching also requires the diagnostician to be culturally competent (Baca & Valenzuela, 1994) and familiar with instructional variables that can be used differently in conjunction with various curricular approaches. Among these are engaged time, the immediacy and nature of performance feedback, grouping practices, and presentation and questioning techniques. For example, one exploratory combination within the diagnostic teaching process might be an increase in the engaged time a student spends being directly taught (instructional variables) phonics (curricular approach). If student learning did not meet expectations, one or more of the critical variables would be systematically altered.

Historically, the effects of different instructional combinations have been judged subjectively by the diagnostic teacher. The decision whether to continue instruction or to test another combination of variables was equally subjective. During the past two decades, there has been a growing sophistication in the use of student performance data to judge instructional effect more effectively. There has also been an increase in the sophistication of decision rules that can be used to guide the course of diagnostic teaching.

Procedures for the collection of student performance data are integral to most models of diagnostic teaching. These range from the use of special recording paper and elaborate techniques for performance analysis (White & Haring, 1980) to the use of checklists and behavioral tallies (Zigmond, Vallecorsa, & Silverman, 1983). Decision rules are usually presented within the context of a particular model but generally indicate what to do if student performance is deficient and how long instruction should continue before some systematic modification in instruction is made.

REFERENCES

Baca, L., & de Valenzuela, J. S. (1994). *Reconstructing the bilingual special education interface.* Washington, DC: National Clearinghouse for Bilingual Education.

Howell, K. W., & Kaplan, J. S. (1980). *Diagnosing basic skills.* Columbus, OH: Merrill.

Reisman, F. K. (1982). *A guide to the diagnostic teaching of arithmetic.* Columbus, OH: Merrill.

Reynolds, M. C., & Birch, J. W. (1977). *Teaching exceptional children in all America's schools.* Reston, VA: Council for Exceptional Children.

Walker, B. J. (1988). *Diagnostic teaching of reading; Techniques for instruction and assessment.* (ERIC Clearinghouse No. CS0103329)

White, O. R., & Haring, N. G. (1980). *Exceptional teaching.* Columbus, OH: Merrill.

Wixson, K. K. (1991). Diagnostic teaching. *Reading Teacher, 44*(6), 420–422.

Zigmond, N., Vallecorsa, A., & Silverman, R. (1983). *Assessment for instructional planning in special education.* Englewood Cliffs, NJ: Prentice Hall.

STEVEN A. CARLSON
Beaverton Schools, Beaverton, Oregon

DIAGNOSTIC PRESCRIPTIVE TEACHING
DIRECT INSTRUCTION
TEACHER EFFECTIVENESS

DIALYSIS AND SPECIAL EDUCATION

Dialysis, the process of flushing kidney wastes by artificial means in cases of acute or chronic renal failure, has been increasingly used with children during the last 35 years. Dialysis methodology is viewed as a drastic mode of treatment for children, necessitated in advanced cases of kidney disease prior to, or as the result of, failed transplantation (Czaczkes & De-Nour, 1979).

While individual differences make generalization difficult, Whitt (1984) indicates that the complex and time-consuming dialysis schedule places most children at educational and emotional risk, as the time spent in hemodialysis treatment interrupts the normal pace and progress of the child's schooling. Hobbs and Perrin (1985) found the result of this loss of school time and educational opportunity to be academic underachievement and missed and splintered basic skills. In addition, the disruption of normal school progress and success weakens children's emotional stability and their feelings of competence and control (Stapleton, 1983).

During periods of school attendance, the primary role of special education is to maintain the independence of the child in dialysis. This is best accomplished by providing resource assistance to allow that child to function effectively within the regular classroom whenever possible while remediating educational weaknesses and gaps (Kleinberg, 1982). As the school experience for the dialysis child represents one of the few opportunities for that child to be in control of the environment, to gain competence and skill, and to prepare for the future in a normalized setting, special education must be used to modify programs, instruction, and the learning environment to ensure optimal educational progress (Sirvis, 1989; Van Osdol, 1982).

Special education services are also required for those periods of time (each week) during which a child is undergoing hemodialysis. Children in such treatment report concerns with the boredom imposed by the length of the sessions and the anxiety associated with the process and its discomforts (Amonette, 1984). Special education must provide instructional materials and programs for children to be used during treatment to relieve anxiety and boredom and effective home and hospital instructors to apply them. Technological advances in computer and telecommunication strategies hold promise for upgrading the educational experience for the dialysis student during nonattendance periods.

REFERENCES

Amonette, L. (1984). *Kidney dialysis patients discover new hope through ABE Program.* Paper presented at the National Adult Education Conference, Louisville, KY.

Czaczkes, J. W., & De-Nour, A. K. (1979). *Chronic hemodialysis as a way of life.* New York: Brunner/Mazel.

Hobbs, N., & Perrin, J. M. (Eds.). (1985). *Issues in the care of children with chronic illness.* San Francisco: Jossey-Bass.

Kleinberg, S. (1982). *Educating the chronically ill child.* Baltimore: Aspen Systems.

Sirvis, B. (1989). *Students with specialized health care needs.* ERIC Clearinghouse on Handicapped and Gifted Children. Reston, VA: Council for Exceptional Children. (ERIC Digest No. 458)

Stapleton, S. (1983). Recognizing powerlessness: Causes and indicators in patients with chronic renal failure. In J. F. Miller (Ed.), *Coping with chronic illness: Overcoming powerlessness.* Philadelphia: Davis.

Van Osdol, W. R. (1982). *Introduction to exceptional children* (3rd ed.). Dubuque, IA: Brown.

Whitt, J. K. (1984). End stage renal disease. In M. G. Eisenberg, L. C. Sutkin, & M. A. Jansen (Eds.), *Chronic illness and disability through the life span: Effects on self and family.* New York: Springer.

RONALD S. LENKOWSKY
Hunter College, City University of New York

PHYSICAL DISABILITIES

DIANA v. STATE BOARD OF EDUCATION

Diana v. *State Board of Education* (1970) and *Guadalupe* v. *Tempe Elementary School District* (1972) were highly similar cases that were never actually brought to trial but that have nevertheless had a significant impact on special education assessment and placement procedures. In each case, civil rights organizations filed suit in federal courts on behalf of all bilingual students attending classes for the mildly mentally retarded (or the respective state's cognate designation). Both cases noted disproportionate representation of bilingual, Spanish-surnamed children in programs for the mentally retarded. Additionally, the plaintiffs in each case argued that intelligence tests administered in English to Spanish-speaking children were the principal reason for the overrepresentation. Other charges were made raising concerns about the quality of programs for the mentally retarded in both cases and violations of the equal protection clause of the Fourteenth Amendment to the U.S. Constitution, including lack of due process considerations. As Reschly (1979) has noted, in both cases the school districts involved were engaged in unsound, unprofessional assessment procedures and had developed much of their special education processes around what most in the field would consider bad professional practice.

Each case was resolved on the basis of similar consent decrees, agreements entered into by each party and then certified by the court to avoid further litigation. Issues regarding the quality of direct service were virtually ignored in the decrees, which centered on assessment and placement procedures. In *Diana,* for example, the consent decree certified by the court required assessment of each child's primary language competence; if the primary language was found to be other than English, tests used in the assessment had to be nonverbal, translated, or administered using an interpreter. The decree also required that unfair portions of English-language tests were to be deleted and more influence accorded to the results of nonverbal intelligence tests when placement decisions were being made.

Guadalupe, in the consent decree, mandated the same changes in testing practices as *Diana. Guadalupe* went on to add four additional statements:

1. IQ tests were not to be the exclusive or the primary basis for the diagnosis of Mild Mental Retardation.
2. Adaptive behavior in other than school settings would be assessed.
3. Due process procedures were to be developed and instituted before individual assessment or any movement toward diagnosis and placement could occur.
4. Special education would be provided to each child in the most normal setting or environment possible.

Since *Diana* and *Guadalupe* were settled by consent decrees, no judicial opinion is available and there are no findings to be reviewed and discussed. Neither case set legal precedent. Both were strongly influential, however, in subsequent legislation passed at the state and federal levels. Wording from the two decrees is now commonplace in many state and federal regulations governing the education of the handicapped.

REFERENCE

Reschly, D. J. (1979). Nonbiased assessment. In G. Phye & D. Reschly (Eds.), *School psychology: Perspectives and issues.* New York: Academic.

CECIL R. REYNOLDS
Texas A&M University

CONSENT DECREE
EQUAL PROTECTION
INDIVIDUALS WITH DISABILITIES EDUCATION
    IMPROVEMENT ACT OF 2004 (IDEIA)
LARRY P.
MARSHALL v. GEORGIA

DIAZEPAM

Diazepam (Valium) is a minor tranquilizer with relatively few side effects compared with other psychotropic medications. It is prescribed primarily with adult populations for symptoms of anxiety. Clinically, diazepam seems to be prescribed infrequently as a psychotropic, particularly as an antianxiety drug in children.

While diazepam is used only infrequently as a psychotropic agent in pediatric populations, it is often used as an adjunct in the treatment of seizure disorders. When administered intravenously in repeated dosages as deemed necessary, diazepam has been found to be effective in the initial management of uncontrolled, continuous seizures, or status epilepticus (Behrman, Vaughn, Victor, & Nelson, 1983). In general, diazepam is not used in the long-term management of seizure disorders because of the likelihood of the development of tolerance to the drug. Tolerance often develops very rapidly, sometimes as quickly as 3 to 14 days after initiation of therapy (Behrman et al., 1983). Increasing the dosage when the tolerance develops may help control the seizures, but, frequently, side effects such as drowsiness, ataxia, and slurred speech make the increased dosage intolerable. Occasionally, diazepam may be indicated therapeutically in the treatment of petit mal seizures, refractory to Zarontin and other agents, and in combination with phenobarbital and phenytoin in the treatment of seizures associated with central nervous system disease (Behrman et al., 1983).

Diazepam has been used to some extent in the treatment of sleep disturbances in children. It should be noted that insomnia and night waking, although common in childhood, are typically transitory. The practitioner must carefully rule out other dysfunctions such as phobic and separation disorders, as well as psychosocial stressors that may result in sleep disturbances. Further, psychostimulant medications used during the day for the treatment of hyperactivity may also cause sleep disturbances (Brown & Borden, 1989). However, if the etiology of the sleep disturbance is an identifiable stressor that cannot be alleviated, the short-term use of diazepam at low dosages, administered in a single dose at bedtime, may be a temporary treatment for both the child and the parent (Shaffer & Ambrosini, 1985). Diazepam may also be particularly effective for those sleep disturbances termed parasomnias; they include nightmares, sleep terrors, and sleepwalking. Because these disorders typically dissipate with age, the need for continued medication must be reassessed frequently.

The side effects attributed to diazepam are often further elaborations of the desired therapeutic effects. Those of primary concern include confusion, disinhibition, incoordination, drowsiness, and depression (Jaffe & Magnuson, 1985; Konopasek, 2004; Rapoport, Mikkelsen, & Werry, 1978). Both physiological and psychological dependence may also develop as a function of prolonged usage (Rapoport et al., 1978). Following prolonged usage, diazepam should be discontinued slowly with decreasing dosages because seizures may occur in response to abrupt withdrawal.

REFERENCES

Behrman, R. E., Vaughn, V. C., Victor, B., & Nelson, W. E. (1983). Convulsive disorders. In R. Behrman & V. Vaughn (Eds.), *Nelson textbook of pediatrics* (pp. 1531–1545). Philadelphia: Saunders.

Brown, R. T., & Borden, K. A. (1989). Neuropsychological effects of stimulant medication on children's learning and behavior. In C. R. Reynolds (Ed.), *Child neuropsychology: Techniques of diagnosis and treatment*. New York: Plenum.

Jaffe, S., & Magnuson, J. V. (1985). Anxiety disorders. In J. Wiener (Ed.), *Diagnosis and psychopharmacology of childhood and adolescent disorders* (pp. 199–214). New York: Wiley.

Konopasek, D. E. (2004). *Medication factsheets.* Longmont, CO: Sopris West.

Rapoport, J. L., Mikkelsen, E. J., & Werry, J. S. (1978). Antimanic, antianxiety, hallucinogenic, and miscellaneous drugs. In J. Werry (Ed.), *Pediatric psychopharmacology* (pp. 316–355). New York: Brunner/Mazel.

Shaffer, D., & Ambrosini, P. J. (1985). Enuresis and sleep disorders. In J. Wiener (Ed.), *Diagnosis and psychopharmacology of childhood and adolescent disorders* (pp. 305–331). New York: Wiley.

Yaffe, S. J., & Danish, M. (1977). The classification and pharmacology of psychoactive drugs in childhood and adolescence. In J. Wiener (Ed.), *Psychopharmacology in childhood and adolescence* (pp. 41–57). New York: Basic Books.

RONALD T. BROWN
SANDRA B. SEXSON
Emory University School of Medicine

ANTICONVULSANTS
PHENOBARBITAL
TRANQUILIZERS
ZARONTIN

DICHOTIC LISTENING

Dichotic listening is an auditory task used in clinical practice and research. The paradigms use simultaneous presentation of differing auditory stimuli to both ears. It has been used in the assessment of selective attention as well as for determination of cerebral hemisphere specialization of language. In the free-recall consonant-vowel (CV) syllable paradigm, for example, presentation to the right ear might be /ba/ simultaneous with presentation to the left ear of /ta/. The child is asked to repeat what he or she hears (e.g., Cohen, Riccio, & Hynd, 1999). Based on the accuracy of free recall for right and left ear presentations, a dominant ear or "ear advantage" is determined. To control for potential differences in absolute hearing between left and right ears, some dichotic listening tasks, such as the Staggered Spondaic Word test (SSW; Katz, 1962), require pure tone testing first, and then presentation of the auditory stimulus at a set decibel level above hearing level for each ear. In contrast to the CV paradigm, the SSW presents a single word to one ear, then different words simultaneously to each ear, and then a single word to the second ear. Thus, the SSW yields right only, competing, and left only conditions for evaluation of ear advantage.

Regardless of the specific task, results of dichotic listening tasks are presumed to provide information on hemispheric lateralization of language (Hugdahl, Carlsson, Uvebrant, & Lundervold, 1997; Kimura, 1961). In the normal population, the typical person demonstrates a right ear advantage on dichotic listening tasks, consistent with left hemisphere specialization for language. In clinical populations, particularly those with involvement of the central auditory system, the laterality ratio or extent of ear advantage is not as great, or the population may evidence a left ear advantage. For example, Cohen et al. (1999) found that children with speech-language impairments demonstrated one of three patterns: (1) weak right ear advantage; (2) left ear advantage or right ear deficiency; or (3) bilateral deficits. Similarly, in comparing children with expected reading levels to those with dyslexia, Asbjornsen, Helland, Obrzut, and Boliek (2003) found that children with dyslexia demonstrated lower laterality indexes (i.e., less pronounced right ear advantage) than would be expected.

At the same time, it is important to remember that dichotic listening tasks also involve attentional processes and memory; performance is not solely determined by language. For this reason, attentional priming has been investigated to determine effects of attention on CV tasks (e.g., Asbjornsen & Bryden, 1998; Obrzut, Horgesheimer, & Boliek, 1999; Riccio, Hynd, Cohen, & Molt, 1996; Riccio, Cohen, Garrison, & Smith, 2005). Additional research is needed before it is possible to dissociate attention, memory, and language components of the various dichotic listening tasks. Until then, caution should be used when making inferences related to cerebral lateralization or localization of function using dichotic listening tasks. Further, if there is no control for potential pure tone differences between right and left ear, additional caution is needed in determining ear advantage for language (or attention or memory).

REFERENCES

Asbjornsen, A. E., & Bryden, M. P. (1998). Auditory attentional shifts in reading-disabled students: Quantification of attentional effectiveness by the Attentional Shift Index. *Neuropsychologia, 36,* 143–148.

Asbjornsen, A. E., Helland, T., Obrzut, J. E., & Boliek, C. A. (2003). The role of dichotic listening performance and tasks of executive functions in reading impairment: A discriminant function analysis. *Child Neuropsychology, 9,* 277–288.

Cohen, M. J., Riccio, C. A., & Hynd, G. W. (1999). Children with specific language impairment: Quantitative and qualitative analysis of dichotic listening performance. *Developmental Neuropsychology, 16,* 243–252.

Hugdahl, K., Carlsson, G., Uvebrant, P., & Lundervold, A. J. (1997). Dichotic listening performance and intracarotid injections of amobarbital in children and adolescents: Preoperative and postoperative comparisons. *Archives of Neurology, 54,* 1494–1500.

Katz, J. (1962). The use of staggered spondaic words for assessing the integrity of the central auditory nervous system. *Journal of Auditory Research, 2,* 237–337.

Kimura, D. (1961). Cerebral dominance and the perception of verbal stimuli. *Canadian Journal of Psychology, 15,* 166–171.

Obrzut, J. E., Horgesheimer, J., & Boliek, C. A. (1999). A "threshold effect" of selective attention on the dichotic REA with children. *Developmental Neuropsychology, 16,* 127–137.

Riccio, C. A., Cohen, M. J., Garrison, T., & Smith, B. (2005). Auditory processing measures: correlation with neuropsychological measures of attention, memory, and behavior. *Child Neuropsychology, 11,* 363–372.

Riccio, C. A., Cohen, M. J., Hynd, G. W., & Molt, L. (1996). The staggered spondaic word test: Performance of children with attention deficit hyperactivity disorder. *American Journal of Audiology, 5,* 55–62.

CYNTHIA A. RICCIO
Texas A&M University

AUDITORY PROCESSING
LANGUAGE DISORDERS
READING DISORDERS

DICTIONARY OF OCCUPATIONAL TITLES

The *Dictionary of Occupational Titles* (DOT) is prepared and published by the U.S. Department of Labor, Employment and Training Administration. It provides comprehensive occupational information to serve the labor market in job placement, employment counseling, and guidance. Concise standardized definitions (12,741) are alphabetized by title with coding arrangements for occupational classifications. Blocks of jobs are assigned to one of 550 occupational groups using 5- or 6-digit code. Skilled, semiskilled, or unskilled categories are specified. The format for each definition is occupational code number; occupational title; industry des-

ignation; alternate title (if any); body of the definitional lead statement; task element statement; undefined related title (if any).

Consumers may reproduce any part of this public document without special permission from the federal government. Source credit is requested but not required. The DOT has 1,404 pages. A computerized version of the DOT is available and provides the benefit of a searchable database.

REFERENCE

U.S. Department of Labor, Employment, and Training Administration. (1996). *Dictionary of occupational titles* (4th ed.). Washington, DC: Author.

C. MILDRED TASHMAN
College of St. Rose

DIFFERENTIAL ABILITIES SCALES

The Differential Abilities Scales (DAS; Elliott, 1990) is an individually administered battery of cognitive and achievement tests designed to be administered to children and adolescents between the ages of 2 years, 6 months through 17 years, 11 months. The British Ability Scales (BAS; Elliott, 1979) was published in Great Britain and was the forerunner to the DAS. In 1984, Colin Elliott began development of the DAS, an American version of the BAS.

The DAS cognitive battery consists of 17 subtests that divide into three levels: Preschool Level (ages 2:6 to 3:5), Upper Preschool Level (3:6 to 5:11), and School-Aged Level (ages 6:0 to 7:11). Depending on the child's age, the core battery consists of four to six subtests. The cognitive battery yields a composite score or General Conceptual Ability score (GCA), in addition to lower-level composite scores, called Cluster scores. For preschool-aged children, two Cluster scores, Verbal Ability and Nonverbal Ability, are yielded from 4 to 6 subtests. For school-aged children, three Cluster scores, Verbal Ability, Nonverbal Reasoning Ability and Spatial Ability, are yielded from 6 subtests. The composite scores are comprised of "core" subtests, only those subtests with relatively high *g* loadings. There are also 2 to 5 "diagnostic" subtests for each level, which measure specific abilities that are less related to *g*, such as speed of information processing and short-term memory; however, the diagnostic subtests do not contribute to the composites. The cognitive battery takes approximately 25 to 65 minutes to administer. The brief school achievement battery consists of 3 subtests that measure basic skills of spelling, arithmetic, and word reading. It is administered only to school-aged children and takes approximately 15 to 25 minutes to administer.

There are some key differences between the DAS and other widely used cognitive batteries such as the Wechsler tests, Kaufman tests, and Stanford-Binet. First, in the DAS, an estimate of the child's ability is based on performance on a set of targeted items, or item set. The DAS does not assume that the child would pass all items below the item set or fail all items above the item set. Thus, children may take different sets of items ranging in difficulty. Second, administration differs in that there is not the use of traditional basal and ceiling rules (e.g., five consecutive failures for ceiling). Rather, if a child passes more than two items and fails more than two items in the item set, the item set would be considered an accurate set of items for the child and the test would be discontinued. A third difference in the DAS concerns scoring. Raw scores are converted to ability scores, which take into account both the difficulty of the items and the number of items answered correctly. However, ability scores are not norm-referenced. Therefore, ability scores for cognitive subtests must then be converted to T-scores ($M = 50$, $SD = 10$) in order to make comparisons with other children or between subtests. T-scores are then summed and converted to a standard score ($M = 100$, $SD = 15$) for both cluster scores and the GCA. Achievement tests yield raw and ability scores, but are directly converted to standard scores (no T-scores). Percentiles and age equivalents are also available for all subtests and composite scores.

The DAS was standardized on a sample of 3,475 children and adolescents. There were 175 children for each age group from 2:6 to 4:11, and 200 children per group for ages 5:00 to 17:11. There were approximately equal distributions of girls and boys per group. Data from the 1988 U.S. Census Bureau was used to stratify the sample on variables including age, sex, race/ethnicity, parent education, geographic location, and (for preschool children) enrollment in preschool. *The Differential Ability Scales Introductory and Technical Handbook* (Elliott, 1990b) contains specific characteristics of the sample.

Reliability and validity data appear to be good and are described in detail in two full chapters of the DAS handbook. Additional studies not included in the handbook have shown high correlations between the DAS and WISC-III, with the highest correlations between DAS GCA and WISC-III FSIQ, DAS Verbal Composite and WISC-III VIQ, DAS Spatial Composite and WISC-III PIQ (correlations ranging from .82 to .92; Wechsler, 1991).

The DAS was designed as a classification and diagnostic tool. For classification purposes, it is intended to provide a single overall score of conceptual and reasoning abilities, in combination with other data, to determine if a child falls into a category such as learning disabled, mentally retarded, or gifted. For diagnostic purposes, the child's profile of cognitive strengths and weaknesses should be examined. The DAS has several strengths that are noteworthy: its division of fluid ability into two factors, nonverbal reasoning and spatial ability; its measurement of nonverbal reasoning without using time limits or requiring visual-motor coordination; and its use of subtests that load high on g for the overall

GCA score. The most notable limitations of the DAS relate to the difficult scoring and conversion system. Five subtests have open-ended responses requiring some judgment by the examiner. Additionally, converting cognitive subtest scores from a raw score to an ability score to a T-score to a standard score is tedious for examiners. The utility of the ability score, which uses an arbitrary numbering system and does not allow for norm-referenced comparisons, does not appear to warrant the "extra" step involved in converting the raw score to its final norm-referenced score.

The DAS is currently being revised.

REFERENCES

Elliott, C. D., Murray, D. J., & Pearson, L. S. (1979). *British Ability Scales.* Windsor, England: National Foundation for Educational Research.

Elliott, C. D. (1990a). *DAS: Administration and scoring manual.* San Antonio, TX: Psychological Corporation.

Elliott, C. D. (1990b). *Differential Ability Scales: Introductory and technical handbook.* San Antonio, TX: Psychological Corporation.

Wechsler, D. (1991). *Manual for the Wechsler Intelligence Scale for Children-Third Edition (WISC-III).* San Antonio, TX: Psychological Corporation.

DEBRA Y. BROADBOOKS
*California School of
Professional Psychology*

RONALD V. SCHMELZER
Eastern Kentucky University

DIFFUSION TENSOR IMAGING

There have been a number of advances in magnetic resonance imaging facilitating access to new opportunities for gathering functional information about the brain. The development of Diffusion Tensor Imaging (DTI) has enabled researchers to go beyond anatomical imaging and study tissue structure at a microscopic level in vivo. DTI was first introduced in the mid 1980s by Le Bihan et al. (1986). DTI is a method of magnetic resonance imaging that measures water diffusion across several tissue axes. With DTI, diffusion anisotropy effects can be fully characterized and exploited providing better details on tissue microstructure (Basser, Mattiello, & Le Bihan, 1994). This is useful in studying the brain because water displacements are not the same throughout the brain. White-matter displacements are smaller or often more restricted than and perpendicular to myelinated fibers as they create physical boundaries that slow the diffusion of water molecules. DTI measures the movement of water in the brain, detecting areas where the normal flow of water is disrupted. A disrupted flow of water indicates the possibility of an underlying abnormality.

One of the most useful applications of DTI has included an understanding of brain ischemia (Warach, 1992). Currently, DTI is useful in the study and diagnosis of white-matter diseases including traumatic brain injuries or neurological insults such as strokes and even epilepsy. DTI may not only be useful in studying white-matter diseases and other neural abnormalities, but it could be used to assess brain maturation in children, newborns, or premature infants (Le Bihan et al., 2001). Increasing research has placed a focus on studying neuronal connectivity (Le Bihan et al., 2001). An important application of DTI is fiber tracking, which allows elucidation of white-matter tracts. DTI is the only noninvasive approach to track brain white-matter fibers. This allows for visualization of various anatomic connections between different parts of the brain on an individual basis. When used in collaboration with fMRI, information about white-matter tracts reveals important information about neurocognitive networks, and provides a quick way to improve our understanding of brain function. Future research will concentrate on improving the accuracy and robustness of the technique, as well as enhanced visualization of the white fiber tracts in three dimensions. Advances in this imaging technique will continue to provide useful information to scientists in better understanding brain function and improving the accuracy and ability to improve the lives of patients.

REFERENCES

Basser, P. J., Mattiello J., & Le Bihan D. (1994). Estimation of the effective self-diffusion tensor from the NMR spin echo. *Journal of Magnetic Resonance Imaging, 103,* 247–254.

Le Bihan, D., Breton, E., Lallemand, D., et al. (1986). MR Imaging of intravoxel incoherent motions: Applications to diffusion and perfusion in neurological disorders. *Radiology, 161,* 401–407.

Le Bihan, D., et al. (2001). Diffusion Tensor Imaging: Concepts and applications. *Journal of Magnetic Resonance Imaging, 13,* 534–546.

Warach, S., Chien, D., Li, W., Ronthal, M., & Edelman, R. R. (1992). Fast magnetic resonance diffusion-weighted imaging of acute human stroke. *Neurology, 42,* 1717–1723.

ADAM J. SCHWEBACH
University of Utah

BIOFEEDBACK
MAGNETIC RESONANCE IMAGING
SPECT

DIGEORGE SYNDROME

See VELO-CARDIO-FACIAL SYNDROME (SHPRINTZEN SYNDROME).

DILANTIN

Dilantin is an antiepileptic drug that can be useful in the treatment of seizure disorders. Generically, it is known as phenytoin. It was introduced in 1938 by Merritt and Putnam, who discovered its anticonvulsant activity in animals. It has proven remarkably effective in treating both partial seizures and generalized tonic-clonic seizure activity. Dilantin appears to work primarily in the motor cortex of the brain; it acts to inhibit the spread of seizure activity by preventing the extension of seizure activity from abnormally discharging neurons to surrounding cells (Mosby, 1997). It is thought that Dilantin tends to stabilize the threshold of neurons against the hyperexcitability caused by excessive stimulation or environmental changes that can lead to seizures. Additionally, Dilantin appears to reduce brain stem center activity responsible for the tonic phase of tonic clonic (grand mal) seizures.

Some minor toxic symptoms such as gastric discomfort and nausea are frequent at the onset of Dilantin therapy. These tend to disappear rapidly. In children, a common effect of chronic use is gingival hyperplasia, which may cause bleeding gums. This condition generally can be prevented by good oral hygiene. Hirsutism occurs frequently, and may be aesthetically distressing, especially in girls. Toxic reactions to Dilantin include blurring of vision or ataxia. The onset of pruritus (severe itching), rash, or fever is an indication for immediate drug withdrawal, as liver damage or bone marrow suppression may occur, as may a syndrome resembling systemic lupus. However, drug withdrawal should always be done on physician's orders. Abrupt withdrawal of Dilantin may precipitate status epilepticus (Mosby, 1997).

REFERENCES

Goldensohn, E. S., Glaser, G. H., & Goldberg, M. A. (1984). Epilepsy. In L. P. Rowland (Ed.), *Merritt's textbook of neurology* (7th ed., pp. 629–650). Philadelphia: Lea & Febiger.

Mosby's GenRx. (1997). *Phenytoin Sodium.* Rx List Monographs. Linn, MO: Mosby.

RICHARD A. BERG
*West Virginia University
Medical Center, Charleston
Division*

ANTICONVULSANTS
EPILEPSY

DIPLEGIA

Diplegia is a topographic term used to describe a movement disorder predominantly affecting the lower extremities, with only mild involvement of the upper extremities. The term diplegia frequently is used as a description of a kind of cerebral palsy in which the arms are less involved than in a quadriplegia and more involved than in a paraplegia (McCloskey, 2003). The term quadriplegia indicates both arms and both legs are involved to a similar degree, and the term paraplegia denotes involvement of both legs only.

Clinical practice suggests the term diplegia is somewhat misleading, as the primary emphasis truly is on the movement disorder of the lower extremities; however, the upper extremities show so little involvement that a casual observer may not detect deficits that could impair function seriously. Often these deficits are sensory-motor-vestibular in nature and interfere with acquisition of fine motor skills such as dressing and handwriting.

The etiology of diplegia may be developmental delay, anoxia, trauma, jaundice, neonatal seizures, reflex suppression, or other factors that suggest the possibility of certain progressive biochemical disorders or spinocerebellar degenerative diseases. Differential diagnosis by a skilled pediatric neurologist, with ongoing follow-up by appropriate therapists, is essential to provide appropriate medical and educational intervention for children with diplegia.

REFERENCES

Berkow, R. (Ed.). (1982). *The Merck manual of diagnosis and therapy* (14th ed.). Rahway, NJ: Merck, Sharp & Dohme.

McCloskey, D. (2003). Diplegia. In E. Fletcher-Janzen & C. R. Reynolds (Eds.), *Childhood disorders diagnostic desk reference* (pp. 183–184). New York: Wiley.

RACHAEL J. STEVENSON
Bedford, Ohio

CHOREA
DYSKINESIA
NEUROPSYCHOLOGY

DIPLOPIA

The basis for understanding diplopia (double vision) requires an appreciation of the physiologic mechanisms of binocularity within the visual cortex (Records, 1979). Evidence suggests there are four classes of cortical neuronal receptive fields for common visual direction—monocular left eye, monocular right eye, binocular corresponding, and binocular disparate. Presumably, each neuron derives stimulation from a specific visual direction; the visual direction is unambiguous for all classes except binocular disparate, where it falls between the visual directions of the two monocular receptive fields for that neuron. Consider stimuli to two eyes, presented on corresponding retinal points and moved gradually away in disparity; in time, fusion breaks

and diplopia is perceived. When stimuli are presented to corresponding points only, as with a point of light, binocular corresponding neurons and monocular right and left neurons are stimulated. All three types have the same visual direction label and there is no conflict, resulting in single vision. When a small disparity is introduced, some binocular disparate neurons are stimulated and binocular corresponding neurons should cease responding. However, the monocular right and left neurons each are stimulated for a visual direction slightly to either side of the mean visual direction for binocular disparate neurons. These are integrated with a third set of responses from the binocular disparate neuron; therefore there should be a range of small disparities for which binocular response gives a unitary perception of a fused stimulus. In essence, it is this disparity that permits stereopsis, a specialized form of depth perception.

Diplopia may be physiologic or pathologic (McCloskey, 2003; Von Noorden, 1985). Physiologic diplopia is normal and results from stimulation and appreciation of objects simultaneously with the area of disparities that may be fused within the cortex and those outside. Object points in visual space stimulating corresponding retinal elements may be constructed to form a plane known as horopter. Both in front of and behind this plane is Panum's fusional space, an area in space that can be integrated cortically without perceiving objects as double. Physiologic diplopia occurs outside this space, and may be appreciated by observing an object in the distance and holding a pencil near. While attending to the distant object, the pencil will be seen as double. Most of the time, physiologic diplopia is cortically suppressed and not appreciated. Its clinical significance is twofold. Occasionally, schoolchildren become aware of and concerned about physiologic diplopia; reassurance is warranted. Second, diplopia may be useful from a diagnostic and therapeutic perspective in the presence of strabismus.

Pathological diplopia may be characterized as either monocular or binocular. Monocular diplopia results from defects in the refractive media or retinal pathology. Examples are high astigmatic refractive error, cataract, ectopic lens position, or macular edema. If diplopia is binocular, image positions may be separated horizontally, vertically, or obliquely; may vary with different directions of gaze and head position; and may be constant or variable.

Extraocular muscle paresis in adults almost always yields diplopia. However, patients with strabismus from early life rarely perceive diplopia. A series of adaptive mechanisms in infancy and childhood avoid this symptom: abnormal head position, binocular rivalry, suppression, and abnormal retinal correspondence. In the presence of a weak extraocular muscle, moving the head to a position that avoids the field of action of the paretic muscle often will prevent diplopia; therefore, an abnormal head position may be an indicator of extraocular muscle paresis. Binocular rivalry is a function that can be present normally or abnormally. When viewing with one eye through a monocular telescope or microscope, it often is unnecessary to close the other eye to avoid confusion of images. This cortical phenomenon, known as retinal rivalry, is a normal adaptation to avoid diplopia. In the presence of strabismus, particularly in a strabismic circumstance where there is alternation of fixation from one eye to the other, retinal rivalry is apparently the operant mechanism. In a constant strabismic circumstance, one eye assumes fixation to the exclusion of the other, and the image from the deviating eye is suppressed (McCloskey, 2003). Suppression is a mechanism, largely limited to infancy and youth, one consequence of which is decreased vision (amblyopia). Thus, amblyopia develops and is treatable in infancy and early childhood; however, once maturation of the system is complete (about age 9 years), amblyopia is neither a threat nor effectively treated.

Where strabismus is of early onset and longstanding duration, the cortical adaptation of abnormal retinal correspondence may ensue. In this instance, noncorresponding retinal points are cortically integrated, presumably to avoid diplopia. Thus diplopia may be monocular or binocular, physiologic or pathologic (McCloskey, 2003). The presence of diplopia may be detrimental to school performance.

REFERENCES

McCloskey, D. (2003). Diplopia. In E. Fletcher-Janzen & C. R. Reynolds (Eds.), *Childhood disorders diagnostic desk reference* (pp. 184–185). New York: Wiley.

Records, R. E. (1979). *Physiology of the human eye and visual system.* Hagerstown, MD: Harper & Row.

Von Noorden, G. K. (1985). *Binocular vision and ocular motility.* St. Louis, MO: Mosby.

GEORGE R. BEAUCHAMP
Cleveland Clinic Foundation

DIRECT INSTRUCTION

The term direct instruction arose from two complementary lines of research and development. Rosenshine (1976) introduced the term into the mainstream of educational research. His synthesis of many classroom observation studies indicated that students consistently demonstrate higher reading achievement scores when their teachers do the following:

1. Devote substantial time to active instruction
2. Break complex skills and concepts into small, easy-to-understand steps and systematically teach in a step-by-step fashion
3. Ensure that all students operate at a high rate of success

4. Provide immediate feedback to students about the accuracy of their work
5. Conduct much of the instruction in small groups to allow for frequent student-teacher interactions

The other source of direct instruction derives from the work of curriculum developers rather than researchers. In the early 1960s in Israel, Smilarsky taught preschoolers from peasant immigrant families from surrounding Arab nations. The method, called direct promotion, taught in a direct manner toward specific goals. In the mid-1960s Bereiter and Engelmann (1966) formed an academically oriented preschool based on direct-instruction principles. In the late 1960s, Engelmann articulated the concept of direct instruction in the form of specific curricular materials and in a comprehensive model for teaching low-performing students. Direct instruction was incorporated as part of the acronym for DISTAR (Direct Instruction System for Teaching and Remediation) and as part of the title of the direct instruction model that took part in the U.S. Office of Education Follow Through Project. The key to direct instruction, as envisioned by Engelmann and his colleagues, is a comprehensive intervention, addressing teacher expectations for student learning, the curriculum, teaching skills, time spent engaged in academic activities, administrative support, and parental involvement.

At the heart of the direct instruction intervention was the conviction that student failure could be prevented or at least remedied, regardless of the label placed on the child. The empirical basis for this conviction is found in a number of sources, ranging from an annotated bibliography of 188 articles and books on direct instruction in special education (Fabre, 1983) to an article reviewing 20 direct instruction studies in special education in Australia (Maggs & Maggs, 1979). Other sources include a review of special education studies in the United States (Gersten, 1985) and an overview of articles on direct instruction (Carnine, 1983). These various reports frequently emphasize the academic gains of students in direct instruction (ABT Associates, 1977).

The national evaluation of the Follow Through (FT) Project yielded another finding that surprised many educators:

> The performance of FT children in direct instruction sites on the affective measures is an unexpected result. The direct instruction model does not explicitly emphasize affective outcomes of instruction, but the sponsor has asserted that they will be the consequence of effective teaching. Critics of the model have predicted that the emphasis on tightly controlled instruction might discourage children from freely expressing themselves, and thus inhibit the development of self-esteem and other affective skills. In fact, this is not the case. (ABT Associates, 1977, p. 73)

These outcomes reflect the basic philosophy of direct instruction: student failures are school failures. School failures are not remedied by showing teachers research findings in an attempt to increase teacher expectations; however, teachers need well-designed curricular materials, substantial instructional time to teach students, and teaching techniques for motivating and helping students who are making numerous mistakes.

Curricular materials guide teachers in explaining, reviewing, and giving practice on academic content. Direct instruction materials are designed in part to minimize student confusions. In a simple example, subtracting 3,942 from 6,000 often confuses students as they try to rename in one column at a time. In direct instruction, students rewrite 600 tens as 599 tens and 1 ten in a single step:

$$
\begin{array}{r}
599{+}1 \\
6{,}000 \\
-3{,}942.
\end{array}
$$

Recognizing that 600 = 599 + 1 is much less confusing than crossing out successive zeroes and rewriting the value represented by each renamed zero.

Direct instruction materials also teach students strategies that allow them to handle a wide range of tasks. In intermediate spelling, students learn a few rules and 655 word roots; they then can spell over 10,000 words. The instructional design principles are articulated in several books: *Theory of Instruction* (Engelmann & Carnine, 1982); *Direct Instruction Reading* (Carnine & Silbert, 1979); *Direct Instruction Mathematics* (Silbert, Carnine, & Stein, 1981); and *Applied Psychology for Teachers: A Behavioral Cognitive Approach* (Becker, 1986).

Direct instruction teaching techniques are designed to maximize the quality and amount of academic engaged time. The amount of time is increased by showing teachers how to schedule instructional time more effectively and how to keep students attending by using reinforcement, rapid pacing, challenges, etc. The quality of learning is particularly influenced by how teachers react to student errors. For memorization errors, teachers give the answers and periodically review the missed questions. For errors reflecting inappropriate strategy selection or application, the teacher asks questions based on prior instruction to guide the student in using the strategy to arrive at an appropriate answer.

Familiarity with direct instruction curriculas and teaching techniques requires intensive staff development. Staff development occurs primarily in individual teachers' classrooms. A supervisor observes and sets priorities for training on teaching techniques. A supervisor might model a correction procedure with a teacher's students one day, observe the teacher applying the procedure immediately, and then return a few days later to see whether the teacher is comfortable with the procedure. If the teacher has mastered the correction procedure, the supervisor will commence training in the next teaching technique on the priority list.

Supervision of direct instruction can be difficult. Supervisors must have tact as well as skill in diagnosing teaching deficiencies, identifying and prioritizing remedies, modeling and prompting remedies, and managing their time efficiently in order to spend sufficient time making classroom observations.

Although some sources point to the success (broadranged) of direct instruction (Adams & Siegfried, 1996; White, 2005), others have suggested that there are no significant differences between direct instruction and regular classroom reading outcomes (Mosley, 1997). Findings suggest that students have to be taught by direct instruction for 2 years or more before effects are noted (Mosley, 1997).

On the other hand, one recent study about Direct Instruction conducted in Milwaukee Public Schools (MPS; White, 2005) examined third- through fifth-grade students' progress and found:

- Despite students being exposed to DI being even lower income, on average, than other MPS low-income students, those individuals with long-term exposure to DI (defined as 5 years) do better, on average, than all low-income MPS students. In fourth grade, students with 5 years of DI had higher average scores, four points in reading and three points in math, than non-DI students and eight points in reading and seven points in math among relatively comparable students with 1 or 2 years of DI. These differences reflect several months of learning.

- Among low-income students tracked between third and fourth grades 2002–03 to 2003–04, those with 5 years of DI increased their math scores by 6.6 percent whereas nonlow-income students increased their scores by 4.7 percent. This difference is statistically significant and is evidence of substantial progress.

- Among students moving from fourth to fifth grade on reading those same years, low-income students with 5 years of DI gained 4.2 percent on their test scores versus 3.9 percent for nonlow-income. The differences are not statistically significant. But it is significant in the sense that these are very different sets of students making about the same academic progress.

- Those low-income, fourth-grade, regular education (no special education) students with 5 years of DI averaged 633 in reading versus 625 for all low-income students, again a substantial difference, especially when one knows the DI students are lower income and more likely to have limited English proficiency.

- Among fifth graders, those with 5 years of DI averaged 660 on reading (and 630 on math) compared to all low-income fifth graders who averaged 646 on reading (626 on math). The difference in reading is about equivalent to 1/2 year of progress, and the 660 is again earned by a lower-income population, suggesting an even greater achievement.

- These and other higher scores and gains by those with long-term DI experience developed despite these students having more challenges to success and attending schools that usually did not have the resources to fully implement DI.

- In the few schools that did completely implement DI, defined as DI in every grade and continuous professional development for the staff, students did even better, on average. Among low-income students, with a mix of regular and special education, students scored an average of 654 on reading and 647 on math versus other low-income students who averaged 648 in reading and 622 on math. These differences suggest that full implementation leads to even greater academic gains. (pp. 1–2)

These data are impressive when considering the special needs of low-income children and the pressures of accountability induced by current legislation.

REFERENCES

ABT Associates. (1977). *Education as experimentation: A planned variation model* (Vol. 4). Cambridge, MA: Authors.

Adams, G. L., & Siegfried, L. (1996). *Research on direct instruction: 25 years beyond DISTAR.* Seattle, WA: Educational Achievement Systems.

Becker, W. C. (1986). *Applied psychology for families.* Chicago: Science Research Associates.

Bereiter, C., & Engelmann, S. (1966). *Teaching disadvantaged children in the preschool.* Englewood Cliffs, NJ: Prentice Hall.

Carnine, D. W., & Silbert, J. (1979). *Direct instruction reading.* Columbus, OH: Merrill.

Carnine, D. (1983). Direct instruction: In search of instructional solutions for educational problems. In D. Carnine, D. Elkind, D. Melchenbaum, R. Lisieben, & F. Smith (Eds.), *Interdisciplinary voices in learning disabilities and remedial education* (pp. 1–66). Austin, TX: PRO-ED.

Engelmann, S., & Carnine, D. W. (1982). *Theory of instruction.* New York: Irvington.

Fabre, T. (1983). *The application of direct instruction in special education: An annotated bibliography.* University of Oregon.

Gersten, R. (1985). Direct instruction with special education students: A review of evaluation research. *Journal of Special Education, 19,* 42–58.

Maggs, A., & Maggs, R. K. (1979). Direct instruction research in Australia. *Journal of Special Education Technology, 81*(3), 26–34.

Mosley, A. M. (1997). *The effectiveness of direct instruction on reading achievement.* (ERIC Clearinghouse No. CS012664)

Rosenshine, B. (1976). Classroom instruction. In N. L. Gage (Ed.), *Psychology of teaching. The 77th yearbook of the National Society for the Study of Education.* Chicago: National Society for the Study of Education.

Silbert, J., Carnine, D. W., & Stein, M. (1981). *Direct instruction mathematics.* Columbus, OH: Merrill.

White, S. (2005). *The benefits from phonics and direct instruction. Wisconsin Policy Research Institute, Inc.* Retrieved January 21, 2006, from http://www.wpri.org

Douglas Carnine
University of Oregon
First edition

Elaine Fletcher-Janzen
*University of Colorado at
Colorado Springs*
Second edition

DISTAR
READING DISORDERS
READING REMEDIATION
RESPONSE TO INTERVENTION

DISABILITY

The term disability is derived from the Latin prefix *dis-,* meaning negation, separation, lack of, or opposite of; and the Latin *habilitas,* meaning fitness, and *habere,* indicating to have or to be easily handled. Disability today indicates the lack of power or ability to do something. It is usually regarded as a negative attribute. The prefix contributes to our English word some of the connotations of its association with Dis, the god of the underworld in Roman mythology with whom the Greeks identified Pluto, and with Hades and the realm of the dead.

Some writers distinguished disability from impairment and handicap. Wright (1960) viewed a disability as mainly a medical condition; however, she saw a handicap reflecting the demands placed on an individual in a particular situation. An individual may indeed have a disability but may not have a handicap except in certain situations. Wright's elaboration on the significance of physical disability is essential reading for persons interested in a psychological perspective of body physique.

Stevens (1962) formulated a taxonomy for special education in which he distinguished among disability, impairment, and handicap. Stevens regarded disability as a loss of function, impairment as tissue damage or disease, and handicap as "the burden which is imposed on the learner when confronted with educational situations which cannot be resolved by reason of body dysfunction or impairment" (p. 65). While the progression may be from tissue damage to loss of function to certain situational difficulties, Stevens argued that the extent or severity of any disability cannot be directly predicted from evaluation of the impairment only. Nor can the behavior one exhibits, or the burden that one elects to carry or that is assigned by society to a person with a certain disability or impairment, be accurately determined from knowledge about the disability only. Disabilities in motion, sensation, intelligence, emotion, and physiological processes do not necessarily translate into specific handicaps in situations requiring mobility, communication, healthy self-concept, or social interaction skills.

The World Health Organization (WHO) has made many efforts over the past 30 years to clarify terms and extend the medical model of disease per se to account for the consequences of disease (1980). In 1980, the International Classification of Impairments, Disabilities, and Handicaps (ICIDH) was formed. The ICIDH bridged the former medical model with a social model and facilitated the recognition of the contributions of medical services, rehabilitation agencies, and social welfare personnel to the care of people with conditions that interfere with everyday life, especially those people who have chronic, progressive, and irreversible conditions. The medical model of disease (WHO, 1980, p. 10) was illustrated as:

$$etiology \rightarrow pathology \rightarrow manifestation$$

The extended model, a biopsychosocial model (WHO, 1980, p. 11), was presented as:

$$disease \rightarrow impairment \rightarrow disability \rightarrow handicap$$

Disability in the WHO classification system denoted the "consequences of impairment in terms of functional performance and activity by the individual" (p. 14). An impairment was defined as "any loss or abnormality of psychological, physiological, or anatomical structure or function" (p. 47). Handicap was defined as "a disadvantage for a given individual, resulting from an impairment or a disability, that limits or prevents the fulfillment of a role that is normal (depending on age, sex, and social and cultural factors) for that individual" (p. 183). Thus impairment represents "exteriorization of a pathological state" (p. 47) and occurs at the tissue level; disability refers to "excesses or deficiencies of customarily expected activity, performance, and behavior" (p. 142) and was located at the level of the person; and handicap "reflects the consequences for the individual—cultural, social, economic, and environmental—that stem from the presence of impairment and disability" (p. 183).

After 9 years of international revision efforts coordinated by the WHO, the World Health Assembly on May 22, 2001, approved the International Classification of Functioning, Disability and Health and its abbreviation of "ICF." This classification was first created in 1980 (and then called the International Classification of Impairments, Disabilities, and Handicaps, or ICIDH) by WHO to provide a unifying framework for classifying the consequences of disease.

Revision activities for ICIDH in the United States and Canada have been under the auspices of the WHO Collaborating Center for the Classification of Diseases for North America since 1993. The North American Collaborating Center (NACC), which recently has been renamed the WHO Collaborating Center for the Family of International Classifications for North America, is housed at the National Center for Health Statistics (NCHS). The Collaborating

Center for the Family of International Classifications for North America (NACC):

- represents the United States and Canada in international activities related to study and revision of the ICIDH/IC

- works with U.S. researchers conducting ICIDH/ICF studies and evaluations

- collaborates with Canadian researchers through the Canadian Institute for Health Information (CIHI)

The ICF classification complements WHO's International Classification of Diseases–10th Revision (ICD), which contains information on diagnosis and health condition, but not on functional status. The ICD and ICF constitute the core classifications in the WHO Family of International Classifications (WHO-FIC). The NACC has responsibilities to WHO in its "Terms of Reference" to promote the development and use of ICF in the light of practical experience.

The ICF is structured around the following broad components: Body functions and structure, Activities (related to tasks and actions by an individual), and Participation (involvement in a life situation), and Additional information on severity and environmental factors.

Functioning and disability are viewed as a complex interaction between the health condition of the individual and the contextual factors of the environment, as well as personal factors. The picture produced by this combination of factors and dimensions is of "the person in his or her world." The classification treats these dimensions as interactive and dynamic rather than linear or static. It allows for an assessment of the degree of disability, although it is not a measurement instrument. It is applicable to all people, whatever their health condition. The language of the ICF is neutral as to etiology, placing the emphasis on function rather than condition or disease. It also is carefully designed to be relevant across cultures as well as age groups and genders, making it highly appropriate for heterogeneous populations.

The NACC has sponsored 10 annual ICF revision meetings in the United States and Canada from 1993 to 2004, hosted the annual WHO ICD meeting in 1993, and did so again in October 2001. The North American Collaborating Center also has sponsored several other ICF activities, such as the development of web-based training for ICF (called "CODE ICF"), the production of ICF videos, and the production of internationally comparable disability tabulations from six national disability surveys (called "DISTAB") back coded to ICF. In this effort, the DISTAB group worked closely with the United Nations (U.N.) in New York, which in June 2001 sponsored a Seminar on the Measurement of Disability. The background papers, and many of the papers presented, are on the U.N. web site. A searchable version of the ICF is available at the WHO web site at http://www.who.org.

In the present context of special education and rehabilitation, the term disability is frequently changed to the adjectival form and used to describe individuals. Thus we hear talk about disabled persons. Note, however, the affect of this change; instead of considering a disability or the lack of power to act, attention is directed to people who are characterized as not having power to act, with no distinction as to what actions might be limited. Wright (1960), in her discussion of physical disabilities, has pointed out the distinction between calling someone a physically disabled person as opposed to a person with a physical disability: "it is precisely the perception of a person with a physical disability as a *physically disabled person* that has reduced all his life to the disability aspects of his physique. The short cut distorts and undermines" (p. 8). Consider the impact of further streamlining our language when we talk about the disabled and characterize as disabled an entire group of people who may share nothing other than their membership in the amorphous group labeled disabled. A common example is the group called the learning disabled (LD); the extreme heterogeneity among the individual group members is obscured by the blanket term or its abbreviation to LD.

Attempts to define the term disability and differentiate it from related terms is more than an exercise in semantics. Precise definitions are needed for determining who is eligible for services; what the incidence and prevalence of conditions are; what projected health care, educational, rehabilitation, and welfare assistance may be required from a local, state, national, or international perspective; and what efforts might facilitate the development of appropriate housing and employment opportunities. It seems likely that as long as the term disability carries a strong pejorative connotation, attempts will be made to limit its denotation and increase the objectivity of its meaning.

REFERENCES

Stevens, G. D. (1962). *Taxonomy in special education for children with body disorders.* Pittsburgh, PA: Department of Special Education and Rehabilitation, University of Pittsburgh.

World Health Organization (WHO). (1980). *International classification of impairments, disabilities, and handicaps: A manual of classification relating to the consequences of disease.* Geneva, Switzerland: Author.

World Health Organization (WHO). (1998). *ICIDH-2 Beta 1 Field Trials.* Retrieved from www.who.org

World Health Organization (WHO). (2006). *International classification of functionality.* Retrieved January 21, 2006, from http://www.who.org

Wright, B. (1960). *Physical disability—A psychological approach.* New York: Harper & Row.

MARJORIE E. WARD
The Ohio State University
First edition

ELAINE FLETCHER-JANZEN
University of Colorado at Colorado Springs
Second edition

CHILD WITH A DISABILITY, DEFINITION OF INDIVIDUALS WITH DISABILITIES IMPROVEMENT EDUCATION ACT OF 2004 (IDEIA)

LABELING

DISABILITY ETIQUETTE

The following text consists of excerpts from the City of San Antonio's (Texas) Planning Department *Disability Etiquette Handbook.* The *Handbook* is featured on the city's web site (http://www.sanantonio.gov/planning/disability_handbook/disability_handbook.asp?res=1280&ver=true) and has won a great deal of positive comments and is being used by other city governments, such as the city of Sacramento, California. It is a positive example of institutional respect and support of individuals with disabilities.

People with Disabilities

People with disabilities are not conditions or diseases. They are individual human beings. For example, a person is not an epileptic, but rather a person who has epilepsy. First and foremost they are people. Only secondarily do they have one or more disabling conditions. Hence, they prefer to be referred to in print or broadcast media as People with Disabilities.

In any story, article, announcement, or advertisement, *people with disabilities* should be used either exclusively or, at a minimum, as the initial reference. Subsequent references can use the terms *person with a disability* or *individuals with disabilities* for grammatical or narrative reasons. In conclusion, the appropriate and preferred initial reference is *people with disabilities.*

Distinction between Disability and Handicap

A *Disability* is a condition caused by an accident, trauma, genetics, or disease that may limit a person's mobility, hearing, vision, speech, or mental function. Some people with disabilities have one or more disabilities.

A *Handicap* is a physical or attitudinal constraint that is imposed upon a person, regardless of whether that person has a disability. Webster's Ninth New Collegiate Dictionary defines handicap as "to put at a disadvantage."

For example, some people with disabilities use wheelchairs. Stairs, narrow doorways, and curbs are handicaps imposed upon people with disabilities who use wheelchairs. People with disabilities have all manners of disabling conditions:

- mobility impairments
- blindness and vision impairments

- deafness and hearing impairments
- speech and language impairments
- mental and learning disabilities

Conversation Etiquette

- When talking to a person with a disability, look at and speak directly to that person, rather than through a companion who may be along.

- Relax. Don't be embarrassed if you happen to use accepted common expressions, such as "See you later" or "Got to be running along," that seem to relate to the person's disability.

- To get the attention of a person with a hearing impairment, tap the person on the shoulder or wave your hand. Look directly at the person and speak clearly, naturally, and slowly to establish if the person can read lips. Not all persons with hearing impairments can lip read. Those who cannot will rely on facial expression and other body language to help in understanding. Show consideration by placing yourself facing the light source and keeping your hands, cigarettes, and food away from your mouth when speaking. Keep mustaches well-trimmed. Shouting won't help. Written notes may.

- When talking with a person in a wheelchair for more than a few minutes, use a chair, whenever possible, in order to place yourself at the person's eye level to facilitate conversation.

- When greeting a person with a severe loss of vision, always identify yourself and others who may be with you. For example: "On my right is Penelope Potts."

- When conversing in a group, give a vocal cue by announcing the name of the person to whom you are speaking. Speak in a normal tone of voice, indicate in advance when you will be moving from one place to another, and let it be known when the conversation is at an end.

- Listen attentively when you're talking to a person who has a speech impairment. Keep your manner encouraging rather than correcting. Exercise patience rather than attempting to speak for a person with speech difficulty. When necessary, ask short questions that require short answers or a nod or a shake of the head. Never pretend to understand if you are having difficulty doing so. Repeat what you understand, or incorporate the interviewee's statements into each of the following questions. The person's reactions will clue you in and guide you to understanding.

- If you have difficulty communicating, be willing to repeat or rephrase a question. Open-ended questions are more appropriate than closed-ended questions. For example:

- *Closed-Ended Question.* You were a tax accountant in XYZ Company in the corporate planning department for 7 years. What did you do there?

- *Open-Ended Question.* Tell me about your recent position as a tax accountant.

- Do not shout at a hearing impaired person. Shouting distorts sounds accepted through hearing aids and inhibits lip reading. Do not shout at a person who is blind or visually impaired—he or she can hear you!

- To facilitate conversation, be prepared to offer a visual cue to a hearing impaired person or an audible cue to a vision impaired person, especially when more than one person is speaking.

Glossary of Acceptable Terms

Acceptable terms	Unacceptable terms
Person with a disability.	Cripple, cripples—the image conveyed is of a twisted, deformed, useless body.
Disability, a general term used for functional limitation that interferes with a person's ability, for example, to walk, hear, or lift. It may refer to a physical, mental, or sensory condition.	Handicap, handicapped person, or handicapped.
People with cerebral palsy, people with spinal cord injuries.	Cerebral palsied, spinal cord injured, and so on. Never identify people solely by their disability.
Person who had a spinal cord injury, polio, a stroke, and so on, or a person who has multiple sclerosis, muscular dystrophy, arthritis, and so on.	Victim. People with disabilities do not like to be perceived as victims for the rest of their lives, long after any victimization has occurred.
Has a disability, has a condition of (spina bifida, etc.), or born without legs, and so on.	Defective, defect, deformed, vegetable. These words are offensive, dehumanizing, degrading, and stigmatizing.
Deafness/hearing impairment. Deafness refers to a person who has a total loss of hearing. Hearing impairment refers to a person who has a partial loss of hearing within a range from slight to severe.	

Acceptable terms	Unacceptable terms
Hard of hearing describes a hearing-impaired person who communicates through speaking and speech-reading, and who usually has listening and hearing abilities adequate for ordinary telephone communication. Many hard of hearing individuals use a hearing aid.	Deaf and Dumb is as bad as it sounds. The inability to hear or speak does not indicate intelligence.
Person who has a mental or developmental disability.	Retarded, moron, imbecile, idiot. These are offensive to people who bear the label.
Uses a wheelchair or crutches; a wheelchair user; walks with crutches.	Confined/restricted to a wheelchair; wheelchair bound. Most people who use a wheelchair or mobility devices do not regard them as confining. They are viewed as liberating; a means of getting around.
Able-bodied; able to walk, see, hear, and so on; people who are not disabled.	Healthy, when used to contrast with "disabled." Healthy implies that the person with a disability is unhealthy. Many people with disabilities have excellent health.
People who do not have a disability.	Normal. When used as the opposite of disabled, this implies that the person is abnormal. No one wants to be labeled as abnormal.
A person who has (name of disability.) Example: A person who has multiple sclerosis.	Afflicted with, suffers from. Most people with disabilities do not regard themselves as afflicted or suffering continually. Afflicted: a disability is not an affliction.

Reasonable Accommodations in the Work Place

Reasonable accommodations enhance the opportunity for qualified persons with disabilities who may not otherwise be considered for reasons unrelated to actual job requirements to be or remain employed. The purpose of providing reasonable accommodations is to enable employers to hire or retain qualified job candidates regardless of their disability by eliminating barriers in the work place.

Types of accommodations include:

- assistive devices
- reassignment
- modified work schedules
- job modifications
- relocation
- or a change in the physical plant

Examples of assistive devices often used in the work place include:

- teletypewriter (TTY) or telephone amplifier, often used by persons with hearing impairments
- wooden blocks to elevate desks and tables for wheelchair users
- large-type computer terminals and braille printers to assist persons with vision impairments

Decisions to implement an accommodation should include making a choice that will best meet the needs of the individual by minimizing limitation and enhancing his or her ability to perform job tasks, while serving the interests of your majority work force.

Reception Etiquette

Know where accessible restrooms, drinking fountains, and telephones are located. If such facilities are not available, be ready to offer alternatives, such as the private or employee restroom, a glass of water, or your desk phone.

Use a normal tone of voice when extending a verbal welcome. Do not raise your voice unless requested.

When introduced to a person with a disability, it is appropriate to offer to shake hands. People with limited hand use or who wear an artificial limb can usually shake hands.

- Shaking hands with the left hand is acceptable.
- For those who cannot shake hands, touch the person on the shoulder or arm to welcome and acknowledge their presence.
- Treat adults in a manner befitting adults
- Call a person by his or her first name only when extending that familiarity to all others present.
- Never patronize people using wheelchairs by patting them on the head or shoulder.
- When addressing a person who uses a wheelchair, never lean on the person's wheelchair. The chair is part of the space that belongs to the person who uses it.
- When talking with a person with a disability, look at and speak directly to that person rather than through a companion who may be along.

- If an interpreter is present, speak to the person who has scheduled the appointment, not to the interpreter. Always maintain eye contact with the applicant, not the interpreter.
- Offer assistance in a dignified manner with sensitivity and respect. Be prepared to have the offer declined. Do not proceed to assist if your offer to assist is declined. If the offer is accepted, listen to and accept instructions.
- Allow a person with a visual impairment to take your arm (at or about the elbow). This will enable you to guide rather than propel or lead the person.
- Offer to hold or carry packages in a welcoming manner. For example: "May I help you with your packages?"
- When offering to hand a coat or umbrella, do not offer to hand a cane or crutches unless the individual requests otherwise.

Service Animals

Background

Over 12,000 people with disabilities use the aid of service animals. Although the most familiar types of service animals are guide dogs used by people who are blind, service animals are assisting persons who have other disabilities as well. Many disabling conditions are invisible. Therefore, every person who is accompanied by a service animal may or may not "look" disabled. A service animal is NOT required to have any special certification.

What is a service animal?

A service animal is NOT a pet! According to the Americans with Disabilities Act of 1990 (ADA) a service animal is any animal that has been individually trained to provide assistance or perform tasks for the benefit of a person with a physical or mental disability that substantially limits one or more major life functions.

Service dog etiquette

- Do not touch the Service Animal, or the person it assists, without permission.
- Do not make noises at the Service Animal—it may distract the animal from doing its job.
- Do not feed the Service Animal—it may disrupt his or her schedule.
- Do not be offended if the person does not feel like discussing his or her disability or the assistance the Service Animal provides. Not everyone wants to be a walking-talking "show and tell" exhibit.

Sign Language Interpreters

The professional interpreter is always considered to be an extension of and part of the event. Interpreters are part of the team meant to deliver accurate and intended messages given by the presenters or performers. The further in advance notice is provided to the interpreter, the more prepared they will be. This process will allow the interpreter to have the proper time needed for an event and prevent "cold" interpreting. Time for preparation is essential to allow accurate dissemination of the intended messages to the audience.

For instance, an interpreter needs to spend an average of 15 to 20 hours of practice for a 2 hour musical concert. With this in mind, the following information given to the interpreter will enhance the quality of the interpreted performance/event.

- name and type of event
- name of event contact person with a phone number
- correct billing address
- clear address and directions to the event and the location where the interpreter is to check-in
- parking passes or information on any kind of special arrangements for parking
- correct spellings of all names of those speaking or performing
- a summary of subjects that will be presented by each speaker
- a list of any musical lyrics in advance, ideally at the time of request
- communication and shared information to all persons directly involved with the event regarding the arrangements for the interpreter

If any information to be presented is other than English, a written interpretation in English will be needed in advance, or an advance notice of at least 3 weeks will be needed to allow adequate time to secure an appropriate interpreter.

STAFF

DISADVANTAGED CHILD

Most writings about disadvantaged children first gained attention during the 1940s and 1950s; lower-class youths and racial minorities were identified as the populace of this educationally disenfranchised group of learners. Historically we can identify the roots of this population in terms of their educational needs, but it was not until the mid 1960s that writers such as Riessman and Havighurst had their turns at defining the characteristics that constitute this deprived population. As indicated by Riessman (1962), the terms culturally deprived, educationally deprived, deprived, underprivileged, disadvantaged, lower class, and lower socioeconomic group, could all be used interchangeably.

Ornstein (1976) has presented an interesting and basic critique of the attempts made by Havighurst and Riessman to provide us with the characteristics of the disadvantaged. Havighurst began by attempting to provide the traditional conceptualization of the disadvantaged that grew out of the earliest of writings. The disadvantaged youth is seen as coming primarily from a low-income family and most likely from a racial minority. Havighurst emphasizes the social, economic, and personal handicaps of the disadvantaged and sees this youth at the lowest end of several strata. Ornstein interprets this as providing the unwary reader with a convenient label that is essentially laden with negativism.

On the other hand, we have Ornstein's interpretation of what he refers to as a positive trend exemplified in Riessman's (1962) classic book *The Culturally Deprived Child,* in which he views the disadvantaged youth as having many positive characteristics. With the emphasis now on a more positive outlook, readers are encouraged to note and develop qualities within this population such as physical orientation, hidden verbal ability, creative potential, group cohesiveness informality, and sense of humor.

Although Riessman has made great efforts to identify some characteristics that might be construed as potentially positive qualities, he also is cognizant of the negative criteria used by Havighurst and others. An examination of *The Culturally Deprived Child* (1962) results in the reader's awareness that Reissman understood the enormity of the problems encountered by the deprived children of our nation.

Karnes, Reid, and Jones (1971), in the Guidance Monograph Series, provide us with an approach to the identification process in that they refer to a difference between middle class and lower class in only the six areas of: (1) self-concept, (2) motivation, (3) social behavior, (4) language, (5) intellectual functioning, and (6) physical fitness. With such broad categories, each educator can conceivably provide us with information applicable to either the Havighurst or Riessman model. In addition, the term disadvantaged youth is also seen as being too nebulous and having a degree of relativism that in turn reduces the selection process for innovative educational programs to confront this issue. Loss of objectivity in the identification and ultimate selection of students for educational enrichment often results in failure to meet the program's goals.

Without many of the precise criteria needed to identify the disadvantaged population, the educational community moved ahead with special programs with a financial base from congressional legislation. In 1965, Congress passed the Elementary and Secondary Education Act (ESEA) and for the first time in U.S. history, federal financial support was provided to both public and nonpublic schools. From this legislation came Title I—Education of Children of Low-Income Families. Title I was designed to support and provide financial incentives for special programs to meet the special needs of socially and educationally deprived children of low-income families. Congress amended and expanded the ESEA many times over the next 30 years. The major criticism of the Act was that funds were spread thinly instead of being focused in areas of most need (Department of Education, 1993). In 2001, the ESEA was again amended and heavily revised by the No Child Left Behind Act, which shifted the focus of funding from schools with a high concentration of low-income families to underperforming schools without regard to the socioeconomic status of children attending such schools. The impact of this change remains unclear, and the ultimate effect in terms of educational outcomes will likely not be known for several more years.

In addition, a crisis developed in urban schools, where an exodus of White middle-class families from the city to private and/or suburban schools created a buildup of educationally disadvantaged minority students (Ornstein, 1989). Issues of cultural competence have also been included recently to the evaluation of services to disadvantaged children. There have been requests (Lake, 1990) to distinguish between the terms "culturally disadvantaged" and "culturally different."

Specific learning characteristics of the deprived or disadvantaged student might include many of the following: (1) oriented to the physical and visual rather than to the oral; (2) content-centered rather than form-centered; (3) externally oriented rather than introspective; (4) problem-centered rather than abstract-centered; (5) inductive rather than deductive; (6) spatial rather than temporal; (7) slow, careful, patient, and persevering (in areas of importance) rather than quick, clever, facile, and flexible; (8) inclined to communicate through actions rather than words; (9) deficient in auditory attention and interpretation skills; (10) oriented toward concrete application of what is learned; (11) short attention span; (12) characteristic gaps in knowledge and learning; (13) lacking experiences of receiving approval for success in tasks (Conte & Grimes, 1969).

Meeting the needs of the disadvantaged child is a relatively new educational approach when viewed within the context of America's education history. Efforts to define this population have not been without conflict, and massive expenditures of monies by the federal government have also stirred controversy. However, studies indicate that enrichment programs (Kaniel & Richtenberg, 1992), mentoring (Shaughnessy, 1992), and appropriate curricula design (Gemma, 1989) have very positive outcomes with children who are disadvantaged.

REFERENCES

Conte, J. M., & Grimes, G. H. (1969). *Media and the culturally different.* Washington, DC: National Education Association.

Gemma, A. (1989). *A comparison of the child-centered curriculum model, the direct instruction curriculum model, and the open-*

framework curriculum model: Three curriculum models for disadvantaged preschool children. (ERIC Clearinghouse No. PS018905)

Kaniel, S., & Richtenberg, R. (1992). Instrumental enrichment: Effects of generalization and durability with talented adolescents. *Gifted Education International, 8*(3), 128–35.

Karnes, M. B., Reid, J., & Jones, G. R. (1971). *The culturally disadvantaged student and guidance.* Boston: Houghton Mifflin.

Lake, R. (1990). An Indian father's plea. *Teacher Magazine, 2*(1), 48–53.

Ornstein, A. C. (1976). Who are the disadvantaged? In J. H. Cull & R. E. Hardy (Eds.), *Problems of disadvantaged and deprived youth* (pp. 5–15). Springfield, IL: Thomas.

Ornstein, A. C. (1989). Enrollment trends in big city schools. *Peabody Journal of Education, 66*(4), 64–71.

Riessman, F. (1962). *The culturally deprived child.* New York: Harper & Row.

Shaughnessy, M. F. (1992). *Mentoring disadvantaged gifted children and youth.* (ERIC Clearinghouse No. UD028765)

U.S. Department of Education. (1993). *Improving America's Schools Act of 1993: The Reauthorization of the Elementary and Secondary Education Act.* Washington, DC: Author.

RICHARD E. HALMSTAD
University of Wisconsin at Stout
Second edition

KIMBERLY F. APPLEQUIST
*University of Colorado at
Colorado Springs*
Third edition

NO CHILD LEFT BEHIND ACT

DISCIPLINE

The noun discipline comes from the Latin word *disciplina,* meaning teaching, learning. However, a more common use of the word connotes either training that corrects or molds or punishment for transgressions against societal or parental rules.

Discipline begins with the efforts of parents to teach the mores of their culture. Almost all of this early discipline begins when the infant becomes mobile and can therefore behave in ways that parents believe need to be changed. Early parental discipline usually focuses on behavioral control (e.g., not touching the untouchable or not running in the street). Difficulties can arise if parents think that the child can control a behavior that the child in fact cannot—at least not at that age. A good example of this is toilet training of toddlers. Parents continue to carry the responsibility for disciplining children until they enter school. From the time children enter school until they leave, a partnership

begins with others, such as teachers to discipline children as well (Foster & Robin, 1998).

Parents seem to discipline their children either through power-assertion techniques or through love-oriented techniques (Hoffman, 1970). In the former style of parental discipline, power-assertion, the parent uses physical punishment, deprives the child of material objects or privileges, directly applies force, or threatens. Control is exercised by taking advantage of greater physical strength and/or control of home environment.

Love withdrawal, a form of love-oriented discipline, uses direct but nonphysical expressions of anger or disappointment when the child misbehaves. For example, the parent may discipline by explicitly stating negative feelings, ignoring, isolating, or turning away from the child.

The use of power-assertive discipline such as spanking or love-oriented techniques such as withdrawal of affection may produce resentment or anxiety and cause the child to focus attention on his or her own negative consequences. These procedures are punitive rather than altruistic, that is, they decrease the child's appreciation of another person's distress.

Through induction, another form of love-oriented parental discipline, the parent appeals to the child's affection or respect for another. In essence, the child may be reminded that someone else will be hurt, disappointed, or suffer from his or her actions.

In comparison, inductive discipline is a nonpunitive technique that communicates the harm caused by a child's actions and encourages the child to place himself or herself in the victim's place. Hoffman (1975) believes that children are likely to develop a strong altruistic orientation if their parents often use inductive disciplinary techniques.

A popular perspective on discipline in the educational setting was espoused by William Glasser (1969). Glasser suggested that children be allowed to determine their own discipline and to set consequences for their behavior. Adults (parents, teachers, etc.) who use Glasser's style of discipline often play a low-key role that reduces immediate application of reward and punishment and supplants both with discussion in which the adult serves as mediator for decision making.

While Glasser's approach may be effective with bright, middle-class, high-school students, it may not be effective with young children or with older adolescents who have grown up in a lower-class setting. If children have not developed the requisite skills for deciding on a socially competent course of action when disciplinary decisions are required, this approach is not suggested. The effectiveness of each technique varies, perhaps influenced most by such factors as the age, verbal reasoning abilities, and cultural background of the child.

On entering the school setting, previously learned behavior patterns emerge when children are faced with adapting to participating in a room where waiting, sharing, instruction, and learning must take place. The term control is often viewed as a convenient catch all for what should be termed classroom management. One is never sure whether the meaning is intended in the broad sense (to cover all of classroom management), or the literal sense, that of keeping pupil behavior so curbed that the classroom is totally teacher-dominated.

Discipline, like control, is often incorrectly used to mean various aspects of classroom management. Good discipline may be considered maintaining an orderly classroom. A classroom and/or school environment that supports good student behavior must also expect the student to make good choices. Students that only respond to external structures such as rewards or punishments learn very little self-discipline and the gains are usually only short-term (Short, 1994).

A more acceptable use of the term in the educational setting would describe discipline as an imposition of self-control in order to promote efficient habits of learning, proper conduct, consideration for others, and a positive learning environment. From the educator's point of view, preventing misbehavior is much more important than imposing control after the fact (Baron, 1992). Teachers working in teams to create positive classroom climates have much better support and success than individual efforts (Bell-Ruppert, 1994). In addition, democratic rather than authoritarian values have emerged in recent classroom discipline models. However, democratic values require flexible problem-solving skills that both the teacher and the students must value (Lewis, 1997).

To maintain discipline in the classroom, the student must be given as much independence as the teacher and child can tolerate. Classroom management should yield neither highly structured teacher-dominated environments nor completely permissive ones. To facilitate the development of self-control and discipline, a teacher's managerial style should attempt to promote active participation and a positive learning environment.

REFERENCES

Baron, E. B. (1992). *Discipline strategies for teachers.* (ERIC Clearinghouse No. SP034413)

Bell-Ruppert, N. (1994, November). *Discipline plans in middle schools.* Paper presented at the Annual Conference and Exhibit of the National Middle School Association.

Foster, S. L., & Robin, A. L. (1998). Parent-adolescent conflict and relationship discord. In E. J. Mash & R. A. Barkley (Eds.), *Treatment of childhood disorders* (2nd ed., pp. 601–646). New York: Guilford.

Glasser, W. (1969). *Schools without failure.* New York: Harper & Row.

Hoffman, M. L. (1970). Moral development. In P. H. Mussen (Ed.), *Carmicheal's manual of child psychology* (Vol. 2, 3rd ed.). New York: Wiley.

Hoffman, M. L. (1975). Altruistic behavior and the parent-child relationships: *Journal of Personality & Social Psychology, 40,* 121–137.

Lewis, R. (1997). *The discipline dilemma: Control Management, Influence* (2nd ed.). Melbourne: Australian Council for Educational Research.

Short, P. (1994). *Rethinking student discipline: Alternatives that work.* (ERIC Clearinghouse No. EA026417)

MICHAEL J. ASH
JOSE LUIS TORRES
Texas A&M University
First edition

ELAINE FLETCHER-JANZEN
University of Colorado at Colorado Springs
Second edition

CLASSROOM MANAGEMENT
SELF-CONTROL CURRICULUM
SELF-MONITORING

DISCOURSE

Discourse are oral and literate units of language that are usually larger than a sentence and show a common theme as well as local and global cohesion and coherence patterns (Schiffrin, 1994). It creates representation of events, objects, beliefs, personalities, and experiences. Discourse includes a variety of cues that include not only words and sentences, but also the tone, the overall purpose, and the relative formality of a communication event. In addition, oral discourse involves gestures, body positions, facial expressions of the speaker, and context (Brownell & Joanette, 1993). Two major types of discourse exist: Basic Interpersonal Communication Skills (BICS) or "everyday language," and Cognitive-Academic Language Proficiency (CALP) or "instructional language" (Chamot & O'Malley, 1994; Cummins, 1983). Both BICS and CALP contribute to education success. Characteristics of discourse associated with BICS and CALP are divided into three categories that occur across a developmental continuum: (1) Conversation, (2) Narration, and (3) Exposition (Larson & McKinley, 1995; Merritt & Culatta, 1998; Naremore, Densmore, & Harman, 1995; Nelson, 1998; Wallach & Butler, 1994).

Conversation is used to request and report concrete items and actions (informal or personal oral or written interactions; Halliday, 1975; Hoskins, 1996; Naremore et al., 1995; Nelson, 1998; Tough, 1979). Conversation is a type of BICS that can be oral (e.g., social group, family conferences, telephone calls, "rap" sessions, gossip) or literate (e.g., personal notes, a diary, e-mail). Conversational discourse is context-embedded and has a structure of topics, initiations, responses, turns, exchanges, topic maintenance, reaction time latency, breakdowns, repairs, pacing/leading, and closure. Conversation competence is measured by quantity, quality, relationship, and manner, as well as nonverbal dimensions of communication. Individuals who do not develop conversational skills may experience difficulty with the second level of discourse, narration.

Narration is used to report what happened, to talk or write about, or to read about the there and then (recounts, eventcasts, accounts, fictional stories; Esterreicher, 1995; Hedberg & Westby, 1993; Hughes, McGillivray, & Schmidek, 1997; Naremore et al., 1995; Nelson, 1998). Narrative competence includes the understanding and use of *story grammars* (characters, place, time, initiating event, problem, internal response, resolution, and ending). Story grammars develop through the process of centering and chaining involved in learning *story types* (heaps, sequences, primitive narratives, unfocused chains, focused chains, and eventually true narratives represented by complex, multiple, embedded, or interactive episodes). Narration, a combination of BICS and CALP discourse, is a bridge between conversation and exposition because narration develops the cognitive, linguistic, and contextual structures introduced in conversation and required by exposition. For some individuals, reading problems may be related to poorly developed productive narrative abilities.

Exposition, an oral and literate CALP communication form, is a context-reduced and abstract form of language used to generalize about and infer what happens in the there and then (Chamot & O'Malley, 1994; Cummins, 1983; Larson & McKinley, 1995; Merritt & Culatta, 1998; Naremore et al., 1995; Nelson, 1998; Ripich & Creaghead, 1994; Wallach & Butler, 1994). Expository language includes understanding and producing speeches, lectures, discussions, classroom discourse, textbooks, reaction papers, essays, and technical, (research, or term papers). Expository forms are structured through genres such as description, collection, sequence/procedure, compare-contrast, cause-effect, problem-solution, and argue-persuade. Exposition competence requires the understanding and use of precise vocabulary (often associated with academic content or career areas), pronunciation, grammar, organization, sequencing, transitions, cohesion, coherence, spelling, proofreading, and editing. Individuals who have not developed the oral and literate communication skills associated with narration may experience difficulties with expository language.

Critical elements that serve as building blocks for successful discourse abilities include *communication-learning functions* (instrumental, regulatory, interactional, personal, heuristic, imaginative, informational/representational, performatives, responsives, expressive; Halliday, 1975), *language-thinking functions* (maintaining, reporting, applying, analyzing, logical reasoning, evaluating, synthesizing, imagining, projecting, predicting, inferencing; Tough, 1979), and *executive functions* (awareness, goal setting, planning, self-initiating, self-inhibiting, self-monitoring,

self-evaluating, ability to change set, strategic behavior; Ylvisaker & Szekeres, 1989). These various communication-learning functions are used in the process of *heuristics,* the reciprocal system of requesting information (asking questions) and responding (answering questions).

Discourse problems may be caused by developmental or acquired conditions. Oral and literate discourse rules and use vary from culture to culture (Hedberg & Westby, 1993). However, the consensus is that for social and academic success throughout life, individuals must be able to understand and use the communication-learning conventions associated with conversation, narration, and exposition (Nelson, 1998; Wallach & Butler, 1994).

REFERENCES

Brownell, H. H., & Joanette, Y. (Eds). (1993). *Narrative discourse in neurologically impaired and normal aging adults.* San Diego, CA: Singular.

Chamot, A. U., & O'Malley, J. M. (1994). *The CALLA handbook: Implementing the cognitive academic language learning approach.* Reading, MA: Addison-Wesley.

Cummins, J. (1983). Language proficiency and academic achievement. In J. W. Oller, Jr. (Ed.), *Issues in language testing research.* Boston: Newbury House.

Esterreicher, C. A. (1995). *Scamper Strategies: FUNdamental activities for narrative development.* Eau Claire, WI: Thinking Publications.

Halliday, M. A. K. (1975). *Learning how to mean: Exploration in the development of language.* London: Edward Arnold.

Hedberg, N. L., & Westby, C. E. (1993). *Analyzing storytelling skills: Theory to practice.* Tucson, AZ: Communication Skill Builders.

Hoskins, B. (1996). *Conversations: A framework for language intervention.* Eau Claire, WI: Thinking Publications.

Hughes, D., McGillivray, L., & Schmidek, M. (1997). *Guide to narrative language.* Eau Claire, WI: Thinking Publications.

Larson, V. L., & McKinley, N. (1995). *Language disorders in older students: Preadolescents and adolescents.* Eau Claire, WI: Thinking Publications.

Merritt, D. D., & Culatta, B. (1998). *Language intervention in the classroom.* San Diego, CA: Singular.

Naremore, R. C., Densmore, A. E., & Harman, D. R. (1995). *Language intervention with school-aged children: Conversation, narrative, and text.* San Diego, CA: Singular.

Nelson, N. W. (1998). *Childhood language disorders in context: Infancy through adolescence* (2nd ed.). Boston: Allyn & Bacon.

Ripich, D. N., & Creaghead, N. A. (Eds.). (1994). *School discourse problems* (2nd ed.). San Diego, CA: Singular.

Schiffrin, D. (1994). *Approaches to discourse.* Cambridge, MA: Blackwell.

Tough, J. (1979). *Talk for teaching and learning.* Portsmouth, NJ: Heinemann.

Wallach, G. P., & Butler, K. G. (1994). *Language learning disabilities in school-age children and adolescents: Some principles and applications.* New York: Merrill/Macmillan College.

Ylvisaker, M., & Szekeres, S. (1989). Metacognitive and executive impairments in head injured children and adults. *Topics in Language Disorders, 9,* 34–49.

STEPHEN S. FARMER
New Mexico State University

DISCREPANCY ANALYSIS

See LEARNING DISABILITIES, SEVERE DISCREPANCY ANALYSIS IN.

DISCREPANCY FROM GRADE

Discrepancy model analysis is used in the assessment of learning disabilities to determine if a difference exists between the level of achievement and ability. Levels of achievement and intelligence are measured reliably by using standardized tests. Results, however, may not always be accurate owing to error in measurement (Connell, 1991). Attempts to measure discrepancy may also be complicated by age or grade level. A discrepancy of 1 year at the third grade for a 9-year-old is more severe than a similar discrepancy for a 16-year-old. In addition, cognitive language relationships change over time, which may make eligibility decision-making inappropriate using these models (Cole, 1992).

Several techniques using expectancy analysis are used in quantifying learning disabilities (Mercer, 1983). They are the mental grade method, the learning quotient method, and the Harris method. Harris (1961) provided a method to determine an individual's reading expectancy grade (RE). The examiner subtracts 5 years from the individual's mental age:

$$RE = MA - 5$$

To determine if a discrepancy exists, a comparison is made between the individual's reading expectancy and the present reading level. The learning quotient method was developed by Myklebust (1968); it includes mental age, chronological age, and grade age (GA). The learning quotient is the ratio between the present achievement age and expectancy age with a score of 89 or below resulting in classification as learning disabled.

A third technique once commonly used to determine discrepancy in learning disabilities was proposed by Harris (1970). This method includes both mental age and chronological age but gives priority to mental age:

$$EA = \frac{2MA + CA}{3}$$

These methods for determining discrepancy have been criticized in that difference scores between two tests were less reliable than each score separately (Salvia & Clark, 1973). It has also been noted that a large number of children might exhibit discrepancy by pure chance. These techniques were also criticized because of their failure with nonreaders.

REFERENCES

Cole, K. (1992). Stability of the intelligence quotient-language quotient relation. *American Journal of Mental Retardation, 97*(2), 131–143.

Connell, P. H. (1991). *An analysis of aptitude-achievement discrepancy formulas in learning disability assessment.* (ERIC Clearinghouse No. TM017793)

Harris, I. (1961). *Emotional blocks to learning.* New York: Free Press.

Harris, A. J. (1970). *How to increase reading ability* (5th ed.). New York: McKay.

Mercer, C. D. (1983). *Students with learning disabilities* (2nd ed.). Columbus, OH: Merrill.

Myklebust, H. (1968). Learning disabilities: Definition and overview. In H. Myklebust (Ed.), *Progress in learning disabilities.* New York: Grune & Stratton.

Salvia, J., & Clark, J. (1973). Use of deficits to identify the learning disabled. *Exceptional Children, 39,* 305–308.

CRAIG D. SMITH
Georgia College

GRADE EQUIVALENTS
LEARNING DISABILITIES
LEARNING DISABILITIES, PROBLEMS IN DEFINITION OF
LEARNING DISABILITIES, SEVERE DISCREPANCY ANALYSIS
IN

DISCRIMINANT ANALYSIS

Discriminant analysis is a statistical technique used to predict group membership from two or more interval dependent variables. It is similar to multiple regression in conception. For example, a researcher might be interested in determining if dyslexic students are distinguishable from other learning-disabled students using the subtests of the Wechsler Intelligence Scale for Children–Revised (WISC-R). Discriminant analysis can be used to determine the optimal set of weights for the WISC-R subtests that maximally separate the two groups on a new variable composed of the weighted sum of the WISC-R subtests.

Discriminant analysis may also be viewed as a data reduction technique. Instead of needing a large number of variables to categorize subjects, the researcher applies discriminant analysis so that a new variable or set of variables is created that uses the information of the original variables. The new variables are linear combinations, or weighted sums, of the original variables. It is anticipated that fewer new variables are needed than in the original set, hence the idea of data reduction. Mathematically, more than one unique solution to the problem is possible. The number of solutions will be equal to the smaller of two numbers: the number of predictors or the degrees of freedom for groups (number of groups minus one). Each solution corresponds to a new variable independent statistically of all the other new solution variables. For two groups there is only one solution since the smaller of the two numbers is equal to one (two groups minus one). This solution is also equal to the multiple regression of the group variable (mathematically defined as, for example, one or two on the predictor variables). The regression weights and the discriminant analysis weights in this case are identical.

For three or more groups, there will be two or more solutions to the problem of maximally distinguishing between the groups. Each solution corresponds to constructing a straight line on which the groups differ most in the sense of squared distance from the mean of the groups on the line. Each solution line is perpendicular in a Euclidean geometric sense from each other solution line. Computer programs are used to solve these problems, and the programs are designed to find the best solution first. The best solution is one in which the variance between the groups is greatest in relation to average variance within the groups for all possible lines. Once this solution is found, the next one is found from the residuals of fit to the first solution. A statistical test, Wilks lambda, is a multivariate analog to the ratio of the sum of squares within groups to the sum of the squares' total. An F-test may be used to test significance. For each new solution, test the additional error reduced in a manner similar to that employed in multiple regression to test a new predictor's additional contribution to prediction. Also, stepwise procedures can be employed in discriminant analysis to select the subset of predictors that maximally separate the groups. Predictors that do not contribute to separation in a given solution are dropped.

Discriminant analysis is widely used in both social and physical sciences. Its mathematical solutions are straightforward for a computer; discriminant analysis programs for computers are widely used (Huberty & Lowman, 1997).

REFERENCES

Cohen, J., & Cohen, P. (1983). *Applied multiple regression/correlation analysis for the social sciences* (3rd ed.). Hillsdale, NJ: Erlbaum.

Huberty, C., & Lowman, L. L. (1997). Discriminant analysis via statistical packages. *Educational and Psychological Management, 57*, 759–784.

Pedhazur, E. (1982). *Multiple regression in behavioral research* (2nd ed.). New York: Holt, Rinehart & Winston.

VICTOR L. WILLSON
Texas A&M University

FACTOR ANALYSIS
MULTIPLE REGRESSION

DISCRIMINATION LEARNING

Discrimination learning refers to the process of learning to respond differentially to relevant dimensions of a stimulus event. As a fundamental construct of behaviorally oriented learning explanations, this type of learning emphasizes events that occur before a behavior(s); the relationship of these events to the strength and contextual appropriateness of the behavior(s); and the resulting consequences that serve to maintain, strengthen, or punish the behavior(s).

During the teaching of discriminations, a stimulus event is presented to the student. Following this presentation, the student independently or, if necessary, with prompts, exhibits a behavioral response. If the behavior that the individual engages in is appropriate relative to the stimulus event, the learner is rewarded with a potentially reinforcing outcome. If the behavior is not appropriate with regard to the stimulus event, the consequent alternatives might include not attending to the response (ignoring), or systematic presentation of consequences aimed at reducing the future probability of the behavior occurring (punishment).

As a function of the consequences that occur in this S > R > C relationship, the stimulus events that have historically led to reinforcement become cues for the learner to engage in particular behaviors that will result in rewarding consequences. These stimulus events are referred to as discriminative stimuli (S^D). Conversely, those stimulus events that have not resulted in reinforcement (S^Δ) do not cue the individual to respond. Discrimination learning, then, teaches an individual when to engage in a particular behavior to obtain desirable outcomes, and by contrast clarifies when behavior will not lead to desirable consequences.

The teaching of discriminations constitutes one of the major tasks for individuals who are involved in educating the exceptional needs learner. While this type of learning is often assumed to take place in an almost incidental fashion, with most exceptional learners this outcome is not as likely. A host of variables, including diverse cognitive skills, inconsistent learning opportunities, and nefarious reinforcement contingencies, may interact to limit such individual's development of accurate discriminations. Effective educational service delivery for the exceptional child or youth often necessitates the use of more systematic methods of teaching discriminations.

Planned teaching of discriminations has involved simple to complex presentations of the attributes of the stimulus events (e.g., size, shape, volume, color, or combinations of these) and varied reinforcement schedules (e.g., movement from fixed to variable schedules of reinforcement) aimed at strengthening the discriminative potential of the stimulus event. Following accurate individualized assessment, discriminations are taught beginning at a level that increases the opportunity for success. Based on continuing assessment, teaching complexity is systematically moved in the direction of more normative skill development.

Teaching of discriminated responses has been used in vocationally oriented curricula, social skills programs, and many other curriculum areas targeted for the exceptional needs learner. By teaching individuals to exhibit specified behaviors under certain stimulus conditions, many of the inconsistent and inappropriate behaviors exhibited by this diverse group have been strengthened or replaced with more environmentally appropriate responses. For a comprehensive explanation of discrimination learning, the reader is referred to texts by Alberto and Troutman (1977) and Sulzer-Azaroff and Mayer (1977). Both texts provide clear examples of the application of this learning principle to educational programming. McDonald and Martin (1993) recommend the use of the Assessment of Basic Learning Abilities Test to assess discrimination acquisition with individuals who have profound disabilities.

REFERENCES

Alberto, P. A., & Troutman, A. C. (1977). *Applied behavior analysis for teachers: Influencing student performance.* Columbus, OH: Merrill.

McDonald, L., & Martin, G. L. (1993). Facilitating discrimination learning for persons with developmental disabilities. *International Journal of Rehabilitation Research, 16*(2), 160–164.

Sulzer-Azaroff, B., & Mayer, G. R. (1977). *Applying behavior-analysis procedures with children and youth.* New York: Holt, Rinehart & Winston.

J. TODD STEPHENS
*University of Wisconsin–
Madison*

APPLIED BEHAVIOR ANALYSIS
BEHAVIOR MODIFICATION
DATA-BASED INSTRUCTION
PRECISION TEACHING

DISPROPORTIONALITY

Disproportionality in special education denotes unequal percentages of students with various demographic characteristics in special education classifications and programs. Disproportionality most often occurs in the mildly handicapping classifications of Mild Mental Retardation (MMR), emotionally disturbed (ED), and specific learning disability (SLD), or in programs for the talented and gifted (TAG). The demographic variables in which disproportionality is most often observed, and sometimes seen as a problem, are ethnic/racial status, sex, and socioeconomic status. Disproportionality related to these student characteristics is well known, but highly controversial (Reschly, 1986, 1991, 1997).

The most widely studied disproportionality phenomenon is the overrepresentation of minorities, males, and economically disadvantaged students in the exceptional child classification of MMR. The same groups are also overrepresented, according to some studies, in programs for the SLD and ED. However, the overrepresentation in SLD and ED is rarely of the same magnitude as in MMR.

In Table 1, data compiled from a Federal Office of Civil Rights (OCR) survey of school districts in the United States, reported in a National Academy of Sciences monograph (Heller, Holtzman, & Messick, 1982), are presented. In 1978, these national results indicated that the only significant area of disproportionality was MMR, where the percentage of black students classified as MMR was three times the percentage of white students so classified. Relatively equal percentages of black, white, and Hispanic students were found in all other classifications except for ED, where black students were again overrepresented, but the numbers of students were small. The national results also indicated that Hispanic students were not overrepresented in special education programs for the mildly handicapped, an apparent reversal of a phenomenon that led earlier to placement bias litigation in Arizona and California.

Other studies have indicated minority disproportionality in SLD and ED. For example, data for the state of Florida presented in the *S1* v. *Turlington* trial (1986) indicated that black students were overrepresented in SLD, ED, and MMR.

Males and economically disadvantaged students generally are overrepresented in special education programs for the MMR. This overrepresentation sometimes approaches a ratio of two males for every female in SLD, ED, and MMR programs. Although studied far less frequently, overrepresentation of economically disadvantaged students is at least as ubiquitous as minority overrepresentation. Indeed, minority overrepresentation is probably best understood as reflecting the effects of poverty circumstances (Reschly, 1986).

Table 1 National projections from 1978 OCR survey (%)

Classification	Minority	Anglo-American	Hispanic	African-American
Mildly mentally retarded	2.54	1.07	0.98	3.46
Seriously emotionally disturbed	0.42	0.29	0.29	0.50
Learning disabled	2.29	2.04	1.78	2.23
Speech impaired	1.82	2.04	1.78	1.87
Totally (mildly handicapped)	7.07	5.72	5.63	8.06

Source: Based on Finn (1982), Table 1, p. 324, and Table 3, p. 330.

The disproportionate representation of students in TAG programs is a virtual mirror image of representation in programs for the mildly handicapped. Economically disadvantaged minority students are underrepresented in programs for the gifted. The degree of underrepresentation is highly variable, but for black students, it is approximately the same as the degree of overrepresentation in programs for the mildly handicapped. The representation of males and females is approximately equal in TAG programs except in very specialized programs that attempt to select the markedly gifted (IQ greater than 150) or in programs for markedly advanced students in the areas of science and mathematics. In the latter kinds of programs, there is considerable underrepresentation of females, a phenomenon that also evokes considerable controversy.

Disproportionality statistics are easily confused and often distorted. In the *Larry P.* case, undisputed facts established that black students constituted 10 percent of the total enrollment in California, but 25 percent of the MMR enrollment. However, only 1 percent of all California black students were in MMR programs. These seeming disparities arise from the low base rate of MMR (and other exceptional conditions) and the failure to clearly distinguish between percent of group in the general population (10 percent), percent of group in the program (1 percent), and percent of the program by group (25 percent; Reschly, 1986). Interpretation of disproportionality statistics must carefully distinguish among these different percentages.

The two general causes of disproportionality suggested in the literature are bias or discrimination and genuine individual differences. In short, the disproportionality is seen by some as a reflection of genuine differences among students and by others as a reflection of pernicious bias and discrimination from a variety of sources.

Allegations of bias or discrimination generally implicate the processes and procedures in which students are selected to be considered for placement in various kinds of programs. Thus bias or discrimination has been alleged in referral procedures, in the assessment process and assessment instruments (especially in intelligence tests), and in decision making by persons responsible for classification and placement decisions. Results of research on referral, assessment process and procedures, and decision making are far from definitive or unequivocal. Thus far, there is little evidence that intentional bias or discrimination is a primary cause of disproportionality (Bickel, 1982; Reschly, 1986).

There is ample evidence establishing an association between extreme poverty and the incidence of Mild Mental Retardation. This evidence has been gathered over the past 80 years with different racial or ethnic groups throughout western Europe and the United States. The MMR is to a large degree a phenomenon of poverty, but the vast majority of poor persons are not mildly mentally retarded (Reschly, 1986, 1991). The mechanisms whereby poverty increases risk for MMR are not clearly understood, but a variety of conditions are implicated (Robinson & Robinson, 1976).

Explanations for the sex disproportionality within the mildly handicapped and in certain types of programs for the gifted are far less clear, but no less controversial. These explanations range from constitutional factors (e.g., suggesting that the greater susceptibility of males to various constitutional disorders explains the overrepresentation of males in the mildly handicapped classifications) to the hypothesis that lower amounts of testosterone in females might account for the underrepresentation of women in programs for extremely advanced students in science and mathematics. Experiential or environmental influences are also suggested for sex disproportionality (e.g., suggestions that sex-typed behavior accounts for greater male referral for learning problems as well as fewer females excelling in math and science). Again, definitive, unequivocal results have not been established, and probably cannot be established in the foreseeable future.

Disproportionality, whether it involves overrepresentation of black students in programs for the mildly retarded or underrepresentation of women in programs for mathematically precocious youths, should be seen as a symptom, but only a symptom. Factors that might lead to disproportionality should be investigated, including possible bias or discrimination in procedures and processes whereby students are selected or placed in various programs.

Disproportionality, particularly overrepresentation of minority students in programs for the mildly mentally retarded, has provoked extensive and enormously expensive litigation beginning in about 1968 and continuing through present day (Bersoff, 1982; Prasse & Reschly, 1986; Reschly, 1986, 1991). The common features of the placement bias cases are: (1) overrepresentation of minority students, usually blacks, in self-contained MMR special classes; (2) class-action suits filed in federal district courts; and (3) allegations of bias in various aspects of the referral, preplacement evaluation, and classification/placement decision making. The outcomes of these cases have been extremely diverse, ranging from judicial decrees banning overrepresentation and forbidding the use of individually administered intelligence tests in certain circumstances to judicial decrees indicating that overrepresentation as such is not discriminatory and upholding the use of IQ tests along with other measures as an important protection for all children in the referral and classification/placement process. Federal circuit courts have upheld trial decisions in two cases, *Larry P.* v. *Riles* (1984) and *Marshall* v. *Georgia* (1985). However, the *Larry P.* and *Marshall* opinions reached opposite conclusions on a similar set of issues. Further litigation is likely.

Research methods designed to develop valid ways to screen, refer, and classify/place students that also eliminate disproportionality have been unsuccessful to date, although significant strides have been made toward reducing the cultural bias of some screening tools, such as the Kaufman

Assessment Battery for Children. However, inclusive programming (Kovach, 1997; Markowitz, 1997) has reduced many instances of placement from service provision to special education outcomes. Processes and procedures that maintain the integrity of programs in meeting the needs of students; apply reliable and valid screening, referral, and classification/placement procedures; and are being consistently implemented and assessed. Centers such as COMRISE (Center of Minority Research in Special Education) are attempting to increase the number and research capacity of minority scholars in institutions of higher education with high minority enrollments. They are building a community of minority scholars within the larger special education research community and are trying to improve the quality and effectiveness of culturally competent special education services for minority students (COMRISE, 1998). The U.S. Department of Education reports disproportionality statistics on an annual basis, and is currently focusing much attention to the less than adequate special education services delivered to inner-city students (U.S. Dept. of Education, 1996). The Office of Civil Rights (OCR) conducts compliance reviews on such issues as ensuring nondiscriminatory practices are followed in the placement of minority students in special education and low-track courses, ensuring that access to English language instruction as well as content courses and other educational benefits are afforded to limited-English proficient students, ensuring student assessment practices are nondiscriminatory, and providing nondiscriminatory access to gifted and talented and other high-ability programs (OCR, 1998). There also has been a national shift toward prereferral intervention, better interventions in regular education, orienting assessment procedures toward intervention rather than classification, the use of court orders, and the use of alternative criteria and assessment procedures (Reschly, 1991, 1997).

Recent years have seen a legislative effort to address the phenomenon of disproportionality in special education. Indeed, the major federal statute in this area, the Individuals with Disabilities Education Act, includes requirements that states develop policies and procedures to prevent overidentification as children with disabilities or disproportionality by student race or ethnicity in this regard, that they collect and report data regarding any such disproportionality, and that they review and revise any relevant policies upon detecting any such disproportionality.

REFERENCES

Bersoff, D. N. (1982). The legal regulation of school psychology. In C. R. Reynolds & T. B. Gutkin (Eds.), *The handbook of school psychology* (pp. 1043–1074). New York: Wiley.

Bickel, W. E. (1982). Classifying mentally retarded students: A review of placement practice in special education. In K. A. Heller, W. H. Holtzman, & S. Messick (Eds.), *Placing children in special education: A strategy for equity* (pp. 182–229). Washington, DC: National Academy.

COMRISE. (1998). *Center of Minority Research in Special Education*. Charlottesville: University of Virginia, Curry School of Education.

Finn, J. D. (1982). Patterns in special education placement as revealed by OCR surveys. In R. A. Heller, W. H. Holtzman, & S. Messick (Eds.), *Placing children in special education: A strategy for equity* (pp. 322–381). Washington, DC: National Academy.

Heller, K., Holtzman, W., & Messick, S. (Eds.). (1982). *Placing children in special education: A strategy for equity*. Washington, DC: National Academy.

Kovach, J. A., & Gordon, D. E. (1997). Inclusive education: A modern-day civil-rights struggle. *Educational Forum, 6*(3), 247–57.

Markowitz, J. (1997). *Addressing the disproportionale representation of students from racial and ethnic minority groups in special education: A resource document*. Alexandria, VA: National Association of State Directors of Special Education.

Office of Civil Rights. (1998). *Annual report to Congress, fiscal year 1996*. Washington, DC: U.S. Department of Education.

Prasse, D. P., & Reschly, D. J. (1986). *Larry P:* A case of segregation, testing, or program efficacy? *Exceptional Children, 52,* 333–346.

Reschly, D. J. (1986). Economic and cultural factors in childhood exceptionality. In R. T. Brown & C. R. Reynolds (Eds.), *Psychological perspectives on childhood exceptionality: A handbook* (pp. 423–466). New York: Wiley-Interscience.

Reschly, D. J. (1991). Bias in cognitive assessment: Implications for future litigation and professional practices. *Diagnostique, 17*(1), 86–90.

Reschly, D. J. (1997). *Disproportionate minority representation in general and special education: Patterns, issues, and alternatives*. Des Moines: Iowa State Department of Education.

Robinson, N., & Robinson, H. (1976). *The mentally retarded child* (2nd ed.). New York: McGraw-Hill.

U.S. Department of Education. (1996). *Eighteenth annual report to Congress: To assure the free appropriate public education of all children with disabilities: Implementation of the Individuals with Disabilities Education Act (IDEA)*. Washington, DC: Author.

Daniel J. Reschly
Iowa State University
Second edition

Kimberly F. Applequist
University of Colorado at Colorado Springs
Third edition

**CULTURAL BIAS IN TESTING
CULTURALLY/LINGUISTICALLY DIVERSE STUDENTS IN SPECIAL EDUCATION, REPRESENTATION OF
INDIVIDUALS WITH DISABILITIES EDUCATION IMPROVEMENT ACT OF 2004 (IDEIA)
LARRY P.
MARSHALL v. GEORGIA
NONDISCRIMINATORY ASSESSMENT**

DISTAR

DISTAR (Direct Instructional System for Teaching and Remediation) was a product name for an instructional system published by Science Research Associates Inc. (SRA). From 1964 to 1966, Siegfried Engelmann and Carl Bereiter developed the teaching methods used in the DISTAR program, which is based on a task analysis of basic skills and presentation of materials in a direct teaching model. In 1967 SRA contracted with Engelmann to develop, write, and test DISTAR reading, language, and arithmetic materials. His coauthors were Elaine Bruner, reading; Douglas Carnine, arithmetic; and Jean Osborn and Therese Engelmann, language. In 1968 Wesley Becker joined Engelmann's Follow-Through Project and in 1969 they formed the Engelmann-Becker Corporation, a private nonprofit organization providing teacher training in the Engelmann-Becker instructional model and the production of materials for Follow-Through sites. Although developmental work took place at the Engelmann-Becker Corporation, product development for DISTAR per se was performed under contract between SRA and the individual authors involved.

The DISTAR system was originally designed to teach basic skills and concepts in reading, arithmetic, and language to disadvantaged preschoolers (Guinet, 1971). However, the scope broadened to include average, above average, learning-disabled, and educable and trainable mentally retarded children (Kim, Berger, & Kratochvil, 1972). Reviews of research (Cotton & Savard, 1982; Gersten, 1981) revealed that the direct instruction method was proven successful with socioeconomically disadvantaged primary age children and special education students through age 13.

Research results comparing the DISTAR program with other direct instruction curricula indicated that DISTAR was comparable in outcomes (Kuder, 1990; Traweek & Berniger, 1997).

REFERENCES

Brinckerhoff, L. (1983, Spring). Siegfried Engleman-Prophet or Profiteer. *ADI NEWS*, p. 1.

Cotton, K., & Savard, W. G. (1982). *Direct instruction: Research on school effectiveness project.* Portland, OR: Northwest Regional Educational Lab. (ERIC Document Reproduction Service No. ED 214 909)

Direct instruction management handbook. (1981). Chicago: Science Research Associates.

Gersten, R. M. (1981, April). *Direct instruction programs in special education settings: A review of evaluation research findings.* Paper presented at the annual international convention of the Council for Exceptional Children, New York. (ERIC Document Reproduction Service No. ED 204 957)

Guinet, L. (1971). *Evaluation of DISTAR materials in three junior learning assistance classes* (Report No. 71-16). Vancouver, BC: Board of School Trustees, Department of Planning and Evaluation. (ERIC Document Reproduction Service No. ED 057 105)

Kim, Y., Berger, B. J., & Kratochvil, D. W. (1972). *DISTAR instructional system* (Report No. OEC-0-70-4892). Washington, DC: Office of Education, Office of Program Planning and Evaluation. (ERIC Document Reproduction Service No. ED 061 632)

Kuder, S. J. (1990). Effectiveness of the DISTAR reading program for children with learning disabilities. *Journal of Learning Disabilities, 23*(1), 69–71.

Moodie, A., & Hoen, R. (1972). *Evaluation of DISTAR programs in learning assistance classes of Vancouver 1971–72* (Report No. 72-18). Vancouver, BC: Board of School Trustees, Department of Planning and Evaluation. (ERIC Document Reproduction Service No. ED 088 911)

Traweek, D., & Berniger, V. (1997). Comparison of beginning literacy programs. *Learning Disability Quarterly, 20*(2), 160–168.

MARY D'IPPOLITO
*Montgomery County
Intermediate Unit,
Norristown, Pennsylvania*

DIRECT INSTRUCTION
FOLLOW THROUGH

DISTRACTIBILITY

Distractibility refers to difficulties in sustaining attention to tasks, concentrating, tracking, and screening out interfering distractions (Lezak, 1995). A child who is distractible may appear to be daydreaming, doodling, or paying unnecessary attention to what others are doing (Children and Adults with Attention Deficit Disorders [CHADD], 2000). Children described as distractible typically display shorter attention spans than do their same-age peers, and they usually have difficulty completing assignments when multitasking is involved. Their inability to focus attention may result in uncompleted assignments and forgotten items. Distractibility negatively impacts a child's ability successfully to complete school and household tasks.

Characteristics of distractibility may be:

1. Difficulty maintaining attention to expected tasks or activities
2. Limited follow-through of required tasks
3. Slow response to directions
4. Failure to devote sufficient attention to tasks so that crucial components of the task are left out and finished products are often messy and unorganized
5. Difficulty listening and apparent inability to follow directions
6. High susceptibility to environmental distractions
7. Limitations in organizing tasks and activities; frequently loss of items needed for task completion or day-to-day items (e.g., homework or lunch money)

8. Avoidance or inability to complete assignments involving continued concentration

9. Appearance of forgetfulness with daily activities

10. Sluggish reaction time

Much of the information and research related to the topic of distractibility is derived from the inattentive subtype of Attention-Deficit/Hyperactivity Disorder (ADHD). The term ADHD is a relatively common neurobiological disorder that affects between 3 and 7 percent of school-aged children, with males being between 2 to 9 times more likely to exhibit these concerns than females (American Psychiatric Association, 2000). Between 40 and 60 percent of children with ADHD also exhibit characteristics of other disorders including learning disabilities, emotional-behavioral disorders, mood disorders, tics or Tourette syndrome, and anxiety disorders (CHADD, 2000). Additionally, frontal lobe injuries or deficits have been associated with limitations in focusing and shifting attention (Mirsky, 1989).

A multimodal treatment approach incorporating medical, psychological, educational, and behavior management interventions has been found to produce the best results in treating children who are distractible (Gaddes & Edgell, 1994). Psychostimulant medication is effective with 70 to 80 percent of children diagnosed with ADHD (CHADD, 2000); methylphenidate (Ritalin), dextroamphetamine (Dexedrine), and pemoline (Cylert) are usually prescribed. These medications are used to improve a child's ability to attend to tasks and to decrease off-task behavior. Frequently reported side effects of stimulant medication include insomnia, headaches, appetite suppression, and irritability when the dose wears off. Growth suppression can be an issue with long-term medication usage. Overall, research indicates that medication helps students with distractibility obtain maximum benefit from educational and behavioral interventions (Bohlmeyer, 1998).

Psychological interventions often include group or individual counseling. The focus of counseling interventions may include social skills development, behavioral self-monitoring, and classroom management regarding the nature of this condition. Parents are also targeted for intervention by providing them with information about distractibility and connecting them with available support groups. Parents, teachers, and others involved with the child on a daily basis can also receive training on using behavioral signals that redirect a child back to the task at hand. Behavioral contracts that outline expectations and rewards for meeting expectations are also effective in many cases (Bohlmeyer, 1998). The use of a coach who offers reminders, feedback, and encouragement may improve a child's work-completion rate and time on task (Hallowell & Ratey, 1994).

Educational techniques designed to reduce a student's level of distractibility generally involve interventions in which the child's teacher implements classroom accommodations to address the child's needs. Efficacious techniques include: (a) providing brief, clear, and specific directions; (b) establishing eye contact prior to giving directions; (c) asking the child to repeat verbal directions for clarification; (d) providing the child with frequent feedback regarding performance; (e) breaking down lengthy assignments into small steps; (f) allowing students a choice of academic assignments; and (g) maintaining a consistent structure so that the child understands the expectations. Peer tutoring and self-monitoring are also school interventions that have been helpful in reducing distractibility by providing children who are distractible with exposure to a model of appropriate behavior and a source of frequent feedback (Brock, 1998).

Other alternative approaches to treating distractibility have been developed to help children stay on task. However, there is no credible scientific evidence to support the use of alternative treatments, such as dietary intervention (e.g., the Feingold diet), electroencephalogram biofeedback, applied kinesiology, optometric vision training, mineral supplements, candida yeast, or anti–motion sickness medications (CHADD, 2000).

Children who have difficulty sustaining attention are at risk for academic difficulties and emotional concerns such as lowered self-esteem. Although it once was thought that children outgrew ADHD in adolescence, it is now understood that the effects of the disability may continue into adulthood. The long-term prognosis is hopeful for those children who receive individual interventions early in life designed to meet their needs and help them succeed at home and school. Longitudinal research indicates that children who obtain appropriate interventions for ADHD exhibit fewer school, substance abuse, and interpersonal problems while demonstrating greater overall functioning than do those who do not receive individualized treatment. Although some children may continue to display distractible behaviors as adults, most can learn compensation strategies and access sources of support that help them remain on task and attain their goals.

REFERENCES

American Psychiatric Association. (2000). *Diagnostic and statistical manual of mental disorders* (4th ed., Text Revision). Washington, DC: Author.

Bohlmeyer, E. M. (1998). Attention deficit disorder: A primer for parents. In A. S. Canter & S. A. Carroll (Eds.), *Helping children at home and school: Handouts from your school psychologist* (pp. 539–541). Bethesda, MD: National Association of School Psychologists.

Brock, S. E. (1998, February). Classroom-based interventions for students with ADHD. *Communiqué*, 8–10.

Children and Adults with Attention Deficit Disorders (CHADD). (2000, November 18). Retrieved from http://www.chadd.org/facts/add_facts.htm

Gaddes, W. H., & Edgell, D. (1994). *Learning disabilities and brain function: A neuropsychological approach.* New York: Springer.

Hallowell, E. M., & Ratey, J. J. (1994). *Driven to distraction.* New York: Pantheon Books.

Lezak, M. D. (1995). *Neuropsychological assessment* (3rd ed.). New York: Oxford University Press.

Mirsky, A. S. (1989). The neuropsychology of attention: Elements of a complex behavior. In E. Perecman (Ed.), *Integrating theory and practice in clinical neuropsychology.* Hillsdale, NJ: Erlbaum.

BOB KIRCHNER
University of Northern Colorado

SHAWN POWELL
United States Air Force Academy

ATTENTION DEFICIT/HYPERACTIVITY DISORDER
ATTENTION SPAN
CONNERS RATING SCALES
FREEDOM FROM DISTRACTIBILITY
HYPERKINESIS
IMPULSE CONTROL

DIVORCE AND SPECIAL EDUCATION

Since the mid 1970s, the impact of parental divorce on children has been an area of concern for professionals in psychology and education. This interdisciplinary consensus has been generated in part by alarming Census descriptions of rapidly changing adult lifestyles. For example, Census reports indicate that the divorce rate more than quadrupled from 1970 to 1994. Since these figures did not account for those who were divorced and remarried at the time of the survey, they actually underestimate the total incidence of divorce in our society. Similarly, the incidence of single-parent child rearing also increased markedly from 11.9 percent in 1970 to 29 percent in 1994. These figures did not include those who have previously experienced a single-parent situation but were living in reconstituted two-parent families.

A central issue is whether adjustment to divorce represents a transitory stressor or is associated with long-term disorders. Longitudinal studies provide a consensus that divorce should be conceptualized as a multistage process (Hetherington, Cox, & Cox, 1978, 1985; Wallerstein, 1985; Wallerstein & Kelly, 1974). These studies, conducted over periods of 6 and 10 years, respectively, reveal complex interactions and altered family relationships that result in long-term maladjustment for children. They also illustrate substantial age and sex differences in adjustment.

Wallerstein and Kelly (Kelly & Wallerstein, 1976; Wallerstein, 1984, 1985; Wallerstein & Kelly, 1974, 1975, 1976, 1980a, 1980b) conducted a 10-year longitudinal study of 131 children residing in Marin County, California, whose parents were divorced. This was a nonclinical sample of children, ages 2½ to 18 years, from white, middle-class families. Clinical interviews were conducted just after separation, and at 1-, 5-, and 10-year intervals following divorce. Initial results revealed that children responded differently by age. At the 1-year follow-up, adjustment problems persisted, although most adolescents had made adequate adjustments (attributed to distancing from parents and successful mastery experiences during the past year). At the 5-year follow-up, variables that mediate children's adjustment to divorce were identified—resolution of parental conflict, child's relationship with noncustodial parent, quality of parenting by custodial parent, personality and coping skills of the child, child's support system, diminished anger and depression in the child, and age and sex of the child. A positive relationship with the father was more important for boys than girls. Results of the 10-year follow-up (of 113 original subjects) confirmed the long-term impact of divorce. Difficulties at 10 years were characterized by poor parenting (diminished capacity to parent) and an overburdened child (taking on of adult responsibility).

Hetherington, Cox, and Cox (Hetherington, 1979; Hetherington et al., 1978, 1979a, 1979b, 1982, 1985) used a sample of 96 divorced- and intact-family preschool-age children from white, middle-class families in Virginia. Children were assessed at 2 months, and 1, 2, and 6 years after divorce. A comprehensive, multifactored, multisource approach to assessment was used to assess sex-role typing and cognitive and social development of the child.

Results indicated severe disorganization and stress during the first year. Difficulties were evident in parenting behavior and child adjustment. Divorced parents were less able than nondivorced parents to cope with parenting. They made fewer maturity demands, were less consistent in discipline, used less reasoning, communicated less with the child, and displayed less interaction with and affection toward the child. Children were more dependent, disobedient, aggressive, demanding, unaffectionate, and whining. Mother-son relationships were particularly affected, characterized by a cycle of poor parenting, child aggression, coercive parenting, increased negative child behavior, and parental feelings of helplessness and incompetence. By 2 years, most of the negative effects had abated. Factors that facilitated adjustment included low parental conflict and parental agreement on child rearing. Results at 6 years (which included a remarried sample) indicated that divorce had a more negative impact on boys and remarriage had a more negative impact on girls. Externalizing problems were more stable across time for boys and internalizing problems more stable for girls. Divorced-family children experienced more negative life changes, which were, in turn, related to more behavior problems at follow-up.

Kurdek et al. (Kurdek, 1981, 1983, 1985, 1987; Kurdek & Berg, 1983; Kurdek, Blisk, & Siesky, 1981; Kurdek & Siesky, 1980a, 1980b; Kurdek & Sinclair, 1985) examined the role of cognitive mediators in children's adjustment to divorce. Their initial study included a sample of 70 divorced-family children, mean age of 9.92 years, from white middle-class families in Dayton, Ohio, whose parents were members of Parents Without Partners. Results revealed that children's adjustment to divorce was facilitated by an internal locus of control, accurate perceptions of social situations (i.e., understanding of interpersonal relations), low interpersonal stress, and good father-child relationships. They found that children's reasoning about divorce was linked to the development of logical and social reasoning. Further, the level of cognitive understanding determined whether the child's thinking about divorce was nonegocentric; focused on parents' thoughts, feelings, and intentions; and was grounded in an appreciation of the complex dynamics of interpersonal relations.

Using a national sample of 18,000 elementary and secondary students from 14 states, Brown (1980) compared one-parent (divorced, separated, widowed, unmarried) and two-parent families. Global measures of adjustment such as grade point average, attendance, suspensions, truancy, and referral for discipline problems were obtained from school records. Findings indicated that the impact for elementary-aged children was evident on behavioral (e.g., suspensions and truancy) and academic indexes. For high-school children, differences were evident on behavioral indexes (e.g., expulsions, tardiness, suspensions); however, there appeared to be little impact on academic achievement.

The research of Stolberg et al. (Stolberg, 1987; Stolberg & Anker, 1983; Stolberg & Bush, 1985; Stolberg & Cullen, 1983; Stolberg, Kiluk, & Garrison, 1986) has focused on environmental factors that mediate children's adjustment to divorce, including such factors as parenting skills, visitation, and family changes associated with divorce. Local samples obtained through Parents Without Partners, newspaper ads, and schools were used. They found parenting skills, frequency of life changes, and marital hostility to be successful predictors of prosocial skills and psychopathology of divorced-family children. Parenting skills (of the mother/custodial parent) were found to be the single most significant influence on child adjustment, particularly affecting prosocial skills. There was no direct relationship between parent and child adjustment when effects of parenting skills were removed.

Furstenberg et al. (Furstenberg, Nord, Peterson, & Zill, 1983; Furstenberg & Spanier, 1984) used data from a national sociological study of children's well being. The representative sample included 1,300 U.S. children (ages 11 to 16) and their families, and subsequent subsamples of divorced and remarried families. Findings from this study revealed a racial difference in divorce and remarriage rates, with blacks one and a half times as likely to divorce but less likely to remarry than whites (remarriage rate: one out of eight for blacks, four out of seven for whites). Frequent contact (at least once per week) of the child with the noncustodial parent was evident in only 17 percent of the divorced sample. Those variables that best predicted amount of contact with the noncustodial parent, irrespective of the child's sex, included provision of child support and residential propinquity, which were positively related to amount of contact, and length of time since separation, which was negatively related.

Findings from other studies relevant to determinants of children's postdivorce adjustment indicate that adjustment is facilitated by availability of the noncustodial parent and a positive relationship with the custodial parent (Hess & Camara, 1979); parent-child discussion of divorce-related topics (Jacobson, 1978a, 1978b); low interpersonal hostility prior to separation (Berg & Kelly, 1979; Jacobson, 1978a, 1978b, 1978c); and more time spent with the father (Jacobson, 1978a, 1978c).

In reviewing the literature on remarriage, Kurdek and Sinclair (1985) conclude that similarities exist between children's adjustment to divorce and to remarriage in that children from both situations (compared with those in intact families) exhibit higher deviance rates, more difficulty in management, and lower self-esteem, as do their parents. Although findings are conflicting, past research generally indicates that (1) remarriage does not necessarily stabilize the family; (2) children reexperience the disruption associated with divorce when parents remarry; and (3) the parent's situation in reference to role strain does not necessarily improve with remarriage.

Critical reviews of past research have consistently indicated severe methodological limitations (Atkeson, Forehand, & Rickard, 1982; Clingempeel & Reppucci, 1982; Kurdek, 1981, 1983). Major limitations include (1) small and biased samples that limit generalizability of the findings; (2) inadequate or nonexistent control groups, which precludes the study of divorce-specific effects, (3) failure to control for socioeconomic status in comparisons between divorced and intact families; and (4) failure to include multimethod, multifactored criteria to control for measurement bias.

The NASP-KSU (National Association of School Psychologists—Kent State University) Impact of Divorce Project was directed at minimizing the limitations of the cited research in order to provide more definitive conclusions about the long-term impact of divorce on children (Guidubaldi, 1983, 1985; Guidubaldi & Cleminshaw, 1985; Guidubaldi, Cleminshaw, & Perry, 1985; Guidubaldi, Cleminshaw, Perry, & Mcloughlin, 1983; Guidubaldi, Cleminshaw, Perry, & Nastasi, 1984; Guidubaldi, Cleminshaw, Perry, Nastasi, & Lightel, 1986; Guidubaldi & Nastasi, 1984; Guidubaldi & Perry, 1985, 1987; Guidubaldi, Perry, & Cleminshaw, 1984; Guidubaldi, Perry, & Nastasi, 1986). Results on 699 children from 38 states at the initial data-gathering period (Time-1) demonstrated more conclusively than previous studies that, during middle childhood (ages 6 to 11), youths are adversely affected by divorce. Because the average length of time in a single-parent home at Time-1 was 3.98 years (SD = 2.54), these effects were interpreted as long term. Specific criteria on which children from divorced homes performed more poorly than those from intact homes are as follows: (1) social-behavioral measures from parent and teacher ratings of peer popularity status, anxiety, dependency, aggression, withdrawal, inattention, and locus of control; (2) Wechsler IQ scores; (3) Wide Range Achievement Test scores in reading, spelling, and math; (4) school performance indexes, including grades in reading and math and repeating of a school grade; (5) adaptive behaviors (measured by the Vineland Teacher Rating Scale) in the areas of daily living, social skills, and communication; and (6) physical health ratings of the children in the study as well as of parents and siblings. Intact-family children showed superior performance on 21 of 27 social competence criteria and 8 of 9 academic competence criteria. Additionally, analyses revealed that divorced-family children were far more likely to have been previously referred to a school psychologist, to have been retained in grade, and to be in special class placements, including programs for reading difficulties.

Definition of the sequelae of divorce is a complex process, and assessment must therefore include not only multidimensional aspects of child and parent adjustment but also a longitudinal-ecological approach. The NASP-KSU study thus included follow-up samples of 229 children at 2- and 3-year intervals, and examined environmental factors as mediators of children's postdivorce adjustment. Major findings from this nationwide study are as follows:

1. The negative, differential effects of divorce on children and young adolescents are long term where the average length of time since divorce was 6.41 years (SD = 2.35) at Time-2 of this study.

2. Children's reactions to divorce are especially influenced by sex and age, with boys during late childhood and early adolescence being more adversely affected on multiple criteria than 6- and 7-year-old boys. Late childhood and young adolescent girls were much better adjusted than those at the 6- and 7-year age levels.

3. Single-parent, divorced-family households have significantly less income than intact families. This difference accounts for significant academic achievement variance between divorced- and intact-family children.

4. The socioeconomic measures of parents' educational and occupational levels moderate some of children's divorce adjustment. This is especially apparent in regard to the educational level of the same sex parent.

5. A positive relationship with both the custodial and noncustodial parent predicted positive adjustment for both girls and boys of divorce concurrently and across time. The noncustodial parent-child relationship was noticeably more important for boys.

6. More frequent and reliable visitation with the noncustodial parent (typically, the father) was associated with better adjustment for both girls and boys.

7. Diminished degree of conflict between parents predicted improved children's adjustment, especially for boys across time to early adolescence.

8. Authoritarian (i.e., punitive) child-rearing styles in comparison with authoritative (i.e., more democratic) and permissive styles predicted more adverse child adjustment, especially for boys.

9. The home routines of less television viewing, regular bedtimes, maternal employment, and helpfulness of maternal grandfather predict positive adjustment for both boys and girls.

10. Family support factors that promote positive postdivorce adjustment are availability of helpful relatives, including in-laws, availability of friends, paid child care assistance such as nursery schools and babysitters, and participation in occupational and educational endeavors by the custodial parent.

11. When the total sample of male and female divorced-family children are considered, school environment variables of smaller school population, safe and orderly atmosphere, fewer miles bused to school, and traditional rather than open classroom structure are associated with better adjustment. However, several school and classroom climate factors relate to better adjustment for girls only. These include safe and orderly environment, frequent monitoring of student progress, high expectations for academic achievement, and time on task.

The impact of divorce on children has appropriately become a central concern of mainstream education. Special educators perhaps need to focus even more on this rapidly increasing disruption of children's lives. As evidenced in the NASP-KSU nationwide study and in Beattie and Maniscalo (1985), children in special education programs disproportionately come from divorced, single-parent homes. Income levels, home routines, and parental supports are adversely affected by this condition and children from these homes, particularly boys, show overwhelming evidence of maladjustment in both academic and social-emotional areas of performance. Understanding conditions that can ameliorate the negative impact of divorce on children may be one of the most critical bases for development of preventive mental health interventions as well as remedial techniques for children already identified as special.

REFERENCES

Atkeson, B. M., Forehand, R. L., & Rickard, K. M. (1982). The effects of divorce on children. In B. B. Lahey & A. E. Kazdin (Eds.), *Advances in clinical child psychology* (Vol. 5). New York: Plenum.

Baumrind, D. (1972). Socialization and instrumental competence in young children. In I. B. Weiner & D. Elkind (Eds.), *Readings in child development* (pp. 178–195). New York: Wiley.

Beattie, J. R., & Maniscalo, G. O. (1985). Special education and divorce. Is there a line? *Techniques, 1*(5), 342–345.

Berg, B., & Kelly, R. (1979). The measured self-esteem of children from broken, rejected, and accepted families. *Journal of Divorce, 2,* 263–369.

Brown, B. F. (1980). A study of the school needs of children from one-parent families. *Phi Delta Kappa, 62,* 537–540.

Clingempeel, W. G., & Reppucci, N. D. (1982). Joint custody after divorce: Major issues and goals for research. *Psychological Bulletin, 91,* 102–127.

Furstenberg, F. F., Nord, C. W., Peterson, J. L., & Zill, N. (1983) The life course of children of divorce: Marital disruption and parental contact. *American Sociological Review, 48,* 656–668.

Furstenberg, F. F., & Spanier, G. B. (1984). *Recycling the family.* Beverly Hills, CA: Sage.

Glick, P. C., & Norton, A. J. (1977). Marrying, divorcing and living together in the U.S. today. *Population Bulletin, 5,* 32.

Guidubaldi, J. (1983, July). Divorce research clarifies issues: A report on NASP's nationwide study. *Communiqué, 10,* 1–3.

Guidubaldi, J. (1985). Differences in children's divorce adjustment across grade level and gender: A report from the NASP-Kent State University Nationwide Project. In S. Wolchik & P. Karoly (Eds.), *Children of divorce: Perspectives on adjustment.* Lexington, MA: Lexington.

Guidubaldi, J., & Cleminshaw, H. (1985). Divorce, family health and child adjustment. *Family Relations, 34,* 35–41.

Guidubaldi, J., Cleminshaw, H., & Perry, J. (1985). The relationship of parental divorce to health status of parents and children. *Special Services in the Schools, 1,* 73–81.

Guidubaldi, J., Cleminshaw, H. K., Perry, J. D., & Mcloughlin, C. S. (1983). The impact of parental divorce on children: Report of the nationwide NASP study. *School Psychology Review, 12,* 300–323.

Guidubaldi, J., Cleminshaw, H. K., Perry, J., & Nastasi, B. (1984). Impact of family support systems on children's academic and social functioning after divorce. In G. Rowe, J. DeFrain, H. Lingrin, R. MacDonald, N. Stinnet, S. Van Zandt, & R. Williams (Eds.), *Family strengths 5: Continuity and diversity* (pp. 191–207). Newton, MA: Education Development Center.

Guidubaldi, J., Cleminshaw, H. K., Perry, J. D., Nastasi, B. K., & Lightel, J. (1986). The role of selected family environment factors in, children's post-divorce adjustment. *Family Relations, 35,* 141–151.

Guidubaldi, J., & Nastasi, B. (1984, April). Classroom climate and post-divorce child adjustment. In J. Guidubaldi (Chair), *Factors related to academic and social adjustment of elementary grade divorced-family children.* Symposium conducted at the annual convention of the American Educational Research Association, New Orleans.

Guidubaldi, J., & Perry, J. D. (1985). Divorce and mental health sequelae for children: A two-year follow-up of a nationwide sample. *Journal of the American Academy of Child Psychiatry, 24,* 531–537.

Guidubaldi, J., & Perry, J. D. (1987). Assessment of adolescents' divorce adjustment and custody arrangements. In R. G. Harrington (Ed.), *Testing adolescents.* Kansas City, MO: Test Corporation of America.

Guidubaldi, J., Perry, J. D., & Cleminshaw, H. K. (1984). The legacy of parental divorce: A nationwide study of family status and selected mediating variables on children's academic and social competencies. In B. B. Lahey & A. E. Kazdin (Eds.), *Advances in clinical child psychology* (Vol. 7, pp. 109–151). New York: Plenum.

Guidubaldi, J., Perry, J. D., & Nastasi, B. K. (1986). Growing up in a divorced family: Initial and long-term perspectives on children's adjustment. In S. Oskamp (Ed.), *Annual review of social psychology.* Beverly Hills, CA: Sage.

Hess, R. D., & Camara, K. A. (1979). Post-divorce family relationships as mediating factors in the consequences of divorce for children. *Journal of Social Issues, 35*(4), 79–96.

Hetherington, E. M. (1979). Divorce: A child's perspective. *American Psychologist, 34,* 851–858.

Hetherington, E. M., Cox, M., & Cox, R. (1978). The aftermath of divorce. In J. H. Stevens, Jr., & M. Mathews (Eds.), *Mother-child, father-child relationships* (pp. 149–176). Washington, DC: National Association for Education of Young Children.

Hetherington, E. M., Cox, M., & Cox, R. (1979a). Family interaction and the social-emotional and cognitive development of children following divorce. In V. Vaughn & T. Brazelton (Eds.), *The family setting priorities.* New York: Science and Medicine.

Hetherington, E. M., Cox, M., & Cox, R. (1979b). Play and social interaction in children following divorce. *Journal of Social Issues, 35,* 26–49.

Hetherington, E. M., Cox, M., & Cox, R. (1982). Effects of divorce on parents and children. In M. E. Lamb (Ed.), *Nontraditional families: Parenting and child development* (pp. 233–288). Hillsdale, NJ: Erlbaum.

Hetherington, E. M., Cox, M., & Cox, R. (1985). Long-term effects of divorce and remarriage on the adjustment of children. *Journal of the American Academy of Child Psychiatry, 24,* 518–530.

Jacobson, D. S. (1978a). The impact of marital separation/divorce on children. I. Parent-child separation and child adjustment. *Journal of Divorce, 1*(4), 341–360.

Jacobson, D. S. (1978b). The impact of marital separation/divorce on children: II. Interparent hostility and child adjustment. *Journal of Divorce, 2,* 3–19.

Jacobson, D. S. (1978c). The impact of marital separation/divorce on children: III. Parent-child communication and child adjustment, and regression analysis of findings from overall study. *Journal of Divorce, 2,* 175–194.

Jenkins, J. E., & Guidubaldi, J. (1997). Nature-nurture controversy revisited: Divorce and gender as factors in children's racial group differences. *Child Study Journal, 27*(2), 145–160.

Kelly, J. B., & Wallerstein, J. S. (1976). The effects of parental divorce: Experiences of the child in early latency. *American Journal of Orthopsychiatry, 46,* 20–23.

Kurdek, L. A. (1981). An integrative perspective on children's divorce adjustment. *American Psychologist, 36,* 856–866.

Kurdek, L. A. (Ed.). (1983). *Children and divorce.* San Francisco: Jossey-Bass.

Kurdek, L. A. (1985). Children's reasoning about parental divorce. In R. D. Ashmore & D. M. Brodzinsky (Eds.), *Perspectives on the family* (pp. 1–48). Hillsdale, NJ: Erlbaum.

Kurdek, L. A. (1987). Cognitive mediators of children's adjustment to divorce. In S. Wolchick & D. Karoly (Eds.), *Children of divorce: Perspectives on adjustment.* New York: Gardner.

Kurdek, L. A., & Berg, B. (1983). Correlates of children's adjustment to their parents' divorces. In L. A. Kurdek (Ed.), *Children and divorce* (pp. 47–60). San Francisco: Jossey-Bass.

Kurdek, L. A., Blisk, D., & Siesky, A. E. (1981). Correlates of children's long-term adjustment to their parents' divorce. *Developmental Psychology, 17,* 565–579.

Kurdek, L. A., & Siesky, A. E. (1980a). Sex role self-concepts of single divorced parents and their children. *Journal of Divorce, 3,* 249–261.

Kurdek, L. A., & Siesky, A. E. (1980b). Children's perceptions of their parents' divorce. *Journal of Divorce, 3,* 339–378.

Kurdek, L. A., & Sinclair, R. (1985). *The relation between adolescent adjustment and family structure, grade, and gender.* Unpublished manuscript, Wright State University, Department of Psychology, Dayton, OH.

Stolberg, A. L. (1987). Prevention programs for divorcing families. In L. Bond (Ed.), *Vermont Conference on the Primary Prevention of Psychopathology.* Burlington, VT: Author.

Stolberg, A., & Anker, J. (1983). Cognitive and behavioral changes in children resulting from parental divorce and consequent environmental changes. *Journal of Divorce, 7,* 23–41.

Stolberg, A. L., & Bush, J. P. (1985). A path analysis of factors predicting children's divorce adjustment. *Journal of Clinical Child Psychology, 14,* 49–54.

Stolberg, A. L., & Cullen, P. M. (1983). Preventive interventions for families of divorce: Divorce Adjustment Project. In L. A. Kurdek (Ed.), *Children and divorce* (pp. 71–82). San Francisco: Jossey-Bass.

Stolberg, A. L., Kiluk, D., & Garrison, K. M. (1986). A temporal model of divorce adjustment with implications for primary prevention. In S. M. Auerbach & A. L. Stolberg (Eds.), *Issues in clinical and community psychology: Crisis intervention with children and families.* Washington, DC: Hemisphere.

U.S. Bureau of the Census. (1979). *Divorce, child custody, and child support* (Current Population Reports, Series P-23, No. 84). Washington, DC: U.S. Government Printing Office.

U.S. Bureau of the Census. (1982a). *Household and family characteristics: March 1981* (Current Population Reports, Series P-20, No. 371). Washington, DC: U.S. Government Printing Office.

U.S. Bureau of the Census. (1982b). *Marital status and living arrangements: March 1981* (Current Population Reports, Series P-20, No. 372). Washington, DC: U.S. Government Printing Office.

U.S. Bureau of the Census. (1984). *Marital status and living arrangements: March 1983* (Current Population Reports, Series P-20). Washington, DC: U.S. Government Printing Office.

Wallerstein, J. S. (1984). Children of divorce: Preliminary report of a ten-year follow-up of young children. *American Journal of Orthopsychiatry, 54,* 444–453.

Wallerstein, J. S. (1985). Children of divorce: Preliminary report of a ten-year follow-up of older children and adolescents. *Journal of the American Academy of Child Psychiatry, 24,* 545–553.

Wallerstein, J. S., & Kelly, J. B. (1974). The effects of parental divorce: The adolescent experience. In E. Anthony & C. Koupanik (Eds.), *The child and his family* (Vol. 3, pp. 479–505). New York: Wiley.

Wallerstein, J. S., & Kelly, J. B. (1975). The effects of parental divorce: Experiences of the preschool child. *Journal of the American Academy of Child Psychiatry, 14,* 600–616.

Wallerstein, J. S., & Kelly, J. B. (1976). The effects of parental divorce experiences of the child in later latency. *American Journal of Orthopsychiatry, 46,* 256–267.

Wallerstein, J. S., & Kelly, J. B. (1980a). California's children of divorce. *Psychology Today, 13,* 66–67.

Wallerstein, J. S., & Kelly, J. B. (1980b). *Surviving the break-up: How children and parents cope with divorce.* New York: Basic Books.

JOHN GUIDUBALDI
BONNIE K. NASTASI
Kent State University

DIX, DOROTHEA L. (1802–1887)

Dorothea Dix, a humanitarian and social reformer, was responsible for major reforms in the care of the mentally ill in the United States and abroad. Shocked by the common practice of incarcerating mentally ill people in jails with criminals, she spent a year and a half investigating conditions in her home state of Massachusetts and, in 1843, reported her findings to the state legislature. Her description of the abhorrent conditions that existed (including the use of chains for restraint) and her argument that mentally ill persons could be properly treated and cared for only in hospitals, resulted in substantial enlargement of the state

Dorthea L. Dix

hospital at Worcester, which was one of only eight mental hospitals in the United States at that time. Capitalizing on her success in Massachusetts, Dix turned her attention to other states and countries. She was responsible for the construction of 32 hospitals in the United States and others in Canada, Europe, and Japan.

During the Civil War, Dix served as superintendent of women nurses, the highest office held by a woman during the war. After the war she returned, at age 65, to her work with hospitals. In 1881 she retired to the New Jersey State Hospital at Trenton, the first hospital established through her efforts, where she remained until her death.

REFERENCE

Marshall, H. E. (1937). *Dorothea Dix, forgotten samaritan.* Chapel Hill: University of North Carolina Press.

PAUL IRVINE
Katonah, New York

DOCTORAL TRAINING IN SPECIAL EDUCATION

The common purpose of doctoral-level education training programs is to prepare leaders for the field, but the programs themselves are as diverse as the roles their graduates assume. Many local, state, and federal administrators, college and university teacher trainers, scholars, and researchers hold the doctorate in special education. Both the doctor of philosophy (PhD) and the doctor of education (DEd or EdD) are awarded. Although the PhD is considered an academic degree and the DEd a professional degree, this distinction does not hold up in practice because many prominent scholars hold the DEd and many practitioners the PhD.

Students are typically selected for doctoral training on the basis of their potential for success in advanced graduate training and the potential they exhibit as special education leaders. Programs frequently use the previous academic achievement of their applicants and Graduate Record Examination scores (or both) to predict success in advanced graduate work. Leadership potential is evaluated through previous professional experience, professional references, and, occasionally, statements of professional goals (by which the seriousness of an applicant's intent may be judged). Typically, admission is competitive.

A program of study is planned under the direction of an advisor (or major professor) and a supervisory committee. The program typically derives from the aspirations of the student and the strengths of the program offerings. In addition to special education course work, doctoral programs may include concentrations in a related field of study or cognate area and work in research methodology and statistics. The successful completion of course work, however, represents only a fraction of the formal requirements that a doctoral candidate must meet. Many programs require a qualifying examination before formal admission to candidacy and, later in the program, a comprehensive examination to determine mastery of the program of studies. Doctoral programs culminate with the completion of an independent research project and the preparation and defense of the dissertation. The supervisory committee evaluates the student's performance at each of these checkpoints.

These formal requirements represent only part of what students learn during their doctoral studies. Many have the opportunity (often as graduate assistants) to develop skills in teaching, supervision, administration, and research. Initially, their participation in these activities is guided by the faculty. With experience, candidates may take on more responsibility and operate with greater independence. Many programs provide financial support for graduate assistants with funds from leadership preparation grants awarded by the U.S. Department of Education's Office of Special Education and Rehabilitative Services.

The importance of these informal experiences in the full preparation of doctoral students was established in an analysis of the credentials of recent graduates. Rose, Cullinan, and Heller (1984) reported that recent graduates who were considered competitive applicants for college and university positions had published at least three articles, presented more than four papers at national conferences, written or assisted in the writing of two grant applications, taught at least one course independently, and conducted numerous workshops and consultancies. Clearly, there is much to be accomplished beyond the formal requirements of a doctoral program for its graduates to compete successfully in the academic job market.

Finally, it must be emphasized that leadership preparation programs have undertaken a critical self-evaluation in response to the common and difficult problems they face: the quantity and quality of students, the poor focus of their offerings, faculty dissatisfaction, and low faculty productivity (Prehm, 1984). With regard to this final concern, research (Schloss & Sindelar, 1985) has shown that productive researchers are the exception and not the rule, even for faculties of doctoral-granting programs. The recent efforts of the Higher Education Consortium for Special Education, an organization representing institutions with comprehensive programs in special education, in developing indicators of quality in leadership training represent a positive first step in addressing these issues. There has been a call for a national data collection system to address a critical shortage of doctoral-level specialists (Smith, 1990).

REFERENCES

Prehm, H. J. (1984). Preparation for leadership in personnel preparation. *Teacher Education & Special Education, 7,* 59–65.

Rose, T. L., Cullinan, D., & Heller, H. W. (1984). A consumer's report of special education doctoral programs. *Teacher Education & Special Education, 7,* 88–91.

Schloss, P. J., & Sindelar, P. T. (1985). Publication frequencies of departments conferring the PhD in special education. *Teacher Education and Special Education, 8,* 67–76.

Sindelar, P. T., & Schloss, P. J. (1986). The reputations of doctoral training program in special education. *Journal of Special Education, 20,* 49–59.

Smith, D. D. (1990) *History and future needs of doctoral training in special education.* (ERIC Clearinghouse No. EC301042)

PAUL T. SINDELAR
Florida State University

SPECIALNET
SUPERVISION IN SPECIAL EDUCATION
TEACHER CENTERS

DOG GUIDES FOR THE BLIND

The use of dogs to guide blind persons has a long history. However, it was not until after World War I that the dog was systematically trained to guide blinded German veterans. The veterans were taught to follow the trained dog's movements through the use of a specially designed harness.

An American, Dorothy Harrison Eustis, living in Switzerland, described the use of German shepherds as dog guides for the blind in a 1927 article published in the *Saturday Evening Post.* One of the Americans who got in touch with Eustis after the publication of the article was Morris Frank, a young man from Tennessee who had been recently blinded. He persuaded Eustis to have a dog trained for him and traveled to Switzerland to be trained with the dog.

After Frank's success with the first American dog guide, the legendary Buddy, Eustis returned to the United States in 1929 and established The Seeing Eye Inc., the first school to train dog guides for the blind in America. The twenty-second edition of the American Foundation for the Blind *Directory of Agencies Serving the Blind in the United States* lists a dozen programs in the United States that prepare dog guides. There are similar training programs throughout the world.

The dog guide, because of a variety of limitations, provides mobility assistance to only about 1 percent of the blind population (Whitstock, 1980). However, the introduction of guide dogs has led to a greater acceptance of blind travelers and has helped a shift in perception of the blind (Blasch & Stuckey, 1995). Personal preferences, remaining vision, vocation, and life circumstances often dictate the advisability of the use of a dog guide. Very few school-aged visually impaired persons use dog guides, although the practice is not prohibited.

REFERENCES

American Foundation for the Blind. (1984). *Directory of agencies serving the visually handicapped in the U.S.* (22nd ed.). New York: Author.

Blasch, B. B., & Stuckey, R. A. (1995). Accessibility and mobility of persons who are visually impaired: A historical analysis. *Journal of Visual Impairment, 89*(5), 417–422.

Whitstock, R. H. (1980). Dog guides. In R. L. Welsh & B. B. Blasch (Eds.), *Foundations of orientation and mobility.* New York: American Foundation for the Blind.

GIDEON JONES
Florida State University

AMERICAN FOUNDATION FOR THE BLIND
MOBILITY TRAINERS

DOLCH WORD LIST

The Dolch Word List of 220 common words constitutes over 65 percent of the words found in elementary reading materials and 50 percent of all reading materials (Dolch, 1960). These high-frequency words form the framework for all reading materials. The list, developed by Edward W. Dolch, includes prepositions, conjunctions, pronouns, adjectives, adverbs, and the most common verbs. There are no nouns included in this list since each noun, according to Dolch, is tied to subject matter (Johns, 1971). The list is comprised of structure words, words that hold language together, as opposed to content words.

The average third-grade reader should be able to identify these 220 service words at sight. Many of the words have irregular spellings and cannot be learned by picture cues. Dolch (1939) reports that if the reader is able to recognize more than half the words at the sight reading rate of 120 words per minute, he or she will have confidence and will be able focus on the meaning of the material.

The Dolch Word List is frequently used as a diagnostic tool to identify poor readers (Elmquist, 1987). Many retarded readers are deficient in recognizing and understanding the proper use of these words. The list also serves as the basis of remedial instruction. Garrard Publishers produces several materials, Popper Words, Basic Sight Vocabulary Cards, and Basic Sight Word Test, based on the list. The actual list can be found at http://www.kidzone.ws/dolch/or on many other web sites.

REFERENCES

Dolch, E. W. (1939). *A manual of remedial reading.* Champaign, IL: Garrard.

Dolch, E. W. (1960). *Teaching primary reading.* Champaign, IL: Garrard.

Elmquist, E. (1987). *Improving reading skills and attitudes through the reading and writing connection.* (ERIC Clearinghouse No. CS010210)

Johns, J. L. (1971). The Dolch Basic Word List—Then and now. *Journal of Reading Behavior, 3,* 35–40.

JOYCE E. NESS
*Montgomery County
Intermediate Unit,
Norristown, Pennsylvania*

**READING DISORDERS
READING REMEDIATION**

DOLL, EDGAR A. (1889–1968)

Edgar A. Doll joined the staff of the Training School at Vineland, New Jersey, as a research and clinical psychologist in 1913. There he worked with E. R. Johnstone and H. H. Goddard in the Vineland Laboratory: the first laboratory devoted solely to the study of mental retardation.

Following service in World War I, three years with New Jersey's State Department of Classification and Education, completion of the doctorate in psychology at Princeton University, and two years of teaching at Ohio State University, Doll returned to Vineland as director of research. His studies of social competence led to the publication, in 1935, of the *Vineland Social Maturity Scale,* a revolutionary instrument that provided an objective basis for measuring social functioning that was more useful than mental age for classifying people for purposes of training and care.

Doll left Vineland in 1949 to serve as coordinator of research for the Devereux Schools. He was later consulting psychologist for the Bellingham, Washington public schools. He served as president of the American Association of Applied Psychology, the American Association on Mental Deficiency, and the American Orthopsychiatric Association.

REFERENCES

Doll, E. A. (1953). *The measurement of social competence: A manual for the Vineland Social Maturity Scale.* Minneapolis, MN: Educational Test Bureau.

Doll, E. E. (1969). Edgar Arnold Doll, 1889–1968. *American Journal of Mental Deficiency, 73,* 680–682.

PAUL IRVINE
Katonah, New York

DOMAN, GLENN (1919–   )

Glenn Doman is internationally known for his interest and pioneering work in child brain development and function. He attended Drexel Institute in 1938, graduated from the University of Pennsylvania in 1940 and in 1965 went on to graduate from the University of Pennsylvania School of Physical Therapy. He was certified at the perceptor level in human brain development in 1969.

Doman has studied children for over 40 years. He founded The Institutes for the Achievement of Human Potential in 1955 and served as its director until 1981; subsequently, he has served as the chairman of its board. He is known for the

Edgar A. Doll

Glenn Doman

formulation of the Doman-Delacato treatment method for children with neurological disabilities, a treatment that was popular during the 1960s. The theory stresses that an individual's development in mobility, vision, audition, and language follows specific neurological stages that are correlated with anatomical progress. The Institutes have worked with thousands of brain-injured children.

Doman's publications include *How to Teach Your Baby to Read* (1964/1994), *What to Do About Your Brain-Injured Child* (1974/1994), *How to Teach Your Baby Math* (1979/1994), *How to Multiply Your Baby's Intelligence* (1984/1994), and *How to Teach Your Baby to Be Physically Superb* (1988/1994). These books are available in 20 languages.

Among his numerous honors, Doman was knighted by the Brazilian government for his work on behalf of the children of the world. In 1994, he was presented with the European prize "Lorenzo, the Magnificent" by the Accademia Internazionale Medicea for his work in the field of science. In 1996, The Institutes for Functional Medicine awarded Doman the first annual Linus Pauling Functional Medicine Award.

REFERENCES

Doman, G. (1994). *How to teach your baby to read* (2nd ed.). New York: Avery.

Doman, G. (1994). *What to do about your brain-injured child* (2nd ed.). New York: Avery.

Doman, G. (1994). *How to teach your baby math* (2nd ed.). New York: Avery.

Doman, G. (1994). *How to multiply your baby's intelligence* (2nd ed.). New York: Avery.

Doman, G. (1994). *How to teach your baby to be physically superb* (2nd ed.). New York: Avery.

ROBERTA C. STOKES
Texas A&M University
First edition

TAMARA J. MARTIN
The University of Texas of the Permian Basin
Second edition

DOPAMINE

Dopamine (DA) is a catecholamine class neurotransmitter. Dopamine has been one of the most studied neurotransmitters because of observed roles for DA in schizophrenia, obsessive-compulsive behavior (Lewis, 1996), conduct disorder (Galvin, 1995) tardive dyskinesia, and Parkinson's disease. Dopaminergic pathways are located throughout the limbic system (area of the brain often associated with

emotional reactivity and memory), the basal ganglia (area of the brain associated with motor timing and complex integration), and frontal brain areas. Animal studies of DA depletion and studies of neurological disorders with motor manifestations (i.e., Parkinson's disease) produce results supportive of DA's contributory role in brain systems involved in normal locomotion (Seiden & Dykstra, 1977). Similarly, researchers working with drugs that stimulate DA in animal brains have noted increases in spontaneous aggression during chemical stimulation of DA receptor sites (Senault, 1970). Introduction of haloperidol (Haldol), a DA-blocking agent, reduces the frequency of such fighting (Leavitt, 1982). The role of DA in sexual activity appears similar, that is, increased availability of DA increases sexual behavior in rats. In humans, however, the latter effect appears more indirect. When L-Dopa, a precursor of DA, was administered to male Parkinson's patients, its observed effect on sexual potency appeared more the result of removing other disabling motor symptoms than a result of direct stimulation of libido (Leavitt, 1982). In addition, DA appears to play a role in the regulation of food intake. Investigators (Seiden & Dykstra, 1977) also have noted a role for DA in the maintenance of avoidance behavior and in the facilitation of behavior on positive reinforcement schedules.

REFERENCES

Galvin, M. (1995). Serum dopamine beta Hydroxylase and maltreatment in psychiatrically hospitalized boys. *Child Abuse & Neglect: The International Journal, 19*(7), 821–832.

Leavitt, F. (1982). *Drugs and behavior.* New York: Wiley.

Lewis, M. H. (1996). Plasma HVA in adults with mental retardation and stereotyped behaviors: Biochemical evidence for a dopamine deficiency model. *American Journal on Mental Retardation, 100*(4), 413–418.

Seiden, L. S., & Dykstra, L. A. (1977). *Psychopharmacology: A biochemical and behavioral approach.* New York: Van Nostrand Reinhold.

Senault, B. (1970). Comportement d'aggressivité intraspécifique induit par l'apomorphine chez le rat. *Psychopharmacologia, 18*, 271–287.

ROBERT F. SAWICKI
Lake Erie Institute of Rehabilitation

HALDOL
TRANQUILIZERS

DOUBLE-BLIND DESIGN

One frequently encountered problem in research involving the administration of medication, particularly psychotropic drugs, is that some children or adults may be improved solely as a function of their knowledge that a drug has been administered. The degree to which this effect, frequently referred to as a placebo effect, is present and affecting the outcome of research is unknown and uncontrolled in any specific situation. Experimenters may also be influenced by administration of medication, particularly if the researcher developed the pharmaceutical agent or has other subjective reasons to be biased toward a particular outcome. In such cases, investigators may observe differential rates of behavioral or physiological change in those subjects receiving medication in comparison with those individuals receiving no drug therapy (Babbie, 1979). In either of these cases, the subject's or experimenter's expectation of a certain outcome represents a threat to the validity of the research design. Validity is compromised when the effect of the drug administered is confounded with the expectation of what, if any, the effects of the drug might be.

To control for the effect of patients merely taking medication, as would be the case if those taking medication were compared with a nonmedicated control group, subjects who are not receiving an active drug substance are administered a placebo that appears identical to the active medication in every regard, with the exception that its active ingredients are inert. Thus, the drug under study is not present in the placebo dose and the patients are unaware of whether their medication is in fact active or a placebo. In research terminology, then, the patients are blind to their own drug condition. In order to control for the effect of experimenter bias, it is also necessary for the investigators who administer medication and those who evaluate the outcome (the presence or absence of the drug effect) to be blind to the drug condition of the patients. When these precautions are followed, the research design is said to employ a double-blind procedure, since neither the patients nor the researchers are cognizant of the drug condition to which patients may be assigned (Sprague, 1979).

Obviously, there must be records of which patients have received active medication and which have received placebos in order for the results of the study to be interpretable. However, it is critical that this information not be available to researchers who may have contact with the patients or to the patients themselves until after the study has been completed. Thus, by following a strict double-blind research design, drug effects may be distinguished from actual patient and experimenter expectations regarding the drug under investigation (Sprague, 1979). Unless these two types of effects can be separated, the validity of such a study would be compromised seriously (Sprague, 1979; Sprague & Werry, 1971).

In summary, the double-blind condition exists when neither the subject involved nor the investigator evaluating the drug trial is cognizant of the control condition (placebo) or the active pharmacological intervention. Such a proce-dure precludes the investigator's expectations and hopes from influencing any physiological or behavioral changes that may occur as a function of active pharmacotherapy (Sprague, 1979).

In reviews of the massive literature pertaining to the psychopharmacology of hyperactive and mentally retarded populations, Sprague (Sprague, 1979; Sprague & Werry, 1971) has underscored that the use of double-blind procedures is a minimum requisite in evaluating psychotropic drugs for these groups. Nonetheless, ethical considerations may preclude withholding an effective medication for a child despite the requirements of rigorous empirical research. Thus, investigators must carefully weigh the mandates of controlled clinical trials research with the special needs of some children. Moreover, some research (Whalen & Henker, 1980) in the field of pediatric psychopharmacology has provided rather convincing evidence to suggest that the notion of being administered any pill, whether placebo or active medication, exerts a specific effect on children's views of personal causality (Margraf, 1991). This is particularly true for hyperactive or conduct-disordered children (Ross & Ross, 1982). Should these findings be upheld in future research, the use of active medication as well as both a placebo and a no-pill condition will in fact be necessary in clinical trials, particularly those that involve stimulant medications or other psychotropic drugs prescribed for behavior disorders in children.

REFERENCES

Babbie, E. R. (1979). *The practice of social research*. Belmont, CA: Wadsworth.

Margraf, J. (1991). How "blind" are doubled blind studies? *Journal of Consulting and Clinical Psychology, 59*(1), 184–187.

Ross, D. M., & Ross, S. A. (1982). *Hyperactivity*. New York: Wiley.

Sprague, R. L. (1979). Assessment of intervention. In R. L. Trites (Ed.), *Hyperactivity in children: Etiology, measurement and treatment implications* (pp. 217–229). Baltimore: University Park Press.

Sprague, R. L., & Werry, J. S. (1971). Methodology of psychopharmacological studies with the retarded. In N. R. Ellis (Ed.), *International review of research in mental retardation* (Vol. 5). New York: Academic.

Whalen, C. K., & Henker, B. (1980). *Hyperactive children: The social ecology of identification and treatment*. New York: Academic.

MARTHA ELLEN WYNNE
Loyola University of Chicago

RONALD T. BROWN
Emory University School of Medicine

**ABAB DESIGN
HAWTHORNE EFFECT
RESEARCH IN SPECIAL EDUCATION**

DOWN, J. (JOHN) LANGDON, (1828–1896)

J. (John) Langdon Down, an English physician, in 1866 described the condition that he called mongolism and that is now known as Down syndrome. Although there had been earlier descriptions in the medical literature of individuals who appeared to belong to the same category, Down is credited with the discovery and description of this clinical entity.

Down was concerned with the prevention of mental retardation. He recommended attention to good parental health and sound prenatal care and child-rearing practices. He advocated education for mentally retarded individuals and recognized the efficacy of early training.

REFERENCES

Down, J. L. (1866). Observations on an ethnic classification of idiots. *London Hospital Clinical Lecture Reports, 3,* 259–262.

Down, J. L. (1887). *Mental affectations of childhood and youth.* London: Churchill.

Penrose, L. S., & Smith, G. F. (1966). *Down's anomaly.* Boston: Little, Brown.

PAUL IRVINE
Katonah, New York

DOWN SYNDROME

Down syndrome, occurring in approximately 1 out of 800 to 1,000 live births (National Dissemination Center for Children with Disabilities, 2004), is the most frequent genetic cause for Mild to Moderate Mental Retardation and associated medical problems (National Institute of Health and Human Development, 2005). Down syndrome is a genetic disorder caused by a chromosomal abnormality. An English physician, John Langdon Down, first identified the condition in 1866. Dr. Down did not understand the cause of the disorder and attributed its physical manifestations as regression to a Mongolian and primitive racial type (Selikowitz, 1997). Thus, he coined the term *mongolism.* Down syndrome is unrelated to race, nationality, religion, or socioeconomic status (National Association for Down Syndrome, 2005). Advanced maternal age is the only substantiated risk factor for babies with Down syndrome (Center for Disease Control, 2005). The probability that a woman under 30 will have a baby with Down syndrome is less than 1 in 1,000, but for a woman who is 35, the chance increases to 1 in 400 (National Institute of Health, 2005).

In 1959, Lejeune, a French geneticist, discovered that Down syndrome is caused by an extra copy of chromosome 21 (Down Syndrome Association United Kingdom, 2005). People with the disorder have an extra, crucial portion of the number 21 chromosome in some or all of their cells. Thus, Down syndrome is commonly known as Trisomy 21. The additional genetic material modifies the course of prenatal development and results in the characteristics associated with the syndrome. Methods for identifying Down syndrome in the prenatal period are screening tests (e.g., triple screen, alphafetoprotein plus, the quad test) that measure the amounts of certain hormones and proteins in the blood, and diagnostic tests (including amniocentesis, chorionic villus sampling, and percutaneous umbilical blood sampling; National Down Syndrome Congress, 2005).

Down syndrome typically is identified at birth or shortly thereafter due to the physical features that frequently are

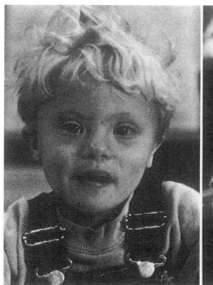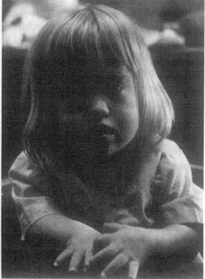

Figure 1 Children with Down syndrome often, but not always, have appealing features as do these children

associated with the disorder. The most common physical characteristics include muscle hypotonia (i.e., low muscle tone), flat facial profile (i.e., somewhat depressed nasal bridge and small nose), oblique palperbral fissures (i.e., upward slant to the eyes), an abnormal shape of the ear, a single crease across the center of the palm as opposed to the average double crease, hyperflexibility (i.e., excessive ability to extend the joints), dysplastic middle phalanx of the fifth finger (i.e., little finger curved inward), epicanthal folds (i.e., small skin folds on the inner corner of the eyes), excessive space between the large and the second toe, and enlargement of the tongue in relationship to the size of the mouth (National Down Syndrome Society, 2005). A test of one's chromosomal karyotype analyzes the child's chromosomes to determine whether an extra chromosome 21 is present in some or all of the cells, confirming a diagnosis that has been made at birth (National Institute of Health, 2005).

Nondisjunction, the most common chromosomal abnormality, refers to faulty cell division resulting in three rather than two number 21 chromosomes. This extra chromosome originates in the development of either the egg or the sperm, and is replicated in every cell of the body as the embryo develops. Therefore, three copies of chromosome 21 exist in all cells of the individual. Nondisjunction is responsible for roughly 95 percent of all cases of Down syndrome (National Down Syndrome Society, 2005).

Mosaicism takes place when nondisjunction of the 21st chromosome occurs in one of the initial cell divisions after fertilization. Mosaicism involves a mixture of two types of cells, some with 46 chromosomes, and some with 47. Mosaicism is responsible for about 1 to 2 percent of Down syndrome cases (National Down Syndrome Society, 2005).

The third type of abnormality, translocation, occurs when part of the 21st chromosome breaks off during cell division and attaches to another chromosome, typically the 14th chromosome. About 3 to 4 percent of Down syndrome cases are accounted for by translocation (National Down Syndrome Society, 2005). Translocation may occur spontaneously and may be passed from parent to child. One or both parents may be a balanced carrier of translocation (e.g., they exhibit no symptoms yet can pass the condition to their offspring). The mother transmits 88 percent of the cases of translocation, fathers transmit 8 percent of the cases, and mitotic errors comprise the remaining 2 percent (National Institute of Health and Human Development, 2005).

Individuals with Down syndrome usually are smaller, develop more slowly intellectually than their peers, and have health-related problems, including respiratory difficulties due to a lowered resistance to infection, rates of mild to moderate hearing loss, speech difficulty, and visual problems including crossed eyes and far- or nearsightedness. Babies with Down syndrome frequently have heart defects, the majority of which are surgically correctable. Some with Down syndrome may have atlantoaxial instability, a misalignment of the top two vertebrae of the neck that can result in

neck injuries (National Dissemination Center for Children with Disabilities, 2004). Those with Down syndrome have a greater likelihood to develop leukemia in childhood, dementia later in life, gastrointestinal blockage, and thyroid problems (Mayo Clinic, 2005). There is a tenfold greater incidence of seizure disorders in individuals with Down syndrome than in the regular population (National Institute of Child Health and Human Development, 2005).

The National Association for Down Syndrome stresses the crucial need for early intervention services for children with the condition and recommends physical, speech, and developmental therapies should be started shortly after birth. Academic placement should consider the strengths, limitations, and needs of the individual child. Partial or full inclusion is somewhat common (National Down Syndrome Society, 2005). Families and schools are encouraged not to place limitations on potential abilities of children with Down syndrome in light of their large range of abilities (National Dissemination Center for Children with Disabilities, 2005). Life expectancy for individuals with Down syndrome is age 50 or older (National Institute of Child Health and Human Development, 2005).

REFERENCES

Canadian Down Syndrome Society. (2001). *Types of Down syndrome.* Retrieved August 31, 2005, from http://www.cdss.ca/types_of_down_syndrome.html

Center for Disease Control. (2005, June 17). *Risk factors for Down syndrome (Trisomy 21): Maternal cigarette smoking and oral contraceptive use in a population-based case-control study.* Retrieved September 20, 2005, from http://www.cdc.gov/ncbddd/bd/ds.htm

Down Syndrome Association United Kingdom. (2005). *New parents.* Retrieved September 20, 2005, from http://www.downs-syndrome.org.uk/DSA_NewParents.aspx#yourbabyhas

Mayo Clinic. (2005, April 7). *Down syndrome.* Retrieved September 5, 2005, from http://www.mayoclinic.com/invoke.cfm?objectid=E0DEA2FF-04FA-4D85-9326CDE6AD3F96DD&dsection=6

National Association for Down Syndrome. (2005). *Down syndrome facts.* Retrieved September 10, 2005, from http://www.nads.org/pages/facts.htm

National Down Syndrome Congress. (2001). *Facts about Down syndrome.* Retrieved September 13, 2005, from http://www.ndsccenter.org/about/about.htm

National Institute of Child Health and Human Development: National Institutes of Health. (March 29, 2005). *Facts about Down syndrome.* Retrieved September 19, 2005, from http://www.nichd.nih.gov/publications/pubs/downsyndrome/down.htm#Prenatal

National Dissemination Center for Children with Disabilities. (2004, January). *Fact sheet four.* Retrieved September 15, 2005, from http://www.nichcy.org/pubs/factshe/fs4txt.htm#edimps

National Down Syndrome Society. (2005). *General information.* Retrieved September 9, 2005, from http://www.ndss.org

Peuschel, S., Canning, C., Murphy, A., & Zausner, E. (1978). *Down syndrome growing and learning.* Kansas City, MO: Andrews, McMeel, & Parker.

Selikowitz, Mark. (1997). *Down syndrome: The facts.* Oxford, UK: Oxford University Press.

MARNI R. FINBERG
University of Florida

DEVELOPMENTAL DELAY
GENETIC COUNSELING
MENTAL RETARDATION
MOSAICISM
TRISOMY 21

DRAW-A-PERSON TEST

The draw-a-person (DAP) is an assessment technique used with both children and adults for a variety of purposes. Harris (1963) provided a set of instructions, a scoring system, and norms for using the technique as a measure of children's intelligence. The test has also been widely used as a projective personality assessment technique following a suggestion by Machover (1949). Although specific instructions vary, the examinee is typically asked to draw a picture of a person. The examiner provides as little structure as possible; however, if necessary, the subject is encouraged to draw an entire person and not to use stick figures. The subject is then asked to draw a person of the opposite sex. These basic instructions are often embellished to include a drawing of oneself and an inquiry phase during which the subject may be asked to make up a story about the person in the drawing or to explain various details included in the picture. Several scoring systems are available (Naglieri, 1988; Shaffer, Duszynski, & Thomas, 1984), and they have moderate to high test-retest reliability based on global quantitative ratings (Naglieri, 1988; Swenson, 1968).

However, the DAP, along with other projective tests, has serious validity problems as a tool for diagnosing emotional disorders. The problems have two sources. First, subjects are drawing the person at only one point in time, and their drawings may vary from one test to another owing to a variety of circumstances. Second, clinical interpreters or researchers may be biased owing to their own theoretical perspective (e.g., psychoanalysis) or desired outcome.

Even with its drawbacks, the DAP is still popular and may provide a reasonable estimate of the cognitive abilities of people across a wide age range. Unfortunately, its effectiveness in diagnosing emotional disorders is limited at best (Groth-Marnat, 1997). Commonly used with standardized tests such as the MMPI, the DAP can be used alone as a means of initiating a conversation with a child or adult in a counseling situation (Groth-Marnat, 1997). A standardized version of the draw-a-person test has been developed to assist with estimations of an individual's cognitive ability. The Draw-a-Person Intellectual Ability Test (DAP:IQ) was published in 2005 (Reynold & Hickman, 2005).

REFERENCES

Groth-Marnat, G. (1997). *Handbook of psychological assessment* (3rd ed.). New York: Wiley.

Harris, D. B. (1963). *Children's drawings as measures of intellectual maturity.* New York: Harcourt, Brace, & World.

Machover, K. (1949). *Personality projection in the drawing of the human figure.* Springfield, IL: Thomas.

Naglieri, J. A. (1988). *Draw a person: A quantitative scoring system.* San Antonio, TX: Psychological Corporation.

Reynolds, C. R., & Hickman, J. A. (2005). *The draw-a-person intellectual ability test for children, adolescents, and adults.* Lutz, FL: PAR, Inc.

Shaffer, J., Duszynski, K., & Thomas, C. (1984). A comparison of three methods for scoring figure drawings. *Journal of Personality Assessment, 48,* 245–254.

Swenson, C. H. (1968). Empirical evaluation of human figure drawings. 1957–1966. *Psychological Bulletin, 70,* 20–44.

ROBERT G. BRUBAKER
Eastern Kentucky University
First edition

WENDY L. FLYNN
Staffordshire University
Second edition

BENDER VISUAL-MOTOR GESTALT TEST
HOUSE-TREE-PERSON
KINETIC-FAMILY-DRAWING

THE DRAW-A-PERSON INTELLECTUAL ABILITY TEST FOR CHILDREN, ADOLESCENTS, AND ADULTS

The DAP:IQ (Reynolds & Hickman, 2003) provides an objective scoring system that is applied to a standardized method for obtaining a drawing of a human figure from which an IQ estimate is then derived. The test is normed for ages 4 years 0 months 0 days through 89 years 11 months 30 days on a population proportionate representative sample of 2,295 individuals from across the United States. All that is necessary for administration and scoring of the DAP:IQ is the test manual, the Administration/Scoring Form, and a sharpened pencil. The examinee is asked to draw a picture of him or herself using the standard instructions provided in the manual. The drawing is not timed but most examinees (children and adults) complete the drawing in 5 minutes or less. Once the examiner has learned the scoring system and is comfortable with the examples in the Manual, scoring is completed typically in only 2 to 3 minutes. In most cases, the total time required to collect the drawing, score it, and interpret it will be less than 10–12 minutes. The DAP:IQ may be administered individually or in groups, the latter being primarily for screening purposes.

The DAP:IQ provides a common set of scoring criteria across its full age range of 4 years through 89 years and is the first draw-a-person test to do so. This not only eases the burden on the examiner but allows for more direct, continuous measurement of a common construct across the age range.

The value of using human figure drawings (HFDs) as a component of the psychoeducational and psychological evaluation has been recognized across 3 centuries. Goodenough (1926), in her groundbreaking, comprehensive study also reviews prior research on using human figure drawings in psychological assessment, going back to at least 1885. Exposure to human figures and the commonality of our fundamental features are universal phenomena among humans. Humans drawing pictures of humans is a common, universal activity as well. Cave drawings and petroglyphs that predate recorded history commonly contain pictures of humans of the era as well as abstract depictions.

Standardized instructions for the task are easy to derive. The drawings are collected in a rapid, efficient manner, and standardized scoring systems emphasize conceptual aspects of the drawings, not their artistic qualities. Drawing itself is a universal activity and few people are resistant to providing a drawing of the human figure once reassured the artistic qualities of their efforts are not being evaluated. Human figure drawings typically can be obtained in even the most challenging of clinical situations, such as the assessment of individuals with Pervasive Developmental Disorder or severely hyperactive children, or when a large number of nonreading or non-English speaking persons must be examined.

As a measure of cognitive ability, scoring criteria for the DAP:IQ should not include motor coordination as a salient component, and subsequently the DAP:IQ does not include or emphasize motor coordination in deriving the scores. Instead it emphasizes the conceptual aspects of the drawing.

REFERENCES

Reynolds, C. R., & Hickman, J. A. (2003). *DAP:IQ, The Draw-A-Person Intellectual Ability Test for Children, Adolescents, and Adults.* Austin, TX: PRO-ED.

Goodenough, F. (1926). *Measurement of intelligence by drawings.* Chicago: World Book Company.

CECIL R. REYNOLDS
Texas A&M University

INTELLIGENCE
INTELLIGENT TESTING

DROPOUT

A dropout is generally considered to be an individual who leaves school before graduation. Yet, Block, Covill-Servo, and Rosen (1978) found a serious problem with this definition and the reporting of dropouts. They found many inconsistencies in the way school districts define and report dropouts. New York defines a dropout as "any pupil who leaves school prior to graduation for any reason except death and does not enter another school" (p. 15). Under this definition, an average of 25 percent of the students entering high school drop out.

In recent years the dropout rate has been declining. For example, the event dropout rate for ages 15 through 24 in grades 10 through 12 has fallen from 6.1 percent in 1972 to 4.5 percent in 1993. However, these figures still constitute a large number of individuals. In 1993, approximately 381,000 students in grades 10 through 12 dropped out of school (National Center for Education Statistics, 1993).

For special education students and children with disabilities, the dropout rate is twice that of their nondisabled peers (Office of Special Education [OSERS], 1997). In addition, dropouts with disabilities do not return to school, and females became unwed mothers at a much higher rate than nondisabled peers (OSERS, 1997).

One of the six national education goals for the United States was to achieve a 90 percent graduation rate by the year 2000 (Dorn, 1996). Reasons for leaving school include a dislike of school, involuntary exclusion, academic problems, problems with teachers, marriage, and pregnancy. These reasons are determined ex post facto and do not have a high predictive value in identifying potential dropouts. Most dropouts are 16 years old and from families with lower socioeconomic status where parental attitudes toward education and parental supervision are low. Dropouts generally are of lower intellectual ability, have poor personal-social skills, and have academic problems.

The consequences of dropping out of school are seen when compared with the results of graduating. Dropouts generally earn significantly less money and are more likely to be unemployed. Contributing to these effects is the finding that dropouts have no postsecondary training because, as an entrance requirement, most postsecondary training programs require a high-school diploma or equivalent.

Dorn (1996) argues that "instead of seeing different educational outcomes as evidence of remaining equities in schooling, Americans have focused instead on the social costs of dropping out." Schools are expected to ameliorate problems that are essentially socioeconomic in nature and many times beyond their scope and jurisdiction.

The National Dropout Prevention Center for Students with Disabilities (NDPC-SD) was created to assist in dropout prevention and reentry programs for students with disabilities. The center is a convenient resource for information about effective dropout-prevention strategies, technical assistance, and program replication. Assistance is available for state and local education agencies, policymakers, administrators, researchers, parents, teachers, and other practitioners. NDPC-SD is housed at the National Dropout Prevention Center/Network (NDPC/N) at Clemson University and is part of OSEP's Technical Assistance and Dissemination (TA&D) Center Network.

NDPC-SD identifies evidence-based programs through research synthesis and assists state agencies to support local education agencies that implement model programs and effective practices. NDPC-SD partners with the Education Development Corporation (EDC) Inc. of Newton, MA, and the Intercultural Development Research Association (IDRA) of San Antonio, TX, to carry out its activities.

A major goal of NDPC-SD is to provide effective technical assistance activities to "scale up" the use of research-validated programs and interventions in dropout prevention. NDPC-SD employs various strategies to transfer knowledge and to support systems change. One strategy used by NDPC-SD is to assist states in building infrastructures by using local districts as implementation sites. This is a part of OSEP's concept of continuous improvement through focused monitoring and technical assistance processes. This strategy reflects research's best-known evidence about sustaining systemic reform efforts and is on point with the 2004 Individuals with Disabilities Education Improvement Act (IDEIA 2004), which calls for aligning all monitoring and technical assistance efforts. These include direct consultation in conducting root/cause analysis, designing state-level initiatives based on state-identified needs, and offering professional development institutes and Web-based resources.

NDPC-SD has access to a broad range of expertise and experience through its national partners and other collaborators, including the What Works Clearinghouse, the What Works Synthesis Center, the National Center for Secondary Education and Transition, the Exiting Community of Practice, and other OSEP-supported TA&D projects. Many NDPC-SD programs and services receive guidance from a national advisory committee that includes members of special and regular education practices, administrators at the state and local levels, parents, and researchers.

NDPC-SD is funded by the U.S. Department of Education's Office of Special Education Programs Cooperative Agreement No. H326Q030002. It can be reached at National Dropout Prevention Center for Students with Disabilities, Clemson University, 209 Martin Street, Clemson, SC 29631-1555, Telephone: (800) 443-6392, TDD/TDY: (866) 212-2775, fax: (864) 656-0136, e-mail: NDPCSD-L@clemson.edu, web site: www.dropoutprevention.org.

REFERENCES

Block, E. E., Covill-Servo, J., & Rosen, M. F. (1978). *Failing students—Failing schools: A study of dropouts and discipline in New York State.* Rochester, NY: Statewide Youth Advocacy Project.

Dorn, S. (1996). *Creating the dropout: An institutional and social history of school failure.* Westport, CT: Praeger.

Office of Special Education. (1997). *An overview of the bill to provide a broad understanding of some of the changes in IDEA '97.* Retrieved from http://www.ed.gov/offices/OSERS/IDEA/overview.html

U.S. Department of Education National Center for Education Statistics. (1993). *High school dropout rates.* Washington, DC: National Institute on the Education of At-Risk Students.

DANIEL R. PAULSON
University of Wisconsin at Stout
First edition

ELAINE FLETCHER-JANZEN
*University of Colorado at
Colorado Springs*
Second edition

DRUG ABUSE

Drug abuse, or more currently substance abuse, is defined by the *Diagnostic and Statistical Manual of Mental Disorders,* fourth edition, text revision (*DSM-IV-TR;* American Psychiatric Association, 2000) as a "a maladaptive pattern of substance use manifested by recurrent and significant adverse consequences related to the repeated use of substances" (p. 182). The criteria for a substance abuse diagnosis are the following:

A. A maladaptive pattern of substance use leading to clinically significant impairment or distress, as manifested by one (or more) of the following, occurring within a 12-month period:

(1) recurrent substance use resulting in a failure to fulfill major role obligations at work, school, or home (e.g., repeated absences or poor work performance related to substance use; substance-related absences, suspensions, or expulsions from school; neglect of children or household)

(2) recurrent substance use in situations in which it is physically hazardous (e.g., driving an automobile or operating a machine when impaired by substance use)

(3) recurrent substance-related legal problems (e.g., arrests for substance-related disorderly conduct)

(4) continued substance use despite having persistent or recurrent social or interpersonal problems caused or exacerbated by the effects of the substance (e.g., arguments with spouse about consequences of intoxication, physical fights)

B. The symptoms have never met the criteria for Substance Dependence for this class of substance (pp. 182–183)

Drug abuse is one of the six categories of behaviors that contribute to the leading causes of morbidity and mortality in the United States (National Clearinghouse for Alcohol and Drug Information [NCADI], 1998). It has only been in the 1980s and 1990s that the neuropsychological effects of drug abuse have started to be understood. This new understanding has been due to technological advances in the study of the brain, and the rise and development of pediatric neurology and neuropsychology. It is during adolescence that the more abstract and sophisticated cognitive skills develop in the human brain. Planning, evaluation, flexibility, internalized behavioral controls, higher-level abstracting skills, and higher levels of moral awareness are some of these sophisticated skills. The use of drugs during this period many have long-lasting effects on frontal and prefrontal regions of the brain (Elliott, 1998). For each insult to the brain there is a concomitant negative consequence for cognitive functions and behavior; therefore, the prevention of drug abuse in youth is extremely important if individual and social consequences are to be avoided.

The Centers for Disease Control (CDC) has developed a Youth Risk Behavior Surveillance System (YRBSS) to monitor the health-risk behaviors among youth and young adults (CDC, 1996). The system includes national, state, and local school-based surveys of high school students and gives a shocking picture of how students in the United States are involved in drug abuse.

According to the 1995 YRBSS, over 80 percent of high school students have used alcohol; over 40 percent have used marijuana; 16 percent have used cocaine, crack, or freebase; and over 20 percent have sniffed or inhaled intoxicating substances. Of the students who had experienced drug abuse, 40 percent initiated drug-related behaviors before the age of 13. Over 30 percent of the students reported using alcohol or drugs at the last episode of sexual intercourse. In addition, over 40 percent of the students had ridden with a driver who had been drinking alcohol.

For the past 30 years, significant efforts have been made with private and public monies to prevent drug abuse. Schools have been a primary vehicle for prevention monies because education has been shown to assist in prevention, and education is a compatible goal with school missions (Bosworth, 1997). Education programs begin as early as the elementary years, and try to eliminate myths that support student use (such as "everybody is doing it") with normative information that gives students statistics. There is no conclusive evidence on what types of programs or strategies are effective or ineffective; however, there is some evidence that scare tactics, providing only information on drugs and their effects, self-esteem building, values clarification, large assemblies, and didactic presentation of material have not

been shown to be particularly effective (Tobler & Stratton, 1997, cited in Bosworth, 1997). Skill building and experiential teaching techniques (role-playing, simulations, and so on) have been successful in helping students utilize positive approaches to avoiding drug use (Bosworth, 1997).

The following resources are cited in Bosworth (1997):

For educators exploring possible drug prevention approaches and curricula, several excellent guides to curriculum selection are available from the National Clearinghouse for Alcohol and Drug Information (NCADI), P.O. Box 2345, Rockville, MD 20852, (800) 729-6686. NCADI is the public information arm of the U.S. Department of Health and Human Services. Free titles include:

Drug Prevention Curricula: A Guide to Selection and Implementation

Community Creating Change: Exemplary Alcohol and Other Drug Prevention Programs

Prevention Plus II: Tools for Creating and Sustaining Drug-Free Communities

Learning to Live Drug Free: A Curriculum Model for Prevention

Prevention Resource Guide's for Elementary Youth and Secondary School Students

Also serving as a programming resource are the Drug-Free Schools and Communities Regional Centers established in 1986 as part of the Drug-Free Schools and Communities Act to help schools and communities eliminate drug and alcohol use among youth. The five regional centers are:

Northeast Regional Center, Sayville, NY, (516) 589-7022
Southeast Regional Center, Louisville, KY, (502) 588-0052
Midwest Regional Center, Oak Brook, IL, (708) 571-4710

An organization dedicated to the promotion and improvement of peer leader programs may also be of help:

The National Peer Helpers Association
P.O. Box 2684
Greenville, NC
(919) 328-6923

REFERENCES

American Psychiatric Association. (1994). *Diagnostic and statistical manual of mental disorders* (4th ed.). Washington, DC: Author.

Bosworth, K. (1997). Drug abuse prevention: School-based strategies that work. *ERIC Clearinghouse on Teaching and Teacher Education.* Washington, DC. (ERIC Digest No. ED409316)

Centers for Disease Control (CDC). (1996). *Youth risk behavior surveillance United States, 1995, 45,* SS-4.

Elliot, R. (1998). Neuropsychological sequelae of substance abuse by youths. In C. R. Reynolds & E. Fletcher-Janzen (Eds.), *Handbook of clinical child neuropsychology* (pp. 311–331). New York: Plenum.

National Clearinghouse for Alcohol and Drug Information (NCADI). (1998). *Youth risk behavior surveillance United States, 1995.* Retrieved from http://www.health.org/pubs/yrbbs/index.htm

ELAINE FLETCHER-JANZEN
*University of Colorado at
Colorado Springs*

AL-ANON
ALCOHOL AND DRUG ABUSE PATTERNS
CHEMICALLY DEPENDENT YOUTHS
SUBSTANCE ABUSE

DRUGS

See SPECIFIC DRUGS.

DUE PROCESS

"Due process" in the field of special education has its roots in the U.S. Constitution. The Fifth and Fourteenth Amendments prohibit the deprivation of any person's life, liberty, or property without due process of law by, respectively, the federal and state governments. More commonly in the field of special education, due process is the shorthand term applied to the procedural safeguards and due process procedures stated in the Individuals with Disabilities Education Act (IDEA) reauthorizations and regulations. These procedures offer parents the right to share with schools in decision making that could result in their child's being found eligible for and placed in special education classes. Because these placements may segregate children from the typical school environment, courts and laws have mandated that schools follow particular procedures to ensure that parents and other guardians have the opportunity to review and give their consent to changes in their child's educational program. Bersoff (1978) and Kotin (1978) provide a discussion of the legal theory underlying the due process requirements.

The due process requirements in special education can be classified under six headings addressed by the IDEA: prior notice requirements, opportunity to examine records, independent educational evaluation, informed consent, impartial due process hearing and appeal (including opportunity for mediation), and requirements for when parents cannot be located. First, the educational agency must provide written notice within a reasonable time frame before any action is initiated to propose or reject (e.g., when parents request special education for their child) a change in the identification, evaluation, or educational placement of a child. The notice must be written in the parents' native language or other mode of communication, such as braille, and in a way that results in parents understanding the notice. The notice must contain a description of the action proposed or refused by the agency, an explanation of why such action was considered, a description of any options to be considered in making a decision, and a full explanation of all procedural safeguards available to the parents. These procedural safeguards allow the parents, at no cost, the opportunity to inspect and review all education records of their child and to obtain an independent educational evaluation conducted by a qualified examiner who is not employed by the agency. The intent of these provisions is to fully inform parents.

With this information, the parents are presumed able to give voluntary informed consent to the actions proposed. Consent must be obtained before the agency conducts a preplacement evaluation and before initial special education placement.

When parents and schools disagree about any issue concerning the evaluation, placement, or educational program for a special education student, either party may request an impartial due process hearing. A hearing officer is presented evidence under conditions that are similar to those in a court. Either party can call witnesses and cross-examine the other party's witnesses. A verbatim record is taken of the proceedings. The hearing officer writes a decision that may be appealed to the state education agency and, if desired, to a civil court. Given the emotional and financial costs of this procedure, several states have initiated a mediation process as an alternative for settling disputes before a due process hearing is conducted; however, mediation is not a substitute for a due process hearing. As noted previously, the IDEA now permits mediation, as well.

Finally, public agencies are required to identify surrogate parents to represent a disabled child when no parent or guardian can be located. Several issues have been raised about this requirement, such as qualifications to be a surrogate parent, training for this role, and liability protection, among others (U.S. Department of Education, 1977).

REFERENCES

Bersoff, D. N. (1978). Procedural safeguards. In L. G. Morra (Ed.), *Developing criteria for the evaluation of due process procedural safeguards provision of Public Law 94-142* (pp. 63–142). Washington, DC: U.S. Office of Education.

Kotin, L. (1978). Recommended criteria and assessment techniques for the evaluation by LEAs of their compliance with the notice and consent requirements of PL 94-142. In L. G. Morra (Ed.),

Developing criteria for the evaluation of due process procedural safeguards provision of Public Law 94-142 (pp. 143–178). Washington, DC: U.S. Office of Education.

U.S. Department of Education. (1984). *Fifth annual report to Congress on the implementation of Public Law 94-142: The Education for All Handicapped Children Act.* Washington, DC: Author.

U.S. Department of Education. (1985). *Sixth annual report to Congress on the implementation of Public Law 94-142: The Education for All Handicapped Children Act.* Washington, DC: Author.

U.S. Department of Education. (1986). *Seventh annual report to Congress on the implementation of Public Law 94-142: The Education for All Handicapped Children Act.* Washington, DC: Author.

U.S. Department of Health, Education, and Welfare. (1977). Education of handicapped children: Implementation of Part B of the Education of the Handicapped Act. *Federal Register, 42*(163), 42474–42518.

ROLAND K. YOSHIDA
Fordham University
First edition

KIMBERLY F. APPLEQUIST
*University of Colorado at
Colorado Springs*
Third edition

INDIVIDUALS WITH DISABILITIES EDUCATION IMPROVEMENT ACT OF 2004 (IDEIA)
INFORMED CONSENT
SURROGATE PARENTS

DUNN, LLOYD M. (1917–   )

Lloyd Dunn was born in Saskatchewan, Canada, and received his U.S. citizenship in 1963. He obtained his BEd (1949) and MEd (1950) from the University of Saskatchewan, later earning his PhD in special education at the University of Illinois. From 1953 to 1969, he was a faculty member of Peabody College, now part of Vanderbilt University. Dunn has served as affiliate professor of education at the University of Hawaii, and was past president and recipient of the Wallin Award of the Council for Exceptional Children.

His major works are in the areas of psychometrics, language development, and education of the mentally retarded. Dunn (1968) has taken the position that much of the past and present practices of special education for minority children who are labeled mildly retarded are morally and educationally wrong. He believes that regular class placement without special education services is needed for most such children (Dunn, 1968). He was an early advocate of small,

special-purpose residential facilities for the more severely retarded, rather than large, impersonal state residential institutions (Dunn, 1963).

Dunn is best known for the textbook, *Exceptional Children in the Schools;* the article, "Special Education for the Mildly Retarded—Is Much of It Justifiable!"; and various assessment tools and instructional programs, including the Peabody Picture Vocabulary Test, the Peabody Individual Achievement Test, and the Peabody Early Languages Kit. His work, outlining a progressive plan to improve special education by merging it with general education, has been extensively analyzed and very influential on policy change and legislation in Canada and the United States (Dahl & Sanche, 1997; Hallahan & Kauffman, 1994; Snell & Drake, 1994).

Dunn was one of the founders of the Kennedy Center in 1965. He was director of Peabody's Mental Retardation Research Training Program, the first doctoral program in the nation for training researchers in this field. He conceived of the Institute on Mental Retardation and Intellectual Development, which came to be known IMRID, and was its first director. The Kennedy Center continues to bring expertise in the biomedical and behavioral sciences to bear in understanding and preventing problems of development and learning.

REFERENCES

Dahl, H., & Sanche, R. (1997). *Special education policy: A retrospective and future prospective—A view from Saskatchewan.* Salt Lake City, UT: Council for Exceptional Children.

Dunn, L. M. (1963). *Exceptional children in the schools.* New York: Holt, Rinehart, & Winston.

Dunn, L. M. (1968). Special education for the mildly retarded—Is much of it justifiable! *Exceptional Children, 35,* 5–22.

Dunn, L. M. & Dunn, L. M. (1981). *Peabody Picture Vocabulary Test–Revised.* Circle Pines, MN: American Guidance Service.

Hallahan, D. P., & Kaufmann, J. M. (1994). Toward a culture of disability in the aftermath of Deno and Dunn. *Journal of Special Education, 27*(4), 496–508.

Snell, M. E., & Drake, George, P. (1994). Replacing cascades with supported education. *Journal of Special Education, 27*(4), 393–409.

ELIZABETH JONES
Texas A&M University
First edition

TAMARA J. MARTIN
*The University of Texas of the
Permian Basin*
Second edition

JESSI K. WHEATLEY
*Falcon School District 49,
Colorado Springs, Colorado*

DURATION RECORDING

Duration recording is a direct observation method that is used in a systematic fashion to determine how long a person engages in a behavior. Duration recording is used for behaviors that have a distinguishable beginning and end, that is, discrete behaviors (Alberto & Troutman, 2006). Examples of behaviors that are suitable for measurement using duration recording include academic engagement, remaining in seat, time participating as a member of a group, engaging in an activity, and tantruming.

To record behavior using duration recording, you first need to operationally define the target behavior. An operational definition is a written statement that precisely defines the behavior you wish to measure in terms that are observable, measurable, and replicable (Fletcher-Janzen & De Pry, 2003). Next, the observer should define the observation period, including recording the start and stop times. A device for measuring time, such as a stopwatch, is used to measure the amount of time the person engages in the targeted behavior. The stopwatch should be allowed to run when the person is meeting the operational definition and stopped when the person does not meet the operational definition. This method continues throughout the observation session.

For example, a sixth-grade teacher has expressed concern about a student who has low levels of academic engagement. In collaboration with her paraprofessional, they operationally define academic engagement as "eyes on the teacher, eyes on the assigned instructional task, or being engaged in a task-related activity." The paraprofessional positions herself so that she can fully observe the student of concern. During several instructional periods, observations are made. The stopwatch is allowed to run as long as the student meets the operational definition of academic engagement, however, the paraprofessional stops the stopwatch each time the student is not meeting the definition, that is, when he is not academically engaged. This method continues until the observation period has concluded. When the observation session is finished, the paraprofessional records the amount of minutes and seconds that she has on the stopwatch. This number is converted to seconds and divided by the total number of seconds for the observation period. In our example, the paraprofessional observed the student for 30 minutes, or 1,800 seconds. Data from her stopwatch indicated that the student was academically engaged for 22 minutes and 30 seconds (1,350 seconds) during one of her observation sessions. She takes the observation total and divides by the observation period (1,350/1,800 = .75 × 100 = 75 percent) and learns that the student was academically engaged for 75 percent of the observation period. The data for this observation period is then recorded and graphed for future reference. In some cases, the teacher or researcher might collect data at several times throughout the day. At the end of the day, the totals would be averaged and recorded as the average duration of the targeted behavior for that day (Alberto & Troutman, 2006). As with all direct observation systems, collecting interobserver reliability data is critical. The formula for calculating interobserver reliability for duration recording is taking the shorter number of minutes (or total seconds) and dividing by the larger number of minutes (or total seconds) then multiplying by 100. This formula will give you the percentage of agreement between the primary observer and an independent observer.

REFERENCES

Alberto, P. A., & Troutman, A. C. (2006). *Applied behavior analysis for teachers* (7th ed.). Upper Saddle River, NJ: Prentice Hall.

Fletcher-Janzen, E., & De Pry, R. L. (2003). *Teaching social competence and character: An IEP planner with goals, objectives, and interventions.* Longmont, CO: Sopris West Educational Services.

RANDALL L. DE PRY
*University of Colorado at
Colorado Springs*

BEHAVIORAL ASSESSMENT
RESEARCH IN SPECIAL EDUCATION

DWARFISM

Dwarfism is a genetic condition that results in an extremely short stature. There are several hundred different diagnosed types of dwarfism. The most common form of short limb dwarfism is Achondroplasia. Achondroplasia occurs in approximately 1 in 26,000–40,000 births, results in disproportionately short arms and legs ("Little people in America," n.d.), and affects about 80 percent of all Little People with equal frequency in males and females in all races ("Reaching new heights," n.d.). The average height of adults with this condition is about 4 feet. Other less-frequent types of dwarfism include spondyloepiphyseal dysplasia congenital (SED) and diastrophic dysplasia ("Little people in America," n.d.). Advances in genetics have lead to the identification of the genes that result in the characteristics of the different types of dwarfism; however, mass genetic testing for this genetic condition is not practiced. Proportionate dwarfism, another commonly recognized type of dwarfism, is often the result of hormonal deficiency and can be treated medically ("Little people in America," n.d.), yet neonatal testing for growth hormone deficiency is controversial (Gandrud & Wilson, 2004).

There is variability in the extent to which a person is affected by the condition; however, for the most part those with dwarfism have normal intelligence, normal life spans, and are in good health ("Little people in America," n.d.). A small number of those with dwarfism may be affected by compression of the brain stem, hydrocephalus, and obstructive apnea. Motor development may be delayed in infants and young children, often resulting in delays in sitting, standing, and walking ("Achondroplasia," n.d). Often, those with dwarfism have a prominent forehead, short fingers, and a flat nose due to abnormalities in cartilage development ("Achondroplasia," n.d.). The small stature that characterizes dwarfism is generally untreatable, however some people opt to undergo limb-lengthening surgery that is often painful and is still extremely controversial in Little People circles ("Little people in America," n.d.). Currently, dwarfism is recognized as a disability under the Americans with Disabilities Act ("Little people in America," n.d.).

When working with those affected by dwarfism one should keep in mind that with the exception of height-related challenges, they are equally productive citizens who engage in similar activities and careers as other average-height individuals. The biggest challenge is to encourage acceptance and understanding, while working to dismiss stereotypes that have historically been intertwined with this condition. Furthermore, a person with dwarfism may experience self-esteem issues that could be addressed with therapy or support groups (Theunissen et al., 2002).

REFERENCES

Achondroplasia. (n.d.). *March of Dimes quick reference and fact sheets.* Retrieved September 10, 2005, from http://www.marchofdimes.com/professionals/681_1204.asp

Gandrud, L. M., & Wilson, D. M. (2004). Is growth hormone stimulation testing in children still appropriate? *Growth Hormone & IGF Research, 14,* 185–194.

Little people in America. (n.d.). *LPA online.* Retrieved August 31, 2005, from http://www.lpaonline.org/resources_faq.html

Reaching new heights. (n.d.). Retrieved August 31, 2005, from http://www.dwarfism.org

Theunissen, N. C. M., Kamp, G. A., Koopman, H. M., Zwinderman, K. A. H., Vogels, T., & Wit, J. M. (2002). Quality of life and self-esteem in children treated for idiopathic short stature. *Journal of Pediatrics, 140,* 507–515.

MICHELLE T. BUSS
Texas A&M University

PHYSICAL ANOMALIES

DYSCALCULIA

Calculation ability, like reading ability, can be impaired in some individuals. When there is a developmental pattern of difficulty in the acquisition of math skills, this is referred to as developmental dyscalculia or dyscalculia (Ardila & Rosselli, 2002) in the neuropsychology literature. More recently, this same constellation of difficulties is referred to as Mathematics Disorder in the psychiatric literature (American Psychiatric Association, 2000), or a specific learning disability in mathematics in the special educational literature. It is estimated that 6 percent of school-age children evidence difficulty in mathematics of sufficient severity to be identified as having dyscalculia (Gross-Tsur, Manor, & Shalev, 1996). Among children with dyscalculia (or Mathematics Disorder), it is not uncommon for many of them also to evidence dyslexia (reading disability) or other disorders (Gross-Tsur et al., 1996). Although there is some evidence that males generally do better on math tasks than females (see Halperin, 1992), dyscalculia is found equally as often in males and females (Gross-Tsur et al., 1996; Lewis, Hitch, & Walker, 1994). No ethnic or racial differences in prevalence have been identified. The prognosis for individuals with dyscalculia varies depending on the severity of the disorder, when it is identified and intervention provided, the effectiveness of the interventions provided, and the motivation of the child and family members (Ardila & Rosselli, 2002).

Although mathematical abilities are routinely included as part of psychoeducational and neuropsychological assessments, and calculation is one of the areas considered in determination of a specific learning disability, there is limited research specific to dyscalculia. Different developmental stages in the acquisition of knowledge related to mathematics have been studied (e.g., Klein & Starkey, 1987). This includes the understanding of counting, one-to-one correspondence, stable order principle, cardinal principle and arithmetic skills of addition, subtraction, and so on. There is a sequenced pattern of skill and knowledge acquisition that begins in early childhood and continues through school age. Dyscalculia often refers to difficulty in any of the aspects of arithmetic functioning including difficulty performing arithmetical operations and inability to apply numerical reasoning. Multiple systems for analyzing errors made in conjunction with dyscalculia have been offered (e.g., Kosc, 1970; Rourke, 1989). Subtypes of dyscalculia, associated with the types of errors, have been proposed as well (e.g., Badian, 1983; Kosc, 1970; Strang & Rourke, 1985).

Factors associated with dyscalculia include possible neurological or genetic etiology (Rourke, 1989) and environmental factors (Fergusson, Horwood, & Lawton, 1990). The similarity of deficits between dyscalculia and acalculia, with identified brain damage support the contention of underlying neurological deficits to dyscalculia as well as acalculia. Hernadek and Rourke (1994) theorized that dyscalculia was one component of developmental right hemisphere syndrome or nonverbal learning disability. This disorder is associated with deficits in visuo-spatial abilities, visual-motor coordination, nonverbal reasoning, and mathematics. Behaviorally, these children have difficulty with nonverbal social cues and social situations. When right hemisphere deficits underlie the dyscalculia, these children and adults do not evidence comorbid language disorders or reading disability (Ardila & Rosselli, 2002). This suggests the existence of at least two differing groups of individuals with dyscalculia—those with right hemisphere dysfunction and those with dyslexic dyscalculia and left hemisphere dysfunction (Shalev, Auerbach, & Gross-Tsur, 1995; Sokol, McCloskey, Cohen, & Aminiosa, 1994). Others have postulated that dyscalculia is part of Gerstmann syndrome (Gerstmann, 1940). With Gerstmann syndrome, there is co-occurring digital agnosia, dysgraphia, and left-right disorientation; it is associated with diffuse and bilateral brain dysfunction.

Intervention for children with dyscalculia should include systematic and concrete verbalizations of the procedures being taught (Strang & Rourke, 1985). Because of potential spatial problems, operations and concepts should be presented as verbal tasks that allow the child to break the operation into component parts. Teaching should follow the normal developmental progression, beginning with early numerical concepts (counting, one-to-one correspondence) and number recognition. As these concepts are mastered, calculation skills (math operations) should be introduced in a systematic manner. Strategy instruction and verbalization of what the task is asking, what the steps are to be followed, and so on can be used to facilitate learning (Strang & Rourke, 1985). For children with difficulty lining up columns and working from right to left, graph paper and color coding may be helpful as cues (Ardila & Rosselli, 1994). Depending on the skill and types of errors the child evidences, different interventions may be appropriate.

REFERENCES

American Psychiatric Association. (2000). *Diagnostic and statistical manual of mental disorders* (4th ed., Text Revision). Washington, DC: Author.

Ardila, A., & Rosselli, M. (2002). Acalculia and dyscalculia. *Neuropsychology Review, 12,* 179–231.

Ardila, A., & Rosselli, M. (1994). Spatial acalculia. *International Journal of Neuroscience, 78,* 177–184.

Badian, N. A. (1983). Dyscalculia and nonverbal disorders of learning. In H. R. Miklebust (Ed.), *Progress in learning disabilities* (Vol. 5, pp. 129–146). New York: Grune & Stratton.

Fergusson, D. M., Horwood, L. J., & Lawton, J. M. (1990). Vulnerability to childhood problems and family social background. *Journal of Child Psychology and Psychiatry, 31,* 1145–1160.

Gerstmann, J. (1940). The syndrome of finger agnosia, disorientation for right and left, agraphia, and acalculia. *Archives of Neurology and Psychiatry, 44,* 398–404.

Gross-Tsur, V., Manor, O., & Shalev, R. S. (1996). Developmental dyscalculia: Prevalence and demographic features. *Developmental Medicine and Clinical Neurology, 38,* 25–33.

Halperin, D. F. (1992). *Sex differences in cognitive abilities* (2nd ed.). Hillsdale, NJ: Erlbaum.

Hernadek, M. C. S., & Rourke, B. P. (1994). Principal identifying features of the syndrome of nonverbal learning disabilities in children. *Journal of Learning Disabilities, 27,* 144–148.

Klein, A., & Starkey, P. S. (1987). The origins and development of numerical cognition: A comparative analysis. In J. A. Sloboda & D. Rogers (Eds.), *Cognitive processes in mathematics* (pp. 1–25). Oxford, MA: Clarendon Press.

Kosc, L. (1970). Psychology and psychopathology of mathematical abilities. *Studies in Psychology, 12,* 159–162.

Lewis, C., Hitch, G. J., & Walker, P. (1994). The prevalence of specific arithmetic difficulties and specific reading disabilities in 9 to 10 year old boys and girls. *Journal of Child Psychology and Psychiatry, 35,* 283–292.

Rourke, B. P. (1989). *Nonverbal learning disabilities: The syndrome and the model.* New York: Guilford.

Shalev, R. S., Auerbach, J., & Gross-Tsur, V. (1995). Developmental dyscalculia behavioral and attentional aspects: A research note. *Journal of Child Psychology and Psychiatry, 36,* 1261–1268.

Sokol, S. M., McCloskey, M., Cohen, N. J., & Alminiosa, D. (1991). Cognitive representations and processes in arithmetic: Inferences from the performance of brain-damaged subjects. *Journal of Experimental Psychology: Learning, Memory, and Cognition, 17,* 355–376.

Strang, J. D., & Rourke, B. P. (1985). Arithmetic disabilities subtypes: The neuropsychological significance of specific arithmetic impairment in childhood. In B. P. Rourke (Ed.), *Neuropsychology of learning disabilities* (pp. 87–101). New York: Guilford.

CYNTHIA A. RICCIO
Texas A&M University

ACALCULIA
ARITHMETIC REMEDIATION
DEVELOPMENTAL DYSLEXIA, HISTORY OF
LEARNING DISABILITIES
MATHEMATICS, LEARNING DISABILITIES IN

DYSCOPIA

See APRAXIA.

DYSFLUENCY

See STUTTERING.

DYSGRAPHIA

Dysgraphia is a disorder characterized by writing difficulties. More specifically, it is defined as difficulty in automatically remembering and mastering the sequence of muscle motor movements needed in writing letters or numbers. The difficulty writing is incongruent with the person's ability and is not due to poor instruction. The disorder varies in terms of severity, ranging from mild to severe.

Problems in writing and difficulty with other motor skills related to instruction are not uncommon among school-age children. Although the prevalence of dysgraphia is unknown, it is estimated that 5–20 percent of children demonstrate some form of deficient writing behavior (Smits-Engelman & Van Galen, 1997). Although a neurologic basis is suspected, the exact cause is unknown. What is known is that it is a problem that results from an integration failure, that is, a deficit in visual-motor integration rather than a deficit in either visual skill or motor skill alone (Bain, Bailet, & Moats, 1991). Dysgraphia is also considered to be caused by difficulty sequencing information as well as a more general auditory or language-processing problem.

Dysgraphia seldom exists in isolation but more commonly occurs with other coordination and learning problems (e.g., dyslexia, dyscalculia, and developmental coordination disorder). The problem has also been found among children who have attention problems and hyperactivity. Because fine motor coordination improves with maturation and instruction, dysgraphia is seldom recognized before the end of the first grade. In fact, the *Diagnostic and Statistical Manual of Mental Disorders,* fourth edition's (*DSM-IV*) diagnosis of Disorders of Written Expression, which dysgraphia may be a part of, stipulates that in order to be diagnosed with a disorder, the individual's writing problem must interfere with learning. In other words, children whose only problem is poor handwriting (i.e., they have no other problem with written expression) are not given a *DSM-IV* diagnosis.

Characteristics of dysgraphia may include:

1. Generally illegible writing despite appropriate attention and time given to the task
2. Mix of print and cursive and upper and lower case and changes in shapes, size, and slant
3. Failure to attend to writing details, unfinished words and letters, and omitted words
4. Irregular spacing between words and letters
5. Standard lines and margins not adhered to
6. Unusual grip on writing tool and unusual wrist/body/paper position
7. Excessive erasures
8. Self-talking while writing or close observation of the writing hand
9. Slow or labored writing and copying even if neat and legible

Although writing samples and behavioral observations of the child are often used to diagnose the problem, a number of standardized assessment instruments may also be helpful. This includes the Developmental Test of Visual-Motor Integration, Coding/Digit Symbol and Symbol Search subtests of the Wechsler intelligence scales (WISC-III/WAIS-III), Bender-Gestalt, and Jordan Left-Right Reversal Test. A variety of written language achievement measures may also be useful, including tests such as the Woodcock Johnson Achievement Test (WJ-3) and Test of Written Language (TOWL). In addition to assessing student characteristics, it is also important to assess the type of instruction that has been provided to the child and his or her response to the writing task. Classroom observations may be helpful in ruling out contextual variables as a significant factor in the writing problem.

Treatment of dysgraphia may include interventions to assist the child in better controlling fine motor skill. Although the classroom teacher and parent may be helpful in this regard, in some cases the child may need to be evaluated and seen by the occupational therapist to work on controlling the writing movements. Few children with dysgraphia actually qualify for special education services under the Individuals with Disabilities in Education Act (IDEA) of 1997; however, some may if the problem in writing is associated with other learning problems (e.g., written language). In the cases where dysgraphia is comorbid with other learning disabilities, children may be served under the category Specific Learning Disabilities. In most cases, children can be accommodated in the regular classroom.

Educators can employ a number of accommodations, modifications, and remediation strategies to help students with dysgraphia. Some of these include allowing the student to use a computer or typewriter to do written work, having them use special writing implements (e.g., grippers or extra-large pencils and pens), or allowing the child to write in whatever form of manuscript is easiest and most legible (e.g., print or cursive). Giving children extra time for writing assignments and allowing them to audiotape assignments, take oral tests, and do more self-correction of their written work may be beneficial. Some children, however, may need further instruction and practice in handwriting. For an excellent resource refer to the Resource Room web site (Jones, 1998).

If untreated, the prognosis for dysgraphia is generally thought to be poor. Although some writing problems persist regardless of intervention, many children can be helped by attention paid to the problem. Not only do children need to be made aware of the problem, but also specific strategies need to be put in place to assist the child. Knowing what strategies are most effective, however, is unclear. Perhaps further studies of other associated conditions will shed light on this otherwise neglected disorder.

REFERENCES

Bain, A. M., Bailet, L. L., & Moats, L. C. (1991). *Written language disorders: Theory into practice.* Austin, TX: PRO-ED.

Jones, S. (1998). *Accommodations and modifications for students with handwriting problems and / or dysgraphia.* Retrieved from http://www.resourceroom.net

Smits-Engelman, B. C. M., & Van Galen, G. P. (1997). Dysgraphia in children: Lasting psychomotor deficiency or transient developmental delay? *Journal of Experimental Child Psychology, 67*(2), 164–184.

Lindsey A. Phillips
Elaine Clark
University of Utah

VISUAL-MOTOR AND VISUAL-PERCEPTUAL PROBLEMS
WRITING DISORDERS
WRITING REMEDIATION

DYSKINESIA

Dyskinesia is a collection of movement disorders involving impairment of central nervous system motor control. It is thought to be due to damage or abnormal development of the basal ganglia, the deep subcortical nuclei in the cerebral cortex. Involuntary movement, irregular motions, or lack of coordinated voluntary movement characterizes dyskinesia (Fredericks & Saladin, 1996). Dyskinetic movement disorders include dystonia, tremor, chorea, tics, and myoclonus. Each movement disorder is uniquely characterized. For example, dystonia is characterized by involuntary, sustained posturing. Small oscillating movements at rest or with effort characterize tremor. Random, excessive, irregularly timed movements characterize chorea. Tics are brief, repetitive, involuntary movements. Involuntary movements that are rapid, shock-like, and arrhythmic (unpatterned) characterize myoclonus (Weiner & Goetz, 1999).

Each movement disorder is unique in regard to the somatic distribution and quality of movement, the age of onset, and etiology. Dyskinesia may be the primary sign or symptom or may be included with the other signs or symptoms of a syndrome. Childhood dyskinetic movement disorders include Tourette syndrome, choreoathetoid cerebral palsy, Wilson's disease, Lesch-Nyhan syndrome, and dystonia. The etiology of a dyskinetic movement disorder is variable and may be due to genetic transmission, brain anoxia, infection, or neoplasm (Weiner & Goetz, 1999).

Prevalence and incidence of dyskinesia in childhood is not documented due to the varied nature of the etiology.

Characteristics of dyskinesia may be:

1. Involuntary sustained muscle contractions producing unusual postures
2. Involuntary oscillating movement at rest or during effort
3. Excessive, irregularly timed involuntary movement
4. Repetitive, brief, purposeless involuntary movement
5. Rapid, often repetitive involuntary movement

Medical intervention includes pharmacologic treatment or intramuscular injections to control the involuntary movement (Kurlan, 1995). Supportive counseling services may be helpful in educating families, peers, and school personnel regarding the nature of the dyskinesia. The school and home environment may need to be restructured or adapted to improve function depending on the severity of the dyskinesia.

In older children and adults tic disorders are a fairly common type of dyskinesia. They may include rapid repetitive facial movements such as blinking, coughing, sniffing, or lip smacking. These too are typically treated symptomatically. They may be treated through the use of relaxation techniques or antianxiety medications in an effort to reduce the stress associated with increased demonstration of this type of dyskinesia (Fredericks & Saladin, 1996). In patients treated with neuroleptic drugs, tardive dyskinesia may develop as a result of this family of drugs. This is more common in adults but may also occur in older adolescents. Unfortunately, this condition may be irreversible (NIH Health Information Index, 2000).

The impact this group of movement disorders may have on the development of children depends in part on the age at onset, the range and severity of symptoms exhibited, and the developmental level of the child. One of the key components of movement and exploration is stability and predictability of postural tone. Without this stability in the trunk, a child may be unwilling or unable to maintain a sitting position necessary to reach, grasp, and explore objects. Cognitive and perceptual motor skills exhibited in refined searching also require stability of movement. Success in this skill depends on the infant's ability to watch an item being hidden, remember where it went, and retrieve it (Piaget, 1952). Without adequate support and predictable movement patterns, this behavior may be difficult or impossible.

Moving independently in the environment, using independent self-help behaviors such as eating and fine motor skills such as stacking blocks and puzzles also requires stable and predictable movements. A very young infant just learning to crawl may be hesitant to proceed if he or she is unable to maintain stability necessary for movement. Moving out into the environment provides opportunities to explore and increase social and language development. Without this ability, the secondary disabilities that may result include delayed cognitive, language, and social skills necessary for smooth transition to the next levels of development.

Thus, delays in development resulting from dyskinesia may not only potentially affect motor development but also impact development in social and cognitive areas as well as other areas depending on the severity of the dyskinesia. Special education placement will depend on the nature of the disability and the level of involvement for each child. A variety of special education service categories (e.g., Mental Disability, Preschool Services, Traumatic Brain Injury, and Physical Disability) may be considered, and services provided should stem from the special needs of each child. Therefore, it is critical that intervention programs address all areas potentially impacted, such as speech, occupational, and physical therapy in addition to academic areas. The ideal program would include a transdisciplinary model in which counseling, physical, occupational, and speech therapy are incorporated into the child's daily activities.

REFERENCES

Fredericks, C. M., & Saladin, L. K. (1996). *Pathophysiology of the motor systems.* Philadelphia: F. A. Davis.

Kurlan, R. (1995). *Treatment of movement disorders.* Philadelphia: J. B. Lippincott.

NIH Health Information Index: National Institute of Neurological Disorders and Stroke. (2000). *Dyskinesias.* Retrieved from http://www.ninds.nih.gov/health_and_medical/disorder/dyskinesias_doc.htm

Piaget, J. (1952). *The origin of intelligence in children.* New York: International Universities Press.

Weiner, W. W., & Goetz, C. G. (1999). *Neurology for the non-neurologist* (4th ed.). Philadelphia: Lippincott Williams & Wilkins.

PATRICIA WORK
MARILYN URQUHART
LANA SVIEN-SENNE
University of South Dakota

DYSLEXIA

See DEVELOPMENTAL DYSLEXIA, HISTORY OF; READING DISORDERS

DYSLOGIC SYNDROME

Dyslogic syndrome, sometimes referred to as developmental or congenital aphasia, consists of the inability to express oneself through language due to a central nervous system dysfunction. Symptoms may not be the result of a sensory or cognitive deficit, nor may they occur due to loss of prior linguistic abilities (Eisenson, 1972; Nicolosi, Harryman, &

Kresheck, 1983; Telzrow, 2000). The primary characteristic of dyslogia is difficulty with communication, which is likely to make learning more difficult and to cause frustration to the child. At times children with dyslogia may be misdiagnosed with mental retardation, deafness, auditory deficit, or psychological disorder due to similarities in behavioral patterns (Telzrow, 2000). True dyslogia is believed to be quite rare, although epidemiological information is not available (Eisenson, 1972).

Eisenson (1972) cited several diagnostic criteria for dyslogia that differentiate it from other language disorders. Children with dyslogia often have difficulty with integrating sensory information. This can occur across sensory modalities but in all cases includes the auditory modality. It appears that those with dyslogia have a particularly difficult time making sense of auditory information. More specifically, he suggested that they struggle to find meaningful patterns in auditory input (Chappell, 1970; Eisenson, 1972).

Characteristics of dyslogia can include:

1. Perceptual dysfunction within or across sensory modalities. In nearly all cases auditory perception is impaired.

2. Auditory perceptual difficulties despite intact hearing.

3. Sequencing difficulties for auditory and sometimes visual events.

4. Child's performance on intellectual tasks below that of children of a similar age. Eisenson (1972) described this as intellectual inefficiency rather than impairment.

5. Delayed language development. Children may be effectively nonverbal until the age of 4 or 5 years. Subsequent language is lacking in vocabulary and syntax.

In addition to their struggles with language, Eisenson (1972) believes that those with dyslogia have difficulty with sequencing in general. Children with dyslogia may also exhibit symptoms of inattention and distractibility that can prevent them from working up to their cognitive ability. As these children approach ages where higher cognitive functioning is more frequently required, their difficulties with sequencing become more apparent.

It appears that with patient training, children with dyslogia may learn to recognize and understand simple words, especially nouns that can be represented by physical objects. There is less evidence for the acquisition of understanding of words that represent less concrete concepts such as feelings or actions. With some training, these children may learn to respond to specific, short directive sentences (e.g., "Come, Mary"). However, it appears that these children have a hard time generalizing their understanding, and responses may be situationally specific. Thus, a child who learns to come to the teacher may not respond to the same command when spoken at home (Chappell, 1970).

Prognosis in cases of dyslogia is varied. In some cases, the ability to communicate effectively by language may never develop. In others, the development of language will be permanently impaired, but improvement does occur (Chappell, 1970; Eisenson, 1972). It should be noted that development or recovery of language among those with dyslogia is generally less successful than is that of children with acquired aphasia (Eisenson, 1972).

The language impairment in these children may be so great that when language does begin to develop, it is likely to be impaired in its syntax and complexity. The pattern of language development is likely to be somewhat idiosyncratic and is unlikely to present as merely delayed. These children may be able to speak, but their ability to communicate verbally is likely to remain impaired (Chappell, 1970; Eisenson, 1972).

In an educational environment, care should be taken to provide these children with nonauditory cues for learning. Attempts to teach language should include simple (two to three word) sentences, extensive and patient repetition, and the pairing of vocabulary with concrete objects. It appears that these children require an optimal environment in order to reach their intellectual potentials. Eisenson (1972) suggested that factors such as irrelevant stimuli, fatigue, and frustration may be especially detrimental to children struggling with dyslogia. In such cases, common accommodations for children with attentional difficulties would likely be helpful.

REFERENCES

Chappell, G. E. (1970). Developmental aphasia revisited. *Journal of Communication Disorders, 3,* 181–197.

Eisenson, J. (1972). *Aphasia in children.* New York: Harper and Row.

Nicolosi, L., Harryman, E., & Kresheck, J. (1983). *Terminology of communication disorders.* Baltimore: Williams & Wilkins.

Telzrow, C. T. (2000). Dyslogic syndrome. In C. Reynolds & E. Fletcher-Janzen (Eds.), *Encyclopedia of special education: A reference for the education of the handicapped and other exceptional children and adults* (2nd ed., Vol. 1, pp. 636–637). New York: Wiley.

MELANIE E. BALLATORE
University of Texas at Austin

CHILDHOOD APHASIA
LANGUAGE DISORDERS

DYSMETRIA

Dysmetria is defined as an aspect of ataxia in which the ability to control the distance, power, and speed of an act is impaired (Stedman, 2000). The term originates from the Greek *dys,* meaning difficult or disordered, and *metron,* meaning measure. Individuals with dysmetria have problems judging the extent to which they must move their body to reach a desired goal and often have difficulty stopping their movement in a precise manner to reach the goal. Movements, therefore, undershoot (hypometria) or overshoot (hypermetria) the distance (Telzrow, 2000). Individuals with dysmetria may have difficulty raising their arms parallel to the floor (i.e., arms extended at the shoulder level). Some may also have problems moving their arms above their heads from their shoulders and back down while keeping their eyes closed.

The prevalence of dysmetria is unknown, but it has been shown to co-occur with other conditions. Some of these associated conditions include neurologic disorders (e.g., cerebellar dysfunction), learning problems (e.g., dyslexia), and psychiatric conditions (e.g., schizophrenia). Unless dysmetria is detected while evaluating for problems associated with related conditions, it is likely to remain undiagnosed. There have been cases of children with traumatic brain injury (TBI) who after being hit by a vehicle are found to have a cerebellar tumor thought to be responsible for the initial misjudgment of distance, and thus the accident. Had imaging not been done to evaluate the TBI, it is likely that the tumor would not have been detected and that the dysmetria would not have been diagnosed.

Characteristics of dysmetria include:

1. Disturbance in the ability to judge distance and control the range of movement in muscle action to reach precisely a desired goal
2. Rapid, brusque movements with more force than is typical
3. Often associated with other conditions (e.g., neurologic and psychiatric)
4. Difficult to diagnose

There is no prescribed treatment for dysmetria, and the literature is almost nonexistent. Frank and Levinson (1976) studied the effectiveness of seasick medications to treat "dysmetric dyslexia." The researchers hypothesize that dysmetric dyslexia may be due to vestibular dysfunction and respond to a specific intervention of the eyes being prevented from moving beyond printed letters and words. In the end, it may be that interventions used to correct dysmetria will be those that are designed to address related problems, including reading disabilities and other learning difficulties. Research is clearly needed to understand this condition better and to find ways to determine when dysmetria signals a more serious problem (e.g., brain tumors).

REFERENCES

Frank, J., & Levinson, H. N. (1976). Seasickness mechanisms and medications in dysmetric dyslexia and dyspraxia. *Academic Therapy, 12*(2), 133–153.

Stedman, T. L. (2000). *Stedman's medical dictionary* (27th ed., p. 553). Baltimore: Lippincott Williams & Wilkins.

Telzrow, C. F. (2000). In C. R. Reynolds & E. Fletcher-Janzen (Eds.), *Encyclopedia of special education* (2nd ed., p. 637). New York: Wiley.

LINDSEY A. PHILLIPS
ELAINE CLARK
University of Utah

MOBILITY INSTRUCTION

DYSMORPHIC FEATURES

Dysmorphic features are those physical anomalies that identify the presence of congenital syndromes or acquired disabilities. Dysmorphic features may be present in a variety of body parts, including the head, face, hands, and feet. Most congenital syndromes are associated with dysmorphic features that are specific to and, in fact, represent signs of the condition. Dysmorphic features associated with Down syndrome, for example, include a single palmar crease (Simian crease) on one or both hands, epicanthus, and microcephaly (Kelly, 1975). Apert's syndrome, another condition frequently associated with mental retardation, is characterized by syndactyly (webbing) of the hands and feet and a flat, narrow head owing to closure of the bony sutures (Batshaw & Perret, 1981). Some dysmorphic features (e.g., anencephaly or absence of the cortical brain tissues) are severe and typically result in death (Batshaw & Perret, 1981).

While dysmorphic features may occur in the absence of any known syndrome and without apparent mental or physical impairment, in most cases such anomalies are suggestive of moderate to severe impairment. Dysmorphic features may represent malformations that occur during the first trimester (Batshaw & Perret, 1981). Malformations may result from genetic abnormalities (e.g., Down syndrome, phenylketonuria); cell migration defects (e.g., cleft palate, spina bifida); maternal infection (e.g., rubella, cytomegalovirus); drugs (e.g., fetal alcohol syndrome, fetal dilantin syndrome); and other teratogens (Batshaw & Perret, 1981; Casey & Collie, 1984). The presence of dysmorphic features often is used to infer level and type of associated impairment. A study of the relationship between physical appearance and mental retardation syndromes reported that atypical appearance increases with the severity of mental retardation; greater atypical appearance is associated with more severe organic impairment in populations of severely and profoundly retarded persons; and mildly retarded persons with positive neurologic findings demonstrated greater degrees of atypical appearance (Richardson, Koller, & Katz, 1985).

Dysmorphic features of a less severe nature also have been identified in populations of mildly handicapped children. Waldrop and Halverson (1971) described findings from five separate studies in which congenital anomalies such as epicanthus, curved fifth digits, and a wide gap between the first and second toes were associated with hyperactive behavior in children. The authors suggest that "the same factors operating in the first weeks of pregnancy influenced the occurrence of *both* the morphological aberrations and the predisposition for impulsive, fast-moving behavior" (Waldrop & Halverson, 1971, p. 343). Subsequent studies demonstrated such minor physical anomalies could be identified in infants, were stable overtime, and were associated with infant irritability (Quinn, Renfield, Burg, & Rapaport, 1977). While these and other authors (e.g., Rosenberg & Weller, 1973) suggest minor congenital anomalies may be useful in predicting at-risk status for mild learning problems, other findings suggest the quality of the child's environment may represent an important intervening variable (LaVeck, Hammond, Telzrow, & LaVeck, 1983).

REFERENCES

Batshaw, M. L., & Perret, Y. M. (1981). *Children with handicaps: A medical primer*. Baltimore: Brooks.

Casey, P. H., & Collie, W. R. (1984). Severe mental retardation and multiple congenital anomalies of uncertain cause after extreme parental exposure to 2, 4-D. *The Journal of Pediatrics, 104,* 313–315.

Kelly, T. E. (1975). The role of genetic mechanisms in childhood handicaps. In R. H. A. Haslam & P. J. Valletutti (Eds.), *Medical problems in the classroom* (pp. 193–215). Baltimore: University Park Press.

LaVeck, F., Hammond, M. A., Telzrow, R., & LaVeck, G. D. (1983). Further observations on minor anomalies and behavior in different home environments. *Journal of Pediatric Psychology, 8,* 171–179.

Quinn, P. O., Renfield, M., Burg, C., & Rapaport, J. L. (1977). Minor physical anomalies: A newborn screening and 1-year follow-up. *Journal of Child Psychiatry, 16,* 662–669.

Richardson, S. A., Koller, H., & Katz, M. (1985). Appearance and mental retardation: Some first steps in the development and application of a measure. *American Journal of Mental Deficiency, 89,* 475–484.

Rosenberg, J. B., & Weller, G. M. (1973). Minor physical anomalies and academic performance in young school-children. *Developmental Medicine & Child Neurology, 15,* 131–135.

Waldrop, M. F., & Halverson, C. F. (1971). Minor physical anomalies and hyperactive behavior in young children. In J. Hellmuth (Ed.), *The exceptional infant* (Vol. 2, pp. 343–380). New York: Brunner/Mazel.

CATHY F. TELZROW
Kent State University

CONGENITAL DISORDERS
MINOR PHYSICAL ANOMALIES
PHYSICAL ANOMALIES

DYSNOMIA

Dysnomia and anomia are used interchangeably to denote problems in finding and using an intended word. Eisenson (1973) defines dysnomia as "difficulty in invoking an appropriate term regardless of its part of speech" (p. 19). It is frequently evidenced in dysphasic patients as a residual of central nervous system dysfunction. The dysphasic individual may substitute a word related by class or function to the intended word (e.g., knife for ford; Eisenson, 1973). Fewer problems were noted on common words than those used less frequently in the language (Jenkins, Jiménez-Pabón, Shaw, & Sefer, 1975).

A dysphasic individual tends to talk around the elusive word and sometimes may remark that he or she knows it but cannot say it. He or she may attempt a gesture to illustrate the word's meaning or may give several functional cues, sometimes achieving successful recall through associations. Some dysphasics recognize the word when it is said to them. Word-finding difficulties also have been found among learning-disabled children with language disorders (Wiig & Semel, 1984) and among children diagnosed as being developmentally dysphasic (Myklebust, 1971). In such cases, the child cannot name an object or picture, but is aware of the error and can recognize the intended word when it is supplied because auditory monitoring processes are intact (Myklebust, 1971).

Dysnomic difficulties are evident in picture-naming tasks, characterized by use of an associated word (e.g., door for key). Use of an opposite such as "brother" for "sister" also is a common error in both children and adults. Verbal association tasks that require a child to name items within categories (e.g., animals) may produce rapid naming of several items and then either silence or incorrect responses. Errors may occur on words that a child has evidenced knowing on previous occasions (Wiig & Semel, 1984). German (1982) studied 8-to-11-year-old learning-disabled children to identify types of substitutions unique to this group when the children were unable to retrieve words. The strongest pattern noted was the substitution of a word of lesser complexity and with wider application (e.g., "string" for "rein"); the weakest pattern was the repetition of initial sound(s) of a related word before the target word was uttered (e.g., "br, br, comb").

Word-finding problems in spontaneous speech may be signaled by inappropriate pauses, use of filler ("um" and "er") and nonmeaningful phrases ("whatchama call it"), substitution of a functional description (circumlocution), or overuse of nonspecific words ("stuff," "place," "something," "thing"; Wiig & Semel, 1984). Classroom tasks involving rhyming words, silent picture naming, matching initial-, medical-, and final-consonant sounds, and look-say methods of reading may prove troublesome for dysnomic children (Wiig, Semel, & Nystrom, 1982). German (1982) suggests that a thorough evaluation of a child's pattern of word substitutions may prove helpful in intervention techniques.

REFERENCES

Eisenson, J. (1973). *Adult aphasia: Assessment and treatment.* New York: Appleton-Century-Crofts.

German, D. (1982). Word-finding substitutions in children with learning disabilities. *Language, Speech & Hearing Services in Schools, 13,* 223–230.

Jenkins, J. J., Jiménez-Pabón, E., Shaw, R. E., & Sefer, J. W. (1975). *Schuell's aphasia in adults: Diagnosis, prognosis, and treatment.* Hagerstown, MD: Harper & Row.

Myklebust, H. (1971). Childhood aphasia: An evolving concept. In L. E. Travis (Ed.), *The handbook of speech pathology and audiology* (pp. 1181–1201). New York: Appleton-Century-Crofts.

Wiig, E., & Semel, E. (1984). *Language assessment and intervention for the learning disabled* (2nd ed.). Columbus, OH: Merrill.

Wiig, E., Semel, E., & Nystrom, L. A. (1982). Comparison of rapid naming abilities in language learning disabled and academically achieving eight-year olds. *Language, Speech & Hearing Services in Schools, 13,* 11–25.

K. Sandra Vanta
Cleveland Public Schools,
Cleveland, Ohio

APHASIA
COMMUNICATION DISORDERS
LANGUAGE DISORDERS

DYSPEDAGOGIA

Dyspedagogia refers to poor teaching. It has been cited as a major cause of reading retardation and other learning disorders. Though the term is used as one of the etiological agents for a wide array of problems, dyspedagogia is commonly associated with the field of learning disabilities (Epstein, Cullinan, Hessen, & Lloyd, 1980), mathematics (Maree, 1992), and currently in general areas that require cross-cultural competency for learners outcomes (Truscott & Truscott, 2005). Indeed, general and special education has been placed under great scrutiny by the No Child Left Behind law and the reauthorization of IDEA in 2004.

Early research in reading disorders and learning disabilities looked for psychophysiological dysfunctions or psychological information-processing deficits as the cause of a child's inefficient learning. Once various forms of testing established a supposed etiology, specific treatment regimens were to flow directly from the diagnosis. Although this approach to special and remedial education, often referred to as ability training, has been questioned (Ysseldyke, 1973), it remains a dominant force in practice. Learning problems were seen as based in the individual child, whether because of psychoneurological dysfunction or sociocultural disadvantage. Improper choice of teaching materials or methodology, or an inappropriate match between learning style and pedagogy, were rarely viewed as contributing factors in a student's academic retardation.

Cohen (1971) cites Harris's research (1968) on teaching beginning reading as an early example of dyspedagogia as an etiological agent in poor reading achievement. When comparisons were made between different beginning reading programs, matching classrooms across and within each program, the achievement discrepancies were greater between classrooms using the same program than across the different types of beginning reading programs. This was generally interpreted to indicate that the teacher variable is a more powerful determinant of student achievement than the actual programs or materials employed.

Cohen (1971) believed that dyspedagogia is the norm for most children, both in regular and special education. Many children, however, learn well enough despite poor or inappropriate teaching. The problem lies in the fact that those children who come to the educational setting with negatively predisposing social, psychological, neurological, or linguistic differences need effective, intensive teaching, and will suffer inordinately from dyspedagogia (Wertsch, 1985). The presenting background problems are not ignored, but the burden falls on educators to minimize their deleterious effects on learning by providing sound, skill-oriented instruction.

As a result of research in regular education on effective teaching (e.g., Brophy, 1979; Lyon, 2003; Rosenshine, 1978), a good deal of attention is being given to issues such as direct instruction, time on task, academically engaged time, instructional management, performance monitoring, success-oriented learning, feedback, reflective teaching, and related practices. This research has offered promise for special and general education (Englert, 1984; Goodman, 1985; Rieth, Edsgrove, & Semmel, 1979).

REFERENCES

Brophy, J. E. (1979). Teacher behavior and its effects. *Journal of Educational Psychology, 71,* 733–750.

Cohen, S. A. (1971). Dyspedagogia as a cause of reading retardation: Definition and treatment. In B. Bateman (Ed.), *Learning disorders* (Vol. 4). Seattle, WA: Special Child Publications.

Englert, C. S. (1984). Effective direct instruction practices in special education settings. *Remedial & Special Education, 5*(2), 38–47.

Epstein, M. H., Cullinan, D., Hessen, E. L., & Lloyd, J. (1980). Understanding children with learning disabilities. *Child Welfare, 59*(1), 3–14.

Goodman, L. (1985). The effective schools movement and special education. *Teaching Exceptional Children, 17,* 102–105.

Harris, A., Morrison, C., Serwa, B., & Gold, L. (1968). *A continuation of the craft project: Comparing approaches with disadvantaged urban Negro children in primary grades* (U.S.O.E. #6-10-063). New York: City University of New York.

Lyon, R. (2003). Reading disabilities: Why do some children have difficulty learning to read? *International Dyslexia Association Perspectives, 29*(2), 111–114.

Maree, J. G. (1992). Problems in mathematics: Moving towards a holistic approach. *Journal of Special Education, 16*(2), 174–182.

Rieth, H. J., Edsgrove, L., & Semmel, M. I. (1979). Relationship between instructional time and academic achievement: Implications for research and practice. *Education Unlimited, 1*(6), 53–56.

Rosenshine, B. (1978). *Academic engaged time, content covered and direct instruction* (ERIC Document No. 152 776). Champaign: University of Illinois.

Truscott, S. D., & Truscott, D. M. (2005). Challenges in urban and rural education. In C. L. Frisby & C. R. Reynolds (Eds.), *Multicultural school psychology* (pp. 357–393). New York: Wiley.

Wertsch, J. (1985). *Vygotsky and the social formation of mind.* London: Harvard University Press.

Ysseldyke, J. E. (1973). Diagnostic-prescriptive teaching: The search for aptitude-treatment interactions. In L. Mann & D. Sabatino (Eds.), *First review of special education.* New York: Grune & Stratton.

JOHN D. WILSON
Elwyn Institutes

DYSPHAGIA

Dysphagia has been defined in several different ways. For example, Buchholz (1996) offered a broad definition in which dysphagia is considered a condition resulting from some interference in eating or the maintenance of nutrition and hydration; Groher (1997) stated that dysphagia is an "abnormality in the transfer of a bolus from the mouth to the stomach" (p. 1). However, a general definition of dysphagia is having difficulty swallowing. This difficulty could be caused by a number of different conditions. The more common causes of swallowing difficulty are neurologic damage such as stroke or progressive neurologic disease such as Parkinson's disease, head and neck tumors and their treatment, medical problems such as rheumatoid arthritis, scleroderma, diabetes, and induced trauma to the esophagus, larynx, tongue, or pharynx (New York Eye and Ear Infirmary [NYEEI], 2000).

Dysphagia typically falls into one of two categories. Oropharyngeal dysphagia is the result of a stroke or neuromuscular disorder that leaves the throat muscles weakened, making it difficult to get food from the mouth into the throat. This condition is often accompanied by choking or coughing when attempting to swallow and the sensation of food going down the windpipe. The most common type of dysphagia, however, is esophageal dysphagia, which refers to the sensation of food sticking or getting caught in the base of one's throat or chest and may be accompanied by pressure or pain in the chest (Mayo Foundation for Medical Education and Research [MFMER], 1998).

A narrowing of the lower esophagus, known as peptic stricture, is a common cause of esophageal dysphagia. The resulting condition, known as gastroesophageal reflux, is a result of stomach acid bubbling up into the esophagus, causing inflammation and scarring in the esophagus. Another cause of esophageal dysphagia is a formation of a pouch in the back of the throat or esophagus, known as diverticulum.

Despite the many medically identifiable causes of dysphagia, many people experience swallowing problems that seem to have no medical basis (e.g., difficulty swallowing pills or the feeling of a lump in the throat). These problems persist in some people even though they have no other difficulty swallowing.

The incidence of dysphagia is approximately 13–14 percent in inpatient hospital settings, 40–50 percent in nursing homes, and approximately 33 percent in rehabilitation centers (NYEEI, 2000).

Acute forms of dysphagia are typically diagnosed by tests such as drinking a barium solution that coats the esophagus and enables an X-ray to show abnormalities in the esophagus; an endoscopy, in which a tube with a special camera at the tip allows the esophagus to be viewed from the inside; or a procedure known as a manometry test, in which an instrument is inserted into the esophagus and pressure readings of esophageal muscle contractions are taken.

Characteristics of dysphagia may include:

1. Pain while swallowing
2. Coughing while eating or drinking or very soon after eating or drinking
3. Wet-sounding voice during or after eating
4. Increased congestion in the chest after eating or drinking
5. Slow eating
6. Multiple swallows on a single mouthful of food
7. Obvious extra effort or difficulty while chewing or swallowing
8. Fatigue or shortness of breath while eating
9. Temperature rise 30 minutes to 1 hour after eating
10. Weight loss associated with increased slowness in eating
11. Frequent heartburn
12. Repetitive pneumonias

The causes of dysphagia determine the course of treatment. Pharyngeal dysphagia may be treated by a throat specialist, neurologist, or a speech pathologist for therapy. Typically, special throat exercises, liquid diets, and in severe cases a feeding tube may be recommended. Esophageal stricture may be treated by a procedure known as dilata-

tion, in which an endoscope is inserted into the esophagus and a special balloon attached to the endoscope is inflated to expand the constricted areas of the esophagus. Acid reflux or esophageal spasms that result in dysphagia may be treated with prescription medication. In some cases, such as diverticulum or the presence of a tumor, surgery may be necessary (MFMER, 1998).

Children with dysphagia may require extra care at lunch and snack times, such as additional time to eat, adult supervision, and education of peers about the disorder.

REFERENCES

Buchholz, D. (1996). Editorial: What is dysphagia? *Dysphagia, 11,* 23.

Groher, M. E. (1997). *Dysphagia: Diagnosis and management* (3rd ed.). Boston: Butterworth-Heinemann.

Mayo Foundation for Medical Education and Research (MFMER). (1998). Dysphagia: When swallowing becomes difficult. *Condition Centers.* Retrieved from http://www.mayoclinic.com/home?id=HQ00590

New York Eye and Ear Infirmary (NYEEI). (2000). Dysphagia: What is a normal swallow? *Health matters.* Retrieved from http://www.nyee.edu

TRACY A. MUENZ
Alliant International University

DYSPHASIA

See LANGUAGE DISORDERS.

DYSPHONIA

See VOICE DISORDERS.

DYSPRAXIA

See APRAXIA.

DYSTONIA

Dystonia is a neurologic movement disorder characterized by sustained muscle contractions that frequently cause twisting or repetitive movements and abnormal, sometimes painful, postures or positions. This disorder may involve any voluntary muscle in the body. Defined as a syndrome of sustained muscle contractions, dystonia encompasses motor syndromes that vary as a function of age of onset, cause, and body distribution (King, Tsui, & Calne, 1995). The symptoms of dystonia may begin during early childhood, in adolescence, or during adulthood. Dystonia may frequently be misdiagnosed or confused with other disorders. The diagnosis may be missed as the movements and resulting postures are often unusual and the condition is rare. The exact prevalence of dystonia in the general population is not known; however, an estimate of 330 cases per million has been made (King et al., 1995).

Characteristics of dystonia may include:

1. Movement is characterized by an excess of involuntary muscle activity (Rothwell, 1995).
2. Childhood dystonia often presents as abnormal foot inversions, awkward gait, and contractions of many different muscle groups and may involve one or more limbs of the proximal or distal muscle groups.
3. Dystonic movements tend to increase with fatigue, stress, and emotional states; they tend to be suppressed with relaxation, hypnosis, and sleep.
4. Dystonia is usually present continually throughout the day whenever the affected body part is in use and disappears with deep sleep.
5. Common misdiagnoses are clubfoot, scoliosis, stress, and psychogenic disorder.
6. Pain is common in some individuals.

Although dystonia has no cure, there are successful treatments that greatly reduce the symptoms and restore individuals to many daily living activities. The first step in treatment is attempting to determine the cause of the dystonia. Dystonia is classified as being primary or idiopathic, in which there is no known organic lesion, but is believed to be hereditary and to occur as the result of a faulty genes (King et al., 1995). It is also classified as being secondary, which generally arises from some insult to the basal ganglia of the central nervous system such as trauma, toxins, drugs, neoplasm, or infarction; another underlying disease process such as Wilson disease, multiple sclerosis, or stroke; or as a result of the use of certain neuroleptic or antipsychotic drugs. For secondary dystonias, treating the underlying cause may improve the dystonia. For instance, treatments for neurological conditions such as multiple sclerosis may reduce dystonic symptoms. Withdrawing or reducing neuroleptic drugs leads to slow improvement in some cases.

There are three main approaches to the treatment of primary dystonia: drug therapy, injections of therapeutic agents (botulinum toxin) directly into dystonic muscle, and surgery (Greene & Fahn, 1992). Drug therapy may include benzodiazepines, which are a class of drugs that interfere with chemical activities in the nervous system and brain, serving to reduce communication between nerve cells; baclofen, which is a drug that is used to treat individuals with spasticity; and anticholinergics, which block the action of the neurotransmitter acetylcholine, thereby deactivating

muscle contractions (King et al., 1995). Surgical intervention may be considered in those individuals with severe dystonia who have not responded or have become nonresponders to drug therapy. The goal of surgery for individuals with dystonia is to attempt to rebalance movement and posture control by destroying specific regions in the brain (King et al., 1995).

Special education services may be available to children with dystonia under the handicapping condition of Other Health Impairment or Physical Disability. Movement problems usually start on the lower limbs and can progress to other parts of the body. At times they may then reach a plateau. Therefore, input from a physical therapist may be required to provide advice, monitoring, and exercises. An occupational therapist may be necessary to identify areas of concern in regard to work, play, and self-care. Speech therapy is often warranted and varies depending on the type of dystonia. A therapy program is then designed to meet individual needs, and information can be provided to the child and family about ways to promote optimal communication. Due to extensive medical intervention, school absences may require home schooling or tutoring by a special educator. Counseling services may be appropriate due to the psychosocial aspects of the physical distortions caused by muscular contractions. Finally, for the dystonic child, most all life activities take longer; this and the effect of the medication may cause fatigue. Consequently, it is important to have realistic expectations of the child's physical performance. The overall goal should be to foster a feeling of successful achievement, emphasizing the activities that children can accomplish rather than focusing on their limitations.

Research evaluating the ideology and a potential cure for dystonia has begun. Some professionals research the effects of dystonia such as the short- and long-term outcomes for afflicted children. Will the child's abilities decline over time? Will there be some psychosocial problems? What is the appropriate educational placement for children with dystonia? Reflecting on the implications of this disorder, these simple questions need further empirical study before clear answers can be provided.

REFERENCES

Greene, P. E., & Fahn, S. (1992). Baclofen in the treatment of idiopathic dystonia in children. *Movement Disorders, 7,* 48–52.

King, J., Tsui, C., & Calne, D. B. (1995). *Handbook of dystonia.* New York: Marcel Dekker.

Rothwell, J. C. (1995). *The physiology of dystonia.* New York: Marcel Dekker.

KENDRA J. BJORAKER
University of Northern Colorado

MOBILITY INSTRUCTION